CQ's Politics in America 2008

THE 110TH CONGRESS

By Congressional Quarterly Staff
Jackie Koszczuk and Martha Angle, Editors

★

In-depth Profiles of Members of Congress

Biographical Data and Key Votes

Election Results and District Snapshots

★

Robert W. Merry, President and Editor-in-Chief
Michael Riley, Editor and Senior Vice President
Keith White, Publisher and Senior Vice President
John A. Jenkins, Publisher and Senior Vice President, CQ Press

Published by Congressional Quarterly Inc.
Paul C. Tash, Chairman
Andrew P. Corty, Vice Chairman
Nelson Poynter (1903–1978), Founder

Congressional Quarterly Inc.
1255 22nd Street N.W.
Washington, DC 20037
202-419-8500; toll-free, 1-800-432-2250
www.cq.com

The paper used in this publication exceeds the requirements of the American National Standard for Information Sciences — Permanence of Paper for Printed Library Materials, ANSI Z39.48-1992.

Printed and bound in the United States of America

11 10 09 08 07 5 4 3 2 1

ISBN 978-0-87289-545-4 (cloth) ISBN 978-0-87289-547-8 (paper)

ISSN 1064-6809

The Library of Congress catalogued an earlier edition of this title as follows:

Congressional Quarterly's Politics in America: 1994, the 103rd Congress / by CQ's political staff: Phil Duncan, Editor

p. cm.

Includes index.

1. United States. Congress — Biography. 2. United States. Congress — Committees. 3. United States. Congress — Election districts — Handbooks, manuals, etc. I. Duncan, Phil. II. Congressional Quarterly Inc. III. Title: Politics in America.
JK1010.C67 1993 328.73'073'45'0202

Politics in America 2008

THE 110TH CONGRESS

EDITORS
Jackie Koszczuk, Martha Angle

MANAGING EDITORS
Susan Shipp, Kimberly Hallock

SENIOR EDITORS
Peter H. King, Brian Nutting, Katrina Van Duyn

CONTRIBUTING EDITORS
Christine C. Lawrence, Amy Stern, Christina L. Lyons, Amanda H. Allen, Arwen Bicknell

SENIOR WRITERS
Greg Giroux, Seth Stern

CONTRIBUTORS
Rebecca Adams, Jonathan Allen, Drew Armstrong, Kate Barrett, Matthew Berger, Laura Blinkhorn, Jonathan Broder, Mary Agnes Carey, Jean Chemnick, John Cochran, Jessica Benton Cooney, John Cranford, Michael R. Crittenden, Chris Dally, Coral Davenport, John M. Donnelly, Marilyn Dickey, Karen Foerstel, Jacob Freedman, Lydia Gensheimer,Libby George, Tom Hannett, Judi Hasson, David Hawkings, Caitlin Hendel, Liriel Higa, Cheyenne Hopkins, Marie Horrigan, Charles Hoskinson, Kathleen Hunter, Colby Itkowitz, Matthew Johnson, Martin Kady II, Rachel Kapochunas, Angela Kim, Rebecca Kimitch, Adrianne Kroepsch, Jon Lewallen, Gebe Martinez, Chuck McCutcheon, Victoria McGrane, David Nather, Frank Oliveri, Alan K. Ota, Keith Perine, Marc Rehmann, Daphne Retter, Catharine Richert, Katherine Rizzo, Michael Sandler, Brendan Spiegel, Eleanor Stables, Tim Starks, Michael Teitelbaum, Jeff Tollefson, Robert Tomkin, Greg Vadala, Rachel Van Dongen, Alex Wayne, Caitlin Webber, Kathryn A. Wolfe, Christopher Wright, Patrick Yoest, Margo Zaneski, Shawn Zeller

RESEARCHERS
Nell Benton (Chief), Alan Ahlrich, Sasha Bartolf, Rachel Bloom, Miranda Blue, Philip Burrowes, Nathaniel Decker, Loren Duggan, Shweta Govindarajan, C. Daniel Guerra, Amanda Harris, Ryan Kelly, Noella Kertes, Sarah Molencamp, Neil Ripley, Heather M. Rothman, Margaret Sammon, Matthew Spieler

PHOTOGRAPHY
Scott J. Ferrell

COPY EDITORS
Marian Jarlenski, Lara Hearnburg Johnson, Tom Whitmire

INTERNS
Rachael Estes, Dyane Fils

HURRICANE STATISTICS
Amanda H. Allen

DISTRICT MAPS
SpatiaLogic Mapping (Charlottesville, Va.), Kimberly Hallock

ONLINE EDITION
Marc Segers, Mary Grace Palumbo, Poya Golriz, Jerry Orvedahl

ACQUISITIONS EDITOR
Margot W. Ziperman

BUSINESS MANAGER
Paul Zurawski

Politics in America

THE 14TH EDITION

As the winds of electoral change swept across the country in the fall of 2006, they prompted a reshuffling of the balance of power in the nation's capital. A newly constituted Democratic Congress, emerging in the final two years of President George W. Bush's tenure, promised to create a political equation different from that of the first six years of the Bush presidency.

While it would be foolhardy to attempt to predict the full impact of this divided government, it's clear that the 535 members of Congress will play a much more central role in determining the nation's course in the next two years than they did in the past six. That fact alone makes this 14th edition of "Politics in America" an essential resource for understanding the key players, issues and politics that will inform our national discourse and public policy making through the 2008 presidential campaign.

The 2006 election also was historic. After winning a majority in the House with 233 seats, Democrats installed the first female Speaker of the House, Nancy Pelosi of California. Pelosi brings energy and a new agenda, along with a smart sense of style, to the leadership role, and early on she did not hesitate to challenge the president, particularly over the war in Iraq. In the Senate, Democrats find themselves with a slim majority (51-49, with two independents who typically side with the Democrats) under the direction of Majority Leader Harry Reid of Nevada. The election also ushered in a large freshman class — 52 new faces in the House and 10 in the Senate.

Already swirling on Capitol Hill are political forces certain to influence the 2008 election. Beyond the war, other perennial factors are in play, among them health care, education, the economy and a handful of hot button social issues. As part of our effort to understand these dynamics, our staffers fanned out across the Capitol for interviews with members of Congress. Our quest: to learn as much as we could about their goals, experiences and perspectives.

Since 1945, Congressional Quarterly, operating at the nexus of politics, legislation and policy, has been an authoritative chronicler of Washington's governmental business. In a city often polarized by extremes, we play it down the middle. We don't say where members of Congress should stand on issues; we simply assess, as nearly as possible, how effective they are at achieving their stated goals. To that end, we carefully examine their public pronouncements, work habits and background.

In 1981, CQ published the first version of "Politics in America," an insider's guide to the people who participate in one of the world's largest democracies. Look inside and you'll find that each lawmaker's section contains an in-depth political profile, key statistics on votes and positions, and a demographic description of the district the member represents.

Day in and day out, CQ's newsroom of more than 130 reporters, editors and researchers brings an unparalleled expertise to the information published in our online news service, CQ.com, and in our many print publications. One change worth noting: This print edition of "Politics in America" is tied closely to an online twin, the Members section of CQ.com. These profiles live on the Web, and, during the next two years, many will be updated to reflect the latest turn of significant events.

Under the editorial direction of Jackie Koszczuk and Martha Angle, we think we have produced the most objective, authoritative, comprehensive and insightful volume of political analysis on the 110th Congress. We trust you'll agree.

Michael Riley
Editor and Senior Vice President
Congressional Quarterly Inc.

A Declaration of Independents

American politics has had its share of voter mood swings over the past quarter-century, each with an identity and a name that quickly entered the vernacular to define the latest agent of change. There were the Reagan Democrats of 1984, the religious right voters of 1988, the Republican "revolutionaries" of 1994 and the soccer moms of 1996. Legions of pollsters, journalists and political candidates analyzed them for their impact on picking winners and losers in national elections.

No longer a sleeping giant, unaligned voters chose Democrats to take charge of Congress. Who will they prefer in 2008?

Now, attention has shifted to another cohort — independent voters. It was their might at the ballot box that handed control of the 110th Congress to the Democrats after a dozen years of Republican rule. For several elections, these voters had neither shown much independence nor behaved as true swing voters. While steadily growing in number, voters who declined to identify with one of the two major political parties actually divided fairly evenly between Republicans and Democrats when casting their ballots. In 2000, about half went for Republican George W. Bush and half for Democrat Al Gore, and it took several months, many lawyers, a national discussion of hanging chads and ultimately the Supreme Court to decide one of the closest presidential contests in U.S. history.

In the next two elections, independent voters, roughly 25 percent of the electorate, remained a sleeping giant. The Sept. 11 attacks drove them in 2002 slightly toward the GOP, the party perceived as more adept at fighting terrorism. But two years later, they again split down the middle between President Bush and Democratic presidential nominee John Kerry.

Then came 2006. By 57 percent to 39 percent, independent voters cast their ballots for Democratic candidates, a 9 percentage point drop for the Republicans from the last midterm election and an assertion of independent-vote power not seen since the Watergate scandal in the 1970s.

Democrats captured six seats in the Senate to secure a bare 51-49 majority when factoring in two independent senators who align with the Democrats. In the House, independent voters turned a comfortable Republican majority into a comfortable Democratic majority; the party balance went from 229-202 (with four vacancies) in the GOP's favor to 233-202 in the Democrats' favor — a real "thumping," as Bush summed up the election.

Democrats held big advantages over Republicans on most of the issues that voters said were important to them, particularly the war in Iraq, concern about the economy and what the Democrats had effectively labeled a "culture of corruption" in the GOP-controlled Congress. "You really have to go back to 1974 to get as great an advantage for a political party among the independents," said Thomas E. Mann, senior fellow at the Brookings Institution. "Independents acted much more like Democrats than Republicans, and that's the story of 2006."

The results had an immediate impact on the 2008 presidential contest. With no incumbent in the running, the race was wide open anyway. Evidence that a large segment of voters was up for grabs — and not simply masking stable party allegiances behind an "independent" registration label — added a new element. Independents were not necessarily going to go to the Democrats again: While the Republicans' standing with the public had plummeted over the previous five years, positive views of the Democrats had also declined, according to the Pew Research Center.

Within a few weeks of the 2006 election, the presidential field was crowded with senators, governors, House members and a former big city mayor, many of them vying to attract the centrists and independents.

About the Editors

Jackie Koszczuk has covered Congress since 1989, when Jim Wright ran the House and George Mitchell led the Senate. She has been both an editor and senior writer for Congressional Quarterly. Earlier, she was a correspondent for the Knight Ridder Washington Bureau and for the Fort Worth Star-Telegram. Born in Chicago, Koszczuk has a degree in communications from Southern Illinois University. She lives in Bethesda, Md., with her husband, Joe Sobczyk, also a journalist, and their two children, Nicholas and Eleanor. This is her third edition of Politics in America.

Martha Angle is Congressional Quarterly's associate editor. She joined the company in 1981 and has held a variety of senior editing positions for its daily, weekly and Web-based publications. She earlier reported on local, state and congressional politics for the Washington Star. A native of Ohio, she graduated from Oberlin College. She is married to fellow journalist Robert M. Walters, and lives in Washington, D.C. Their two daughters, Erica and Dana, are her proudest achievement. Angle wrote for the first Politics in America in 1982. This is her fourteenth edition.

On the Republican side, Sen. John McCain of Arizona was back to try to revive the maverick feel of his 2000 campaign, and former New York Mayor Rudy Giuliani was running on the national reputation he built with his response to Sept. 11. On the Democratic side, freshman Sen. Barack Obama of Illinois, a national unknown before a rousing speech at the 2004 party convention, entered the contest even though New York Sen. Hillary Rodham Clinton, the former first lady, was months ahead of him in organizing, fundraising and visits to early primary states. He pitched his appeal directly to voters yearning for a third way.

In spite of the hoopla surrounding their takeover of Congress, Democrats had to sustain their momentum into 2008 if they were to reset the policy agenda. After all, the White House was still in GOP hands, and though the Democrats controlled the House by a healthy margin of 31 seats, their hold on the Senate was tenuous. The death or resignation of one senator would send them back to the minority, and Republicans had sufficient votes to sustain filibusters and stop bills they opposed. Bush, who vetoed only one bill in his first six years as president, threatened to invoke his power liberally against Democratic bills that did manage to get to his desk.

SUCCESSFUL CENTRISTS

The Democrats in 2006 scored most of their victories by touting centrist positions and successfully dodging the previously fatal "liberal" label applied by Republicans. Unlike the GOP "revolutionaries" a dozen years earlier, they were not unified by a single agenda or pronounced ideology. Many were moderate or conservative Democrats.

Typical of the newcomers was county Sheriff Brad Ellsworth in Indiana, who defeated conservative Republican Rep. John Hostettler by emphasizing his opposition to abortion and gun control. Democratic senators who toppled conservative GOP incumbents displayed notable independence from liberal orthodoxy. Sens. Jim Webb of Virginia, Jon Tester of Montana and Claire McCaskill of Missouri went their own way on budget issues in the first part of the 110th Congress.

Like other large freshman classes elected in times of voter discontent, many in the Class of 2006 began their terms focused on congressional ethics. A few had knocked off powerful incumbents by capitalizing on the anti-corruption theme, including Jerry McNerney, a wind turbine company owner, who toppled California Republican Richard W. Pombo, the chairman of the House Resources Committee.

Democratic challengers also succeeded by reminding voters of Bush administration policies they didn't like. In a Florida district packed with senior citizens, state Sen. Ron Klein unseated veteran Republican Rep. E. Clay Shaw Jr. by focusing on Shaw's support for Bush's unsuccessful proposal to partially privatize the Social Security program.

The Democratic newcomers also had an "outsider" bent reminiscent of the Class of 1994, when Republicans took control of the House after being out of power for four decades. Nineteen of the 38 Democrats sworn in for the first time in January 2007 had never before held political office. The group included a social worker, an allergist, two college professors and a publisher of an alternative newspaper. Celebrities joining Congress for the 110th included former professional football quarterback Heath Shuler and former pop singer John Hall.

THE NEW CONGRESS

The 110th Congress made history by electing a woman as Speaker of the House. Nancy Pelosi of California became the highest-ranking woman in the U.S. government and the highest-ranking female elected official in

American history. Her elevation was part of a pattern of steady, but slow expansion in the power of women and minorities on Capitol Hill. In spite of Pelosi's historic first, the membership of the House and Senate continued to look much as it always had: white, middle-aged, well-educated, wealthy and male.

There were 74 women in the House (including three delegates) and 16 in the Senate, eight more than at the start of the 109th Congress. They constituted just 17 percent of the total membership, far short of their 51 percent share of U.S. population.

The numerical strength of African-Americans and Hispanics in Congress was essentially unchanged. The number of African-American lawmakers, at 41, was the same as in the previous Congress, and there were 26 Hispanics, one more than before.

The Democratic victory did yield an increase in clout for African-Americans in the House, however. Rep. James E. Clyburn of South Carolina was chosen majority whip, the No. 3 post in the leadership, and five black lawmakers claimed committee chairmanships in 2007, although one of them, California's Juanita Millender-McDonald, died of cancer a few months later.

There were a couple firsts in religious diversity. The Class of 2006 included the first Muslim congressman, Keith Ellison, an African-American from Minnesota, and the first two Buddhists, Democrats Mazie K. Hirono of Hawaii, who is Asian-American, and Hank Johnson of Georgia, who is black. The number of Jewish members increased to 30 in the House, up from 26 two years earlier, and to 13 in the Senate, two more than before.

One trend had no regard for gender, race or ethnicity. With advances in medicine and healthful changes in lifestyle, Congress got grayer. The average age of senators at the start of the 110th Congress was just under 62, breaking the record set in the previous Congress by about 18 months. The average age of House members was 56, a full year older.

Four of the seven longest-serving senators in U.S. history were members of the 110th Congress. The oldest of this group is also the longest-serving: West Virginia Democrat Robert C. Byrd won a record ninth six-year term in 2006, two weeks before his 89th birthday.

As Congress got under way, the overriding issue was the war in Iraq, with newly empowered Democrats intent on ending it expeditiously and Bush and the Republican minority looking for a possible path to victory.

But coming on strong was the economy, as an inchoate anxiety about the country's economic health took hold despite relatively low unemployment and a robust stock market. The Pew Center and other polling agents were tracking an increasing number of Americans who felt uneasy about the widening gap between rich and poor.

Tax policy had been predictable while the GOP controlled both the White House and Congress: The more tax cuts the better. Democrats were groping for a substitute to that approach. But the return of large annual deficits in the first half of the decade gave them little room to maneuver on tax and spending issues. Addressing the ever-climbing costs that permeate the health care system and covering the millions of Americans who lack insurance were priorities for the Democrats, though ones with no easy solutions.

Like the dog that chased the car, Democrats were confronted with potential consequences of their successful pursuit of power. Factor in a restive electorate that might not be willing to split the difference between the two political parties any longer, and politics in America in 2008 was shaping up to be interesting indeed.

Jackie Koszczuk
April 2007

As the 110th Congress got under way, the biggest issue by far was the war in Iraq. Democrats wanted to end it; President Bush looked for a path to victory.

Table of Contents

KENTUCKY

LOUISIANA

MAINE

MARYLAND

MASSACHUSETTS

MICHIGAN

MINNESOTA

MISSISSIPPI

MISSOURI

MONTANA

NEBRASKA

NEVADA

NEW HAMPSHIRE

NEW JERSEY

NEW MEXICO

NEW YORK

NORTH CAROLINA

NORTH DAKOTA

OHIO

OKLAHOMA

OREGON

PENNSYLVANIA

PUERTO RICO

RHODE ISLAND

SOUTH CAROLINA

SOUTH DAKOTA

TENNESSEE

TEXAS

UTAH

VERMONT

VIRGIN ISLANDS

VIRGINIA

WASHINGTON

WEST VIRGINIA

WISCONSIN

WYOMING

MEMBER STATISTICS

ELECTIONS

CAMPAIGN FINANCE

COMMITTEES

MEMBER NAME INDEX

Explanation of Statistics

State Profiles

State profile pages contain information on governors, compositions of state legislatures and information about major cities. Information on state legislatures reflects their status as of April 2007. Details about the makeup of the state legislatures, salaries of members, the legislative schedule, registered voters and state term limits were obtained from state officials.

POPULATION AND URBAN STATISTICS

Demographic information for each state and congressional district was obtained from the U.S. Census Bureau and the Bureau of Economic Analysis, both within the Department of Commerce.

On the state pages, violent crime rates are from 2000. The poverty rate is from 1999. Federal workers and military personnel statistics are from 2001.

STATISTICS BY DISTRICT

The tables include the popular vote for the major candidates for president in 2004 in each congressional district. The totals have been calculated to reflect the results within the House district lines in effect for the 2006 election (for the 110th Congress). Greg Giroux of Congressional Quarterly calculated the election results for 36 states. Calculations by state election officials were used for seven states — Connecticut, Georgia, Maine, Minnesota, Nebraska, Texas and Virginia. The remaining seven states have only one House seat.

Demographic information relates to current district lines, including districts in Georgia and Texas whose reconfigured borders did not take effect until the 2006 election.

The figures for racial composition, Hispanic origin, median household income, types of employment, age, education, urban vs. rural residence and size of each congressional district are from the Census Bureau.

The racial composition figures reflect census respondents who described themselves as of one race. The white population figure is for non-Hispanic whites. The median household income figure is for 1999.

The occupational breakdown combines figures from the Census Bureau's management, professional and relations occupations category and its sales and office occupations category to make up the white-collar category we have presented. The blue-collar category includes three Census Bureau categories: farming, fishing and forestry; construction, extraction and maintenance; and production, transportation and material moving occupations.

The college education table shows the percentage of people, age 25 and older, who have completed at least a bachelor's degree. The district's area is presented in square miles of land area.

District Descriptions

In most states, congressional district lines were redrawn in 2001 or 2002 to reflect reapportionment and changes in population patterns revealed in the 2000 census. Maine's constitution calls for redistricting in the third year of each decade and so new lines were drawn in 2003 for the 2004 election. Other mid-decade changes were in response to legal challenges.

A second set of Pennsylvania district lines drawn in 2002 was not effective until the 2004 election. Georgia districts were reconfigured in 2005 for the 2006 election. Texas had five districts — the 15th, 21st, 23rd, 25th and 28th — redrawn by a federal court for the 2006 election.

The district description briefly sets forth the economic, sociological, demographic and political forces that are the keys to elections and that influence

Presidential Vote by District

CQ determined the 2004 presidential vote in each House district by acquiring and recalculating vote returns from state and county election offices in the 43 states that have more than one House district. In seven of those states — Connecticut, Georgia, Maine, Minnesota, Nebraska, Texas and Virginia — CQ used the presidential district vote calculations produced by state election officials. Seven states — Alaska, Delaware, Montana, North Dakota, South Dakota, Vermont and Wyoming — have only one House district.

Key to Party Abbreviations

ABC	Anti-Bushist
AC	American Constitution
AIV	An Independent Voice
AKI	Alaskan Independence
AM	American
AMH	American Heritage
AMI	American Independent
AMP	The American Party
AND	A New Direction
C	Conservative
CC	Concerned Citizens
CFL	Connecticut for Lieberman
CNSTP	Constitution
D	Democratic
DG	Desert Greens
DIS	Diversity is Strength
ENC	Education Not Corruption
FDM	Freedom Party
GR	Grassroots
GREEN	Green
I	Independent
IA	Independent American
IBN	Impeach Bush Now
IGWT	In God We Trust
IGREEN	Independent Green
IMP	Impeach Now!
INDC	Independence
IMC	Independent Maine Course
LIBERT	Libertarian
LMP	Legalize Marijuana
LU	Liberty Union
MC	The Moderate Choice
MOUNT	Mountain
NEB	Nebraska
NJC	New Jersey Conservative Party
NL	Natural Law
NP	New Progressive

continued on next page

the legislative agenda of the district's member of Congress. City population figures are from the U.S. Census Bureau. Additional information on hurricane-affected districts begins on page xxiii.

Military base figures are compiled by CQ from information provided by each base. Military base listings do not include Coast Guard, National Guard or reserve bases, and do not include all depots and arsenals because of space limitations.

Member Profiles

Committees

Standing and select committee assignments as of April 2007 are listed for Senate and House members, as are assignments to major joint committees. Full committee and subcommittee chairmanships are noted.

A complete roster of committee and subcommittee assignments is in the back of the book.

Career and Political Highlights

The member's principal occupations before becoming a full-time public official are given, with the most recent occupation listed first. Often, the political offices listed were part-time jobs and the member continued working at his or her "career" job. Where available, the member's college major is given. Political highlights listed include elected positions in government, high party posts, posts requiring legislative confirmation and unsuccessful candidacies for public office. Dates given cover years of service, not election dates.

Elections

General election returns for 2004 and 2006 are listed for House members, with primary results for 2006 as well. For senators and governors, the most recent election results are listed in detail. Returns do not include candidates who received less than 1 percent of the vote. Because percentages have been rounded and some minor candidates have been excluded, election results do not always add up to 100 percent.

Earlier election victories are noted for members of the House and Senate, with the member's percentage of the vote given. If no percentage is given for a year, the member either did not run or lost the election.

For special elections and primaries where a candidate would have won outright if he or she had received a majority of the votes, two election tallies are given, one for the initial election and one for the subsequent runoff.

PRIMARY ELECTIONS

Louisiana holds its primary on Election Day. It is an open primary, with candidates from all parties on the ballot. Any candidate who receives more than half the votes, or who is unopposed, is elected. If no candidate receives an outright majority, the top two vote-getters, regardless of party, advance to a runoff election later.

Key Votes

Profiles of members who served in the 109th Congress (2005-06) are accompanied by a sampling of key votes chosen by CQ editors from that Congress.

The following vote descriptions provide the vote number, bill number, a brief summary of the matter being voted on, a breakdown of the vote, the date of the vote and President Bush's position on that particular vote, if he unambiguously took one beforehand.

continued from previous page

PAC	Politicians Are Crooks
PACGRN	Pacific Green
PC	Personal Choice
PFP	Peace and Freedom
PGS	Preserve Green Space
PIR	Pirate
PLC	Pro Life Conservative
POP	Populist
POPDEM	Popular Democratic
PPC	Poor People's Campaign
PRI	Puerto Rican Independence
PRO	Progressive
QRT	Quit Raising Taxes
R	Republican
REF	Reform
RMN	Remove Medical Negligence
RTH	Rent is too High
S	Socialist
SE	Socialist Equality
SOL	Solidarity
SW	Socialist Workers
TPM	The Patriot Movement
UNT	Unity
USTAX	U.S. Taxpayers
VGE	Vermont Green
VL	Vermont Localist
WFM	Working Families
WG	Wisconsin Greens
WTN	Withdraw Troops Now
WTP	We The People
X	Not applicable

Key Votes

CQ editors selected key votes from roll-call votes taken during the 109th Congress. The following symbols are used:

- Y voted for (yes)
- N voted against (no)
- # paired for
- + announced for
- X paired against
- – announced against
- P voted "present"
- C voted "present" to avoid possible conflict of interest
- ? did not vote or otherwise make a position known
- I ineligible
- S Speaker exercised his discretion to not vote

Senate Key Votes

2006

Confirm Samuel A. Alito Jr. to the Supreme Court (Senate Vote 2): Confirmation of President Bush's nomination of Samuel A. Alito Jr. of New Jersey to be an associate justice of the U.S. Supreme Court. A yes was a vote in support of the president's position. Confirmed 58-42: R 54-1; D 4-40; I 0-1. Jan. 31, 2006.

Allow consideration of a bill to establish a $140 billion trust fund to compensate victims of asbestos exposure (Senate Vote 21): Specter, R-Pa., motion to waive the Budget Act with respect to the Ensign, R-Nev., point of order against the bill (S 852) that would establish a $140 billion trust fund to compensate victims of asbestos exposure. A three-fifths majority vote (60) of the total Senate is required to waive the Budget Act. (Subsequently, the chair upheld the point of order, and the bill was recommitted to the Judiciary Committee.) Motion rejected 58-41: R 44-11; D 13-30; I 1-0. Feb. 14, 2006.

Extend tax cuts for two years at a cost of $70 billion over five years (Senate Vote 118): Adoption of the conference report on the bill (HR 4297) that would extend about $70 billion in tax cuts over a five-year period. Reduced tax rates on capital gains and dividends would be extended through 2010. It would extend through 2009 a tax provision that allows small businesses to write off up to $100,000 in depreciable assets in the year they are made. It would extend and increase alternative minimum tax exemption amounts for 2006 of $62,550 for a joint return, $42,500 for individuals, and $31,275 for married individuals who file separate returns. A yes was a vote in support of the president's position. Adopted (thus cleared for the president) 54-44: R 51-3; D 3-40; I 0-1. May 11, 2006.

Overhaul immigration policy with border security, enforcement and guest worker program (Senate Vote 157): Passage of the bill (S 2611) that would overhaul U.S. immigration policies and offer a path to citizenship for most illegal immigrants in the country. It would subdivide illegal immigrants into three groups based on how long they had been in the United States. Illegal immigrants in the country more than five years would be able to stay and earn citizenship; those here between two and five years would have three years to file paperwork for a temporary work visa, after which they would be eligible for permanent legal residency; and those here less than two years would have to return to their native country and go through normal channels if they want to return. It would create a guest worker program that could accommodate an additional 200,000 immigrants a year. It also would authorize increased border security and enforcement provisions, including a requirement for businesses to verify documents of all prospective employees through an electronic system managed by the Department of Homeland Security. A yes was a vote in support of the president's position. Passed 62-36: R 23-32; D 38-4; I 1-0. May 25, 2006.

Allow consideration of a bill to permanently repeal the estate tax (Senate Vote 164): Motion to invoke cloture (thus limiting debate) on the motion to proceed to a bill (HR 8) that would permanently repeal the estate tax. Three-fifths of the total Senate (60) is required to invoke cloture. A yes was a vote in support of the president's position. Motion rejected 57-41: R 53-2; D 4-38; I 0-1. June 8, 2006.

Urge President Bush to begin troop withdrawals from Iraq in 2006 (Senate Vote 182): Levin, D-Mich., amendment to HR 2766 that would express the sense of Congress that the president should begin phased redeployment of U.S. troops from Iraq starting in 2006 and submit to Congress by the end of 2006 a plan with estimated dates for continued phased withdrawal. Rejected 39-60: R 1-54; D 37-6 ; I 1-0. June 22, 2006.

Lift President Bush's restrictions on stem cell research funding (Senate Vote 206): Passage of the bill (HR 810) that would allow the use of federal funds in research on embryonic stem cell lines derived from surplus embryos at invitro fertilization clinics, but only if donors give their consent and are not paid for the embryos. The bill would require the Health and Human Services Department to conduct and support research involving human embryonic stem cells that meet certain criteria, regardless of when stem cells were derived from a human embryo. By unanimous consent, the Senate agreed to raise the majority requirement for passage of the bill to 60 votes. A no was a vote in support of the president's position. Passed (thus cleared for the president) 63-37: R 19-36; D 43-1; I 1-0. July 18, 2006.

Authorize military tribunals for suspected terrorists (Senate Vote 259): Passage of the bill (S 3930) that would authorize military tribunals to try detainees designated as unlawful enemy combatants, defined as a person who has "engaged in hostilities or who has purposefully and materially supported hostilities against the United States" in the war on terror. Cases in which the accused is found guilty would be reviewed by a new Court of Military Commission Review. It also would allow prisoners to contest their classification as enemy combatants. It would eliminate habeas corpus rights retroactive to Sept. 11, 2001. The legislation would allow for the use of some coerced testimony and evidence seized without a warrant. Evidence obtained through torture could not be used. Classified evidence, including the sources and methods used to acquire it, would not be disclosed if it would be detrimental to national security. A yes was a vote in support of the president's position. Passed 65-34: R 53-1; D 12-32; I 0-1. Sept. 28, 2006.

2005

Curb class action lawsuits by shifting them from state to federal courts (Senate Vote 9): Passage of the bill (S 5) that would give federal courts jurisdiction over class action cases involving at least 100 plaintiffs if at least $5 million was at stake and two-thirds of the plaintiffs lived in different states. It would require judges to review all non-cash settlements, such as coupons for goods and services, and limit attorney's fees paid in such settlements. It also would prohibit federal judges from approving a net loss settlement without finding that the loss is outweighed by non-monetary benefits. A yes was a vote in support of the president's position. Passed 72-26: R 53-0; D 18-26; I 1-0. Feb. 10, 2005.

Allow confirmation vote on Priscilla R. Owen to the U.S. Court of Appeals for the 5th Circuit (Senate Vote 127): Motion to invoke cloture (thus limiting debate) on President Bush's nomination of Priscilla R. Owen of Texas to be a judge for the U.S. Court of Appeals for the 5th Circuit. Three-fifths of the total Senate (60) is required to invoke cloture. Motion agreed to 81-18: R 55-0; D 26-17; I 0-1. May 24, 2005.

Oppose mandatory emissions limits and block recognition of global warming as a threat (Senate Vote 149): Inhofe, R-Okla., motion to table (kill) the Bingaman, D-N.M., amendment to HR 6 that would express the sense of the Senate that Congress should enact a national program of mandatory, market-based limits and incentives on greenhouse gas emissions that slow, stop and reverse their growth at a rate that would not harm the economy, and would encourage comparable action by other nations. Subsequently, the amendment was adopted by voice vote. A yes was a vote in support of the president's position. Motion rejected 44-53: R 42-12; D 2-40; I 0-1. June 22, 2005.

Approve free-trade pact with five Central American countries (Senate Vote 170): Passage of the bill (S 1370) that would implement a

Key Votes

CQ editors selected key votes from roll-call votes taken during the 109th Congress. The following symbols are used:

- Y voted for (yes)
- N voted against (no)
- # paired for
- + announced for
- X paired against
- – announced against
- P voted "present"
- C voted "present" to avoid possible conflict of interest
- ? did not vote or otherwise make a position known
- I ineligible
- S Speaker exercised his discretion to not vote

free-trade agreement between the United States and Costa Rica, El Salvador, Guatemala, Honduras and Nicaragua and a separate pact with the Dominican Republic. It also would eliminate customs duties on all originating goods traded among the participating nations within 10 days. A yes was a vote in support of the president's position. Passed 54-45: R 43-12; D 10-33; I 1-0. June 30, 2005.

Pass energy policy overhaul favored by President Bush emphasizing domestic oil and gas production (Senate Vote 213): Adoption of the conference report on the bill (HR 6) that would overhaul the nation's energy policy and provide for $14.6 billion in energy-related tax incentives. It would allow lawsuits involving the gasoline additive methyl tertiary butyl ether (MTBE) to be moved to a federal district court and require refiners to use annually 7.5 billion gallons of renewable fuels by 2012. It would grant the Federal Energy Regulatory Commission jurisdiction over reliability standards for electricity transmission networks and extend daylight-saving time by one month. It would allow the Federal Energy Regulatory Commission to approve the construction, expansion or operation of any facility that imports or processes natural gas, including liquefied natural gas. A yes was a vote in support of the president's position. Adopted (thus cleared for the president) 74-26: R 49-6; D 25-19; I 0-1. July 29, 2005.

Shield gunmakers from lawsuits when their products are used in crimes (Senate Vote 219): Passage of the bill (S 397) that would bar certain civil lawsuits against manufacturers, distributors, dealers and importers of firearms and ammunition, principally those lawsuits aimed at making them liable for gun violence. Trade groups also would be protected, and all pending legal action against gunmakers would be dismissed. It also would, with certain exceptions, make it unlawful for licensed gun importers, manufacturers or dealers to sell, deliver or transfer handguns without a secure gun storage or safety device. As amended, it would establish penalties for non-compliance, including a six-month suspension of a license, the revocation of a license, or a $2,500 fine. It would require the attorney general to commission a study on the feasibility of uniform standards for the testing of projectiles against body armor. Penalties for violent or drug trafficking crimes in which the perpetrator uses or possesses armor-piercing ammunition would be increased to a minimum of 15 years imprisonment. If death resulted from the use of such ammunition, a person could be imprisoned up to life or face the death penalty. A yes was a vote in support of the president's position. Passed 65-31: R 50-2; D 14-29; I 1-0. July 29, 2005.

Ban torture of prisoners in U.S. custody (Senate Vote 249): McCain, R-Ariz., amendment to HR 2863 that would establish the U.S. Army Field Manual on Intelligence Interrogation as the uniform standard for interrogating persons detained by the Department of Defense, and prohibit cruel, inhumane or degrading treatment of any prisoner detained by the U.S. government. A no was a vote in support of the president's position. Adopted 90-9: R 46-9; D 43-0; I 1-0. Oct. 5, 2005.

Renew 16 provisions of the Patriot Act (Senate Vote 358): Motion to invoke cloture (thus limiting debate) on the conference report on the bill that would reauthorize the law known as the Patriot Act, and make permanent 14 of the 16 provisions of the act set to expire at the end of the year, and extend for four years the two provisions on access to business and other records and "roving" wiretaps. Three-fifths of the total Senate (60) is required to invoke cloture. A yes was a vote in support of the president's position. Motion rejected 52-47: R 50-5; D 2-41; I 0-1. Dec. 16, 2005.

Allow final vote on opening the Arctic National Wildlife Refuge to oil and gas exploration (Senate Vote 364): Motion to invoke cloture (thus limiting debate) on the conference report on the bill (HR 2863) that would appropriate $453.5 billion for Defense spending in fiscal 2006, including $50 billion for operations in Iraq and Afghanistan. It also would require a 1 percent across-the-board cut to all fiscal 2006 discretionary spending except Veterans Administration funding that was added to the legislation. It would provide $29 billion for disaster assistance to hurricane-damaged areas and $3.8 billion for flu preparedness. It would allow oil and gas leasing in the Arctic National Wildlife Refuge. Three-fifths of the total Senate (60) is required to invoke cloture. A yes was a vote in support of the president's position. Motion rejected 56-44: R 52-3; D 4-40; I 0-1. Dec. 21, 2005.

House Key Votes

2006

Stop broadband companies from favoring select Internet traffic (House Vote 239): Markey, D-Mass., amendment to HR 5252 that would establish network neutrality requirements for broadband providers, including the duty to not block, impair, degrade or discriminate against lawful content, applications or services; to operate its network in a non-discriminatory manner; and to offer all providers equal prioritization of data of a set type if such priority is offered to any one provider. A no was a vote in support of the president's position. Rejected 152-269: R 11-211; D 140-58; I 1-0. June 8, 2006.

Affirm U.S. commitment to war in Iraq and reject setting a withdrawal date for troops (House Vote 288): Adoption of the resolution (H Res 861) that would declare it is not in the national security interest of the United States to set an arbitrary date for the withdrawal or redeployment of U.S. armed forces from Iraq and affirm U.S. commitment to establishing democracy in Iraq. It also would honor Americans taking an active part in the war on terrorism and the sacrifices of the U.S. armed forces who have died or been wounded. The resolution would congratulate Prime Minister Nuri Al-Maliki and the Iraqi people for the formation of their new government. A yes was a vote in support of the president's position. Adopted 256-153: R 214-3; D 42-149; I 0-1. June 16, 2006.

Repeal requirement for bilingual ballots at the polls (House Vote 372): King, R-Iowa, amendment that would strike a provision in the bill (HR 9) that would reauthorize, for 25 years, the requirement that states provide bilingual voting assistance as well as the use of American Community Survey census data. Rejected 185-238: R 181-44; D 4-193; I 0-1. July 13, 2006.

Permit U.S. sale of civilian nuclear technology to India (House Vote 411): Passage of the bill (HR 5682) that would permit the president to waive certain provisions of the Atomic Energy Act of 1954 to seek congressional approval for civilian nuclear cooperation agreements with India if the president makes certain determinations, including that India would provide the United States and the International Atomic Energy Agency with a plan to separate civilian and military nuclear facilities and programs. The bill would require a joint resolution of approval by Congress for a nuclear cooperation agreement with India to enforce the agreement. A yes was a vote in favor of the president's position. Passed 359-68: R 219-9; D 140-58; I 0-1. July 26, 2006.

Build a 700-mile fence on the U.S.-Mexico border to curb illegal crossings (House Vote 446): Passage of the bill (HR 6061) that would require the Homeland Security Department to prevent the entry of terrorists, unlawful aliens, instruments of terrorism, narcotics, and other contraband along the nation's international borders. It would authorize the construction of approximately 700 miles of fencing along the U.S.-Mexico bor-

Key Votes

CQ editors selected key votes from roll-call votes taken during the 109th Congress. The following symbols are used:

- Y voted for (yes)
- N voted against (no)
- # paired for
- + announced for
- X paired against
- – announced against
- P voted "present"
- C voted "present" to avoid possible conflict of interest
- ? did not vote or otherwise make a position known
- I ineligible
- S Speaker exercised his discretion to not vote

der. The bill would require a study of implementing security systems along the U.S.-Canada border and direct the agency to evaluate the ability of personnel to stop fleeing vehicles at the border. Passed 283-138: R 219-6; D 64-131; I 0-1. Sept. 4, 2006.

Permit warrantless wiretaps of suspected terrorists (House Vote 502): Passage of the bill (HR 5825) that would authorize electronic surveillance of communications by suspected terrorists for specified periods without first obtaining approval from the secret court established by the 1978 Foreign Intelligence Surveillance Act (FISA). Warrantless surveillance could be conducted for up to 90 days if an armed or terrorist attack against the United States has occurred, or if there is an "imminent threat." The president would have to notify congressional Intelligence committees and the FISA court of such surveillance. The bill would extend to seven days the time intelligence agencies can conduct warrantless electronic surveillance in "emergency situations" before seeking FISA court approval. A yes was a vote in support of the president's position. Passed 232-191: R 214-13; D 18-177; I 0-1. Sept. 28, 2006.

2005

Intervene in the life-support case of Terri Schiavo (House Vote 90): Sensenbrenner, R-Wis., motion to suspend the rules and pass the bill (S 686) that would give the parents of Theresa Marie Schiavo, a severely brain-damaged Florida woman, the right to file a lawsuit in the U.S. District Court for the Middle District of Florida alleging that Schiavo's rights related to life-sustaining medical treatment have been violated under the Constitution or federal law. A two-thirds majority of those present and voting (174 in this case) is required for passage under suspension of the rules. Motion agreed to (thus clearing the bill for the president) 203-58: R 156-5; D 47-53; I 0-0. March 21, 2005.

Lift President Bush's restrictions on stem cell research funding (House Vote 204): Passage of the bill (HR 810)that would allow the use of federal funds in research on embryonic stem cell lines derived from surplus embryos at invitro fertilization clinics, but only if donors give their consent and are not paid for the embryos. The bill would authorize the Health and Human Services Department to conduct and support research involving human embryonic stem cells that meet certain criteria, regardless of when stem cells were derived from a human embryo. A no was a vote in support of the president's position. Passed 238-194: R 50-180; D 187-14; I 1-0. May 24, 2005.

Prohibit FBI access to library and bookstore records (House Vote 258): Sanders, I-Vt., amendment to HR 2862 that would prohibit the use of funds in the bill to make an application under the Foreign Intelligence Surveillance Act to acquire library circulation records, library patron lists, bookseller sales records or bookseller customer lists. A no was a vote in support of the president's position. Adopted 238-187: R 38-186; D 199-1; I 1-0. June 15, 2005.

Approve free-trade pact with five Central American countries (House Vote 443): Passage of the bill (HR 3045) that would implement a free-trade agreement between the United States and Costa Rica, El Salvador, Guatemala, Honduras and Nicaragua and a separate pact with the Dominican Republic. A yes was a vote in support of the president's position. Passed 217-215: R 202-27; D 15-187; I 0-1. July 28, 2005.

Pass energy policy overhaul favored by President Bush emphasizing domestic oil and gas production (House Vote 445): Adoption of the conference report on the bill (HR 6) that would overhaul the nation's energy policy and provide for $14.6 billion in energy-related tax incentives.

It would allow lawsuits involving the gasoline additive methyl tertiary butyl ether (MTBE) to be moved to a federal district court and require refiners to use annually 7.5 billion gallons of renewable fuels by 2012. The measure would grant the Federal Energy Regulatory Commission jurisdiction over reliability standards for electricity transmission networks and extend daylight-saving time by one month. It would allow the Federal Energy Regulatory Commission to approve the construction, expansion or operation of any facility that imports or processes natural gas, including liquefied natural gas. A yes was a vote in support of the president's position. Adopted (thus sent to the Senate) 275-156: R 200-31; D 75-124; I 0-1. July 28, 2005.

End mandatory preservation of habitat of endangered animal and plant species (House Vote 506): Passage of the bill (HR 3824) that would overhaul and reauthorize the Endangered Species Act through 2010. It would replace the critical habitat designation with expanded authority to develop recovery plans for species that take into account areas of "special value" in conserving an endangered or threatened species. The Interior Department would be required to reimburse landowners who are not allowed to develop their land because of protections for endangered species. It also would authorize grants for private landowners to protect endangered species. Passed 229-193: R 193-34; D 36-158 ; I 0-1. Sept. 29, 2005.

Ban torture of prisoners in U.S. custody (House Vote 630): Murtha, D-Pa., motion to instruct House conferees to include Senate-passed language in the fiscal 2006 Defense appropriations bill (HR 2863) that would establish the U.S. Army Field Manual on Intelligence Interrogation as the uniform standard for interrogating persons detained by the Defense Department, and prohibit cruel, inhumane or degrading treatment of any prisoner detained by the U.S. government. A no was a vote in support of the president's position. Motion agreed to 308-122: R 107-121; D 200-1; I 1-0. Dec. 14, 2005.

Vote Studies

Each year, Congressional Quarterly studies the frequency with which each member of Congress supports or opposes a given position. For example, a score of 25 percent under the support column in the presidential support study would indicate that the member supported the president 25 percent of the time on the votes that were used in the study. Scores are based only on votes cast; failure to vote does not alter a member's score, and all votes have equal statistical weight in the analysis. An explanation of each of the vote studies follows.

PARTY UNITY

Party unity votes are defined as votes in the Senate and House that split the parties, a majority of voting Democrats opposing a majority of voting Republicans. Votes on which the parties agree, or on which either party divides evenly, are excluded. Party unity scores represent the percentage of party unity votes on which a member voted yes or no in agreement with a majority of the member's party. Opposition-to-party scores represent the percentage of party unity votes on which a member voted yes or no in disagreement with a majority of the member's party. The score is based only on votes cast; failure to vote did not alter a member's score. All votes have equal statistical weight in the analysis.

PRESIDENTIAL SUPPORT

CQ tries to determine what the president personally, as distinct from other administration officials, does and does not want in the way of legislative action. This is done by analyzing his messages to Congress, news conference remarks and other public statements and documents.

Congress by its Numbers

A new Congress is elected in each even-numbered year and convenes at the beginning of each odd-numbered year. As a shorthand, this book frequently refers to the actions of a particular Congress by its number. The sequence began with the 1st Congress, which was elected in 1788.

	Elected:	Met in:
110th Congress	2006	2007 and 2008
109th Congress	2004	2005 and 2006
108th Congress	2002	2003 and 2004
107th Congress	2000	2001 and 2002
106th Congress	1998	1999 and 2000
105th Congress	1996	1997 and 1998
104th Congress	1994	1995 and 1996
103rd Congress	1992	1993 and 1994
102nd Congress	1990	1991 and 1992
101st Congress	1988	1989 and 1990
100th Congress	1986	1987 and 1988
99th Congress	1984	1985 and 1986

Occasionally, important measures are so extensively amended that it is impossible to characterize final passage as a victory or a defeat for the president. These votes have been excluded from the study. Votes on motions to recommit, to reconsider or to table (kill) often are key tests that govern the outcome. Such votes are included in the presidential support tabulations.

The score is based only on votes cast; failure to vote did not lower a member's score. All votes have equal statistical weight in the analysis.

Interest Group Ratings

Ratings for members of Congress by four advocacy groups are chosen to represent liberal, conservative, business and labor viewpoints. Following is a description of each group in the order they appear.

AMERICAN FEDERATION OF LABOR-CONGRESS OF INDUSTRIAL ORGANIZATIONS (AFL-CIO)

The AFL-CIO was formed when the American Federation of Labor and the Congress of Industrial Organizations merged in 1955. With affiliates claiming roughly 10 million members, the AFL-CIO accounts for about two-thirds of national union membership. For senators, the ratings are based on seven votes in 1997, eight in 1998, nine in 1999, eight in 2000, 16 in 2001, 13 in 2002 and 2003, 12 in 2004, 14 in 2005 and 15 in 2006. For members of the House, the ratings are based on nine votes in 2002, 16 in 2003, 15 in 2004 and 2005 and 14 in 2006. (www.aflcio.org)

AMERICANS FOR DEMOCRATIC ACTION (ADA)

Americans for Democratic Action was founded in 1947 by a group of liberal Democrats that included Minnesota Sen. Hubert H. Humphrey and Eleanor Roosevelt. The ADA ratings are based on 20 votes each year in each chamber of Congress. (www.adaction.org)

CHAMBER OF COMMERCE OF THE UNITED STATES (CCUS)

The Chamber of Commerce of the United States represents local, regional and state chambers as well as trade and professional organizations. It was founded in 1912 to be "a voice for organized business." For senators, the ratings are based on 18 votes in 1998, 17 in 1999, 15 in 2000, 14 in 2001, 20 in 2002, 23 in 2003, 17 in 2004, 18 in 2005 and 12 in 2006. For members of the House, the ratings are based on 20 votes in 2002, 30 in 2003, 21 in 2004, 27 in 2005 and 15 in 2006. (www.uschamber.com)

AMERICAN CONSERVATIVE UNION (ACU)

The American Conservative Union was founded in 1964 "to mobilize resources of responsible conservative thought across the country and further the general cause of conservatism." The organization intends to provide education in political activity, "prejudice in the press," foreign and military policy, domestic economic policy, the arts, professions and sciences. For senators, the ratings are based on 24 votes in 1997, 25 in 1998, 1999 and 2000, 24 in 2001, 20 in 2002, 19 in 2003, 25 in 2004, 2005 and 2006. For members of the House, the ratings are based on 25 votes each year, except for 24 votes in 2003. (www.conservative.org)

Hurricane Statistics

The annual hurricane season, which runs from June through November, set records in 2005 for the sheer number of hurricanes and the intensity of several of them. The most devastating, by far, was Hurricane Katrina in late August, which laid waste to the Gulf Coast in southeastern Louisiana, Mississippi and Alabama. Hurricane Rita followed a month later, slamming Louisiana and parts of Texas. Other storms — Arlene, Cindy, Dennis, Ophelia, Tammy and Wilma — did significant but lesser damage to Florida, North Carolina and other areas.

Nothing compared with Katrina, which made its initial landfall south of Fort Lauderdale, Fla., on Aug. 25, 2005, then crossed Florida and the Gulf of Mexico, hitting peak Category 5 intensity over water before making new landfalls Aug. 29 as a Category 3 hurricane — first in Plaquemines Parish, La., and then in Hancock County, Miss. By the time the winds ended and the rains stopped, huge sections of New Orleans and its suburbs were under water. Hundreds of homes, hotels, restaurants, casinos and other businesses in Gulfport, Biloxi, and Pascagoula, Miss., were gone. More than a thousand people had lost their lives and hundreds of thousands of people had fled, taking refuge in other parts of their home states, in Texas, and elsewhere across the country. The storm decimated crops, forests and the seafood industry. Tourism, an economic mainstay, came to a halt. Government aid was excruciatingly slow and uneven, payments from private insurers were often denied, and rebuilding efforts lagged, especially in Louisiana.

Data in this section and in the individual district descriptions for hurricane-affected areas were drawn from multiple sources, among them: The Brookings Institution's Metropolitan Policy Program Katrina Index, which features post-hurricane recovery and redevelopment statistics focused on the Greater New Orleans area; The Times-Picayune newspaper and its online coverage of the storms, their aftermath and the ongoing recovery effort; the U.S. Census Bureau American Community Survey, completed under different methodologies from the decennial population census; and the U.S. Census Bureau Special Population Estimates for Impacted Counties in the Gulf Coast Area, which provides data for counties deemed hurricane-affected, including some in Texas. That chart is reproduced here on pp. xxv-xxvii. The last two columns of the chart reflect the percentage change and the net change in population for affected counties and parishes. Data for any county or parish that is split among more than one congressional district appears in full for each district that the county or parish belongs to.

Gulf Coast Politics

Members of Congress from hurricane-affected districts will continue to focus on recovery and reconstruction efforts for years to come, seeking to maximize federal assistance as they have ever since the storms struck. But some politicians now represent constituencies that were dramatically altered by Hurricane Katrina and the population shifts it produced.

Despite overall population growth between the 2000 census and mid-2005, Louisiana now is likely to lose one of its seven House seats after the 2010 census. Due to the storm, Louisiana lost nearly 345,000 residents, mostly from the New Orleans area. And the city already has seen a significant change in several demographic categories since Katrina. The political balance may be affected by a higher percentage of white and wealthy residents, as well as what could turn out to be a permanent reduction in the number of black residents, who typically vote Democratic. The

Storm Diaspora

Most victims of hurricanes Katrina and Rita who left the Gulf Coast in 2005 settled, at least temporarily, in other Southern states, though some traveled much farther. Every state had some evacuees apply for federal assistance and as of the latest FEMA estimates almost 2.6 million people have applied to the agency for federal assistance. Below are the top 15 states ranked by the number of applicants residing in their state.

	State:	Applicants:
1.	Louisiana	1,068,675
2.	Texas	637,915
3.	Mississippi	502,820
4.	Alabama	135,395
5.	Georgia	41,533
6.	Florida	29,282
7.	Tennessee	17,062
8.	California	16,806
9.	Arkansas	14,555
10.	Iowa	9,241
11.	Illinois	7,359
12.	North Carolina	6,633
13.	Missouri	5,929
14.	Virginia	5,907
15.	Oklahoma	5,314

Source: The Federal Emergency Management Agency (CQ Weekly April 10, 2006)

2005 Hurricanes by Landfall

The year 2005 set a record for hurricanes and tropical storms making landfall in the United States. Below are the eight storms, the date and location of each storm's landfall and the congressional district in which it occurred.

Storm	Date	Landfall	District
Arlene *	June 8-13	Panhandle	FL-1
Cindy	July 5-9	Plaquemines Parish	LA-3
Dennis	July 10	Pensacola	FL-1
Katrina	Aug. 25-29	Hallandale Beach	FL-20
		Plaquemines Parish	LA-3
		Hancock County	MS-4
Ophelia	Sept. 14	Cape Fear	NC-7
Rita	Sept. 24	Sabine's Pass	TX-2
		Johnson's Bayou	LA-7
Tammy *	Oct. 5-6	Mayport	FL-4
Wilma	Oct. 24	Southern Florida	FL-25

* Tropical storm

Source: National Oceanic and Atmospheric Administration

2012 election cycle may pit two Louisiana incumbents against each other for a U.S. House seat.

In the Senate, Democrat Mary L. Landrieu won narrowly in 2002 and is up for re-election in 2008. She has fought tenaciously for federal assistance to Louisiana, but it remains to be seen whether she can hold onto her seat. Two reasons her seat might be vulnerable are that some voters from loyally Democratic New Orleans, the base of her political support, were compelled to leave, and that Landrieu's narrow 52 percent to 48 percent 2002 victory is unlikely to deter GOP challengers.

The Biloxi and Pascagoula metropolitan areas on the Mississippi coast suffered the second-largest population loss due to Hurricane Katrina. In that state, the demographic changes swung the other way, resulting in a higher proportion of blacks overall and less of a change in poverty levels and homeownership than in New Orleans.

The political impact of these demographic changes appears to be minimal in Mississippi, however. Republican Gov. Haley Barbour, a former chairman of the Republican National Committee, capitalized on his close contacts with the Bush administration to get federal aid flowing to his state. In contrast, Louisiana Democratic Gov. Kathleen Babineaux Blanco was excoriated for what many in her state considered an ineffectual response. With her popularity plummeting, in 2005 she dropped her planned bid for re-election in 2007. Republican Rep. Bobby Jindal has announced for the race.

Louisiana appointed a state-level recovery czar, an office that leaders hope will spearhead redevelopment of commercial and residential areas. As of April 2007, the indicators used by the Brookings Institution to measure recovery in New Orleans showed that infrastructure rebuilding had stalled. On the state level, legislatures in Louisiana and Mississippi, in particular, have tried to address changing needs for post-hurricane redevelopment. For example, the Louisiana legislature planned to vote on additional judges for suburban areas north of New Orleans that have seen their populations grow as they welcomed evacuees who settled permanently in those parishes. And parish-level elections in Louisiana have turned on issues related to continued recovery efforts and the success of incumbents' attempts to provide stability to devastated neighborhoods.

The recovery and rebuilding efforts across the Gulf Coast were shaping up to be a major topic during the 2008 presidential campaigns. The slow pace of rebuilding in New Orleans in particular is being invoked by politicians and government officials to draw attention to the larger problems of the region. Regardless of whether the city wins a candidate-backed bid to host a national presidential debate, continued funding for the Gulf Coast, as well as the efficiency of federal agencies, will be primary topics of concern for the presidential hopefuls.

Census Population Estimates for Impacted Counties, by District

Shared counties appear once for each congressional district; no district-specific estimates exist.

Alabama

District	County	July 2004	July 2005	Jan. 2006	Change	Net
1	Baldwin	154,456	160,354	160,573	0.14%	219
1 (pt.)	Clarke	26,984	26,882	27,047	0.61	165
1	Mobile	392,265	393,585	391,251	-0.59	-2,334
1	Washington	17,736	17,689	17,628	-0.34	-61
4 (pt.)	Pickens	20,134	19,967	19,956	-0.06	-11
6 (pt.)	Tuscaloosa	159,217	160,947	162,845	1.18	1,898
7	Choctaw	15,005	14,674	14,408	-1.81	-266
7 (pt.)	Clarke	26,984	26,882	27,047	0.61	165
7	Greene	9,619	9,583	9,603	0.21	20
7	Hale	16,837	16,925	17,035	0.65	110
7	Marengo	21,833	21,686	21,777	0.42	91
7 (pt.)	Pickens	20,134	19,967	19,956	-0.06	-11
7	Sumter	13,841	13,582	13,558	-0.18	-24
7 (pt.)	Tuscaloosa	159,217	160,947	162,845	1.18	1,898
State total		**847,927**	**855,874**	**855,681**	**-0.02**	**-193**

Louisiana

District	Parish	July 2004	July 2005	Jan. 2006	Change	Net
1 (pt.)	Jefferson	448,843	448,578	411,305	-8.31%	-37,273
1 (pt.)	Orleans	443,430	437,186	158,353	-63.78	-278,833
1 (pt.)	St. Charles	49,525	50,203	52,269	4.12	2,066
1	St. Tammany	211,398	217,999	220,651	1.22	2,652
1	Tangipahoa	101,761	103,261	109,501	6.04	6,240
1	Washington	42,439	42,966	43,523	1.30	557
2 (pt.)	Jefferson	448,843	448,578	411,305	-8.31	-37,273
2 (pt.)	Orleans	443,430	437,186	158,353	-63.78	-278,833
3 (pt.)	Ascension	86,373	89,855	94,128	4.76	4,273
3	Assumption	23,006	22,996	23,361	1.59	365
3	Iberia	72,551	72,773	72,804	0.04	31
3 (pt.)	Jefferson	448,843	448,578	411,305	-8.31	-37,273
3	Lafourche	90,319	90,543	91,153	0.67	610
3	Plaquemines	28,258	28,282	20,164	-28.70	-8,118
3	St. Bernard	64,848	64,576	3,361	-94.80	-61,215
3 (pt.)	St. Charles	49,525	50,203	52,269	4.12	2,066
3	St. James	20,801	20,885	21,773	4.25	888
3	St. John the Baptist	45,087	45,950	48,642	5.86	2,692
3	St. Martin	49,526	49,642	49,993	0.71	351
3	St. Mary	51,379	50,787	50,744	-0.08	-43
3	Terrebonne	105,041	106,078	107,291	1.14	1,213
4 (pt.)	Allen	21,245	21,252	21,435	0.86	183
4	Beauregard	32,822	33,372	33,009	-1.09	-363
4	Sabine	23,160	23,369	23,809	1.88	440
4	Vernon	46,100	45,323	45,828	1.11	505
5 (pt.)	Allen	21,245	21,252	21,435	0.86	183
5 (pt.)	Evangeline	33,486	33,768	33,778	0.03	10
6 (pt.)	Iberville	29,204	29,107	29,729	2.14	622
5 (pt.)	Pointe Coupee	22,107	22,040	22,649	2.76	609
6 (pt.)	Ascension	86,373	89,855	94,128	4.76	4,273
6	East Baton Rouge	396,882	396,735	413,700	4.28	16,965
6	East Feliciana	18,284	18,237	18,503	1.46	266

6 (pt.)	Iberville	29,204	29,107	29,729	2.14	622
6	Livingston	105,174	108,622	111,863	2.98	3,241
6 (pt.)	Pointe Coupee	22,107	22,040	22,649	2.76	609
6	St. Helena	10,237	10,187	10,920	7.20	733
6	West Baton Rouge	21,285	21,064	20,836	-1.08	-228
6	West Feliciana	9,962	10,050	10,296	2.45	246
7	Acadia	58,182	58,570	58,697	0.22	127
7	Calcasieu	179,925	180,709	174,639	-3.36	-6,070
7	Cameron	9,561	9,493	7,532	-20.66	-1,961
7 (pt.)	Evangeline	33,486	33,768	33,778	0.03	10
7	Jefferson Davis	30,764	30,857	30,624	-0.76	-233
7	Lafayette	190,459	192,448	194,938	1.29	2,490
7	St. Landry	87,794	88,409	89,555	1.30	1,146
7	Vermilion	53,857	54,428	54,463	0.06	35
State total		**3,315,075**	**3,330,600**	**2,985,819**	**-10.35**	**-344,781**

Mississippi

District	County	July 2004	July 2005	Jan. 2006	Change	Net
1	Choctaw	9,273	9,268	9,161	-1.15%	-107
1	Lowndes	58,464	58,061	58,117	0.10	56
1 (pt.)	Winston	19,336	19,300	19,153	-0.76	-147
2	Attala	19,231	19,178	19,022	-0.81	-156
2	Claiborne	9,945	9,962	10,008	0.46	46
2	Copiah	27,844	27,891	28,108	0.78	217
2 (pt.)	Hinds	240,384	239,901	238,234	-0.69	-1,667
2	Jefferson	8,852	8,772	8,838	0.75	66
2 (pt.)	Leake	20,908	20,960	20,879	-0.39	-81
2 (pt.)	Madison	79,720	82,071	83,800	2.11	1,729
2	Warren	48,628	48,538	47,963	-1.18	-575
2	Yazoo	25,739	25,605	25,366	-0.93	-239
3	Adams	31,988	31,640	31,506	-0.42	-134
3	Amite	13,322	13,337	13,702	2.74	365
3	Covington	19,947	19,983	20,009	0.13	26
3	Franklin	8,322	8,318	8,329	0.13	11
3 (pt.)	Hinds	240,384	239,901	238,234	-0.69	-1,667
3 (pt.)	Jasper	17,980	17,998	18,263	1.47	265
3	Jefferson Davis	13,054	13,054	13,099	0.34	45
3 (pt.)	Jones	63,863	64,380	64,259	-0.19	-121
3	Kemper	9,730	9,603	9,571	-0.33	-32
3	Lauderdale	73,925	73,647	72,592	-1.43	-1,055
3	Lawrence	13,392	13,409	13,467	0.43	58
3 (pt.)	Leake	20,908	20,960	20,879	-0.39	-81
3	Lincoln	33,057	33,255	33,441	0.56	186
3 (pt.)	Madison	79,720	82,071	83,800	2.11	1,729
3 (pt.)	Marion	24,292	24,277	24,261	-0.07	-16
3	Neshoba	28,971	29,281	29,321	0.14	40
3	Newton	21,438	21,656	21,514	-0.66	-142
3	Noxubee	12,064	12,009	11,908	-0.84	-101
3	Oktibbeha	37,430	37,541	38,243	1.87	702
3	Pike	38,219	38,548	39,297	1.94	749
3	Rankin	123,321	126,569	128,045	1.17	1,476
3	Scott	28,290	28,419	28,295	-0.44	-124
3	Simpson	26,599	26,956	26,955	0.00	-1
3	Smith	15,773	15,927	16,077	0.94	150
3	Walthall	15,056	15,276	15,724	2.93	448
3	Wilkinson	9,052	9,069	9,444	4.13	375

3 (pt.)	Winston	19,336	19,300	19,153	-0.76	-147
4	Clarke	17,522	17,489	17,444	-0.26	-45
4	Forrest	68,977	69,608	69,292	-0.45	-316
4	George	20,075	20,584	21,074	2.38	490
4	Greene	10,708	10,739	10,836	0.90	97
4	Hancock	45,428	46,240	35,129	-24.03	-11,111
4	Harrison	185,178	186,530	155,817	-16.47	-30,713
4	Jackson	133,020	134,249	126,311	-5.91	-7,938
4 (pt.)	Jasper	17,980	17,998	18,263	1.47	265
4 (pt.)	Jones	63,863	64,380	64,259	-0.19	-121
4	Lamar	42,777	44,148	45,005	1.94	857
4 (pt.)	Marion	24,292	24,277	24,261	-0.07	-16
4	Pearl River	51,039	51,913	55,719	7.33	3,806
4	Perry	12,127	12,052	11,960	-0.76	-92
4	Stone	13,511	13,904	14,211	2.21	307
4	Wayne	20,945	21,083	21,039	-0.21	-44
State total		**1,868,716**	**1,882,198**	**1,839,808**	**-2.25**	**-42,390**

Texas

District	County	July 2004	July 2005	Jan. 2006	Change	Net
1	Angelina	78,554	78,839	79,187	0.44%	348
1	Nacogdoches	55,622	56,066	56,750	1.22	684
1	Sabine	10,267	10,322	10,427	1.02	105
1	San Augustine	8,577	8,557	8,553	-0.05	-4
1	Shelby	25,712	26,008	26,231	0.86	223
2 (pt.)	Harris	3,595,720	3,647,656	3,740,480	2.54	92,824
2	Jefferson	232,048	231,311	233,620	1.00	2,309
2 (pt.)	Liberty	69,937	70,116	70,458	0.49	342
6 (pt.)	Trinity	14,070	14,166	14,254	0.62	88
7 (pt.)	Harris	3,595,720	3,647,656	3,740,480	2.54	92,824
8	Hardin	49,773	50,531	51,212	1.35	681
8	Jasper	34,729	34,699	34,893	0.56	194
8 (pt.)	Liberty	69,937	70,116	70,458	0.49	342
8	Montgomery	360,210	376,051	387,278	2.99	11,227
8	Newton	13,705	13,711	13,865	1.12	154
8	Orange	83,738	83,996	85,043	1.25	1,047
8	Polk	42,849	43,311	43,652	0.79	341
8	San Jacinto	24,427	24,666	24,809	0.58	143
8 (pt.)	Trinity	14,070	14,166	14,254	0.62	88
8	Tyler	19,205	19,025	19,001	-0.13	-24
8	Walker	44,659	44,633	44,771	0.31	138
9 (pt.)	Fort Bend	435,964	457,225	472,635	3.37	15,410
9 (pt.)	Harris	3,595,720	3,647,656	3,740,480	2.54	92,824
10 (pt.)	Harris	3,595,720	3,647,656	3,740,480	2.54	92,824
14 (pt.)	Brazoria	259,762	267,376	273,012	2.11	5,636
14	Chambers	27,859	28,141	28,439	1.06	298
14 (pt.)	Fort Bend	435,964	457,225	472,635	3.37	15,410
14 (pt.)	Galveston	267,623	273,162	277,885	1.73	4,723
18 (pt.)	Harris	3,595,720	3,647,656	3,740,480	2.54	92,824
22 (pt.)	Brazoria	259,762	267,376	273,012	2.11	5,636
22 (pt.)	Fort Bend	435,964	457,225	472,635	3.37	15,410
22 (pt.)	Galveston	267,623	273,162	277,885	1.73	4,723
22 (pt.)	Harris	3,595,720	3,647,656	3,740,480	2.54	92,824
29 (pt.)	Harris	3,595,720	3,647,656	3,740,480	2.54	92,824
State total		**5,755,010**	**5,859,568**	**5,996,455**	**2.34**	**136,887**

Source: U.S. Census Bureau

Recovery by Agency

After the hurricanes, many agencies undertook rebuilding efforts in the Gulf Coast region. Below is a list of some relevant state and federal organizations with their Web addresses. Information about ongoing rebuilding efforts can be found on these sites.

Federal Coordinator for Gulf Coast Rebuilding

www.dhs.gov/officeforgulfcoastrebuilding

Federal Emergency Management Agency

www.fema.gov

National Oceanographic and Atmospheric Administration

www.ncdc.noaa.gov/oa/climate/research/2005/hurricanes05.html

Project Recovery (Miss.)

www.projectrecovery.ms.gov

The Road Home (La.)

www.road2la.org

U.S. Census Bureau

www.census.gov/acs/www/Products/Profiles/gulf_coast

Louisiana and Mississippi State Profiles

The state profile pages for Louisiana and Mississippi contain the most recent official data with respect to urban, racial and overall population, voter registration, income and other demographic statistics. The data for those two states are provided in the same format as those for the other 48 states. The Louisiana and Mississippi pages also include details obtained from state officials about the makeup of the state legislatures, legislative members' salaries, legislative terms and term limits. Because of the economic, sociopolitical and demographic shifts caused by hurricane-related devastation in 2005, however, much of the information in the state tables will remain outdated until it is recalculated as part of the 2010 census.

Demographic information for each state and congressional district was obtained from the Census Bureau and the Bureau of Economic Analysis, both within the U.S. Department of Commerce. An asterisk next to a congressional district indicates that the official data available from the Census Bureau's decennial census are no longer representative of the district because of hurricane-related changes.

Coastal areas in Louisiana and Mississippi were not the only areas of the country whose districts felt the impact of the 2005 hurricane season. The Texas Gulf Coast, Alabama's Mobile Bay area, and Florida's Panhandle were affected. In Texas, Georgia, Tennessee and California, the impact was indirect, measured by the influx of evacuees from the Gulf Coast and other economic factors. Data for Texas, Alabama, Florida and the other affected states do not reflect any major hurricane-related shifts in demographics, which await the 2010 census.

ALABAMA

Gov. Bob Riley (R)

First elected: 2002
Length of term: 4 years
Term expires: 1/11
Salary: $101,433
Phone: (334) 242-7100

Residence: Ashland
Born: Oct. 3, 1944; Ashland, Ala.
Religion: Baptist
Family: Wife, Patsy Riley; four children (one deceased)
Education: U. of Alabama, B.A. 1965 (business administration)
Career: Auto dealer; trucking company executive; farmer
Political highlights: Ashland City Council, 1972-76; candidate for mayor of Ashland, 1976; U.S. House, 1997-2003

Election results:

2006 GENERAL		
Bob Riley (R)	718,327	57.4%
Lucy Baxley (D)	519,827	41.6%
write-ins	12,247	1.0%

Lt. Gov. Jim Folsom Jr. (D)

First elected: 2006
Length of term: 4 years
Term expires: 1/11
Salary: $48,620
Phone: (334) 242-7900

LEGISLATURE

Legislature: Annually, limit of 30 legislative days within 105 calendar days

Senate: 35 members, 4-year terms
2007 ratios: 23 D, 12 R; 31 men, 4 women
Salary: $10/day; $50 for each 3-day week; $2,280/month expenses
Phone: (334) 242-7800

House: 105 members, 4-year terms
2007 ratios: 62 D, 43 R; 91 men, 14 women
Salary: $10/day; $50 for each 3-day week; $2,280/month expenses
Phone: (334) 242-7600

TERM LIMITS

Governor: 2 consecutive terms
Senate: No
House: No

URBAN STATISTICS

CITY	POPULATION
Birmingham	242,820
Montgomery	201,568
Mobile	198,915
Huntsville	158,216
Tuscaloosa	77,906

REGISTERED VOTERS

Voters do not register by party.

POPULATION

2006 population (est.)	4,599,030
2000 population	4,447,100
1990 population	4,040,587
Percent change (1990-2000)	+10.1%
Rank among states (2006)	23
Median age	35.8
Born in state	73.4%
Foreign born	2%
Violent crime rate	486/100,000
Poverty level	16.1%
Federal workers	50,081
Military	38,706

ELECTIONS

STATE ELECTION OFFICIAL
(334) 242-7210
DEMOCRATIC PARTY
(334) 262-2221
REPUBLICAN PARTY
(205) 212-5900

MISCELLANEOUS

Web: www.alabama.gov
Capital: Montgomery

U.S. CONGRESS

Senate: 2 Republicans
House: 5 Republicans, 2 Democrats

2000 Census Statistics by District

DIST.	2004 VOTE FOR PRESIDENT BUSH	KERRY	WHITE	BLACK	ASIAN	HISP	MEDIAN INCOME	WHITE COLLAR	BLUE COLLAR	SERVICE INDUSTRY	OVER 64	UNDER 18	COLLEGE EDUCATION	RURAL	SQ. MILES
1	64%	35%	68%	28%	1%	1%	$34,739	55%	31%	15%	13%	27%	19%	36%	6,317
2	66	33	67	29	1	2	$32,460	55	31	14	13	26	18	50	10,502
3	58	41	65	32	1	1	$30,806	52	34	14	13	25	17	47	7,834
4	71	28	90	5	0	3	$31,344	46	42	12	15	24	11	73	8,372
5	60	39	78	17	1	2	$38,054	57	30	13	12	25	24	41	4,486
6	78	22	89	8	1	2	$46,946	68	22	10	12	24	30	38	4,564
7	35	64	36	62	1	1	$26,672	53	29	17	13	26	15	28	8,669
STATE	62	37	70	26	1	2	$34,135	55	31	13	13	25	19	45	50,744
U.S.	50.7	48.3	69	12	4	13	$41,994	60	25	15	12	26	24	21	3,537,438

Statistical information related to Hurricane Katrina and its impact on Alabama and other states has been collected by Congressional Quarterly and may be found on pages xxiii through xxviii.

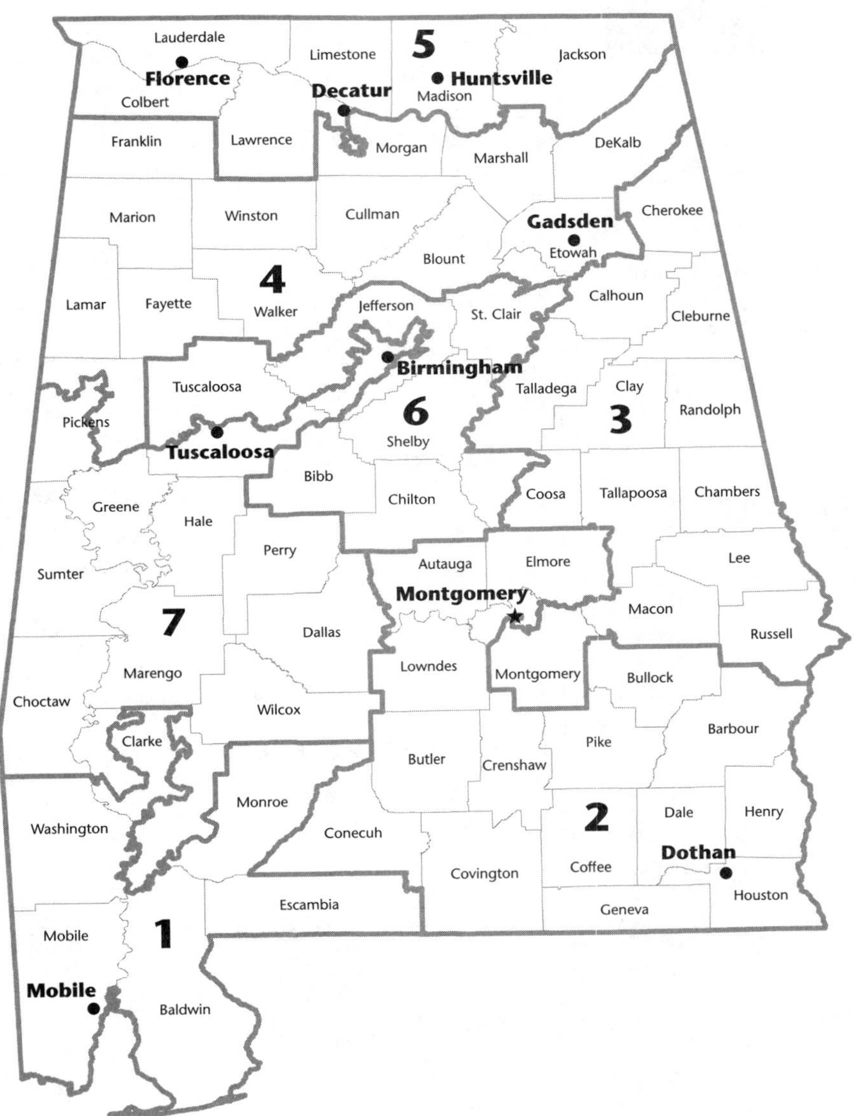
Lauderdale
Limestone
5
Jackson
Florence
Huntsville
Decatur
Madison
Colbert
Franklin
Lawrence
Morgan
Marshall
DeKalb
Marion
Winston
Cullman
Gadsden
Cherokee
Etowah
Blount
4
Lamar
Fayette
Walker
Jefferson
St. Clair
Calhoun
Cleburne
Birmingham
Tuscaloosa
Talladega
Clay
6
3
Randolph
Pickens
Shelby
Tuscaloosa
Bibb
Greene
Chilton
Coosa
Tallapoosa
Chambers
Hale
Perry
Autauga
Elmore
Lee
Sumter
Montgomery
Macon
7
Dallas
Russell
Lowndes
Montgomery
Bullock
Marengo
Choctaw
Wilcox
Clarke
Barbour
Pike
Butler
Crenshaw
Monroe
Washington
Conecuh
2
Dale
Henry
Dothan
Covington
Coffee
Houston
Escambia
Geneva
Mobile
1
Mobile
Baldwin

Sen. Richard C. Shelby (R)

CAPITOL OFFICE
224-5744
senator@shelby.senate.gov
shelby.senate.gov
110 Hart 20510-0103; fax 224-3416

COMMITTEES
Appropriations
Banking, Housing & Urban Affairs - ranking member
Special Aging

RESIDENCE
Tuscaloosa

BORN
May 6, 1934, Birmingham, Ala.

RELIGION
Presbyterian

FAMILY
Wife, Annette Nevin Shelby; two children

EDUCATION
U. of Alabama, A.B. 1957, LL.B. 1963

CAREER
Lawyer; city prosecutor

POLITICAL HIGHLIGHTS
Ala. Senate, 1971-79 (served as a Democrat); U.S. House, 1979-87 (served as a Democrat)

ELECTION RESULTS

2004 GENERAL		
Richard C. Shelby (R)	1,242,200	67.6%
Wayne Sowell (D)	595,018	32.4%
2004 PRIMARY		
Richard C. Shelby (R)		unopposed

PREVIOUS WINNING PERCENTAGES *
1998 (63%); 1992 (65%); 1986 (50%); 1984 House Election (97%); 1982 House Election (97%); 1980 House Election (73%); 1978 House Election (94%)
* Elected as a Democrat 1978-92

Elected 1986; 4th term

The genial Shelby may not be the best known member of the Senate, but he's a cagey legislator who has left his mark on regulation of the financial services industry and has used his power as a senior appropriator to steer millions of federal dollars to Alabama.

Bumped from the chairmanship of the Banking, Housing and Urban Affairs Committee when Democrats took control of the Senate in 2007, he is now the panel's senior Republican. Topping his list of objectives is a goal he pursued in vain during four years as chairman: tighter regulation of mortgage finance giants Fannie Mae and Freddie Mac, the government-sponsored enterprises scarred by accounting scandals earlier this decade. Partisan bickering, disagreements between GOP lawmakers and the White House, and the lobbying prowess of the two companies all thwarted overhaul legislation. But Shelby is nothing if not persistent.

He rarely moves quickly on an issue, preferring to conduct exhaustive hearings and offstage reviews before drafting legislation. "I try to be thorough, to approach issues completely," he says. "The more knowledge you have, the wiser you are." His deliberate approach avoids roiling the financial markets with quick fixes to problems, but it also can slow legislative response to serious abuses. It took Congress more than two years to crack down on unscrupulous financial services and insurance companies that prey on members of the military, in large part because Shelby insisted on waiting for a series of reports on the abuses from government agencies. A bill finally was enacted in September 2006.

Shelby also won passage that year of his bill establishing new rules for the Securities and Exchange Commission when it grants recognition to credit rating agencies that rank the riskiness of bonds, notes and other instruments. But legislation on arguably more significant issues foundered, including proposed changes to the federal flood insurance program in the wake of devastating hurricanes along the Gulf Coast in 2005 and an overhaul of the law governing foreign investments in the United States.

While he prefers free-market solutions to government regulation, Shelby occasionally behaves like the Democrat he once was. One of Congress' first party-switchers in the mid-1990s, he departs from the GOP mainstream most often on questions of privacy, predatory lending and stock market regulation. "People have to have confidence in the banking system and financial markets," he says. "That's why transparency is so important." Legislation is not always the answer, he says; sometimes vigorous oversight alone can spur change in targeted industries.

Shelby's pet issue is consumer privacy. His immersion in the subject dates to the 106th Congress (1999-2000), when he learned that some states were providing information from driver's licenses to marketing firms without motorists' knowledge. In 1999, Shelby won enactment of a law requiring states to obtain permission before sharing personal data such as Social Security numbers.

Shelby took the helm of the Banking panel in 2003, after earlier holding the chairmanship and then the vice chairmanship of the Intelligence Committee, on which he served at the time of the Sept. 11 terrorist attacks. Shelby was one of Capitol Hill's harshest critics of perceived failures by the intelligence community to detect evidence of the plot in advance. He called the attacks "an intelligence failure of unprecedented magnitude," and singled out the Central Intelligence Agency for relying too much on technological tools and not enough on agents in the field. He was given to lengthy critiques of the agency's shortcomings, and regularly called for the resignation of then CIA Director George J. Tenet.

Shelby pushed for greater sharing of intelligence information among federal agencies as part of the law that created the Department of Homeland Security.

Fallout from that period in his career continued into the 109th Congress (2005-06) with a Senate Ethics Committee investigation into allegations that Shelby leaked secret government information to the media. The information, which infuriated top Bush administration officials when it was made public, was the National Security Agency's interception of two messages on the eve of the attacks that were not translated until the next day, Sept. 12, 2001. The Arabic-language messages said, "The match is about to begin" and "Tomorrow is zero hour." The committee cleared Shelby of any wrongdoing in 2005.

Shelby's ability to deliver federal money to Alabama has fueled his popularity back home. As a senior member of the Appropriations Committee and chairman in the 109th Congress of its Commerce, Justice and Science Subcommittee, he has poured money into the state. In the 110th Congress (2007-08), he is the ranking minority member of that panel. He has helped foster the booming space and defense economy in Huntsville, home to NASA's Marshall Space Flight Center and the Army's Redstone Arsenal. The Army was so grateful for Shelby's help in securing a new 200,000-square-foot, $33 million scientific and technical center that it named the facility the Richard C. Shelby Center for Missile Intelligence. A building at the biomedical research complex at the University of Alabama-Birmingham also is named for Shelby and his wife, Annette, in gratitude for the millions of dollars the senator steered to the complex.

Shelby is not a fan of efforts by his Republican colleagues to curb such spending earmarks for home-state projects. Nor does he support their drive to give President Bush power to strike specific line items from appropriations bills. In 2007, Shelby was the sole Republican to side with Senate Democrats in killing a GOP proposal to give the president that power.

Shelby got his Appropriations seat after he switched parties following the Republican takeover of Congress in 1994. Although the switch struck many as opportunistic — just a few months earlier he told the New York Times he had "no intention of switching parties" — he said he made the move because of what he described as the demise of the pro-defense, conservative wing of the Democratic Party. His move also followed an attempt by the Clinton administration to move some space programs out of Alabama after Shelby had audaciously criticized President Bill Clinton's budget while standing next to Vice President Al Gore in front of television cameras.

Shelby spent most of the 1960s as a municipal prosecutor in Tuscaloosa, and sometimes he still cites his law enforcement background. He entered electoral politics by serving eight years in the state Senate, where he often was at odds with Gov. George C. Wallace Jr. Though he was initially interested in running for lieutenant governor in 1978, more than a dozen other Democrats had the same idea. When one of his former law partners, Democrat Walter Flowers, gave up his House seat that year to run for the Senate, Shelby was easily persuaded to change course and run for Congress.

Shelby operated largely behind the scenes in the House for eight years, working on federal projects for his district. But he often sided with Republicans. His election to the Senate as a Democrat in 1986 was a 1 percentage point victory over one-term incumbent Jeremiah Denton, the first Republican elected statewide in Alabama since Reconstruction. Shelby has won re-election twice since his switch, never dropping below 60 percent.

KEY VOTES

2006

- Yes Confirm Samuel A. Alito Jr. to the Supreme Court
- Yes Allow consideration of a bill to establish a $140 billion trust fund to compensate victims of asbestos exposure
- Yes Extend tax cuts for two years at a cost of $70 billion over five years
- No Overhaul immigration policy with border security, enforcement and guest worker program
- Yes Allow consideration of a bill to permanently repeal the estate tax
- No Urge President Bush to begin troop withdrawals from Iraq in 2006
- No Lift President Bush's restrictions on stem cell research funding
- Yes Authorize military tribunals for suspected terrorists

2005

- Yes Curb class action lawsuits by shifting them from state to federal courts
- Yes Allow confirmation vote on Priscilla R. Owen to the U.S. Court of Appeals for the 5th Circuit
- Yes Oppose mandatory emissions limits and block recognition of global warming as a threat
- No Approve free-trade pact with five Central American countries
- Yes Pass energy policy overhaul favored by President Bush emphasizing domestic oil and gas production
- Yes Shield gunmakers from lawsuits when their products are used in crimes
- Yes Ban torture of prisoners in U.S. custody
- Yes Renew 16 provisions of the Patriot Act
- Yes Allow final vote on opening the Arctic National Wildlife Refuge to oil and gas exploration

CQ VOTE STUDIES

	PARTY UNITY		PRESIDENTIAL SUPPORT	
	Support	Oppose	Support	Oppose
2006	88%	12%	86%	14%
2005	94%	6%	89%	11%
2004	94%	6%	86%	14%
2003	96%	4%	95%	5%
2002	80%	20%	87%	13%
2001	88%	12%	97%	3%
2000	97%	3%	45%	55%
1999	89%	11%	38%	62%
1998	91%	9%	34%	66%
1997	93%	7%	57%	43%

INTEREST GROUPS

	AFL-CIO	ADA	CCUS	ACU
2006	7%	10%	83%	74%
2005	23%	10%	89%	88%
2004	25%	20%	88%	84%
2003	15%	10%	82%	90%
2002	38%	10%	85%	80%
2001	19%	5%	93%	100%
2000	0%	0%	93%	100%
1999	22%	10%	71%	84%
1998	0%	5%	78%	92%
1997	14%	5%	90%	92%

Sen. Jeff Sessions (R)

CAPITOL OFFICE
224-4124
sessions.senate.gov
335 Russell 20510-0104; fax 224-3149

COMMITTEES
Armed Services
Budget
Energy & Natural Resources
Judiciary

RESIDENCE
Mobile

BORN
Dec. 24, 1946, Hybart, Ala.

RELIGION
Methodist

FAMILY
Wife, Mary Sessions; three children

EDUCATION
Huntingdon College, B.A. 1969 (history);
U. of Alabama, J.D. 1973

MILITARY SERVICE
Army Reserve, 1973-86

CAREER
Lawyer; teacher

POLITICAL HIGHLIGHTS
Assistant U.S. attorney, 1975-77; U.S. attorney, 1981-93; Ala. attorney general, 1995-97

ELECTION RESULTS

2002 GENERAL		
Jeff Sessions (R)	792,561	58.6%
Susan Parker (D)	538,878	39.8%
Jeff Allen (LIBERT)	20,234	1.5%
2002 PRIMARY		
Jeff Sessions (R)		unopposed

PREVIOUS WINNING PERCENTAGES
1996 (52%)

Elected 1996; 2nd term

At a glance, Sessions does not cut an imposing figure; he is slight in stature and not given to blustery speeches on the Senate floor. But the Alabama Republican can be a conservative pit bull in a pound full of poodles.

A former Alabama attorney general, Sessions is a fierce proponent of executive authority in the war on terrorism and a defender of President Bush's judicial nominees. But he is distinctly cool to the president's proposals to offer guest worker permits and a path to legalization for illegal immigrants. When a bipartisan Senate majority passed an immigration bill in 2006 embodying the Bush approach, Sessions called it "the worst piece of legislation to come before the Senate since I've been here." After the measure died in a standoff with the House, Sessions was among those who pushed through legislation calling for a fence along the Mexican border instead. He also won adoption of a floor amendment to the defense spending bill providing $1.8 billion for the border fence and vehicle barriers.

A deficit hawk, Sessions shares the deep fiscal and social conservatism of many of his Republican colleagues from the South and West. As he nears the end of his second term, he is part of a new generation of Southern GOP senators focused not just on the rural concerns of their populist Democratic predecessors but on conservative Christian values, a muscular foreign policy and a tight-fisted economic policy.

A member of the Budget Committee, Sessions has long promoted spending controls, smaller government and tax cuts. In 2005, he helped lead a push to pare entitlement spending in order to allow more funding for the military and other discretionary programs. Sessions also called for legislation to enforce a cap on spending on the new Medicare prescription drug benefit enacted in 2003, after criticizing the administration for underestimating the program's cost. In 2006, he was one of the leaders of a band of conservative GOP senators who blocked action on a military construction and veterans spending bill that could have become the vehicle for a year-end omnibus spending package. For veterans, the delay put billions of dollars in increases for benefits and health care on hold until 2007.

Sessions also serves on the Judiciary Committee, where he has been an ardent advocate of sweeping executive authority in the war on terrorism. In 2005, he was one of nine Senate Republicans to vote against a ban on "cruel, inhuman or degrading treatment" of suspected terrorists. In 2006, he split with moderate Republican Judiciary Chairman Arlen Specter of Pennsylvania to deny detainees held at Guantánamo Bay in Cuba the right to challenge their imprisonment in U.S. courts. He also defended the National Security Administration's secret domestic wiretapping program.

The Senate's role in confirming judges has absorbed Sessions since he arrived in 1997. He and other conservatives briefly held up Specter's 2005 elevation to Judiciary chairman after the Pennsylvania Republican expressed doubts about the political viability of judicial candidates with strong socially conservative views. But Sessions helped resolve the dispute by extracting a vow from Specter to move all nominations to the floor.

Sessions then promoted the confirmation of William H. Pryor Jr., a former Alabama attorney general, to a permanent seat on the 11th Circuit Court of Appeals. Bush had used a recess appointment in 2004 to put Pryor on the 11th Circuit bench through the end of 2005. Critics said Pryor was hostile to civil rights, federal environmental law and the rights of the disabled. Sessions stressed that Pryor had the "strong support of the entire spectrum of Alabama political leaders." A bipartisan group of senators, the Gang of 14, struck a deal in May 2005 that minimized filibusters of judicial nominations, and Pryor was confirmed the following month.

Sessions has a unique perspective on judicial confirmations. In 1986, he was only the second federal judicial nominee in 48 years whose nomination was killed by the Judiciary Committee. President Ronald Reagan nominated Sessions, then chief prosecutor for the Southern District of Alabama, but critics accused Sessions of "gross insensitivity" on racial issues. According to sworn statements by Justice Department lawyers, he called the NAACP and the American Civil Liberties Union "communist-inspired" and said they tried to "force civil rights down the throats of people." Sessions said his words were misrepresented.

After voting 8-10 against his confirmation, the panel refused, 9-9, to send the nomination to the floor for a vote. On Judiciary, Sessions now serves with several Democratic senators who prevented him from becoming a federal judge, including Chairman Patrick J. Leahy of Vermont, Joseph R. Biden Jr. of Delaware and Edward M. Kennedy of Massachusetts, as well as Specter.

Sessions also sits on Armed Services, where he keeps an eye out for military installations in his state, including Maxwell Air Force Base near Montgomery. An advocate for a missile defense system, Sessions has pushed for more development of space-based devices, which could be a boon to his state's aerospace industry near Huntsville. "We're going to be looking as time goes by to space-based systems that may be even more effective and may be even less expensive," Sessions said in 2004.

At the start of the 110th Congress (2007-08), he gave up his seat on the Health, Education, Labor and Pensions Committee and took a seat on the Energy and Natural Resources panel.

Sessions and his wife both taught school long ago, and he lists education as a top priority. He helped win passage in 2004 of a new law giving schools greater leeway in dealing with disruptive students with disabilities.

A history buff, Sessions takes pride in his middle name — Beauregard, from Gen. P.G.T. Beauregard, the Confederate commander who was the "hero of Fort Sumter" at the Civil War's start. Sessions grew up in the tiny towns of Hybart and Camden, southwest of Montgomery. His father owned a general store and then a farm equipment dealership. Sessions worked in the stores and had what he describes as an idyllic childhood.

A student of political science and history, he joined the Young Republicans and served as student body president at Huntingdon College in Alabama. After earning his law degree, Sessions was a lawyer for a firm in Russellville, Ala., becoming assistant U.S. attorney in 1975. He was named U.S. attorney for the Southern District of Alabama in 1981 and eventually won the notice of the Reagan White House.

After the Senate blocked his nomination, Sessions returned to his work as a federal prosecutor. In 1994, he ran for state attorney general, and with a corruption scandal raging in Montgomery, he rode to victory on a vow to clean up the mess. Two years later, Sessions was lured into the Senate race by Democrat Howell Heflin's retirement after 18 years in Washington. Six other Republicans also entered the primary, but Sessions won in a runoff.

In the general election, Sessions faced Roger Bedford, chairman of the state Senate Judiciary Committee. Sessions appealed to Alabama's conservative Christian activists with his advocacy of a constitutional amendment permitting school prayer. He prevailed over Bedford with 52 percent of the vote, giving Alabama two Republican senators for the first time since Reconstruction. In 2002, he cruised past Democrat Susan Parker, the state auditor, by 19 percentage points.

KEY VOTES

2006

- Yes Confirm Samuel A. Alito Jr. to the Supreme Court
- Yes Allow consideration of a bill to establish a $140 billion trust fund to compensate victims of asbestos exposure
- Yes Extend tax cuts for two years at a cost of $70 billion over five years
- No Overhaul immigration policy with border security, enforcement and guest worker program
- Yes Allow consideration of a bill to permanently repeal the estate tax
- No Urge President Bush to begin troop withdrawals from Iraq in 2006
- No Lift President Bush's restrictions on stem cell research funding
- Yes Authorize military tribunals for suspected terrorists

2005

- Yes Curb class action lawsuits by shifting them from state to federal courts
- Yes Allow confirmation vote on Priscilla R. Owen to the U.S. Court of Appeals for the 5th Circuit
- Yes Oppose mandatory emissions limits and block recognition of global warming as a threat
- Yes Approve free-trade pact with five Central American countries
- Yes Pass energy policy overhaul favored by President Bush emphasizing domestic oil and gas production
- Yes Shield gunmakers from lawsuits when their products are used in crimes
- No Ban torture of prisoners in U.S. custody
- Yes Renew 16 provisions of the Patriot Act
- Yes Allow final vote on opening the Arctic National Wildlife Refuge to oil and gas exploration

CQ VOTE STUDIES

	PARTY UNITY		PRESIDENTIAL SUPPORT	
	Support	Oppose	Support	Oppose
2006	96%	4%	91%	9%
2005	97%	3%	90%	10%
2004	97%	3%	96%	4%
2003	98%	2%	99%	1%
2002	87%	13%	88%	12%
2001	95%	5%	97%	3%
2000	97%	3%	42%	58%
1999	94%	6%	24%	76%
1998	98%	2%	28%	72%
1997	99%	1%	56%	44%

INTEREST GROUPS

	AFL-CIO	ADA	CCUS	ACU
2006	20%	0%	92%	92%
2005	14%	0%	78%	100%
2004	8%	10%	88%	96%
2003	0%	0%	100%	75%
2002	25%	10%	84%	90%
2001	20%	5%	86%	96%
2000	0%	0%	86%	100%
1999	11%	0%	88%	100%
1998	0%	0%	89%	100%
1997	0%	0%	70%	100%

Rep. Jo Bonner (R)

CAPITOL OFFICE
225-4931
bonner.house.gov
422 Cannon 20515-0101; fax 225-0562

COMMITTEES
Agriculture
Budget
Science & Technology
Standards of Official Conduct

RESIDENCE
Mobile

BORN
Nov. 19, 1959, Selma, Ala.

RELIGION
Episcopalian

FAMILY
Wife, Janée Bonner; two children

EDUCATION
U. of Alabama, B.A. 1982 (journalism), attended 1998 (law)

CAREER
Congressional chief of staff; congressional and campaign aide

POLITICAL HIGHLIGHTS
No previous office

ELECTION RESULTS

2006 GENERAL		
Jo Bonner (R)	112,944	68.1%
Vivian Sheffield Beckerle (D)	52,770	31.8%
2006 PRIMARY		
Jo Bonner (R)		unopposed
2004 GENERAL		
Jo Bonner (R)	161,067	63.1%
Judy McCain Belk (D)	93,938	36.8%

PREVIOUS WINNING PERCENTAGES
2002 (61%)

Elected 2002; 3rd term

Bonner is a self-proclaimed backbencher who is focused intently on providing for his constituents in his Mobile-based district. Despite years as a Washington insider, he has zero interest in creating a national profile or gaining a toehold in the political society of the nation's capital.

"I live in Alabama; I work in Washington," he says. "I don't think the founding fathers imagined the House of Representatives as a place where you got elected, then went back to your district before the next Election Day, hoping to get a good report card."

A scion of an old Southern family, Bonner came to Congress in 2003 bent on perpetuating a tradition in his Alabama district of sending federal dollars back home. He took over the seat from Republican Sonny Callahan, an Appropriations chairman on energy and water projects who groomed Bonner as his successor. Bonner had been Callahan's aide for almost 18 years, and before that he interned for long-time appropriator Republican Jack Edwards. "They both made a name for themselves by taking care of the people back home, so I've had two very good teachers," Bonner said.

Bonner kept most of his predecessor's staff. "I know the importance of having a good staff," he says. "I can safely say I was the only member of the freshman class in the 108th Congress [2003-04] . . . who had a staff with a combined experience of 120 years."

Bonner has made no secret of his desire for a seat on Appropriations, a plum assignment viewed almost as an entitlement by voters in his district. But he has been handicapped by his lack of seniority and, ironically, his political good health. Seats on the panel are often used by leaders to shore up vulnerable House members, which Bonner is not. And after their defeat in the 2006 elections, Republicans had no Appropriations seats to offer.

Instead, Bonner has kept his seats on Agriculture, Budget and Science and Technology, and added a seat on the ethics committee — where he can collect a chit from the leadership for his service on a less-than-desirable panel.

Bonner's family is among the most prominent in southern Alabama. His grandfather was a banker in Wilcox County and his great-uncles a doctor, a lawyer and a local newspaper publisher. Bonner, whose given name is Josiah Robins Bonner Jr., is named for his father, a Georgetown-trained attorney who was a county judge, a powerful local post.

The district is anchored by Mobile, an old Confederate port city that exudes charm and Southern gentility and hosts an annual Mardi Gras celebration that predates its more famous sister in New Orleans. North of the city are dense pine forests where timber harvesting is a mainstay. To the north are also Mayberry-style towns, which have produced a remarkable number of great Southern writers. Monroeville was home to both Truman Capote and Harper Lee, who used the town as inspiration for the fictional Maycomb in her classic novel "To Kill a Mockingbird." Bonner's father used to take his sister to visit the Lees, to demonstrate to her that women could have interesting careers.

Like many Southern politicians, Bonner began his career as a Democrat but switched to the Republican Party in the 1990s. He has been a reliable supporter of President Bush and has voted with a majority of his party at least 95 percent of the time since he took office.

At one time, Bonner thought he'd be a journalist, not a member of Congress. As a kid in Camden, which he calls a "storybook hometown," Bonner launched a community newspaper with the loan of a press from the local newspaper editor, whose son was a playmate. In high school, Bonner was a broadcast announcer at basketball games and student council president.

Like Selma and Montgomery a few miles to the north, Camden boiled with racial strife during the 1960s, with blacks boycotting white-owned businesses. Bonner's parents took him out of the integrating Wilcox County public schools to attend the newly formed and mostly white Ft. Dale Academy.

After getting a college degree in journalism, Bonner followed his expanding interest in politics to the 1982 gubernatorial campaign of Democrat George McMillan, who was challenging Democratic incumbent George C. Wallace Jr. To young professionals such as Bonner, McMillan represented a "new chapter" for Alabama after the race-tinged politics of Wallace and the state's history of violence during the civil rights movement.

McMillan lost to Wallace, but Bonner had met Callahan, who was a candidate for lieutenant governor. Callahan also lost, but two years later he won a race for the House seat and hired Bonner to be his press secretary. Bonner eventually rose to become chief of staff.

Callahan quietly encouraged his trusted aide to run for the seat himself when the congressman was ready to step down. In 1997, Bonner moved from Washington to the state district, a rarity for a chief of staff, most of whom work on Capitol Hill. He paid close attention to constituent service, joining the local Rotary Club and board of the local Junior League. By the time Callahan announced his retirement in 2002, Bonner was primed to run.

His toughest competition came from Tom Young, a Mobile native and a fellow Republican who, like Bonner, was a career congressional aide. Young was chief of staff for the state's Republican Sen. Richard C. Shelby. Despite their similarities, Bonner managed to portray Young as a Washington insider not in touch with voters. It became one of the most expensive and hotly contested races of the season. Bonner led in a seven-way June primary but fell short of a majority, forcing a runoff. He went on to win 62 percent of the vote to Young's 38 percent. In November, Bonner easily defeated Democratic businesswoman Judy McCain Belk in the GOP-dominated district.

Setting up shop was a breeze for Bonner. He kept all but two of Callahan's staff, whom he had helped hire through the years. He also took over from his former boss a weekly television talk show called "The Gulf Coast Congressional Report," which aired for years on Sunday mornings. Bonner got good reviews as a smooth, telegenic interviewer.

In 2004, after Belk challenged him in a rematch, Bonner won with 63 percent of the vote. Two years later, he boosted his total to 68 percent.

KEY VOTES

2006

- No Stop broadband companies from favoring select Internet traffic
- Yes Affirm U.S. commitment to war in Iraq and reject setting a withdrawal date for troops
- Yes Repeal requirement for bilingual ballots at the polls
- Yes Permit U.S. sale of civilian nuclear technology to India
- Yes Build a 700-mile fence on the U.S.-Mexico border to curb illegal crossings
- Yes Permit warrantless wiretaps of suspected terrorists

2005

- Yes Intervene in the life-support case of Terri Schiavo
- No Lift President Bush's restrictions on stem cell research funding
- No Prohibit FBI access to library and bookstore records
- Yes Approve free-trade pact with five Central American countries
- No Pass energy policy overhaul favored by President Bush emphasizing domestic oil and gas production
- Yes End mandatory preservation of habitat of endangered animal and plant species
- No Ban torture of prisoners in U.S. custody

CQ VOTE STUDIES

	PARTY UNITY		PRESIDENTIAL SUPPORT	
	Support	Oppose	Support	Oppose
2006	96%	4%	93%	7%
2005	96%	4%	83%	17%
2004	97%	3%	92%	8%
2003	97%	3%	98%	2%

INTEREST GROUPS

	AFL-CIO	ADA	CCUS	ACU
2006	7%	0%	100%	88%
2005	7%	0%	89%	100%
2004	15%	0%	100%	95%
2003	7%	5%	97%	88%

ALABAMA 1

Southwest – Mobile

The beaches of still-ravaged coastal areas in Mobile County and resorts in Baldwin County give way to pine forests and cotton and soybean fields in the northern reaches of the 1st. The city of Mobile anchors the solidly GOP 1st, Alabama's only Gulf Coast district, and has enjoyed recent economic growth that continued even after the 2005 hurricane season.

The coastal communities that suffered direct damage from Hurricane Katrina's storm surge faced well more than a year of rebuilding, relying on state and federal aid, as well as volunteer assistance from national, regional and religious charities. Along the coast, debris lingered inland and in shallow waters, and residents lived in FEMA trailers into 2007. Some communities, like Bayou La Batre, received attention and grant awards for infrastructure and housing redevelopment, while smaller, unincorporated communities have struggled in relative obscurity.

Comparatively unharmed by Hurricane Katrina, Mobile, unlike other areas along the Gulf, was able to re-establish commercial activity within months of the disaster. In the storm's aftermath, the city's port welcomed companies in the shipping industry and the local retail sector served a swath of the greater Gulf Coast area. As part of a barrage of new and expanding shipping and manufacturing business in Mobile, International Shipholding relocated from New Orleans and ST Mobile Aerospace Engineering — the county's largest private employer — signed a deal with FedEx to convert planes at its Mobile facility. Strong shipping, fishing and container industries, along with rising housing prices and tax revenues, place Mobile at the vanguard of growth in Alabama.

Hurricane Katrina had no direct impact on the coast of growing Baldwin County, but tourism at its beaches has not yet recovered from damage caused by Hurricane Ivan in 2004, and condominium and resort development has slowed as buyers are deterred by high homeowner's and flood insurance rates.

MAJOR INDUSTRY

Commercial shipping, aerospace, timber, distribution, agriculture

CITIES

Mobile, 198,915; Prichard, 28,633; Daphne, 16,581; Tillmans Corner, 15,685

NOTABLE

Author Harper Lee based the fictional setting of "To Kill a Mockingbird" on her hometown of Monroeville.

Rep. Terry Everett (R)

CAPITOL OFFICE
225-2901
www.house.gov/everett
2312 Rayburn 20515-0102; fax 225-8913

COMMITTEES
Agriculture
Armed Services
Select Intelligence

RESIDENCE
Rehobeth

BORN
Feb. 15, 1937, Dothan, Ala.

RELIGION
Baptist

FAMILY
Wife, Barbara Everett

EDUCATION
Dale County H.S., graduated 1955

MILITARY SERVICE
Air Force, 1955-59

CAREER
Newspaper executive; construction company owner; farm owner; real estate developer; newspaper reporter

POLITICAL HIGHLIGHTS
No previous office

ELECTION RESULTS

2006 GENERAL		
Terry Everett (R)	124,302	69.5%
Charles D. "Chuck" James (D)	54,450	30.4%
2006 PRIMARY		
Terry Everett (R)	unopposed	
2004 GENERAL		
Terry Everett (R)	177,086	71.4%
Charles D. "Chuck" James (D)	70,562	28.5%

PREVIOUS WINNING PERCENTAGES
2002 (69%); 2000 (68%); 1998 (69%); 1996 (63%); 1994 (74%); 1992 (49%)

Elected 1992; 8th term

Everett was 55 and a self-made millionaire when he won his first election to the House as a conservative from a district whose economy is reliant on agriculture and its military bases. But his attempts to move up the ranks in Congress were thwarted for years by his refusal to raise large amounts of cash for the Republican Party at election time.

GOP leaders passed him over for chairman of the Veterans' Affairs Committee in 2005, in favor of a more junior lawmaker. Two years earlier, Everett lost a bid for Agriculture Committee chairman to Robert W. Goodlatte of Virginia.

Everett remained peeved that the National Republican Congressional Committee, the House GOP's political arm, had backed another candidate in his first run for Congress in 1992. But in the run-up to the 2006 elections, Everett reconciled with the NRCC and contributed $71,000 to its coffers.

Everett is the second-ranking Republican on both the Agriculture and Intelligence committees. He also is the top-ranking Republican on Armed Services' Strategic Forces Subcommittee. There, Everett's interest has been the frequently overlooked issue of protecting the country's space-based technology. "Most members of Congress have only a vague idea of what space means to our military and to our economy," he says.

Everett was one of the major proponents of the so-called bunker buster program, a multimillion-dollar effort to determine whether a nuclear weapon encased in a hardened shell could burrow into the ground and destroy an enemy's buried targets. Democrats balked, saying the program could trigger a new nuclear arms race or lower the threshold for use of a nuclear weapon.

He is a booster of the Bush administration's policies in Iraq, though he has been among the Republicans to express doubts about the way the war has been conducted. In October 2006, Everett joined 32 members of Armed Services in a letter to President Bush urging him to send more troops to Baghdad to try to quell an expanding civil war.

Parochially, Everett looks out for his district's numerous defense contractors and two major military bases, Maxwell-Gunter Air Force Base and Fort Rucker, where Air Force and Army helicopter crews train.

An Air Force intelligence analyst in the 1950s, Everett won a seat on the Intelligence panel in 2002, as the war on terror took center stage. He has consistently called for tougher measures than Congress as a whole has been willing to adopt, insisting that a 2004 intelligence reform bill should have allowed expedited deportation of illegal aliens without judicial review and prevented states from giving driver's licenses to illegal aliens. Both ideas passed the House but were dropped in the final legislation, which Everett voted against. He has opposed efforts to limit the executive branch's ability to conduct domestic surveillance of terrorism suspects.

From 1997 through 2000, he chaired the Veterans' Affairs Subcommittee on Oversight and Investigations, where he aggressively investigated problems reported within the VA. His probes of favoritism in burial policies, delays in payment of disability claims and complaints about substandard medical care put Everett in the news nationally.

His other major interest in the House is agriculture, especially federal policy on peanut farming, an economic mainstay of his district in southeastern Alabama. When Republicans introduced their Freedom to Farm legislation in 1995, Everett was one of the key lawmakers who fended off efforts to eliminate generous price supports for peanut farmers, a significant achievement considering that the new GOP leadership was flexing its muscle to end them. Later, during the 2002 rewrite of the farm bill, Everett again was up against a strong political current to eliminate the 30-cents-a-pound peanut subsidy. As chairman of the Agriculture Subcommittee on Specialty Crops, he formed a coalition with colleagues from peanut-growing Georgia to negotiate a phaseout of the program.

A former peanut farmer himself, Everett was the object of some derision after the Washington Post, New York Times and Wall Street Journal quoted an Everett press release insisting peanut farmers were essential to "fight terrorism." Everett says he was misquoted; his comment was that agriculture ensures a steady supply of food and fiber, which is vital to national security.

A solid conservative vote on social issues, Everett cosponsored a measure in the 108th Congress (2003-04) that would have allowed Congress, by a two-thirds majority vote, to override the Supreme Court if the justices ruled that a particular law was unconstitutional.

Growing up in Dothan, Ala., Everett had a tough start in life. His mother died of brain cancer when he was a senior in high school. Unable to afford college, Everett signed up with the Air Force, where he learned Russian and joined an intelligence unit. When he got back from his service in 1959, his father suffered a fatal heart attack. Everett took charge of the care of his 17-year-old brother and 12-year-old sister, getting by on his small salary as a sports reporter for The Dothan Eagle.

After several years of learning the newspaper business, Everett scraped together the capital to start his own newspaper, then gradually bought up five small papers in the region. He says he sold them in the late 1980s "for more money than I ever thought I could have," and indulged his dream of starting a construction business.

Although successful in business, he was virtually unknown in political circles in 1992 when Republican Bill Dickinson retired after 14 terms. Everett decided to run even though the party establishment was backing a state senator. Spending $600,000 of his own money, Everett won the primary and prevailed in the fall against Democratic state Treasurer George C. Wallace III, son of the former governor. Everett proved to have both the means and a message. He blanketed the district in billboards and TV ads saying: "Send a message, not a politician."

Everett won with a bare plurality of 49 percent of the vote that year but has had no trouble winning re-election since.

KEY VOTES

2006

- No Stop broadband companies from favoring select Internet traffic
- Yes Affirm U.S. commitment to war in Iraq and reject setting a withdrawal date for troops
- Yes Repeal requirement for bilingual ballots at the polls
- Yes Permit U.S. sale of civilian nuclear technology to India
- Yes Build a 700-mile fence on the U.S.-Mexico border to curb illegal crossings
- Yes Permit warrantless wiretaps of suspected terrorists

2005

- ? Intervene in the life-support case of Terri Schiavo
- No Lift President Bush's restrictions on stem cell research funding
- No Prohibit FBI access to library and bookstore records
- Yes Approve free-trade pact with five Central American countries
- Yes Pass energy policy overhaul favored by President Bush emphasizing domestic oil and gas production
- Yes End mandatory preservation of habitat of endangered animal and plant species
- No Ban torture of prisoners in U.S. custody

CQ VOTE STUDIES

	PARTY UNITY		PRESIDENTIAL SUPPORT	
	Support	Oppose	Support	Oppose
2006	95%	5%	87%	13%
2005	96%	4%	85%	15%
2004	93%	7%	76%	24%
2003	97%	3%	89%	11%
2002	99%	1%	85%	15%

INTEREST GROUPS

	AFL-CIO	ADA	CCUS	ACU
2006	14%	5%	93%	88%
2005	14%	0%	85%	96%
2004	13%	0%	100%	92%
2003	13%	10%	90%	84%
2002	0%	0%	84%	100%

ALABAMA 2

Southeast – part of Montgomery, Dothan

The 2nd takes in a chunk of Montgomery, the industrial city of Dothan, and small towns that dot the rural southern Alabama coastal plain. The inland district did not sustain heavy damage when Hurricane Katrina hit the Gulf Coast in late 2005, but it absorbed thousands of evacuees from the storm, mostly in the state capital of Montgomery (split with the 3rd).

Defense and state government provide many jobs in the Montgomery area. Maxwell Air Force Base and its Gunter Annex are responsible for many of the Air Force's computer systems, but the area is bracing for the loss of more than 1,000 jobs on the base as a result of the 2005 round of BRAC recommendations. The State Capitol Complex, nestled in a curling slice of the neighboring 3rd District, serves as a major area job center.

Dothan, in the 2nd's southeast, relies on diverse manufacturing interests and operates as a regional distribution hub. Fort Rucker, 20 miles to the northwest, is an Army aviation training center and supports activities at the Dothan Regional Airport, which is known less for passenger traffic and more for its military presence and the industrial park on its premises.

Agriculture is vital to the economy of the district's vast rural areas, and major crops include peanuts, cotton and soybeans — the 2nd is the nation's second-highest peanut-producing district. Tourism is a steadily increasing business, and large antebellum homes in Eufaula and fishing on Lake Eufaula, on the border with Georgia, lure visitors to the area.

A large military retiree population underscores the 2nd's conservative bent. In 2006, Republican Gov. Bob Riley won every county here except Barbour, Conecuh and black-majority Lowndes and Bullock, but the 2nd's residents have sent conservative Democrats to the state legislature.

MAJOR INDUSTRY
Agriculture, defense, manufacturing, government

MILITARY BASES
Fort Rucker (Army), 4,900 military, 7,200 civilian (2006); Maxwell-Gunter Air Force Base, 4,018 military, 3,652 civilian (2005)

CITIES
Montgomery (pt.), 127,986; Dothan, 57,737; Prattville, 24,303

NOTABLE
The Hank Williams Sr. museum in Georgiana; The Boll Weevil Monument in Enterprise honors the insect, whose taste for cotton induced farmers to grow peanuts; Dothan hosts a national peanut festival annually.

Rep. Mike D. Rogers (R)

CAPITOL OFFICE
225-3261
www.house.gov/mike-rogers
324 Cannon 20515-0103; fax 226-8485

COMMITTEES
Agriculture
Armed Services
Homeland Security

RESIDENCE
Anniston

BORN
July 16, 1958, Hammond, Ind.

RELIGION
Baptist

FAMILY
Wife, Donna Elizabeth "Beth" Rogers; three children

EDUCATION
Jacksonville State U., B.A. 1981 (political science & psychology), M.P.A. 1985; Birmingham School of Law, J.D. 1991

CAREER
Lawyer; laid-off worker assistance program director; psychiatric counselor

POLITICAL HIGHLIGHTS
Calhoun County Commission, 1987-91; candidate for Ala. House, 1990; Ala. House, 1995-2002 (minority leader, 1998-2000)

ELECTION RESULTS

2006 GENERAL		
Mike D. Rogers (R)	98,257	59.4%
Greg A. Pierce (D)	63,559	38.4%
Mark Edwin Layfield (I)	3,414	2.1%
2006 PRIMARY		
Mike D. Rogers (R)		unopposed
2004 GENERAL		
Mike D. Rogers (R)	150,411	61.2%
Bill Fuller (D)	95,240	38.8%

PREVIOUS WINNING PERCENTAGES
2002 (50%)

Elected 2002; 3rd term

Rogers is a diehard supporter of President Bush and a dutiful foot soldier for the Republican leadership in the House. Long after many of his colleagues began distancing themselves from the president on the war in Iraq, he stood fast. "In my world, there is no waning support," he said in 2006. "I'm not getting any push to pull people back before the job's done."

Rogers' world is conservative, culturally and politically. Even though his district in eastern Alabama has a fair number of Democrats, it also is home to many military families, including a large share with someone serving in Iraq. He says support for the U.S. effort in Iraq is "rock solid" in his area. "Folks know that I'm representing their view of the world."

Rogers serves on the Armed Services Committee, where he looks out for the interests of Anniston Army Depot, in his hometown, and of nearby Maxwell-Gunter Air Force Base northwest of Montgomery and Fort Benning, across the border in Georgia. While Republicans were in power, he helped secure $24 million for building Army ground combat vehicles at the Anniston Depot. He also worked to get $55 million in homeland security funds for domestic security training at the old Fort McClellan base, shuttered in 1999.

Homeland security issues occupy a growing share of his attention. He is the top-ranking Republican on the Homeland Security panel's Management, Investigations and Oversight Subcommittee, which he chaired in the 109th Congress (2005-06). Of the Homeland Security Department he says: "This agency is going to be with us for generations, and it's going to become larger and a more important part of our lives than anyone realizes right now." He has targeted border security procurement contracts for special scrutiny.

Border security is an issue that riles his constituents, Rogers says. "People are upset about the fact that we have so many millions of illegals here and nobody knows who they are." He voted in 2005 to make it a crime to be in the United States without legal documentation and in 2006 for legislation calling for a 700-mile fence along the border with Mexico.

The son of a textile worker and a defender of that diminished industry in his state, Rogers opposes free trade with China and is wary of any trade pacts that might hurt the domestic textile industry. He opposed the Morocco Free Trade Agreement in 2004, saying the country has become a conduit for the many Chinese manufacturers there. And he voted against a 2006 bill granting Vietnam normal trade status and extending trade preferences for Haiti and other countries, saying it might open a "back door" for importing "increased numbers of state-subsidized foreign goods." But he voted for the 2005 Central American Free Trade Agreement after he and fellow Alabama Republican Spencer Bachus secured some protections for their state's textile industry.

Rogers is a fervent social conservative and supports an amendment to the Constitution allowing prayer in public schools, which he calls "restoring religious freedom." He is outspoken in the movement for more restrictions on content in broadcast programming, cosponsoring a bill in the 108th Congress (2003-04) raising penalties for violations of federal standards of decency.

The one bump for him during his first term came on a local issue that aroused passions in the district. Rogers supported the burning of chemical agents and munitions at a new federal incinerator at the Anniston Depot, even though local school officials said they had not adequately prepared their buildings for an accidental release of air toxins. GOP Sen. Richard C. Shelby of Alabama came out in favor of a delay. Ultimately, all sides agreed to a timetable to begin destroying more than 2,000 tons of chemicals being stored in aging, leaky igloos. Rogers weathered the controversy, handily winning re-election in 2004.

Rogers traces his ancestry back five generations in eastern Alabama, where his mother worked in a textile factory for 33 years. His father was a federal fireman. Neither graduated from high school, but Rogers made it all the way through law school. While working for the United Way as a career counselor, he met his wife, who worked for a local power company. They attended law school at night and after graduating, she stayed at the power company while he started his own law practice in Anniston.

Rogers says his parents were conservatives who supported Gov. George C. Wallace Jr. and President Richard Nixon. "My dad was a very strong supporter of President Nixon, and that made an impression on me," he says. He volunteered for Ronald Reagan and recalls, "working in his presidential campaign and thinking when my contemporaries became adults, this would be a Republican South because he had so captivated people in the South."

At age 28, Rogers became the first Republican elected to the Calhoun County Commission, long dominated by conservative Democrats. He was elected to the Alabama House in 1994, where he focused on health care and wrote a bill forcing every insurance plan to cover payments to doctors not in their networks. He eventually became House minority leader.

In 2002, when Republican Rep. Bob Riley ran, successfully, for governor, Rogers jumped into the race for his House seat. He got a big helping hand from top Republicans, including Bush, who stumped for him in Auburn. His competition was Joe Turnham, a businessman aided by national Democratic Party organizations, which saw an opportunity to take away a GOP seat. But Rogers won by a slim 2 percentage points.

In 2004, Democrats fielded an impressive candidate in Bill Fuller, a veteran state legislator who chaired the Alabama House Ways and Means Committee. The district is a third African-American, and two of the state's leading black political groups endorsed Fuller. But Rogers raised more than $2 million, with the help of GOP leaders who put him on their list of 10 most vulnerable House members. He beat Fuller, capturing 61 percent of the vote. In 2006, Rogers cruised to re-election by more than 20 percentage points.

In Congress, Rogers often has to deal with the confusion caused by the presence of another House Republican named Mike Rogers. While the two have similar voting records, the other Rogers is from Michigan.

KEY VOTES

2006

- No Stop broadband companies from favoring select Internet traffic
- Yes Affirm U.S. commitment to war in Iraq and reject setting a withdrawal date for troops
- Yes Repeal requirement for bilingual ballots at the polls
- Yes Permit U.S. sale of civilian nuclear technology to India
- Yes Build a 700-mile fence on the U.S.-Mexico border to curb illegal crossings
- Yes Permit warrantless wiretaps of suspected terrorists

2005

- Yes Intervene in the life-support case of Terri Schiavo
- No Lift President Bush's restrictions on stem cell research funding
- No Prohibit FBI access to library and bookstore records
- Yes Approve free-trade pact with five Central American countries
- Yes Pass energy policy overhaul favored by President Bush emphasizing domestic oil and gas production
- Yes End mandatory preservation of habitat of endangered animal and plant species
- No Ban torture of prisoners in U.S. custody

CQ VOTE STUDIES

	PARTY UNITY		PRESIDENTIAL SUPPORT	
	Support	Oppose	Support	Oppose
2006	96%	4%	83%	17%
2005	94%	6%	83%	17%
2004	95%	5%	76%	24%
2003	97%	3%	94%	6%

INTEREST GROUPS

	AFL-CIO	ADA	CCUS	ACU
2006	36%	10%	87%	84%
2005	31%	10%	85%	88%
2004	13%	10%	100%	88%
2003	7%	5%	97%	88%

ALABAMA 3

East – part of Montgomery, Auburn, Anniston

A microcosm of the state, the 3rd enjoys a diversified economy that includes agriculture, industry, government and universities. The district escaped most of the damage caused by Hurricane Katrina in 2005, but the capital city of Montgomery (shared with the 2nd) took in thousands of evacuees. The 3rd's section of Montgomery is home to many significant historical sites and tourist attractions, including the State Capitol Complex, the first White House of the Confederacy and the Dexter Avenue Baptist Church, where the 1955 bus boycott was launched.

Anniston, the Calhoun County seat, relies heavily on federal government jobs. The Justice Department turned former Army base Fort McClellan into a training site for first-responders to chemical, biological and nuclear terrorist attacks. A chemical weapons incinerator at the Anniston Army Depot raised environmental concerns, but has operated without incident.

Auburn University, one of the state's largest employers and a national leader in agricultural research, is developing a research park that is part of a joint venture with the city of Auburn and the state of Alabama. The city has undertaken efforts over the past two decades to lure technology firms and diversify economically beyond reliance on the university. The local industrial base includes a Honda plant in Lincoln and Hyundai's first U.S. plant, south of Montgomery. Area textile mills still struggle to compete with cheap imports.

The Republican-leaning 3rd, the state's most competitive district on paper, has many longtime conservative Democrats who now favor GOP presidential candidates, as well as blacks and small pockets of university liberals who support Democrats at all levels.

MAJOR INDUSTRY
Higher education, technology, manufacturing, defense, textiles

MILITARY BASES
Anniston Army Depot, 57 military, 6,900 civilian (2007)

CITIES
Montgomery (pt.), 73,582; Auburn, 42,987; Phenix City, 28,265; Anniston, 24,276; Opelika, 23,498

NOTABLE
Tuskegee University, founded in 1881, was the first historically black college to be recognized as a National Historic Landmark; Talladega Superspeedway and the International Motorsports Hall of Fame.

Rep. Robert B. Aderholt (R)

CAPITOL OFFICE
225-4876
aderholt.house.gov
1433 Longworth 20515-0104; fax 225-5587

COMMITTEES
Appropriations

RESIDENCE
Haleyville

BORN
July 22, 1965, Haleyville, Ala.

RELIGION
Congregationalist Baptist

FAMILY
Wife, Caroline Aderholt; two children

EDUCATION
Birmingham Southern U., B.A. 1987 (history & political science); Samford U., J.D. 1990

CAREER
Lawyer; gubernatorial aide

POLITICAL HIGHLIGHTS
Republican nominee for Ala. House, 1990; Haleyville municipal judge, 1992-96

ELECTION RESULTS

2006 GENERAL		
Robert B. Aderholt (R)	128,484	70.2%
Barbara Bobo (D)	54,382	29.7%
2006 PRIMARY		
Robert B. Aderholt (R)		unopposed
2004 GENERAL		
Robert B. Aderholt (R)	191,110	74.7%
Carl Cole (D)	64,278	25.1%

PREVIOUS WINNING PERCENTAGES
2002 (87%); 2000 (61%); 1998 (56%); 1996 (50%)

Elected 1996; 6th term

An economic and social conservative, Aderholt wants to see the government tax and spend less. Nonetheless, he works hard to steer a share of federal money to his district and state. As a member of the Appropriations Committee, he has defended the congressional power of the purse, even when fellow Republicans sought to crimp it.

In 2006, Aderholt (ADD-er-holt) was one of just 15 House Republicans to vote against legislation giving the president enhanced power to eliminate line items in spending bills, subject to a final vote of Congress. He said he agreed with the goal of controlling spending but that the line-item veto was not the right way of going about it. "Congress needs to continue to take responsibility for spending and not pass the buck to the president."

A member of the conservative Republican Study Committee, Aderholt believes that Congress and the president should be more aggressive in moving toward a balanced budget. However, the Alabama Republican has resisted efforts by many in his party to crack down on earmarks, the special projects that lawmakers insert into spending bills for their home districts.

In 2006, he reluctantly voted for a measure that included a requirement that the sponsors of earmarks in appropriations bills be made public. Like other GOP appropriators, he did so only after winning a promise that similar disclosure requirements would be applied to earmarks in other types of bills, such as tax legislation. But in 2007, when House Democrats put forward a rules package broadening the disclosure to all bills, Aderholt voted against it.

The son of a judge who also was a Baptist pastor, Aderholt's own judicious and strait-laced demeanor was nurtured not only in his home but also all around it. Northern Alabama has long been one of the most religiously conservative areas of the nation.

Aderholt is best known for his efforts to bring religious values into the public sphere. His most publicized cause in Washington has been to permit public displays of the Ten Commandments. It is a mission he embraced soon after he arrived in 1997 when a federal judge, citing the First Amendment, ordered a judge in Aderholt's district to remove a copy of the commandments from his courtroom wall.

In 2003, when another federal judge ordered the removal of a stone display of the Ten Commandments from Montgomery's state judicial complex, Aderholt said it was a "scene one would expect to see in the former Soviet Union, not the United States of America." In 2005, he introduced legislation that would bar court action against government officials as a result of their "acknowledgement of God as the sovereign source of law, liberty or government."

Aderholt argues that the Constitution has been misinterpreted over the past 40 years by activist judges who have denied the freedom of expression of faith. "Discrimination against religion under the guise of separation of church and state needs to end," he says.

Aderholt is staunchly opposed to abortion; he favors constitutional amendments to outlaw all abortions except to save the life of the woman and has supported all legislation limiting abortion rights. He also opposes human cloning and embryonic stem cell research.

As a member of the Helsinki Commission monitoring human rights in Europe and the countries of the former Soviet Union, Aderholt has extended his campaign for freedom of religious expression overseas, particularly in Georgia and Turkmenistan.

Ever since GOP leaders awarded him a prized appointment to the Appropriations Committee in 1997, Aderholt has quietly steered federal dollars to northern Alabama. He has waged more combative — though less successful — efforts to protect the regionally important steel and textile industries that have been clobbered by foreign competition. After a Gulf States Steel plant in Gadsden closed in 2000, eliminating 1,700 jobs, Aderholt backed legislation providing loan guarantees for steel companies hurt by foreign imports, part of an effort to attract a buyer to reopen the plant.

The next year, when VF Corp., manufacturer of Lee and Wrangler jeans, closed four factories in and around the 4th District, Aderholt voted against granting the president fast-track authority to negotiate trade deals. Seven months later, he voted for the final version of the bill, reversing course after House leaders promised to fight against lifting tariffs on socks made in the Caribbean — an issue of parochial importance because of the major role textile mills play in the local economy.

He voted for the 2005 Central American Free Trade Agreement, which barely squeaked through the Republican-controlled House, but only after receiving written assurances from top administration officials — and a personal phone call from President Bush — vowing that they would help protect domestic sockmakers from import surges. The trade pact passed the House by two votes. But in 2006, Aderholt voted against trade agreements with Haiti and Vietnam.

Aderholt grew up with politics. When he was 5, he wrote a campaign letter touting his father, a judge, in a local election, and he recalls meeting Republican Sen. Bob Dole of Kansas when he was about 11. A month after his law school graduation, Aderholt was nominated for a state House seat but lost the general election. Appointed to a municipal court judgeship in 1992, he went to work for Republican Gov. Fob James Jr. in 1995.

When Democratic Rep. Tom Bevill retired in 1996 after 15 terms, Aderholt decided to try for the seat, believing that it shared demographic and political characteristics with the neighboring 1st District of Mississippi, a longtime Democratic bastion that Republican Roger Wicker had won two years before. In the GOP primary, Aderholt took 49 percent of the vote against four rivals; he won the nomination when the second-place finisher declined to demand a runoff.

Democrats put up a strong candidate in former state Sen. Robert T. "Bob" Wilson Jr., who was nearly as conservative as Aderholt on social issues. Aderholt prevailed by 2 percentage points. He has won handily since.

KEY VOTES

2006

- No Stop broadband companies from favoring select Internet traffic
- Yes Affirm U.S. commitment to war in Iraq and reject setting a withdrawal date for troops
- Yes Repeal requirement for bilingual ballots at the polls
- Yes Permit U.S. sale of civilian nuclear technology to India
- Yes Build a 700-mile fence on the U.S.-Mexico border to curb illegal crossings
- Yes Permit warrantless wiretaps of suspected terrorists

2005

- Yes Intervene in the life-support case of Terri Schiavo
- No Lift President Bush's restrictions on stem cell research funding
- No Prohibit FBI access to library and bookstore records
- Yes Approve free-trade pact with five Central American countries
- Yes Pass energy policy overhaul favored by President Bush emphasizing domestic oil and gas production
- Yes End mandatory preservation of habitat of endangered animal and plant species
- No Ban torture of prisoners in U.S. custody

CQ VOTE STUDIES

	PARTY UNITY		PRESIDENTIAL SUPPORT	
	Support	Oppose	Support	Oppose
2006	95%	5%	87%	13%
2005	97%	3%	93%	7%
2004	93%	7%	85%	15%
2003	96%	4%	92%	8%
2002	96%	4%	82%	18%

INTEREST GROUPS

	AFL-CIO	ADA	CCUS	ACU
2006	21%	10%	87%	84%
2005	13%	0%	85%	92%
2004	7%	0%	100%	92%
2003	20%	10%	89%	83%
2002	11%	0%	90%	92%

ALABAMA 4

North central – Gadsden, part of Decatur

Taking in mountains, foothills, flatlands and large waterways, the rural 4th runs the width of the state, bordering both Mississippi and Georgia. A small black population and the absence of a major city distinguish the relatively poor district from the rest of Alabama.

The 4th relies on assistance from the Appalachian Regional Commission, a decades-old federal-state partnership to aid development and reduce poverty in the area. Completion of "Corridor X," an interstate route following U.S. 78 across the 4th from Mississippi, is a priority of the commission and of local officials, who hope the route will attract new midsize businesses. Many local residents work in nearby metropolitan areas, such as Huntsville (in the 5th) and Birmingham (in the 6th and 7th).

Despite volatility in the coal market and the loss of manufacturing and textile jobs abroad, textiles, mining and rubber and other manufacturing are still major job sources here. The industrial sector has diversified beyond steel and textiles to include food processing and wood products. The Tennessee Valley Authority's Guntersville Reservoir, shared with the 5th, supports a shipping-based economy in Guntersville. Gadsden, the district's only sizable city, has had some success with economic diversification efforts following manufacturing plant closures.

Agribusinesses, especially cattle and poultry enterprises, form a significant sector of the local economy, and tourism is growing. The mountainous landscape provides opportunities for outdoor recreation, and Smith Lake — a 21,000-acre man-made body of water shared by Cullman, Walker and Winston counties — lures visitors to the 4th.

Once a Democratic stronghold, the 4th's conservative population tends to support GOP candidates nationally, but still elects Democrats to state and local offices. In 1996, voters sent a Republican to Congress for just the second time since Reconstruction, and have re-elected him since.

MAJOR INDUSTRY

Manufacturing, textiles, mining, agriculture, tourism

CITIES

Gadsden, 38,978; Albertville, 17,247; Jasper, 14,052; Cullman, 13,995

NOTABLE

Albertville, home to a Mueller fire hydrant plant, calls itself the Fire Hydrant Capital of the World.

Rep. Robert E. 'Bud' Cramer (D)

Elected 1990; 9th term

One of the most conservative Democrats in the House, Cramer sides with members of his own party in major policy disputes only about 60 percent of the time. He votes more often with President Bush than even some Republicans. In spite of the president's eroding popularity in recent years, Cramer supported the White House position more often than 11 Republicans in the House in the 109th Congress (2005-06).

And on votes that pitted the two parties against each other during the two-year span, only one Democrat defected from his party leadership more often, Dan Boren of Oklahoma.

Cramer's independence often frustrates the liberal Democratic leadership, but it suits his constituents. Republicans didn't bother to field a candidate against him in 2006, even though Bush carried the district with 60 percent of the vote two years earlier. Jimmy Carter was the last Democratic presidential candidate to win Alabama's northernmost district.

After revelations that the administration had authorized domestic spying without court warrants, Cramer was among only 18 House Democrats who voted to sanction the practice. He voted to limit the scope of the Endangered Species Act, one of 36 Democrats to do so, and he voted in favor of a constitutional amendment to outlaw same-sex marriage. In 2005, he was among the Democrats supporting the conservative-led effort to intervene in the right-to-die legal case of Terri Schiavo, a severely brain-damaged Florida woman. Meddling by Congress proved highly unpopular, with most polls showing a majority of Americans holding the opinion that the decision to remove the woman's feeding tube should have been left to the courts.

A founding member of the Blue Dogs, a coalition of more than 40 conservative House Democrats, Cramer was one of just seven House Democrats who voted for the 2003 tax cut bill, and he was the chief Democratic cosponsor of legislation to permanently repeal the estate tax.

For years he's been a recruitment target of the GOP as it gained hegemony in the deep South, but Cramer resisted entreaties from Alabama's senior senator, Richard C. Shelby, to follow his example and switch to the Republican Party. House Democratic leaders may not like his lack of loyalty, but they are careful to keep him on the team. Early in 2002, shortly after it was reported that Republicans were dangling an assignment to the House Intelligence Committee as an enticement, Democrats arranged for Cramer to get a seat on the panel.

In 2007, he got a seat on the powerful Defense Appropriations Subcommittee, a plum he calls a "career-long dream." He also was appointed to a newly created Select Intelligence Oversight Panel housed within the Appropriations panel. In 2006, Cramer joined with Republican William M. "Mac" Thornberry of Texas in issuing a report that criticized the Bush administration for moving too slowly in implementing a 2004 intelligence community overhaul that restructured the nation's spy operations.

Cramer has some parochial interest in intelligence matters, too. When the House passed the fiscal 2006 intelligence authorization bill, the mission of the Missile and Space Intelligence Center in Huntsville was expanded to include analyzing the threats posed by foreign missiles to commercial and military aircraft and developing defenses against those threats.

On a handful of big issues, Cramer stuck with his party in the 109th Congress. He joined most Democrats in voting to override Bush's veto of leg-

CAPITOL OFFICE
225-4801
budmail@mail.house.gov
cramer.house.gov
2184 Rayburn 20515-0105; fax 225-4392

COMMITTEES
Appropriations
Select Intelligence
(Oversight & Investigations - chairman)

RESIDENCE
Huntsville

BORN
Aug. 22, 1947, Huntsville, Ala.

RELIGION
Methodist

FAMILY
Widowed; one child

EDUCATION
U. of Alabama, B.A. 1969 (English), J.D. 1972

MILITARY SERVICE
Army, 1972; Army Reserve, 1976-78

CAREER
Lawyer

POLITICAL HIGHLIGHTS
Madison County district attorney, 1981-91

ELECTION RESULTS

2006 GENERAL		
Robert E. "Bud" Cramer (D)	143,015	98.2%
write-ins	2,540	1.7%
2006 PRIMARY		
Robert E. "Bud" Cramer (D)		unopposed
2004 GENERAL		
Robert E. "Bud" Cramer (D)	200,999	73.0%
Gerald "Gerry" Wallace (R)	74,145	26.9%

PREVIOUS WINNING PERCENTAGES
2002 (73%); 2000 (89%); 1998 (70%); 1996 (56%); 1994 (50%); 1992 (66%); 1990 (67%)

islation expanding federal funding of stem cell research, and supported a ban on cruel and inhuman treatment of detainees in U.S. custody. Earlier, he joined Democrats in backing a bill to permit importation of American-made prescription drugs from other countries and in opposing private school vouchers in the District of Columbia.

"This place has often driven me crazy because it's a difficult place to organize," Cramer said in early 2007, reflecting on his 16 years in the House. "I like to think out of the box. This place, partisanship runs strong. It bothers me we don't work together on these issues. I'm a good networker across the aisle."

Cramer has a keen interest in children's issues, which dates to the beginning of his career as an assistant district attorney in Huntsville more than 25 years ago, when he was in charge of juvenile cases. "I learned more about child abuse than I wanted to learn," he says.

Cramer went on to serve 10 years as district attorney, founding the Children's Advocacy Center to shelter and counsel abused children. In Congress, he was responsible for legislation in 1992 to provide federal assistance to a national network of centers modeled on the Huntsville program. Cramer has been able to ensure funding for the centers from his seat on the Appropriations panel.

Local economic development is one of Cramer's priorities. He says he likes to "knock on the doors of businesses" to tout northern Alabama as an attractive destination. In 2004, Cramer announced that Toyota would undertake a major expansion of its engine manufacturing plant in Huntsville, a plant he had worked to attract to the area in 2001. In the 1990s, he helped persuade McDonnell-Douglas, since merged with Boeing Corp., to build a $450 million rocket booster plant in Decatur.

Cramer was born and raised in Huntsville. His parents started the first travel agency there in the 1950s, and though it struggled at first, the business prospered as the city grew. After law school, Cramer married a woman from Huntsville, and the two settled there. (Cramer is now widowed.)

After his stint as district attorney, Cramer saw a chance to move up when Democrat Ronnie G. Flippo left the House seat open in 1990 to run for governor. Cramer won with two-thirds of the vote.

Four years later, as the GOP landslide swept other white Southern Democrats from the House, he narrowly survived. Cramer won by just 1,770 votes over well-funded and well-connected Wayne Parker, the son-in-law of then influential Texas Republican Rep. Bill Archer. Cramer has since won by wide margins and drew no GOP opponent in 2006.

KEY VOTES

2006

- No Stop broadband companies from favoring select Internet traffic
- Yes Affirm U.S. commitment to war in Iraq and reject setting a withdrawal date for troops
- No Repeal requirement for bilingual ballots at the polls
- Yes Permit U.S. sale of civilian nuclear technology to India
- Yes Build a 700-mile fence on the U.S.-Mexico border to curb illegal crossings
- Yes Permit warrantless wiretaps of suspected terrorists

2005

- Yes Intervene in the life-support case of Terri Schiavo
- Yes Lift President Bush's restrictions on stem cell research funding
- Yes Prohibit FBI access to library and bookstore records
- No Approve free-trade pact with five Central American countries
- Yes Pass energy policy overhaul favored by President Bush emphasizing domestic oil and gas production
- Yes End mandatory preservation of habitat of endangered animal and plant species
- Yes Ban torture of prisoners in U.S. custody

CQ VOTE STUDIES

	PARTY UNITY		PRESIDENTIAL SUPPORT	
	Support	Oppose	Support	Oppose
2006	60%	40%	72%	28%
2005	60%	40%	66%	34%
2004	61%	39%	64%	36%
2003	62%	38%	73%	27%
2002	61%	39%	62%	38%

INTEREST GROUPS

	AFL-CIO	ADA	CCUS	ACU
2006	79%	50%	93%	68%
2005	57%	75%	81%	54%
2004	60%	75%	86%	50%
2003	58%	45%	89%	52%
2002	44%	45%	80%	56%

ALABAMA 5

North – Huntsville

The Tennessee River winds through the 5th, which stretches across the state's northern tier and borders Mississippi, Tennessee and Georgia. The Tennessee Valley Authority maintains a strong presence along the waterway, and the government and industrial facilities lining the famous river's shores are vital to the economic well-being of the district.

The federal government fuels the 5th's employment engine, with many government, defense and contracting jobs here. Huntsville hosts the NASA Marshall Space Flight Center, which develops rocket propulsion technology and space flight vehicles, and the Army's Redstone Arsenal. Home to Army rocket and missile programs, Redstone will gain about 4,800 civilian and contractor jobs as a result of the 2005 BRAC round.

The district's government jobs are complemented by strong manufacturing, research and technology sectors. Toyota's first V-8 engine plant outside of Japan opened in Huntsville in 2003 and has since expanded. Huntsville's 3,843-acre Cummings Research Park has 285 tenants with 25,000 employees, and boasts that it is the second-largest research park in the nation and the fourth-largest in the world.

Among an array of manufacturers, Decatur's industrial economy includes a Boeing satellite rocket booster plant, a 3M chemical plant and a Nucor steel mill. Agriculture represents a healthy portion of the 5th's rural economy, and crops include cotton, soybeans and corn.

Voters in the 5th have never sent a Republican to Congress, but GOP presidential candidates are successful here, with George W. Bush winning the district in the 2000 and 2004 elections. Generally, residents are conservative, and Democrats hold many state and local offices.

MAJOR INDUSTRY
Defense, government, manufacturing, technology, agriculture

MILITARY BASES
Redstone Arsenal (Army), 2,000 military, 14,528 civilian (2007)

CITIES
Huntsville, 158,216; Decatur (pt.), 44,655; Florence, 36,264; Madison, 29,329; Athens, 18,967

NOTABLE
"Muscle Shoals Sound" combined country, gospel and rhythm and blues and early hits were cut at Fame Recording Studios in Muscle Shoals.

Rep. Spencer Bachus (R)

CAPITOL OFFICE
225-4921
bachus.house.gov
2246 Rayburn 20515-0106; fax 225-2082

COMMITTEES
Financial Services - ranking member

RESIDENCE
Vestavia Hills

BORN
Dec. 28, 1947, Birmingham, Ala.

RELIGION
Baptist

FAMILY
Wife, Linda Bachus; five children

EDUCATION
Auburn U., B.A. 1969; U. of Alabama, J.D. 1972

MILITARY SERVICE
Ala. National Guard, 1969-71

CAREER
Lawyer; sawmill owner

POLITICAL HIGHLIGHTS
Ala. Senate, 1983; Ala. House, 1983-87; Ala. Board of Education, 1987-91; candidate for Ala. attorney general, 1990; Ala. Republican Party chairman, 1991-92

ELECTION RESULTS

2006 GENERAL		
Spencer Bachus (R)	163,514	98.3%
write-ins	2,786	1.7%
2006 PRIMARY		
Spencer Bachus (R)		unopposed
2004 GENERAL		
Spencer Bachus (R)	264,819	98.8%
write-ins	3,224	1.2%

PREVIOUS WINNING PERCENTAGES
2002 (90%); 2000 (88%); 1998 (72%); 1996 (71%); 1994 (79%); 1992 (52%)

Elected 1992; 8th term

Bachus secured the top-ranking Republican spot on the House Financial Services Committee in the 110th Congress (2007-08) by stepping up his involvement in party political affairs, including raising large sums for Republicans in tight races. Philosophically, he is right at home with the conservatives who dominate the GOP leadership and likes to remind people that the American Civil Liberties Union rates him one of the worst Alabama congressmen. "I'm proud of it," he says.

Bachus (BACK-us) contributed more than $550,000 of his own campaign funds in 2006 to the National Republican Congressional Committee, the House GOP's political arm. And he has been a reliable vote for the leadership on issues such as tax cuts, same-sex marriage and abortion rights. Those factors enabled him to leapfrog over the more senior Richard H. Baker of Louisiana to capture the top GOP post on Financial Services.

In 2006, Bachus succeeded in raising federal deposit insurance coverage for bank accounts. Banks had complained that a ceiling of $100,000 for government-protected deposits was too low and had been unchanged since 1980. Bachus worked out a bill with the Senate Banking Committee that indexes insured amounts to inflation starting in 2010.

Bachus is a steadfast defender of the Sarbanes-Oxley law, which has been controversial in the business community since it was enacted in 2002 to deter corporate fraud. Complaints are premature, he says, because the law hasn't been completely implemented and the Financial Services Committee and regulators are closely monitoring that process.

His other major interest is the rapidly changing environment for handling confidential financial information, driven by advances in computer and Internet technology. Bachus wants the Financial Services panel to address problems with e-mail scams, the burgeoning use of the Internet for financial transactions, and security issues involving personal information. He also wants to crack down on lenders who prey on consumers with high-interest, low-value loans. "Predatory lending is unconscionable," says Bachus, who has teamed up to draft legislation with liberal Massachusetts Democrat Barney Frank, the panel's new chairman.

Bachus sponsored legislation, which became law in 2003, blocking states from imposing financial privacy rules that are tougher than those set by the federal government. He worked to develop strong bipartisan support for the measure, and it passed the House overwhelmingly. Democrats supported the bill after provisions were added to give consumers more tools to combat identity theft and access to free information about their credit reports.

For several years, Bachus has pushed a measure by liberal Democrat Maxine Waters of California that encourages banks to offer so-called basic lifeline accounts to make banking more accessible to poor people. The House passed the bill in 2002, but the Senate never took it up.

A devout Baptist, Bachus' religious beliefs have led to his support of Third World debt relief. In recent years, he also sought to impose economic sanctions on Sudan in the hope of halting the killings of Christians in the southern region. He sponsored legislation in 2004 to prevent foreign oil companies from raising capital through American financial markets if the companies continue to do business in Sudan. The Bush administration said it preferred to negotiate with the oil companies, and the bill went nowhere.

Bachus keeps an eye on local concerns as well. He helped secure a new national veterans' center in Birmingham, and won a provision setting aside

30,000 acres for a wildlife refuge along a stretch of the Cahaba River. A $25 million appropriation in 2004 for an upgrade of U.S. 78, the highway between Birmingham and Memphis, also bears his imprint. And he and others in the Alabama congressional delegation successfully lobbied the Base Realignment and Closure Commission to retain the Birmingham International Airport Air Guard Station, home to the 117th Air Refueling Wing.

He initiated a Judiciary Committee hearing in 2004 on how the National Collegiate Athletic Association investigates rules violations. Bachus criticized NCAA officials for the association's enforcement process, which is closed to the public and relies on faculty from NCAA member schools to set penalties. Two Alabama schools — the University of Alabama and Auburn University — had been placed on probation by the NCAA in the preceding three years.

His committee work is influenced by his conservative views on social policy issues such as abortion rights. During a 2004 debate in the Judiciary panel on a bill to toughen penalties for the promotion of animal fighting, Bachus condemned the panel for having "chosen to protect the rights of a chicken but not those of a child that is three months away from being born." He has pushed bills to curb Internet gambling and target online child pornography.

To take the top GOP post on Financial Services in the 110th Congress, Bachus had to relinquish his seats on the Judiciary and Transportation and Infrastructure panels.

Bachus was an early proponent of making permanent the Bush administration's $1.35 trillion package of tax cuts, passed by Congress in 2001. The tax law contained measures, akin to those proposed by Bachus, to double the child adoption tax credit and to eliminate federal taxes on state-sponsored college tuition savings plans.

Early in his career, Bachus owned a sawmill, but for the most part, he earned a living as a trial lawyer for two decades. He began his career in elective office in 1983, serving first in the state legislature, then on the state board of education and then as chairman of the Alabama GOP.

In his first House bid, Bachus benefited handsomely from the post-1990 census remapping of Alabama's congressional districts, which eviscerated the district held for five terms by Democratic Rep. Ben Erdreich and transformed it into a Republican bastion. Bachus won with 52 percent of the vote in 1992 and since then has been re-elected with at least 70 percent.

In redistricting after the 2000 census, Bachus' district became even more securely Republican. He had no major party opposition in 2002 and ran unopposed in 2004 and 2006.

KEY VOTES

2006

- No — Stop broadband companies from favoring select Internet traffic
- \+ — Affirm U.S. commitment to war in Iraq and reject setting a withdrawal date for troops
- Yes — Repeal requirement for bilingual ballots at the polls
- Yes — Permit U.S. sale of civilian nuclear technology to India
- Yes — Build a 700-mile fence on the U.S.-Mexico border to curb illegal crossings
- Yes — Permit warrantless wiretaps of suspected terrorists

2005

- Yes — Intervene in the life-support case of Terri Schiavo
- No — Lift President Bush's restrictions on stem cell research funding
- No — Prohibit FBI access to library and bookstore records
- Yes — Approve free-trade pact with five Central American countries
- Yes — Pass energy policy overhaul favored by President Bush emphasizing domestic oil and gas production
- Yes — End mandatory preservation of habitat of endangered animal and plant species
- Yes — Ban torture of prisoners in U.S. custody

CQ VOTE STUDIES

	PARTY UNITY		PRESIDENTIAL SUPPORT	
	Support	Oppose	Support	Oppose
2006	97%	3%	97%	3%
2005	98%	2%	88%	12%
2004	95%	5%	88%	12%
2003	96%	4%	98%	2%
2002	98%	2%	89%	11%

INTEREST GROUPS

	AFL-CIO	ADA	CCUS	ACU
2006	21%	0%	93%	88%
2005	20%	5%	93%	92%
2004	13%	5%	100%	96%
2003	13%	10%	96%	88%
2002	11%	0%	100%	100%

ALABAMA 6

Central – suburban Birmingham and Tuscaloosa

Alabama's most prosperous district, the 6th is a mix of white and wealthy parts of Birmingham and Tuscaloosa, their suburbs and nearby rural areas in central Alabama. The district surrounds a thin slice of land in the adjacent 7th that stretches from Tuscaloosa to downtown Birmingham.

Although Birmingham's population has decreased since the 1960s, suburban growth has bolstered the overall population of the metropolitan area. The 6th takes in much of the area's suburbs, while most of the city is in the 7th. Many commuters reside in wealthy suburbs in southern Jefferson County, particularly Mountain Brook, Hoover and Homewood. Shelby County, mainly south of Birmingham, has experienced significant suburban growth over the past three decades and now has the highest median income of any county in the state.

The 6th takes in a section of Tuscaloosa north of the Black Warrior River, which bisects the city. Most of the manufacturing plants that characterize the city's industrial sector are located along the south bank of the river, in the neighboring 7th. Undoubtedly, the area's signature is University of Alabama football, which attracts fans statewide to watch the "Crimson Tide" play just south of the river in the 7th.

Birmingham's suburbs are encroaching on the district's rural areas, but agriculture — mainly fruits and vegetables — and mining remain important to the economic health in some areas. Between Birmingham and Tuscaloosa, the 6th includes a small part of Appalachia, and coal mining provides many jobs here, near small towns such as Brookwood.

The growing conservative, white-collar Birmingham suburbs that account for much of the district's population have kept the 6th reliably Republican. George W. Bush won 78 percent of the district's vote in the 2004 presidential election, his best showing in the state.

MAJOR INDUSTRY

Manufacturing, higher education, mining, agriculture

CITIES

Hoover, 62,742; Birmingham (pt.), 26,723; Vestavia Hills, 24,476; Alabaster, 22,619; Mountain Brook, 20,604

NOTABLE

A 55-foot cast-iron statue in Birmingham of Vulcan, the Roman god of fire and metalworking, is one of the world's largest iron figures.

Rep. Artur Davis (D)

CAPITOL OFFICE
225-2665
www.house.gov/arturdavis
208 Cannon 20515-0107; fax 226-9567

COMMITTEES
House Administration
Judiciary
Ways & Means

RESIDENCE
Birmingham

BORN
Oct. 9, 1967, Montgomery, Ala.

RELIGION
Lutheran

FAMILY
Single

EDUCATION
Harvard U., A.B. 1990 (government), J.D. 1993

CAREER
Lawyer

POLITICAL HIGHLIGHTS
Assistant U.S. attorney, 1994-98; sought Democratic nomination for U.S. House, 2000

ELECTION RESULTS

2006 GENERAL		
Artur Davis (D)		unopposed
2006 PRIMARY		
Artur Davis (D)	93,586	90.9%
Eddison T. Walters (D)	9,358	9.1%
2004 GENERAL		
Artur Davis (D)	183,408	75.0%
Steve F. Cameron (R)	61,019	24.9%

PREVIOUS WINNING PERCENTAGES
2002 (92%)

Elected 2002; 3rd term

Davis advocates an activist federal government but is culturally conservative and more supportive of business interests than many Democrats. His views and voting record, he says, represent the mainstream in his district and in the country.

He says that the government should help lift people out of poverty — his district is the fifth-poorest in the nation — but he supports a constitutional amendment to ban same-sex marriage. "We lose our ability as Southern Democrats to reach voters because they see us as so out of touch on cultural issues, they tune us out on economic issues," Davis says.

In the 110th Congress (2007-08), Davis (his first name is pronounced ar-TOUR) won seats on the Ways and Means and Judiciary committees and a post on the Democratic Steering Committee, all indications that he is regarded as an up-and-comer in House Democratic ranks.

Davis briefly contemplated a bid for the Senate in 2008 against Republican Jeff Sessions, despite the tough challenge he would face in a state that has never elected an African-American as governor or to the Senate. But in early January 2007, he announced that 2008 "is the wrong time for me to seek higher office." He noted that a Senate bid also would hinder him "from actively helping a candidate in the 2008 presidential election cycle." He issued an early endorsement of the presidential candidacy of Democratic Sen. Barack Obama of Illinois, an African-American.

But Davis acknowledged an interest in seeking higher office at some point. He insists he could win over voters based on shared views and values. "When I drive down I-95 to visit my mother in Montgomery, I see a giant Confederate flag. That's part of our history that we live with every day. We were simultaneously the first Confederate capital and the first capital of the civil rights movement. It's not my task to repudiate history; it's my task to find common ground based on our shared history," he says.

Arriving in Congress in 2003, Davis joined both the liberal Congressional Black Caucus and the politically moderate New Democrat Coalition, which he co-chaired in the 109th Congress. He is one of four vice chairmen of the New Democrats in the 110th Congress.

Davis showed a knack for identifying common ground in a House controlled by Republicans for the first four years of his tenure. In 2004, he was a chief sponsor of a measure to help people trying to buy their first homes.

Davis also worked with Charles B. Rangel of New York, then the top-ranking Democrat on the Ways and Means Committee and the most influential African-American in the House, on expanding the child tax credit for poor families, though it is rare for a freshman to take such a prominent role in tax legislation. While their efforts failed to expand President Bush's $1,000 per child tax credit to all families who pay little or no taxes, they won a modified version of the proposal that made it possible for 6.5 million low-income families to get a refundable credit.

As a junior member of the Budget Committee in the 108th Congress (2003-04), Davis engineered a change in the funding formula for black colleges that earned him kudos at home and nationally. He noted that Bush's 2004 budget would have cut funding for 1890 land-grant schools, which are predominately black, while keeping levels the same for 1862 land-grant colleges, which are predominately white. Two of the country's 17 black schools are in Alabama. Casting it as an issue of racial fairness, he won approval of a House amendment that reversed the proposed cuts.

In 2006, Davis secured renewal of the HOPE VI program for rebuilding dilapidated public housing, a program Bush wanted to kill. The measure garnered 64 Republican votes, as well as the support of all Democrats.

Davis votes most often with House liberals, but they can't always rely on him on hot-button issues. He was one of 63 Democrats in 2003 to vote for a conservative-backed ban on what opponents call "partial birth" abortion, a controversial procedure for ending pregnancies. In 2005, he was one of 44 Democrats supporting a renewal of the 2001 anti-terrorism law known as the Patriot Act. And he was among just 27 House Democrats voting in 2006 to allow oil and gas drilling in Alaska's Arctic National Wildlife Refuge.

Davis' personal history is one of the House's remarkable bootstraps stories. He grew up in the hard-pressed west end of Montgomery near downtown. His parents divorced when he was young, and Davis, an only child, was raised by his grandmother and his mother, an elementary school teacher. As a boy, he was a voracious reader, loved history and excelled in school. Admitted to Harvard, he graduated magna cum laude in 1990, and went on to get his law degree there. Davis worked his way through college and took out student loans that he's still paying back.

After graduation, Davis probably would have been welcomed by a dozen corporate law firms. But he had already decided on a life in politics. He went home to Montgomery, working as an assistant U.S. attorney from 1994 to 1998. He launched his first bid for the House in 2000. He lost that race.

But two years later, voters in the 7th District had grown weary of Democratic Rep. Earl F. Hilliard, who after five terms had accrued little influence and was weakened by ethics scandals and by his decision to visit terrorist-friendly Libya. Two locally prominent black political groups — the Alabama Democratic Conference and the Alabama New South Coalition — backed Hilliard anyway and were cool to Davis for taking on an African-American incumbent. But Davis had support from the mayors of Selma and Birmingham; he raised more than $1.5 million, helped in large part by pro-Israel groups who felt Hilliard had been too pro-Palestinian.

Davis finished second to Hilliard in a three-candidate primary and won the runoff with 56 percent of the vote. With no Republican challenger in a heavily Democratic district, his general-election win was a foregone conclusion.

By the time of his first re-election campaign, Davis had opened five offices across the district and hired eight times as many staff as his predecessor. He also launched a private-public initiative aimed at bringing new businesses to the district. He handily turned back primary challengers and sailed to re-election in 2004 and 2006.

KEY VOTES

2006

No Stop broadband companies from favoring select Internet traffic
No Affirm U.S. commitment to war in Iraq and reject setting a withdrawal date for troops
No Repeal requirement for bilingual ballots at the polls
Yes Permit U.S. sale of civilian nuclear technology to India
Yes Build a 700-mile fence on the U.S.-Mexico border to curb illegal crossings
No Permit warrantless wiretaps of suspected terrorists

2005

? Intervene in the life-support case of Terri Schiavo
Yes Lift President Bush's restrictions on stem cell research funding
Yes Prohibit FBI access to library and bookstore records
No Approve free-trade pact with five Central American countries
Yes Pass energy policy overhaul favored by President Bush emphasizing domestic oil and gas production
Yes End mandatory preservation of habitat of endangered animal and plant species
Yes Ban torture of prisoners in U.S. custody

CQ VOTE STUDIES

	PARTY UNITY		PRESIDENTIAL SUPPORT	
	Support	Oppose	Support	Oppose
2006	80%	20%	53%	47%
2005	83%	17%	46%	54%
2004	87%	13%	44%	56%
2003	86%	14%	40%	60%

INTEREST GROUPS

	AFL-CIO	ADA	CCUS	ACU
2006	100%	75%	73%	44%
2005	87%	80%	70%	28%
2004	73%	75%	71%	24%
2003	87%	90%	50%	28%

ALABAMA 7

West central – parts of Birmingham and Tuscaloosa

Marked by stark regional contrasts, the 7th includes chunks of Birmingham and Tuscaloosa, as well as struggling rural areas in west-central Alabama. Although landlocked, the 7th suffered damage from Hurricane Katrina in 2005; FEMA declared eight of the 12 counties here, most of them poor, as disaster areas, thus qualifying residents for public and individual assistance. Most of the eight fall in the watershed of the Tombigbee River, which flows south toward Mobile, and its tributaries.

Economic growth in the 7th's part of Birmingham, the densely populated downtown area, has trailed the rest of the city and its suburbs. Decades of redevelopment efforts have brought some change to downtown, and local leaders still aim to lure technology firms. With a thriving, diversified economy, Tuscaloosa hosts many health care and manufacturing businesses and the University of Alabama, one of the state's largest employers. Nearby Vance is home to a Mercedes-Benz plant.

Almost all of the rest of the 7th is part of Alabama's portion of the Black Belt, a region of rich soil that stretches from Texas to Virginia. This poverty-filled area has not known prosperity since before the Civil War, when cotton plantation owners made fortunes from slave labor. Although agricultural diversification efforts have been modestly successful, local leaders are still searching for assistance for the area.

In contrast to its white, well-to-do neighbor — the Republican 6th — the 7th's residents tend to be lower- to middle-class blacks who vote overwhelmingly Democratic. The 7th was the only Alabama district won by Democratic presidential nominees in either 2000 or 2004, highlighting the district's decidedly Democratic lean.

MAJOR INDUSTRY
Agriculture, manufacturing, higher education, health care

CITIES
Birmingham (pt.), 216,097; Tuscaloosa (pt.), 68,928; Bessemer (pt.), 27,599

NOTABLE
Edmund Pettus Bridge in Selma was the site of "Bloody Sunday," when Alabama state troopers beat and gassed peaceful civil rights marchers — who were co-led by current Georgia Democratic Rep. John Lewis — on their way from Selma to Montgomery in 1965.

ALASKA

Gov. Sarah Palin (R)

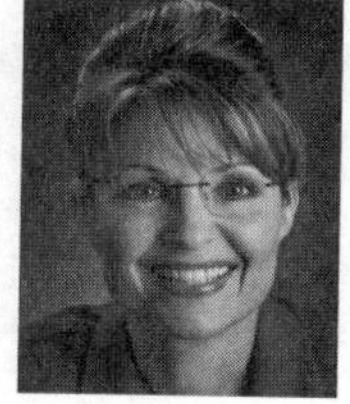

Pronounced: PAL-in (rhymes with "Allen")
First elected: 2006
Length of term: 4 years
Term expires: 12/10
Salary: $125,000
Phone: (907) 465-3500

Residence: Wasilla
Born: Feb. 11, 1964; Sandpoint, Idaho
Religion: Protestant
Family: Husband, Todd Palin; four children
Education: U. of Idaho, B.S. 1987 (journalism)
Career: Commercial fishing company owner; outdoor recreational equipment company owner; sports reporter
Political highlights: Wasilla City Council, 1992-96; mayor of Wasilla, 1996-2002; sought Republican nomination for lieutenant governor, 2002; Alaska Oil and Gas Conservation Commission, 2003-04

Election results:

2006 GENERAL		
Sarah Palin (R)	114,697	48.3%
Tony Knowles (D)	97,238	41.0%
Andrew Halcro (I)	22,443	9.5%

Lt. Gov. Sean Parnell (R)

First elected: 2006
Length of term: 4 years
Term expires: 12/10
Salary: $100,000
Phone: (907) 465-3520

LEGISLATURE

Legislature: January-May, limit of 120 calendar days

Senate: 20 members, 4-year terms
2007 ratios: 11 R, 9 D; 17 men, 3 women
Salary: $24,012
Phone: (907) 465-3701

House: 40 members, 2-year terms
2007 ratios: 23 R, 17 D; 31 men, 9 women
Salary: $24,012
Phone: (907) 465-3725

TERM LIMITS

Governor: 2 consecutive terms
Senate: No
House: No

URBAN STATISTICS

CITY	POPULATION
Anchorage	260,283
Juneau	30,711
Fairbanks	30,224
Sitka	8,835
Ketchikan	7,922

REGISTERED VOTERS

Unaffiliated	38%
Republican	25%
Others	23%
Democrat	14%

POPULATION

2006 population (est.)	670,053
2000 population	626,932
1990 population	550,043
Percent change (1990-2000)	+14%
Rank among states (2006)	47
Median age	32.4
Born in state	38.1%
Foreign born	5.9%
Violent crime rate	567/100,000
Poverty level	9.4%
Federal workers	16,363
Military	22,786

ELECTIONS

STATE ELECTION OFFICIAL
(907) 465-4611
DEMOCRATIC PARTY
(907) 258-3050
REPUBLICAN PARTY
(907) 276-4467

MISCELLANEOUS

Web: www.state.ak.us
Capital: Juneau

U.S. CONGRESS

Senate: 2 Republicans
House: 1 Republican

2000 Census Statistics by District

DIST.	2004 VOTE FOR PRESIDENT BUSH	KERRY	WHITE	BLACK	ASIAN	HISP	MEDIAN INCOME	WHITE COLLAR	BLUE COLLAR	SERVICE INDUSTRY	OVER 64	UNDER 18	COLLEGE EDUCATION	RURAL	SQ. MILES
AL	61%	36%	68%	3%	4%	4%	$51,571	61%	24%	16%	6%	30%	25%	34%	571,951
STATE	61	36	68	3	4	4	$51,571	61	24	16	6	30	25	34	571,951
U.S.	50.7	48.3	69	12	4	13	$41,994	60	25	15	12	26	24	21	3,537,438

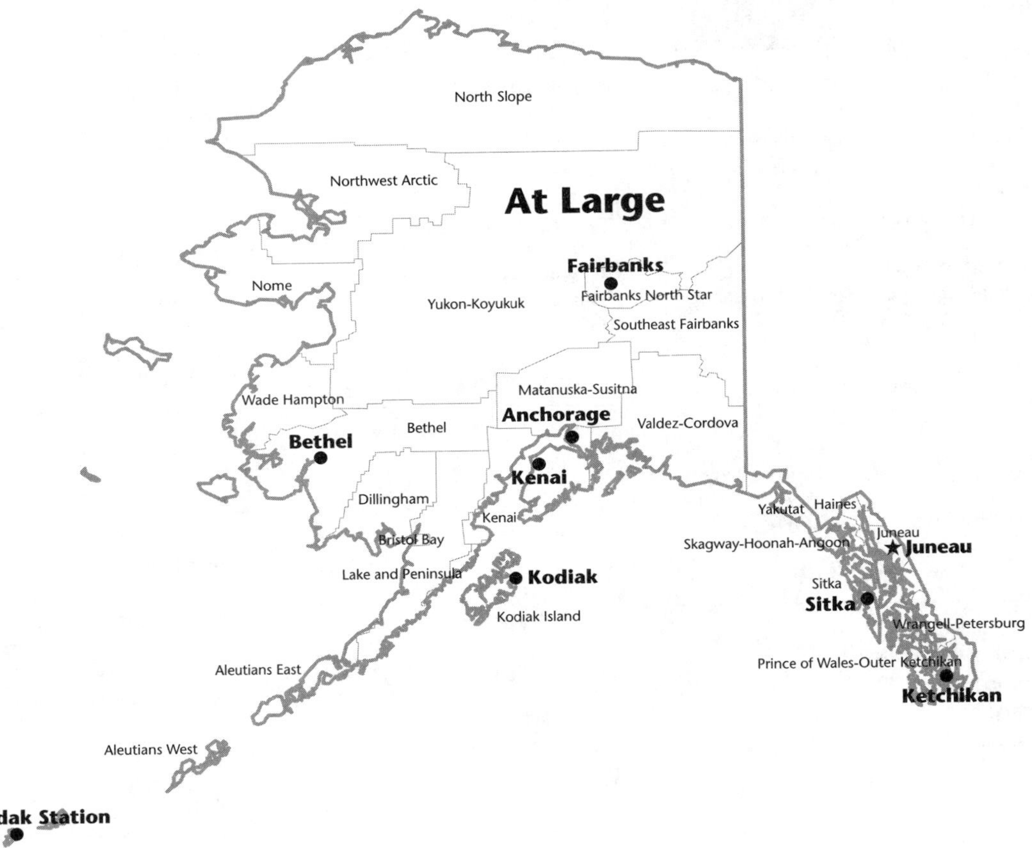
North Slope
Northwest Arctic
At Large
Fairbanks
Fairbanks North Star
Nome
Yukon-Koyukuk
Southeast Fairbanks
Matanuska-Susitna
Wade Hampton
Anchorage
Bethel
Valdez-Cordova
Bethel
Kenai
Dillingham
Kenai
Yakutat
Haines
Bristol Bay
Juneau
Juneau
Skagway-Hoonah-Angoon
Lake and Peninsula
Kodiak
Sitka
Sitka
Kodiak Island
Wrangell-Petersburg
Prince of Wales-Outer Ketchikan
Ketchikan
Aleutians East
Aleutians West
Adak Station

Sen. Ted Stevens (R)

CAPITOL OFFICE
224-3004
stevens.senate.gov
522 Hart 20510-0201; fax 224-2354

COMMITTEES
Appropriations
Commerce, Science & Transportation - ranking member
Homeland Security & Governmental Affairs
Rules & Administration
Joint Library

RESIDENCE
Girdwood

BORN
Nov. 18, 1923, Indianapolis, Ind.

RELIGION
Episcopalian

FAMILY
Wife, Catherine Stevens; six children

EDUCATION
U. of California, Los Angeles, B.A. 1947 (political science); Harvard U., LL.B. 1950

MILITARY SERVICE
Army Air Corps, 1943-46

CAREER
Lawyer

POLITICAL HIGHLIGHTS
U.S. attorney, 1953-56; Republican nominee for U.S. Senate, 1962; Alaska House, 1965-68 (majority leader and Speaker pro tempore, 1967-68); sought Republican nomination for U.S. Senate, 1968

ELECTION RESULTS

2002 GENERAL		
Ted Stevens (R)	179,438	78.2%
Frank Vondersaar (D)	24,133	10.5%
Jim Sykes (GREEN)	16,608	7.2%
Jim Dore (AKI)	6,724	2.9%
Leonard Karpinski (LIBERT)	2,354	1.0%
2002 PRIMARY		
Ted Stevens (R)	64,315	88.9%
Mike Aubrey (R)	7,997	11.1%

PREVIOUS WINNING PERCENTAGES
1996 (77%); 1990 (66%); 1984 (71%); 1978 (76%); 1972 (77%); 1970 Special Election (60%)

Elected 1970; 6th full term

Appointed December 1968

These are frustrating times for Stevens, a gruff, hot-tempered "old bull" who finds himself without a gavel for the first time in many years and out of step with many of his GOP colleagues over the virtues of federal spending for politically popular special projects targeted to the districts and states of individual lawmakers.

Stevens is the longest-serving Senate Republican, and ranks seventh on the all-time tenure list. He is fiercely attached to the Senate, and determined to use his seniority to help his state. He announced soon after the 2006 elections that he would seek a seventh full term in 2008, when he will turn 85. Regarded as an icon back home, he faces little electoral risk.

Stevens detests the partisan polarization that has plagued Congress in recent years, preferring offstage cooperation to public confrontation. He will fight it out with anyone who insists on challenging him, with fireworks galore, but he'd rather cut a deal that satisfies everyone.

Since 1969, Stevens has kept a framed copy of Rotary International's "Four-Way Test" on his Senate chamber desk. He says he tries to live by its maxims, written in 1932: "Is it the truth? Is it fair to all concerned? Will it build goodwill and better friendships? Will it be beneficial to all concerned?"

Stevens was chairman of the Commerce, Science and Transportation Committee in the 109th Congress (2005-06). Before that, he had spent his career on the Appropriations Committee, which he chaired from 1997 to 2005 except for an 18-month interlude in 2001 and 2002 when Democrats controlled the Senate. He remains the top-ranking Republican on Commerce and on the Defense Appropriations Subcommittee.

On both panels, Stevens is paired with Democratic Chairman Daniel K. Inouye of Hawaii. Representing the nation's newest states, the two share a concern for native populations and a commitment to securing federal funds for their isolated states. They have grown so personally close over the years that they refer to themselves as "co-chairmen."

In the 109th Congress, as other Republicans assailed spending earmarks, Stevens bristled. He says these provisions — which direct federal funds to home-state projects — are misunderstood, especially in Alaska's case. Unlike other states that have legions of executive agency officials serving in regional and local offices where they can assess program needs, Alaska depends on its two senators and one at-large House member to look out for its interests, he maintains. "We just don't have people in Nome who represent the Department of Housing and Urban Development," Steven says.

Instead, Alaska has Stevens, and that has been quite enough. His hand is felt everywhere in the state. A grateful state legislature named the Anchorage International Airport for him in 2000. But the dollar chase is getting harder every year, as President Bush insists on tighter caps on domestic spending and conservative Republicans attack earmarks as wasteful. In fact, it was an Alaska project that created such a stink that all lawmakers may find it harder to obtain earmarks in the future.

In 2005, a furor erupted over a proposed bridge to connect Ketchikan, population circa 8,000, with Gravina Island, population 50, at a cost of $223 million. When the Senate debated the annual transportation appropriations bill in October, Republican Tom Coburn of Oklahoma tried to redirect funds for the so-called bridge to nowhere to a rebuilding project for the Interstate 10 bridge in New Orleans, destroyed by Hurricane Katrina. "This amendment is an offense to me!" Stevens shouted on the floor. "It's not only an offense to me, it's a threat to every person in my state." He threatened to resign if the amendment carried. Coburn got only 15 votes.

But conservative attacks on earmarks didn't cease. By 2006, Stevens was grousing that tagging money for projects back home was "going to be almost impossible" in the newly hostile climate. "I have no way to explain this to my people," he lamented. "I really don't know how to handle this."

In another 2005 battle, Stevens lost what may have been his last, best chance to persuade Congress to open Alaska's Arctic National Wildlife Refuge to oil and gas drilling. After years of falling just short, he steered a drilling provision through the Senate as part of a budget bill. But GOP moderates in the House balked. When Stevens tried attaching the drilling provision to the must-pass defense appropriations bill in December 2005, he was unable to surmount a filibuster, even after stuffing the bill with Gulf Coast recovery funds and other enticements to win over senators. "This has been the saddest day of my life," he said.

Stevens also met with frustration on a telecommunications law overhaul, his top priority as Commerce chairman. He was a few votes shy of the 60 he needed to overcome a potential filibuster by Democrats, who said the bill's so-called network neutrality provision failed to prevent broadband operators from discriminating among Internet content providers. "That is really an absolute shame that we are going to lose 18 months of hard work after we almost have complete agreement on the rest of the bill," Stevens said.

His two-year chairmanship succeeded in some ways, however. At the end of 2006, Stevens steered to enactment a reauthorization of the 1976 Magnuson-Stevens Act, which he helped write 30 years earlier. The law governs the nation's commercial fisheries, a vital industry in Alaska.

Stevens' reputation at home and nationally suffered in 2003 after a front-page story in the Los Angeles Times said he had become a millionaire through investments with businessmen who had gotten government contracts and other favors with his help. In one instance, the Times reported, Stevens helped save a $450 million housing contract for an Alaska businessman who had made the senator a partner in other real estate investments. Stevens denied wrongdoing, saying his actions were aimed at helping his state. But he eventually sold off his real estate interests, saying his investment partners were coming under too much scrutiny.

His dream of being at the top of the GOP leadership has been frustrated over the years. In 1984, after eight years as Republican whip, he ran a strong race for Senate majority leader, losing to Bob Dole of Kansas by three votes.

With his typical concern for the Senate as an institution, Stevens in 1999 helped broker a bipartisan agreement on procedures to conduct the impeachment trial of President Bill Clinton in a way that avoided the partisanship that marked the House proceedings.

As a young man, Stevens flew C-46 transports throughout China during World War II and earned the Distinguished Flying Cross. After the war, he got a law degree and worked as a federal prosecutor for three years. He began his pursuit of a Senate seat not long after Alaska became a state in 1959. He got the party's nomination in 1962, but took just 41 percent of the vote against Democrat Ernest J. Gruening that fall.

Stevens won election to the Alaska House, including a stint as majority leader. He tried for the Senate again in 1968 but lost in the primary. Later that year, Democratic Sen. E.L. Bartlett died and Stevens was appointed by GOP Gov. Walter J. Hickel. In the 1970 contest to serve the final two years of Bartlett's term, Stevens beat liberal Democrat Wendell P. Kay with 60 percent of the vote. He has been re-elected easily since then.

His 1978 election was followed by great personal pain. A plane crash killed his first wife and seriously injured Stevens.

KEY VOTES

2006

Yes Confirm Samuel A. Alito Jr. to the Supreme Court
Yes Allow consideration of a bill to establish a $140 billion trust fund to compensate victims of asbestos exposure
Yes Extend tax cuts for two years at a cost of $70 billion over five years
Yes Overhaul immigration policy with border security, enforcement and guest worker program
Yes Allow consideration of a bill to permanently repeal the estate tax
No Urge President Bush to begin troop withdrawals from Iraq in 2006
Yes Lift President Bush's restrictions on stem cell research funding
Yes Authorize military tribunals for suspected terrorists

2005

Yes Curb class action lawsuits by shifting them from state to federal courts
Yes Allow confirmation vote on Priscilla R. Owen to the U.S. Court of Appeals for the 5th Circuit
Yes Oppose mandatory emissions limits and block recognition of global warming as a threat
Yes Approve free-trade pact with five Central American countries
Yes Pass energy policy overhaul favored by President Bush emphasizing domestic oil and gas production
Yes Shield gunmakers from lawsuits when their products are used in crimes
No Ban torture of prisoners in U.S. custody
Yes Renew 16 provisions of the Patriot Act
Yes Allow final vote on opening the Arctic National Wildlife Refuge to oil and gas exploration

CQ VOTE STUDIES

	PARTY UNITY		PRESIDENTIAL SUPPORT	
	Support	Oppose	Support	Oppose
2006	80%	20%	93%	7%
2005	95%	5%	93%	7%
2004	97%	3%	92%	8%
2003	95%	5%	96%	4%
2002	89%	11%	95%	5%
2001	88%	12%	97%	3%
2000	92%	8%	56%	44%
1999	90%	10%	36%	64%
1998	82%	18%	54%	46%
1997	79%	21%	71%	29%

INTEREST GROUPS

	AFL-CIO	ADA	CCUS	ACU
2006	13%	5%	100%	64%
2005	14%	5%	100%	80%
2004	8%	20%	100%	92%
2003	15%	10%	91%	70%
2002	23%	10%	100%	83%
2001	25%	20%	86%	92%
2000	0%	5%	100%	92%
1999	33%	10%	88%	84%
1998	25%	20%	94%	56%
1997	14%	30%	80%	58%

Sen. Lisa Murkowski (R)

CAPITOL OFFICE
224-6665
murkowski.senate.gov
709 Hart 20510-0202; fax 224-5301

COMMITTEES
Energy & Natural Resources
Foreign Relations
Health, Education, Labor & Pensions
Indian Affairs

RESIDENCE
Girdwood

BORN
May 22, 1957, Ketchikan, Alaska

RELIGION
Roman Catholic

FAMILY
Husband, Verne Martell; two children

EDUCATION
Willamette U., attended 1975-77; Georgetown U., B.A. 1980 (economics); Willamette U., J.D. 1985

CAREER
Lawyer; state legislative aide

POLITICAL HIGHLIGHTS
Anchorage district attorney, 1987-89; Alaska House, 1999-2002

ELECTION RESULTS

2004 GENERAL		
Lisa Murkowski (R)	149,773	48.6%
Tony Knowles (D)	140,424	45.6%
Marc J. Millican (NON)	8,885	2.9%
Jerry Sanders (AKI)	3,785	1.2%
2004 PRIMARY		
Lisa Murkowski (R)	45,710	58.1%
Mike Miller (R)	29,313	37.3%
Wev Shea (R)	2,857	3.6%

Elected 2004; 1st full term

Appointed December 2002

Murkowski is the youngster in the three-person Alaska delegation. The state's senior senator, Republican Ted Stevens, is in his 80s, and its only House member, GOP Rep. Don Young, is in his 70s. More than 20 years younger than her colleagues, Murkowski brought "not only a little bit of youth but a different perspective as a woman" to the state's presence in Washington, she told the Anchorage Daily News.

That is evident in Murkowski's legislative interests. She has introduced or cosponsored a number of health-related bills, including one to combat fetal alcohol syndrome, a major problem in her state. Often teaming up with Democrats on legislation, she has pushed proposals to improve prevention and treatment of cardiovascular disease in women and to get junk food out of schools. After waiting for years, she finally won a seat in the 110th Congress (2007-08) on the Health, Education, Labor and Pensions Committee.

She began her first full term in 2005 in a strengthened position politically after winning the seat in her own right. The election lifted the nepotism cloud from her appointment to the Senate two years earlier by her father, Frank H. Murkowski, who quit the Senate when he was elected governor in 2002. In her stint as an appointed senator, she had been able to chalk up several legislative victories with the help of Stevens, for whom she once interned. He calls Murkowski "a hell of a lot better senator than her dad ever was."

Her biggest win came just a few weeks before the election, when President Bush signed a military spending bill that included federal loan guarantees for a 3,500-mile natural gas pipeline to carry Alaska's abundant natural gas to the Midwest. Under the bill, the government would cover 80 percent of the pipeline's costs, up to $18 billion, should builders default on the project, a potential source of thousands of jobs in Alaska.

In late 2004, the Alaska delegation scored one of its biggest parochial legislative victories of recent years, thanks to Murkowski. The House passed her bill to transfer 89 million acres from the federal government to the state of Alaska and Alaska natives. The measure had already passed in the Senate and was supported by the Bush administration.

Like most of the state's politicians, Murkowski wants to open up the Arctic National Wildlife Refuge to oil and gas drilling, an issue she inherited from her father. So far, she's had no more luck than he in convincing pro-environment senators to see it her way. Opening ANWR to drilling would enable an oil pipeline that bisects the state to operate at full capacity; it's at about half-capacity now as production in Prudhoe Bay wanes. Alaska relies heavily on revenues from oil for education, transportation and other governmental basics. Murkowski says most members of Congress have already made up their minds on the issue, just as her father had warned. "It's so emotional. It has become kind of the icon for the environmental cause," she says.

In 2006, she was an aggressive questioner of the actions of energy giant BP, which had to curtail production at its Prudhoe Bay fields because of corrosion in its pipeline. Murkowski said her faith in the industry had "been shattered."

Although more moderate than the senior Murkowski, she usually votes with Bush and the GOP leadership. However, she supports abortion rights and in 2003 joined eight other Senate Republicans voting to affirm support of the Supreme Court decision in *Roe v. Wade*, which legalized abortion. She backs some abortion restrictions, however, voting in 2003 to ban a procedure opponents call "partial birth" abortion. And in 2006, she voted to confirm Supreme Court Justice Samuel A. Alito Jr., despite concerns that he had declined to endorse *Roe v. Wade*.

Murkowski also is more labor-friendly than most Republican senators. She voted against the Bush White House over whether to restrict overtime pay for some classes of workers. She backed Democratic proposals to extend unemployment benefits by 26 weeks and cosponsored a Republican bill to give workers looking for jobs an extra 13 weeks of pay. When GOP leaders in 2006 tried to use a federal minimum wage increase as leverage to win a reduction in estate taxes, Murkowski refused to back the bill until the Labor Department assured her that it wouldn't reduce the pay of workers in Alaska who receive tips in addition to an hourly wage.

Murkowski displays Alaska's libertarian streak at times. She was one of four Republicans joining Democrats in a 2005 filibuster against a bill renewing the Patriot Act, the 2001 anti-terrorism law, arguing that it would infringe too deeply on civil liberties. The filibuster forced the White House to accept modifications to the bill.

Murkowski can claim several Senate firsts. She is the first native-born Alaskan to serve in the chamber and the first daughter of a senator to serve. She is also the only senator to be appointed by a parent, though other offspring have followed their parents to the Senate via the ballot box.

Married and the mother of two teenage sons, Murkowski and her husband, Verne Martell, faced a difficult choice when she first became a senator — move the boys to Washington, or keep them in their familiar home and schools. Murkowski chose the latter course at first, but worried constantly about being so far from her children when she was in Washington. During her first months in office, she missed a Senate vote on the child tax credit in order to speak at her older son's sixth grade graduation ceremony. After the 2004 election, the family moved East. "I'm homesick every day for Alaska and they are too," she says.

The second of six children, Murkowski grew up in Ketchikan in the Alaskan Panhandle and attended high school in Fairbanks. She interned for Stevens in her senior year, then went to Georgetown University in Washington, D.C., graduating in 1980. Her father was just launching his first Senate campaign, and she and her siblings joined the effort. "That's why he had six kids, I'm convinced of it," she jokes. Later, with a law degree from Willamette University in Oregon, she spent two years in the Anchorage district attorney's office before opening a solo law practice.

She ran successfully for the state House in 1998, was re-elected twice and was chosen by her peers in 2002 as majority leader, a post she never filled because of her subsequent appointment to the U.S. Senate.

When the state suffered a funding shortfall, she joined a bipartisan coalition that advocated raising taxes and was instrumental in the passage of a boost in the state's alcohol tax to a dime a drink, at the time the highest rate in the nation. She also supported public funding for abortions.

Facing election in 2004, Murkowski looked vulnerable. Her Democratic challenger, Tony Knowles, was a former two-term governor, a former mayor of Anchorage, a Vietnam veteran, and a onetime oil rig worker who could relate to everyday Alaskans. The nepotism issue weakened her campaign, and Murkowski tried to distance herself politically from her father. By then, he was proving to be an unpopular governor, hurt by his support for a tax increase and for attempting to use federal homeland security funds for a jet to carry him around the state.

Under the banner "Team Alaska," Murkowski played up her working relationships with Stevens and Young, who chaired the Transportation and Infrastructure Committee. As Bush swept 61 percent of Alaska's vote, Murkowski squeaked past Knowles by 3 percentage points.

KEY VOTES

2006

- Yes Confirm Samuel A. Alito Jr. to the Supreme Court
- Yes Allow consideration of a bill to establish a $140 billion trust fund to compensate victims of asbestos exposure
- Yes Extend tax cuts for two years at a cost of $70 billion over five years
- Yes Overhaul immigration policy with border security, enforcement and guest worker program
- Yes Allow consideration of a bill to permanently repeal the estate tax
- No Urge President Bush to begin troop withdrawals from Iraq in 2006
- Yes Lift President Bush's restrictions on stem cell research funding
- Yes Authorize military tribunals for suspected terrorists

2005

- Yes Curb class action lawsuits by shifting them from state to federal courts
- Yes Allow confirmation vote on Priscilla R. Owen to the U.S. Court of Appeals for the 5th Circuit
- Yes Oppose mandatory emissions limits and block recognition of global warming as a threat
- Yes Approve free-trade pact with five Central American countries
- Yes Pass energy policy overhaul favored by President Bush emphasizing domestic oil and gas production
- Yes Shield gunmakers from lawsuits when their products are used in crimes
- Yes Ban torture of prisoners in U.S. custody
- No Renew 16 provisions of the Patriot Act
- Yes Allow final vote on opening the Arctic National Wildlife Refuge to oil and gas exploration

CQ VOTE STUDIES

	PARTY UNITY		PRESIDENTIAL SUPPORT	
	Support	Oppose	Support	Oppose
2006	82%	18%	89%	11%
2005	93%	7%	87%	13%
2004	92%	8%	87%	13%
2003	94%	6%	93%	7%

INTEREST GROUPS

	AFL-CIO	ADA	CCUS	ACU
2006	13%	5%	100%	71%
2005	14%	20%	100%	83%
2004	50%	35%	94%	74%
2003	15%	20%	86%	70%

Rep. Don Young (R)

CAPITOL OFFICE
225-5765
donyoung.house.gov
2111 Rayburn 20515-0201; fax 225-0425

COMMITTEES
Natural Resources - ranking member
Transportation & Infrastructure

RESIDENCE
Fort Yukon

BORN
June 9, 1933, Meridian, Calif.

RELIGION
Episcopalian

FAMILY
Wife, Lula Young; two children

EDUCATION
Yuba Junior College, A.A. 1952; California State U., Chico, B.A. 1958

MILITARY SERVICE
Army, 1955-57

CAREER
Elementary school teacher; riverboat captain

POLITICAL HIGHLIGHTS
Fort Yukon City Council, 1960-64; mayor of Fort Yukon, 1964-68; Alaska House, 1967-70; Alaska Senate, 1971-73; Republican nominee for U.S. House, 1972

ELECTION RESULTS

2006 GENERAL		
Don Young (R)	132,743	56.6%
Diane E. Benson (D)	93,879	40.0%
Alexander Crawford (LIBERT)	4,029	1.7%
2006 PRIMARY		
Don Young (R)		unopposed
2004 GENERAL		
Don Young (R)	213,216	71.1%
Thomas M. Higgins (D)	67,074	22.4%
Timothy A. Feller (GREEN)	11,434	3.8%
Alvin A. Anders (LIBERT)	7,157	2.4%

PREVIOUS WINNING PERCENTAGES
2002 (75%); 2000 (70%); 1998 (63%); 1996 (59%); 1994 (57%); 1992 (47%); 1990 (52%); 1988 (63%); 1986 (56%); 1984 (55%); 1982 (71%); 1980 (74%); 1978 (55%); 1976 (71%); 1974 (54%); 1973 Special Election (51%)

Elected March 1973; 17th full term

Impatient, blunt and irascible, Young is a perfect fit for America's last frontier. His individualism, certainty of opinion and outsize personality make him stand out from the general mix of House lawmakers, just as his giant state stands out from the rest of the country.

Midway through his fourth decade in Congress, Young is the third-most-senior Republican in the House and the eighth-most-senior member overall. As Alaska's lone representative, he has mastered the intricacies of public lands policy, an issue vital in a state overwhelmingly made up of public lands. He served for six years (1995-2001) as chairman of what is now the Natural Resources Committee, which sets land policy, and currently is the panel's top-ranking Republican. Like most Western Republicans, Young is an eager ally of energy, mining and timber interests and a vigorous advocate of the rights of private property holders. His zeal for loosening the government's grip on federal lands puts him squarely at odds with environmentalists, who regularly denounce him. Young, in turn, has likened environmentalists to communists.

He has pushed in vain to open Alaska's Arctic National Wildlife Refuge to oil and gas drilling, which he insists can be done without harm to the environment. "It is right for my people in the state of Alaska," he declared on the House floor in 2001. "It is the best thing we have going, and how dare members talk about something when they have never been there. Shame on them."

More recently, Young served from 2001 through 2006 as chairman of the Transportation and Infrastructure Committee. He steered a six-year, $286.5 billion renewal of highway and mass transit programs to enactment in 2005, though it took him two Congresses to do so and he had to settle for a far smaller package than he wanted. In the 108th Congress (2003-04), he proposed a $375 billion bill that would have increased the 18.4-cents-per-gallon federal tax on gasoline to help pay for transportation projects. But President Bush refused to support a gas tax increase, and GOP leaders forced Young to cut the proposed spending significantly.

During work on the highway bill, Young drew some unwanted attention to Alaska and to the practice of lawmaker earmarks, legislative provisions directing federal funds to home-state projects. It was Young who wrote earmarks into the 2005 highway bill for what became known as two bridges to nowhere in Alaska — one of which was to be named for him. The earmarks were deleted eventually, but the funds remained available for use as Alaska's state transportation officials deemed necessary.

As chairman of the Transportation panel, Young was frequently embroiled in turf battles with other committee chairmen. At the start of the 109th Congress (2005-06), GOP leaders placed control of the Transportation Security Administration under the new Homeland Security Committee, diminishing Young's empire a bit. Though he also served on the Homeland Security panel, he tussled frequently with its chairman, Republican Peter T. King of New York, over the Coast Guard and the Federal Emergency Management Agency, among other issues. Both agencies have a mix of homeland security and other functions, and the turf war between the two chairmen was so ferocious and distracting that the new Democratic chairmen of the panels signed what amounted to a non-aggression pact early in 2007.

In the 108th Congress, Young also engaged in a public intraparty fight with the chairman of the House Appropriations Committee, C.W. Bill Young of

Florida, over the spending panel's lack of funds for certain transportation programs. In 2004, the two fought bitterly over which items to protect in the annual spending measure for transportation. When the bill was on the floor, they took turns eliminating provisions important to each other. Most of the money was put back during House-Senate negotiations on the legislation.

Although he supports Bush and sides with his fellow Republicans on most issues, he parts company with both on selected matters, especially those involving civil liberties. In 2006, for example, he voted against legislation to authorize the National Security Agency's warrantless electronic surveillance program. "I still believe that we can go after the terrorists without the invasion of privacy this bill advocates," he declared.

Born in California, Young was raised on his family's farm there. As a youth, his favorite book was Jack London's "Call of the Wild," which fired his imagination. After completing college and military service, he headed for Alaska in 1959. He worked in construction, commercial fishing, trapping and other odd jobs before settling in as a fifth-grade teacher for Alaska Native students at a school in Fort Yukon, a remote village of about 700 people located on the Yukon River seven miles above the Arctic Circle. There, Young taught school in the winter and captained his own tug and barge operation along the Yukon in the summers, ferrying supplies to villages along the river. He remains the only licensed mariner in Congress.

He was elected mayor of Fort Yukon in 1964 and won a seat in the state House in 1966. He moved up to a state Senate seat in 1970. The only election he has ever lost was his first U.S. House race, in 1972. His opponent, freshman Democrat Nick Begich, disappeared without a trace along with House Majority Leader Hale Boggs during an October airplane flight from Anchorage to Juneau. Begich still beat Young by almost 12,000 votes in November.

When Begich's seat was declared vacant a few weeks later, Young edged out Emil Notti, the former state Democratic chairman, in a 1973 special election. In his first year in the House, he helped win approval of the Trans-Alaska Pipeline, which carries oil from Alaska's North Slope to Valdez. He still cites that as the single most important achievement of his career.

Surviving a vigorous challenge in the post-Watergate election of 1974, Young enjoyed relatively comfortable re-election margins until 1990. That year and in 1992, he barely withstood challenges from John E. Devens, the former Democratic mayor of Valdez. Young conceded in advertisements that he was "abrasive" and "arrogant" but a worthy fighter for Alaska's interests. He has not had a serious scare since, though his 2006 re-election with just less than 57 percent of the vote was his lowest vote share since 1992.

KEY VOTES

2006

- No — Stop broadband companies from favoring select Internet traffic
- Yes — Affirm U.S. commitment to war in Iraq and reject setting a withdrawal date for troops
- No — Repeal requirement for bilingual ballots at the polls
- Yes — Permit U.S. sale of civilian nuclear technology to India
- No — Build a 700-mile fence on the U.S.-Mexico border to curb illegal crossings
- No — Permit warrantless wiretaps of suspected terrorists

2005

- ? — Intervene in the life-support case of Terri Schiavo
- Yes — Lift President Bush's restrictions on stem cell research funding
- Yes — Prohibit FBI access to library and bookstore records
- Yes — Approve free-trade pact with five Central American countries
- Yes — Pass energy policy overhaul favored by President Bush emphasizing domestic oil and gas production
- Yes — End mandatory preservation of habitat of endangered animal and plant species
- No — Ban torture of prisoners in U.S. custody

CQ VOTE STUDIES

	PARTY UNITY		PRESIDENTIAL SUPPORT	
	Support	Oppose	Support	Oppose
2006	92%	8%	90%	10%
2005	91%	9%	78%	22%
2004	92%	8%	87%	13%
2003	96%	4%	92%	8%
2002	94%	6%	86%	14%

INTEREST GROUPS

	AFL-CIO	ADA	CCUS	ACU
2006	36%	25%	100%	72%
2005	21%	5%	96%	83%
2004	17%	0%	100%	95%
2003	21%	5%	93%	79%
2002	13%	10%	90%	86%

ALASKA
At large

Alaska's remoteness belies its dependence on Washington, D.C. The state's proximity to Russia and the Far East makes it a military stronghold, and its economic boosters, such as oil and gas, minerals and timber, lie mostly on federally owned land.

While state and local government is Alaska's largest employer, a never-ending battle for control over the local economy has made voters hostile to Washington. Local lawmakers remain outspoken advocates of opening land to oil and gas exploration and join most Alaskans in support of constructing a natural gas pipeline from Prudhoe Bay through Canada to the lower 48 states.

Most Alaskans view oil and gas exploration as the best way to independence and heavily favor drilling in the Arctic National Wildlife Refuge. Alaska has not had state sales and income taxes since black gold was discovered near Prudhoe Bay in the 1970s. The state continues to build a privatized economy through its thriving tourism industry.

Alaska generally supports Republicans and has not elected a Democrat to Congress since 1974. Voters in some cities, the panhandle and the sparsely populated tundra vote more Democratic. Third parties abound in this cold, conservative frontier state, where most voters register as either independent or nonpartisan, but still mainly vote Republican. Anti-machine GOP candidate Sarah Palin defeated the incumbent governor in the 2006 primary and became the state's first female governor.

MAJOR INDUSTRY
Oil and gas, defense, government, tourism, fishing, timber, mining

MILITARY BASES
Fort Wainwright (Army), 6,500 military, 1,700 civilian (2007); Elmendorf Air Force Base, 6,485 military, 1,077 civilian (2006); Fort Richardson (Army), 5,000 military, 1,200 civilian (2007); Eielson Air Force Base, 2,400 military, 789 civilian (2005); Fort Greely (Army), 200 military, 1,000 civilian (2007); Clear Air Force Station, 90 military, 57 civilian (2007)

CITIES
Anchorage, 260,283; Juneau, 30,711; Fairbanks, 30,224

NOTABLE
Mt. McKinley is the highest point in North America, at 20,320 feet; Juneau, the state capital, is only accessible by ship or air.

ARIZONA

Gov. Janet Napolitano (D)

First elected: 2002
Length of term: 4 years
Term expires: 1/11
Salary: $95,000
Phone: (602) 542-4331

Residence: Phoenix
Born: Nov. 29, 1957; Manhattan, N.Y.
Religion: Methodist
Family: Single
Education: U. of Santa Clara, B.S. 1979 (political science); U. of Virginia, J.D. 1983
Career: Lawyer
Political highlights: U.S. attorney, 1993-97; Ariz. attorney general, 1999-2003

Election results:

2006 GENERAL		
Janet Napolitano (D)	959,830	62.6%
Len Munsil (R)	543,528	35.4%
Barry Hess (LIBERT)	30,268	2.0%

Secretary of State Jan Brewer (R)

(no lieutenant governor)
First elected: 2002
Length of term: 4 years
Term expires: 1/11
Salary: $70,000
Phone: (602) 542-4285

LEGISLATURE

Legislature: 100 days January-April

Senate: 30 members, 2-year terms
2007 ratios: 17 R, 13 D; 17 men, 13 women
Salary: $24,000
Phone: (602) 926-3559

House: 60 members, 2-year terms
2007 ratios: 33 R, 27 D; 42 men, 18 women
Salary: $24,000
Phone: (602) 926-4221

TERM LIMITS

Governor: 2 consecutive terms
Senate: 4 consecutive terms
House: 4 consecutive terms

URBAN STATISTICS

CITY	POPULATION
Phoenix	1,321,045
Tucson	486,699
Mesa	396,375
Glendale	218,812
Scottsdale	202,705

REGISTERED VOTERS

Republican	39%
Democrat	33%
Others	28%

POPULATION

2006 population (est.)	6,166,318
2000 population	5,130,632
1990 population	3,665,228
Percent change (1990-2000)	+40%
Rank among states (2006)	17
Median age	34.2
Born in state	34.7%
Foreign born	12.8%
Violent crime rate	532/100,000
Poverty level	13.9%
Federal workers	46,967
Military	33,485

ELECTIONS

STATE ELECTION OFFICIAL
(602) 542-8683
DEMOCRATIC PARTY
(602) 298-4200
REPUBLICAN PARTY
(602) 957-7770

MISCELLANEOUS

Web: www.az.gov
Capital: Phoenix

U.S. CONGRESS

Senate: 2 Republicans
House: 4 Democrats, 4 Republicans

2000 Census Statistics by District

DIST.	2004 VOTE FOR PRESIDENT BUSH	2004 VOTE FOR PRESIDENT KERRY	WHITE	BLACK	ASIAN	HISP	MEDIAN INCOME	WHITE COLLAR	BLUE COLLAR	SERVICE INDUSTRY	OVER 64	UNDER 18	COLLEGE EDUCATION	RURAL	SQ. MILES
1	54%	45%	58%	1%	1%	16%	$32,979	53%	27%	20%	14%	28%	18%	45%	58,608
2	61	38	78	2	2	14	$42,432	60	23	17	20	24	19	11	20,220
3	58	41	79	2	2	14	$48,108	68	18	14	10	25	30	4	598
4	38	62	29	7	1	58	$30,624	44	36	20	7	33	10	0	199
5	54	45	77	3	3	13	$51,780	73	14	13	10	23	40	3	1,406
6	64	35	77	2	2	17	$47,976	63	23	14	14	28	24	3	724
7	43	57	39	3	1	51	$30,828	51	29	20	11	30	13	16	22,873
8	53	46	74	3	2	18	$40,656	67	17	16	17	23	31	13	9,007
STATE	55	44	64	3	2	25	$40,558	61	23	16	13	27	24	12	113,635
U.S.	50.7	48.3	69	12	4	13	$41,994	60	25	15	12	26	24	21	3,537,438

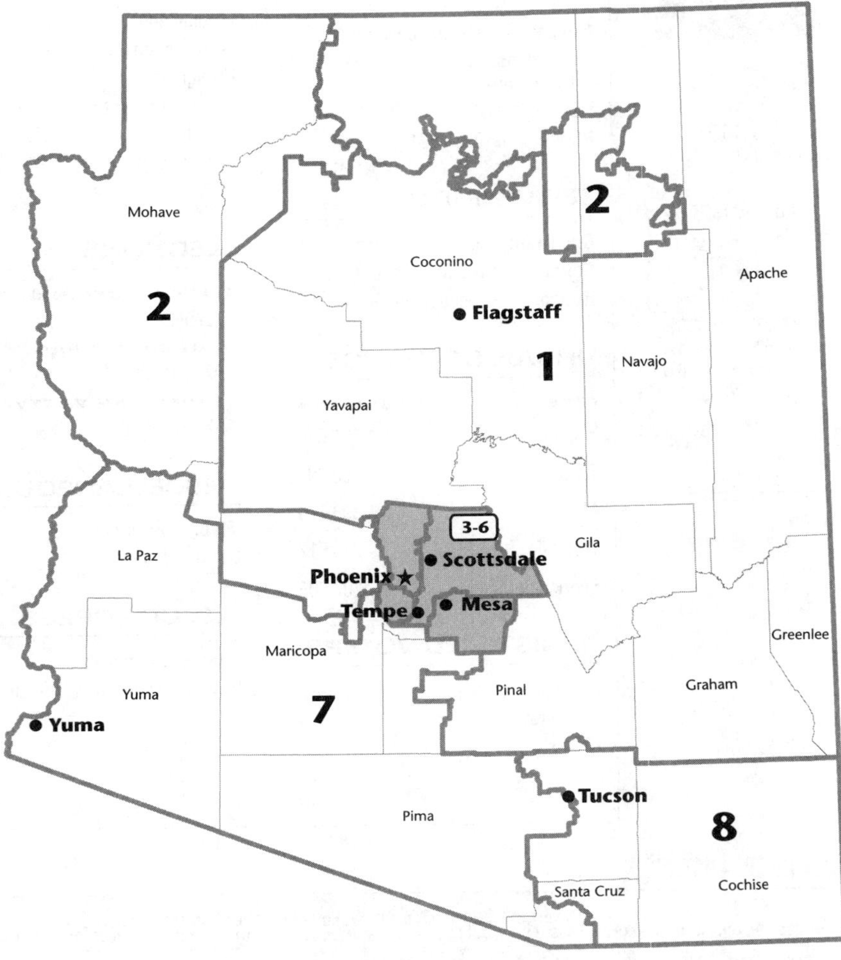
Mohave
2
Coconino
2
Apache
Flagstaff
1
Navajo
Yavapai
3-6
Gila
Scottsdale
La Paz
Phoenix
Tempe
Mesa
Greenlee
Maricopa
Pinal
Graham
Yuma
7
Yuma
Tucson
Pima
8
Santa Cruz
Cochise

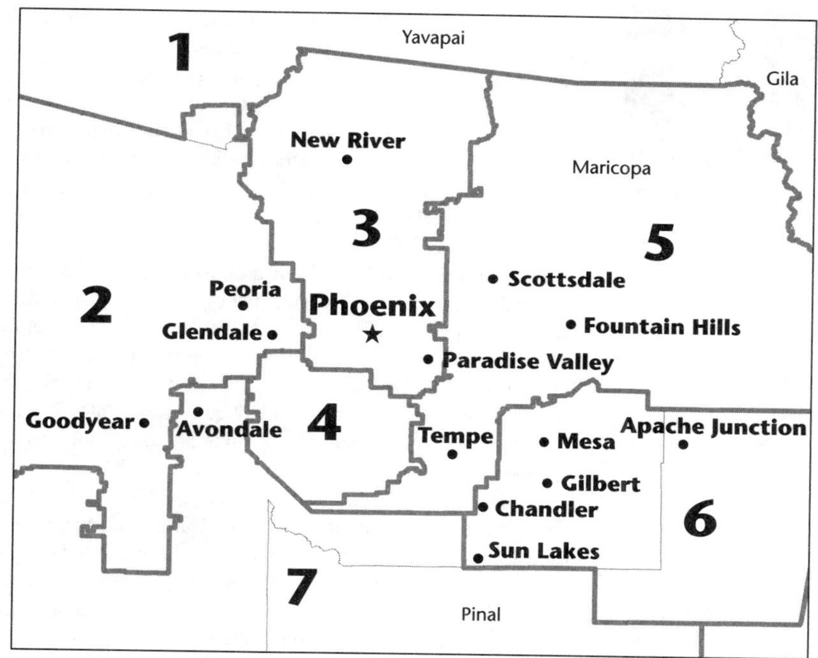
1
Yavapai
Gila
New River
Maricopa
3
5
2
Peoria
Phoenix
Scottsdale
Glendale
Fountain Hills
Paradise Valley
Goodyear
Avondale
4
Tempe
Mesa
Apache Junction
Gilbert
Chandler
6
Sun Lakes
7
Pinal

Sen. John McCain (R)

CAPITOL OFFICE
224-2235
mccain.senate.gov
241 Russell 20510-0303; fax 228-2862

COMMITTEES
Armed Services - ranking member
Commerce, Science & Transportation
Indian Affairs

RESIDENCE
Phoenix

BORN
Aug. 29, 1936, Panama Canal Zone, Panama

RELIGION
Episcopalian

FAMILY
Wife, Cindy McCain; seven children

EDUCATION
U.S. Naval Academy, B.S. 1958; National War College, attended 1973-74

MILITARY SERVICE
Navy, 1958-81

CAREER
Navy officer; Navy Senate liaison; beer distributor

POLITICAL HIGHLIGHTS
U.S. House, 1983-87; sought Republican nomination for president, 2000

ELECTION RESULTS

2004 GENERAL		
John McCain (R)	1,505,372	76.7%
Stuart Starky (D)	404,507	20.6%
Ernest Hancock (LIBERT)	51,798	2.6%
2004 PRIMARY		
John McCain (R)		unopposed

PREVIOUS WINNING PERCENTAGES
1998 (69%); 1992 (56%); 1986 (61%); 1984 House Election (78%); 1982 House Election (66%)

Elected 1986; 4th term

McCain is at the top of the White House watch list for 2008, and every move he makes gets analyzed for its potential impact on the presidential contest. His quandary is whether to spend his Senate days emphasizing his conservative credentials or burnishing the maverick streak that has made him so appealing to Democrats and independents.

The best seats for watching the drama play out are in the Senate Armed Services Committee hearing room. McCain is the top-ranking Republican on the panel, potential Democratic rival Hillary Rodham Clinton is a prominent member, and the war in Iraq dominates the agenda. The senior committee post could help McCain woo conservatives, given his hawkish views on defense in general and on Iraq in particular.

McCain has been an unflagging supporter of the war, even as other Republicans have edged away from President Bush's proposal for a troop "surge" to try to bring an end to American involvement. But he's not an ally for the president on the war. He has said Bush "terribly mishandled" the war, and has called for boosting troop strength far beyond the level the White House considers acceptable.

McCain has long been both a conservative and a maverick. A vocal advocate of a muscular foreign policy and lower spending, he is also a strong-willed senator who works with Democrats and refuses to hold his tongue when he thinks GOP leaders are straying off course. A high-energy man who can be blunt, funny and testy — often in the same sitting — McCain is frequently mislabeled as a moderate Republican, largely because his departures from the party line often put him in the company of moderates.

In May 2005, for example, McCain helped broker a deal among a bipartisan group of senators, known as the Gang of 14, to prevent a showdown over Democrats' ability to filibuster conservative judicial nominees. The seven Republicans and seven Democrats, mostly moderates, pledged to vote against the GOP leadership's "nuclear option," a procedural force play that could have barred all future filibusters of judicial nominations. But the group also vowed to defeat any filibusters of nominees unless "extraordinary circumstances" were involved — a term each Gang member was left to define individually. Social conservatives decried the deal, but it led to confirmation of some of Bush's long-stalled picks.

Later that year, McCain, who endured five and a half years of brutal physical abuse as a prisoner of war in Vietnam, pushed Congress to ban torture of overseas detainees, a move that Bush initially opposed. The president eventually backed down and signed the legislation.

McCain bucked Bush on several other fronts. He voted against both of the president's major tax cuts, in 2001 and 2003. He pushed for stricter fuel efficiency standards and caps on greenhouse gases to combat global warming. He opposed energy exploration in the Arctic National Wildlife Refuge.

But he aligned with the president in 2006, when he teamed up with Edward M. Kennedy of Massachusetts, one of the most liberal Democrats, to push for an immigration overhaul that would create a guest worker program similar to the one Bush advocated and give longtime illegal immigrants a chance to become citizens.

McCain's maverick voting record does not perturb his colleagues as much as his attitude does. In a chamber where members of the club are expected to treat each other with deference, McCain comes off as self-righteous and too quick to discard customary courtesies. He angers GOP leaders and individual senators by repeatedly attempting to eliminate spending projects that he labels "pork," saying the money would be better spent on building up the military. He voted against the Medicare prescription drug bill in 2003 because of its cost.

Even his criticisms of Bush sometimes come from the right rather than the left. He says the administration needs to take a harder line with Russian President Vladimir V. Putin, who he says is endangering democracy in Russia and has failed to help stop Iran from acquiring nuclear weapons.

McCain describes himself as a "pro-life, small-government, anti-spending, foreign-policy-hawk conservative." But he's also a fan of Theodore Roosevelt, and doesn't worry about conservative attacks when he emulates TR's progressivism. "When I know what the right thing to do is, and I do it, it always turns out fine," McCain said in April 2006. "If I do something for political reasons, it always turns out badly. It's just the way my political life has unfolded."

One thing McCain now says he did for political reasons, and wishes he had not, was take back his criticism of the Confederate flag during the South Carolina primary in 2000, when he was battling Bush for the GOP nomination. After suggesting the flag was "a symbol of racism and slavery" — his real view on the subject — McCain later tried to limit political damage in the state by calling it "a symbol of heritage." In his memoir, "Worth the Fighting For," McCain writes that in doing so, he failed to live up to his promise "to tell the truth no matter what." He lost the primary, and the defeat marked the beginning of the end of his presidential campaign that year.

Some of McCain's more recent moves have been interpreted as a politically motivated shift to the right. In 2005, he made amends with the Rev. Jerry Falwell, the religious conservative leader whom he once described as an "agent of intolerance." McCain says, however, that Falwell reached out to him rather than the other way around, an account Falwell did not dispute. McCain also says he voted to extend Bush's tax cuts because letting them expire would effectively be a tax increase.

The son — and grandson — of an admiral, McCain went to the Naval Academy in Annapolis with great family expectations, but didn't prove to be admiral material. He finished fifth from the bottom in the class of 1958. But he was a good Navy flier and, it turned out, a good patriot. Nine years after graduation, his plane was shot down and he was captured by the North Vietnamese. Both arms and a leg broken, McCain was dragged from the crash and thrown, without benefit of medical treatment, into a cell. He spent the next five and a half years enduring torture and solitary confinement, an experience recounted in his best-selling memoir, "Faith of My Fathers," and also the subject of a 2005 movie on the A&E cable network.

After a stint as the Navy's Senate liaison, McCain ran for Congress in 1982, winning the seat of retiring House Minority Leader John J. Rhodes. After two terms, McCain drew 61 percent of the vote to succeed retiring GOP Sen. Barry Goldwater in 1986. During his first Senate term, McCain was one of five senators accused of interceding with federal regulators in behalf of wealthy savings and loan operator Charles H. Keating Jr. After a protracted Ethics Committee investigation, McCain received a mild rebuke in 1991, the low point of his Senate career.

The black mark hurt; in 1992, he won re-election with only 56 percent. But he rebounded in 1998, with 69 percent. And two years later, 5 million people, including a majority of New Hampshire's first-in-the-nation voters, chose McCain over Bush in the GOP primary. Bush ultimately overtook McCain in South Carolina, and the Arizonan returned to the Senate. In 2004, he won his fourth term with 77 percent of the vote.

KEY VOTES

2006

- Yes Confirm Samuel A. Alito Jr. to the Supreme Court
- No Allow consideration of a bill to establish a $140 billion trust fund to compensate victims of asbestos exposure
- Yes Extend tax cuts for two years at a cost of $70 billion over five years
- Yes Overhaul immigration policy with border security, enforcement and guest worker program
- Yes Allow consideration of a bill to permanently repeal the estate tax
- No Urge President Bush to begin troop withdrawals from Iraq in 2006
- Yes Lift President Bush's restrictions on stem cell research funding
- Yes Authorize military tribunals for suspected terrorists

2005

- Yes Curb class action lawsuits by shifting them from state to federal courts
- Yes Allow confirmation vote on Priscilla R. Owen to the U.S. Court of Appeals for the 5th Circuit
- No Oppose mandatory emissions limits and block recognition of global warming as a threat
- Yes Approve free-trade pact with five Central American countries
- No Pass energy policy overhaul favored by President Bush emphasizing domestic oil and gas production
- Yes Shield gunmakers from lawsuits when their products are used in crimes
- Yes Ban torture of prisoners in U.S. custody
- Yes Renew 16 provisions of the Patriot Act
- Yes Allow final vote on opening the Arctic National Wildlife Refuge to oil and gas exploration

CQ VOTE STUDIES

	PARTY UNITY		PRESIDENTIAL SUPPORT	
	Support	Oppose	Support	Oppose
2006	76%	24%	89%	11%
2005	84%	16%	77%	23%
2004	79%	21%	92%	8%
2003	86%	14%	91%	9%
2002	80%	20%	90%	10%
2001	67%	33%	91%	9%
2000	83%	17%	38%	62%
1999	90%	10%	38%	62%
1998	84%	16%	49%	51%
1997	84%	16%	70%	30%

INTEREST GROUPS

	AFL-CIO	ADA	CCUS	ACU
2006	7%	15%	100%	65%
2005	7%	10%	72%	80%
2004	33%	35%	67%	72%
2003	15%	35%	61%	75%
2002	33%	20%	79%	78%
2001	27%	40%	50%	68%
2000	14%	5%	75%	81%
1999	0%	5%	75%	77%
1998	29%	20%	76%	68%
1997	14%	5%	100%	80%

Sen. Jon Kyl (R)

CAPITOL OFFICE
224-4521
info@kyl.senate.gov
kyl.senate.gov
730 Hart 20510-0304; fax 224-2207

COMMITTEES
Finance
Judiciary

RESIDENCE
Phoenix

BORN
April 25, 1942, Oakland, Neb.

RELIGION
Presbyterian

FAMILY
Wife, Caryll Kyl; two children

EDUCATION
U. of Arizona, B.A. 1964 (political science), LL.B. 1966

CAREER
Lawyer

POLITICAL HIGHLIGHTS
U.S. House, 1987-95

ELECTION RESULTS

2006 GENERAL

Jon Kyl (R)	814,398	53.3%
Jim Pederson (D)	664,141	43.5%
Richard Mack (LIBERT)	48,231	3.2%

2006 PRIMARY

Jon Kyl (R)	unopposed

PREVIOUS WINNING PERCENTAGES
2000 (79%); 1994 (54%); 1992 House Election (59%); 1990 House Election (61%); 1988 House Election (87%); 1986 House Election (65%)

Elected 1994; 3rd term

A crafty insider, Kyl has been overshadowed on the national stage by his senior GOP colleague, Arizona Sen. John McCain, a 2008 presidential hopeful. But among senators, he is more influential than McCain, who is often regarded as a show horse. Kyl's standing with his colleagues was affirmed when they elected him chairman of the Republican Conference, the party's No. 3 leadership post, for the 110th Congress (2007-08).

Republicans are looking to Kyl (KILE), long one of the chamber's most stalwart conservatives, to get their message out. The role of public spokesman does not come naturally to Kyl, who, unlike other senators, has typically avoided the television cameras. But his colleagues think his low-key ways may be effective after the polarizing performance of his predecessor, Republican Sen. Rick Santorum of Pennsylvania, a sometimes abrasive conservative who lost his re-election bid. Kyl was easily re-elected to a third term, and now is in position to help plot the GOP's countermoves to the new Democratic majority in Congress.

Dubbed "The Operator" by Time magazine, which named him one of the 10 Best Senators in 2006, Kyl explains his success this way: "You can accomplish a lot if you're not necessarily out in front on everything."

The Arizonan has long been one of the clearest voices among the Senate's most conservative Republicans. His quiet, behind-the-scenes operating style resembles that of the man Kyl considers his political mentor from their days together in the House, Vice President Dick Cheney. "My father said you should find somebody you can trust," Kyl recalls. "So I went to Dick Cheney." The two stayed in touch over the years.

His impact has been most apparent on the Judiciary Committee, where he repeatedly thwarted the panel's moderate Republican chairman, Arlen Specter of Pennsylvania, when the GOP controlled the Senate. Operating in the shadows, Kyl helped bring down the Supreme Court nomination of President Bush's White House counsel, Harriet Miers, whom conservatives viewed as unreliable. He also torpedoed Specter's efforts to oversee the president's domestic surveillance programs.

Kyl split with Specter, Bush and colleague McCain on another key issue — immigration. He opposed their efforts in 2006 to pass a comprehensive bill that tightened border security, created a guest worker program and provided a path to eventual citizenship for 12 million illegal immigrants in the United States. Kyl said illegal immigrants should be forced to return to their home countries before being considered for citizenship.

Despite their disagreement over immigration, Kyl is typically one of the president's most reliable backers. He is also a staunch supporter of the GOP leadership, ranking among the top scorers in party unity on votes that divide the two parties.

Kyl is one of the GOP's pre-eminent advocates of a robust national security posture. Since his time in the House, where he served on the Armed Services Committee, he has advocated a national missile defense system. He strongly supported Bush's decision in 2002 to withdraw from the 1972 Anti-Ballistic Missile Treaty, which banned nationwide antimissile defense. Kyl successfully pushed to include $7.4 billion for missile defenses in the 2002 defense spending law.

Kyl favors unilateral steps rather than negotiated agreements to neutralize emerging military threats, contending that the United States should rely on its military to guarantee its national security rather than on diplomatic agreements. He called the U.S. invasion of Iraq "one of the most ambitious and important missions in world history."

Despite increasing bipartisan concern over Bush's Iraq strategy, Kyl's support for the war effort is unwavering and he strongly opposes Congress weighing in. "You cannot micromanage a war from the United States Senate. Once we authorize it, then we need to see it through until its conclusion," he noted on CNN in February 2007.

He demonstrated an interest in combating terrorism at home long before the attacks of Sept. 11, 2001. As chairman of the Judiciary Subcommittee on Terrorism, Technology and Homeland Security, Kyl led the effort to rewrite wiretapping laws to make it easier for law enforcement officials to track and capture terrorists. Ideas he had long advocated, such as allowing investigators to use roving wiretaps to follow suspects using multiple cell phones, were included in the 2001 anti-terrorism law known as the Patriot Act.

In a rare mind-meld with a Democrat, Kyl worked with California Sen. Dianne Feinstein to win passage of a constitutional amendment to guarantee crime victims the right to speak at proceedings that determine prison sentences and consider the potential release of a convict. In 2004, they decided to abandon the amendment in favor of a stand-alone victims' rights bill. At the same time Kyl led Senate opposition to a measure giving federal inmates access to DNA testing and improving legal representation for state and federal inmates. He said it would become too easy for federal inmates to secure post-conviction DNA tests and win new trials. House Republicans overcame Kyl's opposition to the criminal justice measure by folding into it his victims' rights bill, and the combined measure became law.

Kyl was born in northeastern Nebraska near the small college town of Wayne, where his father, John H. Kyl, was a school principal and led the local Chamber of Commerce. In the 1950s, the family moved to Iowa, where the elder Kyl joined his brother in a clothing business, and later, was elected to the U.S. House, serving 11 years. He helped prepare his son for a life in politics by coaching him in public speaking, and he brought young Kyl to spend the summer of 1963 with him in Washington.

Kyl went to college at the University of Arizona, drawing inspiration from the state's conservative GOP icon, Sen. Barry Goldwater. He read, and reread, Goldwater's "Conscience of a Conservative," and William F. Buckley's "Up from Liberalism." Both had "a huge impact on me," Kyl says.

After graduating from law school, he joined a top Phoenix law firm, Jennings, Strouss and Salmon. Following his father's career model, in 1985 he became president of the Phoenix Chamber of Commerce, building strong ties with the business community.

The following year, he decided to run for the House rather than take a lucrative partnership in the firm. His business ties helped him win a 1986 GOP primary over John Conlan, a former House member trying for a comeback. Kyl handily won the general election in the then traditionally Republican 4th District.

Kyl won three easy re-elections to the House and launched a Senate bid in 1994 even before incumbent Democrat Dennis DeConcini announced his retirement. He breezed to the GOP nomination as first-term Rep. Sam Coppersmith struggled to secure the Democratic nomination. Voters in Arizona liked the themes Kyl stressed — smaller government, lower taxes and reduced regulation. He prevailed over Coppersmith by 14 percentage points. Six years later, the Democrats did not even field a candidate.

But in 2006, Kyl faced millionaire shopping mall developer Jim Pederson, a former state Democratic Party chairman. Bush, Cheney and other GOP bigwigs went all out to help him, and he bucked the year's strong Democratic tide to win a third term by almost 10 percentage points.

KEY VOTES

2006

- Yes Confirm Samuel A. Alito Jr. to the Supreme Court
- Yes Allow consideration of a bill to establish a $140 billion trust fund to compensate victims of asbestos exposure
- Yes Extend tax cuts for two years at a cost of $70 billion over five years
- No Overhaul immigration policy with border security, enforcement and guest worker program
- Yes Allow consideration of a bill to permanently repeal the estate tax
- No Urge President Bush to begin troop withdrawals from Iraq in 2006
- No Lift President Bush's restrictions on stem cell research funding
- Yes Authorize military tribunals for suspected terrorists

2005

- Yes Curb class action lawsuits by shifting them from state to federal courts
- Yes Allow confirmation vote on Priscilla R. Owen to the U.S. Court of Appeals for the 5th Circuit
- Yes Oppose mandatory emissions limits and block recognition of global warming as a threat
- Yes Approve free-trade pact with five Central American countries
- No Pass energy policy overhaul favored by President Bush emphasizing domestic oil and gas production
- Yes Shield gunmakers from lawsuits when their products are used in crimes
- Yes Ban torture of prisoners in U.S. custody
- Yes Renew 16 provisions of the Patriot Act
- Yes Allow final vote on opening the Arctic National Wildlife Refuge to oil and gas exploration

CQ VOTE STUDIES

	PARTY UNITY		PRESIDENTIAL SUPPORT	
	Support	Oppose	Support	Oppose
2006	95%	5%	90%	10%
2005	98%	2%	89%	11%
2004	98%	2%	100%	0%
2003	99%	1%	99%	1%
2002	96%	4%	96%	4%
2001	98%	2%	99%	1%
2000	99%	1%	41%	59%
1999	97%	3%	34%	66%
1998	96%	4%	33%	67%
1997	99%	1%	57%	43%

INTEREST GROUPS

	AFL-CIO	ADA	CCUS	ACU
2006	13%	0%	92%	92%
2005	0%	5%	83%	100%
2004	0%	5%	88%	100%
2003	0%	10%	96%	90%
2002	15%	0%	90%	100%
2001	6%	5%	100%	100%
2000	0%	0%	85%	100%
1999	0%	0%	82%	100%
1998	0%	0%	76%	96%
1997	0%	0%	70%	96%

Rep. Rick Renzi (R)

CAPITOL OFFICE
225-2315
www.house.gov/renzi
418 Cannon 20515-0301; fax 226-9739

COMMITTEES
No committee assignments

RESIDENCE
Flagstaff

BORN
June 11, 1958, Fort Monmouth, N.J.

RELIGION
Roman Catholic

FAMILY
Wife, Roberta Renzi; 12 children

EDUCATION
Northern Arizona U., B.S. 1980 (criminal justice); Catholic U. of America, J.D. 2002

CAREER
Insurance company owner; U.S. Defense Department counterintelligence contractor; real estate agent

POLITICAL HIGHLIGHTS
No previous office

ELECTION RESULTS

2006 GENERAL		
Rick Renzi (R)	105,646	51.8%
Ellen Simon (D)	88,691	43.4%
David Schlosser (LIBERT)	9,802	4.8%
2006 PRIMARY		
Rick Renzi (R)		unopposed
2004 GENERAL		
Rick Renzi (R)	148,315	58.5%
Paul Babbitt (D)	91,776	36.2%
John Crockett (LIBERT)	13,260	5.2%

PREVIOUS WINNING PERCENTAGES
2002 (49%)

Elected 2002; 3rd term

Renzi is a social and fiscal conservative who carves out a big exemption in his ideology for American Indian tribes, a powerful political force in his sprawling, eastern Arizona district that is home to more American Indians than any other congressional district. While he generally champions smaller government, Renzi quietly advocates for as much federal spending as possible for anti-poverty programs for the tribes.

Support from American Indians has been key to Renzi's re-election victories, helping him maintain an edge, albeit a small one, in a district generally favoring Democrats. While other incumbents enjoyed voter support of 59 percent or better, he was returned to the House in 2006 with just 52 percent of the vote. American Indians typically vote Democratic, but they have supported Renzi since his election in 2002. They also are among his major contributors, donating $29,000 to his 2006 campaign.

Renzi's aggressive securing of federal projects, grants and loan guarantees for the folks back home prompted the conservative National Taxpayers Union to give him a low score on spending issues. Renzi told The Arizona Republic's editorial board: "I would defy any politician to travel with me across parts of my district that are without running water, electricity and passable roads and try and call money for them 'pork.' "

He is a perennial target for Democrats at election time, and his 2006 struggle for a third term was complicated by a federal probe into whether he misused his office for a real estate deal in which a former business partner made a large profit. Renzi denied wrongdoing.

In April 2007, his legal problems worsened. The Federal Bureau of Investigation raided an insurance business owned by his wife. Renzi, under pressure by GOP leaders, temporarily gave up his assignments on the House Intelligence Committee and on the Natural Resources and Financial Services panels.

Renzi's district, the largest geographically in the state, is home to the Navajo and four other tribes. In 2006, Renzi pushed through Congress a change in federal housing formulas that resulted in an $84.5 million grant to the Navajo Housing Authority. Another of his bills that became law boosted support for home loans to American Indians, raising the portion of a loan guaranteed by the government from 80 percent to 95 percent.

After a 40-year-old land dispute between the Navajo and the Hopi tribes was finally settled in 2006, Renzi sponsored legislation to convert a $50 million fund now used for relocation into one that also could be used for reconstruction of roads, water lines and schools.

Renzi is a social conservative who touts so-called family values, something he is able to experience daily. The devout Roman Catholic and his wife, Roberta, have the distinction of having more children than any other congressional family — a total of 12 ranging in age from 6 to 24 years in 2006. Renzi jokes that any outing involving his kids is "very loud, like a rock concert." In his first major re-election test in 2004, his opponent tried to make an issue of Renzi's children living and attending school in a Virginia suburb close to Washington, D.C., rather than in his home district. Renzi responded that he needed to be close to his children to be an involved parent.

His conservatism notwithstanding, Renzi has a history of breaking with Republican leaders on personal priorities and political needs. He was the only Arizona Republican to back three of the Democrats' six bills in their "first 100 hours" agenda at the start of the 110th Congress (2007-08). The three bills Renzi supported were a minimum wage increase, requiring the federal government to negotiate with drug companies for lower Medicare prescription prices, and interest cuts on student loans.

In 2003, he first backed a Democratic measure to give a one-time, $1,500 bonus to soldiers in Iraq and Afghanistan but then switched his vote after GOP leaders convinced him Democrats were using the bonus to politicize the war on terror. Renzi took on party leaders in 2004 in a fight over more money for veterans, organizing 20 freshmen to hold out their votes on the Republicans' proposed budget. But the leadership ultimately got enough votes to approve both the budget and an appropriations bill that did not include the big boost in veterans' funding that Renzi wanted.

Renzi's border state is greatly affected by immigration policy. In the 109th Congress (2005-06), during the debate over Bush's proposed guest worker program for illegal immigrants, Renzi backed a conservative bill that dealt only with enforcement and construction of a fence. He said a guest worker program should wait until the government achieved "operational control of the border."

Renzi grew up near the Arizona-Mexico border in Sierra Vista, where his father, a two-star general, was stationed at Fort Huachuca. As a teenager, he crossed into Mexico for dances, bullfights and baseball games. His wife is the great-granddaughter of a Mexican government official who fled that country's political revolution in 1910. When Renzi talks about Mexicans, he refers to them as his "brothers and sisters to the South."

He went to Northern Arizona University in Flagstaff on an athletic scholarship, was elected captain of the football team and led the Lumberjacks to the Big Sky Conference championship.

He graduated with a degree in criminal justice and soon afterward married and started a family. He bought a ranch in southern Arizona in Sonoita, then moved to Virginia to start an insurance brokerage. He got a law degree from Catholic University and interned for Arizona GOP Sen. Jon Kyl while in school.

In 2002, Renzi waged his first campaign for office in a district drawn to be politically competitive. The strongest Democratic challengers, Apache County Attorney Steve Udall and former Clinton aide Fred DuVal, were defeated in the primary by relatively unknown businessman George Cordova. In 2004, Democrats fielded a stronger and better-financed candidate in Paul Babbitt, brother of former Arizona Gov. and Clinton-era Interior Secretary Bruce Babbitt. Renzi prevailed with 59 percent of the vote. Two years later, Renzi won against Democrat and civil rights lawyer Ellen Simon.

KEY VOTES

2006

No Stop broadband companies from favoring select Internet traffic
Yes Affirm U.S. commitment to war in Iraq and reject setting a withdrawal date for troops
No Repeal requirement for bilingual ballots at the polls
Yes Permit U.S. sale of civilian nuclear technology to India
Yes Build a 700-mile fence on the U.S.-Mexico border to curb illegal crossings
Yes Permit warrantless wiretaps of suspected terrorists

2005

Yes Intervene in the life-support case of Terri Schiavo
No Lift President Bush's restrictions on stem cell research funding
No Prohibit FBI access to library and bookstore records
Yes Approve free-trade pact with five Central American countries
Yes Pass energy policy overhaul favored by President Bush emphasizing domestic oil and gas production
Yes End mandatory preservation of habitat of endangered animal and plant species
No Ban torture of prisoners in U.S. custody

CQ VOTE STUDIES

	PARTY UNITY		PRESIDENTIAL SUPPORT	
	Support	Oppose	Support	Oppose
2006	87%	13%	85%	15%
2005	92%	8%	91%	9%
2004	92%	8%	82%	18%
2003	91%	9%	93%	7%

INTEREST GROUPS

	AFL-CIO	ADA	CCUS	ACU
2006	36%	15%	93%	84%
2005	27%	15%	93%	92%
2004	20%	10%	95%	88%
2003	20%	10%	90%	84%

ARIZONA 1

North and east – Flagstaff, Prescott, Navajo reservation

A mix of rural conservatives, artistic liberals and a large American Indian population makes the immense 1st appear ripe for unpredictable elections, but that does not mean the residents have nothing in common.

The eight counties of the 1st, freed partly from Phoenix's influence after gaining their own district following the 2000 census, take in a 58,608-square-mile swath of Arizona that is larger than 30 states. Democrats have a slight voter registration advantage here, and most locals call themselves environmentalists in a district that includes both sides of the Grand Canyon. Despite the Democrats' seeming advantage, George W. Bush captured 54 percent of the 1st's vote in 2004 and Republican Rep. Renzi was re-elected with 52 percent of the 2006 vote.

The district, which exhibits great natural beauty, is a popular destination for tourists, artists and art enthusiasts. Sedona, a renowned tourist destination, is home to numerous art galleries and luxury resorts. The 1st also features mining and timber operations over its vast terrain. Residents are constantly worried about drought, which has hit the area particularly hard in recent years. Drought conditions led to forest fires in 2002 and 2003, which struck severe blows to the area's many timber and agricultural operations, strained the resources of the state and local governments, and qualified the area for disaster relief from FEMA.

The district has the largest American Indian population (23 percent) in the nation, and high rates of poverty and unemployment continue to be problems in the American Indian communities. Because of longstanding land disputes, the 1st is missing a chunk of land in its northern section to avoid placing the Hopi Nation in the same district as the Navajo Nation.

MAJOR INDUSTRY

Tourism, agriculture, timber, mining

CITIES

Flagstaff, 52,894; Prescott, 33,938; Casa Grande, 25,224; Prescott Valley, 23,535

NOTABLE

Lowell Observatory, in Flagstaff, is where Clyde Tombaugh discovered Pluto in 1930; Casa Grande Ruins National Monument near Coolidge features the remains of a large prehistoric building.

Rep. Trent Franks (R)

CAPITOL OFFICE
225-4576
www.house.gov/franks
1237 Longworth 20515-0302; fax 225-6328

COMMITTEES
Armed Services
Judiciary

RESIDENCE
Glendale

BORN
June 19, 1957, Uravan, Colo.

RELIGION
Baptist

FAMILY
Wife, Josephine Franks

EDUCATION
Ottawa U. (Ariz.), attended 1989-90

CAREER
Oil company executive; conservative think tank president; state children's programs director

POLITICAL HIGHLIGHTS
Ariz. House, 1985-87; defeated for re-election to Ariz. House, 1986; sought Republican nomination for U.S. House, 1994

ELECTION RESULTS

2006 GENERAL		
Trent Franks (R)	135,150	58.6%
John Thrasher (D)	89,671	38.9%
Powell Gammill (LIBERT)	5,734	2.5%
2006 PRIMARY		
Trent Franks (R)		unopposed
2004 GENERAL		
Trent Franks (R)	165,260	59.2%
Randy Camacho (D)	107,406	38.5%
Powell Gammill (LIBERT)	6,625	2.4%

PREVIOUS WINNING PERCENTAGES
2002 (60%)

Elected 2002; 3rd term

Franks gets a little miffed when interest groups every year rank him as one of the five most conservative members of the House. He wouldn't mind being No. 1 on that list.

And indeed there isn't a lot of sunlight to the right of Franks. He would freeze the federal budget to get it to balance, he would repeal *Roe v. Wade* and outlaw abortion except to save the life of the woman, and he would get rid of some sitting federal judges. "Nearly all the great social crises in the country are because of some Supreme Court decision that was imposed by judges with an oligarchy mind-set," Franks says.

Franks wages his battle against liberal judges as a senior Republican on the Judiciary Committee. From that perch, he also has been helpful to the White House in rallying support for President Bush's conservative Supreme Court appointments and is a staunch supporter of the administration's Iraq War strategy.

But his legislative scorecard is modest, a reflection of ideas out of the political mainstream and his inexperience as a legislator. Before his 2002 election to Congress, Franks' only previous stint in elective office was as a one-term state House representative. His major endeavor in the House has been trying to gather support for an idea he successfully promoted while he was a state representative: tax credits for charitable contributions to groups that provide tuition vouchers for children enrolled in private or parochial schools. Franks drafted an Arizona law in 1997 creating such scholarships, and has repeatedly sponsored legislation to create a similar national program. So far, he has been unsuccessful in getting it to the floor.

His other signature social issue is abortion. Franks supports rolling back the Supreme Court decision legalizing abortion, which he calls "the greatest holocaust in the history of mankind." Back home, he was known around the statehouse for wearing a tie tack in the shape of a fetus's feet.

Franks is among the Republicans skeptical of government's ability to solve thorny social problems. He opposed Bush's 2003 expansion of the Medicare program with a new prescription drug benefit for the elderly until the very last minute, when, in a dramatic vote tally that lasted through the night, he changed his mind. Franks, along with GOP colleague C.L. "Butch" Otter of Idaho, switched his vote from no to yes, saving the bill from defeat.

Franks went to bat for the leadership again the next year. In late 2004, as a campaign fundraising scandal was bearing down on Majority Leader Tom DeLay, Franks helped draft a rule allowing DeLay to keep his leadership post even if indicted. The rules change provoked such an uproar that Republicans scrapped it in early 2005. Franks says he got involved because of his great respect for DeLay, who helped him in his campaigns for Congress.

Franks may be an ally of the leadership, but he is unpopular with another powerful group within the party: the Republicans who chair the Appropriations subcommittees. He has conducted a creative if quixotic campaign to limit Appropriations Committee membership to six years. And he has repeatedly attacked their earmarks for member projects back home.

From his seat on the Budget Committee in the 108th Congress (2003-04), Franks pushed for deep spending cuts to reduce the deficit. With fellow Arizona Republican Jeff Flake, he sponsored a bill to take money spent on pork barrel projects and put it into defense and homeland security. Unlike many who decry excessive spending while quietly lobbying for every federal dollar they can get, Franks doesn't try to earmark funds for projects for his district. Instead, he focuses on a handful of items important to his constituents. The biggest of these is Luke Air Force Base, a major hub for training fighter pilots. In 2003, working from his seat on the Armed Services Committee, he secured $14 million for land acquisition around the base to keep local development from encroaching on the facility.

Before he got into politics, Franks made a living in the oil and gas exploration business. Right out of high school and starting with nothing — just a truck-mounted rig and a dream — he and his brother went looking for oil in Texas and actually found some. The two were so young they had to hire an 18-year-old friend to get a drilling permit. They drilled a lot of dry holes and lived out of a trailer. But when Franks was just 17, they struck oil, a modest well that produced a few barrels and earnings of $100 a day. "We were in tall cotton then," he recalls with a laugh. Today, Liberty Petroleum Corp. — with Franks' two brothers at the helm — is going strong with exploration projects around the world.

Franks grew up in the small vanadium and uranium mining town of Uravan, Colo. (now a ghost town), the son of a geologist and a nurse. The eldest of five children, Franks was born with a severe cleft lip and palate that took nine surgeries to correct, beginning at just two weeks old. In school, he suffered the taunts of other children, which later inspired his work in children's policy. He is an active booster of Operation Smile, which provides free surgeries to babies with birth defects in 25 countries.

Busy with his growing business, Franks never finished college. He finally settled in the Phoenix suburbs after he married. Josephine Franks, who is from the Philippines, liked the weather and vegetation.

He got into politics with a successful 1984 bid for a statehouse seat, which he lost after one term. He founded a think tank called Arizona Family Research Institute, a group affiliated with Christian syndicated radio host James Dobson and his Focus on the Family organization.

He tried in 1994 for a seat in the U.S. House, but lost the GOP primary to John Shadegg with whom he now serves in the Arizona delegation. When Franks decided to try again in 2002, he wasn't considered a top candidate in the primary, the key event in the heavily Republican district. But he edged past Lisa Atkins, former chief of staff for retiring GOP Rep. Bob Stump, by just 797 votes and handily won the November election.

In early 2004, Franks appeared the most endangered of the first-term Republican incumbents. He took 64 percent of the vote in the GOP primary against radio station owner Rick L. Murphy and went on to win in November with 59 percent — a vote share he matched in his 2006 re-election.

KEY VOTES

2006

- No — Stop broadband companies from favoring select Internet traffic
- Yes — Affirm U.S. commitment to war in Iraq and reject setting a withdrawal date for troops
- Yes — Repeal requirement for bilingual ballots at the polls
- Yes — Permit U.S. sale of civilian nuclear technology to India
- Yes — Build a 700-mile fence on the U.S.-Mexico border to curb illegal crossings
- Yes — Permit warrantless wiretaps of suspected terrorists

2005

- Yes — Intervene in the life-support case of Terri Schiavo
- No — Lift President Bush's restrictions on stem cell research funding
- No — Prohibit FBI access to library and bookstore records
- Yes — Approve free-trade pact with five Central American countries
- Yes — Pass energy policy overhaul favored by President Bush emphasizing domestic oil and gas production
- Yes — End mandatory preservation of habitat of endangered animal and plant species
- No — Ban torture of prisoners in U.S. custody

CQ VOTE STUDIES

	PARTY UNITY		PRESIDENTIAL SUPPORT	
	Support	Oppose	Support	Oppose
2006	96%	4%	90%	10%
2005	98%	2%	91%	9%
2004	98%	2%	91%	9%
2003	97%	3%	93%	7%

INTEREST GROUPS

	AFL-CIO	ADA	CCUS	ACU
2006	7%	10%	93%	100%
2005	14%	5%	81%	100%
2004	0%	0%	95%	100%
2003	7%	10%	93%	88%

ARIZONA 2

Northwest and central – most of Glendale, Peoria, Lake Havasu City; Hopi reservation

The 2nd spans the northwest corner of Arizona, but Republicans living in the booming western Phoenix suburbs in the district's southeast dominate its politics. This area — home to the vast majority of the 2nd's residents — takes in a small corner of the city and suburbs such as Peoria, most of Glendale and the retirement community of Sun City.

The district's economy has diversified beyond agriculture to include manufacturing jobs in the aerospace, electronics, communications and chemical industries. A Honeywell Aerospace division, based in Glendale, is responsible for many of these jobs. Luke Air Force Base, a training center for F-16 pilots approximately 20 miles west of downtown Phoenix, is the district's largest employer and contributes well more than $1 billion to the economy annually. Conservation efforts aim to prevent the Phoenix metropolitan area from encroaching on the base as the area expands.

Most of the district's land is in Mohave County, where Lake Havasu City, Bullhead City and Kingman are located. Democrats maintain isolated areas of influence among American Indians in the northwest, where younger, lower-income and larger minority populations live. Overall, the district is almost 80 percent white and gave Republican George W. Bush 61 percent of its vote in the 2004 presidential election.

The 2nd also includes the Hopi reservation, an appendage separated from the surrounding Navajo reservation (located in the 1st). Redistricting following the 2000 census kept the tribes in different districts due to historical tensions between them. To reach the Hopi land in northeastern Arizona, the 2nd follows the Colorado River through the Grand Canyon, although both sides of the canyon are in the 1st.

MAJOR INDUSTRY
Retail, manufacturing, tourism

MILITARY BASES
Luke Air Force Base, 4,982 military, 1,376 civilian (2007)

CITIES
Glendale (pt.), 146,483; Peoria, 108,364; Phoenix (pt.), 47,199; Lake Havasu City, 41,938; Sun City (unincorporated), 38,309; Bullhead City, 33,769

NOTABLE
The Hopi have authenticated their presence here to the 6th century.

Rep. John Shadegg (R)

CAPITOL OFFICE
225-3361
johnshadegg.house.gov
306 Cannon 20515-0303; fax 225-3462

COMMITTEES
Energy & Commerce
Select Energy Independence & Global Warming

RESIDENCE
Phoenix

BORN
Oct. 22, 1949, Phoenix, Ariz.

RELIGION
Episcopalian

FAMILY
Wife, Shirley Shadegg; two children

EDUCATION
U. of Arizona, B.A. 1972, J.D. 1975

MILITARY SERVICE
Ariz. Air National Guard, 1969-75

CAREER
State prosecutor; lawyer

POLITICAL HIGHLIGHTS
No previous office

ELECTION RESULTS

2006 GENERAL		
John Shadegg (R)	112,519	59.3%
Herb Paine (D)	72,586	38.2%
Mark Yannone (LIBERT)	4,744	2.5%
2006 PRIMARY		
John Shadegg (R)		unopposed
2004 GENERAL		
John Shadegg (R)	181,012	80.1%
Mark Yannone (LIBERT)	44,962	19.9%

PREVIOUS WINNING PERCENTAGES
2002 (67%); 2000 (64%); 1998 (65%); 1996 (67%); 1994 (60%)

Elected 1994; 7th term

Shadegg says he would rather lose on principle than win on politics, and he practices what he preaches. His stubborn adherence to principle cost him his House Republican leadership slots in 2006, but Shadegg says he feels more "liberated" than disappointed.

When Tom DeLay of Texas was indicted on state campaign finance charges, Shadegg (SHAD-egg) got into the race to replace him as House majority leader. As a matter of principle, he resigned as chairman of the Republican Policy Committee, the No. 5 leadership post he had held for just over a year, in order to make the race — in pointed contrast to Majority Whip Roy Blunt of Missouri, who was also running for DeLay's job but refused to give up the whip's position to do so.

Although Shadegg had backing from many conservatives in the influential Republican Study Committee, a group he once headed, he waited too long to jump into the contest. John A. Boehner of Ohio had been quietly lining up support for months in case DeLay resigned. In the initial balloting, Blunt and Boehner were the top two finishers, with 110 votes and 79 votes respectively. Shadegg, a distant third with 40 votes, was eliminated. On the second ballot, Boehner surged to victory. Blunt still had the whip's job to fall back on, but Shadegg was off the team.

Three months later, Shadegg lost his remaining leadership post — a deputy whip's slot — when Blunt tossed him out for voting with other RSC members against the rule governing debate of a supplemental appropriations bill for the war in Iraq and Gulf Coast recovery efforts. The group was protesting the Rules Committee's refusal to allow them to offer amendments to the bill, but Blunt made clear that his deputies would not get away with voting against a leadership-backed rule.

Shadegg tried one more time, challenging Blunt for the whip's job in leadership elections following the November 2006 elections. Blunt handily defeated him, 137-57, as House Republicans opted to stick with an experienced leadership team for their unwelcome journey into minority status.

Stymied in his efforts to advance in the House, Shadegg is considered likely to run for the Senate if either of Arizona's senators retire or if Sen. John McCain is elected president in 2008.

In the meantime, he is pressing his longstanding crusade against member earmarks in appropriations bills, funds targeted to projects benefiting an individual lawmaker's district or campaign backers. With other RSC members, Shadegg in 2006 pushed earmark disclosure requirements through the House as part of a lobbying overhaul bill. He has repeatedly sought without success to delete earmarks from spending bills on the floor.

Shadegg has no qualms about refusing to spend taxpayer dollars on popular programs. He was one of only 25 Republicans to vote in 2003 against expanding the Medicare program to cover prescription drugs. In 2004, he opposed the popular $283 billion transportation bill and an extension of workers' unemployment benefits for an additional 13 weeks.

His penchant for going against the grain shows up in his personal life as well. He and his wife built a house on a golf course, even though they don't golf. They like the location, he says, and enjoy walking the course in the mornings when "those golfers aren't out there" spoiling things.

Despite his independent streak, Shadegg has been useful at times to the GOP leadership. In 1999, he drafted a patients' rights measure designed to stake out a middle ground on managed care regulation. His proposal soared above two other GOP bills and came nearest to toppling the Democratic measure the House ultimately passed.

Speaker J. Dennis Hastert tapped Shadegg as one of his representatives to negotiate with Senate leaders on the managed care issue. Those talks came to naught in 2000. But Shadegg secured a reputation as an eloquent spokesman for the GOP view that, with health care costs rising, any move to increase the legal rights of managed care patients should not lead to a flood of new lawsuits that ultimately could increase insurance prices.

A skilled lawyer who relishes the details of the legislative process, Shadegg has served since 1999 on the Energy and Commerce Committee, which has a major role in shaping health policy. But his own market-oriented proposals often fall under the jurisdiction of the Ways and Means Committee. He advocates tax credits to help people buy insurance, as well as medical savings accounts and new insurance risk pools, exempt from state regulation, for small-business owners and their workers.

One of his ongoing priorities is an overhaul of Indian gambling regulations. With McCain, Shadegg has worked to impose some transparency on the financial workings of tribal casinos, saying that under current law, "Indian tribes are not required to disclose to any regulator or even to their own tribal members the amount of money they make from gaming."

Shadegg's family name is well-known in Arizona GOP circles. His late father, Stephen, was a longtime political adviser to Barry Goldwater, the five-term Arizona senator and 1964 Republican presidential nominee. The younger Shadegg developed his own political connections, working in the state attorney general's office and then serving as counsel to the House Republican Caucus in the Arizona Legislature.

The election law expertise Shadegg gained in Phoenix came in handy when he wrote a position paper for House Republican leaders on the application of law in the disputed 2000 presidential contest. He went to Florida, the locus of the dispute, and was a prominent spokesman for George W. Bush's position.

Shadegg has faced a struggle for election only once, in his initial primary election contest in 1994. For most of the race, he was thought to be trailing former Maricopa County Supervisor Jim Bruner and former state Rep. Trent Franks, now his colleague in Congress. But Shadegg closed strong, winning with 43 percent of the vote to 30 percent for Franks and 21 percent for Bruner. He took the general election with 60 percent, capturing the House seat vacated when Republican Jon Kyl won election to the Senate. He has won re-election handily ever since.

KEY VOTES

2006

No Stop broadband companies from favoring select Internet traffic
Yes Affirm U.S. commitment to war in Iraq and reject setting a withdrawal date for troops
No Repeal requirement for bilingual ballots at the polls
Yes Permit U.S. sale of civilian nuclear technology to India
Yes Build a 700-mile fence on the U.S.-Mexico border to curb illegal crossings
Yes Permit warrantless wiretaps of suspected terrorists

2005

? Intervene in the life-support case of Terri Schiavo
No Lift President Bush's restrictions on stem cell research funding
No Prohibit FBI access to library and bookstore records
Yes Approve free-trade pact with five Central American countries
Yes Pass energy policy overhaul favored by President Bush emphasizing domestic oil and gas production
Yes End mandatory preservation of habitat of endangered animal and plant species
No Ban torture of prisoners in U.S. custody

CQ VOTE STUDIES

	PARTY UNITY		PRESIDENTIAL SUPPORT	
	Support	Oppose	Support	Oppose
2006	95%	5%	90%	10%
2005	98%	2%	96%	4%
2004	99%	1%	97%	3%
2003	97%	3%	89%	11%
2002	98%	2%	87%	13%

INTEREST GROUPS

	AFL-CIO	ADA	CCUS	ACU
2006	7%	10%	100%	100%
2005	8%	0%	81%	100%
2004	7%	0%	95%	100%
2003	7%	20%	90%	96%
2002	11%	0%	90%	100%

ARIZONA 3

Northern Phoenix; Paradise Valley

The 3rd, which encompasses a large chunk of northern Phoenix and the hills and suburbs north of the city, is Arizona's least minority-influenced district. Still, while 79 percent of its residents are white, the district is changing with the rest of the state as the number of Hispanics increases.

Northern Phoenix is home to many new, large planned communities, including North Gateway Village — 45 square miles of what was mostly open land approximately 25 miles north of downtown Phoenix. Significant population growth has caused the political dynamics of the northern part of the district to fluctuate. Young liberal professionals moving into planned communities such as New River are mixed with conservative residents in such areas as the large community of Anthem.

Many of the state's most affluent and politically active residents live east of Phoenix in the posh community of Paradise Valley, where the median household income is more than $150,000. The town is exclusively zoned for single-family residential use and collects no property taxes.

Overall, most district voters consistently support economically and socially conservative candidates at the local and federal levels. George W. Bush captured 58 percent of the presidential vote here in 2004. Democrats are concentrated in the southern part of the 3rd, where the district extends to downtown Phoenix.

Resorts and tourist attractions provide many district jobs, but the economy relies on manufacturing companies, including producers of semiconductors, electronics and aerospace equipment. Aerospace manufacturer Honeywell, which has locations throughout the area, is one of the district's largest employers. The 3rd also is home to the Mayo Clinic Hospital, and health care accounts for a significant portion of the district's economy.

MAJOR INDUSTRY

Technology, manufacturing, electronics, health care, construction

CITIES

Phoenix (pt.), 603,604; Paradise Valley, 13,664; New River, 10,740

NOTABLE

Locally brewed Cave Creek Chili Beer has a pepper in every bottle; Carefree is home to a sundial that locals call one of the largest working sundials in the Western Hemisphere.

Rep. Ed Pastor (D)

CAPITOL OFFICE
225-4065
www.house.gov/pastor
2465 Rayburn 20515-0304; fax 225-1655

COMMITTEES
Appropriations

RESIDENCE
Phoenix

BORN
June 28, 1943, Claypool, Ariz.

RELIGION
Roman Catholic

FAMILY
Wife, Verma Mendez Pastor; two children

EDUCATION
Arizona State U., B.A. 1966 (chemistry), J.D. 1974

CAREER
Teacher; gubernatorial aide; public policy consultant

POLITICAL HIGHLIGHTS
Maricopa County Board of Supervisors, 1977-91

ELECTION RESULTS

2006 GENERAL		
Ed Pastor (D)	56,464	72.5%
Don Karg (R)	18,627	23.9%
Ronald Harders (LIBERT)	2,770	3.6%
2006 PRIMARY		
Ed Pastor (D)		unopposed
2004 GENERAL		
Ed Pastor (D)	77,150	70.1%
Don Karg (R)	28,238	25.7%
Gary Fallon (LIBERT)	4,639	4.2%

PREVIOUS WINNING PERCENTAGES
2002 (67%); 2000 (69%); 1998 (68%); 1996 (65%); 1994 (62%); 1992 (66%); 1991 Special Election (56%)

Elected September 1991; 8th full term

The first Hispanic member of Congress from Arizona, Pastor is a trusted insider in the Democratic leadership. He has been one of his party's chief deputy whips since 1999, and he sits on the Appropriations Committee.

With Democrats in control of the House, Pastor's chief focus in the 110th Congress (2007-08) is rekindling efforts to overhaul immigration policy. Nowhere are tensions higher over the issue than in Pastor's home state, and its congressional delegation is split between those who want more border security and those who, like Pastor (pas-TORE), tend to view immigrants as an important economic engine in Arizona.

Pastor roundly criticized the House Republican majority's immigration proposal in the 109th Congress (2005-06), which made it a felony to be in the United States illegally or to hire undocumented workers. It also created a mandatory employee verification system with identification cards for all workers. He backed a bill by two Arizona GOP colleagues, Jim Kolbe and Jeff Flake, that was similar to an approach taken by the Senate combining border security and work-site enforcement with a guest worker program and a path to citizenship for most illegal immigrants living in the country. The Senate passed the bipartisan measure, but House Republicans deemed it too lenient and refused to negotiate a final bill.

Pastor is among the Democrats who want to revisit the immigration issue. "With a Democratic majority and moderate Republicans I think we'll be able to do something very similar to the Senate bill," Pastor said.

When many lawmakers insisted that immigration and border restrictions be tightened after the Sept. 11 terrorist attacks, Pastor dissented. "Fear and suspicion lead to discrimination and racial profiling," he wrote in an op-ed article in The Arizona Republic. "Attacks on freedom, in the name of terrorism or in the name of security, are attacks on our way of life." Later, Pastor introduced amnesty legislation to allow illegal immigrants who had been in the United States since Jan. 1, 2000, to apply to be legal residents.

Pastor was chairman of the Congressional Hispanic Caucus in 1995-96, and he has opposed recurrent Republican efforts to make English the official language of the federal government, which he thinks would be unconstitutional. His wife, Verma, was the longtime director of bilingual programs for the Arizona Department of Education.

Mild-mannered and calm, Pastor has quietly and efficiently directed millions of dollars home to Phoenix. His seats on the Appropriations subcommittees dealing with transportation, energy and water funding have enabled him to keep a steady flow of grants and contracts to his district. When endorsing him in October 2006 for an eighth full term, The Arizona Republic called him the " 'go to' guy" for Phoenix.

He helped get a federal commitment of $587 million for a light-rail project for the city, which promises to create 1,600 jobs. And from his seat on the energy and water panel, Pastor has helped direct funds to several local habitat restoration programs, including $8.4 million to restore animal habitat and control flooding along the Salt River.

The oldest son of a copper miner, Pastor grew up in a working-class household about 85 miles east of Phoenix. Many of his peers were destined for jobs in the mines, but Pastor's parents had other ideas. They wanted him to go to college, so they saved their money and bought encyclopedias for him to read. His father pushed him to deliver newspapers for The Arizona Republic so he could qualify for a college scholarship that the newspaper was sponsoring. From sixth grade through high school, Pastor delivered papers. He also lettered in football and baseball and was elected senior class president. He went to Arizona State University on a scholarship, becoming the first member of his family to attend college. He worked in the mines during the summers to help pay his expenses.

Graduating with an undergraduate degree in chemistry and a teaching certificate, Pastor taught high school for a time and worked nights helping adults learn to read and write. He got involved with a nonprofit, The Guadalupe Organization Inc., and eventually became its deputy director.

During that time, Pastor got interested in the Chicano movement and its charismatic leader, César Chávez. Believing Mexican-Americans needed more decisive political leadership, he started volunteering for Mexican-American candidates in south Phoenix. He also went to law school.

After working for the successful gubernatorial campaign of Democrat Raul Castro, he became one of the governor's aides.

Pastor was elected to the Maricopa County Board of Supervisors in 1976. During his years there — often as the only Democrat — he generally got along with the GOP majority and was able to achieve much of his legislative agenda. "I said I would never attack them personally," he told the Arizona Daily Star. "In return, I expected them to respect my positions and to listen when I made my pitch." He said his minority-party status on the board of supervisors taught him patience and sharpened his negotiating skills.

Pastor had been eyeing a run for the 2nd District ever since it was drawn in 1982 as the state's most Hispanic district. But he had to wait for venerable Democratic Rep. Morris K. Udall to step down. Udall suffered from Parkinson's disease for more than a decade but stayed in the House until May 1991, when his health finally forced his resignation.

Two days after Udall's resignation, Pastor quit his post on the board to mount a full-time quest to win the special election. He was the establishment's choice, having built up a healthy war chest and solid name recognition as a supervisor. In the five-person special primary, he prevailed by 5 percentage points over Tucson Mayor Tom Volgy. His 11 percentage point victory in the special election over Republican Pat Conner, a Yuma County supervisor, remains his closest House election.

Reapportionment after the 2000 census gave Arizona two additional House seats, and Pastor chose to run in the newly drawn 4th District nestled in the suburbs of Phoenix. Its population is slightly less Hispanic than his old one, but that has caused him no difficulty. He won with more than 70 percent of the vote in 2006.

KEY VOTES

2006

- No Stop broadband companies from favoring select Internet traffic
- No Affirm U.S. commitment to war in Iraq and reject setting a withdrawal date for troops
- No Repeal requirement for bilingual ballots at the polls
- No Permit U.S. sale of civilian nuclear technology to India
- No Build a 700-mile fence on the U.S.-Mexico border to curb illegal crossings
- No Permit warrantless wiretaps of suspected terrorists

2005

- ? Intervene in the life-support case of Terri Schiavo
- Yes Lift President Bush's restrictions on stem cell research funding
- Yes Prohibit FBI access to library and bookstore records
- No Approve free-trade pact with five Central American countries
- No Pass energy policy overhaul favored by President Bush emphasizing domestic oil and gas production
- No End mandatory preservation of habitat of endangered animal and plant species
- Yes Ban torture of prisoners in U.S. custody

CQ VOTE STUDIES

	PARTY UNITY		PRESIDENTIAL SUPPORT	
	Support	Oppose	Support	Oppose
2006	90%	10%	20%	80%
2005	93%	7%	15%	85%
2004	93%	7%	18%	82%
2003	95%	5%	23%	77%
2002	92%	8%	28%	72%

INTEREST GROUPS

	AFL-CIO	ADA	CCUS	ACU
2006	93%	100%	33%	8%
2005	93%	100%	37%	8%
2004	100%	100%	29%	4%
2003	100%	80%	37%	25%
2002	100%	95%	40%	0%

ARIZONA 4

Downtown and south Phoenix; part of Glendale

Centered around Phoenix in Arizona's rapidly growing "Valley of the Sun," the mostly urban, Hispanic-majority 4th remains a Democratic stronghold in an increasingly politically competitive state.

The district is dominated by lower-income neighborhoods in downtown Phoenix that tend to elect Democrats. These areas have undergone a slow economic change as more white-collar workers buy up housing, but the influx has yet to shake the 4th's solidly liberal base.

Local officials are in the process of trying to revitalize downtown Phoenix. Plans are under way to create new office space and hotel rooms, encourage more residents to relocate here and bring a grocery store to the city's core for the first time in almost a quarter-century. Other downtown projects include construction of Arizona State University's downtown campus, the Copper Square urban development district and the construction of the Valley Metro light-rail line that will connect Tempe and Mesa to downtown Phoenix. The initial 20-mile segment is scheduled to cost $1.4 billion and begin service by December 2008.

Glendale — shared with the 2nd District — is a rapidly growing, conservative, prosperous community. A few agricultural or undeveloped areas remain in the southwestern edge of the district, but they are being pushed out by development as the city continues to sprawl outward.

Arizona's Hispanic voters tend to break from the Democratic Party on some social issues, opposing abortion rights and favoring some traditionally Republican "family values" -type legislation. The 4th has the state's highest percentage of Hispanic residents (58 percent) and its highest percentage of black residents (7 percent). John Kerry took 62 percent of the presidential vote here in the 2004 election.

MAJOR INDUSTRY

Retail, government, manufacturing, education

CITIES

Phoenix (pt.) 558,408; Glendale (pt.), 72,329; Guadalupe, 5,228

NOTABLE

The 4th's portion of Phoenix includes the city's airport, city hall, the state Capitol, Chase Field, US Airways Center and Mystery Castle.

Rep. Harry E. Mitchell (D)

CAPITOL OFFICE
225-2190
mitchell.house.gov
2434 Rayburn 20515-0305; fax 225-3263

COMMITTEES
Science & Technology
Transportation & Infrastructure
Veterans' Affairs
(Oversight & Investigations - chairman)

RESIDENCE
Tempe

BORN
July 18, 1940, Phoenix, Ariz.

RELIGION
Roman Catholic

FAMILY
Wife, Marianne Mitchell; two children

EDUCATION
Arizona State U., B.A. 1962 (political science), M.P.A. 1980

CAREER
High school teacher; college instructor

POLITICAL HIGHLIGHTS
Tempe City Council, 1970-78; mayor of Tempe, 1978-94; sought Democratic nomination for superintendent of public instruction, 1994; Ariz. Senate, 1999-2006 (assistant minority leader, 2005-06); Ariz. Democratic Party chairman, 2005-06

ELECTION RESULTS

2006 GENERAL		
Harry E. Mitchell (D)	101,838	50.4%
J.D. Hayworth (R)	93,815	46.4%
Warren Severin (LIBERT)	6,357	3.2%
2006 PRIMARY		
Harry E. Mitchell (D)		unopposed

Elected 2006; 1st term

A seasoned politician and the oldest member of the 2007 freshman class at 66, Mitchell was such a popular mayor in his hometown of Tempe, Ariz., that city officials established the Harry E. Mitchell Government Complex and erected a 35-foot abstract steel statue of him near City Hall.

His defeat of six-term GOP Rep. J.D. Hayworth, a hard-liner on immigration, puts Mitchell in a position to push for his preferred plan, which couples heightened border security and surveillance with a guest worker program. His district, with just 3 percent unemployment, relies heavily on immigrant labor.

Mitchell has posts on three committees that he says are pivotal to his constituents: Transportation and Infrastructure, Science and Technology and Veterans' Affairs. In a coup for a freshman, he was made a subcommittee chairman on Veterans' Affairs. His priorities in the 110th Congress (2007-08) include securing more funds for Arizona wastewater treatment facilities, improving health care for the state's 600,000 veterans and promoting solar technology research. A former teacher, he favors more money for English programs and to help districts deal with the No Child Left Behind law.

A city councilman for eight years, Tempe mayor for 16 years and a state legislator for eight years, Mitchell says he considered the House race only after seeing Hayworth's favorability ratings falling in district polls. "To tell you the truth, I wasn't out there looking for this job," he said.

Mitchell knows a thing or two about challenging powerful incumbents. During his 32 years in public office, he has faced a GOP incumbent in a heavily Republican area each time he has run for a new position.

In the 2006 race, Hayworth, a boisterous veteran of the GOP Class of '94, sought to play to the conservative leanings of voters in the suburban Phoenix district by focusing on his tough approach to illegal immigration. But his aggressive demeanor in debates and other forums turned problematic in his contest with the affable Mitchell. Capitalizing on nationwide voter dissatisfaction with Republicans — as well as a link between Hayworth and disgraced lobbyist Jack Abramoff — Mitchell prevailed by 4 percentage points.

ARIZONA 5

Scottsdale; Tempe; part of Phoenix and Mesa

Wealth, beautiful sunsets and conservative politics abound in the 5th, which takes in a sliver of Phoenix and then spreads east to Tempe, Scottsdale and the western parts of Chandler and Mesa.

With luxury resorts, golf courses, museums, art galleries, spring baseball and warm air, the 5th relies on the success of its hospitality and tourism industries, and caters to both business travelers and vacationers. Scottsdale has been successful, hosting the PGA Tour's FBR Open and its 500,000 fans. The 5th's part of Phoenix includes the zoo and the Desert Botanical Garden. Salt River and Fort McDowell Indian reservations bring guests to casinos, and Scottsdale Pavilions shopping mall, inside Salt River, is an example of development between private business and American Indian communities.

Health care represents a growing sector of the 5th's economy, and health businesses — including Mayo Clinic research facilities and Caremark, a pharmaceutical benefits management firm — employ many here.

Scottsdale and Fountain Hills draw retirees and their bank accounts — both places have higher incomes and median ages than the state and nation. Farther south, Tempe, home of Arizona State University, has a median age under 30. Its more liberal voters offset, but do not heavily endanger, the 5th's GOP bent. Republicans hold a 16-point voter registration edge here, and George W. Bush won the district by 9 points in 2004.

MAJOR INDUSTRY
Tourism, education, health care

CITIES
Scottsdale, 202,705; Tempe, 158,625; Mesa (pt.), 96,622; Phoenix (pt.), 85,765

NOTABLE
Taliesin West in Scottsdale was Frank Lloyd Wright's winter home, and the Taliesin Fellowship seeks to continue his work.

Rep. Jeff Flake (R)

CAPITOL OFFICE
225-2635
jeff.flake@mail.house.gov
www.house.gov/flake
240 Cannon 20515-0306; fax 226-4386

COMMITTEES
Foreign Affairs
Natural Resources

RESIDENCE
Mesa

BORN
Dec. 31, 1962, Snowflake, Ariz.

RELIGION
Mormon

FAMILY
Wife, Cheryl Flake; five children

EDUCATION
Brigham Young U., B.A. 1986 (international relations), M.A. 1987 (political science)

CAREER
Public policy think tank director;
African business trade representative; lobbyist

POLITICAL HIGHLIGHTS
No previous office

ELECTION RESULTS

2006 GENERAL		
Jeff Flake (R)	152,201	74.8%
Jason M. Blair (LIBERT)	51,285	25.2%
2006 PRIMARY		
Jeff Flake (R)		unopposed
2004 GENERAL		
Jeff Flake (R)	202,822	79.4%
Craig Stritar (LIBERT)	52,695	20.6%

PREVIOUS WINNING PERCENTAGES
2002 (66%); 2000 (54%)

Elected 2000; 4th term

The revolution is over but someone forgot to tell Jeff Flake. Long after Republicans stopped crusading against the dangers of deficits and too much federal power, the Goldwater conservative continues to wage war on what he sees as fiscal profligacy and federal intrusiveness. His favorite target is earmarks, the special provisions written into appropriations bills each year that fund lawmakers' pet projects.

Since late 2004, Flake has issued a weekly press release spotlighting an "egregious earmark," such as the one on Dec. 21, 2006, lambasting $500,000 for a Road Extension Project in North Pole, Alaska. His anti-earmark crusade makes him a regular on the House floor and landed him on the CBS news show "60 Minutes" in the fall of 2006.

Flake bemoans the lack of enthusiasm that he and fellow members of the Republican Study Committee, the most conservative bloc of House members, can drum up for their causes, compared with the early days of the 1995 House takeover by Republicans espousing balanced budgets and less federal interference with state and local governments. "We feel like we have been called up for the revolution and we are armed and we're 10 years too late," he says. "The war is over and we lost it."

He and his allies have tried repeatedly, largely without success, to amend appropriations bills to cut spending, especially earmarks. In 2004, Flake took a stab at stopping a $9.6 billion taxpayer-funded buyout of tobacco farmers, but his amendment was dropped from the final version of the agriculture spending bill. "There's never a good time to spend $10 billion bailing out the tobacco industry, but in the midst of a war, a deficit and an economic recovery, this is the worst time," Flake said.

He did eke out a small victory during debate on the huge surface transportation bill in 2005, when the House agreed to count earmarked projects against each state's highway funding allocation.

It's not just earmarks and deficits that upset him. Flake also says his fellow Republicans in Congress too often have trampled on the principle of federalism, overriding state laws and wishes on everything from social policy to regulatory matters. "You can't be a fair weather federalist," he says.

Flake generally supports his president and the GOP leadership. But he defied both in 2003 to vote against creating a Medicare prescription drug benefit for the elderly and disabled. And once it became law, he twice introduced bills to delay its 2006 implementation. Flake voted in 2001 against President Bush's signature No Child Left Behind overhaul of federal education policy, saying he did not see a substantial role for the federal government in education. He also opposed the federal bailout of the airline industry and the creation of the Homeland Security Department.

Flake was among the minority of Republicans who tried to keep the government from using the 2001 anti-terrorism law known as the Patriot Act to obtain library circulation records. And he criticized the Bush administration in 2006 for eavesdropping on Americans without first getting court permission, cosponsoring a bill to curb National Security Agency wiretapping. The executive branch will snatch all the power it can, Flake says, and it's up to Congress to curb the impulse. "It is not their responsibility to balance civil liberties," he says. "They don't see it as their responsibility — that's ours."

He did agree with Bush on immigration, espousing a comprehensive approach combining toughened border security with a guest worker program and a path to eventual legal status for the millions of illegal immigrants already in the United States. Republicans in Congress — and within the Arizona delegation — were deeply divided on the issue. The House in 2005 passed a strict border security and law enforcement bill, while the Senate later passed a measure more like Bush's proposal.

Flake has been a leader among Republicans seeking to end restrictions on travel to Cuba by U.S. citizens. Cuban-American members, mostly from Florida, adamantly oppose any easing of sanctions against the communist regime, but Flake says the longstanding U.S. embargo hasn't worked and should be replaced by a policy of robust economic engagement.

As consistent as he seems, Flake has changed his view on one score. Elected in 2000 on a promise to limit himself to three terms, he said that he'd made a "mistake" and would run again in 2006.

Although he is a hard-liner politically, Flake is easygoing and personable. When he's not with his wife and five children, he spends his free time in the House gym playing basketball with colleagues and he is a star of the GOP's team in the annual congressional charity baseball game.

Flake and 10 siblings grew up on the family ranch near Snowflake, about 100 miles northeast of Phoenix. Established in 1878, the town is named after its Mormon settler founders, Erastus Snow and William Flake, Flake's great-great-grandfather. A Mormon himself, Flake went on a two-year church mission to Zimbabwe and South Africa in 1982. He majored in international relations at Brigham Young University, and in 1989, moved to Namibia as director of the Foundation for Democracy, a group trying to help the country develop a constitution after its break from South Africa.

He returned to Arizona in 1992 to take the helm of the Goldwater Institute, a think tank that led the way to create charter schools and a tax credit plan to fund private school scholarships in Arizona and named for the state's famed conservative trailblazer, Barry Goldwater.

When GOP Rep. Matt Salmon adhered to his own three-term limit and retired in 2000, Flake ran in a primary against four opponents to replace him. Salmon endorsed Flake, giving him an important boost, and he secured the nomination. In the general election, buoyed by significant financial support from the Club for Growth, a fiscally conservative group advocating lower taxes, Flake bested Democratic labor lobbyist David Mendoza.

Redistricting after the 2000 census gave the GOP a tailor-made district for Flake in the eastern Phoenix suburbs. Flake crushed his Democratic opponent in 2002 election — winning by 34 percentage points. The Democrats opted not to field a candidate in 2004 or 2006.

KEY VOTES

2006

No Stop broadband companies from favoring select Internet traffic
Yes Affirm U.S. commitment to war in Iraq and reject setting a withdrawal date for troops
No Repeal requirement for bilingual ballots at the polls
Yes Permit U.S. sale of civilian nuclear technology to India
Yes Build a 700-mile fence on the U.S.-Mexico border to curb illegal crossings
No Permit warrantless wiretaps of suspected terrorists

2005

? Intervene in the life-support case of Terri Schiavo
No Lift President Bush's restrictions on stem cell research funding
Yes Prohibit FBI access to library and bookstore records
Yes Approve free-trade pact with five Central American countries
No Pass energy policy overhaul favored by President Bush emphasizing domestic oil and gas production
Yes End mandatory preservation of habitat of endangered animal and plant species
Yes Ban torture of prisoners in U.S. custody

CQ VOTE STUDIES

	PARTY UNITY		PRESIDENTIAL SUPPORT	
	Support	Oppose	Support	Oppose
2006	86%	14%	72%	28%
2005	91%	9%	74%	26%
2004	93%	7%	74%	26%
2003	90%	10%	70%	30%
2002	89%	11%	70%	30%

INTEREST GROUPS

	AFL-CIO	ADA	CCUS	ACU
2006	0%	20%	79%	100%
2005	7%	0%	70%	96%
2004	13%	15%	81%	96%
2003	13%	25%	67%	92%
2002	22%	5%	65%	96%

ARIZONA 6

Southeast Phoenix suburbs – most of Mesa and Chandler, Gilbert, Apache Junction

Rooted in the conservative leanings of an affluent, historically Mormon population, the suburban 6th favors Republican candidates. The district still has a significant population of Mormons, as well as a mix of young couples who commute to Phoenix. The area's warm sunny days have helped draw an established population of retirees from other states.

The district begins east of Phoenix, where it takes in all but the westernmost segments of Mesa and Chandler. Between the two cities is Gilbert, and the district expands east to take in part of largely agricultural Pinal County, including Apache Junction on the county's northern border.

The southeastern Phoenix suburbs continue to experience the population growth that is characteristic of the area, and construction of the Santan Freeway through Chandler, Gilbert and Mesa serves as a catalyst for further growth. Not surprisingly, the area supports a vibrant construction industry, and retail also is an important and growing sector of the district's economy, with companies such as Wal-Mart and Kroger becoming major employers in the 6th. Manufacturing aids the economy in fast-growing Mesa, and the city hosts a large Boeing facility. Technology manufacturing plays a roll here as well: Intel has two locations in Chandler and employs 10,000 people. Agriculture, especially alfalfa and dairy operations, still plays a role in the district's economy but is being replaced due to sprawling development.

Republicans hold an almost 25-point edge in party registration, and the 6th gave George W. Bush 64 percent of its 2004 presidential vote — his statewide high. In 2006, GOP Sen. Jon Kyl received his highest statewide percentage (62 percent) in the district, while Democratic Gov. Janet Napolitano received her lowest statewide percentage (54 percent) here.

MAJOR INDUSTRY
Manufacturing, technology, retail, construction

CITIES
Mesa (pt.), 299,753; Chandler (pt.), 109,758; Gilbert, 109,697; Apache Junction, 31,814

NOTABLE
Chandler's Ostrich Festival, held each March, features ostrich races and a parade.

Rep. Raúl M. Grijalva (D)

CAPITOL OFFICE
225-2435
www.house.gov/grijalva
1440 Longworth 20515-0307; fax 225-1541

COMMITTEES
Education & Labor
Natural Resources
(National Parks, Forests & Public Lands - chairman)
Small Business

RESIDENCE
Tucson

BORN
Feb. 19, 1948, Tucson, Ariz.

RELIGION
Roman Catholic

FAMILY
Wife, Mona Grijalva; three children

EDUCATION
U. of Arizona, B.A. 1987 (sociology)

CAREER
University dean; community center director

POLITICAL HIGHLIGHTS
Tucson Unified School District Governing Board, 1974-86; Pima County Board of Supervisors, 1989-2002 (chairman, 1997, 2001-02)

ELECTION RESULTS

2006 GENERAL		
Raúl M. Grijalva (D)	80,354	61.1%
Ron Drake (R)	46,498	35.4%
Joe Cobb (LIBERT)	4,673	3.6%
2006 PRIMARY		
Raúl M. Grijalva (D)		unopposed
2004 GENERAL		
Raúl M. Grijalva (D)	108,868	62.1%
Joseph "Joe" Sweeney (R)	59,066	33.7%
Dave Kaplan (LIBERT)	7,503	4.3%

PREVIOUS WINNING PERCENTAGES
2002 (59%)

Elected 2002; 3rd term

Grijalva has a keen interest in immigration and border issues. His southwestern Arizona district shares 300 miles with Mexico and is the second-longest contiguous district after Texas' 23rd. In recent years, hundreds of people trying to evade border police have died in the vast Sonoran Desert, many of them in the brutal heat of August.

Grijalva (gree-HAHL-va) has been a leading opponent of President Bush's guest worker proposal to allow illegal workers to remain in the United States for three years with no guarantee of residency or citizenship. The idea, he says, is reminiscent of the bracero program, which roughly translates to "worker" and refers to the joint U.S.-Mexico agreement under which migrant workers flocked to low-wage farm jobs created by World War II labor shortages. Grijalva's father came to the United States as a bracero. Workers were often mistreated, housed in shacks and cheated out of wages. The program ended under public pressure in 1964.

During the immigration debate in the 109th Congress (2005-06), Grijalva backed legislation by Republican Sen. John McCain — a fellow Arizonan — and Democratic Sen. Edward M. Kennedy of Massachusetts to create a guest worker program with a chance of citizenship. But the GOP-controlled House passed tougher legislation making it a felony to be in the United States illegally or to hire undocumented workers, a bill Grijalva opposed. Congress could not agree on an approach, and the legislation died. "We must never forget that we are a country of immigrants," Grijalva says.

In advance of the 2006 elections, Republicans salvaged one of their ideas — 700 miles of fence along the border with Mexico and a virtual fence of cameras, sensors and unmanned vehicles. Grijalva attacked it as both ineffective and bad for the desert environment. "Building a wall along this rugged wilderness will be impossible in places and will cut off important migratory routes for wildlife and mar the landscape for hundreds of miles," he said. The bill passed and Bush signed it into law.

Grijalva also opposed the president's legislation to implement free-trade agreements with the Dominican Republic and five Central American countries — Costa Rica, El Salvador, Guatemala, Honduras and Nicaragua. It passed with narrow House and Senate tallies and was signed into law in 2005. "'Free trade as it has been practiced has hurt Latinos in the U.S. and widened the gap between rich and poor," Grijalva said in 2005.

The 7th District is more than half Latino and largely poor and undereducated. Staff members in Grijalva's district offices speak Spanish, as do half his aides in Washington. When he arrived in Congress in 2003, Grijalva got a seat on the Education Committee, where he has pushed to fully fund the federal effort to improve test scores in public schools. In 2003, he fought GOP-inspired changes to Head Start giving states more control over the federal program for preschool-age children. He sponsored an unsuccessful amendment to increase Head Start money for children of migrant and seasonal workers, falling short in a 203-227 vote.

In the 110th Congress (2007-08), he became chairman of the Natural Resources subcommittee that oversees public lands. One priority for the subcommittee will be a review of the 1872 Mining Law, which governs hard rock mining on public lands.

Among the most liberal lawmakers, Grijalva voted against Bush more than most other House members, supporting the president only 12 percent of the time in the 109th Congress. He opposes the war in Iraq and was one of only a dozen House members in 2003 to vote against the administration's $78 billion emergency bill to fund the U.S. occupation.

On health care issues, Grijalva supports efforts to expand the Clinton-era Children's Health Insurance Program to include not only poor children but their parents, a multibillion-dollar proposition that Republicans have long dismissed as unrealistic. He also would extend Medicare to people between the ages of 55 and 64, an idea popular among liberals.

Grijalva has had more tangible success with a bill of local interest. In 2005, Bush signed into law his bill returning to four Colorado River Indian tribes 16,000 acres of land they had lost to the government in 1915 after they refused to lease the land for mining. He also steered to passage a bill to spur economic growth on Gila River Indian lands. There are a total of seven tribes in Grijalva's district. On his office wall, he displays a carved mask from the Yaquis.

Personally, Grijalva reflects the more casual ways of the Southwest. His friends donated neckties after he won election to the House, figuring he would have to wear them regularly for the first time. His speech is still lightly accented by Spanish. Grijalva dislikes the nonstop fundraising of modern campaigns and has to be badgered by his staff to keep at it. Advised to hold a golf tournament to raise money, Grijalva instead threw a bowl-a-thon. Roughly a third of his campaign financing comes from labor groups.

Grijalva still lives in the working-class, heavily Latino section of south Tucson where he was born and raised. He attended the University of Arizona, but quit to get married. Grijalva and his school librarian wife, Mona, had three daughters, and he became a social worker and community activist.

He was elected in 1974 to the Tucson school board, where he served 12 years, and later to the Pima County Board of Supervisors. He eventually became chairman of the county board. During his years in local government, he frequently advised young people to stay in school. To set the right example, he went back to school to finish nine credit hours left on his sociology degree, graduating from the University of Arizona at age 39.

When once-a-decade redistricting created a new Hispanic-majority district in southern Arizona, Grijalva jumped into the crowded 2002 primary race. He prevailed despite stiff competition from one incumbent and two former state senators.

In the general election, the makeup of the district ensured Grijalva's victory. The 7th is heavily Democratic and 45 percent of eligible voters are Hispanic. He easily bested Republican Ross Hieb, a farmer and forester. In 2004 and 2006, he was re-elected with more than 60 percent of the vote.

KEY VOTES

2006

Yes Stop broadband companies from favoring select Internet traffic

No Affirm U.S. commitment to war in Iraq and reject setting a withdrawal date for troops

No Repeal requirement for bilingual ballots at the polls

No Permit U.S. sale of civilian nuclear technology to India

No Build a 700-mile fence on the U.S.-Mexico border to curb illegal crossings

No Permit warrantless wiretaps of suspected terrorists

2005

? Intervene in the life-support case of Terri Schiavo

Yes Lift President Bush's restrictions on stem cell research funding

Yes Prohibit FBI access to library and bookstore records

No Approve free-trade pact with five Central American countries

No Pass energy policy overhaul favored by President Bush emphasizing domestic oil and gas production

No End mandatory preservation of habitat of endangered animal and plant species

Yes Ban torture of prisoners in U.S. custody

CQ VOTE STUDIES

	PARTY UNITY		PRESIDENTIAL SUPPORT	
	Support	Oppose	Support	Oppose
2006	99%	1%	10%	90%
2005	98%	2%	13%	87%
2004	99%	1%	12%	88%
2003	99%	1%	16%	84%

INTEREST GROUPS

	AFL-CIO	ADA	CCUS	ACU
2006	93%	100%	27%	4%
2005	93%	100%	30%	0%
2004	100%	100%	10%	0%
2003	100%	100%	20%	12%

ARIZONA 7

Southwest – part of Tucson, Yuma, Avondale

Stretching mainly south and west from Phoenix, the Hispanic-majority, strongly Democratic 7th crosses large reservations and rural areas to take in Yuma, downtown Tucson and most of Arizona's border with Mexico. The district is home to the University of Arizona — southern Arizona's top employer — in Tucson. It also includes the Mexican border town of Nogales and climbs up the state's border with California.

A large population of seasonal immigrant workers — particularly in vegetable farming — buttresses the agriculture and service industries but boosts the district's poverty statistics. The 7th has more blue-collar workers and fewer college graduates than most Arizona districts. Illegal immigration is a major problem here. Crossing the border in this vast desert region is especially dangerous, due to the extreme heat and lack of water, and it also hampers military training activities on the Barry M. Goldwater Range, which stretches across 100 miles of the border.

The Tohono O'odham and Gila River reservations are the 7th's largest, and American Indians make up 6 percent of the district's population. The Gila River reservation, south of Phoenix, has several resorts and casinos, but also has invested in commercial and industrial parks to diversify its economic growth.

Republicans are competitive in most of the 7th's counties, but Democrats dominate in Pima County, the district's most populous, which includes the 7th's portion of Tucson and many American Indian residents. Overall, Democrats have an almost 2-to-1 party registration advantage, and John Kerry took 57 percent of the vote here in the 2004 presidential election.

MAJOR INDUSTRY

Agriculture, tourism, education

MILITARY BASES

Marine Corps Air Station Yuma, 5,000 military, 1,294 civilian (2005); Yuma Proving Ground (Army), 115 military, 636 civilian (2006)

CITIES

Tucson (pt.), 230,164; Yuma, 77,515; Avondale, 35,883; Phoenix (pt.), 26,069

NOTABLE

Yuma Territorial Prison — a late 19th century penitentiary — was turned into a high school, then a shelter for railroad vagrants, and now is a state historic park.

Rep. Gabrielle Giffords (D)

CAPITOL OFFICE
225-2542
giffords.house.gov
502 Cannon 20515-0308; fax 225-0378

COMMITTEES
Armed Services
Foreign Affairs
Science & Technology

RESIDENCE
Tucson

BORN
June 8, 1970, Tucson, Ariz.

RELIGION
Jewish

FAMILY
Engaged to Mark Kelly

EDUCATION
Scripps College, B.A. 1993 (sociology & Latin American history); Cornell U., M.R.P. 1997 (regional planning)

CAREER
Property management company owner; retail tire company president; regional economic and employment analyst

POLITICAL HIGHLIGHTS
Ariz. House, 2001-03; Ariz. Senate, 2003-05

ELECTION RESULTS

2006 GENERAL		
Gabrielle Giffords (D)	137,655	54.3%
Randy Graf (R)	106,790	42.1%
David F. Nolan (LIBERT)	4,849	1.9%
Jay Quick (I)	4,408	1.7%
2006 PRIMARY		
Gabrielle Giffords (D)	33,375	54.3%
Patty Weiss (D)	19,148	31.2%
Jeffrey Lynn "Jeff" Latas (D)	3,687	6.0%
Alex Rodriguez (D)	2,855	4.6%
William "Bill" Johnson (D)	1,768	2.9%

Elected 2006; 1st term

A Fulbright scholar who returned to her hometown of Tucson to run the family tire business, Giffords got into politics out of concern over how poorly Arizona ranked nationally on many social indicators — teenage pregnancy, dropout rates and teen suicide, to name a few. "On issue after issue, my home state was at the bottom of the list," she says. "I looked around and thought, 'Who is making the choices here and where are their values?' "

As a state legislator and the youngest woman elected to the state Senate, Giffords worked to expand health care coverage for families, create and attract high wage jobs, and protect Arizona's environment and open spaces.

On arrival in Congress, she was assigned to three committees: Armed Services, Foreign Affairs and Science and Technology. Giffords can use her spot on Armed Services to look out for the interests of the two military installations in her district. On Science, she says she'll work to promote increased renewable and alternative sources of energy. And on Foreign Affairs, her focus will be on relations with Latin America and Mexico, where she spent a year as a Fulbright scholar.

The 8th District shares a 100-mile-plus border with Mexico, and a top priority for Giffords is an overhaul of immigration law. Fluent in Spanish, Giffords argues for stronger penalties against employers who hire illegal immigrants and for a guest worker program where foreign citizens could work seasonally and return to their home countries during the off-season.

Giffords left a New York consulting job to take over the family tire and automotive business in Tucson when her father became ill in the mid-1990s. During those years, she developed a taste for politics. She sold the family business in 2000 and ran successfully for a seat in the Arizona House. In 2002, she won election to the state Senate.

Giffords decided to run for Congress when 11-term Republican Rep. Jim Kolbe announced he wouldn't seek re-election. She beat out five primary challengers and in the general election faced former state Rep. Randy Graf, a conservative Republican who touted a tough enforcement-first approach to immigration. Giffords prevailed with 54 percent of the vote.

ARIZONA 8

Southeast – part of Tucson and northern suburbs

Nestled in the state's southeast corner, the 8th is home to many swing voters and independents who often favor moderates in national elections. Cochise County takes up most of the 8th's land, but most people live in the Tucson area (Pima County). Border security and an influx of residents are of increasing concern in the district.

Tucson is surrounded by mountain ranges, but the majestic Santa Catalinas north of the city are the local landmark. Suburbs in the north are seeing heavy growth as affluent, retired and military residents move in. This growth has sparked fears that development will mar the scenic vistas. Central Tucson is in the adjacent 7th, but growth is spreading southeast, toward Davis-Monthan Air Force Base, where locals seek to slow building.

Military jets flying past Tucson on their way to or from the base reveal two of the area's economic engines: manufacturing and military. Defense technology contractors and aerospace firms include Raytheon Missile Systems. Fort Huachuca, in Sierra Vista, drives its area's economy. But despite the defense presence, the 8th is increasingly dependent on service industries, including tourism, to support its economic base.

In the state's closest presidential contest in 2004, George W. Bush took 53 percent of the 8th's vote. The U.S. House seat flipped from GOP to Democratic control in 2006.

MAJOR INDUSTRY
Service, manufacturing, military, aerospace

MILITARY BASES
Davis-Monthan Air Force Base, 6,900 military, 2,000 civilian (2005); Fort Huachuca (Army), 3,939 military, 2,717 civilian (2007)

CITIES
Tucson (pt.), 256,535; Casas Adobes (unincorporated), 54,011

NOTABLE
Historic Tombstone is in Cochise County.

ARKANSAS

Gov. Mike Beebe (D)

Pronounced: BEE-bee
First elected: 2006
Length of term: 4 years
Term expires: 1/11
Salary: $80,848
Phone: (501) 682-2345

Residence: Searcy
Born: Dec. 28, 1946; Amagon, Ark.
Religion: Episcopalian
Family: Wife, Ginger Beebe; three children
Education: Arkansas State U., B.A. 1968 (political science); U. of Arkansas, J.D. 1972
Military service: Army Reserve, 1968-74
Career: Lawyer
Political highlights: Ark. Senate, 1983-2003 (president pro tempore, 2001-03); Ark. attorney general, 2003-07

Election results:

2006 GENERAL		
Mike Beebe (D)	430,765	55.6%
Asa Hutchinson (R)	315,040	40.7%
Rod Bryan (I)	15,767	2.0%
Jim Lendall (GREEN)	12,774	1.6%

Lt. Gov. Bill Halter (D)

First elected: 2006
Length of term: 4 years
Term expires: 1/11
Salary: $39,075
Phone: (501) 682-2144

LEGISLATURE

General Assembly: At least 60 calendar days January-March in odd-numbered years

Senate: 35 members, mixed 4-year and two-year terms
2007 ratios: 27 D, 8 R; 29 men, 6 women
Salary: $14,765
Phone: (501) 682-6107

House: 100 members, 2-year terms
2007 ratios: 75 D, 25 R; 78 men, 22 women
Salary: $14,765
Phone: (501) 682-7771

TERM LIMITS

Governor: 2 terms
Senate: 2 terms
House: 3 terms

URBAN STATISTICS

CITY	POPULATION
Little Rock	183,133
Fort Smith	80,268
North Little Rock	60,433
Fayetteville	58,047
Jonesboro	55,515

REGISTERED VOTERS

Voters do not register by party.

POPULATION

2006 population (est.)	2,810,872
2000 population	2,673,400
1990 population	2,350,725
Percent change (1990-2000)	+13.7%
Rank among states (2006)	32
Median age	36
Born in state	63.9%
Foreign born	2.8%
Violent crime rate	445/100,000
Poverty level	15.8%
Federal workers	20,543
Military	18,894

ELECTIONS

STATE ELECTION OFFICIAL
(501) 682-5070
DEMOCRATIC PARTY
(501) 374-2361
REPUBLICAN PARTY
(501) 372-7301

MISCELLANEOUS

Web: www.arkansas.gov
Capital: Little Rock

U.S. CONGRESS

Senate: 2 Democrats
House: 3 Democrats, 1 Republican

2000 Census Statistics by District

DIST.	2004 VOTE FOR PRESIDENT BUSH	KERRY	WHITE	BLACK	ASIAN	HISP	MEDIAN INCOME	WHITE COLLAR	BLUE COLLAR	SERVICE INDUSTRY	OVER 64	UNDER 18	COLLEGE EDUCATION	RURAL	SQ. MILES
1	52%	47%	80%	17%	0%	2%	$28,940	49%	37%	14%	15%	26%	12%	56%	17,151
2	51	48	76	19	1	2	$37,221	60	26	14	12	25	23	34	5,922
3	62	36	87	2	1	6	$33,915	53	33	14	13	26	18	46	8,490
4	51	48	71	24	0	3	$29,675	48	37	15	16	25	13	55	20,505
STATE	54	45	79	16	1	3	$32,182	53	33	14	14	25	17	47	52,068
U.S.	50.7	48.3	69	12	4	13	$41,994	60	25	15	12	26	24	21	3,537,438

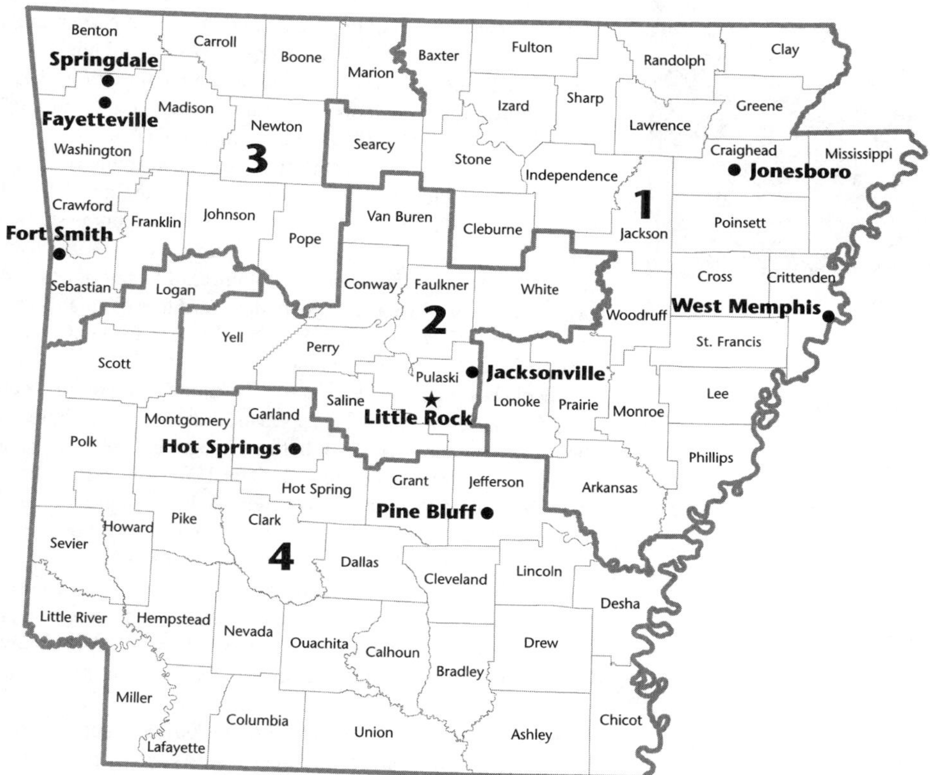
Benton
Springdale
Fayetteville
Washington
Carroll
Madison
Boone
Newton
Marion
Searcy
Baxter
Fulton
Izard
Stone
Sharp
Randolph
Clay
Greene
Lawrence
Craighead
Jonesboro
Mississippi
Independence
1
Jackson
Poinsett
Cross
Crittenden
West Memphis
Woodruff
St. Francis
Lee
Phillips
Monroe
Prairie
Arkansas
3
Crawford
Fort Smith
Sebastian
Franklin
Johnson
Pope
Van Buren
Cleburne
Logan
Conway
Faulkner
White
2
Yell
Perry
Scott
Pulaski
Jacksonville
Saline
Little Rock
Lonoke
Montgomery
Garland
Hot Springs
Polk
Grant
Jefferson
Pine Bluff
Hot Spring
Howard
Pike
Clark
Sevier
4
Dallas
Cleveland
Lincoln
Desha
Little River
Hempstead
Nevada
Ouachita
Calhoun
Drew
Bradley
Miller
Columbia
Union
Ashley
Chicot
Lafayette

Sen. Blanche Lincoln (D)

CAPITOL OFFICE
224-4843
lincoln.senate.gov
355 Dirksen 20510-0404; fax 228-1371

COMMITTEES
Agriculture, Nutrition & Forestry
(Production, Income Protection & Price Support - chairwoman)
Energy & Natural Resources
Finance
(International Trade & Global Competitiveness - chairwoman)
Special Aging

RESIDENCE
Little Rock

BORN
Sept. 30, 1960, Helena, Ark.

RELIGION
Episcopalian

FAMILY
Husband, Steve Lincoln; two children

EDUCATION
Randolph-Macon Woman's College, B.A. 1982 (biology)

CAREER
Lobbyist; congressional aide

POLITICAL HIGHLIGHTS
U.S. House, 1993-97

ELECTION RESULTS

2004 GENERAL		
Blanche Lincoln (D)	580,973	55.8%
Jim Holt (R)	458,036	44.2%
2004 PRIMARY		
Blanche Lincoln (D)	231,037	83.1%
Lisa Burks (D)	47,010	16.9%

PREVIOUS WINNING PERCENTAGES
1998 (55%); 1994 House Election (53%); 1992 House Election (70%)

Elected 1998; 2nd term

Midway through her second term, Lincoln has become a leading Senate advocate for rural America and a forceful voice on the influential Finance Committee for small businesses and working families. Her centrist philosophy and search for bipartisan, "common sense" solutions make her a pivotal vote on many issues.

The wife of a physician and the mother of preteen twin boys, she is a role model for parents trying to juggle the demands of career and family. In a city filled with workaholics, she skips an occasional business meeting to make it to a school play. "It's hard to be high and mighty when you've got peanut butter on your sleeve," she said in "Nine and Counting," a collaborative book written in 2000 by nine women senators.

She says her balancing act is nothing special; millions of Americans do the same thing, often with fewer resources to help them. "A working mother who may not have had all the advantages I had but is still working desperately as she can to provide for her children is just as much an important part of the fabric of this country as I am. And I want her to succeed," she says, explaining why she has pushed so hard for refundable child tax credits, Internet safety measures, health insurance for small businesses and other policies that benefit families.

Lincoln is among the Democrats advocating a greater focus on faith, family and pocketbook issues that appeal to rural voters — a strategy that helped the party recapture control of both chambers in 2006. She launched a legislative advocacy group, dubbed the Third Way, with Sens. Thomas R. Carper of Delaware and Evan Bayh of Indiana. Formed as a nonprofit lobbying group in January 2005, it pushes initiatives backed by moderate Democrats.

Lincoln is a founding member of the moderate New Democrats in the Senate. She often works closely with the state's junior senator, Democrat Mark Pryor, another moderate, and in the 2004 presidential primary season, Lincoln backed a moderate home-state ally, retired Army Gen. Wesley K. Clark, rather than her liberal colleague, Sen. John Kerry of Massachusetts.

She sided with President Bush on the 2001 education overhaul that tied federal funds to student performance on tests and on the 2003 Medicare bill that created a prescription drug benefit for the elderly. She was one of just 11 Senate Democrats supporting the final Medicare measure, which she said "wasn't perfect" but was a step in the right direction. She brings that same perspective to issues ranging from a Social Security overhaul to updating the Endangered Species Act, saying it is important to get things done, even if compromises are required. "My philosophy is really that we don't produce a work of art here, we produce a work in progress," she says.

Her outgoing personality and ability to relate to her constituents — duck hunting is among her leisure pursuits — have made her a popular politician in a state that backed Bush in two elections. In its annual survey of staff attitudes about their bosses, Washingtonian magazine said she ranks high in the "just plain nice" category.

Raised in eastern Arkansas, where her family has farmed for seven generations, Lincoln describes herself as a "daughter of the east Arkansas Delta" and speaks passionately about the need to improve tax breaks, health care and other services in rural areas. In 2002, she backed a six-year farm bill, with a $441 billion price tag, after working to raise the Senate's cap on payments to farmers. A subcommittee chairwoman on the Agriculture

Committee, which began a rewrite of the law in 2007, she is wary of making major changes in the law's support structure for U.S. farmers until and unless global trade talks provide a more even playing field. She is eager to boost incentives promoting the use of corn-based ethanol, biodiesel and other renewable energy developed from farm products.

In 2001, she helped win authorization of the eight-state Delta Regional Authority, modeled after the Appalachian Regional Commission, with initial funding of $20 million to spur economic development in the South. During a trip on Air Force One in 2001, when Bush lobbied her to support his first major tax cut, Lincoln requested disaster relief for Arkansas farmers and increased anti-poverty efforts in the Mississippi Delta region. "Agriculture is really my base, not only for my state's economy but also my heritage," she says.

In the 108th Congress (2003-04), she helped cut a deal on the GOP's so-called Healthy Forests legislation aimed at expediting forest thinning to prevent wildfires. She also pushed for a proposal to shift responsibility for migratory birds to the Agriculture Department from the U.S. Fish and Wildlife Service to help control double-crested cormorants that prey upon catfish farms, a major industry in the state.

Also in the 108th, Lincoln served on the Ethics Committee, which led to a potentially embarrassing close call at the Democratic National Convention in 2004. She backed out of plans to host a rock concert paid for by lobbyists after the watchdog group Citizens for Responsibility and Ethics filed a complaint alleging it would skirt a ban on such arrangements.

Shortly after graduating from college, Lincoln (then Blanche Lambert) got her start on Capitol Hill in 1982 as a staff assistant for Democratic Arkansas Rep. Bill Alexander. She left after two years for a series of research jobs with lobbying firms. In 1991, she decided to challenge Alexander in a race that drew little notice until news broke that Alexander was among the top 10 abusers in the House bank overdraft scandal. She took 61 percent of the vote in the 1992 primary and coasted to victory in November. She married Steve Lincoln, an obstetrician and gynecologist, in 1993 and won re-election to the House the next year.

Seen as a rising star in Arkansas, she decided not to seek a third House term in 1996 after becoming pregnant with twins. But her career pause did not last long. When Democratic Sen. Dale Bumpers announced his retirement in 1998, Lincoln jumped at the chance to run for a Senate seat. In the general election, she benefited from a stumble by her Republican opponent, state Sen. Fay Boozman, who said a woman was unlikely to become pregnant when she is raped because of hormonal responses in her body that he referred to as "God's little protective shield." Lincoln accused Boozman of insensitivity to rape victims, and he later apologized for the remarks. Lincoln won by 13 percentage points, becoming at age 38 the youngest woman ever elected to the Senate.

She told her constituents she was moving to Washington with her family. "I want to watch my family grow up. I want to see their school plays. We'll be back here every holiday and every chance I get, but I'm not going to sacrifice my family for this job," she said.

In 2004, Lincoln raised $6 million for her re-election campaign. She won 56 percent of the vote to defeat Republican state Sen. Jim Holt.

Lincoln says she takes inspiration from Hattie Caraway of Arkansas, the first woman to be popularly elected to the Senate in 1932 and the only other woman senator ever elected from Arkansas. Lincoln carried a quote from Caraway with her when she ran in 1998. It said, "If I can hold on to my sense of humor and a modicum of dignity, I shall have a wonderful time running for office whether I get there or not."

KEY VOTES

2006

- No Confirm Samuel A. Alito Jr. to the Supreme Court
- Yes Allow consideration of a bill to establish a $140 billion trust fund to compensate victims of asbestos exposure
- No Extend tax cuts for two years at a cost of $70 billion over five years
- Yes Overhaul immigration policy with border security, enforcement and guest worker program
- Yes Allow consideration of a bill to permanently repeal the estate tax
- Yes Urge President Bush to begin troop withdrawals from Iraq in 2006
- Yes Lift President Bush's restrictions on stem cell research funding
- No Authorize military tribunals for suspected terrorists

2005

- Yes Curb class action lawsuits by shifting them from state to federal courts
- No Allow confirmation vote on Priscilla R. Owen to the U.S. Court of Appeals for the 5th Circuit
- No Oppose mandatory emissions limits and block recognition of global warming as a threat
- Yes Approve free-trade pact with five Central American countries
- Yes Pass energy policy overhaul favored by President Bush emphasizing domestic oil and gas production
- Yes Shield gunmakers from lawsuits when their products are used in crimes
- Yes Ban torture of prisoners in U.S. custody
- No Renew 16 provisions of the Patriot Act
- No Allow final vote on opening the Arctic National Wildlife Refuge to oil and gas exploration

CQ VOTE STUDIES

	PARTY UNITY		PRESIDENTIAL SUPPORT	
	Support	Oppose	Support	Oppose
2006	81%	19%	59%	41%
2005	81%	19%	50%	50%
2004	79%	21%	72%	28%
2003	81%	19%	61%	39%
2002	61%	39%	89%	11%
2001	79%	21%	71%	29%
2000	80%	20%	84%	16%
1999	83%	17%	80%	20%
House Service:				
1996	66%	34%	63%	37%
1995	64%	36%	63%	37%

INTEREST GROUPS

	AFL-CIO	ADA	CCUS	ACU
2006	73%	90%	67%	8%
2005	79%	95%	89%	16%
2004	100%	95%	71%	20%
2003	77%	75%	78%	20%
2002	77%	70%	75%	40%
2001	88%	85%	79%	28%
2000	50%	70%	86%	20%
1999	89%	95%	65%	12%
House Service:				
1996	57%	30%	64%	36%
1995	58%	60%	63%	20%

Sen. Mark Pryor (D)

CAPITOL OFFICE
224-2353
pryor.senate.gov
257 Dirksen 20510-0403; fax 228-0908

COMMITTEES
Armed Services
Commerce, Science & Transportation
(Consumer Affairs, Insurance & Automotive Safety - chairman)
Homeland Security & Governmental Affairs
(State, Local & Private Sector Preparedness - chairman)
Rules & Administration
Small Business & Entrepreneurship
Select Ethics

RESIDENCE
Little Rock

BORN
Jan. 10, 1963, Fayetteville, Ark.

RELIGION
Christian

FAMILY
Wife, Jill Pryor; two children

EDUCATION
U. of Arkansas, B.A. 1985 (history), J.D. 1988

CAREER
Lawyer

POLITICAL HIGHLIGHTS
Ark. House, 1991-95; sought Democratic nomination for Ark. attorney general, 1994; Ark. attorney general, 1999-2003; U.S. Senate

ELECTION RESULTS

2002 GENERAL		
Mark Pryor (D)	433,386	53.9%
Tim Hutchinson (R)	370,735	46.1%
2002 PRIMARY		
Mark Pryor (D)		unopposed

Elected 2002; 1st term

In the narrowly divided Senate, Democrats have to look to the center to get legislation passed in the 110th Congress (2007-08), and that's where Pryor is usually found. By temperament, training and political necessity, he is a classic centrist — a bridge-builder, not a bomb-thrower.

Pryor was elected to the Arkansas House at age 27, became state attorney general at 35 and won his U.S. Senate seat at 39. Still one of the youngest senators, and the son of the respected former Democratic Sen. David H. Pryor of Arkansas, Mark Pryor's influence on Capitol Hill is growing. In an April 2006 ranking of "best and worst" senators, Time Magazine called him an "up and comer."

In May 2005, Pryor was one of seven Democrats and seven Republicans who joined forces to forestall an all-out political war in the Senate over President Bush's conservative judicial nominees. The so-called Gang of 14 united against a threat by Republican Majority Leader Bill Frist to trigger a parliamentary "nuclear option" that would have precluded traditional Senate filibusters against judicial nominees. The group agreed to prevent filibusters except in "extraordinary circumstances," which they did not precisely define. Most of the Bush nominees won confirmation, though some of the most controversial were ultimately withdrawn or blocked.

Despite his pivotal role in that battle, and his background as a state attorney general, Pryor declined an invitation to serve on the Judiciary Committee "because that's where the ideological fights were. I just didn't want to spend my time in that partisan quagmire."

Pryor likes to focus on defense issues. After a two-year hiatus, he got back on the Armed Services Committee in 2007, an assignment he relishes. His biggest disappointment was losing his Armed Services seat in the 109th Congress (2005-06). As the panel's most junior Democrat, he had been bounced when Republicans made gains in the 2004 elections. From a military-friendly state that is home to the Army's Pine Bluff Arsenal and Little Rock Air Force Base, Pryor had immersed himself in defense issues, consistently showing up at sparsely attended committee hearings, taking briefing papers home to read, lugging around a book of Pentagon acronyms and holding face-to-face meetings with military brass on homeland security issues.

His proudest early accomplishments were changes in law that allowed U.S. soldiers to qualify more easily for child tax credits and the earned-income tax credit, which the government gives to people whose incomes are too low to be taxed.

Pryor serves on six committees, an unusually large number, including the Homeland Security and Governmental Affairs panel and the Commerce, Science and Transportation Committee. Both have a history of bipartisanship. "After the Gang of 14, I had a lot of people reach out to me on both sides of the aisle. A Democrat would say, 'Hey, we're putting together this bipartisan group. Why don't you help me round up some votes on both sides.' I get a lot of offers to do that," Pryor says. "I fill a role here, which I think is a role that the Senate needs."

He parts with his liberal colleagues in the party on some fiscal matters and on flash-point social issues such as gun control and abortion rights. During his first campaign for the Senate, in which he drove Republican incumbent Tim Hutchinson from office in 2002, Pryor declined to declare himself either "pro-choice" or "pro-life," because he said neither label fit.

His voting record since then has tilted to the anti-abortion side. In 2006, he was one of just six Democrats to support a bill making it a crime to take a minor across state lines to obtain an abortion in order to circumvent state parental consent laws. He also backed a bill in 2004 making it a crime to injure a fetus in the course of violence against a woman. And in another vote, Pryor declined to affirm the principles of *Roe v. Wade*, the Supreme Court case that legalized abortion. "I can't in good conscience say that *Roe v. Wade* should never be overturned," he told the Arkansas Democrat-Gazette.

Pryor is more sympathetic to business concerns than many Democrats. The U.S. Chamber of Commerce ranked him third among all Senate Democrats in 2005 as a result of his support for the Central American Free Trade Agreement and an overhaul of bankruptcy law that clamped down on debtors. He calls himself a deficit hawk and says the deficit should be brought under control to keep interest rates low. When he first came to the Senate in 2003, he voted against an omnibus spending bill that contained nearly $300 million in projects for Arkansas. In 2006, he was one of just two Democrats who sided with Republicans to block drought relief funding that would have added $4.8 billion to the deficit.

Political aspiration is a family trait. When his father was elected to the Senate in 1978, Pryor was 15. The family moved to the Washington area, and he quickly established himself in his new environment, becoming class president at the academically competitive Walt Whitman High School in the affluent Maryland suburb of Bethesda. He also was a congressional page, as his father had been. After high school, Pryor, hoping for a career in politics, returned to his hometown of Fayetteville, earning undergraduate and law degrees from the University of Arkansas.

Elected to the state House two years out of law school, Pryor suffered a career setback when he lost the Democratic primary for attorney general in 1994. Shortly thereafter, he was diagnosed with sarcoma, a rare form of cancer that left him unable to walk unassisted for more than a year after surgery. Then the disease went into remission, and Pryor relaunched his career. After he was elected attorney general in 1998, he sued tobacco companies for smoking-related health care costs and made it possible for Arkansans to block telemarketing calls.

Pryor had a familiar name and a centrist profile when he took on a vulnerable, conservative Hutchinson in 2002. The one-term senator, a Baptist minister who had campaigned as a so-called traditional values Republican, had divorced his wife of 29 years and married a former Senate aide. Pryor never spoke directly about Hutchinson's divorce, but frequently touted his own commitment to his religion and his family.

Pryor also emphasized his intention to be less partisan than Hutchinson. "That was one of my major themes of the race, trying to bring people out of the trench warfare around here. That really resonated in Arkansas," he says. Pryor won by 8 percentage points.

Like his father, Pryor chose to move his family to Washington, which is something few members of Congress do these days. At the end of the congressional workweek, senators race for the airports instead of building personal relationships with other Senate families as they once did. Pryor says, "That's a family decision that you have to make, and everybody's different. There's really not a right or wrong."

His children are about the same age as those of home-state Democrat Blanche Lincoln, and the two families are close. The Pryors also socialize with the family of Indiana Democrat Evan Bayh, whose father preceded him in the Senate as well, and that of Minnesota Democratic Sen. Amy Klobuchar, newly elected in 2006. Klobuchar's daughter attends the same middle school as Pryor's children.

KEY VOTES

2006

- No Confirm Samuel A. Alito Jr. to the Supreme Court
- No Allow consideration of a bill to establish a $140 billion trust fund to compensate victims of asbestos exposure
- Yes Extend tax cuts for two years at a cost of $70 billion over five years
- Yes Overhaul immigration policy with border security, enforcement and guest worker program
- No Allow consideration of a bill to permanently repeal the estate tax
- No Urge President Bush to begin troop withdrawals from Iraq in 2006
- Yes Lift President Bush's restrictions on stem cell research funding
- Yes Authorize military tribunals for suspected terrorists

2005

- No Curb class action lawsuits by shifting them from state to federal courts
- Yes Allow confirmation vote on Priscilla R. Owen to the U.S. Court of Appeals for the 5th Circuit
- No Oppose mandatory emissions limits and block recognition of global warming as a threat
- Yes Approve free-trade pact with five Central American countries
- Yes Pass energy policy overhaul favored by President Bush emphasizing domestic oil and gas production
- Yes Shield gunmakers from lawsuits when their products are used in crimes
- Yes Ban torture of prisoners in U.S. custody
- No Renew 16 provisions of the Patriot Act
- No Allow final vote on opening the Arctic National Wildlife Refuge to oil and gas exploration

CQ VOTE STUDIES

	PARTY UNITY		PRESIDENTIAL SUPPORT	
	Support	Oppose	Support	Oppose
2006	76%	24%	64%	36%
2005	80%	20%	58%	42%
2004	81%	19%	68%	32%
2003	84%	16%	60%	40%

INTEREST GROUPS

	AFL-CIO	ADA	CCUS	ACU
2006	73%	75%	75%	20%
2005	79%	90%	78%	24%
2004	92%	85%	71%	20%
2003	85%	70%	61%	30%

Rep. Marion Berry (D)

CAPITOL OFFICE
225-4076
www.house.gov/berry
2305 Rayburn 20515-0401; fax 225-5602

COMMITTEES
Appropriations
Budget

RESIDENCE
Jonesboro

BORN
Aug. 27, 1942, Stuttgart, Ark.

RELIGION
Methodist

FAMILY
Wife, Carolyn Berry; two children

EDUCATION
U. of Arkansas, attended 1960-62 (pre-pharmacy); U. of Arkansas, Little Rock, B.S. 1965 (pharmacy)

CAREER
Farmer; White House aide; pharmacist

POLITICAL HIGHLIGHTS
Gillett City Council, 1976-80; Ark. Soil and Water Conservation Commission, 1986-94 (chairman, 1992)

ELECTION RESULTS

2006 GENERAL		
Marion Berry (D)	127,577	69.3%
Mickey Stumbaugh (R)	56,611	30.7%
2006 PRIMARY		
Marion Berry (D)		unopposed
2004 GENERAL		
Marion Berry (D)	162,388	66.6%
Vernon Humphrey (R)	81,556	33.4%

PREVIOUS WINNING PERCENTAGES
2002 (67%); 2000 (60%); 1998 (100%); 1996 (53%)

Elected 1996; 6th term

Representing one of the poorest regions in the country, Berry aggressively pursues federal aid for the rural economy and farmers in the former sharecropping communities across the Delta. Among national issues, Congress' only pharmacist is focused on curbing prescription drug and health care insurance costs.

Berry is a longtime member of the fiscally conservative Blue Dog Coalition of House Democrats. But like many of the more than 40 members, he struggles with the contradiction of saying he wants a balanced budget while advocating for hundreds of millions of federal dollars for his district, which he is positioned to deliver from his Appropriations Committee seat.

Farm aid is a top priority for the congressman, who spent most of his life on a rice farm and with his brothers co-owns a soybean and rice farm in Gillett, Ark. With the multibillion-dollar farm bill up for renewal in 2007, Berry asked Democratic leaders for a waiver to let him sit on both the Agriculture Committee and the exclusive Appropriations panel in the 110th Congress (2007-08). His request was denied, but he was named one of two vice chairmen of the Democratic Steering and Policy Committee, and was tapped as a senior whip, placing him in positions to help shape long-range farm policy.

He also was named as one of the Appropriations Committee's designees to serve on the Budget Committee in the 110th Congress.

Berry plays up his rural background. He once described himself to a local audience as a "farmer who got more involved in politics than maybe I should have." But he is as passionate about lowering prescription drug costs as he is about farm issues. When Republicans objected in 2007 to a bill he cosponsored that would force the federal government to negotiate with drugmakers for lower Medicare prescription drug costs, Berry said his GOP opponents "don't know turnip greens from butter greens about what they are talking about." He sharply opposed the GOP legislation in 2003 that established a drug benefit under Medicare, calling it "the single sorriest piece of legislation written in my lifetime."

The then-majority Republicans refused to let Democrats even attend negotiations on the final bill, and Berry and New York Democrat Charles B. Rangel, who were Democratic conferees, dramatically barged into a room where the GOP-only talks were being held. When Democrats took control of the House in 2007, they changed the rules to promise more bipartisan legislating, citing the dust-up involving Berry and Rangel.

Berry also drew attention in 2005 during an acrimonious budget debate on the House floor. He took issue with one Republican's characterization of the Blue Dogs as "lap dogs." Berry looked at Florida GOP Rep. Adam H. Putnam, then 31, and declared: "I wonder what you're going to be when you grow up." He then turned to Republican Jeb Hensarling of Texas and called him a "Howdy Doody-looking nimrod." The Arkansas Democrat-Gazette withheld its endorsement of Berry in the 2006 election, citing the name-calling incident.

As a youth, Berry recalls going with his father to the One Horse Store general store in the town of Bayou Meto, where men gathered to talk about politics. Though his father and grandfather never held elective office, Berry said their involvement in civic affairs set an example. While attending pharmacy school at the University of Arkansas, Berry frequented a family friend's drugstore in Little Rock, where many of the state's movers and shakers often gathered. That drugstore, Berry told the Democrat-Gazette, "is where I cut my political teeth."

He worked as a pharmacist for only two years after college, but that background appealed to party leaders years later when they tapped him to represent the rural and conservative factions among House Democrats on health care and prescription drug issues.

Berry tends to be more conservative than his party on certain social and budget issues. He voted in agreement with President Bush's position 43 percent of the time in the 109th Congress (2005-06). He backs gun owners' rights, a constitutional amendment permitting prayer in schools and a mandate for a two-thirds majority vote to raise taxes. He also is an immigration policy hard-liner, arguing that fencing along the U.S.-Mexico border and other security controls must be in place before Congress considers a bipartisan immigration bill that would create a guest worker program for illegal immigrants.

In the 110th Congress, Berry picked up a seat on the Appropriations subcommittee for transportation and housing and urban development projects, an assignment tailored to getting federal help for his district, the state's poorest. As an original backer of the Delta Regional Authority, established in 2000 to spur economic development in the eight-state Mississippi Delta region, Berry pushes for his state's share. One of his goals is to bring commercial air service to the Ozark Regional Airport in Mountain Home, Ark.

Before moving to the Appropriations panel in 2003, Berry was on the Agriculture Committee, which provided the platform for his work on the 2002 farm bill. Though forced to give up the seat for the Appropriations assignment, he remains a fierce advocate for farmers.

Berry began his political career in 1976, when he was elected to the Gillett City Council. In 1982, he became Bill Clinton's gubernatorial campaign coordinator in Arkansas County, a post he also held in 1986 and 1990. As governor, Clinton in 1986 named Berry to the state Soil and Water Conservation Commission, where he served for eight years. He moved to Washington when President Bill Clinton appointed him special assistant to the president for agricultural trade and food assistance issues.

When Democratic Rep. Blanche Lincoln became pregnant with twins and decided to leave the House in 1996, Berry won a close contest to fill her seat against Republican Warren Dupwe, who had held Lincoln to 53 percent of the vote in 1994. In a district that has not elected a Republican since Reconstruction, Berry has easily sailed through five re-election campaigns, usually winning by a 2-1 margin or better.

KEY VOTES

2006

- No Stop broadband companies from favoring select Internet traffic
- Yes Affirm U.S. commitment to war in Iraq and reject setting a withdrawal date for troops
- No Repeal requirement for bilingual ballots at the polls
- Yes Permit U.S. sale of civilian nuclear technology to India
- Yes Build a 700-mile fence on the U.S.-Mexico border to curb illegal crossings
- Yes Permit warrantless wiretaps of suspected terrorists

2005

- Yes Intervene in the life-support case of Terri Schiavo
- Yes Lift President Bush's restrictions on stem cell research funding
- Yes Prohibit FBI access to library and bookstore records
- No Approve free-trade pact with five Central American countries
- Yes Pass energy policy overhaul favored by President Bush emphasizing domestic oil and gas production
- Yes End mandatory preservation of habitat of endangered animal and plant species
- Yes Ban torture of prisoners in U.S. custody

CQ VOTE STUDIES

	PARTY UNITY		PRESIDENTIAL SUPPORT	
	Support	Oppose	Support	Oppose
2006	76%	24%	50%	50%
2005	75%	25%	37%	63%
2004	81%	19%	36%	64%
2003	79%	21%	45%	55%
2002	79%	21%	42%	58%

INTEREST GROUPS

	AFL-CIO	ADA	CCUS	ACU
2006	93%	50%	73%	56%
2005	87%	65%	63%	52%
2004	100%	60%	45%	36%
2003	93%	85%	47%	52%
2002	78%	70%	50%	32%

ARKANSAS 1

Northeast – Jonesboro, West Memphis

Settled in the Natural State's northeastern corner, the 1st stretches from the Mississippi Delta through fertile plains and into the hilly north where the Ozark Mountains begin. The district, the poorest in the state, borders Missouri to the north and Tennessee and Mississippi to the east.

Jonesboro, the district's most populous city, is the perennial hub for northeast Arkansas' agricultural production from the alluvial cotton delta and fertile rice lands. Riceland Foods, one of the world's leading rice millers, is based in Stuttgart. Cattle and poultry businesses prosper in the north, and manufacturing is strong in Stuttgart, Jonesboro and Batesville. Steel production plants near Blytheville aid the area economy.

Poverty is most notably present in the largely white, older populations in the northwest and within the former sharecropping communities in the Democratic Delta. The Delta Regional Authority, which seeks to increase economic development in the areas around the Mississippi River, gives government support to some of the 1st's nonprofit organizations and local communities. These communities continually rank below national averages, with many residents undereducated and unemployed.

The White River National Wildlife Refuge, located in the southeastern portion of the 1st and shared with the 4th, is one of the few areas in the district that routinely attracts tourists. Each year, thousands of fishermen, hunters and watchers travel to the migratory bird preserve.

Despite electing few Republicans at either the state or federal level, the socially conservative and heavily Christian 1st gave George W. Bush 52 percent of its 2004 presidential vote. Western Lonoke County, home to Little Rock suburbanites and some military personnel, leans Republican, although no Republican has represented the district since 1875.

MAJOR INDUSTRY

Agriculture, manufacturing, steel production

CITIES

Jonesboro, 55,515; West Memphis, 27,666; Paragould, 22,017; Blytheville, 18,272; Cabot, 15,261; Forrest City, 14,774

NOTABLE

Hattie Caraway, who in 1932 became the first woman elected to the U.S. Senate, lived in Jonesboro; The world duck calling championship is held annually in Stuttgart.

Rep. Vic Snyder (D)

Elected 1996; 6th term

CAPITOL OFFICE
225-2506
snyder.congress@mail.house.gov
www.house.gov/snyder
1330 Longworth 20515-0402; fax 225-5903

COMMITTEES
Armed Services
(Military Personnel - chairman)
Veterans' Affairs

RESIDENCE
Little Rock

BORN
Sept. 27, 1947, Medford, Ore.

RELIGION
Methodist

FAMILY
Wife, Betsy Singleton; one child

EDUCATION
Willamette U., B.A. 1975 (chemistry); U. of Oregon, M.D. 1979; U. of Arkansas, Little Rock, J.D. 1988

MILITARY SERVICE
Marine Corps, 1967-69

CAREER
Physician

POLITICAL HIGHLIGHTS
Ark. Senate, 1991-96

ELECTION RESULTS

2006 GENERAL		
Vic Snyder (D)	124,871	60.5%
Andy Mayberry (R)	81,432	39.5%
2006 PRIMARY		
Vic Snyder (D)		unopposed
2004 GENERAL		
Vic Snyder (D)	160,834	58.2%
Marvin Parks (R)	115,655	41.8%

PREVIOUS WINNING PERCENTAGES
2002 (93%); 2000 (58%); 1998 (58%); 1996 (52%)

A former Marine with degrees in medicine and law, Snyder is the House champion of the G.I. Bill and chairman of the Armed Services Subcommittee on Military Personnel. Now in the majority, he is positioned to use his power to push his longtime goal of raising benefits for National Guard and Reserve soldiers to the same levels as those of active duty forces.

Snyder is a family practice doctor who has volunteered extensively abroad in refugee camps. In the Marines, he served 13 months in Vietnam at the height of the war in the late 1960s. Today, his work in Congress is almost entirely devoted to defense and veterans' issues.

Snyder is a vocal critic of the Bush administration's conduct of the war in Iraq and he is among the Democrats who will scrutinize developments there as a member of the newly formed Armed Services Oversight and Investigations Subcommittee. As the Military Personnel Subcommittee chairman, he is weighing a potential expansion of the size of the Marine Corps, examining military health costs and working to beef up benefits.

In 2006 and again in 2007, he introduced a bill to ensure that G.I. benefits for the Reserves would rise in proportion to increases in active-duty benefits. As it stands, jurisdiction over benefits is split, with Armed Services handling the Reserves and the Veterans' Affairs Committee responsible for active-duty forces. Snyder would like to combine the two under the Veterans' panel.

During his own medical training, Snyder worked at two Veterans' Administration hospitals, and he is a strong advocate for the VA health care system. Snyder pressured the Defense and Veterans Affairs departments to do more to address the problems of Gulf War syndrome, a mysterious range of ailments reported by veterans of the 1991 military campaign in the Persian Gulf. He also has been persistent in efforts to get veterans tested and treated for a serious type of hepatitis, a liver disease that affects about one-tenth of all veterans in central Arkansas, according to a VA study.

In the 108th Congress (2003-04), Snyder fought a Pentagon plan to issue a single medal for service in Afghanistan and Iraq, successfully pressing a bill for separate medals. "As a Vietnam veteran and former Marine, one of the first things I look for on a soldier's uniform is the campaign ribbon that notes where the soldier served," he says. "There is just a camaraderie that comes about by recognizing that campaign ribbon on a uniform."

Snyder counts as a major achievement his role in the 106th Congress (1999-2000) in overturning a Medicare regulation that halted coverage for immunosuppressive drugs after less than four years. When organ transplant recipients stopped buying the expensive drugs, it sometimes led to organ rejection and another costly transplant — which Medicare covered.

Over the years, Snyder has been among the lawmakers from agribusiness states agitating for an end to the more than 40-year-old economic embargo against Cuba, a change that could create a new market for poultry, rice and soybeans. Snyder contends that U.S. credibility is undermined by the inconsistency of trading with communist-led China and Vietnam.

Snyder's parents divorced when he was 2, and his mother raised him in Medford, Ore. After high school, Snyder attended Willamette University in Salem for two years, then dropped out to join the Marines. He says he wasn't ready to continue college and had always admired the Marines. Plus, he says, he had never been out of the country before, except to Canada.

Snyder got his first taste of politics in high school, as a member of the Teenage Republican Club. He signed up because of family friends he admired who were Republicans of the liberal Rockefeller-style. But by the time he cast his first vote in the 1968 presidential election — from Vietnam — he had switched his allegiance, and Snyder voted that year for Democrat Hubert H. Humphrey over Republican Richard Nixon.

Home from the war, Snyder spent four years working odd jobs. He was an aide at a Colorado school for children with mental health problems and worked at a gas station in Colorado. Returning to Oregon, he became an emergency medical technician, which triggered his interest in medicine. He worked in a nursing home and as a part-time nurse's aide at a hospital.

He went back to Willamette University in 1973, got a degree in chemistry, and then went to medical school at the University of Oregon Health Services Center in Portland. Under the G.I. Bill, most of his education was paid for by the federal government. Snyder did his residency in Little Rock, then settled in Arkansas as a family practitioner. He served as a volunteer doctor in refugee camps abroad, often for months at a time, in Thailand, Honduras, Sudan and Sierra Leone.

Snyder also got a law degree in 1988, and although he's never practiced, he put the knowledge to use as a member of the Arkansas Senate from 1991-96. He sponsored two strict drunken-driving bills that became law.

When Democratic U.S. Rep. Ray Thornton announced his retirement in 1996, Snyder entered the 2nd District race as an underdog, facing two tough opponents in the primary, prosecuting attorney Mark Stodola and John Edwards, former aide to U.S. Sen. David Pryor. Snyder finished second to Stodola, but surged in the runoff to narrowly edge out his foe.

Snyder embraced national Democratic themes in the fall campaign, pledging to oppose GOP initiatives on Medicare, education and the environment. He squeaked past Republican Bud Cummins, a businessman and lawyer, with 52 percent of the vote as President Bill Clinton carried the 2nd District by 18 percentage points.

In his re-election campaigns, Snyder has won by double-digit margins. He likes to defer fundraising until three months before the primary. Acknowledging the approach is risky, he told the Arkansas Democrat-Gazette: "If it helps shorten the campaign, that's an improvement."

In 2003, Snyder ended his long bachelorhood by marrying the Rev. Betsy Singleton, pastor of the United Methodist Church in Little Rock. The two met at a social event, and Snyder recognized Singleton from her sermons on television. The same year, Snyder underwent heart surgery for a faulty mitral valve. The Snyders had a son in 2005, named Charles Pennington Snyder, Penn for short.

KEY VOTES

2006

- Yes Stop broadband companies from favoring select Internet traffic
- Yes Affirm U.S. commitment to war in Iraq and reject setting a withdrawal date for troops
- No Repeal requirement for bilingual ballots at the polls
- Yes Permit U.S. sale of civilian nuclear technology to India
- No Build a 700-mile fence on the U.S.-Mexico border to curb illegal crossings
- No Permit warrantless wiretaps of suspected terrorists

2005

- Yes Intervene in the life-support case of Terri Schiavo
- Yes Lift President Bush's restrictions on stem cell research funding
- Yes Prohibit FBI access to library and bookstore records
- Yes Approve free-trade pact with five Central American countries
- Yes Pass energy policy overhaul favored by President Bush emphasizing domestic oil and gas production
- No End mandatory preservation of habitat of endangered animal and plant species
- Yes Ban torture of prisoners in U.S. custody

CQ VOTE STUDIES

	PARTY UNITY		PRESIDENTIAL SUPPORT	
	Support	Oppose	Support	Oppose
2006	86%	14%	45%	55%
2005	86%	14%	33%	67%
2004	85%	15%	41%	59%
2003	84%	16%	33%	67%
2002	85%	15%	41%	59%

INTEREST GROUPS

	AFL-CIO	ADA	CCUS	ACU
2006	93%	75%	43%	17%
2005	80%	80%	59%	8%
2004	80%	95%	57%	20%
2003	79%	85%	52%	13%
2002	67%	80%	60%	12%

ARKANSAS 2

Central — Little Rock

An urban hub in a relatively rural state, the state capital of Little Rock is the focal point of the 2nd District. More than half of the district's population is concentrated in the Little Rock area — the governmental and economic center of the state. The district has the state's largest white-collar population and its highest median income.

Recent developments in Little Rock's River Market District have transformed the area into a haven for both historians interested in the city's rich Victorian past and partygoers looking for nighttime club and bar venues. The area's vibrant entertainment district now spills over to North Little Rock's side of the Arkansas River, where the 18,000-seat multipurpose Alltel Arena is located. A University of Arkansas campus and the system's medical school lead an education, health care and research sector that employs thousands of 2nd District residents.

Just south and west of Little Rock's Pulaski County, along the foothills of the Ouachita Mountains, is fast-growing Saline County. Pulaski, and Faulkner County to the north, also have gained residents, with Republicans increasing in popularity as the suburbs in all three counties expand. GOP candidates also fare better in White County, where Church of Christ-affiliated Harding University is located.

Democratic support is concentrated in poor and working-class neighborhoods in east Little Rock, which is heavily black, and in strong union and university populations. The district twice supported favorite-son Bill Clinton in presidential elections, but George W. Bush narrowly carried it in 2000 and 2004.

MAJOR INDUSTRY

Government, higher education, military

MILITARY BASES

Little Rock Air Force Base, 6,000 military, 1,200 civilian (2005)

CITIES

Little Rock, 183,133; North Little Rock, 60,433; Conway, 43,167; Jacksonville, 29,916; Benton, 21,906; Sherwood, 21,511; Searcy, 18,928

NOTABLE

The Clinton Presidential Center is located along the river in Little Rock; Little Rock Air Force Base has the largest C-130 training and airlift facility in the world; The cheese dog — a hot dog with cheese in the middle — was invented in 1956 at the Finkbeiner Meat Packing Co. in Little Rock.

Rep. John Boozman (R)

CAPITOL OFFICE
225-4301
www.boozman.house.gov
1519 Longworth 20515-0403; fax 225-5713

COMMITTEES
Foreign Affairs
Transportation & Infrastructure
Veterans' Affairs

RESIDENCE
Rogers

BORN
Dec. 10, 1950, Shreveport, La.

RELIGION
Baptist

FAMILY
Wife, Cathy Boozman; three children

EDUCATION
U. of Arkansas, attended 1969-72; Southern College of Optometry, O.D. 1977

CAREER
Optometrist; cattle farm owner

POLITICAL HIGHLIGHTS
Rogers Public Schools Board of Education, 1994-2001

ELECTION RESULTS

2006 GENERAL		
John Boozman (R)	125,039	62.2%
Woodrow Anderson (D)	75,885	37.8%
2006 PRIMARY		
John Boozman (R)		unopposed
2004 GENERAL		
John Boozman (R)	160,629	59.3%
Jan Judy (D)	103,158	38.1%
Dale Morfey (I)	7,016	2.6%

PREVIOUS WINNING PERCENTAGES
2002 (99%); 2001 Special Election (56%)

Elected 2001; 3rd full term

Boozman continues a long Republican tradition for the rural and small-town district covering the northwest corner of Arkansas. It's been in GOP hands for nearly 40 years; its footnote in history is its snub of Bill Clinton in 1974, when the future Democratic president was defeated in a bid for the House seat, his first loss of a political race. Arkansas has trended toward Republicans in recent decades but at a slower pace than other Southern states, due in part to Clinton's legacy there.

Boozman (BOZE-man) reflects the conservative impulse of the region. On fiscal issues, he has called for abolition of the tax code and supported President Bush's broad tax-cutting agenda. On the array of cultural issues that concern many in his party, he supports a constitutional amendment barring same-sex marriage and he favors allowing the display of the Ten Commandments in public places, backing an Alabama judge's refusal to remove such a monument from the state's judicial building in Montgomery.

Among the medical professionals pursuing second careers in Congress, Boozman is the only doctor of optometry. He and his older brother, Fay, founded an eye clinic in Arkansas.

Boozman says that though he grew up among Southern Democrats, he was drawn to the Republican Party by President Ronald Reagan in the 1980s. Boozman calls himself "pro-life, pro-gun, conservative on social issues and pretty conservative fiscally."

"The Boozman boys have been called a lot of things, but liberal wasn't one of them," he says.

He has patterned his career after another locally well-known politician who devoted himself to parochial concerns of the district, former Republican Rep. John Paul Hammerschmidt, who held the seat from 1967 until 1993. Boozman has focused mainly on issues affecting two big companies headquartered in the 3rd District, Wal-Mart Stores Inc. in Bentonville and Tyson Foods Inc. in Springdale. Both companies are driving economic growth in the area; executives and political action committees associated with the two are among Boozman's biggest political contributors.

Boozman came under fire in March 2005 for an amendment to the surface transportation bill that year that would have extended the maximum workday for truckers to 16 hours, including an unpaid two-hour break. Truckers' workdays are legally held to 14 hours, with 11 consecutive hours of driving allowed. The law was of great interest to trucking-dependent retailers such as Wal-Mart. Critics dubbed Boozman's proposal the "sweatshop-on-wheels amendment," saying it would compromise truckers' safety by forcing them to work longer hours without an increase in pay. Boozman was eventually forced to withdraw it.

In his first term, GOP leaders gave him a seat on the Transportation and Infrastructure Committee, from which he has been able to secure politically popular funding for the Interstate 49 project. Planned to be a main north-south artery between Kansas City, Mo., and port cities in Louisiana, its route cuts through western Arkansas. Boozman's other focus on the committee is securing federal funds for the Northwest Arkansas Regional Airport.

In the 109th Congress (2005-06), Boozman got a seat on the International Relations Committee (renamed Foreign Affairs in the 110th Congress), where he focuses on trade issues and ways to combat drug smuggling. He has pushed for more federal aid to stamp out the rapid growth of methamphetamine drug labs. He is also an advocate of ending the U.S. trade embargo against Cuba, a priority for the state's rice and poultry farmers, who view the country as a potentially lucrative market.

On the Veterans' Affairs panel, Boozman is the senior minority member of the Economic Opportunity Subcommittee. In the 109th Congress, Boozman and Stephanie Herseth-Sandlin, a South Dakota Democrat, cosponsored a bill, passed by the House, requiring the VA to set annual contracting goals for small businesses owned by former military service members.

Boozman is the second of three children of an Air Force master sergeant stationed at Barksdale Air Force Base in Shreveport, La. The family moved around with his father's Air Force assignments, and Boozman spent his early childhood in London, attending an all-boys British school.

Eventually, the family returned to Fort Smith, Ark., where it had roots dating to the late 19th century. The 6-foot, 3-inch Boozman was a standout football player at Northside High School in Fort Smith, population 80,000, and went on to be an offensive tackle for the University of Arkansas' vaunted Razorbacks football team.

He was going to be a dentist until his brother, Fay, who was studying ophthalmology, convinced him to go to optometry school so they could practice together. They co-founded Boozman-Hof Regional Eye Clinic in 1977 in their hometown of Rogers.

Fay Boozman, who died in a March 2005 accident while working on his farm in Rogers, was always the higher-profile politician, serving in the state Senate and eventually running against Democrat Blanche Lincoln in the 1998 open-seat Senate race, but losing. John Boozman started his political career on the Rogers school board, where he served roughly six years. When GOP Rep. Asa Hutchinson was appointed by Bush to head the Drug Enforcement Administration, Fay Boozman was the obvious choice to seek the seat. But he decided to remain in Little Rock as head of the Arkansas Department of Health, so John jumped in.

Boozman finished first in the four-candidate GOP field but was forced into a runoff race by state Sen. Gunner DeLay, a distant cousin of then-Majority Leader Tom DeLay. Endorsed by GOP Gov. Mike Huckabee, Boozman won both the primary runoff and the 2001 special election. In 2002, Boozman's only competition was a write-in candidate.

In 2004, Boozman faced a spirited challenge from State House Rep. Jan Judy, but he outdid her 2-to-1 in campaign fundraising and was heavily favored in the district, the most Republican of Arkansas' four congressional districts. He was re-elected with 59 percent of the vote and won by an even larger margin in 2006.

KEY VOTES

2006

No Stop broadband companies from favoring select Internet traffic

Yes Affirm U.S. commitment to war in Iraq and reject setting a withdrawal date for troops

Yes Repeal requirement for bilingual ballots at the polls

Yes Permit U.S. sale of civilian nuclear technology to India

Yes Build a 700-mile fence on the U.S.-Mexico border to curb illegal crossings

Yes Permit warrantless wiretaps of suspected terrorists

2005

? Intervene in the life-support case of Terri Schiavo

No Lift President Bush's restrictions on stem cell research funding

Yes Prohibit FBI access to library and bookstore records

Yes Approve free-trade pact with five Central American countries

Yes Pass energy policy overhaul favored by President Bush emphasizing domestic oil and gas production

Yes End mandatory preservation of habitat of endangered animal and plant species

Yes Ban torture of prisoners in U.S. custody

CQ VOTE STUDIES

	PARTY UNITY		PRESIDENTIAL SUPPORT	
	Support	Oppose	Support	Oppose
2006	97%	3%	92%	8%
2005	96%	4%	77%	23%
2004	96%	4%	82%	18%
2003	97%	3%	93%	7%
2002	95%	5%	85%	15%

INTEREST GROUPS

	AFL-CIO	ADA	CCUS	ACU
2006	21%	5%	100%	92%
2005	15%	0%	93%	96%
2004	13%	10%	100%	96%
2003	7%	10%	97%	84%
2002	11%	0%	95%	96%

ARKANSAS 3

Northwest – Fort Smith, Fayetteville

Arkansas' hilly northwest subscribes to a rugged conservatism unique in this Democratic state, and its Republican bent remains despite an influx of newcomers.

Bentonville, Rogers, Springdale and Fayetteville, all in the state's northwest corner, represent the wealthier part of the 3rd, where history, religious tradition and an influx of retirees have created a solid GOP base. The 2000 census rated this corridor one of the 10 fastest-growing metropolitan areas in the nation. Hometown giants Tyson Foods in Springdale and Wal-Mart in Bentonville provide economic stability, as does the University of Arkansas' flagship campus in Fayetteville. Farther south and nestled in a bend of the Arkansas River, Fort Smith is a regional manufacturing center; major investment by local government and investors has led to commercial and residential redevelopment here.

Overall, the 3rd has prospered recently from tourism. Anchored by the lush Ozark National Forest, located in the district's south, and Beaver Lake, located in the north, the area attracts thousands of visitors each year. Outdoor enthusiasts take in the gorgeous scenery and history buffs visit Civil War sites such as Pea Ridge National Military Park, as well as the museums and landmarks in Fort Smith, which cover everything from the founding of the namesake fort to the Belle Grove Historic District.

Although the GOP-leaning northwest sets the political tone, the rest of the 3rd — particularly farming communities and the city of Fort Smith — is more open to electing Democrats. The 3rd was the only Arkansas district to give George W. Bush more than 52 percent in the 2004 presidential election (he captured 62 percent here) and it was the state's only district to withhold hearty support from native son Bill Clinton in 1996. The 3rd has sent a Republican to Congress since the 1966 election.

MAJOR INDUSTRY

Agriculture, livestock, retail, tourism

CITIES

Fort Smith, 80,268; Fayetteville, 58,047; Springdale, 45,798; Rogers, 38,829; Russellville, 23,682; Bentonville, 19,730

NOTABLE

Eureka Springs hosts an outdoor drama, The Great Passion Play, which boasts the seven-story Christ of the Ozarks Statue; Atkins is Picklecity, USA, and hosts a Picklefest event each May.

Rep. Mike Ross (D)

CAPITOL OFFICE
225-3772
www.house.gov/ross
314 Cannon 20515-0404; fax 225-1314

COMMITTEES
Energy & Commerce
Science & Technology

RESIDENCE
Prescott

BORN
Aug. 2, 1961, Texarkana, Ark.

RELIGION
Methodist

FAMILY
Wife, Holly Ross; two children

EDUCATION
Texarkana Community College, attended 1979-81; U. of Arkansas, Little Rock, B.A. 1987 (political science)

CAREER
Pharmacy owner; wholesale drug and medical supply company field representative; aide to lieutenant governor

POLITICAL HIGHLIGHTS
Nevada County Quorum Court, 1983-85; Ark. Senate, 1991-2001

ELECTION RESULTS

2006 GENERAL		
Mike Ross (D)	128,236	74.7%
Joe Ross (R)	43,360	25.3%
2006 PRIMARY		
Mike Ross (D)		unopposed
2004 GENERAL		
Mike Ross (D)		unopposed

PREVIOUS WINNING PERCENTAGES
2002 (61%); 2000 (51%)

Elected 2000; 4th term

As a leader of the centrist Blue Dog Coalition, Ross holds the megaphone warning fellow Democrats not to abandon the fiscally conservative policies that he says helped them win control of Congress in 2006. He is the communications co-chairman of the 40-plus-member group of conservative Democrats, who have considerable clout in the new majority. "In no way do we plan to be obstructionist," Ross says. "But we're not going to be a rubber stamp either."

Indeed, Speaker Nancy Pelosi struck a centrist tone at the start of the 110th Congress (2007-08), and some of the major planks in the party's "first 100 hours" agenda were long-held priorities of the Blue Dogs, and Ross in particular. He favored budget rules to ban new deficit spending, greater disclosure of earmarks in appropriations bills, a hike in the minimum wage and government-negotiated prescription drug prices for seniors.

Ross' agenda reflects his middle-class, Southern Democrat upbringing and early political mentoring by President Bill Clinton. At the age of 21, Ross drove Clinton around the state for more than a year as Clinton campaigned for governor, while Ross ran for a term on Nevada County's legislative body, the Quorum Court. Both of them won. "It was me and him in a Chevy Citation," Ross recalls. "I learned a lot. . . . He never forgot where he was from and he never forgot about trying to help the little people." Clinton, who was the governor of Arkansas before becoming president, still sometimes refers constituent problems to Ross.

In the 109th Congress (2005-06), Ross voted with his party 76 percent of the time on votes that divided the two parties, making him one of the least loyal Democrats in the House. The 4th District is socially conservative, and Ross tends to move to the right on social issues. He opposes same-sex marriage and abortion rights, though he voted to lift restrictions on federally funded embryonic stem cell research, which is likened by religious conservatives to abortion.

But he solidly aligns with his party on issues affecting families and children, including education and health care. The only pharmacy owner in Congress, he has a strong interest in reining in prescription drug costs.

Ross has voted with President Bush about half the time on votes that the White House got involved in, also in contrast to most Democrats who voted against Bush much more frequently. Yet Ross disagreed with the president on one big issue: tax cuts. He opposed the president's push to make the 2001 tax cut permanent, citing increased deficit spending and the costs of fighting the war in Iraq.

Ross attracted national media attention in 2006 when he criticized the Federal Emergency Management Agency for parking almost 10,000 new manufactured homes in a hay meadow near Hope's airport, in his district, after they failed to reach Hurricane Katrina victims in Louisiana. Ross said they would sink into the pasture if FEMA did not act, and rather than move them, the agency spent millions of dollars to re-gravel the surface. Ross and Arkansas Democratic Sen. Mark Pryor won approval for the homes to be sold or donated to local governments and nonprofit organizations. But as the year ended, the trailers were still in Hope.

Ross' main committee assignment is on the exclusive Energy and Commerce panel. He says his main goal there is to be Arkansas' "economic ambassador" by attracting new industries to his economically lagging district, where 25 percent of the residents live below the poverty line. A top priority is development of alternative renewable fuels. In the 110th Congress, Ross received permission to also serve on the Science and Technology panel.

Ross has renewed his proposal for the Army's Pine Bluff Arsenal to become the site of a government-owned vaccine production facility. He made a similar pitch in 2004, but the contract was awarded to a California firm. The government later canceled the contract for 75 million doses of anthrax vaccine when the company failed to start clinical trials. Ross said the outcome showed that the government cannot rely on the private sector to produce vaccine stockpiles and has to consider a facility at Pine Bluff.

Ross hunted quail and deer as a young boy, and he is a fierce opponent of gun control legislation. But he backs laws that would keep weapons out of schools. Proving his allegiance to the National Rifle Association, Ross was the lead Democrat on a 2004 measure to overturn gun control laws in the District of Columbia. Ross said he wanted to restore Second Amendment rights in the nation's capital, but city officials called it an election year tactic and a violation of the district's right to home rule.

Ross was born in Texarkana, the son of two schoolteachers who encouraged him to get involved in public service. In 1980, while Ross was still in college and active in a young Democrats club, then-Arkansas Sen. Dale Bumpers wrote him a note of encouragement that now hangs near his desk in his Capitol Hill office.

Ross worked his way through college as a radio announcer. He earned his political science degree from the University of Arkansas at Little Rock when he was 25, while working as a top aide to Arkansas' lieutenant governor, Winston Bryant. In 1988, he was a regional coordinator for Democrat Michael S. Dukakis' presidential campaign.

Ross made a living as a field representative for a wholesale drug and medical supply company, and later he and his pharmacist wife, Holly Ross, opened their own pharmacy in the small town of Prescott. But he stayed active in politics, winning election to the state Senate in 1990.

In 2000, Ross challenged four-term GOP Rep. Jay Dickey. Ross' status as the widely regarded front-runner for the Democratic nomination made him the target of attacks by three opponents in a bitter primary. Two of his primary foes later endorsed Dickey. Ross won by 2 percentage points, making his the Democrats' only victory over an incumbent outside California that year.

In 2002, Dickey was back for a rematch, but Ross won handily, with 61 percent of the vote. Ross drew no opponent in 2004. Although there was speculation that he would run for governor in 2006, he decided to remain in Congress and won re-election with 75 percent of the vote.

KEY VOTES

2006

Yes Stop broadband companies from favoring select Internet traffic
Yes Affirm U.S. commitment to war in Iraq and reject setting a withdrawal date for troops
No Repeal requirement for bilingual ballots at the polls
Yes Permit U.S. sale of civilian nuclear technology to India
Yes Build a 700-mile fence on the U.S.-Mexico border to curb illegal crossings
No Permit warrantless wiretaps of suspected terrorists

2005

Yes Intervene in the life-support case of Terri Schiavo
Yes Lift President Bush's restrictions on stem cell research funding
Yes Prohibit FBI access to library and bookstore records
No Approve free-trade pact with five Central American countries
Yes Pass energy policy overhaul favored by President Bush emphasizing domestic oil and gas production
Yes End mandatory preservation of habitat of endangered animal and plant species
Yes Ban torture of prisoners in U.S. custody

CQ VOTE STUDIES

	PARTY UNITY		PRESIDENTIAL SUPPORT	
	Support	Oppose	Support	Oppose
2006	74%	26%	53%	47%
2005	78%	22%	49%	51%
2004	82%	18%	53%	47%
2003	81%	19%	44%	56%
2002	73%	27%	50%	50%

INTEREST GROUPS

	AFL-CIO	ADA	CCUS	ACU
2006	86%	50%	67%	60%
2005	85%	75%	65%	52%
2004	87%	65%	62%	44%
2003	93%	80%	50%	44%
2002	78%	65%	55%	32%

ARKANSAS 4
South – Pine Bluff, Hot Springs

Planted across most of Arkansas' southern half, the 4th is the state's largest district in area and features an abundant timber industry, small farming communities and one of the state's most lucrative tourist areas.

Local tourism revolves around Hot Springs and the nearby Ouachita Mountains. Hot Springs, heralded as America's first resort, attracts tourists to its national park, and visitors hope the warm waters that were once used to treat illness will still promote relaxation.

The timber industry, located mostly in the district's western portion in and around the Ouachita Mountains, employs thousands of district residents. East of Hot Springs, the Pine Bluff Arsenal, which once produced the nation's supply of biological weapons, is home to an emergency preparedness center and a center for toxicological research, as well as a chemical weapons disposal facility.

Rice, soybeans, cotton and rural poverty characterize the eastern edge of the 4th, where many Mississippi River communities have black-majority populations. Democrats receive their most faithful support from this area. Republicans fare better in the district's oil- and chemical-producing south, as well as in military and white-collar areas near Pine Bluff and Hot Springs.

The socially conservative 4th elected its first GOP representative of the 20th century in 1992, but overwhelmingly supported Hope-born and Hot Springs-raised Bill Clinton in both of his presidential bids. The district gave George W. Bush 51 percent of its presidential vote in 2004, but most of the area's state legislators are Democrats.

MAJOR INDUSTRY
Timber, agriculture, livestock, tourism

MILITARY BASES
Pine Bluff Arsenal (Army), 200 military, 1,366 civilian (2007)

CITIES
Pine Bluff, 55,085; Hot Springs, 35,750; Texarkana, 26,448; El Dorado, 21,530; Camden, 13,154

NOTABLE
Hot Springs was a getaway for mobsters such as Charles "Lucky" Luciano and Al Capone in the 1930s; Nearly 4,000 steaks are cooked each year for Magnolia's World Championship Steak Cook-off.

CALIFORNIA

Gov. Arnold Schwarzenegger (R)

First elected: 2003
Length of term: 4 years
Term expires: 1/11
Salary: $175,000
Phone: (916) 445-2841

Residence: Los Angeles
Born: July 30, 1947; Thal, Austria
Religion: Unspecified
Family: Wife, Maria Shriver; four children
Education: U. of Wisconsin, Superior, B.A. 1979 (business & international economics)
Career: Actor; real estate investor; bodybuilder; weight training supplies salesman
Political highlights: No previous office

Election results:

2006 GENERAL		
Arnold Schwarzenegger (R)	4,850,157	55.9%
Phil Angelides (D)	3,376,732	38.9%
Peter Miguel Camejo (GREEN)	205,995	2.4%
Art Olivier (LIBERT)	114,329	1.3%

Lt. Gov. John Garamendi (D)

First elected: 2006
Length of term: 4 years
Term expires: 1/11
Salary: $154,875
Phone: (916) 445-8994

LEGISLATURE

Legislature: Year-round with recess

Senate: 40 members, 4-year terms
2007 ratios: 25 D, 15 R; 30 men, 10 women
Salary: $113,098
Phone: (916) 445-4251

Assembly: 80 members, 2-year terms
2007 ratios: 47 D, 32 R, 1 vacancy; 53 men, 26 women
Salary: $113,098
Phone: (916) 445-3614

TERM LIMITS

Governor: 2 terms
Senate: 2 terms
Assembly: 3 terms

URBAN STATISTICS

CITY	POPULATION
Los Angeles	3,694,820
San Diego	1,223,400
San Jose	894,943
San Francisco	776,733
Long Beach	461,522

REGISTERED VOTERS

Democrat	43%
Republican	34%
Unaffiliated	19%
Others	5%

POPULATION

2006 population (est.)	36,457,549
2000 population	33,871,648
1990 population	29,760,021
Percent change (1990-2000)	+13.8%
Rank among states (2006)	1
Median age	33.3
Born in state	50.2%
Foreign born	26.2%
Violent crime rate	622/100,000
Poverty level	14.2%
Federal workers	246,152
Military	228,903

ELECTIONS

STATE ELECTION OFFICIAL
(916) 657-2166
DEMOCRATIC PARTY
(916) 442-5707
REPUBLICAN PARTY
(818) 841-5210

MISCELLANEOUS

Web: www.ca.gov
Capital: Sacramento

U.S. CONGRESS

Senate: 2 Democrats
House: 33 Democrats, 19 Republicans
The 37th District seat is vacant.

2000 Census Statistics by District

DIST.	2004 VOTE FOR PRESIDENT BUSH	KERRY	WHITE	BLACK	ASIAN	HISP	MEDIAN INCOME	WHITE COLLAR	BLUE COLLAR	SERVICE INDUSTRY	OVER 64	UNDER 18	COLLEGE EDUCATION	RURAL	SQ. MILES
1	38%	60%	71%	1%	4%	18%	$38,918	58%	24%	18%	13%	25%	25%	24%	11,006
2	62	37	76	1	4	14	$33,559	55	27	18	15	26	17	32	21,758
3	58	41	74	4	6	11	$51,313	68	19	13	12	26	27	14	3,374
4	61	37	84	1	2	9	$49,387	63	20	16	14	26	25	33	16,453
5	38	61	43	14	15	21	$36,719	63	20	17	11	28	21	0	147
6	28	70	76	2	4	15	$59,115	68	18	14	13	23	38	10	1,625
7	32	67	43	17	13	21	$52,778	60	23	17	10	27	22	1	349
8	14	84	43	9	29	16	$52,322	73	12	15	13	14	44	0	35
9	13	86	35	26	15	19	$44,314	69	17	14	11	23	37	0	132
10	40	58	65	6	9	15	$65,245	69	18	13	12	27	36	3	1,013
11	54	45	64	3	9	20	$61,996	68	21	11	10	29	29	10	2,277
12	27	72	48	3	29	16	$70,307	73	15	12	14	21	41	0	117
13	28	71	38	6	28	21	$62,415	67	22	11	10	25	32	1	221
14	30	68	60	3	16	18	$77,985	77	13	10	12	22	52	6	826
15	36	63	47	2	29	17	$74,947	74	17	9	10	24	42	1	286

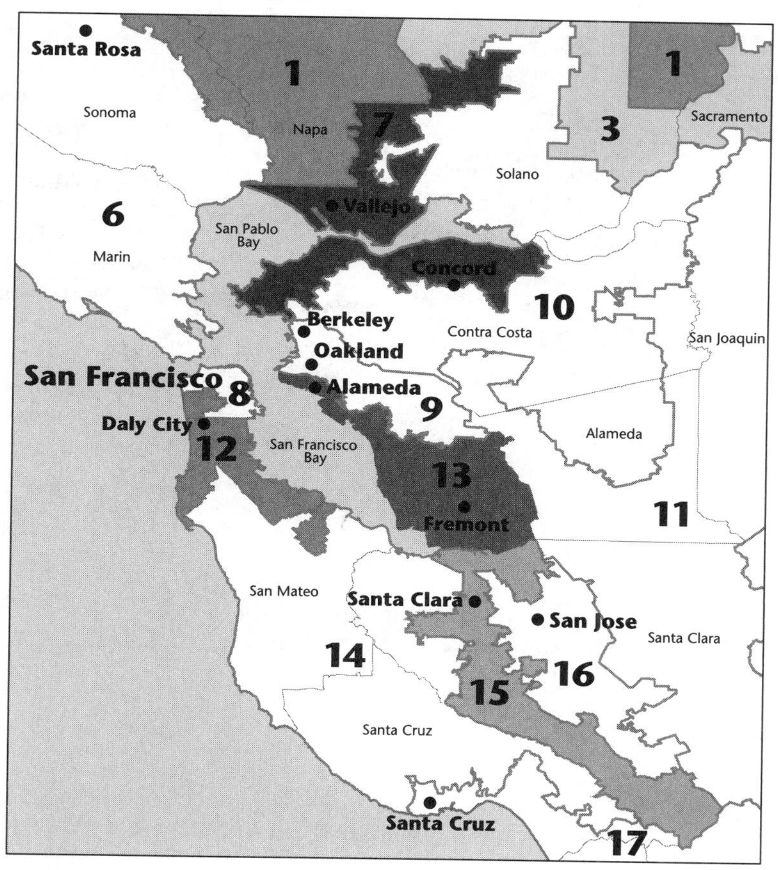

2000 Census Statistics by District

DIST.	2004 VOTE FOR PRESIDENT BUSH	KERRY	WHITE	BLACK	ASIAN	HISP	MEDIAN INCOME	WHITE COLLAR	BLUE COLLAR	SERVICE INDUSTRY	OVER 64	UNDER 18	COLLEGE EDUCATION	RURAL	SQ. MILES
16	36%	63%	32%	3%	23%	38%	$67,689	61%	25%	14%	8%	27%	27%	1%	230
17	33	66	46	3	5	43	$49,234	55	28	16	10	27	25	10	4,820
18	50	49	39	6	9	42	$34,211	46	37	17	10	34	10	9	3,052
19	61	38	60	3	4	28	$41,225	59	25	15	12	28	20	19	6,692
20	48	51	21	7	6	63	$26,800	38	43	19	7	35	6	9	4,982
21	65	34	46	2	5	43	$36,047	53	31	16	10	32	15	20	8,026
22	68	31	67	6	3	21	$41,801	58	25	17	11	29	18	18	10,417
23	40	58	49	2	5	42	$44,874	57	26	17	12	25	26	2	1,042
24	56	43	69	2	4	22	$61,453	68	19	14	11	28	30	6	3,883
25	59	40	57	8	4	27	$49,002	60	24	16	8	32	19	12	21,484
26	55	44	53	4	15	24	$58,968	71	17	12	11	27	32	1	752
27	39	59	45	4	11	36	$46,781	66	20	14	11	26	26	0	151
28	28	71	31	4	6	56	$40,439	58	26	16	9	29	24	0	77
29	37	61	39	6	24	26	$43,895	70	16	14	13	23	33	1	101
30	33	66	76	3	9	8	$60,713	84	7	9	15	17	54	2	286

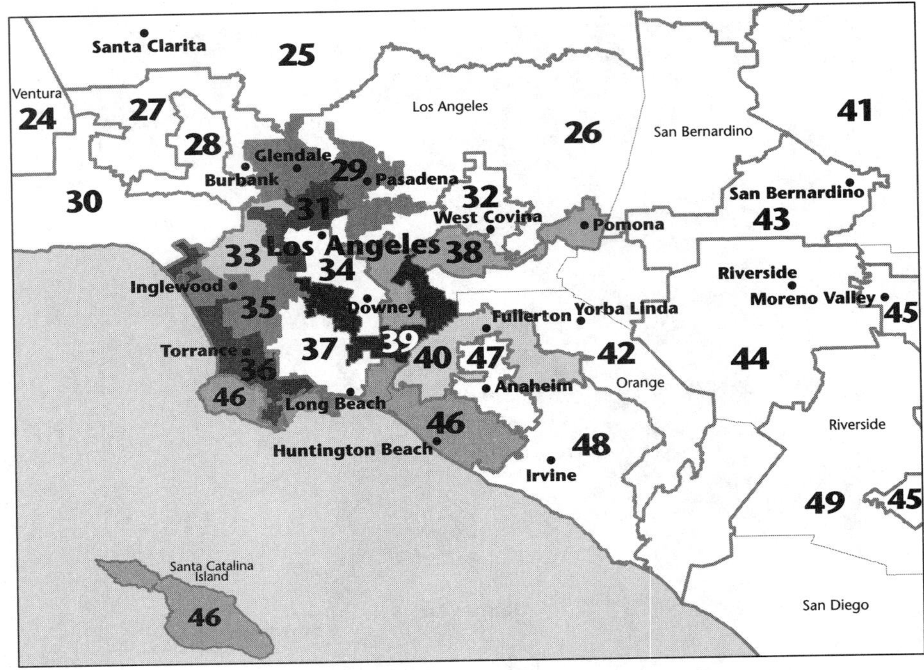

2000 Census Statistics by District

DIST.	2004 VOTE FOR PRESIDENT BUSH	KERRY	WHITE	BLACK	ASIAN	HISP	MEDIAN INCOME	WHITE COLLAR	BLUE COLLAR	SERVICE INDUSTRY	OVER 64	UNDER 18	COLLEGE EDUCATION	RURAL	SQ. MILES
31	22%	77%	10%	4%	14%	70%	$26,093	44%	34%	22%	7%	30%	14%	0%	39
32	37	62	15	3	18	62	$41,394	51	33	16	9	31	14	0	92
33	16	83	20	30	12	35	$31,655	64	18	18	10	24	27	0	48
34	30	69	11	4	5	77	$29,863	44	40	16	8	32	9	0	58
35	20	79	10	34	6	47	$32,156	53	28	19	8	33	13	0	55
36	40	59	48	4	13	30	$51,633	71	16	13	10	23	37	0	75
37	25	74	17	25	11	43	$34,006	54	29	17	8	33	15	0	75
38	34	65	14	4	10	71	$42,488	51	34	15	9	32	13	0	104
39	40	59	21	6	10	61	$45,307	55	31	14	8	33	15	0	65
40	60	39	49	2	16	30	$54,356	65	22	13	11	27	26	0	100
41	62	37	64	5	4	23	$38,721	57	25	17	14	28	18	11	13,314
42	62	37	54	3	16	24	$70,463	74	15	11	8	28	35	1	314
43	41	58	23	12	3	58	$37,390	46	37	17	6	37	9	1	191

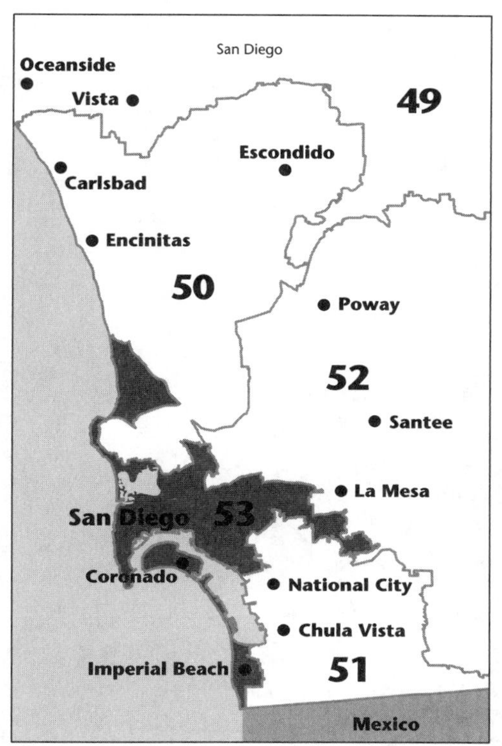

2000 Census Statistics by District

DIST.	2004 VOTE FOR PRESIDENT BUSH	KERRY	WHITE	BLACK	ASIAN	HISP	MEDIAN INCOME	WHITE COLLAR	BLUE COLLAR	SERVICE INDUSTRY	OVER 64	UNDER 18	COLLEGE EDUCATION	RURAL	SQ. MILES
44	59%	40%	51%	5%	5%	35%	$51,578	59%	27%	14%	8%	31%	21%	2%	522
45	56	43	50	6	3	38	$40,468	53	26	21	16	29	17	10	5,980
46	57	42	63	1	15	17	$61,567	73	16	12	13	22	36	0	264
47	50	49	17	1	14	65	$41,618	41	39	20	6	33	10	0	55
48	58	40	68	1	13	15	$69,663	80	10	10	12	23	47	0	212
49	62	36	58	5	3	30	$46,445	58	26	16	13	29	21	10	1,690
50	55	44	66	2	10	19	$59,813	71	16	13	12	25	40	2	300
51	46	53	21	9	12	53	$39,243	55	26	20	10	31	15	4	4,582
52	61	38	73	4	5	14	$52,940	68	18	14	11	27	29	6	2,113
53	38	61	51	7	8	29	$36,637	65	17	19	10	21	32	0	95
STATE	44	54	47	6	11	32	$47,493	63	22	15	11	27	27	6	155,959
U.S.	50.7	48.3	69	12	4	13	$41,994	60	25	15	12	26	24	21	3,537,438

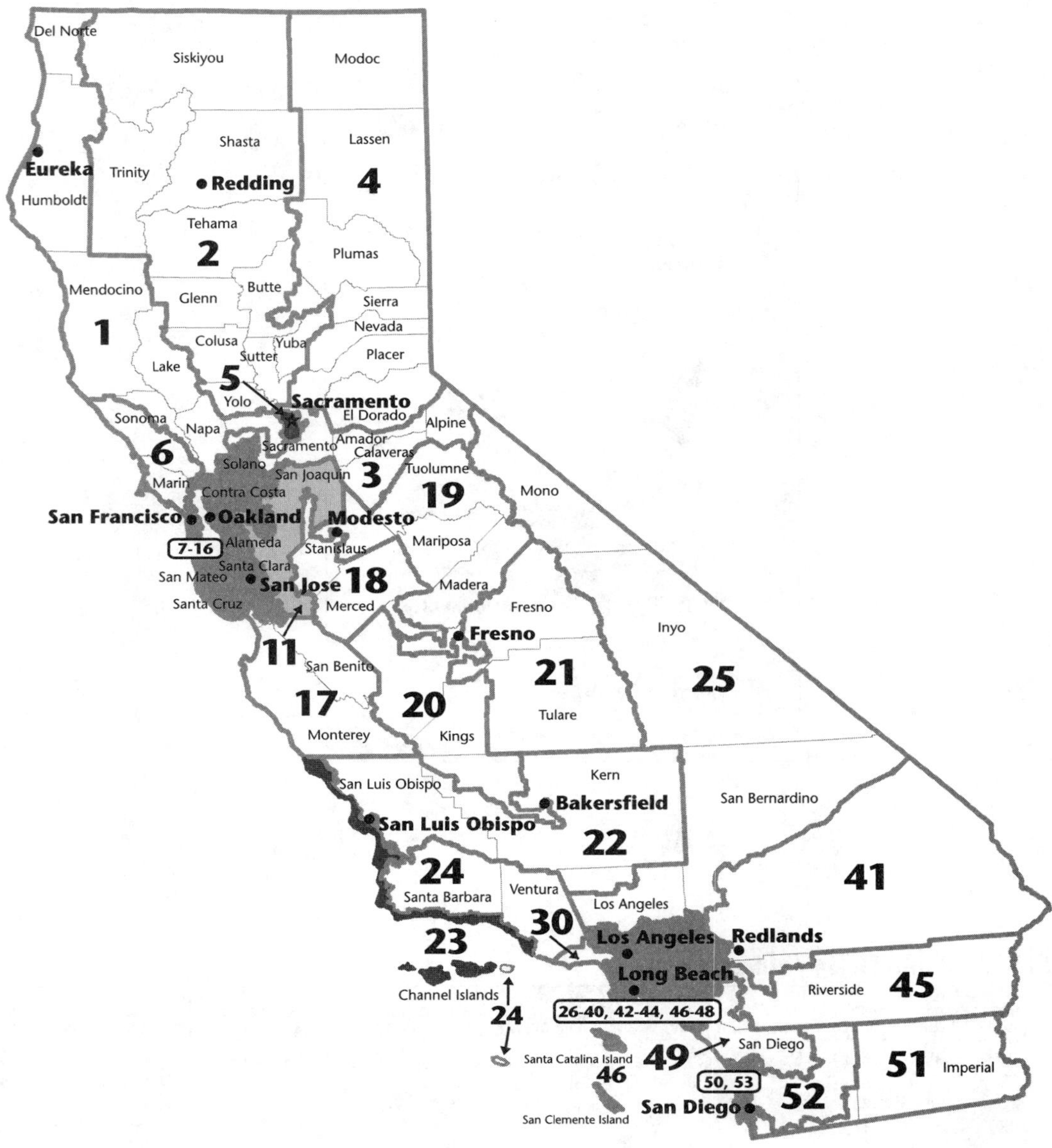
Del Norte
Siskiyou
Modoc
Eureka
Humboldt
Trinity
Shasta
Redding
Lassen
4
Tehama
2
Plumas
Mendocino
1
Glenn
Butte
Sierra
Nevada
Colusa
Yuba
Sutter
Placer
Lake
5
Sacramento
Yolo
El Dorado
Sonoma
Napa
Alpine
6
Amador
Sacramento
Calaveras
Solano
San Joaquin
3
Marin
Tuolumne
Contra Costa
19
Mono
San Francisco
Oakland
Modesto
7-16
Alameda
Stanislaus
Mariposa
Santa Clara
San Mateo
San Jose
18
Santa Cruz
Merced
Madera
Fresno
Inyo
Fresno
11
San Benito
21
25
17
20
Tulare
Monterey
Kings
Kern
San Luis Obispo
Bakersfield
San Bernardino
San Luis Obispo
22
24
41
Santa Barbara
Ventura
Los Angeles
30
Los Angeles
Redlands
23
Long Beach
45
Riverside
Channel Islands
24
26-40, 42-44, 46-48
San Diego
Santa Catalina Island
49
46
51
Imperial
50, 53
52
San Diego
San Clemente Island

Sen. Dianne Feinstein (D)

CAPITOL OFFICE
224-3841
feinstein.senate.gov
331 Hart 20510-0504; fax 228-3954

COMMITTEES
Appropriations
(Interior-Environment - chairwoman)
Judiciary
(Terrorism, Technology & Homeland Security - chairwoman)
Rules & Administration - chairwoman
Select Intelligence
Joint Library - chairwoman
Joint Printing

RESIDENCE
San Francisco

BORN
June 22, 1933, San Francisco, Calif.

RELIGION
Jewish

FAMILY
Husband, Richard Blum; one child, three stepchildren

EDUCATION
Stanford U., A.B. 1955 (history)

CAREER
Civic board official

POLITICAL HIGHLIGHTS
San Francisco Board of Supervisors, 1970-78 (president, 1970-71, 1974-75, 1978); candidate for mayor of San Francisco, 1971, 1975; mayor of San Francisco, 1978-89; Democratic nominee for governor, 1990

ELECTION RESULTS

2006 GENERAL		
Dianne Feinstein (D)	5,076,289	59.4%
Richard "Dick" Mountjoy (R)	2,990,822	35.0%
Todd Chretien (GREEN)	147,074	1.7%
Michael S. Metti (LIBERT)	133,851	1.6%
Marsha Feinland (PFP)	117,764	1.4%
2006 PRIMARY		
Dianne Feinstein (D)	2,176,888	87.0%
Colleen Fernald (D)	199,180	8.0%
Martin Luther Church (D)	127,301	5.1%

PREVIOUS WINNING PERCENTAGES
2000 (56%); 1994 (47%); 1992 Special Election (54%)

Elected 1992; 3rd full term

Feinstein's moderation, personal appeal and high name recognition have made her one of California's most enduring political figures. Thoughtful and pragmatic, she is able to straddle the Senate's ideological divide without making career-long enemies.

A member of six committees — she chairs the Rules and Administration panel — Feinstein (FINE-stine) has an impact on a diverse array of issues, in large measure because of her ability to conduct business calmly in the Senate's often partisan atmosphere. Though she has been as tough on President Bush's judicial nominees as other Democrats, her composed, deliberative debating style gives her more credibility, even though she is one of the few Judiciary Committee members without a law degree.

She is not the loudest member of her party, but that often enhances her effectiveness. When the Bush administration came under fire in 2006 for conducting electronic surveillance of U.S. citizens without court orders, her warning of a looming constitutional confrontation with the executive branch seemed less like political theater than a real possibility. She proposed legislation, which Judiciary Committee Chairman Arlen Specter, a Pennsylvania Republican, cosponsored, making clear that electronic spying had to be conducted under the rules of the 1978 Foreign Intelligence Surveillance Act, which requires investigators to seek individual warrants for surveillance targets.

She also has expressed concerns about the administration's interpretation of executive authority, particularly the use of presidential signing statements to comment on laws passed by Congress. The president has inserted statements into the Federal Register underscoring his belief that the law does not restrict his authority to command the armed forces, conduct foreign policy or supervise the executive branch. Feinstein stated in a 2006 speech that, "The president is usurping power from both the legislative and judicial branches and destroying this balance that has served our country so well," reported the San Francisco Chronicle.

During the two confirmation hearings of Bush's nominees to the Supreme Court, Feinstein ultimately came to the same conclusion as her more liberal Judiciary colleagues, voting against both John G. Roberts Jr. and Samuel A. Alito Jr. Yet she seemed to genuinely consider each nominee's answers rather than coming to the hearings with her mind made up. She ended up voting against Roberts, she said, because "I know as little about what Judge Roberts really thought after the hearings as I did before the hearings." Over time, she has supported, although sometimes reluctantly, her party's filibusters of 10 of the president's conservative judicial nominees, saying their views were out of the mainstream.

Feinstein often goes her own way. She was the sole Judiciary Democrat in 2006 to support a constitutional amendment to protect the flag. As the committee was drafting the bill, she described how, as a 12-year-old, she saw on the front page of the San Francisco Chronicle in February 1945 a big picture of the Marines raising the American flag at Iwo Jima. "I was never the same ever after with respect to the flag," said Feinstein.

Even though she was mayor of the city for more than a decade, Feinstein doesn't operate as the stereotypical "San Francisco liberal" who prizes ideological purity over getting bills passed. That helped her get a key provision into the 2004 overhaul of the country's spy agencies, heralded as one of the most significant bills of Bush's first term. A senior member of the

Intelligence Committee, Feinstein had introduced a bill in 2002 to create a Cabinet-level director of national intelligence with far more control over the 15 intelligence agencies than the CIA director had. The proposal attracted a number of cosponsors but didn't take off until the Sept. 11 commission released a report in 2004 endorsing the idea. It was later folded into a comprehensive intelligence overhaul measure that passed.

In 2001, when both parties were on the verge of throwing in the towel on a contentious overhaul of campaign finance law, Feinstein teamed with Republican Fred Thompson of Tennessee on a compromise amendment that saved the bill. In another instance, she worked with House Republicans to rescue legislation to prevent forest fires that was mired in a partisan dispute over minority party participation in conference committees, marking a rare agreement between the parties on environmental legislation.

Feinstein says she developed her political mantra — "govern from the center" — while serving as San Francisco mayor and trying to work out solutions to satisfy the diverse political forces in her city. A member of the moderate Senate New Democrats, she largely avoids alienating Republicans with the kind of stinging verbal assaults for which the state's other senator, Democrat Barbara Boxer, is known.

Feinstein takes a strong liberal stand, however, in her support for gun control. "I've lived a life that has been impacted by weapons," she wrote in "Nine and Counting," a book by the women senators serving in 2000. "So this is not an esoteric, academic exercise for me. Nor is it a political exercise."

In November 1978, while serving on the San Francisco Board of Supervisors, Feinstein discovered the body of Mayor George Moscone after he and Harvey Milk, the city's first openly gay supervisor, were shot to death in City Hall by former Supervisor Dan White. Feinstein succeeded Moscone and won plaudits for the dignified way she held the city together in the wake of the killings. Feinstein's role, recalled in the 1984 documentary "The Life and Times of Harvey Milk," has given her credibility in the gun debate. When GOP Sen. Larry E. Craig of Idaho, a National Rifle Association board member, once hinted that Feinstein did not have much weapons knowledge, she recounted how she had tried to find Milk's pulse after he was shot.

Feinstein works closely with her female colleagues. She was a prominent skeptic during the Rules Committee's investigation of a GOP challenge to Louisiana Democrat Mary L. Landrieu's slim 1996 Senate victory. "Hell hath no fury like a man beaten by a woman," she said. "Women have to fight our way in this process all the way up. No one hands us anything." Fond of seersucker suits, she gave one to each of the 13 other women senators in 2004 so they'd have no excuse for not wearing one on "Seersucker Suit Day."

Feinstein first won her Senate seat in a 1992 special election against Republican John Seymour, who had been appointed by GOP Sen. Pete Wilson when Wilson became governor in 1990. Boxer was also running and despite differences in style and philosophy, the pair campaigned as "Thelma and Louise," evoking 1992's Best Screenplay Oscar winner.

Two years later, Feinstein had to defend the seat against a tough challenge from millionaire GOP Rep. Michael Huffington, who outspent her by more than 2-to-1 in what was at the time the most expensive Senate contest ever. Not until she and other Democrats turned attack ads against him — and it was revealed that Huffington had hired an illegal immigrant as a household employee — did Feinstein pull ahead.

Her Republican opponent in 2000, former Rep. Tom Campbell, had trouble raising money and did little to inspire his party's conservatives, offering centrist views and even calling Feinstein an effective senator. She cruised to re-election. In 2006, Feinstein handily beat her GOP challenger, former state senator Richard "Dick" Mountjoy, with 59 percent of the vote.

KEY VOTES

2006

No Confirm Samuel A. Alito Jr. to the Supreme Court

Yes Allow consideration of a bill to establish a $140 billion trust fund to compensate victims of asbestos exposure

No Extend tax cuts for two years at a cost of $70 billion over five years

Yes Overhaul immigration policy with border security, enforcement and guest worker program

No Allow consideration of a bill to permanently repeal the estate tax

Yes Urge President Bush to begin troop withdrawals from Iraq in 2006

Yes Lift President Bush's restrictions on stem cell research funding

No Authorize military tribunals for suspected terrorists

2005

Yes Curb class action lawsuits by shifting them from state to federal courts

Yes Allow confirmation vote on Priscilla R. Owen to the U.S. Court of Appeals for the 5th Circuit

No Oppose mandatory emissions limits and block recognition of global warming as a threat

Yes Approve free-trade pact with five Central American countries

No Pass energy policy overhaul favored by President Bush emphasizing domestic oil and gas production

\- Shield gunmakers from lawsuits when their products are used in crimes

Yes Ban torture of prisoners in U.S. custody

No Renew 16 provisions of the Patriot Act

No Allow final vote on opening the Arctic National Wildlife Refuge to oil and gas exploration

CQ VOTE STUDIES

	PARTY UNITY		PRESIDENTIAL SUPPORT	
	Support	Oppose	Support	Oppose
2006	90%	10%	54%	46%
2005	92%	8%	40%	60%
2004	95%	5%	62%	38%
2003	91%	9%	49%	51%
2002	83%	17%	76%	24%
2001	85%	15%	71%	29%
2000	88%	12%	84%	16%
1999	91%	9%	87%	13%
1998	87%	13%	88%	12%
1997	86%	14%	89%	11%

INTEREST GROUPS

	AFL-CIO	ADA	CCUS	ACU
2006	100%	90%	50%	0%
2005	62%	95%	50%	12%
2004	100%	100%	65%	4%
2003	92%	90%	39%	5%
2002	92%	80%	55%	20%
2001	94%	85%	71%	12%
2000	50%	70%	54%	28%
1999	78%	100%	53%	4%
1998	88%	90%	61%	4%
1997	57%	85%	50%	4%

Sen. Barbara Boxer (D)

Elected 1992; 3rd term

For most of her adult life, Boxer has been sniping at the powerful from the left flank of the political spectrum. Now she is among the movers and shakers, but her elevated stature has not led her to moderate her rhetoric.

Halfway through her third term in the Senate, Boxer remains the iconoclastic feminist, environmentalist, anti-war and anti-corporate crusader that has made her a hero to liberals in her home state and around the country.

Just as the 110th Congress (2007-08) got under way, Boxer inflamed passions on both sides of the Iraq War debate when she suggested Secretary of State Condoleezza Rice had little at risk in the war because she is unmarried and childless. "You're not going to pay a particular price, as I understand it, with an immediate family," Boxer told Rice. "So who pays the price? The American military and their families."

Boxer was one of 23 senators who voted against authorizing President Bush to use force in Iraq in 2002. She also voted against the 1991 Gulf War when she served in the House, and she is often sought out by reporters to articulate the liberal position on foreign policy and other issues.

"My political style is to be extremely candid and straight from the shoulders, and not to be mealy-mouthed or waffle," says the 1960s-era war protester. "When I believe in something, I believe in it strongly."

Boxer's belief in the gravity of the threat posed by global warming explains why that issue is her top legislative priority. As chairwoman of the Environment and Public Works Committee, she is uniquely positioned to advance legislation that would reduce greenhouse gas emissions that contribute to global warming.

"I am an optimist. I believe in our ability to act, and I am counting on this committee, which has a distinguished history, to move us forward," she said in January 2007. If she is successful, it would likely be Boxer's most significant contribution to federal law since her 1993 arrival in the Senate. But she will have to make significant compromises in order to get a bill through a divided Senate and secure the signature of the president, who opposes the kind of mandatory caps on emissions that she supports.

Heading into the 110th Congress, only one Boxer-sponsored Senate bill had ever been enacted. That 1994 law allowed states to conduct seismic retrofitting of bridges without regard to whether the bridges were eligible for reconstruction or replacement under an existing federal program.

Despite her thin legislative record, Boxer's contributions to the national political discussion have been robust.

In early 2005, Boxer provided the necessary senatorial signature to contest the certification by Congress of Ohio's electoral votes in the 2004 presidential election. Four years earlier, no senator would support House Democrats' objection to Florida's disputed presidential election results. Boxer's protest forced the Senate to withdraw from a joint session in the House chamber so the two bodies could separately debate the validity of Ohio's election results. The certification was never in doubt, but Boxer forced a debate on the issue of voting irregularities.

On the wall of her Capitol Hill office hangs a picture of Boxer as a House member, leading six other female representatives up the steps of the Senate in 1991 to demand public hearings on law professor Anita Hill's sexual harassment allegations against Supreme Court nominee Clarence Thomas. Looking back, she believes the attention-grabbing stunt helped spark a voter backlash against the overwhelmingly white, male makeup of the

CAPITOL OFFICE
224-3553
boxer.senate.gov
112 Hart 20510-0505; fax 228-3972

COMMITTEES
Commerce, Science & Transportation
Environment & Public Works - chairwoman
(Public Sector Solutions to Global Warming & Children's Health Protection - chairwoman)
Foreign Relations
(East Asian & Pacific Affairs - chairwoman)
Select Ethics - acting chairwoman

RESIDENCE
Millbrae

BORN
Nov. 11, 1940, Brooklyn, N.Y.

RELIGION
Jewish

FAMILY
Husband, Stewart Boxer; two children

EDUCATION
Brooklyn College, B.A. 1962 (economics)

CAREER
Congressional aide; journalist; stockbroker

POLITICAL HIGHLIGHTS
Candidate for Marin County Board of Supervisors, 1972; Marin County Board of Supervisors, 1977-83 (president, 1980); U.S. House, 1983-93

ELECTION RESULTS

2004 GENERAL		
Barbara Boxer (D)	6,955,728	57.7%
Bill Jones (R)	4,555,922	37.8%
Marsha Feinland (PFP)	243,846	2.0%
James P. "Jim" Gray (LIBERT)	216,522	1.8%
2004 PRIMARY		
Barbara Boxer (D)	unopposed	

PREVIOUS WINNING PERCENTAGES
1998 (53%); 1992 (48%); 1990 House Election (68%); 1988 House Election (73%); 1986 House Election (74%); 1984 House Election (68%); 1982 House Election (52%)

Senate that contributed to gains by women in the 1992 elections, which became known as the "Year of the Woman" in politics.

She is known to raise her voice on television and in news conferences when she feels passionately about an issue, sometimes with the help of her "Boxer Box" — a portable platform that boosts the 4-foot, 11-inch senator to microphone level.

Early in her House career, Boxer helped lead efforts to cut wasteful spending from the Pentagon's budget, using the memorable $600 toilet seat as a prop.

On the Environment and Public Works Committee, she led efforts in 2001 to help communities clean up abandoned industrial sites known as brownfields. She has pushed since the 1990s for a ban on the gasoline additive MTBE, a suspected carcinogen. And she has sharply criticized the Bush administration for its proposed rollbacks of clean air regulations, changes to toxic chemical inventories, rules allowing more logging in national forests and its interpretation of "dolphin-safe" tuna fishing regulations.

Boxer has taken on the cause of putting anti-missile technology on U.S. commercial aircraft. In legislation and in letters, she is calling on the government to require the anti-missile devices on all new airplanes.

A seasoned pol, Boxer finds time to address home-state concerns. At the end of 2004, she pushed through a tax provision sought by California's high-tech firms that grants a tax holiday on overseas earnings if the money is reinvested back home. That sort of stance gives her broad popularity in California. Boxer drew more votes in her 2004 re-election than anyone other than the presidential candidates, winning by a 20 percentage point margin over GOP challenger Bill Jones.

Her friendship with House Speaker Nancy Pelosi, a fellow California Democrat, was forged when they represented nearby districts in the House in the 1980s and early 1990s. And it would be hard for her to disavow ties to the "liberal Hollywood elite" after songstress Barbra Streisand gave Boxer a shout-out during a 2006 concert in Los Angeles.

In her first and most difficult re-election campaign, in 1998 against conservative GOP State Treasurer Matt Fong, The Sacramento Bee described Boxer as "a high-profile, high-energy politician with a bent for partisanship and self-promotion." Former Senate Majority Leader Bob Dole of Kansas once called her "the most partisan senator I've ever known." She sided with a majority of her fellow Democrats on 98 percent of the votes that split the two parties in the 109th Congress (2005-06).

In addition to her own political experiences, Boxer had a window into the Clinton White House. Her daughter was married to Tony Rodham, brother of former first lady and current Sen. Hillary Rodham Clinton. Boxer noted in an interview with The New York Times that her grandson is the only person ever to have a grandmother and an aunt serving in the Senate.

Boxer, a Brooklyn-born former stockbroker, has not limited her energies to politics. She published a novel, "A Time to Run," with author Mary-Rose Hayes in 2005. It tells the story of a female senator whose former lover attempts to sabotage her career, and it provides ample fodder for those who like to guess which real-life lawmakers the characters are based on.

Boxer got her political start in Marin County, where she moved when she was 27 with her husband, Stewart, an Oakland labor lawyer. (They met at Brooklyn College.) She was elected to the county board of supervisors in 1976, on her second try, and won a House seat in 1982. A decade later, Boxer beat out fellow House Democrat Mel Levine and Lt. Gov. Leo T. McCarthy to claim the Senate nomination. Then in November 1992, she held off the GOP nominee, conservative TV commentator Bruce Herschensohn, by 5 percentage points.

KEY VOTES

2006

- No Confirm Samuel A. Alito Jr. to the Supreme Court
- No Allow consideration of a bill to establish a $140 billion trust fund to compensate victims of asbestos exposure
- No Extend tax cuts for two years at a cost of $70 billion over five years
- Yes Overhaul immigration policy with border security, enforcement and guest worker program
- No Allow consideration of a bill to permanently repeal the estate tax
- Yes Urge President Bush to begin troop withdrawals from Iraq in 2006
- Yes Lift President Bush's restrictions on stem cell research funding
- No Authorize military tribunals for suspected terrorists

2005

- No Curb class action lawsuits by shifting them from state to federal courts
- No Allow confirmation vote on Priscilla R. Owen to the U.S. Court of Appeals for the 5th Circuit
- No Oppose mandatory emissions limits and block recognition of global warming as a threat
- No Approve free-trade pact with five Central American countries
- No Pass energy policy overhaul favored by President Bush emphasizing domestic oil and gas production
- No Shield gunmakers from lawsuits when their products are used in crimes
- Yes Ban torture of prisoners in U.S. custody
- No Renew 16 provisions of the Patriot Act
- No Allow final vote on opening the Arctic National Wildlife Refuge to oil and gas exploration

CQ VOTE STUDIES

	PARTY UNITY		PRESIDENTIAL SUPPORT	
	Support	Oppose	Support	Oppose
2006	97%	3%	47%	53%
2005	99%	1%	30%	70%
2004	96%	4%	65%	35%
2003	99%	1%	44%	56%
2002	95%	5%	65%	35%
2001	98%	2%	64%	36%
2000	100%	0%	92%	8%
1999	97%	3%	84%	16%
1998	90%	10%	90%	10%
1997	97%	3%	89%	11%

INTEREST GROUPS

	AFL-CIO	ADA	CCUS	ACU
2006	100%	95%	25%	8%
2005	92%	100%	24%	12%
2004	100%	95%	56%	4%
2003	100%	95%	22%	10%
2002	100%	90%	40%	5%
2001	100%	95%	42%	0%
2000	67%	85%	41%	4%
1999	100%	100%	47%	4%
1998	88%	95%	59%	4%
1997	86%	100%	50%	0%

Rep. Mike Thompson (D)

CAPITOL OFFICE
225-3311
mikethompson.house.gov
231 Cannon 20515-0501; fax 225-4335

COMMITTEES
Select Intelligence
(Terrorism, Human Intelligence, Analysis & Counterintelligence - chairman)
Ways & Means

RESIDENCE
St. Helena

BORN
Jan. 24, 1951, St. Helena, Calif.

RELIGION
Roman Catholic

FAMILY
Wife, Janet Thompson; two children

EDUCATION
California State U., Chico, B.A. 1982 (political science), M.A. 1996 (public administration)

MILITARY SERVICE
Army, 1969-73

CAREER
Vintner; winery maintenance supervisor; state legislative aide; college instructor

POLITICAL HIGHLIGHTS
Calif. Senate, 1990-98

ELECTION RESULTS

2006 GENERAL		
Mike Thompson (D)	144,409	66.2%
John W. Jones (R)	63,194	29.0%
Pamela Elizondo (GREEN)	6,899	3.2%
Timothy J. Stock (PFP)	3,503	1.6%
2006 PRIMARY		
Mike Thompson (D)		unopposed
2004 GENERAL		
Mike Thompson (D)	189,366	66.9%
Lawrence Wiesner (R)	79,970	28.3%
Pamela Elizondo (GREEN)	13,635	4.8%

PREVIOUS WINNING PERCENTAGES
2002 (64%); 2000 (65%); 1998 (62%)

Elected 1998; 5th term

A third-generation grape grower, Thompson has proved as adept at cultivating political relationships in Congress as cultivating sauvignon blanc grapes on his 20-acre vineyard in the Napa Valley. A good friend of House Speaker Nancy Pelosi, Thompson serves as a bridge between the more liberal Pelosi and the party's conservative faction, the Blue Dog Coalition.

Backed by Pelosi, Thompson snared a seat on the Budget Committee in 2003 and won assignment to Ways and Means in 2005. He is a loyal ally for the Speaker on some of her priorities, but he can diverge from the party mainstream on certain fiscal matters.

Thompson led the Democratic Congressional Campaign Committee's effort to protect endangered incumbents in the 2006 elections. He also helped launch the DCCC's business council, an outreach program designed to bring the party closer to the business community. As a result of his DCCC work, Thompson emerged in early 2007 as a candidate to chair the campaign committee, but Pelosi instead chose Chris Van Hollen of Maryland.

As a consolation prize, Thompson was given a coveted seat on the Intelligence Committee and the gavel for the Terrorism, Human Intelligence, Analysis and Counterintelligence Subcommittee. Thompson vowed to be aggressive in raising questions about the performance of U.S. intelligence agencies in the war against terrorism and in Iraq.

As a former Vietnam combat veteran, Thompson has a deep interest in the state of the war in Iraq. He opposed the war's authorization in 2002 and has argued against President Bush's proposal to send a surge of more troops. He says Iraq must now police itself and contends the war is overshadowing other American budget priorities. "We simply do not have the resources to continue this war," he said. "The best thing for our country is to end this war as swiftly as possible." After returning from a visit to Iraq in early 2006, he offered an unsuccessful bill calling for the withdrawal of troops by September 2006.

In early 2007, Thompson introduced similar legislation, this time mandating that redeployment of U.S. troops begin by May 2007, with the last troops out by March 2008.

On Ways and Means, Thompson has argued for measures to improve rural health care and its support, including legislation to fund tele-health programs that offer health care advice and doctor consultations via computer and telephone. He has been a champion of increased deductions for home mortgage and state income taxes, which he says are needed to help Californians deal with an expensive housing market and high state and local tax rates.

Thompson will break ranks with his party on pro-business issues and is a firm believer in many of the Blue Dog budget priorities, such as pay-as-you-go rules requiring offsets for tax cuts and spending increases. He has also worked to expand trade markets for California's wine and produce, and he has pressed hard for federal dollars to fight insect-borne crop diseases.

Thompson scored a coup in 2006 when he worked with California Democratic Sen. Barbara Boxer to gain enactment of a bill setting aside 273,000 acres of northern California as wilderness land, spanning parts of five counties in his district. Thompson won over a key ally in California Republican Richard W. Pombo, then-chairman of the Resources Committee, by including provisions to allow access in certain areas for off-road vehicles and to retain some roads. "America's wilderness represents the things we love about being American — our free spirit, our sense of adventure and our passion for exploring the unknown," Thompson said when the measure was signed.

He also has sought to reverse the sharp reduction in salmon runs in the Klamath River. Early in 2007, he urged the government to follow through on a plan for restoring salmon runs, as required by a 2006 measure he helped enact. In 2002, Thompson had criticized federal salmon management efforts by dumping a 500-pound load of dead salmon on the doorstep of the Interior Department.

Thompson became interested in public service as a young man working as a maintenance supervisor at the Beringer Vineyard in Napa Valley. "I was the guy the Hispanic field laborers would come to with their problems," he said. When he once sought to intervene in behalf of a Hispanic worker who had been cheated by a mechanic, Thompson recalled, "The guy in the repair shop said: 'What do you care — the guy's just a Mexican.' "

Outraged by the incident, Thompson says he realized that to be able to help people effectively, he would have to complete his education. He had dropped out of high school and joined the Army, serving as a staff sergeant and platoon leader with the 173rd Airborne Brigade in Vietnam, where he was wounded and received a Purple Heart. In his late 20s and early 30s, he earned his high school diploma and then a college degree.

A political science professor suggested he apply for a fellowship working with the state legislature, which led to a second career as a staff member. Thompson ran for elective office himself in 1990, winning a seat in the state Senate. During his tenure in the California Senate, he built coalitions across party lines on budget and other matters. In tandem with a Republican state senator, he sponsored a welfare overhaul bill that provided recipients with child care aid, job training and education to move them off the public assistance rolls.

Because of California's legislative term limits, Thompson gained seniority quickly in Sacramento. But those same limits meant that he would be out of a job after the 1998 elections, so he set his sights on Congress. The prospect of facing the popular Thompson, it was widely speculated, was the reason GOP incumbent Rep. Frank Riggs abandoned his seat in favor of a quixotic, late bid for the Senate. Thompson easily defeated his underfunded Republican opponent, Napa County Supervisor Mark Luce.

Thompson has gone on to win re-election easily, and redistricting following the 2000 census made the 1st even more favorable to Democrats.

KEY VOTES

2006

- Yes Stop broadband companies from favoring select Internet traffic
- No Affirm U.S. commitment to war in Iraq and reject setting a withdrawal date for troops
- No Repeal requirement for bilingual ballots at the polls
- No Permit U.S. sale of civilian nuclear technology to India
- No Build a 700-mile fence on the U.S.-Mexico border to curb illegal crossings
- No Permit warrantless wiretaps of suspected terrorists

2005

- ? Intervene in the life-support case of Terri Schiavo
- Yes Lift President Bush's restrictions on stem cell research funding
- Yes Prohibit FBI access to library and bookstore records
- No Approve free-trade pact with five Central American countries
- No Pass energy policy overhaul favored by President Bush emphasizing domestic oil and gas production
- No End mandatory preservation of habitat of endangered animal and plant species
- Yes Ban torture of prisoners in U.S. custody

CQ VOTE STUDIES

	PARTY UNITY		PRESIDENTIAL SUPPORT	
	Support	Oppose	Support	Oppose
2006	93%	7%	23%	77%
2005	92%	8%	18%	82%
2004	91%	9%	24%	76%
2003	90%	10%	27%	73%
2002	93%	7%	26%	74%

INTEREST GROUPS

	AFL-CIO	ADA	CCUS	ACU
2006	86%	90%	47%	20%
2005	87%	90%	48%	16%
2004	87%	90%	48%	13%
2003	87%	90%	50%	28%
2002	100%	90%	53%	8%

CALIFORNIA 1
Northern Coast – Eureka; Napa, Davis

The 1st is notable for its breadth and diversity. Even the weather patterns vary across the district, with a rainy north and arid farmland in the south. It takes about nine hours to travel the length of the 1st, a journey that starts in Yolo County, across the river from Sacramento, moves through Napa Valley's famous wineries and the northern coast's majestic redwood forests, and ends at the Oregon border in Del Norte County, one of the district's three coastal counties. In 2006, more than 270,000 acres across the district were designated as new federal wilderness land.

In the north, Mendocino, Humboldt and Del Norte counties have been a battleground for environmentalists and the timber industry, although the isolated protests are less intense than they were two decades ago. East of Mendocino, Lake County has a mix of ranching, farming and tourism, centered on Clearlake. Its relatively low cost of living, compared with Bay Area cities, makes it a retirees' haven. South of Mendocino, the 1st takes in part of wine-producing Sonoma County and all of Napa County. More than 400 wineries are in the 1st, a large segment of the state's total. In addition to wine sales, winery tours also bring revenue. Napa is the second-most popular tourist destination in California after Disneyland.

Apart from wine, timber and tourism, the 1st's economy includes commercial fishing — in Crescent City, Eureka and Fort Bragg. And the University of California, Davis, in Yolo County is a major employer, although just one-quarter of district residents have a college degree.

Politically, the district has an independent streak, and Mendocino and Humboldt counties were Green Party presidential nominee Ralph Nader's two best counties nationwide in 2000. Del Norte is more conservative, and was the only county in the 1st to support George W. Bush in 2000 and 2004. The 1st as a whole, however, supported Democrat John Kerry in 2004, giving him 60 percent of its vote.

MAJOR INDUSTRY
Timber, agriculture, tourism

CITIES
Napa, 72,585; Davis, 60,308; Woodland (pt.), 39,455

NOTABLE
Davis is home to Toad Hollow, a miniature village for toads, and the Toad Tunnel, which allows toads to cross a nearby road overpass safely.

Rep. Wally Herger (R)

Elected 1986; 11th term

CAPITOL OFFICE
225-3076
www.house.gov/herger
2268 Rayburn 20515-0502; fax 226-8852

COMMITTEES
Ways & Means
Joint Taxation

RESIDENCE
Chico

BORN
May 20, 1945, Sutter County, Calif.

RELIGION
Mormon

FAMILY
Wife, Pamela Herger; nine children (one deceased)

EDUCATION
American River College, A.A. 1967; California State U., Sacramento, attended 1969

CAREER
Rancher; gas company executive

POLITICAL HIGHLIGHTS
Calif. Assembly, 1980-86

ELECTION RESULTS

2006 GENERAL		
Wally Herger (R)	134,911	64.2%
A.J. Sekhon (D)	68,234	32.5%
E. Kent Hinesley (LIBERT)	7,057	3.3%
2006 PRIMARY		
Wally Herger (R)		unopposed
2004 GENERAL		
Wally Herger (R)	182,119	66.9%
Mike Johnson (D)	90,310	33.2%

PREVIOUS WINNING PERCENTAGES
2002 (66%); 2000 (66%); 1998 (63%); 1996 (61%); 1994 (64%); 1992 (65%); 1990 (64%); 1988 (59%); 1986 (58%)

A strong supporter of free trade, Herger is the Republicans' standard-bearer on the issue as the senior minority member of the House Ways and Means Subcommittee on Trade. His job in the Democratically controlled 110th Congress (2007-08) is to shepherd the Bush administration's efforts to lower trade barriers and to try to preserve executive branch authority to negotiate trade deals with limited congressional interference.

After two decades in Congress, Herger has advanced in seniority on Ways and Means to become the second-most senior Republican, after Louisiana's Jim McCrery. His focus on trade is a good fit for his central California district, where agriculture dominates the economy. "Free and fair trade is incredibly important to my district and to the nation. We need to export," he said, noting that his district is the third-largest exporter of rice in the United States. It also produces half the world's supply of prunes.

Herger has been immersed in agriculture all of his life, having grown up on his family's 200-acre cattle ranch and plum farm in the northern California town of Rio Oso. His grandparents purchased the land after their arrival from Switzerland in 1907. Financially well-to-do, Herger made his money in ranching and propane gas, running Herger Gas, a propane company in Rio Oso, with his father.

One of his goals is working with Ways and Means Chairman Charles B. Rangel, a New York Democrat, and Sander M. Levin of Michigan, the Democratic chairman of the Trade Subcommittee, to continue the president's authority to negotiate free-trade deals with only an up-or-down vote in Congress. Newly empowered Democrats such as Rangel and Levin want to force U.S. trading partners to meet developed-world labor and environmental standards as a way of equalizing the playing field for U.S. exporters.

Herger is in his first term as the top-ranking Republican on the Trade Subcommittee. In the 109th Congress (2005-06), he was chairman of the Ways and Means subcommittee on welfare. Herger tried to impose tougher work requirements on recipients, continuing a trend that started in the mid-1990s when congressional conservatives struck an agreement with President Bill Clinton that ended 60 years of guaranteed federal assistance and created work requirements. But Herger was blocked by GOP moderates who thought his work rules went too far. Moderates also wanted to pair additional work hours with more federal money for child care.

It was not the first time that Herger was stymied in his welfare reform efforts. Conservatives had an opportunity to tinker with the program when the law came up for renewal in 2002. But Senate moderates objected to conservative proposals coming out of Herger's committee, and the GOP majority was unable to produce a bill.

A Mormon with a large family, Herger says he wants to remain active in the welfare debate and believes preserving traditional family structure is the surest way to reduce the welfare rolls. He takes particular interest in federal programs aimed at children, especially the more than 500,000 children in foster care.

In 2001, he was the chief sponsor of legislation, which became law, to increase funding for adoption, foster care and post-adoption services. In 2006, Herger's subcommittee produced a bill renewing several programs to combat child abuse and neglect. It gave the states $345 million annually, including $40 million that Herger insisted be set aside to pay for once-a-month visits by social workers.

Herger is a member of the Republican Study Committee, a group of the most conservative House Republicans, and GOP leaders can usually count on his support. Herger backed his party positions 99 percent of the time on contentious issues that polarized the two major political parties in the 109th Congress.

He is often among a bloc of Republicans active on Western land issues. In 2005, he was one of 41 House Republicans who threatened to vote against an important budget bill if it did not include a provision to open the Arctic National Wildlife Refuge to oil and gas exploration. The gambit ultimately failed in the face of opposition by Democrats and GOP moderates.

One of Herger's main missions is to prevent environmentalists from encroaching on the interests of loggers, ranchers and private property owners. He's taken a particular interest in what he calls the "government-caused disaster" in the Klamath River basin of northern California and southern Oregon, in which water needed by farmers for irrigation was withheld to protect two species of fish.

Another parochial issue of prime concern is Beale Air Force Base in northern California, where the Air Force in 2002 began basing the Global Hawk unmanned aerial reconnaissance plane. Beale also hosts the U-2 and SR-71 spy planes. In 2004, the Air Force announced that a California Air National Guard intelligence unit also would move to Beale.

While still young, Herger married and had two children, but the marriage broke up. The hippie counterculture was in full flower in the mid-1970s, but Herger's politics and lifestyle tended toward the traditional. He remarried months after meeting his present wife, Pamela, a nurse who, like him, was divorced, had a child and had converted to the Mormon faith. They both wanted a big family, and eventually, the couple had six children, one of whom died of a stroke at age 2.

In 1976, Herger was the Sutter County Republican Central Committee chairman. Four years later, he won election to the state Assembly on the wings of the Reagan revolution. He was in his third term when GOP Rep. Gene Chappie announced his retirement from the House in 1986.

Linking himself to President Ronald Reagan, Herger won the general election with 58 percent of the vote. He has had little electoral difficulty since. Redistricting in 2001 shifted Herger's district to the west — it looks much the same as it did during the 1980s — but left him with his two major population centers, Redding and Chico, and presented him with no re-election worries.

KEY VOTES

2006

No Stop broadband companies from favoring select Internet traffic
Yes Affirm U.S. commitment to war in Iraq and reject setting a withdrawal date for troops
Yes Repeal requirement for bilingual ballots at the polls
Yes Permit U.S. sale of civilian nuclear technology to India
Yes Build a 700-mile fence on the U.S.-Mexico border to curb illegal crossings
Yes Permit warrantless wiretaps of suspected terrorists

2005

? Intervene in the life-support case of Terri Schiavo
No Lift President Bush's restrictions on stem cell research funding
No Prohibit FBI access to library and bookstore records
Yes Approve free-trade pact with five Central American countries
Yes Pass energy policy overhaul favored by President Bush emphasizing domestic oil and gas production
Yes End mandatory preservation of habitat of endangered animal and plant species
No Ban torture of prisoners in U.S. custody

CQ VOTE STUDIES

	PARTY UNITY		PRESIDENTIAL SUPPORT	
	Support	Oppose	Support	Oppose
2006	100%	0%	95%	5%
2005	97%	3%	85%	15%
2004	99%	1%	88%	12%
2003	98%	2%	98%	2%
2002	98%	2%	82%	18%

INTEREST GROUPS

	AFL-CIO	ADA	CCUS	ACU
2006	14%	0%	93%	92%
2005	13%	0%	93%	96%
2004	7%	5%	100%	100%
2003	0%	5%	97%	84%
2002	11%	0%	100%	100%

CALIFORNIA 2

North central — Redding, Chico

The mountainous 2nd forms a north-south strip down the center of northern California, from the Oregon border through the Sacramento Valley. It includes the Sutter Buttes mountain range west of Yuba City.

Agriculture dominates the sprawling 2nd, the largest district in California at almost 22,000 square miles. Almost one-third of the district is rural, with rice farms and orchards that produce walnuts, almonds, olives and peaches. Sunsweet Growers, headquartered in Yuba City, operates the world's largest dried fruit packing plant.

The 2nd endures harsh weather, and wildfires cause at least one major fire every summer, especially in the northernmost counties of Shasta, Trinity and Siskiyou. Water also is a perennial issue: Two-thirds of the state's supply comes from the upper third of the state, which over the years has caused tensions between northern and southern California.

Much of the district's economic activity is centered in Shasta County, home to mining and forestry interests. Redding, the 2nd's largest city, is about 160 miles north of Sacramento in Shasta County and attracts tourists who visit nearby Shasta Lake, the state's largest man-made reservoir. In Butte County, health care is a major employer in Chico.

The 2nd is largely white and Republican, although relatively poor, with the median income here less than $34,000, sixth-lowest in the state. The district has seen a steady influx of Sikhs in the Yuba City area, as well as an infusion of Democratic-leaning Hispanic farm workers. Still, George W. Bush took 62 percent of the district's presidential vote in 2004, one of his best showings in California, and GOP Gov. Arnold Schwarzenegger won 70 percent of the vote here in 2006.

MAJOR INDUSTRY
Agriculture, timber, tourism, health care

MILITARY BASES
Beale Air Force Base, 4,290 military, 1,267 civilian (2006)

CITIES
Redding, 80,865; Chico, 59,954; Yuba City, 36,758

NOTABLE
Redding's Sundial Bridge at Turtle Bay, a pedestrian bridge that spans the Sacramento River, functions as a working sundial but only gives the accurate time one day a year — on the summer solstice in June.

Rep. Dan Lungren (R)

CAPITOL OFFICE
225-5716
www.house.gov/lungren
2448 Rayburn 20515-0503; fax 226-1298

COMMITTEES
Budget
Homeland Security
House Administration
Judiciary
Joint Library

RESIDENCE
Gold River

BORN
Sept. 22, 1946, Long Beach, Calif.

RELIGION
Roman Catholic

FAMILY
Wife, Bobbi Lungren; three children

EDUCATION
U. of Notre Dame, B.A. 1968 (English); Georgetown U., J.D. 1971

CAREER
Lawyer

POLITICAL HIGHLIGHTS
Republican nominee for U.S. House, 1976; U.S. House, 1979-89; Calif. attorney general, 1991-99; Republican nominee for governor, 1998

ELECTION RESULTS

2006 GENERAL		
Dan Lungren (R)	135,709	59.5%
Bill Durston (D)	86,318	37.8%
Douglas Arthur Tuma (LIBERT)	3,772	1.7%
Michael Roskey (PFP)	2,370	1.0%
2006 PRIMARY		
Dan Lungren (R)	unopposed	
2004 GENERAL		
Dan Lungren (R)	177,738	61.9%
Gabe Castillo (D)	100,025	34.8%
Douglas Arthur Tuma (LIBERT)	9,310	3.2%

PREVIOUS WINNING PERCENTAGES
1986 (73%); 1984 (73%); 1982 (69%); 1980 (72%); 1978 (54%)

Elected 2004; 7th term
Also served 1979-89

No typical beginner, Lungren has shown a knack for leaving his imprint on legislation dealing with the national security issues that he says propelled his return to the House in 2004. The self-described "Reagan conservative" was in Congress for a decade — from 1979 to 1989. "It's kind of like riding a bike," Lungren says. "You get back into the rhythm of things."

Political observers once said Lungren was clinging to a political career whose time had passed, but a lot of that grousing has been put to rest by his work since. In the 109th Congress (2005-06), while Republicans still controlled the House, he was the chief sponsor, with California Democrat Jane Harman, of a massive port security bill that was signed into law in 2006. The legislation authorized billions of dollars for new security mandates. He also sponsored a bill, approved in subcommittee, to tighten chemical plant security. While it never made it into law, his push and a comparable one in the Senate created pressure for appropriators to add chemical facility security provisions in a fiscal 2007 spending bill.

In the 110th Congress (2007-08), Lungren is the top-ranking Republican on the Homeland Security panel's Subcommittee on Transportation Security.

Immigration is another important issue for him. In his first House stint, Lungren pushed for sanctions against employers who hire illegal immigrants, but he also supported limited amnesty programs. In 2005, he cosponsored a border security bill to add thousands of enforcement agents at the borders, a provision later incorporated into the House immigration bill.

Lungren's previous experience in a Democratically controlled Congress proved formative. Though he sometimes responds to his Democratic colleagues with smirks and condescending remarks, suggesting that the fiery partisan of old is not entirely gone, he is just as likely to give them a friendly ribbing and collaborate across the aisle. "I think we have a better vision for America than does the other side. But there are ways to combine our legislative approaches," he says.

A former state attorney general, Lungren returned to a familiar seat on the Judiciary panel, where his previous service now makes him seventh in seniority among 17 Republicans. While Lungren generally backs President Bush on national security matters, he angered the administration with amendments to the renewal of the 2001 anti-terrorism law known as the Patriot Act, imposing 10-year expiration dates on roving wiretaps and on expanded police powers to obtain business records. Lungren said the expiration dates would make the administration more likely to cooperate with congressional oversight. In another instance, Lungren cooperated with Democrats by narrowing the scope of a bill sanctioning the National Security Agency's controversial warrantless wiretapping program.

Lungren has tried without great success to get into the GOP leadership. In 2006, he ran for chairman of the Republican Conference, the third-ranking job in the minority, and placed last of four candidates. Also that year, he joined forces with Republican John E. Sweeney of New York in calling for every Republican leader except then Speaker J. Dennis Hastert to stand for re-election. That proposal was rejected by the caucus, 85-107. He and other Republicans thought leaders should be held accountable after a series of ethics scandals caused substantial political damage to the GOP.

Lungren complained publicly that his party had succumbed to the same temptations of power for which they had long criticized Democrats. But he was unwilling to go along with a major change in ethics rules — a ban on privately financed travel for lawmakers, a practice that had led to members of Congress taking lavish trips paid for by lobbyists. Lungren cosponsored an amendment with California Democrat George Miller allowing lawmakers to keep accepting free, privately paid travel. Lungren, who had taken a number of such trips to locales that included Hawaii, said the trips allow lawmakers to get to know each other better.

Lungren has dabbled in issues close to the hearts of social conservatives. He introduced one of several House resolutions calling for a constitutional amendment to ban same-sex marriage. GOP leaders considered bringing the resolution to the floor in 2006, but a vote never materialized. He also voted against a bill permitting federal research using embryonic stem cells, which uses surplus embryos harvested at in vitro fertilization clinics. Lungren argued that an embryo constitutes a life that should not be destroyed.

The second of seven children, Lungren grew up around politics. He remembers walking precincts for Republican candidates at age 6, when his father was President Richard Nixon's personal physician. While Lungren originally wanted to follow his dad into medicine, he found out early in college that he wasn't academically cut out for medical school. "I went to Notre Dame and God sent me a strong message that year called organic chemistry," Lungren says.

He ran for Congress unsuccessfully in 1976 before winning a Long Beach-area congressional district on his second try two years later. Although he came in with a confrontational freshman class of conservative Republicans, he says some of the perceived abrasiveness was misinterpreted. He projected his voice on the House floor, he says, unaware that the sensitive microphones made him seem louder and harsher than he had intended.

He left Congress in 1989 to take a job as California's treasurer, but he was accused of being overly partisan and could not win state Senate confirmation. He bounced back, winning election to become California attorney general. He had that post from 1991 to 1999.

In 1998, he made a failed bid for the governorship, suffering a crushing 20 percentage point defeat that had most political observers writing him off for good. After that race, he stayed in the Sacramento area and was able to jump into the 2004 House race when three-term Republican incumbent Doug Ose announced his retirement. Lungren faced two well-financed candidates in the primary, including Mary Ose, the sister of the incumbent, but he won in a close race. He cruised to a general election victory in the GOP-dominated district. In the 2006 race against Democrat Bill Durston, a physician and Vietnam veteran, he garnered 59 percent of the vote.

KEY VOTES

2006

No Stop broadband companies from favoring select Internet traffic

Yes Affirm U.S. commitment to war in Iraq and reject setting a withdrawal date for troops

Yes Repeal requirement for bilingual ballots at the polls

Yes Permit U.S. sale of civilian nuclear technology to India

Yes Build a 700-mile fence on the U.S.-Mexico border to curb illegal crossings

Yes Permit warrantless wiretaps of suspected terrorists

2005

? Intervene in the life-support case of Terri Schiavo

No Lift President Bush's restrictions on stem cell research funding

No Prohibit FBI access to library and bookstore records

Yes Approve free-trade pact with five Central American countries

Yes Pass energy policy overhaul favored by President Bush emphasizing domestic oil and gas production

Yes End mandatory preservation of habitat of endangered animal and plant species

No Ban torture of prisoners in U.S. custody

CQ VOTE STUDIES

	PARTY UNITY		PRESIDENTIAL SUPPORT	
	Support	Oppose	Support	Oppose
2006	94%	6%	93%	7%
2005	97%	3%	91%	9%

INTEREST GROUPS

	AFL-CIO	ADA	CCUS	ACU
2006	21%	10%	80%	84%
2005	13%	0%	93%	92%

CALIFORNIA 3
Central – Sacramento suburbs

The 3rd stretches west from Alpine County on the Nevada border, bends around Sacramento and reaches Solano County, near Napa. The district is predominately white, white-collar and Republican. It experiences periodic flooding from the Sacramento and American rivers, making water and flood control important local issues.

About 85 percent of the 3rd's population comes from a chunk of Sacramento County that includes the affluent Sacramento suburbs of Citrus Heights and Rio Linda. Many residents here have moved to the 3rd in order to work in state government or to escape the state's more crowded urban areas while still working in the technology industries. Folsom, to Sacramento's northeast, is home to an Intel campus that hosts the company's information technology division, although the campus has seen recent layoffs in the wake of company restructuring.

Wineries and agriculture dominate the 3rd's economy. Amador County, 45 minutes southeast of Sacramento, is home to several large wineries. Elsewhere, grape, almond and prune production dominate, except in forestry-heavy Alpine County, where mountains and skiing are prevalent. McClellan Air Force Base, which closed in 2001, has been converted into a business park (shared with the 5th) that has sought to attract technology businesses, although roughly half of the available square footage in the park remains unleased.

While Sacramento County in the district's western arm is the politically competitive heart of the district, its surrounding areas are largely rural and Republican. Overall, the district gave George W. Bush 58 percent of its presidential vote in 2004 and GOP Gov. Arnold Schwarzenegger 69 percent of its gubernatorial vote in 2006.

MAJOR INDUSTRY

Agriculture, timber, technology

CITIES

Citrus Heights, 85,071; Arden-Arcade (unincorporated) (pt.), 53,597; Folsom, 51,884; Carmichael, 49,742

NOTABLE

Folsom State Prison, depicted in the Johnny Cash song "Folsom Prison Blues" and home to a state license plate factory, is the state's second-oldest prison; Folsom Powerhouse, finished in 1895 and now a state park, was the nation's first long-distance hydroelectric power plant.

Rep. John T. Doolittle (R)

CAPITOL OFFICE
225-2511
doolittle.house.gov
2410 Rayburn 20515-0504; fax 225-5444

COMMITTEES
No committee assignments

RESIDENCE
Roseville

BORN
Oct. 30, 1950, Glendale, Calif.

RELIGION
Mormon

FAMILY
Wife, Julie Doolittle; two children

EDUCATION
U. of California, Santa Cruz, B.A. 1972 (history); U. of the Pacific, J.D. 1978

CAREER
Lawyer; state legislative aide

POLITICAL HIGHLIGHTS
Calif. Senate, 1980-90

ELECTION RESULTS

2006 GENERAL		
John T. Doolittle (R)	135,818	49.0%
Charlie Brown (D)	126,999	45.9%
Dan Warren (LIBERT)	14,076	5.1%
2006 PRIMARY		
John T. Doolittle (R)	63,731	67.2%
J.M. "Mike" Holmes (R)	31,162	32.8%
2004 GENERAL		
John T. Doolittle (R)	221,926	65.4%
David L. Winters (D)	117,443	34.6%

PREVIOUS WINNING PERCENTAGES
2002 (65%); 2000 (63%); 1998 (63%); 1996 (60%); 1994 (61%); 1992 (50%); 1990 (51%)

Elected 1990; 9th term

Doolittle's once-formidable influence in the House diminished in the 110th Congress (2007-08), and not just because his party is now in the minority. The former member of the Republican leadership has come under scrutiny for his ties to lobbyist Jack Abramoff, who pleaded guilty to charges that included bribing public officials. Doolittle also drew unwanted attention for paying his wife, Julie, hundreds of thousands of dollars in fundraising commissions from his campaign coffers and political action committee funds.

As secretary of the Republican Conference, Doolittle was the sixth-ranking member of the House GOP leadership and a protégé of the powerful majority leader, Tom DeLay of Texas, at the start of the 109th Congress (2005-06). But the Justice Department investigation into Abramoff's lavish gifts to lawmakers in exchange for favors for his clients cast suspicion on anyone associated with the lobbyist. In addition, DeLay was forced to relinquish his seat in mid-2006 after his indictment in Texas over alleged campaign finance improprieties.

Doolittle found himself in the spotlight because Abramoff and Indian tribes he represented had given the congressman campaign contributions. Abramoff also paid more than $66,000 in consulting fees to Doolittle's wife.

Furthermore, Doolittle, who had hired his wife as a campaign fundraiser, drew heat for paying her in commissions rather than the usual flat fee. Julie Doolittle claimed a 15 percent cut of the money she raised — nearly $224,000 for the 2006 election alone. The Doolittles said the arrangement was intended to ensure she wasn't paid for work she didn't do.

A Sacramento Bee editorial concluded that Doolittle "has used his power for personal profit and by doing so placed himself among those who have deeply corrupted national politics." Doolittle blames the press and the Democrats for his troubles. "I've suffered a media assault of the kind I've never seen anyone go through," he says. "The press operated like an arm of the Democrat Party."

Despite his difficulties, Doolittle was re-elected by a narrow margin. After the election, he started holding more events with constituents, saying he was in "listening mode."

And in a significant shift, he began to voice skepticism about the Iraq War. In September 2005, Doolittle had sponsored a resolution that linked the Sept. 11 terrorist attacks on the United States with the subsequent invasion of Iraq, saying American forces are "shielding the nation from further terrorist attacks" by battling "terrorist forces" overseas.

Now he says the White House focused too much on Iraq's alleged possession of weapons of mass destruction as a public rationale for the war. He also acknowledges "miscalculations" by war planners and says the war has been "far more difficult" than expected. In early 2007, Doolittle expressed reservations about President Bush's plan to send more than 21,000 additional combat troops to Iraq, calling it a "major gamble" that he hopes is successful.

Although his party no longer controls Congress, Doolittle has vowed to continue to press the traditional conservative agenda of smaller government, fiscal restraint, lower taxes and less regulation. One area in which Doolittle maintains there should be less regulation is campaign financing, arguing that restrictions on money in politics are a violation of the First Amendment right to free speech. He suggests that the focus be on disclosure and that the voters be the judge. He tried, unsuccessfully, to stop the

2002 overhaul of campaign finance law that banned unlimited corporate and labor donations to political parties.

Doolittle has pushed for a diminished federal role in people's lives. In an effort to hold his party's leadership to a firm conservative line on economic and social policy issues, Doolittle in 1997 co-founded the Conservative Action Team, now known as the Republican Study Committee.

On a matter of local concern, Doolittle long has supported completing the huge Auburn Dam in his district, which has been at the center of a bruising battle over federal water development policy. A Bureau of Reclamation report released in January 2007 contended that costs for the dam could approach $10 billion, twice the previous estimates, and that the project could yield less water for drinking and irrigation than previously believed and could damage nearby recreation areas. But Doolittle said that in the wake of Hurricane Katrina, the project was worth its cost since it would provide flood protection.

Raised in a conservative household in Southern California, Doolittle was 13 when he was inspired by Barry Goldwater, the 1964 GOP presidential nominee. But his family had moved to the northern part of the state by then, and Doolittle remembers being perhaps "the only Goldwater supporter in my freshman class" at Cupertino High School.

For college, Doolittle chose the University of California at Santa Cruz, where he was one of only 15 Young Republicans. He says the experience taught him to take independent stances and think for himself.

After a two-year stint as a Mormon missionary in Argentina, Doolittle went to law school, then headed to Sacramento in search of a job with the state legislature. He worked for state Sen. H.L. Richardson, who was not only an influential conservative lawmaker but also a mentor and adviser when Doolittle launched his own bid for the state Senate in 1980. Richardson persuaded Doolittle to run against an entrenched Democratic incumbent. With California favorite son Ronald Reagan heading the GOP ticket that year, Doolittle won a narrow upset. He quickly made himself known in Sacramento, particularly as a dogged proponent of expanded testing for AIDS.

In 1990, Doolittle inherited what had been a safe district from retiring Republican Rep. Norman D. Shumway, who also had positioned himself on the GOP's right flank. Doolittle narrowly beat Democrat Patricia Malberg, a former junior college teacher, that year and again in 1992. He won subsequent races handily until 2006 when his connection to Abramoff became an issue. Nevertheless, in the GOP stronghold, Doolittle eked out a victory with 49 percent of the vote over retired Air Force Lt. Col. Charlie Brown.

KEY VOTES

2006

No Stop broadband companies from favoring select Internet traffic
Yes Affirm U.S. commitment to war in Iraq and reject setting a withdrawal date for troops
Yes Repeal requirement for bilingual ballots at the polls
Yes Permit U.S. sale of civilian nuclear technology to India
Yes Build a 700-mile fence on the U.S.-Mexico border to curb illegal crossings
Yes Permit warrantless wiretaps of suspected terrorists

2005

Yes Intervene in the life-support case of Terri Schiavo
No Lift President Bush's restrictions on stem cell research funding
No Prohibit FBI access to library and bookstore records
Yes Approve free-trade pact with five Central American countries
Yes Pass energy policy overhaul favored by President Bush emphasizing domestic oil and gas production
Yes End mandatory preservation of habitat of endangered animal and plant species
No Ban torture of prisoners in U.S. custody

CQ VOTE STUDIES

	PARTY UNITY		PRESIDENTIAL SUPPORT	
	Support	Oppose	Support	Oppose
2006	98%	2%	90%	10%
2005	97%	3%	86%	14%
2004	96%	4%	85%	15%
2003	98%	2%	94%	6%
2002	98%	2%	84%	16%

INTEREST GROUPS

	AFL-CIO	ADA	CCUS	ACU
2006	14%	5%	93%	84%
2005	13%	0%	85%	92%
2004	13%	0%	90%	92%
2003	7%	5%	93%	74%
2002	13%	5%	84%	91%

CALIFORNIA 4
Northeast – Roseville, Rocklin

Laden with rivers, lakes and the mountain ranges that give their names to Sierra and Nevada counties, the largely rural 4th starts at the Oregon border in the state's northeast corner, then drops down along the Nevada border to Lake Tahoe in the east and near Sacramento in the district's southwest corner.

The mining counties of Placer and El Dorado lend the 4th its Gold Rush feel, although technology drives one of the fastest growth rates in the state. Placer, El Dorado and Nevada counties are home to facilities of big technology names like Hewlett-Packard and Oracle, and are home to more than three-fourths of the district's population. These areas continue to draw those who want to leave California's crowded cities but still work in technology fields.

Timber and agriculture also play important roles in the district's economy, and the 4th is a popular vacation destination. Numerous ski resorts dot the Sierra Nevada mountain range, and Lake Tahoe in eastern El Dorado and Placer counties offers skiing, hiking, golf and shopping. Here, visitors may choose from resorts, condominiums and cabins. Placer, with cheap property and abundant natural beauty, is rapidly becoming a draw for retirees. Despite Roseville's relatively small size, the Placer County city has a strong retail sector, and often ranks among California's top 10 cities (top 3 percent) in retail sales.

The 4th has California's highest percentage of white residents (84 percent) and is safe Republican territory. Republicans hold a 17 percentage point edge in party registration, and George W. Bush took 61 percent of the vote here in the 2004 presidential election. The district gave GOP Gov. Arnold Schwarzenegger 72 percent of its vote in 2006.

MAJOR INDUSTRY
Technology, agriculture, mining, tourism

MILITARY BASES
Sierra Army Depot, 1 military, 640 civilian (2007)

CITIES
Roseville, 79,921; Rocklin, 36,330; Orangevale (unincorporated), 26,705

NOTABLE
According to the U.S. Geological Survey, Lake Tahoe is the second-deepest lake in the United States and the tenth-deepest lake in the world.

Rep. Doris Matsui (D)

CAPITOL OFFICE
225-7163
matsui.house.gov
222 Cannon 20515-0505; fax 225-0566

COMMITTEES
Rules
Transportation & Infrastructure

RESIDENCE
Sacramento

BORN
Sept. 25, 1944, Poston, Ariz.

RELIGION
Methodist

FAMILY
Widowed; one child

EDUCATION
U. of California, Berkeley, B.A. 1966 (psychology)

CAREER
Lobbyist; White House aide; homemaker; state computer systems analyst

POLITICAL HIGHLIGHTS
No previous office

ELECTION RESULTS

2006 GENERAL		
Doris Matsui (D)	105,676	70.8%
Claire Yan (R)	35,106	23.5%
Jeff Kravitz (GREEN)	6,466	4.3%
John C. Reiger (PFP)	2,018	1.4%
2006 PRIMARY		
Doris Matsui (D)		unopposed
2005 SPECIAL		
Doris Matsui (D)	56,175	68.1%
Julie Padilla (D)	7,158	8.7%
John Thomas Flynn (R)	6,559	8.0%
Serge A. Chernay (R)	3,742	4.5%
Michael O'Brien (R)	2,591	3.1%
Shane Singh (R)	1,753	2.1%
Bruce Robert Stevens (R)	1,124	1.4%
Pat Driscoll (GREEN)	976	1.2%
Leonard Padilla (I)	916	1.1%

Elected March 2005; 1st full term

Matsui was hardly a novice when she came to Congress to replace her husband, Robert T. Matsui, who died just days before he was to be sworn in for a 14th term. She had spent decades in Washington as a congressional spouse, a White House aide and a lobbyist. Yet her first committee assignment on the exclusive Rules Committee was an eye-opener.

Matsui says watching Republican lawmakers approve procedures for floor debate strictly along party lines convinced her that Congress needs to make its work more transparent and collegial. It also heightened her appreciation for her late husband's skills as a legislator. "I appreciated that, but I didn't really know until I was in Congress myself," Matsui says.

Taking her husband's seat was an unexpected turn for Matsui. Though he had been diagnosed with a rare bone disease, he had been re-elected in November 2004. A few weeks later, the Matsuis brought their 18-month-old granddaughter, Anna, to the House floor to prepare the toddler for attending the congressman's swearing-in. The next day, he was admitted to the hospital with pneumonia. He died just eight days later, on New Year's Day 2005.

As he lay in the hospital with an increasingly grim prognosis, Matsui says he broached the possibility of her running for his seat. "He told me that I'd be fabulous," she told The Sacramento Bee. " 'But I don't want you to do it for me,' he said. 'Do it because you feel you can make a contribution to Sacramento.' "

Some eight weeks later, she emerged victorious in a special election from a crowded field of a dozen candidates, winning 68 percent of the vote. The night of her victory, her campaign staff took some campaign buttons and an early edition of The Sacramento Bee declaring her victory to the cemetery and placed them on Robert Matsui's grave, officially giving the news. "It was very sweet," Matsui told The Bee.

Her husband's stature in Congress eased her transition. Minority Leader Nancy Pelosi of California, who considered Matsui's husband a close ally, gave her a slot on the exclusive Rules panel, a post rarely given to freshmen. The committee sets the rules for amendments and debate on major bills, and Matsui is often called upon to argue the Democrats' case on the floor. She has done so with increasing confidence as she has settled into the role.

In May 2006, she got a waiver from party leaders to take a second assignment, on the Science Committee. Her priority there was getting full funding for the National Children's Study, a 20-year study of children from birth to age 21, which Matsui says could lead to a better understanding of illnesses including obesity, autism and diabetes.

As part of her husband's legacy, Matsui promotes legislation to preserve the World War II internment camps as historic sites. But she broke with him on one of his signature issues: free trade. Matsui voted against the Central American Free Trade Agreement in 2005, saying it lacked adequate labor and environmental protections. She said her husband had similar reservations before his death.

Matsui and her husband came from similar backgrounds, both having spent part of their childhoods in internment camps that housed detained Japanese-Americans during World War II. She was born in the Poston internment camp in Arizona, but was too young to remember the experience; her family moved out when she was three months old. Her parents tried to shield her from their painful memories. "They never lost hope in the idea that this country is the best country in the world," she said.

Matsui drew on that experience in 2006 while speaking out against legislation allowing the Bush administration to aggressively interrogate and prosecute terrorism suspects. "From my family's perspective, I know something about what can happen to the rights of Americans when the executive branch overreaches in a time of war," she said.

She has opposed the war in Iraq and President Bush's 2007 plan to increase troop levels. But she did not want to vote against funding the increase for fear of endangering troops, and she was not dissuaded by anti-war protesters staging a "peace-in" in her district office during business hours for months.

Matsui met her husband at a college dance, while she attended the University of California at Berkeley and he studied law at the University of California at Hastings. They married in 1966. While her husband pursued a political career, Matsui raised their son and assisted Sacramento-area non-profit organizations. The family moved to Washington when he was elected to Congress in 1978.

Her first full-time political job was with President Bill Clinton, who in 1992 rewarded her for her early support of his campaign with a spot on his eight-member presidential transition committee. She became a deputy assistant to the president and the highest-ranking Asian-American official in the White House. During that time, a New York Times story suggested Matsui had conspired with controversial fundraiser John Huang to improperly solicit campaign contributions from Asian-Americans. She was ultimately cleared of wrongdoing by government investigators, and says the experience left her feeling "very protective of my integrity and my reputation."

After leaving the White House in 1998, she went to work as a lobbyist and government-relations director at the law firm of Collier Shannon Scott in Washington, representing communications and high-technology companies, a job she held until running for Congress.

Like most new members, she has devoted herself to local issues. She wants to restore the region's eligibility for homeland security funding. As a member of the Transportation and Infrastructure Committee, she wants to rebuild deteriorating levees in Sacramento, having learned from the Hurricane Katrina disaster in Gulf Coast states. "She has learned (frankly with a passion that her husband, a tax policy wonk, never had) and then some," the Bee said in endorsing her re-election in 2006. She won easily against a 25-year-old GOP opponent, Claire Yan, a first-year law student.

KEY VOTES

2006

- Yes Stop broadband companies from favoring select Internet traffic
- No Affirm U.S. commitment to war in Iraq and reject setting a withdrawal date for troops
- No Repeal requirement for bilingual ballots at the polls
- No Permit U.S. sale of civilian nuclear technology to India
- No Build a 700-mile fence on the U.S.-Mexico border to curb illegal crossings
- No Permit warrantless wiretaps of suspected terrorists

2005

- No Intervene in the life-support case of Terri Schiavo
- Yes Lift President Bush's restrictions on stem cell research funding
- Yes Prohibit FBI access to library and bookstore records
- No Approve free-trade pact with five Central American countries
- No Pass energy policy overhaul favored by President Bush emphasizing domestic oil and gas production
- No End mandatory preservation of habitat of endangered animal and plant species
- Yes Ban torture of prisoners in U.S. custody

CQ VOTE STUDIES

	PARTY UNITY		PRESIDENTIAL SUPPORT	
	Support	Oppose	Support	Oppose
2006	97%	3%	25%	75%
2005	98%	2%	14%	86%

INTEREST GROUPS

	AFL-CIO	ADA	CCUS	ACU
2006	93%	95%	33%	4%
2005	93%	100%	46%	0%

CALIFORNIA 5
Sacramento

Two things tend to dominate the 5th — state politics and triple-digit temperatures. Located in California's hot Central Valley, the 5th is home to the state capital, Sacramento, and reaches east and south to include a few upper-middle-class suburbs such as Arden-Arcade and Elk Grove (both of which are shared with the 3rd District).

Sacramento first attracted fortune hunters as the starting point of the Gold Rush of 1849. State government now provides the lion's share of employment here, and the 5th has the nation's sixth-highest proportion of government workers at nearly 25 percent. Outside of government, the city's largest employer is the University of California, Davis, medical center, and other major employers include large technology companies such as Intel and Hewlett-Packard. The nearby Port of Sacramento (located in the 1st), which handles approximately 1.3 million tons of cargo each year, is another positive influence on the district's stable economy.

The city has worked to lure tourists to the Old Sacramento neighborhood on the waterfront, home to museums, restaurants, shopping and an annual jazz festival. In addition, Sacramento is home to a California State University campus, and the presence of cheaper land has kept local housing prices below those of San Francisco and elsewhere in the area. The city also attracts visitors to the annual California State Fair.

Although whites form a solid plurality of the overall district's residents, the 5th is racially diverse, with Hispanics making up 21 percent of residents and Asians and blacks each accounting for at least 14 percent of the total population. Democrats hold a 2-1 advantage in voter registration, and John Kerry won 61 percent of the 5th's vote in the 2004 presidential election. Republican Gov. Arnold Schwarzenegger captured slightly less than half of the 5th's vote in the 2006 gubernatorial race — 6 percentage points less than his statewide total of 56 percent.

MAJOR INDUSTRY

State government, technology, health care

CITIES

Sacramento, 407,018; Arden-Arcade (unincorporated) (pt.), 42,428; Parkway-South Sacramento (unincorporated), 36,468

NOTABLE

Founded in 1885, the Crocker Art Museum in Sacramento is the oldest public art museum west of the Mississippi River.

Rep. Lynn Woolsey (D)

CAPITOL OFFICE
225-5161
woolsey.house.gov
2263 Rayburn 20515-0506; fax 225-5163

COMMITTEES
Education & Labor
(Workforce Protections - chairwoman)
Foreign Affairs
Science & Technology

RESIDENCE
Petaluma

BORN
Nov. 3, 1937, Seattle, Wash.

RELIGION
Presbyterian

FAMILY
Divorced; four children

EDUCATION
U. of Washington, attended 1955-57 (business); U. of San Francisco, B.S. 1980 (human resources & organizational behavior)

CAREER
Employment placement company owner; human resources manager

POLITICAL HIGHLIGHTS
Petaluma City Council, 1985-93

ELECTION RESULTS

2006 GENERAL		
Lynn Woolsey (D)	173,190	70.2%
Todd Hooper (R)	64,405	26.1%
Richard W. Friesen (LIBERT)	9,028	3.7%
2006 PRIMARY		
Lynn Woolsey (D)	72,058	66.2%
Joe Nation (D)	36,845	33.8%
2004 GENERAL		
Lynn Woolsey (D)	226,423	72.7%
Paul L. Erickson (R)	85,244	27.4%

PREVIOUS WINNING PERCENTAGES
2002 (67%); 2000 (64%); 1998 (68%); 1996 (62%); 1994 (58%); 1992 (65%)

Elected 1992; 8th term

Woolsey revels in her unambiguous liberalism and has become one of the House's staunchest opponents of the war in Iraq. But her far-left views leave her vulnerable to primary challenges at election time, even in a San Francisco Bay-area congressional district that is home to many affluent former hippies. She continually has to fend off suggestions that her politics are too extreme to make her effective in Washington.

Woolsey (WOOL-zee) drew Democratic opponents in three straight elections, and though she handily prevailed each time, her percentage of the primary vote declined in 2006 to 66 percent from 84 percent in 2004 and 81 percent in 2002. The area's largest newspaper, The San Francisco Chronicle, endorsed her competitor, California State Assemblyman Joe Nation, who made an issue of her anti-war activities, highlighting her invitation to activist Cindy Sheehan to the State of the Union address in 2006.

Sheehan wore a T-shirt bearing an anti-war message and was arrested by Capitol police. Woolsey was unbowed. "Since when is free speech conditioned on whether you agree with the president?" she said. "Stifling the truth will not blind Americans to the immorality of sending young Americans to die in an unnecessary war."

In March 2006, Woolsey introduced a bill to shift $60 billion out of the Pentagon's budget into health care programs for low-income families, school construction and deficit reduction. When the Bush administration in 2003 asked for $87 billion in additional spending for Iraq and Afghanistan, Woolsey demanded a detailed accounting. In the 110th Congress (2007-08), as more Democrats have joined the Out of Iraq Caucus to which she belongs, her views on the war are more mainstream.

To her admirers, Woolsey represents a rare voice of conscience in behalf of racial minorities and women, and for liberal ideas that get little attention anymore, such as her support for a single-payer national health care system. To her detractors, she is an ineffective backbencher, influential neither in shaping national policy nor in bringing federal money home.

One of her most famous moments in Congress was in 1999, when she was booted out of a Senate hearing room by conservative Sen. Jesse Helms of North Carolina for attempting to protest Helms' failure to support a global treaty condemning discrimination against women. During the House debate in 2003 on President Bush's bill to create a Medicare prescription drug benefit for the elderly — a bill Woolsey considered inadequate — she led 84 Democratic lawmakers in publicly renouncing their membership in the AARP to protest the organization's support of the bill.

A member of the Education and Labor Committee, she has twice introduced "Go Girl" legislation to encourage girls to study science and math, but the measure has gone nowhere. She has continually fought Bush administration efforts to allow faith-based groups to get federal money for their anti-poverty and education programs, which she says would lead to discriminatory hiring based on religion and sexual orientation. The mother of a gay man, she condemns what she calls a "shameful discriminatory policy toward gays" by Republicans. She is now chairwoman of the Workforce Protections Subcommittee.

Woolsey has a personal perspective on the federal safety net, as she was once a single parent on welfare. A product of the 1950s, when few women worked outside the home, Woolsey grew up in Seattle, dropped out of the University of Washington to get married and then moved with her stockbroker husband to the suburbs of San Francisco. But the marriage fractured, abruptly ending what Woolsey calls her "Leave It to Beaver" phase of life. At age 29, she was divorced with three children ages 5 and younger. She sold her house, returned a new station wagon and took a job as a secretary, supplementing her income for three years with Aid to Families with Dependent Children, the national welfare program. "I know firsthand what a difference it makes," says Woolsey, who opposed the 1996 welfare overhaul, which set limits on benefits.

She went back to school and at age 42 graduated from the University of San Francisco when her kids were teenagers. When a group of engineers left the company she worked for to start a telecommunications company, they took Woolsey with them. She rose through the ranks to become the human resources manager of Harris Digital Telephone Systems. Later, she started her own human resources consulting company.

Woolsey made the transition into politics in 1981, getting involved in a local effort to control fast-paced development in Petaluma. "After that I tried to get appointed to the planning commission. I couldn't, so I ran for city council," she says. But she traces her interest in politics to an earlier time, when she won a campaign for vice president of her junior high girls' club. "I'm a good team player but I usually ended up being the chair or president," Woolsey says.

Her family, she says, was Republican — her mother and her stepfather, a veterinarian, ran a small-animal clinic. (Her biological father was not involved in her life after her parents divorced.) But Woolsey as a young adult was greatly influenced by the election of President John F. Kennedy and drawn to the Democratic Party.

She was elected to the House in 1992, the "Year of the Woman," in which a record number of women came to Congress for the first time. She won the nomination in a field of eight other candidates for an open seat vacated by Democrat Barbara Boxer, who was elected to the Senate. Woolsey faced a tough general election against Republican Bill Filante, a liberal Republican assemblyman, until Filante fell ill with cancer and curtailed his campaign.

Though she typically has easy re-elections post-primary, her campaign in 2004 suffered from news reports that she had tried to persuade a Marin County judge to reduce the sentence for an aide's son, convicted of rape. She later apologized, saying, "Given my outspoken support for both women's rights and victims' rights, my constituents and my community are right to be shocked by my action." She won with 73 percent of the vote that year and was easily re-elected in 2006.

KEY VOTES

2006

Yes Stop broadband companies from favoring select Internet traffic
No Affirm U.S. commitment to war in Iraq and reject setting a withdrawal date for troops
No Repeal requirement for bilingual ballots at the polls
No Permit U.S. sale of civilian nuclear technology to India
No Build a 700-mile fence on the U.S.-Mexico border to curb illegal crossings
No Permit warrantless wiretaps of suspected terrorists

2005

? Intervene in the life-support case of Terri Schiavo
Yes Lift President Bush's restrictions on stem cell research funding
Yes Prohibit FBI access to library and bookstore records
No Approve free-trade pact with five Central American countries
No Pass energy policy overhaul favored by President Bush emphasizing domestic oil and gas production
No End mandatory preservation of habitat of endangered animal and plant species
Yes Ban torture of prisoners in U.S. custody

CQ VOTE STUDIES

	PARTY UNITY		PRESIDENTIAL SUPPORT	
	Support	Oppose	Support	Oppose
2006	98%	2%	7%	93%
2005	99%	1%	13%	87%
2004	98%	2%	15%	85%
2003	98%	2%	14%	86%
2002	99%	1%	25%	75%

INTEREST GROUPS

	AFL-CIO	ADA	CCUS	ACU
2006	93%	100%	20%	4%
2005	93%	100%	33%	8%
2004	93%	95%	0%	8%
2003	100%	100%	12%	13%
2002	100%	95%	35%	0%

CALIFORNIA 6

Northern Bay Area — Sonoma and Marin counties

Travel north across the Golden Gate Bridge and the scenery changes from the cityscape of San Francisco to the Pacific coastline and inland hills that make up the 6th. This area north of the city is home to upper-middle-class suburbanites who commute to San Francisco and the "Telecom Valley," which extends north from San Rafael to Santa Rosa.

The 6th includes all of Marin County and most of Sonoma County. While migration from San Francisco created a tight housing market in the area — median home prices in Marin are approaching one million dollars — home values in Sonoma are falling. Prices for Sausalito houseboats on Richardson Bay also range up to one million dollars.

Marin is home to San Quentin State Prison — the oldest correctional facility in California — as well as San Rafael and popular getaway spots such as Point Reyes National Seashore, Sausalito and Muir Woods. To the north, Sonoma County is home to a California State University campus and Santa Rosa, the largest city in the district. Wine and dairy ranching dominate the economy; Sonoma County (shared with the 1st) has more than 200 wineries. Technology companies have made inroads here, although many of the video game developers who were based out of San Rafael — including George Lucas-owned LucasArts — have moved to San Francisco in recent years.

The 6th is solid Democratic territory, although conservative currents exist here. The district's affluent residents, despite their wealth, tend to have progressive views. Democrats outnumber Republicans 2-to-1 in voter registration, and Democrat John Kerry received 70 percent of the 6th's vote in the 2004 presidential election.

MAJOR INDUSTRY
Telecommunications, agriculture, tourism

CITIES
Santa Rosa, 147,595; San Rafael, 56,063; Petaluma, 54,548

NOTABLE
The Charles M. Schulz Museum in Santa Rosa celebrates the work of the Peanuts creator; The sport of organized arm-wrestling was founded in Petaluma in 1952; The Marin County Civic Center was Frank Lloyd Wright's last architectural work.

Rep. George Miller (D)

CAPITOL OFFICE
225-2095
george.miller@mail.house.gov
www.house.gov/georgemiller
2205 Rayburn 20515-0507; fax 225-5609

COMMITTEES
Education & Labor - chairman
Natural Resources

RESIDENCE
Martinez

BORN
May 17, 1945, Richmond, Calif.

RELIGION
Roman Catholic

FAMILY
Wife, Cynthia Miller; two children

EDUCATION
San Francisco State U., B.A. 1968;
U. of California, Davis, J.D. 1972

CAREER
Lawyer; state legislative aide

POLITICAL HIGHLIGHTS
Democratic nominee for Calif. Senate, 1969

ELECTION RESULTS

2006 GENERAL		
George Miller (D)	118,000	84.0%
Camden McConnell (LIBERT)	22,486	16.0%
2006 PRIMARY		
George Miller (D)		unopposed
2004 GENERAL		
George Miller (D)	166,831	76.1%
Charles R. Hargrave (R)	52,446	23.9%

PREVIOUS WINNING PERCENTAGES
2002 (71%); 2000 (76%); 1998 (77%); 1996 (72%); 1994 (70%); 1992 (70%); 1990 (61%); 1988 (68%); 1986 (67%); 1984 (66%); 1982 (67%); 1980 (63%); 1978 (63%); 1976 (75%); 1974 (56%)

Elected 1974; 17th term

Miller is an anchor for the liberal wing of his party, a firebrand shaped by the era when Democrats dominated the House. Through thick and thin — and there has been mostly the latter in recent years — Miller has pushed for more funding for public education, stronger worker rights, and tougher consumer safety and environmental regulation.

He is a close ally of Speaker Nancy Pelosi, who represents a district just across the San Francisco Bay from his. Miller was one of her earliest backers, and Pelosi puts a premium on personal loyalty. He encouraged her to run for whip in 2001, which put her on a track to becoming the Democrats' top-ranking leader in the House. He didn't much care for the inclusive leadership style of her predecessor, Richard A. Gephardt of Missouri, saying it resulted in a weak party message.

Pelosi, whose chief of staff used to work for Miller, made Miller co-chairman of the Democratic Steering and Policy Committee, where he has headed the policy side of the operation since 2003. He also was put in charge of shepherding major pieces of the new Democratic majority's agenda through the House, including an increase in the federal minimum wage and a proposal to cut student loan interest rates in half.

As chairman of the Education and Labor Committee, Miller is a central player in a major rewrite of higher education policy that was to get under way in 2007. Miller plans to use the opportunity to advance Democratic ideas for making college more affordable for the working and middle classes.

And Miller is determined to make the landmark 2001 No Child Left Behind Act more workable. He helped write the law, but Miller and the Democrats contend it has been underfunded; the act calls for $20 billion annually to raise test scores in elementary and secondary school programs, but actual federal appropriations during the GOP years were about $12 billion.

In the Labor panel, Miller has taken on companies that give executives lavish retirement packages while trimming or dumping workers' pension plans. In the 109th Congress (2005-06), he tried to strengthen benefit protections for employees as part of an overhaul of private pension regulations. In the end, Miller opposed the final version of the bill, saying it put pension plans in even more jeopardy.

He also helped write an ethics proposal championed by House and Senate Democrats in 2006 in a bid to outdo Republicans in the wake of several influence-peddling scandals involving lobbyists and lawmakers. The proposal became the basis for a host of rules changes put together by Democrats for the 110th Congress (2007-08).

A founder of the Progressive Caucus who came to the House in the "Watergate baby" Class of 1974, Miller is a fierce partisan known for railing against the Republicans on the floor. But he can be a scold to Democrats as well when he thinks they are drifting too far to the ideological center. "There just can't be two Republican Parties," he says.

Miller wants to do more oversight of the executive branch, a function he believes languished during the period of Republican control of both Congress and the White House. After a series of deadly mine disasters in early 2006, Miller set up a Democratic forum to hear from victims' families and other witnesses after Republicans failed to hold hearings. GOP leaders ultimately were shamed into drafting mine safety legislation, which Miller opposed for providing too few new protections for miners.

Miller was one of four authors of the landmark education overhaul of 2001, a bipartisan undertaking that was President Bush's signature domestic initiative. In early meetings on the legislation, Bush took to calling him "Big George," an acknowledgement of his importance to House passage.

Before taking the senior slot on Education in 2001, Miller was the top Democrat on the Resources Committee and he stays involved in environmental issues. The Sierra Club dubbed him a "green giant," and his voting record gets praise from the League of Conservation Voters each year.

Miller had chaired the committee for four years before Republicans won control of Congress in the 1994 elections. For the next six years, he battled his similarly blustery and sharp-tongued GOP successor, Don Young of Alaska, his ideological opposite. Miller not only fought Young's attempts to revise major environmental laws, he blocked some of the chairman's non-controversial proposals, just to show he would not be easily shut out of the process.

As time passed, Miller sometimes found it more productive to work with his nemesis. He joined Young to push the Conservation and Reinvestment Act, which guaranteed that oil royalties would be spent for land conservation. When Young stepped down as chairman in 2000, Miller called him "a very, very caring individual" and "a real pain in the rear."

Miller's occasionally hot temper earned him a place in congressional lore in 1995 when he and Virginia Democrat James P. Moran got into a shoving match with two Republican lawmakers over a bill to bar the use of funds for deploying troops in Bosnia without prior congressional approval.

He is the third George Miller in his family to earn a living in government. His grandfather, George Miller Sr., was the assistant civil engineer in Richmond. His father, George Jr., was a state senator for 20 years. Miller, whose full name is George Miller III, was a law student in 1969 when his father died, and he won the Democratic nomination to succeed him in the state Senate. But he lost the general election.

Miller went to work as a legislative aide to state Sen. George Moscone, the Democratic floor leader and one-time mayor of San Francisco. He was 29 when he was elected to succeed Democratic Rep. Jerome Waldie, who decided to run for governor. Miller won his seat, in part, by exploiting the Watergate scandal that sank Richard Nixon's presidency, which was fresh in voters' minds. He regularly disclosed his campaign donors and political expenses and chided his opponent for not doing the same. He took 56 percent of the vote and has won re-election easily ever since — making him one of just 11 lawmakers who have served more than half their life in Congress.

KEY VOTES

2006

Yes Stop broadband companies from favoring select Internet traffic

No Affirm U.S. commitment to war in Iraq and reject setting a withdrawal date for troops

No Repeal requirement for bilingual ballots at the polls

No Permit U.S. sale of civilian nuclear technology to India

No Build a 700-mile fence on the U.S.-Mexico border to curb illegal crossings

No Permit warrantless wiretaps of suspected terrorists

2005

? Intervene in the life-support case of Terri Schiavo

Yes Lift President Bush's restrictions on stem cell research funding

Yes Prohibit FBI access to library and bookstore records

No Approve free-trade pact with five Central American countries

No Pass energy policy overhaul favored by President Bush emphasizing domestic oil and gas production

No End mandatory preservation of habitat of endangered animal and plant species

Yes Ban torture of prisoners in U.S. custody

CQ VOTE STUDIES

	PARTY UNITY		PRESIDENTIAL SUPPORT	
	Support	Oppose	Support	Oppose
2006	98%	2%	13%	87%
2005	99%	1%	16%	84%
2004	98%	2%	21%	79%
2003	99%	1%	11%	89%
2002	97%	3%	22%	78%

INTEREST GROUPS

	AFL-CIO	ADA	CCUS	ACU
2006	92%	90%	29%	4%
2005	93%	100%	35%	0%
2004	93%	100%	21%	4%
2003	100%	100%	18%	12%
2002	100%	100%	30%	4%

CALIFORNIA 7

Northeastern Bay Area — Vallejo, Richmond

Situated along the San Pablo Bay and home to marshes and wetlands where the Sacramento and San Joaquin deltas feed into the bay, the 7th combines industrial and suburban areas of north Contra Costa County with the western end of more rural Solano County.

In Contra Costa County, the district takes in residential Concord (shared with the 10th) and the industrial cities of Richmond and Martinez along San Pablo Bay, home to oil, steel and biotechnology interests. Richmond was home to four of the Kaiser Shipyards — one of the largest World War II shipbuilding operations — but some of those shipyards have been redeveloped over the past several decades for residential or retail purposes. Chevron is now a major employer, with a refinery and facility in Richmond. Martinez, the Contra Costa County seat, relies in part on the petroleum processing industry.

Health care also is important to the 7th's economy. The medical system implemented during World War II at the Kaiser Shipyards was the foundation for the modern Kaiser Permanente health organization. A Kaiser Permanente medical center in Vallejo, the district's largest city, is the city's largest employer, and the government also employs many workers here. Pittsburg, known for its steel industry, was home to the first nail mill in the Western United States, and the city's USS-POSCO steel mill employs approximately 1,000 workers. Vallejo and other Solano County communities are home to farm-support services.

The 7th, safe Democratic territory, gave John Kerry 67 percent of its 2004 presidential vote. In 2006, Democratic gubernatorial candidate Phil Angelides won a majority here while taking only 39 percent statewide.

MAJOR INDUSTRY
Petrochemicals, steel, biotechnology, agriculture, health care

MILITARY BASES
Naval Weapons Station Seal Beach, Detachment Concord, 152 military, 530 civilian (2006)

CITIES
Vallejo, 116,760; Richmond, 99,216; Vacaville, 88,625; Pittsburg, 56,769

NOTABLE
The Rosie the Riveter World War II Home Front National Historical Park in Richmond commemorates the contributions of women who held industrial jobs in support of the war effort.

Rep. Nancy Pelosi (D)

CAPITOL OFFICE
225-4965
sf.nancy@mail.house.gov
www.house.gov/pelosi
235 Cannon 20515-0508; fax 225-8259

COMMITTEES
Speaker of the House - no committee assignments

RESIDENCE
San Francisco

BORN
March 26, 1940, Baltimore, Md.

RELIGION
Roman Catholic

FAMILY
Husband, Paul Pelosi; five children

EDUCATION
Trinity College (D.C.), A.B. 1962

CAREER
Public relations consultant; senatorial campaign committee finance chairwoman; homemaker

POLITICAL HIGHLIGHTS
Calif. Democratic Party chairwoman, 1981-83

ELECTION RESULTS

2006 GENERAL		
Nancy Pelosi (D)	148,435	80.4%
Mike DeNunzio (R)	19,800	10.7%
Krissy Keefer (GREEN)	13,653	7.4%
Philip Zimt Berg (LIBERT)	2,751	1.5%
2006 PRIMARY		
Nancy Pelosi (D)		unopposed
2004 GENERAL		
Nancy Pelosi (D)	224,017	83.0%
Jennifer Depalma (R)	31,074	11.5%
Leilani Dowell (PF)	9,527	3.5%
Terry Baum - write-in	5,446	2.0%

PREVIOUS WINNING PERCENTAGES
2002 (80%); 2000 (84%); 1998 (86%); 1996 (84%); 1994 (82%); 1992 (82%); 1990 (77%); 1988 (76%); 1987 Special Runoff Election (63%)

Elected June 1987; 10th full term

With her elevation to Speaker of the House, Pelosi made history as the highest-ranking woman ever in U.S. government. Her barrier-shattering rise was the most remarkable personal story of a dramatic midterm election that gave Democrats control of both the House and the Senate in the 110th Congress (2007-08). The 52nd Speaker of the House is a former stay-at-home mother who waited to run for office until her children reached their teens. Now she is second in the constitutional line of presidential succession and arguably the most powerful woman in American politics.

Republicans have a tough opponent in Pelosi (pa-LO-see) despite her ready smile and studied graciousness. Petite and impeccably turned out in an Armani business suit, she has the style of Jackie Kennedy and the iron will of Margaret Thatcher. She demands discipline from the ranks, and punishes those who cross her. When a member tries to dodge her on a tough vote with, "I'm sorry, but I can't be with you this time," Pelosi's response is, "Then we can't be with you." During her triumphant march to deliver a Democratic majority to the House in 2006, she told the Los Angeles Times, "I'm fighting a battle here. I'm not getting my hair done."

She is indeed the "San Francisco liberal" her GOP detractors say she is. But she's a bleeding heart with a ward-boss mentality, inherited from her machine-Democrat father, a former Baltimore mayor who maintained an old-fashioned system of favors and patronage jobs. In the run-up to the 2006 elections, Pelosi worked tirelessly, flying to several cities a week and ultimately raising $50 million for fellow Democrats.

Pelosi demands absolute loyalty in return, and that trait can lead her astray. Just four days before Democrats elected their leaders for the 110th Congress, she intervened in the contest for majority leader by publicly endorsing her longtime ally John P. Murtha of Pennsylvania. She tried to pressure members into choosing him over Maryland's Steny H. Hoyer, the minority whip who had earned the respect of many Democrats. Irked at her heavy-handedness, Democrats chose Hoyer by a vote of 149 to 86.

After more than a dozen years in the minority, Pelosi lost no time resetting the House agenda. She successfully pushed through a "first 100 hours" set of six bills focused on long-held party goals, such as increasing the minimum wage and letting the government use its purchasing power to negotiate with manufacturers for lower Medicare drug prices. She held Democrats together on nearly all of the bills, losing the greatest number — 16 of them — on expanding embryonic stem cell research, which many conservatives oppose. Some bills also won a significant number of GOP votes.

She also left the door open to compromise with Republicans on some issues, such as a guest worker program for illegal immigrants. And she shut down talk of possible political retaliation against the Republican president, saying, "Impeachment is off the table." But Pelosi moved aggressively against the White House on the war in Iraq, threatening to cut the flow of money to the war effort unless President Bush began troop withdrawals.

As minority leader for the four years preceding the election, Pelosi consolidated power by showering rewards on allies and opening up opportunities for junior members. She pressed several senior Democrats to part with coveted committee assignments so that she could give them to junior lawmakers, moderates, Hispanics and African-Americans. When she became Speaker, she quietly left in place a Republican policy of six-year term limits for committee chairmen, a move sure to enhance her power at the expense of the chairmen. Several of them objected to no avail.

Throughout her career, Pelosi has demonstrated the political skills learned from her father, Thomas D'Alesandro Jr., a New Deal-era House member who went on to be Baltimore mayor. In the working-class enclave near downtown called Little Italy, the D'Alesandro row house on Albemarle Street was a refuge for people who needed food, some wood for heat or a job on the city payroll.

With her five brothers, "Little Nancy" took turns at the desk near the door, keeping a "favor file" to be consulted at re-election time. Copies of the daily Congressional Record were stacked beneath her bed. Pelosi's mother, Annunciata, balanced caring for the kids with political organizing, a model her daughter would adopt.

After graduating from Trinity College, an all-women Catholic school in Washington, D.C., Pelosi worked briefly in 1963 as a receptionist for U.S. Sen. Daniel B. Brewster of Maryland. But she left the job after a few months to marry college sweetheart Paul Pelosi. The couple moved to his native San Francisco, where he became a successful investment banker and she a stay-at-home mother of five, albeit a wealthy one with live-in help.

Pelosi juggled caring for her family with political activism, developing into a crack Democratic fundraiser by keeping lists, memorizing names and faces, and meticulously hand-writing thank-you notes to donors. Her five kids served food at political events and canvassed door-to-door as soon as they could walk. In the 1980s, Pelosi rose to chair the California Democratic Party. But she waited until she was 47, and her youngest was in high school, to run for office. When San Francisco's main House seat came open with the death of Rep. Sala Burton, Pelosi used her insider's contacts to nail the nomination, which was tantamount to election in one of the nation's most Democratic districts. She has won re-election easily since.

Pelosi took a big step upward in 2001, when she was elected party whip over Hoyer, 118-95. Some Democrats trace her cool relationship with Hoyer to that race. When Richard A. Gephardt of Missouri stepped aside as minority leader after the party's losses in the 2002 election, Pelosi was ready to make a play for the top job.

Martin Frost, a Texan with more seniority who chaired the Democratic Caucus, ran against her, promising leadership from the center. But Democrats embraced Pelosi's more confrontational politics, which made no apologies for liberal ideology. Ultimately, Frost bowed out of the race, and Pelosi was chosen, 177 to 29, over Harold E. Ford Jr. of Tennessee, a late entrant. She is the first woman elected to the top leadership post of either party.

KEY VOTES

2006

Yes Stop broadband companies from favoring select Internet traffic

No Affirm U.S. commitment to war in Iraq and reject setting a withdrawal date for troops

No Repeal requirement for bilingual ballots at the polls

Yes Permit U.S. sale of civilian nuclear technology to India

No Build a 700-mile fence on the U.S.-Mexico border to curb illegal crossings

No Permit warrantless wiretaps of suspected terrorists

2005

? Intervene in the life-support case of Terri Schiavo

Yes Lift President Bush's restrictions on stem cell research funding

Yes Prohibit FBI access to library and bookstore records

No Approve free-trade pact with five Central American countries

No Pass energy policy overhaul favored by President Bush emphasizing domestic oil and gas production

No End mandatory preservation of habitat of endangered animal and plant species

Yes Ban torture of prisoners in U.S. custody

CQ VOTE STUDIES

	PARTY UNITY		PRESIDENTIAL SUPPORT	
	Support	Oppose	Support	Oppose
2006	98%	2%	25%	75%
2005	99%	1%	16%	84%
2004	97%	3%	21%	79%
2003	98%	2%	20%	80%
2002	99%	1%	23%	77%

INTEREST GROUPS

	AFL-CIO	ADA	CCUS	ACU
2006	93%	95%	40%	8%
2005	93%	95%	36%	0%
2004	93%	100%	35%	8%
2003	87%	100%	34%	12%
2002	100%	100%	37%	0%

CALIFORNIA 8

Most of San Francisco

San Francisco is famous for its landmarks, food and diverse collection of neighborhoods, from the Italian and Hispanic centers of North Beach and the Mission District to spots such as Chinatown, hippie haven Haight-Ashbury and the gay mecca of Castro.

More than 80 percent of the city's residents live in the 8th, which takes in the city's north and east and at 35 square miles is the state's smallest district. The 8th's sizable Asian population (29 percent) is the third-largest in the country. San Francisco's Chinatown neighborhood is one of the largest Chinese communities in North America.

The city boasts many tourist destinations. Alcatraz prison — used as a federal maximum-security facility from 1934 to 1963 and where Al Capone, George "Machine Gun" Kelly and Robert "Birdman" Stroud were once jailed — receives more than one million visitors annually. Fisherman's Wharf, on the city's northern waterfront, the Golden Gate Bridge, which connects San Francisco to Marin County, and the Bay Bridge, which traverses the neck of the bay over Treasure Island to Oakland, are other popular attractions. The city's part of the Golden Gate National Recreation Area hosts a Lucasfilm facility that opened in 2005 on the site of the former Letterman Army Medical Center at the Presidio.

The 8th also is home to San Francisco's financial district along Montgomery Street, known as the "Wall Street of the West." The Federal Reserve Bank of San Francisco is there, as is the Transamerica Pyramid and the headquarters of brokerage firm Charles Schwab and financial company Wells Fargo. The city also has a biomedical industry led by the University of California at San Francisco, the city's second-largest employer after local government.

The 8th is safely Democratic, and Phil Angelides took 64 percent of the 2006 gubernatorial vote here, despite winning only 39 percent statewide.

MAJOR INDUSTRY

Tourism, financial services, health care

CITIES

San Francisco (pt.), 639,088

NOTABLE

The city's famous cable cars were developed by Andrew Smith Hallidie after he witnessed an accident involving a horse-drawn streetcar.

Rep. Barbara Lee (D)

CAPITOL OFFICE
225-2661
barbara.lee@mail.house.gov
www.house.gov/lee
2444 Rayburn 20515-0509; fax 225-9817

COMMITTEES
Appropriations

RESIDENCE
Oakland

BORN
July 16, 1946, El Paso, Texas

RELIGION
Baptist

FAMILY
Husband, Michael Millben; two children

EDUCATION
Mills College, B.A. 1973 (psychology); U. of California, Berkeley, M.S.W. 1975

CAREER
Congressional aide

POLITICAL HIGHLIGHTS
Calif. Assembly, 1990-96; Calif. Senate, 1996-98

ELECTION RESULTS

2006 GENERAL		
Barbara Lee (D)	167,245	86.3%
John "J.D." denDulk (R)	20,786	10.7%
James Eyer (LIBERT)	5,655	2.9%
2006 PRIMARY		
Barbara Lee (D)		unopposed
2004 GENERAL		
Barbara Lee (D)	215,630	84.6%
Claudia Bermudez (R)	31,278	12.3%
James Eyer (LIBERT)	8,131	3.2%

PREVIOUS WINNING PERCENTAGES
2002 (81%); 2000 (85%); 1998 (83%); 1998 Special Election (67%)

Elected April 1998; 5th full term

Lee has a strong disdain for social injustice, shaped, she says, by her early-life recollections of discrimination. Her public high school in Southern California had never chosen a black cheerleader, so Lee set about becoming the first. She enlisted the help of the National Association for the Advancement of Colored People to put pressure on the selection committee before her tryout. Once she was selected, a riot broke out at the school. "I will never be relegated to a minority status in terms of my behavior or what I do," she says. "If it's not right, I will try to right it."

Lee represents the cities of Oakland and Berkeley, two of the most liberal communities in the state. More than one-third of Oakland's residents are black. Her voting record reflects her district, and in 2006, she voted 99 percent of the time in agreement with a majority of her party. In the 110th Congress (2007-08), she serves as co-chairwoman of the Progressive Caucus, the most liberal faction of House Democrats, and is second in command at the Congressional Black Caucus.

She is an insistent voice for the economic, health care and education needs of her constituency. Some of the needs are urgent, she argues, such as recognizing the devastating impact of AIDS on the African-American community, both nationally and internationally.

A leader in the global war on AIDS, Lee helped write many of the provisions of an international AIDS measure that President Bush signed into law in 2003. But she has been less happy with some of the restrictions placed on international AIDS funding, specifically a requirement that one-third of all AIDS prevention money be set aside for abstinence-until-marriage programs. Lee objected that Republicans added the requirement after a hard-fought compromise had been worked out. "Both sides made major concessions with the understanding that those dying of AIDS would trump our political differences," Lee said.

Lee chairs the Black Caucus task force on HIV/AIDS, and she has sponsored several bills that address AIDS issues, including one that would coordinate treatment, care and housing for people living with AIDS who were displaced by Hurricane Katrina. She also wants the government to provide grants to states so that contraception as well as abstinence education can be incorporated in the family-life curriculum.

She has been a strong voice against the Sudanese government for its support of the violence carried out in the Darfur region by the Janjaweed militias. In May 2006, Lee was one of seven members of the Black Caucus arrested at the Sudanese Embassy for disorderly conduct in protest of the government's policies. She joined with fellow Californians Nancy Pelosi, then minority leader, and Tom Lantos, then the top-ranking Democrat on International Relations, on legislation to bar foreign companies from receiving U.S. government contracts if they invested in Sudan. "This bill is designed to wash the blood off our federal contracts," she said.

Lee is a hero of the American peace movement because of her lone "no" vote in Congress on Sept. 14, 2001, against a resolution authorizing Bush to use "all necessary and appropriate force" to retaliate against the terrorist attacks that had occurred three days earlier. Lee said she agonized over her vote and did not make up her mind until she attended a memorial service at the Washington National Cathedral earlier in the day. She decided on her course after hearing an invocation by the Rev. Nathan D. Baxter, the cathedral dean, who prayed that "despite our grief we may not become the evil we deplore."

Lee's vote brought in sacks of hate mail and death threats and at one point she required police protection. But she has never second-guessed herself. "If I had to do it again, I would do it again," she said in a 2006 interview. "For the life of me, I can't understand blind faith in a president, Democrat or Republican."

Her office became a rallying point in 2002 for those opposed to the war in Iraq. She said a pre-emptive invasion to remove Saddam Hussein from power would set "a dangerous precedent." Lee was also one of the original sponsors of a bill to establish a Cabinet-level Department of Peace. Since her appointment to the Appropriations Committee in 2007, she is in a better position to try to pare the defense budget as well as funding for the Iraq War.

Lee's politics grew out of her early memories of discrimination. Her grandmother told her that her mother initially was refused treatment at an El Paso hospital when in labor with her, and then was left unattended for so long that Lee had to be delivered using forceps. She said for many years she had a mark on her forehead from the forceps. Lee spent her early years in El Paso, where the school system was segregated. Her parents sent her and her sister to a Catholic school where Lee said they were often the only black students. In 1960, the family moved to California.

Lee had never even registered to vote when, while studying at Oakland's Mills College, she was faced with a course requirement to work for a political campaign during the presidential election year of 1972. She signed on with Democratic Rep. Shirley Chisholm of New York, the nation's first notable black candidate for president. Lee rose quickly through the ranks, eventually running Chisholm's northern California campaign and, as she proudly recalled a quarter-century later, receiving an "A" in the course.

While earning a master's degree in social work, Lee helped start a community health center in Berkeley before going to work for Democrat Ronald V. Dellums, her predecessor in the House, in 1975. She worked for him in both California and Washington before running for the state legislature, where she served six years in the Assembly and 17 months in the Senate. When Dellums revealed his plans to resign from the House in early 1998, he endorsed Lee to succeed him and she easily won the special election.

Lee's vote in 2001 against the war did nothing to weaken her political standing. She remains enormously popular at home, winning each election since then with more than 80 percent of the vote.

KEY VOTES

2006

- Yes Stop broadband companies from favoring select Internet traffic
- No Affirm U.S. commitment to war in Iraq and reject setting a withdrawal date for troops
- No Repeal requirement for bilingual ballots at the polls
- No Permit U.S. sale of civilian nuclear technology to India
- No Build a 700-mile fence on the U.S.-Mexico border to curb illegal crossings
- No Permit warrantless wiretaps of suspected terrorists

2005

- ? Intervene in the life-support case of Terri Schiavo
- Yes Lift President Bush's restrictions on stem cell research funding
- Yes Prohibit FBI access to library and bookstore records
- No Approve free-trade pact with five Central American countries
- No Pass energy policy overhaul favored by President Bush emphasizing domestic oil and gas production
- \- End mandatory preservation of habitat of endangered animal and plant species
- Yes Ban torture of prisoners in U.S. custody

CQ VOTE STUDIES

	PARTY UNITY		PRESIDENTIAL SUPPORT	
	Support	Oppose	Support	Oppose
2006	99%	1%	7%	93%
2005	98%	2%	13%	87%
2004	99%	1%	15%	85%
2003	99%	1%	11%	89%
2002	99%	1%	25%	75%

INTEREST GROUPS

	AFL-CIO	ADA	CCUS	ACU
2006	93%	100%	20%	4%
2005	93%	100%	31%	4%
2004	100%	95%	5%	0%
2003	100%	100%	17%	12%
2002	100%	90%	30%	0%

CALIFORNIA 9

Northwest Alameda County — Oakland, Berkeley

Across the bay from San Francisco, the 9th is anchored by Oakland and Berkeley, two racially diverse, liberal communities.

More than 60 percent of district residents live in Oakland, which is more than one-third black. Neighborhoods in the city's eastern hills tend to be wealthy and less diverse. Oakland's unemployment rate is slightly above the national average, and crime is a major concern here, but urban revitalization efforts and the development of downtown residential areas have encouraged new residents to move into the area and have bolstered the local economy.

Just north of Oakland, Berkeley is home to the flagship campus of the University of California system and looks out over the bay from the Berkeley Hills. The rest of the district includes smaller communities such as Albany, a suburb at the north end of the district; Piedmont, a residential "suburb in the city" in Oakland's hills; and unincorporated sections of Alameda County southeast of Oakland — Ashland, Castro Valley, Cherryland and Fairview.

The 9th also includes the fast-growing bayside city of Emeryville, which is home to biotechnology firms and high-technology companies, including animation studio Pixar, educational technology developer LeapFrog and Chiron's blood testing laboratories, where the hepatitis C virus was first identified.

With a core constituency in left-leaning Oakland and Berkeley, the 9th is a Democratic stronghold where Republicans account for only 10 percent of registered voters. John Kerry had his best showing in the state here, capturing 86 percent of the 2004 presidential vote. In his 2006 re-election, Gov. Arnold Schwarzenegger took less than one-fourth of the 9th's vote — his lowest percentage statewide.

MAJOR INDUSTRY

Biotechnology, shipping

CITIES

Oakland, 399,484; Berkeley, 102,743; Castro Valley (unincorporated) (pt.), 57,224

NOTABLE

Wham-O Toys, based in Emeryville, marketed many famous toys, including the Frisbee, Hula Hoop, Hacky Sack and Slip 'N Slide; The synthetic element Berkelium was created at UC-Berkeley.

Rep. Ellen O. Tauscher (D)

CAPITOL OFFICE
225-1880
www.house.gov/tauscher
2459 Rayburn 20515-0510; fax 225-5914

COMMITTEES
Armed Services
(Strategic Forces - chairwoman)
Transportation & Infrastructure

RESIDENCE
Alamo

BORN
Nov. 15, 1951, Newark, N.J.

RELIGION
Roman Catholic

FAMILY
Divorced; one child

EDUCATION
Seton Hall U., B.A. 1974 (early childhood education)

CAREER
Child care screening executive; marketing executive; investment banker

POLITICAL HIGHLIGHTS
No previous office

ELECTION RESULTS

2006 GENERAL		
Ellen O. Tauscher (D)	130,859	66.4%
Darcy Linn (R)	66,069	33.5%
2006 PRIMARY		
Ellen O. Tauscher (D)		unopposed
2004 GENERAL		
Ellen O. Tauscher (D)	182,750	65.7%
Jeff Ketelson (R)	95,349	34.3%

PREVIOUS WINNING PERCENTAGES
2002 (76%); 2000 (53%); 1998 (53%); 1996 (49%)

Elected 1996; 6th term

Raised in New Jersey, Tauscher remembers watching the twin towers of the World Trade Center going up across the Hudson River during her high school and college years. Later, she went in and out of those buildings "three or four thousand times" as a stockbroker and investment banker. Now, as a member of the Armed Services Committee, she helps shape national security policy in a political landscape that was altered on Sept. 11, 2001, every bit as dramatically as the skyline she once admired.

Tauscher (TAU — rhymes with "now" — sher) initially sought the committee assignment to watch out for the interests of California's Lawrence Livermore and Sandia national laboratories in her district, which both conduct defense-related research. But she also has used the opportunity to develop an expertise on military strength and preparedness, the war on terror and the spread of nuclear, biological and chemical weapons.

In 2003, she began to fight for an increase in the size of the armed forces, arguing more troops were needed to sustain the U.S. war effort in Iraq and equip the military for a long battle against terrorism. In the 109th Congress (2005-06), she offered a bill to increase the size of the Army by 20,000 troops, the Marines by 12,000, and the Air Force and Navy by 2,000 each.

Yet Tauscher has sharply criticized President Bush's conduct of the Iraq War. "This is about faulty analysis and a failed strategy," she said in 2004. "We've never had enough troops on the ground since the fall of Saddam Hussein's government to deal with the insurgency because we didn't expect one." She urged conferees on the 2005 defense authorization bill to retain a Senate provision requiring quarterly reports to Congress on progress in Iraq and declaring 2006 a "year of transition" toward a withdrawal of U.S. troops.

As chairwoman of the Armed Services Strategic Forces Subcommittee, she told new Secretary of Defense Robert M. Gates in early 2007 that Bush's plan to increase troop levels was "absolutely ridiculous after the colossal and catastrophic failures of your predecessor." But the statement did nothing to mollify liberal activists who bashed her as a traitor to her party, with some accusing her of helping Bush send more troops to Iraq.

A priority for her panel for the 110th Congress (2007-08) is to assess the need for a new generation of nuclear weapons. She has led efforts to stop the Energy Department from developing more, particularly when the United States is trying to persuade other nations to abandon their nuclear programs. Though she lost a close vote in 2004 on an amendment to kill a controversial "bunker buster" tactical nuclear weapon sought by the White House, appropriators subsequently refused to fund the program. Her main parochial interest is Travis Air Force Base, and keeping alive the production of the C-17 transport, which the administration wants to stop building.

A centrist once described by the San Francisco Chronicle as "about the closest thing the Bay Area has to a Republican," Tauscher has been siding with her party's majority — and against Bush — more often the past few years. In 2001, she supported Bush on 40 percent of the roll call votes on which he had staked out a position. By 2005, her presidential support score had dropped to 18 percent. It crept to 25 percent in 2006. She says her early career was good training for legislating. "I understand the art of the deal. Compromise is not a dirty word."

Tauscher serves on the Transportation and Infrastructure Committee, and has aggressively pursued funds to ease congestion in her district, which has some of the country's worst traffic. "It's hard to wrap your heart around a highway," she says wryly. But transportation is the No. 1 concern in a district where people spend a lot of time commuting, she says.

Early in 2001, Tauscher was elected vice chairwoman of the Democratic Leadership Council, an organization of centrist Democrats. Later that year, she was chosen vice chairwoman of a Democratic task force on homeland security, adding to a résumé that led Washingtonian magazine to call her one of the 100 most powerful women in the capital.

Since 2005, she has chaired the House's New Democrat Coalition of moderate, pro-business Democrats. But on most social policy issues, Tauscher is a traditional Democrat. She favors abortion rights, robust environmental protection, federal arts funding and an active federal role in education.

Tauscher came to the House with a wealth of experience in business. The eldest daughter of an Irish-Catholic grocery store manager in New Jersey, she was the first person in her family to attend college, majoring in early childhood education. After graduating from Seton Hall University in 1974, she found it difficult to land a teaching job that earned her enough money to pay off her student loans. She looked across the river at Wall Street and asked herself, "Why not?" By age 25, she was one of the first women to hold a seat on the New York Stock Exchange. During a 14-year career, she was a vice president of the investment banking firm Bear Stearns and a vice president of the American Stock Exchange.

Tauscher moved to northern California in 1989 after marrying ComputerLand executive Bill Tauscher. They had a daughter in 1991 and subsequently divorced. In 1992, unhappy with the child care options available, Tauscher founded a business that screened prospective child care workers. She also published a child care guidebook.

She first got active in politics by helping Sen. Dianne Feinstein in her 1992 and 1994 campaigns, eventually becoming the California Democrat's finance chairwoman. Tauscher considered seeking a House seat in 1994, but her daughter was still a toddler then and so she held off for two years.

In 1996, incumbent Republican Bill Baker looked vulnerable, having alienated some of the 10th District's liberal-leaning voters with a hard line against abortion and in favor of gun owners' rights. With $1.7 million of her own money, Tauscher outspent Baker almost 2-to-1. She won by less than 2 percentage points. In the past three elections, she has enjoyed margins of at least 30 percentage points.

KEY VOTES

2006

Yes Stop broadband companies from favoring select Internet traffic
No Affirm U.S. commitment to war in Iraq and reject setting a withdrawal date for troops
No Repeal requirement for bilingual ballots at the polls
No Permit U.S. sale of civilian nuclear technology to India
No Build a 700-mile fence on the U.S.-Mexico border to curb illegal crossings
No Permit warrantless wiretaps of suspected terrorists

2005

? Intervene in the life-support case of Terri Schiavo
Yes Lift President Bush's restrictions on stem cell research funding
Yes Prohibit FBI access to library and bookstore records
No Approve free-trade pact with five Central American countries
No Pass energy policy overhaul favored by President Bush emphasizing domestic oil and gas production
No End mandatory preservation of habitat of endangered animal and plant species
Yes Ban torture of prisoners in U.S. custody

CQ VOTE STUDIES

	PARTY UNITY		PRESIDENTIAL SUPPORT	
	Support	Oppose	Support	Oppose
2006	93%	7%	25%	75%
2005	95%	5%	18%	82%
2004	93%	7%	35%	65%
2003	92%	8%	20%	80%
2002	86%	14%	35%	65%

INTEREST GROUPS

	AFL-CIO	ADA	CCUS	ACU
2006	86%	95%	40%	12%
2005	93%	90%	52%	8%
2004	93%	100%	48%	16%
2003	80%	90%	40%	12%
2002	78%	85%	65%	8%

CALIFORNIA 10
East Bay suburbs — Fairfield, Antioch, Livermore

Travel through the Caldecott Tunnel across the Alameda-Contra Costa county line, or on Interstate 680 during rush hour, and 10th District residents commuting to and from San Francisco or San Jose probably will surround your car. Separated from the rest of the Bay Area by the hills east of Oakland, the 10th's residents are mainly well-educated, wealthy professionals who work outside the district.

Residents here are a mix of an older generation that moved in from Oakland and newer, younger commuters that identify more with San Francisco or Berkeley. Almost two-thirds of residents live in the 10th's portion of Contra Costa County, including Antioch and most of Concord (shared with the 7th District). The district's Solano County portion, which includes Fairfield, is a growing but still largely agricultural area where commuters may head south to the Bay Area or north to Sacramento.

Although many residents leave the district for work, the 10th is home to two Energy Department defense program laboratories: Lawrence Livermore National Laboratory — one of the country's leading centers of experimental physics research and defense analysis — and the California branch of the Sandia National Laboratory, which provides engineering support and systems integration for nuclear weapons.

The district retains a moderate political character — residents tend to be more fiscally conservative but share their Bay Area neighbors' views on the environment and other quality-of-life issues. The combination of the working-class agricultural sector and more moderate, but still largely liberal, suburbanites helps tilt the 10th Democratic. John Kerry received 58 percent of the district's presidential vote in 2004, although Gov. Arnold Schwarzenegger's percentage in the 10th matched his statewide total of 56 percent in 2006.

MAJOR INDUSTRY
Research, health care, agriculture, service

MILITARY BASES
Travis Air Force Base, 7,900 military, 3,500 civilian (2006)

CITIES
Fairfield, 96,178; Antioch, 90,532; Livermore, 73,345; Concord (pt.), 72,540

NOTABLE
The world's oldest known working lightbulb, first installed in 1901, is housed by the Livermore-Pleasanton Fire Department.

Rep. Jerry McNerney (D)

Elected 2006; 1st term

In his first term in elective office, McNerney wants to be a leading voice on the issue that helped him land his upset victory and the field in which he has spent much of his career — renewable energy. The wind turbine company executive is committed to pushing for greater use of ethanol, biodiesel and other renewable energy sources, though he did not acquire a spot on the Energy and Commerce Committee as he had hoped.

Not only would an increase in renewable energy usage benefit his largely agricultural district east of San Francisco; it would help decrease America's dependence on foreign oil, he says. He is also a proponent of advanced technologies, such as plug-in hybrids, to significantly improve the fuel efficiency of automobiles.

McNerney won assignment to the Transportation and Infrastructure Committee, his second choice. Traffic congestion is one of the 11th District's biggest headaches for commuters who travel Interstates 580 and 680.

Although McNerney has spent much of the past 22 years working in the energy industry, he is quick to dispel any perceptions that he's a one-issue legislator. He says that his frustration with the Iraq War and his son's service in the military also spurred his candidacy. Securing more funds for states to implement federal education mandates as well as overhauling the health care system are other priorities for McNerney.

A quiet frustration with national politics probably would have remained masked had McNerney's son not urged him to challenge Republican Richard W. Pombo in the 2004 election. An Air Force reservist, McNerney's son had received an absentee ballot and was furious to see Pombo was running unopposed.

With enough coaxing and counsel, McNerney, a Ph.D. engineer with no previous political aspirations, began a last-minute write-in campaign and won the Democratic primary. He lost to Pombo in the general election, but was back in 2006. With strong backing from environmental groups, he defeated the seven-term Pombo, who was the House Resources Committee chairman, by 7 percentage points.

CAPITOL OFFICE
225-1947
mcnerney.house.gov
312 Cannon 20515-0511; fax 226-0861

COMMITTEES
Science & Technology
Select Energy Independence & Global Warming
Transportation & Infrastructure
Veterans' Affairs

RESIDENCE
Pleasanton

BORN
June 18, 1951, Albuquerque, N.M.

RELIGION
Roman Catholic

FAMILY
Wife, Mary McNerney; three children

EDUCATION
U.S. Military Academy, attended 1969-71; U. of New Mexico, B.S. 1973 (mathematics), M.S. 1975 (mathematics), Ph.D. 1981 (mathematics)

CAREER
Wind engineering company owner; wind engineer; renewable energy consultant and researcher

POLITICAL HIGHLIGHTS
Democratic nominee for U.S. House, 2004

ELECTION RESULTS

2006 GENERAL		
Jerry McNerney (D)	109,868	53.3%
Richard W. Pombo (R)	96,396	46.7%
2006 PRIMARY		
Jerry McNerney (D)	23,598	52.7%
Steve Filson (D)	12,744	28.5%
Steve Thomas (D)	8,390	18.8%

CALIFORNIA 11

San Joaquin Valley; inland East Bay; part of Stockton

A mix of commuter bedroom communities east of the San Francisco Bay and developing agricultural country inland, the wrench-shaped 11th runs along Interstate 680 and south past San Jose, while the north end surrounds Stockton on three sides (central Stockton is in the 18th District). The diverse city leans Democratic, but the 11th's portion leans Republican.

The 11th includes more than 40 percent of Stockton's residents and almost all of surrounding San Joaquin County, where high-end development is overtaking farmland. Gridlock plagued Stockton during the technology boom, as Bay Area commuters were pushed to the city. Traffic remains a concern here as the economy rebounds from the ensuing downturn.

Dairy products and wine grapes are the primary agricultural goods here. Lodi and Woodbridge produce 40 percent of the state's premium wine grapes, many of which are shipped to the Napa Valley for bottling.

Agricultural exports travel through the trucking centers of Lodi and Tracy on their way out of the 11th. The port of Stockton on the San Joaquin River specializes in bulk cargo, and cement is the main import.

The 11th is conservative, but GOP support is not concrete. In 2004, George W. Bush took 54 percent of the 11th's presidential vote, but Rep. Pombo lost to a Democrat in 2006.

MAJOR INDUSTRY
Agriculture, technology, service

MILITARY BASES
Defense Distribution Depot San Joaquin, 27 military, 2,677 civilian (2007)

CITIES
Stockton (pt.), 104,409; Pleasanton (pt.), 58,432; Lodi, 56,999; Tracy, 56,929

NOTABLE
George W. Bush Elementary School, in Stockton, is named for the sitting president.

Rep. Tom Lantos (D)

CAPITOL OFFICE
225-3531
www.house.gov/lantos
2413 Rayburn 20515-0512; fax 226-4183

COMMITTEES
Foreign Affairs - chairman
Oversight & Government Reform

RESIDENCE
Burlingame

BORN
Feb. 1, 1928, Budapest, Hungary

RELIGION
Jewish

FAMILY
Wife, Annette Lantos; two children

EDUCATION
U. of Washington, B.A. 1949 (economics), M.A. 1950 (economics); U. of California, Berkeley, Ph.D. 1953 (economics)

CAREER
Professor; congressional aide

POLITICAL HIGHLIGHTS
Millbrae School District Board of Trustees, 1959-66 (president, 1960-61, 1965-66)

ELECTION RESULTS

2006 GENERAL		
Tom Lantos (D)	138,650	76.0%
Michael Moloney (R)	43,674	24.0%
2006 PRIMARY		
Tom Lantos (D)	61,510	83.3%
Kevin Hearle (D)	6,973	9.4%
Robert M. Barrows (D)	5,401	7.3%
2004 GENERAL		
Tom Lantos (D)	171,852	68.0%
Mike Garza (R)	52,593	20.8%
Pat Gray (GREEN)	23,038	9.1%
Harland Harrison (LIBERT)	5,116	2.0%

PREVIOUS WINNING PERCENTAGES
2002 (68%); 2000 (75%); 1998 (74%); 1996 (72%); 1994 (67%); 1992 (69%); 1990 (66%); 1988 (71%); 1986 (74%); 1984 (70%); 1982 (57%); 1980 (46%)

Elected 1980; 14th term

A native of Hungary, Lantos is the only Holocaust survivor in Congress. His life experiences have made him an ardent crusader for human rights across the globe and a supporter of a muscular U.S. foreign policy. In the 110th Congress (2007-08), Lantos is chairman of the Foreign Affairs Committee. He was the panel's senior Democrat from 2001 to 2006, and took the helm after his party won control of Congress, vowing to do his part to "change the way our country conducts itself in the world."

His interests span the globe: the wars in Iraq and Afghanistan, genocide in Sudan, funding for the United Nations, nuclear proliferation in North Korea and Iran and the Israeli-Palestinian conflict all drew the Foreign Affairs panel's attentions early in the new Congress. Lantos says that assertion of U.S. power can help steer the Middle East toward democracy. He takes a hard line in support of Israel, backs a tougher stance against Palestinian terrorists and has criticized Saudi Arabia for financing terrorism.

Lantos played an important behind-the-scenes role helping write the 2002 resolution authorizing war against Iraq. He worked with then Republican committee Chairman Henry J. Hyde of Illinois to steer the measure through the House with significant Democratic support. "Had the United States and its allies confronted Hitler earlier, had we acted sooner to stymie his evil designs, the 51 million lives needlessly lost during that war could have been saved," he said.

Lantos now says his vote for authorizing force against Iraq was based on "inaccurate intelligence information." And he has been sharply critical of the way the Bush administration has carried out the war.

Lantos wrote laws in the 1980s imposing sanctions on Libya, but in 2004 he was the first member of Congress to call for those sanctions to be lifted after traveling to the country for a 90-minute session with leader Muammar el-Qaddafi. Lantos was convinced that Qaddafi's pledge to dismantle his programs to make chemical, biological and nuclear weapons was real, and the Bush administration soon agreed. Lantos has visited Libya a half-dozen times in recent years, holding a number of meetings with Qaddafi.

Lantos also has visited North Korea, and he has worked with former U.N. Secretary General Kofi Annan, a close family friend, to set up a visit to Iran, even as he has pressed sanctions legislation — including a tougher version that his committee approved in 2007 — to push Iran into abandoning its nuclear program.

Secretary of State Condoleezza Rice has also been a friend since the days when she was provost at Stanford University, which is just outside Lantos' district. Lantos says he's disappointed with Rice over her role in the Bush administration's foreign policy.

Lantos is eloquent and intellectual — some say haughty — with the courtly air of a man bred in prewar Central Europe. He can be friendly but at times uses his bearing to his advantage to make a point. His sometimes sharp comments cause discomfort for Democratic colleagues. Lantos once described Republicans as "goose-stepping" along with whatever their leaders demanded, a reference to the gait of Nazi soldiers in Hitler's Germany.

Always at the forefront of efforts to prevent genocide and aid its victims, Lantos has battled for humanitarian relief in Sudan. In April 2006, he was arrested for trespassing during a protest demonstration at the embassy of Sudan against the violence in Darfur. "My whole congressional career, if it has an overarching theme, it is an active involvement in human rights," he says. He founded the Congressional Human Rights Caucus in 1983.

His passion for rescuing the powerless extends beyond people to animals. After hundreds of New Orleans residents refused to leave their homes following Hurricane Katrina because they would not abandon their pets, Lantos won passage of a bill in 2006 requiring authorities to include accommodations for pets in disaster evacuation plans. He is a self-described "crazy pet owner" and often brings a neighbor's dog, Max, which Lantos calls Macko ("little teddy bear" in Hungarian), to the office with him.

Lantos was only 16 when the Nazis swept into Budapest, Hungary, and began rounding up Jews. He was sent to a forced labor camp in Szob, a village north of the capital city, escaped, and was captured and severely beaten. He escaped a second time, this time making it back to Budapest and seeking refuge in a safe house, one of the apartment buildings under Swedish diplomat Raoul Wallenberg's protection. Because of his "Aryan" coloring — blond hair and blue eyes — Lantos was able to move around Budapest in a military cadet's uniform, acquiring food and secretly delivering it to Jews in other safe houses. Lantos recalls that he believed he was going to be killed anyway, so that he "might as well be of some use."

After house-to-house fighting for control of the city in 1945, Lantos was liberated when a Soviet soldier burst through the door of his building. He searched in vain for his mother and other members of his family, who had perished. Later he was able to locate childhood friend Annette Tillemann, a Jew who had fled to Switzerland. The two married and have been together since; Annette Lantos is a full-time volunteer in his office. Their experience is featured in the Steven Spielberg documentary "The Last Days."

In 1947, Lantos won a scholarship to study in the United States. He earned a master's degree in economics from the University of Washington, then a doctorate at the University of California at Berkeley. The couple settled in San Francisco, where he was an economics professor at San Francisco State University.

Lantos was working as a consultant to the Senate Foreign Relations Committee when Republican Bill Royer won a 1979 special House election to replace Democrat Leo J. Ryan, who was assassinated in Jonestown, Guyana, by a religious cult that then engineered a notorious mass suicide. Lantos left his job to begin preparing to challenge Royer for the seat.

Lantos' only elective office until then had been as a suburban school board president, but he exploited the incumbent's overconfidence and won by 3 percentage points in 1980. He put down Royer's comeback attempt by 17 points in 1982 and has since won with more than 65 percent of the vote.

KEY VOTES

2006

- Yes Stop broadband companies from favoring select Internet traffic
- No Affirm U.S. commitment to war in Iraq and reject setting a withdrawal date for troops
- No Repeal requirement for bilingual ballots at the polls
- Yes Permit U.S. sale of civilian nuclear technology to India
- No Build a 700-mile fence on the U.S.-Mexico border to curb illegal crossings
- No Permit warrantless wiretaps of suspected terrorists

2005

- ? Intervene in the life-support case of Terri Schiavo
- Yes Lift President Bush's restrictions on stem cell research funding
- Yes Prohibit FBI access to library and bookstore records
- No Approve free-trade pact with five Central American countries
- No Pass energy policy overhaul favored by President Bush emphasizing domestic oil and gas production
- No End mandatory preservation of habitat of endangered animal and plant species
- Yes Ban torture of prisoners in U.S. custody

CQ VOTE STUDIES

	PARTY UNITY		PRESIDENTIAL SUPPORT	
	Support	Oppose	Support	Oppose
2006	97%	3%	24%	76%
2005	96%	4%	15%	85%
2004	96%	4%	23%	77%
2003	96%	4%	16%	84%
2002	94%	6%	20%	80%

INTEREST GROUPS

	AFL-CIO	ADA	CCUS	ACU
2006	100%	100%	33%	9%
2005	93%	95%	38%	0%
2004	93%	95%	37%	9%
2003	100%	80%	28%	8%
2002	100%	95%	30%	4%

CALIFORNIA 12

Part of San Mateo County; most of western San Francisco

A mix of scenic coastal mountains and bayside commuter traffic jams, the 12th lies between its two well-known neighbors, San Francisco and the Silicon Valley.

The district includes southwestern San Francisco, but most residents live in heavily populated San Mateo County suburbs, either in Daly City or between two main commuter routes — the Junipero Serra and Bayshore freeways. The 12th also covers a portion of Pacific coastline from the Great Highway in San Francisco through Pacifica to Moss Beach, and the district stretches southeast to San Carlos and part of Redwood City, about halfway to San Jose.

After an early-2000s downturn in the 12th's technology economy and in Silicon Valley to the south, the region has begun to rebound. Software giant Oracle's corporate headquarters are in Redwood Shores, and the popular Internet video site YouTube was founded in San Mateo. The district's largest employer is still San Francisco International Airport, although several biotechnology firms have set up shop in the South San Francisco area, making biotechnology a leading industry.

The 12th has the fourth-largest Asian population in the nation at more than 28 percent, and Daly City has the largest concentration of Filipinos in the United States. The Farallon Islands, a national wildlife refuge about 30 miles west of San Francisco, also belong to the district.

Wealthy residents in Burlingame and Hillsborough at the district's southern end tend to be conservative, while voters in the San Francisco area are more liberal. Overall, Democrats hold a strong voter registration edge here, and the 12th was one of only 13 districts to give 2006 gubernatorial candidate Phil Angelides a majority of its vote.

MAJOR INDUSTRY

Biotechnology, airport, software

CITIES

San Francisco (pt.), 137,645; Daly City, 103,621; San Mateo, 92,482

NOTABLE

Bay Meadows Racetrack, in San Mateo, is the longest continuously operating racetrack in California.

Rep. Pete Stark (D)

Elected 1972; 18th term

CAPITOL OFFICE
225-5065
www.house.gov/stark
239 Cannon 20515-0513; fax 226-3805

COMMITTEES
Ways & Means
(Health - chairman)
Joint Taxation

RESIDENCE
Fremont

BORN
Nov. 11, 1931, Milwaukee, Wis.

RELIGION
Unitarian

FAMILY
Wife, Deborah Roderick Stark; seven children

EDUCATION
Massachusetts Institute of Technology, B.S. 1953 (engineering); U. of California, Berkeley, M.B.A. 1960

MILITARY SERVICE
Air Force, 1955-57

CAREER
Banker

POLITICAL HIGHLIGHTS
Sought Democratic nomination for Calif. Senate, 1969

ELECTION RESULTS

2006 GENERAL		
Pete Stark (D)	110,756	74.9%
George I. Bruno (R)	37,141	25.1%
2006 PRIMARY		
Pete Stark (D)		unopposed
2004 GENERAL		
Pete Stark (D)	144,605	71.6%
George I. Bruno (R)	48,439	24.0%
Mark W. Stroberg (LIBERT)	8,877	4.4%

PREVIOUS WINNING PERCENTAGES
2002 (71%); 2000 (70%); 1998 (71%); 1996 (65%); 1994 (65%); 1992 (60%); 1990 (58%); 1988 (73%); 1986 (70%); 1984 (70%); 1982 (61%); 1980 (55%); 1978 (65%); 1976 (71%); 1974 (71%); 1972 (53%)

With a liberal's faith in the ability of government to improve the lot of the underprivileged, Stark for more than 34 years has been a leader of Democratic efforts to provide universal health coverage for all Americans. The second-ranking Democrat on the powerful Ways and Means Committee and chairman of its Health Subcommittee, Stark is one of Congress' premier experts on health policy.

But all of that seasoning hasn't saved him from the occasional over-the-top comment that delights the media but undermines his effectiveness as a legislator. Stark has little patience with people who don't share his views, and his abrasive style can make even fellow Democrats squirm.

When the party fared poorly in the 2002 congressional elections, he urged House Minority Leader Richard A. Gephardt to resign, saying he'd done "a lousy job." He once called former Republican Rep. Bill Thomas of California a "fascist," former Republican Rep. Scott McInnis of Colorado a "little wimp" and "fruitcake," and former GOP Rep. Nancy L. Johnson of Connecticut a "whore for the insurance industry." President Bush's decision to declare war on Iraq was the work of "an inexperienced, desperate young man," he said.

"If I really think that what someone is doing will harm people, it becomes a personal matter to me," Stark told the San Jose Mercury News in 2005. "I shouldn't let my emotions get the best of me, but they do."

One of his biggest disappointments under Republican rule was Congress' failure to pass a generous prescription drug benefit for people enrolled in Medicare. His vision of a new drug benefit was derailed, and Congress passed a more limited bill in late 2003 that gave private insurers rather than the government the responsibility to negotiate drug prices for seniors.

Since then, Stark has been the biggest critic of the Republican plan as it has gone from concept to implementation. In early 2006, he accused private companies of predatory marketing for paying higher commission rates to sales people who enrolled beneficiaries in the most expensive plans. He also slammed Thomas for not holding oversight hearings on the roll-out. "Turning over the Medicare prescription drug program to private insurance companies was a bad idea from the start," Stark said.

When Congress was drafting the legislation, Stark tried to force the GOP and the Bush administration to release White House estimates of the cost of the benefit to taxpayers, figures that were far higher than those of the Congressional Budget Office. An internal Department of Health and Human Services investigation found some estimates were withheld from Congress. As Health Subcommittee chairman in 2007, he championed his party's efforts to force the administration to negotiate Medicare drug prices, and quickly rejected a health care tax plan Bush rolled out: "If I could just deep-six it, they'd build a statue of me in Health Care Square."

Yet Stark is willing sometimes to hold his nose and work with Republicans. During the 12 years the GOP held majority control, he helped win new preventative care benefits for Medicare beneficiaries and pushed Congress to reduce out-of-pocket costs for hospital outpatient services. And he won passage of a bill requiring medical facilities to use safer blood-drawing devices. He may be best known for two laws enacted in 1989 and 1993, known as "Stark I" and "Stark II." They strictly regulate physician referrals of Medicare patients to medical facilities in which the doctors have a financial interest, such as laboratories and physical therapy clinics.

On other issues, Stark usually toes the Democratic line. He sided with his party more than 98 percent of the time in the 109th Congress (2005-06) on votes that pitted the two parties against each other. He crusaded against Bush's plan to overhaul Social Security by allowing workers born after 1949 to establish private accounts as part of their retirement plans. During a hearing on Bush's proposal, Stark unleashed a blistering attack on Republicans, saying they were part of "a cynical and diabolical plan to demolish all our entitlement programs."

Stark is more than willing to be the party's pit bull on other issues. In late 2005, he decried published reports that the Bush administration had been spying on U.S. citizens since 2002 as part of the war on terrorism. As a member of the Joint Taxation Committee, he criticizes the administration's economic policies every chance he gets. Stark also opposed the White House's free trade initiative with Central America, putting him at odds with the Bay Area's technology industry. Stark said, "Democrats support labor rights, environmental standards and affordable medications for all citizens. CAFTA does nothing to promote these values."

On occasion, however, Stark's independent nature splits him from the party. In 2002, he was one of three lawmakers who declined to condemn a controversial court decision declaring the words "under God" in the Pledge of Allegiance to be unconstitutional.

Stark grew up in Wisconsin and graduated from the Massachusetts Institute of Technology. After serving in the Air Force in the 1950s, he moved West and got a master's degree in business from the University of California at Berkeley. Though he chose a traditional line of work — at age 31 he had already founded two banks — he became a rabid opponent of the war in Vietnam. He raised a huge neon peace symbol over one of his banks in suburban Walnut Creek.

In 1969, he made his first bid for public office, losing a primary race for a state legislative seat to George Miller, then a young law school student and now a House colleague. Three years later, Stark decided to take on another George Miller, this one an old-school conservative who had represented Oakland in Congress as a Democrat for 28 years.

Stark spent his money generously and made Miller's support of the Vietnam War a major issue on the way to a primary win, followed by an election in which he managed 53 percent of the vote. Only once since has he had a close call. Lulled by years of easy elections, he made only a token effort in 1980, while conservative Republican William J. Kennedy rode Ronald Reagan's first presidential landslide and held Stark to 55 percent. But Stark has won his past five elections with at least 70 percent of the vote.

KEY VOTES

2006

- Yes Stop broadband companies from favoring select Internet traffic
- No Affirm U.S. commitment to war in Iraq and reject setting a withdrawal date for troops
- No Repeal requirement for bilingual ballots at the polls
- No Permit U.S. sale of civilian nuclear technology to India
- No Build a 700-mile fence on the U.S.-Mexico border to curb illegal crossings
- No Permit warrantless wiretaps of suspected terrorists

2005

- ? Intervene in the life-support case of Terri Schiavo
- Yes Lift President Bush's restrictions on stem cell research funding
- Yes Prohibit FBI access to library and bookstore records
- No Approve free-trade pact with five Central American countries
- No Pass energy policy overhaul favored by President Bush emphasizing domestic oil and gas production
- No End mandatory preservation of habitat of endangered animal and plant species
- Yes Ban torture of prisoners in U.S. custody

CQ VOTE STUDIES

	PARTY UNITY		PRESIDENTIAL SUPPORT	
	Support	Oppose	Support	Oppose
2006	99%	1%	5%	95%
2005	98%	2%	11%	89%
2004	99%	1%	15%	85%
2003	98%	2%	11%	89%
2002	99%	1%	23%	77%

INTEREST GROUPS

	AFL-CIO	ADA	CCUS	ACU
2006	92%	95%	8%	4%
2005	93%	90%	32%	0%
2004	100%	90%	5%	0%
2003	100%	100%	17%	12%
2002	100%	100%	26%	0%

CALIFORNIA 13

East Bay — Fremont, Hayward, Alameda

Tucked between the San Francisco Bay to the west, Silicon Valley to the south and Oakland to the north, the 13th is an industrially and culturally diverse suburban area. The district is dotted with working-class communities and although it is described as the less glamorous side of the bay, its large Hispanic and Asian populations — including immigrants from India, China, Afghanistan and the Philippines — have flourished culturally. Asians, concentrated in Fremont, make up 28 percent of the population, which gives the 13th the nation's fifth-largest percentage of Asian residents.

Fremont's joint General Motors-Toyota auto plant employs almost 6,000 workers and is the city's largest employer. Both Fremont and Hayward have become more oriented toward technology industries as Silicon Valley has extended its influence to the East Bay, and Corsair and Lexar, manufacturers of computer memory devices, are based in Fremont. Hayward also is home to a California State University campus.

San Leandro, just south of Oakland, is home to a Coca-Cola plant, Ghirardelli Chocolate, which is the nation's longest continuously operating chocolate manufacturer, Otis Spunkmeyer's cookie empire, and The North Face, which produces outdoor equipment. Cargill Salt has a refinery and production facility in Newark.

The 13th includes Oakland International Airport, although Oakland itself is located in the neighboring 9th. The airport has expanded its terminals and operations in recent years, and FedEx operates an air freight hub, which employs nearly 1,700.

Two-thirds of the district's workers are considered white collar, but the area's blue-collar industry historically has given Democrats a solid base of support. Democrat Phil Angelides received 52 percent of the 13th's gubernatorial vote in 2006, while garnering only 39 percent statewide.

MAJOR INDUSTRY

Electronics, manufacturing, food product processing

CITIES

Fremont, 203,413; Hayward, 140,030; San Leandro, 79,452

NOTABLE

The Oakland Athletics baseball team and Cisco Systems announced in November 2006 that they plan to build a new ballpark in Fremont.

Rep. Anna G. Eshoo (D)

CAPITOL OFFICE
225-8104
eshoo.house.gov
205 Cannon 20515-0514; fax 225-8890

COMMITTEES
Energy & Commerce
Select Intelligence
(Intelligence Community Management - chairwoman)

RESIDENCE
Menlo Park

BORN
Dec. 13, 1942, New Britain, Conn.

RELIGION
Roman Catholic

FAMILY
Divorced; two children

EDUCATION
Canada College, A.A. 1975 (English literature)

CAREER
State legislative aide; homemaker

POLITICAL HIGHLIGHTS
Candidate for San Mateo County Community College Board of Trustees, 1977; Democratic National Committee, 1980-92; San Mateo County Board of Supervisors, 1982-92 (president, 1986); Democratic nominee for U.S. House, 1988

ELECTION RESULTS

2006 GENERAL		
Anna G. Eshoo (D)	141,153	71.1%
Rob Smith (R)	48,097	24.2%
Brian Holtz (LIBERT)	4,692	2.4%
Carol Brouillet (GREEN)	4,633	2.3%
2006 PRIMARY		
Anna G. Eshoo (D)		unopposed
2004 GENERAL		
Anna G. Eshoo (D)	182,712	69.8%
John C. "Chris" Haugen (R)	69,564	26.6%
Brian Holtz (LIBERT)	9,588	3.7%

PREVIOUS WINNING PERCENTAGES
2002 (68%); 2000 (70%); 1998 (69%); 1996 (65%); 1994 (61%); 1992 (57%)

Elected 1992; 8th term

A member of Speaker Nancy Pelosi's inner circle, Eshoo is likely to wield increasing influence as House Democrats work to transform their 2006 victory into a lasting majority. Her talent for building relationships and bridging differences has paid off over her House career, and her Silicon Valley connections are helping Democrats burnish their credentials with the high-technology industry.

Eshoo (EH-shoo) and Pelosi met more than 30 years ago, when both were homemakers active in the California Democratic Party and the Democratic National Committee. Their shared passion for politics (and chocolate) still spices their occasional escapes for ice cream or a meal together in Georgetown or the Bay Area.

Eshoo is one of three Democrats whom Pelosi lined up to preside over the House in the 110th Congress (2007-08) whenever the Speaker needs an experienced hand on the gavel. It is a role Eshoo played in 1993 and 1994 when the Democrats last controlled the chamber, and one she would like to teach new members to perform. "They don't know what it's like to hold the gavel," she said. "It would be a good idea to give them some training."

Eshoo holds a coveted seat on the Energy and Commerce Committee, where she sits on the Health Subcommittee and the Telecommunications and the Internet Subcommittee. Although other panels had chairmanships available at the start of the 110th Congress, Eshoo made no attempt to claim one, preferring to keep her place in line on the two subcommittees that most interest her.

Representing some of Silicon Valley, Eshoo is a champion for the high-tech industry, saying the Internet and related technology not only create jobs at home but also can play a "transformative" role in promoting freedom and democracy abroad. In 2005, she helped persuade Pelosi to develop an agenda highlighting innovation that, among other things, could help Democrats raise campaign cash in Silicon Valley. Eshoo arranged a private summit at Stanford University that brought Pelosi and other lawmakers together with high-tech executives such as Cisco Systems Chairman and CEO John Chambers to kick around ideas for legislation. The resulting agenda included proposals to permanently extend the research and development tax credit and to create incentives encouraging broadband deployment.

In 2007, Eshoo introduced legislation to continue indefinitely a ban on Internet access taxes that was due to expire later that year. She also continued her efforts to advance so-called network neutrality legislation barring broadband providers from granting favored treatment to some content providers in return for payments or other special arrangements. And she resumed a push to require doctors, hospitals and other health care providers to shift to electronic medical records.

Earlier in her career, Eshoo had championed a law to allow the use of electronic signatures to seal some contracts. She joined Republicans in the 108th Congress (2003-04) and subsequently in an unsuccessful effort to block a proposed rule by the Financial Accounting Standards Board requiring companies to treat employee stock options as an expense that had to be deducted from earnings, which would slam the bottom line of many technology companies that distribute options liberally.

Eshoo's pro-business stands have at times put her at odds with her party leaders. In 1995, she helped override President Bill Clinton's veto of a measure to limit lawsuits by disgruntled investors — one of only two laws enacted over his veto. On broader legislation to limit class action lawsuits, Eshoo — after voting no in 1999 with the majority of Democrats — did not vote when the House again passed the bill in 2002, 2003 and finally, 2005.

During the Clinton administration, Eshoo supported free-trade legislation. But like a majority of her fellow Democrats, she has voted against many trade deals negotiated by the Bush administration, saying they lacked adequate labor protections.

Eshoo is reliably liberal on social issues. She favors gun control and supports abortion rights. She and other Catholic Democrats spearheaded efforts earlier this decade to reach out to church leaders who fiercely oppose abortion, and she helped develop an informal caucus of Catholic House Democrats who issued a "statement of principle" in 2006 affirming their strong faith while defending the "primacy of conscience" and noting their "disagreement with the Church in some areas," such as abortion.

Eshoo's childhood prepared her well for a life of public service. Her parents were immigrants from Armenia and modern-day Iran. "In our prayers at dinner, we thanked God for the food and also thanked God for this country," she said.

Eshoo was first drawn to Democratic politics in her native New Britain, Conn. Her father, a jeweler and watchmaker, took the family to political rallies and hung portraits of Franklin D. Roosevelt and Harry S Truman in their home. One day as she walked home from grade school, a man in a big car drove by with a police escort, stopped and offered her a ride. Eshoo accepted the lift — from Truman. As a high school senior, she organized more than 800 students to work for presidential candidate John F. Kennedy. "Back then, I really thought that I was the one who put him over the top."

The family moved to California. Eshoo married young (she has been divorced since the 1980s), and devoted herself to motherhood as she earned a two-year associate's degree in English literature and became active in civic groups.

Eshoo took an internship with then California Assembly Speaker Leo McCarthy and eventually became his chief of staff. Active in local party politics, she won appointment to the Democratic National Committee. In 1982, McCarthy urged her to run for the San Mateo County Board of Supervisors. That post, which she held for a decade, shaped her pragmatic philosophy.

In 1988, Eshoo lost a House race against Republican Tom Campbell, but took 46 percent of the vote. Four years later, in 1992, she won, boosted by Campbell's absence as he ran for the Senate and by a redrawn district map that added more Democratic voters. She has won comfortably ever since.

KEY VOTES

2006

- Yes Stop broadband companies from favoring select Internet traffic
- No Affirm U.S. commitment to war in Iraq and reject setting a withdrawal date for troops
- No Repeal requirement for bilingual ballots at the polls
- Yes Permit U.S. sale of civilian nuclear technology to India
- No Build a 700-mile fence on the U.S.-Mexico border to curb illegal crossings
- No Permit warrantless wiretaps of suspected terrorists

2005

- ? Intervene in the life-support case of Terri Schiavo
- Yes Lift President Bush's restrictions on stem cell research funding
- Yes Prohibit FBI access to library and bookstore records
- No Approve free-trade pact with five Central American countries
- No Pass energy policy overhaul favored by President Bush emphasizing domestic oil and gas production
- No End mandatory preservation of habitat of endangered animal and plant species
- Yes Ban torture of prisoners in U.S. custody

CQ VOTE STUDIES

	PARTY UNITY		PRESIDENTIAL SUPPORT	
	Support	Oppose	Support	Oppose
2006	96%	4%	23%	77%
2005	97%	3%	19%	81%
2004	94%	6%	35%	65%
2003	96%	4%	20%	80%
2002	95%	5%	24%	76%

INTEREST GROUPS

	AFL-CIO	ADA	CCUS	ACU
2006	93%	95%	40%	4%
2005	93%	100%	38%	4%
2004	93%	100%	38%	12%
2003	85%	90%	24%	13%
2002	100%	100%	42%	0%

CALIFORNIA 14

Southern San Mateo and northwestern Santa Clara counties; most of Santa Cruz County

The 14th stretches south from northern San Mateo County on the Pacific coast, taking in the majority of Santa Cruz County and a C-shaped arc of northwestern Santa Clara County just south of the San Francisco Bay. The district is home to Stanford University, technology firms, fruit orchards and some of the nation's most expensive housing — the 14th's median home value was $626,500, according to the 2000 census.

Workers in the 14th are largely wealthy, educated and professional. The district has the highest median income in California, and the third-highest in the country, at close to $78,000. It also has the state's third-highest percentage of white-collar workers (77 percent) and has among the state's lowest percentages of service industry workers (10 percent).

Technology is a dominant industry in the district. Several major firms have their headquarters in the 14th, including Google in Mountain View, Hewlett-Packard in Palo Alto, and Yahoo, Palm and AMD in Sunnyvale.

The 14th also has the fifth-largest percentage of college-educated residents in the United States (52 percent).

Voters in the 14th are liberal on many social and environmental issues, particularly in Santa Cruz County. Many residents are more conservative economically, however, and conservative voting blocs exist in wealthy areas such as Saratoga and Monte Sereno in Santa Clara County. Democrats hold an overall 18 percentage point edge in voter registration, and the district gave Democrat John Kerry 68 percent of its vote in the 2004 presidential election.

MAJOR INDUSTRY

Computers, biotechnology, defense, agriculture

MILITARY BASES

Onizuka Air Force Station, 9 military, 150 civilian (2007)

CITIES

Sunnyvale, 131,760; Mountain View, 70,708; Palo Alto, 58,598; Redwood City (pt.), 52,873; Menlo Park, 30,785

NOTABLE

Stanford University's Rodin Sculpture Garden has the world's largest public concentration of bronze sculptures by Auguste Rodin; Stanford's Linear Accelerator Center claims to be the "world's straightest object."

Rep. Michael M. Honda (D)

CAPITOL OFFICE
225-2631
www.honda.house.gov
1713 Longworth 20515-0515; fax 225-2699

COMMITTEES
Appropriations
Science & Technology

RESIDENCE
San Jose

BORN
June 27, 1941, Stockton, Calif.

RELIGION
Protestant

FAMILY
Widowed; two children

EDUCATION
San Jose State U., B.S. 1969 (biological sciences), B.A. 1970 (Spanish), M.A. 1973 (education)

CAREER
Teacher; principal; Peace Corps volunteer

POLITICAL HIGHLIGHTS
San Jose School Board, 1981-90; Santa Clara County Board of Supervisors, 1990-96; Calif. Assembly, 1996-2000

ELECTION RESULTS

2006 GENERAL		
Michael M. Honda (D)	115,532	72.3%
Raymond L. Chukwu (R)	44,186	27.7%
2006 PRIMARY		
Michael M. Honda (D)		unopposed
2004 GENERAL		
Michael M. Honda (D)	154,385	72.0%
Raymond L. Chukwu (R)	59,953	28.0%

PREVIOUS WINNING PERCENTAGES
2002 (66%); 2000 (54%)

Elected 2000; 4th term

Honda is gaining more visibility in the House as a result of his close connection to a fellow northern California lawmaker, Speaker Nancy Pelosi. After Democrats won back the House majority in 2006, Honda was given a coveted seat on the Appropriations Committee. A year earlier, Pelosi had backed Honda's bid to become one of five vice chairmen of the Democratic National Committee.

As a DNC vice chairman, Honda has focused on reaching out to immigrant communities, particularly Asian-Americans, which was not a surprising priority since the 15th District includes the second-largest population of Asian-Americans in the country. The immigrant experience is also an important part of Honda's own identity.

Born to Nisei farm workers in what is now called Silicon Valley, Honda was just a few months old when the Japanese launched a surprise attack on Pearl Harbor. He and his family were shipped off to an internment camp in Colorado, where they spent about two and a half years before they were able to move to Chicago when his father joined Navy intelligence.

Sixty years later, when terrorists carried out the Sept. 11 attacks against the United States, Honda was one of the most outspoken members of the House in working to ensure that other Americans were not treated like his family was in 1941, only because "we looked like the enemy." Honda wrote President Bush expressing concern about "government-sanctioned racial profiling." And he spoke out against reports of harassment and attacks on Arab-Americans, Muslims and members of other ethnic groups.

In 2006, Honda came to the defense of Minnesota Democrat Keith Ellison, Congress' first Muslim member, who was criticized by some lawmakers for using a Koran to be sworn in ceremonially. Honda wrote to Virginia Republican Virgil H. Goode Jr., one of Ellison's critics, saying, "As one of the many Japanese Americans who were interned during World War II because of war hysteria and racial prejudice, I find it particularly offensive that you are equating Representative-elect Ellison's beliefs with those of radical extremists and condemning him based on their actions."

He also chided California Gov. Arnold Schwarzenegger in October 2006 for suggesting Mexican immigrants have trouble assimilating because they are so close to their country of birth. At a press conference, Honda called that idea a "misunderstanding of the history of the Southwest. The Southwest was part of Mexico," the San José Mercury News reported.

After joining the Appropriations Committee, Honda received a seat on the subcommittee that provides funding for science and space programs. He is likely to work to make sure the NASA-Ames Research Center, near his district, receives its share of government funds. He also has a seat on the Science and Technology Committee, which authorizes the space program.

Representing a district with a healthy slice of California's Silicon Valley, Honda's congressional agenda is centered on the high-technology industry. He favors the repeal of export controls on high-performance computers and permanent renewal of the research and development tax credit. In 2003, he was a lead sponsor of a bill, which the House passed, calling for a beefed-up federal effort in nanotechnology research, the manipulation of matter at the level of a single atom. Honda says nanotechnology will spur profound technological advances over the next two decades.

Honda was one of 126 House Democrats to vote against the 2002 authorization for the war in Iraq. He has also sought to curb military recruiters' access to high school students. He introduced legislation in 2005 that would require schools to release contact information of only those students whose parents opt to participate. Under the No Child Left Behind education law, contact information is provided unless parents specifically say they don't want their child's information given to military recruiters.

Honda remembers little of his internment. He was too young, and he said his parents were reluctant to talk about it afterward. But he was a key participant in the Japanese-American community's effort that resulted in the 1988 law providing a formal apology and compensation to Japanese-Americans who were interned during World War II. That effort inspired Honda, once he reached Congress, to work for reparations for Americans who were prisoners of the Japanese during the war. He was also a leading sponsor of legislation signed into law by Bush in late 2006 to provide $38 million in grant money to preserve the remnants of the internment camps.

Honda said his parents were always civic-minded despite their internment experience. The family moved back to California in 1953, and his parents became strawberry sharecroppers. Honda took janitorial and delivery jobs to pay his way through San Jose State University. He was one credit shy of graduation when he joined a new overseas volunteer effort called the Peace Corps. After a two-year stint in El Salvador, where he built schools and medical clinics, he returned to California to finish college. He took a job as a science teacher and later served as a principal.

Fluent in Spanish from his years in El Salvador, Honda developed strong ties to San Jose's Hispanic community. He went to Norman Y. Mineta, then a city councilman, to volunteer his services to the city. When Mineta was elected mayor, Honda received an appointment to the city planning commission. Mineta, who went on to serve in Congress and as a member of the Cabinet in both the Clinton and George W. Bush administrations, has remained Honda's friend and mentor.

Honda's 1971 appointment to the planning commission led to elected posts on the local school board, the county board of supervisors, and in 1996, election to the California Assembly. When moderate Republican Rep. Tom Campbell left the 15th District open in 2000 to run for the Senate, Democrats viewed it as a prime opportunity. Honda entered the race after a phone call from President Bill Clinton convinced him that the national party would back his bid. He won the election by 12 percentage points.

Bolstered by redistricting and his ties to the Asian and Hispanic communities in a district where almost half the residents are from those constituencies, Honda has cruised to re-election since.

KEY VOTES

2006

- Yes Stop broadband companies from favoring select Internet traffic
- No Affirm U.S. commitment to war in Iraq and reject setting a withdrawal date for troops
- No Repeal requirement for bilingual ballots at the polls
- Yes Permit U.S. sale of civilian nuclear technology to India
- No Build a 700-mile fence on the U.S.-Mexico border to curb illegal crossings
- No Permit warrantless wiretaps of suspected terrorists

2005

- ? Intervene in the life-support case of Terri Schiavo
- Yes Lift President Bush's restrictions on stem cell research funding
- Yes Prohibit FBI access to library and bookstore records
- No Approve free-trade pact with five Central American countries
- No Pass energy policy overhaul favored by President Bush emphasizing domestic oil and gas production
- No End mandatory preservation of habitat of endangered animal and plant species
- Yes Ban torture of prisoners in U.S. custody

CQ VOTE STUDIES

	PARTY UNITY		PRESIDENTIAL SUPPORT	
	Support	Oppose	Support	Oppose
2006	97%	3%	23%	77%
2005	99%	1%	18%	82%
2004	97%	3%	23%	77%
2003	97%	3%	17%	83%
2002	99%	1%	21%	79%

INTEREST GROUPS

	AFL-CIO	ADA	CCUS	ACU
2006	93%	95%	33%	4%
2005	93%	100%	37%	4%
2004	93%	95%	39%	10%
2003	100%	95%	20%	12%
2002	100%	95%	30%	0%

CALIFORNIA 15

Santa Clara County — part of San Jose

Home to one-third of San Jose's residents, the 15th touches the southern tip of the San Francisco Bay in the north, then descends inland through Silicon Valley to still-rural but fast-growing farm towns and the San Benito County border. Fruit orchards that once covered much of the district were converted into housing and businesses after World War II.

Lying in the heart of Silicon Valley, the 15th is home to several prominent technology firms — Apple in Cupertino and Intel and Sun Microsystems in Santa Clara — and Internet ventures like online auction house eBay in San Jose and Netflix in Los Gatos. The downturn in the area's technology industry earlier this decade, particularly within smaller companies, increased unemployment rates in the affluent suburbs west of San Jose.

Recent steady demand from research universities and the federal government have helped the software and semiconductor sectors rebound, although employment levels have not quite matched the increase in production. Agriculture also is important here. Gilroy, located in the southern part of the district and known as the "Garlic Capital of the World," is home to a ConAgra processing plant.

The diverse 15th includes the nation's second-highest percentage of Asian residents (29 percent). The population here is predominately affluent; the district has the fifth-highest median income in the country (nearly $75,000). It also has a high percentage of white-collar workers (74 percent) and has one of the state's lowest percentages of service industry workers (9 percent).

Although some residents are concerned about illegal immigration, voters in the 15th tend to be liberal on social and environmental issues. John Kerry won 63 percent of the district's 2004 presidential vote.

MAJOR INDUSTRY

Computers, biotechnology, health care, agriculture

CITIES

San Jose (pt.), 295,018; Santa Clara, 102,361; Milpitas, 62,698

NOTABLE

Two tons of garlic are consumed during Gilroy's annual Garlic Festival, which features garlic french fries, garlic ice cream — and free gum; The Winchester Mansion in San Jose, designed by the Winchester heiress, took 38 years to build, has 160 rooms and contains structural oddities.

Rep. Zoe Lofgren (D)

CAPITOL OFFICE
225-3072
www.house.gov/lofgren
102 Cannon 20515-0516; fax 225-3336

COMMITTEESS
Homeland Security
House Administration
(Elections - chairwoman)
Judiciary
(Immigration, Citizenship, Refugees, Border Security & International Law - chairwoman)
Joint Library

RESIDENCE
San Jose

BORN
Dec. 21, 1947, San Mateo, Calif.

RELIGION
Lutheran

FAMILY
Husband, John Marshall Collins; two children

EDUCATION
Stanford U., A.B. 1970 (political science);
U. of Santa Clara, J.D. 1975

CAREER
Lawyer; nonprofit housing development director; professor; congressional aide

POLITICAL HIGHLIGHTS
San Jose-Evergreen Community College District Board of Trustees, 1979-81; Santa Clara County Board of Supervisors, 1981-95

ELECTION RESULTS

2006 GENERAL		
Zoe Lofgren (D)	98,929	72.7%
Charel Winston (R)	37,130	27.3%
2006 PRIMARY		
Zoe Lofgren (D)		unopposed
2004 GENERAL		
Zoe Lofgren (D)	129,222	70.9%
Douglas Adams McNea (R)	47,992	26.3%
Markus Welch (LIBERT)	5,067	2.8%

PREVIOUS WINNING PERCENTAGES
2002 (67%); 2000 (72%); 1998 (73%); 1996 (66%); 1994 (65%)

Elected 1994; 7th term

As a young intern on Capitol Hill, Lofgren was chagrined when a draft of a bill she had written in an unlawyerly way was "ripped to shreds" by the House legislative counsel, as she tells it. So Lofgren went back to school and got a law degree. She went on to become quite a bill-shredder herself, rhetorically ripping GOP legislation to pieces during the long period of Republican rule on Capitol Hill. With Democrats in control in the 110th Congress (2007-08), Lofgren finally gets to write bills again.

Lofgren (full name: ZO LOFF-gren) chairs the Judiciary panel's Subcommittee on Immigration, where the national debate over forgiveness policies for illegal workers is expected to play out. A former immigration lawyer herself, she is more sympathetic to providing a path to legalization for immigrants than were the conservative Republicans who wrote the last major immigration bill in 2006, which passed the House but stalled in the Senate.

Lofgren challenged as "very foolish" parts of the get-tough Republican bill that sought to change illegal immigration from a civil to a criminal offense, make it a crime to assist illegal immigrants and called for hundreds of miles of fencing along the U.S. border with Mexico. As a member of the Democrats' immigration task force in the early 2000s, she was also highly critical of the Immigration and Naturalization Service's handling of citizenship requests, calling it "dismal."

Lofgren came to the House in 1995, the first year of Republican control. Her legislative track record shows the frustrations of 12 years in the minority; she introduced 16 bills in the 109th Congress (2005-06), but none saw the light of day as a stand-alone bill. She had more success with amendments to other people's bills. Her provision to accelerate the development of fusion as a long-term energy source was included in the GOP-authored energy bill of 2005. And a Lofgren amendment tacked onto the anti-terrorism law revision of 2005 requires the Justice Department to review the detention of material witnesses who are held without charges.

As the senior Democrat on the Homeland Security panel's Intelligence Subcommittee, she stormed out of a hearing in 2006 in protest after Republican Chairman Rob Simmons decided the panel lacked jurisdiction to investigate allegations of domestic spying by the National Security Agency. Lofgren said, "I think it's important that as we fight terrorism, we also embrace the Constitution."

She has persistently sought to enhance the authority of the cybersecurity arm of the Homeland Security Department, and she backed a bill to replace color-coded terrorism threat warnings with more specific warnings targeted to a region or sector of the economy. Both of those efforts became part of a department reauthorization bill in 2006.

She generally finds herself agreeing with Republicans in just one policy arena — issues that affect her technology-driven district in and around San Jose, the capital of Silicon Valley. Though not an expert in computer technology — she was a political science major in college — she has boned up and made herself knowledgeable.

In 1995, she joined Republicans in voting to override President Bill Clinton's veto of a bill limiting shareholder lawsuits, which had plagued technology companies. The tech industry was particularly hard hit by big declines in stock prices in 2001, and she supported legislation in 2004 to allow companies to offer stock options to employees without recording them as an expense. She is a proponent of more federal support for scientific research and development, arguing that increased funding for agencies such as the National Science Foundation is crucial at a time jobs are moving overseas.

On the social issues that get her attention, Lofgren will not shy from a fight. In 2004, she tried unsuccessfully to stop House approval of a GOP-backed measure giving distinct legal status to fetuses and establishing a separate offense for a crime against a pregnant woman that harms the fetus. She said the Republicans' ultimate aim was to reclassify a fetus as a human. "The real rationale behind this bill is not to protect pregnant women," she said. "It is to define a zygote as a person under law." Lofgren sponsored a Democratic alternative creating additional penalties for crimes against pregnant women, but without separate legal status for fetuses.

Lofgren grew up in a blue-collar neighborhood in south Palo Alto. Her father was a truck driver and her mother was a secretary and a school cafeteria cook. "I didn't meet a Republican until I went to junior high school," she says. While other mothers went door-to-door collecting for the March of Dimes, Lofgren's mother went after "dollars for Democrats." Lofgren would spend hours talking politics with her Swedish immigrant grandfather. Instead of going to dances, she and her friends went to political rallies.

After completing her undergraduate studies at Stanford University on a scholarship, she headed to Washington, D.C., landing an internship with Democratic Rep. Don Edwards. She stayed on as a staffer through the 1970s. (Lofgren's husband is a lawyer in San Jose whom she met one election night while working for Edwards.) She returned to California to study law and practiced immigration law as a partner in the firm of Webber & Lofgren. She also taught immigration law at the University of Santa Clara.

Lofgren was the first executive director of San Jose's Community Housing Developers, a nonprofit organization that created low-income housing. In 1979, a colleague urged her to run for the local community college board of trustees, and she won. A year later, she was elected to the Santa Clara County Board of Supervisors, where she stayed for 14 years and was often in conflict with San Jose Mayor Tom McEnery, a Democrat, who pushed downtown redevelopment while Lofgren argued for more money for education and human services.

When Edwards retired from the House after 32 years, the 1994 Democratic primary saw a face-off between Lofgren and McEnery. She benefited from an uproar that ensued when state election officials barred her from describing herself as "county supervisor/mother" on the ballot. The flap drew national attention to her candidacy, and she went on to win the primary. She won handily that November and has coasted to re-election since.

KEY VOTES

2006

- Yes Stop broadband companies from favoring select Internet traffic
- No Affirm U.S. commitment to war in Iraq and reject setting a withdrawal date for troops
- No Repeal requirement for bilingual ballots at the polls
- Yes Permit U.S. sale of civilian nuclear technology to India
- No Build a 700-mile fence on the U.S.-Mexico border to curb illegal crossings
- No Permit warrantless wiretaps of suspected terrorists

2005

- ? Intervene in the life-support case of Terri Schiavo
- Yes Lift President Bush's restrictions on stem cell research funding
- Yes Prohibit FBI access to library and bookstore records
- No Approve free-trade pact with five Central American countries
- No Pass energy policy overhaul favored by President Bush emphasizing domestic oil and gas production
- No End mandatory preservation of habitat of endangered animal and plant species
- Yes Ban torture of prisoners in U.S. custody

CQ VOTE STUDIES

	PARTY UNITY		PRESIDENTIAL SUPPORT	
	Support	Oppose	Support	Oppose
2006	97%	3%	23%	77%
2005	97%	3%	13%	87%
2004	94%	6%	30%	70%
2003	96%	4%	20%	80%
2002	94%	6%	15%	85%

INTEREST GROUPS

	AFL-CIO	ADA	CCUS	ACU
2006	93%	100%	33%	4%
2005	93%	100%	37%	4%
2004	93%	95%	33%	12%
2003	87%	85%	26%	17%
2002	100%	100%	26%	0%

CALIFORNIA 16
Most of San Jose

The 16th includes two-thirds of San Jose, California's third-largest city, where 92 percent of district residents live. The remainder live in unincorporated areas of Santa Clara County.

The tremendous growth during the technology boom of the 1990s — which earned San Jose the reputation as "the capital of Silicon Valley" — created a largely white-collar workforce and helped to establish the area as a leading exporter of high-technology goods. After an economic downturn earlier this decade, unemployment levels rebounded to roughly 5 percent by the end of 2004. Housing prices remained high, and Santa Clara County has the area's highest median income.

Major technology firms in the 16th include Cisco Systems, Adobe, IBM's Almaden research facility and a Hitachi unit focused on supply chain management. San Jose also has several large medical centers — Good Samaritan Hospital employs nearly 2,000 people — and is home to financial management software company Intacct. Local government and San Jose State University are major public sector employers.

One of the most ethnically diverse districts in the Bay Area, the 16th's Asian population — the ninth-highest in the country at more than 23 percent — includes the nation's second-largest Vietnamese community. Hispanics constitute a plurality of district residents (38 percent), and whites make up 32 percent of the population. The district's recent growth has resulted in one of the state's lowest populations over the age of 64.

The 16th is solidly Democratic, and an influx of Hispanics has helped to keep it that way. White-collar workers are becoming more common and could begin to shift the district's politics to the right, but John Kerry still commanded 63 percent of the district's vote in the 2004 presidential election, and Gov. Arnold Schwarzenegger was held under 50 percent of the vote here in 2006 while capturing 56 percent of the vote statewide.

MAJOR INDUSTRY
Technology, health care, finance

CITIES
San Jose (pt.), 590,306; Alum Rock (unincorporated), 13,479

NOTABLE
The Tech Museum of Innovation, a mango-colored building in downtown San Jose, welcomes hundreds of thousands of visitors to its exhibits, galleries and educational center.

Rep. Sam Farr (D)

CAPITOL OFFICE
225-2861
www.farr.house.gov
1221 Longworth 20515-0517; fax 225-6791

COMMITTEES
Appropriations

RESIDENCE
Carmel

BORN
July 4, 1941, San Francisco, Calif.

RELIGION
Episcopalian

FAMILY
Wife, Shary Baldwin Farr; one child

EDUCATION
Willamette U., B.S. 1963 (biology)

CAREER
State legislative aide; Peace Corps volunteer

POLITICAL HIGHLIGHTS
Monterey County Board of Supervisors, 1975-80; Calif. Assembly, 1980-93

ELECTION RESULTS

2006 GENERAL		
Sam Farr (D)	120,750	75.8%
Anthony R. De Maio (R)	35,932	22.6%
Jeff Edward Taylor (I)	2,611	1.6%
2006 PRIMARY		
Sam Farr (D)		unopposed
2004 GENERAL		
Sam Farr (D)	148,958	66.7%
Mark Risley (R)	65,117	29.2%
Ray Glock-Grueneich (GREEN)	3,645	1.6%
Joe Williams (PF)	2,823	1.3%
Jim Smolen (LIBERT)	2,607	1.2%

PREVIOUS WINNING PERCENTAGES
2002 (68%); 2000 (69%); 1998 (65%); 1996 (59%); 1994 (52%); 1993 Special Runoff Election (54%)

Elected June 1993; 7th full term

Farr's work in Congress is all about natural resources. The former biology major divides his time between trying to preserve some of the most scenic stretches of coastline in the country and fostering the giant agribusiness economy of the inland Salinas Valley, a richly productive region immortalized in John Steinbeck's classic novel, "East of Eden." Farr says, "This is a district where the economy and environment run hand in hand."

Among the area's natural assets are the Big Sur coastline and the second-largest national marine sanctuary outside of Hawaii. Farr has a strong interest in ocean protection and introduced bipartisan legislation on the first day of the 110th Congress (2007-08) to implement recommendations of the U.S. Commission on Ocean Policy, which he helped create.

As a member of the Resources Committee in the late 1990s, Farr was outspoken in urging Congress and the Clinton administration to initiate a comprehensive review of the national policy on maritime and coastal protection, which resulted in the establishment of the ocean commission. That 16-member bipartisan body released its final report in 2004 calling for, among other things, a stronger ocean agency that uses an ecosystem-based approach to better protect oceans and coasts.

Farr, with Illinois Democratic Sen. Richard J. Durbin, also proposed legislation to limit cruise ship pollution damage done to the ocean by prohibiting cruise ships from dumping waste within a 12 mile-wide coastal zone.

In 2002, Farr successfully sponsored a bill classifying 55,000 acres as wilderness in the Los Padres National Forest in the Big Sur area. And he persuaded President Bill Clinton to designate the rocky coastline from Oregon to Mexico as a national monument.

Another main interest for Farr is government regulation of organic farming. As a member of the California Assembly, in 1990 he wrote a bill establishing organic standards for agriculture. Since then, he has been involved in developing guidelines at the federal level.

His district grows 85 crops, including lettuce, spinach, broccoli, celery, peppers and strawberries, and has come a long way economically since Steinbeck's dreamer-protagonist Adam Trask tried shipping lettuce across the country in the days before refrigeration. Trask's investment was lost in freight-train cars full of wilted produce, but today the output of the Salinas Valley salad bowl is $3 billion a year.

Farr dabbles legislatively in another crop — marijuana for medical purposes. He has cosponsored a bill that would allow individuals accused of violating federal marijuana laws to introduce evidence in federal court that they followed state law in using the marijuana for medicinal reasons. He also has cosponsored legislation to reclassify medical marijuana under federal law so it can be legally prescribed.

Farr represents a collection of personnel-oriented military facilities, including the Defense Language Institute Foreign Language Center and the Naval Postgraduate School, which is a center for computer research in intelligence gathering. From his seat on the Appropriations Subcommittee dealing with military construction and quality of life, he added a provision to the military construction bill that the House passed in 2004 requiring houses on Fort Ord land to be sold or rented at below-market rates. "The housing crisis in our area is undeniable, and in order to have a strong and diverse local workforce, we need to have housing for them to live in," Farr said. On Iraq, Farr has refused to support any of President Bush's funding requests for the war, a popular stance with his generally liberal, anti-war constituency. When House Republicans wanted to retaliate in 2003 against countries that opposed the U.S. invasion, Farr protested an amendment that sought to block reconstruction funds from going to companies located in countries that publicly opposed the United Nations' Iraq resolution. The amendment targeted companies in China, Russia, Germany, France and Syria. "The way we're headed, we're not going to have any friends [in the world] tomorrow," he said.

Across the spectrum of issues, Farr is a dependable vote for the Democratic leadership, voting with his party 97 percent of the time on votes that polarized the two parties in the 109th Congress (2005-06).

Farr was born on July Fourth into a political family. His father was a longtime California state senator and the first national director of highway beautification under President Lyndon B. Johnson, an appointive post that grew out of Lady Bird Johnson's highway beautification program. There were always interesting people around the house, like then-California Gov. Edmund G. "Pat" Brown and famed landscape photographer Ansel Adams.

Farr went to Willamette College in the early 1960s. "The '50s and '60s were a lot of conformity, then the breaking out of flower power," he recalls. "What came out the most was a sense of service." After graduating, he spent two years with the Peace Corps in Colombia. "My basic politics came out of being a Peace Corps volunteer and learning about the culture of poverty, which is essentially when you lack access to education, health care and housing, you are forever destined to be poor," Farr says.

Also during that period, he lost his mother to cancer. When he returned home to see her, his mother insisted Farr go back to his work in Colombia when his leave was over. She died the day after Farr left.

When his volunteer stint ended, Farr took a job as a staff member in the California Assembly. He later won election to the Monterey County Board of Supervisors. After five years, he was elected to the Assembly, ultimately serving more than a dozen years in Sacramento.

In 1993, he won a House special election to replace Democratic Rep. Leon E. Panetta, who had become Clinton's White House budget director. Farr was a strong candidate in the Democratic-leaning district and prevailed by 9 percentage points over Pebble Beach lawyer Bill McCampbell, a Republican.

After winning a 1994 rematch by 8 percentage points, Farr has won subsequent elections by wide margins.

KEY VOTES

2006

- Yes Stop broadband companies from favoring select Internet traffic
- No Affirm U.S. commitment to war in Iraq and reject setting a withdrawal date for troops
- No Repeal requirement for bilingual ballots at the polls
- No Permit U.S. sale of civilian nuclear technology to India
- No Build a 700-mile fence on the U.S.-Mexico border to curb illegal crossings
- No Permit warrantless wiretaps of suspected terrorists

2005

- ? Intervene in the life-support case of Terri Schiavo
- Yes Lift President Bush's restrictions on stem cell research funding
- Yes Prohibit FBI access to library and bookstore records
- No Approve free-trade pact with five Central American countries
- No Pass energy policy overhaul favored by President Bush emphasizing domestic oil and gas production
- No End mandatory preservation of habitat of endangered animal and plant species
- Yes Ban torture of prisoners in U.S. custody

CQ VOTE STUDIES

	PARTY UNITY		PRESIDENTIAL SUPPORT	
	Support	Oppose	Support	Oppose
2006	97%	3%	13%	87%
2005	98%	2%	18%	82%
2004	96%	4%	24%	76%
2003	98%	2%	15%	85%
2002	99%	1%	25%	75%

INTEREST GROUPS

	AFL-CIO	ADA	CCUS	ACU
2006	93%	95%	27%	4%
2005	93%	100%	42%	8%
2004	93%	100%	43%	4%
2003	100%	95%	23%	20%
2002	100%	95%	35%	0%

CALIFORNIA 17

Monterey, San Benito and Santa Cruz counties — Salinas, Santa Cruz

The Democratic 17th takes in the most populated part of Santa Cruz County, with its namesake city and several sizable seaside communities, and stretches south to include San Benito and Monterey counties, where Monterey attracts tourists and exclusive Pebble Beach is home to celebrities and Silicon Valley executives.

South of Santa Cruz County, agriculture drives the economy. The Salinas Valley supplies 80 percent of America's artichokes, as well as lettuce, spinach, cauliflower, cut flowers and other crops. Major wineries and vineyards also dot the landscape. The valley is home to most of the district's 43 percent Hispanic population.

More than 60 percent of district residents live in Monterey County. The region has developed as a center for marine sciences, with more than a dozen major research institutions located near the Monterey Bay coastline. The county also attracts tourists to its coastline, wineries and Cannery Row, a former site of fishing and canning businesses and now a shopping center. Several colleges and universities are in the 17th, including the University of California, Santa Cruz, and California State University Monterey Bay.

Santa Cruz County is a Democratic stronghold, and the party holds a voter registration edge in Monterey and San Benito counties. John Kerry easily won the district in 2004 with 66 percent of the presidential vote.

MAJOR INDUSTRY
Agriculture, tourism, higher education

MILITARY BASES
Fort Hunter Liggett (Army), 2,993 military, 2,257 civilian (2007); Defense Language Institute Foreign Language Center/Presidio of Monterey (Army), 3,300 military, 1,100 civilian (2007); Naval Postgraduate School, 1,500 military, 1,307 civilian (2004); Fleet Numerical Meteorology and Oceanography Center, 61 military, 173 civilian (2007)

CITIES
Salinas, 151,060; Santa Cruz, 54,593; Watsonville, 44,265; Hollister, 34,413

NOTABLE
Monterey Canyon is the deepest submarine canyon off the North American coast of the Pacific Ocean.

Rep. Dennis Cardoza (D)

CAPITOL OFFICE
225-6131
www.house.gov/cardoza
435 Cannon 20515-0518; fax 225-0819

COMMITTEES
Agriculture
(Horticulture & Organic Agriculture - chairman)
Rules

RESIDENCE
Atwater

BORN
March 31, 1959, Merced, Calif.

RELIGION
Roman Catholic

FAMILY
Wife, Kathleen McLoughlin; three children

EDUCATION
U. of Maryland, B.A. 1982 (government & politics)

CAREER
Bowling alley executive; realtor; congressional aide; state legislative aide

POLITICAL HIGHLIGHTS
Atwater City Council, 1984-87; Merced City Council, 1994-95; Calif. Assembly, 1996-2002

ELECTION RESULTS

2006 GENERAL		
Dennis Cardoza (D)	71,182	65.5%
John A. Kanno (R)	37,531	34.5%
2006 PRIMARY		
Dennis Cardoza (D)		unopposed
2004 GENERAL		
Dennis Cardoza (D)	103,732	67.5%
Charles F. Pringle Sr. (R)	49,973	32.5%

PREVIOUS WINNING PERCENTAGES
2002 (51%)

Elected 2002; 3rd term

A leader of the conservative Democratic Blue Dog Coalition, Cardoza in 2007 got a plum spot on the Rules Committee, a leadership-driven panel that puts him on the front lines of the big legislative battles on Capitol Hill. Just in his third term, he has been able to break out of the pack and distinguish himself on a handful of issues.

Cardoza was co-chairman of the Blue Dogs in the 109th Congress (2005-06). The group of more than 40 of the most conservative House Democrats often disagrees with the party's liberal leadership in that chamber. Now, with a Democratic majority, Cardoza says the Blue Dogs "are going to act as a moderating influence on both parties."

Cardoza and the Blue Dogs pushed for adoption early in the 110th Congress (2007-08) of pay-as-you-go rule requiring Congress to find offsets when it boosts entitlement program spending or cuts taxes. Cardoza backs an even tougher measure, giving pay-as-you-go rules the force of law.

His votes on budget bills are driven by his distaste for federal deficits. Cardoza voted against President Bush's tax cut bill in 2003, though he does favor reductions in the inheritance tax, which he says disproportionately affects farmers and ranchers. Likewise, he contends that American farmers are placed at a disadvantage by free-trade pacts with countries that don't have to meet the same labor and environmental standards. He voted against the Central American Free Trade Agreement in 2005.

He frequently sides with Republicans on energy and environmental issues. In the 109th Congress, he supported Bush 44 percent of the time — the second-highest support score for a Democrat in the California delegation. Cardoza describes himself as "a raging moderate." A policy wonk, he says he hates campaigning but loves legislating.

On the Resources Committee (now Natural Resources), he often aligned in the 109th Congress with then Chairman Richard W. Pombo, a California Republican who, like Cardoza, came from a Portuguese-American farm family in the state's Central Valley, known for its dairy, fruit and wine output. Both were ardent about protecting the interests of landowners. Cardoza was chief sponsor in 2005 of a bill to make it harder for the federal government to designate vast tracts of land as "critical habitat" for endangered species.

In his first term, Cardoza also had sided with committee Republicans in 2003 in favor of Bush's proposal to open Alaska's Arctic National Wildlife Refuge to oil drilling. And he teamed with GOP Whip Roy Blunt of Missouri to pass a bill requiring the Agriculture Department to work more closely with local governments during crop disasters. Blunt and Cardoza's breadbasket districts had similar problems with local-federal coordination.

Though he had to give up other committee assignments to serve on the Rules panel, Cardoza was allowed to stay on Agriculture and became chairman of its Subcommittee on Horticulture and Organic Agriculture, which oversees bills on fruits and vegetables. With a say in drafting a new farm bill, he can work to get more federal support for such specialty crops.

Cardoza's pet project in the House is fixing the foster care system. He and his wife, Kathleen McLoughlin, a physician with a family practice in Merced, adopted a sibling pair when the children were 6 and 3. (They have one biological child.) The couple was appalled that the agency they worked with did not take children from Los Angeles County because they had been bounced around foster homes, resulting in lasting psychological problems. In his first term, Cardoza introduced a bill to establish a congressionally appointed commission to recommend legislative fixes to the system. "Every day is a challenge," Cardoza says of his adoption experience. "But to take children who would have had almost no opportunity whatsoever, to make them part of our lives, that's a real blessing."

Another of his endeavors is federal funding for a new campus of the University of California system at Merced, which he worked on for years as a state assemblyman. He says education could alleviate some of the social problems in his district, which has a large immigrant population that feeds the seasonal farm labor force. It is 42 percent Hispanic, has double-digit unemployment and a big-city-scale drug problem.

Cardoza grew up in the small town of Atwater, Calif., the grandson of immigrants who came from Portugal's Azores Islands in the 1920s. They revered President Franklin D. Roosevelt, whose programs they believed got them through the Depression. "Back then, if you were Catholic and an immigrant, you were a Democrat," Cardoza says. "They told me they owed their existence to FDR." When the government began minting Roosevelt dimes, his grandmother refused to spend any of them. "When she died, there were bags of them in her closet," he says.

Cardoza's parents were dairy and sweet potato farmers who later opened bowling alleys in Atwater and Merced. Interested in politics as a youth, he got a degree in government and politics from the University of Maryland, then interned for Democratic Rep. Martin Frost of Texas.

After college, Cardoza went home to manage the family's bowling business, but his real desire was to run for office. In 1984, he was elected to the Atwater City Council. He volunteered in the campaign of then California Assemblyman Gary A. Condit, who became a political mentor. Cardoza spent six years in the California Assembly, where, in a foreshadowing of his service in the U.S. House, he was a leader of a moderate Democratic faction and chaired the Rules Committee.

Condit, in the meantime, had begun a long tenure in the U.S. House. But his career was undone by a sex scandal, in which he was forced to admit to an extramarital affair with Chandra Levy, a young woman from Modesto who disappeared and was later found slain in a Washington, D.C., park, the victim of an assault while she was jogging. Condit refused to bow out of the 2002 Democratic primary, so Cardoza challenged him. The relationship with Condit turned bitter, with both of Condit's grown children circulating letters in the district calling Cardoza a "traitor." But he had the Democratic establishment on his side. He won the primary, then prevailed over GOP state Sen. Dick Monteith by 8 percentage points that November.

KEY VOTES

2006

- No Stop broadband companies from favoring select Internet traffic
- Yes Affirm U.S. commitment to war in Iraq and reject setting a withdrawal date for troops
- No Repeal requirement for bilingual ballots at the polls
- Yes Permit U.S. sale of civilian nuclear technology to India
- Yes Build a 700-mile fence on the U.S.-Mexico border to curb illegal crossings
- No Permit warrantless wiretaps of suspected terrorists

2005

- ? Intervene in the life-support case of Terri Schiavo
- Yes Lift President Bush's restrictions on stem cell research funding
- Yes Prohibit FBI access to library and bookstore records
- No Approve free-trade pact with five Central American countries
- Yes Pass energy policy overhaul favored by President Bush emphasizing domestic oil and gas production
- Yes End mandatory preservation of habitat of endangered animal and plant species
- Yes Ban torture of prisoners in U.S. custody

CQ VOTE STUDIES

	PARTY UNITY		PRESIDENTIAL SUPPORT	
	Support	Oppose	Support	Oppose
2006	79%	21%	50%	50%
2005	79%	21%	39%	61%
2004	81%	19%	45%	55%
2003	82%	18%	40%	60%

INTEREST GROUPS

	AFL-CIO	ADA	CCUS	ACU
2006	85%	60%	79%	46%
2005	100%	85%	67%	44%
2004	93%	85%	65%	25%
2003	93%	80%	50%	40%

CALIFORNIA 18

Central Valley – Merced, part of Stockton and Modesto

The politically competitive 18th takes in most of Stockton in San Joaquin County, then dives south to pick up half of Stanislaus County and Merced County, which make up the district's agricultural base. A narrow strip stretches through Madera and Fresno counties to almost reach Fresno.

Growth in Modesto, the Stanislaus County seat, has been spurred by businesses fleeing California's congested coastal cities and by the Central Valley's successful agriculture industry. The city has its own canning and food-processing industry, as well as the Gallo Winery — the nation's second-largest winery. The district's portion of Modesto includes the headquarters of Foster Farms Dairy, the largest privately owned dairy in the state, as well as a full-service plant. National companies such as Del Monte and Frito-Lay also have facilities in the district. These industries help give the 18th one of California's highest percentages of blue-collar workers (37 percent).

Although dominated by agriculture, the district also includes the central portion of the diverse and Democratic port city of Stockton (shared with the 11th), which is a transportation hub on the San Joaquin River. Almost 60 percent of Stockton's residents live in the 18th. In 2005, a University of California campus opened in Merced, the system's 10th and the first U.S. public research university to be built in the 21st century.

The area has a long history of sending Democrats to Congress, having done so for decades, but the district often votes for Republican presidential candidates. George W. Bush carried the 18th with 50 percent of the vote in the 2004 presidential election. Hispanics enjoy a plurality of the district's population (42 percent), while whites make up 39 percent of residents. Stockton has one of the largest Sikh populations in the United States.

MAJOR INDUSTRY

Agriculture, wine, food processing

CITIES

Stockton (pt.), 139,362; Modesto (pt.), 133,975; Merced, 63,893

NOTABLE

Stockton hosts an annual asparagus festival, during which more than 40,000 pounds of asparagus are consumed.

Rep. George Radanovich (R)

CAPITOL OFFICE
225-4540
www.house.gov/radanovich
2367 Rayburn 20515-0519; fax 225-3402

COMMITTEES
Energy & Commerce

RESIDENCE
Mariposa

BORN
June 20, 1955, Mariposa, Calif.

RELIGION
Roman Catholic

FAMILY
Wife, Ethie Radanovich; one child

EDUCATION
California Polytechnic State U., San Luis Obispo, B.S. 1978 (agriculture business management)

CAREER
Vintner; bank manager; carpenter

POLITICAL HIGHLIGHTS
Mariposa County Board of Supervisors, 1989-92 (chairman, 1991); sought Republican nomination for U.S. House, 1992

ELECTION RESULTS

2006 GENERAL		
George Radanovich (R)	110,246	60.6%
TJ Cox (D)	71,748	39.4%
2006 PRIMARY		
George Radanovich (R)		unopposed
2004 GENERAL		
George Radanovich (R)	155,354	66.0%
James Lex Bufford (D)	64,047	27.2%
Larry R. Mullen (GREEN)	15,863	6.7%

PREVIOUS WINNING PERCENTAGES
2002 (67%); 2000 (65%); 1998 (79%); 1996 (67%); 1994 (57%)

Elected 1994; 7th term

Radanovich says Easterners, particularly government bureaucrats, are fairly clueless about issues confronting the West, where the government owns huge tracts of land and private access to water is crucial to local economies.

As chairman of the Resources Committee's Water and Power Subcommittee in the 109th Congress (2005-06), Radanovich (ruh-DON-o-vitch) held sway over an issue vital to Westerners — the availability of water. With Democrats in control in the 110th congress (2007-08), Republicans lost committee seats and Radanovich lost influence over water issues after he had to choose between the Resources seat he had held since his first term and a slot on the powerful Energy and Commerce panel, on which he has served since 2001. In what he called a "tough decision," he picked the latter.

His biggest legislative push on Resources involved efforts to modify a 1992 law that has been controversial with California farmers and that helped propel Radanovich to national office more than a dozen years ago. The Central Valley Project Improvement Act guarantees that 800,000 acre-feet of water annually will be given over to fish and wildlife protection, but farmers say this robs them of water for irrigation. A bill Radanovich backs demands that an equal amount of replacement water be distributed to farmers by 2012 at the "lowest cost reasonably achievable."

Another priority in the 110th Congress is getting federal approval for a negotiated settlement of an 18-year-old legal battle over the use of San Joaquin River water. Radanovich in March 2007 praised negotiators who had reached the settlement and said, "Let's make it happen."

Radanovich and his rural constituents are of one mind on a more limited role for the federal government, and his positions are driven by the tenets of the large GOP Class of '94 — shift authority from the federal to state and local governments and get rid of regulations that hinder business growth.

But he has backed away from one principle espoused by the Class of '94: term limits. When he was first elected, Radanovich promised to serve just five terms, which would have put him out of a job in 2004. But he told the Fresno Bee, "There are issues that are really important to me, like water and power, and reform of the Endangered Species Act, and that hasn't happened yet. I just don't feel that my job is done yet."

Radanovich scored a victory in 2005 when the House passed his proposal to give local communities more say in policy at national parks, particularly Yosemite National Park in his district. Federal proposals to address park overcrowding could hurt tourist-dependent towns and businesses near the park, he says. Radanovich proposed his own plan for Yosemite in the 108th Congress (2003-04) to restore campsites washed away in a 1997 flood and to add more parking along the Merced River. His measure also sought to remove the national landmark status of the park's LeConte Memorial Lodge. That was a jab at the Sierra Club, which had built the lodge in 1903-04. The group opposed the added campsites and parking.

With his district's farmers in mind, Radanovich sponsored a bill allowing the United States to ignore an international environmental treaty calling for a ban in 2005 on methyl bromide, a popular killer of insects, weeds and diseases. The bill became moot when the Bush administration approved exemptions allowing the chemical's continued use.

Radanovich is a party loyalist, only rarely bucking his leaders. In 2005, Resources Committee Chairman Richard W. Pombo, who represented the neighboring 11th District, gave him his "Golden Cowboy Boot" award, reserved for committee members with perfect attendance who vote "perfectly in sync with the chairman."

Radanovich did abandon the leadership on the immigration issue in 2005 as one of just 17 Republicans who voted against a GOP bill cracking down on illegal immigrants. He wanted, but didn't get, a provision for a guest worker program for agriculture, heavily dependent on migrant labor.

He has tried for years to push through Congress a resolution calling on the president to "accurately characterize" as genocide the killing of more than a million Armenians from 1915 to 1923 by the Ottoman Empire, centered in what is now Turkey. Radanovich represents a large population of Armenian-Americans in the Fresno area. But the White House, under both parties, has not wanted to anger Turkey, a strategic ally in the Middle East.

A former vintner, Radanovich gets involved in issues affecting the domestic wine industry. News reports in 2004 suggested that Radanovich received special treatment in a land swap with a local developer and political contributor. The Fresno Bee reported on a financial agreement that allowed Radanovich to reacquire a seven-acre vineyard and barn that had once belonged to his family's winery business. Radanovich told the Associated Press: "I traded 27 acres of land with great development potential for seven land-locked acres owned by the new winery owner that were part of my family's farm where the winery was located." He said suggestions that he got the better part of the deal defied logic.

The fifth of eight children of a Croatian immigrant who owned a clothing store in Mariposa, Radanovich spent his teen years on the family's small ranch outside town. He got his college degree in agriculture business management, and after working a few years as a banker, a carpenter and a substitute teacher, pursued his first love, farming. Inspired by memories of his grandfather making wine in the cellar, Radanovich established a winery in the Mariposa County foothills of the Sierra Nevada. At one time the Radanovich Winery shipped about 6,000 cases of wine annually, but after big financial losses, he closed it in 2003.

Radanovich won a seat on the Mariposa County Board of Supervisors in 1989, and in 1992 made a bid for Congress. Mariposa is far from the district's population center in Fresno County, where he was largely unknown. But Radanovich did well, losing a close primary to eventual GOP nominee Tal Cloud, who lost in November. In 1994, aided by a GOP tilt in the district from the post-1990 census remapping, Radanovich beat incumbent Democratic Rep. Richard H. Lehman. He has won easily since.

KEY VOTES

2006

No Stop broadband companies from favoring select Internet traffic

Yes Affirm U.S. commitment to war in Iraq and reject setting a withdrawal date for troops

Yes Repeal requirement for bilingual ballots at the polls

Yes Permit U.S. sale of civilian nuclear technology to India

Yes Build a 700-mile fence on the U.S.-Mexico border to curb illegal crossings

Yes Permit warrantless wiretaps of suspected terrorists

2005

? Intervene in the life-support case of Terri Schiavo

No Lift President Bush's restrictions on stem cell research funding

No Prohibit FBI access to library and bookstore records

Yes Approve free-trade pact with five Central American countries

Yes Pass energy policy overhaul favored by President Bush emphasizing domestic oil and gas production

Yes End mandatory preservation of habitat of endangered animal and plant species

No Ban torture of prisoners in U.S. custody

CQ VOTE STUDIES

	PARTY UNITY		PRESIDENTIAL SUPPORT	
	Support	Oppose	Support	Oppose
2006	97%	3%	95%	5%
2005	96%	4%	86%	14%
2004	95%	5%	91%	9%
2003	97%	3%	100%	0%
2002	96%	4%	89%	11%

INTEREST GROUPS

	AFL-CIO	ADA	CCUS	ACU
2006	7%	5%	100%	88%
2005	21%	0%	96%	92%
2004	7%	0%	100%	100%
2003	0%	5%	96%	88%
2002	11%	5%	95%	88%

CALIFORNIA 19

Central Valley — part of Fresno and Modesto, Turlock, Madera

A fertile farm district, the 19th includes the heart of Central California's San Joaquin Valley. It takes in about half of Stanislaus County, grabbing a portion of Modesto. East of Stanislaus, it moves south from Tuolumne to Mariposa County into almost all of Madera County and part of the city of Fresno, home to large Hispanic, Hmong and Armenian populations.

The district's portion of Stanislaus County includes less than one-third of Modesto's population and the growing city of Turlock. Tuolumne and Mariposa counties, which along with Madera County to the south are home to Yosemite National Park, are sparsely populated areas that make up only roughly one-tenth of the 19th's population. The counties feature ski slopes and forests of the Sierra Nevada range in the east and former Gold Rush towns such as Jamestown, Sonora and Mariposa in the west.

This agricultural district — boasting the nation's third-highest orchard acreage and tenth-highest number of milk cows — has a Foster Farms Dairy milk and juice processing plant in the 19th's portion of Fresno and a ConAgra plant in Oakdale. Madera County, whose vines account for 10 percent of the state's wine grapes, has several notable wineries, and Yosemite National Park brings tourists here. Turlock's status as a growing bedroom community for San Jose and San Francisco has spurred local debate over issues of smart growth and business development to the north and west.

The 19th is rural, reliably Republican and white, although Hispanics make up 28 percent of residents. Republicans hold a double-digit lead in party registration here, and the district gave George W. Bush 61 percent of its 2004 presidential vote and Arnold Schwarzenegger 69 percent of its 2006 gubernatorial vote.

MAJOR INDUSTRY

Agriculture, dairy, tourism

CITIES

Fresno (pt.), 189,836; Turlock, 55,810; Modesto (pt.), 54,881; Madera, 43,207

NOTABLE

Yosemite National Park was created in 1890, and its El Capitan rock formation is the world's largest granite monolith; Fresno's Forestiere Underground Gardens features plants growing 22 feet below ground.

Rep. Jim Costa (D)

CAPITOL OFFICE
225-3341
congressmanjimcosta@mail.house.gov
www.house.gov/costa
1314 Longworth 20515-0520; fax 225-9308

COMMITTEES
Agriculture
Foreign Affairs
Natural Resources
(Energy & Mineral Resources - chairman)

RESIDENCE
Fresno

BORN
April 13, 1952, Fresno, Calif.

RELIGION
Roman Catholic

FAMILY
Single

EDUCATION
California State U., Fresno, B.A. 1974 (political science)

CAREER
Lobbyist; state legislative aide; congressional district aide; almond orchard owner

POLITICAL HIGHLIGHTS
Calif. Assembly, 1978-94; Democratic nominee for Calif. Senate, 1993; Calif. Senate, 1994-2002

ELECTION RESULTS

2006 GENERAL		
Jim Costa (D)		unopposed
2006 PRIMARY		
Jim Costa (D)		unopposed
2004 GENERAL		
Jim Costa (D)	61,005	53.4%
Roy Ashburn (R)	53,231	46.6%

Elected 2004; 2nd term

It's no surprise that Costa focuses on agriculture, given his family history and the Central Valley district he represents, which includes some of the most productive agricultural areas in the country. Costa's immigrant grandfather started milking cows on the very day he arrived in the Central Valley a century ago from the Portuguese Azores island of Terceira.

Costa's father and uncle later ran the roughly 500-acre farm, located nine miles west of Fresno. They lived next door to each other for 57 years. Costa started helping out at the age of 7. The family sold its dairy herd in the 1970s, and after his father and uncle died, divided up the farm. Costa still owns 240 acres of the property, now an almond orchard. He gives out one-pound bags of his almonds to visitors to his congressional office.

Costa hasn't lost interest in the dairy industry. He looks out for the region's many dairy farmers from his seat on the Agriculture Committee. He has joined fellow California Democrat Devin Nunes (another third-generation Portuguese-American dairyman) in seeking to limit the ability of dairies outside California to sell their milk in the state if they circumvent state and federal rules. And as Congress tackles a rewrite of the basic farm law in the 110th Congress (2007-08), Costa wants to make sure that California farmers and those elsewhere in the United States can be competitive in the global marketplace.

Costa also continues to push for a guest farm-worker program, a proposal that died in 2006 after being attached to a broader immigration overhaul. The bill would allow at least 1.5 million farm workers currently living in the United States to obtain temporary legal status if they can prove they have worked in agriculture long enough. He hopes the bill will fare better in the Democratically controlled 110th Congress.

In addition to looking out for farmers, Costa in recent years has helped get funding for a Fresno veterans' home, a federal penitentiary in his district and a newly renovated Amtrak station in Fresno.

Politics and government are nothing new for the Costa family. The congressman's father served as treasurer for a friend running for the local county board of supervisors. His mother, who died at age 90 in 2006, served on a county social services board and as a school trustee. She joined Democratic clubs and thought Harry S Truman was "a heck of a guy," Costa told the Fresno Bee when his mother died.

Despite his parents' civic involvement, working on the farm and skiing occupied most of Costa's attention in high school and college. It wasn't until he interned in the office of Democratic Rep. B.F. Sisk in the summer of 1973 and attended the Senate Watergate hearings that Costa caught the political bug. "That was like a soap opera for me, reading and staying on top of that," Costa said in an oral history interview with California State University at Sacramento. "I was genuinely hooked by this time."

He worked on the winning 1974 House campaign of California Democrat John Krebs, and then was an aide in his Washington office before returning to California to help on a state legislative race. After 18 months as the state legislator's administrative assistant, Costa decided to run for the Assembly himself in 1978, when the incumbent in the district where he grew up made a run for governor. He was only 26 when he was elected.

He served in the legislature for 24 years, first in the Assembly and then in the state Senate, earning a reputation for expertise on the concerns of local farmers, particularly water issues. Both in Sacramento and on Capitol Hill, his moderate pro-business positions have not always endeared him to organized labor leaders or environmentalists.

In Congress, he is a member of the Blue Dog Coalition of conservative House Democrats. He has voted in favor of Republican bills to permanently repeal the estate tax, weaken the Endangered Species Act and stop minors from crossing state borders to get an abortion without parental consent. In 2006, he was one of only two California Democrats to vote for legislation calling for a double-layered fence along the border with Mexico.

At the same time, however, he sided with most Democrats in opposing the 2005 Central American Free Trade Agreement and voted in 2006 against authorization of the Bush administration's warrantless electronic surveillance program. He also voted to override President Bush's veto of a bill expanding federal funding of embryonic stem cell research.

Early in his first term, The Fresno Bee noted that Costa is "defying labels. Conservative? Moderate? Liberal? In today's political climate, where everyone wants a simple, black-or-white description of every politician, none really seems to fit Costa." That suits Costa just fine. "I don't like being labeled," he says.

In the 110th Congress, Costa gained a seat on the Foreign Affairs Committee, a longtime interest of his. The entryway to his House office includes photos of him with both Pakistani President Pervez Musharraf and Cuba's Fidel Castro.

When term limits forced him out of the state Senate in 2002, Costa opened his own lobbying firm. Having flirted with a House run three previous times, Costa quickly declared his candidacy after six-term Democratic Rep. Cal Dooley announced he would not run again. Getting to know the electorate was not a problem; the state Senate district Costa represented for eight years included the entire congressional district. "I'm like an old shoe who's been working with those folks for a long time," Costa says.

Costa trounced former Dooley chief of staff Lisa Quigley in the primary, which turned ugly when she ran a television ad citing Costa's 1986 arrest in a prostitution sting, for which he had earlier apologized, and a 1994 incident in which police found marijuana in his apartment. (The drug was never linked to him and no charges were filed.) He faced a tough challenge in November from well-funded Republican state Sen. Roy Ashburn. But Costa won by 7 percentage points and was re-elected without opposition in 2006.

KEY VOTES

2006

- No Stop broadband companies from favoring select Internet traffic
- Yes Affirm U.S. commitment to war in Iraq and reject setting a withdrawal date for troops
- No Repeal requirement for bilingual ballots at the polls
- Yes Permit U.S. sale of civilian nuclear technology to India
- Yes Build a 700-mile fence on the U.S.-Mexico border to curb illegal crossings
- No Permit warrantless wiretaps of suspected terrorists

2005

- ? Intervene in the life-support case of Terri Schiavo
- Yes Lift President Bush's restrictions on stem cell research funding
- Yes Prohibit FBI access to library and bookstore records
- No Approve free-trade pact with five Central American countries
- Yes Pass energy policy overhaul favored by President Bush emphasizing domestic oil and gas production
- Yes End mandatory preservation of habitat of endangered animal and plant species
- \+ Ban torture of prisoners in U.S. custody

CQ VOTE STUDIES

	PARTY UNITY		PRESIDENTIAL SUPPORT	
	Support	Oppose	Support	Oppose
2006	76%	24%	47%	53%
2005	79%	21%	42%	58%

INTEREST GROUPS

	AFL-CIO	ADA	CCUS	ACU
2006	86%	70%	93%	56%
2005	93%	80%	70%	32%

CALIFORNIA 20

Central Valley — Kings County, part of Fresno and Bakersfield

The Hispanic-majority 20th reaches from Fresno to Bakersfield, through rural portions of Fresno, Kings and Kern counties. Roughly 40 percent of Fresno's residents live in the 20th, which takes in much of downtown and Hispanic areas in the southern section of the city.

Federal water projects in the Westlands have spawned vast farms with battalions of workers and a wide variety of crops, including alfalfa, cotton, fruits, sugar beets, wheat and nuts. Fresno's agricultural contribution is more industrial, with a Sun-Maid fig plant, a Foster Farms hatchery, several dairy farms and a Kraft Foods plant that manufactures Capri Sun, Tang and Kool-Aid. The district also has attracted public and privately run prisons that assist the area's economy.

The 20th bears much of the burden of the San Joaquin Valley's urban and rural poor and is beset by unemployment and crime. Its residents have the nation's sixth-lowest median income ($26,800), and the district has the state's lowest rate of college education (6 percent), as well as the country's third-highest number of residents (just under 50 percent) without a high school diploma. With the only blue-collar plurality in the state, many district workers are Hispanic and Hmong immigrants who work in the local farming communities that were hurt by agricultural losses after freezing temperatures in early 2007. Overall, the district has the nation's fourth-largest orchard acreage.

Democrats enjoy a distinct voter registration advantage in the 20th, although John Kerry only narrowly won the district's 2004 presidential vote with 51 percent. The 20th is the nation's third-youngest district, with its median age just a shade under 27.

MAJOR INDUSTRY
Agriculture, dairy, prisons

MILITARY BASES
Naval Air Station Lemoore, 7,197 military, 1,650 civilian (2007)

CITIES
Fresno (pt.), 154,998; Bakersfield (pt.), 43,284; Hanford, 41,686; Delano, 38,824

NOTABLE
The Fresno Sanitary Landfill is the country's oldest sanitary landfill.

Rep. Devin Nunes (R)

CAPITOL OFFICE
225-2523
nunes.house.gov
1013 Longworth 20515-0521; fax 225-3404

COMMITTEES
Ways & Means

RESIDENCE
Visalia

BORN
Oct. 1, 1973, Tulare, Calif.

RELIGION
Roman Catholic

FAMILY
Wife, Elizabeth Nunes

EDUCATION
College of the Sequoias, A.A. 1993 (agriculture); California Polytechnic State U., San Luis Obispo, B.S. 1995 (agricultural business), M.S. 1996 (agriculture)

CAREER
Farmer; U.S. Agriculture Department program administrator

POLITICAL HIGHLIGHTS
College of the Sequoias Board of Trustees, 1996-2002; sought Republican nomination for U.S. House, 1998

ELECTION RESULTS

2006 GENERAL		
Devin Nunes (R)	95,214	66.7%
Steven Haze (D)	42,718	29.9%
John Roger Miller (GREEN)	4,729	3.3%
2006 PRIMARY		
Devin Nunes (R)		unopposed
2004 GENERAL		
Devin Nunes (R)	140,721	73.2%
Fred B. Davis (D)	51,594	26.8%

PREVIOUS WINNING PERCENTAGES
2002 (70%)

Elected 2002; 3rd term

Attentive to party fundraising and strategic about building alliances, Nunes appears to be positioning himself for a place in the Republican leadership. A third-generation dairy farmer from the unglamorous, rural midsection of California, he focuses on water, agricultural and transportation issues vital to his district, but has moved increasingly into national issues.

Nunes (NEW-ness) shared $493,000 of his campaign wealth with other Republicans in 2006, and the following year, helped spearhead House GOP fundraising for 2008. Nunes also was part of a small group that successfully backed underdog John A. Boehner of Ohio in his winning contest over Roy Blunt of Missouri for Republican leader in 2006.

"I don't care about being in the leadership, but I want to be a leader," he says. He told the Fresno Bee newspaper that his decision to back Boehner would prove advantageous. "When you help a guy become the fourth-most-powerful person in the United States, it's a good thing," he said.

It was not the first time Nunes picked the right ally. His political mentor was former Rep. Bill Thomas, a fellow California Republican and the powerful chairman of the House Ways and Means Committee in the last years of the Republican majority. In the 109th Congress (2005-06), Nunes snagged a rare vacancy on the tax writing panel despite stiff competition from Republican Pat Tiberi of Ohio, who had two years more seniority.

To take a seat on the exclusive panel, Nunes had to give up the senior GOP slot on the National Parks Subcommittee of the Resources Committee, where he had typically sided with landowners in their frequent disputes with environmentalists.

Nunes is a conservative who voted with his party 97 percent of the time in the 109th Congress, but, like many Republicans, was increasingly dissatisfied with the White House and its handling of the war in Iraq. Nunes publicly criticized the Bush administration for not firing Defense Secretary Donald H. Rumsfeld prior to the midterm elections.

In 2006, Nunes won passage of an important dairy bill in his district, a controversial measure forcing dairy producers to operate in a federally regulated system and aimed at an Arizona-based dairy, Sarah Farms, which was operating outside the system and selling milk for a lower price in California. Nunes' district is a top milk producer; the Nunes family dairy was started by his grandfather. He also has received substantial campaign contributions from the dairy industry and its lobbyists.

Nunes won election to Congress in 2002 on a promise to deliver more water to an underquenched slice of the state that would revert to desert if not for irrigation. His prime focus has been securing federal funding for a dam on the San Joaquin River, which would help chronic water shortages in Tulare County and a portion of Fresno County, two of the most agriculturally rich counties in the United States. In 2006, a group of California lawmakers, including Nunes, agreed on legislation to implement a court settlement restoring water flows to a 60-mile dry stretch of the lower San Joaquin River, which could return salmon to the river.

Nunes is an advocate for the Sequoia and Kings Canyon national parks in his district, but is frequently at odds with environmental groups who oppose commercial logging. He supports the thinning and clearing of national forests as a check on wildfires that have plagued California in recent years, including a 2002 fire that destroyed thousands of acres in Sequoia National Forest, the 1.1 million-acre park named for its giant trees.

As scenic as parts of his district are, it suffers from high unemployment and below-average education levels, a legacy of the area's seasonal economy, its reliance on immigrants for farm work and an abundance of cheap housing for people fleeing California's high-priced coastal cities. It also is a major source of illegal methamphetamine, and Nunes is pushing for more federal funds to combat increasingly organized groups producing the drug in hidden, illegal factories. He and others in the California congressional delegation secured $1.5 million for the state in fiscal 2006.

Nunes' family hails from the Azores, the nine-island chain off the coast of Portugal. His immigrant grandfather established the 640-acre family farm, where his father still has a dairy operation. Two uncles also work there; Nunes and his brother, Anthony, once ran an alfalfa hay harvesting business. Nunes can trace his agrarian roots back several hundred years. "Everyone on the Azores had three cows, fished and made wine," he says.

The district is home to a concentration of Portuguese-Americans, many of them related by blood or marriage and most Roman Catholic. They share food traditions, festivals and other cultural elements. In 2003, Nunes married Elizabeth Tamariz, a Portuguese-American who teaches elementary school and whom he's known since childhood.

After graduating from California Polytechnic State University in 1996, Nunes volunteered to help a candidate for the board of the two-year College of the Sequoias, which he had attended. The candidate unexpectedly quit, and Nunes, then 22, decided to run himself. He wound up ousting a seasoned incumbent. The next day Nunes, wearing work clothes and fixing his grandmother's water heater, was surprised when a local television crew drove out to interview him. He was hooked on politics.

While on the school board, he met Thomas, the local congressman. In 1998, he agreed to an all-but-hopeless challenge to Democratic incumbent Cal Dooley in the 20th District and lost. In 2000, Nunes campaigned for George W. Bush, and was rewarded when Thomas helped him get appointed state director for the U.S. Agriculture Department's rural development program when Bush became president in 2001.

Reapportionment gave California an additional seat, and the 21st District was created. In 2002, Nunes beat two better-known Republicans in the primary, Fresno Mayor Jim Patterson and state Rep. Mike Briggs. His two competitors split the GOP vote in the Fresno area, to Nunes' advantage. He also benefited from a Hispanic-sounding name and the solid support of Portuguese-American voters in Tulare County. He cruised to victory in the general election. He easily won re-election in 2004 and 2006.

KEY VOTES

2006

No Stop broadband companies from favoring select Internet traffic
Yes Affirm U.S. commitment to war in Iraq and reject setting a withdrawal date for troops
Yes Repeal requirement for bilingual ballots at the polls
Yes Permit U.S. sale of civilian nuclear technology to India
Yes Build a 700-mile fence on the U.S.-Mexico border to curb illegal crossings
Yes Permit warrantless wiretaps of suspected terrorists

2005

? Intervene in the life-support case of Terri Schiavo
No Lift President Bush's restrictions on stem cell research funding
No Prohibit FBI access to library and bookstore records
Yes Approve free-trade pact with five Central American countries
Yes Pass energy policy overhaul favored by President Bush emphasizing domestic oil and gas production
Yes End mandatory preservation of habitat of endangered animal and plant species
No Ban torture of prisoners in U.S. custody

CQ VOTE STUDIES

	PARTY UNITY		PRESIDENTIAL SUPPORT	
	Support	Oppose	Support	Oppose
2006	98%	2%	95%	5%
2005	96%	4%	87%	13%
2004	95%	5%	91%	9%
2003	98%	2%	100%	0%

INTEREST GROUPS

	AFL-CIO	ADA	CCUS	ACU
2006	8%	0%	100%	84%
2005	29%	5%	96%	84%
2004	13%	0%	100%	96%
2003	7%	5%	100%	88%

CALIFORNIA 21
Central Valley — Tulare County, part of Fresno

The agriculture-dominated 21st is home to all of Tulare and part of Fresno counties, which vie each year for the title of top farm goods-producing county in the nation. The 21st ranks first in the country in both orchard acreage and total number of milk cows. In addition to about 20 percent of the city of Fresno, the district takes in some of the mountains and forests of the Sierra Nevada chain on its eastern edge.

Tulare County is the world's largest dairy-producing area and the nation's second-largest agricultural county. The Land O'Lakes creamery here is the largest dairy processing plant in the United States. The county also produces more than 250 other agricultural goods, including oranges, grapes, nuts and cotton — although freezing conditions in early 2007 hurt production. Tulare also is developing an ethanol industry.

The city of Tulare hosts the annual World Ag Expo, the world's largest agricultural exposition, which draws an annual attendance of more than 100,000 people from more than 60 countries. Visalia is the site of a Kraft Foods cheese and sour cream manufacturing plant.

The 21st includes the eastern portion of Fresno, including Fresno Yosemite International Airport. Fresno also is home to a Gap clothing distribution center and the Foster Farms turkey hatchery. Tourists are attracted to the district's location in the Sequoia Valley: The Giant Sequoia National Monument and the Sequoia National Forest are located east of Porterville and offer camping, hiking, kayaking or mountain biking either in the forest or in the nearby Sierra Nevada range.

The district's share of Fresno is the more conservative area of the city, and the rest of the 21st is reliably Republican. District residents gave George W. Bush 65 percent of the vote in the 2004 presidential election, his second-best showing in the state, and gave Arnold Schwarzenegger 72 percent of the gubernatorial vote here in 2006.

MAJOR INDUSTRY
Agriculture, dairy, transportation, tourism

CITIES
Visalia, 91,565; Fresno (pt.), 82,818; Clovis, 68,468; Tulare, 43,994; Porterville, 39,615

NOTABLE
The Porterville High School marching band is said to be the oldest high school band in California.

Rep. Kevin McCarthy (R)

Elected 2006; 1st term

McCarthy was groomed for the House by his powerful predecessor, Republican Bill Thomas, the former chairman of the House Ways and Means Committee whose retirement from Congress paved the way for McCarthy. He was an aide to Thomas for 15 years, beginning while in college, and working his way up to be Thomas' district director.

The two are also friends and share an interest in cars and car shows. When the 14-term congressman decided to step down in 2006, McCarthy, by then a seasoned state legislator as well, was the obvious successor.

He was a virtual shoo-in after winning the GOP primary against two little-known competitors. He went on to easily best Democratic businesswoman Sharon M. Beery in the Republican-friendly district.

Except for a stint as a small-business owner in college, McCarthy has spent his life in politics. At age 19, he won $5,000 in the California state lottery, invested it successfully in the stock market and opened a restaurant called Kevin O's Deli — all before his 21st birthday.

His first public office was on the Kern County Community College Board. He was elected to the California Assembly in 2002. As a freshman, he was chosen by his colleagues to be Republican leader. In that role, he was a member of California's "Big 5," an informal decision-making group also including Gov. Arnold Schwarzenegger, the Senate president pro tempore, the GOP Senate leader and the speaker of the Assembly.

"Serving in the minority and being the leader gave me a whole different perspective," McCarthy says. "It gave me the ability to know what you should fight for, when to fight, and why you have to work so closely as a team to be effective."

When he got to Congress, McCarthy was chosen as freshman representative to the House Republican Steering Committee, which makes the all-important committee assignments. McCarthy got a seat on the Agriculture Committee, giving him a hand in the redrafting of farm policy in the 110th Congress (2007-08). He is the only Republican on the committee from California, the largest agricultural producer in the nation.

CAPITOL OFFICE
225-2915
kevinmccarthy.house.gov
1523 Longworth 20515-0522; fax 225-8798

COMMITTEES
Agriculture
Homeland Security
House Administration
Natural Resources
Joint Printing

RESIDENCE
Bakersfield

BORN
Jan. 26, 1965, Bakersfield, Calif.

RELIGION
Baptist

FAMILY
Wife, Judy McCarthy; two children

EDUCATION
Bakersfield College, attended 1984-85; California State U., Bakersfield, B.S. 1989 (business administration), M.B.A. 1994

CAREER
Congressional district aide; deli owner

POLITICAL HIGHLIGHTS
Kern County Republican Central Committee, 1992-2002; Kern County Community College District Board of Trustees, 2000-02; Calif. Assembly, 2002-06 (minority leader, 2004-06)

ELECTION RESULTS

2006 GENERAL		
Kevin McCarthy (R)	133,278	70.7%
Sharon M. Beery (D)	55,226	29.3%
2006 PRIMARY		
Kevin McCarthy (R)	63,399	85.6%
Steven W. Nichols (R)	5,995	8.1%
David W. Evans (R)	4,637	6.3%

CALIFORNIA 22

Kern and San Luis Obispo counties — Bakersfield

The 22nd stretches inland from San Luis Obispo County near the coast to Ridgecrest in Kern County before dipping south into northwest Los Angeles County. It then turns north again to take in most of Bakersfield and most of the rest of Kern. More than two-thirds of its residents live in Kern County.

Kern is known for oil production and a strong agricultural base, although early 2007 crop production was hurt by freezing weather in the San Joaquin Valley. Along with vineyards and cattle in the San Luis Obispo area (the city itself is in the coastal 23rd), the two counties produce billions of dollars each year in crops such as grapes, citrus, cotton and nuts. Kern also is home to the Hyundai-Kia California Proving Ground testing facility.

Bakersfield (shared with the 20th) is Kern County's largest city and sits in the southern end of the San Joaquin Valley. The city, along with Lancaster (shared with the 25th) in Los Angeles County, continues to grow. Oil and agriculture dominate, but the city is trying to diversify with a technology sector.

Northern San Luis Obispo County is home to many conservative Democrats, but the 22nd is GOP territory. President George W. Bush in 2004 and Gov. Arnold Schwarzenegger in 2006 won their highest vote percentages in the state here during their respective runs.

MAJOR INDUSTRY
Agriculture, oil, military

MILITARY BASES
Edwards Air Force Base, 2,707 military, 9,132 civilian (2006) (shared with the 25th); Naval Air Warfare Center Weapons Division, China Lake, 951 military, 3,920 civilian (2006) (shared with the 25th)

CITIES
Bakersfield (pt.), 203,773; Lancaster (pt.), 65,976; Oildale (unincorporated), 27,885

NOTABLE
Edwards AFB was the site of Chuck Yeager's 1947 flight that broke the sound barrier.

Rep. Lois Capps (D)

CAPITOL OFFICE
225-3601
www.house.gov/capps
1110 Longworth 20515-0523; fax 225-5632

COMMITTEES
Energy & Commerce
Natural Resources

RESIDENCE
Santa Barbara

BORN
Jan. 10, 1938, Ladysmith, Wis.

RELIGION
Lutheran

FAMILY
Widowed; three children (one deceased)

EDUCATION
Pacific Lutheran U., B.S. 1959 (nursing); Yale U., M.A. 1964 (religion); U. of California, Santa Barbara, M.A. 1990 (education)

CAREER
Elementary school nurse; college instructor

POLITICAL HIGHLIGHTS
No previous office

ELECTION RESULTS

2006 GENERAL		
Lois Capps (D)	114,661	65.2%
Victor D. Tognazzini (R)	61,272	34.8%
2006 PRIMARY		
Lois Capps (D)		unopposed
2004 GENERAL		
Lois Capps (D)	153,980	63.0%
Donald E. Regan (R)	83,926	34.4%
Michael Favorite (LIBERT)	6,391	2.6%

PREVIOUS WINNING PERCENTAGES
2002 (59%); 2000 (53%); 1998 (55%); 1998 Special Runoff Election (53%)

Elected March 1998; 5th full term

Capps' influence on Capitol Hill is on the rise. Her two signature issues, health care and environmental protection, rank high on the agenda in the Democratically controlled Congress. And she has shown an ability to outmaneuver more powerful lawmakers to further her legislative goals.

A solid Democrat who voted with her party 98 percent of the time in the 109th Congress (2005-06), Capps has evolved from a politically inexperienced widow who claimed her late husband's seat in 1998 to a seasoned legislator whose position on the Energy and Commerce Committee gives her influence over a sweep of issues from telecommunications to health care.

She represents a strip of the southern California coast that includes Santa Barbara, whose beaches were fouled in 1969 by a ruptured underwater oil well. That has made her a determined foe of offshore oil drilling. In 2006, she voted against a GOP bill to allow drilling off most of the nation's coasts, and she is pressing for a permanent ban on new drilling.

Capps exudes the warmth of the school nurse she once was, but she's capable of steely resolve as well. In 2005, she nearly outmaneuvered former Republican Majority Leader Tom DeLay of Texas over potential liability for cleanup costs of water contaminated by a fuel additive made mostly in Texas. When the GOP's energy policy bill was on the House floor, Capps ambushed DeLay and his fellow Texas Republican Joe L. Barton, chairman of the Energy and Commerce Committee, by challenging a provision exempting U.S. producers of the fuel additive methyl tertiary butyl ether (MTBE) from lawsuits over water contamination. Capps had an example of MTBE contamination in her own district, where Cambria's drinking water has been affected.

Democrats led by Capps caught GOP leaders off guard with their argument that, because a liability shield would shift potentially billions of dollars in cleanup costs to local governments, it violated the 1995 unfunded mandates law. That law bars imposition of new costs on states and localities without federal money to help meet the mandates. Barton "had no idea until I spoke" that the MTBE shield risked being derailed, Capps says.

Though her challenge failed, 213-219, the House debate called new attention to MTBE contamination. The Senate refused to include the liability shield in its version of the bill, and House Republicans, mindful that the same issue had killed a GOP energy bill in 2004, finally relented in order to get the legislation enacted.

In late 2006, Capps lost a different showdown with House Armed Services Committee Chairman Duncan Hunter, a California Republican who won enactment of legislation limiting public access to Santa Rosa Island, part of Channel Islands National Park, so military veterans can hunt there. She is trying to reverse that action in the 110th Congress (2007-08).

On health care, Capps' goal is to boost federal funds for cancer prevention, research and public education, and to ensure greater access to health care. She readily acknowledges that she is motivated by the loss of her 35-year-old daughter, Lisa, to lung cancer in 2000. "We do it better when it's personal," she says.

She keeps her registered nurse's license current, studying and taking a new exam every two years. Asked why she bothers now that she's firmly entrenched in Congress, she says simply, "It's who I am." Plus, she knows being a nurse enhances her credibility on health care issues.

She wants to use the Congressional Women's Caucus to build support for two measures she could not get through the GOP Congress. One directs the National Institutes of Health to explore possible links between the environment and breast cancer; the other calls for more study of heart disease in women. With a bipartisan push, she says, "we can make our presence more keenly felt" in an institution that remains male-dominated.

Capps' interests extend to foreign affairs. She is part of the House Democracy Assistance Commission, which works with parliaments in emerging democracies, and has long been concerned about the Israeli-Palestinian conflict. She supports funding for Israel, "but not in terms of repressive actions toward the Palestinians." She backed President Bush during debate on a fiscal 2005 supplemental spending bill, opposing any move by lawmakers to limit the president's flexibility to distribute financial aid to the Palestinians. But she criticized Bush's handling of the 2006 fighting between Israel and the militant Shiite group Hezbollah in Lebanon, calling for a cease-fire after Lebanese civilians were killed.

Capps sometimes breaks with her party on tax cuts. She voted to override President Bill Clinton's veto of Republican bills that slashed estate taxes and eliminated the so-called marriage penalty. And in 2001, she was one of only 28 House Democrats to vote for Bush's $1.35 trillion tax cut package. But she voted against the 2003 GOP tax cuts.

The daughter and granddaughter of Lutheran ministers, Capps grew up in small towns in Wisconsin and Montana. She has a master's degree in religion from Yale. She worked as a nurse for many years in Santa Barbara schools and also ran the county's teen pregnancy counseling project.

When her husband, Walter Capps, ran for the House in 1996, she stood in for him at campaign events while he recovered from injuries suffered in a car accident caused by a drunken driver. When he had a fatal heart attack less than a year into his first term, Lois Capps ran for his seat in what was then the 22nd District. She benefited from his political organization and from disunity among Republicans. A primary contest on the GOP side between conservative state Rep. Tom Bordonaro and moderate state Rep. Brooks Firestone was a bitter struggle that Bordonaro finally won.

Capps stayed focused on local issues and stressed Democratic themes of protecting the environment and improving education and health care. She won by 9 percentage points over Bordonaro, becoming the 35th widow to win a House seat after the death of a husband. She won a full term in November 1998, again besting Bordonaro, this time by 12 percentage points. In 2000, Republicans targeted her district, but she held on. Redistricting gave her a boost, and she has won easily since 2002.

KEY VOTES

2006

- Yes Stop broadband companies from favoring select Internet traffic
- No Affirm U.S. commitment to war in Iraq and reject setting a withdrawal date for troops
- No Repeal requirement for bilingual ballots at the polls
- No Permit U.S. sale of civilian nuclear technology to India
- No Build a 700-mile fence on the U.S.-Mexico border to curb illegal crossings
- No Permit warrantless wiretaps of suspected terrorists

2005

- ? Intervene in the life-support case of Terri Schiavo
- Yes Lift President Bush's restrictions on stem cell research funding
- Yes Prohibit FBI access to library and bookstore records
- No Approve free-trade pact with five Central American countries
- No Pass energy policy overhaul favored by President Bush emphasizing domestic oil and gas production
- No End mandatory preservation of habitat of endangered animal and plant species
- Yes Ban torture of prisoners in U.S. custody

CQ VOTE STUDIES

	PARTY UNITY		PRESIDENTIAL SUPPORT	
	Support	Oppose	Support	Oppose
2006	98%	2%	15%	85%
2005	98%	2%	11%	89%
2004	98%	2%	21%	79%
2003	97%	3%	20%	80%
2002	93%	7%	32%	68%

INTEREST GROUPS

	AFL-CIO	ADA	CCUS	ACU
2006	93%	95%	27%	4%
2005	93%	95%	32%	0%
2004	100%	100%	24%	0%
2003	87%	100%	33%	16%
2002	89%	90%	45%	12%

CALIFORNIA 23

Central Coast – Oxnard, Santa Barbara, Santa Maria, San Luis Obispo

The Democratic 23rd is a sliver of coastline stretching south from the Monterey County line through San Luis Obispo, Santa Barbara and Oxnard into Ventura County, which lies northwest of Los Angeles.

Agriculture is a mainstay in the San Luis Obispo area. Santa Maria is known for both manufacturing and agriculture, especially broccoli, celery and lettuce. The Goleta Valley, just north of Santa Barbara, was previously a farming region but is now attracting high-technology research. Oxnard is home to large biotechnology companies and the Port of Hueneme, the only international port on the central coast, which imports the majority of bananas and cars into California. Tourism also bolsters this beachfront district's economy.

Students at the district's colleges, including California Polytechnic State University in San Luis Obispo and the University of California, Santa Barbara, combine with wealthy members of Hollywood's elite in Santa Barbara County to tilt the 23rd to the left. John Kerry received 58 percent of the district's 2004 presidential vote. Strongly Democratic Oxnard is home to a significant portion of the 23rd's Hispanic population — 42 percent of district residents are Hispanic.

MAJOR INDUSTRY

Agriculture, military, tourism

MILITARY BASES

Naval Base Ventura County, 7,646 military, 6,936 civilian (2005) (shared with the 24th); Vandenberg Air Force Base, 5,221 military, 4,240 civilian (2005) (shared with the 24th)

CITIES

Oxnard, 170,358; Santa Barbara, 92,325; Santa Maria, 77,423; Goleta (unincorporated), 55,204; San Luis Obispo, 44,174

NOTABLE

Santa Barbara was the birthplace of the Egg McMuffin; Hearst Castle, a historic house museum at San Simeon, was home to William Randolph Hearst; Oxnard, called the Strawberry Capital of California, hosts an annual strawberry festival and yields roughly $100 million annually from its berry acres; San Luis Obispo was the site of the first Jamba Juice store in 1990; Channel Islands National Park.

Rep. Elton Gallegly (R)

CAPITOL OFFICE
225-5811
www.house.gov/gallegly
2309 Rayburn 20515-0524; fax 225-1100

COMMITTEES
Foreign Affairs
Judiciary
Natural Resources
Select Intelligence

RESIDENCE
Simi Valley

BORN
March 7, 1944, Huntington Park, Calif.

RELIGION
Protestant

FAMILY
Wife, Janice Gallegly; four children

EDUCATION
California State U., Los Angeles, attended 1962-63

CAREER
Real estate broker

POLITICAL HIGHLIGHTS
Simi Valley City Council, 1979-86;
mayor of Simi Valley, 1980-86

ELECTION RESULTS

2006 GENERAL		
Elton Gallegly (R)	129,812	62.0%
Jill M. Martinez (D)	79,461	38.0%
2006 PRIMARY		
Elton Gallegly (R)	51,923	80.1%
Michael Tenenbaum (R)	12,903	19.9%
2004 GENERAL		
Elton Gallegly (R)	178,660	62.8%
Brett Wagner (D)	96,397	33.9%
Stuart A. Bechman (GREEN)	9,321	3.3%

PREVIOUS WINNING PERCENTAGES
2002 (65%); 2000 (54%); 1998 (60%); 1996 (60%); 1994 (66%); 1992 (54%); 1990 (58%); 1988 (69%); 1986 (68%)

Elected 1986; 11th term

No doubt Gallegly has mixed feelings about being a member of the 110th Congress (2007-08). He had announced just before California's March 2006 filing deadline that he was retiring from the House, only to be persuaded by GOP officials that he needed to stay. They said his retirement would endanger Republican control of the district.

A good soldier, Gallegly (GAL-uh-glee) returned to the campaign trail and won easily in his Republican-leaning suburban Los Angeles district. He saved the seat but his party lost the House. His loyalty notwithstanding, his own party leaders do not always treat him that well.

Gallegly was passed over for the chairmanship of the Resources Committee in the 108th Congress (2003-04). He had waged an aggressive campaign to become chairman while being careful to pay homage to the seniority of H. James Saxton of New Jersey, the highest-ranking Republican on the committee who also had an interest in the chairmanship. Gallegly, who ranked just below Saxton in seniority, promoted himself as a Westerner more in tune with the property rights views of Republican leaders.

But GOP leaders skipped over Gallegly, Saxton and three other senior Republicans to elevate Richard W. Pombo of California, a protégé of Majority Leader Tom DeLay, to the chairmanship. "That process was one that left a bitter taste in a lot of mouths," Gallegly said in 2006. "Tom DeLay was never my first pick to go fishing with. I'm sure that didn't help me." In 2007, the top GOP spot on the panel, now known as Natural Resources, went to Alaska's Don Young, who chaired the panel from 1995-2001.

Gallegly also sits on Foreign Affairs, where in the 109th Congress (2005-06) he was chairman of the Europe and Emerging Threats Subcommittee, with the task of monitoring new terrorist threats around the world.

During 2005, Gallegly achieved some success pushing a national security measure, known as the Real ID Act, which set minimum security requirements that states must meet for their driver's licenses to be accepted as identification to board commercial flights or enter federal facilities.

Gallegly said curtailing identification fraud is a major security issue because people who are in the United States illegally often use fake IDs to obtain valid documents, such as a driver's license. The legitimate documents then can be used to stay in the country. "The 'Real ID' has made it a lot more complicated for those who want to live off counterfeit documents," Gallegly told the Ventura County Star. "Identification is vital, particularly in keeping tabs on people who want to do us great harm."

A traditional Western conservative, Gallegly first came to the House to fight federal restrictions on land use. He has looked after his state's water interests and helped landowners butting up against federal environmental laws that protect certain species of animals.

Gallegly is one of the few non-lawyers to sit on the Judiciary Committee, where he takes a hard line on illegal immigrants, a signature issue. He may be best remembered for his unsuccessful 1996 effort to allow local school districts to decide whether to provide a public school education to the children of illegal immigrants. He argued that states such as California could not afford public education for those children and that the promise of free schooling was a magnet drawing illegal immigrants into the country.

In the early days of the 110th Congress, he introduced a host of immigration-related bills, including measures on education, identification and employment, and one prohibiting automatic citizenship for children born to people who are not citizens or permanent resident aliens.

While maintaining a conservative voting record overall, Gallegly occasionally casts his lot with Democrats. As the former mayor of Simi Valley, a community close enough to Los Angeles that many of its residents are concerned about the spread of urban crime, Gallegly has voted for gun restrictions opposed by many Republicans.

But he joins other conservative Republicans in continuing to support the war in Iraq, saying that setting a specific date for withdrawal of troops would simply encourage Iraqi insurgents. "I don't like war anywhere, and I don't think anybody does," he told the Ventura County Star. "But it's better on foreign than on domestic soil. Just ask the people in New York City."

On the local front, Gallegly spent much of 2005 trying to spare Naval Base Ventura County from the Pentagon's latest downsizing effort. Although the base will remain open, many thousands of jobs will be moved to the Naval Air Warfare Center Weapons Division in China Lake. And he takes great pride in representing the district that contains the Ronald Reagan Presidential Library. Among his prized possessions is a photo with the former president taken aboard Air Force One. The two are looking out the window at the future site of the library in Simi Valley.

When he was growing up in Southeast Los Angeles, Gallegly followed the political persuasions of his father, a lifelong Democrat. He described his father in an interview with the Los Angeles Times as "an FDR Democrat, and they're much different from the Democrats of today. He believed in government helping people who couldn't help themselves, but not those who could." His parents were poor Dust Bowl migrants from southeastern Oklahoma, he said, who never "worked for a penny above minimum wage."

After dropping out of college, Gallegly went into the real estate business and built a successful brokerage. Frustrated in his dealings with local government, he decided to run for office himself in 1979.

Gallegly won a seat on the Simi Valley City Council and served concurrently as mayor for six years before running for Congress in 1986. Touting his record of boosting Simi Valley's economic development, Gallegly defeated Tony Hope, the comedian's son, in the GOP primary and then won the general election by 40 percentage points. The area Gallegly represented in the 1990s was more competitive politically; in 2000, Al Gore carried the district and Gallegly was held to 54 percent of the vote.

Congressional district lines were redrawn for the current decade with incumbent protection in mind, and Gallegly's district is more reliably Republican. Despite his effort to retire, he won handily in 2006.

KEY VOTES

2006

- No Stop broadband companies from favoring select Internet traffic
- Yes Affirm U.S. commitment to war in Iraq and reject setting a withdrawal date for troops
- Yes Repeal requirement for bilingual ballots at the polls
- Yes Permit U.S. sale of civilian nuclear technology to India
- Yes Build a 700-mile fence on the U.S.-Mexico border to curb illegal crossings
- Yes Permit warrantless wiretaps of suspected terrorists

2005

- ? Intervene in the life-support case of Terri Schiavo
- No Lift President Bush's restrictions on stem cell research funding
- No Prohibit FBI access to library and bookstore records
- Yes Approve free-trade pact with five Central American countries
- Yes Pass energy policy overhaul favored by President Bush emphasizing domestic oil and gas production
- Yes End mandatory preservation of habitat of endangered animal and plant species
- No Ban torture of prisoners in U.S. custody

CQ VOTE STUDIES

	PARTY UNITY		PRESIDENTIAL SUPPORT	
	Support	Oppose	Support	Oppose
2006	96%	4%	94%	6%
2005	97%	3%	85%	15%
2004	94%	6%	82%	18%
2003	96%	4%	98%	2%
2002	94%	6%	82%	18%

INTEREST GROUPS

	AFL-CIO	ADA	CCUS	ACU
2006	14%	0%	100%	84%
2005	13%	0%	92%	80%
2004	13%	0%	100%	96%
2003	7%	5%	97%	84%
2002	11%	5%	95%	100%

CALIFORNIA 24

Ventura and Santa Barbara counties — Thousand Oaks, Simi Valley

North and west of the close-in Los Angeles suburbs, the 24th includes ski-friendly mountains, fertile valleys and a slice of coastline with excellent surfing. The district takes in nearly all of Ventura County and inland Santa Barbara County.

Ventura County, where more than four-fifths of district residents live, is a mix of lower-income farming communities — many workers in the local agricultural industry are immigrants — and more-upscale residential neighborhoods, such as fast-growing Moorpark. Ventura has large insurance, finance and electronics sectors, and the health care, biotechnology and construction industries have bolstered a growing economy — growth that has caused skyrocketing home values.

Citrus fruit thrives in the sunshine and fertile soil of Ventura County, while the central and western portions of the 24th in Santa Barbara County produce grapes, broccoli and strawberries. Western Ventura includes most of the Los Padres National Forest. San Nicolas Island, the Anacapa Islands and part of the Santa Monica Mountains National Recreation Area also fall within the 24th's boundaries.

The 24th's conservatism comes from interior Santa Barbara. Military retirees and Vandenberg Air Force Base, as well as southern Ventura cities such as Simi Valley and Thousand Oaks, also contribute to the GOP base.

MAJOR INDUSTRY

Biotechnology, aerospace, service, agriculture

MILITARY BASES

Naval Base Ventura County, 7,646 military, 6,936 civilian (2005) (shared with the 23rd); Vandenberg Air Force Base, 5,221 military, 4,240 civilian (2005) (shared with the 23rd)

CITIES

Thousand Oaks, 117,005; Simi Valley, 111,351; Ventura (pt.), 79,416; Camarillo, 57,077; Lompoc, 41,103; Moorpark, 31,415

NOTABLE

The Ronald Reagan Presidential Library is in Simi Valley; An all-white Simi Valley jury acquitted three police officers accused of beating motorist Rodney King, touching off Los Angeles riots in 1992.

Rep. Howard P. "Buck" McKeon (R)

CAPITOL OFFICE
225-1956
mckeon.house.gov
2351 Rayburn 20515-0525; fax 226-0683

COMMITTEES
Armed Services
Education & Labor - ranking member

RESIDENCE
Santa Clarita

BORN
Sept. 9, 1939, Los Angeles, Calif.

RELIGION
Mormon

FAMILY
Wife, Patricia McKeon; six children

EDUCATION
Brigham Young U., B.S. 1985

CAREER
Clothing store owner

POLITICAL HIGHLIGHTS
William S. Hart School Board, 1978-87; Santa Clarita City Council, 1987-92 (mayor, 1987-88)

ELECTION RESULTS

2006 GENERAL		
Howard P. "Buck" McKeon (R)	93,987	60.0%
Robert Rodriguez (D)	55,913	35.7%
David W. Erickson (LIBERT)	6,873	4.4%
2006 PRIMARY		
Howard P. "Buck" McKeon (R)		unopposed
2004 GENERAL		
Howard P. "Buck" McKeon (R)	145,575	64.4%
Fred "Tim" Willoughby (D)	80,395	35.6%

PREVIOUS WINNING PERCENTAGES
2002 (65%); 2000 (62%); 1998 (75%); 1996 (62%); 1994 (65%); 1992 (52%)

Elected 1992; 8th term

McKeon has seen more than his share of ups and downs over the past few years. As a result of upheavals in his own party, in early 2006 he unexpectedly found himself chairing the House committee in charge of education, bringing full circle a political career that began with service on his local school board. But less than a year later, the Democratic sweep in the November elections stripped away his gavel.

McKeon is still the top-ranking Republican on the Education and Labor Committee, which sets federal policies that touch every school in the nation. And he still thinks his committee job is easier than that first one on the school board. Local politics is up close and personal, says McKeon. "City council and school boards, those are tough votes, because you've got your friends and your neighbors, they're sitting right there watching you vote. Half of them are going to be mad at you — if you're fortunate."

McKeon took over the helm at Education in February 2006 after his predecessor, John A. Boehner of Ohio, was elected House majority leader to replace indicted Republican Tom DeLay of Texas. McKeon inherited a full agenda, which he struggled to clear away at the end of the 109th Congress (2005-06) in hopes the committee could concentrate in 2007 on reauthorization of President Bush's signature No Child Left Behind elementary and secondary education programs.

He had mixed success. On the plus side, he steered to enactment a renewal of vocational education programs, which Bush had wanted to eliminate. He also was a key negotiator on a bill that renewed a variety of social service programs for seniors.

He also participated in the House-Senate negotiations that resulted in a major overhaul of federal regulations governing pension plans. But Boehner, the chief architect of that bill, continued to call the shots during months of tough bargaining, even though he no longer chaired the committee.

Before assuming the full committee gavel, McKeon chaired the 21st Century Competitiveness Subcommittee, which had jurisdiction over higher education and job training programs. In 2006, he won House passage of a Boehner-sponsored bill reauthorizing most of the Higher Education Act, which governs federal aid to colleges and college students. But he was unable to get bipartisan backing for the legislation and it stalled in the Senate. Democrats objected to $12 billion in cuts in the student loan program imposed by a budget-savings bill that Republicans had pushed through a few days before McKeon became chairman.

Also hung up in a standoff with the Senate was a reauthorization of the Workforce Investment Act, which governs federal job training programs. McKeon sponsored the House version of that measure, which passed in 2005. But it too caused a partisan split and a clash with the Senate. Democrats objected to a provision in the McKeon bill to allow religious faith-based groups that receive federal grants to use religious preferences in hiring.

McKeon has long been concerned with rapidly increasing college tuition, a prime issue in his suburban Los Angeles district. He won inclusion in the 2006 higher education bill of a requirement that the Education Department assign an "affordability index" to every college that uses federal financial aid programs and to compile reports on their tuition increases. McKeon hoped that public exposure would drive down costs. But two floor amendments adopted by the House significantly weakened his provision.

But he has also made friends in the education community. He was honored in 2002 by the National Association of Independent Colleges and Universities. "No one in Congress has done more to keep higher education accessible and affordable for millions of students of all backgrounds," the group's president said.

In one of his more unusual pursuits, McKeon won enactment in 2003 of a bill making it illegal to buy, sell or possess lions, tigers and other wild cats. He said actress Tippi Hedren, star of Alfred Hitchcock's film "The Birds" and mother of actress Melanie Griffith, got him interested in the issue. She runs an animal sanctuary near Acton, Calif., that houses large cats, including two tigers once owned by pop star Michael Jackson.

McKeon has served on the Education Committee since he first arrived in Congress in 1993, and the Armed Services Committee since his second term. In 2006, he took a leave of absence from the latter panel to make room for Republican Brian P. Bilbray of California, who won a special election to succeed convicted Republican Randy "Duke" Cunningham. But McKeon reclaimed the seat in 2007, and Bilbray was bumped.

An important local issue for McKeon is a proposal by Mexican mining company Cemex Inc. to expand a sand and gravel mine in the Soledad Canyon to produce concrete, which the city of Santa Clarita has fought. McKeon, a former mayor of Santa Clarita, introduced a bill in 2006 to prevent the Bureau of Land Management from granting the company mining rights and to limit mining in the area. The city hung a banner over its roads reading, "Thank you, Buck, for HR 5471."

Before he became immersed in politics, McKeon worked in his family's business, a chain of Western-wear stores based in Santa Clarita that was founded by his parents in 1962 and that at its peak had 500 employees and 52 stores. But Howard & Phil's Western Wear fell on hard times in the 1990s, a casualty, the family said, of declining Japanese tourism and the drop in popularity of country line-dancing. The business closed in 1999, though McKeon still has a soft spot for ostrich skin cowboy boots.

He got his start on the local school board when his oldest daughter was in high school. He became the first mayor of Santa Clarita after it incorporated in 1987, and served two terms on its city council. He was reluctantly gearing up to run for a third term in 1991 when redistricting created a new House seat around his Santa Clarita base. McKeon jumped at the chance to run, and was the surprise GOP primary winner over Phillip D. Wyman, a 14-year state Assembly veteran. In November, McKeon had a sizable spending edge and defeated Democratic lawyer and rancher James H. "Gil" Gilmartin by 19 percentage points. His re-elections have been easy.

KEY VOTES

2006

- No — Stop broadband companies from favoring select Internet traffic
- Yes — Affirm U.S. commitment to war in Iraq and reject setting a withdrawal date for troops
- Yes — Repeal requirement for bilingual ballots at the polls
- Yes — Permit U.S. sale of civilian nuclear technology to India
- Yes — Build a 700-mile fence on the U.S.-Mexico border to curb illegal crossings
- Yes — Permit warrantless wiretaps of suspected terrorists

2005

- ? — Intervene in the life-support case of Terri Schiavo
- Yes — Lift President Bush's restrictions on stem cell research funding
- No — Prohibit FBI access to library and bookstore records
- Yes — Approve free-trade pact with five Central American countries
- Yes — Pass energy policy overhaul favored by President Bush emphasizing domestic oil and gas production
- Yes — End mandatory preservation of habitat of endangered animal and plant species
- No — Ban torture of prisoners in U.S. custody

CQ VOTE STUDIES

	PARTY UNITY		PRESIDENTIAL SUPPORT	
	Support	Oppose	Support	Oppose
2006	96%	4%	95%	5%
2005	97%	3%	89%	11%
2004	96%	4%	85%	15%
2003	95%	5%	96%	4%
2002	95%	5%	90%	10%

INTEREST GROUPS

	AFL-CIO	ADA	CCUS	ACU
2006	14%	5%	100%	80%
2005	13%	0%	93%	84%
2004	20%	0%	100%	88%
2003	7%	10%	97%	76%
2002	11%	5%	90%	88%

CALIFORNIA 25

Northern Los Angeles and San Bernardino counties; Inyo and Mono counties

The vast 25th stretches from east-central California on the Nevada border south along the mountains and through Death Valley before crossing the Mojave Desert and San Bernardino County into northern suburban Los Angeles County, where nearly three-fourths of residents live.

The district's fastest-growing area is the Antelope Valley desert due north of Los Angeles, home to Lancaster (shared with the 22nd) and Palmdale, which is California's largest "desert city" and is the commercial and transportation center for the high desert. Special state and federal tax breaks encourage businesses to relocate to Palmdale, which also has been a major research, development and flight testing site for the aerospace industry, and is home to major Lockheed Martin and Boeing facilities. Lancaster's inexpensive land and business-friendly policies attract national and local companies. Victorville also has grown, with a 45 percent population increase in the first five years of the 2000s.

Most of the land in Inyo and Mono counties is government-owned, and a few towns rely on mining, agriculture and tourism. The Santa Clarita Valley on the district's southwestern edge is suburban, and Six Flags Magic Mountain is the largest employer. The valley also has active manufacturing, aerospace and defense industries.

The district is solidly Republican, and includes a mix of upper-middle-class residents and more-conservative working-class whites.

MAJOR INDUSTRY

Tourism, manufacturing, construction, aerospace, military

MILITARY BASES

Edwards Air Force Base, 2,707 military, 9,132 civilian (2006) (shared with the 22nd); Fort Irwin (Army), 4,765 military, 4,040 civilian (2006); Naval Air Warfare Center Weapons Division, China Lake, 951 military, 3,920 civilian (2006) (shared with the 22nd); Marine Corps Logistics Base Barstow, 187 military, 1,709 civilian (2007)

CITIES

Santa Clarita, 151,088; Palmdale, 116,670; Victorville, 64,029; Lancaster (pt.), 52,742; Los Angeles (pt.), 22,882

NOTABLE

Badwater Basin in Death Valley is the lowest point in the United States.

Rep. David Dreier (R)

CAPITOL OFFICE
225-2305
dreier.house.gov
233 Cannon 20515-0526; fax 225-7018

COMMITTEES
Rules - ranking member

RESIDENCE
San Dimas

BORN
July 5, 1952, Kansas City, Mo.

RELIGION
Christian Scientist

FAMILY
Single

EDUCATION
Claremont Men's College, B.A. 1975 (political science); Claremont Graduate U., M.A. 1976 (American government)

CAREER
Real estate developer; university fundraiser

POLITICAL HIGHLIGHTS
Republican nominee for U.S. House, 1978

ELECTION RESULTS

2006 GENERAL		
David Dreier (R)	102,028	57.0%
Cynthia Rodriguez Matthews (D)	67,878	37.9%
Ted Brown (LIBERT)	5,887	3.3%
Elliott Graham (AMI)	3,351	1.9%
2006 PRIMARY		
David Dreier (R)	29,569	64.9%
S. Sonny Sardo (R)	12,186	26.7%
Melvin C. "Mel" Milton (R)	3,826	8.4%
2004 GENERAL		
David Dreier (R)	134,596	53.6%
Cynthia Rodriguez Matthews (D)	107,522	42.8%
Randall Weissbuch (LIBERT)	9,089	3.6%

PREVIOUS WINNING PERCENTAGES
2002 (64%); 2000 (57%); 1998 (58%); 1996 (61%); 1994 (67%); 1992 (58%); 1990 (64%); 1988 (69%); 1986 (72%); 1984 (71%); 1982 (65%); 1980 (52%)

Elected 1980; 14th term

After eight years as Speaker J. Dennis Hastert's right-hand man at the helm of the powerful House Rules Committee, Dreier is reacclimating himself to life in the minority, where he faces the Sisyphean task of battling Democrats on a committee that is stacked 9-4 in the majority's favor.

Some see the new role as just desserts for an unrepentant insider who used his gavel to advance the Republican agenda by shutting the Democratic minority out of the legislative process. The affable Californian, a master of parliamentary procedure, was such a natural at that job that Hastert waived a three-term chairmanship limit at the start of the 109th Congress (2005-06) to keep Dreier in control of the panel.

Now he is on the short end of the dais, but he has wasted little time complaining. Instead, he began life in the minority by roasting Democrats for failing to live up to their promises to conduct a more open process. "It's my job to hold them accountable for what they promised," Dreier said a few weeks into the 110th Congress (2007-08). "I'm loving it."

Even though Democrats cursed the rules Dreier produced as chairman, most of his colleagues find him quite agreeable personally. Dreier's preternatural ability to remember names, hometowns and details about the lives of colleagues, staffers and journalists is remarkable even in Washington. The personal touch seemed to soften the blow, if ever so slightly, when he told colleagues their amendments would never be discussed on the House floor.

His mix of personal grace, procedural know-how and relentless enthusiasm for his work have made him a vital player in the Capitol, even as social conservatives have repeatedly questioned the "small-l" libertarian's commitment to their orthodoxy. His legislative philosophy can be reduced to four principles: economic freedom, small government, strong national defense and personal liberty.

Though a GOP loyalist on most issues, Dreier has split with his party's majority on some high-profile issues. He twice voted against proposed constitutional amendments to outlaw same-sex marriage, and he voted in 2006 to override President Bush's veto of legislation expanding federal funding for embryonic stem cell research.

In 2005, Hastert decided to appoint Dreier as temporary majority leader when Tom DeLay of Texas was forced to step down after his indictment on campaign finance-related charges. Dreier says he didn't really want the job, rejected multiple entreaties and finally agreed to take it under pressure. "I said, very late at night, 'I guess so; if I have to.' "

By the next day, he didn't have to.

Roy Blunt of Missouri, then the majority whip, had begged Hastert to reconsider. Social conservatives argued vehemently that Dreier could not be trusted. The job went to Blunt.

"Mr. Blunt made it very clear that he wanted it, and I clearly didn't want it," Dreier says.

All Dreier has ever wanted, he says, is to be chairman of the Rules Committee. A history buff, Dreier says a relative, Richard Bland Lee of Virginia, served on the first Rules panel near the end of the 18th century.

While the Rules panel doesn't legislate directly, Dreier has put his skills to work on some of the most important issues of the post-Sept. 11 era, including the creation of the Department of Homeland Security. And as befits someone representing a growing Los Angeles high-tech area, he has promoted the use of new technologies on the Hill, advocating more aggressive and sophisticated use of the Internet.

In 2004, after he had helped elect his pal Arnold Schwarzenegger to the governorship of California the previous year, Dreier was seen as a potentially strong challenger to liberal Democratic Sen. Barbara Boxer. But Dreier passed on that race and on a possible shot at running the Motion Picture Association of America. The House is his home.

Dreier first fell in love with the institution in college, when he was an intern for former GOP Rep. Barry Goldwater Jr. of California in the mid-1970s. That was followed by an internship with another California Republican, one-term Sen. S.I. Hayakawa.

Dreier launched his first House bid in 1978 from a dorm at Claremont University, his alma mater, where he was working in the planning and development office. His seatmate at Republican candidate school was a young Texan with a healthy political bloodline named George W. Bush. Both would lose that year. Dreier's father, a Marine Corps drill instructor whose emphasis on discipline is evident in the younger Dreier's consistent workout regimen, figured his son would come home to Kansas City, Mo., to work in the family's real estate development business.

But Dreier, whose stake in the company makes him one of the richest members of Congress, had been bitten by the political bug. Two years after he lost to Democratic incumbent James F. Lloyd, he was back, swamping the incumbent in fundraising and riding the Reagan wave to victory.

Outside the Capitol, Dreier hobnobs with a California political crowd that includes the actor-turned-governor Schwarzenegger. Dreier, who jogs and does 200 pushups daily, trades fitness tips with the former body-builder.

Dreier co-chaired Bush's 2000 presidential campaign in California, one of the nation's biggest electoral prizes, and served as parliamentarian of the Republican National Convention in Philadelphia that year.

But his pro-business embrace of Bush's immigration plan nearly cost him his seat in 2004, after he "won" a contest run by Los Angeles radio talk show hosts "John and Ken" to single out lawmakers they claimed had done little to stop the flow of undocumented immigrants across the border. John and Ken launched an aggressive "Fire Dreier" campaign.

He managed to top Democrat Cynthia Rodriguez Matthews but recorded his lowest-ever winning vote share, at just 54 percent, since unseating Lloyd. In 2006, after taking a harder line against illegal immigration, Dreier rebounded in a rematch with Matthews, increasing his share of the vote to 57 percent to win by a margin of 19 percentage points.

KEY VOTES

2006

- No Stop broadband companies from favoring select Internet traffic
- Yes Affirm U.S. commitment to war in Iraq and reject setting a withdrawal date for troops
- Yes Repeal requirement for bilingual ballots at the polls
- Yes Permit U.S. sale of civilian nuclear technology to India
- Yes Build a 700-mile fence on the U.S.-Mexico border to curb illegal crossings
- Yes Permit warrantless wiretaps of suspected terrorists

2005

- Yes Intervene in the life-support case of Terri Schiavo
- Yes Lift President Bush's restrictions on stem cell research funding
- No Prohibit FBI access to library and bookstore records
- Yes Approve free-trade pact with five Central American countries
- Yes Pass energy policy overhaul favored by President Bush emphasizing domestic oil and gas production
- Yes End mandatory preservation of habitat of endangered animal and plant species
- No Ban torture of prisoners in U.S. custody

CQ VOTE STUDIES

	PARTY UNITY		PRESIDENTIAL SUPPORT	
	Support	Oppose	Support	Oppose
2006	94%	6%	93%	7%
2005	96%	4%	89%	11%
2004	92%	8%	94%	6%
2003	95%	5%	100%	0%
2002	93%	7%	92%	8%

INTEREST GROUPS

	AFL-CIO	ADA	CCUS	ACU
2006	14%	10%	100%	72%
2005	13%	0%	93%	84%
2004	13%	5%	100%	88%
2003	7%	5%	100%	83%
2002	11%	5%	100%	84%

CALIFORNIA 26
Northeastern Los Angeles suburbs

Set in the foothills of the San Gabriel Mountains, the 26th is a mix of Los Angeles bedroom communities and the mountainous Angeles National Forest, which makes up its northern half. The commuter-heavy district takes in middle- to upper-class suburbs, many of which have retained their own identities and quaint downtowns.

In the far western part of the 26th, a high-technology flavor is set by La Cañada Flintridge and Pasadena (in the neighboring 29th), which is home to NASA's Jet Propulsion Laboratory and the California Institute of Technology. Monrovia boasts engineering firms and start-up technology companies that employ a highly educated workforce, and Glendora is experiencing rising home values. Arcadia has seen an increase in its Asian population (45 percent), and revenue from the Santa Anita racetrack has supported capital improvements for the city. The traffic congestion caused by district residents who commute to Los Angeles or technology jobs in the areas surrounding the 26th has become a hot issue locally.

Rancho Cucamonga, in the 26th's chunk of San Bernardino County, is a destination for young, middle-class families. Corporate call centers and technology firms fill the San Bernardino Inland Valley suburbs. Small defense subcontractors also provide jobs, and the area is a trade-related import and export manufacturing and distribution hub.

Rapid development in communities surrounding Pasadena and in other Los Angeles County cities — particularly Arcadia, Glendora, Monrovia and San Dimas — has brought young, wealthy, fiscally minded, socially moderate Republicans to the district. The district gave George W. Bush 55 percent of its 2004 presidential vote and Arnold Schwarzenegger 65 percent of its 2006 gubernatorial vote. While not as diverse as most of its neighbors, the 26th is one-fourth Hispanic.

MAJOR INDUSTRY
Service, manufacturing, health care, biotechnology

CITIES
Rancho Cucamonga, 127,743; Upland, 68,393; Arcadia, 53,054; Glendora, 49,415; Monrovia, 36,929; San Dimas, 34,980; Claremont, 33,998

NOTABLE
The collection at the Huntington Library in San Marino includes Thomas Gainsborough's painting, The Blue Boy, and a Gutenberg Bible.

Rep. Brad Sherman (D)

CAPITOL OFFICE
225-5911
www.house.gov/sherman
2242 Rayburn 20515-0527; fax 225-5879

COMMITTEES
Financial Services
Foreign Affairs
(Terrorism, Nonproliferation & Trade - chairman)
Judiciary

RESIDENCE
Sherman Oaks

BORN
Oct. 24, 1954, Los Angeles, Calif.

RELIGION
Jewish

FAMILY
Wife, Lisa N. K. Sherman

EDUCATION
U. of California, Los Angeles, B.A. 1974 (political communication); Harvard U., J.D. 1979

CAREER
Accountant; lawyer

POLITICAL HIGHLIGHTS
Calif. State Board of Equalization, 1991-97 (chairman, 1991-95)

ELECTION RESULTS

2006 GENERAL		
Brad Sherman (D)	92,650	68.8%
Peter Hankwitz (R)	42,074	31.2%
2006 PRIMARY		
Brad Sherman (D)		unopposed
2004 GENERAL		
Brad Sherman (D)	125,296	62.3%
Robert M. Levy (R)	66,946	33.3%
Eric J. Carter (GREEN)	8,956	4.5%

PREVIOUS WINNING PERCENTAGES
2002 (62%); 2000 (66%); 1998 (57%); 1996 (50%)

Elected 1996; 6th term

Smart, funny and self-deprecating, Sherman is a self-described "recovering nerd" who is willing to wave off handlers and just be himself, whether by risking an election year appearance on the comedy show, "The Colbert Report," or earnestly warning of the dangers posed by a nuclear Iran.

He jokes that he has been drawn to jobs held in the lowest possible public esteem, which explains why he's a certified public accountant, a lawyer and a politician.

A strong defender of Israel, Sherman favors an aggressive U.S. foreign policy, but regrets his 2002 vote authorizing the U.S. invasion of Iraq. He says that at some point, he would consider curtailing funding for the war if President Bush does not start bringing home the troops.

His chief preoccupation is nuclear non-proliferation. As chairman in the 110th Congress (2007-08) of the Foreign Affairs panel's Subcommittee on Terrorism, Nonproliferation and Trade, Sherman sees Iran as the No. 1 security threat in the world, with North Korea as a close second. "It's all about the nuclear weapons," he says.

For years, Sherman has badgered Bush about the threat posed by Iran, talking to him about the issue whenever he saw the president — including holiday parties, according to the Los Angeles Daily News. In the 109th Congress (2005-06), Sherman supported GOP-sponsored legislation dramatically tightening sanctions on Iran. After a watered-down version was enacted, he started over in 2007, quickly moving the tougher version through the Foreign Affairs Committee. "Iran is roughly five years from acquiring nuclear weapons," he wrote in a 2006 brief on his Web site. "While Bush has often talked about the problem, we have done virtually nothing to thwart Iran's nuclear program."

In the summer of 2006, Sherman defended Israeli air strikes against Lebanon as a justified response to the Iran-backed group Hezbollah's kidnapping of two Israeli soldiers. Earlier the same year, he advocated cutting off funding for the Palestinian government after the militant group Hamas won a majority vote in the Palestinian elections.

Sherman has found his background as a CPA invaluable in his work on the Financial Services Committee, especially during its investigations and response to corporate accounting scandals such as Enron earlier this decade. In the 108th Congress (2003-04), he pushed for new federal rules forcing companies to account for stock options on their annual reports of revenues and expenses. And he rallied Democrats to stop an attempt in committee to tie the hands of officials such as New York State Attorney General Eliot Spitzer (now governor), who were actively prosecuting fraud in the securities industry. Some lawmakers said the federal Securities and Exchange Commission should remain the dominant regulator. With characteristic edge, Sherman argued that while he normally agrees that a national approach is best, the SEC "has done such a phenomenally poor job," perhaps the oversight duties should go to localities and states.

A hard-liner on a balanced budget and a former member of the Budget Committee, Sherman expressed exasperation over Bush's tax cuts at a time of deepening deficits. When Federal Reserve Chairman Alan Greenspan told Congress in 2003 that he "would prefer to find the situation in which spending was constrained, the economy was growing, and tax cuts were capable of being initiated without creating fiscal problems," Sherman shot back: "I would prefer a world in which Julia Roberts was calling me, but that is not likely to occur."

What did occur — "miraculously," as Sherman put it — was his December 2006 marriage to Lisa Nicola Kaplan, a State Department expert on global anti-Semitism. The pair met two years earlier while picking up take-out at a Chinese restaurant on Capitol Hill.

Sherman says Congress has a responsibility to use taxpayer money carefully. In 2003, he spearheaded a vote on the Iraq supplemental spending bill that embarrassed the Bush administration on no-bid contracts awarded to Vice President Dick Cheney's old employer, Halliburton Co. The amendment requiring normal competitive bidding procedures for oil-related contracts in Iraq carried easily in the GOP-controlled House, surprising even Sherman. In 2004, when House Resources Chairman Richard W. Pombo requested $500,000 for postage for national mailings touting the panel's work, Sherman noted that such spending in the previous Congress was only $3,000. He argued that unlike members of Congress, committees don't have constituents and so should not have franking privileges.

For the 110th Congress, Sherman gave up his seat on the Science Committee for one on Judiciary, where he can address intellectual property issues such as protecting movies from unauthorized copying. His Los Angeles-area district is, among other things, the capital of the adult film industry. In his 2006 appearance on "The Colbert Report," Sherman riffed on his nerdiness and feigned shock when host Stephen Colbert quizzed him on the pornography industry in his district.

One of Sherman's pet projects is altering the order of presidential succession. In 2007, he reintroduced his bill to ensure that the presidency remains in the hands of the same political party by allowing the president to designate either the Speaker of the House or the House minority leader as second in line after the vice president, followed by either the majority or minority leader of the Senate, rather than the Senate president pro tempore.

Sherman got his start in politics as a child, stuffing envelopes for Democratic Rep. George E. Brown Jr., a longtime family friend. A tax law specialist, Sherman was elected to the five-member California State Board of Equalization in 1990 and 1994. The board administers tax programs that account for more than a third of the state's revenues, and Sherman led a successful drive during his tenure to repeal the unpopular tax on snacks. In 1996, Sherman ran for the seat of retiring Democratic Rep. Anthony C. Beilenson, who endorsed him. He won the nomination with 54 percent of the vote, besting six other candidates, and carried the general election by 6 percentage points. Since then, he has won re-election comfortably.

KEY VOTES

2006

- Yes Stop broadband companies from favoring select Internet traffic
- P Affirm U.S. commitment to war in Iraq and reject setting a withdrawal date for troops
- No Repeal requirement for bilingual ballots at the polls
- Yes Permit U.S. sale of civilian nuclear technology to India
- No Build a 700-mile fence on the U.S.-Mexico border to curb illegal crossings
- No Permit warrantless wiretaps of suspected terrorists

2005

- ? Intervene in the life-support case of Terri Schiavo
- Yes Lift President Bush's restrictions on stem cell research funding
- Yes Prohibit FBI access to library and bookstore records
- No Approve free-trade pact with five Central American countries
- No Pass energy policy overhaul favored by President Bush emphasizing domestic oil and gas production
- No End mandatory preservation of habitat of endangered animal and plant species
- Yes Ban torture of prisoners in U.S. custody

CQ VOTE STUDIES

	PARTY UNITY		PRESIDENTIAL SUPPORT	
	Support	Oppose	Support	Oppose
2006	94%	6%	28%	72%
2005	95%	5%	15%	85%
2004	96%	4%	27%	73%
2003	97%	3%	16%	84%
2002	95%	5%	28%	72%

INTEREST GROUPS

	AFL-CIO	ADA	CCUS	ACU
2006	100%	95%	33%	4%
2005	93%	100%	41%	0%
2004	100%	95%	33%	4%
2003	100%	90%	30%	9%
2002	89%	100%	35%	4%

CALIFORNIA 27

Part of the San Fernando Valley; part of Burbank

While most of the 27th is within Los Angeles, people who live here do not generally think of themselves as residents of the city. Instead, they view themselves as part of the growing Los Angeles communities of Van Nuys, Encino or Sherman Oaks in the San Fernando Valley north of central Los Angeles. The valley's portion of the city lies primarily in the 27th and 28th districts.

Biomedical firms and entertainment ventures located just outside of Hollywood drive the economy here. Diagnostic testing company Quest Diagnostics has a laboratory in Tarzana and a Northridge site devoted to clinical trials. Other firms are scattered across Sylmar, Van Nuys and North Hollywood. Toymaker MGA Entertainment has its corporate office in Van Nuys. The San Fernando Valley also is home to much of the nation's adult entertainment industry.

Real estate developers see the valley as a prime location for expansion of the area's hospitality industry — particularly hotels and small conference sites — because of its proximity to Hollywood and the local airports. The flat, grid-like streets of the 27th hold both the Bob Hope (Burbank) and Van Nuys airports. There are several colleges here as well, including California State University, Northridge. Reservoirs and aqueducts in the northwest provide water to millions of Los Angeles County residents.

Forty-five percent white and 36 percent Hispanic, the district also has experienced a rapid increase in Asian immigrants, particularly from India and Pakistan. This rise of immigration has increased demand for housing, which in turn has led to higher housing rates — the median home price here can be as much as three times the national average.

Two-thirds of the district's workers are employed in white-collar jobs, and the district is solidly Democratic. Residents here gave Democrat John Kerry 59 percent of the vote in the 2004 presidential election.

MAJOR INDUSTRY
Biotechnology, service

CITIES
Los Angeles (pt.), 591,573; Burbank (pt.), 45,436

NOTABLE
Van Nuys Airport is the world's busiest general aviation airport.

Rep. Howard L. Berman (D)

CAPITOL OFFICE
225-4695
www.house.gov/berman
2221 Rayburn 20515-0528; fax 225-3196

COMMITTEES
Foreign Affairs
Judiciary
(Courts, the Internet & Intellectual Property - chairman)

RESIDENCE
Valley Village

BORN
April 15, 1941, Los Angeles, Calif.

RELIGION
Jewish

FAMILY
Wife, Janis Berman; two children

EDUCATION
U. of California, Los Angeles, B.A. 1962 (international relations), LL.B. 1965

CAREER
Lawyer

POLITICAL HIGHLIGHTS
Calif. Assembly, 1972-82 (majority leader, 1973-1979)

ELECTION RESULTS

2006 GENERAL		
Howard L. Berman (D)	79,866	73.9%
Stanley Kimmel Kesselman (R)	20,629	19.1%
Byron De Lear (GREEN)	3,868	3.6%
Kelley L. Ross (LIBERT)	3,679	3.4%
2006 PRIMARY		
Howard L. Berman (D)	31,048	80.5%
Charles R. Coleman Jr. (D)	7,547	19.6%
2004 GENERAL		
Howard L. Berman (D)	115,303	71.0%
David R. Hernandez Jr. (R)	37,868	23.3%
Kelley L. Ross (LIBERT)	9,339	5.8%

PREVIOUS WINNING PERCENTAGES
2002 (71%); 2000 (84%); 1998 (82%); 1996 (66%); 1994 (63%); 1992 (61%); 1990 (61%); 1988 (70%); 1986 (65%); 1984 (63%); 1982 (60%)

Elected 1982; 13th term

A UCLA law school graduate who started out in politics helping César Chávez organize farmworkers in the 1960s, Berman is a rare breed of House member — a liberal trusted by Republicans. Berman is known as an institutionalist, someone who puts his concern for the integrity of the institution of Congress above politics. He also has a track record of being able to work with the opposition on high-profile legislation.

He was the choice of Democratic Leader Nancy Pelosi when she needed someone in 2006 to step into the party's senior slot on the House ethics committee, which had broken down amid intense partisan warfare. When the Democratic ranking member, Alan B. Mollohan of West Virginia, was forced to step aside amid questions about his own ethics, Pelosi returned Berman to the spot he had occupied with distinction from 1997 to 2003, when the committee investigated several high-profile cases.

"This is an honor I could have done without," was Berman's response, a reflection of the generally mixed feelings that come with service on the committee that investigates fellow lawmakers. Nonetheless, Berman's selection had the immediate intended effect of reassuring Republicans, and the committee resumed its work. In just a few weeks, Berman and Republican Chairman Doc Hastings of Washington were able to agree on cases that had languished for most of the 109th Congress (2005-06). Late in 2006, Berman served on an ad hoc investigative subcommittee that examined and criticized the way GOP leaders and staff handled allegations about Florida GOP Rep. Mark Foley's inappropriate dealings with young pages. Foley had resigned Sept. 29 after his sexually explicit e-mails to former pages became public.

Berman has been the senior Democrat since 1999 on Judiciary's Subcommittee on Courts, the Internet and Intellectual Property, and he chairs the panel in the 110th Congress (2007-08). He also serves on the Judiciary Committee's new antitrust task force. He is an expert on copyrights and patents and a defender of online freedom of speech. In 2005, Pelosi made him the House Democrats' chief liaison to the entertainment industry, which has a vital stake in protecting intellectual property and is an important constituency in Berman's San Fernando Valley district.

Berman is passionate about immigration issues. In 2005, he and Republican moderate Jim Kolbe of Arizona tried to bridge the polarized debate on immigration with a proposal to create a guest worker program similar to a plan offered by President Bush. It would have allowed more immigrants to come in legally to work in low-skill, low-paid jobs that American workers tend to shun, like meat processing, crop harvesting and domestic service. Their effort failed when the House adopted a more conservative, law-and-order bill cracking down on illegal immigration. Berman then tried in vain to persuade the Senate to make it easier for agricultural workers to enter and stay in the United States.

While Judiciary is known for its hot-blooded debates on social issues, disagreements in Berman's subcommittee are seldom overtly partisan and tend to divide according to competing industries affected by rapidly developing technologies. Berman's role on the subcommittee is important to southern California's many writers, composers and other content creators, and Berman has taken their side in efforts to curb pirating over the Internet. In 2004, Congress passed a bill he cosponsored with conservative Texas GOP Rep. Lamar Smith establishing three special judgeships to determine copyright royalty rates and the distribution of royalties.

Berman's other committee is Foreign Affairs, where he focuses on support for Israel, an issue important to the liberal Jews in Westside Los Angeles, and on ways to stop the spread of weapons of mass destruction. He was an early advocate of sanctions against Saddam Hussein and voted to authorize the Iraq War. "I was convinced that Hussein had chemical and biological weapons and was trying to acquire nuclear weapons, based on his behavior and activities in the past. . . . Turns out I was wrong," Berman says.

In 1996, he played a key role in the passage of legislation imposing sanctions on foreign companies that did business with Libya and Iran, countries then linked with international terrorism. Berman tried unsuccessfully to limit the reach of the Patriot Act, the anti-terrorism law enacted in 2001 that permitted federal authorities to detain immigrants indefinitely.

The son of a Polish immigrant who sold textiles in Los Angeles, Berman credits a favorite high school teacher with igniting his career in politics. "My parents weren't political, so she was the person who moved me to challenge assumptions and to debate issues," he once said. At the University of California at Los Angeles, he had an internship with the California Assembly's Agriculture Committee, where he worked on labor issues with Chávez's United Farm Workers. "From then on, I was hooked," he says.

In college, he met Henry A. Waxman, then president of the school's Federation of Young Democrats. The two became fast friends and card-playing buddies. Berman helped Waxman win a seat in the state Assembly, marking the start of the Berman-Waxman political network of like-minded politicians and activists who helped their hand-picked candidates with money and organization. The alliance was a power in Los Angeles County for years.

In 1972, Berman won an Assembly seat by defeating an incumbent Republican. A consummate facilitator and tactician with a relaxed style, he rose to majority leader. He lost a bid for speaker to Democrat Willie L. Brown Jr., but Brown repaid him by approving a congressional map with an ideal district for Berman. Since his first win in 1982, he has won re-election easily. He contemplated running for mayor of Los Angeles in 1993 and 1997, but decided against it although he had the political heft to compete.

In California redistricting after 2000, the House Democratic delegation hired Berman's brother, Michael Berman, as a consultant to draft new post-census lines. The map eventually approved protected most incumbents, including Republicans, and carved out of Berman's district several Hispanic communities, making it less likely he would face a primary challenge by a Hispanic candidate in future elections. But it angered Hispanics in the state who wanted a map that would favor election of a Hispanic.

KEY VOTES

2006

- Yes Stop broadband companies from favoring select Internet traffic
- Yes Affirm U.S. commitment to war in Iraq and reject setting a withdrawal date for troops
- No Repeal requirement for bilingual ballots at the polls
- Yes Permit U.S. sale of civilian nuclear technology to India
- No Build a 700-mile fence on the U.S.-Mexico border to curb illegal crossings
- No Permit warrantless wiretaps of suspected terrorists

2005

- ? Intervene in the life-support case of Terri Schiavo
- Yes Lift President Bush's restrictions on stem cell research funding
- Yes Prohibit FBI access to library and bookstore records
- No Approve free-trade pact with five Central American countries
- No Pass energy policy overhaul favored by President Bush emphasizing domestic oil and gas production
- No End mandatory preservation of habitat of endangered animal and plant species
- Yes Ban torture of prisoners in U.S. custody

CQ VOTE STUDIES

	PARTY UNITY		PRESIDENTIAL SUPPORT	
	Support	Oppose	Support	Oppose
2006	96%	4%	29%	71%
2005	96%	4%	18%	82%
2004	97%	3%	31%	69%
2003	94%	6%	17%	83%
2002	96%	4%	24%	76%

INTEREST GROUPS

	AFL-CIO	ADA	CCUS	ACU
2006	92%	90%	43%	8%
2005	93%	95%	41%	4%
2004	100%	90%	29%	0%
2003	87%	5%	34%	17%
2002	100%	90%	37%	10%

CALIFORNIA 28
Part of the San Fernando Valley

The 28th is centered in the San Fernando Valley north of Los Angeles, where it takes in the small city of San Fernando and includes parts of the Los Angeles communities of Pacoima, Arleta, Panorama City, Van Nuys and North Hollywood. The southern border follows in part famed Mulholland Drive, taking in Encino, Sherman Oaks and Studio City in the Hollywood Hills north of Beverly Hills.

The 28th's thriving commercial district, centered on financial services, is just south of Route 101, along Ventura Boulevard, where bank branches in office towers compete with miles of strip malls, fast-food outlets and trendy restaurants. Traffic congestion is a major concern in the area, and Interstate 405, one of the most congested highways in the country, runs through the southwestern arm of the district.

The technology and entertainment industries have fueled the district's resurgent economy for the last decade. The CBS Studio Center in Studio City is off Ventura Boulevard just south of the Los Angeles River. Local officials and environmentalists have targeted the river for conservation and urban revitalization. Several biomedical and medical equipment firms are in the district, including manufacturers of medical devices and hospital supplies. While the district's manufacturing industry declined after the closure of a General Motors plant in 1992, the Pepsi Bottling Group still has a facility in San Fernando.

New immigrants are driving service industry growth here. Once mainly white, suburban city communities have attracted many Hispanics, who make up 56 percent of the 28th's population. This influx keeps the 28th in the Democratic column, and the district gave John Kerry 71 percent of its 2004 presidential vote. Overall, 44 percent of residents were born outside of the United States, the eighth-highest percentage in the nation.

MAJOR INDUSTRY
Service, entertainment, manufacturing, health care

CITIES
Los Angeles (pt.), 615,523; San Fernando, 23,564

NOTABLE
The Academy of Television Arts and Sciences, which presents the annual Emmy Awards, is based in North Hollywood; Rock & Roll Hall of Famer Ritchie Valens ("La Bamba") was a native of Pacoima, which renamed a local park in his honor.

Rep. Adam B. Schiff (D)

CAPITOL OFFICE
225-4176
schiff.house.gov/hor/ca29
326 Cannon 20515-0529; fax 225-5828

COMMITTEES
Appropriations
Judiciary

RESIDENCE
Burbank

BORN
June 22, 1960, Framingham, Mass.

RELIGION
Jewish

FAMILY
Wife, Eve Schiff; two children

EDUCATION
Stanford U., A.B. 1982 (political science & pre-med); Harvard U., J.D. 1985

CAREER
Federal prosecutor; lawyer

POLITICAL HIGHLIGHTS
Assistant U.S. attorney, 1987-93; Democratic nominee for Calif. Assembly (special election), 1994; Democratic nominee for Calif. Assembly, 1994; Calif. Senate, 1996-2000

ELECTION RESULTS

2006 GENERAL		
Adam B. Schiff (D)	91,014	63.5%
William J. Bodell (R)	39,321	27.4%
William M. Paparian (GREEN)	8,197	5.7%
Lynda L. Llamas (PFP)	2,599	1.8%
Jim Keller (LIBERT)	2,258	1.6%
2006 PRIMARY		
Adam B. Schiff (D)	33,750	82.6%
Bob McCloskey (D)	7,102	17.4%
2004 GENERAL		
Adam B. Schiff (D)	133,670	64.6%
Harry Frank Scolinos (R)	62,871	30.4%
Philip Koebel (GREEN)	5,715	2.8%
Ted Brown (LIBERT)	4,570	2.2%

PREVIOUS WINNING PERCENTAGES
2002 (63%); 2000 (53%)

Elected 2000; 4th term

A former federal prosecutor and Harvard law graduate, Schiff is one of the Democrats trying to remake the party's image on national security issues. He is thoughtful and moderate in his views, useful traits for telegraphing a message of reassurance, and he is one of the most outspoken critics of the Bush administration's war on terrorism. He founded a group called the Democratic Study Group on National Security "to get Democrats to speak more knowledgeably, more forcefully" on those issues.

In the 110th Congress (2007-08), Schiff won a seat on the Appropriations Committee, where he has posts on the State-Foreign Operations and Commerce-Justice-Science subcommittees.

His other focus is trying to moderate the fight between congressional conservatives and judges. From his seat on the Judiciary Committee, Schiff launched a series of meetings between lawmakers and state and federal judges, including Supreme Court Chief Justice William H. Rehnquist. "This protracted war against the judicial branch will only denigrate both Congress and the courts," he says.

While he supports tough anti-terror laws, Schiff also wants to protect civil liberties. In 2006 and again in 2007, he teamed with conservative Republican Jeff Flake of Arizona on a bill to rein in a controversial warrantless surveillance program. They contended that domestic surveillance to catch terrorists should be conducted under the careful watch of a special court.

During his freshman year in Congress, Schiff took an active part in Judiciary panel deliberations on the Patriot Act anti-terrorism law, which was written in the weeks following the Sept. 11 attacks. Five years later, legislation reauthorizing the law included provisions by Schiff addressing port security, rail security and the transport of weapons of mass destruction.

In 2003, he sponsored legislation to authorize military tribunals for prosecuting terrorists, setting specific rules aimed at averting abuses of suspects, including granting public access and providing for Supreme Court review. This, and a bill authorizing the president to detain U.S. citizens as so-called enemy combatants, were made highly relevant by two 2004 high court rulings stressing Congress' authority to set detention ground rules. In 2005, he attached to another bill a requirement that the attorney general report annually to Congress on the status of detained U.S. citizens or residents.

Although he considers himself a moderate, Schiff's voting record has moved closer to that of his party's liberal core. In 2001, his first year in office, he sided with President Bush 40 percent of the time. By the 109th Congress (2005-06), his support for Bush had fallen to 30 percent. "My views on issues have been pretty consistent," he said. "What we've seen is the president and the GOP moving harder and harder to the right. They've been leaving a lot of moderate Democrats behind."

His votes on tax legislation typify this changing perspective. Schiff was one of 28 Democrats who voted to enact the Bush tax cuts in 2001, but he opposed the next round in 2003, saying it was "fiscally irresponsible" to pass additional tax cuts when the nation was at war and racking up large annual deficits. He also opposed the 2004 corporate tax package and the 2005 tax cut extensions.

In 2003 and 2004, Schiff's bill increasing criminal penalties for identity theft was signed into law, and he cosponsored successful legislation to foster the use of DNA analysis in criminal investigations and to expand the national DNA database.

Schiff's melting pot district outside Los Angeles is home to one of the largest group of Armenians in the United States, and he has championed a longstanding effort to persuade the president to formally recognize as genocide the deaths of millions of Armenians that began in 1915 at the hands of the Ottoman Empire, in what is now Turkey.

A central goal of Schiff's agenda is the promotion of early childhood education, from preschool through third grade. In 2003 and 2004, he helped organize opposition to the proposed cutbacks in the Head Start program, saying the GOP-backed legislation would "close the door of the Head Start program to tens of thousands of deserving children and their families."

Schiff was born in Massachusetts, but when he was 11, his family moved to northern California where his father bought a lumber yard. He and his brother had to help out in the business. "There's nothing like working in a lumber yard to make you want to go to grad school," Schiff says.

When he entered Stanford, Schiff could not decide between medicine and law, so he majored in both pre-med and political science and was accepted to both medical school and law school. Although his parents urged him to become a doctor, Schiff chose law. "All my doctor friends say I made the right decision, and all my lawyer friends say I messed up," Schiff says. "Now that I'm in politics, everyone says I messed up."

After getting his law degree, he returned to California and clerked for a federal judge, then worked in the U.S. Attorney's office for six years. A colleague there, Tom Umberg, who was elected to the California Assembly, was the inspiration for his shift into politics. "I wanted to deal with the root causes of the problems I was dealing with as a U.S. attorney," Schiff says.

He was unsuccessful at first, losing to Republican James E. Rogan in 1994 in a contest for an Assembly seat. He rebounded in 1996, winning a state Senate district that included the old 27th Congressional District.

Schiff in 2000 again faced Rogan, by then a U.S. House member who had become a prime Democratic target because of his high-profile role in the GOP-orchestrated impeachment of President Bill Clinton. Schiff and Rogan raised more than $11 million between them, a House race record. And their race was viewed nationally as a referendum on Clinton's impeachment. But Schiff says the race actually turned on local concerns like whether Rogan provided adequate constituent service. The district, Schiff says, was split down the middle on impeachment and the calculation was, "if either one of us raised impeachment, the voters would punish us."

He defeated Rogan by 9 percentage points and has been re-elected easily every two years since then.

KEY VOTES

2006

Yes Stop broadband companies from favoring select Internet traffic

No Affirm U.S. commitment to war in Iraq and reject setting a withdrawal date for troops

No Repeal requirement for bilingual ballots at the polls

Yes Permit U.S. sale of civilian nuclear technology to India

No Build a 700-mile fence on the U.S.-Mexico border to curb illegal crossings

No Permit warrantless wiretaps of suspected terrorists

2005

No Intervene in the life-support case of Terri Schiavo

Yes Lift President Bush's restrictions on stem cell research funding

Yes Prohibit FBI access to library and bookstore records

No Approve free-trade pact with five Central American countries

No Pass energy policy overhaul favored by President Bush emphasizing domestic oil and gas production

No End mandatory preservation of habitat of endangered animal and plant species

Yes Ban torture of prisoners in U.S. custody

CQ VOTE STUDIES

	PARTY UNITY		PRESIDENTIAL SUPPORT	
	Support	Oppose	Support	Oppose
2006	94%	6%	35%	65%
2005	94%	6%	24%	76%
2004	93%	7%	38%	62%
2003	96%	4%	16%	84%
2002	92%	8%	32%	68%

INTEREST GROUPS

	AFL-CIO	ADA	CCUS	ACU
2006	86%	85%	47%	12%
2005	93%	85%	42%	0%
2004	93%	95%	43%	12%
2003	87%	100%	33%	16%
2002	88%	95%	45%	8%

CALIFORNIA 29

Glendale; Pasadena; Alhambra; part of Burbank

Set in the foothills of the San Gabriel Mountains, the 29th includes the largely residential Los Angeles suburbs of Glendale, Pasadena, Alhambra and part of Burbank. Although part of the Los Angeles area, Glendale and Pasadena have their own downtowns.

Television and movie production studios drive the economy in Burbank, home to Walt Disney's studios, and Glendale, home to DreamWorks Animation SKG. Glendale also is home to the corporate headquarters of Nestlé USA and the International House of Pancakes. A technology community has sprung up near a number of colleges and universities in the area, including the California Institute of Technology, and NASA's Jet Propulsion Laboratory. The area suffers from heavy traffic congestion, and some residents hope that a planned streetcar line through Glendale and into Burbank will help alleviate the problem.

The region includes a wide mix of ethnicities, with none holding a majority of district residents. The 29th has the fifth-highest percentage of Asian residents in California (and the eighth-largest in the nation) at 24 percent, and is slightly more than one-fourth Hispanic. Monterey Park (shared with the 32nd) is known as "Little Taipei" for its Taiwanese and other Asian immigrants. Glendale is home to about 75,000 Armenians, one of the largest such communities outside of Armenia, and Alhambra is heavily Asian and Hispanic.

Over the years, immigration and the growing nearby Hollywood economy have transformed once-WASPish neighborhoods, giving the district a Democratic lean. The 29th gave Democrat John Kerry 61 percent of its vote in the 2004 presidential election.

MAJOR INDUSTRY

Entertainment, technology, engineering

CITIES

Glendale, 194,973; Pasadena, 133,936; Alhambra, 85,804; Burbank (pt.), 54,880; San Gabriel, 39,804; Altadena (unincorporated) (pt.), 38,306

NOTABLE

More people have looked through the Zeiss Telescope at the Griffith Observatory than any other telescope in the world; Pasadena's annual Tournament of Roses Parade is never held on a Sunday; The first Church of Scientology was founded in Glendale in 1954; The first satellite launched by the United States was built at the Jet Propulsion Laboratory.

Rep. Henry A. Waxman (D)

CAPITOL OFFICE
225-3976
www.house.gov/waxman
2204 Rayburn 20515-0530; fax 225-4099

COMMITTEES
Energy & Commerce
Oversight & Government Reform - chairman

RESIDENCE
Beverly Hills

BORN
Sept. 12, 1939, Los Angeles, Calif.

RELIGION
Jewish

FAMILY
Wife, Janet Waxman; two children

EDUCATION
U. of California, Los Angeles, B.A. 1961 (political science), J.D. 1964

CAREER
Lawyer

POLITICAL HIGHLIGHTS
Calif. Assembly, 1968-74

ELECTION RESULTS

2006 GENERAL		
Henry A. Waxman (D)	151,284	71.5%
David Nelson Jones (R)	55,904	26.4%
Adele M. Cannon (PFP)	4,546	2.1%
2006 PRIMARY		
Henry A. Waxman (D)		unopposed
2004 GENERAL		
Henry A. Waxman (D)	216,682	71.2%
Victor Elizalde (R)	87,465	28.8%

PREVIOUS WINNING PERCENTAGES
2002 (70%); 2000 (76%); 1998 (74%); 1996 (68%); 1994 (68%); 1992 (61%); 1990 (69%); 1988 (72%); 1986 (88%); 1984 (63%); 1982 (65%); 1980 (64%); 1978 (63%); 1976 (68%); 1974 (64%)

Elected 1974; 17th term

If there is one outcome from the 2006 Democratic sweep of Congress sure to give the Bush administration heartburn, it is the ascension of Waxman to the chairmanship of the Oversight and Government Reform Committee. Even in the minority, Waxman harried federal executives and agencies and did his utmost to investigate administration policies. Armed now with subpoena power, he will be an even sharper thorn in the side of the White House.

Waxman has always pushed for transparency and accountability — in government and industry alike. He is not physically intimidating, standing five-foot-five with wire-rimmed glasses and a bald head, yet his precise and pointed style of questioning witnesses can be brutally effective. Even those who like him often describe him as a "pit bull."

His panel has broad jurisdiction to oversee the executive branch and Waxman intends to use this power. "Done right, congressional oversight can be exceptionally effective in shaping national policy," he said at a September 2006 panel discussion on congressional oversight. "Simply by holding hearings, asking questions and releasing information, Congress can influence the direction of the nation even without passing legislation."

As the committee's top-ranking minority member, he hounded the White House on Iraq's elusive nuclear weapons, Halliburton's contracts in the war zone, Vice President Dick Cheney's 2001 energy task force, the cost of drugs under Medicare and the government's response to the 2005 hurricanes Katrina and Rita. But in the minority, he could not compel White House officials to appear before the committee. As chairman, he will not hesitate to wield his subpoena power if the administration seeks to ignore or defy his requests for documents or testimony. He has sponsored legislation to set up a special commission, modeled after the Sept. 11 commission, to investigate abuses of detainees at Abu Ghraib and Guantánamo Bay. And he has specifically cited subjects like the Medicare prescription drug benefit and border security as targets for greater oversight.

But Waxman has said he will not go to the extremes that Republicans pursued in President Bill Clinton's second term, when GOP Rep. Dan Burton of Indiana, then chairman of the Government Reform panel, issued more than 1,000 subpoenas to the Clinton administration and the Democratic Party. "Our jurisdiction knows no bounds. We can investigate anything," Waxman said at the 2006 panel discussion. "But I think we need to approach it with balance and without duplication of effort."

Waxman has a good relationship with the committee's top Republican, Virginia's Thomas M. Davis III. The two have teamed up to send pointed inquiries to federal agencies on such subjects as flu vaccine shortages. They also released a report on former lobbyist Jack Abramoff's dealings with the executive branch. And they worked well in March 2005 when Davis subpoenaed Major League Baseball stars to investigate steroid use in the sport. Although no legislation was enacted, the panel's hearings pushed the league to adopt more stringent penalties for athletes who use steroids.

Waxman is among the House's most adroit political practitioners. While he brings his extensive knowledge on a broad policy portfolio into behind-the-scenes negotiations, he can be a forceful partisan combatant in front of the television cameras. But he is patient and willing to cut deals with Republicans when necessary, as his pragmatic relationship with Davis suggests. Compromise, Waxman said, "can further your ideas and even help you improve your ideas."

Waxman's main base of operations before Government Reform was the Energy and Commerce Committee, where he chaired the Health and Environment Subcommittee for 16 years before the GOP takeover of 1995. He remains the second-ranking Democrat on the full committee and is a major force on health policy. He has excoriated a provision of the 2003 Medicare prescription drug law that barred the government from negotiating with pharmaceutical companies to obtain discounts for seniors. The GOP-sponsored law instead allowed private insurance companies to negotiate prices with the drugmakers. "It's not surprising that the interests of the drug companies and the health insurers who gave millions of dollars to Republican members of Congress came first — and seniors last," Waxman said in a January 2006 speech. "Corruption, incompetence, and an ideology that favors private profits over public programs all played a role."

A one-time smoker, Waxman is a leading congressional crusader against the tobacco industry. He convened the 1994 hearing during which the chief executives of the nation's seven largest tobacco companies testified under oath that they did not believe nicotine was addictive.

Waxman grew up in an apartment above a Los Angeles grocery store run by his father, who was the son of Russian immigrants and a New Deal Democrat who influenced his son's early thinking about politics and government. Waxman's political career began at UCLA in the 1960s, when he and fellow student — and now House colleague — Howard L. Berman became active in California's Federation of Young Democrats. In 1968, after a term as chairman of the state federation, Waxman, with Berman's support, challenged Democratic state Assemblyman Lester McMillan in a primary. McMillan was nearing retirement after 26 years in office. Waxman beat him with 64 percent of the vote.

It was the start of the so-called Waxman-Berman machine, an informal network of like-minded politicians who pooled resources to back candidates with money, organization and savvy. The "machine" was functioning so smoothly in 1974 that Waxman had little trouble winning a House seat created with him in mind. Berman waltzed into his own seat eight years later.

Waxman's constituents in Beverly Hills and part of West Hollywood are not only politically involved, many are also wealthy and have been generous with donations to Waxman's political action committee. In turn, the committee's contributions to other House members have broadened Waxman's influence among his colleagues. His own campaigns are formalities; he has never won re-election with less than 61 percent of the vote.

KEY VOTES

2006

Yes Stop broadband companies from favoring select Internet traffic

? Affirm U.S. commitment to war in Iraq and reject setting a withdrawal date for troops

No Repeal requirement for bilingual ballots at the polls

No Permit U.S. sale of civilian nuclear technology to India

No Build a 700-mile fence on the U.S.-Mexico border to curb illegal crossings

No Permit warrantless wiretaps of suspected terrorists

2005

? Intervene in the life-support case of Terri Schiavo

Yes Lift President Bush's restrictions on stem cell research funding

Yes Prohibit FBI access to library and bookstore records

No Approve free-trade pact with five Central American countries

No Pass energy policy overhaul favored by President Bush emphasizing domestic oil and gas production

No End mandatory preservation of habitat of endangered animal and plant species

Yes Ban torture of prisoners in U.S. custody

CQ VOTE STUDIES

	PARTY UNITY		PRESIDENTIAL SUPPORT	
	Support	Oppose	Support	Oppose
2006	98%	2%	8%	92%
2005	98%	2%	16%	84%
2004	97%	3%	13%	87%
2003	97%	3%	16%	84%
2002	98%	2%	25%	75%

INTEREST GROUPS

	AFL-CIO	ADA	CCUS	ACU
2006	100%	95%	33%	4%
2005	93%	100%	38%	0%
2004	100%	100%	20%	0%
2003	85%	95%	34%	17%
2002	100%	80%	33%	5%

CALIFORNIA 30

West Los Angeles County – Santa Monica, West Hollywood, part of Los Angeles

With such glamorous locales as Beverly Hills, Malibu, Bel Air and Pacific Palisades, few places in the 30th have not been immortalized by a movie or television show. The Democratic district stretches west from Santa Monica along the Pacific Coast Highway, past Malibu to the Ventura County line. It also extends north across the Santa Monica Mountains to Calabasas and Hidden Hills on the north side of the range.

The entertainment industry drives the economy here. Many movie and television studios have facilities in the 30th, including MGM, HBO Films, Fox Broadcasting and King World Productions. Tourism also brings revenue to the district. The 30th is home to attractions such as Grauman's Chinese Theater and several blocks of the Hollywood Walk of Fame. The famed Hollywood Bowl also is in the district.

Exclusive Rodeo Drive offers ample high-end shopping, and health care also is a major economic contributor. The 30th has six medical campuses, including the Cedars-Sinai Medical Center and a Department of Veterans Affairs-run site.

The district, about three-fourths white, has an active gay community in West Hollywood and a large Jewish population. Its economy is overwhelmingly white-collar, and it has the state's highest percentage (54 percent) of college-educated residents, which also is the fourth-largest percentage in the country. The district's colleges and universities, including Pepperdine University and the University of California, Los Angeles, together provide tens of thousands of jobs.

The district votes overwhelmingly Democratic in elections at all levels, and gave John Kerry 66 percent of its presidential vote in 2004.

MAJOR INDUSTRY

Entertainment, higher education, health care, tourism

CITIES

Los Angeles (pt.), 399,622; Santa Monica, 84,084; West Hollywood, 35,716

NOTABLE

The Rancho La Brea Tar Pits Museum boasts three million Ice Age fossils; Santa Monica Airport, formerly Clover Field, was the takeoff and landing point in 1924 for the first circumnavigation of the Earth by air.

Rep. Xavier Becerra (D)

CAPITOL OFFICE
225-6235
becerra.house.gov/hor/ca31
1119 Longworth 20515-0531; fax 225-2202

COMMITTEES
Budget
Ways & Means

RESIDENCE
Los Angeles

BORN
Jan. 26, 1958, Sacramento, Calif.

RELIGION
Roman Catholic

FAMILY
Wife, Carolina Reyes; three children

EDUCATION
Stanford U., A.B. 1980 (economics), J.D. 1984

CAREER
State prosecutor; state legislative aide; lawyer

POLITICAL HIGHLIGHTS
Calif. Assembly, 1990-92; candidate for mayor of Los Angeles, 2001

ELECTION RESULTS

2006 GENERAL		
Xavier Becerra (D)		unopposed
2006 PRIMARY		
Xavier Becerra (D)	26,904	89.5%
Sal Genovese (D)	3,227	10.5%
2004 GENERAL		
Xavier Becerra (D)	89,363	80.2%
Luis Vega (R)	22,048	19.8%

PREVIOUS WINNING PERCENTAGES
2002 (81%); 2000 (83%); 1998 (81%); 1996 (72%); 1994 (66%); 1992 (58%)

Elected 1992; 8th term

As the first Hispanic ever on the Ways and Means Committee, the Stanford-educated Becerra has made himself a champion of the working class. His Los Angeles district has the state's lowest median income and numerous hospitals, and Becerra's work often is divided between providing health and tax benefits to low-income families and keeping an eye out for the city's sprawling entertainment industry, including Paramount Studios.

Becerra (full name: HAH-vee-air beh-SEH-ra) also is campaigning for the Smithsonian Institution to build a National Museum of the American Latino on the National Mall in Washington. His legislation to create a bipartisan, 23-member commission to plan the facility easily passed in the House in 2006. A former chairman of the Congressional Hispanic Caucus, Becerra is a prominent backer of a broad immigration bill combining stricter immigration controls with a legalization process for illegal immigrants.

Becerra vigorously campaigned for vice chairman of the party's caucus weeks before Democrats won the House in 2006, but he dropped his bid when Rep. John B. Larson of Connecticut, a close ally of Speaker Nancy Pelosi of California, decided to keep the post. Pelosi created a new leadership spot for Becerra, assistant to the Speaker.

Becerra is a member of the Progressive Caucus, the group of the most liberal House Democrats, and is a loyal Democratic vote. But in 2001, he voted for the sweeping anti-terrorism law that most members of the Progressives said went too far in restricting civil liberties. "Extraordinary times call for extraordinary measures," Becerra said.

His seats on the Ways and Means subcommittees on Social Security and human resources issues have placed him at the fore of debates on tax, trade, health care and welfare policies, such as increasing the minimum wage and Medicare prescription drug benefits. Becerra adamantly opposed President Bush's plan to let workers divert some of the payroll tax they now pay into private investment accounts. He noted that three in four Hispanics who receive Social Security benefits depend on them for half their income.

With the nation's largest seaport in the Los Angeles area, Becerra generally backed trade deals — including the 1993 North American Free Trade Agreement — until 2005, when he opposed the U.S. free-trade pact with Central America, citing a lack of worker protections. Months later, he voted against the Oman Free Trade Agreement, again citing labor rights and port security concerns. "We protect property and products more than we protect people, and I don't think that's wise policy," he said.

Becerra says tax policy should reward workers, a view shaped by "seeing how hard my parents worked and how little they got paid and never complaining about it." His tax agenda would make filing income tax returns simpler and less costly for modest-income families, whom he says get cheated by refund anticipation loans carrying high interest rates. Another of his legislative goals is to expand the earned income tax credit for families with children, and he has called for tax incentives for developers to clean up small, contaminated sites, such as abandoned gasoline stations.

The entertainment industry also is a major interest. Becerra and Hollywood were disappointed in 2004 when the House passed a $137 billion corporate tax relief bill that left out the film industry. Becerra told The Daily News of Los Angeles that he believed the industry lost out because GOP leaders, then in the majority, calculated they could get more votes by wooing Southern lawmakers with a $10 billion tobacco buyout.

Los Angeles' high gun violence rate led Becerra to push for "gun fingerprinting" legislation requiring the Justice Department to test-fire every gun sold in the United States to record ballistics data that could be used by local law enforcement agencies investigating gun-related crimes.

Becerra can count a number of successes in behalf of his immigrant constituents. In 2002, Becerra's proposal to make community libraries eligible for federal after-school funds was enacted as part of a federal education bill.

Immigration issues dominated Becerra's early years in Congress, when he sat on the Judiciary Committee and chaired the Hispanic Caucus in 1997 and 1998. His interest in the issue is also personal. His mother was born in Mexico, and his father, though born in the United States, spent much of his early life moving back and forth across the border, earning a living by shining shoes, cleaning hulls on ships, canning tomatoes and working on highway construction crews. Becerra says he wears his father's wedding ring to remind himself of his modest beginnings.

Becerra's application to Stanford came from a friend who chose not to fill out the form himself. "I didn't know where Stanford was, living only two hours away from it," Becerra said. He worked his way through college, becoming the first member of his family to earn a four-year college degree.

He wanted to be a biochemist. But his college years coincided with the 1978 U.S. Supreme Court case of University of California at Davis medical school applicant Allan Bakke, in which the court found affirmative action constitutional but invalidated the use of racial quotas. "I remember participating in student rallies and marching at the federal courthouse in San Francisco. It made me start to think more about advocacy," Becerra says.

A state Senate fellowship cemented that interest and he opted for law school. His first job post-college was with a legal services office in Worcester, Mass., helping mentally ill clients. Returning to California, Becerra worked for a state senator and then for the state attorney general's office.

In 1990, urged on by friends, he won a campaign for the California Assembly. During his first term in Sacramento, Becerra was recruited to run for the U.S. House in the newly drawn, overwhelmingly Hispanic 30th District. He outdistanced nine other candidates in the 1992 primary and easily won in November, with 58 percent of the vote, against Republican Morry Waksberg and three minor-party candidates.

In 2001, Becerra raised and spent $1.7 million in a bid to become Los Angeles' mayor, but finished fifth in the 14-candidate primary. In subsequent re-election campaigns for the House seat, Becerra has won by large margins, and he was unopposed in 2006.

KEY VOTES

2006

Yes Stop broadband companies from favoring select Internet traffic

No Affirm U.S. commitment to war in Iraq and reject setting a withdrawal date for troops

No Repeal requirement for bilingual ballots at the polls

No Permit U.S. sale of civilian nuclear technology to India

No Build a 700-mile fence on the U.S.-Mexico border to curb illegal crossings

No Permit warrantless wiretaps of suspected terrorists

2005

\- Intervene in the life-support case of Terri Schiavo

Yes Lift President Bush's restrictions on stem cell research funding

Yes Prohibit FBI access to library and bookstore records

No Approve free-trade pact with five Central American countries

No Pass energy policy overhaul favored by President Bush emphasizing domestic oil and gas production

No End mandatory preservation of habitat of endangered animal and plant species

Yes Ban torture of prisoners in U.S. custody

CQ VOTE STUDIES

	PARTY UNITY		PRESIDENTIAL SUPPORT	
	Support	Oppose	Support	Oppose
2006	99%	1%	21%	79%
2005	99%	1%	16%	84%
2004	99%	1%	18%	82%
2003	98%	2%	17%	83%
2002	100%	0%	23%	77%

INTEREST GROUPS

	AFL-CIO	ADA	CCUS	ACU
2006	100%	95%	21%	4%
2005	92%	100%	37%	0%
2004	93%	95%	29%	0%
2003	87%	95%	31%	16%
2002	88%	100%	32%	0%

CALIFORNIA 31

Northeast and South Los Angeles

The only district set entirely within the city of Los Angeles, the 31st is densely populated, heavily Hispanic and staunchly Democratic. The district wraps around west of downtown to extend south into South Los Angeles (south central) and northeast toward Pasadena. Hispanics (70 percent) and Asians (14 percent) outnumber whites (10 percent).

Rapid immigration has changed many of the district's already diverse communities, and some newcomers are finding a mixed reception. Many Hispanics are among the new residents, and Pico Union and Westlake are dominated by Central American and Mexican immigrants. Other heavily Hispanic communities include Highland Park and Glassell Park. The eastern side of the district includes Lincoln Heights and El Sereno — heavily Hispanic, blue-collar areas with a significant Mexican immigrant presence. Filipinotown, between Echo Park and Westlake, also has a predominately Mexican and Central American presence.

Directly west of Elysian Park, where Dodger Stadium is located, is the artsy and gentrifying Echo Park. In the northeast sits Eagle Rock, a hilly, middle-class pocket of relative affluence that votes Democratic but leans more toward the political center than other parts of the 31st.

Despite economic contributions from Paramount Studios, a slew of area hospitals, and white-collar businesses along the Wilshire Boulevard central business corridor, the 31st has the lowest median income in the state, and fourth-lowest in the country, at slightly more than $26,000 per year. Only 14 percent of residents here have a college education, and more than 52 percent do not have a high school diploma, which is the second-highest percentage in the country.

The 31st supports Democrats, although voter turnout is usually low. John Kerry received 77 percent of the district's 2004 presidential vote, and Democrat Phil Angelides received 67 percent of the vote here in the 2006 gubernatorial race, even though he took less than 40 percent statewide.

MAJOR INDUSTRY

Service, entertainment, tourism, health care

CITIES

Los Angeles (pt.), 639,088

NOTABLE

Dedicated in 1886, 575-acre Elysian Park is the city's oldest public park.

Rep. Hilda L. Solis (D)

CAPITOL OFFICE
225-5464
solis.house.gov
1414 Longworth 20515-0532; fax 225-5467

COMMITTEES
Energy & Commerce
Natural Resources
Select Energy Independence & Global Warming

RESIDENCE
El Monte

BORN
Oct. 20, 1957, Los Angeles, Calif.

RELIGION
Roman Catholic

FAMILY
Husband, Sam H. Sayyad

EDUCATION
California State Polytechnic U., Pomona, B.A. 1979 (political science); U. of Southern California, M.P.A. 1981

CAREER
State college preparation program director; White House aide

POLITICAL HIGHLIGHTS
Rio Hondo Community College Board of Trustees, 1985-92; Los Angeles County Insurance Commission, 1991-93; Calif. Assembly, 1992-94; Calif. Senate, 1994-2000

ELECTION RESULTS

2006 GENERAL		
Hilda L. Solis (D)	76,059	83.0%
Leland Faegre (LIBERT)	15,627	17.0%
2006 PRIMARY		
Hilda L. Solis (D)		unopposed
2004 GENERAL		
Hilda L. Solis (D)	119,144	85.0%
Leland Faegre (LIBERT)	21,002	15.0%

PREVIOUS WINNING PERCENTAGES
2002 (69%); 2000 (79%)

Elected 2000; 4th term

Solis' political style and her agenda evolved from her upbringing as the daughter of naturalized citizens. Her father, a worker at a battery recycling plant in the San Gabriel Valley, organized immigrant co-workers for the Teamsters Union to gain improved health care benefits. Solis herself broke through cultural barriers to be the first in her family to finish college.

An energetic lawmaker in her fourth term, she advocates for women, immigrants' rights, education, worker safety and better access to health care. Central to her career in the California Legislature and now in Congress has been eradication of toxic waste in poor neighborhoods and other "environmental justice" issues, earning Solis (soh-LEEZ) a Kennedy Profile in Courage Award from the Kennedy Library in 2000. She belongs to the Progressive Caucus, the group of the most liberal House Democrats.

In Solis' second term, her close alliance with then Democratic Minority Leader Nancy Pelosi of California led to a coveted seat on the Energy and Commerce Committee. Solis became the top-ranking Democrat on its environment subcommittee, but on a panel where seniority matters, her relatively junior status kept her from securing the gavel when Democrats took control of the House in 2007 and instead she was made vice chairwoman.

Still, her loyalty to Pelosi and her aggressive fundraising for the Democratic Congressional Campaign Committee earned her a spot as one of two vice chairmen of the Democratic Steering and Policy Committee, which makes all-important committee assignments. She also is a senior member of the leadership's whip team.

As the 110th Congress (2007-08) opened, Solis was part of a rebellion by women in the Congressional Hispanic Caucus who objected that Chairman Joe Baca, a California Democrat, had been demeaning to women and had abused the group's political action committee. Solis was among six caucus members in 2006 who cut ties to the group's political action committee after it made campaign contributions to Baca's two sons in their unsuccessful races for seats in the California Legislature. Solis said there was a general "lack of respect afforded to women members of the Hispanic Caucus." Baca called the claims "categorically untrue."

On Energy and Commerce, one of her top targets is the Environmental Protection Agency, which has delayed cleanup of superfund hazardous waste sites and enforcement of the leaky underground storage tank program. Solis' district includes dozens of drinking water wells that have been shut down because of the presence of perchlorate, a rocket fuel and munitions component. The Bush administration is "siding too much with the industries that need to be regulated," she says.

In 2006, Solis and New Jersey Democrat Frank Pallone Jr. won House support to block the EPA's plan to scale back public disclosure of chemical and waste releases under the Toxics Release Inventory. The administration argued that the process was burdensome for small businesses.

In her early days in the House, Solis was on the Education and the Workforce Committee, where she defied then GOP Chairman John A. Boehner of Ohio over his proposal to combine minority-serving institutions with special education programs in one subcommittee. She organized her network of college presidents to block the move.

Solis' agenda is rooted in the San Gabriel Valley where she grew up. "In places like the assembly plant my father worked at, where they recycled batteries, there were a lot of contaminants and people were getting ill," she says. While in the California Legislature, she overcame opposition from GOP Gov. Pete Wilson and the business community to win passage of "environmental justice" legislation to address pollution in poor neighborhoods, which Wilson vetoed and Democratic Gov. Gray Davis later signed.

Solis is the third of seven children of immigrants who met in a citizenship class. Her father arrived in the United States from Mexico and worked blue-collar jobs. Her mother came from Nicaragua and worked for a toymaker after her last children, twins, were born. Solis and her siblings were in charge of the babies and chores. "It wasn't what you would call the all-American life for a young girl growing up," she says. "We had to mature very quickly."

Her mother stressed education, sometimes using a jar of uncooked pinto beans to teach the children addition and multiplication — "our abacus, Latino-style," Solis quips. She was the first in her family to go to college, encouraged by a school counselor, who came to her house to help her fill out college and financial aid applications.

Solis earned a bachelor's degree in political science and a graduate degree in public administration. As part of her graduate studies, Solis wrote dozens of letters and landed a job as a newsletter editor for the Carter administration's White House Office of Hispanic Affairs. At the start of the Reagan administration, she moved to the Office of Management and Budget's civil rights division, but the undoing of Carter's policies drove her back home. She got a job with a state program helping disadvantaged students prepare for college.

Her first election was in 1985, to the Rio Hondo Community College board. She moved on to the California Assembly in 1992 and to the state Senate in 1994, becoming its youngest member and first Hispanic woman.

In 2000, she took on incumbent U.S. Rep. Matthew G. Martinez, a Democrat whose views on issues such as abortion rights and gun control were considerably more conservative than hers. She ignored warnings that she was breaking "the golden rule" by taking on a fellow Democratic officeholder. She got support from Democratic Sen. Barbara Boxer and only one other House Democratic member, Loretta Sanchez of California.

Solis won the primary with 62 percent of the vote. The general election did not include a Republican, and she captured 79 percent of the vote against three minor-party candidates. In 2002, redistricting did not alter the Democratic or Hispanic bent of the district, and she won by 41 percentage points. She easily won re-election in 2004 and 2006 against minor-party opposition.

KEY VOTES

2006

Yes	Stop broadband companies from favoring select Internet traffic
No	Affirm U.S. commitment to war in Iraq and reject setting a withdrawal date for troops
No	Repeal requirement for bilingual ballots at the polls
No	Permit U.S. sale of civilian nuclear technology to India
No	Build a 700-mile fence on the U.S.-Mexico border to curb illegal crossings
No	Permit warrantless wiretaps of suspected terrorists

2005

?	Intervene in the life-support case of Terri Schiavo
Yes	Lift President Bush's restrictions on stem cell research funding
Yes	Prohibit FBI access to library and bookstore records
No	Approve free-trade pact with five Central American countries
No	Pass energy policy overhaul favored by President Bush emphasizing domestic oil and gas production
No	End mandatory preservation of habitat of endangered animal and plant species
Yes	Ban torture of prisoners in U.S. custody

CQ VOTE STUDIES

	PARTY UNITY		PRESIDENTIAL SUPPORT	
	Support	Oppose	Support	Oppose
2006	99%	1%	13%	87%
2005	99%	1%	17%	83%
2004	99%	1%	18%	82%
2003	99%	1%	16%	84%
2002	100%	0%	18%	82%

INTEREST GROUPS

	AFL-CIO	ADA	CCUS	ACU
2006	93%	100%	27%	4%
2005	93%	100%	35%	0%
2004	93%	100%	25%	0%
2003	100%	100%	21%	12%
2002	100%	100%	28%	0%

CALIFORNIA 32

East Los Angeles; El Monte; West Covina

The 32nd takes in a small chunk of the city of Los Angeles and extends east into largely Hispanic and Asian working-class suburbs. It includes the southern and central San Gabriel Valley, and reaches east to Azusa and Covina, capturing a few good-size cities.

The district lacks a dominant industry, and many residents commute out of the 32nd for work. The San Gabriel Valley has suffered from higher unemployment rates than the rest of the nation despite population growth. Once a small farming town, El Monte became home to some small aerospace factories, and is now a light manufacturing area with a huge retail auto complex. Irwindale, dominated by rock quarries and landfills, is among the district's industrial centers. Rosemead has a large ethnic Chinese population, and it is the headquarters for the Panda Express food chain. The 32nd's small piece of the city of Los Angeles hosts a California State University campus.

As city dwellers continue to leave Los Angeles, the 32nd has seen an increase in residential development over the past five years. Two-fifths of the population here is foreign-born, and many residents speak a language other than English at home. The area has several daily Spanish- and Chinese-language papers. Monterey Park (shared with the 29th) is known as "Little Taipei" for its Taiwanese and other Asian immigrants. Another large Asian population lives in wealthy West Covina.

El Monte, in the heart of the San Gabriel Valley, and Baldwin Park to the east are blue-collar cities that form the 32nd's Democratic base. Although there are pockets of Republicans and older white voters in Azusa, these groups are shrinking. The 32nd gave John Kerry 62 percent of its 2004 presidential vote, and was one of only 13 districts statewide to give Democrat Phil Angelides a majority of the 2006 gubernatorial vote.

MAJOR INDUSTRY
Service, light manufacturing, higher education

CITIES
El Monte, 115,965; West Covina, 105,080; Baldwin Park, 75,837; Rosemead, 53,505; Covina, 46,837; Azusa, 44,712

NOTABLE
MGM's trademark roaring lion came from Gay's Lion Farm in El Monte, where animal trainer Charles Gay kept African lions until 1942; The first In-N-Out Burger restaurant opened in 1948 in Baldwin Park.

Rep. Diane Watson (D)

CAPITOL OFFICE
225-7084
www.house.gov/watson
125 Cannon 20515-0533; fax 225-2422

COMMITTEES
Foreign Affairs
Oversight & Government Reform

RESIDENCE
Los Angeles

BORN
Nov. 12, 1933, Los Angeles, Calif.

RELIGION
Roman Catholic

FAMILY
Single

EDUCATION
U. of California, Los Angeles, B.A. 1954 (education); California State U., Los Angeles, M.S. 1968 (school psychology); Harvard U., attended 1981-82; Claremont Graduate School, Ph.D. 1987 (educational administration)

CAREER
School administrator; state education department official; teacher; school psychologist

POLITICAL HIGHLIGHTS
Los Angeles County Board of Education, 1975-78; Calif. Senate, 1978-98; candidate for Los Angeles County Board of Supervisors, 1992; U.S. ambassador to the Federal States of Micronesia, 1999-2001

ELECTION RESULTS

2006 GENERAL		
Diane Watson (D)		unopposed
2006 PRIMARY		
Diane Watson (D)	47,461	90.9%
Mervin Leon Evans (D)	4,774	9.1%
2004 GENERAL		
Diane Watson (D)	166,801	88.6%
Bob Weber (LIBERT)	21,513	11.4%

PREVIOUS WINNING PERCENTAGES
2002 (83%); 2001 Special Runoff Election (75%)

Elected June 2001; 3rd full term

As one of the most liberal members of the House, Watson sees in the Democratic takeover of Congress an opportunity to put some muscle behind legislation aimed at helping people in poverty.

A former Los Angeles public school teacher and the first African-American woman elected to the Los Angeles County school board, Watson has positioned herself as an advocate for inner-city children in the Head Start preschool program, youths threatened by gang violence, and New Orleans residents displaced by Hurricane Katrina.

Watson fumed in the wake of Katrina about the Bush administration's bungled response to the August 2005 storm that devastated New Orleans and a large swath of the Gulf Coast. She called it "dysfunctional." With the party in control of both houses of Congress as a result of the 2006 midterm election, Watson wants to boost federal aid to restore New Orleans, especially the hard-hit, predominately black Lower 9th Ward. And, as a member of the Domestic Policy Subcommittee of the House Oversight and Government Reform Committee, she is urging a committee investigation of the government's response to Katrina.

Watson is not afraid of confrontation. While attending the United Nations World Conference Against Racism during her first term, Watson proclaimed, "America is a racist state." In 2005, Watson, along with other African-American leaders, objected to descriptions of displaced New Orleans residents as refugees. "These are American citizens, plus they are the sons and daughters of slaves," she told the Los Angeles Times. "Calling them refugees coming from a foreign country does not apply to their status. This shows disdain for them. I'm almost calling this a hate crime."

Watson is a seasoned legislator. She spent 20 years in the California Senate, most of them as a committee chairwoman. She knows how to employ bipartisan pragmatism in her self-described role as an agitator for constituencies with little voice in government. In the legislative arena, she knows how to shelve rhetoric and work quietly to achieve her goals.

Watson can point to a better-than-average success rate in winning approval of her legislative offerings, largely because while in the minority, she concentrated on a limited number of achievable goals.

In the 108th Congress (2003-04), she won favorable House action on almost half of the 14 measures she authored, but they were relatively minor, like one that awarded a congressional gold medal to civil rights activist Dorothy Height. In the 109th Congress (2005-06), her bill to authorize $5 million to protect intellectual property from piracy was wrapped into a foreign aid bill enacted in 2005. Also in that period, the House approved her amendment to anti-gang legislation that added 200 federal agents to combat gang violence.

In the 110th Congress (2007-08), Watson wants the government to get more involved in combating gang violence. She favors early intervention programs for at-risk young people, and says a rehabilitative approach is more likely to succeed than a punitive one. "These are still developing young people, they're not adults, and we have to look at them this way," she says. "Are we going to throw them all into lockups at the expense of taxpayers?"

Watson is also a big believer in boosting federal funding for Head Start, a program she contends is one of the best strategies for helping children from troubled families.

On the Oversight and Government Reform Committee, Watson continues an effort, begun while she was in the state Senate, to get rid of mercury amalgam in dental fillings, which she says is a health risk. She has a bipartisan ally in Republican Dan Burton of Indiana, who chaired the committee in the 107th Congress (2001-02) when Watson first arrived on Capitol Hill.

The downtown Los Angeles section of Watson's district was once the hub for the movie industry, and many of her constituents are still involved in the entertainment industry. She fought Federal Communications Commission rules allowing consolidation of media ownership, arguing that reducing the number of media outlets limited expression for creative artists.

Watson's father was a police officer and her mother was a postal worker. She says she put in time at the local post office, sorting Christmas mail for seven seasons. But her career choice was education. She earned bachelor's and master's degrees and a Ph.D. in education-related disciplines, and went on to become a teacher and psychologist in the Los Angeles school system for more than a decade.

She entered politics in 1975, winning election to the Los Angeles County school board, the first black woman elected to the post. Three years later, she achieved another first, becoming the first black woman elected to the California Senate, where she shook up the mostly white male institution. The California Political Almanac said Watson "seemed to specialize in crashing the party and opening the windows." She chaired the body's Health and Human Services Committee for 17 years, and she was the first non-lawyer to serve on its Judiciary Committee. She was credited with helping rebuild her community after the 1992 riots sparked by the acquittal of police officers charged with beating motorist Rodney King.

After term limits ended her state Senate career in 1998, President Bill Clinton named Watson ambassador to Micronesia, a federation of more than 600 islands in the Pacific.

When 12-term Democratic Rep. Julian C. Dixon died in December 2000, Watson was urged by Dixon's supporters to run for the seat. In her special-election bid, she took 33 percent of the vote, defeating 10 other Democrats in the primary. The primary win virtually guaranteed victory in the overwhelmingly Democratic 32nd District. In the June general election, Watson took 75 percent of the vote, besting Republican Noel Irwin Hentschel.

Redistricting shifted the boundaries of Watson's district slightly east and north and renumbered it the 33rd, but its essential Democratic character was unchanged. Since besting her Republican opponent with 83 percent of the vote in 2002, she has not faced a GOP challenger.

KEY VOTES

2006

Yes Stop broadband companies from favoring select Internet traffic
No Affirm U.S. commitment to war in Iraq and reject setting a withdrawal date for troops
No Repeal requirement for bilingual ballots at the polls
No Permit U.S. sale of civilian nuclear technology to India
No Build a 700-mile fence on the U.S.-Mexico border to curb illegal crossings
No Permit warrantless wiretaps of suspected terrorists

2005

? Intervene in the life-support case of Terri Schiavo
Yes Lift President Bush's restrictions on stem cell research funding
Yes Prohibit FBI access to library and bookstore records
No Approve free-trade pact with five Central American countries
No Pass energy policy overhaul favored by President Bush emphasizing domestic oil and gas production
No End mandatory preservation of habitat of endangered animal and plant species
Yes Ban torture of prisoners in U.S. custody

CQ VOTE STUDIES

	PARTY UNITY		PRESIDENTIAL SUPPORT	
	Support	Oppose	Support	Oppose
2006	98%	2%	9%	91%
2005	98%	2%	9%	91%
2004	98%	2%	23%	77%
2003	98%	2%	17%	83%
2002	98%	2%	16%	84%

INTEREST GROUPS

	AFL-CIO	ADA	CCUS	ACU
2006	100%	80%	33%	0%
2005	93%	95%	37%	4%
2004	92%	85%	16%	0%
2003	87%	100%	21%	17%
2002	100%	85%	26%	0%

CALIFORNIA 33
West Los Angeles; Culver City

The 33rd is an ethnically diverse, Democratic district that begins about one mile inland from Venice Beach, runs east through Culver City and ends up in South Los Angeles (south central). From there it runs north through Koreatown, the "Miracle Mile" district and Hollywood.

Blacks, Hispanics and Asians account for more than three-fourths of the population, but the 33rd has no single racial majority. Over the past decade there has been an influx of Hispanics, who now account for the largest part of the population, at 35 percent. The 33rd has a solid middle class, as well as some sharply contrasting areas such as wealthy Hancock Park — where the Los Angeles mayor's official residence is located — and the city's poor South Los Angeles neighborhood.

The largest business sector is the service industry, with health care also providing jobs for many residents. The University of Southern California is in the 33rd's portion of Los Angeles, along with university-affiliated hospitals such as Children's Hospital Los Angeles. Although the 33rd is no longer the film production hub it used to be, it is home to the real Tinseltown — Hollywood — and entertainment continues to be a factor in its overall economy. Sony Pictures Studios (formerly MGM Studios) makes its home in Culver City, which now has a blossoming art scene. The Kodak Theater is the site of the annual Academy Awards.

For recreation, residents and tourists flock to Exposition Park in downtown Los Angeles. In addition to the Los Angeles County Natural History Museum and the California Science Center, the park boasts the Los Angeles Memorial Coliseum, which hosted two Olympiads.

Democrats have an overwhelming advantage in the 32nd, and John Kerry took 83 percent of the district's 2004 presidential vote. Democrat Phil Angelides won 69 percent of the gubernatorial vote here in 2006, his highest vote percentage in the state.

MAJOR INDUSTRY
Service, entertainment, health care

CITIES
Los Angeles (pt.), 582,746; Culver City, 38,816

NOTABLE
Howard Hughes built the huge H-4 Hercules "Spruce Goose" aircraft at his Culver City facility — the infamous wooden plane flew only once.

Rep. Lucille Roybal-Allard (D)

CAPITOL OFFICE
225-1766
www.house.gov/roybal-allard
2330 Rayburn 20515-0534; fax 226-0350

COMMITTEES
Appropriations
Standards of Official Conduct

RESIDENCE
East Los Angeles

BORN
June 12, 1941, Boyle Heights, Calif.

RELIGION
Roman Catholic

FAMILY
Husband, Edward Allard; four children

EDUCATION
California State U., Los Angeles, B.A. 1965 (speech)

CAREER
Nonprofit worker

POLITICAL HIGHLIGHTS
Calif. Assembly, 1986-92

ELECTION RESULTS

2006 GENERAL		
Lucille Roybal-Allard (D)	57,459	76.8%
Wayne Miller (R)	17,359	23.2%
2006 PRIMARY		
Lucille Roybal-Allard (D)		unopposed
2004 GENERAL		
Lucille Roybal-Allard (D)	82,282	74.5%
Wayne Miller (R)	28,175	25.5%

PREVIOUS WINNING PERCENTAGES
2002 (74%); 2000 (85%); 1998 (87%); 1996 (82%); 1994 (81%); 1992 (63%)

Elected 1992; 8th term

Roybal-Allard personifies some of the most significant changes in U.S. politics of the last half-century. The first Mexican-American woman ever elected to Congress and the first woman to head the Congressional Hispanic Caucus, she has seen the political strength of both women and Hispanics climb to record levels in the current Congress.

Over the years, many sons have followed their fathers to Congress; Roybal-Allard is one of just three women currently in the House to have followed their father there. (The others are Speaker Nancy Pelosi, also a California Democrat, and Republican Shelley Moore Capito of West Virginia.)

Her father was Edward R. Roybal, one of only three Hispanic members of the House when he arrived in 1963. In the 110th Congress (2007-08), there are 23 Hispanic members of the House (not counting non-voting delegates), seven from California. Edward R. Roybal, who died in 2005, co-founded the Congressional Hispanic Caucus, which his daughter later chaired.

Despite her political pedigree, Roybal-Allard says she grew up facing discrimination and discouragement. She recalls being punished as a child for speaking Spanish in school. She also remembers how her parents would be stopped and questioned when they tried to enter hotels.

Her own family tried to dampen her ambitions. Her father's relatives ridiculed him for sending his daughters to college, saying all that was expected of them was marriage and children. Later, her siblings discouraged her from entering politics, citing the difficulties their father faced.

Roybal-Allard says the treatment she and her family received made her particularly sensitive to the problems of immigrants. She voted against bills that Republicans pushed through the House in the 109th Congress (2005-06) to authorize a 700-mile fence along the border with Mexico, to tighten asylum requirements and to make it a felony to be in the United States without valid legal papers. "Instead of a comprehensive immigration reform bill that provides real security to our nation's borders, these bills are Band-Aids with harmful provisions that will not make us safer or fix our broken immigration system," she said on the House floor.

In the 108th Congress (2003-04), Roybal-Allard pressed for legislation to make it easier for children of illegal immigrants to qualify for in-state tuition rates at public universities if they meet other residency criteria.

Like her father before her, Roybal-Allard serves on the Appropriations Committee, where she looks out for her district and the surrounding area. After joining the Appropriations Subcommittee on Homeland Security in 2003, she urged her colleagues to boost funding for state and local governments, including high-threat urban areas such as Los Angeles, that bear much of the cost whenever terror threats require heightened security. In 2006, Los Angeles Mayor Antonio Villaraigosa singled her out for special thanks after the award of more than $80 million to boost local efforts to prepare for and respond to a terrorist attack.

Before entering politics, Roybal-Allard worked for the United Way and then served as an assistant director on the Alcoholism Council of East Los Angeles. In Congress, she has focused much of her legislative energy on fighting underage drinking. "While we have an extensive campaign to combat illegal drug use, the fact remains that alcohol kills more teens than all other drugs combined," she says. Her efforts have drawn praise from Mothers Against Drunk Driving and other organizations.

A member of the Appropriations Labor, Health and Human Services and

Education Subcommittee, Roybal-Allard won a $1 million provision in 2001 for the Health and Human Services Department to develop new programs to curb underage drinking. She built on that over the years, and in 2006 she won enactment of legislation to coordinate all federal programs and research efforts on underage drinking and to provide grants to colleges, states and nonprofit organizations to combat the problem.

Another of her priorities has been to improve the lot of women victimized by domestic violence. Beginning in the 104th Congress (1995-96), Roybal-Allard has offered a bill every two years to give unemployment benefits to women forced to leave jobs because of domestic violence.

Roybal-Allard drew plaudits in the late 1990s for her role in awakening the power of the California congressional delegation, which had been divided and ineffective. As the first elected chairwoman of the California Democratic delegation, she worked with her GOP counterpart, Jerry Lewis, to find issues on which the majority of the delegation could agree.

In 2003, she agreed to take a seat on the House ethics committee at the request of her California colleague, then Minority Leader Pelosi. The committee is the least popular assignment in the House. Members generally serve for a maximum of three two-year terms, and this is her final one.

In her legislative work, Roybal-Allard tries to balance the related but not always overlapping needs of her two chief constituencies: a minority underclass mired in chronic poverty and a substantial Latino working class of laborers and shop owners. In recent years, Roybal-Allard and other community leaders have been working to encourage citizenship applications and to help speed the process.

On the biggest foreign policy issue in recent years, Roybal-Allard voted against the 2002 resolution authorizing the use of force in Iraq, and remains fiercely opposed to the U.S. involvement there. The wife of a Marine who did two tours in Vietnam and the stepmother of a son who served in Iraq with the Army, she said in 2007 that President Bush's decision to commit a sizable contingent of troops to Iraq "defies common sense."

Roybal-Allard served six years in the California state Assembly before winning election to the House in 1992. As a result of redistricting, her father had hoped that she could serve beside him in Congress. But her mother's poor health and the strain of constant travel prompted him to retire instead. Democrat Xavier Becerra won her father's old seat that year, while she captured a neighboring Hispanic district by a 2-to-1 margin.

She has won with no less than 74 percent of the vote in each re-election since in the heavily Democratic district.

KEY VOTES

2006

Yes Stop broadband companies from favoring select Internet traffic
No Affirm U.S. commitment to war in Iraq and reject setting a withdrawal date for troops
No Repeal requirement for bilingual ballots at the polls
Yes Permit U.S. sale of civilian nuclear technology to India
No Build a 700-mile fence on the U.S.-Mexico border to curb illegal crossings
No Permit warrantless wiretaps of suspected terrorists

2005

? Intervene in the life-support case of Terri Schiavo
Yes Lift President Bush's restrictions on stem cell research funding
Yes Prohibit FBI access to library and bookstore records
No Approve free-trade pact with five Central American countries
No Pass energy policy overhaul favored by President Bush emphasizing domestic oil and gas production
No End mandatory preservation of habitat of endangered animal and plant species
Yes Ban torture of prisoners in U.S. custody

CQ VOTE STUDIES

	PARTY UNITY		PRESIDENTIAL SUPPORT	
	Support	Oppose	Support	Oppose
2006	93%	7%	27%	73%
2005	97%	3%	15%	85%
2004	98%	2%	24%	76%
2003	99%	1%	15%	85%
2002	99%	1%	22%	78%

INTEREST GROUPS

	AFL-CIO	ADA	CCUS	ACU
2006	100%	100%	33%	4%
2005	93%	95%	43%	0%
2004	100%	100%	35%	0%
2003	100%	100%	27%	12%
2002	100%	100%	35%	0%

CALIFORNIA 34

East central Los Angeles; Downey; Bellflower

The Democratic 34th takes in the heart and southeastern part of Los Angeles and has an overwhelming Hispanic majority. At 77 percent, the district has the largest concentration of Hispanics in California and the fourth-largest percentage in the country. Nearly 54 percent of residents here do not have a high school diploma, the highest rate in the nation.

The local economy revolves around businesses in revitalized downtown areas and in nearby light manufacturing centers such as Vernon and Commerce. Downtown businesses include toy, jewelry and garment manufacturers and retailers. Some space downtown is being converted into lofts. Many of Los Angeles' civic buildings, including city hall, the county prison and courthouses, are in the 34th. Despite redevelopment and many small businesses, the area's crime rates have increased.

Brighter spots include Walt Disney Concert Hall, home of the Los Angeles Philharmonic; the Dorothy Chandler Pavilion, home of the Los Angeles Opera; the Los Angeles Convention Center; and Staples Center, home to basketball's Lakers, Clippers and Sparks, and hockey's Kings. Transportation hub Union Station and the terminus of the 20-mile Alameda Corridor rail link connecting the city to the ports of Los Angeles and Long Beach also are in the district.

Vernon's population explodes during the workday as workers stream into its food-processing and furniture plants. Southeast of the city, Downey's economy is driven in part by the Rancho Los Amigos National Rehabilitation Center. The district also is attracting new "green" industries, such as recycling companies.

The 34th averages some of California's youngest, poorest and least-educated residents, and generally has low voter turnout. Democrat Phil Angelides captured 63 percent of the district's 2006 gubernatorial vote here, despite the presence of slightly more suburban and conservative Bellflower and Downey in the south, where there are fewer Hispanics.

MAJOR INDUSTRY
Government, manufacturing, service, retail

CITIES
Los Angeles (pt.), 188,018; Downey, 107,323; Bellflower, 72,878

NOTABLE
The first Taco Bell opened in 1962 in Downey.

Rep. Maxine Waters (D)

CAPITOL OFFICE
225-2201
www.house.gov/waters
2344 Rayburn 20515-0535; fax 225-7854

COMMITTEES
Financial Services
(Housing & Community Opportunity - chairwoman)
Judiciary

RESIDENCE
Los Angeles

BORN
Aug. 15, 1938, St. Louis, Mo.

RELIGION
Christian

FAMILY
Husband, Sidney Williams; two children

EDUCATION
California State U., Los Angeles, B.A. 1970

CAREER
City council staffer; public relations firm owner; Head Start program coordinator; telephone company service representative

POLITICAL HIGHLIGHTS
Calif. Assembly, 1976-90

ELECTION RESULTS

2006 GENERAL		
Maxine Waters (D)	82,498	83.7%
Gordon Michael Mego (AMI)	8,343	8.5%
Paul T. Ireland (LIBERT)	7,665	7.8%
2006 PRIMARY		
Maxine Waters (D)	34,338	86.1%
Carl McGill (D)	5,538	13.9%
2004 GENERAL		
Maxine Waters (D)	125,949	80.5%
Ross Moen (R)	23,591	15.1%
Gordon Michael Mego (AMI)	3,440	2.2%
Charles Tate (LIBERT)	3,427	2.2%

PREVIOUS WINNING PERCENTAGES
2002 (78%); 2000 (87%); 1998 (89%); 1996 (86%); 1994 (78%); 1992 (83%); 1990 (79%)

Elected 1990; 9th term

Waters is an old-school liberal, and while none of her colleagues doubt her commitment to her ideals, they are sometimes put off by her prickliness. When she is fired up about something, Waters has been known to verbally blast opponents and even allies, telling them to "shut up." She says that if she softened her stance and engaged in the give-and-take typical of Washington, her constituents would be let down. And Waters is relentless in pressing for government assistance for her poor, minority-dominated district in South Los Angeles.

When Republicans were in the majority, Waters seldom found sympathy for her repeated pleas for federal dollars for inner cities. But over the years, she has won a few battles over job training, community development funding and the fight against AIDS, which she says has become an epidemic in Los Angeles County. And in the 110th Congress (2007-08), she chairs the Financial Services Housing and Community Opportunity Subcommittee, a post she uses to advance legislation to expand the availability of housing for low-income Americans, including victims of the devastating 2005 Gulf Coast hurricanes. She is an advocate of Community Block Grants, for housing and infrastructure improvements in poor communities.

She also has worked to stop banks from charging transaction fees to small depositors and from engaging in predatory lending practices, in which customers in low-income communities pay higher rates and fees than customers in wealthier localities.

An ally of House Speaker Nancy Pelosi, her fellow Californian, Waters is one of nine chief deputy whips and serves on the leadership's Steering and Policy Committee, which makes all-important committee assignments.

Waters is also a force to be reckoned with in her 90 percent minority district. Since 2004, she has been fighting a plan by Los Angeles County to close a trauma center at King/Drew Medical Center, a public hospital established to improve local health care after riots in the Watts neighborhood in 1965. When the board of supervisors held a public hearing in 2004, she packed it with an overflow crowd that included the Rev. Jesse Jackson and Yolanda King, daughter of the Rev. Martin Luther King Jr., for whom the center was named. According to the Los Angeles Times, "The supervisors appeared especially rattled by Waters, who seemed at times to have taken control of the hearing away from its chairman."

In Washington, President Bush is a favorite target. Waters critiques his performance in unvarnished terms on issues ranging from the war in Iraq to the state of the economy — although it is the war that has fired her rage the most in recent years. In the 109th Congress (2005-06), she cosponsored a bill to ban funding for the war and in June 2005 founded the Out of Iraq Caucus with a group of fellow liberals to press for a redeployment of U.S. troops.

During an abortion rights rally in 2005, Waters laid verbal waste to a goodly segment of Bush's Cabinet, including the former attorney general, the Defense secretary and the secretary of State. "George W. Bush, go to hell! And while you're at it, we want you to take Ashcroft with you," she said. "And don't forget Rumsfeld. And please carry along Condi Rice." In January 2006, Waters called for Bush's impeachment for authorizing warrantless surveillance of Americans in terrorism investigations.

On the Judiciary Committee, Waters often jumps headfirst into the boisterous discussions on one of Capitol Hill's most partisan committees. During a hearing on the warrantless wiretapping program, Waters asked Steve Bradbury, acting assistant attorney general, "Were you involved in advising the president in any way when he decided to undermine the Constitution of the United States of America?"

In the aftermath of the contested presidential election in 2000, Democratic leaders named Waters to head a task force on the election process. Saying many citizens were denied their right to participate, she called the election "the first major civil rights issue of the 21st century." Waters' Democrats-only panel held a series of hearings and made recommendations, and the group played an important role in keeping up pressure for eventual congressional action. In 1998, Waters was one of President Bill Clinton's staunchest defenders during impeachment proceedings.

In addition to her battles with Republicans, Waters can mix it up with the conservatives in her own party. She campaigned for Democrat Ned Lamont when he challenged incumbent Connecticut Sen. Joseph I. Lieberman in 2006. Waters had clashed earlier with Lieberman in 2000 when he was Al Gore's presidential running mate. "We want to win, but we don't want to win at any cost," She said of Lieberman at a Democratic National Committee meeting.

Born in St. Louis as one of 13 children in a family on welfare, Waters bused tables in a segregated restaurant when she was a teenager. Married just after high school, she moved in 1961 with her first husband and two children to Los Angeles, where she worked in a clothing factory and for the telephone company.

Waters' public career began in 1965, when she took a job as program coordinator in the new Head Start program. Meanwhile, she was working her way through college. She got involved in community organizing, which led her to politics. After working as a volunteer and a consultant to several candidates, she won an upset victory in 1976 for a seat in the California state Assembly, representing many of the same neighborhoods that are part of her congressional district today.

Waters got her chance to run for Congress in 1990, when Democratic Rep. Augustus F. Hawkins retired after 14 terms. She had been preparing for the move for years. During redistricting debates in the Assembly in 1982, Waters maneuvered to remove from Hawkins' district a blue-collar, mainly white suburb she saw as unfriendly territory. Waters' 1990 election to the U.S. House was never in doubt, and since then she has had a virtual lock on her seat — winning each election with at least 75 percent of the vote. She had no Republican opponent in 2006.

KEY VOTES

2006

- Yes Stop broadband companies from favoring select Internet traffic
- No Affirm U.S. commitment to war in Iraq and reject setting a withdrawal date for troops
- No Repeal requirement for bilingual ballots at the polls
- No Permit U.S. sale of civilian nuclear technology to India
- No Build a 700-mile fence on the U.S.-Mexico border to curb illegal crossings
- No Permit warrantless wiretaps of suspected terrorists

2005

- ? Intervene in the life-support case of Terri Schiavo
- Yes Lift President Bush's restrictions on stem cell research funding
- Yes Prohibit FBI access to library and bookstore records
- No Approve free-trade pact with five Central American countries
- No Pass energy policy overhaul favored by President Bush emphasizing domestic oil and gas production
- No End mandatory preservation of habitat of endangered animal and plant species
- Yes Ban torture of prisoners in U.S. custody

CQ VOTE STUDIES

	PARTY UNITY		PRESIDENTIAL SUPPORT	
	Support	Oppose	Support	Oppose
2006	96%	4%	13%	87%
2005	96%	4%	14%	86%
2004	97%	3%	13%	87%
2003	98%	2%	12%	88%
2002	97%	3%	21%	79%

INTEREST GROUPS

	AFL-CIO	ADA	CCUS	ACU
2006	100%	90%	31%	4%
2005	93%	95%	32%	8%
2004	100%	95%	12%	4%
2003	100%	100%	17%	17%
2002	100%	95%	22%	0%

CALIFORNIA 35

South and Southeast Los Angeles; Inglewood

The Democratic 35th is centered in South and Southeast Los Angeles (south central), and is bordered by downtown Los Angeles to the north, beaches to the west, Torrance to the south and the industrial Alameda Corridor to the east.

Although the 35th is mostly poor, Inglewood and the South Bay cities of Hawthorne, Gardena and Lawndale have middle-class areas. Gardena allows poker parlors, and enjoys a revenue stream from gambling. The 1999 move of the Los Angeles Lakers and Kings from Inglewood to the Staples Center in the nearby 34th was a disappointment for the 35th, but Hollywood Park racetrack remains in Inglewood. West of Inglewood, Los Angeles International Airport is one of the region's largest employers.

A precipitous decline in the district's manufacturing base has allowed poverty, crime and street gangs to dominate the area. Police-community relations, public safety and economic development are central public policy concerns. Riots put the 35th in the headlines in 1992, following the acquittal of white police officers accused of beating black motorist Rodney King. Subsequently, the area became part of a successful federal empowerment zone and local revitalization zone to help areas affected by the riots. The tax credits and incentives available to local employers have helped increase the number of jobs and aided in the rebuilding of damaged areas.

The 35th leads the state in Democratic party registration — almost 65 percent of voters have aligned themselves with the party — and Democrat Phil Angelides captured 67 percent of the district's 2006 gubernatorial vote. Once predominately black, the district is seeing a huge influx of Hispanics (47 percent of the population), but it still has the state's largest black population at 34 percent. Gardena also has a large and politically influential Japanese community.

MAJOR INDUSTRY

Aerospace, service, manufacturing

CITIES

Los Angeles (pt.), 280,597; Inglewood, 112,580; Hawthorne, 84,112

NOTABLE

Central Avenue, on the district's eastern edge, was the West Coast hub of African-American entertainment during the jazz age; Hawthorne was the birthplace of The Beach Boys.

Rep. Jane Harman (D)

CAPITOL OFFICE
225-8220
www.house.gov/harman
2400 Rayburn 20515-0536; fax 226-7290

COMMITTEES
Energy & Commerce
Homeland Security
(Intelligence, Information Sharing & Terrorism Risk Assessment - chairwoman)

RESIDENCE
Venice

BORN
June 28, 1945, Queens, N.Y.

RELIGION
Jewish

FAMILY
Husband, Sidney Harman; four children

EDUCATION
Smith College, B.A. 1966 (government); Harvard U., J.D. 1969

CAREER
Lawyer; White House aide; congressional aide

POLITICAL HIGHLIGHTS
U.S. House, 1993-99; sought Democratic nomination for governor, 1998

ELECTION RESULTS

2006 GENERAL		
Jane Harman (D)	105,323	63.4%
Brian Gibson (R)	53,068	31.9%
James R. Smith (PFP)	4,592	2.8%
Mike Binkley (LIBERT)	3,170	1.9%
2006 PRIMARY		
Jane Harman (D)	30,333	62.5%
Marcy Winograd (D)	18,227	37.5%
2004 GENERAL		
Jane Harman (D)	151,208	62.0%
Paul Whitehead (R)	81,666	33.5%
Alice Stek (PF)	6,105	2.5%
Mike Binkley (LIBERT)	5,065	2.1%

PREVIOUS WINNING PERCENTAGES
2002 (61%); 2000 (48%); 1996 (52%); 1994 (48%); 1992 (48%)

Elected 1992; 7th term

Did not serve 1999-2001

Harman had a rough start in the new House majority. On the outs with Speaker Nancy Pelosi of California, she was denied promotion as chairwoman of the Intelligence Committee. But she had a relatively soft landing with her return to the powerful Energy and Commerce Committee, albeit as a rank-and-file member.

An expert on national intelligence, Harman remains active on those issues from another new perch: as chairwoman of the Homeland Security Intelligence Subcommittee, a significantly smaller platform than she would have had heading the Intelligence Committee. The subcommittee focuses on intelligence operations of the Homeland Security Department, which coordinates with state and local governments on terrorism information-sharing. Harman has a strong interest in improving communications systems for first-responders.

Although Pelosi said she removed Harman from the Intelligence slot because of term limits, she was privately unhappy with her. Pelosi viewed Harman as too close to the Bush administration and too hawkish on defense. Liberal Alcee L. Hastings of Florida emerged as an alternative to Harman, but his chances were hurt by a public rehash of a roughly two-decades-old case in which he was impeached as a federal judge. Pelosi eventually chose neither of them, tapping Silvestre Reyes of Texas instead.

Harman told CNN, "It was her choice. Obviously, I had hoped to stay. I thought I'd earned it and that it had been promised. But I think Silvestre Reyes is an excellent choice. He has my support."

Harman had pursued the chairmanship so doggedly that she drew the attention of federal investigators. Time magazine reported that the Federal Bureau of Investigation looked into whether the American Israel Public Affairs Committee had lobbied House leaders to keep Harman as top-ranking Democrat on Intelligence in exchange for the promise of favors from Harman. Nothing had come of the probe by early 2007.

With Pelosi's blessing, Harman got a seat on the Energy and Commerce panel, where she can focus on entertainment and broadcast issues important to her Los Angeles district. She also is interested in energy independence and global warming.

While she was the ranking Democrat on Intelligence, Harman initially worked closely with Republican Chairman Peter Hoekstra of Michigan, whom she viewed as more collegial than his predecessor, Porter J. Goss of Florida. In 2004, the two steered to enactment a major reorganization of intelligence agencies in line with recommendations of the commission that investigated the terrorist attacks of Sept. 11, 2001.

But the Harman-Hoekstra alliance deteriorated in 2006. Tensions boiled over when Harman released an unclassified summary of a report on the committee activities of former Rep. Randy "Duke" Cunningham, a California Republican who was convicted on bribery charges. A furious Hoekstra said Harman broke a promise by releasing the report without his consent.

Harman was an early advocate of the creation of a Homeland Security Department, well before President Bush proposed one. During her first six years in Congress, "terrorism was not on my radar," she told an interviewer for the Harvard Law Bulletin. But that changed with her service on the 10-member, congressionally mandated National Commission on Terrorism. She joined the panel after finding herself temporarily unemployed in 1999. She had left her House seat to run for California governor, but lost a three-way primary to Lt. Gov. Gray Davis, who won that November. Harman helped write the commission's report warning that the terrorist threat to the United States was increasing and that "today's terrorists seek to inflict mass casualties." It was released a little over a year before the attacks.

In 2000, Democrats pleaded with her to run for her old seat, then held by Republican Steven T. Kuykendall. She agreed, but only after she was promised a return to the Intelligence panel if she won.

Harman is among the wealthiest members of Congress; her second husband is electronics executive Sidney Harman, and the couple's net worth is in the millions. A disciplined runner and athlete, she can be similarly driven in her job. A former aide told the Los Angeles Times that working for her is "a survival-of-the-fittest kind of game, Jane being the fittest."

Harman appeals to the swing voters in her upscale, suburban Los Angeles district with moderate fiscal stands and liberal social views, including unflagging support for abortion rights. During her gubernatorial campaign, she marketed herself to Republican women who supported abortion rights as "the best Republican in the Democratic Party."

Harman's father, a doctor, fled Nazi Germany and came to the United States. She was born in New York City, but the family moved to west Los Angeles when she was 4 years old.

She caught the politics bug in 1964 when, as a Smith College student, she did an internship in Washington. After getting a law degree from Harvard, she returned to Washington to work for Democratic Sen. John V. Tunney of California and the Senate Judiciary Committee. In 1977, she worked in the Carter White House, then served as a special counsel at the Pentagon.

In 1991, she and her husband returned to California and settled in the 36th District, where incumbent Rep. Democrat Mel Levine had announced plans to run for the Senate. Her move to the district was branded opportunism by the opposition, but Harman made an issue of the anti-abortion position of GOP candidate Joan Milke Flores. She also spent a considerable amount of her own money, and won by 6 percentage points.

The 36th was a swing district throughout the 1990s, and her re-elections in 1994 and 1996 were hard-fought affairs. In 2000, Harman won back the seat from Kuykendall by just less than 2 percentage points. Remapping before the 2002 election gave the district a much more Democratic tilt, and Harman has won handily since then. But she had to stave off a vigorous 2006 primary challenge from Marcy Winograd, a teacher and anti-war activist, who assailed Harman as too cozy with Bush. Harman took 62 percent of the primary vote and easily won the general election.

KEY VOTES

2006

- Yes Stop broadband companies from favoring select Internet traffic
- No Affirm U.S. commitment to war in Iraq and reject setting a withdrawal date for troops
- No Repeal requirement for bilingual ballots at the polls
- No Permit U.S. sale of civilian nuclear technology to India
- No Build a 700-mile fence on the U.S.-Mexico border to curb illegal crossings
- No Permit warrantless wiretaps of suspected terrorists

2005

- ? Intervene in the life-support case of Terri Schiavo
- Yes Lift President Bush's restrictions on stem cell research funding
- Yes Prohibit FBI access to library and bookstore records
- No Approve free-trade pact with five Central American countries
- No Pass energy policy overhaul favored by President Bush emphasizing domestic oil and gas production
- \- End mandatory preservation of habitat of endangered animal and plant species
- Yes Ban torture of prisoners in U.S. custody

CQ VOTE STUDIES

	PARTY UNITY		PRESIDENTIAL SUPPORT	
	Support	Oppose	Support	Oppose
2006	91%	9%	25%	75%
2005	90%	10%	26%	74%
2004	91%	9%	34%	66%
2003	91%	9%	25%	75%
2002	83%	17%	42%	58%

INTEREST GROUPS

	AFL-CIO	ADA	CCUS	ACU
2006	93%	90%	40%	12%
2005	82%	75%	58%	5%
2004	87%	95%	55%	13%
2003	75%	85%	45%	16%
2002	50%	60%	65%	36%

CALIFORNIA 36

Southwest Los Angeles County — Torrance, Redondo Beach, part of Los Angeles

The 36th is home to some of Los Angeles' most famous beaches and biggest aerospace firms. The district begins in the Venice area of the city, then runs along the Pacific coast south through El Segundo to Manhattan, Hermosa and Redondo beaches before hitting Torrance.

Torrance, the district's largest whole city, is dotted with oil wells and derricks. The ExxonMobil refinery in the north end of the city, along with Chevron in El Segundo, help fuel southern California. Torrance also is the sales headquarters of several major automakers, and its Del Amo Fashion Center is one of the largest malls in the country.

Several major companies maintain headquarters here, and aerospace firms in Torrance and El Segundo drive the economy. The district has some of the state's most-educated residents, some of whom lost jobs due to decreases in defense and aerospace spending. Many firms, such as Northrop Grumman, have converted some jobs to non-defense projects. Such efforts to diversify the economy and encourage dual-use technology have provided an economic boost.

Torrance is split politically: It is wealthier toward the coast, but inland sections include middle- and working-class areas that have conservative and labor-heavy pockets. Venice's eclectic beaches are considered the state's most liberal havens outside of Berkeley, while Manhattan Beach and Marina del Rey are ritzier. In 2006, Gov. Arnold Schwarzenegger took 53 percent of the district's gubernatorial vote, 3 percentage points below his statewide total, but overall the 36th leans Democratic and the party holds a 12-point voter registration edge.

MAJOR INDUSTRY
Aerospace, technology, manufacturing

MILITARY BASES
Los Angeles Air Force Base, 1,357 military, 2,236 civilian (2005)

CITIES
Los Angeles (pt.), 295,807; Torrance, 137,946; Redondo Beach, 63,261; Manhattan Beach, 33,852

NOTABLE
The Hyperion sewage treatment plant in Playa del Rey, the former focus of a lengthy lawsuit, is now one of the cleanest plants in the region.

Vacant Seat

Rep. Juanita Millender-McDonald (D) Died April 22, 2007

Juanita Millender-McDonald began the 110th Congress (2007-08) as the new chairwoman of the House Administration Committee with a heavy agenda planned for her panel. She had barely begun work when she succumbed to cancer, leaving open the 37th District seat she had occupied since March 1996. She died April 22, 2007, at the age of 68.

California Gov. Arnold Schwarzenegger, a Republican, called a June 26, 2007, special election to choose a successor.

The minority-majority 37th District — whites make up 17 percent of the population based on the 2000 census — is overwhelmingly Democratic. Massachusetts Sen. John Kerry carried 74 percent of the district's vote over President Bush in the 2004 presidential election.

State Rep. Laura Richardson, a one-time Long Beach city councilwoman and former field deputy for Millender-McDonald, jumped into the contest within days. She was soon followed by state Sen. Jenny Oropeza of Carson and a number of other contenders. There was some talk that Valerie McDonald, the congresswoman's daughter, might join the race.

Richardson's roots in Long Beach were a likely plus in the special election. Roughly 370,000 residents of Long Beach live in the 37th District, making it the district's dominant jurisdiction. But the contest threatened to expose demographic rivalries within the 37th.

Richardson, like Millender-McDonald, is African-American. Hispanics now outnumber black residents in the district, and that was seen as a potential advantage for Oropeza, who is Hispanic. Oropeza served six years in the California Assembly before winning election to the state Senate in November 2006. Richardson's staff, however, said that based on historical patterns, the district's African-Americans were more likely to vote than its Hispanics, many of whom were not U.S. citizens.

A multitude of other contenders were eyeing the race, including Republican minister L. J. "Bishop" Guillory, who said he had intended to run against Millender-McDonald in 2008 and was prepared to spend millions of dollars of his own money on a campaign.

Candidates of all parties were to compete on a single ballot on June 26, 2007. Anyone receiving an outright majority of the votes that day would be elected. If no one met that test, the top vote-getters from each party were to face off in an Aug. 21, 2007, special election. At that point, the Democratic nominee would be the prohibitive favorite.

Whoever replaces Millender-McDonald, the new member is not likely to be assigned to the House Administration Committee. Its Democratic members are appointed directly by House Speaker Nancy Pelosi, and typically are seasoned lawmakers well versed in the internal politics of the House. The panel oversees the day-to-day operations of Congress, including perquisites such as office space, a useful tool for rewarding friends and punishing enemies. It also handles federal election-related legislation.

Millender-McDonald also served on the Transportation and Infrastructure and Small Business committees, assignments critical to her district, which borders two large seaports and includes major highways that carry cargo from the ports inland.

Her successor might well inherit those seats, although the final decision rests primarily with Pelosi, a fellow California Democrat.

CALIFORNIA 37

Southern Los Angeles County — most of Long Beach, Compton, Carson

The 37th combines some of the state's poorest and most Democratic communities with a large chunk of middle-class Long Beach. Minorities make up almost 85 percent of the population, with Hispanics as the dominant group, totaling 43 percent of residents. The district is one-fourth black and more than one-tenth Asian.

The district contains a sliver of Los Angeles itself, and then spreads to the lower- and middle-class suburbs of Compton and Carson south of Los Angeles. These communities boost Democratic presidential candidates to high margins of victory in the 37th: John Kerry garnered 74 percent of the district's vote in the 2004 presidential election.

Compton has a multiracial and ethnic population, and its poverty, crime rate and ongoing gang activity often lead it to be labeled as an "inner-city" community. Factories, petroleum refineries and other industrial sites occupy about half of Carson, and several national retailers and fast-food chains have moved into communities once considered undevelopable.

The non-coastal portion of Long Beach (the port is in the 46th) contains a more suburban, politically mixed community. It has a sizable Cambodian population, and dozens of languages are spoken in local schools. The area has grown with the development of high-tech and aerospace industries, although Boeing's C-17 jet facility is slated for closure in 2009. The multibillion-dollar Alameda Corridor project, which runs through the district linking the ports of Long Beach and Los Angeles to the south with distribution areas in the city of Los Angeles to the north, created construction jobs in the 37th, and local leaders hope transportation and warehousing jobs will continue to provide an economic boost.

MAJOR INDUSTRY

Service, manufacturing, oil

CITIES

Long Beach (pt.), 368,591; Compton, 93,493; Carson, 89,730; Los Angeles (pt.), 33,808

NOTABLE

Major League Baseball's Urban Youth Academy in Compton provides free baseball and softball instruction; The Home Depot Center's multi-use sports complex in Carson is home to soccer's Chivas USA and LA Galaxy.

PRIOR ELECTION RESULTS

2006 GENERAL		
Juanita Millender-McDonald (D)	80,716	82.4%
Herb Peters (LIBERT)	17,246	17.6%
2004 GENERAL		
Juanita Millender-McDonald (D)	118,823	75.1%
Vernon Van (R)	31,960	20.2%
Herb Peters (LIBERT)	7,535	4.8%
2002 GENERAL		
Juanita Millender-McDonald (D)	63,445	72.9%
Oscar A. Velasco (R)	20,154	23.2%
Herb Peters (LIBERT)	3,413	3.9%

Rep. Grace F. Napolitano (D)

CAPITOL OFFICE
225-5256
grace@mail.house.gov
www.napolitano.house.gov
1610 Longworth 20515-0538; fax 225-0027

COMMITTEES
Natural Resources
(Water & Power - chairwoman)
Transportation & Infrastructure

RESIDENCE
Norwalk

BORN
Dec. 4, 1936, Brownsville, Texas

RELIGION
Roman Catholic

FAMILY
Husband, Frank Napolitano; five children

EDUCATION
Brownsville H.S., graduated 1954

CAREER
Regional transportation claims agent

POLITICAL HIGHLIGHTS
Norwalk City Council, 1986-92 (mayor, 1989-90); Calif. Assembly, 1992-98

ELECTION RESULTS

2006 GENERAL		
Grace F. Napolitano (D)	75,181	75.3%
Sidney W. Street (R)	24,620	24.7%
2006 PRIMARY		
Grace F. Napolitano (D)		unopposed
2004 GENERAL		
Grace F. Napolitano (D)		unopposed

PREVIOUS WINNING PERCENTAGES
2002 (71%); 2000 (71%); 1998 (68%)

Elected 1998; 5th term

Napolitano's grandmotherly image, enhanced by her silvery hair, is sometimes deceptive. She can be a fierce political fighter who is protective of the interests of her mostly Hispanic constituency. Her political mantra: "Constituents are the most important thing." And if those constituents call her office, it is not uncommon for her to call them back.

In the 109th Congress (2005-06), Napolitano chaired the Congressional Hispanic Caucus. In one of her first actions on behalf of the group, she sent a letter to the Senate saying the caucus would not endorse Alberto R. Gonzales, President Bush's nominee for attorney general. Although caucus members had always supported "the advancement of Latinos into high levels of public office," Napolitano said they could not support Gonzales because he never took the time to meet with them. Napolitano added that the Latino community lacked clear information on how Gonzales, as attorney general, would influence certain policies, such as the Voting Rights Act, affirmative action and due process rights of immigrants.

As co-chairwoman of the Congressional Mental Health Caucus in the 109th Congress, Napolitano bristled at Hollywood star Tom Cruise's contention that mental health treatment is "pseudoscience," and that women with postpartum depression should take vitamins instead of anti-depressants. "He's never been pregnant or delivered a child," Napolitano, a mother of five, said later. She said women need more help and doctors more education about postpartum depression and other mental health concerns.

Lessening the stigma of mental health and gaining insurance parity for its treatment are priorities for Napolitano. "It hits every segment of society," she says. "It doesn't stop at race or ethnicity." With Minnesota Republican Jim Ramstad and Rhode Island Democrat Patrick J. Kennedy, she is pressing legislation to require insurance companies to offer the same reimbursements for mental health care as for treatment of other conditions.

After Napolitano expressed disappointment that Democrats did not include immigration in their "Six for '06" platform for the 2006 campaign, she said House Speaker Nancy Pelosi asked her to help craft a comprehensive immigration reform package in 2007. Napolitano wants to bolster security at the U.S.-Mexico border, but she opposes a fence authorized by Congress in 2006. She supports a guest worker program and a path to citizenship for illegal immigrants already in the United States.

Napolitano has served on the Natural Resources Committee since she arrived in the House and in 110th Congress (2007-08), she chairs its Subcommittee on Water and Power, a post that will help her watch out for her district's water needs. In January 2007, she cosponsored legislation with California Republican David Dreier to authorize federal funds for recycling facilities to help supply water to San Bernardino County for watering lawns, irrigation and industry.

In 2004, Congress passed a pared-back version of her bill to increase funding for cleaning up groundwater in the San Gabriel Basin, an important piece of southern California's strategy to protect its water supply. She also weighed in on legislation to help fund the CalFed Bay-Delta Program, developed by the state of California to improve water quality and storage systems, increase its water supply and restore state fisheries.

At the start of the 110th Congress in 2007, Napolitano won a seat on the Transportation and Infrastructure Committee, which has jurisdiction over many water projects as well as all modes of transportation. She brings considerable expertise to the panel, having served on the transportation committee in the state legislature for six years before coming to Congress.

Napolitano was one of 36 House Democrats who supported a 2004 resolution declaring the world safer with the removal of Saddam Hussein from power in Iraq but who voted against the 2002 law authorizing force in Iraq. She also opposed a 2003 administration request for an additional $87 billion in spending for Iraq, saying it would take away from badly needed federal funds at home. In 2007, she opposed Bush's plan to send additional troops to Iraq, saying early that year, "I want my kids back."

Napolitano grew up in Brownsville, Texas, the daughter of a Mexican immigrant who raised her two children on a shoestring budget. Napolitano has cultivated a strong connection to her mother's homeland as a public official. As chairwoman of the state legislature's committee on international trade and development, she traveled to Mexico many times.

Napolitano married at age 18, and she had five children by age 23. She spent the first part of her adult life attending to their needs, while also working at the Ford Motor Co. She caught the political bug as a volunteer in Norwalk's efforts to cultivate a sister-city relationship with Hermosillo, Mexico. She first joined the group to show her children and "other youngsters on this side how lucky they were" compared with Mexican children, but became immersed in the project and managed the organization's budget.

In her first run for political office, Napolitano challenged the Norwalk establishment and won a seat on the city council by 28 votes. She capitalized on outrage over an expensive city council trip to Palm Springs and campaigned with $35,000 she borrowed using her home as collateral. She says it was in that race that she learned the importance of constituent service — which her opponent had neglected. She served six years on the council, two of them as mayor, before moving up to the state legislature for six years.

Nonetheless, she was overlooked when Democrat Esteban E. Torres in 1997 announced his retirement from the House. Torres threw his support to his top aide and son-in-law, James Casso. But Napolitano won the primary by 618 votes, then took just over two-thirds of the vote to win in November. She has sailed to re-election ever since, with 75 percent of the vote in 2006.

In Washington, she has tried to win over her political opponents in much the same way that she and her second husband, Frank, won customers to their Italian restaurant — through their stomachs. She prides herself on catering her own fundraisers with homemade Mexican molés, guacamole and other dishes. She says such personal involvement is the best way to express her thanks to her supporters. "I treat them like I would my family," she says.

KEY VOTES

2006

Yes Stop broadband companies from favoring select Internet traffic

No Affirm U.S. commitment to war in Iraq and reject setting a withdrawal date for troops

No Repeal requirement for bilingual ballots at the polls

Yes Permit U.S. sale of civilian nuclear technology to India

No Build a 700-mile fence on the U.S.-Mexico border to curb illegal crossings

No Permit warrantless wiretaps of suspected terrorists

2005

? Intervene in the life-support case of Terri Schiavo

Yes Lift President Bush's restrictions on stem cell research funding

Yes Prohibit FBI access to library and bookstore records

No Approve free-trade pact with five Central American countries

Yes Pass energy policy overhaul favored by President Bush emphasizing domestic oil and gas production

No End mandatory preservation of habitat of endangered animal and plant species

Yes Ban torture of prisoners in U.S. custody

CQ VOTE STUDIES

	PARTY UNITY		PRESIDENTIAL SUPPORT	
	Support	Oppose	Support	Oppose
2006	98%	2%	21%	79%
2005	98%	2%	14%	86%
2004	98%	2%	21%	79%
2003	99%	1%	13%	87%
2002	98%	2%	21%	79%

INTEREST GROUPS

	AFL-CIO	ADA	CCUS	ACU
2006	100%	100%	33%	8%
2005	100%	100%	35%	0%
2004	100%	95%	33%	0%
2003	100%	95%	24%	12%
2002	89%	100%	40%	0%

CALIFORNIA 38

East Los Angeles County – Pomona, Norwalk

The Democratic 38th is a middle- and working-class Hispanic-majority district. A sideways "L" shape, the district takes in the city of Norwalk in southeastern Los Angeles County, then stretches north along Interstate 5 to include nearly half of East Los Angeles. It then runs east through Montebello, Pico Rivera and La Puente, before extending a thin arm parallel to the 60 Freeway into the Inland Valley to take in Pomona, the district's largest city, at the county's eastern edge.

Small businesses dominate the 38th, which includes the heart of East Los Angeles' business district, and many are owned or operated by Hispanics. The city of Industry, an almost entirely industrial area with no business tax, is home to a few thousand businesses that the city claims provides more than 80,000 jobs. Like the many commuter towns around Industry, Norwalk, the district's second-largest city, is a bedroom community. The city received a publicity boost in 2006 when the multi-agency Joint Regional Intelligence Center opened. The center will coordinate analysis of possible terrorist threats to area counties.

Although it has a large blue-collar workforce, the district contains some affluent and conservative areas such as Hacienda Heights, Rowland Heights (shared with the 42nd) and a narrow sliver of Whittier. Montebello is a middle-class Hispanic area with an Armenian community. Southeast Pomona is densely populated and has experienced some crime problems in recent years. Efforts to revitalize the city's dilapidated downtown and to renovate the Fox Theater are ongoing.

The 38th's working-class residents ensure that the district votes reliably Democratic. John Kerry received 65 percent of the 2004 presidential vote here. California State Polytechnic University, Pomona, and Cerritos College (shared with the 39th) add students to the Democratic mix.

MAJOR INDUSTRY

Manufacturing, oil

CITIES

Pomona, 149,473; Norwalk, 103,298; Pico Rivera, 63,428; Montebello, 62,150; East Los Angeles (unincorporated) (pt.), 53,349

NOTABLE

The Pomona Swap Meet and Car Show is billed as the largest collection of antique cars, parts and accessories on the West Coast.

Rep. Linda T. Sánchez (D)

CAPITOL OFFICE
225-6676
www.lindasanchez.house.gov
1222 Longworth 20515-0539; fax 226-1012

COMMITTEES
Education & Labor
Foreign Affairs
Judiciary
(Commercial & Administrative Law - chairwoman)

RESIDENCE
Lakewood

BORN
Jan. 28, 1969, Orange, Calif.

RELIGION
Roman Catholic

FAMILY
Divorced

EDUCATION
U. of California, Berkeley, B.A. 1991 (Spanish literature); U. of California, Los Angeles, J.D. 1995

CAREER
Union official; campaign aide; lawyer

POLITICAL HIGHLIGHTS
No previous office

ELECTION RESULTS

2006 GENERAL		
Linda T. Sánchez (D)	72,149	65.9%
James L. Andion (R)	37,384	34.1%
2006 PRIMARY		
Linda T. Sánchez (D)	23,893	77.8%
Ken Graham (D)	5,083	16.6%
Frank Amador (D)	1,738	5.7%
2004 GENERAL		
Linda T. Sánchez (D)	100,132	60.7%
Tim Escobar (R)	64,832	39.3%

PREVIOUS WINNING PERCENTAGES
2002 (55%)

Elected 2002; 3rd term

One of the most liberal members of the House, Sánchez is also one of the funniest. In her relatively brief congressional career, she has become a hit on the charity fundraiser circuit, doing a standup comedy routine that won her the 2006 title of "Funniest Celebrity in Washington, D.C."

In a town that takes itself painfully seriously, that might not seem like much of a prize. But colleagues and staff say Sánchez really can crack them up. "I grew up in a family of seven and my brothers teased me unmercifully, so I learned to be quick with a comeback," she says. Her material ranges from the political to the personal, the latter often a riff on her life as a single woman in search of dates. She is careful not to stray too far across the line of good taste, despite her very safe seat.

Sánchez may joke about her social life, but she is entirely serious about her career. She never has to look far to remember her roots as the sixth of seven children of Mexican immigrants. Her older sister, Democratic Rep. Loretta Sanchez, represents a nearby Santa Ana-based district. The two are the first, and so far only, sisters to serve in Congress together.

A former labor union leader, Linda T. Sánchez has concentrated in the House on the concerns of her Hispanic-majority district south of Los Angeles. Instead of the standard photograph collection of grinning and famous politicians on the wall, a self-portrait of Mexican artist Frida Kahlo hangs next to Sánchez's desk.

She favors increasing the federally mandated minimum wage and has opposed the Bush administration's free-trade agreements, arguing they failed to protect workers' rights. "We cannot preach about spreading freedom and opportunity around the world while ignoring the lack of labor and human rights standards in our trade bills," she said in 2006.

Her interest in immigration policy led her to seek and secure a seat on the Judiciary Committee, where she fought the enforcement-oriented immigration bill passed by the House in 2005, calling it a "laundry list of very mean-spirited and unenforceable anti-immigrant measures." She also did not think much of President Bush's proposal for a guest worker program allowing illegal immigrants to continue working in the United States for several years, provided they went home afterward. With other panel Democrats, Sánchez argued that such a program was a better deal for the businesses employing illegal help than for the workers, who would not have a chance to become permanent residents or citizens.

Sánchez took an active role in the 2006 reauthorization of the landmark Voting Rights Act, opposing unsuccessful GOP attempts to repeal the law's bilingual ballot requirements. She cited her mother, now an elementary school teacher, who finds it easier to be an informed voter because California's long and often complex ballots are available in Spanish. Sánchez also joined other Democrats in a battle against legislation passed by the House to require presentation of an official photo identification card and proof of citizenship in order to vote. She called such a requirement "the equivalent of a 21st century poll tax," warning it would disenfranchise millions of elderly Americans, the poor, and the disabled who might not have a driver's license, passport or other official ID. The bill died in the Senate.

Some of Sánchez's House colleagues got a sense of her views on gender equality when she joined the all-male roster of players in the annual House baseball game between Democrats and Republicans. The back of her shirt bore the numerals IX, for Title IX, shorthand for the landmark 1972 law that mandated equal treatment for women in education programs, a measure that had a dramatic impact on the growth of women's sports.

Sánchez had no experience in local or state government before her election in 2002, but she has begun to carve out an identity separate from that of "Loretta's sister." Though they are both Democrats, Linda, who is in her 30s, is no political clone of Loretta, in her 40s. Before coming to the House, Linda practiced civil rights and labor law; Loretta was a businesswoman with an MBA. Their personal styles are different, too. Linda, nine years younger, is a night owl; Loretta an early riser. Linda is messy, Loretta neat. They even spell their last name differently: Linda uses an accent and Loretta does not. (They pronounce it the same way: SAN-chez.)

But the sisterly bond between the two was obvious in 2007 when Linda quit the Congressional Hispanic Caucus in protest after Loretta accused caucus Chairman Joe Baca, D-Calif., of calling her a derogatory name.

Growing up, Linda was the more rebellious of the two. Her father, Ignacio, was a mechanic at a tire shop, where he met her mother, Maria Macias, who was working in the shop's accounting office. Her mother began organizing for a union, and met her father as she sought workers to sign up.

Sánchez often questioned why their traditional Latino family gave boys special status. "There was a very clear distinction between what boys could do and what girls could do," she says. "Boys were served first and girls served them. They had a lot more freedom and a lot fewer responsibilities."

Her mother told Sánchez to either accept the way things were or try to change them. She once took Sánchez to hear farm labor organizer César Chávez speak. Sánchez, who had worked her way through college as a nanny, security guard, bilingual teacher's aide and ESL instructor, was inspired by Chávez's words to go back to school for a law degree and to get involved in labor organizing. She later became executive secretary-treasurer of the AFL-CIO in Orange County, the county's top union post.

Her political activism started in high school in Anaheim. Upset by her gaffe-prone local congressman, conservative Republican Robert K. Dornan, Sánchez knocked on doors for Democratic challenger Dave Carter. Carter lost, but Sánchez's efforts eventually paid off. In 1996, she was the field organizer for sister Loretta's successful campaign against Dornan.

In 2000, after the census, the California Legislature drew a new district south of downtown Los Angeles that favored a Hispanic Democratic candidate. In 2002, incumbent Republican Rep. Steve Horn declined to run for the seat. Sánchez jumped in, winning a six-way contest with help from Loretta's fundraising network and vigorous campaigning by her family.

KEY VOTES

2006

- Yes Stop broadband companies from favoring select Internet traffic
- No Affirm U.S. commitment to war in Iraq and reject setting a withdrawal date for troops
- No Repeal requirement for bilingual ballots at the polls
- Yes Permit U.S. sale of civilian nuclear technology to India
- No Build a 700-mile fence on the U.S.-Mexico border to curb illegal crossings
- No Permit warrantless wiretaps of suspected terrorists

2005

- ? Intervene in the life-support case of Terri Schiavo
- Yes Lift President Bush's restrictions on stem cell research funding
- Yes Prohibit FBI access to library and bookstore records
- No Approve free-trade pact with five Central American countries
- No Pass energy policy overhaul favored by President Bush emphasizing domestic oil and gas production
- No End mandatory preservation of habitat of endangered animal and plant species
- Yes Ban torture of prisoners in U.S. custody

CQ VOTE STUDIES

	PARTY UNITY		PRESIDENTIAL SUPPORT	
	Support	Oppose	Support	Oppose
2006	98%	2%	15%	85%
2005	99%	1%	13%	87%
2004	99%	1%	15%	85%
2003	99%	1%	15%	85%

INTEREST GROUPS

	AFL-CIO	ADA	CCUS	ACU
2006	93%	100%	33%	4%
2005	93%	100%	30%	0%
2004	100%	100%	20%	0%
2003	100%	100%	24%	12%

CALIFORNIA 39

Southeast Los Angeles County – South Gate, Lakewood

The U-shaped 39th starts in South Gate and Lynwood, just south of Los Angeles, before stretching south and east to take in Lakewood and Cerritos, then northeast through La Mirada to South Whittier and Whittier. Despite external similarities — ethnic populations and working-class economic bases — most of these communities have little interaction with one another. The district is 61 percent Hispanic.

Whittier (shared mainly with the 42nd) and South Whittier are home to many second- and third-generation Latino families, and pockets of wealth exist there. La Mirada and the Asian American-heavy Cerritos are slightly more conservative communities that resemble cities in neighboring, wealthier Orange County — former farm areas now dependent on a diverse array of aerospace and technology jobs, including metals processing, semiconductors, and the manufacturing of air and spacecraft harnesses and jet engine components. Lakewood is more blue-collar, while South Gate, Lynwood and Paramount are heavily working-class and include many new immigrants.

The district has a strong organized-labor movement. Towns like Whittier and Lakewood have a number of industrial centers, and most residents work in the district or nearby rather than commuting to downtown Los Angeles, Orange County or Long Beach.

Democrats control the 39th, which gave John Kerry 59 percent of its 2004 presidential vote, but the support is not as strong as in most of Los Angeles County. Kerry's victory margin here (18 points) was the smallest margin among the 13 districts contained entirely in the county.

MAJOR INDUSTRY

Manufacturing, aerospace

CITIES

South Gate, 96,375; Lakewood, 79,345; Lynwood, 69,845; Whittier (pt.), 56,918; Paramount, 55,266; South Whittier (unincorporated), 55,193

NOTABLE

Paramount is home to Zamboni, maker of the ice resurfacing machines used at skating and hockey rinks; The home of California's last Mexican governor is in Whittier's Pio Pico Historical Park.

Rep. Ed Royce (R)

CAPITOL OFFICE
225-4111
www.house.gov/royce
2185 Rayburn 20515-0540; fax 226-0335

COMMITTEES
Financial Services
Foreign Affairs

RESIDENCE
Fullerton

BORN
Oct. 12, 1951, Los Angeles, Calif.

RELIGION
Roman Catholic

FAMILY
Wife, Marie Royce

EDUCATION
California State U., Fullerton, B.A. 1977 (accounting & finance)

CAREER
Tax manager

POLITICAL HIGHLIGHTS
Calif. Senate, 1982-92

ELECTION RESULTS

2006 GENERAL		
Ed Royce (R)	100,995	66.8%
Florice Orea Hoffman (D)	46,418	30.7%
Philip H. Inman (LIBERT)	3,876	2.6%
2006 PRIMARY		
Ed Royce (R)		unopposed
2004 GENERAL		
Ed Royce (R)	147,617	67.9%
J. Tilman Williams (D)	69,684	32.1%

PREVIOUS WINNING PERCENTAGES
2002 (68%); 2000 (63%); 1998 (63%); 1996 (63%); 1994 (66%); 1992 (57%)

Elected 1992; 8th term

The Democratic takeover in the 110th Congress (2007-08) is likely to reduce Royce's influence to some degree, but not on a topic that has been his passion for years — the promotion of robust trade with Africa. He sees trade as a way to help lift nations out of poverty and keep totalitarian regimes out of power.

A member of the Foreign Affairs Committee, Royce served four terms as chairman of the subcommittee on Africa, winning a waiver from House GOP leaders to stay on beyond the usual six-year limit. He gave up that gavel in 2005, taking the top spot on the Terrorism and Nonproliferation subcommittee. He continues to serve as the top-ranking Republican on that panel, but that does not mean he has lost interest in Africa. With Democrat Charles B. Rangel of New York, another champion of trade with Africa, now chairing the Ways and Means Committee, Royce is confident that such efforts will not disappear from the agenda.

"The United States needs to encourage African nations to move toward the free market and steer them in the direction of self-sufficiency. Markets work and subsidies don't," Royce says. He maintains that Western nations must engage with Africa to counter the growing Chinese influence on the continent. "The U.S. and Europe are attempting to offer a liberalized trade and investment system for Africa," he says. "China is trying to bribe the heads of state, saying, 'we'd like your raw materials and in exchange we'll help provide you security so you can stay in power without elections.' "

Royce's successes on Africa include a 2004 law authorizing $18.6 million to help protect the African rain forest along the Congo River basin and to promote eco-tourism. In 2000, he helped win a reduction in tariffs and quotas on imports from sub-Saharan Africa.

In the 109th Congress (2005-06), Royce championed efforts to sanction Sudan for the genocide in its Darfur region. To help raise awareness about the atrocities in the region, he enlisted actor Don Cheadle, star of the movie "Hotel Rwanda," a film about the 1994 genocide in that East African nation. In January 2005, he led a bipartisan congressional delegation to Darfur. Upon their return, Royce, Cheadle and others held a news conference to condemn the atrocities and call for more international action. In 2006, Royce was one of 45 Republicans backing a Democratic effort to shift some foreign aid funds from Egypt to Darfur refugees.

Royce also sought to target the proliferation of shoulder-fired missiles that terrorists could use to bring down airliners. In 2006, Royce-authored provisions regarding sanctions on nations that knowingly transfer shoulder-fired surface-to-air missiles were enacted, though his own bill on the topic never made it to the floor. As a member of the Financial Services Committee, he cosponsored a bill in 2004 to crack down on foreign governments whose citizens or banks finance domestic or international terrorism.

A staunch supporter of India, Royce drew criticism in 2001 when on a congressional delegation to India he left the group rather than visit Pakistan. Critics said he bent to the will of Indian-American groups that raised funds for his re-election efforts, but Royce said he did not want to legitimize President Pervez Musharraf, who had come to power in a coup.

He takes pride in his efforts in 2006 helping steer to enactment legislation permitting the president to complete negotiations with India on a nuclear cooperation treaty. The measure allows the United States to export nuclear materials to India but requires that country to open its civilian nuclear sites to international inspection.

Royce has been an ardent tax cutter while attacking government largess, even if it means going against his own party. Throughout the 1990s, he co-chaired the Congressional Porkbusters Coalition, and in 2006 he was one of just eight House members, all Republicans, to vote against a highway bill stuffed with funding for lawmakers' individual projects.

Although Royce grew up in a blue-collar Democratic household, he developed a conservative economic viewpoint early on. In high school, he became intrigued by the free-market message in the book "Economics in One Lesson," by Henry Hazlitt. The author challenged prevailing economic thinking that gave the government a central role, and that spurred Royce to read similar books on economic theory. He found himself defending the unorthodox viewpoints to fellow students and teachers, honing his debating skills as a result.

In college, he went to the aid of a young woman staffing a College Republicans recruiting table when three young men overturned it and caused a disturbance. "I stepped in and was explaining the concept of free speech and nonviolence on campus," he recalls. He wound up joining the College Republicans.

Royce spent 10 years in the California Senate, where he wrote the nation's first law making it a felony to stalk or threaten someone with injury — giving the police recourse when a stalker has not yet attacked an intended victim. He also was the guiding force behind a 1990 ballot proposition, approved by voters, setting forth rights for crime victims.

In Washington, Royce has continued his anti-stalking campaign, winning enactment of a measure similar to the one he sponsored in California. The federal law, signed in 1996, made it a crime to cross state lines with the intent to stalk or harass. In 1999, Royce and other lawmakers won enactment of a bill expanding the definition of stalking. In subsequent years, he introduced a victim's rights amendment to the Constitution.

After a decade in Sacramento, Royce jumped at the chance to run for the House in 1992 when iconoclastic Republican William E. Dannemeyer gave up his seat to run for the Senate. Royce had represented a sizable slice of the House district in the state Senate, and he drew no primary opposition. His Democratic opponent, Molly McClanahan, proved too liberal for Orange County, and Royce prevailed by almost 20 percentage points.

In redistricting after the 2000 census, the Los Angeles County portion of Royce's old 39th District was removed and the district was renumbered the 40th. Regardless of the remapping, Royce continues to win with ease.

KEY VOTES

2006

- No Stop broadband companies from favoring select Internet traffic
- Yes Affirm U.S. commitment to war in Iraq and reject setting a withdrawal date for troops
- Yes Repeal requirement for bilingual ballots at the polls
- Yes Permit U.S. sale of civilian nuclear technology to India
- Yes Build a 700-mile fence on the U.S.-Mexico border to curb illegal crossings
- Yes Permit warrantless wiretaps of suspected terrorists

2005

- ? Intervene in the life-support case of Terri Schiavo
- No Lift President Bush's restrictions on stem cell research funding
- No Prohibit FBI access to library and bookstore records
- Yes Approve free-trade pact with five Central American countries
- No Pass energy policy overhaul favored by President Bush emphasizing domestic oil and gas production
- Yes End mandatory preservation of habitat of endangered animal and plant species
- No Ban torture of prisoners in U.S. custody

CQ VOTE STUDIES

	PARTY UNITY		PRESIDENTIAL SUPPORT	
	Support	Oppose	Support	Oppose
2006	94%	6%	93%	7%
2005	97%	3%	89%	11%
2004	94%	6%	82%	18%
2003	95%	5%	93%	7%
2002	97%	3%	82%	18%

INTEREST GROUPS

	AFL-CIO	ADA	CCUS	ACU
2006	7%	5%	100%	96%
2005	0%	0%	77%	96%
2004	20%	15%	90%	96%
2003	7%	10%	87%	88%
2002	11%	0%	85%	100%

CALIFORNIA 40

North central Orange County — Orange, Fullerton

Like most of Orange County, the 40th is largely wealthy and Republican, although these inland areas are less affluent than the coast. The district forms a half circle that contains Orange County's northern and western mid-size cities. It extends north from Los Alamitos on the Los Angeles County border to take in most of Fullerton before turning southeast to reach Orange and Villa Park. It wraps around Anaheim and Garden Grove, taking in small chunks of each.

Before massive growth a generation ago, Orange County was largely agricultural and blanketed with orange and lemon groves, and many cities were dairy farm communities. Relying heavily on aerospace and defense, the 40th's economy is now more diverse. New technology firms have settled in the district, and tourists continue to head to Knott's Berry Farm amusement park and other entertainment venues in Buena Park.

Fullerton is home to a Raytheon facility and a Kimberly-Clark paper mill, as well as a California State University campus that is one of the city's major employers. Adams Rite Aerospace in Fullerton makes airplane cockpit security doors, which Congress mandated after the Sept. 11, 2001, terrorist attacks. Orange is a health care center, and the district is home to four major hospitals. Cypress is the headquarters of Pacificare Health Systems.

Orange, the solidly suburban district's largest city, and Fullerton are both upper-middle class; Stanton is a more blue-collar community. While whites make up about half of the district's population, an influx of wealthier Hispanics and Asians are shifting the 40th's demographics. District officials now boast of the area's diversity.

Republicans dominate the 40th at local, state and national levels. George W. Bush earned 60 percent of the 2004 presidential vote here, and Gov. Arnold Schwarzenegger took 69 percent here during his 2006 re-election.

MAJOR INDUSTRY

Aerospace, defense, manufacturing, health care, tourism

CITIES

Orange, 128,821; Fullerton (pt.), 108,151; Anaheim (pt.), 87,082; Buena Park, 78,282; Cypress, 46,229; Stanton, 37,403; Placentia (pt.), 37,356

NOTABLE

Fullerton is the center of the influential Orange County punk rock scene.

Rep. Jerry Lewis (R)

CAPITOL OFFICE
225-5861
www.house.gov/jerrylewis
2112 Rayburn 20515-0541; fax 225-6498

COMMITTEES
Appropriations - ranking member

RESIDENCE
Redlands

BORN
Oct. 21, 1934, Seattle, Wash.

RELIGION
Presbyterian

FAMILY
Wife, Arlene Willis; seven children

EDUCATION
U. of California, Los Angeles, B.A. 1956 (government)

CAREER
Insurance executive

POLITICAL HIGHLIGHTS
San Bernardino School Board, 1965-68; Calif. Assembly, 1968-78; Republican nominee for Calif. Senate, 1973

ELECTION RESULTS

2006 GENERAL		
Jerry Lewis (R)	109,761	66.9%
Louie A. Contreras (D)	54,235	33.1%
2006 PRIMARY		
Jerry Lewis (R)		unopposed
2004 GENERAL		
Jerry Lewis (R)	181,605	83.0%
Peymon Mottahedek (LIBERT)	37,332	17.1%

PREVIOUS WINNING PERCENTAGES
2002 (67%); 2000 (80%); 1998 (65%); 1996 (65%); 1994 (71%); 1992 (63%); 1990 (61%); 1988 (70%); 1986 (77%); 1984 (85%); 1982 (68%); 1980 (72%); 1978 (61%)

Elected 1978; 15th term

Few can beat Lewis at the insider's game on the most insider of committees, House Appropriations. But his stature as the top-ranking Republican on the influential panel has been hurt by a federal investigation into influence peddling involving his staff, family members and lobbyists.

Lewis has been in the House for nearly 30 years, most of them as an appropriator. He finally got his dream job of Appropriations Committee chairman in 2005, then lost it just two years later when Republicans were swept out of power. His short tenure was marked by the extremes of professional achievement and personal scandal. He presided over a major reorganization of the hidebound appropriations subcommittees and then coordinated with the Senate to get every spending bill through Congress in 2005, something appropriators rarely accomplish. But those milestones were overshadowed by ongoing issues about his personal ethics.

A federal grand jury was looking into Lewis' relationship with Bill Lowery, a lobbyist and close friend who hired several Lewis aides and their relatives while seeking favors in spending bills. In October 2006, as Lewis' legal defense bills topped $750,000, spokeswoman Barbara J. Comstock told the Los Angeles Times that he would be "fully exonerated once this investigation is completed."

Lewis also came under unflattering scrutiny in the media in late 2006 after he fired 60 committee investigators who had been working on uncovering waste and fraud in relief spending for Hurricane Katrina and in expensive security upgrades at the Capitol.

A big challenge for Lewis in the 109th Congress (2005-06) was dealing with conservatives in his own party who were trying to eliminate the practice of earmarks, in which projects and grants for individual lawmakers are tucked into spending bills outside the normal vetting process. The longstanding custom contributes to the great influence of appropriators, who decide whose projects get funded.

The Republican Study Committee, a group of the most conservative lawmakers, challenged Lewis and other appropriators with repeated amendments to strip earmarks from the spending bills. Although they failed, they put a public spotlight on the secretive practice. In a strategy aimed at silencing critics, Lewis insisted that any change in earmarking also apply to lawmakers who slip provisions into tax bills or other legislation. The House agreed only to a rule change affecting appropriations bills, requiring earmark sponsors to be identified.

In 2005, his first year as chairman, Lewis stuck to a disciplined schedule, getting all the annual spending bills through the House and working with Senate Appropriations Committee Chairman Thad Cochran of Mississippi to get them to the president's desk. It marked the first time Congress managed to clear all the appropriations measures since 2001, when the process was facilitated by the surge of patriotism following the Sept. 11 attacks. In 2006, Lewis got 10 of the 11 spending bills through the House, while the Senate passed only two, making it necessary for Congress to adopt temporary funding resolutions to keep the government operating.

Lewis became chairman after beating out a more senior Republican, Ralph Regula of Ohio, to succeed C.W. Bill Young of Florida, who relinquished the gavel under party-mandated term limits. House GOP leaders chose Lewis for his track record of raising money for the party and for his willingness to let them exert more control over appropriations.

As soon as Lewis became chairman, the longtime staff director left and Lewis reorganized the subcommittees in line with a plan by then Majority Leader Tom DeLay, scaling them back from 13 to 10 and reshuffling their jurisdictions. He also had to squire to passage several multibillion-dollar bills funding the war in Iraq at a time when both Republicans and Democrats were growing increasingly nervous about the costs of the war and the quality of the intelligence that led to the 2003 U.S. invasion. Back in the minority in 2007, he sought ways to portray Democrats as big spenders.

With a distinguishing, toothpaste-commercial smile and a buoyant personality, Lewis, a former insurance salesman, can turn on the charm. But it can disappear in an instant, as Pentagon officials learned the hard way during the six years he presided over the Defense Appropriations Subcommittee and repeatedly challenged their budgets.

He has been a force in demanding that the Department of Defense modernize more quickly to meet post-Cold War threats to security, even if it means scrapping revered projects. In 1999, he waged a losing battle to deny $1.9 billion for the chronically overbudget F-22 jet fighter, designed to fight a vanquished enemy, the Soviet Union. Ultimately, lobbying by the Air Force and the plane's contractors led Congress to approve the money.

In more than two decades on the Appropriations panel, Lewis generally has pushed to limit the growth of government spending. From 1995 to 1999, when he was in charge of the subcommittee that funds housing and veterans programs, Lewis cut spending more deeply than any of the other "cardinals," as the subcommittee chairmen are known. He feels differently about defense needs. When he moved over to the Defense Subcommittee, Lewis secured double the amount sought by the Clinton administration in 2000 to beef up the Army's mobile fighting force.

Over the years, Lewis tried to move up the leadership ladder but was edged out by conservatives who were more confrontational in dealing with the Democrats. After Republicans took control of the House in 1995, Lewis strained his relations with Democratic appropriators by dutifully enforcing the new GOP leadership's cuts in domestic programs.

Lewis dates his interest in government to a trip he made to Washington in 1955. He left the insurance business to enter GOP politics in the early 1960s, winning a seat on the San Bernardino School Board. After three years there, he won a state Assembly seat that he held for a decade.

Lewis' House seat is usually safe. His San Bernardino County-based district has given him at least 61 percent of the vote in 15 elections. Despite his ethics troubles, he won in 2006 with 67 percent of the vote.

KEY VOTES

2006

No	Stop broadband companies from favoring select Internet traffic
?	Affirm U.S. commitment to war in Iraq and reject setting a withdrawal date for troops
No	Repeal requirement for bilingual ballots at the polls
Yes	Permit U.S. sale of civilian nuclear technology to India
Yes	Build a 700-mile fence on the U.S.-Mexico border to curb illegal crossings
Yes	Permit warrantless wiretaps of suspected terrorists

2005

Yes	Intervene in the life-support case of Terri Schiavo
Yes	Lift President Bush's restrictions on stem cell research funding
No	Prohibit FBI access to library and bookstore records
Yes	Approve free-trade pact with five Central American countries
Yes	Pass energy policy overhaul favored by President Bush emphasizing domestic oil and gas production
Yes	End mandatory preservation of habitat of endangered animal and plant species
No	Ban torture of prisoners in U.S. custody

CQ VOTE STUDIES

	PARTY UNITY		PRESIDENTIAL SUPPORT	
	Support	Oppose	Support	Oppose
2006	94%	6%	90%	10%
2005	95%	5%	89%	11%
2004	93%	7%	91%	9%
2003	96%	4%	96%	4%
2002	92%	8%	87%	13%

INTEREST GROUPS

	AFL-CIO	ADA	CCUS	ACU
2006	21%	15%	93%	67%
2005	13%	0%	93%	76%
2004	13%	0%	100%	88%
2003	7%	5%	100%	80%
2002	11%	10%	84%	88%

CALIFORNIA 41

Most of San Bernardino County — Redlands

The 41st includes vast desert and mountain stretches and most of the nation's largest county, San Bernardino, although it is home to less than one-third of the massive county's residents. The western quarter of the 41st, where the district's Inland Empire, Victor Valley and Riverside County areas are located, contains the vast majority of its population.

The district begins in a sliver of northwestern Riverside County, including the San Jacinto Valley, Banning, San Jacinto, Beaumont and Calimesa, before crossing into San Bernardino County to pick up communities south of the San Bernardino Mountains. Redlands (the district's largest city), Highland, Yucaipa and part of San Bernardino (shared with the 43rd) are here, and Highland's San Manuel Indian Reservation, with a resort casino, is now a primary employer.

The 41st has a large population of day laborers, many of whom are Hispanic immigrants. Voters supported a tax increase on the 2006 ballot to expand the local police force, and deportation efforts are expanding in the region. Gang activity has caused increased crime in San Bernardino.

On the north side of the mountains are the rapidly growing Victor Valley cities of Hesperia and Apple Valley, where affordable land and housing make the area attractive to Los Angeles and Orange county commuters. As the 41st moves east, development is difficult, as high desert, dry lakes and mountains dominate the landscape to the Arizona and Nevada state lines. Local hospitals, government and the military are major employers.

Republicans enjoy a 16-point edge in voter registration, and Gov. Arnold Schwarzenegger won 69 percent of the vote here in his 2006 re-election.

MAJOR INDUSTRY

Service, manufacturing, military

MILITARY BASES

Marine Corps Air Ground Combat Center, Twentynine Palms, 10,761 military, 1,582 civilian (2005)

CITIES

Redlands, 63,591; Hesperia, 62,582; San Bernardino (pt.), 54,789; Apple Valley, 54,239; Highland, 44,605; Yucaipa, 41,207

NOTABLE

The Mojave National Preserve features the Devils Playground dunes; Roy Rogers' former ranch was in Apple Valley, and state Route 18 is known locally as the "Happy Trails Highway."

Rep. Gary G. Miller (R)

CAPITOL OFFICE
225-3201
gary.miller@mail.house.gov
www.house.gov/garymiller
2438 Rayburn 20515-0542; fax 226-6962

COMMITTEES
Financial Services
Transportation & Infrastructure

RESIDENCE
Diamond Bar

BORN
Oct. 16, 1948, Huntsville, Ark.

RELIGION
Protestant

FAMILY
Wife, Cathy Miller; four children

EDUCATION
Mt. San Antonio Community College, attended 1968-70

MILITARY SERVICE
Army, 1967-68

CAREER
Real estate developer

POLITICAL HIGHLIGHTS
Diamond Bar Municipal Advisory Council, 1988-89; Diamond Bar City Council, 1989-90; sought Republican nomination for Calif. Senate, 1990; Diamond Bar City Council, 1991-95 (mayor, 1993-94); sought Republican nomination for Calif. Senate (special election), 1994; Calif. Assembly, 1995-98

ELECTION RESULTS

2006 GENERAL		
Gary G. Miller (R)		unopposed
2006 PRIMARY		
Gary G. Miller (R)		unopposed
2004 GENERAL		
Gary G. Miller (R)	167,632	68.1%
Lewis Myers (D)	78,393	31.9%

PREVIOUS WINNING PERCENTAGES
2002 (68%); 2000 (59%); 1998 (53%)

Elected 1998; 5th term

A successful real estate developer, Miller's focus in Congress is curbing environmental and business regulations he says hinder business. A conservative and strong ally for President Bush on Capitol Hill, his impact was diminished by a federal investigation into some of his land deals at the beginning of the 110th Congress (2007-08).

After easily winning re-election in 2006, Miller came under scrutiny by the Federal Bureau of Investigation for a provision he added to a 2005 highway bill that improved land a mile from property he owned. The bureau also was looking into Miller's deferral of capital gains taxes on land sales he made to the city of Monrovia in 2002 and to Fontana in 2005 and 2006. Miller contended he sold the land under threat of eminent domain; city officials disputed that account. Miller says he paid all necessary taxes and blamed the controversy on the media. He said he had provided House Republican leaders with documents showing he did nothing wrong.

Miller has extensive real estate investments in his fast-growing Orange County district, according to the Orange County Register newspaper.

A fiscal and social conservative, Miller subscribes to Republican tenets of shrinking the federal government, overhauling the tax code and advancing a "pro-family" agenda. Though ideologically on the far right, Miller is usually less confrontational than other lawmakers at the extremes on the political spectrum. Easygoing by nature, Miller has made friends and formed legislative alliances with Democrats.

With a seat on the House Financial Services Committee, Miller cosponsored a bill in the 109th Congress (2005-06) with liberal Massachusetts Rep. Barney Frank to help communities clean up property contaminated by pollutants. Miller's brownfields plan passed in the House but failed to get through the Senate. He started over in 2007, when the House again passed the bill. Miller also has tried to make homeownership in his district more affordable, describing a crisis of the "new homeless" — middle-class families whose incomes are less than what is needed to buy a home in the area.

Miller has been outspoken on illegal immigration, a big issue for voters in the Los Angeles exurbs in his district. Miller says the burden of undocumented workers falls most heavily on his state. "Illegal immigration places a strain on our society and I want everyone in this body to understand, California bears the brunt of the burden of the failed immigration policies of the federal government," he said in a floor speech.

When the House in 2004 voted overwhelmingly against a measure that would have required hospital workers in emergency rooms to investigate the immigration status of their patients, Miller and seven other Republicans were the only members of the California delegation to support the legislation, which failed, 88-331.

From his seat on the Transportation and Infrastructure Committee, Miller supported the committee's six-year, $283 billion transportation bill, which the House passed in 2004. Miller voted for it despite calls from other conservatives to rein in spending in the face of a burgeoning federal deficit.

During House-Senate conference negotiations on the bill, Miller added a provision to rename a stretch of the Imperial Highway in southern California after President Richard Nixon. The renamed road increases the visibility of the Nixon Library, located in Yorba Linda in Miller's district. He later secured $4 million to house Nixon's presidential papers and tapes.

Concerned that Nixon, in light of the Watergate scandal, might destroy some materials from his presidency, Congress passed a law after he resigned giving the government possession of the records, which had been stored at a National Archives facility in Maryland since the 1970s. The funds secured by Miller paid for the transfer of the papers to California and for a new building. "Thirty years have elapsed since President Nixon left the White House," Miller told the Los Angeles Times. "It is time to bring these historical documents home to California."

A Civil War history buff, Miller in 2002 won enactment of his bill to provide federal grants to states and localities to preserve battle sites.

On foreign affairs issues, he is generally skeptical of using government money for international aid. When the House in 2003 overwhelmingly approved Bush's plan for $15 billion to combat AIDS worldwide, Miller was one of 41 members, and the only lawmaker from California, to vote against it. He said he was "concerned that this proposal could shortchange health care needs here at home."

Miller was raised by his mother and grandparents. At an early age, his family moved from Arkansas, where he was born, to Whittier, east of Los Angeles, where many other poor families from Oklahoma and Arkansas had settled. He attended community college for a while, but did not get a degree. After leaving school, he started a partnership with a building contractor, and they bid on home improvement contracts with the U.S. Housing and Urban Development Department. He says he learned construction skills on the job, and moved on to building single-family homes and eventually to developing planned communities.

Miller began his political career on the Diamond Bar Municipal Advisory Council and then was a member of Diamond Bar's first city council after the city was incorporated in 1989. He became mayor in 1993.

He lost primary bids for the California Senate in 1990 and 1994. Early in 1995, when voters forced a recall election of state Assemblyman Paul Horcher, who left the Republican Party and backed liberal Democrat Willie L. Brown Jr. for Assembly speaker, Miller ran for the seat and won.

In 1998, three-term U.S. Rep. Jay C. Kim was convicted on campaign finance charges, and Miller challenged him in the GOP primary. He won by almost 4,000 votes, and went on to win the general election by 13 percentage points. Miller helped bankroll his campaign with his own money. In remapping after the 2000 census, the district shifted to the south and west and was renumbered the 42nd. Miller won by 39 percentage points in 2002, and almost as much in 2004. In 2006, he was unopposed.

KEY VOTES

2006

- No Stop broadband companies from favoring select Internet traffic
- Yes Affirm U.S. commitment to war in Iraq and reject setting a withdrawal date for troops
- Yes Repeal requirement for bilingual ballots at the polls
- Yes Permit U.S. sale of civilian nuclear technology to India
- Yes Build a 700-mile fence on the U.S.-Mexico border to curb illegal crossings
- Yes Permit warrantless wiretaps of suspected terrorists

2005

- ? Intervene in the life-support case of Terri Schiavo
- No Lift President Bush's restrictions on stem cell research funding
- No Prohibit FBI access to library and bookstore records
- Yes Approve free-trade pact with five Central American countries
- Yes Pass energy policy overhaul favored by President Bush emphasizing domestic oil and gas production
- Yes End mandatory preservation of habitat of endangered animal and plant species
- No Ban torture of prisoners in U.S. custody

CQ VOTE STUDIES

	PARTY UNITY		PRESIDENTIAL SUPPORT	
	Support	Oppose	Support	Oppose
2006	98%	2%	95%	5%
2005	98%	2%	89%	11%
2004	98%	2%	85%	15%
2003	99%	1%	92%	8%
2002	99%	1%	90%	10%

INTEREST GROUPS

	AFL-CIO	ADA	CCUS	ACU
2006	7%	0%	100%	88%
2005	14%	0%	92%	96%
2004	13%	0%	100%	100%
2003	0%	5%	100%	87%
2002	0%	0%	95%	100%

CALIFORNIA 42

Parts of Orange, Los Angeles and San Bernardino counties — Mission Viejo, Chino

Although most of its population lives in Orange County, the Republican 42nd is centered around the suburbs where Orange, Los Angeles and San Bernardino counties come together east of Los Angeles proper. From there, the 42nd has a long arm that stretches southeast and then southwest farther into Orange County to Mission Viejo and Rancho Santa Margarita. A chunk of eastern Anaheim also falls within the district's borders.

Chino and Chino Hills in San Bernardino County have an agricultural heritage, but the economic influence of dairy production is waning due to rapid residential development and growth in the manufacturing and service sectors. Diamond Bar and Rowland Heights (shared with the 38th) in Los Angeles County have large Asian populations. Hispanics and Asians also live in the northern Orange County cities of Brea — a fast-growing major retail center with a recently redeveloped downtown — La Habra and Placentia (shared with the 40th), although this segment of Orange County is predominately white-collar and white. Conservatism persists even among non-whites, and Republicans maintain a significant lead in voter registration. The district gave George W. Bush 62 percent of its 2004 presidential vote, and Arnold Schwarzenegger took 71 percent of the 42nd's vote in the 2006 gubernatorial election.

Overall, the district is mostly middle- and upper-class and dominated by residential communities. Many residents work in technology firms and commute to Los Angeles or Irvine (which is located in the 48th). Unemployment is low, and housing prices, particularly in Orange County, are above average.

MAJOR INDUSTRY

Service, light manufacturing, dairy

CITIES

Mission Viejo, 93,102; Chino, 67,168; Chino Hills, 66,787; La Habra, 58,974; Yorba Linda, 58,918; Diamond Bar, 56,287; Anaheim (pt.), 55,395

NOTABLE

Yorba Linda, the birthplace and burial site of President Richard Nixon, is the home of the Nixon Library; La Habra has hosted an annual Corn Festival since 1949; Chino is home to the Planes of Fame museum.

Rep. Joe Baca (D)

CAPITOL OFFICE
225-6161
www.house.gov/baca
1527 Longworth 20515-0543; fax 225-8671

COMMITTEES
Agriculture
(Operations, Oversight, Nutrition & Forestry - chairman)
Financial Services
Natural Resources

RESIDENCE
Rialto

BORN
Jan. 23, 1947, Belen, N.M.

RELIGION
Roman Catholic

FAMILY
Wife, Barbara Baca; four children

EDUCATION
California State U., Los Angeles, B.A. 1971 (sociology)

MILITARY SERVICE
Army, 1966-68

CAREER
Travel agency owner; corporate community relations executive

POLITICAL HIGHLIGHTS
San Bernardino Community College District Board of Trustees, 1979-93; sought Democratic nomination for Calif. Assembly, 1988, 1990; Calif. Assembly, 1992-98 (Speaker pro tempore, 1995); Calif. Senate, 1998-99

ELECTION RESULTS

2006 GENERAL		
Joe Baca (D)	52,791	64.5%
Scott Folkens (R)	29,069	35.5%
2006 PRIMARY		
Joe Baca (D)		unopposed
2004 GENERAL		
Joe Baca (D)	86,830	66.4%
Ed Laning (R)	44,004	33.6%

PREVIOUS WINNING PERCENTAGES
2002 (66%); 2000 (60%); 1999 Special Runoff Election (51%)

Elected 1999; 4th full term

Baca was elected chairman of the Congressional Hispanic Caucus for the 110th Congress (2007-08), but he quickly found himself in hot water with its female members. One of his California colleagues accused him of insulting her and quit the caucus in protest early in 2007. Other women in the caucus complained of dismissive treatment.

Baca denied the allegation by Democrat Loretta Sanchez that he had referred to her as a "whore" in a conversation with a California state legislator. But he admitted calling Hilda L. Solis, another California Hispanic Democrat, a "kiss-up" to Speaker Nancy Pelosi. He apologized to Solis, but the grumbling continued within the Hispanic Caucus.

He had already upset many in the caucus in 2006, when he headed its political action committee and approved contributions to a number of non-federal candidates, including two of his own sons who ran unsuccessfully for the California Legislature. His sons returned the money after six caucus members resigned from the PAC in protest.

Baca's district is close to 60 percent Hispanic, and he is the first Hispanic to be elected to Congress from the part of southern California known as the Inland Empire, a region east of Los Angeles anchored by the city of San Bernardino. With single-minded ambition, Baca rose from hardscrabble beginnings — he started working at age 10 as a shoeshine boy — to Congress. "I'm a fighter because I know what it's like to struggle," he says.

But Baca's drive can rub some of his colleagues the wrong way. He has ruffled feathers during his political ascent, and other lawmakers complain that he sometimes hogs the credit for joint endeavors. His local newspaper, the San Bernardino Sun, called him "a follower more than a leader" in a 2006 editorial offering a lukewarm re-election endorsement.

The congressman refers to himself as "working Joe Baca," which could apply to both his work ethic and his strong backing for (and from) organized labor. The AFL-CIO gives him a lifetime voting score of 97 percent.

In 2004, however, Baca drew sharp criticism from one local union. After 12 Border Patrol agents arrested 492 illegal aliens during sweeps at shopping malls and other public places in San Bernardino and San Diego counties, Baca said the agents overstepped their authority. The sweeps caused fear and unrest in the Latino community. "I am doing everything I can to make sure that sweeps like the ones last week do not happen again," he told residents at a community meeting, according to the Los Angeles Times.

The union representing southern California Border Patrol agents responded angrily that Baca had falsely accused the agents of racial profiling. His Republican challenger in the 2004 campaign said the incident showed Baca supported illegal immigration. Baca is unrepentant, saying there is still lingering fear in his area. "You should go after the hard criminals," he says, not people "who work hard and are applying for citizenship."

Baca, like most House Democrats, voted against both a 2006 law calling for a 700-mile fence along the border with Mexico and a 2005 House bill that made it a felony to reside in the United States without legal papers. "This legislation has a face," he said. "It's the face of a nanny, a gardener, the cook at your favorite restaurant, the cleaning crew at your workplace."

While he is a guaranteed pro-labor vote, Baca affiliates with the Blue Dog Coalition of conservative House Democrats and sides with Republicans on some issues, including supporting gun owners' rights. He also has broken with his party on environmental issues. He supports oil drilling in Alaska's

Arctic National Wildlife Refuge, aligning himself with the Teamsters, who value the jobs the drilling would create, and he voted with Republicans in 2005 to relax the Endangered Species Act.

Baca does want the federal government to help protect the water quality in his district. In 2004, the House passed his bill authorizing $50 million to help inland cities clean up perchlorate-contaminated groundwater in the Santa Ana River Watershed. Perchlorate, a chemical used in rocket fuel, had been found in at least 20 drinking-water wells. He won additional money for cleanup in the fiscal 2007 defense spending bill.

Baca was born in tiny Belen, N.M., just south of Albuquerque. The son of a railroad laborer and the youngest of 15 children in a house where little English was spoken, Baca as a boy moved with his family to Barstow, Calif. He shined shoes, delivered newspapers and worked as a janitor. He was a laborer for the Santa Fe Railroad between his high school graduation and getting drafted into the Army in 1966. He served as a paratrooper with the 101st and 82nd Airborne divisions but was not sent to Vietnam.

After completing his service, Baca got a degree in sociology from California State University at Los Angeles, then landed a job as a community affairs representative for a local phone company.

His political career began in 1979 with election to the San Bernardino Community College District Board of Trustees, where he served 14 years. After two failed attempts to oust a fellow Democrat in the state Assembly, he finally won the seat in 1992 when the incumbent retired. He was re-elected twice and then won a state Senate seat in 1998.

By then, he was more interested in Washington, D.C., than in Sacramento. He toyed with challenging U.S. Rep. George Brown in the Democratic primary, boasting he could beat him in every precinct. When Brown died midway through his 18th term, Baca ran against his widow, Marta Macias Brown, in the 1999 special-election primary. She said it was inappropriate for Baca to run after the party had just helped him win an expensive state Senate contest, but he defeated her in the primary and posted a 6 percentage point win over GOP businessman Elia Pirozzi in the special runoff. He has won handily ever since.

As a child, Baca aspired to a career in baseball. Well into his 30s, he played catcher for the San Bernardino Stars, a semi-pro fast-pitch softball team. Playing on the Democratic team in the annual congressional ball game, he ruptured a ligament in his right elbow in 2003. Now golf is his game; with a 2 handicap, Golf Digest in 2005 rated him one of the top golfers in Washington.

KEY VOTES

2006

- No Stop broadband companies from favoring select Internet traffic
- No Affirm U.S. commitment to war in Iraq and reject setting a withdrawal date for troops
- No Repeal requirement for bilingual ballots at the polls
- Yes Permit U.S. sale of civilian nuclear technology to India
- No Build a 700-mile fence on the U.S.-Mexico border to curb illegal crossings
- No Permit warrantless wiretaps of suspected terrorists

2005

- Yes Intervene in the life-support case of Terri Schiavo
- Yes Lift President Bush's restrictions on stem cell research funding
- Yes Prohibit FBI access to library and bookstore records
- No Approve free-trade pact with five Central American countries
- Yes Pass energy policy overhaul favored by President Bush emphasizing domestic oil and gas production
- Yes End mandatory preservation of habitat of endangered animal and plant species
- Yes Ban torture of prisoners in U.S. custody

CQ VOTE STUDIES

	PARTY UNITY		PRESIDENTIAL SUPPORT	
	Support	Oppose	Support	Oppose
2006	91%	9%	35%	65%
2005	88%	12%	34%	66%
2004	92%	8%	32%	68%
2003	89%	11%	30%	70%
2002	91%	9%	28%	72%

INTEREST GROUPS

	AFL-CIO	ADA	CCUS	ACU
2006	100%	95%	47%	20%
2005	100%	90%	58%	32%
2004	93%	90%	43%	12%
2003	100%	85%	40%	29%
2002	89%	95%	42%	13%

CALIFORNIA 43

Southwest San Bernardino County — Ontario, Fontana, most of San Bernardino

The San Bernardino County communities of Ontario, Fontana and San Bernardino form the base of the 43rd, which lies in the heart of the Inland Valley east of Los Angeles. Although the district has prospered like its neighbors in Orange and Los Angeles counties, it retains a diverse and working-class feel.

The 43rd is part of California's fastest-growing region, and some residents commute into Los Angeles along the Pomona and San Bernardino freeways. Growing technology, manufacturing and aerospace industries have allowed the local economy to recover from a steel mill closure and the loss of a nearby Air Force base a decade ago.

The renovated Ontario airport is part of a growing transportation hub — particularly for FedEx and UPS — and the large Ontario Mills mall hosts major retail anchors. Sunkist Growers has a processing plant in Ontario, and a robust manufacturing sector supports companies such as Mag Instrument, the makers of the Maglite flashlight.

Rialto, which is half Hispanic, is experiencing population and housing growth, and is home to regional distribution centers for Staples and Toys "R" Us. Fontana is growing as well, as residents and investors see area housing as a good place to put their money.

The district is nearly 60 percent Hispanic, and registered Democrats outnumber Republicans by 13 percentage points. The 43rd favors Democrats on all levels, and gave Phil Angelides 49 percent of the vote in the 2006 gubernatorial race, even as he won only 39 percent statewide. Congestion and illegal immigration are big issues among residents here.

MAJOR INDUSTRY

Manufacturing, electronics, construction, agriculture

CITIES

Ontario, 158,007; San Bernardino (pt.), 130,612; Fontana, 128,929; Rialto, 91,873; Colton (pt.), 43,349

NOTABLE

Fontana is the birthplace of the Hells Angels motorcycle club; The steel mill scene in now-Gov. Arnold Schwarzenegger's movie "Terminator 2" was filmed at the old Kaiser mill in Fontana.

Rep. Ken Calvert (R)

CAPITOL OFFICE
225-1986
www.house.gov/calvert
2201 Rayburn 20515-0544; fax 225-2004

COMMITTEES
Appropriations

RESIDENCE
Corona

BORN
June 8, 1953, Corona, Calif.

RELIGION
Protestant

FAMILY
Divorced

EDUCATION
Chaffey College, A.A. 1973 (business);
San Diego State U., B.A. 1975 (economics)

CAREER
Real estate executive; restaurant executive

POLITICAL HIGHLIGHTS
Sought Republican nomination for U.S. House, 1982; Riverside County Republican Party chairman, 1984-88

ELECTION RESULTS

2006 GENERAL		
Ken Calvert (R)	89,555	60.0%
Louis Vandenberg (D)	55,275	37.0%
Kevin Akin (PFP)	4,486	3.0%
2006 PRIMARY		
Ken Calvert (R)		unopposed
2004 GENERAL		
Ken Calvert (R)	138,768	61.6%
Louis Vandenberg (D)	78,796	35.0%
Kevin Akin (PFP)	7,559	3.4%

PREVIOUS WINNING PERCENTAGES
2002 (64%); 2000 (74%); 1998 (56%); 1996 (55%); 1994 (55%); 1992 (47%)

Elected 1992; 8th term

A seasoned legislator, Calvert has been a fairly typical House Republican — conservative on fiscal and social policy, except where water rights vital to his district are concerned. In the 110th Congress (2007-08), Calvert secured a coveted spot on the House Appropriations Committee, which controls the federal purse strings.

Conservative bloggers in May 2007 objected to the GOP leadership's choice of Calvert because of ethical questions raised about his real estate holdings in a 2006 story in the Los Angeles Times. The newspaper reported that he and a partner held numerous properties near transportation projects that Calvert had supported with federal earmarks, appropriations for specific projects in a lawmaker's district. Some of the properties sold for substantial profits. Calvert denied wrongdoing, telling the Times he has never "done anything to enrich myself using the position I hold."

Calvert also responded to the conservative critics with a letter saying he had faced "tough questions" in a private meeting with fellow Republicans and had allayed any concerns about his ethics. "We had a candid, frank discussion, and I answered all of the questions I was asked and was approved by both the Steering Committee and the Republican Conference," Calvert wrote. The conference is composed of all House Republicans.

To take the seat on Appropriations, he gave up the top-ranking minority slot on the Science and Technology Committee's Space and Aeronautics Subcommittee. He had chaired the Space Subcommittee in the 109th Congress (2005-06).

A lifelong resident of southern California, where the aviation and aerospace industry has a rich history, Calvert steered to enactment a bill that largely endorsed President Bush's plan to send astronauts back to the moon and to Mars. Although subcommittee Democrats complained that Calvert shut them out of the drafting process, the full Science Committee unanimously approved a bipartisan version.

Before taking the top GOP spot on the Science Subcommittee, Calvert served as chairman of Resources' Water and Power Subcommittee. He won enactment in 2004 of his legislation to reauthorize and restructure the California Federal Bay-Delta Program, which aims to enhance the state's water supply, reliability and quality. The CalFed legislation was his top priority, and Calvert worked closely with California Democratic Sen. Dianne Feinstein to write a bill acceptable to both chambers. "Water is not and should not be a partisan issue," Calvert says.

The CalFed project stretches over the enormous delta that begins in the San Francisco Bay area and extends from the Sacramento Valley in the north to the San Joaquin Valley in the south, providing irrigation and drinking water for two-thirds of the state's population.

Calvert represents an area with a diverse economy, where agriculture, manufacturing, the military and tourism interests can clash with environmental advocates over issues of land use and urban sprawl. Calvert typically sides with property owners against the environmentalists.

A real estate agent before coming to Congress, Calvert sponsored legislation passed in 2003 to ensure that competitive adjustable-rate mortgages (ARMs) are available to first-time homebuyers. He also has repeatedly introduced legislation, cosponsored by more than half of his House colleagues, to keep banks permanently out of the real estate business.

Calvert is a native son of the area he now represents, not all that common in the rapidly growing region that is now part of the Los Angeles megalopolis. He was born in Corona, just west of Riverside. His family owned the Jolly Fox restaurant for nearly half a century, diversifying into other ventures such as a motel and bowling alley. After closing the businesses, they kept the land. "My father was a believer in owning real estate," Calvert says. "That way you control your own destiny."

His father, who had changed parties to become a Republican in the mid-1960s, won election to the city council and then served as Corona's mayor. The younger Calvert remembers working on Richard Nixon's 1968 presidential campaign, and as a college student, he interned in the Capitol Hill office of GOP Rep. Victor Veysey.

At age 28, Calvert in 1982 jumped into an open-seat race for Congress, in a district that contained most of Riverside County. Relying on door-to-door campaigning, he did surprisingly well against a large field headed by Riverside County Supervisor Al McCandless, losing the GOP primary by just 868 votes. Calvert stayed active in party affairs, significantly increasing GOP registration in Riverside County and helping run the gubernatorial campaigns of Republicans George Deukmejian and Pete Wilson.

When reapportionment created a new 43rd District for western Riverside County in 1992, Calvert ran again. This time he won, but personal tragedy marred his triumph. In September, at the height of the campaign season, Calvert's father committed suicide. "It leaves a big hole in your life," he says. "I ate breakfast every morning with my father, and I still miss him every day."

Calvert's congressional tenure got off to a rough start. In his first term, a tryst with a prostitute drew widespread notice. He said his "inappropriate" behavior stemmed from depression over his recent divorce and his father's suicide.

Following the publicity, Calvert won the 1994 Republican primary by 2 percentage points, but the national surge that delivered the House to the GOP carried him to victory with 55 percent of the vote. Since then, Calvert's toughest challenges have come from his own party. In 2000, he won the nomination with 58 percent. In 2002, in redistricted territory, now numbered the 44th but politically similar to his previous district, Calvert took 70 percent in a three-way primary and cruised to a sixth term.

When he was first elected, Calvert, like other Republicans touting reform of Congress that year, pledged to limit his tenure in the House. But he changed his mind and ran again in 2004. Voters don't seem to care. He won his last two elections with comfortable margins.

KEY VOTES

2006

No Stop broadband companies from favoring select Internet traffic
Yes Affirm U.S. commitment to war in Iraq and reject setting a withdrawal date for troops
Yes Repeal requirement for bilingual ballots at the polls
Yes Permit U.S. sale of civilian nuclear technology to India
Yes Build a 700-mile fence on the U.S.-Mexico border to curb illegal crossings
Yes Permit warrantless wiretaps of suspected terrorists

2005

Yes Intervene in the life-support case of Terri Schiavo
Yes Lift President Bush's restrictions on stem cell research funding
No Prohibit FBI access to library and bookstore records
Yes Approve free-trade pact with five Central American countries
Yes Pass energy policy overhaul favored by President Bush emphasizing domestic oil and gas production
Yes End mandatory preservation of habitat of endangered animal and plant species
No Ban torture of prisoners in U.S. custody

CQ VOTE STUDIES

	PARTY UNITY		PRESIDENTIAL SUPPORT	
	Support	Oppose	Support	Oppose
2006	95%	5%	95%	5%
2005	98%	2%	89%	11%
2004	93%	7%	82%	18%
2003	98%	2%	98%	2%
2002	96%	4%	89%	11%

INTEREST GROUPS

	AFL-CIO	ADA	CCUS	ACU
2006	14%	5%	100%	80%
2005	13%	0%	93%	84%
2004	21%	0%	100%	88%
2003	7%	5%	100%	88%
2002	11%	0%	100%	92%

CALIFORNIA 44

Northwestern Riverside County – Riverside, Corona

The 44th is a fast-growing residential district that lies east of Los Angeles and north of San Diego. It contains about one-third of Riverside County's residents and takes in the southeastern portion of Orange County that borders San Diego County. The Orange County areas include coastal San Clemente, a premier surfing spot, and Santa Ana Mountain forests.

The district is experiencing major growth, as young, white-collar families move into its cities. The trend is especially true in Norco and Corona, where low real estate prices have created attractive bedroom communities for residents who work in Orange or Los Angeles counties. These commuters have increased traffic along Route 91, however, and congestion is an issue. The area's high levels of air pollution make it part of the greater-Los Angeles "smog belt."

Despite the population influx, manufacturing and agriculture — including dairy, citrus, grapes, dates and avocados — still contribute to the economy. Riverside began growing navel oranges — still one of the area's major crops — in the 19th century. These industries are being driven farther east and out of the district, however, as the Los Angeles area continues to expand. Local officials are trying to halt illegal drug production in the Riverside County portions of the Inland Empire, dubbed by some as the methamphetamine capital of the world.

The 44th leans Republican, although the more blue-collar Riverside communities and the areas around the University of California, Riverside, lean Democratic. Registered Republicans outnumber Democrats, and Gov. Arnold Schwarzenegger took two-thirds of the district's vote in 2006.

MAJOR INDUSTRY
Manufacturing, agriculture, health care

MILITARY BASES
Naval Surface Warfare Center, Corona Division, 5 military, 1,142 civilian (2006)

CITIES
Riverside, 255,166; Corona, 124,966; San Clemente, 49,936

NOTABLE
Riverside's Mission Inn was where Richard and Pat Nixon were married and Ronald and Nancy Reagan stopped on their honeymoon.

Rep. Mary Bono (R)

CAPITOL OFFICE
225-5330
www.house.gov/bono
104 Cannon 20515-0545; fax 225-2961

COMMITTEES
Energy & Commerce

RESIDENCE
Palm Springs

BORN
Oct. 24, 1961, Cleveland, Ohio

RELIGION
Protestant

FAMILY
Divorced; two children

EDUCATION
U. of Southern California, B.F.A. 1984 (art history)

CAREER
Homemaker; restaurateur

POLITICAL HIGHLIGHTS
No previous office

ELECTION RESULTS

2006 GENERAL		
Mary Bono (R)	99,638	60.7%
David Roth (D)	64,613	39.3%
2006 PRIMARY		
Mary Bono (R)		unopposed
2004 GENERAL		
Mary Bono (R)	153,523	66.6%
Richard J. Meyer (D)	76,967	33.4%

PREVIOUS WINNING PERCENTAGES
2002 (65%); 2000 (59%); 1998 (60%); 1998 Special Election (64%)

Elected April 1998; 5th full term

Now in her fifth full term, Bono has established herself as a moderate-to-conservative Republican whose celebrity drawing power is matched by political competence. Though she was once a classic widow-legislator, succeeding her late husband, entertainer-turned-politician Sonny Bono, she has proved a capable lawmaker in her own right. She also is one of the most popular guests on the campaign fundraising circuit, making public appearances across the country in behalf of Republican colleagues.

In the 109th Congress (2005-06), Bono focused on two health issues: AIDS and autism. She pushed for a bill, signed into law by President Bush, shifting AIDS funding from urban centers to less-populated areas, which helped districts like hers. Bono says she took up autism as a priority at the request of former Rep. Jim Greenwood (1993-2005), a Pennsylvania moderate Republican who asked her to carry on his work on the issue when he retired from Congress. "So many of my friends are touched by autism, it became an easy issue to champion," Bono says.

In her early years in the House, Bono pursued legacy issues of her late husband, who died in a 1998 skiing accident. An early effort was helping to pass a copyright extension bill, first championed by and eventually named for Sonny. In the 108th Congress (2003-04), she focused on intellectual property issues of interest to the entertainment industry. In 2004, she wrote a bill regulating "spyware," software that monitors the behavior of computer users while collecting sensitive information about them. The House passed her bill, but the Senate did not.

Bono usually toes the Republican Party line, but has an independent streak on a handful of social issues. On abortion, she sometimes votes with pro-abortion rights groups, and she opposed the GOP's effort in 2004 to amend the Constitution to ban same-sex marriage.

She strongly supports federal funding for medical research using embryonic stem cells, which are harvested from surplus embryos at in vitro fertilization clinics. Opponents liken their use to abortion. "Issues of bioethics are really difficult, but I believe there is a great deal of hope in embryonic stem cell research," Bono told the Desert Sun newspaper. She says her physician father and chemist mother influenced her thinking on the issue.

In 2005, with her party engulfed in multiple ethics scandals, Bono joined a group of House Republicans calling on their leaders, including then House Speaker J. Dennis Hastert, to stand for re-election. The rebellion fizzled out, and most of the leaders kept their jobs. Also that year, she was the sole Republican to join Democrats on the Energy and Commerce Committee in opposing GOP legislation creating uniform food safety and labeling standards, out of concern the bill would undermine stricter state laws.

In Washington, Bono has cultivated an image of a plain-speaking, unpretentious lawmaker who is ready to roll up her sleeves. She focuses on the day-to-day issues of her Inland Empire and Coachella Valley constituents, such as high energy bills, the availability of low-income housing, access to water, and resolution of longstanding American Indian land claims. Over time, she also has learned to be resourceful in securing federal dollars for projects back home.

An influx of immigrants into her district put her in a difficult spot during the immigration debate of 2005-06. She voted for the House Republicans' tough border security bill but said she also liked an alternative by Senate moderates creating a guest worker program for illegal immigrants. "Unfortunately, the people who believe in stronger border enforcement and a guest worker program, they've been left out of the debate," Bono said. "It's been focused on the extremists on both sides."

Bono has continued her husband's work on preserving the Salton Sea, a southern California man-made lake threatened by pollution from agricultural and industrial runoff. There have been widespread deaths of fish and birds there. Despite these efforts, she generally has gotten low marks from the League of Conservation Voters, including for her vote supporting the Bush administration's controversial forest fire prevention plan that called for forest thinning. Critics charged it would mainly benefit the timber industry.

Bono grew up in South Pasadena, Calif., the daughter of a surgeon, who taught at the University of Southern California, and a chemist, who put her husband through medical school. Bono worked her way through college as a cocktail waitress, majoring in art history.

As she was celebrating her college graduation at Sonny Bono's West Hollywood restaurant, she met the owner and the two began a relationship. They married two years later, in 1986, when she was 24 years old and about half Sonny's age. Mary Bono helped manage the restaurant, which he relocated to their new home in Palm Springs, and other companies associated with his entertainment royalties. The first time she voted was for Sonny, as mayor of Palm Springs in 1988.

She came to Washington with Sonny after he was elected to the House in 1994, becoming a stay-at-home mother of their two children and working on a brown belt in karate. When he died in the skiing accident four years later, GOP leaders urged her to run for his seat.

The race proved to be unusual. Sonny's 83-year-old mother criticized her decision to run because it would take time away from the children. Her Democratic opponent, Ralph Waite, was an actor who appeared as television's Pa Walton; he campaigned in the district only two days a week due to a commitment to appear in a play in New Jersey.

Bono won a special election in April with almost two-thirds of the vote. She has not been seriously threatened in her re-election bids, and redistricting in 2001 increased the GOP tilt of the 45th District.

Her romantic life remains fodder for the tabloids. In September 2005, Bono announced her divorce from her second husband, Glenn Baxley, the founder of a Western wear company, after a little less than four years of marriage. Three months later, she was romantically linked to Rep. Connie Mack, a Florida Republican who had announced his divorce from his wife in August 2005.

KEY VOTES

2006

? Stop broadband companies from favoring select Internet traffic
Yes Affirm U.S. commitment to war in Iraq and reject setting a withdrawal date for troops
No Repeal requirement for bilingual ballots at the polls
Yes Permit U.S. sale of civilian nuclear technology to India
Yes Build a 700-mile fence on the U.S.-Mexico border to curb illegal crossings
Yes Permit warrantless wiretaps of suspected terrorists

2005

? Intervene in the life-support case of Terri Schiavo
Yes Lift President Bush's restrictions on stem cell research funding
? Prohibit FBI access to library and bookstore records
Yes Approve free-trade pact with five Central American countries
Yes Pass energy policy overhaul favored by President Bush emphasizing domestic oil and gas production
Yes End mandatory preservation of habitat of endangered animal and plant species
No Ban torture of prisoners in U.S. custody

CQ VOTE STUDIES

	PARTY UNITY		PRESIDENTIAL SUPPORT	
	Support	Oppose	Support	Oppose
2006	85%	15%	81%	19%
2005	93%	7%	80%	20%
2004	86%	14%	58%	42%
2003	91%	9%	89%	11%
2002	89%	11%	84%	16%

INTEREST GROUPS

	AFL-CIO	ADA	CCUS	ACU
2006	17%	25%	86%	68%
2005	20%	15%	93%	71%
2004	27%	35%	100%	56%
2003	7%	10%	93%	68%
2002	11%	10%	95%	71%

CALIFORNIA 45

Riverside County — Moreno Valley, Palm Springs

Ritzy desert resorts, a booming service industry and agriculture fuel the economy of the 45th, whose residents generally are split between Riverside County's rapidly growing Inland Empire areas, such as Moreno Valley, Hemet and Murrieta, and the resort-filled Coachella Valley cities farther east.

The Palm Springs area, including Cathedral City, Indian Wells, La Quinta and Indio, draws visitors to its golf courses. Once known as a playground for the rich and retired, the area has seen an influx of younger, middle-class families. Still, the 45th retains the state's highest percentage of residents over age 64 (16 percent). Beyond tourism and service, the resort region also boasts strong real estate, health care, shopping and gambling industries. Wind turbine generators are becoming more common in the area as alternate energy sources.

Fiscally conservative and socially liberal, Palm Springs has a growing gay population — the city elected its first gay mayor in 2003 — and has sizable Jewish and Hispanic communities. Migrant farm laborers, the majority of whom are Hispanic, work in the agricultural communities of the Coachella and San Jacinto valleys — producing citrus, dates, alfalfa and grapes — and the Temecula wine country. The gambling industry boosts the economies of the district's American Indian reservations. Health care service providers and small educational institutions have begun to settle in the 45th, attracting professionals. Moreno Valley has become one of Los Angeles' largest exurbs, but air pollution issues may slow further growth.

Although the district leans Republican, pockets in Rancho Mirage and Palm Springs tend to vote Democratic. Overall, the district gave George W. Bush 56 percent of its presidential vote in 2004, and Republicans hold a 10-point voter registration advantage.

MAJOR INDUSTRY

Service, tourism, agriculture, manufacturing

CITIES

Moreno Valley, 142,381; Hemet, 58,812; Indio, 49,116; Murrieta, 44,282

NOTABLE

The Palm Springs International Festival of Short Films is the largest festival of its kind in North America; The world's largest rotating tramcars can be found at the Palm Springs Aerial Tramway.

Rep. Dana Rohrabacher (R)

Elected 1988; 10th term

CAPITOL OFFICE
225-2415
dana@mail.house.gov
www.house.gov/rohrabacher
2300 Rayburn 20515-0546; fax 225-0145

COMMITTEES
Foreign Affairs
Science & Technology

RESIDENCE
Huntington Beach

BORN
June 21, 1947, Coronado, Calif.

RELIGION
Baptist

FAMILY
Wife, Rhonda Rohrabacher; three children

EDUCATION
Los Angeles Harbor College, attended 1965-67; California State U., Long Beach, B.A. 1969 (history); U. of Southern California, M.A. 1971 (American studies)

CAREER
White House speechwriter; newspaper reporter

POLITICAL HIGHLIGHTS
No previous office

ELECTION RESULTS

2006 GENERAL		
Dana Rohrabacher (R)	116,176	59.6%
Jim Brandt (D)	71,573	36.7%
Dennis Chang (LIBERT)	7,303	3.7%
2006 PRIMARY		
Dana Rohrabacher (R)		unopposed
2004 GENERAL		
Dana Rohrabacher (R)	171,318	61.9%
Jim Brandt (D)	90,129	32.6%
Tom Lash (GREEN)	10,238	3.7%
Keith Gann (LIBERT)	5,005	1.8%

PREVIOUS WINNING PERCENTAGES
2002 (62%); 2000 (62%); 1998 (59%); 1996 (61%); 1994 (69%); 1992 (55%); 1990 (59%); 1988 (64%)

A free spirit and a bit of a dreamer, Rohrabacher is a table-thumping conservative with a libertarian streak that sometimes puts him at odds with his party and his president. He is not exactly a team player.

A plaque in his office reads, "Fighting for Freedom . . . and Having Fun." Rohrabacher (ROAR-ah-BAH-ker) represents Huntington Beach, a surfing community in coastal southern California, and he is an avid surfer. Among his friends are writers, artists and musicians from his era, including heavy metal vocalist Sammy Hagar and folk singer Joan Baez.

For more than two decades, one of those friends was lobbyist Jack Abramoff, whose influence-peddling activities were at the heart of the corruption scandals that helped drive congressional Republicans from power in 2006. Unlike others who had known Abramoff and accepted his campaign contributions for years, Rohrabacher publicly stood by him after his criminal conviction, saying Abramoff was a good man who had done some bad things. "The last thing I'm going to do is kick a friend when they're down," he told the Los Angeles Times.

Rohrabacher took up the cause of a pair of Border Patrol agents sentenced in October 2006 to long terms in prison for the non-fatal 2005 shooting in Texas of a man who turned out to be a drug smuggler attempting to flee across the Mexican border. The trial showed the agents hid evidence of the shooting, and the suspect was given immunity from prosecution for his testimony against them. The case swiftly became a cause for conservatives, and Rohrabacher angrily denounced President Bush for refusing to intervene, calling him arrogant and aloof. He invited the wife of one of the imprisoned agents to be his guest at the president's 2007 State of the Union address, and rounded up lawmakers to press for a pardon of the two agents.

Rohrabacher sees illegal immigration as an "invasion of the United States," and urges aggressive steps to combat it at every point from the border to the workplace. He voted for a series of GOP bills and amendments in the 109th Congress (2005-06) that ordered stepped-up border security and internal enforcement of immigration laws.

In the previous Congress, he unsuccessfully sought to pass a bill that would have required hospitals to report to authorities the names of illegal aliens they treated. House leaders promised him a floor vote on the controversial measure in return for his yes vote for a 2003 bill creating a new federal program, a prescription drug benefit under Medicare. But the GOP leadership showed little enthusiasm for Rohrabacher's bill, and more Republicans voted against it than for it.

Rohrabacher split with his party in the 109th Congress on some other high-profile issues. He was one of 18 House Republicans opposing renewal of the 2001 anti-terrorism law called the Patriot Act, saying in a floor speech, "We should not be required to live in peacetime under the extraordinary laws that were passed during times of war and crisis."

He was part of an equally small group of Republicans voting to protect states that chose to permit medical use of marijuana. And, as the father of triplets conceived through in vitro fertilization, he voted to override Bush's veto of a bill expanding embryonic stem cell research. The Los Angeles Times reported that despite his anti-abortion views, Rohrabacher said his experience had convinced him that a "sperm is not potential life until it's put into a woman's body."

Science fascinates Rohrabacher, particularly space. As entrepreneurs began building private aircraft capable of reaching altitudes previously seen only by government spacecraft, Rohrabacher decided to help these businessmen-explorers reach space. He was driven by his own interest in space in addition to the well-being of his district. Boeing Co.'s space division is one of the 46th District's largest employers.

As chairman of the Science Committee's Space and Aeronautics Subcommittee from 1997 to 2005, Rohrabacher introduced a number of bills intended to foster private space flight, including one to offer a prize of up to $100 million for the first private spacecraft to make three orbits of the Earth. That one went nowhere, but he did push through a law supporting the development of commercial space projects and allowing the Federal Aviation Administration to regulate private spacecraft.

His timing was good. Only months before Bush signed the new law in late 2004, a private aircraft known as SpaceShipOne had reached low Earth orbit, presaging a new era of space tourism.

It wasn't the first instance of uncanny timing for Rohrabacher. He was one of a few members of Congress who, after the terrorist attacks of Sept. 11, could accurately declare "I told you so" about the dangers emanating from global terrorists. On the day of the attacks, Rohrabacher had been scheduled to meet with National Security Council officials at the White House to warn them to expect a possible terrorist attack from Osama bin Laden and the ruling Taliban regime of Afghanistan.

When Congress reconvened a few days later, he took to the House floor and described his many trips to Central Asia, including an undercover sojourn to Afghanistan before he was sworn into Congress in 1989.

During his younger days, Rohrabacher was a hard-drinking, banjo-playing wanderer who worked as a house-painter. He later found steady work as a reporter and editorial writer for the Orange County Register newspaper. He served as assistant press secretary for Ronald Reagan's 1976 and 1980 presidential campaigns, then became a White House speechwriter for President Reagan.

In his first bid for elective office, in 1988, Rohrabacher ran for the House seat being vacated by GOP Rep. Dan Lungren. He won despite primary competitors who had both name recognition and Lungren's support, and has won every successive election with no less than 54 percent of the vote. In 2002, his newly drawn district included the port of Long Beach. But the new constituency was no problem; he won with 62 percent. In 2004, he beat back a primary challenge from former Rep. Robert K. Dornan, then easily won in November. He had no trouble winning re-election in 2006.

KEY VOTES

2006

- No Stop broadband companies from favoring select Internet traffic
- Yes Affirm U.S. commitment to war in Iraq and reject setting a withdrawal date for troops
- Yes Repeal requirement for bilingual ballots at the polls
- Yes Permit U.S. sale of civilian nuclear technology to India
- Yes Build a 700-mile fence on the U.S.-Mexico border to curb illegal crossings
- Yes Permit warrantless wiretaps of suspected terrorists

2005

- ? Intervene in the life-support case of Terri Schiavo
- Yes Lift President Bush's restrictions on stem cell research funding
- No Prohibit FBI access to library and bookstore records
- Yes Approve free-trade pact with five Central American countries
- No Pass energy policy overhaul favored by President Bush emphasizing domestic oil and gas production
- Yes End mandatory preservation of habitat of endangered animal and plant species
- No Ban torture of prisoners in U.S. custody

CQ VOTE STUDIES

	PARTY UNITY		PRESIDENTIAL SUPPORT	
	Support	Oppose	Support	Oppose
2006	90%	10%	90%	10%
2005	94%	6%	80%	20%
2004	91%	9%	84%	16%
2003	92%	8%	87%	13%
2002	94%	6%	77%	23%

INTEREST GROUPS

	AFL-CIO	ADA	CCUS	ACU
2006	7%	15%	93%	88%
2005	7%	5%	81%	96%
2004	29%	15%	85%	91%
2003	13%	15%	80%	84%
2002	22%	5%	85%	96%

CALIFORNIA 46

Coastal Los Angeles and Orange counties — Huntington Beach, Costa Mesa

The 46th is a comfortably conservative district that runs along the coast south of Los Angeles with an eclectic mix of residents, including senior citizens, surfers and aerospace workers, that live in several different areas. The mountainous peninsula in the district's northwest is home to ultra-wealthy areas such as Rancho Palos Verdes. In the center is a more blue-collar community around Long Beach Harbor, home to one of the nation's largest port complexes. To the southeast, the district takes in Orange County communities such as Huntington Beach and Costa Mesa.

Aerospace, technology and residential construction dominate the 46th's industry. Wealthy Huntington Beach is a hub for both water sports enthusiasts and aerospace workers. Boeing's Huntington Beach plant employs thousands in defense, space and research programs. The construction sector, benefiting from the residential real estate boom in Orange County, has generated many jobs here. Manufacturing remains important to many residents as well, although highly skilled aircraft assemblage and technology development positions have replaced textile factory jobs.

The 46th is more than three-fifths white and senior citizens are a significant constituency. Some areas in the district's interior, which includes most of Westminster — home to a large Vietnamese population and shared with the 40th District — tend to be less affluent than coastal cities. The coastal areas generally vote more Republican than the inland communities do, but overall the 46th leans Republican. The district gave Arnold Schwarzenegger 69 percent of its gubernatorial vote in 2006.

MAJOR INDUSTRY

Aerospace, technology, manufacturing, construction

MILITARY BASES

Naval Weapons Station Seal Beach, 166 military, 600 civilian (2006)

CITIES

Huntington Beach, 189,594; Costa Mesa, 108,724; Long Beach (pt.), 83,666; Westminster (pt.), 60,399; Fountain Valley, 54,978

NOTABLE

Huntington Beach is home to the International Surfing Museum; The 46th includes two channel islands: Santa Catalina and San Clemente.

Rep. Loretta Sanchez (D)

CAPITOL OFFICE
225-2965
loretta@mail.house.gov
www.house.gov/sanchez
1230 Longworth 20515-0547; fax 225-5859

COMMITTEES
Armed Services
Homeland Security
(Border, Maritime & Global Counterterrorism - chairwoman)
Joint Economic

RESIDENCE
Garden Grove

BORN
Jan. 7, 1960, Lynwood, Calif.

RELIGION
Roman Catholic

FAMILY
Divorced

EDUCATION
Chapman U., B.S. 1982 (economics); American U., M.B.A. 1984 (finance)

CAREER
Financial adviser; strategic management associate

POLITICAL HIGHLIGHTS
Candidate for Anaheim City Council, 1994

ELECTION RESULTS

2006 GENERAL		
Loretta Sanchez (D)	47,134	62.3%
Tan Nguyen (R)	28,485	37.7%
2006 PRIMARY		
Loretta Sanchez (D)		unopposed
2004 GENERAL		
Loretta Sanchez (D)	65,684	60.4%
Alexandria A. Coronado (R)	43,099	39.6%

PREVIOUS WINNING PERCENTAGES
2002 (61%); 2000 (60%); 1998 (56%); 1996 (47%)

Elected 1996; 6th term

A telegenic defender of women, government social programs and organized labor, Sanchez has a feisty side that attracts controversy. Most recently, it was her highly public feud with the chairman of the Congressional Hispanic Caucus, Joe Baca, a fellow Californian and fellow Democrat.

Sanchez resigned her membership in the caucus in February 2007, charging that Baca had been demeaning to women, had abused the group's political action committee and had held improper elections. She also made the explosive claim that Baca had called her a "whore" to a mutual political acquaintance. Baca denied it, but the episode bitterly divided Hispanic Democrats as they were about to assert greater power in the Democratically controlled 110th Congress (2007-08).

Sanchez can be aggressively partisan, and sometimes makes headlines for unconventional behavior. In 2000, she embarrassed fellow Democrats on the eve of their national convention in Los Angeles by refusing to cancel a fundraiser at the Playboy mansion, relenting only at the last minute. Her annual offbeat Christmas card usually generates a buzz; the 2006 version featured her lounging in her bed with her pet cat.

Thanks in part to her outspoken, spirited style, Sanchez has become a master fundraiser. In the 2006 campaign, she gave $280,000 to other Democrats running for office. Sanchez also was an early ally of fellow Californian Nancy Pelosi, now Speaker of the House.

With the Democratic takeover of Congress, Sanchez chairs the Homeland Security Subcommittee on Border, Maritime and Global Counterterrorism, putting her in a better position to push her bills that languished in the Republican House, including one setting security performance standards for the country's chemical facilities.

She has used her seat on the Armed Services Committee to focus attention on the sensitive topic of sexual assault in the military and service academies. In 2005, her proposal to make it easier to press sexual assault charges in the military, particularly in cases of date rape, acquaintance rape and sexual extortion by commanders of their subordinates, won approval.

Her district has one of the largest Vietnamese communities outside Vietnam, and Sanchez has waged an ongoing battle with communist Hanoi. She has opposed expanding trade with Vietnam, citing poor political and human rights conditions. Officials in Hanoi have not made it feasible for her to visit.

In her fight with Baca, Sanchez forced into the open a simmering gender conflict in the 21-member Hispanic caucus. As it organized for the new Congress, Sanchez raised the issue of the treatment of women, then resigned. Her sister, Linda Sánchez, also a House member from California, resigned in protest as well. In 2006, Loretta Sanchez and five other caucus members cut ties to the group's political action committee after it made campaign contributions to Baca's sons, Joe Jr. and Jeremy, in their unsuccessful races for seats in the California legislature.

Though Sanchez is allied with the Democratic left on most social issues, she follows a more centrist course on fiscal policy, as a member of the Democratic Blue Dog Coalition. She also has sided with conservatives on such issues as amending the Constitution to outlaw flag desecration and encouraging states to prosecute violent juvenile offenders as adults.

A daughter of working-class Mexican immigrants, Sanchez says she grew up a "shy, quiet girl" who did not speak English. She credits government with her success. "I am a Head Start child, a public school kid, a Pell

Grant recipient," she says. She opposed the GOP's unsuccessful effort to restructure the Head Start program in the 108th Congress (2003-04), invoking her experience growing up poor and challenged by a speech impediment. "I know about these kids, because I am one of those kids," she said during debate on the bill. "It hurts to hear you talk about how we are not successful, or how we are losers. But we are very successful. We have had a lot of successes with Head Start."

Her father was a unionized machinist and her mother a secretary who worked to organize plant workers into a union. Sanchez joined the United Food and Commercial Workers after getting a job in high school scooping ice cream, and she had a union-paid scholarship to college. She traces her ambitions to a first-grade catechism class. A nun asked what she wanted to be when she grew up. "I answered, 'The pope. He's the head of everyone, the one making the rules,' " she told the Orange County Register.

Sanchez's childhood shyness was so extreme that her mother took her to doctors for advice. Her father forced her to take speech and drama classes in school. She worked her way through college and earned a master's degree in business administration. Feeling isolated as a Hispanic woman in the investment world, she made her first foray into politics in 1994, losing a race for an Anaheim City Council seat.

In 1996, she brazenly took on GOP Rep. Robert K. Dornan, a controversial conservative icon. After winning a four-way primary with 35 percent of the vote, she drew attention from liberal groups who played a hunch that their archenemy might not have his guard up. Thanks to the increasing number of Hispanics in the district and a backlash against a ballot initiative to end state affirmative action programs, Sanchez scored a 984-vote upset.

Dornan claimed he lost to illegal voting by non-citizens. A House task force later said it found such instances, but not enough to prove they affected the outcome. In a 1998 rematch, Sanchez defeated Dornan by 17 percentage points. Her re-elections since have been by larger margins.

Sanchez is the older of the first sister duo ever to serve in Congress. Six years after she had won her seat in the House, Sanchez drew on her accumulated political capital to help her younger sister, Linda T. Sánchez, a civil rights and labor lawyer, win a seat of her own in the reconfigured 39th District in nearby Los Angeles County.

Sanchez is considering running for governor in 2010, or for the Senate if Democrat Barbara Boxer declines to seek re-election that year. She has formed a political action committee to begin raising money for a possible statewide race.

KEY VOTES

2006

No Stop broadband companies from favoring select Internet traffic
No Affirm U.S. commitment to war in Iraq and reject setting a withdrawal date for troops
No Repeal requirement for bilingual ballots at the polls
Yes Permit U.S. sale of civilian nuclear technology to India
No Build a 700-mile fence on the U.S.-Mexico border to curb illegal crossings
No Permit warrantless wiretaps of suspected terrorists

2005

? Intervene in the life-support case of Terri Schiavo
Yes Lift President Bush's restrictions on stem cell research funding
Yes Prohibit FBI access to library and bookstore records
No Approve free-trade pact with five Central American countries
No Pass energy policy overhaul favored by President Bush emphasizing domestic oil and gas production
No End mandatory preservation of habitat of endangered animal and plant species
Yes Ban torture of prisoners in U.S. custody

CQ VOTE STUDIES

	PARTY UNITY		PRESIDENTIAL SUPPORT	
	Support	Oppose	Support	Oppose
2006	95%	5%	26%	74%
2005	93%	7%	24%	76%
2004	94%	6%	33%	67%
2003	97%	3%	22%	78%
2002	96%	4%	21%	79%

INTEREST GROUPS

	AFL-CIO	ADA	CCUS	ACU
2006	93%	100%	47%	12%
2005	87%	90%	52%	16%
2004	93%	100%	40%	12%
2003	100%	90%	34%	12%
2002	100%	100%	32%	4%

CALIFORNIA 47

Orange County – most of Santa Ana, Anaheim and Garden Grove

An inland chunk of Orange County full of older suburban homes and younger families, the Hispanic-majority 47th is unlike its mostly affluent, Republican neighbors in the county. Located roughly 30 miles southeast of Los Angeles, it takes in parts of four cities: Santa Ana, Anaheim, Garden Grove and Fullerton. A growing number of Hispanics, Vietnamese and other ethnic minorities are changing the demographics here and creating a strong Democratic base.

Almost half of the district's population is in Santa Ana (the Orange County seat), which has higher unemployment and more blue-collar jobs than surrounding areas. Defense subcontractors and small businesses are scattered throughout the district, but apart from Disneyland, no single employer drives the area's economy.

Three-fourths of Garden Grove's culturally diverse residents live in the 47th, which has distinct central (a mix of Arabs, Vietnamese, Koreans and Hispanics) and east (heavily Hispanic) sections. An influx of refugees from Southeast Asia has spurred a conservative backlash from some residents who worry that increased demand for social services will lead to higher taxes. The Asian community, some of which is heavily Christian, also has a conservative side.

Santa Ana is one of only two Orange County cities with more registered Democrats than Republicans. The 47th also has some of Anaheim's most Democratic areas. The small part of Fullerton in the district's northern end is heavily Hispanic, although the city overall leans Republican. George W. Bush managed a narrow win here in the 2004 presidential election with 50 percent of the 47th's vote.

MAJOR INDUSTRY

Small business, service, defense, tourism

CITIES

Santa Ana (pt.), 299,552; Anaheim (pt.), 185,537; Garden Grove (pt.), 125,336; Fullerton (pt.), 17,852

NOTABLE

The 47th's part of Anaheim is home to Disneyland, baseball's Angels and hockey's Ducks; The 10,000-member Crystal Cathedral Ministries mega-church is located in Garden Grove.

Rep. John Campbell (R)

CAPITOL OFFICE
225-5611
www.house.gov/campbell
1728 Longworth 20515-0548; fax 225-9177

COMMITTEES
Budget
Financial Services

RESIDENCE
Irvine

BORN
July 19, 1955, Los Angeles, Calif.

RELIGION
Presbyterian

FAMILY
Wife, Catherine Campbell; two children

EDUCATION
U. of California, Los Angeles, B.A. 1976 (economics); U. of Southern California, M.S. 1977 (business taxation)

CAREER
Car dealership president; accountant

POLITICAL HIGHLIGHTS
Calif. Assembly, 2000-04; Calif. Senate, 2004-05

ELECTION RESULTS

2006 GENERAL		
John Campbell (R)	120,130	59.9%
Steve Young (D)	74,647	37.2%
Bruce Cohen (LIBERT)	5,750	2.9%
2006 PRIMARY		
John Campbell (R)		unopposed
2005 SPECIAL		
John Campbell (R)	46,184	44.4%
Steve Young (D)	28,853	27.8%
Jim Gilchrist (AMI)	26,507	25.5%
Bea Tiritilli (GREEN)	1,430	1.4%

Elected December 2005; 1st full term

There is much about Campbell that is reminiscent of his predecessor, Republican Christopher Cox, who left a 17-year career in the House in mid-2005 to become chairman of the Securities and Exchange Commission.

Like Cox, Campbell is a button-down conservative who assiduously looks out for the needs of his pro-business, affluent coastal district in Orange County. Both men are federal budget hawks seeking to simplify the tax code and limit spending. When Cox led the congressional effort to extend the moratorium on the federal Internet tax, for example, Campbell was taking similar steps in the state legislature.

Both also are known for their tenacity and ambition. But while Cox relied on his meticulous, intellectual personality over the back-slapping style of the House to push his ideas, Campbell — also hands-on in his work — likes to loosen his collar every once in a while. His Capitol Hill office is accented with photographs of cars and a model of a 1957 Corvette convertible (he has three Corvettes in California), representing a boyhood passion that turned into a career owning automobile dealerships. Campbell spent almost 25 years in the automobile business, as a corporate officer and owner of franchises that sold Nissan, Mazda, Ford, Saturn, Porsche and Saab models.

His cell phone ring tone plays "California" by Phantom Planet, the theme song to "The OC," the former Orange County-based television show on Fox. "Devastating," Campbell says with a chuckle of the show's demise in 2007.

While playful, he is nonetheless considered a serious-minded legislator with a keen eye on government spending. Campbell is a certified public accountant and before he sold cars he was a tax accountant with what is now Ernst & Young in Los Angeles. When he came to Congress in December 2005, his background — including service in the California Legislature — made him an easy pick for appointments to the House Budget and Financial Services committees. He was also given a seat on Veterans' Affairs that he had to give up at the start of the 110th Congress (2007-08).

Campbell heads the budget task force for the conservative House Republican Study Committee, making him a high-profile critic of the Democratic majority's spending policies. Budgeting terms such as "dynamic scoring" and "pay-go" rules are part of his lexicon. He favors a proposal to tie federal spending to some measurement, such as increases in population and inflation or gross domestic product growth. He wants to make permanent the tax cuts advanced during President Bush's first term.

He has scaled back his ideas for tough immigration control. Though the House passed his proposal in 2006 to deny funding to "sanctuary cities" that do not let local police enforce federal immigration law, he said it would be useless to resurrect the measure in the 110th Congress, controlled by Democrats who are opposed.

His district lies about 80 miles from the Mexican border, and Campbell's conservative immigration views were challenged during the 2005 House special-election campaign. His chief opponent was Republican Jim Gilchrist, co-founder of the Minuteman Project, a group that looks for illegal crossings on the U.S.-Mexico border.

Gilchrist, running as an American Independent Party candidate, criticized Campbell's support in Sacramento for offering in-state tuition to illegal immigrants at state colleges and universities, and also for letting immigrants use Mexican consulate cards as identification. Campbell said he erred in voting for the tuition bill out of a belief that students had to be applying for citizenship to qualify. He said his support for the consulate cards was based on appeals from the law enforcement community, which wanted the cards to better track immigrants.

Energy and the environment also are key issues for Campbell. He joined a bipartisan California coalition in 2006 that blocked an effort to ease a moratorium that prohibits oil and natural gas drilling offshore in the Atlantic and Pacific oceans and part of the Gulf of Mexico. He also is working with California Democratic Sen. Dianne Feinstein to increase tax incentives for environmentally friendly solar technology. Before he was elected, Campbell drove an electric car for two years to promote low-emission vehicles.

A fourth-generation Californian, Campbell is a member of the Sons of Union Veterans and has occasionally played in Civil War re-enactments. He grew up in the Hancock Park area of Los Angeles, in a house built in 1922 by his maternal grandfather.

Campbell's great-grandfather on his father's side, Alexander, was elected to the California Assembly in 1860 on the same Republican ticket as Abraham Lincoln. He chaired the Judiciary Committee that wrote the state Constitution in 1887. The congressman's father, also named Alexander, ran unsuccessfully for the state Senate when John Campbell was 11. Campbell's father also was a classic car collector and dealership investor, spurring Campbell's own interest in cars.

In 1978, after receiving an economics degree from the University of California in Los Angeles and a graduate degree in business taxation from the University of Southern California, Campbell moved to Orange County to be a corporate comptroller for car dealerships. He became a GOP volunteer and campaign donor, and a second tenor for the Irvine Presbyterian Church.

In 2000, Campbell was recruited to run for the state Assembly and won. Four years later, when term limits forced out the sitting GOP state senator, Campbell moved up. He cites as top state legislative accomplishments, "Keeping the people of California from suffering any tax increases and the recall of [Democratic Gov.] Gray Davis," a campaign Campbell helped lead.

In the 11-candidate open special primary to fill Cox's House seat in 2005, Campbell got 45 percent of the vote. He prevailed in the special election with 44 percent — a relatively modest share in a district where Republicans regularly get 60 percent or more. Gilchrist took 26 percent. Democrat Steve Young, a lawyer with a low-key campaign, drew 28 percent. In a 2006 rematch with Young, Campbell won with 60 percent of the vote.

KEY VOTES

2006

No Stop broadband companies from favoring select Internet traffic

Yes Affirm U.S. commitment to war in Iraq and reject setting a withdrawal date for troops

Yes Repeal requirement for bilingual ballots at the polls

Yes Permit U.S. sale of civilian nuclear technology to India

Yes Build a 700-mile fence on the U.S.-Mexico border to curb illegal crossings

Yes Permit warrantless wiretaps of suspected terrorists

2005

No Ban torture of prisoners in U.S. custody

CQ VOTE STUDIES

	PARTY UNITY		PRESIDENTIAL SUPPORT	
	Support	Oppose	Support	Oppose
2006	95%	5%	90%	10%
2005	100%	0%	100%	0%

INTEREST GROUPS

	AFL-CIO	ADA	CCUS	ACU
2006	7%	0%	87%	88%
2005	0%	0%	50%	100%

CALIFORNIA 48

Southern Orange County – Irvine, Newport Beach

The 48th covers the Orange County coast from Newport Beach south through Laguna Beach to Dana Point, and it takes in a chunk of the inland county from the coast through Irvine to the foothills of the Santa Ana mountains. Registered Republicans outnumber Democrats nearly 2-to-1 here, and the district is distinguished by its large white-collar labor force and its high median income. Many workers commute in from the north or east, where the cost of living is cheaper.

Newport Beach is a wealthy enclave noted for its beautiful sandy beaches, luxurious housing and solid Republicanism. Picturesque Laguna Beach attracts tourists and scuba divers, and while it has more registered Republicans than Democrats, it is home to a liberal enclave known as "the arts colony." Inland is Laguna Woods, home to a significant number of senior citizens, Laguna Niguel and Laguna Hills. Nearly 70 percent of district residents are white.

Smog, crime and other problems endemic to Los Angeles generally do not affect these areas. Irvine was the nation's safest city with more than 100,000 people, based on the FBI's 2005 crime reporting statistics. But the sheer number of people who commute into the district makes transportation among the toughest problems here, as traffic backs up and increases the threat of pollution. Toll roads in the area have helped, and a successful county ballot initiative in 2006 to extend dedicated tax revenues for road improvements aims to ease congestion. Many residents continue to oppose construction of a new commuter train line.

While Republicans dominate the 48th, pockets of Democratic strength can be found in the district's inland sections and in the more liberal-leaning community surrounding the University of California, Irvine. The university's engineering and biomedical research programs have attracted a large number of thriving high-technology and biotechnology firms to the area, and the university is the district's largest employer.

MAJOR INDUSTRY

Technology, research, tourism

CITIES

Irvine, 143,072; Newport Beach, 70,032; Tustin, 67,504

NOTABLE

The Ayn Rand Institute is located in Irvine; Balboa Island is an artificial island in the Newport Harbor that was filled before World War I.

Rep. Darrell Issa (R)

CAPITOL OFFICE
225-3906
www.house.gov/issa
211 Cannon 20515-0549; fax 225-3303

COMMITTEES
Judiciary
Oversight & Government Reform
Select Intelligence

RESIDENCE
Vista

BORN
Nov. 1, 1953, Cleveland, Ohio

RELIGION
Antioch Orthodox Christian Church

FAMILY
Wife, Kathy Issa; one child

EDUCATION
Kent State U., A.A. 1976 (general studies); Siena Heights College, B.A. 1976 (business)

MILITARY SERVICE
Army, 1970-72, 1976-80; Army Reserve, 1980-88

CAREER
Car alarm company owner; electronics manufacturing company executive

POLITICAL HIGHLIGHTS
Sought Republican nomination for U.S. Senate, 1998

ELECTION RESULTS

2006 GENERAL		
Darrell Issa (R)	98,831	63.3%
Jeeni Criscenzo (D)	52,227	33.4%
Lars R. Grossmith (LIBERT)	4,952	3.2%
2006 PRIMARY		
Darrell Issa (R)		unopposed
2004 GENERAL		
Darrell Issa (R)	141,658	62.6%
Mike Byron (D)	79,057	34.9%
Lars R. Grossman (LIBERT)	5,751	2.5%

PREVIOUS WINNING PERCENTAGES
2002 (77%); 2000 (61%)

Elected 2000; 4th term

Issa's Lebanese Christian heritage gives him a perspective on the roiling conflicts in the Middle East that few other members possess. "When your last name is Arabic for Jesus, you sort of get a natural ability to go through the region and be accepted a little bit more quickly," he told the Washington Post in 2006.

He vigorously condemns terrorists while urging U.S. policymakers to reach out to friendly Arab nations. His sympathetic approach to Arab nations draws condemnations from pro-Israel advocates, while Arab commentators complain about his pro-Israel votes. "If you're an honest broker, you're not going to side 100 percent with either antagonist," he says.

Issa (EYE-sah), the grandson of Lebanese immigrants, was in a unique position in 2006, when Hezbollah fighters operating from southern Lebanon crossed into Israel and captured Israeli soldiers. Israel retaliated with air attacks and then invaded Lebanon. The House swiftly passed a resolution condemning the Hezbollah attacks. Although Issa voted for it, he tried in vain, with three other lawmakers of Lebanese descent, to add language urging "all parties to protect innocent life and civilian infrastructure."

Issa was the only member of Congress to travel to Lebanon during the conflict. On returning, he urged the United States to act quickly to help rebuild Lebanon or risk losing the "hearts and minds" of the people to Hezbollah, which moved swiftly to help the Lebanese rebuild their damaged homes.

Issa also has called for more trade agreements with moderate Arab nations, such as the pacts with Bahrain and Oman that Congress approved in 2005 and 2006. "We're not exactly swimming in friends in that region. The fact that these are friendly nations to the United States and not particularly antagonistic to Israel, those are big pluses," he said.

Issa has had firsthand experience with the fallout from the Sept. 11 terrorist attacks. Three weeks after the attacks, he was barred from boarding an Air France plane on an official trip to the Middle East, even as another lawmaker was permitted to board. "I had an Arab surname and a one-way ticket to Saudi Arabia," he said. He started the trip the next day.

Issa is a loud critic of illegal immigration and an advocate of tougher border security measures. In 2005, he took a leave of absence from the Energy and Commerce Committee, which he had joined just two years earlier, to return to his old assignments on the Judiciary and International Relations panels as Congress was tackling immigration overhaul and the United States was trying to promote democracy in Iraq and elsewhere in the Middle East. In 2007, he once again left the international panel, renamed Foreign Affairs, but was unable to return to Energy; there were no GOP openings.

Unlike some GOP hard-liners, Issa would support a guest worker program that allowed immigrants to work in the United States temporarily. "If you say all we're going to do is secure our borders — what I call the tag 'em, bag 'em and deport 'em attitude — you're not mindful of the problem. We have to be realistic about how we solve the problem."

Issa would like to advance in his party's leadership ranks, but as the GOP organized itself for the 110th Congress (2007-08) he lost the election for chairman of the Policy Committee by a better than 2-1 ratio to Michigan's Thaddeus McCotter.

Issa may not be the most prominent member of the California delegation, but he is the only one who can be called a kingmaker. It was Issa's millions that bankrolled the California recall effort in 2003 that ousted Democratic

Gov. Gray Davis and put Republican Arnold Schwarzenegger in his place. Although Issa wanted to replace Davis himself, several of his GOP House colleagues were convinced Issa could not defeat Davis. They urged Schwarzenegger to run. Issa was upset but swallowed his pride and bowed out.

Long before he engineered the recall, Issa was the frontman for business in a 1996 campaign to overturn racial and gender preferences in California state contracting and college admissions. The authors of Proposition 209, the "California Civil Rights Initiative," were having trouble finding a prominent businessman to take the lead on an issue that might get him branded a racist, but Issa took on the role and the initiative passed narrowly.

Issa was born into a working-class family in Cleveland, where his father worked as a salesman and an X-ray technician. On his 17th birthday, just two months into his senior year, Issa quit high school and joined the Army. After he had served two years, the Army paid for Issa's college education with the understanding that he would return to active duty upon graduation.

Along the way, he and his older brother, William, got into trouble. In 1972, they were arrested for allegedly stealing a Maserati from a car dealership. The charges were dropped. In 1980, the two were charged with faking the theft of Issa's Mercedes Benz. Again, the charges were dropped. In both cases, Issa blamed his brother.

After fulfilling his Army obligation, Issa went back to Cleveland and used his $7,000 in life savings to invest in a small car alarm business. He and his wife, Kathy, eventually took control of the business, the maker of the popular Viper anti-theft device. In 1985, they moved the business to Vista, about 30 miles north of San Diego. Issa immersed himself in industry activities, and in 1999 and 2000 he was chairman of the board of the Consumer Electronics Association, an industry trade group. "When people ask me why I got into the car alarm business, I tell them the truth," he said in a statement to the San Francisco Chronicle. "It was because my brother was a car thief." He sold the business, which made him an extremely wealthy man.

In California, Issa became involved behind the scenes in local GOP politics. He briefly considered challenging 49th District Democratic Rep. Lynn Schenk in 1994, but remained on the sidelines. Four years later, he spent $11 million on a failed bid for the 1998 GOP Senate nomination.

Issa was back in 2000 when Republican Ron Packard announced his retirement from the 48th District, a reliably GOP district that was home to President Richard Nixon. Issa weathered a nine-candidate primary, sinking $2 million into the race, then won the general election easily with 61 percent of the vote. His re-elections have been easy in what is now the 49th District.

KEY VOTES

2006

No Stop broadband companies from favoring select Internet traffic
Yes Affirm U.S. commitment to war in Iraq and reject setting a withdrawal date for troops
Yes Repeal requirement for bilingual ballots at the polls
Yes Permit U.S. sale of civilian nuclear technology to India
Yes Build a 700-mile fence on the U.S.-Mexico border to curb illegal crossings
Yes Permit warrantless wiretaps of suspected terrorists

2005

\+ Intervene in the life-support case of Terri Schiavo
Yes Lift President Bush's restrictions on stem cell research funding
No Prohibit FBI access to library and bookstore records
Yes Approve free-trade pact with five Central American countries
Yes Pass energy policy overhaul favored by President Bush emphasizing domestic oil and gas production
Yes End mandatory preservation of habitat of endangered animal and plant species
Yes Ban torture of prisoners in U.S. custody

CQ VOTE STUDIES

	PARTY UNITY		PRESIDENTIAL SUPPORT	
	Support	Oppose	Support	Oppose
2006	94%	6%	95%	5%
2005	95%	5%	89%	11%
2004	95%	5%	85%	15%
2003	97%	3%	98%	2%
2002	94%	6%	85%	15%

INTEREST GROUPS

	AFL-CIO	ADA	CCUS	ACU
2006	21%	5%	100%	80%
2005	13%	0%	93%	84%
2004	20%	0%	100%	92%
2003	7%	5%	97%	83%
2002	13%	0%	100%	96%

CALIFORNIA 49

North San Diego County; West Riverside County

Based in fast-growing northwestern San Diego County and western Riverside County, the heavily residential 49th is home to many bedroom communities, including Vista and Oceanside. New residents are being lured to the area by comparatively affordable land and housing prices.

While some residents work in the district, others commute to jobs in San Diego (a sliver of which falls in the 49th) or, to a lesser extent, Orange County. The massive Camp Pendleton Marine Corps Base sits near Oceanside, on the largest undeveloped portion of coast in southern California, but the local economy relies less on military contracts than its San Diego or Orange County neighbors. In northeast San Diego, Rancho Bernardo has manufacturing and defense sectors, including Hewlett-Packard and Northrop Grumman, many of which are located at a large industrial park in the nearby 50th. Visitors to Oceanside and the beaches along the coast also boost the local economy.

Most residents live in San Diego County, but growth has been prodigious in Temecula in Riverside County. Old Town Temecula welcomes tourists who visit the area's wineries. The desert terrain of the Temecula Valley also has become known for balloon rides, skydiving and golf. The Pechanga Resort and Casino near Temecula employs thousands.

Some areas here have considerable Hispanic populations, but nearly 60 percent of the district is white. The district supports Republicans, and it gave George W. Bush 62 percent of its 2004 presidential vote and Arnold Schwarzenegger 71 percent of its 2006 gubernatorial vote. Perris, with a large retirement community, is one of the few places Democrats hold an edge.

MAJOR INDUSTRY
Medical devices, services, manufacturing, tourism, defense

MILITARY BASES
Camp Pendleton Marine Corps Base, Air Station and Naval Hospital, 38,000 military, 65,000 civilian (2007); Naval Weapons Station Seal Beach, Detachment Fallbrook, 64 military, 224 civilian (2006)

CITIES
Oceanside, 161,029; Vista, 89,857; Temecula, 57,716; Perris, 36,189

NOTABLE
The Oceanside Pier, at 1,954 feet, is the longest wooden pier on the western United States coastline.

Rep. Brian P. Bilbray (R)

CAPITOL OFFICE
225-0508
www.house.gov/bilbray
227 Cannon 20515-0550; fax 225-2558

COMMITTEES
Oversight & Government Reform
Science & Technology
Veterans' Affairs

RESIDENCE
Carlsbad

BORN
Jan. 28, 1951, Coronado, Calif.

RELIGION
Roman Catholic

FAMILY
Wife, Karen Bilbray; six children (one deceased)

EDUCATION
Southwestern College (Calif.), attended 1970-74 (history)

CAREER
Lobbyist; tax firm owner; lifeguard

POLITICAL HIGHLIGHTS
Imperial Beach City Council, 1976-78; mayor of Imperial Beach, 1978-85; San Diego County Board of Supervisors, 1985-95; U.S. House, 1995-2001; defeated for re-election to U.S. House, 2000

ELECTION RESULTS

2006 GENERAL		
Brian P. Bilbray (R)	118,018	53.1%
Francine Busby (D)	96,612	43.5%
Paul King (LIBERT)	4,119	1.9%
Miriam E. Clark (PFP)	3,353	1.5%
2006 PRIMARY		
Brian P. Bilbray (R)	41,545	54.0%
Eric Roach (R)	10,617	13.8%
Bill Hauf (R)	9,952	12.9%
Bill Morrow (R)	4,788	6.2%
2006 SPECIAL		
Brian P. Bilbray (R)	78,341	49.6%
Francine Busby (D)	71,146	45.0%
William Griffith (I)	6,027	3.8%
Paul King (LIBERT)	2,519	1.6%

PREVIOUS WINNING PERCENTAGES
1998 (49%); 1996 (53%); 1994 (49%)

Elected June 2006; 4th full term

Also served 1995-2001

Bilbray was the Republican Party's white knight in the chaotic 2006 election season. Returning to the House after a hiatus of almost five and a half years, he managed to keep the San Diego-based district in GOP hands in spite of a bribery scandal that forced the Republican incumbent out of office in late 2005.

He prevailed in the June 2006 special election called to replace GOP Rep. Randy "Duke" Cunningham, who was sent to prison after admitting to taking more than $2 million in bribes from defense contractors. Democrats saw a chance to snatch the seat in the traditionally Republican district, and put up a well-financed candidate in local school board member Francine Busby.

Bilbray defeated her first in the special election to fill the remainder of Cunningham's term. She challenged him again in November for a full, two-year term, and he prevailed. Bilbray had represented a similar slice of southern California from 1995 until 2001, the old 49th District, which had some of the same political turf as the present-day 50th.

Upon Bilbray's triumphant return to Congress, grateful Republican leaders persuaded fellow Californian Howard P. "Buck" McKeon to take a leave from the Armed Services panel to make room for Bilbray. But Bilbray had to give up that prize in 2007, after Democrats took control of the House and the GOP lost seats on every committee.

Bilbray's San Diego-area district is home to the Marine Corps Air Station Miramar, many active members of the military and more than 64,000 veterans. A multitude of defense contractors underpin the local economy.

Bilbray continues to pursue his trademark issue: the fight against illegal immigration. It was central to both contests with Busby, and of paramount interest to a district just 25 miles from the border with Mexico. Though he is a moderate on a number of domestic issues, Bilbray joined with conservative hard-liners in 2006 to stop President Bush's guest worker proposal.

"I will not vote for any bill that offers something to somebody who broke our immigration laws that is not offered to the 100 million people waiting to immigrate legally. The fact is that rewarding somebody for breaking the laws and the rules is not only stupid, it is immoral," Bilbray said in an interview with MSNBC.

In 2007, he took over the chairmanship of the Republican-dominated Immigration Reform Caucus from Tom Tancredo of Colorado, the longtime leading House advocate of a crackdown on illegal immigration.

During his first stint in the House, Bilbray sponsored legislation to deny citizenship to U.S.-born children of illegal immigrants, and he says the federal government ought to help with costs that the states incur because of illegal immigration.

A member of the radicalized Republican Class of '94, Bilbray endorsed its legislation to cut Medicare spending by $270 billion, to make it harder to get on welfare, and to amend the Constitution to guarantee the right to prayer in public schools. "There was a real feeling of having to show Democrats how it could be done better," Bilbray told the San Diego Union Tribune in 2006. "But I think we've lost a lot of that revolutionary fire that made the 'Contract With America' so worth being involved in."

Bilbray's politics are more moderate on some other social issues; he has supported some gun control measures and generally voted for abortion rights. He was one of the few Republicans to vote against repealing the ban on semiautomatic assault-style weapons in 1996. And while he opposed what critics call "partial birth" abortion, and federal funding for most abortions, he did not support overturning *Roe v. Wade*, which legalized abortion.

A former lifeguard who still surfs the coastal waters of southern California, Bilbray tends to take the side of environmentalists. A staple of his political biography is the story of how, as the young mayor of Imperial Beach, he became so frustrated with the federal response to complaints that the Tijuana River was carrying pollution from Mexico onto U.S. beaches, he climbed aboard a bulldozer and dammed the offending stream.

In 1996, Bilbray voted to protect a threatened sea bird species, the marbled murrelet, though most Republicans favored lifting protections on 40,000 acres of private land in northern California. But he came under fire from green groups and surfing organizations for voting in 1995 to relax regulatory provisions of the Clean Water Act. Bilbray had sought to exempt San Diego from a rule under the act requiring the city to treat its sewage twice before discharging it into the ocean.

Once the owner of a tax preparation service, Bilbray was first elected to the Imperial Beach City Council at age 24, and became the city's mayor at 27. He served for 10 years on the San Diego County Board of Supervisors, the job he had when he decided to run for the House in 1994.

That first race generated as many sparks as his 2006 comeback. He ousted a Democratic freshman, Lynn Schenk, despite her ample campaign treasury of $1.4 million. Bilbray raised less than half that. But he appealed to bedrock Republicans and to the old 49th District's swing voters to eke out victory with a 49 percent plurality. Schenk had 46 percent.

In 1996, he spiked to nearly 53 percent of the vote in his first re-election contest, but dropped to 49 percent in 1998. Finally, he lost the seat in 2000 to Democrat Susan A. Davis in a strong year for Democrats in California.

Bilbray left electoral politics for a spell, but stayed involved in Washington as co-chairman of the National Board of Advisors for the Federation for American Immigration Reform (FAIR), a group that advocates limiting immigration and beefing up border security.

Cunningham's fall from grace gave Bilbray the opportunity to stage a comeback. Many voters in the 50th District knew him, and though conservative activists mistrusted him on social issues, they liked his tough stance on illegal immigration. The new district was more Republican than his old one, with a 15 percentage point edge over Democrats in voter registration. Democrats hoped the taint from the Cunningham scandal would overcome that tilt, but Bilbray defeated Busby by 5 percentage points in June, then beat her by 10 points in a rematch in November.

KEY VOTES

2006

- Yes Affirm U.S. commitment to war in Iraq and reject setting a withdrawal date for troops
- Yes Repeal requirement for bilingual ballots at the polls
- Yes Permit U.S. sale of civilian nuclear technology to India
- Yes Build a 700-mile fence on the U.S.-Mexico border to curb illegal crossings
- Yes Permit warrantless wiretaps of suspected terrorists

CQ VOTE STUDIES

	PARTY UNITY		PRESIDENTIAL SUPPORT	
	Support	Oppose	Support	Oppose
2006	93%	7%	93%	7%
2000	76%	24%	38%	62%
1999	72%	28%	39%	61%
1998	74%	26%	35%	65%
1997	87%	13%	36%	64%

INTEREST GROUPS

	AFL-CIO	ADA	CCUS	ACU
2006	11%	5%	100%	94%
2000	10%	25%	80%	68%
1999	38%	50%	68%	68%
1998	20%	20%	61%	64%
1997	13%	15%	80%	76%

CALIFORNIA 50

North San Diego; Escondido; Carlsbad

With its beautiful beach communities and upper-class suburbs, the San Diego-area 50th is a steadily growing GOP stronghold. It combines affluent suburbs like Carlsbad, beach communities such as Encinitas, the northern part of San Diego itself, and inland Escondido and San Marcos, which are tucked within the district's northeast curve.

The area's wealth is a testament to a still booming technology industry north of San Diego that has been likened to a mini-Silicon Valley. The growth of cellular technology companies and computer firms, combined with military and defense contracting, has helped the area's image and diversified the economy. Home construction abounds in the north San Diego region, and the mild climate of the coastal area is friendly to commercial production of flowers and fruits.

Unlike San Diego's south side, the 50th is two-thirds white and heavily Republican, although there is a growing Hispanic population here. The 50th's conservative corridor, which runs north and south through the district along Interstate 15, includes the Marine Corps base in Miramar (shared with the 52nd). Coastal cities such as Del Mar, Carlsbad and Encinitas, where beach pollution and the environment are issues, add some liberals to the district, but they are outweighed by inland voters. Illegal immigration also is a large issue in the 50th. Republican Arnold Schwarzenegger took 70 percent of the district's vote in the 2006 gubernatorial election.

MAJOR INDUSTRY

Technology, defense, manufacturing, tourism, agriculture

MILITARY BASES

Marine Corps Air Station Miramar, 8,850 military, 1,150 civilian (2007) (shared with the 52nd)

CITIES

San Diego (pt.), 262,523; Escondido, 133,559; Carlsbad, 78,247; Encinitas, 58,014; San Marcos, 54,977

NOTABLE

The Flower Fields in Carlsbad features a blooming 50-acre hillside; Carlsbad is home to several major golf equipment manufacturers, as well as the Legoland theme park; The Paul Ecke Ranch produces more than half the world's poinsettias; The Quail Botanical Garden in Encinitas has the largest bamboo collection in the nation.

Rep. Bob Filner (D)

CAPITOL OFFICE
225-8045
www.house.gov/filner
2428 Rayburn 20515-0551; fax 225-9073

COMMITTEES
Transportation & Infrastructure
Veterans' Affairs - chairman

RESIDENCE
Chula Vista

BORN
Sept. 4, 1942, Pittsburgh, Pa.

RELIGION
Jewish

FAMILY
Wife, Jane Filner; two children

EDUCATION
Cornell U., B.A. 1963 (chemistry);
U. of Delaware, M.A. 1969 (history);
Cornell U., Ph.D. 1973 (history of science)

CAREER
Congressional aide; professor

POLITICAL HIGHLIGHTS
San Diego Unified School District Board of Education, 1979-83 (president, 1982); candidate for San Diego City Council, 1983; San Diego City Council, 1987-92 (deputy mayor, 1990-91)

ELECTION RESULTS

2006 GENERAL		
Bob Filner (D)	78,114	67.4%
Blake L. Miles (R)	34,931	30.2%
Dan Litwin (LIBERT)	2,790	2.4%
2006 PRIMARY		
Bob Filner (D)	23,312	51.2%
Juan Vargas (D)	19,364	42.5%
Daniel C. "Danny" Ramirez (D)	2,862	6.3%
2004 GENERAL		
Bob Filner (D)	111,441	61.6%
Michael Giorgino (R)	63,526	35.1%
Michael S. Metti (LIBERT)	5,912	3.3%

PREVIOUS WINNING PERCENTAGES
2002 (58%); 2000 (68%); 1998 (99%); 1996 (62%); 1994 (57%); 1992 (57%)

Elected 1992; 8th term

A fiery liberal with a short fuse, Filner is finally in a position to win some of the battles he has fought to help the nation's veterans. As the chairman of the Veterans' Affairs Committee, he is determined to enhance benefits for veterans of the Iraq War and to ensure that the United States keeps its promises to those who don the uniform.

He has been a vehement critic of the Bush administration's efforts to charge increased fees to veterans to offset the soaring costs of their health care. He has pressed to expand treatment for veterans with combat-related stress and other mental health problems. He has assailed the Veterans Affairs Department for failing to protect the personal data of the nation's veterans from computer theft and other potential threats. And he fought for years to grant full benefits to Filipino veterans who served with U.S. forces in World War II.

His efforts, inspired by the large Filipino community in his area, won him the gratitude of the Philippine government, especially when he was arrested with Filipino-American protesters who chained themselves to the White House fence in 1997. His work paid off in 2003 when his measure was signed by President Bush. The legislation gave U.S.-Filipino veterans full access to VA medical facilities, restored burial benefits to Philippine scouts, and boosted the compensation for Filipino veterans and their widows.

But his hot temper earned him a challenge to the chairmanship for the 110th Congress (2007-08). Critics cited his fights with former GOP chairman Steve Buyer of Indiana, and a profanity-laced tirade outside VA headquarters in June. Filner said you have to be loud sometimes to get things done.

A 1960s civil rights activist who by his own account avoided the draft with repeated student deferments, Filner landed on the Veterans' Affairs Committee almost by accident. Soon after his first election in 1992, he ran into Democratic Sen. Alan Cranston of California, who was heading into retirement. Cranston, who had chaired the veterans' committee in the Senate, urged Filner to seek the House assignment, telling him it was good politics for a liberal to champion the cause of veterans. Filner took the advice.

The newly minted panel member showed up at a reception hosted by then Chairman G.V. Sonny Montgomery of Mississippi, a legend in the veterans' community. Filner had never heard of him. "Mr. Chairman," he said, "I was once a tourist through your state. I took a Greyhound bus to your capital, Jackson. I got off and the police chief showed me around his jail. The sheriff in Hines County showed me around his jail, and then I spent a couple of months in your state penitentiary. I was one of the first Freedom Riders." Montgomery did not bat an eyelash. "I was the head of the National Guard that arrested you," he replied.

Filner, convinced he had wrecked his relations with the chairman, went to the panel's first meeting filled with dread. Montgomery introduced him to his new colleagues. "This here distinguished gentleman from California, we've been close friends for 35 years," Montgomery said, according to Filner. "All the other freshmen looked at me like, how does he even know who you are? I became like his pet on the committee."

Filner makes no apology for his liberal views. In fact, he and other like-minded Democrats started a small organizing group called the Moving All Democrats caucus, which goes by the moniker "MAD dogs." Lamenting the declining influence of liberals within the party, Filner said, "One day, we'll come out of the kennel."

Filner joined Congressional Black Caucus members in their parliamentary attempt at a January 2001 joint session to prevent Congress from certifying the Electoral College's 2000 presidential results that resolved the contested election in favor of George W. Bush. Incensed by a Supreme Court ruling the previous month that effectively decided the election, Filner said he considered offering a resolution of impeachment against some of the justices. And during California's electricity crisis at the start of the decade, which hurt Filner's hometown of San Diego, he filed court motions calling utility companies guilty of murder, extortion and grand larceny.

Filner also sits on the Transportation and Infrastructure Committee, where he has worked to get as much money as possible for California projects. He focuses particularly on transportation projects near the Mexican border, where facilities were strained by increased traffic under the North American Free Trade Agreement, which he opposed. The Sept. 11 terrorist attacks worsened congestion as border security was beefed up.

Filner has little patience for the anti-immigration views of many conservative Republicans. Representing a Hispanic-majority border district, he has urged an increase in economic aid and infrastructure support for Mexico to help it create jobs and raise living standards. He also advocates issuance of "smart cards" with biometric data that citizens of both countries could use when they cross the border to shop, work or vacation. "We could then focus on the people we don't know. That would be smart," he says.

A native Pennsylvanian, Filner is the son of a former union organizer and businessman who was an early fundraiser for the Rev. Dr. Martin Luther King Jr. Filner met King as a teenager, and participated in his first civil rights march in 1957. He left college to join the Freedom Riders in 1961. He was arrested during a sit-in at a Mississippi lunch counter with John Lewis, now a House colleague from Georgia. After his release from prison, he finished college and later earned a doctorate in the history of science.

As a young academic, Filner had never been west of Chicago. His colleagues thought he was "going to the frontier" when he accepted a teaching position in San Diego. He taught history at San Diego State University starting in the 1970s. After working for former senator and vice president Hubert H. Humphrey and Rep. Donald M. Fraser, both Minnesota Democrats, he spent four years on the San Diego school board and five on the city council. He then ran for a newly created 50th District House seat in 1992. His single-minded devotion to fundraising and tireless campaigning helped him overcome five Democratic primary foes. The Democratic makeup of his now 51st District has allowed him a string of easy general-election victories.

KEY VOTES

2006

Yes Stop broadband companies from favoring select Internet traffic

No Affirm U.S. commitment to war in Iraq and reject setting a withdrawal date for troops

No Repeal requirement for bilingual ballots at the polls

Yes Permit U.S. sale of civilian nuclear technology to India

No Build a 700-mile fence on the U.S.-Mexico border to curb illegal crossings

No Permit warrantless wiretaps of suspected terrorists

2005

? Intervene in the life-support case of Terri Schiavo

Yes Lift President Bush's restrictions on stem cell research funding

Yes Prohibit FBI access to library and bookstore records

No Approve free-trade pact with five Central American countries

No Pass energy policy overhaul favored by President Bush emphasizing domestic oil and gas production

No End mandatory preservation of habitat of endangered animal and plant species

Yes Ban torture of prisoners in U.S. custody

CQ VOTE STUDIES

	PARTY UNITY		PRESIDENTIAL SUPPORT	
	Support	Oppose	Support	Oppose
2006	97%	3%	18%	82%
2005	98%	2%	15%	85%
2004	98%	2%	23%	77%
2003	99%	1%	11%	89%
2002	99%	1%	22%	78%

INTEREST GROUPS

	AFL-CIO	ADA	CCUS	ACU
2006	92%	95%	33%	12%
2005	93%	100%	37%	4%
2004	93%	95%	22%	9%
2003	100%	100%	17%	13%
2002	89%	100%	25%	0%

CALIFORNIA 51

Central and southern San Diego; Imperial County

The part-urban, part-rural 51st runs east along the entire length of California's border with Mexico, except for the western tip at the Pacific Ocean. In the east, it takes in all of Imperial County, and near the Pacific, it climbs north from the border to include part of central San Diego and some close-in suburbs.

The 51st's part of San Diego, which starts south and east of downtown, is working-class and heavily Hispanic. Mexican shoppers, drawn to the large shopping centers, continue to cross the border to spend money at local malls. Chula Vista is becoming an upscale housing development hot spot with rising industrial and commercial growth. South of Chula Vista and across the border from Tijuana, Otay Mesa hosts several major manufacturing plants that have twin sites in the Mexican city.

Imperial County is heavily agricultural, with an annual crop yield of about $1 billion, and tends to have high unemployment. The county is more than two-thirds Hispanic. Voters here are more conservative than their city cousins, but still lean Democratic.

The Hispanic-majority 51st gave 53 percent to presidential nominee John Kerry in 2004. Border issues, particularly illegal immigration — which fills agricultural labor jobs — was a key issue here in the 2006 elections. Ranchers and growers see illegal immigration as a necessary source of labor, while others say it threatens the district's quality of life.

Water is another concern in the 51st. Both San Diego and Imperial counties are under pressure to reduce their dependency on the Colorado River, and a proposed solution — to lower the Salton Sea's high salinity and pesticide levels — has environmentalists concerned about the local ecosystem and migratory birds.

MAJOR INDUSTRY

Service, manufacturing, agriculture, retail

MILITARY BASES

Naval Station San Diego (shared with the 53rd), 28,460 military, 8,423 civilian (2005); El Centro Naval Air Facility, 330 military, 500 civilian (2007)

CITIES

San Diego (pt.), 239,457; Chula Vista, 173,556; National City, 54,260

NOTABLE

The San Ysidro-Tijuana border crossing is the world's busiest; El Centro is the winter training home of the Navy's Blue Angels.

Rep. Duncan Hunter (R)

CAPITOL OFFICE
225-5672
www.house.gov/hunter
2265 Rayburn 20515-0552; fax 225-0235

COMMITTEES
Armed Services - ranking member

RESIDENCE
Alpine

BORN
May 31, 1948, Riverside, Calif.

RELIGION
Baptist

FAMILY
Wife, Lynne Hunter; two children

EDUCATION
U. of Montana, attended 1966-67;
U. of California, Santa Barbara, attended 1967-68;
Western State U., B.S.L. 1976, J.D. 1976

MILITARY SERVICE
Army, 1969-71

CAREER
Lawyer

POLITICAL HIGHLIGHTS
No previous office

ELECTION RESULTS

2006 GENERAL		
Duncan Hunter (R)	123,696	64.6%
John Rinaldi (D)	61,208	32.0%
Michael Benoit (LIBERT)	6,465	3.4%
2006 PRIMARY		
Duncan Hunter (R)		unopposed
2004 GENERAL		
Duncan Hunter (R)	187,799	69.2%
Brian S. Keliher (D)	74,857	27.6%
Michael Benoit (LIBERT)	8,782	3.2%

PREVIOUS WINNING PERCENTAGES
2002 (70%); 2000 (65%); 1998 (76%); 1996 (65%); 1994 (64%); 1992 (53%); 1990 (73%); 1988 (74%); 1986 (77%); 1984 (75%); 1982 (69%); 1980 (53%)

Elected 1980; 14th term

The changeover to a Democratically controlled House abruptly ended Hunter's chairmanship of Armed Services, where the decorated Vietnam War veteran has served for more than 25 years. But with his deep knowledge of defense-related issues, Hunter, as the committee's top-ranking Republican, is likely to be a force in the debate over strategy in Iraq until 2008, when he plans to retire from Congress.

In early 2007, Hunter made it known that he planned to leave the House whether or not his long-shot bid for president in 2008 was successful. That paved the way for his son, Marine 1st Lt. Duncan Duane Hunter, to run for the seat. The younger Duncan served in Iraq.

Although he often won't toe the Bush administration line, Hunter has backed the president 100 percent on the war in Iraq. When House Democrats called for a phased withdrawal of U.S. troops, the senior Hunter led the charge with a stunt that temporarily silenced the war critics. In November 2005, he sponsored a resolution calling for the deployment of U.S. troops in Iraq to end immediately. Hunter, of course, held the opposite view, as did most Republicans. But he made his point — that the House at large supported the war — with a 3-403 vote against his proposal.

Hunter was also an important ally for President Bush in the fall of 2005 when Sen. John McCain, a Republican from Arizona and also a Vietnam War hero, sought to pass a ban on "cruel, inhuman, or degrading treatment or punishment" of suspected terrorists in U.S. custody, which the administration maintained would have crimped its intelligence gathering operation. Hunter unsuccessfully tried to get rid of the provision during the House-Senate conference on the annual defense authorization bill. He refused to sign the final document until then Director of National Intelligence John D. Negroponte assured him it would not "degrade" the country's ability to collect valuable intelligence information.

On other aspects of the annual defense bill, the 14-term House veteran feels entitled to go his own way. Hunter usually insists on "Buy America" rules that make it more difficult for the Pentagon to do business with foreign firms and that have drawn veto threats in the past. And for Hunter there is never enough money in military budgets for troop quality-of-life expenses. He added to the fiscal 2007 defense spending bill a provision giving heavily discounted health care benefits to military reservists.

Hunter's bill also took a different tack on a variety of weapons programs. He wanted less money for the new F-35 Joint Strike Fighter than the president and more for the C-17 Globemaster III transport plane, which the administration wanted to terminate.

In 2004, Hunter took a high-profile role in blocking a wide-ranging intelligence overhaul bill until he was satisfied it would allow U.S. troops untrammeled access to spying data. He regarded the creation of a new national intelligence director as a potential threat to the link between the Pentagon and intelligence provided by satellites and other means.

His independence sometimes makes him an uncomfortable ally for the defense establishment. He sounds out independent experts and occasionally challenges the armed services. In the early 1990s, he battled to make the Navy explore more novel designs and missions for nuclear-powered submarines. And over the Pentagon's objections, he has pushed for a pilot program to let small companies bid to take over some weapons programs.

A member of the Armed Services panel since he was elected to the

House at age 32, Hunter supported President Ronald Reagan's military buildup in the 1980s and was a critic of President Bill Clinton's reduced defense budgets in the 1990s. Now in his late 50s, Hunter is relatively young for one with his legislative seniority. He is tied as the seventh-longest-serving House Republican. His sometimes boisterous informality contrasts with the courtliness of his counterpart, Senate Armed Services senior Republican John W. Warner of Virginia. Still, Hunter has a solid grasp of the arguments and a forceful style of presentation.

On fiscal and social issues, he casts a reliably conservative vote. In the early 1980s, he was a leader of the Conservative Opportunity Society, founded by then GOP Rep. and later Speaker Newt Gingrich. On trade and border security issues, Hunter's views blend conservative populism with a concern for keeping U.S.-developed technology out of hostile hands. When the House voted in 2000 to grant China normal trade status, Hunter led a band of Republicans warning that the vote would help Beijing rebuild its military. Hunter opposed the 1993 North American Free Trade Agreement and has worked to upgrade fences along the Mexican border.

The biggest influence in Hunter's life was his father, Robert O. Hunter, a former Marine who joined up after the Japanese attack on Pearl Harbor. After the war, his father settled in Riverside, Calif., and ran a cattle ranch and construction firm. He ran once unsuccessfully for the House.

Hunter's early life followed a similar pattern. He dropped out of the University of California at Santa Barbara to join the Army because he felt compelled to serve in Vietnam. Furthermore, he wasn't that interested in school; he was "the proud bearer of a 1.7 grade point average," he says. Hunter won a Bronze Star for participating in 25 helicopter combat assaults.

After the service, Hunter buckled down to academics and got a law degree. For three years in the late 1970s, he ran a storefront legal office in San Diego's Barrio Logan, often giving free legal advice to poor Hispanics.

In 1980, his father urged him to challenge nine-term Democrat Lionel Van Deerlin in what was then California's 42nd District. Hunter's work in the usually Democratic inner city and his tireless campaigning helped produce an upset victory over Van Deerlin, whom he portrayed as "anti-defense." He promised that a pro-Pentagon stance would keep jobs in the San Diego area, which has the nation's largest naval base and numerous defense industries. With a boost from the Reagan landslide that year, he won with 53 percent of the vote.

He secured his hold on the district in ensuing campaigns, except for a difficult run in 1992, when he was held to 53 percent.

KEY VOTES

2006

No Stop broadband companies from favoring select Internet traffic
Yes Affirm U.S. commitment to war in Iraq and reject setting a withdrawal date for troops
Yes Repeal requirement for bilingual ballots at the polls
Yes Permit U.S. sale of civilian nuclear technology to India
Yes Build a 700-mile fence on the U.S.-Mexico border to curb illegal crossings
Yes Permit warrantless wiretaps of suspected terrorists

2005

? Intervene in the life-support case of Terri Schiavo
No Lift President Bush's restrictions on stem cell research funding
No Prohibit FBI access to library and bookstore records
No Approve free-trade pact with five Central American countries
Yes Pass energy policy overhaul favored by President Bush emphasizing domestic oil and gas production
Yes End mandatory preservation of habitat of endangered animal and plant species
No Ban torture of prisoners in U.S. custody

CQ VOTE STUDIES

	PARTY UNITY		PRESIDENTIAL SUPPORT	
	Support	Oppose	Support	Oppose
2006	94%	6%	92%	8%
2005	97%	3%	89%	11%
2004	95%	5%	84%	16%
2003	96%	4%	91%	9%
2002	94%	6%	78%	22%

INTEREST GROUPS

	AFL-CIO	ADA	CCUS	ACU
2006	15%	5%	93%	88%
2005	20%	5%	88%	92%
2004	7%	5%	95%	87%
2003	20%	10%	83%	83%
2002	33%	10%	75%	88%

CALIFORNIA 52

Eastern San Diego; inland San Diego County

The 52nd wraps around the east side of San Diego from Poway in the north to east of Otay Mesa in the south, and stretches about 100 miles east and north through mountains and protected desert parks to reach San Diego County's borders with Riverside and Imperial counties. The overwhelming majority of residents either live in predominately wealthy, conservative suburbs, or are among the roughly 15 percent of the city of San Diego's population included in the 52nd.

After years of slow economic growth, El Cajon and Santee are in the midst of a housing boom, as property values have increased over the last decade. Poway, whose economic roots lie in agriculture, has a more wealthy, rural feel to it than the surrounding suburban sprawl, where growth is becoming a hot issue. Just outside of Poway is an expanse of evenly developed "suburbs" that includes part of Rancho Bernardo (shared with the 49th and 50th) and Scripps Ranch. Those areas, within San Diego's city limits, have attracted both retirees and young families.

San Diego's large military and defense-related workforce contributes to both the district's conservatism and its robust economy. Although most of the area's military bases are in the 53rd, many residents commute to nearby defense contracting jobs. In 2006, San Diego County voters rejected a ballot proposal to move commercial flight operations from Lindbergh Field (in the 53rd) to the current site of the Miramar air station.

The district is nearly three-fourths white, and blue- and white-collar workers alike tend to vote Republican. Arnold Schwarzenegger took 72 percent of the 2006 gubernatorial vote here — his second-best showing.

MAJOR INDUSTRY

Technology, manufacturing, defense

MILITARY BASES

Marine Corps Air Station Miramar, 8,850 military, 1,150 civilian (2007) (shared with the 50th)

CITIES

San Diego (pt.), 164,554; El Cajon, 94,869; La Mesa, 54,749; Santee, 52,975; Poway, 48,044

NOTABLE

The Unarius Academy of Science, based in El Cajon, believes UFOs will bring new technologies that will enable humanity to begin a new civilization without pollution or poverty.

Rep. Susan A. Davis (D)

CAPITOL OFFICE
225-2040
susan.davis@mail.house.gov
www.house.gov/susandavis
1526 Longworth 20515-0553; fax 225-2948

COMMITTEES
Armed Services
Education & Labor
House Administration

RESIDENCE
San Diego

BORN
April 13, 1944, Cambridge, Mass.

RELIGION
Jewish

FAMILY
Husband, Steve Davis; two children

EDUCATION
U. of California, Berkeley, B.A. 1965 (sociology); U. of North Carolina, M.A. 1968 (social work)

CAREER
High school leadership program director; public television producer; social worker

POLITICAL HIGHLIGHTS
San Diego Unified School District Board of Education, 1983-92 (president, 1989-92); Calif. Assembly, 1994-2000

ELECTION RESULTS

2006 GENERAL		
Susan A. Davis (D)	97,541	67.6%
John "Woody" Woodrum (R)	43,312	30.0%
Ernie Lippe (LIBERT)	3,534	2.4%
2006 PRIMARY		
Susan A. Davis (D)		unopposed
2004 GENERAL		
Susan A. Davis (D)	146,449	66.1%
Darin Hunzeker (R)	63,897	28.9%
Lawrence P. Rockwood (GREEN)	7,523	3.4%
Adam Van Susteren (LIBERT)	3,567	1.6%

PREVIOUS WINNING PERCENTAGES
2002 (62%); 2000 (50%)

Elected 2000; 4th term

A former local school board member, Davis makes education her focus in Congress, though she also has a strong interest in military issues. Her district is home to three universities, and she represents most of San Diego's numerous military bases.

On the Education and Labor Committee, Davis is an ally of fellow Californian and House Speaker Nancy Pelosi, who first urged Davis to run for the House and helped her raise money. Davis is a proponent of the Democratic position that demands imposed on schools by President Bush's much-touted No Child Left Behind Act of 2001 should be fully funded by the federal government. In 2005, she was a vocal opponent of the administration's efforts to cut vocational education funds. She told the San Diego Union-Tribune, "Education cuts are sending the wrong message to our kids."

On the Armed Services Committee, Davis has been active in efforts to improve the troops' quality of life in housing, pay and health care. She has sponsored bills to maintain military families' eligibility for such government programs as free or reduced-cost school lunches and supplementary security income, which provides payments to the poor, elderly and disabled.

Often, she combines her interests in education and the military: In the 109th Congress (2005-06), she offered a bill to prevent veterans' contributions to education benefits from reducing other federal student aid.

She has been successful with legislation expanding veterans' home loans and disability benefits. Her proposal was part of a veterans' benefits package that also contained Davis-authored protections for veterans who have to rely on someone else to manage their federal benefits, citing evidence that these fiduciaries embezzled thousands of dollars from veterans.

In the 110th Congress (2007-08), Davis expanded her issues portfolio to include election reform. She was appointed to the House Administration Committee, which oversees federal elections as well as internal operations of the House. From her new perch, Davis offered legislation to lift restrictions on absentee ballots and another bill to prohibit state elections officials from campaigning for federal candidates if they have a role in overseeing the candidates' election.

One of Davis' longstanding concerns is the regulation of diet supplements, an interest that dates to her service in the California Assembly. Davis wrote state legislation to restrict sales of supplements containing ephedrine and to more closely regulate supplements in general. An ephedrine-labeling bill written by Davis passed, only to be vetoed by Democratic Gov. Gray Davis, who called it a federal matter. Once in Congress, she took the governor's hint: She wrote bills requiring dietary supplement manufacturers to provide the Food and Drug Administration with a list of their products and reports of serious adverse reactions. Late in 2003, the FDA announced it was banning the sale of ephedrine.

She is a loyal Democrat; in the 109th Congress, she voted with her party 95 percent of the time on votes in which the parties held different positions.

Davis has supported Bush on some international trade issues, which has sometimes gotten her into hot water with organized labor. In 2001, she voted in favor of giving the president authority to negotiate trade agreements that cannot be amended by Congress. Several of her pro-trade colleagues in the moderate New Democrat Coalition voted against it, saying that the timing was wrong. Davis was among only 21 members of her party — and one of only two from California — voting yes. She said that on balance the bill would benefit her district. Still, she called it the "most agonizing vote of my first year in Washington." She also broke with her party in 2003 to back trade agreements with Chile and Singapore, but in 2005, she opposed the Central American Free Trade Agreement.

Davis was raised in Richmond, Calif., the daughter of a pediatrician father. She was studying social work in graduate school in North Carolina when she met Steve Davis, who was studying to be a psychiatrist. They married, and spent two years in Japan while he served in the Air Force.

When the family returned stateside and eventually settled in San Diego, Davis became active in community affairs. She joined the League of Women Voters, serving as the president of the San Diego chapter. She also worked at the local public television station.

In 1983, when California Democrat Robert Filner, who now represents the neighboring 51st District, left the San Diego school board to run for the city council, Davis won the election to replace him. While still on the school board, she helped start a local fellowship program for preteens and teenagers to learn about how business and government work. She did not seek re-election to the school board in 1992 and became the fellowship program's first executive director.

Two years later, she won the first of three terms in the California Assembly. She worked on a state law that allows women to directly access an obstetrician-gynecologist, rather than first having to obtain a referral. Once in the U.S. House, she introduced similar legislation at the federal level.

A California law on term limits barred Davis from running again for the Assembly in 2000. Pelosi urged her to run for Congress instead, inviting Davis to shadow her for a day at the Capitol, mentoring her and providing fundraising contacts.

The political vulnerability of the 49th District's GOP incumbent, Brian P. Bilbray, who had twice won with less than 50 percent of the vote, provided Davis with an opportunity. She took advantage of it, capturing the seat by a narrow 3 percentage point margin.

Davis' vote in favor of the president's trade legislation cost her the support of the AFL-CIO, which had pumped almost a quarter million dollars into the 2000 campaign.

But in 2002, without the labor group's backing, Davis benefited from the newly drawn 53rd District lines that transformed her previously marginal district into a safer one. She won with 62 percent of the vote and was easily re-elected in 2004 and 2006.

KEY VOTES

2006

- Yes Stop broadband companies from favoring select Internet traffic
- No Affirm U.S. commitment to war in Iraq and reject setting a withdrawal date for troops
- No Repeal requirement for bilingual ballots at the polls
- Yes Permit U.S. sale of civilian nuclear technology to India
- No Build a 700-mile fence on the U.S.-Mexico border to curb illegal crossings
- No Permit warrantless wiretaps of suspected terrorists

2005

- ? Intervene in the life-support case of Terri Schiavo
- Yes Lift President Bush's restrictions on stem cell research funding
- Yes Prohibit FBI access to library and bookstore records
- No Approve free-trade pact with five Central American countries
- No Pass energy policy overhaul favored by President Bush emphasizing domestic oil and gas production
- No End mandatory preservation of habitat of endangered animal and plant species
- Yes Ban torture of prisoners in U.S. custody

CQ VOTE STUDIES

	PARTY UNITY		PRESIDENTIAL SUPPORT	
	Support	Oppose	Support	Oppose
2006	94%	6%	26%	74%
2005	96%	4%	20%	80%
2004	95%	5%	33%	67%
2003	93%	7%	18%	82%
2002	92%	8%	35%	65%

INTEREST GROUPS

	AFL-CIO	ADA	CCUS	ACU
2006	86%	90%	33%	8%
2005	93%	90%	41%	0%
2004	93%	100%	43%	4%
2003	87%	90%	33%	12%
2002	89%	90%	50%	8%

CALIFORNIA 53

Downtown San Diego; Imperial Beach

The coastal 53rd is the economic engine that drives surrounding districts. It includes San Diego's downtown, large employers and most of its military bases. The district also runs south along the Pacific Coast through Coronado and Imperial Beach to the Mexican border.

The defense industry, based around the military installations, is a major economic contributor. Tourists also flock to the area to enjoy the mild climate, wide beaches and attractions, such as SeaWorld, Balboa Park (including the San Diego Zoo) and PETCO Park, where baseball's Padres play. Condos, hotels and restaurants in the revived downtown attract young professionals and suburban residents who work nearby. Local environmentalists are split over long-term solutions to pollution and sewage that still cause occasional beach closures.

Colleges in the district include the University of California, San Diego in the north, San Diego State University and the University of San Diego. Some private companies have formed research agreements with the schools, and the district's economy also has benefited from biotechnology and telecommunications firms, such as Qualcomm.

The 53rd includes Hispanic Democratic sections east of the city in places such as Lemon Grove, as well as blue-collar, central city areas like North Park, City Heights, Barrio Logan and Hillcrest, one of the area's most liberal and Democratic neighborhoods and the center of the city's gay community. Overall, the district is less than one-third Hispanic, and residents here gave John Kerry 61 percent of the 2004 presidential vote.

MAJOR INDUSTRY

Defense, tourism, biotechnology, telecommunications, higher education

MILITARY BASES

Naval Station San Diego (shared with the 51st), 28,460 military, 8,423 civilian (2005); Naval Air Station North Island/Naval Amphibious Base Coronado, 27,000 military, 8,000 civilian (2006); Naval Base Point Loma, 5,942 military, 13,631 civilian (2005); Naval Medical Center San Diego, 3,270 military, 2,260 civilian (2007); Marine Corps Recruit Depot San Diego, 1,450 military, 1,230 civilian (2007)

CITIES

San Diego (pt.), 542,356; Imperial Beach, 26,992; Lemon Grove, 24,918

NOTABLE

Imperial Beach is home to the U.S. Open Sandcastle Competition.

COLORADO

Gov. Bill Ritter Jr. (D)

First elected: 2006
Length of term: 4 years
Term expires: 1/11
Salary: $90,000
Phone: (303) 866-2471

Residence: Denver
Born: Sept. 6, 1956; Aurora, Colo.
Religion: Roman Catholic
Family: Wife, Jeannie Ritter; four children
Education: Colorado State U., B.A. 1978 (political science); U. of Colorado, J.D. 1981
Career: Lawyer; state prosecutor
Political highlights: Assistant U.S. attorney, 1990-92; Denver district attorney, 1993-2005

Election results:

2006 GENERAL		
Bill Ritter Jr. (D)	888,096	57.0%
Bob Beauprez (R)	625,886	40.2%
D. Winkler-Kinateder (LIBERT)	23,323	1.5%

Lt. Gov. Barbara O'Brien (D)

First elected: 2006
Length of term: 4 years
Term expires: 1/11
Salary: $68,500
Phone: (303) 866-2087

LEGISLATURE

General Assembly: 120 days January-May

Senate: 35 members, 4-year terms
2007 ratios: 20 D, 15 R; 24 men, 11 women
Salary: $30,000
Phone: (303) 866-2316

House: 65 members, 2-year terms
2007 ratios: 39 D, 26 R; 42 men, 23 women
Salary: $30,000
Phone: (303) 866-2904

TERM LIMITS

Governor: 2 terms
Senate: 2 consecutive terms
House: 4 consecutive terms

URBAN STATISTICS

CITY	POPULATION
Denver	554,636
Colorado Springs	360,890
Aurora	276,393
Lakewood	144,126
Fort Collins	118,652

REGISTERED VOTERS

Republican	36%
Unaffiliated	34%
Democrat	30%

POPULATION

2006 population (est.)	4,753,377
2000 population	4,301,261
1990 population	3,294,394
Percent change (1990-2000)	+30.6%
Rank among states (2006)	22
Median age	34.3
Born in state	41.1%
Foreign born	8.6%
Violent crime rate	334/100,000
Poverty level	9.3%
Federal workers	51,455
Military	42,802

ELECTIONS

STATE ELECTION OFFICIAL
(303) 894-2200
DEMOCRATIC PARTY
(303) 623-4762
REPUBLICAN PARTY
(303) 758-3333

MISCELLANEOUS

Web: www.colorado.gov
Capital: Denver

U.S. CONGRESS

Senate: 1 Democrat, 1 Republican
House: 4 Democrats, 3 Republicans

2000 Census Statistics by District

DIST.	2004 VOTE FOR PRESIDENT BUSH	KERRY	WHITE	BLACK	ASIAN	HISP	MEDIAN INCOME	WHITE COLLAR	BLUE COLLAR	SERVICE INDUSTRY	OVER 64	UNDER 18	COLLEGE EDUCATION	RURAL	SQ. MILES
1	31%	68%	54%	10%	3%	30%	$39,658	64%	21%	15%	11%	22%	34%	0%	171
2	41	58	79	1	3	15	$55,204	66	21	13	7	25	39	13	5,615
3	55	44	75	1	0	21	$35,970	56	26	17	13	25	24	39	53,963
4	58	41	79	1	1	17	$43,389	60	26	14	10	26	29	25	30,898
5	66	33	77	6	2	11	$45,454	63	21	15	9	27	30	14	7,708
6	60	39	88	2	3	6	$73,393	77	13	9	7	29	47	15	4,104
7	48	51	69	6	3	20	$46,149	63	24	13	10	25	26	2	1,258
STATE	52	47	74	4	2	17	$47,203	65	22	14	10	26	33	16	103,718
U.S.	50.7	48.3	69	12	4	13	$41,994	60	25	15	12	26	24	21	3,537,438

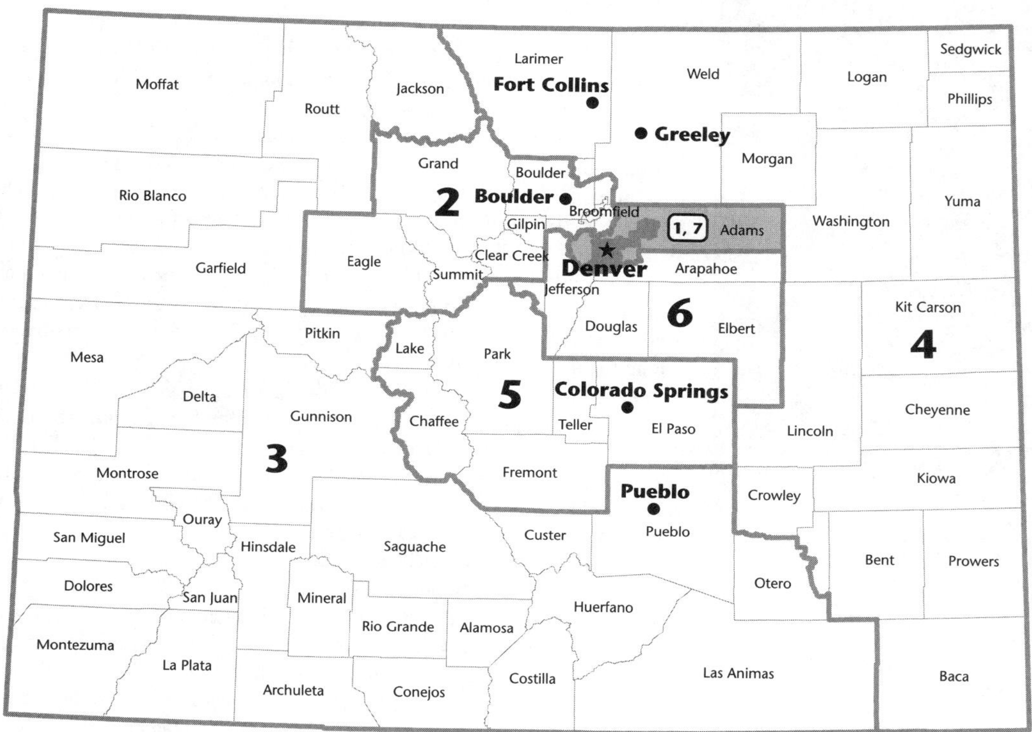
Moffat
Routt
Jackson
Larimer
Fort Collins
Weld
Logan
Sedgwick
Phillips
Greeley
Morgan
Rio Blanco
Grand
Boulder
2
Boulder
Broomfield
Gilpin
1, 7
Adams
Yuma
Washington
Garfield
Eagle
Summit
Clear Creek
Denver
Arapahoe
Jefferson
Kit Carson
4
Douglas
6
Elbert
Mesa
Pitkin
Lake
Park
Delta
5
Colorado Springs
Gunnison
Chaffee
Teller
El Paso
Lincoln
Cheyenne
3
Montrose
Fremont
Pueblo
Kiowa
Crowley
Ouray
San Miguel
Hinsdale
Saguache
Custer
Pueblo
Bent
Prowers
Dolores
San Juan
Mineral
Otero
Huerfano
Montezuma
Rio Grande
Alamosa
La Plata
Costilla
Las Animas
Baca
Archuleta
Conejos

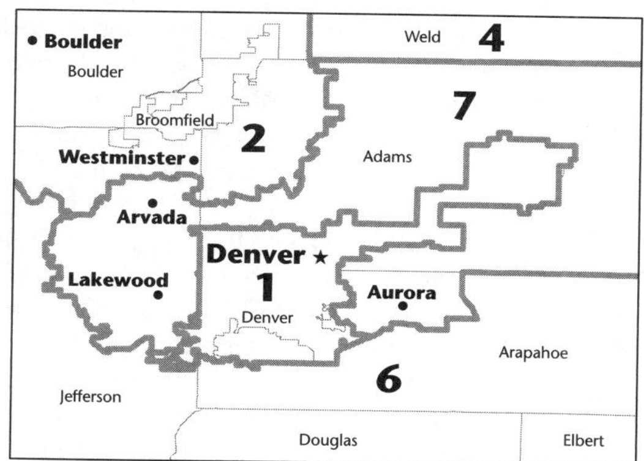
Boulder
Boulder
Weld
4
7
Broomfield
2
Westminster
Adams
Arvada
Denver
1
Lakewood
Aurora
Denver
Arapahoe
6
Jefferson
Douglas
Elbert

Sen. Wayne Allard (R)

CAPITOL OFFICE
224-5941
allard.senate.gov/public
521 Dirksen 20510-0606; fax 224-6471

COMMITTEES
Appropriations
Banking, Housing & Urban Affairs
Budget
Health, Education, Labor & Pensions

RESIDENCE
Loveland

BORN
Dec. 2, 1943, Fort Collins, Colo.

RELIGION
Protestant

FAMILY
Wife, Joan Allard; two children

EDUCATION
Colorado State U., D.V.M. 1968

CAREER
Veterinarian

POLITICAL HIGHLIGHTS
Colo. Senate, 1983-91; U.S. House, 1991-97

ELECTION RESULTS

2002 GENERAL		
Wayne Allard (R)	717,892	50.7%
Tom Strickland (D)	648,129	45.8%
Douglas Campbell (AC)	21,547	1.5%
Rick Stanley (LIBERT)	20,776	1.5%
2002 PRIMARY		
Wayne Allard (R)		unopposed

PREVIOUS WINNING PERCENTAGES
1996 (51%); 1994 House Election (72%); 1992 House Election (58%); 1990 House Election (54%)

Elected 1996; 2nd term

Allard's fans regularly describe the fifth-generation Colorado native as "a workhorse, not a showhorse." His campaign staff began to use that term more than a decade ago, when the affable senator with a plodding style was building a reputation in the House for a unique brand of pro-business environmentalism coupled with fiscal and social conservatism.

But Colorado's shifting demographics and political landscape — Democrats scored major gains in the state over the past two elections — left Allard increasingly vulnerable. His announcement in early 2007 that he would honor his term limit pledge and retire at the end of his second term came as no surprise. Democrats had already targeted the seat as a top 2008 takeover prospect, with Rep. Mark Udall signaling his intent to go after it long before Allard said he would retire.

In 2006, Allard's low profile on national issues helped land him on Time Magazine's list of the five worst members of the U.S. Senate. The cutting article said Allard is so bland that he is known by some as "Dullard." He says he doesn't mind being assailed for a lack of pizzazz because Colorado voters did not send him to Washington to make a media splash. He is well-liked by colleagues across the political spectrum, and his resolve often is underestimated by his political foes.

A product of the modern West, Allard is a states' rights-loving conservative with an innate skepticism of the federal government. But he sometimes is confoundingly pro-environment, to the distraction of his liberal critics who derisively describe him as "environmental lite."

Raised on a ranch near Walden, in one of Colorado's most isolated areas, Allard started his career as a veterinarian. His anti-tax and anti-regulatory positions are among the most conservative in the Senate. But despite the Senate's push to the right after the 2004 election, the low-key Allard was passed over for the chairmanship of the Budget Committee in favor of Judd Gregg of New Hampshire, a more assertive fiscal conservative.

Allard proudly declares on his Web site that he is "the most frugal member of the Colorado delegation," having returned more than $4.2 million in unspent office funds to the national treasury. He supported President Bush's massive tax cuts in 2001 and 2003, and as the 2010 expiration date for several of those tax cuts looms, Allard says renewing them will be among his highest priorities in his final two years in office.

Allard started the 110th Congress (2007-08) battling Democratic efforts to raise the federal minimum wage for the first time in a decade. He offered a floor amendment to exempt states with a minimum wage rate below the proposed $7.25 per hour federal level, but it was overwhelmingly defeated.

The Republicans' loss of the majority in the 2006 elections diminished the likelihood of another vote on the one issue that garnered national attention for Allard during his current term: a proposed constitutional amendment to outlaw same-sex marriage. Allard was the chief Senate sponsor of the amendment, which Colorado Republican Marilyn Musgrave offered in the House. He trumpeted it as an effort to protect the institution of marriage from "activist judges," but in both 2004 and 2006 the measure fell far short of the 60 votes needed to overcome a filibuster.

Allard gave up his seats on the Armed Services and Environment and Public Works committees in the 109th Congress (2005-06) to join the Appropriations Committee. As chairman of the Legislative Branch Subcommittee during that two-year Congress, he had the thankless task of overseeing construction of the Capitol Visitor Center. Lawmakers' frustration with massive cost overruns and constant construction delays reached a new high just as Allard became responsible for the project's funding. As some of his colleagues howled at management decisions of Architect of the Capitol Alan M. Hantman and demanded his resignation, Allard began holding monthly hearings on the center's progress. The hearings forced a new level of accountability from Hantman, who had to explain each delay and cost overrun as it occurred.

Of his years serving on the Environment panel, Allard is proudest of his success in establishing the Great Sand Dunes National Park in south-central Colorado and converting the radioactivity-tainted Rocky Flats, a former nuclear weapons facility outside Denver, to a national wildlife refuge. In the 109th Congress, he also won enactment of a measure to establish a pristine quarter-mile area of land on each side of the Rio Grande River as it flows through Colorado. The law also seeks to prevent a federal water right from being asserted in the protected area.

Still, national environmental groups assail Allard for his anti-regulatory stands on clean water mandates and the protection of endangered species. The League of Conservation Voters labeled Allard one of its "dirty dozen" and supported his opponent in the 2002 election.

Allard says he tries to strike a balance between economic development and protection of the environment. "You have to be sensitive to the environment but also protect private property rights and Colorado's water rights as well," he says. "That's where I get crosswise with the environmental groups in Washington."

In his three House terms, Allard compiled a solidly conservative record. He advocated eliminating the Education, Energy and Commerce departments and backed a constitutional amendment banning abortion.

The senator subscribes to the concept of the citizen-politician. He grew up on his family's ranch, rising at dawn and working until sunset baling hay. His great-great-grandfather, a trapper and explorer, was among the first permanent settlers of northern Colorado.

Allard wanted to be a veterinarian from the time he was in grade school. So after getting his degree in veterinary medicine from Colorado State University, he and his microbiologist wife, Joan, opened their own small-animal practice in Loveland, northwest of Denver.

Allard's first government job was as Loveland's part-time health officer. Later, he divided his time between the Colorado state Senate and his veterinary practice for eight years. In 1990, Republican Hank Brown, then the 4th District representative, decided to run for the Senate, and Allard successfully sought Brown's seat.

Brown gave Allard another opening by retiring from the Senate after just one term. The 1996 GOP primary became a showdown between Allard and state Attorney General Gale A. Norton. Norton had greater statewide name recognition, but Allard had better fundraising. He easily won the primary. (Norton went on to become Interior secretary in 2001.)

Allard created a stir in the 1996 general election when, during a televised debate with Democratic nominee Tom Strickland, he responded affirmatively to a hypothetical question about whether he would support public hanging to deter crime. Allard also drew vigorous opposition from environmentalists but won strong support from conservative Christian groups, and went on to win by 5 percentage points.

In a 2002 rematch, Strickland tried again to make the environment an issue. Allard fought back with a campaign that summed up the election as a choice between a "lawyer lobbyist or a veterinarian who loves animals." He won with just 51 percent of the vote, no improvement over 1996.

KEY VOTES

2006

- Yes Confirm Samuel A. Alito Jr. to the Supreme Court
- Yes Allow consideration of a bill to establish a $140 billion trust fund to compensate victims of asbestos exposure
- Yes Extend tax cuts for two years at a cost of $70 billion over five years
- No Overhaul immigration policy with border security, enforcement and guest worker program
- Yes Allow consideration of a bill to permanently repeal the estate tax
- No Urge President Bush to begin troop withdrawals from Iraq in 2006
- No Lift President Bush's restrictions on stem cell research funding
- Yes Authorize military tribunals for suspected terrorists

2005

- Yes Curb class action lawsuits by shifting them from state to federal courts
- Yes Allow confirmation vote on Priscilla R. Owen to the U.S. Court of Appeals for the 5th Circuit
- Yes Oppose mandatory emissions limits and block recognition of global warming as a threat
- Yes Approve free-trade pact with five Central American countries
- Yes Pass energy policy overhaul favored by President Bush emphasizing domestic oil and gas production
- Yes Shield gunmakers from lawsuits when their products are used in crimes
- No Ban torture of prisoners in U.S. custody
- Yes Renew 16 provisions of the Patriot Act
- Yes Allow final vote on opening the Arctic National Wildlife Refuge to oil and gas exploration

CQ VOTE STUDIES

	PARTY UNITY		PRESIDENTIAL SUPPORT	
	Support	Oppose	Support	Oppose
2006	95%	5%	91%	9%
2005	97%	3%	98%	2%
2004	98%	2%	98%	2%
2003	98%	2%	97%	3%
2002	91%	9%	96%	4%
2001	98%	2%	97%	3%
2000	98%	2%	35%	65%
1999	97%	3%	23%	77%
1998	97%	3%	28%	72%
1997	98%	2%	48%	52%

INTEREST GROUPS

	AFL-CIO	ADA	CCUS	ACU
2006	13%	0%	92%	88%
2005	21%	0%	89%	96%
2004	8%	5%	94%	96%
2003	0%	10%	100%	70%
2002	17%	5%	100%	100%
2001	6%	5%	100%	100%
2000	0%	0%	93%	100%
1999	0%	0%	100%	95%
1998	0%	5%	83%	100%
1997	0%	0%	80%	100%

Sen. Ken Salazar (D)

CAPITOL OFFICE
224-5852
salazar.senate.gov
702 Hart 20510-0605; fax 228-5036

COMMITTEES
Agriculture, Nutrition & Forestry
Energy & Natural Resources
Finance
Select Ethics
Special Aging

RESIDENCE
Denver

BORN
March 2, 1955, Alamosa, Colo.

RELIGION
Roman Catholic

FAMILY
Wife, Hope Salazar; two children

EDUCATION
Colorado College, B.A. 1977 (political science); U. of Michigan, J.D. 1981

CAREER
Lawyer; ice cream shop owner; gubernatorial aide; farmer

POLITICAL HIGHLIGHTS
Colo. Natural Resources Department executive director, 1990-94; Colo. attorney general, 1999-2005

ELECTION RESULTS

2004 GENERAL		
Ken Salazar (D)	1,081,188	51.3%
Pete Coors (R)	980,668	46.5%
2004 PRIMARY		
Ken Salazar (D)	173,167	73.0%
Mike Miles (D)	63,973	27.0%

Elected 2004; 1st term

With his wire-rim glasses and thinning gray hair, Salazar looks more like a college professor than a rancher-politician. But his family has owned a ranch in Colorado's San Luis Valley since the 1850s. And he and his brother John, a member of the House, are at once beneficiaries and architects of their state's recent political shift toward the Democratic Party.

Both were elected in 2004. Both are centrists who have avoided polarizing positions and found ways to appeal to the independent-minded, hardworking, live-and-let-live voters of their rapidly changing state. Ken, the younger of the two, is the more seasoned politician. He served as state director of natural resources and as Colorado's attorney general before his election to the Senate. Midway through his first term, he was already turning up on lists of potential 2008 Democratic vice presidential possibilities.

The brothers' simultaneous election made their triumph all the sweeter. They rented a Capitol Hill apartment together when they first arrived in Washington and later bought a condo about a mile and a half away. They wanted a place closer, but, the senator said, "It's just too expensive!"

Although Salazar and Florida Republican Mel Martinez, also elected in 2004, became the first Hispanics to serve in the Senate since Democrat Joseph M. Montoya of New Mexico left in 1977, the Coloradan resists being pigeonholed as a spokesman for Hispanic issues. "I'm a U.S. senator for all the people of Colorado," he says firmly.

In his first two years, he focused on agriculture and energy issues crucial to his state. At the start of the 110th Congress (2007-08), he was awarded a coveted seat on the Finance Committee. He uses it to press for an end to the alternative minimum tax, for tax incentives for renewable energy and for breaks for small businesses, including a permanent overhaul of the federal estate tax to protect family farms and businesses.

The estate tax repeal is an issue more often championed by Republicans, but Salazar is a different breed of Democrat. He picks his way carefully through the legislative minefield, siding with the business community and Republicans on some measures, such as a 2005 bill to limit class action lawsuits, while backing labor and the Democrats on others, such as opposition to the Central American Free Trade Agreement.

He has a unique perspective on small-business issues, having owned a Dairy Queen in Westminster, Colo., with his wife, Hope. Salazar and his wife also have invested in radio stations in Denver and Pueblo. One of eight children, Salazar grew up on a ranch in Colorado's mountainous San Luis Valley where his Mexican ancestors settled in 1850. Their home did not have electricity until after Salazar graduated from law school in 1981.

When he first arrived on Capitol Hill, he was surprised by the level of partisanship. "This is a town of divided camps," he says. But Majority Leader Harry Reid of Nevada "understands that I came from a moderate Western state. I've been given a lot of flexibility to do what I need to do."

Salazar in turn has helped persuade national Democratic leaders that a flexible, centrist approach can win over moderate voters in Colorado and other Western states once seen as hostile territory. The senator, along with Colorado's Democratic governor and Denver's mayor, succeeded in nabbing the party's 2008 national convention for Denver.

Salazar signaled his willingness to put partisanship aside early in the 109th Congress (2005-06) when he backed the high-profile Cabinet nominations of two of President Bush's closest allies: Condoleezza Rice as secretary of state and Alberto R. Gonzales as attorney general. In fact, Salazar introduced Gonzales at the start of his confirmation hearing before the Judiciary Committee. Salazar said he was "honored" to do so and noted that "he and I come from similar backgrounds." He was one of just six Democrats who voted to confirm Gonzales.

His praise turned to criticism in early 2007, amidst a growing uproar over the Justice Department's dismissal of eight U.S. attorneys. Salazar, who served as chief counsel for Colorado's then Gov. Roy Romer and later as Colorado attorney general, noted in a floor speech that if Justice allowed portions of the U.S. attorneys corps "to become a vehicle for political patronage," then Gonzales has "forfeited his right to lead the department."

In May 2005, Salazar cemented his centrist credentials as part of the Gang of 14 — seven Democrats and seven Republicans who formed a pivotal voting bloc to deter the bulk of Democratic filibusters against Bush's judicial nominees but also to block a Republican leadership plan to permanently end such filibusters.

Salazar sits on the Agriculture and Energy and Natural Resources committees. His understanding of agriculture issues is bone deep. A lifelong sportsman, he backs conservation efforts and opposes oil drilling in Alaska's Arctic National Wildlife Refuge. However, he supports increasing petroleum production as long as environmental concerns are adequately addressed.

On Iraq, Salazar has agreed with most Democrats that the war has been mishandled. In early 2007, he backed party leaders in seeking to put the Senate on record against Bush's new troop buildup.

Salazar was pegged early on as a rising star by Sen. Ben Nighthorse Campbell, the Democrat-turned-Republican whose seat he ultimately won when Campbell retired. Campbell had recommended him in 1994 to head the Bureau of Land Management. That was after Salazar had distinguished himself as a lawyer specializing in water and resources issues and had interrupted his quick rise at a well-heeled Denver law firm to become the governor's chief counsel.

Salazar got his first taste of Capitol Hill in the early 1990s as Colorado's director of natural resources, when he testified before Congress about water bills that would benefit his state. He won plaudits from both parties for crafting a program that used lottery funds for land conservation. But rather than take up Campbell's suggestion to join the federal government as the Bureau of Land Management chief, Salazar heeded the call of family and routine and returned to private practice. He also made time to coach his young daughters' basketball team.

Although he is sometimes accused of grandstanding, Salazar has mostly won praise from Republicans and Democrats for being a straight shooter and sharp negotiator. He won his first elective office in 1998, as state attorney general. He led a successful effort to squelch a ballot initiative to fund $2 million in water projects that Western Coloradans worried would benefit urban Denver at the expense of rural areas.

Salazar's national stature rose in 1999, when he joined GOP Gov. Bill Owens in a bipartisan response to the Columbine High School tragedy. The two organized a summit on youth violence and pushed through a ballot measure to limit firearms sales at gun shows. He broke with Owens, however, in 2003 to oppose a GOP redistricting effort, which ultimately failed.

Campbell's surprise retirement in 2004 gave Salazar an opening to run for the Senate, but he faced an uphill battle against well-financed beer magnate Pete Coors, a handsome political neophyte with unrivaled name recognition. Ultimately, Salazar's up-from-the-bootstraps biography and his independent image compared favorably with Coors' more privileged upbringing and Salazar won by almost 5 percentage points.

KEY VOTES

2006

- No Confirm Samuel A. Alito Jr. to the Supreme Court
- No Allow consideration of a bill to establish a $140 billion trust fund to compensate victims of asbestos exposure
- No Extend tax cuts for two years at a cost of $70 billion over five years
- \+ Overhaul immigration policy with border security, enforcement and guest worker program
- No Allow consideration of a bill to permanently repeal the estate tax
- Yes Urge President Bush to begin troop withdrawals from Iraq in 2006
- Yes Lift President Bush's restrictions on stem cell research funding
- Yes Authorize military tribunals for suspected terrorists

2005

- Yes Curb class action lawsuits by shifting them from state to federal courts
- Yes Allow confirmation vote on Priscilla R. Owen to the U.S. Court of Appeals for the 5th Circuit
- No Oppose mandatory emissions limits and block recognition of global warming as a threat
- No Approve free-trade pact with five Central American countries
- Yes Pass energy policy overhaul favored by President Bush emphasizing domestic oil and gas production
- Yes Shield gunmakers from lawsuits when their products are used in crimes
- Yes Ban torture of prisoners in U.S. custody
- No Renew 16 provisions of the Patriot Act
- No Allow final vote on opening the Arctic National Wildlife Refuge to oil and gas exploration

CQ VOTE STUDIES

	PARTY UNITY		PRESIDENTIAL SUPPORT	
	Support	Oppose	Support	Oppose
2006	90%	10%	58%	42%
2005	84%	16%	49%	51%

INTEREST GROUPS

	AFL-CIO	ADA	CCUS	ACU
2006	80%	85%	64%	17%
2005	86%	100%	72%	32%

Rep. Diana DeGette (D)

CAPITOL OFFICE
225-4431
www.house.gov/degette
2421 Rayburn 20515-0601; fax 225-5657

COMMITTEES
Energy & Commerce

RESIDENCE
Denver

BORN
July 29, 1957, Tachikawa, Japan

RELIGION
Presbyterian

FAMILY
Husband, Lino Lipinsky; two children

EDUCATION
Colorado College, B.A. 1979 (political science); New York U., J.D. 1982

CAREER
Lawyer; state public defender

POLITICAL HIGHLIGHTS
Colo. House, 1993-96 (assistant minority leader, 1995-96)

ELECTION RESULTS

2006 GENERAL		
Diana DeGette (D)	129,446	79.8%
Thomas D. Kelly (GREEN)	32,825	20.2%
2006 PRIMARY		
Diana DeGette (D)		unopposed
2004 GENERAL		
Diana DeGette (D)	177,077	73.5%
Roland Chicas (R)	58,659	24.4%
George C. Lilly (AC)	5,193	2.2%

PREVIOUS WINNING PERCENTAGES
2002 (66%); 2000 (69%); 1998 (67%); 1996 (57%)

Elected 1996; 6th term

DeGette's unflinching legislative style is like that of a practiced attorney, which she also is. She presents her case with passion and fights to win. She may compromise to get results, but she does not give in easily.

For years, she has fought to lift President Bush's restrictions on federally funded embryonic stem cell research. Despite its promise for developing treatments for many serious diseases, Bush opposes it, saying such research would "support and encourage the destruction of human life." He vetoed a stem cell bill that cleared Congress in 2006.

Undeterred, DeGette (de-GET) reintroduced the measure and the House passed it again in the opening days of the new Democratically controlled 110th Congress (2007-08). But the final count was still 37 votes short of the two-thirds majority required to override a veto. Bush refused to meet with DeGette and other bill supporters, and she would not pare back her measure. "My attitude is — having been a litigator for 15 years — I am not going to negotiate against myself," she said. "The next president of the United States will be pro-stem cell research."

She also moved to build the majorities in Congress for federally supported research, renaming her political action committee the Stem Cell Action Fund. Contributions have taken off since she announced that the money raised would be doled out to candidates who support the research.

Now in her sixth term, DeGette is one of nine chief deputy Democratic whips, and she is a member of the party's Steering and Policy Committee, which develops strategy and makes committee assignments. She briefly considered running for majority whip against South Carolina's James E. Clyburn, but backed off. "I am young enough and new enough in my career that I will have opportunities," she said.

DeGette had an auspicious arrival on Capitol Hill in 1997, when she was the only freshman to win a coveted assignment to the Energy and Commerce Committee. She soon made her presence felt on a broad array of topics: the budget, abortion rights, gun control, health care and tobacco regulation. At the start of the 110th Congress, her mentor, Chairman John D. Dingell, a Michigan Democrat, named her the panel's vice chairwoman.

Earlier this decade, DeGette was a fierce advocate of corporate responsibility, beginning with the 2002 bankruptcy of the energy behemoth Enron Corp. She took on one of her district's biggest employers, the regional telephone giant Qwest Communications International Inc. Some lawmakers would have tried to defend the hometown company, but DeGette used Qwest to demonstrate her pro-consumer views.

Her activism on embryonic stem cell research is shaped in part by personal experience: one of her daughters has diabetes. In the 108th Congress (2003-04), the House passed her plan to authorize $1 million to help those with juvenile diabetes by increasing access to islet cell transplantation, a procedure that infuses new insulin-producing cells into a patient. In the 107th Congress (2001-02), DeGette won enactment of a law requiring that pediatric experts review medical devices for children before they are put on the market.

DeGette is a defender of abortion rights, including the right of a woman to have a late-term procedure described by critics as "partial birth" abortion. "To assume that any woman would choose this tragic procedure after carrying a healthy fetus for 8 or 9 months is offensive to the women who are facing this gruesome decision," she has said.

Her longtime support of gun control intensified after 15 people died in the 1999 rampage at Columbine High School, just outside her district.

Although a loyal Democrat — she sided with a majority of her party 97 percent of the time in the 109th Congress of 2005-06 — she parted ways with most of her colleagues on legislation to make it easier to import prescription drugs. On the House floor in 2003, she held up a plastic bag of brand-name, brightly colored pills, which she said were all fakes. "I used to think I supported this legislation," she said, but she changed her mind after learning that "tons" of counterfeit drugs were entering the country.

Born in Japan where her father was stationed with the Air Force, DeGette spent most of her childhood in the Denver area. The eldest of five children, DeGette took some after-school jobs to help pay the bills when her parents divorced. She was deeply affected, at age 10, by the news coverage of the assassination of the Rev. Dr. Martin Luther King Jr. and the civil rights movement he led. "It hit me, the whole idea of social justice and fighting for equality. I decided I was going to become a lawyer."

After earning a law degree at New York University, DeGette became public defender in Denver and then went into private practice, specializing in cases of discrimination based on disability, sex and age.

She volunteered in the mayoral campaign of Federico Peña, who later served in President Bill Clinton's Cabinet. That spurred her interest in public office. "I can do these cases one at a time," she recalls thinking, "or I can get elected to office and I can affect many people by changing the laws."

She won a Colorado House seat in 1992. As a freshman member of the minority party, DeGette won enactment of a law — upheld by the Supreme Court in 2000 — requiring protesters to stay 8 feet from anyone within 100 feet of entrances to clinics where abortions are performed.

That so-called bubble bill made her a target of abortion opponents who have continued to protest at her home over the years. The demonstrations taught her to stand up to fierce criticism, she says, and "I think it's a good civics lesson for my kids. They understand the First Amendment and freedom of speech."

While in the state House, DeGette moved up to the party leadership. But she resigned from the legislature in early 1996 to concentrate on her bid to succeed liberal Democratic Rep. Patricia Schroeder in Congress.

DeGette won a highly publicized battle with Republican nominee Joe Rogers, a lawyer and former aide to Colorado GOP Sen. Hank Brown. Outspending her opponent 2-to-1, she prevailed by 17 percentage points. Her five re-elections have been with two-thirds or more of the vote.

KEY VOTES

2006

- Yes Stop broadband companies from favoring select Internet traffic
- No Affirm U.S. commitment to war in Iraq and reject setting a withdrawal date for troops
- No Repeal requirement for bilingual ballots at the polls
- Yes Permit U.S. sale of civilian nuclear technology to India
- No Build a 700-mile fence on the U.S.-Mexico border to curb illegal crossings
- No Permit warrantless wiretaps of suspected terrorists

2005

- ? Intervene in the life-support case of Terri Schiavo
- Yes Lift President Bush's restrictions on stem cell research funding
- Yes Prohibit FBI access to library and bookstore records
- No Approve free-trade pact with five Central American countries
- No Pass energy policy overhaul favored by President Bush emphasizing domestic oil and gas production
- No End mandatory preservation of habitat of endangered animal and plant species
- Yes Ban torture of prisoners in U.S. custody

CQ VOTE STUDIES

	PARTY UNITY		PRESIDENTIAL SUPPORT	
	Support	Oppose	Support	Oppose
2006	98%	2%	25%	75%
2005	96%	4%	16%	84%
2004	97%	3%	29%	71%
2003	96%	4%	30%	70%
2002	98%	2%	25%	75%

INTEREST GROUPS

	AFL-CIO	ADA	CCUS	ACU
2006	100%	95%	33%	4%
2005	87%	90%	37%	0%
2004	100%	90%	37%	0%
2003	86%	90%	31%	17%
2002	100%	95%	35%	0%

COLORADO 1

Denver

Shaped somewhat like a golfer's driver, the head of the 1st is the capital city of Denver, and its handle stretches north and east following the city limits to reach the airport. The 1st, a bastion of liberalism in a conservative-leaning state, is Colorado's smallest district in size, but Denver's presence allows the district to set the tone for the Centennial State's economic future.

Denver was once dependent on the region's oil and gas industries, but the city boomed during the 1990s as its economy became more diverse from technology and telecommunications companies. These industries now rival state government as the major employers here.

Health care also is important to Denver's economic well-being. There are several hospitals and service providers downtown or in surrounding areas, but the region's health industry is anchored by the University of Colorado at Denver and Health Sciences Center campus and bioscience research park at the former Fitzsimons Army Medical Center, located just outside the district's borders in Aurora (in the neighboring 7th).

Denver maintains a healthy tourism industry. Recent revitalization efforts to the city's lower downtown district, known by locals as "LoDo," have helped attract visitors. Large entertainment venues and a robust nightlife make Denver one of premier cities to visit between the West Coast and Midwest. Denver International Airport, which opened in 1995, has become one of the nation's busiest.

Denver has the most diverse population in Colorado — the district's fast-growing Hispanic community makes up nearly one-third of residents while blacks make up one-tenth. Ninety percent of the 1st's residents live in Denver, which has not sent a Republican to the U.S. House since 1970. John Kerry won 68 percent of the district's 2004 presidential vote, easily his highest percentage in the state.

MAJOR INDUSTRY

Telecommunications, computers, government, health care, tourism

CITIES

Denver, 554,636; Englewood, 31,727

NOTABLE

The Great American Beer Festival is the nation's largest and oldest annual brewing competition; The U.S. Mint coin production facility in Denver offers free tours to visitors.

Rep. Mark Udall (D)

CAPITOL OFFICE
225-2161
markudall.house.gov/hor/co02
100 Cannon 20515-0602; fax 226-7840

COMMITTEES
Armed Services
Natural Resources
Science & Technology
(Space & Aeronautics - chairman)

RESIDENCE
Eldorado Springs

BORN
July 18, 1950, Tucson, Ariz.

RELIGION
Unspecified

FAMILY
Wife, Maggie Fox; two children

EDUCATION
Williams College, B.A. 1972 (American civilization)

CAREER
Colo. Outward Bound School executive director

POLITICAL HIGHLIGHTS
Colo. House, 1997-99

ELECTION RESULTS

2006 GENERAL		
Mark Udall (D)	157,850	68.2%
Rich Mancuso (R)	65,481	28.3%
Norm Olsen (LIBERT)	5,025	2.2%
J.A. Calhoun (GREEN)	2,951	1.3%
2006 PRIMARY		
Mark Udall (D)		unopposed
2004 GENERAL		
Mark Udall (D)	207,900	67.2%
Stephen M. Hackman (R)	94,160	30.4%
Norm Olsen (LIBERT)	7,304	2.4%

PREVIOUS WINNING PERCENTAGES
2002 (60%); 2000 (55%); 1998 (50%)

Elected 1998; 5th term

With a likely Senate race in his future, Udall is following the well-worn political trail to the ideological center in anticipation of a statewide contest. His famous father, the late liberal Rep. Morris K. Udall, remains the chief influence in his life, but today he's just as likely to take his political cues from Republican Sen. John McCain, the opposing party's notorious maverick.

As Udall prepares to run for Colorado's open Senate seat in 2008, he has assumed more-moderate positions on immigration, the budget and even the environment, the signature issue for generations of Udalls. He angered Colorado environmentalists in 2006 by sponsoring a bill to ease environmental reviews of tree-cutting in forests damaged by an overabundance of bark beetles. Local officials wanted to get rid of dying trees that could lead to forest fires, but environmentalists feared it would hasten timber harvests without adequate review of the impact on the environment.

A few years earlier, when wildfires scorched large sections of Colorado in 2002, Udall helped broker a compromise with the Bush administration to ease some environmental rules for forest clearing. "I've looked to be a problem-solver and not blindly embrace a philosophy," he says.

In 2005, Udall voted for a get-tough immigration bill that was mainly written by conservatives and that encouraged local police to arrest immigration violators. He has to be politically sensitive to the wide swath of Coloradans who support Colorado conservative lawmaker and possible presidential candidate Tom Tancredo and his call for a crackdown on illegal immigration.

Also in 2005, Udall joined with some of the House's most conservative members in backing legislation to give the White House new authority over spending. In an unlikely alliance with the Republican Study Committee, he supported legislation allowing the president to remove specific items from appropriations bills, followed by an up-or-down vote by Congress. Udall says Democrats deserve as much credit as Republicans for the idea, noting he had introduced a similar bill earlier that year. Early in the 110th Congress (2007-08), he offered the bill again.

Like McCain, Udall is not hesitant to cross party lines to form alliances on legislation he wants to pass. The tall, telegenic lawmaker is popular with colleagues from both parties and regarded as thoughtful, principled and deliberative. He says McCain was a friend of his father's and someone he considers a role model. McCain often teams with Democrats on bills against the wishes of GOP leaders.

But on tough votes, Udall sticks with his party. He voted with a majority of Democrats 92 percent of the time on issues that polarized the parties in the 109th Congress (2005-06). In 2007, he became chairman of the Science and Technology panel's Space and Aeronautics Subcommittee.

He also has been a longstanding opponent of going to war with Iraq — Udall voted against the Bush administration's war resolution in 2002 — but he conspicuously did not join in calls for an immediate withdrawal. In 2005, Udall and Tom Osborne, a Nebraska Republican, wrote a letter to colleagues working on the defense bill urging them to accept the Senate's position prodding the administration to start bringing U.S. troops home in 2006. "We are overextended financially, militarily and diplomatically, and we're certainly not stronger for the invasion but weaker," says Udall, a member of the Armed Services Committee.

No issue hits home for a Udall like environmental protection. His uncle, Stewart Udall, was Interior secretary in the Kennedy and Johnson administrations. And from his seat on the Natural Resources Committee, Udall can see a portrait of his father, who chaired the panel (then known as Interior) from 1977 to 1991 and wrote legislation doubling the size of the national park system and tripling the extent of the national wilderness system.

In 2004, Udall helped lead a successful ballot initiative boosting the portion of electricity produced by in-state utilities that is derived from renewable energy sources. He and his cousin, Democratic Rep. Tom Udall of New Mexico, have promoted bills to create a program encouraging volunteers to help federal agencies preserve parks, forests and other sensitive tracts.

Udall was 10 years old when his father, a legendarily witty and energetic liberal, first won election to the House from Arizona in 1961. He remembers being rousted from sleep to join his five pajama-clad siblings to celebrate their father's first House victory. One of his proudest moments was witnessing "Mo" Udall, as he was known, become the first prominent House Democrat to come out against President Lyndon B. Johnson's troop buildup in Vietnam, during a speech at the University of Arizona in 1967.

The junior Udall purposely waited until later in life to get into politics. He says he wanted to step in when he felt ready, not simply to follow his father. After graduating from Williams College in 1972 with a degree in American civilization, Udall didn't go home to Arizona, but rather moved to Colorado's Western Slope and launched a career with the Colorado Outward Bound School. He was a course director for 10 years, then served as executive director from 1985 to 1995.

He was an avid mountain climber, scaling Kanchenjunga, the world's third-highest peak and attempting to reach the summit of Mount Everest in 1994 via a route that has been climbed only once. He says he gave up mountain climbing out of concern for his two young children.

In his first House race for the seat that Democrat David E. Skaggs gave up after a dozen years, Udall hammered hard when his GOP opponent, former Boulder Mayor Bob Greenlee, questioned the scientific validity of global warming. Udall also campaigned door-to-door to prove he was a "legitimate Coloradan" and not trying to capitalize on a famous name. In one of the more costly House races that year, Udall prevailed by just 5,500 votes, less than 3 percent. A month after the election, Mo Udall died of Parkinson's disease.

In subsequent elections, Udall's victory margins steadily increased to comfortably safe levels. He briefly entered the 2004 Colorado Senate race when Republican Sen. Ben Nighthorse Campbell retired, but withdrew once state Attorney General Ken Salazar decided to run. Udall announced in early 2005 that he would try for the Senate seat in 2008.

KEY VOTES

2006

- Yes Stop broadband companies from favoring select Internet traffic
- No Affirm U.S. commitment to war in Iraq and reject setting a withdrawal date for troops
- No Repeal requirement for bilingual ballots at the polls
- Yes Permit U.S. sale of civilian nuclear technology to India
- No Build a 700-mile fence on the U.S.-Mexico border to curb illegal crossings
- No Permit warrantless wiretaps of suspected terrorists

2005

- ? Intervene in the life-support case of Terri Schiavo
- Yes Lift President Bush's restrictions on stem cell research funding
- Yes Prohibit FBI access to library and bookstore records
- No Approve free-trade pact with five Central American countries
- No Pass energy policy overhaul favored by President Bush emphasizing domestic oil and gas production
- No End mandatory preservation of habitat of endangered animal and plant species
- Yes Ban torture of prisoners in U.S. custody

CQ VOTE STUDIES

	PARTY UNITY		PRESIDENTIAL SUPPORT	
	Support	Oppose	Support	Oppose
2006	92%	8%	30%	70%
2005	91%	9%	20%	80%
2004	94%	6%	32%	68%
2003	95%	5%	24%	76%
2002	93%	7%	33%	67%

INTEREST GROUPS

	AFL-CIO	ADA	CCUS	ACU
2006	93%	85%	53%	16%
2005	87%	90%	37%	8%
2004	93%	100%	53%	8%
2003	83%	80%	32%	18%
2002	89%	95%	40%	4%

COLORADO 2

Northwest Denver suburbs; Boulder

The 2nd takes in some suburbs north and west of Denver, along with Boulder, before heading into the mountains, crossing the Continental Divide and scooping up national forests, wilderness areas, reservoirs and part of ski country. Boulder's liberal culture pulls the district to the left, but overall the 2nd is mostly moderate with a Democratic lean.

Boulder is home to the University of Colorado's flagship campus and a committed corps of environmentalists. At the foothills of the Rocky Mountains, outdoor sports remain the city's most popular pastime, and Outside Magazine named Boulder the best "all-around" sports town in 2006. By day, the eclectic Pearl Street Mall is home to the city's shopping district, and by sunset, bars and clubs give it a vibrant nightlife.

The district includes the northern part of Jefferson and western Adams counties, where a plurality of residents live. This area includes nearly all of Westminster, the district's most populated city, as well as growing suburbs between Boulder and Denver. The 2nd also includes some growing communities north of Denver in southwestern Weld County.

Skiing is king in the mountain counties of Eagle, Grand and Summit, located in the western part of the district; the resort city of Vail is in Eagle County. These skiing communities and other towns along Interstate 70 make it a tourist magnet year-round. Rocky Mountain National Park (shared with the 4th) also draws visitors for its majestic scenery.

Environmental issues play heavily here, and because Boulder has been one of the fastest-growing cities in the state, urban sprawl has gained attention. Bicycling is highly regarded in snowy Boulder, and the city's plows often clear the Boulder Creek bike path. Several federal research laboratories and biotechnology companies have facilities in the district in order to take advantage of the well-educated workforce.

MAJOR INDUSTRY

Technology, research, higher education, tourism

CITIES

Westminster (pt.), 100,850; Boulder, 94,673; Thornton (pt.), 82,378

NOTABLE

The Eisenhower Memorial Tunnel, which takes Interstate 70 across the Continental Divide, is the highest vehicular tunnel in the world; The atomic clock at the National Institute of Standards and Technology in Boulder is the nation's official timekeeper.

Rep. John Salazar (D)

CAPITOL OFFICE
225-4761
www.house.gov/salazar
1531 Longworth 20515-0603; fax 226-9669

COMMITTEES
Agriculture
Transportation & Infrastructure
Veterans' Affairs

RESIDENCE
Manassa

BORN
July 21, 1953, Alamosa, Colo.

RELIGION
Roman Catholic

FAMILY
Wife, Mary Lou Salazar; three children

EDUCATION
Colorado State U., attended 1971-72;
Adams State College, B.S. 1981 (business)

MILITARY SERVICE
Army, 1973-76

CAREER
Farmer; rancher; seed potato business owner

POLITICAL HIGHLIGHTS
Colo. Agricultural Commission, 1999-2002;
Colo. House, 2003-04

ELECTION RESULTS

2006 GENERAL		
John Salazar (D)	146,488	61.6%
Scott Tipton (R)	86,930	36.5%
Bert L. Sargent (LIBERT)	4,417	1.9%
2006 PRIMARY		
John Salazar (D)		unopposed
2004 GENERAL		
John Salazar (D)	153,500	50.6%
Greg Walcher (R)	141,376	46.6%
Jim Krug (X)	8,770	2.9%

Elected 2004; 2nd term

Though Salazar's father had hoped at least one of his five sons would enter the priesthood, that dream went unfulfilled. Instead, two of the five wound up in Congress — one in each chamber. Their simultaneous election in 2004 was a remarkable triumph for a family of Mexican-American farmers who first arrived in Colorado's San Luis Valley in the 1850s.

John Salazar is not as well known as his younger brother, Ken, Colorado's junior senator. But he doesn't seem to mind. He says his brother is the politician in the family; he'd rather be known as a farmer and rancher who fell unexpectedly into public service.

The Salazar brothers and their three sisters grew up in a tiny house on the family's 52-acre homestead ranch; the five boys slept in a single room. Their mother stored food in an old-fashioned icebox; electricity didn't arrive until the 1980s. Their father grew alfalfa and potatoes using a horse-drawn cultivator. "We were raised very poor," says Salazar, who, along with his siblings, rode the family plow as ballast.

That childhood — and his own experience as a potato seed farmer — informs Salazar's priorities in Congress. He has worked to ensure that water from the snowmelt of Colorado's Western Slope is retained instead of being sent to growing populations elsewhere in the state or to California and Nevada — a paramount issue for ranchers and farmers in his sprawling district, which is larger than Florida. "We have to get cities like Colorado Springs and Aurora to admit there is massive destruction when water leaves the basin," he told the Colorado Springs Business Journal.

Salazar is a member of the Agriculture and Transportation and Infrastructure committees, serving on the latter's Water Resources and Environment Subcommittee. He has proposed a federally funded water easement program for Colorado's agricultural land, and presses for development of renewable energy from biofuels. Salazar can attest to the pinch of rising energy costs; the fuel bill for his potato farm rose from $50,000 in 2004 to $113,000 in 2005.

Salazar, the only military veteran in Colorado's congressional delegation, serves on the Veterans' Affairs Committee, where he feels a deep personal commitment. He has a son who served in the Colorado National Guard, and his father, a World War II veteran, came to him at age 84 after contracting Alzheimer's disease and asked Salazar to promise that he'd be buried in his uniform. Salazar says his father's last word to him after suffering what proved to be a fatal heart attack was "uniform."

Like his brother, Salazar has carved out a centrist voting record during his first term, in line with his Republican-leaning district. A lifelong hunter, he voted for Republican legislation shielding the gun industry from lawsuits.

He also supported elimination of the estate tax, an overhaul of bankruptcy laws, and legislation to bar transport of minors across state lines to evade parental-notification abortion laws. "I've never been a pawn for any party," Salazar told the Rocky Mountain News.

Salazar and his brother share a Washington apartment, and he says they could use some housekeeping help. "I think we're both Oscars," he quipped, referring to the sloppy half of "The Odd Couple."

But the two brothers don't necessarily share all the same views. For example, they split over whether Defense Secretary Donald H. Rumsfeld should have been forced from office in the fall of 2006. Salazar argued that U.S. problems in Iraq were "greater than one person," while his senator brother called for Rumsfeld's immediate firing.

Salazar, like all of his brothers, spent time at a Catholic seminary in Cincinnati, where Franciscan priests woke them daily at 5:30 a.m. with cowbells and packed almost every minute with study or prayer. After that three-year experience, Salazar says, when he later joined the military, "basic training was a piece of cake."

After nearly four years in the Army's Criminal Investigations Division, Salazar earned a business degree from Adams State College in Alamosa, Colo. He settled in as a potato farmer on part of the family land where he grew up, developing niche potato seeds still sold on a Web site, spudseed.com. "Agriculture is a pretty tough business unless you find a niche," he says. Salazar landed on the cover of Spudman, the potato-growers' journal, in 1990 and was named Colorado seed potato grower of the year for 1995-96.

His first exposure to politics came in a Colorado leadership program for people in agriculture that took him to Washington, D.C., and the Soviet Union.

He returned home and served on the Rio Grande Water Conservation District, fighting off a private company's attempts to buy up rights to ship local water to Denver's suburbs. He was appointed to the Colorado Agriculture Commission in 1999, and won a seat in the state legislature in 2002.

Salazar was unopposed for the Democratic U.S. House nomination in 2004, while Republican Greg Walcher, a former director of the state Department of Natural Resources, survived a fractious primary. Despite a strong showing by President Bush in the 3rd District, Salazar won by 4 percentage points. He emphasized his agricultural roots, using the campaign slogan, "Send a farmer to Congress."

He also capitalized on his role as a leader of the opposition to a 2003 state referendum that many voters feared would divert water from their region to Colorado's Front Range cities. Walcher supported the plan, but district voters overwhelmingly did not.

In 2006, he soundly defeated Republican challenger Scott Tipton, a Cortez businessman, who had to curtail his ad purchases in the weeks before the election because of a lack of funds.

In 2005, Salazar had briefly left the door open to a possible gubernatorial bid before announcing, "Under no circumstances will I run for governor." But when asked in 2007, he said he would not rule out such a run in the future. "I think the Lord has a plan for each and every one of us," he says. "Whatever his will is, is probably what I'll do."

KEY VOTES

2006

Yes Stop broadband companies from favoring select Internet traffic
Yes Affirm U.S. commitment to war in Iraq and reject setting a withdrawal date for troops
No Repeal requirement for bilingual ballots at the polls
Yes Permit U.S. sale of civilian nuclear technology to India
No Build a 700-mile fence on the U.S.-Mexico border to curb illegal crossings
No Permit warrantless wiretaps of suspected terrorists

2005

? Intervene in the life-support case of Terri Schiavo
Yes Lift President Bush's restrictions on stem cell research funding
Yes Prohibit FBI access to library and bookstore records
No Approve free-trade pact with five Central American countries
Yes Pass energy policy overhaul favored by President Bush emphasizing domestic oil and gas production
Yes End mandatory preservation of habitat of endangered animal and plant species
Yes Ban torture of prisoners in U.S. custody

CQ VOTE STUDIES

	PARTY UNITY		PRESIDENTIAL SUPPORT	
	Support	Oppose	Support	Oppose
2006	76%	24%	57%	43%
2005	81%	19%	46%	54%

INTEREST GROUPS

	AFL-CIO	ADA	CCUS	ACU
2006	77%	60%	64%	44%
2005	80%	75%	67%	44%

COLORADO 3
Western Slope; Pueblo

Spanning 29 counties, the 3rd includes more than half of Colorado's land area, moving from the Wyoming border in the north to the Ute Mountain Indian Reservation and Four Corners area in the southwest, before heading east to include all but one county on the state's southern edge. It displays some of the variety found outside the state's urban centers: rural poor, resort rich, old steel mill towns and isolated Hispanic counties.

Most of the state's rivers flow down the Western Slope to Nevada and California, and farmers here would like to see more of the water stored for local use. The 3rd's manufacturing sector has declined, and the district is hoping to diversify its economy by creating a more educated workforce, as other areas in the state have accomplished. Former robust mining areas have dwindled into small, struggling towns, and western cattle ranchers have seen their profits shrink. The San Luis Valley and rural areas west of Interstate 25 have been hardest hit.

Pueblo, the district's most populous county, was once dependent on its steel industry but is beginning to attract people back to its namesake city's downtown area. Both the Historic Arkansas Riverwalk and Union Avenue Historic District lure in locals and tourists. In the north and west part of the district, national parks, such as Black Canyon of the Gunnison, and ski resorts combine to support the area's hottest economic mainstay: tourism. Visitors who hike, bike or raft find themselves enthusiastically touring the San Juan or Sawatch Mountains, the latter of which includes Aspen and its ski resort.

Residential Colorado has spilled over the Continental Divide onto the Western Slope. Baby boomers building rustic retirement homes along this mountainous terrain tend to give the 3rd a Republican lean. But Pueblo County, heavily unionized and more than one-third Hispanic, helps keep the district competitive. Overall, Republican George W. Bush took 55 percent of the presidential vote here in 2004 while the U.S. House seat flipped from GOP to Democratic control.

MAJOR INDUSTRY
Tourism, skiing, agriculture

CITIES
Pueblo, 102,121; Grand Junction, 41,986; Clifton (unincorporated), 17,345

NOTABLE
The Federal Citizen Information Center is in Pueblo.

Rep. Marilyn Musgrave (R)

Elected 2002; 3rd term

CAPITOL OFFICE
225-4676
musgrave.house.gov
1507 Longworth 20515-0604; fax 225-5870

COMMITTEES
Agriculture
Small Business

RESIDENCE
Fort Morgan

BORN
Jan. 27, 1949, Greeley, Colo.

RELIGION
Assemblies of God

FAMILY
Husband, Steve Musgrave; four children

EDUCATION
Colorado State U., B.A. 1972 (social studies)

CAREER
Homemaker; teacher

POLITICAL HIGHLIGHTS
Morgan County School Board, 1990-94;
Colo. House, 1995-99; Colo. Senate, 1999-2003

ELECTION RESULTS

2006 GENERAL		
Marilyn Musgrave (R)	109,732	45.6%
Angie Paccione (D)	103,748	43.1%
Eric Eidsness (REF)	27,133	11.3%
2006 PRIMARY		
Marilyn Musgrave (R)		unopposed
2004 GENERAL		
Marilyn Musgrave (R)	155,958	51.1%
Stan Matsunaka (D)	136,812	44.8%
Bob Kinsey (GREEN)	12,739	4.2%

PREVIOUS WINNING PERCENTAGES
2002 (55%)

A social conservative who has been identified almost entirely with the battle to outlaw same-sex marriage, Musgrave has seen her victory margins dwindle with each election. In 2006, she held the dubious distinction of winning with the lowest vote share of any House member — just 45.6 percent versus 43.1 percent for her Democratic opponent.

Colorado has been edging to the left in recent years, while Musgrave occupies the far right of the political spectrum. She is anti-tax, anti-abortion and anti-regulation and opposes gay rights and gun control. She has a career 99 percent rating from the American Conservative Union and the National Rifle Association awards her an "A" grade.

Hailing from the wide-open eastern third of Colorado, where people generally are skeptical of the federal government and disdainful of what they view as an overly permissive society, she is not one to compromise on her positions. In the state legislature, Musgrave led the fight for citizens to carry concealed weapons but voted against the final version of the bill because it required gun owners to pass a background check and a handgun safety course. Those were conditions the NRA found acceptable but she didn't.

President Bush got a taste of Musgrave's intransigence when he tried, without success, to get her vote on his 2003 Medicare prescription drug bill, a top domestic initiative of his first term. Musgrave was one of only 25 Republicans who refused to support the legislation despite intense lobbying by the White House and a decision by GOP leaders to hold open the evening floor vote until nearly dawn while they worked to win over the last votes needed for passage.

A former schoolteacher and grandmother of five who married her high school sweetheart, Musgrave has a friendly, non-threatening personality that serves to soften any resentment about her unyielding policy stances. A former colleague in the Colorado legislature recalls how once, in the heat of political battle, Musgrave produced a needle and thread and mended the unraveled hem of his suit jacket at her desk on the state Senate floor.

Musgrave shot to prominence in Congress during her first term as the chief House sponsor of a proposed constitutional amendment banning same-sex marriage, an issue that gained unexpected momentum when Bush endorsed it in his 2004 re-election campaign. Overnight, Musgrave was being quoted on the radio by conservative guru Rush Limbaugh and courted by The Wall Street Journal and other national media. She pursued the amendment again in the 109th Congress (2005-06), only to see it defeated a second time.

After the Democratic takeover of the House and her own close call in the 2006 election, Musgrave decided to forgo introduction of the gay marriage amendment in the 110th Congress (2007-08). Instead, she turned her attention to local issues and to work on a new farm bill. She serves on the Agriculture Committee, where she is the top-ranking Republican on the Specialty Crops Subcommittee. She is working to help ranchers and farmers who were hard-hit by blizzards in December 2006. She also is pushing for new incentives for renewable fuels such as ethanol; corn is a major crop in her heavily rural district.

Musgrave's early life in tiny rural Eaton, Colo. was marked with challenges. Her father, a laborer in a meatpacking plant, struggled with alcoholism. The family moved frequently and never seemed to have enough money. Musgrave cleaned houses and waited tables to earn a degree from Colorado State University.

She rejected the liberal campus philosophy of the 1960s, eschewed student protests and wondered at a professor who asserted that every citizen deserved a guaranteed income. She felt that people were entitled to an income but only if they worked. While still in school, she married childhood sweetheart Steve Musgrave, a Colorado Farm Bureau insurance agent; she taught school for a while but quit to raise the couple's four children. She volunteered at a local anti-abortion center, then decided to run for the Morgan County School Board because she thought students needed more academic rigor and discipline.

She went on to serve a total of eight years in the Colorado General Assembly, first getting elected to the House in 1994 and later to the Senate. She was instrumental in passing the state's same-sex marriage law, continually reintroducing the measure though Democratic Gov. Roy Romer vetoed it twice. It was finally signed into law by Republican Gov. Bill Owens. She also led a push to exempt farm and ranch equipment from sales taxes and was a steadfast defender of gun owners' rights.

When Republican Rep. Bob Schaffer announced in late 2001 that he would honor a term limit pledge and retire, Musgrave ran for the open seat in 2002. She won the GOP nod by defeating former Weld County GOP Chairman Jeff Bedingfield, with 65 percent of the vote.

In the general-election campaign, Democrats put up a formidable candidate in state Senate President Stan Matsunaka, who had blocked many of Musgrave's initiatives and who had a history of winning in Republican-leaning areas. He portrayed Musgrave as an extremist; she countered by denouncing him as the too liberal "Stan the Tax Man." Musgrave had a big fundraising advantage, with support from Gun Owners of America, the National Pro-Life Alliance and giant retailer Wal-Mart's political action committee. She won by 13 percentage points, continuing a Republican streak in the district dating to 1972.

In 2004, Matsunaka was back for a rematch. Musgrave defeated him again, winning re-election but by a smaller, 6 percentage point margin.

Two years later, Democrats targeted her as vulnerable, putting up state Rep. Angie Paccione, who accused Musgrave of being a single-issue lawmaker. Many voters didn't like either major party candidate; 11 percent voted for Reform Party nominee Eric Eidsness, a former EPA official in the Reagan administration. Musgrave barely survived, winning by less than 3 percentage points.

KEY VOTES

2006

No	Stop broadband companies from favoring select Internet traffic
Yes	Affirm U.S. commitment to war in Iraq and reject setting a withdrawal date for troops
Yes	Repeal requirement for bilingual ballots at the polls
Yes	Permit U.S. sale of civilian nuclear technology to India
Yes	Build a 700-mile fence on the U.S.-Mexico border to curb illegal crossings
Yes	Permit warrantless wiretaps of suspected terrorists

2005

Yes	Intervene in the life-support case of Terri Schiavo
No	Lift President Bush's restrictions on stem cell research funding
Yes	Prohibit FBI access to library and bookstore records
Yes	Approve free-trade pact with five Central American countries
Yes	Pass energy policy overhaul favored by President Bush emphasizing domestic oil and gas production
Yes	End mandatory preservation of habitat of endangered animal and plant species
No	Ban torture of prisoners in U.S. custody

CQ VOTE STUDIES

	PARTY UNITY		PRESIDENTIAL SUPPORT	
	Support	Oppose	Support	Oppose
2006	98%	2%	90%	10%
2005	99%	1%	89%	11%
2004	98%	2%	85%	15%
2003	96%	4%	85%	15%

INTEREST GROUPS

	AFL-CIO	ADA	CCUS	ACU
2006	7%	0%	100%	96%
2005	13%	0%	92%	100%
2004	7%	0%	100%	100%
2003	7%	15%	93%	96%

COLORADO 4

North and east – Fort Collins, Greeley

The 4th, which covers Colorado's eastern plains and touches five other states, looks more like the Kansas prairies than the rugged Rockies, differentiating it from the Centennial State's other districts.

Thanks to intensive irrigation, the 4th's southern and eastern portions include productive wheat and corn fields, and the district is one of the nation's top 10 in cattle and calves. But as demand for beef has fallen and wheat prices have declined, some ranchers and farmers have faced hard times, and the area has suffered from recent droughts. The southern part of the district is spread across mainly small rural communities, and with roughly 9,000 residents, Lamar is the only town or city in the 4th's southern half with more than 3,000 people.

The northwestern part of the district, including Larimer and almost all of Weld counties, along with the 4th's small part of Boulder County, holds 80 percent of the district's population while occupying less than a third of its land. Fort Collins, the district's most populous city, was voted Money Magazine's 2006 best small city to live in, cashing in on job growth, low crime and surrounding natural beauty. Home to Colorado State University and its research facilities, Fort Collins' workforce has attracted technology firms to the city, which continues to experience population growth.

The 4th has a long history of sending GOP members to the House, and most of the district is rural Republican territory. Almost every county entirely in the 4th gave George W. Bush more than two-thirds of its vote in the 2004 presidential election, with Cheyenne County awarding Bush a statewide high of 81 percent and Washington County giving him his second-highest total. Fort Collins is an exception to that strong GOP tilt and tends to support Democrats in local elections. Overall, Bush took 58 percent of the 4th's vote.

MAJOR INDUSTRY

Agriculture, meatpacking, higher education, manufacturing

CITIES

Fort Collins, 118,652; Greeley, 76,930; Longmont, 71,093; Loveland, 50,608

NOTABLE

Greeley hosts the Greeley Stampede, a rodeo and music festival held each year leading up to July 4th; Estes Park's Stanley Hotel inspired Stephen King's "The Shining."

Rep. Doug Lamborn (R)

Elected 2006; 1st term

Lamborn is a far-right conservative on all social and fiscal policy, though opposition to taxes probably is his signature issue. According to the Rocky Mountain News, Lamborn would begin campaign appearances by saying, "I am Doug Lamborn, and I will never raise your taxes."

He wants to make all of President Bush's tax cuts permanent. In early 2007, Lamborn (LAMB-born) praised Bush's budget blueprint, which aims to balance the federal budget in five years without tax hikes.

Lamborn supports legislation to establish association health plans to allow small businesses to band together to buy health insurance. He backs Bush's plan to give tax deductions to individuals and families who purchase health insurance. He says the 2003 Medicare drug law is a "costly mistake."

A Western conservative, Lamborn vigorously defends private property rights and denounces increased governmental powers of eminent domain. He opposes abortion, embryonic stem cell research and gun control measures. He backs laws that permit carrying a concealed weapon and takes a hard line against illegal immigration.

The defense industry is a dominant presence in Colorado's 5th. Lamborn says he has been promised a seat on the Armed Services Committee, on which his predecessor served, once Republicans have vacancies to fill. Meanwhile, he vows to use his seat on the Veterans' Affairs Committee to help secure a veterans' cemetery in the Pikes Peak region of Colorado. Lamborn also serves on the Natural Resources Committee.

An acolyte of President Ronald Reagan, Lamborn was a veteran Colorado legislator when Republican Joel Hefley's retirement announcement early in 2006 sparked a free-for-all in the August GOP primary — the definitive election in the strongly conservative 5th. With the backing of the conservative Club for Growth, Lamborn edged ex-Hefley aide Jeff Crank in the primary, though Hefley denounced the tenor of Lamborn's campaign and refused to endorse him in the general election. Nonetheless, Lamborn won by nearly 20 percentage points over retired Air Force Lt. Col. Jay Fawcett. Crank is expected to challenge Lamborn's bid for renomination in 2008.

CAPITOL OFFICE
225-4422
lamborn.house.gov
437 Cannon 20515-0605; fax 225-1942

COMMITTEES
Natural Resources
Veterans' Affairs

RESIDENCE
Colorado Springs

BORN
May 24, 1954, Leavenworth, Kan.

RELIGION
Christian

FAMILY
Wife, Jeanie Lamborn; five children

EDUCATION
U. of Kansas, B.S. 1978 (journalism), J.D. 1985

CAREER
Lawyer

POLITICAL HIGHLIGHTS
Republican nominee for Kan. House, 1982; Colo. House, 1995-98; Colo. Senate, 1998-2007 (president pro tempore, 1999-2000)

ELECTION RESULTS

2006 GENERAL		
Doug Lamborn (R)	123,264	59.6%
Jay Fawcett (D)	83,431	40.3%
2006 PRIMARY		
Doug Lamborn (R)	15,126	27.0%
Jeff Crank (R)	14,234	25.4%
Bentley B. Rayburn (R)	9,735	17.4%
Lionel Rivera (R)	7,213	12.9%
John Wesley Anderson (R)	6,474	11.5%
Duncan Bremer (R)	3,310	5.9%

COLORADO 5

Central — Colorado Springs

God and country dominate the 5th, an overwhelmingly conservative district in Colorado's center that gave George W. Bush his highest statewide percentage (66 percent) in the 2004 presidential election. Military bases employ tens of thousands in the Colorado Springs area, and James Dobson's Focus on the Family and other evangelical groups are based in the 5th.

The district has made itself an indispensable arm of the modern military, and Colorado Springs houses the U.S. Space Command, the North American Aerospace Defense Command and some of the country's satellite defense research. The city has broadened its economic base beyond the military, although much of the 5th's new industry, including superconductor and computer development, depends on the defense industry. More than 80 percent of district residents live in El Paso County (Colorado Springs), and the city was selected by Money Magazine in 2006 as the nation's best big city to live in.

The Colorado Springs area is a prime destination for retired military personnel and other tourists, who stop at local spots such as the U.S. Air Force Academy, Pikes Peak — the most visited mountain in North America — and Garden of the Gods.

MAJOR INDUSTRY
Military, defense, tourism, technology

MILITARY BASES
Fort Carson (Army), 17,381 military, 2,959 civilian; U.S. Air Force Academy, 6,695 military, 3,381 civilian; Peterson Air Force Base, 2,910 military, 3,815 civilian (2007); Schriever Air Force Base, 1,710 military, 4,703 civilian (2006); Cheyenne Mountain Air Force Station, 581 military, 251 civilian (2006)

CITIES
Colorado Springs, 360,890

NOTABLE
The U.S. Olympic Headquarters is in Colorado Springs.

Rep. Tom Tancredo (R)

CAPITOL OFFICE
225-7882
tancredo.house.gov
1131 Longworth 20515-0606; fax 226-4623

COMMITTEES
Foreign Affairs
Natural Resources

RESIDENCE
Littleton

BORN
Dec. 20, 1945, North Denver, Colo.

RELIGION
Presbyterian

FAMILY
Wife, Jackie Tancredo; two children

EDUCATION
U. of North Colorado, B.A. 1968

CAREER
Think tank president; teacher

POLITICAL HIGHLIGHTS
Colo. House, 1977-81; U.S. Education Department regional representative, 1981-93

ELECTION RESULTS

2006 GENERAL		
Tom Tancredo (R)	158,806	58.6%
Bill Winter (D)	108,007	39.9%
Jack J. Woehr (LIBERT)	4,093	1.5%
2006 PRIMARY		
Tom Tancredo (R)		unopposed
2004 GENERAL		
Tom Tancredo (R)	212,778	59.5%
Joanna L. Conti (D)	139,870	39.1%
Jack J. Woehr (LIBERT)	3,857	1.1%

PREVIOUS WINNING PERCENTAGES
2002 (67%); 2000 (54%); 1998 (56%)

Elected 1998; 5th term

After making his mark in Congress on the immigration issue, Tancredo took his show on the road in hopes of influencing the outcome of the presidential nominating season in 2008. Though he's sometimes dismissed as a gadfly, his get-tough views on stemming the flow of illegal migrants have had a major impact on the debate in recent years.

By the time he set up a presidential exploratory committee in early 2007, Tancredo (tan-CRAY-doe) had already made repeat visits to Iowa, New Hampshire and South Carolina, which host early presidential nominating contests. While he conceded his one-note message and lack of national identity made him a longshot, his aim was to influence the platform of the eventual GOP nominee, much as commentator Pat Buchanan pushed the party to the right by winning the New Hampshire primary in 1996. "My focus from this time on is going to be on the presidential election," Tancredo said. "That's where all the marbles will be."

Tancredo relishes his rebel status, which transformed him in the 109th Congress (2005-06) from a relative unknown to a regular on television news shows and Internet blogs. "When I got here, somebody told me, 'There's only one way to get something done — talk about it constantly.' I remember saying, 'I can do that,'" he says. Along the way, Tancredo has alienated a few prominent fellow Republicans. President Bush won't invite him to the White House and former Majority Leader Tom DeLay of Texas once warned he'd have "no career" if he kept challenging the leadership.

While Bush and other leading Republicans were pushing for establishment of a guest worker program and an earned path to eventual citizenship for illegal workers already in the country, Tancredo was pulling in the other direction. He had much to do with the 2005 House passage of a bill calling for tighter border security and stepped-up workplace enforcement of immigration laws, with no guest worker or legalization provisions. Tancredo urged even tougher steps, such as jail terms for those who hire illegal immigrants.

His penchant for inflammatory rhetoric gets him in trouble, too. In 2005, Tancredo angered Arab-American groups when he suggested on a talk show that the United States "could take out their holy sites," including Mecca, in response to a hypothetical nuclear terrorist attack within the United States. He also tried to get the National Park Service to halt work on a memorial to victims of Sept. 11, 2001, because its crescent shape could be mistaken for an Islamic symbol. The design was chosen with help from the families of United Flight 93 passengers who foiled a terrorist hijacking in Pennsylvania, and was intended to evoke the flight path of the plane and arms cradling the crash victims.

In 2006, Tancredo got into a near fistfight with another lawmaker after the two appeared on CNBC to discuss immigration. Democratic Rep. Luis V. Gutierrez of Illinois noted that Tancredo had arrived late and remarked: "The immigrant shows up on time. The gringo was late. I guess that's why we get the jobs." A shouting match ensued, with both men calling the other "racist." Gutierrez claimed Tancredo tried to block his path; Tancredo maintained he put his hand on Gutierrez's shoulder, the Denver Post reported.

Representing Denver's successful and conservative southern suburbs, Tancredo was warning of the fallout from illegal immigration long before the issue caught fire after the Sept. 11 attacks. As a member of the Colorado House in the 1970s, Tancredo pushed to curtail taxpayer funding for bilingual school programs and, though it never got off the ground, proposed a state constitutional amendment denying services to illegal immigrants.

Tancredo himself is a product of America's melting pot, and, for all his dark warnings about "multiculturalism," he has invoked his family's ethnicity in political campaigns. All four of his grandparents came from Italy, arriving in the late 1800s, when the United States had no immigration quotas. His grandfather came through Ellis Island at age 9 with a note pinned to his shirt asking he be safely delivered to family friends. His mother, Adeline Lombardi Tancredo, raised her children in an Italian section of North Denver, shopping only at Italian butchers, cheese sellers and bakers. Son "Tommy" featured her spaghetti sauce recipe on campaign flyers.

Tancredo draws a distinction between the assimilation that families like his made — they learned English and called themselves Americans — and the presumption today of bilingual accommodations, heritage loyalty and cross-border ties. "I was taught to take great pride in what America was all about," he says. "Today I think we have been captured by multiculturalism."

In college, Tancredo spoke out in favor of the Vietnam War (though after graduating in 1968, he accepted a medical deferment based on earlier treatment for depression). He was a junior high school teacher in the 1970s, then served two terms in the state legislature. In 1981, he began a 12-year tenure as the Education Department's regional manager. He advocated dismantling the department and cut his own staff by 75 percent. In the 1990s, he was president of the libertarian Independence Institute think tank.

In his first House race, Tancredo bested four other Republicans in the primary, then breezed to victory in November to succeed retiring GOP Rep. Dan Schaefer. Tancredo was held to 54 percent of the vote in 2000, but redistricting in 2002 made the 6th District more Republican and Tancredo coasted that year. Two years later, he announced that "after much prayer and soul searching" he would run for re-election, breaking a pledge to serve no more than six years. That year, 2004, he faced a well-funded Democratic foe but prevailed by 20 percentage points. He did almost as well in 2006.

In his early terms, Tancredo staked out conservative ground and not just on immigration. He supported vouchers for private school tuition, gun owners' rights and a plan to scrap the income tax system for a national sales tax or a flat tax. His advocacy for gun owners has been tested in dramatic ways. The fatal Columbine High School shootings in 1999 took place just blocks from his suburban Denver home. And in 2006, another school shooting, in Bailey, Colo., when a gunman took six female students hostage, was just outside his district. Though still a foe of most gun control, Tancredo has endorsed some limits on gun purchases.

KEY VOTES

2006

No Stop broadband companies from favoring select Internet traffic
Yes Affirm U.S. commitment to war in Iraq and reject setting a withdrawal date for troops
Yes Repeal requirement for bilingual ballots at the polls
Yes Permit U.S. sale of civilian nuclear technology to India
Yes Build a 700-mile fence on the U.S.-Mexico border to curb illegal crossings
Yes Permit warrantless wiretaps of suspected terrorists

2005

Yes Intervene in the life-support case of Terri Schiavo
No Lift President Bush's restrictions on stem cell research funding
No Prohibit FBI access to library and bookstore records
No Approve free-trade pact with five Central American countries
Yes Pass energy policy overhaul favored by President Bush emphasizing domestic oil and gas production
Yes End mandatory preservation of habitat of endangered animal and plant species
Yes Ban torture of prisoners in U.S. custody

CQ VOTE STUDIES

	PARTY UNITY		PRESIDENTIAL SUPPORT	
	Support	Oppose	Support	Oppose
2006	91%	9%	79%	21%
2005	93%	7%	80%	20%
2004	94%	6%	81%	19%
2003	90%	10%	84%	16%
2002	96%	4%	76%	24%

INTEREST GROUPS

	AFL-CIO	ADA	CCUS	ACU
2006	21%	10%	100%	92%
2005	33%	5%	77%	100%
2004	21%	10%	95%	100%
2003	20%	25%	77%	92%
2002	11%	5%	79%	100%

COLORADO 6

Denver suburbs — part of Aurora; Douglas County

Managing growth is a top priority for the affluent, white-collar suburbs that lie south of Denver and make up the heart of the 6th. As in much of Colorado, the 6th has experienced dramatic population growth in recent years. Douglas County's growth in the 1990s, when it increased its population by 191 percent, continues this decade, and Coloradans' commute to and from the Mile High City is a serious problem. Officials hope a 19-mile extension of the Southeast Light Rail and Bus System that opened in 2006 will help ease the gridlock.

Manufacturing remains the 6th's largest industry, but unlike in Midwest and Rust Belt cities, the jobs are in the technology sector. Employers include Lockheed Martin and First Data, whose corporate headquarters are in Greenwood Village.

North and east of Douglas, a plurality of district residents live in overwhelmingly rural Arapahoe County. The urban, western portion of Arapahoe, which includes the county seat of Littleton just south of Denver, has many residential and retail areas. Columbine High School, site of a 1999 shooting that left 15 dead, is in Littleton, which makes gun control an emotional issue in the area. Less than one-third of Aurora, Colorado's third-most-populous city, is in the 6th.

Douglas accounts for only 30 percent of the 6th's residents, but the county's suburban population solidifies the district as a GOP stronghold. George W. Bush won 60 percent of the 6th's presidential vote in 2004. The district has the state's largest white-collar workforce, highest median income and largest percentage of residents with at least a bachelor's degree (47 percent). Minorities total 12 percent of residents, making the 6th Colorado's only district where minorities represent less than 20 percent of the population.

MAJOR INDUSTRY
Manufacturing, technology

CITIES
Aurora (pt.), 78,878; Highlands Ranch (unincorporated), 70,931; Southglenn (unincorporated), 43,520; Littleton, 40,340

NOTABLE
The Comanche Crossing Railroad Site near Strasburg marks the place where the last spike was driven in 1870 to create the first continuous transcontinental railroad.

Rep. Ed Perlmutter (D)

CAPITOL OFFICE
225-2645
perlmutter.house.gov
415 Cannon 20515-0607; fax 225-5278

COMMITTEES
Financial Services
Homeland Security

RESIDENCE
Golden

BORN
May 1, 1953, Denver, Colo.

RELIGION
Protestant

FAMILY
Wife, Deana Perlmutter; three children

EDUCATION
U. of Colorado, B.A. 1975 (political science), J.D. 1978

CAREER
Lawyer

POLITICAL HIGHLIGHTS
Colo. Senate, 1995-2003 (president pro tempore, 2001-03)

ELECTION RESULTS

2006 GENERAL		
Ed Perlmutter (D)	103,918	54.9%
Rick O'Donnell (R)	79,571	42.1%
Dave Chandler (GREEN)	3,073	1.6%
Roger McCarville (AC)	2,605	1.4%
2006 PRIMARY		
Ed Perlmutter (D)	15,598	53.3%
Peggy Lamm (D)	11,047	37.7%
Herb Rubenstein (D)	2,625	9.0%

Elected 2006; 1st term

With a moderate image burnished as a state legislator, Perlmutter reflects the centrism of his suburban Denver district. His constituents are an almost equal mix of Democrats, Republicans and independents, so his legislative positions aim for the middle ground.

Perlmutter's willingness to cross party lines in the Colorado Senate on certain issues is likely to continue in Congress. He supports an immigration bill introduced by Republican David Dreier of California and a guest worker program similar to President Bush's proposal.

A longtime champion of renewable energy, Perlmutter likens the goal of energy independence to John F. Kennedy's challenge to land a man on the moon. To this end, he advocates the creation of a federal research program akin to the Apollo Project. One likely beneficiary of such a program would be the National Renewable Energy Lab, the nation's premier renewable energy research facility, located in Perlmutter's district.

Stem cell research is another top priority for Perlmutter, whose eldest daughter has epilepsy.

A Colorado native, Perlmutter worked his way through law school as a laborer on construction projects. He boasts an extensive history handling bankruptcy cases as a lawyer and plans to put his financial background to use with his seat on the Financial Services Committee.

Perlmutter was elected to the Colorado state Senate in 1994, served two terms and became president pro tempore. In 2004, he co-chaired John Kerry's presidential campaign operation in Colorado.

He saw an opportunity to run for the House in 2006 when GOP Rep. Bob Beauprez launched a bid for governor rather than seeking re-election to the 7th District seat. Perlmutter's GOP opponent was the articulate Rick O'Donnell, a former state education commissioner. But O'Donnell's suggestion that high school boys spend part of their senior year in public service, such as securing the border, hurt him, as did the anti-Republican tide. What was originally a tossup race turned into a resounding victory for Perlmutter.

COLORADO 7

Denver suburbs — Lakewood, parts of Aurora and Arvada

Surrounding Denver (and the 1st District) on three sides, the suburban 7th has nearly equal numbers of Democrats, Republicans and unaffiliated voters, making it the state's most politically competitive district.

The 7th includes parts of Adams, Arapahoe and Jefferson counties, with more than half its residents in Jefferson. The 7th's portion of Jefferson includes Lakewood, a middle-class area just west of Denver, Golden and most of Arvada. Commerce City, a Hispanic-majority, lower-middle-class area just north of Denver, and most of Aurora (shared with the 6th) also are in the 7th. Minorities total nearly one-third of residents, giving the 7th the second-highest percentage in the state.

Former military facilities have received new life here, as the former Fitzsimons Army Medical Center is the site of the region's health industry anchor — a University of Colorado at Denver and Health Sciences Center campus. Also, the former weapons-producing Rocky Mountain Arsenal is now a national wildlife refuge and the largest contiguous open space in the Denver area. Adjacent to the refuge is the new Colorado Rapids soccer stadium, which opened in 2007. Buckley Air Force Base remains a link in the Air Force Space Command satellite tracking system.

MAJOR INDUSTRY
Telecommunications, aerospace, manufacturing, health care

MILITARY BASES
Buckley Air Force Base, 2,971 military, 3,240 civilian (2007)

CITIES
Aurora (pt.), 197,515; Lakewood, 144,126; Arvada (pt.), 98,941; Wheat Ridge, 32,913

NOTABLE
The Coors Brewing Co., based in Golden, features free brewery tours and tastings.

CONNECTICUT

Gov. M. Jodi Rell (R)

First elected: 2006; assumed office July 1, 2004, due to resignation of John G. Rowland, R
Length of term: 4 years
Term expires: 1/11
Salary: $150,000
Phone: (860) 566-4840

Residence: Brookfield
Born: June 16, 1946; Norfolk, Va.
Religion: Protestant
Family: Husband, Lou Rell; two children
Education: Old Dominion College, attended 1965-66; Western Connecticut State U., attended 1982-84
Career: Homemaker; investment firm office clerk
Political highlights: Conn. House, 1985-95 (deputy minority leader 1991-1995); lieutenant governor, 1995-2004

Election results:

2006 GENERAL		
M. Jodi Rell (R)	710,048	63.2%
John DeStefano (D)	398,220	35.4%

Lt. Gov. Michael Fedele (R)

First elected: 2006
Length of term: 4 years
Term expires: 1/11
Salary: $110,000
Phone: (860) 524-7384

LEGISLATURE

General Assembly: January-June in odd-numbered years; February-May in even-numbered years

Senate: 36 members, 2-year terms
2007 ratios: 24 D, 12 R; 28 men, 8 women
Salary: $28,000
Phone: (860) 240-0500

House: 151 members, 2-year terms
2007 ratios: 107 D, 44 R; 106 men, 45 women
Salary: $28,000
Phone: (860) 240-0400

TERM LIMITS

Governor: No
Senate: No
House: No

URBAN STATISTICS

CITY	POPULATION
Bridgeport	139,529
New Haven	123,626
Hartford	121,578
Stamford	117,083

REGISTERED VOTERS

Unaffiliated	44%
Democrat	34%
Republican	21%

POPULATION

2006 population (est.)	3,504,809
2000 population	3,405,565
1990 population	3,287,116
Percent change (1990-2000)	+3.6%
Rank among states (2006)	29
Median age	37.4
Born in state	57%
Foreign born	10.9%
Violent crime rate	325/100,000
Poverty level	7.9%
Federal workers	21,296
Military	16,675

ELECTIONS

STATE ELECTION OFFICIAL
(860) 509-6100
DEMOCRATIC PARTY
(860) 560-1775
REPUBLICAN PARTY
(860) 547-0589

MISCELLANEOUS

Web: www.ct.gov
Capital: Hartford

U.S. CONGRESS

Senate: 1 Democrat, 1 independent
House: 4 Democrats, 1 Republican

2000 Census Statistics by District

DIST.	2004 VOTE FOR PRESIDENT BUSH	KERRY	WHITE	BLACK	ASIAN	HISP	MEDIAN INCOME	WHITE COLLAR	BLUE COLLAR	SERVICE INDUSTRY	OVER 64	UNDER 18	COLLEGE EDUCATION	RURAL	SQ. MILES
1	39%	60%	72%	13%	2%	11%	$50,227	66%	20%	14%	15%	24%	28%	7%	653
2	44	54	89	3	2	4	$54,498	63	21	16	12	24	29	33	2,028
3	42	56	76	11	3	8	$49,752	65	21	14	15	24	28	3	459
4	46	52	71	11	3	13	$66,598	72	16	13	13	26	42	4	457
5	49.0	49.3	80	5	2	11	$53,118	63	23	14	14	25	30	14	1,248
STATE	44	54	77	9	2	9	$53,935	66	20	14	14	25	31	12	4,845
U.S.	50.7	48.3	69	12	4	13	$41,994	60	25	15	12	26	24	21	3,537,438

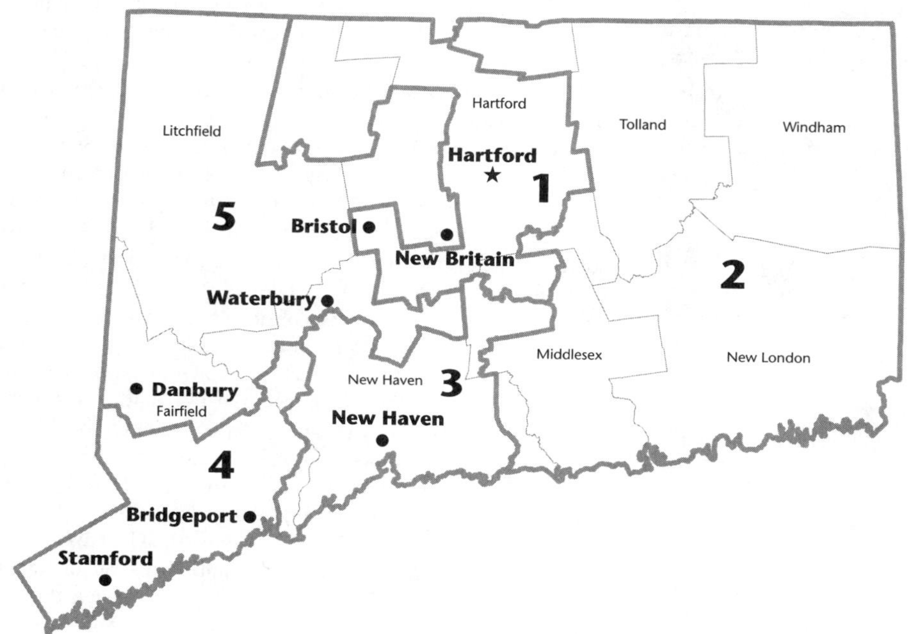
Hartford
Litchfield
Tolland
Windham
Hartford
1
5
Bristol
New Britain
2
Waterbury
Middlesex
New London
New Haven
3
Danbury
Fairfield
New Haven
4
Bridgeport
Stamford

Sen. Christopher J. Dodd (D)

CAPITOL OFFICE
224-2823
dodd.senate.gov
448 Russell 20510-0702; fax 224-1083

COMMITTEES
Banking, Housing & Urban Affairs - chairman
Foreign Relations
(Western Hemisphere, Peace Corps & Narcotics Affairs - chairman)
Health, Education, Labor & Pensions
(Children & Families - chairman)
Rules & Administration
Joint Library

RESIDENCE
East Haddam

BORN
May 27, 1944, Willimantic, Conn.

RELIGION
Roman Catholic

FAMILY
Wife, Jackie Clegg Dodd; two children

EDUCATION
Providence College, B.A. 1966;
U. of Louisville, J.D. 1972

MILITARY SERVICE
Army Reserve, 1969-75

CAREER
Lawyer; Peace Corps volunteer

POLITICAL HIGHLIGHTS
U.S. House, 1975-81

ELECTION RESULTS

2004 GENERAL

Christopher J. Dodd (D)	945,347	66.4%
Jack Orchulli (R)	457,749	32.1%

2004 PRIMARY

Christopher J. Dodd (D)	unopposed

PREVIOUS WINNING PERCENTAGES
1998 (65%); 1992 (59%); 1986 (65%); 1980 (56%); 1978 House Election (70%); 1976 House Election (65%); 1974 House Election (59%)

Elected 1980; 5th term

An influential liberal long frustrated in his ambition for higher office, Dodd faced a tough personal choice at the opening of the 110th Congress (2007-08). When Democrats took control of the Senate, he landed a job he had wanted for years, as chairman of the Senate Banking, Housing and Urban Affairs Committee. But the wide-open contest for president was also heating up, and Dodd, having passed up a chance to run four years earlier, made a now-or-never decision to get in.

He entered as a dark horse in a nominating contest that had already attracted national stars such as Democratic Sens. Hillary Rodham Clinton of New York and Barack Obama of Illinois and former Sen. John Edwards of North Carolina. But Dodd calculated that as chairman of the committee overseeing banks and Wall Street investment houses, he would be competitive in fundraising in the early primaries. Early on, Dodd also attracted some top-shelf professional help, including Jim Jordan, former campaign manager for 2004 Democratic nominee John Kerry of Massachusetts.

Dodd had other assets not as obvious at first glance. He has long been a pro at one-on-one politicking in Democratic circles, and is well-liked by party activists, especially in intimate political settings like the Iowa precinct caucuses, the first-in-the-nation test of fortitude in the presidential nominating season, said David Lightman, the Washington bureau chief of the Hartford Courant who has covered Dodd closely for many years.

Dodd gambled that the public, after its experience with a former governor from Texas, would be looking for someone with experience in national governance. In fact, Dodd has spent more than half his life in Congress.

"On every major foreign policy and domestic debate of the last quarter-century, I've been there," Dodd said. "I happen to believe this time around that matters, that you demonstrably can get things done."

On the Banking panel, where he has served since he first arrived in the Senate in 1981, Dodd has balanced the interests of consumers with those of the banking, investment and insurance industries. Consumer advocates say he has been with them on many issues, but has opposed them on some of their top priorities. Industry groups offer the same assessment.

His approach represents a shift from that of Paul S. Sarbanes of Maryland, the panel's former senior Democrat who retired at the end of 2006. Dodd is more sympathetic to business, especially the insurance industry, a big presence in Connecticut. The state also has the highest per capita income in the United States and is home to a number of the nation's hedge funds and major financial firms. Its proximity to Manhattan makes it a popular place to live for traders, financial advisers and executives.

In 1995, Dodd was instrumental in passing a law limiting shareholders' ability to bring class action securities fraud lawsuits against publicly traded companies. A decade later, he backed limits on class action suits in general. But he also was one of the authors of the 2002 Sarbanes-Oxley Act, an overhaul of accounting practices enacted after a series of corporate scandals hurt shareholders.

In the 110th Congress, Dodd said he would seek to extend the Terrorism Risk Insurance Act, which provides a federal backstop for private property insurers writing policies against the threat of terrorism. Critics say the program, which was set to expire in 2007, puts the federal government on the hook for losses that insurers should cover. Insurers counter that it is impossible to accurately insure a random risk like a large-scale attack.

Dodd played a critical role in writing the original legislation.

The senator also wants to explore creation of a federal charter option for the nation's larger insurance companies, which would spare them from having to comply with 50 different state insurance laws.

At the same time, Dodd stood up for consumers, holding early 2007 hearings taking aim at abusive credit card and predatory lending practices. He also vowed that his Banking panel would tighten standards for the security of private financial information.

Liberal party activists by and large like Dodd's position on Iraq. Though he supported the resolution in 2002 authorizing the invasion of Iraq, he has been critical of the Bush administration's handling of the war and has called for the withdrawal of troops.

Dodd's congressional career dates to his days as a member of the U.S. House, and includes such milestones as sponsorship of the Family and Medical Leave Act, which guaranteed time off to care for children and elderly family members. He also has a solid civil rights record, and led the fight to strengthen voting procedures after the bitterly contested 2000 election. The resulting law set the first federal standards for the conduct of elections and authorized nearly $4 billion to carry them out.

Although he chaired the Democratic National Committee in the mid-1990s, Dodd has been disappointed in attempts to move up in the leadership. He explored a run against Nevada's Harry Reid for minority leader in the 109th Congress (2005-06) after Tom Daschle of South Dakota lost his 2004 re-election bid, but bowed out when it became clear Reid had the votes locked up. Ten years earlier, Daschle bested Dodd for the job by just one vote.

In 2004, Dodd considered seeking the nomination for president but deferred to home-state colleague Sen. Joseph I. Lieberman, who had been Al Gore's running mate four years earlier and wanted his own shot. "It's getting beyond the point where it's my time," Dodd lamented to the Courant.

Dodd may be hounded on the campaign trail by questions about his past. In the 1980s, when he was divorced and socializing frequently with Sen. Edward M. Kennedy of Massachusetts, also divorced at the time, the pair's womanizing was fodder for the tabloids. Over the years, however, Dodd quit the heavy partying and in 1999, married Jackie Marie Clegg, an Export-Import Bank official more than 10 years his junior. The couple now has two small children.

The joke-loving, white-maned Dodd has an easy, comfortable way with people, in part derived from his background as a child of the Senate. His father, Thomas J. Dodd, was a Democratic senator from Connecticut for two terms, though his career declined after his censure in 1967 for misusing political contributions. (To this day, the senator believes his father was mistreated by his colleagues, and so casts memorable votes to signal his belief that fellow senators should get the benefit of the doubt. He was among just eight Democrats to vote to confirm arch-conservative Sen. John Ashcroft of Missouri as attorney general in 2001.)

Dodd won his first House election in 1974 at age 30 on a family name that still resonated with older voters in the state. It was the post-Watergate election, and he captured an open seat that had been held by a Republican.

When Democrat Abraham Ribicoff retired six years later, Dodd became the youngest person ever elected to the Senate from Connecticut. He took 56 percent of the vote against former New York Sen. James L. Buckley, who carried the standard of the newly resurgent conservative wing of the state GOP and whose family homestead is in Connecticut. Dodd has since won re-election more easily, taking almost two-thirds of the vote in his 1998 contest and again in 2004, when he defeated his GOP foe, former clothing company executive Jack Orchulli, with 66 percent of the vote.

KEY VOTES

2006

- No Confirm Samuel A. Alito Jr. to the Supreme Court
- Yes Allow consideration of a bill to establish a $140 billion trust fund to compensate victims of asbestos exposure
- No Extend tax cuts for two years at a cost of $70 billion over five years
- Yes Overhaul immigration policy with border security, enforcement and guest worker program
- No Allow consideration of a bill to permanently repeal the estate tax
- Yes Urge President Bush to begin troop withdrawals from Iraq in 2006
- Yes Lift President Bush's restrictions on stem cell research funding
- No Authorize military tribunals for suspected terrorists

2005

- Yes Curb class action lawsuits by shifting them from state to federal courts
- No Allow confirmation vote on Priscilla R. Owen to the U.S. Court of Appeals for the 5th Circuit
- No Oppose mandatory emissions limits and block recognition of global warming as a threat
- No Approve free-trade pact with five Central American countries
- No Pass energy policy overhaul favored by President Bush emphasizing domestic oil and gas production
- No Shield gunmakers from lawsuits when their products are used in crimes
- Yes Ban torture of prisoners in U.S. custody
- ? Renew 16 provisions of the Patriot Act
- No Allow final vote on opening the Arctic National Wildlife Refuge to oil and gas exploration

CQ VOTE STUDIES

	PARTY UNITY		PRESIDENTIAL SUPPORT	
	Support	Oppose	Support	Oppose
2006	95%	5%	49%	51%
2005	94%	6%	33%	67%
2004	95%	5%	60%	40%
2003	95%	5%	47%	53%
2002	94%	6%	68%	32%
2001	98%	2%	66%	34%
2000	95%	5%	98%	2%
1999	90%	10%	86%	14%
1998	91%	9%	93%	7%
1997	87%	13%	94%	6%

INTEREST GROUPS

	AFL-CIO	ADA	CCUS	ACU
2006	100%	95%	42%	8%
2005	79%	95%	39%	8%
2004	100%	100%	41%	4%
2003	100%	95%	32%	15%
2002	100%	80%	40%	5%
2001	94%	95%	36%	16%
2000	75%	95%	53%	13%
1999	88%	95%	53%	0%
1998	88%	95%	61%	4%
1997	57%	90%	50%	4%

Sen. Joseph I. Lieberman (I)

CAPITOL OFFICE
224-4041
lieberman.senate.gov
706 Hart 20510-0703; fax 224-9750

COMMITTEES
Armed Services
(Airland - chairman)
Environment & Public Works
(Private Sector & Consumer Solutions to Global Warming and Wildlife Protection - chairman)
Homeland Security & Governmental Affairs - chairman
Small Business & Entrepreneurship

RESIDENCE
New Haven

BORN
Feb. 24, 1942, Stamford, Conn.

RELIGION
Jewish

FAMILY
Wife, Hadassah Lieberman; four children

EDUCATION
Yale U., B.A. 1964 (politics & economics), LL.B. 1967

CAREER
Lawyer

POLITICAL HIGHLIGHTS
Conn. Senate, 1971-80 (served as a Democrat; majority leader, 1975-80); Democratic nominee for U.S. House, 1980; Conn. attorney general, 1983-89 (served as a Democrat); Democratic nominee for vice president, 2000; sought Democratic nomination for president, 2004

ELECTION RESULTS

2006 GENERAL		
Joseph I. Lieberman (CFL)	564,095	49.7%
Ned Lamont (D)	450,844	39.7%
Alan Schlesinger (R)	109,198	9.6%
2006 PRIMARY		
Ned Lamont (D)	146,404	51.8%
Joseph I. Lieberman (D)	136,490	48.2%

PREVIOUS WINNING PERCENTAGES *
2000 (63%); 1994 (67%); 1988 (50%)
* Elected as a Democrat 1988-2000

Elected 1988; 4th term

Lieberman is the Senate's wild card, coveted by both political parties but irrevocably committed to neither. After a lifetime as a Democrat, including a stint as the party's vice presidential nominee, he lost the Democratic nomination in the 2006 primary election because of his unwavering support for the war in Iraq. He won a fourth term anyway, running without party backing, but the experience estranged him from the party.

At the start of the 110th Congress (2007-08), Lieberman and independent Bernard Sanders of Vermont sided with the Democrats for organizational purposes, giving the party a bare 51-49 operational edge. But unlike Sanders, Lieberman hinted that his allegiance was tenuous. "I'm beholden to no particular political group," he said. "I was elected as an independent, and the majority of my votes were from independents and Republicans."

Many of his Senate colleagues publicly backed Democrat Ned Lamont, who defeated Lieberman in the primary. After winning the November general election in spite of them, Lieberman wanted to be known as an Independent Democrat, but official Senate record-keepers forced him to choose between Democrat and independent. He opted for the latter. And he said it was possible he could someday switch to the GOP.

Worried Democratic leaders wooed him. He was named chairman of the Homeland Security and Governmental Affairs Committee. He'd been the panel's top Democrat during the Republican majority, and Democratic leaders weren't about to deny him the gavel when the flip of a single seat could switch party control back to the GOP. He served as floor manager for two high-profile bills at the forefront of the new Democratic agenda, one tightening ethics rules and one implementing recommendations by the independent Sept. 11 commission to shore up defenses against terrorism.

When Democratic leaders pressed for adoption of resolutions condemning President Bush's decision in January 2007 to deploy thousands more U.S. troops to Iraq, Lieberman voted with Republicans against the measures. He began skipping the weekly Democratic Party lunches, which were spiced by carping about the war. His absence was noted, and in early March, Majority Leader Harry Reid coaxed him back to the table, literally. "It was kind of awkward, you know? It felt like me, and then everybody else," Lieberman said of the tensions that prompted his boycott. But Reid "just called me, and he said, 'Come on back,'" Lieberman said. "He's a straightforward guy."

It's not just the war that finds Lieberman to the right of his party; he's more hawkish than the typical Democrat on national security issues in general. And he has occasionally sided with business interests, as in 2005, when he voted to limit class action lawsuits. But on most domestic issues, from taxes to civil rights, the New Englander is a reliable Democratic vote. He is pro-labor, supports abortion rights, opposes the Bush tax cuts and is a strong environmentalist. In fact, Lieberman and Republican John McCain of Arizona are chief sponsors of one of the most aggressive legislative proposals to reduce greenhouse gas emissions that contribute to global warming. When describing his advocacy of environmental stewardship, he often cites "tikkun olam," the Jewish belief that it is every person's duty to protect all of God's creations.

Lieberman works to build company in the center of the Senate's political spectrum. In the 109th Congress (2005-06), he was one of seven Democrats and seven Republicans who formed a pivotal Gang of 14 to deter Democratic filibusters against Bush's conservative judicial nominees while blocking Republican leadership threats to use a parliamentary "nuclear option" ending such filibusters forever. With Democrats in control in the 110th Congress, they have more direct ways to stop judicial nominees they oppose. But Lieberman and other members of the Gang decided to continue their loose coalition and expand it. Indeed, Lieberman and Republican Lamar Alexander of Tennessee formed a new bipartisan group to hold dutch-treat social sessions aimed at getting to know one another better "so that we can work better together."

As chairman of the Homeland Security Committee, Lieberman already works closely with top-ranking Republican Susan Collins of Maine, one of the GOP's few remaining moderates. In 2004, when Collins held the gavel, the pair pushed to enactment an overhaul of the nation's intelligence agencies after a conservative uprising had stalled it for months. Early in 2007, Lieberman and Collins announced a new seating plan for the committee hearing room dais, alternating members by party, rather than Republicans on one side and Democrats on the other.

Lieberman was an early proponent of creating a Homeland Security Department, unveiling his proposal long before Bush embraced the idea in 2002. Lieberman also pressed Bush to accept the creation of the independent commission to investigate government failures that may have opened the nation to the Sept. 11 terrorist attacks. The commission's recommendations ultimately shaped the intelligence overhaul and other homeland security legislation that Lieberman has advanced. He continues to criticize the Bush administration for what he sees as inadequate funding of the Homeland Security Department.

Lieberman soared to national prominence in the 2000 presidential campaign, when Al Gore tapped him as his running mate, the first Jewish politician to be on a national ticket. Lieberman charmed voters with his broad smile and gee-whiz attitude. But four years later, when he attempted to win the presidential nomination himself after Gore decided against a second try, his campaign never caught fire. He dropped out in early February 2004 after losing in seven primary states, including Delaware, which he had targeted most heavily.

His religious faith is a driving force for Lieberman. He has been a fervent supporter of Israel, and has been more open than most Democrats to Bush's proposal to give faith-based organizations federal funds to provide social services. In 2000, he was one of nine Senate Democrats supporting a bill to create tax-deferred education savings accounts that parents could use for tutoring, supplies or private school tuition — a backdoor approach, in the view of liberal Democrats, to the GOP idea of creating vouchers that would drain money from the public schools.

Before the 2000 campaign, Lieberman was perhaps best known to the nation for a September 1998 speech criticizing President Bill Clinton's behavior in the Monica Lewinsky sex scandal as "immoral." But he never called for the president's resignation and like all other Senate Democrats, he voted against convicting Clinton in the 1999 impeachment trial.

Lieberman always has been politically ambitious. He won a state Senate seat in 1970 — helped by 24-year-old campaign aide Clinton, who was then at Yale Law School — and soon rose to majority leader. He lost a race for the U.S. House in the Reagan landslide of 1980, but rebounded in 1982 to become Connecticut attorney general.

Six years later, Lieberman mounted a tough and sometimes negative campaign for the Senate and won a narrow upset victory over Lowell P. Weicker Jr., a three-term liberal Republican. To win, he had to rally core liberal Democratic supporters while running to the right of Weicker on school prayer and foreign policy. He has prevailed comfortably ever since, with the exception of the 2006 election.

KEY VOTES

2006

No Confirm Samuel A. Alito Jr. to the Supreme Court

Yes Allow consideration of a bill to establish a $140 billion trust fund to compensate victims of asbestos exposure

No Extend tax cuts for two years at a cost of $70 billion over five years

Yes Overhaul immigration policy with border security, enforcement and guest worker program

No Allow consideration of a bill to permanently repeal the estate tax

No Urge President Bush to begin troop withdrawals from Iraq in 2006

Yes Lift President Bush's restrictions on stem cell research funding

Yes Authorize military tribunals for suspected terrorists

2005

Yes Curb class action lawsuits by shifting them from state to federal courts

Yes Allow confirmation vote on Priscilla R. Owen to the U.S. Court of Appeals for the 5th Circuit

No Oppose mandatory emissions limits and block recognition of global warming as a threat

? Approve free-trade pact with five Central American countries

Yes Pass energy policy overhaul favored by President Bush emphasizing domestic oil and gas production

No Shield gunmakers from lawsuits when their products are used in crimes

Yes Ban torture of prisoners in U.S. custody

No Renew 16 provisions of the Patriot Act

No Allow final vote on opening the Arctic National Wildlife Refuge to oil and gas exploration

CQ VOTE STUDIES

	PARTY UNITY		PRESIDENTIAL SUPPORT	
	Support	Oppose	Support	Oppose
2006	85%	15%	62%	38%
2005	90%	10%	46%	54%
2004	89%	11%	63%	37%
2003	95%	5%	32%	68%
2002	85%	15%	77%	23%
2001	93%	7%	69%	31%
2000	88%	12%	94%	6%
1999	87%	13%	89%	11%
1998	80%	20%	83%	17%
1997	77%	23%	93%	7%

INTEREST GROUPS

	AFL-CIO	ADA	CCUS	ACU
2006	77%	75%	44%	17%
2005	92%	80%	61%	8%
2004	83%	75%	79%	0%
2003	100%	70%	25%	0%
2002	92%	85%	60%	20%
2001	93%	95%	43%	28%
2000	80%	75%	33%	20%
1999	78%	95%	47%	0%
1998	75%	80%	56%	16%
1997	29%	75%	60%	20%

Rep. John B. Larson (D)

CAPITOL OFFICE
225-2265
www.house.gov/larson
1005 Longworth 20515-0701; fax 225-1031

COMMITTEES
Select Energy Independence & Global Warming
Ways & Means

RESIDENCE
East Hartford

BORN
July 22, 1948, Hartford, Conn.

RELIGION
Roman Catholic

FAMILY
Wife, Leslie Larson; three children

EDUCATION
Central Connecticut State U., B.S. 1971 (history)

CAREER
Insurance company owner; high school teacher

POLITICAL HIGHLIGHTS
East Hartford Board of Education, 1978-79; East Hartford Town Council, 1979-83; Conn. Senate, 1983-95 (president pro tempore, 1987-95); sought Democratic nomination for governor, 1994

ELECTION RESULTS

2006 GENERAL		
John B. Larson (D)	154,539	74.4%
Scott MacLean (R)	53,010	25.5%
2006 PRIMARY		
John B. Larson (D)		unopposed
2004 GENERAL		
John B. Larson (D)	198,802	73.0%
John M. Halstead (R)	73,601	27.0%

PREVIOUS WINNING PERCENTAGES
2002 (67%); 2000 (72%); 1998 (58%)

Elected 1998; 5th term

An affable insider, Larson is the vice chairman of the Democratic Caucus, the lowest rung in the party's elected leadership in the House. He was elected to the post in early 2006, after outmaneuvering two better-known candidates, Jan Schakowsky of Illinois and Joseph Crowley of New York. Larson benefited from a split in the caucus between supporters of Democratic Leader Nancy Pelosi of California, who favored liberal Schakowsky, and those of then Whip Steny H. Hoyer of Maryland, who backed centrist Crowley.

During the race, Larson quietly picked off votes one by one, aided by John P. Murtha of Pennsylvania, the senior Democrat on the Defense Appropriations Subcommittee and a consummate behind-the-scenes operator. Larson also was able to cash chits he had earned by doing favors for colleagues as the top-ranking Democrat on the perks-disbursing House Administration Committee from 2003 to 2005.

"We worked both Joe's list and Jan's list," Larson said. "Our strategy was a second-ballot strategy." When Schakowsky came in third on the first ballot, she threw her support to Larson, who went on to beat Crowley, 116-87, on the second.

Larson was inspired to enter public service by President John F. Kennedy, another Catholic from a large New England family, yet his views reflect more the middle of the Democratic Party than Kennedy's ever did. A member of the New Democrat Coalition, a centrist group, Larson says he was influenced by his experiences as an insurance business owner.

"I'm not a person who thinks the federal government should be interfering in everything," he said. "But . . . when jobs are outsourced, and your pension is being pulled out and you have no health benefits, then you need government to level the playing field for you, so you're not the one getting the short end of the stick."

During his first three terms, Larson served on the Armed Services Committee, using the post to protect his hometown's largest employer, Pratt & Whitney Aircraft, which makes engines for military aircraft. He also fought proposed funding cuts for the F-22 jet fighter, whose engine is made by Pratt & Whitney.

Earlier in his House career, Larson was also on the Science Committee, where he championed legislation to increase funding for aerospace research and development. In 2004, Larson and Connecticut's two senators obtained funding to create a National Center for Aerospace Leadership in the 1st District, which is anchored by Hartford, an overwhelmingly minority city that lost population in the 1990s.

In 2003, Pelosi made Larson the top-ranking Democrat on the House Administration panel and appointed him to the Democratic Steering Committee, which makes committee assignments. Two years later, he gave up his seats on Armed Services and House Administration to take a coveted seat on the influential Ways and Means Committee. He joined fellow Democrats there in successfully fighting off President Bush's proposal to carve out private accounts from Social Security payroll taxes. He pushed unsuccessfully to allow Medicare to negotiate lower prescription drug prices for seniors and he sided with labor-oriented Democrats in battling virtually all trade agreements, including the 2005 Central American Free Trade Agreement.

Closely aligned with Murtha, the first prominent House Democrat to call for a prompt withdrawal from Iraq, Larson is a critic of U.S. strategy in the war. "The military phase of this operation is over," he wrote in a 2005 opinion piece for the Hartford Courant newspaper. "The Iraqi government, however, will never stand on its own as long as we remain there."

A former high school football coach, Larson often emphasizes the importance of teamwork, particularly in the partisan atmosphere of the House. One of his earliest successes in Congress came during his first term, when he lined up both Republican Speaker J. Dennis Hastert and Democratic Leader Richard A. Gephardt as cosponsors of a measure directing the librarian of Congress to prepare a history of the House.

Larson grew up in an East Hartford public housing project originally built for workers for United Aircraft, precursor to United Technologies Corp., the parent company of Pratt & Whitney. His father was a Pratt & Whitney fireman who moonlighted as an auto mechanic and butcher to support the family. His mother, a state employee, served on the town council. Larson and his seven siblings shared a single bathroom in what they laughingly refer to as the "brick mansion at 10 Chandler Street."

After graduating from Central Connecticut State University, Larson taught high school history and coached for about five years. He left teaching to join an insurance company that he eventually bought. After stints on the local school board and town council, he was elected in 1982 to the state Senate, where he served a dozen years, including a record eight years as president pro tempore, the state's third-highest office. His proudest achievement as a state legislator was Connecticut's Family and Medical Leave Act, the first such law enacted in the country.

Larson made an unsuccessful bid for governor in 1994, gaining the endorsements of party leaders but losing the primary to state Comptroller Bill Curry. "After being in a fetal position for three months, I went back to work," he said. In 1996, he led a statewide volunteer drive, "ConneCT '96," to wire schools and libraries to the Internet. In Congress, he founded the Digital Divide Caucus, which aims to make technology available to all Americans, regardless of income or location.

When veteran 1st District Democratic Rep. Barbara B. Kennelly announced she was running for governor in 1998, Larson was the first Democrat to file for her seat. He edged past Connecticut Secretary of State Miles S. Rapoport in the primary and then built on the lessons from his 1994 defeat to win the general election. "We did not target the likely voter, the prime voter, and saturate that list. We had to go beyond that list, and reach out to Republicans and independents and Democrat who don't normally vote," he said. He rolled to a 17 percentage point victory and has not been seriously threatened since.

KEY VOTES

2006

- Yes Stop broadband companies from favoring select Internet traffic
- No Affirm U.S. commitment to war in Iraq and reject setting a withdrawal date for troops
- No Repeal requirement for bilingual ballots at the polls
- Yes Permit U.S. sale of civilian nuclear technology to India
- No Build a 700-mile fence on the U.S.-Mexico border to curb illegal crossings
- No Permit warrantless wiretaps of suspected terrorists

2005

- No Intervene in the life-support case of Terri Schiavo
- Yes Lift President Bush's restrictions on stem cell research funding
- Yes Prohibit FBI access to library and bookstore records
- No Approve free-trade pact with five Central American countries
- No Pass energy policy overhaul favored by President Bush emphasizing domestic oil and gas production
- No End mandatory preservation of habitat of endangered animal and plant species
- Yes Ban torture of prisoners in U.S. custody

CQ VOTE STUDIES

	PARTY UNITY		PRESIDENTIAL SUPPORT	
	Support	Oppose	Support	Oppose
2006	97%	3%	24%	76%
2005	98%	2%	15%	85%
2004	95%	5%	24%	76%
2003	96%	4%	18%	82%
2002	95%	5%	30%	70%

INTEREST GROUPS

	AFL-CIO	ADA	CCUS	ACU
2006	100%	95%	43%	8%
2005	93%	100%	44%	0%
2004	93%	100%	38%	16%
2003	100%	100%	21%	20%
2002	100%	95%	50%	0%

CONNECTICUT 1

Central – Hartford, Bristol

Resembling a backward "C," the 1st carves a path from the state's sparsely populated northwestern towns along the Massachusetts border to the capital of Hartford before winding west to occupy the central city of Bristol. Situated midway between Boston and New York — roughly 100 miles from each — the staunchly Democratic district is an attractive commercial center straddling the Northeast Corridor.

Once recognized as the international insurance capital, Hartford still hosts the headquarters or offices of several major firms. The insurance industry combines with the financial services sector and state government to form the backbone of the 1st's economy. Aerospace and defense firms also provide a significant source of employment, as United Technologies' Pratt & Whitney, which builds aircraft engines, is headquartered in East Hartford. Bristol is the home of ESPN, and the network is a job source.

The bustle of the capital's central business district belies the economic struggle of many city residents. Reflecting a state trend, the 1st's predominately white and wealthy suburbs thrive, while cities such as Hartford depopulate and decay. Unemployment hovers above 9 percent, and Hartford's school system is floundering with test scores that lag behind the rest of the region. Significant efforts are under way to renew Hartford's historic downtown and riverfront, and development programs aim to aid the city's troubled manufacturing industry. Hometown companies Stanley tools and Colt firearms continue Hartford area operations, but other manufacturers have undergone downsizing.

Hartford area voters have not sent a Republican to the U.S. House since 1956, and the 1st gave Democrat John Kerry his largest statewide presidential vote percentage in 2004. The city's large minority population, mostly Hispanics of Puerto Rican descent, is firmly Democratic.

MAJOR INDUSTRY

Insurance, banking, defense, government

CITIES

Hartford, 121,578; West Hartford (unincorporated), 63,589; Bristol, 60,062; East Hartford (unincorporated), 49,575

NOTABLE

Hartford's Wadsworth Atheneum is the oldest public art museum in the United States.

Rep. Joe Courtney (D)

CAPITOL OFFICE
225-2076
courtney.house.gov
215 Cannon 20515-0702; fax 225-4977

COMMITTEES
Armed Services
Education & Labor

RESIDENCE
Vernon

BORN
April 6, 1953, Hartford, Conn.

RELIGION
Roman Catholic

FAMILY
Wife, Audrey Budarz Courtney; two children

EDUCATION
Tufts U., B.A. 1975 (history); U. of Connecticut, J.D. 1978

CAREER
Lawyer; public defender

POLITICAL HIGHLIGHTS
Conn. House, 1987-95; Democratic nominee for lieutenant governor, 1998; Democratic nominee for U.S. House, 2002

ELECTION RESULTS

2006 GENERAL		
Joe Courtney (D)	121,248	50.02%
Rob Simmons (R)	121,165	49.98%
2006 PRIMARY		
Joe Courtney (D)		unopposed

Elected 2006; 1st term

Courtney has the dubious distinction of winning the closest House race in 2006. The former state representative unseated three-term Republican Rep. Rob Simmons by 83 votes out of more than 242,000 votes cast. The race was a rematch of a 2002 contest in which Simmons bested Courtney by 8 percentage points.

A leader on health issues in the state legislature, Courtney says he hopes to use his expertise to bring Connecticut-style reforms to Washington. In the state House, he chaired the Public Health and Human Services committees. In Congress, his seat on the Education and Labor panel's Health Subcommittee gives him the opportunity to help shape health care policy at the federal level. He wants to create a Child Health Insurance Program like the one implemented in Connecticut.

Courtney also advocates changes to the No Child Left Behind Act, which ties federal aid to student performance. He says the law sets unfair standards for measuring schools' success. Courtney favors the idea of a "growth model" that would establish a continuum for grading teachers and schools. He has also called for adequate funding from Washington to meet the law's requirements, an issue over which his state is suing in court.

The youngest of five boys, Courtney grew up in West Hartford. He says he was influenced more by the "Camelot" era of the early 1960s than his father's mildly Republican stance. "I was an Irish Catholic kid who remembered John F. Kennedy — the nuns actually prayed for him during the election in second grade," he says.

Courtney served as a staffer for Democrat Sam Gejdenson when Gejdenson was a state representative and Courtney was in law school. Gejdenson went on to serve for two decades in Congress, losing his seat to Simmons in 2000. In 2006, Connecticut politics came full circle with Courtney ousting Simmons.

Courtney had the national political environment on his side: The anti-Republican mood was too much for Simmons, but barely. Courtney's razor-thin victory puts him near the top of the GOP's target list for 2008.

CONNECTICUT 2

East – Norwich, New London

Predominately middle-class and politically moderate, the 2nd is the state's largest district. It runs from the waterfront of Middlesex and New London counties north to the Massachusetts border through small former mill towns and the main campus of the University of Connecticut in Storrs.

Defense and tourism now steer the 2nd's ship. Groton's General Dynamics' Electric Boat shipyard and the New London Naval Submarine Base are major employers. But declining Navy demand for subs is forcing shipyard layoffs, and the New London base has fought to survive recent BRAC rounds.

Coastal attractions such as historic Mystic Seaport draw visitors, but the massive American Indian-owned casino resorts are the rainmakers of the 2nd's economy. The large casino Foxwoods, the state's leading taxpayer, makes more than $1 billion in annual profit. Mohegan Sun, the resort casino in Uncasville, hosts the state's only professional sports team, the WNBA's Connecticut Sun. The influx of gamblers and casino workers has strained highways here, making transportation a chronic political issue. Casinos and surrounding towns also have quarreled over taxes and which regulations shall apply to reservation land.

The 2nd is largely white, with growing black and Hispanic communities. The competitive district's U.S. House seat changed hands in 2006, and Democrat John Kerry took 54 percent of the 2004 presidential vote here.

MAJOR INDUSTRY
Casinos, defense, tourism, health care

MILITARY BASES
New London Naval Submarine Base, 7,500 military, 2,400 civilian (2006)

CITIES
Norwich, 36,117; New London, 25,671

NOTABLE
U.S. Coast Guard Academy in New London.

Rep. Rosa DeLauro (D)

CAPITOL OFFICE
225-3661
www.house.gov/delauro
2262 Rayburn 20515-0703; fax 225-4890

COMMITTEES
Appropriations
(Agriculture - chairwoman)
Budget

RESIDENCE
New Haven

BORN
March 2, 1943, New Haven, Conn.

RELIGION
Roman Catholic

FAMILY
Husband, Stanley Greenberg; three children

EDUCATION
London School of Economics, attended 1962-63; Marymount College (N.Y.), B.A. 1964; Columbia U., M.A. 1966 (international politics)

CAREER
Political activist; congressional and mayoral aide

POLITICAL HIGHLIGHTS
No previous office

ELECTION RESULTS

2006 GENERAL		
Rosa DeLauro (D)	150,436	76.0%
Joseph Vollano (R)	44,386	22.4%
Daniel A. Sumrall (GREEN)	3,089	1.6%
2006 PRIMARY		
Rosa DeLauro (D)		unopposed
2004 GENERAL		
Rosa DeLauro (D)	200,638	72.4%
Richter Elser (R)	69,160	25.0%
Ralph A. Ferrucci (GREEN)	7,182	2.6%

PREVIOUS WINNING PERCENTAGES
2002 (66%); 2000 (72%); 1998 (71%); 1996 (71%); 1994 (63%); 1992 (66%); 1990 (52%)

Elected 1990; 9th term

DeLauro is one of her party's fiercest liberal champions. Steeped in kitchen-table politics and community activism from her childhood in a working-class Italian neighborhood, she is also a smart politician — one of a circle of leaders working to reframe the party's traditional positions to put it on an aggressive footing after more than a decade in the minority.

For DeLauro, a lifelong Catholic, that work has included Democratic efforts to refocus the "values debate" onto an array of issues where the party is strongest, such as poverty and the environment. In the process, she has taken on the Catholic Church hierarchy, arguing that her party's agenda speaks to the heart of Catholic social teachings. "We all take our religion seriously," she said. "It's part of who we are."

DeLauro (da-LAUR-o) has long been a voice for the party on national issues such as abortion rights, equal pay for women and women's health parity. DeLauro knows she can speak out on national issues as long as she tends to business at home. She is hawkish on federal funding for the Black Hawk helicopter, product of the Stratford, Conn.-based Sikorsky Aircraft Corp.

DeLauro is easily one of the most recognizable faces in the House. Her floor speeches are highly partisan and are often accompanied by strong podium-pounding. She also stands out in her bright colors, bold prints and chunky jewelry. Washingtonian magazine has named her one of the "workhorses" of Congress.

During her 16 years in the House, DeLauro has broken gender barriers to climb the Democratic leadership ladder. In that quest, she has had both successes and setbacks. In the 107th Congress (2001-02), she ran the party's communications arm as the hand-picked assistant of Minority Leader Richard A. Gephardt. But as Democrats met late in 2002 to organize for the 108th Congress (2003-04), she lost a race for Democratic Caucus chief to Robert Menendez of New Jersey by a lone vote, 104-103. Though she is among the most influential House Democrats, all of her leadership roles so far have been appointed.

In the 108th Congress, Democratic Leader Nancy Pelosi made her the co-chairwoman of the Democratic Steering Committee, which makes committee assignments. She has continued in that spot through the 110th Congress (2007-08) as well. DeLauro also gained a seat on the Budget Committee in addition to her slot on Appropriations.

In 2004, she led her fellow Catholic representatives to speak out against church leaders who threatened to deny Communion to politicians who favored abortion rights. They also urged the Catholic Church to weigh in on a broader array of national issues — such as hunger, housing and wages. In 2006, she and others signed a statement urging church leaders to work with them on such social issues and leave room for disagreement on abortion rights and other matters.

DeLauro is the chairwoman of the Agriculture Appropriations Subcommittee, where she has focused much of her energy on food safety and drug approval and oversight. She is a persistent critic of the government's safeguards against diseases potentially affecting the nation's beef and poultry supplies and supports the consolidation of all federal food safety efforts into one agency. She also champions country-of-origin food labeling, which had been delayed for years by the former chairman, Henry Bonilla of Texas.

She has confronted the Food and Drug Administration over its backlog in approving cheaper generic drugs and criticized the agency's reluctance to require tougher oversight of drugs once they reach the market.

DeLauro works to ensure that her party does not take for granted the women voters who are one of its strongest constituencies. In 2005, after the Bureau of Labor Statistics stopped collecting data on women in the workforce, she and other lawmakers got the survey restarted, saying it was essential to gauge how women are faring. She also advocates tough penalties against employers who do not pay women and men equally for the same work. In 2000, she successfully pushed for legislation requiring insurers to pay for hospital stays after a mastectomy — ending a practice commonly known as "drive-through mastectomies." Her interest in women's health issues stems in part from her own battle with ovarian cancer more than 20 years ago.

All of the significant figures in DeLauro's life are passionately political. Her parents were both blue-collar activists on the New Haven City Council, and her husband is Stanley Greenberg, a prominent Democratic pollster and former adviser to President Bill Clinton.

DeLauro developed her liberal views and political smarts growing up in Wooster Square, a tight-knit Italian neighborhood in New Haven. Her father, Ted, was an immigrant, and her mother, Luisa, was a factory worker who got her high school diploma studying at night. Her parents' home was the hub of neighborhood meetings about happenings in the schools, the availability of jobs, and hassles with immigration officials. When her father decided to run for the city council, he kept a file box filled with voters' names and their concerns, then walked door-to-door to seek their votes.

In the 1960s, DeLauro became a community organizer in President Lyndon B. Johnson's War on Poverty, then worked for the mayor of New Haven. She proved her mettle running Democrat Christopher J. Dodd's first Senate campaign. When he won, she became his chief of staff for seven years. She expanded her political network by taking the helm of EMILY's List, the fundraising group that supports female candidates for higher office.

In 1990, when Democratic Rep. Bruce Morrison gave up his 3rd District seat to run for governor of Connecticut, DeLauro was ready to step out of supporting roles and become a candidate herself. Her political contacts enabled her to raise money quickly and shoo away intraparty competition.

Republicans put up state Sen. Thomas Scott, an energetic conservative opposed to gun control and abortion rights. He made some headway portraying DeLauro as a far-left radical, but her coalition of activist liberals and blue-collar voters gave her the win. Scott came back for a rematch in 1992, but DeLauro was ready with a healthy campaign war chest. She won with 66 percent of the vote and has been re-elected easily ever since.

KEY VOTES

2006

- Yes Stop broadband companies from favoring select Internet traffic
- No Affirm U.S. commitment to war in Iraq and reject setting a withdrawal date for troops
- No Repeal requirement for bilingual ballots at the polls
- No Permit U.S. sale of civilian nuclear technology to India
- No Build a 700-mile fence on the U.S.-Mexico border to curb illegal crossings
- No Permit warrantless wiretaps of suspected terrorists

2005

- ? Intervene in the life-support case of Terri Schiavo
- Yes Lift President Bush's restrictions on stem cell research funding
- Yes Prohibit FBI access to library and bookstore records
- No Approve free-trade pact with five Central American countries
- No Pass energy policy overhaul favored by President Bush emphasizing domestic oil and gas production
- No End mandatory preservation of habitat of endangered animal and plant species
- Yes Ban torture of prisoners in U.S. custody

CQ VOTE STUDIES

	PARTY UNITY		PRESIDENTIAL SUPPORT	
	Support	Oppose	Support	Oppose
2006	98%	2%	13%	87%
2005	98%	2%	9%	91%
2004	98%	2%	21%	79%
2003	99%	1%	18%	82%
2002	96%	4%	22%	78%

INTEREST GROUPS

	AFL-CIO	ADA	CCUS	ACU
2006	100%	100%	27%	8%
2005	93%	95%	37%	0%
2004	100%	100%	29%	4%
2003	93%	100%	30%	20%
2002	100%	100%	35%	0%

CONNECTICUT 3
South – New Haven, Milford

The 3rd includes coastal New Haven County towns such as Guilford on Long Island Sound and the port city of New Haven, and takes in Stratford in Fairfield County and part of inland Middletown in Middlesex County.

Like other cities in the state, New Haven is far poorer than its affluent suburbs. Yale University is the city's largest employer, but labor issues cause tension between the school and the city's blue-collar workers. In order to ease that tension, Yale invested tens of millions of dollars into civic development and has promised more. One initiative, to find private outlets for Yale's scientific research, brought biotechnology start-ups to the city. Some firms grew and contracted with pharmaceutical giants, but critics charge that the companies do not provide jobs for the city's working-class residents.

Beyond Yale's influence, the economy here relies on the defense industry, manufacturing and technology. Sikorsky Aircraft, a helicopter manufacturer based in Stratford, depends on military contracts, and it suffered after the Defense Department terminated the Comanche helicopter program and did not award Sikorsky the contract for the Marine One presidential helicopter. Suburban industrial parks have drawn in manufacturing and technology firms. Also, the city has begun revitalizing downtown, but attempts to lure tourists to the waterfront and groups to its convention centers have achieved only minor success. Professionals commute from the district's suburbs throughout the state and as far away as New York City.

The 3rd's working-class constituents and liberal ivory-tower elite, along with New Haven's Hispanic and black residents, combine to make the district strongly Democratic. Many Italian-Americans reside in the district's suburbs. Overall, the 3rd gave Democrat John Kerry a comfortable 14-point margin of victory in the 2004 presidential election.

MAJOR INDUSTRY
Higher education, defense, biotechnology, manufacturing

CITIES
New Haven, 123,626; West Haven, 52,360; Milford, 52,305; Stratford (unincorporated), 49,976; Middletown (pt.), 34,329; Naugatuck, 30,989

NOTABLE
New Haven, home to strong Italian communities, claims to be the birthplace of pizza in America.

Rep. Christopher Shays (R)

CAPITOL OFFICE
225-5541
www.house.gov/shays
1126 Longworth 20515-0704; fax 225-9629

COMMITTEES
Financial Services
Homeland Security
Oversight & Government Reform

RESIDENCE
Bridgeport

BORN
Oct. 18, 1945, Darien, Conn.

RELIGION
Christian Scientist

FAMILY
Wife, Betsi deRaismes Shays; one child

EDUCATION
Principia College, B.A. 1968 (American history & political science); New York U., M.B.A. 1974 (urban affairs & economics), M.P.A. 1978

CAREER
Real estate broker; public official; Peace Corps volunteer

POLITICAL HIGHLIGHTS
Conn. House, 1975-87; Republican candidate for mayor of Stamford, 1983

ELECTION RESULTS

2006 GENERAL		
Christopher Shays (R)	106,510	51.0%
Diane Farrell (D)	99,450	47.6%
Philip Z. Maymin (LIBERT)	3,058	1.5%
2006 PRIMARY		
Christopher Shays (R)		unopposed
2004 GENERAL		
Christopher Shays (R)	152,493	52.4%
Diane Farrell (D)	138,333	47.6%

PREVIOUS WINNING PERCENTAGES
2002 (64%); 2000 (58%); 1998 (69%); 1996 (60%); 1994 (74%); 1992 (67%); 1990 (77%); 1988 (72%); 1987 Special Election (57%)

Elected August 1987; 10th full term

During his long political career, the moderate Shays has carved out a reputation as a maverick, well practiced in political theater, who carefully tracks the pulse of his district. Those attributes helped him achieve an unwanted distinction: He was the only House Republican from New England to survive the Democratic sweep in the 2006 elections.

In an election in which voters rejected the Iraq War, Shays deftly turned his 2002 vote for the war and early support for President Bush into strident critiques of the administration's handling of Iraq and a call for a plan to withdraw U.S. troops. He also reminded voters weary of congressional corruption that he had long been at odds with the most powerful House GOP leaders. He underscored his points with a 54-page campaign booklet that charted his war policy, his declining support of Bush and the millions of federal dollars sent to the district the previous two years.

A Democratic-controlled Congress may be kinder to Shays' priorities than the ones controlled by his own party. He advocates increased national security intelligence oversight (which he pursued as the past chairman of the Government Reform Subcommittee on National Security), tighter ethics rules and energy independence, including repeal of $8 billion in tax breaks for energy producers. "I will be working with the Democrats on a lot of issues that they and I feel strongly about," Shays said, adding after a pause, "to the extent [House Speaker] Nancy Pelosi allows them."

Shays can be a GOP partisan. When then Speaker J. Dennis Hastert came under fire in 2006 for his handling of the congressional page sex scandal, Shays defended Hastert by referring to the 1969 incident in which a young woman drowned in a car driven by Massachusetts Democratic Sen. Edward M. Kennedy. "Dennis Hastert didn't kill anybody," Shays said.

During debate on the 2002 law creating the Homeland Security Department, he offered a key amendment on the rights of federal unionized workers. It gave GOP moderates a chance to vote for something that seemed to favor labor, but essentially preserved the expanded management authority the White House sought.

Initially a strong backer of the Iraq War, Shays nonetheless stood out as the rare Republican who demanded oversight. By the end of 2006, he had visited Iraq 15 times to track Pentagon and State Department programs under his subcommittee's jurisdiction.

Shays often frustrates GOP leaders. In 2006, he voted with his party a mere 57 percent of the time, the lowest score among House Republicans and a 10 percentage point drop from 2005. His support for Bush's positions has declined from a high of 82 percent in 2002 to a low of 53 percent in 2006.

Shays opposes oil drilling in Alaska's Arctic National Wildlife Refuge and a constitutional ban on same-sex marriage. He supports abortion rights, expanded stem cell research, raising the minimum wage and gun control.

After dozens of his constituents died in the Sept. 11 attacks, Shays sought, against Bush's wishes, an independent inquiry into government lapses in tracking terrorists. He pushed for the intelligence overhaul enacted in 2004 and worked with Virginia Republican Frank R. Wolf to create the independent Iraq Study Group that recommended a course correction in 2006.

Shays scored his biggest legislative triumph in 2002, with enactment of new federal campaign finance limits he cosponsored with Democrat Martin T. Meehan of Massachusetts. (A similar bill by Arizona Republican John McCain and Democrat Russ Feingold of Wisconsin passed the Senate.) He continues to push for more campaign restrictions, with little luck so far.

Angry GOP leaders, who had fought the 2002 campaign law, denied Shays chairmanship of the Government Reform Committee in 2003. But he continued speaking out. After Republicans temporarily relaxed ethics rules in 2005 to help then Majority Leader Tom DeLay of Texas, Shays accused his party of "prostituting the ethics rules" and was the first to call for DeLay's resignation from the leadership team.

Shays' positions flow naturally from the Rockefeller Republicanism that, while dying elsewhere, is still alive in the 4th District where he was born. They also appeal to struggling residents of Bridgeport, the state's biggest city. He remains a Republican, he says, because "I believe that dollars are better spent in the private sector than in the public sector." He adds, "I believe in a strong national defense, and I think the terrorist threat is for real. I think a lot of my Democratic colleagues don't."

Shays, a Christian Scientist, was a conscientious objector during the Vietnam War. Marrying right out of college, he and Betsi deRaismes Shays spent two years in the Fiji Islands as Peace Corps volunteers. "Having served two years in the Peace Corps, I concluded there was no way I was going to kill anybody," he recalled. But he voted for the 1991 Persian Gulf War and the 2002 resolution authorizing use of force against Saddam Hussein's regime. He says, "I realized that when you vote, your own personal views are separate from what you have to do for the good of the country."

Shays' interest in government goes back to the third grade, where his public school teacher led him to biographies of historic figures like George Washington and Davy Crockett.

At 29, Shays was elected to the state House in the post-Watergate election of 1974. He became a prominent advocate for victims' rights after the 1979 rape and murder of a 14-year-old Stamford girl. He also developed an anti-establishment reputation. In 1985, he was jailed for several days on a contempt citation after refusing to leave the witness stand during a hearing on misconduct charges against two lawyers.

Name recognition from that event helped propel him to the House two years later, when veteran Republican Stewart B. McKinney died. With an extensive grass-roots network, Shays defeated the anointed GOP candidate in the primary and took the special election with 57 percent of the vote.

His first serious challenge came in 2004, when Democrat Diane Farrell, the First Selectman, or mayor, of Westport, criticized his war stance. Shays won with 52 percent of the vote. During a rematch with Farrell in 2006, Shays defended his record in 11 campaign debates and won with 51 percent.

KEY VOTES

2006

- Yes Stop broadband companies from favoring select Internet traffic
- Yes Affirm U.S. commitment to war in Iraq and reject setting a withdrawal date for troops
- No Repeal requirement for bilingual ballots at the polls
- Yes Permit U.S. sale of civilian nuclear technology to India
- Yes Build a 700-mile fence on the U.S.-Mexico border to curb illegal crossings
- No Permit warrantless wiretaps of suspected terrorists

2005

- No Intervene in the life-support case of Terri Schiavo
- Yes Lift President Bush's restrictions on stem cell research funding
- No Prohibit FBI access to library and bookstore records
- Yes Approve free-trade pact with five Central American countries
- No Pass energy policy overhaul favored by President Bush emphasizing domestic oil and gas production
- No End mandatory preservation of habitat of endangered animal and plant species
- Yes Ban torture of prisoners in U.S. custody

CQ VOTE STUDIES

	PARTY UNITY		PRESIDENTIAL SUPPORT	
	Support	Oppose	Support	Oppose
2006	57%	43%	53%	47%
2005	67%	33%	57%	43%
2004	69%	31%	59%	41%
2003	78%	22%	67%	33%
2002	80%	20%	82%	18%

INTEREST GROUPS

	AFL-CIO	ADA	CCUS	ACU
2006	58%	65%	62%	36%
2005	27%	55%	70%	20%
2004	57%	70%	86%	38%
2003	27%	30%	77%	48%
2002	11%	20%	95%	76%

CONNECTICUT 4
Southwest — Bridgeport, Stamford

The 4th extends from the outskirts of New York City and runs along the spectacularly wealthy "Gold Coast" towns on Long Island Sound. It also takes in the industrial city of Norwalk and white-collar Stamford, and, in stark contrast to the coastal affluence, Bridgeport, the state's largest city. The district's extremes create difficult terrain for politicians to navigate, as polo clubs rub elbows with the decayed city.

Financial workers riding commuter trains and Interstate 95 long brought wealth from Wall Street to the district's tony suburbs, but with the burgeoning hedge fund industry centered in Greenwich, the trains and roads are experiencing rising occupancy in both directions. As some New York City residents commute to the 4th for work, traffic issues already permeating the public debate have been exacerbated. Some relief may come once a high-speed ferry service from Bridgeport to LaGuardia Airport and Lower Manhattan is established.

Bridgeport has suffered the fate of many post-industrial cities and registers a poverty rate far above the national average. Crime and drugs plague the city and development efforts have achieved mixed success. The South End, however, has seen marked progress, as apartments and businesses take over abandoned factories.

The suburban elite drive the political landscape here. Darien, New Canaan and Oxford were three of the seven jurisdictions in the state to give George W. Bush more than 60 percent of the vote in 2004. Still, the 4th preferred the last three Democratic presidential candidates overall, and most of the urban poor votes Democratic — John Kerry's 71 percent showing in Bridgeport was his fifth-highest percentage in the state in 2004. GOP mayors continue to dominate local politics in the affluent suburbs, while Stamford and Bridgeport have Democratic mayors.

MAJOR INDUSTRY

Banking, manufacturing, health care

CITIES

Bridgeport, 139,529; Stamford, 117,083; Norwalk, 82,951; Trumbull (unincorporated), 34,243; Shelton (pt.), 28,192

NOTABLE

General Electric's corporate headquarters are in Fairfield; The World Wrestling Entertainment corporate headquarters is in Stamford; The Barnum Museum in Bridgeport houses many of the showman's exhibits.

Rep. Christopher S. Murphy (D)

CAPITOL OFFICE
225-4476
chrismurphy.house.gov
501 Cannon 20515-0705; fax 225-4488

COMMITTEES
Financial Services
Oversight & Government Reform

RESIDENCE
Cheshire

BORN
Aug. 3, 1973, White Plains, N.Y.

RELIGION
Protestant

FAMILY
Engaged to Cathy Holahan

EDUCATION
Williams College, B.A. 1996 (history & political science); U. of Connecticut, J.D. 2002

CAREER
Lawyer; state legislative and campaign aide

POLITICAL HIGHLIGHTS
Southington Planning & Zoning Commission, 1997-99; Conn. House, 1999-2003; Conn. Senate, 2003-07

ELECTION RESULTS

2006 GENERAL		
Christopher S. Murphy (D, WFM)	122,980	56.5%
Nancy L. Johnson (R)	94,824	43.5%
2006 PRIMARY		
Christopher S. Murphy (D, WFM)	unopposed	

Elected 2006; 1st term

Murphy is a young man in a hurry, an irrepressible multi-tasker who never sees any goal as beyond his reach. In 1996, at the ripe age of 23, he managed the congressional campaign of a virtual unknown who came within 1,600 votes of unseating veteran Republican Nancy L. Johnson. Ten years later, Murphy finished the job, ousting Johnson by a solid margin.

In between, he captured a seat in the state House, unseating a 14-year incumbent, and then won election to the state Senate four years later. He did it all while working and attending law school. "I think it's a miracle that I passed the bar," he says, because on the first day of the exam, "I left immediately to cast a vote, and the second day I left immediately to announce I was running for state Senate."

That kind of drive is characteristic. "I just think that I discovered early on that there were things that people said couldn't be done that could be done, it was just that no one had tried," he says.

Murphy is a member of the 30-Something Working Group, a collection of young lawmakers who take to the House floor regularly to sound off about the issues of the day. He serves on the Oversight and Government Reform Committee, which he says gives him a chance to learn about a broad sweep of issues, and on Financial Services, a strong fit for a Connecticut lawmaker, given the state's insurance industry and Wall Street ties.

In the state Senate, he chaired the Public Health Committee. He advocates universal health coverage but thinks the big push on that issue will have to wait until after the 2008 presidential elections. In the meantime, he has volunteered to help organize constituent pressure for reform.

Murphy's grandfather and great-grandfather worked at a New Britain ball bearing factory; he is a staunch supporter of organized labor. His mother grew up in public housing, while his father came from a more affluent background. He credits his mother with instilling a sense of obligation to give back to society in all three of her children. His brother works for Save the Children, and his sister is a social worker. In high school, he picked politics as his focus. He's never looked back.

CONNECTICUT 5

West — Danbury, New Britain, most of Waterbury

Based in the hilly western part of the state, the 5th is a mix of rolling bucolic farmland and mid-size industrial cities. Its longstanding manufacturing cities are making the difficult transition into successful centers of technology and skilled manufacturing.

Waterbury is the district's most populous city, with about 80 percent of residents living in the 5th (the rest live in the 3rd). It is middle-class and diverse, with blacks and Hispanics together totaling 40 percent of the population. East of Waterbury, on the 5th's southeastern edge, are Cheshire, an upper-income, Republican-leaning area, and Meriden, a Democratic-voting area.

North and east of Waterbury, the district branches off to take in New Britain, where the Hand Tools Division of Stanley Works is a major employer. New Britain votes Democratic and is home to a very large Polish community, in addition to an ample Hispanic community. Growing Danbury, located in the 5th's southwestern corner, has experienced a recent influx of immigrants. Employers in Danbury include Praxair, which makes industrial gases, and Scholastic Library Publishing.

The 5th is politically competitive. John Kerry barely won the 2004 presidential vote here, and the House seat changed hands in 2006. George W. Bush carried several towns north and east of Danbury, including burgeoning New Milford and Newtown, in 2004.

MAJOR INDUSTRY
Manufacturing, health care

CITIES
Waterbury (pt.), 88,624; Danbury, 74,848; New Britain, 71,538; Meriden, 58,244

NOTABLE
Cheshire was designated the "Bedding Plant Capital of Connecticut" by the state legislature.

DELAWARE

Gov. Ruth Ann Minner (D)

First elected: 2000
Length of term: 4 years
Term expires: 1/09
Salary: $132,500
Phone: (302) 739-4101

Residence: Milford
Born: Jan. 17, 1935; Milford, Del.
Religion: Methodist
Family: Widowed; three children
Education: Delaware Technical and Community College, G.E.D. 1968
Career: Towing company owner; state legislative aide
Political highlights: Del. House, 1975-83; Del. Senate, 1983-93; lieutenant governor, 1993-2001

Election results:

2004 GENERAL		
Ruth Ann Minner (D)	185,687	50.9%
William Swain Lee (R)	167,115	45.8%
Frank Infante (LIBERT, INDC)	12,206	3.3%

Lt. Gov. John Carney (D)

First elected: 2000
Length of term: 4 years
Term expires: 1/09
Salary: $75,500
Phone: (302) 744-4333

LEGISLATURE

General Assembly: January-June

Senate: 21 members, 4-year terms
2007 ratios: 13 D, 8 R; 14 men, 7 women
Salary: $42,000
Phone: (302) 744-4087

House: 41 members, two-year terms
2007 ratios: 22 R, 19 D; 32 men, 9 women
Salary: $42,000
Phone: (302) 744-4087

TERM LIMITS

Governor: 2 terms
Senate: No
House: No

URBAN STATISTICS

CITY	POPULATION
Wilmington	72,664
Dover	32,135
Newark	28,547
Milford	6,732
Seaford	6,699

REGISTERED VOTERS

Democrat	44%
Republican	32%
Others/unaffiliated	24%

POPULATION

2006 population (est.)	853,476
2000 population	783,600
1990 population	666,168
Percent change (1990-2000)	+17.6%
Rank among states (2006)	45
Median age	36
Born in state	48.3%
Foreign born	5.7%
Violent crime rate	684/100,000
Poverty level	9.2%
Federal workers	5,438
Military	8,799

ELECTIONS

STATE ELECTION OFFICIAL
(302) 739-4277
DEMOCRATIC PARTY
(302) 328-9036
REPUBLICAN PARTY
(302) 651-0260

MISCELLANEOUS

Web: www.delaware.gov
Capital: Dover

U.S. CONGRESS

Senate: 2 Democrats
House: 1 Republican

2000 Census Statistics by District

DIST.	2004 VOTE FOR PRESIDENT BUSH	KERRY	WHITE	BLACK	ASIAN	HISP	MEDIAN INCOME	WHITE COLLAR	BLUE COLLAR	SERVICE INDUSTRY	OVER 64	UNDER 18	COLLEGE EDUCATION	RURAL	SQ. MILES
AL	46%	53%	72%	19%	2%	5%	$47,381	63%	23%	15%	13%	25%	25%	20%	1,954
STATE	46	53	72	19	2	5	$47,381	63	23	15	13	25	25	20	1,954
U.S.	50.7	48.3	69	12	4	13	$41,994	60	25	15	12	26	24	21	3,537,438

Wilmington
Newark
New Castle
Dover
Kent
At Large
Sussex

Sen. Joseph R. Biden Jr. (D)

CAPITOL OFFICE
224-5042
biden.senate.gov
201 Russell 20510-0802; fax 224-0139

COMMITTEES
Foreign Relations - chairman
Judiciary
(Crime & Drugs - chairman)

RESIDENCE
Wilmington

BORN
Nov. 20, 1942, Scranton, Pa.

RELIGION
Roman Catholic

FAMILY
Wife, Jill Biden; four children (one deceased)

EDUCATION
U. of Delaware, B.A. 1965 (history & political science); Syracuse U., J.D. 1968

CAREER
Lawyer

POLITICAL HIGHLIGHTS
New Castle County Council, 1970-72

ELECTION RESULTS

2002 GENERAL		
Joseph R. Biden Jr. (D)	135,253	58.2%
Raymond J. Clatworthy (R)	94,793	40.8%
2002 PRIMARY		
Joseph R. Biden Jr. (D)		unopposed

PREVIOUS WINNING PERCENTAGES
1996 (60%); 1990 (63%); 1984 (60%); 1978 (58%); 1972 (50%)

Elected 1972; 6th term

Biden has a seemingly unquenchable ambition that his prominence as chairman of the Senate Foreign Relations Committee doesn't entirely satisfy. Two decades after his first bid for the presidency fizzled, Biden again has set his sights on the White House. He hopes his vast expertise in foreign policy, will help him stand out in a crowded 2008 field as the Iraq War continues to dominate the political landscape. But he faces very long odds.

Biden uses his Foreign Relations chairmanship regularly to blast the Bush administration's handling of the war. He has a deeper understanding of foreign policy than most lawmakers, and can be eloquent in critiquing President Bush's policies while still maintaining working relationships with key officials such as Secretary of State Condoleezza Rice. But his seemingly incurable loquacity brings embarrassing verbal slips that make it hard for him to gain traction on a broader playing field.

Nearing the end of his sixth term, Biden has spent more than half his life in the Senate, a distinction held by just three other current senators — fellow Democrats Robert C. Byrd of West Virginia, Edward M. Kennedy of Massachusetts and Daniel K. Inouye of Hawaii. The American public, at least the portion that watches public affairs programs, knows him as a frequent guest on the Sunday television talk shows, where he can be sometimes profound and sometimes long-winded, even for a politician.

Although he voted for the 2002 resolution approving the use of force against Iraq, Biden has since used television appearances and floor speeches to castigate the administration for a lack of planning prior to the invasion, poor field intelligence, insufficient troops and ill-conceived strategies. Biden often voices criticisms that the panel's top-ranking Republican, Richard G. Lugar of Indiana, agrees with but is reluctant to say publicly.

On the hustings and in the Senate, Biden in early 2007 brandished a plan for Iraq that called in part for partitioning the country into mostly autonomous Kurdish, Shiite and Sunni regions. "There is no other way to end this cycle of sectarian violence, absent giving the parties breathing room — control over the fabric of their daily lives," Biden said.

Biden has a history of deal-cutting with Republicans, which helped him cultivate a rapport with both Rice and former Secretary of State Colin L. Powell. He chaired Foreign Relations during a transformational moment in U.S. foreign policy — the aftermath of the Sept. 11 terrorist attacks. Not only did he have decades of experience in foreign policy, but as a former chairman of the Judiciary Committee, he brought together many strands of knowledge important to the country's new war on terrorism. Indeed, on the day before Sept. 11, Biden warned in a speech that the United States faced a grave threat from a terrorist attack.

In the turbulent weeks after the attacks, Biden's Senate colleagues looked to him to help draft the resolution that gave Bush authority to wage war against the al Qaeda terrorist network and the Taliban regime in Afghanistan. Biden steered a course between giving Bush sufficient authority to prosecute terrorists and surrendering congressional oversight over foreign policy.

Biden had mixed results from his other high-profile endeavor, which was attempting to slow Bush's rush to war with Iraq. Biden insisted that any action required both congressional and United Nations approval, and he took credit when the president chose to at least ask Congress to sanction war. But in 2002, the president rebuffed Biden's effort to pass legislation requiring a go-slow approach and instead bypassed his panel to cut a deal with House Democratic Leader Richard A. Gephardt of Missouri.

Biden's tendency to say exactly what is on his mind has tripped him up on occasion. On the day he announced his 2008 presidential campaign, Biden was forced to explain why, in an interview with the New York Observer, he had referred to Illinois Democratic Sen. Barack Obama, another presidential contender, as the "first mainstream African-American [presidential candidate] who is articulate and bright and clean." Biden said he meant to praise Obama as an appealing fresh face on the political scene and meant no slight to previous black presidential aspirants, and he apologized profusely.

Biden has been outspoken as a member of the Judiciary Committee, which he chaired from 1987 to 1995. His stewardship at Judiciary probably is best remembered for his handling of the 1991 nomination of Clarence Thomas for the Supreme Court. The nationally televised committee hearings at which professor Anita F. Hill accused Thomas of sexual harassment were an embarrassment to Biden, whose committee had not conducted more than a cursory investigation of Hill's charges until after they were leaked to the media.

But Biden also compiled a substantial legislative record wielding the Judiciary gavel, including a comprehensive anti-crime law in 1994 and an anti-terrorism law in 1996. Indeed, Biden is quick to point out that six years before the Sept. 11 attacks, he had proposed many of the provisions included in the subsequent anti-terrorism law, but that his ideas had been derailed by civil libertarians.

When Democrats regained control of the Senate in June 2001, upon the defection of Vermont's James M. Jeffords from the GOP, Biden had his pick of the Foreign Relations or Judiciary chairmanships. After a period of calculated public indecision, Biden took the Foreign Relations gavel and pressed the new Judiciary chairman, Democrat Patrick J. Leahy of Vermont, to name him chairman of the Crime and Drugs Subcommittee. That allowed Biden to pursue his long-held interest in anti-narcotics efforts.

The son of a Scranton, Pa., automobile dealer, Biden overcame a childhood stutter and often speaks with charming self-deprecation. But what has made him a compelling political figure are the tragedies and dramas of his private life. As a 29-year-old county councilman, Biden in 1972 summoned the brashness to challenge Republican Sen. J. Caleb Boggs in a campaign run by his sister. Running on a dovish Vietnam platform and accusing the incumbent of being a do-nothing, Biden won by 3,162 votes.

Five weeks later, Biden's wife, Neilia, and their infant daughter, Amy, were killed and their two sons seriously injured in an automobile accident. Biden at first said he would not take the job he had just won. Persuaded by Democratic Leader Mike Mansfield of Montana, Biden was sworn in at the bedside of one of his sons. Biden later remarried, had another child and commutes by train from Wilmington to Washington every day.

A short presidential bid in the 1988 race resulted in Biden's most humiliating political moment. He withdrew from contention for the Democratic nomination in September 1987 after reports that he had plagiarized passages in speeches and in a 1965 law school paper, and had exaggerated his résumé. Later, in 1988, a brain aneurysm nearly killed him.

Biden's return to good health bolstered Delaware's affections, and he won his 1990 Senate race with 63 percent of the vote — a career best. He is likely to be re-elected easily in 2008 if his presidential bid falters. And his son Beau has taken the first step toward what could be a Biden dynasty in Delaware, winning election in 2006 as state attorney general.

KEY VOTES

2006

- No Confirm Samuel A. Alito Jr. to the Supreme Court
- No Allow consideration of a bill to establish a $140 billion trust fund to compensate victims of asbestos exposure
- No Extend tax cuts for two years at a cost of $70 billion over five years
- Yes Overhaul immigration policy with border security, enforcement and guest worker program
- No Allow consideration of a bill to permanently repeal the estate tax
- Yes Urge President Bush to begin troop withdrawals from Iraq in 2006
- Yes Lift President Bush's restrictions on stem cell research funding
- No Authorize military tribunals for suspected terrorists

2005

- No Curb class action lawsuits by shifting them from state to federal courts
- No Allow confirmation vote on Priscilla R. Owen to the U.S. Court of Appeals for the 5th Circuit
- No Oppose mandatory emissions limits and block recognition of global warming as a threat
- No Approve free-trade pact with five Central American countries
- No Pass energy policy overhaul favored by President Bush emphasizing domestic oil and gas production
- No Shield gunmakers from lawsuits when their products are used in crimes
- Yes Ban torture of prisoners in U.S. custody
- No Renew 16 provisions of the Patriot Act
- No Allow final vote on opening the Arctic National Wildlife Refuge to oil and gas exploration

CQ VOTE STUDIES

	PARTY UNITY		PRESIDENTIAL SUPPORT	
	Support	Oppose	Support	Oppose
2006	91%	9%	55%	45%
2005	89%	11%	27%	73%
2004	95%	5%	70%	30%
2003	90%	10%	46%	54%
2002	89%	11%	77%	23%
2001	94%	6%	65%	35%
2000	88%	12%	91%	9%
1999	93%	7%	89%	11%
1998	87%	13%	91%	9%
1997	82%	18%	84%	16%

INTEREST GROUPS

	AFL-CIO	ADA	CCUS	ACU
2006	93%	100%	45%	4%
2005	93%	100%	44%	8%
2004	100%	95%	63%	0%
2003	100%	75%	32%	26%
2002	100%	80%	50%	10%
2001	100%	100%	38%	12%
2000	63%	80%	60%	16%
1999	89%	95%	47%	4%
1998	88%	85%	56%	4%
1997	57%	70%	70%	16%

Sen. Thomas R. Carper (D)

Elected 2000; 2nd term

CAPITOL OFFICE
224-2441
carper.senate.gov
513 Hart 20510-0803; fax 228-2190

COMMITTEES
Banking, Housing & Urban Affairs
(Economic Policy - chairman)
Commerce, Science & Transportation
Environment & Public Works
(Clean Air & Nuclear Safety - chairman)
Homeland Security & Governmental Affairs
(Federal Financial Management - chairman)
Special Aging

RESIDENCE
Wilmington

BORN
Jan. 23, 1947, Beckley, W.Va.

RELIGION
Presbyterian

FAMILY
Wife, Martha Carper; two children

EDUCATION
Ohio State U., B.A. 1968 (economics);
U. of Delaware, M.B.A. 1975

MILITARY SERVICE
Navy, 1968-73; Naval Reserve, 1973-91

CAREER
State economic development official

POLITICAL HIGHLIGHTS
Del. treasurer, 1977-83; U.S. House, 1983-93; governor, 1993-2001

ELECTION RESULTS

2006 GENERAL		
Thomas R. Carper (D)	170,567	67.1%
Jan Ting (R)	69,734	27.4%
Christine O'Donnell (X)	11,127	4.4%
William E. Morris (LIBERT)	2,671	1.1%
2006 PRIMARY		
Thomas R. Carper (D)		unopposed

PREVIOUS WINNING PERCENTAGES
2000 (56%); 1990 House Election (66%); 1988 House Election (68%); 1986 House Election (66%); 1984 House Election (58%); 1982 House Election (52%)

Carper has won more statewide elections than anyone in Delaware's history, and he's running out of worlds to conquer. His senior Democratic colleague, Joseph R. Biden Jr., has dipped a toe into the presidential campaign waters, but Carper professes no interest in that course, often musing in speeches that he has his sights set on vice president. "There's a job I'm interested in. There's a lot less competition," he likes to say, regularly evoking laughter.

Carper is a centrist, committed to finding what he calls "common sense positions." In 2004, he co-founded a group called the Third Way, with the idea of giving moderates a higher profile and serving as a think tank to generate middle-of-the-road legislation.

Democratic leaders tapped him to serve as a deputy whip. And in mid-2005, he was named vice chairman of the moderate Democratic Leadership Council once headed by Bill Clinton. "I was a New Democrat before it was fashionable," Carper says. "I really think that we need more people in Congress who think like governors, who are results-oriented, who are not so ideologically driven, people who are impatient with gridlock, and maybe a little less partisan."

Carper applies his statehouse experience every day. He says his consensus-building skills were sharpened by his work with the National Governors Association, where he and Republican Gov. John Engler of Michigan developed a set of radical changes to welfare that formed the basis for the federal welfare overhaul of 1996. He organizes brainstorming sessions with the seven other senators who are also former governors. In 2004, he joined with them to fight a proposed four-year ban on taxes on Internet access that he argued would drain state treasuries of telecommunication taxes. They pushed a two-year ban instead, winning some concessions.

Carper was quick to take the lead in 2005 in opposing the Bush administration's attempts to trim the federal deficit with cuts to local and state governments. He is just as quick to object to bills imposing new mandates on the states without providing the federal money to pay for them.

While he supports President Bush more often than most other Democrats, he is voting with the president considerably less often than he did when Bush first took office. In the 107th Congress (2001-02), he backed Bush on 75 percent of the votes on which the president had staked out a position. By the 109th Congress (2005-06), his support score had dwindled to 54 percent.

Carper's backing was crucial in 2005 to a successful GOP bill tightening the rules for class action lawsuits and shifting them from state to federal courts, which many fellow Democrats opposed as a bad deal for plaintiffs. With the credit card industry a major force in Delaware, he also was one of 18 Senate Democrats who supported a 2005 bankruptcy overhaul that made it harder for consumers to wipe out their debts by declaring bankruptcy.

In 2004, the conservative U.S. Chamber of Commerce gave him its Legal Reform Award. The following year, he ranked fifth among Senate Democrats on the chamber's annual scorecard rating business-friendly votes, with a 72 percent score.

A member of the Environment and Public Works Committee, Carper has been deeply engaged in the panel's struggle to rewrite the landmark Clean Air Act. In the 110th Congress (2007-08), he was given the gavel of the panel's Clean Air Subcommittee. In the 109th Congress, Bush pushed to create a market-based system of curbing power plant emissions of three pollutants — sulfur dioxide, nitrogen oxides and mercury. Carper led panel Democrats in pressing the Environmental Protection Agency to provide an analysis of the health and economic benefits of the administration's approach compared with a rival bill he had introduced and another one by Vermont independent James M. Jeffords. When the administration stonewalled, Carper put a hold on the 2005 nomination of EPA Administrator Stephen L. Johnson.

A colleague suggested the tactic, which he initially rebuffed as not his style, saying, "That's not the way I work." When he continued to be ignored, however, Carper decided to take his friend's advice. He put a hold on Johnson's nomination until he got the data he wanted. Carper then introduced a tougher clean air bill that included regulation of carbon dioxide emissions, which were not covered by Bush's plan.

Carper is a strong supporter of Amtrak, the federally subsidized passenger railroad. He and Biden both spend nights at home in Wilmington and take an early morning Amtrak train to Washington. Carper fights an annual battle against the Bush administration's attempts to turn over unprofitable lines outside the Northeast to the states and private businesses. In 2002, he helped secure a $1.2 billion security upgrade for the railroad.

Carper was raised in southern Virginia. When he was in high school, his family moved to Columbus, Ohio, and he went to Ohio State University on an ROTC scholarship. In college, he underwent a political transformation. In 1964, he had campaigned for Republican presidential candidate Barry Goldwater. But by 1968, his senior year, his skepticism about the Vietnam War led him to volunteer in the anti-war presidential campaign of Democratic Sen. Eugene McCarthy. Yet he wore his Navy uniform to his college graduation, and went on to serve in the Navy for five years, flying P-3 submarine-hunting planes in Southeast Asia. He served another 18 years in the Naval Reserve, retiring as a captain in 1991.

He was smitten by Delaware during his first year in the Navy, flying into Dover aboard a military transport plane. He looked out the window just as the sun was coming up and thought, "What a beautiful place." Later, he told a friend, he'd "like to move to a little state where you would not need a lot of money and fame, and maybe run for office."

Carper enrolled in the University of Delaware's business school, earning a master's degree in business administration. He decided to stay in Delaware and launch a career in economic development. One day in 1976, he was lying on a beach, listening to the radio, when a news report said Democrats could not find a candidate for state treasurer. He entered the race, and at age 29, beat a strongly favored Republican.

In 1982, Carper ran for the House after Democrats again had trouble finding someone to take on Republican Rep. Thomas B. Evans. Delaware's economic woes at the time and revelations that Evans was romantically involved with lobbyist Paula Parkinson boosted Carper's campaign, and Delaware's House seat went Democratic for the first time since 1966.

He ran successfully for governor in 1992, swapping jobs with moderate Republican Michael N. Castle, who is still in the House. After two terms as governor, Carper in 2000 sought to return to Washington in a battle-of-the-titans challenge to five-term Republican Sen. William V. Roth Jr., the Senate Finance Committee chairman who was the architect of the Individual Retirement Account named for him.

Carper found ways to distinguish himself from Roth on health care and in other policy areas. Although he did not directly make a point of it, age was a factor. Carper was 53, Roth was 79. Voters gave Carper a surprisingly large 12 percentage point victory. In 2006, he faced nominal opposition.

KEY VOTES

2006

No Confirm Samuel A. Alito Jr. to the Supreme Court
Yes Allow consideration of a bill to establish a $140 billion trust fund to compensate victims of asbestos exposure
No Extend tax cuts for two years at a cost of $70 billion over five years
Yes Overhaul immigration policy with border security, enforcement and guest worker program
No Allow consideration of a bill to permanently repeal the estate tax
Yes Urge President Bush to begin troop withdrawals from Iraq in 2006
Yes Lift President Bush's restrictions on stem cell research funding
Yes Authorize military tribunals for suspected terrorists

2005

Yes Curb class action lawsuits by shifting them from state to federal courts
Yes Allow confirmation vote on Priscilla R. Owen to the U.S. Court of Appeals for the 5th Circuit
No Oppose mandatory emissions limits and block recognition of global warming as a threat
Yes Approve free-trade pact with five Central American countries
No Pass energy policy overhaul favored by President Bush emphasizing domestic oil and gas production
No Shield gunmakers from lawsuits when their products are used in crimes
Yes Ban torture of prisoners in U.S. custody
No Renew 16 provisions of the Patriot Act
No Allow final vote on opening the Arctic National Wildlife Refuge to oil and gas exploration

CQ VOTE STUDIES

	PARTY UNITY		PRESIDENTIAL SUPPORT	
	Support	Oppose	Support	Oppose
2006	79%	21%	64%	36%
2005	77%	23%	38%	62%
2004	86%	14%	66%	34%
2003	81%	19%	53%	47%
2002	74%	26%	79%	21%
2001	80%	20%	72%	28%
House Service:				
1992	76%	24%	32%	68%
1991	76%	24%	37%	63%
1990	89%	11%	23%	77%
1989	85%	15%	41%	59%

INTEREST GROUPS

	AFL-CIO	ADA	CCUS	ACU
2006	87%	90%	58%	20%
2005	64%	90%	72%	8%
2004	100%	95%	71%	12%
2003	77%	75%	70%	10%
2002	85%	80%	50%	25%
2001	93%	90%	58%	24%
House Service:				
1992	67%	75%	63%	40%
1991	92%	55%	40%	20%
1990	92%	78%	21%	17%
1989	83%	80%	50%	21%

Rep. Michael N. Castle (R)

CAPITOL OFFICE
225-4165
www.castle.house.gov
1233 Longworth 20515-0801; fax 225-2291

COMMITTEES
Education & Labor
Financial Services

RESIDENCE
Wilmington

BORN
July 2, 1939, Wilmington, Del.

RELIGION
Roman Catholic

FAMILY
Wife, Jane Castle

EDUCATION
Hamilton College, B.A. 1961 (economics);
Georgetown U., LL.B. 1964

CAREER
Lawyer; state prosecutor

POLITICAL HIGHLIGHTS
Del. House, 1967-69; Del. Senate, 1969-77 (minority leader, 1976-77); lieutenant governor, 1981-85; governor, 1985-93

ELECTION RESULTS

2006 GENERAL		
Michael N. Castle (R)	143,897	57.2%
Denni Spivack (D)	97,565	38.8%
Karen M. Hartley-Nagle (I)	5,769	2.3%
Michael Berg (GREEN)	4,463	1.8%
2006 PRIMARY		
Michael N. Castle (R)		unopposed
2004 GENERAL		
Michael N. Castle (R)	245,978	69.1%
Paul Donnelly (D)	105,716	29.7%

PREVIOUS WINNING PERCENTAGES
2002 (72%); 2000 (68%); 1998 (66%); 1996 (70%); 1994 (71%); 1992 (55%)

Elected 1992; 8th term

Castle, who has been increasingly at odds with his party and President Bush, may find himself breathing a little easier in the minority despite the fact that he will be even more isolated within the GOP.

The leader of the diminished band of House Republican moderates, Castle has been a leader of the Republican Main Street Partnership and the affiliated Tuesday Group. The 2006 elections thinned the already meager ranks of both, but the Democratic takeover of the House means he will no longer be under constant pressure from Republican leaders to toe the party line. And he hopes to find common ground with some of the conservative Democrats who make up a sizable bloc within the new majority.

A former governor who remains extremely popular in his home state, Castle breaks with GOP leaders on issues where he feels they are too far to the right, including the size of tax cuts, environmental protection and federal funding for stem cell research. He regularly ranks in the top tier of Republicans bucking both the president and the party leadership. "My politics fit Delaware's politics," he says. "They appreciate the fact that I'm independent." Castle was one of only three House Republicans to vote for all six of the new Democratic majority's signature bills at the start of the 110th Congress (2007-08).

He calls himself a "pragmatist," believing that being a social moderate with fiscally conservative views is the only way to get things done in Congress. His middle-of-the-road positioning, combined with the political savvy gained from eight years in the governor's mansion, have landed Castle in the middle of some of the country's most contentious debates. On big issues, Castle often carries a substantial bloc of moderate votes with him.

He has scored some notable successes, although they are few and far between. In 2005, Republicans eager to open up Alaska's Arctic National Wildlife Refuge to oil drilling included such a provision in a filibuster-proof budget savings bill, pushing it through the Senate. But Castle and other moderates threatened to sink the entire budget measure unless the drilling provision was dropped. They forced its removal from the final budget bill.

Even though Castle is one of the most senior Republicans on two committees — Financial Services and Education and Labor — his moderate views cost him any chance of chairing either. When Republican John A. Boehner of Ohio stepped down as chairman of the Education Committee after being elected majority leader in early 2006, Castle briefly considered a bid for the gavel. He quickly dropped the idea, telling the Wilmington News-Journal, "The bottom line is I wouldn't make it."

As chairman of the Education Reform Subcommittee, however, Castle was one of the architects of federal education policy in recent years. He was a lead sponsor of the No Child Left Behind law, the 2001 legislation initiated by Bush that for the first time tied federal education aid to improvements in student test scores. Castle also shepherded through Congress a bill calling for disabled students to be treated the same as non-disabled students when being punished for violations of school policy. Advocates for the disabled decried the move as a potential violation of civil rights, but Castle said it would give localities more flexibility.

One of his more recent crusades is the troubling trend in childhood obesity in the United States, which Castle believes can be fought in part by providing healthier foods in schools. He sponsored a bill in the 108th Congress (2003-04) directing the Agriculture Department to develop nutrition guidelines for foods sold in schools and to make $30 million available for nutrition awareness and physical fitness programs.

Castle is deeply involved in the push by Democrats and GOP moderates to relax limits that Bush has imposed on federal funding of embryonic stem cell research.

Amiable and relatively quiet, Castle nonetheless is forceful in his opinions and sometimes bold in confronting his leadership. In 2001, he was one of six Republicans who signed a petition to force Speaker J. Dennis Hastert to bring campaign finance legislation to the floor. Before that, in 1998, Castle was among the dozen GOP lawmakers who voted against three of the four articles of impeachment against President Bill Clinton, who was embroiled in a sex scandal involving a White House intern. In 2006, Castle fought to toughen a lobbying and ethics bill put together by GOP leaders. He almost voted against it, considering it "not strong enough," but finally cast a yes vote.

A fan of coin collecting, Castle has used his seat on the Financial Services Committee to promote creation of new collectible U.S. coins. He was the lead House sponsor of a 2005 law that authorized the minting of a series of $1 coins, starting in 2007, that will bear the likenesses of all U.S. presidents. Four coins a year will be issued, with presidents featured in chronological order. Earlier, Castle was the principal author of the law that put commemorations of each of the 50 states on quarters. Because of collectors, that program raised nearly $5 billion in its first six years, and Castle is hoping the presidential coin program nets $4 billion to $5 billion for the Treasury.

The 6-foot, 4-inch Castle was a basketball star in high school. He went to Georgetown University Law School after college "sort of because I didn't know what I was doing." In private practice, he worked for a former Delaware attorney general who encouraged him to take the part-time position of deputy attorney general, a post he assumed at age 26. In 1966, he ran for the state House in a Democratic-leaning district. He won and later ousted an incumbent state senator. After 10 years in the General Assembly, he won election as lieutenant governor for one term and governor for two terms.

With his stint as governor ending, Castle ran for the state's at-large congressional seat in 1992. He won a tough, four-way GOP primary and in November prevailed with 55 percent of the vote. Castle has coasted to reelection since. He was slowed only briefly in his 2006 campaign by two small strokes he suffered in September. His next step could be a Senate race, but only if Democrat Joseph R. Biden Jr. decides to relinquish his seat in his 2008 presidential bid. Castle has no plans to challenge Biden or the state's other Democratic senator, Thomas R. Carper.

KEY VOTES

2006

No Stop broadband companies from favoring select Internet traffic
Yes Affirm U.S. commitment to war in Iraq and reject setting a withdrawal date for troops
No Repeal requirement for bilingual ballots at the polls
Yes Permit U.S. sale of civilian nuclear technology to India
Yes Build a 700-mile fence on the U.S.-Mexico border to curb illegal crossings
? Permit warrantless wiretaps of suspected terrorists

2005

No Intervene in the life-support case of Terri Schiavo
Yes Lift President Bush's restrictions on stem cell research funding
Yes Prohibit FBI access to library and bookstore records
Yes Approve free-trade pact with five Central American countries
No Pass energy policy overhaul favored by President Bush emphasizing domestic oil and gas production
No End mandatory preservation of habitat of endangered animal and plant species
Yes Ban torture of prisoners in U.S. custody

CQ VOTE STUDIES

	PARTY UNITY		PRESIDENTIAL SUPPORT	
	Support	Oppose	Support	Oppose
2006	77%	23%	78%	22%
2005	76%	24%	65%	35%
2004	79%	21%	74%	26%
2003	77%	23%	69%	31%
2002	79%	21%	78%	22%

INTEREST GROUPS

	AFL-CIO	ADA	CCUS	ACU
2006	36%	40%	83%	52%
2005	20%	40%	78%	28%
2004	35%	50%	85%	52%
2003	20%	40%	76%	40%
2002	11%	25%	95%	76%

DELAWARE

At large

Delaware's coastal terrain and inland agricultural sector contrasts with the state's corporate center near Wilmington and its suburbs. A string of beach resorts in the state's southeast corner — from Rehoboth to Fenwick Island — draws hundreds of thousands of tourists each year.

The state enjoys relatively low unemployment, and its favorable tax rates attract financial services companies, especially credit card firms. Due to liberal incorporation rules, Delaware is the on-paper home to 60 percent of the Fortune 500 companies, which keeps the state's specialized business court busy.

Wilmington is the state's economic hub — many manufacturing plants and banking firms are based in and around the city — and it is the very real home of the DuPont Company, one of Delaware's largest private employers. Fifty years ago, almost half the state's population lived in the city, which now casts only about 10 percent of Delaware's vote. Recent projects to transform areas along the Delaware River into new neighborhoods have lured some people back to Wilmington.

Set in the state's Kent County midsection, the state capital of Dover previously was known for manufacturing. The city has benefited from an expansion of the local tourism industry, particularly at Dover Downs, a gambling and racing facility.

The GOP's strength lies in Wilmington's growing suburbs and south of the Chesapeake and Delaware canal, in the poultry farms and coastal marshes of the Delmarva Peninsula. Wilmington and Dover have Democratic constituencies. Immigration, legal and illegal, is changing communities across the state as new residents, many from Guatemala and China, recently have made the traditionally dominant Anglo-Saxon population a minority in some towns.

MAJOR INDUSTRY
Financial services, manufacturing, tourism, chemicals

MILITARY BASES
Dover Air Force Base, 6,100 military, 1,800 civilian (2006)

CITIES
Wilmington, 72,664; Dover, 32,135; Newark, 28,547

NOTABLE
In 1787, Delaware was the first state to ratify the U.S. Constitution; Dover is the only U.S. state capital with a volunteer fire department.

FLORIDA

Gov. Charlie Crist (R)

First elected: 2006
Length of term: 4 years
Term expires: 1/11
Salary: $132,932
Phone: (850) 488-4441

Residence: St. Petersburg
Born: July 24, 1956; Altoona, Pa.
Religion: Methodist
Family: Divorced
Education: Wake Forest U., attended 1974-76; Florida State U., B.S. 1978 (government); Samford U., J.D. 1981
Career: State government official; lawyer; congressional state aide
Political highlights: Sought Republican nomination for Fla. Senate, 1986; Fla. Senate, 1992-98; Republican nominee for U.S. Senate, 1998; Fla. Education commissioner, 2001-03; Fla. attorney general, 2003-07

Election results:

2006 GENERAL		
Charlie Crist (R)	2,519,845	52.2%
Jim Davis (D)	2,178,289	45.1%
Max Linn (REF)	92,595	1.9%

Lt. Gov. Jeff Kottkamp (R)

First Elected: 2006
Length of term: 4 years
Term expires: 1/11
Salary: $127,399
Phone: (850) 488-4711

LEGISLATURE

Legislature: 60 days March-May; session is often extended

Senate: 40 members; 4-year terms
2007 ratios: 26 R, 14 D; 29 men, 11 women
Salary: $30,996
Phone: (850) 487-5270

House: 120 members; 2-year terms
2007 ratios: 78 R, 42 D; 93 men, 27 women
Salary: $30,996
Phone: (850) 488-1157

TERM LIMITS

Governor: 2 terms
Senate: 2 consecutive terms
House: 4 consecutive terms

URBAN STATISTICS

CITY	POPULATION
Jacksonville	735,617
Miami	362,470
Tampa	303,447
St. Petersburg	248,232
Hialeah	226,419

REGISTERED VOTERS

Democrat	40%
Republican	38%
Unaffiliated	19%
Others	3%

POPULATION

2006 population (est.)	18,089,888
2000 population	15,982,378
1990 population	12,937,926
Percent change (1990-2000)	+23.5%
Rank among states (2006)	4

Median age	38.7
Born in state	32.7%
Foreign born	16.7%
Violent crime rate	812/100,000
Poverty level	12.5%
Federal workers	118,600
Military	106,092

ELECTIONS

STATE ELECTION OFFICIAL
(850) 245-6200
DEMOCRATIC PARTY
(850) 222-3411
REPUBLICAN PARTY
(850) 222-7920

MISCELLANEOUS

Web: www.myflorida.com
Capital: Tallahassee

U.S. CONGRESS

Senate: 1 Democrat, 1 Republican
House: 16 Republicans, 9 Democrats

2000 Census Statistics by District

DIST.	2004 VOTE FOR PRESIDENT BUSH	KERRY	WHITE	BLACK	ASIAN	HISP	MEDIAN INCOME	WHITE COLLAR	BLUE COLLAR	SERVICE INDUSTRY	OVER 64	UNDER 18	COLLEGE EDUCATION	RURAL	SQ. MILES
1	72%	28%	78%	14%	2%	3%	$36,738	57%	25%	18%	13%	24%	20%	23%	4,642
2	54	45	72	22	1	3	$34,718	62	21	18	12	23	24	38	9,425
3	35	65	38	49	2	8	$29,785	52	27	21	11	28	13	10	1,796
4	67	32	78	14	2	4	$43,947	65	21	14	11	24	24	22	4,118
5	58	41	88	5	1	6	$34,815	55	27	17	26	20	14	36	4,044
6	61	38	79	12	2	5	$36,846	61	23	16	15	23	21	31	2,912
7	57	43	81	9	1	7	$40,525	63	21	16	18	22	25	13	1,797
8	55	44	70	7	3	18	$41,568	64	20	17	14	23	26	8	987
9	57	42	85	4	2	8	$40,742	68	18	14	20	22	25	6	634
10	51	48	88	4	2	4	$37,168	65	20	15	23	18	23	0	175
11	40	60	48	27	2	20	$33,559	61	22	17	12	25	21	0	244
12	58	42	72	13	1	12	$37,769	56	28	16	17	25	17	16	1,956
13	56	43	86	4	1	8	$40,187	59	24	18	29	18	24	11	2,599
14	61	38	84	5	1	9	$42,541	60	22	19	27	18	24	9	1,057
15	57	43	78	7	2	11	$39,397	58	22	19	20	22	22	10	2,545

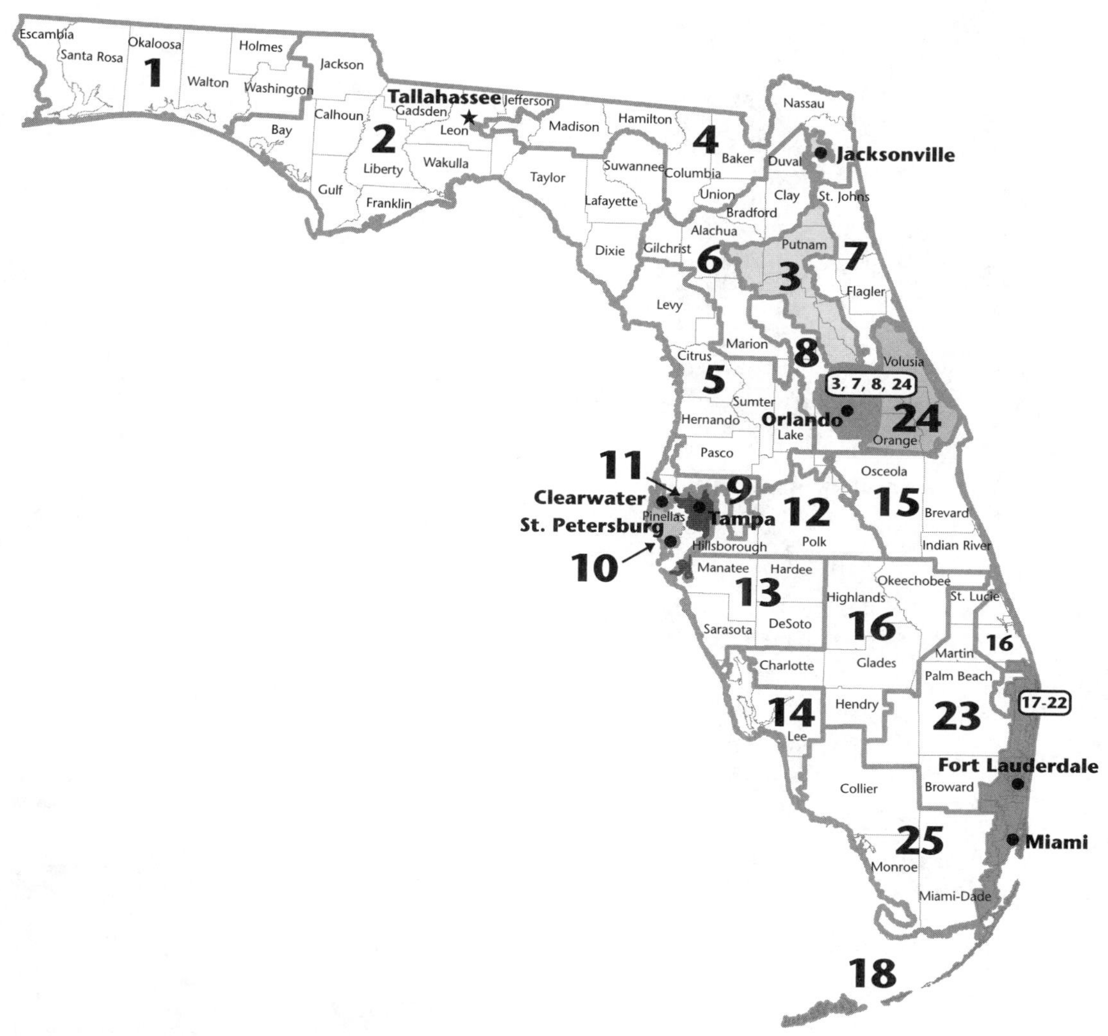

2000 Census Statistics by District

DIST.	2004 VOTE FOR PRESIDENT BUSH	KERRY	WHITE	BLACK	ASIAN	HISP	MEDIAN INCOME	WHITE COLLAR	BLUE COLLAR	SERVICE INDUSTRY	OVER 64	UNDER 18	COLLEGE EDUCATION	RURAL	SQ. MILES
16	55%	45%	82%	6%	1%	10%	$39,408	58%	25%	17%	25%	21%	20%	15%	4,538
17	17	83	18	55	2	21	$30,426	52	24	23	11	29	14	0	97
18	54	45	30	6	1	63	$32,298	60	21	18	18	19	26	1	355
19	33	66	77	6	2	13	$42,237	67	17	15	30	19	26	0	231
20	36	63	67	8	2	21	$44,034	69	16	14	17	21	30	0	160
21	57	43	21	7	2	70	$41,426	64	23	14	13	24	23	0	135
22	49	51	82	4	2	11	$51,200	69	16	14	21	19	34	1	268
23	21	78	29	51	1	14	$31,309	48	28	24	12	28	13	2	3,362
24	56	44	80	6	2	10	$43,954	65	20	15	15	23	26	9	1,583
25	56	44	24	10	2	62	$44,489	62	23	15	9	29	20	6	4,268
STATE	52	47	65	14	2	17	$38,819	61	22	17	18	23	22	11	53,927
U.S.	50.7	48.3	69	12	4	13	$41,994	60	25	15	12	26	24	21	3,537,438

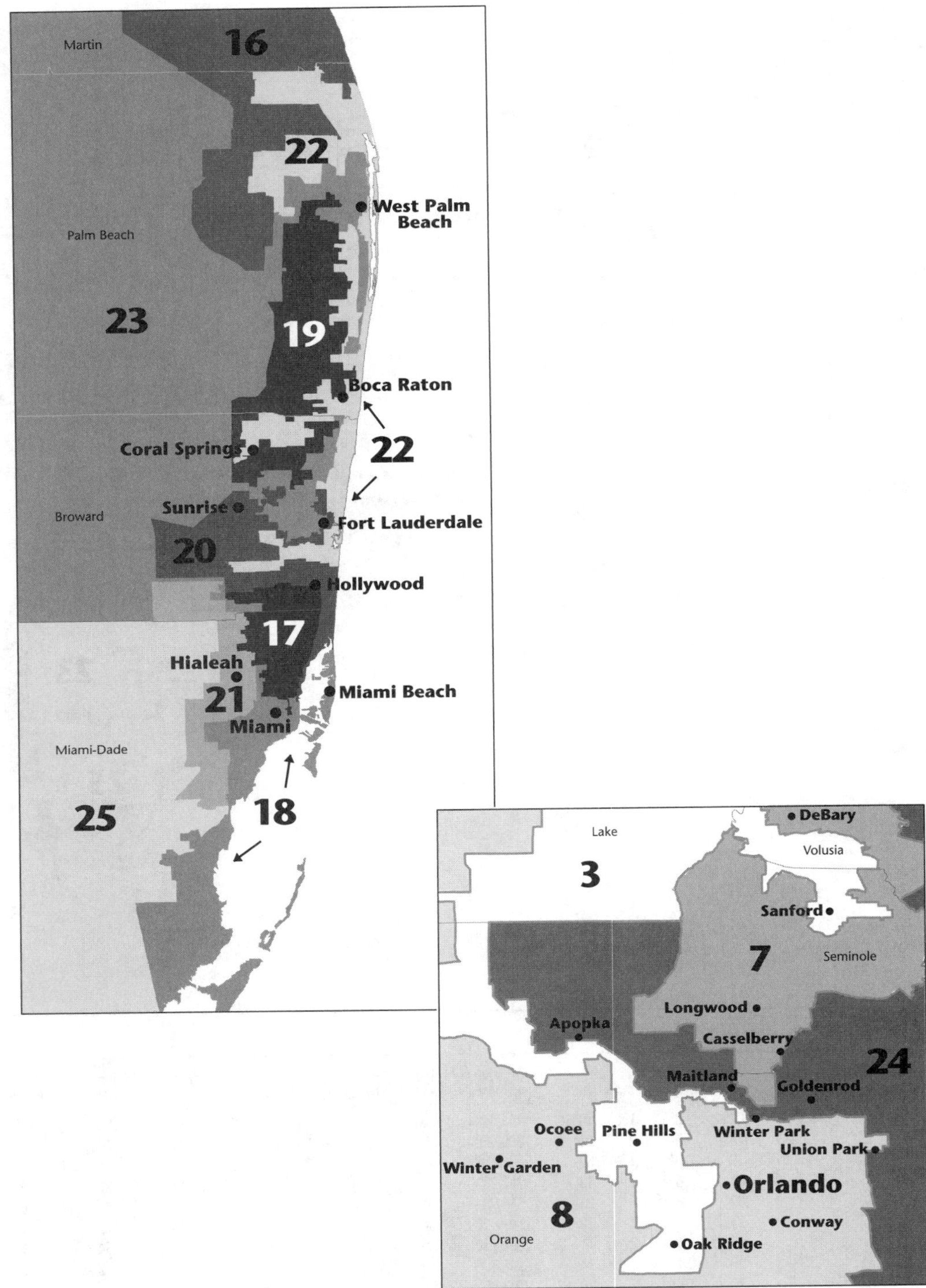

16
Martin
22
West Palm Beach
Palm Beach
23
19
Boca Raton
22
Coral Springs
Sunrise
Broward
Fort Lauderdale
20
Hollywood
17
Hialeah
Miami Beach
21
Miami
Miami-Dade
18
25
DeBary
Lake
Volusia
3
Sanford
7
Seminole
Longwood
Apopka
Casselberry
24
Maitland
Goldenrod
Ocoee
Pine Hills
Winter Park
Union Park
Winter Garden
Orlando
8
Conway
Orange
Oak Ridge

Sen. Bill Nelson (D)

CAPITOL OFFICE
224-5274
billnelson.senate.gov
716 Hart 20510-0905; fax 228-2183

COMMITTEES
Armed Services
(Strategic Forces - chairman)
Budget
Commerce, Science & Transportation
(Space, Aeronautics & Related Sciences - chairman)
Foreign Relations
(International Operations & Organizations - chairman)
Select Intelligence
Special Aging

RESIDENCE
Orlando

BORN
Sept. 29, 1942, Miami, Fla.

RELIGION
Episcopalian

FAMILY
Wife, Grace H. Nelson; two children

EDUCATION
Yale U., B.A. 1965 (political science);
U. of Virginia, J.D. 1968

MILITARY SERVICE
Army, 1968-70; Army Reserve, 1965-71

CAREER
Lawyer

POLITICAL HIGHLIGHTS
Fla. House, 1972-78; U.S. House, 1979-91; sought Democratic nomination for governor, 1990; Fla. treasurer and insurance commissioner, 1995-2001

ELECTION RESULTS

2006 GENERAL		
Bill Nelson (D)	2,890,548	60.3%
Katherine Harris (R)	1,826,127	38.1%
2006 PRIMARY		
Bill Nelson (D)		unopposed

PREVIOUS WINNING PERCENTAGES
2000 (51%); 1988 House Election (61%); 1986 House Election (73%); 1984 House Election (61%); 1982 House Election (71%); 1980 House Election (70%); 1978 House Election (61%)

Elected 2000; 2nd term

Nelson is one of the Senate's least known members, a low-profile politician whom colleagues describe as "nice" and "careful." But he does a solid job taking care of his state. And he is a political moderate unburdened by the extreme liberalism that tends to play poorly in Florida.

Nelson secured a second term after a ballyhooed challenge to his seat ended with a whimper in 2006. Republicans had targeted him for defeat that November, hoping voters could be persuaded to replace the bland Democratic centrist. But their candidate, GOP conservative Katherine Harris of Florida recount fame, turned out to be a little too colorful; she ran the year's worst campaign, and Nelson coasted to re-election.

Even without Harris' self-immolation, the state's voters might have sent Nelson back to Washington in recognition of his parochial attentiveness and deliberative, middle-of-the-road style. "Too careful? That's criticism I can live with," Nelson told The Miami Herald in 2006.

In his first term, Nelson used Senate rules to block legislation that would have opened coastal areas of the Gulf of Mexico to energy drilling. He threatened a filibuster and held up one of President Bush's Interior Department appointments. But when gas prices hit $3 a gallon, and Congress came under pressure to allow more exploration, Nelson negotiated the best deal he could. The bill that came out of the Senate in 2006 opened the eastern Gulf to drilling but banned wells along the Florida coast. It also guaranteed Gulf states a share of the new revenue for coastal preservation. Nelson's support helped Majority Leader Bill Frist, a Republican from Tennessee, bring other Democrats along.

As a member of the centrist New Democrats, Nelson often deviates from the party line. During the 109th Congress (2005-06), he supported Bush's position on issues a little more than half the time. He was one of only five Democrats to support permanent repeal of the estate tax, the federal levy on inherited wealth. And he voted for the Central American Free Trade Agreement in spite of two powerful political forces aligned against it — organized labor and the state's influential sugar lobby.

In 2002, Nelson voted for the use of force against Iraq, but later changed his tune as popular opinion against the war increased. In early 2007, he cosponsored a resolution opposing the president's decision to further boost troop levels for the Iraq War. Speaking before the Council on Foreign Relations, he said he believed the sectarian violence could be brought to a close only by "an aggressive diplomatic effort, not military might." He also cosponsored a resolution urging Bush to set clear benchmarks to determine military and political progress in Iraq.

His relationship with fellow Florida Sen. Mel Martinez, a Republican who is also relatively new to the Senate, is a work in progress after getting off to a rough start. In 2005, the press was given an internal memo from a Martinez staffer spelling out a strategy to use the Terri Schiavo right-to-die case against Nelson in his re-election bid. Nelson had opposed Republican efforts to force a judge to keep the comatose woman alive in spite of her husband's wishes. Martinez apologized to Nelson, and the two later worked together on the coastal drilling issue and on securing federal money for Everglades restoration.

Nelson also is a protector of Florida's Space Coast, home of the Kennedy Space Center, and is now chairman of the Space Subcommittee, part of the full Commerce, Science and Transportation Committee. Back in 1986, when he chaired the House's Space Subcommittee, Nelson had the opportunity to fly aboard the space shuttle *Columbia*. He has been a vocal advocate for funding increases for NASA, and was one of the first in Congress to warn of the dangers of delaying upgrades to the space shuttles, a point tragically driven home in 2003 when the *Columbia* exploded while attempting to re-enter Earth's atmosphere. In 2004, when Bush proposed sending humans to Mars, an enthusiastic Nelson appeared with him at the announcement. His only gripe about Bush's proposal was that it didn't call for enough money to accomplish the goals, in his view.

Appealing to Florida's senior citizen population, Nelson has cultivated an expertise in consumer protection and privacy issues. He has sought to prevent insurance companies and financial institutions from sharing customers' medical and financial information without their consent. He also has worked to block pharmaceutical manufacturers and pharmacies from trying to persuade customers to buy alternative drugs to those recommended by their doctors.

On the Foreign Relations Committee, Nelson has focused on Latin America, whose affairs are closely tied to Florida, a magnet for Spanish-speaking people resettling in the United States. He is now chairman of the International Operations and Organizations Subcommittee.

Nelson is a fifth-generation Floridian. His great-great-grandfather immigrated to America from Denmark in 1829, settling near Chipley in the Florida Panhandle, where much of Nelson's family still lives. Nelson's father was a lawyer, among the first to graduate from the University of Miami law school in 1929. His mother was a schoolteacher.

Nelson set an early course in politics, majoring in political science at Yale and writing his senior thesis about the Kennedy Space Center. He met his wife at a meeting of the Key Club, a high school community service club, and they honeymooned by campaigning for Nelson in his first race for the Florida Legislature.

In 1978, Nelson won a bid for an open U.S. House seat, taking conservative stands on economic issues and advocating more military spending. He was an early member of the moderate Democratic Leadership Council that helped boost Bill Clinton to the national stage. Yet, despite a string of House re-elections and the positive publicity attending his adventure as an astronaut, Nelson lost the 1990 Democratic primary for governor, his only electoral defeat.

Four years later, he was elected state insurance commissioner, and he dealt with the aftermath of Hurricane Andrew, which ravaged southern Florida and the state's insurance market in 1992. He also helped obtain a $206 million settlement for African-Americans who had been overcharged for life insurance and burial policies, bolstering his image as a consumer watchdog and his appeal among black voters.

From the time he announced his run for the Senate, Nelson was the front-runner for the seat Republican Connie Mack had held for two terms. He portrayed his opponent, 10-term congressman Bill McCollum, as too far to the right for Florida, and won with 51 percent of the vote.

When he sought re-election, the GOP felt Nelson was vulnerable in a state led by the president's brother, Gov. Jeb Bush, and the site of the historically close presidential contest of 2000. The GOP primary produced Harris, a House member who, as the Florida secretary of state, was a leading figure in the 2000 drama. But Harris' campaign was beset by disorganization, disillusionment among her staff and controversy over her public comments, including her suggestion that voters should elect only "tried and true" Christians. Jeb Bush tried to recruit a replacement, but Harris refused to get out of the race, and Nelson glided to a 22 percentage point victory.

KEY VOTES

2006

No Confirm Samuel A. Alito Jr. to the Supreme Court
No Allow consideration of a bill to establish a $140 billion trust fund to compensate victims of asbestos exposure
Yes Extend tax cuts for two years at a cost of $70 billion over five years
Yes Overhaul immigration policy with border security, enforcement and guest worker program
Yes Allow consideration of a bill to permanently repeal the estate tax
No Urge President Bush to begin troop withdrawals from Iraq in 2006
Yes Lift President Bush's restrictions on stem cell research funding
Yes Authorize military tribunals for suspected terrorists

2005

No Curb class action lawsuits by shifting them from state to federal courts
Yes Allow confirmation vote on Priscilla R. Owen to the U.S. Court of Appeals for the 5th Circuit
No Oppose mandatory emissions limits and block recognition of global warming as a threat
Yes Approve free-trade pact with five Central American countries
No Pass energy policy overhaul favored by President Bush emphasizing domestic oil and gas production
Yes Shield gunmakers from lawsuits when their products are used in crimes
Yes Ban torture of prisoners in U.S. custody
No Renew 16 provisions of the Patriot Act
No Allow final vote on opening the Arctic National Wildlife Refuge to oil and gas exploration

CQ VOTE STUDIES

	PARTY UNITY		PRESIDENTIAL SUPPORT	
	Support	Oppose	Support	Oppose
2006	76%	24%	60%	40%
2005	84%	16%	47%	53%
2004	92%	8%	62%	38%
2003	90%	10%	56%	44%
2002	77%	23%	78%	22%
2001	92%	8%	70%	30%
House Service:				
1990	77%	23%	40%	60%
1989	80%	20%	47%	53%
1988	72%	28%	46%	54%
1987	76%	24%	42%	58%

INTEREST GROUPS

	AFL-CIO	ADA	CCUS	ACU
2006	60%	60%	83%	40%
2005	71%	80%	50%	20%
2004	100%	80%	65%	4%
2003	77%	80%	48%	20%
2002	85%	70%	70%	30%
2001	100%	95%	43%	16%
House Service:				
1990	86%	50%	0%	27%
1989	91%	60%	50%	31%
1988	71%	45%	43%	56%
1987	63%	52%	53%	35%

Sen. Mel Martinez (R)

CAPITOL OFFICE
224-3041
martinez.senate.gov
356 Russell 20510-0303; fax 228-5171

COMMITTEES
Armed Services
Banking, Housing & Urban Affairs
Energy & Natural Resources
Special Aging

RESIDENCE
Orlando

BORN
Oct. 23, 1946, Sagua La Grande, Cuba

RELIGION
Roman Catholic

FAMILY
Wife, Kitty Martinez; three children

EDUCATION
Orlando Junior College, A.A. 1967; Florida State U., B.A. 1969 (international affairs), J.D. 1973

CAREER
Lawyer

POLITICAL HIGHLIGHTS
Sought Republican nomination for lieutenant governor, 1994; Orange County chairman, 1998-2001; Housing and Urban Development secretary, 2001-03

ELECTION RESULTS

2004 GENERAL		
Mel Martinez (R)	3,672,864	49.4%
Betty Castor (D)	3,590,201	48.3%
Dennis F. Bradley (VET)	166,642	2.2%
2004 PRIMARY		
Mel Martinez (R)	522,994	44.9%
Bill McCollum (R)	360,474	30.9%
Doug Gallagher (R)	158,360	13.6%
Johnnie Byrd (R)	68,982	5.9%
Karen Saull (R)	20,365	1.8%
Sonya March (R)	17,804	1.5%
Larry Klayman (R)	13,257	1.1%

Elected 2004; 1st term

The soft-spoken Martinez, who knew little English when he arrived in the United States as a teenage Cuban refugee, is now the Republican Party's chief ambassador. The Florida senator was chosen general chairman of the Republican National Committee in January 2007, a reflection of the prominence he has gained and of the party establishment's desire to appeal to Hispanic voters after a harrowing loss at the polls in 2006.

Like the life-changing 1962 airlift that carried him from Fidel Castro's Cuba to Orlando at the age of 15, Martinez's journey to the Senate and the RNC has been swift. He has been helped along by an up-from-the-bootstraps work ethic and a series of fortuitous turns.

He befriended President Bush during the 2000 election, when he served as one of the Bush campaign's multiple chairmen in Florida, and was later tapped by the newly elected president to be secretary of Housing and Urban Development. "Mel, it touches my heart to know that this man, who could have been living in repression and tyranny, is now in the Cabinet of the President of the United States," Bush said at a 2003 re-election fundraiser.

Later that year, the White House helped persuade Martinez to run for the Senate, a move Republican strategists hoped would help Bush tally more votes in Florida's politically formidable Cuban-American community.

Since becoming the first Cuban-American in the Senate, Martinez has been one of Bush's strongest allies on headline issues such as immigration, national security and judicial nominations — demonstrating commitment both to social conservatism and to the pro-business GOP establishment.

In 2006, Martinez helped resurrect a stalled immigration overhaul proposal, teaming with Republican Sen. Chuck Hagel of Nebraska to offer a compromise that the Senate passed. House GOP opposition ultimately doomed the plan, which would have beefed up border security, established a guest worker program and created a path to citizenship for many illegal immigrants.

Conservative critics of the Senate's immigration bill opposed Martinez's election to the chairmanship of the RNC, but with the backing of the White House and others in the GOP establishment he captured the post of general chairman — Mike Duncan, a veteran RNC official and its former general counsel, is national chairman — with ease.

"I think some people may see it as some sort of position taken on immigration, and they are not happy with that," said Sen. Jeff Sessions, an Alabama Republican who opposed the Senate bill. "But Mel is so talented, and such an articulate Republican spokesman, I think he'll be fine."

Martinez also played a critical role in 2006 on a bill that opened more offshore areas to oil and gas drilling. After the House passed a sweeping measure that permitted drilling off virtually any U.S. coast, Martinez helped write a far more restrictive plan that opened 8.3 million more acres in the Gulf of Mexico to drilling, but protected Florida's beaches and shared drilling revenue with the Gulf Coast states. House Republicans complained that the bill did little more than what the Bush administration could do administratively, but the compromise became law as part of a year-end tax bill.

Going forward, Martinez, like Bush, wants to encourage Americans to purchase health insurance on their own, rather than through their employers. The president's plan to give tax breaks to those who do so was pronounced "dead on arrival" by Democrats when he proposed it in early

2007. But Martinez, who in the 109th Congress (2005-06) had introduced his own bill offering refundable tax credits to those buying health insurance on their own, unveiled in 2007 a hybrid combining his version and Bush's. Also in the 109th Congress, Martinez took a similar approach toward education, offering legislation to give tax credits of up to $4,500 to parents who enroll their children in religious schools.

Martinez is a devout Catholic who opposes abortion and same-sex marriage. In 2005, he cosponsored legislation to give federal courts jurisdiction over the case of Terri Schiavo, a brain-damaged Florida woman. But the federal courts ultimately refused to order that her feeding tube be reinstated and Schiavo died.

Martinez then was embarrassed by the actions of his legal counsel, who resigned after admitting that he wrote a memo citing the political advantages of the GOP weighing in on the case.

Martinez, a Democrat until the Reagan administration, is a former trial attorney who once specialized in helping poor clients and fellow immigrants win handsome settlements from companies. He now says that he supports limiting jury awards for "pain and suffering," although his preferred $500,000 ceiling is twice as high as the one Bush has advocated.

As HUD secretary, he launched a Center for Faith-Based and Community Services, an office intended to help religious-oriented organizations compete for federal grants. Martinez was a forceful advocate for home ownership, one of Bush's favorite initiatives, but his effort to simplify the purchasing process for would-be homebuyers fell flat in Congress. Critics faulted him for failing to increase rental housing for poor people.

Martinez's life story proved a compelling backdrop for his 2004 campaign, especially in the context of a Bush re-election bid that focused on attracting Hispanic support. Martinez arrived in Florida by himself as part of "Operation Pedro Pan," a joint effort of the U.S. government and the Roman Catholic Church to spirit some 14,000 Cubans to the mainland.

He was moved from one foster home to another — it was a foster mother who shortened his given name, Melquiades, to Mel — while he worked to save money for college, and later for his family, with whom he was eventually reunited. Martinez later called the program that brought him to the United States one of the first public-private "faith based" initiatives.

Martinez supports Bush's approach to foreign policy, from the war on terrorism to the embargo against Cuba. "My understanding of good and evil in the world was based on that experience," he said of his personal history. "My understanding of America being a beacon of hope in the world, a positive force in the world, comes from that immigrant experience."

Martinez is known for his charisma, approachability and talent for networking. But he has sometimes appeared to lose his cool in fast-developing situations. In a 2000 press release, Martinez called government agents "armed thugs" for their handling of 5-year-old Elián Gonzalez, a Cuban boy who sparked an international incident when he was plucked from an inner tube in U.S. waters off Miami.

During the 2004 campaign, Martinez had to apologize to former Rep. Bill McCollum, his GOP primary opponent, for calling McCollum "anti-family" and saying in ads that McCollum sided with the "radical homosexual lobby."

In the general election, he accused his Democratic opponent, Betty Castor, the state's former education commissioner, of being soft on terrorism because she did not suspend a professor with suspected ties to Islamic Jihad while she was president of the University of Southern Florida. Martinez edged Castor with 49 percent of the vote.

KEY VOTES

2006

- Yes Confirm Samuel A. Alito Jr. to the Supreme Court
- Yes Allow consideration of a bill to establish a $140 billion trust fund to compensate victims of asbestos exposure
- Yes Extend tax cuts for two years at a cost of $70 billion over five years
- Yes Overhaul immigration policy with border security, enforcement and guest worker program
- Yes Allow consideration of a bill to permanently repeal the estate tax
- No Urge President Bush to begin troop withdrawals from Iraq in 2006
- No Lift President Bush's restrictions on stem cell research funding
- Yes Authorize military tribunals for suspected terrorists

2005

- Yes Curb class action lawsuits by shifting them from state to federal courts
- Yes Allow confirmation vote on Priscilla R. Owen to the U.S. Court of Appeals for the 5th Circuit
- Yes Oppose mandatory emissions limits and block recognition of global warming as a threat
- Yes Approve free-trade pact with five Central American countries
- No Pass energy policy overhaul favored by President Bush emphasizing domestic oil and gas production
- Yes Shield gunmakers from lawsuits when their products are used in crimes
- Yes Ban torture of prisoners in U.S. custody
- Yes Renew 16 provisions of the Patriot Act
- Yes Allow final vote on opening the Arctic National Wildlife Refuge to oil and gas exploration

CQ VOTE STUDIES

	PARTY UNITY		PRESIDENTIAL SUPPORT	
	Support	Oppose	Support	Oppose
2006	86%	14%	92%	8%
2005	94%	6%	91%	9%

INTEREST GROUPS

	AFL-CIO	ADA	CCUS	ACU
2006	7%	0%	100%	84%
2005	14%	5%	83%	100%

Rep. Jeff Miller (R)

CAPITOL OFFICE
225-4136
jeffmiller.house.gov
1535 Longworth 20515-0901; fax 225-3414

COMMITTEES
Armed Services
Veterans' Affairs

RESIDENCE
Chumuckla

BORN
June 27, 1959, St. Petersburg, Fla.

RELIGION
Methodist

FAMILY
Wife, Vicki Miller; two children

EDUCATION
U. of Florida, B.A. 1984 (journalism)

CAREER
Real estate broker; state agriculture department official; deputy county sheriff

POLITICAL HIGHLIGHTS
Fla. House, 1998-2001

ELECTION RESULTS

2006 GENERAL		
Jeff Miller (R)	135,786	68.5%
Jeff Roberts (D)	62,340	31.5%
2006 PRIMARY		
Jeff Miller (R)		unopposed
2004 GENERAL		
Jeff Miller (R)	236,604	76.5%
Mark S. Coutu (D)	72,506	23.5%

PREVIOUS WINNING PERCENTAGES
2002 (75%); 2001 Special Election (66%)

Elected October 2001; 3rd full term

Miller's district is home to a number of military installations and more than 100,000 veterans, and he is an ardent advocate for both. A defender of the war in Iraq, he supports both the president who ordered U.S. troops into battle and the men and women who have waged the war.

The Florida Republican serves on both the Armed Services and Veterans' Affairs committees, which gives him a good grasp of the challenges facing the military and its veterans. In the 110th Congress (2007-08), he became the top-ranking Republican on the Veterans' Affairs Subcommittee on Health — just as the quality of care for those wounded in Iraq came under fire.

After The Washington Post in early 2007 disclosed widespread problems at Walter Reed Army Medical Center, Miller criticized the Pentagon's failure to address the shortcomings sooner. And in a letter to Defense Secretary Robert M. Gates, he "strongly recommended" the firing of the Army's surgeon general, Lt. Gen. Kevin Kiley, the former commander at Walter Reed. Miller was just one of many calling for Kiley's head; the general soon retired under pressure.

Miller's district in the Florida Panhandle is home to the Naval Air Station in Pensacola, the Air Force's Hurlburt Field and Eglin Air Force Base. He has worked to improve benefits for military personnel and their families since he arrived in Congress. In 2004, he was successful in adding an amendment to the annual defense authorization bill that eliminated the so-called widows' tax on surviving spouses of military retirees.

Under the military's Survivor Benefit Plan, enacted in the 1970s, spouses of deceased career military retirees initially received 55 percent of the soldier's annual retirement pay, but that payment was cut to 35 percent when the spouse reached age 62. That is when individuals first become eligible for Social Security, but anyone starting Social Security at age 62 faces reduced benefits for life. Miller's provision allowed military spouses over 62 to retain 55 percent of their deceased spouse's military retirement pay.

In 2003, Miller cosponsored a measure allowing disabled veterans to simultaneously receive both military pension checks and veterans' disability benefits. A version of the plan was ultimately rolled into that year's defense authorization bill.

Miller delivers for his district in other ways. He was able to gain federal emergency funds in the 2004 catchall appropriations bill for the replacement of the Interstate 10 bridge spanning Escambia Bay. The bridge, which was severely damaged by Hurricane Ivan in the fall of 2004, is expected to cost more than $300 million to replace.

A sixth-generation Floridian whose parents sold real estate and operated a cattle ranch near Clearwater, Miller understands the needs of the 1st District, which is dotted with rural farm towns, such as his hometown of Chumuckla. A former deputy sheriff, Miller appears as comfortable in cowboy boots as in a business suit.

Conservative on both social and fiscal policy, Miller opposes abortion and embryonic stem cell research, supports school vouchers and favors strict immigration controls. He wants to make permanent President Bush's first-term tax cuts and enact new reductions, particularly for small businesses.

A former small-businessman himself, Miller is close to the business leaders in his community, many of whom rely on a robust tourism economy. He opposes drilling for oil and gas off the Florida coast, not only because of the potential detrimental environmental impact on beaches, but also to maintain the areas used for training exercises by pilots from Eglin Air Force Base. But in 2006, he voted for a House bill expanding offshore drilling elsewhere across the nation.

In January 2003, Miller was one of just four House lawmakers to vote against an extension of unemployment benefits that had expired Dec. 28, 2002. "At what point do we quit providing a check to someone without a job?" he asked. "I'm afraid that extending these benefits will diminish the desire to go out and find a job," he said, according to The Associated Press.

Miller also wanted to make sure that one group of unemployed workers — lawmakers expelled from Congress — were cut off from the government-financed portion of their pensions. He introduced legislation in 2003 directed at Ohio Democrat James A. Traficant, who was expelled from the House in July 2002 just before he was convicted of 10 counts of bribery, racketeering and tax evasion. Traficant was sentenced to eight years in prison but continues to receive an annual pension of more than $35,000. Miller's bill went nowhere in 2003, but in early 2007, the House passed legislation stripping pensions from members of Congress convicted of crimes related to their official duties. The move came after corruption convictions of two GOP members of Congress in the 109th Congress (2005-06).

A former real estate broker and political aide, Miller has an eclectic résumé. While in high school, he was a disc jockey for the local radio station. Later, he had a stint as a deputy county sheriff and held part-time jobs as a stock car racer and auctioneer.

As a journalism major at the University of Florida, he was elected president of college fraternities for southeast Florida. This distinction came after he had become president of the university's agriculture fraternity, Alpha Gamma Rho, and then president of the school's fraternity system. He remains an enthusiastic supporter of the Florida Gators football team, a passion he shares with his two grown sons.

After college, Miller joined the staff of Florida Agriculture Commissioner Doyle Connor, later serving as a state representative for the heavily Republican north Florida district that he now represents in Congress.

Miller came to Congress in October 2001, after winning a special election to replace GOP Rep. Joe Scarborough, who had resigned from the House to spend more time with his family. (Scarborough later began a television career.) Miller had no trouble winning the special election, garnering 66 percent of the vote. He has coasted to re-election since then.

KEY VOTES

2006

- No Stop broadband companies from favoring select Internet traffic
- Yes Affirm U.S. commitment to war in Iraq and reject setting a withdrawal date for troops
- Yes Repeal requirement for bilingual ballots at the polls
- Yes Permit U.S. sale of civilian nuclear technology to India
- Yes Build a 700-mile fence on the U.S.-Mexico border to curb illegal crossings
- Yes Permit warrantless wiretaps of suspected terrorists

2005

- Yes Intervene in the life-support case of Terri Schiavo
- No Lift President Bush's restrictions on stem cell research funding
- Yes Prohibit FBI access to library and bookstore records
- Yes Approve free-trade pact with five Central American countries
- No Pass energy policy overhaul favored by President Bush emphasizing domestic oil and gas production
- Yes End mandatory preservation of habitat of endangered animal and plant species
- No Ban torture of prisoners in U.S. custody

CQ VOTE STUDIES

	PARTY UNITY		PRESIDENTIAL SUPPORT	
	Support	Oppose	Support	Oppose
2006	97%	3%	92%	8%
2005	96%	4%	85%	15%
2004	99%	1%	92%	8%
2003	96%	4%	85%	15%
2002	98%	2%	85%	15%

INTEREST GROUPS

	AFL-CIO	ADA	CCUS	ACU
2006	14%	5%	93%	92%
2005	15%	0%	80%	92%
2004	8%	5%	100%	100%
2003	7%	15%	83%	92%
2002	0%	0%	84%	100%

FLORIDA 1

Panhandle — Pensacola, Fort Walton Beach

Occupying the western portion of the Panhandle — wedged between Alabama and the Gulf of Mexico — the 1st stretches from Washington County north of Panama City to Pensacola and the Perdido River. Often dubbed "Lower Alabama," the 1st's Bible Belt culture is much closer to the Old South than to Florida's big cities.

The 1st is home to several large military bases, and the strong defense presence stabilizes its economy. Eglin Air Force Base is the military's center for air-delivered weaponry, and, including contractors and civilians, the base is slated to add 5,000 people by 2012. Tourism and the area's building boom also create economic and population growth here, as the district transitions from manufacturing. Developers continue to break ground on condominiums in Pensacola and on retirement communities in previously rural settings.

Bucolic open spaces and the white sand beaches of Emerald Coast towns such as Destin (a small part of which is in the 2nd) draw vacationers. Although the district was spared major physical destruction from the 2004 and 2005 hurricanes, coastal homes and businesses were damaged and the storms halted the tourism industry's strong growth by disrupting the flow of visitors from other parts of the South.

The 1st, even more conservative than its GOP registration edge would indicate, gave George W. Bush 72 percent of its 2004 presidential vote, Bush's highest total in Florida. The 1st's Democrats are more "Dixiecrat" than liberal, and the political ideology of the predominately white district is heavily influenced by the military.

MAJOR INDUSTRY

Defense, tourism, construction, health care

MILITARY BASES

Naval Air Station Pensacola, 14,952 military, 4,218 civilian (2006); Eglin Air Force Base, 11,000 military, 5,000 civilian (2007); Hurlburt Field (Air Force), 6,000 military, 2,000 civilian (2007); Naval Technical Training Center Corry Station, 2,620 military, 411 civilian; Naval Air Station Whiting Field, 1,738 military, 1,382 civilian (2006)

CITIES

Pensacola, 56,255; Ferry Pass (unincorporated), 27,176

NOTABLE

The Blue Angels flight group is housed at Naval Air Station Pensacola.

Rep. Allen Boyd (D)

CAPITOL OFFICE
225-5235
www.house.gov/boyd
1227 Longworth 20515-0902; fax 225-5615

COMMITTEES
Appropriations
Budget

RESIDENCE
Monticello

BORN
June 6, 1945, Valdosta, Ga.

RELIGION
Methodist

FAMILY
Wife, Cissy Boyd; three children

EDUCATION
North Florida Junior College, A.A. 1966;
Florida State U., B.S. 1969 (accounting)

MILITARY SERVICE
Army, 1969-71

CAREER
Farmer

POLITICAL HIGHLIGHTS
Sought Democratic nomination for Jefferson County Board of County Commissioners, 1972; Fla. House, 1989-96

ELECTION RESULTS

2006 GENERAL		
Allen Boyd (D)	unopposed	
2006 PRIMARY		
Allen Boyd (D)	unopposed	
2004 GENERAL		
Allen Boyd (D)	201,577	61.7%
Bev Kilmer (R)	125,399	38.4%

PREVIOUS WINNING PERCENTAGES
2002 (67%); 2000 (72%); 1998 (95%); 1996 (59%)

Elected 1996; 6th term

After a decade as a backbencher, Boyd finds himself in the influential role of co-chairman of the conservative Blue Dog Coalition in a new Democratic majority. The party's leaders must pay attention to the growing group of moderate-to-conservative House members if they want to stay in power. Boyd's conservative stands and focus on parochial concerns have enabled him to solidify his position in the Tallahassee-based 2nd District while many similar Southern districts have gone Republican.

As a Blue Dog leader — he founded a similar group in the Florida Legislature — Boyd will keep pressure on his party leadership to move an agenda that is palatable to conservative Democrats and swing voters in districts like his. Boyd's voting record is among the most conservative of the House Democrats. In 2006, he strayed from his party on one-third of all party-line votes, and in the 109th Congress (2005-06) he backed President Bush's position more than half the time.

But while he initially voted to authorize the president to wage war in Iraq, in early 2007 he spoke out against Bush's plan to send more than 21,000 additional combat troops to Iraq. "The men and women serving in Iraq are counting on their political leaders to develop a successful strategy in Iraq, and interjecting more young American men and women in uniform into the crossfire of an Iraqi civil war is simply not the right approach," Boyd told his colleagues on the House floor. He says, however, that he will vote to provide funds for the U.S. effort even though he thinks the mission is misguided.

A rifle platoon leader during the Vietnam War, Boyd's views on Iraq have particular significance in the 110th Congress (2007-08) because he sits on the Defense Appropriations Subcommittee, which writes the annual Pentagon spending bills and legislation to provide supplemental funding for the war.

That seat, coupled with a spot on Appropriations' Military Construction-VA Subcommittee, gives him a perch from which to protect the interests of Tyndall Air Force Base and other nearby military installations. Although he considers himself a fiscal conservative, Boyd is not shy about pushing for government spending for his district. He has worked to speed runway upgrades and other improvements at Tyndall in preparation for the arrival of a second squadron of the Air Force's F-22 air-to-air combat planes.

A fifth-generation farmer, his seat on the Agriculture Appropriations Subcommittee makes him a powerful advocate for Florida's farmers and an influential player in the state's congressional delegation.

Boyd is not afraid to break from his party on hot-button issues. At the beginning of the 109th Congress, he was the first Democrat to back Bush's plan to add personal investment accounts to Social Security, even teaming up with Republican Jim Kolbe of Arizona to draft a bill. His defection denied House Democrats a unified opposition on the issue.

In the tax arena, however, Boyd often opposes the president's agenda. He favors paying down the national debt over major tax reductions. When the nation returned to deficit spending during Bush's first term, Boyd said the $1.35 trillion, 10-year tax cut package enacted in 2001 should be reconsidered. But six weeks before Election Day 2004, Boyd was in the midst of the toughest re-election fight of his congressional career and voted for a tax cut extension plan. In 2006, though, he voted against extending some of Bush's tax cuts at a cost of $70 billion over five years.

Boyd has taken a tough stance on immigration, voting in the 109th Congress to impose stricter identification and asylum requirements on immigrants and to build 700 miles of fencing along the U.S. border with Mexico. But he voted against repealing bilingual voting-assistance programs.

A lifelong hunter, Boyd opposes gun control legislation. The position is reflective of a broader record of voting to protect individual liberties from government encroachment. In the 109th Congress, he voted to give property owners greater access to federal courts in eminent domain cases and against authorizing the president's warrantless wiretapping program.

A product of rural Jefferson County, just east of Tallahassee, Boyd was raised on a farm. He went to Florida State University just down the road, spent two years in the Army, and then returned home to help his family raise cattle, cotton, sod and peanuts. He became involved in agricultural organizations and civic groups.

A failed bid in 1972 for an open county commission seat seemed to have rid him of his inclination toward elective office, but more than a decade later, another open seat beckoned him. He won a 1989 special election to the state House and served seven years, cultivating good relations with the business community.

He first won his U.S. House seat in 1996 after the retirement of three-term Democrat Pete Peterson. Boyd demonstrated that he could hold together the 2nd District's traditional Democratic coalition: Tallahassee-area voters with jobs in state and local government and higher education, African-Americans, and the portion of the white electorate still clinging to an inherited aversion to the GOP dating back to the Civil War. Boyd defeated Republican Bill Sutton, a former bank president and one-time state commerce secretary, by 19 percentage points.

Boyd won re-election easily until 2004 when he drew a well-funded challenger in state Rep. Bev Kilmer, who tried to cast him as a liberal. Boyd was the only incumbent Democrat in Florida with a GOP foe, and it was the state's only truly competitive House race. But his popularity took him to a comfortable 62 percent victory; he was unopposed in 2006.

Boyd briefly pursued a run for the Senate when Democrat Bob Graham announced he would retire at the end of the 108th Congress (2003-04), but his lack of statewide recognition convinced him to seek re-election to the House instead. His newfound status in the majority and enhanced position on the Appropriations Committee mean Boyd is likely to stay put for the time being. "I don't know what the future holds, but being in the majority gives us a new lease on life. I'm enjoying this work a lot more than I was two years ago," he says.

KEY VOTES

2006

- No Stop broadband companies from favoring select Internet traffic
- P Affirm U.S. commitment to war in Iraq and reject setting a withdrawal date for troops
- No Repeal requirement for bilingual ballots at the polls
- Yes Permit U.S. sale of civilian nuclear technology to India
- Yes Build a 700-mile fence on the U.S.-Mexico border to curb illegal crossings
- No Permit warrantless wiretaps of suspected terrorists

2005

- ? Intervene in the life-support case of Terri Schiavo
- Yes Lift President Bush's restrictions on stem cell research funding
- Yes Prohibit FBI access to library and bookstore records
- No Approve free-trade pact with five Central American countries
- No Pass energy policy overhaul favored by President Bush emphasizing domestic oil and gas production
- Yes End mandatory preservation of habitat of endangered animal and plant species
- Yes Ban torture of prisoners in U.S. custody

CQ VOTE STUDIES

	PARTY UNITY		PRESIDENTIAL SUPPORT	
	Support	Oppose	Support	Oppose
2006	67%	33%	62%	38%
2005	75%	25%	42%	58%
2004	67%	33%	61%	39%
2003	74%	26%	50%	50%
2002	71%	29%	50%	50%

INTEREST GROUPS

	AFL-CIO	ADA	CCUS	ACU
2006	86%	50%	93%	63%
2005	77%	80%	70%	42%
2004	60%	70%	75%	46%
2003	71%	70%	71%	38%
2002	75%	70%	58%	40%

FLORIDA 2

Panhandle — part of Tallahassee, Panama City

The 2nd stretches around Florida's Big Bend, connecting the Panhandle and the state capital of Tallahassee (a sliver of which is in the 4th District) to the north-central part of the state. Taking in all or part of 16 counties, the 2nd features tobacco and peanut farms, forests and small towns.

The district's natural resources — from the Gulf Coast beaches where oysters are harvested to abundant farmland — drive its economy. Although agriculture has struggled occasionally due to drought and high energy prices, a steady base of government employees working in the state capital buffers any long-term economic effects. Florida's forestry industry also maintains a strong presence in the district. Panama City, in Bay County, relies on tourism and the economic benefits of the military community around Tyndall Air Force Base. The 2nd has the third-largest percentage (28 percent) of government workers in any district in the nation. Not surprisingly, given its reliance on farming and the military, agriculture and veterans' affairs dominate the district's politics.

While Democratic, the 2nd is not as liberal as districts in southeast Florida. Many of the district's Democrats, including farmers and retirees, often hold conservative views on fiscal and social issues. The exception is the Tallahassee area (Leon County), home to Florida State University and Florida A&M University. Bay County has a stronger conservative element, as do the smaller communities that ring the Gulf Coast. Black residents — the majority of whom live in the Tallahassee area or in neighboring Gadsden County — make up more than one-fifth of the district's population. John Kerry took at least 60 percent of the 2004 presidential vote in Gadsden and Leon counties, but George W. Bush won the district with 54 percent.

MAJOR INDUSTRY
Agriculture, government, manufacturing

MILITARY BASES
Tyndall Air Force Base, 4,120 military, 1,081 civilian (2004)

CITIES
Tallahassee (pt.), 147,167; Panama City, 36,417; Callaway, 14,233

NOTABLE
The Suwannee River was made famous by Stephen Foster's song, "Old Folks at Home"; Tallahassee's National High Magnetic Field Laboratory is the highest-powered magnet laboratory in the world.

Rep. Corrine Brown (D)

CAPITOL OFFICE
225-0123
www.house.gov/corrinebrown
2336 Rayburn 20515-0903; fax 225-2256

COMMITTEES
Transportation & Infrastructure
(Railroads, Pipelines & Hazardous Materials - chairwoman)
Veterans' Affairs

RESIDENCE
Jacksonville

BORN
Nov. 11, 1946, Jacksonville, Fla.

RELIGION
Baptist

FAMILY
Divorced; one child

EDUCATION
Florida A&M U., B.S. 1969 (sociology), M.A. 1971 (education); U. of Florida, Ed.S. 1974

CAREER
College guidance counselor; travel agency owner

POLITICAL HIGHLIGHTS
Candidate for Fla. House, 1980; Fla. House, 1982-92

ELECTION RESULTS

2006 GENERAL	
Corrine Brown (D)	unopposed
2006 PRIMARY	
Corrine Brown (D)	unopposed
2004 GENERAL	
Corrine Brown (D)	unopposed

PREVIOUS WINNING PERCENTAGES
2002 (59%); 2000 (58%); 1998 (55%); 1996 (61%); 1994 (58%); 1992 (59%)

Elected 1992; 8th term

Combative and partisan, Brown shows little sign of mellowing, even as she has built up seniority and gained sufficient power to shape policy instead of simply criticizing it. She now chairs a subcommittee on one House committee and is the No. 2 Democrat on a second committee.

Brown is an unrelenting antagonist of President Bush, saying his budget priorities have "dangerous flaws" that sacrifice a commitment to the poor and elderly in favor of defense and tax cuts. She was an early critic of the war in Iraq, voting against the 2002 resolution authorizing Bush to use force against Saddam Hussein's regime. In the 110th Congress (2007-08), she is a member of the Out of Iraq Caucus, an increasingly vocal band of House members pressing for a withdrawal of U.S. troops from Iraq.

There are several military installations near the 3rd District, and Jacksonville is home to many retired military personnel. Brown keeps an eye on their needs as the No. 2 Democrat on the Veterans' Affairs Committee and its Health Subcommittee, which has been increasingly busy in recent years as Congress tackles the strains placed on the VA medical system by returning Iraq War veterans.

In the 109th Congress (2005-06), Brown assailed the White House and Republicans for what she saw as inadequate funding for veterans' health care. At a March 2005 hearing, she listened impatiently as the committee's Republican chairman, Steve Buyer of Indiana, tried to convince veterans groups that he was sympathetic to their needs. "We've heard a lot of talk up here," Brown snapped, "and frankly, a lot of it is bulls- - -."

Her sharp tongue briefly cost her speaking privileges on the House floor in 2004. She accused Buyer and others of participating in a "coup d'état" and of stealing the contested 2000 presidential election in Florida. Unapologetic after the incident, she said, "If they're going to take my words down for telling the truth, that's OK. . . . We had a coup d'état. Straight out, they stole the election."

Brown may be acerbic, but she is attentive to her district and her committee duties. In 2007, she became chairwoman of the Transportation and Infrastructure panel's Railroads Subcommittee, after serving four years as top-ranking Democrat. She used her new power to push some old priorities, including stepped-up rail security and greater stability for Amtrak, the financially troubled federally subsidized passenger rail system.

From her seat on Transportation, she also has been able to direct a good share of federal funding to her district and state. During the 2004 renewal of federal transportation programs, she served on the House-Senate committee negotiating the final bill and won tens of millions of dollars for road and transit projects in Jacksonville and Orlando. She also has worked to make minority hiring a priority at the Transportation Security Administration since its creation in 2001.

After the 2000 election controversy in Florida — when voters, including many minorities, were turned away from some polling places and thousands of ballots were miscast or uncounted — Brown joined in the volley of criticism and began working to overhaul the election process. She backed the election standards law enacted in 2002, unlike several colleagues in the Black Caucus who felt the measure did not do enough.

Brown has a long history of fending off allegations of ethical lapses. One of her 1992 primary opponents, former state Rep. Andrew E. Johnson, filed charges with the Florida Commission on Ethics claiming that Brown had received illegal campaign donations and made a staff member from her state representative's office work in her travel agency. She agreed in February 1994 to pay Florida $5,000 to settle the ethics probe but denied any wrongdoing.

In 1998, the Committee on Standards of Official Conduct began investigating her financial dealings with West African businessman Foutanga Dit Babani Sissoko after he provided Brown lodging in his luxury Miami condominium. Sissoko's chief financial officer also gave Brown's daughter, Shantrel, a $50,000 Lexus automobile. The Lexus was given to Brown's daughter just weeks after Brown aggressively lobbied the Clinton administration to have Sissoko released from a U.S. prison where he was serving time in a bribery case.

In 2000, the ethics panel concluded it could not find sufficient evidence to prove improper conduct, in large measure because key witnesses "were beyond the reach of the committee's subpoena power." But the committee ruled that Brown had "demonstrated, at the least, poor judgment."

In 2005, the Florida Times-Union in Jacksonville said Brown's daughter had lobbied in behalf of a private Jacksonville school, Edward Waters College, while her mother was steering millions in federal dollars to the school. The younger Brown was a registered lobbyist for Alcalde & Fay, a suburban Washington law firm with numerous Florida clients. Brown's spokesman said the congresswoman was not lobbied by her daughter.

Brown was steered into politics by one of her sorority sisters at Florida A&M University, Gwendolyn Sawyer Cherry, who went on to become Florida's first black state representative. Although Brown lost her first state House race in 1980, Cherry kept after her to try again, and Brown won a seat in 1982. She served in the state House for a decade.

When a black-majority 3rd District was created by redistricting for the 1990s, Brown was one of four candidates in the bitter 1992 Democratic primary for the seat. She survived a runoff with 64 percent of the vote. Latent acrimony over ethics charges raised in the primary helped hold her share of the vote to 59 percent in November against Republican Don Weidner.

Until recently, Brown had to work for most of her election victories. She won more than three-fifths of the vote — a traditional threshold for having a safe seat — in only one of her first six races, when she got a lift on President Bill Clinton's coattails in 1996. Republicans ran a black candidate against Brown in three of her re-election contests, seeking to eliminate race as a factor. Her fortunes have since improved. In 2004, Brown faced only a write-in opponent, and in 2006 she was unopposed.

KEY VOTES

2006

No Stop broadband companies from favoring select Internet traffic

No Affirm U.S. commitment to war in Iraq and reject setting a withdrawal date for troops

No Repeal requirement for bilingual ballots at the polls

Yes Permit U.S. sale of civilian nuclear technology to India

Yes Build a 700-mile fence on the U.S.-Mexico border to curb illegal crossings

No Permit warrantless wiretaps of suspected terrorists

2005

? Intervene in the life-support case of Terri Schiavo

Yes Lift President Bush's restrictions on stem cell research funding

Yes Prohibit FBI access to library and bookstore records

No Approve free-trade pact with five Central American countries

No Pass energy policy overhaul favored by President Bush emphasizing domestic oil and gas production

No End mandatory preservation of habitat of endangered animal and plant species

Yes Ban torture of prisoners in U.S. custody

CQ VOTE STUDIES

	PARTY UNITY		PRESIDENTIAL SUPPORT	
	Support	Oppose	Support	Oppose
2006	95%	5%	33%	67%
2005	96%	4%	16%	84%
2004	94%	6%	32%	68%
2003	95%	5%	20%	80%
2002	95%	5%	29%	71%

INTEREST GROUPS

	AFL-CIO	ADA	CCUS	ACU
2006	100%	100%	40%	20%
2005	92%	95%	42%	0%
2004	92%	90%	37%	8%
2003	100%	95%	33%	22%
2002	100%	95%	42%	0%

FLORIDA 3

North — parts of Jacksonville, Orlando and Gainesville

The Democratic, blue-collar 3rd bounces among three of Florida's northern cities and includes both heavily urban areas and long stretches of swamps and lakes along the St. Johns River. It slithers south along the river into a large portion of highly working-class Putnam County, where bass fishing is prevalent, before taking in part of Gainesville, home to the University of Florida (in the 6th District), and continuing southeast to Orlando (shared with the 8th and 24th districts). Blacks make up a plurality (49 percent) of district residents, and the 3rd has the lowest median income (just under $30,000) of any Florida district.

The district relies on Jacksonville's port, Naval Air Station Jacksonville (in the 4th District) and other area government facilities for jobs. Transportation company CSX also is based in Jacksonville. The growth of the financial services sector has helped the city's economic outlook.

At the district's southern end, many Orlando residents work in tourism jobs at locations such as Walt Disney World (in the 8th District). Renovations to the Florida Citrus Bowl and construction of a new arena for basketball's Magic in downtown Orlando should bring increased revenue for the city. Most of the area in between the northern cities is dominated by agricultural land and lacks major private employers, contributing to the 3rd's overall underdeveloped economic profile.

Democrats dominate the 3rd — outnumbering Republicans 3-to-1 in registration. Some rural areas in Clay County and in the Palatka area (shared with the 7th) on the St. Johns River are home to Republicans and old-line conservative Democrats, but not enough to counter the 3rd's strong proclivity toward Democratic candidates for federal office. John Kerry won the 2004 presidential vote here by 30 percentage points.

MAJOR INDUSTRY

Defense, government, transportation, higher education

CITIES

Jacksonville (pt.), 251,892; Orlando (pt.), 61,906; Pine Hills (unincorporated), 41,764; Gainesville (pt.), 35,540

NOTABLE

Eatonville was the hometown of Harlem Renaissance author Zora Neale Hurston; The St. Johns River and its tributaries flow north to Jacksonville.

Rep. Ander Crenshaw (R)

CAPITOL OFFICE
225-2501
crenshaw.house.gov
127 Cannon 20515-0904; fax 225-2504

COMMITTEES
Appropriations

RESIDENCE
Jacksonville

BORN
Sept. 1, 1944, Jacksonville, Fla.

RELIGION
Episcopalian

FAMILY
Wife, Kitty Crenshaw; two children

EDUCATION
U. of Georgia, A.B. 1966 (political science);
U. of Florida, J.D. 1969

CAREER
Investment bank executive; lawyer

POLITICAL HIGHLIGHTS
Fla. House, 1972-78; candidate for Fla. secretary of state, 1978; sought Republican nomination for U.S. Senate, 1980; Fla. Senate, 1986-94 (president, 1992-93); sought Republican nomination for governor, 1994

ELECTION RESULTS

2006 GENERAL		
Ander Crenshaw (R)	141,759	69.7%
Robert J. Harms (D)	61,704	30.3%
2006 PRIMARY		
Ander Crenshaw (R)		unopposed
2004 GENERAL		
Ander Crenshaw (R)		unopposed

PREVIOUS WINNING PERCENTAGES
2002 (100%); 2000 (67%)

Elected 2000; 4th term

A loyal Republican who has helped the GOP leadership out of a jam or two, Crenshaw suffered some career setbacks after he was swept up in an ethics scandal in the 109th Congress (2005-06) involving overseas trips sponsored by lobbyists. When Republican leaders organized late in 2006 for the new 110th Congress (2007-08), they passed him over for the ranking minority spot of the Budget Committee.

Crenshaw accompanied Majority Leader Tom DeLay, his wife and others on an expense-paid trip to South Korea in 2001, sponsored by a nonprofit Korean group later identified as a front for a foreign lobbying campaign. According to media reports, the group was operated by a Washington lobbying firm run by DeLay's former chief of staff. House rules prohibit lawmakers from taking trips paid for by lobbyists or foreign agents. Crenshaw said in a letter to the House Committee on Standards of Official Conduct that the trip was a chance to bring together policymakers from the United States and South Korea. DeLay resigned under an ethics cloud in 2006.

Crenshaw's shot at the top minority post on Budget was not helped by his earlier decision to back the wrong horse in a hotly contested race to succeed DeLay. He supported Roy Blunt of Missouri over John A. Boehner of Ohio. Boehner is the GOP leader in the 110th Congress, giving him great influence over the selection of committee leadership posts.

In his early years in the House, Crenshaw advanced quickly. In only his second term, the former college basketball player secured a seat on the powerful Appropriations Committee by doing his "pregame homework."

He lined up support early within the Florida delegation, the fourth-largest after California, Texas and New York. And he let GOP leaders know they could count on him on tough votes, close calls and turf battles. To prove his worth in his freshman term, Crenshaw, though generally a supporter of larger military budgets, urged the Armed Services Committee to back a leadership-drafted budget that called for less spending than committee members wanted. Crenshaw has been loyal to his party on big votes, siding with his leadership more than 95 percent of the time on issues that polarized the parties.

He is a conservative across the board on fiscal and social issues. He advocates replacing the federal income tax system with a flat sales tax, and he votes with conservatives on hot-button social issues such as restricting federal funding for medical research on stem cells taken from surplus embryos at in vitro fertilization clinics, which conservatives liken to abortion. "On balance, I'd start with the proposition that government doesn't solve problems very well," he once told the Orlando Sentinel.

After losing his bid to be ranking member on the Budget panel to Paul D. Ryan of Wisconsin, who had less seniority, Crenshaw left the committee. But he kept his seat on the Appropriations panel, where his focus is delivering dollars to his district. His official congressional biography touts his "securing billions of dollars in defense projects for Northeast Florida."

In the 109th Congress, he joined with others in the Florida delegation in a furious attempt to keep the Navy from retiring the *USS John F. Kennedy*, an aircraft carrier docked at the Naval Station Mayport. The Pentagon proposed in 2005 to retire one of its 12 carriers to save $1 billion and chose the *Kennedy*, the oldest and likeliest target for retirement. Crenshaw lost that battle and turned his attention to replacing the *Kennedy* with a new nuclear carrier homeported at Mayport, a $100 million project requiring upgrades to the facilities.

Also important to Crenshaw's district is tourism at Atlantic Coast beaches. In 2005 and 2006, he helped secure approximately $8 million to help restore beaches in Nassau County damaged by severe weather. One of his enduring acts was passage of a law designating American Beach as part of a historic preserve. American Beach was a popular vacation spot for African-Americans during segregation. At one time larger than 200 acres, it has shrunk to half that size because of development.

Crenshaw's family has been in the Jacksonville area since 1901. The son of a lawyer, he grew up comfortably middle-class and was senior class president at Robert E. Lee High School. A lanky 6-foot-4, he went to the University of Georgia on a basketball scholarship and was the third member of his family, following his father and brother, to letter in a sport for the Bulldogs. The first name he uses, Ander, is a shortened version of his given name Alexander and was coined by his older brother.

Of draft age during the Vietnam War, Crenshaw served in the ROTC but avoided combat through a student deferment and then a high number in the draft lottery.

While working on a law degree at the University of Florida, he formed a Campus Crusade for Christ chapter. He eventually found he was not interested in practicing law after all and turned to investment banking. He says he began thinking about running for political office after he started dating Kitty Kirk, the daughter of former Florida Gov. Claude R. Kirk Jr. The two got married.

In 1972, Crenshaw won election to the state House, where he served six years. He moved up to the state Senate in 1986. In 1993, Crenshaw became the first Republican to preside over the Florida Senate in 118 years, leading a chamber split evenly between the two parties. His reputation as someone who would seek consensus kept the power-sharing agreement from descending into sheer acrimony.

Despite his success in the legislature, Crenshaw lost three statewide elections — a bid for secretary of state in 1978, the Republican primary for Senate in 1980 and the GOP primary for governor in 1994. In the latter race, he drew attention for condemning homosexuals but said he would hire gay people if elected.

After leaving the state Senate in 1994, he stayed out of politics until an opportunity to run for Congress came in 2000, when GOP Rep. Tillie Fowler stuck to her term-limit pledge and retired. Crenshaw won the primary easily, guaranteeing him victory in the solidly Republican district.

KEY VOTES

2006

- No Stop broadband companies from favoring select Internet traffic
- Yes Affirm U.S. commitment to war in Iraq and reject setting a withdrawal date for troops
- Yes Repeal requirement for bilingual ballots at the polls
- Yes Permit U.S. sale of civilian nuclear technology to India
- Yes Build a 700-mile fence on the U.S.-Mexico border to curb illegal crossings
- Yes Permit warrantless wiretaps of suspected terrorists

2005

- Yes Intervene in the life-support case of Terri Schiavo
- No Lift President Bush's restrictions on stem cell research funding
- No Prohibit FBI access to library and bookstore records
- Yes Approve free-trade pact with five Central American countries
- No Pass energy policy overhaul favored by President Bush emphasizing domestic oil and gas production
- Yes End mandatory preservation of habitat of endangered animal and plant species
- No Ban torture of prisoners in U.S. custody

CQ VOTE STUDIES

	PARTY UNITY		PRESIDENTIAL SUPPORT	
	Support	Oppose	Support	Oppose
2006	96%	4%	97%	3%
2005	97%	3%	89%	11%
2004	95%	5%	88%	12%
2003	98%	2%	98%	2%
2002	98%	2%	90%	10%

INTEREST GROUPS

	AFL-CIO	ADA	CCUS	ACU
2006	7%	0%	100%	84%
2005	13%	5%	89%	92%
2004	13%	0%	100%	92%
2003	7%	5%	97%	88%
2002	11%	0%	100%	96%

FLORIDA 4
North – part of Jacksonville, sliver of Tallahassee

The solidly Republican 4th is anchored in Jacksonville and the surrounding beach communities of Duval County. It wraps around the northeast corner of the state and then runs across the northern border counties as far west as Leon County, where it narrows to a finger to take in a small eastern part of Tallahassee, the state capital. Much of the 4th shadows Interstate 10, a highway that bridges the 150 miles of rural territory between Jacksonville and Tallahassee.

Defense, agriculture, inland water and coastal issues dominate the 4th's politics. Republicans now hold a slight but growing edge in voter registration after decades of Democratic dominance. Many nominal Democrats in the more rural areas of the district are old-line conservatives who now side with GOP candidates. One such example is Baker County, where Democrats hold a better than 2-1 voter registration advantage, but George W. Bush won 78 percent of the county's vote in the 2004 presidential election. Overall, the 4th gave Bush 67 percent of the vote.

Jacksonville is a major city, with health care and financial services sectors, and the local economy is still partly supported by manufacturing. The Port of Jacksonville (located in the 3rd District) is the southern hub for international importers and exporters. The Navy's strong presence along the St. Johns River — slashing through the center of Jacksonville — bolsters the city's economy and provides many jobs. This area's plentiful beaches and golf courses are big tourist draws, and many residents are employed in the hospitality industry.

MAJOR INDUSTRY

Defense, financial services, tourism, health care

MILITARY BASES

Naval Air Station Jacksonville, 9,549 military, 10,325 civilian (2004); Naval Station Mayport, 15,000 military, 2,000 civilian (2006)

CITIES

Jacksonville (pt.), 396,879; Jacksonville Beach, 20,990

NOTABLE

Fernandina Beach is the only part of the current United States to have existed under eight flags: France, Spain (twice), England, "Patriot," "Green Cross of Florida," Mexico, Confederate and United States.

Rep. Ginny Brown-Waite (R)

CAPITOL OFFICE
225-1002
brown-waite.house.gov
414 Cannon 20515-0905; fax 226-6559

COMMITTEES
Financial Services
Homeland Security
Veterans' Affairs

RESIDENCE
Brooksville

BORN
Oct. 5, 1943, Albany, N.Y.

RELIGION
Roman Catholic

FAMILY
Husband, Harvey Waite; three children

EDUCATION
State U. of New York, Albany, B.S. 1976; Russell Sage College, M.A. 1984 (public administration)

CAREER
Health care consultant; state legislative aide

POLITICAL HIGHLIGHTS
Hernando County Board of Commissioners, 1991-93; Fla. Senate, 1992-2002 (president pro tempore, 2001-02)

ELECTION RESULTS

2006 GENERAL		
Ginny Brown-Waite (R)	162,421	59.9%
John Russell (D)	108,959	40.1%
2006 PRIMARY		
Ginny Brown-Waite (R)		unopposed
2004 GENERAL		
Ginny Brown-Waite (R)	240,315	65.9%
Robert G. Whittel (D)	124,140	34.1%

PREVIOUS WINNING PERCENTAGES
2002 (48%)

Elected 2002; 3rd term

Brown-Waite is a loyal Republican most of the time, but her reputation has been defined by exceptions, just as it was earlier when she served in the Florida Legislature. She may appear to be a sweet, pint-size grandmother, but she is forceful, driven, straight-talking and not easily intimidated.

In defiance of the GOP leadership, she voted for five of six signature bills that the Democrats rushed to the floor in the early days of their majority in 2007. (She did not support their proposal to force drug companies to negotiate their prices with the Medicare program.)

Two years earlier, when House Republicans rushed to block the removal of a feeding tube from Terri Schiavo, a severely brain-damaged Florida woman, Brown-Waite took a public stand against her party. She marched into the House chamber and sat down next to Florida Democrat Debbie Wasserman-Schultz, a leading opponent of the GOP-sponsored bill. As Republicans glared, she spoke out against the measure, then cast one of just five Republican no votes. "The woman has a backbone of steel," Wasserman-Schultz told the Miami Herald.

A transplanted Yankee, Brown-Waite jumped into local politics in her adopted state of Florida at midlife and, in short order, rose from a seat on the county commission to a top post in the GOP-dominated statehouse. When the Florida nursing home industry tried to slip into one of her bills a provision relaxing standards for family notification when a patient is released, Brown-Waite denounced nursing home lobbyists as "slimy bastards," according to the Herald. And when the tobacco lobby looked to her in 1996 to help fight a lawsuit that Democratic Gov. Lawton Chiles had engineered against the industry, she instead stood up on the floor of the state Senate and said she refused to "play the tobacco game." Her vote helped turn the tide against Big Tobacco.

With a track record of getting bills passed in a big, populous state, Brown-Waite adapted quickly to legislating at the national level. But she has kept her focus on issues important to her constituents. Her district has one of the largest contingents of veterans in the nation, and she uses her seat on the Veterans' Affairs Committee to look after their needs.

The signature effort of her first term was a proposal to require that VA hospitals provide treatment to veterans within 30 days of their seeking care or allow them to be treated by a private facility. In the 109th Congress (2005-06), she helped push through a $100,000 increase in the death benefit paid to survivors of those killed in action. She also lobbied successfully for two new VA clinics in her district and major improvements at three others. She faithfully attends medal award ceremonies in her district.

With many retirement communities in the 5th District, Brown-Waite reacted warily to the changes to Social Security proposed by President Bush in 2005, opposing any cuts in benefits. She said Bush's plan for private accounts within Social Security left too many "unanswered questions."

She parted with the president again in 2006, when she was one of 51 Republicans voting to override his veto of legislation expanding federally funded embryonic stem cell research. She supported the legislation again early in 2007.

On most issues, however, Brown-Waite votes the party line. She supports some restrictions on abortion and a constitutional ban on same-sex marriage. She voted for Bush's 2003 tax cut, and in 2005 and 2006 backed renewal of the 2001 anti-terrorism law known as the Patriot Act. She supports gun owners' rights and carries a .38-caliber handgun.

At home, Brown-Waite's favorite getaway is cruising Florida's scenic coast in her red 1959 MG. But she says it is hard to find replacement parts for a vehicle that is almost 50 years old.

In the 109th Congress (2005-06), she was elected co-chairwoman, along with California Democrat Hilda L. Solis, of the Congressional Women's Caucus. Brown-Waite worked for the reauthorization of the Violence Against Women Act, among other efforts. Her interest in that topic is both deep and personal. She grew up in Albany, N.Y., the daughter of a file clerk who threw her abusive husband out of the house. "It has made me . . . a very strong, outspoken person who believes we need to provide the kind of funds so that abuse victims have a place to get away from the abuser," she says.

She married young, divorced and later married Harvey Waite, then a New York state trooper. For 17 years, she served as an aide in the New York state Senate. Even after her husband retired and the couple moved to Florida in 1985, she continued to commute to the job in New York, quitting only when her mother became ill and moved in with them in Florida.

Brown-Waite won election in 1990 to the Hernando County Board of Commissioners, a post she sought after getting involved in a dispute over the building of a hazardous waste incinerator. She went on to serve a decade in the state Senate, rising to GOP whip and chairing major committees. She pushed bills to give patients more access to information through physician profiles and to tighten controls on health maintenance organizations. Her record on health care was marred, however, by a 2000 Tampa Tribune story about a too-cozy relationship with a Tampa HMO that paid her an annual salary of nearly $24,000 to "interpret" legislation that she had had a hand in passing.

She developed a pro-consumer record for fighting water and sewer rate hikes. And she backed a bill requiring mothers to wait 48 hours after giving birth before signing consent for adoption, an issue of personal interest to her. Brown-Waite adopted her daughter when the girl was 10 and living in an abusive home. The birth mother initially resisted giving her up.

When she was barred by term limits from continuing in the state Senate, her GOP allies redrew the lines of Democratic Rep. Karen L. Thurman's district to favor a 2002 challenge by Brown-Waite. After an easy GOP primary win, Brown-Waite prevailed in November by a scant 2 percentage points. Two years later, Thurman declined a rematch, and Brown-Waite had only nominal Democratic opposition. In 2006, a year when Democrats made strong gains elsewhere, Brown-Waite was re-elected easily.

KEY VOTES

2006

- No Stop broadband companies from favoring select Internet traffic
- Yes Affirm U.S. commitment to war in Iraq and reject setting a withdrawal date for troops
- Yes Repeal requirement for bilingual ballots at the polls
- Yes Permit U.S. sale of civilian nuclear technology to India
- Yes Build a 700-mile fence on the U.S.-Mexico border to curb illegal crossings
- Yes Permit warrantless wiretaps of suspected terrorists

2005

- No Intervene in the life-support case of Terri Schiavo
- Yes Lift President Bush's restrictions on stem cell research funding
- No Prohibit FBI access to library and bookstore records
- Yes Approve free-trade pact with five Central American countries
- No Pass energy policy overhaul favored by President Bush emphasizing domestic oil and gas production
- Yes End mandatory preservation of habitat of endangered animal and plant species
- Yes Ban torture of prisoners in U.S. custody

CQ VOTE STUDIES

	PARTY UNITY		PRESIDENTIAL SUPPORT	
	Support	Oppose	Support	Oppose
2006	89%	11%	90%	10%
2005	91%	9%	83%	17%
2004	95%	5%	87%	13%
2003	95%	5%	96%	4%

INTEREST GROUPS

	AFL-CIO	ADA	CCUS	ACU
2006	29%	15%	87%	88%
2005	14%	10%	88%	87%
2004	14%	5%	100%	96%
2003	7%	10%	87%	83%

FLORIDA 5

Northern west coast — Pasco, Hernando counties

Located north of Tampa on Florida's west coast, the 5th includes Hernando, Citrus, Sumter and part of Pasco counties and portions of four other counties. The district takes in the southern half of Florida's Nature Coast along the Gulf of Mexico, and the district's eastern edge, in Lake County, extends to the greater Orlando area.

Tourism, integral to the 5th's economy, is centered on the Nature Coast. Gated communities and golf courses clustered on the coast are havens for retirees, while the area's beaches, snorkeling spots and historic towns attract visitors. The Nature Coast also is home to numerous preserves and parks, which boast panthers, bears and manatees.

Agriculture is a mainstay in the district's less developed areas. Levy County in the north depends on cattle, dairy and peanuts, while the southeast part of the 5th has a large citrus crop. Housing developers and retail businesses continue to buy up land in Pasco County, and industrial parks in Pasco and Hernando host small manufacturing companies.

Social Security, prescription drugs and veterans' affairs dominate politics in the 5th, where more than one-fourth of residents are 65 or older. While controlled growth remains important to district residents, the region is expanding rapidly with a steady influx of retirees and young professionals. Parts of Pasco and Lake counties serve as bedroom communities for Tampa and Orlando, respectively.

The 5th's electorate is largely conservative, especially on fiscal issues. Republicans slightly outnumber Democrats in voter registration — although many Democrats are conservative Southern Democrats — and 17 percent of voters are registered independents. George W. Bush took 58 percent of the 5th's 2004 presidential vote.

MAJOR INDUSTRY

Tourism, service, agriculture, health care, manufacturing

CITIES

Spring Hill (unincorporated), 69,078; Land O' Lakes (unincorp.), 20,971

NOTABLE

Weeki Wachee Springs water park, established in 1947, is known for its live, underwater performances by "mermaids."

Rep. Cliff Stearns (R)

CAPITOL OFFICE
225-5744
www.house.gov/stearns
2370 Rayburn 20515-0906; fax 225-3973

COMMITTEES
Energy & Commerce
Veterans' Affairs

RESIDENCE
Ocala

BORN
April 16, 1941, Washington, D.C.

RELIGION
Presbyterian

FAMILY
Wife, Joan Stearns; three children

EDUCATION
George Washington U., B.S. 1963 (electrical engineering)

MILITARY SERVICE
Air Force, 1963-67

CAREER
Hotel and restaurant executive; advertising account executive

POLITICAL HIGHLIGHTS
No previous office

ELECTION RESULTS

2006 GENERAL		
Cliff Stearns (R)	136,601	59.9%
David E. Bruderly (D)	91,528	40.1%
2006 PRIMARY		
Cliff Stearns (R)		unopposed
2004 GENERAL		
Cliff Stearns (R)	211,137	64.4%
David E. Bruderly (D)	116,680	35.6%

PREVIOUS WINNING PERCENTAGES
2002 (65%); 2000 (100%); 1998 (100%); 1996 (67%); 1994 (99%); 1992 (65%); 1990 (59%); 1988 (53%)

Elected 1988; 10th term

As a key player in the House on technology, Stearns has been at the center of efforts by Congress to keep a step ahead of Internet pirates in protecting the privacy of consumers and the security of their personal information. He is a committed social conservative who does not let ideology stand in the way of legislating when he zeroes in on an issue.

In the 110th Congress (2007-08), Stearns is the senior Republican on the Energy and Commerce subcommittee that deals with consumer protection, after chairing the panel for six years during the GOP majority. He has an inclusive, business-like style and he does his homework. He may propose, as he has with every new Congress, a measure requiring the Ten Commandments to be prominently displayed in the Capitol, but he also can distinguish between a bill going nowhere for lack of bipartisan support and legislation he can get enacted. Generally, he lets pragmatism rule the day.

Stearns is also fiscally conservative. On the few occasions on which he strays from the party line, it is often because he objects to the price tag. In 2003, he was one of only 18 House Republicans who voted to require that half of all reconstruction aid to Iraq be in the form of loans, rather than grants. He is the perennial sponsor of a bill to prevent members of Congress from receiving their automatic pay adjustments in any year following a fiscal year in which the government runs a deficit. It has about as much chance of passing as his Ten Commandments resolution, but it's another example of Stearns making his point.

He consistently earns plaudits from budget watchdog groups, such as the National Taxpayers Union, the Council of Citizens Against Government Waste and Americans for Tax Reform. The Florida Times-Union (Jacksonville) approvingly called him the "biggest tightwad" in the state's congressional delegation.

Stearns said he would work with liberal Democrat Bobby L. Rush of Illinois, who in the 110th Congress replaced him as chairman of the Subcommittee on Commerce, Trade and Consumer Protection, to pass legislation bolstering data security on the Internet and requiring software companies to get a computer user's permission before installing programs that can collect personal information. Stearns says the two can also come to terms on a bill regulating the use of steroids in sports.

Stearns was the chief sponsor of a controversial bill enacted in 2005 that shielded firearms manufacturers and dealers from liability lawsuits when their products are used in crimes. Stearns worked on the legislation for six years prior to its enactment.

His conservative stripes also showed through in the 108th Congress (2003-04) when he championed a provision in broadcast decency legislation to make it easier for the Federal Communications Commission to fine individual performers for indecent actions. In 2006, he was among a group of conservative Republicans who tried but failed to drop from the Voting Rights Act renewal requirements for bilingual assistance at the polls.

Although his primary focus has been on issues before his Commerce Subcommittee, Stearns has remained a member of the Veterans' Affairs Committee, where he was chairman of the Health Subcommittee from 1997 through 2000. In that period, he won passage of a bill to improve access to long-term care for disabled veterans and expanded the VA's obligation to provide alternatives to nursing home care.

The son of a U.S. Justice Department lawyer, Stearns was born and raised in Washington, D.C., where he was a basketball and track star at Woodrow Wilson High School. Stearns attended George Washington University on an Air Force ROTC scholarship. Despite growing up in the capital, Stearns says he didn't have much interest in politics. His first foray came while in engineering school, when he was the campaign manager for a student who was elected president of the university student council.

After graduation, the Air Force stationed Stearns at Vandenberg Air Force base in California. He served four years as a specialist in aerospace engineering and satellite reconnaissance.

When he got out of the service, Stearns worked in advertising before going into business for himself. He took over a dilapidated motel in Massachusetts and renovated it. In the 1970s, spotting what he viewed as an undervalued Howard Johnson motel for sale in northern Florida, Stearns moved to the Sunshine State. He built a small motel and restaurant management business in Ocala that ultimately employed 120 people.

Ronald Reagan's dominance of national politics in the early 1980s inspired Stearns to join the GOP and to get more involved in civic life. From Reagan, he took "the belief in the importance of freedom and the opportunity to choose, free markets and owning your own property."

He served on the board of the Monroe, Fla., regional hospital and was director of the local Chamber of Commerce. He also joined church and civic groups.

In 1988, Stearns ran for an open U.S. House seat and, through his local alliances and political savvy, was able to beat two better-connected candidates for the Republican nomination.

Though he was an underdog in the general election against Democratic state House Speaker Jon Mills, Stearns' limited political background gave him a salient, populist theme as what he called "a citizen congressman." Stearns went on to out-hustle an overconfident Mills for the seat, aided by George H. W. Bush's strong showing in the 6th District that year. In his last eight elections, he has never failed to capture at least 60 percent of the vote.

In his early years on Capitol Hill, Stearns was a forerunner of the tough-talking fiscal and social conservatives who came to Congress in droves in the 1990s. Back then, as a backbencher in the minority party, much of his effort was devoted to speaking out for conservative social causes and spearheading battles against abortion rights, pornography and funding for the National Endowment for the Arts. Although his views have not changed and he still votes to curb abortion rights, he lets others take the lead on those issues.

KEY VOTES

2006

- No Stop broadband companies from favoring select Internet traffic
- Yes Affirm U.S. commitment to war in Iraq and reject setting a withdrawal date for troops
- Yes Repeal requirement for bilingual ballots at the polls
- Yes Permit U.S. sale of civilian nuclear technology to India
- Yes Build a 700-mile fence on the U.S.-Mexico border to curb illegal crossings
- Yes Permit warrantless wiretaps of suspected terrorists

2005

- ? Intervene in the life-support case of Terri Schiavo
- No Lift President Bush's restrictions on stem cell research funding
- No Prohibit FBI access to library and bookstore records
- Yes Approve free-trade pact with five Central American countries
- Yes Pass energy policy overhaul favored by President Bush emphasizing domestic oil and gas production
- Yes End mandatory preservation of habitat of endangered animal and plant species
- No Ban torture of prisoners in U.S. custody

CQ VOTE STUDIES

	PARTY UNITY		PRESIDENTIAL SUPPORT	
	Support	Oppose	Support	Oppose
2006	93%	7%	85%	15%
2005	94%	6%	87%	13%
2004	96%	4%	85%	15%
2003	94%	6%	91%	9%
2002	96%	4%	82%	18%

INTEREST GROUPS

	AFL-CIO	ADA	CCUS	ACU
2006	21%	10%	93%	96%
2005	33%	10%	89%	88%
2004	20%	0%	100%	96%
2003	7%	5%	90%	92%
2002	22%	5%	82%	96%

FLORIDA 6

North central – parts of Jacksonville, Gainesville and Ocala

The landlocked and boomerang-shaped 6th takes in large swaths of rural territory along with suburbs of northern cities. Stretching from western Duval County (Jacksonville), the district takes in portions of Gainesville before swinging southeast into Marion County. The 6th's southern tip is in Leesburg, which is within Orlando's sphere in central Florida.

The 6th contains three regions with distinct interests. The northern end, centered in Jacksonville (shared with the 3rd and 4th districts), is heavily influenced by the military and the busy port. Gainesville, shared with the 3rd in the middle of the district, is home to the University of Florida and the Malcolm Randall VA Medical Center, a major veterans' hospital. The area south of Ocala, famed for its thoroughbred horse farms, is a haven for retirees and roughly an hour from either Florida coast.

The district includes all of two small counties — Gilchrist and Bradford — and parts of six others, including Alachua and Marion, each of which contains about one-fourth of the 6th's population. Alachua is the biggest Democratic outpost in the district, while Republicans have their strongest registration edge in the Clay County Jacksonville suburbs and exurbs west of the St. Johns River. The district's political agenda is dominated by defense interests.

The 6th is firmly conservative and although the GOP maintains a clear edge in most federal races, registered Republicans maintain only a slight advantage over Democrats. Regardless of party affiliation, voters are willing to support some moderate Democratic candidates. George W. Bush took 61 percent of the district's vote in the 2004 presidential election — 4 percentage points more than in 2000.

MAJOR INDUSTRY

Higher education, defense, health care, agriculture

CITIES

Jacksonville (pt.), 86,846; Gainesville (pt.), 59,907; Lakeside (unincorporated), 30,927; Ocala (pt.), 29,559

NOTABLE

The Florida Museum of Natural History is located on the campus of the University of Florida in Gainesville.

Rep. John L. Mica (R)

CAPITOL OFFICE
225-4035
www.house.gov/mica
2313 Rayburn 20515-0907; fax 226-0821

COMMITTEES
Oversight & Government Reform
Transportation & Infrastructure - ranking member

RESIDENCE
Winter Park

BORN
Jan. 27, 1943, Binghamton, N.Y.

RELIGION
Episcopalian

FAMILY
Wife, Pat Mica; two children

EDUCATION
Miami-Dade Community College, A.A. 1965; U. of Florida, B.A. 1967 (political science & education)

CAREER
Cellular telephone company executive; lobbyist; trade consultant; real estate investor; congressional aide

POLITICAL HIGHLIGHTS
Fla. House, 1976-80; Republican nominee for Fla. Senate, 1980

ELECTION RESULTS

2006 GENERAL		
John L. Mica (R)	149,656	63.1%
John F. Chagnon (D)	87,584	36.9%
2006 PRIMARY		
John L. Mica (R)		unopposed
2004 GENERAL		
John L. Mica (R)		unopposed

PREVIOUS WINNING PERCENTAGES
2002 (60%); 2000 (63%); 1998 (100%); 1996 (62%); 1994 (73%); 1992 (56%)

Elected 1992; 8th term

Mica says he has no particular hobbies or recreational interests. He doesn't like sports — not even golf, a huge industry in his home state. "I'm a pretty dull guy," he says. "I don't have a lot of hobby activities. But I love politics."

Given that, it comes as no surprise that even in the minority, the Florida Republican is still a force to be reckoned with on Capitol Hill and back home. Mica (MY-cah) is the top-ranking Republican on the Transportation and Infrastructure Committee in the 110th Congress (2007-08), and a senior member of the Oversight and Government Reform panel. He is also a formidable GOP fundraiser. During the 2006 election cycle, when he was hoping to gain the Transportation Committee chairmanship, he distributed nearly $1 million through his leadership political action committee and traveled to about 50 districts to stump for fellow Republicans.

Mica is a House leader on aviation issues; he chaired the Transportation Aviation Subcommittee from 2001 through 2006. Following the Sept. 11 terrorist attacks he took what had been a legislative backwater and made it a hub of new laws and security measures that have changed the way Americans travel. He championed the effort to arm airline pilots, and he would like to see cargo pilots armed as well. He helped write the law establishing the Transportation Security Administration (TSA) under the Homeland Security Department. But Mica has criticized the agency repeatedly for being unresponsive to local concerns and slow to utilize high technology. He delights in calling the TSA a "Soviet-style bureaucracy."

In the 108th Congress (2003-04), Mica's panel contributed to a major intelligence overhaul, adding provisions speeding federal approval of devices on airplanes to foil shoulder-fired missiles and mandating a new system of identifying travelers through biometric means, such as retinal scans.

The Transportation Committee prides itself on its bipartisanship and Mica has maintained friendly relationships with panel Democrats. But his views drastically diverge from theirs on issues involving organized labor and federal spending. In 2006, his final year as panel chairman, Mica helped quash a bill that would have forced the Federal Aviation Administration (FAA) back to the bargaining table with its air traffic controllers.

In the 110th Congress, with unions pushing for redress of a long list of grievances from a dozen years of GOP control, Mica swiftly locked horns with Democrats. As the House considered a homeland security bill extending collective bargaining rights and whistleblower protections to TSA screeners in February 2007, Mica announced he had lined up enough votes to sustain a threatened presidential veto. The next month, he warned that Republicans also could sustain a threatened veto of a clean water bill that sought to apply the Davis-Bacon prevailing wage law to construction of federally funded wastewater treatment plants. Few doubted that the pattern would continue throughout the two-year Congress.

Mica also regularly clashes with Democrats over the fate of Amtrak, the nation's financially troubled passenger rail system. He has proposed splitting off the profitable Northeast Corridor and Virginia-to-Florida Auto Train routes for management by an interstate compact of states or a private company. The other, money-losing routes across the country would continue to be subsidized by the government. President Bush has long sought to privatize Amtrak, but the Democrats' 2006 takeover of Congress put Mica's proposal and the president's plan on ice.

The Transportation Committee's top priority for the 110th Congress is reauthorizing the FAA, and changing the way it is funded in order to finance an upgrade of the air traffic control system. In early 2007, Mica indicated he was open to a Bush administration plan that sought to shift the FAA's funding base from commercial airline ticket fees to all aircraft that use the system, including corporate jets and other private planes. Democrats roundly panned the proposal.

Mica has described his political style as a combination of the pushiness of former Republican House Speaker Newt Gingrich and the "political wisdom" of Robert H. Michel of Illinois, an even-tempered pragmatist who was the House GOP leader from 1981 to 1995, when Republicans were last in the minority. These days, he says, it is Michel's approach that remains the more dominant influence. "I've tempered a bit," he says.

Though Mica calls Florida home now, he grew up in upstate New York. He ended up in the Sunshine State when his parents decided to head south for warmer weather better suited for their health. "My parents used to keep a trailer in Florida in the Miami area," Mica says, noting that "in those days you didn't have a condo, but people would buy a trailer." After years of trips back and forth, the family settled in Florida when Mica was high school age. His father's health was poor, and Mica and his brothers interrupted their schooling to work and help support the family.

Ironically, Mica's other family members are largely Democrats, including his brother Daniel A. Mica, who served in the House from 1979 to 1989. His other brother worked for Lawton Chiles, a former Democratic U.S. senator and Florida governor. "Those are the crosses I have to bear," he said wryly. "But we pretty much agree on stuff."

His family's Democratic tilt didn't sway Mica. The first campaign he worked in was Republican Richard Nixon's 1960 presidential race against John F. Kennedy. A photograph of him with Nixon is one of the few political pictures hanging in his Capitol Hill office.

Mica served in the state legislature from 1976 to 1980. He then came to Washington as chief of staff for U.S. Sen. Paula Hawkins, a Republican who served one term. After she lost her re-election bid to Democrat Bob Graham in 1986, Mica turned to business ventures, including international trade consulting and the cellular telephone business, and became a millionaire.

Redistricting and a retirement gave him an opening to run for Congress in 1992. GOP Rep. Craig T. James decided not to seek a third House term, and the new Florida map gave the 7th District a clear Republican tilt. Mica won by 13 percentage points, and he has been re-elected with ease since. He was unopposed in 2004 and prevailed by 26 percentage points in 2006.

KEY VOTES

2006

No Stop broadband companies from favoring select Internet traffic
Yes Affirm U.S. commitment to war in Iraq and reject setting a withdrawal date for troops
Yes Repeal requirement for bilingual ballots at the polls
Yes Permit U.S. sale of civilian nuclear technology to India
Yes Build a 700-mile fence on the U.S.-Mexico border to curb illegal crossings
Yes Permit warrantless wiretaps of suspected terrorists

2005

? Intervene in the life-support case of Terri Schiavo
No Lift President Bush's restrictions on stem cell research funding
No Prohibit FBI access to library and bookstore records
Yes Approve free-trade pact with five Central American countries
Yes Pass energy policy overhaul favored by President Bush emphasizing domestic oil and gas production
Yes End mandatory preservation of habitat of endangered animal and plant species
No Ban torture of prisoners in U.S. custody

CQ VOTE STUDIES

	PARTY UNITY		PRESIDENTIAL SUPPORT	
	Support	Oppose	Support	Oppose
2006	99%	1%	95%	5%
2005	97%	3%	91%	9%
2004	95%	5%	85%	15%
2003	98%	2%	98%	2%
2002	96%	4%	90%	10%

INTEREST GROUPS

	AFL-CIO	ADA	CCUS	ACU
2006	14%	0%	100%	92%
2005	7%	0%	92%	100%
2004	13%	0%	100%	84%
2003	7%	10%	97%	88%
2002	0%	0%	95%	96%

FLORIDA 7
East – St. Johns County, Daytona Beach

The 7th parallels Interstate 95 from southeast of Jacksonville to northern Daytona Beach, where it turns to follow Interstate 4 southwest into the Orlando area. It includes all of fast-growing Flagler and St. Johns counties, as well as much of Volusia County, parts of Putnam and Seminole counties and a tiny sliver of Orange County. Two-fifths of the district's population lives in Volusia, mostly on the strip of coast stretching from Ormond Beach to Daytona Beach.

Once a major agricultural area, Seminole County now serves as the suburban home to middle- and upper-class Orlando commuters and their families. But some inland portions of the district maintain some agrarian heritage, especially in bucolic Flagler County. The Daytona Beach area attracts more than eight million visitors annually, and although its popularity as a spring break destination for college students has decreased, it continues to draw bikers and race car fans to its beaches and sporting events, including the Daytona 500 stock car race, which is held in the nearby 24th District.

A steady influx of people into the 7th has translated into a sustained economic boom, but also has pushed growth-management issues to the top of the local agenda. Retirees have flocked to once-small towns near the ocean, drawing retail shops but not as many larger employers. The tourism-based economy is broadened by a growing aerospace industry near Daytona Beach, helped by Embry-Riddle Aeronautical University.

Republicans hold a party-registration edge and have won the 7th's presidential vote since 1992, with George W. Bush taking 57 percent of the vote here in 2004. Some moderate Democratic candidates also have success with the 7th's voters.

MAJOR INDUSTRY
Tourism, aerospace, service

CITIES
Daytona Beach (pt.), 53,629; Deltona, 47,033; Ormond Beach, 36,301; Palm Coast, 32,732; Wekiwa Springs (unincorporated), 23,169

NOTABLE
St. Augustine is the oldest continuously inhabited city in the United States; Jackie Robinson Stadium is a minor league park in Daytona Beach, where Robinson was the first black baseball player to play in a spring training game.

Rep. Ric Keller (R)

CAPITOL OFFICE
225-2176
www.house.gov/keller
419 Cannon 20515-0908; fax 225-0999

COMMITTEES
Education & Labor
Judiciary

RESIDENCE
Orlando

BORN
Sept. 5, 1964, Johnson City, Tenn.

RELIGION
Methodist

FAMILY
Wife, Dee Dee Keller; three children

EDUCATION
East Tennessee State U., B.S. 1986 (speech communications); Vanderbilt U., J.D. 1992

CAREER
Lawyer

POLITICAL HIGHLIGHTS
No previous office

ELECTION RESULTS

2006 GENERAL		
Ric Keller (R)	95,258	52.8%
Charlie Stuart (D)	82,526	45.7%
Wes Hoaglund (X)	2,640	1.5%
2006 PRIMARY		
Ric Keller (R)	30,707	72.5%
Elizabeth Doran (R)	11,661	27.5%
2004 GENERAL		
Ric Keller (R)	172,232	60.5%
Stephen Murray (D)	112,343	39.5%

PREVIOUS WINNING PERCENTAGES
2002 (65%); 2000 (51%)

Elected 2000; 4th term

Unlike many of his conservative colleagues, Keller is willing to join forces with Democrats to advance legislation he supports. Indeed, he already sees significant opportunities for cooperation in two areas in the 110th Congress (2007-08) — education and law enforcement.

Keller, the top-ranking Republican on the Education and Labor subcommittee that handles higher education, is one of the leading champions of Pell grants, federal grants for low-income college students. He was raised, along with two siblings, by a single mother on a secretary's salary, and he says Pell grants helped pay for his college education. As soon as he got to the House in 2001, Keller introduced a bill to increase the size of Pell grants.

He then organized a Pell Grant Caucus, and as its chairman, pushed successfully to raise the maximum grant from $3,750 to $4,050 a year. In the 109th Congress (2005-06), he sponsored a bill to increase the maximum to $6,000. Although it failed to win enactment, he is optimistic that he can achieve that goal in the Democratically controlled 110th Congress.

Keller did succeed in pushing through legislation in the 109th Congress that relieves Pell grant recipients of certain repayment obligations when their college educations are disrupted by natural disasters such as 2005's Hurricane Katrina. He says his interest in the issue was sparked in 2004, when four hurricanes disrupted community colleges in his district.

From his seat on the Education Committee, Keller takes pride in pressing measures he says will enhance the dignity and well-being of disadvantaged students. One such bill requires school systems to implement a school lunch payment system that protects the privacy of students getting free or reduced-price lunches. He also worked to authorize federal grants to local mentoring programs. That legislation, which became law as part of the 2001 No Child Left Behind education overhaul, grew out of Keller's precongressional experience as a volunteer with Orlando-area mentoring and social support organizations for troubled young people.

Keller is hoping to make several changes to the No Child Left Behind Act when the Education panel tackles a rewrite in 2007. But he does not favor President Bush's proposal to extend the law's testing requirements to 11th and 12th graders. "I'm frankly tested out at this point," he says.

A member of the Judiciary Committee, Keller is eager to work with Democrats to reauthorize and boost funding for the COPS program, a local policing initiative launched by President Bill Clinton that the Bush administration has repeatedly tried to scale back. He calls it "one of the single most successful law enforcement programs" in history.

But Keller is a realist about other issues he has pushed in the Judiciary Committee. "What I'm not going to do is spend a lot of time on bills we know won't pass anymore, such as various tort reform bills," he said after the 2006 elections. That includes his pet project, the "cheeseburger bill" for which he is best known outside his Florida district. The bill — which passed in the House in 2004 and 2005 but died in the Senate — would shield food manufacturers and restaurants from lawsuits by overweight customers seeking to blame them for their obesity.

Keller himself has struggled with his weight, fighting an often losing battle of the bulge. "I'm still too chubby," he admitted in late 2006. But he insists it is his responsibility — and not a restaurant's — to control his caloric intake. He said losing weight was a 2007 New Year's resolution, and he's started exercising and "eating right."

Like many of his conservative colleagues, Keller initially believed in term limits and pledged to serve no more than eight years in the House. But less than two weeks after the 2006 elections, he announced a change of heart. "As a rookie candidate, I underestimated the value of experience and seniority," he said, explaining his decision to run again in 2008.

Back home in his district, two of the largest businesses are The Walt Disney Co. and NBC Universal Inc., and Keller is strategically placed to protect their interests as a member of the Judiciary Subcommittee on Courts, the Internet and Intellectual Property. He has pressed the Justice Department to make cracking down on copyright violations a higher priority.

As a private lawyer in Orlando, Keller helped write two state constitutional amendments to finance the cleanup of Everglades National Park. One, dubbed "Polluter Pays" and passed in 1996, held that sugar companies should contribute to Everglades restoration. In Congress, Keller was among the minority of Florida lawmakers who voted to reduce the sugar subsidy for the industry, a political power in the state.

In 2006, when the Bush administration announced plans to sell off 300,000 acres of national forest land across the country, including 973 acres of Ocala National Forest in Florida's 8th District, Keller took the lead in fighting the plan and succeeded in killing it through an amendment on an appropriations bill.

Keller had just made partner at his Orlando law firm when he jumped into the 8th District House race to replace 10-term Republican Bill McCollum, who waged an unsuccessful bid for the Senate in 2000. It was his initial foray into politics, and at first he was not taken seriously by the political pros. He got their attention when he finished second in a three-way GOP primary and then won an October runoff against veteran state Rep. Bill Sublette.

Democrats made a strong bid to capture the normally Republican 8th District seat by running a well-known local figure, former Orange County Commission Chairwoman Linda Chapin. But Chapin saw her comfortable lead in the polls shrink as Keller gathered steam with the help of conservative groups including the Club for Growth, an anti-tax organization that put over $400,000 into the campaign.

Keller won by fewer than 4,000 votes. He immediately set to work raising money to shore himself up for re-election, and his next two races were much easier. In 2006, a Democratic year, he stressed his splits with the Bush administration, especially on the Ocala National Forest issue, and won by 7 percentage points over Charlie Stuart, a member of a prominent Orlando family.

KEY VOTES

2006

- No Stop broadband companies from favoring select Internet traffic
- Yes Affirm U.S. commitment to war in Iraq and reject setting a withdrawal date for troops
- Yes Repeal requirement for bilingual ballots at the polls
- Yes Permit U.S. sale of civilian nuclear technology to India
- \+ Build a 700-mile fence on the U.S.-Mexico border to curb illegal crossings
- Yes Permit warrantless wiretaps of suspected terrorists

2005

- ? Intervene in the life-support case of Terri Schiavo
- No Lift President Bush's restrictions on stem cell research funding
- No Prohibit FBI access to library and bookstore records
- Yes Approve free-trade pact with five Central American countries
- No Pass energy policy overhaul favored by President Bush emphasizing domestic oil and gas production
- Yes End mandatory preservation of habitat of endangered animal and plant species
- Yes Ban torture of prisoners in U.S. custody

CQ VOTE STUDIES

	PARTY UNITY		PRESIDENTIAL SUPPORT	
	Support	Oppose	Support	Oppose
2006	94%	6%	95%	5%
2005	96%	4%	84%	16%
2004	98%	2%	91%	9%
2003	99%	1%	96%	4%
2002	99%	1%	87%	13%

INTEREST GROUPS

	AFL-CIO	ADA	CCUS	ACU
2006	15%	0%	100%	88%
2005	13%	5%	88%	96%
2004	0%	0%	100%	100%
2003	0%	5%	96%	86%
2002	11%	0%	100%	100%

FLORIDA 8

Central – most of Orlando

One of Florida's few landlocked districts, the 8th is thriving nonetheless, powered by the presence of Walt Disney World, Sea World and Universal Studios' resort in the Orlando area. The district surrounds western Orlando and includes upscale parts of the region, a large chunk of the city — including much of the downtown area — and the Walt Disney World complex. It then pushes north to take in parts of Lake and Marion counties, giving it a rural element.

The Orlando economy is booming and boasts a very low unemployment rate. While tourism is still the 8th's undisputed leader — the Orlando area is the world's top vacation destination and receives around 50 million visitors each year — the district's economy is diverse and increasingly relies on a growing technology sector headed by Oracle and defense and aerospace contractor Lockheed Martin. The research park of the University of Central Florida's Institute for Simulation and Training is an economic engine for the area. While the economic growth and redevelopment of downtown Orlando has brought new office parks and upscale condominiums to the city, housing prices have skyrocketed and affordable housing for workers in the tourism industry is scarce.

Residents of Orlando's suburbs — from middle-class areas near the city to well-heeled Winter Park and Windermere — support conservative Republicans on social and economic issues. The population here is younger, wealthier and more educated than in most Florida districts. Republicans mostly prevail in Orange County elections, but the county's surging Hispanic population has put Orange within political reach of Democratic statewide candidates. Many Orlando-area Hispanics are of Puerto Rican heritage and vote Democratic. Al Gore in 2000 was the first Democratic presidential nominee to carry Orange County since Franklin D. Roosevelt in 1944, and John Kerry captured the county in 2004.

MAJOR INDUSTRY

Tourism, technology, aerospace

CITIES

Orlando (pt.), 123,842; Ocoee (pt.), 23,591; Ocala (pt.), 16,384; Eustis, 15,106

NOTABLE

Dozens of celebrities — including golf's Tiger Woods and basketball's Shaquille O'Neal — have homes at Isleworth in Windermere; There are more than 100 lakes in the Orlando metropolitan area.

Rep. Gus Bilirakis (R)

CAPITOL OFFICE
225-5755
bilirakis.house.gov
1630 Longworth 20515-0909; fax 225-4085

COMMITTEES
Foreign Affairs
Homeland Security
Veterans' Affairs

RESIDENCE
Palm Harbor

BORN
Feb. 8, 1963, Gainesville, Fla.

RELIGION
Greek Orthodox

FAMILY
Wife, Eva Bilirakis; four children

EDUCATION
St. Petersburg Junior College, attended 1981-83; U. of Florida, B.A. 1986 (political science); Stetson U., J.D. 1989

CAREER
Lawyer; college instructor

POLITICAL HIGHLIGHTS
Fla. House, 1998-2006

ELECTION RESULTS

2006 GENERAL		
Gus Bilirakis (R)	123,016	55.9%
Phyllis Busansky (D)	96,978	44.1%
2006 PRIMARY		
Gus Bilirakis (R)	40,603	82.0%
David Langheier (R)	8,915	18.0%

Elected 2006; 1st term

Bilirakis stepped into the House seat vacated by his father, Michael Bilirakis, who represented the Tampa-area district for 24 years. The Bilirakis roots run deep in the district; the family settled there after leaving Greece a century ago. Gus Bilirakis' first taste of politics came at age 7, when he volunteered in a gubernatorial campaign.

Assigned to the Veterans' Affairs Committee for the 110th Congress (2007-08), Bilirakis (bil-uh-RACK-iss) wasted no time in pressing for bills to aid veterans. In early 2007, he introduced legislation to boost veterans' benefits, as well as a pair of measures to provide tax incentives for businesses that hire reservists or National Guard members. "I understand that for many small businesses the burden of hiring someone that may be out for extended periods can be tough and strain resources, but I believe this 10 percent credit, up to $2,000 per reservist or National Guardsman per year, helps offset the added costs and burdens," Bilirakis said when he offered the legislation.

A lawyer who specialized in estate planning, Bilirakis has a particular interest in health care and other issues important to seniors, who make up almost a quarter of the district's population. Other priorities include issues he advocated in the Florida Legislature, most notably making catastrophic homeowners' insurance and health insurance for low-income people more widely available.

Elected to the Florida House in 1998, he served there eight years, where he chaired committees on crime prevention and public safety. In Congress, he has a seat on the Homeland Security Committee.

His opportunity to move to the U.S. House came in 2006 with his father's retirement. The younger Bilirakis inherited valuable name recognition and a strong political legacy from a veteran lawmaker who rarely faced a serious Democratic challenge and ran unopposed four times. Gus Bilirakis breezed past his primary opponent, then went on to defeat Democrat Phyllis Busansky, a former Hillsborough County commissioner, winning by 12 percentage points.

FLORIDA 9

North Tampa suburbs

Suburban and rural areas north of Tampa form the bulk of the 9th, which encompasses coastal areas of Pinellas and Pasco counties as well as a large chunk of mostly suburban Hillsborough County.

The 9th is mostly residential. With a large number of retirees from the North, one-fifth of the population is 65 or older. Clearwater (shared with the 10th) is known as a beach resort and is the "spiritual headquarters" of the Church of Scientology, which has a large community here. Palm Harbor and Tarpon Springs have Greek Orthodox populations.

The 9th's economy is driven by tourism, fueled by "snowbirds" who spend winters here and visitors to its beaches. Many year-round residents commute to Tampa or St. Petersburg. Service-oriented industries add to the mix, but the prevalence of shopping centers and strip malls has created growth issues along the coast. The 9th's economy has grown along with its residents, although the northeast portions lag behind the Clearwater area. Plant City is the exception, as families move in from out of state.

The 9th long has been home for mostly GOP retirees, and Republicans retain an edge here due to their dominance in Hillsborough. Many of the county's most heavily GOP precincts are in the 9th, in towns like Valrico east of Interstate 75 and in the upscale Westchase area in western Hillsborough. The 9th's part of Pinellas also is decidedly Republican, while the two parties are even in registration in its share of Pasco County.

MAJOR INDUSTRY
Tourism, service, health care, technology

CITIES
Clearwater (pt.), 79,189; Palm Harbor (unincorporated) (pt.), 30,806

NOTABLE
Tarpon Springs is known as the "Sponge Capital of the World" for its natural sponges.

Rep. C.W. Bill Young (R)

CAPITOL OFFICE
225-5961
bill.young@mail.house.gov
www.house.gov/young
2407 Rayburn 20515-0910; fax 225-9764

COMMITTEES
Appropriations

RESIDENCE
Indian Shores

BORN
Dec. 16, 1930, Harmarville, Pa.

RELIGION
Methodist

FAMILY
Wife, Beverly Young; three children

EDUCATION
St. Petersburg H.S., graduated 1948

MILITARY SERVICE
Fla. National Guard, 1948-57

CAREER
Insurance executive; public official

POLITICAL HIGHLIGHTS
Fla. Senate, 1960-70 (minority leader, 1966-70)

ELECTION RESULTS

2006 GENERAL		
C.W. Bill Young (R)	131,488	65.9%
Samm Simpson (D)	67,950	34.1%
2006 PRIMARY		
C.W. Bill Young (R)		unopposed
2004 GENERAL		
C.W. Bill Young (R)	207,175	69.3%
Robert D. "Bob" Derry (D)	91,658	30.7%

PREVIOUS WINNING PERCENTAGES
2002 (100%); 2000 (76%); 1998 (100%); 1996 (67%); 1994 (100%); 1992 (57%); 1990 (100%); 1988 (73%); 1986 (100%); 1984 (80%); 1982 (100%); 1980 (100%); 1978 (79%); 1976 (65%); 1974 (76%); 1972 (76%); 1970 (67%)

Elected 1970; 19th term

Although he is the chamber's longest-serving Republican, Young no longer finds the House a comfortable home. He is weary of the unrelenting partisanship, ethics scandals and the political money chase. But he says he feels duty bound to remain as long as there are U.S. troops in Iraq. "As long as this war is raging, I feel a responsibility to make sure the troops have whatever it is they need to carry out their mission and protect themselves while they're doing it," he said in 2006.

As chairman of the Defense Appropriations Subcommittee in 2005 and 2006 — and of the full Appropriations Committee for six years before that — Young directed nearly $400 billion to the military for the war in Iraq and Afghanistan in a series of supplemental spending bills. He provided billions more defense dollars through regular appropriations bills. As the panel's ranking member in the 110th Congress (2007-08), he battled Democrats' desires to put conditions on such funding.

The war is personal for Young. He and his wife Beverly visit wounded soldiers at National Naval Medical Center in Maryland two or three times a week. Despite the sad human toll he witnesses, Young says he would again vote to go to war in Iraq. "But I probably would have been more outspoken about going there with overwhelming force, as opposed to just-barely-enough force," he says. Nevertheless, during 2007 debate on another supplemental, he opposed Democrats' desire to condition deployments on troop readiness. "I don't think Congress can micromanage any battle," he said.

He found himself on the defensive when concerns arose about mismanagement and soldiers' poor living conditions at Walter Reed Army Medical Center. Young said he knew of the problems as early as 2003, but said he preferred to privately confront the hospital commander rather than wield his clout as an Appropriations subcommittee chairman.

The Youngs' devotion to the troops also drew attention in early 2006, when Beverly Young was ejected from the House spectators' gallery during President Bush's State of the Union address for wearing a T-shirt with the words, "Support the Troops: Defending Our Freedom." Young chastised the Capitol police from the House floor the next day, saying they had insulted him and his wife. The police apologized.

Young is a consummate team player. But when he was full committee chairman, he resisted the leadership's unwritten decree for chairmen to raise large amounts of political cash for the party. And later he dug in his heels when GOP conservatives pushed a lobbying and ethics bill requiring public disclosure of the names of lawmakers who quietly pack spending bills with earmarks — funds for projects requested by an individual member. Feeling their turf threatened, appropriators led by Young refused to back the bill until GOP leaders promised it would apply to tax bills and authorizing legislation as well.

Young steers a moderate course on various issues, breaking with the party's dominant conservatives to support a minimum wage increase, a ban on semiautomatic assault-style weapons, and protection of Florida's beaches from erosion and offshore oil and gas drilling. And he uses his power as an appropriator to help Florida in other ways. Following a devastating quartet of hurricanes, he delivered more than $13 billion in federal aid, mostly for his state. With the 2004 presidential election approaching, Young persuaded the White House to increase its relief request to Congress by almost $2 billion, warning of potentially unhappy Floridians in the voting booths.

Young's normally non-confrontational style personifies the go-along, get-along culture of Appropriations. But it is also a product of a legislative attitude forged during 24 years in the House minority before the GOP takeover in 1995. He learned then that working with Democrats was a prerequisite for getting legislation passed.

When Republicans took the majority, Speaker Newt Gingrich skipped over Young and two other senior members he considered too willing to hike spending. Young settled for chairing the Defense Subcommittee. When he finally got the full panel's gavel in 1999, he allowed conservatives to dominate the early stages of budget negotiations until legislative reality — the need to gain Democratic President Bill Clinton's signature — set in. Clinton refused to sign bills he said cut spending too far, so Young and the GOP met his demands rather than risk a politically unacceptable government shutdown.

He has been untouched by the spate of congressional ethics scandals in recent years, but the careers of some old friends have been damaged or destroyed. Former California Rep. Randy "Duke" Cunningham's admission that he took bribes "really hit me hard," Young told the St. Petersburg Times, which also reported that Young turned down a $300,000 job to stay in Congress. The Youngs for years have lived in a modest home 30 miles from the Capitol. Beverly Young once said they can't afford to live closer because her husband "doesn't take bribes like all the others." Young, in an interview, said playfully that his wife "has a big mouth."

Close to Young's heart is his work funding bone marrow transplant research and a federally sponsored bone marrow donor registry. Young became interested in the issue in the 1980s after he met a 10-year-old constituent at risk of dying for lack of a bone marrow donor. After adopting the cause, Young learned in 1990 that his eldest daughter had a leukemia treatable only by a bone marrow transplant that ultimately saved her life.

Young was born into hardscrabble poverty in Pennsylvania's coal country during the Depression. His father, an alcoholic, abandoned the family when Young was a boy, and after his mother became ill, the family stayed with relatives in St. Petersburg. Young never went to college, but worked his way to success in the insurance business. He got into politics in 1960, when he was elected as the sole Republican in the Florida Senate. By 1967, there were 20 others, and Young was minority leader.

In 1970, he inherited Florida's most dependable Republican House seat from William C. Cramer, who ran for the Senate. The 10th District has tilted Democratic, but more often than not, Young has been re-elected with ease. Since 1982, Democrats have fielded a candidate only about half the time.

KEY VOTES

2006

No Stop broadband companies from favoring select Internet traffic
Yes Affirm U.S. commitment to war in Iraq and reject setting a withdrawal date for troops
Yes Repeal requirement for bilingual ballots at the polls
Yes Permit U.S. sale of civilian nuclear technology to India
Yes Build a 700-mile fence on the U.S.-Mexico border to curb illegal crossings
Yes Permit warrantless wiretaps of suspected terrorists

2005

? Intervene in the life-support case of Terri Schiavo
Yes Lift President Bush's restrictions on stem cell research funding
No Prohibit FBI access to library and bookstore records
Yes Approve free-trade pact with five Central American countries
No Pass energy policy overhaul favored by President Bush emphasizing domestic oil and gas production
Yes End mandatory preservation of habitat of endangered animal and plant species
No Ban torture of prisoners in U.S. custody

CQ VOTE STUDIES

	PARTY UNITY		PRESIDENTIAL SUPPORT	
	Support	Oppose	Support	Oppose
2006	90%	10%	87%	13%
2005	92%	8%	82%	18%
2004	91%	9%	87%	13%
2003	95%	5%	94%	6%
2002	94%	6%	88%	12%

INTEREST GROUPS

	AFL-CIO	ADA	CCUS	ACU
2006	43%	10%	87%	84%
2005	15%	5%	92%	87%
2004	20%	10%	95%	87%
2003	7%	10%	93%	87%
2002	13%	0%	85%	96%

FLORIDA 10

West – most of Pinellas County, St. Petersburg

The 10th takes in about 70 percent of Pinellas County's residents, including most of St. Petersburg and its upscale beachfront communities. From the southern portion of Pinellas, it excludes most of Clearwater (shared with the 9th) in the central part of the county and captures Dunedin and half of Palm Harbor at its northern tip.

Nearly one-fourth of the district's residents are 65 or older, and many retirees reside in Largo and the Gulf Coast towns. Younger residents tend to live in Pinellas Park and St. Petersburg to be closer to major employers and Tampa. Because Pinellas County is the most densely populated county in the state, the 10th did not see its population boom in the 1990s like many other areas in Florida.

The tourism industry, an economic mainstay for the district, takes in about $2 billion per year from area hotels and attractions such as The Pier and Sunken Gardens. A growing technology sector centered around the computer and defense industries, and a strong financial services sector, have diversified the 10th's economy and brought more white-collar jobs to the area. The district also includes two airports.

Downtown St. Petersburg has experienced a cultural revival — the Mahaffey Theater has been renovated, and residents flock to the area's museums and orchestra and theater performances. A new art facility is planned that will house a Dale Chihuly gallery along with condominium and retail space. District residents also take pride in the preservation of the area's white sand beaches and wildlife areas.

Republicans hold a slight advantage over Democrats in the 10th and the majority of locally elected officials are Republican. However, 20 percent of district voters are registered as independent, and the 10th's loyalties often flip between parties in presidential elections. George W. Bush edged out John Kerry with 51 percent of the vote here in 2004.

MAJOR INDUSTRY
Tourism, health care, retail, technology

CITIES
St. Petersburg (pt.), 179,087; Largo, 69,371; Pinellas Park, 45,658

NOTABLE
The Salvador Dalí Museum in St. Petersburg houses the world's largest collection of art by the Spanish surrealist.

Rep. Kathy Castor (D)

CAPITOL OFFICE
225-3376
castor.house.gov
317 Cannon 20515-0911; fax 225-5652

COMMITTEES
Armed Services
Rules

RESIDENCE
Tampa

BORN
Aug. 20, 1966, Miami, Fla.

RELIGION
Presbyterian

FAMILY
Husband, Bill Lewis; two children

EDUCATION
Emory U., B.A. 1988 (political science);
Florida State U., J.D. 1991

CAREER
Lawyer

POLITICAL HIGHLIGHTS
Democratic nominee for Fla. Senate, 2000; Hillsborough County Board of Commissioners, 2002-06

ELECTION RESULTS

2006 GENERAL		
Kathy Castor (D)	97,470	69.7%
Eddie Adams Jr. (R)	42,454	30.3%
2006 PRIMARY		
Kathy Castor (D)	21,310	54.0%
Leslie Miller (D)	13,474	34.1%
Scott Farrell (D)	1,721	4.4%
Al Fox (D)	1,653	4.2%
Michael Steinberg (D)	1,336	3.4%

Elected 2006; 1st term

Her family political fortunes brightened sharply with Castor's 2006 election to the House. Two years earlier, her mother, Democrat Betty Castor, lost a Senate bid to Florida Republican Mel Martinez by just 1 percentage point.

The congresswoman attributes some of her success to her family name: Castor's mother was a local officeholder, state education commissioner and president of the University of South Florida before running for Senate. Her father was a county judge. But Castor built a solid reputation of her own during four years as a Hillsborough County Commissioner. "I loved public policy from a very early age, and my parents taught me to stand up for folks that do not have a voice," she says.

Castor will get a broad overview of public policy as a member of the Rules Committee, an arm of the leadership that sets guidelines for floor consideration of all major bills in the House. She welcomed the assignment for exactly that opportunity. She also serves on the Armed Services Committee, where she looks out for MacDill Air Force Base, headquarters for the U.S. Central Command and U.S. Special Operations Command. And House Speaker Nancy Pelosi made Castor the freshman class representative on the Democratic Steering and Policy Committee, which makes committee assignments. Castor asked for that plum even before she was elected, according to the Tampa Tribune. Pelosi told her no one else had done so.

Castor has a special interest in health care; Florida's many retirees depend upon Medicare, and she is a strong supporter of the joint federal-state State Children's Health Insurance Program. She assailed President Bush's fiscal 2008 budget, complaining that its funding restrictions would "sock it to the most vulnerable, our seniors and our kids."

Castor's path to the House was opened when Democratic Rep. Jim Davis made a failed bid for governor. She capitalized on her strong name recognition and financial support from EMILY's List, a political committee that backs Democratic women who support abortion rights, to win a five-way primary. She trounced GOP architect Eddie Adams Jr. in November.

FLORIDA 11

West – Tampa, south St. Petersburg

The 11th, one of the younger and more racially diverse districts in the state, ranges from Tampa and part of Bradenton across the bay to south St. Petersburg. The Tampa area's strong service and technology sectors help to make it the commercial, industrial and financial hub of Florida's west coast.

Tampa is experiencing rapid growth — the city's skyline is expected to double in volume by the time Tampa hosts the 2009 Super Bowl. The city's airport and seaport make it a major shipping and transit hub; Tampa's port is Florida's largest cargo volume seaport and is home to three cruise lines. The University of South Florida is one of the state's largest schools and an economic engine for the city.

Tampa's traditional cigar industry has made a comeback in Ybor City, a downtown Tampa neighborhood. The influence of Cuban and Spanish culture is pronounced here, and its success at reinventing itself as a nighttime hot spot has given the area new life.

Blacks and Hispanics combined total about half of the 11th's population, with heavy concentrations of blacks in south St. Petersburg, east Tampa and parts of Bradenton, and Hispanics in west Tampa and the Egypt Lake-Leto and Town 'n' Country areas just northwest of the city. Democrats outnumber Republicans 2-to-1 in the strongly Democratic 11th.

MAJOR INDUSTRY
Service, health care, finance, tourism

MILITARY BASES
MacDill Air Force Base, 12,000 military, 7,000 civilian (2004)

CITIES
Tampa (pt.), 284,199; Town 'n' Country (unincorp.), 72,523; St. Petersburg (pt.), 69,145

NOTABLE
The Sunshine Skyway Bridge is the world's longest cable-stayed concrete bridge.

Rep. Adam H. Putnam (R)

CAPITOL OFFICE
225-1252
www.house.gov/putnam
1725 Longworth 20515-0912; fax 226-0585

COMMITTEES
Financial Services

RESIDENCE
Bartow

BORN
July 31, 1974, Bartow, Fla.

RELIGION
Episcopalian

FAMILY
Wife, Melissa Putnam; four children

EDUCATION
U. of Florida, B.S. 1995 (economics)

CAREER
State legislator; citrus farmer and cattle rancher

POLITICAL HIGHLIGHTS
Fla. House, 1996-2000

ELECTION RESULTS

2006 GENERAL		
Adam H. Putnam (R)	124,452	69.1%
Joe Viscusi (X)	34,976	19.4%
Ed Bowlin (X)	20,636	11.5%
2006 PRIMARY		
Adam H. Putnam (R)		unopposed
2004 GENERAL		
Adam H. Putnam (R)	179,204	64.9%
Bob Hagenmaier (D)	96,965	35.1%

PREVIOUS WINNING PERCENTAGES
2002 (100%); 2000 (57%)

Elected 2000; 4th term

Putnam is the House Republicans' prodigy. The 30-something Floridian has rapidly climbed the leadership ladder, taking the No. 3 position of GOP Conference chairman at the beginning of the 110th Congress (2007-08). It was the second time within a year that he had defeated older and generally more seasoned candidates for a leadership post.

Putnam beat out Jack Kingston of Georgia for the conference chairman slot, 100-91, after dispatching Dan Lungren of California and Marsha Blackburn of Tennessee on the first two ballots. Nine months earlier, he had captured the chairmanship of the Republican Policy Committee, placing him fifth in the House GOP hierarchy, by defeating Darrell Issa of California, Phil Gingrey of Georgia and Thaddeus McCotter of Michigan.

The youngest member of Congress when he was elected in 2000 (a distinction he did not lose until four years later), he has been stopped occasionally by the Capitol police and asked for identification. Putnam caught the eye of former Speaker J. Dennis Hastert early on. His cool temperament, grasp of policy and loyalty to the Republican Party made him Hastert's choice to fill a vacancy on the influential Rules Committee in 2004 after Florida Republican Porter J. Goss departed to become CIA director.

He quickly mastered the multi-layered parliamentary intricacies of managing bills on the floor. His first assignment was handling rules governing debate for a high-profile hurricane relief bill for Florida. Since then, he has taken the lead on a number of rules. "Adam is one of the brightest young members of the caucus," said Rep. Mike Simpson, an Idaho Republican. "I've seen him down there fighting for a rule while the other side is beating the heck out of you. I can see Adam one day being Speaker of the House." In the 110th Congress, Putnam took a seat on the Financial Services Committee.

As the GOP Conference chairman, he is the party's chief spokesman from the House, responsible for guiding the rank and file about GOP positions on issues. His first tasks included protecting President Bush's plans for extended tax breaks in the fiscal 2008 budget, supporting Bush's increase of troops for the Iraq War over the objections of the majority of Americans, then responding to Democratic efforts to set restrictions on war funding.

Pressured to help the party regain the majority in 2008, Putnam said he would focus closely on the details of each message. He hired what he called an "all-star staff," set up a "war room" to provide party members research material for the Iraq debate, and helped set up weekly radio addresses. "It has to be more than just obstructionism and saying no all the time. We have to be competitive in the field of ideas," he told the St. Petersburg Times.

Being a member of the leadership means Putnam is expected to toe the party line, and he usually does, voting with a majority of his party about 97 percent of the time. He is among the most conservative Republicans in the House, opposing abortion and same-sex marriage. On the rare occasions he does stray, it is typically on free-trade bills. In 2005, he initially opposed the Bush administration on the Central American Free Trade Agreement, but ended up voting for it after pressing for, and getting, a provision protecting the sugar industry, which was threatened by Latin American imports.

Four years earlier, he had opposed Bush on fast-track authority to sign trade deals that lawmakers could not later amend. Putnam, who is from a prominent central Florida citrus and cattle ranching family, said it put the state's orange growers at risk. At a closed-door meeting, Bush singled out Putnam, whose red hair is easy to spot in a crowd, saying, "I'm talking about you, Red." House leaders also pressured Putnam, but he refused to yield. Afterward, he said, "I feel like I'm going to throw up."

The next year, when the final version of the trade bill returned to the floor for a vote, Putnam agreed to go along if he could get a few small revisions to help citrus growers. "By the time the second vote came around, I had learned there's a fine line between raising an issue and being marginalized," he said. "We came pretty close to being marginalized."

Putnam is a fifth-generation Floridian, scion of a family of cattle ranchers and citrus growers. He comes from the small town of Bartow, southwest of Orlando, and remains deeply rooted there. His brother lives across the street and his parents just down the road. In 2001, when a compost plant operator sought permission to operate on land next to 3,000 acres of Putnam land, the congressman attended the local planning board meeting and the plan was scrapped. The plant operator accused Putnam of throwing his weight around, but Putnam told the local Ledger newspaper that many residents objected to the plant. "Nobody wants to live next door to a poop plant," Putnam said.

He has loved politics all his life. When Putnam was 11 years old, he told his grandfather he would run for governor some day, an ambition he still harbors. "I consider myself a creature of the House," he said. "If I'm inclined to run statewide, it would be for governor and not to go to the other side of the Capitol."

He began planning for his first political race during his last year at the University of Florida, where he got a degree in economics. A year later, in 1996, he was elected to the state legislature and stayed for four years, chairing the House Agriculture Committee. He was 26 when he was elected to Congress.

In 2000, Republican Rep. Charles T. Canady, for whom Putnam had interned as a college student, stepped down. The Democratic candidate, auto dealer Michael Stedem, tried to make Putnam's youth an issue, but Putnam avoided the trap. He declined MTV's request to follow him on the campaign trail, saying he didn't want any "purple-hair yahoo" asking whether he wore "boxers or briefs." Putnam won with 57 percent of the vote. He was unopposed for re-election in 2002 and has won easily since then, taking 69 percent of the vote in 2006.

KEY VOTES

2006

No Stop broadband companies from favoring select Internet traffic
Yes Affirm U.S. commitment to war in Iraq and reject setting a withdrawal date for troops
Yes Repeal requirement for bilingual ballots at the polls
Yes Permit U.S. sale of civilian nuclear technology to India
Yes Build a 700-mile fence on the U.S.-Mexico border to curb illegal crossings
Yes Permit warrantless wiretaps of suspected terrorists

2005

Yes Intervene in the life-support case of Terri Schiavo
No Lift President Bush's restrictions on stem cell research funding
No Prohibit FBI access to library and bookstore records
Yes Approve free-trade pact with five Central American countries
No Pass energy policy overhaul favored by President Bush emphasizing domestic oil and gas production
Yes End mandatory preservation of habitat of endangered animal and plant species
No Ban torture of prisoners in U.S. custody

CQ VOTE STUDIES

	PARTY UNITY		PRESIDENTIAL SUPPORT	
	Support	Oppose	Support	Oppose
2006	97%	3%	97%	3%
2005	97%	3%	89%	11%
2004	97%	3%	91%	9%
2003	98%	2%	100%	0%
2002	98%	2%	88%	12%

INTEREST GROUPS

	AFL-CIO	ADA	CCUS	ACU
2006	7%	0%	100%	84%
2005	13%	5%	85%	92%
2004	13%	0%	100%	100%
2003	7%	5%	97%	88%
2002	0%	0%	95%	96%

FLORIDA 12
West central – Polk and Hillsborough counties

The 12th has plenty of land, but much of it is covered by citrus groves and natural lakes rather than beaches and developments. Centered east of Tampa and southwest of Orlando, the district includes almost all of Polk County, suburban and exurban portions of southern and eastern Hillsborough County, and a very small slice of western Osceola County.

Agriculture in Polk County drives the 12th's economy. Polk is the state's top producer of citrus, while the Hillsborough County portion of the district cultivates tomatoes and strawberries. Three hurricanes criss-crossed the district in 2004, but its inland location, along with massive federal aid, allowed all but the smallest farms to recover.

The 12th's secondary industries grew steadily over the past decade, and unemployment here has dropped. Publix Supermarkets is headquartered in Lakeland, and financial and insurance companies also have large offices in the area. The district's central location makes it a distribution hub, as well as home to a sizable health care sector. However, employment in Florida's phosphate mining industry, in the area around Bartow and Mulberry, has decreased by half over the past decade. As another slice of the economic pie, the district continues to attract retirees to its sizable retirement communities, including Sun City Center.

A slight Democratic registration advantage belies the social and economic conservatism of most residents. The GOP has the edge among the third of the district's population in Hillsborough County, and the 12th has backed Republican presidential candidates since 1992. Traditional Southern Democratic voters could make state and local elections here more competitive, but Republicans have had better success recently recruiting top-quality candidates for important offices.

MAJOR INDUSTRY
Agriculture, mining, financial services

CITIES
Brandon (unincorporated) (pt.), 72,878; Lakeland (pt.), 71,079; Winter Haven, 26,487

NOTABLE
A water tower in front of the Publix bakery headquarters in Lakeland is shaped like a birthday cake with candles; Cypress Gardens Adventure Park in Winter Haven was Florida's first theme park.

Rep. Vern Buchanan (R)

CAPITOL OFFICE
225-5015
buchanan.house.gov
1516 Longworth 20515-0913; fax 226-0828

COMMITTEES
Small Business
Transportation & Infrastructure
Veterans' Affairs

RESIDENCE
Sarasota

BORN
May 8, 1951, Detroit, Mich.

RELIGION
Baptist

FAMILY
Wife, Sandy Buchanan; two children

EDUCATION
Cleary College, B.B.A. 1975 (business administration); U. of Detroit, M.B.A. 1986

MILITARY SERVICE
Mich. Air National Guard, 1970-76

CAREER
Car dealership owner; copy and printing company owner; marketing representative

POLITICAL HIGHLIGHTS
No previous office

ELECTION RESULTS

2006 GENERAL		
Vern Buchanan (R)	119,309	50.1%
Christine Jennings (D)	118,940	49.9%
2006 PRIMARY		
Vern Buchanan (R)	20,918	32.3%
Nancy Detert (R)	15,804	24.4%
Tramm Hudson (R)	15,535	24.0%
Mark Flanagan (R)	6,465	10.0%
Donna Clarke (R)	5,972	9.2%

Elected 2006; 1st term

A wealthy Florida auto dealer, Buchanan had never before held public office, and his first days on Capitol Hill were tenuous ones.

He won his seat by 369 votes and his election foe, Democratic banker Christine Jennings, contested the results, claiming widespread voting irregularities, including malfunctions of electronic voting machines, which were responsible for 18,000 "undervotes" in Sarasota County. Still, the Florida secretary of state certified Buchanan the winner and he was sworn in with the other House members in January 2007.

Even though he is a first-time office holder, Buchanan is not without some political experience. He was co-chairman of the Republican National Committee's Finance Committee and state finance chairman for Florida Sen. Mel Martinez's 2004 election campaign.

Buchanan has seats on the Small Business, Transportation and Infrastructure and Veterans' Affairs committees. The 13th District includes a large number of retired veterans, and Buchanan hopes to use his Veterans' Affairs assignment to secure an ambulatory surgery and specialty care clinic for veterans in Sarasota.

Buchanan says his political philosophy is aligned with Reagan-era conservatism in that he believes in small government and that "everyone who can work should work." He says national defense should be the federal government's highest priority. "Border security first," he says. "Everything else comes after."

Buchanan grew up with five siblings in a small town near Detroit. He earned an MBA from the University of Detroit after working his way through college. He served six years in the Air National Guard, and moved to Florida from Michigan in 1990.

He and Jennings ran neck and neck in the weeks before the election in this conservative-leaning district. Jennings took a pro-business and centrist stance, but Buchanan attacked her as being weak on taxes and immigration. Of the more than $8 million in Buchanan's campaign receipts, $5.5 million came from his personal accounts; Jennings raised nearly $3 million.

FLORIDA 13

Southwest — Sarasota, most of Bradenton

Retirees from the North flock to the Gulf Coast cities of Sarasota and Bradenton, making the 13th a reliably Republican district. Sarasota and Manatee counties have nearly 90 percent of the district's population; the more affluent tend to live near Sarasota, with middle-class residents more prevalent around Bradenton.

Most residents live near the coast, while farmland and citrus groves are inland. Coastal Sarasota County cultivates a refined image with its art museums, theater and symphony performances. It generally draws a more highly educated and wealthier class of retirees than most other west coast communities in Florida. Bradenton (shared with the 11th) is the retail center of Manatee County. The city is partly a Tampa-St. Petersburg-area suburb, and has a more noticeable mix of incomes and ethnic groups than Sarasota. Overall, the 13th has the nation's highest median age and is a popular home for older part-time residents.

Service industries, including investment companies, and trade make up much of the labor force. The district's agricultural industry is strong, with large tomato and citrus crops, although disease is an ongoing threat. The area's Gulf beaches, barrier islands and state park make environmental policy a bipartisan concern here.

Republicans hold an advantage in party registration, and voters here decidedly favor GOP candidates in statewide races.

MAJOR INDUSTRY
Agriculture, tourism, health care, service

CITIES
Sarasota, 52,715; Bradenton (pt.), 39,385

NOTABLE
In 1927, the Ringling Bros. circus began setting up shop in Sarasota each winter.

Rep. Connie Mack (R)

CAPITOL OFFICE
225-2536
mack.house.gov
115 Cannon 20515-0914; fax 226-0439

COMMITTEES
Budget
Foreign Affairs
Transportation & Infrastructure

RESIDENCE
Fort Myers

BORN
Aug. 12, 1967, Fort Myers, Fla.

RELIGION
Roman Catholic

FAMILY
Divorced; two children

EDUCATION
U. of Florida, B.S. 1993 (advertising)

CAREER
Marketing consultant; health products sales representative

POLITICAL HIGHLIGHTS
Fla. House, 2000-03

ELECTION RESULTS

2006 GENERAL		
Connie Mack (R)	151,615	64.4%
Robert M. Neeld (D)	83,920	35.6%
2006 PRIMARY		
Connie Mack (R)		unopposed
2004 GENERAL		
Connie Mack (R)	226,662	67.6%
Robert M. Neeld (D)	108,672	32.4%

Elected 2004; 2nd term

Though he's the son of a respected former senator of the same name, Mack's early taste of politics was anything but positive. He hated the sometimes critical appraisals of his father in the press. "I think that some of the shots taken at my father really had a negative impact on me," he says. "I thought, 'They don't even know who my father is, he's such an honorable, good man.' But as you get older, you realize that's just part of politics these days."

Mack's 14th District consists almost entirely of a portion of Florida's Gulf Coast that was represented from 1983 to 1989 by his father, Connie Mack III, who went on to serve in the Senate from 1989 to 2001. His son also is carrying on the family tradition of going by the nickname initiated by his great-grandfather, the manager and owner of the old Philadelphia Athletics baseball team. The congressman's given name is actually Cornelius McGillicuddy IV.

Mack says he did not have much interest in public office until he had his own family. "I wanted to be where the decisions were being made so I could make sure that my children and grandchildren have opportunity," he says.

An emphasis on "family values" also defined Mack's initial race for Congress in 2004. But his first term in Washington turned out to be difficult for his own family. Mack split from Ann, his wife of nine years, in August 2005, and weeks later, he was linked romantically to another member of Congress, Republican Mary Bono of California — the widow of Sonny Bono, a pop star-turned-congressman — who was divorcing her second husband. The Macks waged a court battle over where the children, then ages 3 and 5, would live. His former wife wanted to move to Fort Lauderdale, where she said she had more of a support system. But that city is outside of Mack's Cape Coral-based congressional district.

Mack's personal difficulties had little impact on his 2006 re-election as it turned out. He faced Democrat Robert M. Neeld, a Cape Coral accountant, in a rematch of 2004, but prevailed with a safe 64 percent of the vote.

Like any savvy freshman who tries to shore up his hold on his seat, Mack focused on district concerns his first two years. He snagged a seat on the Transportation and Infrastructure Committee, and focused on promoting projects popular with constituents. Mack was instrumental in getting $81 million included in the 2005 surface transportation bill for Interstate 75, a major artery through southwestern Florida. Congestion along I-75 was the largest single issue in Mack's first House campaign.

On another important parochial issue, Mack fought efforts to expand offshore oil and gas leasing. A potential oil spill would be disastrous to a local economy that depends on its Gulf Coast beaches for tourist dollars, he said. Mack and other members of the Florida delegation managed to get an offshore drilling provision removed after it was tacked onto a budget bill in 2005. A narrow bill that finally passed Congress in 2006 prohibits drilling within 125 miles of Florida's coast. Mack would like to go further by letting the state make the decisions. In 2007, Mack introduced legislation to increase funds for research on red tides — toxic blooms of algae, which have affected the southwest Florida coast.

While attuned to local concerns, Mack also began to build an international portfolio with a focus on Latin American issues. With Washington preoccupied with the war in Iraq, Mack, from his seat on the International Relations (now Foreign Affairs) Committee, carved out a niche as a vocal and oft-quoted critic of Venezuela's leftist dictator, Hugo Chávez. "He's a bad guy," Mack says. "I don't think the Congress really understands the negative potential that Hugo Chávez presents, whether it's from an economic standpoint or whether it's about the health and welfare of his own country."

In July 2005, Mack sponsored an amendment on the House floor to create broadcast programming for a Venezuelan audience similar to Radio and TV Marti programs aimed at communist-ruled Cuba. It passed by voice vote. He also blasted former Rep. Joseph P. Kennedy II, the nephew of the former president, in February 2007 for a television ad by his nonprofit Citizens Energy Corp. in which he appears saying discounted oil is on its way to poor families courtesy of "our good friends in Venezuela at Citgo."

A tax-cutting conservative on fiscal issues, Mack was fairly independent from his party in other key battles, for a relative newcomer. He voted against renewing key portions of the Patriot Act, the Bush administration's anti-terrorism law, citing provisions allowing eavesdropping of suspects without a court warrant. "I believe the Patriot Act tramples on the civil liberties that are part of the foundation of this country," he says. He also voted against the Republican president's major trade initiative of 2005, the Central American Free Trade Agreement. Mack breaks with the national GOP to support expanding federal funding for embryonic stem cell research, which uses cells harvested from surplus embryos at in vitro fertilization clinics.

Mack grew up in southwestern Florida, and was a student at Cape Coral High School when his father was elected to Congress. The Macks moved to the nation's capital, settling in the affluent suburb of McLean, Va. Mack graduated from Massanutten Military Academy in Woodstock, Va.

Mack says he "stuffed envelopes and walked precincts" for his father but wasn't interested in politics himself until after college. He returned to the family's home state to attend the University of Florida, where he got a degree in advertising. He was a health products salesman and marketing consultant, but soon thought of following in his father's footsteps.

At age 33, Mack was elected to the Florida House in 2000 from Ft. Lauderdale. During three years as a state legislator, Mack organized a group of members opposed to all new taxes and government fees.

When Republican Porter J. Goss decided to retire after eight terms, Mack moved from Ft. Lauderdale to Fort Myers to run in the 2004 race in the overwhelmingly Republican 14th District. He eked out a primary victory in a four-way race marked by opponents' jabs about his ties to the area. Voters didn't seem to care, and after winning the primary, he cruised to a lopsided general-election victory.

KEY VOTES

2006

- No Stop broadband companies from favoring select Internet traffic
- Yes Affirm U.S. commitment to war in Iraq and reject setting a withdrawal date for troops
- Yes Repeal requirement for bilingual ballots at the polls
- Yes Permit U.S. sale of civilian nuclear technology to India
- Yes Build a 700-mile fence on the U.S.-Mexico border to curb illegal crossings
- No Permit warrantless wiretaps of suspected terrorists

2005

- Yes Intervene in the life-support case of Terri Schiavo
- Yes Lift President Bush's restrictions on stem cell research funding
- No Prohibit FBI access to library and bookstore records
- No Approve free-trade pact with five Central American countries
- No Pass energy policy overhaul favored by President Bush emphasizing domestic oil and gas production
- Yes End mandatory preservation of habitat of endangered animal and plant species
- Yes Ban torture of prisoners in U.S. custody

CQ VOTE STUDIES

	PARTY UNITY		PRESIDENTIAL SUPPORT	
	Support	Oppose	Support	Oppose
2006	93%	7%	87%	13%
2005	96%	4%	80%	20%

INTEREST GROUPS

	AFL-CIO	ADA	CCUS	ACU
2006	8%	25%	93%	84%
2005	13%	5%	81%	92%

FLORIDA 14

Southwest — Cape Coral, Fort Myers, Naples

Traditionally a haven for retirees and tourists, the solidly Republican 14th features Gulf Coast beaches and a rapidly expanding population centered in Lee County, where migration of families and young professionals from the North and from Florida's east coast adds to the mix. The 14th also takes in the coastal edge of Collier County and a small slice of Charlotte County. Most residents live near the coast, between the shore and Interstate 75, which runs through the district before turning east into the Everglades.

The population in Collier and Lee counties grew significantly in the 1990s and continues to rise — Cape Coral in Lee County has seen its population grow by at least another one-third already this decade. Originally a retirement community, Cape Coral has attracted young professionals with new white-collar job opportunities and many business relocations to the area. The city's service industry continues to grow, and new housing developments are expanding at a rapid rate. Wealthier retirees live around Naples, where golf courses and high-rise condominiums are plentiful and new construction has helped put the area in the state's top 10 in taxable property value.

Fort Myers' Florida Gulf Coast University, with its environmental and science research centers, and the nearby Everglades help promote marine biology and a bustling eco-tourism industry. The barrier islands act as a magnet for tourists — Sanibel Island is renowned for the seashells that wash up on its beaches from the Gulf of Mexico.

Small Democratic pockets exist within Lee County, but the 14th has the largest Republican voter registration advantage in the state, and residents here regularly give GOP candidates large vote percentages. George W. Bush won the district's 2004 presidential vote with 61 percent.

MAJOR INDUSTRY

Tourism, health care, service, construction

CITIES

Cape Coral, 102,286; Fort Myers, 48,208; North Fort Myers (unincorporated), 40,214; Lehigh Acres (unincorporated), 33,430

NOTABLE

Naples has more than 100 golf courses, and southwest Florida boasts that it leads the United States in golf holes per capita.

Rep. Dave Weldon (R)

CAPITOL OFFICE
225-3671
weldon.house.gov
2347 Rayburn 20515-0915; fax 225-3516

COMMITTEES
Appropriations

RESIDENCE
Indiatlantic

BORN
Aug. 31, 1953, Amityville, N.Y.

RELIGION
Christian

FAMILY
Wife, Nancy Weldon; two children

EDUCATION
State U. of New York, Stony Brook, B.S. 1978 (biochemistry); State U. of New York, Buffalo, M.D. 1981

MILITARY SERVICE
Army Medical Corps, 1981-87; Army Reserve, 1987-92

CAREER
Physician

POLITICAL HIGHLIGHTS
No previous office

ELECTION RESULTS

2006 GENERAL		
Dave Weldon (R)	125,965	56.3%
Bob Bowman (D)	97,834	43.7%
2006 PRIMARY		
Dave Weldon (R)		unopposed
2004 GENERAL		
Dave Weldon (R)	210,388	65.4%
Simon Pristoop (D)	111,538	34.7%

PREVIOUS WINNING PERCENTAGES
2002 (63%); 2000 (59%); 1998 (63%); 1996 (51%); 1994 (54%)

Elected 1994; 7th term

Weldon tries to advance his socially conservative values any chance he gets, although his opportunities may be more limited now that the Democrats are running the House. A physician whose specialty is internal medicine, he has taken a high-profile role on medically related social issues such as embryonic stem cell research and the right to die. He also does his best to limit access to abortion.

The day before the House passed a measure in January 2007 to expand federal spending on embryonic stem cell research, Weldon held a news conference condemning it. Under the bill, federal grants could be used for research on embryos donated by in vitro fertility clinics, as long as they were not created for scientific purposes and would otherwise be discarded. "What has been forced upon us by the left in the United States is getting the federal government to fund the destruction of more embryos — and that has been the debate, and that has been the line that the president has drawn and said that he does not want crossed," Weldon said. President Bush had vetoed an identical bill in July 2006, and the House fell 51 votes short of an override.

Weldon was also active in the 2005 debate on whether to intervene in the case of Terri Schiavo, a brain-damaged Florida woman in a vegetative state whose husband's request to remove her feeding tube was backed by state and federal courts. The courts' decision outraged many social conservatives, and Weldon introduced a bill to require doctors and hospitals to provide food and fluids to incapacitated patients unless they have living wills.

In 2004, Weldon inserted a provision in a catchall spending bill to deny federal aid to states and localities that compel health care providers, facilities or insurance companies to provide, fund or refer abortion services. The provision significantly expanded the "conscience clause" under federal law that shields doctors and other health care providers from discrimination lawsuits when they refuse to perform abortions and cite their personal opposition to the procedure.

A member of the Appropriations Committee, Weldon gained a seat in the 110th Congress (2007-08) on the Labor, Health and Human Services, and Education Subcommittee. The Labor-HHS spending bill is often a battleground for provisions dealing with medical issues and abortion.

In addition to his medical interests, Weldon has another legislative passion: space. Until redistricting in 2002, his Space Coast district included the Kennedy Space Center. His district's economy still depends greatly on NASA and the private companies attracted there by space-related work.

He has not been shy about getting money directed home to help the space industry. And he was pleased in June 2006 when an effort to eliminate the Bush administration's funding for the mission to Mars program failed during debate on the Commerce, Justice, State spending bill. The $3.8 billion program seeks to return astronauts to the moon by 2020 in preparation for future missions to Mars. Weldon and other supporters said the United States cannot afford to lose the lead in space exploration. "This is the United States of America. We are the nation of pioneers and explorers," said Weldon. "For us to say, 'No we don't want to do that, we can't afford it, we have too many problems,' would be a very unfortunate thing."

Protecting NASA's space programs can trump Weldon's concern about controlling federal spending. When the conservative Republican Study Committee, of which he is a member, also proposed cancelling NASA's moon and Mars initiative to help pay for Hurricane Katrina recovery, Weldon made clear he did not agree with the suggestion. But in most cases, he is a loyal party soldier. In the 109th Congress (2005-06), he voted in agreement with his party 96 percent of the time on votes that pitted Republicans against Democrats.

Weldon is musically bipartisan, however. He plays bass guitar with Minnesota Democrat Collin C. Peterson and three other GOP lawmakers in a rock band called the Second Amendments that entertained U.S. troops in Afghanistan, Iraq, Kuwait and Germany during a 2005 Christmas tour.

Weldon began his involvement in politics in the late 1980s as the cofounder of a conservative group, the Space Coast Family Forum, that endorsed candidates based on their stances on abortion, sex education and other social issues. Religion plays an important part in Weldon's life. He says he tries to read the Bible and pray every day, and he lists among his political influences his "idol . . . Jesus Christ." His values sit well with the culturally conservative voters along central Florida's eastern coast.

Like many Floridians, Weldon is a transplant from the North. He grew up on Long Island, the son of a postal clerk. He worked his way through his undergraduate days as an X-ray technician, and the Army paid his way through medical school. After a stint as an Army doctor, he moved to Florida in 1987 and went into private practice.

Other than the Space Coast Family Forum, Weldon's only taste of political life until his run for Congress came when he was president of his local homeowners association. But when two-term Democratic Rep. Jim Bacchus unexpectedly decided to retire in 1994, Weldon entered the race, overcoming criticism that he was too conservative for the district. Weldon's Family Forum ties gave him a ready-made base of support among conservatives, and he won the GOP nomination in a runoff.

That year found the district's voters in a conservative mood, and Weldon emphasized his support for mainstream GOP fare: tax cuts, welfare reform and other aspects of the House GOP's policy manifesto, the "Contract with America." An extensive get-out-the-vote effort by such groups as the Christian Coalition helped him beat Democrat Sue Munsey, a former head of the Cocoa Beach Area Chamber of Commerce, with 54 percent of the vote.

In 2000, Weldon handed then House Democratic Leader Richard A. Gephardt a double defeat: Not only did he win re-election, but his unexpectedly large victory came over Gephardt's cousin, state Sen. Patsy Kurth. Weldon flirted with a run for the Senate in 2004 but ultimately decided against it. He then coasted to re-election. In 2006, he won by close to 13 percentage points.

KEY VOTES

2006

No Stop broadband companies from favoring select Internet traffic

Yes Affirm U.S. commitment to war in Iraq and reject setting a withdrawal date for troops

Yes Repeal requirement for bilingual ballots at the polls

Yes Permit U.S. sale of civilian nuclear technology to India

Yes Build a 700-mile fence on the U.S.-Mexico border to curb illegal crossings

Yes Permit warrantless wiretaps of suspected terrorists

2005

Yes Intervene in the life-support case of Terri Schiavo

No Lift President Bush's restrictions on stem cell research funding

No Prohibit FBI access to library and bookstore records

Yes Approve free-trade pact with five Central American countries

No Pass energy policy overhaul favored by President Bush emphasizing domestic oil and gas production

Yes End mandatory preservation of habitat of endangered animal and plant species

No Ban torture of prisoners in U.S. custody

CQ VOTE STUDIES

	PARTY UNITY		PRESIDENTIAL SUPPORT	
	Support	Oppose	Support	Oppose
2006	97%	3%	90%	10%
2005	95%	5%	91%	9%
2004	95%	5%	88%	12%
2003	97%	3%	96%	4%
2002	98%	2%	85%	15%

INTEREST GROUPS

	AFL-CIO	ADA	CCUS	ACU
2006	14%	5%	93%	88%
2005	7%	0%	81%	88%
2004	7%	0%	100%	91%
2003	7%	5%	93%	71%
2002	11%	0%	90%	100%

FLORIDA 15

East central – Indian River County; parts of Brevard, Osceola and Polk counties

Most residents of the 15th live along the Atlantic Coast in Brevard and Indian River counties between the conservative strongholds of Merritt Island and Vero Beach. In addition to all of Indian River and three-fourths of Brevard, the 15th contains regional agricultural hubs in inland Osceola County and in the district's slice of Polk County. Melbourne and Palm Bay, on the Treasure Coast along the district's central shore, form a major population center.

In the northeastern corner of the district, the Cape Canaveral Air Force Station and Patrick Air Force Base — along with the Kennedy Space Center (located in the neighboring 24th) — are the Space Coast's economic engine, propelling the thriving technology and aerospace industries. NASA's presence, despite an uncertain future, is an enormous economic boost, providing the district with high-paying jobs, lucrative contracts and popular tourist attractions.

Tourism is an important secondary economy, and the15th is home to beautiful beaches, including Sebastian Inlet, which claims some of the best surfing on the Atlantic seaboard. Disney's Vero Beach Resort is becoming a high-profile destination, and fast-growing Kissimmee, which has a large Hispanic population, depends on Orlando's tourism industry.

Although Democrats hold slight registration edges in the 15th's portions of Osceola and Polk, the GOP has a significant registration edge overall in the district. Voters have favored GOP presidential candidates since 1992, and in 2004, George W. Bush captured 57 percent of the vote here.

MAJOR INDUSTRY

Technology, defense, tourism, agriculture

MILITARY BASES

Patrick Air Force Base, 2,300 military, 8,600 civilian (2005)

CITIES

Palm Bay, 79,413; Melbourne, 71,382; Kissimmee, 47,814; Merritt Island (unincorporated) (pt.), 27,291

NOTABLE

Jim Morrison, singer-songwriter for The Doors, was born in Melbourne; The original name of Yeehaw Junction, at a crossroads of what is now the Florida turnpike, was "Jackass Crossing."

Rep. Tim Mahoney (D)

Elected 2006; 1st term

Mahoney captured this traditionally Republican district with just less than 50 percent of the vote. The residents of the 16th were ready for a change as their six-term representative, Republican Mark Foley, left the House in a hurry in 2006 once his sexually explicit online messages to House teenage pages were splashed across the news.

Mahoney is a wealthy investment banking firm owner and a political neophyte. He was given a seat on the Financial Services Committee, a good fit with his business background. Mahoney says he wants to reduce homeowners' insurance rates by creating a national catastrophe program to assist state and private insurance programs in covering losses related to natural disasters. Florida homeowners have high insurance rates as a result of hurricane-related property damage.

Mahoney says he also wants to take a close look at the estate tax and its effect on family-owned farms and ranches. He says cash-strapped families can be forced to sell their land because they cannot afford the tax. Mahoney also has a seat on the Agriculture Committee — another good fit as he owns a 98-acre ranch where he raises 40 head of cattle.

Aware that he represents a GOP-leaning district, Mahoney has taken pains to align himself with the more centrist Democrats in the House. He joined the Blue Dog Coalition, a group of fiscally conservative Democrats.

Mahoney had raised more than $1 million to challenge Foley in 2006, yet his campaign was thought to be a long shot. Foley's overall conservative record and his more moderate social positions had made him so entrenched that Democrats didn't seriously recruit for most of his elections.

But Mahoney suddenly went from underdog to favorite on Sept. 29, when Foley abruptly resigned after his e-mail messages were made public. Though Foley quit the race too late to have his name removed from the ballot, Republicans chose state Rep. Joe Negron as a replacement nominee and made a major effort to inform voters that any votes cast for Foley would be recorded as votes for Negron. Nonetheless, Mahoney ended up winning by some 4,400 votes — a roughly 2 percentage point margin.

CAPITOL OFFICE
225-5792
mahoney.house.gov
1541 Longworth 20515-0916; fax 225-3132

COMMITTEES
Agriculture
Financial Services

RESIDENCE
Palm Beach Gardens

BORN
Aug. 15, 1956, Aurora, Ill.

RELIGION
Methodist

FAMILY
Wife, Terry Mahoney; one child

EDUCATION
West Virginia U., B.A. 1978 (international studies & computer marketing); George Washington U., M.B.A. 1983

CAREER
Investment banking firm owner; computer hardware company executive; sales and marketing executive

POLITICAL HIGHLIGHTS
No previous office

ELECTION RESULTS

2006 GENERAL		
Tim Mahoney (D)	115,832	49.5%
Joe Negron (R) (Mark Foley, R)	111,415	47.7%
Emmie Ross (X)	6,526	2.8%
2006 PRIMARY		
Tim Mahoney (D)	unopposed	

FLORIDA 16

South central – Port St. Lucie, parts of Port Charlotte and Wellington

The 16th sprawls over south-central Florida, connecting wealthy east coast communities with Charlotte Harbor on the west coast. In between, rural Floridians raise cattle and grow sugar cane, particularly around Lake Okeechobee. The 16th envelops the west side of the lake and also takes in most of St. Lucie County's white population near the Atlantic Ocean. With the lake and beaches, the environment is a significant issue here.

The district's coast-to-coast geography has proved to be more of a curse than a blessing in recent years as three hurricanes — Frances, Jeanne and Wilma — have come ashore in the 16th, causing billions of dollars in damage. Although armed with federal aid, local agriculture is still vulnerable.

St. Lucie County, the 16th's most populous jurisdiction, accounts for about one-fourth of residents. The 16th's share of St. Lucie — including all of Port St. Lucie and some of Fort Pierce and Lakewood Park — has a slight Republican lean. The district's portion of Martin County is older and more Republican. Two months after a scandal involving its GOP House member, the usually Republican 16th, known for high voter turnout, elected a Democrat to the House.

Fast-growing Port St. Lucie is within commuting distance to major area cities, and its affordable housing market has attracted many new residents who are fleeing skyrocketing housing prices in southern Florida.

MAJOR INDUSTRY
Agriculture, government, health care

CITIES
Port St. Lucie, 88,769; Port Charlotte (pt.) (unincorp.), 39,610; Wellington (pt.), 35,797

NOTABLE
LaBelle hosts the Swamp Cabbage Festival at the end of each February.

Rep. Kendrick B. Meek (D)

CAPITOL OFFICE
225-4506
kendrickmeek.house.gov
1039 Longworth 20515-0917; fax 226-0777

COMMITTEES
Armed Services
Ways & Means

RESIDENCE
Miami

BORN
Sept. 6, 1966, Miami, Fla.

RELIGION
Baptist

FAMILY
Wife, Leslie A. Meek; two children

EDUCATION
Florida A&M U., B.S. 1988 (criminal justice)

CAREER
Security firm business development aide; state trooper

POLITICAL HIGHLIGHTS
Fla. House, 1994-98; Fla. Senate, 1998-2002

ELECTION RESULTS

2006 GENERAL		
Kendrick B. Meek (D)		unopposed
2006 PRIMARY		
Kendrick B. Meek (D)	32,426	89.4%
Dufirstson Neree (D)	3,850	10.6%
2004 GENERAL		
Kendrick B. Meek (D)		unopposed

PREVIOUS WINNING PERCENTAGES
2002 (100%)

Elected 2002; 3rd term

Meek is a man on the move, a rising star among House Democrats who has carved out a reputation as a serious legislator with a particular expertise on Haiti. Going forward, he is likely to broaden his focus significantly.

As he began his third term, Meek won a coveted assignment to the Ways and Means Committee, where he is now Florida's lone representative. That is a weighty responsibility, given Florida's role as the trade-reliant gateway to Latin America and its large senior population that depends on Medicare and Social Security. All are issues addressed by Ways and Means.

Heading into the 110th Congress (2007-08), Democratic Leader Nancy Pelosi also gave Meek a seat on the Democratic Steering Committee, which makes committee assignments. And he is chairman of the Congressional Black Caucus Foundation, the policy and educational arm of the caucus. "Kendrick is one of our brightest young members," Pelosi said. "He's been a leader in the House since the first day he arrived in Washington.

Meek initially sought a spot on the Appropriations Committee — where his mother, whom he succeeded in the House, had served. But he concluded that he could accomplish more on Ways and Means, given its broad reach. To take the Ways and Means post, Meek had to relinquish a seat on the Homeland Security panel, but was able to retain his Armed Services seat.

Meek's district is 55 percent black and has the largest Haitian population in the United States, including residents of Miami's Little Haiti neighborhood. (He issues news releases on Haiti-related topics in both English and Haitian Creole.) Many constituents have friends or relatives on the destitute island nation 600 miles southeast of Florida. Meek visits the country frequently and has fought to liberalize treatment for Haitian refugees. He has been a vocal critic of President Bush's policies on Haitian immigrants, whom he claims are unfairly singled out for detention and deportation.

When Haitian President Jean-Bertrand Aristide was toppled in a coup in 2004, Meek tried in vain to get Attorney General John Ashcroft to approve temporary protective status for people fleeing the violence. Meek wants to broaden a 1998 law his mother, Democrat Carrie P. Meek, wrote that grants immigration protection to Haitians who were living in the country before 1996 and are applying to become permanent residents. His efforts were blocked during the GOP reign, but he is hoping for success in the Democratically controlled Congress.

Meek did win approval of a measure giving Haitian-made apparel duty-free access to U.S. markets even if it was made with fabric from third countries such as China. A catchall tax and trade bill cleared by Congress in December 2006 granted such access, within certain limits.

Meek represents the mostly poor and working-class neighborhoods of northeast Miami-Dade and southeastern Broward counties. He is well-known back home for his very public fights with Florida's former governor, presidential brother Jeb Bush, over education and affirmative action during his days in the state legislature.

He advocates smaller class sizes in public schools as a way to raise test scores and deter dropouts. He introduced a bill in 2003 that built on efforts he led in Florida that resulted in a state constitutional amendment mandating class sizes from preschool through high school. His federal legislation would give states with class-size reduction programs up to $200 million in matching grants to build new classrooms or to hire more teachers.

Meek was born into politics the way some children inherit the family business. His mother was the first African-American elected to Congress from Florida since Reconstruction. Kendrick remembers curling up to sleep under her desk in the Florida House as she read bills late into the night. Carrie P. Meek, a divorced mother of three, was a strong role model, coaching young Kendrick through early learning difficulties stemming from dyslexia. When he was 12, she made him a page at the state Capitol.

Meek graduated from his mother's alma mater, Florida A&M University, where he studied criminal justice. He went to work as a state trooper, and with his mother's help, rose quickly to captain and got onto Democratic Lt. Gov. Buddy MacKay's security detail.

After just five years on the force, in 1994, he decided to challenge a veteran Democratic state House member who was a leader on women's issues. Rep. Elaine Gordon retired, avoiding a primary battle, and Meek was elected. In 1998, Meek, at age 32, elbowed out another Democratic incumbent to capture his mother's old state Senate seat.

Kendrick soon drew notice in his own right. When Gov. Bush refused to meet with him to discuss a proposal to eliminate minority preferences in state contracts and university admissions, Meek staged a well-publicized, overnight "sit in" at Bush's office. The move galvanized opponents, leading to the state's largest-ever protest march on the Capitol.

Capitalizing on the momentum, Meek traveled the state promoting an "Arrive with Five" campaign urging women and minorities to register to vote in 2000 and to bring five new voters with them. It helped turn out the largest number of black voters in state history, according to the Orlando Sentinel.

Meek then reconstituted his forces into the successful campaign to amend the state constitution in 2002 to make smaller classes mandatory, overcoming fierce opposition from Gov. Bush.

In 2002, Carrie P. Meek announced her retirement less than two weeks before the candidate filing deadline, giving her son a jump-start. Would-be challengers stayed away, and Meek was easily elected.

In 2006, Meek faced the first primary opposition of his House career. He was challenged by Dufirstson Neree, a Haitian-born international development expert who grew up in Miami. Meek campaigned aggressively against the political newcomer, visiting churches, barbershops, street corners and youth football fields. He trounced the challenger with almost 90 percent of the vote and was unopposed in November.

KEY VOTES

2006

- No — Stop broadband companies from favoring select Internet traffic
- No — Affirm U.S. commitment to war in Iraq and reject setting a withdrawal date for troops
- No — Repeal requirement for bilingual ballots at the polls
- Yes — Permit U.S. sale of civilian nuclear technology to India
- No — Build a 700-mile fence on the U.S.-Mexico border to curb illegal crossings
- No — Permit warrantless wiretaps of suspected terrorists

2005

- Yes — Intervene in the life-support case of Terri Schiavo
- Yes — Lift President Bush's restrictions on stem cell research funding
- Yes — Prohibit FBI access to library and bookstore records
- No — Approve free-trade pact with five Central American countries
- No — Pass energy policy overhaul favored by President Bush emphasizing domestic oil and gas production
- No — End mandatory preservation of habitat of endangered animal and plant species
- Yes — Ban torture of prisoners in U.S. custody

CQ VOTE STUDIES

	PARTY UNITY		PRESIDENTIAL SUPPORT	
	Support	Oppose	Support	Oppose
2006	89%	11%	37%	63%
2005	93%	7%	26%	74%
2004	94%	6%	39%	61%
2003	93%	7%	26%	74%

INTEREST GROUPS

	AFL-CIO	ADA	CCUS	ACU
2006	100%	95%	57%	8%
2005	93%	95%	52%	9%
2004	93%	85%	45%	9%
2003	87%	85%	47%	23%

FLORIDA 17

Southeast – parts of Miami and Hollywood

The black-majority and solidly Democratic 17th is a compact district that takes in part of northeast Miami-Dade County and a slice of southeast Broward County. It stretches south from Hollywood and Pembroke Pines into Miami, taking in part of Miramar and North Miami, and it includes an array of neighborhoods that are ethnically and economically diverse.

The district has the state's highest percentage of black residents (55 percent), including many from the West Indies. Whites and Hispanics each make up about one-fifth of the residents. Little Haiti, the cultural heart of southern Florida's thriving Haitian community, is located in the 17th. There is a sizable population of Cuban-Americans, although the community is not as large here as elsewhere in southern Florida. More than 40 percent of district residents speak a language other than English at home, and more than one-third were born outside of the United States.

Overtown, once the region's hub of African-American wealth, spent decades in decline, but the area is now part of Miami-Dade's federal empowerment zone. Although improvement efforts had stalled, the city pledged millions of dollars in 2006 to complete development of affordable housing and new business space in Overtown and to revitalize the historic neighborhood in the area around the Lyric Theater.

Infrastructure is important to the district: Miami International Airport is located just outside the 17th, and the Opa-Locka airport serves as a base for civilian pilots. Interstate 95 — a major hurricane evacuation route — runs through the district. Health concerns are a major topic for residents, many of whom are uninsured. In addition, the HIV/AIDS epidemic has hit the 17th hard, particularly in the black community.

Democrats win at all levels in the 17th, where statewide GOP candidates often receive less than 25 percent of the vote. In 2004, John Kerry won 83 percent here in the presidential race — his best showing in the state.

MAJOR INDUSTRY

Transportation, service, entertainment

CITIES

Miami (pt.), 81,688; Hollywood (pt.), 57,267; North Miami (pt.), 50,514; Miramar (pt.), 41,272; Carol City (unincorporated) (pt.), 35,858

NOTABLE

Opa-Locka's architecture is based on an Arabian theme.

Rep. Ileana Ros-Lehtinen (R)

CAPITOL OFFICE
225-3931
www.house.gov/ros-lehtinen
2160 Rayburn 20515-0918; fax 225-5620

COMMITTEES
Foreign Affairs - ranking member

RESIDENCE
Miami

BORN
July 15, 1952, Havana, Cuba

RELIGION
Episcopalian

FAMILY
Husband, Dexter Lehtinen; two children, two stepchildren

EDUCATION
Miami-Dade Community College, A.A. 1972 (English); Florida International U., B.A. 1975 (English & education), M.S. 1976-86 (education); U. of Miami, Ph.D. 2004 (education)

CAREER
Teacher; private school administrator

POLITICAL HIGHLIGHTS
Fla. House, 1982-86; Fla. Senate, 1986-89

ELECTION RESULTS

2006 GENERAL		
Ileana Ros-Lehtinen (R)	79,631	62.1%
David "Big Dave" Patlak (D)	48,499	37.9%
2006 PRIMARY		
Ileana Ros-Lehtinen (R)		unopposed
2004 GENERAL		
Ileana Ros-Lehtinen (R)	143,647	64.7%
Sam Sheldon (D)	78,281	35.3%

PREVIOUS WINNING PERCENTAGES
2002 (69%); 2000 (100%); 1998 (100%); 1996 (100%); 1994 (100%); 1992 (67%); 1990 (60%); 1989 Special Election (53%)

Elected August 1989; 9th full term

Ros-Lehtinen had hoped to claim the gavel of the House Foreign Affairs Committee in 2007, but she had to settle for the top-ranking minority slot instead. Even so, her rise to that position was a significant achievement. She leapfrogged over three more-senior Republicans to become the only GOP woman to hold a top House committee post.

The first Cuban-American and first Hispanic woman elected to Congress, Ros-Lehtinen (full name: il-ee-AH-na ross-LAY-tin-nen) spent her early years in the House focused on U.S. policy toward Cuba and on immigration. But she has expanded her portfolio to other international arenas in recent years. A strong supporter of Israel and an ardent human rights advocate, she finds her views on both topics nicely aligned with those of the new Foreign Affairs chairman, Democrat Tom Lantos of California.

During the 109th Congress (2005-06), Ros-Lehtinen chaired the Middle East and Central Asia Subcommittee. She took aim at countries suspected of supporting terrorists, advocating a hard line against Iran over its nuclear policy and against Saudi Arabia over lingering concerns about whether it is financing terrorist groups. A law enacted in 2006 extending sanctions against Iran was a watered-down version of legislation that Ros-Lehtinen had steered through the House with the support of Lantos.

The two also teamed up on a 2006 law restricting U.S. aid to the Hamas-led Palestinian government. The House had again passed a stronger version sponsored by Ros-Lehtinen. She called the final law "just the beginning of our efforts to deny Hamas or any other terrorist organization the economic resources, the political legitimacy and the excuses to pursue their threatening agenda."

Unlike Lantos, Ros-Lehtinen has continued to defend President Bush's conduct of the war in Iraq. "We've got to be victorious in this," she said in November 2006. She had a personal stake in the fighting: Her stepson, a Marine, served in Iraq in 2006, as did his wife.

Ros-Lehtinen continues to preach the wisdom of keeping Cuba isolated, even as the island faces a transition from the rule of President Fidel Castro. She has not softened her stance despite increasing divisions within the Republican Party on the issue.

Her prominent role in the Elián González episode in 1999 and 2000 caused some consternation in her party. Social conservatives wanted the 5-year-old boy to be returned to his father in Cuba after he was pulled from the sea by rescuers helping a disabled boat full of refugees. Elián's mother drowned in the tragedy. Ros-Lehtinen and other Florida politicians made the case a cause célèbre, insisting — in vain — that the boy be allowed to stay with his U.S. relatives.

Ros-Lehtinen visited Elián several times, even attending his birthday party, and her efforts received the ultimate accolade for a Cuban-American legislator — a direct personal attack from Cuba's state-run newspaper, Granma, which called her a "ferocious wolf disguised as a woman." She had "loba feroz" (shortened to "loba frz") stamped on a vanity license plate.

Ros-Lehtinen's concern about Cuba is what originally motivated her to run for Congress. As chairwoman of the International Relations panel's Human Rights Subcommittee in the early 2000s, she pressed Cuba on its treatment of political dissidents and drew attention to the plight of dissidents in such countries as Pakistan, Northern Ireland and the Congo.

Ros-Lehtinen has clashed with the majority in her party who have pushed restrictive immigration policies. She and fellow Floridian Lincoln Diaz-Balart, also a Cuban-American, were among 17 House Republicans voting against a 2005 immigration bill that would have made it a crime to be in the United States without legal documents. In 2006, they were among six GOP members voting against construction of a 700-mile fence along the Mexican border. And in 1996, the two were the only House Republicans to vote against the final version of the welfare overhaul because it sharply restricted certain federal benefits to legal immigrants.

Although she opposes abortion and sides with social conservatives on most other issues, she parts ways with them on gay rights. The Florida Keys, home to a large gay population, were added to her district after the 2000 census, and Ros-Lehtinen has moved to cultivate her new constituents. In 2004, she did not participate in a House vote on a proposed constitutional amendment to ban same-sex marriage. Two years later, she was one of 27 Republicans to vote against a similar measure.

Ros-Lehtinen switched her tune on trade issues once Bush took office. In 1995, she voted against granting President Bill Clinton the power to negotiate trade agreements that Congress must consider on an expedited basis, without amendment; in 2002, she backed such authority for Bush. In 2000, she voted against granting China normal trade status. After Bush was in office, she supported most of his major trade proposals, including the controversial 2005 Central American Free Trade Agreement.

Ros-Lehtinen was 7 years old when her family fled Cuba for Florida. After growing up in Miami and graduating from college, she became a teacher and ran a bilingual private school in southern Florida. She fulfilled a 14-year dream in 2004 by completing a doctorate in education. Her dissertation topic: perspectives of U.S. House members on educational testing.

In 1982, at age 30, she was the first Hispanic elected to the state legislature. In a 1989 special election to replace the late Democratic Rep. Claude Pepper, Ros-Lehtinen defeated three other candidates to win the Republican nomination. With generous support from the national party, she beat Democrat Gerald Richman, a Jewish Miami Beach lawyer with limited political experience. She prepared well for her re-election campaign a year later, and several formidable Democrats declined to challenge her. Reapportionment in 2002 gave her a more demographically diverse district that includes the Keys, territory she welcomed because it is a common destination for Cuban refugees seeking asylum in the United States. She won in 2002 with 69 percent of the vote and prevailed in the past two elections with more than 60 percent.

KEY VOTES

2006

- No — Stop broadband companies from favoring select Internet traffic
- Yes — Affirm U.S. commitment to war in Iraq and reject setting a withdrawal date for troops
- No — Repeal requirement for bilingual ballots at the polls
- Yes — Permit U.S. sale of civilian nuclear technology to India
- No — Build a 700-mile fence on the U.S.-Mexico border to curb illegal crossings
- Yes — Permit warrantless wiretaps of suspected terrorists

2005

- Yes — Intervene in the life-support case of Terri Schiavo
- No — Lift President Bush's restrictions on stem cell research funding
- No — Prohibit FBI access to library and bookstore records
- Yes — Approve free-trade pact with five Central American countries
- No — Pass energy policy overhaul favored by President Bush emphasizing domestic oil and gas production
- Yes — End mandatory preservation of habitat of endangered animal and plant species
- Yes — Ban torture of prisoners in U.S. custody

CQ VOTE STUDIES

	PARTY UNITY		PRESIDENTIAL SUPPORT	
	Support	Oppose	Support	Oppose
2006	89%	11%	85%	15%
2005	91%	9%	79%	21%
2004	89%	11%	84%	16%
2003	93%	7%	96%	4%
2002	93%	7%	85%	15%

INTEREST GROUPS

	AFL-CIO	ADA	CCUS	ACU
2006	15%	15%	87%	63%
2005	20%	10%	93%	88%
2004	14%	15%	95%	80%
2003	13%	5%	90%	78%
2002	11%	10%	75%	88%

FLORIDA 18
Southeast – most of Miami; Florida Keys

The 18th features the glitz of downtown Miami and the southern part of Miami Beach, but its political base comes from the Hispanic-dominated areas west of downtown. The 18th winds its way south along the coast from Miami and follows U.S. 1 through the Florida Keys. A majority of residents were born outside of the United States, and more than three-fifths of the population is Hispanic, with many stridently anti-Castro.

The 18th's wide mix of areas includes downtrodden sections of Little Havana, where there has been some new residential development, as well as wealthy Coral Gables (home to the University of Miami), Key Biscayne and Fisher Island. Residents tend to be conservative on foreign policy issues but more in line with Democrats on welfare and other social issues. A strong economy that is not solely dependent on tourism has translated into little opposition for incumbents.

The Keys — a 120-mile-long island chain between the Gulf of Mexico and the Atlantic Ocean — and in particular Key West, have a significant gay and lesbian population, in addition to older natives who adhere to the independence and environmentalism of the "Conch Republic." The islands, as well as downtown Miami, suffered high winds, heavy rain and power outages from hurricanes Katrina, Rita and Wilma in 2005, and tourists and many residents evacuated during that storm season.

The Port of Miami and Miami International Airport, which is nearby in the 21st, are major transportation centers that feed the thriving trade and tourism industries. Concerns about port security have mounted since Sept. 11, as has the Port of Miami's traffic, particularly with the Pacific Rim. The port's trade with China has increased, and expanded service on routes to Europe began in late 2006. Local officials are concerned that the federal and state governments will not provide sufficient funds to meet the port's rising security needs.

MAJOR INDUSTRY
Trade, transportation, tourism

CITIES
Miami (pt.), 270,214; Miami Beach (pt.), 75,172; Coral Gables, 42,249; Westchester (unincorporated), 30,271; Key West, 25,478

NOTABLE
"Independence Day" celebrations in the Conch Republic honor the one-minute rebellion of Key West residents against a 1982 federal blockade.

Rep. Robert Wexler (D)

CAPITOL OFFICE
225-3001
www.house.gov/wexler
2241 Rayburn 20515-0919; fax 225-5974

COMMITTEES
Financial Services
Foreign Affairs
(Europe - chairman)
Judiciary

RESIDENCE
Boca Raton

BORN
Jan. 2, 1961, Queens, N.Y.

RELIGION
Jewish

FAMILY
Wife, Laurie Wexler; three children

EDUCATION
Emory U., attended 1978-79; U. of Florida, B.A. 1982 (political science); George Washington U., J.D. 1985

CAREER
Lawyer

POLITICAL HIGHLIGHTS
Fla. Senate, 1990-96

ELECTION RESULTS

2006 GENERAL

Robert Wexler (D)	unopposed

2006 PRIMARY

Robert Wexler (D)	unopposed

2004 GENERAL

Robert Wexler (D)	unopposed

PREVIOUS WINNING PERCENTAGES
2002 (72%); 2000 (72%); 1998 (100%); 1996 (66%)

Elected 1996; 6th term

Wexler has rarely seen a camera he didn't like, or a microphone that didn't merit a sound bite. He is so comfortable in the glare of media attention that he allowed a film crew from the Sundance Channel to shadow him and his staff for a year and a half for a six-part cable TV reality series called "The Hill" that began airing in August 2006. He did so, he said, to give the public a chance to "try to unlock, to a degree, the mystery of Congress."

There's no mystery to Wexler's views. He shares them readily, on subjects ranging from prescription drug prices to U.S. policy on Iraq to Palm Beach County's difficulties in administering elections in 2000 and 2002.

But it is on the subject of the Middle East that Wexler, who sits on the Foreign Affairs Committee, has been most vocal. For the Florida Democrat, whose district includes the heavily Jewish community of Boca Raton and parts of Palm Beach County, Middle East policy is virtually local politics. "That is the stuff I love talking about," Wexler says. He is the chairman of the Subcommittee on Europe.

He vigorously defended Israel's 2006 effort to root out Hezbollah fighters in Lebanon who had captured two Israeli soldiers. Wexler visited Israel three times over the summer, meeting with the brother of one of the captured soldiers. He also visited Boca Raton's sister city in northern Israel, Kiryat Bialik, which had been hit by rockets. He said he wanted to assure its residents that the United States would stand with them. "This conflict needs to be viewed in the much larger context of the fuller war on terror," he said.

Although he voted in 2002 to authorize the use of military force against Iraq, Wexler has lambasted the Bush administration's handling of the conflict. He voted against a 2004 resolution that said the United States and the world are safer with the removal of Saddam Hussein and his regime. And in 2005, he was one of just three House members to vote for a resolution calling for an immediate withdrawal from Iraq. Republicans had engineered the vote in an attempt to put Democrats in a bind, but Wexler said he was determined never to be trapped into a vote that could be construed as support for President Bush's "stay the course" war policy.

Florida's voting problems in 2000 and 2002 infuriated the congressman. He filed lawsuits challenging use of the new touchscreen voting machines in the state because they do not provide a paper record of ballots cast. He also introduced legislation to require that all electronic voting machines print paper records. Although the 11th U.S. Circuit Court of Appeals in June 2006 upheld a lower court ruling against his position, he appealed to the Supreme Court. "This is my greatest passion," Wexler said. "I won't stop." After the high court declined to hear the case, Wexler cosponsored a new bill requiring voting machines to produce a paper trail.

Wexler usually votes with a majority of House Democrats, but he irked party leaders in 2005 on a core issue — Social Security. They wanted to concentrate on bashing Bush's proposal for private accounts within Social Security, but he offered a bill to shore up the system's solvency by raising the payroll tax by 3 percentage points for people earning more than $90,000 a year. That amount, matched by similar employer contributions, would protect guaranteed benefits indefinitely, he said. He argued it wasn't enough to attack the Bush plan but that Democrats needed an alternative. "My view was Social Security was our home court advantage, and if we can't beat George Bush in a debate on Social Security, then I don't think I deserve to be in the U.S. Congress," he explained.

A member of the Judiciary Committee, Wexler made his first media splash during President Bill Clinton's impeachment. His staff estimates he was interviewed on television about 100 times during the six months the impeachment wars raged in Congress.

Wexler's penchant for publicity sometimes trips him up. In July 2006, during an appearance on The Comedy Channel's "Colbert Report," he was asked to say a few things that would "really lose the election for you if you were contested." It resulted in him saying, "I enjoy cocaine because it's a fun thing to do." Numerous people scolded him afterward, but the worst blow came from his teenage children. "They thought I was foolish," he said.

Wexler is one of Congress' most frequent travelers. The Center for Public Integrity ranked him 10th among lawmakers in the cost of privately paid trips between 2000 and 2005. He racked up the second-most costly trip of any member — a $29,951 five-day trip to Kazakhstan in 2002. Most of the expense was airfare for the congressman and his wife. He defended the trip as a way to foster ties with Kazakhstan, a moderate Muslim nation.

Born in Queens, Wexler was best friends as a young boy with the son of Republican Rep. Norman Lent. He recalls that at age 8 or 9 the two used to play a board game in which they pretended to run a presidential campaign. "I knew every state's electoral college vote count when I was 9 years old," Wexler says. A year later, when he was 10, his family moved to southern Florida. There was no special reason for the move; they just fell in love with the climate. "It must have been a particularly bad winter in New York," he says.

After earning his law degree at George Washington University, Wexler returned to Florida and practiced law in Boca Raton. In 1990, he unseated a 16-year veteran of the state Senate. During the ensuing six years, Wexler won generally favorable reviews, but he also drew fire for some controversial proposals. As chairman of the state Senate's Criminal Justice Committee, he proposed castration (via a chemical process, not surgery) for two-time rapists and electrocution for a third rape conviction. The head of the Florida chapter of the American Civil Liberties Union said, "He wants to adopt Islamic-style justice." But Wexler told the Orlando Sentinel, "What I'm proposing is just common sense."

When four-term Democratic Rep. Harry A. Johnston announced he would not seek re-election in 1996, Wexler leaped at the opening. In the ensuing four-way primary, he won a plurality of the vote, then handily defeated state Senate Majority Leader Peter Weinstein in the runoff. He rolled up two-thirds of the general-election vote against Republican Beverly Kennedy, a Pompano Beach financial consultant. He has won re-election easily since.

KEY VOTES

2006

- Yes Stop broadband companies from favoring select Internet traffic
- No Affirm U.S. commitment to war in Iraq and reject setting a withdrawal date for troops
- No Repeal requirement for bilingual ballots at the polls
- ? Permit U.S. sale of civilian nuclear technology to India
- Yes Build a 700-mile fence on the U.S.-Mexico border to curb illegal crossings
- No Permit warrantless wiretaps of suspected terrorists

2005

- No Intervene in the life-support case of Terri Schiavo
- Yes Lift President Bush's restrictions on stem cell research funding
- Yes Prohibit FBI access to library and bookstore records
- No Approve free-trade pact with five Central American countries
- No Pass energy policy overhaul favored by President Bush emphasizing domestic oil and gas production
- No End mandatory preservation of habitat of endangered animal and plant species
- Yes Ban torture of prisoners in U.S. custody

CQ VOTE STUDIES

	PARTY UNITY		PRESIDENTIAL SUPPORT	
	Support	Oppose	Support	Oppose
2006	93%	7%	30%	70%
2005	97%	3%	22%	78%
2004	97%	3%	32%	68%
2003	97%	3%	22%	78%
2002	89%	11%	29%	71%

INTEREST GROUPS

	AFL-CIO	ADA	CCUS	ACU
2006	100%	90%	33%	8%
2005	93%	100%	26%	0%
2004	85%	95%	37%	0%
2003	100%	95%	27%	16%
2002	100%	100%	32%	9%

FLORIDA 19

Southeast — parts of Coral Springs, Margate and Boca Raton

Two-thirds of the heavily Democratic 19th's residents live in Palm Beach County and one-third live in Broward County, mostly west of Interstate 95, where subdivisions and gated communities dot the landscape. The 19th has no coastline in either county, and it stretches from a small part of West Palm Beach as far south as a sliver of Fort Lauderdale, taking in parts of Boca Raton, Margate and Deerfield Beach. Older, upper-middle-class residents make it one of the most-educated and white-collar districts in the state.

The 19th has the highest percentage of residents age 65 or older (30 percent) of any district in the nation, and elderly voters make up more than 80 percent of the electorate in the 19th's portion of Palm Beach County. Also, the 19th's aging residents make health care an important industry in the district, and, along with Social Security, it dominates the political agenda.

The district's portion of Boca Raton long has been home to corporate headquarters and has a strong business atmosphere. Rexall Sundown, a vitamin producer, has a major facility here. Near the Florida Turnpike in Palm Beach County, new developments are replacing previously rural land in areas such as Boynton Beach.

The 19th, which excludes some of the wealthy gated communities in Boca Raton, is more than three-fourths white, and the 19th supports Democrats by overwhelming margins at state and national levels. Retirees, including many Jewish condominium residents, provide a consistent base of Democratic support throughout much of the district.

MAJOR INDUSTRY

Health care, financial services

CITIES

Coral Springs (pt.), 74,195; Margate (pt.), 42,284; Greenacres, 27,569; Tamarac (pt.), 25,756; Coconut Creek (pt.), 24,901

NOTABLE

A photo editor for The Sun, a supermarket tabloid, contracted the first fatal case of anthrax in 2001 while working at the newspaper's Boca Raton office; Cococut Creek is home to the world's largest butterfly aviary, called Butterfly World.

Rep. Debbie Wasserman-Schultz (D)

CAPITOL OFFICE
225-7931
www.house.gov/schultz
118 Cannon 20515-0920; fax 226-2052

COMMITTEES
Appropriations
(Legislative Branch - chairwoman)
Judiciary
Joint Printing

RESIDENCE
Weston

BORN
Sept. 27, 1966, Queens, N.Y.

RELIGION
Jewish

FAMILY
Husband, Steve Schultz; three children

EDUCATION
U. of Florida, B.A. 1988 (political science), M.A. 1990 (political science)

CAREER
University program administrator; college instructor; state legislative aide

POLITICAL HIGHLIGHTS
Fla. House, 1992-2000 (Democratic leader pro tempore, 2000); Fla. Senate, 2000-04

ELECTION RESULTS

2006 GENERAL		
Debbie Wasserman-Schultz (D)	unopposed	
2006 PRIMARY		
Debbie Wasserman-Schultz (D)	unopposed	
2004 GENERAL		
Debbie Wasserman-Schultz (D)	191,195	70.2%
Margaret Hostetter (R)	81,213	29.8%

Elected 2004; 2nd term

Wasserman-Schultz had a precocious freshman term in Congress, setting the stage for even more opportunities for her to impress Democratic leaders in her second term.

Speaker Nancy Pelosi recognized her potential as a standout among young members by giving her a seat on the Appropriations Committee, where she wound up as the chairwoman of the Legislative Branch Subcommittee, making her a member of the powerful "college of cardinals" who write the all-important spending bills. All of the other chairmen have served at least 16 years in the House.

She also was named one of nine chief deputy whips and chairs the "Frontline" program of the Democratic Congressional Campaign Committee, which focuses logistical and financial resources on key 2008 House races.

In her first term, she took a leading role in trying to stop conservatives in Congress from intervening in the case of Terri Schiavo, a severely brain-damaged Florida woman who was the subject of a major court case over end-of-life medical decisions. Well-versed in the long legal battle from her days in the Florida State Legislature, Wasserman-Schultz became a forceful opponent of intervention in the nationally watched Schiavo case in 2005.

By that time, Wasserman-Schultz had become a familiar figure on television programs such as "Face the Nation" and the "Today Show." She says that, "I had a lot of specific knowledge that kind of thrust me into a more public spotlight. . . . And then there was just momentum that built from there."

In June 2005, she landed a coveted seat on the Judiciary Committee. And she was asked by Patrick J. Leahy, the top-ranking Democrat on the Senate Judiciary panel, to be a witness in the closely watched Supreme Court confirmation hearing of Samuel A. Alito Jr., where a portion of the debate focused on his record on privacy issues. In the 110th Congress (2007-08), she was able to keep her seat on Judiciary while adding the Appropriations post.

Her first year on the Hill was dubbed "a political fairy tale" by The Miami Herald. The Jewish Daily Forward, a respected New York-based Yiddish and English newspaper, named her one of its 50 most-influential Jewish Americans of 2005, describing Wasserman-Schultz as "articulate with a trademark halo of curly blond locks."

Her youthful looks belie a tough partisanship, which she has shown on the Judiciary Committee by holding her own with conservatives on some of her priorities, such as the issue of separation of church and state. During committee debate in 2006 on a bill aimed at preserving the phrase "under God" in the Pledge of Allegiance, which had been ruled unconstitutional by a federal court, she scolded Republicans for ignoring "the things that people actually have to deal with in their daily lives, like gas prices, health care costs, fiscal responsibility, a real debate on Iraq."

Wasserman-Schultz has been knee-deep in politics since college and plays the Washington game with ease. Even before her own election to the House, she had donated $100,000 from her campaign funds to help other candidates during the 2004 election season, exceeding amounts given by many senior House Democrats. (She had cash to spare; she was unopposed in her primary and a shoo-in in the general election in the overwhelmingly Democratic 20th District.) Since then, she's kept up the practice, considered a prerequisite for landing a leadership job, donating more than $170,000 to Democrats with tough re-election battles in 2006.

Before her Frontline assignment with the DCCC, she had co-chaired its

"Red to Blue" initiative to recruit candidates in Republican-held districts for the 2006 elections. Wasserman-Schultz helped candidates raise money, offered advice and helped them find mentors among current House members.

In her first term, Wasserman-Schultz pursued her pet issue, swimming pool safety. She pressed for legislation giving federal grants to states that require fences around pools and devices that prevent children from becoming trapped in drains. On her favorite foreign affairs topic, Wasserman-Schultz is a vocal defender of Israel; her district includes the third-largest concentration of Jewish Americans in the country.

Policy affecting children is important to Wasserman-Schultz, who has a toddler and twins who were 7 in 2006. She flies to Washington on Tuesday mornings and back home to Weston on Thursday nights to maximize her time with her family. Her husband, Steve Schultz, a banker, stays with their children in Florida during the week.

She grew up in Lido Beach on the southern shore of Long Island. Her father was the chief financial officer for a girls' clothing company, Roanna Togs; her mother was a horticulturist. Wasserman-Schultz left the suburbs to attend college at the University of Florida, her father's alma mater. There, she abandoned her childhood dream of becoming a veterinarian — chemistry was her undoing — and shifted her studies to public policy. Since then, she says, she has "never really wanted to do anything other than be a member of a legislative body."

After graduation, she took a job as chief of staff with state Rep. Peter Deutsch, who became her mentor. When he left to campaign for the U.S. House, he persuaded her to run to replace him in the state legislature.

That first race in 1992 proved her toughest. Local party bosses dismissed her, and she raised only $21,000. Deutsch told her to ignore all that and apply shoe leather. Wasserman-Schultz estimates she knocked on 25,000 doors, taking notes about the conversations after she left, then mailing personal follow-up letters, sometimes cooing over a homeowner's dog or cat. She prevailed in a six-way Democratic primary, avoiding a runoff, and went on to become, at age 26, the youngest woman ever to serve in the Florida House. Eight years later, she moved up to the state Senate.

When Deutsch decided to run for the U.S. Senate in 2004, Wasserman-Schultz again ran for his seat. Name recognition and early fundraising deterred potential Democratic primary foes and her general election win over Republican Margaret Hostetter, a social-conservative activist, was never in doubt. The GOP didn't bother to field a challenger in 2006.

KEY VOTES

2006

- Yes Stop broadband companies from favoring select Internet traffic
- No Affirm U.S. commitment to war in Iraq and reject setting a withdrawal date for troops
- No Repeal requirement for bilingual ballots at the polls
- Yes Permit U.S. sale of civilian nuclear technology to India
- No Build a 700-mile fence on the U.S.-Mexico border to curb illegal crossings
- No Permit warrantless wiretaps of suspected terrorists

2005

- No Intervene in the life-support case of Terri Schiavo
- Yes Lift President Bush's restrictions on stem cell research funding
- Yes Prohibit FBI access to library and bookstore records
- No Approve free-trade pact with five Central American countries
- No Pass energy policy overhaul favored by President Bush emphasizing domestic oil and gas production
- No End mandatory preservation of habitat of endangered animal and plant species
- Yes Ban torture of prisoners in U.S. custody

CQ VOTE STUDIES

	PARTY UNITY		PRESIDENTIAL SUPPORT	
	Support	Oppose	Support	Oppose
2006	94%	6%	33%	67%
2005	94%	6%	24%	76%

INTEREST GROUPS

	AFL-CIO	ADA	CCUS	ACU
2006	100%	95%	40%	4%
2005	93%	100%	44%	0%

FLORIDA 20

Southeast — parts of Hollywood, Sunrise, Davie and Fort Lauderdale

Middle-class suburbs mix with beach communities as the 20th snakes through heavily Democratic territory in Broward and Miami-Dade counties from as far north as Tamarac to as far south as Miami Beach. The district takes in a slice of Fort Lauderdale and accounts for about one-third of Broward's population, much of it in suburbs such as Sunrise, Plantation and Davie. The westernmost areas in Broward teem with shopping centers and development as many former Miami residents have moved north in search of suburban life and reduced living costs.

In addition to those western Broward suburbs, the 20th wraps around to reach some coastal northeastern Miami suburbs, with their golf courses and condominium developments. It twists through portions of Hollywood and Hallandale and moves south into Aventura, which has a growing community of young professionals working in the booming financial and business services sector, and North Miami before jumping the Intracoastal Waterway to take in highly developed Bal Harbor and a chunk of northern Miami Beach. In August 2005, Hurricane Katrina made its first landfall over this coastal arm of the 20th.

Two-thirds of residents are white and about one-fifth are Hispanic, most of Cuban descent and strongly anti-Castro. The 20th's large Jewish population makes U.S.-Israel relations politically important. Wilton Manors has a significant gay and lesbian community, and Dania Beach is becoming a more prominent gay resort area.

Davie, with its cattle ranches in the central part of the 20th, has retained some of its rural feel. Plantation has more-expensive homes and light industry. Democrats tend to win elections in the 20th at all levels.

MAJOR INDUSTRY

Tourism, business services, retail

CITIES

Hollywood (pt.), 81,921; Sunrise (pt.), 71,670; Davie (pt.), 70,142; Plantation (pt.), 66,264; Weston, 49,286; Pembroke Pines (pt.), 37,466

NOTABLE

Dania Beach has an active community for the Basque game jai-alai, and its fronton, or playing arena, opened in 1953.

Rep. Lincoln Diaz-Balart (R)

Elected 1992; 8th term

Diaz-Balart's career-long quest to block archenemy Fidel Castro from getting any economic advantages from the United States got a little harder with the Democratic takeover of Congress. Some leading Democrats wanted to revisit the issue of sanctions that deny the ailing communist dictator access to tourism dollars and U.S. food supplies.

Diaz-Balart (DEE-az ba-LART) is a savvy inside operator on the Rules Committee, a leadership-backed panel heavily engaged in most major floor fights. But his passion is Cuban-American relations. He and Castro share a long and colorful personal and political history. Diaz-Balart hails from a prominent family of pre-revolutionary politicians who fled Cuba when Castro took power. And Diaz-Balart represents the fervently anti-Castro, Cuban-American community in south Florida. Castro's terminal illness, made public in 2006, did not soften those sentiments. Diaz-Balart expressed no sympathy for the "murderous thug."

Democrats want to review the hard-line policy toward Cuba that Diaz-Balart and his coalition in Congress have struggled to maintain: a ban on U.S. citizens traveling to Cuba and a four-decade-old embargo on trade with Cuba, which many farm-state lawmakers would like to suspend. "Our job will be tougher now," Diaz-Balart told the Sun Sentinel. "The Cuban dictator is going to have strong allies in positions of power in Congress."

Three other Cuban-American members of Congress share Diaz-Balart's feelings about Cuba, though he remains the ringleader — his younger brother, Rep. Mario Diaz-Balart, Republican Rep. Ileana Ros-Lehtinen, who represents parts of Miami, and Democratic Sen. Robert Menendez of New Jersey. Diaz-Balart believes there should be no easing of sanctions until Cuba frees its political prisoners, legalizes opposition parties and promises free elections.

So far, Diaz-Balart has been able to count on steady support from the White House. President Bush's political aides credited Diaz-Balart's Cuban-American constituents for putting Bush over the top in Florida in the 2000 presidential election. The White House in 2003 threatened to veto a year-end spending bill if it contained a provision easing travel to Cuba — a provision opposed by Diaz-Balart. The tactic worked; the provision was removed.

But even the Bush administration has occasionally disappointed Diaz-Balart. In 2006, he objected to a Treasury Department decision to allow Cuba to participate in a baseball tournament on American soil.

During the 109th Congress (2005-06), Diaz-Balart successfully pressed the administration to adopt a program aimed at allowing the defection of Cuban doctors living outside of Cuba. He also lobbied the Coast Guard to notify the Cuban-American relatives of people caught at sea trying to reach the United States. In 2001, Attorney General John Ashcroft yielded to pleas from Diaz-Balart and Ros-Lehtinen to try to strip Eriberto Mederos, a Cuban-American in Miami, of his U.S. citizenship for allegedly torturing political prisoners at a psychiatric hospital in Havana in the 1970s. It was the first such case in more than two decades.

Diaz-Balart is a skillful inside player. Drawing on his background as a prosecutor, he can be persuasive in face-to-face meetings. He moves easily in the arcane world of House rules and congressional organization. He is the second-ranking Republican on the Rules Committee, which sets the ground rules for floor debate. But his influence was much diminished when the Democrats took over in 2007. He calls his changed circum-

CAPITOL OFFICE
225-4211
diaz-balart.house.gov
2244 Rayburn 20515-0921; fax 225-8576

COMMITTEES
Rules

RESIDENCE
Miami

BORN
Aug. 13, 1954, Havana, Cuba

RELIGION
Roman Catholic

FAMILY
Wife, Cristina Diaz-Balart; two children

EDUCATION
U. of South Florida, B.A. 1976 (international relations); Case Western Reserve U., J.D. 1979

CAREER
Lawyer; state prosecutor

POLITICAL HIGHLIGHTS
Democratic nominee for Fla. House, 1982; Fla. House, 1986-89; Fla. Senate, 1989-92

ELECTION RESULTS

2006 GENERAL		
Lincoln Diaz-Balart (R)	66,784	59.5%
Frank J. Gonzalez (D)	45,522	40.5%
2006 PRIMARY		
Lincoln Diaz-Balart (R)		unopposed
2004 GENERAL		
Lincoln Diaz-Balart (R)	146,507	72.8%
Frank J. Gonzalez (LIBERT)	54,736	27.2%

PREVIOUS WINNING PERCENTAGES
2002 (100%); 2000 (100%); 1998 (75%); 1996 (100%); 1994 (100%); 1992 (100%)

stances in the minority "not necessarily pleasant."

On Rules, Diaz-Balart frequently led House floor debates for the Republicans, a plus for a party eager to showcase one of only four Hispanic members of their party in the House. He in turn leveraged the party's interest in wooing Hispanic voters to press for liberalized immigration policies out of the Republican mainstream.

In 2006, he was among a small minority of Republicans who voted against legislation to build a 700-mile fence along the U.S.-Mexico border and to classify illegal immigrants as criminals. He says "the immigration debate did hurt Republicans," particularly among Latino voters. He also broke with conservatives in his party in 2006 to support renewing a provision of the landmark 1965 Voting Rights Act that requires local governments to offer assistance to non-English speakers.

Florida's Cuban-American community is heavily Republican, but the working-class nature of his constituency can lead Diaz-Balart to stray from the party line. He was one of the few Republican House candidates in 1994 who declined to sign the "Contract with America," the GOP's political manifesto that year, and he bucked his party on the 1996 welfare overhaul, which imposed new restrictions on benefits to legal as well as illegal immigrants.

Diaz-Balart's grandfather, father and uncle served in Cuba's House before the family fled to the United States in 1959, the year of the revolution. The future congressman was 5 years old. His father's sister was married to Castro in the late 1940s and early 1950s, but they divorced and a falling-out between the families ensued. His father, Rafael Diaz-Balart, remained an exile leader of distinction. More than 1,000 people attended his funeral in Miami's Little Havana neighborhood in 2005 after he died of leukemia at age 79.

Diaz-Balart completed law school, then worked for a Miami legal services organization providing free legal help for the poor. He was a Dade County prosecutor in the early 1980s under Janet Reno, whom he frequently criticized during her time as attorney general under President Bill Clinton.

A Democrat in his early days in politics, Diaz-Balart was a co-chairman of the Democrats for Reagan campaign in Florida in 1984 and switched to the GOP in 1985, easily winning a state House seat in 1986. He served three years in the House and three in the state Senate.

When the courts redrew Florida's congressional maps after the 1990 census, a second Hispanic-majority district was created. Diaz-Balart easily bested a fellow Cuban-American state senator in a two-way Republican primary. He drew no Democratic foe that November, and since then has not faced a serious challenge.

KEY VOTES

2006

No Stop broadband companies from favoring select Internet traffic
Yes Affirm U.S. commitment to war in Iraq and reject setting a withdrawal date for troops
No Repeal requirement for bilingual ballots at the polls
Yes Permit U.S. sale of civilian nuclear technology to India
No Build a 700-mile fence on the U.S.-Mexico border to curb illegal crossings
Yes Permit warrantless wiretaps of suspected terrorists

2005

Yes Intervene in the life-support case of Terri Schiavo
No Lift President Bush's restrictions on stem cell research funding
No Prohibit FBI access to library and bookstore records
Yes Approve free-trade pact with five Central American countries
No Pass energy policy overhaul favored by President Bush emphasizing domestic oil and gas production
Yes End mandatory preservation of habitat of endangered animal and plant species
Yes Ban torture of prisoners in U.S. custody

CQ VOTE STUDIES

	PARTY UNITY		PRESIDENTIAL SUPPORT	
	Support	Oppose	Support	Oppose
2006	90%	10%	87%	13%
2005	90%	10%	81%	19%
2004	90%	10%	91%	9%
2003	95%	5%	94%	6%
2002	94%	6%	87%	13%

INTEREST GROUPS

	AFL-CIO	ADA	CCUS	ACU
2006	21%	15%	93%	60%
2005	14%	5%	89%	87%
2004	7%	10%	84%	83%
2003	13%	5%	90%	71%
2002	14%	15%	83%	88%

FLORIDA 21

Southeast – most of Hialeah and Kendall

The Hispanic-majority 21st is a Republican district on the eastern edge of the Florida Everglades that includes middle-class suburbs in Miami-Dade County and a slice of Broward County, from parts of Pembroke Pines and Miramar in the north through most of Hialeah in its center and much of the Colombian-American area of Kendall to the south. It includes one-fourth of Miami-Dade's population.

Many residents commute from Hialeah to other parts of the Miami area for work. Hialeah is Florida's fifth-largest city by population and is a vibrant, blue-collar residential area filled with Cuban-Americans. Miramar and Pembroke Pines host many young professionals from Latin America, and the 21st has the nation's largest percentage (57 percent) of foreign-born residents. Southern Florida's healthy economy has led to steady job creation and residential development in the district.

Transportation-related businesses, including Carnival Cruise Lines, have set up facilities close to Miami International Airport in Fountainbleau. The airport — a major international hub that carries more than 30 million passengers annually, many of them to Latin America — is a major employment source and economic driver in southern Florida. In late 2005, Hurricane Wilma damaged airport infrastructure and caused a several-day closure.

Traditionally, the 21st's politics center around immigration issues and opposition to Fidel Castro. Economic and foreign policy conservatism, however, are balanced somewhat by residents' more moderate views on labor and social policy matters. The district's large, suburban Cuban-American community accounts for its GOP bent in statewide and federal elections. Few areas in Florida are as heavily Republican as Hialeah, with its large base of elderly Cuban-American voters. George W. Bush carried the 21st by 16 percentage points in 2000 and by 14 points in 2004.

MAJOR INDUSTRY

Transportation, trade, small business

CITIES

Hialeah (pt.), 208,552; Kendall (unincorporated) (pt.), 59,676; Pembroke Pines (pt.), 54,246; Fountainbleau (unincorporated) (pt.), 52,244

NOTABLE

Amelia Earhart's final flight (1937) began in Hialeah; The Audubon Society has designated Hialeah Park as a sanctuary for the American flamingo.

Rep. Ron Klein (D)

CAPITOL OFFICE
225-3026
klein.house.gov
313 Cannon 20515-0922; fax 225-8398

COMMITTEES
Financial Services
Foreign Affairs

RESIDENCE
Boca Raton

BORN
July 10, 1957, Cleveland, Ohio

RELIGION
Jewish

FAMILY
Wife, Dori Klein; two children

EDUCATION
Ohio State U., B.A. 1979 (political science); Case Western Reserve U., J.D. 1982

CAREER
Lawyer; lobbyist

POLITICAL HIGHLIGHTS
Fla. House, 1992-96; Fla. Senate, 1996-2006 (minority leader, 2002-04)

ELECTION RESULTS

2006 GENERAL		
Ron Klein (D)	108,688	50.9%
E. Clay Shaw Jr. (R)	100,663	47.1%
Neil Evangelista (X)	4,254	2.0%
2006 PRIMARY		
Ron Klein (D)		unopposed

Elected 2006; 1st term

The minority leader of the Florida Senate for two years, Klein will be happy to be part of the House majority. In fact, he helped bring about the majority by toppling Republican E. Clay Shaw Jr., a 26-year House veteran.

Klein calls himself a "pro-business Democrat," and was rewarded for his election victory with a seat on the Financial Services Committee. Klein wanted the seat in order to focus on the issue of homeowners' insurance, a perennial problem in Florida. He hopes to come up with solutions that provide stability and competition in the Florida insurance market.

He also gained a seat on Foreign Affairs, where he expects to be an active participant in the Iraq War debate. He is a member of the Western Hemisphere Subcommittee, which he said was an important assignment for his area, home to many South and Central American immigrants. "Although the federal government has had pretty much a hands-off policy for the last number of years on South America, that is going to be changing," Klein said, citing changes in the governments of Venezuela, Nicaragua and Cuba.

Klein was born in Cleveland. He attended Ohio State University and Case Western Reserve. He worked as a lawyer but found himself drawn back to politics when he became involved in community organizations in Boca Raton. During college, he had interned for the Ohio General Assembly and later for Democratic Rep. Tom Luken.

Because of Shaw's status as a conservative Republican in a district that narrowly favored Massachusetts Sen. John Kerry for president in 2004, and the Democrats' recruitment of Klein — who had solid experience and strong fundraising skills — Democratic strategists targeted the race. Shaw had won over the years because of his focus on issues relevant to his large elderly constituency, including the future of Social Security.

But Klein made headway by criticizing Shaw's support for establishing personal savings accounts in the Social Security program, a plan favored by President Bush that drew little interest from Congress or the public. That fit into Klein's theme of tying Shaw closely to Bush. Klein won, taking 51 percent of the vote to Shaw's 47 percent.

FLORIDA 22

Southeast — coastal Broward and Palm Beach counties

The 22nd follows picturesque Route A1A down a sliver of Atlantic coastline from northern Palm Beach County to Fort Lauderdale in Broward County. Although its projections reach inland in places to pick up middle-class suburbs and gated communities, the district is recognized by its upscale beachfront areas, including parts of Boca Raton. Overwhelmingly white and mostly well-off, the 22nd has the highest median income in Florida and one of the nation's largest Jewish populations.

Republicans hold a slim voter registration edge here — strongest in the 22nd's portion of Palm Beach County — but overall, the district is politically competitive. John Kerry won the 22nd by 2 percentage points in the 2004 presidential election and the U.S. House seat flipped party control in 2006. Social Security, the Middle East and port issues top the political agenda here. Residents also are concerned about roads, as urbanization and development stretch the aging infrastructure and exacerbate heavy traffic problems.

The district has a corporate presence and is home to major transportation centers — Fort Lauderdale/Hollywood International Airport, Port Everglades and the Port of Palm Beach. It boasts ritzy hotels and shopping centers, and the ports attract cruise line and shipping business. Its elderly population, including many military veterans, supports several large hospitals. The wealth of many residents helps insulate them from economic pressures, but tourism is still vital to the area.

MAJOR INDUSTRY
Health care, tourism, shipping

CITIES
Fort Lauderdale (pt.), 61,509; Boca Raton (pt.), 55,946; Coral Springs (pt.), 43,354

NOTABLE
The International Swimming Hall of Fame Museum is in Fort Lauderdale.

Rep. Alcee L. Hastings (D)

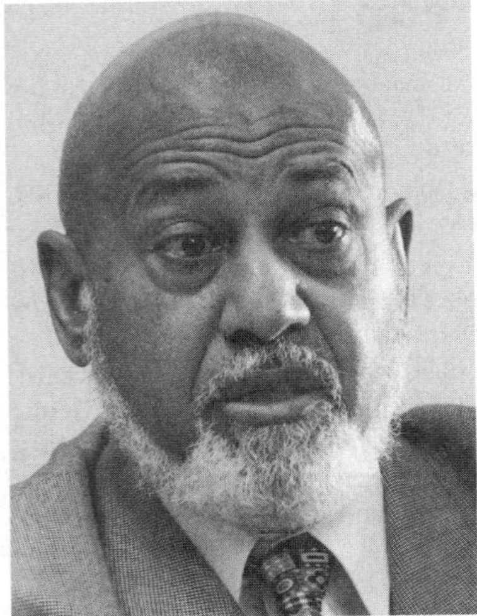

CAPITOL OFFICE
225-1313
alceehastings.house.gov
2353 Rayburn 20515-0923; fax 225-1171

COMMITTEES
Rules
(Legislative & Budget Process - chairman)
Select Intelligence

RESIDENCE
Miramar

BORN
Sept. 5, 1936, Altamonte Springs, Fla.

RELIGION
African Methodist Episcopal

FAMILY
Divorced; three children

EDUCATION
Fisk U., B.S. 1958 (zoology & botany); Howard U., attended 1958-60 (law); Florida A&M U., J.D. 1963

CAREER
Judge; lawyer

POLITICAL HIGHLIGHTS
Sought Democratic nomination for U.S. Senate, 1970; U.S. District Court judge, 1979-89; Democratic nominee for Fla. secretary of state, 1990

ELECTION RESULTS

2006 GENERAL

Alcee L. Hastings (D)	unopposed

2006 PRIMARY

Alcee L. Hastings (D)	unopposed

2004 GENERAL

Alcee L. Hastings (D)	unopposed

PREVIOUS WINNING PERCENTAGES
2002 (77%); 2000 (76%); 1998 (100%); 1996 (73%); 1994 (100%); 1992 (59%)

Elected 1992; 8th term

Though he is a nationally recognized champion of liberal causes and an inside player in the House, Hastings does not have the influence he might have were it not for a 1980s bribery case that resurfaces every time he goes for a promotion.

With the Democrats once again in the majority, the 110th Congress (2007-08) looked to be his chance for a top-tier role. But Hastings was denied the chairmanship of the Intelligence Committee after Republicans raised the issue of his past. While serving as a federal judge, Hastings was impeached by the U.S. House in 1988 and removed from office by the Senate the following year even though he had been acquitted of criminal charges related to the alleged bribery conspiracy.

Hastings lobbied hard for the Intelligence gavel, making the case that he was the best-qualified candidate. But in November 2006, President Bill Clinton called him and convinced Hastings to drop his bid for the sake of his party, which had campaigned against a "culture of corruption" in the Republican Congress. Hastings said he met with incoming Speaker Nancy Pelosi and told her he would bow out. She "thanked me, and she hugged me," he said. He had spared her a bruising battle with the Congressional Black Caucus, which was backing Hastings. (She later named Silvestre Reyes of Texas to the Intelligence chairmanship.) Still, he felt bitter about the outcome. "No one ever cared that I was found not guilty in a court of law, that I was innocent of what I was charged with," he said.

As consolation, in February 2007 Pelosi appointed Hastings chairman of the U.S. Commission on Security and Cooperation in Europe, better known as the Helsinki Commission. The previous year, he had wrapped up a second one-year term as the first American president of the Parliamentary Assembly of the OSCE, a 56-nation organization of mostly European nations that focuses on security issues, ranging from arms control to human rights. In that position, he visited nearly three dozen foreign countries, continuing his long-time interest in election monitoring in countries such as Azerbaijan, Ukraine and Belarus, where he led a group of 400 election monitors in March 2006.

His foreign trips cause him to miss many votes — at least two dozen on the final passage of legislation in 2005 alone, according to the Palm Beach Post. But Hastings told the Post that the trips are beneficial to voters back home and they allow him to present to other countries an alternative voice for the United States to that of the Bush administration.

Hastings is a sharp critic of President Bush's policies both at home and abroad. During the last half-dozen years of GOP control, he used his seat on the powerful Rules Committee to protest the substance of Republican legislation as well as the floor procedures used by GOP leaders against the minority. Two hours before Bush's 2005 State of the Union address, Hastings released a statement saying Bush should "tell the corporations and executives who bankrolled his re-election campaign and record-breaking $40 million inauguration spectacle that America's no longer for sale."

On Intelligence, his questions were among the most pointed in the House about the veracity of the administration's intelligence assessments of Iraq's possession of weapons of mass destruction. Hastings has also pushed for more cultural and ethnic diversity in recruiting new intelligence agents.

As a liberal Democrat from Florida, Hastings was not happy with the results of the past two presidential elections. After the bitter 2000 presidential contest, he led a walkout by members of the Congressional Black

Caucus to protest George W. Bush's victory over Al Gore, who, as vice president, presided over the House's formal election session. "We did all we could," Hastings called out to Gore. Hastings was also among the 31 House members to vote to challenge the results of Ohio's 2004 presidential vote, and thus the presidential election, when the electoral votes were counted in Congress.

Hastings arrived in the House in 1993 determined to impress the lawmakers who had impeached him five years before. "Succeeding is the best revenge," he once said. "My goal was to get beyond people viewing me as an impeached judge." To that end, in addition to focusing on foreign affairs, he concentrated on issues of particular concern to his constituents — funding for Medicare, job training, Head Start and sugar subsidies. In the 109th Congress (2005-06), he forcefully criticized the administration's response to hurricanes that struck Florida in 2004 and 2005 and opposed a Federal Aviation Administration plan to consolidate air traffic radar facilities in Miami and Palm Beach.

The congressman's local activism includes resisting what he sees as efforts by some white Florida Democrats to shift the state party to the right, diminishing the influence of black voters. He has several times urged African-Americans to consider voting for Republicans to send the party a signal that it should not take their support for granted.

The only child of undereducated parents who mostly toiled as domestic workers, Hastings earned a degree in zoology and botany at Fisk University, a predominately African-American college in Nashville, and was accepted to medical school. He chose to pursue a career in law instead. In 1979, President Jimmy Carter nominated Hastings for a U.S. District Court seat in Miami, and he became the first black federal judge in Florida.

In 1983, a jury acquitted Hastings of charges that he solicited a $150,000 bribe in exchange for granting a lenient sentence, but a federal judicial panel later concluded he had lied and made up evidence to secure that verdict. The vote was 413-3 in the House to impeach him and 69-26 in the Senate to remove him from office.

After losing a bid for Florida secretary of state in 1990, Hastings made a successful play in 1992 for the House seat representing the new 23rd District — drawn for the 1990s with a slight black majority. State Rep. Lois Frankel, a liberal white Democrat, took 35 percent of the vote to his 28 percent in the primary, but Hastings won the nomination in a runoff with 58 percent. Since then, he has run unopposed in four of the last seven elections, including 2004 and 2006.

KEY VOTES

2006

- No — Stop broadband companies from favoring select Internet traffic
- No — Affirm U.S. commitment to war in Iraq and reject setting a withdrawal date for troops
- No — Repeal requirement for bilingual ballots at the polls
- Yes — Permit U.S. sale of civilian nuclear technology to India
- No — Build a 700-mile fence on the U.S.-Mexico border to curb illegal crossings
- No — Permit warrantless wiretaps of suspected terrorists

2005

- No — Intervene in the life-support case of Terri Schiavo
- Yes — Lift President Bush's restrictions on stem cell research funding
- Yes — Prohibit FBI access to library and bookstore records
- No — Approve free-trade pact with five Central American countries
- No — Pass energy policy overhaul favored by President Bush emphasizing domestic oil and gas production
- No — End mandatory preservation of habitat of endangered animal and plant species
- Yes — Ban torture of prisoners in U.S. custody

CQ VOTE STUDIES

	PARTY UNITY		PRESIDENTIAL SUPPORT	
	Support	Oppose	Support	Oppose
2006	94%	6%	31%	69%
2005	96%	4%	21%	79%
2004	97%	3%	23%	77%
2003	96%	4%	23%	77%
2002	93%	7%	27%	73%

INTEREST GROUPS

	AFL-CIO	ADA	CCUS	ACU
2006	100%	95%	33%	8%
2005	93%	90%	31%	4%
2004	92%	55%	21%	0%
2003	100%	100%	19%	17%
2002	100%	95%	42%	0%

FLORIDA 23

Southeast – parts of Fort Lauderdale, West Palm Beach and Lauderhill

One of two black-majority districts in the state, the heavily Democratic 23rd stretches southwest from working-class Fort Pierce to the eastern shores of Lake Okeechobee and back east toward coastal hubs such as West Palm Beach and Fort Lauderdale. Most residents live in Broward County, and much of the area west of the Florida Turnpike, including a significant portion of the Everglades, is rural. The eastern borders of the 23rd tend to be several blocks off the coast, with the neighboring 22nd taking in much of the prime beachfront property.

Most urban areas in the 23rd — such as Lauderhill, Lauderdale Lakes, Riviera Beach and portions of West Palm Beach — contain largely black neighborhoods and attract local government employees, educators and other middle-class professionals. The 23rd is growing more diverse, drawing in many Hispanic and Caribbean immigrants. Citrus, sugar cane and rice growers work the large but sparsely populated rural portions of the district. The 23rd lacks a major employment sector, and the vulnerability of citrus crops to bad weather contributes to making it one of the poorest districts in the state. District residents, especially in Fort Lauderdale and towns bordering Lake Okeechobee, such as Pahokee, suffered significant property damage and home losses after Hurricane Wilma in 2005 and the ongoing recovery has been slow.

Democrats outnumber Republicans by a ratio of nearly 4-to-1, and voters routinely give Democratic candidates more than 75 percent of the vote in competitive statewide elections. Indeed, many heavily black precincts — including some in western Fort Lauderdale and Lauderdale Lakes — give Democratic candidates more than 90 percent of the vote. Overall, the district gave John Kerry 78 percent of its presidential vote in 2004.

MAJOR INDUSTRY

Agriculture, local government, small business

CITIES

Fort Lauderdale (pt.), 57,387; West Palm Beach (pt.), 52,330; Lauderhill (pt.), 47,371; North Lauderdale, 32,264; Lauderdale Lakes (pt.), 30,895

NOTABLE

Lake Okeechobee, part of which is in the 23rd, is the second-largest freshwater lake contained wholly within the United States.

Rep. Tom Feeney (R)

Elected 2002; 3rd term

CAPITOL OFFICE
225-2706
www.house.gov/feeney
323 Cannon 20515-0924; fax 226-6299

COMMITTEES
Financial Services
Judiciary
Science & Technology

RESIDENCE
Oviedo

BORN
May 21, 1958, Abington, Pa.

RELIGION
Presbyterian

FAMILY
Wife, Ellen Feeney; two children

EDUCATION
Pennsylvania State U., B.A. 1980 (political science); U. of Pittsburgh, J.D. 1983

CAREER
Lawyer

POLITICAL HIGHLIGHTS
Fla. House, 1990-94; Republican nominee for lieutenant governor, 1994; Fla. House, 1996-2002 (Speaker, 2000-02)

ELECTION RESULTS

2006 GENERAL		
Tom Feeney (R)	123,795	57.9%
Clint Curtis (D)	89,863	42.1%
2006 PRIMARY		
Tom Feeney (R)		unopposed
2004 GENERAL		
Tom Feeney (R)		unopposed

PREVIOUS WINNING PERCENTAGES
2002 (62%)

Feeney saw his star dim considerably in recent years after he was connected to disgraced lobbyist Jack Abramoff. It didn't help that he played a prominent role in the unpopular congressional effort to intervene in the case of Terri Schiavo, a brain-damaged Florida woman whom the courts ruled should not be kept alive by means of a feeding tube.

His biggest setback was the disclosure that he had accepted a golf trip to Scotland in 2003 from Abramoff, who was later convicted of fraud and other crimes. Feeney acknowledged he'd "gotten a black eye and been embarrassed" by his part in the influence-peddling scandal that unfolded in 2005 and 2006. After a House ethics committee investigation, Feeney agreed to pay the Treasury $5,643 for the trip. He was also hurt by his close alliance with former GOP Majority Leader Tom DeLay, who was indicted in Texas on campaign finance-related charges. "I thought Tom was the most important conservative congressman of our time," he said after DeLay resigned.

Earlier, in 2005, Feeney was out front among Republicans in siding with Schiavo's parents in a court fight with her husband, who wanted to remove the feeding tube that kept her alive. Congress tried to intervene, with Feeney declaring it had a "moral obligation" to do so, but the courts ruled that the tube could be removed, and Schiavo died. Polls showed that the public felt Congress should have stayed out of it.

Brash and ambitious, Feeney no doubt has a future in Republican politics if he can put the Abramoff affair behind him. He is a sharp legislative tactician, thanks to his years in the rough-and-tumble Florida House, and is unfazed by the nitty-gritty of legislating. Infatuated with politics since grade school, when Richard Nixon was his hero, Feeney rose to power at a precocious pace in Florida, ultimately becoming House Speaker and a pal of Gov. Jeb Bush, the president's brother.

His talent for a pithy quote gets him more than the usual share of media exposure for one relatively new to Capitol Hill, and he is a prolific fundraiser for the National Republican Congressional Committee, which helps elect fellow Republicans.

Feeney is an outspoken member of the Republican Study Committee, the most conservative bloc of House Republicans. He is a favorite of both the Christian Coalition and the Club for Growth, which advocates lower taxes and smaller government. In his office, Feeney keeps an early edition of economist Adam Smith's seminal 1776 book "Wealth of Nations," one of the classics he is fond of citing. He often mentions Plato and Aristotle at Judiciary Committee sessions, and tosses in Edmund Burke when an opening arises.

Believing in a limited role for government, he was one of 25 House Republicans to vote against President Bush's top domestic priority in 2003 — expanding Medicare to add a prescription drug benefit. He bucked a majority of his party in 2005 when he voted against a national energy policy overhaul featuring subsidies and tax breaks. In 2006, he opposed a combined estate tax reduction and minimum wage increase he said was too costly.

But he is not as adamant about government thrift when it comes to the space program, which employs thousands of people in his district. Feeney is a booster of the space shuttle and of Bush's call for a manned mission to the moon and to Mars. In May 2007 Feeney became the ranking Republican on the Science Committee's Space and Aeronautics Subcommittee.

A critic of "judicial activism," Feeney in his first term got legislation through Congress that made it harder for judges to depart from sentencing guidelines, a notable accomplishment for a freshman. The so-called Feeney Amendment was opposed by the American Bar Association and criticized by Chief Justice William H. Rehnquist. After a 2005 Supreme Court ruling rendered federal sentencing guidelines optional, Feeney denounced the decision and launched a new effort to curb the discretion of judges.

Feeney grew up in Glenside, a suburb of Philadelphia, the son of a community college dean and elementary schoolteacher. He played ice hockey and got hooked on politics at age 10, after portraying Nixon in a mock school election in 1968.

Liberalism may have been the fashionable campus philosophy during Feeney's undergraduate years at Penn State, but he was enamored of a Californian named Ronald Reagan. After graduation, he chose a law school — the University of Pittsburgh — for its reputation for turning out prominent Pennsylvania politicians. But with only middling grades in law school, Feeney abandoned his political plans and moved to Florida, where the economy was booming. He became a real estate lawyer and his wife Ellen — his law school-era sweetheart — became an engineer with a space contractor. The couple started a family.

Politics was still a fascination, however. "I was unsure whether a transplanted Yankee could make it in the Deep South," he recalls. "Then I get to Orlando and find out everybody's a transplanted Yankee." At age 32, he won his first election, to the Florida House in 1990. As a state legislator, he advocated parental consent for schools to teach yoga, which he said "hypnotized" children, and called for the state to secede if the national debt topped $6 trillion.

Feeney caught the eye of Jeb Bush, who was being talked about as a future governor and was leading an effort to establish tax-paid vouchers for education, Feeney's pet issue. In 1994, Bush picked Feeney as his lieutenant-governor running mate. Bush lost, but he and Feeney forged a strong political bond. In 1998, Bush became governor, and in 2000 Feeney rose to Florida House Speaker. He cemented his friend-of-the-Bushes status in the famously contested 2000 presidential election. After the state Supreme Court ruled against George W. Bush, Feeney asserted that the House had the power to appoint presidential electors for Bush. The U.S. Supreme Court later gave Bush the victory, rendering Feeney's move unnecessary.

When reapportionment in 2000 provided Florida two new congressional seats, Feeney used his power as Speaker to ensure one of the new districts was tailor-made for him. After a ferocious contest with Democrat Harry Jacobs, a personal-injury lawyer, Feeney won with 62 percent of the vote. He was unopposed in 2004, and in 2006 won with 58 percent of the vote.

KEY VOTES

2006

- No Stop broadband companies from favoring select Internet traffic
- Yes Affirm U.S. commitment to war in Iraq and reject setting a withdrawal date for troops
- Yes Repeal requirement for bilingual ballots at the polls
- Yes Permit U.S. sale of civilian nuclear technology to India
- Yes Build a 700-mile fence on the U.S.-Mexico border to curb illegal crossings
- Yes Permit warrantless wiretaps of suspected terrorists

2005

- Yes Intervene in the life-support case of Terri Schiavo
- No Lift President Bush's restrictions on stem cell research funding
- No Prohibit FBI access to library and bookstore records
- Yes Approve free-trade pact with five Central American countries
- No Pass energy policy overhaul favored by President Bush emphasizing domestic oil and gas production
- Yes End mandatory preservation of habitat of endangered animal and plant species
- No Ban torture of prisoners in U.S. custody

CQ VOTE STUDIES

	PARTY UNITY		PRESIDENTIAL SUPPORT	
	Support	Oppose	Support	Oppose
2006	96%	4%	90%	10%
2005	98%	2%	89%	11%
2004	99%	1%	88%	12%
2003	98%	2%	91%	9%

INTEREST GROUPS

	AFL-CIO	ADA	CCUS	ACU
2006	21%	10%	93%	96%
2005	14%	0%	81%	96%
2004	7%	0%	100%	100%
2003	8%	10%	93%	96%

FLORIDA 24

East central – Orlando suburbs, part of Space Coast

The 24th includes nearly 60 miles of Atlantic coastline before it sweeps west to take in much of the area between the so-called Space Coast and the Republican-leaning Orlando suburbs. It draws nearly equally from Orange, Seminole and Volusia counties, with just a bit less than one-fifth of its population coming from its portion of Brevard County. It picks up several suburban communities north or east of Orlando, including most of Altamonte Springs and all of Oviedo.

The Kennedy Space Center is the region's economic engine. The 2003 *Columbia* shuttle disaster and the troubled return-to-flight missions resulted in a re-examination of the future of a federally funded space program. Residents are concerned about how the retirement of NASA's Space Shuttle program in 2010, as well as the proposed Orion replacement program set to launch in 2014, will impact the thousands of district jobs that rely on the aerospace and technology industries.

Tourism is another important pillar of the local economy. Launches at Cape Canaveral are a huge draw, and the district's coastline and nature preserves attract eco-tourists and beach-seeking visitors from Orlando's resorts. In the north are popular beach communities and the city of Daytona Beach, most of which is in the neighboring 7th District. The 24th takes in one of Daytona Beach's jewels — Daytona International Speedway, home to NASCAR's Daytona 500 stock car race.

The district, with a relatively young population for Florida, is potentially politically competitive but has a distinct Republican lean in voter registration. The GOP nominee does well in presidential contests here, and George W. Bush captured 52 percent of the area's vote in 2000 before increasing his percentage by 4 points in 2004.

MAJOR INDUSTRY

Aerospace, tourism, technology

CITIES

Port Orange, 45,823; Titusville, 40,670; Altamonte Springs (pt.), 30,130; Oviedo, 26,316; Deltona (pt.), 22,510

NOTABLE

One of the Space Coast region's area codes is 321, deliberately chosen to mimic the countdown to liftoff.

Rep. Mario Diaz-Balart (R)

CAPITOL OFFICE
225-2778
www.house.gov/mariodiaz-balart
328 Cannon 20515-0925; fax 226-0346

COMMITTEES
Budget
Science & Technology
Transportation & Infrastructure

RESIDENCE
Miami

BORN
Sept. 25, 1961, Fort Lauderdale, Fla.

RELIGION
Roman Catholic

FAMILY
Wife, Tia Diaz-Balart; one child

EDUCATION
U. of South Florida, attended 1979-82

CAREER
Marketing firm executive; mayoral aide

POLITICAL HIGHLIGHTS
Fla. House, 1988-92; Fla. Senate, 1992-2000; Fla. House, 2000-02

ELECTION RESULTS

2006 GENERAL		
Mario Diaz-Balart (R)	60,765	58.5%
Michael Calderin (D)	43,168	41.5%
2006 PRIMARY		
Mario Diaz-Balart (R)		unopposed
2004 GENERAL		
Mario Diaz-Balart (R)		unopposed

PREVIOUS WINNING PERCENTAGES
2002 (65%)

Elected 2002; 3rd term

Diaz-Balart is not as prominent in the House as his older, better-known brother, Lincoln, but he is just as dedicated to maintaining the hard line against the Castro regime in Cuba — an article of faith for much of the Cuban-American community in Florida.

Unlike his brother, who was born in Cuba and lived there until the Diaz-Balart (DEE-az ba-LART) family was forced into exile by Fidel Castro, Mario was born in Fort Lauderdale. His district is heavily Cuban, but less so than the two other Hispanic-majority districts in southern Florida, represented by Lincoln and fellow Republican Ileana Ros-Lehtinen.

Like them, he often disagrees with the majority of his fellow Republicans on immigration issues. In 2005, he voted with Democrats against a bill that tightened rules for immigrants trying to obtain asylum, and he sharply criticized House GOP immigration legislation that would have made being an illegal immigrant a felony. Diaz-Balart said that was "offensive, excessive and demonized hardworking immigrants."

He has also pressed the Bush administration to renew temporary protected status for Hondurans, Nicaraguans and Salvadorans.

As a Florida House member heading the legislature's post-census reapportionment in 2000, Diaz-Balart drew the district himself, carving out a Republican slice of Miami-Dade County and rural areas to the west. Non-Cubans in gated communities miles from Miami's borders initially objected to being included. But Diaz-Balart has worked to win over constituents who are more concerned about their tax burdens than about Castro.

Diaz-Balart says cutting waste and fraud in government spending is a priority. But he isn't shy about seeking federal money for Florida projects. A member of the Transportation and Infrastructure Committee, he proudly trumpeted the $81.1 million authorized in the 2005 highway bill for expansion of Interstate 75 in southwest Florida. He also pushed for a provision in that bill designed to help Miami construct new metrorail routes worth $2.2 billion, plus $50 million aimed at returning trolleys to downtown. He told the Miami Herald that "both of these items are huge wins for the community."

An important parochial topic is the $7.8 billion Everglades restoration project. Within his district are vast tracts of Florida swamp, including Everglades National Park. The U.S. Army Corps of Engineers project seeks to restore an ecosystem that little by little has been destroyed by development, and Diaz-Balart regularly pursues appropriations for the project.

Diaz-Balart faced his first tough test as a junior House member in 2003 when senior Republicans on the Appropriations Committee restricted release of Everglades money — and he was unaware of the threat until the bill was less than 24 hours from a scheduled floor vote. His brother, a senior member of the Rules Committee who is close to GOP leaders, held up the bill while Mario scurried to assuage concerns about the project. He was able to reopen the funding spigot, claiming a victory back home.

He is quick-talking and gregarious in contrast to the more reserved Lincoln. The two are among four sibling pairs in Congress; the others are House Democrats Linda T. Sánchez and Loretta Sanchez of California, Colorado Democrats Sen. Ken Salazar and Rep. John Salazar and Sen. Carl Levin and Rep. Sander M. Levin, both Michigan Democrats.

Diaz-Balart will always be influenced by the politics of his family, sometimes called the Cuban Kennedys. Florida International University's new

$40 million law school building was named in honor of Diaz-Balart's grandfather, a decision school officials say was made as a tribute to Mario Diaz-Balart, who supported the school while serving in the state legislature. His father, Rafael Diaz-Balart, who died in 2005 at age 79, was once majority leader of the Cuban House, and his aunt was Castro's first wife and mother of Castro's son. According to Ann Louise Bardach's book, "Cuba Confidential: Love and Vengeance in Miami and Havana," the Cuban leader has jokingly boasted to foreign guests about having two nephews serving in Congress though he has also called the Diaz-Balarts his "most repulsive enemies." The Diaz-Balarts were a wealthy and politically prominent family under Cuban leader Fulgencio Batista, before Castro toppled Batista's government in 1959. Their home was looted and burned as the family vacationed in Paris.

As word of Castro's failing health spread in 2006, Diaz-Balart suggested the world was witnessing the regime's death throes. "If Cuba is a sugar cube, it is already in the water. It may not have disintegrated, but it's in the water." He urged the United States to maintain its strict embargo, arguing that lifting it would be akin to "putting an IV into the corpse of the regime."

He also strongly criticizes other regimes he considers oppressive. He voted against a proposed free-trade agreement with Vietnam in 2006. "I am in favor of free trade with free people, not with slave owners," he said. "It is an issue of human rights."

The youngest of four brothers, Diaz-Balart dropped out of the University of South Florida to work for the campaign of Miami Mayor Xavier Suarez. In 1988, he was elected to the Florida House, and four years later, to the state Senate. Forced out of the Senate by term limits in 2000, he ran successfully to return to the state House, which was not the step back it appeared to be. Florida got two new seats in Congress as a result of the once-a-decade census. Diaz-Balart was appointed by Florida House Speaker Tom Feeney to head the panel drawing a new congressional map. In some old-fashioned log-rolling, Diaz-Balart drew a Hispanic-majority district for himself and another GOP-leaning district in central Florida that Feeney ultimately won.

In Diaz-Balart's first House race, Annie Betancourt, a Democratic state representative who was also Cuban-American, challenged him in a contest that became a referendum on Cuba policy. Diaz-Balart supported continued U.S. sanctions while Betancourt, although equally anti-Castro, called for loosening economic and travel restrictions. Diaz-Balart outspent Betancourt 6-to-1, and won with 65 percent of the vote. Two years later, he was unopposed, and in 2006, he easily defeated his Democrat opponent.

KEY VOTES

2006

No Stop broadband companies from favoring select Internet traffic
Yes Affirm U.S. commitment to war in Iraq and reject setting a withdrawal date for troops
No Repeal requirement for bilingual ballots at the polls
Yes Permit U.S. sale of civilian nuclear technology to India
No Build a 700-mile fence on the U.S.-Mexico border to curb illegal crossings
Yes Permit warrantless wiretaps of suspected terrorists

2005

Yes Intervene in the life-support case of Terri Schiavo
No Lift President Bush's restrictions on stem cell research funding
No Prohibit FBI access to library and bookstore records
Yes Approve free-trade pact with five Central American countries
No Pass energy policy overhaul favored by President Bush emphasizing domestic oil and gas production
Yes End mandatory preservation of habitat of endangered animal and plant species
\+ Ban torture of prisoners in U.S. custody

CQ VOTE STUDIES

	PARTY UNITY		PRESIDENTIAL SUPPORT	
	Support	Oppose	Support	Oppose
2006	90%	10%	90%	10%
2005	94%	6%	87%	13%
2004	94%	6%	94%	6%
2003	97%	3%	98%	2%

INTEREST GROUPS

	AFL-CIO	ADA	CCUS	ACU
2006	14%	15%	93%	64%
2005	8%	5%	96%	92%
2004	7%	5%	95%	96%
2003	7%	10%	93%	88%

FLORIDA 25

South – western Miami-Dade County, the Everglades

The Hispanic-majority 25th takes in a broad swath of land covering the western portion of Miami-Dade County and almost all of Collier and Monroe counties' land area. Although geographically centered in Everglades National Park and Big Cypress National Preserve, nearly 90 percent of the population lives in Miami-Dade County, mostly on the western edge of the Miami region and in communities south of the city.

Although many residents commute to Miami for work, agriculture — especially the nursery and landscaping sector — is a mainstay for the local economy. The industry suffered a considerable blow in 2005 after hurricanes Katrina and Wilma caused hundreds of millions of dollars of damage to winter vegetables, fruit trees, sugar cane and nurseries; the industry is still recovering with the aid of federal disaster relief grants.

National parks give the 25th an ecosystem and array of wildlife — everything from manatees to panthers — not commonly found in North America, and they are significant tourist draws. Restoration of the Everglades, oil drilling and the pace of development will remain contentious issues here for the foreseeable future.

Many district residents are Cuban-American, and Republicans hold a party registration edge over Democrats here. Republican support for a hard line against Fidel Castro-led Cuba has helped the GOP forge a longstanding alliance with southern Florida's large Cuban-American community. Republicans have won the area in most statewide elections, especially those involving members of the Bush family. The 2004 presidential election was no different, as George W. Bush won the district with 56 percent of the vote.

MAJOR INDUSTRY
Agriculture, tourism

CITIES
Kendale Lakes (unincorporated), 56,901; Tamiami (unincorporated), 54,788; The Hammocks (unincorporated), 47,379

NOTABLE
Everglades National Park covers 1.5 million acres — which is just a small portion of the Everglades; The Coral Castle, located in Homestead, is a castle made from 1,100 tons of coral.

GEORGIA

Gov. Sonny Perdue (R)

First elected: 2002
Length of term: 4 years
Term expires: 1/11
Salary: $135,000
Phone: (404) 656-1776

Residence: Bonaire
Born: Dec. 20, 1946; Perry, Ga.
Religion: Baptist
Family: Wife, Mary Perdue; four children
Education: U. of Georgia, D.V.M. 1971
Military service: Air Force, 1971-74
Career: Fertilizer and grain business owner; veterinarian
Political highlights: Houston County Planning and Zoning Board, 1978-90; Ga. Senate, 1991-2001 (president pro tempore, 1997-99)

Election results:

2006 GENERAL		
Sonny Perdue (R)	1,229,724	57.9%
Mark Taylor (D)	811,049	38.2%
G. Michael Hayes (LIBERT)	81,412	3.8%

Lt. Gov. Casey Cagle (R)

First elected: 2006
Length of term: 4 years
Term expires: 1/11
Salary: $88,941
Phone: (404) 656-5030

LEGISLATURE

General Assembly: January-March, limit of 40 days

Senate: 56 members, 2-year terms
2007 ratios: 34 R, 22 D; 48 men, 8 women
Salary: $17,342
Phone: (404) 656-0028

House: 180 members, 2-year terms
2007 ratios: 106 R, 74 D; 142 men, 38 women
Salary: $17,342
Phone: (404) 656-0305

TERM LIMITS

Governor: 2 terms
Senate: No
House: No

URBAN STATISTICS

CITY	POPULATION
Atlanta	416,474
Augusta-Richmond	199,775
Columbus	186,291
Savannah	131,510
Athens-Clarke	101,489

REGISTERED VOTERS

Voters do not register by party.

POPULATION

2006 population (est.)	9,363,941
2000 population	8,186,453
1990 population	6,478,216
Percent change (1990-2000)	+26.4%
Rank among states (2006)	9
Median age	33.4
Born in state	57.8%
Foreign born	7.1%
Violent crime rate	505/100,000
Poverty level	13%
Federal workers	93,207
Military	96,952

REDISTRICTING

A new 13-district map was signed in to law by Gov. Perdue on May 3, 2005.

ELECTIONS

STATE ELECTION OFFICIAL
(404) 656-2871
DEMOCRATIC PARTY
(404) 870-8201
REPUBLICAN PARTY
(404) 257-5559

MISCELLANEOUS

Web: www.georgia.gov
Capital: Atlanta

U.S. CONGRESS

Senate: 2 Republicans
House: 6 Republicans, 6 Democrats
The 10th District seat is vacant.

2000 Census Statistics by District

DIST.	2004 VOTE FOR PRESIDENT BUSH	KERRY	WHITE	BLACK	ASIAN	HISP	MEDIAN INCOME	WHITE COLLAR	BLUE COLLAR	SERVICE INDUSTRY	OVER 64	UNDER 18	COLLEGE EDUCATION	RURAL	SQ. MILES
1	67%	33%	69%	25%	1%	4%	$34,912	53%	32%	16%	11%	27%	17%	43%	11,406
2	48	51	48	48	1	3	$29,843	50	34	17	12	28	14	42	10,841
3	70	29	76	19	1	2	$47,553	58	30	12	10	27	21	44	4,112
4	28	72	30	53	5	11	$47,943	62	24	14	7	27	29	2	330
5	25	74	34	56	2	6	$37,802	67	18	16	10	22	37	0	246
6	70	30	81	7	4	6	$71,699	78	13	9	7	26	51	7	681
7	69	30	76	12	5	6	$60,450	69	21	10	6	29	32	13	972
8	61	39	63	32	1	3	$36,294	53	32	15	12	27	16	43	7,171
9	77	22	86	3	1	9	$41,116	51	37	11	11	26	16	53	4,334
10	65	34	74	20	2	3	$36,615	56	30	14	12	24	23	50	5,892
11	71	29	80	12	1	5	$45,710	58	30	12	9	27	22	30	2,693
12	49.6	50.2	51	45	1	3	$30,383	49	33	18	11	27	14	40	8,657
13	39	61	47	41	3	8	$46,477	61	26	13	7	28	23	4	572
STATE	58	41	63	28	2	5	$42,433	59	27	13	10	27	24	28	57,906
U.S.	50.7	48.3	69	12	4	13	$41,994	60	25	15	12	26	24	21	3,537,438

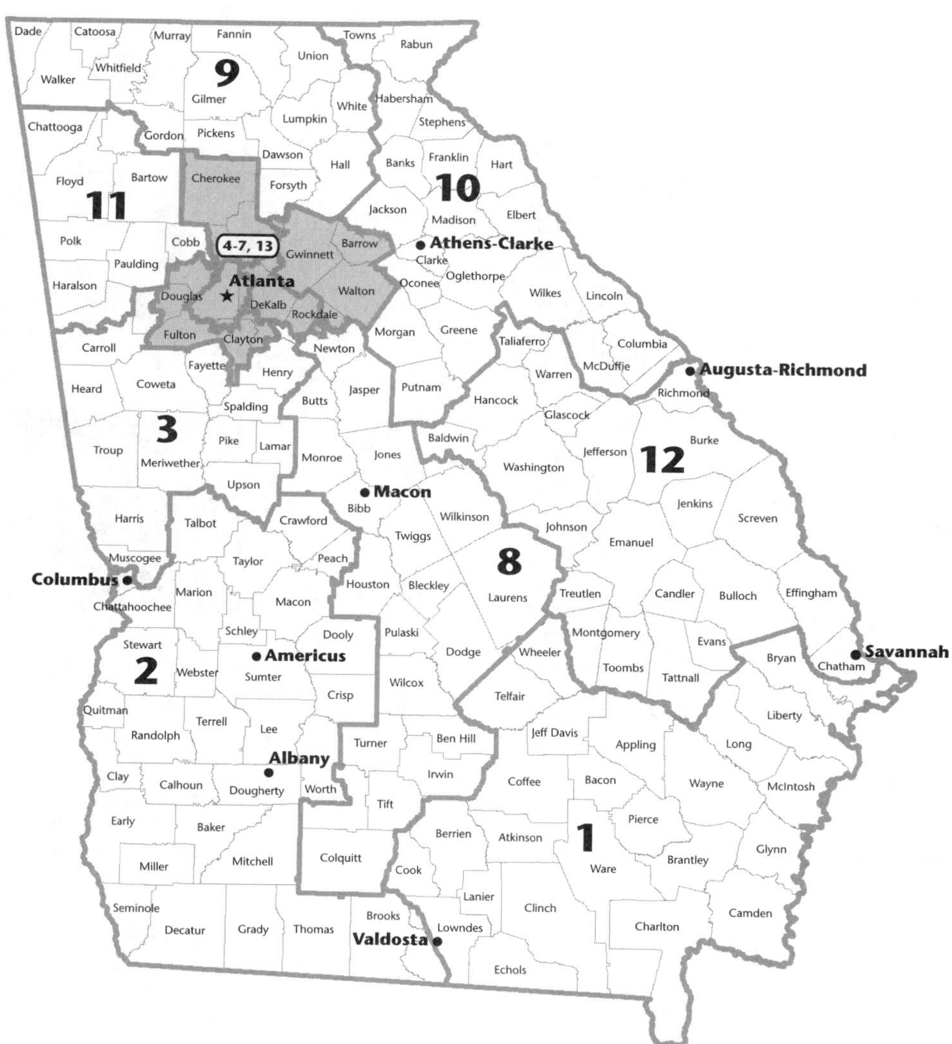
Dade
Catoosa
Murray
Fannin
Towns
Rabun
Union
Walker
Whitfield
9
Gilmer
White
Habersham
Stephens
Chattooga
Gordon
Pickens
Lumpkin
Dawson
Hall
Banks
Franklin
Hart
Floyd
Bartow
Cherokee
Forsyth
10
11
Jackson
Madison
Elbert
Polk
Cobb
4-7, 13
Gwinnett
Barrow
Athens-Clarke
Clarke
Paulding
Haralson
Atlanta
Douglas
DeKalb
Rockdale
Walton
Oconee
Oglethorpe
Wilkes
Lincoln
Carroll
Fulton
Clayton
Newton
Morgan
Greene
Taliaferro
Columbia
McDuffie
Augusta-Richmond
Richmond
Fayette
Henry
Heard
Coweta
Butts
Jasper
Putnam
Warren
Hancock
Glascock
Spalding
3
Troup
Pike
Lamar
Meriwether
Monroe
Jones
Baldwin
Washington
Jefferson
12
Burke
Upson
Macon
Bibb
Wilkinson
Harris
Talbot
Crawford
Twiggs
Johnson
Emanuel
Jenkins
Screven
Muscogee
Taylor
Peach
8
Columbus
Marion
Houston
Bleckley
Laurens
Treutlen
Candler
Bulloch
Effingham
Chattahoochee
Macon
Schley
Dooly
Pulaski
Montgomery
Evans
Stewart
Americus
Dodge
Wheeler
Toombs
Tattnall
Bryan
Savannah
Chatham
2
Webster
Sumter
Crisp
Wilcox
Telfair
Quitman
Terrell
Lee
Randolph
Turner
Ben Hill
Jeff Davis
Appling
Liberty
Long
Albany
Clay
Calhoun
Dougherty
Worth
Irwin
Coffee
Bacon
Wayne
McIntosh
Tift
Early
Baker
Berrien
Atkinson
1
Pierce
Glynn
Miller
Mitchell
Colquitt
Cook
Ware
Brantley
Lanier
Clinch
Camden
Seminole
Decatur
Grady
Thomas
Brooks
Lowndes
Charlton
Valdosta
Echols

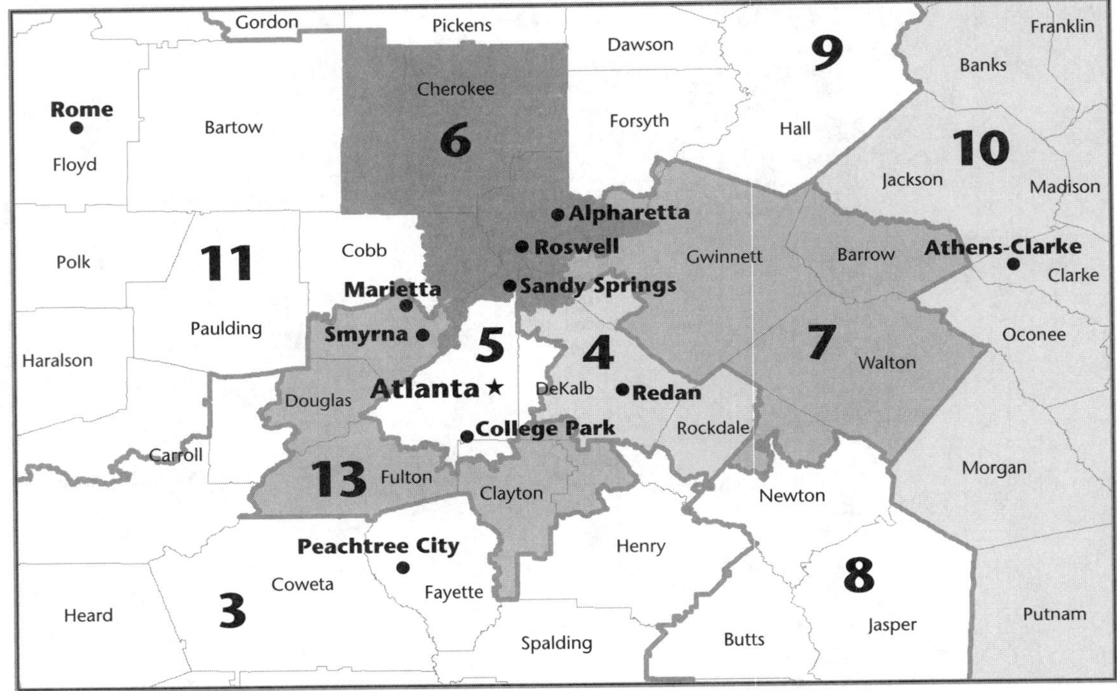
Gordon
Pickens
Dawson
Franklin
9
Banks
Cherokee
Rome
Bartow
Forsyth
Hall
6
10
Floyd
Jackson
Madison
Alpharetta
Roswell
Polk
11
Cobb
Gwinnett
Barrow
Athens-Clarke
Clarke
Marietta
Sandy Springs
Paulding
Smyrna
5
4
7
Oconee
Haralson
Walton
Atlanta
DeKalb
Redan
Douglas
College Park
Rockdale
Carroll
13
Fulton
Morgan
Clayton
Newton
Peachtree City
Henry
Coweta
8
Fayette
Heard
3
Putnam
Jasper
Butts
Spalding

Sen. Saxby Chambliss (R)

CAPITOL OFFICE
224-3521
chambliss.senate.gov
416 Russell 20510-1005; fax 224-0103

COMMITTEES
Agriculture, Nutrition & Forestry - ranking member
Armed Services
Rules & Administration
Select Intelligence
Joint Printing

RESIDENCE
Moultrie

BORN
Nov. 10, 1943, Warrenton, N.C.

RELIGION
Episcopalian

FAMILY
Wife, Julianne Chambliss; two children

EDUCATION
Louisiana Tech U., attended 1961-62; U. of Georgia, B.B.A. 1966 (business administration); U. of Tennessee, J.D. 1968

CAREER
Lawyer; hotel owner; firefighter; construction worker

POLITICAL HIGHLIGHTS
Sought Republican nomination for U.S. House, 1992; U.S. House, 1995-2003

ELECTION RESULTS

2002 GENERAL		
Saxby Chambliss (R)	1,071,352	52.7%
Max Cleland (D)	932,422	45.9%
Claude Thomas (LIBERT)	27,830	1.4%
2002 PRIMARY		
Saxby Chambliss (R)	300,371	61.1%
Bob Irvin (R)	132,132	26.9%
Robert "Bob" Brown (R)	59,109	12.0%

PREVIOUS WINNING PERCENTAGES
2000 House Election (59%); 1998 House Election (62%); 1996 House Election (53%); 1994 House Election (63%)

Elected 2002; 1st term

Chambliss is relatively new to the Senate, but he's an old hand at parsing farm policy, which is his primary focus as the Agriculture Committee undertakes a major overhaul of the farm bill governing commodity programs, conservation, farm credit and food stamps.

The Georgian is the top-ranking Republican on the panel, fresh from two years as its chairman in the 109th Congress (2005-06), when the GOP ran the Senate. He got the gavel a scant two years after he arrived in the Senate from the House, because more-senior panel Republicans held other chairmanships or leadership posts. His promotion was no doubt also helped by his 2002 defeat of incumbent Democratic Sen. Max Cleland in one of the most hotly contested races of the year.

Chambliss (SAX-bee CHAM-bliss) watches out for his agriculture-heavy state, a major producer of peanuts, cotton and tobacco. But regional differences, rather than party affiliations, often drive farm policy decision-making and the new chairman, Democrat Tom Harkin, is from Iowa.

Chambliss is especially focused on peanut farmers, whom he thinks were wronged in the last rewrite of the farm bill in 2002. Then, the old peanut subsidy program was ended and farmers were guaranteed no more than coverage of their losses for five years. At the time, Chambliss chaired the House Agriculture Subcommittee on General Farm Commodities and Risk Management. He was not afraid to mix it up with leaders of his own party, but he couldn't save the peanut subsidy program in spite of his influence as a negotiator on the final version.

Chambliss makes sure committee members have peanuts in mind when drafting bills. When he was chairman, he distributed the salty snacks during hearings and business sessions of the panel. But it takes more than a steady supply of peanuts to resolve the perennial intraparty fights over farm bills. Other powerful farm-state senators in late 2006 were calling for a cap of $250,000 on payments to individual farmers. Chambliss and other Southerners oppose caps because their staple crops, such as cotton and rice, cost more to produce than wheat and corn.

Chambliss had eight years of experience as a House member before coming to the Senate. Once there, he picked up where he had left off, landing assignments to three committees — Armed Services, Intelligence and Agriculture — directly paralleling those he had had in the House. He also was named to the Rules and Administration Committee, which tends to the Senate's operational needs. Chambliss quickly positioned himself as a loyal GOP foot soldier, consistently supporting President Bush's agenda and the Republican Party leadership. He is a down-the-line conservative on social issues, fiscal policy and regulatory matters.

In his first two years in the Senate, Chambliss served on the Judiciary Committee, where he headed the subcommittee that handles immigration policy. Although no longer on the panel, he played an active role in the Senate's 2006 debate on an immigration overhaul, focusing in particular on provisions affecting farm workers.

He opposed the bill that finally passed, objecting that it could eventually lead to citizenship for immigrants who are in the United States illegally. Chambliss says that when he spoke at a naturalization ceremony in 2005, he was approached by several of the new citizens, who all told him in effect, "Don't let someone who came here illegally get in line ahead of people like me who have worked so hard" to achieve citizenship. "That made a significant impression on me," Chambliss says.

On Armed Services, he looks out for the state's military installations, which have thrived since World War II, thanks partly to a nearly continuous presence of a Georgian on the committee. Cleland spent his one term there, succeeding Sam Nunn, who chaired the panel for eight years ending in 1994. Before him, Richard B. Russell was chairman in the 1950s and 1960s.

An avid quail, duck and dove hunter, Chambliss is a member of the Congressional Sportsmen's Caucus and sponsored legislation to establish a federal policy to promote hunting. He also is a big NASCAR fan.

The son of an Episcopal priest, Chambliss says his family's frequent moves to new church assignments when he was young made him learn to make friends quickly. "I grew up in a home where we didn't have a lot of money, but we had a lot of love and a lot of discipline," he says. "And I think those types of values helped shape me."

When he was five, his dad was the announcer for the Rock Hill Chicks, a minor league baseball club in North Carolina. Chambliss dreamed of becoming a baseball star. "I almost got there," he says wistfully: He played second base on the University of Georgia baseball team. In the year after college, he worked as a firefighter and as a construction worker to pay for law school. He also coached YMCA basketball and Little League baseball.

Chambliss spent much of his adult life before Congress as a small-town lawyer in rural southern Georgia, representing local farmers who grew commodity crops like peanuts and cotton. He got to know federal farm bills inside out. "I just kind of backed into this," he says of his agri-legal expertise. "No one else in town wanted to take the time to read the regulations and study the law and figure out how the farm bill operates. As a result, I developed a clientele all across south Georgia."

He lost his first bid for public office, when in 1992 he sought the Republican nomination to challenge Democratic Rep. J. Roy Rowland. But when Rowland retired in 1994, Chambliss captured an easy pickup for the GOP in that landslide year by defeating Democrat Craig Mathis, a lawyer and the son of former Rep. Dawson Mathis. Chambliss was the first Republican since Reconstruction to represent the rural middle Georgia district.

He declined entreaties to run for the Senate against Democrat Zell Miller in 2000. Chambliss chose to stay in the House at the urging of Speaker J. Dennis Hastert, and expected to be rewarded with the chairmanship of the Budget Committee. When that prize went instead to Jim Nussle of Iowa, Chambliss again began thinking about the Senate.

Three days after the Sept. 11 terrorist attacks, Chambliss' nascent challenge to Cleland got an important boost when Hastert picked Chambliss to chair a new Intelligence Subcommittee on Terrorism and Homeland Security. The panel was assigned one of the hottest topics on the national agenda — recommending ways that the CIA, FBI and National Security Agency could prevent future attacks.

Chambliss made one slip that could have cost him the election had he not turned things around. In an offhand remark viewed as insensitive, he quipped that one route to security would be for local sheriffs to "arrest every Muslim that comes across the state line."

Chambliss went on the attack against Cleland on the terrorism issue, alleging that the incumbent had gone soft on defense by opposing portions of Bush's plans to create a Department of Homeland Security. Democrats charged him with unfairly impugning the patriotism of Cleland, who had lost both legs and an arm in the Vietnam War. To this day, no congressional campaign of recent times rankles Democrats more. But Chambliss' focused campaign strategy, combined with a massive Republican voter turnout effort, propelled him to a 7 percentage point victory.

KEY VOTES

2006

Yes Confirm Samuel A. Alito Jr. to the Supreme Court

Yes Allow consideration of a bill to establish a $140 billion trust fund to compensate victims of asbestos exposure

Yes Extend tax cuts for two years at a cost of $70 billion over five years

No Overhaul immigration policy with border security, enforcement and guest worker program

Yes Allow consideration of a bill to permanently repeal the estate tax

No Urge President Bush to begin troop withdrawals from Iraq in 2006

No Lift President Bush's restrictions on stem cell research funding

Yes Authorize military tribunals for suspected terrorists

2005

Yes Curb class action lawsuits by shifting them from state to federal courts

Yes Allow confirmation vote on Priscilla R. Owen to the U.S. Court of Appeals for the 5th Circuit

Yes Oppose mandatory emissions limits and block recognition of global warming as a threat

Yes Approve free-trade pact with five Central American countries

Yes Pass energy policy overhaul favored by President Bush emphasizing domestic oil and gas production

Yes Shield gunmakers from lawsuits when their products are used in crimes

Yes Ban torture of prisoners in U.S. custody

Yes Renew 16 provisions of the Patriot Act

Yes Allow final vote on opening the Arctic National Wildlife Refuge to oil and gas exploration

CQ VOTE STUDIES

	PARTY UNITY		PRESIDENTIAL SUPPORT	
	Support	Oppose	Support	Oppose
2006	94%	6%	93%	7%
2005	95%	5%	91%	9%
2004	99%	1%	100%	0%
2003	97%	3%	97%	3%
House Service:				
2002	98%	2%	90%	10%
2001	98%	2%	93%	7%
2000	95%	5%	24%	76%
1999	94%	6%	26%	74%
1998	95%	5%	22%	78%
1997	96%	4%	26%	74%

INTEREST GROUPS

	AFL-CIO	ADA	CCUS	ACU
2006	13%	0%	92%	96%
2005	21%	5%	94%	96%
2004	0%	5%	93%	96%
2003	15%	5%	91%	90%
House Service:				
2002	0%	0%	90%	100%
2001	17%	0%	95%	100%
2000	0%	0%	90%	91%
1999	33%	10%	80%	80%
1998	0%	0%	94%	96%
1997	0%	5%	88%	88%

Sen. Johnny Isakson (R)

CAPITOL OFFICE
224-3643
www.isakson.senate.gov
120 Russell 20510-1006; fax 228-0724

COMMITTEES
Environment & Public Works
Foreign Relations
Health, Education, Labor & Pensions
Small Business & Entrepreneurship
Veterans' Affairs

RESIDENCE
Marietta

BORN
Dec. 28, 1944, Atlanta, Ga.

RELIGION
Methodist

FAMILY
Wife, Dianne Isakson; three children

EDUCATION
U. of Georgia, B.B.A. 1966 (real estate)

MILITARY SERVICE
Ga. Air National Guard, 1966-72

CAREER
Real estate company president

POLITICAL HIGHLIGHTS
Candidate for Cobb County Commission, 1974; Ga. House, 1977-90 (Republican leader, 1983-90); Republican nominee for governor, 1990; Ga. Senate, 1993-96; sought Republican nomination for U.S. Senate, 1996; Ga. Board of Education chairman, 1996-99; U.S. House, 1999-2005

ELECTION RESULTS

2004 GENERAL		
Johnny Isakson (R)	1,864,202	57.9%
Denise L. Majette (D)	1,287,690	40.0%
Allen Buckley (LIBERT)	69,051	2.1%
2004 PRIMARY		
Johnny Isakson (R)	346,670	53.3%
Herman Cain (R)	170,370	26.2%
Mac Collins (R)	133,952	20.6%

PREVIOUS WINNING PERCENTAGES
2002 House Election (80%); 2000 House Election (75%); 1999 Special House Election (65%)

Elected 2004; 1st term

Friendly, folksy and committed to consensus-building, Isakson has never pursued a hard-line approach to legislating. His determination to do whatever it takes to get a job done has helped him navigate the political shoals in Georgia and in Congress, whether his party is in control or not.

"I try to be pragmatic on the issues and conservative in my philosophy," he says. "You can beat your chest all you want to, but if four is a majority, then three equals zero." He'd rather "try to make things happen" than demand ideological purity and wind up with nothing.

He has made quite a bit happen during his Senate term and the nearly three House terms that preceded it, not to mention earlier in his career back home. His years as a leader in Georgia politics and in Congress have been characterized by a passion for education reform, which remains a top priority. He was chairman of the Georgia Board of Education from 1996 to 1999, and as a member of the House he helped write the final version of the landmark 2001 No Child Left Behind education law, working closely with Democratic Sen. Edward M. Kennedy, among others. He is eager to revise and renew the law during the 110th Congress (2007-08).

Isakson also worked closely with Kennedy, now chairman of the Health, Education, Labor and Pensions Committee on which both men serve, on two major issues in 2006 — an overhaul of the federal law governing private pension plans and a rewrite of mine safety standards. He labored successfully to ensure that the final pension measure included provisions to help Atlanta-based Delta Air Lines, which was operating under bankruptcy court protection. The law gave Delta and other financially strapped airlines extra time to fully fund their pension plans, which otherwise could have been dumped on the federal Pension Benefit Guaranty Corporation, shifting the burden to taxpayers.

In the days before the final vote, Isakson prowled the halls of the Capitol, tracking down senators who had placed "holds" on the bill, blocking a floor vote. "I tried to open a dialogue," he told The Atlanta Journal-Constitution. "Slowly, each one dropped their holds." When the measure finally cleared by a 93-5 vote on the eve of the August recess, Isakson went back to his Capitol Hill apartment to do his laundry before leaving town for the month. He celebrated with a gin and tonic in the laundry room.

Earlier in 2006, Isakson, then chairman of the Employment and Workplace Safety Subcommittee, went to West Virginia two days after an explosion at the Sago Mine killed a dozen coal miners. Isakson, Kennedy, West Virginia Democrat John D. Rockefeller IV and Wyoming Republican Michael B. Enzi talked to miners' families, the company and other experts. Within months, they had steered a new mine safety law to enactment.

Isakson, a multimillionaire former real estate executive, attributes his passion for education to his father, Edwin Andrew Isakson, a high school dropout. After his older sister died as a young child, his father repeatedly told Isakson he was destined to be the first in the family to attend college. The elder Isakson bought season tickets to Georgia Tech football games, then deliberately parked two miles away so he could walk his son across the campus to the stadium. Isakson's father would point to the buildings and say, "One day you're going to go to a school like this."

Isakson began his focus on education early in his House career. Though he was the lowest-ranking Republican on the Education and the Workforce Committee in the 106th Congress (1999-2000), he was the driving force behind a proposal to help states pay for federally mandated school modernization costs such as asbestos removal and outfitting buildings for disabled students. Committee Republicans were resisting Democratic plans for the federal government to pay for the school repairs, but Isakson saw the potential political impact of the construction issue and convinced GOP leaders that they would lose the debate without their own proposal.

Meanwhile, he kept an eye on district concerns. He promoted federal grants for programs like one in Dalton, Ga., that hired Mexican teachers to teach immigrant students who cannot speak English. He used his seat on the Transportation and Infrastructure panel to get more funds for traffic-clogged Atlanta. He also badgered Georgia officials to bring Atlanta into compliance with the Clean Air Act, a requirement for getting federal highway funds.

He has continued to pursue local highway funding as a Senate Environment and Public Works Committee member, snagging $92 million for Atlanta-area projects in the 2005 surface transportation bill.

Isakson ranked among the top 10 Senate Republicans in the 109th Congress (2005-06) in his support of President Bush and his loyalty to the Republican Party. In the 110th Congress, he was granted a seat on the Foreign Relations Committee, where he backed Bush's plan to commit more than 21,000 additional U.S. combat troops to the war in Iraq.

But Isakson sometimes is even more conservative on fiscal matters than GOP leaders. Despite his own efforts to bring federal funds to his district, he has sought to curb the practice of larding measures with last-minute earmarks, funds directed to home-state projects. In the House, he registered his opposition to earmarks by voting against catchall spending measures, which he said made it easier to stuff pet projects into the federal budget.

Isakson has cut a national profile only recently, but has long been a fixture in Georgia politics. He was in the General Assembly for almost 17 years and was the GOP candidate for governor in 1990. He was defeated by Zell Miller, the Democratic lieutenant governor at the time. In 1996, he sought the Republican nomination for the U.S. Senate but lost. "I pretty much figured my political career was over," he says. "That was two statewide races I had lost." But Miller fired the state school board members and asked Isakson to take the chairman's job. "So I say, well, heck, I'll do that . . . and I was pretty successful."

In 1999, Isakson was the immediate front-runner to succeed House Speaker Newt Gingrich, who resigned from his seat under fire from his Republican colleagues after the party's loss of seats in the 1998 midterm elections. Enjoying a huge advantage in name recognition and campaign funds, Isakson carried 65 percent of the vote against five opponents in the 1999 special election. He easily cruised to re-election in 2000 and 2002.

Miller, meanwhile, had completed two terms as governor when he was appointed and then later elected to serve out the term of GOP Sen. Paul Coverdell, who died July 18, 2000. The conservative Democrat, who voted with Republicans more often than not, chose to retire rather than run in 2004. Isakson jumped into the race, challenged by two Republicans — businessman Herman Cain and 8th District Rep. Mac Collins — who claimed he was too liberal. Isakson took 53 percent of the vote, avoiding a runoff, and defeated one-term Democratic Rep. Denise L. Majette with 58 percent.

Isakson and Republican Saxby Chambliss, Georgia's senior senator, share a friendship dating back to their days as students at the University of Georgia in 1962. "We know a lot on each other we can never tell," Isakson says with a smile, noting that their sorority-sister wives also have been fast friends since 1963. Chambliss helped in Isakson's unsuccessful campaign for governor against Miller.

KEY VOTES

2006

Yes Confirm Samuel A. Alito Jr. to the Supreme Court
Yes Allow consideration of a bill to establish a $140 billion trust fund to compensate victims of asbestos exposure
Yes Extend tax cuts for two years at a cost of $70 billion over five years
No Overhaul immigration policy with border security, enforcement and guest worker program
Yes Allow consideration of a bill to permanently repeal the estate tax
No Urge President Bush to begin troop withdrawals from Iraq in 2006
No Lift President Bush's restrictions on stem cell research funding
Yes Authorize military tribunals for suspected terrorists

2005

Yes Curb class action lawsuits by shifting them from state to federal courts
Yes Allow confirmation vote on Priscilla R. Owen to the U.S. Court of Appeals for the 5th Circuit
Yes Oppose mandatory emissions limits and block recognition of global warming as a threat
Yes Approve free-trade pact with five Central American countries
Yes Pass energy policy overhaul favored by President Bush emphasizing domestic oil and gas production
Yes Shield gunmakers from lawsuits when their products are used in crimes
Yes Ban torture of prisoners in U.S. custody
Yes Renew 16 provisions of the Patriot Act
Yes Allow final vote on opening the Arctic National Wildlife Refuge to oil and gas exploration

CQ VOTE STUDIES

	PARTY UNITY		PRESIDENTIAL SUPPORT	
	Support	Oppose	Support	Oppose
2006	97%	3%	93%	7%
2005	95%	5%	91%	9%
House Service:				
2004	99%	1%	89%	11%
2003	99%	1%	96%	4%
2002	94%	6%	85%	15%
2001	97%	3%	90%	10%
2000	91%	9%	30%	70%
1999	87%	13%	29%	71%

INTEREST GROUPS

	AFL-CIO	ADA	CCUS	ACU
2006	13%	0%	92%	96%
2005	21%	5%	94%	100%
House Service:				
2004	8%	5%	100%	95%
2003	0%	5%	100%	84%
2002	0%	5%	100%	96%
2001	9%	5%	100%	88%
2000	0%	5%	85%	72%
1999	13%	10%	91%	66%

Rep. Jack Kingston (R)

CAPITOL OFFICE
225-5831
jack.kingston@mail.house.gov
www.house.gov/kingston
2368 Rayburn 20515-1001; fax 226-2269

COMMITTEES
Appropriations

RESIDENCE
Savannah

BORN
April 24, 1955, Bryan, Texas

RELIGION
Episcopalian

FAMILY
Wife, Libby Kingston; four children

EDUCATION
U. of Georgia, B.A. 1978 (economics)

CAREER
Insurance broker

POLITICAL HIGHLIGHTS
Ga. House, 1984-92

ELECTION RESULTS

2006 GENERAL		
Jack Kingston (R)	94,961	68.5%
Jim Nelson (D)	43,668	31.5%
2006 PRIMARY		
Jack Kingston (R)		unopposed
2004 GENERAL		
Jack Kingston (R)		unopposed

PREVIOUS WINNING PERCENTAGES
2002 (72%); 2000 (69%); 1998 (100%); 1996 (68%); 1994 (77%); 1992 (58%)

Elected 1992; 8th term

With a quick wit and informal, easygoing personality, Kingston is a regular on the late-night talk and comedy show circuit. He may need his sense of humor in the 110th Congress (2007-08) now that Democrats control the agenda and he is no longer in the House Republican leadership.

In the 109th Congress (2005-06), he served as vice chairman of the Republican Conference, the organization of all House Republicans that, among other things, seeks to enhance the GOP's public image. But he fell short in a bid for the conference chairmanship in November 2006, losing to fellow conservative Adam Putnam of Florida by 100-91 on the third ballot.

Kingston, who chaired the House GOP's "Theme Team," a group responsible for spreading the party's message in the 109th Congress, is finding other ways to publicize Republican viewpoints. He is ahead of many colleagues in using and appearing on alternative media, saying it is the best way to reach unaffiliated voters. Kingston was a regular guest on "Politically Incorrect," the old late-night ABC talk show with liberal host Bill Maher, and he also appears on Maher's new HBO show, "Real Time with Bill Maher." Kingston was also the first congressman to go on "Better Know a District," a recurring segment on "The Colbert Report," comedian Stephen Colbert's fake-news show on Comedy Central. He also is a frequent guest on conservative mainstays such as Rush Limbaugh's radio show.

Kingston has embraced the new media world by blogging on his congressional Web site and producing podcasts, audio programs that can be downloaded, on which he discusses legislation and current events. His legislative interns produce an occasional amateur video documentary, called "Journeys with Jack," and post it on the video Web site YouTube.com. "Blogs are like political gasoline," Kingston says. "If you have a blog in place, when something happens you can react quickly and it's unfettered access. On a day-to-day message, blogs might not sometimes drive the message like you want, but when there's a crisis or a hot issue they will."

As a member of the Appropriations Committee, Kingston does his best to protect Georgia's interests. He tried, unsuccessfully, to add a provision to the fiscal 2007 agriculture appropriations bill to help peanut farmers pay for crop storage. Peanut and cotton crops help sustain his district's economy. On the Agriculture Appropriations Subcommittee, where he is the top Republican in the 110th Congress, Kingston is sometimes at odds with fellow Republicans who view federal crop subsidy programs for crops like peanuts as antithetical to free enterprise.

Georgia is home to 12 military bases, and Kingston took on former President Jimmy Carter over Carter's defense of the New London Naval Submarine Base in Groton, Conn., where Carter had served in the submarine force. The Pentagon recommended that the Connecticut base be closed, but the Base Realignment and Closure Commission voted to keep it open, with some commissioners citing a letter from Carter in the base's behalf. If the Connecticut base had closed, more than 3,000 jobs would have gone to Kings Bay Naval Submarine Base in Kingston's district.

In an August 2005 op-ed in the Atlanta Journal-Constitution, Kingston wrote, "It is disappointing for anyone, including Carter, to inject an emotional attachment, however heartfelt, into a decision that should be made on the facts and what is best for the future, not the past, of our military forces."

Kingston and Democrat Sanford D. Bishop Jr. are the only Georgians on Appropriations, where they both serve on the Agriculture and Defense subcommittees. Kingston's influence took a hit even before the Democratic takeover in 2007. When Republicans restructured the Appropriations subcommittees in 2005, they eliminated the Legislative Branch Subcommittee, which Kingston had chaired. He was left without a gavel. A strong fiscal conservative, he had used the legislative branch spending bill as an example of restraint. His final bill, produced in 2004, was one of the few spending bills that came close to honoring President Bush's request for increases of less than 1 percent in spending — a point of pride for Kingston.

Although he voted with a majority of his party on 96 percent of votes splitting the two parties in the 109th Congress, Kingston sometimes goes his own way. He was one of 38 Republicans in 2005 to vote in favor of a proposal preventing law enforcement officers from using funds to search library and bookstore records. On a different issue, he sided with House party leaders against his fellow Georgia Republicans. Georgia and Texas Republicans led the revolt in 2006 against efforts to renew the 1965 Voting Rights Act without amendment. Kingston was the only Georgia Republican to vote in favor of its renewal, siding with top leaders of both political parties.

He credits the voting rights law with opening up the political process to Southern Republicans as well as African-Americans. "If not for the Voting Rights Act, I don't think I would be in Congress," he said. He was also a key Republican to sign on to Georgia Democrat John Lewis' proposal for an African-American museum on the National Mall, approved in 2003.

Born in Texas, where his father was an art professor, Kingston and his family spent a few months in Ethiopia — his father was working with the Education Department to help set up schools in the African country — before settling in Georgia when Kingston was a toddler.

After earning an undergraduate degree in economics, Kingston moved to Savannah to sell insurance. He won election in 1984 to the state House, where he served eight years. When Democrat Lindsay Thomas retired in 1992, Kingston was well positioned to woo voters into the Republican column in a House race; many of them already had been voting Republican for president. Kingston drew minor primary opposition, then dispatched Democrat Barbara Christmas, a school principal. His 58 percent share of the vote that year remains his lowest election percentage.

Redistricting after the 2000 census put Kingston and GOP colleague Saxby Chambliss in the same House district, but Chambliss opted for the Senate. The new 1st District had an even more Republican flavor and Kingston won easily in 2002 and 2004. More redistricting in 2006 didn't really alter the district and he prevailed with more than two-thirds of the vote.

KEY VOTES

2006

? Stop broadband companies from favoring select Internet traffic

Yes Affirm U.S. commitment to war in Iraq and reject setting a withdrawal date for troops

Yes Repeal requirement for bilingual ballots at the polls

Yes Permit U.S. sale of civilian nuclear technology to India

Yes Build a 700-mile fence on the U.S.-Mexico border to curb illegal crossings

Yes Permit warrantless wiretaps of suspected terrorists

2005

Yes Intervene in the life-support case of Terri Schiavo

No Lift President Bush's restrictions on stem cell research funding

Yes Prohibit FBI access to library and bookstore records

Yes Approve free-trade pact with five Central American countries

Yes Pass energy policy overhaul favored by President Bush emphasizing domestic oil and gas production

Yes End mandatory preservation of habitat of endangered animal and plant species

No Ban torture of prisoners in U.S. custody

CQ VOTE STUDIES

	PARTY UNITY		PRESIDENTIAL SUPPORT	
	Support	Oppose	Support	Oppose
2006	95%	5%	97%	3%
2005	98%	2%	85%	15%
2004	97%	3%	91%	9%
2003	98%	2%	94%	6%
2002	98%	2%	85%	15%

INTEREST GROUPS

	AFL-CIO	ADA	CCUS	ACU
2006	7%	5%	100%	92%
2005	15%	0%	92%	88%
2004	0%	0%	100%	96%
2003	0%	10%	97%	88%
2002	0%	0%	85%	96%

GEORGIA 1

Southeast – Valdosta, Savannah suburbs

As recently as two decades ago, the 1st was a Democratic stronghold of peanut and tobacco farmers. Today, the 1st still relies heavily on agriculture, but its voters now overwhelmingly favor Republicans. Spanning 25 counties in southeast Georgia, the 1st takes in all of the state's coastline to the east, part of the border with Florida to the south, and primarily rural areas to the north and west. After mid-decade redistricting prior to the 2006 election, the 1st shed a sliver of land running north almost to Macon and acquired two rural northern counties and the rest of Bryan County, near Savannah.

The 1st's economy is wedded to agriculture — tobacco, peanuts, cotton, carrots and blueberries are among the important crops here. Valdosta, almost all of which is now in the 1st, is a growing city that is home to health care facilities, a state university and major retailers. Manufacturing also retains a presence in the district, and the 1st's military influence is strong, with three of the state's major military bases.

Tourism is important here, as retirees and well-off visitors flock to a string of islands known for golf courses and resorts off the coast of Brunswick. Regional tourism hubs Savannah and Brunswick also have active ports (Savannah's is in the neighboring 12th). The district's ports and coastline make trade and coastal conservation dominant issues.

The 1st is reliably Republican, with GOP strength in Camden and Glynn counties on the coast and Chatham and Bryan counties near Savannah. Democrats can win, especially at the local level, in Liberty and McIntosh counties and in the 1st's newly acquired Telfair and Wheeler counties. Rep. Kingston won every county except Telfair in 2006.

MAJOR INDUSTRY

Agriculture, military, manufacturing, tourism

MILITARY BASES

Fort Stewart (Army), 17,760 military, 3,170 civilian (2007) (shared with the 12th); Kings Bay Naval Submarine Base, 4,426 military, 3,635 civilian (2006); Moody Air Force Base, 4,278 military, 375 civilian (2006)

CITIES

Valdosta (pt.), 43,708; Hinesville, 30,392; Savannah (pt.), 20,894

NOTABLE

The Okefenokee Swamp — roughly 7000 years old — covers 438,000 acres and is home to about 10,000 alligators and 233 species of birds.

Rep. Sanford D. Bishop Jr. (D)

CAPITOL OFFICE
225-3631
bishop.email@mail.house.gov
www.house.gov/bishop
2429 Rayburn 20515-1002; fax 225-2203

COMMITTEES
Appropriations

RESIDENCE
Columbus

BORN
Feb. 4, 1947, Mobile, Ala.

RELIGION
Baptist

FAMILY
Wife, Vivian Creighton Bishop; one stepchild

EDUCATION
Morehouse College, B.A. 1968 (political science); Emory U., J.D. 1971

MILITARY SERVICE
Army, 1971

CAREER
Lawyer

POLITICAL HIGHLIGHTS
Ga. House, 1977-91; Ga. Senate, 1991-93

ELECTION RESULTS

2006 GENERAL		
Sanford D. Bishop Jr. (D)	88,662	67.9%
Bradley C. Hughes (R)	41,967	32.1%
2006 PRIMARY		
Sanford D. Bishop Jr. (D)		unopposed
2004 GENERAL		
Sanford D. Bishop Jr. (D)	129,984	66.8%
Dave Eversman (R)	64,645	33.2%

PREVIOUS WINNING PERCENTAGES
2002 (100%); 2000 (53%); 1998 (57%); 1996 (54%); 1994 (66%); 1992 (64%)

Elected 1992; 8th term

With his independent voting record, Bishop has resisted pigeonholing throughout his congressional career. A centrist in a predominately liberal party, he has built a durable base of support in his diverse constituency by paying close attention to his district's agriculture and military interests.

Bishop's voting record paints him as the most conservative black member of Congress, with a middle-of-the-road philosophy that cuts across a variety of economic and social issues. He breaks ranks with his fellow Democrats more often than any other member of the Congressional Black Caucus, and is the caucus member who most often votes in support of President Bush. But then, he represents a district that twice voted for Bush.

Bishop and fellow Georgia Democrat David Scott are the only black members of the coalition of conservative House Democrats known as the Blue Dogs. Bishop has won commendations from the National Federation of Independent Business and the American Legion for his legislative stands, and in the 109th Congress (2005-06) he was named by the U.S. Chamber of Commerce as one of 10 House Democrats with the most probusiness voting records.

Bishop did not vote for Bush's 2001 and 2003 tax cuts, but in 2004, he was one of the first Democrats to indicate he would vote for the corporate tax overhaul bill. In 2006, he was one of just 27 Democrats voting to permit oil drilling in the Arctic National Wildlife Refuge. He was one of 34 in his party who voted that year for a proposed constitutional amendment to ban same-sex marriage.

On certain core issues, however, Bishop aligns with his fellow Democrats. He supports abortion rights and has taken labor's side on certain issues, such as his opposition to the 2005 Central American Free Trade Agreement.

Bishop and another Blue Dog, Marion Berry of Arkansas, were named to the Appropriations Committee in 2003 as part of an effort by then Minority Leader Nancy Pelosi to award choice committee assignments to all factions of the party. To take the seat, Bishop had to leave the Agriculture and Intelligence panels.

He had served on Intelligence since 1997 and had been in line to be its top-ranking Democrat in both the 107th (2001-02) and the 108th (2003-04) Congresses. On the first occasion, Pelosi, who ranked just ahead of Bishop, declined to step down from the top slot when she became Democratic whip late in 2001. A year later, he was passed over when the top spot went to Jane Harman of California. After the 2006 elections, Bishop's name figured in speculation about the chairmanship, though he no longer served on Intelligence. But Pelosi settled on Silvestre Reyes of Texas instead.

In the 110th Congress (2007-08), Bishop's assignments on Appropriations include the Agriculture, Defense and Military Construction-VA subcommittees. Bishop supports a healthy defense budget and looks out for the interests of the 2nd District's Fort Benning, the Army's huge infantry training base, as well as Moody Air Force Base, which was in the 2nd before redistricting put it just across the 1st District line in 2001.

Fort Benning was a winner in the 2005 round of military base closures and consolidations. It will be taking in additional units from other bases, and the area around the base is expected to grow by as many as 30,000 people. Bishop has worked to funnel more dollars to the region to prepare for the influx.

More peanuts are grown in the 2nd District than in any other congressional district — considerably more than a quarter of the nation's output — and on Agriculture, Bishop played a crucial role in protecting peanut farmers when their subsidy program was overhauled in 2002. The farm bill that year did away with the Depression-era peanut program, which had kept prices high by effectively limiting who could grow peanuts to those who held a government quota. But Bishop was able to include a new market support program, in addition to a cash payment as a buyout of the quota, and requirements that foreign peanuts be labeled.

Bishop grew up in Mobile, Ala., where his parents were both educators. His father was the president of a community college that is now named for him — Bishop State Community College. His mother was the college librarian. In 2003, his first year as an appropriator, the younger Bishop secured $75,000 for a technology center at the college.

While he was at Emory University Law School, Bishop spent a summer interning with the NAACP's Legal Defense Fund in New York. After earning his law degree, he practiced civil rights law in Columbus, Ga., representing inmates at a state prison whose 1972 lawsuit resulted in a Supreme Court decision ordering reforms at the overcrowded facility.

Bishop was elected to the state legislature in 1976, serving for 16 years. He was on the Reapportionment Committee that, with stern urgings from the Justice Department, in 1992 drew new congressional district maps that made the 2nd District the state's third black-majority district. Columbus business leaders persuaded Bishop to seek the new seat and helped finance his challenge to white Democratic Rep. Charles Hatcher, who had been identified as one of the chief abusers of the House's private bank, with 819 overdrafts. In a primary runoff against Hatcher, Bishop won the nomination with 53 percent of the vote; in November, he coasted past Republican physician Jim Dudley.

In 1995, a federal court found the new lines to be an unconstitutional "racial gerrymander" and handed down a revised map that put Columbus in the 3rd District. The black share of the population in the redrawn 2nd dropped from 51 percent to 39 percent. Bishop moved about 90 miles southeast to Albany, in the center of the 2nd.

He weathered some tough re-election fights in 1996, 1998 and 2000. But redistricting following the 2000 census was good to Bishop, putting part of Muscogee County, his longtime home, back in the 2nd District and increasing the black share of the population to 44 percent. He was unopposed in 2002 and, in subsequent redistricting for the 2006 election, his district was made even more Democratic.

KEY VOTES

2006

No Stop broadband companies from favoring select Internet traffic
Yes Affirm U.S. commitment to war in Iraq and reject setting a withdrawal date for troops
No Repeal requirement for bilingual ballots at the polls
Yes Permit U.S. sale of civilian nuclear technology to India
Yes Build a 700-mile fence on the U.S.-Mexico border to curb illegal crossings
No Permit warrantless wiretaps of suspected terrorists

2005

Yes Intervene in the life-support case of Terri Schiavo
Yes Lift President Bush's restrictions on stem cell research funding
Yes Prohibit FBI access to library and bookstore records
No Approve free-trade pact with five Central American countries
Yes Pass energy policy overhaul favored by President Bush emphasizing domestic oil and gas production
Yes End mandatory preservation of habitat of endangered animal and plant species
Yes Ban torture of prisoners in U.S. custody

CQ VOTE STUDIES

	PARTY UNITY		PRESIDENTIAL SUPPORT	
	Support	Oppose	Support	Oppose
2006	72%	28%	63%	37%
2005	77%	23%	47%	53%
2004	78%	22%	57%	43%
2003	80%	20%	44%	56%
2002	80%	20%	52%	48%

INTEREST GROUPS

	AFL-CIO	ADA	CCUS	ACU
2006	93%	65%	87%	64%
2005	80%	85%	74%	45%
2004	69%	55%	79%	35%
2003	100%	75%	57%	44%
2002	78%	75%	55%	40%

GEORGIA 2

Southwest – Albany, part of Columbus, Valdosta suburbs

The racially diverse and Democratic-leaning 2nd sits in southwestern Georgia, extending south from Talbot and Crawford counties and running along the Alabama border on the west before reaching the Florida line. Although mostly rural, the 2nd takes in the cities of Albany and Americus and more than half of Columbus.

Despite losing three heavily agricultural counties in redistricting prior to the 2006 election, the struggling farming industry is still the economic lifeline of the 2nd — more than 25 percent of the nation's peanuts are grown in the district. Farmers here also grow wheat, cotton, soybeans and tobacco, and a new $170 million ethanol plant in Mitchell County is expected to produce 100 million gallons of ethanol annually.

Big-name manufacturers and retailers increasingly factor into the 2nd's economy, and the district's two military bases also play a vital role. Fort Benning (shared with the 3rd) and the Marine Corps base in Albany have begun expanding operations as a result of the 2005 BRAC round.

Slightly less than half of the 2nd's population is black, and the mid-decade redistricting led to a stronger Democratic lean here. The 2nd gained Democratic Macon, Marion and Peach counties, and lost Turner, Tift and Colquitt counties, which all lean Republican. Pockets of GOP strength exist in centrally located Lee County, as well as in Thomasville and other southern parts of the district. Dougherty County, whose county seat is Albany, is the district's most populous and is reliably Democratic. John Kerry would have narrowly won the new 2nd with 51 percent of the vote here in the 2004 presidential election.

MAJOR INDUSTRY
Agriculture, military, manufacturing, health care

MILITARY BASES
Fort Benning (Army), 49,149 military, 7,140 civilian (shared with the 3rd); Marine Corps Logistics Base, 516 military, 1,854 civilian (2004)

CITIES
Columbus (pt.), 119,135; Albany, 76,939; Thomasville, 18,162

NOTABLE
Jackie Robinson, who broke baseball's color barrier in 1947, was born in Cairo; Sylvester hosts the annual Georgia Peanut Festival every October.

Rep. Lynn Westmoreland (R)

CAPITOL OFFICE
225-5901
westmoreland.house.gov
1213 Longworth 20515-1008; fax 225-2515

COMMITTEES
Oversight & Government Reform
Small Business
Transportation & Infrastructure

RESIDENCE
Grantville

BORN
April 2, 1950, Atlanta, Ga.

RELIGION
Baptist

FAMILY
Wife, Joan Westmoreland; three children

EDUCATION
Georgia State U., attended 1969-70

CAREER
Construction company owner;
real estate developer

POLITICAL HIGHLIGHTS
Sought Republican nomination for Ga. Senate, 1988; Republican nominee for Ga. Senate, 1990; Ga. House, 1993-2005 (minority leader, 2001-03)

ELECTION RESULTS

2006 GENERAL		
Lynn Westmoreland (R)	130,428	67.6%
Mike McGraw (D)	62,371	32.4%
2006 PRIMARY		
Lynn Westmoreland (R)		unopposed
2004 GENERAL		
Lynn Westmoreland (R)	227,524	75.6%
Silvia Delamar (D)	73,632	24.5%

Elected 2004; 2nd term

Apparently no one told Westmoreland that freshmen are supposed to sit in the back and defer to the wisdom of their party elders. In his first term in Congress, Westmoreland picked fights with several powerful committee chairmen, lost his title as a deputy whip on the second day on the job, and forced Republican leaders to repeatedly postpone a bipartisan bill renewing the landmark Voting Rights Act.

Westmoreland says he didn't intentionally make mischief, rather he felt his positions were "important enough to fight for." And in his view, bipartisanship is overrated. "I'm not a bipartisan kind of guy," he says. "I'm not saying if [the Democrats] didn't have a good idea, I wouldn't vote for it. I just haven't heard them have a good idea." His independence won him plaudits from conservatives back home, and his name has cropped up as a possible candidate for governor in 2010. An Atlanta Journal-Constitution columnist called him a "breath of fresh air that politics needs."

In the House, senior GOP lawmakers were not as impressed. Rep. Joe L. Barton, the Texas Republican who chaired the House Energy and Commerce Committee from 2004 to 2006, denounced Westmoreland for opposing his bill requiring automakers to share information about their technologically sophisticated cars with independent auto-repair shops. In an unusual act of retaliation by a senior lawmaker against a member of the same party, an advocacy group affiliated with Barton ran radio ads in 2005 in Westmoreland's district saying he was "working against car owners like you." Westmoreland said the bill unnecessarily federalized car repairs.

Another powerful Republican, Appropriations Committee Chairman Jerry Lewis of California, went after Westmoreland after he and a small group of Republican conservatives called for an end to earmarks, the additions slipped into spending bills by individual lawmakers to benefit their districts. Lewis' staff leaked to the press a list of earmarks that Westmoreland and his allies had quietly requested.

In 2006, Westmoreland may have set a short-timer's record for service as a deputy whip, an appointive post helping leaders gather votes for important bills. He was removed the day after getting the job for voting against a leadership-backed rule governing debate of a major spending bill. Under GOP conference rules, all members of the whip team must vote for the rules, which are often manipulated to the advantage of the majority party.

Westmoreland's biggest battle with the leadership was over the Voting Rights extension in 2006. He and other conservatives insisted that one of the act's protections for minority voting rights was outmoded and should be dropped. It forced some states to get permission from the Justice Department or a federal judge to change their election procedures. "It doesn't make sense to subjugate Georgia to the whims of federal bureaucrats until 2031 based on turnout of an election featuring Barry Goldwater and Lyndon Johnson," Westmoreland wrote in the Journal-Constitution.

Exasperated GOP leaders had hoped to pass the bill quickly in an election year to mollify Hispanic voters unhappy with the party's tough stance on illegal immigration. But they had to pull it from the floor just as it was about to come up for a vote. Ultimately, they agreed to allow Westmoreland and other Southern Republicans to offer amendments, which all failed but attracted significant GOP support. Before the votes, Westmoreland faced off with fellow Georgian John Lewis, a Democrat and a respected former civil rights leader, who accused him of misconstruing his words.

Focusing on stopping bills he didn't like, Westmoreland introduced only one measure of his own in his first term — a resolution congratulating a Columbus, Ga., baseball team for winning the 2006 Little League World Series. But he did cosponsor a bill — in both the 109th (2005-06) and 110th Congresses (2007-08) — requiring the Ten Commandments be displayed in the Capitol. The proposal led to a testy exchange in June 2006 with host Stephen Colbert of Comedy Central's "Colbert Report," a late-night show that pokes fun at members of Congress. In one of his trademark ambushes, Colbert asked Westmoreland to name all of the Commandments, which he could not do. The experience, says Westmoreland, taught him, "Don't ever try to be funnier than the comedian hosting the show."

Westmoreland, a successful real estate builder and developer, honed his sparring skills in a dozen years in the Georgia State Legislature, where he faced off against Republican Gov. Sonny Purdue over proposals to raise taxes on alcoholic beverages and tobacco products. After Westmoreland rallied opposition to the tax increases, Purdue had to settle for a scaled-down tax increase on tobacco and no increase on alcohol.

Westmoreland hails from a family of Atlanta mill workers. His father was a firefighter in the Atlanta suburbs, who died on the job while responding to an early-morning alarm at a warehouse fire in freezing cold weather. Westmoreland spent one year at Georgia State University, but left to work full time. He was married at the time, to a woman he first flirted with in the eighth grade by asking her for a pencil, and his father-in-law hired him in his home-building business. After a few years, he started his own construction business and later expanded into real estate development and sales in the late 1980s.

Westmoreland grew up in a family of conservative Democrats, but had little interest in politics until the mid-1980s, when he was inspired by another Georgian, Newt Gingrich, the fiery conservative who was emerging as a leader and later helped Republicans win majority control of Congress.

Westmoreland tried but failed twice to win a state House seat, but finally prevailed in 1992, helped by a reapportionment that gave him a more favorable Republican district. He rose through the leadership ranks himself, and had the chance to become the first Republican Speaker of the Georgia House. But he decided instead to run for Congress in 2004.

Westmoreland won a GOP primary runoff over a Gingrich-backed candidate, Dylan Glenn — a former White House and gubernatorial aide who sought to become the House's only black Republican. In 2006, he easily beat Democratic challenger Mike McGraw by 35 percentage points.

KEY VOTES

2006

No Stop broadband companies from favoring select Internet traffic
Yes Affirm U.S. commitment to war in Iraq and reject setting a withdrawal date for troops
Yes Repeal requirement for bilingual ballots at the polls
Yes Permit U.S. sale of civilian nuclear technology to India
Yes Build a 700-mile fence on the U.S.-Mexico border to curb illegal crossings
Yes Permit warrantless wiretaps of suspected terrorists

2005

Yes Intervene in the life-support case of Terri Schiavo
No Lift President Bush's restrictions on stem cell research funding
No Prohibit FBI access to library and bookstore records
Yes Approve free-trade pact with five Central American countries
Yes Pass energy policy overhaul favored by President Bush emphasizing domestic oil and gas production
Yes End mandatory preservation of habitat of endangered animal and plant species
No Ban torture of prisoners in U.S. custody

CQ VOTE STUDIES

	PARTY UNITY		PRESIDENTIAL SUPPORT	
	Support	Oppose	Support	Oppose
2006	97%	3%	83%	17%
2005	98%	2%	90%	10%

INTEREST GROUPS

	AFL-CIO	ADA	CCUS	ACU
2006	14%	5%	100%	92%
2005	20%	5%	85%	96%

GEORGIA 3

West central – Atlanta and Columbus suburbs

Solidly Republican, the 3rd takes in all or part of 15 counties, beginning in overflow areas near Atlanta and ranging south and west through rural areas to reach the Alabama border and part of Columbus.

Burgeoning Atlanta suburbs in Fayette, Coweta and Henry counties account for growth in the northeastern part of the district, as new homes and subdivisions replace previously rural areas. The population of Henry County (shared with the 13th) grew by more than 40 percent this decade, but as residents have left Atlanta to escape urban congestion, Henry has started to experience traffic problems of its own. Peachtree City in Fayette County is a planned community of more than 30,000 inhabitants that is known for golf cart paths that snake through the city.

In the 3rd's more rural counties, agriculture remains a mainstay. Textile and poultry processing plants dot the landscape, and the timber industry flourishes here. LaGrange, which is nearly half black and was once famous for its textile industry, is now a manufacturing center and will be the site of a Kia Motors plant. To the south, the 3rd's portion of Muscogee County includes part of Columbus, Fort Benning (shared with the 2nd and expanding as a result of the 2005 BRAC process) and regional health care providers. The northern portion of Muscogee in the 3rd hosts many of Columbus' residential communities.

The 3rd is dependably Republican, despite being nearly one-fifth black. Redistricted prior to the 2006 election, George W. Bush would have earned 70 percent of the new 3rd's vote in the 2004 presidential election. In 2006, the district's GOP representative carried the parts of each county wholly or partially in the 3rd.

MAJOR INDUSTRY
Agriculture, services, home building, timber, poultry processing, textiles

MILITARY BASES
Fort Benning (Army), 49,149 military, 7,140 civilian (2004) (shared with the 2nd)

CITIES
Columbus (pt.), 67,156; Peachtree City, 31,580; LaGrange, 25,998

NOTABLE
Franklin D. Roosevelt's Little White House, in Warm Springs, is where the president died on April 12, 1945, while posing for the "Unfinished Portrait," which is now on display in the home's museum.

Rep. Hank Johnson (D)

CAPITOL OFFICE
225-1605
hankjohnson.house.gov
1133 Longworth 20515-1004; fax 226-0691

COMMITTEES
Armed Services
Judiciary
Small Business

RESIDENCE
Lithonia

BORN
Oct. 2, 1954, Washington, D.C.

RELIGION
Buddhist

FAMILY
Wife, Mereda Davis Johnson; two children

EDUCATION
Clark College, B.A. 1976 (political science); Texas Southern U., J.D. 1979

CAREER
Lawyer; county judge

POLITICAL HIGHLIGHTS
Sought Democratic nomination for Ga. House, 1986; DeKalb County Board of Commissioners, 2001-06

ELECTION RESULTS

2006 GENERAL		
Hank Johnson (D)	106,352	75.3%
Catherine Davis (R)	34,778	24.6%
2006 PRIMARY RUNOFF		
Hank Johnson (D)	41,281	58.8%
Cynthia A. McKinney (D)	28,915	41.2%
2006 PRIMARY		
Cynthia A. McKinney (D)	29,216	47.1%
Hank Johnson (D)	27,529	44.4%
John F. Coyne III (D)	5,253	8.5%

Elected 2006; 1st term

An associate judge in DeKalb County for 10 years and a criminal and civil attorney for 25 years, Johnson is well versed in the law. He also spent five years as a DeKalb county commissioner.

Soft-spoken and calm, Johnson's judicial demeanor gives him a drastically different style from that of his predecessor, former Democratic Rep. Cynthia A. McKinney, who was often a confrontational advocate for liberal causes. "I'm not going to be one to make a lot of headlines," Johnson said. "But in the final analysis, I expect people to see results in my activities."

Johnson serves on the Armed Services Committee, as did McKinney, where he said he looks forward to weighing in on the war in Iraq. After President Bush gave his 2007 State of the Union address, Johnson said, "I'm a little unsettled that the president is still linking 9-11 to the war in Iraq. There is no linkage." He also sits on the Judiciary Committee, which should be a good fit with his extensive legal background. And he successfully lobbied for a seat on Small Business, where he said he hopes to "shift some attention back to the needs of working people and away from big business and wealthy individuals."

Johnson, who was born and raised in Washington, D.C., went south for college and law school. He is one of the first two Buddhists ever to be elected to Congress; the other is another Democratic freshman, Mazie K. Hirono of Hawaii.

Johnson said he decided to run for the House because he viewed McKinney as "ineffective and divisive." He was able to hold McKinney to less than 50 percent of the vote in the July 2006 primary in part because a third Democrat in the race, John F. Coyne, captured more than 8 percent of the vote. This pushed McKinney into a runoff with Johnson, who won that contest in August.

Winning the primary is tantamount to being elected in the strongly Democratic black-majority 4th District. Johnson cruised in the general election, beating Republican Catherine Davis, a human resources manager, by more than 50 percentage points.

GEORGIA 4

Atlanta suburbs — most of DeKalb County

The Democratic, suburban DeKalb County-based 4th grabs most of DeKalb, half of Rockdale and part of Gwinnett counties. One of Georgia's two black-majority districts, African-Americans make up 53 percent of residents here.

Like the rest of the Atlanta area, southern DeKalb and northern Rockdale are growing rapidly. Decatur (shared with the 5th) is fighting to retain its small-town feel but is filling up with condos and commuters. Residential development is transforming previously unpopulated land from Lithonia east through Conyers, in Rockdale County.

Most residents commute to Atlanta or work in service-oriented firms in the 4th. Emory University and Centers for Disease Control and Prevention, both on the eastern edge of the 5th, employ many 4th District residents.

South DeKalb is home to some wealthy black communities. To the north, towns like Doraville (split with the 6th) are increasingly home to large foreign-born populations, and as many as half of Clarkston's residents are refugees. The 4th's part of Gwinnett has many Hispanic residents.

The 4th, redistricted prior to the 2006 election, is Democratic at all levels, and would have given John Kerry 72 percent of its 2004 presidential vote. DeKalb is heavily Democratic, but some voters in the portions of Rockdale and Gwinnett, and in DeKalb's more white, affluent areas, favor the GOP.

MAJOR INDUSTRY
Service, health care, government

CITIES
Redan (unincorporated), 33,841; Candler-McAfee (unincorporated), 28,294

NOTABLE
Stone Mountain Park has a huge granite rock face onto which a sculpture of Robert E. Lee and other Confederate leaders is carved.

Rep. John Lewis (D)

CAPITOL OFFICE
225-3801
www.house.gov/johnlewis
343 Cannon 20515-1005; fax 225-0351

COMMITTEES
Ways & Means
(Oversight - chairman)

RESIDENCE
Atlanta

BORN
Feb. 21, 1940, Troy, Ala.

RELIGION
Baptist

FAMILY
Wife, Lillian Lewis; one child

EDUCATION
American Baptist Theological Seminary, B.A. 1961 (theology); Fisk U., B.A. 1963 (religion & philosophy)

CAREER
Civil rights activist

POLITICAL HIGHLIGHTS
Sought Democratic nomination for U.S. House (special election), 1977; Atlanta City Council, 1982-86

ELECTION RESULTS

2006 GENERAL
John Lewis (D) unopposed

2006 PRIMARY
John Lewis (D) unopposed

2004 GENERAL
John Lewis (D) unopposed

PREVIOUS WINNING PERCENTAGES
2002 (100%); 2000 (77%); 1998 (79%); 1996 (100%); 1994 (69%); 1992 (72%); 1990 (76%); 1988 (78%); 1986 (75%)

Elected 1986; 11th term

A leader of the nonviolent protests of the 1960s, Lewis is the keeper of the flame of the civil rights movement in Congress, and its single most influential voice on race relations. He is also trusted by Democratic leaders, who consider him to be unencumbered by ego and ambition and "absolutely intellectually honest," as Democratic Whip Steny H. Hoyer puts it.

Lewis became famous as one of the leaders of the 1965 "Bloody Sunday" protest in Selma, Ala., an event that inspired passage of the landmark Voting Rights Act. Now he leads members of Congress each year on a tour of civil rights sites in the South, and he is among the top 10 lawmakers sought by colleagues to speak in their districts. "John is one of the most respected, if not the most respected member" of the House, Hoyer says. In the Democratic leadership, Lewis holds the appointive post of senior chief deputy whip.

By the usual measure, Lewis is not a productive lawmaker. He doesn't introduce many bills or push for amendments. Those he does advance are in keeping with his civil rights background. His legislation creating the National Museum of African American History and Culture was signed into law by President Bush in 2003 after years of effort.

More recently, Lewis spoke out in 2005 against the Senate confirmation of John G. Roberts Jr. as chief justice of the United States based on memos Roberts wrote that suggested he opposed affirmative action and the voting rights law. Lewis was also highly critical that year of the level of federal aid for the mostly black victims of Hurricane Katrina, saying the administration put too much faith in private charities. "But when we get ready to go to war, we don't go around soliciting resources with a bucket or an offering plate," he said. "We have the courage to come before Congress and debate the issue, authorize money. That's what we need to do here."

Lewis has a coveted seat on the Ways and Means Committee, where he is chairman of the Oversight Subcommittee and has continued to push the issue of federal aid for hurricane-devastated areas. He also has promoted bills to reduce racial disparities in health care and to provide medical services for the poor and the uninsured. He finds much to dislike in Republican tax policy and argues that liberalized trade undermines the quest for labor rights in the Third World. When Congress approved sweeping new surveillance powers for law enforcement after the Sept. 11 terrorist attacks, Lewis voted no, saying he feared a return to the days when the government spied on him and other civil rights leaders.

His preacher's voice, with its thundering timbre and a cadence similar to that of the Rev. Martin Luther King Jr., is one of the House's most familiar. Lewis is among the few in the chamber with a past worthy of a book. His autobiography, "Walking With the Wind," recounts the day in March 1965 when he stood at the front of hundreds of marchers on the Edmund Pettus Bridge in Selma and faced down state troopers without moving a muscle. The police attacked the peaceful crowd — Lewis suffered a severe concussion from a crack of a trooper's billy club — and images from the march helped jolt Congress into giving minorities full voting rights.

Earnest and serious, Lewis writes in his book: "I've never been the kind of person who naturally attracts the limelight. I'm not a handsome guy. I'm not flamboyant. I'm not what you would call elegant."

But activist groups and Democratic Party leaders call on him for everything from ribbon-cuttings to fundraising dinners. Mississippi Sen. Trent Lott, trying to salvage his job as Senate Republican leader, sought forgiveness from Lewis in 2002 after his off-the-cuff remarks praising Sen. Strom Thurmond's 1948 pro-segregation presidential campaign. Since 1997, Lewis has been involved in the Faith and Politics Institute, an interfaith, nonpartisan organization that sponsors forums on racial issues and the annual congressional pilgrimage to Selma.

One of 10 children of sharecroppers, Lewis recalls that he was shy as a boy attending segregated schools in rural Alabama. He was inspired by hearing King's sermons on the radio and developed a sense of outrage at the brutal lynching of 15-year-old Emmett Till in Mississippi in 1955. Lewis was the same age as Till at the time. Later, as a student at the American Baptist Theological Seminary in Nashville, he attended workshops on nonviolent resistance and says he developed a sense of mission. He joined the Student Nonviolent Coordinating Committee, a youthful fulcrum of the civil rights movement that sought to go beyond trying to effect change through strictly legal channels by moving to the next level of protest, civil disobedience.

As a Freedom Rider, Lewis sat at segregated lunch counters and took dangerous bus rides through the Deep South. In 1963, with 24 arrests under his belt, he was chosen chairman of the SNCC. Over the next three years, he led the group's effort for voting rights, including the Selma march. But a rift formed between Lewis' old guard, with its emphasis on nonviolence, and newer activists led by Stokely Carmichael. In 1966, Lewis was replaced by Carmichael as chairman and the SNCC's philosophy changed, culminating in the 1968 riots in Washington, D.C., after King's assassination.

Lewis first ran for Congress in 1977, for the seat Andrew Young left to become U.N. ambassador, but lost to Wyche Fowler. He went to Washington instead to head the federal volunteer agency ACTION. Returning to Atlanta, he won a seat on the city council in 1981. He made his next bid for the House in 1986, when Fowler ran for the Senate. He beat out state Sen. Julian Bond for the Democratic nomination, and breezed to a 3-1 victory in November. He has won re-election with ease. In 2002, 2004 and 2006, the GOP did not bother to field a candidate.

In 2006, Lewis lost a good friend with the death of Coretta Scott King, the wife of his mentor. In an interview with National Public Radio, he recalled, "She would call me late at night, and we would talk, and especially right after the assassination of Dr. King, because she was planning the Martin Luther King Center. . . . And one night, she called and talked so long and so late I fell asleep on the telephone, and I heard myself snoring. And she fell asleep. And I woke up and I said, 'Mrs. King, Mrs. King!' She was not there. And [later] we would laugh about it."

KEY VOTES

2006

Yes Stop broadband companies from favoring select Internet traffic
No Affirm U.S. commitment to war in Iraq and reject setting a withdrawal date for troops
No Repeal requirement for bilingual ballots at the polls
No Permit U.S. sale of civilian nuclear technology to India
No Build a 700-mile fence on the U.S.-Mexico border to curb illegal crossings
\- Permit warrantless wiretaps of suspected terrorists

2005

No Intervene in the life-support case of Terri Schiavo
Yes Lift President Bush's restrictions on stem cell research funding
Yes Prohibit FBI access to library and bookstore records
No Approve free-trade pact with five Central American countries
No Pass energy policy overhaul favored by President Bush emphasizing domestic oil and gas production
No End mandatory preservation of habitat of endangered animal and plant species
Yes Ban torture of prisoners in U.S. custody

CQ VOTE STUDIES

	PARTY UNITY		PRESIDENTIAL SUPPORT	
	Support	Oppose	Support	Oppose
2006	99%	1%	15%	85%
2005	99%	1%	9%	91%
2004	98%	2%	18%	82%
2003	99%	1%	13%	87%
2002	96%	4%	21%	79%

INTEREST GROUPS

	AFL-CIO	ADA	CCUS	ACU
2006	85%	80%	10%	4%
2005	92%	100%	33%	0%
2004	100%	100%	10%	4%
2003	100%	90%	17%	13%
2002	100%	80%	31%	0%

GEORGIA 5

Atlanta

The heart of the 5th lies in Atlanta, the symbolic capital of the New South and the commercial center of the Southeast. The black-majority and reliably Democratic 5th takes in all of the city of Atlanta, much of surrounding Fulton County and slices of DeKalb and Clayton counties to the east and south.

Atlanta is a transportation hub, and Hartsfield-Jackson Atlanta International Airport has a nearly $20 billion annual economic impact on the region. Delta Air Lines, Coca-Cola and CNN all have headquarters in the 5th. AT&T's purchase of BellSouth in 2006 will result in job loss here, although AT&T will retain a regional hub in the city.

Atlanta's population remained fairly constant for years, but renovation of the city's business district and development of downtown areas has helped fuel explosive growth. New condominiums are luring residents, while hotel construction and attractions such as the World of Coca-Cola venue and Georgia Aquarium are popular tourist destinations.

Atlanta has a plethora of cultural and entertainment sites — the Georgia World Congress Center (including Centennial Olympic Park and the Georgia Dome); Woodruff Arts Center; and Turner Field, home of baseball's Braves. The 5th also boasts a slew of universities — Emory University, Georgia State University and Georgia Institute of Technology. Under 2005 BRAC rules, Fort McPherson is slated to close by late 2011.

Republicans have some luck in Atlanta's affluent outlying areas such as Buckhead, a neighborhood full of old money and trendy shops. John Kerry would have received 74 percent of the redistricted 5th's 2004 presidential vote, his highest percentage in Georgia.

MAJOR INDUSTRY

Transportation, distribution, higher education

MILITARY BASES

Fort McPherson (Army), 2,104 military, 2,391 civilian (2006)

CITIES

Atlanta, 416,474; East Point, 39,595; Sandy Springs (pt.) (unincorporated), 27,359

NOTABLE

The Rev. Martin Luther King Jr.'s childhood home and the Ebenezer Baptist Church, where he was a pastor, are in the Sweet Auburn neighborhood.

Rep. Tom Price (R)

CAPITOL OFFICE
225-4501
tom.house.gov
424 Cannon 20515-1006; fax 225-4656

COMMITTEES
Education & Labor
Financial Services

RESIDENCE
Roswell

BORN
Oct. 8, 1954, Lansing, Mich.

RELIGION
Presbyterian

FAMILY
Wife, Elizabeth Clark Price; one child

EDUCATION
U. of Michigan, B.A. 1976 (general studies), M.D. 1979

CAREER
Surgeon

POLITICAL HIGHLIGHTS
Ga. Senate, 1997-2005 (minority whip, 1999-2002; majority leader, 2003); U.S. House

ELECTION RESULTS

2006 GENERAL		
Tom Price (R)	144,958	72.4%
Steve Sinton (D)	55,294	27.6%
2006 PRIMARY		
Tom Price (R)	47,925	82.3%
John Konop (R)	10,322	17.7%
2004 GENERAL		
Tom Price (R)		unopposed

Elected 2004; 2nd term

Price belongs to the generation of Republicans who drove the Democrats out of the state capitols in the South. When the GOP came to power in the Georgia General Assembly in 2002, Price became the state's first-ever Republican state Senate majority leader. Not bad for a Yankee.

Price grew up in Michigan, the son of an emergency room doctor. But he felt a stronger affinity for Virginia, his mother's ancestral home and the place where he spent many contented summer vacations. After following in his father's footsteps by graduating from medical school, Price says one of his first independent decisions as an adult was to move to Atlanta for a residency in orthopedic surgery at Emory University. There, he met his anesthesiologist wife, Elizabeth, and the two settled in the Atlanta area.

He is among several physician politicians drawn to Congress in recent years after getting fed up with the high cost of malpractice insurance. He advocates a cap of $250,000 in damages for pain and suffering due to malpractice, an idea popular with Republicans but opposed by the powerful trial lawyers' lobby, an ally of the majority Democrats. Price says malpractice limits should be part of more sweeping changes to the health care system and that individuals should be allowed to buy medical insurance on the free market, with employers and the government subsidizing whatever plan an individual chooses.

As the congressman from the district once represented by former Speaker Newt Gingrich, Price's politics are distinctly conservative. He would abolish the Internal Revenue Service and replace virtually all taxes — including income, corporate, dividend and capital gains — with a 23 percent national sales tax. During the immigration debate in 2005, he won a provision in the House bill directing the executive branch to secure the country's porous borders in 18 months. But the bill had a short shelf life; it was rejected by the Senate.

In 2006, Price joined a band of conservatives in the House calling for a clampdown on earmarks, the special projects that lawmakers tuck quietly into appropriations bills to curry favor with voters. The group pushed successfully for public disclosure of the sponsors of earmarks in the House.

Price opposes abortion rights and takes a conservative line on embryonic stem cell research, though the medical community generally supports such research. He says scientists are close to being able to extract cells without destroying embryos, which will mitigate the ethical issues that their use poses now for him and other anti-abortion lawmakers.

As a freshman, Price rallied other GOP rookies to form a group called the Official Truth Squad. During the 109th Congress (2005-06), its members regularly took to the House floor just before adjournment for an hour of discussion on what Price called "the disinformation from our colleagues across the aisle." With the Republicans in the minority in the 110th Congress (2007-08), the group has said its theme would be "tracking broken promises."

With thousands of airline workers in his district, Price pushed for a change in pension law to help Delta Air Lines meet billions of dollars in pension obligations. As a member of what was then the Education and the Workforce Committee, he proposed in 2005 giving airlines more time to make up shortfalls in their pension plans.

Price represents north suburban Atlanta, one of the nation's wealthiest enclaves. The seat was held for 20 years by Gingrich, the pugnacious

Republican who led the GOP takeover of Congress in 1994. By contrast, Price comes off more as an affable "country club" Republican than a conservative firebrand. He told the Atlanta Journal-Constitution that he has "a surgeon's mentality." "Instead of creating controversy, I get things done."

During his childhood in Michigan, Price recalls going on rounds with his grandfather, who was also a doctor. With a strong academic performance in high school, Price went directly into an accelerated medical program at the University of Michigan, graduating in 1979. When he finished his residency at Emory, he and his new wife decided to stay in rapidly growing Atlanta. Price practiced solo for six years, then, with a $150,000 loan, established an orthopedic clinic north of the city. Over time, it grew into a 475-person business with revenues of $50 million a year.

Price became increasingly involved in civic organizations like the Rotary Club and in Republican politics as an organizer and fundraiser. When a friend in the state Senate decided to retire in 1996, she urged Price to run. In the Assembly, he was known as a quick study on the details of policy and the rules and mechanics of passing bills. Within two years, he was chosen minority whip, and when Republicans took control of the state Senate in 2003, he became the majority leader. With the legislature in session during only part of the year, he continued to practice medicine.

After Gingrich resigned from Congress, the seat was held for almost three terms by Republican Johnny Isakson. When Isakson ran (successfully) for the Senate in 2004, it created an opening for Price. Democrats wrote off the district as a GOP monopoly and did not bother fielding a candidate.

The real contest was the primary. Price finished first in a seven-candidate race, then went into a runoff against fellow GOP state Sen. Robert Lamutt, a real estate developer. Both politicians were wealthy and conservative and shared many political views, making it hard for voters to make distinctions. Both campaigned on less government and an end to the federal income tax. Each sank significant sums of personal funds into their campaigns — with Price spending $500,000 and Lamutt $1.6 million. Lamutt got Gingrich's endorsement. Price had the support of doctors and health care groups. He prevailed, 54 percent to 46 percent. He was easily re-elected in 2006.

Once in office, Price learned the fundraising ropes quickly. He raised $100,000 for Republicans in tight races in 2006, making him competitive in the future for a plum committee assignment or entry-level leadership role. He also formed a "suburban strategy caucus" with other House Republicans from suburban districts to help the party tap into the growing number of suburban voters who don't align consistently with one party.

KEY VOTES

2006

- No Stop broadband companies from favoring select Internet traffic
- Yes Affirm U.S. commitment to war in Iraq and reject setting a withdrawal date for troops
- Yes Repeal requirement for bilingual ballots at the polls
- Yes Permit U.S. sale of civilian nuclear technology to India
- Yes Build a 700-mile fence on the U.S.-Mexico border to curb illegal crossings
- Yes Permit warrantless wiretaps of suspected terrorists

2005

- Yes Intervene in the life-support case of Terri Schiavo
- No Lift President Bush's restrictions on stem cell research funding
- No Prohibit FBI access to library and bookstore records
- Yes Approve free-trade pact with five Central American countries
- Yes Pass energy policy overhaul favored by President Bush emphasizing domestic oil and gas production
- Yes End mandatory preservation of habitat of endangered animal and plant species
- No Ban torture of prisoners in U.S. custody

CQ VOTE STUDIES

	PARTY UNITY		PRESIDENTIAL SUPPORT	
	Support	Oppose	Support	Oppose
2006	96%	4%	97%	3%
2005	97%	3%	87%	13%

INTEREST GROUPS

	AFL-CIO	ADA	CCUS	ACU
2006	7%	0%	100%	92%
2005	13%	0%	93%	96%

GEORGIA 6

North Atlanta suburbs — Roswell, Alpharetta

Anchored in Atlanta's burgeoning northern suburbs, the 6th takes in all of Cherokee County and parts of three other counties, and is home to corporate headquarters and Republican voters who commute to Atlanta. The overwhelmingly white 6th is Georgia's most affluent and educated district. Office parks, malls, golf courses and housing subdivisions dominate most of the landscape, and the foothills of the Blue Ridge Mountains rise from northern Cherokee County.

Northern Fulton County, the center of the 6th, hosts UPS' corporate headquarters between Sandy Springs and Dunwoody, which is in adjacent DeKalb County. Alpharetta is a technology center — Verizon's southeast regional headquarters are located here, as are large offices for Hewlett Packard, ADP and ChoicePoint. Roswell, formerly a cotton-milling center, is now a booming Fulton County bedroom community and home to the regional headquarters of the city's largest employer, Kimberly-Clark. Roswell's historic district lures visitors with historic landmarks, outdoor recreation, and shopping and dining venues.

While northern Cherokee County remains largely rural, the southern portion of the county is experiencing rapid growth and becoming increasingly suburban. Eastern Cobb County serves as a bedroom community for downtown Atlanta, and GE Energy has its headquarters in the southern tip of the district.

The 6th is full of fiscally conservative Republican voters, and the district is a GOP stronghold throughout. North DeKalb County is home to Atlanta's older, more traditional suburbs, and the area's voters include more minorities and residents who tend to be socially moderate. Voters in the new 6th, redistricted prior to the 2006 election, would have given George W. Bush 70 percent of their 2004 presidential vote.

MAJOR INDUSTRY

Technology, distribution, finance, healthcare

CITIES

Roswell, 79,334; Sandy Springs (pt.) (unincorporated), 58,422; Alpharetta, 34,854; Dunwoody (unincorporated), 32,808

NOTABLE

The city of Mountain Park (Fulton County) is home to Indian Spring — Cherokee Indians would venture from the hills to the spring, believing the waters had healing powers.

Rep. John Linder (R)

CAPITOL OFFICE
225-4272
linder.house.gov
1026 Longworth 20515-1007; fax 225-4696

COMMITTEES
Ways & Means

RESIDENCE
Duluth

BORN
Sept. 9, 1942, Deer River, Minn.

RELIGION
Presbyterian

FAMILY
Wife, Lynne Linder; two children

EDUCATION
U. of Minnesota, Duluth, B.S. 1963;
U. of Minnesota, D.D.S. 1967

MILITARY SERVICE
Air Force, 1967-69

CAREER
Financial executive; dentist

POLITICAL HIGHLIGHTS
Ga. House, 1975-81; Republican nominee for Ga. Senate, 1980; Ga. House, 1983-91; Republican nominee for U.S. House, 1990

ELECTION RESULTS

2006 GENERAL		
John Linder (R)	130,561	70.9%
Allan Burns (D)	53,553	29.1%
2006 PRIMARY		
John Linder (R)		unopposed
2004 GENERAL		
John Linder (R)		unopposed

PREVIOUS WINNING PERCENTAGES
2002 (79%); 2000 (100%); 1998 (69%); 1996 (64%); 1994 (58%); 1992 (51%)

Elected 1992; 8th term

Linder has spent the past decade trying to regain his footing in the leadership of his own party. A friend and ally of former House Speaker Newt Gingrich, his own fortunes declined when Gingrich was forced to resign under an ethics cloud in 1998. Linder then lost the chairmanship of the National Republican Congressional Committee, the organization that helps recruit and fund GOP candidates for the House.

He also was in line to chair the Rules Committee in the 109th Congress (2005-06) until Speaker J. Dennis Hastert granted a term limit waiver to Chairman David Dreier of California, allowing him a fourth two-year stint at the helm. (Ironically, Linder had written the "Linder Rule," which set term limits on committee chairmanships.) Linder then left Rules for a seat on the Ways and Means Committee.

On Ways and Means, he continues to press his case for replacing the income tax with a national sales tax, his signature issue. He wants to see the U.S. government institute a 23 percent national sales tax as a replacement for all federal income, estate and payroll taxes. He says the national sales tax, which he calls the FairTax, is a way to broaden the tax base, eliminate fraud and bureaucracy and solve long-term deficits in federal entitlement programs.

"Under the FairTax, the number of people paying into Social Security and Medicare more than doubles from 158 million workers to 300 million Americans and 45 million foreign tourists and visitors," Linder said in a statement after the 2007 State of the Union. "Until we change our nation's mechanism of raising revenue, our fiscal future will continue to be at risk."

To better explain his FairTax proposal, Linder wrote a book, along with radio talk show host Neil Boortz, entitled, "The FairTax Book: Saying Goodbye to the Income Tax and the IRS." The book, which was published in 2005, reached No. 1 on the New York Times' nonfiction bestseller list. But the New York Times itself was far less supportive. In its review of the book, the Times wrote, "For a book that claims in its introduction to be 'about honesty,' this statement falls far short. No reputable economist of any political stripe would support it." Still, Linder said he expected the book to sell 30,000 to 40,000 copies, and it has sold millions. "To do something large, you have to move the country first, and then move the Congress," he said.

Despite his removal from its leadership ranks, Linder remains a loyal party member. He voted with his party 97 percent of the time in the 109th Congress on votes that pitted Republicans against Democrats. And even though he pushes his own anti-income tax plan, he remains an ardent supporter of President Bush's tax proposals as well. He voted for the $70 billion five-year tax cuts extension measure of 2006, and the $137 billion corporate tax cut approved in 2004.

Linder is as conservative socially as he is fiscally. He opposes abortion and cosponsored legislation that became law in 2003 banning a procedure critics call "partial birth" abortion. He also supported Bush's 2006 veto of a bill to allow the use of federal funds for research on embryonic stem cells derived from surplus embryos at in vitro fertilization clinics.

As a member of the Homeland Security Committee in the 109th Congress, Linder chaired the Prevention of Nuclear and Biological Attack Subcommittee. He advocated for the establishment of a bio-intelligence agency at the Homeland Security Department and attempted to bring such homeland security contracting to Fort Gordon, then a military base in his district.

At a 2006 subcommittee hearing, Linder said the nation needs to improve its community health and hospital preparedness systems to bolster the national response to a pandemic, and added that such systems would have benefits beyond the current threat of avian flu. "Clearly, if we are successful in implementing these strategies, our nation will be better equipped to face the threat of biological terrorism," Linder said.

Linder grew up in a small Minnesota town, the son of a car salesman. He worked his way through college at the University of Minnesota in Duluth, starting in pre-med but switching to dentistry after being inspired by observing dentists at a speech clinic working with children with cleft palates.

After graduating from dental school, Linder joined the Air Force, where he practiced dentistry in San Antonio. Linder and his wife then moved to suburban Atlanta. He set up a dentistry practice, but was increasingly interested in politics. He subscribed to the Congressional Record, a daily digest of activities on the House and Senate floors, and was fascinated, he says, by the good ideas he found in the Extension of Remarks section, where lawmakers expound on issues of the day. He also said he was moved by the writings of National Review founder William F. Buckley.

Linder ran successfully for a seat in the Georgia House in 1974 and wound up serving a total of 14 years in the state legislature. In 1977, he founded a lending institution that specialized in providing financial assistance to small businesses, and eventually he left dentistry. While in the state House, he earned a reputation for battling the Democratic leadership.

Linder first ran for Congress in 1990, losing a tight battle with Democratic Rep. Ben Jones in the 4th District. Two years later, redistricting gave the district a more Republican tilt, and Linder tried again. He narrowly edged out Democratic state Sen. Cathey Steinberg, with 51 percent of the vote, while Jones sought re-election in the 10th District.

After a Supreme Court decision invalidated Georgia's congressional map as racial gerrymandering, Linder in 1995 wound up representing a redrawn 11th District including some Atlanta suburbs and rural areas.

He enjoyed easy re-elections until forced to face off against GOP Rep. Bob Barr — a fellow conservative with a higher national profile — in the 2002 primary in the newly drawn 7th District. Barr was known for his role as a leader in the House GOP effort to impeach President Bill Clinton.

But Republican voters ultimately rejected Barr's acerbic style and polarizing politics in favor of the button-down Linder, who prevailed by 29 percentage points. Linder went on to win in November with 79 percent of the vote. He was unopposed in 2004 and won easily in 2006 .

KEY VOTES

2006

- No Stop broadband companies from favoring select Internet traffic
- Yes Affirm U.S. commitment to war in Iraq and reject setting a withdrawal date for troops
- Yes Repeal requirement for bilingual ballots at the polls
- Yes Permit U.S. sale of civilian nuclear technology to India
- Yes Build a 700-mile fence on the U.S.-Mexico border to curb illegal crossings
- Yes Permit warrantless wiretaps of suspected terrorists

2005

- Yes Intervene in the life-support case of Terri Schiavo
- No Lift President Bush's restrictions on stem cell research funding
- No Prohibit FBI access to library and bookstore records
- Yes Approve free-trade pact with five Central American countries
- Yes Pass energy policy overhaul favored by President Bush emphasizing domestic oil and gas production
- Yes End mandatory preservation of habitat of endangered animal and plant species
- No Ban torture of prisoners in U.S. custody

CQ VOTE STUDIES

	PARTY UNITY		PRESIDENTIAL SUPPORT	
	Support	Oppose	Support	Oppose
2006	98%	2%	93%	7%
2005	97%	3%	89%	11%
2004	98%	2%	94%	6%
2003	98%	2%	100%	0%
2002	98%	2%	90%	10%

INTEREST GROUPS

	AFL-CIO	ADA	CCUS	ACU
2006	8%	0%	100%	96%
2005	13%	0%	93%	96%
2004	7%	0%	100%	100%
2003	0%	5%	100%	88%
2002	11%	0%	100%	100%

GEORGIA 7

East of Atlanta – outer Atlanta suburbs

A mix of eastern Atlanta suburbs and less-populous areas west of Athens, the solidly Republican 7th is centered in Gwinnett County (shared with the 4th), a fast-growing and increasingly diverse county with a rapidly developing economy. In redistricting prior to the 2006 election, northern suburbs were replaced with eastern outer suburbs.

Some district residents still commute to Atlanta for work, but job growth in Gwinnett County keeps a rising number of locals here during the day. Gwinnett boasts a diverse economy, with an emerging science corridor along Interstate 85 that houses several technology firms. Retail and service jobs have replaced manufacturing, and the two sectors now account for roughly half the county's employment. The Gwinnett Center, with an arena and performing arts center, is the cultural hub.

Gwinnett, which accounts for more than three-fourths of the 7th's population, is transforming — almost one-fourth of residents were born abroad, and more Hispanics and Asians are registered to vote in Gwinnett than in any other Georgia county. The international flavor is spicing up the school system, local businesses and politics.

The remainder of the 7th is split between suburban and rural areas, which include small parts of Newton and Forsyth counties and all of more sparsely populated Barrow and Walton counties. Despite their historically rural composition, western Walton, Barrow and Newton counties also are filling up with new bedroom communities.

Republican support in the 7th is anchored in Gwinnett County. The district's small portion of Newton County is more friendly to Democrats, but Gwinnett's Republican support puts the district solidly in the GOP corner. Changing demographics in Gwinnett, however, may alter the 7th's political makeup in the coming years. George W. Bush would have won 69 percent of the redistricted 7th's vote in 2004.

MAJOR INDUSTRY

Service, retail, technology, construction, manufacturing

CITIES

Lawrenceville, 22,397; Duluth, 22,122; Snellville, 15,351

NOTABLE

The town of Between, in Walton County, was named by a postmaster because of its location halfway between Loganville and Monroe.

Rep. Jim Marshall (D)

CAPITOL OFFICE
225-6531
jimmarshall.house.gov
504 Cannon 20515-1003; fax 225-3013

COMMITTEES
Agriculture
Armed Services
Financial Services

RESIDENCE
Macon

BORN
March 31, 1948, Ithaca, N.Y.

RELIGION
Roman Catholic

FAMILY
Wife, Camille Hope; two children

EDUCATION
Princeton U., A.B. 1972 (politics); Boston U., J.D. 1977

MILITARY SERVICE
Army, 1968-70

CAREER
Lawyer; professor; logging business owner

POLITICAL HIGHLIGHTS
Mayor of Macon, 1995-99; Democratic nominee for U.S. House, 2000

ELECTION RESULTS

2006 GENERAL		
Jim Marshall (D)	80,660	50.5%
Mac Collins (R)	78,908	49.5%
2006 PRIMARY		
Jim Marshall (D)		unopposed
2004 GENERAL		
Jim Marshall (D)	136,273	62.9%
Calder Clay (R)	80,435	37.1%

PREVIOUS WINNING PERCENTAGES
2002 (51%)

Elected 2002; 3rd term

A war hero who dropped out of Princeton to fight in Vietnam, Marshall is a gung-ho supporter of the war in Iraq, a defender of the flag, an avid hunter and a conservative Democrat. Often out of step with his party, Marshall had to fight to keep his job in 2006, a year otherwise favorable to Democrats.

The son and grandson of Army generals, Marshall has been one of President Bush's most reliable Democratic boosters of the Iraq War, hanging in long after others changed or modified their positions. Marshall was one of only two Democrats in the House to vote no on the party's resolution opposing Bush's plan in 2007 to send more troops to Iraq. He also opposed Speaker Nancy Pelosi's call for congressional investigations of White House decision-making before the war.

He has attacked critics of the war, including the media, for being indirectly responsible for the deaths of U.S. soldiers. Negativity about the U.S. role, he says, weakens Iraqi resolve for self-governance and emboldens insurgents. In an impassioned floor speech on his party's anti-troop surge resolution, Marshall said, "To those soldiers and Marines who are engaged, I would say the following: Don't be discouraged by this debate and vote. It is birthed in the very democracy that you are defending."

By early 2007, Marshall had visited the troops in Iraq 10 times since the war began in 2003. During a Thanksgiving 2005 trip, Marshall and two other congressmen traveling with him, Republican Tim Murphy of Pennsylvania and Democrat Ike Skelton of Missouri, escaped serious injury when their military vehicle flipped over en route to the Baghdad airport. An oncoming tanker truck refused to yield as it approached the U.S. convoy in the middle of the road. Marshall told the Macon Telegraph newspaper, "Then all of a sudden brakes get slammed on. Then we hit something and go off the side of the road and tip over."

He is not much of a Democratic team player on domestic issues, either. In the 110th Congress (2007-08), when Pelosi rushed the party's "first 100 hours" agenda to the floor with fanfare, most Democrats voted for all six bills, which included an increase in the federal minimum wage and greater leverage for the government to negotiate prescription drug prices. Marshall was the only Democrat to vote against two of the six bills, opposing funding for embryonic stem cell research and a rollback of tax breaks and subsidies for oil and gas companies.

Democratic leaders grudgingly tolerate his independence. To do otherwise could further endanger Marshall politically in a district that could easily fall to the GOP in 2008. He hung on to the seat in 2006 by only 1,752 votes out of about 160,000 cast; his contest with former Rep. Mac Collins, a Republican, was one of the 10 closest House races of the year.

A GOP-drawn district remap that took effect for the 2006 election renumbered his district as the 8th (from the 3rd) and excluded many of his old constituents while bringing in voters unfamiliar with him. Marshall countered Republican efforts to cast him as a liberal by emphasizing his military background and his record as a center-right Southern Democrat.

He and Rep. John Barrow, another conservative who survived a very close election in 2006, are Georgia's only two white Democrats. The military drives the economy in Marshall's district, with Robins Air Force Base there and Fort Benning and its famed Army Infantry school nearby.

In the 109th Congress (2005-06), Marshall supported the position of the president 62 percent of the time, more often than all but four other Democrats. He was one of only 18 Democrats to vote to authorize warrantless wiretapping and among the 64 who supported a Republican bill to build 700 miles of fence along the Mexican border to help stem illegal crossings.

Marshall was born in Ithaca, N.Y., but grew up on Army bases around the world. His family moved 22 times. He was a National Merit Scholar in high school in Mobile, Ala., and was admitted to Princeton University. In 1968, he left school to become an Army ranger. Marshall says he felt it was wrong for him to sit out the war on an academic deferment. He was wounded twice in combat and earned a Purple Heart.

Marshall has survived several bouts of skin cancer, a condition he attributes to his exposure to the herbicide Agent Orange in Vietnam. In 2003, he had successful surgery to treat prostate cancer.

When his Army service ended in 1970, Marshall finished his degree in politics at Princeton and then worked a series of jobs, including as a wilderness instructor, a short-order cook, a welder and a high school economics teacher. He also owned and operated a small logging business in Idaho, during which time he was badly injured when a tree fell on his leg. While recovering, Marshall got a law degree from Boston University, where he met his wife, Camille, also a law student. (Her father, John Hope, a meteorologist, named Hurricane Camille for her.)

The two moved south, where her family roots were, and Marshall joined the faculty of Mercer University's law school in Macon. In 1995, at age 47, he ran for office for the first time, becoming mayor of Macon. In that role, he was credited with shoring up the city financially. A fitness buff and jogger, he earned local public affection in 1997 by chasing down a man who had broken into the women's locker room at his health club. Apparently in superior shape, Marshall overtook the suspect, who was later arrested.

Marshall first ran for the House in 2000, challenging GOP Rep. Saxby Chambliss. He lost by 18 percentage points, then came back in 2002 in a redrawn district that included Macon. His Republican opponent was Calder Clay, a Macon city councilman. Marshall edged out Clay by only 1,528 votes in the third-closest House race that year.

Marshall looked vulnerable for re-election in 2004. Polls showed him in a dead heat in a rematch with Clay, who was well-financed. But Clay failed to make a compelling case for ousting Marshall, who won with 63 percent of the vote. Republicans gained control of the statehouse in 2005 and plotted their revenge, drawing up a new map that changed the district's boundaries to make it more GOP-friendly.

KEY VOTES

2006

- Yes Stop broadband companies from favoring select Internet traffic
- Yes Affirm U.S. commitment to war in Iraq and reject setting a withdrawal date for troops
- No Repeal requirement for bilingual ballots at the polls
- No Permit U.S. sale of civilian nuclear technology to India
- Yes Build a 700-mile fence on the U.S.-Mexico border to curb illegal crossings
- Yes Permit warrantless wiretaps of suspected terrorists

2005

- Yes Intervene in the life-support case of Terri Schiavo
- No Lift President Bush's restrictions on stem cell research funding
- Yes Prohibit FBI access to library and bookstore records
- No Approve free-trade pact with five Central American countries
- Yes Pass energy policy overhaul favored by President Bush emphasizing domestic oil and gas production
- Yes End mandatory preservation of habitat of endangered animal and plant species
- No Ban torture of prisoners in U.S. custody

CQ VOTE STUDIES

	PARTY UNITY		PRESIDENTIAL SUPPORT	
	Support	Oppose	Support	Oppose
2006	65%	35%	65%	35%
2005	67%	33%	59%	41%
2004	69%	31%	53%	47%
2003	73%	27%	53%	47%

INTEREST GROUPS

	AFL-CIO	ADA	CCUS	ACU
2006	64%	35%	73%	72%
2005	67%	70%	63%	46%
2004	80%	55%	55%	48%
2003	87%	70%	48%	24%

GEORGIA 8

Middle Georgia – Macon

The 8th, a long vertical strip in central Georgia, extends from outer Atlanta suburbs in Newton County south through Macon to Colquitt County near the Florida border. The district is politically, economically and racially diverse and includes urban, suburban and rural areas. About one-third of residents are black, and although the district is generally middle-class, pockets of poverty dot the 8th.

Macon has a diverse economy — with regional distribution centers, a university and a hospital system — that serves central Georgia. The city's economy remained stable in recent years despite job loss after the closure of a large Brown & Williamson tobacco plant. South of Macon, Robins Air Force Base is the area's economic engine; the base employs more than 25,000 people, including military and civilian personnel and aerospace contractors and manufacturers.

In the 8th's north, fast-growing Newton County serves as a bedroom community for Atlanta, and some of the old-line rural counties to the south of Newton also now house commuters. The 8th relies heavily on agriculture, especially in the southern tier of the district where cotton and peanuts are grown. Timber, peaches and pecans also are harvested in the 8th, and every county here has some agricultural production.

Many residents are traditional Southern "Yellow Dog" Democrats who still support Democrats at the local level but back the GOP in national races. Macon, more than 60 percent black, is a Democratic stronghold. Colquitt and Tift, in the southern tip, have become solidly GOP counties. While the district's portion of Newton is Republican, increases in black and younger residents are shifting it to the left. The 8th, most of whose residents lived in the old 3rd before redistricting prior to 2006, would have given George W. Bush 61 percent of its presidential vote in 2004.

MAJOR INDUSTRY

Agriculture, aerospace, distribution, timber

MILITARY BASES

Robins Air Force Base, 6,329 military, 13,431 civilian (2006)

CITIES

Macon, 97,255; Warner Robins (pt.), 48,787; Dublin, 15,857

NOTABLE

Macon's Wesleyan College, one of the first degree-granting colleges for women, was founded in 1836.

Rep. Nathan Deal (R)

CAPITOL OFFICE
225-5211
www.house.gov/deal
2133 Rayburn 20515-1010; fax 225-8272

COMMITTEES
Energy & Commerce

RESIDENCE
Gainesville

BORN
Aug. 25, 1942, Millen, Ga.

RELIGION
Baptist

FAMILY
Wife, Sandra Dunagan Deal; four children

EDUCATION
Mercer U., B.A. 1964, J.D. 1966

MILITARY SERVICE
Army, 1966-68

CAREER
Lawyer; state prosecutor

POLITICAL HIGHLIGHTS
Hall County Juvenile Court judge, 1971-72; Hall County attorney, 1977-79; Ga. Senate, 1981-93 (served as a Democrat; president pro tempore, 1991-93)

ELECTION RESULTS

2006 GENERAL		
Nathan Deal (R)	128,685	76.6%
John D. Bradbury (D)	39,240	23.4%
2006 PRIMARY		
Nathan Deal (R)		unopposed
2004 GENERAL		
Nathan Deal (R)		unopposed

PREVIOUS WINNING PERCENTAGES *
2002 (100%); 2000 (75%); 1998 (100%); 1996 (66%); 1994 (58%); 1992 (59%)
* Elected as a Democrat 1992-94

Elected 1992; 8th term

Deal held the chairmanship of an important House subcommittee on health care policy for just two years before the Democrats took over in 2007 and bumped him to minority status. He then became the top-ranking Republican on the Energy and Commerce Health Subcommittee.

In his short stint as chairman, Deal was often overshadowed by bigger players in the health care arena, especially given his relatively slight background in the legislatively complex issue. Among Republicans, Rep. Bill Thomas of California, the former chairman of the Ways and Means Committee, dominated the subject with both his grasp of the substance of health policy and his great influence in the Republican caucus.

A lawyer by trade, Deal acknowledged at the start of his tenure as chairman that he knew little about health care beyond what he had learned with his wife providing in-home care to his elderly in-laws. Members of Congress who take the lead on health care tend to have many years of experience with the issue and a deep knowledge of the many-layered U.S. medical system. But Deal showed signs of coming into his own, managing to push a handful of substantial bills through the House.

He won some changes in Medicaid, the country's main health care program for the poor, that gave states more flexibility, such as letting them set the amount of co-payments charged to patients.

He also succeeded in winning approval of a requirement for people on Medicaid to show proof of U.S. citizenship in order to receive benefits. Before the change, 46 states allowed Medicaid beneficiaries to verify their citizenship with a verbal "yes." Both ideas were controversial, and Deal had to overcome objections from advocates for the poor.

Another of Deal's successful efforts was a law prohibiting people from getting Viagra through Medicaid. But his attempt to put the same restriction on coverage under Medicare was struck from a fiscal 2006 appropriations bill.

Deal proved an able ally for Energy and Commerce panel Chairman Joe L. Barton, a Texas Republican, in helping enact a law giving the National Institutes of Health director the authority to allot funding for disease research, so that groups representing diabetes research or cancer research, for example, were not pitted against each other at the Appropriations Committee.

Deal's greatest disappointment in the 109th Congress (2005-06) was his inability to force greater reforms in Medicaid. He wanted to introduce health savings accounts to the program. He also would have liked to pass restrictions on the use of hospital emergency rooms, permitting doctors to send non-emergency patients to other medical facilities. And he and his GOP allies were unable to win final passage of a bill prodding doctors and hospitals to use electronic medical records, a Bush administration priority. The bill passed in the House, but stalled in the Senate in 2006.

His challenge in the 110th Congress (2007-08) is to try to put curbs on the more liberal approach to health care of new Health Subcommittee Chairman Frank Pallone Jr., a New Jersey Democrat, and especially on any expansions of twin medical behemoths Medicare and Medicaid.

The courtly Deal, thoroughly Southern in his conservative politics, was once a Democrat himself. He switched parties in 1995, after the Republicans took control of the House for the first time in four decades. He said at the time, "The Democratic Party's attitude wasn't in tune with me or my constituents' beliefs."

The switch enhanced Deal's political security. As a Democrat, he won his initial congressional election and then re-election with slightly less than 60 percent of the vote — the threshold often used to assess whether a lawmaker is safe in his next re-election bid. He has enjoyed easier victories since switching to the GOP, even running unopposed in two of the last three elections.

Once a supporter of term limits, Deal reneged on a pledge to serve no more than 12 years, which would have made 2004 his last year in the House. "The reality is, it still takes a while to be able to affect legislation," he told the Atlanta Journal-Constitution newspaper.

Deal briefly found himself in the national spotlight in 2003 when Speaker J. Dennis Hastert slipped a provision for him into that year's catchall spending bill to allow beef and poultry producers to give their animals non-organic feed and still label the meat as organic. Deal, who had been pushing for the organic chicken feed exemption in behalf of Baldwin-based Fieldale Farms in his district, said the standards for organic producers were too strict. Amid an outcry from organic food producers, the provision was repealed.

Deal looks out for the area's businesses in other ways. At first glance, the landlocked and mostly rural district seems an unlikely hot spot for concern about immigration. But the poultry and carpet businesses rely on foreign workers, and Deal has long been an advocate of tougher enforcement against illegal immigrants, including those who enter the United States legally but stay longer than permitted.

Deal is the only child of two public school teachers (his wife is also a teacher), and although his parents were not active in politics, they impressed upon him the importance of being active in public life. "After all, teaching is a type of public service," he says.

He was a successful high school and college debater, and he went on to law school. Fulfilling a commitment he made as a four-year ROTC member during college, he joined the Army and served two years in the Judge Advocate General corps before opening his law practice in Gainesville. He served as a prosecutor and a juvenile court judge and then ran successfully for an open state Senate seat in 1980.

Deal had a string of effortless re-elections in the legislature by the time U.S. Rep. Ed Jenkins, a fellow conservative Democrat, announced his retirement in 1992. Deal's GOP opponent that year was Daniel Becker, who made abortion the focus of a "morality in government" campaign. Becker's appeal proved to be limited and Deal prevailed.

KEY VOTES

2006

No Stop broadband companies from favoring select Internet traffic
Yes Affirm U.S. commitment to war in Iraq and reject setting a withdrawal date for troops
Yes Repeal requirement for bilingual ballots at the polls
? Permit U.S. sale of civilian nuclear technology to India
Yes Build a 700-mile fence on the U.S.-Mexico border to curb illegal crossings
Yes Permit warrantless wiretaps of suspected terrorists

2005

? Intervene in the life-support case of Terri Schiavo
No Lift President Bush's restrictions on stem cell research funding
No Prohibit FBI access to library and bookstore records
Yes Approve free-trade pact with five Central American countries
Yes Pass energy policy overhaul favored by President Bush emphasizing domestic oil and gas production
Yes End mandatory preservation of habitat of endangered animal and plant species
No Ban torture of prisoners in U.S. custody

CQ VOTE STUDIES

	PARTY UNITY		PRESIDENTIAL SUPPORT	
	Support	Oppose	Support	Oppose
2006	97%	3%	80%	20%
2005	98%	2%	87%	13%
2004	100%	0%	87%	13%
2003	99%	1%	93%	7%
2002	96%	4%	82%	18%

INTEREST GROUPS

	AFL-CIO	ADA	CCUS	ACU
2006	15%	5%	92%	92%
2005	20%	5%	89%	96%
2004	7%	0%	94%	100%
2003	20%	5%	93%	84%
2002	11%	0%	90%	100%

GEORGIA 9

North — Dalton, Gainesville

Anchored by North Georgia's mountains, the 9th runs across most of the state's northern border. It includes Cloudland Canyon State Park, the man-made Lake Lanier, a chunk of the Chattahoochee National Forest and several growing Atlanta suburbs, as well as bedroom communities outside of Chattanooga, Tenn.

The 9th's economy has long depended on poultry processing and carpet manufacturing industries rooted in Gainesville and Dalton. As Atlanta expands northward, a surge of new residents in the district's south has brought white-collar and service sector jobs to the 9th and has helped diversify the local economy. The southern portions of Forsyth and Hall counties host suburbs full of Republicans and housing subdivisions.

Gainesville is home to the Northeast Georgia Medical Center, a regional healthcare hub. Near the state's northwestern corner, Catoosa and Walker counties continue to grow with residents who commute to Chattanooga. In the northeast, mountainous Fannin, Union and White counties are popular destinations for tourists and retirees.

The 9th has the state's smallest proportion of black residents (3 percent), although its Hispanic population is expanding due to job opportunities in both the poultry processing and carpet manufacturing industries. More than half the schoolchildren in Dalton and Gainesville are Hispanic.

As a whole, the 9th's population is overwhelmingly white and strongly Republican, at both the national and local levels. The GOP allegiance in some north-central counties dates to the Civil War. In mid-decade redistricting prior to the 2006 election, the old 9th and 10th districts swapped corners of the state, with the new 9th gaining a few northeastern counties and shedding some eastern Atlanta suburbs. Republican George W. Bush would have received 77 percent of the new 9th's vote in the 2004 presidential election — a statewide high.

MAJOR INDUSTRY

Poultry processing, carpet manufacturing, service

CITIES

Dalton, 27,912; Gainesville, 25,578

NOTABLE

Gainesville, the "poultry capital of the world," displays an obelisk in the center of town that has a chicken statue on top; Springer Mountain is the southern terminus of the 2,174-mile Appalachian National Scenic Trail.

Vacant Seat

Rep. Charlie Norwood (R)
Died Feb. 13, 2007

Six days after announcing his decision to enter hospice care, Republican Rep. Charlie Norwood succumbed to cancer on Feb. 13, 2007. The 65-year-old Georgian was diagnosed with lung cancer, which had metastasized to his liver, shortly after winning re-election to a seventh House term in November 2006.

Republican Gov. Sonny Perdue of Georgia scheduled a June 19 special election for the seat, in which all candidates, regardless of party, were to compete on one ballot. The crowded 10-person field was topped by Republican Jim Whitehead, who according to state law automatically vacated his state Senate seat after filing for the congressional race. Whitehead was the best-known candidate and the only elected officeholder in the field. He also reported strong fundraising totals and hired a few former Norwood aides. Whitehead also was a personal friend of the congressman's.

Despite front-runner status for Whitehead, it was uncertain whether he could nab a majority of all votes needed for an outright victory in the single-ballot election. It seemed certain that Whitehead and one other candidate, regardless of party affiliation, would compete in a July 17 runoff.

Other Republicans who filed for the race were physician Paul Broun, who had run three unsuccessful campaigns for Congress; conservative activist Bill Greene, who was backed by the Minuteman PAC and other groups that advocate tougher immigration law enforcement; Nate Pulliam, a realtor and Iraq War veteran; Erik M. Underwood, who had mounted a failed write-in campaign for a Georgia state House seat in 2006; and real estate executive Mark Myers, who was waging his fourth bid for Congress.

Georgia's 10th District, which includes part of Augusta and borders North Carolina and South Carolina, was highly likely to remain in Republican hands. The state's congressional map was redrawn in 2005, when Democratic areas formerly contained in Democratic Rep. John Barrow's district were annexed to the renumbered 10th.

But Democrats were planning a credible effort for the seat. Their top candidate was James Marlow Jr., a former sales director for Yahoo! Inc. who had the backing of many Democratic county chairmen. The other Democratic candidates out of the gate were attorney Evita Paschall and Marion "Denise" Freeman, who had lost decisively to Norwood in 1998 and 2000. The Libertarian candidate was psychotherapist Jim Sendelbach.

Norwood had had health problems for a number of years. In 2004, he had a lung transplant, and in 2000, he survived a serious car accident that shattered several of his ribs and bones in his hands.

Norwood was into middle age when he entered the political arena. His successful run for the House in 1994 was his first bid for public office.

A dentist, Norwood was heavily involved in health care policy during his dozen years in office. He was known as the leading House Republican advocate of a patients' "bill of rights" that would have allowed consumers to sue their health maintenance organizations and insurance companies in state courts for medical decisions or improper denials of care that resulted in injury or death. The bill was widely debated but never passed.

A day before his death, Norwood reintroduced the original legislation he sponsored in 1999 with Democratic Rep. John D. Dingell of Michigan. It "would be a good start" for the 110th Congress (2007-08), he said.

GEORGIA 10

Northeast – Athens; part of Augusta

The Republican 10th contains the state's mountainous northeastern corner and follows Georgia's eastern border south to Augusta's GOP-heavy suburbs. In the west, Athens is home to the University of Georgia.

Higher education jobs lend stability to the district's economy, and the University of Georgia provides service and health care jobs. Agriculture remains an economic mainstay for many in the 10th; dairy, cattle, corn, soybeans and some cotton are produced in the district. The district's northern tier is largely rural, but the Blue Ridge Mountains and a chain of lakes along the South Carolina border are popular destinations for tourists, retirees and Atlanta-area residents with weekend homes.

The 10th's southeastern arm takes in Augusta's northern and western suburbs in Richmond County and includes all of fast-growing Columbia County, home to many Augusta commuters. Fort Gordon, mostly in Richmond County and home to the Army Signal Center, was spared from BRAC closures, although the 2005 BRAC round targeted Athens' Navy Supply Corps School. The Savannah River Site, a nuclear facility located across the river in South Carolina, remains a major employer in the region, despite significant personnel reductions since the mid-1990s. Augusta also is a major manufacturing and retail center.

Mid-decade redistricting prior to the 2006 election added Athens to the 10th District while removing some counties on the old district's western border. The remapping also changed the number of the district, renumbering the old 9th as the new 10th.

The 10th is decidedly Republican, and the majority of the district's population lives in rural areas that support Republicans. GOP Rep. Charlie Norwood won every county in the district in 2006 except for Clarke County, home to Athens and its liberal university community. The 10th's portion of Richmond includes the county's most GOP-friendly area, and the suburbs in Columbia County are overwhelmingly Republican. In 2004, George W. Bush would have captured 65 percent of the current 10th's presidential vote.

MAJOR INDUSTRY
Higher education, service, agriculture, manufacturing

MILITARY BASES
Fort Gordon (Army), 11,998 military, 2,814 civilian (2007) (shared with the 12th); Navy Supply Corps School, 416 military, 174 civilian (2007)

CITIES
Athens-Clarke, 101,489; Augusta-Richmond (pt.), 79,910; Martinez (unincorporated), 27,749

NOTABLE
The annual Masters golf tournament is held at Augusta National Golf Club; The Ty Cobb Museum, honoring the Hall of Fame "Georgia Peach" baseball player, is in Royston.

PRIOR ELECTION RESULTS

2006 GENERAL		
Charlie Norwood (R)	117,721	67.4%
Terry Holley (D)	57,032	32.6%
2004 GENERAL		
Charlie Norwood (R)	197,869	74.3%
Bob Ellis (D)	68,462	25.7%

Rep. Phil Gingrey (R)

CAPITOL OFFICE
225-2931
gingrey.ga@mail.house.gov
www.house.gov/gingrey
119 Cannon 20515-1011; fax 225-2944

COMMITTEES
Armed Services
Science & Technology

RESIDENCE
Marietta

BORN
July 10, 1942, Augusta, Ga.

RELIGION
Roman Catholic

FAMILY
Wife, Billie Gingrey; four children

EDUCATION
Georgia Institute of Technology, B.S. 1965 (chemistry); Medical College of Georgia, M.D. 1969

CAREER
Physician

POLITICAL HIGHLIGHTS
Marietta Board of Education, 1993-97 (chairman, 1994-97); Ga. Senate, 1999-2003

ELECTION RESULTS

2006 GENERAL		
Phil Gingrey (R)	118,524	71.1%
Patrick Samuel Pillion (D)	48,261	28.9%
2006 PRIMARY		
Phil Gingrey (R)		unopposed
2004 GENERAL		
Phil Gingrey (R)	120,696	57.4%
Rick Crawford (D)	89,591	42.6%

PREVIOUS WINNING PERCENTAGES
2002 (52%)

Elected 2002; 3rd term

Gingrey doesn't intend to sit back and complain with Democrats in control of the House. He's been in the minority before, in the Georgia legislature, and he says it just requires a different set of skills. He has no plans to "wait for the crumbs to fall off the table." That isn't the way this obstetrician-politician operates.

Gingrey is goal-oriented; he boasts he delivered 5,200 babies before coming to the House. He ran for Congress on the slogan, "He Delivers," and he isn't happy unless he's crossing items off his to-do list.

One item still on that list is legislation to curb medical malpractice lawsuits, which Gingrey says drive up insurance premiums for doctors and force some to abandon their practices. His desire to limit such suits was one of his main reasons for seeking a seat in Congress in 2002. The House in 2005 approved his legislation to cap punitive damage awards at $250,000, but the bill, like similar measures before it, died in the Senate.

Gingrey has faced some medical concerns of his own. In December 2002, he had double coronary bypass surgery. Once his health rebounded, he resumed a rigorous exercise schedule.

He had hoped to win a seat on the Ways and Means Committee in the 110th Congress (2007-08) after losing out in the 109th Congress to fellow Georgia Republican John Linder. But Republicans lost slots on all committees with the change in House control. Gingrey was bounced off the Rules Committee, where he had served in the 109th, and returned to the Armed Services and Science and Technology panels, where he served in his first term before joining Rules. His state has a heavy military presence, though his district will lose a naval air station due to the 2005 round of base closings.

Gingrey suspects his bid for Ways and Means may also have suffered from his ambivalence about free-trade agreements. With a Republican in the White House, GOP leaders want trade supporters on the committee, which has jurisdiction over all trade issues. Gingrey did back President Bush's Central American Free Trade Agreement in 2005, but the following year he voted against bills granting permanent normal trade relations to Vietnam, implementing a free trade deal with Oman, and giving trade breaks to Haiti. He said he was worried about their impact on the domestic textile industry.

While in the majority, Gingrey's farthest-reaching effort was a bill setting stricter standards for reporting on and measuring the effectiveness of teacher training programs at the college level. Gingrey's bill built on Bush's 2001 overhaul of public education, the No Child Left Behind Act, by making federal grants to colleges and universities contingent on producing teachers who are highly qualified in their core subjects.

He also has sponsored legislation, which passed the House in 2004 and again in 2006, to create within the Environmental Protection Agency a research and development program for "green" chemistry, an emerging field of making products that generate the least amount of hazardous waste.

Gingrey is one of the House's staunchest opponents of abortion, even in cases of rape or incest. He also quickly joined Bush in calling for a constitutional ban on same-sex marriage, an issue the president used to rally social conservatives in his 2004 re-election campaign.

He drew some unfavorable media attention during the 2005 congressional intervention in the case of Terri Schiavo, a Florida woman whose family fought in court over withdrawal of life support. Gingrey argued during a debate on the floor that Schiavo could improve "with proper treatment, now denied." He drew on his background as a doctor to justify intervention. (An autopsy later showed that Schiavo's brain had deteriorated beyond any possibility of recovery.)

Gingrey's mother was the daughter of Irish immigrants who grew up in Queens. His father, who grew up in South Carolina, owned a series of small businesses, including a drive-through restaurant, a liquor store and a motel in Augusta, Ga., none of which did particularly well. Gingrey worked his way through the Georgia Institute of Technology with a factory job. He intended to become an engineer, but after visiting an operating room with a family friend who was a neurosurgeon, he decided to go to medical school. He chose obstetrics because "I like the upbeatness of delivering babies and having that situation almost always a happy one," he once told the Atlanta Journal-Constitution.

Gingrey served about four years as Marietta school board chairman when his children were in school (the four Gingrey children are now grown), then went on to two terms in the Georgia Senate while continuing with his medical practice. He became well-known for advocating tighter teen driving laws; Gingrey said he was motivated by reading obituaries of teenagers he had helped deliver as babies.

In 2001, he toyed with running against Democratic incumbent Sen. Max Cleland. But after redistricting gave Georgia two new seats in the House as a result of population growth, he decided to run for the House. The Democratic legislature had designed the 11th District to favor one of their own, so much so that Republican Rep. Bob Barr, who then represented a portion of it, chose to run instead in the GOP primary against fellow Republican Linder. With Barr out of the way, Gingrey jumped in and won the primary. He had a hard fight in the general election against Roger Kahn, a wealthy wholesale liquor distributor who lent his own campaign $2.5 million. Gingrey got help from the American Medical Association, which paid for polling and radio ads.

He won with 52 percent of the vote, mainly by appealing to right-leaning and religious conservatives from rural areas. But the Georgia Ethics Commission found him guilty of violating state ethics codes by funneling money from his state campaign committee to his congressional race. He paid a $250 fine and returned $3,500 in contributions.

By the time of his 2004 race, Gingrey had caught on to fundraising. He amassed $1.5 million in 2003 and won with 57 percent of the vote. Mid-decade redistricting in 2005 was favorable to the GOP, and Gingrey won going away in 2006.

KEY VOTES

2006

No Stop broadband companies from favoring select Internet traffic

Yes Affirm U.S. commitment to war in Iraq and reject setting a withdrawal date for troops

Yes Repeal requirement for bilingual ballots at the polls

Yes Permit U.S. sale of civilian nuclear technology to India

Yes Build a 700-mile fence on the U.S.-Mexico border to curb illegal crossings

Yes Permit warrantless wiretaps of suspected terrorists

2005

Yes Intervene in the life-support case of Terri Schiavo

No Lift President Bush's restrictions on stem cell research funding

No Prohibit FBI access to library and bookstore records

Yes Approve free-trade pact with five Central American countries

Yes Pass energy policy overhaul favored by President Bush emphasizing domestic oil and gas production

Yes End mandatory preservation of habitat of endangered animal and plant species

No Ban torture of prisoners in U.S. custody

CQ VOTE STUDIES

	PARTY UNITY		PRESIDENTIAL SUPPORT	
	Support	Oppose	Support	Oppose
2006	96%	4%	87%	13%
2005	97%	3%	87%	13%
2004	98%	2%	85%	15%
2003	99%	1%	95%	5%

INTEREST GROUPS

	AFL-CIO	ADA	CCUS	ACU
2006	14%	5%	87%	92%
2005	13%	0%	89%	100%
2004	7%	5%	100%	96%
2003	0%	5%	100%	84%

GEORGIA 11

Northwest – Rome, most of Marietta

Nestled against the Alabama border in northwest Georgia, the 11th runs south from Chattooga County into Carroll County and east into the western Atlanta suburbs in Cobb County. The conservative district takes in all of six counties and parts of three others, spanning rural areas in the west, small cities such as Rome and suburbs such as Marietta.

The 11th's chunk of Cobb hosts white-collar, middle-income suburbs and most of the city of Marietta (shared with the 13th and 6th districts), where aerospace and military jobs spur the economy. The local Lockheed Martin plant, next to a Naval air station, builds C-130J and F-22 planes, although the air station is closing under 2005 BRAC recommendations. Paulding County is filling up with residents who commute to Atlanta, and its population grew by an estimated 40 percent since the 2000 census.

To the west, the string of rural counties along the Alabama border still depend on agriculture — mainly hay, cotton, corn and soybeans. Haralson County also has a Honda plant, and Rome, in Floyd County, is home to three colleges, several medical centers and manufacturing plants — Kellogg Company and Pirelli Tires both have large factories in the area. Textiles and carpet manufacturing remain important in the 11th's northern counties.

Until redistricting prior to the 2006 election, the 11th included all or part of 17 counties, was 28 percent black and was politically competitive. After the mid-decade remap, it is 12 percent black and its residents favor GOP candidates in federal and state elections. Some conservative Southern Democrats in rural counties still vote for Democrats locally. The 11th's portion of Cobb, which accounts for roughly one-third of the district's population, remains a GOP stronghold. George W. Bush would have won the new 11th with 71 percent of the presidential vote in 2004.

MAJOR INDUSTRY
Defense, manufacturing, textiles, agriculture, construction

MILITARY BASES
Naval Air Station Atlanta, 1,233 military, 139 civilian (2005)

CITIES
Marietta (pt.), 47,721; Rome, 34,980; Kennesaw, 21,675

NOTABLE
Like its Italian namesake, Rome is built on seven hills; A Kennesaw law requires each household to own a gun and the appropriate ammunition.

Rep. John Barrow (D)

CAPITOL OFFICE
225-2823
barrow.house.gov
213 Cannon 20515-1012; fax 225-3377

COMMITTEES
Agriculture
Energy & Commerce

RESIDENCE
Savannah

BORN
Oct. 31, 1955, Athens, Ga.

RELIGION
Baptist

FAMILY
Divorced; two children

EDUCATION
U. of Georgia, B.A. 1976 (history & political science); Harvard U., J.D. 1979

CAREER
Lawyer

POLITICAL HIGHLIGHTS
Sought Democratic nomination for Ga. House, 1986; Athens-Clarke County Commission, 1991-2005

ELECTION RESULTS

2006 GENERAL		
John Barrow (D)	71,651	50.3%
Max Burns (R)	70,787	49.7%
2006 PRIMARY		
John Barrow (D)		unopposed
2004 GENERAL		
John Barrow (D)	113,036	51.8%
Max Burns (R)	105,132	48.2%

Elected 2004; 2nd term

Barrow had one of the closest election contests of any Democrat in 2006, and party leaders wasted no time shoring up his chances for 2008. They gave him a pair of choice committee assignments and tagged him for special campaign help in the next cycle.

Barrow (BEAR-oh — rhymes with "arrow"), who affiliates with the Blue Dog Coalition, a group of conservative Democrats, gained a seat on the powerful Energy and Commerce Committee, where he can pursue the health care issues that he championed in his campaign. Although most Energy and Commerce members are not allowed to serve on any other committee, House Speaker Nancy Pelosi allowed Barrow to keep his seat on the Agriculture Committee as well. That guarantees him a voice in the scheduled farm policy rewrite in the 110th Congress (2007-08), which is important to his constituents in rural portions of the sprawling 12th District.

A native of Athens, Barrow worked there as a trial lawyer and spent 14 years as an Athens-Clarke County commissioner before ousting Republican Rep. Max Burns in 2004. The district had been drawn to favor Democrats following the last decennial census, which worked in his favor. But a 2005 redistricting after Republicans took control of the state legislature stripped away his Athens hometown and much of his Democratic base.

Burns set out to retake the seat, but Barrow fought to hold it. He moved to Savannah, raised $2.5 million and built a centrist voting record that helped him withstand the challenge. Burns tried to make an issue of Barrow's Harvard Law degree and his occasional use of big words like "assimilate." Barrow painted himself as a gun-toting conservative with deep Georgia roots. He closed one commercial by saying, "I approve of this message, and I approve of them Dawgs, too," a statement sure to win nods from the district's true political base — University of Georgia fans. Barrow is an alumnus, which helped offset any elitist taint from Harvard Law.

Barrows is one of two white Democrats in the Georgia congressional delegation. He is friends with the other one, third-term Rep. Jim Marshall, who also squeaked to re-election in 2006. "Jim Marshall and I had to stand in the same fire," he says, noting that President Bush made four visits to their districts to drum up support for their opponents.

Like Marshall, Barrow votes with Republicans more than most Democrats in Congress. During the 109th Congress (2005-06), he voted more frequently in support of Bush than all but 10 of his Democratic colleagues. (Marshall was one of those who rebelled even more often.)

Barrow joined Republicans in voting to build a 700-mile fence along the border with Mexico and to make it a felony to be in the United States without legal papers. He was one of 18 Democrats voting to authorize the Bush administration's warrantless electronic surveillance program, and one of just four supporting an end to bilingual voting assistance.

He voted to extend through 2010 the reduced tax rate on capital gains and dividend income favored by Republicans, and he backed GOP efforts to limit the scope of the Endangered Species Act. He also sided with Republicans in supporting repeal of the federal estate tax. He was one of just six Democrats voting to keep an estate tax provision linked to an increase in the federal minimum wage. In all, he broke ranks to side with Republicans 28 percent of the time on votes that pitted the two parties against each other.

The pattern continued in the 110th Congress. He was one of just two

Democrats voting early in 2007 to shift more than $500 million in a catchall appropriations bill from various domestic projects to military housing, anti-drug efforts and deficit reduction.

But Barrow sticks with his fellow Democrats on most issues. He voted to expand federally funded embryonic stem cell research and to override Bush's 2006 veto of stem cell legislation. With the exception of an alternative energy bill, he supported the Democratic agenda in early 2007, including an increase in the federal minimum wage. He also backed legislation to make it easier for workers to organize a union at their workplace.

In his first term, Barrow was more supportive of Bush's Iraq policy than most Democratic members of Congress, but in 2007 he voted with his party in opposition to the president's decision to send more than 21,000 additional combat troops to Iraq. "I do not believe that this plan represents the change in strategy that we need in Iraq, nor does it offer a good enough chance for success to be worth the sacrifices that it will cost," he said on the House floor.

Barrow is a big booster of the military. Both his parents served in the Army, and both were captains. His father was in a tank destroyer battalion, his mother in military intelligence. "They were pacing each other," he says. "They'd call each other and Daddy said, 'Well, I just made captain.' And Mama said, 'Me too.' "

His parents were also both civil rights advocates. In the early 1960s, Barrow says, they were co-chairmen of the local chapter of HOPE, which stood for Help Our Public Education, fighting for integration. They wrote to the parents of students at the University of Georgia, asking them to support integration. "They got death threats. Daddy kept a Mauser [a German rifle] next to the door," he recalls. "My life was part 'To Kill a Mockingbird,' with my dad Atticus Finch, and part 'Remember the Titans,' " a movie about a football team that integrated.

In 1986, Barrow made a failed bid for the state House, losing by 30 votes in a special-election runoff. He ran successfully for election to the Athens-Clarke County Commission in 1990 and went on to serve for 14 years.

In his first U.S. House race in 2004, Barrow took 51 percent of the vote in a four-way Democratic primary, and with strong backing from national Democratic officials, he staved off the well-financed and aggressive Burns by 7,904 votes — a 4 percentage point margin. That was a landslide compared with his 2006 victory in their rematch, which Barrow won by just 864 votes. Only four House contests nationwide were closer.

KEY VOTES

2006

- No Stop broadband companies from favoring select Internet traffic
- Yes Affirm U.S. commitment to war in Iraq and reject setting a withdrawal date for troops
- Yes Repeal requirement for bilingual ballots at the polls
- Yes Permit U.S. sale of civilian nuclear technology to India
- Yes Build a 700-mile fence on the U.S.-Mexico border to curb illegal crossings
- Yes Permit warrantless wiretaps of suspected terrorists

2005

- Yes Intervene in the life-support case of Terri Schiavo
- Yes Lift President Bush's restrictions on stem cell research funding
- Yes Prohibit FBI access to library and bookstore records
- No Approve free-trade pact with five Central American countries
- Yes Pass energy policy overhaul favored by President Bush emphasizing domestic oil and gas production
- Yes End mandatory preservation of habitat of endangered animal and plant species
- Yes Ban torture of prisoners in U.S. custody

CQ VOTE STUDIES

	PARTY UNITY		PRESIDENTIAL SUPPORT	
	Support	Oppose	Support	Oppose
2006	65%	35%	65%	35%
2005	78%	22%	47%	53%

INTEREST GROUPS

	AFL-CIO	ADA	CCUS	ACU
2006	64%	45%	87%	76%
2005	87%	75%	56%	40%

GEORGIA 12

East – most of Augusta and Savannah

The 12th reaches from Augusta to Savannah along the South Carolina border, taking in a string of sparsely populated counties on its western edge that were added during redistricting prior to the 2006 election. The politically competitive district includes urban Democratic strongholds, socially conservative rural counties and GOP-friendly suburbs.

Savannah's port, the East Coast's second-largest container port, fuels the 12th's economy, and Fort Stewart (shared with the 1st) and Hunter Army Airfield together employ tens of thousands of people. Savannah's downtown has a vibrant tourism industry. Many in Richmond County (Augusta) work at Fort Gordon (shared with the 10th) or at the Energy Department's Savannah River Site, across the river in South Carolina.

Many textile factories in the center of the district have shut down. The rest of the 12th mainly relies on agriculture. Toombs County's Vidalia grows its famous sweet onion; Bulloch and Emanuel counties are timber-growing areas.

Effingham County, north of Savannah, now hosts many white residents who have left urban areas of Chatham County (Savannah). GOP strength is rooted in Effingham and the southern counties of Toombs, Tattnall and Bulloch. The 12th's portions of Chatham and Richmond are reliably Democratic, as are Hancock and Washington counties. Hancock County, in the district's northwest, is one of Georgia's most heavily black counties and one of its poorest. Democrats narrowly held the 12th in 2006, and Democrat John Kerry would have eked out a 50.2 percent majority of the new 12th's 2004 presidential vote.

MAJOR INDUSTRY

Agriculture, manufacturing, timber

MILITARY BASES

Fort Stewart (Army), 17,760 military, 3,170 civilian (2007) (shared with the 1st); Fort Gordon (Army), 11,998 military, 2,814 civilian (2007) (shared with the 10th); Hunter Army Airfield, 7,900 military, 730 civilian (2007)

CITIES

Augusta-Richmond (pt.), 119,865; Savannah (pt.), 110,616; Statesboro, 22,698

NOTABLE

Vidalia onions were named the official state vegetable in 1990.

Rep. David Scott (D)

CAPITOL OFFICE
225-2939
davidscott.house.gov
417 Cannon 20515-1013; fax 225-4628

COMMITTEES
Agriculture
Financial Services
Foreign Affairs

RESIDENCE
Atlanta

BORN
June 27, 1946, Aynor, S.C.

RELIGION
Baptist

FAMILY
Wife, Alfredia Scott; two children

EDUCATION
Florida A&M U., B.A. 1967 (English & speech); U. of Pennsylvania, M.B.A. 1969

CAREER
Advertising agency owner; recruiting firm executive; defense contracting company manager

POLITICAL HIGHLIGHTS
Ga. House, 1975-83; Ga. Senate, 1983-2003

ELECTION RESULTS

2006 GENERAL		
David Scott (D)	103,019	69.2%
Deborah Travis Honeycutt (R)	45,770	30.8%
2006 PRIMARY		
David Scott (D)	29,179	67.3%
Donzella J. James (D)	14,157	32.7%
2004 GENERAL		
David Scott (D)		unopposed

PREVIOUS WINNING PERCENTAGES
2002 (60%)

Elected 2002; 3rd term

Scott defies the conventional wisdom about African-Americans in Congress. He is neither consistently liberal nor always loyal to the Democratic Party. Scott is pro-military, he likes tax cuts and he voted for President Bush's Medicare prescription drug plan, facing down Democratic leaders who opposed it. "He who controls the center controls the political debate," he says. "You can't lead from the left; you can't lead from the right."

Scott says he got to Congress in spite of his party, not because of it. Establishment Democrats in this suburban Atlanta district backed a rival in the 2002 primary when Scott, after more than 25 years in the Georgia General Assembly, decided to run for the new 13th District seat. Nevertheless, Scott got the nomination with strong support from affluent suburbanites, business leaders, doctors and big health care companies.

Over the years, Scott was closely associated with Atlanta's black and liberal leaders — former mayors Andrew Young and Maynard Jackson as well as Jimmy Carter, the governor who became president — but he calculated correctly that only a centrist could win the district. The 13th is a mix of urban and rural areas with nearly even numbers of black and white voters.

When he arrived in Washington, Scott joined the coalition of conservative Democrats called the Blue Dogs. He gets high ratings from the business lobby; he was among the 10 House Democrats in 2006 whose voting records were ranked most business-friendly by the Chamber of Commerce. In the 109th Congress (2005-06), he voted for the Republican bankruptcy overhaul bill and for permanent repeal of the estate tax.

A component of Scott's appeal to white voters is his support for the military, which has a major presence in Georgia. He is a co-founder of the Democrats' national security study group, and he says Democrats can once again be the party associated with a strong military by returning to the hawkish defense postures of presidents Franklin D. Roosevelt and John F. Kennedy.

He was one of only seven Democrats to vote for Bush's $350 billion, 10-year tax bill in 2003. He also favors a flat tax, an idea typically pushed by conservatives that would replace the present graduated income tax with a single rate for everyone. Scott says that such a tax, while regressive, would greatly simplify the labyrinthine tax code. "The tax cut was not just for white folks paying taxes," he says. "I have a district where a lot of African-Americans with money are paying taxes."

On other big issues, Scott votes a more traditional liberal line. In late 2005, he called on Bush to start drawing down American forces in Iraq. "What's in the best interest of American security is not losing more and more of our soldiers in an unfocused effort," Scott said in a 2006 interview. "What's in the best interest of American security is to find a political solution to what is a political problem."

On the Financial Services Committee in the 108th Congress (2003-04), Scott protested proposed Republican cuts in housing programs for the poor, but sided with the GOP on a bill favoring brokerage firms and investment banks when states seek to punish them for corporate fraud.

Scott's background is a lesson in adaptation. Born in Aynor, S.C., an impoverished country town, he attended elementary school in Pennsylvania. When he was in sixth grade, his family moved to Scarsdale, N.Y., where his father and mother went to work for a wealthy family as a chauffeur and a maid. An only child, Scott was also the only black child in his school. His classmates had money, while he lived in an apartment over the garage on the estate owned by his parents' employer. Civil rights protests raged across the country, and though Scott says he encountered surprisingly little overt bigotry among Scarsdale's upper crust, his racial isolation was stressful. "I learned at a very young age how to have confidence in myself and how to get along with people who don't look like me," he says.

Scott finished high school in Daytona Beach, Fla., then went on to Florida A&M University. During an internship in Washington with the Labor Department, Scott by chance met George W. Taylor, the noted labor-management expert. Taylor suggested Scott apply to the University of Pennsylvania's Wharton School of Finance, where Taylor was on the faculty. "Well, maybe I will," Scott replied. "What's the Wharton school?"

With a Wharton MBA in hand, in the early 1970s Scott was attracted to Atlanta and its emerging crop of black leaders. He was a volunteer with Young's campaign for the House in 1972.

Two years later, Scott won his first election to the Georgia House, launching a 28-year career in the legislature. He chaired the state Senate Rules Committee, leading the Atlanta Journal-Constitution in 1993 to describe him as "the second-most-powerful black politician in the state, behind only the mayor of Atlanta," who was Jackson.

A religious man who sometimes sees the hand of divine intervention in his legislative successes, Scott authored the Georgia law requiring a moment of silence at the beginning of the public school day. He has sponsored a national version of the bill in the House. He says the moment of silence has the effect of calming children and giving them "inner strength." Scott quotes liberally from both the Bible and Shakespeare.

In the state legislature, he clashed frequently with the National Rifle Association, pushing to passage a law requiring background checks for handgun purchases and championing a bill aimed at keeping guns away from children. Scott wrote the state's sex-education law and fended off conservatives who tried to restrict curricula to sixth grade and beyond. He once stopped Waste Management Inc., the garbage-hauling giant, from expanding a landfill in a poor black neighborhood that already had several dumps.

Scott won a decisive primary victory in the new 13th District in 2002 despite the party's decision to back state Sen. Greg Hecht. He also outpolled David Worley, a former state Democratic Party chairman who had run twice against former GOP House Speaker Newt Gingrich.

Scott easily defeated businessman Clay Cox in the general election. His campaign featured ads by his wife's brother, baseball great Hank Aaron, holder of the record for career home runs.

KEY VOTES

2006

No Stop broadband companies from favoring select Internet traffic

No Affirm U.S. commitment to war in Iraq and reject setting a withdrawal date for troops

No Repeal requirement for bilingual ballots at the polls

Yes Permit U.S. sale of civilian nuclear technology to India

No Build a 700-mile fence on the U.S.-Mexico border to curb illegal crossings

No Permit warrantless wiretaps of suspected terrorists

2005

Yes Intervene in the life-support case of Terri Schiavo

Yes Lift President Bush's restrictions on stem cell research funding

Yes Prohibit FBI access to library and bookstore records

No Approve free-trade pact with five Central American countries

Yes Pass energy policy overhaul favored by President Bush emphasizing domestic oil and gas production

Yes End mandatory preservation of habitat of endangered animal and plant species

Yes Ban torture of prisoners in U.S. custody

CQ VOTE STUDIES

	PARTY UNITY		PRESIDENTIAL SUPPORT	
	Support	Oppose	Support	Oppose
2006	85%	15%	45%	55%
2005	79%	21%	43%	57%
2004	79%	21%	47%	53%
2003	76%	24%	38%	62%

INTEREST GROUPS

	AFL-CIO	ADA	CCUS	ACU
2006	86%	85%	60%	32%
2005	100%	80%	74%	38%
2004	86%	75%	78%	30%
2003	87%	75%	60%	32%

GEORGIA 13

Atlanta suburbs — parts of Clayton, Cobb and Douglas counties

Before mid-decade redistricting, the spidery 13th spanned parts of 11 counties circling Atlanta. Since redistricting prior to the 2006 election, the 13th forms a crescent shape that cradles the southwest corner of Atlanta and takes in parts of six counties, including sizable chunks of Cobb and Clayton.

The 13th includes an array of middle-income urban, suburban and rural areas. A significant number of residents commute to Atlanta, where major corporations employ large numbers of district residents. Regional health care providers are large employers in the 13th, as are universities nearby in the 5th (in Fulton County). The 13th is experiencing rapid growth in southern Fulton and eastern Douglas counties where working-class families and retirees are pouring in to once less-populated areas.

Cobb County accounts for about one-third of the district's population and has a growing black population. Many residents in southern Cobb work in defense-related industries near Marietta, or for Home Depot, which has headquarters in the 13th. South of Atlanta, Clayton County, which also has one-third of the population, suffered with the 2006 closure of a Ford plant in Hapeville (nearby in the 5th), and expects job loss from the 2005 BRAC round's closure of Fort Gillem. Many of the commuters from Clayton still rely on transportation and warehousing sectors around the busy Hartsfield-Jackson Atlanta International Airport (in the 5th).

Minorities make up more than half of the 13th's population, although whites form a plurality, and the district is dependably Democratic. Republicans have some success in eastern Douglas, but John Kerry would have won 61 percent of the new 13th's 2004 presidential vote.

MAJOR INDUSTRY
Distribution, aerospace, health care, services

MILITARY BASES
Fort Gillem (Army), 398 military, 1,796 civilian (2004)

CITIES
Smyrna (pt.), 38,195; Mableton (unincorporated), 29,733

NOTABLE
Jonesboro was the setting for Tara, the plantation in Margaret Mitchell's novel "Gone With the Wind."

HAWAII

Gov. Linda Lingle (R)

First elected: 2002
Length of term: 4 years
Term expires: 12/10
Salary: $112,000
Phone: (808) 586-0034

Residence: Honolulu
Born: June 4, 1953; St. Louis, Mo.
Religion: Jewish
Family: Divorced
Education: California State U., Northridge, B.A. 1975 (journalism)
Career: Newspaper owner; journalist
Political highlights: Maui County Council, 1981-91; mayor of Maui, 1991-98; Republican nominee for governor, 1998; Hawaii Republican Party chairwoman, 1999-2002

Election results:

2006 GENERAL		
Linda Lingle (R)	215,313	62.5%
Randy Iwase (D)	121,717	35.4%
Jim Brewer (GREEN)	5,435	1.6%

Lt. Gov. James "Duke" Aiona (R)

First elected: 2002
Length of term: 4 years
Term expires: 12/10
Salary: $100,000
Phone: (808) 586-0255

LEGISLATURE

Legislature: 60 days January-April

Senate: 25 members, 4-year terms
2007 ratios: 20 D, 5 R; 18 men, 7 women
Salary: $35,900
Phone: (808) 586-6720

House: 51 members, 2-year terms
2007 ratios: 43 D, 8 R; 33 men, 18 women
Salary: $35,900
Phone: (808) 586-6400

TERM LIMITS

Governor: 2 consecutive terms
Senate: No
House: No

URBAN STATISTICS

CITY	POPULATION
Honolulu	371,657
Hilo	40,759
Kailua	36,513
Kaneohe	34,970
Waipahu	33,108

REGISTERED VOTERS

Voters do not register by party.

POPULATION

2006 population (est.)	1,285,498
2000 population	1,211,537
1990 population	1,108,229
Percent change (1990-2000)	+9.3%
Rank among states (2006)	42
Median age	36.2
Born in state	56.9%
Foreign born	17.5%
Violent crime rate	244/100,000
Poverty level	10.7%
Federal workers	29,276
Military	53,632

ELECTIONS

STATE ELECTION OFFICIAL
(808) 453-8683
DEMOCRATIC PARTY
(808) 596-2980
REPUBLICAN PARTY
(808) 593-8180

MISCELLANEOUS

Web: www.hawaii.gov
Capital: Honolulu

U.S. CONGRESS

Senate: 2 Democrats
House: 2 Democrats

2000 Census Statistics by District

DIST.	2004 VOTE FOR PRESIDENT BUSH	KERRY	WHITE	BLACK	ASIAN	HISP	MEDIAN INCOME	WHITE COLLAR	BLUE COLLAR	SERVICE INDUSTRY	OVER 64	UNDER 18	COLLEGE EDUCATION	RURAL	SQ. MILES
1	47%	52%	18%	2%	54%	5%	$50,798	64%	16%	20%	15%	22%	29%	1%	191
2	44	56	28	2	28	9	$48,686	57	21	22	11	27	23	16	6,232
STATE	45	54	23	2	41	7	$49,820	60	19	21	13	24	26	9	6,423
U.S.	50.7	48.3	69	12	4	13	$41,994	60	25	15	12	26	24	21	3,537,438

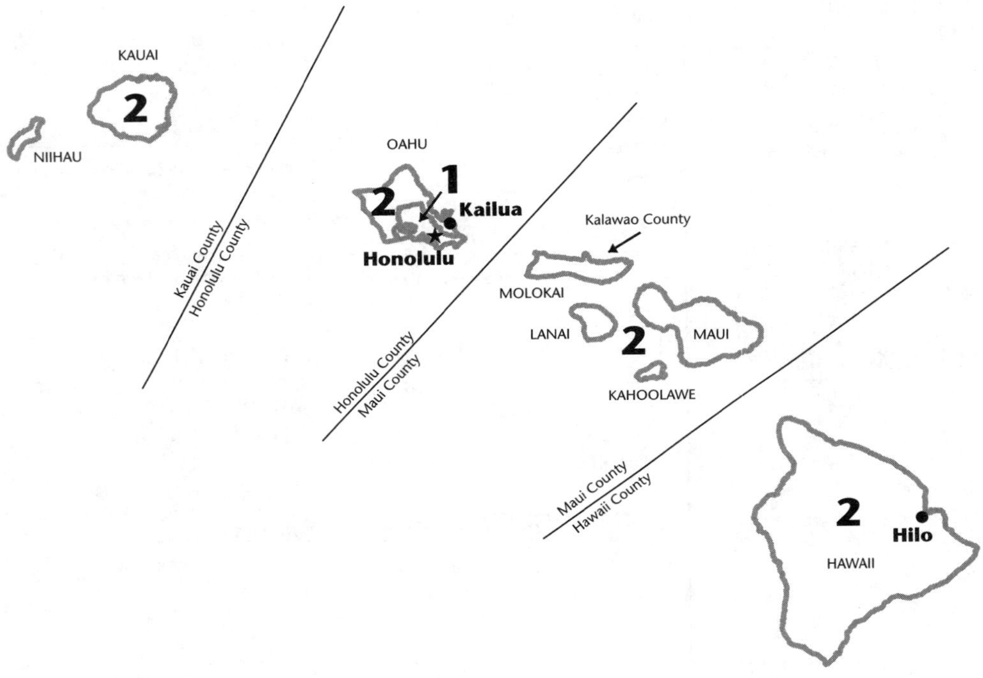
KAUAI
2
NIIHAU
Kauai County
Honolulu County
OAHU
1
2
Kailua
Honolulu
Honolulu County
Maui County
Kalawao County
MOLOKAI
LANAI
2
MAUI
KAHOOLAWE
Maui County
Hawaii County
2
Hilo
HAWAII

Sen. Daniel K. Inouye (D)

CAPITOL OFFICE
224-3934
senator@inouye.senate.gov
inouye.senate.gov
722 Hart 20510-1102; fax 224-6747

COMMITTEES
Appropriations
(Defense - chairman)
Commerce, Science & Transportation - chairman
Indian Affairs
Rules & Administration
Joint Printing

RESIDENCE
Honolulu

BORN
Sept. 7, 1924, Honolulu, Hawaii

RELIGION
Methodist

FAMILY
Widowed; one child

EDUCATION
U. of Hawaii, A.B. 1950 (government & economics); George Washington U., J.D. 1952

MILITARY SERVICE
Army, 1943-47

CAREER
Lawyer; city prosecutor

POLITICAL HIGHLIGHTS
Hawaii Territorial House, 1954-58 (majority leader); Hawaii Territorial Senate, 1958-59; U.S. House, 1959-63

ELECTION RESULTS

2004 GENERAL		
Daniel K. Inouye (D)	313,629	75.5%
Cam Cavasso (R)	87,172	21.0%
Jim Brewer (NON)	9,269	2.2%
Jeff Mallan (LIBERT)	5,277	1.3%
2004 PRIMARY		
Daniel K. Inouye (D)	157,367	93.8%
Brian Evans (D)	8,051	4.8%
Eddie Yoon (D)	2,437	1.5%

PREVIOUS WINNING PERCENTAGES
1998 (79%); 1992 (57%); 1986 (74%); 1980 (78%); 1974 (83%); 1968 (83%); 1962 (69%); 1960 House Election (74%); 1959 Special House Election (68%)

Elected 1962; 8th term

The first Japanese-American elected to Congress, Inouye is first and foremost a man of honor, one of the attributes that mark him as the product of an earlier political era, when collegiality was valued over partisan combativeness and reverence for the Senate as an institution was the norm.

He does not give his word lightly, and once he does, he keeps it. Inouye (in-NO-ay) declined to cast a tie-breaking vote for a Democratic amendment to President Bush's 2001 tax bill in order to keep his promise to "pair" his votes that day with his best friend, Ted Stevens, a Republican who would have voted the other way but was home in Alaska speaking at his granddaughter's high school graduation ceremony.

In the 110th Congress (2007-08), Inouye chairs the Commerce, Science and Transportation Committee, and also wields the gavel of the Appropriations Defense Subcommittee. He essentially swapped titles with Stevens, who stepped down to the ranking minority job on both panels after Democrats claimed the majority in 2006.

Their unusually close, cross-party partnership was likely to continue under the new arrangement. Inouye and Stevens regularly refer to themselves as "co-chairmen." They like to deal with differences behind the scenes and before the committee votes publicly. That personal dynamic was sure to affect the fate of a sweeping telecommunications bill that was left unfinished in the 109th Congress (2005-06), and along with it, the partisan fight over so-called network neutrality, the idea that phone and cable companies should have to treat similar types of Internet traffic equally.

Inouye shares with Stevens an interest in shifting military priorities away from a longstanding concentration on Europe and toward the Pacific. The two also see eye to eye on issues affecting indigenous populations. The prospect that native Alaskans might benefit from oil exploration in the Arctic National Wildlife Refuge prompted Inouye to consistently support Stevens' efforts to open the refuge to oil drilling. Most Democrats oppose the proposal as a threat to Alaska's wildlife.

The taciturn Inouye and the temperamental Stevens are an unlikely match in personality, but share a bond as representatives of the two newest states. Inouye said their relationship is a model for others. "Many of our colleagues realize that if they're able to set aside some of the partisanship, much can be done. And we have proven that," he said.

An extremely private man, Inouye is a living link between Hawaii's past as a U.S. territory and its future as the nation's vibrant, multicultural bridge to the Pacific Rim. He has represented Hawaii in Congress since the archipelago joined the union in 1959, and is the fourth-longest-serving senator in history. Among current senators, only Robert C. Byrd of West Virginia and Edward M. Kennedy of Massachusetts have been in the Senate longer. Kennedy in March 2006 described Inouye as "our rock, our steady hand, our wise counselor."

On the rare occasions when Inouye speaks out publicly, his words command attention. When the Senate was debating in 2002 whether to grant Bush authority to attack Iraq, Inouye made headlines when he took exception to a Bush comment that Democrats were not sufficiently concerned about national security. Inouye, who lost an arm while fighting Nazi Germany in World War II and who was awarded the Congressional Medal of Honor in 2000 for bravery, rose on the Senate floor to protest. "It grieves me when my president makes statements that would divide this nation," he said. "This is not a time for Democrats and Republicans to say we got more medals than you, we've lost more limbs than you, we've shed more blood than you."

Inouye stepped aside in 2005 as the top Democrat on the Indian Affairs panel to take the ranking minority slot on Commerce, but he continued to advance legislation for American Indians and ethnic Native Hawaiians. In 2006, he and fellow Hawaii Democrat Daniel K. Akaka got a long-sought vote to try to force a floor debate on legislation to grant sovereign status to Native Hawaiians, like that enjoyed by Alaska Natives and American Indians. But with Republicans balking, their effort fell four votes short of the 60 votes needed to limit debate. They hope to fare better in the Democratically controlled 110th Congress.

Inouye's colleagues have come to rely on him to handle delicate tasks that require impartiality and unquestioned probity. His 1987 appointment to chair the Senate committee investigating the Iran-contra affair stemmed not only from his evenhanded manner but also from the esteem he won during the 1973 Watergate hearings leading to the resignation of President Richard Nixon. When then Minority Leader Harry Reid recused himself in 2002, Inouye stepped in to head the Ethics Committee's investigation of fellow Democrat Robert G. Torricelli of New Jersey.

In 2005, when Senate Majority Leader Bill Frist was threatening a parliamentary power play to eliminate filibusters against Bush's judicial nominees, Inouye, a devout institutionalist, was one of the bipartisan Gang of 14 — seven Democrats and seven Republicans who joined together to thwart Frist's plan, while also limiting filibusters against nominees to "extraordinary circumstances."

On Appropriations, Inouye has secured billions of federal dollars for his state. In the fiscal 2007 defense spending bill alone, he snared $372 million for Hawaii, ranging from $25 million for the Maui Space Surveillance System, which tracks satellites, to $1 million for a buoy study in Kaneohe Bay to seek ways to turn wave energy into electricity.

Inouye is revered by Hawaii's large Japanese-American community. In 1943, as an 18-year-old pre-med student at the University of Hawaii, he enlisted in the famed all-Nisei "Go for Broke" 442nd Regimental Combat Team and fought across Italy and France. When he advanced alone to take out a machine gun that had pinned down his men, he lost his right arm and spent 20 months in military hospitals.

At the Percy Jones Hospital in Michigan, he met another recuperating soldier with an arm injury — Bob Dole of Kansas, who later became Senate majority leader. Dole told Inouye he planned to be in Congress someday. Prevented by his injury from becoming a surgeon, Inouye decided he too would try politics.

He won his first election in 1954, to Hawaii's territorial House. Inouye helped guide Hawaii to statehood in 1959, and was elected that year as its first U.S. House member. In 1962, Inouye won election to the Senate.

He has been seriously threatened only once since then. In 1992, state Sen. Rick Reed, his Republican opponent, ran a radio ad featuring claims by Inouye's barber that Inouye had made unwanted sexual advances. Inouye called the accusation "unmitigated lies," and the Ethics Committee dropped a review of the charges. But the bad press likely contributed to his lowest winning percentage ever in a congressional race, 57 percent.

Inouye suffered a grievous personal loss in March 2006 when Maggie, his wife of almost 57 years whom he described as "my inspiration," died of cancer. It speaks volumes about his deep sense of duty that he was back at his Senate desk the day after her death to vote on amendments to the annual budget resolution, and remained on duty until the Senate completed work on the budget at week's end.

KEY VOTES

2006

No Confirm Samuel A. Alito Jr. to the Supreme Court
? Allow consideration of a bill to establish a $140 billion trust fund to compensate victims of asbestos exposure
No Extend tax cuts for two years at a cost of $70 billion over five years
Yes Overhaul immigration policy with border security, enforcement and guest worker program
No Allow consideration of a bill to permanently repeal the estate tax
Yes Urge President Bush to begin troop withdrawals from Iraq in 2006
Yes Lift President Bush's restrictions on stem cell research funding
No Authorize military tribunals for suspected terrorists

2005

No Curb class action lawsuits by shifting them from state to federal courts
? Allow confirmation vote on Priscilla R. Owen to the U.S. Court of Appeals for the 5th Circuit
No Oppose mandatory emissions limits and block recognition of global warming as a threat
No Approve free-trade pact with five Central American countries
Yes Pass energy policy overhaul favored by President Bush emphasizing domestic oil and gas production
No Shield gunmakers from lawsuits when their products are used in crimes
Yes Ban torture of prisoners in U.S. custody
No Renew 16 provisions of the Patriot Act
Yes Allow final vote on opening the Arctic National Wildlife Refuge to oil and gas exploration

CQ VOTE STUDIES

	PARTY UNITY		PRESIDENTIAL SUPPORT	
	Support	Oppose	Support	Oppose
2006	90%	10%	56%	44%
2005	90%	10%	44%	56%
2004	95%	5%	59%	41%
2003	93%	7%	48%	52%
2002	90%	10%	76%	24%
2001	98%	2%	66%	34%
2000	91%	9%	94%	6%
1999	91%	9%	86%	14%
1998	93%	7%	87%	13%
1997	91%	9%	87%	13%

INTEREST GROUPS

	AFL-CIO	ADA	CCUS	ACU
2006	100%	95%	50%	8%
2005	100%	90%	44%	5%
2004	100%	100%	50%	8%
2003	100%	85%	40%	15%
2002	92%	80%	41%	0%
2001	100%	90%	43%	9%
2000	60%	60%	69%	23%
1999	88%	95%	50%	0%
1998	88%	80%	44%	9%
1997	83%	75%	50%	4%

Sen. Daniel K. Akaka (D)

CAPITOL OFFICE
224-6361
akaka.senate.gov
141 Hart 20510-1103; fax 224-2126

COMMITTEES
Armed Services
(Readiness & Management Support - chairman)
Banking, Housing & Urban Affairs
Energy & Natural Resources
(National Parks - chairman)
Homeland Security & Governmental Affairs
(Oversight of Government Management - chairman)
Indian Affairs
Veterans' Affairs - chairman

RESIDENCE
Honolulu

BORN
Sept. 11, 1924, Honolulu, Hawaii

RELIGION
Congregationalist

FAMILY
Wife, Millie Akaka; five children

EDUCATION
U. of Hawaii, B.Ed. 1952, M.Ed. 1966

MILITARY SERVICE
Army Corps of Engineers, 1945-47

CAREER
Gubernatorial aide; state economic grants official; elementary school principal and teacher

POLITICAL HIGHLIGHTS
Sought Democratic nomination for lieutenant governor, 1974; U.S. House, 1977-90

ELECTION RESULTS

2006 GENERAL		
Daniel K. Akaka (D)	210,330	61.3%
Cynthia Thielen (R)	126,097	36.8%
Lloyd Jeffery Mallan (LIBERT)	6,415	1.9%
2006 PRIMARY		
Daniel K. Akaka (D)	129,158	54.7%
Ed Case (D)	107,163	45.3%

PREVIOUS WINNING PERCENTAGES
2000 (73%); 1994 (72%); 1990 Special Election (54%); 1988 House Election (89%); 1986 House Election (76%); 1984 House Election (82%); 1982 House Election (89%); 1980 House Election (90%); 1978 House Election (86%); 1976 House Election (80%)

Elected 1990; 3rd full term

Appointed April 1990

His name comes first on every roll call vote in the Senate, but that's pretty much the extent of Akaka's fame on Capitol Hill. He is rarely out front in national debates, viewing his role in Washington as a defender of the interests of his Pacific island state, with its complicated relationship with the mainland.

Now in his 80s, Akaka (uh-KAH-kuh) drew his first serious political challenge in years when Democratic Rep. Ed Case, almost 30 years his junior, decided to take him on in the 2006 primary. While expressing respect and "the deepest aloha" for the incumbent, Case said that it was time for "the next generation" of leadership. (The state's other senator, Democrat Daniel K. Inouye, is also in his 80s.) Akaka retorted that Hawaii benefited from his depth of experience, and his Senate colleagues rushed to his aid. So did the voters; he took almost 55 percent of the vote against Case in the primary and easily won re-election in November, although his 61 percent share of the general election vote was his lowest since his initial Senate election.

Akaka is the only native Hawaiian ever to serve in the Senate — his mother was Hawaiian and his father was of Chinese and Hawaiian ancestry — and he focuses most intently on home-state issues, ranging from the islands' role in national security to creation of an honorary postage stamp for surfing and swimming legend Duke Kahanamoku.

"It brings me back to what my mother and dad used to tell me when I was little: 'We don't want you to be a showhorse. We want you to be a workhorse,'" Akaka says. "So I wanted to be a workhorse of service to people, especially to the people of Hawaii and our country."

His signature legislation, known locally as the Akaka Bill, would recognize ethnic Native Hawaiians as an indigenous group and give them a status similar to that held by Alaska Natives and American Indians. That would allow them to negotiate with the state and federal governments over land use, a major source of contention in Hawaii. About 20 percent of residents trace at least part of their ancestry to indigenous Polynesian inhabitants.

Akaka has sponsored the bill every Congress since 2000, when the House passed a similar measure. It has been blocked by conservative Republicans, who argue that it could bring gambling to the state, disrupt military operations and discriminate against Hawaiians of other ethnicities.

In 2005, Akaka's bill won approval from the Indian Affairs Committee and Majority Leader Bill Frist promised to bring it to the floor. But then Hurricane Katrina struck, and legislation aiding Gulf Coast reconstruction took precedence. At Akaka's behest, Frist finally tried to call up the bill in 2006, but Akaka fell four votes short of the 60 needed to overcome a filibuster. He promptly reintroduced it in 2007, hoping that the new Democratic majority would finally be enough to push the bill through the Senate.

Akaka had to publicly clarify remarks he made on National Public Radio in 2005 that were interpreted as a suggestion that Hawaii might want to secede. He said he meant no such thing when he told a radio interviewer, "I believe the people of Hawaii need to have the flexibility to address the long-standing issues resulting from the overthrow" of the Hawaiian monarchy.

Hawaii's last monarch, Queen Liliuokalani, was dethroned in 1893 in a rebellion led by the U.S. minister to Hawaii and supported by U.S.-owned business interests on the islands and the U.S. military. A century later, President Bill Clinton signed a resolution sponsored by Akaka officially apologizing. An Akaka law enacted in 1995 compensates native Hawaiians by transferring federal land to a trust in return for lands seized by the United States during the state's territorial period.

When Akaka does venture into national issues, it's typically on matters affecting the military and its veterans. He chairs the Veterans' Affairs Committee in the 110th Congress (2007-08), and is a senior member and subcommittee chairman on the Armed Services Committee. He frequently offers amendments to boost funding for veterans' programs, declaring, "Care for veterans must be viewed as a cost of war." In 2004, he cosponsored a bill to permanently add 30,000 soldiers to the Army, but it died in the Senate.

Akaka took part in one of the most closely watched events of the 108th Congress (2003-04), a 2004 hearing in which top defense officials were grilled over the abuse of Iraqi prisoners. Akaka proved an able interrogator, asking Joint Chiefs of Staff Chairman Gen. Richard B. Myers, "How is it that an entire brigade could be deployed to Iraq and not trained for their mission?"

A solid Democrat who votes with his party more than 90 percent of the time, Akaka will take on monied interests when he is outraged, as he was in 2003 after a series of trading abuses in the mutual fund industry. He was the first senator to introduce legislation that would curtail conflicts of interest on mutual fund boards, though the Senate took no action on the bill.

Akaka has a quiet, deliberative approach — described by islander politicos as "island style" — more in tune with traditional Hawaiian ways than with the modern media operations common in politics now. The 12-hour plane rides from Washington to Honolulu make it difficult for Akaka to return home, so every morning he meets in his D.C. office with visiting constituents over coffee and pastries.

In 2005, his empathy for indigenous people made him one of only four Democrats to vote in support of President Bush's proposal to allow oil drilling in Alaska's Arctic National Wildlife Refuge. (Inouye was another.) Akaka cited the support of some Alaska Natives for economic development of the refuge. Democratic Leader Tom Daschle maneuvered to keep Akaka off the conference committee on a similar bill in 2002, even though he was the second-ranking Democrat on the Energy and Natural Resources panel.

A protector of Hawaii's sugar industry, Akaka has successfully fought recurrent efforts to do away with sugar subsidy programs. In 1990, he fought an attempt by Democrat Bill Bradley of New Jersey, a lanky former basketball star. Akaka said, "I'm only 5-feet-7, but I slam-dunked him."

Akaka's career is a study in quiet perseverance. After graduating from the Kamehameha School for Boys, he served in the Army Corps of Engineers during World War II. Returning home, he got a degree in education from the University of Hawaii and became a teacher, then a principal. He rose through the Honolulu education bureaucracy, and in 1976 prevailed in a tough primary contest for the 2nd District seat in the House. He rose to the middle tier of seniority on the House Appropriations Committee, where he concentrated almost entirely on parochial needs.

When Democratic Sen. Spark M. Matsunaga died in April 1990, Akaka was a logical choice to fill the vacancy. He was on good terms with Democratic Gov. John Waihee III, who made the appointment. He also was close to the state party leadership and had the support of Japanese-Americans.

But in the special election that fall to fill out Matsunaga's term, he faced a serious challenge from GOP Rep. Patricia F. Saiki. Akaka had been a sedate figure during his House career and was not readily identifiable to many Hawaiians. But by stressing his ability to deliver federal largess to Hawaii, he prevailed with 54 percent of the vote. He won his next two Senate elections easily, and then battled his way to a third full term in 2006.

KEY VOTES

2006

No Confirm Samuel A. Alito Jr. to the Supreme Court
No Allow consideration of a bill to establish a $140 billion trust fund to compensate victims of asbestos exposure
No Extend tax cuts for two years at a cost of $70 billion over five years
Yes Overhaul immigration policy with border security, enforcement and guest worker program
No Allow consideration of a bill to permanently repeal the estate tax
Yes Urge President Bush to begin troop withdrawals from Iraq in 2006
Yes Lift President Bush's restrictions on stem cell research funding
No Authorize military tribunals for suspected terrorists

2005

No Curb class action lawsuits by shifting them from state to federal courts
Yes Allow confirmation vote on Priscilla R. Owen to the U.S. Court of Appeals for the 5th Circuit
No Oppose mandatory emissions limits and block recognition of global warming as a threat
No Approve free-trade pact with five Central American countries
Yes Pass energy policy overhaul favored by President Bush emphasizing domestic oil and gas production
No Shield gunmakers from lawsuits when their products are used in crimes
Yes Ban torture of prisoners in U.S. custody
No Renew 16 provisions of the Patriot Act
Yes Allow final vote on opening the Arctic National Wildlife Refuge to oil and gas exploration

CQ VOTE STUDIES

	PARTY UNITY		PRESIDENTIAL SUPPORT	
	Support	Oppose	Support	Oppose
2006	96%	4%	48%	52%
2005	96%	4%	40%	60%
2004	97%	3%	56%	44%
2003	97%	3%	51%	49%
2002	91%	9%	63%	37%
2001	98%	2%	70%	30%
2000	98%	2%	97%	3%
1999	96%	4%	89%	11%
1998	96%	4%	91%	9%
1997	97%	3%	90%	10%

INTEREST GROUPS

	AFL-CIO	ADA	CCUS	ACU
2006	93%	95%	30%	0%
2005	100%	95%	39%	8%
2004	100%	95%	29%	5%
2003	100%	90%	30%	11%
2002	100%	80%	53%	0%
2001	100%	95%	50%	13%
2000	86%	85%	46%	12%
1999	89%	100%	41%	4%
1998	100%	85%	41%	10%
1997	71%	95%	60%	4%

Rep. Neil Abercrombie (D)

CAPITOL OFFICE
225-2726
neil.abercrombie@mail.house.gov
www.house.gov/abercrombie
1502 Longworth 20515-1101; fax 225-4580

COMMITTEES
Armed Services
(Air & Land Forces - chairman)
Natural Resources

RESIDENCE
Honolulu

BORN
June 26, 1938, Buffalo, N.Y.

RELIGION
Unspecified

FAMILY
Wife, Nancie Caraway

EDUCATION
Union College, B.A. 1959; U. of Hawaii, M.A. 1964, Ph.D. 1974 (American studies)

CAREER
Educator

POLITICAL HIGHLIGHTS
Sought Democratic nomination for U.S. Senate, 1970; Hawaii House, 1974-78; Hawaii Senate, 1978-86; U.S. House, 1986-87; defeated in primary for re-election to U.S. House, 1986; Honolulu City Council, 1988-90

ELECTION RESULTS

2006 GENERAL		
Neil Abercrombie (D)	112,904	69.4%
Richard "Noah" Hough (R)	49,890	30.6%
2006 PRIMARY		
Neil Abercrombie (D)	82,169	79.1%
Alexandra Kaan (D)	21,667	20.9%
2004 GENERAL		
Neil Abercrombie (D)	128,567	63.0%
Dalton Tanonaka (R)	69,371	34.0%
Elyssa Young (LIBERT)	6,243	3.1%

PREVIOUS WINNING PERCENTAGES
2002 (73%); 2000 (69%); 1998 (62%); 1996 (50%); 1994 (54%); 1992 (73%); 1990 (61%); 1986 Special Election (30%)

Elected 1990; 9th full term

Also served Sept. 1986-Jan. 1987

Abercrombie is a fierce critic of the war in Iraq, which he has opposed from the outset. The one-time Vietnam War protester is a member of the Out of Iraq Caucus, even as he chairs a subcommittee of the House Armed Services Committee. He sees no contradiction in his roles: He is a strong supporter of the U.S. military, which he feels has been severely overextended in Iraq and Afghanistan.

He is amused at the emphasis others put on his past as a Vietnam War protester, saying people assume "that you must have been against the military. And I wasn't, I never was. . . . I felt that the military was being misused for political purposes, and that always infuriated me."

He has the same objections to the war in Iraq. He has consistently voted against spending measures and resolutions that supported the Iraq War, and for measures calling for a timetable for the return of troops. In a February 2007 floor speech opposing President Bush's "surge" of thousands more U.S. troops, he called the war "the greatest strategic foreign policy folly in our nation's history." He said, "Smugly self-righteous in its belief that U.S. troops would be targeted with nothing more lethal than rose petals, this administration has been complacent in leaving the burden of their war on the men and women of our armed forces, active, reserve and National Guard." He said the extensive use of reserve and National Guards troops, in particular, was profoundly affecting whole communities. "Why have they been so misused?" he asked. "Because there isn't anybody else."

Abercrombie says that although many label him a liberal, he sees himself as a "radical conservative" and a "strict constitutionalist." He says his politics are based not on ideology, but rather on a determination "to go on offense for those who are being misused and mistreated. And that is the way I grew up, so I don't feel that I have changed."

When Abercrombie made his congressional debut years ago, he seemed to have stepped out of a 1960s time capsule. His outspoken demeanor — and his long hair — were verbal and visual cues of a lawmaker pushing the leftward edge of the ideological envelope at every turn. Minus the ponytail (it was shorn in 1997), Abercrombie retains much of his early intensity.

But his opposition to the Iraq War has not kept him from looking out for Hawaii's interests in a robust Pentagon budget, and as a senior member of the Armed Services Committee, he is in a position to deliver. He chairs the Air and Land Forces Subcommittee, and he counts among his proudest achievements in Congress the hundreds of millions of dollars he has procured for military research and construction in his district's numerous bases and installations, which include Pearl Harbor. His efforts have not gone unnoticed; in 2002, a new tugboat that services Navy vessels at Pearl Harbor was named after him.

His efforts are not limited to the military budget. In the 110th Congress (2007-08), he is working to coordinate federal, state and military officials in a drive to obtain federal funds to build a multibillion-dollar transit system on Oahu. He says such a rail system not only is the answer to Honolulu's traffic woes but also will "completely transform the urban landscape . . . and all of the social and economic implications that come from that."

In such observations, Abercrombie sometimes sounds like the professor he once was. When a federal appeals court ruled that schoolchildren could not be required to recite the Pledge of Allegiance because it contains the phrase "under God," Abercrombie joined all but three House members in voting to condemn the decision. But Abercrombie explained his vote in terms of the sociological importance of rituals such as the pledge in promoting values such as freedom and patriotism.

Abercrombie generally votes with his fellow Democrats, but he deviates on some tax policies important to the travel and tourism industries that account for a large share of his state's employment. He has pushed hard for legislation allowing a tax deduction for the full cost of business meals and entertainment as well as for travel costs of an accompanying spouse on a business trip. He also has backed GOP efforts to repeal the estate tax, which he says is harmful to Hawaii's many family-owned businesses. "They're right on this issue," he says of the Republicans.

The 2001 tax cut law included an Abercrombie-sponsored provision allowing shareholders in the Campbell Estate — Hawaii's seventh-largest private landowner — up to 14 years to pay the taxes they will owe when the trust is dissolved in 2007.

He has also pushed legislation that would grant ethnic Native Hawaiians sovereign status similar to that held by American Indians and Alaska Natives. A bid to call up such legislation in the Senate, after years of inaction by GOP leaders, fell short by four votes in 2006. But Hawaii's lawmakers hope the new Democratic majority will be more favorable to their cause.

The man who now represents Waikiki got his start in Buffalo, N.Y. After college, he moved to Hawaii for graduate school. Along the way to his advanced degrees, he traveled widely and worked as a teaching assistant, a probation officer, a waiter and a custodian. Soon after he earned his Ph.D., he became a practitioner of protest politics, taking 13 percent of the 1970 Democratic Senate primary vote as an anti-Vietnam War candidate. Four years later, he won election to the state House.

After 11-plus years in the state legislature, Abercrombie briefly served in the House when he won a special election in 1986 to fill a vacancy. But he narrowly lost the primary election for a full term, which was held the same day. He got a second chance when the seat opened up in 1990, winning the Democratic primary with 46 percent of the vote and cruising to an easy victory in November.

He faced difficult re-election battles in 1994 and 1996 and struggled to fend off charges that he was an extreme liberal. Since then, however, he has won by comfortable margins, carrying 69 percent of the vote in 2006. But he never takes a race for granted. "I was dismissed as a candidate in 1974, and I won," he says. "So believe me, I have an indelible lesson in front of me — that I won an election I wasn't supposed to."

KEY VOTES

2006

- Yes Stop broadband companies from favoring select Internet traffic
- No Affirm U.S. commitment to war in Iraq and reject setting a withdrawal date for troops
- No Repeal requirement for bilingual ballots at the polls
- No Permit U.S. sale of civilian nuclear technology to India
- No Build a 700-mile fence on the U.S.-Mexico border to curb illegal crossings
- No Permit warrantless wiretaps of suspected terrorists

2005

- ? Intervene in the life-support case of Terri Schiavo
- Yes Lift President Bush's restrictions on stem cell research funding
- Yes Prohibit FBI access to library and bookstore records
- No Approve free-trade pact with five Central American countries
- Yes Pass energy policy overhaul favored by President Bush emphasizing domestic oil and gas production
- Yes End mandatory preservation of habitat of endangered animal and plant species
- Yes Ban torture of prisoners in U.S. custody

CQ VOTE STUDIES

	PARTY UNITY		PRESIDENTIAL SUPPORT	
	Support	Oppose	Support	Oppose
2006	92%	8%	17%	83%
2005	92%	8%	15%	85%
2004	94%	6%	15%	85%
2003	94%	6%	16%	84%
2002	89%	11%	32%	68%

INTEREST GROUPS

	AFL-CIO	ADA	CCUS	ACU
2006	86%	90%	40%	12%
2005	100%	100%	42%	12%
2004	93%	85%	32%	0%
2003	100%	95%	30%	16%
2002	100%	85%	45%	12%

HAWAII 1

Oahu — Honolulu, Waipahu, Pearl City

Located on the southern coast of the island of Oahu, the compact 1st takes in the narrow plain south of the Koolau mountain range, encompassing the city of Honolulu — the engine that drives all of Hawaii — and Waipahu to the west of Honolulu.

Honolulu is Hawaii's capital, home to most of its business and about one-third of its people. In Honolulu's east lies Waikiki and the heart of the state's leading industry: tourism. The industry slumped following Asia's mid-1990s economic problems and the Sept. 11 attacks, but it has largely regained its dominant economic footing. The legacy of World War II remains etched in the 1st's consciousness, and Pearl Harbor anchors a strong military presence in the district.

Democrats are entrenched in the 1st, and the district has elected only one Republican to Congress in its history. Japanese-Americans, particularly of the older generation, dominate the Democratic Party here and are joined by many other non-white constituents to form the majority of the 1st's residents. The district has the highest percentage (54 percent) of Asian residents in the nation, and ethnic Native Hawaiians make up less than 7 percent of the population. Locally, Democrats also do very well, although some moderate Republican enclaves exist in the suburbs of East Honolulu and Waikiki. George W. Bush held John Kerry to 52 percent here in the 2004 presidential election, showing that a Republican candidate can make the vote close.

MAJOR INDUSTRY
Tourism, military, construction

MILITARY BASES
Hickam Air Force Base, 5,205 military, 1,945 civilian (2004); Fort Shafter, 3,000 military, 1,950 civilian (2005); Pearl Harbor Naval Shipyard and IMF, 525 military, 3,757 civilian (2003); Tripler Army Medical Center, 1,500 military, 1,500 civilian; Naval Submarine Base Pearl Harbor, 2,500 military, 175 civilian; Naval Station Pearl Harbor, 524 military, 501 civilian (2006); Camp H.M. Smith, 730 military, 160 civilian (2004)

CITIES
Honolulu, 371,657; Waipahu, 33,108; Pearl City, 30,976; Waimalu, 29,371

NOTABLE
Iolani Palace in downtown Honolulu was the official residence of the Hawaiian Kingdom's last two monarchs.

Rep. Mazie K. Hirono (D)

Elected 2006; 1st term

A native of Fukushima, Japan, Hirono came to Hawaii as a child and became a U.S. citizen in 1959, the year Hawaii became a state. She said she's proud to be among the small number of foreign-born members of Congress. "I think that I truly exemplify the American dream as an immigrant who came here with nothing, not speaking the language," she said.

An attorney, Hirono (full name: may-ZEE hee-RO-no) served for nearly 14 years in the Hawaii state House. She was elected twice as Hawaii's lieutenant governor, but was thwarted in her effort to move to the governor's mansion in 2002, upset by Republican Linda Lingle, whose victory ended 40 years of Democratic control of the governorship.

Hirono sits on the Education and Labor Committee, where she says she intends to take a hard look at the No Child Left Behind law, which she says overemphasizes the use of testing. She also has a seat on the Transportation and Infrastructure panel. Transportation is a hot topic in Hawaii, which she says needs federal funds for infrastructure repairs.

Although winning Hawaii's 2nd District seat is Hirono's first national office, she is not a newcomer to the nation's capital. She earned her law degree from Georgetown University in 1978, where she focused on public interest law. Hirono and freshman Democrat Hank Johnson of Georgia are the first two Buddhists ever to be elected to Congress.

In 2006, Hirono used her statewide name recognition to run for the open 2nd seat, after Democrat Ed Case decided to challenge Sen. Daniel K. Akaka. Hirono competed against nine other Democrats in the September primary but gained an edge with fundraising support from EMILY's List. She placed first in the primary with 22 percent, beating out the next-highest contender by 844 votes. She won the general election easily over GOP state Sen. Bob Hogue, with 61 percent of the tally.

Hirono says she sees herself as a successor to the late Democratic Rep. Patsy T. Mink, who was known as an activist liberal. "Patsy fought for working men and women and she fought for education," said Hirono. "Those are the issues that are really important to me."

CAPITOL OFFICE
225-4906
hirono.house.gov
1229 Longworth 20515-1102; fax 225-4987

COMMITTEES
Education & Labor
Transportation & Infrastructure

RESIDENCE
Honolulu

BORN
Nov. 3, 1947, Fukushima, Japan

RELIGION
Buddhist

FAMILY
Husband, Leighton Kim Oshima; one stepchild

EDUCATION
U. of Hawaii, B.A. 1970 (psychology); Georgetown U., J.D. 1978

CAREER
Lawyer; campaign and state legislative aide

POLITICAL HIGHLIGHTS
Hawaii House, 1981-94; lieutenant governor, 1994-2002; Democratic nominee for governor, 2002

ELECTION RESULTS

2006 GENERAL		
Mazie K. Hirono (D)	106,906	61.0%
Bob Hogue (R)	68,244	39.0%
2006 PRIMARY		
Mazie K. Hirono (D)	24,487	21.8%
Colleen Hanabusa (D)	23,643	21.1%
Matt Matsunaga (D)	16,001	14.3%
Clayton Hee (D)	12,649	11.3%
Gary L. Hooser (D)	10,730	9.6%
Brian Schatz (D)	8,254	7.4%
Ron Menor (D)	8,030	7.2%
Nestor R. Garcia (D)	4,479	4.0%
Hanalei Y. Aipoalani (D)	2,688	2.4%
Joe Zuiker (D)	1,174	1.0%

HAWAII 2

Suburban and Outer Oahu; 'Neighbor Islands'

The 2nd's islands are amazing in their geographic diversity, with sandy beaches, volcanoes, tropical rain forests and deserts. The district includes part of Oahu and all of Hawaii's other seven major islands.

Tourism and agriculture, the 2nd's leading industries, struggled through rough times in the 1990s. While tourism has bounced back, the closure of numerous sugar plantations continues to hurt agricultural prospects. Growers have turned to coffee, macadamia nuts and bananas to counter the industry's recent job losses. Tax incentives have helped attract technology companies.

The 2nd has a large Asian population (28 percent) and is heavily Democratic. While there are some predominately white, conservative-leaning communities on Oahu and Maui, these areas usually are not strong enough to push Republicans to victory in federal races. Economic problems offer the GOP an opening at the local level, but the 2nd has kept Democrats in office, and John Kerry captured 56 percent of the 2nd's 2004 presidential vote. In 2006, GOP Gov. Linda Lingle did well in Honolulu County while winning only 51 percent in Kauai County.

MAJOR INDUSTRY
Tourism, agriculture, military

MILITARY BASES
Schofield Barracks (Army), 16,500 military, 3,950 civilian (2005); Marine Corps Base Hawaii, 7,014 military, 1,905 civilian (2004); Naval Computer and Telecommunications Area Master Station Pacific, 769 military, 257 civilian; Lualualei Naval Magazine, 200 military, 435 civilian (2003)

CITIES
Hilo, 40,759; Kailua, 36,513; Kaneohe, 34,970

NOTABLE
The Northwestern Hawaiian Islands Marine National Monument conservation area, at more than 137,000 square miles, is larger than all U.S. national parks combined.

IDAHO

Gov. C. L. "Butch" Otter (R)

First elected: 2006
Length of term: 4 years
Term expires: 1/11
Salary: $105,000
Phone: (208) 334-2100

Residence: Star
Born: May 3, 1942; Caldwell, Idaho
Religion: Roman Catholic
Family: Wife, Lori Otter; four children
Education: College of Idaho, B.A. 1967 (political science)
Military service: Idaho National Guard, 1967-73
Career: Agribusiness company executive; oil company partner
Political highlights: Idaho House, 1972-76; sought Republican nomination for governor, 1978; lieutenant governor, 1987-2001; U.S. House, 2001-07

Election results:

2006 GENERAL		
C. L. "Butch" Otter (R)	237,437	52.7%
Jerry M. Brady (D)	198,845	44.1%
Marvin Richardson (CNSTP)	7,309	1.6%
Ted Dunlap (LIBERT)	7,241	1.6%

Lt. Gov. Jim Risch (R)

First elected: 2002
Length of term: 4 years
Term expires: 1/11
Salary: $27,820
Phone: (208) 334-2200

LEGISLATURE

Legislature: January-March or April

Senate: 35 members, 2-year terms
2007 ratios: 28 R, 7 D; 29 men, 6 women
Salary: $16,116
Phone: (208) 332-1309

House: 70 members, 2-year terms
2007 ratios: 51 R, 19 D; 52 men, 18 women
Salary: $16,116
Phone: (208) 332-1140

TERM LIMITS

Governor: No
Senate: No
House: No

URBAN STATISTICS

CITY	POPULATION
Boise	185,787
Nampa	51,867
Pocatello	51,466
Idaho Falls	50,730
Meridian	34,919

REGISTERED VOTERS

Voters do not register by party.

POPULATION

2006 population (est.)	1,466,465
2000 population	1,293,953
1990 population	1,006,749
Percent change (1990-2000)	+28.5%
Rank among states (2006)	39
Median age	33.2
Born in state	47.2%
Foreign born	5%
Violent crime rate	253/100,000
Poverty level	11.8%
Federal workers	12,939
Military	9,730

ELECTIONS

STATE ELECTION OFFICIAL
(208) 334-2852
DEMOCRATIC PARTY
(208) 336-1815
REPUBLICAN PARTY
(208) 343-6405

MISCELLANEOUS

Web: www.idaho.gov
Capital: Boise

U.S. CONGRESS

Senate: 2 Republicans
House: 2 Republicans

2000 Census Statistics by District

DIST.	2004 VOTE FOR PRESIDENT BUSH	KERRY	WHITE	BLACK	ASIAN	HISP	MEDIAN INCOME	WHITE COLLAR	BLUE COLLAR	SERVICE INDUSTRY	OVER 64	UNDER 18	COLLEGE EDUCATION	RURAL	SQ. MILES
1	68%	30%	89%	0%	1%	7%	$38,364	56%	28%	15%	12%	28%	20%	34%	39,525
2	68	30	87	0	1	9	$36,934	57	27	16	11	29	23	33	43,222
STATE	68	30	88	0	1	8	$37,572	57	28	16	11	29	22	34	82,747
U.S.	50.7	48.3	69	12	4	13	$41,994	60	25	15	12	26	24	21	3,537,438

Boundary
Bonner
Coeur d'Alene
Kootenai
Benewah
Shoshone
Latah
Moscow
Clearwater
Nez Perce
Lewiston
Lewis
Idaho
1
Adams
Valley
Lemhi
Washington
Custer
Clark
Fremont
Payette
Gem
Boise
2
Jefferson
Madison
Teton
Canyon
Butte
Boise
Idaho Falls
Bonneville
Camas
Blaine
Ada
Elmore
Bingham
Gooding
Lincoln
Caribou
Jerome
Minidoka
Power
Bannock
Owyhee
Twin Falls
Cassia
Twin Falls
Oneida
Bear Lake
Franklin

Sen. Larry E. Craig (R)

CAPITOL OFFICE
224-2752
craig.senate.gov
520 Hart 20510-1203; fax 228-1067

COMMITTEES
Appropriations
Energy & Natural Resources
Environment & Public Works
Veterans' Affairs - ranking member
Special Aging

RESIDENCE
Eagle

BORN
July 20, 1945, Council, Idaho

RELIGION
Methodist

FAMILY
Wife, Suzanne Craig; three children

EDUCATION
U. of Idaho, B.A. 1969 (political science); George Washington U., attended 1969-70 (U.S. foreign policy)

MILITARY SERVICE
Idaho National Guard, 1970-72

CAREER
Farmer; rancher

POLITICAL HIGHLIGHTS
Idaho Senate, 1974-80; U.S. House, 1981-91

ELECTION RESULTS

2002 GENERAL		
Larry E. Craig (R)	266,215	65.2%
Alan Blinken (D)	132,975	32.6%
Donovan Bramwell (LIBERT)	9,354	2.3%
2002 PRIMARY		
Larry E. Craig (R)		unopposed

PREVIOUS WINNING PERCENTAGES
1996 (57%); 1990 (61%); 1988 House Election (66%); 1986 House Election (65%); 1984 House Election (69%); 1982 House Election (54%); 1980 House Election (54%)

Elected 1990; 3rd term

With a bit of mischief, Craig calls himself a "right-wing pragmatist." The unlikely combination of terms captures his approach to his job: He's unquestionably conservative, both fiscally and socially, but he wastes little time standing on abstract principles if bending a little gets the job done.

He is willing to bide his time when things don't break his way initially, and he will sometimes work with Democrats. That represents a political evolution for a formerly confrontational and controversy-prone lawmaker, a foot soldier in the Reagan revolution who raised eyebrows with stunts like his 1995 reference to national forest, fish and wildlife police as a potentially "armed federal entity" that should lay down its weapons. Today, Craig is every bit the conservative he was then, but has mellowed in style and consequently has more impact on policy. He is now one of the Senate's most influential Western Republicans, a group often identified with anti-regulation positions.

"When a problem can't be solved by any other means, I believe government, in a non-intrusive way, should become involved," Craig says. "I believe states should play a dominant role, but sometimes states need assistance. Most importantly, I don't want government to ever be feared by its citizenry."

Though land use issues continue to be important to him, Craig's signature topic in recent years has been immigration, a rare case in which he takes a more liberal position than President Bush and most GOP conservatives. He has pushed amnesty-style proposals for illegal migrant farm workers, and some of his ideas became part of the immigration bill debated in 2006. The year before, that development was foretold when his proposals nearly made it into law as part of a must-do supplemental appropriations bill. With as many as 12 million immigrants estimated to be living and working illegally in the United States, Craig says deporting them all is impractical and potentially devastating to states, particularly those with big farm economies like Idaho that are dependent on seasonal labor.

Craig will take on the White House on occasion. He refused to vote for a sweeping rewrite of the 2001 Patriot Act, the country's major anti-terrorism law, because he viewed it as a threat to civil liberties. With three other Republicans and most Democrats, he dug in for a Senate filibuster that forced the White House and leaders to negotiate a new bill in 2006.

Earlier, Craig broke with Bush in 2002 when the Senate debated legislation giving the president fast-track authority to negotiate trade agreements that Congress must approve or reject without amendment. He teamed with Minnesota Democrat Mark Dayton to win adoption of a provision giving the Senate power to vote separately on parts of trade pacts that weaken U.S. anti-dumping laws. Bush threatened a veto unless the provision was removed. In the end, Craig settled for a requirement that trade negotiators keep anti-dumping laws intact if possible.

In the 109th Congress (2005-06), Craig was chairman of the Veterans' Affairs Committee. To get a handle on soaring VA health care costs attributed to a growing number of veterans from the Iraq and Afghanistan wars, Craig was willing to embrace White House proposals to charge higher enrollment fees and prescription drug co-payments to financially well-off veterans who were not disabled during military service. He backed off, however, when the plan ran into furious opposition from veterans' groups. Craig then opened discussions with the groups in the hope of finding compromise. In 2006, the president signed into law Craig's $3.2 billion measure authorizing major medical projects, mandating an information technology overhaul at the Veterans Affairs Department, and allowing veterans to hire attorneys to help them navigate the benefit claims process.

Craig has served on the Appropriations Committee since 1997, but has not chaired a subcommittee. In 2005, he could have taken the gavel of the District of Columbia or Legislative Branch panels, but said he was not interested. In the 110th Congress (2007-08), he is the top-ranking Republican on the Interior Appropriations Subcommittee.

As a member of the Energy and Natural Resources Committee, he has fought efforts by Democrats and moderate Republicans to limit or ban livestock grazing, mining, drilling and road-building on the millions of acres owned by the U.S. government. He also has worked to rewrite the Endangered Species Act, which he says tramples on private property rights and inhibits job growth. And he helped write the comprehensive energy overhaul passed by Congress in 2005. Although he sided with the oil industry on most issues in the legislation, Craig bluntly told oil executives at a hearing that their record profits were making it "not terribly fun defending you."

In the 110th Congress, he became a member of the Environment and Public Works Committee, which, like Energy and Commerce, has jurisdiction over issues related to global warming. Craig says he believes the Earth is warming, but he has challenged the idea that the emission of greenhouse gases is a major factor. Yet he told The Idaho Statesman newspaper in early 2007 that as the science has become clearer, he'd rather err on the side of safety and encourage the development of climate-friendly energy technology — provided it does not restrict economic growth.

His unwavering conservatism, combined with flawless diction and masterful debating skills, lifted Craig to the chairmanship of the Republican Policy Committee, the fourth-ranking GOP leadership position, at the start of his second term in 1997. He had to give up the post at the end of 2002 because of party-imposed term limits. His efforts to move up since then have been bested by other senior Republicans.

A member of the National Rifle Association board, Craig zealously guards the rights of gun owners. After a student massacre at Colorado's Columbine High School in 1999, he led the campaign against proposals to require background checks at gun shows. In 2002, Craig joined Democrats on a bill strengthening instant background checks, and in 2005 he won enactment of his bill to shield gun manufacturers from lawsuits.

Away from Washington, Craig is on the board of the Center for the New West, a conservative think tank based in Boise. He has pushed the center to focus its work on the problem of keeping the rapidly growing region supplied with water.

Water happens to be essential for Craig's favorite off-duty activity. He calls himself "an uncontrolled gardener," and is thankful that his hobby gives him a chance to spend time with his eight grandchildren. "My wife knows she's not a golf widow or a skiing or a hunting widow," he says. "She's a gardening widow."

Craig showed an early inclination toward politics. Born on his family's ranch, which was homesteaded in 1899 by his grandfather, he headed the Idaho Young Republicans and was national vice president of the Future Farmers of America. In 1974, he won election to the state Senate, and has never lost an election since.

In 1980, he ran for an open House seat and won with 54 percent of the vote. The retirement of Republican Sen. James A. McClure after three terms in 1990 then opened a Senate seat, and Craig easily bested state Attorney General Jim Jones in the GOP primary, and went on to win the general election with 61 percent of the vote. He won two more terms with relative ease.

KEY VOTES

2006

Yes Confirm Samuel A. Alito Jr. to the Supreme Court

Yes Allow consideration of a bill to establish a $140 billion trust fund to compensate victims of asbestos exposure

Yes Extend tax cuts for two years at a cost of $70 billion over five years

Yes Overhaul immigration policy with border security, enforcement and guest worker program

Yes Allow consideration of a bill to permanently repeal the estate tax

No Urge President Bush to begin troop withdrawals from Iraq in 2006

No Lift President Bush's restrictions on stem cell research funding

Yes Authorize military tribunals for suspected terrorists

2005

Yes Curb class action lawsuits by shifting them from state to federal courts

Yes Allow confirmation vote on Priscilla R. Owen to the U.S. Court of Appeals for the 5th Circuit

Yes Oppose mandatory emissions limits and block recognition of global warming as a threat

No Approve free-trade pact with five Central American countries

Yes Pass energy policy overhaul favored by President Bush emphasizing domestic oil and gas production

Yes Shield gunmakers from lawsuits when their products are used in crimes

Yes Ban torture of prisoners in U.S. custody

No Renew 16 provisions of the Patriot Act

Yes Allow final vote on opening the Arctic National Wildlife Refuge to oil and gas exploration

CQ VOTE STUDIES

	PARTY UNITY		PRESIDENTIAL SUPPORT	
	Support	Oppose	Support	Oppose
2006	91%	9%	94%	6%
2005	93%	7%	82%	18%
2004	98%	2%	96%	4%
2003	98%	2%	97%	3%
2002	93%	7%	95%	5%
2001	96%	4%	97%	3%
2000	100%	0%	40%	60%
1999	97%	3%	29%	71%
1998	99%	1%	29%	71%
1997	97%	3%	54%	46%

INTEREST GROUPS

	AFL-CIO	ADA	CCUS	ACU
2006	13%	0%	100%	88%
2005	36%	15%	89%	96%
2004	8%	5%	88%	96%
2003	15%	5%	91%	90%
2002	8%	5%	90%	100%
2001	13%	0%	100%	96%
2000	0%	0%	93%	100%
1999	0%	0%	88%	96%
1998	0%	5%	100%	84%
1997	0%	5%	100%	84%

Sen. Michael D. Crapo (R)

CAPITOL OFFICE
224-6142
crapo.senate.gov
239 Dirksen 20510-1205; fax 228-1375

COMMITTEES
Agriculture, Nutrition & Forestry
Banking, Housing & Urban Affairs
Budget
Finance

RESIDENCE
Idaho Falls

BORN
May 20, 1951, Idaho Falls, Idaho

RELIGION
Mormon

FAMILY
Wife, Susan Crapo; five children

EDUCATION
Brigham Young U., B.A. 1973 (political science); Harvard U., J.D. 1977

CAREER
Lawyer

POLITICAL HIGHLIGHTS
Idaho Senate, 1984-92 (president pro tempore, 1988-92); U.S. House, 1993-99

ELECTION RESULTS

2004 GENERAL

Michael D. Crapo (R)	499,796	99.2%
Scott F. McClure (D) - write-in	4,136	0.8%

2004 PRIMARY

Michael D. Crapo (R)	unopposed

PREVIOUS WINNING PERCENTAGES
1998 (70%); 1996 House Election (69%); 1994 House Election (75%); 1992 House Election (61%)

Elected 1998; 2nd term

Among the most well-liked senators, Crapo is known by his colleagues as "a nice guy," and not by accident. He works at it. He says he learned as a freshman in high school that little gestures, such as making eye contact with people, can make a big difference in building relationships.

Conservative in philosophy but moderate in demeanor, Crapo (CRAY-poe) was aptly described in 2003 by former GOP Sen. James A. McClure in the Idaho Statesman newspaper. "He's not flamboyant, he's not seeking headlines, he is thoughtful, and he works," McClure said. "That's a good combination. You're not threatening anybody, you're not pushing anybody, you're not embarrassing anybody."

Crapo is not merely reluctant to personalize political disagreements, he thinks that the practice is a major negative in modern politics. "I really do believe that this country is made strong by a real strong clash of ideas," he says. "But it's the clash of ideas, not the clash of personalities, that is what counts and what generates good public policy."

His sunny manner belies an ambition — fueled in part by his dedication to a deceased older brother — that is reflected in his climb up the political ladder. A cum laude graduate of Harvard Law School, Crapo was elected to the Idaho Senate at age 33 and chosen its president pro tempore just four years later. He won the 2nd District seat in the U.S. House in 1992 and in his first term, landed a sought-after seat on the House Energy and Commerce Committee.

Crapo has been in the Senate since 1998. He is on the Finance Committee, where he works to advance the GOP tax-cutting agenda. He also serves on the Banking, Housing and Urban Affairs panel, an unusual choice for a senator from a rural Western state. "The issues that we deal with in Banking and Finance, in particular, are as critical to a farmer as they are to a banker on Wall Street," he says. "The farmers are interested in financing for their farming operations, they're interested in estate tax law." Crapo took the lead in 2006 on a wide-ranging banking regulation bill to ease restrictions on banks, credit unions and other financial institutions. That bill became law.

Crapo lost his oldest brother to cancer. An Idaho state legislator and wunderkind who was also his mentor and law partner, Terry Crapo died just two weeks after being diagnosed with leukemia in 1982. Crapo faced his own trial with cancer starting in 2000, when doctors diagnosed prostate cancer and operated. Early in 2005, the cancer returned and Crapo underwent radiation treatments while he continued to work in the Senate. By mid-2006, regular blood tests indicated he was cancer-free. "It's been a very sobering experience," he says. Crapo now sponsors regular prostate and breast cancer screening fairs in Idaho. In the past three Congresses, he has authored a bill to create an Office of Men's Health, to coordinate and promote the status of men's health in the United States.

When he got his Finance Committee assignment in 2005, Crapo had to relinquish his seat on Environment and Public Works, where in 2003 and 2004 he had chaired the Fisheries, Wildlife and Water Subcommittee. He did not make the decision lightly, because an overhaul of the Endangered Species Act has been a priority of his for years. Crapo says he received assurances from senior Republicans on the Environment Committee that he could continue working on endangered species matters.

Crapo long has taken an interest in water issues, ranging from pollution from agricultural runoff to helping small communities with improvements to water systems. On the Agriculture, Nutrition and Forestry Committee, he also took an active role in legislation enacted in 2003 aimed at preventing wildfires. It authorized the thinning of 20 million acres of national forests and restricted legal challenges to logging.

Crapo sometimes bucks his party and the president on trade issues. Like many Westerners, he is wary of Canadian policies toward timber and agricultural trade with the United States, and opposed legislation to implement both the 1993 North American Free Trade Agreement and the 1994 General Agreement on Tariffs and Trade. Since then, he voted to enact the 2000 law making permanent the normalized U.S.-China trade relationship but he opposed the 2005 Central American Free Trade Agreement out of concern over its potential impact on Idaho sugar beet producers.

Crapo is generally supportive of party positions, voting with the majority of Senate Republicans 95 percent of the time on party-line votes in the 109th Congress (2005-06). But he strays on occasion. He has voted against measures to limit medical malpractice awards, which would have pre-empted an Idaho law, and to provide tax incentives for charitable donations. He is among the minority of Senate Republicans who favor lifting the ban on travel to Cuba.

Crapo grew up in Idaho Falls, the youngest of six children of the local postmaster and his homemaker wife. In addition to his post office job, his father farmed 200 acres of potatoes, grain and pasture for cattle-grazing, and the children pitched in to help. The family farm expanded over the years and today is run by Crapo's uncles and cousins.

Crapo made his political debut in a bid for student body president of his high school, showing a flair for organization and media-grabbing. He and seven other candidates ran as the Bonnie and Clyde slate, dressing up like robbers and getting the local police to chase them across town after a mock clothing store holdup. The stunt made the evening news. "I don't know why we thought that staging a robbery would get us elected, but it did," he recalls. He learned another valuable political lesson. "I always made a point in high school of just making eye contact with people as I was passing them in the hall," says Crapo, who has kept up the practice as a senator.

At Brigham Young University, he earned a degree in political science and indulged a passion for dirt bike racing. After graduation, he went East to be a Washington intern for Idaho GOP Rep. Orval Hansen. He considered a career in medicine, but changed his mind after gaining admission to Harvard Law School, an institution he found "very exhilarating and challenging."

More at ease in boots and jeans than a business suit, Crapo got his law degree and returned to his hometown to practice. A devout Mormon, he says his experiences with the church, which gives its lay leaders considerable responsibilities in dealing with personal and community issues, helped prepare him for public office.

In 1992, he ran for the House seat being vacated by Democrat Richard Stallings, who ran unsuccessfully for the Senate. In the GOP-leaning 2nd District, Crapo was aided by George H.W. Bush's presence on the ticket, and he defeated Democrat J.D. Williams by 26 percentage points.

Crapo has never faced a tough election. When Republican Sen. Dirk Kempthorne decided to run for governor in 1998, Crapo quickly became the ordained front-runner to succeed him. Crapo's popularity and a strong Republican tide enabled him to crush Bill Mauk, a former Democratic state chairman, by more than 40 points.

In 2004, for the first time in the state's history, Idaho's Democratic Party declined to field a Senate candidate. An opponent, Jerome businessman Scott F. McClure, surfaced late in the campaign, claiming that democracy was not well served if voters had no choice at all. He ran as a write-in candidate. Crapo captured 99 percent of the vote.

KEY VOTES

2006

- Yes Confirm Samuel A. Alito Jr. to the Supreme Court
- No Allow consideration of a bill to establish a $140 billion trust fund to compensate victims of asbestos exposure
- Yes Extend tax cuts for two years at a cost of $70 billion over five years
- No Overhaul immigration policy with border security, enforcement and guest worker program
- Yes Allow consideration of a bill to permanently repeal the estate tax
- No Urge President Bush to begin troop withdrawals from Iraq in 2006
- No Lift President Bush's restrictions on stem cell research funding
- Yes Authorize military tribunals for suspected terrorists

2005

- Yes Curb class action lawsuits by shifting them from state to federal courts
- Yes Allow confirmation vote on Priscilla R. Owen to the U.S. Court of Appeals for the 5th Circuit
- Yes Oppose mandatory emissions limits and block recognition of global warming as a threat
- No Approve free-trade pact with five Central American countries
- Yes Pass energy policy overhaul favored by President Bush emphasizing domestic oil and gas production
- Yes Shield gunmakers from lawsuits when their products are used in crimes
- Yes Ban torture of prisoners in U.S. custody
- Yes Renew 16 provisions of the Patriot Act
- Yes Allow final vote on opening the Arctic National Wildlife Refuge to oil and gas exploration

CQ VOTE STUDIES

	PARTY UNITY		PRESIDENTIAL SUPPORT	
	Support	Oppose	Support	Oppose
2006	95%	5%	88%	12%
2005	95%	5%	84%	16%
2004	96%	4%	90%	10%
2003	98%	2%	97%	3%
2002	92%	8%	96%	4%
2001	94%	6%	96%	4%
2000	100%	0%	41%	59%
1999	97%	3%	30%	70%
House Service:				
1998	89%	11%	30%	70%
1997	94%	6%	20%	80%

INTEREST GROUPS

	AFL-CIO	ADA	CCUS	ACU
2006	7%	0%	83%	88%
2005	21%	10%	94%	100%
2004	8%	10%	94%	92%
2003	15%	5%	91%	89%
2002	9%	10%	94%	94%
2001	19%	10%	100%	92%
2000	0%	0%	93%	100%
1999	0%	0%	88%	100%
House Service:				
1998	22%	10%	94%	83%
1997	13%	0%	70%	92%

Rep. Bill Sali (R)

CAPITOL OFFICE
225-6611
sali.house.gov
508 Cannon 20515-1201; fax 225-3029

COMMITTEES
Natural Resources
Oversight & Government Reform

RESIDENCE
Kuna

BORN
Feb. 17, 1954, Portsmouth, Ohio

RELIGION
Evangelical

FAMILY
Wife, Terry Sali; six children

EDUCATION
Boise State U., B.B.A. 1981 (economics); U. of Idaho, J.D. 1984

CAREER
Lawyer; musician; heavy equipment warehouse clerk

POLITICAL HIGHLIGHTS
Idaho House, 1990-2006

ELECTION RESULTS

2006 GENERAL		
Bill Sali (R)	115,843	49.9%
Larry E. Grant (D)	103,935	44.8%
Dave Olson (I)	6,857	3.0%
Andy Hedden-Nicely (NL)	2,882	1.2%
Paul Smith (CNSTP)	2,457	1.1%
2006 PRIMARY		
Bill Sali (R)	18,985	25.8%
Robert Vasquez (R)	13,624	18.5%
Sheila Sorenson (R)	13,472	18.3%
Keith Johnson (R)	13,186	17.9%
Norman M. Semanko (R)	7,976	10.9%
R. Skipper "Skip" Brandt (R)	6,289	8.6%

Elected 2006; 1st term

Known in Idaho for his hard-line conservatism and blunt rhetoric, Sali wasted no time making his mark in Congress. As House Democrats in January 2007 voted to increase the federal minimum wage, Sali mockingly proposed legislation to combat obesity by reducing the Earth's gravity by 10 percent. He said the two were equally absurd — that Congress can no more modify the workings of the free market than it can alter the laws of nature.

While the move was good for some chuckles, Sali (pronounced "Sally") hasn't always inspired such a benign reaction. In Idaho's state legislature, he was known for infuriating other lawmakers, including fellow Republicans. At various times in his career, he has publicly feuded with Idaho Republicans such as Sen. Larry E. Craig, former Rep. Helen Chenoweth, who held the 1st District seat from 1995-2001, and Rep. Mike Simpson, who represents the adjacent 2nd District. Simpson, a former Speaker of the Idaho House, was once so angry at Sali he threatened to throw him out a third-floor window.

Although Sali's take-no-prisoners attitude may hurt his legislative efforts at times, he said during his campaign, "If you want a go-along-to-get-along guy in Congress, that ain't me." That didn't bother other GOP newcomers to Congress; they elected him president of their 13-member freshman class, making him the liaison between the new members and party leaders.

Heralded by conservative organizations in Idaho for his vehement opposition to abortion, Sali opposes same-sex marriage, supports strict immigration laws, and favors allowing religious displays on public property. Antitax and anti-regulation, he argues for a smaller, less obtrusive government.

When Republican Rep. C.L. "Butch" Otter ran for governor in 2006, Sali jumped into the race for the 1st District seat. Concerned that almost three-quarters of Idaho Republican voters had preferred another candidate, national GOP leaders poured money into Sali's campaign and sent top names like Vice President Dick Cheney to stump for him. Sali also capitalized on support from the conservative Club for Growth, a national anti-tax group, to win a six-way primary. He then edged past Democrat Larry E. Grant, a former Micron Technology executive, by 5 percentage points in November.

IDAHO 1

West – Nampa, Panhandle, part of Boise

From its smokestack-shaped panhandle that opens into British Columbia in the north, the 1st travels 500 miles south to the Nevada state line, bordering both Washington and Oregon to the west. Rural and rugged, the 1st features winding rivers, deep canyons and trails that trace the historic expedition of Lewis and Clark as they sought a route to the Pacific Ocean.

The area west of Boise, in Ada and Canyon counties, is the most populated region of the 1st. Boise (shared with the 2nd) has lured new technology firms, such as Hewlett-Packard, which complement the white-collar economy already established at companies such as Micron Technology, located nearby in the 2nd. Also west of Boise, agriculture, lumber, paper, construction, electronics and food processing companies employ thousands of residents.

There are manufacturing, call center and casino-based jobs in the northern part of the district near the Democratic-leaning area of Coeur d' Alene. The land between that city and Boise is home to rural communities that promote a growing tourism industry by marketing the scenic byways that tower over sapphire lakes and thick forests. Struggling small timber mills also are spread throughout this heavily forested region.

Since 1967, Democrats have held the U.S. House seat for only four years (1991-95), making the 1st one of the strongest GOP seats in the northwest. In both the 2000 and 2004 presidential elections, George W. Bush swept every county in the 1st.

MAJOR INDUSTRY
Manufacturing, agriculture, timber

CITIES
Boise City (pt.), 59,680; Nampa, 51,867; Meridian, 34,919; Coeur d'Alene, 34,514

NOTABLE
Near Riggins in Idaho County, Hells Canyon separates Idaho from Oregon and is the nation's deepest river gorge.

Rep. Mike Simpson (R)

CAPITOL OFFICE
225-5531
www.house.gov/simpson
1339 Longworth 20515-1202; fax 225-8216

COMMITTEES
Appropriations
Budget

RESIDENCE
Blackfoot

BORN
Sept. 8, 1950, Burley, Idaho

RELIGION
Mormon

FAMILY
Wife, Kathy Simpson

EDUCATION
Utah State U., attended 1968-72 (pre-dentistry); Washington U. (Mo.), D.M.D. 1977; Utah State U., B.S. 2002 (pre-dentistry)

CAREER
Dentist

POLITICAL HIGHLIGHTS
Blackfoot City Council, 1980-84; Idaho House, 1984-98 (Speaker, 1992-98)

ELECTION RESULTS

2006 GENERAL		
Mike Simpson (R)	132,262	62.0%
Jim Hansen (D)	73,441	34.4%
Cameron Forth (I)	5,113	2.4%
Travis J. Hedrick (CNSTP)	2,516	1.2%
2006 PRIMARY		
Mike Simpson (R)		unopposed
2004 GENERAL		
Mike Simpson (R)	193,704	70.7%
Lin Whitworth (D)	80,133	29.3%

PREVIOUS WINNING PERCENTAGES
2002 (68%); 2000 (71%); 1998 (53%)

Elected 1998; 5th term

Superficially, Simpson is indistinguishable from many Republican conservatives. He is anti-abortion, anti-regulation, anti-tax and pro-energy development. But he is also determined to try to understand the point of view of those who differ with him.

Since the days when he served in the Idaho House, Simpson has kept in his office a 12-point set of "Simpson's Rules," which include "hear both sides before judging" and "never, never make an enemy needlessly." In his quest to understand other viewpoints, he briefly joined the American Civil Liberties Union and the Idaho Conservation League, and he regularly attends meetings with environmental groups who disagree with him.

No. 1 on the list of Simpson's rules: "Never compromise your integrity." Simpson doesn't criticize his colleagues often, but will do so when he thinks they're out of line. At the start of the 110th Congress (2007-08), Republicans complained loudly as the Democrats created one big, unamendable package of the slew of fiscal 2007 spending bills that GOP leaders had left unfinished the year before. Simpson was the exception. He was the only Republican to vote for the rule governing debate of the legislation, and one of a tiny handful opposing the procedural protest votes that Republicans forced. "I have a really hard time criticizing the Democrats in general when it's a result of our inability to pass the budget," he said. As for the "obstructionist" procedural moves, he said, "I objected when the Democrats did it. How could I not object when Republicans do it?"

In the 108th Congress (2003-04), Simpson won a seat on the Appropriations Committee, a panel where bipartisan relationships are important because they can provide votes for spending on hometown projects. After the Democrats won control of the House in the 2006 elections, he was in danger of losing his spot on the Energy and Water Development Subcommittee, where he looks out for local priorities, including the Idaho National Laboratory. But thanks to his good relationships with the committee's new Democratic chairman, David R. Obey of Wisconsin, and top Republican Jerry Lewis of California, a deal was reached that kept Simpson on the panel.

During his first term, Simpson set an ambitious goal of meeting every one of his 434 House peers. He actually met about 350 of them, underscoring his vow to work with ideological soul mates and partisan opposites alike. "A legislative body functions on relationships. You may have the best idea in the world, but if you can't convince 218 people to agree with you, you're out of luck," he told the Idaho Statesman soon after arriving.

Simpson will need all his consensus-building skills as he tries again to win enactment of legislation overhauling how public lands in central Idaho can be used. For more than half his years in Congress, he has been trying to push through a bill that would create three new wilderness areas while releasing other federal land for development. The House passed his measure in July 2006, but in December, at the end of the two-year Congress, it was removed at the last minute from a catchall tax bill as outgoing Speaker J. Dennis Hastert of Illinois substituted some provisions aimed at helping his own state. Simpson was deeply disappointed but vowed to start over in 2007. He reintroduced his bill on the first day of the new Congress.

Simpson says he represents the views of rural Western lawmakers, whose perspectives on water and land-use issues are often misunderstood by Easterners. As an example, he cites with exasperation efforts in the 109th Congress (2005-06) to ban the sale of wild horses for slaughter if no one adopts them. Simpson warned the House that wild horse herds can double in five years, with animals growing sick and dying as their population outpaces available forage.

Simpson grew up in the eastern Idaho town of Blackfoot, where his father and uncle had a dental practice. He met his wife, Kathy, in high school. He was on the football team and she was a cheerleader. They both attended Utah State. (Simpson did not collect his degree there until 2002, when a professor suggested he have some credits from dental school at Washington University in St. Louis transferred to Utah State.)

Returning to Blackfoot to join the family dental business, Simpson decided to run for a city council seat, a nonpartisan job, after he noticed that no one else was. He says his interest in politics was first sparked by a high school teacher who was a Democrat, but when he decided to run for the state legislature four years later, Simpson had to choose a party affiliation and concluded he was more comfortable with the GOP.

Simpson started out with a reputation as an occasionally angry maverick but mellowed and made a name for himself in Boise, rising through the ranks in the state House and serving as Speaker during his last six years there. He gave some thought to seeking the governorship in 1998 but decided against it when Republican Sen. Dirk Kempthorne chose to run. Republican Rep. Michael D. Crapo made a bid for Kempthorne's Senate seat, which created an opening for Simpson in the 2nd District. He won a four-way GOP primary despite criticism from social conservatives that he was insufficiently ardent on their issues.

During the campaign, Simpson was more worried about voters learning of his memberships in the ACLU and the Idaho Conservation League than of his use of marijuana in college 30 years earlier. He made no effort to hide that he is a lapsed Mormon who once smoked and still drinks occasionally, but these personal details seemed to have little effect on the heavily Mormon, but also Republican, electorate. He went on to defeat conservative Democrat Richard Stallings, who had held the seat from 1985 to 1993.

When he was first elected to Congress, Simpson had intended to work for free in Washington, D.C., dental clinics, but he found that licensing requirements made that too complicated. He also discovered that he did not have time to see patients during his visits back home, so he reluctantly sold his share of a dental practice.

Simpson has easily won re-election every two years. He has not ruled out a future run for governor or Senate, and is often mentioned as a likely contender if GOP Sen. Larry E. Craig does not seek re-election in 2008.

KEY VOTES

2006

No Stop broadband companies from favoring select Internet traffic
Yes Affirm U.S. commitment to war in Iraq and reject setting a withdrawal date for troops
Yes Repeal requirement for bilingual ballots at the polls
Yes Permit U.S. sale of civilian nuclear technology to India
Yes Build a 700-mile fence on the U.S.-Mexico border to curb illegal crossings
Yes Permit warrantless wiretaps of suspected terrorists

2005

Yes Intervene in the life-support case of Terri Schiavo
No Lift President Bush's restrictions on stem cell research funding
No Prohibit FBI access to library and bookstore records
No Approve free-trade pact with five Central American countries
Yes Pass energy policy overhaul favored by President Bush emphasizing domestic oil and gas production
Yes End mandatory preservation of habitat of endangered animal and plant species
No Ban torture of prisoners in U.S. custody

CQ VOTE STUDIES

	PARTY UNITY		PRESIDENTIAL SUPPORT	
	Support	Oppose	Support	Oppose
2006	95%	5%	89%	11%
2005	94%	6%	91%	9%
2004	94%	6%	79%	21%
2003	94%	6%	95%	5%
2002	95%	5%	92%	8%

INTEREST GROUPS

	AFL-CIO	ADA	CCUS	ACU
2006	21%	5%	93%	80%
2005	20%	10%	89%	92%
2004	7%	0%	95%	92%
2003	7%	10%	97%	92%
2002	11%	0%	100%	92%

IDAHO 2

East – Pocatello, Idaho Falls, part of Boise

Covering the Gem State's eastern and central portions, the 2nd includes most of Boise, a few midsize towns and a vast swath of agricultural land fed by the Snake River. The district's central and north are full of mountain ranges, rivers and fishing sites.

Elmore County, in the district's west, is home to Mountain Home Air Force Base, but most of the district relies on agriculture, primarily potatoes, sugar beets and grain. Blackfoot, in Bingham County, is known as the potato-producing capital of the world and supplies some of the 2nd's food processing plants, including a McCain (Ore-Ida) frozen french fries facility. Some farmers have expanded into dairy, beef and cheese processing as well, and the district also hosts technology firms, including Micron Technology, which is the state's largest private employer.

Tourism is another leading industry, and with natural wonders such as Shoshone Falls and ski resorts such as Sun Valley, the 2nd attracts a steady stream of vacationers. Waterfalls, snowmobile trails and spectacular views leave tourists with Idaho's motto, "Esto Perpetua," (Let it be perpetual), in mind.

The district consistently votes Republican at the state and national level. Members of The Church of Jesus Christ of Latter-day Saints make up the district's largest religious group, and like most Mormon areas, the district is strongly conservative. Since 1992, only Blaine County, a resort area, has voted for Democratic candidates in presidential elections. George W. Bush took 68 percent of the 2nd's vote in the 2004 presidential election.

MAJOR INDUSTRY

Agriculture, food processing, tourism, technology

MILITARY BASES

Mountain Home Air Force Base, 3,985 military, 882 civilian (2006)

CITIES

Boise City (pt.), 126,107; Pocatello, 51,466; Idaho Falls, 50,730; Twin Falls, 34,469; Rexburg, 17,257

NOTABLE

The vast majority of all commercial trout sold in the United States is produced in the Hagerman Valley near Twin Falls; Sun Valley was America's first ski resort; In 1955, Arco became the first town powered solely by atomic energy — for one hour.

ILLINOIS

Gov. Rod R. Blagojevich (D)

Pronounced: bla-GOY-a-vich
First elected: 2002
Length of term: 4 years
Term expires: 1/11
Salary: $156,091
Phone: (217) 782-0244

Residence: Chicago
Born: Dec. 10, 1956; Chicago, Ill.
Religion: Eastern Orthodox
Family: Wife, Patricia Blagojevich; two children
Education: Northwestern U., B.A. 1979 (history); Pepperdine U., J.D. 1983
Career: Lawyer
Political highlights: Assistant Cook County state's attorney, 1986-88; Ill. House, 1993-97; U.S. House, 1997-2003

Election results:

2006 GENERAL		
Rod R. Blagojevich (D)	1,736,731	49.8%
Judy Baar Topinka (R)	1,369,315	39.3%
Rich Whitney (GREEN)	361,336	10.4%

Lt. Gov. Pat Quinn (D)

First elected: 2002
Length of term: 4 years
Term expires: 1/11
Salary: $117,800
Phone: (217) 782-7884

LEGISLATURE

General Assembly: January-May; meets in October or November to consider vetoes

Senate: 59 members, rotates between 2 and 4-year terms
2007 ratios: 37 D, 22 R; 46 men, 13 women
Salary: $57,619
Phone: (217) 782-5715

House: 118 members, 2-year terms
2007 ratios: 66 D, 52 R; 83 men, 35 women
Salary: $57,619
Phone: (217) 782-8223

TERM LIMITS

Governor: No
Senate: No
House: No

URBAN STATISTICS

CITY	POPULATION
Chicago	2,896,016
Rockford	150,115
Aurora	142,990
Naperville	128,358
Peoria	112,936

REGISTERED VOTERS

Voters do not register by party.

POPULATION

2006 population (est.)	12,831,970
2000 population	12,419,293
1990 population	11,430,602
Percent change (1990-2000)	+8.6%
Rank among states (2006)	5
Median age	34.7
Born in state	67.1%
Foreign born	12.3%
Violent crime rate	657/100,000
Poverty level	10.7%
Federal workers	91,284
Military	57,753

ELECTIONS

STATE ELECTION OFFICIAL
(217) 782-4141
DEMOCRATIC PARTY
(217) 546-7404
REPUBLICAN PARTY
(217) 525-0011

MISCELLANEOUS

Web: www.illinois.gov
Capital: Springfield

U.S. CONGRESS

Senate: 2 Democrats
House: 10 Democrats, 9 Republicans

2000 Census Statistics by District

DIST.	2004 VOTE FOR PRESIDENT BUSH	KERRY	WHITE	BLACK	ASIAN	HISP	MEDIAN INCOME	WHITE COLLAR	BLUE COLLAR	SERVICE INDUSTRY	OVER 64	UNDER 18	COLLEGE EDUCATION	RURAL	SQ. MILES
1	17%	83%	27%	65%	1%	5%	$37,222	61%	22%	17%	13%	28%	19%	0%	98
2	16	84	26	62	1	10	$41,330	60	24	16	12	29	18	0	185
3	41	59	68	6	3	21	$48,048	58	28	14	14	26	21	0	124
4	21	79	18	4	2	74	$35,935	43	39	17	6	32	14	0	39
5	33	67	66	2	6	23	$48,531	65	22	14	12	20	34	0	57
6	53	46	75	3	8	12	$62,640	70	20	10	10	26	35	0	213
7	16	83	27	62	4	6	$40,361	71	16	14	10	27	32	0	56
8	55	44	79	3	6	11	$62,762	67	22	11	8	28	32	4	618
9	31	68	62	11	12	12	$46,531	70	16	14	16	21	40	0	75
10	47	52	75	5	6	12	$71,663	76	15	10	12	27	48	0	250
11	53	46	84	8	1	7	$47,800	55	30	15	12	27	19	22	4,241
12	48	52	80	16	1	2	$35,198	55	27	18	14	25	17	23	4,425
13	55	45	82	5	7	5	$71,686	75	16	9	9	28	42	1	355
14	55	44	74	5	2	18	$56,314	60	27	13	9	29	26	14	2,852
15	58	41	88	6	2	2	$38,583	58	27	15	14	23	23	36	10,072

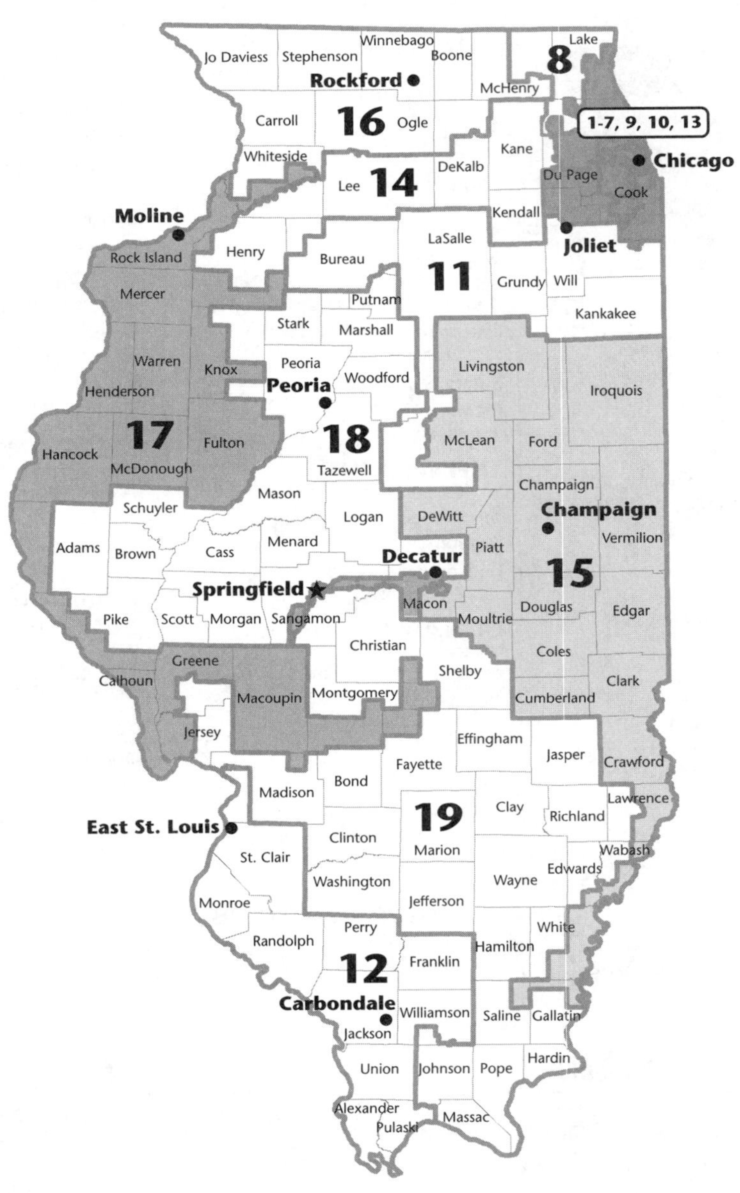

2000 Census Statistics by District

DIST.	2004 VOTE FOR PRESIDENT BUSH	KERRY	WHITE	BLACK	ASIAN	HISP	MEDIAN INCOME	WHITE COLLAR	BLUE COLLAR	SERVICE INDUSTRY	OVER 64	UNDER 18	COLLEGE EDUCATION	RURAL	SQ. MILES
16	55%	44%	86%	5%	1%	6%	$48,960	57%	30%	13%	12%	28%	21%	22%	4,098
17	48	51	87	7	1	4	$35,066	52	31	18	16	24	15	29	8,120
18	58	42	90	6	1	2	$41,934	59	25	15	15	24	21	32	8,186
19	61	39	94	3	0	1	$38,955	55	29	16	15	24	17	48	11,519
STATE	44	55	68	15	3	12	$46,590	62	24	14	12	26	26	12	55,584
U.S.	50.7	48.3	69	12	4	13	$41,994	60	25	15	12	26	24	21	3,537,438

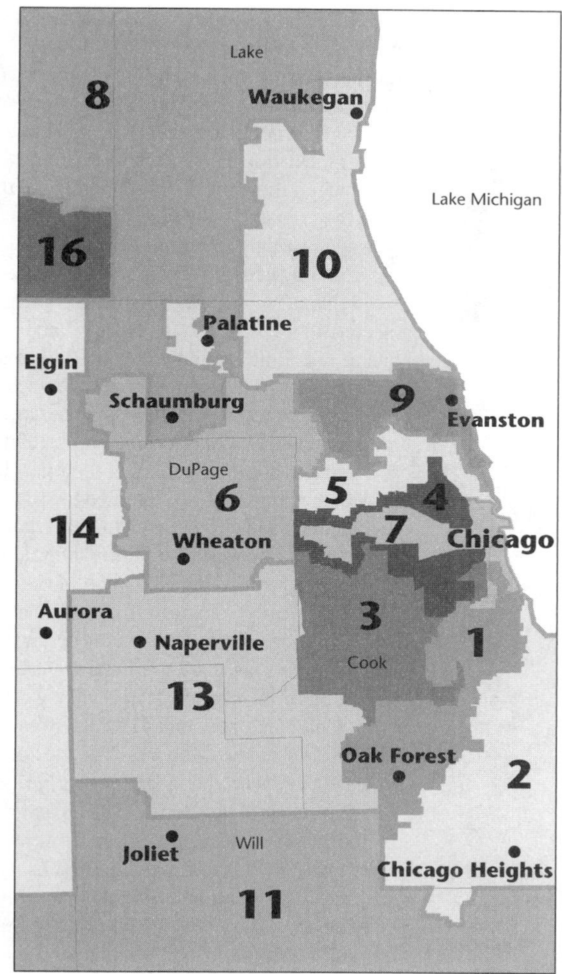
Lake
8
Waukegan
Lake Michigan
16
10
Palatine
Elgin
Schaumburg
9
Evanston
DuPage
5
4
6
14
7
Chicago
Wheaton
3
Aurora
Naperville
1
Cook
13
Oak Forest
2
Joliet
Will
Chicago Heights
11

Sen. Richard J. Durbin (D)

CAPITOL OFFICE
224-2152
durbin.senate.gov
309 Hart 20510-1304; fax 228-0400

COMMITTEES
Appropriations
(Financial Services - chairman)
Judiciary
(Human Rights & the Law - chairman)
Rules & Administration

RESIDENCE
Springfield

BORN
Nov. 21, 1944, East St. Louis, Ill.

RELIGION
Roman Catholic

FAMILY
Wife, Loretta Durbin; three children

EDUCATION
Georgetown U., B.S.F.S. 1966 (international affairs & economics), J.D. 1969

CAREER
Gubernatorial and state legislative aide; lawyer

POLITICAL HIGHLIGHTS
Democratic nominee for Ill. Senate, 1976; Democratic nominee for lieutenant governor, 1978; U.S. House, 1983-97

ELECTION RESULTS

2002 GENERAL

Richard J. Durbin (D)	2,103,766	60.3%
Jim Durkin (R)	1,325,703	38.0%
Steven Burgauer (LIBERT)	57,382	1.7%

2002 PRIMARY

Richard J. Durbin (D)	unopposed

PREVIOUS WINNING PERCENTAGES
1996 (56%); 1994 House Election (55%); 1992 House Election (57%); 1990 House Election (66%); 1988 House Election (69%); 1986 House Election (68%); 1984 House Election (61%); 1982 House Election (50%)

Elected 1996; 2nd term

Smart, combative and quick on his feet, Durbin has settled in easily as the Senate Democrats' second-ranking leader. He is diligent about the duties of a party whip — counting votes and standing guard against surprise procedural moves by the other party — even as he remains a prolific sponsor of bills and amendments. And while he's not immune from public relations gaffes, as he proved with an ill-considered Nazi reference during his first year as whip, he has largely put that incident behind him and returned to his role as one of the Democrats' most skilled debaters.

A longtime political insider who still has a regular-guy manner and sense of humor, Durbin has a knack for matching his rhetoric to the occasion — catchy when the subject is broad political themes, detailed when the subject is the nuts and bolts of legislation. He can shift gears between the two in a way few other lawmakers can.

Durbin was a natural choice for whip when Harry Reid of Nevada moved up to replace Minority Leader Tom Daschle after the South Dakotan was defeated at the polls in 2004. Durbin had been around legislatures for nearly all of his adult life and had honed his leadership skills under Daschle, heading a group of senators that met weekly to set the party's message.

Durbin takes pride in how well he and Reid held Senate Democrats together against GOP priorities in the 109th Congress (2005-06). It wasn't easy, he said, because leaders of the minority have few carrots or sticks to use with senators who are tempted to stray. "All we can do is tell them how much better it will be if we stick together, and how that will improve our odds of winning the majority next time," he said presciently in August 2006.

As majority whip, Durbin is one of the most prominent leaders in Congress, but he is overshadowed in the public eye by the state's junior senator, Barack Obama, whose decision to run for president in 2008 merely intensified the media's fascination with him. Durbin seems to take his younger colleague's stardom in stride. "I'm in what we call the designated-driver caucus in the Senate," Durbin told The State Journal-Register in Illinois in August 2006. "We're the ones who will drive the Senate while all our colleagues who are intoxicated with the idea of [being] president are in the back seat."

Unlike many of his Democratic colleagues, Durbin doesn't try to mask his liberalism; instead, he embraces it and tries to force Republicans to explain why they don't share his values. Often, his speeches are packed with eye-rolling sarcasm. "Oh, you just want to pull up a chair by the fireplace, relax, look at the ceiling and think: 'Thank God prosperity has arrived,'" Durbin said in 2006 after Senate Republicans linked an estate tax reduction to a minimum wage increase and called the bill the "Family Prosperity Act." He voted against it, as did nearly all Senate Democrats.

Durbin's domestic policy priorities tend toward the education and health care issues that appeal most broadly to Democrats. In the 109th Congress, he sponsored a bill to reduce college costs by cutting interest rates on subsidized student loans. Democrats quickly began advancing similar legislation in 2007. He also cosponsored a measure with Democrat Blanche Lincoln of Arkansas to let small businesses join a large insurance pool in an arrangement modeled after the health care program for federal employees.

Durbin's wordplay can be clever, but his tendency to wing it landed him in trouble in 2005. In a floor speech about reports of abuses of detainees at Guantánamo Bay in Cuba, Durbin said that if an outsider didn't know the actions had been committed by U.S. troops, "you would most certainly believe this must have been done by Nazis, Soviets in their gulags, or some mad regime — Pol Pot or others — that had no concern for human beings." Republicans and conservative commentators called his remarks an insult to American soldiers. Eventually, Durbin delivered an emotional apology on the Senate floor, admitting to "a very poor choice of words."

Strongly pro-union, Durbin took heat from unions in 1993 for supporting the North American Free Trade Agreement, and again in 2000 for backing the Clinton administration on granting China permanent normal trade status. By 2002, with a Republican in the White House, he was back on labor's side, opposing revival of fast-track procedures for congressional consideration of trade deals and cosponsoring a measure to impose stiff tariffs on imports from China unless it reformed its currency policy.

While Congress is in session, Durbin shares a Capitol Hill row house with three other veteran Democrats: Sen. Charles E. Schumer of New York, Rep. Bill Delahunt of Massachusetts and Rep. George Miller of California, the owner. Its distinctive ambience — unmade beds, beer bottles jostling an ancient jug of olives in the fridge, golf shoes left behind by a former colleague in 1992 — is so notorious that it merited a New York Times write-up and a visit from an ABC News television crew in early 2007. Durbin proudly told ABC about the night he killed a large rat with a golf club. "I'm not a good golfer," he quipped. "I had to three-putt."

By the time he reached the Senate in 1997, Durbin had seven House terms under his belt. He led the successful effort in the late 1980s to ban smoking on most domestic airline flights. Later, as chairman and then top-ranking Democrat on the House Agriculture Appropriations Subcommittee, he tried unsuccessfully to scale back government support for tobacco farmers and to exempt tobacco-related cases from new rules making it harder to bring class action lawsuits.

His interest in the tobacco issue was deeply personal. The youngest of three brothers raised in East St. Louis by a father who was a railroad night watchman and a mother who was a switchboard operator, Durbin was just 14 years old when his chain-smoking father died of lung cancer. He has dedicated much of his congressional career to crusading against tobacco use.

"I didn't stand by his bedside and vow to get even with the tobacco companies," Durbin said. But when tobacco issues came up in Congress, he said, "I really had the personal experience of loss. I think it made me fight a little harder." To make matters worse, shortly after his father was diagnosed, his mother learned she had colon cancer. "She looked me in the eye and said, 'I'm going to get through this,'" he said. She did, and was able to watch him begin his congressional career.

Durbin caught the politics bug in college, when he was an intern for Democratic Sen. Paul Douglas, whose Senate seat he now holds. He walked the hallways with legendary senators such as Robert F. Kennedy and held long conversations with Douglas, who used to tell Durbin stories as the young intern handed him letters to sign. One of Durbin's sons is named after Douglas.

After law school, Durbin went back home and had a number of jobs in politics, including state Senate parliamentarian and aide to Lt. Gov. Paul Simon, who later became a U.S. senator and presidential candidate. In 1982, Durbin unseated 11-term GOP Rep. Paul N. Findley by 1,410 votes in a Springfield-based House district. He won re-election six times.

When his old mentor, Simon, announced he would not seek re-election in 1996, Durbin got into the race. He won by 15 percentage points against state Rep. Al Salvi, a little-known conservative who campaigned as a staunch foe of abortion rights and defender of gun ownership. In 2002, Durbin coasted to a second term.

KEY VOTES

2006

- No Confirm Samuel A. Alito Jr. to the Supreme Court
- No Allow consideration of a bill to establish a $140 billion trust fund to compensate victims of asbestos exposure
- No Extend tax cuts for two years at a cost of $70 billion over five years
- Yes Overhaul immigration policy with border security, enforcement and guest worker program
- No Allow consideration of a bill to permanently repeal the estate tax
- Yes Urge President Bush to begin troop withdrawals from Iraq in 2006
- Yes Lift President Bush's restrictions on stem cell research funding
- No Authorize military tribunals for suspected terrorists

2005

- No Curb class action lawsuits by shifting them from state to federal courts
- Yes Allow confirmation vote on Priscilla R. Owen to the U.S. Court of Appeals for the 5th Circuit
- No Oppose mandatory emissions limits and block recognition of global warming as a threat
- No Approve free-trade pact with five Central American countries
- Yes Pass energy policy overhaul favored by President Bush emphasizing domestic oil and gas production
- No Shield gunmakers from lawsuits when their products are used in crimes
- Yes Ban torture of prisoners in U.S. custody
- No Renew 16 provisions of the Patriot Act
- No Allow final vote on opening the Arctic National Wildlife Refuge to oil and gas exploration

CQ VOTE STUDIES

	PARTY UNITY		PRESIDENTIAL SUPPORT	
	Support	Oppose	Support	Oppose
2006	98%	2%	47%	53%
2005	99%	1%	33%	67%
2004	96%	4%	54%	46%
2003	97%	3%	46%	54%
2002	97%	3%	67%	33%
2001	95%	5%	62%	38%
2000	99%	1%	97%	3%
1999	95%	5%	87%	13%
1998	95%	5%	90%	10%
1997	97%	3%	92%	8%

INTEREST GROUPS

	AFL-CIO	ADA	CCUS	ACU
2006	100%	100%	45%	4%
2005	100%	100%	28%	0%
2004	92%	95%	47%	4%
2003	85%	95%	35%	10%
2002	100%	95%	50%	0%
2001	94%	95%	31%	0%
2000	75%	95%	50%	4%
1999	89%	100%	35%	4%
1998	100%	95%	50%	8%
1997	100%	100%	40%	4%

Sen. Barack Obama (D)

CAPITOL OFFICE
224-2854
barack_obama@obama.senate.gov
obama.senate.gov
713 Hart 20510-1305; fax 228-4320

COMMITTEES
Foreign Relations
(European Affairs - ranking member)
Homeland Security & Governmental Affairs
Health, Education, Labor & Pensions
Veterans' Affairs

RESIDENCE
Chicago

BORN
Aug. 4, 1961, Honolulu, Hawaii

RELIGION
United Church of Christ

FAMILY
Wife, Michelle Obama; two children

EDUCATION
Occidental College, attended 1979-81; Columbia U., B.A. 1983 (political science); Harvard U., J.D. 1991

CAREER
Lawyer; voter registration and education project director; community outreach organizer; business reporter

POLITICAL HIGHLIGHTS
Ill. Senate, 1997-2004; sought Democratic nomination for U.S. House, 2000

ELECTION RESULTS

2004 GENERAL		
Barack Obama (D)	3,597,456	70.0%
Alan L. Keyes (R)	1,390,690	27.1%
Albert J. Franzen (I)	81,164	1.6%
Jerry Kohn (LIBERT)	69,253	1.4%
2004 PRIMARY		
Barack Obama (D)	655,923	52.8%
Daniel Hynes (D)	294,717	23.7%
Blair Hull (D)	134,453	10.8%
Maria Pappas (D)	74,987	6.0%
Gery Chico (D)	53,433	4.3%
Nancy Skinner (D)	16,098	1.3%
Joyce Washington (D)	13,375	1.1%

Elected 2004; 1st term

Long on charisma but short on experience governing at the national level, Obama looked into the mirror and saw a president looking back earlier than most members of the Senate, a well-established incubator of White House ambition. During the 109th Congress (2005-06), Obama spent his first term toiling at a few high-profile issues and a few unglamorous ones, but as a freshman in the minority party, his bills did not get far.

Still, among fellow senators, Obama (full name: buh-ROCK o-BAH-mah) earned a reputation as a hard worker, a good listener and a quick study who has a bright future in Congress if his race for the White House falls short. His diligence proved he has more to offer than the communication skills that fueled his quick rise to national stardom in 2004.

He has made an effort to stay in the Senate game despite the demands of a presidential run. He bookends his weeks on Capitol Hill with campaign speeches and fundraisers on the road. When the Senate is in session, he lingers at hearings long after he has had his turn to question the witnesses. His legislative output also increased noticeably in early 2007, after he declared his candidacy for president in February.

Within days, he called for a phased withdrawal of all combat troops from Iraq by March 31, 2008, a proposal designed to draw a contrast between himself and the front-runner for the Democratic presidential nomination, Sen. Hillary Rodham Clinton of New York. She was under fire from the party's activists for being vague about when and how to withdraw from Iraq.

With a cool but self-deprecating manner, Obama likes to depict himself as a pragmatic politician who shares the public's weariness with partisan and ideological fights. His actual Senate voting record is more partisan than he would care to admit. In the 109th Congress, he stuck with his party on 97 percent of the votes that pitted a majority of Democrats against a majority of Republicans. That's a higher score than all but five other Senate Democrats. All three of his Senate rivals for the 2008 nomination — Clinton, Joseph R. Biden Jr. of Delaware, and Christopher J. Dodd of Connecticut — broke ranks more frequently.

But some of the "good government" causes he adopted allowed him to show a non-ideological side. In 2006, then Minority Leader Harry Reid made Obama the spokesman for the Democrats' congressional ethics overhaul, citing his work on a similar initiative as an Illinois state senator. Ultimately, Obama voted against the bill the Senate passed that year because it didn't create an independent entity to enforce the new rules or curb lawmakers' use of private jets, two proposals closely identified with him.

He did better on the next round, in 2007, after the Democrats had taken control of the Senate. Working with Democrat Russ Feingold of Wisconsin, Obama persuaded Reid to push for legislation that included many of the strongest elements that ethics watchdog groups had recommended, including one to make senators pay the full charter rate, rather than first-class airfare, on corporate jets. He still had no luck on his toughest proposal: outside enforcement of ethics standards. After initially calling for an independent ethics commission, Obama scaled back his goals and endorsed an Office of Public Integrity within Congress. Even that raised alarm among members of Congress, who are skittish about being judged by outsiders, and the Senate voted it down.

Obama has partnered with Republicans, including frequent collaborations with Tom Coburn of Oklahoma, whose hard-core conservative views normally would have put him and Obama on opposite sides. The two discovered a shared interest in government transparency and teamed up on a bill, signed into law in 2006, creating a single, searchable database of all federal contracts, grants and loans. Another Obama measure that became law was the result of a partnership with Republican Richard G. Lugar of Indiana, former chairman of the Senate Foreign Relations panel. They cosponsored legislation to strengthen international efforts to destroy conventional weapons.

Obama is a liberal, but not one on the furthest end of party ideology. He supports abortion rights and expanded health care for the poor and opposes President Bush's tax policies. In early 2005, he voted with liberal Democrats to oppose oil drilling in the Alaskan wilderness.

But he is against same-sex marriage and favors work requirements and time limits for welfare recipients. He also voted for a Republican bill that discourages some class action lawsuits and limits attorneys' fees in such lawsuits. "I am rooted in the African-American community, but I am not limited to it," Obama likes to say.

The son of a white mother from Kansas and a black Kenyan father, Obama, whose first name in Swahili means "blessed by God," was raised in Hawaii by his mother and maternal grandparents. His father left the family to attend Harvard when Obama was 2, and the couple divorced. Determined that her son advance in life, Obama's mother, Ann Dunham, sent him to Punahou Academy, an elite private school in Honolulu. He went on to earn degrees from Columbia University and Harvard Law School, where he became the first African-American president of the Harvard Law Review.

His early adulthood was marked by confusion about his place in African-American society and a period of using drugs and alcohol, a time chronicled in a 1995 book, "Dreams from My Father: A Story of Race and Inheritance" that became a bestseller. Obama went to work on Wall Street for a time, and when that did not suit him, he applied for community organizer jobs around the country, finally landing one on Chicago's hard-pressed South Side.

There, he went from activist to politician, running for state senator and spending about eight years in the Illinois General Assembly. Obama is credited with bills that created a state income tax credit for the working poor and required police agencies to videotape interrogations and confessions in all murder cases.

In 2000, Obama made his first run at a seat in Congress, challenging Democratic Rep. Bobby L. Rush. He was trounced by the popular incumbent and former civil rights leader. Four years later, Obama found himself on an unexpectedly easy path to the Senate seat vacated by retiring GOP Sen. Peter G. Fitzgerald. A series of setbacks for the GOP turned fortune Obama's way. The Republican front-runner, multimillionaire Jack Ryan, dropped out amid allegations he had pressured his wife to go to sex clubs. Desperate for a quick replacement, Republicans settled on Alan L. Keyes, a bombastic social conservative who moved from Maryland to Illinois to run.

Suddenly, Obama was favored to capture the seat. He gave the keynote speech that year for presidential nominee John Kerry of Massachusetts and wowed the convention with a high-minded speech calling on Americans to put aside their ideological and cultural differences. The nationally televised address kicked off what one GOP operative bemoaned as an "Obamapalooza" of positive media coverage. He won the race with 70 percent of the vote, becoming the Senate's only current black senator, and the third since Reconstruction.

His heroes, he says, are Gandhi, the Rev. Martin Luther King Jr., Picasso and jazz musician John Coltrane. "I'm enamored with people who change the framework, who don't take something as a given, but scramble it," Obama says.

KEY VOTES

2006

No Confirm Samuel A. Alito Jr. to the Supreme Court
No Allow consideration of a bill to establish a $140 billion trust fund to compensate victims of asbestos exposure
No Extend tax cuts for two years at a cost of $70 billion over five years
Yes Overhaul immigration policy with border security, enforcement and guest worker program
No Allow consideration of a bill to permanently repeal the estate tax
Yes Urge President Bush to begin troop withdrawals from Iraq in 2006
Yes Lift President Bush's restrictions on stem cell research funding
No Authorize military tribunals for suspected terrorists

2005

Yes Curb class action lawsuits by shifting them from state to federal courts
Yes Allow confirmation vote on Priscilla R. Owen to the U.S. Court of Appeals for the 5th Circuit
No Oppose mandatory emissions limits and block recognition of global warming as a threat
No Approve free-trade pact with five Central American countries
Yes Pass energy policy overhaul favored by President Bush emphasizing domestic oil and gas production
No Shield gunmakers from lawsuits when their products are used in crimes
Yes Ban torture of prisoners in U.S. custody
No Renew 16 provisions of the Patriot Act
No Allow final vote on opening the Arctic National Wildlife Refuge to oil and gas exploration

CQ VOTE STUDIES

	PARTY UNITY		PRESIDENTIAL SUPPORT	
	Support	Oppose	Support	Oppose
2006	96%	4%	49%	51%
2005	97%	3%	33%	67%

INTEREST GROUPS

	AFL-CIO	ADA	CCUS	ACU
2006	93%	95%	55%	8%
2005	100%	100%	39%	8%

Rep. Bobby L. Rush (D)

CAPITOL OFFICE
225-4372
www.house.gov/rush
2416 Rayburn 20515-1301; fax 226-0333

COMMITTEES
Energy & Commerce
(Commerce, Trade & Consumer Protection - chairman)

RESIDENCE
Chicago

BORN
Nov. 23, 1946, Albany, Ga.

RELIGION
Protestant

FAMILY
Wife, Carolyn Rush; five children (one deceased)

EDUCATION
Roosevelt U., B.A. 1973 (political science); U. of Illinois, Chicago, attended 1975-77 (political science), M.A. 1994 (political science); McCormick Seminary, M.A. 1998 (theological studies)

MILITARY SERVICE
Army, 1963-68

CAREER
Insurance broker; political activist

POLITICAL HIGHLIGHTS
Candidate for Chicago City Council, 1975; sought Democratic nomination for Ill. House, 1978; Chicago City Council, 1983-93; candidate for mayor of Chicago, 1999

ELECTION RESULTS

2006 GENERAL		
Bobby L. Rush (D)	146,623	84.1%
Jason E. Tabor (R)	27,804	15.9%
2006 PRIMARY		
Bobby L. Rush (D)	81,593	81.6%
Phillip Jackson (D)	18,427	18.4%
2004 GENERAL		
Bobby L. Rush (D)	212,109	84.9%
Raymond G. Wardingley (R)	37,840	15.1%

PREVIOUS WINNING PERCENTAGES
2002 (81%); 2000 (88%); 1998 (87%); 1996 (86%); 1994 (76%); 1992 (83%)

Elected 1992; 8th term

Rush has taken many different paths in life, including community activist, Black Panther, city councilman, U.S. congressman and ordained pastor. He says the thread connecting all of them is a belief in public service and a desire for social justice. He is among the most liberal House members, active in both the Progressive Caucus and the Congressional Black Caucus. His main goal in Congress, he says, is to better the lives of his South Side Chicago constituents, among the city's poorest residents.

In the 110th Congress (2007-08), Rush chairs a subcommittee with a wide reach in the regulation of the fast-growing technology sector. When Democrats came to power, he took the gavel of the Subcommittee on Commerce, Trade and Consumer Protection, which is part of the influential Energy and Commerce Committee. He is a proponent of bringing technology to underserved areas, and in the early 2000s was the driving force in an unsuccessful effort to force regional Bell companies to offer high-speed Internet service in low-income neighborhoods. In 2006, he was the only Democratic sponsor of a bill to draw telephone companies into the video market. "This legislation represents a huge step in bringing lower prices and more choices, not only to my hard-pressed constituents, but to the entire nation," Rush said.

Although the GOP-drafted measure passed in the House, it faltered in the Senate. Republicans and Democrats split over the need for so-called network neutrality rules that would prevent the phone and cable giants from using their control over the broadband market to favor certain online traffic or discriminate against Internet phone companies, video sites and other competing online services. Rush was one of 58 Democrats to vote against a Democratic attempt to include network neutrality requirements.

Rush's support of the telecommunications bill brought him some criticism at home. The Chicago Sun-Times reported in 2006 that Rush had secured a $1 million grant from a phone company for a community center he had founded in his district. Rush countered that there was no conflict of interest because he had received no personal benefit from the grant, which he said was used to provide technology resources to the people and businesses of Englewood and Chicago's South Side. "The real conflict here is America's unwillingness to invest much-needed capital in communities such as Englewood," Rush wrote. "Rather than the Sun-Times asking me to step down, perhaps it should ask our nation to step it up."

Rush's own financial situation was scrutinized in 2005 when the Sun-Times reported in November that his South Side home was being foreclosed on. Rush said that "over the past three years, I have used considerable personal assets in building a church. I do not apologize. As with any worthwhile endeavor of this magnitude, personal sacrifices must be made." Rush is the pastor of the Beloved Community Christian Church.

Rush's life took numerous twists and turns before landing him in Congress. Born in southern Georgia, he grew up in Chicago, where his mother moved when he was 7 after her marriage broke up. She worked as a Republican activist because whites dominated the city's Democratic machine. Rush volunteered for the Army, but when he became disillusioned by a commanding officer whom he viewed as racist, he joined the Student Non-Violent Coordinating Committee.

He soon founded the Illinois chapter of the militant Black Panthers organization. Rush coordinated a Panthers-run program that provided free breakfasts for children and a medical clinic that developed a mass screening effort for sickle cell anemia. But of his life as a Black Panther, Rush says, "Fear was a constant companion," and he worried about encounters with white police officers. "I thought I would be killed by the Chicago Police Department," he says. "I never thought that I would see my 30th birthday."

When he was in his 20s, Rush was imprisoned for six months for illegal possession of weapons. In Congress, however, he has been an advocate of strict controls on firearms. His commitment to tighter gun restrictions has been strengthened by personal experience. In 1999, his son Huey (named after Black Panther leader Huey Newton) was shot and killed in a Chicago sidewalk robbery. The assailants were identified, arrested and convicted in 2002. More hardship struck his family that year. Rush's nephew was charged with murder in what police said was a drug deal gone bad. "These kinds of stories have no winners, only losers, and occur far too often in our communities," Rush said.

After graduating from college, Rush quit the Black Panthers, sold insurance and entered local politics, challenging the party machine and losing races for the Chicago City Council and the state House. In 1983, however, he won election to the city council on the coattails of 1st District Democratic Rep. Harold Washington, who was elected in an upset as Chicago's first black mayor.

Rush won a seat in Congress in 1992, ousting Democrat Charles A. Hayes, who had replaced Washington in the House but who was susceptible to Rush's charge that he had not provided sufficient leadership. Because of his past association with the Black Panthers, the media instantly focused on Rush after the 1992 election, making him a TV celebrity before his term even began. But Rush seldom mentions that part of his past, except on issues concerning increased police powers. He was a vocal opponent of legislation swept to enactment soon after the Sept. 11 terrorist attacks that increased law enforcement's ability to investigate and prosecute suspected terrorists.

Rush has won every general election for Congress with ease. However, he had a poor showing when he sought to oust Democrat Richard M. Daley as mayor in 1999, receiving just 28 percent in the primary. In the race, Rush accused Daley of neglecting the city's poorer neighborhoods.

Following that defeat, Rush had to face an emboldened field of primary challengers in 2000 but was renominated with 61 percent of the vote. In that campaign, he defeated Barack Obama, the future Illinois senator elected to the 109th Congress. In subsequent elections Rush has won overwhelmingly.

KEY VOTES

2006

No Stop broadband companies from favoring select Internet traffic
No Affirm U.S. commitment to war in Iraq and reject setting a withdrawal date for troops
No Repeal requirement for bilingual ballots at the polls
Yes Permit U.S. sale of civilian nuclear technology to India
No Build a 700-mile fence on the U.S.-Mexico border to curb illegal crossings
No Permit warrantless wiretaps of suspected terrorists

2005

? Intervene in the life-support case of Terri Schiavo
Yes Lift President Bush's restrictions on stem cell research funding
Yes Prohibit FBI access to library and bookstore records
No Approve free-trade pact with five Central American countries
Yes Pass energy policy overhaul favored by President Bush emphasizing domestic oil and gas production
No End mandatory preservation of habitat of endangered animal and plant species
Yes Ban torture of prisoners in U.S. custody

CQ VOTE STUDIES

	PARTY UNITY		PRESIDENTIAL SUPPORT	
	Support	Oppose	Support	Oppose
2006	93%	7%	32%	68%
2005	97%	3%	20%	80%
2004	97%	3%	21%	79%
2003	96%	4%	15%	85%
2002	95%	5%	28%	72%

INTEREST GROUPS

	AFL-CIO	ADA	CCUS	ACU
2006	92%	80%	46%	9%
2005	100%	100%	44%	4%
2004	100%	100%	24%	0%
2003	100%	95%	29%	12%
2002	100%	85%	50%	0%

ILLINOIS 1

Chicago — South Side and southwest

The nation's first black-majority district, the 1st covers much of Chicago's South Side. Starting at 26th Street in the historic black hub, the district spreads out to the south and west through residential areas. It narrows through the southwestern neighborhoods of Washington Heights, Beverly and Morgan Park, then expands outside the city to scoop up close-in suburbs as it extends south to Cook County's border with Will County. About 70 percent of the 1st's residents live in Chicago.

The 1st is home to some of the city's largest subsidized housing projects, and about 20 percent of its population lives in poverty. Its median income, at roughly $37,000, is one of the lowest in Illinois. Many people work in the service industry, and residents here face the longest travel times to work of any district outside of New York. Despite the presence of the University of Chicago in the Hyde Park neighborhood, only 19 percent of district residents have a college education.

The district has several solidly middle-class black neighborhoods, including Chatham and Avalon Park. Its north end takes in part of Bronzeville, which has attracted many black-owned businesses and young black professionals who move in and rehabilitate old houses instead of leaving the city. This has led to a shortage of available housing for poorer residents. The area is trying to use its rich history to attract tourism by refurbishing old buildings and investing in heritage sites.

The 1st, represented by black congressmen since 1929, has the nation's largest percentage of African-American residents at 65 percent. Blue Island, a southwest suburb, has a large Hispanic population, and also is one-fourth black. White voters are concentrated outside of the city or in some southwest neighborhoods. The 1st is one of the state's most Democratic districts, and it gave 2004 presidential nominee John Kerry his third-best showing in Illinois with 83 percent.

MAJOR INDUSTRY

Hospitals, higher education, manufacturing

CITIES

Chicago (pt.), 451,488; Oak Forest (pt.), 28,041; Orland Park (pt.), 27,342; Tinley Park (pt.), 23,863; Blue Island (pt.), 23,436

NOTABLE

The first self-sustaining nuclear reaction took place at the University of Chicago under the stands at Stagg Field in 1942.

Rep. Jesse L. Jackson Jr. (D)

CAPITOL OFFICE
225-0773
www.house.gov/jackson
2419 Rayburn 20515-1302; fax 225-0899

COMMITTEES
Appropriations

RESIDENCE
Chicago

BORN
March 11, 1965, Greenville, S.C.

RELIGION
Baptist

FAMILY
Wife, Sandi Jackson; two children

EDUCATION
North Carolina A&T U., B.S. 1987 (business management); Chicago Theological Seminary, M.A. 1990 (theology); U. of Illinois, J.D. 1993

CAREER
Political activist

POLITICAL HIGHLIGHTS
No previous office

ELECTION RESULTS

2006 GENERAL		
Jesse L. Jackson Jr. (D)	146,347	84.8%
Robert Belin (R)	20,395	11.8%
Anthony W. Williams (LIBERT)	5,748	3.3%
2006 PRIMARY		
Jesse L. Jackson Jr. (D)		unopposed
2004 GENERAL		
Jesse L. Jackson Jr. (D)	207,535	88.5%
Stephanie Sailor (LIBERT)	26,990	11.5%

PREVIOUS WINNING PERCENTAGES
2002 (82%); 2000 (90%); 1998 (89%); 1996 (94%); 1995 Special Election (76%)

Elected December 1995; 6th full term

As the son of the famous civil rights leader, Jackson has lived with the expectation that one day he would aspire to a national role in his party. He has acknowledged that it is both a blessing and a curse to be the son of the Rev. Jesse L. Jackson. "I inherited my parents' friends and detractors, neither of which I have earned," he said in 2006.

Yet at the start of his second decade in Congress, Jackson seems content to focus on the needs of his 2nd District constituents. "If it doesn't immediately impact the people of the 2nd District," he said, "it's not what I wake up thinking about."

To that end, he has done his best to bring economic development to his South Side and suburban Chicago district where unemployment remains high. Jackson was given a seat on the Appropriations Committee in his second term, and he has helped to fund a variety of projects in his district. Over the past five years, he has helped direct more than $148 million for the Deep Tunnel Project, which is designed to improve flood protection and water quality for the Chicago metropolitan area. In 2006, he brought money home to ensure more reliable bus service, to build a new senior community center, and to develop better water supply systems.

Jackson also has been the leading advocate for the construction of a third airport for the Chicago area, which he says will provide economic expansion for his district as well as relieve the overcrowding at Chicago's O'Hare Airport. He wants the new airport to be located on rural land outside of Peotone, just south of his district. It would aim to attract discount air carriers. His plan has run into opposition from some of his state colleagues, however, including Republican Jerry Weller, in whose district the airport would be built, and Chicago Democratic Mayor Richard M. Daley, who favors an expansion of O'Hare.

Weller inserted language in a defense bill in 2005 mandating that a majority of the new airport's governing board reside in Will County, which is in his district. He wanted to ensure that Will County officials and not Jackson's coalition of mostly southern Cook County towns would govern the airport project. Jackson accused Weller of trying to sabotage years of work that he and state transportation officials had put into planning the airfield.

But now that Jackson's party runs the House, he may have better luck overturning Weller's language. Jackson is not seeking federal money for the airport; he says it will be completely financed by private interests. "The beauty of private financing is that it comes with no cost or risk to taxpayers, yet airport revenues can be used to improve local communities," Jackson said. "It's a win-win for taxpayers." He said he already has attracted more than $200 million in private funding for the airport.

Jackson also has explored the option of inviting an Indian gaming casino to his district to bring in jobs and revenue. At a 2005 hearing of the House Resources Committee, Jackson pleaded the case of the Ho-Chunk Nation of Wisconsin, which wants to put a casino in his district. Although he decried the practice of "reservation shopping," in which tribes hunt for prime casino real estate outside of reservation lands, he said his case was different because the Ho-Chunk Indians have historic ties to his district. The tribe roamed across his part of Illinois, he said, before they were forced back to their present home by white settlers.

Jackson said the Ho-Chunk project would be a "family entertainment destination" and would bring tourists and jobs. "In my congressional district, there are 60 people for every one job," he said.

Although he is intent on addressing local concerns, Jackson is also an advocate and spokesman for the liberal values of his party. He may not have his father's physical presence nor the cadences of the civil rights leader's oratory, but he is full of energy and can equal his father's partisan rhetoric.

At a September 2005 news briefing by the Congressional Black Caucus, he joined other members in offering stinging criticism of the federal relief effort for hurricane-damaged New Orleans. "A few short years ago, we saw in the Persian Gulf something that was described by this administration as shock and awe," he said. "But here on the shores of the United States of America, in the last 140 or so hours, we have witnessed something shockingly awful, and that is the lack of response — the quick response — from our government to those Americans who are suffering, who are dying."

Jackson sits on the State-Foreign Operations Appropriations Subcommittee, where he has paid particular attention to aid for African nations. In an emergency spending bill in June 2006, he secured $64 million for Liberia and $197 million for Sudan, of which $173 million was to be used for the African Union peacekeeping operation in the Darfur region.

The congressman takes voting seriously: In his first decade in the House, he missed just two roll call votes. When he missed the first vote, on March 1, 2001, he says he was talking to a reporter in the Rayburn Building and did not hear the bells signifying a vote. He rushed to the floor but was too late.

At one point in 2006, Jackson seemed interested in extending his area of influence and flirted with the idea of challenging Mayor Daley for a shot at running the Windy City. But once the Democrats took over the House, Jackson dropped the idea, and Daley won re-election in a landslide.

Jackson graduated from Washington, D.C.'s elite St. Albans School, and he has earned degrees in both theology and law. He followed in his father's footsteps, serving as vice president at-large of Operation PUSH (People United to Serve Humanity) and as national field director for the Rainbow Coalition.

Jackson came to Congress in a 1995 special election to replace Democrat Mel Reynolds, who resigned after being convicted of sexual misconduct. Jackson countered criticism that he was too young for the job by arguing that being the son of Jesse Jackson amounted to a lifetime of political experience. After winning a hard-fought primary against state Sen. Emil Jones Jr., Jackson had no difficulty in the general election. His subsequent elections have been a breeze.

KEY VOTES

2006

Yes Stop broadband companies from favoring select Internet traffic
No Affirm U.S. commitment to war in Iraq and reject setting a withdrawal date for troops
No Repeal requirement for bilingual ballots at the polls
Yes Permit U.S. sale of civilian nuclear technology to India
No Build a 700-mile fence on the U.S.-Mexico border to curb illegal crossings
No Permit warrantless wiretaps of suspected terrorists

2005

Yes Intervene in the life-support case of Terri Schiavo
Yes Lift President Bush's restrictions on stem cell research funding
Yes Prohibit FBI access to library and bookstore records
No Approve free-trade pact with five Central American countries
No Pass energy policy overhaul favored by President Bush emphasizing domestic oil and gas production
No End mandatory preservation of habitat of endangered animal and plant species
Yes Ban torture of prisoners in U.S. custody

CQ VOTE STUDIES

	PARTY UNITY		PRESIDENTIAL SUPPORT	
	Support	Oppose	Support	Oppose
2006	98%	2%	23%	77%
2005	98%	2%	13%	87%
2004	98%	2%	15%	85%
2003	98%	2%	9%	91%
2002	96%	4%	25%	75%

INTEREST GROUPS

	AFL-CIO	ADA	CCUS	ACU
2006	100%	100%	27%	4%
2005	93%	100%	30%	0%
2004	100%	100%	14%	0%
2003	100%	100%	17%	12%
2002	100%	90%	25%	0%

ILLINOIS 2

Chicago — far South Side; Chicago Heights

The 2nd begins on Chicago's South Side along Lake Michigan and extends south along the Indiana border, as well as southwest, to take in Chicago Heights and other Cook County suburbs before reaching across the Will County line to snatch up University Park.

The Chicago portion of the district starts in the Hyde Park area near the University of Chicago (located in the 1st) and takes in the South Shore, South Chicago, Roseland, Pullman and heavily Hispanic East Side neighborhoods. About 40 percent of the 2nd's residents live in the city.

The district's economy once was built on steel, but when the industry collapsed in the late 1970s, it devastated the district's industrial-based economy. Ford Motor Co. is one of the few large manufacturing businesses remaining in the district, with a stamping plant in Chicago Heights and an assembly plant north of Calumet City — the company's oldest operating facility in the world. Unemployment remains high in the district, and many residents have fled the South Side to find jobs.

Several south suburbs are trying to bring new construction, retail and service jobs to the region by developing entertainment venues on now-vacant commercial and industrial sites. But Dolton's deal to refurbish an abandoned plant stalled in 2006 over corruption accusations, and ongoing attempts by the Ho-Chunk Indian nation to build a casino and shopping complex have not yet yielded construction.

The district's suburbs are a mix of heavily black areas such as Harvey, Dolton and Ford Heights, and largely white areas like Homewood, Flossmoor and Thornton. Overall, the 2nd is largely black (62 percent) and working-class. This staunchly Democratic base helped the district give John Kerry his highest 2004 presidential vote percentage (84 percent) in the state.

MAJOR INDUSTRY

Automotive and wire manufacturing, health care

CITIES

Chicago (pt.), 265,814; Calumet City, 39,071; Chicago Heights, 32,776

NOTABLE

Pullman, a factory town now part of Chicago that was built by the Pullman Palace Car Co. in the 1880s, was the first company-planned industrial town in the United States.

Rep. Daniel Lipinski (D)

Elected 2004; 2nd term

CAPITOL OFFICE
225-5701
www.house.gov/lipinski
1717 Longworth 20515-1303; fax 225-1012

COMMITTEES
Science & Technology
Small Business
Transportation & Infrastructure

RESIDENCE
Western Springs

BORN
July 15, 1966, Chicago, Ill.

RELIGION
Roman Catholic

FAMILY
Wife, Judy Lipinski

EDUCATION
Northwestern U., B.S. 1988 (mechanical engineering); Stanford U., M.S. 1989 (engineering-economic systems); Duke U., Ph.D. 1998 (political science)

CAREER
Professor; congressional aide; campaign aide

POLITICAL HIGHLIGHTS
No previous office

ELECTION RESULTS

2006 GENERAL		
Daniel Lipinski (D)	127,768	77.1%
Raymond G. Wardingley (R)	37,954	22.9%
2006 PRIMARY		
Daniel Lipinski (D)	44,401	54.4%
John T. Kelly (D)	20,918	25.7%
John P. Sullivan (D)	16,231	19.9%
2004 GENERAL		
Daniel Lipinski (D)	167,034	72.6%
Ryan Chlada (R)	57,845	25.2%
Krista Grimm ()	5,077	2.2%

Lipinski finally landed the spot he had wanted since winning his father's seat in 2004. The new Democratic leadership appointed him in 2007 to the Transportation and Infrastructure Committee, which was where his father had fortified his political base brick by brick over two decades in Congress.

Like his father, William O. Lipinski, Daniel Lipinski is an economic populist, a social conservative, and an admirer of Republican icon Ronald Reagan. He is also devoted to addressing the transportation issues important to Chicago and its inner suburbs. "My positions on issues are very similar to my father's positions, and I don't feel like I need to make any apologies for that," Lipinski says.

A seat on the Transportation Committee, and specifically its Aviation and Railroads subcommittees, may not be every politician's dream job, but it is where Lipinski has wanted to sit since succeeding his father. From there, he can focus on federal projects affecting Chicago's Midway Airport and its robust railroad sector.

Lipinski wants to boost funding for the Chicago Region Environmental and Transportation Efficiency program, a $1.5 billion partnership between the state, the city and its transit system, and freight railroads to improve rail infrastructure in the region. "This is something very critical for me," he says. "I grew up about 100 yards from railroad tracks and right now I live about 60 yards from railroad tracks, so that is my No. 1 project."

He also is likely to have a hand in revising the federal rail safety system, which was scheduled to be considered in the 110th Congress (2007-08) for the first time since 1994. Safety watchdog groups were calling for greater regulation of the industry, including more track inspections and fines for companies that break the rules. William O. Lipinski is now a lobbyist for the Association of American Railroads, and a Washington Post story in 2007 raised questions as to whether he was hired to influence his son.

The Lipinski father-son political team has attracted attention before. The senior Lipinski all but assured his son would succeed him by the way in which he timed his retirement in 2004. He first filed to run for re-election and was unopposed in the March Democratic primary. Then, he announced during the August recess that he would retire from the House after 11 terms. As permitted by state law, a committee of 3rd District Democrats, which included the senior Lipinski and several of his allies, met and unanimously selected Daniel Lipinski to fill the vacated slot. In November, the younger Lipinski defeated Republican political unknown Ryan Chlada by almost 3-to-1.

At the time, Lipinski was 38, and it had been 15 years since he lived in the Chicago area. He was an associate professor at the University of Tennessee in Knoxville. He moved back to the Chicago area to run for the seat. He told the local press, "My heart has always been here. I've always wanted to come back. This is my home. I'm not a carpetbagger."

When Lipinski ran for re-election in 2006, all was not forgotten. Some Democratic activists who thought the earlier selection process smacked of nepotism backed other candidates in the primary. Lipinski won with 54 percent of the vote over financial consultant John T. Kelly, who took 26 percent, and local prosecutor John P. Sullivan, who got 20 percent. Still, Lipinski's share of the Democratic primary vote was subpar for an incumbent. In November, however, he cruised to re-election, winning by 54 percentage points.

In Washington, Lipinski sticks with his Democratic colleagues on labor matters, but generally is more conservative on social issues. In the 109th Congress (2005-06), he sided with most Republicans in favoring a bill that criminalized transporting minors across state lines to obtain an abortion, and he voted against federal funding for embryonic stem cell research. Such research is often opposed by anti-abortion forces because it uses cells harvested from surplus embryos at in vitro fertilization clinics. He also voted to build a 700-mile fence along the U.S. border with Mexico.

Lipinski joined the majority of Democrats in voting against the implementation of the Central American Free Trade Agreement, which labor unions opposed, and he voted no on limiting the scope of the Endangered Species Act.

On the Iraq War, Lipinski first supported President Bush's efforts in Iraq, voting for a Republican-sponsored resolution that rejected setting an "arbitrary" date for troop withdrawals. But in 2007, with public sentiment turning against the war, Lipinski supported a Democratic resolution disapproving of Bush's plan to send more troops to Iraq. "It is painfully clear that a change in strategy in Iraq is needed now," Lipinski said on the House floor.

Lipinski was born and raised in the district, a working-class swath of the city and close-in suburbs with an industrial feel and populated with cookie-cutter bungalows. There are generational differences between the father and son. The elder Lipinski attended college for two years and trained for Congress as a city councilman and ward boss. Daniel Lipinski went to prep school, earned a degree in mechanical engineering from Northwestern University and later earned a doctorate in political science from Duke University. He never had run for office before his successful House race.

He wasn't a total novice though. Lipinski had not only worked on numerous Illinois campaigns, he had also served as a congressional aide to Gov. Rod R. Blagojevich and had had a fellowship in the office of House Minority Leader Richard A. Gephardt of Missouri.

His career in academia was devoted to politics as well. He has published several papers on how politicians communicate with constituents, including their increasing use of the Internet. In person, his style is that of the enthusiastic lecturer he once was, peppering his conversation with examples and facts and then describing dissenting opinions of others to give the fullest possible picture of the debate.

Lipinski is a good friend of Rep. David E. Price, a North Carolina Democrat who was on his dissertation committee. Also a career educator and former political science professor, Price was in between congressional stints at the time, having lost in the Republican sweep of 1994 only to be returned to the House in the 1996 election.

KEY VOTES

2006

Yes Stop broadband companies from favoring select Internet traffic
Yes Affirm U.S. commitment to war in Iraq and reject setting a withdrawal date for troops
No Repeal requirement for bilingual ballots at the polls
Yes Permit U.S. sale of civilian nuclear technology to India
Yes Build a 700-mile fence on the U.S.-Mexico border to curb illegal crossings
No Permit warrantless wiretaps of suspected terrorists

2005

Yes Intervene in the life-support case of Terri Schiavo
No Lift President Bush's restrictions on stem cell research funding
Yes Prohibit FBI access to library and bookstore records
No Approve free-trade pact with five Central American countries
Yes Pass energy policy overhaul favored by President Bush emphasizing domestic oil and gas production
No End mandatory preservation of habitat of endangered animal and plant species
Yes Ban torture of prisoners in U.S. custody

CQ VOTE STUDIES

	PARTY UNITY		PRESIDENTIAL SUPPORT	
	Support	Oppose	Support	Oppose
2006	86%	14%	49%	51%
2005	86%	14%	43%	57%

INTEREST GROUPS

	AFL-CIO	ADA	CCUS	ACU
2006	100%	70%	47%	33%
2005	87%	85%	46%	16%

ILLINOIS 3

Chicago — southwest side; south and west suburbs

The 3rd covers the southwest corner of Chicago and adjacent suburbs, part of a working-class region known as the Bungalow Belt that is stocked with voters of Eastern European, Italian and Irish descent.

Chicago residents make up about 40 percent of the district population. The 3rd includes the historically Irish neighborhood of Bridgeport, which is the political base of the powerful Daley family, and southwest Chicago neighborhoods such as Beverly, West Lawn, Clearing and Garfield Ridge, where Midway Airport is located. The largely Hispanic West Lawn and West Eldson neighborhoods have experienced rapid growth.

Crisscrossed by highways, railroads and the Chicago Sanitary and Ship Canal, the 3rd has historically served as a manufacturing and distribution center. The district is home to the Nabisco bakery, the largest "biscuit" bakery in the world, and the Nabisco Distribution Center, responsible for nearly 30 percent of all Nabisco product shipments. Expansion at Midway in the early 2000s broadened the district's retail and service base and created new jobs for district residents. Although several "legacy carriers," such as American Airlines and United Airlines, scaled back operations here to concentrate on nearby O'Hare International Airport (in the 6th), Southwest Airlines has expanded to fill the void.

In national elections, the 3rd typically votes Democratic, but not by the same wide margins as other Chicago-based districts — John Kerry won 59 percent of the 2004 presidential vote here. Many working- and middle-class voters lean to the right on social issues, and there is an ample GOP vote in the district's more affluent western Cook County suburbs.

MAJOR INDUSTRY

Transportation, warehouses, manufacturing

CITIES

Chicago (pt.), 266,264; Oak Lawn, 55,245; Berwyn (pt.), 51,179; Burbank, 27,902

NOTABLE

Berwyn is home to the world's largest laundromat, with roughly 300 washers and dryers combined, which runs on solar power; The South Side Irish parade, in Chicago's Beverly neighborhood, calls itself the largest neighborhood-based St. Patrick's Day parade outside of Dublin.

Rep. Luis V. Gutierrez (D)

CAPITOL OFFICE
225-8203
luisgutierrez.house.gov
2266 Rayburn 20515-1304; fax 225-7810

COMMITTEES
Financial Services
(Domestic & International Monetary Policy, Trade & Technology - chairman)
Judiciary

RESIDENCE
Chicago

BORN
Dec. 10, 1953, Chicago, Ill.

RELIGION
Roman Catholic

FAMILY
Wife, Soraida Arocho Gutierrez; two children

EDUCATION
Northeastern Illinois U., B.A. 1975 (liberal arts)

CAREER
Teacher; social worker

POLITICAL HIGHLIGHTS
Chicago City Council, 1986-93

ELECTION RESULTS

2006 GENERAL		
Luis V. Gutierrez (D)	69,910	85.8%
Ann Melichar (R)	11,532	14.2%
2006 PRIMARY		
Luis V. Gutierrez (D)		unopposed
2004 GENERAL		
Luis V. Gutierrez (D)	104,761	83.7%
Tony Cisneros (R)	15,536	12.4%
Jake Whitmer (LIBERT)	4,845	3.9%

PREVIOUS WINNING PERCENTAGES
2002 (80%); 2000 (89%); 1998 (82%); 1996 (94%); 1994 (75%); 1992 (78%)

Elected 1992; 8th term

In what he says will be his last term, Gutierrez has his sights set on immigration reform, one of the few issues that has a chance of being resolved by the Republican White House and the Democratic Congress. He cosponsored bipartisan, bicameral legislation that began gaining traction with both political parties early in the 110th Congress (2007-08).

Gutierrez (full name: loo-EES goo-tee-AIR-ez) announced in March 2007 that the current House term — his eighth — would be his last.

In his remaining time, he plans to work for passage of a bill admitting illegal immigrants into a guest worker program, with a path to eventual citizenship. The idea was endorsed by the Senate in 2006 and attracted many House adherents as well. Count on Gutierrez to inject himself into a rekindled effort. In the 110th Congress, his newly gained seat on the Judiciary panel puts him in the middle of the action.

He learned the ropes of dealmaking on the rough-and-tumble Chicago City Council, where his tenacity earned him the nickname "El Gallito," Spanish for "the little fighting rooster."

In the highly charged debate over immigration in the 109th Congress (2005-06), the battle became personal for Gutierrez. At one point, he got into an angry argument on an MSNBC broadcast with Rep. Tom Tancredo, the Colorado Republican who was leading the opposition to a guest worker program. Their argument continued off-air and escalated into a shoving match, including the use of foul language and charges of racism. "I feel passionately about this and I lost my temper," Gutierrez says of the March 2006 incident. "It wasn't my best moment."

The feisty congressman has courted the other side in gentler ways. He appeared on CNN's "Moneyline," a platform for anchor Lou Dobbs' conservative views on immigration, and once invited Dobbs to a luncheon with 15 members of the Congressional Hispanic Caucus.

Gutierrez favors what he calls a "holistic approach" that would create a guest worker program, improve enforcement of existing laws, enhance border security, and make additional visas available to reunite families.

In the 108th Congress (2003-04), Gutierrez's bill was a Democratic alternative to President Bush's proposal offering undocumented immigrants a temporary guest worker visa, with no guarantee of a green card. "Unlike the president's plan that says, 'Come, work and adios,' our legislation respects workers," said Gutierrez. But he was also hopeful of a compromise solution. "The president of the United States has made an offer," he said. "We're responding. Let's engage in some constructive dialogue."

The first Hispanic member of Congress from Illinois, Gutierrez represents one of the poorest, least-educated districts in the nation. He can be passionate in his defense of society's underdogs. Seventy-five percent of his constituent casework is related to immigration, and he says his office has facilitated more than 40,000 citizenship applications. A 2002 Chicago Sun-Times editorial called Gutierrez "arguably . . . the most influential Latino political leader in Chicago history."

Gutierrez has been a member of the Financial Services Committee since coming to Congress in 1993, and in the 110th Congress he became chairman of the Domestic and International Monetary Policy, Trade and Technology Subcommittee. In 2006, he backed legislation designed to protect members of the military from unscrupulous financial services firms that use aggressive tactics to sell mutual funds, insurance policies and other investment products. He also pressed for greater disclosure from institutions selling high-interest "payday" loans.

He likes to remind lawmakers of the difficulties faced by non-white Americans. He often cites something that happened to him at the Capitol in 1996. Returning to his office from a reception with his daughter and niece, Gutierrez was confronted by a security officer who questioned whether he indeed was a member of Congress and then made insulting remarks.

Gutierrez's first year in the House was marked by his nationally televised criticism of Congress, which drew angry responses from both sides of the aisle. Gutierrez denounced Congress' shortcomings in an appearance on the CBS program "60 Minutes." He drew raves from congressional critics, and his office logged more than 500 phone calls and faxes praising his candor. But his House colleagues called his performance self-serving.

Born in Chicago to Puerto Rican immigrants, Gutierrez went to high school in their home country and says he was nearly expelled for agitating for Puerto Rican independence. Later, at Northeastern Illinois University in the 1970s, he was part of a group of students that took over the university president's office to protest a lack of basic English language classes for incoming students.

He worked for more than a decade as a teacher, social worker and community activist. In 1983, he joined the campaign of Democratic Rep. Harold Washington, who defeated incumbent Mayor Jane Byrne and Illinois States Attorney Richard M. Daley, son of the longtime mayor, to become the city's first African-American mayor. "This man was different," Gutierrez says of Washington, who raised issues of affordable housing, ending police brutality and improving schools in ways that Gutierrez says moved him.

The same year, Gutierrez ran against then Rep. Dan Rostenkowski, the powerful Democratic chairman of the House Ways and Means Committee, for ward boss for the 32nd Ward. He lost, then went to work in Washington's administration. Three years later, he was elected to the City Council, where he spent nearly seven years.

After Washington died and Daley became mayor, he and Gutierrez reconciled. When the oddly shaped Hispanic-majority 4th District was created for the 1992 election, Daley backed Gutierrez for the seat and former foe Rostenkowski contributed $5,000 to his campaign. Rival alderman Juan Soliz labeled Gutierrez a machine Democrat, but Daley's support practically guaranteed Gutierrez the non-Hispanic white vote. He won easily in the heavily Democratic district. Since then, he has often faced a primary challenge but has breezed to re-election in the fall.

KEY VOTES

2006

Yes Stop broadband companies from favoring select Internet traffic

? Affirm U.S. commitment to war in Iraq and reject setting a withdrawal date for troops

No Repeal requirement for bilingual ballots at the polls

Yes Permit U.S. sale of civilian nuclear technology to India

No Build a 700-mile fence on the U.S.-Mexico border to curb illegal crossings

? Permit warrantless wiretaps of suspected terrorists

2005

No Intervene in the life-support case of Terri Schiavo

Yes Lift President Bush's restrictions on stem cell research funding

Yes Prohibit FBI access to library and bookstore records

No Approve free-trade pact with five Central American countries

No Pass energy policy overhaul favored by President Bush emphasizing domestic oil and gas production

\- End mandatory preservation of habitat of endangered animal and plant species

Yes Ban torture of prisoners in U.S. custody

CQ VOTE STUDIES

	PARTY UNITY		PRESIDENTIAL SUPPORT	
	Support	Oppose	Support	Oppose
2006	97%	3%	23%	77%
2005	98%	2%	18%	82%
2004	99%	1%	24%	76%
2003	97%	3%	14%	86%
2002	95%	5%	31%	69%

INTEREST GROUPS

	AFL-CIO	ADA	CCUS	ACU
2006	100%	80%	31%	4%
2005	92%	100%	38%	0%
2004	100%	90%	22%	0%
2003	100%	90%	31%	12%
2002	100%	95%	42%	0%

ILLINOIS 4

Chicago – parts of North Side, southwest side

Surrounding the black-majority 7th District in the center of Chicago, the small, horseshoe-shaped 4th was drawn to unite the city's Hispanic neighborhoods into one voting bloc. Slightly less than 90 percent of district residents live in Chicago.

The district boasts the state's largest Hispanic population, and the nation's fifth-largest, at 74 percent. The 4th is largely young and poor, with the nation's fifth-lowest median age (27.2 years) and a median income slightly less than $36,000. Nearly half of the district's residents age 25 or older do not have a high school diploma.

A narrow strip of land — about 10 miles in length and running along railroad tracks, highways and cemeteries — attaches the Puerto Rican neighborhood of Logan Square in the northern part of the 4th to Mexican-American populations in Little Village and Pilsen in the southern portion. More than 90 percent of residents are Hispanic in these parts of the South Lawndale and Lower West Side communities around Cermak Road in the southern arm of the district. Close-in Chicago suburbs such as Cicero and Stone Park, formerly home to Slavic and Italian populations, respectively, also have seen rapid Hispanic growth.

The 4th has the state's largest percentage of blue-collar workers, many of whom are immigrants living in the district's Hispanic, Ukrainian and Polish neighborhoods. Most jobs in the district are in the transportation and manufacturing sectors, and the warehousing industry is strong.

The district is plagued by low voter turnout, but is solidly Democratic at all levels. Democrat John Kerry garnered 79 percent of the 4th's presidential vote in 2004.

MAJOR INDUSTRY
Light manufacturing, transportation

CITIES
Chicago (pt.), 560,373; Cicero (pt.), 73,209; Melrose Park (pt.), 5,756

NOTABLE
Cermak Road is named for former Chicago Mayor Anton Cermak, who was killed in 1933 by a bullet meant for President-elect Franklin Delano Roosevelt; The Back of the Yards neighborhood in Chicago was the subject of Upton Sinclair's 1906 novel "The Jungle."

Rep. Rahm Emanuel (D)

CAPITOL OFFICE
225-4061
rahm.emanuel@mail.house.gov
www.house.gov/emanuel
1319 Longworth 20515-1305; fax 225-5603

COMMITTEES
Ways & Means

RESIDENCE
Chicago

BORN
Nov. 29, 1959, Chicago, Ill.

RELIGION
Jewish

FAMILY
Wife, Amy Rule; three children

EDUCATION
Sarah Lawrence College, B.A. 1981 (liberal arts); Northwestern U., M.A. 1985 (speech & communication)

CAREER
Investment bank executive; senior White House official; campaign aide and finance director

POLITICAL HIGHLIGHTS
No previous office

ELECTION RESULTS

2006 GENERAL		
Rahm Emanuel (D)	114,319	78.0%
Kevin Edward White (R)	32,250	22.0%
2006 PRIMARY		
Rahm Emanuel (D)	53,727	83.1%
Mark A. Fredrickson (D)	6,050	9.4%
John Haptonstall (D)	4,876	7.5%
2004 GENERAL		
Rahm Emanuel (D)	158,400	76.2%
Bruce Best (R)	49,530	23.8%

PREVIOUS WINNING PERCENTAGES
2002 (67%)

Elected 2002; 3rd term

Emanuel's mix of political and policy smarts has made him one of the most important Democratic players on Capitol Hill. As head of the Democratic Congressional Campaign Committee, he got some of the credit for the party's spectacular takeover of the House in the 2006 elections. His grateful colleagues promptly elected him to the chairmanship of the House Democratic Caucus, the No. 4 leadership post.

Emanuel pairs a thorough knowledge of campaigns with a deep interest in new policy ideas. A former top official in the Clinton White House, he understands how to use the media, excels at fundraising and is one of the party's best strategists. The former president once described him as a breath of fresh air "blowing at gale force speed."

Under Emanuel, the DCCC in 2005-06 raised and spent $64 million on House races, less than the $82 million its GOP counterpart raised but an increase of nearly 75 percent over the previous two-year election cycle. Emanuel required candidates to meet specific goals to qualify for fundraising help, to demonstrate an ability to raise money on their own and to generate media coverage. Early on, he kept DCCC resources targeted on the most promising take-away districts. Then, as Republicans were weakened by influence-peddling scandals and Democratic challengers began to climb in the polls, he spread the largess to once-marginal races around the country.

No less a GOP stalwart than Newt Gingrich of Georgia, who once plotted a successful takeover of the House himself, told Fox News: "Every Republican should respect what [Speaker] Nancy Pelosi and Rahm Emanuel have done. They put together a campaign team. They recruited people who are fairly centrist. They learned a big lesson out of being too far to the left."

The man known as "Rahmbo" for his frequent outbursts is an intense, high-energy personality with a legendary disregard for what others think of him. He doesn't mind knocking heads to get things done, his colleagues say, because he counts on patching up relationships later.

Emanuel has ambitions for himself as well. After the election, he considered challenging James E. Clyburn of South Carolina for Democratic whip, the third-ranking leadership job. But that would have riled the Congressional Black Caucus (Clyburn is a former chairman), and cost him the goodwill he had just earned by helping lead Democrats to the majority. He settled for an uncontested election as Democratic Caucus chairman, which Clyburn was vacating.

In his first two terms in the House, Emanuel used his seat on the Ways and Means Committee to promote health care and tax policies, such as a "Fair Flat Tax" plan he says would provide more relief to middle-class families than flat tax proposals by conservatives. In early 2007, he assembled a bipartisan group of lawmakers behind a major expansion of Medicaid and the State Children's Health Insurance Program to cover 6 million children who are estimated to be eligible for public insurance but not enrolled. He combined it with a new tax credit to encourage middle-income families to buy private insurance.

Emanuel's district takes in the trendy, rowhouse neighborhoods along Chicago's lakefront but is dominated by the sprawling working-class sections northwest of downtown, where Polish, and increasingly Spanish, is a first language for many. Having grown up in the well-heeled suburb of Wilmette, Emanuel had to fend off suggestions in his first campaign in 2002 that he had moved to the district out of political opportunism.

He is one of four children of a Chicago pediatrician. His father, Benjamin, is a native of what is now Israel and fought in the Zionist movement in the 1940s; he emigrated to the United States in 1959 after marrying Emanuel's mother, Marsha, an American Jew and civil rights activist whom he had met during his medical training. Emanuel's family experience inspires his passionate interest in Middle East policy.

At New Trier High School, Emanuel was small for a boy — he's still just 5 feet 8 inches tall and 150 pounds — and drawn to soccer. He took a ballet class to improve his agility and liked it so much that he continued to study dance while at Sarah Lawrence College in New York.

Emanuel discovered politics by accident. During a semester off, he worked on the campaign staff of a Democratic House candidate in a district near Springfield, Ill., and befriended David Wilhelm, another young, idealistic campaign worker. Emanuel returned to Chicago to get a master's degree in speech and communication and to pursue a political career.

He worked on the 1984 Senate campaign of Illinois Democrat Paul Simon, then as national campaign director for the DCCC and later as a fundraiser in the first campaign of Chicago Mayor Richard M. Daley Jr. By 1991, Wilhelm had become campaign manager for the fledgling presidential campaign of Arkansas Gov. Bill Clinton. He recruited Emanuel to head fundraising, and his old friend turned an anemic operation into a vaunted money machine.

Clinton took Emanuel to the White House as political director. Only 33, Emanuel was a star, but he was blunt to a fault. He jumped on tables to lecture aides and he screamed at political donors he thought stingy. When he alienated other senior aides, he was demoted to manager of special legislative efforts. He worked hard to rehabilitate himself, and when senior adviser George Stephanopoulos left in 1996, Emanuel was given the job.

He left Washington in 1999 and became an investment banker, though he had no training in that field. He built a stable of clients who had been big Democratic donors, raking in $16 million in less than three years, the Chicago Tribune reported. Having made his fortune, he jumped into the 2002 race to succeed Democratic Rep. Rod R. Blagojevich, who ran, successfully, for governor.

Emanuel's biggest obstacle was primary opponent Nancy Kaszak, a former state representative with a Polish surname who depicted him as a carpetbagger. But Emanuel had the backing of Daley and of the labor unions. He also got walking-around help from a police sergeant uncle in a district where many police officers and firefighters live. He won easily and cruised to re-election in 2004 and 2006.

KEY VOTES

2006

Yes	Stop broadband companies from favoring select Internet traffic
No	Affirm U.S. commitment to war in Iraq and reject setting a withdrawal date for troops
No	Repeal requirement for bilingual ballots at the polls
Yes	Permit U.S. sale of civilian nuclear technology to India
No	Build a 700-mile fence on the U.S.-Mexico border to curb illegal crossings
No	Permit warrantless wiretaps of suspected terrorists

2005

?	Intervene in the life-support case of Terri Schiavo
Yes	Lift President Bush's restrictions on stem cell research funding
Yes	Prohibit FBI access to library and bookstore records
No	Approve free-trade pact with five Central American countries
No	Pass energy policy overhaul favored by President Bush emphasizing domestic oil and gas production
No	End mandatory preservation of habitat of endangered animal and plant species
Yes	Ban torture of prisoners in U.S. custody

CQ VOTE STUDIES

	PARTY UNITY		PRESIDENTIAL SUPPORT	
	Support	Oppose	Support	Oppose
2006	92%	8%	33%	67%
2005	95%	5%	24%	76%
2004	97%	3%	18%	82%
2003	95%	5%	26%	74%

INTEREST GROUPS

	AFL-CIO	ADA	CCUS	ACU
2006	93%	90%	47%	4%
2005	93%	100%	48%	0%
2004	100%	100%	29%	0%
2003	87%	95%	39%	24%

ILLINOIS 5

Chicago – North Side

The 5th spans Chicago's North Side, stretching from Lake Michigan in the east to near O'Hare International Airport (located in the 6th) in the west. The district is home to one of the city's few remaining active industrial sectors, running through the middle of the 5th along the north branch of the Chicago River.

DePaul University students and "lakefront liberals" inhabit wealthy east-side communities such as Lincoln Park. The district includes the historic Lincoln Park beach, ethnic restaurants and local entertainment venues, which provide a weekend and evening destination for residents from other parts of the north side, the west side and the north suburbs.

The district's west covers part of the "Bungalow Belt," a stretch of 1930s brick homes separating the suburbs from downtown Chicago. The west's working-class base routinely supports populist-style Democrats, but far west-side neighborhoods and some portions of the Bungalow Belt also have elected a few Republicans to local offices in the past. This section of town is still dominated by middle- and working-class neighborhoods and second- and third-generation German and Polish residents, but there is an increasing number of Hispanic newcomers.

The combination of these voting habits makes for a constituency that leans Democratic. On the federal level, the 5th supports Democrats for president and Congress, and Democratic statewide candidates also generally do well here. The district gave Democrat John Kerry 67 percent of its 2004 presidential vote.

Although far behind the Hispanic-majority 4th, the 5th District has the state's second-largest percentage of Hispanics at 23 percent. The district's black population (2 percent) is the lowest in the state.

MAJOR INDUSTRY
Manufacturing, warehousing and storage, electronics, health care

CITIES
Chicago (pt.), 549,762; Elmwood Park (pt.), 23,741; Franklin Park, 19,434

NOTABLE
Wrigley Field is home to baseball's Chicago Cubs; Chicago's Music Box Theatre, a restored movie theater that first opened in 1929 and now presents roughly 300 shows annually in various formats, allegedly has been haunted since 1977 by the ghost of its original manager.

Rep. Peter Roskam (R)

Elected 2006; 1st term

Roskam hopes to follow in the footsteps of two powerful House Republicans on whose staffs he worked: former Majority Leader Tom DeLay of Texas, and Henry J. Hyde, Roskam's predecessor in the 6th District and past chairman of both the Judiciary and International Relations committees.

Roskam has said there is "no finer role model in public life" than Hyde. The two men share a similarly conservative social agenda, including opposing abortion. As a state senator, Roskam led the opposition to state funding for a procedure opponents call "partial birth" abortion. Roskam also fought state funding of embryonic stem cell research, and says he will continue to oppose it at the federal level.

A fiscal conservative, he wants to ease the tax burden and rein in government spending. He favors giving the president the line-item veto. He also supports making the 2003 tax cuts permanent. But he does not object to the practice of earmarking federal funds for projects back home.

Roskam sits on the Financial Services Committee, where he wants to work to create jobs in the financial services industry. More than 50,000 of his constituents work in some area of the financial services sector, he says.

Roskam has a good deal of legislative experience. He served in the Illinois House for six years, and the state Senate for about seven. His first political office was serving as the president of the student senate at Glenbard West High School, where he was also a varsity gymnast.

Roskam won one of the nation's most hotly contested races. In the heyday of Hyde's long House career, GOP victory was a sure thing in this suburban Chicago district. But Roskam barely eked out a win over Democrat Tammy Duckworth, an Illinois Army National Guardswoman — and sharp critic of President Bush's handling of the Iraq War — who lost her legs when a rocket-propelled grenade hit her helicopter in Iraq.

Roskam emphasized his ties to the district and portrayed himself as a more local candidate than Duckworth, who had attracted substantial financial support from outside of Illinois. Roskam won by less than 3 percentage points.

CAPITOL OFFICE
225-4561
roskam.house.gov
507 Cannon 20515-1306; fax 225-1166

COMMITTEES
Financial Services

RESIDENCE
Wheaton

BORN
Sept. 13, 1961, Hinsdale, Ill.

RELIGION
Anglican

FAMILY
Wife, Elizabeth Roskam; four children

EDUCATION
U. of Illinois, B.A. 1983 (political science); Illinois Institute of Technology, J.D. 1989

CAREER
Lawyer; education scholarship nonprofit executive director; congressional aide; teacher

POLITICAL HIGHLIGHTS
Ill. House, 1993-99; sought Republican nomination for U.S. House, 1998; Ill. Senate, 2000-07

ELECTION RESULTS

2006 GENERAL		
Peter Roskam (R)	91,382	51.4%
Tammy Duckworth (D)	86,572	48.6%
2006 PRIMARY		
Peter Roskam (R)		unopposed

ILLINOIS 6

Northwest and west Chicago suburbs

Just west of Chicago, the 6th includes northern DuPage County and northwestern Cook County. Residents are mostly wealthy, white-collar workers who live in the older, mostly built-out suburbs along commuter rail lines that run into the city.

Residents here commute both to Chicago and to the booming northwest satellite cities. O'Hare International Airport (an extension of the city of Chicago and the district's eastern border) is one of the busiest airports in the world and is the center of the 6th's commercial district. Hotels and other travel-related businesses, and firms seeking close airport access, are located nearby. United Airlines plans to retain a major operations center in Elk Grove despite moving its headquarters to downtown Chicago.

Most workers in the 6th are professionals, and the district has the second-lowest proportion of service industry workers in Illinois. Overall, the 6th is one-eighth Hispanic, and areas in DuPage County, such as Addison, Bensenville and Glendale Heights, are becoming more racially diverse.

The district has a reputation as a Republican bastion, historically working in opposition to Chicago's Democrats. This is particularly true of DuPage, which accounts for three-fourths of the district's population, but the Cook County portions of the district also have a conservative lean. The district's conservatism has moderated in recent years, but the 6th gave George W. Bush 53 percent of its presidential vote in 2004.

MAJOR INDUSTRY
Airport, light manufacturing, health care

CITIES
Wheaton, 55,416; Elmhurst, 42,762; Lombard, 42,322; Carol Stream, 40,438; Addison, 35,914

NOTABLE
Barnes & Noble traces its beginning to 1873, when Charles M. Barnes sold books from his home in Wheaton.

Rep. Danny K. Davis (D)

CAPITOL OFFICE
225-5006
www.house.gov/davis
2159 Rayburn 20515-1307; fax 225-5641

COMMITTEES
Education & Labor
Oversight & Government Reform
(Federal Workforce, Postal Service & the District of Columbia - chairman)

RESIDENCE
Chicago

BORN
Sept. 6, 1941, Parkdale, Ark.

RELIGION
Baptist

FAMILY
Wife, Vera G. Davis; two children

EDUCATION
Arkansas AM&N College, B.A. 1961 (history & education); Chicago State U., M.A. 1968 (guidance); Union Institute, Ph.D. 1977 (public administration)

CAREER
Health care association executive; teacher; postal clerk

POLITICAL HIGHLIGHTS
Chicago City Council, 1979-90; sought Democratic nomination for U.S. House, 1984, 1986; Cook County Commission, 1990-97; sought Democratic nomination for mayor of Chicago, 1991

ELECTION RESULTS

2006 GENERAL		
Danny K. Davis (D)	143,071	86.7%
Charles Hutchinson (R)	21,939	13.3%
2006 PRIMARY		
Danny K. Davis (D)	77,287	89.0%
Jim Ascot (D)	6,646	7.7%
Robert Dallas (D)	2,921	3.4%
2004 GENERAL		
Danny K. Davis (D)	221,133	86.1%
Antonio Davis-Fairman (R)	35,603	13.9%

PREVIOUS WINNING PERCENTAGES
2002 (83%); 2000 (86%); 1998 (93%); 1996 (82%)

Elected 1996; 6th term

A lot of the people who get out of prison in Illinois wind up in Davis' district on Chicago's west side, making him one of the few advocates in Congress for former criminals. With his deep, melodious voice, Davis is given to impassioned speeches about boosting the federal commitment to housing, drug rehabilitation and other programs aimed at the underclass.

His own life is a study in overcoming adversity. Davis was one of 11 children of sharecroppers who picked cotton in southeastern Arkansas. He and his siblings went to a segregated school four or five months of the year, spending the rest of the time in the fields. Before coming to Congress, he made his mark in the rough-and-tumble world of Chicago politics, becoming the first African-American alderman who was not part of the Democratic Party machine.

Though his district takes in tonier parts of the city, including trendy new developments near the Loop, it is dominated by poor, drug-ravaged neighborhoods with the highest percentage of felons released in Illinois. "All of the issues associated with poverty are pronounced in my district," Davis says. "Rather than run from it, or hope someone else is going to do it, we took [up] the ex-offender issue."

Davis promotes legislation aimed at helping ex-cons make a transition to productive lives, particularly drug treatment programs that he says have gone begging during the Bush administration. He often teams up with Democrat Charles B. Rangel of New York, who as chairman of the Ways and Means Committee has more influence over dollars-and-cents issues and whose Harlem district has many of the same social problems.

Like Rangel, Davis also promotes the idea of reducing taxes and regulations on companies operating in designated urban and rural renewal areas. Davis, a member of the Congressional Black Caucus, has pushed for federal review of police brutality and racial profiling.

From his seat on the Education and Labor Committee, Davis is a big believer in the federal Head Start program, which provides preschool education to disadvantaged children. He has sponsored legislation to give stipends to Head Start teachers and to increase the numbers of African-American and Hispanic men hired as teachers or sought as role models.

He is an equally strong advocate for historically black colleges, like the one he attended, the University of Arkansas at Pine Bluff. A number of his siblings also attended the college. "I strongly believe that perhaps none of us would have been able to attend college had it not been for the fact that the University of Arkansas at Pine Bluff, which then was Arkansas AM&N College, existed," he said in remarks on the House floor in 2006.

"Public education has been the greatest equalizer that has existed in this country," said Davis in opposing GOP attempts a few years ago to create government-financed vouchers for private school tuition. "I'm suspect when I see anything that is going to seriously impact or erode that system."

Davis also sits on the Oversight and Government Reform Committee, where he is the chairman of the subcommittee on the U.S. Postal Service and the federal workforce. While the assignment is "not all that sexy," he says, he has an affinity for the postal system. Davis once worked as a postal clerk for a year.

A member of the Congressional Progressive Caucus, he votes a consistently liberal line on most issues. On the major foreign policy issue before the 110th Congress (2007-08), Davis also sticks with the liberals in his party.

He voted against the 2002 resolution authorizing the military invasion of Iraq and has been a vocal opponent of the war.

Davis received some negative scrutiny from the press in 2006 when he was named by PoliticalMoneyLine as Congress' 15th-most-frequent traveler at the expense of private interests. A trip he made that year to Sri Lanka was funded by an organization associated with the Tamil Tigers, which the State Department considers a terrorist organization, the Chicago Tribune reported. Davis told the newspaper that the $13,000 trip he took with an aide was to investigate how the country was using reconstruction aid after the 2004 tsunami, and that he thought the sponsor was a cultural group.

Before Democrats won the House in November 2006, Davis had let it be known he was interested in becoming Cook County Board president, one of the most powerful jobs in Chicago politics, after President John Stroger suffered a debilitating stroke. To Davis' disappointment, the Democratic party regulars chose the former board president's son, Todd Stroger.

Davis started his career thinking he would be a teacher. After his graduation from college, with $50 from his father, Davis left Arkansas for California. He got as far as Chicago when his money ran out. He stayed with an older sister, and got a job teaching high school language arts and social studies during school hours, then moonlighted at the post office from 3 p.m. until 9 p.m.

Davis got involved in the community, and his activism eventually led him to become president of the National Association of Community Health Centers. In 1979, Davis headed a committee of neighborhood leaders looking for a candidate to challenge the Democratic machine in a Chicago City Council race, but he failed to turn up anyone. "So I said, 'What the hell,' and decided to run myself," he says.

On the council in the early 1980s, Davis was a close associate of Harold Washington, a former House member and the city's first black mayor, who also had challenged the mostly white Democratic machine.

In 1984, Davis opposed U.S. Rep. Cardiss Collins in the Democratic primary for the 7th District seat; he lost by 10 percentage points but held her to less than a majority. Davis opposed Collins again in 1986 but lost decisively. And in 1991, Davis was the decided underdog in a Democratic primary campaign for mayor against the incumbent, Richard M. Daley.

When Collins announced plans to retire in 1996, Davis jumped into the race. He faced a crowded primary field and opposition from some regular machine Democrats, but he cleared those hurdles and coasted to victory with 82 percent of the vote. He has had equally decisive wins ever since.

KEY VOTES

2006

- No Stop broadband companies from favoring select Internet traffic
- No Affirm U.S. commitment to war in Iraq and reject setting a withdrawal date for troops
- No Repeal requirement for bilingual ballots at the polls
- Yes Permit U.S. sale of civilian nuclear technology to India
- No Build a 700-mile fence on the U.S.-Mexico border to curb illegal crossings
- No Permit warrantless wiretaps of suspected terrorists

2005

- ? Intervene in the life-support case of Terri Schiavo
- Yes Lift President Bush's restrictions on stem cell research funding
- Yes Prohibit FBI access to library and bookstore records
- No Approve free-trade pact with five Central American countries
- No Pass energy policy overhaul favored by President Bush emphasizing domestic oil and gas production
- No End mandatory preservation of habitat of endangered animal and plant species
- Yes Ban torture of prisoners in U.S. custody

CQ VOTE STUDIES

	PARTY UNITY		PRESIDENTIAL SUPPORT	
	Support	Oppose	Support	Oppose
2006	97%	3%	25%	75%
2005	97%	3%	20%	80%
2004	98%	2%	16%	84%
2003	99%	1%	13%	87%
2002	96%	4%	24%	76%

INTEREST GROUPS

	AFL-CIO	ADA	CCUS	ACU
2006	100%	90%	40%	8%
2005	93%	100%	41%	4%
2004	87%	90%	30%	0%
2003	100%	100%	19%	12%
2002	100%	90%	42%	0%

ILLINOIS 7

Chicago — downtown, West Side; west suburbs

East to west, the 7th stretches from the Loop, Chicago's downtown business district, almost to the DuPage County line, taking in the well-to-do western suburbs of River Forest and Oak Park. North to south, the district runs from the upscale Lincoln Park neighborhood (shared with the 5th) to 57th Street on the South Side.

The eastern end of the 7th houses some of Chicago's gems, including the Sears Tower, the plush high-rises of River North, several museums and about a dozen colleges and universities. Chicago's "Magnificent Mile" on Michigan Avenue includes some high-end shops and first-rate hotels. Most people employed in the district commute from surrounding suburbs to the downtown headquarters of business giants such as Boeing, United Airlines, Quaker and Hyatt, as well as to Chicago's financial center.

In contrast, most of the district lives in the poverty-stricken neighborhoods that stretch from the western Loop to the edge of the county. Except for a few communities of middle-class blacks, the West Side has had problems with gang violence, unemployment and crumbling infrastructure. The 7th is home to two-thirds of Chicago's public housing projects, but improvements are ongoing, with some once-dilapidated areas now home to lofts and galleries. The district also is home to most of Chicago's professional sports teams.

The 7th fills with white commuters during the day, but more than 60 percent of district residents are black. A reliably Democratic district at all levels, the only genuine political contests in the 7th are the Democratic primaries. John Kerry won 83 percent of the 2004 presidential vote here — his second-highest percentage in the state.

MAJOR INDUSTRY

Insurance, financial services, health care

CITIES

Chicago (pt.), 502,445; Oak Park, 52,524; Maywood (pt.), 24,895

NOTABLE

The Cook County Jail is the largest single-site county pre-detention facility in the nation; The Home Insurance Building, constructed in Chicago in 1885 and demolished in 1931, is considered the first skyscraper in the United States; The Grant Park Music Festival, held each year in Millennium Park, is a free outdoor classical music series.

Rep. Melissa Bean (D)

CAPITOL OFFICE
225-3711
melissa@mail.house.gov
www.house.gov/bean
318 Cannon 20515-1308; fax 225-7830

COMMITTEES
Financial Services
Small Business
(Finance & Tax - chairwoman)

RESIDENCE
Barrington

BORN
Jan. 22, 1962, Chicago, Ill.

RELIGION
Serbian Orthodox

FAMILY
Husband, Alan Bean; two children

EDUCATION
Oakton Community College, A.A. 1982 (business); Roosevelt U., B.A. 2002 (political science)

CAREER
Technology consulting firm president; telecommunications sales manager

POLITICAL HIGHLIGHTS
Democratic nominee for U.S. House, 2002

ELECTION RESULTS

2006 GENERAL		
Melissa Bean (D)	93,355	50.9%
David McSweeney (R)	80,720	44.0%
William C. Scheurer (X)	9,312	5.1%
2006 PRIMARY		
Melissa Bean (D)		unopposed
2004 GENERAL		
Melissa Bean (D)	139,792	51.7%
Philip M. Crane (R)	130,601	48.3%

Elected 2004; 2nd term

Melissa Bean had a lot to prove her first term in Congress. After winning arguably the biggest upset victory of 2004, she had to demonstrate her ability to satisfy her Republican-leaning constituency north and west of Chicago. According to the Chicago Tribune's editorial page when it endorsed her in 2006, "She has delivered."

One of the few female members of the Blue Dogs, a coalition of fiscally conservative Democrats, the mother of two describes her budget philosophy as "tough love." She praised passage of pay-as-you-go budget rules, which require offsets for spending increases or tax cuts. Like parents and business leaders, she says, lawmakers have to make the difficult decisions to eliminate wasteful spending, even in well-intentioned programs that aren't performing.

Bean's committee assignments are on Financial Services and Small Business, and her priorities include a bill designed to protect families from Internet crime and child predators.

The bills she wrote as a freshman went nowhere, not unusual for a minority-party freshman. Bean may have more success in the 110th Congress (2007-08) as a member of the majority with influential friends in the Senate, including Majority Whip Richard J. Durbin, Illinois' senior senator. She chairs the Small Business Subcommittee on Finance and Tax.

A fiscal conservative, Bean says she's socially more moderate. She backs federal funding for embryonic stem cell research and voted against a constitutional ban on same-sex marriage.

Yet she still lands to the right on some social issues, voting, for instance, to limit the legal liability of gun manufacturers when guns are used in crimes.

A suburban businesswoman for 20 years, Bean says she doesn't buy into the "false choices" between business and labor, or business and the environment. Her support for business angered state labor interests, a core Democratic constituency, however, who felt betrayed when she voted in favor of the 2005 Central American Free Trade Agreement. State union leaders promptly reversed a decision to give her a "Person of the Year" award, and the Illinois AFL-CIO did not endorse her 2006 campaign.

Her business background informs both her policy stands and how she approaches the job of being a lawmaker. She applies the language of boardrooms to her congressional role, speaking of "bringing value" to her committees, setting goals and measuring performance. In one's early years in the House, she says, "You have to build your infrastructure and build your team and create your best practices."

She started the job with some operational disadvantages. Bitter from his 3 percentage point defeat in 2004, veteran Republican Philip M. Crane didn't leave behind a single constituent case file, Bean says. Each had to be restarted from scratch, as did 500 routine form letters.

Bean's more localized interests are environmental protection for the Great Lakes and easing the district's considerable commuter traffic problems.

The oldest of four children, Bean was adopted as an infant, though her mother later gave birth to her three siblings. That background inspired her to introduce legislation in 2005 to provide an additional $2,000 tax credit to families who adopt children age 9 or older.

Her adoptive parents were Serbian; Bean's grandfather on her father's side immigrated to Chicago from Yugoslavia, working for three years as a laborer before he could afford the ticket for his wife to join him. Bean was raised in the Orthodox Church and surrounded by Serbian culture, music and food.

She grew up exploring the shop floor and drafting room of the engineering and manufacturing firm her father owned, and Bean says she knew she'd go into business herself one day. She recalls playing office there with her younger brother. From the purchasing office, she'd call him in engineering, shouting, "I have an order and I need it quick!"

While pursuing her associate's degree, Bean worked part-time for a technology company called Data Access Systems, then one of the country's fastest-growing companies. When the firm made her a full-time job offer, she switched her classes to the evenings. Bean was in sales, her desired field, by the age of 21 and a branch manager by age 23. In 1995, she founded her own technology consulting firm.

She never gave up school, however, working on and off throughout her career — and two pregnancies — toward a bachelor's degree in political science, which she earned in 2002. It just took longer than she'd originally planned, she says, recalling how she finished one class just in time to give birth to her oldest daughter, Victoria, a mere 10 days later.

Motherhood motivated Bean to become active in politics beyond the voting booth. "It totally changes your priorities, and issues like air quality and school quality become paramount in your life," she says.

After collecting a respectable 43 percent of the vote in her long-shot bid against Crane in 2002, Bean came into 2004 armed with a far larger campaign treasury and stronger national party support. She convinced many voters that Crane, who had represented the region since 1969, was more interested in foreign travel than the concerns of his constituents.

The GOP targeted her seat from the day she won it, but in 2006 she held on with about 51 percent, beating well-funded GOP challenger David McSweeney, an investment banker, by almost 7 percentage points.

Bean is a pro at juggling family and work. Even on a busy day, she finds time to plan a surprise dance party for her daughter's sweet 16. When Congress is in session, she lives in a Capitol Hill row house with Democratic Reps. Carolyn B. Maloney of New York and Debbie Wasserman-Schultz of Florida, flying back home every weekend. Her family comes to Washington for spring and summer breaks. Sometimes, all three women have their kids visit and the house is crammed with air mattresses. It's a zoo, but a lot of fun, Bean says.

KEY VOTES

2006

- Yes Stop broadband companies from favoring select Internet traffic
- Yes Affirm U.S. commitment to war in Iraq and reject setting a withdrawal date for troops
- No Repeal requirement for bilingual ballots at the polls
- Yes Permit U.S. sale of civilian nuclear technology to India
- Yes Build a 700-mile fence on the U.S.-Mexico border to curb illegal crossings
- Yes Permit warrantless wiretaps of suspected terrorists

2005

- Yes Intervene in the life-support case of Terri Schiavo
- Yes Lift President Bush's restrictions on stem cell research funding
- Yes Prohibit FBI access to library and bookstore records
- Yes Approve free-trade pact with five Central American countries
- Yes Pass energy policy overhaul favored by President Bush emphasizing domestic oil and gas production
- No End mandatory preservation of habitat of endangered animal and plant species
- Yes Ban torture of prisoners in U.S. custody

CQ VOTE STUDIES

	PARTY UNITY		PRESIDENTIAL SUPPORT	
	Support	Oppose	Support	Oppose
2006	76%	24%	50%	50%
2005	83%	17%	48%	52%

INTEREST GROUPS

	AFL-CIO	ADA	CCUS	ACU
2006	64%	60%	80%	48%
2005	73%	80%	73%	12%

ILLINOIS 8

Northwest Cook County – Schaumburg; parts of Lake and McHenry counties

The 8th, located in the northeastern corner of the state, takes in northwestern Cook County and parts of Lake and McHenry counties. Most residents live in the affluent, well-established suburbs just northwest of Chicago or farther north through western Lake County and toward the Chain O' Lakes vacation communities near the Wisconsin border.

The district is home to many white-collar employers, including sales and health care companies. The 8th's range of industry provides varied employment and attracts residents to the area. As in other northwestern Chicago suburban districts, some of the 8th's cities, such as Palatine (shared with the 10th) and Schaumburg (a small part of which is in the 6th and 10th districts), have lured corporate headquarters. A major shopping mall in Schaumburg draws business from across the northwest and west exurbs. Cook County benefits from its access to interstates and proximity to O'Hare International Airport (in the 6th).

The 8th contains a significant portion of Lake County, where a slight majority of district residents live. This growing area is largely upscale and well-educated; in the southwest Lake villages of North Barrington and Kildeer, the median family income is more than $100,000. The northeastern part of McHenry County, which is west of Lake, is home to some sparsely populated, affluent towns.

Despite the northeast corner of Illinois' strong tradition of sending Republicans to the U.S. House — having done so for more than a half century until 2004 — the 8th's voters picked a Democrat for the second straight House election in 2006. In 2004, Republican George W. Bush captured 55 percent of the district's presidential vote.

MAJOR INDUSTRY
Health care, insurance, retail, government

CITIES
Schaumburg (pt.), 71,577; Palatine (pt.), 47,077; Hoffman Estates (pt.), 39,568; Mundelein (pt.), 28,416

NOTABLE
The Volo Illinois Auto Museum features classic and celebrity cars.

Rep. Jan Schakowsky (D)

CAPITOL OFFICE
225-2111
jan.schakowsky@mail.house.gov
www.house.gov/schakowsky
1027 Longworth 20515-1309; fax 226-6890

COMMITTEES
Energy & Commerce
Select Intelligence

RESIDENCE
Evanston

BORN
May 26, 1944, Chicago, Ill.

RELIGION
Jewish

FAMILY
Husband, Robert Creamer; three children

EDUCATION
U. of Illinois, B.S. 1965 (elementary education)

CAREER
Senior citizens group director; consumer advocate; homemaker; teacher

POLITICAL HIGHLIGHTS
Candidate for Cook County Commission, 1986; Ill. House, 1991-99 (floor leader, 1994-99)

ELECTION RESULTS

2006 GENERAL		
Jan Schakowsky (D)	122,852	74.6%
Michael P. Shannon (R)	41,858	25.4%
2006 PRIMARY		
Jan Schakowsky (D)		unopposed
2004 GENERAL		
Jan Schakowsky (D)	175,282	75.7%
Kurt J. Eckhardt (R)	56,135	24.3%

PREVIOUS WINNING PERCENTAGES
2002 (70%); 2000 (76%); 1998 (75%)

Elected 1998; 5th term

A member of the Congressional Progressive Caucus, the most liberal group of House Democrats, Schakowsky is a firm believer in the power of government to improve the lives of Americans. And despite the setbacks of the Bush era, she continues trying to push the public agenda to the left. "It's more important than ever for there to be a very clear, unapologetic progressive voice," she has said.

Schakowsky (shuh-KOW-ski) is one of the most loyal House Democrats. Since 2001, she has backed her party 99 percent of the time on votes that pitted the two parties against each other. When she splits with her party's majority, as she did by voting against a major pension overhaul bill in 2006, it is usually because she thinks a bill does not do enough to protect consumers or workers.

Schakowsky is an ally of Speaker Nancy Pelosi of California and serves as one of nine chief deputy whips. But even though she was seen as Pelosi's candidate, she failed in a 2006 bid to become vice chairwoman of the Democratic Caucus, her party's No. 4 leadership post. She came in third on the first ballot behind moderate Joseph Crowley of New York and John B. Larson of Connecticut. Schakowsky then threw her support to Larson, who won handily on the second ballot.

Despite that disappointment, in the 110th Congress (2007-08) she added a seat on the Intelligence Committee to her portfolio and retained her post on the Steering and Policy Committee, which plays a large role in making Democratic committee assignments.

And she continues to draw attention within Democratic circles for her fundraising prowess. With a safe seat, she was by far the biggest party fundraiser among first-term House members in 2000 and one of the biggest among all Democrats. It is a pattern she has repeated, focusing her fundraising efforts on women candidates in particular. In the 2004 election cycle, she made donations to 75 House Democratic incumbents and challengers, and raised $1.3 million for Women LEAD, a group aimed at female donors that she headed. During the 2006 election cycle, she contributed more than $350,000 to the Democratic Congressional Campaign Committee, the party's political arm in the House, and individual candidates.

Schakowsky gained a coveted assignment to the Energy and Commerce Committee in 2003, where she ranks second in seniority on the Commerce, Trade and Consumer Protection Subcommittee. The post enables her to continue the work she began three decades ago in behalf of consumers. In 2006, a bill she introduced to make it illegal to pose as someone else in order to obtain that person's phone records was included in a measure the full committee approved to impose criminal penalties for fraudulently gaining access to phone records. She also has introduced legislation to end automatic-teller surcharges and what she calls excessive bank fees.

She is wary of handing over too much authority to the government. In early 2005, when GOP leaders revived legislation to give federal regulators more authority to punish broadcasters and performers for sexually explicit or vulgar programming, Schakowsky said, "We are heading down a slippery slope when Big Brother decides what constitutes free speech and artistic expression." She was one of two Democrats on Energy and Commerce voting against the bill. The following year, she led calls for committee hearings to grill telephone company executives about why they had turned over customers' call records to the National Security Agency without first demanding to see a subpoena or court order.

Schakowsky is a vehement critic of the 2003 Medicare prescription drug law, which she says is far too complicated and contains too many coverage gaps. She fought for a delay of its initial May 15, 2006, enrollment deadline, and when that failed, she continued to push to revamp the program entirely. She wants the government to offer drug coverage directly, rather than forcing seniors to sign up with private insurance companies to obtain benefits.

Schakowsky has been a sharp critic of U.S. intervention in Iraq, voting against the resolution authorizing the war there. Although she supported the Bush administration's fight against terrorism in Afghanistan, she said it must be coupled with increased foreign aid to economically distressed nations. "That has to be included in the calculation of the war on terrorism," she said. "There is no security in the world without economic justice."

Schakowsky does not just espouse progressive causes. A veteran activist of more than 25 years, she seeks to teach organizing skills to others. With her husband, Robert Creamer, she set up a training program for political advocates that has been replicated nationwide. The program brought volunteers to Chicago to a "campaign school," where they were given instruction and political tools and then put to work on several House races.

In 2006, her husband was sentenced to five months in prison for writing bad checks to generate cash for his failing Illinois nonprofit, Illinois Public Action, and for failing to withhold taxes from employees' paychecks. The judge said the sentence was lighter than normal for such a case because Creamer had not enriched himself. Schakowsky stood by him, even as she acknowledged he had made a mistake.

Schakowsky was a stay-at-home mother in the early 1970s, when she helped launch a successful nationwide campaign to require freshness dates on food products. She said six women got together and decided they wanted to know how old the food was in their local grocery. "You would bring home cottage cheese and it would be green around the edges," she said. "We would find infant formula that was sometimes years beyond the [expiration] date." She continued as a community activist and was elected to the Illinois House in 1990. She rose to become chairwoman of the state House Labor and Commerce Committee and Democratic floor leader.

Liberal Democrat Sidney R. Yates held the 9th District seat for 48 years before retiring in 1998. Schakowsky bested state Sen. Howard W. Carroll and Hyatt hotel heir Jay "J.B." Pritzker in the primary and easily won the general election in the heavily Democratic district. She has won each election since with more than 70 percent of the vote.

KEY VOTES

2006

- Yes Stop broadband companies from favoring select Internet traffic
- No Affirm U.S. commitment to war in Iraq and reject setting a withdrawal date for troops
- No Repeal requirement for bilingual ballots at the polls
- Yes Permit U.S. sale of civilian nuclear technology to India
- No Build a 700-mile fence on the U.S.-Mexico border to curb illegal crossings
- No Permit warrantless wiretaps of suspected terrorists

2005

- ? Intervene in the life-support case of Terri Schiavo
- Yes Lift President Bush's restrictions on stem cell research funding
- Yes Prohibit FBI access to library and bookstore records
- No Approve free-trade pact with five Central American countries
- ? Pass energy policy overhaul favored by President Bush emphasizing domestic oil and gas production
- No End mandatory preservation of habitat of endangered animal and plant species
- Yes Ban torture of prisoners in U.S. custody

CQ VOTE STUDIES

	PARTY UNITY		PRESIDENTIAL SUPPORT	
	Support	Oppose	Support	Oppose
2006	99%	1%	15%	85%
2005	99%	1%	9%	91%
2004	99%	1%	12%	88%
2003	99%	1%	15%	85%
2002	99%	1%	25%	75%

INTEREST GROUPS

	AFL-CIO	ADA	CCUS	ACU
2006	100%	95%	20%	0%
2005	100%	100%	29%	0%
2004	100%	100%	5%	0%
2003	100%	100%	20%	12%
2002	100%	100%	30%	0%

ILLINOIS 9
Chicago — North Side lakefront; Evanston

The 9th starts in upscale Wilmette (shared with the 10th), runs south through the liberal suburbs of Evanston and Skokie and Chicago's multiethnic North Side, and then drops into one of the city's most prosperous lakefront neighborhoods. It also extends west to blue-collar Des Plaines (shared with the 6th and 10th districts) and Rosemont (shared with the 6th).

Slightly less than half of the district's population lives in Chicago. The neighborhoods of Uptown, Edgewater and Rogers Park — home to Loyola University — once housed Eastern European and Irish immigrants, but are now an eclectic mix of Asian, European and African immigrants. Uptown in particular has experienced rapid gentrification, and residents are now at odds over the future of what previously was a working-class enclave. The 9th also has the largest percentage of Asian residents in the state, and the district's suburbs contain a sizable Jewish population. The district includes a significant elderly population as well.

Lakeview, the district's southernmost point, includes a large gay population. Many young professionals have moved into the area near Wrigley Field (in the adjacent 5th), and most of the other Chicagoans in the 9th live in the far northwestern part of the city, near O'Hare International Airport (in the neighboring 6th).

Evanston is home to Northwestern University, which provides the bulk of jobs in that area. Health care also is a major employer here, with several large hospitals such as Evanston Northwestern Healthcare. Most of the district's jobs are concentrated in a few major industries, and the district contains a mix of the very wealthy and the very poor.

Its mix of immigrants, affluent urbanites and college students makes the 9th solidly Democratic. The district awarded Democrat John Kerry 68 percent of its 2004 presidential vote, his fifth-best showing in the state.

MAJOR INDUSTRY
Health care, higher education, insurance, light manufacturing

CITIES
Chicago (pt.), 299,868; Evanston, 74,239; Skokie, 63,348; Des Plains (pt.), 39,632; Park Ridge, 37,775; Niles, 30,068

NOTABLE
Tinkertoy sets were invented by an Evanston stonemason in 1913.

Rep. Mark Steven Kirk (R)

CAPITOL OFFICE
225-4835
www.house.gov/kirk
1030 Longworth 20515-1310; fax 225-0837

COMMITTEES
Appropriations

RESIDENCE
Highland Park

BORN
Sept. 15, 1959, Champaign, Ill.

RELIGION
Congregationalist

FAMILY
Wife, Kimberly Vertolli-Kirk

EDUCATION
Cornell U., B.A. 1981 (history); London School of Economics, M.S. 1982; Georgetown U., J.D. 1992

MILITARY SERVICE
Naval Reserve, 1989-present

CAREER
Congressional aide; lawyer; U.S. State Department aide; World Bank officer

POLITICAL HIGHLIGHTS
No previous office

ELECTION RESULTS

2006 GENERAL		
Mark Steven Kirk (R)	107,929	53.4%
Daniel J. Seals (D)	94,278	46.6%
2006 PRIMARY		
Mark Steven Kirk (R)		unopposed
2004 GENERAL		
Mark Steven Kirk (R)	177,493	64.1%
Lee Goodman (D)	99,218	35.9%

PREVIOUS WINNING PERCENTAGES
2002 (69%); 2000 (51%)

Elected 2000; 4th term

Kirk is a quintessential Republican moderate — a congressional demographic that thinned considerably in the 2006 elections but which could be influential in the 110th Congress (2007-08) when Democratic leaders need to trawl for an occasional GOP vote. Kirk is the co-chairman of the Tuesday Group of centrist Republicans, and he says he will use his position to "build partnerships with key Democratic leaders to make this Congress a success."

Representing a centrist-minded district anchored in the suburbs north of Chicago, Kirk parts with Republican doctrine on a number of big issues. In January 2007, he backed all six signature bills espoused by the new Democratic majority, including initiatives to promote embryonic stem cell research and increase the federal minimum wage. Kirk also was among the 17 Republicans who voted in February 2007 for a nonbinding resolution disapproving of a Bush administration initiative to increase U.S. troop strength in Iraq. Kirk's voting record consistently earns strong marks from abortion rights and environmental organizations.

Congressional ethics also are an abiding concern for Kirk. He promoted legislation in early 2007 to cancel pension benefits of any member of Congress who is convicted of a felony — a response to scandals in the 109th Congress (2005-06) that tarnished Congress' image and contributed to GOP losses in the 2006 elections. But Kirk's interest in ethics overhauls predates Democratic control of the House. At the outset of the 109th Congress, when GOP leaders sought to change House ethics rules to protect embattled Majority Leader Tom DeLay, Kirk threatened to vote against the changes and to try to take others with him. The leadership backed down.

Now in his fourth term, Kirk commands respect on Capitol Hill. He is well-educated and polished. GOP Whip Roy Blunt made Kirk one of his deputies, to help the leadership round up votes on hotly contested bills. Kirk also gained a seat on the Appropriations Committee after only one term.

After the 2006 elections overturned the GOP's majority, Kirk contemplated but ruled out a run for the chairmanship of the House Republican Conference, the third-ranking position in the party hierarchy. Kirk, who faced an expectedly close race in 2006, said his constituents sent him "a strong message that they want an independent voice."

In the 109th Congress, Kirk spearheaded an informal "suburban caucus" of Republican members that worked to identify policy prescriptions and address the concerns of a burgeoning group of suburban voters who do not align monolithically with one party. The group promoted legislation to combat suburban drug gangs, protect open spaces and allow local school districts to access national crime information databases to determine whether prospective school employees might endanger children.

Kirk is well versed in international issues, having been an intelligence officer in the Naval Reserve for more than 15 years. That gives him cachet on a priority issue — fighting terrorism and protecting the homeland. With the Navy, Kirk did seven tours of duty in hot spots around the world, including Panama, Haiti, Bosnia and Iraq. He has a degree from the London School of Economics, he once worked for a member of Parliament, and he has traveled in more than 40 countries.

Kirk previously was legislative counsel for the House International Relations Committee and worked at the World Bank. His boss on International Relations, former New York Republican Rep. Benjamin A. Gilman, said

Kirk "has a great leadership potential. Give him as many responsibilities as possible."

Kirk's idea of attacking a heroin problem in the Chicago suburbs was to travel to Afghanistan in 2005 to bolster President Hamid Karzai's promise to stem the country's large output of heroin — an effort that has a $700 million commitment in aid from the United States. Kirk considers such root treatment of the problem key to stopping not only addiction but the giant profits from the heroin trade suspected to be going to fugitive Osama bin Laden, mastermind of the Sept. 11 terrorist attacks.

Key parochial issues for him include securing funds for an expansion of the Metra commuter rail system, which connects suburbs in his district to the Loop. He also has pushed for pollution cleanup of the Great Lakes. Anything affecting the Great Lakes Naval base gets Kirk's attention, too.

The son of a telephone company executive, Kirk grew up in Kenilworth, a wealthy suburb on Chicago's North Shore along Lake Michigan. A brush with death at age 16 — he nearly drowned in the lake during a boating accident — shaped his future. "To be given a second chance means it has to mean something," he told the Chicago Tribune. "For me, that means making a difference through public service."

After graduating from New Trier High School, Kirk built an impressive résumé, including a stint in Mexico learning to speak fluent Spanish, degrees from three universities, combat service in Kosovo and a career in military intelligence. He spent several years on the staff of GOP Rep. John Edward Porter, prior to working at the State Department and the World Bank.

When Porter retired in 2000, Kirk jumped into a primary contest with 10 other Republicans, most of whom had substantial personal wealth. But Kirk impressed voters with his grasp of policy, and was helped by Porter's endorsement. He beat his closest competitor, printing company heiress Shawn Donnelley, by 16 percentage points. In the general election, he faced a formidable opponent in state Rep. Lauren Beth Gash, but prevailed by 2 percentage points.

Kirk was overwhelmingly re-elected in 2002 and 2004 but faced a close race in 2006, when antipathy to President Bush and his policies held Kirk to 53 percent of the vote against Democrat Daniel J. Seals, a marketing executive who raised nearly $2 million and who drew comparisons to Illinois Democratic Sen. Barack Obama. But Kirk remains popular and his 2006 showing may have been an aberration and not predictive of future close contests. Kirk often is mentioned as a potential candidate for the U.S. Senate someday, yet he ruled out challenging Democratic Sen. Richard J. Durbin in 2008.

KEY VOTES

2006

- No Stop broadband companies from favoring select Internet traffic
- Yes Affirm U.S. commitment to war in Iraq and reject setting a withdrawal date for troops
- No Repeal requirement for bilingual ballots at the polls
- Yes Permit U.S. sale of civilian nuclear technology to India
- Yes Build a 700-mile fence on the U.S.-Mexico border to curb illegal crossings
- Yes Permit warrantless wiretaps of suspected terrorists

2005

- Yes Intervene in the life-support case of Terri Schiavo
- Yes Lift President Bush's restrictions on stem cell research funding
- Yes Prohibit FBI access to library and bookstore records
- Yes Approve free-trade pact with five Central American countries
- Yes Pass energy policy overhaul favored by President Bush emphasizing domestic oil and gas production
- No End mandatory preservation of habitat of endangered animal and plant species
- Yes Ban torture of prisoners in U.S. custody

CQ VOTE STUDIES

	PARTY UNITY		PRESIDENTIAL SUPPORT	
	Support	Oppose	Support	Oppose
2006	79%	21%	80%	20%
2005	80%	20%	67%	33%
2004	84%	16%	63%	37%
2003	87%	13%	81%	19%
2002	85%	15%	85%	15%

INTEREST GROUPS

	AFL-CIO	ADA	CCUS	ACU
2006	36%	45%	80%	54%
2005	20%	30%	81%	36%
2004	29%	45%	90%	63%
2003	7%	10%	89%	58%
2002	11%	20%	95%	76%

ILLINOIS 10

North and northwest Chicago suburbs — Waukegan

The mostly upscale 10th hugs Lake Michigan, taking in southeast Lake County and northeast Cook County. Along the lakefront, Chicagoland's old-money elite live in tony areas such as Wilmette (shared with the 9th), Kenilworth and Winnetka.

The 10th has the state's highest percentage of college-educated (48 percent) and white-collar (76 percent) workers, and the wealth of the district's workforce mirrors the wealth of local industry. The 10th is home to several Fortune 500 companies, including Abbott Laboratories in North Chicago, Allstate Insurance in Northbrook and Walgreen in Deerfield.

Most of the 10th's minorities live in the northern area between Highwood and Waukegan (a small part of which is in the 8th). That area also is home to the Great Lakes Naval base, the nation's only naval recruit training command, which may lose roughly 2,000 jobs in the coming years. Waukegan is roughly 45 percent Hispanic and 20 percent black, and North Chicago, just south of Waukegan, also is minority-majority. The 10th also has a large Jewish constituency.

Suburban white-collar workers and the more working-class residents of Waukegan combine to make the 10th a moderate "swing" district — fiscally conservative but socially liberal, especially on abortion rights and gun control. Its proximity to Lake Michigan makes environmental issues important here. While area residents have sent a Republican to the U.S. House for decades, the area generally supports Democratic presidential candidates, and narrowly backed John Kerry in 2004 with 52 percent of its vote. Democrats also enjoy electoral success at the local level.

MAJOR INDUSTRY

Pharmaceutical research, insurance, military

MILITARY BASES

Naval Station Great Lakes, 4,050 military, 2,452 civilian (2004)

CITIES

Waukegan (pt.), 79,726; Arlington Heights (pt.), 69,414; Buffalo Grove, 42,909; North Chicago, 35,918; Wheeling, 34,496; Northbrook, 33,435

NOTABLE

The Ravinia Festival, held every summer in Highland Park, is the oldest outdoor music festival in North America.

Rep. Jerry Weller (R)

CAPITOL OFFICE
225-3635
www.house.gov/weller
108 Cannon 20515-1311; fax 225-3521

COMMITTEES
Ways & Means

RESIDENCE
Morris

BORN
July 7, 1957, Streator, Ill.

RELIGION
Christian

FAMILY
Wife, Zury de Weller; one child

EDUCATION
Joliet Junior College, attended 1977;
U. of Illinois, B.S. 1979 (agriculture)

CAREER
Hog farmer; U.S. Agriculture Department aide; congressional aide; health and beauty products salesman

POLITICAL HIGHLIGHTS
Republican nominee for Ill. House, 1986;
Ill. House, 1989-95

ELECTION RESULTS

2006 GENERAL		
Jerry Weller (R)	109,009	55.1%
John Pavich (D)	88,846	44.9%
2006 PRIMARY		
Jerry Weller (R)		unopposed
2004 GENERAL		
Jerry Weller (R)	173,057	58.7%
Tari Renner (D)	121,903	41.3%

PREVIOUS WINNING PERCENTAGES
2002 (64%); 2000 (56%); 1998 (59%); 1996 (52%); 1994 (61%)

Elected 1994; 7th term

A member of the large Class of '94 that gave Republicans control of the House for the first time in four decades, Weller now has to learn how to operate in the minority. Like the other 22 remaining members of that House GOP class, he is likely to find the experience frustrating, especially as he seeks to promote tax breaks for businesses, a favorite cause.

Still, Weller can take satisfaction in the mark he has already left on the tax code. He was the leading champion of a popular 2001 change erasing the longstanding "marriage penalty," which left many two-earner married couples owing more taxes than they would have filing as singles. Weller's persistence on the topic sometimes tried the patience of even his allies. When he appeared before the Ways and Means Committee to present his plan to eliminate the marriage penalty, he brought his familiar props — poster-size photos of a young couple from Joliet, Ill., who were affected by the tax differential. But before Weller could deliver his well-rehearsed speech about the plight of Shad and Michelle Hallihan, Republican Ways and Means Chairman Bill Thomas of California jokingly declared that Weller's time had expired, adding, "I believe I know them."

Weller has sought to make the marriage penalty change a permanent part of the tax code. He had some success in 2004, when Congress extended the tax break through 2010, and one of his first bills in the 110th Congress (2007-08) was to make the 2001 changes permanent. He blasted the House Democrats' budget blueprint, which would permit them to expire.

While the GOP was running Congress, Weller also won approval of a provision to cut excise taxes for a manufacturer of fishing tackle boxes in his district. In the 109th Congress (2005-06), Weller pushed successfully for faster write-offs for business investment. He also won inclusion of a provision in a 2006 pension overhaul measure allowing people over age 50 to make "catchup contributions" to their tax-deferred retirement savings plans, beyond the usual dollar limits.

Weller is an expert on Latin American issues, but the Democratic takeover at the start of the 110th Congress bumped him from his seat on the newly renamed Foreign Affairs Committee. In 2004, he made headlines with his marriage to Guatemalan legislator Zury Rios Sosa, daughter of the former Guatemalan dictator, Efrain Rios Montt. A Democratic rival and the Chicago Sun-Times urged him to resign from the committee, arguing that his marriage would present a conflict of interest on issues affecting U.S. policy in Latin America. Weller insisted there was no conflict and refused to leave the panel. He said he would not vote on bills related to Guatemala. The Federal Election Commission issued a ruling the same year to allow Weller's wife, a foreign national, to be an unpaid campaign adviser for him. Their infant daughter, Marizú Catherine, was born in Guatemala in August 2006.

Weller is close to former Speaker J. Dennis Hastert, who is from a neighboring district. With Hastert's backing, Weller as a freshman served on the Steering Committee, which makes GOP committee assignments. Two years later, he won his coveted Ways and Means seat and was elected president of his sophomore class. But a bid to climb the leadership ladder failed when he finished last in a four-way race for Republican Conference secretary.

Nevertheless, Weller has made himself useful to the party, raising money for Republican candidates and working to boost GOP support among Hispanic Americans. In 2006, he moved $100,000 into the party coffers in October alone. As finance chairman of the National Republican

Congressional Committee, Weller helped the party raise a record $163 million for the 2002 campaign cycle. He would have liked to chair the NRCC, a leadership role, but House Republicans instead gave the job to New York's Thomas M. Reynolds for the 2004 and 2006 cycles.

Weller sided with a majority of his fellow Republicans 91 percent of the time on party-line votes in the 109th Congress, but he occasionally goes his own way. He balked at President Bush's 2005 proposal to create individual investment accounts within Social Security, and he was one of 43 Republicans urging budget writers that year not to make cuts in Medicaid, the joint federal-state health insurance program for the poor. In 2007, he was one of 82 Republicans voting with Democrats to raise the minimum wage for the first time in a decade.

One of his key district issues is the establishment of a third Chicago-area airport in Peotone. It's a rare point of disagreement with Hastert, who wants to enlarge Chicago's O'Hare Airport instead. Weller in 2007 found himself locked in a dispute with an Illinois colleague, Jesse L. Jackson Jr., over the governance of the proposed third airport.

Raised on a hog farm, Weller got his first taste of politics in high school, winning election as class president. While in college, he worked as a volunteer in the successful campaign of Republican Tom Corcoran and became the new congressman's first intern in 1977. Following graduation from college, he joined Proctor and Gamble's toiletries division as a product salesman, helping to introduce, among other things, Pert shampoo. But he missed politics and signed on in 1981 as an aide to President Ronald Reagan's first Agriculture secretary, John R. Block. "I was the youngest member of the staff and a runner," Weller recalls. "He was a marathoner, so I traveled with him and was his running partner."

In 1986, Weller ran for the Illinois House. Declared the winner by four votes, he took office in January. But a recount showed him losing by four votes, and he soon departed. He won the seat two years later, however, and stayed until his election to the U.S. House in 1994. Democratic Rep. George E. Sangmeister paved the way for his move up, retiring after four terms, and Weller took 61 percent of the vote against Democratic state Rep. Frank Giglio.

He held off a stiff Democratic challenge in 1996 from former state Rep. Clem Balanoff, winning by less than 4 percentage points. He had little difficulty in the next four elections, scoring comfortable wins. Then in 2006, Democratic lawyer John Pavich held him to 55 percent, despite being outspent by better than 3-to-1. That was Weller's closest call in a decade.

KEY VOTES

2006

- No — Stop broadband companies from favoring select Internet traffic
- Yes — Affirm U.S. commitment to war in Iraq and reject setting a withdrawal date for troops
- Yes — Repeal requirement for bilingual ballots at the polls
- Yes — Permit U.S. sale of civilian nuclear technology to India
- Yes — Build a 700-mile fence on the U.S.-Mexico border to curb illegal crossings
- Yes — Permit warrantless wiretaps of suspected terrorists

2005

- ? — Intervene in the life-support case of Terri Schiavo
- No — Lift President Bush's restrictions on stem cell research funding
- No — Prohibit FBI access to library and bookstore records
- Yes — Approve free-trade pact with five Central American countries
- Yes — Pass energy policy overhaul favored by President Bush emphasizing domestic oil and gas production
- Yes — End mandatory preservation of habitat of endangered animal and plant species
- Yes — Ban torture of prisoners in U.S. custody

CQ VOTE STUDIES

	PARTY UNITY		PRESIDENTIAL SUPPORT	
	Support	Oppose	Support	Oppose
2006	89%	11%	95%	5%
2005	94%	6%	86%	14%
2004	92%	8%	88%	12%
2003	95%	5%	100%	0%
2002	96%	4%	88%	12%

INTEREST GROUPS

	AFL-CIO	ADA	CCUS	ACU
2006	36%	5%	100%	80%
2005	13%	5%	93%	92%
2004	20%	15%	100%	84%
2003	7%	5%	97%	84%
2002	11%	5%	95%	92%

ILLINOIS 11

South Chicago exurbs — Joliet; part of Bloomington-Normal

Beginning south of Chicago in suburban Will County, the 11th heads west through the old industrial city of Joliet and into farming country, with a sliver making a southward turn in LaSalle County to run parallel to Interstate 39 as it heads to Bloomington-Normal.

Will County (shared mainly with the 13th) has seen an influx of young families, and fast-growing Joliet's proximity to the Chicago metropolitan area has helped alleviate past economic troubles there. Many visitors to Joliet come to the Harrah's Casino and Hotel, the newly built Silver Cross Field — home to the Joliet JackHammers independent baseball team — and the Rialto Square Theatre.

Ongoing debate over construction of a third Chicago metro-area airport in Peotone, southeast of Joliet, pits residents in the 11th's northern areas, who say a new airport would bring an economic boost to the suburbs, against rural residents, who worry it would disrupt their way of life.

South of Will, the 11th includes Kankakee County, still in the ambit of Chicagoland, before assuming a more rural posture west of those two counties as it takes in a small corner of Livingston County, all of Grundy and LaSalle counties, and most of Bureau County. A jaunt south takes it to Bloomington-Normal (shared with the 15th), which is another fast-growing metropolitan area where the population has grown 30 percent since 1990. Illinois State University is here.

The 11th remains politically competitive, although in recent years it has supported Republicans. The district handed George W. Bush 53 percent of its 2004 presidential vote.

MAJOR INDUSTRY

Farm equipment manufacturing, agriculture, insurance

CITIES

Joliet (pt.), 105,052; Normal (pt.), 30,662; Bloomington (pt.), 30,298; Kankakee, 27,491

NOTABLE

The Midewin National Tallgrass Prairie, the first national tallgrass prairie, is in Will County; The now-closed Joliet Correctional Center is featured in the television show "Prison Break" and also was used for the opening scene of "The Blues Brothers."

Rep. Jerry F. Costello (D)

CAPITOL OFFICE
225-5661
www.house.gov/costello
2408 Rayburn 20515-1312; fax 225-0285

COMMITTEES
Science & Technology
Transportation & Infrastructure
(Aviation - chairman)

RESIDENCE
Belleville

BORN
Sept. 25, 1949, East St. Louis, Ill.

RELIGION
Roman Catholic

FAMILY
Wife, Georgia Cockrum Costello; three children

EDUCATION
Belleville Area College, A.A. 1971; Maryville College of the Sacred Heart, B.A. 1973

CAREER
Law enforcement official

POLITICAL HIGHLIGHTS
St. Clair County Board chairman, 1980-88

ELECTION RESULTS

2006 GENERAL		
Jerry F. Costello (D)		unopposed
2006 PRIMARY		
Jerry F. Costello (D)	45,600	90.1%
Kenneth Charles Wiezer (D)	4,991	9.9%
2004 GENERAL		
Jerry F. Costello (D)	198,962	69.5%
Erin R. Zweigart (R)	82,677	28.9%
Walter B. Steel (LIBERT)	4,794	1.7%

PREVIOUS WINNING PERCENTAGES
2002 (69%); 2000 (100%); 1998 (60%); 1996 (72%); 1994 (66%); 1992 (71%); 1990 (66%); 1988 (53%); 1988 Special Election (51%)

Elected August 1988; 10th full term

Costello is a bridge builder, literally. As one of just three Illinois lawmakers on the 75-member Transportation and Infrastructure Committee, he looks out for the state's interests in highway construction, mass transit, aviation, bridges and tunnels. In the 110th Congress (2007-08), he holds the gavel as chairman of the Transportation panel's Aviation Subcommittee.

He pursues his dollars-and-cents mission with gusto, and is generally not a player in the big national debates that engage Congress. For Costello, all politics truly is local.

He believes that improving the region's transportation infrastructure is the key to attracting new jobs to East St. Louis, Ill., where he grew up and which he remembers as a prosperous, bustling manufacturing center. "If you couldn't get a job in East St. Louis, you couldn't get a job anywhere," he recalls. The city went into a steep decline as plants closed and workers at steel mills, meatpacking houses and rail yards moved away, and today it is one of Illinois' most impoverished cities.

Among the millions of federal dollars Costello has secured for his district and the state was $600 million in federal funding for the MetroLink light rail, which connects St. Louis with the Metro East area in Illinois. A new stop in East St. Louis resulted in construction nearby of the first new housing development in 30 years. In the 2005 surface transportation reauthorization law, Costello helped snag $239 million to pay part of the cost of building a new bridge across the Mississippi River between St. Louis and eastern Illinois.

Costello also won approval of legislation to set aside federal land for a visitor center devoted to the journey of explorers Meriwether Lewis and William Clark, near the site where the expedition departed on its westward journey in 1804. And Costello looks out for Scott Air Force Base, a major local employer, which he and Democratic Gov. Rod R. Blagojevich worked to protect from the 2005 round of military base closings. The base was not only spared, it was awarded new missions producing 800 new jobs. In 2006, Costello and Republican John Shimkus of the adjacent 19th District trumpeted their success in getting $34.6 million for new facilities at the base.

Costello and Shimkus are also leading efforts to place a clean-coal research facility in the southern part of the state, to help revive the region's sagging coal industry. Early in the 110th Congress, Costello introduced legislation aimed at increasing the use of coal as a fuel source in ethanol plants: a twofer for Illinois mainstay products of coal and corn.

Costello, who rarely speaks on the House floor, is not a completely dependable vote for Democratic leaders. On social policy issues, he reflects his constituency's cultural conservatism. He opposes abortion and supports gun owners' rights. He voted for a ban on a procedure that opponents call "partial birth" abortion, and for a proposed constitutional amendment to ban same-sex marriage. On business issues, though, he typically supports labor. In 2006, he took the lead on the side of the nation's air traffic controllers in their contract dispute with the Federal Aviation Administration over pay and work rules. He has been a consistent anti-war vote, opposing resolutions authorizing the use of force against Iraq in 1991 and in 2002.

He has received his share of unfavorable publicity. Media reports in 2002 revealed that Illinois Secretary of State Jesse White hired Costello's 26-year-old son for a $50,000-a-year job over a more experienced candidate after Costello called in his son's behalf. Costello described it as a routine job reference call, and attributed the flap, in part, to a long-running feud with his hometown newspaper, the Belleville News-Democrat.

In 1997, he was named an "unindicted co-conspirator" in the trial of his childhood friend and former business partner Amiel Cueto, who was convicted of trying to block the federal investigation of a convicted racketeer. Witnesses testified that Costello was a silent partner in two casino deals and that he helped pass a bill to aid an Indian tribe that owned the land where one of the casinos was to be built. Costello denied wrongdoing. Republicans tried to use the case against him in the 1998 campaign, to no avail.

Costello lived in East St. Louis until he was in high school. Then the family moved to nearby Belleville. His father had been elected county sheriff, and that job required him to live near the jail. "We literally lived in an apartment next to the county jail for four years, and after that moved back to East St. Louis when most people were moving out," he recalls.

The experience piqued his interest in law enforcement, and while attending a local community college, Costello took a job as a court bailiff. He eventually rose to become administrator of the local court system. In 1980, he was elected chairman of the St. Clair County Board, a job he held for eight years and that established his name in the heavily Democratic area.

As a county official, he developed his talent for snaring federal grants. One of his projects was a new regional airport. But there was an insufficient market for the facility and it went largely vacant. In endorsing his GOP opponent in 2004, the Chicago Tribune said of Costello, "He fashions himself a bring-home-the-bacon congressman, but his biggest accomplishment — winning federal money for MidAmerica Airport outside St. Louis — has turned out to be an expensive flop."

Costello ran his first race for the House in 1988 after elderly Democratic Rep. Melvin Price decided against seeking re-election. But in the primary, Madison County Auditor Pete Fields portrayed Costello as an old-style, hardball "boss" in the county Democratic Party. Costello survived because of a huge financial advantage but with only a 46 percent plurality.

When Price died in April, Costello squared off against Republican college official Robert H. Gaffner in a special election. Gaffner suggested voters call Costello and quiz him about his ethics. Costello barely won the special election, then went on to win in November with 53 percent of the vote.

He was not seriously challenged again until 1998, when Republican Bill Price, an orthopedic surgeon and the son of Melvin Price, gave him a contest. Costello overcame questions about his connections with Cueto and charged that Price represented a threat to Social Security and Medicare. Costello took 60 percent of the vote and has not dipped below 66 percent since.

KEY VOTES

2006

Yes Stop broadband companies from favoring select Internet traffic
Yes Affirm U.S. commitment to war in Iraq and reject setting a withdrawal date for troops
No Repeal requirement for bilingual ballots at the polls
No Permit U.S. sale of civilian nuclear technology to India
Yes Build a 700-mile fence on the U.S.-Mexico border to curb illegal crossings
No Permit warrantless wiretaps of suspected terrorists

2005

Yes Intervene in the life-support case of Terri Schiavo
No Lift President Bush's restrictions on stem cell research funding
Yes Prohibit FBI access to library and bookstore records
No Approve free-trade pact with five Central American countries
Yes Pass energy policy overhaul favored by President Bush emphasizing domestic oil and gas production
Yes End mandatory preservation of habitat of endangered animal and plant species
Yes Ban torture of prisoners in U.S. custody

CQ VOTE STUDIES

	PARTY UNITY		PRESIDENTIAL SUPPORT	
	Support	Oppose	Support	Oppose
2006	87%	13%	37%	63%
2005	82%	18%	37%	63%
2004	82%	18%	41%	59%
2003	84%	16%	41%	59%
2002	80%	20%	40%	60%

INTEREST GROUPS

	AFL-CIO	ADA	CCUS	ACU
2006	93%	70%	40%	48%
2005	87%	80%	52%	40%
2004	93%	70%	38%	36%
2003	93%	80%	38%	48%
2002	100%	70%	50%	36%

ILLINOIS 12

Southwest – Belleville, East St. Louis, Carbondale

The 12th begins in the St. Louis suburbs along the Mississippi River and extends south along the river to Cairo at the southern tip of Illinois, where the Mississippi and Ohio rivers converge.

East St. Louis, an overwhelmingly black city in St. Clair County, has experienced declining population and some of the state's worst urban blight for years, and crime rates remain high. Federal and state aid, along with new revenue from casino gambling, provided income for the city, but residents still face high unemployment and poverty rates.

Other cities in the 12th also are attempting to overcome difficult economic situations. Alton is in the midst of a major revitalization aimed at providing jobs, growing industry and creating new tourism. The city, along with Clark Properties, converted the long-vacant Owens-Illinois Glass factory into usable warehouse and light industrial space. Belleville, worried about defense cutbacks, recently found out that nearby Scott Air Force Base, the area's major employer, will gain 800 new jobs as a result of the 2005 BRAC round. Higher education remains one of the area's few steadfast employers, with Carbondale's Southern Illinois University, and its 21,500 students, bolstering Jackson County's economy.

The district's economic anxiety and minority population (blacks make up 16 percent) make it solid Democratic turf. St. Clair County has voted Democratic in the past eight presidential elections. Despite only carrying St. Clair, Jackson and Alexander counties among the nine counties entirely in the 12th, Democrat John Kerry still captured 52 percent of the 12th's 2004 presidential vote. Some corn and hog farmers in western counties lean Republican, but they are too few to sway the district.

MAJOR INDUSTRY

Manufacturing, higher education, casinos, agriculture

MILITARY BASES

Scott Air Force Base, 7,829 military, 5,604 civilian (2005)

CITIES

Belleville, 41,410; East St. Louis, 31,542; Granite City, 31,301; Alton, 30,496; O'Fallon, 21,910; Carbondale, 20,681

NOTABLE

Cahokia Mounds, a prehistoric civilization, was designated by the United Nations as a World Heritage Site in 1982; The Gateway Geyser, which stands at 600 feet, is a man-made fountain in East St. Louis.

Rep. Judy Biggert (R)

CAPITOL OFFICE
225-3515
www.house.gov/biggert
1034 Longworth 20515-1313; fax 225-9420

COMMITTEES
Education & Labor
Financial Services
Science & Technology

RESIDENCE
Hinsdale

BORN
Aug. 15, 1937, Chicago, Ill.

RELIGION
Episcopalian

FAMILY
Husband, Rody Biggert; four children

EDUCATION
Stanford U., A.B. 1959 (international relations); Northwestern U., J.D. 1963

CAREER
Lawyer

POLITICAL HIGHLIGHTS
Hinsdale Board of Education, 1982-85 (president, 1983-85); Village of Hinsdale Plan Commission, 1989-93; Ill. House, 1993-99

ELECTION RESULTS

2006 GENERAL		
Judy Biggert (R)	119,720	58.3%
Joseph Shannon (D)	85,507	41.7%
2006 PRIMARY		
Judy Biggert (R)	52,900	79.6%
Bob Hart (R)	13,564	20.4%
2004 GENERAL		
Judy Biggert (R)	200,472	65.0%
Gloria Schor Andersen (D)	107,836	35.0%

PREVIOUS WINNING PERCENTAGES
2002 (70%); 2000 (66%); 1998 (61%)

Elected 1998; 5th term

Biggert is from a generation when career choices for women were limited. Her sister wanted to be a nurse and considered medical school only after their business executive father convinced her that girls could be doctors. When Biggert applied to a master's in business degree program, she received a letter saying women were not accepted, but that she was welcome to take a few night classes.

Today, Biggert is a lawyer by training, a mother of four and a fifth-term congresswoman with a solid legislative track record on the family and social welfare issues that interest her. Her tendency to favor federal involvement in areas such as childhood education and health care puts her in the House's relatively small moderate Republican camp.

When she arrived in Congress in 1999, Fortune magazine identified Biggert as one of the newcomers most likely to be a star. But her moderate tendencies confounded her efforts to get into the GOP leadership in the House, dominated by conservatives. She ran for Republican Conference secretary in 2001, reminding her colleagues that she had been a prolific fundraiser for them. She lost to conservative Barbara Cubin of Wyoming, 123-76. In 2002, Biggert made a second bid for the conference secretary post, but dropped out when she concluded Californian John T. Doolittle, a conservative close to Majority Leader Tom DeLay of Texas, had the election wrapped up.

Once an advocate of term limits, Biggert is now a believer in the seniority system, which has given her more power to advance her legislative agenda. "The longer I've been here, the more I like seniority," she says. Of her now abandoned pledge to serve only six years, she says, "I realized the first term that there was really so much more to this job than I expected. I just said, 'I made a mistake.' . . . I really like doing the work. I really like the law."

Biggert has focused on two priorities — education and energy research. The former is a natural fit; she is a former school board president. And the latter is vital to her district, which is home to the Argonne National Laboratory, one of the Energy Department's largest facilities.

From her seat on the Education and Labor Committee, she has championed programs for homeless children. In 2006, her provision to help homeless youth access student aid for colleges made it into the final House version of a higher education bill. In 2005, as a budget bill was being assembled, she was one of four committee Republicans who crossed party lines to defeat a plan that would have let families displaced by Hurricane Katrina use federal funds for private or parochial school tuition. In the 110th Congress (2007-08), her position as ranking Republican on the Financial Services Committee's Housing Subcommittee adds to her clout on such issues.

In the 109th Congress (2005-06), she chaired the Energy Subcommittee on the Science Committee. She remains on the renamed Science and Technology panel and continues to focus on the development of advanced technologies, especially hydrogen-fueled cars. The 2005 energy policy overhaul included her provisions to expand nuclear fuel reprocessing research at Argonne, plus $2 billion to put hydrogen fuel cell vehicles on the road by 2020, with much of that research taking place at Argonne.

Though she affiliates with GOP moderates in the Tuesday Group and the Republican Main Street Partnership, Biggert has taken a conservative line on some issues. She did not support the 2002 campaign finance law, she voted against creation of the independent Sept. 11 commission and she supported opening Alaska's Arctic National Wildlife Refuge to oil drilling.

In 2003, she sponsored "flex time" legislation to let employers replace overtime pay with compensatory time off. She argued that the change would help women juggling the competing demands of work and family. But the bill was scorned by women's groups and unions, who said employers would coerce employees to work overtime without extra pay.

Biggert has been at odds with President Bush somewhat more often than the typical House Republican, but her party unity score is about average for a GOP member. And she is known for party loyalty. When Speaker J. Dennis Hastert cleaned house at the ethics committee in 2005, removing Republicans who had fallen into disfavor because they admonished his ally DeLay for ethical lapses, Biggert was one of only two Republicans that Hastert kept on the committee. However, late in 2006 she was on an ethics subcommittee that was critical of the way that Hastert and other House leaders responded to inappropriate behavior of former Florida GOP Rep. Mark Foley toward underage male House pages.

Biggert graduated from Stanford in 1959, and after her disappointing letter from business school, enrolled at Northwestern to study law. She met her husband, Rody Biggert, there and later clerked for a federal appeals court judge. (Still interested in legal issues, she has joined with California Democrat Adam B. Schiff in an effort to improve relations between Congress and the federal judiciary.) After school, both she and Rody got offers from a downtown Chicago law firm, but Biggert decided to start her own home-based law practice specializing in real estate and estate planning. She worked at home for 20 years, while helping raise their four children, now all grown. "Quiet time was about quarter to four in the morning until they got up," she recalls.

Biggert volunteered in civic groups, including lending a hand in a new federal program for at-risk children called Head Start. She served on the Hinsdale planning commission and the board of education, including a stint as board president from 1983 to 1985. Elected to the Illinois House in 1992, she focused on women's and children's issues and was elected assistant Republican leader after just one term in Springfield.

Biggert was the hand-picked successor of Republican Harris W. Fawell when he retired in 1998. She defeated five men vying for the GOP nomination and went on to win the seat with 61 percent of the vote.

In 2004, she passed up entreaties to run for the Senate after party leaders were desperate to replace a GOP primary winner who withdrew amid a sex scandal, leaving the field open to an attractive newcomer, a Democrat named Barack Obama. Biggert's solidly Republican 13th District — its tilt was maintained by redistricting — keeps her safe right where she is.

KEY VOTES

2006

- No Stop broadband companies from favoring select Internet traffic
- Yes Affirm U.S. commitment to war in Iraq and reject setting a withdrawal date for troops
- No Repeal requirement for bilingual ballots at the polls
- Yes Permit U.S. sale of civilian nuclear technology to India
- Yes Build a 700-mile fence on the U.S.-Mexico border to curb illegal crossings
- Yes Permit warrantless wiretaps of suspected terrorists

2005

- Yes Intervene in the life-support case of Terri Schiavo
- Yes Lift President Bush's restrictions on stem cell research funding
- No Prohibit FBI access to library and bookstore records
- Yes Approve free-trade pact with five Central American countries
- Yes Pass energy policy overhaul favored by President Bush emphasizing domestic oil and gas production
- No End mandatory preservation of habitat of endangered animal and plant species
- Yes Ban torture of prisoners in U.S. custody

CQ VOTE STUDIES

	PARTY UNITY		PRESIDENTIAL SUPPORT	
	Support	Oppose	Support	Oppose
2006	88%	12%	80%	20%
2005	87%	13%	72%	28%
2004	88%	12%	74%	26%
2003	90%	10%	85%	15%
2002	89%	11%	82%	18%

INTEREST GROUPS

	AFL-CIO	ADA	CCUS	ACU
2006	21%	30%	93%	64%
2005	13%	20%	89%	60%
2004	13%	35%	100%	64%
2003	13%	10%	100%	60%
2002	11%	15%	100%	84%

ILLINOIS 13

Southwest Chicago suburbs – Naperville

More than half of the suburban Chicago-based 13th's population lives in the district's booming southern part of DuPage County, an area that includes Naperville. Nearly one-third of district residents live in northern Will County communities such as Bolingbrook and Romeoville, with the rest living in the southwestern edge of Cook County.

Naperville, Downers Grove (a small part of which is in the 6th) and Oak Brook (shared with the 6th) have become leading suburban Chicago business centers, and companies such as OfficeMax, Sara Lee and McDonald's have corporate headquarters here. These large corporations and other high-paying employers have been attracted to the district by Chicago's busy O'Hare International Airport (nearby in the 6th) as well as the state's second-highest percentage of white collar workers. The presence of these corporations has helped the 13th achieve the highest median income in the state, and one of the top 10 nationwide, at nearly $72,000.

The Argonne National Laboratory, in southeast DuPage, and the Fermi National Accelerator Laboratory, in the neighboring 14th, have made the area into a scientific research and technology hub. DePaul University also has a campus in Naperville.

The district's growth over the past decade has created serious traffic problems for its suburban residents. But despite two-thirds growth since 1990 and long commutes for those who work in Chicago, Naperville routinely ranks among the nation's best places to live.

Voters in the 13th tend to vote Republican. While many residents are fiscally conservative, they generally hold moderate views on social and environmental issues. George W. Bush won the 13th with 55 percent of the vote in both the 2000 and 2004 presidential elections.

MAJOR INDUSTRY

Scientific research, health care, insurance

CITIES

Naperville, 128,358; Bolingbrook, 56,321; Downers Grove (pt.), 45,139

NOTABLE

The Millennium Carillon in Naperville is among the four largest such structures in the world, with a system of 72 bronze bells weighing up to six tons each.

Rep. J. Dennis Hastert (R)

CAPITOL OFFICE
225-2976
www.house.gov/hastert
2304 Rayburn 20515-1314; fax 225-0697

COMMITTEES
Energy & Commerce

RESIDENCE
Plano

BORN
Jan. 2, 1942, Aurora, Ill.

RELIGION
Methodist

FAMILY
Wife, Jean Hastert; two children

EDUCATION
Wheaton College (Ill.), A.B. 1964 (economics); Northern Illinois U., M.A. 1967 (education)

CAREER
Teacher; restaurateur

POLITICAL HIGHLIGHTS
Ill. House, 1981-86

ELECTION RESULTS

2006 GENERAL		
J. Dennis Hastert (R)	117,870	59.8%
Jonathan "John" Laesch (D)	79,274	40.2%
2006 PRIMARY		
J. Dennis Hastert (R)		unopposed
2004 GENERAL		
J. Dennis Hastert (R)	191,618	68.6%
Ruben K. Zamora (D)	87,590	31.4%

PREVIOUS WINNING PERCENTAGES
2002 (74%); 2000 (74%); 1998 (70%); 1996 (64%); 1994 (76%); 1992 (67%); 1990 (67%); 1988 (74%); 1986 (52%)

Elected 1986; 11th term

Well-loved by his troops, Hastert nonetheless had a disappointing conclusion to his long run as Speaker of the House. Republicans were tossed out of their majorities in both houses of Congress in November 2006, after months of turmoil and scandal. A share of the blame trickled up, as it usually does, to Hastert and the rest of the GOP leadership.

The final chapter of his speakership also was marred by a scandal involving young congressional pages that broke just before the election and raised serious questions about Hastert's response to a sensitive problem.

When the House changed hands in early 2007, the portly Illinoisan, who has been battling health problems in recent years, left the Republican leadership but stayed on in the House. He became the ranking member of the Energy and Commerce Subcommittee on Energy and Air Quality, a job that lets him express his conservative, anti-government regulation views, albeit with a much lower profile than he had.

For a man who was virtually unknown before becoming Speaker, Hastert was one of the most durable lawmakers to hold the office. In June 2006, when he had been Speaker for more than seven years, he became the longest-serving Republican Speaker since Joe Cannon, also from Illinois, in the early 1900s. If Hastert had remained as Speaker in the 110th Congress (2007-08), he would have closed in on Democrat Thomas P. "Tip" O'Neill's record of 10 years of continuous service. (Democrat Sam Rayburn served longer, but his reign was interrupted by a brief period of Republican rule.)

Hastert survived by staying above the fray, getting involved in crises when he had to, but generally prodding members of the Republican Conference to work problems out for themselves. The hands-off approach had a downside, particularly when his mentor, former Majority Leader Tom DeLay of Texas, damaged the House GOP's credibility with one scandal after another, drawing little obvious reaction from Hastert, who considered him an ally and a friend. DeLay ultimately resigned in disgrace. Though many Republicans felt he had ceded too much power to DeLay, Hastert remained personally popular with the rank and file, who never saw him as part of the ethics problem. House Republicans also did not have a clear successor who could easily bridge the party's conservative and moderate factions.

Then came the page scandal, and Hastert for the first time was viewed as a liability. Florida Republican Mark Foley abruptly resigned in September 2006 amid news reports of sexually explicit e-mails he sent former congressional pages. In the ensuing uproar, Hastert acknowledged that he had known Foley sent questionable e-mails, and had not launched a thorough investigation into the messages or Foley's habit of spending large amounts of time with male pages. Democrats portrayed him as a leader more interested in protecting Foley's district seat and the tottering GOP majority.

After a nine-week inquiry, the House ethics committee in December concluded that Hastert and other leaders broke no rules but took them to task for failing to do more to protect pages from Foley's inappropriate behavior.

Hastert has generally been loyal to President Bush and his agenda. He even agreed to run for another term in 2006 at Bush's request, postponing a retirement that had long been rumored because of his health. Suffering from diabetes, he was hospitalized twice during the 109th Congress (2005-06), once for kidney stones and once for a skin infection.

During Bush's second term, Hastert had to head off rank-and-file rebellions from conservatives who said Republicans had become too free spending, and from moderates who said the party was indifferent to the social safety net. He appeased conservatives in 2005 by proposing to offset costs of Hurricane Katrina reconstruction, and in 2006 he gave moderates a vote on a minimum wage increase by tying it to a permanent estate tax increase.

Although many conservative Republicans say it was a mistake to expand an entitlement program, Hastert takes particular pride in his role in the 2003 passage of the Medicare prescription drug legislation. As a health care policy expert, he says the legislation ultimately will help the program's finances by allowing people to maintain their health with prescription drugs, rather than needing expensive surgeries later.

To get the final bill through the House, Hastert famously held the vote open for three hours while he cajoled, lobbied and pleaded with conservatives who opposed it. Just before dawn, he got the final votes he needed. Democrats accused him of cheating, but Hastert insisted the normal 15-minute span for a vote was a minimum under House rules, not a maximum.

The oldest of three boys, Hastert grew up in Aurora, Ill., helping his father make deliveries from the family's farm supply store. His mother, who helped run the store, made friends easily but could also be strict with her children. "I learned pretty quickly that if I broke the rules, I'd probably get a smack across the face," Hastert recalled in his 2004 autobiography.

In high school, Hastert played football and wrestled, suffering a shoulder injury that later forced him to leave the ROTC in college. Inspired by the athletics directors he admired, he decided to become a coach, a career choice that meant he would have to teach as well. He got a master's degree in education from Northern Illinois University and became a high school social studies teacher and wrestling coach.

Hastert stayed on that track for 16 years before being appointed in 1981 to a vacancy in the Illinois General Assembly, where he served about six years. When GOP Rep. John E. Grotberg retired from the U.S. House in 1986, Hastert was elected to succeed him with 52 percent of the vote. He has been re-elected by comfortable margins ever since.

In 1994, when Republicans gained control of the House, Hastert ran DeLay's successful upset campaign for majority whip. In turn, DeLay appointed Hastert as his chief deputy. In 1998, Newt Gingrich stepped down as Speaker after Republicans lost seats in the mid-term elections. Robert L. Livingston, the influential Appropriations Committee chairman, was set to run for the job but withdrew suddenly after admitting to an extramarital affair. With the help of DeLay's whip team, Hastert took less than 24 hours to lock up the support to become Speaker.

KEY VOTES

2006

- S Stop broadband companies from favoring select Internet traffic
- Yes Affirm U.S. commitment to war in Iraq and reject setting a withdrawal date for troops
- S Repeal requirement for bilingual ballots at the polls
- Yes Permit U.S. sale of civilian nuclear technology to India
- S Build a 700-mile fence on the U.S.-Mexico border to curb illegal crossings
- S Permit warrantless wiretaps of suspected terrorists

2005

- Yes Intervene in the life-support case of Terri Schiavo
- No Lift President Bush's restrictions on stem cell research funding
- S Prohibit FBI access to library and bookstore records
- Yes Approve free-trade pact with five Central American countries
- Yes Pass energy policy overhaul favored by President Bush emphasizing domestic oil and gas production
- S End mandatory preservation of habitat of endangered animal and plant species
- S Ban torture of prisoners in U.S. custody

CQ VOTE STUDIES

	PARTY UNITY		PRESIDENTIAL SUPPORT	
	Support	Oppose	Support	Oppose
2006	98%	2%	100%	0%
2005	100%	0%	100%	0%
2004	100%	0%	100%	0%
2003	100%	0%	100%	0%
2002	100%	0%	100%	0%

INTEREST GROUPS

	AFL-CIO	ADA	CCUS	ACU
2006	0%	0%	100%	88%
2005	29%	0%	90%	100%
2004	0%	0%	100%	100%
2003	0%	0%	100%	75%
2002	0%	--%	100%	8%

ILLINOIS 14
North Central – Aurora, Elgin, DeKalb

The majority of the 14th's residents live in Kane County on the district's eastern side, in established towns along the Fox River valley. West of the river, prairies and farms stretch to Henry County, nearly to the Mississippi River. Rich in hay, soybeans and corn, the flat landscape is interrupted only by Northern Illinois University in DeKalb.

The district's population center in Kane County is on the outskirts of Chicago. Aurora (shared with the 13th) continues to grow rapidly and has recently passed Rockford to become the state's second-largest city. Kendall County, into which some Aurora residents spill across the county line, is the nation's second-fastest-growing county this decade based on census information released in 2007. Aurora has a long history of manufacturing, and its largest employer is the heavy-equipment manufacturer Caterpillar.

Aurora and Elgin (small parts of which are in the 8th and 6th) have benefited from job growth in nearby Naperville and Schaumburg, suburban cities that have emerged as Chicagoland business centers.

Aurora and Elgin also each host one of the state's nine riverboat casinos, attracting thousands of visitors annually to their downtown areas.

Elgin and Aurora are about one-third Hispanic, and many of these residents work in blue-collar jobs in the area. Only three other Illinois districts — the Chicago-area 3rd, 4th and 5th — have a greater Hispanic population than the 14th, which is almost one-fifth Hispanic.

While its minority influence tends to help Democrats, the 14th overall has a strong Republican tilt, due mostly to the GOP leanings of Kane, Kendall and northwestern DuPage counties. GOP-friendly suburban and rural voters far outnumber the cities' blue-collar and minority Democrats. In 2004, George W. Bush won 55 percent of the 14th's presidential vote.

MAJOR INDUSTRY

Farm machinery and other manufacturing, casinos, agriculture

CITIES

Aurora (pt.), 102,144; Elgin (pt.), 74,013; DeKalb, 39,018; Carpentersville, 30,586; St. Charles, 27,896; Batavia, 23,866; West Chicago (pt.), 23,449

NOTABLE

Former President Ronald Reagan's birthplace in Tampico and boyhood home in Dixon are operated as local museums.

Rep. Timothy V. Johnson (R)

CAPITOL OFFICE
225-2371
www.house.gov/timjohnson
1207 Longworth 20515-1315; fax 226-0791

COMMITTEES
Agriculture
Transportation & Infrastructure

RESIDENCE
Urbana

BORN
July 23, 1946, Champaign, Ill.

RELIGION
Assemblies of God

FAMILY
Divorced; nine children

EDUCATION
U.S. Military Academy, attended 1964;
U. of Illinois, B.A. 1969, J.D. 1972

CAREER
Lawyer; realtor

POLITICAL HIGHLIGHTS
Urbana City Council, 1971-75; Ill. House, 1977-2000

ELECTION RESULTS

2006 GENERAL		
Timothy V. Johnson (R)	116,810	57.6%
David Gill (D)	86,025	42.4%
2006 PRIMARY		
Timothy V. Johnson (R)		unopposed
2004 GENERAL		
Timothy V. Johnson (R)	178,114	61.1%
David Gill (D)	113,625	39.0%

PREVIOUS WINNING PERCENTAGES
2002 (65%); 2000 (53%)

Elected 2000; 4th term

Johnson frequently breaks from the conservatives that dominate the Republican Party. In the 109th Congress (2005-06), he was among the least loyal members of the GOP on party-line votes, and he bucked his president more often than all but seven other Republicans.

He does tend to side with his party on social issues. He generally supports efforts to restrict abortion, and he voted in 2005 against expanding federal funding for embryonic stem cell research, which uses cells harvested from surplus embryos at in vitro fertilization clinics. He also voted in 2004 for a constitutional amendment to ban same-sex marriage.

Johnson belongs to the Main Street Partnership, a group of moderate and pro-business Republicans. He parts from conservatives most notably on environmental issues. In 2005, he voted against scaling back the Endangered Species Act of 1973 and opposed a plan to open Alaska's Arctic National Wildlife Refuge to oil and gas exploration. He was one of only a handful of Republicans to win an endorsement from the Sierra Club in 2006.

Johnson is a leader in the effort to ban MTBE, a gasoline additive blamed for polluting groundwater. He advocates greater use of two MTBE rivals: ethanol, which is made from corn, and biodiesel, which is derived from soybeans. Both plants are grown in abundance in the agriculture-driven 15th District in central Illinois.

Johnson started the 110th Congress (2007-08) by splitting with his party on a high-profile vote on the Iraq War. In February 2007, he was one of just 17 Republicans to support a resolution disapproving of President Bush's plan to boost U.S. combat forces by more than 21,000. "It was a difficult vote, and I support the president generally and the troops specifically," Johnson said. "But I think we have achieved for the most part what we can achieve."

His most in-your-face defiance of GOP leaders in the 109th Congress was on a fiscal vote. In 2005, Johnson was one of only 12 Republicans to oppose the budget bill, which is typically a test of party loyalty. The rank and file are expected to support their leadership's big-picture blueprint for spending each year. Johnson objected to an $844 million cut in food stamps over five years, which he said prompted his no vote.

On another important vote for the House GOP in 2005, Johnson bucked the party to vote for a Democratic amendment that restricted federal law enforcement agents' access to library and bookstore records. And he was one of just 13 Republicans to vote against sanctioning the administration's use of warrantless wiretaps of terrorism suspects.

His nonpartisan approach to voting fits in with his interest in building comity. He bemoans the rancorous atmosphere in the House, telling the Bloomington (Ill.) Pantagraph newspaper in 2004 that the lack of civility is "offensive to me" and that "both sides are guilty." In 2005, Johnson and New York Democrat Steve Israel formed the Center Aisle Caucus, to encourage members of Congress to respect other points of view and to rebuke lawmakers who take an uncivil tone in floor debate.

Agriculture policy is Johnson's leading parochial interest, since crops and food processing are the economic lifeblood for thousands of his constituents. He's been on the Agriculture Committee since his first term.

Johnson is known around the House for his healthy habits and his love of basketball. He spends a chunk of his day in the House gym, swimming laps or pounding out miles on a treadmill while catching up on his reading or returning phone calls to constituents — with a self-described compulsion to make phone calls, he sometimes places several hundred calls a day. He says he wants his self-discipline to be an example for others at a time when Americans' lifestyles are often blamed for illness, premature death and diminished productivity.

He also has what he admits are "very, very eccentric eating habits." Johnson skips breakfast and lunch and survives on a diet of fruit, rice cakes, granola, vitamin supplements, juice and farmer's cheese. "I eat the same thing every single meal of my life," he told Illinois Magazine. His thin physique evokes comments that he resembles another central Illinois politician, Abraham Lincoln, but the resemblance was more striking when Johnson had a beard. He shaved it off in late 2001.

Johnson's mother and her parents were active in McLean County GOP politics. His father, originally a Democrat, switched parties and became a Republican who served on the Urbana City Council. Johnson says he began passing out campaign literature when he was 3 or 4 years old.

He became a GOP precinct committeeman at age 21 while still in college. By 24, he was on the Urbana City Council, and at 30, he was elected to the Illinois House, where he stayed for nearly 24 years. Outside the legislature, Johnson worked in real estate and founded a law practice.

During his long tenure in Springfield, Johnson worked to toughen penalties for drunken driving and sex offenses. By 2000, he was looking for something new, and he leapt at the chance to run for the U.S. House when Republican Rep. Thomas W. Ewing announced his retirement.

An indefatigable campaigner, Johnson was the first candidate in the race. But the GOP primary field grew to four, and three influential Illinois Republicans backed different candidates. Gov. George Ryan endorsed Johnson, Speaker J. Dennis Hastert backed state Rep. Bill Brady, and incumbent Ewing supported his son, Sam. Running on high name recognition and ample personal funds, Johnson won with 44 percent of the vote.

The 15th District leans Republican, and Johnson entered the fall race as a strong favorite. But he faced a tougher-than-expected battle with his Democratic foe, university instructor Mike Kelleher, a first-time candidate and former Capitol Hill aide. Johnson prevailed, though with a modest 53 percent. He promised to limit himself to three two-year terms, but right before the 2002 election, he revoked that pledge.

Redistricting that year put Democratic Rep. David Phelps' home in the 15th District, but Phelps decided to run against Republican John Shimkus in the 19th instead. Johnson cruised to a 2-1 victory over political novice Joshua T. Hartke. He has been easily re-elected since.

KEY VOTES

2006

- No Stop broadband companies from favoring select Internet traffic
- Yes Affirm U.S. commitment to war in Iraq and reject setting a withdrawal date for troops
- Yes Repeal requirement for bilingual ballots at the polls
- Yes Permit U.S. sale of civilian nuclear technology to India
- Yes Build a 700-mile fence on the U.S.-Mexico border to curb illegal crossings
- No Permit warrantless wiretaps of suspected terrorists

2005

- Yes Intervene in the life-support case of Terri Schiavo
- No Lift President Bush's restrictions on stem cell research funding
- Yes Prohibit FBI access to library and bookstore records
- Yes Approve free-trade pact with five Central American countries
- Yes Pass energy policy overhaul favored by President Bush emphasizing domestic oil and gas production
- No End mandatory preservation of habitat of endangered animal and plant species
- Yes Ban torture of prisoners in U.S. custody

CQ VOTE STUDIES

	PARTY UNITY		PRESIDENTIAL SUPPORT	
	Support	Oppose	Support	Oppose
2006	79%	21%	74%	26%
2005	77%	23%	54%	46%
2004	77%	23%	62%	38%
2003	82%	18%	74%	26%
2002	85%	15%	80%	20%

INTEREST GROUPS

	AFL-CIO	ADA	CCUS	ACU
2006	50%	20%	86%	76%
2005	33%	40%	70%	52%
2004	60%	40%	86%	64%
2003	47%	30%	79%	60%
2002	11%	15%	85%	76%

ILLINOIS 15

East central — Champaign, Bloomington, Danville

Agriculture is the dominant industry in the 15th, which takes in all or part of 22 counties, including Champaign — the district's main city. The 15th runs nearly 250 miles north to south, with a long, narrow appendage that hugs the Indiana border on the western bank of the Wabash River down to Gallatin County. The district's roughly 10,000 square miles encompass several population centers separated by expansive farmland.

Corn and soybean fields cover much of the territory, and the land both around Bloomington-Normal and in counties south of Champaign produces high crop yields. Both the district's family and commercial farms produce feed and raw material for food products manufactured just over the district border at Decatur-based, worldwide distributor Archer Daniels Midland (in the 17th).

Scattered amid the farms are several midsize towns, including Danville, that are centered around agribusiness and manufacturing. Higher education is big business in the 15th, with more than 40,000 students at the University of Illinois flagship campus in Urbana-Champaign. Bloomington-Normal's Illinois State and Illinois Wesleyan universities are just outside the district (in the 11th). Bloomington, home to State Farm Insurance, leads downstate Illinois in insurance and finance.

The district has a solid GOP lean, and Republicans typically run strongest in counties north of Champaign, including Iroquois and Ford. Both counties gave Republican George W. Bush at least 70 percent of their vote in the 2004 presidential election. Champaign County's academic community keeps Democrats competitive in the county, and Champaign was the only Illinois county east of Decatur and south of Chicago that Bush lost in the 2004 presidential election, although by a slim margin. Overall, Bush won the 15th with 58 percent of the vote in 2004.

MAJOR INDUSTRY

Agriculture, higher education, food processing, insurance

CITIES

Champaign, 67,518; Urbana, 36,395; Bloomington (pt.), 34,510; Danville, 33,904; Charleston, 21,039; Mattoon, 18,291

NOTABLE

The Lincoln Log Cabin State Historic Site in Coles County preserves the last home of Abraham Lincoln's father and stepmother.

Rep. Donald Manzullo (R)

CAPITOL OFFICE
225-5676
www.house.gov/manzullo
2228 Rayburn 20515-1316; fax 225-5284

COMMITTEES
Financial Services
Foreign Affairs

RESIDENCE
Egan

BORN
March 24, 1944, Rockford, Ill.

RELIGION
Baptist

FAMILY
Wife, Freda Manzullo; three children

EDUCATION
American U., B.A. 1967 (political science); Marquette U., J.D. 1970

CAREER
Lawyer

POLITICAL HIGHLIGHTS
Sought Republican nomination for U.S. House, 1990

ELECTION RESULTS

2006 GENERAL		
Donald Manzullo (R)	125,951	63.6%
Richard D. Auman (D)	63,627	32.1%
General John Borling - write-in	8,523	4.3%
2006 PRIMARY		
Donald Manzullo (R)		unopposed
2004 GENERAL		
Donald Manzullo (R)	204,350	69.1%
John Kutsch (D)	91,452	30.9%

PREVIOUS WINNING PERCENTAGES
2002 (71%); 2000 (67%); 1998 (100%); 1996 (60%); 1994 (71%); 1992 (56%)

Elected 1992; 8th term

Manzullo is sometimes dismissed as a loose cannon, but he can be an effective legislator. A champion of the manufacturing industry and small business, his brazen moves occasionally change the course of legislative affairs, to the irritation of the Republican leadership.

That was the case in the summer of 2005 when he led a highly unusual floor revolt against legislation by an influential committee chairman, Henry J. Hyde, a fellow Illinois Republican who headed the International Relations panel. Hyde's bill would have punished companies that illegally sold arms to China, but Manzullo (man-ZOO-low) feared it would hurt U.S. businesses that unknowingly did so, including the Chicago-based Boeing, which employs 2,300 people in his district. More than 60 lawmakers switched their votes on the bill, embarrassing GOP leaders trying to maintain discipline. The bill later passed, but with a revision making it clear that companies had to knowingly break U.S. law to be sanctioned; Manzullo proclaimed himself satisfied.

In 2003 and 2004, Manzullo helped lead another intraparty rebellion, against Republican Ways and Means Chairman Bill Thomas of California. With the blessing of Speaker J. Dennis Hastert, another Illinoisan protective of manufacturing interests, Manzullo allied with Democrats and rounded up GOP lawmakers to deny Thomas a majority on a corporate tax bill, forcing the powerful chairman to include $77 billion in tax breaks for manufacturers and small businesses. At one point, Thomas had made enough compromises to satisfy Hastert, but not Manzullo, and reluctantly dispatched an emissary to placate him. In the end, Manzullo got what he wanted and Thomas got some tax breaks for multinationals that he wanted.

As Small Business chairman, Manzullo made a splash in 2002 by confronting Tom Scully, head of the Centers for Medicare and Medicaid, when Scully refused to testify on the same panel with medical industry witnesses who had been critical of his agency. Manzullo subpoenaed Scully, and threatened to hold him in contempt of Congress if he didn't comply. Scully relented and apologized to the committee.

GOP term limits ended Manzullo's run as the top-ranking Republican on the Small Business panel in the 110th Congress (2007-08). He left the panel and rejoined the newly renamed Foreign Affairs Committee, where he last served in 2000. He is the top Republican on the panel's Asia Subcommittee, enabling him to keep his focus on manufacturing and trade issues, particularly relations with China.

Manzullo's strong views on helping small business date to his boyhood, when his family lived in a one-room apartment above their struggling grocery store in Rockford in the late 1940s. Manzullo's father, Frank, extended store credit to newly arrived immigrants from Poland, Latvia and Lithuania and, handy with tools, he converted thick packing boxes from his potato chip deliveries into insulation for the newcomers' drafty houses. "He was a one-man social welfare agency," recalls Manzullo. "It was just a tremendous sense of love. He taught me more about public service just the way he lived his life."

Later, in 1964, Frank Manzullo started a restaurant, eventually bringing Manzullo's brother into the business. The Italian eatery remained in operation for nearly four decades, until his brother was forced to close because of the high cost of providing health insurance to his employees. "He had to sell $70,000 of spaghetti in a year just to afford it for himself and his wife. That's in gross sales," says Manzullo, who has cosponsored several bills to help small business with the cost of health insurance, including one allowing trade groups to sponsor plans for their members.

Manzullo recalls deciding at age 4 that he wanted to be a lawyer. And at age 10, he decided he wanted to be in Congress. He spent 20 years as a small-town lawyer in Oregon, Ill., handling family cases, writing deeds and wills and advising small companies. Over the years, he watched the once vibrant region around the city of Rockford in the industrial heartland disintegrate as machine tool, automobile parts and tire plants closed their doors and unemployment became a chronic problem.

When Republican Rep. Lynn Martin decided to try for the Senate in 1990, Manzullo ran for her seat, with the intention of devoting himself to helping the manufacturing sector. He campaigned door-to-door, and got a respectable 46 percent of the vote in the GOP primary, but Democrat John W. Cox Jr. won the general election. Two years later, Manzullo tried again, winning the GOP primary with 56 percent of the vote. In November, the district reverted to its traditional GOP form; Manzullo ejected Cox by 12 percentage points. He has not had a serious challenge since.

One of the most ardent social conservatives in Congress, Manzullo early in his career helped start pregnancy crisis centers in Rockford and picketed clinics that performed abortions. His wife, Freda, a microbiologist, taught their three children at home until eighth grade, when they went to a small Christian high school in suburban Washington. When the House is in recess, the family heads for their small beef cattle farm in Illinois.

Every year, Manzullo leads the fight to convince Congress to adopt buy-American policies requiring the Pentagon to purchase only products that have at least 50 percent U.S.-made components. But lawmakers usually succumb to arguments that it is impractical because much of the technology the Pentagon buys is no longer made in the United States.

Unlike other friends of manufacturing in Congress, Manzullo is anti-protectionist and a defender of free trade. The way to help small firms survive competition with big companies and foreign rivals, he says, is to cut regulation and give them access to government contracts and foreign markets. Manzullo is a strong backer of the Export-Import Bank and the Overseas Private Investment Corporation, two government agencies that assist businesses in expanding exports. Manzullo says they are essential to counterbalance the help foreign governments give their business communities.

He also lobbied the administration to pressure China to end the low fixed exchange rate for its currency, the yuan, which makes Chinese goods less expensive in the United States and U.S. goods more expensive in China.

KEY VOTES

2006

? Stop broadband companies from favoring select Internet traffic
Yes Affirm U.S. commitment to war in Iraq and reject setting a withdrawal date for troops
Yes Repeal requirement for bilingual ballots at the polls
Yes Permit U.S. sale of civilian nuclear technology to India
Yes Build a 700-mile fence on the U.S.-Mexico border to curb illegal crossings
Yes Permit warrantless wiretaps of suspected terrorists

2005

Yes Intervene in the life-support case of Terri Schiavo
No Lift President Bush's restrictions on stem cell research funding
Yes Prohibit FBI access to library and bookstore records
Yes Approve free-trade pact with five Central American countries
Yes Pass energy policy overhaul favored by President Bush emphasizing domestic oil and gas production
Yes End mandatory preservation of habitat of endangered animal and plant species
Yes Ban torture of prisoners in U.S. custody

CQ VOTE STUDIES

	PARTY UNITY		PRESIDENTIAL SUPPORT	
	Support	Oppose	Support	Oppose
2006	95%	5%	94%	6%
2005	94%	6%	70%	30%
2004	93%	7%	84%	16%
2003	95%	5%	95%	5%
2002	95%	5%	82%	18%

INTEREST GROUPS

	AFL-CIO	ADA	CCUS	ACU
2006	9%	10%	100%	91%
2005	13%	0%	93%	100%
2004	14%	5%	100%	100%
2003	13%	10%	97%	88%
2002	13%	5%	95%	100%

ILLINOIS 16

North — Rockford, part of McHenry County

The 16th spans most of the Illinois-Wisconsin border, taking in Rockford and covering the rolling northern prairie where family farmers grow corn and raise dairy cows. It includes all of six counties and parts of three others, including all of Winnebago and the majority of McHenry counties.

McHenry County (shared with the 8th) contains large expanses of farmland, and the proximity of Chicago draws many residents to the county's suburban enclaves. Although McHenry continues a several-decades-long pattern of growth, Boone County, to its west, is among the nation's fastest-growing counties this decade. Solidly GOP, McHenry as a whole voted for George W. Bush by 20 percentage points in the 2004 presidential election, and Bush won Boone by nearly 15 points.

Roughly one-fourth of the 16th's voters live in the industrial hub of Rockford in Winnebago County. At one time a major machine-tool manufacturing center, Rockford suffered a typical Rust Belt decline. Although the transition away from traditional manufacturing was difficult, the city has upgraded to technology manufacturing and expanded its exports to China, Mexico and Canada. It is still one of the most densely populated manufacturing communities in the United States.

The 16th includes Illinois' leading dairy producers, and Jo Daviess County, in the northwest corner, is a state leader in raising beef cattle and producing hay. Galena, in the rolling hills of Jo Daviess near the Mississippi River, has a tourist-based economy.

Three-fourths of the district's black residents live in Rockford, giving the city a base of loyal Democrats. But the 16th overall covers mostly conservative, Republican territory. Only once in the 20th century did voters here elect a Democrat to the House. Bush received 55 percent of the district's vote in the 2004 presidential election.

MAJOR INDUSTRY

Manufacturing, aircraft and machine parts, agriculture, trade

CITIES

Rockford,150,115; Crystal Lake (pt.), 37,740; Freeport, 26,443

NOTABLE

The Ulysses S. Grant Home is in Galena; The Rockford Peaches, three-time winners of the league, were one of only two teams to play every season of the All-American Girls Professional Baseball League (1943-54).

Rep. Phil Hare (D)

Elected 2006; 1st term

Hare spent roughly 24 years as the district director for Lane Evans, who retired from the 17th District seat in 2006 because of the effects of the Parkinson's disease he had been battling for years. Hare's knowledge of the district combined with his political connections enabled him to raise money quickly, and he went into the November election with a considerable edge over his GOP opponent, television broadcaster Andrea Zinga. He won with 57 percent of the vote.

Hare said his background as Evans' aide "prepared me very well for this job." He will follow in Evans' footsteps as a strong advocate for labor and liberal causes. Hare was once a union steward at a clothing factory, and he supports prevailing wage laws and an increase in the federal minimum wage. The district has suffered from the loss of manufacturing jobs, and Hare is backing a bill by his Illinois colleague, Democrat Jan Schakowsky, that aims to curb the outsourcing of jobs overseas.

Hare mentioned Evans after voting in 2007 to allow federal funding for embryonic stem cell research, saying on the House floor that "Lane is just one of millions of Americans struggling with chronic illnesses that are curable with the advancement of stem cell research." He has opposed the war in Iraq from the start and complained that President Bush's "failed 'stay the course' strategy over the last four years has left our troops refereeing a civil war with no end in sight."

Hare received assignments to the Veterans' Affairs Committee — where Evans had served as the top-ranking Democrat in the 109th Congress (2005-06) — and the Education and Labor Committee. He said that any attempt by the Bush administration to underfund veterans' health care would be "over my dead body."

Hare has lived his whole life in the 17th District. His mother was active in local politics and volunteered on John F. Kennedy's campaign for president. His father was a machinist and member of his local union. In 1969, Hare went to work at the Seaford Clothing Factory, where he cut lining for men's suits and served as a union leader. He went to work for Evans in 1982.

CAPITOL OFFICE
225-5905
hare.house.gov
1118 Longworth 20515-1317; fax 225-5396

COMMITTEES
Education & Labor
Veterans' Affairs

RESIDENCE
Rock Island

BORN
Feb. 21, 1949, Galesburg, Ill.

RELIGION
Roman Catholic

FAMILY
Wife, Beckie Hare; two children

EDUCATION
Alleman H.S., graduated 1967; Moline Community College, attended 1967-68, attended 1974-74 (business administration & accounting)

MILITARY SERVICE
Army Reserve, 1969-75

CAREER
Congressional district director; campaign aide; clothing factory worker

POLITICAL HIGHLIGHTS
No previous office

ELECTION RESULTS

2006 GENERAL		
Phil Hare (D)	115,025	57.2%
Andrea Zinga (R)	86,161	42.8%

ILLINOIS 17

West — Moline; parts of Decatur and Springfield

The 17th is one of the state's most expansive districts. Winding over nine full counties and parts of 14 others, it hugs much of the border along the Mississippi River and reaches its tentacle-like arms past Springfield as far inland as Decatur. The 17th includes rich farmland along the Mississippi, as well as Rock Island and Moline — Illinois' half of the industrial Quad Cities that straddle the river across from Iowa.

Moline is a retail hub for the Illinois Quad Cities, and the development of the John Deere Commons revitalized the city's downtown. It contains the John Deere Pavilion, a visitor center, and shopping, dining and lodging. The cornerstone of the Commons is the MARK of the Quad Cities, a 12,000-seat arena and convention center.

Corn, soybeans and hogs fuel most of the rest of the 17th's economy, and even the industrial sector here, which is dominated by John Deere and Archer Daniels Midland, depends on agriculture. The Rock Island Arsenal is a major employer, although the installation stands to lose jobs from BRAC.

The 17th has a Democratic tilt. Democratic votes in Rock Island, coupled with the lean in the 17th's parts of Springfield and Decatur, are enough to overcome GOP tendencies in some rural areas. John Kerry captured 51 percent of the 2004 presidential vote here.

MAJOR INDUSTRY
Farm equipment manufacturing, agriculture, defense, food processing

MILITARY BASES
Rock Island Arsenal (Army), 272 military, 6,695 civilian (2007)

CITIES
Decatur (pt.), 58,701; Moline, 43,768; Quincy, 40,366; Rock Island, 39,684; Galesburg, 33,706; Springfield (pt.), 28,952; East Moline, 20,333

NOTABLE
Moline is known as the "Farm Implement Capital of the World."

Rep. Ray LaHood (R)

CAPITOL OFFICE
225-6201
www.house.gov/lahood
1424 Longworth 20515-1318; fax 225-9249

COMMITTEES
Appropriations

RESIDENCE
Peoria

BORN
Dec. 6, 1945, Peoria, Ill.

RELIGION
Roman Catholic

FAMILY
Wife, Kathy LaHood; four children

EDUCATION
Spoon River Community College, attended 1963-65; Bradley U., B.S. 1971 (education)

CAREER
Congressional aide; youth bureau director; urban planning commission director; teacher

POLITICAL HIGHLIGHTS
Ill. House, 1982-83; defeated for election to Ill. House, 1982

ELECTION RESULTS

2006 GENERAL		
Ray LaHood (R)	150,194	67.3%
Steve Waterworth (D)	73,052	32.7%
2006 PRIMARY		
Ray LaHood (R)		unopposed
2004 GENERAL		
Ray LaHood (R)	216,047	70.2%
Steve Waterworth (D)	91,548	29.8%

PREVIOUS WINNING PERCENTAGES
2002 (100%); 2000 (67%); 1998 (100%); 1996 (59%); 1994 (60%)

Elected 1994; 7th term

Like his mentor and one-time boss, former House Republican leader Robert H. Michel, LaHood is a low-key moderate with a reputation for getting along well with members of both parties. He's also an institutionalist, a man of the House — and proud of it.

When listing his priorities, he puts the needs of the House alongside the needs of his heavily agricultural district, and he is well positioned to look after both. A member of the Appropriations Committee, he sits on both the Agriculture and Legislative Branch subcommittees. And his reputation for bipartisanship and civility may hold him in good stead as he pursues his goals under a Democratic majority.

LaHood had plenty of reasons to enter the 110th Congress (2007-08) frustrated and disappointed. For years, he has organized bipartisan "civility retreats" in the hope of easing the mounting partisan distrust in the House, but he had to discontinue them for lack of interest. Then, his party's majority fell apart under the weight of ethics scandals, and he watched his friend and Illinois colleague, J. Dennis Hastert, lose the Speaker's gavel to Democratic Leader Nancy Pelosi.

LaHood had stood with Hastert to the end, although he made it known when he disagreed with how the leadership was dealing with the GOP's problems. LaHood spoke out against a change to House ethics rules that would have allowed then Majority Leader Tom DeLay to keep his leadership position after he was indicted on felony charges in Texas. "It sent the wrong message, and it's one of the reasons we lost the House," he said.

Yet he remains committed to bipartisanship. Early in 2007, he joined with Illinois Democrat Rahm Emanuel and Minnesota Republican Jim Ramstad to sponsor a $60 billion plan aimed at providing health insurance to most American children without it. Extending health insurance to those who do not have it — especially children — is a high-profile issue nationally and a priority for congressional Democrats. Many Republicans are supportive, although they acknowledge that the issue was not a priority when their party was in control. "I doubt if we were the majority party, we'd be standing here today talking about this bill, or this issue," LaHood said.

A master of parliamentary procedure, LaHood was often chosen by Hastert to preside in the chamber over contentious floor proceedings. The leadership had faith that LaHood's quick and confident rulings from the chair would keep order during emotionally charged debates.

He also was part of a small, informal group of advisers to Hastert. The two are close friends, having served in the state legislature together. But neither that relationship nor his prowess in managing floor debate has translated to increased power within the GOP leadership.

LaHood is now in his second decade in the House, and he spent another decade before his 1994 election as the chief of staff to Michel, whose district he stepped in to represent when Michel retired. Like his former boss, LaHood is moderate, and he occasionally seems out of step with the hard-charging conservatives from his Class of '94. He was one of only three Republicans in his class who refused to sign the "Contract with America," the GOP's policy manifesto that year. He said he was unwilling to pledge automatic support for tax cuts or increases in defense spending, adding that he was concerned with controlling the federal budget deficit.

LaHood also has paid attention to the practical aspects of constituent service for his district. Funding for agriculture in particular is important to his district's farmers who grow or sell corn and soybeans. Among other things, he wants broader use of ethanol, the corn-based fuel additive.

LaHood was passed over as chairman of the Intelligence Committee in 2004 even though he had more seniority on the panel than Peter Hoekstra of Michigan, who was tapped by Hastert for the post. LaHood rotated off the panel in 2007. He now serves as the top-ranking Republican on the new Appropriations panel created to oversee spending on intelligence.

LaHood usually is a reliable vote for his party on core issues. Yet at times, he splits from the GOP leadership. He voted no in 2004 on a measure reorganizing the nation's 15 intelligence agencies and creating a new position of national intelligence director. He was one of 67 Republicans to vote against the bill, and one of only three members of the Illinois delegation to vote no. LaHood said the reorganization measure would add a new and unneeded layer of bureaucracy to the federal government.

Although LaHood may not always vote the way the GOP leadership wants, he occasionally will be the frontman for certain party needs. Even though he later spoke out against the rule change for DeLay, LaHood tried to find a legislative way in 2004 to shelve an ethics complaint filed against the leader. He offered an amendment, which failed in committee, to that year's legislative branch spending bill to prohibit lame-duck lawmakers from filing complaints with the House ethics committee. The move came one day after freshman Democrat Chris Bell of Texas filed a complaint accusing DeLay of improper and illegal behavior. Bell lost his bid for a second House term in a March Democratic primary forced by the off-year congressional redistricting engineered largely by DeLay. LaHood's proposed rule change would have applied to Bell and blocked his complaint.

In 2005, LaHood seriously explored running for governor back home against incumbent Democrat Rod R. Blagojevich, himself a former House member, but abandoned the idea, saying people in his district told him they wanted him to stay in the House.

The grandson of an immigrant from Lebanon and a one-time junior high school teacher, LaHood watches out for minority rights. He worries about the level of sophistication among his colleagues in their knowledge of the Middle East. "There is a pretty fair understanding about Israel and the Palestinians," he says, "but there is only a sketchy understanding of other countries in the region, including Syria, Egypt and Lebanon."

LaHood first declared his candidacy for Congress in 1993, one day after Michel announced his retirement after 30 years in the House. He won with 60 percent of the vote and has not faced a serious challenge since.

KEY VOTES

2006

- No Stop broadband companies from favoring select Internet traffic
- Yes Affirm U.S. commitment to war in Iraq and reject setting a withdrawal date for troops
- Yes Repeal requirement for bilingual ballots at the polls
- Yes Permit U.S. sale of civilian nuclear technology to India
- Yes Build a 700-mile fence on the U.S.-Mexico border to curb illegal crossings
- Yes Permit warrantless wiretaps of suspected terrorists

2005

- Yes Intervene in the life-support case of Terri Schiavo
- No Lift President Bush's restrictions on stem cell research funding
- Yes Prohibit FBI access to library and bookstore records
- Yes Approve free-trade pact with five Central American countries
- Yes Pass energy policy overhaul favored by President Bush emphasizing domestic oil and gas production
- No End mandatory preservation of habitat of endangered animal and plant species
- No Ban torture of prisoners in U.S. custody

CQ VOTE STUDIES

	PARTY UNITY		PRESIDENTIAL SUPPORT	
	Support	Oppose	Support	Oppose
2006	89%	11%	93%	7%
2005	89%	11%	69%	31%
2004	86%	14%	75%	25%
2003	90%	10%	89%	11%
2002	92%	8%	82%	18%

INTEREST GROUPS

	AFL-CIO	ADA	CCUS	ACU
2006	36%	5%	87%	80%
2005	21%	5%	92%	65%
2004	40%	20%	85%	71%
2003	29%	15%	89%	72%
2002	11%	0%	89%	92%

ILLINOIS 18

Central — Peoria, parts of Springfield and Decatur

The 18th takes in all or part of 20 counties in central and western Illinois, with Peoria County accounting for nearly 30 percent of the population. In the south, it takes in the northern part of Springfield (the state capital), some Republican-leaning suburbs north and west of the city and rural turf that stretches west of the capital almost to the Mississippi River. In the southeast, the 18th runs to northern Decatur.

Peoria, an American Everytown filled with hard-working, middle-class folks, is the district's population center and hosts five hospitals, a University of Illinois College of Medicine campus and Bradley University. The downtown area has remained vibrant, with corporate, government, medical, convention and educational facilities. Peoria Museum Square is slated for completion in 2009, and the civic center is expanding. Most of Peoria's downtown residents live in high-rise condominiums, riverfront lofts or converted office and warehouse apartments.

In much of this predominately agricultural district, voters worry about crop prices, ethanol, free trade and estate taxes. The district's economic health still depends largely on Peoria-based manufacturer Caterpillar, which makes earth-moving equipment and other heavy machinery; the manufacturer is the largest employer in the city, providing tens of thousands of jobs and economic stability.

The Republican lean of the rural areas, primarily those expanses north and east of Peoria and north of Springfield, tips the 18th to the GOP. Woodford County, which abuts Peoria to the east, gave George W. Bush 68 percent of its vote in the 2004 presidential election, as did Logan County. Peoria, with its strong manufacturing base, tends to vote Democratic, but in the 2004 presidential election, Democrat John Kerry won the city by only 4 percentage points. Overall, Bush captured 58 percent of the 18th's 2004 presidential vote.

MAJOR INDUSTRY

Manufacturing, ethanol and grain products, agriculture, health care

CITIES

Peoria, 112,936; Springfield (pt.), 57,209; Pekin, 33,857; East Peoria, 22,638; Jacksonville, 18,940; Decatur (pt.), 15,571

NOTABLE

Abraham Lincoln's tomb in Springfield is a state historic site.

Rep. John Shimkus (R)

CAPITOL OFFICE
225-5271
www.house.gov/shimkus
2452 Rayburn 20515-1319; fax 225-5880

COMMITTEES
Energy & Commerce

RESIDENCE
Collinsville

BORN
Feb. 21, 1958, Collinsville, Ill.

RELIGION
Lutheran

FAMILY
Wife, Karen Muth Shimkus; three children

EDUCATION
U.S. Military Academy, B.S. 1980;
Southern Illinois U., M.B.A. 1997

MILITARY SERVICE
Army, 1980-86; Army Reserve, 1986-present

CAREER
Teacher

POLITICAL HIGHLIGHTS
Candidate for Madison County Board, 1988; Collinsville Township Board of Trustees, 1989-93; Madison County treasurer, 1990-97; Republican nominee for U.S. House, 1992

ELECTION RESULTS

2006 GENERAL		
John Shimkus (R)	143,491	60.7%
Danny L. Stover (D)	92,861	39.3%
2006 PRIMARY		
John Shimkus (R)		unopposed
2004 GENERAL		
John Shimkus (R)	213,451	69.4%
Tim Bagwell (D)	94,303	30.6%

PREVIOUS WINNING PERCENTAGES
2002 (55%); 2000 (63%); 1998 (61%); 1996 (50%)

Elected 1996; 6th term

During a decade in the House, Shimkus rarely received media attention outside of his southern Illinois district, at least not of the type and intensity that erupted during the House page scandal that broke just before Republicans lost control of Congress in 2006. Given a choice, he would probably prefer obscurity.

Shimkus (SHIM-kus) was the chairman of the three-member board that oversees the high school page program when ABC News revealed that Republican Rep. Mark Foley of Florida had sent sexually explicit e-mails to young male pages. As public pressure for a full accounting grew, Shimkus acknowledged that a parent had complained about Foley, but that he had accepted Foley's assurances the messages were harmless.

In 2005, Shimkus was notified by the House clerk of a parent's complaint about an e-mail from Foley to a young man in Louisiana. Shimkus confronted Foley, who told him the message was an innocent inquiry about the boy's well-being after Hurricane Katrina hit the Gulf Coast. Shimkus says he told Foley to have no further communication with the former page.

Several months later, in 2006, ABC News reported that Foley had been sending not innocent but sexually explicit e-mails. Shimkus came under fire for failing to fully investigate Foley. Shimkus also conceded that he had not alerted the other two members of the page oversight board, Democrat Dale E. Kildee of Michigan and Republican Shelley Moore Capito of West Virginia.

Reflecting on the episode months later, Shimkus said, "It was like walking around the corner and getting hit by a two-by-four. I had to get an attorney and I never had to get one before. The attorney advises you to say nothing. You can't say nothing in politics. If you say nothing, people will assume you are guilty."

The Foley scandal broke just weeks before the November election, and further eroded support for the Republicans already weakened by earlier ethics scandals and President Bush's unpopularity. In early 2007, Shimkus declined to return to the page board. "I think I have been tarnished by it," he told the St. Louis Post-Dispatch newspaper. "I'm done with it, and not because I don't love the kids. If you're going to have a new look at it, in all honesty, you ought to have some new eyes looking at it."

Shimkus' main focus is on the Energy and Commerce panel, a major committee with a broad portfolio. He is the senior Republican on the Environment and Hazardous Materials Subcommittee. Shimkus generally favors easing environmental restrictions on refineries and power plants. In the 109th Congress (2005-06), he pushed legislation to give incentives to coal-to-liquid refineries to benefit coal-producing areas like his district.

With other farm-state lawmakers, Shimkus advocates greater use of ethanol, a gasoline additive made from corn that is used to reduce emissions. He also supports greater use of an alternative fuel called biodiesel, which is refined from soybeans, a crop also grown in his district.

A 1980 graduate of West Point, Shimkus is a lieutenant colonel in the U.S. Army Reserve and extremely interested in issues affecting U.S. troops. He has been an unwavering supporter of the war in Iraq, and in 2007 he voted no on a Democratic resolution that disapproved of Bush's decision to increase U.S. troop strength in Iraq.

Shimkus was in the first West Point class to include women, and he is a strong voice for women in combat. In 2005, he fought a proposal that would have limited women's role in combat, joining Rep. Heather A. Wilson, a New Mexico Republican and the only female military veteran in Congress. "As long as the women can do the mission demanded of them, they should not be excluded," he says. "That's not a difficult one for me."

Shimkus is a social conservative who calls himself "a pro-life Christian." But he will side with Democrats on labor issues. In 2007, he voted for the Democratic majority's increase in the federal minimum wage. Three years earlier, he supported a Democratic amendment to extend unemployment insurance benefits for jobless workers. He is often torn on trade votes. His district has a large population of factory workers wary of foreign competition. But Shimkus also wants to promote agricultural products from Illinois, which ranks among the top 10 states in agricultural exports.

Shimkus grew up in Collinsville. His father worked at a local telephone company for 50 years and his mother worked at home rearing seven children. In college, Shimkus was burly and athletic, playing junior varsity baseball at West Point. He was in the Army from 1980 to 1986, then returned to Collinsville to teach high school history and government.

In 1989, he won his first election, to the Collinsville Township Board of Trustees, and from there went on to be Madison County treasurer. In 1992, he challenged Democratic Rep. Richard J. Durbin, who had represented the 20th District for 10 years, and lost, getting 44 percent of the vote. When Durbin was elected to the Senate in 1996, Shimkus was ready to try again.

In the general election, he faced state Rep. Jay C. Hoffman, who emphasized his work on anti-crime legislation in the Assembly. Shimkus portrayed Hoffman as an opponent of tax relief and billed himself as a pro-business candidate favoring fewer taxes and government regulations. Although President Bill Clinton carried the district by 7 percentage points, Shimkus managed to win narrowly by 1,238 votes.

In 2002, reapportionment cost Illinois one of its House seats. Ultimately Shimkus and Democrat David Phelps wound up running against each other in the new 19th District. The district's demographics favored Shimkus, and he won the incumbent-versus-incumbent matchup by almost 10 percentage points. Two years later, he was re-elected with more than two-thirds of the vote against businessman Tim Bagwell. But his share of the vote dropped to 61 percent in 2006.

The year before, Shimkus broke his pledge to serve no more than six terms, which would have put him out of office in 2008. "It was a mistake at the time, and it's a mistake today," Shimkus told the Springfield State Journal-Register, adding "the voters are the final arbiters, and if they want to hold me accountable, then they will."

KEY VOTES

2006

- No Stop broadband companies from favoring select Internet traffic
- Yes Affirm U.S. commitment to war in Iraq and reject setting a withdrawal date for troops
- Yes Repeal requirement for bilingual ballots at the polls
- Yes Permit U.S. sale of civilian nuclear technology to India
- Yes Build a 700-mile fence on the U.S.-Mexico border to curb illegal crossings
- Yes Permit warrantless wiretaps of suspected terrorists

2005

- ? Intervene in the life-support case of Terri Schiavo
- No Lift President Bush's restrictions on stem cell research funding
- No Prohibit FBI access to library and bookstore records
- Yes Approve free-trade pact with five Central American countries
- Yes Pass energy policy overhaul favored by President Bush emphasizing domestic oil and gas production
- Yes End mandatory preservation of habitat of endangered animal and plant species
- Yes Ban torture of prisoners in U.S. custody

CQ VOTE STUDIES

	PARTY UNITY		PRESIDENTIAL SUPPORT	
	Support	Oppose	Support	Oppose
2006	93%	7%	92%	8%
2005	92%	8%	80%	20%
2004	91%	9%	76%	24%
2003	95%	5%	89%	11%
2002	94%	6%	80%	20%

INTEREST GROUPS

	AFL-CIO	ADA	CCUS	ACU
2006	29%	0%	93%	83%
2005	27%	10%	89%	92%
2004	43%	20%	95%	88%
2003	27%	10%	90%	80%
2002	11%	0%	90%	100%

ILLINOIS 19

South — southern rural counties; part of Springfield

The 19th sprawls across southern Illinois, meandering over all or part of 30 counties to create the largest congressional district in the state. The district reaches from Springfield, in central Illinois, south to Metropolis, which borders Kentucky. In the east, it reaches from the Ohio River in Gallatin, Hardin, Pope and Massac counties across the state to the Mississippi River in Jersey and Madison counties.

The 19th's part of Madison County contains roughly 20 percent of the district's population, and its portion of Sangamon County (Springfield) holds 10 percent. The rest of the population is spread widely across the remaining counties. Pope County, the state's least populous, is almost entirely within the Shawnee National Forest.

The northern counties cover typical Midwestern country — acres of corn and soybean fields dotted by small towns. The southern half, however, looks more like Appalachia than Midwestern prairie. The hilly, forested counties here once contained rich deposits of coal and were one of the nation's chief coal mining regions. Despite a recent uptick in mining, the economy is now predominately agricultural, with the 19th earning Illinois' top ranking in soybean yield and land used for farms.

Factory jobs account for most employment in Edwardsville, Collinsville, Glen Carbon and Godfrey, all of which are within Madison County. Edwardsville hosts a Southern Illinois University campus. In Sangamon, the state capital of Springfield is sustained mainly by the state government and the University of Illinois-Springfield and the Southern Illinois University Medical School (in the nearby 17th).

The district has a historically conservative Democratic tradition, but went Republican in the last two presidential elections, backing George W. Bush with a statewide-high 61 percent of the vote in 2004.

MAJOR INDUSTRY

Agriculture, coal mining, manufacturing, food products

CITIES

Springfield (pt.), 25,293; Collinsville (pt.), 21,803; Edwardsville (pt.), 21,478

NOTABLE

Metropolis was declared the official hometown of Superman in 1972.

INDIANA

Gov. Mitch Daniels (R)

First elected: 2004
Length of term: 4 years
Term expires: 1/09
Salary: $95,000
Phone: (317) 232-4567

Residence: Indianapolis
Born: April 7, 1949; Monongahela, Pa.
Religion: Presbyterian
Family: Wife, Cheri Daniels; four children
Education: Princeton U., A.B. 1971 (urban studies); Indiana U., attended 1975-76 (law); Georgetown U., J.D. 1979
Career: Pharmaceutical company executive; public policy institute executive; lawyer; White House aide; congressional and campaign aide; mayoral aide
Political highlights: U.S. Office of Management and Budget director, 2001-03

Election results:

2004 GENERAL		
Mitch Daniels (R)	1,302,912	53.2%
Joseph E. Kernan (D)	1,113,900	45.5%
Ken Gividen (LIBERT)	31,664	1.3%

Lt. Gov. Rebecca Skillman (R)

First elected: 2004
Length of term: 4 years
Term expires: 1/09
Salary: $76,000
Phone: (317) 232-4545

LEGISLATURE

General Assembly: January-April in odd-numbered years; January-March in even-numbered years

Senate: 50 members, 4-year terms
2007 ratios: 33 R, 17 D; 37 men, 13 women
Salary: $11,600
Phone: (317) 232-9400

House: 100 members, 2-year terms
2007 ratios: 51 D, 49 R; 85 men, 15 women
Salary: $11,600
Phone: (317) 232-9600

TERM LIMITS

Governor: 2 terms
Senate: No
House: No

URBAN STATISTICS

CITY	POPULATION
Indianapolis	791,926
Fort Wayne	205,727
Evansville	121,582
South Bend	107,789
Gary	102,746

REGISTERED VOTERS

Voters do not register by party.

POPULATION

2006 population (est.)	6,313,520
2000 population	6,080,485
1990 population	5,544,159
Percent change (1990-2000)	+9.7%
Rank among states (2006)	15
Median age	35.2
Born in state	69.3%
Foreign born	3.1%
Violent crime rate	349/100,000
Poverty level	9.5%
Federal workers	37,567
Military	22,639

ELECTIONS

STATE ELECTION OFFICIAL
(317) 232-3939
DEMOCRATIC PARTY
(317) 231-7100
REPUBLICAN PARTY
(317) 635-7561

MISCELLANEOUS

Web: www.in.gov
Capital: Indianapolis

U.S. CONGRESS

Senate: 1 Democrat, 1 Republican
House: 5 Democrats, 4 Republicans

2000 Census Statistics by District

DIST.	2004 VOTE FOR PRESIDENT BUSH	KERRY	WHITE	BLACK	ASIAN	HISP	MEDIAN INCOME	WHITE COLLAR	BLUE COLLAR	SERVICE INDUSTRY	OVER 64	UNDER 18	COLLEGE EDUCATION	RURAL	SQ. MILES
1	44%	55%	70%	18%	1%	10%	$44,087	53%	31%	15%	13%	27%	17%	13%	2,209
2	56	43	84	8	1	5	$40,381	51	35	14	13	26	17	27	3,679
3	68	31	88	6	1	4	$44,013	52	36	12	11	28	18	35	3,240
4	69	30	94	1	1	3	$45,947	57	30	13	11	26	22	32	4,016
5	71	28	93	3	1	2	$52,800	63	25	12	11	27	31	26	3,266
6	64	35	93	4	0	1	$39,002	50	35	15	14	25	15	41	5,550
7	41	58	63	29	1	4	$36,522	58	26	16	11	26	21	0	262
8	62	38	94	4	1	1	$36,732	52	32	16	14	24	16	42	7,042
9	59	40	94	2	1	2	$39,011	51	35	14	12	24	17	48	6,603
STATE	60	39	86	8	1	4	$41,567	54	32	14	12	26	19	29	35,867
U.S.	50.7	48.3	69	12	4	13	$41,994	60	25	15	12	26	24	21	3,537,438

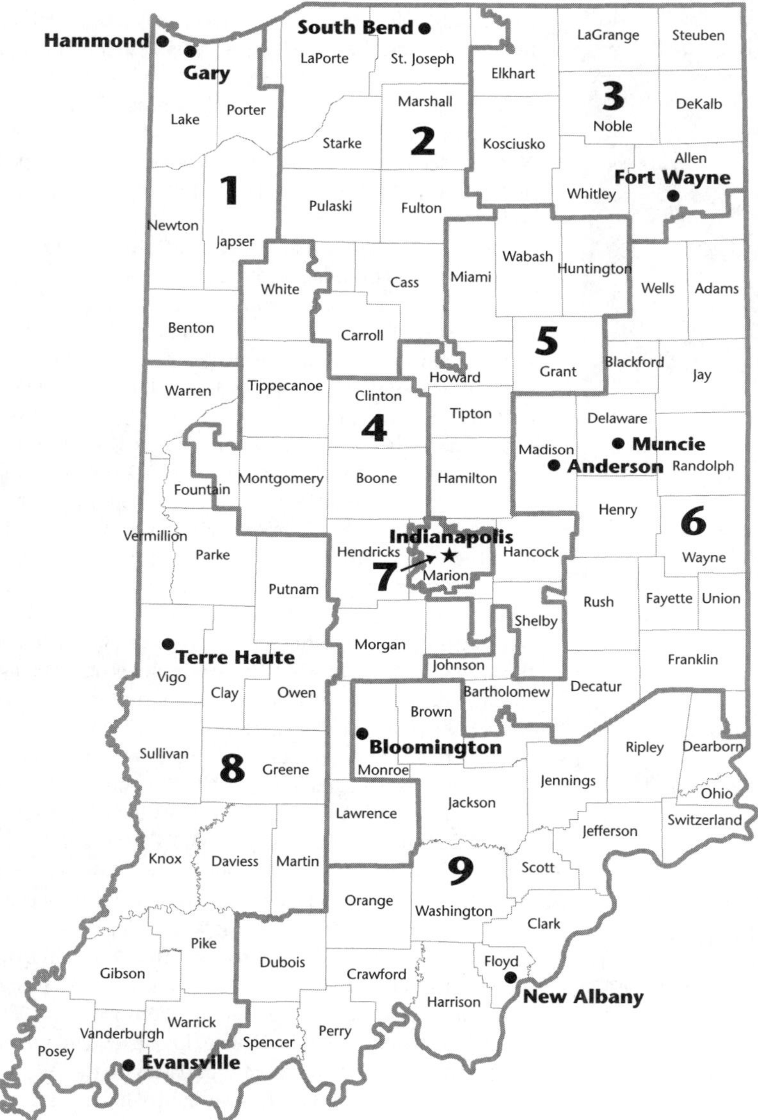
Hammond
Gary
South Bend
LaPorte
St. Joseph
Elkhart
LaGrange
Steuben
Lake
Porter
Marshall
3
DeKalb
Noble
Starke
2
Kosciusko
Allen
1
Fort Wayne
Whitley
Pulaski
Fulton
Newton
Japser
Wabash
Miami
Huntington
Cass
White
Wells
Adams
Benton
Carroll
5
Grant
Blackford
Howard
Jay
Warren
Tippecanoe
Clinton
Tipton
Delaware
4
Muncie
Madison
Anderson
Randolph
Montgomery
Boone
Hamilton
Fountain
Henry
6
Indianapolis
Vermillion
Parke
Hendricks
Hancock
Wayne
7
Marion
Putnam
Rush
Fayette
Union
Shelby
Terre Haute
Morgan
Franklin
Vigo
Johnson
Clay
Owen
Decatur
Bartholomew
Brown
Sullivan
Bloomington
Ripley
Dearborn
8
Greene
Monroe
Jennings
Ohio
Jackson
Lawrence
Switzerland
Jefferson
Knox
Daviess
Martin
9
Scott
Orange
Washington
Clark
Pike
Dubois
Floyd
Gibson
Crawford
New Albany
Harrison
Warrick
Perry
Vanderburgh
Posey
Spencer
Evansville

Sen. Richard G. Lugar (R)

CAPITOL OFFICE
224-4814
senator_lugar@lugar.senate.gov
lugar.senate.gov
306 Hart 20510-1401; fax 228-0360

COMMITTEES
Agriculture, Nutrition & Forestry
Foreign Relations - ranking member

RESIDENCE
Indianapolis

BORN
April 4, 1932, Indianapolis, Ind.

RELIGION
Methodist

FAMILY
Wife, Charlene Lugar; four children

EDUCATION
Denison U., B.A. 1954; Oxford U., M.A. 1956 (Rhodes scholar)

MILITARY SERVICE
Navy, 1957-60

CAREER
Farm manager; manufacturing executive

POLITICAL HIGHLIGHTS
Indianapolis School Board, 1964-67; mayor of Indianapolis, 1968-75; Republican nominee for U.S. Senate, 1974; sought Republican nomination for president, 1996

ELECTION RESULTS

2006 GENERAL

Richard G. Lugar (R)	1,171,553	87.4%
Steve Osborne (LIBERT)	168,820	12.6%

2006 PRIMARY

Richard G. Lugar (R)	unopposed

PREVIOUS WINNING PERCENTAGES
2000 (67%); 1994 (67%); 1988 (68%); 1982 (54%); 1976 (59%)

Elected 1976; 6th term

It speaks volumes about Lugar's standing back home that he was the only senator granted a free ride to re-election in 2006, when not a single Democrat in Indiana was willing to play sacrificial lamb. The veteran Republican, now the third-longest-serving member of his party in the Senate, commands enormous respect both at home and in Washington.

A fifth-generation Hoosier with a passion for foreign policy, Lugar embodies the phrase, "a gentleman and a scholar." Nominated for the Nobel Peace Prize in 2000 for his work on nuclear nonproliferation, he was dubbed "The Wise Man" by Time Magazine, which named him one of the 10 best senators in 2006.

Although he admits that the intricacies of foreign policy do not capture the imagination of Indiana voters, his meticulous work on his campaigns and his diligent attention to constituent service give him license to steer his own course in Washington. "Let's be honest," Dan Parker, chairman of the Indiana state Democratic Party, said in June 2006. "Richard Lugar is beloved not only by Republicans but by independents and Democrats."

With his ready smile and quiet manner, Lugar might seem to be the last senator to cause problems for the White House. But as chairman, and now top-ranking Republican, of the Foreign Relations Committee, Lugar has been a polite but persistent critic of President Bush's foreign policy.

In 2003, when the U.S. mission in Iraq seemed to be foundering, Lugar declared that it was time for the White House and Congress to "level" with the American people about what it would take to stabilize Iraq. Lugar announced he would hold hearings on the administration's plans for postwar Iraq and bluntly dismissed the message Bush had been delivering that the military operation would be over quickly and cleanly.

"This idea that we will be in just as long as we need to and not a day more, we've got to get over that rhetoric. It is rubbish!" Lugar said. "We're going to be there a long time." The following week, Bush publicly conceded that the nation was engaged in a "massive and long-term undertaking" in Iraq.

Lugar held more than 30 oversight hearings on Iraq after becoming chairman in 2003, probing the failures of U.S. efforts there, even as he backed Bush's refusal to set a timetable for U.S. withdrawal. He has also opposed a fixed deadline for Iran to comply with demands that it cease development of its nuclear program. And he split with Bush in 2006 over the president's refusal to engage in one-on-one talks with North Korea over its nuclear program. Diplomacy, in his view, involves more than drawing lines in the sand.

Lugar first chaired the Foreign Relations panel in 1985-86, when Republicans briefly controlled the Senate. In subsequent years, he was both the chairman and the top-ranking Republican on the Agriculture Committee, and was the architect of a 1996 overhaul of federal farm policy. When Jesse Helms of North Carolina retired, Lugar reclaimed the helm of the Foreign Relations Committee.

Lugar struggled to restore the prestige of a committee whose luster had faded since the end of the Cold War. But the White House largely ignored the committee — and most of Congress — as it pursued an aggressive foreign policy built around a global war against terrorism.

Lugar's signature issue is nuclear arms nonproliferation. In 1991, he teamed with Democrat Sam Nunn of Georgia, then chairman of the Senate Armed Services Committee, to create a cooperative threat reduction program to help the countries of the former Soviet Union secure and dispose of weapons of mass destruction. By the mid-2000s, the Nunn-Lugar program had deactivated more than 6,800 Soviet nuclear warheads.

Politics is an intellectual calling for Lugar. With all the energy and self-discipline of a long-distance runner — in his 70s, he still runs 12 to 15 miles a week — he has racked up an impressive list of accomplishments. He was first in his class in high school and at Denison University, where he was co-president of the student body with his wife-to-be, Charlene Smeltzer; a Rhodes Scholar at Oxford; a naval intelligence officer; two-time mayor of Indianapolis; and the longest-serving senator in Indiana history.

Lugar participated in some of the dramatic foreign policy events of the past three decades. In 1986, he headed a U.S. delegation monitoring the Philippine contest between President Ferdinand E. Marcos and challenger Corazon C. Aquino. Lugar helped persuade President Ronald Reagan that Marcos had stolen the election and should step down. The same year, Lugar dealt Reagan one of his worst foreign policy defeats when he joined with Democrats in voting for sanctions against South Africa. When Reagan vetoed the measure, Lugar led the successful effort to override his veto.

On the domestic front, Lugar has employed his own experience as a farmer to shape agriculture policy. For almost a half-century, he has run a 604-acre corn, soybean and walnut farm that belonged to his father. He helped steer to enactment in 1996 a sweeping farm bill that replaced New Deal-era crop subsidies and moved farmers toward a free-market system. But pressure from farmers prompted Congress in 2002 to undo most of the changes.

With the Agriculture Committee preparing to tackle a new farm bill in 2007, Lugar is increasingly focused on promoting the development of renewable energy. Working with Democrats such as Tom Harkin of Iowa and Barack Obama of Illinois, he spent much of the 109th Congress (2005-06) on energy issues. "Dependence on imported oil has put the United States in a position that no great power should tolerate," he told the Senate. "We must respond to our energy vulnerability as a crisis." In September 2006, he introduced a five-part National Fuels Initiative designed to expand production of renewable fuels such as biomass or corn-based ethanol by 100 billion gallons a year by 2025 through a combination of regulatory mandates and tax credits. On the first day of the 110th Congress (2007-08), Lugar reintroduced the legislation.

Lugar, a sickly child plagued by allergies and ear infections, was an avid reader of biographies who published a family newspaper on a toy printing press. He learned piano and cello at his mother's urging, showing a flair for improvisation and composition. The young Hoosier, with his brother Tom, also learned the vagaries of farming from their father, who paid them 10 cents an hour during hard summers of work. One year, the boys invested their savings in an acre of wheat, only to see it wiped out by a flood just before harvest.

Lugar first ran for office in 1963, winning a school board race. He became mayor of Indianapolis in 1968 and went on to merge the city and surrounding Marion County into a single governmental unit. In 1974, running for the Senate in a Watergate-dominated year with a reputation as "Richard Nixon's favorite mayor," Lugar came within a respectable 75,000 votes of Democratic incumbent Birch Bayh (whose son, Evan, is now Indiana's junior senator). In 1976, he handily defeated a much weaker Democratic incumbent, Vance Hartke, and he has been re-elected five times since.

Briefly considered as a vice presidential prospect in 1980, Lugar was stung eight years later when the No. 2 spot on the GOP ticket went to the junior senator from Indiana, Dan Quayle. Lugar ran an abbreviated presidential campaign in 1996 but was doomed by his complex policy speeches on international affairs and a campaign style that borders on lecturing.

KEY VOTES

2006

Yes Confirm Samuel A. Alito Jr. to the Supreme Court
Yes Allow consideration of a bill to establish a $140 billion trust fund to compensate victims of asbestos exposure
Yes Extend tax cuts for two years at a cost of $70 billion over five years
Yes Overhaul immigration policy with border security, enforcement and guest worker program
Yes Allow consideration of a bill to permanently repeal the estate tax
No Urge President Bush to begin troop withdrawals from Iraq in 2006
Yes Lift President Bush's restrictions on stem cell research funding
Yes Authorize military tribunals for suspected terrorists

2005

Yes Curb class action lawsuits by shifting them from state to federal courts
Yes Allow confirmation vote on Priscilla R. Owen to the U.S. Court of Appeals for the 5th Circuit
No Oppose mandatory emissions limits and block recognition of global warming as a threat
Yes Approve free-trade pact with five Central American countries
Yes Pass energy policy overhaul favored by President Bush emphasizing domestic oil and gas production
Yes Shield gunmakers from lawsuits when their products are used in crimes
Yes Ban torture of prisoners in U.S. custody
Yes Renew 16 provisions of the Patriot Act
Yes Allow final vote on opening the Arctic National Wildlife Refuge to oil and gas exploration

CQ VOTE STUDIES

	PARTY UNITY		PRESIDENTIAL SUPPORT	
	Support	Oppose	Support	Oppose
2006	82%	18%	91%	9%
2005	84%	16%	84%	16%
2004	94%	6%	93%	7%
2003	97%	3%	98%	2%
2002	91%	9%	100%	0%
2001	92%	8%	100%	0%
2000	86%	14%	65%	35%
1999	88%	12%	40%	60%
1998	84%	16%	54%	46%
1997	83%	17%	62%	38%

INTEREST GROUPS

	AFL-CIO	ADA	CCUS	ACU
2006	20%	15%	100%	64%
2005	21%	10%	100%	88%
2004	8%	20%	100%	84%
2003	0%	10%	96%	80%
2002	31%	5%	95%	90%
2001	13%	15%	100%	92%
2000	0%	10%	100%	84%
1999	0%	5%	100%	88%
1998	0%	0%	94%	68%
1997	0%	30%	90%	64%

Sen. Evan Bayh (D)

CAPITOL OFFICE
224-5623
bayh.senate.gov
313 Russell 20510-1404; fax 228-1377

COMMITTEES
Armed Services
Banking, Housing & Urban Affairs
(Security & International Trade - chairman)
Small Business & Entrepreneurship
Select Intelligence
Special Aging

RESIDENCE
Indianapolis

BORN
Dec. 26, 1955, Shirkieville, Ind.

RELIGION
Episcopalian

FAMILY
Wife, Susan Bayh; two children

EDUCATION
Indiana U., B.S. 1978 (business economics);
U. of Virginia, J.D. 1981

CAREER
Lawyer

POLITICAL HIGHLIGHTS
Ind. secretary of state, 1986-89; governor, 1989-97

ELECTION RESULTS

2004 GENERAL

Evan Bayh (D)	1,496,976	61.7%
Marvin B. Scott (R)	903,913	37.2%
Albert Barger (LIBERT)	27,344	1.1%

2004 PRIMARY

Evan Bayh (D)	unopposed

PREVIOUS WINNING PERCENTAGES
1998 (64%)

Elected 1998; 2nd term

Bayh took himself out of the early jockeying for the 2008 presidential race, but he didn't completely shelve his ambition for a promotion. In his early 50s, he is young enough to consider a future race, and he also made it clear that he would not turn up his nose at the job of running mate.

The son of another Democratic senator from Indiana — Birch Bayh, who ran for president in 1976 — Bayh (BY) is a telegenic graduate of Washington's prestigious St. Albans School and a proven vote-getter in red-state Indiana. He won two terms as governor, serving from 1989 to 1997, in a state Democrats have not carried in a presidential campaign since the Johnson landslide of 1964.

Bayh was in the pack of would-be contenders for the wide-open presidential contest of 2008, but a cold-eyed assessment of his viability in late 2006 told him he would have difficulty breaking out. He did not have the fundraising agility of Hillary Rodham Clinton of New York, the charisma of Barack Obama of Illinois or the name recognition of John Edwards of North Carolina. Despite repeated trips to early battleground states, Bayh was weak in the early polling in Iowa. "The odds were longer than I felt I could responsibly pursue," he said.

He is still a leading centrist in Congress, a past chairman of the Democratic Leadership Council, the middle-of-the-road group that launched Bill Clinton and Joseph I. Lieberman. In the 110th Congress (2007-08), Bayh continued to focus on his work on national security-related committees, making him potentially attractive to a presidential nominee wanting to send the message that the ticket is strong on national defense.

He left the door open to a vice presidential selection. "I love being in the Senate, and I'd like to think I make a difference here," Bayh told National Public Radio in February 2007. "But you know, if you're president or vice president, I think you have an even greater opportunity to help our country, and that's what I'm all about."

With seats on both the Armed Services and Intelligence committees, Bayh was an early backer of the war in Iraq and of a pre-emptive strike to stop Saddam Hussein from developing weapons of mass destruction. "I'm not sure we'll find a smoking gun here," he had said. "But if we wait until it's cocked and loaded, it's probably too late."

By late 2004, Bayh said the administration had mishandled the war, and he called for the resignation of Defense Secretary Donald H. Rumsfeld. In the 109th Congress (2005-06), he called for a flexible withdrawal date for U.S. troops, saying Congress should not micromanage the president. Overall, he has charged that the war in Iraq is a distraction from pressing foreign policy issues in Iran and Afghanistan, particularly pushing tougher sanctions against Iran to pressure it to abandon its nuclear program. "They're hard, fanatical individuals who, I think, will only respect forceful action," he said of Iran to The Indianapolis Star. "So we need to start with diplomatic, cultural and economic forceful action so that, God willing, they don't resort to something else one day."

In a move aimed at better equipping the troops in the field, Bayh won the addition of more than $213 million to a defense spending bill in 2006 for "up-armored" Humvees. The funding was also a boon to an Indiana company, AM General, which produces the Humvees.

Bayh is now the chairman of the Banking, Housing and Urban Affairs Subcommittee on Security and International Trade, where he has focused on China's increasingly controversial trade practices. In 2005, he delayed Senate action on the nomination of Rob Portman as U.S. trade representative not because he opposed Portman, but to call attention to what he viewed as foot-dragging by the administration against confronting China trade practices that he considered unfair, especially the government's refusal to subject its currency to the open market, as other countries do.

His call for tariffs on China was greeted favorably by the United Auto Workers at a 2006 conference. In another bridge to labor groups, the generally business-friendly Bayh joined in an August 2006 bus tour protesting labor practices at Wal-Mart, the behemoth retailer that keeps its prices down by providing cheap wages and paltry benefits for its employees.

Though his father was one of the Senate's leading liberal Democratic voices during an 18-year career, the younger Bayh is more in tune with the Hoosier State's conservative bent. He says he always looks for the center, because that is where deals are made. In 2004, he co-founded a group called the Third Way to generate middle-of-the-road legislative proposals.

Bayh generally takes a cautious approach to politics. He tends to inch ahead rather than rush forward. His floor speeches are rare and prosaic events, filled with calls for compromise and a reliance on "Hoosier values." While many fellow senators gave impassioned speeches before voting on President Clinton's fate in the 1999 Senate impeachment trial, Bayh, who voted to acquit, delivered remarks that sounded like a legal brief. However, he was an early critic of Bush's tax cut policies, and voted against the first, $1.35 trillion installment in 2001.

Critics say Bayh's caution comes from his attempts to accumulate political capital rather than risk his neck on bold initiatives. In the 108th Congress (2003-04), he pushed the male equivalent of mom's apple pie with legislation promoting responsible fatherhood. He and conservative GOP Sen. Rick Santorum of Pennsylvania tried but failed to attach to a welfare bill $100 million to educate men about taking care of their children and $200 million to promote marriage through education and counseling programs for low-income couples.

Born in the small town of Shirkieville, Ind., Bayh moved to Washington at age 7, when his father was elected to the Senate. While attending St. Albans School, among his babysitters was Lynda Bird Johnson, the president's older daughter. Bayh met his wife, Susan, while she was a summer intern for the House Ways and Means Committee. In law school, he managed his father's losing campaign for a fourth term in 1980, when Birch Bayh was swept out in the Reagan landslide.

After clerking for a federal judge and practicing law, at age 30 Bayh was elected Indiana secretary of state. Two years later, in 1988, he became the youngest governor in the nation and stayed popular for eight years, in part by riding the crest of a robust economy.

He delivered the keynote address at the 1996 Democratic convention. Term limits barred him from running for governor again, so Bayh began preparing to challenge GOP incumbent Sen. Daniel R. Coats, who decided to retire in 1998 rather than face Bayh. In November, Bayh trounced Mayor Paul Helmke of Fort Wayne by a nearly 2-1 margin.

Bayh's movie-star good looks and cross-party appeal keep his favorability ratings high in Indiana. He briefly considered a 2004 campaign for the White House, publishing the requisite pre-campaign memoir. Also, opposition from abortion rights groups who questioned his suitability for a vice presidential slot in 2000 had weakened over the preceding two years.

But Bayh concluded his children were too young for him to be an absent father for the better part of two years. Bayh is the father of school-age twins. He won re-election to the Senate that year with 62 percent of the vote.

KEY VOTES

2006

- No Confirm Samuel A. Alito Jr. to the Supreme Court
- Yes Allow consideration of a bill to establish a $140 billion trust fund to compensate victims of asbestos exposure
- No Extend tax cuts for two years at a cost of $70 billion over five years
- Yes Overhaul immigration policy with border security, enforcement and guest worker program
- No Allow consideration of a bill to permanently repeal the estate tax
- Yes Urge President Bush to begin troop withdrawals from Iraq in 2006
- Yes Lift President Bush's restrictions on stem cell research funding
- No Authorize military tribunals for suspected terrorists

2005

- Yes Curb class action lawsuits by shifting them from state to federal courts
- Yes Allow confirmation vote on Priscilla R. Owen to the U.S. Court of Appeals for the 5th Circuit
- No Oppose mandatory emissions limits and block recognition of global warming as a threat
- No Approve free-trade pact with five Central American countries
- Yes Pass energy policy overhaul favored by President Bush emphasizing domestic oil and gas production
- No Shield gunmakers from lawsuits when their products are used in crimes
- Yes Ban torture of prisoners in U.S. custody
- No Renew 16 provisions of the Patriot Act
- No Allow final vote on opening the Arctic National Wildlife Refuge to oil and gas exploration

CQ VOTE STUDIES

	PARTY UNITY		PRESIDENTIAL SUPPORT	
	Support	Oppose	Support	Oppose
2006	89%	11%	58%	42%
2005	90%	10%	36%	64%
2004	78%	22%	64%	36%
2003	82%	18%	55%	45%
2002	70%	30%	79%	21%
2001	82%	18%	69%	31%
2000	92%	8%	98%	2%
1999	88%	12%	89%	11%

INTEREST GROUPS

	AFL-CIO	ADA	CCUS	ACU
2006	100%	85%	45%	16%
2005	100%	95%	56%	20%
2004	100%	90%	65%	20%
2003	85%	75%	43%	30%
2002	85%	70%	65%	30%
2001	100%	100%	50%	32%
2000	75%	80%	60%	16%
1999	89%	90%	59%	12%

Rep. Peter J. Visclosky (D)

CAPITOL OFFICE
225-2461
www.house.gov/visclosky
2256 Rayburn 20515-1401; fax 225-2493

COMMITTEES
Appropriations
(Energy-Water - chairman)

RESIDENCE
Merrillville

BORN
Aug. 13, 1949, Gary, Ind.

RELIGION
Roman Catholic

FAMILY
Divorced; two children

EDUCATION
Indiana U. Northwest, B.S. 1970 (accounting); U. of Notre Dame, J.D. 1973; Georgetown U., LL.M. 1982

CAREER
Lawyer; congressional aide

POLITICAL HIGHLIGHTS
No previous office

ELECTION RESULTS

2006 GENERAL		
Peter J. Visclosky (D)	104,195	69.7%
Mark J. Leyva (R)	40,146	26.8%
Charles E. Barman (I)	5,266	3.5%
2006 PRIMARY		
Peter J. Visclosky (D)		unopposed
2004 GENERAL		
Peter J. Visclosky (D)	178,406	68.3%
Mark J. Leyva (R)	82,858	31.7%

PREVIOUS WINNING PERCENTAGES
2002 (67%); 2000 (72%); 1998 (73%); 1996 (69%); 1994 (56%); 1992 (69%); 1990 (66%); 1988 (77%); 1986 (73%); 1984 (71%)

Elected 1984; 12th term

Visclosky's chances of becoming a cardinal looked bleak when he dropped out of Roman Catholic seminary at age 15. But Congress afforded him a second opportunity: When Democrats took control of the House in 2007, the quintessential old-school appropriator became a member of the "college of cardinals," as the chairmen of the spending panel's subcommittees are known. In the 110th Congress (2007-08), he wields the gavel of Appropriations' Energy-Water Subcommittee.

Despite his influential role on energy and defense policy, Visclosky (vis-KLOSS-key) assiduously skirts the national spotlight. His floor speeches are as rare as mentions of his name in national newspapers, and he acknowledges an aversion to publicity. "I try to avoid that like the plague," he says. Indeed, while many of his less powerful colleagues try to prove their influence by sending press releases back home, Visclosky quietly sends federal dollars.

A straightforward, head-down approach to attaining goals has served him well. The son of John Visclosky, former mayor of Gary, Ind., he knew when he gave up the seminary that he, too, wanted to get into public service. He started out as an aide to Democrat Adam Benjamin Jr., a state senator at the time, went on to work in Benjamin's congressional office, then eventually took his place in the House.

Once in Congress, Visclosky began a long quest to win a seat on the Appropriations Committee, where Benjamin had served. He finally made it onto the panel in October 1991 — six years, nine months and nine days after he made his first bid for such an appointment, Visclosky later recalled. "I'm an appropriator," he said recently. "Money makes policy."

In the 110th Congress, Visclosky is not just an appropriator but a chairman with power over the Energy Department and the politically popular water development projects undertaken by the Army Corps of Engineers. He also sits on the Defense Appropriations Subcommittee, which oversees funding for the Pentagon and the Iraq War.

Visclosky's low-key approach should not be confused with a lack of determination. He showed early on in his chairmanship that the Energy Department could expect a focused watchdog as its overseer. "Since the history of cost estimates is so incredibly rotten, how would you suggest Congress evaluate major projects?" Visclosky asked Energy Secretary Samuel W. Bodman at a hearing in March 2007.

In particular, Visclosky chastised the administration for requesting $405 million for a program to develop technologies for converting nuclear waste into fuel for nuclear reactors without providing a full cost estimate for the multidecade project and also for seeking new warheads after spending billions of dollars to preserve existing warheads.

On another front, Visclosky has battled with presidents — both Democratic and Republican — who he believes have not done enough to protect the domestic steel industry from unfair foreign competition. His effort to revive the flagging steel industry has been a defining issue of his congressional career. His hope is that he can slow or even reverse the continued decline of steel, which is the main industry of his northwestern district. His father was an ironworker.

Visclosky urged President Bush in 2002 to impose tariffs of 40 percent on foreign steel imports, saying anything less would be "meaningless and unacceptable." Bush set lower tariffs and then, just 21 months later, revoked them. Visclosky and his allies in the Congressional Steel Caucus introduced legislation to reinstate the tariffs, but to no avail. He chairs the Congressional Steel Caucus in the 110th Congress.

Visclosky's other abiding interest in Congress is delivering money for Indiana transportation and infrastructure projects and for efforts to diversify his district's economy. He is the only Hoosier on the Appropriations panel, and he must watch out for his colleagues' interests as well as his own district's needs.

In recent Congresses, he has sought millions of dollars for improvements to the Gary/Chicago International Airport to help make it a more viable alternative to crowded O'Hare and Midway airports in Chicago. He also backs the extension of commuter rail lines from Chicago, redevelopment efforts along the Lake Michigan shore and a technology "incubator" center affiliated with Purdue University.

In representing his reliably Democratic district, Visclosky generally votes the party line. But he is a fiscal conservative who will break with his leadership on some budgetary matters. Visclosky says that the government has "a moral responsibility" to balance the budget.

After dropping out of seminary, Visclosky went on to get degrees at two Catholic institutions, Notre Dame and Georgetown. Despite a passion for history, he made the practical decision to pursue an accounting degree as an undergraduate. After graduating from Notre Dame law school in 1973, he linked his fortunes to Benjamin, then a state senator and rising political star in Indiana. Visclosky coordinated Benjamin's successful campaign for Congress in 1976 and served as one of his top aides in Washington for nearly six years.

When Benjamin died in September 1982, Democrats were without a candidate for the November election. As the 1st District Democratic chairman, Richard G. Hatcher — Gary's longtime mayor — was in a position to choose the Democratic nominee, and he picked Katie Hall, a state senator and loyal ally. She won easily, but when she sought renomination in 1984, Visclosky and another candidate challenged her.

Visclosky put on dozens of $2 "dog and bean" dinners to attract the young, the elderly and the unemployed. His "Slovak kid" background helped, as did the memory that older voters had of the candidate's father — Gary's comptroller in the 1950s and its mayor in 1962-63. Visclosky bested Hall in the primary by 2 percentage points, then swamped Republican Joseph B. Grenchik, the mayor of Whiting, in November. He has won handily ever since, including garnering nearly 70 percent of the vote in 2006.

KEY VOTES

2006

Yes Stop broadband companies from favoring select Internet traffic

No Affirm U.S. commitment to war in Iraq and reject setting a withdrawal date for troops

No Repeal requirement for bilingual ballots at the polls

Yes Permit U.S. sale of civilian nuclear technology to India

No Build a 700-mile fence on the U.S.-Mexico border to curb illegal crossings

No Permit warrantless wiretaps of suspected terrorists

2005

No Intervene in the life-support case of Terri Schiavo

Yes Lift President Bush's restrictions on stem cell research funding

Yes Prohibit FBI access to library and bookstore records

No Approve free-trade pact with five Central American countries

Yes Pass energy policy overhaul favored by President Bush emphasizing domestic oil and gas production

No End mandatory preservation of habitat of endangered animal and plant species

Yes Ban torture of prisoners in U.S. custody

CQ VOTE STUDIES

	PARTY UNITY		PRESIDENTIAL SUPPORT	
	Support	Oppose	Support	Oppose
2006	90%	10%	20%	80%
2005	91%	9%	26%	74%
2004	90%	10%	19%	81%
2003	91%	9%	25%	75%
2002	92%	8%	22%	78%

INTEREST GROUPS

	AFL-CIO	ADA	CCUS	ACU
2006	100%	100%	27%	12%
2005	93%	85%	37%	8%
2004	100%	95%	35%	4%
2003	100%	85%	37%	24%
2002	100%	90%	35%	12%

INDIANA 1

Northwest – Gary, Hammond

A Rust Belt district bordered by Lake Michigan to the north and Illinois to the west, the Democratic 1st is home to steelworkers, a large union presence and some large minority populations in Lake County.

In contrast to the farming that dominates other Indiana districts, the steel industry has been a mainstay in the 1st for decades. More steel is produced here than in any other district in the nation. Competition in the global economy, however, has hindered recent production, and the late 1990s saw poor output relative to previous local standards. Nevertheless, there are still more than 30,000 steelworkers residing in Gary, Hammond and East Chicago.

Most of the 1st's population is in Lake County, which includes Gary, where more than 80 percent of residents are black, and East Chicago, where more than half of the population is Hispanic. The 1st also is home to many Eastern European ethnic neighborhoods.

Residents in and around Gary still struggle with the effects of unemployment, and now count on Lake Michigan-based tourism to lure people to the 1st. The region's lake boat gambling has brought in some jobs and attracted tourists, but has not countered the cutbacks and lower production in the steel industry and manufacturing.

The 1st generally supports Democratic candidates by large margins. There are GOP pockets in Lake County suburbs such as Crown Point and Merrillville, but the northern cities are mostly Democratic. Lake County gave Democrat John Kerry 61 percent of its 2004 presidential vote — his best county statewide — and despite some Republican support in growing Porter County and in farming communities farther south, the 1st overall gave Kerry 55 percent of its 2004 vote.

MAJOR INDUSTRY

Steel, manufacturing, gambling

CITIES

Gary, 102,746; Hammond, 83,048; Portage, 33,496; East Chicago, 32,414; Merrillville, 30,560; Valparaiso (pt.), 27,362; Hobart, 25,363

NOTABLE

Singer Michael Jackson was raised in Gary; "Gary, Indiana" was a hit song in Meredith Willson's 1957 Broadway musical, "The Music Man"; "A Christmas Story" is based on life in Hammond in the early 1940s.

Rep. Joe Donnelly (D)

Elected 2006; 1st term

Donnelly is the founder and owner of a company that makes rubber stamps, but the Democratic leadership cannot count on him to sign off automatically on traditional party positions. A socially conservative centrist who won a district that leans Republican, Donnelly is against gun control, abortion rights, amnesty for illegal immigrants and same-sex marriage.

In his first week in the House, Donnelly was one of four freshman Democrats to vote no on a measure to lift restrictions on federally funded embryonic stem cell research. Donnelly said that "in light of the ethical concerns still surrounding embryonic stem cell research," he could not vote for the bill. Although he is critical of the Bush administration's handling of the war in Iraq, he has cautioned against a specific timetable for exiting. "We can't walk out of Iraq," he said. "We have to stabilize that country, and we have to win."

He is likely to be more in step with his party on labor issues and was a cosponsor of an early Democratic measure to increase the federal minimum wage. He also says he will demand that labor and environmental standards be included in any future trade agreements.

Donnelly sits on the Agriculture, Financial Services and Veterans' Affairs committees. He said he plans to use his Veterans' Affairs seat to investigate the dilapidated conditions and administrative inefficiencies of the outpatient facilities at the Walter Reed Army Medical Center, as reported by The Washington Post. "These men and women have fought and shed blood on the battlefield for us," Donnelly said. "They deserve the level of care and housing befitting their service and sacrifice for America."

Donnelly was successful in 2006 with a rematch against GOP incumbent Chris Chocola, who had defeated him by 10 percentage points in 2004. The political atmosphere in the 2nd District was strikingly different in 2006. President Bush's job approval ratings had plunged, and Donnelly pointed out frequently that Chocola seldom disagreed with the president's position on House votes. Donnelly's success at raising about twice as much money for this campaign than his first helped him seal his victory: He earned 54 percent of the vote to Chocola's 46 percent.

CAPITOL OFFICE
225-3915
donnelly.house.gov
1218 Longworth 20515-1402; fax 225-6798

COMMITTEES
Agriculture
Financial Services
Veterans' Affairs

RESIDENCE
Granger

BORN
Sept. 28, 1955, Queens, N.Y.

RELIGION
Roman Catholic

FAMILY
Wife, Jill Donnelly; two children

EDUCATION
U. of Notre Dame, B.A. 1977 (government), J.D. 1981

CAREER
Customized office products company owner; lawyer

POLITICAL HIGHLIGHTS
Democratic nominee for Ind. Senate, 1990; Democratic nominee for U.S. House, 2004

ELECTION RESULTS

2006 GENERAL		
Joe Donnelly (D)	103,561	54.0%
Chris Chocola (R)	88,300	46.0%
2006 PRIMARY		
Joe Donnelly (D)	30,589	83.0%
Steve Francis (D)	6,280	17.0%

INDIANA 2

North central — South Bend, parts of Elkhart and Kokomo

The 2nd begins in Kokomo and moves north through small farming communities before reaching counties on the state's northern border, which include the cities of South Bend, Mishawaka and Elkhart and are home to more than two-thirds of district residents.

South Bend, in St. Joseph County, is home to an ideologically and economically diverse population. The wealthy, white-collar, Catholic Notre Dame community that hosts faculty and professionals is joined by low-income, minority residents downtown, as well as blue-collar areas east of the city. Neighboring Mishawaka has grown as some South Bend residents have left downtown.

East of Mishawaka, communities in Elkhart County (shared with the 3rd) round out the 2nd's heavily populated northeast. Farming and business in Elkhart — a national center for the manufactured housing industry — create a faithful conservative constituency.

Michigan City's steel manufacturers in the district's northwest create a strong northern Democratic-leaning region: LaPorte County was one of only four Indiana counties won by John Kerry in the 2004 presidential election. Kokomo (shared with the 5th) is another mainly white, blue-collar area; it relies on the auto industry, with Delphi and DaimlerChrysler as major employers. But these Democratic pockets can be overmatched by GOP support from the rest of the 2nd. George W. Bush won the district's 2004 presidential vote with 56 percent, but the 2nd's U.S. House seat changed hands from Republican to Democrat in 2006.

MAJOR INDUSTRY
Manufacturing, higher education, agriculture

CITIES
South Bend, 107,789; Elkhart (pt.), 48,783; Mishawaka, 46,557; Michigan City, 32,900

NOTABLE
The World Whiffleball Championship is played every year in Mishawaka.

Rep. Mark Souder (R)

CAPITOL OFFICE
225-4436
souder@mail.house.gov
www.house.gov/souder
2231 Rayburn 20515-1403; fax 225-3479

COMMITTEES
Education & Labor
Homeland Security
Oversight & Government Reform

RESIDENCE
Fort Wayne

BORN
July 18, 1950, Fort Wayne, Ind.

RELIGION
Evangelical

FAMILY
Wife, Diane Souder; three children

EDUCATION
Indiana U., Fort Wayne, B.S. 1972 (business administration); U. of Notre Dame, M.B.A. 1974

CAREER
Congressional aide; furniture company executive; general store owner

POLITICAL HIGHLIGHTS
No previous office

ELECTION RESULTS

2006 GENERAL		
Mark Souder (R)	95,421	54.3%
Thomas Hayhurst (D)	80,357	45.7%
2006 PRIMARY		
Mark Souder (R)	39,449	71.3%
William Larsen (R)	15,845	28.7%
2004 GENERAL		
Mark Souder (R)	171,389	69.2%
Maria M. Parra (D)	76,232	30.8%

PREVIOUS WINNING PERCENTAGES
2002 (63%); 2000 (62%); 1998 (63%); 1996 (58%); 1994 (55%)

Elected 1994; 7th term

Souder's career in Congress is driven by his religious beliefs. Yet while his voting record paints him as a party loyalist and a social conservative, the complete portrait is more nuanced. He aligns with liberals when his faith tells him that government should help those in need.

"I'm defined more by where I come from in my evangelical tradition" than by political orthodoxy, says Souder (SOW — rhymes with "now" — dur). Being a faith-based lawmaker, he says, isn't just about opposing abortion and homosexuality but is a "holistic" exercise in letting his beliefs guide him on all the issues. He sometimes supports bills protecting the environment, helping people in poverty or providing treatment, not merely punishment, to drug abusers. Souder calls his 2002 vote to go to war in Iraq, with its inevitable toll in human life, the most difficult decision in his six terms, one he made only after concluding the Bible says that "governments are to punish evildoers."

In the 109th Congress (2005-06), with the GOP in charge, Souder used his post as chairman of a Government Reform panel subcommittee to exert a considerable impact on federal drug policy. In 2006, he was the chief House sponsor of a law that limits access to pseudoephedrine, a chemical precursor to methamphetamine that had been widely available in over-the-counter cold medicines. The year before, he won enactment of a bill correcting an unintended consequence in the law that restricted the number of drug-addicted patients who could be treated in group doctor practices.

Souder was also out front in pushing a new federal mandate for drug testing of professional athletes in baseball, football, basketball and hockey. He successfully steered it through the Government Reform Committee but it was dropped by other panels before the bill got to the floor. He is the author of a 1998 law barring federal student loans to people convicted of selling or possessing illegal drugs. Congress modified the law in 2006 by making it apply only to people convicted of drug offenses while attending school.

Souder is a force behind the perennial effort by conservatives to relax strict gun control laws in Washington, D.C. The city's delegate in Congress, Democrat Eleanor Holmes Norton, has called him an "incorrigible extremist."

Souder is usually a dependable vote for business interests. He was one of just three House members to receive a 100 percent score from the U.S. Chamber of Commerce for his 2005 voting record. But one of those votes, in favor of the Central American Free Trade Agreement, came after Souder and others pressured House leaders to allow a vote on a bill to address allegedly unfair trade practices by China.

A former congressional aide, Souder often works behind the scenes. Friendly, talkative and wonkish, he immerses himself in the details of his issues, is rarely caught flat-footed on the facts and loves to explain legislative politics at length, without seeming imperious. His passion for policy, however, has not translated into leadership roles, perhaps because he has no appetite for the year-round fundraising demanded of leaders. "I don't like to raise money, and I never will," Souder says.

Instead of running for a leadership post himself, in early 2006 he delivered a nominating speech for John Shadegg of Arizona, a fellow member of the conservative Republican Study Committee, in the midterm race for majority leader that elevated John A. Boehner of Ohio to the No. 2 job in the House GOP leadership. Souder's bigger disappointment was losing out in an intraparty competition to replace Boehner as chairman of the Education and the Workforce Committee. The post went to Howard P. "Buck" McKeon of California, who had more seniority and who had backed Boehner for majority leader.

When he is not on duty, Souder likes to visit national parks. Inspired by a love of the outdoors and an interest in history, he has traveled to about 160 Park Service sites since he was elected to Congress in 1994. He also still finds time for following his beloved Notre Dame football team and the Chicago White Sox. A Sox fan since 1958, he is part of a tradition of Indianans adopting Chicago teams as their own.

The Souders were among the earliest settlers of Allen County, Indiana, in the 1840s. The family's harness shop grew into a series of family businesses in Grabill that made the Souder name well known. The modern-day Souders, many of them religious conservatives, for the most part avoided the gritty, temporal realm of politics.

That changed the day then Rep. Daniel R. Coats, a conservative Indiana Republican who later served in the Senate, dropped by the family store to buy some furniture and met Mark Souder. Coats' beliefs, such as using the tax code to further conservative causes, appealed to Souder. In 1985, he became Coats' staff director on the Select Committee on Children, Youth and Families. He later was deputy chief of staff in Coats' Senate office.

In 1994, Souder decided to run for Coats' former House seat, fortuitously picking a year Republicans were destined to take control of both houses of Congress from the Democrats. He triumphed in a tough, six-candidate GOP primary field, and then went on the attack early for the general-election campaign. Starting with summer radio ads, he portrayed incumbent Democratic Rep. Jill L. Long as a Washington insider beholden to special interests and the Clinton administration. The strategy paid off; Souder beat Long by 11 percentage points.

In 1998, Souder declared his opposition to impeaching President Bill Clinton, saying he should be prosecuted as a private citizen. That stance earned him a serious primary opponent in 2000, but Souder eventually bested Allen County chief deputy prosecutor Michael Loomis. He attracted stiff primary competition again in 2002, this time as a result of redistricting, but Souder handily defeated former Fort Wayne Mayor Paul Helmke.

In 2006, he joined a string of lawmakers — at least eight in the 2006 election cycle alone, according to U.S. Term Limits, an advocacy group — to break an earlier term limit pledge. He survived a Democratic surge in Indiana that ousted three GOP House colleagues, winning by 9 points over Fort Wayne City Councilman Thomas Hayhurst, Souder's closest race yet.

KEY VOTES

2006

No Stop broadband companies from favoring select Internet traffic
Yes Affirm U.S. commitment to war in Iraq and reject setting a withdrawal date for troops
Yes Repeal requirement for bilingual ballots at the polls
Yes Permit U.S. sale of civilian nuclear technology to India
Yes Build a 700-mile fence on the U.S.-Mexico border to curb illegal crossings
Yes Permit warrantless wiretaps of suspected terrorists

2005

Yes Intervene in the life-support case of Terri Schiavo
No Lift President Bush's restrictions on stem cell research funding
No Prohibit FBI access to library and bookstore records
Yes Approve free-trade pact with five Central American countries
Yes Pass energy policy overhaul favored by President Bush emphasizing domestic oil and gas production
Yes End mandatory preservation of habitat of endangered animal and plant species
No Ban torture of prisoners in U.S. custody

CQ VOTE STUDIES

	PARTY UNITY		PRESIDENTIAL SUPPORT	
	Support	Oppose	Support	Oppose
2006	94%	6%	92%	8%
2005	97%	3%	87%	13%
2004	94%	6%	79%	21%
2003	97%	3%	98%	2%
2002	94%	6%	89%	11%

INTEREST GROUPS

	AFL-CIO	ADA	CCUS	ACU
2006	21%	0%	100%	88%
2005	27%	5%	100%	96%
2004	13%	5%	100%	88%
2003	7%	5%	100%	88%
2002	11%	10%	85%	88%

INDIANA 3
Northeast – Fort Wayne

While the manufacturing center located around Fort Wayne may drive the 3rd's economy, it is conservative farmers living across the vast agricultural land that influence local politics and make the district Republican. Allen County (Fort Wayne) is the 3rd's population center, and nearly half of the district's population lives in the county.

Like other Midwestern cities, Fort Wayne has suffered from a downturn in the manufacturing industry. Nevertheless, the 3rd remains a leading producer of recreational vehicles, manufactured homes and orthopedic products, such as knee replacement devices. Its white-collar businesses, supported by growing health care technology and financial-service industries, have prevented the 3rd's economy from slipping.

Fort Wayne has a rich entertainment history and attracts musical and theater performers to venues in the city. Educators and students visit Fort Wayne's Science Central, an interactive educational station that is recognized statewide and designed to help Indiana become a leader in science and math. In the 3rd's northwest, particularly near Shipshewana, Indiana's Amish Country draws tourists each year. Various lakes throughout the district, including the state's deepest in Kosciusko County, become summer hotspots.

Despite union ties, social conservatism tends to have more influence over voters in the 3rd, and many district residents hold deep-rooted religious beliefs driven by traditional values. Rural voters, especially in Kosciusko County — which gave George W. Bush a statewide high of 78 percent in the 2004 presidential election — bolster the state's Republican leanings. Bush won every county in the 3rd with at least 63 percent of the vote.

MAJOR INDUSTRY

Manufacturing, agriculture, health care

CITIES

Fort Wayne (pt.), 202,769; Goshen (pt.), 26,611

NOTABLE

Author and naturalist Gene Stratton-Porter's former home is a state historical site on Sylvan Lake in Noble County; Warsaw, which calls itself the Orthopedic Manufacturing Capital of the World, was home to the first orthopedic device manufacturer, established in 1895; Kendallville hosts the annual Mid-America Windmill Festival.

Rep. Steve Buyer (R)

CAPITOL OFFICE
225-5037
www.house.gov/buyer
2230 Rayburn 20515-1404; fax 225-2267

COMMITTEES
Energy & Commerce
Veterans' Affairs - ranking member

RESIDENCE
Monticello

BORN
Nov. 26, 1958, Rensselaer, Ind.

RELIGION
Methodist

FAMILY
Wife, Joni Buyer; two children

EDUCATION
The Citadel, B.S. 1980 (business administration); Valparaiso U., J.D. 1984

MILITARY SERVICE
Army Reserve, 1980-84; Army, 1984-87; Army Reserve, 1987-present

CAREER
Lawyer; Army prosecutor

POLITICAL HIGHLIGHTS
No previous office

ELECTION RESULTS

2006 GENERAL		
Steve Buyer (R)	111,057	62.4%
David Sanders (D)	66,986	37.6%
2006 PRIMARY		
Steve Buyer (R)	50,695	73.0%
Mike Campbell (R)	18,799	27.1%
2004 GENERAL		
Steve Buyer (R)	190,445	69.5%
David Sanders (D)	77,574	28.3%
Kevin R. Fleming (LIBERT)	6,117	2.2%

PREVIOUS WINNING PERCENTAGES
2002 (71%); 2000 (61%); 1998 (63%); 1996 (65%); 1994 (70%); 1992 (51%)

Elected 1992; 8th term

Buyer had the thankless distinction of leading President Bush's efforts to make veterans pay more out of pocket for their government health care plans, while wartime public and political sentiment strongly favored veterans. Not surprisingly, his proposals have gone nowhere.

Like Bush, Buyer (BOO-yer) thinks the medical system of the Veterans Affairs Department has been on an unsustainable course since benefits were significantly expanded in 1996 to provide care for all veterans, not just those with service-connected maladies. The VA's finances threaten to deteriorate further as thousands of Iraq War veterans return and look to the VA for care. The White House proposed enrollment fees and increased drug co-payments for veterans who are neither poor nor combat-disabled.

When Buyer, as the chairman of the Veterans' Affairs Committee, tried to advance the Bush plan in the House in 2005, he got his hat handed to him by veterans' groups that mobilized against the proposal. In 2006, Bush resubmitted the fee plan, but Buyer took a pass. "What am I going to do?" he asked. "Bring something up we voted down?"

Though Buyer is a Persian Gulf War veteran and a colonel in the Army Reserve, he has a rocky relationship with veterans' groups. In addition to the medical fees clash, he antagonized them by scrapping traditional joint House and Senate committee hearings on the veterans' budget that had been timed to coincide with the groups' annual D.C. conferences, allowing them to pack the meetings with their supporters. But he did win their praise in 2006 for working to expand GI Bill education benefits for reservists.

Buyer was elevated to chairman at Veterans' Affairs in 2005, after former Chairman Christopher H. Smith of New Jersey was ousted for bucking Bush and the leadership on veterans spending. He held it for only two years before the Democrats took control of the House in 2007. Buyer and new Democratic Chairman Bob Filner of California frequently clash.

Buyer is a tough-talking conservative who enjoys sparring with liberals on abortion, gun control and other polarizing issues. Sometimes, his sharp elbows jab fellow Republicans as well.

As a member of the Energy and Commerce Committee, he broke with Chairman Joe L. Barton of Texas to win adoption of an amendment to the 2005 budget-cutting bill that excluded mental health drugs from Medicaid cuts. Eli Lilly, the Indiana company that makes the anti-depressant Prozac, stood to benefit, but Buyer bristled at media suggestions that his amendment was aimed at helping the company. His amendment was later dropped in conference with the Senate. When Barton put forth his plan for a telecommunications overhaul, Buyer so disliked it that he threatened to submit a competing version.

A feisty partisan, Buyer stepped into the fray over the contested 2000 presidential election, and ended up the target of an ethics complaint. Florida Democratic Rep. Peter Deutsch accused Buyer, at the time chairman of the Armed Services Subcommittee on Military Personnel, of using his influence to obtain information on military absentee voters and passing on the data to the Republican Party in Florida. The House ethics committee dismissed the complaint but concluded that one of Buyer's subcommittee aides improperly shared government information for political purposes.

Buyer came to Congress fresh from duty with the Army Reserve in the Persian Gulf War, where he was a lawyer specializing in the treatment of prisoners, detained civilians and refugees. He was still in the reserves when the United States invaded Iraq in 2003, and was notified that he would be called for active duty. But the Pentagon decided that the presence of a congressman in the region would cause security problems.

During his tour of duty in 1991, Buyer was near an enemy munitions depot when it was destroyed by U.S. forces. He suffered a series of mysterious illnesses for years afterward, including breathing difficulty, kidney problems and two bouts of pneumonia. In 2000, Buyer was notified by the Defense Department that he likely had been exposed to chemical agents that drifted in the smoke cloud from the depot.

Buyer's father was a dentist who also operated a small farm along the banks of the Tippecanoe River in Indiana, where Buyer spent his childhood. Buyer recalls that his grandfather died of cancer and his father would not put chemicals on anything, convinced they were causing cancer. "Everything was organic. My father was a conservative Republican. If you saw the farm, you would've asked, 'Are you from California?' "

Buyer majored in business administration at The Citadel, the military college of South Carolina, then attended law school in Indiana. He worked his way through by painting fairgrounds buildings and churches. "You name it, I painted it, so long as it didn't move," he said.

When he returned from the Gulf War, Buyer ran for Congress against three-term Democrat Jim Jontz. He criticized Jontz's vote in 1991 against giving President George Bush authority to commit troops to the Gulf and drew attention to Jontz's four overdrafts at the private House bank during a scandal that caught up a number of members with overdrawn accounts. Buyer's 4,500-vote win was among the biggest House upsets of 1992. He easily won his next four re-election bids.

Reapportionment after the 2000 census took one House seat away from Indiana, forcing a substantial redrawing of district lines. Buyer's 5th District was parceled out among six districts. Only 3 percent of his former constituents were put in the 4th, but his hometown was there, so Buyer decided to run for re-election there in 2002. To introduce himself to his new constituents, he staged a 260-mile run across the new district. He declared the journey a success, reporting that he went through two pairs of shoes and encountered one angry pit bull and 51 dead opossums.

Buyer's energetic campaign was a contrast to that of his chief GOP opponent, first-term Rep. Brian Kerns, who put up a lackluster fight. Buyer won the primary and cruised to a 45 percentage point win in November in the GOP district. He enjoyed a similar margin of victory in 2004, but saw his margin drop to a still comfortable 24 percentage points in 2006.

KEY VOTES

2006

No Stop broadband companies from favoring select Internet traffic
Yes Affirm U.S. commitment to war in Iraq and reject setting a withdrawal date for troops
Yes Repeal requirement for bilingual ballots at the polls
Yes Permit U.S. sale of civilian nuclear technology to India
Yes Build a 700-mile fence on the U.S.-Mexico border to curb illegal crossings
Yes Permit warrantless wiretaps of suspected terrorists

2005

Yes Intervene in the life-support case of Terri Schiavo
No Lift President Bush's restrictions on stem cell research funding
No Prohibit FBI access to library and bookstore records
Yes Approve free-trade pact with five Central American countries
Yes Pass energy policy overhaul favored by President Bush emphasizing domestic oil and gas production
Yes End mandatory preservation of habitat of endangered animal and plant species
No Ban torture of prisoners in U.S. custody

CQ VOTE STUDIES

	PARTY UNITY		PRESIDENTIAL SUPPORT	
	Support	Oppose	Support	Oppose
2006	97%	3%	90%	10%
2005	98%	2%	86%	14%
2004	96%	4%	87%	13%
2003	97%	3%	96%	4%
2002	97%	3%	83%	17%

INTEREST GROUPS

	AFL-CIO	ADA	CCUS	ACU
2006	33%	10%	87%	83%
2005	20%	0%	93%	96%
2004	13%	5%	100%	96%
2003	7%	10%	97%	92%
2002	13%	0%	94%	91%

INDIANA 4

West central — Indianapolis suburbs, Lafayette

Traversing the 4th by car requires a nearly 175-mile trip through a slender district that takes in a mixture of farmland, small towns and suburbs. It spans from White County, which is roughly halfway between Chicago and Indianapolis, south to Lawrence County, which is about halfway between Indianapolis and Louisville.

Tippecanoe County, just south of White, takes in the 4th's largest metropolitan area — Lafayette and West Lafayette. The latter is home to the main campus of Purdue University, and its enrollment of more than 38,000 students. Known for its engineering school, Purdue grooms students to lead the district's influential manufacturing industry. Beyond Purdue's campus, both the area's signature architecture and its historic neighborhoods make West Lafayette much more than a college town in the middle of expansive cornfields.

Montgomery, White (shared with the 2nd) and Boone counties, arrayed across the district's north near Tippecanoe, are some of the top Indiana counties in soybean production and are near the top in corn production.

Moving south and east, the 4th cuts into a western sliver of Marion County (Indianapolis) and takes in fast-growing Hendricks County suburbs west of the city and Johnson County suburbs as it curves south of the city. Johnson is filling up with young, well-educated families.

The remaining southern counties of the 4th consist of smaller farming communities similar to those found elsewhere across the state. The 4th's agriculture industry and rural areas make it overwhelmingly Republican territory. In the 2004 presidential election, Montgomery and Boone gave George W. Bush 75 percent of their vote, and Bush did not lose a single county entirely in the 4th in either 2000 or 2004.

MAJOR INDUSTRY
Higher education, agriculture, manufacturing

CITIES
Lafayette, 56,397; Indianapolis (pt.), 40,207; Greenwood, 36,037

NOTABLE
The General Lew Wallace Study and Museum, which honors the Ben-Hur author, is in Crawfordsville; Tippecanoe Battlefield was where troops led by then governor, and later president, William Henry Harrison fought off an American Indian attack in 1811; The first official U.S. airmail flight took off from Lafayette via balloon in 1859.

Rep. Dan Burton (R)

CAPITOL OFFICE
225-2276
www.house.gov/burton
2308 Rayburn 20515-1405; fax 225-0016

COMMITTEES
Foreign Affairs
Oversight & Government Reform

RESIDENCE
Indianapolis

BORN
June 21, 1938, Indianapolis, Ind.

RELIGION
Christian

FAMILY
Wife, Samia Burton; four children

EDUCATION
Indiana U., attended 1958-59; Cincinnati Bible College, attended 1959-60

MILITARY SERVICE
Army, 1956-57; Army Reserve, 1957-62

CAREER
Real estate and insurance agent

POLITICAL HIGHLIGHTS
Ind. House, 1967-69; Ind. Senate, 1969-71; Republican nominee for U.S. House, 1970; sought Republican nomination for U.S. House, 1972; Ind. House, 1977-81; Ind. Senate, 1981-83

ELECTION RESULTS

2006 GENERAL		
Dan Burton (R)	133,118	65.0%
Katherine Fox Carr (D)	64,362	31.4%
Sheri Conover Sharlow (LIBERT)	7,431	3.6%
2006 PRIMARY		
Dan Burton (R)	61,150	84.0%
Clayton L. "C.L. Jim" Alfred (R)	6,869	9.4%
Victor D. Wakley (R)	4,822	6.6%
2004 GENERAL		
Dan Burton (R)	228,718	71.8%
Katherine Fox Carr (D)	82,637	26.0%
Rick Hodkin (LIBERT)	7,008	2.2%

PREVIOUS WINNING PERCENTAGES
2002 (72%); 2000 (70%); 1998 (72%); 1996 (75%); 1994 (77%); 1992 (72%); 1990 (63%); 1988 (73%); 1986 (68%); 1984 (73%); 1982 (65%)

Elected 1982; 13th term

Despite consistently high party unity scores, Burton sometimes strays from his Republican colleagues on issues ranging from foreign policy to prescription drug prices. He has been passed over in recent years for committee leadership posts and marginalized by Republican leaders.

Burton has found himself at odds with his fellow Republicans on a number of foreign policy issues, such as taking up Pakistan's cause in its dispute with India over Kashmir. Earlier this decade, he called attention to alleged kidnappings of Americans in Saudi Arabia when the Bush White House was taking a softer line toward a key Middle East ally. He has, however, backed the president's conduct of the war in Iraq.

Only a dozen Republicans have served in the House longer than Burton, but his seniority has not been much help to him of late. House GOP leaders passed him over for the top Republican spot on the Foreign Affairs Committee in the 110th Congress (2007-08), choosing the more junior Ileana Ros-Lehtinen of Florida instead. In the 108th Congress (2003-04), Burton was blocked from assuming the chairmanship of the panel's South Asia Subcommittee, though his seniority put him in line for it, because he was thought to be too pro-Pakistan. Two years later, he was given the gavel of the Western Hemisphere Subcommittee, covering the half of the globe where his agenda was least distressing to his colleagues.

Burton continues to champion the cause of Pakistan. In 2006, as other panel members pressed the Bush administration for more information about a proposed arms sale to Pakistan, Burton declared, "Pakistan is a friend and ally of the United States in the global war on terror, and we need to work together to solidify our relationship."

His more publicized departures from the party line involve a high-profile domestic issue: prescription drug prices. Despite the fact that thousands of employees of pharmaceutical giant Eli Lilly live in his district, Burton sides with Democrats in their efforts to force down prices of prescription drugs. His concerns date back to the days when his first wife was battling the breast cancer that took her life in 2002, and he met other patients who could not afford their cancer-fighting drugs. In 2007, Burton was one of just 24 Republicans voting with Democrats to require the government to negotiate prices for Medicare's prescription drug benefit. Four years earlier, he was in the minority of Republicans voting to allow imports of lower-priced prescription drugs from Canada and selected other countries.

Burton doesn't mind going his own way. Early in 2007, he was the only House member of either party to vote against an ethics package that tightened gift and travel rules. He insisted the rules were too complicated, and that full disclosure was the best way to prevent abuses by lawmakers.

From 1997 to 2003, Burton chaired the Government Reform Committee, where he led repeated investigations of the Clinton White House. Most famously, he suggested presidential counsel Vincent W. Foster Jr.'s suicide in 1994 was a murder. He conducted his own investigation in his backyard assisted by a homicide detective, firing a gun into what he would describe only as "a head-like object" — reportedly a pumpkin or watermelon — to see whether the sound could be heard at a distance. Burton once called his Democratic critics "squealing pigs" and President Bill Clinton a "scumbag."

Burton bombarded the White House with subpoenas and investigations into campaign fundraising and other areas. But he suffered some loss of credibility with the revelation in 1998 that he had fathered a son out of wedlock in the early 1980s. At the time of his disclosure, he was leading the House investigation of Clinton's attempts to cover up a sexual relationship with a young White House intern.

It is a sign of how distant those days are that one of Burton's chief allies on the 2003 drug importation bill was former top Clinton White House adviser Rahm Emanuel, now a Democratic House leader from Illinois. "It's great to work with you without my lawyer present," Emanuel quipped.

Burton remains one of the House's most conservative members, although others often occupy the spotlight these days. He was a co-founder of the Conservative Action Team, now known as the Republican Study Committee, but is no longer one of its leaders. In fact, as the RSC elected its chairman for the 110th Congress, Burton and some other founders of the organization were on the losing side. Jeb Hensarling of Texas was chosen over their preferred candidate, Todd Tiahrt of Kansas.

Burton endured a difficult early life. His 6-foot, 8-inch tall father regularly beat him and his mother, and was eventually jailed for abuse. His family lived in hotels and trailer parks, and by the time he was 12, Burton had lived in 38 states, Mexico and Canada. "I never stopped worrying that Dad would come back after he got out of jail," he told People magazine in 1994. "One day, when I was 13, he did. I was baby-sitting my younger brother and sister when I saw him come up the front walk. I was petrified and yelled, 'Don't come up here.' . . . I grabbed a shotgun we kept beside the front door. When he saw the gun, he turned around. I'm glad he did because I might have shot him."

After a stint in the Army and a couple years of college, Burton worked as an insurance agent. At that time, he considered himself an independent but often voted Democratic. But in 1964 he read an interview with Norman Thomas, a socialist presidential candidate who espoused the idea that the socialist philosophy was infiltrating American politics through the Democratic Party. Burton went to the library, read the Congressional Record and studied the legislation Democrats supported. Concluding that Thomas was right, Burton called the local GOP and joined.

Two years later, at age 28, he won a seat in the state legislature as a Republican. He served a total of 10 years there, interrupted by losing congressional bids in 1970 and 1972. In 1982, he finally won the U.S. House seat he had been seeking, and he has coasted to re-election ever since.

However, by early 2007, he was already facing a potential 2008 challenge in the GOP primary from John McGoff, a former county coroner who began an "outsider" campaign. At the same time, Burton was receiving criticism for missing 19 roll call votes while playing in a golf tournament in California.

KEY VOTES

2006

- Yes Stop broadband companies from favoring select Internet traffic
- \+ Affirm U.S. commitment to war in Iraq and reject setting a withdrawal date for troops
- Yes Repeal requirement for bilingual ballots at the polls
- Yes Permit U.S. sale of civilian nuclear technology to India
- Yes Build a 700-mile fence on the U.S.-Mexico border to curb illegal crossings
- Yes Permit warrantless wiretaps of suspected terrorists

2005

- Yes Intervene in the life-support case of Terri Schiavo
- No Lift President Bush's restrictions on stem cell research funding
- No Prohibit FBI access to library and bookstore records
- Yes Approve free-trade pact with five Central American countries
- Yes Pass energy policy overhaul favored by President Bush emphasizing domestic oil and gas production
- Yes End mandatory preservation of habitat of endangered animal and plant species
- No Ban torture of prisoners in U.S. custody

CQ VOTE STUDIES

	PARTY UNITY		PRESIDENTIAL SUPPORT	
	Support	Oppose	Support	Oppose
2006	96%	4%	91%	9%
2005	97%	3%	89%	11%
2004	96%	4%	76%	24%
2003	94%	6%	86%	14%
2002	97%	3%	84%	16%

INTEREST GROUPS

	AFL-CIO	ADA	CCUS	ACU
2006	21%	0%	92%	88%
2005	13%	0%	92%	96%
2004	21%	0%	95%	100%
2003	13%	20%	93%	92%
2002	13%	0%	80%	100%

INDIANA 5
East central – part of Indianapolis and suburbs

Dominated by Indianapolis suburbanites and rural farmers, the 5th is Indiana's wealthiest district and is staunchly Republican turf. Although Hamilton, Hancock and the district's portion of Marion counties, which surround the state capital on three sides, make up a small percentage of the 5th's land area, half of the district's population lives there.

The district's most affluent residents live in northern Indianapolis (Marion County) and in the Hamilton County suburbs of Carmel, Fishers and Noblesville. Here, growing populations of white-collar workers in electronics and financial services bring median incomes well above state and national averages. Hamilton and Hancock in particular have used an increase in white-collar residents to boost income levels. Southeast of Indianapolis, the district takes in most of Shelby County and a chunk of northeastern Johnson County.

The northern part of the 5th includes small cities that are closer to Fort Wayne than Indianapolis and are much different from the district's suburban southern portion. These residents earn modest incomes from the area's solid farming industry, based mostly in corn, and from operating small businesses. Miami, Wabash and Grant counties all lost population in the 1990s and have lost residents thus far this decade. The 5th also takes in most of Howard County, including part of working-class Kokomo (shared with the 2nd).

Suburban Indianapolis residents have made the 5th into the Hoosier state's most Republican district. While the rural communities are not as affluent as their suburban counterparts, they too solidly support GOP candidates. Republican George W. Bush captured 71 percent of the district's 2004 presidential vote — his best showing in the state.

MAJOR INDUSTRY

Financial services, electronics, agriculture

CITIES

Indianapolis (pt.), 131,892; Fishers, 37,835; Carmel, 37,733; Marion, 31,320

NOTABLE

The International Circus Hall of Fame is in Peru; The Elwood Haynes Museum, in Kokomo, honors the hometown inventor who was among the first to build a gasoline-powered automobile; Each September, Fairmount hosts the James Dean Festival to honor their beloved rebel without a cause.

Rep. Mike Pence (R)

CAPITOL OFFICE
225-3021
mikepence.house.gov
1317 Longworth 20515-1406; fax 225-3382

COMMITTEES
Foreign Affairs
Judiciary

RESIDENCE
Columbus

BORN
June 7, 1959, Columbus, Ind.

RELIGION
Christian

FAMILY
Wife, Karen Pence; three children

EDUCATION
Hanover College, B.A. 1981 (history);
Indiana U., J.D. 1986

CAREER
Radio and television broadcaster; think tank president; lawyer

POLITICAL HIGHLIGHTS
Republican nominee for U.S. House, 1988, 1990

ELECTION RESULTS

2006 GENERAL		
Mike Pence (R)	115,266	60.0%
Barry A. Welsh (D)	76,812	40.0%
2006 PRIMARY		
Mike Pence (R)	52,188	86.1%
George T. Holland (R)	8,406	13.9%
2004 GENERAL		
Mike Pence (R)	182,529	67.1%
Melina Ann "Mel" Fox (D)	85,123	31.3%
Chad "Wick" Roots (LIBERT)	4,397	1.6%

PREVIOUS WINNING PERCENTAGES
2002 (64%); 2000 (51%)

Elected 2000; 4th term

As a former talk radio host who describes himself as "Rush Limbaugh on decaf," Pence is one of the most articulate communicators of the conservative message, maybe too articulate for his own good. His influence in the House waned after the GOP did poorly at the polls in 2006, and Pence's harping on the budget deficit just before the election was deemed decidedly unhelpful to the party in retrospect.

As Republicans regrouped after the election, Pence challenged Republican Leader John A. Boehner of Ohio for the party's top job but was rejected by a lopsided 168-27. He failed to get the support of most of the more than 100 members of the conservative Republican Study Committee, despite coming off a two-year stint as its chairman. Pence had the backing of conservative writers, commentators and bloggers but had difficulty building support among colleagues, some of whom groused that he had made them look bad before the election with his focus on the GOP majority's lack of restraint in the annual spending bills and its failure to rein in earmarks, the special projects that lawmakers tuck into the bills for their home districts.

If some Republicans say Pence has a political tin ear, they can't deny his tendency to vote his principles, which manages to rankle people on both the right and the left. "You've got to be willing to go in there and turn your face like flint to the wind," Pence says. "And I think too few of my colleagues in the conservative caucus are willing to do that."

Pence led the charge in 2003 against a $400 billion-plus Medicare prescription drug bill as an unwarranted expansion of government, in spite of immense pressure to vote for it from GOP leaders and President Bush. Pence also split with the president on another signature initiative, the 2001 No Child Left Behind education bill, because it would increase federal spending. Pence is frequently in the face of appropriators, who tend to favor the status quo on spending, and he is usually among the loudest to complain about the perennial vote to hike up the federal debt limit when Congress wants to spend more money. In 2005, the conservative weekly Human Events named him its man of the year.

But then he turned around and disappointed conservatives in 2006 by proposing a compromise immigration bill that would have required illegal immigrants to leave the country but allowed them to eventually return and become eligible for U.S. citizenship. Conservatives considered the move a capitulation to liberal demands for amnesty for illegal workers and harshly attacked Pence in public comments. Pence merely said that the thrift and hard work of today's immigrants reminded him of a beloved grandfather, who emigrated from Ireland and came to Ellis Island in 1923.

Conservatives found it downright bewildering when Pence offered a bill in 2006 to make it tougher to subpoena news reporters, who are widely viewed by conservatives as too liberal. Pence said, "There is nothing more consistent with my belief in limited government than maintaining a free and independent press."

In 2002, Pence had a public spat with popular Arizona Republican Sen. John McCain over McCain's campaign finance legislation. The Indianapolis Star reported Pence saying, "McCain is so deep in bed with the Democrats that his feet are coming out of the bottom of the sheets."

A social conservative, Pence opposes abortion and embryonic stem cell research. He was active in the debate on a constitutional amendment to ban same-sex marriage. Pence calls himself "a Christian, a conservative and a

Republican, in that order." Despite his zeal, he personally has a soft-spoken, placid manner, and he remains in the good graces of his party's leaders in spite of his periodic rebellions.

Pence grew up in Columbus, Ind., where his father ran a group of gas stations. The family was Irish Catholic and Democratic, and President John F. Kennedy was practically an icon. But Pence's views changed after he joined an evangelical fellowship group at Hanover College. His new religion pulled him to the right politically, especially in his distaste for the Democratic Party's support for abortion rights. He met his wife, Karen, at an evangelical church service, where she was playing the guitar.

In 1988, at age 29, Pence made a run for the House in a challenge to veteran Democratic Rep. Philip R. Sharp. He lost by 6 percentage points. Two years later, he tried again, this time losing by almost 19 points. In the latter race, Pence ran a harshly negative campaign against Sharp. Pence later repented with an article called, "Confessions of a Negative Campaigner," in which he said, "Negative campaigning, I now know, is wrong."

It was during that period that Limbaugh captured Pence's imagination. "I was inspired by those dulcet tones to seek a career in radio and television," he recalls. Pence's first radio show aired in 1989 in Rushville, Ind. He eventually built up a syndicated talk show that was heard on 18 stations across the state, sometimes as Limbaugh's "warm-up act." Pence has a small radio studio in his House office where he records commentaries that he posts on a Web site. He devotes several hours most weeks to appearing on local talk radio and cable television programs.

His years as a radio broadcaster and as host of a public affairs television show in Indianapolis kept his name before the public. When he decided in 2000 to run for the seat of GOP Rep. David M. McIntosh, who ran unsuccessfully for governor, Pence easily beat state Rep. Jeff Linder and four other opponents in the GOP primary. He then topped Democratic lawyer Bob Rock by 12 percentage points in November.

Democrats who controlled the remapping process after the 2000 census sought to bolster vulnerable Democratic Rep. Baron P. Hill in the neighboring 9th District. In shaping the new 6th District, the Democrats gave Pence some of Hill's Republican-leaning rural territory in southeastern Indiana. In 2002, they fielded an active challenger in Melina Ann "Mel" Fox, a farmer and party activist running for office for the first time. Pence won by 29 percentage points in a race that was noted for its civility. He won by a larger margin in a 2004 rematch. In 2006, even as three other Hoosier State Republicans lost their re-election bids, Pence captured a 20 percentage point victory.

KEY VOTES

2006

- No — Stop broadband companies from favoring select Internet traffic
- Yes — Affirm U.S. commitment to war in Iraq and reject setting a withdrawal date for troops
- No — Repeal requirement for bilingual ballots at the polls
- Yes — Permit U.S. sale of civilian nuclear technology to India
- Yes — Build a 700-mile fence on the U.S.-Mexico border to curb illegal crossings
- Yes — Permit warrantless wiretaps of suspected terrorists

2005

- Yes — Intervene in the life-support case of Terri Schiavo
- No — Lift President Bush's restrictions on stem cell research funding
- No — Prohibit FBI access to library and bookstore records
- Yes — Approve free-trade pact with five Central American countries
- Yes — Pass energy policy overhaul favored by President Bush emphasizing domestic oil and gas production
- Yes — End mandatory preservation of habitat of endangered animal and plant species
- No — Ban torture of prisoners in U.S. custody

CQ VOTE STUDIES

	PARTY UNITY		PRESIDENTIAL SUPPORT	
	Support	Oppose	Support	Oppose
2006	96%	4%	90%	10%
2005	98%	2%	91%	9%
2004	99%	1%	94%	6%
2003	98%	2%	94%	6%
2002	99%	1%	84%	16%

INTEREST GROUPS

	AFL-CIO	ADA	CCUS	ACU
2006	8%	15%	100%	100%
2005	13%	0%	92%	100%
2004	0%	0%	100%	100%
2003	7%	10%	96%	100%
2002	11%	5%	84%	100%

INDIANA 6

East — Muncie, Anderson, Richmond

Covering most of Indiana's eastern border with Ohio, the 6th combines a mix of farmland, midsize cities and suburban populations. The district's economy, anchored in Muncie, is driven by the auto manufacturing industry.

The auto industry has declined in the 6th, which in turn has hurt the economies of the district's most populous cities — Muncie and Anderson. But there has been some positive news, as MAGNA Powertrain announced plans in 2004 to build a complex in Muncie to manufacture parts for General Motors, employing hundreds of local residents, and Honda plans to build a new automobile plant in Decatur County near Greensburg by 2008.

The 6th's largest cities also are its educational hubs. Muncie is home to Ball State University, and Anderson University is in nearby Anderson. The centerpiece of Anderson's revitalized downtown arts and culture center is the Paramount Theatre. South and east of Muncie and Anderson, the 6th takes in Wayne and Henry counties, where the percentage of residents over age 65 is among the highest in Indiana. This fertile land also hosts rich corn and soybean farms, as well as dairy silos and hog barns.

The 6th has a Democratic past that was fueled by its union population, but like most of rural Indiana, its residents now lean conservative and the district is more Republican today. George W. Bush carried all 19 counties that lie wholly or partly in the 6th in both the 2000 and 2004 presidential elections, earning 64 percent of the vote overall in 2004.

MAJOR INDUSTRY
Auto manufacturing, agriculture, light manufacturing

CITIES
Muncie, 67,430; Anderson, 59,734; Richmond, 39,124

NOTABLE
The Wilbur Wright Birthplace and Museum is in Millville; Famous Ball State University alumni include late-night talk show host David Letterman and Garfield cartoonist Jim Davis; The Academy of Model Aeronautics is located in Muncie, which in the 1920s was the model for "Middletown," a study of small-town American life; The Indiana Basketball Hall of Fame is in New Castle.

Rep. Julia Carson (D)

CAPITOL OFFICE
225-4011
rep.carson@mail.house.gov
www.house.gov/carson
2455 Rayburn 20515-1407; fax 225-5633

COMMITTEES
Financial Services
Transportation & Infrastructure

RESIDENCE
Indianapolis

BORN
July 8, 1938, Louisville, Ky.

RELIGION
Baptist

FAMILY
Divorced; two children

EDUCATION
Martin U., attended 1994-95 (political science)

CAREER
Clothing store owner; human resources manager; congressional district aide

POLITICAL HIGHLIGHTS
Ind. House, 1973-77; Ind. Senate, 1977-91; Center Township trustee, 1991-97

ELECTION RESULTS

2006 GENERAL		
Julia Carson (D)	74,750	53.8%
Eric Dickerson (R)	64,304	46.2%
2006 PRIMARY		
Julia Carson (D)	29,503	81.3%
Kris Kiser (D)	4,052	11.2%
Bobby Hidalgo (D)	1,690	4.7%
Joseph Charles Stockett III (D)	730	2.0%
2004 GENERAL		
Julia Carson (D)	121,303	54.4%
Andrew "Andy" Horning (R)	97,491	43.7%
Barry Campbell (LIBERT)	4,381	2.0%

PREVIOUS WINNING PERCENTAGES
2002 (53%); 2000 (59%); 1998 (58%); 1996 (53%)

Elected 1996; 6th term

Dogged by health problems, this feisty Democrat with a history of underperforming in elections refuted skeptics calling for her retirement by running again and winning in 2006 — albeit by a narrower margin than she's used to. "People thought I was too sick to run," she said. "I'm not too sick for anything."

Carson has battled a number of ailments through the years, including heart disease (she had bypass surgery in 1997), high blood pressure, asthma and diabetes. She missed almost a third of the House roll call votes in 2004 and had to answer tough campaign questions about her health. Nevertheless, she won re-election by 11 percentage points that year, and by 8 points in 2006.

She is a loyal Democrat who stuck with her party on 98 percent of votes in the 109th Congress (2005-06). She speaks out insistently for poor people, victims of discrimination and the homeless. And she will often disregard her ideological differences with conservatives to work on issues that affect her district or help her bring home federal cash.

Her weapons of choice are blunt talk and a dollop of charm. In a 2005 Indianapolis Star article, President Bush said of Carson, "She's not afraid to speak her mind. She's kind of like my mother." Five years earlier, President Bill Clinton said, "I've just sort of learned to do what she asks me without her having to argue it now."

In her district, she is often known just as "Julia," and supporters carry "I [heart shape] Julia" signs. Many feel they know her, and that she pays attention to their concerns.

In 2005, her office set up briefings to explain the new Medicare prescription drug program to senior citizens. The same year, she used her position on the Transportation and Infrastructure Committee to land $12.5 million for improvements to the Children's Museum of Indianapolis. Critics called it pork, but defenders hailed the museum as an "economic engine" that would help revitalize surrounding neighborhoods.

In early 2007, she teamed with Kentucky Republican Geoff Davis on legislation to help people on the verge of homelessness and to protect victims of domestic violence by banning the disclosure of certain information.

Carson has been a fairly reliable supporter of organized labor, environmental protection, abortion rights, gun control and government health care programs. From her seat on the Financial Services Committee, she has resisted such GOP initiatives as an overhaul of the federal public housing program, which included a requirement that unemployed tenants perform eight hours of community service per month.

Carson's personal background has informed her policy views. Born to a teenage single mother, she waited tables, delivered newspapers and did farm labor to earn money as a youth. Later, as a divorced young mother of two, she pinched every penny. While Carson's self-reliance might seem to fit right in with the philosophy of the typical conservative, her experiences have led her to very different conclusions about how to help the poor.

Right before her election to Congress in 1996, she held the job of Center Township trustee, administering municipal social services to low-income people in downtown Indianapolis. "We got people off of welfare and put them into jobs and into training and into educational experiences," Carson says. "We did not do that by being cruel." She uses adjectives like "cruel" and "regressive" to describe many GOP proposals.

In 2002, Carson opposed Bush's request for authority to wage war against Iraq, and in 2007 she opposed the administration's plans to send in more combat troops. In 2005, she voted against an $82 billion supplemental spending bill for the war, even though it contained $1.4 billion in funding for Indiana-made Humvees. Carson was the only member of the Indiana delegation to vote against the measure, which passed.

Carson's record on trade liberalization has been mixed. She typically joins Democrats in opposing Bush's free-trade agreements. But in 2000, she bowed to intense lobbying by the Clinton White House, put aside her concerns about human rights violations and voted to make permanent the normal trade relations between the United States and China.

She has been a staunch foe of Bush's economic policies, arguing that the administration had "perpetrated a fraud upon the people" by maintaining that the budget could accommodate not only his tax cuts but also adequate social spending and a reduction of the national debt. She opposed making the Bush tax cuts permanent, noting that Vice President Dick Cheney received $31,000 in tax deductions.

Carson characterized it as "incomprehensible" when Republicans sought to close the Legal Services Corporation in the 1990s and leave legal representation for the indigent to private attorneys. She has said providing government vouchers parents can use to pay tuition at private or religious schools is a "cruel hoax" on the public school system.

In 1999, Carson won enactment of a measure awarding the Congressional Gold Medal to civil rights figure Rosa Parks. The bill initially won little support beyond members of the Congressional Black Caucus, but Carson stirred up media coverage and eventually enlisted more than 300 cosponsors in her successful campaign.

Carson began her congressional career as a secretary, and then a district aide, for Democratic Rep. Andrew Jacobs Jr. of Indianapolis. In 1972, she won the first of two state House terms, and in 1976 she moved up to the state Senate, where she served until 1991. During her years in the General Assembly, she worked as human resources director at Cummins Engine and later opened a dress shop that failed and left her saddled with debt. (She had her state Senate wages garnished to partially pay off the debts.)

When Jacobs retired in 1996 after 15 terms, he endorsed Carson to succeed him, helping her win a difficult nomination battle and hold off a vigorous GOP attempt to capture the 10th District. She won her next two re-election contests by comfortable margins. Redistricting for this decade made her district — which was formerly the 10th — somewhat less Democratic.

KEY VOTES

2006

- Yes Stop broadband companies from favoring select Internet traffic
- No Affirm U.S. commitment to war in Iraq and reject setting a withdrawal date for troops
- \- Repeal requirement for bilingual ballots at the polls
- Yes Permit U.S. sale of civilian nuclear technology to India
- No Build a 700-mile fence on the U.S.-Mexico border to curb illegal crossings
- No Permit warrantless wiretaps of suspected terrorists

2005

- No Intervene in the life-support case of Terri Schiavo
- Yes Lift President Bush's restrictions on stem cell research funding
- Yes Prohibit FBI access to library and bookstore records
- No Approve free-trade pact with five Central American countries
- Yes Pass energy policy overhaul favored by President Bush emphasizing domestic oil and gas production
- No End mandatory preservation of habitat of endangered animal and plant species
- Yes Ban torture of prisoners in U.S. custody

CQ VOTE STUDIES

	PARTY UNITY		PRESIDENTIAL SUPPORT	
	Support	Oppose	Support	Oppose
2006	99%	1%	21%	79%
2005	97%	3%	16%	84%
2004	97%	3%	17%	83%
2003	97%	3%	20%	80%
2002	96%	4%	19%	81%

INTEREST GROUPS

	AFL-CIO	ADA	CCUS	ACU
2006	100%	90%	43%	4%
2005	100%	100%	40%	0%
2004	100%	75%	29%	0%
2003	93%	95%	33%	38%
2002	100%	100%	37%	0%

INDIANA 7
Most of Indianapolis

The 7th, Indiana's smallest district in size, is the only one not to have a rural, farming identity. Despite the district's largely white-collar workforce, it has the state's lowest median income, and is the conservative state's most Democratic; it gave John Kerry a statewide high of 58 percent of the 2004 presidential vote.

Almost four times bigger than Fort Wayne, the state's next-most-populous city, Indianapolis is the state's banking and commercial center. Heavy industry also plays a role in the city's economy, with a few automotive plants hanging on despite industry downturns. The joint Indiana University-Purdue University at Indianapolis campus and Butler University make it a hub for higher education. The medical school at IUPUI supports the district's established health care industry.

Indianapolis also is home to the state's major professional sports teams: football's Colts and basketball's Pacers and Fever. Despite the teams' local support, the 7th's biggest pro sport is auto racing — the Indianapolis Motor Speedway hosts the annual Indianapolis 500 race.

Indianapolis also is home to the national headquarters of The American Legion, the largest veterans organization in the world. The Soldiers' and Sailors' Monument, located in Monument Circle, complements a skyline graced by the state Capitol. The city has undergone considerable revitalization, particularly in the Fountain Square area.

Large minority populations in central Indianapolis — where some neighborhoods are up to 65 percent black — form the 7th's core and the base of its strong Democratic support. In the city's northern tier, white-collar residents are some of the wealthiest in the state and are more receptive to Republican candidates. Overall, the 7th has a Democratic tilt, although some residents tend toward social conservatism.

MAJOR INDUSTRY
Manufacturing, health care, higher education

CITIES
Indianapolis (pt.), 619,827; Lawrence (pt.), 28,086

NOTABLE
The NCAA Hall of Champions is on the western edge of downtown Indianapolis; President Benjamin Harrison, John Dillinger, poet James Whitcomb Riley, three vice presidents and 10 Indiana governors are buried in Indianapolis' Crown Hill cemetery.

Rep. Brad Ellsworth (D)

CAPITOL OFFICE
225-4636
ellsworth.house.gov
513 Cannon 20515-1408; fax 225-3284

COMMITTEES
Agriculture
Armed Services
Small Business

RESIDENCE
Evansville

BORN
Sept. 11, 1958, Jasper, Ind.

RELIGION
Roman Catholic

FAMILY
Wife, Beth Ellsworth; one child

EDUCATION
Indiana State U., Evansville, B.S. 1981 (sociology); Indiana State U., M.S. 1993 (criminology)

CAREER
Police officer

POLITICAL HIGHLIGHTS
Vanderburgh County sheriff, 1999-2006

ELECTION RESULTS

2006 GENERAL		
Brad Ellsworth (D)	131,019	61.0%
John Hostettler (R)	83,704	39.0%
2006 PRIMARY		
Brad Ellsworth (D)		unopposed

Elected 2006; 1st term

The telegenic Ellsworth, a local sheriff who campaigned as an anti-abortion, pro-gun moderate tough on crime, was one of the more prominent Democratic conservatives helping the party regain House control in 2006.

Ellsworth's first House floor speech delved into the need to curb budget deficits and the national debt, and he considers scrutiny of federal spending among his top priorities. He voted early on against expanded federal funding of embryonic stem cell research, but he sided with his fellow Democrats on a range of other issues from requiring the government to negotiate Medicare prescription drug prices to raising the minimum wage.

"It's kind of funny," he said during his campaign, "because the people who are more liberal say I'm way too conservative for them, and I see these [Republican Party] commercials that say I'm a liberal, so I guess I'm in no man's land." He vowed to "bridge the gap between the two extremes."

With a seat on the Armed Services Committee, he can look out for the Crane Naval Surface Warfare Center, a major employer in his district. Ellsworth calls the Iraq War "the most important thing in the world," and he voted in early 2007 for a war funding bill calling for a withdrawal of U.S. combat troops by August 2008.

Ellsworth also serves on the Agriculture Committee, where he will have a say in rewriting the nation's farm policy law in the 110th Congress (2007-08). Highway 41, which stretches the length of his 8th District, is lined with corn and soybean farms.

National Democrats had frequently tried to talk him into running for Congress. Ellsworth, prone to self-deprecation, said he finally decided to go for it after his heart, head and stomach agreed he could handle the race.

Ellsworth argued that incumbent Republican John Hostettler's views had fallen out of line with those of his district. Hostettler returned fire, equating a vote for Ellsworth as a vote for California's Nancy Pelosi to be Speaker of the House. But 8th District voters weren't worried; Ellsworth won by 22 percentage points. National party leaders quickly put him on their list for additional help in 2008.

INDIANA 8

West — Evansville, Terre Haute

Indiana's southwest corner, formed by the converging Wabash and Ohio rivers, houses the 8th, a district characterized by laborers and social conservatives. Evansville, an Ohio River port and the state's third-largest city, is southern Indiana's industrial center. It is located in Vanderburgh County, the district's most populous, and is home to the 8th's only substantial minority and liberal populations.

North of Evansville the district takes on a more rural and culturally conservative flavor. Gibson and Knox counties are among Indiana's top corn-producing areas. This region also grows soybeans, wheat and various fruits and vegetables. Daviess County has a large Amish population.

Terre Haute, farther north in Vigo County, is the district's other manufacturing center, and the 8th produces appliances and machinery. Terre Haute gets some Democratic votes from Indiana State University's faculty and students, and Evansville is home to Southern Indiana and Evansville universities. Having refurbished its downtown, Evansville is trying to establish tourism revenue, and the Casino Aztar is docked on the Ohio River.

Known in political circles as the "Bloody Eighth" for its aggressive and close races, the 8th's manufacturing base and history as a mining center long gave Democrats an edge. Cultural issues moved the district to the right, but local elections continue to be split between the two parties. George W. Bush carried every county here in taking 62 percent of the 8th's 2004 presidential vote, but the U.S. House seat flipped from GOP to Democratic control in 2006.

MAJOR INDUSTRY
Manufacturing, agriculture, higher education

MILITARY BASES
Naval Surface Warfare Center, Crane Division, 15 military, 2,756 civilian (2007)

CITES
Evansville, 121,582; Terre Haute, 59,614

NOTABLE
Vincennes is the oldest city in Indiana.

Rep. Baron P. Hill (D)

CAPITOL OFFICE
225-5315
baronhill.house.gov
223 Cannon 20515-1409; fax 226-6866

COMMITTEES
Energy & Commerce
Science & Technology
Joint Economic

RESIDENCE
Seymour

BORN
June 23, 1953, Seymour, Ind.

RELIGION
Methodist

FAMILY
Wife, Betty Hill; three children

EDUCATION
Furman U., B.A. 1975 (history)

CAREER
Financial adviser; state student assistance commission executive director; state legislative aide; insurance company manager

POLITICAL HIGHLIGHTS
Ind. House, 1982-90; Democratic nominee for U.S. Senate, 1990; U.S. House, 1999-2005; defeated for re-election to U.S. House, 2004

ELECTION RESULTS

2006 GENERAL		
Baron P. Hill (D)	110,454	50.0%
Mike Sodrel (R)	100,469	45.5%
D. Eric Schansberg (LIBERT)	9,893	4.5%
2006 PRIMARY		
Baron P. Hill (D)	53,883	79.2%
Gretchen Clearwater (D)	9,415	13.8%
Lendall B. Terry (D)	2,501	3.7%
John "Cosmo" Hockersmith (D)	2,267	3.3%

PREVIOUS WINNING PERCENTAGES
2002 (51%); 2000 (54%); 1998 (51%)

Elected 1998; 4th term

Did not serve 2005-07

The latest election helped Hill with some self-esteem issues. He had not considered running for his old seat in 2006, having been tossed out of office two years earlier by 9th District voters who chose Republican Mike Sodrel. "I had it in my mind that once you are a loser, you are tagged as a loser," Hill says.

A chance meeting near the Capitol with an old colleague, Democratic Rep. David E. Price of North Carolina, made Hill view things differently. Price related that he, too, was once turned out by voters only to come back in the next election. Hills says, "I remember leaving that conversation thinking, 'Oh my goodness, I'm really thinking about doing this now.' "

Hill went on to take the seat back from Sodrel, but he isn't out of the woods. He beat Sodrel with just 50 percent of the vote, and though he's a right-leaning Democrat, the socially conservative residents of Indiana's southeastern hill country could be talked into voting for a Republican again. The Democratic Congressional Campaign Committee put Hill on its list of vulnerable incumbents who will need fundraising help in 2008. House Democratic leaders also gave Hill a seat on the Energy and Commerce Committee, a high-profile posting and generally a lucrative source for campaign contributions from business and industry.

Hill, whose first House stint was from 1999 to 2005, rejoined the Blue Dog Coalition, the group of fiscally conservative House Democrats. He says he used to have more in common on those issues with Republicans but that now "they don't care about these huge deficits like I care about them." Deficit spending grew considerably under the Bush administration when Republicans controlled Congress.

Hill says his political philosophy is that "government should be used as a tool to lessen the dangers of our society and increase opportunities." It lessens the dangers through programs such as Medicare, he says, and increases opportunities by improving public education. Hill is married to a middle-school math teacher.

He breaks with his party on some social issues. He supports gun owners' rights and splits his votes on abortion. He doesn't think the Supreme Court's landmark *Roe v. Wade* decision legalizing abortion should be overturned. And in 2007, he supported federal funding for embryonic stem cell research, which uses cells harvested from surplus embryos at in vitro fertilization clinics and is opposed by anti-abortion groups. But Hill has voted for laws requiring parental notification and consent for a minor seeking an abortion.

Hill says his focus is affordable health care insurance and energy independence. Having experienced Washington political gridlock before, he thinks that nothing short of a constitutional amendment will fix the problem of millions of uninsured Americans. His amendment would make health care a fundamental right, which he says is "the only way to force something to happen."

Achieving energy independence from oil companies is also a major theme for him. On the Energy and Commerce Committee, he wants to pass legislation promoting the use of ethanol, biodiesel and wind energy. And he favors increased tax credits for owners of hybrid vehicles.

Hill says the House ethics panel should be made up of retired members of Congress so current members wouldn't be in the position of investigating their colleagues. "Former members of Congress can take one step back but still have institutional knowledge."

Hill is the youngest of seven children whose parents worked in a shoe factory. A basketball star at Seymour High School, he was inducted into the Indiana Basketball Hall of Fame in 2000, along with National Basketball Association legend Larry Bird. "When I was growing up in Seymour, all I could think of was basketball and girls," Hill says. "Politics was the furthest thing from my mind."

He went to Furman University on a basketball scholarship, which he says is the only way he could have gone to college. In those years, he picked up the political bug watching the Watergate hearings on television and becoming fascinated by the process of government. He also liked the competitive aspect of politics, which reminded him of sports.

After getting his degree in history, Hill returned home to the small town of Seymour and ran an insurance and real estate business. Elected to the Indiana House in 1982, he served there for eight years. He left the legislature in 1990 to wage an uphill battle for the U.S. Senate. Hill attracted some notice by walking the length of Indiana — from the Ohio River to Lake Michigan — where he celebrated by jumping into the 60-degree water. He lost to Republican Daniel R. Coats, who had been appointed to the seat two years earlier to replace Republican Dan Quayle, the party's vice presidential candidate that year. Hill did surprisingly well against Coats, capturing 46 percent of the vote.

He lost interest in politics for a spell after Democrats in the Indiana House, like their national colleagues, lost control of the chamber in 1994. He went to work as a financial analyst for Merrill Lynch. But Hill didn't hesitate when Democratic Rep. Lee Hamilton let him know he'd be retiring from the 9th District seat in 1998 after 17 terms.

Hill beat former state Sen. Jean Leising, who had made enemies in the state GOP and had difficulty raising money. Hill was remembered for his high school basketball exploits in the hoops-crazy state and was able to outspend Leising, $1 million to $650,000. He won by about 3 percentage points.

Republicans targeted him for defeat two years later with challenger Kevin Kellems, a former aide to Indiana GOP Sen. Richard G. Lugar. But Kellems lost the primary to Michael Everett Bailey, who had gained notoriety in 1992 by running graphic TV ads about abortion. Bailey ran the same ads against Hill, to no effect. He was re-elected.

In 2002, Sodrel challenged him unsuccessfully, but then came back two years later with a better campaign organization, ample financing and help from the national party. Sodrel won that race by a half percentage point.

CQ VOTE STUDIES>

	PARTY UNITY		PRESIDENTIAL SUPPORT	
	Support	Oppose	Support	Oppose
2004	83%	17%	32%	68%
2003	83%	17%	38%	62%
2002	76%	24%	45%	55%
2001	72%	28%	34%	66%
2000	81%	19%	76%	24%

INTEREST GROUPS

	AFL-CIO	ADA	CCUS	ACU
2004	87%	85%	48%	20%
2003	80%	90%	53%	40%
2002	44%	70%	65%	28%
2001	82%	75%	50%	32%
2000	70%	70%	60%	16%

INDIANA 9

Southeast – Bloomington, New Albany

Bordering the Ohio River to the south, the 9th shares socially conservative roots and, more recently, competitive politics with Indiana's other river valley district (the 8th). Manufacturing forms the economic foundation, although agriculture and retail trade also are prevalent in Indiana's southeastern quadrant. The district extends as far north as Monroe County to take in almost all of Bloomington.

The 9th's northeastern counties are seeing an increase in Cincinnati migrants, who have started to change the area from rural to slightly suburban. To the southwest, Clark and Floyd counties are growing as the Louisville metropolitan area grows. More of the 9th's residents live in Clark than in any of the district's other 19 counties. Opportunities — in manufacturing, retail and health care — in these growing areas have helped these counties stave off high unemployment and poverty levels that run well above the state average in some of the 9th's other counties. Elizabeth, in Harrison County south of Louisville, is home to a riverboat casino and resort that is a primary employer in the region. Factories also provide jobs for residents of the small and midsize cities, while corn and soybean fields occupy most of the rural landscape.

Bloomington is home to Indiana University and gives Monroe County a Democratic lean. While the university helps make Monroe one of Indiana's best-educated counties, the 9th as a whole is blue-collar with a low percentage of college graduates. Despite the district's Democratic heritage, the area's social conservatism propelled George W. Bush to double-digit victories here in the 2000 and 2004 presidential elections. In 2006, party control of the U.S. House seat flipped for the second straight election, with voters giving the Democratic winner 50 percent of the vote.

MAJOR INDUSTRY
Manufacturing, agriculture, retail

CITIES
Bloomington (pt.), 66,459; New Albany, 37,603; Jeffersonville, 27,362

NOTABLE
Larry Bird is from French Lick; The bicycling movie "Breaking Away" features Bloomington's love for cycling, which is celebrated each October during the Hilly Hundred Bicycle Weekend; The movie "Hoosiers" was based on the state championship success of the 1954 Milan High School basketball team.

IOWA

Gov. Chet Culver (D)

First elected: 2006
Length of term: 4 years
Term expires: 1/11
Salary: $130,000
Phone: (515) 281-5211

Residence West Des Moines
Born: Jan. 25, 1966; Washington, D.C.
Religion: Presbyterian
Family: Wife, Mari Culver; two children
Education: Virginia Polytechnic Institute and State U., B.A. 1988 (political science); Drake U., M.A. 1994 (teaching)
Career: Teacher; state justice department consumer and environmental analyst; campaign aide; lobbyist
Political highlights: Iowa secretary of state, 1999-2007

Election results:

2006 GENERAL

Chet Culver (D)	569,021	54.0%
Jim Nussle (R)	467,425	44.4%

Lt. Gov. Patty Judge (D)

First elected: 2006
Length of term: 4 years
Term expires: 1/11
Salary: $103,212
Phone: (515) 281-0225

LEGISLATURE

General Assembly: January-May

Senate: 50 members, 4-year terms
2007 ratios: 30 D, 20 R; 44 men, 6 women
Salary: $25,000
Phone: (515) 281-3371

House: 100 members, 2-year terms
2007 ratios: 54 D, 46 R; 72 men, 28 women
Salary: $25,000
Phone: (515) 281-3221

TERM LIMITS

Governor: No
Senate: No
House: No

URBAN STATISTICS

CITY	POPULATION
Des Moines	198,682
Cedar Rapids	120,758
Davenport	98,359
Sioux City	85,013
Waterloo	68,747

REGISTERED VOTERS

Unaffiliated	43%
Democrat	31%
Republican	30%

POPULATION

2006 population (est.)	2,982,085
2000 population	2,926,324
1990 population	2,776,755
Percent change (1990-2000)	+5.4%
Rank among states (2006)	30
Median age	36.6
Born in state	74.8%
Foreign born	3.1%
Violent crime rate	266/100,000
Poverty level	9.1%
Federal workers	18,928
Military	14,329

ELECTIONS

STATE ELECTION OFFICIAL
(515) 281-0145
DEMOCRATIC PARTY
(515) 244-7292
REPUBLICAN PARTY
(515) 282-8105

MISCELLANEOUS

Web: www.iowa.gov
Capital: Des Moines

U.S. CONGRESS

Senate: 1 Democrat, 1 Republican
House: 3 Democrats, 2 Republicans

2000 Census Statistics by District

DIST.	2004 VOTE FOR PRESIDENT BUSH	KERRY	WHITE	BLACK	ASIAN	HISP	MEDIAN INCOME	WHITE COLLAR	BLUE COLLAR	SERVICE INDUSTRY	OVER 64	UNDER 18	COLLEGE EDUCATION	RURAL	SQ. MILES
1	46%	53%	92%	4%	1%	2%	$38,727	56%	29%	15%	14%	25%	20%	34%	7,217
2	44	55	92	2	2	3	$40,121	59	27	14	13	24	25	34	7,566
3	49.7	49.6	90	3	2	3	$43,176	62	24	14	13	26	25	27	6,979
4	51	48	95	1	1	3	$38,242	56	29	15	16	24	20	49	15,760
5	60	39	94	1	1	4	$36,773	53	31	16	17	26	16	51	18,348
STATE	50	49	93	2	1	3	$39,469	57	28	15	15	25	21	39	55,869
U.S.	50.7	48.3	69	12	4	13	$41,994	60	25	15	12	26	24	21	3,537,438

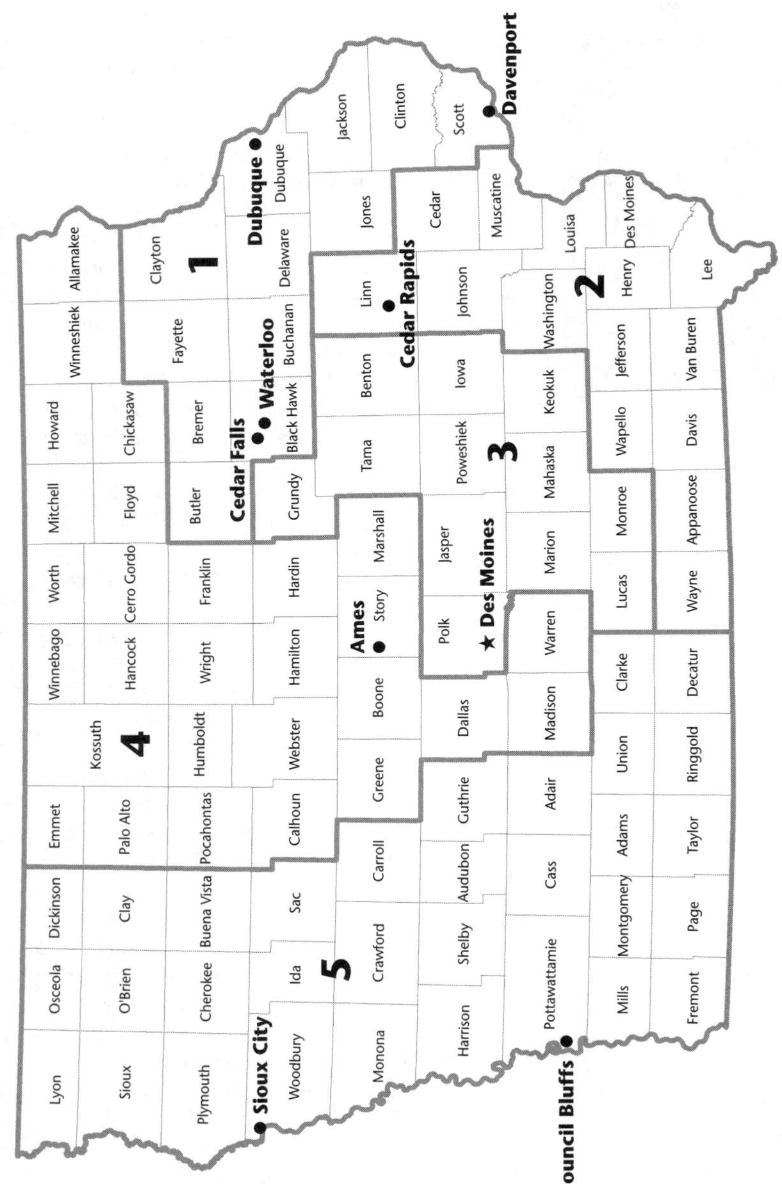
1
2
3
4
5
Dubuque
Waterloo
Cedar Falls
Cedar Rapids
Davenport
Des Moines
Ames
Sioux City
Council Bluffs
Allamakee
Winneshiek
Howard
Mitchell
Worth
Winnebago
Kossuth
Emmet
Dickinson
Osceola
Lyon
Clayton
Fayette
Chickasaw
Floyd
Cerro Gordo
Hancock
Palo Alto
Clay
O'Brien
Sioux
Bremer
Butler
Franklin
Wright
Humboldt
Pocahontas
Buena Vista
Cherokee
Plymouth
Dubuque
Delaware
Buchanan
Black Hawk
Grundy
Hardin
Hamilton
Webster
Calhoun
Sac
Ida
Woodbury
Jackson
Jones
Linn
Benton
Tama
Marshall
Story
Boone
Greene
Carroll
Crawford
Monona
Clinton
Scott
Cedar
Johnson
Iowa
Poweshiek
Jasper
Polk
Dallas
Guthrie
Audubon
Shelby
Harrison
Muscatine
Louisa
Washington
Keokuk
Mahaska
Marion
Warren
Madison
Adair
Cass
Pottawattamie
Des Moines
Henry
Jefferson
Wapello
Monroe
Lucas
Clarke
Union
Adams
Montgomery
Mills
Lee
Van Buren
Davis
Appanoose
Wayne
Decatur
Ringgold
Taylor
Page
Fremont

Sen. Charles E. Grassley (R)

CAPITOL OFFICE
224-3744
grassley.senate.gov
135 Hart 20510-1501; fax 224-6020

COMMITTEES
Agriculture, Nutrition & Forestry
Budget
Finance - ranking member
Judiciary

RESIDENCE
New Hartford

BORN
Sept. 17, 1933, New Hartford, Iowa

RELIGION
Baptist

FAMILY
Wife, Barbara Grassley; five children

EDUCATION
U. of Northern Iowa, B.A. 1955, M.A. 1956 (political science); U. of Iowa, attended 1957-58 (graduate studies)

CAREER
Farmer

POLITICAL HIGHLIGHTS
Republican nominee for Iowa House, 1956; Iowa House, 1959-75; U.S. House, 1975-81

ELECTION RESULTS

2004 GENERAL

Charles E. Grassley (R)	1,038,175	70.2%
Arthur Small (D)	412,365	27.9%
Christy Welty (LIBERT)	15,218	1.0%

2004 PRIMARY

Charles E. Grassley (R)	unopposed

PREVIOUS WINNING PERCENTAGES
1998 (68%); 1992 (70%); 1986 (66%); 1980 (54%); 1978 House Election (75%); 1976 House Election (57%); 1974 House Election (51%)

Elected 1980; 5th term

Grassley has an independent streak that drives the White House to distraction, and his more ideological Republican colleagues on the right often pressure him to stay with the program. But while his attitude can infuriate many in the GOP, his insistence on collaborating with Democrats often garners him legislative success.

With more than a quarter-century in Congress, and as the top-ranking Republican of the Finance Committee, his cooperation is key to advancing White House initiatives on taxes, Medicare, Social Security, trade and welfare. But he will do the president's bidding only to a point. He is an old-style fiscal conservative who demands the Bush administration's tax cuts be offset with revenue increases or spending cuts. The prairie populist in him lashes out at the Food and Drug Administration (FDA) for being too soft on big pharmaceutical companies, and he is a champion of government whistleblowers. And at the start of President Bush's second term in 2005, Grassley announced he didn't agree with Bush's approach to overhauling the Social Security program, arguing that Congress should be left to write the bill.

His rebellious streak is cushioned by a disarming candor, and his adversaries must find it tough to stay mad at him. Once, after concluding he was wrong to publicly question a proposed Bush tax cut on corporate dividends, Grassley said, "I think I should have kept my mouth shut."

At the same time, Grassley's drive to write bills through consensus often gets legislative results. As a senior member of the Judiciary Committee, Grassley in 2005 won enactment of laws to limit class action lawsuits and overhaul bankruptcy standards — after working for years to steer the bills through Congress. "The difference between being an ideologue and a realistic conservative is, I want to get things done. In order to get things done, you can't be a consistent ideologue," says Grassley.

When he was chairman of the Finance panel, Grassley was able to draw support for tax measures from moderates in both parties, especially Max Baucus of Montana, then the panel's top-ranking Democrat, who has been a constant ally. In a sea of bitter partisanship in the Senate, they operate as a nonpartisan island, sharing office staff and issuing joint statements.

Agreements between the pair helped clear the way for some of Bush's biggest victories in tax policy, beginning with the 10-year, $1.35 trillion tax cut of 2001. Grassley and Baucus were also central to passage of the administration's 2003 Medicare prescription drug benefit. And the two planned to work together during the 110th Congress (2007-08) — when their roles switched and Baucus became chairman — to fix the alternative minimum tax to keep it from ensnaring millions more middle-class taxpayers.

The senators' working relationship with the House got off to a rocky start in early 2007 after they tried to attach legislation for small-business tax breaks to a House-passed minimum wage bill. Grassley rejected House leaders' demands for an unencumbered wage bill. "It's one thing to live in political and ideological fantasy land, and it's quite another to make law," he said.

He is a social conservative who opposes abortion and gun control, and he votes the party line when it comes to approving conservative judges. On fiscal matters, he's not as conservative as some Republicans would like, but they can't argue with his personal thrift. For 23 years, he ordered only the complimentary side salad, roll and coffee at the Senate GOP weekly business lunch. When the party in 2003 started charging for those, he says he began arriving after the meal "so I don't have to watch my colleagues eat."

Grassley has led many high-profile investigations into government waste and misconduct. As chairman, he used the Finance panel's muscle to investigate government agencies, including the Internal Revenue Service and the Federal Bureau of Investigation. "Frankly, it takes too much time to pass legislation on some issues," he says. "With oversight, it's direct and immediate, and you see results much more quickly." In early 2007, he supported a probe into the firings of eight U.S. attorneys who alleged the administration fired them for political reasons.

For several years, he has targeted the FDA's drug approval office. "It's no secret that the FDA is too cozy with the drug industry," he once said. He was the most vocal opponent of Andrew C. von Eschenbach's confirmation as FDA commissioner in December 2006. "A vote for this nominee would be an endorsement of the stonewalling and disrespect he has shown for congressional oversight," he said. Grassley had been investigating the FDA's handling of an antibiotic called Ketek. He said von Eschenbach and the administration barred access to documents and FDA employees involved in the case.

Grassley gained allies in his battle with the FDA when the Democrats took control of Congress in 2007. In February, testifying at a House Energy and Commerce Committee hearing, he reflected that, "Sometimes I wonder why I spent two days in the car with President Bush, riding around in the cold of Iowa to help him get nominated in the year 2000."

In 2003 and 2004, he staged dramatic hearings with anonymous witnesses sitting behind screens recounting schemes by U.S. corporations to shelter billions of dollars from taxation. He also was a force behind the 1995 law making Congress abide by the same labor and safety rules as private business. He considers one of his greatest accomplishments a 1986 law allowing private citizens to sue in behalf of the government if they discover someone defrauding the government and to share in any damages awarded.

Grassley's devotion to fair and efficient government made him especially sensitive to criticism in 2006 that he helped advance a federal boondoggle by earmarking $50 million for an indoor, man-made "rainforest" on Iowa's flatlands. The project was the brainchild of a longtime Grassley donor. After it was ridiculed in the press, Grassley sponsored a provision tying the federal funds to matching investments from business or local governments.

The son of Waterloo-area farmers, Grassley has deep rural roots and is a fierce defender of farming interests. From his seats on the Agriculture and Finance committees, he has fought for federal incentives to boost corn-based ethanol use, for tax credits and subsidies for farmers, and to open new markets for U.S. commodities through free-trade agreements.

Grassley, who views himself as one of the few farmer-statesmen left in a country founded by them, often returns home to work the family corn and soybean fields. He has been known to haul grain with a cell phone tucked inside his cap so he can feel the vibrations of an incoming call.

He had dreamed of a career in politics since high school, though initially aimed only to make it to the Iowa House. After graduating from the University of Northern Iowa, he continued with graduate work there and at another Iowa university and paid the bills by working in a factory, where he was a Machinists union member. A few years later, he and his wife, Barbara, took over his family's grain and livestock operation.

At the age of 25, he began a 16-year stint in the Iowa House, where he became Appropriations Committee chairman. He was elected to the U.S. House in 1974, succeeding H.R. Gross, a revered Republican figure in the state who retired. Six years later, he moved to the Senate after unseating liberal Democrat John C. Culver. He has won with ease ever since.

Now in his 70s, Grassley runs almost daily, usually two to three miles at a 9 1/2 minute pace, a habit he adopted in 1999 as a New Year's resolution.

KEY VOTES

2006

- Yes Confirm Samuel A. Alito Jr. to the Supreme Court
- Yes Allow consideration of a bill to establish a $140 billion trust fund to compensate victims of asbestos exposure
- Yes Extend tax cuts for two years at a cost of $70 billion over five years
- No Overhaul immigration policy with border security, enforcement and guest worker program
- Yes Allow consideration of a bill to permanently repeal the estate tax
- No Urge President Bush to begin troop withdrawals from Iraq in 2006
- No Lift President Bush's restrictions on stem cell research funding
- Yes Authorize military tribunals for suspected terrorists

2005

- Yes Curb class action lawsuits by shifting them from state to federal courts
- Yes Allow confirmation vote on Priscilla R. Owen to the U.S. Court of Appeals for the 5th Circuit
- Yes Oppose mandatory emissions limits and block recognition of global warming as a threat
- Yes Approve free-trade pact with five Central American countries
- Yes Pass energy policy overhaul favored by President Bush emphasizing domestic oil and gas production
- Yes Shield gunmakers from lawsuits when their products are used in crimes
- Yes Ban torture of prisoners in U.S. custody
- Yes Renew 16 provisions of the Patriot Act
- Yes Allow final vote on opening the Arctic National Wildlife Refuge to oil and gas exploration

CQ VOTE STUDIES

	PARTY UNITY		PRESIDENTIAL SUPPORT	
	Support	Oppose	Support	Oppose
2006	93%	7%	87%	13%
2005	96%	4%	89%	11%
2004	97%	3%	94%	6%
2003	96%	4%	99%	1%
2002	88%	12%	95%	5%
2001	93%	7%	99%	1%
2000	94%	6%	42%	58%
1999	90%	10%	33%	67%
1998	86%	14%	39%	61%
1997	91%	9%	60%	40%

INTEREST GROUPS

	AFL-CIO	ADA	CCUS	ACU
2006	20%	5%	92%	88%
2005	14%	5%	100%	96%
2004	17%	20%	100%	96%
2003	0%	5%	100%	80%
2002	15%	10%	95%	95%
2001	13%	5%	100%	92%
2000	0%	0%	100%	96%
1999	0%	0%	94%	92%
1998	0%	5%	83%	80%
1997	0%	5%	100%	80%

Sen. Tom Harkin (D)

CAPITOL OFFICE
224-3254
harkin.senate.gov
731 Hart 20510-1502; fax 224-9369

COMMITTEES
Agriculture, Nutrition & Forestry - chairman
Appropriations
(Labor-HHS-Education - chairman)
Health, Education, Labor & Pensions
Small Business & Entrepreneurship

RESIDENCE
Cumming

BORN
Nov. 19, 1939, Cumming, Iowa

RELIGION
Roman Catholic

FAMILY
Wife, Ruth Harkin; two children

EDUCATION
Iowa State U., B.S. 1962 (government & economics); Catholic U. of America, J.D. 1972

MILITARY SERVICE
Navy, 1962-67; Naval Reserve, 1968-74

CAREER
Lawyer; congressional aide

POLITICAL HIGHLIGHTS
Democratic nominee for U.S. House, 1972; U.S. House, 1975-85; sought Democratic nomination for president, 1992

ELECTION RESULTS

2002 GENERAL		
Tom Harkin (D)	554,278	54.2%
Greg Ganske (R)	447,892	43.8%
Timothy A. Harthan (GREEN)	11,340	1.1%
2002 PRIMARY		
Tom Harkin (D)		unopposed

PREVIOUS WINNING PERCENTAGES
1996 (52%); 1990 (54%); 1984 (56%); 1982 House Election (59%); 1980 House Election (60%); 1978 House Election (59%); 1976 House Election (65%); 1974 House Election (51%)

Elected 1984; 4th term

The longest-serving Democratic senator in Iowa's history, Harkin finds his philosophical anchor in Franklin D. Roosevelt's activist view of government. He cites Roosevelt's proclamation: "Better the occasional faults of a government that lives in a spirit of charity than the constant omission of a government frozen in the ice of its own indifference."

In Harkin's view, government should intervene to help the poor, the disabled and family farmers. With his party now in control, Harkin is likely to push hard to fulfill his liberal vision. As chairman of the Agriculture, Nutrition and Forestry Committee, he will be in charge of crafting a new multi-year, multibillion-dollar farm bill for the Senate that satisfies both crop growers and environmentalists. He also chaired the panel for an 18-month period in 2001 and 2002, when the Democrats briefly controlled the Senate, and was a force behind the 2002 farm bill, which preserved many government subsidies.

Harkin's challenge in 2007 will be managing the allocation of federal money. The old-line commodities groups want to protect their subsidies; new groups representing specialty-crop growers will be on the scene; and ethanol and conservation initiatives will have a higher profile than before. In Iowa, corn and soybean production rules, and Harkin says he supports continued commodity-crop subsidies. At the same time, environmental responsibility is close to Harkin's heart. He was the creator of the Conservation Security Program in the 2002 farm law, which pays farmers for following specific land and water conservation practices, and he says strengthening the farm law's conservation title is one of his top priorities. Harkin is also a champion of disaster relief for crops lost to drought, flood and fire.

He will have to deal too with the usual tug of war within his own party between farm-state senators who support stronger land conservation efforts and urban liberals who want more money for school lunches and low-income food programs. Harkin also chairs the Appropriations panel's Labor, Health and Human Services, and Education Subcommittee, which oversees the largest of the 12 spending bills. Harkin shares many of the priorities of former Chairman Arlen Specter of Pennsylvania, including health care policy and increased funding for the National Institutes of Health. Working together, Harkin and Specter doubled funding for medical research at the NIH between 1998 and 2003. Harkin is also a champion of funding for special education programs.

Specter and Harkin joined forces on another major health initiative, a bill to lift Bush's restrictions on embryonic stem cell research, which some scientists say holds promise in the treatment of disease. After years of fruitless attempts, the pair saw the legislation pass in 2006 only to draw the first veto of Bush's presidency. An override attempt failed.

Harkin is a good friend of organized labor, often drawing 100 percent ratings on the AFL-CIO's annual scorecard. But he occasionally votes for free-trade agreements in deference to Iowa farmers eager to boost their exports. Also with his farmers in mind, Harkin in 2005 joined with ag-state Republicans to win a provision in the energy bill requiring refiners to boost renewable fuels such as corn-based ethanol to 7.5 billion gallons by 2012, a move helped along by steep increases in gasoline prices at the time. Ethanol is key to Harkin's vision of making agriculture a vital component of the nation's energy security.

While he promotes the fuel potential of Iowa corn, Harkin finds a more delectable use for it in his Senate office, where he has kept a vintage red-

and-white popcorn maker by the front door since 1986. Visitors, aides and Harkin regularly help themselves.

Harkin's signal legislative achievement was the 1990 Americans with Disabilities Act, which extended broad civil rights protections to an estimated 54 million Americans with mental and physical disabilities. Harkin says he was inspired by his deaf brother, Frank, and he gave part of his floor speech in sign language in Frank's honor.

The son of a coal miner, Harkin grew up in a small, crowded house in Cumming, Iowa, a town, as he puts it, "with no stop lights, no police and no crime. . . . In summer, there was always something to pick and eat — wild plums along the road, huge raspberry and blackberry patches along the railroad tracks, black walnuts by the gunnysackful in the fall." As a boy, he liked to watch the coal-powered train engines as they passed his house; on Halloween night, he and his pals had a ritual of pushing over all of Cumming's outhouses, until one neighbor got wise and built his of concrete.

Life for Harkin took a tragic turn when he turned 10 and lost his mother, a Slovenian immigrant. After working his way through college and law school, Harkin spent five years as a Navy pilot during the Vietnam War. Being a pilot fulfilled a lifelong dream: Harkin still holds a pilot's license.

Though interested in politics since college — he was president of Young Democrats at Iowa State — he stumbled into the field as a career. In 1968, out of the Navy and out of work, he was watching TV over a beer and a burger at a diner when President Lyndon B. Johnson startled him by announcing that he would not seek a second term. The next morning, a friend working for the Iowa Democratic Party offered him a job. "I thought, 'I'm going broke, I've got no prospects for the future. Why not?' " Harkin recalls.

In 1969, he was hired by Iowa Democratic Rep. Neal Smith as an aide on the House select committee investigating the U.S. military's progress in Vietnam. He made a name for himself with his discovery of South Vietnam's "tiger cages." Outwitting a government official on a guided tour of a prison camp, Harkin found, behind a hidden door, hundreds of men, women and children crammed into underground cells, with open grates on top through which guards poured skin-searing doses of lime. Harkin photographed the political prisoners and tape-recorded their stories.

Skittish members of the committee sought to suppress his documentation of abuses by America's ally. But Harkin insisted on going public, and his photographs and story in Life magazine energized the anti-war movement, and forced South Vietnam to shutter the tiger cages. The move cost the 30-year-old Harkin his Hill job.

In 1972, Harkin ran for the U.S. House against entrenched GOP incumbent William Scherle. He attracted publicity with his "work days," toiling alongside farmers, teachers and welfare caseworkers. He lost narrowly but tried again and toppled Scherle by a slim margin in 1974. In four House re-elections, he captured about 60 percent of the vote.

His Senate campaigns have been tougher. He won his seat in 1984 by ousting GOP Sen. Roger W. Jepsen with 56 percent of the vote. In 1990, his Republican challenger, Rep. Tom Tauke, accused Harkin of abusing congressional mailing privileges and voting for excessive spending. Harkin eventually won by 9 percentage points. In 1996, he won a third term by defeating GOP Rep. Jim Ross Lightfoot by 5 percentage points.

The farm bill's enactment just before the 2002 elections helped him stave off a tough challenge from Republican Rep. Greg Ganske. Considered one of the most vulnerable incumbents because of Iowa's swing politics, Harkin defeated Ganske by 10 points.

Harkin's four terms in the Senate far surpass the second-place Democrat in Iowa history — George W. Jones, who served 10-plus years (1848-59).

KEY VOTES

2006

No Confirm Samuel A. Alito Jr. to the Supreme Court
Yes Allow consideration of a bill to establish a $140 billion trust fund to compensate victims of asbestos exposure
No Extend tax cuts for two years at a cost of $70 billion over five years
Yes Overhaul immigration policy with border security, enforcement and guest worker program
No Allow consideration of a bill to permanently repeal the estate tax
Yes Urge President Bush to begin troop withdrawals from Iraq in 2006
Yes Lift President Bush's restrictions on stem cell research funding
No Authorize military tribunals for suspected terrorists

2005

No Curb class action lawsuits by shifting them from state to federal courts
Yes Allow confirmation vote on Priscilla R. Owen to the U.S. Court of Appeals for the 5th Circuit
No Oppose mandatory emissions limits and block recognition of global warming as a threat
No Approve free-trade pact with five Central American countries
Yes Pass energy policy overhaul favored by President Bush emphasizing domestic oil and gas production
No Shield gunmakers from lawsuits when their products are used in crimes
Yes Ban torture of prisoners in U.S. custody
No Renew 16 provisions of the Patriot Act
No Allow final vote on opening the Arctic National Wildlife Refuge to oil and gas exploration

CQ VOTE STUDIES

	PARTY UNITY		PRESIDENTIAL SUPPORT	
	Support	Oppose	Support	Oppose
2006	95%	5%	46%	54%
2005	98%	2%	27%	73%
2004	94%	6%	52%	48%
2003	98%	2%	46%	54%
2002	92%	8%	69%	31%
2001	97%	3%	63%	37%
2000	97%	3%	92%	8%
1999	97%	3%	91%	9%
1998	98%	2%	88%	12%
1997	92%	8%	87%	13%

INTEREST GROUPS

	AFL-CIO	ADA	CCUS	ACU
2006	100%	100%	36%	8%
2005	100%	100%	33%	4%
2004	100%	100%	59%	8%
2003	100%	95%	32%	15%
2002	100%	80%	45%	15%
2001	100%	100%	38%	8%
2000	75%	95%	57%	4%
1999	89%	100%	47%	4%
1998	100%	95%	50%	5%
1997	71%	85%	70%	12%

Rep. Bruce Braley (D)

CAPITOL OFFICE
225-2911
braley.house.gov
1408 Longworth 20515-1501; fax 226-5051

COMMITTEES
Oversight & Government Reform
Small Business
(Contracting & Technology - chairman)
Transportation & Infrastructure

RESIDENCE
Waterloo

BORN
Oct. 30, 1957, Grinnell, Iowa

RELIGION
Presbyterian

FAMILY
Wife, Carolyn Braley; three children

EDUCATION
Iowa State U., B.A. 1980 (political science); U. of Iowa, J.D. 1983

CAREER
Lawyer

POLITICAL HIGHLIGHTS
No previous office

ELECTION RESULTS

2006 GENERAL		
Bruce Braley (D)	113,724	55.0%
Mike Whalen (R)	89,471	43.3%
James F. Hill (PIR)	2,184	1.1%
2006 PRIMARY		
Bruce Braley (D)	10,489	36.1%
Rick Dickinson (D)	9,971	34.3%
Bill Gluba (D)	7,453	25.6%
Denny Heath (D)	1,161	4.0%

Elected 2006; 1st term

Although Braley has spent the past two decades as a trial lawyer, he knows what work is like outside the courtroom. Braley said he applied for his first job in third grade and has been working ever since. He has delivered newspapers, baled hay, detassled corn, worked at a grain elevator and driven dump trucks. To help pay his way through college and law school, he worked as a restaurant server and in highway maintenance.

Not surprisingly, he is a strong supporter of the labor movement and voted early in 2007 to increase the federal minimum wage and to make it easier for unions to organize employees. On the day the House passed the union organizing bill, Braley donned the same pair of boots he wore working for a county road department one summer in the early 1980s.

Braley gained a seat on the Transportation and Infrastructure Committee, where he may have a better understanding than many of his colleagues of what it actually takes to build a road. He also sits on Small Business, where he chairs the Contracting and Technology Subcommittee.

Affordable health insurance is also a concern for Braley. In early 2007, he voted to allow the federal government to negotiate lower drug prices for Medicare.

Braley proudly claims a family heritage that includes 150 years in Iowa agriculture. His first bill as a congressman would authorize education grants to train technicians in the fields of bioenergy and other agriculture-based renewable energy resources.

Braley won the seat of former GOP Rep. Jim Nussle, who ran for governor and lost. In the general election, he faced GOP businessman Mike Whalen. Braley's campaign referred to Whalen — who owns hotels and restaurants — as a "millionaire CEO," while Whalen described Braley as a "liberal trial lawyer" who would do more "suing" than "doing."

District voters have Democratic leanings and favored Sen. John Kerry over President Bush in the 2004 presidential election. So Braley's opposition to Bush's Iraq policy and his support for increasing the federal minimum wage resonated in the district. He won by 12 percentage points.

IOWA 1

East — Davenport, Waterloo, Dubuque

Taking in half of Iowa's Mississippi River counties as well as farmland to the west, the 1st is dominated by three midsize industrial cities: Dubuque and Davenport on the river, and Waterloo in inland Black Hawk County.

Located at the 1st's southern tip, Davenport and Bettendorf make up Iowa's half of the Quad Cities. Davenport is a district health care hub. Its downtown is in the midst of a river redevelopment project, which the city hopes will stimulate the local economy. Already drawing in revenue are the area's minor league baseball team — the Swing of the Quad Cities — and the five-story high pedestrian skybridge that offers visitors a sweeping view of the Mississippi River.

North of the Quad Cities and built against the bluffs facing the Mississippi River, Dubuque is Iowa's oldest city. Once dependent on manufacturing and meatpacking, the city has experienced growth in the finance, insurance and information technology industries.

West along Route 20, Waterloo diversified its traditional meatpacking and farm implement industries to include finance and insurance businesses. Black Hawk County, which also includes Cedar Falls and the University of Northern Iowa, has a strong Democratic base from its academic and labor workforce.

There are many GOP voters in the rural farmland between the three main cities, but overall, Democrats outnumber Republicans. The GOP's Jim Nussle won only 41 percent of his former district's 2006 gubernatorial vote.

MAJOR INDUSTRY
Farm machinery, meatpacking, health care, agriculture

CITIES
Davenport, 98,359; Waterloo, 68,747; Dubuque, 57,686; Cedar Falls, 36,145

NOTABLE
The National Farm Toy Museum in Dyersville.

Rep. Dave Loebsack (D)

CAPITOL OFFICE
225-6576
loebsack.house.gov
1513 Longworth 20515-1502; fax 226-1278

COMMITTEES
Armed Services
Education & Labor

RESIDENCE
Mount Vernon

BORN
Dec. 23, 1952, Sioux City, Iowa

RELIGION
Methodist

FAMILY
Wife, Teresa Loebsack; four children

EDUCATION
Iowa State U., B.S. 1974 (political science), M.A. 1976 (political science); U. of California, Davis, Ph.D. 1985 (political science)

CAREER
Professor

POLITICAL HIGHLIGHTS
No previous office

ELECTION RESULTS

2006 GENERAL		
Dave Loebsack (D)	107,683	51.3%
Jim Leach (R)	101,707	48.5%
2006 PRIMARY		
Dave Loebsack (D) - write-in	501	34.9%
Other write-ins	936	65.1%

Elected 2006; 1st term

Loebsack taught college-level foreign policy courses for 24 years and has traveled extensively overseas — a background that informs his opposition to the Bush administration's Iraq policy. As a candidate, he called for a gradual withdrawal of troops and the removal of Defense Secretary Donald H. Rumsfeld, who resigned right after a 2006 election in which Loebsack and other opponents of the Iraq War were victorious.

Loebsack (LOBE-sack) brings his foreign policy credentials to bear on the Armed Services Committee. In 2007, he backed a war funding bill requiring withdrawal of U.S. combat troops from Iraq by August 2008.

In keeping with his experience, Loebsack was appointed to the Education and Labor Committee. Iowa's 2nd District is honeycombed with colleges and universities — including the University of Iowa and Cornell College, a small school where Loebsack taught. Loebsack vowed during the campaign to protect student financial aid. Voting in January 2007 to cut interest rates for undergraduates with subsidized loans, Loebsack recalled his own poverty and his reliance on loans and grants to pay for his education.

Loebsack supports "greater transparency" in government, including an overhaul of campaign laws that would include public financing of campaigns. "I think we've got to get it to the point where we don't have to worry about big money influencing campaigns in particular," he said.

Iowa has one of the nation's largest percentages of elderly residents, so Social Security and Medicare are important to Loebsack. He says the 2003 Medicare prescription drug law is confusing and must be simplified if not scrapped. He opposes private accounts under Social Security and supports increasing to $150,000 the wage level subject to the payroll tax.

Loebsack was one of the 2006 election's unlikeliest winners. He upset 15-term Republican Jim Leach, a mild-mannered moderate widely respected in both parties who eschewed attacks on Loebsack. Despite Leach's image as a GOP iconoclast, Loebsack apparently convinced enough voters that a vote for Leach was tantamount to endorsing continued Republican control of Congress. Loebsack won by about 5,900 votes.

IOWA 2

Southeast — Cedar Rapids, Iowa City

The Democratic-leaning 2nd spreads across corn fields to take in 15 southeastern Iowa counties, bending from Cedar Rapids in its north to Wayne County in its southwest.

Cedar Rapids, in Linn County, is the state's second-most-populous city. Long a grain-processing center, the city now is home to a large Quaker Food and Beverage plant. Recently, the local economy has diversified as technology firms have moved to the area south of Cedar Rapids between it and Iowa City. Defense electronics and telecommunications equipment firms are among the fastest-growing sectors here.

Iowa City, in Johnson County, is home to the University of Iowa, as well as a growing number of technology companies and a strong health care industry. The academic community gives the city a strong liberal tilt.

The 2nd's other population center runs along the Mississippi River in the southeast, in Des Moines and Lee counties. Unions retain some influence here, but a growing ethanol industry and riverboat casino-based tourism now contribute to the economy. The land in the 2nd's southwestern arm is predominately rural, depending mainly on corn, tomatoes, pork and soybeans. With the exception of Wapello County (Ottumwa), this rural area leans Republican.

Johnson, Linn and the river counties give the 2nd a decidedly Democratic tilt. Democrat Chet Culver's three best statewide counties in the 2006 gubernatorial race were here, and he received 60 percent of the 2nd's vote.

MAJOR INDUSTRY
Technology, telecommunications, health care, grain processing, higher education

CITIES
Cedar Rapids, 120,758; Iowa City, 62,220

NOTABLE
The Cedar Rapids Museum of Art houses the largest collection of art by "American Gothic" painter Grant Wood.

Rep. Leonard L. Boswell (D)

CAPITOL OFFICE
225-3806
rep.boswell.ia03@mail.house.gov
www.house.gov/boswell
1427 Longworth 20515-1503; fax 225-5608

COMMITTEES
Agriculture
(Livestock, Dairy & Poultry - chairman)
Select Intelligence
Transportation & Infrastructure

RESIDENCE
Des Moines

BORN
Jan. 10, 1934, Harrison County, Mo.

RELIGION
Community of Christ

FAMILY
Wife, Dody Boswell; three children

EDUCATION
Graceland College, B.A. 1969 (business administration)

MILITARY SERVICE
Army, 1956-76

CAREER
Farmer; Army officer

POLITICAL HIGHLIGHTS
Iowa Senate, 1985-97 (president, 1992-97); sought Democratic nomination for U.S. House, 1986; Iowa Democratic Central Committee, 1992-96; Democratic nominee for lieutenant governor, 1994

ELECTION RESULTS

2006 GENERAL		
Leonard L. Boswell (D)	114,558	51.8%
Jeff Lamberti (R)	103,166	46.6%
Helen Meyers (SW)	3,426	1.5%
2006 PRIMARY		
Leonard L. Boswell (D)	31,602	98.8%
write-ins (D)	391	1.2%
2004 GENERAL		
Leonard L. Boswell (D)	168,007	55.2%
Stan Thompson (R)	136,099	44.7%

PREVIOUS WINNING PERCENTAGES
2002 (53%); 2000 (63%); 1998 (57%); 1996 (49%)

Elected 1996; 6th term

Livestock farmer Boswell gained the gavel of the Agriculture subcommittee on livestock and dairy after his party took control of the House in 2007, just as Congress was embarking on the first major revamp of farm policy in six years. As a subcommittee chairman, he should have a significant impact on the issues he and his rural Iowa district care about the most. Boswell raises about 140 cows a year and also grows corn and soybeans.

Raised on a tenant farm, Boswell is a believer in government support for farmers. He credits farm subsidies with the relatively affordable bounty available at most U.S. supermarkets. "Some of our urban neighbors think farmers shouldn't get help," he says. "But we all have to eat."

An issue in the 2007 farm bill rewrite is the fuel-versus-feed debate. Livestock owners worry that the ethanol boom will mean a jump in corn prices and more expensive feed. Boswell acknowledges that the issue has "got us all stirred up," but he says "the market will adjust," an opinion shared by committee Chairman Collin C. Peterson, a Minnesota Democrat. "There's a new era in agriculture with alternative fuels, and it's the right thing for the environment," Boswell said in a 2007 interview. "It's also the right thing to get out of the clutches of OPEC. I feel very confident that we'll work our way through this."

He was the only Iowan to vote against the last six-year farm bill rewrite passed by the House in 2001. He said it did not provide enough for small family farms and it did not take steps to minimize livestock ownership by meatpackers in order to improve market access for smaller operators. But Boswell supported the final legislation the following year.

On non-farm issues, Boswell trends more conservative than many in his party. He belongs to the Blue Dog Coalition of fiscally conservative Democrats. In the 109th Congress (2005-06), he voted with his party 80 percent of the time on issues that polarized the parties, and he backed President Bush's policies about half the time, a relatively high rate for a Democrat.

With his calm demeanor, Boswell, now in his early 70s, is from a more civil era in politics, and so he was the unlikely actor in one of 2006's nastier campaigns. Viewing him as vulnerable, national Republicans targeted him for defeat that year. They put up a strong challenger in Jeff Lamberti, the GOP president of the Iowa Senate, and poured thousands of dollars in negative ads into the district. Information about Boswell's attendance at Select Intelligence Committee briefings was leaked, and Republicans accused him of missing meetings vital to national security.

The Democratic Congressional Campaign Committee stepped into the race with its own large expenditures on negative advertising against Lamberti, including a commercial that tried to link him to factory farms that are bad for the environment. Boswell called the contest "one of the worst experiences I've ever been through." With the backlash against the Republican president and Congress that year, Boswell prevailed, but with only 52 percent of the vote, an unimpressive showing for a five-term incumbent. The campaign arm of the House Democratic Caucus early in 2007 picked Boswell's district as a 2008 "Frontline" race to get additional party support.

He may have been hurt by his vote for the 2002 Iraq War resolution. In 2006, he was one of 42 Democrats who voted with the Republican majority against setting a date for the withdrawal of troops. After the 2006 election, Boswell opposed Bush's plan to send more than 21,000 additional U.S. combat troops to Iraq. "As one member of Congress who voted in support of the Iraq resolution of 2002, I recognize the pretext for going to war was based on faulty, misleading intelligence," Boswell said on the House floor in early 2007. "I cannot reverse that vote, but I can no longer acquiesce to a failed and tragic military exercise in Iraq."

Boswell has an interest in federal support for law enforcement. In the 109th Congress, he pushed a bill to give states $300 million to strengthen sex offender registries, and another to secure more money to crack down on methamphetamine labs plaguing rural areas.

Boswell's parents, tenant farmers in Iowa during the Great Depression, were able to buy land as a result of subsidies created by President Franklin D. Roosevelt. "Roosevelt was a very special person to them and to me," says Boswell, a lifelong Democrat who rebuffed overtures in the early 2000s to switch to the GOP.

In 1956, Boswell married and was drafted into the Army, then went to officer training school. "Here I was, this green farm guy coming into all of this," he recalls. "Someone said, 'Do you want to go into flight school?' And I thought, 'Whoa, I've always wanted to fly airplanes!' " He became a lieutenant colonel and ultimately served 20 years. He did two one-year tours of duty as an assault helicopter pilot in Vietnam, earning two Distinguished Flying Crosses and two Bronze Stars.

After his military service, Boswell returned home to raise cattle on 475 acres in his native Decatur County. He also earned a college degree in business administration and became involved in local politics, spending 12 years in the Iowa Senate and rising to become its president.

In 1996, Boswell ran for the U.S. House, seeking the seat of Republican Jim Ross Lightfoot, who was running for the Senate. He won the primary easily. In the general election, he won the endorsement of the Iowa Farm Bureau, and eked out a win against Mike Mahaffey, a county prosecutor and former state GOP chairman.

The breadth of his life experience set him apart from his classmates when, at 63, he arrived in Congress in 1997, the oldest House freshman that year.

Redistricting in 2002 compelled him to move to Des Moines. In the 2002 race against Republican lawyer Stan Thompson, Boswell was attacked as a liberal who opposed school prayer. He used his hefty campaign war chest to counter campaign appearances by Bush administration heavyweights in behalf of Thompson and won with 53 percent of the vote.

In 2004, Boswell broke a pledge to serve only four terms by running for and winning a fifth. In 2005, he spent 11 weeks recovering from a noncancerous tumor in his stomach and lost 70 pounds.

KEY VOTES

2006

No Stop broadband companies from favoring select Internet traffic
Yes Affirm U.S. commitment to war in Iraq and reject setting a withdrawal date for troops
No Repeal requirement for bilingual ballots at the polls
Yes Permit U.S. sale of civilian nuclear technology to India
Yes Build a 700-mile fence on the U.S.-Mexico border to curb illegal crossings
Yes Permit warrantless wiretaps of suspected terrorists

2005

? Intervene in the life-support case of Terri Schiavo
Yes Lift President Bush's restrictions on stem cell research funding
Yes Prohibit FBI access to library and bookstore records
No Approve free-trade pact with five Central American countries
Yes Pass energy policy overhaul favored by President Bush emphasizing domestic oil and gas production
? End mandatory preservation of habitat of endangered animal and plant species
Yes Ban torture of prisoners in U.S. custody

CQ VOTE STUDIES

	PARTY UNITY		PRESIDENTIAL SUPPORT	
	Support	Oppose	Support	Oppose
2006	78%	22%	47%	53%
2005	82%	18%	39%	61%
2004	83%	17%	39%	61%
2003	85%	15%	42%	58%
2002	81%	19%	40%	60%

INTEREST GROUPS

	AFL-CIO	ADA	CCUS	ACU
2006	86%	70%	67%	44%
2005	93%	60%	55%	32%
2004	87%	80%	55%	20%
2003	80%	80%	45%	23%
2002	78%	80%	55%	32%

IOWA 3

Central and east central – Des Moines

Squeezed between the state's other four districts, the 3rd is Iowa's only district not to border another state and is in some ways a microcosm of the Hawkeye state. It includes relatively well-off urban and suburban areas, as well as rural counties, industrial cities and scattered towns still yearning for economic development.

Almost two-thirds of the district's residents live in Des Moines or surrounding Polk County. Unlike the rest of Iowa's urban centers, the capital city is not dependent on agriculture and the economy is stable without it. The city is an anchor for insurance and financial companies. Some firms, such as Wells Fargo Financial, have headquarters in the city, and others have regional offices in the metropolitan area. A bustling health care industry complements the smaller, but significant, manufacturing industry. The city's black and Hispanic residents help make the 3rd Iowa's most minority-populated district, although whites still compose 90 percent of the district's population.

Perhaps the only thing growing faster in Des Moines than its economy is its skyline. Opened in 2005, the Iowa Events Center — a four-venue, multipurpose complex under one interconnected roof — is already bolstering the area's economy. The city's three miles of skywalk allows residents to move quickly between new downtown developments, commercial centers and historical areas, such as East Village, where the state Capitol is located.

The rest of the 3rd takes on a more rural flavor, and no county outside of Polk has more than 40,000 residents. Although George W. Bush won a slight plurality of the 3rd's vote in the 2004 presidential election, the influence of Des Moines and surrounding Polk County gives the 3rd its slight Democratic lean overall. Democrat Chet Culver took 54 percent of the district's vote in the 2006 gubernatorial election.

MAJOR INDUSTRY
Insurance, health care, manufacturing, government

CITIES
Des Moines, 198,682; West Des Moines (pt.), 42,525; Urbandale (pt.), 28,745; Ankeny, 27,117; Newton, 15,579

NOTABLE
Each year, more than one million tourists visit the Amana Colonies, seven villages originally settled in 1855 by the Community of True Inspiration.

Rep. Tom Latham (R)

CAPITOL OFFICE
225-5476
tom.latham@mail.house.gov
www.house.gov/latham
2447 Rayburn 20515-1504; fax 225-3301

COMMITTEES
Appropriations

RESIDENCE
Alexander

BORN
July 14, 1948, Hampton, Iowa

RELIGION
Lutheran

FAMILY
Wife, Kathy Latham; three children

EDUCATION
Wartburg College, attended 1967; Iowa State U., attended 1967-70 (agriculture & business)

CAREER
Seed company executive; insurance agency marketing representative; insurance agent; bank teller

POLITICAL HIGHLIGHTS
Franklin County Republican Party chairman, 1984-91

ELECTION RESULTS

2006 GENERAL		
Tom Latham (R)	120,984	57.3%
Selden E. Spencer (D)	90,359	42.8%
2006 PRIMARY		
Tom Latham (R)		unopposed
2004 GENERAL		
Tom Latham (R)	181,294	60.9%
Paul W. Johnson (D)	116,121	39.0%

PREVIOUS WINNING PERCENTAGES
2002 (55%); 2000 (69%); 1998 (99%); 1996 (65%); 1994 (61%)

Elected 1994; 7th term

Latham is a close ally of House Minority Leader John A. Boehner and a member of the Appropriations Committee. He can be counted on to be loyal to the GOP leadership in its battles with the Democrats over national policy, while legislatively he pursues a mostly local agenda focused on the agrarian economy of central Iowa, home to some of the country's most productive farmland. Latham and his brothers own three farms and a seed company.

Latham backed his good friend Boehner, an Ohioan, in a ferocious intraparty contest against Roy Blunt of Missouri for majority leader in early 2006, when Republicans still controlled the House. In an upset, Boehner narrowly defeated Blunt, who was majority whip at the time and the presumed favorite for the top job. Boehner is often found just off the House floor holding court with Latham and four other members of his "kitchen cabinet," a strategy committee that worked with Boehner during his leadership campaign.

As the only Iowan on the Appropriations Committee, Latham looks out for the entire state delegation. "I have a tremendous amount of pressure from all five districts . . . to help out with their projects," says Latham, who sits on the powerful spending panel's Agriculture Subcommittee.

Latham has directed millions of dollars to the National Animal Disease Center, a livestock health research facility in Ames in his district. The facility — which Latham says is "like the CDC [Centers for Disease Control], only for livestock" — tests for diseases such as mad cow and anthrax.

In the 109th Congress (2005-06), Latham obtained the last $59 million of a $462 million modernization of the center, one of the largest public works projects in Iowa history. Ames is home to several other federally funded agriculture research facilities as well, and Latham has been able to direct funds their way, including to a lab that researches the use of corn and soybeans for pharmaceuticals. One of his priorities in the 110th Congress (2007-08) is securing funds for a renewable fuels facility to develop cellulose ethanol.

Latham has no apologies for his earmarks — provisions quietly slipped into spending bills to fund special projects in lawmakers' districts. The Democratic leadership and Republican conservatives have clamored for public disclosure of the sponsors of earmarks, though neither political party has gone so far as to try to stop them.

When it comes to parts of the budget not earmarked for Iowa, Latham considers himself a fiscal conservative. He wants to see Congress roll back federal regulations and taxes, to create "a smaller and smarter federal government." He has supported President Bush's tax cut proposals, and he pushed for permanent repeal of the estate tax, which he says forces farm families to sell their assets rather than passing them down.

Another of his priorities is improving military health care. Iowa has one of the highest percentages of National Guard and reserve troops that have been deployed to Iraq. In 2005, he partnered with Republican Sen. Lindsey Graham of South Carolina on a bill to give Guard and reserve troops the same health benefits as regular duty soldiers. Critics said it would add to the military's skyrocketing health care costs, but the measure passed after a heated debate, as part of the annual defense bill for 2006.

In early 2007, Latham sponsored legislation, which had died in the previous Congress, to allow veterans to get routine medical care from a local doctor or hospital rather than traveling great distances to a Department of Veterans Affairs facility. Known as the VALOR bill, Latham said the measure would relieve pressure on stressed VA clinics.

Early in 2007, responding to the news that death benefits for a servicewoman from his district who was killed in Iraq were not going to her daughter, Latham introduced a bill to rectify the matter.

Though he has been a steadfast backer of the war in Iraq, Latham expresses dissatisfaction. "There is no question that there's been some real mistakes made," he said. In 2007, however, he supported Bush's plan to send more than 21,000 additional U.S. combat troops to Iraq.

Latham grew up doing farm chores and helping in the family seed business. He stayed close to home for his first 20 years, attending Wartburg College about 50 miles east of his hometown of Alexander and then going to Iowa State University, about 60 miles south in Ames. Today, he jokes that he lives in the suburbs — his home is a mile from downtown Alexander, with a population of less than 200.

He says his interest in politics was sparked by a trip he took in 1990, as a member of a farm delegation that visited Russia and Poland. He was appalled at the primitive agricultural methods and machinery in the former communist countries, whose governments, he said, not only had mismanaged the economy but had "destroyed individual freedom and dignity." He remembers one Polish farmer who tearfully told him that farmers hadn't owned their land since the Nazis seized it in World War II.

Back in Iowa, Latham chaired the Franklin County Republican Party for seven years but rebuffed entreaties to run for the legislature because the seasonal nature of the seed business conflicted with legislative sessions. In 1994, however, when GOP Rep. Fred Grandy gave up the 5th District seat to seek the governorship, Latham decided to run. He was a good fit for the district in a strong GOP year, and he breezed to election.

He was returned to the House easily in three subsequent elections, but in 2002 new district lines drafted by a nonpartisan state agency made the district more competitive. The new map put Latham's home in the 4th District, while more than half his constituents lived in the 5th District.

Latham decided to run in the 4th anyway. He was well-known to many of the new district's residents, owing to his days as a traveling farm seed salesman. He wound up winning by almost 12 percentage points against Democrat John Norris, a former state party chairman. He cruised to re-election in 2004, winning by almost 22 points. In 2006, he was re-elected by a still-comfortable margin of more than 14 points. Latham has been mentioned as a possible contender in 2008 for Iowa Sen. Tom Harkin's seat should the Democrat appear vulnerable.

KEY VOTES

2006

No Stop broadband companies from favoring select Internet traffic
Yes Affirm U.S. commitment to war in Iraq and reject setting a withdrawal date for troops
Yes Repeal requirement for bilingual ballots at the polls
Yes Permit U.S. sale of civilian nuclear technology to India
Yes Build a 700-mile fence on the U.S.-Mexico border to curb illegal crossings
Yes Permit warrantless wiretaps of suspected terrorists

2005

Yes Intervene in the life-support case of Terri Schiavo
No Lift President Bush's restrictions on stem cell research funding
No Prohibit FBI access to library and bookstore records
Yes Approve free-trade pact with five Central American countries
Yes Pass energy policy overhaul favored by President Bush emphasizing domestic oil and gas production
Yes End mandatory preservation of habitat of endangered animal and plant species
Yes Ban torture of prisoners in U.S. custody

CQ VOTE STUDIES

	PARTY UNITY		PRESIDENTIAL SUPPORT	
	Support	Oppose	Support	Oppose
2006	95%	5%	97%	3%
2005	96%	4%	87%	13%
2004	92%	8%	88%	12%
2003	95%	5%	93%	7%
2002	92%	8%	85%	15%

INTEREST GROUPS

	AFL-CIO	ADA	CCUS	ACU
2006	21%	5%	100%	84%
2005	20%	5%	93%	84%
2004	20%	10%	100%	72%
2003	13%	5%	97%	84%
2002	11%	5%	100%	88%

IOWA 4

North and central – Ames, Mason City

The vast 4th takes up most of the state's northern border and dips deeply south, past the state capital of Des Moines (in the 3rd District), to reach the Republican-leaning counties of Dallas, Madison and Warren.

Ames, nestled along the Skunk River, is about 30 miles north of the capital city and represents the district's largest population center. It is home to Iowa State University, and the university has become a renowned agricultural economics institution. The university's influence gives the city a Democratic lean, although surrounding Story County only gave John Kerry 52 percent of its 2004 presidential vote.

Rural, farming communities and smaller cities make up the rest of the 4th. Marshalltown, east of Ames, is home to a large meatpacking industry, which has brought many Hispanic immigrants to the city. Mason City, the 4th's second-most-populous city, is heavily dependent on manufacturing. Fort Dodge in Webster County is home to trucking firms, gypsum factories and veterinary pharmaceuticals. Southwest of Ames, Dallas County is a big exception to Iowa's generally sluggish population growth. Suburban growth in this area west of Des Moines has fueled Dallas' skyrocketing, and sustained, population increase since the 1990s, at by far the fastest clip in the state, and the county has a median household income well above the district or state average.

The 4th divides Republican-leaning western Iowa and Democratic-leaning eastern Iowa, and has a slight GOP lean itself. George W. Bush won the district with 51 percent of the 2004 presidential vote, capturing 15 of the 20 counties that have fewer than 20,000 residents. Democrat Chet Culver won the 4th's 2006 gubernatorial vote with 54 percent — roughly the same percentage that he captured statewide.

MAJOR INDUSTRY

Meatpacking, health care, veterinary pharmaceuticals, agriculture

CITIES

Ames, 50,731; Mason City, 29,172; Marshalltown, 26,009

NOTABLE

Madison County's covered bridges were popularized in Robert James Waller's book; In 1959, after playing a last concert, Buddy Holly, Ritchie Valens and J.P. "The Big Bopper" Richardson died in a plane crash near Clear Lake; Kraft Foods' refrigerated Jell-O pudding snacks are only produced in Mason City.

Rep. Steve King (R)

CAPITOL OFFICE
225-4426
steve.king@mail.house.gov
www.house.gov/steveking
1609 Longworth 20515-1505; fax 225-3193

COMMITTEES
Agriculture
Judiciary
Small Business

RESIDENCE
Kiron

BORN
May 28, 1949, Storm Lake, Iowa

RELIGION
Roman Catholic

FAMILY
Wife, Marilyn King; three children

EDUCATION
Northwest Missouri State U., attended 1967-70

CAREER
Construction company owner

POLITICAL HIGHLIGHTS
Iowa Senate, 1997-2002

ELECTION RESULTS

2006 GENERAL		
Steve King (R)	105,712	58.4%
Joyce Schulte (D)	64,516	35.7%
Roy Nielsen (X)	8,194	4.5%
Cheryl L. Brodersen (X)	2,490	1.4%
2006 PRIMARY		
Steve King (R)		unopposed
2004 GENERAL		
Steve King (R)	168,583	63.3%
Joyce Schulte (D)	97,597	36.6%

PREVIOUS WINNING PERCENTAGES
2002 (62%)

Elected 2002; 3rd term

King gets a lot of ink for a junior member of Congress, mostly for the controversial things he says. In his short time in the House, he has called former communist-baiting Sen. Joe McCarthy a hero, pushed for the construction of a fence to keep out illegal Mexican immigrants and threatened to cut the budgets of judges he thinks are too liberal.

A self-described "family values" Republican, King is disdainful of liberal views in the culture wars. Longtime Des Moines Register political columnist David Yepsen dubbed him "the Pat Buchanan of Iowa."

His rhetorical edginess belies a "kindly uncle" manner; in person, he is meticulously polite and self-deprecating. He is at home, however, with the hardball tactics of former Majority Leader Tom DeLay, who regularly knocked heads to get votes for conservative causes.

From his seat on the Judiciary Committee, he has taken aim at judges he considers too activist and too liberal. After the courts rebuffed Congress' attempt in 2005 to intervene in the case of Terri Schiavo, a severely brain-damaged Florida woman being kept alive by a feeding tube, King asserted Congress had the power to retaliate against the courts that allowed the tube to be removed. "We have the constitutional authority to eliminate any and all inferior courts," he told The Washington Post.

After Supreme Court Justice Sandra Day O'Connor invited King and a few other lawmakers to lunch, he said the meeting "did not change my position as to which branch of government has the constitutional authority to restrict the other branches." In 2005, King proposed cutting the Supreme Court's budget by $1.5 million; the attempt failed, as have most of his proposals.

As top-ranking member of Judiciary's Immigration Subcommittee, King is outspoken about cracking down on illegal immigration and opposes President Bush's proposed guest worker program. In 2005, he proposed building a fence along the entire 2,000-mile border with Mexico. Congress in late 2006 did clear a bill to build 700 miles of fencing. Early the next year, he joined an effort to keep Sen. Mel Martinez of Florida from the top job at the Republican National Committee because he was too lenient on immigration. He suggested Martinez "take an oath to refrain from a mention of the president's immigration plan any time he makes a public statement." He changed his tune on the administration slightly after a tour of the U.S.-Mexico border in February 2007, telling the Register he saw progress in the U.S. efforts to crack down on illegal immigration.

King also has pushed for English to be the nation's primary language. As an Iowa state senator he had sponsored a bill, which became law, making English the state's official language. His effort to make it the nation's official language came to naught in the 109th Congress (2005-06), but he offered another bill in 2007. At the same time, he was embroiled in a lawsuit he filed against Iowa Governor Chet Culver and Secretary of State Michael Mauro, in which he charged that Culver, as secretary of state, violated the state's English-only law by providing voter registration forms in other languages.

He has made his views on other issues just as clear. In 2005, he picked a fight with Rep. Barbara Lee, an African-American Democrat from California, over her proposal to name a post office after Maudelle Shirek, a 94-year-old former Berkeley city councilwoman and left-leaning community activist. When Lee accused King of acting like McCarthy, the Wisconsin senator who in the 1950s sought to expose communist sympathizers, King called him "a hero for America." He also raised eyebrows when he likened the abuse of prisoners by U.S. soldiers at the Abu Ghraib prison in Iraq to college fraternity hazing.

King generally dislikes federal entitlement programs and initially resisted Bush's 2003 expansion of the Medicare program to create a prescription drug benefit for the elderly. He eventually voted for the bill under heavy pressure from GOP leaders. On foreign policy, he follows other conservatives in harboring a deep suspicion of the United Nations, which he calls a "Third World class-envy society." He wants to reduce the U.S. share of the U.N. budget.

King has had some luck with district-focused legislation. As an Agriculture Committee member, he inserted in a 2003 energy bill a provision granting a tax credit for small ethanol producers. The provision was aimed at making the half-dozen small producers in his district more competitive with ethanol giants Archer Daniels Midland and Cargill.

Born in tiny Storm Lake, King has deep roots in the district, which covers the predominately rural western third of Iowa. His maternal great-grandparents were among the original homesteaders there after the Civil War.

In 1975, he started the King Construction Company, a small earth-moving firm that specialized in soil erosion solutions for farmers. His annual sales were about $700,000. (His son now owns the business.) He says he became increasingly angry at rising federal taxes, burdensome government regulations and Internal Revenue Service audits of his business. "After they picked my pocket, I went to work and sat there every day, thinking about how to get rid of them," he says.

In 1996, he won a seat in the Iowa Senate, where he became known for a culturally conservative agenda. His God and Country law requires Iowa public schools to teach that the United States has "derived its strength from Biblical values." In 2000, King fought an executive order by Democratic Gov. Tom Vilsack banning discrimination against homosexuals in state jobs, arguing it gave preferential treatment to certain groups of people. He took the fight to the Iowa Supreme Court and won, overturning Vilsack's order.

King's opportunity to run for Congress came in 2002 after redistricting put 5th District GOP Rep. Tom Latham's home in the 4th District. Latham chose to run in the 4th, leaving the 5th District seat open.

During the primary, King had to overcome formidable competition from state House Speaker Brent Siegrist of Council Bluffs and fellow state Sen. John Redwine. When no candidate received the required 35 percent of the vote to prevail, the outcome was decided by a nominating convention — and King won. He easily took the general election with 62 percent of the vote and has been re-elected with comfortable margins ever since.

KEY VOTES

2006

- No Stop broadband companies from favoring select Internet traffic
- Yes Affirm U.S. commitment to war in Iraq and reject setting a withdrawal date for troops
- Yes Repeal requirement for bilingual ballots at the polls
- Yes Permit U.S. sale of civilian nuclear technology to India
- Yes Build a 700-mile fence on the U.S.-Mexico border to curb illegal crossings
- Yes Permit warrantless wiretaps of suspected terrorists

2005

- Yes Intervene in the life-support case of Terri Schiavo
- No Lift President Bush's restrictions on stem cell research funding
- No Prohibit FBI access to library and bookstore records
- Yes Approve free-trade pact with five Central American countries
- Yes Pass energy policy overhaul favored by President Bush emphasizing domestic oil and gas production
- Yes End mandatory preservation of habitat of endangered animal and plant species
- No Ban torture of prisoners in U.S. custody

CQ VOTE STUDIES

	PARTY UNITY		PRESIDENTIAL SUPPORT	
	Support	Oppose	Support	Oppose
2006	96%	4%	83%	17%
2005	98%	2%	87%	13%
2004	99%	1%	85%	15%
2003	98%	2%	91%	9%

INTEREST GROUPS

	AFL-CIO	ADA	CCUS	ACU
2006	21%	15%	93%	100%
2005	13%	0%	93%	100%
2004	13%	5%	100%	96%
2003	0%	10%	96%	88%

IOWA 5

West – Sioux City, Council Bluffs

The 32-county 5th takes in miles of fertile soil and gently undulating hills in the western part of the state. This bountiful land has allowed the region to remain more like the Iowa of old than any other part of the state. The 5th has the most farmland in Iowa and grows the most corn and soybeans in the state.

Sioux City is the district's largest metropolitan center and has a rich link to America's history — Lewis and Clark passed through it on their way to the Pacific Northwest. Bordering South Dakota and Nebraska to its west, Sioux City has become a major trading center for the tri-state area. Home of the original annual "Corn Palaces" in the late 19th century, Sioux City is now a distribution center for the state's primary crop and also for the local meatpacking industry, which is supported by livestock raised locally. Bedroom communities, such as growing Sergeant Bluff, are now home to some white-collar workers leaving the city.

Council Bluffs, nicknamed "Iowa's Leading Edge," also is located on the state's western border, farther south along the Missouri River. Unlike Sioux City, Council Bluffs is growing. Many residents here commute across the river to work for Omaha businesses that have been lured to Nebraska by lower tax rates. Public improvement projects underway since the mid-1990s are attracting new health care and distribution businesses to the city. Also, a trio of casinos have added a gaming industry to the region.

The two large cities lean Republican, and the Corn Belt farmland found in the rest of the 5th makes it Iowa's strongest GOP district. The socially conservative farm towns helped George W. Bush earn 60 percent of the district's 2004 presidential vote, making it his best Iowa district. In 2006, the 5th was the only district won by Republican Jim Nussle in his unsuccessful gubernatorial campaign. Nussle took 55 percent of the 2006 vote here, and his six best Iowa counties all were in the 5th.

MAJOR INDUSTRY

Meatpacking, agriculture, distribution

CITIES

Sioux City, 85,013; Council Bluffs, 58,268; Spencer, 11,317

NOTABLE

The annual Donna Reed Festival is held in the actress' hometown of Denison; The Union Pacific Railroad Museum is located in Council Bluffs.

KANSAS

Gov. Kathleen Sebelius (D)

Pronounced: SUH-beel-yus
First elected: 2002
Length of term: 4 years
Term expires: 1/11
Salary: $105,889
Phone: (785) 296-3232

Residence: Topeka
Born: May 15, 1948; Cincinnati, Ohio
Religion: Roman Catholic
Family: Husband, Gary Sebelius; two children
Education: Trinity College (D.C.), B.A. 1970 (political science); U. of Kansas, M.P.A. 1977
Career: Law association director; state corrections department official
Political highlights: Kansas Governmental Ethics Commission, 1975-77; Kan. House, 1987-95; Kan. insurance commissioner, 1995-2003

Election results:

2006 GENERAL		
Kathleen Sebelius (D)	491,993	57.9%
Jim Barnett (R)	343,586	40.4%
Carl Kramer (LIBERT)	8,896	1.0%

Lt. Gov. Mark Parkinson (D)

First elected: 2006
Length of term: 4 years
Term expires: 1/11
Salary: $29,900
Phone: (785) 296-2213

LEGISLATURE

Legislature: January to spring, limit of 90 days in even-numbered years

Senate: 40 members, 4-year terms
2007 ratios: 30 R, 10 D; 27 men, 13 women
Salary: $85/day in session; $99/day expenses; $8,480/year allowance
Phone: (785) 296-7344

House: 125 members, 2-year terms
2007 ratios: 78 R, 47 D; 90 men, 35 women
Salary: $85/day in session; $99/day expenses; $8,480/year allowance
Phone: (785) 296-7633

TERM LIMITS

Governor: 2 terms
Senate: No
House: No

URBAN STATISTICS

CITY	POPULATION
Wichita	344,284
Overland Park	149,080
Kansas City	146,866
Topeka	122,377

REGISTERED VOTERS

Republican	46%
Unaffiliated/others	28%
Democrat	27%

POPULATION

2006 population (est.)	2,764,075
2000 population	2,688,418
1990 population	2,477,574
Percent change (1990-2000)	+8.5%
Rank among states (2006)	33
Median age	35.2
Born in state	59.5%
Foreign born	5%
Violent crime rate	389/100,000
Poverty level	9.9%
Federal workers	25,639
Military	29,103

ELECTIONS

STATE ELECTION OFFICIAL
(785) 296-4561
DEMOCRATIC PARTY
(785) 234-0425
REPUBLICAN PARTY
(785) 234-3456

MISCELLANEOUS

Web: www.accesskansas.org
Capital: Topeka

U.S. CONGRESS

Senate: 2 Republicans
House: 2 Democrats, 2 Republicans

2000 Census Statistics by District

DIST.	2004 VOTE FOR PRESIDENT BUSH	KERRY	WHITE	BLACK	ASIAN	HISP	MEDIAN INCOME	WHITE COLLAR	BLUE COLLAR	SERVICE INDUSTRY	OVER 64	UNDER 18	COLLEGE EDUCATION	RURAL	SQ. MILES
1	72%	26%	85%	2%	1%	11%	$34,869	53%	31%	16%	16%	26%	18%	48%	57,373
2	59	39	87	5	1	4	$37,855	58	27	16	14	25	23	40	14,134
3	55	44	80	9	3	7	$51,118	70	17	12	10	27	39	5	778
4	64	34	81	7	2	7	$40,917	57	29	14	13	28	23	21	9,531
STATE	62	37	83	6	2	7	$40,624	60	26	14	13	27	26	29	81,815
U.S.	50.7	48.3	69	12	4	13	$41,994	60	25	15	12	26	24	21	3,537,438

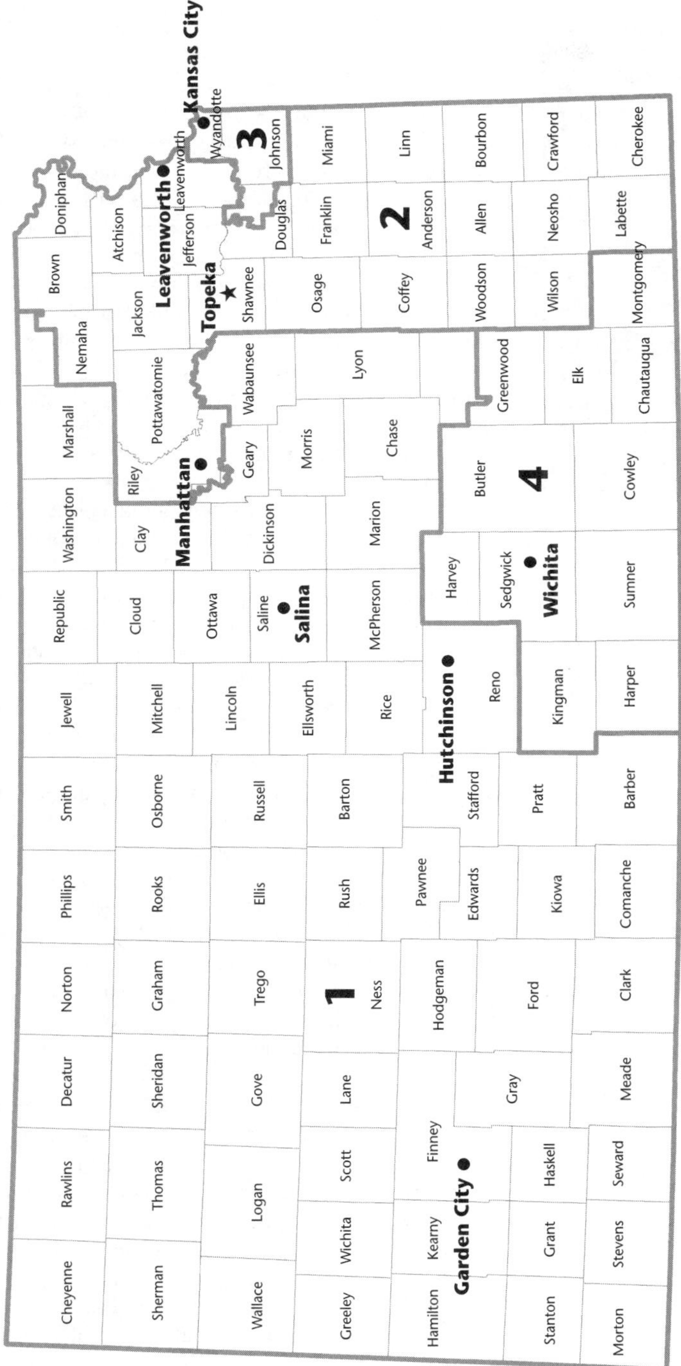
Kansas City
Wyandotte
Leavenworth
Doniphan
Atchison
Leavenworth
Jefferson
Brown
Jackson
Topeka
Shawnee
Douglas
Johnson
3
Miami
Linn
Bourbon
Crawford
Cherokee
Franklin
2
Anderson
Allen
Neosho
Labette
Osage
Coffey
Woodson
Wilson
Montgomery
Nemaha
Pottawatomie
Wabaunsee
Lyon
Greenwood
Elk
Chautauqua
Marshall
Riley
Manhattan
Geary
Morris
Chase
Butler
4
Cowley
Washington
Clay
Dickinson
Marion
Harvey
Sedgwick
Wichita
Sumner
Republic
Cloud
Ottawa
Saline
Salina
McPherson
Hutchinson
Reno
Kingman
Harper
Jewell
Mitchell
Lincoln
Ellsworth
Rice
Smith
Osborne
Russell
Barton
Stafford
Pratt
Barber
Phillips
Rooks
Ellis
Rush
Pawnee
Edwards
Kiowa
Comanche
Norton
Graham
Trego
1
Ness
Hodgeman
Ford
Clark
Decatur
Sheridan
Gove
Lane
Gray
Meade
Rawlins
Thomas
Logan
Scott
Finney
Haskell
Seward
Garden City
Cheyenne
Sherman
Wallace
Wichita
Kearny
Grant
Stevens
Greeley
Hamilton
Stanton
Morton

Sen. Sam Brownback (R)

CAPITOL OFFICE
224-6521
sam_brownback@brownback.senate.gov
brownback.senate.gov
303 Hart 20510-1604; fax 228-1265

COMMITTEES
Appropriations
Judiciary
Joint Economic

RESIDENCE
Topeka

BORN
Sept. 12, 1956, Garnett, Kan.

RELIGION
Roman Catholic

FAMILY
Wife, Mary Brownback; five children

EDUCATION
Kansas State U., B.S. 1979 (agricultural economics); U. of Kansas, J.D. 1982

CAREER
Lawyer; college instrutor; White House fellow

POLITICAL HIGHLIGHTS
Kan. secretary of Agriculture, 1986-93;
U.S. House, 1995-96

ELECTION RESULTS

2004 GENERAL		
Sam Brownback (R)	780,863	69.2%
Lee Jones (D)	310,337	27.5%
Steven A. Rosile (LIBERT)	21,842	1.9%
George Cook (REF)	15,980	1.4%
2004 PRIMARY		
Sam Brownback (R)	286,839	87.0%
Arch Naramore (R)	42,880	13.0%

PREVIOUS WINNING PERCENTAGES
1998 (65%); 1996 Special Election (54%);
1994 House Election (66%)

Elected 1996; 2nd full term

Brownback considers politics a calling, and his religious beliefs inform everything he does in that arena. A former evangelical Christian who is now a Catholic, he is given to passionate denunciations of what he views as the decay of American culture. He has led campaigns for media indecency laws and against the use of embryonic stem cells and cloning for research. As a presidential aspirant, he says he wants to "renew the society and the culture."

Yet Brownback parts with conservatives on some issues. He backed President Bush's comprehensive immigration plan in 2006 even though conservatives condemned it as amnesty for illegal immigrants. "They did not come here for handouts. Like us, they are looking for the American dream," Brownback said. "Social conservatives and people of faith should welcome what these immigrants bring to America." Nevertheless, he backed a bill that became law, which authorizes the construction of 700 miles of fencing and surveillance technology along the border. He said the plan would further discussion toward comprehensive immigration reform.

Although Brownback has generally supported the war effort, including a vote opposing a March 2007 resolution that would have set a timetable for U.S troop withdrawal, he did speak out against Bush's 2007 plan to send more than 21,000 additional U.S. combat troops to Iraq. "Iraq requires a political rather than a military solution," he said.

He also goes his own way on human rights. After visiting Sudan in 2004, Brownback pressed a resolution condemning ethnic cleansing in the Darfur region as "genocide" and said the United States should help supply the African Union peacekeeping mission with equipment and technical advisers. In recent years, he has teamed with Democrats on bills to reduce recidivism among released prisoners, to curb sex trafficking and to build an African-American history museum on the Mall. Next to photographs of Ronald Reagan and Margaret Thatcher on his office wall are framed pictures of the Rev. Martin Luther King Jr., Mother Teresa and Franklin D. Roosevelt.

In August 2006, he reproached the Bush administration for approving a visa for former Iranian President Mohammad Khatami. Brownback, a member of the Senate Appropriations panel dealing with the State Department and foreign operations, said Khatami's government was responsible for brutal crackdowns against political reformers and systematic persecution of religious minorities.

Most of the time, Brownback's views are in line with the GOP right, and he gets out front on social issues. He is a leading critic of medical research using embryonic stem cells, which he equates with taking a human life. Each year, he introduces the Unborn Child Pain Awareness Act, requiring women who seek an abortion after 20 weeks of pregnancy to sign a form saying they have been informed that a fetus can feel pain. He also has sponsored a bill that would make human cloning a crime and championed a constitutional amendment that would ban same-sex marriage.

Brownback was active on a number of social fronts in 2006. After trying for several years, he succeeding in turning into law his proposal to increase fines — to $325,000 per incident — against television broadcasters that air indecent, violent or other objectionable programming. He also cosponsored a bill, passed by the Senate, authorizing the Centers for Disease Control and Prevention to study the effect of electronic media on children. In late September, Brownback announced he was spearheading a task force to investigate how fast-food advertising may promote obesity in kids.

As head of the GOP Values Action Team in the Senate, Brownback regularly meets with representatives from 60 conservative groups, including the Family Research Council and Concerned Women for America. He attends midweek Bible readings and prayer sessions and has close personal and political connections to religious conservative activists. His conversion to Catholicism by a priest who is prominent in the ultra-conservative Opus Dei prelature, where members practice self-mortification and live in communal housing, sparked editorials at home calling on him to explain the relationship. Brownback said he is not a member of the group.

When Brownback started his career in Congress, he was known as a small-government crusader and a leader of the young, change-minded Republicans in the watershed election of 1994. As a House member in 1995 and 1996, he was a founder of the New Federalists, a group that called for abolishing the departments of Education, Housing and Urban Development, and Energy and Commerce. He also advocated balancing the federal budget.

In 1995, a doctor's diagnosis of melanoma, which required two surgeries, launched Brownback on a spiritual odyssey. "As the doctors took a 'wait and see' attitude, I began to examine my life in a new light," says Brownback. Brownback had been raised a Methodist, but as adults he and his wife joined a nondenominational evangelical church. He converted to Catholicism in 2002 with the help of Sen. Rick Santorum of Pennsylvania.

He grew up in a white, one-story farmhouse in Parker, Kan., (population 280) on 1,400 acres where his family grew corn, wheat, soybean, cattle and hogs. His parents still live on the farm and Brownback goes back a couple times a year to help. His own economic circumstances changed dramatically when he married Mary Stauffer, heiress to a family media fortune that included the Topeka Capitol-Journal and several TV stations. His wife's family fortune explains why he regularly ranks as the Kansas delegation's wealthiest member, with publicly disclosed assets between $1.6 million and $7.2 million. The Brownbacks had three children and adopted two more, a girl from China and a boy from Guatemala.

Brownback has been inclined toward politics since he was president of his eighth-grade class. He was student body president at Kansas State University and a national officer of the Future Farmers of America. He was Kansas' secretary of agriculture, an appointive post, for about six years before running for office. He planned a bid for governor in 1994, but instead chose to run for Democratic Rep. Jim Slattery's seat in the 2nd District when Slattery ran for governor. In that year's GOP tidal wave, Brownback easily defeated Democratic candidate John Carlin, a former two-term governor.

Brownback declared a plan to run for Senate the day after Republican Bob Dole announced his retirement in 1996. But GOP Gov. Bill Graves asked Brownback to wait and appointed Lt. Gov. Sheila Frahm to fill the seat until the special election. Brownback beat Frahm in the primary by 13 percentage points, then took 54 percent of the vote in the general election. His campaign fundraising came under investigation later that year; his in-laws had given money to his campaign in excess of legal limits using third-party organizations, including one called Triad. The Federal Election Commission imposed $28,000 in fines against his campaign and his in-laws.

He was easily re-elected in 2004 with 69 percent. In January 2007, he announced his candidacy for president, saying he would advocate a compassionate brand of conservatism. While better-known Republicans were getting in position for 2008, he began targeting religious and social conservatives. He said he believes Americans are hungry for a conservative in office, and that the perception that Republicans in general had strayed from conservative principles contributed to large GOP losses in the 2006 elections.

KEY VOTES

2006

- Yes Confirm Samuel A. Alito Jr. to the Supreme Court
- Yes Allow consideration of a bill to establish a $140 billion trust fund to compensate victims of asbestos exposure
- Yes Extend tax cuts for two years at a cost of $70 billion over five years
- Yes Overhaul immigration policy with border security, enforcement and guest worker program
- Yes Allow consideration of a bill to permanently repeal the estate tax
- No Urge President Bush to begin troop withdrawals from Iraq in 2006
- No Lift President Bush's restrictions on stem cell research funding
- Yes Authorize military tribunals for suspected terrorists

2005

- Yes Curb class action lawsuits by shifting them from state to federal courts
- Yes Allow confirmation vote on Priscilla R. Owen to the U.S. Court of Appeals for the 5th Circuit
- Yes Oppose mandatory emissions limits and block recognition of global warming as a threat
- Yes Approve free-trade pact with five Central American countries
- Yes Pass energy policy overhaul favored by President Bush emphasizing domestic oil and gas production
- Yes Shield gunmakers from lawsuits when their products are used in crimes
- Yes Ban torture of prisoners in U.S. custody
- Yes Renew 16 provisions of the Patriot Act
- Yes Allow final vote on opening the Arctic National Wildlife Refuge to oil and gas exploration

CQ VOTE STUDIES

	PARTY UNITY		PRESIDENTIAL SUPPORT	
	Support	Oppose	Support	Oppose
2006	83%	17%	92%	8%
2005	97%	3%	93%	7%
2004	98%	2%	98%	2%
2003	96%	4%	97%	3%
2002	94%	6%	98%	2%
2001	94%	6%	99%	1%
2000	98%	2%	40%	60%
1999	95%	5%	31%	69%
1998	96%	4%	37%	63%
1997	96%	4%	56%	44%

INTEREST GROUPS

	AFL-CIO	ADA	CCUS	ACU
2006	7%	5%	100%	87%
2005	14%	10%	89%	100%
2004	0%	15%	94%	96%
2003	0%	5%	100%	80%
2002	15%	5%	100%	100%
2001	19%	0%	93%	96%
2000	0%	0%	100%	100%
1999	0%	5%	94%	95%
1998	0%	0%	94%	92%
1997	0%	0%	100%	100%

Sen. Pat Roberts (R)

CAPITOL OFFICE
224-4774
roberts.senate.gov
109 Hart 20510-1605; fax 224-3514

COMMITTEES
Agriculture, Nutrition & Forestry
Finance
Health, Education, Labor & Pensions
Select Ethics

RESIDENCE
Dodge City

BORN
April 20, 1936, Topeka, Kan.

RELIGION
Methodist

FAMILY
Wife, Franki Roberts; three children

EDUCATION
Kansas State U., B.A. 1958 (journalism)

MILITARY SERVICE
Marine Corps, 1958-62

CAREER
Congressional aide; newspaper owner; reporter

POLITICAL HIGHLIGHTS
U.S. House, 1981-97

ELECTION RESULTS

2002 GENERAL		
Pat Roberts (R)	641,075	82.5%
Steven A. Rosile (LIBERT)	70,725	9.1%
George Cook (REF)	65,050	8.4%
2002 PRIMARY		
Pat Roberts (R)	233,642	83.7%
Thomas L. "Tom" Oyler (R)	45,491	16.3%

PREVIOUS WINNING PERCENTAGES
1996 (62%); 1994 House Election (77%); 1992 House Election (68%); 1990 House Election (63%); 1988 House Election (100%); 1986 House Election (77%); 1984 House Election (76%); 1982 House Election (68%); 1980 House Election (62%)

Elected 1996; 2nd term

After a tempestuous, often frustrating four-year stint as chairman of the Senate Intelligence Committee, Roberts seemed almost relieved when the 2006 Democratic electoral sweep stripped him of his gavel. In fact, he left the panel altogether, opting for a less stressful spot as the lowest-ranking Republican on the Finance Committee.

To take the Finance slot, he had to give up his seat on the Armed Services Committee as well. Roberts was ready for a break from the strain of dealing with national security issues while the United States was bogged down in a messy war in Iraq and striving to prevent future terrorist attacks at home. "I'm very happy," he told the Kansas City Star. The Finance Committee, he noted, handles "everything that affects our daily lives," from taxes and trade to Social Security and Medicare.

Roberts, a former House Agriculture Committee chairman, had the seniority to claim the top GOP slot at Senate Agriculture in the 110th Congress (2007-08), when the committee was expected to write an overhaul of the nation's farm policy. But he deferred to Saxby Chambliss of Georgia, declaring, "I intend to be his wingman."

Roberts was a prime architect of the 1996 Freedom to Farm law, which replaced traditional crop subsidies with a system of fixed but declining payments to farmers. He voted against the 2002 farm bill, which undid a number of the changes he and other Republicans had written into law in 1996.

As Intelligence chairman, Roberts was largely sidelined during the biggest restructuring of the nation's intelligence community in 60 years. His panel was bypassed in favor of the Homeland Security and Governmental Affairs Committee, which wrote the bill that became law in 2004.

During the 109th Congress (2005-06), Roberts found himself in near-constant battles with John D. Rockefeller IV of West Virginia, the Intelligence panel's top Democrat. The two tussled repeatedly over a long-running investigation of prewar intelligence about Iraq and the uses made of it by top Bush administration policymakers.

Roberts guided the first phase of the inquiry to a successful conclusion, with the panel issuing a bipartisan report in 2004 concluding that the CIA relied on flawed and outdated intelligence regarding Saddam Hussein's weapons of mass destruction. Although Roberts repeatedly set deadlines for concluding the second phase of the inquiry, it remained unfinished as the 109th Congress came to an end. Rockefeller charged that "any time the Intelligence Committee pursued a line of inquiry that brought us close to the role of the White House in the use of intelligence prior to the war, our efforts have been thwarted." Roberts countered that Democrats were trying to expand the probe and were politicizing it. Some, he said in 2006, "make clear that they believe the gravest threat we face is not Osama bin Laden and al Qaeda, but rather the president of the United States."

Roberts is known for unleashing verbal zingers on the floor and off. More than once, he was voted "funniest senator" in Washingtonian magazine's annual survey of congressional staff. Lamenting his lack of input on the 2004 intelligence overhaul, Robert said, "I'm like a one-legged chicken." In 2003, he said asking the federal agency that administers Medicare and Medicaid for help would be akin to "asking the Boston Strangler for a neck rub."

Though he does not tout the fact, few members have as good a claim as Roberts to foreseeing the threat of a terrorist attack before Sept. 11, 2001. As the first chairman of the Armed Services Subcommittee on Emerging

Threats and Capabilities, which focuses on the terrorism threat, Roberts in 1999 started pressing the Pentagon and Congress to get beyond a Cold War mentality and prepare for military attacks that would use novel weapons. He urged preparedness for a gamut of possible terrorist assaults — attacks on civilian populations with nuclear, chemical or biological weapons and cyber-attacks on critical computer networks.

While he is a reliable GOP vote on such issues as abortion rights and cutting taxes, he is less confrontational than some younger Republicans. He often tries to build alliances with Democrats on issues that interest him. Early in the 110th Congress, Roberts teamed with Edward M. Kennedy of Massachusetts on a proposal to tighten regulation of pharmacists who hand-mix prescription drugs, a practice known as "compounding." Kennedy's home-state colleague, Rep. Barney Frank, once told the Kansas City Star that Roberts was "not one of the impossible ideologues."

For a decade while Republicans ran Congress, Roberts tried in vain to move a bill providing grants to help small businesses offer child care for their workers. In early 2007, with Democrats in control, his measure was added as an amendment to the Senate minimum wage bill.

Since 1999, Roberts has been on the Ethics Committee, where he was the chairman from late 1999 to mid-2001. In 2002, he helped mete out the harshest punishment of a senator in years when Democrat Robert G. Torricelli was severely admonished for accepting gifts from a campaign donor.

Roberts, a former Marine like his father, has deep ties to the military and continues to be loyal to the Marines. His uncle was a military attaché to the U.S. embassy in China who survived the 1937 sinking by Japanese planes of the U.S. gunboat *Panay*. Roberts' office is decorated with Marine regalia though it has been more than 40 years since his service.

A fourth-generation Kansan, Roberts earned a journalism degree from Kansas State University, intending to follow a family tradition in the news business. His great-grandfather, J.W. Roberts, founded the Oskaloosa Independent, the second-oldest newspaper in Kansas, after moving to the Kansas Territory from Ohio with "a Bible, a six-shooter and printing press in tow," according to a 1996 profile of Roberts in the Star. Politics ran in the family, too; Roberts' father, Wes, was chairman of the Republican National Committee under President Dwight D. Eisenhower.

After graduation, Roberts was drafted, so he joined the Marines. Returning home in 1962, he worked as a reporter and then co-owned a weekly newspaper in the Phoenix suburbs. He learned about zoning boards, city councils, boards of education, and developed, as he told the Star later, "a healthy respect and a degree of cynicism in a lot of federal programs."

He first came to Washington to work as a Senate aide and later ran the office of Republican Rep. Keith G. Sebelius of Kansas. When Sebelius announced his retirement in 1980, Roberts was ready. He cruised to victory in the general election, capitalizing on Sebelius' popularity and referring to "our record" so frequently he sounded like an incumbent.

As he became one of the most popular politicians in Kansas, Roberts was often likened to Majority Leader Bob Dole, another Kansan known for his caustic humor and conservative outlook.

Roberts initially balked at making a Senate bid in 1996 when Republican Nancy Landon Kassebaum retired, saying he wanted to focus on shepherding the farm bill into law. But he eventually entered the race and handily won the GOP nod. Facing Democratic state Treasurer Sally Thompson in the fall, he won with 62 percent of the vote. In 2002, Democrats didn't field a candidate.

But Roberts is unlikely to be that fortunate when he faces election in 2008. Democrats made gains in Kansas in 2006, and could sense an opportunity.

KEY VOTES

2006

Yes Confirm Samuel A. Alito Jr. to the Supreme Court
Yes Allow consideration of a bill to establish a $140 billion trust fund to compensate victims of asbestos exposure
Yes Extend tax cuts for two years at a cost of $70 billion over five years
No Overhaul immigration policy with border security, enforcement and guest worker program
Yes Allow consideration of a bill to permanently repeal the estate tax
No Urge President Bush to begin troop withdrawals from Iraq in 2006
No Lift President Bush's restrictions on stem cell research funding
Yes Authorize military tribunals for suspected terrorists

2005

Yes Curb class action lawsuits by shifting them from state to federal courts
Yes Allow confirmation vote on Priscilla R. Owen to the U.S. Court of Appeals for the 5th Circuit
Yes Oppose mandatory emissions limits and block recognition of global warming as a threat
Yes Approve free-trade pact with five Central American countries
Yes Pass energy policy overhaul favored by President Bush emphasizing domestic oil and gas production
\+ Shield gunmakers from lawsuits when their products are used in crimes
No Ban torture of prisoners in U.S. custody
Yes Renew 16 provisions of the Patriot Act
Yes Allow final vote on opening the Arctic National Wildlife Refuge to oil and gas exploration

CQ VOTE STUDIES

	PARTY UNITY		PRESIDENTIAL SUPPORT	
	Support	Oppose	Support	Oppose
2006	94%	6%	88%	12%
2005	94%	6%	93%	7%
2004	99%	1%	92%	8%
2003	96%	4%	97%	3%
2002	96%	4%	96%	4%
2001	95%	5%	99%	1%
2000	97%	3%	38%	62%
1999	94%	6%	29%	71%
1998	95%	5%	35%	65%
1997	90%	10%	59%	41%

INTEREST GROUPS

	AFL-CIO	ADA	CCUS	ACU
2006	27%	5%	92%	84%
2005	8%	0%	100%	88%
2004	17%	15%	100%	92%
2003	0%	15%	100%	90%
2002	15%	0%	100%	100%
2001	13%	0%	93%	100%
2000	0%	0%	100%	92%
1999	0%	0%	94%	88%
1998	0%	0%	100%	84%
1997	0%	15%	90%	68%

Rep. Jerry Moran (R)

CAPITOL OFFICE
225-2715
www.jerrymoran.house.gov
2202 Rayburn 20515-1601; fax 225-5124

COMMITTEES
Agriculture
Transportation & Infrastructure
Veterans' Affairs

RESIDENCE
Hays

BORN
May 29, 1954, Great Bend, Kan.

RELIGION
Protestant

FAMILY
Wife, Robba Moran; two children

EDUCATION
Fort Hays State U., attended 1972-73;
U. of Kansas, B.S. 1976 (economics), J.D. 1981

CAREER
Lawyer; banker

POLITICAL HIGHLIGHTS
Kan. Senate, 1989-97 (vice president, 1993-95; majority leader, 1995-97)

ELECTION RESULTS

2006 GENERAL		
Jerry Moran (R)	156,728	78.6%
John Doll (D)	39,781	20.0%
Sylvester Cain (REF)	2,869	1.4%
2006 PRIMARY		
Jerry Moran (R)		unopposed
2004 GENERAL		
Jerry Moran (R)	239,776	90.7%
Jack W. Warner (LIBERT)	24,517	9.3%

PREVIOUS WINNING PERCENTAGES
2002 (91%); 2000 (89%); 1998 (81%); 1996 (73%)

Elected 1996; 6th term

Moran has his eye on higher office after an unusually strong showing at the ballot box in an otherwise gloomy year for most Republicans. Moran was returned for a sixth term with 79 percent of the vote, one of only three GOP House members who had contested races to achieve numbers that high as the party's majorities came crashing down in Congress.

A buoyant Moran told local reporters after the election that he was leaving his options open for a run for the U.S. Senate or for governor of Kansas. Republican Sen. Sam Brownback announced that he would make a 2008 bid for the White House, and Democratic Gov. Kathleen Sebelius reaches the end of her second four-year term in 2010.

In the anti-Republican tide of 2006, only two other GOP House members, Louisianans Bobby Jindal and Richard Baker, earned more than 79 percent of the vote. Moran defeated Democrat John Doll, who took 20 percent, and Reform Party candidate Sylvester Cain, with 1 percent. Moran was one of the few Republican incumbents immune to Democratic efforts to hang President Bush's unpopularity around their necks. In the 109th Congress (2005-06), his support for Bush's policies was relatively weak; he voted with the president only 73 percent of the time the administration staked out a position on legislation.

In the past few years, Moran has defied the White House on some of its biggest initiatives. In 2003, he opposed Bush's Medicare prescription drug bill as too costly and not good for his rural constituents. Though not naming Moran, then Republican House Speaker J. Dennis Hastert complained in a 2004 autobiography about a fourth-term "Prairie State" member who "voted no, then ran and hid." Moran won plaudits from conservative and libertarian groups for his vote.

Before that, Moran voted against Bush's No Child Left Behind Act, which imposed mandatory testing on public schools hoping to qualify for federal aid. Moran insisted education was a state and local issue. "The law is based on the false premise that we can all perform at the same level, and that's just not true. I also think it's ruining the teaching profession," said Moran, who has sponsored a bill giving schools an additional year to improve before being labeled a failing school under the act.

When the administration, in response to terrorism threats, stopped giving visas to foreign doctors who agreed to work in rural outposts, Moran rallied opposition among rural lawmakers and the visa program resumed.

Hailing from a state that boasts a strong wheat, corn and soybean industry, Moran's seat on the Agriculture Committee gives him a say in the 2007 rewrite of farm policy. He has pushed for more incentives to boost the burgeoning corn and ethanol markets, but needs to balance that with the interests of the state's cattle and pork producers, who worry that demand for ethanol could lead to a spike in feed costs. "That's all the more reason we need to open our livestock markets to Japan and Korea and Europe," says Moran, a supporter of free trade and the opening of world markets to U.S. farm exports.

He joined with other farm-state lawmakers in the 109th Congress in pushing to ease restrictions on trade with Cuba, despite opposition from Bush. He is the senior Republican on a key Agriculture subcommittee, General Farm Commodities and Risk Management. During the last major revision of the farm law, in 2002, Moran worked on provisions to increase production of ethanol and to speed access to broadband cable in rural areas, which many see as essential to small-town economic survival.

Moran is a native of the 1st District, which, at 57,373 square miles, is among the nation's largest. His father was a laborer in the oil fields and his mother worked as a secretary at an electric utility.

When Moran was 5, the family moved from the country to Plainville, population 2,000, a place Moran calls a "pretty typical Kansas community." In fourth grade, he wanted to be a geologist. "I grew up loving the outdoors," he says. "I would scout, camp, hike and fossil hunt."

In high school, he discovered politics. As a student body officer, Moran was in charge of inviting the local congressman, Republican Keith G. Sebelius, to speak at a fundraising dinner. They kept in touch, and several years later Moran went to Washington as an intern for Sebelius (father-in-law of the current governor). It was the summer of 1974, the height of the Watergate scandal, and Moran remembers feeling like an eyewitness to history as the House Judiciary Committee held hearings to consider the impeachment of President Richard Nixon.

"Leaving Kansas was a big deal. Our family vacations usually consisted of going to the Badlands and Mount Rushmore, or Pike's Peak," Moran says. "That was the extent that most kids I knew traveled."

In 1976, Moran graduated from the University of Kansas with a degree in economics and took a job as a banker. He earned his law degree five years later and opened his own practice in Hays, where he now lives with his wife and two daughters.

In 1988, he made a long-shot race for the state Senate against an 18-year incumbent and won by just a couple hundred votes. Moran went on to become chairman of the state Senate Judiciary Committee and then ascended to majority leader in 1995, thanks to his ability to appeal to both the conservative and moderate wings of the Kansas GOP.

He ran for Congress in 1996 when Republican Pat Roberts left the House seat to succeed Nancy Landon Kassebaum in the Senate. Moran quickly became the front-runner, portraying himself as a pragmatic conservative. In a district with a long Republican tradition, and with Kansas Republican Bob Dole topping the GOP ticket as its presidential nominee, Moran rolled to an easy victory with 73 percent of the vote against John Divine, the former mayor of Salina.

In redistricting following the 2000 census, the Big First, as the district is called, got even larger geographically, as the legislature had to expand the boundaries to make up for population losses in many of the western and central counties. Regardless, Moran keeps racking up decisive wins.

KEY VOTES

2006

No	Stop broadband companies from favoring select Internet traffic
Yes	Affirm U.S. commitment to war in Iraq and reject setting a withdrawal date for troops
Yes	Repeal requirement for bilingual ballots at the polls
No	Permit U.S. sale of civilian nuclear technology to India
Yes	Build a 700-mile fence on the U.S.-Mexico border to curb illegal crossings
No	Permit warrantless wiretaps of suspected terrorists

2005

?	Intervene in the life-support case of Terri Schiavo
No	Lift President Bush's restrictions on stem cell research funding
Yes	Prohibit FBI access to library and bookstore records
Yes	Approve free-trade pact with five Central American countries
Yes	Pass energy policy overhaul favored by President Bush emphasizing domestic oil and gas production
Yes	End mandatory preservation of habitat of endangered animal and plant species
Yes	Ban torture of prisoners in U.S. custody

CQ VOTE STUDIES

	PARTY UNITY		PRESIDENTIAL SUPPORT	
	Support	Oppose	Support	Oppose
2006	87%	13%	70%	30%
2005	92%	8%	76%	24%
2004	92%	8%	68%	32%
2003	92%	8%	82%	18%
2002	89%	11%	72%	28%

INTEREST GROUPS

	AFL-CIO	ADA	CCUS	ACU
2006	29%	5%	93%	84%
2005	29%	15%	93%	96%
2004	21%	10%	95%	92%
2003	27%	25%	90%	92%
2002	0%	5%	90%	96%

KANSAS 1

West and central — Salina, Hutchinson, Garden City, Emporia

In the 1960s, Truman Capote described western Kansas as a "lonesome area that other Kansans call 'out there.'" The fiscally conservative Big First takes in all of western Kansas and stretches as far east as Nemaha County in the north and the city of Emporia farther south, covering most of rural Kansas in the process. The district covers 70 percent of the state and has more land area than most U.S. states (including 25 of the 26 states east of the Mississippi River).

The 1st's economy depends on agriculture, but several years of drought have hurt local wheat, sorghum and corn yields. Young people leaving the rural areas and an aging population have stalled growth — many counties have smaller populations now than they did a century ago.

The largest population center, Salina, is in the district's eastern portion and relies on agriculture and manufacturing. Food-related industry, manufacturing and a growing health care sector dominate Hutchinson, site of the annual Kansas State Fair. The return of the Army's Big Red One brigade to Fort Riley (in the 2nd) has sparked a population boom in Junction City and the surrounding counties. In the west, towns such as Garden City and Dodge City rely on meatpacking and tourism. Despite suffering nationally, the cattle industry in Kansas remains strong and draws large numbers of Mexican immigrants — over half of all school children in Garden City are Hispanic.

The 1st is comfortably Republican and overwhelmingly voted for George W. Bush in the 2004 presidential contest, giving him his highest percentage in the state (72 percent). The GOP also dominates local offices, and many counties have no Democratic Party organizations.

MAJOR INDUSTRY

Agriculture, manufacturing, oil and gas

CITIES

Salina, 45,679; Hutchinson, 40,787; Garden City, 28,451; Emporia, 26,760; Dodge City, 25,176; Hays, 20,013; Liberal, 19,666; Junction City, 18,886

NOTABLE

Dwight D. Eisenhower's burial place and presidential library are in Abilene; The Kansas Cosmosphere in Hutchinson has a U.S. space artifact collection second only to the National Air and Space Museum's.

Rep. Nancy Boyda (D)

Elected 2006; 1st term

CAPITOL OFFICE
225-6601
boyda.house.gov
1711 Longworth 20515-1602; fax 225-7986

COMMITTEES
Agriculture
Armed Services

RESIDENCE
Topeka

BORN
Aug. 2, 1955, Clayton, Mo.

RELIGION
Methodist

FAMILY
Husband, Steve Boyda; two children, five stepchildren

EDUCATION
William Jewell College, B.S. 1977 (chemistry & education)

CAREER
Pharmaceutical company executive; teacher; U.S. Environmental Protection Agency chemist

POLITICAL HIGHLIGHTS
Democratic nominee for U.S. House, 2004

ELECTION RESULTS

2006 GENERAL		
Nancy Boyda (D)	114,139	50.6%
Jim Ryun (R)	106,329	47.1%
Roger D. Tucker (REF)	5,094	2.3%
2006 PRIMARY		
Nancy Boyda (D)		unopposed

Boyda scored one of the most surprising upsets of the 2006 elections, ousting an incumbent on her second try. To hang onto the seat, however, she will need to apply the sort of grass-roots attention that helped her get elected in the mostly conservative, Republican-leaning 2nd District.

House Democratic leaders, eager to reward her, handed Boyda (BOY-duh) a pair of plum committee assignments — Agriculture and Armed Services. The Agriculture seat will give her a say in rewriting the 2002 farm law, which is up for renewal in 2007. And on Armed Services, she can look after the interests of Fort Riley and Fort Leavenworth, the district's big military bases, just as her GOP predecessor, five-term Rep. Jim Ryun, did.

A former pharmaceutical company executive and onetime Republican who switched parties in 2003, Boyda describes herself as a centrist. She will pick her path carefully through the partisan minefields on Capitol Hill.

She learned almost immediately how hard that could be. In a nationally televised ABC news interview just days after she was sworn in, she stumbled when asked about President Bush's planned troop increase in Iraq — seeming to suggest that Congress had no say on funding the deployment and that those who wanted the troops to come home "should have thought about that before they voted for President Bush not once, but twice."

After complaints by anti-war voters who had supported her, Boyda apologized, blaming her choice of words on "first-week jitters," according to the Topeka Capital-Journal. But she stuck by her plan to support funds for the troops, despite her sharp criticism of the war during her campaign.

Boyda's campaign against Ryun was a classic, under-the-radar effort that drew little notice until the last minute. She and her husband Steve ran a grass-roots operation built around personal contact, newspaper inserts, radio ads, and thousands of yard signs asking, "Had Enough?"

It was the opposite strategy from her first race against Ryun, when she raised more money and hired big-time consultants — only to lose by 15 percentage points. In 2006, Boyda sneaked up on Ryun, nudging him out by less than 4 points. Ryun said he would seek a third matchup in 2008.

KANSAS 2

East – Topeka, Manhattan, Leavenworth

The 2nd runs the length of east Kansas from Nebraska to Oklahoma, passing west of Kansas City. This district combines rural farm communities and urbanized areas, including the state capital of Topeka. One-fourth of the 2nd's residents live in Topeka or surrounding Shawnee County, where state government is the largest employer.

The 2nd has enjoyed steady economic growth and low unemployment over recent years. The district's rural areas rely on cattle, corn, soybeans and wheat, but farming has suffered from recent droughts that have had a strong impact in the state's southeast.

Fort Riley and Fort Leavenworth are integral to the 2nd's economy. The return of the Army's famed Big Red One infantry division to Fort Riley, in Manhattan, is expected to bring revenue and new residents to the 2nd.

Republican support here is anchored in the rural areas, while Democrats find more success in Topeka, western Lawrence (the liberal University of Kansas is in the 3rd's portion of the city), the blue-collar southeast corner, and Manhattan, home to Kansas State University. The 2nd is conservative, but not overwhelmingly Republican, and the population boom in Riley and Douglas counties is pulling it toward the center. The 2nd gave George W. Bush 59 percent of its 2004 presidential vote, but the U.S. House seat switched to Democratic control in 2006.

MAJOR INDUSTRY
Agriculture, defense, higher education, government

MILITARY BASES
Fort Riley (Army), 20,000 military, 2,000 civilian (2007); Fort Leavenworth (Army), 2,900 military, 2,156 civilian (2006)

CITIES
Topeka, 122,377; Manhattan, 44,831; Leavenworth, 35,420; Lawrence (pt.), 25,768

NOTABLE
The Kansas Museum of History is in Topeka.

Rep. Dennis Moore (D)

CAPITOL OFFICE
225-2865
www.house.gov/moore
1727 Longworth 20515-1603; fax 225-2807

COMMITTEES
Budget
Financial Services

RESIDENCE
Lenexa

BORN
Nov. 8, 1945, Anthony, Kan.

RELIGION
Protestant

FAMILY
Wife, Stephene Moore; seven children

EDUCATION
Southern Methodist U., attended 1965;
U. of Kansas, B.A. 1967; Washburn U., J.D. 1970

MILITARY SERVICE
Army, 1970; Army Reserve, 1970-73

CAREER
Lawyer

POLITICAL HIGHLIGHTS
Johnson County district attorney, 1977-89;
Democratic nominee for Kan. attorney general, 1986

ELECTION RESULTS

2006 GENERAL		
Dennis Moore (D)	153,105	64.6%
Chuck Ahner (R)	79,824	33.7%
Robert A. Conroy (REF)	4,051	1.7%
2006 PRIMARY		
Dennis Moore (D)		unopposed
2004 GENERAL		
Dennis Moore (D)	184,050	54.8%
Kris Kobach (R)	145,542	43.4%

PREVIOUS WINNING PERCENTAGES
2002 (50%); 2000 (50%); 1998 (52%)

Elected 1998; 5th term

During his re-election campaign, Moore met a man in the grocery store who recognized him, and, in a whisper, told the congressman, "I'm a Republican. You're the only Democrat I've ever voted for." With his party's takeover of Congress, it's finally OK for Moore to be a Democrat in Kansas' notoriously competitive 3rd District.

While the vast majority of incumbents breeze to re-election, Moore always had to sweat it out against tough challengers just to break the 50 percent mark. But the anti-Republican wave of 2006 swept him to a personal best of almost 65 percent of the vote against businessman Chuck Ahner, an endorsement of the careful, moderate politics that has kept Moore returning every two years. He says he succeeds in the swing district because local people remember him from his days as the Johnson County district attorney and think, "Well, he's a Democrat, but he's not a crazy Democrat."

Moore belongs to both the centrist New Democrat Coalition and the Blue Dogs, a coalition of conservative House Democrats. He supported Blue Dog colleague Harold E. Ford Jr. of Tennessee in his unsuccessful 2002 race against Nancy Pelosi of California to become Democratic leader — a bit of history that could haunt Moore if he ever needs a favor from Pelosi, who is now Speaker of the House and is known for keeping score.

He sides with Republicans a tad more often than do other Democrats. Moore supported President Bush's decision to go to war with Iraq in 2002 and voted for the president's first big, $1.35 trillion tax cut bill in 2001. But when the government slipped into yearly deficits, Moore opposed making the tax cuts permanent. He uses the phrase "debt tax" to describe the interest the United States pays on the national debt.

Relatively powerless during the years of GOP rule on the Hill, Moore nevertheless got some bills passed by working with Republicans. One of his first bills, which raised the allowable contribution to IRAs from $2,000 to $5,000, was going nowhere in Congress until Republican Rep. Rob Portman of Ohio asked Moore to add it to a larger retirement security bill that he was sponsoring. Moore agreed.

He says his proudest accomplishment was a bipartisan bill he steered to passage in 2005 with Alabama Republican Rep. Spencer Bachus that increased the military death benefit from $12,000 to $100,000, applied retroactively to soldiers who had died since October 2001.

Moore is a member of the Center Aisle Caucus, a bipartisan group that works to establish dialogue between the parties, and he has urged the Democratic leadership to reinstate bipartisan retreats, the weekend events that usually include family members.

Despite the conservative lean of his constituents, Moore is a reliable vote for Democratic Party leaders on a handful of core issues, including gun control. He was among the Democrats who pushed for a bill in 2003 calling on the government to negotiate lower drug prices in behalf of Medicare beneficiaries. The bill was blocked by the GOP majority then; when Democrats came to power in 2007, they immediately passed the measure.

Moore grew up in Wichita. His father, Warner Moore, was Sedgwick County attorney and the most influential person in Moore's life. He was a lawyer, so Moore became a lawyer, even graduating from the same law school, Washburn in Topeka. He followed his father's career path by becoming a prosecuting attorney. His father was a Democrat, so Moore is a Democrat. To be otherwise "wasn't an option," he says. Warner Moore, who died in 2006, ran twice for the House, in 1958 and 1960, both times unsuccessfully. A framed "Warner Moore for Congress" poster hangs in his son's Capitol Hill office.

In college, Moore joined the ROTC and was slated for two years in the service afterward. He went to Fort Benning, Ga., in 1970 for infantry officers basic training, expecting to be sent to Vietnam. But just before he graduated from law school, he got a letter saying the war was winding down and he could choose active duty or the reserves. He chose the reserves.

Like many of his generation, Moore was drawn to politics by the civil rights movement and the political activism of the 1960s. He campaigned in Nebraska for presidential hopeful Robert F. Kennedy. In 1965, friends visiting his dorm encouraged him to join them on their drive to Selma, Ala., to take part in a civil rights march. Moore took his father's advice and skipped the trip. He says he is glad that later, as a congressman, he was able to return to the scene of the historic march with former civil rights leader John Lewis, a Democratic House colleague from Georgia.

For a dozen years, Moore was the Johnson County district attorney, known for his personal touch. Barbara Daniels, the mother of a teenager murdered by three men, asked Moore if she could testify whenever one of the killers came up for parole. "If I call, he answers," Daniels told The Kansas City Star. "He's really been a good friend." Moore took the lead in creating a county victims assistance program.

The 3rd District had long been represented by GOP moderates when, in 1998, Moore unseated conservative Republican Vince Snowbarger after one term. Snowbarger had not raised much money, a mistake Moore was careful not to make. In his first re-election campaign, Moore raised $1.5 million to defeat state Rep. Phill Kline, another conservative.

In 2002, odds seemed to be against Moore. The district had been redrawn to be slightly more Republican, and GOP nominee Adam Taff was more moderate than Moore's past challengers. Moore organized a get-out-the-vote drive in Democratic areas, and he may have benefited from the National Republican Congressional Committee's decision not to pump money into the race until late in the campaign. Moore won, but with just 50 percent of the vote.

Moore loves to play guitar, and his staff often hears him on the guitar in his office. In 2006, he played and sang "This Land Is Your Land" for a group of 5th- and 6th-graders back in the district. One of them sent him a letter, which he has kept. It says, "If it didn't work out in Congress, you could have been a country singer."

KEY VOTES

2006

No Stop broadband companies from favoring select Internet traffic
Yes Affirm U.S. commitment to war in Iraq and reject setting a withdrawal date for troops
No Repeal requirement for bilingual ballots at the polls
Yes Permit U.S. sale of civilian nuclear technology to India
Yes Build a 700-mile fence on the U.S.-Mexico border to curb illegal crossings
No Permit warrantless wiretaps of suspected terrorists

2005

\- Intervene in the life-support case of Terri Schiavo
Yes Lift President Bush's restrictions on stem cell research funding
Yes Prohibit FBI access to library and bookstore records
Yes Approve free-trade pact with five Central American countries
Yes Pass energy policy overhaul favored by President Bush emphasizing domestic oil and gas production
No End mandatory preservation of habitat of endangered animal and plant species
Yes Ban torture of prisoners in U.S. custody

CQ VOTE STUDIES

	PARTY UNITY		PRESIDENTIAL SUPPORT	
	Support	Oppose	Support	Oppose
2006	87%	13%	37%	63%
2005	85%	15%	30%	70%
2004	83%	17%	38%	62%
2003	87%	13%	29%	71%
2002	82%	18%	40%	60%

INTEREST GROUPS

	AFL-CIO	ADA	CCUS	ACU
2006	92%	85%	60%	23%
2005	80%	80%	59%	16%
2004	87%	90%	62%	20%
2003	80%	90%	52%	28%
2002	78%	85%	60%	20%

KANSAS 3

Kansas City region – Overland Park, eastern Lawrence

Eastern Kansas' 3rd differs markedly from the state's other districts. Compact, it is almost entirely within the sphere of Kansas City, Mo., and roughly 90 percent of residents live either in Kansas City, Kan., or in its Johnson County suburbs. The district boasts Overland Park, Kansas City and Olathe, three of the state's most populous cities. Heading west, the 3rd takes in eastern Douglas County and most of Lawrence, Kansas' liberal bastion and home to the University of Kansas.

The district has a disparate economic character, containing both the state's richest and poorest counties. Poverty and unemployment are prevalent in Kansas City, Kan., and in surrounding Wyandotte County. But the Kansas Speedway, which opened in 2001 in western Wyandotte, has fueled a renaissance in the area. Kansas City, an industrial town that has had its share of Rust Belt blues, still maintains a large industrial base and has attracted growth in its bioscience sector.

Johnson County is the economic engine of Kansas — it is the state's richest county, with telecommunications company headquarters, suburban developments and a strong service sector. While Kansas City has lost population over the past decade, Johnson is booming, and its largest city, Overland Park, is now the second largest in the state. Johnson accounted for half of job growth in Kansas over the past decade and nearly two-thirds of population growth in the state.

Populous, wealthy Johnson County tends to be strongly Republican, and gives the 3rd a GOP lean, but socially moderate Republicans often exhibit an independent streak. Democratic strength in Wyandotte and parts of Douglas keep the 3rd competitive — these were the only two counties in Kansas won by John Kerry in the 2004 presidential election.

MAJOR INDUSTRY

Telecommunications, auto manufacturing, service

CITIES

Overland Park, 149,080; Kansas City, 146,866; Olathe, 92,962; Lawrence (pt.), 54,330; Shawnee, 47,996; Lenexa, 40,238; Leawood, 27,656

NOTABLE

The Mahaffie Stagecoach Stop in Olathe is the last remaining Santa Fe Trail stagecoach stop that is still open to the public.

Rep. Todd Tiahrt (R)

CAPITOL OFFICE
225-6216
www.house.gov/tiahrt
2441 Rayburn 20515-1604; fax 225-3489

COMMITTEES
Appropriations
Select Intelligence

RESIDENCE
Goddard

BORN
June 15, 1951, Vermillion, S.D.

RELIGION
Assemblies of God

FAMILY
Wife, Vicki Tiahrt; three children (one deceased)

EDUCATION
South Dakota School of Mines and Technology, attended 1969-71; Evangel College, B.A. 1975 (business administration); Southwest Missouri State U., M.B.A. 1989 (marketing)

CAREER
College instructor; airline company project manager

POLITICAL HIGHLIGHTS
Republican nominee for Kan. House, 1990; Kan. Senate, 1993-95

ELECTION RESULTS

2006 GENERAL		
Todd Tiahrt (R)	116,386	63.5%
Garth J. McGinn (D)	62,166	33.9%
Joy R. Holt (REF)	4,655	2.5%
2006 PRIMARY		
Todd Tiahrt (R)		unopposed
2004 GENERAL		
Todd Tiahrt (R)	173,151	66.1%
Michael R. Kinard (D)	81,388	31.1%
David Loomis (LIBERT)	7,376	2.8%

PREVIOUS WINNING PERCENTAGES
2002 (61%); 2000 (54%); 1998 (58%); 1996 (50%); 1994 (53%)

Elected 1994; 7th term

A onetime contract manager with Boeing Co., Tiahrt focuses on issues affecting the aviation industry in Congress. It's no wonder: About half of all the general aviation aircraft sold in the world is produced in his home base of Wichita.

In recent years, Tiahrt (TEE-hart) has tried without success to break into the Republican leadership ranks in the House. He is seriously contemplating a run for the Senate — possibly in 2008, if GOP Sen. Sam Brownback's long-shot presidential bid leads to a spot on a successful GOP ticket. It seems likelier, however, that he will run in 2010 if Brownback decides not to seek re-election.

In the 110th Congress (2007-08), Tiahrt is the top-ranking Republican on the Interior Appropriations Subcommittee.

Although he says he's an advocate of government spending restraint, Tiahrt makes frequent use of earmarks, the special projects tucked into appropriations bills by individual lawmakers for their districts. The practice came under fire in the 109th Congress (2005-06) after some projects were tied to bribery scandals. He has used his seat to win an array of federal contracts and grants for his district, particularly for defense, transportation and water development projects. In 2004, Tiahrt inserted $1 million into a catchall spending bill for the Wichita police force's effort to catch a serial killer. He also designated funding to buy laptops for special education teachers in Kansas.

On the Defense Appropriations Subcommittee, Tiahrt teamed with Washington Democrat Norm Dicks to try to win congressional approval for a plan allowing the Air Force to lease 100 Boeing 767 aircraft for use as aerial refueling tankers. The modifications on the planes were to be done at Boeing's Wichita facility, and the city stood to gain about 1,000 jobs. But the Pentagon shelved the deal in 2004 after the $21 billion, no-bid contract came under fire from GOP Sen. John McCain of Arizona and an Air Force procurement official admitted to illegally helping the company while negotiating a lucrative job offer.

Tiahrt is less enthusiastic about federal funding for the Environmental Protection Agency. As the new senior Republican on the Appropriations Subcommittee on the Interior and Environment in the 110th Congress, Tiahrt says he wants to cut the amount that EPA can spend on the regulatory process and on pursuing polluters in court.

With the hope of breaking into the GOP leadership in early 2006, Tiahrt spent a month campaigning and lobbying his colleagues for the job of Republican whip, then the third-ranking post among the majority House Republicans. But when Whip Roy Blunt of Missouri was upset in his bid to move up to majority leader, losing to John A. Boehner of Ohio, Blunt decided to hang on to the whip's job, denying Tiahrt and other interested candidates the opportunity to run as his replacement.

Later in 2006, Tiahrt vied for the chairmanship of the Republican Study Committee, the group of the most conservative House Republicans. He lost to Jeb Hensarling of Texas on a 57-42 vote. Tiahrt later quit the group.

A social conservative who is guided by his religious convictions, Tiahrt frequently tries to advance conservative ideas by adding social policy proposals to the annual appropriations bills. In 2004, he inserted a provision in one bill limiting the disclosure of federally stored information about firearms that are used in crimes. His other amendments have targeted abortion services at family planning organizations overseas, needle-exchange programs for drug abusers and adoptions by same-sex couples. "People accuse me of being a social conservative with a vengeance, but I really haven't been," Tiahrt says. "These are just common-sense initiatives."

Born in South Dakota, Tiahrt grew up on a family farm in the southeastern part of the state. He learned to hunt and fish as a boy, and his father served on the local school board. Tiahrt played football in college, getting a scholarship to the South Dakota School of Mines and Technology. But he lost the scholarship after a knee injury ended his sports career, and he transferred to Evangel College in Springfield, Mo., a Christian liberal arts school run by the Assemblies of God church, of which Tiahrt is a member. He worked his way through college at a bank.

Tiahrt majored in business administration. After graduation, his first job was as a project engineer for Zenith Electronics Corp. studying the assembly line process. One assignment was to figure out how high boxes of TVs could be stacked. He later worked as a contract manager for Boeing, dealing mostly with Air Force contracts.

He originally registered as a Democrat. His grandfather had impressed him with the story of how the federal government had helped with the purchase of the family farm during the Depression. The congressman says he didn't give his party affiliation much thought until he set out to run for the Kansas House in 1990. He decided then that the Republican Party was a better match for his strong religious views.

Tiahrt lost that race for the state House, succumbing in a recount after initial tallies had shown him with a 24-vote lead. He remained active in local politics and two years later was elected to the state Senate, where he was best known for pushing legislation allowing people to carry concealed weapons.

In 1994, Tiahrt waged a long-shot challenge to popular nine-term Democratic Rep. Dan Glickman. Glickman's polls throughout that summer showed him with a lead of 30 percentage points. But Tiahrt mobilized a grass-roots network that drew heavily from the ranks of the anti-abortion movement, in which his wife was active. He chipped away at Glickman's lead, linking him to the unpopular Clinton administration, and won by 6 percentage points.

Tiahrt had a serious re-election battle in 1996, eventually defeating moderate Democrat Randy Rathbun, a former U.S. attorney, by just 3 points. Democrats continue to harbor some hope of capturing the district again, but Tiahrt has won subsequent elections by comfortable margins.

Tiahrt faced a personal tragedy in 2004, when his 16-year-old son, Luke, committed suicide in July at the family's home in a Washington suburb.

KEY VOTES

2006

No Stop broadband companies from favoring select Internet traffic
Yes Affirm U.S. commitment to war in Iraq and reject setting a withdrawal date for troops
? Repeal requirement for bilingual ballots at the polls
Yes Permit U.S. sale of civilian nuclear technology to India
Yes Build a 700-mile fence on the U.S.-Mexico border to curb illegal crossings
Yes Permit warrantless wiretaps of suspected terrorists

2005

Yes Intervene in the life-support case of Terri Schiavo
No Lift President Bush's restrictions on stem cell research funding
No Prohibit FBI access to library and bookstore records
Yes Approve free-trade pact with five Central American countries
Yes Pass energy policy overhaul favored by President Bush emphasizing domestic oil and gas production
Yes End mandatory preservation of habitat of endangered animal and plant species
No Ban torture of prisoners in U.S. custody

CQ VOTE STUDIES

	PARTY UNITY		PRESIDENTIAL SUPPORT	
	Support	Oppose	Support	Oppose
2006	96%	4%	87%	13%
2005	97%	3%	91%	9%
2004	96%	4%	85%	15%
2003	99%	1%	98%	2%
2002	96%	4%	88%	12%

INTEREST GROUPS

	AFL-CIO	ADA	CCUS	ACU
2006	33%	5%	93%	84%
2005	13%	0%	93%	96%
2004	13%	5%	100%	92%
2003	14%	5%	100%	88%
2002	11%	5%	95%	96%

KANSAS 4
South central — Wichita

Wichita, the state's largest city, is called the "Air Capital of the World"— nearly half of the world's general aviation aircraft are built here and the industry powers the district's economy. The moderately conservative 4th is centered on Wichita and much of the rest of the district is farmland.

The aviation industry that Wichita and the district depend on suffered an economic downturn following the Sept. 11, 2001, terrorist attacks, but the industry, and Wichita's economy, have rebounded. Aerostructures manufacturer Spirit AeroSystems, which was purchased by Onex from Boeing Commercial Airplanes in 2005, is headquartered in Wichita and its plant has increased production.

Cessna Aircraft, Raytheon Aircraft, Bombardier Aerospace, Boeing's Integrated Defense Systems and other airplane manufacturers have operations in the area. Although the industry keeps the local economy healthy, the city continually looks for ways to diversify, most recently through its growing health care sector. Wichita also benefits from its universities and a strong food manufacturing sector.

Sumner County, on the Oklahoma border, is Kansas' leading wheat-growing county. Harper and Kingman counties to the west also rely heavily on their wheat production. Cattle graze in sparsely populated Greenwood, Elk and Chautauqua counties to the east.

Republicans won the 4th's U.S. House seat in 1994 and have kept control of the GOP-leaning district since. Despite higher Republican voter registration, Democrats — aided by a strong union presence in Wichita — do capture some local offices. George W. Bush took 64 percent of the 4th's presidential vote in 2004.

MAJOR INDUSTRY
Aviation, defense, agriculture, health care

MILITARY BASES
McConnell Air Force Base, 2,641 military, 960 civilian (2005)

CITIES
Wichita, 344,284; Derby, 17,807; Newton, 17,190

NOTABLE
Pizza Hut was founded in Wichita in 1958 by students at the University of Wichita (now called Wichita State University), and the original Pizza Hut restaurant has been moved onto the university's campus.

KENTUCKY

Gov. Ernie Fletcher (R)

First elected: 2003
Length of term: 4 years
Term expires: 1/08
Salary: $119,505
Phone: (502) 564-2611

Residence: Frankfort
Born: Nov. 12, 1952; Mount Sterling, Ky.
Religion: Baptist
Family: Wife, Glenna Fletcher; two children
Education: U. of Kentucky, B.S 1974 (mechanical engineering), M.D. 1984
Military service: Air Force, 1974-80
Career: Physician
Political highlights: Ky. House, 1995-96; Republican nominee for U.S. House, 1996; U.S. House, 1999-2003

Election results:

2003 GENERAL		
Ernie Fletcher (R)	596,284	55.0%
Ben Chandler (D)	487,159	45.0%

Lt. Gov. Stephen Pence (R)

First elected: 2003
Length of term: 4 years
Term expires: 1/08
Salary: $101,596
Phone: (502) 564-2611

LEGISLATURE

General Assembly: January-April in even-numbered years, limit of 60 days; January-March in odd-numbered years, limit of 30 days

Senate: 38 members, 4-year terms
2007 ratios: 21 R, 16 D, 1 I; 33 men, 5 women
Salary: $181/day in session; $1,715/month out of session
Phone: (502) 564-8100

House: 100 members, 2-year terms
2007 ratios: 61 D, 39 R; 88 men, 12 women
Salary: $181/day in session; $1,715/month out of session
Phone: (502) 564-8100

TERM LIMITS

Governor: 2 terms
Senate: No
House: No

URBAN STATISTICS

CITY	POPULATION
Lexington-Fayette	260,512
Louisville Metro	674,032
Owensboro	54,067

REGISTERED VOTERS

Democrat	57%
Republican	37%
Unaffiliated/others	6%

POPULATION

2006 population (est.)	4,206,074
2000 population	4,041,769
1990 population	3,685,296
Percent change (1990-2000)	+9.7%
Rank among states (2006)	26
Median age	35.9
Born in state	73.7%
Foreign born	2%
Violent crime rate	295/100,000
Poverty level	15.8%
Federal workers	36,234
Military	50,134

ELECTIONS

STATE ELECTION OFFICIAL
(502) 573-7100
DEMOCRATIC PARTY
(502) 695-4828
REPUBLICAN PARTY
(502) 875-5130

MISCELLANEOUS

Web: www.kentucky.gov
Capital: Frankfort

U.S. CONGRESS

Senate: 2 Republicans
House: 4 Republicans, 2 Democrats

2000 Census Statistics by District

DIST.	2004 VOTE FOR PRESIDENT BUSH	KERRY	WHITE	BLACK	ASIAN	HISP	MEDIAN INCOME	WHITE COLLAR	BLUE COLLAR	SERVICE INDUSTRY	OVER 64	UNDER 18	COLLEGE EDUCATION	RURAL	SQ. MILES
1	63%	36%	90%	7%	0%	1%	$30,360	47%	39%	15%	15%	24%	12%	63%	11,683
2	65	34	91	6	1	2	$35,724	50	36	14	12	26	14	53	7,567
3	49	51	76	19	1	2	$39,468	62	24	14	14	24	25	2	367
4	63	36	95	2	0	1	$40,150	56	30	14	12	26	18	40	5,679
5	61	39	97	1	0	1	$21,915	48	36	15	12	25	10	79	10,676
6	58	41	87	8	1	2	$37,544	59	27	14	11	23	25	29	3,757
STATE	60	40	89	7	1	1	$33,672	54	32	14	13	25	17	44	39,728
U.S.	50.7	48.3	69	12	4	13	$41,994	60	25	15	12	26	24	21	3,537,438

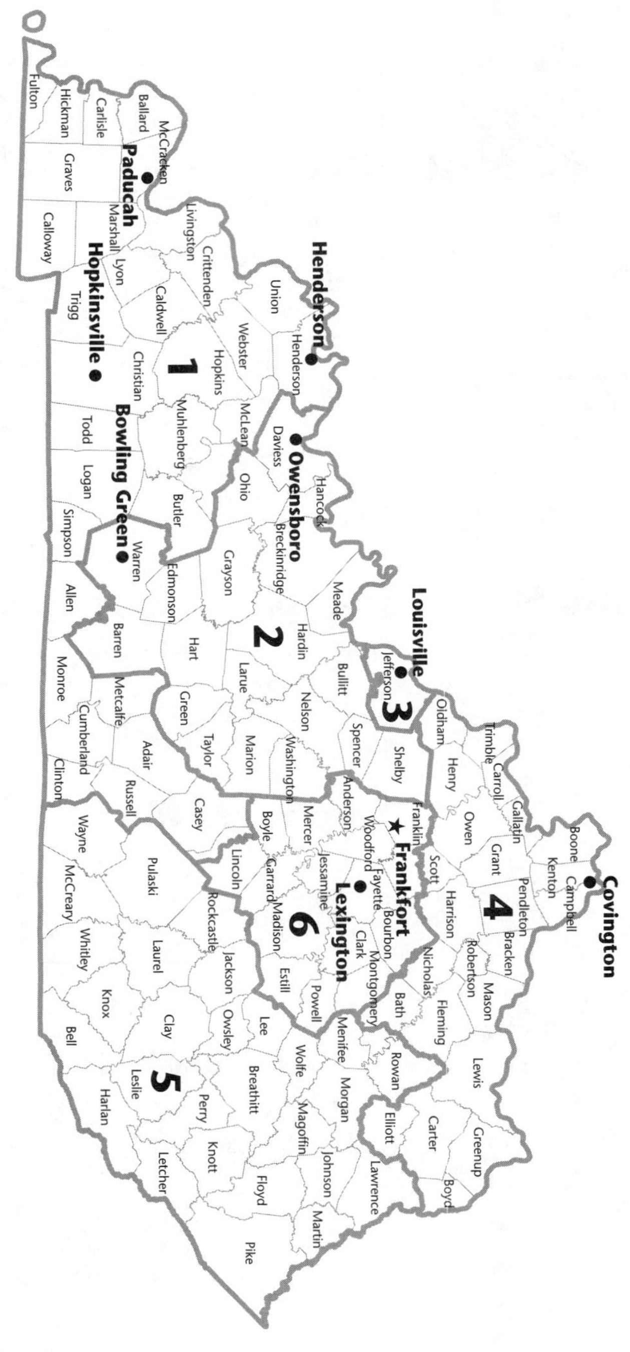

Fulton
Hickman
Carlisle
Ballard
McCracken
Paducah
Graves
Calloway
Marshall
Livingston
Lyon
Crittenden
Trigg
Caldwell
Hopkinsville
Union
Henderson
Henderson
Webster
Hopkins
Christian
1
Todd
Muhlenberg
McLean
Daviess
Owensboro
Logan
Bowling Green
Butler
Ohio
Hancock
Simpson
Warren
Edmonson
Grayson
Breckinridge
Allen
Barren
Hart
Meade
2
Hardin
Louisville
Jefferson
3
Monroe
Metcalfe
Green
Larue
Bullitt
Nelson
Oldham
Cumberland
Adair
Taylor
Marion
Washington
Spencer
Shelby
Henry
Trimble
Carroll
Clinton
Russell
Casey
Boyle
Mercer
Anderson
Franklin
Frankfort
Owen
Gallatin
Boone
Wayne
Pulaski
Lincoln
Garrard
Jessamine
Woodford
Fayette
Lexington
Scott
Grant
Kenton
Covington
Campbell
McCreary
Rockcastle
Madison
6
Bourbon
Harrison
Pendleton
4
Whitley
Laurel
Jackson
Estill
Clark
Montgomery
Nicholas
Robertson
Bracken
Knox
Clay
Owsley
Lee
Powell
Bath
Fleming
Mason
Bell
Leslie
5
Perry
Breathitt
Wolfe
Menifee
Rowan
Lewis
Harlan
Magoffin
Morgan
Elliott
Carter
Greenup
Letcher
Knott
Floyd
Johnson
Lawrence
Boyd
Pike
Martin

Sen. Mitch McConnell (R)

CAPITOL OFFICE
224-2541
mcconnell.senate.gov
361A Russell 20510-1702; fax 224-2499

COMMITTEES
Agriculture, Nutrition & Forestry
Appropriations
Rules & Administration

RESIDENCE
Louisville

BORN
Feb. 20, 1942, Sheffield, Ala.

RELIGION
Baptist

FAMILY
Wife, Elaine L. Chao; three children

EDUCATION
U. of Louisville, B.A. 1964; U. of Kentucky, J.D. 1967

CAREER
Lawyer; U.S. Justice Department official; congressional aide

POLITICAL HIGHLIGHTS
Jefferson County judge-executive, 1978-85

ELECTION RESULTS

2002 GENERAL		
Mitch McConnell (R)	731,679	64.7%
Lois Combs Weinberg (D)	399,634	35.3%
2002 PRIMARY		
Mitch McConnell (R)		unopposed

PREVIOUS WINNING PERCENTAGES
1996 (55%); 1990 (52%); 1984 (50%)

Elected 1984; 4th term

McConnell is a consummate pragmatist and inside player who can cut deals and accept less than a full loaf to get a job done. In the 110th Congress (2007-08), McConnell was elected minority leader, pitting him against Harry Reid of Nevada, an equally skilled parliamentary chess player who was elected majority leader after Democrats captured the Senate.

"I'm a conservative Republican. On most issues, I would like to see a right-of-center result," McConnell has long said. "But I've also been in legislative politics long enough to know that rarely do you get exactly what you want. Our whole process is about accepting less than what you want in order to advance the ball."

The Kentucky conservative represents a major shift from his predecessor, Bill Frist of Tennessee, a telegenic majority leader and former heart surgeon who spent much of the 109th Congress (2005-06) preparing to run for president. McConnell, who served for four years as whip under Frist, possesses a deeper understanding of the levers of power and how the institution operates. He is most comfortable working behind the scenes.

McConnell is also intensely loyal to President Bush. As Republicans distanced themselves from the White House with every new negative poll, McConnell stood out as an unshakable supporter. His wife, Elaine L. Chao, is Bush's Labor secretary. He first met the president as a supporter of his father's first race for president in 1988, when the younger Bush was working in the campaign's Washington office.

As the top-ranking Senate Republican, McConnell prefers to guide his party caucus through persuasion rather than threats. "I start with the notion that everyone in the Senate is smart or they wouldn't have made it this far in politics. So I spend a lot of time listening," he says. "In a body that simply cannot be operated top-down for a variety of institutional reasons, the only way to be effective is to be a good listener."

Individual members in the Senate have more autonomy than they do in the House, and lining them up for an important vote requires, in McConnell's well-known phrase, "almost all carrot and no stick."

Philosophically, McConnell is a conservative devoted to tradition and constitutional principles as he sees them. In 2006, he parted ways with most Senate Republicans to oppose a constitutional amendment that would allow Congress to ban flag burning. The measure failed by a single vote. He voted against it for the same reason he led the fight in 2002 against a major rewrite of campaign finance rules. McConnell, a self-described "First Amendment hawk," said both measures were violations of freedom of speech. "I think the Constitution and the Bill of Rights have served us well for more than 200 years," he said, "and we ought not to be modifying them."

He is best known for his prowess at leveraging power and his ability to sniff out a deal. In 2006, he managed to avert an embarrassing loss for Bush on a big budget bill. Faced with possible defections by Republicans who disagreed with Bush's spending priorities, McConnell secretly wooed a Democrat, Mary L. Landrieu of Louisiana, just days before a showdown Senate floor vote. McConnell persuaded Frist to make an overture to Landrieu, and then, in his role as an Appropriations subcommittee chairman, he and other Republicans on the committee put together a package of recovery spending for Landrieu's state, heavily damaged by hurricanes the summer before. Landrieu's lone Democratic vote for Bush's budget gave political cover to wavering moderate Republicans, who fell in line behind the plan, providing a narrow but decisive 51-vote majority on the floor.

The growing public dissatisfaction with the war in Iraq has presented McConnell with his greatest challenge. In 2007, he had trouble holding together his GOP troops in the face of heavy pressure from Democrats for a withdrawal date for U.S. soldiers from Iraq. Chuck Hagel of Nebraska and Gordon H. Smith of Oregon joined Democrats in agreeing to tie further funding for the war to a troop withdrawal.

During his Senate career, McConnell has served in a variety of insider roles, some more pleasant than others. From 1999-2002, he chaired the Rules Committee, which handles internal Senate housekeeping matters as well as campaign finance and election legislation. He also chaired the Ethics Committee in 1995 when it voted to expel Republican Bob Packwood of Oregon over charges of sexual misconduct. Packwood subsequently resigned. McConnell also did a stint during the 1998 and 2000 election cycles as the head of the National Republican Senatorial Committee, the party's Senate campaign arm.

McConnell blocked a rewrite of campaign finance rules for 15 years, mounting more than 20 filibusters against various iterations of the legislation. When the measure finally was enacted in 2002, he assembled some of the nation's best legal minds and took the battle to the Supreme Court, which narrowly upheld the law in 2003. He was vilified by government watchdog groups as the chief defender of a corrupt status quo, but he was indifferent to the notoriety and made no apologies.

An only child, McConnell was born in Alabama, lived in Georgia for part of his childhood and moved to Kentucky at age 13. His father, an Army officer who fought in World War II, became a civilian Army employee after the war and then a human resources director for DuPont in Louisville.

While the family was living in Alabama, McConnell, at age 2, was stricken with polio, a disease that easily could have left him with a permanent disability. His mother learned a physical therapy regimen that she administered several times a week, and took him to nearby Warm Springs, Ga., to the same specialists who were treating Franklin D. Roosevelt. At their urging, she kept the child from walking until he was 4, a seemingly impossible task that saved McConnell from permanent damage to his afflicted left leg. "She was a true saint," McConnell says. The episode taught him the value of "tenacity and discipline," he says, and though he still has trouble walking down flights of stairs, he has no other lasting effects.

McConnell showed an early taste for politics. He was student body president in high school and in college, and president of his law school class. After law school, he worked on Capitol Hill for GOP Sen. Marlow W. Cook of Kentucky, and then served as a deputy assistant attorney general in the Ford administration. He served two terms as the chief executive of Jefferson County, now Louisville Metro, before waging his winning 1984 Senate race.

His campaign against two-term Democratic Sen. Walter D. Huddleston struggled until McConnell hit upon a gimmick to demonstrate that the incumbent had limited influence and was often absent from committee meetings. He aired television ads showing bloodhounds sniffing around Washington in search of Huddleston. Aided by President Ronald Reagan's re-election coattails, McConnell won by four-tenths of a percentage point.

In 1990, McConnell brought back the TV bloodhounds, this time to bark up the fact that he had made 99 percent of the votes cast during his first term. He won with 52 percent of the vote. His margin of victory has grown in each of his subsequent races: 55 percent in 1996 against former Lt. Gov. Steven L. Beshear and 65 percent in 2002 against Lois Combs Weinberg, an education activist.

KEY VOTES

2006

- Yes Confirm Samuel A. Alito Jr. to the Supreme Court
- Yes Allow consideration of a bill to establish a $140 billion trust fund to compensate victims of asbestos exposure
- Yes Extend tax cuts for two years at a cost of $70 billion over five years
- Yes Overhaul immigration policy with border security, enforcement and guest worker program
- Yes Allow consideration of a bill to permanently repeal the estate tax
- No Urge President Bush to begin troop withdrawals from Iraq in 2006
- No Lift President Bush's restrictions on stem cell research funding
- Yes Authorize military tribunals for suspected terrorists

2005

- Yes Curb class action lawsuits by shifting them from state to federal courts
- Yes Allow confirmation vote on Priscilla R. Owen to the U.S. Court of Appeals for the 5th Circuit
- Yes Oppose mandatory emissions limits and block recognition of global warming as a threat
- Yes Approve free-trade pact with five Central American countries
- Yes Pass energy policy overhaul favored by President Bush emphasizing domestic oil and gas production
- Yes Shield gunmakers from lawsuits when their products are used in crimes
- Yes Ban torture of prisoners in U.S. custody
- Yes Renew 16 provisions of the Patriot Act
- Yes Allow final vote on opening the Arctic National Wildlife Refuge to oil and gas exploration

CQ VOTE STUDIES

	PARTY UNITY		PRESIDENTIAL SUPPORT	
	Support	Oppose	Support	Oppose
2006	96%	4%	91%	9%
2005	99%	1%	93%	7%
2004	99%	1%	98%	2%
2003	99%	1%	100%	0%
2002	97%	3%	96%	4%
2001	98%	2%	97%	3%
2000	99%	1%	42%	58%
1999	95%	5%	33%	67%
1998	95%	5%	39%	61%
1997	97%	3%	59%	41%

INTEREST GROUPS

	AFL-CIO	ADA	CCUS	ACU
2006	13%	5%	100%	84%
2005	14%	5%	94%	100%
2004	8%	15%	94%	96%
2003	0%	10%	100%	84%
2002	23%	0%	95%	100%
2001	6%	5%	93%	96%
2000	0%	5%	92%	100%
1999	0%	0%	88%	84%
1998	0%	0%	94%	92%
1997	0%	5%	100%	88%

Sen. Jim Bunning (R)

CAPITOL OFFICE
224-4343
bunning.senate.gov
316 Hart 20510-1703; fax 228-1373

COMMITTEES
Banking, Housing & Urban Affairs
Budget
Energy & Natural Resources
Finance

RESIDENCE
Southgate

BORN
Oct. 23, 1931, Southgate, Ky.

RELIGION
Roman Catholic

FAMILY
Wife, Mary Bunning; nine children

EDUCATION
Xavier U., B.S. 1953 (economics)

CAREER
Investment broker; sports agent; professional baseball player

POLITICAL HIGHLIGHTS
Fort Thomas City Council, 1977-79; Ky. Senate, 1979-83; Republican nominee for governor, 1983; U.S. House, 1987-99

ELECTION RESULTS

2004 GENERAL		
Jim Bunning (R)	873,507	50.7%
Daniel Mongiardo (D)	850,855	49.3%
2004 PRIMARY		
Jim Bunning (R)	96,545	84.0%
Barry Metcalf (R)	18,395	16.0%

PREVIOUS WINNING PERCENTAGES
1998 (50%); 1996 House Election (68%); 1994 House Election (74%); 1992 House Election (62%); 1990 House Election (69%); 1988 House Election (74%); 1986 House Election (55%)

Elected 1998; 2nd term

An eight-time All-Star pitcher and member of baseball's Hall of Fame, Bunning was known for his fastball on the mound but throws more curves in Congress. As a conservative, he is a strong supporter of President Bush's agenda but goes his own way on occasion.

Bunning was among the Republicans who stuck with Bush on the war in Iraq as the conflict bogged down and grew increasingly unpopular with the public. "Failure in Iraq is not an option," Bunning said. "A safe and secure Iraq is vital to our overall success in the war on terror and the president is asking us to work with him to get the job done. That's exactly what I intend to do."

But Bunning was one of only two senators in 2006 to oppose Robert M. Gates as Defense secretary though Gates had been hand-picked by the president to replace Donald H. Rumsfeld. Bunning contended that Gates had been critical of American efforts in Iraq and Afghanistan "without providing any viable solutions to the problems our troops currently face," and said, "We need a secretary of defense to think forward with solutions and not backward on history we cannot change." Bunning also opposed the nomination of Federal Reserve Chairman Ben Bernanke, although he later commended him for improving the Fed's responsiveness to Congress.

For a diehard conservative, Bunning crossed the aisle a number of times to sponsor bills with Democrats. He joined with Sen. Barack Obama of Illinois in cosponsoring an energy bill that would create infrastructure for transforming coal into liquid fuel as a way of easing U.S. dependency on foreign oil. He cosponsored legislation with Democratic Sen. Debbie Stabenow of Michigan that would give companies the ability to fight back against countries that artificially inflate their currency.

And he joined with Nebraska Democrat Ben Nelson in legislation that would make permanent tax incentives for adoption. The father of nine children, Bunning has a personal interest in foster care and adoption issues. Two of his daughters have adopted children.

Bunning secured his Senate seat in 1998 by fewer than 7,000 votes, and was re-elected in 2004 with a bit wider margin — 22,652 votes out of more than 1.7 million ballots cast — but against a relatively unknown state senator who should have been an easy mark for an incumbent U.S. senator.

The squeakers are a testament to the strong feelings evoked by Bunning's stubborn and competitive political style — the same style that left batters swinging ineffectually during his baseball days. His admirers point to his diligence and conservative convictions. His detractors see him as needlessly abrasive and prone to the kind of impolitic comments that contributed to his weak showing in the last election. During remarks to a Republican audience, Bunning told a joke in which he commented that his Democratic opponent, Daniel Mongiardo, an Italian-American state senator, resembled one of Saddam Hussein's sons. The widely circulated comment was an embarrassment for Bunning.

Yet even his critics acknowledge that there is more to Bunning than a celebrity senator with a Hall-of-Fame name in sports. With a degree in economics from Xavier University, Bunning seems as much at ease tangling with Bernanke over monetary policy as he does reminiscing about his days with the Philadelphia Phillies.

A former House member, Bunning was chairman of the Ways and Means Social Security Subcommittee from 1995-98 and favored using the budget surplus to shore up the Social Security trust fund. Later, he backed Bush's unsuccessful proposal in 2005 to allow younger workers to privately invest a portion of what they pay into the program.

In the 110th Congress (2007-08), Bunning was positioned to have a say in nearly all of the tax and spending issues on the horizon from his seats on two pivotal committees: Finance and Budget.

As a former athlete, Bunning took an avid interest in the debate over the use of steroids in professional sports in the 109th Congress (2005-06). He is a strong supporter of penalties for professional athletes who use steroids. "I remember players didn't get better as they got older. We all got worse. When I played with Hank Aaron and Willie Mays and Ted Williams, they didn't put on 40 pounds to bulk up . . . and they didn't hit more homers in their late 30s than they did in their late 20s," he said.

When it comes to advocacy in behalf of Kentucky's economic interests, Bunning has yet to match the reputation of his Senate colleague, Minority Leader Mitch McConnell, who has a 14-year head start on him and a seat on the Appropriations Committee. But Bunning has been effective defending home-state interests as a leading supporter in the 108th Congress (2003-04) of a 10-year, $10 billion buyout for tobacco farmers.

A strong opponent of abortion and gun control, Bunning fits in comfortably with the Senate's ideological conservatives. His voting record typically rates 90 percent-plus scores from the American Conservative Union.

Bunning was born and reared in the Kentucky suburbs of Cincinnati. His major league career spanned 17 years, primarily with the Phillies and the Detroit Tigers. He played in both the American and National leagues and was the first pitcher to record 100 wins and 1,000 strikeouts in each league. He had 224 career wins and pitched two no-hitters. The 6-foot-3-inch athlete pitched a perfect game on June 21, 1964, against the Mets while playing for Philadelphia.

He was inducted into the Hall of Fame in 1996, and the Phillies retired his No. 14 uniform five years later. For several seasons, he managed minor-league teams, then returned to Kentucky to work as an agent to professional athletes.

Bunning launched his political career with a seat on the Fort Thomas City Council in 1977. Two years later, he unseated a longtime Democratic state senator, and eventually rose to Republican floor leader in the Kentucky Senate. He ran for governor in 1983, losing to Democratic Lt. Gov. Martha Layne Collins. But he got a respectable 44 percent of the vote in a state that usually elects Democratic governors.

In 1986, GOP officials enlisted Bunning to run for the seat of retiring Republican Rep. Gene Snyder in the 4th District, an area connecting the Louisville and Cincinnati suburbs. Bunning won with 55 percent, and was re-elected to the House five times.

The 1998 Senate election to succeed retiring Democrat Wendell H. Ford pitted Bunning against Democrat Scotty Baesler, a three-term House member from the adjacent 6th District.

Outside groups including the Christian Coalition intervened to attack Baesler's support of abortion rights. Bunning ultimately won the general election by 6,766 votes out of more than 1.1 million cast.

In 2004, Bunning faced Mongiardo, a physician and state senator who started out far behind Bunning in both name recognition and cash. In a campaign that was highly negative on both sides, Bunning was trounced in the major urban centers of Louisville and Lexington, but he reaped votes from rural conservatives who came out to vote in favor of a state constitutional amendment banning same-sex marriage, which Bunning made a signature issue.

KEY VOTES

2006

- Yes Confirm Samuel A. Alito Jr. to the Supreme Court
- No Allow consideration of a bill to establish a $140 billion trust fund to compensate victims of asbestos exposure
- Yes Extend tax cuts for two years at a cost of $70 billion over five years
- No Overhaul immigration policy with border security, enforcement and guest worker program
- Yes Allow consideration of a bill to permanently repeal the estate tax
- No Urge President Bush to begin troop withdrawals from Iraq in 2006
- No Lift President Bush's restrictions on stem cell research funding
- Yes Authorize military tribunals for suspected terrorists

2005

- Yes Curb class action lawsuits by shifting them from state to federal courts
- Yes Allow confirmation vote on Priscilla R. Owen to the U.S. Court of Appeals for the 5th Circuit
- Yes Oppose mandatory emissions limits and block recognition of global warming as a threat
- Yes Approve free-trade pact with five Central American countries
- Yes Pass energy policy overhaul favored by President Bush emphasizing domestic oil and gas production
- Yes Shield gunmakers from lawsuits when their products are used in crimes
- Yes Ban torture of prisoners in U.S. custody
- Yes Renew 16 provisions of the Patriot Act
- Yes Allow final vote on opening the Arctic National Wildlife Refuge to oil and gas exploration

CQ VOTE STUDIES

	PARTY UNITY		PRESIDENTIAL SUPPORT	
	Support	Oppose	Support	Oppose
2006	97%	3%	90%	10%
2005	98%	2%	91%	9%
2004	98%	2%	94%	6%
2003	99%	1%	100%	0%
2002	97%	3%	96%	4%
2001	97%	3%	96%	4%
2000	98%	2%	33%	67%
1999	95%	5%	24%	76%
House Service:				
1998	92%	8%	20%	80%
1997	95%	5%	27%	73%

INTEREST GROUPS

	AFL-CIO	ADA	CCUS	ACU
2006	13%	0%	91%	96%
2005	14%	5%	94%	92%
2004	17%	15%	100%	100%
2003	0%	10%	100%	85%
2002	31%	0%	95%	100%
2001	13%	0%	93%	100%
2000	13%	5%	78%	100%
1999	11%	0%	82%	100%
House Service:				
1998	0%	0%	94%	92%
1997	0%	0%	90%	92%

Rep. Edward Whitfield (R)

CAPITOL OFFICE
225-3115
www.house.gov/whitfield
2411 Rayburn 20515-1701; fax 225-3547

COMMITTEES
Energy & Commerce

RESIDENCE
Hopkinsville

BORN
May 25, 1943, Hopkinsville, Ky.

RELIGION
Methodist

FAMILY
Wife, Constance Whitfield; one child

EDUCATION
U. of Kentucky, B.S. 1965 (business); Wesley Theological Seminary, attended 1966; U. of Kentucky, J.D. 1969

MILITARY SERVICE
Army Reserve, 1967-73

CAREER
Lawyer; oil distributor; railroad executive

POLITICAL HIGHLIGHTS
Ky. House, 1974-75 (served as a Democrat)

ELECTION RESULTS

2006 GENERAL		
Edward Whitfield (R)	123,618	59.6%
Tom Barlow (D)	83,865	40.4%
2006 PRIMARY		
Edward Whitfield (R)		unopposed
2004 GENERAL		
Edward Whitfield (R)	175,972	67.4%
Billy R. Cartwright (D)	85,229	32.6%

PREVIOUS WINNING PERCENTAGES
2002 (65%); 2000 (58%); 1998 (55%); 1996 (54%); 1994 (51%)

Elected 1994; 7th term

Whitfield is a fierce defender of two of Kentucky's homegrown industries — horses and tobacco. He has led a campaign to stop the slaughter of American-bred horses for export as food, setting off a spirited lobbying battle that continued into the 110th Congress (2007-08). He also has been influential in blocking Food and Drug Administration (FDA) regulation of tobacco; his western Kentucky district has been economically dependent on tobacco since the days of slavery.

It is his anti-horse slaughter campaign, however, that has gotten him the most attention in recent years. He and his wife, Constance, are horse lovers who have rescued several animals from an early demise. Two of those animals, a giant white draft horse named Mr. Ed and a pony with a bushy mane named Spitfire, they bought at auction in 2004 before the horses could be sold for slaughter.

Constance Whitfield is the vice chairwoman of the Kentucky Horse Racing Authority. The couple began working on the issue after their experience at the 2004 horse auction in Pennsylvania. They got into a shouting match with auction operators when they witnessed a horse, too sick and feeble to travel, being loaded onto a trailer for a 1,500-mile trip to Texas, where one of three horse slaughterhouses in the United States is located. The Whitfields felt the humane approach would have been to euthanize the animal.

Whitfield then introduced a bill in the 109th Congress (2005-06) to make it a crime to transport, sell or buy horses with the intent of killing them for human consumption. The measure targets three facilities, two in the Dallas-Fort Worth area and one in rural Illinois, that slaughter horses primarily for sale in France and Belgium, where horse meat is a delicacy.

But Whitfield came up against farm-state lawmakers on the Agriculture Committee, who almost universally opposed the bill because of the precedent it might set for other livestock, such as cattle. Indeed, the bill seemed headed for the scrap heap when the Agriculture panel voted against it, 37-3.

Whitfield enjoined animal rights activists, as well as some famous horse lovers, including country singer Willie Nelson, pop icon Paul McCartney and oil tycoon T. Boone Pickens. The slaughter plants hired former Democratic Rep. Charlie Stenholm of Texas, an old friend of many ag-state lawmakers who once chaired the Agriculture Committee.

Whitfield turned to his friend, then House Speaker J. Dennis Hastert of Illinois, and even though one of the slaughter plants was in Hastert's home state, he agreed to let the bill come up for a floor vote. When it did, it passed overwhelmingly in September 2006. The Senate, however, never took up the bill, and Whitfield has planned a renewed effort in the 110th Congress. "The whole process of slaughter just seemed to me to be not right, particularly when every slaughterhouse operating in America is owned by some foreign company," he says.

Whitfield is the top-ranking Republican on a key subcommittee involved in the regulation of tobacco, the Energy and Commerce Subcommittee on Oversight and Investigations. The panel has oversight of the FDA, which has tried over the years to restrict tobacco products because of their adverse health effects. Whitfield has been on Energy and Commerce since 1995, when the GOP took control of the House and an influential Republican colleague from another tobacco state, Thomas J. Bliley Jr. of Virginia, was looking to bring friends of the industry onto the committee, which he chaired. Whitfield fought Clinton administration attempts in the latter half of the 1990s to sue tobacco companies for selling hazardous products. Later, in 2004, he pushed for provisions in a comprehensive corporate tax bill giving tobacco farmers a 10-year, $10 billion buyout. Congress passed the measure and President Bush signed it.

Whitfield also has been active in shaping health care legislation. In 2005, Congress passed his bill to allow electronic monitoring of prescription drugs, which discourages the overprescribing of medicines and "doctor shopping" by drug addicts. Legislation he sponsored and that Congress passed in 2001 compensated nuclear plant workers for the adverse health effects of exposure to radiation, which helped employees at the uranium enrichment plant in Paducah in his district.

Born in Hopkinsville, near the Tennessee border, Whitfield is the son of a railroad conductor; his mother worked in finance at a local hospital. Whitfield spent a year at Wesley Theological Seminary in Washington, D.C., before switching to law school. He spent much of his early career doing regulatory and legislative work for major railroads, including CSX Corp. He lived many of those years in Washington, and in the early 1990s was a lawyer for the Interstate Commerce Commission.

When Republicans sought to capture a majority in Congress in 1994, Whitfield was recruited to run for the House by Kentucky GOP Sen. Mitch McConnell. Challenging Democratic Rep. Tom Barlow seemed like a long shot, with Democrats greatly outnumbering Republicans in registered voters. Plus, Whitfield had not lived in Kentucky for a dozen years; he moved from CSX headquarters in Jacksonville, Fla., to make the race.

But efforts to paint him as a carpetbagger were offset by the strength of his family roots in the 1st District. His extended family had farmed in the area since 1799, and a great uncle was president of the Kentucky Farm Bureau. Furthermore, Whitfield was a friend of Democrat Edward Breathitt, who was a Kentucky governor in the 1960s.

Whitfield won that race with 51 percent of the vote. He is the first Republican to represent the 1st District, and in each election he has added to his margin of victory and tightened his hold on the seat. He was threatened by the anti-Republican tide of the 2006 election, but ended up winning re-election with 60 percent in a rematch with Democrat Barlow.

Whitfield was once a Democrat and served for two years in the state House as a member of that party shortly after law school. "That whole area is Democratic. Everyone grew up a Democrat," he says. He switched parties during the Reagan revolution of the 1980s.

KEY VOTES

2006

- No Stop broadband companies from favoring select Internet traffic
- Yes Affirm U.S. commitment to war in Iraq and reject setting a withdrawal date for troops
- Yes Repeal requirement for bilingual ballots at the polls
- Yes Permit U.S. sale of civilian nuclear technology to India
- Yes Build a 700-mile fence on the U.S.-Mexico border to curb illegal crossings
- Yes Permit warrantless wiretaps of suspected terrorists

2005

- Yes Intervene in the life-support case of Terri Schiavo
- No Lift President Bush's restrictions on stem cell research funding
- Yes Prohibit FBI access to library and bookstore records
- Yes Approve free-trade pact with five Central American countries
- Yes Pass energy policy overhaul favored by President Bush emphasizing domestic oil and gas production
- Yes End mandatory preservation of habitat of endangered animal and plant species
- Yes Ban torture of prisoners in U.S. custody

CQ VOTE STUDIES

	PARTY UNITY		PRESIDENTIAL SUPPORT	
	Support	Oppose	Support	Oppose
2006	90%	10%	87%	13%
2005	94%	6%	87%	13%
2004	91%	9%	85%	15%
2003	94%	6%	94%	6%
2002	94%	6%	87%	13%

INTEREST GROUPS

	AFL-CIO	ADA	CCUS	ACU
2006	21%	0%	93%	76%
2005	21%	10%	85%	88%
2004	14%	5%	100%	88%
2003	21%	10%	100%	84%
2002	0%	0%	94%	100%

KENTUCKY 1

West — Hopkinsville, Henderson, Paducah

Located in the western part of the Bluegrass state, Kentucky's rural 1st is a hub of agricultural activity. Tobacco still dominates the economy, particularly in the counties south of the Ohio River city of Henderson.

The Ohio River port of Paducah (McCracken County) traditionally has been western Kentucky's political and population center, although its population has been surpassed by both Henderson and Hopkinsville. Hopkinsville is an agricultural market center and has an ethanol plant, owned by two collectives of farmer investors, that expects to produce up to 33 million gallons of fuel ethanol annually. The city also is heavily dependent on nearby Fort Campbell, much of which is in Tennessee.

Tobacco yields have increased in most of the 1st, but have decreased in the area around Paducah. The industry has faced uncertainty since the federal government's buyout of local tobacco farmers, which ended longstanding production quotas and price controls. The 1st also has an abundance of coal. Despite a generally volatile market, the coal mining industry is experiencing growth after years of decline. Tourism and recreation also play a role in the economy, especially near the 170,000-acre forested Land Between the Lakes area.

The 1st is no longer the Democratic stronghold that it once was, and the 1994 GOP wave sent the district's first Republican to Congress. While conservative Democrats continue to dominate local offices in western Kentucky, the region votes for Republican presidential candidates. George W. Bush carried all of the district's 34 counties in the 2004 election, including Ballard and Muhlenberg counties, which last voted for a GOP presidential candidate in 1972.

MAJOR INDUSTRY

Tobacco, agriculture, manufacturing, coal

MILITARY BASES

Fort Campbell, 30,334 military, 4,388 civilian (2006) (shared with Tennessee's 7th District)

CITIES

Hopkinsville, 30,089; Henderson, 27,373; Paducah, 26,307

NOTABLE

The Jefferson Davis Monument, located at his birthplace in Fairview, is a 351-foot obelisk; The nation's only plant that turns uranium into nuclear fuel is operated by USEC in Paducah.

Rep. Ron Lewis (R)

CAPITOL OFFICE
225-3501
www.house.gov/ronlewis
2418 Rayburn 20515-1702; fax 226-2019

COMMITTEES
Ways & Means

RESIDENCE
Cecilia

BORN
Sept. 14, 1946, Greenup County, Ky.

RELIGION
Baptist

FAMILY
Wife, Kayi Lewis; two children

EDUCATION
Morehead State U., attended 1964-67; U. of Kentucky, B.A. 1969 (political science & history); Southern Baptist Theological Seminary, attended 1980 (divinity); Morehead State U., M.A. 1981 (higher education)

MILITARY SERVICE
Navy, 1972

CAREER
Christian bookstore owner; minister; college instructor; oil company sales representative

POLITICAL HIGHLIGHTS
Sought Republican nomination for Ky. House, 1971

ELECTION RESULTS

2006 GENERAL		
Ron Lewis (R)	118,548	55.4%
Mike Weaver (D)	95,415	44.6%
2006 PRIMARY		
Ron Lewis (R)		unopposed
2004 GENERAL		
Ron Lewis (R)	185,394	67.9%
Adam Smith (D)	87,585	32.1%

PREVIOUS WINNING PERCENTAGES
2002 (70%); 2000 (68%); 1998 (64%); 1996 (58%); 1994 (60%); 1994 Special Election (55%)

Elected May 1994; 7th full term

Faced with an unusually strong challenge to his seat in the last election, Lewis switched his focus from the social issues that usually get the former Baptist preacher fired up to more local, dollars-and-cents concerns in his heartland district, where the economy is in transition. Tobacco farmers are by necessity switching to other crops and military bases are downsizing.

In his initial years in the House, Lewis often used the pulpit of the House floor to sermonize about the decline of moral values in America. His focus of late has been on the difficult economic situation of many of his constituents. He has used his seat on the influential, tax-writing Ways and Means Committee to come up with tax incentives helpful back home and to push for fewer trade barriers for the district's farm products.

In 2006, Lewis sponsored the Rural Communities Investment Act, which provides tax incentives to make interest income on farm real estate and certain rural housing loans exempt from federal taxation. And he introduced a proposal to extend a federal program to provide capital for businesses.

Lewis also successfully joined with the Kentucky delegation in 2005 to fight the closing of Fort Knox, which houses most of the U.S. gold reserves and employs nearly 9,000 personnel in his district. The base is being realigned, with some new functions, but it was designated to stay open and to keep the gold reserves in the last round of base closings.

With his attentiveness to folks at home, Lewis was able to beat back the most serious challenge to his seat since he won it in a special election in 1994. The Democrats in 2006 put up a good challenger in Mike Weaver, a retired Army colonel as conservative as Lewis on many issues and able to make the case that he was unaligned with the liberal Democratic leadership in Congress. As a former member of the military, Weaver also had credibility on national security issues, where Democrats are often weakest.

Lewis aired campaign commercials suggesting that Weaver would vote to raise taxes, and Vice President Dick Cheney and First Lady Laura Bush made campaign appearances for him. In the end, Lewis won re-election to a seventh full term by almost 11 percentage points.

He was helped by some of his earlier work for tobacco farming, a declining mainstay in rural central Kentucky. The son of a tobacco farmer, Lewis worked in 2004 for passage of a 10-year, $10 billion buyout of tobacco farmers to encourage crop diversification. He defended the buyout against critics who called it a boon for large growers, saying it would help the 8,000 tobacco growers in his district. "Recipient payments are a simple case of economics. Those who have invested more also have had more to lose; those less, less," Lewis said.

A free-trade advocate who voted for President Bush's Central American Free Trade initiative in 2005, Lewis tries to persuade colleagues that communities can surmount the trade pact's adverse effects. He once brought some of his GOP colleagues on Ways and Means to his district to see for themselves how a once-industrialized community can survive. He took them to Campbellsville, where a Fruit of the Loom plant shut down in 1997 — its production moved overseas — causing hundreds of layoffs. But now, Lewis says, Campbellsville is a hub of new jobs, with 13 recently arrived companies that collectively employ 3,700, including distributors such as Amazon.com and international companies such as Murakami, an auto parts producer. The town is an example of how to not "put all your eggs in one basket and [to] diversify your economy," he says.

Lewis also champions the development of alternative fuels that make use of crops grown in his district. Backed by Kentucky farm organizations, he introduced legislation to promote increased use of ethanol and biodiesel, made from corn and soybeans.

And he still enjoys a good social policy fight now and then. With a national debate raging over same-sex marriage, Lewis introduced controversial legislation in 2004 to allow a two-thirds majority in Congress to overrule the Supreme Court in any case in which the high court declared an act of Congress unconstitutional. "America's judicial branch has become increasingly overreaching and disconnected from the values of everyday Americans," he said. "Congress, as the people's branch of representative government, should take steps to equally affirm our authority to interpret constitutional issues."

Once the owner of a Christian bookstore, Lewis has a perfect career score from the Christian Coalition. He blames the Democratic Party for a decline in moral values, and has been active in groups such as the House Family Caucus and the Pro-Life Caucus.

Lewis worked his way through college, doing stints at a steel company, a hospital and the highway department. After graduating from the University of Kentucky, Lewis worked as a salesman, and then moved on to a teaching job for five years at a small Louisville business college. He later attended seminary and became an ordained Baptist minister.

Lewis had never before held office when he sought the 1994 GOP nomination for a race against Democratic Rep. William H. Natcher. When Natcher died that March, in his 41st year in the House, party officials chose Lewis to run in the resulting special election.

Although west-central Kentucky had been represented by a Democrat for more than a century, Democratic voters did not have to make a big ideological leap to support Lewis; his culturally conservative views are the norm in this part of the country. Lewis effectively tied his Democratic opponent, former state Sen. Joseph Prather, to the unpopular Clinton White House. With about $200,000 from the national GOP, Lewis won with 55 percent of the vote in the special election, an outcome that presaged the Republican electoral tide that would sweep the GOP into control of the House that fall.

He had easy re-elections until Weaver came on the scene in 2006, but Lewis prevailed with 55 percent of the vote. He is among the lawmakers who came to Congress promising to limit their service, in his case to no more than four terms, but in 1998 he broke that pledge, saying it had been a mistake.

KEY VOTES

2006

- No — Stop broadband companies from favoring select Internet traffic
- Yes — Affirm U.S. commitment to war in Iraq and reject setting a withdrawal date for troops
- Yes — Repeal requirement for bilingual ballots at the polls
- Yes — Permit U.S. sale of civilian nuclear technology to India
- Yes — Build a 700-mile fence on the U.S.-Mexico border to curb illegal crossings
- Yes — Permit warrantless wiretaps of suspected terrorists

2005

- Yes — Intervene in the life-support case of Terri Schiavo
- No — Lift President Bush's restrictions on stem cell research funding
- No — Prohibit FBI access to library and bookstore records
- Yes — Approve free-trade pact with five Central American countries
- Yes — Pass energy policy overhaul favored by President Bush emphasizing domestic oil and gas production
- Yes — End mandatory preservation of habitat of endangered animal and plant species
- No — Ban torture of prisoners in U.S. custody

CQ VOTE STUDIES

	PARTY UNITY		PRESIDENTIAL SUPPORT	
	Support	Oppose	Support	Oppose
2006	97%	3%	95%	5%
2005	96%	4%	89%	11%
2004	96%	4%	82%	18%
2003	96%	4%	90%	10%
2002	98%	2%	85%	15%

INTEREST GROUPS

	AFL-CIO	ADA	CCUS	ACU
2006	29%	5%	100%	84%
2005	20%	10%	85%	88%
2004	27%	5%	95%	84%
2003	13%	15%	97%	84%
2002	11%	0%	90%	96%

KENTUCKY 2

West central — Owensboro, Bowling Green

The mostly rural 2nd, anchored in Kentucky's west-central heartland, takes in some suburban areas near Louisville and runs through rolling tobacco country, ending in the river country to the west.

Tobacco remains the 2nd's dominant crop, but production in some areas has decreased here as crop areas moved west following the federal buyout of tobacco farms and the end of the quota system. Coal and oil east of Owensboro make it western Kentucky's leading trade center and provide jobs throughout the district. An Amazon.com distribution center in Campbellsville has brought stability to an otherwise grim economy in the 2nd's rural areas, which have been subject to the highs and lows of the coal industry. The General Motors Corvette plant in Bowling Green employs around 1,200. Tourism is a growing sector of the economy, and Mammoth Cave National Park, which has the most extensive known cave system in the world, draws more than 2 million visitors annually.

The eastern portion of the district includes several of the distilleries on Kentucky's "Bourbon Trail." Bardstown, in Nelson County, bills itself as the heart of the Bourbon Trail and boasts a whiskey museum. The 2nd is home to many distilleries that produce famous brands such as Jim Beam, in Clermont, and Maker's Mark, in Loretto.

The 2nd includes the birthplace (in Larue County) of Abraham Lincoln, the first Republican president, and district voters now side with the GOP in federal elections after a long period of Democratic dominance. In the 2004 presidential election, George W. Bush won all 19 counties that lie wholly within the 2nd, and just two gave him less than 60 percent of the vote. The 2nd was Bush's best district (65 percent) in Kentucky in 2004.

MAJOR INDUSTRY

Tobacco, coal, oil, tourism, manufacturing

MILITARY BASES

Fort Knox, 5,473 military, 3,319 civilian (2006)

CITIES

Owensboro, 54,067; Bowling Green, 49,296; Elizabethtown, 22,542

NOTABLE

The U.S. Bullion Depository, or "Gold Vault," at Fort Knox houses the largest portion of the U.S. gold reserve; Bardstown's Federal Hill Mansion inspired Stephen Foster to compose the ballad "My Old Kentucky Home" and is on the state's commemorative quarter.

Rep. John Yarmuth (D)

CAPITOL OFFICE
225-5401
yarmuth.house.gov
319 Cannon 20515-1703; fax 225-5776

COMMITTEES
Education & Labor
Oversight & Government Reform

RESIDENCE
Louisville

BORN
Nov. 4, 1947, Louisville, Ky.

RELIGION
Jewish

FAMILY
Wife, Cathy Yarmuth; one child

EDUCATION
Yale U., B.A. 1969 (American studies); Georgetown U. Law School, attended 1971-72

CAREER
Periodical publisher and columnist; television commentator; public relations executive; congressional aide; stockbroker

POLITICAL HIGHLIGHTS
Republican nominee for Louisville Board of Alderman, 1975; Republican nominee for Jefferson County Board of Commissioners, 1981

ELECTION RESULTS

2006 GENERAL		
John Yarmuth (D)	122,489	50.6%
Anne M. Northup (R)	116,568	48.2%
2006 PRIMARY		
John Yarmuth (D)	30,962	53.8%
Andrew Horne (D)	18,662	32.4%
James Walter Moore (D)	4,582	8.0%
Burrel Charles Farnsley (D)	3,322	5.8%

Elected 2006; 1st term

One of the first signs of the Democratic tidal wave in the November 2006 elections came when television networks reported that Yarmuth had defeated five-term Republican incumbent Anne M. Northup to represent Kentucky's 3rd District.

Yarmuth says he mounted his successful challenge to Northup to address the needs of ordinary Americans on issues such as health care, education and the minimum wage. "Our government has made the rich and powerful its priority, and I think it is time that changed," Yarmuth says.

Yarmuth's political awakening came in 1960, when John F. Kennedy was elected president. "I was 13 years old when he was elected," Yarmuth recalls. "Those were my formative years." Nonetheless, Yarmuth's initial foray into politics came as a legislative aide to Kentucky Republican Sen. Marlow W. Cook from 1971-75. It was not until 1985 that he became a Democrat, deciding the party more closely reflected his views.

Yarmuth founded Louisville Today magazine in 1976, publishing it until 1982, along with an alternative newspaper, City Paper. After a stint in public relations in the 1980s, he founded and edited the weekly Louisville Eccentric Observer in the 1990s and appeared as a commentator on Kentucky radio and television. He also was editor and owner of Kentucky Golfer, a statewide publication, and rated golf courses for Golf Digest.

"Probably the greatest benefit of having a journalistic background is [having] a healthy skepticism and the ability and willingness to ask the right questions about things," Yarmuth says.

On the Education and Labor Committee, he will play a role in rewriting the landmark 2001 No Child Left Behind Act, which is up for renewal in the 110th Congress (2007-08). Yarmuth is a critic of the education law, saying his urban district has "very serious problems" with its reporting requirements and measurements of progress.

Yarmuth edged Northup by just 2 percentage points, and Democratic campaign strategists in early 2007 put him on their "Frontline" list for extra financial and logistical support heading into the 2008 election cycle.

KENTUCKY 3

Louisville Metro

With the Ohio River to the west, the 3rd sprawls across ethnically and economically diverse neighborhoods of Louisville Metro. Compared to the rest of the state, Louisville has a sizable black population — more than one-third of Kentucky's blacks live here.

Although statewide staple tobacco still aids the 3rd's hearty economy, other sectors now rival it. Local officials have focused on attracting new businesses to the area, and Louisville now has many health care and insurance firms. Louisville's airport is an international hub for United Parcel Service, one of the area's largest private employers.

Manufacturing still retains a large local presence: Two Ford assembly plants provide nearly 9,000 jobs, although many worry about the company's future plans to close plants. General Electric Consumer & Industrial employs 5,000 at its Louisville plant. Tourism is a large contributor to the local economy.

The 3rd is Kentucky's most Democratic district, but John Kerry took only 51 percent of the district's 2004 presidential vote. The party runs well at the local level, especially downtown, and labor strength runs deep among the blue-collar residents of the city's South End, despite job losses from industrial decline. Blacks living in the West End also back Democrats. Republicans near the river in the affluent East End, coupled with the growing number of white-collar suburbanites east of downtown, appear to be pulling the district to the right, although a Democrat won the House seat in 2006.

MAJOR INDUSTRY
Service, trade, manufacturing, health care

CITIES
Louisville Metro, 674,032

NOTABLE
The Kentucky Derby, called "the greatest two minutes in sports," is held at Churchill Downs in south Louisville.

Rep. Geoff Davis (R)

CAPITOL OFFICE
225-3465
www.house.gov/geoffdavis
1108 Longworth 20515-1704; fax 225-0003

COMMITTEES
Armed Services
Financial Services

RESIDENCE
Hebron

BORN
Oct. 26, 1958, Montreal, Canada

RELIGION
Baptist

FAMILY
Wife, Pat Davis; six children

EDUCATION
U.S. Military Academy, B.S. 1981

MILITARY SERVICE
Army, 1976-87

CAREER
Manufacturing productivity consulting firm owner; aerospace technology consultant

POLITICAL HIGHLIGHTS
Republican nominee for U.S. House, 2002

ELECTION RESULTS

2006 GENERAL		
Geoff Davis (R)	105,845	51.7%
Ken Lucas (D)	88,822	43.4%
Brian Houillion (LIBERT)	10,100	4.9%
2006 PRIMARY		
Geoff Davis (R)		unopposed
2004 GENERAL		
Geoff Davis (R)	160,982	54.4%
Nick Clooney (D)	129,876	43.9%
Michael E. Slider (I)	5,069	1.7%

Elected 2004; 2nd term

A business-oriented conservative, Davis served in the Army for more than a decade where he was a flight commander with the 82nd Airborne. A West Point graduate, he is unfailing in his support of the war in Iraq.

But in the run-up to his 2006 re-election, Davis faced stinging criticism for his answer in an October debate in which he badly underestimated the number of casualties in Iraq during the month, one of the deadliest since the war began in March 2003. Davis said 17 American military personnel serving in Iraq had died, while the number was 71 on the day of the debate.

Davis' campaign said he misspoke as a result of nervousness. But his opponent, former 4th District Democratic Rep. Ken Lucas, used the incident to paint Davis as out of touch with reality and beholden to the Bush administration. It was another example of how the Iraq War colored most of the 2006 campaigns. Although Davis was re-elected, Lucas held him to just less than 52 percent of the vote.

Davis remains committed to the war and spoke out against a February 2007 Democratic resolution offering a timetable for withdrawal of U.S. troops from Iraq. "This non-binding resolution serves no purpose other than pacifying the Democrats' political base and lowering morale in our military," Davis said. But he is aware of the toll the Iraq War has taken on the U.S. military. He has called for an increase in current force structure of about 100,000 soldiers over the next five years to reduce the pressure on National Guard and Reserve forces.

Davis sits on the Armed Services Committee and also on the Financial Services panel, where in 2006 he was successful with a measure aimed at protecting members of the military from abusive or misleading sales practices by financial services companies. The legislation gives state insurance regulators jurisdiction on military bases and prohibits the sale of certain products to members of the military. Davis said the bill "is an important first step to safeguarding the financial futures of our service members."

Also from his Financial Services seat, he sponsored legislation passed by the House in February 2007 to require federal financial regulators to report to Congress annually on efforts to simplify reporting requirements for corporations. Davis said the goal of the bill is "to hold federal agencies, as well as Congress, more accountable for making swift progress in reducing the complexity and costs of financial reporting for businesses and increasing transparency for investors." The House had passed a similar measure in the 109th Congress (2005-06), but the Senate never acted on it.

Davis' conservative social views match his fiscal ones. He opposes abortion and efforts to restrict gun ownership. He supports extending President Bush's tax cuts. He says health care costs could be lowered by curbing lawsuits. And he believes schools should be allowed to search students.

He sponsored a bill, passed by the House in September 2006, to require local school systems to create policies that allow searches of students on "reasonable suspicion" that they might be carrying drugs or weapons. School systems that didn't create such policies could lose federal money for programs preventing drug use and violence, a provision that has angered local school administrators and school boards. And Democrats criticized Republicans for backing the bill while simultaneously cutting spending on the program grants.

Davis is a solid vote for his party, backing the GOP in the 109th Congress on 95 percent of votes in which a majority of one party was aligned against a majority of the other. He supported Bush 91 percent of the time on votes on which the president had expressed his preference.

Davis disagreed with the president on immigration, however. A strong proponent of better border control, Davis said the battle to control the U.S. border is of paramount importance in dealing with terrorism. He supported erecting a 700-mile fence along the U.S.-Mexico border, and opposed Bush's proposal to grant amnesty to many illegal aliens. "The unfortunate fact is that we live in a time when terrorists want to hit us as hard as they can," Davis said. "And it is elementary that to defend ourselves against these determined and resourceful enemies, our border must be secure."

Davis says limited government is desirable. But personal experiences have sensitized him to the help government can provide: Social Security survivor benefits enabled his family to make ends meet after his stepfather died, and a government-subsidized loan made it possible for his mother to buy a house. Davis worked as a janitor while in high school to help his family pay the bills.

After leaving the Army, Davis worked as an aerospace consultant before starting his own manufacturing and technology consulting firm. He also served as a volunteer chaplain with the state correctional agency.

Davis made his political debut in 2002 by nearly defeating Democratic Rep. Ken Lucas, whose conservative views had enabled him to prevail in the socially conservative district. After the 4 percentage point defeat, Davis immediately began preparing for a second campaign. In late 2003, Lucas announced that he would not seek re-election.

Davis comfortably won the 2004 GOP primary, then squared off against Democratic nominee Nick Clooney — the father of actor George Clooney — who was almost universally known as a longtime local newscaster and columnist. A close race was forecast, but the strong GOP underpinnings of the district helped Davis post a solid 10 percentage point victory.

The 2006 contest was a rematch of 2002, though under reversed circumstances. Lucas, after some courting by national Democratic recruiters, surprised Davis by announcing just before the January candidate filing deadline that he was coming out of retirement and seeking to reclaim the seat. Lucas was uniquely suited to challenge Davis on this conservative turf. His party unity score was regularly one of the lowest among House Democrats during his six-year tenure.

Though there is a slight majority of registered Democrats, GOP candidates still fare well, especially at the presidential level — in 2004, Bush took 63 percent of the vote. In 2006, Davis defeated Lucas with 52 percent.

KEY VOTES

2006

No Stop broadband companies from favoring select Internet traffic
Yes Affirm U.S. commitment to war in Iraq and reject setting a withdrawal date for troops
Yes Repeal requirement for bilingual ballots at the polls
Yes Permit U.S. sale of civilian nuclear technology to India
Yes Build a 700-mile fence on the U.S.-Mexico border to curb illegal crossings
Yes Permit warrantless wiretaps of suspected terrorists

2005

Yes Intervene in the life-support case of Terri Schiavo
No Lift President Bush's restrictions on stem cell research funding
No Prohibit FBI access to library and bookstore records
Yes Approve free-trade pact with five Central American countries
Yes Pass energy policy overhaul favored by President Bush emphasizing domestic oil and gas production
Yes End mandatory preservation of habitat of endangered animal and plant species
Yes Ban torture of prisoners in U.S. custody

CQ VOTE STUDIES

	PARTY UNITY		PRESIDENTIAL SUPPORT	
	Support	Oppose	Support	Oppose
2006	94%	6%	95%	5%
2005	96%	4%	87%	13%

INTEREST GROUPS

	AFL-CIO	ADA	CCUS	ACU
2006	29%	5%	93%	84%
2005	13%	0%	93%	88%

KENTUCKY 4

North — Covington, Florence, Ashland

The 4th travels across northern Kentucky, from the industrial city of Ashland along the Ohio River, past tobacco farms and small towns, through the Ohio commuters' region before reaching the Oldham County suburbs northeast of Louisville Metro. Nearly half of district residents live in the Cincinnati suburbs.

The city of Covington and other parts of northern Kentucky in Boone, Campbell and Kenton counties — which include Cincinnati suburbs — have enjoyed steady economic growth for more than a decade. Cincinnati-Northern Kentucky International Airport, located in Boone County, is the largest economic driving force in the region, and is expanding domestic and international service. Delta Airlines and its regional partner Comair are major area employers, as is air freight carrier DHL. Covington also serves as a regional processing center for the IRS.

The economy in the eastern part of the district, however, has not done as well. Ashland struggled to cope after businesses relocated and downsized in the late 1980s, and the city has declined as an industrial hub. Boyd County, which includes Ashland, was the only county in the 4th to lose population in the 1990s, and the county is experiencing continued slow, but steady, population loss. Other regional jurisdictions, including those across the Ohio and Big Sandy rivers in Ohio and West Virginia, respectively, are cooperating to try to attract more industrial firms to this tri-state area. Local Ashland leaders also are predicting some property redevelopment and some job growth, especially in the retail and service sectors.

Oldham joins the Cincinnati-area counties in voting reliably Republican, and the 4th steadfastly backs GOP presidential candidates. George W. Bush took 63 percent of the 4th's 2004 presidential vote, and John Kerry carried just three counties — Elliott, which has voted Democratic for president since before 1920, Bath and Carter, which Bush narrowly lost.

MAJOR INDUSTRY
Transportation, manufacturing, health care, service

CITIES
Covington, 43,370; Florence, 23,551; Ashland, 21,981

NOTABLE
The Kentucky Speedway racetrack is located near Sparta.

Rep. Harold Rogers (R)

CAPITOL OFFICE
225-4601
talk2hal@mail.house.gov
www.house.gov/rogers
2406 Rayburn 20515-1705; fax 225-0940

COMMITTEES
Appropriations

RESIDENCE
Somerset

BORN
Dec. 31, 1937, Barrier, Ky.

RELIGION
Baptist

FAMILY
Wife, Cynthia Doyle Rogers; three children

EDUCATION
Western Kentucky U., attended 1956-57;
U. of Kentucky, B.A. 1962, LL.B. 1964

MILITARY SERVICE
Ky. National Guard, 1956-57; N.C. National Guard, 1957-58; Ky. National Guard, 1958-63

CAREER
Lawyer

POLITICAL HIGHLIGHTS
Pulaski and Rockcastle counties commonwealth attorney, 1969-80; Republican nominee for lieutenant governor, 1979

ELECTION RESULTS

2006 GENERAL		
Harold Rogers (R)	147,201	73.8%
Kenneth Stepp (D)	52,367	26.2%
2006 PRIMARY		
Harold Rogers (R)		unopposed
2004 GENERAL		
Harold Rogers (R)		unopposed

PREVIOUS WINNING PERCENTAGES
2002 (78%); 2000 (74%); 1998 (78%); 1996 (100%); 1994 (79%); 1992 (55%); 1990 (100%); 1988 (100%); 1986 (100%); 1984 (76%); 1982 (65%); 1980 (68%)

Elected 1980; 14th term

Even if Rogers weren't an old-style congressman in real life, he could play one on TV, with his stark-white hair, generous midsection and passion for cigars. Wielding the power that comes with being an appropriator is second nature to Rogers after a quarter-century in the House, though his tendency to use that power to reward friends and political supporters brings him unwanted attention at times.

That was the case in the 109th Congress (2005-06), when he was the subject of several newspaper and government watchdog investigations in the aftermath of the influence-peddling scandal that brought down his former ally, Majority Leader Tom DeLay of Texas. But while DeLay was forced to resign from Congress, Rogers remained immensely popular in his poor southeastern Kentucky district, the beneficiary of his experienced hand on the federal spigot.

Still, it was not a banner period in his long House career. News organizations documented his relationships with companies doing business with the Homeland Security Department, including a small Massachusetts firm whose executives donated more than $120,000 to Rogers' campaign after he helped the company secure a contract worth up to $463 million for explosives detection devices. The firm also agreed to move $15 million worth of business to Rogers' district. The congressman and the company said the campaign donations were unrelated to the contract.

Other news accounts chronicled expensive trips Rogers took to Hawaii, Palm Springs and Las Vegas paid for by private interests, some of whom benefited from his Appropriations Committee work. In 2005, the Lexington Herald-Leader reported that some of Rogers' allocations went to marginal projects, including $500,000 to pave a parking lot for Lee's Ford Marina Resort, owned by a campaign donor. The conservative National Review magazine described Rogers as "an exemplary figure of congressional disgrace."

But the free use of his power over spending has endeared him to local officials and constituents. The 5th District is by far the poorest district in the state. The Lexington paper estimates that half the adults in Rogers' district don't work and nearly a third live in poverty. Since 1999, Rogers has helped facilitate more than $2 billion in investment, the newspaper said. Over the years, he has secured money for highways, industrial parks, new prisons and waterworks, plus federal incentives for homeland security-related companies to headquarter there. In 2004, Rogers announced that a new National Institute for Hometown Security, a nonprofit research group, would be housed in his hometown of Somerset.

Rogers is the senior Republican on the Appropriations panel's Homeland Security Subcommittee, which controls the budget for more than 22 government agencies. Prior to Democrats taking control of the House in 2007, he was the chairman of the subcommittee, with authority over about $35 billion in federal spending each year. Before that, he chaired the panel's Transportation Subcommittee, which controls another deep pot of federal money.

As chairman, Rogers frequently pressured the struggling Department of Homeland Security to shape up as he guided the annual homeland security spending bills through the House. In 2005, angry that the Coast Guard had not done enough on its long-term modernization program called Deepwater, Rogers drafted a bill that provided $466 million less than the Bush administration had requested for the Guard. He relented in final negotiations on the bill, once he was satisfied with the service's progress.

During consideration of the next year's spending bill, Rogers said that the administration had put too much emphasis on border security at the expense of other parts of the country's anti-terrorism defenses. He reallocated money in the bill from border security to other needs, such as transportation security and first-responder grants.

Rogers was peeved when Democrats began to lard the appropriations bills with some of the same kind of narrow earmarks for individual districts that they had criticized him for during the years of GOP rule. When Democrats in early 2007 tucked several such provisions into a supplemental spending bill for the war in Iraq, Rogers called it "an attempt to buy votes."

A gregarious, old-style Republican pol who understands the art of cutting a legislative deal, Rogers has been the chairman of three different Appropriations subcommittees since joining the panel in his second term in 1983. But his popularity with colleagues did not help him ascend to the chairmanship of the full committee at the start of the 109th Congress in 2005, a job he very much wanted. GOP leaders instead gave the gavel to Republican Jerry Lewis of California, whom they saw as more willing to let them curb the power of the Appropriations subcommittee chairmen.

The 2002 law creating the Department of Homeland Security settled a longstanding debate, in which Rogers played a leading role, over how to improve the performance of the Immigration and Naturalization Service. The agency was split in half, with one bureau to guard the nation's borders and another to process immigration paperwork. Both bureaus were placed in the new security agency. Rogers had promoted such a plan, with little success, during the six years he was chairman of Appropriations' Commerce, Justice and State Subcommittee, which provided funding for the INS.

After earning undergraduate and law degrees at the University of Kentucky, Rogers made a name for himself in the southeastern part of the state as a civic activist, promoting industrial development. In 1969, he took over as the commonwealth's attorney in that part of the state and continued to play a conspicuous role in politics as prosecutor for Pulaski and Rockcastle counties.

Although he lost a 1979 campaign for lieutenant governor, the name recognition he earned paid off when he ran for the House in 1980 to succeed retiring Republican Tim Lee Carter. Rogers won a 10-person GOP primary and then waltzed to victory in November with 68 percent of the vote. He has posted a lower vote percentage only twice, most notably in 1992 when, running in a district made more Democratic by redistricting, he was held to 55 percent. In 2006, he won re-election with nearly 74 percent of the vote.

KEY VOTES

2006

No Stop broadband companies from favoring select Internet traffic
Yes Affirm U.S. commitment to war in Iraq and reject setting a withdrawal date for troops
Yes Repeal requirement for bilingual ballots at the polls
Yes Permit U.S. sale of civilian nuclear technology to India
Yes Build a 700-mile fence on the U.S.-Mexico border to curb illegal crossings
Yes Permit warrantless wiretaps of suspected terrorists

2005

? Intervene in the life-support case of Terri Schiavo
No Lift President Bush's restrictions on stem cell research funding
No Prohibit FBI access to library and bookstore records
Yes Approve free-trade pact with five Central American countries
Yes Pass energy policy overhaul favored by President Bush emphasizing domestic oil and gas production
Yes End mandatory preservation of habitat of endangered animal and plant species
No Ban torture of prisoners in U.S. custody

CQ VOTE STUDIES

	PARTY UNITY		PRESIDENTIAL SUPPORT	
	Support	Oppose	Support	Oppose
2006	96%	4%	93%	7%
2005	96%	4%	91%	9%
2004	95%	5%	88%	12%
2003	98%	2%	95%	5%
2002	95%	5%	87%	13%

INTEREST GROUPS

	AFL-CIO	ADA	CCUS	ACU
2006	29%	10%	87%	80%
2005	13%	0%	93%	92%
2004	20%	0%	100%	88%
2003	7%	5%	97%	84%
2002	13%	0%	100%	88%

KENTUCKY 5

East and southeast – Somerset, Middlesborough

The rural 5th, which takes in eastern Kentucky's hardscrabble coal country, has struggled with poverty, undereducation and a lack of economic diversity. The district has the nation's highest percentage of white residents (97 percent) and its second-lowest median income.

Coal mining once was a thriving industry in this sparsely populated Appalachian region. Mining still provides thousands of jobs in the area, particularly in places such as Pike, Perry, Harlan and Knott counties, but despite some increased demand due to exports and coal power generation, these eastern counties are trying to diversify their economies. Some community leaders are trying to attract tourists by highlighting the area's country music heritage, building new arts centers and showcasing the area's coal history.

Population in the western portion of the district is concentrated in Pulaski and Laurel counties. Somerset, in Pulaski, relies heavily on tourism and recreation. Lake Cumberland is nearby, as is the Big South Fork National River and Recreation Area. The Daniel Boone National Forest extends from Rowan County in the north to the Tennessee border.

Methamphetamine abuse, a major problem in surrounding states, has become an issue in the 5th, but groups are attempting to improve local public awareness and drug enforcement efforts. Education also is a concern, as the 5th has the state's lowest percentage (10 percent) of residents with a bachelor's degree or more.

The 5th is secure GOP territory — no Democrat has represented the southeast Kentucky district since 1889. Republicans run particularly well in the more populous central and western areas. Democrats maintain a strong presence in the far eastern coal counties, where the United Mine Workers of America union is strong, but in 2004, George W. Bush carried the 5th with 61 percent of the presidential vote.

MAJOR INDUSTRY
Coal, service, tourism

CITIES
Somerset, 11,352; Middlesborough, 10,384

NOTABLE
Colonel Harland Sanders began making what would later be known as Kentucky Fried Chicken at his service station in Corbin.

Rep. Ben Chandler (D)

CAPITOL OFFICE
225-4706
chandler.house.gov
1504 Longworth 20515-1706; fax 225-2122

COMMITTEES
Appropriations
Science & Technology

RESIDENCE
Versailles

BORN
Sept. 12, 1959, Versailles, Ky.

RELIGION
Presbyterian

FAMILY
Wife, Jennifer Chandler; three children

EDUCATION
U. of Kentucky, B.A. 1983 (history), J.D. 1986

CAREER
Lawyer

POLITICAL HIGHLIGHTS
Ky. auditor, 1992-96; Ky. attorney general, 1996-2004; Democratic nominee for governor, 2003

ELECTION RESULTS

2006 GENERAL		
Ben Chandler (D)	158,765	85.5%
Paul Ard (LIBERT)	27,015	14.5%
2006 PRIMARY		
Ben Chandler (D)		unopposed
2004 GENERAL		
Ben Chandler (D)	175,355	58.6%
Tom Buford (R)	119,716	40.0%

PREVIOUS WINNING PERCENTAGES
2004 Special Election (55%)

Elected February 2004; 2nd full term

Now in his second full term in the House, Chandler was picked by Democratic leaders for a spot on the powerful Appropriations Committee in 2007 as a reward for making sure the competitive 6th District stayed in the Democratic column. His conservatism can give them fits, and his vote is not always theirs for the asking, but he did his part to put them in the majority by taking the 6th District seat away from the Republicans in a special election in 2004, and then warding off a serious challenge later that year. In 2006, with Chandler safely ensconced, the GOP did not even field a challenger.

Chandler is further to the right on certain social and economic issues than many of his Democratic colleagues, in keeping with the general sentiment of his Bluegrass Kentucky district. He will stick with his party on broad concerns such as the Iraq War, but overall he is a centrist. He belongs to the Blue Dog Coalition, a group of fiscally conservative Democrats.

In the 109th Congress (2005-06), he voted with his party 81 percent of the time on votes on which the parties disagreed. And he supported President Bush's position relatively frequently. He voted with Bush 53 percent of the time on bills on which the president took a firm position, placing Chandler among the top 15 Democrats favoring the White House point of view. "I disagree with a lot of things that the national Democrats do. I disagree with plenty of things that the Republicans do," he says. "The point is, on an issue, I'm going to be my own man."

Socially, he is opposed to same-sex marriage, and supports some curbs on abortion but opposes an outright ban. He backs the rights of gun owners. But he joined with most Democrats when he voted in 2005 and 2007 for a measure to expand federal funding for embryonic stem cell research, which uses cells harvested from surplus embryos at in vitro fertilization clinics.

He opposes giving tax cuts to the wealthy, saying tax relief should be directed to middle- and lower-income taxpayers because "those are the very people who would have plugged it right back into the economy." He voted against a 2006 bill to extend about $70 billion of Bush's 2001 and 2003 tax breaks over five years. The bill also included capital gains and dividend tax cuts important to the White House.

In 2005, Chandler found himself at the center of a dispute with the Bush administration over a locally sensitive issue. Bush's 2006 budget proposed reducing funds for destroying chemical weapons stockpiles at the Blue Grass Army Depot just southeast of Richmond. The weapons have long been a concern to the surrounding communities in Chandler's district.

Chandler joins with his party in calling for an end to the Iraq War, which he says has become a "fiasco" and "badly managed." He supported a February 2007 resolution by the Democratic leadership opposing Bush's call for more troops for Iraq. Chandler said, "In my judgment, this war is beyond the scope of our men and women in uniform. The situation in Iraq is in dire need of a diplomatic solution."

Chandler got a seat on the Appropriations State-Foreign Operations Subcommittee, which is a good fit for him and his longtime interest in foreign affairs. As a college student, he served as an intern in the British Parliament, an experience that he says gave him a global view of the world. "You just cannot afford to be on bad terms with 95 percent of the world," he says. "You need allies and friends." Chandler also serves with 11 other members of Congress in the NATO Parliamentary Assembly, which aims to improve relationships among the NATO partners.

In 2005, as a member of the International Relations Committee, he objected to a bill to withhold U.S. funds from the United Nations if the organization did not make a series of sweeping changes in how it does business. The bill would have mandated withholding up to 50 percent of U.S. assessed dues if the United Nations did not reach 39 goals laid out in the bill. Democrats supported the idea of a U.N. overhaul but opposed holding back U.S. dues, saying that step was "draconian." Chandler agreed. "This bill is akin to the child who takes his ball home when he doesn't get his way," he said.

Chandler also sits on the Science and Technology Committee, where he says he wants to work to ensure "we are good stewards of the environment."

Chandler lives in Woodford County on land that has been in his family since 1784, eight years before Kentucky became a state. The area is home to some of the finest thoroughbred horse farms in the world. He was born in Versailles, and he says he can trace his ancestors on his mother's side back to the second boat that arrived at Jamestown in 1609.

Chandler also has deep political roots in Kentucky. His grandfather and namesake, A.B. "Happy" Chandler, was a two-time governor and a U.S. senator and may be best remembered for his five-year stint as commissioner of Major League Baseball.

In 1991, Chandler was elected Kentucky auditor, and then won elections for attorney general in 1995 and 1999, becoming the state's youngest-ever attorney general. As Kentucky's top law enforcement officer, he oversaw the establishment of the state's "do not call" telemarketing list.

He ran for governor in 2003 but was defeated by Republican Rep. Ernie Fletcher. After his loss, Chandler ran in the special-election contest for the House seat vacated by Fletcher. His race against GOP state Sen. Alice Forgy Kerr drew widespread attention. The candidates were financially competitive. Both national parties recognized that the contest would be perceived as a bellwether and spent heavily on them. The nine-week campaign cost more than $4 million. Chandler won by 12 percentage points. A little more than eight months later, he won election to a full term.

After besting Chandler, Fletcher went on to have a tough first term as governor. His budget and tax reform plans were rejected by the legislature, and state employees protested his changes in their health benefits. Meanwhile, Chandler was being celebrated as a party hero for capturing Fletcher's old seat. "I love this job. I wouldn't trade," he told the Lexington Herald-Leader in 2004. "Ernie might want to, but I don't think I'd let him."

KEY VOTES

2006

- Yes Stop broadband companies from favoring select Internet traffic
- Yes Affirm U.S. commitment to war in Iraq and reject setting a withdrawal date for troops
- No Repeal requirement for bilingual ballots at the polls
- Yes Permit U.S. sale of civilian nuclear technology to India
- Yes Build a 700-mile fence on the U.S.-Mexico border to curb illegal crossings
- No Permit warrantless wiretaps of suspected terrorists

2005

- Yes Intervene in the life-support case of Terri Schiavo
- Yes Lift President Bush's restrictions on stem cell research funding
- Yes Prohibit FBI access to library and bookstore records
- No Approve free-trade pact with five Central American countries
- No Pass energy policy overhaul favored by President Bush emphasizing domestic oil and gas production
- No End mandatory preservation of habitat of endangered animal and plant species
- Yes Ban torture of prisoners in U.S. custody

CQ VOTE STUDIES

	PARTY UNITY		PRESIDENTIAL SUPPORT	
	Support	Oppose	Support	Oppose
2006	83%	17%	56%	44%
2005	80%	20%	50%	50%
2004	79%	21%	45%	55%

INTEREST GROUPS

	AFL-CIO	ADA	CCUS	ACU
2006	86%	60%	57%	50%
2005	87%	85%	52%	36%
2004	86%	70%	55%	32%

KENTUCKY 6

East central — Lexington, Frankfort

The 6th embodies the culture and economic pursuits that most outsiders associate with Kentucky. This is the heart of the Bluegrass region, which spawns Kentucky Derby champions and is host to considerable tobacco and liquor interests.

A patchwork of urban, suburban and rural areas, the 6th has experienced steady economic growth and now has a robust economy. Lexington has a strong equine industry and is known as the thoroughbred capital of the world. The city is home to the University of Kentucky, which is central Kentucky's largest employer. Just north of Lexington in Georgetown, at Toyota's largest plant in North America, the company's first hybrid vehicle produced in the United States rolled off the line in 2006. The state capital, Frankfort, is located about 30 miles northwest of Lexington.

Tobacco, always a highly charged subject in this region, continues to be a strong economic force, although there has been a gradual decline in production. The end of the quota system — which controlled the supply and price of tobacco — and the government's tobacco buyout have prompted many tobacco operations to consolidate or leave the newly competitive industry. Production also has generally shifted away from the 6th in favor of the state's western regions.

The 6th is a politically competitive district. Republican George W. Bush won the area's 2004 presidential vote, but the 6th's House seat flipped from Republican to Democrat in 2004 and has remained so. Voters here, who tend to be socially conservative, will support candidates from either party. Frankfort's government workers contribute to Franklin County's Democratic lean, although the county voted for Bush in 2004. Democratic support dips in Scott (shared with the 4th) and Woodford counties. The GOP runs up big margins in the farmland south of Lexington.

MAJOR INDUSTRY

Manufacturing, service, tobacco, retail

MILITARY BASES

Blue Grass Army Depot, 4 military, 1,200 civilian (2007)

CITIES

Lexington-Fayette, 260,512; Frankfort, 27,741; Richmond, 27,152

NOTABLE

Bourbon whiskey was named after Bourbon County.

LOUISIANA

Gov. Kathleen Babineaux Blanco (D)

Pronounced: Bab-in-oh BLAHN-ko
First elected: 2003
Length of term: 4 years
Term expires: 1/08
Salary: $95,000
Phone: (225) 342-7015

Residence: Lafayette
Born: Dec. 15, 1942; Coteau, La.
Religion: Roman Catholic
Family: Husband, Raymond Blanco; six children (one deceased)
Education: U. of Southwestern Louisiana, B.S. 1964 (business education)
Career: Political marketing firm partner; U.S. Census Bureau district manager; homemaker; teacher
Political highlights: La. House, 1984-89; La. Public Service Commission, 1989-95 (chairwoman, 1993-94); lieutenant governor, 1996-2004

Election results:

2003 GENERAL RUNOFF		
Kathleen Babineaux Blanco (D)	731,358	52.0%
Bobby Jindal (R)	676,484	48.1%

Lt. Gov. Mitch Landrieu (D)

First elected: 2003
Length of term: 4 years
Term expires: 1/08
Salary: $85,000
Phone: (225) 342-7009

LEGISLATURE

Legislature: March-June in odd-numbered years; April-June in even-numbered years

Senate: 39 members, 4-year terms
2007 ratios: 24 D, 15 R; 32 men, 7 women
Salary: $16,800
Phone: (225) 342-2040

House: 105 members, 4-year terms
2007 ratios: 61 D, 43 R, 1 I; 87 men, 18 women
Salary: $16,800
Phone: (225) 342-6945

TERM LIMITS

Governor: 2 terms
Senate: 3 consecutive terms
House: 3 consecutive terms

URBAN STATISTICS

CITY	POPULATION
New Orleans	484,674
Baton Rouge	227,818
Shreveport	200,145
Lafayette	110,257
Lake Charles	71,757

REGISTERED VOTERS

Democrat	55%
Republican	23%
Unaffiliated/others	22%

POPULATION

2006 population (est.)	4,287,768
2000 population	4,468,976
1990 population	4,219,973
Percent change (1990-2000)	+5.9%
Rank among states (2006)	24
Median age	34
Born in state	79.4%
Foreign born	2.6%
Violent crime rate	681/100,000
Poverty level	19.6%
Federal workers	34,590
Military	41,392

ELECTIONS

STATE ELECTION OFFICIAL
(225) 922-0900
DEMOCRATIC PARTY
(225) 336-4155
REPUBLICAN PARTY
(225) 928-2998

MISCELLANEOUS

Web: www.louisiana.gov
Capital: Baton Rouge

U.S. CONGRESS

Senate: 1 Democrat, 1 Republican
House: 5 Republicans, 2 Democrats

2000 Census Statistics by District

DIST.	2004 VOTE FOR PRESIDENT BUSH	KERRY	WHITE	BLACK	ASIAN	HISP	MEDIAN INCOME	WHITE COLLAR	BLUE COLLAR	SERVICE INDUSTRY	OVER 64	UNDER 18	COLLEGE EDUCATION	RURAL	SQ. MILES
1 *	70%	29%	80%	13%	2%	5%	$40,948	65%	21%	14%	13%	25%	27%	20%	2,402
2 *	24	75	28	64	3	4	$27,514	56	22	22	10	28	19	1	266
3 *	58	41	70	25	1	2	$34,463	50	35	15	11	29	11	27	7,010
4	59	40	62	33	1	2	$31,085	53	29	18	13	27	17	41	10,765
5	62	37	63	34	1	1	$27,453	54	29	18	13	27	16	47	13,775
6 *	59	40	63	33	1	2	$37,931	61	24	15	10	27	24	24	3,076
7 *	60	39	72	25	1	1	$31,453	55	29	17	12	28	17	31	6,268
STATE	57	42	63	32	1	2	$32,566	57	27	17	12	27	19	27	43,562
U.S.	50.7	48.3	69	12	4	13	$41,994	60	25	15	12	26	24	21	3,537,438

The districts with an asterisk in the above table experienced significant changes in population and demographics due to hurricanes Katrina and Rita in 2005. The statistics published here reflect information collected as part of the 2000 census. This information is the most recent comprehensive U.S. Census Bureau data broken down by congressional district. It is included here for the purpose of comparing pre-hurricane district information with available post-hurricane data. Additional statistical information collected by Congressional Quarterly may be found on pages xxiii through xxviii.

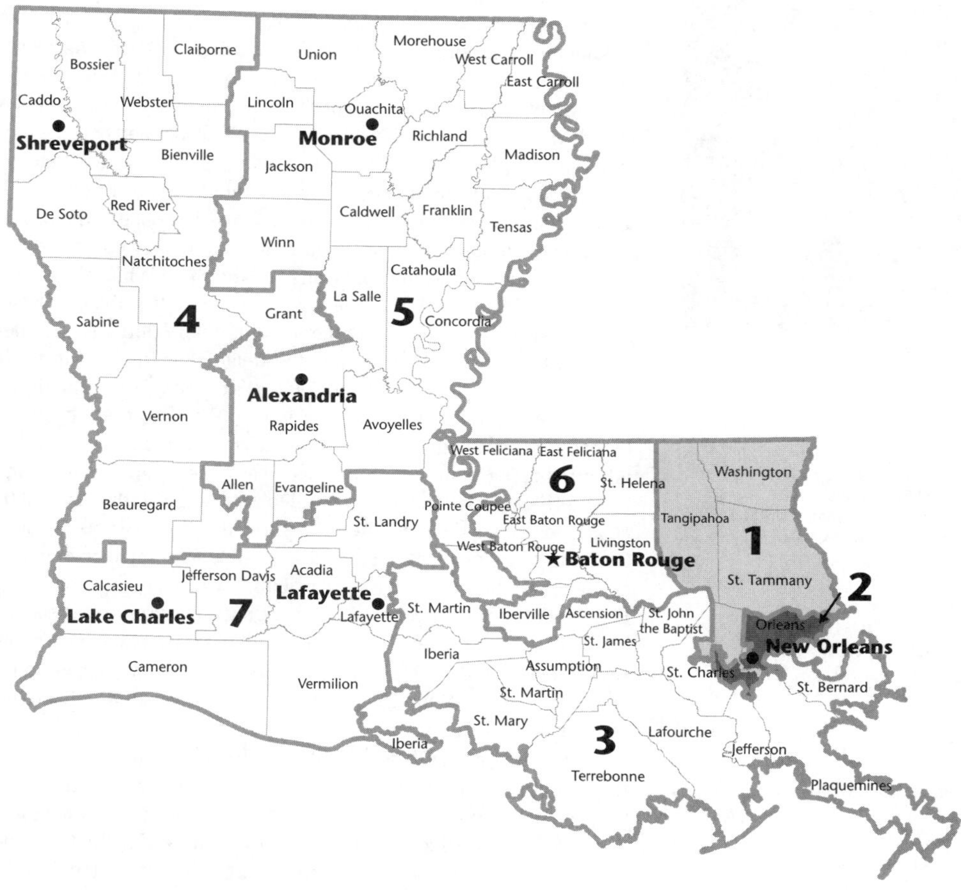
Claiborne
Bossier
Union
Morehouse
West Carroll
East Carroll
Caddo
Webster
Lincoln
Ouachita
Shreveport
Monroe
Richland
Bienville
Jackson
Madison
De Soto
Red River
Caldwell
Franklin
Tensas
Winn
Natchitoches
Catahoula
La Salle
Grant
Sabine
4
5
Concordia
Alexandria
Vernon
Rapides
Avoyelles
West Feliciana
East Feliciana
Washington
6
St. Helena
Allen
Evangeline
Beauregard
Pointe Coupee
St. Landry
East Baton Rouge
Tangipahoa
1
West Baton Rouge
Livingston
Baton Rouge
Acadia
Jefferson Davis
St. Tammany
2
Calcasieu
Lafayette
Lake Charles
7
Lafayette
St. Martin
Iberville
Ascension
St. John the Baptist
Orleans
New Orleans
St. James
Iberia
Cameron
Assumption
St. Charles
St. Bernard
Vermilion
St. Martin
St. Mary
Lafourche
3
Iberia
Jefferson
Terrebonne
Plaquemines

Sen. Mary L. Landrieu (D)

CAPITOL OFFICE
224-5824
landrieu.senate.gov
724 Hart 20510-1804; fax 224-9735

COMMITTEES
Appropriations
(Legislative Branch - chairwoman)
Energy & Natural Resources
Homeland Security & Governmental Affairs
(Disaster Recovery - chairwoman)
Small Business & Entrepreneurship

RESIDENCE
New Orleans

BORN
Nov. 23, 1955, Arlington, Va.

RELIGION
Roman Catholic

FAMILY
Husband, Frank Snellings; two children

EDUCATION
Louisiana State U., B.A. 1977 (sociology)

CAREER
Realtor

POLITICAL HIGHLIGHTS
La. House, 1980-88; La. treasurer, 1988-96; candidate for governor, 1995

ELECTION RESULTS

2002 GENERAL RUNOFF		
Mary L. Landrieu (D)	638,654	51.7%
Suzanne Haik Terrell (R)	596,642	48.3%
2002 GENERAL		
Mary L. Landrieu (D)	573,347	46.0%
Suzanne Haik Terrell (R)	339,506	27.2%
John Cooksey (R)	171,752	13.8%
Tony Perkins (R)	119,776	9.6%
Raymond Brown (D)	23,553	1.9%

PREVIOUS WINNING PERCENTAGES
1996 (50%)

Elected 1996; 2nd term

With a long bloodline in the civic life of New Orleans, Landrieu has become the unofficial delegate for the city's effort to secure tens of billions of dollars in federal reconstruction money in the wake of Hurricane Katrina. Her performance in the once-in-a-career role likely will be critical to the outcome of her 2008 re-election campaign.

After an initial stumble following Katrina's Aug. 29, 2005, landfall, when she was upbraided by a television reporter for praising federal emergency response officials as thousands of city residents remained stranded or were already dead, Landrieu (LAN-drew) did an about-face and became the administration's toughest critic. The senator, who lost a home to the storm's catastrophic flooding, threatened to punch out President Bush if he blamed local fire and police officials for an inadequate response to the disaster.

While the tough talk cheered down-and-out flood victims, it deepened a chasm between Louisiana politicians and the Bush White House. Landrieu also openly feuded with the state's junior senator, Republican David Vitter, over the size and specifics of relief funding bills. Ultimately, former Democratic Sen. John B. Breaux, a noted dealmaker, stepped in to mediate, which fed perceptions that Landrieu was not ready for prime time.

At other times, however, Landrieu — the daughter of former New Orleans Mayor Maurice "Moon" Landrieu — has demonstrated that she inherited at least some of her father's savvy as a power broker. In March 2006, as Senate GOP leaders struggled to push through a fiscal 2007 budget, Landrieu cut a deal with them. She provided the final vote needed to pass the budget bill, which called for subsequent legislation to open Alaska's Arctic National Wildlife Refuge to oil drilling, a cause she had long supported. But she delivered her vote only after winning a provision to create a $10 billion Gulf Coast recovery fund that would draw some of the revenue from ANWR leases and offshore drilling. "I was sent here to represent my state, and that's what I'm doing," Landrieu said. She was the only Democrat to vote for the resolution.

Ever since Katrina struck, in fact, Landrieu has pursued help for the battered Gulf Coast from any and all sources. Scarcely a bill moves through the Senate without a bid by Landrieu to amend it with new aid for the hurricane zone. While her efforts did not always succeed in the GOP-controlled Congress, she expects to prevail more often with her fellow Democrats in charge of the 110th Congress (2007-08).

Landrieu is a moderate who departs from her party on many crucial votes. Only one other Senate Democrat split from the party's majority more often in the 109th Congress (2005-06) and the early months of the 110th Congress. Her independence has helped her get elected in her conservative Southern state, but it often leaves liberals wary of her next move.

In 2005, Landrieu was one of the Gang of 14, a group of seven Democrats and seven Republicans who seized the Senate's balance of power on judicial nominations. They vowed to prevent filibusters of the president's nominees except under "extraordinary circumstances," a term they left up to each senator to define. But they also vowed to block GOP leaders from using a parliamentary force play to end all judicial filibusters. To the dismay of liberals, Gang members found no extraordinary circumstances surrounding Bush's Supreme Court nominees, and the Senate confirmed both Chief Justice John G. Roberts Jr. and Justice Samuel A. Alito Jr. Landrieu voted for Roberts but sided with most Democrats in opposing Alito.

In the 110th Congress, Democrats have no need of filibusters to block nominees they oppose, since they can stop them in committee. But the Gang didn't vanish. Instead, Landrieu and GOP moderate Olympia J. Snowe of Maine moved to combine its remaining members and those of the old Centrist Coalition into a new bipartisan Common Ground Coalition.

Soon after Bush took office, Landrieu split with her party to vote for his $1.35 trillion tax cut in 2001. She also aligned herself with Republicans on a vote to permanently repeal the estate tax. But she opposed the 2003 tax cuts, which reduced maximum rates on capital gains and dividends.

She has little patience for some of the social issues on which there seems no identifiable middle ground. When the Senate considered a constitutional ban on same-sex marriage in 2004, Landrieu was one of 50 senators voting to block it. Her office was bombarded with calls from angry supporters of the ban, but Landrieu said the amendment would violate the Constitution's underlying principle of limiting the role of government in people's lives. In 2006, she voted to block a similar amendment.

That position, along with her opposition to federal vouchers for private school tuition for low-income families, makes her unpopular with some of her state's many Roman Catholic voters. The church hierarchy favors school vouchers, and a group ran ads in the New Orleans Times-Picayune publicizing the fact that Landrieu's two children attend a private school in Washington, D.C. Landrieu argued that private schools that accept vouchers should meet the same tough testing requirements imposed on public schools by the federal government.

Landrieu stepped out on another hot-button social issue in 2005 when she and GOP Sen. George Allen of Virginia cosponsored the Senate's official apology to the victims of lynching in the 19th and 20th centuries. The Senate over the years had filibustered anti-lynching bills passed by the House and endorsed by several presidents.

Landrieu shares a strong bond with her female colleagues in the Senate. In 2000, she collaborated on a book about their rise, "Nine and Counting," and she announced afterward that she would not campaign against any of those women — Democrat or Republican.

Unlike most of her female colleagues, Landrieu still has two children at home. Both are adopted, and Landrieu has fought tirelessly to increase the adoption tax credit, reform the foster care system and ease international adoptions. She co-chairs the Congressional Adoption Coalition.

Landrieu was born to politics. She is the oldest of nine children of Moon Landrieu, who was New Orleans mayor for eight years and secretary of Housing and Urban Development in the Carter administration. Her brother, Mitch Landrieu, was elected Louisiana's lieutenant governor in 2003.

She was elected to the Louisiana House at age 23, went on to become state treasurer, then made an unsuccessful run for governor in 1995. A year later, in a contest to fill the seat of retiring Democratic Sen. J. Bennett Johnston, she won by the slimmest margin ever in a Louisiana Senate race — 5,788 votes out of 1.7 million cast. The loser, conservative Louis "Woody" Jenkins, alleged voter fraud. The Senate Rules Committee, controlled by Republicans, conducted a divisive probe that dragged on for months after the election.

When she ran again in 2002, Landrieu was forced into a runoff after falling short of the 50 percent vote share needed to claim victory in Louisiana's unique nonpartisan primary. She had finished first with 46 percent in the nine-candidate field, which included three well-known Republicans: state elections commissioner Suzanne Haik Terrell, Rep. John Cooksey and state Rep. Tony Perkins. In the runoff, she increased the size of her 1996 victory sevenfold, to 42,012 votes. Bush campaigned for Terrell, but analysts said his efforts looked like overkill and may have helped Landrieu.

KEY VOTES

2006

- No Confirm Samuel A. Alito Jr. to the Supreme Court
- Yes Allow consideration of a bill to establish a $140 billion trust fund to compensate victims of asbestos exposure
- No Extend tax cuts for two years at a cost of $70 billion over five years
- Yes Overhaul immigration policy with border security, enforcement and guest worker program
- No Allow consideration of a bill to permanently repeal the estate tax
- No Urge President Bush to begin troop withdrawals from Iraq in 2006
- Yes Lift President Bush's restrictions on stem cell research funding
- Yes Authorize military tribunals for suspected terrorists

2005

- Yes Curb class action lawsuits by shifting them from state to federal courts
- Yes Allow confirmation vote on Priscilla R. Owen to the U.S. Court of Appeals for the 5th Circuit
- No Oppose mandatory emissions limits and block recognition of global warming as a threat
- No Approve free-trade pact with five Central American countries
- Yes Pass energy policy overhaul favored by President Bush emphasizing domestic oil and gas production
- Yes Shield gunmakers from lawsuits when their products are used in crimes
- Yes Ban torture of prisoners in U.S. custody
- No Renew 16 provisions of the Patriot Act
- Yes Allow final vote on opening the Arctic National Wildlife Refuge to oil and gas exploration

CQ VOTE STUDIES

	PARTY UNITY		PRESIDENTIAL SUPPORT	
	Support	Oppose	Support	Oppose
2006	75%	25%	71%	29%
2005	76%	24%	64%	36%
2004	81%	19%	68%	32%
2003	78%	22%	58%	42%
2002	65%	35%	84%	16%
2001	81%	19%	74%	26%
2000	88%	12%	85%	15%
1999	81%	19%	86%	14%
1998	89%	11%	86%	14%
1997	77%	23%	87%	13%

INTEREST GROUPS

	AFL-CIO	ADA	CCUS	ACU
2006	73%	65%	75%	24%
2005	86%	95%	76%	44%
2004	100%	85%	71%	32%
2003	77%	60%	78%	20%
2002	83%	70%	84%	35%
2001	88%	85%	69%	28%
2000	63%	80%	73%	16%
1999	67%	95%	59%	4%
1998	88%	90%	67%	8%
1997	29%	70%	70%	16%

Sen. David Vitter (R)

CAPITOL OFFICE
224-4623
vitter.senate.gov
516 Hart 20510-1803; fax 228-5061

COMMITTEES
Commerce, Science & Transportation
Environment & Public Works
Foreign Relations
Small Business & Entrepreneurship
Special Aging

RESIDENCE
Metairie

BORN
May 3, 1961, New Orleans, La.

RELIGION
Roman Catholic

FAMILY
Wife, Wendy Baldwin Vitter; four children

EDUCATION
Harvard U., A.B. 1983; Oxford U., B.A. 1985 (Rhodes scholar); Tulane U., J.D. 1988

CAREER
Lawyer; professor

POLITICAL HIGHLIGHTS
La. House, 1992-99; U.S. House, 1999-2005

ELECTION RESULTS

2004 GENERAL		
David Vitter (R)	943,014	51.0%
Chris John (D)	542,150	29.3%
John Kennedy (D)	275,821	14.9%
Arthur A. Morrell (D)	47,222	2.6%
2002 HOUSE GENERAL		
David Vitter (R)	147,117	81.5%
Monica L. Monica (R)	20,268	11.2%
Robert "Bob" Namer (R)	7,229	4.0%
Ian P. Hawkhurst (I)	5,956	3.3%

PREVIOUS WINNING PERCENTAGES
2000 House Election (80%); 1999 Special Runoff Election House Election (51%)

Elected 2004; 1st term

Vitter is the first Republican senator from Louisiana since Reconstruction, and in many ways he represents the changing face of that state's electorate after generations of Democratic machine politics.

A staunch conservative, Vitter has aligned himself with President Bush and GOP leaders in Congress on the war in Iraq, tax policy and a wide range of issues important to social conservatives. On several counts, the youthful Vitter broke the mold for a Louisiana senator when he filled the seat of retiring Sen. John B. Breaux, a smooth Democrat known for his deal-making and his ability to work the backrooms of the Senate.

In some ways, Vitter's arrival in the Senate as an idealistic young Republican was a long time in the making. While he was an undergraduate at Harvard, Vitter wrote in a Rhodes scholarship application that he aspired to change the reputation of cronyism and corruption typified by Louisiana's legendary Gov. Huey Long. Vitter won the scholarship and was eventually elected to the U.S. House in 1999 at age 38.

In his first two years in the Senate, Vitter has remained a faithful foot soldier for Republican leaders. But he has managed to stand out on a handful of issues, showing signs of becoming more independent as he gains seniority and experience in the esoteric ways of the Senate.

In 2005, Vitter introduced a bill, opposed by the Republican White House and most GOP senators, to allow Americans to buy U.S.-made drugs from foreign countries, where they often can be purchased more cheaply than in the United States. Vitter argued that Americans without prescription drug coverage, including many in his home state, should have the option of buying drugs from Canada or other countries if they are cheaper. The bill has gone nowhere in the Senate.

In 2006, Vitter also went his own way in voting against a guest worker program backed by the White House, an idea many conservatives opposed.

Vitter had bucked his party in 2005 when he did not support the Central American Free Trade Agreement, saying that it would hurt Louisiana's sugar farmers. In the House, he had opposed steel tariffs imposed in 2002 by the Bush administration because he worried they would hurt the Port of New Orleans, which derives significant revenue from steel shipments.

When it comes to home-state concerns, Vitter also has tended to part ways with Republicans and has voted with Louisiana's senior senator, Democrat Mary L. Landrieu. Vitter has a cool personal relationship with Landrieu, however, and the two don't always work well together. After Hurricane Katrina devastated New Orleans and other Louisiana coastal areas in 2005, Vitter and Landrieu offered competing measures aimed at helping cash-strapped local governments pay essential workers. The conflict led to a confrontation on the Senate floor that ended only when Vitter walked out of the chamber.

Hard feelings between the two lawmakers go back to Vitter's election night in 2004, when Landrieu called him to say that the other top vote-getter, House Democrat Chris John, would not concede the race until every vote had been counted. Landrieu claims Vitter hung up on her.

On issues not affecting Louisiana, Vitter has been a loyal freshman, voting with Bush 88 percent of the time in the 109th Congress (2005-06) on issues where the president took a position.

Over the past two years, no issue has dominated Vitter's agenda more than the impact of Katrina. Vitter says the failure of governmental agencies at all levels taught him about the need for vigilance and oversight of critical infrastructure. He has been particularly hard on the Army Corps of Engineers, and in a June 2006 letter to Bush complained that the Corps still had not repaired levees so that they could withstand a mild hurricane or even flooding rains. Katrina destroyed entire neighborhoods in Vitter's hometown of New Orleans, where he grew up as the son of a petroleum engineer.

Vitter has used his seat on the Environment and Public Works Committee to press for transportation and coastal restoration projects in Louisiana. In 2006, Vitter and Landrieu successfully pushed for a larger share of Gulf of Mexico oil drilling revenue for Louisiana, with the promise that the money would be used to restore the state's endangered coastal wetlands.

On social issues, Vitter has established himself as one of a cadre of strong social conservatives in the Republican freshman Class of 2004. He has voted against same-sex marriage and in favor of abortion restrictions, reflecting what he calls "Louisiana values."

Echoing his Rhodes scholarship application, Vitter has continued to criticize his state's reputation for corruption. He says that Democratic Rep. William J. Jefferson of New Orleans, who in 2005 was caught with $90,000 in marked bills in his freezer in a corruption investigation, should not have challenged an FBI search of his congressional office.

In an effort to bolster his ethics credentials, Vitter in early 2007 proposed an amendment to prohibit Senate spouses who are lobbyists from directly lobbying senators. The measure was adopted as part of the Senate's congressional ethics bill.

Vitter's views on corruption have long informed his career. When he was in the state legislature, Vitter filed an ethics complaint against a close friend of then Gov. Edwin Edwards and led an effort to recall Edwards, who eventually resigned and was sentenced in 2001 to 10 years in prison for corruption. Also while in the state House, Vitter won passage of a measure limiting the terms of state legislators, and led a successful fight to end a scholarship program at Tulane University that allowed state legislators to choose recipients.

Vitter is a longtime critic of the gambling interests in Louisiana, and, while in the state House, he feuded with fellow Republican and then Gov. Mike Foster over the issue. When Vitter was elected to the U.S. House, however, the two patched things up, and he won Foster's endorsement for his Senate bid.

In 2004, Vitter ran for the Senate seat left open when Breaux retired. He had a tough opponent in John, who was Breaux's protégé. In Louisiana, all comers, regardless of party, are on the same ballot for the all-candidate general election on Election Day. Vitter faced two independents and four Democrats, including John.

Vitter was favored going in, but the question was whether his competitors would hold him to less than the required 50 percent of the vote and force a December runoff between the two top vote-getters. Vitter had won the state GOP's backing and no other Republicans entered the race. John, on the other hand, had stiff competition from three Democratic rivals, who split the vote. Vitter won a rare, outright victory by taking a majority of the votes and capturing the seat without a runoff.

Louisiana has not had a Republican senator since William Pitt Kellogg, who began service in 1868 but was elected to the job by the state legislature, not directly by voters. The 17th Amendment, ratified in 1913, calls for direct election of senators.

KEY VOTES

2006

- Yes Confirm Samuel A. Alito Jr. to the Supreme Court
- Yes Allow consideration of a bill to establish a $140 billion trust fund to compensate victims of asbestos exposure
- Yes Extend tax cuts for two years at a cost of $70 billion over five years
- No Overhaul immigration policy with border security, enforcement and guest worker program
- Yes Allow consideration of a bill to permanently repeal the estate tax
- No Urge President Bush to begin troop withdrawals from Iraq in 2006
- No Lift President Bush's restrictions on stem cell research funding
- Yes Authorize military tribunals for suspected terrorists

2005

- Yes Curb class action lawsuits by shifting them from state to federal courts
- Yes Allow confirmation vote on Priscilla R. Owen to the U.S. Court of Appeals for the 5th Circuit
- Yes Oppose mandatory emissions limits and block recognition of global warming as a threat
- No Approve free-trade pact with five Central American countries
- Yes Pass energy policy overhaul favored by President Bush emphasizing domestic oil and gas production
- Yes Shield gunmakers from lawsuits when their products are used in crimes
- Yes Ban torture of prisoners in U.S. custody
- Yes Renew 16 provisions of the Patriot Act
- Yes Allow final vote on opening the Arctic National Wildlife Refuge to oil and gas exploration

CQ VOTE STUDIES

	PARTY UNITY		PRESIDENTIAL SUPPORT	
	Support	Oppose	Support	Oppose
2006	94%	6%	87%	13%
2005	94%	6%	89%	11%
House Service:				
2004	98%	2%	94%	6%
2003	99%	1%	96%	4%
2002	99%	1%	85%	15%
2001	98%	2%	93%	7%
2000	92%	8%	25%	75%
1999	92%	8%	20%	80%

INTEREST GROUPS

	AFL-CIO	ADA	CCUS	ACU
2006	20%	0%	92%	92%
2005	29%	15%	83%	96%
House Service:				
2004	7%	5%	100%	96%
2003	0%	10%	97%	88%
2002	11%	0%	95%	100%
2001	8%	0%	100%	100%
2000	0%	0%	85%	88%
1999	14%	5%	88%	83%

Rep. Bobby Jindal (R)

CAPITOL OFFICE
225-3015
bobby.jindal@mail.house.gov
jindal.house.gov
1205 Longworth 20515-1801; fax 226-0386

COMMITTEES
Homeland Security
Natural Resources

RESIDENCE
Kenner

BORN
June 10, 1971, Baton Rouge, La.

RELIGION
Roman Catholic

FAMILY
Wife, Supriya Jindal; three children

EDUCATION
Brown U., Sc.B. 1991 (biology & public policy); Oxford U., M.Litt. 1994 (Rhodes scholar)

CAREER
State university system president; management consultant

POLITICAL HIGHLIGHTS
La. Health and Hospitals Department secretary, 1996-98; U.S. Health and Human Services assistant secretary for planning and evaluation, 2001-03; candidate for governor, 2003

ELECTION RESULTS

2006 GENERAL		
Bobby Jindal (R)	130,508	88.1%
David Gereighty (D)	10,919	7.4%
Stacey Tallitsch (D)	5,025	3.4%
Peter Beary (LIBERT)	1,676	1.1%
2004 GENERAL		
Bobby Jindal (R)	225,708	78.4%
Roy Armstrong (D)	19,266	6.7%
M.V. "Vinny" Mendoza (D)	12,779	4.4%
Daniel Zimmerman (D)	12,135	4.2%
Jerry Watts (D)	10,034	3.5%
Mike Rogers (R)	7,975	2.8%

Elected 2004; 2nd term

Nine months after Jindal was first elected to Congress, Hurricane Katrina permanently changed his district, his voters and his career. The hurricane destroyed much of New Orleans and southern Louisiana, including swaths of Jindal's district, on Aug. 29, 2005. Since then, his work in Washington has been dominated by the aftermath of the storm.

About two-thirds of the bills he introduced in the 18 months after Katrina hit were related to that, or similar natural disasters.

"The challenge is to address problems we had before the storm, not to rebuild what we had before," Jindal (JIN-dle) told the New Orleans Times-Picayune in October 2006. The storm appears to have altered even Jindal's usually business-friendly politics, jaundicing him toward insurance companies, criticized by Louisianans for dropping policies and increasing premiums after Katrina. He has signed on as a cosponsor to Democratic legislation that would strip insurance companies of their antitrust exemption and affect their ability to share data on losses. The companies use the information to set rates. "It does not seem right that insurance companies are making record profits while Louisiana residents cannot afford their premiums," he told the House Financial Services Committee in February 2007.

Jindal's signature legislative achievement in his first term was a law that opened 8.3 million acres in the Gulf of Mexico to drilling and dedicated some of the substantial revenue to Gulf Coast states, which were hardest hit in the 2005 hurricane season. Jindal sponsored an early House version of the bill, which passed in June 2006 and was later enacted as part of a larger tax and trade bill. The law splits revenues from drilling 50-50 between the federal government and Gulf states.

Together with Republican Sen. David Vitter of Louisiana, Jindal also wrote a law banning states and cities from taking their citizens' guns during disasters. The city of New Orleans had come under criticism for taking some 700 guns after Katrina struck. The city returned the guns to their owners in April 2006 after the National Rifle Association threatened a lawsuit.

The Louisiana Democratic Party has accused Jindal of exploiting Katrina for political gain. After the storm, Jindal made public statements disparaging the performance of Louisiana Gov. Kathleen Babineaux Blanco, a Democrat who beat him in a runoff for governor in 2003. But even some Democrats lauded Jindal as effective in aiding recovery efforts. "The disappointment that people have registered over the response of government is legitimate from top to bottom, but there were some people who distinguished themselves, and Bobby Jindal was one of them," St. Bernard Parish Sheriff Jack Stephens told the Times-Picayune.

Jindal didn't live in his district before running for his House seat. Yet his legislative work, attention to his constituents, and knack for politics — coupled with Blanco's stumbling performance — greatly elevated Jindal's profile. As a consequence, his second term in the House was shaping up to be possibly his last. Early in 2007, he announced he was running for governor later in the year. Times-Picayune polls showed Jindal to be popular statewide.

Jindal has long been considered a political savant in the Republican Party, as well as a health policy expert. "His résumé is why he's a rock star," says Rep. Jim McCrery, a Louisiana Republican serving as Jindal's 2007 gubernatorial campaign chairman.

As an undergraduate at Brown University, Jindal interned for a month one summer in McCrery's office. About a week after he had started, Jindal asked to meet with McCrery himself. Jindal asked whether he might contribute to some policy work, on top of the menial chores he was performing with other interns. "I'm thinking, 'Aw, gee, this is just what I need — all those interns coming in to ask me for things to do,'" McCrery recalls. So he told Jindal to go research Medicare, the enormous entitlement program that pays for health care for the aged, and to recommend ways to contain the growth of its budget. "I figured, 'That'll take care of him. I'll never see him again,'" McCrery recalled.

Two weeks later, Jindal dropped a thick report on McCrery's desk and asked whether the congressman would read it before his internship ended. "I read it and it was great," McCrery said. Jindal went on to be a Rhodes scholar and attended Oxford.

His career was launched in 1996, when at age 24 he was appointed to lead Louisiana's Health and Hospitals Department. He served as executive director of a commission studying Medicare reform in 1998, answering to co-chairman John B. Breaux, then a Democratic U.S. senator from Louisiana. He was named head of Louisiana's university system in 1999. President Bush appointed him in 2001 as an assistant secretary in the Health and Human Services Department.

He returned to Louisiana in 2003 to challenge Blanco for governor and lost, though narrowly, collecting 48 percent of the vote to her 52 percent. When then Rep. David Vitter, a Republican, left the U.S. House to run successfully for the Senate in 2004, Jindal moved from his home city of Baton Rouge to the New Orleans suburbs to run for Vitter's seat. He won convincingly; he and Vitter are now close political allies.

Jindal, whose parents emigrated from India, prevailed in a district that is conservative and largely white. He is the only member of Indian heritage in Congress, and only the second ever, after Dalip Singh Saund, a California Democrat born in India who served in the House from 1957 to 1963.

Jindal had been preparing to enter Harvard Medical School when former Louisiana Gov. Mike Foster, a Republican, offered him the job steering the state's health department in 1996. As a result, Jindal never earned his medical degree. But one recent summer, he had to play doctor anyway.

His third child was born without much warning on Aug. 15, 2006, forcing Jindal to deliver the boy himself at home. "I made sure he wasn't tangled up in the umbilical cord or that his head didn't hit the floor," Jindal told the Times-Picayune. "I tried to do everything you see in the movies." He tied off the boy's umbilical cord with a shoelace before paramedics arrived, and the delivery was a success.

KEY VOTES

2006

No Stop broadband companies from favoring select Internet traffic
Yes Affirm U.S. commitment to war in Iraq and reject setting a withdrawal date for troops
Yes Repeal requirement for bilingual ballots at the polls
Yes Permit U.S. sale of civilian nuclear technology to India
Yes Build a 700-mile fence on the U.S.-Mexico border to curb illegal crossings
Yes Permit warrantless wiretaps of suspected terrorists

2005

Yes Intervene in the life-support case of Terri Schiavo
No Lift President Bush's restrictions on stem cell research funding
No Prohibit FBI access to library and bookstore records
No Approve free-trade pact with five Central American countries
Yes Pass energy policy overhaul favored by President Bush emphasizing domestic oil and gas production
Yes End mandatory preservation of habitat of endangered animal and plant species
No Ban torture of prisoners in U.S. custody

CQ VOTE STUDIES

	PARTY UNITY		PRESIDENTIAL SUPPORT	
	Support	Oppose	Support	Oppose
2006	88%	12%	90%	10%
2005	97%	3%	85%	15%

INTEREST GROUPS

	AFL-CIO	ADA	CCUS	ACU
2006	21%	0%	100%	92%
2005	27%	10%	89%	100%

LOUISIANA 1

East — Metairie, part of Florida Parishes

A short distance from downtown New Orleans, the conservative 1st skims the edges of the city and reaches north across Lake Pontchartrain to the Mississippi border. Democrats held the 1st for more than a century before 1977, but residents now warmly welcome the GOP on all levels. Prior to Hurricane Katrina in 2005, the 1st's population center was in neighborhoods south of the lake, including upscale Metairie.

Across the Lake Pontchartrain Causeway to the north, the 1st includes three of the "Florida Parishes," so named because they were part of Spanish Florida until 1810. Once a community of seasonal homes, the north shore is now a booming bedroom community, experiencing a population influx as residents from the rest of the state flock to the relatively stable residential area. Slidell and other towns along the northern lakeshore still face rebuilding costs from the damage inflicted by the hurricane's high winds, downed trees and flooding.

South of the lake, Lakeview in western Orleans Parish and parts of historic Old Metairie in Jefferson Parish flooded when the hurricane storm surge broke the levee holding back the 17th Street Canal, the border between Jefferson and Orleans parishes. As with much of the Greater New Orleans area, local officials and residents throughout the 1st hope that rebuilt neighborhoods will retain their unique character. Although available housing was still insufficient into 2007, the reopening of many local schools was viewed as a positive step toward recovery.

As businesses resume operations here and hotels attempt to lure back tourists, a shortage of service industry workers, coupled with high workforce attrition, is hindering growth. Petrochemicals and oil have recovered, and Northrop Grumman's shipbuilding operations, based at the Avondale Shipyard in the 2nd, and other major employers are leading the way in providing housing, salaries and benefits to returning workers.

MAJOR INDUSTRY
Petrochemicals, oil

CITIES
Metairie (unincorporated) (pt.), 140,916; Kenner (pt.), 46,007; New Orleans (pt.), 37,451; Slidell, 25,695

NOTABLE
The Lake Pontchartrain Causeway is the world's longest highway bridge over water.

Rep. William J. Jefferson (D)

CAPITOL OFFICE
225-6636
www.house.gov/jefferson
2113 Rayburn 20515-1802; fax 225-1988

COMMITTEES
Small Business

RESIDENCE
New Orleans

BORN
March 14, 1947, Lake Providence, La.

RELIGION
Baptist

FAMILY
Wife, Andrea Green Jefferson; five children

EDUCATION
Southern U. and A&M College, B.A. 1969 (English & political science); Harvard U., J.D. 1972; Georgetown U., LL.M. 1996 (taxation)

MILITARY SERVICE
Army, 1969-75

CAREER
Lawyer; congressional aide

POLITICAL HIGHLIGHTS
La. Senate, 1980-91; candidate for mayor of New Orleans, 1982, 1986; candidate for governor, 1999

ELECTION RESULTS

2006 GENERAL RUNOFF		
William J. Jefferson (D)	35,153	56.5%
Karen Carter (D)	27,011	43.5%
2006 GENERAL		
William J. Jefferson (D)	28,283	30.1%
Karen Carter (D)	20,364	21.7%
Derrick Shephard (D)	16,799	17.9%
Joseph "Joe" Lavigne (R)	12,511	13.3%
Troy C. Carter (D)	11,304	12.0%
Eric T. Bradley (R)	1,159	1.2%
Regina Bartholomew (D)	1,125	1.2%

PREVIOUS WINNING PERCENTAGES
2004 (79%); 2002 (64%); 2000 (100%); 1998 (86%); 1996 (100%); 1994 (75%); 1992 (73%); 1990 (53%)

Elected 1990; 9th term

Although Jefferson faced allegations that he accepted bribes in exchange for favorable legislative action, voters in hurricane-ravaged New Orleans sent him back to Congress in the last election. Jefferson was accused of using his influence to promote African trade deals in return for cash and other rewards for himself and family members. FBI agents found $90,000 in marked bills in Jefferson's freezer during an August 2005 raid, and then seized documents from his Capitol Hill office in May 2006.

Two of his former associates pleaded guilty to paying him to help secure telecommunications deals in African countries, but Jefferson continued to maintain his innocence. "For over 18 months, the federal government has investigated me and has yet to bring a single charge against me," Jefferson said in a 2006 campaign ad.

House Republican leaders at first sought to capitalize on Jefferson's problems as a way to deflect ethics charges against some members of their own party, but after FBI agents launched the surprise raid on Jefferson's congressional office, then GOP Speaker J. Dennis Hastert angrily denounced the action as an intrusion on the legislative branch. President Bush directed the FBI to seal the records it had obtained during the raid. And Jefferson's own legal challenge to the seizure of the documents held up proceedings in his case for months.

Jefferson's unresolved ethical problems proved to be a major headache for House Democratic leaders, who highlighted the GOP as the party of scandal during the 2006 election. In the 109th Congress (2005-06), Democratic Leader Nancy Pelosi engineered Jefferson's removal from the powerful Ways and Means Committee in the wake of the bribery revelations. The Congressional Black Caucus objected, arguing that if Jefferson were white, he would have been allowed to keep his privileges until his guilt or innocence was decided.

In the 110th Congress (2007-08), Jefferson got a seat on the Small Business Committee and Speaker Pelosi also decided to give Jefferson a spot on the Homeland Security Committee. But she was forced to put that plan on hold once Republicans demanded a potentially embarrassing roll call vote on whether to seat him.

The bribery allegations signaled a rapid reversal of fortune for Jefferson, known for his remarkable rise from poverty. He was born into a family of 10 children in far northeastern Louisiana, where he earned money by chopping cotton. His mother was adamant about the need for education, and Jefferson proved to be a high achiever.

After graduating from Southern University in Baton Rouge, he won a scholarship to Harvard Law School, which his mother had never heard of. He earned her approval when he explained that it was where President John F. Kennedy went to school. He went on to clerk for a federal judge in New Orleans and then worked as an aide to Democratic Sen. J. Bennett Johnston Jr. of Louisiana. He moved to New Orleans in 1976 to practice law.

Elected to the state Senate in 1979, Jefferson represented a racially mixed New Orleans district that included much of the affluent Uptown neighborhood. He became known as a nuts-and-bolts expert on fiscal matters and a promoter of economic development. But he also gained a reputation among fellow state lawmakers as "Dollar Bill" for earning lucrative contracts from state and local agencies for his law firm.

Jefferson's political career began unraveling in 2005, the same year Hurricane Katrina destroyed much of his district, including the heavily affected and predominantly black Lower 9th Ward. Even Jefferson's actions in the aftermath of the hurricane became a source of controversy as press accounts revealed that he used a National Guard truck and personnel to help remove personal items from his home after the storm.

But he has tried to help the district with the little influence he has left in the House. He backed a 2007 measure to overhaul the Small Business Administration's troubled disaster loan program, a rebuilding plan covering major natural disasters that had drawn harsh criticism for delays in getting loans to hurricane victims. Also in 2007, the House passed Jefferson-sponsored legislation giving minority-owned businesses affected by the storms additional time to rebuild under the SBA's business development program.

When he came to the House in 1991, Jefferson stood out as one of the more conservative and business-friendly members of the generally liberal Congressional Black Caucus. Oil and gas interests are big business in Louisiana; Jefferson is a firm supporter of the energy industry and he voted to allow oil drilling in Alaska's Arctic National Wildlife Refuge. He is also more conservative socially than many in his party. He has supported constitutional amendments to ban flag burning and same-sex marriage.

Earlier in his congressional career, Jefferson tried without success to get into the party leadership. In 2003, Pelosi picked fellow Californian Robert T. Matsui over Jefferson to head the party's House re-election organization, the Democratic Congressional Campaign Committee. Jefferson had worked to show his mettle with energetic fundraising in the run-up to the 2002 election, and he had the backing of many members of the Black Caucus.

Jefferson split with Louisiana Democrats in 2004 when he disagreed with retiring Sen. John B. Breaux and Sen. Mary L. Landrieu over who had the best shot at keeping Breaux's seat Democratic. Breaux and Landrieu backed Democratic Rep. Chris John, but Jefferson supported state Treasurer John Kennedy. The divided allegiances helped make David Vitter the first GOP senator from Louisiana since Reconstruction.

In 1990, after serving as a state senator for 11 years, Jefferson finished first in the crowded November race for the 2nd District seat left open when Democratic Rep. Lindy Boggs retired after 18 years. But he was forced into a runoff where he narrowly defeated lawyer Marc Morial, the son of New Orleans' first black mayor. Jefferson became the first African-American elected to Congress from Louisiana since Reconstruction. Even with his legal troubles, in 2006 he was re-elected with almost 57 percent of the vote in another runoff election, this time against Democratic state Rep. Karen Carter.

KEY VOTES

2006

No Stop broadband companies from favoring select Internet traffic
No Affirm U.S. commitment to war in Iraq and reject setting a withdrawal date for troops
No Repeal requirement for bilingual ballots at the polls
Yes Permit U.S. sale of civilian nuclear technology to India
No Build a 700-mile fence on the U.S.-Mexico border to curb illegal crossings
No Permit warrantless wiretaps of suspected terrorists

2005

? Intervene in the life-support case of Terri Schiavo
Yes Lift President Bush's restrictions on stem cell research funding
Yes Prohibit FBI access to library and bookstore records
Yes Approve free-trade pact with five Central American countries
Yes Pass energy policy overhaul favored by President Bush emphasizing domestic oil and gas production
No End mandatory preservation of habitat of endangered animal and plant species
Yes Ban torture of prisoners in U.S. custody

CQ VOTE STUDIES

	PARTY UNITY		PRESIDENTIAL SUPPORT	
	Support	Oppose	Support	Oppose
2006	88%	12%	46%	54%
2005	90%	10%	26%	74%
2004	94%	6%	32%	68%
2003	91%	9%	33%	67%
2002	92%	8%	40%	60%

INTEREST GROUPS

	AFL-CIO	ADA	CCUS	ACU
2006	85%	60%	86%	35%
2005	93%	85%	59%	29%
2004	80%	80%	57%	17%
2003	87%	90%	46%	32%
2002	86%	75%	58%	20%

LOUISIANA 2
New Orleans

New Orleans suffered catastrophic damage in late 2005, as rising waters propelled by the high winds and storm surge of Hurricane Katrina swept over and through the levees surrounding the below-sea-level city. As locals attempt to restore the infrastructure and character of the "Big Easy," they face funding obstacles, rising crime rates, weak education and health sectors, and workforce and housing shortages.

Although the city's population had already declined from its peak in 1960, some post-storm estimates put the new number at less than 200,000. Inexact methodologies and doubts over how many former residents will return have made tracking population and demographic changes tricky.

Floods covered the 9th Ward, Gentilly and other low-lying areas, which were left in shambles into 2007, but higher-ground areas like the French Quarter and Uptown escaped most of the water. The Superdome was heavily damaged and not fully repaired until more than a year later. Schools, hospitals and other services came to a halt immediately after the storm and many areas face protracted efforts to rebuild.

Famed for its food and jazz, the city was a popular tourist spot prior to the storm — Mardi Gras and the Jazz & Heritage Festival alone drew millions of visitors and billions of dollars. By 2007, 90 percent of area hotels had reopened, and local officials actively sought to lure visitors back to the once-humming city. Still, the loss of convention business hurt tourism across the board, from dining to shopping to taxi service.

The port, shipbuilding and petroleum sectors held steady after the storm despite losing some business to other Gulf cities. Northrop Grumman's Avondale Shipyard provides jobs, and the port's cargo and cruise facilities rebounded within a year. Money spent by cruise ship visitors docking at the port should benefit small businesses in the city.

MAJOR INDUSTRY
Shipping, oil and gas, tourism, shipbuilding

MILITARY BASES
Naval Support Activity New Orleans, 2,830 military, 1,809 civilian (2007)

CITIES
New Orleans (pt.), 447,223; Marrero (unincorporated) (pt.), 35,796

NOTABLE
The National Shrine of Our Lady of Prompt Succor (New Orleans) hosts a statue of the state's patron saint, who hears prayers in times of disaster.

Rep. Charlie Melancon (D)

CAPITOL OFFICE
225-4031
www.house.gov/melancon
404 Cannon 20515-1803; fax 226-3944

COMMITTEES
Energy & Commerce
Science & Technology

RESIDENCE
Napoleonville

BORN
Oct. 3, 1947, Napoleonville, La.

RELIGION
Roman Catholic

FAMILY
Wife, Peachy Melancon; two children

EDUCATION
U. of Southwestern Louisiana, B.S. 1971 (agribusiness)

CAREER
Sugar cane trade group president; insurance company owner; storage and housing rental company owner; ice cream shop owner; multi-county planning and development director

POLITICAL HIGHLIGHTS
Candidate for La. House, 1975; La. House, 1987-93

ELECTION RESULTS

2006 GENERAL		
Charlie Melancon (D)	75,023	55.0%
Craig Romero (R)	54,950	40.3%
Olangee "O.J." Breech (D)	4,190	3.1%
James Lee Blake (LIBERT)	2,168	1.6%
2004 GENERAL RUNOFF		
Charlie Melancon (D)	57,611	50.2%
Billy Tauzin III (R)	57,042	49.8%

Elected 2004; 2nd term

Melancon's early congressional career has been defined almost exclusively by hurricanes Katrina and Rita, which tore through opposite ends of his district about a month apart in late August and September 2005.

After Katrina devastated St. Bernard and Plaquemines parishes, Melancon (meh-LAW-sawn) told his colleagues he had a hard time contradicting constituents who said the federal government had failed them.

"As their congressman, it is painfully ironic that the help I have been able to give them has not been from the federal government at all," Melancon said on the House floor. "I have had to work around the system, identifying needs and coordinating resources myself, much of it from private and unofficial sources."

The ensuing battle for federal resources revealed an independent streak in Melancon that has led him to publicly challenge the president, Republicans in Congress and even the leaders of his own party.

He raised eyebrows shortly after Democrats took control of Congress at the start of the 110th Congress (2007-08) when he charged that his own leadership was not doing enough to address the recovery needs of the Gulf Coast. "I am disappointed that Speaker Pelosi hasn't lived up to her commitment to people of Louisiana, Mississippi and the Gulf Coast," Melancon said in a February 2007 interview with the New Orleans Times-Picayune. "I've gotten past the point where I think it's just happenstance."

Melancon's arm's-length relationship with Democratic leaders is an electoral imperative. In 2004, he pulled off a rare feat, a Democratic takeback of a Southern district that had gone Republican, and he managed to build his vote margin from 569 votes that year to more than 20,000 votes in 2006. With the Democratic takeover of the House in 2007, Melancon won assignment to the Energy and Commerce Committee, where his predecessor, Republican W.J. "Billy" Tauzin Jr., had wielded the gavel just a few years earlier.

Despite his relatively junior status, the seat provides Melancon a spot from which to look out for the interests of the district's oil, gas and petrochemical industries.

He also retains an assignment to the Science and Technology Committee, where his place on the Space and Aeronautics Subcommittee gives him the opportunity to engage in debates important to the National Aeronautics and Space Administration's Michoud Assembly Facility.

Even before he made it onto Energy and Commerce, he had a hand in the enactment of a major offshore-drilling law in the 109th Congress (2005-06). The measure expands oil and gas drilling in the Gulf of Mexico, and, for the first time, gives Louisiana and other Gulf Coast states a share of federal offshore drilling revenues. Support for drilling separated Melancon from the liberal orthodoxy of many of his Democratic colleagues. It was not the only issue on which the bayou lawmaker waved goodbye to his party on the floor.

He voted to limit the scope of the Endangered Species Act, authorize the president's warrantless wiretapping program, impose stricter identification and asylum standards on immigrants, and build 700 miles of fencing along the U.S.-Mexico border. He was one of 15 Democrats who voted in 2006 to extend some of President Bush's tax cuts, at a cost of $70 billion over five years. But he voted against a package of $40 billion in spending cuts.

In 2006, he scored a 76 percent rating from the American Conservative Union and a 40 percent rating from the liberal Americans for Democratic Action. He voted with his party only 67 percent of the time in the 109th Congress on votes where the two parties staked out different positions.

Most of Melancon's constituents share his Roman Catholic faith, and he deviates from the party line on most social issues. In 2005, he voted to give the parents of Terri Schiavo, a brain-dead Florida woman, the right to appeal a court decision that eventually resulted in the removal of Schiavo's feeding tube. The following year, he voted to criminalize transporting minors across state lines to get abortions without parental notification.

He also supports gun owners' rights, and he defines marriage exclusively as the union of a man and a woman. He introduced legislation in the 109th Congress expressing the sense of Congress that displaying the Ten Commandments in a public building does not violate the First Amendment.

But Melancon breaks with social conservatives over federal funding for embryonic stem cell research. He voted to expand federal support for such research in the 109th Congress and later to override Bush's successful veto of the bill. He backed similar legislation early in 2007. "This is pro-life in that it will give people a better quality of life," Melancon told the Times-Picayune. "Anyone who says this is anti-pro-life doesn't want to take a real look at it."

Back home, the Napoleonville native has long bolstered the local economy as a state legislator, a planning official, the president of the American Sugar Cane League and a business owner. As a state representative, Melancon was the driving force behind the Louisiana Tourism Taxing District, which dedicated a portion of state sales tax to tourism promotion. The tourism industry will be a prominent component of the region's recovery efforts in the coming years.

Not surprisingly, most of the bills Melancon has introduced relate to the Gulf Coast's recovery efforts. But he began working on coastal restoration issues even before the hurricanes pummeled his district.

In May 2005, he introduced a bill, cosponsored by all of his Louisiana colleagues, to provide a tax credit against income taxes incurred while providing for the protection of coastal land.

Melancon beat Tauzin's son, Billy Tauzin III, in the closest election of 2004 by promising to maintain a rightward agenda. He garnered only 24 percent of the first-round vote in November that year, but it was enough for second place in the first vote of a two-tiered election system and for a spot in the December runoff against Tauzin.

Melancon came into the 2006 election with a clear edge because of his profile as a conservative Democrat, his focus on hurricane repair and his well-funded campaign operation. And despite the district's conservative lean, he won with 55 percent of the vote over GOP state Sen. Craig Romero.

KEY VOTES

2006

- No — Stop broadband companies from favoring select Internet traffic
- Yes — Affirm U.S. commitment to war in Iraq and reject setting a withdrawal date for troops
- No — Repeal requirement for bilingual ballots at the polls
- Yes — Permit U.S. sale of civilian nuclear technology to India
- Yes — Build a 700-mile fence on the U.S.-Mexico border to curb illegal crossings
- Yes — Permit warrantless wiretaps of suspected terrorists

2005

- Yes — Intervene in the life-support case of Terri Schiavo
- Yes — Lift President Bush's restrictions on stem cell research funding
- Yes — Prohibit FBI access to library and bookstore records
- No — Approve free-trade pact with five Central American countries
- Yes — Pass energy policy overhaul favored by President Bush emphasizing domestic oil and gas production
- Yes — End mandatory preservation of habitat of endangered animal and plant species
- Yes — Ban torture of prisoners in U.S. custody

CQ VOTE STUDIES

	PARTY UNITY		PRESIDENTIAL SUPPORT	
	Support	Oppose	Support	Oppose
2006	62%	38%	72%	28%
2005	71%	29%	52%	48%

INTEREST GROUPS

	AFL-CIO	ADA	CCUS	ACU
2006	71%	40%	93%	76%
2005	93%	80%	67%	61%

LOUISIANA 3

South central – New Iberia, Houma, Chalmette

In August 2005, Hurricane Katrina plowed into the 3rd's Plaquemines Parish just south of Buras. The storm drove high winds, torrential rain and a 20-foot surge of water over the bayous, swamps and marshes of eastern Louisiana. A month later, Hurricane Rita swept over Acadiana — or Cajun country — destroying or severely damaging small towns in southwestern Louisiana, including the westernmost portions of the 3rd.

Water submerged the mostly middle-class Plaquemines and St. Bernard parishes when levees failed, and full recovery is not assured. These former bedroom communities now host tiny fractions of pre-storm populations. Some who remained in the area moved north into booming parts of the 1st District.

The 3rd long supported fishing, oystering and shrimping, but the small operations in Plaquemines and west along the coast have not gotten back on the water. West of Plaquemines, rural Lafourche and Terrebonne parishes grew sugar, rice and citrus, but now farmers struggle to renew agricultural production and ranchers have lost cattle. Rita's flooding caused property damage and economic losses to small towns on Route 90 between Houma and Lafayette (in the 7th). Many residents in the state's rural western areas have resettled in the 3rd.

Oil and gas, which spurred a decade of revival, recovered from the storms, and the 3rd continues to support much of the regional offshore drilling economy. Tax credits have attracted manufacturing and retail interests, although some parishes have not received credit extensions.

Democrats dominated the region for most of a century, but the Catholic 3rd now trends Republican. The ability to bring federal and state aid to the district may largely determine future political success here.

MAJOR INDUSTRY

Oil and gas, petrochemicals, shipbuilding, agriculture

MILITARY BASES

Naval Air Station Joint Reserve Base New Orleans, 1,200 military, 1,100 civilian (2004)

CITIES

New Iberia, 32,623; Houma, 32,393; Chalmette (unincorporated), 32,069

NOTABLE

St. John the Baptist Parish holds its annual Andouille Festival in October.

Rep. Jim McCrery (R)

CAPITOL OFFICE
225-2777
jim.mccrery@mail.house.gov
www.house.gov/mccrery
242 Cannon 20515-1804; fax 225-8039

COMMITTEES
Ways & Means - ranking member
Joint Taxation

RESIDENCE
Shreveport

BORN
Sept. 18, 1949, Shreveport, La.

RELIGION
Methodist

FAMILY
Wife, Johnette McCrery; two children

EDUCATION
Louisiana Tech U., B.A. 1971 (English & history); Louisiana State U., J.D. 1975

CAREER
Lobbyist; lawyer; congressional aide

POLITICAL HIGHLIGHTS
Candidate for Leesville City Council, 1978

ELECTION RESULTS

2006 GENERAL

Jim McCrery (R)	77,078	57.4%
Artis R. Cash Sr. (D)	22,757	16.9%
Patti Cox (D)	17,788	13.2%
Chester T. Kelley (R)	16,649	12.4%

2004 GENERAL

Jim McCrery (R)	unopposed

PREVIOUS WINNING PERCENTAGES
2002 (72%); 2000 (71%); 1998 (100%); 1996 (71%); 1994 (80%); 1992 (63%); 1990 (55%); 1988 (69%); 1988 Special Runoff Election (51%)

Elected April 1988; 10th full term

McCrery's ascension to top-ranking Republican on the House Ways and Means Committee brought a marked change in tone to the important tax writing panel. While he can be a fiercely loyal partisan, he is collegial with Democrats, including Chairman Charles B. Rangel of New York. Rangel had a contentious, unproductive relationship with the cantankerous Bill Thomas of California, who chaired the committee from 2001 through 2006.

McCrery likes to immerse himself in the details of legislation and approaches most issues pragmatically. Although as liberal on fiscal policy as McCrery is conservative, Rangel also has a pragmatic streak, which could result in the two getting to the bargaining table once in a while.

In the 109th Congress (2005-06), for instance, McCrery supported President Bush's plan to partially privatize Social Security, but he was willing to shelve it if that's what it took to get legislation to overhaul the financially shaky retirement program. He still thinks a bill is possible. "It can't be done on a partisan basis," he says. "We've got to have the will on both sides of the aisle. We've got to have some give and take." Individual private accounts don't necessarily have to be part of a final deal, he says. "We need to go into a room with a blank sheet of paper and come up with a solution. We know everything there is to know about this issue. It's not magic."

In 2006, the New Orleans Times-Picayune praised McCrery for his ability to work across party lines, noting in an editorial that he got $8 billion in tax credits for the state after Hurricane Katrina. "That legislation is among the most significant tools for this region's recovery," the newspaper said.

McCrery would have been chairman of the committee if the GOP had held onto power after the 2006 elections, because Thomas was due to step down under GOP term limits. McCrery had campaigned for the job for months and spent a lot of time raising money for colleagues' tight re-election races, distributing nearly $1 million in 2006. After the Democrats' success at the polls, he had no competition for the top minority slot, though he didn't have the most seniority. (Wally Herger of California is the most senior Republican.)

After the brutal hurricane season of August and September 2005, McCrery's northwest Louisiana district took in 50,000 evacuees from the New Orleans area — on top of the severe economic damage its timber industry suffered from Hurricane Rita, which downed countless trees. McCrery said he spent 85 percent of his legislative time that fall on hurricane-related issues, working with his staff seven days a week.

He was outspoken in criticizing the Bush administration's response. Communications among local, state and federal agencies responding to the crisis were a serious problem in spite of the enormous amount of money Congress spent after the Sept. 11 terrorist attacks to fix such problems. He said that the command and control structure was nonexistent. "It seemed like everybody was in charge, and therefore nobody was in charge."

Over the years of Republican control on Capitol Hill, McCrery worked closely with Thomas, whom he calls his best friend in the House. As a result, he was able to rack up an impressive list of accomplishments. After Thomas picked him to be the Select Revenue Subcommittee chairman in 2001, McCrery shepherded through the House the president's tax cuts, the economic stimulus package that followed the Sept. 11 attacks, and the 2004 corporate tax law. As chairman of the Social Security panel in the 109th Congress, McCrery was primed to handle Social Security, the most politically sensitive domestic initiative of Bush's second term — a plan to introduce market forces into the Social Security program by allowing younger workers to divert 4 percent of their wages into personal investment accounts. The plan proved unpopular, and the effort stalled.

At the local level, McCrery watches out for the interests of Fort Polk and Barksdale Air Force Base. If the bases were closed, he said the impact on his district's economy would be "cataclysmic." He also was able to secure $150 million in the 2005 surface transportation bill to help complete the long-stalled Interstate 49 project, which is slated to stretch from New Orleans to Kansas City.

McCrery's fascination with politics began at a young age. At 11, growing up in Leesville, he displayed a homemade "Nixon for President" sign in his front yard during the 1960 campaign. As a teenager, McCrery was elected high school student body president, defeating a popular quarterback, by setting up his first phone bank and contacting hundreds of fellow students.

After graduating from law school, McCrery joined a firm in Leesville, then put in two years as an assistant city attorney in Shreveport, the town where he was born. As a Democrat, he signed on with Louisiana Democratic Rep. Buddy Roemer in 1981, working in his district office in Shreveport and later as his legislative director in Washington. McCrery returned to Louisiana in 1984 to lobby for Georgia-Pacific Corp. in the state capital.

In 1987, he joined the list of Southern conservative Democrats switching to the GOP. After Roemer became governor, McCrery jumped into the 1988 special election to succeed him. Although initially the least known candidate, he stood out as the only Republican and impressed voters with his knowledge of issues. He finished first in the primary and took 51 percent of the vote to defeat Democratic state Sen. Foster L. Campbell Jr. in the special-election runoff.

His most significant re-election challenge came in 1992, when redistricting matched him against fellow incumbent Jerry Huckaby, an eight-term Democrat. Huckaby chaired the Agriculture Subcommittee on Cotton, Rice and Sugar — commodities of great importance to Louisiana. But he was put at a disadvantage by the demographics of the new district and also had 88 overdrafts at the private bank for House members. McCrery won with 63 percent and has not been as seriously challenged since.

Before the 2004 elections, McCrery came close to quitting, tired of the travel back and forth to his Shreveport home and of missing his kids' soccer games. He told Bush and then Speaker J. Dennis Hastert that he planned to retire. But his wife, Johnette, urged him to stay and agreed to move the family to Washington. The family now lives in McLean, Va.

KEY VOTES

2006

- No Stop broadband companies from favoring select Internet traffic
- Yes Affirm U.S. commitment to war in Iraq and reject setting a withdrawal date for troops
- Yes Repeal requirement for bilingual ballots at the polls
- Yes Permit U.S. sale of civilian nuclear technology to India
- Yes Build a 700-mile fence on the U.S.-Mexico border to curb illegal crossings
- Yes Permit warrantless wiretaps of suspected terrorists

2005

- ? Intervene in the life-support case of Terri Schiavo
- No Lift President Bush's restrictions on stem cell research funding
- No Prohibit FBI access to library and bookstore records
- Yes Approve free-trade pact with five Central American countries
- Yes Pass energy policy overhaul favored by President Bush emphasizing domestic oil and gas production
- Yes End mandatory preservation of habitat of endangered animal and plant species
- Yes Ban torture of prisoners in U.S. custody

CQ VOTE STUDIES

	PARTY UNITY		PRESIDENTIAL SUPPORT	
	Support	Oppose	Support	Oppose
2006	97%	3%	100%	0%
2005	97%	3%	89%	11%
2004	98%	2%	97%	3%
2003	97%	3%	100%	0%
2002	97%	3%	87%	13%

INTEREST GROUPS

	AFL-CIO	ADA	CCUS	ACU
2006	14%	0%	100%	88%
2005	13%	0%	92%	92%
2004	8%	5%	100%	96%
2003	0%	5%	97%	88%
2002	13%	0%	100%	92%

LOUISIANA 4

Northwest and west — Shreveport, Bossier City

Covering most of western Louisiana, the conservative 4th takes in Shreveport in the north and wanders into timber country in Beauregard and Allen parishes in the south.

The Red River divides Shreveport and Bossier City geographically, but unites them economically. Five riverboat casinos dock on the river, and land-based gambling sites dot the shores. A wave of riverfront renewal, including the Louisiana Boardwalk shopping and entertainment complex that opened in Bossier City in 2005, has brought new businesses to the area, and an influx in service and retail jobs has helped drive the economy in recent years.

Shreveport also is a health care hub for northern Louisiana, eastern Texas and southern Arkansas. General Motors operates a light truck plant in Shreveport, and Barksdale Air Force Base near Bossier City is a major employer for both cities.

Natchitoches, the oldest permanent settlement in the former Louisiana Purchase territory, uses its history and festivals to lure tourists, and more than 100,000 people flock to its Christmas Festival every year. Besides Fort Polk in Vernon County, the rest of the 4th relies on poultry production and forestry interests, which were damaged by Hurricane Rita in 2005.

The 4th is predominately white, but blacks make up one-third of the population. Although registered Democrats outnumber Republicans and have enjoyed local success, the suburbs around Shreveport and Bossier City have elected some Republicans in recent elections, and the 4th overall typically prefers a Republican in the White House. George W. Bush received 59 percent of the district's 2004 presidential vote.

MAJOR INDUSTRY

Military, riverboat gambling, health care, timber, retail

MILITARY BASES

Fort Polk (Army), 8,150 military, 6,781 civilian (2007); Barksdale Air Force Base, 7,442 military, 1,981 civilian (2005)

CITIES

Shreveport, 200,145; Bossier City, 56,461; Natchitoches, 17,865

NOTABLE

Natchitoches hosts an annual Meat Pie Festival featuring a beauty pageant, triathlon and eating contest.

Rep. Rodney Alexander (R)

CAPITOL OFFICE
225-8490
rodney.alexander@mail.house.gov
www.house.gov/alexander
316 Cannon 20515-1805; fax 225-5639

COMMITTEES
Appropriations
Budget

RESIDENCE
Quitman

BORN
Dec. 5, 1946, Quitman, La.

RELIGION
Baptist

FAMILY
Wife, Nancy Alexander; three children

EDUCATION
Louisiana Tech U., attended 1965

MILITARY SERVICE
Air Force Reserve, 1965-71

CAREER
Insurance agent; road construction contractor

POLITICAL HIGHLIGHTS
Jackson Parish Police Jury, 1972-87 (president, 1980-87); La. House, 1988-2002 (served as a Democrat)

ELECTION RESULTS

2006 GENERAL		
Rodney Alexander (R)	78,211	68.3%
Gloria Williams Hearn (D)	33,233	29.0%
Brent Sanders (LIBERT)	1,876	1.6%
John Watts (X)	1,262	1.1%
2004 GENERAL		
Rodney Alexander (R)	141,495	59.4%
Zelma "Tisa" Blakes (D)	58,591	24.6%
John W. "Jock" Scott (R)	37,971	16.0%

PREVIOUS WINNING PERCENTAGES *
2002 (50%)
* Elected as a Democrat

Elected 2002; 3rd term

Unlike the typical politician, Alexander is not someone who likes media attention. "I don't seek publicity," he says. "I don't promote a lot of legislation. I don't talk a lot."

Indeed, Alexander spoke just once on the House floor in all of 2006. During four days of debate in early 2007 on deploying additional U.S. troops to Iraq — debate in which every House member was allotted five minutes to speak — Alexander was one of 37 who declined the invitation.

But Alexander's low-key style could not keep him out of the headlines during one of the most sensational scandals to hit Congress in recent years. He fell into the middle of the 2006 congressional page scandal after revelations that a teenager he had sponsored as a page had received inappropriate e-mail messages from Republican Rep. Mark Foley of Florida.

Alexander's aides learned about the "overly friendly" e-mails in 2005 and soon afterward informed the Speaker's office. They also spoke with the page's parents, who said they did not want to pursue the matter but wanted the interaction with Foley to stop. While the Louisiana page did not receive the type of sexually explicit e-mail Foley sent to other former pages, Alexander was called to testify before the House ethics committee on what he knew about the messages and when. The camera-shy Alexander ended up on cable networks such as Fox and CNN. The ethics committee ultimately cleared GOP leaders and aides of official wrongdoing but found Hastert and others had failed to do enough to protect the chamber's teenage pages.

While Alexander may not seek publicity, it does seem to follow him. First elected to Congress in 2002 as a Democrat, he garnered plenty of media attention two years later when he switched to the Republican Party just minutes before the filing deadline for re-election. The maneuver prevented Democrats from recruiting a strong challenger, and Alexander sailed to an easy victory. While his switch infuriated Democrats, it endeared him to GOP leaders, who awarded him a coveted seat on the Appropriations Committee in the 109th Congress (2005-06). He kept that seat in the 110th Congress (2007-08), and added a plum spot on the Budget Committee as well.

Alexander says he didn't switch to win perks, and that he has no regrets about his move even though Democrats recaptured control of the House in the 2006 elections. "I'm pro-life, pro-family, pro-gun," Alexander says. "That's why I was uncomfortable being a Democrat. I didn't change just to be in the majority."

Nevertheless, Alexander has made the most of his position on Appropriations, securing millions of federal dollars for his impoverished district in northeast Louisiana. An unrepentant expert at earmarking funds for his district in appropriations bills, Alexander brags about the criticism he receives from outside groups that assail pork barrel spending. In 2006, Citizens Against Government Waste awarded Alexander and his Senate colleague, Louisiana Democrat Mary L. Landrieu, "The Flood of Pork Award" for a $100 million energy and water project they secured for their state.

"I'll take that kind of criticism any time," Alexander says. "When a conservative group criticizes me for spending too much, then I say I'm doing my job properly."

Alexander worked particularly hard to win funding for his state in the wake of Hurricane Katrina, which devastated southern Louisiana in 2005.

While Alexander's northern district was not directly hit by the hurricane, the area is dealing with a massive influx of people who fled their homes in New Orleans and other areas devastated by the storm. He wants to make sure his district's schools, hospitals and police stations are properly funded to handle the expanded population.

In particular, Alexander is concerned about health care in his district, a region plagued with large pockets of poverty and unemployment. "Health care issues are the most important thing out there in my district. If you talk to a momma with a sick baby, she doesn't care how many nuclear warheads Kim Jong-il has."

Alexander says he wants to create school-based clinics to ensure children located in rural areas of his district get adequate health care. "We've got some areas where 10- and 12-year-olds have never been to a clinic. We need to make sure health care is available in isolated areas."

Alexander also will be paying close attention in the 110th Congress to a scheduled rewrite of the 2002 farm bill. He intends to use his seat on the Appropriations Agriculture Subcommittee to make sure the farmers of his district do not suffer. He said he also will push to promote ethanol and biofuels programs that would benefit farmers in his district.

Since his party switch, Alexander has voted with a majority of his fellow Republicans 97 percent of the time on votes pitting the parties against each other. But he does not consider himself partisan. In 2005, following Hurricane Katrina, he rose on the House floor — one of just three times he spoke on the floor that year — to defend Democratic Louisiana Gov. Kathleen Babineaux Blanco, who had come under criticism from many Republicans for her handling of the crisis.

"I served with the lady 20 years ago in the state legislature. She had some criticism for me when I changed parties last year, but I understand that. But she is a decent lady," Alexander said. "I would appreciate it if members would refrain from throwing stones at this particular time. We have some devastation down there and a lot of hurt people."

A former construction contractor who dropped out of Louisiana Tech University, Alexander has spent much of his adult life in politics. He was only 25 when he was first elected to the Jackson Parish Police Jury, the Louisiana equivalent of a county board of supervisors, and he later served 14 years in the state House before running for Congress.

He won his first congressional race in 2002 by a mere 974 votes but has had no trouble winning re-election since then. He took 59 percent of the vote after his 2004 party switch and garnered 68 percent in 2006.

KEY VOTES

2006

- No Stop broadband companies from favoring select Internet traffic
- Yes Affirm U.S. commitment to war in Iraq and reject setting a withdrawal date for troops
- Yes Repeal requirement for bilingual ballots at the polls
- Yes Permit U.S. sale of civilian nuclear technology to India
- Yes Build a 700-mile fence on the U.S.-Mexico border to curb illegal crossings
- Yes Permit warrantless wiretaps of suspected terrorists

2005

- Yes Intervene in the life-support case of Terri Schiavo
- No Lift President Bush's restrictions on stem cell research funding
- No Prohibit FBI access to library and bookstore records
- Yes Approve free-trade pact with five Central American countries
- Yes Pass energy policy overhaul favored by President Bush emphasizing domestic oil and gas production
- Yes End mandatory preservation of habitat of endangered animal and plant species
- Yes Ban torture of prisoners in U.S. custody

CQ VOTE STUDIES

	PARTY UNITY		PRESIDENTIAL SUPPORT	
	Support	Oppose	Support	Oppose
2006	97%	3%	93%	7%
2005	97%	3%	89%	11%
2004	97%	3%	67%	33%
2003	69%	31%	56%	44%

INTEREST GROUPS

	AFL-CIO	ADA	CCUS	ACU
2006	21%	5%	100%	80%
2005	13%	0%	93%	92%
2004	80%	40%	70%	48%
2003	87%	60%	67%	48%

LOUISIANA 5

Northeast and central — Monroe, Alexandria

The 5th stretches south from the Arkansas border among the Mississippi River delta parishes in its east and the national forests and midsize cities of central Louisiana in its west. It is conservative throughout, and is plagued by pockets of poverty and unemployment despite numerous efforts to bring more economic opportunities to the area.

Although the rich, black soil along the Mississippi River produces much of the state's cotton and soybeans, poor education and transportation systems slow economic growth — the 5th is the eighth-poorest district in the country, with a median household income of just under $27,500.

The outlook is not entirely bleak, however. Monroe depends increasingly on health care, service and retail industries, and is home to a University of Louisiana campus and CenturyTel, a telecommunications company. Several development projects — including improvements to a Ouachita River port in West Monroe and the building of the NASCAR-affiliated Monroe Motor Speedway scheduled to open in early 2008 — are expected to bring jobs, tourism and revenue to the district.

The 5th's portion of central Louisiana is fueled by Alexandria in Rapides Parish, which is home to a Proctor & Gamble detergent manufacturing plant. In the district's northwest, Lincoln Parish hosts Louisiana Tech University in Ruston and the historically black Grambling State University in Grambling.

This historically Democratic district now leans Republican, but the 5th's voters still support conservatives of either party. Roughly one-third of the district's residents are black, and Democrats hold many local offices, although residents of Baptist- and Pentecostal-dominated northern Louisiana are more likely than the Catholics in the South to vote for Republicans. George W. Bush took 62 percent of the district's vote in the 2004 presidential election.

MAJOR INDUSTRY

Agriculture, health care, higher education

CITIES

Monroe, 53,107; Alexandria, 46,342; Ruston, 20,546

NOTABLE

Grambling State became the first Louisiana college or university to receive a visit from a sitting president when Bill Clinton gave the 1999 commencement address.

Rep. Richard H. Baker (R)

CAPITOL OFFICE
225-3901
www.house.gov/baker
341 Cannon 20515-1806; fax 225-7313

COMMITTEES
Financial Services
Transportation & Infrastructure
Veterans' Affairs

RESIDENCE
Baton Rouge

BORN
May 22, 1948, New Orleans, La.

RELIGION
Methodist

FAMILY
Wife, Kay Baker; two children

EDUCATION
Louisiana State U., B.A. 1971 (political science)

CAREER
Real estate broker

POLITICAL HIGHLIGHTS
La. House, 1972-86 (served as a Democrat, 1972-85)

ELECTION RESULTS

2006 GENERAL		
Richard H. Baker (R)	94,658	82.8%
Richard M. Fontanesi (LIBERT)	19,648	17.2%

2004 GENERAL		
Richard H. Baker (R)	189,106	72.2%
Rufus Holt Craig Jr. (D)	50,732	19.4%
Edward Anthony Galmon (D)	22,031	8.4%

PREVIOUS WINNING PERCENTAGES
2002 (84%); 2000 (68%); 1998 (51%); 1996 (69%); 1994 (81%); 1992 (51%); 1990 (100%); 1988 (100%); 1986 (51%)

Elected 1986; 11th term

After years of focusing on esoteric banking and finance issues that even he admits were often of no interest to his own constituents, Baker turned his attention homeward after the devastation of Hurricane Katrina.

He won praise in Louisiana for his proposal to create a federal agency to buy up property damaged by Hurricane Katrina and combine the land for redevelopment. But the "Baker bill," as it came to be known, died after the White House made clear it opposed the plan to use $20 billion in Treasury bonds to purchase the damaged property. The Bush administration's alternative to provide Louisiana with more community block grant money left Baker dissatisfied.

But Baker, who calls himself a policy wonk, didn't give up. He reached across the aisle and worked with Massachusetts Democrat Barney Frank to find other ways to help his beleaguered state. He and Frank cosponsored a 2006 measure to take away the Federal Emergency Management Agency's role in providing emergency housing after a disaster and to give the responsibility to the Department of Housing and Urban Development.

The bill, among other things, discouraged the creation of "trailer cities" and instead encouraged deployment of what Baker says is more cost-effective modular housing, or "Katrina cottages," 400- to 750-square-foot prefabricated homes. "We need the ability right now to provide folks creative, longer-term options like Katrina cottages," Baker told the New Orleans Times-Picayune. "And to avoid another situation in which we spend $9 billion on cruise ships and trailers instead of putting that money toward our long-term housing solutions." Baker successfully added language to an appropriations bill in 2006 to use the more cost-effective modular housing.

Baker has been a mainstay of the Financial Services Committee, where he has worked before with Frank, who became the committee's chairman in the 110th Congress (2007-08). When the Republicans held the majority, Baker chaired the Capital Markets Subcommittee, which has a wide portfolio covering the securities and insurance industries, capital markets and the secondary mortgage market.

But Baker has yet to attain his long-sought goal of a top post on the Financial Services panel. The Democratic takeover of the House in 2007 ensured he wouldn't become chairman, and he lost the spot of ranking Republican to Spencer Bachus of Alabama, even though Baker had more seniority.

Yet one of Baker's objectives appears to be on the road to completion in the 110th Congress. He signed on to cosponsor a bill drafted by Frank to create a new independent government regulator to oversee Fannie Mae and Freddie Mac, the financiers of nearly half the nation's home loans. The bill would not only provide a regulator for the giant mortgage lenders but also create an affordable housing fund to distribute a small percentage of the companies' investment portfolios to housing concerns.

Baker was the most vociferous critic of Fannie and Freddie long before other lawmakers came to his corner, because of alleged multibillion-dollar accounting improprieties by the two government-sponsored enterprises. Fannie Mae lawyers threatened to sue Baker in 2003 when he sought to disclose the salaries of the company's top executives. In 2006, he asked the Justice Department to investigate two executives for perjury for possibly lying to Congress under oath.

Baker also has signaled a willingness to work with Financial Services Democrats on issues such as forcing hedge funds to disclose more information and overhauling the federal flood insurance program. The House in June 2006 easily passed Baker's bill addressing the nation's flood insurance program, which had to borrow heavily from the government to pay an estimated $23 billion in claims stemming from the 2005 hurricane season.

Baker in the 110th Congress also will address water-related issues from his post as the top-ranking Republican on the Transportation and Infrastructure Committee's Water Resources and Environment Subcommittee. The panel has oversight of the water projects managed by the Army Corps of Engineers. Longstanding criticism of the way the corps managed water projects intensified when the New Orleans levees administered by the agency were breached after Hurricane Katrina.

Baker's staid and decorous style often puts him at odds with the popular perception of the back-slapping Louisiana politician. An amateur astronomer, he prefers stargazing to attending Louisiana State University football games or other venues for political hobnobbing. But he has a sense of humor and often jokes about how his rectitude contrasts with his state's reputation. "I'm beginning my 36th year of continuous elected duty in the state of Louisiana without an indictment," Baker told a Baton Rouge audience in 2006, according to the hometown newspaper, The Advocate.

By age 23, Baker had graduated from LSU and started his own real estate business. He credits his father, a World War II pilot and minister for 47 years, for guiding him philosophically and his mother-in-law for getting him into politics. Baker considered following in his father's footsteps, but realized that a pastoral life required a more patient man. His mother-in-law, who worked in local campaigns and organized political fundraisers over sandwiches and fruit punch at parlor parties, encouraged him to run for office.

He won election to the Louisiana state House in 1972 and made a name for himself by writing a law creating objective criteria for allocation of state highway funds, which had been based on political favoritism. In 1985, Baker switched political allegiance from the Democrats to the GOP, a practical move that instantly made him the favorite to capture the House seat being vacated by Republican Rep. W. Henson Moore, who ran for the Senate.

In 1992, reapportionment cost Louisiana a House seat, and Baker was re-elected by only 2,700 votes after he was forced to run in the same district as GOP Rep. Clyde C. Holloway. Baker's only other close call was in 1998, when he prevailed by 2,800 votes in a race against Democrat Marjorie McKeithen, the daughter and granddaughter of big players in Louisiana politics. In 2002, Baker was the beneficiary of redistricting, and his turf became more securely Republican. He has been re-elected easily every year.

KEY VOTES

2006

- No Stop broadband companies from favoring select Internet traffic
- Yes Affirm U.S. commitment to war in Iraq and reject setting a withdrawal date for troops
- Yes Repeal requirement for bilingual ballots at the polls
- Yes Permit U.S. sale of civilian nuclear technology to India
- Yes Build a 700-mile fence on the U.S.-Mexico border to curb illegal crossings
- Yes Permit warrantless wiretaps of suspected terrorists

2005

- Yes Intervene in the life-support case of Terri Schiavo
- No Lift President Bush's restrictions on stem cell research funding
- No Prohibit FBI access to library and bookstore records
- Yes Approve free-trade pact with five Central American countries
- Yes Pass energy policy overhaul favored by President Bush emphasizing domestic oil and gas production
- Yes End mandatory preservation of habitat of endangered animal and plant species
- No Ban torture of prisoners in U.S. custody

CQ VOTE STUDIES

	PARTY UNITY		PRESIDENTIAL SUPPORT	
	Support	Oppose	Support	Oppose
2006	97%	3%	95%	5%
2005	98%	2%	91%	9%
2004	95%	5%	94%	6%
2003	98%	2%	98%	2%
2002	96%	4%	82%	18%

INTEREST GROUPS

	AFL-CIO	ADA	CCUS	ACU
2006	8%	0%	100%	92%
2005	13%	0%	92%	92%
2004	13%	5%	100%	88%
2003	0%	5%	100%	88%
2002	11%	0%	95%	100%

LOUISIANA 6

East central – Baton Rouge

Centered around Baton Rouge, the socially conservative 6th takes in a slew of petrochemical plants along the Mississippi River as well as rural parishes along the Mississippi border. Baton Rouge's economic and population growth has spilled over into neighboring parishes, which attract commuters with superior schools and lower crime rates.

Government is the primary employer in the state capital of Baton Rouge, providing more than 20 percent of city jobs. Higher education also drives the economy, as Louisiana State University and Southern University are here. Casinos and other ventures, such as the new Shaw Center for the Arts — home to a museum, theater and gallery — have helped Baton Rouge promote tourism. A proposed light-rail system connecting Baton Rouge to New Orleans might help as well, but implementation of those plans are considered a long-term goal.

Although the Port of Greater Baton Rouge in Port Allen is no longer the 6th's economic engine, it still gives the area a boost and ranks among the top 10 U.S. ports by tonnage. The petrochemical industry rebounded in recent years, but agriculture fuels the 6th's rural parishes, with sugar cane in the west and paper mills and potato farms in the northeast.

Baton Rouge has felt ripple effects since hurricanes Katrina and Rita in 2005. The city itself was largely unaffected, but it took in tens of thousands of displaced residents from New Orleans and other areas. The housing market surged as individuals and companies snapped up available units.

Socially conservative suburban and rural voters have shifted toward the GOP, but Baton Rouge's minority and blue-collar residents still vote Democratic. Republican George W. Bush won 59 percent of the 6th's 2004 presidential vote.

MAJOR INDUSTRY

Government, higher education, petrochemicals

CITIES

Baton Rouge, 227,818; Shenandoah (unincorporated), 17,070

NOTABLE

The state Capitol, completed in 1932, is the tallest in the United States; Gov. Huey Long, who led the fight for a new state Capitol, was assassinated there in 1935 and is buried on the Capitol grounds.

Rep. Charles Boustany Jr. (R)

CAPITOL OFFICE
225-2031
boustany.house.gov
1117 Longworth 20515-1807; fax 225-5724

COMMITTEES
Agriculture
Education & Labor
Transportation & Infrastructure

RESIDENCE
Lafayette

BORN
Feb. 21, 1956, Lafayette, La.

RELIGION
Episcopalian

FAMILY
Wife, Bridget Boustany; two children

EDUCATION
U. of Southwestern Louisiana, B.S. 1978 (biology); Louisiana State U., M.D. 1982

CAREER
Surgeon

POLITICAL HIGHLIGHTS
No previous office

ELECTION RESULTS

2006 GENERAL		
Charles Boustany Jr. (R)	113,720	70.7%
Mike Stagg (D)	47,133	29.3%
2004 GENERAL RUNOFF		
Charles Boustany Jr. (R)	75,039	55.0%
Willie Landry Mount (D)	61,493	45.0%

Elected 2004; 2nd term

Boustany, a heart surgeon with no political résumé to speak of before his election to the House, learned legislating by the immersion method. Eight months after he was sworn in, hurricanes Katrina and Rita slammed the Gulf Coast, doing billions of dollars in damage to his coastal district in southwestern Louisiana.

Much of his work in his first term focused on reconstruction. One of his bills, giving the Labor Department more flexibility in providing temporary work and training in disaster areas, made it to President Bush's desk and was signed into law. Although a minor bill compared with other recovery legislation passed by Congress, it was a feat nonetheless for Boustany (boo-STAN-knee) as a freshman lawmaker. Another of his proposals, also enacted, extended the amount of time schools in hurricane-affected areas had to collect $1.4 billion appropriated the previous year.

The imperative of getting results for hurricane-ravaged cities and farms taught Boustany how to cut Congress' red tape, but also took a toll on his emotions and on his wife and two children. "The work consumed my days, every moment of my waking days," he recalls.

Like other members of Congress from Louisiana and Mississippi, the states that suffered the most damage and displacement, Boustany was highly dissatisfied with the Bush administration's response to the crisis, which was marred by long delays and confusion in rescuing survivors, removing debris and rebuilding. Though Congress has sent large infusions of cash to the region, the pace in getting it to the local level has been slow. Cameron Parish, one of the hardest hit areas in his district, had gotten only 13 percent of the federal money obligated to it from the Federal Emergency Management Agency by early 2007. An objective for Boustany in the 110th Congress (2007-08) is legislation to speed the delivery of aid to the region.

Boustany's other preoccupation has been issues affecting the agrarian economy of his district. From his seat on the Agriculture Committee, he looks out for rice and sugar growers in particular. In a major rewrite of farm policy scheduled for the 110th Congress, he opposes any major changes to the sugar subsidy program.

Protection of the sugar cane industry was the reason he voted against Bush's Central American Free Trade Agreement, despite entreaties from GOP leaders to support it. Sugar producers in the United States fear the agreement will allow cheaper sugar from Latin American and Caribbean countries to saturate the U.S. market. "I was under extreme pressure for a member of only six months," he recalls of the free-trade fight in 2005.

Like other freshmen with an eye toward staying awhile, Boustany concentrated on federal projects for his district in his first term. He was chosen for a coveted seat on the Transportation and Infrastructure Committee, which establishes priorities for competing road and building projects. His main goal is securing funding for his district's portion of Interstate 49.

Boustany has strongly conservative positions on most issues. His views on abortion place him to the right even among conservatives. He says he is "100 percent pro-life" without exception. Boustany supports a constitutional ban on same-sex marriage and joined other conservatives on a bill to build a 700-mile fence along the border with Mexico.

He favors Bush's pro-business, tax-cutting agenda, including making permanent the tax cuts for individuals and businesses that the president signed into law during his first term. He also stuck with Bush on the war in Iraq, supporting the president's plan in 2007 to send in additional combat troops, while many other Republicans were backing away.

Boustany grew up in Lafayette, the son of Charles Boustany Sr., a longtime coroner for Lafayette Parish. His mother, a homemaker with 10 children, also did charitable work in the community.

Following in his father's footsteps, Boustany went to medical school, becoming a heart surgeon. As early as 6th grade, he was interested in politics and history and was an avid reader of American political biographies. His family was staunchly Democratic, but Boustany as a young man was influenced by columnist George Will and other conservative thinkers. "It created friction then, and still does," says Boustany of his political split with his father. "We have a lot of arguments over the dinner table."

Boustany practiced medicine for 14 years in Lafayette. He met and married his wife, Bridget, the niece of former Gov. Edwin Edwards, also a Democrat (though she became a Republican as well).

In 2001, Boustany had to give up practicing medicine because of arthritis in his neck and hands. He decided to give politics a shot. "One of the things that compelled me to run was the fact that Louisiana was always last on the list of a lot of good things," he says.

In 2004, after Democratic Rep. Chris John decided to run for the Senate, Boustany talked it over with his wife and with friends who had run for office and mapped out his first campaign plan, starting "with me and a telephone and that was it," he told the Daily Advertiser newspaper.

After finishing first with 39 percent of the vote in the Nov. 2 all-party primary, Boustany cruised to a comfortable 10 percentage point win in the runoff with state Sen. Willie Landry Mount, a Democrat. He made history as the first Republican to be elected from the area since 1884.

Mount was hindered by a conflict with Democratic state Sen. Don Cravins, whom she edged out in the primary race for the second runoff slot. Cravins, who is black, contended that the state Democratic Party showed favoritism toward Mount, who is white. That made it hard for Mount to galvanize support among blacks, who make up a quarter of the district's population and are crucial to Democrats' success in the region.

Boustany, meanwhile, made it difficult for Mount to attract support from the district's conservative majority. The Democrat voiced strongly conservative views throughout her run, casting herself in the same light as outgoing Democrat John. But Boustany portrayed himself as a more stalwart conservative and won one of the last Democratic redoubts in the GOP-dominated South. He was handily re-elected in 2006, with 71 percent.

KEY VOTES

2006

- No Stop broadband companies from favoring select Internet traffic
- Yes Affirm U.S. commitment to war in Iraq and reject setting a withdrawal date for troops
- Yes Repeal requirement for bilingual ballots at the polls
- Yes Permit U.S. sale of civilian nuclear technology to India
- Yes Build a 700-mile fence on the U.S.-Mexico border to curb illegal crossings
- Yes Permit warrantless wiretaps of suspected terrorists

2005

- ? Intervene in the life-support case of Terri Schiavo
- No Lift President Bush's restrictions on stem cell research funding
- No Prohibit FBI access to library and bookstore records
- No Approve free-trade pact with five Central American countries
- Yes Pass energy policy overhaul favored by President Bush emphasizing domestic oil and gas production
- Yes End mandatory preservation of habitat of endangered animal and plant species
- Yes Ban torture of prisoners in U.S. custody

CQ VOTE STUDIES

	PARTY UNITY		PRESIDENTIAL SUPPORT	
	Support	Oppose	Support	Oppose
2006	95%	5%	95%	5%
2005	96%	4%	86%	14%

INTEREST GROUPS

	AFL-CIO	ADA	CCUS	ACU
2006	21%	0%	100%	80%
2005	27%	15%	89%	96%

LOUISIANA 7

Southwest – Lafayette, Lake Charles

Anchored by blue-collar Lake Charles in the west, white-collar Lafayette in the east and the Gulf of Mexico to the south, the 7th boasts both coastal and city life.

While damage to New Orleans and southeastern Louisiana received considerable attention during the 2005 hurricane season, the 7th did not escape the storms unscathed. Hurricane Rita landed in Cameron Parish near Johnsons Bayou, flooded Lake Charles in Calcasieu Parish and demolished smaller towns such as Creole and Cameron, where almost 90 percent of homes were destroyed. Father east, Lafayette welcomed evacuees from other parts of the state.

Agriculture, along with oil and gas production, directs the 7th's economy, although Rita destroyed nearly half of Calcasieu's soybean, sugar and hay crops, 900 acres of rice fields and hundreds of cattle. Lake Charles' oil refineries and chemical production plants fared better, but damaged gas compressors decreased supply in the storm's aftermath. Fishing also saw a downturn, as the storm surge increased salinity and sediment inland, killing fish and vegetation. Cameron Parish, once the nation's fifth-largest fishing port, lost about 60 percent of its commercial fleet.

Area construction and contracting jobs are expected to increase as hurricane-related repairs expand in the 7th. Many residents were provided with temporary trailers and federal disaster loans, and housing is still scarce in the southern areas of the 7th, not only for residents who lost homes but also for workers who came here to help rebuild.

The 7th's sizable Catholic population bolsters its socially conservative leanings. Despite this bent, the area only began electing Republicans to Congress in 2004, and George W. Bush won 60 percent of the 7th's presidential vote that year. Lafayette Parish is the 7th's most GOP-friendly area.

MAJOR INDUSTRY
Agriculture, oil and gas, petrochemicals, fishing

CITIES
Lafayette, 110,257; Lake Charles, 71,757; Opelousas, 22,860

NOTABLE
Southwest Louisiana Institute (now University of Louisiana at Lafayette) in 1954 was the first all-white state college in the South to desegregate.

MAINE

Gov. John Baldacci (D)

Pronounced: ball-DA-chee
First elected: 2002
Length of term: 4 years
Term expires: 1/11
Salary: $70,000
Phone: (207) 287-3531

Residence: Bangor
Born: Jan. 30, 1955; Bangor, Maine
Religion: Roman Catholic
Family: Wife, Karen Baldacci; one child
Education: U. of Maine, B.A. 1986 (history)
Career: Restaurant operator
Political highlights: Bangor City Council, 1978-81; Maine Senate, 1982-94; U.S. House, 1995-2003

Election results:

2006 GENERAL		
John Baldacci (D)	209,927	38.1%
Chandler E. Woodcock (R)	166,425	30.2%
Barbara Merrill (IMC)	118,715	21.6%
Patricia H. LaMarche (GREEN)	52,690	9.6%

Senate President Beth Edmonds (D)

(no lieutenant governor)
Phone: (207) 287-1500

LEGISLATURE

Legislature: January-June in odd-numbered years; January-April in even-numbered years

Senate: 35 members, 2-year terms
2007 ratios: 18 D, 17 R; 23 men, 12 women
Salary: $21,869/2-year term
Phone: (207) 287-1540

House: 151 members, 2-year terms
2007 ratios: 88 D, 60 R, 2 I, 1 vacancy; 106 men, 44 women
Salary: $21,869/2-year term
Phone: (207) 287-1400

TERM LIMITS

Governor: 2 consecutive terms
Senate: 4 consecutive terms
House: 4 consecutive terms

URBAN STATISTICS

CITY	POPULATION
Portland	64,249
Lewiston	35,690
Bangor	31,473
South Portland	23,325
Auburn	23,203

REGISTERED VOTERS

Unaffiliated/others	41%
Democrat	31%
Republican	28%

POPULATION

2006 population (est.)	1,321,574
2000 population	1,274,923
1990 population	1,227,928
Percent change (1990-2000)	+3.8%
Rank among states (2006)	40
Median age	38.6
Born in state	67.3%
Foreign born	2.9%
Violent crime rate	110/100,000
Poverty level	10.9%
Federal workers	13,542
Military	10,200

ELECTIONS

STATE ELECTION OFFICIAL
(207) 624-7736
DEMOCRATIC PARTY
(207) 622-6233
REPUBLICAN PARTY
(207) 622-6247

MISCELLANEOUS

Web: www.maine.gov
Capital: Augusta

U.S. CONGRESS

Senate: 2 Republicans
House: 2 Democrats

2000 Census Statistics by District

DIST.	2004 VOTE FOR PRESIDENT BUSH	KERRY	WHITE	BLACK	ASIAN	HISP	MEDIAN INCOME	WHITE COLLAR	BLUE COLLAR	SERVICE INDUSTRY	OVER 64	UNDER 18	COLLEGE EDUCATION	RURAL	SQ. MILES
1	43%	55%	96%	1%	1%	1%	$42,044	61%	24%	14%	14%	24%	28%	51%	3,535
2	46	52	97	0	0	1	$32,678	53	31	16	15	23	18	71	27,244
STATE	45	54	96	1	1	1	$37,240	57	27	15	14	24	23	60	30,862
U.S.	50.7	48.3	69	12	4	13	$41,994	60	25	15	12	26	24	21	3,537,438

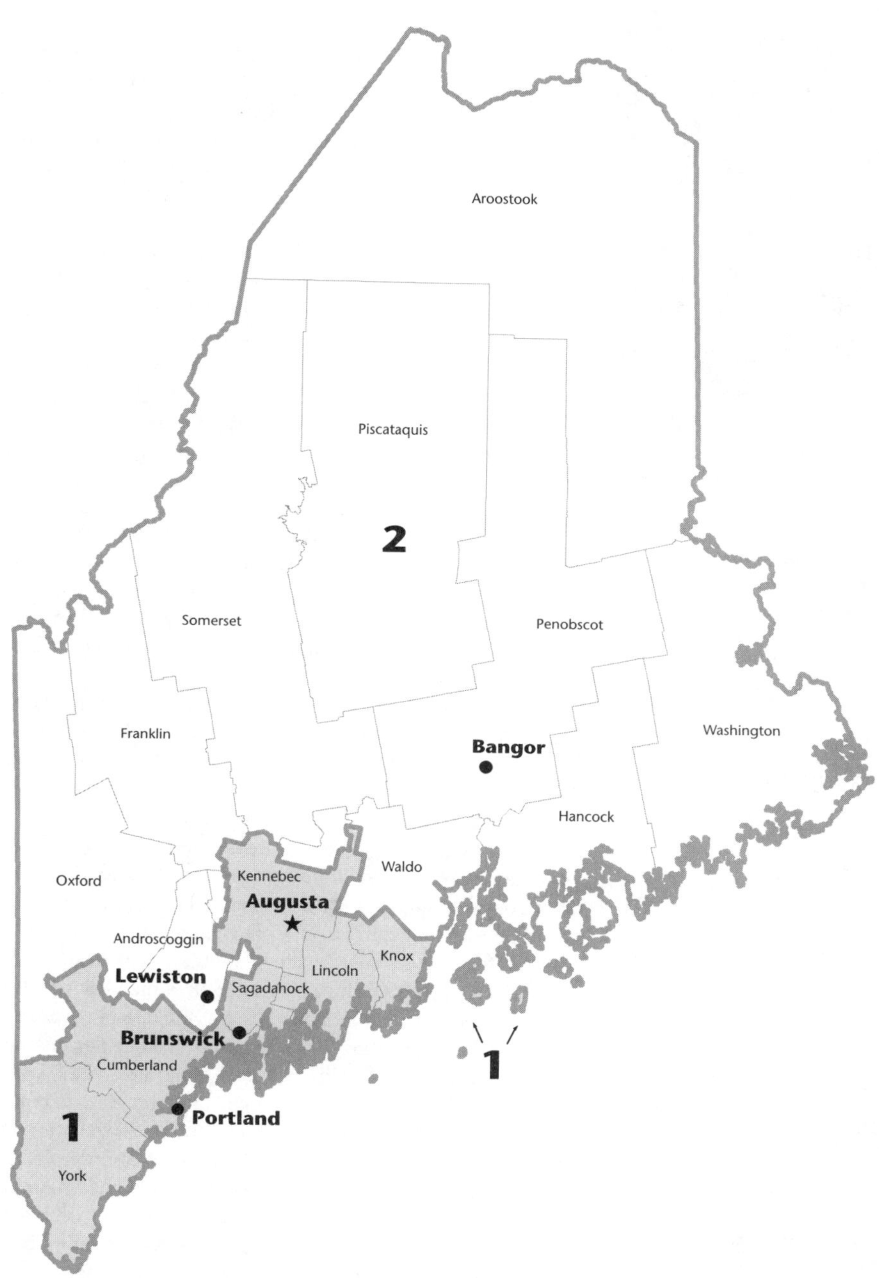
Aroostook
Piscataquis
2
Somerset
Penobscot
Franklin
Washington
Bangor
Hancock
Waldo
Oxford
Kennebec
Augusta
Androscoggin
Knox
Lewiston
Lincoln
Sagadahock
Brunswick
1
Cumberland
Portland
1
York

Sen. Olympia J. Snowe (R)

CAPITOL OFFICE
224-5344
snowe.senate.gov
154 Russell 20510-1903; fax 224-1946

COMMITTEES
Commerce, Science & Transportation
Finance
Small Business & Entrepreneurship - ranking member
Select Intelligence

RESIDENCE
Falmouth

BORN
Feb. 21, 1947, Augusta, Maine

RELIGION
Greek Orthodox

FAMILY
Husband, John R. McKernan Jr.

EDUCATION
U. of Maine, B.A. 1969 (political science)

CAREER
Congressional district aide; city employee

POLITICAL HIGHLIGHTS
Maine House, 1973-77; Maine Senate, 1977-79; U.S. House, 1979-95

ELECTION RESULTS

2006 GENERAL		
Olympia J. Snowe (R)	402,598	74.0%
Jean M. Hay Bright (D)	111,984	20.6%
William H. Slavick (I)	29,220	5.4%
2006 PRIMARY		
Olympia J. Snowe (R)	58,979	98.9%
write-ins (R)	673	1.1%

PREVIOUS WINNING PERCENTAGES
2000 (69%); 1994 (60%); 1992 House Election (49%); 1990 House Election (51%); 1988 House Election (66%); 1986 House Election (77%); 1984 House Election (76%); 1982 House Election (67%); 1980 House Election (79%); 1978 House Election (51%)

Elected 1994; 3rd term

Snowe is one of the Senate's most influential centrists. She is not the only Republican to buck President Bush and the GOP leadership at decisive moments, but her seat on the Finance Committee gives her enormous leverage on tax and budget matters, Social Security, Medicare and other issues. Her pivotal vote is coveted by both parties, regardless of who is in charge of the Senate.

Snowe has served in Congress for nearly three decades, and as the years have passed, her party has increasingly done things she's not happy about — cutting taxes as deficits surged and paying too much attention to divisive social issues. "People don't live by ideology alone. They live by solutions. We've got to be relevant to the average American," says Snowe, named one of the 10 best senators by Time magazine in 2006.

Snowe's biggest break with Bush was over his 2005 proposal to add private savings accounts to Social Security. From her seat on the Finance Committee, she refused to support such accounts or the steep cuts in guaranteed benefits that would accompany them. She told Maine audiences she was proud of obstructing the plan, which died in Congress.

Also that year, she was one of the Senate's Gang of 14 — seven Republicans and seven Democrats who joined forces to block a threat by Majority Leader Bill Frist to use a parliamentary power play to eliminate Democratic filibusters against Bush's conservative judicial nominees. The group also agreed to prevent such filibusters in all but extraordinary cases.

Escalating budget deficits during the Bush era changed Snowe's thinking on tax cuts. When President Ronald Reagan slashed taxes in 1981, she says, Americans really were overtaxed. And when Bush unveiled his sweeping tax cut plan in 2001, Snowe voted for it. But by 2003, with deficits escalating, Snowe was one of the centrists who forced GOP leaders to slash Bush's next tax cut bill in half, from $726 billion to $350 billion. In 2004, she and other moderates insisted on applying pay-as-you-go rules to tax cuts, not just spending increases as GOP leaders wanted. The dispute left Congress unable to adopt its annual budget.

In 2007, Snowe and Susan Collins, her home-state colleague and fellow moderate, were the only Senate Republicans to vote for the new Democratic majority's fiscal 2008 budget resolution, which carried the pay-as-you-go requirement she had long advocated. She cited that provision along with increased funding allowances for programs she has championed, such as the State Children's Health Insurance Program and the Low Income Home Energy Assistance Program, in explaining her vote to constituents.

After the GOP sweep in the 2004 elections, Snowe was among the Republicans who unsuccessfully urged the party to compromise more with Democrats. She and moderate Democrat Mary L. Landrieu of Louisiana paired up in 2007 to create a bipartisan group built on the membership of the Gang of 14 and the old Centrist Coalition, which Snowe had co-chaired.

Although Snowe doesn't get everything she wants, she often succeeds at slipping targeted provisions into final legislation, sometimes playing hardball to prevail. In 2006, Snowe blocked action on a flood insurance bill until she was able to win $1 billion for the Low Income Home Energy Assistance Program, which helps poor families pay their heating bills.

Another local issue she watches closely is the reauthorization of the Magnuson-Stevens fisheries conservation law, important to Maine, with its 3,500 miles of coastline and robust fishing industry. She also looks out for the Bath Iron Works, the giant builder of Navy ships that is one of the state's largest employers. During the 2005 round of military base closings, she successfully fought a proposal to shut down the Portsmouth Naval Shipyard though she was unable to save Brunswick Naval Air Station.

Snowe, one of 16 women in the Senate, likes being a role model for younger generations entering politics. A 2002 Miss America pageant contestant cited her as inspiration. As the top-ranking Republican on the Small Business Committee, she encourages female entrepreneurs. That panel also is an important parochial base for her — more than 95 percent of Maine's 40,000-plus employers are firms with fewer than 20 employees.

Though she strongly supports abortion rights, Snowe seeks to broker compromises with conservatives. She tried but failed in 2003 to find an alternative to the GOP's ban on a procedure opponents call "partial birth" abortion. On environmental matters, she generally votes in favor of strong environmental regulations and against her party's efforts to open Alaska's Arctic National Wildlife Refuge and more of the Gulf of Mexico to oil drilling.

Snowe's father, Greek immigrant George Bouchles, and her mother, Georgia, operated the State Street Diner in Augusta, down the street from the state house. Georgia Bouchles loved politics, and the diner was a magnet for politicians, business people and journalists. Snowe still runs into folks back home who remember her as a kid hanging out at the restaurant.

In 1955, when Olympia was 8, her mother died of breast cancer. The next year, her father died of heart disease. Her 13-year-old brother went to live with relatives and Olympia was sent to St. Basil's Academy, a school for girls run by the Greek Orthodox Church in Garrison, N.Y. She spent summers in Auburn, Maine, with an uncle who was a barber and his textile-worker wife and their five children. Snowe would make the long train ride between Maine and New York by herself, sometimes taking two trains and spending the night at the train station. Once, her suitcases were stolen. "I can identify with people's difficulties and tragedies and impediments in life," Snowe said in 2006. "Having been to the depths of despair, I know what it feels like, and then to overcome those challenges because of the support [from] my family, my church and my school."

Snowe got through the University of Maine on student loans and with summer jobs at a Christmas ornament factory. After graduation, she married Peter Snowe, who, like her, was deeply interested in politics. "I found conflicting choices in my life. At the time I was engaged to be married, yet I also had my own aspirations as an individual. I was anxious that with the words, 'I do,' all my goals and dreams would evaporate," she says in "Nine and Counting," a book she wrote in 2001 with other women senators. Her husband was elected to the Maine legislature and she went to work as a district aide for GOP Rep. William S. Cohen, who later became secretary of Defense. In 1973, Peter Snowe was killed in an automobile accident during a snowstorm, and a still-grieving Olympia was elected to succeed him.

Three years later, in 1976, she won a seat in the Maine Senate. In 1978, when Cohen made a winning race for the U.S. Senate, she captured his House seat. She later fell in love for the second time — with GOP Rep. John R. McKernan Jr., who represented the adjacent 1st District. They married in 1989, while he was serving the first of two terms as governor of Maine.

Snowe enjoyed a series of easy re-election victories until 1990, when a deepening recession led to voter restlessness. She eventually defeated Democratic state Rep. Patrick K. McGowan, 51 percent to 49 percent. A 1992 rematch was even closer; she won with a 49 percent plurality. When Senate Majority Leader George J. Mitchell, a Democrat, retired in 1994, she ran for the seat and prevailed with 60 percent of the vote. In 2000 and 2006, she overwhelmed her Democratic opponents.

KEY VOTES

2006

Yes Confirm Samuel A. Alito Jr. to the Supreme Court

Yes Allow consideration of a bill to establish a $140 billion trust fund to compensate victims of asbestos exposure

No Extend tax cuts for two years at a cost of $70 billion over five years

Yes Overhaul immigration policy with border security, enforcement and guest worker program

Yes Allow consideration of a bill to permanently repeal the estate tax

No Urge President Bush to begin troop withdrawals from Iraq in 2006

Yes Lift President Bush's restrictions on stem cell research funding

\+ Authorize military tribunals for suspected terrorists

2005

Yes Curb class action lawsuits by shifting them from state to federal courts

Yes Allow confirmation vote on Priscilla R. Owen to the U.S. Court of Appeals for the 5th Circuit

No Oppose mandatory emissions limits and block recognition of global warming as a threat

No Approve free-trade pact with five Central American countries

Yes Pass energy policy overhaul favored by President Bush emphasizing domestic oil and gas production

Yes Shield gunmakers from lawsuits when their products are used in crimes

Yes Ban torture of prisoners in U.S. custody

Yes Renew 16 provisions of the Patriot Act

Yes Allow final vote on opening the Arctic National Wildlife Refuge to oil and gas exploration

CQ VOTE STUDIES

	PARTY UNITY		PRESIDENTIAL SUPPORT	
	Support	Oppose	Support	Oppose
2006	56%	44%	75%	25%
2005	56%	44%	67%	33%
2004	71%	29%	74%	26%
2003	75%	25%	82%	18%
2002	57%	43%	90%	10%
2001	64%	36%	84%	16%
2000	71%	29%	62%	38%
1999	69%	31%	49%	51%
1998	65%	35%	55%	45%
1997	59%	41%	78%	22%

INTEREST GROUPS

	AFL-CIO	ADA	CCUS	ACU
2006	47%	45%	75%	36%
2005	64%	65%	78%	32%
2004	67%	65%	71%	60%
2003	0%	55%	65%	45%
2002	31%	30%	85%	65%
2001	50%	40%	79%	60%
2000	0%	30%	73%	80%
1999	33%	45%	59%	60%
1998	38%	35%	78%	40%
1997	43%	55%	70%	44%

Sen. Susan Collins (R)

CAPITOL OFFICE
224-2523
collins.senate.gov
413 Dirksen 20510-1904; fax 224-2693

COMMITTEES
Armed Services
Homeland Security & Governmental Affairs - ranking member
Special Aging

RESIDENCE
Bangor

BORN
Dec. 7, 1952, Caribou, Maine

RELIGION
Roman Catholic

FAMILY
Single

EDUCATION
St. Lawrence U., B.A. 1975 (government)

CAREER
Business center director; congressional aide

POLITICAL HIGHLIGHTS
Maine Department of Professional and Financial Regulation commissioner, 1987-91; Small Business Administration official, 1992-93; Maine deputy treasurer, 1993; Republican nominee for governor, 1994

ELECTION RESULTS

2002 GENERAL		
Susan Collins (R)	295,041	58.4%
Chellie Pingree (D)	209,858	41.6%
2002 PRIMARY		
Susan Collins (R)		unopposed

PREVIOUS WINNING PERCENTAGES
1996 (49%)

Elected 1996; 2nd term

Hailing from the notably independent state of Maine, Collins is a Republican moderate who rarely asserts her independence in a way that would cause critics to question her party loyalty. She usually remains above the fray.

Her centrist credentials earned her key negotiating posts in some of the biggest legislative battles of recent years, including creation of the Homeland Security Department and a rewrite of the nation's intelligence laws.

Collins has always been thought to be politically secure in Maine, but in early 2007 she was already pegged as one of the top five targets by Democrats, who are looking to expand their slim majority in the Senate in 2008. Until the Democratic sweep of congressional elections in 2006, it would have been unheard-of to target the well-liked moderate from Maine. Yet Collins is seen as vulnerable because of her support for the war in Iraq and Maine's increasingly Democratic electorate.

In her two terms in the Senate, Collins has built a résumé that has earned her respect from Democrats and loyalty from Republican leaders. As chairwoman of the Homeland Security and Governmental Affairs Committee in the 108th Congress (2003-04), Collins led the charge to rewrite the nation's intelligence laws to create a more centralized spy infrastructure. On the recommendation of the Sept. 11 commission, Collins wrote legislation that merged the country's 15 intelligence agencies while carefully navigating a series of turf battles between the Pentagon, Congress and the White House.

In the 109th Congress (2005-06), Collins used her committee post to push through an overhaul of the nation's lobbying laws in the wake of the Jack Abramoff influence-peddling scandal, but the legislation never reached a conference with the House. She had bucked her party's leadership by putting in the bill the creation of an independent "Office of Public Integrity," which would have had the authority to investigate Senate ethics violations. Collins and her colleague on the Homeland Security and Governmental Affairs panel, Connecticut independent Joseph I. Lieberman, have tried to cultivate reputations as bipartisan reformers, but their idea of an Office of Public Integrity was shot down by senators who objected to the idea of outsiders investigating the Senate.

Collins' style is soft-spoken and measured, but she has a reputation for being a demanding boss and a fierce negotiator behind the scenes. While some senators are less engaged in the nit-picking details of legislation, Collins, a former congressional aide, seems to relish the nuts and bolts of governing and legislating.

Like any moderate, she maintains independence without necessarily causing her party to lose on major votes. On votes that pitted one party against the other, Collins stood with the GOP 62 percent of the time in the 109th Congress — only her home-state counterpart, Republican Olympia J. Snowe, and Lincoln Chafee, a Rhode Island Republican, voted more often in opposition to the position taken by the GOP.

The war in Iraq has been a crucial test for many GOP moderates, and Collins is no exception. She has criticized the Iraq War, and she opposed President Bush's plan to send in more than 21,000 additional U.S. combat troops. Yet she was unwilling to side with the anti-war Democrats in setting a firm troop withdrawal date from Iraq. Collins has carefully calibrated her views to show that she is not in lockstep with the president but is unwilling to completely withdraw support for the war. "My vote against this rapid withdrawal does not mean that I support an open-ended commitment of U.S. troops to Iraq," Collins said after a critical Senate vote in March 2007 to set a timetable for troop withdrawal. "Indeed, I have repeatedly expressed my opposition to the president's plan to send an additional 21,500 troops to Iraq."

Collins no longer holds a gavel in the 110th Congress (2007-08) now that Democrats are in control of the Senate, but thanks to her close working relationship with Lieberman, the two carry out committee duties in an almost symbiotic co-chairmanship. In fact, Lieberman and Collins made a show of their bipartisanship by creating a seating chart for committee meetings in which Democratic seats alternated with Republican seats along the dais, rather than seating all the Democrats on one side and all the Republicans on the other, which is the Senate tradition.

Collins and Lieberman worked together in March 2007 to advance legislation implementing the unfulfilled recommendations made three years ago by the Sept. 11 commission. As recommended by the commission, the bill would distribute first-responder grants largely on the basis of risk, improve emergency communications and strengthen surface transportation security. The Senate rejected three amendments aimed at changing the grant formula, marking a victory for Lieberman and Collins. The two had argued to leave the homeland security grant provision unchanged. "We need to bring all states to reach minimum levels of preparedness because otherwise terrorists will exploit the weak links," Collins said.

Collins is consistently conservative on fiscal policy, yet she has expressed worries about the impact of tax cuts on the deficit. To that end, Collins joined Snowe as the only two Republicans who voted for the Democratic fiscal 2008 budget resolution in March 2007, helping give Democrats a victory on a 52-47 vote. The Democratic budget was appealing, Collins said, because it included increases in low-income heating assistance and children's health programs. Collins has in the past supported a constitutional amendment that would require a balanced budget.

On social policy, Collins sides with the Democrats, establishing a consistent voting record favoring abortion rights and voting against other social conservative priorities, including a constitutional amendment to define marriage as between a man and a woman.

Collins comes from a political family — her parents each served as mayor of the town of Caribou — yet she has followed a path that has taken her far beyond the woodsy confines of northern Maine. As a high school senior, Collins visited the U.S. Capitol and spent time talking with Sen. Margaret Chase Smith, a Republican trailblazer and one-time presidential candidate. Collins, like Snowe, often cites Smith as her inspiration for running in Maine as a Republican.

After graduating from St. Lawrence University in 1975, Collins took her passion for politics to Washington and worked as an aide to Maine Republican Sen. William Cohen. After learning the ins and outs of legislating in Washington, Collins returned to Maine to serve as commissioner of the state's Department of Professional and Financial Regulation.

In 1994, Collins won the Republican nomination for governor, but finished a disappointing third behind Democratic nominee Joseph E. Brennan, who finished second, and independent Angus King, who won the contest. But in 1996, when Collins' old boss Cohen announced his retirement, Collins regrouped and took the race by 5 percentage points. She won handily in 2002, beating Democratic challenger Chellie Pingree, a former state senator. On the heels of the Democratic successes in the Northeast in the 2006 election cycle, Collins will have a tough race in 2008. Maine's Democratic Rep. Tom Allen is the likely challenger.

KEY VOTES

2006

- Yes Confirm Samuel A. Alito Jr. to the Supreme Court
- Yes Allow consideration of a bill to establish a $140 billion trust fund to compensate victims of asbestos exposure
- Yes Extend tax cuts for two years at a cost of $70 billion over five years
- Yes Overhaul immigration policy with border security, enforcement and guest worker program
- Yes Allow consideration of a bill to permanently repeal the estate tax
- No Urge President Bush to begin troop withdrawals from Iraq in 2006
- Yes Lift President Bush's restrictions on stem cell research funding
- Yes Authorize military tribunals for suspected terrorists

2005

- Yes Curb class action lawsuits by shifting them from state to federal courts
- Yes Allow confirmation vote on Priscilla R. Owen to the U.S. Court of Appeals for the 5th Circuit
- No Oppose mandatory emissions limits and block recognition of global warming as a threat
- No Approve free-trade pact with five Central American countries
- Yes Pass energy policy overhaul favored by President Bush emphasizing domestic oil and gas production
- Yes Shield gunmakers from lawsuits when their products are used in crimes
- Yes Ban torture of prisoners in U.S. custody
- Yes Renew 16 provisions of the Patriot Act
- Yes Allow final vote on opening the Arctic National Wildlife Refuge to oil and gas exploration

CQ VOTE STUDIES

	PARTY UNITY		PRESIDENTIAL SUPPORT	
	Support	Oppose	Support	Oppose
2006	66%	34%	79%	21%
2005	59%	41%	62%	38%
2004	78%	22%	82%	18%
2003	78%	22%	87%	13%
2002	57%	43%	88%	12%
2001	67%	33%	88%	12%
2000	74%	26%	57%	42%
1999	74%	26%	49%	51%
1998	67%	33%	63%	37%
1997	61%	39%	76%	24%

INTEREST GROUPS

	AFL-CIO	ADA	CCUS	ACU
2006	47%	45%	92%	48%
2005	64%	65%	78%	32%
2004	50%	45%	94%	68%
2003	31%	45%	78%	35%
2002	31%	35%	85%	55%
2001	50%	35%	79%	64%
2000	0%	25%	80%	76%
1999	11%	25%	76%	64%
1998	38%	35%	78%	36%
1997	14%	50%	80%	48%

Rep. Tom Allen (D)

CAPITOL OFFICE
225-6116
rep.tomallen@mail.house.gov
www.house.gov/allen
1127 Longworth 20515-1901; fax 225-5590

COMMITTEES
Budget
Energy & Commerce

RESIDENCE
Portland

BORN
April 16, 1945, Portland, Maine

RELIGION
Protestant

FAMILY
Wife, Diana Allen; two children

EDUCATION
Bowdoin College, B.A. 1967 (English);
Oxford U., B.Phil. 1970 (Rhodes scholar);
Harvard U., J.D. 1974

CAREER
Policy consultant; lawyer; congressional aide

POLITICAL HIGHLIGHTS
Portland City Council, 1989-95 (mayor, 1991-92);
sought Democratic nomination for governor, 1994

ELECTION RESULTS

2006 GENERAL		
Tom Allen (D)	170,949	60.8%
Darlene J. Curley (R)	88,009	31.3%
Dexter J. Kamilewicz (I)	22,029	7.8%
2006 PRIMARY		
Tom Allen (D)		unopposed
2004 GENERAL		
Tom Allen (D)	219,077	59.7%
Charles E. Summers Jr. (R)	147,663	40.3%

PREVIOUS WINNING PERCENTAGES
2002 (64%); 2000 (60%); 1998 (60%); 1996 (55%)

Elected 1996; 6th term

An articulate advocate for his liberal causes, Allen has emerged as a leading Democratic voice on health care policy, particularly the high cost of prescription drugs. He says there is a crisis of access and affordability that goes far beyond the price of medicine. "The wheels are coming off this employer-based health care system," Allen says.

As a member of the Energy and Commerce Committee and its Health Subcommittee, Allen has a say on legislation affecting Medicare and Medicaid, the giant health insurance programs for the elderly and the poor. He has fought to empower the government to bargain with drug companies to reduce prescription costs for Medicare beneficiaries. And he has pressed to allow imports of lower-cost drugs from other countries, a closely watched issue in border states such as Maine. Congressional Republicans and the White House had blocked both proposals; but with Democrats in charge in the 110th Congress (2007-08), the House early in 2007 passed a drug-price negotiation bill.

A sharp critic of the 2003 Medicare drug law, Allen sponsored legislation in 2006 to reimburse states for costs they incurred when they rushed to aid low-income seniors left stranded by the spotty implementation of the new Medicare drug benefit.

Allen argues that, while Republicans often pushed "extreme individualism" during their 12 years in power in the House with such notions as personal health savings accounts, the newly in-charge Democrats need to "articulate the other side of the American experience" and promote a collective responsibility to meet basic economic and social needs.

Maine is a poor state with an older population, and with the other three members of the state's small delegation, Allen fights to preserve federal programs that provide assistance and jobs. Two of the most important are the Medicaid program and shipbuilding contracts for Bath Iron Works and the Portsmouth Naval Shipyard. The two shipyards employ many of Allen's constituents, along with Brunswick Naval Air Station. For his first six years in Congress, Allen served on the Armed Services Committee, and he says the Bush administration is buying too few ships to meet the goal of keeping a naval fleet of more than 300 vessels.

Both the Portsmouth shipyard and the Brunswick Naval Air Station were on the Pentagon's hit list in the 2005 round of military base closings. Allen and the Maine delegation to Congress battled furiously to save the two facilities. In the end, they were able to preserve Portsmouth, but lost Brunswick.

On the biggest defense issue of the day, Allen sides with the majority of House Democrats in opposing the war in Iraq, which he calls "a major miscalculation" by the Bush administration.

As a member of Energy and Commerce's Subcommittee on Energy and Air Quality, Allen is positioned to tackle another of the state's big concerns, air pollution. Prevailing winds blow much of the pollution produced in the Midwest to New England, especially to Maine, and the state's lawmakers of both parties tend to be united in demanding tough clean air regulation. Allen fought to overturn Environmental Protection Agency rules issued in 2005 that regulated mercury emissions from power plants, saying they did not do enough to reduce health risks mercury poses to children and women of childbearing age. Early in the 110th Congress, he introduced two bills dealing with mercury exports and areas of severe mercury contamination.

Allen cut his teeth on one of the hottest issues before Congress in the past decade — campaign finance. As co-chairman of the freshman task force on the issue in the 105th Congress (1997-98), Allen pushed to ban "soft money," the unlimited contributions from corporations, unions and wealthy individuals that were becoming a dominant force in federal elections. Allen stayed active in the cause, generally behind the scenes, until changes to campaign finance law were enacted in 2002, with a ban on soft money at the core. In 2006, he joined forces with Republican Charles Bass of New Hampshire to fight legislation to exempt all Internet-based political activity from regulation. Allen and Bass were poised for a floor battle when the Federal Election Commission effectively sided with them, deciding to regulate paid campaign advertising on the Web while exempting blogs, news articles and all other unpaid political discourse.

Allen comes from a political family. His father and grandfather were both on the Portland City Council, and his mother was active in politics as well. He was an exceptional student, a Rhodes scholar who went on to get a law degree from Harvard. During his college years, Allen worked in 1970 for Democratic Sen. Edmund S. Muskie, both on a campaign in Maine and on Muskie's Senate staff.

After practicing law in Portland for almost 20 years, Allen was elected to the city council. He served for six years, including one as the council-elected mayor. He chaired Bill Clinton's 1992 presidential campaign in Maine and was an adviser on agriculture issues during Clinton's transition.

Allen made an unsuccessful bid for the Democratic gubernatorial nomination in 1994, and then two years later challenged freshman GOP Rep. James B. Longley Jr. With financial assistance from the AFL-CIO, the Sierra Club and other groups that ran campaign ads in his behalf, Allen mobilized core Democratic supporters while successfully tying Longley to the "extreme" Contract With America, the policy manifesto that House Republicans pushed in their first two years in power, from 1995 to 1996. He prevailed by 11 percentage points and has won easily ever since.

Allen has had his eye on a race for the Senate for some time. In May 2007, he announced he would challenge moderate Republican Susan Collins, who is seeking a third term in 2008.

When he's home in Portland, Allen hangs out with friends from his high school days at Becky's Diner, a local institution catering to a diverse clientele that ranges from fishermen to college students. During breaks from work, Allen heads to his family's summer place near Sebago Lake. There, he enjoys tending to the farm, growing apples and clearing brush, which he says is about the only thing he has in common with President Bush.

KEY VOTES

2006

- Yes Stop broadband companies from favoring select Internet traffic
- No Affirm U.S. commitment to war in Iraq and reject setting a withdrawal date for troops
- No Repeal requirement for bilingual ballots at the polls
- Yes Permit U.S. sale of civilian nuclear technology to India
- No Build a 700-mile fence on the U.S.-Mexico border to curb illegal crossings
- No Permit warrantless wiretaps of suspected terrorists

2005

- ? Intervene in the life-support case of Terri Schiavo
- Yes Lift President Bush's restrictions on stem cell research funding
- Yes Prohibit FBI access to library and bookstore records
- No Approve free-trade pact with five Central American countries
- No Pass energy policy overhaul favored by President Bush emphasizing domestic oil and gas production
- No End mandatory preservation of habitat of endangered animal and plant species
- Yes Ban torture of prisoners in U.S. custody

CQ VOTE STUDIES

	PARTY UNITY		PRESIDENTIAL SUPPORT	
	Support	Oppose	Support	Oppose
2006	95%	5%	23%	77%
2005	97%	3%	13%	87%
2004	95%	5%	41%	59%
2003	95%	5%	20%	80%
2002	95%	5%	36%	64%

INTEREST GROUPS

	AFL-CIO	ADA	CCUS	ACU
2006	100%	95%	47%	8%
2005	93%	95%	42%	0%
2004	93%	100%	38%	8%
2003	100%	95%	30%	12%
2002	100%	95%	53%	0%

MAINE 1

South – Portland, Augusta

Covering Maine's southern tip, the 1st boasts both rural oceanfront property and high-paying jobs. Residents of the state's largest city, Portland, continue to move into outlying areas, bringing single-family homes to once-uninterrupted forests and farmland.

The technology boom that spread north from Boston during the 1990s has slowed, but software jobs continue to offset manufacturing and textile plant closures. Health care, financial services and insurance firms are here, and Interstate 95 offers a straight shot between the district and Boston for both commuters and seasonal residents, who tend to live on the coast. Tourism is important in the lower part of the state, as residents from across New England and Canada head to popular beaches and shopping areas, including the L.L. Bean flagship store in Freeport, which is open 24 hours a day and has more than 3 million annual visitors.

The military's influence is strong in the 1st. Portsmouth Naval Shipyard escaped the 2005 BRAC round, but Brunswick Naval Air Station was ordered closed by 2011. The Pentagon will stagger the job losses over the next few years, but the economic effects, such as a drop in the area's housing prices, may be immediate.

The district's traditional Yankee Republican tendencies have given way to a solidly Democratic voting preference in federal elections. In 2004, the 1st favored John Kerry by 12 percentage points. Republicans still find some support at the state and local levels, especially in York County towns. In the 2006 gubernatorial election, Democrat John Baldacci ran 14 percentage points ahead of his GOP challenger in both Cumberland and York counties — the district's two most-populous — which was 6 points better than his 8 percentage point win statewide.

MAJOR INDUSTRY
Military shipbuilding, financial services, technology, tourism

MILITARY BASES
Portsmouth Naval Shipyard, 95 military, 3,900 civilian (2007); Brunswick Naval Air Station, 2,880 military, 395 civilian (2005)

CITIES
Portland, 64,249; South Portland, 23,324; Biddeford, 20,942

NOTABLE
Portland businessman Neal Dow, the "father of prohibition," helped push through the 1851 "Maine Law," which banned the sale of liquor in Maine.

Rep. Michael H. Michaud (D)

CAPITOL OFFICE
225-6306
www.house.gov/michaud
1724 Longworth 20515-1902; fax 225-2943

COMMITTEES
Small Business
Transportation & Infrastructure
Veterans' Affairs
(Health - chairman)

RESIDENCE
East Millinocket

BORN
Jan. 18, 1955, Millinocket, Maine

RELIGION
Roman Catholic

FAMILY
Single

EDUCATION
Schenck H.S., graduated 1973

CAREER
Paper mill worker

POLITICAL HIGHLIGHTS
Maine House, 1981-94; Maine Senate, 1995-2002 (president, 2001)

ELECTION RESULTS

2006 GENERAL		
Michael H. Michaud (D)	179,732	70.5%
Laurence S. D'Amboise (R)	75,146	29.5%
2006 PRIMARY		
Michael H. Michaud (D)		unopposed
2004 GENERAL		
Michael H. Michaud (D)	199,303	58.0%
Brian N. Hamel (R)	135,547	39.5%
Carl Cooley (SE)	8,586	2.5%

PREVIOUS WINNING PERCENTAGES
2002 (52%)

Elected 2002; 3rd term

No one can say Michaud lacks confidence. After just two terms, the Maine Democrat made a bid for the chairmanship of the House Veterans' Affairs Committee following the 2006 elections. While he fell short, it did him no apparent harm. He wound up chairing the panel's Health Subcommittee instead.

Michaud (ME-shoo) took a shot at the full committee chairmanship when it became evident there was some uneasiness within the Democratic Caucus about the sometimes fiery temperament of Bob Filner of California, who was in line for the gavel following the retirement of senior Democrat Lane Evans of Illinois. The Democratic Steering Committee, headed by Speaker Nancy Pelosi, decided to go with Filner but Michaud took advantage of a caucus rule that allows anyone receiving at least 14 votes to demand a second ballot. Although Michaud had the endorsement of Evans, Filner prevailed, 112-69.

Michaud served as the Health Subcommittee's top-ranking Democrat in the 109th Congress (2005-06). He has championed measures to increase treatment for veterans suffering post-traumatic stress syndrome and to allow veterans who live in rural areas far from Veterans Affairs hospitals or clinics to obtain treatment locally from private providers. He wasted no time in the 110th Congress (2007-08) advancing legislation addressing the problems of combat veterans returning from Iraq and Afghanistan.

While he presses for improved treatment of those returning from Iraq, Michaud is a critic of the war itself. He was among 14 Democrats who voted against funding for the war in March 2007, even though the bill called for withdrawal of U.S. troops by August 2008.

Since his first term, Michaud has fought to reduce the spiraling cost of prescription drugs. In the 108th Congress (2003-04), he introduced legislation based on the "Maine Rx" policy he helped create as a state legislator. It called for the federal Medicare program to negotiate lower prices for seniors' prescription drugs. The GOP-controlled Congress rejected that idea in passing the 2003 Medicare drug law. But House Democrats made the legislation one of their top priorities in the 110th Congress, and the House passed it as part of its "first 100 hours" opening agenda in 2007.

Most members of Congress claim to be on the side of the working man in America, but Michaud is one of the few who has actually been one. He was a union card-carrying paper mill worker for three decades before being elected to the House in 2002. While many of his House colleagues were pursuing their college degrees, Michaud was punching a clock at the Great Northern Paper Co. in Millinocket, Maine.

Three days after he was sworn in, Great Northern filed for bankruptcy protection and shuttered its two paper mills, including the one in East Millinocket where Michaud, his father and grandfather had worked. His first weeks as a congressman were consumed by the fallout from the surge in unemployment in the district. He cosponsored a bill to extend the length of federal unemployment assistance and to boost the tax deductibility of health care costs. Michaud also helped get $900,000 for the Millinocket Regional Hospital to treat uninsured workers.

House Democrats regularly call on him to speak when labor bills are under consideration. In 2004, party leaders chose him to lead opposition on the floor to a Bush administration initiative limiting some workers' eligibility for overtime pay. In 2007, he took the floor to promote legislation making it easier for workers to unionize.

Michaud is a fierce critic of the free-trade deals of the past decade or so, blaming them for the steep decline in Maine's manufacturing base and unemployment rates of 30 percent in some parts of the state. In a January 2007 floor speech he declared, "The American workforce is sick of these trade deals, these side deals being cut. They don't want more trade adjustment assistance; they want their jobs. . . . My mom always told me, you can't fix what's broken. Our trade policies are broken."

Along with five other members from both parties, he is pressing to establish a Northern Border Economic Development Commission to promote new jobs and development in the most economically distressed border areas of Maine, New Hampshire, Vermont and New York.

Though he votes with Democrats most of the time, Michaud opposes abortion except to save the life of the woman. He is one of the few Democrats from the North to affiliate with the Blue Dogs, a coalition of conservative Democrats.

Michaud grew up in the small rural town of Medway, close to the Great Northern mill. After high school, he considered going to college to study criminal justice, thinking he'd become a state trooper. But Great Northern beckoned with good wages and health benefits, and Michaud followed in the footsteps of his father and grandfather. He became a paper finisher, working on the final stages of papermaking at the mill. He remains a member of what is now United Steelworkers Local 4-00037.

Michaud decided to run for the state House because of his concern about pollution in the Penobscot River, to which his employer, Great Northern, contributed. Elected in 1980, he took advantage of a clause in his union contract that allowed workers to keep their jobs while serving in the legislature. He worked at the mill when the legislature was not in session, and when it was, he chaired the Environment Committee and wrote bills to clean up the river.

Michaud served seven terms in the state House, then ran for the Maine Senate in 1994. Two years later, he became chairman of the Appropriations Committee and in 2000 was elected state Senate president. At that point, he took a leave of absence from the mill.

In 2002, when Democratic Rep. John Baldacci ran successfully for governor, Michaud went after the open 2nd District seat. Support from organized labor helped him eke out a narrow victory over Republican Kevin L. Raye, former chief of staff for Olympia J. Snowe, who held the 2nd District seat from 1979-95 and is now Maine's senior senator. Michaud won re-election easily in 2004 and 2006.

KEY VOTES

2006

No Stop broadband companies from favoring select Internet traffic
No Affirm U.S. commitment to war in Iraq and reject setting a withdrawal date for troops
No Repeal requirement for bilingual ballots at the polls
Yes Permit U.S. sale of civilian nuclear technology to India
No Build a 700-mile fence on the U.S.-Mexico border to curb illegal crossings
No Permit warrantless wiretaps of suspected terrorists

2005

Yes Intervene in the life-support case of Terri Schiavo
Yes Lift President Bush's restrictions on stem cell research funding
Yes Prohibit FBI access to library and bookstore records
No Approve free-trade pact with five Central American countries
No Pass energy policy overhaul favored by President Bush emphasizing domestic oil and gas production
No End mandatory preservation of habitat of endangered animal and plant species
Yes Ban torture of prisoners in U.S. custody

CQ VOTE STUDIES

	PARTY UNITY		PRESIDENTIAL SUPPORT	
	Support	Oppose	Support	Oppose
2006	92%	8%	30%	70%
2005	92%	8%	18%	82%
2004	88%	12%	38%	62%
2003	90%	10%	31%	69%

INTEREST GROUPS

	AFL-CIO	ADA	CCUS	ACU
2006	100%	90%	40%	12%
2005	93%	90%	48%	16%
2004	93%	90%	48%	20%
2003	100%	95%	40%	40%

MAINE 2

North – Lewiston, Bangor, Presque Isle

Millions of acres of trees surround the small towns of northern Maine's 2nd. The largest district in a state east of the Mississippi, the 2nd attracts millions of visitors "from away," or out of state in the local lingo, to Acadia National Park, Baxter State Park and Maine's many lakes and ski slopes. Development of the privately owned timber forests of the North Woods is a major issue, as resorts, single-family homes and in-migration of residents from other states could permanently alter the landscape.

Lobstering dominates the coast, and the timber industry reigns inland. Farming is in decline in parts of the district, although the 2nd remains one of the nation's largest producers of potatoes and blueberries. Sparsely populated in parts, the region is less wealthy than the 1st, which has benefited from a more diverse employment base.

As the national economy has become more service-based, the 2nd has suffered. Manufacturing jobs, especially in shoes and textiles, have gone abroad, and some residents have headed south to find work. Citing the district's easy access to Boston via Interstate 95, some local residents and elected officials have pushed for an east-west highway to promote job growth.

A weak party system throughout the state and a higher proportion of rural voters have helped make the 2nd the more competitive of Maine's two congressional districts. Voters here gave only a 6 percentage point edge to Democrat John Kerry in the 2004 presidential election — just half of the advantage he enjoyed in the 1st District. The 2nd's voters will support candidates from either major party, but the district has developed a Democratic lean, and Rep. Michaud has enjoyed increasing margins of victory since his 2002 election.

MAJOR INDUSTRY

Logging, agriculture, fishing, tourism, textiles

CITIES

Lewiston, 35,690; Bangor, 31,473; Auburn, 23,203; Waterville, 15,605; Presque Isle, 9,511

NOTABLE

Established in 1919, Acadia National Park was the first national park east of the Mississippi River; Since 1992, Harrington-based Worcester Wreath has decorated, donated and delivered 5,000 wreaths every December for graveside ceremonies at Arlington National Cemetery.

MARYLAND

Gov. Martin O'Malley (D)

First elected: 2006
Length of term: 4 years
Term expires: 1/11
Salary: $150,000
Phone: (410) 974-3901

Residence: Baltimore
Born: Jan. 18, 1963; Washington, D.C.
Religion: Roman Catholic
Family: Wife, Catherine Curran O'Malley; four children
Education: Catholic U., B.A. 1985 (political science); U. of Maryland, Baltimore, J.D. 1988
Career: Lawyer; city prosecutor; campaign aide
Political highlights: Democratic nominee for Md. Senate, 1990; Baltimore City Council, 1991-99; mayor of Baltimore, 1999-2007

Election results:

2006 GENERAL		
Martin O'Malley (D)	942,279	52.7%
Robert L. Ehrlich Jr. (R)	825,464	46.2%

Lt. Gov. Anthony G. Brown (D)

First elected: 2006
Length of term: 4 years
Term expires: 1/11
Salary: $125,000
Phone: (410) 974-3901

LEGISLATURE

General Assembly: 90 days January-April

Senate: 47 members, 4-year terms
2007 ratios: 33 D, 14 R; 36 men, 11 women
Salary: $43,500
Phone: (410) 841-3700

House: 141 members, 4-year terms
2007 ratios: 104 D, 37 R; 90 men, 51 women
Salary: $43,500
Phone: (410) 841-3800

TERM LIMITS

Governor: 2 consecutive terms
Senate: No
House: No

URBAN STATISTICS

CITY	POPULATION
Baltimore	651,154
Frederick	52,767
Gaithersburg	52,613
Bowie	50,269
Rockville	47,388

REGISTERED VOTERS

Democrat	55%
Republican	29%
Unaffiliated/others	16%

POPULATION

2006 population (est.)	5,615,727
2000 population	5,296,486
1990 population	4,781,468
Percent change (1990-2000)	+10.8%
Rank among states (2006)	19
Median age	36
Born in state	49.3%
Foreign born	9.8%
Violent crime rate	787/100,000
Poverty level	8.5%
Federal workers	151,044
Military	50,137

ELECTIONS

STATE ELECTION OFFICIAL
(410) 269-2840
DEMOCRATIC PARTY
(410) 269-8818
REPUBLICAN PARTY
(410) 263-2125

MISCELLANEOUS

Web: www.maryland.gov
Capital: Annapolis

U.S. CONGRESS

Senate: 2 Democrats
House: 6 Democrats, 2 Republicans

2000 Census Statistics by District

DIST.	2004 VOTE FOR PRESIDENT BUSH	KERRY	WHITE	BLACK	ASIAN	HISP	MEDIAN INCOME	WHITE COLLAR	BLUE COLLAR	SERVICE INDUSTRY	OVER 64	UNDER 18	COLLEGE EDUCATION	RURAL	SQ. MILES
1	62%	36%	85%	11%	1%	2%	$51,918	63%	23%	14%	13%	25%	27%	36%	3,653
2	45	54	66	27	2	2	$44,309	61	23	15	12	26	20	2	355
3	45	54	76	16	3	3	$52,906	72	16	12	13	23	37	1	293
4	21	78	28	57	6	8	$57,727	71	15	14	7	28	33	2	315
5	42	57	60	30	4	3	$62,661	68	19	13	9	26	29	25	1,504
6	65	34	92	5	1	1	$50,957	61	24	14	12	26	24	39	3,062
7	26	73	34	59	4	2	$38,885	67	16	17	12	26	28	5	294
8	30	69	56	16	11	14	$68,306	77	11	12	12	24	54	1	297
STATE	43	56	62	28	4	4	$52,868	68	18	14	11	26	31	14	9,774
U.S.	50.7	48.3	69	12	4	13	$41,994	60	25	15	12	26	24	21	3,537,438

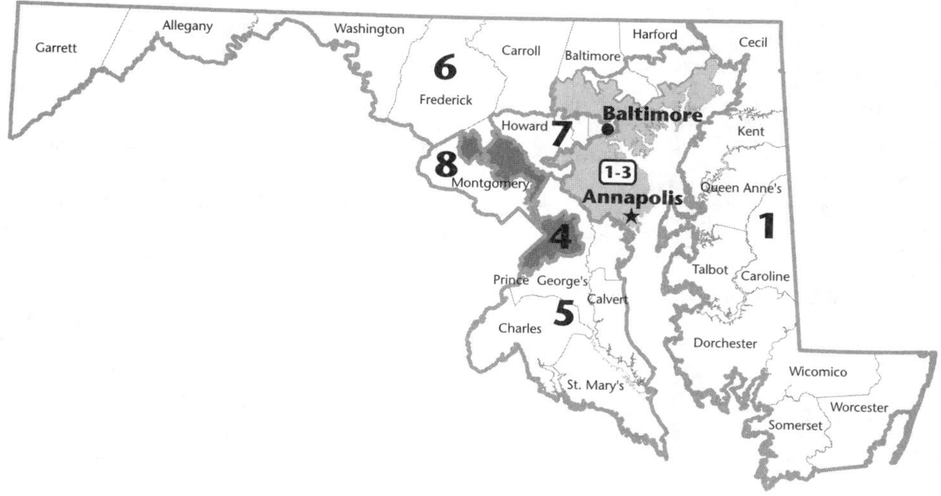
Garrett
Allegany
Washington
Carroll
Baltimore
Harford
Cecil
6
Frederick
Baltimore
Kent
Howard
7
8
1-3
Montgomery
Annapolis
Queen Anne's
1
4
Talbot
Caroline
Prince George's
Calvert
5
Charles
Dorchester
Wicomico
St. Mary's
Worcester
Somerset

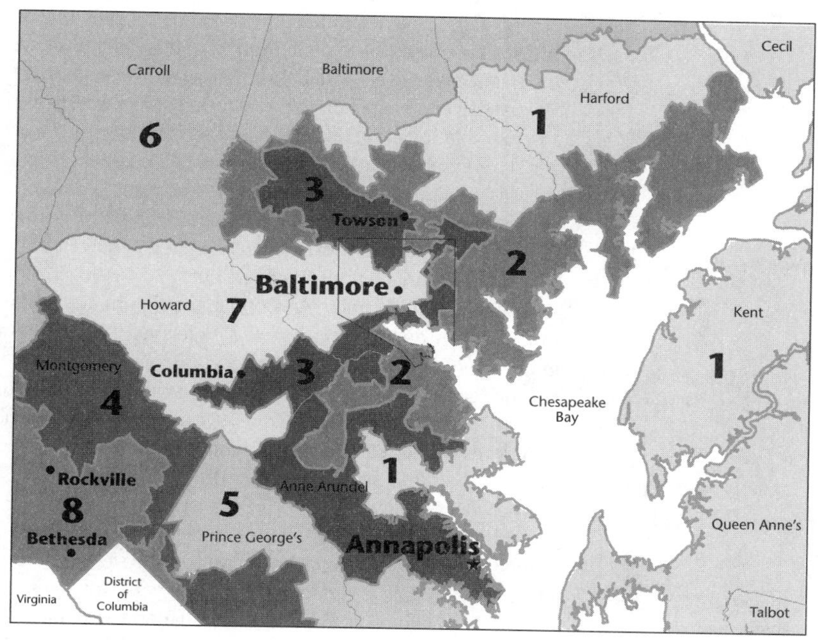
Carroll
Baltimore
Cecil
Harford
1
6
3
Towson
2
Baltimore
Howard
7
Kent
Montgomery
Columbia
3
2
1
4
Chesapeake
Bay
1
Rockville
Anne Arundel
8
5
Queen Anne's
Bethesda
Prince George's
Annapolis
District
of
Columbia
Virginia
Talbot

Sen. Barbara A. Mikulski (D)

CAPITOL OFFICE
224-4654
mikulski.senate.gov
503 Hart 20510-2003; fax 224-8858

COMMITTEES
Appropriations
(Commerce-Justice-Science - chairwoman)
Health, Education, Labor & Pensions
(Retirement & Aging - chairwoman)
Select Intelligence

RESIDENCE
Baltimore

BORN
July 20, 1936, Baltimore, Md.

RELIGION
Roman Catholic

FAMILY
Single

EDUCATION
Mount Saint Agnes College, B.A. 1958 (sociology); U. of Maryland, M.S.W. 1965

CAREER
Social worker

POLITICAL HIGHLIGHTS
Baltimore City Council, 1971-77; Democratic nominee for U.S. Senate, 1974; U.S. House, 1977-87

ELECTION RESULTS

2004 GENERAL		
Barbara A. Mikulski (D)	1,504,691	64.8%
E.J. Pipkin (R)	783,055	33.7%
Maria Allwine (GREEN)	24,816	1.1%
2004 PRIMARY		
Barbara A. Mikulski (D)	408,848	89.9%
A. Robert Kaufman (D)	32,127	7.1%
Sidney Altman (D)	13,901	3.1%

PREVIOUS WINNING PERCENTAGES
1998 (71%); 1992 (71%); 1986 (61%); 1984 House Election (68%); 1982 House Election (74%); 1980 House Election (76%); 1978 House Election (100%); 1976 House Election (75%)

Elected 1986; 4th term

At 4 feet, 11 inches, Mikulski may be the shortest senator, but she could also be the toughest. She is well-known on Capitol Hill for cutting off tongue-tied aides and reporters, brusquely demanding, "What's your question?" And she has proved during a Senate career of two decades that she can go toe-to-toe with any adversary, often walking away triumphant.

Trent Lott of Mississippi, the Senate Republican whip, says that in those rare instances when he and Mikulski are on the same side of a fight, "She's good to take in the trenches with you." Democratic Leader Harry Reid of Nevada, a soft-spoken Mormon who came to the Senate the same year as Mikulski, remembers that she once intervened as he was fending off pressure from fellow Democrats to support abortion rights legislation. " 'Leave him alone. It's a matter of principle,' " he recalls Mikulski saying. "And everybody walked away, because everybody's afraid of her."

Mikulski takes pride in her status as dean of the Senate women and maintains a support network for them. From the time she arrived in 1987 until 1992, Mikulski and Republican Nancy Landon Kassebaum of Kansas were the only female senators. As their ranks jumped to five in 1993, to nine in 1999, to 14 in 2003 and 16 in 2007, Mikulski has offered the newcomers introductory seminars and dispensed advice on everything from organizing their offices to setting long-range goals. Hillary Rodham Clinton of New York was far from a typical freshman when she first took her seat in 2001, but she still needed guidance in the chamber's arcane customs. Mikulski, Clinton says, took her in hand before she was even elected.

Hard-nosed and persistent, much like the east Baltimore neighborhood where she was raised, Mikulski is a fierce advocate for Maryland interests. She used every weapon in her arsenal in 2005 to wrestle through Congress a measure lifting a cap on temporary visas for seasonal workers needed by her state's crab processors and other small businesses, pushing long after she was warned that she was asking the impossible. "I promised small businesses they could count on me to keep fighting until we had a solution and they had the seasonal workers they needed to stay in business," she said. "My promises made are promises kept."

A senior member of the Appropriations Committee, Mikulski also sits on the Health, Education, Labor and Pensions Committee and the Intelligence panel. She served for a decade as caucus secretary, the No. 3 Democratic leadership post, before stepping down in 2004 to give another woman, Michigan's Debbie Stabenow, a boost onto the leadership ladder.

Mikulski first got involved in politics in the early 1970s during a neighborhood battle to stop a highway project. At one point, she recalls, she jumped on a table and gave a fiery speech and everyone in the room cheered. Over the years, experience taught her that good speeches must come with good ideas and the ability to get results.

"If you only talk and don't produce . . . you contribute to the cynicism," she wrote in "Nine and Counting," a collaborative book written by the nine women serving in the Senate in 2000. "When I was a social worker, I wanted to help people, but it was difficult to do because I didn't have all of the resources I wanted. Now I am a social worker with power."

The senator's record has rarely disappointed feminist groups. She is a strong supporter of abortion rights and has tried to ensure that federal health care plans provide abortion coverage. She helped push to enactment the 1990 law that created the women's health research office at the National Institutes of Health. And in 1995, she was the first member of the Ethics Committee to call for public hearings on sexual harassment allegations against Republican Bob Packwood of Oregon, a turning point in a three-year case that ultimately led to Packwood's resignation from the Senate.

She still fights for local interests, including finding money to relieve the state's congested roads, leading efforts to clean up the Chesapeake Bay and finding ways to protect the state's economy. When a General Motors plant located in Baltimore closed in November 2004, Mikulski promised to help laid-off workers find new jobs and recruit a new business to the old plant.

When the Democrats gained the majority in 2006, Mikulski became the chairwoman of the Appropriations panel that funds science programs as well as the departments of Commerce and Justice. She is a longtime supporter of the National Aeronautics and Space Administration, which has a presence in Maryland at the Goddard Space Flight Center, a research facility that employs nearly 9,000 people. In 2005, she won $271 million, $50 million more than President Bush had requested, for a repair mission to keep the Hubble Space Telescope operational.

Mikulski grew up in the working-class Baltimore neighborhood of Highlandtown. Her parents ran a grocery store called Willy's Market, across the street from their row house, opening early every morning so that steel workers could buy lunch before their morning shift. Nearby, her Polish immigrant grandmother operated a bakery legendary for its jelly doughnuts and raisin bread.

Inspired by a movie about Marie Curie, Mikulski decided to become a chemist. Reality set in when she got to college. "I got a 'C' in chemistry and an 'A' in social sciences. I decided that I would go with my strengths," she says. She earned a master's degree in social work in 1965. When parts of her neighborhood were torched in anger after the 1968 assassination of the Rev. Martin Luther King Jr., social worker Mikulski delivered food to families during the riots, sometimes by riding atop a tank.

She jumped into a multiethnic, multiracial fight against a freeway that would have leveled some city neighborhoods. Building on that successful battle, Mikulski won a city council seat in 1971 and became prominent in the feminist movement. When feminist leader Betty Friedan died in 2006, a photo in The Washington Post showed Mikulski marching beside her.

In the post-Watergate election of 1974, Mikulski seized on the public backlash against Republicans by challenging incumbent Sen. Charles McC. Mathias Jr. She lost, but got a respectable 43 percent of the vote. That positioned her for 1976, when Democrat Paul S. Sarbanes gave up his seat as Baltimore's congressman to run for the Senate. Mikulski won and went on to serve five terms in the House. There, from her seat on the Energy and Commerce Committee, she became a champion of consumer causes. She also attracted notice on the national scene, including some support for her possible selection as Walter F. Mondale's running mate in 1984; the nod went to another congresswoman, New York's Geraldine Ferraro.

Mikulski won her Senate seat in 1986, when Mathias retired. She easily defeated Rep. Michael D. Barnes and outgoing Gov. Harry R. Hughes in the primary, and she bested conservative Linda Chavez, a staff director of the U.S. Commission on Civil Rights under President Ronald Reagan, by 22 percentage points in November. Since then, in three re-election campaigns, she has been victorious by at least 30 points.

For many years, Mikulski lived in a two-story Fells Point row house in Baltimore, commuting to the Capitol. In 1995, she was mugged as she walked from her car to her house, and the next year, she moved to a "maintenance free" condo near Johns Hopkins University. "I am changing my address, not changing my roots," she told constituents.

KEY VOTES

2006

No Confirm Samuel A. Alito Jr. to the Supreme Court
No Allow consideration of a bill to establish a $140 billion trust fund to compensate victims of asbestos exposure
No Extend tax cuts for two years at a cost of $70 billion over five years
Yes Overhaul immigration policy with border security, enforcement and guest worker program
No Allow consideration of a bill to permanently repeal the estate tax
Yes Urge President Bush to begin troop withdrawals from Iraq in 2006
Yes Lift President Bush's restrictions on stem cell research funding
No Authorize military tribunals for suspected terrorists

2005

No Curb class action lawsuits by shifting them from state to federal courts
Yes Allow confirmation vote on Priscilla R. Owen to the U.S. Court of Appeals for the 5th Circuit
No Oppose mandatory emissions limits and block recognition of global warming as a threat
No Approve free-trade pact with five Central American countries
Yes Pass energy policy overhaul favored by President Bush emphasizing domestic oil and gas production
No Shield gunmakers from lawsuits when their products are used in crimes
Yes Ban torture of prisoners in U.S. custody
No Renew 16 provisions of the Patriot Act
No Allow final vote on opening the Arctic National Wildlife Refuge to oil and gas exploration

CQ VOTE STUDIES

	PARTY UNITY		PRESIDENTIAL SUPPORT	
	Support	Oppose	Support	Oppose
2006	96%	4%	49%	51%
2005	98%	2%	35%	65%
2004	96%	4%	61%	39%
2003	97%	3%	44%	56%
2002	96%	4%	68%	32%
2001	98%	2%	66%	34%
2000	97%	3%	92%	8%
1999	96%	4%	86%	14%
1998	97%	3%	91%	9%
1997	92%	8%	91%	9%

INTEREST GROUPS

	AFL-CIO	ADA	CCUS	ACU
2006	93%	100%	42%	0%
2005	100%	90%	41%	5%
2004	100%	100%	56%	8%
2003	100%	90%	39%	15%
2002	100%	100%	47%	0%
2001	100%	95%	43%	12%
2000	88%	95%	46%	8%
1999	89%	100%	59%	4%
1998	100%	90%	53%	4%
1997	86%	95%	44%	4%

Sen. Benjamin L. Cardin (D)

Elected 2006; 1st term

CAPITOL OFFICE
224-4524
cardin.senate.gov
509 Hart 20510-2002; fax 224-1651

COMMITTEES
Budget
Environment & Public Works
Foreign Relations
Judiciary
Small Business & Entrepreneurship

RESIDENCE
Baltimore

BORN
Oct. 5, 1943, Baltimore, Md.

RELIGION
Jewish

FAMILY
Wife, Myrna Edelman Cardin; two children (one deceased)

EDUCATION
U. of Pittsburgh, B.A. 1964 (economics); U. of Maryland, Baltimore, LL.B. 1967

CAREER
Lawyer

POLITICAL HIGHLIGHTS
Md. House, 1967-87 (Speaker, 1979-87); U.S. House, 1987-2007

ELECTION RESULTS

2006 GENERAL		
Benjamin L. Cardin (D)	965,477	54.2%
Michael S. Steele (R)	787,182	44.2%
Kevin Zeese (GREEN)	27,564	1.5%
2006 PRIMARY		
Benjamin L. Cardin (D)	257,545	43.7%
Kweisi Mfume (D)	238,957	40.5%
Josh Rales (D)	30,737	5.2%
Dennis F. Rasmussen (D)	10,997	1.9%
Mike Schaefer (D)	7,773	1.3%
Allan Lichtman (D)	6,919	1.2%

PREVIOUS WINNING PERCENTAGES
2004 House Election (63%); 2002 House Election (66%); 2000 House Election (76%); 1998 House Election (78%); 1996 House Election (67%); 1994 House Election (71%); 1992 House Election (74%); 1990 House Election (70%); 1988 House Election (73%); 1986 House Election (79%)

A hard-working career legislator known for his grasp of economic policy, Cardin has a wonkish demeanor that invites comparisons to his professorial predecessor, Democrat Paul S. Sarbanes. At his swearing-in ceremony in January 2007, Cardin mentioned Charles Carroll, the first man to hold the seat in 1788, and repeated several times that he was the 62nd Maryland senator.

In the months that followed, however, Cardin displayed a rhetorical aggressiveness that surprised some observers. In his first speech, he denounced President Bush's plan to send more than 21,000 additional U.S. combat troops to Iraq and called for the withdrawal of U.S. forces. In subsequent speeches, he spoke passionately about global warming and in support of increasing the federal minimum wage, saying, "I believe it is wrong that millions of hard-working Americans who play by the rules still live in poverty and are unable to provide for their families."

Cardin said such remarks show his desire to emulate his hard-nosed fellow Democrat from Maryland, Barbara A. Mikulski, as well as Sarbanes. "I've got a little Mikulski and Sarbanes in me, as well as a lot of other people," he said in February 2007. He said it also reflects his impatient desire for accomplishment after 12 years as a member of the minority in the House. "I don't want to waste any time — I want to get things done," he said. "I'm going to use every opportunity I can to change our policies."

Cardin will have plenty of platforms from which to seek change. In recognition of his broad background of 20 years in the House, he received assignments to five committees, two more than he said he had sought: Foreign Relations, Judiciary, Environment and Public Works, Budget and Small Business. He also co-chairs the Commission on Security and Cooperation in Europe, known as the Helsinki Commission — the U.S. arm of the world's largest regional security organization.

His priorities fit the overall tenor of his party. In addition to finding an exit strategy for Iraq, he wants to work toward gaining more affordable health care. Within hours of being sworn in, he introduced a bill to allow the federal government to negotiate the price of prescription drugs under Medicare. Later, he introduced a measure similar to one he had sponsored as a House member in the 109th Congress (2005-06) to ensure that physical, speech and occupational therapies are fully covered by Medicare.

Energy independence is another issue on which Cardin seeks to be a player. He has called for significantly hiking Corporate Average Fuel Economy standards within a decade, boosting funding for federal energy efficiency programs and increasing tax credits for renewable energy programs. To cut transportation and energy use, he wants Congress to provide tax incentives for employers who offer telecommunicating opportunities to workers.

Closer to home, Cardin wants to improve environmental conditions in the Chesapeake Bay, saying the federal government should make a comprehensive commitment in the same way it did with the Florida Everglades a decade ago. He also plans to devote his energies to improving mass transit in the Baltimore-Washington area, citing "tremendous needs" to deal with the area's rapid growth.

Cardin also has an interest in governmental reform. In 1997, he co-chaired a bipartisan task force in an attempt to reform ethics procedures in the House. He joined Republican Sen. Norm Coleman of Minnesota in adding an amendment to the Senate's ethics bill in January 2007 to establish a Web site enabling the public to access congressional travel records.

Though generally a dependable Democratic vote, Cardin takes pride in being a lawmaker willing to work across party lines to develop consensus. In the Senate, that willingness may mark him as a Democrat whom Republicans will try to woo on certain issues.

As a member of the House Ways and Means Committee, he developed a close relationship with Ohio Republican Rob Portman — the main conduit between the Bush White House and GOP leaders during Bush's first term, who later became Bush's budget director. In the 108th Congress (2003-04), the two lawmakers developed an alternative to the president's ambitious plan to restructure Social Security and allow younger workers to divert a share of their payroll tax payments into personal retirement accounts.

Such endeavors did not always sit well with House Democratic leaders. In 2006, Cardin was passed over for the top Democratic spot on the Ways and Means Social Security Subcommittee after he said he was open to compromise on some GOP proposals for overhauling the benefits program.

Cardin is a one-time "boy wonder" who entered the Maryland House of Delegates at the age of 23, before he had even graduated from the University of Maryland Law School. He was elected to a seat that had been held by his father and his uncle. He went on to become the youngest House Speaker in Maryland in 100 years before being elected to his Baltimore-area House seat in 1986.

Despite becoming a potent figure in a state with a strong Democratic tilt, Cardin did not have an automatic road to the Senate in 2006 after Sarbanes announced his retirement. In a primary with more than a dozen candidates, his chief competition was former Democratic Rep. Kweisi Mfume, a past NAACP president and longtime friend.

Cardin was the presumed favorite throughout the early stages of the campaign because he was backed by much of the state and national party leadership and because of a large fundraising advantage. Yet he was unable to break away from Mfume because of a combination of factors that included Cardin's unprepossessing personality and Mfume's charisma, as well as his support among the Democrats' key African-American constituency. Cardin won the September primary, 44 percent to 41 percent.

In the general election, Cardin was up against another tough competitor — Republican Lt. Gov. Michael S. Steele, Maryland's first statewide black elected official. Steele threatened to take away the votes of black Democrats who felt party leaders had taken them for granted by not supporting Mfume and black candidates for other statewide offices.

Steele tailored his TV and radio ads to black voters and brought in endorsements from several prominent black Democrats, mostly from the Democratic stronghold of Prince George's County. Other Steele ads tried to portray the former chairman of the Maryland GOP as an agent of change, an independent centrist unafraid to criticize both political parties.

Cardin, meanwhile, ran what some pundits described as an unimaginative and plodding campaign. But he and the state's Democrats succeeded in tying Steele to Bush and other prominent Republicans, and Cardin won with 54 percent of the vote.

Cardin accused the Republicans of engaging in dishonest campaign tactics, such as chartering buses carrying black men, mostly poor, from as far as Philadelphia to hand out inaccurate voter guides. The experience led him to cosponsor an anti-voting fraud bill in early 2007 with fellow Democrats Charles E. Schumer of New York and Barack Obama of Illinois. The measure would impose criminal penalties on politicians found guilty of deceptive campaign practices, such as making false claims to voters about who has endorsed a candidate.

KEY VOTES

House Service:

2006

- Yes Stop broadband companies from favoring select Internet traffic
- No Affirm U.S. commitment to war in Iraq and reject setting a withdrawal date for troops
- No Repeal requirement for bilingual ballots at the polls
- Yes Permit U.S. sale of civilian nuclear technology to India
- No Build a 700-mile fence on the U.S.-Mexico border to curb illegal crossings
- No Permit warrantless wiretaps of suspected terrorists

2005

- No Intervene in the life-support case of Terri Schiavo
- Yes Lift President Bush's restrictions on stem cell research funding
- Yes Prohibit FBI access to library and bookstore records
- No Approve free-trade pact with five Central American countries
- No Pass energy policy overhaul favored by President Bush emphasizing domestic oil and gas production
- No End mandatory preservation of habitat of endangered animal and plant species
- Yes Ban torture of prisoners in U.S. custody

CQ VOTE STUDIES

House Service:

	PARTY UNITY		PRESIDENTIAL SUPPORT	
	Support	Oppose	Support	Oppose
2006	95%	5%	25%	75%
2005	95%	5%	22%	78%
2004	94%	6%	35%	65%
2003	93%	7%	24%	76%
2002	90%	10%	35%	65%
2001	89%	11%	35%	65%
2000	92%	8%	94%	6%
1999	92%	8%	83%	17%
1998	91%	9%	78%	22%
1997	85%	15%	83%	17%

INTEREST GROUPS

House Service:

	AFL-CIO	ADA	CCUS	ACU
2006	100%	90%	40%	8%
2005	92%	95%	40%	0%
2004	100%	95%	43%	0%
2003	87%	90%	37%	20%
2002	100%	95%	55%	0%
2001	100%	100%	35%	4%
2000	90%	90%	42%	8%
1999	89%	100%	28%	0%
1998	100%	95%	25%	8%
1997	88%	85%	40%	12%

Rep. Wayne T. Gilchrest (R)

CAPITOL OFFICE
225-5311
www.house.gov/gilchrest
2245 Rayburn 20515-2001; fax 225-0254

COMMITTEES
Natural Resources
Transportation & Infrastructure

RESIDENCE
Kennedyville

BORN
April 15, 1946, Rahway, N.J.

RELIGION
Methodist

FAMILY
Wife, Barbara Gilchrest; three children

EDUCATION
Wesley College, A.A. 1971; Delaware State U., B.A. 1973 (history); Loyola College (Md.), attended 1990

MILITARY SERVICE
Marine Corps, 1964-68

CAREER
Teacher

POLITICAL HIGHLIGHTS
Republican nominee for U.S. House, 1988

ELECTION RESULTS

2006 GENERAL		
Wayne T. Gilchrest (R)	185,177	68.8%
Jim Corwin (D)	83,738	31.1%
2006 PRIMARY		
Wayne T. Gilchrest (R)		unopposed
2004 GENERAL		
Wayne T. Gilchrest (R)	245,149	75.8%
Kostas Alexakis (D)	77,872	24.1%

PREVIOUS WINNING PERCENTAGES
2002 (77%); 2000 (64%); 1998 (69%); 1996 (62%); 1994 (68%); 1992 (51%); 1990 (57%)

Elected 1990; 9th term

A quiet, quirky Republican from Maryland's Eastern Shore, Gilchrest is one of his party's leading environmentalists in Congress. He is also a thorn in the side of the GOP leadership, which has tolerated him to help maintain Republican numbers in the House but has never embraced him.

An avid outdoorsman, he makes no secret of the fact that he prefers wandering the wilderness to strolling the halls of the Capitol. He goes canoeing every weekend, calling it "political dialysis" — getting the week's politics out of his system. He doesn't care whether it's 100 degrees outside or 30, raining or sunny. Canoeing, he says, makes him feel alive.

Gilchrest seems almost entirely without affectation. He meanders around his office, eavesdropping as a receptionist explains his position to a caller. He fetches coffee for a visitor and readily answers any questions without the staff watchdogs many lawmakers keep on hand.

A former public school teacher and house painter who got into politics through "a random set of circumstances," Gilchrest defies his party and his president on a range of issues. He has favored gun control and abortion rights, supported embryonic stem cell research, and opposed efforts to pass a constitutional amendment banning same-sex marriage.

But most of all, he champions environmental protection and conservation efforts. On the then named Resources Committee, he chaired the Fisheries and Oceans Subcommittee from 2001-07. He battled committee Chairman Richard W. Pombo of California, a conservative property rights advocate, over the Endangered Species Act, mining regulation, oil drilling in Alaska's Arctic National Wildlife Refuge and other issues. By 2006, Pombo was so fed up that he stripped Gilchrest's panel of all legislative jurisdiction.

Gilchrest was undeterred. He kept plugging away at efforts to protect the Chesapeake Bay from pollution and to tighten regulation of U.S. fisheries. He is an advocate of renewable fuels and has introduced legislation to limit emissions of greenhouse gases, including carbon dioxide, which the White House does not support. He regularly holds forums in his district on global warming. He sees small signs of progress, although it's slow going. "It's like turning an aircraft carrier with canoe paddles," he says. The solution? "More people with canoe paddles."

Although he supported the invasion of Iraq, Gilchrest was one of the first Republicans to speak out against the U.S. military's abuse of detainees evidenced in photographs from the Abu Ghraib prison. In 2006, he was one of just seven House Republicans to vote against legislation authorizing indefinite detention and trial by military tribunals of suspects captured in the war on terror. In 2007, he was one of only 17 House Republicans to vote for a Democratic-drafted resolution disapproving of sending more troops to Iraq and one of only two in the GOP to back a bill that set a timetable for troop withdrawals.

Gilchrest supports free trade and votes with the GOP majority on labor issues. Unlike many with strong public school ties, he backs conservatives' push to give parents taxpayer-financed vouchers for private school education. He says competition will force public schools to improve.

When Congress debated the last farm bill in 2002, Gilchrest banded with environmentalists to try to divert billions of dollars from commodity subsidy payments into conservation programs, such as those that pay farmers to idle environmentally sensitive land and to protect wildlife and wetlands. The effort was unsuccessful, but it marked the first time in years that suburban and Northeastern lawmakers had worked so actively and come so close to shaping agriculture policy against the wishes of Farm Belt lawmakers. Gilchrest did come away from the 2002 farm bill with a federal pilot program to send agricultural conservation funds to the most environmentally sensitive land on the Chesapeake's eastern Delmarva Peninsula.

Born in New Jersey, Gilchrest traces his passion for wilderness to his youth in farm country not far from New York City where he played in the woods, soaking in sights and smells. By the time he reached high school, the woods were gone — and he felt like he was the only one who cared.

He joined the Marine Corps right out of high school. He plays down the 1967 battle in Vietnam that won him the Bronze Star and the chest and shoulder wound that earned him a Purple Heart, portraying his conduct as more foolhardy than brave. He attended several colleges, mixing in jobs plucking chickens in Maine and studying rural poverty in Kentucky. After graduating from Delaware State University, he held a series of teaching jobs, ending up on Maryland's Eastern Shore in 1979. He supplemented his income painting houses in the summers.

When he hit 40, Gilchrest decided he wanted to escape to the wilderness, which he had loved since his childhood. He quit his job and moved his wife and three young children to a cabin in rural Idaho. His wife and daughter went back before long; the woods weren't for them. He and his sons stayed until he fell off a horse and broke his jaw a year or so after the move. He returned to Maryland, and the family was reunited. He began painting houses again.

He decided to run for the House in 1988 against Rep. Roy Dyson, a conservative Democrat who did not share his concerns about the environment. Gilchrest rushed to Annapolis in paint-covered clothes to file for the election after he read in a newspaper that the GOP was having trouble finding a candidate. He lost that first bid but won their 1990 rematch.

Gilchrest's only general-election scare was two years later, when redistricting pitted him against three-term Democratic Rep. Tom McMillen, a basketball star with the University of Maryland, the U.S. Olympic team and the Washington Bullets. Gilchrest won with 51 percent of the vote.

In 2002, the conservative Club for Growth made one of its first efforts to unseat a moderate incumbent Republican, backing attorney Dave Fischer, who captured 36 percent of the primary vote against Gilchrest. Another conservative, state Sen. Richard F. Colburn, whom Gilchrest had defeated in the 1990 primary, tried again in the 2004, scoring 38 percent. In 2006, Glichrest faced no primary challenger and won the general election with ease.

KEY VOTES

2006

- No Stop broadband companies from favoring select Internet traffic
- Yes Affirm U.S. commitment to war in Iraq and reject setting a withdrawal date for troops
- No Repeal requirement for bilingual ballots at the polls
- Yes Permit U.S. sale of civilian nuclear technology to India
- Yes Build a 700-mile fence on the U.S.-Mexico border to curb illegal crossings
- Yes Permit warrantless wiretaps of suspected terrorists

2005

- Yes Intervene in the life-support case of Terri Schiavo
- Yes Lift President Bush's restrictions on stem cell research funding
- No Prohibit FBI access to library and bookstore records
- Yes Approve free-trade pact with five Central American countries
- Yes Pass energy policy overhaul favored by President Bush emphasizing domestic oil and gas production
- No End mandatory preservation of habitat of endangered animal and plant species
- Yes Ban torture of prisoners in U.S. custody

CQ VOTE STUDIES

	PARTY UNITY		PRESIDENTIAL SUPPORT	
	Support	Oppose	Support	Oppose
2006	75%	25%	57%	43%
2005	80%	20%	72%	28%
2004	85%	15%	74%	26%
2003	88%	12%	80%	20%
2002	86%	14%	80%	20%

INTEREST GROUPS

	AFL-CIO	ADA	CCUS	ACU
2006	43%	40%	77%	48%
2005	20%	25%	89%	42%
2004	27%	35%	95%	56%
2003	7%	25%	82%	63%
2002	13%	10%	94%	78%

MARYLAND 1

East — Eastern Shore, part of Anne Arundel County

The 1st includes the mostly rural Eastern Shore and some fast-growing Anne Arundel County suburbs across the Chesapeake Bay. It also crosses the Susquehanna River in northeastern Maryland and claims chunks of Harford County, including Bel Air, and Baltimore County.

The Eastern Shore, which holds about three-fifths of the district's population, has a steady economic grounding in agriculture, relying mainly on vegetables, fruit and chicken breeding. The central, more rural, part of the Eastern Shore is solidly Republican. The northern counties, closer to Baltimore and Philadelphia, and southern counties, with larger black and working-class populations, are more Democratic, but do not factor heavily in elections. Ocean City is a popular beach town on the Atlantic shore that swells with visitors during the summer months.

Across the bay, the 1st includes some GOP-leaning parts of Anne Arundel, including the predominately white, educated, upper-middle class areas of Arnold, Severna Park and Millersville. Part of Baltimore's conservative northern suburbs also are included in the 1st.

Despite regional differences, all of the 1st's areas share a conservative bent that benefits Republicans. The 1st consistently supports Republican presidential candidates, and George W. Bush won 62 percent of the district's 2004 presidential vote. Two statewide GOP candidates in 2006 — Michael S. Steele running for the U.S. Senate and Gov. Robert L. Ehrlich Jr. running for re-election — captured more than 60 percent of the 1st's vote while garnering roughly 45 percent overall in Maryland.

MAJOR INDUSTRY

Agriculture, manufacturing, tourism

MILITARY BASES

U.S. Naval Academy/Naval Station Annapolis, 700 military, 1,533 civilian (2006) (shared with the 3rd District)

CITIES

Bel Air South (unincorporated) (pt.), 35,353; Severna Park (unincorporated) (pt.), 26,646; Bel Air North (unincorporated) (pt.), 25,372; Salisbury, 23,743; Arnold (unincorporated), 23,422

NOTABLE

Wild ponies roam Assateague Island, a barrier island on the Atlantic Ocean; Smith Island calls itself Maryland's only inhabited offshore island in the Chesapeake Bay.

Rep. C.A. Dutch Ruppersberger (D)

CAPITOL OFFICE
225-3061
dutch.house.gov
1730 Longworth 20515-2002; fax 225-3094

COMMITTEES
Appropriations
Select Intelligence
(Technical & Tactical Intelligence - chairman)

RESIDENCE
Cockeysville

BORN
Jan. 31, 1946, Baltimore, Md.

RELIGION
Methodist

FAMILY
Wife, Kay Ruppersberger; two children

EDUCATION
U. of Maryland, attended 1963-67;
U. of Baltimore, J.D. 1970

CAREER
Collection agency owner; lawyer;
county prosecutor

POLITICAL HIGHLIGHTS
Democratic nominee for Md. Senate, 1978; Baltimore County Council, 1985-94; Baltimore County executive, 1994-2002

ELECTION RESULTS

2006 GENERAL		
C.A. Dutch Ruppersberger (D)	135,818	69.2%
Jimmy Mathis (R)	60,195	30.7%
2006 PRIMARY		
C.A. Dutch Ruppersberger (D)	56,450	82.3%
Christopher C. Boardman (D)	12,118	17.7%
2004 GENERAL		
C.A. Dutch Ruppersberger (D)	164,751	66.6%
Jane Brooks (R)	75,812	30.7%
Keith Salkowski (GREEN)	6,508	2.6%

PREVIOUS WINNING PERCENTAGES
2002 (54%)

Elected 2002; 3rd term

Ruppersberger is an affable former county prosecutor who is at ease with the back-slapping nature of the business. And although he can claim credit for only a couple minor pieces of legislation, he has become known as someone willing to cross party lines to cut a deal — particularly on intelligence issues. The former Republican Intelligence Committee chairman, Peter Hoekstra of Michigan, calls him a "real consensus builder." Ruppersberger says, "The stakes are too high for us to not work together."

At the start of the 110th Congress (2007-08), he gained a seat on the Appropriations Committee — taking the place of fellow Maryland Democrat and new House Majority Leader Steny H. Hoyer. It is a choice assignment where he can play a leading role on federal funding issues as well as look out for his district. In that seat, Hoyer led efforts to raise federal salaries, and Ruppersberger is expected to do the same thing. He represents employees who work at the National Security Agency (NSA) and at the Coast Guard Yard at Curtis Bay. And his district is adding tens of thousands of new jobs as part of the military's Base Realignment and Closure process, primarily at Fort George C. Meade and the Aberdeen Proving Ground.

Yet his first test as a new member of the committee came on the fiscal 2007 war supplemental funding bill. Democratic appropriators were pressured to refrain from amending the leadership's bill, which provided war funding yet set a timeline for troops to be withdrawn from Iraq, and provided funds for items not related to war efforts. Ruppersberger was game.

For much of his career in the House, Ruppersberger has focused on his position on the Intelligence Committee, where he is best known for working across party lines, even when he's unhappy with the Bush administration. He was highly critical of the administration for operating warrantless NSA surveillance programs without informing Congress, and he called for hearings in 2005. But the next year, he felt obliged to support the intelligence community and vote against an amendment to a defense spending bill to withhold funds for surveillance programs that did not undergo a court review. He broke with his party to vote no. Nevertheless, in the 110th Congress, he was granted the chairmanship of the Technical and Tactical Intelligence Subcommittee.

He also has developed expertise on homeland security issues, especially port security. His district is less than an hour's drive from Washington, D.C., and, besides the NSA, is home to Baltimore/Washington International Thurgood Marshall Airport and the Helen Delich Bentley Port of Baltimore. He has championed more spending for first-responders — local fire, police and rescue squads. A former county executive, Ruppersberger says local governments are strained each time the federal government posts a heightened terrorism alert. "Every time the code went up, we had to double our resources," he said.

Ruppersberger has had a couple of legislative victories. The energy policy overhaul enacted in 2005 included his proposal to give tax incentives to drivers of hybrid cars. And after hearing complaints from U.S. soldiers arriving at BWI Airport that they had to pay for connecting flights home out of their own pockets, Ruppersberger set up an offbeat program that allowed civilians to donate their frequent flier miles to soldiers via a Web site. "Operation Hero Miles" got the public's attention, and at Ruppersberger's instigation, Congress directed the Pentagon in 2004 to pay the whole airfare bill for troops returning from Afghanistan and Iraq for rest and recuperation.

In an important parochial battle, Ruppersberger fought successfully to stop plans for a 1,750-bed federal prison in Dundalk, a largely Democratic blue-collar community in his district.

On national issues, he mostly votes with his party. Though he supports abortion rights in most cases, he was among the 62 Democrats who in 2003 voted for a ban on a procedure that critics call "partial birth" abortion.

He was born Charles Albert Ruppersberger III, but goes by Dutch. The son of a Baltimore manufacturing salesman and a schoolteacher, he says the doctor who delivered him described him as a "big, blond Dutchman." (His hair has since turned black.) As practical a politician as they come, Ruppersberger later adopted the nickname legally when he realized his given name was too long for a bumper sticker.

A good athlete as a youth, he played lacrosse at the University of Maryland and made the U.S. team in 1967. During college summers, he was a lifeguard in Ocean City, Md., then worked his way through night school at the University of Baltimore Law School as an insurance claims adjuster.

He began his public career as a Baltimore County assistant state's attorney. In 1985, he won a seat on the county council, then in 1994 got the top job as county executive. Ruppersberger steered the county to triple-A bond ratings while building new schools, roads and parks. Governing magazine called Baltimore one of the nation's four best-managed counties in 2001.

The next year, Ruppersberger planned to run for governor, but was dogged by events that took place two years earlier. In 2000, he had aggressively pushed a bill to allow the county to condemn private property for urban revitalization. People in the affected areas fought back with a referendum that passed by a margin of 2-to-1, an embarrassing renunciation for the county executive. Then in November 2000, The Baltimore Sun reported that he had steered government grants to an apartment rental firm with which he had personal business dealings. Ruppersberger called the report flawed and said he had broken no laws.

But he was too weakened politically to take on a primary fight against the well-financed Kathleen Townsend, daughter of Sen. Robert F. Kennedy. Hoyer urged him to run instead for the newly redrawn House 2nd District, which was 64 percent Democratic. Republicans put up popular former Rep. Helen Delich Bentley, who had represented the 2nd from 1985-95, but Ruppersberger prevailed by almost 9 percentage points. He won re-election with more than 66 percent of the vote in 2004, and with 69 percent two years later. He had flirted with a 2006 run for the Senate seat of retiring Democrat Paul S. Sarbanes, but deferred to 10-term Rep. Benjamin L. Cardin.

KEY VOTES

2006

- No Stop broadband companies from favoring select Internet traffic
- No Affirm U.S. commitment to war in Iraq and reject setting a withdrawal date for troops
- No Repeal requirement for bilingual ballots at the polls
- Yes Permit U.S. sale of civilian nuclear technology to India
- Yes Build a 700-mile fence on the U.S.-Mexico border to curb illegal crossings
- No Permit warrantless wiretaps of suspected terrorists

2005

- ? Intervene in the life-support case of Terri Schiavo
- Yes Lift President Bush's restrictions on stem cell research funding
- Yes Prohibit FBI access to library and bookstore records
- No Approve free-trade pact with five Central American countries
- Yes Pass energy policy overhaul favored by President Bush emphasizing domestic oil and gas production
- No End mandatory preservation of habitat of endangered animal and plant species
- Yes Ban torture of prisoners in U.S. custody

CQ VOTE STUDIES

	PARTY UNITY		PRESIDENTIAL SUPPORT	
	Support	Oppose	Support	Oppose
2006	85%	15%	46%	54%
2005	89%	11%	35%	65%
2004	88%	12%	44%	56%
2003	89%	11%	23%	77%

INTEREST GROUPS

	AFL-CIO	ADA	CCUS	ACU
2006	93%	85%	67%	24%
2005	100%	95%	63%	20%
2004	86%	90%	55%	12%
2003	93%	90%	33%	24%

MARYLAND 2
Part of Baltimore and suburbs — Dundalk, Essex

The 2nd includes parts of northern and eastern Baltimore, suburbs on most sides of the city and most of the land east of Interstate 95 between Baltimore and the Susquehanna River, along the Chesapeake Bay coastline of Baltimore and Harford counties. Its Anne Arundel County portion, south of Baltimore, includes Baltimore-Washington airport and Fort George G. Meade, home of the National Security Agency. Fort Meade is expected to receive additional personnel in the coming years.

In eastern Baltimore County, the blue-collar industrial sector, including Dundalk, has struggled with unemployment. Bethlehem Steel, one of the county's economic engines, filed for bankruptcy in 2001 and was later acquired by a Europe-based company. The Sparrows Point plant is still a major employer, but steelworkers and local officials worry about the impact foreign control of the state's steel industry may have on the Maryland economy. Possible further consolidations, job cuts, and health care and pension reductions have not eased the worry.

The district's northwest branch moves through the GOP-heavy northern suburbs but then hooks into largely African-American suburbs west of Baltimore, such as Randallstown. Blacks overall make up 27 percent of the 2nd's population.

Solidly Democratic voters in Baltimore County and Baltimore city, which together make up nearly three-fourths of the district's population, push the 2nd into the Democratic column. Democrats Martin O'Malley and Benjamin L. Cardin each received 53 percent of the 2nd's vote in their respective 2006 gubernatorial and Senate runs.

MAJOR INDUSTRY

Manufacturing, defense, product distribution

MILITARY BASES

Fort George G. Meade (Army), 10,564 military, 26,982 civilian (2007); Aberdeen Proving Ground (Army), 4,341 military, 11,644 civilian (2006)

CITIES

Baltimore (pt.), 111,715; Dundalk (unincorporated), 62,306; Essex (unincorporated), 39,078; Randallstown (unincorporated) (pt.), 29,097

NOTABLE

Aberdeen is home to Cal Ripken Baseball, a youth division of the amateur Babe Ruth League; The Havre de Grace Decoy Museum contains the nation's largest collection of wooden duck decoys.

Rep. John Sarbanes (D)

CAPITOL OFFICE
225-4016
sarbanes.house.gov
426 Cannon 20515-2003; fax 225-9219

COMMITTEES
Education & Labor
Natural Resources
Oversight & Government Reform

RESIDENCE
Towson

BORN
May 22, 1962, Baltimore, Md.

RELIGION
Greek Orthodox

FAMILY
Wife, Dina Sarbanes; three children

EDUCATION
Princeton U., A.B. 1984 (public & international affairs); Harvard U., J.D. 1988

CAREER
Lawyer; state education consultant

POLITICAL HIGHLIGHTS
No previous office

ELECTION RESULTS

2006 GENERAL		
John Sarbanes (D)	150,142	64.0%
John White (R)	79,174	33.8%
Charles McPeek Sr. (LIBERT)	4,941	2.1%
2006 PRIMARY		
John Sarbanes (D)	26,954	31.9%
Peter Beilenson (D)	21,481	25.4%
Paula C. Hollinger (D)	18,008	21.3%
Andy Barth (D)	7,561	9.0%
Kevin O'Keefe (D)	4,084	4.8%
Oz Bengur (D)	3,774	4.5%
Mishonda Baldwin (D)	2,202	2.6%

Elected 2006; 1st term

A political novice who capitalized on a well-known last name to win his seat, Sarbanes now is bent on carving out his own niche on Capitol Hill.

The oldest son of Maryland Sen. Paul S. Sarbanes, who retired at the end of 2006 after 36 years in Congress, John Sarbanes acknowledges that his father's stellar reputation set a high bar for him. "I think those expectations would be more burdensome if I didn't have a confidence and pride in the things I've been doing myself," he told the Baltimore Sun in January 2007.

Sarbanes, like his father, was educated at Princeton University and Harvard Law School. His dad was a Rhodes Scholar at Oxford; the younger Sarbanes studied law and politics in Greece on a Fulbright scholarship.

He spent 16 years at Baltimore's prestigious Venable law firm, where he served as chairman of the firm's health care practice, representing hospitals and other medical providers. For seven years, he was a special assistant to the state superintendent of schools, serving as a liaison to the troubled Baltimore City schools. The latter experience is likely to prove especially useful, given his assignment to the Education and Labor Committee, which is tackling an overhaul of the 2001 No Child Left Behind elementary and secondary education law in the 110th Congress (2007-08).

While Sarbanes is no fan of the education law, he does not think repeal is necessarily the answer. Instead, he hopes to move the statute away from what he considers its "obsessive focus" on math and reading and encourage studies in the humanities and sciences. He also says factors used to determine whether schools are improving are "too rigid."

John Sarbanes got his shot at Congress when 10-term Democratic Rep. Benjamin L. Cardin launched his successful bid to succeed the senior Sarbanes in the Senate. The primary drew eight candidates. The list included another congressional offspring, Peter Beilenson, a former Baltimore health commissioner whose father, Democrat Anthony Beilenson, represented a California district for 20 years, and state Sen. Paula C. Hollinger of Baltimore County. But the Sarbanes name trumped all, and in the heavily Democratic 3rd, he had no trouble in November.

MARYLAND 3

Part of Baltimore; eastern Columbia; Annapolis

Like a Z-shaped lightning bolt, the 3rd flashes through three of Maryland's largest urban hubs — Baltimore, Columbia and Annapolis.

Starting in traditionally Jewish suburbs northwest of Baltimore, the 3rd snakes east and south, grabbing northeastern suburbs and part of downtown by Fells Point and the stadiums for baseball's Orioles and football's Ravens. Many ethnic areas of eastern Baltimore are here. The 3rd then turns south and west through suburban Arbutus and Elkridge on its way to eastern Columbia. Finally, the district moves southeast to Annapolis. Distinct areas here are unified by trade concerns centered around the port.

State and local governments provide jobs in Annapolis — both the state capital and the Anne Arundel County seat. Technology, financial services and health care push the economy around Columbia. Fort George G. Meade and Baltimore/Washington International Thurgood Marshall Airport (both in the neighboring 2nd) lure defense-related firms to the region.

The district has some GOP-leaning areas in Anne Arundel and Baltimore counties, but overall the 3rd supports Democrats for federal office. John Kerry won 54 percent of the district's 2004 presidential vote.

MAJOR INDUSTRY
Government, technology, defense

MILITARY BASES
U.S. Naval Academy/Naval Station Annapolis, 700 military, 1,533 civilian (2006) (shared with the 1st District)

CITIES
Baltimore (pt.), 168,687; Columbia (unincorporated) (pt.), 40,311; Annapolis, 35,838; Pikesville (unincorporated), 29,123

NOTABLE
The Preakness Stakes is held at Pimlico in northwestern Baltimore.

Rep. Albert R. Wynn (D)

CAPITOL OFFICE
225-8699
www.house.gov/wynn
2470 Rayburn 20515-2004; fax 225-8714

COMMITTEES
Energy & Commerce
(Environment & Hazardous Materials - chairman)

RESIDENCE
Mitchellville

BORN
Sept. 10, 1951, Philadelphia, Pa.

RELIGION
Baptist

FAMILY
Wife, Gaines Clore Wynn; one child, one stepchild

EDUCATION
U. of Pittsburgh, B.S. 1973 (political science); Howard U., attended 1973-74 (public administration); Georgetown U., J.D. 1977

CAREER
Lawyer

POLITICAL HIGHLIGHTS
Md. House, 1983-87; Md. Senate, 1987-93

ELECTION RESULTS

2006 GENERAL		
Albert R. Wynn (D)	141,897	80.7%
Michael Moshe Starkman (R)	32,792	18.6%
2006 PRIMARY		
Albert R. Wynn (D)	40,857	49.7%
Donna Edwards (D)	38,126	46.4%
George E. McDermott (D)	3,200	3.9%
2004 GENERAL		
Albert R. Wynn (D)	196,809	75.2%
John McKinnis (R)	52,907	20.2%
Theresa M. Dudley (GREEN)	11,885	4.5%

PREVIOUS WINNING PERCENTAGES
2002 (79%); 2000 (87%); 1998 (86%); 1996 (85%); 1994 (75%); 1992 (75%)

Elected 1992; 8th term

Long seen as a master of the art of politics, Wynn badly misread his constituents in 2006 and wound up in his closest election battle since his first race for the House. He edged past an anti-war challenger in the Democratic primary election by fewer than 3,000 votes and emerged decidedly chastened, vowing to re-examine his whole approach to his job.

Often referred to as a "kingmaker" in Prince George's County, a black-majority and overwhelmingly Democratic suburb of Washington, D.C., Wynn was caught off guard by a strong challenge from his left. Lawyer and community activist Donna Edwards attacked him for his 2002 vote in favor of the war in Iraq, his support for the GOP energy policy overhaul in 2005 and his backing for a permanent reduction in the estate tax. She said he was too close to President Bush and too close to business interests.

Wynn had renounced his Iraq War vote by 2004, saying he had been misled by erroneous prewar intelligence. "I regret that vote," he said. Edwards said that wasn't good enough. "Leadership is not about regret; it is about leading," said Edwards. Wynn declared during the campaign that he was "not a blind Democrat" but was nonetheless a "true" one.

But given his re-election scare, he may be less inclined in the 110th Congress (2007-08) to split with the majority of his party. "When an incumbent experiences a close election, that's a message from the voters that they're not satisfied or pleased with all the things that you've done," Wynn says. "You have to re-evaluate the things you've done and listen to the sentiment that the voters are expressing." He said in late 2006, for example, that he was looking at his position on repeal of the estate tax and "thinks that will change."

Wynn, who has a seat on the Energy and Commerce Committee, has focused his legislative efforts on what he can do for Maryland in general and the 4th District in particular. In the 110th Congress, he chairs the Energy panel's Environment and Hazardous Materials Subcommittee.

His office regularly touts the federal funding he helps bring home, such as $208 million in the 2004 catchall spending bill for projects in and around the 4th District, including: $800,000 for the Intercounty Connector, a new highway to connect the I-270 corridor in Montgomery County with the I-95/U.S. 1 corridor in Prince George's County; $1 million to reduce pollution in the Anacostia River; and $200,000 for a study of the Potomac River.

He also touts his aid to businesses in his district that compete for federal contracts, boasting in 2006 that the 4th District ranked 12th nationwide in federal contracts received the preceding two years.

When Wynn was first elected to Congress in 1992, he represented a district drawn by state General Assembly Democrats to maximize the clout of minority voters. But when district lines were redrawn for this decade, Wynn put his party loyalty ahead of his personal political security. He encouraged mapmakers to move some suburban Democrats from his 4th District to the neighboring 8th District, which helped force Republican Constance A. Morella from office in 2002. The shift did him no harm in general elections; the 4th remains reliably Democratic.

Wynn earned his reputation as a kingmaker in 1998, when his voter mobilization skills helped Democrat Parris N. Glendening win re-election as governor. In 2002, he played a dominant role in Prince George's County politics, offering key endorsements of the new county executive, Jack Johnson, and most of the new county council members.

Wynn has looked out for his district on a highly divisive issue in Maryland politics — whether to legalize gambling. At mid-decade, when Maryland's GOP Gov. Robert L. Ehrlich Jr. was promoting slot machines to cure the state's budget ills, Wynn favored a casino attached to a four-star hotel in Prince George's County. He argued such a project would create thousands of jobs and spur economic development. But Ehrlich's plans failed, the casino option was not considered, and ultimately Wynn changed his mind. He says he no longer supports any gambling in Prince George's County.

The 4th was the nation's first black-majority district dominated by middle-class suburbanites. As a result, its residents' priorities differ from those in many other districts with large African-American populations. Many of Wynn's constituents are small-business owners who contract with the federal government, and he tends to be more pro-business than most of his colleagues in the Congressional Black Caucus.

Wynn's strong political base has helped him move up in the ranks of the Black Caucus; he has chaired its political action committee, its task force on campaign finance reform and its minority business task force. He has also served as a Democratic regional whip and senior whip. He is closely allied with Democrat Steny H. Hoyer, who represents the adjoining 5th District in Maryland. After the 2006 elections, he helped Hoyer become majority leader in spite of efforts by Nancy Pelosi of California, the incoming Speaker, to push Hoyer aside in favor of John P. Murtha of Pennsylvania.

Born in Philadelphia, Wynn spent his early years in North Carolina, where his father farmed and his mother taught school. When he was 7, his father was hired by the Department of Agriculture and the family moved back north, spending one year in Washington, D.C., before heading to the Maryland suburbs. Wynn attended segregated schools until he was in the ninth grade. He was elected president of his high school senior class. "I have always been pretty good at mobilizing," Wynn recalls.

Wynn excelled at the trombone and was a debater at the University of Pittsburgh. After earning a law degree from Georgetown University in 1977, Wynn ran the Prince George's County Consumer Protection Commission. He became involved in local politics, working on other candidates' campaigns. In 1982, his door-to-door campaigning skills and party contacts helped him unseat an incumbent state representative.

After 10 years in Annapolis, Wynn was one of 13 Democrats who lined up for the newly drawn 4th District. He won the primary, which was tantamount to election, with 1,300 more votes than Alexander Williams Jr., the Prince George's County prosecutor. Until 2006, that was his only tough race.

KEY VOTES

2006

No Stop broadband companies from favoring select Internet traffic

No Affirm U.S. commitment to war in Iraq and reject setting a withdrawal date for troops

No Repeal requirement for bilingual ballots at the polls

Yes Permit U.S. sale of civilian nuclear technology to India

No Build a 700-mile fence on the U.S.-Mexico border to curb illegal crossings

No Permit warrantless wiretaps of suspected terrorists

2005

Yes Intervene in the life-support case of Terri Schiavo

Yes Lift President Bush's restrictions on stem cell research funding

Yes Prohibit FBI access to library and bookstore records

No Approve free-trade pact with five Central American countries

Yes Pass energy policy overhaul favored by President Bush emphasizing domestic oil and gas production

Yes End mandatory preservation of habitat of endangered animal and plant species

Yes Ban torture of prisoners in U.S. custody

CQ VOTE STUDIES

	PARTY UNITY		PRESIDENTIAL SUPPORT	
	Support	Oppose	Support	Oppose
2006	91%	9%	33%	67%
2005	87%	13%	27%	73%
2004	88%	12%	38%	62%
2003	91%	9%	20%	80%
2002	87%	13%	32%	68%

INTEREST GROUPS

	AFL-CIO	ADA	CCUS	ACU
2006	86%	85%	60%	20%
2005	80%	95%	70%	24%
2004	80%	95%	71%	20%
2003	100%	90%	43%	20%
2002	100%	85%	50%	8%

MARYLAND 4

Inner Prince George's County; part of Montgomery County

The first suburban district in the nation with a black majority, the 4th includes Washington, D.C.'s eastern suburbs in Prince George's County and a sizable swath of northern Montgomery County. Democrats have a strong hold on the district's largely middle-class, black population.

The 4th's thriving economy is built on small business and the spillover of technology firms from Montgomery County and the Northern Virginia suburbs. The district includes major portions of the Prince George's County High Technology Triangle, which is home to offices for Raytheon and other companies and is bolstered by the University of Maryland and NASA's Goddard Space Flight Center (both nearby in the 5th).

Prince George's County is a national leader in black business formation, home ownership and education. Many of its residents are federal employees who have moved out of Washington, and the 4th has the nation's highest percentage of federal government employees (29 percent). Despite this, some of Prince George's County's low-income areas inside the Capital Beltway, which surrounds Washington, share the capital's problems of drug trafficking and violent crime.

Nearly 40 percent of the 4th's residents live in Montgomery County outer suburbs and exurbs, such as Burtonsville, Olney and Sandy Spring, and the district has a 57 percent black population. The 4th's solid Democratic tendencies led voters to give John Kerry 78 percent of the 2004 presidential vote here, his highest percentage in Maryland.

MAJOR INDUSTRY
Retail, computers, recreation, technology

MILITARY BASES
Andrews Air Force Base, 5,202 military, 4,798 civilian (2007); Adelphi Army Research Laboratory, 13 military, 617 civilian (2006)

CITIES
Silver Spring (unincorporated) (pt.), 46,910; Oxon Hill-Glassmanor (unincorporated), 35,355; Suitland-Silver Hill (unincorporated), 33,515

NOTABLE
Air Force One is kept at Andrews Air Force Base; Brookeville served as the nation's capital for a day in August 1814, when the British invaded Washington and President James Madison fled the White House.

Rep. Steny H. Hoyer (D)

CAPITOL OFFICE
225-4131
www.house.gov/hoyer
1705 Longworth 20515-2005; fax 225-4300

RESIDENCE
Mechanicsville

BORN
June 14, 1939, Manhattan, N.Y.

RELIGION
Baptist

FAMILY
Widowed; three children

EDUCATION
U. of Maryland, B.S. 1963 (political science); Georgetown U., J.D. 1966

CAREER
Lawyer

POLITICAL HIGHLIGHTS
Md. Senate, 1967-79 (president, 1975-79); sought Democratic nomination for lieutenant governor, 1978; Md. Board of Higher Education, 1978-81

ELECTION RESULTS

2006 GENERAL		
Steny H. Hoyer (D)	168,114	82.7%
Steve Warner (GREEN)	33,464	16.5%
2006 PRIMARY		
Steny H. Hoyer (D)		unopposed
2004 GENERAL		
Steny H. Hoyer (D)	204,867	68.7%
Brad Jewitt (R)	87,189	29.2%
Bob S. Auerbach (GREEN)	4,224	1.4%

PREVIOUS WINNING PERCENTAGES
2002 (69%); 2000 (65%); 1998 (65%); 1996 (57%); 1994 (59%); 1992 (53%); 1990 (81%); 1988 (79%); 1986 (82%); 1984 (72%); 1982 (80%); 1981 Special Election (55%)

Elected May 1981; 13th full term

Considered one of the driving forces behind the Democratic takeover of the House in the 2006 election, Hoyer was rewarded with the job of majority leader, the second-highest leadership post. His selection by fellow Democrats came in spite of an aggressive campaign by Speaker Nancy Pelosi to fill the slot with one of her closest allies. His victory at Pelosi's expense served to enhance Hoyer's independence from the new Speaker.

Their rough start, after a joyous midterm election for the party, raised the question whether they would be an effective team in the 110th Congress (2007-08), considering the challenges posed for the Democrats by a White House in GOP hands and a Senate only barely under their control.

Pelosi says Hoyer is too independent. For example, as she was trying to bring Democrats together on the biggest issue in the last election — the war in Iraq — Hoyer went his own way, issuing a detailed position paper supporting the war effort, which Pelosi did not endorse. After the party took power, Hoyer continued to take a more moderate position on the war than liberals who pushed for a firm troop withdrawal date.

As the 110th Congress organized, Pelosi pressured Democrats to choose as majority leader John P. Murtha of Pennsylvania, a decorated Vietnam combat veteran who had led the charge for a redeployment of troops. But Hoyer, a 25-year House veteran and seasoned leader, had locked up support from his colleagues, most of whom were loath to turn against him after his heroic efforts helping Democratic challengers oust GOP incumbents in the election, including distributing $1 million from his own war chest. He beat Murtha 149-86 in the secret balloting.

Hoyer's uneasy relationship with Pelosi goes back years. She defeated him for the Democratic whip job in 2001, his second try after losing a bid a decade earlier to liberal Democrat David E. Bonior of Michigan. Hoyer went on to be elected in 1989 as caucus chairman, the fourth-ranking job in the Democratically controlled House at that time. But he never stopped campaigning to move up, continuing to raise significant sums of money for Democrats and earning their loyalty. When Pelosi was selected minority leader in late 2002, Hoyer finally nailed down the whip's job.

Inspired by John F. Kennedy, Hoyer takes many of his cues from the 35th president. He made politics his lifelong career after hearing Kennedy tell a college crowd that public service is a noble calling. Unlike many of his Democratic colleagues, Hoyer was influenced by Kennedy's foreign policy views as well, insisting that military strength and international cooperation are equally important in keeping the country safe. He believes Democrats have yet to convince most Americans that they have "the intention, but also the courage, to defeat terrorists."

Hoyer's moderate leanings are a matter of style as well as substance. He holds quiet, back-channel dialogues with conservative Democrats in the Blue Dog Coalition as well as with GOP moderates to try to find legislative middle ground. He is a longtime booster of the Democratic Leadership Council, a centrist group once headed by President Bill Clinton, and he opposed Howard Dean's selection as Democratic National Committee chairman because he considered Dean "a polarizing figure."

Still, no one would mistake Hoyer for a Republican. He was one of the leaders of the Democrats' drive to increase the minimum wage, and he is a persistent advocate of cost-of-living adjustments for federal workers, who make up a large voting bloc in his district. One of the legislative highlights of his career was shepherding to passage the sweeping 1990 Americans with Disabilities Act, which banned discrimination against people with disabilities in employment, public services and accommodations.

Hoyer plays down his differences with Pelosi. When conservative columnist Robert Novak in 2006 floated the idea of Hoyer staging a "coup," he laughed and said Pelosi had nothing to fear. "I think we complement each other," he says, and the proof is in the House Democrats' party unity on roll call votes, which reached its highest level in a half-century in 2005.

Hoyer's top priorities are reducing the budget deficit, cutting college costs and fixing the 2003 Medicare prescription drug law's gaps in coverage. In 2006, he pushed vigorously to rewrite the rules for lobbying members of Congress — a major rallying point for the party — after a string of influence-peddling scandals. His drive for stronger ethical standards in Congress also distinguished him from Murtha, who opposed many of the Democrats' proposed changes in the rules.

Born in New York City, Hoyer was raised in a military family. His stepfather was in the Air Force, his biological parents were divorced, and his mother worked at the Navy Federal Credit Union. He spent much of his childhood in Florida, where his stepfather was stationed at Homestead Air Force Base south of Miami. A transfer to Andrews Air Force Base brought the family to Maryland when Hoyer was in high school.

In 1959, Hoyer was a struggling public relations major in college when he heard then Sen. Kennedy speak at spring convocation. He switched to political science, went on to law school at Georgetown and landed a job as an aide to Sen. Daniel B. Brewster of Maryland. Fatefully, Pelosi also took a job with Brewster in 1963, as his receptionist. Though she too had plenty of potential, the feminist movement had yet to open doors for women; it was Hoyer, not Pelosi, who was groomed for a future in politics. Brewster sent him around the state as his representative, allowing Hoyer to make contacts useful in building a political base. In 1966, at age 27, he was elected to the Maryland Senate, and in two terms became its youngest president ever.

Hoyer suffered a setback in 1978, when he ran for lieutenant governor on a ticket with acting Gov. Blair Lee III and the two lost the primary. Three years later, Hoyer revived his career by claiming the 5th District U.S. House seat after Rep. Gladys Noon Spellman fell ill. He held the seat easily until redistricting in the 1990s added a conservative swath of southern Maryland. Held to 53 percent of the vote in 1992, he has since posted higher margins. In 2006, he had no GOP foe, freeing him to travel around the country in support of other Democratic House candidates.

KEY VOTES

2006

- Yes Stop broadband companies from favoring select Internet traffic
- No Affirm U.S. commitment to war in Iraq and reject setting a withdrawal date for troops
- No Repeal requirement for bilingual ballots at the polls
- Yes Permit U.S. sale of civilian nuclear technology to India
- No Build a 700-mile fence on the U.S.-Mexico border to curb illegal crossings
- No Permit warrantless wiretaps of suspected terrorists

2005

- No Intervene in the life-support case of Terri Schiavo
- Yes Lift President Bush's restrictions on stem cell research funding
- Yes Prohibit FBI access to library and bookstore records
- No Approve free-trade pact with five Central American countries
- Yes Pass energy policy overhaul favored by President Bush emphasizing domestic oil and gas production
- No End mandatory preservation of habitat of endangered animal and plant species
- Yes Ban torture of prisoners in U.S. custody

CQ VOTE STUDIES

	PARTY UNITY		PRESIDENTIAL SUPPORT	
	Support	Oppose	Support	Oppose
2006	92%	8%	27%	73%
2005	93%	7%	24%	76%
2004	95%	5%	24%	76%
2003	92%	8%	24%	76%
2002	89%	11%	32%	68%

INTEREST GROUPS

	AFL-CIO	ADA	CCUS	ACU
2006	100%	90%	40%	4%
2005	100%	95%	52%	12%
2004	100%	100%	38%	0%
2003	87%	90%	40%	20%
2002	100%	95%	42%	4%

MARYLAND 5

Outer Prince George's County; southern Maryland

The 5th includes part of Prince George's County, southern Anne Arundel County, and all of the three rapidly growing southern counties of Charles, Calvert and St. Mary's. The mix of liberals in Prince George's County and conservative Democrats and Republicans throughout much of the rest of the district gives the 5th a broad array of political interests.

The district is enjoying a moderate amount of economic success due to a technology boom since the 1990s, both in Prince George's County and in Southern Maryland. Many residents and companies have left the Washington, D.C., metropolitan area for the southern counties, attracted by the abundance of land and the military presence. Its proximity to Washington gives the 5th the nation's second-highest percentage of government workers (29 percent), behind the neighboring 4th District. The tri-county area retains its Southern rural character, however, despite transitioning away from tobacco as a major crop.

Prince George's County, which accounts for half the district's population and nearly 60 percent of its registered Democrats, includes many liberal black communities as well as College Park, home of the University of Maryland's main campus. Republicans hold a slight registration edge among the 5th's Calvert and Anne Arundel residents, but Democrats have the advantage elsewhere. A growing black population helped John Kerry take largely exurban Charles County while winning the 5th's 2004 presidential vote handily, and statewide Democratic candidates Martin O'Malley and Benjamin L. Cardin each received 56 percent of the 5th's vote in their respective 2006 gubernatorial and U.S. Senate races.

MAJOR INDUSTRY

Defense, agriculture, technology

MILITARY BASES

Naval Air Station Patuxent River, 3,100 military, 7,600 civilian (2007); Naval Surface Warfare Center, Indian Head Division, 6 military, 1,288 civilian

CITIES

Bowie (pt.), 47,714; St. Charles (unincorporated), 33,379; Clinton (unincorporated), 26,064; College Park, 24,657

NOTABLE

NASA Goddard Space Flight Center; St. Mary's City was the first capital of Maryland; The College Park Airport, established in 1909, is the world's oldest continuously operating airport.

Rep. Roscoe G. Bartlett (R)

CAPITOL OFFICE
225-2721
bartlett.house.gov
2412 Rayburn 20515-2006; fax 225-2193

COMMITTEES
Armed Services
Science & Technology
Small Business

RESIDENCE
Frederick

BORN
June 3, 1926, Moreland, Ky.

RELIGION
Seventh-day Adventist

FAMILY
Wife, Ellen Bartlett; 10 children

EDUCATION
Columbia Union College, B.S. 1947 (theology & biology); U. of Maryland, M.S. 1948 (physiology), Ph.D. 1952 (physiology)

CAREER
Real estate developer; scientific research company owner; farmer; biomedical engineer; professor

POLITICAL HIGHLIGHTS
Sought Republican nomination for U.S. Senate, 1980; Republican nominee for U.S. House, 1982

ELECTION RESULTS

2006 GENERAL		
Roscoe G. Bartlett (R)	141,200	59.0%
Andrew Duck (D)	92,030	38.4%
Robert E. Kozak (GREEN)	6,095	2.5%
2006 PRIMARY		
Roscoe G. Bartlett (R)	45,474	79.3%
Joseph T. Krysztoforski (R)	11,889	20.7%
2004 GENERAL		
Roscoe G. Bartlett (R)	206,076	67.4%
Kenneth T. Bosley (D)	90,108	29.5%
Gregory Hemingway (GREEN)	9,324	3.1%

PREVIOUS WINNING PERCENTAGES
2002 (66%); 2000 (61%); 1998 (63%); 1996 (57%); 1994 (66%); 1992 (54%)

Elected 1992; 8th term

Calling himself a citizen-legislator, Bartlett has a laid-back, folksy manner that is a good match for his mostly rural Maryland district. Now an octogenarian, he is considerably older than many of his conservative Republican colleagues first elected in the 1990s, but he is every bit their equal in ideological fervor. Bartlett holds fast to a conservative political philosophy based on self-reliance, strong religious beliefs and a strict constructionist reading of the Constitution. He displays the Ten Commandments in his office beside a mural of the first prayer held in Congress.

Though perhaps a strict constructionist, Bartlett is not against changing the Constitution. He favors constitutional amendments to ban same-sex marriage and flag burning, and he won his own flag-waving victory in 2006 when Congress passed a bill he sponsored barring condominium associations from prohibiting homeowner displays of the U.S. flag. Bartlett said he introduced his bill after a constituent told him some associations had such rules.

A stalwart defense hawk, Bartlett is an equally staunch libertarian who regretted his 2001 vote for the anti-terrorism law known as the Patriot Act, which gave the government sweeping new powers to track, arrest and prosecute suspected terrorists. "Probably the least patriotic thing I've done since I got here," he lamented in an interview several months later. "If the price of catching another terrorist or two is an erosion of our civil liberties, they will have won." In 2005, he voted against reauthorization of the law, and in 2006 he voted against a bill to create military commissions to try suspected terrorists, complaining that it suspended the right of habeas corpus.

Bartlett also has called for closure of the U.S. prison at Guantánamo Bay, Cuba, where captured terrorist suspects are detained. He says the facility is hurting America's image abroad and that "the harm it is doing to us internationally exceeds any benefit we accrue by keeping them there."

The abuse of Iraqi prisoners at the Abu Ghraib prison near Baghdad put an uncomfortable spotlight on Bartlett's district, which includes Cresaptown, Md., the headquarters of the Army's 372nd Military Police Company where several of the reservists implicated in the 2004 scandal were stationed. Bartlett, who believed high-ranking officials ordered the abuse, was careful not to come down too hard on the reservists.

Bartlett has supported the Iraq War and voted against attempts to set a timetable for withdrawal. In 2005, he said President Bush needs to give Americans and Iraqis a specific list of political and security criteria that must be met before U.S. troops can come home. "The American people need to be told, 'We're getting there,' " he said. In early 2007, he was among 28 House Republicans who wrote Bush urging him to reconsider his plan to send more than 21,000 additional combat troops to Iraq. But ultimately he stuck with the president, voting against a Democratic resolution disapproving of the plan, then against a House war supplemental funding bill that set timelines for troop withdrawal — legislation Bush vowed to veto.

Bartlett has long held a seat on the Armed Services Committee, and is the top-ranking member of the Seapower and Expeditionary Forces Subcommittee. Earlier in his career, he made headlines with his defense initiatives. He fought a 1994 Pentagon move to integrate men and women in housing and basic training, vowing to prevent a "powder puff" military. In 1996, he authored a provision to ban sale of "lascivious" materials on military bases — a measure the courts later found unconstitutional.

Bartlett goes his own way on issues that engage his flair for science. On the Science and Technology Committee, he is well-versed in the subject of global energy resources. Unlike most in his party, he opposes drilling for oil in Alaska's Arctic National Wildlife Refuge, saying there is not enough oil there to help end the nation's dependence on foreign oil.

Bartlett believes in the theory of "peak oil" and says the world is nearing a point at which global demand for oil will exceed production, causing prices to skyrocket and a global depression. In 2005, he co-founded the Congressional Peak Oil Caucus, which highlights the need to conserve fossil fuels, invest in alternative energy and prepare for an energy crisis. He practices what he preaches, driving a Toyota Prius hybrid car the 50 miles from his home in Frederick, Md., to Washington, D.C., each day.

Bartlett in 2005 was one of 31 Republicans to vote against the final version of an energy policy bill that provided incentives for greater production of oil, gas, coal and nuclear power and a reduction in regulation of the electric power industry. Later that year, Bartlett at first voted against a bill to encourage new and expanded oil refineries after the energy supply disruptions from Hurricane Katrina. But after extreme pressure from the GOP leadership when the bill was failing on the floor, Bartlett voted yes.

Bartlett was born on his grandfather's farm in Kentucky. His father, who worked as a tenant farmer in western Pennsylvania during the Depression, refused to take any assistance from the government during those hard times — promoting Bartlett's own devotion to self-reliance. He intended to become a minister but instead pursued an education in physiology at the University of Maryland, earning a master's degree and a doctorate in physiology.

He taught in California and Washington, D.C., and did research for the National Institutes of Health and the Navy's School of Aviation Medicine, where his mechanical skill led him into engineering. He holds 20 patents, including for components found in breathing equipment used by pilots, astronauts and rescue workers. Bartlett was honored in 1999 for his lifetime achievements by the American Institute of Aeronautics and Astronautics.

In 1961, Bartlett moved to a dairy farm in Frederick County, which he operated while working at the Johns Hopkins Applied Physics Laboratory in Howard County. He later entered the home building business.

He made an unsuccessful House bid in 1982 but returned a decade later. He narrowly won a three-way GOP primary in 1992 and expected to again face conservative Democrat Beverly B. Byron, a seven-term incumbent, who had heavily defeated him in 1982. But Byron was upset in the primary by former state delegate Thomas H. Hattery, whom Bartlett then beat by 8 percentage points. His re-elections have been easy.

KEY VOTES

2006

- No Stop broadband companies from favoring select Internet traffic
- Yes Affirm U.S. commitment to war in Iraq and reject setting a withdrawal date for troops
- Yes Repeal requirement for bilingual ballots at the polls
- Yes Permit U.S. sale of civilian nuclear technology to India
- Yes Build a 700-mile fence on the U.S.-Mexico border to curb illegal crossings
- Yes Permit warrantless wiretaps of suspected terrorists

2005

- Yes Intervene in the life-support case of Terri Schiavo
- No Lift President Bush's restrictions on stem cell research funding
- Yes Prohibit FBI access to library and bookstore records
- Yes Approve free-trade pact with five Central American countries
- No Pass energy policy overhaul favored by President Bush emphasizing domestic oil and gas production
- Yes End mandatory preservation of habitat of endangered animal and plant species
- Yes Ban torture of prisoners in U.S. custody

CQ VOTE STUDIES

	PARTY UNITY		PRESIDENTIAL SUPPORT	
	Support	Oppose	Support	Oppose
2006	85%	15%	77%	23%
2005	89%	11%	64%	36%
2004	93%	7%	76%	24%
2003	92%	8%	89%	11%
2002	94%	6%	79%	21%

INTEREST GROUPS

	AFL-CIO	ADA	CCUS	ACU
2006	14%	25%	80%	84%
2005	14%	5%	85%	84%
2004	20%	10%	90%	92%
2003	20%	20%	90%	88%
2002	22%	10%	80%	96%

MARYLAND 6

North and west – Frederick, Hagerstown

The 6th reaches across the northern tier of the state from Western Maryland to the Susquehanna River. It takes in all of Garrett, Allegany, Washington, Frederick and Carroll counties, as well as large portions of Baltimore and Harford counties and a small, exurban corner of Montgomery County. The 6th has a rural tradition and a conservative bent that benefits the GOP.

Frederick and Carroll counties are growing rapidly and thriving economically, as new residents escaping urban and inner suburban areas are moving in and commuting to Baltimore and Washington, D.C. BP Solar will spend $70 million to expand its Frederick facility — the largest integrated solar manufacturing plant in the nation. Unlike Frederick County, which has military, government, education and manufacturing industries, Carroll is still mainly agricultural.

The three western counties are less populous and remain solidly conservative. Although the demise of the old-line manufacturing industry in the last decade has harmed much of the Appalachian Mountain area, Washington County, with its strong manufacturing base, still prospers. Hagerstown, the largest city in the county, serves as a junction of several highways, acting as a hub between the Appalachians and the highly populated Mid-Atlantic region. Nestled in the mountains, Allegany County is slightly more than two hours from Baltimore, Washington or Pittsburgh. Allegany and Garrett counties struggle and have become dependent on tourism as companies close their operations here.

The 6th also includes northern portions of Baltimore and Harford counties, where Republicans and conservative Democrats reign. The 6th gave George W. Bush his highest vote share (65 percent) of any Maryland district in the 2004 presidential election.

MAJOR INDUSTRY
Manufacturing, technology, agriculture, tourism

MILITARY BASES
Fort Detrick (Army), 1,050 military, 6,380 civilian (2007)

CITIES
Frederick, 52,767; Hagerstown, 36,687; Eldersburg (unincorporated), 27,741; Cumberland, 21,518; Westminster, 16,731

NOTABLE
Camp David, the president's retreat, is located in Frederick County.

Rep. Elijah E. Cummings (D)

CAPITOL OFFICE
225-4741
www.house.gov/cummings
2235 Rayburn 20515-2007; fax 225-3178

COMMITTEES
Armed Services
Oversight & Government Reform
Transportation & Infrastructure
(Coast Guard & Maritime Transportation - chairman)
Joint Economic

RESIDENCE
Baltimore

BORN
Jan. 18, 1951, Baltimore, Md.

RELIGION
Baptist

FAMILY
Divorced; three children

EDUCATION
Howard U., B.A. 1973 (political science); U. of Maryland, J.D. 1976

CAREER
Lawyer

POLITICAL HIGHLIGHTS
Md. House, 1983-96 (Speaker pro tempore, 1995)

ELECTION RESULTS

2006 GENERAL		
Elijah E. Cummings (D)	158,830	98.1%
write-ins	3,147	1.9%
2006 PRIMARY		
Elijah E. Cummings (D)		unopposed
2004 GENERAL		
Elijah E. Cummings (D)	179,189	73.4%
Tony Salazar (R)	60,102	24.6%
Virginia T. Rodino (GREEN)	4,727	1.9%

PREVIOUS WINNING PERCENTAGES
2002 (74%); 2000 (87%); 1998 (86%); 1996 (83%); 1996 Special Election (81%)

Elected April 1996; 6th full term

The son of South Carolina sharecroppers, Cummings is one of the major voices in Congress on issues affecting the underclass. A liberal with no affection for the Bush administration, he nonetheless has worked effectively with conservatives to address such problems as steroids in baseball and methamphetamine addiction.

Cummings and Mark Souder, a conservative from Indiana and his colleague on the Oversight and Government Reform Committee, share a strong interest in combating drug abuse. When Republicans controlled the House, Souder chaired the panel's subcommittee on crime and drug policy, and Cummings was the senior Democrat. Cummings traveled with Souder to Ohio, Kentucky and Indiana to study the problem of methamphetamine labs. Cummings is one of only a handful of black Democrats to take an interest in the issue, which unlike the crack epidemic of the 1980s, has sprung up in small towns and rural areas, not just the inner city. He also joined Souder in making steroid use in sports a marquee issue in the 109th Congress (2005-06), saying he was particularly concerned about the increased use of steroids among high schoolers.

A former Congressional Black Caucus chairman, Cummings took a lead role in the response to the administration's handling of the Hurricane Katrina disaster, which disproportionately affected African-Americans in New Orleans. Cummings pressed President Bush to increase relief funds immediately after the hurricane and pushed for more money to rebuild the city, telling MSNBC, "If we can rebuild Baghdad, damnit, we can rebuild New Orleans and the Gulf Coast." But in the hurricane aftermath, Cummings said the country needed to confront the issue of poverty as well as race. "This is not so much a black-white issue. This is a green issue," he said.

Cummings opposes the war in Iraq, and in 2005 sided with Pennsylvania Democrat John P. Murtha and signed on to his resolution to redeploy U.S. forces at the earliest possible date. It was Murtha's skepticism about U.S. progress in the war that marked a turning point in congressional support. However, in the contest for majority leader in the 110th Congress (2007-08), Cummings backed fellow Maryland Democrat Steny H. Hoyer over Murtha for the No. 2 leadership post. He gave one of the nominating speeches for Hoyer at the closed Democratic Caucus elections.

From his seat on the Transportation and Infrastructure Committee, Cummings has been active in efforts to improve the government-run passenger train system, Amtrak. He chairs the Coast Guard and Maritime Transportation Subcommittee in the 110th Congress.

After keeping a fairly low profile during his first three terms, Cummings served a two-year stint as chairman of the Black Caucus in the 108th Congress (2003-04). He became an outspoken critic of the president on issues ranging from health care and taxes to foreign policy and Iraq. He described Bush's education plan, passed with bipartisan support in 2001 but never fully funded, as "pious declarations about 'leaving no child behind.' "

Cummings then led the Black Caucus in 2003 in protesting Bush's decision to renominate federal District Judge Charles W. Pickering Sr. to the 5th Circuit Court of Appeals after the Democratically controlled Senate Judiciary Committee had rejected the nomination in 2002.

Cummings also accused Bush in 2003 of refusing to open a dialogue with the all-Democratic Black Caucus, saying the president declined invitations for more than two years. When Bush did meet with the group in early 2005,

Cummings said, "I don't think anything changed other than we had a very cordial meeting." When Bush met with the group again early in 2007, Cummings said, "The meeting did not exceed my expectations, but I was pleased to have a dialogue with him regarding the concerns of my constituents."

On a district level, Cummings fights for more federal assistance to combat violent crime, improve education and health care, and stimulate economic development. In 2002, he won expanded federal support for a nursing program at Coppin State College in Baltimore. In recent years, he got more than $12 million set aside for Baltimore's light-rail project and $2.4 million for drug treatment and combating drug use in the city.

Cummings has been active in trying to improve relations among diverse neighborhoods in the Baltimore area, particularly between the black and Jewish communities. The Elijah Cummings Youth Program in Israel, launched in 1998, takes a dozen non-Jewish students from the 7th District to Israel for four weeks each summer.

He shares a friendship with Maryland Republican Rep. Wayne T. Gilchrest, whose nearby Eastern Shore district, rural and majority white, is a sharp contrast to his own black, urban Baltimore district. The two arranged joint "fact-finding" tours of each other's turf in 2006.

Born in Baltimore, Cummings was one of seven children of working-class parents who had migrated from the South. He recalls a childhood in which "we did not have many opportunities. . . . We did not play on grass. We played on asphalt." But he was set on a productive course by "two very strong parents," who scrimped and saved to buy their own home in a city neighborhood that was integrating.

He graduated Phi Beta Kappa from Howard University, where he was also student government president. He says his mother was hesitant about attending his graduation ceremony because she did not want to embarrass her son in front of "all those sophisticated people" at Howard, but Cummings told her he would be honored to have her there.

He went on to get a law degree from the University of Maryland, and six years later was elected to the Maryland House. In 13 years there, he rose to the chamber's second-ranking position, at the time the highest Maryland office ever held by an African-American. In 1996, he outpaced 26 other Democrats and five Republicans to replace Democrat Kweisi Mfume who resigned his House seat early to become president of the NAACP. Since then, Cummings has won re-election overwhelmingly. In 2004, he and Rep. James E. Clyburn of South Carolina were co-chairmen of African-American issues for Massachusetts Sen. John Kerry's presidential campaign.

KEY VOTES

2006

No Stop broadband companies from favoring select Internet traffic
No Affirm U.S. commitment to war in Iraq and reject setting a withdrawal date for troops
No Repeal requirement for bilingual ballots at the polls
No Permit U.S. sale of civilian nuclear technology to India
No Build a 700-mile fence on the U.S.-Mexico border to curb illegal crossings
No Permit warrantless wiretaps of suspected terrorists

2005

Yes Intervene in the life-support case of Terri Schiavo
Yes Lift President Bush's restrictions on stem cell research funding
Yes Prohibit FBI access to library and bookstore records
No Approve free-trade pact with five Central American countries
No Pass energy policy overhaul favored by President Bush emphasizing domestic oil and gas production
No End mandatory preservation of habitat of endangered animal and plant species
Yes Ban torture of prisoners in U.S. custody

CQ VOTE STUDIES

	PARTY UNITY		PRESIDENTIAL SUPPORT	
	Support	Oppose	Support	Oppose
2006	96%	4%	23%	77%
2005	97%	3%	17%	83%
2004	98%	2%	21%	79%
2003	97%	3%	14%	86%
2002	95%	5%	25%	75%

INTEREST GROUPS

	AFL-CIO	ADA	CCUS	ACU
2006	100%	100%	33%	8%
2005	93%	100%	41%	4%
2004	100%	100%	30%	0%
2003	100%	90%	25%	18%
2002	100%	95%	45%	0%

MARYLAND 7
Downtown Baltimore; part of Columbia

The 7th takes in both the largely poor neighborhoods of West Baltimore and much of downtown, with the bustling retail center of the Inner Harbor. The district then follows the black migration west to include Baltimore County's middle-class southwestern suburbs and the bulk of Howard County, including the western portion of Columbia, a liberal-leaning planned community between Baltimore and Washington, D.C.

Efforts to improve Baltimore's poor neighborhoods have been slow, and urban problems, such as crime, drug abuse, teen pregnancy and unemployment, have prompted many of the city's middle-class residents to head to the suburbs. But the picture within the city is not all bleak. Many of Baltimore's most identifiable landmarks and businesses are in the 7th, and there are middle-class black communities along Liberty Heights Avenue in West Baltimore.

The 7th takes in the gentrified Mount Vernon area, home of the Walters Art Museum and the Peabody Institute, which is affiliated with Johns Hopkins University and is one of the nation's major academies for professionally trained musicians. Farther north are Johns Hopkins University and the Baltimore Museum of Art. West of the downtown hub, the old retail section around Lexington Market and the 1st Mariner Arena still survives. Just southwest of the city, the University of Maryland, Baltimore County campus and its adjacent research area are attracting technology firms. West of Baltimore County are sprawling suburbs in racially diverse and mainly wealthy, well-educated Howard County.

The 7th's black majority, the most in the state at 59 percent, gives Democrats a distinct advantage in national and local contests throughout much of the district. But Republicans regularly win on the local level in the more rural parts of Howard County.

MAJOR INDUSTRY
Health care, manufacturing, technology

CITIES
Baltimore (pt.), 370,752; Ellicott City (unincorporated) (pt.), 56,231; Columbia (unincorporated) (pt.), 47,943; Catonsville (unincorporated), 39,820; Woodlawn (unincorporated), 36,079

NOTABLE
The 7th's portion of Baltimore is home to NAACP national headquarters, author Edgar Allan Poe's gravesite and the National Aquarium.

Rep. Chris Van Hollen (D)

CAPITOL OFFICE
225-5341
chris.vanhollen@mail.house.gov
www.house.gov/vanhollen
1707 Longworth 20515-2008; fax 225-0375

COMMITTEES
Oversight & Government Reform
Ways & Means

RESIDENCE
Kensington

BORN
Jan. 10, 1959, Karachi, Pakistan

RELIGION
Episcopalian

FAMILY
Wife, Katherine Wilkens Van Hollen; three children

EDUCATION
Swarthmore College, B.A. 1983 (philosophy); Harvard U., M.P.P. 1985; Georgetown U., J.D. 1990

CAREER
Lawyer; gubernatorial aide; congressional aide

POLITICAL HIGHLIGHTS
Md. House, 1991-95; Md. Senate, 1995-2003

ELECTION RESULTS

2006 GENERAL		
Chris Van Hollen (D)	168,872	76.5%
Jeffrey M. Stein (R)	48,324	21.9%
Gerard P. Giblin (GREEN)	3,298	1.5%
2006 PRIMARY		
Chris Van Hollen (D)	73,544	91.3%
Deborah A. Vollmer (D)	6,989	8.7%
2004 GENERAL		
Chris Van Hollen (D)	215,129	74.8%
Chuck Floyd (R)	71,989	25.0%

PREVIOUS WINNING PERCENTAGES
2002 (52%)

Elected 2002; 3rd term

Van Hollen is moving up in the ranks of House Democrats, but his ambitions appear to be aimed at the other side of the Capitol. He nearly left the House in 2006 to run for an open Senate seat and could well do so in 2010 if veteran Democrat Barbara A. Mikulski should decide to retire.

Well-educated and well-traveled, Van Hollen is a good match for his district, a swath of demographically elite suburbs just outside Washington, D.C. He has concentrated on education issues, while maintaining a personal interest in foreign policy, and is capable of searing analysis in the latter arena. His critique in 2003 of the Bush administration's handling of the war in Iraq received national attention.

In the 110th Congress (2007-08), Democratic leaders gave Van Hollen two plum assignments: a seat on the Ways and Means Committee and the chairmanship of the Democratic Congressional Campaign Committee, the party's political arm in the House.

Those posts were rewards for his efforts leading up to the successful 2006 elections in which the Democrats picked up 31 seats in the House and gained control of the chamber. Van Hollen was in charge of the DCCC's 10-member candidate recruitment team, a responsibility that contributed to his decision to forgo a bid to succeed retiring Democratic Sen. Paul S. Sarbanes. He and Debbie Wasserman-Schultz of Florida were also named co-chairmen of a "Red to Blue" drive to direct extra resources to Democratic challengers considered strong prospects to oust GOP incumbents.

Van Hollen's top domestic goal is improving public schools, which has appeal in the generally affluent, white-collar area he represents. Many of his constituents work for the federal government, its contractors or lobbyists; others are engaged in biomedical research, technology and other professions. Education is a priority for all of them.

To take the Ways and Means post, Van Hollen had to give up seats on the Judiciary and Education committees. On the latter panel, he had pressed for increased education funding, including for President Bush's signature No Child Left Behind Act, which set tough new testing standards for public schools. He also sought to give mandatory status to federal aid for special-needs students in order to boost it to the 40 percent level envisioned under the Individuals with Disabilities Education Act. He continued that effort in the 110th Congress.

Van Hollen continues to serve on the Oversight and Government Reform Committee, where he looks out for the interests of the numerous federal employees in his district. He teams up with other local lawmakers to press for parity between military personnel and civilian workers when Congress sets annual cost-of-living adjustments. In his first year in Congress, he took GOP leaders by surprise and won House adoption of an amendment to the annual Transportation-Treasury spending bill that blocked funding to streamline the transfer of government jobs to private contractors. (His amendment was weakened in the final bill.) He won a similar amendment two years later, only to see it dropped later as a result of a Bush veto threat.

The views of most House newcomers don't usually draw much attention, but Van Hollen's 2003 critique of Bush's Iraq policy proved an exception. Van Hollen knew something about the troubled nation; in the late 1980s, as a young aide to the Senate Foreign Relations Committee, he had traveled to the border between Iraq and Turkey to interview rebel ethnic Kurds about Saddam Hussein's use of chemical weapons against them. The report he and a colleague produced resulted in an ultimately unsuccessful attempt in Congress to impose economic sanctions against Iraq.

In speeches on the House floor and at the University of Maryland, Van Hollen said the United States' unilateral invasion of Iraq had squandered international sympathy for the United States after the Sept. 11 terrorist attacks, and that the Iraq War would not result in the spread of democracy in the Middle East. "It is just as easy to imagine a scenario where difficulties in Iraq fuel resentment of occupying U.S. troops and inflame the region against us," he said in widely quoted remarks.

Van Hollen is a liberal on most big social issues, favoring abortion rights and restrictions on the availability of guns. He fought in vain to stop a bill shielding gun dealers and manufacturers from lawsuits by gun crime victims and another measure exempting gun sale statistics from public disclosure under the Freedom of Information Act. Six of the 10 people killed by snipers in random attacks in the Washington area in 2002 lived in his district.

The son of a Foreign Service officer, Van Hollen was born in Pakistan and lived in Turkey, India and Sri Lanka, where his father was ambassador. His mother was an expert on Russia. After receiving a graduate degree in public policy and national security studies from Harvard's Kennedy School of Government, he joined the staff of Maryland Sen. Charles McC. Mathias Jr., a Republican moderate. When Mathias retired in 1986, Van Hollen went to work for the Foreign Relations Committee as an arms control and NATO specialist.

He won election to the Maryland House in 1990, serving four years there and eight in the state Senate. He successfully championed a state law mandating trigger locks on guns, two cigarette tax increases opposed by the tobacco lobby and a big boost in funding for Montgomery County schools. He also led a drive to block drilling for gas in the Chesapeake Bay.

A promotion to Congress seemed out of reach, however, as liberal Republican Constance A. Morella regularly won re-election with crossover Democratic votes. But redistricting after the 2000 census changed matters. Minority neighborhoods in Prince George's County, which abuts Montgomery, were added to bolster Democratic registration, and suddenly the district looked better for Van Hollen.

First, he had to survive a four-way primary, narrowly edging state Rep. Mark K. Shriver, a nephew of President John F. Kennedy. He and Morella then waged one of the costliest and most watched contests of the 2002 election. Each spent about $3 million. Van Hollen eked out a 4 percentage point win. In both 2004 and 2006, he got about three-fourths of the vote.

KEY VOTES

2006

Yes Stop broadband companies from favoring select Internet traffic
No Affirm U.S. commitment to war in Iraq and reject setting a withdrawal date for troops
No Repeal requirement for bilingual ballots at the polls
Yes Permit U.S. sale of civilian nuclear technology to India
No Build a 700-mile fence on the U.S.-Mexico border to curb illegal crossings
No Permit warrantless wiretaps of suspected terrorists

2005

No Intervene in the life-support case of Terri Schiavo
Yes Lift President Bush's restrictions on stem cell research funding
Yes Prohibit FBI access to library and bookstore records
No Approve free-trade pact with five Central American countries
No Pass energy policy overhaul favored by President Bush emphasizing domestic oil and gas production
No End mandatory preservation of habitat of endangered animal and plant species
Yes Ban torture of prisoners in U.S. custody

CQ VOTE STUDIES

	PARTY UNITY		PRESIDENTIAL SUPPORT	
	Support	Oppose	Support	Oppose
2006	95%	5%	30%	70%
2005	99%	1%	15%	85%
2004	96%	4%	35%	65%
2003	97%	3%	22%	78%

INTEREST GROUPS

	AFL-CIO	ADA	CCUS	ACU
2006	93%	90%	40%	4%
2005	93%	100%	37%	0%
2004	100%	100%	38%	4%
2003	87%	95%	33%	16%

MARYLAND 8

Part of Montgomery County – Bethesda, Gaithersburg, Rockville

The 8th contains wealthy Montgomery County suburbs northwest of Washington, D.C., such as Bethesda, Chevy Chase and Potomac, as well as less-affluent suburbs in eastern Montgomery and western Prince George's counties. It also includes the Interstate 270 technology corridor, a hotbed for high-technology and biotechnology companies that runs through Rockville and Gaithersburg. In the western part of the district, officials struggle to preserve an agricultural heritage.

Government dominates the 8th, where federal agencies, such as the National Institutes of Health, abound and where federal employees who work in Washington reside. County and state government also provide jobs in Rockville, the Montgomery County seat. The large contingent of highly educated professionals supports a thriving economy that is bolstered by a wide array of big-name business interests, including Lockheed Martin and Marriott.

The district has a strong Democratic lean, helped by liberal Takoma Park and heavily black and Hispanic neighborhoods in western Prince George's County. The 8th has the highest percentage of Asians (11 percent) and Hispanics (14 percent) of any Maryland district, and the support voters here gave Democratic Senate candidate Benjamin L. Cardin in 2006 — 70 percent of the vote — was the second-highest in the state, behind only one of Maryland's two black-majority districts.

MAJOR INDUSTRY

Government, technology, service, retail

MILITARY BASES

National Naval Medical Center, 2,672 military, 1,868 civilian; National Geospatial-Intelligence Agency, 45 military, 1,455 civilian; Naval Surface Warfare Center, Carderock Division, 3 military, 1,340 civilian (2007)

CITIES

Wheaton-Glenmont (unincorporated), 57,694; Bethesda (unincorporated), 55,277; Gaithersburg, 52,613; Rockville, 47,388

NOTABLE

Glen Echo Park has a working Dentzel Carousel — in the menagerie style with handcrafted horses, rabbits and other animals — that turns to the music of an original Wurlitzer band organ, one of only 11 that still exist.

MASSACHUSETTS

Gov. Deval Patrick (D)

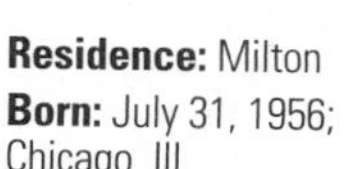

Pronounced: DUH-vahl
First elected: 2006
Length of term: 4 years
Term expires: 1/11
Salary: $135,000
Phone: (617) 725-4005

Residence: Milton
Born: July 31, 1956; Chicago, Ill.
Religion: Presbyterian
Family: Wife, Diane Patrick; two children
Education: Harvard U., A.B. 1978 (English & American literature), J.D. 1982
Career: Lawyer; beverage company executive
Political highlights: Assistant attorney general, Civil Rights Division, 1994-1997

Election results:

2006 GENERAL		
Deval Patrick (D)	1,234,984	55.6%
Kerry Healey (R)	784,342	35.3%
Christy Mihos (I)	154,628	7.0%
Grace Ross (GREEN)	43,193	1.9%

Lt. Gov. Timothy P. Murray (D)

First elected: 2006
Length of term: 4 years
Term expires: 1/11
Salary: $120,000
Phone: (617) 725-4005

LEGISLATURE

General Court: Usually year-round, but meeting time varies

Senate: 40 members, 2-year terms
2007 ratios: 34 D, 5 R, 1 vacancy; 27 men, 12 women
Salary: $58,237
Phone: (617) 722-1276

House: 160 members, 2-year terms
2007 ratios: 140 D, 19 R, 1 vacancy; 122 men, 37 women
Salary: $58,237
Phone: (617) 722-2356

TERM LIMITS

Governor: 2 terms
Senate: No
House: No

URBAN STATISTICS

CITY	POPULATION
Boston	589,141
Worcester	172,648
Springfield	152,082
Lowell	105,167
Cambridge	101,355

REGISTERED VOTERS

Unenrolled	50%
Democrat	37%
Republican	13%

POPULATION

2006 population (est.)	6,437,193
2000 population	6,349,097
1990 population	6,016,425
Percent change (1990-2000)	+5.5%
Rank among states (2006)	13
Median age	36.5
Born in state	66.1%
Foreign born	12.2%
Violent crime rate	476/100,000
Poverty level	9.3%
Federal workers	53,161
Military	23,516

ELECTIONS

STATE ELECTION OFFICIAL
(617) 727-2828
DEMOCRATIC PARTY
(617) 472-0637
REPUBLICAN PARTY
(617) 523-5005

MISCELLANEOUS

Web: www.mass.gov
Capital: Boston

U.S. CONGRESS

Senate: 2 Democrats
House: 10 Democrats

2000 Census Statistics by District

DIST.	2004 VOTE FOR PRESIDENT BUSH	KERRY	WHITE	BLACK	ASIAN	HISP	MEDIAN INCOME	WHITE COLLAR	BLUE COLLAR	SERVICE INDUSTRY	OVER 64	UNDER 18	COLLEGE EDUCATION	RURAL	SQ. MILES
1	35%	63%	89%	2%	2%	6%	$42,570	60%	24%	16%	14%	24%	25%	31%	3,101
2	40	59	82	5	1	9	$44,386	61	24	15	14	26	23	15	922
3	40	59	86	3	3	6	$50,223	66	21	14	13	25	31	7	581
4	34	65	88	2	3	3	$53,169	68	20	13	14	24	37	12	732
5	41	57	80	2	5	12	$56,217	67	21	12	11	27	34	7	566
6	41	58	90	2	2	4	$57,826	70	18	13	14	24	35	5	480
7	33	66	84	3	6	5	$56,110	73	14	13	16	21	40	0	170
8	16	82	49	22	8	16	$39,300	71	13	17	9	18	40	0	41
9	38	61	79	8	4	5	$55,407	69	17	14	14	24	34	2	313
10	43	56	92	2	3	1	$51,928	67	18	15	17	23	34	8	934
STATE	37	62	82	5	4	7	$50,502	67	19	14	14	24	33	9	7,840
U.S.	50.7	48.3	69	12	4	13	$41,994	60	25	15	12	26	24	21	3,537,438

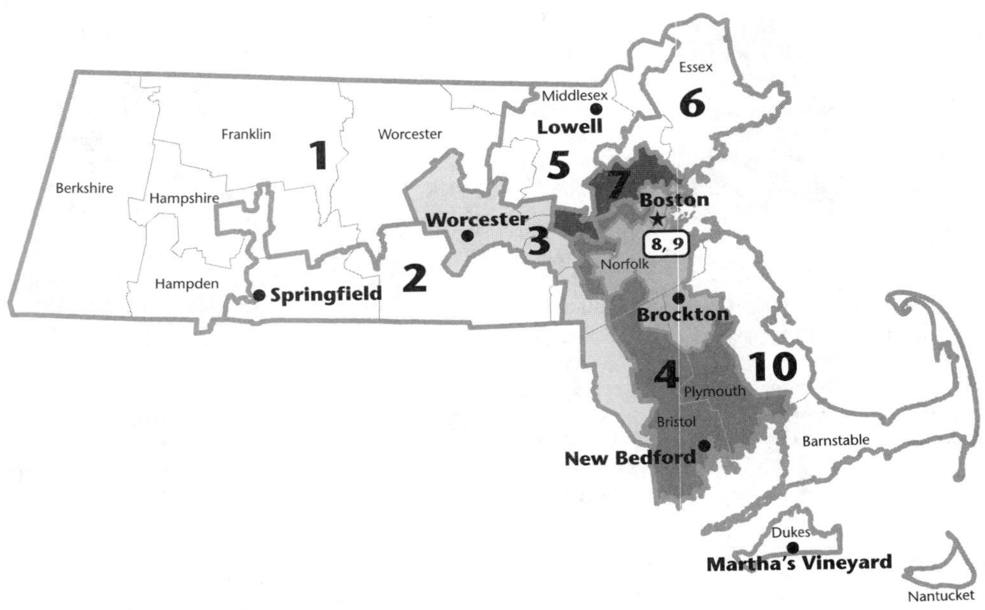

Essex
Middlesex
6
Lowell
Franklin
Worcester
1
5
Berkshire
Hampshire
7
Boston
Worcester
3
8, 9
Norfolk
Hampden
Springfield
2
Brockton
10
4
Plymouth
Bristol
Barnstable
New Bedford
Dukes
Martha's Vineyard
Nantucket

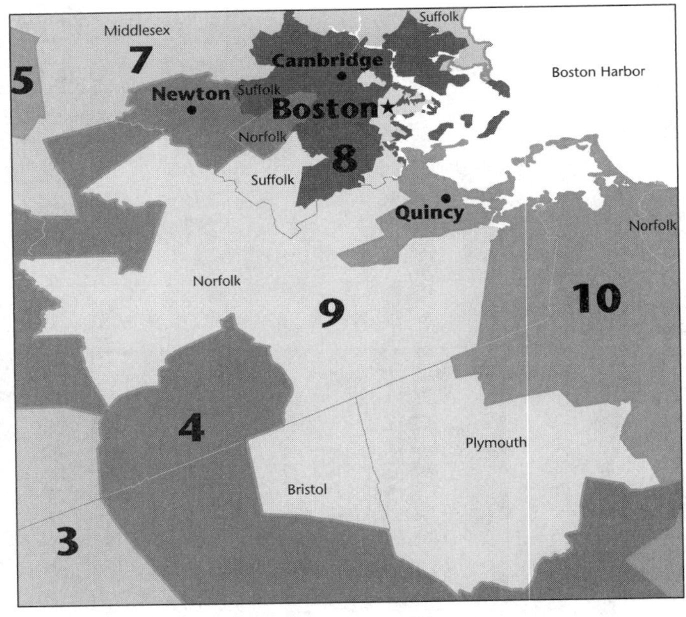

Suffolk
Middlesex
7
Boston Harbor
5
Cambridge
Newton
Suffolk
Boston
Norfolk
8
Suffolk
Quincy
Norfolk
Norfolk
10
9
4
Plymouth
Bristol
3

Sen. Edward M. Kennedy (D)

CAPITOL OFFICE
224-4543
kennedy.senate.gov
317 Russell 20510-2101; fax 224-2417

COMMITTEES
Armed Services
(Seapower - chairman)
Health, Education, Labor & Pensions - chairman
Judiciary
(Immigration, Refugees & Border Security - chairman)
Joint Economic

RESIDENCE
Hyannis Port

BORN
Feb. 22, 1932, Boston, Mass.

RELIGION
Roman Catholic

FAMILY
Wife, Victoria Reggie Kennedy; three children, two stepchildren

EDUCATION
Harvard U., A.B. 1956 (government); International Law School, The Hague (The Netherlands), attended 1958; U. of Virginia, LL.B. 1959

MILITARY SERVICE
Army, 1951-53

CAREER
Lawyer

POLITICAL HIGHLIGHTS
Suffolk County assistant district attorney, 1961-62; sought Democratic nomination for president, 1980

ELECTION RESULTS

2006 GENERAL		
Edward M. Kennedy (D)	1,500,738	69.3%
Kenneth G. Chase (R)	661,532	30.5%
2006 PRIMARY		
Edward M. Kennedy (D)		unopposed

PREVIOUS WINNING PERCENTAGES
2000 (73%); 1994 (58%); 1988 (65%); 1982 (61%); 1976 (69%); 1970 (62%); 1964 (74%); 1962 Special Election (55%)

Elected 1962; 8th full term

Kennedy is one of the giants of American politics over the past half-century. He towers as the Democrats' most recognizable spokesman, the Senate's leading liberal and the author of some of the landmark social legislation of modern times. After fellow Democrat Robert C. Byrd of West Virginia, he is second in seniority in the Senate. And he is the third-longest-serving senator ever.

Kennedy is the embodiment of his famous family's commitment to public service, and with more than four decades in the Congress, he is an anchor for his party's liberal base. Yet unlike many of his left-leaning colleagues, he is more interested in making laws than staying on message, and at the end of the day, will make a deal with Republicans to get a bill passed.

Now in his mid-70s, he has slowed physically and suffers chronic back pain. But few younger legislators can match his impact. With Democrats in control in the 110th Congress (2007-08), it is hard to identify a major domestic issue that Kennedy is not deeply involved in. By dint of his personal influence and his position as chairman of the Health, Education, Labor and Pensions (HELP) Committee, his policy portfolio is bursting.

Kennedy was the party's leader on a renewed effort in 2007 to pass an immigration bill creating a guest worker program for illegal aliens. He was at the fore of a quest to satisfy pent-up Democratic demands for a major increase in federal funding to help public schools meet their obligations under the No Child Left Behind law of 2001. He pushed for boosts in spending for Head Start early education programs for the poor and for Pell grants, the popular college aid program. He was behind a move to make it easier for unions to organize in workplaces, a proposal that gave conservatives fits.

"In the Senate, Ted Kennedy is a force of nature," said Sen. Gordon H. Smith, an Oregon Republican. "He's a bigger-than-life leader around this place, and I think he has tremendous gravitational pull for his party."

Although Kennedy is the ideological opposite of the senior Republican on the HELP panel, conservative Sen. Michael B. Enzi of Wyoming, the two are expected to continue the unusually productive bipartisan relationship they shared when the GOP controlled the Senate and Enzi chaired the panel.

Despite the presence of a Republican in the White House, Kennedy had a hand in shaping the education overhaul of 2001 and the creation of a Medicare prescription drug benefit in 2003. When the immigration debate heated up in 2006, he was in the thick of it, teaming with Republican John McCain of Arizona on a bill offering a path to citizenship for illegal immigrants who agree to pay fines and back taxes. "What's at stake is not just our security but our humanity as well, and we can't set that aside," Kennedy said.

He was a leader of the fruitless Democratic effort to block President Bush's Supreme Court nominations. He opposed John G. Roberts Jr. as chief justice, declaring, "There is ample evidence in John Roberts' record to indicate that he would turn the clock back on this country's great march of progress toward equal opportunity for all." He also sought to derail Samuel A. Alito Jr. for associate justice, but with a strategy that did not show him at his persuasive best. When he criticized Alito's involvement decades earlier in a Princeton alumni group that opposed the admission of women and other affirmative action positions, conservatives publicized Kennedy's alumni membership in the Owl Club, an exclusive all-male club at Harvard. Kennedy dropped his membership.

In 2006, Kennedy published "America Back on Track," in which he attempted to reset the national agenda to focus on guaranteed health care for every American, expanded civil rights, and more educational opportunities. On Iraq, Kennedy wrote that the administration "wrongly used preventive war for a regime change in Iraq, and it did so essentially unilaterally." His brother, President John F. Kennedy, he noted, had resisted pressure to launch a first strike against Cuba during the 1962 missile crisis.

From his desk at the rear of the Senate chamber, he can startle the somnolent with his thunderous roar, his face reddening and his voice needing no microphone. Republicans like to use him as a metaphor for the left, labeling Democrats at election time as "Ted Kennedy liberals." Behind the scenes, though, some of them nurture productive and friendly relationships with Kennedy, in particular conservative Utah Republican Orrin G. Hatch. Kennedy also has an appreciation for the iron law of the Senate: Little can be accomplished without the 60 votes needed to overcome filibusters, the endless speeches aimed at delaying and ultimately killing a bill.

Despite his national profile, Kennedy tends to the parochial needs of Massachusetts like a freshman congressman. In 2005, he was influential in stopping the planned closure of Otis Air Force Base on Cape Cod. And he led a lengthy battle to block a proposed wind farm off the Cape, which would put 130 wind turbines in Nantucket Sound, where some of the country's wealthiest families, including the Kennedys, have homes.

Kennedy's public image has long been defined by family triumph, tragedy and scandal. He once had a penchant for reckless behavior, now apparently outgrown. There was the 1969 auto accident at Chappaquiddick in which the passenger in his car, Mary Jo Kopechne, drowned; the long period of pub-crawling in the 1980s; the 1991 revelry with his son, Democratic Rep. Patrick J. Kennedy of Rhode Island, and nephew William Kennedy Smith at a Florida nightclub that ended with a woman accusing Smith of rape. Smith was acquitted after a highly publicized trial. Kennedy's personal life stabilized after 1992, when he married for the second time, to Washington attorney Victoria Reggie.

Doubts about his judgment fueled Republican hopes of defeating him in 1994, when GOP venture capitalist Mitt Romney — now former Massachusetts governor and 2008 presidential candidate — tapped his personal fortune to mount a campaign tagging the senator as worn, used goods. Kennedy fought back, touring the state delivering federal checks and painting Romney as inexperienced. Bucking the year's GOP tide, Kennedy won with 58 percent of the vote. In 2000, he won his seventh full term with 73 percent against another wealthy businessman, Jack E. Robinson III.

The youngest of nine children of Rose Fitzgerald, a congressman's daughter, and Joseph P. Kennedy, an ambassador to Britain and the first chairman of the Securities and Exchange Commission, Kennedy was elected in 1962, at age 30, to fill the remaining two years of President Kennedy's Senate term. The president had arranged for family friend Benjamin A. Smith to be appointed until his youngest brother was old enough under the Constitution to serve.

After John F. Kennedy was assassinated in 1963 and Sen. Robert F. Kennedy of New York was assassinated while seeking the Democratic presidential nomination in 1968, Kennedy felt intense pressure to take up his brothers' fallen banner. But when he challenged President Jimmy Carter in 1980, questions about Chappaquiddick exploded anew, and Kennedy failed to articulate a clear reason why he wanted to be president. For many, the most memorable moment of his campaign came at its finale, in his concession speech at the Democratic National Convention. "For all those whose cares have been our concern," Kennedy intoned, "the work goes on, the cause endures, the hope still lives, and the dream shall never die."

KEY VOTES

2006

- No Confirm Samuel A. Alito Jr. to the Supreme Court
- No Allow consideration of a bill to establish a $140 billion trust fund to compensate victims of asbestos exposure
- No Extend tax cuts for two years at a cost of $70 billion over five years
- Yes Overhaul immigration policy with border security, enforcement and guest worker program
- No Allow consideration of a bill to permanently repeal the estate tax
- Yes Urge President Bush to begin troop withdrawals from Iraq in 2006
- Yes Lift President Bush's restrictions on stem cell research funding
- No Authorize military tribunals for suspected terrorists

2005

- No Curb class action lawsuits by shifting them from state to federal courts
- No Allow confirmation vote on Priscilla R. Owen to the U.S. Court of Appeals for the 5th Circuit
- No Oppose mandatory emissions limits and block recognition of global warming as a threat
- No Approve free-trade pact with five Central American countries
- No Pass energy policy overhaul favored by President Bush emphasizing domestic oil and gas production
- No Shield gunmakers from lawsuits when their products are used in crimes
- Yes Ban torture of prisoners in U.S. custody
- No Renew 16 provisions of the Patriot Act
- No Allow final vote on opening the Arctic National Wildlife Refuge to oil and gas exploration

CQ VOTE STUDIES

	PARTY UNITY		PRESIDENTIAL SUPPORT	
	Support	Oppose	Support	Oppose
2006	99%	1%	48%	52%
2005	100%	0%	26%	74%
2004	98%	2%	59%	41%
2003	97%	3%	47%	53%
2002	97%	3%	64%	36%
2001	97%	3%	66%	34%
2000	98%	2%	94%	6%
1999	97%	3%	93%	7%
1998	100%	0%	96%	4%
1997	97%	3%	88%	12%

INTEREST GROUPS

	AFL-CIO	ADA	CCUS	ACU
2006	87%	100%	36%	0%
2005	93%	95%	28%	0%
2004	100%	100%	31%	0%
2003	100%	95%	26%	10%
2002	100%	100%	29%	0%
2001	100%	100%	38%	4%
2000	86%	90%	40%	12%
1999	88%	95%	47%	4%
1998	100%	95%	47%	0%
1997	100%	100%	40%	4%

Sen. John Kerry (D)

CAPITOL OFFICE
224-2742
kerry.senate.gov
304 Russell 20510-2102; fax 224-8525

COMMITTEES
Commerce, Science & Transportation
(Science, Technology & Innovation - chairman)
Finance
(Social Security, Pensions & Family Policy - chairman)
Foreign Relations
(Near Eastern & South & Central Asian Affairs - chairman)
Small Business & Entrepreneurship - chairman

RESIDENCE
Boston

BORN
Dec. 11, 1943, Denver, Colo.

RELIGION
Roman Catholic

FAMILY
Wife, Teresa Heinz Kerry; two children, three stepchildren

EDUCATION
Yale U., B.A. 1966 (political science); Boston College, J.D. 1976

MILITARY SERVICE
Navy, 1966-70

CAREER
Lawyer; county prosecutor

POLITICAL HIGHLIGHTS
Democratic nominee for U.S. House, 1972; lieutenant governor, 1983-85; Democratic nominee for president, 2004

ELECTION RESULTS

2002 GENERAL		
John Kerry (D)	1,605,976	80.0%
Michael E. Cloud (LIBERT)	369,807	18.4%
Randall Forsberg - write-in	24,898	1.2%
2002 PRIMARY		
John Kerry (D)		unopposed

PREVIOUS WINNING PERCENTAGES
1996 (52%); 1990 (57%); 1984 (55%)

Elected 1984; 4th term

He doesn't have the platform of a presidential campaign anymore, or even an official leadership position, but Kerry has returned to the Senate with a changed perspective and a single-minded focus: extricating the United States from the war in Iraq.

Although he spent two years preparing for a second presidential bid in 2008, the voters had moved on. Among Democrats, two of his Senate colleagues, Hillary Rodham Clinton and Barack Obama, raced to the front of the early polls. By January 2007, Kerry was far behind, mired in the single digits. In a Senate floor speech Jan. 24, he announced that he would not run again for the White House but instead would concentrate on forcing an end to the war in Iraq. "It is time to put my energy to work as part of the majority in the Senate to do all I can to end this war and strengthen our security and our ability to fight the real war on terror," Kerry declared. He said he would seek a fifth Senate term in 2008, a race he is favored to win.

The administration, he says, has no credibility left on Iraq. "As someone who made the mistake of voting for the resolution that gave the president the authority to go to war, I feel the weight of a personal responsibility to act, to devote time and energy to the national dialogue in an effort to limit this war and bring our participation to a conclusion," he said in his floor speech.

A member of the Foreign Relations Committee, Kerry has taken more aggressive stands on Iraq since his presidential campaign. In the fall of 2005, he called for a withdrawal of 20,000 troops, and a few months later declared that all U.S. troops should be brought home if Iraq failed to have an operational government by May 15, 2006. In 2006, he offered an amendment, defeated 13-86, calling for a troop withdrawal by mid-2007. By March 2007, more Senate Democrats were ready to follow his lead. The Senate passed a war funding bill that required a troop withdrawal to begin within 120 days, with a goal of completing the redeployment within a year.

Kerry also spoke out more forcefully in defense of his opposition to the Vietnam War, a stance that provoked vicious attacks during his presidential race. In a 2006 speech in Boston, Kerry said he was right to criticize that war and that Americans who oppose the Iraq War also should speak out. "It is profoundly wrong to think that fighting for your country overseas and fighting for your country's ideals at home are contradictory or even separate duties," he said. "They are, in fact, two sides of the very same patriotic coin."

The time he spent crisscrossing the country in his 2004 run for the White House opened his eyes to the reality of problems that affect people's lives, he says, and to the silliness of the partisan battles and point-scoring maneuvers that keep the government from solving them.

"It's a very, very different perspective," Kerry says. "It opens up a broader view of the country, other states' views, and a greater urgency about people's problems. It just brings a clarity and a focus that wasn't there before." Kerry says his presidential campaign taught him about the many financial anxieties families deal with today. "Wages are going down. The average worker is getting squeezed. Tuition is going up. Benefits are being squeezed. Pensions are dropping," he said.

Now, when Kerry talks about bills on the Senate floor, he loads his speeches with anecdotes about people he met on the trail. During debate in 2006 on a measure to help small businesses provide health insurance to their workers, Kerry told of a woman who kept working during her chemotherapy for breast cancer because she was afraid she would lose her insurance if she took time off.

Kerry has had a few legislative successes since the campaign. In 2005, three provisions of his "Military Family Bill of Rights" became law. They allow widows and children to stay in military housing for a year after a service member is killed, increase death benefits to $500,000 and give all members of the National Guard and the reserves health care through a special program for military personnel, even those not mobilized.

With Democrats in charge, he has a better chance to pass his top priorities — a measure to provide health care to all children and energy independence legislation. His "Kids Come First" bill, which would expand Medicaid and the State Children's Health Insurance Program, stalled in the Finance Committee while Republicans were in control, because he would pay for it by rolling back some of the Bush tax cuts.

Kerry's actions are not always welcomed by the Democratic leadership. When he and his Massachusetts colleague, Sen. Edward M. Kennedy, announced a 2006 filibuster of Supreme Court nominee Samuel A. Alito Jr., whom Kerry called a "far-right ideologue," they undermined Minority Leader Harry Reid, who opposed the filibuster. Ultimately, it failed, attracting only 25 votes, far short of the 41 votes they needed.

Democrats have embraced him more warmly for his exuberant fundraising. Kerry has used his e-mail list to help raise money for Democratic candidates throughout the country. But even among members of his party, Kerry has always struggled with an aloof, blue-blood image. Largely because of the inherited wealth of his wife, Teresa Heinz Kerry, he is one of the 50 richest members of Congress, with a net worth estimated by the Los Angeles Times to be somewhere between $900 million and $3.2 billion.

In his long Senate career, Kerry has been known more for his investigative skills and foreign relations initiatives than for his legislative efforts. As chairman of the Senate Select Committee on POW/MIA Affairs in the 102nd Congress (1991-92), Kerry joined forces with Republican John McCain of Arizona, a fellow Vietnam veteran, on a report that found no evidence that missing soldiers in Vietnam were still alive and paved the way for President Bill Clinton later to normalize diplomatic relations.

A former prosecutor, Kerry gained early prominence with his inquiry into the Bank of Credit and Commerce International scandal in the late 1980s. He was widely credited with spurring a federal investigation of BCCI officials, including Democratic power broker Clark Clifford.

After rising to the rank of lieutenant in the Navy, Kerry became one of the nation's most prominent demonstrators against the Vietnam War when he returned to the United States. He got front-page coverage in 1971 when he asked the Senate Foreign Relations Committee, "How do you ask a man to be the last man to die for a mistake?" He tried to exploit the publicity by moving to Lowell and running for an open House seat in 1972. He won the primary, but lost in the fall to Republican Paul Cronin.

After his defeat, he went to law school and then worked as an assistant district attorney in Middlesex County. In 1982, he was elected lieutenant governor in a challenge to the Democratic establishment. Two years later, he beat Democratic Rep. James M. Shannon for the nomination to replace retiring Sen. Paul E. Tsongas. He won the general election over conservative businessman Raymond Shamie with 55 percent of the vote.

In 1996, he faced his toughest challenge yet from William F. Weld, then the state's popular GOP governor. On the campaign trail, Weld's affable, down-to-earth style contrasted well with Kerry's stiff persona. But Kerry's late spending and solid performance in a series of debates carried him to victory by 7 percentage points. In 2002, Republicans did not even bother to run a candidate against him.

KEY VOTES

2006

- No Confirm Samuel A. Alito Jr. to the Supreme Court
- No Allow consideration of a bill to establish a $140 billion trust fund to compensate victims of asbestos exposure
- No Extend tax cuts for two years at a cost of $70 billion over five years
- Yes Overhaul immigration policy with border security, enforcement and guest worker program
- No Allow consideration of a bill to permanently repeal the estate tax
- Yes Urge President Bush to begin troop withdrawals from Iraq in 2006
- Yes Lift President Bush's restrictions on stem cell research funding
- No Authorize military tribunals for suspected terrorists

2005

- No Curb class action lawsuits by shifting them from state to federal courts
- No Allow confirmation vote on Priscilla R. Owen to the U.S. Court of Appeals for the 5th Circuit
- No Oppose mandatory emissions limits and block recognition of global warming as a threat
- No Approve free-trade pact with five Central American countries
- No Pass energy policy overhaul favored by President Bush emphasizing domestic oil and gas production
- No Shield gunmakers from lawsuits when their products are used in crimes
- Yes Ban torture of prisoners in U.S. custody
- No Renew 16 provisions of the Patriot Act
- No Allow final vote on opening the Arctic National Wildlife Refuge to oil and gas exploration

CQ VOTE STUDIES

	PARTY UNITY		PRESIDENTIAL SUPPORT	
	Support	Oppose	Support	Oppose
2006	95%	5%	51%	49%
2005	97%	3%	34%	66%
2004	100%	0%	50%	50%
2003	100%	0%	30%	70%
2002	92%	8%	72%	28%
2001	98%	2%	65%	35%
2000	96%	4%	97%	3%
1999	95%	5%	93%	7%
1998	95%	5%	94%	6%
1997	97%	3%	87%	13%

INTEREST GROUPS

	AFL-CIO	ADA	CCUS	ACU
2006	87%	95%	55%	12%
2005	93%	100%	33%	8%
2004	100%	25%	--%	0%
2003	100%	85%	0%	13%
2002	92%	85%	55%	20%
2001	100%	95%	38%	4%
2000	75%	90%	53%	12%
1999	78%	95%	53%	0%
1998	100%	95%	50%	4%
1997	71%	95%	50%	0%

Rep. John W. Olver (D)

CAPITOL OFFICE
225-5335
www.house.gov/olver
1111 Longworth 20515-2101; fax 226-1224

COMMITTEES
Appropriations
(Transportation-HUD - chairman)

RESIDENCE
Amherst

BORN
Sept. 3, 1936, Honesdale, Pa.

RELIGION
Unspecified

FAMILY
Wife, Rose Olver; one child

EDUCATION
Rensselaer Polytechnic Institute, B.S. 1955 (chemistry); Tufts U., M.S. 1956 (chemistry); Massachusetts Institute of Technology, Ph.D. 1961 (chemistry)

CAREER
Professor

POLITICAL HIGHLIGHTS
Mass. House, 1969-73; Mass. Senate, 1973-91

ELECTION RESULTS

2006 GENERAL		
John W. Olver (D)	158,057	76.4%
William H. Szych (X)	48,574	23.5%
2006 PRIMARY		
John W. Olver (D)		unopposed
2004 GENERAL		
John W. Olver (D)		unopposed

PREVIOUS WINNING PERCENTAGES
2002 (68%); 2000 (68%); 1998 (72%); 1996 (53%); 1994 (99%); 1992 (52%); 1991 Special Election (50%)

Elected June 1991; 8th full term

Olver embodies the direct, no-nonsense, hardworking attributes associated with many New Englanders. With eight full terms in the House, he continues to promote certain bedrock principles — balance the budget, protect the environment, work for peace, take the train.

A solitary man, Olver enjoys hiking and rock climbing, and perusing the details of appropriations bills. The Lowell Sun noted in 2006 that the analytical Amherst Democrat "detests attending speeches by visiting dignitaries — calling one that he avoided recently a 'foolish show.' He skips presidential events and dislikes fundraisers."

He is the only member of the Massachusetts House delegation on the Appropriations Committee, where he now chairs the Transportation-HUD Subcommittee. Olver may not be flashy but he knows how the money flows. He has used his Appropriations seat to help his district and state get a share of the federal pie. In the past four years, he has directed money home for bike paths, buses, wildlife refuges and numerous transit and highway improvements. He has helped the University of Massachusetts at Amherst receive more than $4 million for research projects, including $1.2 million in the 2006 spending bill for a microbiological energy harvesting project, which is using microorganisms to convert organic wastes into electricity.

Now that he holds the gavel of an Appropriations subcommittee, he may have to take a broader view of spending issues. He has said certain spending has to be restrained because of the mounting budget deficit and the war in Iraq. "There's no easy pot of money, because we're already running a deficit of $400 billion a year," Olver told the Sun in November 2006. "We cannot continue to build that debt up."

Olver wants to increase federal funding for Amtrak, the national passenger rail system, and for public housing. A committed protector of Amtrak, he has consistently opposed the Bush administration's plan to end subsidies to the railroad absent congressional passage of a restructuring plan. Olver says it is the government's responsibility to solve society's problems and to play a part in economic development. "Better roads, bridges, airports, commuter rail systems and other public transit options are needed to connect people to educational centers, health and social services, and, perhaps most importantly, good jobs," he said after learning he would chair the Transportation spending panel.

A member of the Progressive Caucus, the most liberal faction of House Democrats, Olver has opposed the war in Iraq from the start, voting against the war authorization in 2002. He joined with fellow Massachusetts Democrat Jim McGovern and two other Democratic appropriators — Barbara Lee of California and José E. Serrano of New York — in sponsoring a measure requiring the withdrawal of U.S. troops within six months and barring any funding for the war thereafter. After President Bush announced early in 2007 his plan to send more than 21,000 additional combat troops to Iraq, Olver said, "This strategy is four years too late and at least 100,000 troops too few. If the president carries out this escalation, I believe he will be remembered for the deaths of many more American soldiers and Iraqi civilians."

Olver and McGovern were arrested during a 2006 protest at the Sudanese Embassy over the civil war in Darfur and charged with disorderly conduct. "They are slaughtering people, families, entire villages," Olver said. "What we are doing today is adding weight" to growing international demands for intervention in the troubled west Sudanese region.

A former chemistry professor, Olver long has said the nation must do more to reduce greenhouse gas emissions and to increase automobile fuel economy to help control climate change. Olver and Maryland Republican Wayne T. Gilchrest formed the House's Climate Change Caucus, whose members work to develop bipartisan agreements on climate issues. In early 2007, they reintroduced a measure to set caps on the amount of carbon dioxide emitted from the burning of fossil fuels and create a market-based system that rewards companies for developing new technologies needed to combat climate change.

Olver may have a quiet and low-key personality, but he enjoys a challenge. He is an avid outdoorsman who still spends much of his free time hiking, rock climbing, wind surfing and cross-country skiing. In 2005, when he was in his late 60s, he took an 11-day hiking trek in the Arctic carrying everything he needed in a backpack.

Olver grew up on a farm located in the Pocono area of Pennsylvania. His family ran the farm and a boardinghouse as well. In the summer, young families would take the train from Philadelphia or New York and stay with them at their house for a week or two. The Olver house fronted on a lake and had its own beach. Olver's father ran the farm, which had 20 or 25 milking cows, and his mother tended the boardinghouse.

Olver attended a three-room schoolhouse, graduating at age 15. He finished college when he was 18 and earned a doctorate from the Massachusetts Institute of Technology at age 24. He taught chemistry at the University of Massachusetts' Amherst campus for eight years before making his first foray into elective politics by winning a state House race in 1968.

Four years later, he bucked the national GOP trend, unseating an incumbent Republican state senator. He stayed in the state Senate until 1991, when 17-term Silvio O. Conte, the liberal 1st District Republican, died in February. Olver won a 10-way Democratic primary with surprising ease, then collected endorsements from his defeated rivals as well as from union members, environmentalists, women's groups and abortion rights supporters. He won the special election by fewer than 2,000 votes, marking the first time since 1892 that the area had sent a Democrat to the House.

After that, he alternated close races in 1992 and 1996 (when he defeated Jane Swift, who would later serve as governor) with re-election romps in 1994 and 1998. In the 2000 election, Olver won by 39 percentage points. His territory left largely intact by redistricting, he won by 35 points in 2002 and was unopposed in 2004. With no Republican opponent again in 2006, Olver took 76 percent of the vote against an independent.

KEY VOTES

2006

Yes Stop broadband companies from favoring select Internet traffic

No Affirm U.S. commitment to war in Iraq and reject setting a withdrawal date for troops

No Repeal requirement for bilingual ballots at the polls

Yes Permit U.S. sale of civilian nuclear technology to India

No Build a 700-mile fence on the U.S.-Mexico border to curb illegal crossings

No Permit warrantless wiretaps of suspected terrorists

2005

No Intervene in the life-support case of Terri Schiavo

Yes Lift President Bush's restrictions on stem cell research funding

Yes Prohibit FBI access to library and bookstore records

No Approve free-trade pact with five Central American countries

No Pass energy policy overhaul favored by President Bush emphasizing domestic oil and gas production

No End mandatory preservation of habitat of endangered animal and plant species

Yes Ban torture of prisoners in U.S. custody

CQ VOTE STUDIES

	PARTY UNITY		PRESIDENTIAL SUPPORT	
	Support	Oppose	Support	Oppose
2006	96%	4%	15%	85%
2005	98%	2%	15%	85%
2004	98%	2%	21%	79%
2003	99%	1%	15%	85%
2002	99%	1%	27%	73%

INTEREST GROUPS

	AFL-CIO	ADA	CCUS	ACU
2006	100%	95%	40%	4%
2005	93%	95%	33%	0%
2004	100%	100%	19%	0%
2003	100%	100%	23%	16%
2002	100%	95%	37%	0%

MASSACHUSETTS 1

West – Pittsfield, Leominster, Westfield, Amherst

The oranges of autumn, the whites of winter and the greens of spring and summer attract vacationers to the 1st. With three distinct geographical regions — the Berkshires, the Connecticut River Valley and the larger commuter towns to the northeast — the district embodies three vastly different population centers that rarely interact with each other.

Tourist areas include the kind of serene New England towns depicted in films, books and Norman Rockwell paintings. Tanglewood, the summer home of the Boston Symphony Orchestra, also attracts music fans to its outdoor theater in Lenox. The Yankee Candle Company, one of the largest manufacturers of scented candles and a popular tourist attraction, is based in South Deerfield.

The region suffered closures and heavy downsizing of its once-dominant textile mills and plastics factories during a decades-long industry recession, with Pittsfield and Fitchburg suffering the most. Pittsfield's population continues to shrink 20 years after General Electric's departure and the attendant job loss. A strong retail industry and an influx of Boston commuters has spurred growth in Leominster, a western outgrowth of the Boston suburbs that sits at the junction of two major highways at the eastern edge of the district.

Once a Republican stronghold, the 1st still has some GOP-supporting, sparsely populated rural areas along the Connecticut border, but these last toeholds of Rockefeller Republicanism are overwhelmed by large numbers of Democratic union voters in the northeast and university liberals around Amherst, where the state's flagship university is located. John Kerry took 63 percent of the 2004 presidential vote here, and five of Kerry's top 10 cities or towns are in the district.

MAJOR INDUSTRY

Paper, tourism, higher education, plastics

CITIES

Pittsfield, 45,793; Leominster, 41,303; Westfield, 40,072; Holyoke, 39,838; Fitchburg, 39,102; West Springfield (unincorporated), 27,899

NOTABLE

The oldest house in Berkshire County, the Ashley House, was bought in 1735 by Colonel John Ashley for his wife and named on the National Register of Historic Places in 1975.

Rep. Richard E. Neal (D)

CAPITOL OFFICE
225-5601
www.house.gov/neal
2208 Rayburn 20515-2102; fax 225-8112

COMMITTEES
Ways & Means
(Select Revenue Measures - chairman)

RESIDENCE
Springfield

BORN
Feb. 14, 1949, Worcester, Mass.

RELIGION
Roman Catholic

FAMILY
Wife, Maureen Neal; four children

EDUCATION
American International College, B.A. 1972 (political science); U. of Hartford, M.P.A. 1976

CAREER
College lecturer; teacher; mayoral aide

POLITICAL HIGHLIGHTS
Springfield City Council, 1978-84 (president, 1979); mayor of Springfield, 1984-89

ELECTION RESULTS

2006 GENERAL		
Richard E. Neal (D)	164,939	98.7%
write-ins	2,254	1.3%
2006 PRIMARY		
Richard E. Neal (D)		unopposed
2004 GENERAL		
Richard E. Neal (D)	217,682	98.7%
write-ins	2,802	1.3%

PREVIOUS WINNING PERCENTAGES
2002 (99%); 2000 (99%); 1998 (98%); 1996 (72%); 1994 (59%); 1992 (53%); 1990 (100%); 1988 (80%)

Elected 1988; 10th term

Neal has been pushing for years to overhaul the alternative minimum tax, which is forcing millions more middle-income Americans to shell out extra money to the federal government each year. As chairman of the Ways and Means Select Revenue Measures Subcommittee, he is now in a position to do something about the problem.

In opposing President Bush's tax cuts of 2001 and 2003, Neal repeatedly argued — presciently as it turns out — that lower regular income tax rates would drive millions more people into the alternative minimum tax. The AMT was originally designed to ensure that the very richest people would have to pay some tax despite all the credits and deductions they might claim. Because it was not indexed to inflation, however, it now reaches many middle-class taxpayers, especially those who live in high-tax states or have big families. Democrats and Republicans alike have called for a revamp or repeal of the AMT, but either would cost billions of dollars in lost revenue. That poses a huge challenge for Neal and Ways and Means Chairman Charles B. Rangel, the New York Democrat who is his ally in the effort. "In a perfect world, I would permanently revoke the AMT and overhaul the tax code," Neal says. But he knows he does not live in a perfect world.

Another priority for Neal in the 110th Congress (2007-08) is closing tax loopholes, especially those involving corporations. He introduced legislation aimed at barring reduced-rate treatment of dividends from certain companies that avoid paying either U.S. or foreign income taxes, and has taken aim at corporations that establish offshore headquarters to avoid U.S. taxation. But Neal also backs fair tax treatment for U.S. companies that operate abroad, sponsoring legislation to make permanent a tax incentive that assists U.S. financial services companies with subsidiaries abroad.

Neal is likely to be a key player in defending Social Security. He vehemently opposes Bush's proposal to allow wage earners to divert a portion of their payroll taxes to create individual investment accounts within Social Security. He sees personal accounts as a threat to the guaranteed benefit system millions of Americans depend upon. In 2005, when Bush was pushing his plan aggressively, Neal switched from the Ways and Means Trade Subcommittee to the Social Security panel because of his personal experience. Neal and his two younger sisters received Social Security survivor benefits after the death of their parents. He compares the benefits to jumping on a trampoline: "You hit it and you bounce back up."

The 2nd District residents of Springfield and its surrounding areas tend to be blue-collar and Irish Catholic and are not as liberal as other voters in the state. Neal opposes federal funding of abortions and voted in favor of the 2003 ban on what opponents call "partial birth" abortion. He also voted in 2005 for a constitutional amendment allowing Congress to outlaw desecration of the U.S. flag. Yet in both 2004 and 2006, he voted against amending the Constitution to prohibit same-sex marriage.

Neal has been a leader of congressional efforts to keep the United States involved in the search for peace in Northern Ireland. His paternal grandparents are from Ireland, while his maternal grandparents are from Northern Ireland; both sets were Irish nationalists. Neal is chairman of the congressional Friends of Ireland, and he has met on several occasions with leaders of both sides. He favors a power-sharing arrangement between factions that achieves a "parity of esteem."

Neal voted against the initial resolution supporting the invasion of Iraq and believes the "intelligence [supporting the invasion] was untrue." He also opposed Bush's call in 2006 for more troops, and wants a "more multilateral effort in the nation involving more Arab countries and soldiers."

Although Neal is a party loyalist, he drew some attention in 2001 when he appeared to be thwarting the effort of his Massachusetts colleague and Washington roommate, Martin T. Meehan, to bring campaign finance legislation to the floor. When GOP leaders refused to bring up the bill, Meehan and his Republican cosponsor, Christopher Shays of Connecticut, sought to force the bill to a vote by getting a majority of members to sign a discharge petition. Neal initially declined to sign, arguing that legislative chaos would result if such grass-roots campaigns were to succeed on a regular basis. Still, he promised Meehan that if he gained 217 signatures, he would provide the pivotal 218th — which is what happened in early 2002.

What the golf course is for many businessmen and civic leaders, the basketball court is for Neal — a place to develop personal relationships that go beyond political interests and to cut a deal now and then while working up a healthy sweat. Neal spends plenty of time in the members-only House gymnasium and at the Springfield YMCA competing in what his staff describes as "spirited" full-court games. As a former high school player and the father of two sons good enough to play at the college level, Neal's passion for the game goes well beyond any sense of obligation he may feel as the representative of the city where basketball was invented.

Neal says he has always been fascinated by politics. He majored in political science in college, and later he was co-chairman of George McGovern's 1972 presidential campaign in western Massachusetts. After serving as an aide to Springfield Mayor William C. Sullivan, he won three elections to the city council. He also taught history and government at a high school and area colleges. In 1983, he won the first of three elections as Springfield mayor, drawing favorable notices for stimulating downtown rehabilitation.

In 1988, when Democrat Edward P. Boland announced his retirement after 36 years in the House, Neal was quick off the mark. He won the nomination unopposed and crushed a weak GOP foe. He faced a couple of stiff challenges in the early 1990s — especially in 1994 when anti-incumbent fever was running high and Neal was being chastised for 87 overdrafts at the now-defunct private bank for House members. But Republicans have not fielded a challenger since 1996.

Neal was among the Massachusetts Democrats mentioned as eyeing a Senate race when John Kerry became the party's 2004 presidential nominee, but Kerry held onto his seat after losing to Bush.

KEY VOTES

2006

Yes Stop broadband companies from favoring select Internet traffic

No Affirm U.S. commitment to war in Iraq and reject setting a withdrawal date for troops

No Repeal requirement for bilingual ballots at the polls

Yes Permit U.S. sale of civilian nuclear technology to India

No Build a 700-mile fence on the U.S.-Mexico border to curb illegal crossings

No Permit warrantless wiretaps of suspected terrorists

2005

? Intervene in the life-support case of Terri Schiavo

Yes Lift President Bush's restrictions on stem cell research funding

Yes Prohibit FBI access to library and bookstore records

No Approve free-trade pact with five Central American countries

No Pass energy policy overhaul favored by President Bush emphasizing domestic oil and gas production

No End mandatory preservation of habitat of endangered animal and plant species

Yes Ban torture of prisoners in U.S. custody

CQ VOTE STUDIES

	PARTY UNITY		PRESIDENTIAL SUPPORT	
	Support	Oppose	Support	Oppose
2006	96%	4%	18%	82%
2005	97%	3%	15%	85%
2004	98%	2%	24%	76%
2003	95%	5%	30%	70%
2002	96%	4%	28%	72%

INTEREST GROUPS

	AFL-CIO	ADA	CCUS	ACU
2006	100%	95%	36%	4%
2005	93%	85%	41%	0%
2004	100%	95%	33%	4%
2003	80%	95%	33%	24%
2002	88%	90%	37%	4%

MASSACHUSETTS 2

South central – Springfield, Chicopee, Northampton

The rolling hills and thick forests of the 2nd extend along the state's southern border from Springfield and Northampton in the west to Bellingham in the east. Springfield dwarfs all other communities in the 2nd; small, rural towns and intermittent farms fill out the rest of south-central Massachusetts.

The region's future rests with the insurance and health care industries — most notably Mass Mutual and Baystate Health System — which replaced some of Springfield's shrinking manufacturing base. New business parks are increasing commercial and industrial space. Service jobs and employment related to Chicopee's Westover Air Reserve Base are also important to the area's economy. The 2002 expansion of the Basketball Hall of Fame and the restoration of the MassMutual Center arena have brought more visitors to Springfield.

Hispanics once gravitated to Springfield's North End but are now more dispersed through the city. Most blacks, although significantly fewer in number than Hispanics, live near the city's center. These two populations consist of well over half of the city's total population, making Springfield the district's multicultural region.

Residents in and around Springfield, many of whom are blue-collar and Irish Catholic, vote Democratic and dominate the district's elections. Smith College, a large liberal arts college for women, produces a strongly liberal vote in Northampton. Despite this strong Democratic lean, some Republicans have been competitive, particularly among small-town and rural voters. In 2004, East Brookfield was George W. Bush's best city or town in Massachusetts, giving him 57 percent of its presidential vote.

MAJOR INDUSTRY

Insurance, health care, higher education, tourism

CITIES

Springfield, 152,082; Chicopee, 54,653; Northampton, 28,978

NOTABLE

Theodor Geisel, better known as Dr. Seuss, was born in Springfield, where the Dr. Seuss National Memorial Sculpture Garden now sits at the Springfield Museums.

Rep. Jim McGovern (D)

CAPITOL OFFICE
225-6101
www.house.gov/mcgovern
438 Cannon 20515-2103; fax 225-5759

COMMITTEES
Budget
Rules
(Rules & the Organization of the House - chairman)

RESIDENCE
Worcester

BORN
Nov. 20, 1959, Worcester, Mass.

RELIGION
Roman Catholic

FAMILY
Wife, Lisa McGovern; two children

EDUCATION
American U., B.A. 1981 (history), M.P.A. 1984

CAREER
Congressional aide; campaign aide

POLITICAL HIGHLIGHTS
Sought Democratic nomination for U.S. House, 1994

ELECTION RESULTS

2006 GENERAL		
Jim McGovern (D)	166,973	98.8%
write-ins	1,983	1.2%
2006 PRIMARY		
Jim McGovern (D)		unopposed
2004 GENERAL		
Jim McGovern (D)	192,036	70.5%
Ronald A. Crews (R)	80,197	29.4%

PREVIOUS WINNING PERCENTAGES
2002 (99%); 2000 (99%); 1998 (57%); 1996 (53%)

Elected 1996; 6th term

McGovern's career ambition is to hold the gavel of the House Rules Committee. He's the second-ranking Democrat on the panel, behind Louise M. Slaughter of New York, who became chairwoman in 2007. At 47, and in his sixth term in the House, he knows he's got a good chance to sit in that chair. Certainly, few members can match his knowledge of arcane House rules and procedures, and as a liberal Democrat he doesn't shy from partisan battles.

Before his 1996 election, McGovern spent nearly two decades on Capitol Hill, first as an intern and campaign aide to South Dakota senator and presidential candidate George McGovern (no relation), and later on the staff of Joe Moakley, the Rules Committee chairman for five and a half years and dean of the Massachusetts House delegation until his death in 2001. "McGovern taught me it was OK to be an idealist," he told The Boston Globe. "Moakley taught me how to get things done."

McGovern loves to talk about his days working for the colorful Moakley, an old-fashioned, back-slapping pol who mentored him in politics. During his first Democratic Caucus meeting after winning election, McGovern took a seat just a few feet away from the elder lawmaker, enjoying his moment in the sun and his ascension from staffer to congressman. As McGovern recalls, Moakley called him over and suggested McGovern fetch him a "bologna and cheese sandwich and a diet Coke." When Moakley died, McGovern moved quickly to get the vacancy on the Rules Committee, a powerful arm of the leadership that sets the parameters for floor debate.

He's proved to be an able bare-knuckles fighter in the tartly partisan debates of the committee. He had sharp words for the GOP leadership when it tried but ultimately failed to enact a series of rule changes in 2005, mostly to benefit the scandal-plagued Majority Leader Tom DeLay of Texas. One change would have voided any ethics complaint not acted on within 45 days, which McGovern charged would have allowed the Republican ethics committee chairman to kill complaints by letting the clock run on them. "This should be a place where honesty and integrity are the standard, not a place where the rules are changed merely to protect a powerful few from their own ethical shortcomings," McGovern said.

But like any other House member, McGovern — who also gained a seat on the Budget Committee in 2007 — tries to look out for his home district. He told The Boston Herald that during the 110th Congress (2007-08) he hoped to improve commuter rail service in his district, push for more funding for open space preservation and press for incentives for firms working on renewable energy and the environment.

He embraces multiple humanitarian causes, and is a cosponsor of the Torture Outsourcing Prevention Act, which would prohibit the United States from turning immigrants over to other countries where they are likely to be tortured. He is a critic of the administration's softened stance on U.S. use of land mines. He joined with North Carolina Republican Sen. Elizabeth Dole to promote an international school lunch program. It was a particularly apt congressional pairing, as the program's biggest boosters are George McGovern, a longtime ambassador to the World Food Program, and Dole's husband, former GOP Senate Majority Leader Bob Dole.

McGovern also has a keen interest in foreign affairs, particularly in Latin America. He has traveled to Cuba a number of times, and in 2002 was among the 17 Democrats and 17 Republicans to form the Cuba Working Group, which has pressed for elimination of the ban on travel to Cuba and restrictions on food sales to the island.

While he was a top aide to Moakley, McGovern was a key staff member on a 1990 House task force that looked into the murders the year before of six Jesuit priests and two women in El Salvador. Several of the Salvadoran military officers implicated in the case had graduated from the U.S. Army School of the Americas at Fort Benning, Ga. Since then, McGovern has tried to eliminate funding for the school, now renamed the Western Hemisphere Institute for Security Cooperation. He says the facility "continues to train military officers who harm and kill the innocent people of Latin America."

McGovern belongs to the Progressive Caucus, the most left-leaning faction of House Democrats. He is a vocal opponent of the Iraq War and favors the immediate withdrawal of U.S. troops. He wants to expand the Medicare program to give every American health insurance. He would like the federal government to do far more to fight poverty, regulate polluters and combat greenhouse gases blamed for global warming.

During his childhood in working-class Worcester — his father ran a liquor store and his mother taught dance — the McGoverns followed politics closely, especially where the Kennedy family was involved. When Sen. Robert F. Kennedy was assassinated in 1968, he said, "My father gathered us around the kitchen table and we wrote sympathy cards to Ethel."

He had his first brush with politics as a junior high school student in 1972, when he became involved in the campaign of presidential candidate McGovern. Later, as an American University student, he worked in McGovern's Senate office. In 1984, when the South Dakotan launched another presidential bid, Jim McGovern was his campaign manager in Massachusetts and made the nominating speech at the Democratic National Convention. The elder McGovern returned the favor in 1996, campaigning for him in his House race.

McGovern had made an unsuccessful bid in 1994 for the 3rd District seat, but in 1996 he upset two-term Republican Peter I. Blute, and he has won easily since. During the 2004 presidential campaign, McGovern actively campaigned for John Kerry while many of his colleagues were gearing up to run for Kerry's Senate seat. McGovern was returning a favor; Kerry went out of his way to appear at a campaign event for him when few gave him much chance of beating Blute.

McGovern has started a political trend at home. His former aide, Timothy Murray, the Worcester mayor, ran for lieutenant governor in 2006, and Ed Augustus, a one-time McGovern chief of staff, was elected to the state Senate in 2004, defeating Roberta Blute, the wife of the man McGovern unseated in 1996.

KEY VOTES

2006

- Yes Stop broadband companies from favoring select Internet traffic
- No Affirm U.S. commitment to war in Iraq and reject setting a withdrawal date for troops
- No Repeal requirement for bilingual ballots at the polls
- Yes Permit U.S. sale of civilian nuclear technology to India
- No Build a 700-mile fence on the U.S.-Mexico border to curb illegal crossings
- No Permit warrantless wiretaps of suspected terrorists

2005

- ? Intervene in the life-support case of Terri Schiavo
- Yes Lift President Bush's restrictions on stem cell research funding
- Yes Prohibit FBI access to library and bookstore records
- No Approve free-trade pact with five Central American countries
- No Pass energy policy overhaul favored by President Bush emphasizing domestic oil and gas production
- No End mandatory preservation of habitat of endangered animal and plant species
- Yes Ban torture of prisoners in U.S. custody

CQ VOTE STUDIES

	PARTY UNITY		PRESIDENTIAL SUPPORT	
	Support	Oppose	Support	Oppose
2006	98%	2%	23%	77%
2005	99%	1%	15%	85%
2004	98%	2%	21%	79%
2003	99%	1%	16%	84%
2002	99%	1%	22%	78%

INTEREST GROUPS

	AFL-CIO	ADA	CCUS	ACU
2006	100%	95%	40%	4%
2005	93%	100%	35%	0%
2004	93%	100%	38%	4%
2003	100%	100%	23%	12%
2002	100%	100%	30%	0%

MASSACHUSETTS 3

Central and south – Worcester, Attleboro, part of Fall River

The 3rd cuts a diagonal sliver from the mountains of Princeton to the fishing community of Fall River, winding its way from areas north and west of Boston almost to the Atlantic Ocean far south of the city.

Worcester, a working-class city, has a strong biotechnology presence. The city centralized its health care and research facilities into a medical center, spurring economic development and job growth. The city is the 3rd's population hub, and downtown revitalization and new projects are currently in the works. Despite previously slow population growth, Worcester's employment base is expected to grow in response to its economic expansion, with residents moving here partly due to housing costs that are more reasonable than in the Boston area. To the north and south, suburban communities contain residents who mostly commute to jobs in Boston or Providence, R.I., although Worcester's economic growth has lured some residents to work locally.

At the district's southern tip, Fall River (shared with the 4th District) has long been a bastion of white, blue-collar, ethnic Democrats. The city had one of the state's highest unemployment rates in the 1990s before increased employment lowered the figure to roughly 5 percent in 2000. Unemployment rates have risen this decade, however, and local government officials hope that business partnerships will attract new employers to Fall River.

Democratic dominance in Worcester and Fall River allows Democrats to overcome Republican support in the towns surrounding Worcester. George W. Bush failed to carry a single city or town in the 3rd in the 2000 presidential election, but managed to squeak out wins in Rutland and Wrentham with 50 percent of the vote in 2004.

MAJOR INDUSTRY

Biotechnology, health care, heavy manufacturing, retail

CITIES

Worcester, 172,648; Fall River (pt.), 53,704; Attleboro, 42,068

NOTABLE

The Worcester Art Museum, home to an internationally recognized collection of paintings, sculptures, decorative arts, textiles and photography, boasts the nation's largest collection of Antiochin mosaics.

Rep. Barney Frank (D)

CAPITOL OFFICE
225-5931
www.house.gov/frank
2252 Rayburn 20515-2104; fax 225-0182

COMMITTEES
Financial Services - chairman

RESIDENCE
Newton

BORN
March 31, 1940, Bayonne, N.J.

RELIGION
Jewish

FAMILY
Single

EDUCATION
Harvard U., A.B. 1962 (government), J.D. 1977

CAREER
Lawyer; mayoral and congressional aide

POLITICAL HIGHLIGHTS
Mass. House, 1973-81

ELECTION RESULTS

2006 GENERAL		
Barney Frank (D)	176,513	98.5%
write-ins	2,730	1.5%
2006 PRIMARY		
Barney Frank (D)		unopposed
2004 GENERAL		
Barney Frank (D)	219,260	77.7%
Charles A. Morse (I)	62,293	22.1%

PREVIOUS WINNING PERCENTAGES
2002 (98%); 2000 (75%); 1998 (98%); 1996 (72%); 1994 (100%); 1992 (68%); 1990 (66%); 1988 (70%); 1986 (89%); 1984 (74%); 1982 (60%); 1980 (52%)

Elected 1980; 14th term

Frank is a rarity in the House — a throwback liberal who will cut a deal with a conservative. He is widely acknowledged to be among the smartest members of the House. In a little more than a quarter-century in Congress, he has amassed an encyclopedic knowledge of public policy and parliamentary rules, which he employs with precision. One of the House's most adept debaters, he can also be one of the most abrasive.

Frank revels in catching Republicans off-guard with his biting sarcasm. He chides the GOP for dictating policy to the states at the same time it champions states' rights. He exploits rifts in the opposing party, once observing, "The right hand doesn't know what the far right hand is doing."

Frank is now chairman of the Financial Services Committee, where he is likely to promote legislation designed to protect investors and consumers from corporate excesses without sending the message that Democrats are anti-business. Frank has demonstrated a keen awareness of the distinction, but he has not been reluctant to criticize corporate America for its missteps. He has a financial pragmatism that is grounded in the knowledge that a hands-off approach is sometimes the best choice when dealing with the economy and financial markets. "It's important for us to show the financial community it has nothing to be afraid of from us," he says.

When fellow Democrats decry abuses by corporate America, Frank couches his criticisms of the private sector. One day, he is criticizing conservative efforts to strip away money for affordable housing in a mortgage regulation bill. The next, he's working in favor of legislation reducing the regulatory burden on banks. The willingness to balance the competing interests has gained Frank the loyalty of junior committee members and the respect of Republicans, and the panel is more bipartisan as a result.

But he has not held back his disapproval of the massive compensation packages granted to corporate executives that often include lavish perks and multimillion-dollar salaries. Early in 2007, Frank reintroduced legislation to allow shareholders to cast a non-binding vote on a company's executive pay plans. His measure builds on rules passed by the Securities and Exchange Commission in 2006 that require greater disclosure from companies about their compensation activities, especially deferred compensation such as retirement plans.

Under his leadership, Financial Services is likely to address data security and consumer privacy issues and legislation protecting borrowers from predatory lending practices. Frank would also like to roll back a handful of federal banking regulations that have pre-empted state laws considered more consumer-friendly than the federal rules.

On the issue closest to his heart — federal funding to combat homelessness — Frank has been the Democrats' most potent critic of President Bush's attempts to cut spending on rent assistance for low-income families. He steered a bill through the committee in early 2007 aimed at securing affordable housing for low-income residents displaced in 2005 by the Gulf Coast hurricanes. The bill would block demolition of damaged public housing in New Orleans until the government has a plan to replace it and would grant displaced public housing tenants an absolute right of return. For Frank, the bill was symbolic of a commitment to help the poor no matter what other priorities Congress has. "To put them at the bottom of the list and say . . . you get help only if we don't go to Mars is wrong," he said.

Frank will also want to roll back cuts, pushed by the White House, in affordable housing, Community Development Block Grant and other programs. "What we will do is get back in the business of federal housing construction," he said. He is also a defender of the giant government-backed mortgage financiers Fannie Mae and Freddie Mac, which help keep money for mortgages cheap and plentiful but have been assailed by critics for accounting troubles.

Frank has the distinction of being the first member of Congress in history to announce his homosexuality, and he does not shy away from allusions to his personal life during floor debates. He is on the front line opposing Republican-led attempts to ban same-sex marriage, and has been outspoken in a pitched political battle in Massachusetts, where conservatives want to put a proposed constitutional gay-marriage ban on the 2008 state ballot.

Frank's honesty about his homosexuality since he came out in 1987 helped him survive near political death three years later when the House reprimanded him after a male prostitute revealed he'd had an affair with Frank and had run his business out of the lawmaker's Washington apartment. Though the influential Boston Globe called on him to resign, Frank refused. And his mostly urban constituents took the scandal in stride: They gave him 66 percent of the vote that year and sent him back to Congress.

Frank grew up in Bayonne, N.J., the son of a truck stop operator on the New Jersey Turnpike. The Franks loved to discuss politics, and a decisive event for him was the murder of black teenager Emmett Till in 1955, when Frank was 15. All four of the Frank children went on to careers tied to government service. Frank's sister is Anne Lewis, a Democratic operative who is a longtime campaign adviser for New York Sen. Hillary Rodham Clinton.

Frank graduated from Harvard and considered choosing a life in academia. But then he went to work as an aide to Boston Mayor Kevin White in 1967, joining a team of other young, activist policy wonks. He was a natural, though outwardly he did not fit the establishment model. He was a Jewish kid with a New Jersey accent who was also gay, though he only shared that information with friends at the time. Still, he was elected to the Massachusetts House and stayed for eight years.

When Democratic Rep. Robert F. Drinan, a liberal Catholic priest, bowed to a papal prohibition on clergymen holding public office, Frank ran for his seat, winning in 1980 with 52 percent of the vote against a Republican who portrayed him as too liberal. His hardest re-election battle was his first, when Frank in 1982 ran against GOP Rep. Margaret M. Heckler. He won with 60 percent. His closest contest since was in 1990, following the prostitute scandal. He had no opposition in 2006.

KEY VOTES

2006

Yes Stop broadband companies from favoring select Internet traffic
No Affirm U.S. commitment to war in Iraq and reject setting a withdrawal date for troops
No Repeal requirement for bilingual ballots at the polls
Yes Permit U.S. sale of civilian nuclear technology to India
Yes Build a 700-mile fence on the U.S.-Mexico border to curb illegal crossings
No Permit warrantless wiretaps of suspected terrorists

2005

No Intervene in the life-support case of Terri Schiavo
Yes Lift President Bush's restrictions on stem cell research funding
Yes Prohibit FBI access to library and bookstore records
No Approve free-trade pact with five Central American countries
No Pass energy policy overhaul favored by President Bush emphasizing domestic oil and gas production
No End mandatory preservation of habitat of endangered animal and plant species
Yes Ban torture of prisoners in U.S. custody

CQ VOTE STUDIES

	PARTY UNITY		PRESIDENTIAL SUPPORT	
	Support	Oppose	Support	Oppose
2006	96%	4%	15%	85%
2005	96%	4%	15%	85%
2004	98%	2%	16%	84%
2003	98%	2%	16%	84%
2002	97%	3%	14%	86%

INTEREST GROUPS

	AFL-CIO	ADA	CCUS	ACU
2006	100%	95%	29%	12%
2005	93%	100%	33%	0%
2004	100%	100%	20%	4%
2003	100%	100%	23%	16%
2002	100%	100%	26%	8%

MASSACHUSETTS 4

New Bedford; Boston suburbs – Newton; Taunton; part of Fall River

Downtowns replete with 18th and 19th century town hall buildings dot the Yankee communities in the 4th, several of which have celebrated their 300th or 350th anniversaries. The district encompasses thickly settled Boston suburbs, rural cranberry bogs and urban New Bedford and Fall River (shared with the 3rd District).

The economic health of the 4th reflects a split between the northern and southern tiers of the district. The strong economies of the northern well-to-do towns and Boston suburbs have benefited from the Route 128 technology corridor, although moderate unemployment started to affect the area in the past decade. Today, the northern towns mostly consist of Boston commuters. The southern fishing and former textile mill communities, including Fall River and New Bedford, struggled to stave off double-digit unemployment as the textile industry declined and commercial fishermen faced sparse catches. Nevertheless, fishing remains an important industry and way of life for this section of the district. In the 4th's center, the cranberry bogs in Middleborough and biotechnology firms farther north provide a strong economic base.

The blue-collar, immigrant-laden southern section of the district gives the 4th a strong Democratic lean. New Bedford, which has one of the lowest median household incomes in the state, and Fall River are heavily Portuguese and vote solidly Democratic. So does the district's wealthiest community, Westport, located south of Fall River and west of New Bedford. The wealthy northwestern towns of Wellesley, Dover and Sherborn are more likely to support Republicans, but the well-to-do and densely populated Newton and Brookline opt for liberal Democrats.

MAJOR INDUSTRY

Fishing, cranberries, health care, textile manufacturing

CITIES

New Bedford, 93,768; Newton, 83,829; Brookline (unincorporated), 57,107; Taunton, 55,976; Fall River (pt.), 38,234; Wellesley (unincorporated), 26,613

NOTABLE

Ocean Spray, the first producer of cranberry juice drinks, is headquartered in Lakeville-Middleborough.

Rep. Martin T. Meehan (D)

CAPITOL OFFICE
225-3411
martin.meehan@mail.house.gov
www.house.gov/meehan
2229 Rayburn 20515-2105; fax 226-0771

COMMITTEES
Armed Services
(Oversight & Investigations - chairman)
Judiciary

RESIDENCE
Lowell

BORN
Dec. 30, 1956, Lowell, Mass.

RELIGION
Roman Catholic

FAMILY
Wife, Ellen Murphy; two children

EDUCATION
U. of Massachusetts, Lowell, B.S. 1978 (political science & education); Suffolk U., M.P.A. 1981, J.D. 1986

CAREER
County prosecutor; state securities investigator; state legislative aide; congressional aide

POLITICAL HIGHLIGHTS
No previous office

ELECTION RESULTS

2006 GENERAL		
Martin T. Meehan (D)	159,120	98.7%
write-ins	2,152	1.3%
2006 PRIMARY		
Martin T. Meehan (D)		unopposed
2004 GENERAL		
Martin T. Meehan (D)	179,652	67.0%
Thomas P. Tierney (R)	88,232	32.9%

PREVIOUS WINNING PERCENTAGES
2002 (60%); 2000 (98%); 1998 (71%); 1996 (99%); 1994 (70%); 1992 (52%)

Elected 1992; 8th term

Meehan, in "the most difficult professional decision of my life," decided early in 2007 to trade in his congressional pin for the cap and gown of academia. He accepted an offer to become chancellor of the University of Massachusetts at Lowell, citing a commitment to strengthening a public education system that had underpinned his successes in life.

His decision to start his new job on July 1, 2007, was announced the previous March. He is an alumnus of the school. Meehan said he also welcomed the chance to be home more often with his wife and two young sons. "Serving in Congress has its advantages, but being away from your family three to four nights a week is not one of them," he said.

His Washington, D.C., roommate, fellow Bay State Democrat Richard E. Neal, joked to the Boston Globe newspaper that he'd be glad to see Meehan go. Neal had been sleeping in the living room of their shared apartment, and planned to grab the lone bedroom, which Meehan had occupied because he had moved in first.

Meehan did not endorse a successor for his seat, and possible candidates began lining up immediately. Republican officials said they intended to put up a fight, noting that the 5th District does not typically lean as far in the Democrats' direction as most in Massachusetts. In 2004, 57 percent of the district's voters favored home-state Sen. John Kerry in his challenge to President Bush, compared with 62 percent of voters statewide.

Possible candidates on the Democratic side were Niki Tsongas, widow of former Sen. Paul E. Tsongas who once represented the House district; state Reps. James Miceli of Wilmington, James Eldridge of Acton and Barry Finegold of Andover; Lowell City Councilor Eileen Donoghue; Middlesex Sheriff James DiPaola; developer David O'Brien of Concord; and Middlesex District Attorney Chris Doherty.

Possible Republican contenders included former state Rep. Donna Cuomo of North Andover, Lawrence Mayor Michael Sullivan and businessman Charles McCarthy, the 2002 Republican nominee who took 34 percent and held Meehan to 60 percent — the incumbent's career-low for a reelection contest.

Meehan left his mark in Congress in the area of campaign finance. He spent much of his more than 14-year House career trying to reduce and regulate the flow of cash into national elections as one of his party's leading campaign finance reformers. To Meehan, money isn't the mother's milk of politics, it's the stuff poisoning the well of public policy.

Teaming with Christopher Shays, a Connecticut Republican, Meehan sponsored the House version of the 2002 campaign finance overhaul that was championed in the Senate by Republican John McCain of Arizona and Democrat Russ Feingold of Wisconsin. The law, enacted after a seven-year battle, banned unlimited corporate and labor union donations to political parties and restricted issue advertisements, in the first significant tightening of campaign rules in decades.

At the start of the 109th Congress (2005-06), the self-described "street kid from Lowell" was back on the case. Again joined by Shays, Meehan sued the Federal Election Commission, charging that it was too lax in enforcing the new law. A federal court agreed, and in early 2006 the FEC issued new rules to regulate online political advertising.

Meehan and his allies had less success with legislation to close a loophole in the law that allowed so-called 527 organizations (named after an applicable section of the tax code) to collect vast sums of unregulated money and spend it on political advertising. Democrats who had supported their 2002 legislation were hostile to reining in 527 groups such as MoveOn.org, which backs liberal candidates. The Republican-controlled House narrowly passed the bill in 2006, but it died in the Senate.

As the House was engulfed in influence-peddling scandals that led to the criminal convictions of lobbyist Jack Abramoff and two prominent lawmakers, Meehan and Shays tried to force creation of an independent Office of Public Integrity to investigate ethics complaints, but their proposal was shot down in committee.

He was among the minority of House Democrats voting in October 2002 to authorize Bush to use force against Iraq. But as early as January 2005, Meehan called for an "exit strategy" and a cut in U.S. troops in Iraq, issues that got traction early in 2007. Senior Massachusetts Sen. Edward M. Kennedy and Rep. John P. Murtha of Pennsylvania, a decorated Marine veteran, later joined the call for troop withdrawals.

Meehan was usually within the mainstream of his party, but with some quirks. Like an earlier 5th District congressman and former presidential candidate, Democrat Paul E. Tsongas, he was a social policy liberal and a budget cutter. He often was rated among the most fiscally responsible members of Congress by the moderate Concord Coalition.

Meehan had harbored ambitions for higher office. In the 2004 election cycle, as Massachusetts Sen. John Kerry was running for president, Meehan raised more than $4 million for a possible campaign to replace Kerry. He kept most of it, to the ire of liberal activist groups and some party fundraisers who wanted him to share the wealth to help Democrats regain control of the House and Senate in 2006.

The fast-talking Meehan is the son of working-class Irish Americans; his father was a typesetter at a newspaper in Lowell. Meehan was inspired to pursue politics by President John F. Kennedy in the 1960s, and named his first son Robert Francis after one of the president's younger brothers, who was U.S. attorney general.

In Meehan's first election to the House in 1992, he ousted Rep. Chester G. Atkins in the Democratic primary by branding him an unsavory political insider. In November, Meehan took 52 percent of the vote over former GOP Rep. Paul W. Cronin in a district that at the time had a slight Republican edge. On his way to winning his House seat, Meehan pledged to serve only four terms in Congress, but reneged on the pledge in 2000. In 2006, Republicans opted not to field a challenger.

KEY VOTES

2006

- Yes Stop broadband companies from favoring select Internet traffic
- No Affirm U.S. commitment to war in Iraq and reject setting a withdrawal date for troops
- No Repeal requirement for bilingual ballots at the polls
- Yes Permit U.S. sale of civilian nuclear technology to India
- No Build a 700-mile fence on the U.S.-Mexico border to curb illegal crossings
- ? Permit warrantless wiretaps of suspected terrorists

2005

- ? Intervene in the life-support case of Terri Schiavo
- Yes Lift President Bush's restrictions on stem cell research funding
- Yes Prohibit FBI access to library and bookstore records
- No Approve free-trade pact with five Central American countries
- No Pass energy policy overhaul favored by President Bush emphasizing domestic oil and gas production
- No End mandatory preservation of habitat of endangered animal and plant species
- Yes Ban torture of prisoners in U.S. custody

CQ VOTE STUDIES

	PARTY UNITY		PRESIDENTIAL SUPPORT	
	Support	Oppose	Support	Oppose
2006	98%	2%	22%	78%
2005	99%	1%	15%	85%
2004	98%	2%	22%	78%
2003	96%	4%	20%	80%
2002	98%	2%	26%	74%

INTEREST GROUPS

	AFL-CIO	ADA	CCUS	ACU
2006	100%	80%	25%	0%
2005	93%	100%	41%	0%
2004	93%	100%	22%	4%
2003	87%	100%	31%	20%
2002	100%	75%	44%	9%

MASSACHUSETTS 5

North central — Lowell, Lawrence, Haverhill

More than a generation ago, billowing smokestacks put Lawrence and Lowell among the nation's leading industrial centers. Today, the cities remain blue-collar, strongly Democratic population hubs for the 5th, but the wealthy suburbs and rural communities — home to technology workers and some of the nation's most prestigious preparatory schools — give the district a more upscale flavor.

Manufacturing-based jobs are still vital to struggling Lawrence. Unemployment here reached 15 percent in 1991 before dropping to near 5 percent over the next decade, only to shoot back up above 11 percent in 2007. Immigration has pushed Lawrence's growing Hispanic population, composed mostly of Dominicans and Puerto Ricans, into the majority and given Lawrence a Latin flavor, confirmed by the many ethnic restaurants in the city.

Lowell and its surrounding suburbs, meanwhile, have largely succeeded in reinventing themselves after suffering through declines to once-major area employers. The city's ability to retool its economic base has attracted software firms and other technology companies. The economic upswing spurred growth in small towns, as aging buildings that once housed textile mills, and then defense contractors, became home to start-ups and financial services firms. Lowell also has sought to become a cultural hub, and now boasts the nation's largest free folk festival.

The southern part of the 5th is generally wealthy, with Carlisle, Sudbury, Harvard and Bolton all registering six-figure median household incomes. GOP candidates sometimes win in these areas, as Republican Mitt Romney did in the 2002 gubernatorial election. Nevertheless, Democrat John Kerry was victorious in these towns in the 2004 presidential race, as was Democratic gubernatorial candidate Deval Patrick in 2006.

MAJOR INDUSTRY

Computer software, defense manufacturing, light manufacturing

CITIES

Lowell, 105,167; Lawrence, 72,043; Haverhill, 58,969; Methuen, 43,789

NOTABLE

Concord was the site of the first day of fighting in the Revolutionary War on April 19, 1775 (now celebrated each year as Patriots Day); Paul Revere's ride and the first Revolutionary battles in towns in the 5th and 7th districts are re-enacted every year.

Rep. John F. Tierney (D)

CAPITOL OFFICE
225-8020
www.house.gov/tierney
2238 Rayburn 20515-2106; fax 225-5915

COMMITTEES
Education & Labor
Oversight & Government Reform
(National Security & Foreign Affairs - chairman)
Select Intelligence

RESIDENCE
Salem

BORN
Sept. 18, 1951, Salem, Mass.

RELIGION
Unspecified

FAMILY
Wife, Patrice Tierney

EDUCATION
Salem State College, B.A. 1973 (political science); Suffolk U., J.D. 1976

CAREER
Lawyer; chamber of commerce official

POLITICAL HIGHLIGHTS
Democratic nominee for U.S. House, 1994

ELECTION RESULTS

2006 GENERAL		
John F. Tierney (D)	168,056	69.6%
Richard W. Barton (R)	72,997	30.2%
2006 PRIMARY		
John F. Tierney (D)		unopposed
2004 GENERAL		
John F. Tierney (D)	213,458	69.9%
Steven P. O'Malley Jr. (R)	91,597	30.0%

PREVIOUS WINNING PERCENTAGES
2002 (68%); 2000 (71%); 1998 (55%); 1996 (48%)

Elected 1996; 6th term

Tierney finally has the opportunity to experience the satisfaction of real power. The die-hard liberal had spent his entire House career in a Congress run by conservative Republicans until the Democratic takeover in the 110th Congress (2007-08). He now has a chance not only to see more of his party's initiatives considered, but as chairman of the Oversight and Government Reform Subcommittee on National Security, he also can help shape a part of the new majority's agenda.

He wasted no time finding a place in the spotlight. In early 2007, media reports unveiled patient care problems at Walter Reed Army Medical Center, where injured soldiers from Iraq and Afghanistan and other veterans are treated. As soon as the scandal broke, Tierney called a field hearing at Walter Reed, where he lambasted senior commanders of the Army who suggested they had been unaware of the problems: "I have to tell you, the first thing that pops into my mind is: Where've you been? Where has all the brass been?"

Believing similar substandard living conditions likely exist throughout the military health care system, he said, "We need a sustained focus here, and much more needs to be done." Tierney pursued the matter, posting on his Web site a call to active duty service members and veterans having trouble finding quality care to send in their story.

Tierney has been increasingly interested in national security issues over the past few years. He served on the then-named Government Reform panel for eight years before taking a leave of absence in 2005 for a seat on the Intelligence Committee. On Government Reform, he was a member of the National Security Subcommittee and participated in the legislative creation of the Department of Homeland Security and the Sept. 11 commission.

He has worked to boost funding for first-responder communications training and equipment. In 2002, he cosponsored a bipartisan bill that required the intelligence community to share homeland security information with local officials and directed the president to set up procedures for declassifying that type of information so that state officials can remain informed about threats. "It's not like local fire and police are doing just local things," he said. "They're a part of homeland security response."

Tierney constantly chafed under GOP majority rule and was among its harshest critics. He accused Republicans of twisting facts to achieve their ends, putting wealthy corporate chiefs ahead of everyday people and abusing democratic processes. His liberal politics and tough talk were once considered a risk for a politician who won his first election by just 371 votes. But after a decade on Capitol Hill, he enjoys the security of perpetual incumbency and solid support back home.

Even under GOP rule, Tierney managed to eke out some victories on the Education Committee and its Subcommittee on Competitiveness. He has championed measures to make college more affordable, encourage alternative paths to teaching and help local school districts hire more teachers to reduce class sizes in elementary and secondary schools.

He played an active role in the committee's rewrite of the Higher Education Act in 2005, winning approval of proposals to make it easier for mid-career professionals to switch into teaching and working to preserve campus-based student aid programs. He also has successfully advanced proposals to offer incentives to encourage top college graduates to enter teaching.

Tierney has a good-government bent, and every Congress he quixotically offers a bill called "Clean Money, Clean Elections." It contains many of the dramatic but politically radioactive changes pushed by government watchdog groups, including public financing of elections, free broadcast time for candidates and limits on expenditures by political parties. A few provisions were included in the campaign finance law enacted in 2002, and Tierney continues to push the remaining ones with little hope of success. Still, he won the House Democratic Caucus' backing of public financing of elections, which he says is the only way to clean up campaigns. "For someone filing that bill since 1997, it's good to hear other people finally singing the tune," he says.

Tierney also continues to press for changes to prevent companies from canceling or reducing their retirees' health benefits and to provide incentives to states to develop universal health care programs. He worked in the 109th Congress (2005-06) with top scholars from the conservative Heritage Foundation and the liberal Brookings Institution in search of a consensus approach. Though unsuccessful, he continued this initiative in 2007.

Though Tierney served a year as president of the Salem Chamber of Commerce, he usually does not see eye to eye with the U.S. Chamber, backing the business group's position less than a quarter of the time. But he did work with local business interests as well as other Massachusetts lawmakers in a successful fight to preserve Hanscom Air Force Base from elimination in the 2005 round of military base closings. He argued the base's location close to Boston's high-tech Route 128 corridor was essential to that area's military research facilities that work on surveillance and intelligence electronics.

Tierney first became interested in politics as a boy growing up in Salem. His uncle served as a ward councilor in Peabody, and Tierney used to campaign with him door-to-door. He worked to put himself through college, where he majored in political science. He got a law degree from Suffolk University and was a partner in the law firm of Tierney, Kalis and Lucas for more than 20 years, until his election to the House. Throughout his legal career, he was active in Salem civic affairs. Rather than relocate to Washington, Tierney and his wife, Patrice, continue to make Salem their home.

Tierney launched his first campaign in 1994 and came within 4 percentage points of defeating freshman GOP Rep. Peter G. Torkildsen, who was aided by that year's Republican tide. He tried again in 1996, and with President Bill Clinton sweeping the district by 28 percentage points, he managed a 371-vote win. Torkildsen was back for a rematch in 1998, stressing his moderate positions on abortion and gay rights. GOP party strategists targeted the race as a priority, but Tierney won by 12 points. His re-elections have been a breeze ever since.

KEY VOTES

2006

- Yes Stop broadband companies from favoring select Internet traffic
- No Affirm U.S. commitment to war in Iraq and reject setting a withdrawal date for troops
- No Repeal requirement for bilingual ballots at the polls
- Yes Permit U.S. sale of civilian nuclear technology to India
- No Build a 700-mile fence on the U.S.-Mexico border to curb illegal crossings
- No Permit warrantless wiretaps of suspected terrorists

2005

- ? Intervene in the life-support case of Terri Schiavo
- Yes Lift President Bush's restrictions on stem cell research funding
- Yes Prohibit FBI access to library and bookstore records
- No Approve free-trade pact with five Central American countries
- No Pass energy policy overhaul favored by President Bush emphasizing domestic oil and gas production
- No End mandatory preservation of habitat of endangered animal and plant species
- Yes Ban torture of prisoners in U.S. custody

CQ VOTE STUDIES

	PARTY UNITY		PRESIDENTIAL SUPPORT	
	Support	Oppose	Support	Oppose
2006	96%	4%	13%	87%
2005	98%	2%	13%	87%
2004	99%	1%	12%	88%
2003	99%	1%	15%	85%
2002	99%	1%	23%	77%

INTEREST GROUPS

	AFL-CIO	ADA	CCUS	ACU
2006	100%	100%	33%	8%
2005	93%	100%	30%	0%
2004	100%	100%	19%	0%
2003	100%	100%	23%	12%
2002	100%	100%	32%	0%

MASSACHUSETTS 6

North Shore – Lynn, Peabody

Pristine beaches line the cool ocean of Boston's North Shore, home to some of the state's largest homes. Country clubs, fox hunting and polo are popular diversions for residents of the northern inland, where the population is sparse but wealthy.

The population is denser along the Route 128 technology corridor in the southern part of the district, which developed when communities across the state began to shift from manufacturing to an information-based economy in the 1990s. Fueled in part by Boston's universities, technology firms have flourished from Burlington, where Sun Microsystems has offices, to Gloucester, which also supports a major fishing industry. Burlington's addition of an industrial park reflects the continued growth of the district's economy.

Urban dwellers are concentrated mostly in Lynn and Peabody and provide blue-collar and minority votes for Democrats. Lynn is home to aerospace and defense contractors and hosts a General Electric jet engine plant. Other population centers include the adjacent coastal cities of Beverly — which locals describe as the birthplace of the Navy because the first ship commissioned by the Continental Congress sailed from its harbor in 1775 — and major tourist destination Salem, with its rich history as the site of the 1692 witch trials. Salem is middle-class and has a Democratic slant, while Beverly is more politically independent.

Republicans can do well in upscale towns such as Boxford, Lynnfield, Topsfield and Wenham, which narrowly backed George W. Bush in the 2004 presidential election. While the 6th has a Democratic tilt, it is not overwhelming, and the GOP can win by attracting independent-minded "unenrolled" voters.

MAJOR INDUSTRY

Computer software, defense, fishing

MILITARY BASES

Hanscom Air Force Base, 1,780 military, 3,925 civilian (2005)

CITIES

Lynn, 89,050; Peabody, 48,129; Salem, 40,407; Beverly, 39,862; Gloucester, 30,273; Saugus (unincorporated), 26,078

NOTABLE

The 6th includes territory that spawned the original "gerrymander," a state legislative district named for Gov. Elbridge Gerry in 1812.

Rep. Edward J. Markey (D)

CAPITOL OFFICE
225-2836
www.house.gov/markey
2108 Rayburn 20515-2107; fax 226-0092

COMMITTEES
Energy & Commerce
(Telecommunications & the Internet - chairman)
Homeland Security
Natural Resources
Select Energy Independence & Global Warming - chairman

RESIDENCE
Malden

BORN
July 11, 1946, Malden, Mass.

RELIGION
Roman Catholic

FAMILY
Wife, Susan Blumenthal

EDUCATION
Boston College, B.A. 1968, J.D. 1972

MILITARY SERVICE
Army Reserve, 1968-73

CAREER
Lawyer

POLITICAL HIGHLIGHTS
Mass. House, 1973-77

ELECTION RESULTS

2006 GENERAL		
Edward J. Markey (D)	171,902	98.3%
write-ins	2,889	1.7%
2006 PRIMARY		
Edward J. Markey (D)	unopposed	
2004 GENERAL		
Edward J. Markey (D)	202,399	73.6%
Kenneth G. Chase (R)	60,334	21.9%
James O. Hall (I)	12,139	4.4%

PREVIOUS WINNING PERCENTAGES
2002 (98%); 2000 (99%); 1998 (71%); 1996 (70%); 1994 (64%); 1992 (62%); 1990 (100%); 1988 (100%); 1986 (100%); 1984 (71%); 1982 (78%); 1980 (100%); 1978 (85%); 1976 Combined General & Special Election (77%)

Elected 1976; 16th full term

The social upheaval of the 1960s drove a young, idealistic Markey into politics at age 26 and he has never left. He is now one of the most senior and influential Democrats in Congress, with a potent, forward-looking legislative portfolio on technology issues. His biggest career frustration has been his inability to get to the Senate. There has not been an open seat in Massachusetts in 22 years. Markey almost certainly would have run in 2004 if Sen. John Kerry had beaten President Bush, but it was not to be.

Markey is now chairman of the Energy and Commerce subcommittee responsible for telecommunications issues, where he has had an impact on some of the biggest technology-related legislation in the past 20 years. An effort in 2006 to prevent telecommunications giants such as AT&T and Verizon from gaining too much control over Internet traffic was typical for Markey, who has a passion for initiatives that advance technology but are consumer-friendly. His so-called network neutrality bill demanded that telephone and cable operators controlling the nation's broadband networks provide equal access to rivals and small, independent Web site operators. He also has been a key player in efforts to force cell phone providers to get customers' permission to publish phone numbers, in implementing "v-chips" allowing parents to block programs and in the digital television transition.

His signature legislation was the 1996 telecommunications overhaul that opened local phone markets to competition, set conditions for the powerful Bells to enter new markets, and regulated competition between telephone and cable companies. In 1992, he had engineered the only veto override of President George H.W. Bush's four years in office, leading the House to vote 308-114 to restore a bill he helped write that regulated the booming cable industry. The president previously had vetoed 35 bills successfully.

Markey's stature on the Telecommunications Subcommittee makes him a favorite for campaign contributions from the entertainment industry and telephone, cable and computer companies. And he and his wife, former assistant surgeon general Dr. Susan Blumenthal, enjoy hobnobbing with celebrities and snaring choice seats at the annual Academy Awards show.

His other big push in recent years has been port security. Markey has led a Democratic move on the House Homeland Security Committee to require total scanning of cargo at sea ports, but has faced opposition from Republicans and business groups. That opposition helped defeat his proposal in the 109th Congress (2005-06), but it was revived in 2007 when the Democratic House attached it to broader Sept. 11 legislation.

As a member of the Natural Resources Committee, he has sought a way to force oil companies to renegotiate drilling leases with the government to fix a contract mistake that has allowed them to reap millions of dollars in profit. "Oil companies want to play Uncle Sam for Uncle Sucker," said Markey, known for mixing humor and biting sarcasm. In 2006, the House approved his proposal to renegotiate the leases, but it never became law.

That same year, he became one of Speaker Nancy Pelosi's key players in the global warming debate. As a vocal supporter of mandatory emissions controls, he was named chairman of a new Select Committee on Energy Independence and Global Warming. Pelosi created the panel — over objections by Republicans and some Democratic committee chairmen — to investigate the problems of global warming and make legislative recommendations to the appropriate committees.

The working-class son of a milk truck driver, Markey was greatly influenced in his early years by another Irish Catholic from Massachusetts — President John F. Kennedy. As a student at Malden Catholic High School, he listened to interviews with the Rev. Martin Luther King Jr. and Malcolm X on a radio talk show that aired from 10 p.m. to midnight. At that time, Massachusetts "was alive with the potential of the Kennedy vision of what our country could be," Markey recalls. In 1968, the year Markey graduated from Boston College, he campaigned for liberal Democrat Eugene McCarthy.

After earning his law degree, Markey ran for the state House and won, and quickly became a thorn in the side of the old establishment Democrats. He picked a fight in 1976 with the party leaders over judicial reform, successfully pushing a bill to force judges to give up their law practices while in office. The Massachusetts bar endorsed the bill, but the Speaker kicked him off the Judiciary Committee. When he showed up for work the next day, his office was cleaned out — desk, cabinet, chair, everything gone. He astutely turned the event into a political asset; he ran for an open seat in the U.S. House with the slogan, "The bosses can tell me where to sit, no one can tell me where to stand." He won with his message of reform and change.

In his early years in Washington, Markey crusaded against the domestic use of nuclear power and for a freeze on nuclear weapons during President Ronald Reagan's defense buildup. In 1979, after the Three Mile Island nuclear accident, he pressed for a moratorium on nuclear plant construction, but it was defeated in the House. Even in a Democratic Congress, his leftist views were out of the mainstream, and he had a reputation for staking out the moral high ground but attaining little legislatively.

That began to change in the mid-1980s as Markey grew in seniority and became more open to working with Republicans. He became less of a headline-grabber and more of the legislative workhorse that defines his style today. "I've come to realize that overnight success in legislation is not possible. I also realize that any good idea, if it is worked on consistently over a period of time, has a very good chance of becoming law," he told the Boston Globe in 2001.

Markey got a wake-up call in 1984 after his indecision almost cost him his seat. He initially announced his Senate candidacy when Paul E. Tsongas retired, then changed his mind. Former state Sen. Sam Rotondi, running in the primary for his seat, made an issue of the indecision and Markey won with just 54 percent of the vote. His career hit bottom more than a decade ago when then trendy Spy magazine named him one of the 10 "dumbest" congressmen. But these days he has no trouble getting re-elected, and he has banked more than $2 million for the future.

KEY VOTES

2006

Yes Stop broadband companies from favoring select Internet traffic

No Affirm U.S. commitment to war in Iraq and reject setting a withdrawal date for troops

No Repeal requirement for bilingual ballots at the polls

No Permit U.S. sale of civilian nuclear technology to India

No Build a 700-mile fence on the U.S.-Mexico border to curb illegal crossings

No Permit warrantless wiretaps of suspected terrorists

2005

? Intervene in the life-support case of Terri Schiavo

Yes Lift President Bush's restrictions on stem cell research funding

Yes Prohibit FBI access to library and bookstore records

No Approve free-trade pact with five Central American countries

No Pass energy policy overhaul favored by President Bush emphasizing domestic oil and gas production

No End mandatory preservation of habitat of endangered animal and plant species

Yes Ban torture of prisoners in U.S. custody

CQ VOTE STUDIES

	PARTY UNITY		PRESIDENTIAL SUPPORT	
	Support	Oppose	Support	Oppose
2006	98%	2%	7%	93%
2005	98%	2%	15%	85%
2004	98%	2%	15%	85%
2003	99%	1%	13%	87%
2002	99%	1%	25%	75%

INTEREST GROUPS

	AFL-CIO	ADA	CCUS	ACU
2006	100%	100%	20%	4%
2005	93%	100%	30%	0%
2004	100%	100%	10%	0%
2003	100%	100%	20%	12%
2002	100%	100%	30%	4%

MASSACHUSETTS 7

Northwest Boston suburbs – Framingham

The affluent strip along eastern Massachusetts' technology corridor, sometimes referred to as a Silicon Valley of the East, shapes the 7th's character. The district includes some of the state's most well-to-do communities as it jumps east from an urban retail center in Framingham to Route 128, which rings Boston, then through Medford and Malden to the middle-class coastal town of Revere. The area takes pride in its history: each year, Lexington re-enacts Paul Revere's ride and the first Revolutionary War battles (which took place in towns in the 7th and 5th districts) on Patriots Day in April.

For decades, Revere has attracted vacationers to its beaches, but a strong software and Internet industry drives the 7th's economy. Many Medford and Malden residents commute to blue-collar jobs in Boston. Malden has a growing Asian community, and the 7th is home to the second-largest Asian population in the state, as well as numerous advocacy organizations for Asian-Americans.

The 7th's political roots are a mix of Protestant Yankee Republicans and Irish Democrats. The wealthy sections of the 7th vary from the more conservative Weston to the liberal Lincoln. Democrats also draw votes from a blue-collar, middle-class base in Framingham and in the eastern part of the district, including Revere, Everett and Malden. But like all Massachusetts districts, the 7th votes Democratic in federal races. John Kerry won 66 percent of the district's 2004 presidential vote. George W. Bush's best showing in the district in 2004 was in Woburn, where he received only 43 percent of the vote.

MAJOR INDUSTRY

Computer software, telecommunications, defense

MILITARY BASES

Army Soldier Systems Center (Natick), 150 military, 1,850 civilian (2007)

CITIES

Framingham (unincorporated), 66,910; Waltham, 59,226; Malden, 56,340; Medford, 55,765; Revere, 47,283; Arlington (unincorporated), 42,389

NOTABLE

James Pierpont is said to have written "Jingle Bells" in 1850 while visiting Medford Square; The New England Confectionery Company (NECCO), the oldest multiline candy company in the United States, is located in Revere.

Rep. Michael E. Capuano (D)

CAPITOL OFFICE
225-5111
www.house.gov/capuano
1530 Longworth 20515-2108; fax 225-9322

COMMITTEES
Financial Services
House Administration
Transportation & Infrastructure
Joint Printing

RESIDENCE
Somerville

BORN
Jan. 9, 1952, Somerville, Mass.

RELIGION
Roman Catholic

FAMILY
Wife, Barbara Teebagy Capuano; two children

EDUCATION
Dartmouth College, B.A. 1973 (psychology); Boston College, J.D. 1977

CAREER
Lawyer; state legislative aide

POLITICAL HIGHLIGHTS
Somerville Board of Aldermen, 1977-79; candidate for mayor of Somerville, 1979, 1981; Somerville Board of Aldermen, 1985-89; mayor of Somerville, 1990-99; sought Democratic nomination for Mass. secretary of state, 1994

ELECTION RESULTS

2006 GENERAL		
Michael E. Capuano (D)	125,515	90.7%
Laura Garza (SW)	12,449	9.0%
2006 PRIMARY		
Michael E. Capuano (D)		unopposed
2004 GENERAL		
Michael E. Capuano (D)	165,852	98.7%
write-ins	2,229	1.3%

PREVIOUS WINNING PERCENTAGES
2002 (100%); 2000 (99%); 1998 (82%)

Elected 1998; 5th term

If there is a face to the political class known as the "Massachusetts liberal," it belongs to Capuano. An ethnic surname and thick Boston accent almost would seem to be requirements for the job of representing the district that produced the Kennedy dynasty and well-known House Speaker Thomas P. "Tip" O'Neill Jr.

True to his heritage, Capuano (KAP-you-AH-no) is a politician's pol, quick with a joke and a slap on the back and attuned to the insider's game. He played a key role in the successful 2006 leadership campaign of Connecticut Democrat John B. Larson, helping Larson outmaneuver two better-known candidates for the post of caucus vice chairman. A tart-tongued partisan, he was picked by incoming Speaker Nancy Pelosi in November 2006 to head the House Democratic transition team.

At the start of the 110th Congress (2007-08), Pelosi tapped him for another prominent role as the chairman of a bipartisan task force to weigh the need for an ethics commission composed of people outside Congress. The group was given a May 1 deadline to report their findings, but had yet to wrap up their work at that time.

A member of the Progressive Caucus, a group of the most left-leaning House Democrats, Capuano opposes a constitutional amendment banning same-sex marriage. He voted against authorizing President Bush to wage war in Iraq and opposed the administration's anti-terrorism law known as the Patriot Act, saying it was a threat to civil liberties. In early 2007, while voting for a resolution that set a March 2008 deadline for the start of U.S. troop withdrawal from Iraq, he said that he would have preferred a vote on "a course of action that would have gotten us out of Iraq much sooner."

His singular achievement in Congress has more to do with roads and bridges than with war and peace, however. As the lone Bay State member on the Transportation and Infrastructure Committee, he is credited with reversing the decline in grants to Massachusetts in reaction to the "Big Dig," the over-budget, scandal-ridden Boston tunnel project that had made many in Congress leery of the state's management of transportation projects. When a concrete slab in a Big Dig tunnel fell and killed a motorist in 2006, Capuano led the state's congressional delegation in demanding a federal probe. At the start of the 110th Congress, he introduced a bill that would establish a nationwide highway tunnel inspection program.

Capuano proved adept at the horse-trading that goes on behind the scenes in the stiff competition for earmarked federal grants, and he ultimately secured hundreds of millions of dollars for the state in 2005 as part of a six-year reauthorization of the surface transportation law. "We all have certain skills. . . . I get along with these guys. I'm a compromiser when I need to be," he says.

He may have an Ivy League education (Dartmouth), but Capuano likes to stress his roots in a working-class section of Somerville, the city outside Boston where he launched his political career in the 1970s, as a city alderman. His legislative endeavors usually find him engaged in traditional liberal pursuits to help the underclass. In 2005, Capuano won enactment of a new grant to provide assistance to young witnesses threatened with retaliation. He was inspired by a boy from Roxbury, one of Boston's poorest and most violent sections. The boy cooperated with police after witnessing a friend commit a mugging, and then was harassed to the point that he and his family feared leaving their apartment.

Trained as a tax attorney, Capuano sits on the Financial Services Committee, where he is a strong advocate of affordable housing initiatives. A bill passed by the House during his first term included his provision to allow teachers and uniformed municipal workers to buy homes through subsidized housing programs even if their incomes are above the poverty level.

Capuano drew national notice with his comments on the accounting scandals of the early part of this decade. When officials of Global Crossing Ltd., a bankrupt communications company, appeared before Financial Services, newspapers across the country reported Capuano's unambiguous indictment: "The whole thing you're talking about is nothing more than a much more fancy and larger Ponzi scheme," he said.

Capuano won the 8th District seat after Joseph P. Kennedy II, the son of Robert F. Kennedy and nephew of President John F. Kennedy, gave it up after six terms. The House seat has much of the original territory that it did when President Kennedy represented it for three terms, from 1947-53.

Capuano hails from a more modest political dynasty. His father was the first Italian-American elected to local office in Somerville. While Capuano is half-Irish, his Italian-American name is a change from the Irish identification of the Kennedys, Gov. James Michael Curley and Speaker O'Neill.

Capuano must navigate in a district where political tensions continually bubble to the surface. When he was mayor of Somerville, detractors called him "tyrannical" and said he managed the city like a ward boss, hiring friends and relatives and running enemies out of public agencies. Capuano, who won five elections and held the job for nearly a decade, called the attacks on his leadership style "a sign of a good executive."

Capuano triumphed in a 10-person Democratic donnybrook created by Kennedy's unexpected 1998 retirement in the solidly Democratic district. The presumed front-runner was Raymond L. Flynn, a former Boston mayor and ambassador to the Vatican who had abandoned a flagging run for governor. But Capuano and others ganged up against Flynn and, although greatly outspent by two other candidates, Capuano was lifted to victory by a strong turnout in Somerville and second-place finishes in several other communities. He breezed by a Republican opponent that November, and the GOP has not fielded a candidate since.

He briefly eyed running for governor in 2006 but decided against it.

As he nears a decade on Capitol Hill, Capuano says, "I am one of those guys who is absolutely shocked I'm a member of the House. I still think they're going to tap me on the shoulder and say, 'We didn't mean you.' I still think of myself as just a Somerville kid hanging out around the corner."

KEY VOTES

2006

Yes Stop broadband companies from favoring select Internet traffic

No Affirm U.S. commitment to war in Iraq and reject setting a withdrawal date for troops

No Repeal requirement for bilingual ballots at the polls

Yes Permit U.S. sale of civilian nuclear technology to India

Yes Build a 700-mile fence on the U.S.-Mexico border to curb illegal crossings

No Permit warrantless wiretaps of suspected terrorists

2005

No Intervene in the life-support case of Terri Schiavo

Yes Lift President Bush's restrictions on stem cell research funding

Yes Prohibit FBI access to library and bookstore records

No Approve free-trade pact with five Central American countries

No Pass energy policy overhaul favored by President Bush emphasizing domestic oil and gas production

No End mandatory preservation of habitat of endangered animal and plant species

Yes Ban torture of prisoners in U.S. custody

CQ VOTE STUDIES

	PARTY UNITY		PRESIDENTIAL SUPPORT	
	Support	Oppose	Support	Oppose
2006	96%	4%	25%	75%
2005	96%	4%	17%	83%
2004	96%	4%	24%	76%
2003	97%	3%	19%	81%
2002	98%	2%	21%	79%

INTEREST GROUPS

	AFL-CIO	ADA	CCUS	ACU
2006	100%	90%	40%	8%
2005	93%	95%	37%	4%
2004	93%	90%	19%	4%
2003	100%	100%	20%	16%
2002	89%	95%	28%	4%

MASSACHUSETTS 8

Part of Boston and suburbs — Cambridge, Somerville

The 8th combines Boston's historic Revolutionary War sites with neighborhoods that reflect its evolving future. It grabs approximately 70 percent of the city's population, almost all west of Interstate 93, picking up the Back Bay area, Chinatown and many largely black and Hispanic communities in areas like Roxbury, Dorchester and Jamaica Plain. The 8th is the state's only district where a majority of residents are minorities.

Among the 8th's many oft-visited Beantown sights are Bunker Hill, the Old North Church, the *U.S.S. Constitution* and Logan International Airport (shared with the 7th). Although in 2006 the Massachusetts Transit Authority completed its long-running "Big Dig" transportation project, most of which falls within the 8th, structural deficiencies have caused further closures and logistics problems.

Two of the world's most respected universities — Harvard and the Massachusetts Institute of Technology — lie across the Charles River from Boston in Cambridge. The district also takes in dozens of other colleges, which drive much of the economy, whether through blue-collar service employees who work at the schools and teaching hospitals or through biotechnology software firms that employ local talent.

Somerville, just north of Cambridge, has a thriving arts community, while Chelsea, with more-affordable housing and blue-collar jobs, has seen its Hispanic population expand to make up one-half the city's residents.

Typifying the district's monolithically liberal politics, Cambridge gave George W. Bush just 13 percent of the vote in the 2000 and 2004 presidential elections. Unsurprisingly, John Kerry received 82 percent of the district's presidential vote in 2004, a statewide high.

MAJOR INDUSTRY
Biotechnology, higher education, health care, tourism

CITIES
Boston (pt.), 420,922; Cambridge, 101,355; Somerville, 77,478

NOTABLE
The 8th is the descendant of the district once represented by John F. Kennedy (1947-53) and Thomas P. "Tip" O'Neill Jr. (1953-87); Fenway Park is home to baseball's Boston Red Sox.

Rep. Stephen F. Lynch (D)

CAPITOL OFFICE
225-8273
stephen.lynch@mail.house.gov
www.house.gov/lynch
221 Cannon 20515-2109; fax 225-3984

COMMITTEES
Financial Services
Oversight & Government Reform

RESIDENCE
Boston

BORN
March 31, 1955, Boston, Mass.

RELIGION
Roman Catholic

FAMILY
Wife, Margaret Lynch; one child

EDUCATION
Wentworth Institute of Technology, B.S. 1988 (construction management); Boston College, J.D. 1991; Harvard U., M.A. 1998 (public administration)

CAREER
Lawyer; ironworker

POLITICAL HIGHLIGHTS
Mass. House, 1995-96; Mass. Senate, 1996-2001

ELECTION RESULTS

2006 GENERAL		
Stephen F. Lynch (D)	169,420	78.1%
Jack E. Robinson III (R)	47,114	21.7%
2006 PRIMARY		
Stephen F. Lynch (D)		unopposed
2004 GENERAL		
Stephen F. Lynch (D)		unopposed

PREVIOUS WINNING PERCENTAGES
2002 (100%); 2001 Special Election (65%)

Elected October 2001; 3rd full term

Lynch may have gone to Harvard, but he's at home in any pub or diner in South Boston, or "Southie," as the locals know it. Lynch grew up in one of Southie's poorest housing projects, put himself through school as an ironworker and was elected president of the local union. Like a lot of his constituents, he's a Democrat with a conservative bent on some social issues.

A Roman Catholic, Lynch opposes abortion and was one of only 47 Democrats — and the only lawmaker from Massachusetts — to vote with conservatives on the controversial congressional intervention in the case of Terri Schiavo, a severely brain-damaged Florida woman who was the subject of a major court battle over end-of-life medical decisions. House Republicans successfully pushed for congressional action to try to block a state judge's decision to remove Schiavo's feeding tube, but federal judges refused to order doctors to reinsert the tube.

Lynch has declined to join social conservatives in the battle over civil rights for homosexuals, however. He opposes a constitutional amendment to prohibit same-sex marriage and has expressed support for an extension of medical benefits to domestic partners.

He describes himself as a moderate, and in the 109th congress (2005-06) he voted with a majority of Democrats 91 percent of the time on votes that polarized the two parties. On most fiscal votes, Lynch fits comfortably in the party mainstream. In 2003, he voted with virtually all House Democrats against President Bush's $350 billion tax cut and also against the president's prescription drug benefit under Medicare.

As a former labor leader, Lynch voted in 2003 to block Bush's plans to limit eligibility for overtime pay. He also opposed the law enacted in 2002 granting the president fast-track authority to negotiate trade deals Congress must approve or reject but cannot amend.

Lynch serves on the Oversight and Government Reform Committee. Still a member of its subcommittee with jurisdiction over national security, in May 2003 he traveled with the first congressional delegation to visit Iraq after the U.S.-led invasion in March. He has taken five additional trips to Iraq, the most recent in April 2007. In 2006, and again at the start of the 110th Congress (2007-08), Lynch introduced a bill that aims to speed up the transition of basic public services to the Iraq government.

Lynch regrets his vote in 2002 to authorize the war in Iraq. In hindsight, Lynch says, Congress should have taken more time to verify intelligence the Bush administration used to build the case for invading Iraq. "We took the best information that was available; unfortunately, it was not very good," he says. "We committed our troops prematurely."

Lynch secured the Democratic nomination in his first try for a House seat on an inauspicious date — Sept. 11, 2001. He was campaigning as a Democrat with an independent streak and says the terrorist attacks heightened his willingness to err on the side of using force to head off terrorist threats.

From his seat on the Government Reform panel, Lynch in 2005 took on the role of inquisitor during hearings regarding the use of steroids in baseball, a sport Bostonians are passionate about. He aggressively questioned major league players suspected of steroid use and denounced the league's unwillingness to act. "All I got were a lot of reasons to believe these guys will not and cannot get their arms around this," he said.

He's most proud of his work on a local project, the construction of Cushing House, a 28-bed facility for adolescents with drug problems. Inspired by a spate of drug-related teen suicides in his district, Lynch secured federal funding for the facility, or as he puts it, he "brought back some dough." It was completed in 2005. He talked old union pals into donating labor and a factory owner into donating space. "There's already a waiting list," he said in 2006. "[It's] probably the best thing I've done."

Formerly on the Veterans' Affairs Committee, Lynch continues to look after the interests of the three VA medical facilities in his district and its shelter for homeless veterans. Along with former Rep. Jack Quinn, a moderate Republican from New York, he introduced legislation to improve staffing levels at VA hospitals, which he said are so chronically inadequate that patients' lives are endangered.

Lynch came to the House after winning a special election in the fall of 2001 to replace the district's beloved longtime congressman, Joe Moakley, a Democrat who died of leukemia while still in office. "As high as he went in the ranks of Congress, he always paid attention to the situation for the families in his district," Lynch says. "That's something I've tried to emulate."

Lynch's father was an ironworker for 40 years, as was he for 18 years. At age 30, Lynch was elected the youngest president ever of Ironworkers Local 7. He earned a law degree from Boston College and later a master's degree from Harvard, his tickets out of the unstable and dangerous trade. He joined a law firm and continued a practice he had begun in law school of representing housing project residents for free.

In 1994, Lynch unseated incumbent state Rep. Paul Gannon in the Massachusetts House; two years later, he won a special election for a state Senate seat. That gave him a solid launching pad to run for Congress when Moakley died soon after his 15th term had begun in 2001.

It was not a clear shot. Lynch was up against six other Democrats, several of whom criticized him for his opposition to abortion. Two of them raised questions about an incident from Lynch's attorney days, when he defended 14 white teenagers accused of harassing a white girl and her Hispanic boyfriend. But Lynch benefited from his bootstraps personal story, as well as from publicity over his decision to donate 60 percent of his liver to his brother-in-law, who had liver cancer.

Lynch won the primary with 39 percent of the vote and went on to defeat Republican state Sen. Jo Ann Sprague with 65 percent. In 2002 and 2004, no Republican challenged him for re-election. In 2006, he easily defeated Republican Jack E. Robinson III, taking more than three-quarters of the vote. Robinson, a Harvard-educated lawyer and businessman, had been dealt a similar shellacking in 2000 when he took on Sen. Edward M. Kennedy.

KEY VOTES

2006

- Yes Stop broadband companies from favoring select Internet traffic
- Yes Affirm U.S. commitment to war in Iraq and reject setting a withdrawal date for troops
- No Repeal requirement for bilingual ballots at the polls
- No Permit U.S. sale of civilian nuclear technology to India
- Yes Build a 700-mile fence on the U.S.-Mexico border to curb illegal crossings
- No Permit warrantless wiretaps of suspected terrorists

2005

- Yes Intervene in the life-support case of Terri Schiavo
- Yes Lift President Bush's restrictions on stem cell research funding
- Yes Prohibit FBI access to library and bookstore records
- No Approve free-trade pact with five Central American countries
- No Pass energy policy overhaul favored by President Bush emphasizing domestic oil and gas production
- No End mandatory preservation of habitat of endangered animal and plant species
- Yes Ban torture of prisoners in U.S. custody

CQ VOTE STUDIES

	PARTY UNITY		PRESIDENTIAL SUPPORT	
	Support	Oppose	Support	Oppose
2006	90%	10%	30%	70%
2005	92%	8%	16%	84%
2004	91%	9%	42%	58%
2003	91%	9%	27%	73%
2002	94%	6%	33%	67%

INTEREST GROUPS

	AFL-CIO	ADA	CCUS	ACU
2006	100%	90%	27%	20%
2005	93%	90%	37%	12%
2004	93%	85%	43%	28%
2003	100%	85%	27%	33%
2002	100%	90%	40%	13%

MASSACHUSETTS 9
Part of Boston; southern suburbs — Brockton, Braintree

The 9th begins with a central swath of downtown Boston, covering Beacon Hill, the West End and the financial district. The statehouse and brokerage houses — the 9th is home to one of the world's largest centers for mutual fund investing — dominate this part of Boston and share the area with sprawling Boston Common park and several of New England's major tourist attractions. Faneuil Hall Marketplace anchors the retail industry.

From central Boston the district hops the Fort Point Channel into South Boston, referred to as "Southie," and closely hugs Interstate 93 on its way into Milton. It connects through Dedham to West Roxbury, a mostly white suburban enclave in the southwestern part of Boston.

Some of the wealthiest neighborhoods in the state are along the Charles River, and the "Brahmin" homes of Beacon Hill are counterbalanced by the poor and working-class neighborhoods of traditionally Irish Southie and middle-class suburban communities south and west of the city. Although solidly Democratic, Southie's political tradition is one of supporting pro-labor Democrats who are more socially conservative.

The 9th's areas outside of Boston are relatively conservative for Massachusetts. Although portions of the district's suburbs helped elect GOP governors in the 1990s, Democrat Deval Patrick won Randolph and Needham, and narrowly carried Braintree, while winning the 2006 gubernatorial race. The district's mostly blue-collar base in Boston and Brockton keeps it solidly Democratic in federal elections.

MAJOR INDUSTRY

Financial services, government, tourism

CITIES

Boston (pt.), 168,219; Brockton, 94,304; Braintree (unincorporated), 33,698; Randolph (unincorporated), 30,963; Needham (unincorporated), 28,911

NOTABLE

Patriots tossed boxes of tea into the district's Boston Harbor during the Boston Tea Party in 1773, a catalyst for the Revolutionary War; In the 1640s, Dedham authorized the first solely U.S. taxpayer-funded public school; The John F. Kennedy Library and Museum is in the 9th's portion of Boston.

Rep. Bill Delahunt (D)

CAPITOL OFFICE
225-3111
william.delahunt@mail.house.gov
www.house.gov/delahunt
2454 Rayburn 20515-2110; fax 225-5658

COMMITTEES
Foreign Affairs
(International Organizations, Human Rights & Oversight - chairman)
Judiciary
Standards of Official Conduct

RESIDENCE
Quincy

BORN
July 18, 1941, Quincy, Mass.

RELIGION
Roman Catholic

FAMILY
Divorced; two children

EDUCATION
Middlebury College, B.A. 1963;
Boston College, J.D. 1967

MILITARY SERVICE
Coast Guard, 1963; Coast Guard Reserve, 1963-71

CAREER
Lawyer

POLITICAL HIGHLIGHTS
Quincy City Council, 1971-73; Mass. House, 1973-75; Norfolk County district attorney, 1975-97

ELECTION RESULTS

2006 GENERAL		
Bill Delahunt (D)	171,812	64.3%
Jeffrey K. Beatty (R)	78,439	29.4%
Peter A. White (I)	16,808	6.3%
2006 PRIMARY		
Bill Delahunt (D)		unopposed
2004 GENERAL		
Bill Delahunt (D)	222,013	65.9%
Michael J. Jones (R)	114,879	34.1%

PREVIOUS WINNING PERCENTAGES
2002 (69%); 2000 (74%); 1998 (70%); 1996 (54%)

Elected 1996; 6th term

Delahunt is an affable Yankee pol in an age dominated by polarizing partisanship in Washington. He has a knack for cultivating relationships with colleagues who have far different ideological outlooks, and as a consequence, he's had his name on a few bills that passed in recent years, something that few of his fellow liberal Democrats can claim.

A longtime Democratic voice on the International Relations (now Foreign Affairs) and Judiciary committees, Delahunt (DELL-a-hunt) has been among the most outspoken critics of the war in Iraq. In 2005, he cosponsored with other Democrats a bill demanding that spending on Iraq reconstruction be matched by investments in health care, education and public safety at home. It had no chance of passing the GOP-controlled House, but it spelled out a popular view of the war in his party.

As chairman of the Foreign Affairs oversight subcommittee in the Democratic-controlled 110th Congress (2007-08), Delahunt said he would fight to end U.S. reconstruction grants to Iraq after his subcommittee determined that the Iraqi government had $12 billion it could use for road building and other infrastructure needs. He claims the Bush administration's "ideological approach" to foreign policy has hurt U.S. national security and the economy. In early 2007, he said he would use his chairmanship "to repair this damage and restore America's reputation."

A friend of leftist Venezuelan President Hugo Chávez, Delahunt helped broker a much-publicized November 2005 deal for the country's state-owned oil company Citgo to provide cut-rate heating oil to low-income Massachusetts residents. The conservative Wall Street Journal editorial page called the arrangement an attempt by Chávez — a political adversary of the Bush administration — to buy friends in Washington.

Delahunt defended it as a way of getting affordable fuel to people after Congress and the administration failed to help by increasing home heating assistance for the poor. "It's an embarrassment that we're forced to seek foreign assistance," he fired back.

Delahunt and Arizona Republican Jeff Flake are co-chairmen of the bipartisan Cuba Working Group, a coalition of lawmakers pressing for an end to the trade embargo against the island nation imposed more than four decades ago. In 2007, Delahunt introduced a bill to lift travel restrictions on Americans who want to visit family members in Cuba.

A former prosecutor, Delahunt was tapped to serve on the House ethics committee in the 110th Congress, an assignment few members relish.

Most often, Delahunt is at work on bipartisan deals that give him bragging rights to legislation on the law-and-order issues close to his heart. He partnered with Republican Ray LaHood of Illinois in 2004 in a successful legislative effort that ensured death row inmates have access to DNA evidence that might clear them. In 2005, Delahunt teamed with then GOP Majority Leader Tom DeLay to host a meeting of international relief groups, including UNICEF and the Red Cross, to discuss ways of cracking down on international trafficking in women and children.

Delahunt says he was inspired to enter politics by President John F. Kennedy. While a student at Middlebury College, he was co-chairman of a Vermont college students-for-Kennedy group. The other chairman was the late Ronald H. Brown, secretary of Commerce under President Bill Clinton.

Delahunt spent more than 20 years as a district attorney just south of Boston, and his experience as a prosecutor makes him an influential voice for his party on Judiciary. "Billy has locked up more people than everyone else on the committee put together," Barney Frank of Massachusetts, for years the panel's No. 2 Democrat, told The Boston Globe. "He is a liberal with his head on his shoulders."

During his tenure, Delahunt prosecuted John Salvi, who in 1994 killed two people at Brookline, Mass., abortion clinics. Delahunt himself opposed abortion rights for many years, but switched his position at the urging of his two grown daughters, Kara and Kristin.

Delahunt, who adopted Kara as an abandoned Vietnamese baby in 1975, has been a force behind legislation to ease overseas adoptions. In 2000, he won passage of his bill to grant automatic citizenship to children adopted from abroad, as well as to foreign-born children of U.S. parents.

Although "politics may make odd bedfellows," Delahunt's bedfellows are reliable liberals, too — as was made clear by "The Little House on the Hill," a short-lived television show put together by comedian Al Franken in 2002. It portrayed the domestic hijinks of Delahunt and his three Democratic housemates, Sens. Charles E. Schumer of New York and Richard J. Durbin of Illinois and Rep. George Miller of California.

Delahunt's fondness for the Boston Red Sox has crept into his political work. At a 1999 reception for Venezuelan President Chávez, Delahunt gave him a framed baseball card of Luis Aparicio, a Venezuelan and Hall of Fame shortstop who played for the Red Sox. And in 2003, then International Relations panel Chairman Henry J. Hyde broke into Delahunt's aggressive questioning of a Pentagon official by saying, "I think a more relevant question is how long do we have to wait for the Red Sox to win the pennant." "Only the gods know that," Delahunt said.

A Quincy native, Delahunt became a city councilman at age 30. Elected to the state House in 1972, he shared an office with a couple of other Beacon Hill rookies, Frank and Rep. Edward J. Markey of Massachusetts. Two years later, Gov. Michael S. Dukakis named him the district attorney for suburban Norfolk County, of which Quincy is the major municipality.

In 1996, when Democrat Gerry E. Studds announced his retirement, Delahunt was regarded as the Democratic front-runner from the start. But in a hard-fought September primary, he trailed state Rep. Phil Johnston by about 300 votes. Delahunt went to court, charging that ballots that should have been counted for him were mistakenly counted as blank. A state judge concurred, and Delahunt was certified the primary winner just 28 days before Election Day. He went on to win the general election by 13 percentage points and has had no trouble retaining his seat since.

KEY VOTES

2006

- Yes Stop broadband companies from favoring select Internet traffic
- No Affirm U.S. commitment to war in Iraq and reject setting a withdrawal date for troops
- No Repeal requirement for bilingual ballots at the polls
- Yes Permit U.S. sale of civilian nuclear technology to India
- Yes Build a 700-mile fence on the U.S.-Mexico border to curb illegal crossings
- No Permit warrantless wiretaps of suspected terrorists

2005

- ? Intervene in the life-support case of Terri Schiavo
- Yes Lift President Bush's restrictions on stem cell research funding
- Yes Prohibit FBI access to library and bookstore records
- No Approve free-trade pact with five Central American countries
- No Pass energy policy overhaul favored by President Bush emphasizing domestic oil and gas production
- No End mandatory preservation of habitat of endangered animal and plant species
- Yes Ban torture of prisoners in U.S. custody

CQ VOTE STUDIES

	PARTY UNITY		PRESIDENTIAL SUPPORT	
	Support	Oppose	Support	Oppose
2006	95%	5%	33%	67%
2005	99%	1%	9%	91%
2004	98%	2%	19%	81%
2003	98%	2%	10%	90%
2002	97%	3%	24%	76%

INTEREST GROUPS

	AFL-CIO	ADA	CCUS	ACU
2006	93%	90%	53%	12%
2005	92%	85%	35%	0%
2004	93%	95%	33%	0%
2003	100%	95%	14%	13%
2002	100%	90%	39%	0%

MASSACHUSETTS 10

South Shore — Quincy, Cape Cod, islands

Cool coastal breezes in the summer and warm ocean air in the winter attract retirees and tourists to the 10th, where most towns border the ocean. The area that spawned the nation's puritanical streak and the Thanksgiving holiday still retains a Yankee flavor.

In contrast, the northern part of the 10th has attracted residents from Boston's neighborhoods and now boasts a strong ethnic flavor, as evidenced by the many varied restaurants and cultural celebrations in the area. With the exception of a handful of thriving cranberry bogs, the mainland coastal towns of the 10th, commonly referred to as the South Shore, consist mostly of bedroom communities for Boston's professionals or Quincy's blue-collar workers. Available affordable housing options and a desirable quality of life have caused a substantial population boom here, making it one of the fastest-growing areas in Massachusetts. A thriving software industry helped the northern area recover from a recession in the early 1990s, and health care is now an important economic contributor.

On the Cape, tourism is dominant, but maritime technology and research are growing industries, especially in Woods Hole, home to world-renowned scientific institutions specializing in marine biology.

The 10th tends to be more evenly split politically than any other districts in Massachusetts. While the state's most liberal population lives on the far end of Cape Cod, where Provincetown, a predominately gay artists' colony and resort area, thrives, the district also includes one of the highest concentrations of Republicans in the state on the South Shore and in the wealthier towns on the Cape. As a result, the 10th was the state's least heavily Democratic district in both the 2000 and 2004 presidential races.

MAJOR INDUSTRY

Marine technology, biotechnology, health care, tourism

CITIES

Quincy, 88,025; Weymouth (unincorporated), 53,988; Barnstable, 47,821

NOTABLE

The John Alden House in Duxbury is named for the Pilgrim who sailed on the Mayflower; Quincy was home to the first Dunkin' Donuts and Howard Johnson's.

MICHIGAN

Gov. Jennifer M. Granholm (D)

First elected: 2002
Length of term: 4 years
Term expires: 1/11
Salary: $177,000
Phone: (517) 373-3400

Residence: Lansing
Born: Feb. 5, 1959; Richmond, Canada
Religion: Roman Catholic
Family: Husband, Daniel G. Mulhern; three children
Education: U. of California, Berkeley, B.A. 1984 (political science & French); Harvard U., J.D. 1987
Career: Federal prosecutor; campaign aide; lawyer
Political highlights: Wayne County Corporation Counsel, 1994-98; Mich. attorney general, 1999-2003

Election results:

2006 GENERAL		
Jennifer D. Granholm (D)	2,142,513	56.4%
Dick DeVos (R)	1,608,086	42.3%

Lt. Gov. John Cherry (D)

First elected: 2002
Length of term: 4 years
Term expires: 1/11
Salary: $123,900
Phone: (517) 373-3400

LEGISLATURE

Legislature: Year-round with recess

Senate: 38 members, 4-year terms
2007 ratios: 21 R, 17 D; 29 men, 9 women
Salary: $79,650; $12,000/year expenses
Phone: (517) 373-2400

House: 110 members, 2-year terms
2007 ratios: 58 D, 52 R; 90 men, 20 women
Salary: $79,650; $12,000/year expenses
Phone: (517) 373-0135

TERM LIMITS

Governor: 2 terms
Senate: 2 terms
House: 3 terms

URBAN STATISTICS

CITY	POPULATION
Detroit	951,270
Grand Rapids	197,800
Warren	138,247
Flint	124,943
Sterling Heights	124,471

REGISTERED VOTERS

Voters do not register by party.

POPULATION

2006 population (est.)	10,095,643
2000 population	9,938,444
1990 population	9,295,297
Percent change (1990-2000)	+6.9%
Rank among states (2006)	8
Median age	35.5
Born in state	75.4%
Foreign born	5.3%
Violent crime rate	555/100,000
Poverty level	10.5%
Federal workers	54,604
Military	21,833

ELECTIONS

STATE ELECTION OFFICIAL
(517) 373-2540
DEMOCRATIC PARTY
(517) 371-5410
REPUBLICAN PARTY
(517) 487-5413

MISCELLANEOUS

Web: www.michigan.gov
Capital: Lansing

U.S. CONGRESS

Senate: 2 Democrats
House: 9 Republicans, 6 Democrats

2000 Census Statistics by District

DIST.	2004 VOTE FOR PRESIDENT BUSH	KERRY	WHITE	BLACK	ASIAN	HISP	MEDIAN INCOME	WHITE COLLAR	BLUE COLLAR	SERVICE INDUSTRY	OVER 64	UNDER 18	COLLEGE EDUCATION	RURAL	SQ. MILES
1	53%	46%	94%	1%	0%	1%	$34,076	51%	30%	19%	17%	23%	16%	67%	24,887
2	60	39	87	4	1	5	$42,589	51	34	15	12	28	18	44	5,365
3	59	40	82	8	2	6	$45,936	57	30	13	11	28	24	23	1,854
4	55	44	93	2	1	2	$39,020	54	29	17	14	25	19	59	7,451
5	41	59	75	18	1	4	$39,675	51	32	17	12	27	15	21	1,754
6	53	46	84	9	1	4	$40,943	53	32	15	12	26	21	42	3,331
7	54	45	88	6	1	3	$45,181	54	32	15	12	26	19	46	4,295
8	54	45	88	5	2	3	$52,510	63	23	14	9	26	29	30	2,254
9	50	49	81	8	6	3	$65,358	75	15	10	12	24	44	1	311
10	56	43	94	1	1	2	$52,690	55	32	13	11	27	17	34	3,549
11	52	47	90	4	3	2	$59,177	65	24	12	12	25	29	3	399
12	39	60	82	12	2	1	$46,784	60	27	14	16	23	20	0	160

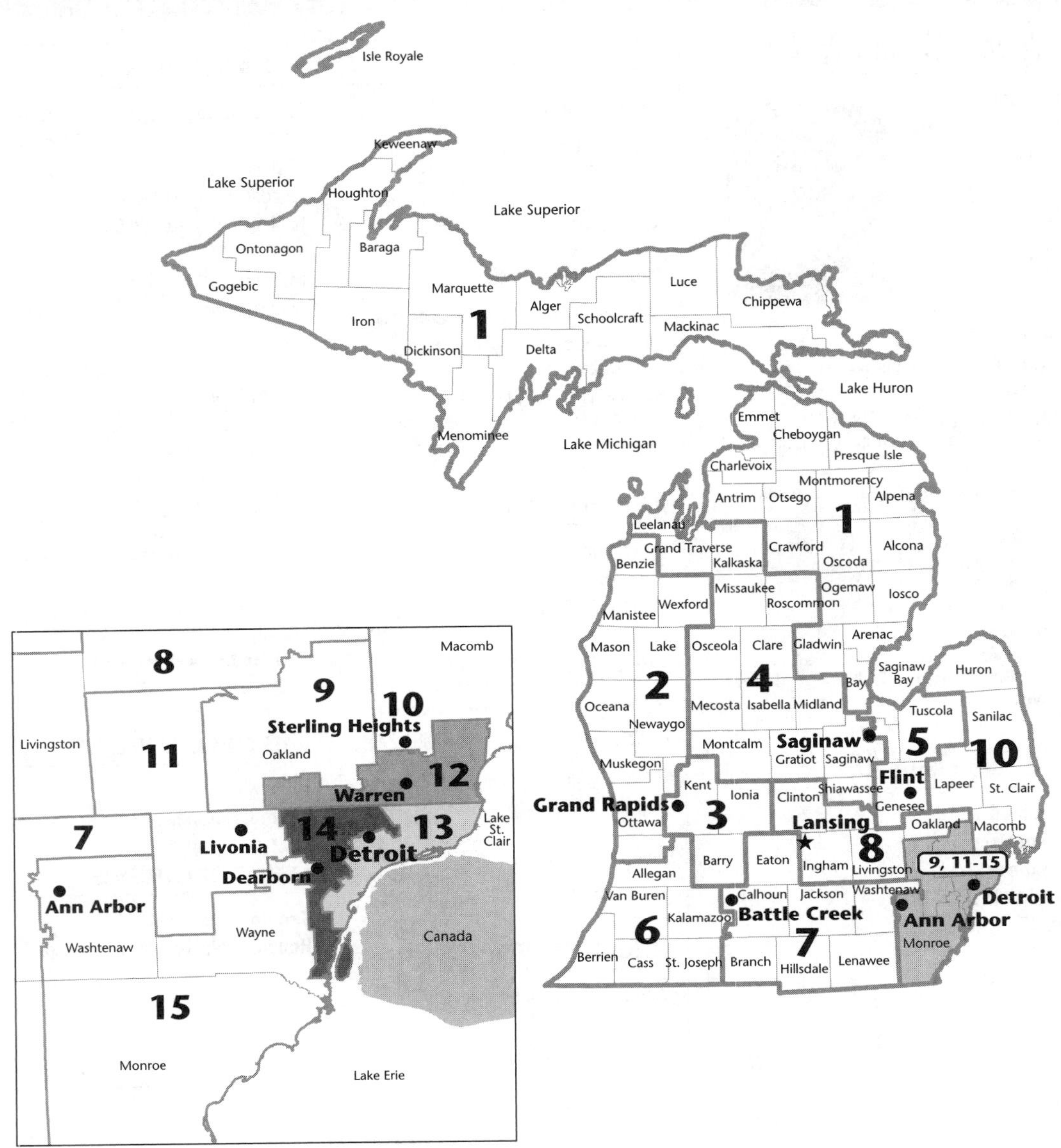

2000 Census Statistics by District

DIST.	2004 VOTE FOR PRESIDENT BUSH	KERRY	WHITE	BLACK	ASIAN	HISP	MEDIAN INCOME	WHITE COLLAR	BLUE COLLAR	SERVICE INDUSTRY	OVER 64	UNDER 18	COLLEGE EDUCATION	RURAL	SQ. MILES
13	19%	80%	29%	60%	1%	7%	$31,165	51%	29%	20%	11%	30%	14%	0%	108
14	18	82	32	61	1	2	$36,099	53	29	18	12	29	14	0	123
15	38	61	79	12	4	3	$48,963	59	26	14	10	25	28	12	961
STATE	48	51	79	14	2	3	$44,667	57	28	15	12	26	22	25	56,804
U.S.	50.7	48.3	69	12	4	13	$41,994	60	25	15	12	26	24	21	3,537,438

Sen. Carl Levin (D)

CAPITOL OFFICE
224-6221
levin.senate.gov
269 Russell 20510-2202; fax 224-1388

COMMITTEES
Armed Services - chairman
Homeland Security & Governmental Affairs
(Permanent Investigations - chairman)
Small Business & Entrepreneurship

RESIDENCE
Detroit

BORN
June 28, 1934, Detroit, Mich.

RELIGION
Jewish

FAMILY
Wife, Barbara Levin; three children

EDUCATION
Swarthmore College, B.A. 1956 (political science); Harvard U., LL.B. 1959

CAREER
Lawyer

POLITICAL HIGHLIGHTS
Michigan Civil Rights Commission general counsel, 1964-67; Detroit chief appellate defender, 1968-69; Detroit City Council, 1970-77 (president, 1974-77)

ELECTION RESULTS

2002 GENERAL		
Carl Levin (D)	1,896,614	60.6%
Andrew Raczkowski (R)	1,185,545	37.9%
2002 PRIMARY		
Carl Levin (D)		unopposed

PREVIOUS WINNING PERCENTAGES
1996 (58%); 1990 (57%); 1984 (52%); 1978 (52%)

Elected 1978; 5th term

The chairman of the Armed Services Committee, Levin is the leading defense expert among Senate Democrats and one of his party's most thoughtful critics of the war in Iraq. He is widely respected by colleagues on both sides of the aisle, who know him for his attention to detail and solid knowledge of policy.

Levin opposed the 2002 resolution authorizing President Bush to use force in Iraq, calling it a "blank check" for Bush to act unilaterally and warning it would cost the United States international support. In the 110th Congress (2007-08), he and Foreign Relations Committee Chairman Joseph R. Biden Jr. of Delaware led the movement to begin withdrawing U.S. troops. In 2007, a resolution they wrote with Senate Majority Leader Harry Reid limited the scope of the mission in Iraq and set a goal for withdrawing all troops by March 31, 2008. Levin said the U.S. refusal to spell out a withdrawal policy "has made the Iraqis less willing to take on responsibility."

Although the resolution failed, very similar wording later passed the Senate as part of a fiscal 2007 supplemental spending bill for the war.

Earlier, in the 109th Congress (2005-06), Levin highlighted the administration's flawed assessment of Iraq's alleged weapons of mass destruction, which Bush cited as a rationale for the war. Levin singled out former CIA Director George J. Tenet for not being assertive enough before the war in stopping senior administration officials from making dire statements about Iraq, especially about its alleged ties to al Qaeda and attempts to reconstitute its nuclear program — claims that U.S. intelligence had not substantiated. More accountability, Levin said, "might have undermined the false sense of urgency for proceeding to war and could have contributed to delay, neither of which fit the administration's policy goals."

Despite his rumpled suits and reading glasses perched precariously at the tip of his nose, Levin is more pit bull than professor when it comes to pursuing his objectives. Whether he is probing offshore tax evasion or picking apart Pentagon policymakers, Levin is both unfailingly polite and utterly relentless. Time Magazine in 2006 put him on its list of the 10 best U.S. senators.

Levin's comprehension of the complicated issues he deals with is the foundation of his clout. He is a master of detail, and is known for preparing for hours before questioning hostile witnesses in order to keep them from evading his questions. He is a dogged but genial interrogator in committee hearings and a tenacious negotiator in legislative drafting sessions.

He had a significant role in the debate over the U.S. terrorist detainee program. Levin worked with then Armed Services Chairman John W. Warner of Virginia and Republicans John McCain of Arizona and Lindsey Graham of South Carolina to craft a law governing the handling of detainees following a June 2006 Supreme Court ruling that the White House's policy of military tribunals violated U.S. and international law. Levin said, "This administration has lost the support of much of the world because of the way we treat detainees," he said. "We've got to win back that support if we are going to win the war on terror." He wound up voting against the final version of the bill because it denied detainees the right of habeas corpus.

Levin has sought to block administration plans for deploying a national missile shield, saying the effort violates laws governing weapons development. He unsuccessfully tried to use the 2005 defense authorization bill to shift some $515 million from the program to other priorities, such as efforts to keep nuclear materials out of the hands of terrorists.

As the chairman of the Homeland Security and Governmental Affairs panel's Permanent Subcommittee on Investigations, and formerly the senior Democrat on the panel, Levin branches out beyond defense issues to delve into such wide-ranging topics as energy market manipulation and contractor abuses on projects in Iraq.

Despite his high profile on national issues, Levin still devotes significant attention to issues affecting Michigan. Levin and his older brother, Sander, who represents Michigan's 12th District in the House, have collaborated on trade issues, focusing particularly on trade with China. The Chinese have little respect for international copyright laws, the two brothers say. This affects Michigan, where state officials complain that China's illegal manufacture of copyrighted auto parts has caused the state to lose jobs.

Like others from his state, Levin splits with a majority of his fellow Democrats when he thinks federal regulations could harm U.S. automakers. When the Senate passed an energy policy overhaul in 2005, Levin thwarted efforts to increase the Corporate Average Fuel Economy standards, arguing such standards are "both arbitrary and discriminatory" since they measure the fuel efficiency of an entire fleet of cars as opposed to individual models. He is pushing for greater government involvement in promoting biofuels, such as the ethanol fuel blend E-85 that can be used by flexible fuel vehicles that Detroit wants to build.

Levin also worked with fellow Michigan Sen. Debbie Stabenow to craft an agreement with Canadian officials to reduce the amount of trash entering Michigan landfills from Canada. The senators cosponsored a provision requiring security inspections of trash at the border.

Although Carl Levin made it to the Senate four years before Sander M. Levin won his House seat, he says he has always looked up to his older brother. Both absorbed a passion for politics from their father, a lawyer active in social justice causes in Detroit. "My older brother was a tremendous role model for me," Levin says. "As a kid, he always involved me in his group. He's sort of a lifelong best buddy for me."

In the 1960s, Levin was general counsel to the Michigan Civil Rights Commission. He had no plans to run for office until riots in 1967 ripped apart Detroit. "After that, there were a lot of people who said I should run for local government," he said. In 1970, he was elected to the Detroit City Council, where he worked to rebuild a shattered city. He butted heads with federal housing officials, and said he decided to run for the Senate in 1978 in part to try to make federal agents "more responsive to local communities."

Levin faced Republican incumbent Robert P. Griffin, who had initially planned to retire after losing a bid to become party leader the previous year. By the time he reversed course and decided to run, Griffin had missed one-third of the Senate votes over a full year. Levin said Griffin was obviously tired of the job, and the voters agreed. Levin won by 4 percentage points.

Levin has an avuncular manner, but he can play political hardball. In 1984, he aired an ad showing his GOP opponent, former astronaut Jack Lousma, warming up a Japanese audience by telling them about the Toyota he owned — a faux pas in a state where the phrase "Japanese car" translates as joblessness. President Ronald Reagan carried Michigan with 59 percent of the vote that year, but Levin held on to win with 52 percent.

In his three succeeding re-election efforts, Levin's margin of victory steadily improved. By 2002, he was entrenched enough that several GOP heavyweights declined to make what they assumed to be a futile run. At one point, Republicans considered nominating a one-time contestant in the TV reality game show "Survivor." Ultimately, state Rep. Andrew Raczkowski took up the GOP banner, but he garnered just 38 percent of the vote.

KEY VOTES

2006

- No Confirm Samuel A. Alito Jr. to the Supreme Court
- Yes Allow consideration of a bill to establish a $140 billion trust fund to compensate victims of asbestos exposure
- No Extend tax cuts for two years at a cost of $70 billion over five years
- Yes Overhaul immigration policy with border security, enforcement and guest worker program
- No Allow consideration of a bill to permanently repeal the estate tax
- Yes Urge President Bush to begin troop withdrawals from Iraq in 2006
- Yes Lift President Bush's restrictions on stem cell research funding
- No Authorize military tribunals for suspected terrorists

2005

- No Curb class action lawsuits by shifting them from state to federal courts
- No Allow confirmation vote on Priscilla R. Owen to the U.S. Court of Appeals for the 5th Circuit
- No Oppose mandatory emissions limits and block recognition of global warming as a threat
- No Approve free-trade pact with five Central American countries
- Yes Pass energy policy overhaul favored by President Bush emphasizing domestic oil and gas production
- No Shield gunmakers from lawsuits when their products are used in crimes
- Yes Ban torture of prisoners in U.S. custody
- No Renew 16 provisions of the Patriot Act
- No Allow final vote on opening the Arctic National Wildlife Refuge to oil and gas exploration

CQ VOTE STUDIES

	PARTY UNITY		PRESIDENTIAL SUPPORT	
	Support	Oppose	Support	Oppose
2006	94%	6%	56%	44%
2005	97%	3%	41%	59%
2004	96%	4%	60%	40%
2003	98%	2%	50%	50%
2002	95%	5%	66%	34%
2001	98%	2%	65%	35%
2000	97%	3%	92%	8%
1999	97%	3%	89%	11%
1998	98%	2%	93%	7%
1997	95%	5%	90%	10%

INTEREST GROUPS

	AFL-CIO	ADA	CCUS	ACU
2006	100%	100%	50%	8%
2005	93%	100%	39%	17%
2004	100%	100%	41%	0%
2003	85%	100%	39%	25%
2002	100%	95%	40%	0%
2001	100%	100%	36%	8%
2000	75%	90%	66%	12%
1999	89%	95%	53%	4%
1998	100%	90%	44%	0%
1997	86%	95%	50%	0%

Sen. Debbie Stabenow (D)

CAPITOL OFFICE
224-4822
senator@stabenow.senate.gov
stabenow.senate.gov
133 Hart 20510-2204; fax 228-0325

COMMITTEES
Agriculture, Nutrition & Forestry
(Rural Revitalization, Conservation, Forestry & Credit - chairwoman)
Budget
Finance

RESIDENCE
Lansing

BORN
April 29, 1950, Clare, Mich.

RELIGION
United Methodist

FAMILY
Husband, Tom Athans; two children

EDUCATION
Michigan State U., B.A. 1972, M.S.W. 1975

CAREER
Leadership training consultant

POLITICAL HIGHLIGHTS
Ingham County Commission, 1975-78 (chairwoman, 1977-1978); Mich. House, 1979-91; Mich. Senate, 1991-94; sought Democratic nomination for governor, 1994; Democratic nominee for lieutenant governor, 1994; U.S. House, 1997-2001

ELECTION RESULTS

2006 GENERAL

Debbie Stabenow (D)	2,151,278	57.0%
Mike Bouchard (R)	1,559,597	41.4%

2006 PRIMARY

Debbie Stabenow (D)	unopposed

PREVIOUS WINNING PERCENTAGES
2000 (49%); 1998 House Election (57%); 1996 House Election (54%)

Elected 2000; 2nd term

Stabenow is moving down the leadership ladder in the Senate but up in legislative influence — a trade she negotiated when Democrats captured majority control of the chamber in the 2006 elections.

In the 110th Congress (2007-08), Stabenow relinquished her leadership post as Democratic conference secretary to Patty Murray of Washington. In exchange, Democratic leaders gave her a coveted seat on the Finance Committee where she can shape health policy, her top legislative interest. She retained a toehold in the leadership as chairwoman of the Democratic Steering and Outreach Committee, an appointed position that helps decide all-important committee assignments.

Stabenow (STAB-uh-now) has substantial input on every aspect of fiscal policy in the new Senate majority. She is one of just three Democrats to serve on both the tax-writing Finance Committee and the Budget Committee, which drafts the annual federal budget.

But it is Finance's jurisdiction over the Medicare program and most health care legislation that Stabenow relishes most. She has spent her congressional career fighting to promote generic drugs over expensive brand-name prescription medicines, and she has battled in vain to persuade the Bush administration to allow imports of cheaper drugs from Canada. With Democrats in charge, she has a better chance of advancing those priorities. (To get onto Finance, she also had to give up her post on Banking, Housing and Urban Affairs, which she had held for six years.)

Stabenow is perpetually sunny, with a warm, maternal way about her that she maintains through the grittiest of political battles. She's a polished pol who's been at the game most of her life. She picks issues that resonate with voters, and frequently gains the tactical advantage over the opposition, as she did in her first Senate campaign by ushering busloads of Michigan senior citizens across the Canadian border to illustrate the plight of the elderly taking desperate measures to find affordable medicines.

But when the fight is over, Stabenow often will turn a political enemy into an ally. After two terms in the House, she narrowly unseated Republican incumbent Sen. Spencer Abraham in 2000, becoming the first woman senator from Michigan. One of her first acts was to help Abraham win Senate confirmation as President Bush's secretary of Energy.

Michigan's flagging auto industry and high unemployment rate are constant concerns for Stabenow. Such worries — and her own re-election battle — influenced her votes on immigration legislation in 2006. She backed several Republican amendments, casting the deciding vote on one that required certification that no U.S. workers were available to take jobs offered to immigrant guest workers. Even after several restrictive amendments were adopted, Stabenow was one of only four Democrats to vote against the final bill.

She has shown a willingness to join with Republicans on a number of other issues. She partnered with moderate Republican Olympia J. Snowe of Maine in a failed attempt to pass legislation that would have delayed future tax cuts if expected budget surpluses did not materialize. When she was in the House, Stabenow voted for GOP-sponsored measures to restructure the nation's public housing system and to encourage states to prosecute violent juvenile offenders as adults. She also supported a Republican-spawned constitutional amendment to outlaw desecration of the U.S. flag.

Yet Stabenow votes a traditional Democratic line on labor issues, abortion rights, education funding, gun control and public support for the arts. She championed a ban on oil and gas drilling in the Great Lakes, and in 2003, she fought for a year's delay of the allotment of $5 billion in rebuilding funds for Iraq, saying the money would be better spent on domestic school construction, veterans' health care, community health clinics and transportation projects. She sets an example for diversity in the workplace with a staff that is roughly two-thirds female and one-third racial minorities.

In 2002, she voted against giving Bush fast-track authority to negotiate trade agreements that Congress cannot amend, which labor strongly opposed. She also opposed the 2005 Central American Free Trade Agreement, though she has supported some bilateral trade pacts such as the 2004 agreements with Morocco and Australia.

Stabenow, with home-state Democratic colleague Carl Levin, clashed with Bush over the president's judicial nominees for the 6th U.S. Circuit Court of Appeals, which includes Michigan. They blocked the nominations for four years to protest the refusal of the Republican-controlled Senate Judiciary Committee to consider President Bill Clinton's picks for that court in the final four years of his tenure. Only after a bipartisan group of senators, the Gang of 14, struck a deal in 2005 on the handling of judicial nominees did Bush win confirmation for most of his 6th Circuit picks.

Stabenow serves on the Agriculture Committee, where she will help rewrite the 2002 farm law, which is up for renewal. She succeeded in getting a provision in that law helping Michigan farmers by mandating a $200 million annual increase in what the government spends on blueberries, cherries and other specialty crops for food programs for the poor.

Stabenow was born and raised in the small town of Clare, Mich. Her father was an Oldsmobile dealer, her mother a nurse. The eldest of three children, she credits her parents with urging her to reach high. "I was very blessed," she told the Detroit News in 2005. "In high school, I would hear 'nurse' or 'teacher' as career options. But dad would say, 'No, doctor or engineer.' He gave me confidence to take risks, to push limits."

She got into politics at an early age. In her mid-20s, Stabenow, trained as a social worker, was angered by the closing of a local nursing home. She successfully challenged an incumbent to win a seat on the Ingham County Commission in 1975, and went on to serve 12 years in the Michigan House and a term in the state Senate.

She had one unhappy year in politics. In 1994, she lost the Democratic gubernatorial primary to veteran Democratic Rep. Howard Wolpe. She then accepted Wolpe's invitation to join his ticket as a candidate for lieutenant governor. But incumbent GOP Gov. John Engler swept to re-election in what turned out to be a good year for Republicans.

Stabenow made a comeback in 1996, ending Republican Rep. Dick Chrysler's one-term tenure in the politically competitive 8th District. She was easily re-elected to the seat in 1998.

That set up Stabenow's 2000 challenge to Abraham, who started out with a big lead in the polls. But Stabenow and allied groups staged a counteroffensive. She had a campaign chest of $8 million and was the top recipient of funds from EMILY's list, a political action committee that supports Democratic women candidates who support abortion rights. Her campaign peaked just in time and she won by less than 2 percentage points.

In 2006, Republicans saw her as vulnerable, encouraged by mediocre approval ratings by the public and an overall negative political climate created by the state's sluggish economy. They nominated Oakland County Sheriff Mike Bouchard and attacked her as ineffective. But Stabenow again piled up the campaign cash, and with a strong Democratic wind at her back that year, won a second term handily.

KEY VOTES

2006

- No Confirm Samuel A. Alito Jr. to the Supreme Court
- Yes Allow consideration of a bill to establish a $140 billion trust fund to compensate victims of asbestos exposure
- No Extend tax cuts for two years at a cost of $70 billion over five years
- No Overhaul immigration policy with border security, enforcement and guest worker program
- No Allow consideration of a bill to permanently repeal the estate tax
- Yes Urge President Bush to begin troop withdrawals from Iraq in 2006
- Yes Lift President Bush's restrictions on stem cell research funding
- Yes Authorize military tribunals for suspected terrorists

2005

- No Curb class action lawsuits by shifting them from state to federal courts
- No Allow confirmation vote on Priscilla R. Owen to the U.S. Court of Appeals for the 5th Circuit
- No Oppose mandatory emissions limits and block recognition of global warming as a threat
- No Approve free-trade pact with five Central American countries
- Yes Pass energy policy overhaul favored by President Bush emphasizing domestic oil and gas production
- No Shield gunmakers from lawsuits when their products are used in crimes
- Yes Ban torture of prisoners in U.S. custody
- No Renew 16 provisions of the Patriot Act
- No Allow final vote on opening the Arctic National Wildlife Refuge to oil and gas exploration

CQ VOTE STUDIES

	PARTY UNITY		PRESIDENTIAL SUPPORT	
	Support	Oppose	Support	Oppose
2006	88%	12%	51%	49%
2005	95%	5%	33%	67%
2004	96%	4%	58%	42%
2003	97%	3%	49%	51%
2002	95%	5%	66%	34%
2001	96%	4%	64%	36%
House Service:				
2000	82%	18%	74%	26%
1999	87%	13%	78%	22%
1998	87%	13%	78%	22%
1997	88%	12%	81%	19%

INTEREST GROUPS

	AFL-CIO	ADA	CCUS	ACU
2006	100%	90%	50%	16%
2005	93%	100%	44%	12%
2004	100%	100%	65%	8%
2003	85%	95%	39%	20%
2002	100%	95%	45%	0%
2001	100%	100%	43%	8%
House Service:				
2000	90%	90%	47%	16%
1999	78%	95%	44%	4%
1998	90%	100%	61%	9%
1997	100%	95%	50%	12%

Rep. Bart Stupak (D)

CAPITOL OFFICE
225-4735
www.house.gov/stupak
2352 Rayburn 20515-2201; fax 225-4744

COMMITTEES
Energy & Commerce
(Oversight & Investigations - chairman)

RESIDENCE
Menominee

BORN
Feb. 29, 1952, Milwaukee, Wis.

RELIGION
Roman Catholic

FAMILY
Wife, Laurie Stupak; two children (one deceased)

EDUCATION
Northwestern Michigan Community College, A.A. 1972; Saginaw Valley State College, B.S. 1977 (criminal justice); Thomas M. Cooley Law School, J.D. 1981

CAREER
Lawyer; state trooper; patrolman

POLITICAL HIGHLIGHTS
Mich. House, 1989-91; sought Democratic nomination for Mich. Senate, 1990

ELECTION RESULTS

2006 GENERAL		
Bart Stupak (D)	180,448	69.4%
Don Hooper (R)	72,753	28.0%
2006 PRIMARY		
Bart Stupak (D)		unopposed
2004 GENERAL		
Bart Stupak (D)	211,571	65.6%
Don Hooper (R)	105,706	32.8%

PREVIOUS WINNING PERCENTAGES
2002 (68%); 2000 (58%); 1998 (59%); 1996 (71%); 1994 (57%); 1992 (54%)

Elected 1992; 8th term

Befitting someone from Michigan's frigid and self-reliant Upper Peninsula, Stupak is a Democrat who goes his own way often enough to preserve his standing as a centrist back home in the rural reaches of the 1st District. A former police officer and state trooper, he favors gun owners' rights, opposes abortion and is a steadfast ally of organized labor. That combination satisfies the region's many social conservatives while pleasing its union-label Democrats.

After serving all but one of his first seven terms in Congress in the minority, Stupak (STU-pack) has an opportunity to raise his profile considerably with his selection in the 110th Congress (2007-08) as chairman of the House Energy and Commerce panel's Oversight and Investigations Subcommittee. That is the subcommittee that his Michigan colleague, John D. Dingell, himself chaired when the Democrats last ran the House in the early 1990s. Dingell, then and now chairman of the full Energy and Commerce Committee, made the Oversight panel a force to be reckoned with, with his aggressive and relentless interrogations. Stupak says his background in law and law enforcement make him a good fit for the job.

Stupak is interested in looking into security lapses at the government's nuclear research labs, outbreaks of bacterial infection in food supplies and possible gas price gouging. "It's interesting that gas drops 60 cents a gallon right before the election . . . and goes right back up after the election," Stupak told the Detroit Free Press in January 2007. "There are so many things, where do you even start?" Early in the 110th Congress, the subcommittee also began looking into health care in New Orleans post-Hurricane Katrina and contamination of pet food.

Stupak is usually a reliable vote for Democratic leaders. In 2005, he voted no on the Central American Free Trade Agreement, which organized labor opposed. However, he has a bit of social conservatism that mirrors his constituency. He sided with the GOP leadership in opposing the use of federal funds for embryonic stem cell research. He also voted for a bill making it a federal crime to take a minor across state lines for an abortion to avoid state parental notification and consent laws.

On the Energy and Commerce panel, Stupak advocates for technology access for rural areas like his district that typically lag behind in multimedia capabilities. After a federal court ruled in 2006 that satellite company DISH Network had been sending distant signals to hundreds of thousands of its customers illegally, many Upper Peninsula inhabitants lost channels. Stupak went to work trying to find a way to restore the service legally.

Like many of his Michigan colleagues, Stupak is very protective of the Great Lakes. He opposes efforts to divert water from the lakes to states where water is in short supply. And his proposal to ban oil drilling in the Great Lakes became part of the 2005 energy law. In early 2007, the House passed his proposal encouraging greater cooperation between Canada and the United States to clean up sewage discharges in the Great Lakes.

Stupak has to be careful on environmental issues, however. Economically struggling communities in his district would like to attract more industry, but encouraging development threatens the natural environment, which attracts much-needed tourist dollars. He has supported road-building subsidies for the logging industry and criticized the National Park Service for proposing a ban on snowmobiles in parks. He says each national park should set its own policy.

A top priority for Stupak is legislation dealing with law enforcement. In the 107th Congress (2001-02), he won enactment of a bill limiting public access to body armor, which emboldens criminals to engage in shootouts with police. Since the 2001 terrorist attacks, and the Sept. 11 commission's finding that local law enforcement often cannot communicate well with emergency services, Stupak has been a leading advocate of federal aid to improve first-responder communications systems.

On a matter close to his heart, Stupak has pressed the Food and Drug Administration to impose tighter regulation on the acne medication Accutane, which he believes was the reason his son B.J. — a popular high school athlete and student leader — committed suicide at age 17 in 2000. Stupak instigated a two-year congressional investigation into the drug's effects, and in 2004 the FDA ordered doctors and pharmacies to inform patients about the drug's risks and get their consent before dispensing it.

Though Stupak has been a member of the National Rifle Association, in the wake of the shootings at Colorado's Columbine High School in 1999 he voted for the strictest of several proposals to require background checks at gun shows. His vote drew opposition from many in northern Michigan, where gun ownership is common and hunting is a popular pastime. The NRA, which had endorsed Stupak in the past, backed his Republican challenger in 2000. Stupak returned to good standing with the association after voting in 2004 for a bill to repeal a ban on gun ownership in the District of Columbia. The NRA endorsed him in his 2006 race.

As a lifelong resident of the Upper Peninsula (known by locals as the U.P.), Stupak prides himself on his "Yooper" background. While serving as an Escanaba police officer, he earned an undergraduate degree in criminal justice. He then got a law degree while working as a trooper. He retired from the force in 1984 after injuring a knee while chasing a suspect on foot. Stupak practiced law and got involved in local politics. He won a state House seat in 1988 but gave it up after two years for a state Senate bid in which he narrowly lost the Democratic primary.

Stupak's opportunity to try for Congress came in 1992, when Republican Rep. Robert W. Davis retired after seven terms. Davis' departure was hastened when the House ethics committee labeled him one of 22 abusers of the private bank then maintained for House members. Stupak defeated former Republican Rep. Philip E. Ruppe with 54 percent of the vote. In subsequent elections in the 1990s, he only once polled more than 60 percent. But decennial redistricting for this decade created a slightly more Democratic 1st District, and Stupak's road to re-election has been easier since.

KEY VOTES

2006

Yes Stop broadband companies from favoring select Internet traffic

No Affirm U.S. commitment to war in Iraq and reject setting a withdrawal date for troops

No Repeal requirement for bilingual ballots at the polls

Yes Permit U.S. sale of civilian nuclear technology to India

Yes Build a 700-mile fence on the U.S.-Mexico border to curb illegal crossings

? Permit warrantless wiretaps of suspected terrorists

2005

Yes Intervene in the life-support case of Terri Schiavo

No Lift President Bush's restrictions on stem cell research funding

Yes Prohibit FBI access to library and bookstore records

No Approve free-trade pact with five Central American countries

Yes Pass energy policy overhaul favored by President Bush emphasizing domestic oil and gas production

No End mandatory preservation of habitat of endangered animal and plant species

Yes Ban torture of prisoners in U.S. custody

CQ VOTE STUDIES

	PARTY UNITY		PRESIDENTIAL SUPPORT	
	Support	Oppose	Support	Oppose
2006	90%	10%	37%	63%
2005	87%	13%	28%	72%
2004	91%	9%	41%	59%
2003	86%	14%	38%	62%
2002	89%	11%	33%	67%

INTEREST GROUPS

	AFL-CIO	ADA	CCUS	ACU
2006	100%	75%	33%	28%
2005	100%	80%	46%	25%
2004	93%	80%	38%	16%
2003	100%	85%	29%	42%
2002	100%	80%	45%	16%

MICHIGAN 1

Upper Peninsula; northern Lower Michigan

Beginning along the shore of the Saginaw Bay, the 1st stretches 25,000 square miles and into Lake Superior to reach the Great Lake State's northernmost outpost on Isle Royale. Full of rolling, forested hills, the 1st takes in 44 percent of Michigan's land mass, but did not contain a single city with more than 20,000 residents at the time of the 2000 census.

Self-proclaimed "Yoopers" from the state's Upper Peninsula (U.P.) are connected to the rest of the district on the Lower Peninsula only by the Mackinac Bridge. Despite being Michiganders, Yoopers, isolated from the rest of their state, tend to identify culturally with nearby Wisconsinites or Canadians.

Touching three of the Great Lakes, the 1st has more freshwater shoreline than any other district in the continental United States and relies heavily on tourism revenue. U.P. residents and visitors spend the winter months atop mountains that get hundreds of inches of lake-effect snow, making the 1st one of the few places suited to skiing in the Midwest. Cabins, beaches and resorts around the Lower Peninsula's Petoskey and Mackinac Island also lure tourists from Detroit, Chicago and Cleveland.

Nearly tapped out resources in the mining industry now provide only modest incomes for district residents. The logging industry also faces uncertain times, and NAFTA has effectively killed most remaining copper, paper and iron production in the area.

There is a strong current of social conservatism in the 1st, particularly with regard to gun rights, that contributes to the Republican shift in recent years, although Democrats still dominate local politics. In 2004, the 1st was the only Michigan district to back a presidential candidate, George W. Bush, and a House candidate, Rep. Stupak, from different political parties.

MAJOR INDUSTRY

Logging, tourism, mining, auto parts

CITIES

Marquette, 19,661; Sault Ste. Marie, 16,542; Escanaba, 13,140

NOTABLE

Gordon Lightfoot's song "Wreck of the Edmund Fitzgerald" was inspired by the crash near Whitefish Point, which is now home to the Great Lakes Shipwreck Museum; The National Ski Hall of Fame is in Ishpeming.

Rep. Peter Hoekstra (R)

CAPITOL OFFICE
225-4401
hoekstra.house.gov
2234 Rayburn 20515-2202; fax 226-0779

COMMITTEES
Appropriations Select Intelligence Oversight Panel
Education & Labor
Select Intelligence - ranking member

RESIDENCE
Holland

BORN
Oct. 30, 1953, Groningen, Netherlands

RELIGION
Christian Reformed Church

FAMILY
Wife, Diane Hoekstra; three children

EDUCATION
Hope College, B.A. 1975 (political science);
U. of Michigan, M.B.A. 1977

CAREER
Furniture company executive

POLITICAL HIGHLIGHTS
No previous office

ELECTION RESULTS

2006 GENERAL		
Peter Hoekstra (R)	183,006	66.5%
Kimon Kotos (D)	86,950	31.6%
2006 PRIMARY		
Peter Hoekstra (R)		unopposed
2004 GENERAL		
Peter Hoekstra (R)	225,343	69.3%
Kimon Kotos (D)	94,040	28.9%

PREVIOUS WINNING PERCENTAGES
2002 (70%); 2000 (64%); 1998 (69%); 1996 (65%); 1994 (75%); 1992 (63%)

Elected 1992; 8th term

After more than two years as chairman of the House Intelligence Committee, where he defended the Bush administration's controversial tactics in the war on terrorism and fought committee Democrats pushing for more scrutiny of the administration's intelligence efforts, Hoekstra in the 110th Congress (2007-08) finds his role in that arena much reduced.

The Democratic takeover of the House took away his chairmanship. Hoekstra (HOOK-struh) is still the top-ranking Republican on the Intelligence panel, and still comes to President Bush's aid when it comes to the president's plans for conducting the war in Iraq. And he is on the new Intelligence Oversight panel of the Appropriations Committee. He maintains that "radical militant Islam is more dangerous and unique than any enemy that the United States has ever faced."

But Hoekstra also reclaimed the seat on the Education and Labor Committee that he had given up for two years to focus on the Intelligence panel duties, and early in 2007 he inserted himself as a key player in the debate over what to do about the 2001 education law, known as No Child Left Behind, that imposed a new testing regimen on elementary and secondary education.

Back then, as a member of what was known as the Education and the Workforce Committee, he unsuccessfully fought to kill a central tenet of Bush's education initiative, mandatory annual testing in the elementary grades, which he called an inappropriate federal mandate.

In the 110th Congress, as the panel started its work on the reauthorization of the education law, Hoekstra took the lead in pushing a bill that would let states come up with their own ways to measure school performance. Although many Democrats have criticized the Bush administration for not providing enough money to carry out the law's mandates, Hoekstra was unable to attract Democratic support to join the dozens of GOP backers.

In his two years as Intelligence chairman, Hoekstra tried to strengthen the committee's oversight role, but stood behind the White House when push came to shove. He vigorously defended the Bush administration's use of wiretaps in terrorism investigations without prior consent from judges. He agreed with Bush's contention that a president had inherent constitutional authority to spy on suspected terrorists.

One of his first moves after taking the gavel from Porter J. Goss of Florida, who was appointed CIA chief in 2004, was to create a new Intelligence subcommittee on oversight to track implementation of the 2004 intelligence overhaul. Several months later, Hoekstra and senior Democrat Jane Harman of California said they were concerned that Director of National Intelligence John D. Negroponte was creating more bureaucracy rather than streamlining the nation's intelligence capabilities as the law intended.

Hoekstra consistently supports conservative positions, voting with Bush 91 percent of the time in the 109th Congress (2005-06). On votes that divide the House along party lines, he sides with the GOP more than 90 percent of the time.

Hoekstra has closer ties to labor than most conservatives. The Michigan Teamsters union routinely endorses him for re-election, and he helped nurture an uneasy political relationship between the union and the White House. That led to the union's backing of Bush's proposal to drill in Alaska's Arctic National Wildlife Refuge, which the union said would create jobs.

As chairman of the Education and the Workforce panel's Oversight Subcommittee for six years (1995-2001), Hoekstra examined the books of the Labor and Education departments and of President Bill Clinton's AmeriCorps community service program. He also headed a probe of election corruption within the Teamsters union for which he was criticized by members of both parties. Democrats said he was seeking partisan advantage while Republicans objected that he wasn't being political enough.

In bearing, Hoekstra is reserved, even stolid, displaying the personal discipline that made him a success as a business executive. Hoekstra lives out of his office when Congress is in session, stowing his clothes, a sleeping bag and a pillow there. He showers at the House gym and eats at the House restaurants; his wife and three children live in Michigan. "I'm about as tight as you can get. I'm frugal in the finest of Dutch traditions," he said.

The child of immigrants from the Netherlands, Hoekstra was born Cornelius Peter Hoekstra, but Cornelius was dropped at the insistence of immigration officials who decreed it was not a familiar name in America. His family settled in the town of Holland in a heavily Dutch part of Michigan, but he has never forgotten the ham-handed welcome. "That's shattering to your self-esteem. You're three years old and they take away your name and give you a new one," he said.

Hoekstra's father ran a local bakery shop for 25 years. The family spoke English and Dutch at home, but he was encouraged to blend into his new surroundings. "There was really a tremendous desire to become American. In some ways, you forgot or you hid your Dutch ancestry."

After getting a master's degree in business administration from the University of Michigan, Hoekstra spent 15 years at the furniture design firm Herman Miller. He started as a project manager and rose to vice president for product management.

The House seat was the first public office he attempted to win. In 1992, he knocked off 13-term GOP Rep. Guy Vander Jagt for whom he once had interned, accusing the incumbent of neglecting his constituents in favor of Washington life. Hoekstra ousted Vander Jagt in the GOP primary by 6 percentage points, which still surprises him. He took five weeks off before primary day and spent just $50,000. His victory presaged the political earthquake of 1994, when entrenched incumbents fell nationwide and Republicans took control of Congress. Hoekstra was typical of the trend, a change-minded novice sweeping his way into political office.

He promised to serve six terms and leave, but later revoked that pledge. The 2nd District voters didn't seem to mind the about-face. He captured about two-thirds of the vote in his re-election bids for his seventh and eighth terms.

KEY VOTES

2006

- No — Stop broadband companies from favoring select Internet traffic
- Yes — Affirm U.S. commitment to war in Iraq and reject setting a withdrawal date for troops
- Yes — Repeal requirement for bilingual ballots at the polls
- Yes — Permit U.S. sale of civilian nuclear technology to India
- Yes — Build a 700-mile fence on the U.S.-Mexico border to curb illegal crossings
- Yes — Permit warrantless wiretaps of suspected terrorists

2005

- ? — Intervene in the life-support case of Terri Schiavo
- No — Lift President Bush's restrictions on stem cell research funding
- No — Prohibit FBI access to library and bookstore records
- Yes — Approve free-trade pact with five Central American countries
- Yes — Pass energy policy overhaul favored by President Bush emphasizing domestic oil and gas production
- Yes — End mandatory preservation of habitat of endangered animal and plant species
- No — Ban torture of prisoners in U.S. custody

CQ VOTE STUDIES

	PARTY UNITY		PRESIDENTIAL SUPPORT	
	Support	Oppose	Support	Oppose
2006	95%	5%	90%	10%
2005	96%	4%	91%	9%
2004	98%	2%	90%	10%
2003	95%	5%	92%	8%
2002	91%	9%	88%	12%

INTEREST GROUPS

	AFL-CIO	ADA	CCUS	ACU
2006	21%	5%	93%	92%
2005	13%	0%	89%	100%
2004	15%	5%	95%	96%
2003	23%	10%	88%	77%
2002	11%	5%	85%	92%

MICHIGAN 2
West — Muskegon, Holland

The 2nd spans 160 miles of the Lake Michigan shoreline, making it an attractive location for tourists and retirees. The district is full of cherry trees, asparagus farms and sandy beaches, and the beaches are bombarded every summer by vacationers hoping for at least one completely sunny day.

Most of the 2nd's land north of Muskegon, the district's largest city, consists of sparsely populated, smaller rural communities, which are nestled in the Manistee National Forest and make up the state's most sprawling school districts south of the Upper Peninsula. Benzie County in the north continues to grow, as baby boomers and young families look to move into communities outside of crowded metropolitan areas.

Opportunities in the once-rich logging industry have been replaced by jobs at smaller manufacturing companies, which are mostly based in the district's south. Muskegon has struggled to keep manufacturing jobs, but western Michigan hosts several of the nation's top office furniture makers, including Herman Miller in Zeeland and Haworth in Holland, both south of Muskegon.

Holland is a conservative, Dutch-settled port town that relies on tourism. Early 20th century lifestyle is recreated in the Dutch Village Theme Park, which features traditional crafts and klompen dancers. Holland's annual tulip festival draws hundreds of thousands of visitors every May.

Traditional Dutch heritage has made the 2nd one of Michigan's most staunchly Republican districts. The district gave George W. Bush 60 percent of its 2004 presidential vote, and Ottawa County — with more than one-third of district residents — gave Bush 72 percent, both statewide highs. Support for Democratic candidates is found among minority voters in Muskegon.

MAJOR INDUSTRY
Metal, furniture, tourism, agriculture

CITIES
Muskegon, 40,105; Holland, 35,048; Norton Shores, 22,527

NOTABLE
Grand Haven, known as Coast Guard City USA, honors the men and women of the U.S. Coast Guard during its annual festival; Oceana County hosts the National Asparagus Festival.

Rep. Vernon J. Ehlers (R)

CAPITOL OFFICE
225-3831
www.house.gov/ehlers
2182 Rayburn 20515-2203; fax 225-5144

COMMITTEES
Education & Labor
House Administration - ranking member
Science & Technology
Transportation & Infrastructure
Joint Library
Joint Printing

RESIDENCE
Grand Rapids

BORN
Feb. 6, 1934, Pipestone, Minn.

RELIGION
Christian Reformed Church

FAMILY
Wife, Jo Ehlers; four children

EDUCATION
Calvin College, attended 1952-55 (physics); U. of California, Berkeley, A.B. 1956 (physics), Ph.D. 1960 (physics)

CAREER
Professor; physicist

POLITICAL HIGHLIGHTS
Kent County Commission, 1975-83 (chairman, 1979-82); Mich. House, 1983-85; Mich. Senate, 1985-93 (president pro tempore, 1990-93)

ELECTION RESULTS

2006 GENERAL		
Vernon J. Ehlers (R)	171,212	63.1%
James Rinck (D)	93,846	34.6%
Jeff A. Steinport (LIBERT)	3,702	1.4%
2006 PRIMARY		
Vernon J. Ehlers (R)		unopposed
2004 GENERAL		
Vernon J. Ehlers (R)	214,465	66.6%
Peter H. Hickey (D)	101,395	31.5%
Warren Adams (LIBERT)	3,695	1.2%

PREVIOUS WINNING PERCENTAGES
2002 (70%); 2000 (65%); 1998 (73%); 1996 (69%); 1994 (74%); 1993 Special Election (67%)

Elected December 1993; 7th full term

The white-haired, grandfatherly Ehlers briefly realized his goal of becoming a full committee chairman in 2006, heading the House's panel on House Administration for a little less than a year before the Democratic takeover of the chamber snatched the gavel away in 2007.

Ehlers (AY-lurz) had ascended in less than ideal circumstances. He was appointed by the GOP leadership to replace scandal-plagued colleague Bob Ney of Ohio, who was caught up in an influence-peddling scandal and eventually resigned.

In the 110th Congress (2007-08), Ehlers is the top-ranking Republican on the House Administration panel and, perhaps more important, the ranking Republican on the Research and Science Education Subcommittee of the Science and Technology Committee. As the first research physicist elected to Congress, Ehlers would like someday to chair the Science panel.

In one sense, the Democratic takeover of the House did not affect Ehlers as much as many of his GOP colleagues. Many of them had to relinquish committee assignments entirely, as the GOP had to downsize its rosters. But Ehlers was able to keep all four of his committees. He also serves on Education and Labor, and Transportation and Infrastructure.

And sometimes, he is able to pursue his interests across committee lines. In the case of improving math and science education, he has offered bills addressing the issue in both the Education and Science panels.

On House Administration, he has had a longstanding interest in bringing the Capitol into the technology age. Ehlers has been using computers since 1957, when working on his doctorate in the structure of the atomic nucleus. When he got to Congress, he found the institution was technologically years, if not decades, behind private industry. He recalls, "It was easier to send an e-mail to Moscow than to send it 20 feet down the hall to a colleague."

When Republicans took control of the House in 1995, Speaker Newt Gingrich of Georgia, also a technology buff, appointed Ehlers to help bring the House into the Internet age. The project eventually consumed more than 700 hours of his time, and established him as a go-to guy on science and technology issues. One of Ehlers' first moves as House Administration chairman was to undertake a review of the House's information technology systems.

His other avid interest is national policy on science. He is a regular at sparsely attended Science panel meetings, where as a trained scientist his opinion carries extra weight. New York Republican Sherwood Boehlert, the committee's chairman from 2001-07, once said, "With Vern, usually it's me asking a question and then listening."

Ehlers frets that the United States is not devoting enough resources to basic science and to science education. "If kids in school now want a good job in the future, they had better know the basics of science, mathematics and engineering," he says. "Most of them are not learning that in elementary and secondary schools right now."

He was able to get a provision in President Bush's 2001 education policy overhaul that ensures students are tested on science as well as reading and math. In 2003, he successfully offered a measure to expand the National Science Foundation's kindergarten through 12th-grade programs.

Ehlers travels extensively to schools and universities to promote science education. "I often tell high school kids, 'Don't laugh at the nerds. If you're not a nerd, you're likely to be working for one in the future,'" he says. When asked in an interview with the American Physical Association what he would like people to know about him, Ehlers said, "Well, I'm a nice guy. So sometimes I feel like a misfit in Congress. There are other nice people there, don't misunderstand me, but it's a pretty tough place. It's a little hard for someone from the world of physics to get used to."

Ehlers and fellow physicist-legislator Rush D. Holt, a New Jersey Democrat, led a group of 155 lawmakers urging appropriators to double the National Science Foundation's budget, money they say has resulted in more than 100 Nobel Prizes and innovations such as Internet browsers, wireless phones and global positioning technology.

He is among the Republican moderates who take a stronger pro-environment stand. An environmental activist who launched his political career on green issues, Ehlers opposes drilling for oil in Alaska's Arctic National Wildlife Refuge. He also supported increasing fuel efficiency standards for sport utility vehicles — an unpopular position in auto-centric Michigan. But he backed the controversial administration decision not to sign the Kyoto Protocol to limit industrial emissions, arguing that the treaty unfairly exempted China and other developing nations.

The son of a minister and a devout Christian himself, Ehlers keeps a Bible in his office, on a shelf next to his Basic Dictionary of Science.

A sickly child who suffered from severe asthma, Ehlers was schooled at home because his parents felt he would be less likely to catch colds from other children. His interest in science was sparked by his sister's free subscription to Popular Science magazine. "I still remember doing some of those experiments at home," he says. His father encouraged him to go to college, and Ehlers excelled academically, completing his doctorate in physics at the University of California at Berkeley at age 26. He stayed on as a research physicist for six years. In 1966, he left for the more conservative, religious-oriented atmosphere of Calvin College in Grand Rapids, which he had attended as an undergraduate.

In 1982, Ehlers won election to the state House, succeeding Republican Paul B. Henry, a former colleague at Calvin, who had moved to the state Senate. Over the next dozen years, Ehlers followed Henry up the political ladder, succeeding him in the state Senate and finally in Congress. In 1993, Ehlers was president pro tempore of the Michigan Senate. Nearly 60 years old, he was looking for a new challenge and weighing a campaign for the Senate seat held by Democrat Donald W. Riegle Jr. But when Henry died of brain cancer that July, Ehlers launched a House bid. He won with 67 percent of the vote in the special election and has never faced a significant challenge to his re-election.

KEY VOTES

2006

- No Stop broadband companies from favoring select Internet traffic
- Yes Affirm U.S. commitment to war in Iraq and reject setting a withdrawal date for troops
- No Repeal requirement for bilingual ballots at the polls
- Yes Permit U.S. sale of civilian nuclear technology to India
- Yes Build a 700-mile fence on the U.S.-Mexico border to curb illegal crossings
- Yes Permit warrantless wiretaps of suspected terrorists

2005

- Yes Intervene in the life-support case of Terri Schiavo
- No Lift President Bush's restrictions on stem cell research funding
- Yes Prohibit FBI access to library and bookstore records
- Yes Approve free-trade pact with five Central American countries
- Yes Pass energy policy overhaul favored by President Bush emphasizing domestic oil and gas production
- No End mandatory preservation of habitat of endangered animal and plant species
- Yes Ban torture of prisoners in U.S. custody

CQ VOTE STUDIES

	PARTY UNITY		PRESIDENTIAL SUPPORT	
	Support	Oppose	Support	Oppose
2006	84%	16%	95%	5%
2005	78%	22%	67%	33%
2004	86%	14%	79%	21%
2003	84%	16%	85%	15%
2002	85%	15%	87%	13%

INTEREST GROUPS

	AFL-CIO	ADA	CCUS	ACU
2006	21%	10%	80%	68%
2005	20%	15%	85%	64%
2004	27%	20%	100%	67%
2003	7%	15%	87%	68%
2002	11%	15%	95%	80%

MICHIGAN 3

West central – Grand Rapids

Grand Rapids, Michigan's second-most-populous city, teems with auto plants and metals manufacturing, but it's a world away from Detroit. Conservative Dutch Republicans — not auto union Democrats — control the 3rd, making it one of the state's strongest GOP districts.

Also unlike Detroit, Grand Rapids escaped complete dependence on the auto industry. The city is a leading producer of metal office furniture, in addition to avionics systems, tools and home appliances. Footwear manufacturer Wolverine World Wide, maker of brands such as Hush Puppies and Sebago, has headquarters in Rockford, north of Grand Rapids. One of the largest employers here, direct sales company Alticor, based in Ada, markets personal- and home-care products. The 3rd's growing health care industry prompted Michigan State University to build a new medical school, to be completed by 2010, in Grand Rapids.

Major efforts to revitalize downtown Grand Rapids have attracted young professionals, who enjoy the 3rd's big city amenities and close proximity to the Lake Michigan shoreline. The new convention center in Grand Rapids complements its rejuvenated business and entertainment district.

Gerald R. Ford made his way to the U.S. House and then the Oval Office from Grand Rapids — the area airport is named for the 38th president — and his brand of small-government Republicanism and fiscal restraint still holds sway in the 3rd. In the 2004 presidential election, the district gave George W. Bush 59 percent of its vote, his second-highest percentage in the state.

More than 80 percent of residents live in Kent County, which grew by 15 percent in the 1990s largely because of rapid growth outside of Grand Rapids, which grew by just 5 percent. The rest live in Ionia and Barry counties, located east and southeast of Kent, respectively.

MAJOR INDUSTRY
Office furniture, auto parts, metals manufacturing, health care

CITIES
Grand Rapids, 197,800; Wyoming, 69,368; Kentwood, 45,255; Walker, 21,842; Forest Hills (unincorporated), 20,942

NOTABLE
The Norton Mound Group, one of the best-preserved burial centers of the Hopewell culture, is in Grand Rapids.

Rep. Dave Camp (R)

CAPITOL OFFICE
225-3561
www.house.gov/camp
137 Cannon 20515-2204; fax 225-9679

COMMITTEES
Ways & Means

RESIDENCE
Midland

BORN
July 9, 1953, Midland, Mich.

RELIGION
Roman Catholic

FAMILY
Wife, Nancy Camp; three children

EDUCATION
Albion College, B.A. 1975 (economics);
U. of San Diego, J.D. 1978

CAREER
Lawyer; congressional aide

POLITICAL HIGHLIGHTS
Mich. House, 1989-91

ELECTION RESULTS

2006 GENERAL		
Dave Camp (R)	160,041	60.6%
Mike Huckleberry (D)	100,260	37.9%
2006 PRIMARY		
Dave Camp (R)		unopposed
2004 GENERAL		
Dave Camp (R)	205,274	64.4%
Mike Huckleberry (D)	110,885	34.8%

PREVIOUS WINNING PERCENTAGES
2002 (68%); 2000 (68%); 1998 (91%); 1996 (65%); 1994 (73%); 1992 (63%); 1990 (65%)

Elected 1990; 9th term

Camp has formed his own one-man House faction: the moderate conservative. He is the only lawmaker on the rosters of both the conservative Republican Study Committee and the moderate Republican Main Street Partnership.

He sees no conflict in planting one foot on each side of House Republicans' ideological divide. "I'm a conservative on fiscal policy, but I'm a moderate on some other issues," he says. Those other issues, however, are few and far between; Camp usually votes with conservatives. Still, he finds it useful to have "as many channels of communication as you can."

With an understated political style and unswerving loyalty to party leaders, Camp has steadily moved up the ranks in the House. He has worked his way onto the top row of the Ways and Means Committee dais, where he served as chairman of the Select Revenue Measures Subcommittee in the 109th Congress (2005-06) and is the top-ranking Republican on the Health Subcommittee in the 110th Congress (2007-08). He was a strong supporter of President Bush's proposal to create private investment accounts within Social Security, promoting it vigorously despite the backlash the plan encountered. He says the debate was "a huge educational issue for everyone" and vows to continue pursuing a solution to the retirement system's long-term fiscal imbalances.

Camp has substantial expertise on retirement issues. During the 109th Congress, he was deeply involved in work on a major pension overhaul bill that included significant new tax incentives for retirement savings. He was one of a handful of lawmakers from both chambers who spent months writing the final bill, which he called among the most difficult issues he has tackled as a legislator. "It was complex politically and complex policywise," he said. "You usually get one, but you don't get both."

When he arrived in the House in 1991, Camp was on the leading edge of the wave of youthful Republican conservatives who since have flooded the chamber. But while many of those lawmakers still cultivate their images as political outsiders, Camp has made his mark the old-fashioned way — landing a choice committee assignment, digging into complex legislative issues and taking on a variety of chores for party elders.

Camp ran J. Dennis Hastert's whirlwind campaign for Speaker at the end of 1998 and remained a part of Hastert's inner circle. When Hastert left the leadership in the 110th Congress, Camp kept his post on the GOP Steering Committee, which makes committee assignments for the party.

But it is on Ways and Means, where Camp has served since his second term, that he has been most influential. He played a key role in the enactment of the 1996 law overhauling the welfare system, supported all the major trade pacts of his tenure and has been a leader in the GOP's quest to make permanent the package of tax cuts enacted in 2001.

Although Camp usually votes the party line, in early 2004 he was one of 39 Republicans to vote for a Democratic amendment extending for six months a federal program offering 13 weeks of supplemental unemployment benefits to jobless workers who have exhausted their state benefits.

He was one of 67 Republicans to vote against a 2004 overhaul of the nation's intelligence agencies. A member of the Homeland Security Committee at the time, Camp said he objected to the omission from the final bill of certain provisions regarding detention of terrorists and illegal aliens thought to be a security risk and the failure to grant border patrol agents greater authority to deport dangerous illegal aliens.

Camp has drawn on his experience as a domestic-law attorney in Michigan to promote the adoption of children in foster care. In 2003, he won enactment of a bill to give states financial incentives to increase the number of adoptions each year, particularly of older children and those with special needs. Camp's measure offered states $4,000 extra for each child adopted beyond the previous year's level.

Frugal with federal monies, Camp has long promoted legislation to apply any lawmaker's unused office and staff funds to paying down the national debt, and during his tenure he has returned to the Treasury more than $1 million in unused office account money, though lawmakers are not required to do so.

In 2006, Camp drew scrutiny for contributions he had received from convicted lobbyist Jack Abramoff and American Indian tribes Abramoff represented. The $35,000 Camp had received was the most of any Michigan lawmaker. He denounced Abramoff and gave to charity the $500 he had received directly from the lobbyist. But he refused to return the tribal contributions, saying he was proud of his work on issues important to the tribes. He is a vice chairman of the Native American Caucus in Congress.

Camp's office in Washington features a rack of several dozen men's neckties — a curiosity for visiting constituents, who paw through the collection looking for a tie that represents a favorite school or organization. He began building the collection when The Detroit News reported that Camp had arrived in Congress with just three ties and invited readers to supplement the congressman's collection.

Camp's interest in politics began at an early age, and he got his initial hands-on experience volunteering on the local judicial campaign of a lawyer for whom he was interning. He then branched out, getting involved in campaigns for Republicans at the local and state levels. "It was a case where my hobby overtook my career," he says.

After practicing law for five years, Camp became chief of staff for Republican Rep. Bill Schuette, a childhood friend. He returned to Michigan in 1986 to manage Schuette's re-election campaign, and two years later Camp won an open state House seat based in Midland, his hometown.

When Schuette ran for the Senate against Democrat Carl Levin in 1990, Camp went after his mentor's congressional seat. With Schuette's endorsement, Camp eked out a primary victory. He went on to win the general election with 65 percent of the vote and has won re-election easily ever since, including his defeat of Democrat Mike Huckleberry in 2006.

KEY VOTES

2006

- No Stop broadband companies from favoring select Internet traffic
- Yes Affirm U.S. commitment to war in Iraq and reject setting a withdrawal date for troops
- Yes Repeal requirement for bilingual ballots at the polls
- Yes Permit U.S. sale of civilian nuclear technology to India
- Yes Build a 700-mile fence on the U.S.-Mexico border to curb illegal crossings
- Yes Permit warrantless wiretaps of suspected terrorists

2005

- Yes Intervene in the life-support case of Terri Schiavo
- No Lift President Bush's restrictions on stem cell research funding
- No Prohibit FBI access to library and bookstore records
- Yes Approve free-trade pact with five Central American countries
- Yes Pass energy policy overhaul favored by President Bush emphasizing domestic oil and gas production
- Yes End mandatory preservation of habitat of endangered animal and plant species
- Yes Ban torture of prisoners in U.S. custody

CQ VOTE STUDIES

	PARTY UNITY		PRESIDENTIAL SUPPORT	
	Support	Oppose	Support	Oppose
2006	95%	5%	100%	0%
2005	95%	5%	83%	17%
2004	94%	6%	82%	18%
2003	97%	3%	94%	6%
2002	95%	5%	85%	15%

INTEREST GROUPS

	AFL-CIO	ADA	CCUS	ACU
2006	14%	0%	100%	84%
2005	21%	10%	89%	83%
2004	27%	10%	100%	88%
2003	7%	5%	100%	84%
2002	11%	0%	100%	96%

MICHIGAN 4
North central – Midland, Traverse City

Stretching from just west of Saginaw northwest to Leelanau Peninsula's lakeshore at the mouth of Grand Traverse Bay, bountiful forests, farms and inland lakes cover much of the 14 central Michigan counties that lie wholly or partly in the 4th, which is the state's second-largest district in land area. The fast-growing but still sparsely populated white pine forests northwest of Midland were once logging lands but now host summer cottages for vacationers and homes for retirees.

Rapid growth in the 4th's northwest shows no signs of stopping. Leelanau and Grand Traverse counties both grew by more than 20 percent during the 1990s and have grown this decade. Recent economic boosts spurred by tourism and new development on the Lake Michigan shore make the northwest a prime summer destination each year.

On the district's eastern border, Midland, the 4th's largest city, is home to Dow Chemical and Dow Corning, makers of chemicals, plastics and silicone products. The city benefits from the company's philanthropy, with churches, schools and libraries built by the Dow fortune. In 2007, the city also gained a minor league baseball team, the Great Lakes Loons, whose stadium is sponsored by the chemical company.

Thirty miles west of Midland, Mount Pleasant hosts Central Michigan University's nearly 30,000 students, many of whom have strong ties to the local community.

West and south of Midland and Mount Pleasant, the district turns agricultural. Farmers — who till fields of sugar beets, dry beans, corn, wheat and oats — worry about free trade, price supports and crop insurance. The number of farms and small towns throughout the 4th gives it a Republican lean.

MAJOR INDUSTRY

Agriculture, chemical and plastics manufacturing, tourism

CITIES

Midland (pt.), 41,463; Mount Pleasant, 25,946; Saginaw Township North (unincorporated), 24,994; Owosson, 15,713; Traverse City, 14,532

NOTABLE

Locals from Traverse City, which calls itself the "Cherry Capital of the World" and is known for its annual Cherry Festival, baked a cherry pie that weighed more than 28,000 pounds.

Rep. Dale E. Kildee (D)

CAPITOL OFFICE
225-3611
dkildee@mail.house.gov
www.house.gov/kildee
2107 Rayburn 20515-2205; fax 225-6393

COMMITTEES
Education & Labor
(Early Childhood, Elementary & Secondary Education - chairman)
Natural Resources

RESIDENCE
Flint

BORN
Sept. 16, 1929, Flint, Mich.

RELIGION
Roman Catholic

FAMILY
Wife, Gayle Kildee; three children

EDUCATION
Sacred Heart Seminary, B.A. 1952; U. of Detroit, attended 1954 (teaching certificate); U. of Peshawar (Pakistan), attended 1958-59 (Rotary fellowship); U. of Michigan, M.A. 1961 (history)

CAREER
Teacher

POLITICAL HIGHLIGHTS
Mich. House, 1965-75; Mich. Senate, 1975-77

ELECTION RESULTS

2006 GENERAL		
Dale E. Kildee (D)	176,171	72.9%
Eric J. Klammer (R)	60,967	25.2%
2006 PRIMARY		
Dale E. Kildee (D)		unopposed
2004 GENERAL		
Dale E. Kildee (D)	208,163	67.2%
Myrah Kirkwood (R)	96,934	31.3%

PREVIOUS WINNING PERCENTAGES
2002 (92%); 2000 (61%); 1998 (56%); 1996 (59%); 1994 (51%); 1992 (54%); 1990 (68%); 1988 (76%); 1986 (80%); 1984 (93%); 1982 (75%); 1980 (93%); 1978 (77%); 1976 (70%)

Elected 1976; 16th term

Kildee got into politics in the 1960s, the heyday of the civil rights movement and the Great Society war on poverty, and his philosophy remains firmly rooted in that era. "The government's role is to promote, protect, defend and enhance human dignity," he says.

The son of an autoworker from Flint, the home of General Motors Corp., Kildee is a fierce protector of the auto industry and labor unions. A seminary graduate, he abandoned the path to the priesthood to become a Latin teacher. "I wasn't sure I could face the loneliness of a priest's life," he says. But his experiences laid the foundation for his strong opposition to abortion and his staunch support for public education. Raised with a deep concern for the plight of American Indians, he remains dedicated to improving their lot.

Kildee is the second-ranking Democrat on the Natural Resources Committee, and also holds that same spot on the Education and Labor panel, good positions from which to press his causes. In 2005, he fought against job training legislation that centered on block grants to the states, arguing that turning federal programs into grants to the states weakens the programs. They lose their identities and hence the advocacy groups that fight for their renewal, Kildee said.

In 2001, he was a negotiator on the final version of President Bush's No Child Left Behind education overhaul, helping to block an effort to combine drug-abuse prevention and after-school programs into one block grant. As the senior Democrat on the subcommittee that handles higher education, he joined other Democrats in 2006 in trying unsuccessfully to amend a Republican-drafted reauthorization bill to make it more generous to student borrowers. In the 110th Congress (2007-08), with the No Child Left Behind law up for renewal, Kildee opted to chair the subcommittee with jurisdiction: Early Childhood, Elementary and Secondary Education.

Convinced that recent trade agreements have contributed to job losses at home and failed to improve labor standards abroad, Kildee voted against the 2005 Central American Free Trade Agreement, just as he voted against other major trade deals. "They have called me a protectionist, and I plead guilty to that," Kildee said. When bankrupt auto parts maker Delphi Corp. announced in 2006 it would shut down operations in his district, Kildee blamed "disastrous trade policies and our president's neglect and indifference to the role of the U.S. automotive industry in our entire economy."

Like fellow Michigan Democrat John D. Dingell, Kildee requires his congressional employees who drive to work to do so in a car manufactured by members of the United Auto Workers. After all, he reasons, you would not expect to see Brazilian oranges in the office of a lawmaker from Florida.

Kildee's foreign policy outlook was profoundly affected by his own life experiences. As a young teacher, he won a Rotary Foundation Fellowship and studied at the University of Peshawar in Pakistan, which he says gave him great insight into the "real Islam," and helped him understand the divisions between Shiites and Sunnis that have roiled Iraq since the U.S.-led invasion there in 2003, which Kildee opposed.

Kildee's grandparents, immigrants from Ireland, had frequent contact with Indians on the reservation near Traverse City. As a child, Kildee often heard his father say that Indians were treated unfairly. When he became a state legislator, Kildee wrote a law allowing Michigan's American Indians to attend its state colleges for free. In his suit pocket are copies not only of the Constitution but also of the landmark 1832 Supreme Court decision that gave the federal government exclusive jurisdiction over Indian affairs.

In the House, that jurisdiction is generally exercised by the Natural Resources Committee, where Kildee has closely monitored a long-running class action lawsuit over mismanagement by the federal government of Indian trust funds. When lawmakers in 1997 started talking about taxing Indian-run gambling operations, Kildee founded the Native American Caucus. In honor of his efforts, the Grand Traverse Band of Ottawa and Chippewa Indians in 1998 named April 15 "Dale Kildee Day."

Kildee made an unusual request when in 2002, he sought to join the all-female Congressional Caucus for Women's Issues. He was gently rebuffed by California Democrat Juanita Millender-McDonald, then the caucus co-chairwoman, who said through an aide, "Regrettably, he's of the wrong gender." She later backtracked and named Kildee an honorary nonvoting member.

Starting in late 1985, Kildee voted yes or no on more than 6,000 consecutive roll call votes on the House floor, the longest streak of any active member. By Congressional Quarterly's accounting, the streak ended in June 1998, when he joined more than 60 lawmakers in voting "present" on a campaign finance bill. The Detroit News contends the streak did not end until 8,141 votes in October 2000, when Kildee was in an Education Committee meeting and missed a routine vote to approve the House journal. Kildee did not miss a single roll call between 2001 and 2007.

Diligent about more than voting, he is frugal with his office account and returns money from his allocation to the U.S. Treasury every year, with the total approaching $1.4 million over his career. He favors a ban on all privately financed travel for members and accepted less of it — less than $1,000 in 2005 — than most members of the Michigan delegation.

Elected to the state House in 1964, Kildee won a state Senate seat in 1974. He won an open U.S. House seat two years later and coasted until 1992 and 1994, when Republican Megan O'Neill, who had worked in the White House under President George H. W. Bush, ran strong campaigns. In 1992, Kildee had become vulnerable after reports that he had 100 overdrafts at the private bank for House members. Plus, redistricting for the 1990s had left him a redrawn 9th District in which almost half the people were new to him.

Redistricting for this decade by the GOP-controlled state legislature pitted Kildee against five-term incumbent Democrat James A. Barcia in a redrawn 5th District. But Barcia ran for the state Senate rather than take on Kildee in a 2002 primary, and Kildee locked up his seat once again.

KEY VOTES

2006

Yes Stop broadband companies from favoring select Internet traffic

No Affirm U.S. commitment to war in Iraq and reject setting a withdrawal date for troops

No Repeal requirement for bilingual ballots at the polls

No Permit U.S. sale of civilian nuclear technology to India

Yes Build a 700-mile fence on the U.S.-Mexico border to curb illegal crossings

No Permit warrantless wiretaps of suspected terrorists

2005

Yes Intervene in the life-support case of Terri Schiavo

No Lift President Bush's restrictions on stem cell research funding

Yes Prohibit FBI access to library and bookstore records

No Approve free-trade pact with five Central American countries

No Pass energy policy overhaul favored by President Bush emphasizing domestic oil and gas production

No End mandatory preservation of habitat of endangered animal and plant species

Yes Ban torture of prisoners in U.S. custody

CQ VOTE STUDIES

	PARTY UNITY		PRESIDENTIAL SUPPORT	
	Support	Oppose	Support	Oppose
2006	96%	4%	33%	67%
2005	91%	9%	22%	78%
2004	93%	7%	35%	65%
2003	92%	8%	29%	71%
2002	89%	11%	38%	62%

INTEREST GROUPS

	AFL-CIO	ADA	CCUS	ACU
2006	100%	80%	27%	20%
2005	93%	80%	33%	20%
2004	100%	90%	38%	16%
2003	100%	90%	27%	32%
2002	100%	80%	40%	8%

MICHIGAN 5
East — Flint, Saginaw, Bay City

Drawn as the only Democratic-leaning district outside of Detroit and its suburbs, the 5th is the birthplace of General Motors, and the district's ties to the United Auto Workers (UAW) union still influence Michigan politics. Auto industry and other manufacturing-based workers live in working-class Flint, Saginaw and Bay City, while the district's northeast section features farmland stretching across Tuscola County on Michigan's "Thumb" to Saginaw Bay.

Flint, the 5th's largest city, grew alongside the U.S. auto industry, and its population had peaked by the late 1960s. As in many of Michigan's cities, industry downsizing caused population losses here. Saginaw, roughly 30 miles north of Flint, has experienced a similar population drop as residents seek jobs outside of the city, with some settling in the western suburbs of Saginaw County (in the 4th District) and others departing the region altogether. Sustained population loss in mid-Michigan threatens to impact housing prices and school systems.

While downsizing at Delphi and General Motors plants has hindered the district's auto parts manufacturing sector, the industry still plays a role in the local economy, drawing suppliers and distributors to the 5th. The district's agricultural community thrives on family-owned farms and the region's rich sugar beat industry, and the Michigan Sugar Company makes its headquarters in Bay City.

The 5th's blue-collar voters adhere to fiscal populism and social conservatism, and they tend to identify strongly with the Democratic Party. Genesee County (Flint), which accounts for two-thirds of the district's population, is strongly influenced by the UAW and gave 60 percent of its vote to Democrat John Kerry in the 2004 presidential election, his third-best showing in Michigan. His Genesee tally was bolstered by overwhelming support from Flint, which is predominately black.

MAJOR INDUSTRY
Auto parts manufacturing, agriculture, sugar processing

CITIES
Flint, 124,943; Saginaw, 61,799; Bay City, 36,817; Burton, 30,308

NOTABLE
Frankenmuth, which calls itself "Michigan's Little Bavaria," was founded as a Lutheran mission and holds annual German-heritage festivals.

Rep. Fred Upton (R)

CAPITOL OFFICE
225-3761
tellupton@mail.house.gov
www.house.gov/upton
2183 Rayburn 20515-2206; fax 225-4986

COMMITTEES
Energy & Commerce

RESIDENCE
St. Joseph

BORN
April 23, 1953, St. Joseph, Mich.

RELIGION
Protestant

FAMILY
Wife, Amey Upton; two children

EDUCATION
U. of Michigan, B.A. 1975 (journalism)

CAREER
Congressional aide; White House budget analyst

POLITICAL HIGHLIGHTS
No previous office

ELECTION RESULTS

2006 GENERAL		
Fred Upton (R)	142,125	60.6%
Kim Clark (D)	88,978	37.9%
Kenneth E. Howe (LIBERT)	3,480	1.5%
2006 PRIMARY		
Fred Upton (R)		unopposed
2004 GENERAL		
Fred Upton (R)	197,425	65.3%
Scott Elliott (D)	97,978	32.4%

PREVIOUS WINNING PERCENTAGES
2002 (69%); 2000 (68%); 1998 (70%); 1996 (68%); 1994 (73%); 1992 (62%); 1990 (58%); 1988 (71%); 1986 (62%)

Elected 1986; 11th term

A genial moderate Republican, Upton could be a key swing vote for the Democrats as they pursue their legislative agenda in the 110th Congress (2007-08). A pragmatist, Upton sees himself as a natural-born compromiser. He will support President Bush and the GOP leadership, but just as likely will go his own way.

Upton has a generally conservative record, but has stood alone on issues ranging from the Iraq War and gun control to environmental and fiscal issues. In February 2007, he was one of 17 Republicans who voted for a resolution disapproving of Bush's plan to increase troop strength in Iraq, although in 2002 he had supported an authorization for Bush to use force. In 2005, he was one of 34 Republicans to vote against legislation to overhaul the Endangered Species Act and one of 50 Republicans to vote for a measure, opposed by Bush, to allow the use of federal funds for embryonic stem cell research. In 2004, he was one of just 12 House Republicans supporting a budget amendment by conservative Blue Dog Coalition Democrats to require new tax cuts to be offset with spending reductions or revenue increases. He also was one of 16 Republicans who voted against a package of corporate tax cuts later in the year.

Now in his 50s, Upton still looks too boyish to be in his 11th term. By telling everyone he meets to "just call me Fred," he perpetuates that image. Bush dubbed him "Freddy Boy" initially and later simply "Freddy."

Upton is the top-ranking Republican on Energy and Commerce's Subcommittee on Telecommunications and the Internet, where he served as chairman from 2001-06 and became an influential voice on communications issues. Under his leadership, the panel pushed forward bills to raise broadcast indecency fines, to extend daylight saving time and to allow telephone companies to compete with cable TV companies in the video market. The 2006 telecommunications bill, as approved by Upton's subcommittee, would have allowed video operators to obtain a national franchise from the Federal Communications Commission instead of negotiating service agreements with individual municipalities. But the bill never became law, and Congress is expected to revisit the issue during the 110th Congress.

The change approved by Upton's panel was important to the big telephone companies, which were spending billions of dollars on new fiber optic networks but said existing rules slowed the rollout of video services over those lines. Upton said the bill was good for consumers because it removed impediments to increased competition, lower prices, greater choice and better service quality in the video marketplace.

But the bill stalled because of a dispute over so-called network neutrality rules intended to prevent the big phone and cable companies from using their control over the broadband market to discriminate against competitors in how they provide access over the Internet. Democrat Edward J. Markey of Massachusetts, now chairman of the panel, sided with consumer groups and the big Internet companies, which warned that stronger protections were needed to preserve the open, egalitarian nature of the Internet. Upton and other Republicans, backed by the phone and cable companies, insisted broadband providers needed flexibility to manage network traffic.

After singer Janet Jackson's "wardrobe malfunction" in the 2004 Super Bowl halftime show, Upton sought to stiffen the fines the FCC could impose for broadcast indecency. He proposed increasing the maximum penalty for indecency violations to $500,000 from $32,500 per offense. He said many broadcasters were deep-pocketed enough to view the existing fine structure as simply the price of doing business. When Congress approved an increase of $325,000 per incident in 2006, Upton said the new cap would give the law some "teeth."

Upton has been frustrated by the violence and sexual imagery contained in video games. He drafted a measure in the 109th Congress (2005-06) to give the Federal Trade Commission the authority to fine game makers that deliberately mislead consumers with ratings labels, including those that make games with hidden content. Video game makers operate under a voluntary rating system, and Upton says his message for the industry is, "If you're not going to do it yourself, get out of the way."

Upton worked with Markey in 2005 on a proposal to extend daylight saving time for eight weeks. Congress ultimately cleared a revised version of their measure that extended daylight saving time for one month beginning in 2007. By allowing one more hour of daylight in the evening, the lawmakers hope to conserve energy used for lighting.

Upton comes from one of Michigan's wealthier Republican families; his grandfather helped found Whirlpool Corp., which is based in Upton's district. A sense of social responsibility was instilled in the young Upton early on. His parents took care of as many as two dozen foster children at various times, and one of Upton's first jobs was in a day care center.

He was first elected to Congress in 1986 after ousting incumbent Mark D. Siljander, a Christian conservative activist, in a Republican primary. But Upton's credentials as a fiscal conservative were solid: He had spent nearly a decade working for David A. Stockman, first on Stockman's 1976 campaign; then in Washington on his congressional staff; and finally at the Office of Management and Budget, where Stockman was President Ronald Reagan's budget director and Upton was the budget office's liaison to Capitol Hill.

In Congress, Upton became a deputy to Newt Gingrich when Gingrich was elected GOP whip in 1989, and the next year joined Gingrich in castigating President George H. W. Bush for agreeing to raise taxes as part of a deal to reduce the deficit. But Upton resigned as a deputy whip in 1993 because he disliked Gingrich's confrontational style.

Upton's political positioning has kept him secure in his House seat; he usually wins with more than 65 percent of the vote. But in 2002, he drew a primary challenge from state Sen. Dale L. Shugars, who charged Upton was not conservative enough. Upton criticized Shugars for waging a negative campaign and urged voters to reject such tactics. Upton was renominated with 66 percent. In 2004 and 2006, he was not challenged in the primary.

KEY VOTES

2006

No Stop broadband companies from favoring select Internet traffic
Yes Affirm U.S. commitment to war in Iraq and reject setting a withdrawal date for troops
Yes Repeal requirement for bilingual ballots at the polls
Yes Permit U.S. sale of civilian nuclear technology to India
Yes Build a 700-mile fence on the U.S.-Mexico border to curb illegal crossings
Yes Permit warrantless wiretaps of suspected terrorists

2005

Yes Intervene in the life-support case of Terri Schiavo
Yes Lift President Bush's restrictions on stem cell research funding
No Prohibit FBI access to library and bookstore records
Yes Approve free-trade pact with five Central American countries
Yes Pass energy policy overhaul favored by President Bush emphasizing domestic oil and gas production
No End mandatory preservation of habitat of endangered animal and plant species
Yes Ban torture of prisoners in U.S. custody

CQ VOTE STUDIES

	PARTY UNITY		PRESIDENTIAL SUPPORT	
	Support	Oppose	Support	Oppose
2006	81%	19%	80%	20%
2005	87%	13%	76%	24%
2004	88%	12%	82%	18%
2003	86%	14%	91%	9%
2002	92%	8%	82%	18%

INTEREST GROUPS

	AFL-CIO	ADA	CCUS	ACU
2006	36%	10%	100%	80%
2005	27%	10%	89%	80%
2004	47%	35%	90%	76%
2003	27%	10%	93%	76%
2002	11%	5%	95%	92%

MICHIGAN 6

Southwest – Kalamazoo, Portage, Benton Harbor

Forests, fertile soil and front-row seats to Lake Michigan in the state's southwestern corner make the 6th a prime spot for tourists in every season. Cherries and peaches grow in a fruit belt that extends north from St. Joseph and Benton Harbor through Van Buren County. Vineyards along the lakeshore produce a strong crop of juice grapes, and area wineries account for nearly half of the state's wine grapes. Affluent Chicagoans keep second homes in the wooded area along the shoreline.

Appliance manufacturer Whirlpool, based in Benton Harbor, and orthopedic company Stryker make their headquarters in the 6th. Other firms are here as well, and the district has become a hub for the state's health care industry. Pharmaceutical maker Pfizer plans to close its research site in Kalamazoo County, the district's most-populous county, by the end of 2008, but will retain its manufacturing site there. Following the latest round of downsizing by Pfizer, local leaders hope to encourage the growing pharmaceutical start-ups that have emerged in the face of repeated industry job cuts.

Education is another pillar of the local economy. Western Michigan University is home, at least for most of the year, to roughly 25,000 students. In a 2006 initiative funded by private donors, the Kalamazoo public school system instituted the "Kalamazoo Promise," a scholarship program aimed at supporting its graduates by offering to sponsor up to 100 percent of tuition to attend an in-state public college.

The 6th's conservative Dutch heritage, white-collar corporate managers and rural conservatives make it a Republican-leaning district. In 2004, Van Buren, St. Joseph, Cass and Berrien counties all favored George W. Bush in the presidential race. Kalamazoo's blue-collar workforce makes it one of the few Democratic parts of the 6th; John Kerry carried the city by 34 percentage points in 2004. Predominately black Benton Harbor gave Kerry more than 95 percent of its presidential vote.

MAJOR INDUSTRY

Manufacturing, agriculture, higher education, tourism, health care

CITIES

Kalamazoo, 77,145; Portage, 44,897; Niles, 12,204; Sturgis, 11,285

NOTABLE

The courthouse in Berrien Springs, built in 1839 and now a museum, is the state's oldest courthouse.

Rep. Tim Walberg (R)

CAPITOL OFFICE
225-6276
walberg.house.gov
325 Cannon 20515-2207; fax 225-6281

COMMITTEES
Agriculture
Education & Labor

RESIDENCE
Tipton

BORN
April 12, 1951, Chicago, Ill.

RELIGION
Protestant

FAMILY
Wife, Sue Walberg; three children

EDUCATION
Western Illinois U., attended 1969-70 (forestry); Fort Wayne Bible College, B.S. 1975 (Christian education); Wheaton College (Ill.), M.A. 1978 (communications)

CAREER
Religious school fundraiser; education think tank president; minister

POLITICAL HIGHLIGHTS
Candidate for Onsted Community Schools Board of Education, 1981; Mich. House, 1983-98; sought Republican nomination for U.S. House, 2004

ELECTION RESULTS

2006 GENERAL		
Tim Walberg (R)	122,348	49.9%
Sharon Marie Renier (D)	112,665	46.0%
David L. Hutchinson (LIBERT)	3,788	1.5%
Dave Horn (USTAX)	3,611	1.5%
Joe Schwarz (X) - write-in	2,614	1.1%
2006 PRIMARY		
Tim Walberg (R)	33,245	53.1%
Joe Schwarz (R)	29,330	46.9%

Elected 2006; 1st term

A minister and former state representative known for his socially conservative views, Walberg says his faith defines who he is. He says he will continue his efforts to reduce taxes, cut spending and promote what he calls "traditional" values.

On fiscal matters, one group Walberg won't have to impress is the Club for Growth. The conservative group best known for its anti-tax stand was one of his biggest supporters during the 2006 campaign, and Walberg has vowed to stay true to the organization's principles. He is quick to point out his record in the Michigan House: In nearly 16 years, Walberg never voted to increase taxes.

As a member of the Agriculture Committee, Walberg will be able to advocate for his heavily rural district, where tractor combines are as common on county roads as General Motors cars built in Michigan. Walberg anticipates playing a role in the rewrite of the farm bill, which is up for renewal in 2007.

He also has been assigned to the Education and Labor Committee, where his priority is finding ways to stimulate Michigan's ailing economy.

In his second quest for the 7th District seat, Walberg won a hard-fought primary campaign against first-term Rep. Joe Schwarz, who had defeated him in the 2004 GOP primary. Walberg called the moderate Schwarz a "RINO" — Republican In Name Only. Schwarz had the backing of virtually all of the state and national Republican establishment, but Walberg had the support of the district's conservative Republican base and the financial backing of the Club for Growth. He defeated Schwarz 53 percent to 47 percent.

Walberg's general-election campaign was plagued by a few setbacks. Schwarz would not endorse him and alleged that the Club for Growth violated campaign finance laws. Also, one of Walberg's staff members resigned after pleading guilty to an act of domestic violence in which he struck his 9-year-old foster child. Walberg raised 20 times more than his Democratic opponent, organic farmer Sharon Marie Renier, but he won the race by barely 4 percentage points in the Republican-leaning district.

MICHIGAN 7

South central – Battle Creek, Jackson

The southern Michigan counties that make up the 7th take in small towns, farming communities and a few midsize cities. Kellogg's Tony the Tiger makes his home in Battle Creek, the district's largest city. The cereal giant is one of the city's largest employers, and its philanthropic organization donates generously to the Battle Creek area.

Auto parts manufacturing drives small-town economies, especially in Jackson. Outside the cities and towns, expansive fields of soybeans and corn dominate the rest of the 7th, which is the state's leading producer of both crops. Lenawee County is at the forefront of both soybean and corn harvesting for the region.

The farming counties of Branch, Eaton, Hillsdale, Jackson and Lenawee have been fertile ground for the GOP, and George W. Bush carried all five in the last two presidential elections, despite losing the state both times. Here, even local blue-collar Democrats tend to be socially conservative. Washtenaw County, in the east, is more Democratic, as some residents of suburban Detroit migrate to the outskirts of heavily Democratic Ann Arbor (located in the neighboring 15th). Overall, Bush took 54 percent of the 7th's 2004 vote.

A Quaker tradition shaped the district's political and social culture. In 1854, Jackson's abolitionists selected anti-slavery candidates in a state convention that has become known as "Under the Oaks," and as the birth of the Republican Party.

MAJOR INDUSTRY
Agriculture, food processing, auto parts manufacturing, health care

CITIES
Battle Creek, 53,364; Jackson, 36,316

NOTABLE
Sojourner Truth lived in Battle Creek; Battle Creek's annual Cereal Festival culminates in the world's longest breakfast table.

Rep. Mike Rogers (R)

CAPITOL OFFICE
225-4872
www.mikerogers.house.gov
133 Cannon 20515-2208; fax 225-5820

COMMITTEES
Energy & Commerce
Select Intelligence

RESIDENCE
Brighton

BORN
June 2, 1963, Livonia, Mich.

RELIGION
Methodist

FAMILY
Wife, Diane Rogers; two children

EDUCATION
Adrian College, B.A. 1985 (sociology & criminal justice)

MILITARY SERVICE
Army, 1985-88

CAREER
Home construction company owner; FBI agent

POLITICAL HIGHLIGHTS
Mich. Senate, 1995-2001 (majority floor leader, 1999-2001)

ELECTION RESULTS

2006 GENERAL		
Mike Rogers (R)	157,237	55.3%
Jim Marcinkowski (D)	122,107	42.9%
2006 PRIMARY		
Mike Rogers (R)	41,839	84.3%
Mike Flynn (R)	7,784	15.7%
2004 GENERAL		
Mike Rogers (R)	207,925	61.1%
Robert Alexander (D)	125,619	36.9%
Will Tyler White (LIBERT)	3,591	1.1%

PREVIOUS WINNING PERCENTAGES
2002 (68%); 2000 (49%)

Elected 2000; 4th term

With four terms under his belt, Rogers has put himself on the Republican leadership track by becoming a prolific fundraiser. The affable, energetic former FBI agent threw himself into the gritty business of raising money for endangered Republicans in the last two election cycles, and keeps his eye on the top job for the party's main fundraising arm in the House, the National Republican Congressional Committee.

For the 2006 election, Rogers' political action committee gave about $530,000 to fellow Republicans in tight races. He called his fund the MIKE R FUND, for Majority Initiative to Keep Electing Republicans. Two years earlier, as finance chairman of the NRCC, he co-chaired the committee's "Battleground" effort that banked $16 million for colleagues in tough races.

He has made other conspicuous moves to build his leadership bonafides. After a series of scandals rocked the GOP in the 109th Congress (2005-06), Rogers announced in 2006 he would run for Republican whip, the No. 3-ranking leadership post, if Roy Blunt of Missouri moved up to majority leader, the second-ranking job. Saying he stood for "bold change," Rogers unveiled an overhaul plan tightening lobbying rules and reining in some campaign finance practices. However, Rep. John A. Boehner of Ohio upset Blunt in the contest, becoming the party's choice to replace disgraced Tom DeLay of Texas. That left Blunt in place and stymied Rogers' hopes of landing one of the top posts.

Blunt in 2002 had briefly considered naming Rogers his chief deputy. But instead, Blunt chose Eric Cantor of Virginia. Rogers' consolation prize was appointment to the Energy and Commerce Committee, an important and productive panel. And he was named one of 18 deputy majority whips.

An Army veteran, Rogers initially urged a go-slow approach when President Bush sought congressional authorization for war with Iraq. Once his concerns were satisfied, Rogers voted for the 2002 war resolution. He remained loyal to the president and the war effort even as popular support plummeted. In early 2007, he opposed Bush's plan for a hefty troop buildup, but voted against the Democrats' non-binding resolution opposing the plan. He offered his own resolution urging that 4,000 troops be brought from existing forces in the Middle East to strengthen efforts against al Qaeda in Al Anbar Province west of Baghdad.

In March 2007, as the House prepared to vote on a war supplemental funding bill setting a U.S. troop withdrawal deadline, Rogers' Lansing office was vandalized. The FBI was called in to help investigate the vandalism, which included the placement of a sign in the front window that read, "Rogers: There Is Blood on Your Hands." Undaunted, Rogers voted against the bill.

When anti-war protesters appeared at funerals of soldiers killed in Iraq, Rogers rushed in with legislation to stop them. His bill, signed into law in 2006, prohibited protests at national cemeteries unless approved by cemetery officials, restricted protests within 500 feet of a cemetery entrance and set penalties of a year in jail and $100,000 in fines.

The Sept. 11 terrorist attacks happened in Rogers' first year in the House and put a premium on his background as a former FBI special agent. He has showcased his knowledge about intelligence gathering and counterterrorism as a member of the Intelligence Committee. Because he has firsthand experience in wiretapping, Rogers was asked for his input as the Justice Department developed its anti-terrorism legislation after the attacks. He is now the top-ranking member of the Terrorism Subcommittee.

On the Energy and Commerce Committee, he is an advocate for the automobile industry, the economic engine of his state. In 2006, and again in 2007, he introduced a bill to give the Big Three automakers up to $20 billion in federally backed loan guarantees to develop "green" technologies, such as hybrid engines and clean diesel fuel. The bill would give domestic automakers cheaper access to capital after a slide in credit ratings in recent years. "This isn't the dreaded bailout word," Rogers told The Detroit News.

He slipped into the 2005 energy bill a provision blocking the Environmental Protection Agency from revising the way fuel economy is measured to account for modern driving habits, such as higher speeds and greater use of air conditioning, since the standards were written in the 1980s. Rogers said the new tests would burden automakers financially.

Rogers grew up in Livingston County, west of Detroit. His father was a high school vice principal and football coach, and a town supervisor. His mother ran the local chamber of commerce and served on the county commission. The youngest of five boys, Rogers says his mother would volunteer the children for civic events. "I remember putting up Christmas light decorations for the city of Brighton. We used to call it forced family fun," he says. "My parents taught me that public service is an honorable thing."

Rogers knew as a teenager that he wanted to be an FBI agent. After graduating from college, he spent three years in the Army and then went to the FBI Academy, finishing first in his class. He got a coveted assignment to the field office in Chicago, where he unraveled a major case involving public officials in the Chicago suburb of Cicero.

In the 1990s, Rogers and his wife returned to Brighton to raise their family. With his father and brothers, he ran a modular home assembly company. He also got into state politics. When a longtime GOP incumbent retired from the state Senate, Rogers won the seat in a strongly Republican district. Re-elected in 1998, he served as majority floor leader in his last term.

When Democrat Debbie Stabenow decided to give up her seat to run for the Senate in 2000, Rogers made a bid and faced Democratic state Senate colleague Dianne Byrum in the general election. The closest House election that year, Rogers' victory was not official until December, when Byrum conceded after a partial recount supported Rogers' slim lead.

Rogers then set out to solidify his hold on the 8th. He raised nearly $750,000 his first six months in office. Redistricting for 2002 added thousands of GOP voters to the district and Byrum declined a rematch. Rogers won with 68 percent of the vote — his highest percentage to date. Since then, he has been returned safely to office, but his victory margins have decreased.

KEY VOTES

2006

No Stop broadband companies from favoring select Internet traffic

Yes Affirm U.S. commitment to war in Iraq and reject setting a withdrawal date for troops

Yes Repeal requirement for bilingual ballots at the polls

Yes Permit U.S. sale of civilian nuclear technology to India

Yes Build a 700-mile fence on the U.S.-Mexico border to curb illegal crossings

Yes Permit warrantless wiretaps of suspected terrorists

2005

? Intervene in the life-support case of Terri Schiavo

No Lift President Bush's restrictions on stem cell research funding

No Prohibit FBI access to library and bookstore records

Yes Approve free-trade pact with five Central American countries

Yes Pass energy policy overhaul favored by President Bush emphasizing domestic oil and gas production

Yes End mandatory preservation of habitat of endangered animal and plant species

No Ban torture of prisoners in U.S. custody

CQ VOTE STUDIES

	PARTY UNITY		PRESIDENTIAL SUPPORT	
	Support	Oppose	Support	Oppose
2006	95%	5%	90%	10%
2005	94%	6%	87%	13%
2004	95%	5%	97%	3%
2003	98%	2%	96%	4%
2002	96%	4%	85%	15%

INTEREST GROUPS

	AFL-CIO	ADA	CCUS	ACU
2006	21%	5%	93%	88%
2005	20%	5%	93%	92%
2004	20%	10%	100%	92%
2003	7%	5%	100%	84%
2002	0%	0%	90%	92%

MICHIGAN 8

Central — Lansing

Stamped with the state seal, the 8th — Michigan's capital district — is dominated by various manufacturing facilities of the influential auto industry. The district, once home to Olds Motor Vehicle Co., includes Lansing, East Lansing and various agricultural communities to the east, but is emerging from its agrarian and industrial past toward a suburban future.

The 2004 death of the Oldsmobile line may have hurt the district's economy, but auto parts suppliers and General Motors, which still makes Chevrolet, Cadillac, Pontiac and other brands, continue to employ many district residents. The dominance of auto manufacturing in the district is rivaled only by the thousands of jobs provided by state government agencies centered in the capital city of Lansing.

Ingham County makes up three-fifths of the 8th's population, mainly in Lansing and East Lansing. Just down the road from the capital, East Lansing caters to one of the most liberal constituencies of the state, the Michigan State University community. The university, founded in 1855 and the nation's pioneer land grant college, has a top-ranked study abroad program. Students and faculty members combine with local autoworkers to make Ingham strongly Democratic, and John Kerry took 58 percent of the county's 2004 presidential vote.

Ingham's Democratic lean is counterbalanced by the 8th's powerful agricultural vote in Clinton, Livingston and Shiawassee counties, which also are new commuter sanctuaries for residents who work in Lansing, Detroit and Flint. George W. Bush won 54 percent of the district's 2004 presidential vote. The remainder of the 8th's voters live in northern Oakland County, one of the wealthiest in the nation, although the 8th's portion of the county remains the least developed.

MAJOR INDUSTRY

Auto manufacturing, state government, higher education

CITIES

Lansing (pt.), 114,321; East Lansing, 46,525; Okemos (unincorporated), 22,805

NOTABLE

Basketball star Earvin "Magic" Johnson hails from Lansing and played college ball at Michigan State University; Howell celebrates the honeydew harvest with its annual Melon Festival.

Rep. Joe Knollenberg (R)

CAPITOL OFFICE
225-5802
www.house.gov/knollenberg
2349 Rayburn 20515-2209; fax 226-2356

COMMITTEES
Appropriations

RESIDENCE
Bloomfield Township

BORN
Nov. 28, 1933, Mattoon, Ill.

RELIGION
Roman Catholic

FAMILY
Wife, Sandie Knollenberg; two children

EDUCATION
Eastern Illinois U., B.S. 1955 (social science)

MILITARY SERVICE
Army, 1955-57

CAREER
Insurance broker

POLITICAL HIGHLIGHTS
Oakland County Republican Party chairman, 1978-86

ELECTION RESULTS

2006 GENERAL		
Joe Knollenberg (R)	142,390	51.6%
Nancy Skinner (D)	127,620	46.2%
Adam Goodman (LIBERT)	3,702	1.3%
2006 PRIMARY		
Joe Knollenberg (R)	46,713	69.8%
Patricia Godchaux (R)	20,211	30.2%
2004 GENERAL		
Joe Knollenberg (R)	199,210	58.5%
Steven Reifman (D)	134,764	39.5%
Robert Schubring (LIBERT)	6,825	2.0%

PREVIOUS WINNING PERCENTAGES
2002 (58%); 2000 (56%); 1998 (64%); 1996 (61%); 1994 (68%); 1992 (58%)

Elected 1992; 8th term

This Congress may be unlike any other for Knollenberg. For the first time in six years, he does not chair an Appropriations subcommittee. And for the first time in his congressional career, his re-election margin in 2006 dropped below double digits, to a scant 5 percentage points. Democrats promptly targeted his seat for 2008.

But Knollenberg, now in his eighth term, probably will make do. He has an easygoing style well suited to the bipartisan deal-making of the Appropriations panel. And he knows his way around the committee, having served as chairman of three of its subcommittees — the District of Columbia, Military Construction, and Transportation, Treasury and Housing.

In the 110th Congress (2007-08), he is the top-ranking Republican on the Transportation-HUD Subcommittee, serving next to the new chairman, Massachusetts Democrat John W. Olver. The two men have spent the majority of their House careers on the panel, and they are equally adept at sending money home. But appropriators are finding it increasingly difficult to come up with money for domestic priorities as the war in Iraq drags on and the Pentagon consumes hundreds of billions of dollars.

Knollenberg knows what it is like to work with limited funds. In the 108th Congress (2003-04), when he served as chairman of the Military Construction Subcommittee, he struggled to write a bill with nearly $1.3 billion less than the year before. The result was a 15-week impasse in a House-Senate conference, as lawmakers toiled over painful cuts and the possibility that their actions would make life harder for troops overseas. Knollenberg eventually fashioned a compromise that trimmed several programs and leveraged government funds to finance privately built military housing.

Knollenberg has supported the Iraq War, but in February 2007, when the House debated a Democratic resolution opposing President Bush's plan to deploy thousands more U.S. troops there, he expressed some reservation. Although he called the resolution "pure politics" and voted against it, he warned, "If the Iraqis do not step up to this challenge in the coming months, then it will be time to re-evaluate."

Despite his growing concern about Iraq, Knollenberg is usually a good Republican soldier. In the 109th Congress (2005-06), he supported the president's position 92 percent of the time and voted with his party 96 percent of the time on votes that divided the two parties. Yet he disagreed with the White House in March 2006 over a proposal to enhance the president's power to rescind individual spending bill items. Knollenberg said he was concerned about "the unlimited nature of this proposal and the possibility that future presidents could use it as a legislative tool, not as a fiscal tool."

In 2006, Knollenberg won enactment of a measure he sponsored to ban trafficking in counterfeit labels, containers or stickers, and require the forfeiture and destruction of equipment used to manufacture fake goods. U.S. auto companies have complained that parts counterfeiting in countries such as China has grown into a $12 billion annual drain on their bottom line and presents a danger to consumers.

Like most Michigan lawmakers, Knollenberg hastens to help the auto manufacturers that are an integral part of his state's economy. He took a leading role in opposing the steel tariffs Bush imposed in 2002. His district contains one of the country's highest concentrations of auto parts manufacturers, and they were affected by steep increases in steel prices.

He also strongly opposes raising automotive fuel economy standards, which he says would cost domestic auto industry jobs. Early in 2007, he even took on California Republican Gov. Arnold Schwarzenegger over fuel efficiency increases. His re-election campaign placed a billboard along a busy interstate in metropolitan Detroit that said, "Arnold to Michigan: Drop Dead!" according to the Detroit News. Knollenberg said Michigan and the Big Three auto companies were being "unfairly bullied by politicians who have no understanding of auto manufacturing."

Knollenberg is socially conservative and earns high ratings from groups such as the Christian Coalition and the American Conservative Union. Knollenberg, whose son, Steve, is gay, usually earns low marks for his voting record from the Human Rights Campaign, an issue advocacy group for homosexuals. But Knollenberg was among the small minority of House Republicans in 2004 and again in 2006 who voted against a proposed constitutional amendment to ban same-sex marriage. He says his son's "sexual orientation is a personal matter," and that he "unequivocally" supports him "with all the love and respect that a family possibly can."

The fifth of 13 children raised on a farm in central Illinois, Knollenberg graduated from Eastern Illinois University. After two years in the Army, he moved to the Detroit area in 1959 to work as an Allstate Insurance agent, eventually opening his own branch office. His community activities in the north Detroit suburbs included chairing a local PTA, chairing the Oakland County GOP organization and heading the campaign of Republican Rep. William S. Broomfield.

When Broomfield retired in 1992 after 18 terms, Knollenberg won the GOP nomination in a three-way race. He then defeated Democrat Walter O. Briggs IV, nephew of former Democratic Sen. Philip A. Hart, by 18 percentage points in the upscale Republican 11th District. His next four re-election wins came easily; his smallest victory margin was 15 points in 2000.

After redistricting for this decade, Knollenberg sought re-election in the 9th District, with a constituency that was 60 percent new. In 2002, he was matched dollar for dollar by wealthy Democratic lawyer David Fink in one of the most expensive House races in Michigan history, but he won by 18 points. In 2004, he upped his winning margin to 19 points.

But 2006 was another story. Knollenberg first faced a primary challenge from former state Rep. Patricia Godchaux, who ran as a moderate. Knollenberg won renomination with 70 percent of the vote. But Godchaux's portrayal of him as too far to the right may have buttressed a central theme of his Democratic opponent, radio talk show host Nancy Skinner. The general-election race was much closer than expected.

KEY VOTES

2006

- No Stop broadband companies from favoring select Internet traffic
- Yes Affirm U.S. commitment to war in Iraq and reject setting a withdrawal date for troops
- Yes Repeal requirement for bilingual ballots at the polls
- Yes Permit U.S. sale of civilian nuclear technology to India
- Yes Build a 700-mile fence on the U.S.-Mexico border to curb illegal crossings
- Yes Permit warrantless wiretaps of suspected terrorists

2005

- ? Intervene in the life-support case of Terri Schiavo
- No Lift President Bush's restrictions on stem cell research funding
- No Prohibit FBI access to library and bookstore records
- Yes Approve free-trade pact with five Central American countries
- Yes Pass energy policy overhaul favored by President Bush emphasizing domestic oil and gas production
- Yes End mandatory preservation of habitat of endangered animal and plant species
- Yes Ban torture of prisoners in U.S. custody

CQ VOTE STUDIES

	PARTY UNITY		PRESIDENTIAL SUPPORT	
	Support	Oppose	Support	Oppose
2006	97%	3%	95%	5%
2005	95%	5%	89%	11%
2004	94%	6%	88%	12%
2003	97%	3%	100%	0%
2002	96%	4%	92%	8%

INTEREST GROUPS

	AFL-CIO	ADA	CCUS	ACU
2006	14%	5%	100%	75%
2005	13%	0%	93%	84%
2004	13%	5%	100%	84%
2003	7%	5%	100%	84%
2002	0%	0%	100%	88%

MICHIGAN 9

Suburban Detroit – eastern Oakland County

Michigan's heavily suburban 9th — the wealthiest and most-educated district in the state — is wholly contained within Oakland County, one of the most affluent counties in the nation and home to the U.S. headquarters for DaimlerChrysler in Auburn Hills. The district includes more than half of Oakland County's residents.

Troy, in the district's southeastern corner, is a major office center and is home to Michigan's growing high-technology automotive research and design industry. But the city did receive some bad news in 2005 when Kmart, which merged with Sears to form Sears Holdings, relocated its headquarters from Troy to Chicago. Troy has a large Asian population, and the 9th has more Asians than any other district in the state. North of Troy, Oakland University in Rochester continues to grow.

Communities such as Farmington Hills, north of the northern Detroit boundary cut by 8 Mile Road, form a corridor between Grand River Avenue and the Northwestern Highway that has served as one of the major routes for white exodus out of Detroit.

Upper-middle-class Troy, Bloomfield Township and Rochester Hills give the district a Republican lean, but Democrats fare well in Pontiac, where blacks have a plurality and John Kerry won 79 percent of the 2004 presidential vote. Kerry also won Farmington Hills, the most-populous city in the 9th, and West Bloomfield Township by comfortable margins.

Republican presidential candidates do not garner the vote percentages in Oakland that they once did. George W. Bush received 49 percent of Oakland's 2004 vote, which was barely higher than his 48 percent showing statewide. Bush won the 9th with 50 percent of the overall vote.

MAJOR INDUSTRY

Auto manufacturing, engineering, health care, insurance

CITIES

Farmington Hills, 82,111; Troy, 80,959; Rochester Hills, 68,825; Pontiac, 66,337; Waterford (unincorporated) (pt.), 66,316; West Bloomfield Township (unincorporated), 64,862; Royal Oak (pt.), 54,536

NOTABLE

The first Holocaust museum built in the United States was in West Bloomfield; The Rev. Charles Coughlin broadcast his controversial weekly radio programs from the Shrine of the Little Flower church in Royal Oak in the 1930s.

Rep. Candice S. Miller (R)

CAPITOL OFFICE
225-2106
candicemiller.house.gov
228 Cannon 20515-2210; fax 226-1169

COMMITTEES
Armed Services
Select Energy Independence & Global Warming
Transportation & Infrastructure

RESIDENCE
Harrison Township

BORN
May 7, 1954, Detroit, Mich.

RELIGION
Presbyterian

FAMILY
Husband, Donald Miller; one child

EDUCATION
Macomb Community College, attended 1973-74; Northwood Institute, attended 1974

CAREER
Boat saleswoman

POLITICAL HIGHLIGHTS
Harrison Township Board of Trustees, 1979-80; Harrison Township supervisor, 1980-92; Republican nominee for U.S. House, 1986; Macomb County treasurer, 1993-95; Mich. secretary of state, 1995-2002

ELECTION RESULTS

2006 GENERAL		
Candice S. Miller (R)	179,072	66.2%
Robert Denison (D)	84,689	31.3%
Mark Byrne (LIBERT)	2,875	1.1%
2006 PRIMARY		
Candice S. Miller (R)		unopposed
2004 GENERAL		
Candice S. Miller (R)	227,720	68.6%
Rob Casey (D)	98,029	29.5%
Phoebe A. Basso (LIBERT)	3,966	1.2%

PREVIOUS WINNING PERCENTAGES
2002 (63%)

Elected 2002; 3rd term

Miller was a member of the first all-woman sailing crew to compete in the prestigious 300-mile Port Huron to Mackinac Island regatta. At first, the local yacht club barred her and other women from the race across Lake Huron, but the women protested until they were allowed to race. They called their boat the Sayonara. Years later, fellow race veterans admitted her to their Old Goat Society, when she completed her 25th race.

As her race experiences show, Miller is not easily intimidated. She is an assertive party loyalist who usually says what's on her mind. She lashed out in 2006 on having to defend herself against what she called the "culture of corruption." She was angry about campaign tactics that tried to link GOP incumbents to Randy "Duke" Cunningham, the California Republican who pleaded guilty in 2005 to accepting at least $2.4 million in bribes from defense contractors. "The atmosphere here in Washington is so unbelievably poisoned right now," she told The Macomb Daily. "We're obviously going to spend a lot of time looking at every penny everyone has received."

The congresswoman also has been outspoken about the effect of immigration on her state. She introduced a measure in 2005 to amend the Constitution so that only the number of U.S. citizens, instead of the total number of people, would be used to determine how many districts each state has after the decennial census. "I don't mind losing a seat because American citizens have moved somewhere," she told the Detroit Free Press. "But to lose a congressional seat because of illegal immigrants is outrageous." She said Michigan and eight other states lost one seat after the 2000 census while California picked up six seats because illegal immigrants were counted. The measure went nowhere in the 109th Congress (2005-06), but Miller reintroduced it early in the 110th Congress (2007-08).

Miller had a relatively high profile in 2004 as President Bush's campaign chairwoman in Michigan, an important swing state courted heavily by both presidential candidates. She had arrived in the House two years earlier, already a well-established statewide political player, having served two terms as secretary of state. Miller immediately landed on Washington's rising star watch list, but in 2004 she received a rebuke from the House ethics committee for threatening political retaliation against a fellow Republican who refused to support a GOP-backed health care bill.

The ethics panel said Miller went too far when, during the battle over Bush's Medicare prescription drug plan, she cornered Republican Nick Smith, also from Michigan, on the House floor and threatened to use her influence in his son's House race unless Smith supported the legislation. At the time, Brad Smith was seeking to take his retiring father's place, a race he ultimately lost. The elder Smith complained to the ethics panel of pressure from Miller and Republican leaders.

Miller is a loyal Republican and a social and fiscal conservative. But as she represents some suburban areas north of Detroit, the nation's automobile-making hub, she sometimes sides with big labor. Her daughter is a Ford assembly worker who belongs to the United Auto Workers.

She has voted to extend federal unemployment benefits, and she was one of 27 Republicans to vote no in 2005 on a measure to implement the Central American Free Trade Agreement, known as CAFTA. The 10th District is the fourth-largest producer of sugar beets in the nation, and CAFTA provided for a modest increase in sugar imports. Miller said she was concerned the trade pact would undermine her district's farmers.

Miller's major committee assignment is Armed Services, where she fiercely protects the interests of Selfridge Air National Guard Base in her district. Her husband, Donald Miller, is a circuit judge and former commander of the base. Miller was thrilled when Selfridge was spared during the 2005 base closing process. "We have survived and we have a net gain of jobs for Macomb County," she told The Macomb Daily. She wants Selfridge to become the Midwest hub of the Homeland Security Department.

In Michigan, Miller is perhaps an improbable icon of feminist ideals, shattering as she has a number of gender barriers in politics and in one of the state's most popular sports. When Miller was growing up in 1960s suburban Detroit, her father, who owned a marina, discouraged his daughter's interest in sailboat racing because he deemed it a better sport for boys, particularly her older brother Gary. "In my family, women's liberation was not discussed," she once told a newspaper profiler. "You were supposed to get married and do your thing."

She joined a high school boating crew anyway. Miller attended a community college but dropped out to sell boats for the family business. By 25, she was a divorced single mother with a toddler. (She later remarried.) When the local township board proposed a tax increase on marinas, she became a "noisy activist" and surprised herself by finding "that whole experience very stimulating."

Miller was elected to the township board and just a year later unseated the Harrison Township supervisor, becoming the first woman to hold the job. In 1994, she was elected Michigan's first female secretary of state, and in two terms was recognized for making the technologically backward office more efficient and for instituting fraud-proof driver's licenses.

Miller had long eyed a seat in Congress but was blocked by the popularity of Democratic Rep. David E. Bonior, whom she had lost to in 1986 when she was relatively green. Though Miller was the favorite to take on Bonior again in 2000, she was more interested in preparing to run for governor. When Republican Gov. John Engler decided to back Lt. Gov. Dick Posthumus as his successor, Miller stayed out of both contests.

The Republican-controlled legislature made it up to her in 2002 with a redrawn congressional district that included several GOP-leaning counties and Miller's base in Macomb County. Her Democratic opponent was popular Macomb County Prosecuting Attorney Carl J. Marlinga. Miller, who enjoyed solid statewide name recognition and greatly outpaced Marlinga in fundraising, won with 63 percent of the vote. She drew only marginal competition in 2004 and won again easily in 2006.

KEY VOTES

2006

No Stop broadband companies from favoring select Internet traffic
Yes Affirm U.S. commitment to war in Iraq and reject setting a withdrawal date for troops
Yes Repeal requirement for bilingual ballots at the polls
Yes Permit U.S. sale of civilian nuclear technology to India
Yes Build a 700-mile fence on the U.S.-Mexico border to curb illegal crossings
Yes Permit warrantless wiretaps of suspected terrorists

2005

Yes Intervene in the life-support case of Terri Schiavo
No Lift President Bush's restrictions on stem cell research funding
No Prohibit FBI access to library and bookstore records
No Approve free-trade pact with five Central American countries
Yes Pass energy policy overhaul favored by President Bush emphasizing domestic oil and gas production
Yes End mandatory preservation of habitat of endangered animal and plant species
Yes Ban torture of prisoners in U.S. custody

CQ VOTE STUDIES

	PARTY UNITY		PRESIDENTIAL SUPPORT	
	Support	Oppose	Support	Oppose
2006	89%	11%	94%	6%
2005	94%	6%	85%	15%
2004	93%	7%	85%	15%
2003	96%	4%	95%	5%

INTEREST GROUPS

	AFL-CIO	ADA	CCUS	ACU
2006	25%	10%	93%	84%
2005	20%	5%	89%	84%
2004	27%	10%	100%	84%
2003	13%	10%	97%	83%

MICHIGAN 10

East – northern Macomb County, Port Huron, most of Michigan 'Thumb'

Stretching from Detroit's northern suburbs in Macomb County to the tip of Michigan's "Thumb," the 10th combines suburban, lakefront and rural communities. Although Macomb long had been an electoral bellwether, the county's recent suburban population growth led it to support Republican George W. Bush in the 2004 presidential election, even as Michigan overall handed Bush a 3 percentage point loss.

Macomb, where half of the district's population resides, largely has shed its blue-collar, "Reagan Democrat" reputation. Suburban growth in Harrison Township, Shelby and Sterling Heights (shared with 12th) has made the area more white-collar. Lapeer County, northwest of Macomb, also has grown, as upwardly mobile residents drift farther away from decaying urban centers in Flint (to the west) and Detroit (to the south).

Northeast of Macomb is St. Clair County, a politically competitive region where one-fourth of district residents live. St. Clair's Port Huron, a source of blue-collar Democratic votes, is the U.S. terminus of the Blue Water bridges, which cross into Ontario, Canada. Bridge traffic into the United States stimulates the area's economy, as Canadian tourists spend money on the U.S. side of the border. Water-quality issues are important to local residents along Lake Huron and other district bays and rivers, and the area has many small businesses based on the boating industry.

Elsewhere in the district, the 10th's rural communities depend on fruit, soybeans, corn, dairy and other crops. The 10th has the most productive sugar beet fields in the state, and the fertile soil of the Thumb is known for its navy bean fields. Huron County leads Michigan in milk production, with Sanilac County also in the top five.

MAJOR INDUSTRY

Auto manufacturing, agriculture, recreation

CITIES

Sterling Heights (pt.), 86,536; Shelby (unincorporated), 65,159; Port Huron, 32,338

NOTABLE

The U.S. Senate's famous navy bean soup uses only Michigan navy beans; Port Huron's Fort Gratiot Lighthouse is the state's oldest and was rebuilt in 1829 by Lucius Lyon, who later became a U.S. senator.

Rep. Thaddeus McCotter (R)

CAPITOL OFFICE
225-8171
thaddeus.mccotter@mail.house.gov
mccotter.house.gov
1632 Longworth 20515-2211; fax 225-2667

COMMITTEES
Financial Services

RESIDENCE
Livonia

BORN
Aug. 22, 1965, Detroit, Mich.

RELIGION
Roman Catholic

FAMILY
Wife, Rita McCotter; three children

EDUCATION
U. of Detroit, B.A. 1987 (political science), J.D. 1990

CAREER
Lawyer

POLITICAL HIGHLIGHTS
Schoolcraft College Board of Trustees, 1989-92; Wayne County Commission, 1993-98; Mich. Senate, 1999-2002

ELECTION RESULTS

2006 GENERAL		
Thaddeus McCotter (R)	143,658	54.1%
Tony Trupiano (D)	114,248	43.0%
John T. Tatar (LIBERT)	4,340	1.6%
Charles E. Tackett (USTAX)	3,538	1.3%
2006 PRIMARY		
Thaddeus McCotter (R)		unopposed
2004 GENERAL		
Thaddeus McCotter (R)	186,431	57.0%
Phillip Truran (D)	134,301	41.0%
Charles I. Basso (LIBERT)	6,484	2.0%

PREVIOUS WINNING PERCENTAGES
2002 (57%)

Elected 2002; 3rd term

McCotter's politics are largely conservative, but his personality is '60s radical fringe. A serious fan of old rock and roll with a rebellious side, McCotter is disinclined toward pious political rhetoric. Passion, he says in his clipped Midwestern way of getting to the point, "is a very bad song by Rod Stewart. At the end of the day, it is hard work."

He's among a growing number of restless, younger Republicans agitating for change after a long season of drooping public confidence in President Bush and scandal-tainted Republican leaders in Congress.

In 2006, McCotter ran twice for a leadership post on a platform of bringing in new blood. "We need a more relaxed, creative environment," he said. "Ideas go up the food chain, and they stay up the food chain. We can't seem to legislate. There's not enough room for individuality."

In February, as the GOP elected new leaders for the year in the aftermath of the departure several months before of Majority Leader Tom DeLay, McCotter finished a distant second to Florida's Adam H. Putnam, with 75 votes to Putnam's 118 in a contest for chairman of the Republican Policy Committee, the party's No. 5 post.

But late in the year, as the GOP organized itself for the 110th Congress (2007-08), McCotter easily defeated Darrell Issa of California, 132-63, for the same Policy Committee post. He vowed that more voices of rank-and-file Republicans would be heard in the development of the party's agenda.

McCotter is a fiscal conservative, favoring lower taxes and smaller government. "My first instinct is to protect people from the power of government," he likes to say. He supported Bush's tax cut policies and favors making some of them permanent. He once got into a heated debate with a fellow Republican state senator in Michigan, a portly fellow who wanted to raise the dollar-a-pack tax on cigarettes. A smoker, McCotter threatened to propose a tax on candy and junk food. "I hate all taxes," he said to the man. "I don't care if it is on your snacks, or beers or cigarettes. Government deals off cigarette tax revenue are wrong. You either make it illegal or leave it alone."

McCotter departs from party orthodoxy on some labor issues, erring in favor of the large segment of his constituency that is working-class. He was among a small band of Republicans to break ranks and support measures in both 2003 and 2004 to extend unemployment benefits for an additional 13 weeks. "My constituents don't enjoy taking unemployment compensation. It's a necessity," he said.

Though most Republicans stayed mum as the war in Iraq turned increasingly sour politically, McCotter in 2006 was one of six House Republicans to call for an independent, bipartisan commission to assess U.S. progress. A long-time rocker who once played the Detroit club circuit, McCotter went overseas in 2005 to entertain the troops in Iraq, Afghanistan and elsewhere with a country rock band, "The Second Amendments," made up of McCotter on lead guitar and four House colleagues. "Everyone thinks that the stereotypical Republican is some Philistine with a limousine. That just doesn't really hold up anymore," he told the Detroit News.

With a district near Detroit, McCotter champions the auto industry above other interests when they conflict. He opposes tougher fuel economy standards for vehicles, saying they are "unfunded mandates" that would spur layoffs and disrupt the auto-dominated local economy. In 2003, he joined other GOP members from Michigan in urging Bush to drop tariffs on foreign steel that tended to drive up prices for Detroit car manufacturers.

The 11th District depends on the hundreds of millions of dollars pumped into southeast Michigan every year by Canadian tourists. McCotter is pressing for changes in a new law requiring a passport to cross into Canada by land or sea, which could take effect as early as Jan. 1, 2008. The northern border should be regulated differently than the U.S.-Mexico border, he says.

The area also depends on the Great Lakes for drinking water, cargo traffic and recreation. McCotter, a self-described conservationist, has signed on to numerous bills to clean up the lakes and eliminate invasive species.

On another issue of local fascination, McCotter and Michigan Democratic Sen. Carl Levin slipped a provision into an appropriations bill that granted citizenship to Canadian ice dancer Tanith Belbin, just in time for Belbin and her partner Ben Agosto to qualify for the 2006 U.S. Olympic team. They ultimately won a silver medal for the United States in Turin, Italy.

A lifelong resident of his district, McCotter still lives in his hometown of Livonia with his wife, who is a registered nurse, and their three children. His parents were both special education teachers in the Detroit public schools. His mother, Joan, was elected to the Livonia City Council in 1985, a campaign he helped manage. In his youth, McCotter was a semi-professional musician playing guitar in several bands, including one called Sir Funk-a-Lot and the Knights of the Terrestrial Jam.

When stardom failed to materialize, McCotter attended the University of Detroit Law School and went into solo law practice. A friend persuaded him to get involved in the 1988 presidential campaign, and McCotter went to the Republican National Convention as a delegate pledged to George H. W. Bush.

In 1992, he won a seat on the Wayne County Commission, where he was the driving force behind a law requiring 60 percent voter approval for any tax increase. Elected to the state Senate in 1998, McCotter was vice chairman of the reapportionment committee that drew new congressional district maps after the 2000 census. That put him in position to draw the new 11th District, which happened to include his entire old state Senate district.

In the 2002 primary, McCotter handily beat businessman David C. Hagerty. In the general election, he easily fended off Democratic nominee Kevin Kelley, a township supervisor who had a long political résumé but got into the race late. McCotter got an infusion of $500,000 when George W. Bush headlined a fundraising dinner.

In 2004, McCotter easily defeated the Democratic nominee, local union president Phillip Truran, by 16 percentage points. In the down year for Republican candidates in 2006, he still prevailed by more than 11 points.

KEY VOTES

2006

- No Stop broadband companies from favoring select Internet traffic
- P Affirm U.S. commitment to war in Iraq and reject setting a withdrawal date for troops
- Yes Repeal requirement for bilingual ballots at the polls
- Yes Permit U.S. sale of civilian nuclear technology to India
- Yes Build a 700-mile fence on the U.S.-Mexico border to curb illegal crossings
- Yes Permit warrantless wiretaps of suspected terrorists

2005

- Yes Intervene in the life-support case of Terri Schiavo
- No Lift President Bush's restrictions on stem cell research funding
- No Prohibit FBI access to library and bookstore records
- No Approve free-trade pact with five Central American countries
- Yes Pass energy policy overhaul favored by President Bush emphasizing domestic oil and gas production
- Yes End mandatory preservation of habitat of endangered animal and plant species
- Yes Ban torture of prisoners in U.S. custody

CQ VOTE STUDIES

	PARTY UNITY		PRESIDENTIAL SUPPORT	
	Support	Oppose	Support	Oppose
2006	87%	13%	82%	18%
2005	89%	11%	78%	22%
2004	91%	9%	82%	18%
2003	96%	4%	96%	4%

INTEREST GROUPS

	AFL-CIO	ADA	CCUS	ACU
2006	50%	15%	93%	83%
2005	40%	20%	81%	88%
2004	27%	15%	95%	88%
2003	7%	50%	100%	88%

MICHIGAN 11

Southeast – Livonia, Westland, Novi

The 11th, which takes in suburbs west and north of Detroit, stands out as a Republican-leaning area in a region known for its support of pro-labor Democrats. As in other Michigan districts that surround the Motor City, auto manufacturing still plays a prominent role in the district despite recent efforts to diversify the area's economy.

Although Detroit's presence makes Wayne County, where 70 percent of the district's residents live, a Democratic stronghold, the 11th's portion of Wayne begins just west of where Detroit proper ends, and the 11th's portion of Wayne is politically competitive. Residents here tend toward fiscal conservatism, and they split their presidential votes almost evenly in 2004 between George W. Bush and John Kerry.

The 11th's overall Republican lean stems from upper-middle-class communities such as Livonia, the most populous city in the district, and Canton, a rapidly growing area near the Wayne County border east of Ann Arbor, which is in the 15th District. The 11th also covers southwestern Oakland County, which is more GOP-leaning than middle-class Wayne areas such as Redford, just west of Detroit, and Westland, a city south of Livonia that gave 58 percent of its 2004 vote to Kerry.

Revitalization efforts in the 11th's smaller communities are attracting younger residents. Novi grew by 47 percent in the 1990s and has increased in population this decade as well. Many district residents are employed in the health care or auto parts manufacturing industries, and population growth has transformed the landscapes of Plymouth, Canton and Novi, where home ownership is now expected to rise. Areas such as Wixom were once almost entirely filled with auto workers, but these communities have been affected by downsized or shuttered auto facilities. In Wixom, a Ford plant is scheduled to close by 2008.

MAJOR INDUSTRY

Auto manufacturing, engineering, health care, insurance, finance

CITIES

Livonia, 100,545; Westland, 86,602; Canton (unincorporated), 76,366; Redford (unincorporated), 51,622; Novi, 47,386; Garden City, 30,047

NOTABLE

Novi, first settled around 1825, is said to have been named for being the sixth stop — No. VI, using the abbreviation and Roman numerals — on a stagecoach route.

Rep. Sander M. Levin (D)

CAPITOL OFFICE
225-4961
www.house.gov/levin
1236 Longworth 20515-2212; fax 226-1033

COMMITTEES
Ways & Means
(Trade - chairman)
Joint Taxation

RESIDENCE
Royal Oak

BORN
Sept. 6, 1931, Detroit, Mich.

RELIGION
Jewish

FAMILY
Wife, Victoria Levin; four children

EDUCATION
U. of Chicago, B.A. 1952; Columbia U., M.A. 1954 (international relations); Harvard U., LL.B. 1957

CAREER
Lawyer; U.S. Agency for International Development official

POLITICAL HIGHLIGHTS
Oakland Board of Supervisors, 1961-64; Mich. Senate, 1965-71 (minority leader, 1969-70); Michigan Democratic Party chairman, 1968-69; Democratic nominee for governor, 1970, 1974

ELECTION RESULTS

2006 GENERAL		
Sander M. Levin (D)	168,494	70.2%
Randell J. Shafer (R)	62,689	26.1%
Andy Lecureaux (LIBERT)	3,259	1.4%
2006 PRIMARY		
Sander M. Levin (D)		unopposed
2004 GENERAL		
Sander M. Levin (D)	210,827	69.3%
Randell J. Shafer (R)	88,256	29.0%
Dick Gach (LIBERT)	5,051	1.7%

PREVIOUS WINNING PERCENTAGES
2002 (68%); 2000 (64%); 1998 (56%); 1996 (57%); 1994 (52%); 1992 (53%); 1990 (70%); 1988 (70%); 1986 (76%); 1984 (100%); 1982 (67%)

Elected 1982; 13th term

Mild-mannered but tenacious, Levin has the look and speaking style of a distracted college professor. He is known for throwing his intellectual might into understanding the details of legislation and their practical implications. By the end of lengthy hearings, he often looks so rumpled, with his white hair strewn about, that he appears to be physically wrestling with the answers to his complex questions.

Levin, known as "Sandy," is the older half of a House-Senate sibling pair, but he was elected four years after Democratic Sen. Carl Levin. The two get together at least once a week to play squash and often consult each other on policy. "When Mom and Dad bought a house, the first thing they did was to knock down the wall between two small rooms," Sander Levin recalls. The brothers roomed together until Sander left for college. Rummaging through a trunk of his childhood belongings in 2006, he found a sign Carl had hand-painted when Sander won the presidency of his high school senior class: "Welcome Mr. President."

A senior member of the Ways and Means Committee, Levin is his party's leading trade expert. He became top-ranking Democrat on the Trade Subcommittee in 1999, and now chairs the panel after a two-year stint guarding the fort at the Social Security Subcommittee. He took the top slot there after the Jan. 1, 2005, death of his close friend, Robert T. Matsui of California. Early reports suggested that the job would go to Benjamin L. Cardin of Maryland, then the No. 2 Democrat on the panel, but Levin outranked Cardin on the full committee and was seen by some Democrats as more certain to hang tough against President Bush's proposal to create private accounts within Social Security. "When some of us talked, the leadership and myself, the feeling was that I should take it," Levin said.

Levin threw himself into the battle and soon became a guiding strategic force in the Democrats' successful effort to kill it. He believes Bush never fully understood the importance of Social Security and its guaranteed retirement benefit — as well as its disability and survivor benefits — to average people. "They call Social Security the third rail [of politics]. That misstates it. It's the electricity that goes into the third rail," he said.

During the 2005 Social Security fight, Levin and his closest aides gathered at a large conference table in his office every morning to talk strategy and policy. There, they hatched plans to increase the number of town hall meetings Democrats were holding with constituents to discuss Social Security — even as Republicans were scaling back their own town halls — and came up with counter-terminology for administration rhetoric. When the administration described a plan to reduce guaranteed Social Security benefits for wealthier future retirees as "progressive price indexing," Levin and his staff renamed it a "sliding-scale benefit cut."

Even with his attention directed toward Social Security issues, Levin helped lead the Democratic charge in 2005 against a free-trade agreement with Central America that passed the House by just two votes. While he earlier had voted for liberalized trade with Chile and Singapore, Levin warned that the Central American agreement was entirely different because of poor labor laws in most Latin American countries. He believes that he and Matsui first formulated what he says is today the basic Democratic position on trade policy: "growth with equity," or expanding trade but dictating the terms, especially in the area of worker rights. In 2007, he started negotiations with the White House over modifying U.S. trade policy to include enforceable labor and environmental standards, among other things.

Levin has become a strong critic of the way U.S. trade with China has evolved, even though he was a central player in securing enactment of the 2000 law making China a permanent normal U.S. trading partner. Passage by the House was deeply in doubt until Levin and Nebraska Republican Doug Bereuter struck a deal to include in the bill the creation of a commission to monitor China's behavior on human rights and compliance with trade rules. Levin later was appointed to the commission, and his work with the group has formed the basis for much of his later criticism.

Earlier in his House career, Levin often was able to find common ground with conservatives. He joined Ohio Republican Rob Portman on legislation to combat illegal drugs, including a bipartisan matching grant initiative that by 2004 supported 713 community anti-drug coalitions nationwide. But he says it is far harder these days to find friendly Republicans. "There's much more polarization," he says.

Levin represents one of the most renowned political proving grounds in the nation: Macomb County outside Detroit, where the term "Reagan Democrat" was coined. After four years as an appointed supervisor in Oakland County, Levin in 1964 won his first elective office, a suburban Detroit state Senate seat. He was minority leader in Lansing, served as state Democratic Party chairman in the late 1960s, and was viewed as a rising star when he was the party's gubernatorial nominee in 1970 and 1974. But his low-key manner did not shine in the statewide races, and he lost both.

After a stint as assistant administrator in the U.S. Agency for International Development, Levin ran for the House seat of retiring Democratic Rep. William M. Brodhead in 1982. With his well-known surname — his younger brother, Carl, had been in the Senate almost four years by then — and support from the party establishment, Levin overcame five primary opponents and went on to win the general election easily.

He had little trouble with re-election until redistricting after the 1990 census removed many metro Detroit Jewish voters from his district and added neighborhoods where he was unknown. In 1992, Republican challenger John Pappageorge, a retired Army colonel, held him to 53 percent of the vote though Levin outspent him by a more than 5-1 ratio. Levin won two rematches, in 1994 and 1996, with 52 percent and 57 percent of the vote.

The GOP-led state legislature redrew Levin's district for this decade to make it more Democratic, and in 2002 Levin easily prevailed with 68 percent of the vote. He has won re-election easily since. His son, Andy, ran for an open state Senate seat in 2006 but lost. The winner: John Pappageorge.

KEY VOTES

2006

- Yes Stop broadband companies from favoring select Internet traffic
- No Affirm U.S. commitment to war in Iraq and reject setting a withdrawal date for troops
- No Repeal requirement for bilingual ballots at the polls
- Yes Permit U.S. sale of civilian nuclear technology to India
- No Build a 700-mile fence on the U.S.-Mexico border to curb illegal crossings
- No Permit warrantless wiretaps of suspected terrorists

2005

- No Intervene in the life-support case of Terri Schiavo
- Yes Lift President Bush's restrictions on stem cell research funding
- Yes Prohibit FBI access to library and bookstore records
- No Approve free-trade pact with five Central American countries
- Yes Pass energy policy overhaul favored by President Bush emphasizing domestic oil and gas production
- No End mandatory preservation of habitat of endangered animal and plant species
- Yes Ban torture of prisoners in U.S. custody

CQ VOTE STUDIES

	PARTY UNITY		PRESIDENTIAL SUPPORT	
	Support	Oppose	Support	Oppose
2006	93%	7%	25%	75%
2005	95%	5%	20%	80%
2004	95%	5%	26%	74%
2003	93%	7%	22%	78%
2002	95%	5%	28%	72%

INTEREST GROUPS

	AFL-CIO	ADA	CCUS	ACU
2006	100%	90%	40%	8%
2005	100%	95%	48%	4%
2004	100%	100%	38%	0%
2003	87%	90%	37%	20%
2002	100%	95%	40%	0%

MICHIGAN 12

Suburban Detroit – Warren, Clinton, Southfield

Heavily Democratic and dependent on the automobile manufacturing industry, the 12th is home to well-settled Macomb and Oakland county suburbs north of 8 Mile Road, Detroit's northern boundary. The shoe-shaped district borders Lake St. Clair at its heel and the city of Detroit at its instep before its toes extend to Southfield.

The district is lined with auto manufacturing facilities, and Warren, in Macomb County, is home to the General Motors Technical Center, a 320-acre design and engineering campus. The Army's Tank-automotive and Armaments Command also is based in Warren, which is the district's most populous city and has been a traditional Democratic safe haven: The city gave John Kerry 56 percent of its presidential vote in 2004.

Nearly 70 percent of the 12th's residents live in Macomb in the district's eastern half. Although the county overall narrowly supported George W. Bush in the 2004 presidential election, the 12th's portion of the county gave Democrat John Kerry 54 percent of the vote.

Sterling Heights (shared with the 10th) continues to grow, and Clinton Township, at slightly less than 100,000 people, claims to be the most populous township in Michigan. St. Clair Shores, the self-proclaimed "boat capital of Michigan," has more than six miles of waterfront and more than 7,000 registered boats.

In its western portion, the 12th takes in several southern Oakland County communities near the Detroit boundary that are heavily Democratic and have large black populations: Southfield, which has become a haven for black urban professionals escaping Detroit's crime, Lathrup Village and Oak Park. Other Oakland County communities in the 12th include Ferndale, Hazel Park and Madison Heights, which also are solidly Democratic but are overwhelmingly white.

MAJOR INDUSTRY

Auto manufacturing, auto and tank research and design

CITIES

Warren, 138,247; Clinton (unincorporated), 95,648; Southfield, 78,296; St. Clair Shores, 63,096; Roseville, 48,129; Sterling Heights (pt.), 37,935

NOTABLE

The Detroit Zoo is in Royal Oak, which received its name in 1819 when then Governor Lewis Cass and his companions christened a large tree.

Rep. Carolyn Cheeks Kilpatrick (D)

CAPITOL OFFICE
225-2261
www.house.gov/kilpatrick
2264 Rayburn 20515-2213; fax 225-5730

COMMITTEES
Appropriations

RESIDENCE
Detroit

BORN
June 25, 1945, Detroit, Mich.

RELIGION
African Methodist Episcopal

FAMILY
Divorced; two children

EDUCATION
Ferris State U., A.A. 1965; Western Michigan U., B.S. 1968 (education); U. of Michigan, M.A. 1972 (education)

CAREER
Teacher

POLITICAL HIGHLIGHTS
Mich. House, 1979-97; candidate for Detroit City Council, 1991; sought Democratic nomination for Mich. Senate, 1994

ELECTION RESULTS

2006 GENERAL		
Carolyn Cheeks Kilpatrick (D)	unopposed	
2006 PRIMARY		
Carolyn Cheeks Kilpatrick (D)	unopposed	
2004 GENERAL		
Carolyn Cheeks Kilpatrick (D)	173,246	78.2%
Cynthia Cassell (R)	40,935	18.5%
Thomas Lavigne (GREEN)	4,261	1.9%
Eric B. Gordon (LIBERT)	3,211	1.5%

PREVIOUS WINNING PERCENTAGES
2002 (92%); 2000 (89%); 1998 (87%); 1996 (88%)

Elected 1996; 6th term

A political force in her native Detroit, Kilpatrick is positioned to raise her national profile considerably with her selection as chairwoman of the Congressional Black Caucus in the first Democratic Congress in a dozen years.

As the leader of the august group of African-American lawmakers, Kilpatrick will shape the agenda for its 43 mostly liberal members for the 110th Congress (2007-08). Only the fifth woman to head the caucus, Kilpatrick said she wanted to focus on its traditional mission of closing the gap between whites and minorities in education, health care and employment. But she also planned to press for more funding for the fight against AIDS and for the victims of Hurricane Katrina, who are disproportionately black.

The caucus in the 110th Congress is potentially in its most influential position in its 38-year existence. Among its members are the chairmen and chairwomen of five committees, including the powerful Judiciary and Ways and Means committees, and of several subcommittees. Democratic Whip James E. Clyburn of South Carolina, the third-ranking House leader, is a caucus member. "We are the conscience of the United States House of Representatives," said Kilpatrick, who was the group's vice chairwoman in the 109th Congress (2005-06). "Watch for us. We will take our caucus to another level."

The group's ability to flex its muscle was constricted in one way. It was confronted with two candidates for the 2008 Democratic presidential nomination with sterling credentials in civil rights — Sen. Barack Obama of Illinois, who is black, and Sen. Hillary Rodham Clinton of New York, a good friend to the caucus on many of its issues. Kilpatrick announced that the caucus would not endorse either of the front-runners in the primaries but would be "lockstep behind" the party's eventual nominee.

With Kilpatrick at the helm, the caucus was poised to be a focal point of Iraq War opposition. She has been strongly opposed to the war since 2002, when she voted against authorizing the U.S. invasion. "Instead of 'Bring them on,' I hope that my colleagues agree that Congress can start to 'Bring them home,' " Kilpatrick said on the House floor. The caucus' other major foreign policy issue was the genocide in the Darfur region of Sudan.

Kilpatrick led the battle with Speaker Nancy Pelosi over Democratic Rep. William J. Jefferson of Louisiana, a caucus member. Jefferson was the subject of a U.S. Justice Department bribery probe in 2005, and FBI officials found $90,000 in marked bills in the freezer of his Washington, D.C., home. Jefferson maintained his innocence. But Pelosi in 2006 pressured the Democratic Caucus to oust him from his seat on the Ways and Means Committee. Kilpatrick insisted that if Jefferson were white, the leadership would have left him in place pending the outcome of the criminal investigation.

Kilpatrick was in the headlines in late 2005, when Detroit resident and civil rights activist Rosa Parks died. Kilpatrick spoke movingly in several forums about Parks, who galvanized the budding civil rights movement in 1955 by refusing to give up her seat to a white man on a public bus. Kilpatrick met Parks as a teen. "I remember thinking, 'How dare I not do all I can after seeing this little, strong woman who took a stand to make life better for me, for all of us. How dare any of us to shirk from any injustice,'" Kilpatrick told the Detroit Free Press. Kilpatrick, with Democratic Rep. John Conyers Jr. of Detroit, led an effort to allow Parks to lie in state in the Capitol Rotunda, where presidents are usually honored in death.

Kilpatrick has long been more influential at home than in Washington.

In 2005, she helped revive the career of her son, Detroit Mayor Kwame Kilpatrick, when he was down by double digits in the polls in his re-election bid. She was criticized in the local press for missing House votes while giving rousing speeches for her son in Detroit. Her son won a second term.

The Detroit News, the more conservative of the city's two major newspapers, refused to endorse Kilpatrick's own re-election campaign the following year, and called her one of Congress' "most ineffective members."

Kilpatrick's other focus is her work on the Appropriations Committee, where she has a seat on the Financial Services Subcommittee and tries to steer federal dollars to her center-city district, the poorest in the state. In 2000, she and New Jersey Democrat Robert Menendez helped persuade President Bill Clinton to sign an executive order aimed at giving minority firms more of the government's advertising business. Kilpatrick has been working since to codify the Clinton order.

Kilpatrick breaks from the liberal ranks when it comes to automobile fuel economy standards, which are anathema to the Detroit-area automobile industry.

A native of Detroit, Kilpatrick holds a master's degree in education. She taught business and vocational classes in the public schools for eight years. She won the first of nine terms in the state House, a full-time job, in 1978. In Lansing, she was the first black woman to serve on the Appropriations Committee, and she once led a bipartisan coalition of lawmakers seeking to block a proposal by popular Republican Gov. John Engler to halt state funding for local transportation programs.

She has hit a few bumps in her political career. She lost a 1991 Detroit City Council bid when questions arose about whether she was sufficiently independent from Mayor Coleman Young; and she failed, after changing her mind several times, to win a spot on the 1994 state Senate ballot.

In 1996, when Democratic Rep. Barbara-Rose Collins became the subject of investigations by the House ethics committee and the Justice Department into allegations of ethical misconduct, Kilpatrick stepped forward to challenge her one-time political ally. She won a majority of the primary vote and beat Collins by 20 percentage points. The November outcome was a foregone conclusion in the heavily Democratic district. Kilpatrick has since won re-election with ease. She had no challenger in 2006.

Kilpatrick's son was once her campaign manager, and he succeeded her in the state House when she came to Congress. In 2001, he was elected mayor of Detroit at 31. He credited his mother and father, a leading Wayne County government official, for instilling in him the belief in public service.

KEY VOTES

2006

Yes Stop broadband companies from favoring select Internet traffic
\- Affirm U.S. commitment to war in Iraq and reject setting a withdrawal date for troops
No Repeal requirement for bilingual ballots at the polls
No Permit U.S. sale of civilian nuclear technology to India
No Build a 700-mile fence on the U.S.-Mexico border to curb illegal crossings
No Permit warrantless wiretaps of suspected terrorists

2005

? Intervene in the life-support case of Terri Schiavo
Yes Lift President Bush's restrictions on stem cell research funding
Yes Prohibit FBI access to library and bookstore records
No Approve free-trade pact with five Central American countries
No Pass energy policy overhaul favored by President Bush emphasizing domestic oil and gas production
No End mandatory preservation of habitat of endangered animal and plant species
Yes Ban torture of prisoners in U.S. custody

CQ VOTE STUDIES

	PARTY UNITY		PRESIDENTIAL SUPPORT	
	Support	Oppose	Support	Oppose
2006	97%	3%	23%	77%
2005	96%	4%	17%	83%
2004	96%	4%	28%	72%
2003	97%	3%	17%	83%
2002	98%	2%	27%	73%

INTEREST GROUPS

	AFL-CIO	ADA	CCUS	ACU
2006	100%	100%	27%	4%
2005	93%	100%	32%	4%
2004	100%	95%	29%	4%
2003	100%	100%	24%	16%
2002	100%	95%	42%	0%

MICHIGAN 13

Part of Detroit; Lincoln Park; Wyandotte

The auto industry and Motown Records kept Detroit humming for decades before economic problems overwhelmed the city, which remains among the most crime-ridden in the nation. Detroit, divided between the 13th and 14th districts, still has a tough reputation and relatively high taxes, and many suburbs have become regional office centers that have lured companies away from the city. Recent revitalization plans, however, are bringing the roar back into the city, and the downtown has new tourist destinations.

A slightly larger share of Detroit's population lives in the black-majority 13th. The city has been steadily losing population for decades, and it fell below one million residents in the 2000 census. Future census figures are expected to show the city out of the top ten most-populous U.S. cities for the first time since the late 19th century. Wealthy communities to the northeast, such as Grosse Pointe, also are losing population.

Detroit remains overwhelmingly Democratic, and John Kerry won the 13th's portion of the city with 93 percent of the vote in the 2004 election. Pockets of poverty exist, and the 13th has the state's highest percentage of households with annual incomes less than $10,000 (18 percent).

Downtown Detroit and the waterfront, which fall in the 13th, are targets for extensive redevelopment. A massive downtown entertainment complex includes two cornerstone sports stadiums — Comerica Park opened in 2000 for baseball's Tigers and Ford Field opened in 2002 for football's Lions. The RiverWalk project, aimed at promoting tourism along the Detroit River, is under way and will stretch for several miles along the waterfront. The city's downtown neighborhoods are luring businesses, and General Motors has relocated its headquarters to the Renaissance Center on the waterfront.

MAJOR INDUSTRY

Auto and auto parts manufacturing, government

CITIES

Detroit (pt.), 511,449; Lincoln Park, 40,008; Wyandotte, 28,006

NOTABLE

The headquarters of Michigan's famous Faygo "pop" is in the 13th; J.W. Westcott Company, a "floating" post office, is located near Ambassador Bridge; The Charles H. Wright Museum of African-American History is in Detroit's cultural center north of downtown.

Rep. John Conyers Jr. (D)

CAPITOL OFFICE
225-5126
www.house.gov/conyers
2426 Rayburn 20515-2214; fax 225-0072

COMMITTEES
Judiciary - chairman
(Anti-Trust Taskforce - chairman)

RESIDENCE
Detroit

BORN
May 16, 1929, Detroit, Mich.

RELIGION
Baptist

FAMILY
Wife, Monica Conyers; two children

EDUCATION
Wayne State U., B.A. 1957, LL.B. 1958

MILITARY SERVICE
Mich. National Guard, 1948-50; Army, 1950-54; Army Reserve, 1954-57

CAREER
Lawyer; congressional aide

POLITICAL HIGHLIGHTS
Candidate for mayor of Detroit, 1989; candidate for mayor of Detroit, 1993

ELECTION RESULTS

2006 GENERAL		
John Conyers Jr. (D)	158,755	85.3%
Chad Miles (R)	27,367	14.7%
2006 PRIMARY		
John Conyers Jr. (D)		unopposed
2004 GENERAL		
John Conyers Jr. (D)	213,681	83.9%
Veronica Pedraza (R)	35,089	13.8%

PREVIOUS WINNING PERCENTAGES
2002 (83%); 2000 (89%); 1998 (87%); 1996 (86%); 1994 (81%); 1992 (82%); 1990 (89%); 1988 (91%); 1986 (89%); 1984 (89%); 1982 (97%); 1980 (95%); 1978 (93%); 1976 (92%); 1974 (91%); 1972 (88%); 1970 (88%); 1968 (100%); 1966 (84%); 1964 (84%)

Elected 1964; 22nd term

Among the most pronounced shifts in power in the new Democratic Congress in 2007 was the ascension of Conyers to the chairmanship of the Judiciary Committee, where the country's social policy dramas play out. The civil rights era lawmaker, as liberal as his GOP predecessors were conservative, has a much different agenda.

With Conyers at the helm, constitutional amendments to ban gay marriage and conservative proposals to curb the power of federal courts are unlikely to see the light of day, as are business-backed efforts to overhaul the civil justice system. Bills that had enjoyed strong House support, to shield the food industry from lawsuits, for example, are a thing of the past.

Oversight of the Bush administration, virtually nonexistent during GOP rule, is bound to consume much more of the panel's time and resources. Conyers objects to the administration's liberal use of executive power, in particular the National Security Agency's controversial warrantless surveillance program. He also is skeptical of recent laws making it easier for law enforcement to detain and interrogate suspected terrorists. And he launched a probe of President Bush's use of signing statements that signal that the president might disregard elements of a bill he just signed into law. Conyers said that such a tactic "is a constitutional issue that no self-respecting federal legislature should tolerate."

Conyers is especially interested in election reform. He wants to address problems in recent elections of eligible voters being thwarted at the polls and possible manipulation of electronic voting machines. He oversaw an investigation of flaws in the voting process in Ohio during the Bush-Kerry election, issuing a report that was turned into a book called, "What Went Wrong in Ohio: The Conyers Report on the 2004 Presidential Election."

In 2005, Conyers was an eloquent spokesman against the decision by House Republican leaders to intervene in a Florida right-to-die case in which the courts ultimately decided to remove the feeding tube of severely brain-damaged Terri Schiavo. "We are no longer a nation of laws but have been reduced to a nation of men," Conyers said.

Among the harshest critics of the war in Iraq, Conyers in 2005 went so far as to call for impeachment proceedings against Bush for manipulating intelligence in the buildup to the war. But Democrats in the 110th Congress (2007-08) were not planning to pursue the matter.

Conyers has served longer than any other current House member except John D. Dingell, his fellow Detroit-area Democrat. Like Dingell, he is a liberal partisan seasoned enough to engage the other side when he wants to get something done and not just score debating points.

In the minority, he worked closely behind the scenes with Republican Chairman F. James Sensenbrenner Jr. of Wisconsin, despite their frequent public disagreements over policy. In 2001, the two were able to forge an agreement giving law enforcement greater legal leeway to fight terrorism, though their bipartisan bill was later scrapped by GOP leaders. For all their ideological differences, Conyers and Sensenbrenner agreed that Congress has a constitutional responsibility to serve as a check on the executive branch. With limited success, the two pressed the Justice Department to account for how it was using powers under the 2001 anti-terrorism law known as the Patriot Act.

Conyers tends to delegate more power to his top lieutenants than did Sensenbrenner. In 2006, he assigned sensitive negotiations on legislation renewing the Voting Rights Act to North Carolina's Melvin Watt, then top-ranking Democrat on one of the Judiciary subcommittees.

In recent years, Conyers was under a cloud as the House ethics committee investigated complaints that he compelled his official staff to do campaign work and personal chores such as babysitting his children. The ethics panel elicited a promise from Conyers in December 2006 to meet six conditions it set generally barring use of his staff for campaign work.

A co-founder of the Congressional Black Caucus, Conyers has championed the causes of civil rights, minorities and the poor. He introduced legislation to make the birthday of the Rev. Martin Luther King Jr. a national holiday just four days after the civil rights leader's assassination in 1968, and he pushed the bill until it was finally enacted in 1983.

In 2001, he pursued a bill to ban racial profiling by law enforcement. And in each Congress for more than a decade, Conyers has introduced legislation to set up a commission to study whether the federal government owes reparations to African-American descendants of slaves.

Conyers won the gratitude of other Democrats for his vociferous defense of President Bill Clinton during the 1998 impeachment. He accused Republicans of a politically inspired attempt to remove a twice-elected president on trivial grounds related to his affair with a White House intern. By that time, Conyers was the only remaining Judiciary Committee member from 1974, when the panel had voted to impeach President Richard Nixon for obstruction of justice and abuse of official powers. Conyers had been on the Nixon administration's infamous "enemies list."

After serving in the Army in Korea, Conyers went home to Detroit and became involved in politics while in law school there. The creation in 1964 of a second black-majority congressional district in the city provided an opening for Conyers, who won a primary race against accountant Richard H. Austin by 108 votes. He won the Democratic district in a rout that November and has won his 21 subsequent terms the same way.

Conyers has sometimes seemed less interested in legislative brokerage than in being a liberal voice of protest. Twice in the early 1970s, he waged symbolic campaigns for Speaker against Carl Albert of Oklahoma, whom he accused of "stagnation and reaction." Two failed bids for mayor of Detroit did not enhance his reputation, including a 1989 challenge to Mayor Coleman A. Young in which he finished third in the nonpartisan primary.

Conyers has a deep interest in jazz and posters of jazz artists are hung in his office. In 1987, he successfully sponsored a House resolution declaring jazz a "rare and valuable national American treasure."

KEY VOTES

2006

Yes Stop broadband companies from favoring select Internet traffic
No Affirm U.S. commitment to war in Iraq and reject setting a withdrawal date for troops
No Repeal requirement for bilingual ballots at the polls
No Permit U.S. sale of civilian nuclear technology to India
No Build a 700-mile fence on the U.S.-Mexico border to curb illegal crossings
No Permit warrantless wiretaps of suspected terrorists

2005

No Intervene in the life-support case of Terri Schiavo
Yes Lift President Bush's restrictions on stem cell research funding
Yes Prohibit FBI access to library and bookstore records
No Approve free-trade pact with five Central American countries
No Pass energy policy overhaul favored by President Bush emphasizing domestic oil and gas production
No End mandatory preservation of habitat of endangered animal and plant species
Yes Ban torture of prisoners in U.S. custody

CQ VOTE STUDIES

	PARTY UNITY		PRESIDENTIAL SUPPORT	
	Support	Oppose	Support	Oppose
2006	98%	2%	8%	92%
2005	97%	3%	15%	85%
2004	98%	2%	7%	93%
2003	98%	2%	10%	90%
2002	99%	1%	21%	79%

INTEREST GROUPS

	AFL-CIO	ADA	CCUS	ACU
2006	93%	100%	20%	4%
2005	92%	95%	35%	13%
2004	100%	90%	11%	0%
2003	100%	90%	19%	15%
2002	100%	100%	21%	0%

MICHIGAN 14

Parts of Detroit and Dearborn

The first half of the 20th century brought great prosperity to Detroit, as General Motors helped make it the "Motor City." But race riots during the summer of 1967 and the oil crisis of the early 1970s sparked an exodus that is still occurring. In 1960, 1.7 million people lived in Detroit; in 2000, its population was 951,000, and more recent census estimates put its population at less than 900,000. Detroit no longer dominates the music scene, many residents have fled to the suburbs, and many automakers have moved plants to Mexico or non-union U.S. towns.

The 14th covers the residential neighborhoods that sprang up north of Detroit's auto plants. It includes slightly less than half of the city's residents (the rest are in the 13th), and Detroit accounts for two-thirds of the district's total population. Redevelopment efforts in the district have stalled, as has demolition of blighted areas, and the violent crime rate remains high. The city's finances also are in disarray — a potential problem in an area with a large public sector workforce.

The 14th includes two-thirds of Dearborn, which is home to Ford Motor Co. and its Rouge Center factory — once the largest in the world. With 30 percent of the city's residents of Arab ancestry, Dearborn helps give the 14th the highest Arab-American population of any district in the nation. The district also includes two cities surrounded entirely by Detroit: Hamtramck, an ethnically diverse enclave, and Highland Park, an overwhelmingly black area that in 2000 had the highest poverty rate (38 percent) in metropolitan Detroit.

The 14th has one of the country's highest percentages of black residents (61 percent) and is safely Democratic. Detroit's unyielding Democratic bent keeps Republicans from carrying the 14th or elections in Wayne County. With 82 percent of the vote, the 14th gave 2004 Democratic presidential candidate John Kerry his largest vote tally in the state.

MAJOR INDUSTRY

Auto and auto parts manufacturing, health care

CITIES

Detroit (pt.), 439,821; Dearborn (pt), 64,759; Southgate, 30,136; Allen Park, 29,376; Hamtramck, 22,976

NOTABLE

Woodward Avenue, between 6 Mile and 7 Mile roads, was the nation's first paved road (1909); Dearborn hosts the Automotive Hall of Fame.

Rep. John D. Dingell (D)

CAPITOL OFFICE
225-4071
www.house.gov/dingell
2328 Rayburn 20515-2215; fax 226-0371

COMMITTEES
Energy & Commerce - chairman

RESIDENCE
Dearborn

BORN
July 8, 1926, Colorado Springs, Colo.

RELIGION
Roman Catholic

FAMILY
Wife, Debbie Dingell; four children

EDUCATION
Georgetown U., B.S. 1949 (chemistry), J.D. 1952

MILITARY SERVICE
Army, 1944-46

CAREER
County prosecutor

POLITICAL HIGHLIGHTS
No previous office

ELECTION RESULTS

2006 GENERAL		
John D. Dingell (D)	181,946	88.0%
Aimee Smith (GREEN)	9,447	4.6%
Gregory Stempfle (LIBERT)	8,410	4.1%
Robert F. Czak (USTAX)	7,064	3.4%
2006 PRIMARY		
John D. Dingell (D)	38,769	97.9%
F. Vernuccio (D)	842	2.1%
2004 GENERAL		
John D. Dingell (D)	218,409	70.9%
Dawn Anne Reamer (R)	81,828	26.6%
Gregory Stempfle (LIBERT)	3,400	1.1%

PREVIOUS WINNING PERCENTAGES
2002 (72%); 2000 (71%); 1998 (67%); 1996 (62%); 1994 (59%); 1992 (65%); 1990 (67%); 1988 (97%); 1986 (78%); 1984 (64%); 1982 (74%); 1980 (70%); 1978 (77%); 1976 (76%); 1974 (78%); 1972 (68%); 1970 (79%); 1968 (74%); 1966 (63%); 1964 (73%); 1962 (83%); 1960 (79%); 1958 (79%); 1956 (74%); 1955 Special Election (76%)

Elected December 1955; 26th full term

Dingell reigns as dean of the House, the longest-serving sitting member, and he is one of Congress' legends. The Michigan Democrat has had a hand in transformational legislation, ranging from the Civil Rights Act to the Endangered Species Act. With Democrats back in control of Congress, he will be one of the majority's most activist and powerful players as the new chairman of the Energy and Commerce Committee.

Dingell is known for tenacity and toughness, a reputation won in his aggressive oversight of the executive branch during his first stint as Energy and Commerce chairman from 1981 to 1995. He built what scholars consider one of the most expansive congressional power centers of the post-World War II era. His staff hung a picture of Earth in the committee office as a representation of the panel's jurisdiction, which spans energy, health care and telecommunications.

Although Speaker Nancy Pelosi is unlikely to allow him that much power again — she's never forgotten that Dingell backed her opponent in her first leadership race — he commands an important committee and has the personal gravitas to have an impact on some big issues.

Pelosi took a step to curb Dingell's power in early 2007 by creating a temporary committee to handle the Democrats' top-priority issue of global warming. She appointed as chairman Edward J. Markey of Massachusetts, who shares her views on mandatory emission controls for cars. Dingell, a defender of Detroit's auto industry, has long opposed them.

Dingell fumed, but declined to oppose the new panel after Pelosi assured him that the power to write the legislation would remain with him and his committee. For his part, Dingell softened his opposition to raising fuel efficiency standards. "It's my view that we need a new approach," he said.

Health care is the issue closest to Dingell's heart. He helped write the law that created the Medicare program in 1965. In the first weeks of the 110th Congress (2007-08), the House passed a Dingell-backed bill to give the federal government negotiating leverage with the drug companies, something Republicans had blocked when they wrote the 2003 Medicare drug bill.

A believer in national health insurance, Dingell in 2007 joined with New York Democrat Sen. Hillary Rodham Clinton, who's making a 2008 presidential bid, on a bill to dramatically expand the federal health insurance program for children in poverty. His committee also drafted legislation to prohibit employers and insurance companies from collecting genetic information and using it in hiring and firing decisions or in setting insurance rates.

Dingell's return to the chairmanship means tougher oversight of the executive branch and the resurrection of the "Dingell-gram," the lengthy letters full of detailed questions and document requests to federal agencies for which he and his staff were known. On the witness stand, an interrogation by a well-briefed and aggrieved Dingell can be brutal. In March 2007, he dragged all five members of the Federal Communications Commission before his committee to complain that they overstepped their authority in easing regulations for the cable industry. Also in his sights is the Food and Drug Administration, which Dingell says is "badly broken."

Even in the minority, he was able to embarrass the Bush administration into responding to his requests, rather than dismissing them with form letters as they initially tried to do. President Bush once called Dingell the "biggest pain in the ass" on Capitol Hill.

First elected in 1955, Dingell marked his 50th year in Congress in 2005.

He is on track to break the all-time House service record of 53 years set by another "old bull" Democrat, former Rep. Jamie L. Whitten of Mississippi. Dingell would surpass Whitten in February 2009.

Age has slowed Dingell physically. Now past 80, he suffers from chronic back pain and walks with a cane. But he retains a thorough grasp of House rules, arcane parliamentary procedure and legislative detail. Dingell once famously said, "If you let me write procedure and I let you write substance, I'll screw you every time."

Republican Joe L. Barton of Texas, chairman of the Energy panel in the 109th Congress (2005-06), brought Dingell into energy policy overhaul discussions in 2005 rather than risk leaving him to lob grenades from the outside — heeding the credo Dingell lives by: "Keep your friends close, but your enemies closer." To his surprise, Barton discovered Dingell to be helpful — tutoring him, for instance, in the ways of preventing the Senate from controlling the final draft of the bill. For his part, Dingell won a few concessions in the legislation, and ended up voting for it.

Dingell on most issues stands with liberal Democrats, supporting Great Society programs and expansion of the federal government's role. He departs on abortion rights and gun control, both of which he opposes. An avid hunter, he displays on his walls a stuffed menagerie of big game conquests and has long been a friend of the powerful National Rifle Association.

Elected to the House in a December special election at age 29, Dingell inherited both his seat and his political philosophy from his father, a New Deal Democrat who represented the Detroit-area district for 22 years. The younger Dingell grew up in Washington, was a congressional page and graduated from Georgetown Law School. He was an assistant county prosecutor in Dearborn, Mich., when his father unexpectedly died in office.

Soon, Dingell's hero, Speaker Sam Rayburn, gave him a seat on what was then the Committee on Interstate and Foreign Commerce. He became chairman in 1981, and ran the committee with an iron fist for 14 years.

In 26 general elections, he drew less than 60 percent of the vote only once, when Republicans won control of Congress in 1994. But in 2002, after the GOP-controlled state legislature redrew boundaries to reflect Michigan's post-census loss of a House seat, Dingell was pitted in the primary against another incumbent Democrat, eight-year veteran Lynn Rivers. Feminists, environmentalists and gun control advocates backed Rivers, as did then Minority Whip Pelosi. But he fought back with a hefty campaign war chest and a muscular coalition of NRA members, auto union members, business lobbyists and grass-roots activists. He won with 59 percent of the vote.

KEY VOTES

2006

- Yes Stop broadband companies from favoring select Internet traffic
- ? Affirm U.S. commitment to war in Iraq and reject setting a withdrawal date for troops
- No Repeal requirement for bilingual ballots at the polls
- No Permit U.S. sale of civilian nuclear technology to India
- No Build a 700-mile fence on the U.S.-Mexico border to curb illegal crossings
- No Permit warrantless wiretaps of suspected terrorists

2005

- ? Intervene in the life-support case of Terri Schiavo
- Yes Lift President Bush's restrictions on stem cell research funding
- Yes Prohibit FBI access to library and bookstore records
- No Approve free-trade pact with five Central American countries
- Yes Pass energy policy overhaul favored by President Bush emphasizing domestic oil and gas production
- No End mandatory preservation of habitat of endangered animal and plant species
- Yes Ban torture of prisoners in U.S. custody

CQ VOTE STUDIES

	PARTY UNITY		PRESIDENTIAL SUPPORT	
	Support	Oppose	Support	Oppose
2006	90%	10%	23%	77%
2005	92%	8%	26%	74%
2004	94%	6%	27%	73%
2003	91%	9%	28%	72%
2002	96%	4%	26%	74%

INTEREST GROUPS

	AFL-CIO	ADA	CCUS	ACU
2006	100%	95%	33%	13%
2005	100%	95%	52%	12%
2004	100%	95%	33%	4%
2003	100%	85%	31%	28%
2002	100%	90%	42%	4%

MICHIGAN 15

Southeast – Ann Arbor, Taylor, parts of Dearborn and Dearborn Heights

Situated in Michigan's southeast corner west and south of Detroit, the 15th's flat land contains a mix of academics, engineers and auto workers. GOP votes from the 15th's rural farming communities in the southwest are overshadowed by Democratic strongholds in Wayne County's urban areas, as well as Ann Arbor, the district's most populous city.

Ann Arbor, in the 15th's northwest corner in Washtenaw County, is home to the University of Michigan and gave John Kerry 76 percent of its 2004 presidential vote. Pfizer plans to close its Ann Arbor plant by the end of 2008, costing the city more than 2,000 research jobs. Officials hope that some members of the highly educated workforce will find work in the academic or research communities, or at Google, which aims to hire 1,000 people here for AdWords, a company advertising vehicle.

Ypsilanti, a working-class town southeast of Ann Arbor, is home to Eastern Michigan University and also reliably backs Democratic candidates. Engineering and robotics firms have emerged south and east of Ann Arbor, developing automated auto manufacturing that has turned Detroit's assembly line jobs into highly skilled, computerized work.

A little more than 40 percent of the 15th's residents live in the blue-collar, reliably Democratic Wayne County suburbs. The 15th's most populous city here is Taylor, located a few miles east of Detroit Metropolitan Wayne County Airport in Romulus. Dearborn, the western third of which is in the 15th, Dearborn Heights (shared with the 11th) and Inkster form the district's northeast corner. Monroe County, south of Wayne and Washtenaw, borders Lake Erie to the east and the Toledo, Ohio, area to the south. George W. Bush narrowly carried the county in the 2004 presidential election.

MAJOR INDUSTRY

Auto and parts manufacturing, higher education, medical research, steel

CITIES

Ann Arbor, 114,024; Taylor, 65,868; Dearborn Heights (pt.), 44,694; Dearborn (pt.), 33,016; Inkster, 30,115; Romulus, 22,979; Ypsilanti, 22,362

NOTABLE

The National Oceanic and Atmospheric Administration's Great Lakes Environmental Research Laboratory is in Ann Arbor.

MINNESOTA

Gov. Tim Pawlenty (R)

First elected: 2002
Length of term: 4 years
Term expires: 1/11
Salary: $120,303
Phone: (651) 296-3391

Residence: Eagan
Born: Nov. 27, 1960; South St. Paul, Minn.
Religion: Protestant
Family: Wife, Mary Pawlenty; two children
Education: U. of Minnesota, B.A. 1983 (political science), J.D. 1986
Career: Internet consulting firm executive; lawyer
Political highlights: Eagan Planning Commission, 1988-89; Eagan City Council, 1990-92; Minn. House, 1993-2003

Election results:

2006 GENERAL		
Tim Pawlenty (R)	1,028,568	46.7%
Mike Hatch (D)	1,007,460	45.7%
Peter Hutchinson (I)	141,735	6.4%

Lt. Gov. Carol Molnau (R)

First elected: 2002
Length of term: 4 years
Term expires: 1/11
Salary: $78,197
Phone: (651) 296-3391

LEGISLATURE

Legislature: January-May in odd-numbered years; February-May in even-numbered years

Senate: 67 members, 4-year terms
2007 ratios: 44 D, 23 R; 40 men, 27 women
Salary: $31,141
Phone: (651) 296-0504

House: 134 members, 2-year terms
2007 ratios: 85 D, 49 R; 91 men, 43 women
Salary: $31,141
Phone: (651) 296-2146

TERM LIMITS

Governor: No
Senate: No
House: No

URBAN STATISTICS

CITY	POPULATION
Minneapolis	382,618
St. Paul	287,151
Duluth	86,918
Rochester	85,806
Bloomington	85,172

REGISTERED VOTERS

Voters do not register by party.

POPULATION

2006 population (est.)	5,167,101
2000 population	4,919,479
1990 population	4,375,099
Percent change (1990-2000)	+12.4%
Rank among states (2006)	21
Median age	35.4
Born in state	70.2%
Foreign born	5.3%
Violent crime rate	281/100,000
Poverty level	7.9%
Federal workers	32,833
Military	19,625

ELECTIONS

STATE ELECTION OFFICIAL
(651) 215-1440
DEMOCRATIC PARTY
(651) 293-1200
REPUBLICAN PARTY
(651) 222-0022

MISCELLANEOUS

Web: www.state.mn.us
Capital: St. Paul

U.S. CONGRESS

Senate: 1 Democrat, 1 Republican
House: 5 Democrats, 3 Republicans

2000 Census Statistics by District

DIST.	2004 VOTE FOR PRESIDENT BUSH	KERRY	WHITE	BLACK	ASIAN	HISP	MEDIAN INCOME	WHITE COLLAR	BLUE COLLAR	SERVICE INDUSTRY	OVER 64	UNDER 18	COLLEGE EDUCATION	RURAL	SQ. MILES
1	51%	47%	93%	1%	2%	3%	$40,941	57%	28%	15%	15%	25%	22%	44%	13,322
2	54	45	92	2	2	3	$61,344	65	23	12	8	30	31	20	3,035
3	51	48	89	4	4	2	$63,816	73	17	10	10	27	40	4	468
4	37	62	78	6	8	5	$46,811	67	19	14	12	26	33	0	202
5	28	71	71	13	5	6	$41,569	67	18	15	12	22	35	0	124
6	57	42	95	1	1	1	$56,862	60	27	12	8	29	25	36	3,081
7	55	43	93	0	1	3	$36,453	53	31	16	17	26	16	66	31,796
8	46	53	95	1	0	1	$37,911	53	30	17	16	25	18	63	27,583
STATE	48	51	88	3	3	3	$47,111	62	24	14	12	26	27	29	79,610
U.S.	50.7	48.3	69	12	4	13	$41,994	60	25	15	12	26	24	21	3,537,438

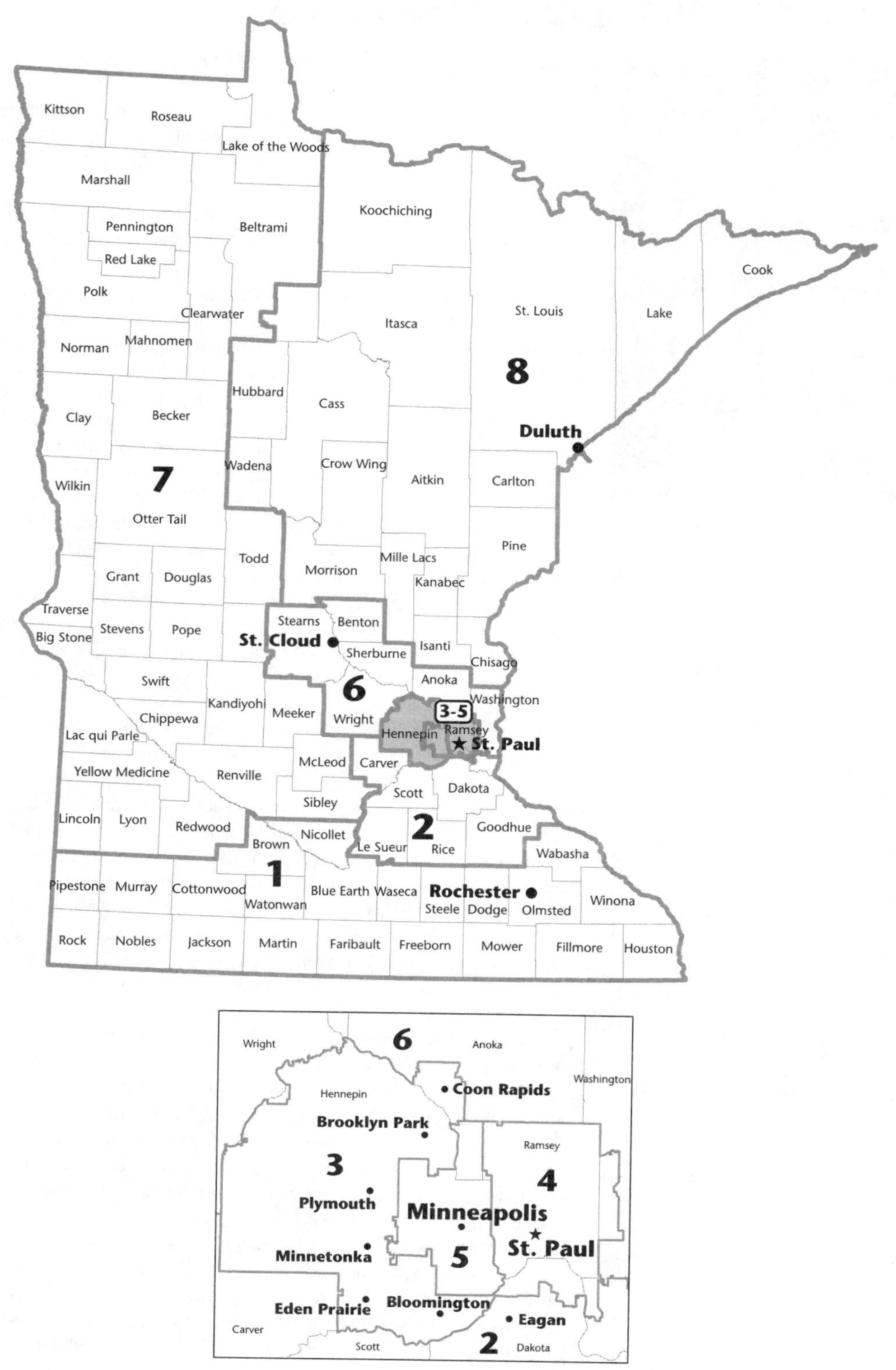
Kittson
Roseau
Lake of the Woods
Marshall
Pennington
Beltrami
Red Lake
Polk
Clearwater
Norman
Mahnomen
Koochiching
Itasca
St. Louis
Lake
Cook
8
Duluth
Hubbard
Cass
Clay
Becker
Wadena
Crow Wing
Aitkin
Carlton
Wilkin
7
Otter Tail
Pine
Todd
Morrison
Mille Lacs
Kanabec
Grant
Douglas
Traverse
Stevens
Pope
Stearns
Benton
St. Cloud
Big Stone
Sherburne
Isanti
Chisago
Swift
Anoka
6
Washington
Kandiyohi
Meeker
Wright
3-5
Chippewa
Hennepin
Ramsey
St. Paul
Lac qui Parle
McLeod
Carver
Yellow Medicine
Renville
Dakota
Scott
Sibley
Lincoln
Lyon
Redwood
2
Goodhue
Nicollet
Brown
Le Sueur
Rice
Wabasha
1
Pipestone
Murray
Cottonwood
Watonwan
Blue Earth
Waseca
Rochester
Steele
Dodge
Olmsted
Winona
Rock
Nobles
Jackson
Martin
Faribault
Freeborn
Mower
Fillmore
Houston
Wright
6
Anoka
Coon Rapids
Washington
Hennepin
Brooklyn Park
Ramsey
3
4
Plymouth
Minneapolis
St. Paul
Minnetonka
5
Eden Prairie
Bloomington
Eagan
Carver
Scott
2
Dakota

Sen. Norm Coleman (R)

CAPITOL OFFICE
224-5641
coleman.senate.gov
320 Hart 20510-2303; fax 224-1152

COMMITTEES
Agriculture, Nutrition & Forestry
Foreign Relations
Homeland Security & Governmental Affairs
Small Business & Entrepreneurship
Special Aging

RESIDENCE
St. Paul

BORN
Aug. 17, 1949, Brooklyn, N.Y.

RELIGION
Jewish

FAMILY
Wife, Laurie Coleman; four children (two deceased)

EDUCATION
Hofstra U., B.A. 1971 (political science); Brooklyn Law School, attended 1972-74; U. of Iowa, J.D. 1976

CAREER
Lawyer; state prosecutor and solicitor general; city welfare aide

POLITICAL HIGHLIGHTS
Sought Democratic nomination for mayor of St. Paul, 1989; mayor of St. Paul, 1994-2002 (served as a Democrat 1994-96); Republican nominee for governor, 1998

ELECTION RESULTS

2002 GENERAL		
Norm Coleman (R)	1,116,697	49.5%
Walter F. Mondale (D)	1,067,246	47.3%
Jim Moore (INDC)	45,139	2.0%
2002 PRIMARY		
Norm Coleman (R)	195,630	94.4%
Jack Shepard (R)	11,678	5.6%

Elected 2002; 1st term

Coleman is an agile politician. His career has been marked by his ability to know when to turn right and when left. Defined by his pragmatism, he also has a keen capacity for reading the prevailing political winds. Neither side is ever sure how he will vote.

Some of this flexibility is necessary in the politically competitive world of Minnesota politics, and some of it is just Coleman. He says he wants to be a moderating voice within the Republican Party.

Once a supporter of President Bush's invasion of Iraq, he began to distance himself from both the war and the president in 2007. He stood on the Senate floor in January and said, "When the current path isn't working, you have to be flexible. You have to shift. You have to make a change." Coleman said Bush's early 2007 plan to send thousands more troops to Iraq was wrong.

As a member of the Foreign Relations Committee, Coleman has visited Iraq twice. But like other Republican moderates, Coleman remains steadfastly opposed to writing a timetable for troop withdrawal into law. "Is there deep concern about the war in Minnesota? Absolutely. There is a lot of frustration," said Coleman, after voting to strip the timetable language from a March 2007 supplemental spending bill. "But to tell the enemy, 'This is when we are going to be leaving' — that's a bad idea."

Coleman also distanced himself from the president in 2006 when he joined with a chorus of Democrats to demand a staff shake-up at the White House. His suggestion was rebuffed, but it was only the beginning of his departures from Bush. He was one of just five GOP lawmakers to support a stand-alone measure to raise the minimum wage — before small business tax breaks were added to attract more Republican support.

Coleman also has gone his own way on oil drilling. He has opposed opening Alaska's Arctic National Wildlife Refuge to oil drilling several times — voting twice to ban drilling in the area and opposing a 2006 budget resolution that would have allowed it. "This is yet another attempt by drilling proponents to slip ANWR drilling through the Senate after they failed to do so in last year's budget process," Coleman said in a statement. Yet in 2006, he supported a bill that expanded drilling in the Gulf of Mexico. "If we open this area up, it will go a long way to, hopefully at least, stabilizing prices for folks on fixed income and farmers who worry about the cost of natural gas and producing fertilizer," Coleman told the Associated Press. "This is a big issue for Minnesota."

With his New York accent, styled hair and glinting smile, Coleman seems an unlikely breadbasket politician but he sits on the Agriculture Committee and has a large portfolio of farm issues. During a 2007 rewrite of the massive farm bill, Coleman will advocate expanding farm loans and extending a milk subsidy program. He has spoken in support of alternative energy sources, particularly ethanol and biodiesel made from Minnesota corn and soybeans.

In the 109th Congress (2005-06), Coleman made a name for himself as the chairman of the Homeland Security and Governmental Affairs panel's Permanent Subcommittee on Investigations, a powerful forum for inquiries into government, business and political malfeasance. He now serves as the panel's ranking member. In 2006, Coleman spearheaded an investigation that uncovered massive gaps in the nation's port security. The probe made headlines when Government Accountability Office investigators were able to smuggle radioactive material into the country. The fallout from the investigation helped Coleman gain Senate approval for a provision in port security legislation that authorized pilot technology for screening all incoming cargo containers for radiation and density.

Coleman is not your typical Midwestern Republican. He went to the hippie music festival Woodstock and was a rock band roadie with the band Ten Years After.

A Brooklyn native, he grew up part of a large, extended family. His high school classmate was New York Democratic Sen. Charles E. Schumer. While student body president at Hofstra University in Hempstead, N.Y., on Long Island, he led anti-war protests and organized a student strike in 1970 after protesters at Kent State University were shot by members of the Ohio National Guard. He brokered a compromise with the university's administration that averted the complete shutdown of the school.

After graduation, a mentor who had become a vice president at the University of Iowa's law school offered Coleman the chance to attend tuition-free by working as a graduate assistant. He earned his law degree. Then he was recruited by the Minnesota attorney general and became a prosecutor.

From the beginning of his political career in 1989, Coleman did not fit comfortably with Democratic Party leaders, and he failed to get the party's endorsement to run for mayor of St. Paul that year. Four years later, he ran against the party's endorsed candidate and won. Coleman has always been more conservative than Minnesota's Democratic-Farmer-Labor Party on fiscal and social issues. He opposes abortion and supports "pro-family" issues, he says, as a result of losing two of his four children in infancy to the incurable genetic disorder known as Zellweger syndrome. The deaths, he has said, gave him resolve to value every life.

In 2007, he offered an alternative stem cell research bill, one that would not harm embryos. The Senate passed his measure, which he said would result in new federal support for stem cell research without crossing moral boundaries, along with a more controversial proposal that drew a veto threat.

As mayor of St. Paul during the economic boom of the 1990s, Coleman developed increasingly pro-business sentiments while working to revitalize the city. Democrats, he said, defended the "status quo" favoring labor, while he tried to keep a lid on wages and benefits.

In December 1996, Coleman switched parties, officially became a Republican, and was re-elected the following year. Democrats accused him of political opportunism, as it was widely anticipated that he was preparing to run for governor in 1998. As expected, he entered the governor's race as the GOP nominee, only to be defeated by Reform Party candidate Jesse Ventura. Yet the statewide name recognition Coleman developed in that race convinced GOP strategists that he should be their pick in 2002 to take on the liberal Democratic Sen. Paul Wellstone.

Coleman ran on his eight years as mayor, during which the city enjoyed job growth, downtown revitalization, and the return of major league hockey to Minnesota for the first time since the North Stars left for Dallas in 1993 — all accomplished without an increase in property taxes. Coleman said his bipartisan approach would make him more effective than Wellstone, who was known more for standing by his principles than for getting bills passed.

The contest seemed deadlocked when Wellstone, his wife, daughter, three aides and two pilots died in the crash of their campaign plane in northern Minnesota. Democrats replaced Wellstone on the ballot with Walter F. Mondale. A Minnesota political icon, Mondale was vice president under President Jimmy Carter and the 1984 Democratic presidential nominee.

After the tragedy, the conventional wisdom was that the seat would stay Democratic, considering the outpouring of public sympathy for the loss of Wellstone and the fame of Mondale. But Coleman eked out a win by just 2 percentage points and helped the GOP clinch control of the Senate.

KEY VOTES

2006

Yes Confirm Samuel A. Alito Jr. to the Supreme Court

Yes Allow consideration of a bill to establish a $140 billion trust fund to compensate victims of asbestos exposure

Yes Extend tax cuts for two years at a cost of $70 billion over five years

Yes Overhaul immigration policy with border security, enforcement and guest worker program

Yes Allow consideration of a bill to permanently repeal the estate tax

No Urge President Bush to begin troop withdrawals from Iraq in 2006

No Lift President Bush's restrictions on stem cell research funding

Yes Authorize military tribunals for suspected terrorists

2005

Yes Curb class action lawsuits by shifting them from state to federal courts

Yes Allow confirmation vote on Priscilla R. Owen to the U.S. Court of Appeals for the 5th Circuit

\- Oppose mandatory emissions limits and block recognition of global warming as a threat

Yes Approve free-trade pact with five Central American countries

Yes Pass energy policy overhaul favored by President Bush emphasizing domestic oil and gas production

Yes Shield gunmakers from lawsuits when their products are used in crimes

Yes Ban torture of prisoners in U.S. custody

Yes Renew 16 provisions of the Patriot Act

Yes Allow final vote on opening the Arctic National Wildlife Refuge to oil and gas exploration

CQ VOTE STUDIES

	PARTY UNITY		PRESIDENTIAL SUPPORT	
	Support	Oppose	Support	Oppose
2006	77%	23%	88%	12%
2005	77%	23%	84%	16%
2004	91%	9%	92%	8%
2003	92%	8%	98%	2%

INTEREST GROUPS

	AFL-CIO	ADA	CCUS	ACU
2006	33%	25%	100%	68%
2005	36%	30%	88%	64%
2004	25%	30%	100%	84%
2003	0%	15%	91%	85%

Sen. Amy Klobuchar (D)

CAPITOL OFFICE
224-3244
senator@klobuchar.senate.gov
klobuchar.senate.gov
302 Hart 20510-2305; fax 228-2186

COMMITTEES
Agriculture, Nutrition & Forestry
Commerce, Science & Transportation
Environment & Public Works
Joint Economic

RESIDENCE
Minneapolis

BORN
May 25, 1960, Plymouth, Minn.

RELIGION
Congregationalist

FAMILY
Husband, John Bessler; one child

EDUCATION
Yale U., B.A. 1982 (political science); U. of Chicago, J.D. 1985

CAREER
Lawyer; lobbyist

POLITICAL HIGHLIGHTS
Hennepin County attorney, 1999-2007

ELECTION RESULTS

2006 GENERAL		
Amy Klobuchar (D)	1,278,849	58.1%
Mark Kennedy (R)	835,653	37.9%
Robert Fitzgerald (INDC)	71,194	3.2%
2006 PRIMARY		
Amy Klobuchar (D)	294,671	92.5%
Darryl Stanton (D)	23,872	7.5%

Elected 2006; 1st term

Though she calls herself a progressive, Klobuchar is more moderate than Mark Dayton and Paul Wellstone, the liberal Democrats who represented Minnesota before her. A fiscal conservative with a populist streak, she focuses on economic matters of concern to middle-class families. She also has an interest in energy and environmental issues, but stresses their benefits for rural farmers and fishing enthusiasts.

A chief prosecutor for Hennepin County for eight years, Klobuchar (KLO-buh-shar) also is concerned with restoring public trust in government. At her inauguration, she boasted of bringing "a Minnesota moral compass" to guide her in decision-making and has spoken in favor of prohibiting members from accepting private meals, gifts and trips.

Klobuchar works on fiscal policy as a member of the Joint Economic Committee. Shrinking the federal deficit and providing middle-class tax relief were cornerstones of her successful 2006 campaign. She advocates a return to the pay-as-you-go model of budgeting, in which proposed tax cuts or spending increases must be offset so as not to enlarge the deficit. She says reductions in spending and cutbacks on tax loopholes could shrink the deficit while paying for tax credits for first-time home buyers.

Klobuchar also campaigned in favor of an increase in the minimum wage, and in a January 2007 floor speech she cited her own experience in working for low pay. "I've had a number of minimum wage-type jobs, as a carhop, as a highway worker and as a pie cutter," she said. "If there are other pie cutters in the U.S. Senate, I'd like to meet them."

As befits someone from a large farm state, Klobuchar serves on the Agriculture Committee. She also has a seat on Environment and Public Works. She wasted little time in expressing her desire to become a player on both panels in finding solutions to global warming. Even in notoriously cold Minnesota, she said, the subject has become a recurring topic in meetings with constituents. In 2006, she noted, "December in Minnesota felt more like October. Our ice fishing seasons are shorter, and our skiers and snowmobilers haven't seen much snow."

She called on the Senate to deal with the issue of global warming in the 2007 farm bill by providing incentives for farmers to grow perennial grasses and other biomass crops for cellulosic ethanol production. She also wants to increase funding for research aimed at helping farmers come up with ways to store carbon in the soil.

She also said she supports some version of a cap-and-trade system for greenhouse gas emissions, renewable fuel content standards for cars and trucks, and strong renewable standards for electricity generation that makes greater use of wind, solar and other alternative sources.

Although she opposed the invasion of Iraq, Klobuchar is against immediate withdrawal. She favors a more gradual redeployment that involves countries in the region. She spoke out against President Bush's plan in February 2007 to deploy thousands of additional troops, saying it contradicted the message that voters had sent a few months earlier when she and other Democrats were elected to Congress.

Klobuchar also has a seat on Commerce, Science and Transportation. She has an interest in providing greater broadband Internet access for rural residents, and she criticized Bush's proposed budget in which he sought to cut grants for that purpose. "You see jobs going to other countries where they have broadband, and yet we've got small towns across this country that don't have that capability," she said.

Since coming to Washington, Klobuchar said, she has been surprised that, for all of the surface partisan infighting, the Senate remains a fairly cordial and civil place. Her assigned "mentor" as a freshman is Olympia J. Snowe, a Republican moderate from Maine, whom Klobuchar admires for her ability to seek bipartisan consensus.

Klobuchar has worked on Minnesota issues with her Republican colleague from the state, Norm Coleman. Given Coleman's desire to get things done as he faces a difficult 2008 re-election fight, that relationship appears to have even more potential.

Klobuchar grew up in the Minneapolis suburb of Plymouth, the daughter of longtime Minneapolis Star Tribune newspaper columnist Jim Klobuchar. She attended Yale, where her senior thesis detailed the 10-year political debate over the building of the Hubert H. Humphrey Metrodome in Minneapolis. It was published as a book, "Uncovering the Dome," that has been used as a text in college courses.

After graduating from the University of Chicago's law school, Klobuchar returned to Minnesota to practice law and worked closely with former Vice President Walter Mondale. She also helped her father recover from alcoholism, a battle he subsequently chronicled in a book of his own.

In 1995, Klobuchar's daughter was born with a health problem. While the baby was kept at the hospital, Klobuchar was discharged after 24 hours because her health plan would not pay for a longer stay. As a private citizen, she lobbied state lawmakers successfully for a law to guarantee new mothers 48 hours at the hospital.

Klobuchar entered the Hennepin County attorney's race in 1998 and defeated Republican Rep. Jim Ramstad's sister, Sheryl. Klobuchar focused on fighting violent crime, particularly crimes involving convicted felons who possessed guns. She also advocated for a felony DWI law enabling prosecutors to target chronic drunken drivers. She was re-elected in 2002 without opposition.

When Dayton announced his retirement from the Senate in early 2005, Klobuchar was recognized as an early favorite to secure the Democratic-Farmer-Labor Party nomination. She racked up the support of the majority of DFL state legislators in Minnesota during the primaries, and her three leading opponents the dropped out of the race and gave her their endorsement.

In the general election, Klobuchar's main opponent was Republican Rep. Mark Kennedy, whom Republicans considered an ideal candidate. Kennedy represented the 6th District, which cuts a wide swath from the Twin Cities suburbs to St. Cloud. He had steered money to his home state as a member of the Transportation and Infrastructure Committee.

However, the tough national political environment facing the GOP proved to be too much for Kennedy. Despite his attempts to downgrade her tough-on-crime image, Klobuchar consistently led throughout the campaign. She won with 58 percent of the vote to Kennedy's 38 percent and Independence Party candidate Robert Fitzgerald's 3 percent. She managed to collect all but eight of Minnesota's 87 counties. Hers was the largest U.S. Senate election margin in Minnesota since 1978, and it made Klobuchar the state's first elected female senator.

For Klobuchar, one significant aspect of her victory was that she could get elected on the same platform as her male Democratic colleagues. Though she did address such issues as child care and after-school care, she said her campaign "was sort of more bread-and-butter. It wasn't that much different than the issues that, say, [Pennsylvania Sen.] Bob Casey ran on."

Rep. Tim Walz (D)

CAPITOL OFFICE
225-2472
walz.house.gov
1529 Longworth 20515-2301; fax 225-3246

COMMITTEES
Agriculture
Transportation & Infrastructure
Veterans' Affairs

RESIDENCE
Mankato

BORN
April 6, 1964, West Point, Neb.

RELIGION
Lutheran

FAMILY
Wife, Gwen Walz; two children

EDUCATION
Chadron State College, B.S. 1989 (social science education); Minnesota State U., Mankato, M.S. 2001 (educational leadership); Saint Mary's U. of Minnesota, attending

MILITARY SERVICE
Neb. National Guard, 1981-96; Minn. National Guard, 1996-2005

CAREER
Teacher; mortgage processor

POLITICAL HIGHLIGHTS
No previous office

ELECTION RESULTS

2006 GENERAL		
Tim Walz (D)	141,556	52.7%
Gil Gutknecht (R)	126,486	47.1%
2006 PRIMARY		
Tim Walz (D)		unopposed

Elected 2006; 1st term

A high school teacher and military veteran, Walz's only venture into politics prior to his long-shot 2006 campaign consisted of some community organizing for Sen. John Kerry's 2004 presidential campaign. But that lack of political experience turned out to be an asset, not a liability, in toppling six-term Republican Rep. Gil Gutknecht. Voters were looking for change.

Ironically, it was President Bush who drove Walz to run. Bush went to Mankato, Walz's hometown, for a 2004 campaign rally — the first visit by a president since Harry S Truman. Walz took a couple of students to see the president, but they were turned away after being grilled about their political leanings. "It's really disappointing," Walz told the Minneapolis Star Tribune. "What happened to being able to listen to the other side?"

Walz (WALLS) retired from the military in 2005 after more than two decades in the Army National Guard, including a deployment to Italy to oversee supply shipments to troops in Afghanistan. He is a critic of Bush's conduct of the war, saying it was shaped by "blind ideology" rather than facts. "As a 24-year veteran of the Army National Guard, I know that our soldiers are trained to fulfill the mission they are given. But having a mission that is achievable is the key to any military success," he told the House in 2007.

Walz grew up in Nebraska and joined the Guard there at age 17 to help pay for college; his father died during his second year of study, and his mother and 8-year-old brother were living on Social Security survivor benefits. That, he says, focused his reasons for becoming a Democrat. "I understood Social Security was an investment in the common good," he says. "That's when I became a firm believer that we're all in this together."

After college, Walz went to China in 1989 to teach U.S. history. "For many of the people I met there, it was their first contact with the Western world," he says. He still speaks some Chinese.

His organizing work for Kerry in 2004 taught him some campaign basics, which he applied to his own race against Gutknecht. He won with 53 percent of the vote. With GOP challengers lining up to take him on in 2008, national Democrats have targeted him for extra financial and logistical help.

MINNESOTA 1

South – Rochester, Mankato

One of the state's three rural districts, the 1st runs across the state's entire southern tier from South Dakota to the Mississippi River, cut horizontally by Interstate 90 and vertically by Interstate 35. While rural areas continue to lose population, cities such as Mankato and Rochester, home to an IBM facility and the Mayo Clinic, thrive. Agriculture and food processing still drive the local economy.

Corn, soybeans, sugar beets, hogs and dairy are staples here. Food processing, from fresh turkey to canned soups, is prevalent throughout the district's land west of Rochester. Winona and Mankato host state universities, and west of Mankato, no town has more than 15,000 residents.

Although the 1st is still more than 90 percent white, Hispanic, Asian and black immigrants have come to the district to work in processing plants and in agriculture. Worthington in particular has a significant immigrant population.

Rochester, the district's largest city, has a historically moderate GOP base. In 2006, however, Rochester aligned itself with the 1st's many smaller towns and farmers that support the Democratic-Farmer-Labor Party. National issues, along with debate about a more than $2 billion rail expansion through Rochester and southern Minnesota, influenced the 2006 local and federal elections, handing Democrats sweeping victories. Although George W. Bush took 51 percent of the 1st's 2004 presidential vote, the area has supported independents in the past, and voters here chose to send a Democrat to the U.S. House in 2006 rather than re-elect their GOP representative.

MAJOR INDUSTRY
Agriculture, food processing, health care

CITIES
Rochester, 85,806; Mankato, 32,427; Winona, 27,069; Austin, 23,314; Owatonna, 22,434

NOTABLE
Austin, the birthplace of SPAM, is home to the SPAM Museum and an annual festival.

Rep. John Kline (R)

CAPITOL OFFICE
225-2271
www.house.gov/kline
1429 Longworth 20515-2302; fax 225-2595

COMMITTEES
Armed Services
Education & Labor
Standards of Official Conduct

RESIDENCE
Lakeville

BORN
Sept. 6, 1947, Allentown, Pa.

RELIGION
Methodist

FAMILY
Wife, Vicky Kline; two children

EDUCATION
Rice U., B.A. 1969 (biology);
Shippensburg U., M.S. 1988 (public administration)

MILITARY SERVICE
Marine Corps, 1969-94

CAREER
Think tank executive; farmer; management consultant; Marine officer

POLITICAL HIGHLIGHTS
Republican nominee for U.S. House, 1998, 2000

ELECTION RESULTS

2006 GENERAL		
John Kline (R)	163,269	56.2%
Coleen Rowley (D)	116,343	40.0%
Douglas Williams (INDC)	10,802	3.7%
2006 PRIMARY		
John Kline (R)	unopposed	
2004 GENERAL		
John Kline (R)	206,313	56.4%
Teresa Daly (D)	147,527	40.3%
Douglas Williams (INDC)	11,822	3.2%

PREVIOUS WINNING PERCENTAGES
2002 (53%)

Elected 2002; 3rd term

Now in his third term, Kline is branching out. The retired Marine colonel is reaching beyond his comfort zone of military issues to develop expertise on other subjects, including pension overhaul that is vital to one of his district's major corporate constituents, Northwest Airlines.

As a member of the Education and the Workforce Committee, Kline served on the 2006 conference committee that negotiated a complex overhaul of the laws governing private pension plans — a plum for a relatively new lawmaker. "More than 9,000 of Northwest Airlines' pension plan participants live in my district," Kline said. "That has had us pretty heavily engaged." The version of the bill that became law included what Kline said was much-needed relief for the airlines.

His effort to become an informed advocate on a range of subjects is a change from his early days in Congress, when he was called on mainly for his expertise in military matters. "I really have broadened my field," he says.

But with the United States at war, Kline remains a go-to guy on defense and is one of the administration's staunchest defenders of the war effort. When critics compare it to the U.S. experience in Vietnam, Kline says the history lesson should be about withdrawing troops before the war is won. A similar pullout from Iraq would be a "horrible breach of faith," said the Vietnam veteran. "I'm not going to let that happen."

A member of the Armed Services Committee, Kline has visited both Iraq and Afghanistan. He is one the few members of Congress with a child who has served in the conflict. His son, John Daniel, is an Army Blackhawk helicopter pilot who had a year-long tour in Iraq in 2006. "I'm worried about him," Kline said. "But I'm worried about them all."

Kline has a straight-arrow military bearing befitting his 25 years in the service along with an easygoing charm that serves him in the political arena. As a Marine officer, he did a stint carrying the "football" — a briefcase containing the codes needed to launch a nuclear attack — for Presidents Jimmy Carter and Ronald Reagan. The military contributed to Kline's salient political trait — persistence. He lost two House bids to the same Democrat before finally winning a seat in 2002 in a newly drawn, GOP-leaning district in the Twin Cities suburbs, where young families moving to outer burgs tend to be socially liberal and fiscally conservative.

He has made headway passing legislation even though he is a relatively junior lawmaker. Just a few months into office, he was able to extend an exemption for active duty personnel from payments on college loans. He also won admirers in the Peace Corps with his successful proposal to bar U.S. troops from using service in the corps to fulfill part of their military obligation. Corps officials feared the safety and effectiveness of their volunteers would be compromised if they came to be seen as soldiers in disguise.

Kline is a strong fiscal and social conservative who wants to see the Bush tax cuts made permanent. He opposes abortion except in cases of rape or incest. His record earned him a "True Blue Award" from the conservative Family Research Council. Liberal interest groups tend to give him their lowest marks. He has a 3 percent lifetime rating from the League of Conservation Voters for his votes on the environment, and the Children's Defense Fund-Minnesota attacked him for supporting cuts in social spending.

Kline grew up in Texas, where his father owned a small-town newspaper. His mother managed the Corpus Christi Symphony Orchestra for 40 years. He joined the ROTC at Rice University in Houston while earning a biology degree and later received a master's in public administration from Shippensburg University in Pennsylvania.

During his military career, Kline was a helicopter pilot in Vietnam, commanded aviation forces in Somalia, and flew the presidential helicopter Marine One. He also worked at Marine headquarters as a program development officer, responsible for developing a long-range spending plan. In 1994, he retired with the rank of colonel, settled in Lakeville, Minn., with his wife, and helped his father-in-law manage the family farm in Houston County, at the southeastern tip of the state.

In 1998, contemplating a run for Congress, he sought advice from friend James A. Baker III, Reagan's former chief of staff, whom he met during his White House duty. Baker administered a "dose of reality," telling Kline, "Well, you don't have your party's nomination, you are running against an incumbent, and you don't have any money. Other than that, you're in good shape."

Kline spent months visiting delegates whose support he would need at the nominating convention. "I would walk up and ring their doorbells," he says. "Sometimes I would be invited in. Sometimes we'd be standing in the doorway talking. Sometimes I'd leave them a note."

Kline got the GOP nomination in 1998 at an old-fashioned, Minnesota-style convention at a local junior high school. He lost in the general election to Democratic incumbent Rep. Bill Luther. In 2000, he challenged Luther again, this time getting help from national Republican groups. He lost again, but by only 5,000 votes.

Redistricting paired Luther with GOP Rep. Mark Kennedy in the new 6th District. Luther moved to the redrawn 2nd District, which held only about 39 percent of his former constituency and was far more Republican than before. Kline challenged him again. Luther tried to portray Kline as an "extremist," and the state Democratic Party ran a radio ad claiming he would "end Social Security as we know it." But Kline's message of lower taxes, smaller government and a strong military prevailed with voters.

In 2004, Kline easily won re-election. In 2006, Democrats found a tough challenger for Kline — FBI whistleblower Coleen Rowley, who won admirers after it became public that she had unsuccessfully appealed to her superiors to crack down on Zacarias Moussaoui, later convicted as a 9/11 conspirator. Rowley's campaign stumbled when she had to apologize to Kline for a photo on her Web site depicting him as Colonel Klink, a Nazi prison camp commander from the 1960s television show, "Hogan's Heroes." Kline raised much more money than Rowley, and prevailed by 16 percentage points.

KEY VOTES

2006

- No Stop broadband companies from favoring select Internet traffic
- Yes Affirm U.S. commitment to war in Iraq and reject setting a withdrawal date for troops
- Yes Repeal requirement for bilingual ballots at the polls
- Yes Permit U.S. sale of civilian nuclear technology to India
- Yes Build a 700-mile fence on the U.S.-Mexico border to curb illegal crossings
- Yes Permit warrantless wiretaps of suspected terrorists

2005

- Yes Intervene in the life-support case of Terri Schiavo
- No Lift President Bush's restrictions on stem cell research funding
- No Prohibit FBI access to library and bookstore records
- Yes Approve free-trade pact with five Central American countries
- Yes Pass energy policy overhaul favored by President Bush emphasizing domestic oil and gas production
- Yes End mandatory preservation of habitat of endangered animal and plant species
- Yes Ban torture of prisoners in U.S. custody

CQ VOTE STUDIES

	PARTY UNITY		PRESIDENTIAL SUPPORT	
	Support	Oppose	Support	Oppose
2006	95%	5%	95%	5%
2005	97%	3%	89%	11%
2004	99%	1%	94%	6%
2003	98%	2%	98%	2%

INTEREST GROUPS

	AFL-CIO	ADA	CCUS	ACU
2006	14%	0%	100%	88%
2005	13%	0%	93%	100%
2004	7%	5%	100%	96%
2003	0%	5%	100%	84%

MINNESOTA 2

Southern Twin Cities suburbs

A blend of rural farmland in the south and a growing suburban north, the 2nd is tucked just south of the Minneapolis-St. Paul metropolitan area. The district includes all or part of seven rapidly growing counties, and reflects the population influx to the Twin Cities region.

Residents can hop on Interstate 35 and shoot into the Twin Cities from Scott, the fastest-growing county in the state, or Dakota counties. New, expensive housing developments underscore the area's higher incomes, and population increases in Carver, Scott and particularly Dakota (shared with the 4th) have made these counties younger and wealthier.

Affordable new housing in the southern counties of Le Sueur, Rice and Goodhue is attracting new residents. This area still has fertile farmland, producing corn and soybeans, among other crops, but development is encroaching on some of the smaller family farms. Agricultural success here tends to rely on larger, incorporated farms.

Despite some fluctuations in the airline industry, Northwest Airlines, which makes its headquarters in Eagan, remains an economic linchpin for the region. Casinos are big business for the Shakopee Mdewakanton Sioux tribe in Prior Lake, and other large employers are Blue Cross/Blue Shield and Lockheed Martin — both in the 2nd's part of northwestern Dakota County — and 3M, headquartered in St. Paul (in the 4th District).

The district leans Republican, propelled by Scott and Carver counties. It has a growing number of young families who tend to vote along socially progressive lines but remain fiscally conservative. Dakota County has some working-class areas that are faithful Democratic-Farmer-Labor Party supporters. The Rice County towns of Northfield — home to St. Olaf and Carleton colleges — and Faribault also provide Democratic votes, while Goodhue County remains a conservative farming area.

MAJOR INDUSTRY

Manufacturing, casinos, aviation, agriculture

CITIES

Eagan, 63,557; Burnsville, 60,220; Apple Valley, 45,527; Lakeville, 43,128

NOTABLE

The late Sen. Paul Wellstone was a political science professor at Carleton College before beginning his political career; The Green Giant food manufacturing company was founded in Le Sueur.

Rep. Jim Ramstad (R)

CAPITOL OFFICE
225-2871
mn03@mail.house.gov
www.house.gov/ramstad
103 Cannon 20515-2303; fax 225-6351

COMMITTEES
Ways & Means

RESIDENCE
Minnetonka

BORN
May 6, 1946, Jamestown, N.D.

RELIGION
Protestant

FAMILY
Wife, Kathryn Ramstad; one child

EDUCATION
U. of Minnesota, B.A. 1968;
George Washington U., J.D. 1973

MILITARY SERVICE
Army Reserve, 1968-74

CAREER
Lawyer; professor; congressional and state legislative aide

POLITICAL HIGHLIGHTS
Minn. Senate, 1981-91

ELECTION RESULTS

2006 GENERAL		
Jim Ramstad (R)	184,333	64.9%
Wendy Wilde (D)	99,588	35.0%
2006 PRIMARY		
Jim Ramstad (R)		unopposed
2004 GENERAL		
Jim Ramstad (R)	231,871	64.6%
Deborah Watts (D)	126,665	35.3%

PREVIOUS WINNING PERCENTAGES
2002 (72%); 2000 (68%); 1998 (72%); 1996 (70%); 1994 (73%); 1992 (64%); 1990 (67%)

Elected 1990; 9th term

A solid centrist, Ramstad reflects his upscale, suburban district, home to the nation's largest shopping mall and to voters who lean Republican while also placing a high value on public education, supporting environmental causes and holding moderate views on social issues.

He is considerably less loyal to President Bush and GOP congressional leaders than the typical Republican. He voted against Bush's positions 31 percent of the time in the 109th Congress (2005-06), and against the party's positions on one out of four votes that divided along partisan lines.

Early in the 110th Congress (2007-08), he voted for all six bills on the Democrats' "first 100 hours" agenda, one of only three Republicans to do so (the others were Michael N. Castle of Delaware and Todd R. Platts of Pennsylvania). And he was one of 17 Republicans who backed a resolution in opposition to Bush's plan to send more troops to Iraq.

While he has endured a stream of appeals to vote more often with his party, he says, "Over the years, the pressure has really lessened because I think most of my colleagues understand." His district outside Minneapolis is the state's most affluent, and includes the 4.2 million-square-foot Mall of America in Bloomington.

A member of the Ways and Means panel, Ramstad has supported Bush's tax cuts, but was unhappy that the president's 2005 and 2006 budget proposals failed to address the problem of the alternative minimum tax. Originally enacted in 1969 to make sure the wealthy did not take too many deductions and pay too little tax, the AMT was never properly adjusted for inflation and now has the unintended effect of hitting many middle-class taxpayers.

In early 2006, he was one of just 12 House Republicans to vote against the final version of a spending bill for labor, health and education programs that he said would reduce the deficit "on the backs of the least amongst us." Later that year, he was one of only a dozen GOP defectors to vote against the annual budget resolution.

A budget bill enacted early in 2006 contained a bright spot for Ramstad — his plan to repeal the so-called Byrd amendment, named for its author, West Virginia's Democratic Sen. Robert C. Byrd. Byrd's provision allowed duties collected in cases involving unfair trade practices to go directly to the aggrieved companies, an arrangement Ramstad argued gave companies an incentive to seek anti-dumping and countervailing duty rewards rather than search for new markets for their products.

Ramstad is among the party moderates who have fought efforts by Republicans to open Alaska's Arctic National Wildlife Refuge to oil drilling. He also has opposed proposals to allow increased motorboat traffic in northern Minnesota's Boundary Waters wilderness area. He was one of only 10 Republican congressional candidates endorsed by the Sierra Club in 2006.

He also steers a more moderate course than many of his Republican colleagues on abortion, backing legalized abortion but supporting "reasonable limits." He voted to ban a procedure opponents call "partial birth" abortion, labeling it "repulsive and extreme." He supports federal funding for embryonic stem cell research, in part, he says, to prevent the private sector from deciding the legal and moral issues surrounding stem cell research.

Ramstad is a firm supporter of free trade and served on the whip team that got the Central American Free Trade Agreement approved in 2005 by a scant two votes. He also helped round up votes for a series of bilateral trade agreements, including pacts with Chile, Singapore, Morocco and Australia.

Ramstad, whose district is home to several medical companies, uses his seat on the Ways and Means panel to pursue his interest in health care. He won enactment in the 2003 Medicare overhaul of provisions to increase access for seniors to medical technology and to extend care for the frail elderly. Concerned that Medicare sometimes takes years to approve reimbursement for new medical devices, he introduced legislation to speed up the process.

A recovering alcoholic, Ramstad is keenly interested in boosting treatment for drug and alcohol addicts, and has repeatedly pressed bipartisan legislation that would require insurance companies to cover the costs of such care. In 2006, after Rhode Island Democratic Rep. Patrick J. Kennedy admitted to being addicted to pain killers, Ramstad took a personal interest in Kennedy, giving him support and advice. The two men have teamed on legislation to require insurers to treat mental illnesses the same way they do physical ailments.

Ramstad speaks freely about his struggles with addiction. He says he slipped into alcoholism as a college senior, and that he recognized the need to do something about it in 1981 when he woke up in jail in Sioux Falls, S.D., after a night of drinking and fighting, with little memory of what had happened. "Every day, I have to recover," he says. "Every day I do healthy, positive things so I won't take another drink."

Ramstad has been fascinated by politics since childhood. As a 10-year-old in Jamestown, N.D., he decorated a little red wagon with "I Like Ike" stickers and hit the streets with a megaphone and literature for Dwight D. Eisenhower's re-election campaign. When he ran for Congress in 1990, his mother dragged the wagon out of storage and his nephew hauled it across a stage, redecorated with Ramstad flyers.

For years, Ramstad's Web page carried a famous photo of a young Bill Clinton shaking hands with President John F. Kennedy at the White House in 1963. Also in that photo is Ramstad, who was with Clinton in the American Legion Boys Nation contingent that day.

Ramstad came to Washington to study law and to work as an aide to North Dakota GOP Rep. Tom Kleppe. In 1980, he won a seat in the Minnesota Senate, serving until he ran for the 3rd District seat vacated in 1990 by Republican Bill Frenzel. His abortion rights stance put him at odds with the party nominating convention, but the impact was mitigated by high-profile endorsements from leading state conservative Vin Weber and former Sen. Rudy Boschwitz. He defeated four candidates after seven ballots, won in November with 67 percent of the vote and has won easily since.

KEY VOTES

2006

No Stop broadband companies from favoring select Internet traffic
Yes Affirm U.S. commitment to war in Iraq and reject setting a withdrawal date for troops
No Repeal requirement for bilingual ballots at the polls
Yes Permit U.S. sale of civilian nuclear technology to India
Yes Build a 700-mile fence on the U.S.-Mexico border to curb illegal crossings
Yes Permit warrantless wiretaps of suspected terrorists

2005

Yes Intervene in the life-support case of Terri Schiavo
Yes Lift President Bush's restrictions on stem cell research funding
No Prohibit FBI access to library and bookstore records
Yes Approve free-trade pact with five Central American countries
Yes Pass energy policy overhaul favored by President Bush emphasizing domestic oil and gas production
No End mandatory preservation of habitat of endangered animal and plant species
Yes Ban torture of prisoners in U.S. custody

CQ VOTE STUDIES

	PARTY UNITY		PRESIDENTIAL SUPPORT	
	Support	Oppose	Support	Oppose
2006	70%	30%	70%	30%
2005	80%	20%	67%	33%
2004	91%	9%	74%	26%
2003	80%	20%	76%	24%
2002	84%	16%	82%	18%

INTEREST GROUPS

	AFL-CIO	ADA	CCUS	ACU
2006	50%	35%	87%	68%
2005	20%	35%	81%	46%
2004	7%	25%	100%	76%
2003	20%	25%	90%	56%
2002	11%	15%	95%	92%

MINNESOTA 3

Hennepin County suburbs – Bloomington, Brooklyn Park, Plymouth

Minnesota's most affluent district, the 3rd takes in Hennepin County suburbs north, west and south of Minneapolis. The primarily white-collar population is grounded in fiscal conservatism, but adheres to moderate views on social issues. The 3rd also is known for its political independence: Brooklyn Park elected Jesse Ventura mayor in the 1990s and the district later supported him in his race for governor.

The 3rd is a classic picture of suburban living, with an abundant technology industry, white-collar workers, golf courses and middle-class homes. The district has the most-educated residents in the state, with 40 percent holding at least a bachelor's degree.

Several Fortune 500 corporations have their headquarters in the district and employ local residents, as do other large companies — such as Northwest Airlines and General Mills — based just outside the 3rd. Traffic backups for commuters driving east from Lake Minnetonka — the largest lake in the Twin Cities area — have worsened considerably due to sustained regional growth. Transportation, and Interstate highway upgrades, are important issues here.

Blue-collar residents from Brooklyn Park, Coon Rapids (a small part of which is in the 6th) and Brooklyn Center are conservative Democratic-Farmer-Labor Party voters, but the affluent, Republican south and west portions of the 3rd cast more votes, giving the district a tilt to the right. The 3rd routinely registers high rates of voter participation, and generally elects Republicans to the state legislature. George W. Bush captured 51 percent of the district's 2004 presidential vote. In 2006, the 3rd gave Republican Gov. Tim Pawlenty 53 percent of its gubernatorial vote while awarding Democrat Amy Klobuchar 56 percent of its U.S. Senate vote.

MAJOR INDUSTRY
Electronics, manufacturing, transportation

CITIES
Bloomington, 85,172; Brooklyn Park, 67,388; Plymouth, 65,894; Coon Rapids (pt.), 58,396; Eden Prairie, 54,901; Minnetonka, 51,301

NOTABLE
Bloomington's Mall of America has 4.2 million square feet of retail and office space, more than 500 stores and employs more than 11,000 people.

Rep. Betty McCollum (D)

CAPITOL OFFICE
225-6631
www.mccollum.house.gov
1714 Longworth 20515-2304; fax 225-1968

COMMITTEES
Appropriations
Oversight & Government Reform

RESIDENCE
St. Paul

BORN
July 12, 1954, Minneapolis, Minn.

RELIGION
Roman Catholic

FAMILY
Divorced; two children

EDUCATION
Inver Hills Community College, A.A. 1980;
College of St. Catherine, B.A. 1987 (education)

CAREER
Teacher; retail saleswoman

POLITICAL HIGHLIGHTS
Candidate for North St. Paul City Council, 1984; North St. Paul City Council, 1987-92; Minn. House, 1993-2001

ELECTION RESULTS

2006 GENERAL		
Betty McCollum (D)	172,096	69.5%
Obi Sium (R)	74,797	30.2%
2006 PRIMARY		
Betty McCollum (D)		unopposed
2004 GENERAL		
Betty McCollum (D)	182,387	57.5%
Patrice Bataglia (R)	105,467	33.2%
Peter F. Vento (INDC)	29,099	9.2%

PREVIOUS WINNING PERCENTAGES
2002 (62%); 2000 (48%)

Elected 2000; 4th term

A former substitute teacher, McCollum keeps an eye on education policy but has broadened her portfolio in recent years by becoming a quiet but serious player on international issues. A consistent critic of the war in Iraq from its inception, McCollum and her liberal views are at home in heavily Democratic St. Paul.

McCollum, the first woman to represent Minnesota in the House in more than 40 years, is an ally of Congress' most prominent woman, Speaker Nancy Pelosi of California. When Pelosi ran for party whip in 2001, she asked McCollum to give the nominating speech. When Pelosi ascended to Democratic leader in 2003, she named McCollum to the Steering Committee, which makes recommendations for committee assignments.

That positioned her to pitch for a seat on the powerful Appropriations Committee, and she asked Pelosi in early 2006 to name her to replace retiring Rep. Martin Olav Sabo, also a Minnesota Democrat.

She got the Appropriations assignment in the 110th Congress (2007-08) and landed on two subcommittees — Labor-HHS-Education and State-Foreign Operations — that enable her to continue working on the same issues that occupied much of her time in the previous Congress. She was on the Education and International Affairs panels in the 109th Congress (2005-06).

McCollum was an early and ardent critic of the war, one of 126 Democrats who opposed the 2002 resolution sanctioning President Bush's decision. After listening to administration officials make their case during several classified briefings that year, she came away convinced there was no need to go to war. McCollum told the Minneapolis Star Tribune newspaper that she was later "stunned" to hear national security adviser Condoleezza Rice talk of ties between Saddam Hussein and the al Qaeda terrorist network and of disarming Iraq before it attacked the United States. "What the American people are learning now is how our intelligence was misused," she said. "Only the intelligence that supported the administration's view was presented to the public."

Interested in world diplomacy since she was a child, McCollum has twice been to Baghdad to assess the war effort, the last time in August 2004. She pressed without much success to force the International Affairs panel to hold oversight hearings on the war and to investigate the alleged disappearance of $1 billion from the Iraqi Ministry of Defense during the tenure of the U.S.-led interim government.

McCollum has also traveled to Africa to try to bring attention to the global AIDS crisis, and in 2003 she won passage of an amendment requiring that at least 10 percent of U.S. funding to fight AIDS internationally be spent on orphans and vulnerable children. In 2006, she joined a bipartisan group urging Secretary of State Rice to appoint a special envoy to Sudan, ripped by alleged government-backed genocide in the western Darfur region.

On an issue that combines local priorities with her committee work, McCollum is the leading advocate of federal funding for the resettlement of Hmong refugees from Laos in Minnesota, securing $19 million in the 2004 catchall spending bill. St. Paul is home to one of the highest concentrations of the Hmong people in the United States. She sponsored a bill passed by both chambers in 2004 to normalize trade relations with Laos. The measure bitterly divided the Hmong community, with foes of the current regime in Laos arguing against rewarding the government with a trade pact. But McCollum said that ending the isolation of Laos would give the United States more influence in the country's future.

Another major policy arena for McCollum is education, an issue she campaigned on to win her first House election in 2000. From her perch on the Education Committee, she criticized the Bush administration for underfunding the No Child Left Behind initiative, the overhaul of federal education policy that tied aid to performance on student achievement tests. McCollum was one of only six House Democrats in 2001 to vote against the final bill.

McCollum has a solid Democratic voting record, backing her party on 97 percent of the votes on which the two parties squared off in the 109th Congress. She has a career rating of 98 percent from the liberal Americans for Democratic Action.

An important local issue for her is the proposed designation of the 3,900-mile Mississippi River as a national scenic trail, opposed by private property rights groups. In 2006, the House passed McCollum's bill calling for a feasibility study.

McCollum was born and raised in the Twin Cities area in what she describes as a frugal middle-class household. Family discussions often included world affairs and far-off places. "My father served in India and China during WWII, so we always had the atlas open at home, talking about countries and food and geography and culture and climate," McCollum said.

She studied at a community college and worked as a sales clerk at J.C. Penney and Sears department stores, and also as a substitute teacher, while raising two children. She got her bachelor's degree at 32, about the time she was venturing into politics. After being rebuffed by the city of North St. Paul in her quest to get immediate repairs at a local playground, McCollum ran for the city council. She lost that first bid, but won in a second attempt. She moved to the state legislature six years later, beating two incumbents thrown into the same district by redistricting.

With 14 years in elective office under her belt, McCollum jumped into the primary race for the seat vacated by Democratic Rep. Bruce F. Vento, who announced in 2000 that he had a rare form of lung cancer. Although six other Democrats were competing, McCollum gained an important edge when she was endorsed by the state Democratic Party.

McCollum drew a seasoned Republican foe in state Sen. Linda Runbeck. She was worried that independent candidate Tom Foley, a former Democrat and longtime Ramsey County attorney, would siphon off Democratic votes, but Foley, who ran as a fiscal conservative, appeared to draw votes from both candidates. Though McCollum missed a majority with 48 percent of the vote, she easily outran Runbeck, who took 31 percent. Foley finished with 21 percent. McCollum has been re-elected since with comfortable margins.

KEY VOTES

2006

- Yes Stop broadband companies from favoring select Internet traffic
- No Affirm U.S. commitment to war in Iraq and reject setting a withdrawal date for troops
- No Repeal requirement for bilingual ballots at the polls
- Yes Permit U.S. sale of civilian nuclear technology to India
- No Build a 700-mile fence on the U.S.-Mexico border to curb illegal crossings
- No Permit warrantless wiretaps of suspected terrorists

2005

- ? Intervene in the life-support case of Terri Schiavo
- Yes Lift President Bush's restrictions on stem cell research funding
- Yes Prohibit FBI access to library and bookstore records
- No Approve free-trade pact with five Central American countries
- No Pass energy policy overhaul favored by President Bush emphasizing domestic oil and gas production
- No End mandatory preservation of habitat of endangered animal and plant species
- Yes Ban torture of prisoners in U.S. custody

CQ VOTE STUDIES

	PARTY UNITY		PRESIDENTIAL SUPPORT	
	Support	Oppose	Support	Oppose
2006	96%	4%	20%	80%
2005	98%	2%	11%	89%
2004	97%	3%	21%	79%
2003	97%	3%	18%	82%
2002	98%	2%	25%	75%

INTEREST GROUPS

	AFL-CIO	ADA	CCUS	ACU
2006	93%	95%	33%	4%
2005	93%	95%	33%	0%
2004	93%	100%	24%	0%
2003	100%	100%	24%	12%
2002	89%	100%	40%	4%

MINNESOTA 4

Ramsey County – St. Paul and suburbs

St. Paul, the state capital and the heart of the 4th, is a collection of distinct neighborhoods, which include liberal university communities, residential areas, labor populations and state government.

St. Paul developed as a major port and railroading center and still has a strong labor tradition. The announced closure of a Ford auto manufacturing plant will affect thousands of union workers, but plans are under way to redevelop the site. Local leaders in St. Paul hope to fill the economic gaps caused by manufacturing downsizing with the growing renewable energy and green building industries.

The 4th has a large percentage of white-collar workers who live in middle- and high-income neighborhoods and work at major district-based corporations such as 3M. Dairy producer Land O' Lakes is the leader of agribusiness in the area. St. Paul and surrounding areas are home to many colleges and universities, including the University of Minnesota's agriculture school.

Represented in the U.S. House by a Democrat since 1949, voters in St. Paul, who make up nearly half of the current 4th, consistently support the Democratic-Farmer-Labor Party at all levels. Today, blue-collar and growing black, Hispanic and Hmong communities — the city has one of the nation's largest Hmong populations — contribute to the Democratic flavor. John Kerry won 62 percent of the 4th's 2004 presidential vote.

As with much of central Minnesota, the 4th has an independent streak demonstrated by its support for Jesse Ventura in the 1998 gubernatorial race. The limited GOP base here is in the growing suburbs to the north of the city. St. Paul will host the 2008 Republican National Convention at the downtown Xcel Energy Center, which is home to hockey's Wild. Fast-growing Washington County and affluent northern suburbs in North Oaks and White Bear Lake have independent and moderate voters.

MAJOR INDUSTRY

State government, higher education, manufacturing

CITIES

St. Paul, 287,151; Maplewood, 34,947; Roseville, 33,690; Oakdale, 26,653

NOTABLE

In 2002, the area elected Mee Moua to the state Senate, making her the first Hmong state legislator in the United States.

Rep. Keith Ellison (D)

CAPITOL OFFICE
225-4755
ellison.house.gov
1130 Longworth 20515-2305; fax 225-4886

COMMITTEES
Financial Services
Judiciary

RESIDENCE
Minneapolis

BORN
Aug. 4, 1963, Detroit, Mich.

RELIGION
Muslim

FAMILY
Wife, Kim Ellison; four children

EDUCATION
Wayne State U., B.A. 1986 (economics), attended 1986-87 (economics); U. of Minnesota, J.D. 1990

CAREER
Lawyer; nonprofit law firm executive director

POLITICAL HIGHLIGHTS
Minn. House, 2003-07

ELECTION RESULTS

2006 GENERAL		
Keith Ellison (D)	136,060	55.6%
Alan Fine (R)	52,263	21.3%
Tammy Lee (INDC)	51,456	21.0%
Jay Pond (GREEN)	4,792	2.0%
2006 PRIMARY		
Keith Ellison (D)	29,003	41.2%
Mike Erlandson (D)	21,857	31.1%
Ember Reichgott Junge (D)	14,454	20.5%
Paul Ostrow (D)	3,795	5.4%

Elected 2006; 1st term

The first Muslim to serve in Congress, Ellison was caught up in a controversy even before attending his first committee meeting. Ellison decided to use a Koran owned by Thomas Jefferson at a ceremonial swearing-in following the official oath in the House chamber.

This prompted Virginia Republican Virgil H. Goode Jr., an advocate of stringent controls on immigration, to write in a letter to his constituents, "If American citizens don't wake up and adopt [my] position on immigration there will likely be many more Muslims elected to office and demanding the use of the Koran." Ellison, who converted to Islam from Catholicism while in college at Wayne State University, said in an interview with CNN that he was not angry about Goode's comments. "I just think it is a learning gap that we have to close," he said.

Ellison has seats on the Financial Services Committee, where he intends to address affordable housing issues, and the Judiciary Committee. A legal rights activist, Ellison was once head of the Legal Rights Center, a public defense organization serving Hennepin County.

Ellison succeeded Democratic Rep. Martin Olav Sabo, who retired after three decades representing the strongly Democratic Minneapolis-based 5th District. Ellison said he wants to emulate Sabo by promoting peace, setting up universal health care — which he calls "the human rights issue of our time" — and fighting for middle-class economic justice by increasing the minimum wage and addressing college affordability.

The biggest election challenge Ellison faced was winning the Democratic primary over longtime Sabo aide Mike Erlandson, a former state Democratic Party chairman, and former state Sen. Ember Reichgott Junge. He won with 41 percent of the vote.

Ellison took 56 percent in November to defeat GOP business consultant Alan Fine, becoming the first African-American to represent Minnesota in Congress. He is one of a small handful of black lawmakers to represent districts with sizable white majorities — the 5th District's population is about 70 percent white and is the state's most racially diverse district.

MINNESOTA 5
Minneapolis and suburbs

Minneapolis is located at the northernmost navigable point on the Mississippi River. The city experienced population growth in the 1990s, and it accounts for most of the 5th's residents. The state's most racially diverse district, the 5th's black and Asian communities help shape its liberal politics.

Minneapolis is home to large corporations, including Target, U.S. Bancorp and General Mills. The 5th lured well-educated white-collar workers during the economic boom of the 1990s, but the shift did not change the area's liberal-mindedness. The local art and theater community's left lean is bolstered by the University of Minnesota and other colleges and universities here. Residents who flock to the area's many lakes also support environmental protections.

Downtown Minneapolis hosts four professional sports teams: basketball's Timberwolves and Lynx, baseball's Twins and football's Vikings. Completion of the Hiawatha Line light rail connecting southern suburbs to downtown has eased traffic congestion, which had been a growing problem. Downtown's lack of affordable housing, however, has pushed poorer communities north, into an area plagued by violent crime despite city prevention efforts.

Although Minneapolis is known for its Scandinavian heritage, the 5th is racially diverse. Hmong, Tibetans and blacks — including a sizable Somali population — add to the Democratic-Farmer-Labor Party voter rolls, as do large American Indian communities. Democrat Amy Klobuchar won 74 percent of the 5th's 2006 U.S. Senate vote — her best showing in the state.

MAJOR INDUSTRY
Corporate offices, banking, higher education

CITIES
Minneapolis, 382,618; St. Louis Park, 44,126

NOTABLE
Prince got his start during the pop music "Minneapolis Sound" surge in the 1980s.

Rep. Michele Bachmann (R)

CAPITOL OFFICE
225-2331
bachmann.house.gov
412 Cannon 20515-2306; fax 225-6475

COMMITTEES
Financial Services

RESIDENCE
Stillwater

BORN
April 6, 1956, Waterloo, Iowa

RELIGION
Evangelical Lutheran

FAMILY
Husband, Marcus Bachmann; five children

EDUCATION
Winona State U., B.A. 1978 (political science & English); Oral Roberts U., J.D. 1986; College of William and Mary, LL.M. 1988 (tax law)

CAREER
Homemaker; U.S. Treasury Department lawyer

POLITICAL HIGHLIGHTS
Candidate for Stillwater Area School District Board, 1999; Minn. Senate, 2001-07

ELECTION RESULTS

2006 GENERAL

Michele Bachmann (R)	151,248	50.1%
Patty Wetterling (D)	127,144	42.1%
John Paul Binkowski (INDC)	23,557	7.8%

2006 PRIMARY

Michele Bachmann (R)	unopposed

Elected 2006; 1st term

One of the few Republicans to defeat a Democrat in an open-seat race in 2006, Bachmann is a social and fiscal conservative. She is also the first Republican woman to be elected to the House from Minnesota.

Bachmann's fiscally conservative views fit neatly with her suburban Twin Cities constituents. While serving in the Minnesota Senate, she also championed conservative stances on social issues. Bachmann was the author of a proposed constitutional amendment to define marriage as between one man and one woman. She opposes abortion rights.

A tax attorney, Bachmann (BOCK-man) sits on the Financial Services Committee. She says she supports making President Bush's tax cuts permanent and repealing the estate tax. She objected that the Democrats' 2008 budget resolution contained the "largest tax increase in history."

At the start of the 110th Congress (2007-08), Bachmann said in an interview that she knew of an Iranian plan to partition Iraq. She later clarified the statement in an op-ed posted on the Minneapolis Star Tribune's Web site. "I said that an agreement had already been made to divide Iraq and create a safe haven for terrorists," she wrote. "Rather, I meant that America's adversaries are in agreement that a divided Iraq benefits their objective to expel America from the region, resulting in Iraq being a safe haven for terrorists." She opposes efforts to cut funding to U.S. troops serving in Iraq or to set a timetable for troop withdrawal.

Bachmann became a local activist after objecting to the state's performance-based Profile of Learning program. She favors local control of schools. "Those closest to our students — not well-intentioned but distant bureaucrats — understand best our students' needs," she said. The Bachmanns have five children and have been foster parents to 23 other children.

Bachmann bested Democrat Patty Wetterling, who gained prominence as a child safety advocate after the 1989 abduction of her 11-year-old son, who never was found. The seat had opened up when GOP Rep. Mark Kennedy ran unsuccessfully for the Senate. Bachmann won by an 8 percentage point margin, collecting 50 percent of the vote to Wetterling's 42 percent.

MINNESOTA 6

North and east Twin Cities suburbs; St. Cloud

One of Minnesota's three suburban-oriented districts, the 6th hooks counterclockwise from eastern Twin Cities suburbs through conservative, rapidly developing areas northwest to the former granite-quarrying city of St. Cloud, the 6th's only major urban center. Development has not yet made fast-growing St. Cloud, in heavily Catholic Stearns County, a Twin Cities suburb. Officials hope a 40-mile commuter train line linking Sherburne County with the Twin Cities, planned for 2009, will help alleviate traffic problems.

Anoka and Wright counties, to the north and west of Minneapolis and its first-ring suburbs, include new, wealthy suburban developments. Washington County, to the east and north of St. Paul, includes Woodbury (a small part of which is in the 2nd), which is growing rapidly, and the small town of Stillwater on the St. Croix River, which marks the Wisconsin border.

The 6th has a GOP lean. It gave George W. Bush his best state showing (57 percent) in the 2004 presidential election, and awarded Republicans Mark Kennedy and Tim Pawlenty their highest percentages in the 2006 U.S. Senate and gubernatorial races, respectively. The young, high-income families that fuel the region's growth tend to favor fiscal conservatism, but are not conservative on social issues such as public safety and education. Blue-collar communities in the suburbs of Anoka and Washington counties are faithful Democratic-Farmer-Labor Party supporters.

MAJOR INDUSTRY
Corporate administration, manufacturing

CITIES
St. Cloud, 59,107; Blaine, 44,942; Woodbury (pt.), 44,767; Andover, 26,588; Ramsey, 18,510

NOTABLE
Writer and radio show host Garrison Keillor was born in Anoka.

Rep. Collin C. Peterson (D)

CAPITOL OFFICE
225-2165
collinpeterson.house.gov
2211 Rayburn 20515-2307; fax 225-1593

COMMITTEES
Agriculture - chairman

RESIDENCE
Detroit Lakes

BORN
June 29, 1944, Fargo, N.D.

RELIGION
Lutheran

FAMILY
Divorced; three children

EDUCATION
Moorhead State U., B.A. 1966 (accounting)

MILITARY SERVICE
Minn. National Guard, 1963-69

CAREER
Accountant

POLITICAL HIGHLIGHTS
Minn. Senate, 1977-87; sought Democratic nomination for U.S. House, 1982; Democratic nominee for U.S. House, 1984, 1986; sought Democratic nomination for U.S. House, 1988

ELECTION RESULTS

2006 GENERAL		
Collin C. Peterson (D)	179,164	69.7%
Michael J. Barrett (R)	74,557	29.0%
Ken Lucier (CNSTP)	3,303	1.3%
2006 PRIMARY		
Collin C. Peterson (D)	33,732	86.0%
Erik Thompson (D)	5,476	14.0%
2004 GENERAL		
Collin C. Peterson (D)	207,628	66.1%
David E. Sturrock (R)	106,349	33.8%

PREVIOUS WINNING PERCENTAGES
2002 (65%); 2000 (69%); 1998 (72%); 1996 (68%); 1994 (51%); 1992 (50%); 1990 (54%)

Elected 1990; 9th term

Peterson is the House Democrats' rebel. He's a conservative in a liberal party, a farm-focused lawmaker in a chamber dominated by members from urban areas. And his first love isn't politics at all, it's music. If life had gone as planned, he'd be a rock star.

Instead, the Minnesota Democrat is chairman of the House Agriculture Committee in the 110th Congress (2007-08), having overcome doubts about his party loyalty. He became the panel's top Democrat in 2005, despite rumblings about his right to the job. "It turned out to be not that big of a deal," Peterson says. "Only three or four [Democrats] voted against me on the Steering Committee."

The concern was understandable. A founding member of the conservative Democratic Blue Dog Coalition, Peterson has consistently voted in opposition to his party's positions. He has ranked for years among the 10 Democrats voting most often against the majority of their party. Peterson also has supported President Bush far more often than the typical Democrat. He says his votes suit his Republican-leaning district while his heart remains in the party. "Democrats do a better job of standing up for ordinary people," he says.

Peterson gets along so well with the opposition that he's the lone Democrat in a five-member country rock band he fronts called "The Second Amendments," which has performed for U.S. troops in Germany, Kuwait, Iraq, Pakistan and Afghanistan. In 2005, the band played at WE Fest in Minnesota and Farm Aid in Illinois. The other members are all Republicans, and Peterson says, "It helps us bridge a lot of political issues."

Peterson is a gun rights advocate, but that doesn't explain the band's name. It's an incarnation of an earlier congressional group he led called "The Amendments." (Before he came to Washington, Peterson played lead guitar in a group called Collin and the Establishment that included a lawyer, an accountant and a businessman.)

First on Peterson's plate at the outset of the 110th Congress was a major rewrite of farm policy, last done in 2002. As work gets under way, the United States faces pressure from its trading partners to cut farm subsidies, an idea unpopular with farmers but one that could give the White House and Congress leverage in forcing other countries to reduce tariffs.

Peterson once maintained that it would be foolhardy to go forward with rewriting farm law until after the next round of international trade talks. But he changed his mind after the 2006 election gave him the gavel, saying some parts are worth revamping. "Farmers like what we did in 2002," he said. "We'd like to maintain the current structure of the bill but tinker with some of the commodity programs and add a disaster relief title."

Though Peterson, like other Blue Dogs, advocates a balanced federal budget, he is a booster of farm subsidies. He opposes Bush's efforts to cut spending on farm programs, and is bitter about White House and GOP resistance to emergency relief for drought-stricken farmers. He also wants a section promoting use of ethanol and biofuels, including federal incentives for farmers who make ethanol from corn.

Peterson was part of the House-Senate conference committee that wrote the 2002 farm bill that boosted spending by $73.5 billion over 10 years. The bill essentially reversed a 1996 law designed to wean farmers from federal price supports, a longtime goal of fiscal conservatives. Peterson considers the 2002 law a success, and he defends the federal subsidies for agriculture-dependent regions. He likes to share in the credit for defeating a perennial amendment to the annual agriculture appropriations bill to kill the sugar price-support program. Sugar beets are a major crop in the 7th District.

Peterson opposed the Bush administration's 2005 Central American Free Trade Agreement, which he thought would increase sugar imports and undercut the price of domestic sugar. He also voted in 2002 against granting the president fast-track authority to negotiate trade agreements that Congress cannot amend. And in 2000, he opposed granting China permanent normal trade status.

On fiscal issues not related to farm policy, Peterson has been more of a typical budget conservative, opposing Bush tax cuts that he thought would lead to deficits. He voted for the $1.35 trillion tax cut in 2001, while also backing an unsuccessful amendment to delay them if Congress did not cut spending sufficiently to keep the budget balanced. When Bush sent more tax cuts to Capitol Hill in 2003, Peterson voted no. As the budget deficit ballooned in 2004, Peterson voiced regrets for having backed the initial round.

Peterson draws high marks from the National Rifle Association. An avid sportsman, he once boasted he has "more dead animals on my wall than anybody in this Congress, except for [Alaska Republican] Don Young."

He grew up on his family's farm near the North Dakota border and learned self-sufficiency at an early age. Once, as a boy, he ran his father's weeder into a telephone pole — he was too weak to turn it quickly enough — and his father and grandfather sat in the yard watching, amused, while the young Peterson figured out how to turn the machine around.

He used the money he made working on the farm to buy a guitar. At 16, he was good enough to join a touring band. But he gave up his dream of stardom when it became clear he'd have to quit college to pursue it. He made a practical choice of accounting as a career.

He got his start in politics with 10 years in the state Senate. In the 1980s, he made four unsuccessful bids for a U.S. House seat; in two attempts, he failed to get even the Democratic nomination. "When I make up my mind to do something, it's hard to dissuade me," he said.

Peterson decided to run again in 1990 when Republican Rep. Arlan Stangeland was weakened by revelations that he had used his House credit card to charge several calls to or from the phone of a female Virginia lobbyist. Peterson finally prevailed, with 54 percent of the vote. After scratching out close re-election victories in 1992 and 1994, Peterson has since won with better than 65 percent of the vote.

KEY VOTES

2006

- Yes Stop broadband companies from favoring select Internet traffic
- Yes Affirm U.S. commitment to war in Iraq and reject setting a withdrawal date for troops
- Yes Repeal requirement for bilingual ballots at the polls
- No Permit U.S. sale of civilian nuclear technology to India
- Yes Build a 700-mile fence on the U.S.-Mexico border to curb illegal crossings
- Yes Permit warrantless wiretaps of suspected terrorists

2005

- ? Intervene in the life-support case of Terri Schiavo
- No Lift President Bush's restrictions on stem cell research funding
- Yes Prohibit FBI access to library and bookstore records
- No Approve free-trade pact with five Central American countries
- Yes Pass energy policy overhaul favored by President Bush emphasizing domestic oil and gas production
- Yes End mandatory preservation of habitat of endangered animal and plant species
- Yes Ban torture of prisoners in U.S. custody

CQ VOTE STUDIES

	PARTY UNITY		PRESIDENTIAL SUPPORT	
	Support	Oppose	Support	Oppose
2006	63%	37%	60%	40%
2005	64%	36%	54%	46%
2004	63%	37%	50%	50%
2003	65%	35%	58%	42%
2002	64%	36%	54%	46%

INTEREST GROUPS

	AFL-CIO	ADA	CCUS	ACU
2006	79%	35%	73%	72%
2005	80%	65%	70%	56%
2004	80%	55%	76%	52%
2003	87%	70%	70%	50%
2002	56%	45%	70%	48%

MINNESOTA 7

West — Moorhead, Willmar

Stretching 330 miles from north to south, the vast 7th spans almost the entire western third of Minnesota. It shifts from flat prairie in the west to hills, lakes and heavy forests in the middle of the state. Apart from Willmar in the southern part of the district, the 7th's main population centers — Moorhead and East Grand Forks — are on the Red River, which forms the border between Minnesota and North Dakota. Both locales have much larger companion cities across the river.

Floods and droughts over the past decade resulted in agricultural struggle in the northwest region. Reductions in crop harvests forced some farmers to subsidize their livelihood with part-time work in other industries and sent younger residents fleeing to the Twin Cities area. Sugar beets, soybeans, wheat, corn and sunflower seeds are thriving in the south. Overall, the district is the nation's top producer of sugar beets, and is among the country's most productive districts in other crops.

The 7th also relies on poultry raising and processing, and leads the nation in turkey raising. Willmar is home to the headquarters of turkey processor Jennie-O, and Schwan Food is based in Marshall. The Prairie Correctional Facility, a private prison with inmates from out of state, is in Appleton. The district's manufacturing firms lend some stability: The 7th produces hockey sticks, windows, snowmobiles and skis. In the north and east, retirees and baby boomers are creating new lake-home construction, changing the dynamics of the local tourism industry.

The 7th tends to be socially conservative and fiscally moderate, but has supported candidates from both parties. It was George W. Bush's second-strongest Minnesota district in 2004, giving him 55 percent of its presidential vote. In 2006, the district backed Republican Tim Pawlenty for governor and Democrat Amy Klobuchar for U.S. senator. Its more conservative voters are along the state's western border and in western Stearns County, while the southern counties support Democrats.

MAJOR INDUSTRY

Agriculture, poultry processing, light manufacturing, recreation

CITIES

Moorhead, 32,177; Willmar, 18,351; Fergus Falls, 13,471

NOTABLE

Writer Sinclair Lewis, who was the first American to win the Nobel Prize in Literature, grew up in Sauk Centre.

Rep. James L. Oberstar (D)

CAPITOL OFFICE
225-6211
www.house.gov/oberstar
2365 Rayburn 20515-2308; fax 225-0699

COMMITTEES
Transportation & Infrastructure - chairman

RESIDENCE
Chisholm

BORN
Sept. 10, 1934, Chisholm, Minn.

RELIGION
Roman Catholic

FAMILY
Wife, Jean Oberstar; six children

EDUCATION
College of St. Thomas, B.A. 1956 (French & political science); College of Europe (Belgium), M.A. 1957 (comparative government)

CAREER
Language teacher; congressional aide

POLITICAL HIGHLIGHTS
Sought Democratic nomination for U.S. Senate, 1984

ELECTION RESULTS

2006 GENERAL		
James L. Oberstar (D)	180,670	63.6%
Rod Grams (R)	97,683	34.4%
Harry Robb Welty (UNT)	5,508	1.9%
2006 PRIMARY		
James L. Oberstar (D)		unopposed
2004 GENERAL		
James L. Oberstar (D)	228,586	65.2%
Mark Groettum (R)	112,693	32.2%
Van Presley (GREEN)	8,933	2.6%

PREVIOUS WINNING PERCENTAGES
2002 (69%); 2000 (68%); 1998 (66%); 1996 (67%); 1994 (66%); 1992 (59%); 1990 (73%); 1988 (75%); 1986 (73%); 1984 (67%); 1982 (77%); 1980 (70%); 1978 (87%); 1976 (100%); 1974 (62%)

Elected 1974; 17th term

After a dozen years as the top-ranking minority member on the Transportation and Infrastructure Committee, Oberstar finally has the gavel at his command. The long apprenticeship made a fast start possible after Democrats captured control of Congress in the 2006 elections.

Under his guidance, the committee plunged almost immediately in early 2007 into a series of hearings on rail, transit, emergency response and aviation issues. Facing a Sept. 30, 2007, expiration of the Federal Aviation Administration's authorization, Oberstar focused much of the panel's initial attention on that topic. He took an early stand against a White House proposal for radically altering the way the FAA and its air traffic control system is funded. He also called for a reopening of a contract the FAA unilaterally imposed on the controllers in 2006 after the Republican-controlled Congress of the time declined to intervene.

Oberstar, now seventh in seniority among House Democrats, is one of just four "Watergate babies" elected in 1974 who are still serving in the House. Unlike other chairmen who often skip subcommittee hearings, Oberstar attends them regularly to ask pointed, detailed questions. Witnesses know they had better come prepared. "What I said in previous Congresses was almost always of interest and valuable and useful and factually accurate," Oberstar told the Minneapolis Star-Tribune after claiming the chairmanship. "Now it has weight."

Oberstar sees generous federal spending on transportation and infrastructure as key to maintaining America's global competitiveness. At a 2005 panel meeting on the highway bill, Oberstar remarked on the vast government spending on highways and rail networks he saw during a 2004 trip to China. "China is investing $150 billion to build the equivalent of our interstate highway system in the next 15 years," he said. As a result, he warned, Chinese goods "are going to be less expensive when they come to our shores" because they will move faster through their own country.

He is concerned by what he sees as a Bush administration effort to minimize federal spending on transportation and to move highway funding away from the long-established Highway Trust Fund, financed through federal gasoline taxes, toward public-private partnerships that rely more on tolls. He is exploring ways to bolster trust fund revenues instead.

Oberstar and the former chairman of the Transportation Committee, Republican Don Young of Alaska, usually worked in concert to help members gain federal funds for their districts' transportation and infrastructure needs. New rules on earmarks, the special set-asides for lawmakers' home-state projects, could make it harder to help colleagues in the 110th Congress (2007-08). But Oberstar will look out for Minnesota, pushing to expand light-rail and commuter train service in his state.

Oberstar and Young successfully defended their committee against efforts to shrink its jurisdiction. They could not derail a bureaucratic transfer of the Federal Emergency Management Agency and the Coast Guard to the new Homeland Security Department created by Congress in 2002. But they succeeded in keeping legislative jurisdiction over both agencies, despite a claim by the new Homeland Security Committee. They also retained oversight of aviation regulation, although not airline security.

Oberstar's father was an iron ore miner who worked in both underground mine shafts and open pits, where Oberstar also labored as a teenager. His mother worked in a shirt factory. Coming from this blue-collar mining family, with a father who was a union official, Oberstar is a fierce ally of unions. He repeatedly sought ways to help airline workers laid off in the aftermath of the Sept. 11 terrorist attacks. And in 2007, he pushed a wastewater treatment bill through the House that applied Davis-Bacon prevailing wage laws to projects constructed under the bill, including those using non-federal funds.

A dedicated bicyclist, Oberstar included in the 1998 transportation law many provisions to encourage biking and enhance bicycle safety and education. He protected those measures when the law was renewed in 2005.

Oberstar strays from most of his fellow Democrats on abortion and gun owners' rights. In 2004, he was one of 52 Democrats who voted in favor of striking down the District of Columbia's gun control law. A devout Roman Catholic, he has proposed a constitutional amendment to ban abortion except where the woman's life is in danger. In 2006, he was one of 14 House Democrats voting to sustain President Bush's veto of a bill expanding federal funding of embryonic stem cell research, which uses cells taken from surplus embryos at in vitro fertilization clinics.

Oberstar co-chairs the Congressional Coalition on Adoption; his oldest child was adopted. He also seeks more federal funding for breast cancer research. His first wife died in 1991 after an eight-year battle with the disease, and he has since married a woman who lost her first husband to cancer. He has pushed to provide financial relief, including a tax credit, to caregivers of sick family members.

A policy wonk with a dry sense of humor, he can converse in six different languages. Oberstar takes delight in demonstrating his facility with language, including French and Creole, which he taught to U.S. Navy personnel in Haiti in the early 1960s. He sometimes breaks into fluent French during committee hearings, and when the French ambassador hosted a reception in 2005 for the Congressional French Caucus, which Oberstar co-chairs, Oberstar delivered a speech in both English and French. The congressman, who has a graduate degree from the College of Europe in Brussels, also speaks some Spanish, Italian, Slovenian and Serbo-Croatian.

Oberstar's mentor and predecessor in the House was Democrat John A. Blatnik, who rose to the chairmanship of what was then the Public Works Committee. Oberstar learned the ropes on Capitol Hill as Blatnik's chief aide for 11 years. When Blatnik retired, Oberstar was elected to succeed him. He has won easily ever since, including in 2006, when he took 64 percent of the vote against Republican Rod Grams, who served in the House from 1993 to 1995 and in the Senate from 1995 to 2001.

KEY VOTES

2006

- Yes Stop broadband companies from favoring select Internet traffic
- No Affirm U.S. commitment to war in Iraq and reject setting a withdrawal date for troops
- No Repeal requirement for bilingual ballots at the polls
- No Permit U.S. sale of civilian nuclear technology to India
- No Build a 700-mile fence on the U.S.-Mexico border to curb illegal crossings
- No Permit warrantless wiretaps of suspected terrorists

2005

- Yes Intervene in the life-support case of Terri Schiavo
- No Lift President Bush's restrictions on stem cell research funding
- \+ Prohibit FBI access to library and bookstore records
- No Approve free-trade pact with five Central American countries
- Yes Pass energy policy overhaul favored by President Bush emphasizing domestic oil and gas production
- No End mandatory preservation of habitat of endangered animal and plant species
- Yes Ban torture of prisoners in U.S. custody

CQ VOTE STUDIES

	PARTY UNITY		PRESIDENTIAL SUPPORT	
	Support	Oppose	Support	Oppose
2006	88%	12%	35%	65%
2005	93%	7%	23%	77%
2004	91%	9%	27%	73%
2003	91%	9%	33%	67%
2002	94%	6%	28%	72%

INTEREST GROUPS

	AFL-CIO	ADA	CCUS	ACU
2006	100%	80%	27%	22%
2005	100%	90%	31%	20%
2004	93%	75%	14%	12%
2003	100%	85%	24%	44%
2002	100%	80%	26%	4%

MINNESOTA 8

Northeast – Duluth, Iron Range

The expansive 8th covers Minnesota's northeast quadrant, including Duluth and the Iron Range — taconite-mining communities that stretch across the middle of the state through Cass, Crow Wing and St. Louis counties. The district has the most varied terrain in the state, from farms in the south and west through the Iron Range and a watery northern border to rugged terrain in the northeastern region.

Timber and mining, traditional economic mainstays in the area, still provide a solid base for the region, and export opportunities for Iron Range-mined ore bolster the industry in the face of decreased domestic demand. Duluth, on Lake Superior, is the shipping point for much of the grain from the Plains states and is the westernmost deep-sea port to the Atlantic. The University of Minnesota has a regional campus in Duluth that serves more than 11,000 students. Northwest Airlines' Iron Range reservation center is located in Chisholm, which is northwest of Duluth.

Resorts and casinos near the Canadian border draw local and out-of-state tourists, helping to buoy the local economy. The district takes in the 61-mile Superior National Forest Scenic Byway, and winter sport tourism, fishing, canoeing and camping draw visitors as well. Huge tracts of land in the 8th are designated as state and national forests, and the Boundary Waters Canoe Area Wilderness along the Canadian border is noted for its motor-free beauty.

Blue-collar workers with strong ties to labor cement the 8th's long affiliation with the Democratic-Farmer-Labor Party. Voters here favor a hands-off approach to federal land management and tend to oppose gun control and abortion. The district is Democratic, and northeastern Minnesota has not been represented by a Republican in the U.S. House since 1947. In 2006, Republican Gov. Tim Pawlenty took only 41 percent of the vote here, making the 8th one of only three districts he did not win.

MAJOR INDUSTRY

Mining, timber, recreation

CITIES

Duluth, 86,918; Hibbing, 17,071; Brainerd, 13,178

NOTABLE

The only operating gas station designed by architect Frank Lloyd Wright is in Cloquet; The U.S. Hockey Hall of Fame is in Eveleth, which also boasts the largest hockey stick in the United States.

MISSISSIPPI

Gov. Haley Barbour (R)

First elected: 2003
Length of term: 4 years
Term expires: 1/08
Salary: $122,160
Phone: (601) 359-3150

Residence: Yazoo City
Born: Oct. 21, 1947; Yazoo City, Miss.
Religion: Presbyterian
Family: Wife, Marsha Barbour; two children
Education: U. of Mississippi, attended 1965-69 (political science), J.D. 1973
Career: Lobbyist; lawyer; White House aide; party official
Political highlights: Republican nominee for U.S. Senate, 1982; Republican National Committee chairman, 1993-97

Election results:

2003 GENERAL		
Haley Barbour (R)	470,404	52.6%
Ronnie Musgrove (D)	409,787	45.8%

Lt. Gov. Amy Tuck (R)

First elected: 1999*
Length of term: 4 years
Term expires: 1/08
Salary: $60,00
Phone: (601) 359-3200
*Elected as a Democrat

LEGISLATURE

Legislature: 90 days January-April

Senate: 52 members, 4-year terms
2007 ratios: 27 R, 25 D, 47 men, 5 women
Salary: $10,000
Phone: (601) 359-3202

House: 122 members, 4-year terms
2007 ratios: 74 D, 48 R; 103 men, 19 women
Salary: $10,000
Phone: (601) 359-3360

TERM LIMITS

Governor: 2 terms
Senate: No
House: No

URBAN STATISTICS

CITY	POPULATION
Jackson	184,256
Gulfport	71,127
Biloxi	50,644
Hattiesburg	44,779
Greenville	41,633

REGISTERED VOTERS

Voters do not register by party.

POPULATION

2006 population (est.)	2,910,540
2000 population	2,844,658
1990 population	2,573,216
Percent change (1990-2000)	+10.5%
Rank among states (2006)	31
Median age	33.8
Born in state	74.3%
Foreign born	1.4%
Violent crime rate	361/100,000
Poverty level	19.9%
Federal workers	25,318
Military	35,850

ELECTIONS

STATE ELECTION OFFICIAL
(601) 359-6357
DEMOCRATIC PARTY
(601) 969-2913
REPUBLICAN PARTY
(601) 948-5191

MISCELLANEOUS

Web: www.state.ms.us
Capital: Jackson

U.S. CONGRESS

Senate: 2 Republicans
House: 2 Democrats, 2 Republicans

2000 Census Statistics by District

DIST.	2004 VOTE FOR PRESIDENT BUSH	KERRY	WHITE	BLACK	ASIAN	HISP	MEDIAN INCOME	WHITE COLLAR	BLUE COLLAR	SERVICE INDUSTRY	OVER 64	UNDER 18	COLLEGE EDUCATION	RURAL	SQ. MILES
1	62%	37%	71%	26%	0%	1%	$32,535	49%	39%	12%	12%	27%	14%	62%	11,413
2	40	58	35	63	0	1	$26,894	52	31	17	11	29	17	37	13,625
3	65	34	64	33	1	1	$31,907	57	30	13	13	26	20	60	13,168
4 *	68	31	73	22	1	2	$33,023	52	31	17	12	27	17	46	8,701
STATE	59	39	61	36	1	1	$31,330	52	33	15	12	27	17	51	46,907
U.S.	50.7	48.3	69	12	4	13	$41,994	60	25	15	12	26	24	21	3,537,438

The district with an asterisk in the above table experienced significant changes in population and demographics due to hurricane Katrina in 2005. The statistics published here reflect information collected as part of the 2000 census. This information is the most recent comprehensive U.S. Census Bureau data broken down by congressional district. It is included here for the purpose of comparing pre-hurricane district information with available post-hurricane data. Additional statistical information collected by Congressional Quarterly may be found on pages xxiii through xxviii.

DeSoto
Benton
Alcorn
Tishomingo
Marshall
Tippah
Tunica
Tate
Prentiss
Union
Lafayette
Lee
Panola
Itawamba
1
Pontotoc
Tupelo
Coahoma
Quitman
Yalobusha
Tallahatchie
Calhoun
Chickasaw
Monroe
Bolivar
Grenada
Clay
Webster
Columbus
Montgomery
Sunflower
Leflore
Carroll
Oktibbeha
Lowndes
Choctaw
Greenville
Holmes
Washington
Humphreys
Attala
Winston
Noxubee
2
Sharkey
Yazoo
Leake
Neshoba
Kemper
Madison
Issaquena
Lauderdale
Warren
Scott
Newton
Jackson
Meridian
Hinds
Rankin
3
Jasper
Clarke
Claiborne
Copiah
Simpson
Smith
Jefferson
Covington
Lawrence
Jones
Wayne
Adams
Franklin
Lincoln
Jefferson Davis
Hattiesburg
Marion
Perry
Lamar
Greene
Wilkinson
Amite
Pike
Forrest
Walthall
4
George
Pearl River
Stone
Harrison
Jackson
Biloxi
Hancock
Gulfport
Pascagoula

Sen. Thad Cochran (R)

CAPITOL OFFICE
224-5054
cochran.senate.gov
113 Dirksen 20510-2402; fax 224-9450

COMMITTEES
Agriculture, Nutrition & Forestry
Appropriations - ranking member
Rules & Administration

RESIDENCE
Jackson

BORN
Dec. 7, 1937, Pontotoc, Miss.

RELIGION
Baptist

FAMILY
Wife, Rose Cochran; two children

EDUCATION
U. of Mississippi, B.A. 1959 (psychology); Trinity College (U. of Dublin, Ireland), attended 1963-64 (international law); U. of Mississippi, J.D. 1965

MILITARY SERVICE
Navy, 1959-61

CAREER
Lawyer

POLITICAL HIGHLIGHTS
U.S. House, 1973-78

ELECTION RESULTS

2002 GENERAL		
Thad Cochran (R)	533,269	84.6%
Shawn O'Hara (REF)	97,226	15.4%
2002 PRIMARY		
Thad Cochran (R)		unopposed

PREVIOUS WINNING PERCENTAGES
1996 (71%); 1990 (100%); 1984 (61%); 1978 (45%); 1976 House Election (76%); 1974 House Election (70%); 1972 House Election (48%)

Elected 1978; 5th term

After waiting his turn for decades, Cochran in 2005 finally claimed the gavel at one of the premier congressional power centers, the Senate Appropriations Committee. But the chairmanship brought him as many headaches as perquisites, and before he could find a cure, the Democrats took his prize away.

Not only did Cochran have to hand over his gavel to Democrat Robert C. Byrd of West Virginia in the 110th Congress (2007-08), he also found himself once again operating in the shadow of Mississippi's junior senator, Trent Lott, who worked his way back into the Senate Republican leadership after getting pushed out in 2002 for a racially insensitive remark.

Unlike Lott, his longtime rival, the courtly Cochran operates quietly behind the scenes to achieve his objectives with a minimum of fuss. But in an era of persistent budget deficits and demands from budget conservatives for domestic spending cuts, Cochran as Appropriations chairman was sharply circumscribed in doling out federal funds. The pinch was so tight that in June 2006 he was unable to hang onto $700 million the Senate had included at his behest in a supplemental spending bill. The money would have paid for relocation of a railroad line in Mississippi, but conservatives singled it out as an unnecessary earmark for an individual lawmaker.

Nonetheless, Cochran has funneled plenty of money to his state. He made sure that Mississippi was at the front of the line for recovery aid after Hurricane Katrina and other storms ravaged the Gulf Coast in 2005. Though he lost out on the rail relocation, he secured millions for hurricane recovery projects in Mississippi. And Cochran's cotton, peanut, rice and sugar farmers get emergency federal relief when they ask for it.

An institutionalist at heart, Cochran made a priority of getting all of the appropriations bills through the Senate his first year as chairman, after several years in which the Republican majority had to rely on eleventh-hour omnibus bills to run the government. But in 2006, the process fell apart as Senate GOP leaders declined to advance most of the annual spending bills, leaving a stack for Democrats to clean up in early 2007.

Cochran nonetheless was back out front for his party in 2007, managing GOP floor opposition to an Iraq War funding bill that included a timetable for withdrawal of all U.S. troops. Though his effort to delete the deadline failed narrowly, Cochran drew the praise of Senate GOP Leader Mitch McConnell of Kentucky "for his usual flawless effort in moving legislation across the floor."

Urbane and thoughtful, Cochran is an anomaly in the modern Senate, where sharp, partisan rhetoric is the norm. His rivalry with Lott probably was inevitable, given that both are smart, adept politicians in the same party in a relatively small state. Cochran was four years ahead of Lott at Ole Miss, where both were fraternity presidents and cheerleaders, an elected post that has been the starting point of many a Mississippi political career.

Though the two were elected to the House the same year, Cochran won election to the Senate a decade before Lott. But when Lott arrived, he was in the vanguard of the young, aggressive conservatives who took control of the Republican caucus. By 1995, Lott had zipped ahead of Cochran to become GOP whip, the job he holds for the 110th Congress.

When Majority Leader Bob Dole resigned to focus on his 1996 presidential campaign, the two Mississippians battled one another for the job.

Lott began collecting votes earlier and won, 44-8.

Cochran ran the Agriculture Committee for two years before he became Appropriations chairman. In 2002, he was a major player in the rewrite of the law that authorizes federal agriculture subsidies and conservation and nutrition programs. But his 2003-04 stint as Agriculture chairman was uneventful. He held few bill markups, in part because panel member Charles E. Grassley, an Iowa Republican, was waiting with amendments to reduce the maximum federal payments a farmer could receive. Grassley wanted to free up money for other farm programs. Cochran opposed lower payment limits. Mississippi's cotton and rice crops are more expensive to grow than some Midwestern crops and thus receive larger subsidies. The two are likely to square off again in a 2007-08 rewrite of the farm law.

Cochran is a member of the Rules Committee, which handles election laws. He played a pivotal role in the long drive to curb large individual donations to campaigns, called soft money. His announcement in 2001 that he had switched sides and would support a bill that GOP leaders opposed began a steady erosion of Republican opposition. The law was enacted 14 months later. "It became obvious to me that the influence of soft money and independent groups was overwhelming the efforts of candidates," Cochran said. A majority of Senate Republicans voted against the bill.

Elected to the House in President Richard Nixon's re-election landslide of 1972, Cochran was one of the bright lights among a new breed of GOP conservatives dissolving the Democrats' "Solid South." But while Nixon's vaunted "Southern Strategy" included a none-too-subtle pitch to whites unhappy about the empowerment of blacks, Cochran avoided alienating African-Americans. Though his electoral base was the Jackson area's young, upwardly mobile white population, he maintained contacts with the black communities that made up almost half his constituency.

Cochran's father was a school principal, his mother a math teacher. He was a standout in high school, valedictorian of his class, a Boy Scout leader, a member of the 4-H Club and an athlete, lettering in football, basketball, baseball and tennis. "There never was any question in my mind of whether I was going to college, it was just a matter of where," he says. "So I benefited greatly from [my parents'] example and their encouragement."

Another legacy of his childhood is musical talent. A baby grand piano sits in his Senate office, transferred there a few years ago when he moved into a Capitol Hill apartment that lacked room for it. He says he's "not a very good pianist," but his aides disagree. "I do enjoy playing," Cochran admits.

In his first year of law school, Cochran posted the highest scholastic average, and later got a Rotary fellowship to study international law at Trinity College in Dublin, Ireland. He joined a Jackson law firm after graduation, and made partner in less than three years.

Cochran was active in local party politics during his law career and was a key state figure in Nixon's 1968 campaign. In 1972, when Democratic Rep. Charles R. Griffin retired, Cochran narrowly won the open seat. Lott was elected to the House the same year, and the two soon became the leaders of warring factions within the state party. The pragmatists, led by Cochran, and the ideologues, led by Lott, feuded with increasing intensity for the better part of two decades.

Although Lott wanted to run for the Senate in 1978, when long-serving Democrat James O. Eastland retired, Cochran muscled him out of the way and became Mississippi's first GOP senator in a century. He won with 45 percent of the vote, as an independent black candidate drew much of the black vote away from Democrat Maurice Dantin, a former Columbia mayor. All of Cochran's Senate re-elections have been cakewalks. Democrats did not even field a challenger in 1990 or 2002.

KEY VOTES

2006

- Yes Confirm Samuel A. Alito Jr. to the Supreme Court
- Yes Allow consideration of a bill to establish a $140 billion trust fund to compensate victims of asbestos exposure
- Yes Extend tax cuts for two years at a cost of $70 billion over five years
- No Overhaul immigration policy with border security, enforcement and guest worker program
- Yes Allow consideration of a bill to permanently repeal the estate tax
- No Urge President Bush to begin troop withdrawals from Iraq in 2006
- Yes Lift President Bush's restrictions on stem cell research funding
- Yes Authorize military tribunals for suspected terrorists

2005

- Yes Curb class action lawsuits by shifting them from state to federal courts
- Yes Allow confirmation vote on Priscilla R. Owen to the U.S. Court of Appeals for the 5th Circuit
- Yes Oppose mandatory emissions limits and block recognition of global warming as a threat
- Yes Approve free-trade pact with five Central American countries
- Yes Pass energy policy overhaul favored by President Bush emphasizing domestic oil and gas production
- Yes Shield gunmakers from lawsuits when their products are used in crimes
- No Ban torture of prisoners in U.S. custody
- Yes Renew 16 provisions of the Patriot Act
- Yes Allow final vote on opening the Arctic National Wildlife Refuge to oil and gas exploration

CQ VOTE STUDIES

	PARTY UNITY		PRESIDENTIAL SUPPORT	
	Support	Oppose	Support	Oppose
2006	87%	13%	89%	11%
2005	97%	3%	96%	4%
2004	98%	2%	92%	8%
2003	98%	2%	98%	2%
2002	86%	14%	96%	4%
2001	84%	16%	96%	4%
2000	98%	2%	45%	55%
1999	94%	6%	38%	62%
1998	86%	14%	53%	47%
1997	82%	18%	68%	32%

INTEREST GROUPS

	AFL-CIO	ADA	CCUS	ACU
2006	15%	10%	92%	67%
2005	21%	0%	100%	88%
2004	8%	15%	100%	92%
2003	0%	5%	100%	85%
2002	23%	25%	100%	90%
2001	25%	15%	86%	88%
2000	0%	0%	100%	92%
1999	0%	0%	88%	84%
1998	0%	0%	100%	76%
1997	0%	15%	90%	56%

Sen. Trent Lott (R)

CAPITOL OFFICE
224-6253
senatorlott@lott.senate.gov
lott.senate.gov
487 Russell 20510-2403; fax 224-2262

COMMITTEES
Commerce, Science & Transportation
Finance
Rules & Administration

RESIDENCE
Pascagoula

BORN
Oct. 9, 1941, Grenada County, Miss.

RELIGION
Baptist

FAMILY
Wife, Patricia Elizabeth Lott; two children

EDUCATION
U. of Mississippi, B.P.A. 1963 (public administration), J.D. 1967

CAREER
Lawyer; congressional aide

POLITICAL HIGHLIGHTS
U.S. House, 1973-89

ELECTION RESULTS

2006 GENERAL

Trent Lott (R)	388,399	63.6%
Eric Fleming (D)	213,000	34.9%
Harold M. Taylor (LIBERT)	9,522	1.6%

2006 PRIMARY

Trent Lott (R)	unopposed

PREVIOUS WINNING PERCENTAGES
2000 (66%); 1994 (69%); 1988 (54%); 1986 House Election (82%); 1984 House Election (85%); 1982 House Election (79%); 1980 House Election (74%); 1978 House Election (100%); 1976 House Election (68%); 1974 House Election (73%); 1972 House Election (55%)

Elected 1988; 4th term

Lott is enjoying a rare political comeback. After getting dumped as Senate leader in 2002 for a racially insensitive remark, he was chosen by his colleagues as Republican whip at the start of the 110th Congress (2007-08). During his exile, Lott had used his chairmanship of the Rules Committee to get involved in brokering agreements on some major bills, and apparently fellow GOP senators felt they did better with him than without him.

In late 2006, as Republicans were reorganizing after a disastrous election that cost them both houses of Congress, Lott upset Lamar Alexander of Tennessee in the race for GOP whip, winning by a single vote. Demoralized senators were restive and newly skeptical of inexperienced leaders after the lackluster performance of Majority Leader Bill Frist of Tennessee in the 109th Congress (2005-06). Lott, a proven tactician who is popular with his colleagues and the press, became the No. 2 GOP leader in the Senate; Mitch McConnell of Kentucky was elected to the top job of minority leader.

Unlike McConnell, a backstage operator with little taste for the media, Lott loves the daily hallway give-and-take with reporters. His pithy assessments of Senate dynamics and the particulars of legislation make him a valuable spokesman for the party's message. He is also a facilitator able to bring rival factions together on legislation, something he did to great effect when he was majority leader.

Lott was Senate Republican leader from June 1996 to December 2002, when his tendency to speak off the cuff got him into trouble. In a speech for retiring GOP Sen. Strom Thurmond of South Carolina, Lott praised Thurmond's segregationist campaign for president in 1948, saying, "I want to say this about my state: When Strom Thurmond ran for president, we voted for him. We're proud of it. And if the rest of the country had followed our lead, we wouldn't have had all these problems over all these years, either."

A political firestorm erupted. Lott repeatedly apologized, even making an appearance on Black Entertainment Television. But Republicans distanced themselves, and behind the scenes the White House maneuvered to replace him with Frist, an ally of President Bush. When Frist announced he would challenge Lott at a special GOP caucus to reconsider the party's leadership, Lott, his political options exhausted, stepped down. He felt betrayed by his colleagues and Bush. In his 2005 memoir, "Herding Cats: A Life in Politics," Lott recalls telling Bush, "You didn't help me when you could have."

To help cushion his fall, Frist gave Lott the chairmanship of the Rules and Administration Committee. Although the panel produces little legislation of its own, Lott used his influence to involve himself in negotiations on bills affecting lobbying and ethics rules, port security and offshore drilling.

In 2003, he joined Democrats opposing the Bush administration's rule allowing greater consolidation of media ownership. He backed GOP moderate Arlen Specter of Pennsylvania in 2004 for the chairmanship of the Judiciary Committee, defending him against social conservatives who objected to his views on abortion. Lott worked with moderates on the 2004 overhaul of the intelligence agencies, whipping votes and helping to settle disputes.

Although he voted the party line less often, he remained a committed conservative. He favored the "nuclear option" on judges — the GOP effort to change the rules to quash Democratic filibusters of conservative nominees. And he opposed the 2003 Medicare prescription drug bill as too expensive, only reluctantly casting the deciding vote preventing Democrats from killing it.

An institutionalist and fierce advocate for the Senate, Lott joined then Speaker J. Dennis Hastert of Illinois in objecting to the Federal Bureau of Investigation's raid on a congressional office in 2006 during a corruption probe of Democratic Rep. William J. Jefferson of Louisiana. Lott insisted that Jefferson's papers be returned and that the FBI notify the sergeant at arms of future raids. "We need to be sure we don't allow a situation where some future administration could use it for intimidation, pilfering through our papers and such," Lott said. "You may say that it wouldn't happen, but you never know."

After Hurricane Katrina laid waste to the Gulf Coast in 2005, wiping out his beachfront Pascagoula home along the way, Lott worked tirelessly to squeeze rebuilding money out of Congress. He joined forces with his Mississippi colleague and longtime rival, Thad Cochran, Appropriations Committee chairman at the time, and Louisiana's two senators, and they muscled through the Senate a $29 billion bill for rebuilding levees, schools and roads. The bill was almost $12 billion more than Bush's request.

Lott also went to war against the insurance industry, which was refusing to pay claims from many Gulf Coast homeowners. Lott sued his own insurance company, and in 2007 he testified before the Senate Judiciary Committee as it began weighing legislation to strip away the insurance industry's exemption from federal antitrust laws. "The good Lord made sure I lost my house so I could feel the pain of everybody else," Lott said.

Lott, the son of a shipyard worker, has been a political animal at least since his days at the University of Mississippi, where he was a cheerleader and president of the Interfraternity Council.

He came to Washington in 1968 as the top aide to House Rules Committee Chairman William M. Colmer, a Mississippi Democrat. When Colmer retired in 1972, Lott switched parties and ran as a Republican to succeed him. He won with 55 percent of the vote against Democratic state Sen. Ben Stone and was easily re-elected seven times. In 1981, he became the first House Republican whip from the deep South.

When Democrat John C. Stennis retired in 1988 after 41 years in the Senate, Lott was elected with 54 percent over Democratic Rep. Wayne Dowdy. Lott arrived on the Capitol's north side with a wave of aggressive conservatives moving over from the House who were eager to push a more overtly conservative agenda in the clubby Senate. Lott won election as Republican Conference secretary in 1993, and two years later he ousted the more moderate Alan K. Simpson of Wyoming to become whip.

Eighteen months after that, when Majority Leader Bob Dole resigned to focus on his 1996 presidential campaign, Lott sought the top job, vowing more aggressive leadership. His opponent was his long-abiding competitor, Cochran, the state's senior senator. The party voted for Lott, 44-8.

As majority leader, he often tried to cut deals with then Democratic Leader Tom Daschle of South Dakota to keep legislation moving. A single-minded focus on forcing bills to passage, and a sometimes dictatorial approach, created tensions in the party. Lott's threat of retribution against those who strayed on Bush's first tax cut proposal backfired badly. Moderate James M. Jeffords of Vermont quit the GOP in a huff, became an independent and sided with Democrats, handing them control of the Senate in June 2001.

Lott considered retiring at the close of the 109th Congress; among other things, he worried about his family finances after the loss of his Pascagoula home. But he felt an obligation to help his state recover from Hurricane Katrina. In December 2005, as he and his wife, Patricia, were celebrating their 42nd wedding anniversary, she observed that her husband was unusually quiet. "You've changed your mind, haven't you?" she said. He admitted that he wanted to run for re-election in 2006. He won handily.

KEY VOTES

2006

- Yes Confirm Samuel A. Alito Jr. to the Supreme Court
- Yes Allow consideration of a bill to establish a $140 billion trust fund to compensate victims of asbestos exposure
- Yes Extend tax cuts for two years at a cost of $70 billion over five years
- No Overhaul immigration policy with border security, enforcement and guest worker program
- Yes Allow consideration of a bill to permanently repeal the estate tax
- No Urge President Bush to begin troop withdrawals from Iraq in 2006
- Yes Lift President Bush's restrictions on stem cell research funding
- Yes Authorize military tribunals for suspected terrorists

2005

- Yes Curb class action lawsuits by shifting them from state to federal courts
- Yes Allow confirmation vote on Priscilla R. Owen to the U.S. Court of Appeals for the 5th Circuit
- Yes Oppose mandatory emissions limits and block recognition of global warming as a threat
- Yes Approve free-trade pact with five Central American countries
- Yes Pass energy policy overhaul favored by President Bush emphasizing domestic oil and gas production
- Yes Shield gunmakers from lawsuits when their products are used in crimes
- Yes Ban torture of prisoners in U.S. custody
- Yes Renew 16 provisions of the Patriot Act
- Yes Allow final vote on opening the Arctic National Wildlife Refuge to oil and gas exploration

CQ VOTE STUDIES

	PARTY UNITY		PRESIDENTIAL SUPPORT	
	Support	Oppose	Support	Oppose
2006	94%	6%	88%	12%
2005	95%	5%	93%	7%
2004	94%	6%	94%	6%
2003	98%	2%	97%	3%
2002	98%	2%	100%	0%
2001	98%	2%	96%	4%
2000	98%	2%	45%	55%
1999	97%	3%	32%	68%
1998	96%	4%	39%	61%
1997	94%	6%	56%	44%

INTEREST GROUPS

	AFL-CIO	ADA	CCUS	ACU
2006	15%	5%	92%	88%
2005	23%	5%	100%	91%
2004	17%	5%	100%	96%
2003	0%	10%	96%	89%
2002	15%	0%	100%	100%
2001	0%	0%	85%	96%
2000	0%	5%	93%	100%
1999	0%	0%	82%	96%
1998	0%	0%	94%	92%
1997	0%	5%	90%	72%

Rep. Roger Wicker (R)

CAPITOL OFFICE
225-4306
roger.wicker@mail.house.gov
www.house.gov/wicker
2350 Rayburn 20515-2401; fax 225-3549

COMMITTEES
Appropriations

RESIDENCE
Tupelo

BORN
July 5, 1951, Pontotoc, Miss.

RELIGION
Southern Baptist

FAMILY
Wife, Gayle Wicker; three children

EDUCATION
U. of Mississippi, B.A. 1973 (political science & journalism), J.D. 1975

MILITARY SERVICE
Air Force, 1976-80; Air Force Reserve, 1980-2004

CAREER
County public defender; lawyer; congressional aide

POLITICAL HIGHLIGHTS
Miss. Senate, 1988-94

ELECTION RESULTS

2006 GENERAL		
Roger Wicker (R)	95,098	65.9%
James K. "Ken" Hurt (D)	49,174	34.1%
2006 PRIMARY		
Roger Wicker (R)		unopposed
2004 GENERAL		
Roger Wicker (R)	219,328	78.9%
Barbara Dale Washer (REF)	58,256	21.1%

PREVIOUS WINNING PERCENTAGES
2002 (71%); 2000 (70%); 1998 (67%); 1996 (68%); 1994 (63%)

Elected 1994; 7th term

In 12 years in Congress, Wicker has gone from revolutionary to comfortable insider. The former president of the historic Republican Class of '94 prefers the quiet, unseen work in the trenches of the Appropriations Committee where he can provide for his district.

Like his compatriots from that era, Wicker is adjusting to life in the minority for the first time in the 110th Congress (2007-08). It may be easier on him than on some others; members of the clubby Appropriations panel take a mutual back-scratching approach that provides something for everyone at the end of the day, regardless of party affiliation.

With the help of Mississippi Republican Sen. Trent Lott, Wicker has had some success turning his impoverished state into a magnet for high-tech defense jobs by sending millions of dollars back home to encourage research, provide tax breaks and build infrastructure. His seats on the Appropriations panel's Defense and Military Construction-VA subcommittees are essential to that effort.

Businesses have relocated to the "Golden Triangle," the area between the towns of Columbus, Starkville and West Point. "Twenty years ago, who would have dreamed that aircraft plants would spring out of the forests and soybean fields of Mississippi?" Wicker says.

Wicker was a member of the Appropriations subcommittee that funds health, education and labor programs for six terms and took a special interest in beefing up spending on medical research. He was active in efforts to double the budget for the National Institutes of Health over five years, and he pressed for more spending to fight polio and muscular dystrophy.

Wicker also has been credited back home with diligence in nailing down reconstruction money for his state, which was hard-hit by hurricanes in 2005. In what is high praise for any local congressman, the Jackson Clarion-Ledger wrote, "Having Roger Wicker on the House Appropriations Committee and on the House negotiating team for the Katrina relief package was a major stroke for the state."

Such activity routinely puts Mississippi as one of the top 10 states for "pork per capita," according to the watchdog group Citizens Against Government Waste, but Wicker nonetheless regards himself as a fiscal conservative willing to rein in federal spending in other areas. In backing a proposed across-the-board spending cut in 1999, he said, "There are no winners and losers, and I don't know of any accounts that couldn't take a small hit."

Wicker has a strong record of loyalty to his party, his leaders and a conservative agenda. He rarely breaks with the GOP leadership on votes, siding with his party more than 95 percent of the time, and is consistently given high scores by the American Conservative Union. And he has remained a solid supporter of President Bush, even as Bush's popularity plunged before the 2006 election.

Wicker supported the president's decision to send additional troops to Iraq in early 2007. Just before Bush's State of the Union address in January, he shot an e-mail message to presidential adviser Karl Rove suggesting the president remind the nation that the troop surge was among the recommendations of the bipartisan Iraq Study Group.

He is proud to have been a leader of the Class of '94 and attended a 10th anniversary reunion intended to rekindle some of the intellectual fires of that election. But Wicker says he never viewed taking control of the House for the first time in 40 years as a revolution. "I didn't come to Washington to burn all the buildings down. We were all unfairly painted with the same brush," he said in 1998. "Most of us in our own ways are much more pragmatic and results-oriented."

Wicker scored one of his biggest legislative victories in the 108th Congress (2003-04). Appalled by the poor understanding most high school students have of American history, Wicker joined with Republican Sen. Lamar Alexander of Tennessee in a two-year effort to create special academies to teach history to both high school students and teachers. "If we expect future generations to appreciate what it means to be an American, we must teach them," he told the Clarion-Ledger. The bill was signed by Bush in 2004.

As Wicker gained seniority on Appropriations, he was close to becoming one of the so-called cardinals, the subcommittee chairmen who write the annual spending bills. But the changeover to a Democratic majority altered his future and thrust him into a minority role on the panel; he can still wheel and deal with other appropriators for federal projects, just not quite as successfully.

Raised in a political family — Wicker's father was a county attorney, a state senator and then a circuit judge for 20 years — Wicker organized the local teenage Republican club in high school. Although his father was a Democrat, as was virtually every officeholder in the South in those days, Wicker says, "There's not a dime's worth of difference in his philosophy of government and mine."

He was the first Republican ever to be elected student body president at Ole Miss. While still in college, he was a delegate to the 1972 Republican National Convention and came to know a young Trent Lott as Lott was making his first run for Congress. Wicker was in the Air Force ROTC and after law school served four years on active duty as both a prosecutor and defense counsel before going to work for Lott in Washington in 1980. He came home to practice law and, in 1987, won a state Senate seat. In Jackson, he helped write Mississippi's strict abortion law and push through an education overhaul that included a controversial school-choice provision.

When Democratic Rep. Jamie L. Whitten retired in 1994 after 53 years in the House — the longest service in the chamber's history — the conservative-minded 1st District was ripe for GOP picking. Wicker emphasized his legislative experience and edged out Grant Fox, a former Senate aide, for the Republican nomination. In November, he won with 63 percent of the vote, and he has not been seriously challenged since.

KEY VOTES

2006

- No Stop broadband companies from favoring select Internet traffic
- Yes Affirm U.S. commitment to war in Iraq and reject setting a withdrawal date for troops
- Yes Repeal requirement for bilingual ballots at the polls
- Yes Permit U.S. sale of civilian nuclear technology to India
- Yes Build a 700-mile fence on the U.S.-Mexico border to curb illegal crossings
- Yes Permit warrantless wiretaps of suspected terrorists

2005

- \+ Intervene in the life-support case of Terri Schiavo
- No Lift President Bush's restrictions on stem cell research funding
- No Prohibit FBI access to library and bookstore records
- Yes Approve free-trade pact with five Central American countries
- Yes Pass energy policy overhaul favored by President Bush emphasizing domestic oil and gas production
- Yes End mandatory preservation of habitat of endangered animal and plant species
- No Ban torture of prisoners in U.S. custody

CQ VOTE STUDIES

	PARTY UNITY		PRESIDENTIAL SUPPORT	
	Support	Oppose	Support	Oppose
2006	97%	3%	97%	3%
2005	97%	3%	84%	16%
2004	95%	5%	86%	14%
2003	97%	3%	96%	4%
2002	99%	1%	85%	15%

INTEREST GROUPS

	AFL-CIO	ADA	CCUS	ACU
2006	7%	0%	100%	88%
2005	20%	5%	93%	96%
2004	8%	0%	100%	87%
2003	0%	10%	97%	88%
2002	11%	0%	90%	100%

MISSISSIPPI 1

North — Tupelo, Southaven, Columbus

The northeastern Hill Country and rich farmland on the edge of the Delta region in northwestern Mississippi support an agricultural economy in the 1st, while manufacturing dominates in Lee County (Tupelo) and surrounding areas. Tupelo is a major producer of upholstered furniture, Columbus has some steel manufacturing and Oxford is home to the University of Mississippi.

The visitors center for the 444-mile Natchez Trace Parkway is in Tupelo, the 1st's largest city. The district also includes Mississippi's entire portion of the soon-to-be completed Interstate 22 (currently Highway 78), which will connect Memphis and Birmingham through Tupelo. In addition to infrastructure development, the area received good news in 2007 when Toyota announced that the company will open a new $1.3 billion manufacturing plant northwest of Tupelo in 2010. The city's status as the birthplace of Elvis Presley attracts hundreds of thousands of visitors each year, and generates millions of dollars in revenue.

DeSoto County, the district's most populous and the state's fastest-growing, is becoming a haven for residents who commute from the 1st's northwestern corner into Memphis over the Tennessee border. To the east, Marshall and Benton counties are home to many of the district's African-Americans, a group that makes up more than one-fourth of the 1st's population.

Democrats — including Jamie L. Whitten, the longest-serving House member — held the congressional seat for more than a century until Republicans took it in 1994. Voters here have gradually turned away from Democrats in federal elections, favoring GOP presidential candidates. George W. Bush won 62 percent of the 1st's 2004 presidential vote.

MAJOR INDUSTRY

Furniture, manufacturing, agriculture

MILITARY BASES

Columbus Air Force Base, 1,440 military, 1,707 civilian (2007)

CITIES

Tupelo, 34,211; Southaven, 28,977; Columbus, 25,944; Olive Branch, 21,054

NOTABLE

Tupelo hosts a biannual national furniture market that draws enough visitors to temporarily double the local population; Columbus lures tourists to its historic antebellum home tours.

Rep. Bennie Thompson (D)

CAPITOL OFFICE
225-5876
benniethompson.house.gov
2432 Rayburn 20515-2402; fax 225-5898

COMMITTEES
Homeland Security - chairman

RESIDENCE
Bolton

BORN
Jan. 28, 1948, Bolton, Miss.

RELIGION
Methodist

FAMILY
Wife, London Thompson; one child

EDUCATION
Tougaloo College, B.A. 1968 (political science); Jackson State College, M.S. 1972 (educational administration)

CAREER
Teacher

POLITICAL HIGHLIGHTS
Bolton Board of Aldermen, 1969-73; mayor of Bolton, 1973-79; Hinds County Board of Supervisors, 1980-93

ELECTION RESULTS

2006 GENERAL		
Bennie Thompson (D)	100,160	64.3%
Yvonne E. Brown (R)	55,672	35.7%
2006 PRIMARY		
Bennie Thompson (D)	58,941	64.4%
Chuck Espy (D)	31,906	34.8%
2004 GENERAL		
Bennie Thompson (D)	154,526	58.4%
Clinton B. LeSueur (R)	107,647	40.7%

PREVIOUS WINNING PERCENTAGES
2002 (55%); 2000 (65%); 1998 (71%); 1996 (60%); 1994 (54%); 1993 Special Runoff Election (55%)

Elected April 1993; 7th full term

Once a relatively obscure lawmaker with a focus on agriculture and rural development, Thompson has become a player on the national stage. He is the chairman of the Homeland Security Committee and his party's point man on emergency preparedness and response. His public statements often thoughtfully credit the work of other Democrats, a sure way to make friends in politics.

His career-making moment came in 2005, when he traded a seat on the Agriculture Committee for the senior Democratic slot on the relatively new Homeland Security panel. "I was No. 4 on Agriculture. I looked up [at more-senior members] and thought, 'They ain't going nowhere,' " he said. "I was convinced that Homeland Security was a major opportunity for me to serve as a ranking member on issues that are vitally important."

Early in the 110th Congress (2007-08), Thompson pushed through the House a bill calling for new regulations, and authorizing more than $6.1 billion over four years, for rail and mass transit security in the hope of protecting against an attack like the March 2004 commuter train bombings in Madrid. The House also passed a bill he cosponsored to create an office to further international cooperation in developing and using technology to fight terrorism. And he quickly saw House passage of his bill to implement recommendations of the Sept. 11 commission, though he was immediately criticized for not including more funding details in his rush to get the bill through. His response: "We'll work it out."

He wants to boost overall spending for homeland security, especially for local and state first-responders. When the administration proposed a 2008 budget that included cuts to first-responder programs, he said, "When 9/11 struck, it was the local firefighters, police, and [emergency medical technicians] who were on the front lines and risked their lives for their nation. Yet, year after year, the president has taken an ax to the resources that they need to protect us." During the 109th Congress (2005-06), he backed legislation to channel more first-responder funds to high-risk areas and he fought to ensure the bill included flood control levees, important in his state, as part of the definition of dams, which qualify for terrorism risk evaluations.

Homeland Security Secretary Michael Chertoff is bound to get more invitations to the Hill under Thompson's rule. When the GOP was in control, Thompson said, Chertoff had become "a stranger" to the panel, and he vowed greater oversight. "Time and time again this committee has requested information regarding the department's contracting decisions, hiring practices, emergency preparedness, and fraud, waste and abuse issues, and time and time again we are either ignored or given the runaround," Thompson said.

Thompson inherited some unresolved turf battles, particularly with the Transportation and Infrastructure Committee, chaired by Minnesota Democrat James L. Oberstar. Some of the jurisdictional differences came to light when the two panels' rail security bills reached the House floor in March 2007, but the chairmen reached a compromise.

His early experiences as a black politician in Mississippi and the makeup of his constituency — largely black, rural and poor — have made him a champion of civil rights and rural development, and an expert at maximizing opportunities that come his way. His first run for public office was in 1968, at age 20, to be an alderman in his hometown of Bolton. The town's whites didn't want a black man on the board, so they barred him from city hall. He got a court order to force them to back down and let him claim his seat.

Every now and then, he faces a primary challenge in his heavily Democratic district, so he keeps a high profile back home, maintaining six district offices, more than the average. And he brings home the bacon. During a 2006 flap over earmarks — the special projects that lawmakers tuck into appropriations bills to curry favor with voters — Thompson was criticized for setting aside nearly $1 million in federal funds for the Jackson Zoo.

Thompson's 2nd District is one of the poorest in the nation, and one of his goals is to secure more federal funding to improve the region's infrastructure, rural housing and health care. He has called for aggressive federal action to combat discrimination, particularly in the Agriculture Department's administration of federal farm and loan programs.

When home-state GOP Sen. Trent Lott lauded Strom Thurmond's segregationist 1948 presidential campaign, Thompson, the state's only black congressman, condemned the remarks and noted Lott had never sought him out in the years he's served in Congress. When conservatives question the need for affirmative action programs, he bristles. He once said, "For most of us who are over 45, we never had new textbooks in our community, we never had the opportunity to play in a public playground or swim in a public swimming pool, and so some of us take very seriously the notion of affirmative action, because this was the only opportunity that many of us ever received."

Born in 1948, Thompson was educated in segregated elementary and secondary schools. His father, a mechanic, died when he was in the 10th grade. His mother was a school teacher. At Tougaloo College, he met civil rights activist Fannie Lou Hamer, who inspired him to pursue politics. He graduated in 1968, the year he was elected an alderman in Bolton. Four years later, he was elected mayor of Bolton. At 32, he was elected to the board of supervisors for Hinds County, which includes the capital city, Jackson. His record led former President Bill Clinton to name Thompson as one of 100 "unsung African-Americans" at the 2004 opening of his presidential library.

He ran for the House in a 1993 special election after Rep. Mike Espy resigned to become Clinton's Agriculture secretary. Thompson triumphed in a runoff, with 55 percent of the vote. One of the candidates he defeated was Clarksdale Mayor Henry Espy, Mike Espy's brother.

In his 1994 bid for a full term, he won by 15 percentage points. His subsequent re-elections were by comfortable margins. In 2006, he faced a primary challenge from Henry Espy's son, Chuck. Touting the advantages of incumbency and raising three times as much money as Espy, Thompson once again prevailed in the family feud.

KEY VOTES

2006

- Yes Stop broadband companies from favoring select Internet traffic
- Yes Affirm U.S. commitment to war in Iraq and reject setting a withdrawal date for troops
- No Repeal requirement for bilingual ballots at the polls
- Yes Permit U.S. sale of civilian nuclear technology to India
- No Build a 700-mile fence on the U.S.-Mexico border to curb illegal crossings
- No Permit warrantless wiretaps of suspected terrorists

2005

- No Intervene in the life-support case of Terri Schiavo
- Yes Lift President Bush's restrictions on stem cell research funding
- Yes Prohibit FBI access to library and bookstore records
- No Approve free-trade pact with five Central American countries
- Yes Pass energy policy overhaul favored by President Bush emphasizing domestic oil and gas production
- Yes End mandatory preservation of habitat of endangered animal and plant species
- Yes Ban torture of prisoners in U.S. custody

CQ VOTE STUDIES

	PARTY UNITY		PRESIDENTIAL SUPPORT	
	Support	Oppose	Support	Oppose
2006	90%	10%	41%	59%
2005	93%	7%	17%	83%
2004	92%	8%	33%	67%
2003	94%	6%	25%	75%
2002	94%	6%	22%	78%

INTEREST GROUPS

	AFL-CIO	ADA	CCUS	ACU
2006	100%	90%	60%	30%
2005	87%	95%	52%	12%
2004	87%	85%	45%	8%
2003	100%	90%	43%	20%
2002	100%	90%	55%	8%

MISSISSIPPI 2

West central – Jackson, Mississippi Delta

Lying mostly west of Interstate 55 and north of Interstate 20, the 2nd combines most of Jackson — the state's capital and largest city — with Vicksburg and the nutrient-rich flatlands of the Mississippi Delta. North of Vicksburg, the road drops 15 feet in Issaquena County, marking the beginning of the Delta.

Agriculture is important both to the state and the district, and the 2nd supports catfish-raising, cotton, rice and soybeans. The cotton and rice crops, in particular, were damaged by Hurricane Katrina's high winds in 2005. The Delta's agricultural economy has promoted landowner/tenant relationships that have made the 2nd one of the nation's poorest districts, with a median income of slightly less than $27,000.

Aside from agriculture, the 2nd's economic underpinnings come from a variety of sources. Successes include Vicksburg, where a mixture of tourism, casinos and a Mississippi River port have fostered local prosperity. A $100 million ethanol plant that will produce 60 million gallons annually also will call Vicksburg home, one of the largest such plants in the South. Outside Canton, a Nissan assembly plant north of Jackson employs approximately 4,000 workers.

Government, service and small-scale manufacturing jobs have kept unemployment in check in Jackson. The city is working to revitalize its downtown, with new convention and conference centers scheduled to open in 2008, and Jackson also hosts the State Fair and annual rodeo.

Although some low-income white residents live in the 2nd, it is the only black-majority district in a state with the highest percentage of black residents in the nation. Despite a Republican foothold in some areas near Jackson and to the northeast, the 2nd was the only Mississippi district to favor John Kerry in the 2004 presidential election, giving him 58 percent of its vote.

MAJOR INDUSTRY

Agriculture, government, casinos

CITIES

Jackson (pt.), 152,424; Greenville, 41,633; Vicksburg, 26,407

NOTABLE

Norris Bookbinding, based in Greenwood, is the largest Bible rebinding plant in the nation.

Rep. Charles W. "Chip" Pickering Jr. (R)

CAPITOL OFFICE
225-5031
www.house.gov/pickering
229 Cannon 20515-2403; fax 225-5797

COMMITTEES
Energy & Commerce

RESIDENCE
Laurel

BORN
Aug. 10, 1963, Laurel, Miss.

RELIGION
Baptist

FAMILY
Wife, Leisha Jane Pickering; five children

EDUCATION
Mississippi College, attended 1981-82; U. of Mississippi, B.A. 1986 (business administration); Baylor U., M.B.A. 1989

CAREER
Congressional aide; U.S. Agriculture Department official

POLITICAL HIGHLIGHTS
No previous office

ELECTION RESULTS

2006 GENERAL		
Charles W. Pickering Jr. (R)	125,421	77.7%
Jim Giles (I)	25,999	16.1%
Lamonica L. Magee (REF)	10,060	6.2%
2006 PRIMARY		
Charles W. Pickering Jr. (R)		unopposed
2004 GENERAL		
Charles W. Pickering Jr. (R)	234,874	80.1%
Jim Giles (I)	40,426	13.8%
Lamonica L. Magee (REF)	18,068	6.2%

PREVIOUS WINNING PERCENTAGES
2002 (64%); 2000 (73%); 1998 (85%); 1996 (61%)

Elected 1996; 6th term

A less-polished politician than Pickering might have been knocked off stride by an unexpected film appearance in which his religious convictions were held up to scorn by a popular comedian.

Instead, the boyish-looking scion of one of Mississippi's leading political families took his 2006 cameo in "Borat: Cultural Learnings of America for Make Benefit Glorious Nation of Kazakhstan" perfectly in stride, offering a trademark aw-shucks smile and a chuckle when asked about the short clip of him addressing a Pentecostal revival. His spokesman said he has no plans to see the comically vulgar movie.

Now entering his second decade in the House, Pickering has proved himself an effective legislator and a deft political operator. He played a crucial role in lobbying fellow Republicans to support the 2003 Medicare prescription-drug law as party leaders held the vote on the measure open for three hours to win its passage, even chasing then Rep. C.L. "Butch" Otter down a hallway so Speaker J. Dennis Hastert could make a last-ditch pitch.

But he has, at times, appeared frustrated by the geriatric nature of the chamber, where it can be hard for talented junior lawmakers to make a mark commensurate with their abilities. A long House career may be even less attractive to Pickering if Republicans remain in the minority, where his conservative views on social and economic issues are not likely to get much consideration from Democratic leaders.

But Pickering is a strong bet to win a seat in the Senate when one of Mississippi's long-serving Republican senators, either Trent Lott or Thad Cochran, retires, though it could take some time. Lott — Pickering's Capitol Hill mentor — abandoned plans to retire after the 109th Congress (2005-06) and later managed a stunning political resurrection by reclaiming the No. 2 leadership spot as Republican whip after being knocked out from the GOP's top spot late in 2002. Meanwhile, at the start of the 110th Congress (2007-08), Cochran still had not committed to running for a sixth term in 2008.

Pickering's considerable strategic skills and ties to multiple generations of the state's political elite make him an important potential ally for those seeking the presidency. He served as co-chairman of George W. Bush's presidential campaigns in Mississippi in 2000 and 2004. He decided early in the process to back Arizona Sen. John McCain in the 2008 GOP primary, lending McCain a degree of legitimacy with state religious conservatives.

But Pickering's influence proved insufficient to overcome the objections Democrats had when his father, Charles W. Pickering Sr., was nominated by President Bush to a seat on the 5th U.S. Circuit Court of Appeals. The elder Pickering's record on civil rights helped sink his nomination in both 2002 and 2003, leading Bush to give him a temporary "recess" appointment while Congress was on break in 2004.

Throughout his career, Pickering has been a reliable Republican vote. He vigorously promoted the Bush tax cuts and embraced the president's call for a constitutional amendment defining marriage as the union of a man and a woman. In 2004, he cosponsored the House version of the amendment. "Protecting the institution of marriage guards the very social fabric of our country," he said. "The encouragement of marriage will be fruitless if the very foundation of marriage is destroyed."

From his seat on the Energy and Commerce Committee, Pickering has been able to use the expertise he developed as the telecommunications aide for Lott. He was one of Lott's pivotal staff players during the debate over the overhaul of telecommunications law in the 104th Congress (1995-96).

When he ran for Congress in 1996, a top campaign benefactor was then WorldCom head Bernard J. Ebbers, who is now serving a 25-year prison term for his involvement in a massive accounting fraud. Pickering later said his advocacy in behalf of Worldcom was simply that of an official doing his best to promote a local company that provided jobs for his constituents.

In 2002, the big telecommunications fight was over whether to allow the four regional Bell companies to offer broadband Internet services over telephone lines without first opening their local markets to competitors, an important requirement of 1996 law. MCI WorldCom, then a long-distance company headquartered near Pickering's district, opposed the bill, and Pickering sided with them. He argued that it would kill competition in the telecommunications market. Though the House easily passed a bill, the Senate did not act.

Pickering, who says he is a seventh-generation Mississippian, comes from a prominent Jones County family, of which his father remains the patriarch. But he says he "kind of rebelled against" politics as a youth. He went to small, Baptist-run Mississippi College for three semesters, then worked for a year on the family dairy and catfish farm before heading to the University of Mississippi to study business. After college, Pickering was a trailblazer in establishing a Baptist missionary presence beyond the Iron Curtain, in Hungary. He returned to another Baptist institution, Baylor University, for a master's degree with an emphasis on international business.

There is a tradition in Mississippi of congressional aides moving into elective office; Lott did so, as did 1st District Republican Rep. Roger Wicker. So when Democrat G.V. "Sonny" Montgomery retired, Pickering jumped at the chance to join that group. His political contacts and well-known name propelled him to first place in the nine-candidate 1996 GOP primary, and he won the runoff against former state Rep. Bill Crawford. In November, Pickering took 61 percent of the vote against Democrat John Arthur Eaves Jr., a lawyer who also grew up in a political family.

Because Mississippi lost a seat in post-2000 census reapportionment, a federal court redistricting plan forced Pickering into a race against Democrat Ronnie Shows, a four-year House veteran. The district lines favored the GOP and Pickering won by 29 percentage points — the most lopsided of the four general-election matchups between incumbents in 2002. After a legal challenge to the redistricting plan that went all the way to the Supreme Court, the 3rd retains its GOP advantage, and Pickering won his last two elections handily, with no Democratic opposition.

KEY VOTES

2006

- No Stop broadband companies from favoring select Internet traffic
- Yes Affirm U.S. commitment to war in Iraq and reject setting a withdrawal date for troops
- Yes Repeal requirement for bilingual ballots at the polls
- Yes Permit U.S. sale of civilian nuclear technology to India
- Yes Build a 700-mile fence on the U.S.-Mexico border to curb illegal crossings
- Yes Permit warrantless wiretaps of suspected terrorists

2005

- Yes Intervene in the life-support case of Terri Schiavo
- No Lift President Bush's restrictions on stem cell research funding
- No Prohibit FBI access to library and bookstore records
- Yes Approve free-trade pact with five Central American countries
- Yes Pass energy policy overhaul favored by President Bush emphasizing domestic oil and gas production
- Yes End mandatory preservation of habitat of endangered animal and plant species
- Yes Ban torture of prisoners in U.S. custody

CQ VOTE STUDIES

	PARTY UNITY		PRESIDENTIAL SUPPORT	
	Support	Oppose	Support	Oppose
2006	92%	8%	97%	3%
2005	94%	6%	82%	18%
2004	94%	6%	85%	15%
2003	95%	5%	96%	4%
2002	97%	3%	85%	15%

INTEREST GROUPS

	AFL-CIO	ADA	CCUS	ACU
2006	14%	0%	100%	84%
2005	29%	10%	92%	92%
2004	20%	5%	100%	92%
2003	0%	5%	97%	83%
2002	11%	0%	90%	100%

MISSISSIPPI 3

East central to southwest – Jackson suburbs

The strongly Republican 3rd picks up Jackson's northeast corner and some of its mostly white northern and eastern suburbs as it sprawls across 28 counties, moving from Oktibbeha and Noxubee counties in the east central part of the state to the Mississippi River in the southwestern corner. This southwest portion was in Hurricane Katrina's path in 2005, and the storm's heavy rain and wind caused significant damage to the district's substantial timber crop.

Timber is dominant in the 3rd, but health care and defense also are important industries, especially in Meridian, home to several medical centers and a Naval Air Station. Peavey Electronics, one of the world's largest manufacturers of guitars and amplifiers, also is based in Meridian. The district's white-collar workers — the 3rd has the state's highest percentage at 57 percent — provide economic stability.

Elsewhere in the district, small rural communities, filled with poultry and dairy farms, are prevalent, and Rankin County's rapid growth over the past two decades has been spurred by an influx of nearby Jackson residents moving to the suburbs. Pearl, in Rankin County, is now home to a minor league baseball team and its $25 million stadium, which, along with a nearby $30 million Bass Pro Shop outdoor store, anchors an entertainment complex that brings tourist revenue to the area. Tourism also is an economic engine in Natchez, on the Mississippi River, which attracts nearly 150,000 visitors annually to its antebellum homes and dockside casinos. Mississippi State University, the state's largest university, is located in Starkville at the district's northeastern tip.

Republicans now dominate the federal politics of the 3rd, as Democrats did for most of the 20th century, and George W. Bush took 65 percent of the district's 2004 presidential vote.

MAJOR INDUSTRY
Timber, poultry, agriculture, defense

MILITARY BASES
Naval Air Station Meridian, 2,200 military, 1,500 civilian (2007)

CITIES
Meridian, 39,968; Jackson (pt.), 31,832; Pearl, 21,961; Starkville, 21,869

NOTABLE
Mississippi State University is home to a large collection of papers from author and alumnus John Grisham.

Rep. Gene Taylor (D)

CAPITOL OFFICE
225-5772
www.house.gov/genetaylor
2269 Rayburn 20515-2404; fax 225-7074

COMMITTEES
Armed Services
(Seapower & Expeditionary Forces - chairman)
Transportation & Infrastructure

RESIDENCE
Bay St. Louis

BORN
Sept. 17, 1953, New Orleans, La.

RELIGION
Roman Catholic

FAMILY
Wife, Margaret Taylor; three children

EDUCATION
Tulane U., B.A. 1976 (history & political science); U. of Southern Mississippi, Gulf Park, attended 1978-80 (business & economics)

MILITARY SERVICE
Coast Guard Reserve, 1971-84

CAREER
Box company sales representative

POLITICAL HIGHLIGHTS
Bay St. Louis City Council, 1981-83; Miss. enate, 1983-89; Democratic nominee for U.S. House, 1988

ELECTION RESULTS

2006 GENERAL		
Gene Taylor (D)	110,996	79.8%
Randy McDonnell (R)	28,117	20.2%
2006 PRIMARY		
Gene Taylor (D)		unopposed
2004 GENERAL		
Gene Taylor (D)	179,979	64.2%
Michael Lott (R)	96,740	34.5%
Tracy Lou O'Hara Hill (REF)	3,663	1.3%

PREVIOUS WINNING PERCENTAGES
2002 (75%); 2000 (79%); 1998 (78%); 1996 (58%); 1994 (60%); 1992 (63%); 1990 (81%); 1989 Special Runoff Election (65%)

Elected October 1989; 9th full term

Taylor is a conservative Democrat known for his leadership on defense issues as well as his constant willingness to defy the party and go his own way on issues ranging from the Iraq War and immigration to stem cell research and same-sex marriage.

And he does not do so quietly. On no other issue has that been more apparent than the aftermath and cleanup from Hurricane Katrina, which ravaged his Gulf Coast district, destroyed his home and has consumed his personal and official energies for the past couple of years.

Soon after the storm made landfall on Aug. 29, 2005, Taylor went after the Federal Emergency Management Agency (FEMA), earning the lasting enmity of its deposed head, Michael D. Brown, with whom he exchanged angry words during a hearing a month after the storm. Taylor accused Brown of being ignorant of the situation and woefully unprepared to respond. "You get an F-minus in my book," he said. A year later, Brown fired back in an interview with Playboy magazine,"For that little twerp to claim I didn't understand death and suffering, he can just bite me for all I care." Taylor retorted, "Had I known before the hearing that he was up in Baton Rouge ordering steaks on his government credit card at the same time the people of South Mississippi were resorting to police-sanctioned looting to feed themselves, I would have done more than just verbally kick his butt."

A dispute with GOP Rep. Tom Price of Georgia during floor debate on a 2007 bill extending certain housing voucher programs led Republicans to invoke a rarely used rule to try to remove Taylor from the debate. Objecting to a Price amendment, Taylor told him he should "have the decency" to visit Mississippi "before you hold them to a standard that you would never hold your own people to and you failed to hold the Bush administration to." The chairman ruled Taylor had impugned Price's character, but members voted to allow him to stay.

For Taylor, the housing issue was personal. His Bay St. Louis house, more than 100 years old and 14 feet above sea level, was washed away when Katrina struck. Just hours before, Taylor and his family had driven 16 miles inland to stay at his brother's house. He had brought only a Rastafarian wig his daughter had brought him from her honeymoon in Jamaica, two pairs of shorts, three t-shirts, a flashlight and a cordless drill.

Next to FEMA on Taylor's enemies list is the insurance industry, which refused to cover damage to thousands of Gulf Coast homes, including Taylor's, claiming that flooding — not wind — was responsible. Taylor and GOP Sen. Trent Lott, also of Mississippi and who also lost his home, both have sued State Farm. "They told me I had not $1 worth [of wind damage] in a place that had eight hours of up to 100-mile-per-hour winds," Taylor said. Taylor's attorney is Lott's brother-in-law, one of the nation's leading trial attorneys.

In 2006, Taylor won adoption of an amendment to a flood insurance bill mandating a federal investigation into whether insurers inappropriately ascribed Katrina damages to flooding instead of excessive wind. Lott inserted similar language in another bill.

Though Katrina has dominated Taylor's life, he has continued to work on defense issues. The fiscal 2007 defense authorization bill included a Taylor provision requiring all U.S. military vehicles operating outside compounds in Iraq and Afghanistan to carry equipment to jam deadly remotely detonated "improvised explosive devices." A foe of the base closure and realignment process, he fought to protect military installations in his district from the 2005 round of closures, but the Naval Station in Pascagoula was on the hit list.

Taylor's voting record is among the most conservative of any House Democrat. In 1998, he was the only Democrat who voted in favor of all House articles of impeachment against President Bill Clinton. In 2006, he was the only Democrat to vote for four amendments Southern Republicans offered to a bill extending the landmark 1965 Voting Rights Act. A year earlier, he sided with the GOP to support a punitive immigration bill and against easing curbs on embryonic stem cell research. He also voted for constitutional amendments to ban same-sex marriage and flag desecration. In March 2007, he was one of 14 Democrats to oppose a Democratic war spending bill that included a timeline for withdrawal of troops from Iraq.

But at the start of the 110th Congress (2007-08), he showed a bit of party unity when he supported Nancy Pelosi of California for Speaker, rather than putting up a more conservative nominee as he had in the past.

Taylor sticks with his party on trade policy, arguing that working people are hurt by trade liberalization while the monied establishment benefits. He has voted against every significant trade law enacted during his tenure, including the 1993 North American Free Trade Agreement, the 2002 legislation restoring the president's fast-track trade negotiating authority, and the 2005 Central American Free Trade Agreement. He also has voted against most of Bush's big tax cuts.

Observing him only in public, one could assume Taylor is a humorless man. "If he was like he appears on TV, none of us would work for the S.O.B.," an aide once said. But in private, Taylor is an easygoing, fun-loving guy.

He went to Catholic schools and recalls the nuns wheeling in a television set so students could watch the inauguration of the first Catholic president, John F. Kennedy. Taylor was only 7 years old, but he recalls that moment as sparking his political interests. His father served with John D. Dingell of Michigan during World War II, and Dingell — now the most senior member of the House — later provided support for Taylor's first House bid.

Taylor majored in political science and history at Tulane and then became a salesman for a box company. In 1981, he won a seat on the Bay St. Louis City Council, and later served six years in the state Senate.

The national Democratic Party had little interest in Taylor when he sought the seat Lott left open in 1988 to run for the Senate. But he surprised them with a strong, 45 percent showing against Republican Larkin Smith. Less than a year later, Smith died in a plane crash. In the special-election campaign, Taylor prevailed over Lott's longtime aide Tom Anderson Jr. and Democratic Attorney General Mike Moore. He has won with ease since.

KEY VOTES

2006

- Yes Stop broadband companies from favoring select Internet traffic
- Yes Affirm U.S. commitment to war in Iraq and reject setting a withdrawal date for troops
- Yes Repeal requirement for bilingual ballots at the polls
- No Permit U.S. sale of civilian nuclear technology to India
- Yes Build a 700-mile fence on the U.S.-Mexico border to curb illegal crossings
- Yes Permit warrantless wiretaps of suspected terrorists

2005

- ? Intervene in the life-support case of Terri Schiavo
- No Lift President Bush's restrictions on stem cell research funding
- Yes Prohibit FBI access to library and bookstore records
- No Approve free-trade pact with five Central American countries
- No Pass energy policy overhaul favored by President Bush emphasizing domestic oil and gas production
- Yes End mandatory preservation of habitat of endangered animal and plant species
- Yes Ban torture of prisoners in U.S. custody

CQ VOTE STUDIES

	PARTY UNITY		PRESIDENTIAL SUPPORT	
	Support	Oppose	Support	Oppose
2006	73%	27%	60%	40%
2005	65%	35%	45%	55%
2004	67%	33%	45%	55%
2003	71%	29%	53%	47%
2002	63%	37%	45%	55%

INTEREST GROUPS

	AFL-CIO	ADA	CCUS	ACU
2006	71%	40%	53%	68%
2005	54%	60%	59%	60%
2004	67%	60%	52%	54%
2003	87%	65%	47%	68%
2002	67%	50%	45%	48%

MISSISSIPPI 4
Southeast – Gulf Coast, Hattiesburg

Mississippi's only Gulf Coast district, the conservative 4th suffered when Hurricane Katrina landed in 2005, bringing severe damage to coastal towns. Some, such as Biloxi and Gulfport, regrouped relatively quickly, while others, like Waveland and Pass Christian, struggled into 2007.

Biloxi's economy is driven by casino resorts, but hurricane damage forced the city's casinos to close. Most reopened by the end of 2005 or in 2006, and some now have plans to build new gaming facilities. The winds, rain and surge also destroyed homes and communities here, as well as fishing reefs in the Mississippi Sound that supported Biloxi's sportfishing industry. Local and state officials are implementing plans for several mixed-use developments to help attract residents and revenue.

About 8,500 homes in Gulfport were destroyed or damaged by the storm, and the city lost roughly $4 million in property taxes. Dozens of municipal buildings also were destroyed, including a veterans hospital and the Armed Forces Retirement Home. Congress designated money to rebuild the home, but gave ownership of the hospital's land to the city. Harbor redevelopment plans include restoring piers and boat launches, adding restaurants and retail areas, and renovating Jones Park. Adding to the coast's economic instability, Naval Station Pascagoula was ordered closed as part of the 2005 BRAC round. Farther north, Hattiesburg experienced an estimated 40 percent increase in population following the hurricane as residents fled inland, despite the fact that many of the city's homes, businesses and roads were destroyed as well.

A Democrat holds the 4th's U.S. House seat, and residents will support conservatives of either party. George W. Bush had his best Mississippi showing here (68 percent of the vote) in the 2004 presidential election.

MAJOR INDUSTRY
Military, shipbuilding, casinos

MILITARY BASES
Keesler Air Force Base, 7,591 military, 3,632 civilian (2006); Naval Construction Training Center Gulfport, 3,800 military, 1,000 civilian (2007); Naval Oceanographic Office, 104 military, 996 civilian (2006)

CITIES
Gulfport, 71,127; Biloxi, 50,644; Hattiesburg, 44,779; Pascagoula, 26,200

NOTABLE
Black Creek is the state's only National Scenic River.

MISSOURI

Gov. Matt Blunt (R)

First elected: 2004
Length of term: 4 years
Term expires: 1/09
Salary: $120,087
Phone: (573) 751-3222

Residence: Springfield
Born: Nov. 20, 1970; Strafford, Mo.
Religion: Baptist
Family: Wife, Melanie Blunt; one child
Education: U.S. Naval Academy, B.S. 1993 (history)
Military service: Navy, 1993-98; Naval Reserve, 1998-present
Career: Coffee company market researcher
Political highlights: Mo. House, 1999-2001; Mo. secretary of state, 2001-05

Election results:

2004 GENERAL		
Matt Blunt (R)	1,382,419	50.8%
Claire McCaskill (D)	1,301,442	47.9%

Lt. Gov. Peter Kinder (R)

First elected: 2004
Length of term: 4 years
Term expires: 1/09
Salary: $77,184
Phone: (573) 751-4727

LEGISLATURE

General Assembly: January-May

Senate: 34 members, 4-year terms
2007 ratios: 21 R, 13 D; 27 men, 7 women
Salary: $31,351
Phone: (573) 751-3766

House: 163 members, 2-year terms
2007 ratios: 92 R, 71 D; 132 men, 31 women
Salary: $31,351
Phone: (573) 751-3659

TERM LIMITS

Governor: 2 terms
Senate: 2 terms
House: 4 terms

URBAN STATISTICS

CITY	POPULATION
Kansas City	441,545
St. Louis	348,189
Springfield	151,580
Independence	113,288
Columbia	84,531

REGISTERED VOTERS

Voters do not register by party.

POPULATION

2006 population (est.)	5,842,713
2000 population	5,595,211
1990 population	5,117,073
Percent change (1990-2000)	+9.3%
Rank among states (2006)	18
Median age	36.1
Born in state	67.8%
Foreign born	2.7%
Violent crime rate	490/100,000
Poverty level	11.7%
Federal workers	57,783
Military	38,091

ELECTIONS

STATE ELECTION OFFICIAL
(573) 751-2301
DEMOCRATIC PARTY
(573) 636-5241
REPUBLICAN PARTY
(573) 636-3146

MISCELLANEOUS

Web: www.state.mo.us
Capital: Jefferson City

U.S. CONGRESS

Senate: 1 Democrat, 1 Republican
House: 5 Republicans, 4 Democrats

2000 Census Statistics by District

DIST.	2004 VOTE FOR PRESIDENT BUSH	KERRY	WHITE	BLACK	ASIAN	HISP	MEDIAN INCOME	WHITE COLLAR	BLUE COLLAR	SERVICE INDUSTRY	OVER 64	UNDER 18	COLLEGE EDUCATION	RURAL	SQ. MILES
1	25%	75%	46%	50%	2%	1%	$36,314	62%	21%	17%	14%	26%	22%	1%	217
2	60	40	93	2	2	1	$61,416	71	18	11	11	27	38	8	1,248
3	43	57	86	9	2	2	$41,091	60	24	15	13	25	23	13	1,247
4	64	35	92	3	1	2	$34,541	51	33	16	14	25	16	60	14,544
5	40	59	66	24	1	6	$38,311	62	23	15	13	26	23	4	512
6	57	42	92	3	1	2	$41,225	59	27	15	13	25	21	34	13,032
7	67	32	93	1	1	3	$32,929	55	29	16	14	24	19	41	5,480
8	63	36	92	4	0	1	$27,865	48	36	16	16	25	12	60	18,681
9	59	41	93	4	1	1	$36,693	54	31	15	13	25	20	54	13,925
STATE	53	46	84	11	1	2	$37,934	58	27	15	14	26	22	31	68,886
U.S.	50.7	48.3	69	12	4	13	$41,994	60	25	15	12	26	24	21	3,537,438

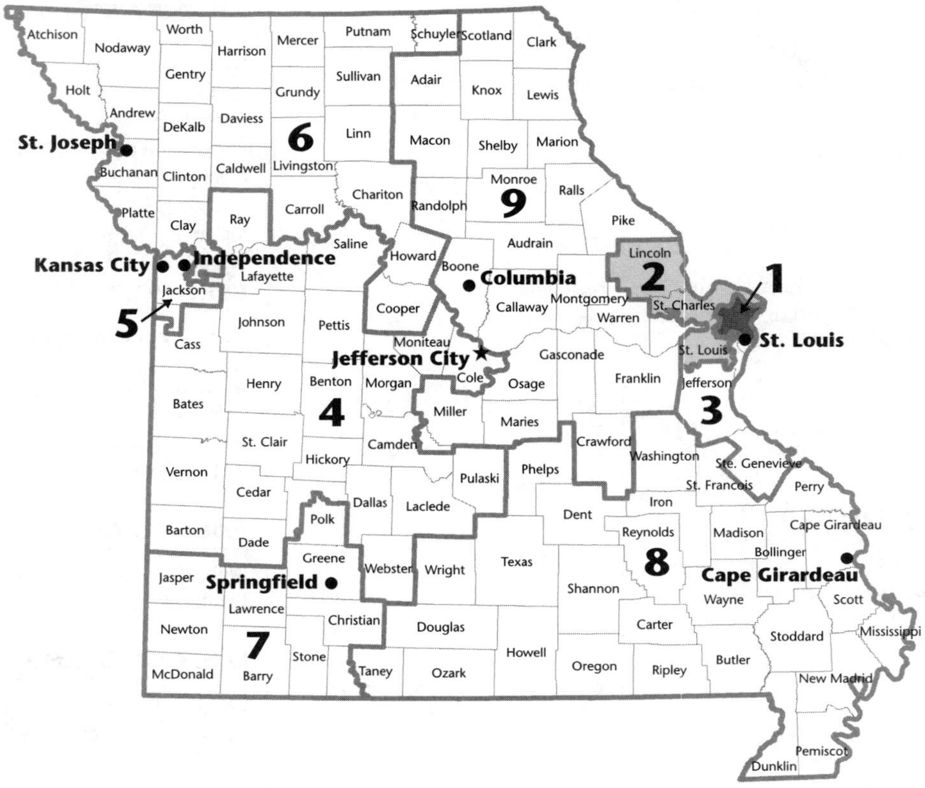
Atchison
Nodaway
Worth
Harrison
Mercer
Putnam
Schuyler
Scotland
Clark
Holt
Gentry
Grundy
Sullivan
Adair
Knox
Lewis
Andrew
DeKalb
Daviess
6
Linn
Macon
Shelby
Marion
St. Joseph
Buchanan
Clinton
Caldwell
Livingston
Chariton
Monroe
Ralls
Platte
Clay
Ray
Carroll
Randolph
9
Pike
Saline
Audrain
Lincoln
Kansas City
Independence
Howard
Boone
2
1
Lafayette
Columbia
Jackson
Cooper
Callaway
Montgomery
St. Charles
5
Johnson
Pettis
Warren
St. Louis
Cass
Moniteau
Jefferson City
Gasconade
Henry
Benton
Morgan
Cole
Osage
Franklin
Jefferson
Bates
4
Miller
3
Maries
St. Clair
Camden
Crawford
Washington
Ste. Genevieve
Vernon
Hickory
Phelps
Pulaski
St. Francois
Perry
Cedar
Dallas
Laclede
Iron
Barton
Polk
Dent
Madison
Cape Girardeau
Dade
Reynolds
Bollinger
Greene
8
Jasper
Springfield
Webster
Wright
Texas
Cape Girardeau
Shannon
Wayne
Scott
Lawrence
Newton
Christian
Douglas
Carter
Stoddard
Mississippi
7
Stone
Howell
Oregon
Ripley
Butler
McDonald
Barry
Taney
Ozark
New Madrid
Pemiscot
Dunklin

Sen. Christopher S. Bond (R)

CAPITOL OFFICE
224-5721
bond.senate.gov
274 Russell 20510-2503; fax 224-8149

COMMITTEES
Appropriations
Environment & Public Works
Small Business & Entrepreneurship
Select Intelligence - vice chairman

RESIDENCE
Mexico

BORN
March 6, 1939, St. Louis, Mo.

RELIGION
Presbyterian

FAMILY
Wife, Linda Bond; one child

EDUCATION
Princeton U., A.B. 1960; U. of Virginia, LL.B. 1963

CAREER
Lawyer

POLITICAL HIGHLIGHTS
Republican nominee for U.S. House, 1968; Mo. auditor, 1971-73; governor, 1973-77; defeated for re-election as governor, 1976; governor, 1981-85

ELECTION RESULTS

2004 GENERAL		
Christopher S. Bond (R)	1,518,089	56.1%
Nancy Farmer (D)	1,158,261	42.8%
2004 PRIMARY		
Christopher S. Bond (R)	541,998	88.1%
Mike Steger (R)	73,354	11.9%

PREVIOUS WINNING PERCENTAGES
1998 (53%); 1992 (52%); 1986 (53%)

Elected 1986; 4th term

Nothing would make Bond happier than to cap his career in the Senate by becoming the chairman of the Intelligence Committee. The job would satisfy both his professional goals and his personal interests, and he tailored his work in the Senate in recent years to becoming the successor to Chairman Pat Roberts, a Kansas Republican.

Roberts did relinquish his top GOP post on the panel in the 110th Congress (2007-08), but the Democratic takeover of the chamber meant that Bond is the vice chairman instead of the man who holds the gavel.

Bond is the Senate point man for the Bush administration's war in Iraq and has been a staunch defender of secret warrantless surveillance on U.S. citizens in the war on terror. In recent years, Bond has developed expertise on the rise of Islamic fundamentalism in Southeast Asia, and has a publishing contract for a book on the topic.

Bond frequently appears on radio and television programs to rebut Democratic attacks on the administration's policies. On the PBS show "NewsHour," he sparred with Joe Wilson, the former U.S. ambassador who disputed the administration's claims that Iraq had tried to buy uranium from Niger. Bond said Wilson's story was a "hoax designed only to smear the president," a welcome spin on the story at a time the White House was under fire for outing Wilson's wife, Valerie Plame, a CIA operative whose identity was supposed to be kept secret.

Bond was a fierce critic of Iraq's former leader Saddam Hussein, causing a stir in 1998 by proposing repeal of an executive branch policy barring U.S. intelligence agencies from sponsoring or carrying out political assassinations.

The war, and issues related to intelligence gathering, are also personal for Bond. His only child, Sam, is a U.S. Marine Corps intelligence officer deployed to Iraq for a second time in 2007. During his first tour in 2005, he lost five members of his unit to a bomb planted by insurgents. In 2006, Bond visited Afghanistan, Pakistan, Kuwait and Qatar as part of his immersion in anti-terrorism issues.

Bond raised hundreds of thousands of dollars for fellow Republicans through his political action committee, KITPAC, which he created in 2005. His wife, Linda, also actively raised money for the party as finance director of the National Republican Senatorial Committee for the 2006 election.

Bond's new profile is a leap from his former focus on the parochial concerns of Missouri and from the work that had previously consumed him as a senior Republican on the Appropriations Committee. He was known for the amount of federal money he could funnel to Missouri, and for his enthusiastic advocacy of more spending on roads, highways and water projects, frequently over the objections of the administration and budget conservatives in his party. When the watchdog group Citizens Against Government Waste gave him a "License to Pork" award in 1999, Bond responded, "If they think it's pork, it's an awfully healthy diet for the people of Missouri, and I'm proud to participate in it."

Early in 2007, when the Environment and Public Works panel approved a multibillion-dollar bill authorizing hundreds of water projects, Bond proudly noted that the measure contained nearly $4 billion for a home-state project on the Mississippi and Illinois rivers.

Bond was a leader of a pack of Senate Republicans who locked horns with the White House over a highway bill in 2005. He helped craft a $319 billion Senate bill that was considerably more expensive than the White House would accept. In 2004, he crossed the administration by producing a bill that contained $2 billion in budget-busting "emergency" spending for veterans' and space programs. That generated a Bush veto threat, and when Bond's handiwork was rolled into a catchall spending bill, the extra money was gone.

Though a conservative on most issues and a loyal Republican on most critical votes, Bond is a moderate on spending issues. He fought Bush's attempts to cut community development block grants in the 2006 budget and also opposed a plan to gut HOPE, a housing program Bond helped create in 1990 that provides money to demolish blighted public housing. He was also a chief sponsor of legislation that created the 1993 Family and Medical Leave Act. "Reducing the deficit almost solely on the back of domestic spending is very troubling and is an ill-conceived strategy that could have disastrous results for many important programs," Bond says.

A booster of the National Guard, Bond in 2006 joined Patrick J. Leahy, a Vermont Democrat, in winning approval of almost $3 billion in a defense spending bill to replenish National Guard equipment used or destroyed in Iraq and Afghanistan and to buy new gear.

Bond won a fourth term at age 65, staying on at an age when some lawmakers choose to leave public life to make more money while still relatively young. He has seen significant changes in his personal life in recent years. In 2002, the divorced Bond made GOP political consultant Linda Pell his second wife. The pair share a comfortable existence in a $2.2 million house they purchased in an exclusive section of Washington in 2005. Bond lost considerable weight on a low-carb diet, and sometimes comes to the floor in athletic garb when unexpected votes interrupt his workouts.

He has a reputation as a low-key workhorse, yet his fellow Republicans have been reluctant to elect him to the leadership; he lost three attempts to become chairman of the Senate Republican caucus.

Bond is not shy about blocking bills that he thinks harm Missouri businesses. In 2005, after he became chairman of the Appropriations subcommittee that handles transportation spending, Bond inserted a last-minute provision in the bill that weakened an effort to crack down on unscrupulous household moving companies. The change benefited Missouri-based UniGroup Inc., owner of United Van Lines and Mayflower.

When Congress overhauled election laws in 2002, the bill contained a Bond provision requiring voters to show proof of residence to vote. It was intended to fix problems like those found in St. Louis in 2000, where thousands of voters had registered in more than one place. But some saw it as a racist impediment to minority voters. Bond negotiated with Democrats for six months on a compromise.

Bond was born into an affluent family that made its fortune in brick manufacturing. For college, it was Princeton, and after that, the University of Virginia for law school, where he graduated first in his class.

Bond won his first statewide race for auditor in 1970 at age 31. Two years later, he became Missouri's first Republican governor since World War II. He had a troubled first term. Democrats in the legislature found him aloof, and Republicans chafed at his efforts to abolish patronage jobs. He lost his bid for re-election in 1976 to Democrat Joseph P. Teasdale. But Teasdale was a weak administrator, and Bond came back and avenged his loss in 1980, helped by President Ronald Reagan's coattails.

In 1986, Bond battled Democratic Lt. Gov. Harriett Woods in a bitter contest for the Senate seat being vacated by Democrat Thomas F. Eagleton. Bond ran as a budget-conscious conservative and painted Woods as a liberal out of sync with Missourians. She called Bond a passive governor and a rubber stamp for Reagan. Bond won with 53 percent of the vote. In his 2004 race, Bond defeated state Treasurer Nancy Farmer by 13 percentage points.

KEY VOTES

2006

- Yes Confirm Samuel A. Alito Jr. to the Supreme Court
- Yes Allow consideration of a bill to establish a $140 billion trust fund to compensate victims of asbestos exposure
- Yes Extend tax cuts for two years at a cost of $70 billion over five years
- No Overhaul immigration policy with border security, enforcement and guest worker program
- Yes Allow consideration of a bill to permanently repeal the estate tax
- No Urge President Bush to begin troop withdrawals from Iraq in 2006
- No Lift President Bush's restrictions on stem cell research funding
- Yes Authorize military tribunals for suspected terrorists

2005

- Yes Curb class action lawsuits by shifting them from state to federal courts
- Yes Allow confirmation vote on Priscilla R. Owen to the U.S. Court of Appeals for the 5th Circuit
- Yes Oppose mandatory emissions limits and block recognition of global warming as a threat
- Yes Approve free-trade pact with five Central American countries
- Yes Pass energy policy overhaul favored by President Bush emphasizing domestic oil and gas production
- Yes Shield gunmakers from lawsuits when their products are used in crimes
- No Ban torture of prisoners in U.S. custody
- Yes Renew 16 provisions of the Patriot Act
- Yes Allow final vote on opening the Arctic National Wildlife Refuge to oil and gas exploration

CQ VOTE STUDIES

	PARTY UNITY		PRESIDENTIAL SUPPORT	
	Support	Oppose	Support	Oppose
2006	91%	9%	89%	11%
2005	94%	6%	93%	7%
2004	94%	6%	92%	8%
2003	97%	3%	97%	3%
2002	89%	11%	98%	2%
2001	94%	6%	99%	1%
2000	96%	4%	46%	54%
1999	93%	7%	34%	66%
1998	88%	12%	38%	62%
1997	89%	11%	62%	38%

INTEREST GROUPS

	AFL-CIO	ADA	CCUS	ACU
2006	7%	5%	92%	80%
2005	21%	0%	100%	88%
2004	42%	20%	100%	96%
2003	8%	5%	100%	80%
2002	15%	10%	100%	84%
2001	19%	10%	93%	88%
2000	0%	0%	100%	92%
1999	0%	0%	94%	84%
1998	13%	15%	89%	72%
1997	0%	15%	100%	76%

Sen. Claire McCaskill (D)

CAPITOL OFFICE
224-6154
mccaskill.senate.gov
717 Hart 20510-2505; fax 228-6326

COMMITTEES
Armed Services
Commerce, Science & Transportation
Homeland Security & Governmental Affairs
Indian Affairs
Special Aging

RESIDENCE
Kirkwood

BORN
July 24, 1953, Rolla, Mo.

RELIGION
Roman Catholic

FAMILY
Husband, Joseph Shepard; seven children

EDUCATION
U. of Missouri, B.A. 1975 (political science), J.D. 1978

CAREER
Lawyer; city prosecutor

POLITICAL HIGHLIGHTS
Mo. House, 1983-89; sought Democratic nomination for Jackson County prosecutor, 1988; Jackson County Legislature, 1991-93; Jackson County prosecutor, 1993-99; Mo. auditor, 1999-2007; Democratic nominee for governor, 2004

ELECTION RESULTS

2006 GENERAL		
Claire McCaskill (D)	1,055,255	49.6%
Jim Talent (R)	1,006,941	47.3%
Frank Gilmour (LIBERT)	47,792	2.2%
2006 PRIMARY		
Claire McCaskill (D)	282,767	80.8%
Bill Clinton Young (D)	67,173	19.2%

Elected 2006; 1st term

There is strong symbolism in the fact that the living room window of McCaskill's condominium in Washington, D.C., features an up-close view of the front yard of the Government Accountability Office building. It's emblematic of the role the former state auditor and prosecutor wants to carve out as a senator. She hopes to be an in-house expert on oversight, including audits and investigations. "GAO is my next-door neighbor, both literally and figuratively, in terms of what I'm going to be doing in the Senate," she says.

Like many Democrats in 2006, McCaskill campaigned heavily on the theme of restoring congressional oversight after years of Republican reluctance to investigate the Bush administration. She called for the creation of a new "Truman committee" to investigate profiteering in the Iraq War, inspired by a special Senate committee in the 1940s headed by Harry S Truman — then a senator from Missouri — that examined fraud and shortages during World War II.

The committee wasn't created in 2007, but McCaskill was assigned to two committees that will allow her to hone her oversight skills on war profiteering and other subjects: Armed Services, which has jurisdiction over the Defense Department, and Homeland Security and Governmental Affairs, which covers a broad swath of federal agencies as well as the massive Homeland Security Department. She is also a member of the latter committee's Permanent Subcommittee on Investigations, the successor to the original Truman committee.

It didn't take long for McCaskill to become a vocal member of both panels. At one Armed Services hearing in February 2007, she asked Defense Secretary Robert M. Gates and the department's comptroller how much defense spending went to contracts that received competitive bids, as opposed to those that were awarded with no competition. Neither could answer the question.

And in March 2007, after the scandal of the poor management of Walter Reed hospital was revealed, McCaskill grilled the Army surgeon general, Lt. Gen. Kevin C. Kiley, who was temporarily put in charge of the hospital for wounded soldiers even though news reports indicated he had been told about the problems. "It would be hard to walk through outpatient at Walter Reed and talk to soldiers and not confront a complaint," she said. The Army's failure to act, she said, "belongs at your doorstep." He was forced out later that month.

McCaskill is happy to dive into the less glamorous oversight subjects as well. Not many senators are known for bragging about how many GAO reports they read, but she claims to have read between 50 and 100 of the reports in her first months in office and has a goal of reading at least 10 a week. McCaskill sees her oversight work in the Senate as a natural extension of her eight years as the state auditor in Missouri, as well as six years as Jackson County prosecutor. "I think the skill sets you get as a prosecutor and an auditor are great for this place," she says. "It is obvious that the federal government is not the most efficiently run place in the world."

She is trying to learn the legislative ropes as well, and she has proposed a tax cut package that would create a larger deduction for college tuition, a bigger child care tax credit and a new tax credit for people buying a home for the first time. The child care tax credit became part of a package of middle-class tax breaks McCaskill cosponsored with Democrat

Charles E. Schumer of New York.

In addition, McCaskill teamed up with Barack Obama of Illinois, the Democratic presidential candidate, to introduce legislation to address Walter Reed's problems by simplifying paperwork for wounded veterans, adding caseworkers and requiring more frequent inspector general inspections of military hospitals. And in March 2007, she helped defuse a standoff over collective bargaining rights that threatened to jeopardize a bill to implement the recommendations of the Sept. 11 commission. The Senate approved an amendment she wrote that would grant collective bargaining rights for airport screeners, but that would not allow them to strike or bargain for higher pay and would require them to do what the Homeland Security Department asks them to do during an emergency — caveats that addressed Bush administration concerns.

McCaskill comes from a politically active family; her father served as state insurance director, and her mother was the first woman to serve on the Columbia City Council. One of four children, she was used to her father giving quizzes on current events at the dinner table. She recalls going to political events wearing sashes and "those obnoxious foam little bowler hats" to advertise candidates' campaigns. She listened to the speeches and caught the political bug, particularly after a teacher urged her to consider becoming a lawyer, noting that she was better at arguing than she was at subjects that had obvious right and wrong answers.

After joining the debate team in her senior year in high school, McCaskill majored in political science at the University of Missouri and went on to law school there. She clerked for the Missouri Court of Appeals and interviewed for jobs as a prosecutor and as a public defender. The prosecutor's office offered her a job first, and soon she was learning the ropes as an assistant prosecutor in Kansas City, specializing in sex crimes, homicide and arson cases.

In 1982, she launched her political career by winning a seat in the Missouri House, where she wrote the state's first minimum sentencing law for repeat offenders. Following an unsuccessful run for Jackson County prosecutor in 1988, McCaskill won the job in 1993, becoming the first woman to hold the office. She focused on punishing domestic violence and created a drug court to help non-violent offenders seek treatment. After six years on the job, McCaskill was elected state auditor, where she examined waste — such as a stash of $1 million worth of state-owned computers that had never been used — and ineffective programs, such as the state's troubled foster care system.

But McCaskill saw a political future for herself that involved more than just performance audits, and in 2004 she took on the Democratic Party establishment by defeating the incumbent governor, Bob Holden, in the primary. She might have been headed for the governor's mansion that year, except for the formidable opposition of Republican Matt Blunt, the son of House Minority Whip Roy Blunt. McCaskill lost the race by just less than 3 percentage points, in part because Blunt had a huge edge in rural areas.

Shortly after that defeat, however, Schumer urged McCaskill to make one more run for higher office, this time against Jim Talent, a Republican senator whom Democratic leaders considered vulnerable. McCaskill campaigned hard to win over the rural voters she had lost in the governor's race, and criticized Talent relentlessly as a passive legislator who had failed to ask tough questions of the Bush administration on the Iraq War. She also was aided by the popularity of a ballot initiative to expand embryonic stem cell research, which she supported and Talent opposed. McCaskill got by Talent by a little more than 2 percentage points, a key victory that helped the Democrats gain control of the Senate.

Rep. William Lacy Clay (D)

CAPITOL OFFICE
225-2406
www.house.gov/clay
434 Cannon 20515-2501; fax 225-1725

COMMITTEES
Financial Services
Oversight & Government Reform
(Information Policy, Census & National Archives - chairman)

RESIDENCE
St. Louis

BORN
July 27, 1956, St. Louis, Mo.

RELIGION
Roman Catholic

FAMILY
Wife, Ivie Lewellen Clay; two children

EDUCATION
U. of Maryland, B.S. 1983 (government & politics)

CAREER
Paralegal; real estate agent; congressional aide

POLITICAL HIGHLIGHTS
Mo. House, 1983-91; Mo. Senate, 1991-2000

ELECTION RESULTS

2006 GENERAL		
William Lacy Clay (D)	141,574	72.9%
Mark J. Byrne (R)	47,893	24.7%
Robb E. Cunningham (LIBERT)	4,768	2.5%
2006 PRIMARY		
William Lacy Clay (D)		unopposed
2004 GENERAL		
William Lacy Clay (D)	213,658	75.3%
Leslie L. Farr II (R)	64,791	22.8%
Terry Chadwick (LIBERT)	3,937	1.4%

PREVIOUS WINNING PERCENTAGES
2002 (70%); 2000 (75%)

Elected 2000; 4th term

The son of a Missouri congressman, Clay grew up in the Washington suburbs, majored in government in college, and soon after went to Jefferson City as a Missouri state legislator. He has spent much of his time in Congress trying to improve the mechanics of government. His focus: eliminating election fraud and opening government records to public scrutiny.

Clay succeeded his father, Democratic Rep. William L. Clay, an African-American political pioneer who served in the House for 32 years. The younger Clay, who shares his father's liberal views but also touts his independence, was quick to press his priorities when Democrats took control in the 110th Congress (2007-08).

In early 2007, as the new chairman of the Oversight and Government Reform panel's subcommittee with jurisdiction over public information and the census, Clay wasted no time pushing legislation ensuring public access to a host of government documents. Over the objections of the Bush administration, Clay won House passage in March 2007 of legislation to stop former presidents and vice presidents from shielding their records from the public. The legislation would overturn President Bush's executive order of 2001 that allowed former Oval Office occupants and their heirs to keep certain records secret. Bush had sought to keep some of his father's records out of the public domain. Another House-passed bill that emerged from Clay's subcommittee would require presidential libraries to disclose the identities of big donors.

Clay was also successful out of the chute with a bill to make it harder for the government to resist Freedom of Information Act requests, which are sometimes delayed for years. The House passed his bill requiring federal agencies to respond to such requests within 20 business days and to establish a system for tracking the requests.

He also vowed to see that the undercount of mostly poor and minority people in the decennial census "never happens again."

Clay has devoted a good deal of effort to monitoring the nation's electoral process, which he says is not always implemented fairly, particularly in poor and predominately Democratic neighborhoods. He complained about the long lines and voting irregularities in Ohio in 2004, and he joined in a lawsuit that kept polls open extra hours in St. Louis in 2000 to permit voters caught in long lines to cast ballots.

On Iraq, Clay is among the most adamant of the anti-war lawmakers. He voted against the resolution in 2002 sanctioning the invasion. In a 2006 speech, he asked why Bush's twin daughters had not enlisted. During the House debate in 2007 over Bush's decision to send more troops to Iraq, Clay said, "Great nations do not start wars as a matter of policy. They exercise diplomacy and negotiation to avert threats and achieve security."

Clay is among a growing number of liberals who are resisting pressure from interest groups to side with them in every instance on hot-button social issues such as abortion. Although an abortion rights supporter, in 2005 Clay supported a bill making it a crime to evade parental notification laws by taking a minor across state lines to get an abortion. Clay said the legislation was a "sensible" approach. "Now, that's going to alienate some of my constituents in the pro-choice community," Clay told the St. Louis Post-Dispatch. "But look, it's time we start telling these constituency groups, 'Hey, don't be so rigid in your stance and hold us to such a litmus test that it costs us seats.' "

On the Financial Services Committee, Clay's interest is in making housing more affordable and cracking down on questionable lending practices in low-income communities, such as subprime lending in which pricier home loans are given to people with patchy credit histories. As the number of subprime mortgages ending in foreclosure climbed to record levels in 2007, Clay called the problem "catastrophic."

Another of Clay's priorities is to spur economic development in urban St. Louis County, where crime and a troubled public school system have contributed to a steady decline in population. Economic development is a family effort. Clay's wife, Ivie, works for the St. Louis Development Corp., the city's economic development agency.

Clay is an avid cook and a golf fanatic, but his mother told a local newspaper that politics "has been his life. That's the only thing he knows." He was 12 when his father was elected to Congress, and he spent his teenage years in suburban Maryland, attending high school in Silver Spring and college at the University of Maryland in College Park. To pay for his college education, Clay was a House of Representatives doorman for six years. The hours he spent watching the action from the cloakrooms and the Speaker's Lobby gave him ample insight into the ways of Congress.

After college, he was just starting law school when an opening in the Missouri House drew him back to St. Louis to run in a special election. He spent the next 17 years in the General Assembly, serving eight years in the House before winning a 1991 special election for a state Senate vacancy. He supplemented his part-time legislator's salary by working in real estate and as a paralegal.

In Jefferson City, Clay helped push through measures benefiting welfare recipients, imposing new penalties for hate crimes and creating tax breaks for those saving for education and home ownership. When the Ku Klux Klan announced that its members would "adopt" a stretch of Interstate 55 to keep it clean, Clay orchestrated legislative action to name that segment of the road after civil rights icon Rosa Parks.

Clay was the presumed heir to the 1st District seat from the moment his father announced his retirement in 1999. The younger Clay both embraced his father and declared his independence when he entered the race to succeed him. "Although I am not my father, I am my father's son, in that we share the same values . . . and commitment to principles, such as fairness and justice," said Clay. He won easily in 2000, with 75 percent of the vote.

The district was altered some by the state legislature in decennial redistricting, but it caused Clay no electoral distress. He won with 70 percent in 2002 and hasn't dipped below that level in subsequent elections.

KEY VOTES

2006

No Stop broadband companies from favoring select Internet traffic
No Affirm U.S. commitment to war in Iraq and reject setting a withdrawal date for troops
No Repeal requirement for bilingual ballots at the polls
Yes Permit U.S. sale of civilian nuclear technology to India
No Build a 700-mile fence on the U.S.-Mexico border to curb illegal crossings
No Permit warrantless wiretaps of suspected terrorists

2005

No Intervene in the life-support case of Terri Schiavo
Yes Lift President Bush's restrictions on stem cell research funding
Yes Prohibit FBI access to library and bookstore records
No Approve free-trade pact with five Central American countries
No Pass energy policy overhaul favored by President Bush emphasizing domestic oil and gas production
No End mandatory preservation of habitat of endangered animal and plant species
Yes Ban torture of prisoners in U.S. custody

CQ VOTE STUDIES

	PARTY UNITY		PRESIDENTIAL SUPPORT	
	Support	Oppose	Support	Oppose
2006	94%	6%	28%	72%
2005	96%	4%	16%	84%
2004	97%	3%	24%	76%
2003	98%	2%	16%	84%
2002	94%	6%	32%	68%

INTEREST GROUPS

	AFL-CIO	ADA	CCUS	ACU
2006	93%	90%	67%	16%
2005	92%	85%	44%	21%
2004	87%	100%	35%	8%
2003	100%	95%	32%	13%
2002	100%	80%	44%	4%

MISSOURI 1
North St. Louis; northeast St. Louis County

Flanked by the Mississippi and Missouri rivers, the heavily Democratic, St. Louis-based 1st is a mixture of poor urban neighborhoods, middle-class suburbs and a business district that once was the center of one of the five largest cities in the United States.

The 1st takes in the northern half of St. Louis, including many of the city's popular attractions, such as the Gateway Arch and Forest Park, which attracts more than 12 million visitors a year and is about 500 acres larger than New York's Central Park. Major area employers, such as Boeing, BJC HealthCare — one of the largest nonprofit health care organizations in the nation — and Monsanto, are scattered throughout the 1st.

Suburbs in St. Louis County include the region's main airport. Once one of the nation's 10 busiest, Lambert International Airport's ranking has fallen significantly, a result of route consolidation following the 2001 merger of American Airlines and TWA, which was formerly based in St. Louis. After years of rumors, Ford in early 2006 idled its SUV assembly plant in Hazelwood, eliminating nearly 1,500 local jobs.

By far the state's most heavily Democratic district, the 1st gave John Kerry 75 percent of its vote in the 2004 presidential election. Local and state contests almost always favor Democrats. The black population, which stood at just less than 60 percent after the 1990 census, has decreased considerably, although African-Americans still make up almost 50 percent of district voters.

St. Louis has hemorrhaged 60 percent of its population between 1950 and 2005. Frustrated by failing schools and aging housing stock, residents were lured to suburbia, where seemingly endless acres were converted from farmland. To slow declines in the city, developers and lawmakers have poured billions of dollars into downtown redevelopment projects, including a new stadium for baseball's St. Louis Cardinals.

MAJOR INDUSTRY
Aircraft and other manufacturing, health care, higher education

CITIES
St. Louis (pt.), 163,020; Florissant, 50,497; Hazelwood, 26,206; University City (pt.), 24,075; Ferguson, 22,406

NOTABLE
The first suit filed by Dred Scott was tried in St Louis' historic Old Courthouse, now part of Jefferson National Expansion Memorial Park.

Rep. Todd Akin (R)

CAPITOL OFFICE
225-2561
rep.akin@mail.house.gov
www.house.gov/akin
117 Cannon 20515-2502; fax 225-2563

COMMITTEES
Armed Services
Science & Technology
Small Business

RESIDENCE
Town & Country

BORN
July 5, 1947, Manhattan, N.Y.

RELIGION
Christian

FAMILY
Wife, Lulli Akin; six children

EDUCATION
Worcester Polytechnic Institute, B.S. 1971 (engineering); Covenant Theological Seminary, M.Div. 1985

MILITARY SERVICE
Army, 1972-72; Army Reserve, 1972-80

CAREER
University lecturer; steel company manager; computer company marketing executive

POLITICAL HIGHLIGHTS
Mo. House, 1989-2000

ELECTION RESULTS

2006 GENERAL		
Todd Akin (R)	176,452	61.3%
George D. "Boots" Weber (D)	105,242	36.6%
Tamara A. Millay (LIBERT)	5,923	2.1%
2006 PRIMARY		
Todd Akin (R)	41,464	88.1%
Sherman Parker (R)	5,597	11.9%
2004 GENERAL		
Todd Akin (R)	228,725	65.4%
George D. "Boots" Weber (D)	115,366	33.0%
Darla R. Maloney (LIBERT)	4,822	1.4%

PREVIOUS WINNING PERCENTAGES
2002 (67%); 2000 (55%)

Elected 2000; 4th term

As one of the House's most conservative and pro-military members, Akin is a bellwether of the loss of confidence in Congress in the Bush administration's handling of the war in Iraq.

He is the top-ranking Republican on a newly created investigative panel of the Armed Services Committee, and in that role in 2007 he joined with the subcommittee's chairman, Democrat Martin T. Meehan of Massachusetts, to open a probe on the training of Iraqi army and police units, one area where the White House had fallen short of its goals in Iraq. It was one of the rare times Akin has found common ground with Democrats.

He expressed regret that his own party had not conducted effective oversight of the war from its start in 2003, when Republicans were in the majority, until Democrats took control of the House in 2007. "We didn't push the oversight aspects of our jobs as much as the Democrats are doing now," Akin told the St. Louis Post-Dispatch newspaper. He also said the administration had conducted the war "on the cheap" and that, "I don't think as a nation we have built the structure we needed for this conflict."

Before reaching his conclusions, Akin had gone to Iraq several times, including to visit his son, Marine Lt. Perry Akin, then 24 and a combat engineer in Iraq. However, he refused to join Democrats in their calls for a date certain for withdrawing troops, and in fact, was highly critical of their attempts to "micromanage" the war with soldiers in the field. "If you have got a better idea, put it on the table," Akin exhorted Democrats on the House floor in February 2007. "But if you don't, shut up. And don't undermine the morale of our troops and encourage our enemies."

Aside from his work on the Armed Services panel on the war, Akin's signature issue in recent years has been a bill to bar federal courts, including the U.S. Supreme Court, from hearing constitutional challenges to the Pledge of Allegiance. Many conservatives were incensed by a 2002 U.S. Court of Appeals ruling that the phrase "under God" in the pledge was an unconstitutional endorsement of religion. The Supreme Court struck down the appeals court decision in June 2004 on technical, not constitutional, grounds, and Akin has pressed for legislation to prevent further rulings against the pledge.

The House in 2004 passed his bill with support from 34 Democrats, but it died in the Senate. Akin won House approval of his bill again in 2006, but it too was ignored by the Senate. He says he is concerned that the Supreme Court will ultimately rule that "under God" has to be removed from the patriotic statement that opens many an American school day. Congress added the words to the pledge in 1954. He offered his bill again early in 2007.

Akin's primary opponent in the 2006 election tried to make an issue of his single-minded focus on the Pledge of Allegiance issue, but was unsuccessful. Missouri state Rep. Sherman Parker, who was waging an uphill challenge, was seriously undercut when he was arrested for failing to appear in court for a speeding ticket and failure to properly register his car.

Akin's voting record often gets a perfect score from the American Conservative Union. He favors restricting abortion, toughening enforcement of obscenity laws, limiting regulations on small businesses and putting the likeness of President Ronald Reagan on the $50 bill. He is steadfastly opposed to same-sex marriage and gun control. His six children have been home-schooled, and he wants to give parents more choice over the schools their children attend. He also advocates local control over school testing.

Akin is suspicious of much of federal spending, with the exception of money for the military. He was one of the few House members — Republican or Democrat — to side with President Bush in 2004 against passage of a massive surface transportation bill, even though it contained projects he sought for his district. He called the bill "a poor use of taxpayers' money," but the measure ultimately passed.

A former Army lieutenant, Akin assiduously looks out for the interests of Boeing Co., which has large plants in St. Charles County in the 2nd District, as well as in St. Louis, in the neighboring 1st. In 2004, he helped ensure that the defense authorization bill included $357 million in funding for research on Boeing's new electronic attack aircraft.

Akin's great-grandfather founded the Laclede Steel Co. of St. Louis, and his father worked there as well. Akin grew up in the St. Louis area and went to the Worcester Polytechnic Institute in Massachusetts, where he studied engineering and joined the Army ROTC. After serving as an Army combat engineer, Akin sold large computers for IBM in Massachusetts, where he met his wife, Lulli. After four years, Akin returned to Missouri and worked for a while at Laclede Steel before getting involved in state politics.

As a member of the Missouri House for 12 years, he unsuccessfully sued the state after the legislature approved a schools bill with $310 million in tax increases. Later, wary of the social impact of expanded gambling, he brought suit against the state's approval of riverboat casino licenses. The court battle eventually led to a referendum on the issue that, while permitting the licenses, resulted in stricter state regulation of the industry.

Akin's reputation as a doctrinaire state legislator spurred opponents to label him as ideologically isolated when he launched his campaign for the House seat vacated by Republican Jim Talent, who ran for governor in 2000. But grass-roots support enabled Akin to narrowly prevail in a five-way primary; he defeated former St. Louis County Executive Gene McNary by just 56 votes. Many credited Akin's victory to inclement weather on Election Day that hurt turnout for McNary. Akin told the St. Louis Post-Dispatch, "My base will show up in earthquakes."

The Democratic nominee, state Sen. Ted House, who held conservative views on social issues, characterized Akin's stands on health care and education as "far extreme." But an energetic campaign and the district's Republican leanings carried Akin to a 13 percentage point victory. He has won with more than 60 percent of the vote in three successive elections.

KEY VOTES

2006

- No Stop broadband companies from favoring select Internet traffic
- Yes Affirm U.S. commitment to war in Iraq and reject setting a withdrawal date for troops
- Yes Repeal requirement for bilingual ballots at the polls
- Yes Permit U.S. sale of civilian nuclear technology to India
- Yes Build a 700-mile fence on the U.S.-Mexico border to curb illegal crossings
- Yes Permit warrantless wiretaps of suspected terrorists

2005

- Yes Intervene in the life-support case of Terri Schiavo
- No Lift President Bush's restrictions on stem cell research funding
- No Prohibit FBI access to library and bookstore records
- Yes Approve free-trade pact with five Central American countries
- Yes Pass energy policy overhaul favored by President Bush emphasizing domestic oil and gas production
- Yes End mandatory preservation of habitat of endangered animal and plant species
- No Ban torture of prisoners in U.S. custody

CQ VOTE STUDIES

	PARTY UNITY		PRESIDENTIAL SUPPORT	
	Support	Oppose	Support	Oppose
2006	97%	3%	95%	5%
2005	99%	1%	91%	9%
2004	99%	1%	94%	6%
2003	97%	3%	89%	11%
2002	98%	2%	90%	10%

INTEREST GROUPS

	AFL-CIO	ADA	CCUS	ACU
2006	14%	0%	100%	92%
2005	14%	0%	89%	100%
2004	7%	0%	95%	100%
2003	29%	5%	90%	88%
2002	11%	0%	85%	100%

MISSOURI 2

West St. Louis County; north and east St. Charles County – St. Charles

Composed mostly of upper-middle-class white suburbanites, the 2nd is the state's richest and one of its fastest-growing districts. The district's population has swelled as a result of residential and commercial migration out of St. Louis.

Commuter traffic into the St. Louis business district from St. Charles County, Missouri's fastest-growing, remains heavy, and state officials are trying to ease the congestion. A $535 million reconstruction and improvement project planned for Interstate 64 in St. Louis County (shared with the 1st) should begin to improve the drive for commuters after its completion in 2010. Also, many local residents have solved their traffic problems by finding jobs away from downtown. Boeing, with plants in the 2nd and on the outskirts of St. Louis (in the 1st), DaimlerChrysler in Fenton, and a General Motors plant in Wentzville are major employers, as are financial services and biotechnology companies.

The district's dwindling but diverse agricultural industry supports the northern fringes of the Mississippi-Missouri river junction. The district's portion of Lincoln County, located in its northwest, is still heavily dependent on both manufacturing and agriculture, and it has steadily grown in population as job opportunities have moved outside of St. Louis.

The district's strong white-collar vote favors Republicans on nearly all levels. Wealthy communities such as Ladue and Frontenac are unshakably Republican. Lincoln County has a Democratic-leaning constituency, but the 2nd gave George W. Bush 60 percent of its vote in the 2004 presidential election.

MAJOR INDUSTRY

Auto manufacturing, biotechnology, agriculture

CITIES

St. Charles, 60,321; St. Peters (pt.), 50,001; Chesterfield, 46,802; O'Fallon (pt.), 44,949; Wildwood, 32,884; Ballwin, 31,283

NOTABLE

Route 66 State Park near Eureka is located on what was Times Beach, the site of an environmental disaster where soil became tainted with dioxin; St. Charles was the last established U.S. town that Lewis and Clark visited as they embarked on their journey.

Rep. Russ Carnahan (D)

CAPITOL OFFICE
225-2671
www.house.gov/carnahan
1710 Longworth 20515-2503; fax 225-7452

COMMITTEES
Foreign Affairs
Science & Technology
Transportation & Infrastructure

RESIDENCE
St. Louis

BORN
July 10, 1958, Columbia, Mo.

RELIGION
Methodist

FAMILY
Wife, Debra Carnahan; two children

EDUCATION
U. of Missouri, B.S. 1979 (public administration), J.D. 1983

CAREER
Lawyer; campaign aide; state legislative aide

POLITICAL HIGHLIGHTS
Democratic nominee for U.S. House, 1990; Mo. House, 2001-05

ELECTION RESULTS

2006 GENERAL		
Russ Carnahan (D)	145,219	65.6%
David Bertelsen (R)	70,189	31.7%
R. Christophel (LIBERT)	4,213	1.9%
2006 PRIMARY		
Russ Carnahan (D)	37,200	76.4%
Jim Frisella (D)	11,517	23.6%
2004 GENERAL		
Russ Carnahan (D)	146,894	52.9%
Bill Federer (R)	125,422	45.1%
Kevin C. Babcock (LIBERT)	4,367	1.6%

Elected 2004; 2nd term

Carnahan has a long political pedigree in Missouri that he shows off in his Capitol Hill office, which doubles as a small museum of the family's political history. On the wall hangs the congressional license plate of his grandfather, A.S.J. Carnahan, who served in the House in the 1940s and 1950s. Also on display, under the glass surface of a coffee table, are campaign buttons for his late father, Mel, the popular former Missouri governor. Mel Carnahan died in a plane crash while campaigning for the Senate in 2000. When he won the race posthumously against Republican John Ashcroft, Carnahan's mother, Jean, was appointed to the seat.

As in other families with deep political roots, Carnahan says he feels like he has always been in politics because it was such a family project. This lifelong immersion perhaps explains some of his early smooth moves as a House newbie. In the 110th Congress (2007-08), he added a seat on the Foreign Affairs Committee, where he can have a voice in the political debate over ending the war in Iraq. "For me, it's going to be a very important jurisdiction in the years ahead as we try to rebuild what I believe is a very low standing and image of the U.S. around the world," Carnahan says.

He was a strong critic of conservative attempts to find offsets for spending aimed at helping Hurricane Katrina victims in 2005. "Why are we trying to find offsets for rebuilding Biloxi but not the cost of rebuilding Baghdad?" Carnahan said, according to the St. Louis Post-Dispatch.

His other assignments in the 110th Congress are the Science and Technology and Transportation and Infrastructure panels. The latter assignment allows him to accomplish the parochial work of bringing home money for roads and bridges while pursuing his interest in world affairs.

Carnahan was one of the rare freshmen to get a bill passed in the House in his first term. But the legislation, which increased funding for stem cell research, became the first bill vetoed by President Bush. Carnahan says he is confident the new Democratic Congress can build veto-proof margins in both chambers to get the legislation enacted. "We must . . . set reasonable, ethical standards to move this medical research forward," he says.

In 2006, he introduced legislation to slash excessive oil company profits. The bill would impose a windfall profits tax on the companies, repeal tax credits given to them by the Republican Congress and redirect the money to develop new alternative energy technologies. Carnahan also has pressed for a measure acknowledging the phenomenon of global warming and encouraging the United States to participate in international treaties addressing the issue.

Health care has been an abiding concern for Carnahan based on his professional experience before politics. He got to know the industry well in nine years as an attorney for the St. Louis-based health care provider, BJC Healthcare. Carnahan supports allowing the importation of prescription drugs from Canada and expanding government medical services to the uninsured.

Carnahan is not as liberal as his predecessor, Richard A. Gephardt, the former Democratic House leader and a 2004 presidential candidate. Carnahan voted in favor of a constitutional amendment to ban flag desecration in 2005. He also voted to renew expiring provisions of the 2001 anti-terrorism law known as the Patriot Act. He says that many but not all of his concerns about the law's impact on civil liberties were addressed by amendments.

Carnahan's start in politics was earlier than most. He remembers at age 8 packing into the family's Pontiac station wagon for the "Caravan for Carnahan" during his father's 1966 campaign for the state legislature. Led by a flatbed truck with a piano on the back and loudspeakers, the caravan traveled to small towns, where the family handed out campaign flyers while a piano player belted out tunes.

Carnahan's first job after graduating in 1979 from the University of Missouri was driving an old Chevy van to take his father around to every county in the state as he campaigned for state treasurer. (Carnahan is a fan of antique cars and motorcycles.)

He attended law school, also at the University of Missouri, where he met his wife, Debra, now a judge in St. Louis' municipal court. After getting his law degree in 1983, he got his first government job working as a legislative aide for the Missouri House Speaker.

He later went to work at a St. Louis law firm before launching his first bid for elective office at age 31. In 1990, he challenged veteran Republican Rep. Bill Emerson for his seat in the U.S. House and lost in a conservative southeastern Missouri district. He lowered his sights and in 2000 was elected to the Missouri House, where he stayed for two terms.

Still, despite his name recognition and four years in the state legislature, his election was hardly a sure thing when he ran to succeed Gephardt in 2004. Carnahan narrowly beat out a crowded field of nine other candidates in the Democratic primary, in which he became the focus of negative attacks. In the general election, he faced Republican Bill Federer, an author who had twice run unsuccessfully against Gephardt. Carnahan won with 53 percent of the vote.

Despite concerns among Democrats that he might be vulnerable in 2006, he won re-election with 66 percent of the vote against Republican David Bertelsen, who got just 32 percent.

Carnahan is not the only family member to be politically inspired by those early campaign caravans. His sister, Robin Carnahan, was elected Missouri secretary of state in 2004 the same day he won a seat in Congress. Their brother, Randy Carnahan, who was serving as an aide in their father's Senate campaign, also died in the plane crash. Jean Carnahan took her husband's seat for two years, but then lost the next election to Republican Jim Talent.

In 2005, Carnahan restarted "Camp Carnahan," a weekend-long training program his father used to run each year for Missouri political activists. "It's a great way to keep his memory alive," Carnahan says.

KEY VOTES

2006

No Stop broadband companies from favoring select Internet traffic

No Affirm U.S. commitment to war in Iraq and reject setting a withdrawal date for troops

No Repeal requirement for bilingual ballots at the polls

Yes Permit U.S. sale of civilian nuclear technology to India

No Build a 700-mile fence on the U.S.-Mexico border to curb illegal crossings

No Permit warrantless wiretaps of suspected terrorists

2005

No Intervene in the life-support case of Terri Schiavo

Yes Lift President Bush's restrictions on stem cell research funding

Yes Prohibit FBI access to library and bookstore records

No Approve free-trade pact with five Central American countries

No Pass energy policy overhaul favored by President Bush emphasizing domestic oil and gas production

No End mandatory preservation of habitat of endangered animal and plant species

Yes Ban torture of prisoners in U.S. custody

CQ VOTE STUDIES

	PARTY UNITY		PRESIDENTIAL SUPPORT	
	Support	Oppose	Support	Oppose
2006	91%	9%	40%	60%
2005	94%	6%	22%	78%

INTEREST GROUPS

	AFL-CIO	ADA	CCUS	ACU
2006	100%	90%	53%	12%
2005	93%	95%	41%	0%

MISSOURI 3

South St. Louis; southeast St. Louis County; Jefferson and Ste. Genevieve counties

Bordered on the east by the Mississippi River, the 3rd includes the southern half of St. Louis, as well as older, established suburbs and newer, sprawling ones. Most of the district's suburban middle-class residents commute to St. Louis County's business district, although there are traces of small-scale farming, manufacturing and river trading.

Whereas St. Louis as a whole (shared with the 1st District) has declined in population, immigrant communities continue to bolster south St. Louis' residential areas. Traditionally German Bevo Mill and Tower Grove neighborhoods now host a large Vietnamese community, as well as one of the nation's largest Bosnian populations. To the south, Jefferson County has been one of the state's fastest-growing areas and has gained national attention for its methamphetamine problem.

Many suburban residents work outside the district, but Anheuser-Busch, headquartered in the 3rd's portion of St. Louis, is a major provider of jobs to the region. Thousands of tourists visit the brewery's historical center each year, and the brewery is a St. Louis icon. The district's other large employers include a National Geospatial-Intelligence Agency defense facility and the St. Louis VA Medical Center-Jefferson Barracks Division, which provides medical assistance for veterans. Farther south, on the fringes of Ste. Genevieve County, small farming complements a sizable trading industry along the Mississippi River.

The district's blue-collar base favors Democrats, although the GOP finds significant support in middle-class communities such as Arnold, and a large Catholic contingent gives the district an anti-abortion tilt. The 3rd gave John Kerry 57 percent of its vote in the 2004 presidential election.

MAJOR INDUSTRY

Beer manufacturing, defense, health care

CITIES

St. Louis (pt.), 185,169; Oakville (unincorporated), 35,309

NOTABLE

Baseball legends Yogi Berra and Joe Garagiola grew up on The Hill, a historically Italian neighborhood in south St. Louis; Built by August A. Busch Sr. and opened in 1917, the still-operating Bevo Mill restaurant served a non-alcoholic drink during prohibition that tasted like beer.

Rep. Ike Skelton (D)

CAPITOL OFFICE
225-2876
www.house.gov/skelton
2206 Rayburn 20515-2504; fax 225-2695

COMMITTEES
Armed Services - chairman

RESIDENCE
Lexington

BORN
Dec. 20, 1931, Lexington, Mo.

RELIGION
Christian Church

FAMILY
Widowed; three children

EDUCATION
Wentworth Military Academy, A.A. 1951;
U. of Edinburgh (United Kingdom), attended 1953;
U. of Missouri, A.B. 1953 (history), LL.B. 1956

CAREER
Lawyer; state prosecutor

POLITICAL HIGHLIGHTS
Lafayette County prosecuting attorney, 1957-60; Mo. Senate, 1971-77

ELECTION RESULTS

2006 GENERAL		
Ike Skelton (D)	159,303	67.6%
James A. "Jim" Noland Jr. (R)	69,254	29.4%
Bryce Holthouse (LIBERT)	4,479	1.9%
Melinda "Mel" Ivey (PRO)	2,459	1.0%
2006 PRIMARY		
Ike Skelton (D)		unopposed
2004 GENERAL		
Ike Skelton (D)	190,800	66.2%
James A. "Jim" Noland Jr. (R)	93,334	32.4%

PREVIOUS WINNING PERCENTAGES
2002 (68%); 2000 (67%); 1998 (71%); 1996 (64%); 1994 (68%); 1992 (70%); 1990 (62%); 1988 (72%); 1986 (100%); 1984 (67%); 1982 (55%); 1980 (68%); 1978 (73%); 1976 (56%)

Elected 1976; 16th term

After three decades in Congress, Skelton, chairman of the Armed Services Committee, takes the long view of the U.S. military and its role in securing America's place in the world. He is deeply disturbed by what he sees these days.

Sixty-one years after Winston Churchill's famous "Iron Curtain" speech at Westminster College in Fulton, Mo., about the march of communism and the need to counter it, Skelton took the same stage in April 2007 to offer his own strategic vision — one built around a mix of economic, diplomatic, military and moral power needed to keep America the "indispensable nation" in a changing world. It is not an easy task, he said. "The horizon is clouded by the smoke rising from Iraq; it stings the eyes and blocks attempts to look beyond that conflict."

Although he voted in 2002 to authorize the use of force against Iraq, Skelton also warned President Bush in advance that the challenge lay not in toppling Saddam Hussein, but in stabilizing Iraq afterward. "I have no doubt that our military would decisively defeat Iraq's forces and remove Saddam," he wrote the president, "but like the proverbial dog chasing the car, we must consider what we would do after we caught it."

Skelton says Bush has made "irretrievable mistakes" in that regard. In February 2007, he sponsored and steered to passage a resolution opposing the deployment of additional U.S. combat forces to Iraq, while affirming support for the troops already there. "We have stretched and strained our forces and their equipment to the breaking point, degrading our military readiness and exposing our nation to unacceptable levels of strategic risk," he told the House. The following month, he voted for a war funding bill that set a timetable for a U.S. withdrawal.

Skelton wants Bush to pay more attention to the "forgotten war" in Afghanistan, which he says has been "under-resourced" for far too long. Failure to reverse deteriorating conditions there, he warns, could jeopardize not only the future of Afghanistan but also that of the NATO alliance, which has struggled to secure the country.

Skelton intends to use his power as chairman to address the strains the war has put on the armed forces. Dismayed by the repeated deployments to the war zone endured by units, he has pushed hard to increase the size of both services. "You can only deploy them so often," Skelton said before passage of the 2004 defense authorization bill that called for the addition of 39,000 soldiers and Marines. The situation has only worsened since then, he says.

A childhood bout with polio kept Skelton out of the service, but he has had a lifelong interest in military history and, specifically, military readiness. He often refers to Task Force Smith, the first U.S. soldiers sent to repel North Korea's invasion of South Korea in 1950. "Undermanned, underequipped and undertrained, the soldiers of Task Force Smith were unprepared for the attack that came their way," he wrote in 2007 in an op-ed piece for The Kansas City Star. The unit suffered terrible casualties and was forced to retreat. "Those soldiers and our nation learned the hard way that sending unready forces to war can have disastrous consequences."

In addition to enlarging the Army and Marine Corps, Skelton wants to tackle broader issues of interagency reform and a revitalization of the entire defense production system. The wars in Iraq and Afghanistan have spotlighted the inadequacies of both, he says. "We need teams of diplomats, development experts and other specialists in fields such as rule of law, engineering and agribusiness to accompany our soldiers in the task of rebuilding Iraq and Afghanistan," he said in his Westminster speech.

Earlier this decade, Skelton supported Bush's decision to deploy a nationwide anti-missile defense system that could fend off small numbers of missiles launched by North Korea or other rogue states. But he insisted that it undergo thorough testing before deployment and that it not be funded at the expense of more-pressing defense requirements, particularly pay and other factors bearing on the troops' quality of life.

Bush isn't the only president to draw fire from Skelton on issues of readiness. The Missouri Democrat often viewed President Bill Clinton's defense budgets as anemic and goaded the administration to request more money and more troops. But he also parried some GOP attacks on Clinton.

On most social issues, Skelton is in tune with his constituents and at odds with his more liberal Democratic colleagues. He has opposed abortion in most cases, voted to repeal the ban on certain semiautomatic assault-style weapons and supported amending the Constitution to prohibit same-sex marriage. On votes pitting most Democrats against most Republicans, he stuck with his party only 75 percent of the time in the 109th Congress (2005-06), while voting in agreement with Bush 61 percent of the time.

Named Isaac Newton Skelton at birth, he was a high school sophomore when he contracted polio, dashing his dream of attending West Point. He became a patient at Warm Springs, Ga., where President Franklin D. Roosevelt went for treatment. He learned there to get on with his life, avoiding self-pity. He worked tirelessly to regain strength and joined the school track team as a two-miler. "He proved there really were no limitations," a teammate told the St. Louis Post-Dispatch in 2007.

Skelton's father, a friend of Harry S Truman's, took his son to Washington for the 1949 inauguration. Truman played a central role in Skelton's political life. He asked Skelton to run for Congress in 1962, against Democratic Rep. Bill Randall, whom the former president disliked. But Skelton demurred; he was a young lawyer who had only recently married. (His wife died in August 2005.)

After serving six years in the state Senate, Skelton did run in 1976 as Randall retired. He was endorsed by Truman's widow, and won with 56 percent of the vote. He chaired a joint session of Congress on the day it observed Truman's 100th birthday, and fought a Smithsonian exhibit on the dropping of the first atomic bomb that he viewed as unfairly questioning Truman's motives. In 2006, Skelton received the Truman Award for Public Service.

In his recent electoral wins, he has taken about two-thirds of the vote.

KEY VOTES

2006

No Stop broadband companies from favoring select Internet traffic

No Affirm U.S. commitment to war in Iraq and reject setting a withdrawal date for troops

No Repeal requirement for bilingual ballots at the polls

Yes Permit U.S. sale of civilian nuclear technology to India

Yes Build a 700-mile fence on the U.S.-Mexico border to curb illegal crossings

No Permit warrantless wiretaps of suspected terrorists

2005

Yes Intervene in the life-support case of Terri Schiavo

Yes Lift President Bush's restrictions on stem cell research funding

Yes Prohibit FBI access to library and bookstore records

Yes Approve free-trade pact with five Central American countries

Yes Pass energy policy overhaul favored by President Bush emphasizing domestic oil and gas production

Yes End mandatory preservation of habitat of endangered animal and plant species

Yes Ban torture of prisoners in U.S. custody

CQ VOTE STUDIES

	PARTY UNITY		PRESIDENTIAL SUPPORT	
	Support	Oppose	Support	Oppose
2006	75%	25%	60%	40%
2005	76%	24%	61%	39%
2004	80%	20%	68%	32%
2003	75%	25%	62%	38%
2002	73%	27%	58%	42%

INTEREST GROUPS

	AFL-CIO	ADA	CCUS	ACU
2006	86%	55%	80%	50%
2005	79%	75%	70%	38%
2004	93%	65%	60%	48%
2003	80%	80%	60%	64%
2002	67%	60%	70%	32%

MISSOURI 4

West central — Kansas City suburbs, Jefferson City

Laden with lakes, rivers and farmland, the 4th's northern border is formed in part by the Missouri River. With the exception of some southeast Kansas City suburbs, the state capital of Jefferson City and medium-size Sedalia, the district typifies rural and small-town Missouri.

Agriculture has been an economic mainstay here for decades. Most residents work at small-scale farming, mainly row crops, with soybeans, corn and wheat, or livestock. Others work for moderate-size manufacturers of household goods. Tourism helps in the rural areas. With miles of shoreline, modern hotels and retail outlets, the Lake of the Ozarks region (shared with the 9th) attracts 300,000 boaters each weekend during peak times. The lake areas also draw retirees and professionals looking to set up second homes.

The 4th's piece of the Kansas City suburbs has not grown as fast as the area north of the city (in the 6th), and the suburbs are not as affluent, but they do provide some blue-collar manufacturing jobs. Moving east, the district picks up the smaller cities of Warrensburg and Sedalia, where the Scott Joplin Ragtime Festival is held each June. State government employs more than 15,000 people in Jefferson City, all but a very small sliver of which is located in the 4th.

Voters in some of the western counties favor Democrats in congressional elections, while Republican votes can be tilled in the east, especially in Webster and Camden counties. The district may be trending Republican: GOP state legislators heavily outnumber their Democratic counterparts in the state districts covering the 4th, and George W. Bush took 64 percent of the 2004 presidential election vote here, winning all 25 counties either wholly or partially in the district.

MAJOR INDUSTRY

Government, defense, agriculture, manufacturing

MILITARY BASES

Fort Leonard Wood, 5,035 military, 6,482 civilian (2007); Whiteman Air Force Base, 3,700 military, 2,200 civilian (2007)

CITIES

Jefferson City (pt.), 39,611; Sedalia, 20,339; Warrensburg, 16,340

NOTABLE

President Harry S Truman was born in Lamar; The restored home of George Caleb Bingham in Arrow Rock honors the American artist.

Rep. Emanuel Cleaver II (D)

CAPITOL OFFICE
225-4535
emanuel.cleaver@mail.house.gov
www.house.gov/cleaver
1641 Longworth 20515-2505; fax 225-4403

COMMITTEES
Financial Services
Select Energy Independence & Global Warming

RESIDENCE
Kansas City

BORN
Oct. 26, 1944, Waxahachie, Texas

RELIGION
Methodist

FAMILY
Wife, Dianne Cleaver; four children

EDUCATION
Murray State College (Okla.), attended 1963-64; Prairie View A&M College, B.S. 1972 (sociology); Saint Paul School of Theology, M.Div. 1974

CAREER
Minister; radio talk show host; civil rights group chapter founder; charitable group manager

POLITICAL HIGHLIGHTS
Sought Democratic nomination for Mo. House, 1970; sought Democratic nomination for Kansas City Council, 1975; Kansas City Council, 1979-91; mayor of Kansas City, 1991-99

ELECTION RESULTS

2006 GENERAL		
Emanuel Cleaver II (D)	136,149	64.2%
Jacob Turk (R)	68,456	32.3%
Randall Langkraehr (LIBERT)	7,314	3.5%
2006 PRIMARY		
Emanuel Cleaver II (D)		unopposed
2004 GENERAL		
Emanuel Cleaver II (D)	161,727	55.2%
Jeanne Patterson (R)	123,431	42.1%
Rick Bailie (LIBERT)	5,827	2.0%

Elected 2004; 2nd term

If Cleaver's speeches sound as though they could be delivered from a pulpit rather than a House podium, it's because the former Kansas City mayor is an ordained Methodist minister who casts many of his liberal positions in religious terms.

As the House prepared to vote on expanding federal funding for embryonic stem cell research in 2007, Cleaver said he saw no conflict between religion and science. "I realize that whenever we are able to use the scientific advancements that we are not becoming the enemies of faith, but rather it is another way to praise God and his constantly evolving creation," he said.

That capacity for marrying religious doctrine with liberal policymaking led House Speaker Nancy Pelosi to appoint Cleaver to the newly created panel on energy independence and global warming with the specific charge to reach out to religious leaders. "Contrary to what many believe, certain elements of the evangelical movement in this country are far ahead of mainline Protestants with regard to the environment," Cleaver told The Kansas City Star. In addition, Pelosi asked him, as a former mayor, to serve as the liaison between the global warming committee and the nation's cities.

In just his second term, Cleaver has claimed the position of second vice chairman in the Congressional Black Caucus and serves as a regional whip, one of the mid-level leadership positions in the Democratic Caucus — testaments to the faith his peers and Democratic leaders have in his ability to build coalitions. When House and Senate Democrats unveiled their campaign plan for the 2006 elections at a rally near the Capitol, Cleaver, despite his junior status, was tapped to be one of a handful of speakers.

His rapid, if somewhat unheralded, advancement in the Democratic ranks follows a long history of achievement in the face of steep odds. Raised in poverty in then segregated Wichita Falls, Texas, Cleaver grew up to represent a district in which only about one-quarter of the residents are black. (His district has the smallest black population of any district represented by an African-American.) He has been a pastor, a civil rights leader and a talk show host, in addition to serving as a city councilman and mayor.

That experience helped him win a seat on the Financial Services Committee, where he has been an advocate for fair housing and government-subsidized homes; he often notes that he grew up in public housing. In the 109th Congress (2005-06), and again in 2007, Cleaver introduced a resolution condemning racially restrictive housing covenants.

He has sponsored legislation aimed at getting members of Congress to drive vehicles that use alternative fuels. But most of the bills he offered in the 109th Congress might raise eyebrows among environmentalists: He secured duty suspensions for a wide variety of chemicals used in pesticides and fungicides. The substances, used by the Bayer Corporation's crop-protection facility in Kansas City, are a local economic lubricant.

Cleaver, the senior pastor at St. James United Methodist Church, in Kansas City, Mo., has a talent for turning a phrase, particularly when it comes to issues of faith and the separation of church and state. "When the church and the state sleep together, the church rises the next day without respect," Cleaver told the San Francisco Chronicle in 2005, after Republican Walter B. Jones of North Carolina introduced a bill allowing clergy to make political endorsements from the pulpit without losing religious-based tax exemptions.

Later that year, Cleaver was one of 22 House members, all Democrats, who voted against a House resolution expressing support for Christmas and its traditions and symbols. "As if Christmas was in danger, and if we did not vote, if the people in here did not vote, Christmas was not going to occur," he said later. "I have a master's degree in theology and never read anything which would suggest that God needed the help of the 109th Congress."

On a constitutional amendment banning same-sex marriage, he told The Kansas City Star: "The institution of marriage is holy and sacred, and this body is not one that ought to come within 100 miles of sacredness and holiness."

On major social issues — from transporting minors across state lines for abortions to allowing Terri Schiavo's parents to appeal the decision to remove her feeding tube — Cleaver has voted with his party's liberals. In 2006, he scored a 95 percent rating from the liberal Americans for Democratic Action and an 8 percent rating from the American Conservative Union.

Like most Democrats, Cleaver opposes continued U.S. troop presence in Iraq. "If this conflict continues, there will be only two classes of young people: one-half in graves and the other half in hospitals," he said in February 2007 when the House was debating a resolution opposing President Bush's plan to send more than 21,000 additional U.S. combat troops into Iraq.

When he came to Congress, Cleaver had an agenda that included higher taxes for high-income taxpayers and increased funding for education. His wife until early 2005 was the chief administrative officer for the Kansas City School District. When he was elected second vice chairman of the Black Caucus for the 110th Congress (2007-08), he said his top priority would be to combat state laws that require voters to produce state-issued identification cards to cast ballots.

Cleaver's early run in Congress has not been without controversy. In 2005, according to The Associated Press, he paid back taxes on his car wash business, addressing an issue that had been raised during his first campaign for Congress the previous year.

In 2004, seeking to succeed retiring Democratic Rep. Karen McCarthy in a district that favors Democrats, Cleaver faced Republican businesswoman Jeanne Patterson, who spent more than $2.8 million of her own money — much of it on ads that raised questions about Cleaver's professional and personal ethics. Cleaver denied Patterson's charges and accused her of trying to buy the seat. He emphasized his record as mayor of Kansas City from 1991 to 1999, when he helped bring firms such as Citicorp and Harley Davidson to the region. He defeated Patterson by a comfortable 13 percentage points and easily won re-election in 2006 with 64 percent of the vote.

KEY VOTES

2006

No Stop broadband companies from favoring select Internet traffic
\- Affirm U.S. commitment to war in Iraq and reject setting a withdrawal date for troops
No Repeal requirement for bilingual ballots at the polls
Yes Permit U.S. sale of civilian nuclear technology to India
? Build a 700-mile fence on the U.S.-Mexico border to curb illegal crossings
No Permit warrantless wiretaps of suspected terrorists

2005

No Intervene in the life-support case of Terri Schiavo
Yes Lift President Bush's restrictions on stem cell research funding
Yes Prohibit FBI access to library and bookstore records
No Approve free-trade pact with five Central American countries
No Pass energy policy overhaul favored by President Bush emphasizing domestic oil and gas production
No End mandatory preservation of habitat of endangered animal and plant species
Yes Ban torture of prisoners in U.S. custody

CQ VOTE STUDIES

	PARTY UNITY		PRESIDENTIAL SUPPORT	
	Support	Oppose	Support	Oppose
2006	93%	7%	32%	68%
2005	96%	4%	22%	78%

INTEREST GROUPS

	AFL-CIO	ADA	CCUS	ACU
2006	100%	95%	50%	8%
2005	93%	100%	48%	8%

MISSOURI 5
Kansas City and suburbs

Kansas City long has been known for its blues style of jazz and its barbeque grilling. The Democratic 5th takes in some minority, lower-income communities in the city and some suburban middle-class areas in Jackson and Cass counties. Today, Kansas City is the nation's second-largest rail hub, and a resurgence in high-end loft communities has lured younger, well-to-do residents to the city.

Most of the 5th's residents live in northern Jackson County cities, with 70 percent of the district's population either in Kansas City (shared with the 6th) or Independence (a small part of which is in the 6th). The 5th has a strong steel and automobile manufacturing base in the urban and suburban areas of northern Jackson. The federal government also is a large employer in Kansas City, as is Hallmark Cards, although the city's Marine Corps Support Activity facility closed as part of the 2005 BRAC round.

Overall, the 5th is almost two-thirds white-collar, with tax preparation and personal finance company H&R Block headquartered in the district, and a diverse economic base has helped the district grow into a transportation and telecommunications hub. Many call centers have relocated to the area, which welcomes electronic-based businesses. Meanwhile, many residents travel out of the 5th to work at companies such as Sprint Communications and General Motors. The southern communities depend on agriculture: Despite economic diversification, the 5th is still a viable market for feeder cattle and winter wheat.

With nearly all of Kansas City's black neighborhoods, the 5th is roughly one-fourth black, and the district is reliably Democratic and socially moderate. Democrats have held the Kansas City seat since 1931, and John Kerry took 59 percent of the district's 2004 presidential vote.

MAJOR INDUSTRY
Auto manufacturing, transportation, agriculture, telecommunications

CITIES
Kansas City (pt.), 322,910; Independence (pt.), 110,822; Lee's Summit (pt.), 65,498; Raytown, 30,388

NOTABLE
Harry S Truman hailed from Independence; The Negro Leagues Baseball Museum is in Kansas City; Walt Disney first produced animated cartoons at his Laugh-O-Gram Studio in Kansas City.

Rep. Sam Graves (R)

CAPITOL OFFICE
225-7041
sam.graves@mail.house.gov
www.house.gov/graves
1415 Longworth 20515-2506; fax 225-8221

COMMITTEES
Agriculture
Small Business
Transportation & Infrastructure

RESIDENCE
Tarkio

BORN
Nov. 7, 1963, Fairfax, Mo.

RELIGION
Baptist

FAMILY
Wife, Lesley Graves; three children

EDUCATION
U. of Missouri, B.S. 1986 (agronomy)

CAREER
Farmer

POLITICAL HIGHLIGHTS
Mo. House, 1993-95; Mo. Senate, 1995-2000

ELECTION RESULTS

2006 GENERAL		
Sam Graves (R)	150,882	61.6%
Mary Jo Shettles (D)	87,477	35.7%
Erik Buck (LIBERT)	4,757	1.9%
2006 PRIMARY		
Sam Graves (R)		unopposed
2004 GENERAL		
Sam Graves (R)	196,516	63.8%
Charles S. Broomfield (D)	106,987	34.8%
Erik Buck (LIBERT)	4,352	1.4%

PREVIOUS WINNING PERCENTAGES
2002 (63%); 2000 (51%)

Elected 2000; 4th term

If you ask Graves, Lady Bird Johnson's Highway Beautification Act of 1965 is just another example of government meddling. As a member of the Small Business Committee, he once proposed exemptions to the law's billboard ban to free up businesses to advertise where they please. "The Highway Beautification Act is an ugly obstacle for small businesses," he says. "If we continue to take away billboards because someone in Washington decides what is pretty to look at, small businesses will continue to suffer."

A sixth-generation farmer from the rural northwest corner of Missouri, Graves is not given to half-measures in his political views. He has called for a halt in all immigration until foreigners already here are accounted for. He sponsored a bill to terminate the federal income tax code, and he wants the federal government to stop acquiring land for national parks and forests.

One of the rare places Graves sees a proper role for the federal government is in helping farmers like himself. He argues that farmers are at the mercy of factors beyond their control — including the imperative of providing low-cost food to consumers — so government involvement is essential. With a seat on the Agriculture Committee, Graves has a hand in a major rewrite of farm law slated for the 110th Congress (2007-08). The last time the law was modified, in 2002, Graves won a provision to boost farmers' earnings by easing their entry into other stages of food production, such as food processing and the transportation of crops.

A lifelong resident of tiny Tarkio, Graves returned to the family farm after graduating with a degree in agronomy from the University of Missouri in 1986. The following year, NBC's "Today" show featured him as an example of a young person willing to stay on the land and farm. He said on the show that he wanted to preserve his family's heritage.

Now, his younger brother Danny and his father, Sam Graves Sr., run the farm, raising corn, soybeans and cattle. Though he spends most days on Capitol Hill, Graves will wax rhapsodic about the many uses of baling wire and of his memories of climbing up on the 1968 John Deere 4020 tractor that his grandfather bought new. When he's in his home district, Graves sometimes helps out. "If I'm out on the combine all day by myself, I take a tape recorder and it clears my head," he says.

Like his views on domestic issues, Graves' outlook on the top foreign policy issue of the day pulls no punches. Don't look for him among the legions of lawmakers re-evaluating their earlier support for the war in Iraq. "This idea of armchair quarterbacking and telling enemies what we are doing is ridiculous," Graves says with his usual candor. "We need to put our trust in the military and the commanders. We've got soldiers defending this country and putting [their] life on the line. This is a war on radical Islam. Every single war we've gotten in trouble with is because politicians stuck their noses in."

As Congress and President Bush search for an immigration policy all can agree on, Graves comes down squarely in favor of tough enforcement; he opposes Bush's plan to give illegal immigrants "guest worker" status. "We've got a sick immigration policy," Graves says. "We need a much more stringent policy. We have to keep illegals out, and we have to do a better job in terms of legal immigration by getting rid of many of the fast-track programs. They should have been done away with right after 9/11."

Although agricultural issues top his agenda, Graves succeeded in passing a couple bills unrelated to farm policy in the 109th Congress (2005-06). He was the principal sponsor of legislation capping at 36 percent so-called payday loans offered near military bases. The loans, typically peddled out of storefronts in low-income neighborhoods, carried rates as high as 400 percent and were considered a form of predatory lending. Graves fended off a vigorous lobbying campaign by the Community Financial Services Association, the trade group for payday lenders.

He also was successful with an amendment to the 2005 transportation bill banning vicarious liability, a legal avenue for people injured by a rental car to sue the rental car company, as well as the driver of the vehicle. The trial lawyer lobby defended vicarious liability.

Earlier, two of Graves' proposals were included in the No Child Left Behind education bill of 2001. One requires that 95 percent of federal education dollars be spent in the classroom and the other protects teachers from frivolous lawsuits arising from disciplining students. His wife, Lesley, is an elementary school teacher.

As a fiscal conservative, Graves raised eyebrows the same year by obtaining a $273,000 grant for the Kansas City suburb of Blue Springs to combat Goth culture among local teenagers. The town gave half the money back in 2004 because it could not find enough of a problem to combat.

The Graves family long has been active in northwest Missouri politics. Graves' great-grandfather, also named Sam, was a Democrat who served on the Atchison County Commission. And Graves' brother Todd was appointed by Bush to be the U.S. attorney for western Missouri.

Graves became involved in politics through the Missouri Farm Bureau, and was once named the organization's national outstanding young farmer. He spent two years in the Missouri House and six in the state Senate. He once staged a filibuster that threatened a school desegregation bill that he thought did not contain enough for rural districts. He sponsored a measure successfully easing state automobile inspection requirements, and proposed that prisoners be required to work on chain gangs.

Six months before the 2000 election, when Rep. Pat Danner, a popular conservative Democrat who had held the 6th District seat for four terms, unexpectedly announced her retirement, Graves jumped into the primary contest and quickly overshadowed several less-known Republican hopefuls.

The Democrats nominated the congresswoman's son, Steve Danner. But Graves' assertive campaign and conservative politics gave him momentum in a district that, other than St. Joseph and its portion of Kansas City, consists mainly of small towns and farms. Though historically Democratic, the district had become competitive, and is now considered Republican. Graves has won re-election easily since.

KEY VOTES

2006

No Stop broadband companies from favoring select Internet traffic

Yes Affirm U.S. commitment to war in Iraq and reject setting a withdrawal date for troops

\+ Repeal requirement for bilingual ballots at the polls

Yes Permit U.S. sale of civilian nuclear technology to India

Yes Build a 700-mile fence on the U.S.-Mexico border to curb illegal crossings

Yes Permit warrantless wiretaps of suspected terrorists

2005

Yes Intervene in the life-support case of Terri Schiavo

No Lift President Bush's restrictions on stem cell research funding

No Prohibit FBI access to library and bookstore records

Yes Approve free-trade pact with five Central American countries

Yes Pass energy policy overhaul favored by President Bush emphasizing domestic oil and gas production

Yes End mandatory preservation of habitat of endangered animal and plant species

No Ban torture of prisoners in U.S. custody

CQ VOTE STUDIES

	PARTY UNITY		PRESIDENTIAL SUPPORT	
	Support	Oppose	Support	Oppose
2006	98%	2%	95%	5%
2005	95%	5%	86%	14%
2004	93%	7%	79%	21%
2003	96%	4%	92%	8%
2002	95%	5%	79%	21%

INTEREST GROUPS

	AFL-CIO	ADA	CCUS	ACU
2006	15%	0%	100%	88%
2005	13%	0%	93%	92%
2004	20%	10%	100%	92%
2003	0%	5%	100%	83%
2002	11%	0%	95%	100%

MISSOURI 6
Northwest – St. Joseph, part of Kansas City

In Missouri's northwest, the 6th is bordered by Iowa to the north and the Missouri River to the west and much of the south. Rich farmland continues to drive the district's economy, while suburban areas surrounding Kansas City and St. Joseph — both located on the Missouri River — provide a solid middle-class workforce for the area's shipping and manufacturing industries.

Platte, Clay and eastern Jackson counties surround Kansas City (shared with the 5th). Platte County's Kansas City International Airport, a major hub for Southwest Airlines, provides many district jobs. A Ford plant in Claycomo employs around 5,000 and is one of the area's largest employers. American Airlines, Citigroup, Farmland and Harley-Davidson employ thousands of other district residents.

The state's largest city north of Kansas City — about an hour's drive — is St. Joseph, which was a Pony Express terminus for riders carrying mail to and from California in the early 1860s. Today, it remains a distribution center and a district economic hub.

Outside of the two metropolitan areas, farmland spreads for miles. Corn and livestock are prevalent here, and new processing plants have created a growing market for soybeans as well. Craig, in Holt County, is home to the Golden Triangle ethanol plant, which produces 19 million gallons of ethanol per year.

Although historically Democratic, the 6th became politically competitive during the last quarter of the 20th century before moving firmly into the Republican column this decade. George W. Bush won all 26 of the district's counties in the 2004 presidential election, earning 57 percent of the 6th's overall vote in the process. Republicans seeking state office also have fared better recently, especially in the northern, rural areas.

MAJOR INDUSTRY
Agriculture, international shipping, manufacturing

CITIES
Kansas City (pt.), 118,635; St. Joseph, 73,990; Blue Springs (pt.), 39,698; Gladstone, 26,365; Liberty, 26,232

NOTABLE
The Jesse James Home in St. Joseph was where the outlaw was shot and killed in 1882; The Camden Point Baptist Church Cemetery is the oldest Confederate cemetery west of the Mississippi River.

Rep. Roy Blunt (R)

CAPITOL OFFICE
225-6536
blunt.house.gov
217 Cannon 20515-2507; fax 225-5604

COMMITTEES
No committee assignments

RESIDENCE
Strafford

BORN
Jan. 10, 1950, Niangua, Mo.

RELIGION
Baptist

FAMILY
Wife, Abigail Blunt; four children

EDUCATION
Southwest Baptist U., B.A. 1970 (history); Southwest Missouri State U., M.A. 1972 (history & government)

CAREER
University president; teacher

POLITICAL HIGHLIGHTS
Greene County clerk, 1973-84; Republican nominee for lieutenant governor, 1980; Mo. secretary of state, 1985-93; sought Republican nomination for governor, 1992

ELECTION RESULTS

2006 GENERAL		
Roy Blunt (R)	160,942	66.7%
Jack Truman (D)	72,592	30.1%
Kevin Craig (LIBERT)	7,566	3.1%
2006 PRIMARY		
Roy Blunt (R)	47,758	79.9%
Clendon L. Kinder (R)	5,197	8.7%
Midge Potts (R)	4,294	7.2%
Bernard F. Kennetz Jr. (R)	2,498	4.2%
2004 GENERAL		
Roy Blunt (R)	210,080	70.5%
Jim Newberry (D)	84,356	28.3%

PREVIOUS WINNING PERCENTAGES
2002 (75%); 2000 (74%); 1998 (73%); 1996 (65%)

Elected 1996; 6th term

Blunt has had an uneven tenure as the GOP whip, a job that in many ways is now easier for him in the minority when defections from the party line don't matter as much as they did when Republicans had the majority. Many of Blunt's colleagues like his cool-headed personal style but others say he hasn't been an effective vote-rustler, which is the chief duty of the whip. Still, he retained sufficient support among the rank and file to be returned to the leadership in the 110th Congress (2007-08).

Not too long ago, Blunt was thought likely to be the next Speaker of the House. Then came the tumultuous events of 2006. Majority Leader Tom DeLay of Texas, one of the most powerful leaders of his time, left Congress under an ethics cloud, leaving a void in the GOP hierarchy. Blunt was the likely successor, but his close ties to DeLay hurt him. Some members harbored doubts that he was as hardworking or as effective as his deputy, Eric Cantor of Virginia, considered a skilled vote-counter.

John A. Boehner of Ohio, chairman of the Education and the Workforce Committee, challenged Blunt for majority leader. Blunt refused to give up the whip's job to run, blocking several Republicans eager to be his replacement and reinforcing a view among some colleagues that he is opportunistic. Todd Tiahrt of Kansas publicly called on Blunt to step aside and clear the field for others, including Tiahrt, Cantor, Zach Wamp of Tennessee and Mike Rogers of Michigan.

In party elections in February 2006, Blunt led Boehner 110-79 on the first ballot while conservative John Shadegg of Arizona drew 40 votes. On a second ballot, most of Shadegg's supporters shifted to Boehner, who defeated Blunt, 122-109. Joel Hefley of Colorado said, "That tie to DeLay was hard for Blunt to overcome."

Blunt continued to work as whip under Boehner, and he ran for the post again after the November 2006 elections swept Republicans from power. His allies praised his "calming manner" during calamitous times. Although Boehner and Blunt were challenged by unhappy conservatives, they both prevailed handily. Blunt rebuffed a challenge by Shadegg, 137-57.

In the minority, Blunt has had to switch to playing defense and picking at Democratic weaknesses — for instance, leading the charge in 2007 when Speaker Nancy Pelosi requested access to an Air Force jet to travel back to her San Francisco district when the House is not in session. Blunt called the plane a "flying Lincoln Bedroom," a reference to President Bill Clinton's use of the White House for fundraising when he was in office.

Minority status has also put Blunt more in touch with his conservative roots. Once among President Bush's closest allies in the House, Blunt introduced a bill in the 110th Congress to seriously weaken Bush's No Child Left Behind education law, enacted in 2002, by letting states opt out and still keep their federal funding. Blunt now says he is troubled that the law's testing mandates dramatically shift authority over schools to the federal government.

Many Republicans find Blunt refreshing after their years under DeLay's thumb. Blunt's approach is to win votes from Republicans by doing favors for them on other bills, not by threatening them. "What the whip needs to understand is what members want to accomplish while they're here, what things about their district define the way they do their job here," he says. "Often, you [are] able to say, 'I've been to your district, and this is not a vote that's a problem for you in your district.'"

Blunt holds regular "listening sessions," bringing into a room a dozen lawmakers from opposing sides of an issue and letting them experience the difficulty leaders face in finding middle ground. Although Blunt is a conservative, others on the right have not always appreciated his conciliatory style. In 2003, the House leadership had to pull from the floor a bill to allow businesses to offer workers compensatory time in lieu of overtime pay. Speaker J. Dennis Hastert and DeLay felt that Blunt had not worked hard enough to get the votes to pass it.

Blunt also does not have a blemish-free ethical record. In 2002, he tried to slip a provision benefiting Philip Morris USA into a homeland security bill at a time he was romantically involved with Philip Morris lobbyist Abigail Perlman, whom he later married after divorcing his first wife of 35 years.

Blunt rose through the ranks quickly by allying himself with DeLay, who made him chief deputy whip in the 106th Congress (1999-2000). That role, the GOP's top non-elective leadership post, helped him run successfully for whip after the 2002 elections. He built his own loyalty base by helping vulnerable Republicans at election time; his political action committee gave $713,000 to candidates in the 2004 election and $945,000 in 2006.

The son of a dairy farmer and a state legislator, Blunt was raised on a farm near Springfield. He still lives on a farm near there, and each summer conducts an agricultural tour of the district, visiting farms and ranches and bringing in foreign trade representatives from Asia.

After college, Blunt became a high school government and history teacher. But he was active in politics at an early age, working in 1972 on an unsuccessful congressional bid by conservative Republican John Ashcroft, who went on to become governor, senator and then U.S. attorney general. A year later, Blunt was appointed Greene County clerk by GOP Gov. Christopher S. Bond, now Missouri's senior senator.

Blunt won the first of two terms as Missouri secretary of state in 1984. That set the stage for his campaign for governor in 1992. After losing the GOP primary, Blunt accepted the presidency of his alma mater, Southwest Baptist University. But he jumped back into public life when GOP Rep. Mel Hancock announced his retirement in 1996. Blunt won a narrow primary victory over Gary Nodler, a former congressional aide. In the general election, Blunt cruised to victory with 65 percent of the vote in the reliably Republican district. He has been easily re-elected since.

In 2006, Blunt, then 56, and his wife adopted a son from Russia. He has three adult children from his previous marriage, including Matt Blunt, a Republican who was elected governor of Missouri in 2004.

KEY VOTES

2006

- No Stop broadband companies from favoring select Internet traffic
- Yes Affirm U.S. commitment to war in Iraq and reject setting a withdrawal date for troops
- Yes Repeal requirement for bilingual ballots at the polls
- Yes Permit U.S. sale of civilian nuclear technology to India
- Yes Build a 700-mile fence on the U.S.-Mexico border to curb illegal crossings
- Yes Permit warrantless wiretaps of suspected terrorists

2005

- Yes Intervene in the life-support case of Terri Schiavo
- No Lift President Bush's restrictions on stem cell research funding
- No Prohibit FBI access to library and bookstore records
- Yes Approve free-trade pact with five Central American countries
- Yes Pass energy policy overhaul favored by President Bush emphasizing domestic oil and gas production
- Yes End mandatory preservation of habitat of endangered animal and plant species
- No Ban torture of prisoners in U.S. custody

CQ VOTE STUDIES

	PARTY UNITY		PRESIDENTIAL SUPPORT	
	Support	Oppose	Support	Oppose
2006	98%	2%	97%	3%
2005	98%	2%	91%	9%
2004	97%	3%	100%	0%
2003	98%	2%	100%	0%
2002	98%	2%	91%	9%

INTEREST GROUPS

	AFL-CIO	ADA	CCUS	ACU
2006	7%	0%	100%	88%
2005	14%	0%	93%	96%
2004	7%	0%	100%	96%
2003	0%	5%	97%	88%
2002	14%	0%	100%	100%

MISSOURI 7
Southwest — Springfield, Joplin

The 7th sits nestled in the southwestern corner of Missouri. Springfield, in Greene County, is the region's industrial and commercial center, while Branson leads the 7th's thriving tourism industry. This part of the "Show Me State" grew by 24 percent in the 1990s and retains a strong agricultural foundation.

Springfield, nicknamed the "Queen City of the Ozarks," is a manufacturing hub, but also is home to a few large national retail chains, including Bass Pro Shops and O'Reilly Auto Parts. Nearly 50 percent of district residents live in either Greene or neighboring Christian County on the 7th's eastern edge. The district's other population center, Joplin, is across the district in Jasper County. Once a lead and zinc mining town, Joplin is now a manufacturing and trucking center.

A family-friendly entertainment destination, Branson is a magnet for country music fans. This town of 6,000 draws more than 6 million visitors a year. The city boasts more than 40 theaters, including the Andy Williams Moon River, Mel Tillis and Dick Clark's American Bandstand theaters. The area also relies on the resort industry around Taneycomo and Table Rock lakes.

The southwestern corner of the district supports beef and dairy cattle, along with poultry farming. Expansion along U.S. Highway 71, which runs from Kansas City into Arkansas, is expected to improve the area's accessibility and economic prospects.

The 7th long has been a GOP bastion. The Assemblies of God, based in Springfield, is among the active religious groups that reflect the area's devout, conservative population. The district gave Republican George W. Bush 67 percent of its vote in the 2004 presidential election — Bush's best showing in the state.

MAJOR INDUSTRY
Agriculture, tourism, manufacturing

CITIES
Springfield, 151,580; Joplin, 45,504; Carthage, 12,668

NOTABLE
George Washington Carver's boyhood home in Diamond (Newton County) is now a national monument; Precious Moments Inspiration Park, devoted to the inspirational figurines, is in Carthage.

Rep. Jo Ann Emerson (R)

CAPITOL OFFICE
225-4404
www.house.gov/emerson
2440 Rayburn 20515-2508; fax 226-0326

COMMITTEES
Appropriations

RESIDENCE
Cape Girardeau

BORN
Sept. 16, 1950, Washington, D.C.

RELIGION
Presbyterian

FAMILY
Husband, Ron Gladney; two children, six stepchildren

EDUCATION
Ohio Wesleyan U., B.A. 1972 (political science)

CAREER
Public affairs executive; lobbyist

POLITICAL HIGHLIGHTS
No previous office

ELECTION RESULTS

2006 GENERAL		
Jo Ann Emerson (R)	156,164	71.6%
Veronica J. Hambacker (D)	57,557	26.4%
Brandon McCullough (LIBERT)	4,268	2.0%
2006 PRIMARY		
Jo Ann Emerson (R)		unopposed
2004 GENERAL		
Jo Ann Emerson (R)	194,039	72.2%
Dean Henderson (D)	71,543	26.6%

PREVIOUS WINNING PERCENTAGES*
2002 (72%); 2000 (69%); 1998 (63%); 1996 (50%); 1996 Special Election (63%)
*Elected as an independent in 1996 general election

Elected 1996; 6th full term

Emerson's party lost the past election, and almost immediately she began to enjoy some real power. The moderate Republican for years had pushed bills aimed at cutting the costs of prescription drugs only to be shut down by conservative GOP leaders who often refused to bring them up for a vote. When Democrats took office, she started getting somewhere.

Emerson was featured at a Democratic event in 2007 to kick off drug importation legislation, which she has long advocated as a way to cut costs for seniors by allowing them to buy U.S.-made drugs from foreign countries where price controls are in effect. The media-friendly event was held by Rep. Rahm Emanuel of Illinois, one of the leaders of the Democratic Party's victory in the 2006 midterm election, and liberal Rosa DeLauro of Connecticut.

Emerson was invited into discussions with Democratic leaders about a bill with a wider reach. It would give the giant Medicare program the authority to negotiate lower drug prices with private industry, something that both the industry and Republican leaders opposed and that was expressly prohibited in the GOP's 2003 Medicare drug bill.

Emerson can be blunt, and she makes no apologies for reaching across party lines on her centerpiece issue. With drug prices soaring, Emerson said lawmakers needed to "stop listening to the scare tactics of drug companies" and pay more attention to average citizens. In arguing for allowing Medicare to negotiate a better deal, Emerson said, "The Department of Defense isn't forced to buy bullets one at a time and we shouldn't force Medicare to buy medicines one pill at a time."

Her involvement in the early Democratic efforts points to the influence Emerson can have as a Republican willing to do business with the other side. She may get satisfaction from her newfound impact on legislation, after the treatment she sometimes got from her own leadership in recent years.

In what was viewed as a deal gone sour for Emerson, her drug importation bill of 2003 was the victim of backroom dealing. Emerson withheld support of a Medicare drug bill that GOP leaders wanted until they agreed to permit a floor vote on her bill allowing drug imports from 25 industrialized countries. Her yes vote allowed the leaders' Medicare bill to pass.

A month later, the House passed Emerson's drug importation bill with a higher number of GOP votes than expected, 87. Despite the show of support, the measure was mysteriously dropped from the final Medicare bill when it went to conference with the Senate, a process controlled by the leaders and the committee chairmen.

Eventually, Republican leaders and President Bush got a Medicare drug bill to the floor, but it was silent on drug importation. Emerson refused to support it. During a dramatic, night-long vote, she voted no, and then hid behind a banister on the Democratic side of the chamber while Republican Whip Roy Blunt, on an arm-twisting mission, searched for her in vain. "At that point, it was high drama. I didn't want to miss anything," Emerson said later. "They didn't talk to me because they didn't find me."

Emerson was among only 20 House Republicans who voted for at least five of the six bills that made up the Democrats' "first 100 hours" agenda of the 110th Congress (2007-08). She voted for increasing the minimum wage and for more federal funding for embryonic stem cell research, which conservatives liken to abortion because it uses surplus embryos from in vitro fertilization clinics. She objected to one bill because it relinquished authority to the United Nations for a security initiative on weapons of mass destruction.

Emerson and 10 other Republicans crossed party lines in 2004 to support a Democratic motion in favor of making both tax cuts and spending subject to pay-as-you-go rules.

Although a moderate in most cases, Emerson has a socially conservative side. She opposes abortion and same-sex marriage. She also voted for the 2002 resolution authorizing the war in Iraq; her stepdaughter Jessica, an Army captain, did a tour in Iraq. Emerson says, "I'm very proud of my stepdaughter, but it's heart-wrenching to send her off." In 2007, she told the St. Louis Post-Dispatch she was "totally against" Bush's plan to send more troops to Iraq, but nevertheless voted against a Democratic resolution in opposition, saying that it "is not going to change one thing."

Emerson represents the southeastern Missouri congressional district, where farming is a mainstay. She has become a self-taught expert on agriculture policy since she succeeded her husband, Bill Emerson, in the 8th District. (He died of lung cancer in 1996.) Early in 2005, she was one of 12 Republicans who voted against the GOP-drafted budget resolution, after leading the opposition to the plan's proposed cuts in farm programs.

As a member of the Appropriations Committee and its Agriculture Subcommittee, Emerson knows the importance of delivering federal dollars to her district, as symbolized by her husband's legacy, a $100 million Mississippi River bridge linking Missouri and Illinois that bears his name.

Emerson was raised in the suburbs of Washington, D.C., where her father, Ab Hermann, was executive director of the Republican National Committee for many years. She says her father taught her to get along with Democrats, including family friend Hale Boggs, the powerful Louisiana representative who rose to majority leader before disappearing on a plane flight in Alaska in 1972. Emerson remained friends with Boggs' widow, Lindy, and drew inspiration from her race to succeed her husband after his death.

After graduating from Ohio Wesleyan, Emerson worked for the National Republican Congressional Committee and then as a lobbyist. In Washington, she met Bill Emerson, a former congressional staffer who also was a lobbyist, and they married. Bill Emerson was elected to the House in 1980, and was a candidate for a ninth House term when he died. Jo Ann Emerson ran as an independent in the general-election race to succeed him, because the partisan filing deadline had passed. She won with 50 percent of the vote, finishing 13 percentage points ahead of Democrat Emily Firebaugh and 39 points ahead of the official GOP candidate, Richard A. Kline. Emerson's re-elections have been by strong margins. In 2000, she married a Democrat, St. Louis labor lawyer Ron Gladney.

KEY VOTES

2006

No Stop broadband companies from favoring select Internet traffic

Yes Affirm U.S. commitment to war in Iraq and reject setting a withdrawal date for troops

Yes Repeal requirement for bilingual ballots at the polls

Yes Permit U.S. sale of civilian nuclear technology to India

Yes Build a 700-mile fence on the U.S.-Mexico border to curb illegal crossings

Yes Permit warrantless wiretaps of suspected terrorists

2005

Yes Intervene in the life-support case of Terri Schiavo

Yes Lift President Bush's restrictions on stem cell research funding

Yes Prohibit FBI access to library and bookstore records

Yes Approve free-trade pact with five Central American countries

Yes Pass energy policy overhaul favored by President Bush emphasizing domestic oil and gas production

Yes End mandatory preservation of habitat of endangered animal and plant species

Yes Ban torture of prisoners in U.S. custody

CQ VOTE STUDIES

	PARTY UNITY		PRESIDENTIAL SUPPORT	
	Support	Oppose	Support	Oppose
2006	89%	11%	74%	26%
2005	90%	10%	68%	32%
2004	89%	11%	61%	39%
2003	91%	9%	93%	7%
2002	93%	7%	81%	19%

INTEREST GROUPS

	AFL-CIO	ADA	CCUS	ACU
2006	50%	15%	93%	72%
2005	27%	15%	89%	88%
2004	50%	20%	86%	76%
2003	31%	10%	92%	95%
2002	22%	0%	95%	96%

MISSOURI 8
Southeast — Cape Girardeau, Ozark Plateau

The 8th is Missouri's largest district in size, and some of the state's most bountiful farmland can be found here alongside mountains, forests and Mississippi Valley towns. The district has the state's lowest median income (less than $28,000), and only 12 percent — Missouri's smallest percentage — of the 8th's residents have at least a bachelor's degree.

Agriculture and lead mining fuel the central counties, while the southeast area, dubbed the boot heel because of its shape, is a former wheat-growing region that now produces soybeans, corn, cotton and rice. Lumber also features heavily in the 8th, and the district includes four-fifths of the 1.5 million-acre Mark Twain National Forest that dots the countryside of southern Missouri.

Major growth centers in the district include the northern counties of Phelps and St. Francois, which have been boosted by light manufacturing and defense subcontracting firms. Located on the Mississippi River, Cape Girardeau is the district's most populous city and is a regional hub for education, commerce and health care.

Frequent flooding and earthquakes from the New Madrid fault line that runs through southeastern Missouri make the 8th a disaster-prone region, although reinforced levees and highways have reduced the risk. Preparation for smaller floods along the Mississippi is still an annual spring ritual in the border towns.

The district spans the political spectrum from solidly Republican counties in the west, and in the northeast along the Mississippi River, to "Yellow Dog" Democratic territory in the boot heel. Voters tend to be conservative on social issues such as abortion and gun control. George W. Bush carried the 8th with 63 percent of the district's 2004 presidential vote.

MAJOR INDUSTRY

Agriculture, lead mining, lumber

CITIES

Cape Girardeau, 35,349; Sikeston, 16,992; Poplar Bluff, 16,651; Rolla, 16,367

NOTABLE

The Laura Ingalls Wilder Historic Home and Museum is in Mansfield, where the author wrote the beloved "Little House" series; The New Madrid region has more earthquakes than any other part of the United States east of the Rocky Mountains.

Rep. Kenny Hulshof (R)

CAPITOL OFFICE
225-2956
rep.hulshof@mail.house.gov
hulshof.house.gov
409 Cannon 20515-2509; fax 225-5712

COMMITTEES
Ways & Means

RESIDENCE
Columbia

BORN
May 22, 1958, Sikeston, Mo.

RELIGION
Roman Catholic

FAMILY
Wife, Renee Hulshof; two children

EDUCATION
U. of Missouri, B.S. 1980 (agriculture economics); U. of Mississippi, J.D. 1983

CAREER
State and city prosecutor; public defender

POLITICAL HIGHLIGHTS
Sought Republican nomination for Boone County prosecutor, 1992; Republican nominee for U.S. House, 1994

ELECTION RESULTS

2006 GENERAL		
Kenny Hulshof (R)	149,114	61.4%
Duane N. Burghard (D)	87,145	35.9%
Steven R. Hedrick (LIBERT)	3,925	1.6%
Bill Hastings (PRO)	2,487	1.0%
2006 PRIMARY		
Kenny Hulshof (R)		unopposed
2004 GENERAL		
Kenny Hulshof (R)	193,429	64.6%
Linda Jacobsen (D)	101,343	33.8%
Tamara A. Millay (LIBERT)	3,228	1.1%

PREVIOUS WINNING PERCENTAGES
2002 (68%); 2000 (59%); 1998 (62%); 1996 (49%)

Elected 1996; 6th term

Hulshof volunteered to take a seat on the House ethics committee — a rare move he likened to offering oneself for jury duty — as party leaders made committee assignments for the 110th Congress (2007-08).

His Republican leadership turned him down, even though he is a party loyalist in most respects and a reliable conservative who supports tax cuts, backs President Bush on the war in Iraq and opposes abortion.

A state prosecutor before he entered politics, Hulshof (HULLZ-hoff) was a member of the House ethics committee that investigated a series of allegations against Republican Majority Leader Tom DeLay of Texas during the 108th Congress (2003-04). The panel voted to reprimand DeLay for three separate incidents, much to the displeasure of House Republican leaders. Hulshof was unceremoniously dumped from the ethics panel at the start of the 109th Congress (2005-06), along with the Republican chairman, Joel T. Hefley of Colorado, and another GOP member who had voted to rebuke DeLay. In 2006, when the House voted on revised ethics rules, Hulshof was one of 20 Republicans to vote against the package, saying it "failed to provide for meaningful enforcement of ethics rules."

By the start of the 110th Congress, DeLay was long gone, Democrats were running the House and John A. Boehner of Ohio was the top-ranking Republican leader. Hulshof asked to be restored to the Committee on Standards of Official Conduct, as the ethics panel is formally titled. Boehner turned him down, without explanation.

Although the Democratic takeover gives him fewer chances to shine, Hulshof is still seen as a rising GOP star in Missouri, where he has been mentioned as a potential Senate candidate if Republican Christopher S. Bond should decide against seeking a fifth term in 2010. His dust-up with his own leadership over ethics is likely to enhance his reputation as a straight-shooter willing to put principle above partisanship.

In the meantime, Hulshof will concentrate on advancing his tax-cutting priorities as a member of the Ways and Means Committee. He supports making Bush's tax cuts permanent, and he sponsored legislation the House passed in 2005 to repeal the federal estate tax. That goal appears out of reach with Democrats in charge, but Hulshof will continue to press for a permanent overhaul of the tax. "The death tax is the most unfair and least productive federal tax," he said in 2006. "It benefits the U.S. Treasury very little, but hits small businesses and farmers very hard."

He has been a major player in farm states' campaign to use tax credits to create markets for renewable fuels, such as ethanol and biodiesel, both of which are derived from agricultural products. He finally succeeded in winning the tax credit for biodiesel — largely made from soybeans, a leading Missouri crop — as part of a corporate tax bill in 2004. The tax break was extended to 2008 in the 2005 energy policy overhaul. Hulshof will continue to push for additional tax incentives for renewable energy.

Hulshof has made a concerted effort to define himself as not only conservative but also pragmatic and cooperative. He may no longer be able to steer his own bills through the House, but he proved early in 2007 that he could work with Ways and Means Democrats to get his provisions added to legislation sponsored by others. He won inclusion of an anti-fraud section in a bill to extend tax breaks for victims of Hurricane Katrina, the 2005 storm that devastated the Gulf Coast. The panel also approved a provision he wrote extending protections against genetic discrimination by insurers or employers to participants in clinical research.

In his first term, Hulshof was a leading force behind the first in a series of biannual and bipartisan "civility" retreats, designed to allow Republicans and Democrats to get acquainted with one another in a non-confrontational setting. In the same vein, Hulshof's wife, Renee, formed a support group with the wife of a state Democratic figure for spouses of those deployed to the Middle East for the Iraq War.

A former high school athlete, Hulshof stars as first baseman for the Republicans in the annual charity baseball game against the Democrats, and as a guard and a forward on the congressional basketball team that plays a team of lobbyists for charity. He also sings and plays the drums in his church choir — and in "The Second Amendments," a bipartisan congressional country rock band fronted by lead singer Collin C. Peterson, a Minnesota Democrat, and including three other Republicans. The band played for the troops in Iraq and Afghanistan in December 2005. "Hopefully they'll overlook our lack of talent and appreciate the effort," he told the St. Louis Post-Dispatch shortly before departing for the Middle East.

Hulshof grew up on a farm near the boot heel of southeastern Missouri and still recalls getting an uncomfortably personal lesson in how politics influences agriculture when his parents almost lost their farm in the early 1980s because of the U.S. embargo on grain sales to the Soviet Union.

An agricultural economics graduate of the University of Missouri, he went on to the University of Mississippi for law school. Upon graduation, he worked as a public defender and then as a prosecutor in Cape Girardeau County before moving to Columbia to work for the state attorney general.

Hulshof was a fill-in candidate in 1994 against Democratic Rep. Harold L. Volkmer, a two-decade incumbent. He was tapped by party leaders when the GOP front-runner bowed out after the filing deadline. Despite being a political neophyte with no name recognition, Hulshof lost by just 5 percentage points. When he tried again in 1996, he first overcame a stiff primary challenge from wealthy ophthalmologist Harry Eggleston, then edged Volkmer by slightly fewer than 6,000 votes in November.

Hulshof has flirted with seeking higher office. Bond and other prominent Republicans tried in 2001 to persuade him to challenge Democrat Jean Carnahan's bid for what was almost a full term in the Senate. He demurred, citing family reasons. Republican Jim Talent entered the race instead and won — only to lose his re-election bid in 2006. After his easy House re-election in 2002, Hulshof briefly considered a run for governor in 2004. He won re-election to the House comfortably in 2004 and 2006.

KEY VOTES

2006

No Stop broadband companies from favoring select Internet traffic

Yes Affirm U.S. commitment to war in Iraq and reject setting a withdrawal date for troops

Yes Repeal requirement for bilingual ballots at the polls

Yes Permit U.S. sale of civilian nuclear technology to India

Yes Build a 700-mile fence on the U.S.-Mexico border to curb illegal crossings

Yes Permit warrantless wiretaps of suspected terrorists

2005

Yes Intervene in the life-support case of Terri Schiavo

No Lift President Bush's restrictions on stem cell research funding

No Prohibit FBI access to library and bookstore records

Yes Approve free-trade pact with five Central American countries

Yes Pass energy policy overhaul favored by President Bush emphasizing domestic oil and gas production

Yes End mandatory preservation of habitat of endangered animal and plant species

Yes Ban torture of prisoners in U.S. custody

CQ VOTE STUDIES

	PARTY UNITY		PRESIDENTIAL SUPPORT	
	Support	Oppose	Support	Oppose
2006	95%	5%	97%	3%
2005	93%	7%	83%	17%
2004	96%	4%	94%	6%
2003	96%	4%	98%	2%
2002	95%	5%	88%	12%

INTEREST GROUPS

	AFL-CIO	ADA	CCUS	ACU
2006	21%	0%	100%	80%
2005	13%	0%	92%	92%
2004	8%	5%	100%	91%
2003	7%	5%	100%	88%
2002	11%	10%	100%	96%

MISSOURI 9

Northeast – Columbia, St. Louis exurbs

Bordering Iowa and Illinois, as well as five other districts in Missouri, the 9th picks up small towns scattered among the farmland areas of northeastern and central Missouri. Columbia, the district's single large city, and some western St. Louis suburbs are the 9th's only population centers.

The 9th splits suburban St. Charles County with the neighboring 2nd District and encompasses all of adjacent Warren and Franklin counties. General Motors and Boeing plants in nearby districts provide jobs, but much of the area's growth has come from small businesses. Nestled along the district's portion of the Missouri River Valley, residents of Gasconade and surrounding counties call their area the state's wine country, and boast a wine industry that dates back to the 19th century. In other rural areas, the district's economy still thrives on cattle, soybeans, corn and winter wheat.

About halfway between St. Louis and Kansas City, Columbia is a steadily growing and mostly middle-class city. Its economy depends on a robust and growing University of Missouri flagship campus, which is a land-grant institution and the state's largest public research university. The city's medical facilities include the Harry S Truman Memorial Veterans Hospital, and Columbia is a regional hub for companies in the insurance industry, such as Shelter Insurance.

Historically Democratic, the 9th has become increasingly Republican over the past two decades with the growth of suburban St. Louis and the decline of "Yellow Dog" Democrats in rural communities. While there are still many middle-class, socially conservative Democrats, an increase in white-collar GOP voters has turned the 9th Republican. George W. Bush won 59 percent of the district's vote in the 2004 presidential election.

MAJOR INDUSTRY

Higher education, agriculture, insurance, health care

CITIES

Columbia, 84,531; Hannibal, 17,757; Kirksville, 16,988

NOTABLE

Samuel Clemens (Mark Twain) was born in the town of Florida in Monroe County and grew up in Hannibal, which attracts visitors to Twain's boyhood home; Westminster College in Fulton was the site of Winston Churchill's "Iron Curtain" speech after World War II.

MONTANA

Gov. Brian Schweitzer (D)

First elected: 2004
Length of term: 4 years
Term expires: 1/09
Salary: $96,462
Phone: (406) 444-3111

Residence: Helena
Born: Sept. 4, 1955; Havre, Mont.
Religion: Roman Catholic
Family: Wife, Nancy Schweitzer; three children
Education: Colorado State U., B.S. 1978 (international agronomy); Montana State U., Bozeman, M.S. 1980 (soil science)
Career: Farmer; rancher; agronomist
Political highlights: Democratic nominee for U.S. Senate, 2000

Election results:

2004 GENERAL		
Brian Schweitzer (D)	225,016	50.4%
Bob Brown (R)	205,313	46.0%
Bob Kelleher (GREEN)	8,393	1.9%
Stanley R. Jones (LIBERT)	7,424	1.7%

Lt. Gov. John Bohlinger (R)

First elected: 2004
Length of term: 4 years
Term expires: 1/09
Salary: $74,173
Phone: (406) 444-3111

LEGISLATURE

Legislature: January-April in odd-numbered years, limit of 90 days

Senate: 50 members, 4-year terms
2007 ratios: 26 D, 24 R; 41 men, 9 women
Salary: $83/day in session; $99/day in session allowance
Phone: (406) 444-4880

House: 100 members, 2-year terms
2007 ratios: 49 D, 50 R, 1 CNSTP; 71 men, 29 women
Salary: $83/day in session; $99/day in session allowance
Phone: (406) 444-4819

TERM LIMITS

Governor: 2 terms in a 16-year period
Senate: 2 terms in a 16-year period
House: 4 terms in a 16-year period

URBAN STATISTICS

CITY	POPULATION
Billings	89,847
Missoula	57,053
Great Falls	56,690
Butte-Silver Bow	34,606
Bozeman	27,509

REGISTERED VOTERS

Voters do not register by party.

POPULATION

2006 population (est.)	944,632
2000 population	902,195
1990 population	799,065
Percent change (1990-2000)	+12.9%
Rank among states (2006)	44
Median age	37.5
Born in state	56.1%
Foreign born	1.8%
Violent crime rate	241/100,000
Poverty level	14.6%
Federal workers	13,044
Military	8,349

ELECTIONS

STATE ELECTION OFFICIAL
(406) 444-4732
DEMOCRATIC PARTY
(406) 442-9520
REPUBLICAN PARTY
(406) 442-6469

MISCELLANEOUS

Web: www.state.mt.us
Capital: Helena

U.S. CONGRESS

Senate: 2 Democrats
House: 1 Republican

2000 Census Statistics by District

DIST.	2004 VOTE FOR PRESIDENT BUSH	KERRY	WHITE	BLACK	ASIAN	HISP	MEDIAN INCOME	WHITE COLLAR	BLUE COLLAR	SERVICE INDUSTRY	OVER 64	UNDER 18	COLLEGE EDUCATION	RURAL	SQ. MILES
AL	59%	39%	90%	0%	1%	2%	$33,024	59%	24%	17%	13%	26%	24%	46%	145,552
STATE	59	39	90	0	1	2	$33,024	59	24	17	13	26	24	46	145,552
U.S.	50.7	48.3	69	12	4	13	$41,994	60	25	15	12	26	24	21	3,537,438

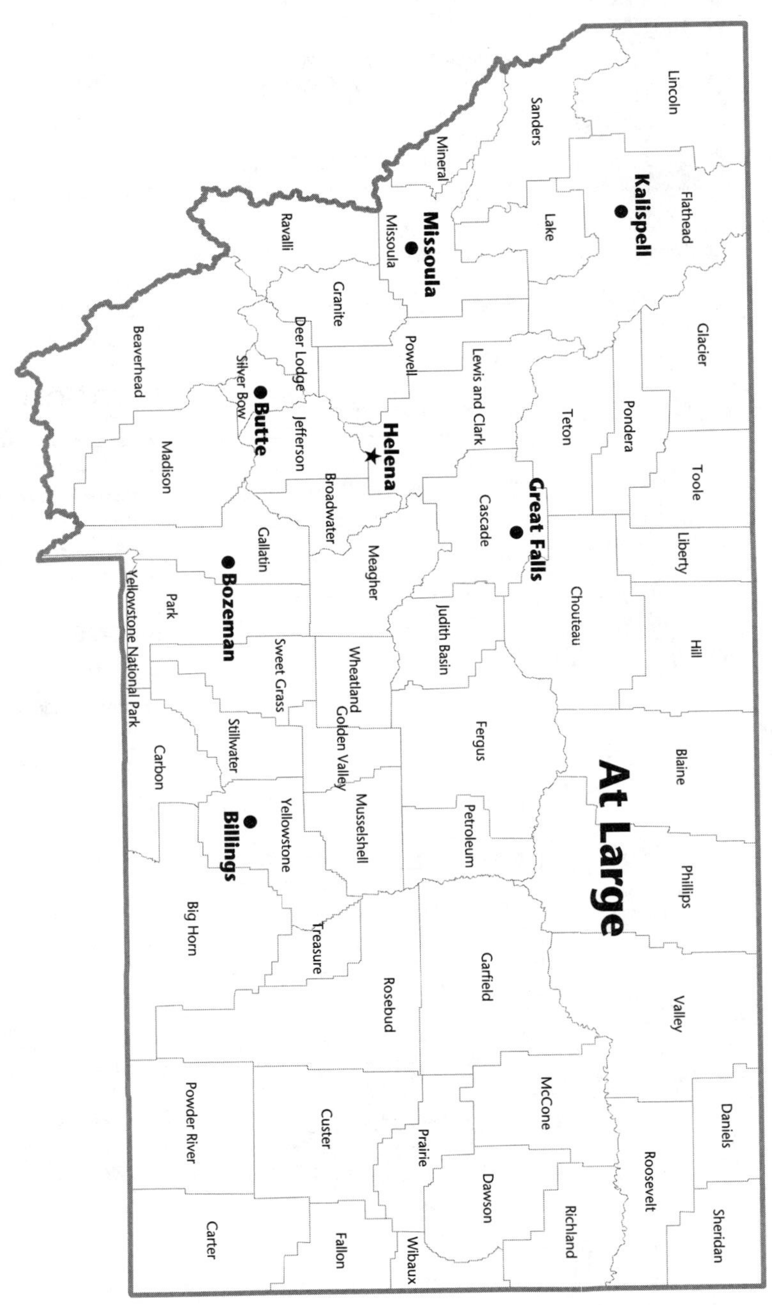
Lincoln
Sanders
Mineral
Kalispell
Flathead
Lake
Missoula
Missoula
Ravalli
Granite
Glacier
Powell
Deer Lodge
Beaverhead
Silver Bow
Butte
Lewis and Clark
Teton
Pondera
Helena
Jefferson
Madison
Toole
Great Falls
Cascade
Broadwater
Gallatin
Liberty
Meagher
Bozeman
Park
Yellowstone National Park
Chouteau
Judith Basin
Hill
Wheatland
Sweet Grass
Golden Valley
Stillwater
Fergus
Carbon
Blaine
At Large
Musselshell
Yellowstone
Billings
Petroleum
Phillips
Big Horn
Treasure
Garfield
Rosebud
Valley
McCone
Custer
Powder River
Daniels
Prairie
Roosevelt
Dawson
Richland
Sheridan
Carter
Fallon
Wibaux

Sen. Max Baucus (D)

CAPITOL OFFICE
224-2651
max@baucus.senate.gov
baucus.senate.gov
511 Hart 20510-2602; fax 224-0515

COMMITTEES
Agriculture, Nutrition & Forestry
(Domestic & Foreign Marketing - chairman)
Environment & Public Works
(Transportation & Infrastructure - chairman)
Finance - chairman
Joint Taxation

RESIDENCE
Helena

BORN
Dec. 11, 1941, Helena, Mont.

RELIGION
United Church of Christ

FAMILY
Wife, Wanda Baucus; one child

EDUCATION
Stanford U., A.B. 1964 (economics), LL.B. 1967

CAREER
Lawyer

POLITICAL HIGHLIGHTS
Mont. House, 1973-75; U.S. House, 1975-78

ELECTION RESULTS

2002 GENERAL		
Max Baucus (D)	204,853	62.7%
Mike Taylor (R)	103,611	31.7%
Stan Jones (LIBERT)	10,420	3.2%
Bob Kelleher (GR)	7,653	2.3%
2002 PRIMARY		
Max Baucus (D)		unopposed

PREVIOUS WINNING PERCENTAGES
1996 (50%); 1990 (68%); 1984 (57%); 1978 (56%); 1976 House Election (66%); 1974 House Election (55%)

Elected 1978; 5th term

Baucus' ability to deal with a wide range of personalities has helped him survive as a Democrat in a conservative-leaning state. He is one of the few Senate Democrats that Republicans look to for support on issues such as taxes, trade and prescription drug coverage under Medicare. Thus, as Baucus assumed the chair of the tax-writing Finance Committee in the 110th Congress (2007-08), there was less angst on the GOP side of the aisle than with some of the other Democrats taking over powerful committees.

"When you negotiate, you usually settle pretty much in the middle," Baucus said in 2007, summing up his approach to legislating.

Baucus has a good working relationship with outgoing chairman and now top-ranking Republican Charles E. Grassley of Iowa. Both men come from rural states and they share many of the same concerns.

As the top-ranking Democrat on Finance at the time, Baucus worked closely with Grassley in 2001 to advance President Bush's $1.35 trillion tax cut legislation through a Senate split 50-50 between Republicans and Democrats. And in 2004, Baucus' participation was critical in passing a $146 billion corporate tax cut package, also a White House priority.

Baucus and Grassley were unhappy that GOP leaders didn't work harder early in the 109th Congress (2005-06) to renew several popular tax breaks, including some that expired — among others, the credit for corporate research and development, the deduction for sales taxes in states with no income tax and a deduction for college expenses. The tax breaks were extended on a temporary basis near the end of 2006, and an effort to further extend them topped Baucus' agenda in the 110th Congress, as did extending some of Bush's tax cuts for the middle class set to expire in 2010.

Baucus' relationship with his House counterpart, liberal Ways and Means Committee Chairman Charles B. Rangel of New York, has been rocky in comparison. The two come from different backgrounds. Baucus grew up on his family's ranch 25 miles from Helena; Rangel represents a heavily minority district in Harlem that gave Bush only 9 percent of its vote in 2004.

Baucus infuriated Rangel by collaborating with the Bush administration and Grassley on the 2003 Medicare bill creating a prescription drug benefit for seniors. Rep. Bill Thomas, the California Republican who chaired Ways and Means, excluded Rangel and all other House Democrats from negotiations on the final bill, instead cutting a deal with Baucus and other senators.

Baucus and Rangel differed on some of the big issues before their committees in the 110th Congress. Baucus favored only a two-year extension of income exemptions from the alternative minimum tax and was more focused on small-business tax cuts. Rangel preferred outright repeal of the AMT, an income tax aimed at the wealthy that has increasingly ensnared middle-class taxpayers. The chairmen were also on opposite sides of a bill that required the government to negotiate prices for drugs provided to Medicare beneficiaries. Rangel supported it; Baucus preferred simply to remove the prohibition on such negotiations.

In 2007, as the new Democratic majority attempted to push an increase in the federal minimum wage through Congress, Baucus called for $8.3 billion worth of tax breaks to get business on board and win GOP votes. Rangel and House Democratic leaders backed a $1.3 billion version.

However, Baucus and Rangel do share some priorities, including trade liberalization and tax benefits for the working poor.

On trade issues, Baucus generally supports proposals intended to relax trade constraints and votes to approve bilateral trade agreements. But he has fiercely criticized the Bush administration for not collaborating more closely with Congress on such pacts.

An ardent champion of Montana beef producers, Baucus could stand in the way of trade agreements if cattle ranchers aren't taken into account. He particularly wants Japan to open its markets to U.S. beef, and he supported a 2006 bill to impose economic sanctions if the Japanese government did not lift its ban on U.S. beef imports.

Baucus' personal crusade is finding a way to close the $340 billion annual tax gap between what is owed to the government and what is actually paid to the Internal Revenue Service. In 2006, he delayed action on the nomination of Eric Solomon to be assistant Treasury secretary for tax policy to pressure the administration to deal with the problem.

Baucus' ability and desire to work with Republicans reflects the historical political divide in his sparsely populated state. Democrats traditionally have dominated in the mountainous western half, while Republicans rule in the open ranch land of the eastern half. His political success is due in part to the intimate access he affords constituents who are used to a one-on-one relationship with their politicians. He still takes all phone calls from constituents, unscreened. "I'm the hired hand," he says.

Now in his 60s, Baucus attempts physical feats that men half his age would never contemplate. In the past four years, he has suffered a motorcycle accident, a major head injury when he fell during a 50-mile ultramarathon (the latter required an operation in which two small holes were drilled into his skull) and heart surgery to implant a pacemaker.

He came to a rough-and-tumble life naturally. His family emigrated from Germany in the late 1800s and eventually settled in Montana. His great-grandfather, Henry Sieben, was named to the Cowboy Hall of Fame. Baucus' brother and sister-in-law now run the sprawling Sieben Ranch north of Helena. Of the ranch, Baucus says, "It's my blood. It's the soil. It's the earth. It's my family." His family faced a tragedy in the summer of 2006 when Baucus' nephew, Marine Cpl. Phillip E. Baucus, 28, was killed in Iraq. His funeral was held at the ranch.

Baucus was adventurous as a young man. He spent part of his junior year in college at an exchange program in France. He then went to England, where he traveled with some Gypsies. He left England and embarked on a global journey that took him across Europe, the Middle East and Africa. He was in the Belgian Congo, he said, when he had an "epiphany" that he should undertake a career in public service.

After finishing Stanford Law School in 1967, he was an attorney for the Securities and Exchange Commission in Washington for three years. He returned home to Montana in 1971 to coordinate the state's constitutional convention, and the next year he won a seat in the state legislature.

Two years later, he dislodged a two-term Republican incumbent to win a U.S. House seat in the post-Watergate election of 1974. He arrived in the Senate in December 1978, four days after his 37th birthday. Although he had just won the Senate seat for the term starting in January 1979, he was appointed to the position in December after Democrat Paul Hatfield resigned. Hatfield had been appointed earlier in the year upon the death of Sen. Lee Metcalf, who had served in Congress for 25 years. Despite Hatfield holding the Senate seat for most of 1978, Baucus was the victor when the two went head to head in the Democratic primary.

Holding his seat in the Senate has not always been easy, and in 1996 Baucus won by fewer than 20,000 votes over Republican Denny Rehberg, then the lieutenant governor and now Montana's sole House member. In 2002, Baucus cruised to victory with 63 percent of the vote.

KEY VOTES

2006

- No Confirm Samuel A. Alito Jr. to the Supreme Court
- Yes Allow consideration of a bill to establish a $140 billion trust fund to compensate victims of asbestos exposure
- No Extend tax cuts for two years at a cost of $70 billion over five years
- Yes Overhaul immigration policy with border security, enforcement and guest worker program
- Yes Allow consideration of a bill to permanently repeal the estate tax
- Yes Urge President Bush to begin troop withdrawals from Iraq in 2006
- Yes Lift President Bush's restrictions on stem cell research funding
- No Authorize military tribunals for suspected terrorists

2005

- No Curb class action lawsuits by shifting them from state to federal courts
- Yes Allow confirmation vote on Priscilla R. Owen to the U.S. Court of Appeals for the 5th Circuit
- Yes Oppose mandatory emissions limits and block recognition of global warming as a threat
- No Approve free-trade pact with five Central American countries
- Yes Pass energy policy overhaul favored by President Bush emphasizing domestic oil and gas production
- Yes Shield gunmakers from lawsuits when their products are used in crimes
- Yes Ban torture of prisoners in U.S. custody
- No Renew 16 provisions of the Patriot Act
- No Allow final vote on opening the Arctic National Wildlife Refuge to oil and gas exploration

CQ VOTE STUDIES

	PARTY UNITY		PRESIDENTIAL SUPPORT	
	Support	Oppose	Support	Oppose
2006	79%	21%	61%	39%
2005	74%	26%	45%	55%
2004	72%	28%	57%	43%
2003	74%	26%	54%	46%
2002	67%	33%	88%	12%
2001	67%	33%	71%	29%
2000	88%	12%	97%	3%
1999	87%	13%	81%	19%
1998	84%	16%	81%	19%
1997	73%	27%	87%	13%

INTEREST GROUPS

	AFL-CIO	ADA	CCUS	ACU
2006	71%	70%	70%	8%
2005	85%	95%	71%	24%
2004	92%	85%	71%	29%
2003	62%	85%	74%	15%
2002	69%	75%	70%	37%
2001	81%	80%	71%	28%
2000	75%	85%	46%	16%
1999	78%	95%	59%	4%
1998	75%	80%	56%	5%
1997	29%	65%	70%	4%

Sen. Jon Tester (D)

CAPITOL OFFICE
224-2644
tester.senate.gov
204 Russell 20510-2603; fax 224-8594

COMMITTEES
Banking, Housing & Urban Affairs
Energy & Natural Resources
Homeland Security & Governmental Affairs
Indian Affairs
Small Business & Entrepreneurship
Veterans' Affairs

RESIDENCE
Big Sandy

BORN
Aug. 21, 1956, Havre, Mont.

RELIGION
Church of God

FAMILY
Wife, Sharla Tester; two children

EDUCATION
College of Great Falls, B.A. 1978 (music education & secondary education)

CAREER
Farmer; teacher

POLITICAL HIGHLIGHTS
Big Sandy School Board of Trustees, 1983-92 (chairman, 1986-91); Mont. Senate, 1999-2007 (minority whip, 2001-03; minority leader, 2003-05; president, 2005-07)

ELECTION RESULTS

2006 GENERAL		
Jon Tester (D)	199,845	49.2%
Conrad Burns (R)	196,283	48.3%
Stan Jones (LIBERT)	10,377	2.6%
2006 PRIMARY		
Jon Tester (D)	65,757	60.8%
John Morrison (D)	38,394	35.5%
Paul Richards (D)	1,636	1.5%
Robert Candee (D)	1,471	1.4%

Elected 2006; 1st term

Tester may rank dead last in seniority among Senate Democrats, but he is near the top of their "most valuable players" list. His narrow 2006 victory over an entrenched Republican incumbent was a major factor in the party's takeover of control for the 110th Congress (2007-08).

In many ways, the burly third-generation Montana farmer with his cowboy boots and 1950s flat-top haircut is a model for Democratic success in the Mountain West — territory Republicans had made their own until the past few years. A pragmatic, independent-minded populist who is comfortable in his own skin, Tester wants to make a difference, not a splash. He is content to listen and learn for now, concentrating on what he knows and building expertise on other topics over time.

Tester was president of the Montana state Senate before his election to Congress, but he's finding the U.S. Senate a very different institution — slower, for one thing, much slower — which Tester finds frustrating. The state Senate dealt with 1,300 to 1,400 bills in a 90-day session every other year. The U.S. Senate spends weeks on a single bill. "Patience is something that I think is probably a good quality to have here," he says.

The differences between the two Senates pale in comparison with the differences between Washington, D.C., and his home near Big Sandy, a town of 703 residents. When he is at his farm, which his grandfather homesteaded in 1916, the nearest neighbor is three-quarters of a mile away. Only the moon and stars break the dark of night; only the wind pierces the silence. "It never gets dark here," Tester said of Washington. "It never gets quiet here. It doesn't matter if it's 3 in the morning or 3 in the afternoon."

Tester has found a stellar way to cast some light of his own on the workings of the Senate: He posts his daily schedule on his Web site, listing all his appointments and activities. The postings name names — and affiliations. The Senate historian's office said his move is unprecedented. Tester doesn't consider it a big deal. He figures his constituents have a right to know who's got his ear. It's important, he says, for government to be transparent. Excessive coziness between lobbyists and lawmakers was a major theme in his successful campaign to oust three-term GOP Sen. Conrad Burns. Burns had accepted $150,000 from disgraced lobbyist Jack Abramoff, his firm or his clients. While Burns later gave the money to charities, Tester rode the issue hard.

Tester's other big domestic issue during his campaign was the health care crisis, which has hit Montana particularly hard: One in five residents is uninsured. "It affects everybody, it cuts across all lines," he says. "And right now it's tough, and the system's broken, and I think we need to do some things to fix it." He favors mechanisms to allow small businesses to form purchasing pools to lower premium costs, and uniform electronic medical records, among other steps.

Although he's not on the Senate committees that tackle the broader problems of health care costs and the uninsured, he did land a seat on the Veterans' Affairs Committee. From that perch, he is looking to address the health care problems facing veterans returning from Iraq and Afghanistan. He is especially concerned about the difficulties faced by veterans living in far-flung rural communities like those that dot Montana.

Another focus for Tester is energy issues, particularly the promotion of renewable fuels — a cause he pursued in the Montana Senate. Renewables, he says, can "take pressure off the Middle East and imported oil overall."

It's a topic he's familiar with. "I come from agriculture. We can raise oilseeds, we can raise a lot of stuff you can make ethanol out of. . . . We have wind, we've got solar, we've got methane. . . . There's just a lot of opportunity out there."

Growing up on an 1,800-acre family farm, Tester and his brothers learned to do almost everything at an early age. But the learning came at a price. Grinding meat as a child, he severed three fingers on his left hand.

He caught the politics bug early. "We went to the Capitol when I was in high school. I got involved in student government my senior year of high school." After graduating from college with a bachelor's degree in music education and secondary education, he taught music for a couple of years at his hometown elementary school. While attending church one day, he spotted a pretty young woman named Sharla. He joined the church youth group to spend more time with her and let her strike him out at a softball game. That apparently was a winning move; they've been married since 1978.

Tester gave up teaching to concentrate on the farm, where the family also operated a custom butcher shop that his parents had started in the 1960s to supplement their meager income. They went organic in 1987, and now grow wheat, barley, lentils, peas, millet, buckwheat, alfalfa and hay. In 2007, Tester's daughter and son-in-law moved back to the farm to run the place in his absence; he also has a son in college.

Tester served as chairman of the Big Sandy school board and of his local Soil Conservation Service Committee before winning election to the Montana Senate, a seat he went after in 1998 because he was infuriated by the soaring rates that followed electricity deregulation approved by a Republican-controlled legislature. He felt free to run because the GOP incumbent — a neighbor — stepped down. "He had known my folks for a long time," Tester says. "I wouldn't have done it. But he retired."

Tester rose to minority whip and minority leader before becoming president of the state Senate in 2005, after Democrats gained control of the chamber. He championed legislation requiring public utilities in the state to use more renewable energy, and supported tax credits for companies that generate wind power in the state.

After two four-year terms, Tester was reaching his state term limit. Democrat Brian Schweitzer, a rancher and friend with a political profile much like his, had been elected governor of Montana in 2004, after losing a Senate race against Burns in 2000. Sentiment in the state was swinging against Republicans, and Tester and his wife traveled to Washington in May 2005 to meet with national Democratic Party officials about a possible run against Burns, who was widely seen as vulnerable. They also wanted to see whether they could imagine living in the nation's capital. They decided they could.

The first test was the primary, in which Tester faced state Auditor John Morrison, a better-known, better-funded candidate backed by the Democratic establishment. Morrison was leading in initial polls, but lost support rapidly after revelations that he had had an affair and allegations that he had allowed the relationship to influence his official conduct — a charge he denied. With Democrats eager to attack Burns on ethics, they wanted a candidate with a spotless reputation. Tester trounced Morrison.

He then plunged into the November campaign, repeatedly attacking Burns over his ties to lobbyists and big money interests. He also spoke out strongly against the war in Iraq, saying President Bush had failed to develop a plan for ending it. Burns suffered from a series of gaffes such as scolding firefighters for a "piss-poor job" fighting a huge fire in eastern Montana and making racially insensitive comments about immigrants. The battle went down to the wire; the Montana Senate race was one of the last to be called. Tester won by 3,562 votes — getting 49 percent of the total cast.

Rep. Denny Rehberg (R)

CAPITOL OFFICE
225-3211
denny.rehberg@mail.house.gov
www.house.gov/rehberg
516 Cannon 20515-2601; fax 225-5687

COMMITTEES
Appropriations

RESIDENCE
Billings

BORN
Oct. 5, 1955, Billings, Mont.

RELIGION
Episcopalian

FAMILY
Wife, Janice Lenhardt Rehberg; three children

EDUCATION
Montana State U., attended 1973-74;
Washington State U., B.A. 1977 (political science)

CAREER
Rancher; congressional aide; realtor

POLITICAL HIGHLIGHTS
Mont. House, 1985-91; lieutenant governor, 1991-97; Republican nominee for U.S. Senate, 1996

ELECTION RESULTS

2006 GENERAL		
Denny Rehberg (R)	239,124	58.9%
Monica Lindeen (D)	158,916	39.1%
Mike Fellows (LIBERT)	8,085	2.0%
2006 PRIMARY		
Denny Rehberg (R)		unopposed
2004 GENERAL		
Denny Rehberg (R)	286,076	64.4%
Tracy Velazquez (D)	145,606	32.8%
Mike Fellows (LIBERT)	12,548	2.8%

PREVIOUS WINNING PERCENTAGES
2002 (65%); 2000 (52%)

Elected 2000; 4th term

Rehberg has been a loyal supporter of the Republican leadership and the Bush White House, but he still felt the need to put some distance between himself and the national GOP as he cruised toward an easy re-election in 2006. "I'm not George Bush and I'm not Dick Cheney," he told the Great Falls Tribune.

Nevertheless, Rehberg — pro-business, pro-development and socially conservative — continues to back most Republican priorities. He voted against a war supplemental spending bill in March 2007 that included an agricultural aid provision because the measure also called for the withdrawal of U.S. troops from Iraq.

Rehberg (REE-berg) usually will cross party lines only if he sees a threat to his state's parochial interests. He was one of just 27 Republicans who voted against the Central American Free Trade Agreement in 2005. He similarly opposed Australia trade legislation in the 108th Congress (2003-04), because he feared more beef imports would threaten the livelihood of Montana ranchers.

He has backed legislation, opposed by the White House, to allow the importation of cheaper prescription drugs from Canada; Montanans often cross the border to purchase medicines. "I have to vote my state," he says.

Still, Rehberg was rewarded for party loyalty at the start of the 109th Congress (2005-06) with a coveted seat on the Appropriations Committee. He has used the position to further address the concerns of his vast, largely rural state. In 2005, for example, he sought to include language in the agricultural appropriations bill to speed up implementation of a country-of-origin labeling law that would distinguish U.S.-produced beef from imports. In early 2007, he again offered similar legislation, this time setting a September 2007 deadline for country-of-origin labels.

Rehberg is a strong protector of Montana's military installations. He voted to delay the scheduled 2005 round of military base closures and introduced a resolution at the start of the 110th Congress (2007-08) to support keeping all 200 Minuteman III intercontinental ballistic missiles in silos at Malmstrom Air Force Base in Great Falls. The Pentagon has said it will eliminate 50 of the missiles.

Issues concerning Montana's large American Indian population are also a priority for Rehberg. In early 2007, he proposed creating an Indian Affairs Committee in the House, like the one in the Senate. "While I don't have a lot of seniority, I think people would listen to me from the perspective of a Republican from a rural state with seven reservations," Rehberg told the Great Falls Tribune.

In the 109th Congress, he worked to combat methamphetamine abuse, which has hit Montana and other rural states particularly hard. He successfully pressed for an amendment on a bill reauthorizing the Office of National Drug Control Policy to require that 10 percent of the money going to the National Youth Anti-Drug Media Campaign each year be used to target methamphetamine abuse.

As the state's lone congressman, Rehberg drives thousands of miles each year across a state that is 500 miles long. He represents more constituents than any of his colleagues in the House — an estimated 944,632 in 2006. Even though Montana's population increased by 13 percent in the 1990s, it did not grow enough to win back a congressional seat that it had lost in the 1990 reapportionment.

Rehberg has consistently put the need for greater energy production ahead of environmental concerns. He was one of 41 House Republicans who threatened to vote against a 2005 budget package if language to allow drilling in Alaska's Arctic National Wildlife Refuge were removed.

Rehberg says he has a keen personal interest in seeing Congress enact a permanent repeal of the estate tax because his family had to sell part of its ranch holdings to pay taxes after his great-grandmother died in 1976.

Rehberg grew up on his family's beef cattle and cashmere goat ranch, competing in gymnastics and playing the drums. His mother taught elementary school, and his father, Jack, ran the ranch and worked a number of other jobs to help support the family. Jack Rehberg was the GOP nominee for a House seat in 1970, but took just 36 percent of the vote against the incumbent, Democrat John Melcher.

After earning a degree in political science, Rehberg worked as an intern in the Montana Senate, sold real estate for two years, and then moved to Washington in 1979 to join the staff of GOP Rep. Ron Marlenee of Montana. He returned to the family ranch three years later and ended up serving six years in the state House. He managed political campaigns for Marlenee in 1986 and Republican Conrad Burns in his successful Senate bid in 1988.

Rehberg was appointed lieutenant governor in 1991 when Lt. Gov. Allen Kolstad quit to join the administration of President George H.W. Bush. Rehberg was elected to a four-year term in 1992. In 1996, he came within 5 percentage points of defeating Democratic Sen. Max Baucus, who outspent him almost 3-to-1.

In 2000, he was unopposed for the House nomination when GOP Rep. Rick Hill retired after two House terms, citing poor health. Rehberg looked to be the underdog against Democratic state school superintendent Nancy Keenan, but after a somewhat vitriolic campaign, he won by 5 percentage points.

During that race, Rehberg removed himself from the management of the family ranch by arranging to move its 600 goats to the Baucus family ranch. The two families now share the profits from the operation.

National GOP strategists sounded out Rehberg about another race against Baucus in 2002, but he nixed that idea. In 2002 and 2004, he won by margins of more than 30 percentage points. In 2006, he was mentioned as a potential replacement for Burns, whose link to convicted lobbyist Jack Abramoff ultimately contributed to his defeat. Rehberg opted to stay in the House, where he easily beat Democratic state Rep. Monica Lindeen by 20 percentage points.

KEY VOTES

2006

- No Stop broadband companies from favoring select Internet traffic
- Yes Affirm U.S. commitment to war in Iraq and reject setting a withdrawal date for troops
- Yes Repeal requirement for bilingual ballots at the polls
- Yes Permit U.S. sale of civilian nuclear technology to India
- Yes Build a 700-mile fence on the U.S.-Mexico border to curb illegal crossings
- Yes Permit warrantless wiretaps of suspected terrorists

2005

- Yes Intervene in the life-support case of Terri Schiavo
- No Lift President Bush's restrictions on stem cell research funding
- Yes Prohibit FBI access to library and bookstore records
- No Approve free-trade pact with five Central American countries
- Yes Pass energy policy overhaul favored by President Bush emphasizing domestic oil and gas production
- Yes End mandatory preservation of habitat of endangered animal and plant species
- No Ban torture of prisoners in U.S. custody

CQ VOTE STUDIES

	PARTY UNITY		PRESIDENTIAL SUPPORT	
	Support	Oppose	Support	Oppose
2006	97%	3%	95%	5%
2005	95%	5%	83%	17%
2004	96%	4%	76%	24%
2003	95%	5%	93%	7%
2002	95%	5%	85%	15%

INTEREST GROUPS

	AFL-CIO	ADA	CCUS	ACU
2006	29%	0%	100%	83%
2005	27%	10%	89%	92%
2004	13%	5%	95%	96%
2003	7%	10%	93%	84%
2002	11%	0%	95%	100%

MONTANA

At large

Montana's Big Sky country has long been a place where pioneers traveled to strike it rich. Once explored by Lewis and Clark and later by fur trappers and gold seekers, Montana is now a prime destination for celebrities and telecommuters who want to purchase their own small piece of the frontier.

The economy is supported by natural resources, forcing Montana to find a balance between exploiting its terrain and protecting it, especially in the face of increased global demand for energy resources. Butte, the site of years of mining, continues to be the center of a massive superfund clean-up effort. The economy also relies on tourism, with three of the five entrances to Yellowstone National Park in southern Montana, and Glacier National Park located in the northwestern part of the state.

The district combines the state's two politically independent halves into an unpredictable voting bloc. The western, mountainous half of the state leans Democratic, with an environmental base and a union tradition in mining and lumber mills. It also is home to the state's university community in Missoula. The area has been shifting to support more natural resources-based development in recent years. The eastern half, a flat plain where wheat and cattle are raised, follows a tradition of rural Republicanism.

Voters here will support both parties. In 2004, only six of the state's 56 counties voted Democratic in the presidential election as George W. Bush earned 59 percent of the vote. At the same time, many voters split their tickets as the state elected a Democratic governor. Montana also elected a Democratic challenger to the U.S. Senate in 2006.

MAJOR INDUSTRY

Agriculture, tourism, forestry

MILITARY BASES

Malmstrom Air Force Base, 3,600 military, 450 civilian (2006)

CITIES

Billings, 89,847; Missoula, 57,053; Great Falls, 56,690; Butte-Silver Bow, 34,606; Bozeman, 27,509; Helena, 25,780

NOTABLE

Montana elected Jeannette Rankin, the first woman in Congress, in 1916; Jordan was the site of a 1996 standoff between federal authorities and an anti-tax group called The Freemen.

NEBRASKA

Gov. Dave Heineman (R)

First elected: 2006; assumed office Jan. 20, 2005, due to appointment of Mike Johanns, R, to be Agriculture secretary
Length of term: 4 years
Term expires: 1/11
Salary: $85,000
Phone: (402) 471-2244

Residence: Fremont
Born: May 12, 1945; Falls City, Neb.
Religion: Eastern Orthodox
Family: Wife, Sally Ganem; one child
Education: U.S. Military Academy, B.S. 1970 (economics)
Military service: Army, 1970-75
Career: Congressional aide; health and beauty products company salesman
Political highlights: Neb. Republican Party executive director, 1979-81; Fremont City Council, 1990-94; Neb. treasurer, 1995-2001; lieutenant governor, 2001-05

Election results:

2006 GENERAL		
Dave Heineman (R)	435,507	73.4%
David Hahn (D)	145,115	24.5%
Barry Richards (NEB)	8,953	1.5%

Lt. Gov. Rick Sheehy (R)

First elected: 2006; assumed office Jan. 24, 2005, due to Heineman's ascension to governor
Length of term: 4 years
Term expires: 1/11
Salary: $75,000
Phone: (402) 471-2256

LEGISLATURE

Unicameral Legislature: 90 days in odd-numbered years; 60 days in even-numbered years

Legislature: 49 nonpartisan members, 4-year terms
2007 ratios: 40 men, 9 women
Salary: $12,000
Phone: (402) 471-2271

TERM LIMITS

Governor: 2 consecutive terms
Legislature: 2 consecutive terms

URBAN STATISTICS

CITY	POPULATION
Omaha	390,007
Lincoln	225,581
Bellevue	44,382
Grand Island	42,940
Kearney	27,431

REGISTERED VOTERS

Republican	50%
Democrat	33%
Nonpartisan/others	17%

POPULATION

2006 population (est.)	1,768,331
2000 population	1,711,263
1990 population	1,578,385
Percent change (1990-2000)	+8.4%
Rank among states (2006)	38
Median age	35.3
Born in state	67.1%
Foreign born	4.4%
Violent crime rate	328/100,000
Poverty level	9.7%
Federal workers	15,620
Military	15,040

ELECTIONS

STATE ELECTION OFFICIAL
(402) 471-2555
DEMOCRATIC PARTY
(402) 434-2180
REPUBLICAN PARTY
(402) 475-2122

MISCELLANEOUS

Web: www.nebraska.gov
Capital: Lincoln

U.S. CONGRESS

Senate: 1 Democrat, 1 Republican
House: 3 Republicans

2000 Census Statistics by District

DIST.	2004 VOTE FOR PRESIDENT BUSH	KERRY	WHITE	BLACK	ASIAN	HISP	MEDIAN INCOME	WHITE COLLAR	BLUE COLLAR	SERVICE INDUSTRY	OVER 64	UNDER 18	COLLEGE EDUCATION	RURAL	SQ. MILES
1	63%	36%	91%	1%	2%	4%	$40,021	58%	27%	15%	13%	25%	24%	35%	11,951
2	61	38	80	10	2	6	$45,235	67	20	13	10	27	31	2	411
3	75	24	92	0	0	6	$33,866	54	31	15	17	26	17	54	64,511
STATE	66	33	87	4	1	6	$39,250	59	26	15	14	26	24	30	76,872
U.S.	50.7	48.3	69	12	4	13	$41,994	60	25	15	12	26	24	21	3,537,438

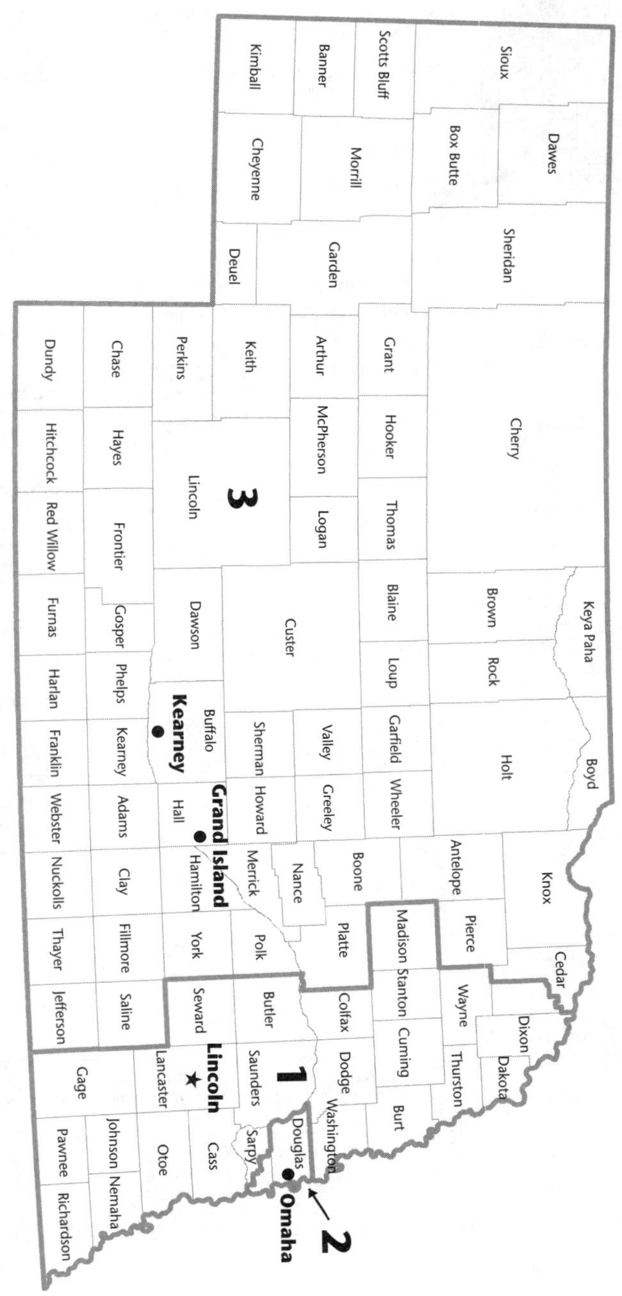

Sioux
Dawes
Box Butte
Sheridan
Scotts Bluff
Banner
Kimball
Morrill
Cheyenne
Garden
Deuel
Cherry
Keya Paha
Boyd
Brown
Rock
Holt
Knox
Cedar
Dixon
Dakota
Grant
Hooker
Thomas
Blaine
Loup
Garfield
Wheeler
Arthur
McPherson
Logan
Keith
Perkins
Chase
Dundy
Hayes
Hitchcock
Lincoln
3
Frontier
Red Willow
Dawson
Custer
Gosper
Furnas
Phelps
Harlan
Buffalo
Kearney
Sherman
Valley
Kearney
Franklin
Howard
Greeley
Hall
Grand Island
Adams
Webster
Antelope
Pierce
Wayne
Thurston
Boone
Nance
Merrick
Hamilton
Clay
Nuckolls
Madison
Stanton
Platte
Polk
York
Fillmore
Thayer
Colfax
Cuming
Burt
Butler
Seward
Saline
Jefferson
Dodge
Washington
Saunders
1
Lincoln
Lancaster
Gage
Douglas
Sarpy
Cass
Otoe
Johnson
Nemaha
Pawnee
Richardson
Omaha
2

Sen. Chuck Hagel (R)

CAPITOL OFFICE
224-4224
chuck_hagel@hagel.senate.gov
hagel.senate.gov
248 Russell 20510-2705; fax 224-5213

COMMITTEES
Banking, Housing & Urban Affairs
Foreign Relations
Rules & Administration
Select Intelligence

RESIDENCE
Omaha

BORN
Oct. 4, 1946, North Platte, Neb.

RELIGION
Episcopalian

FAMILY
Wife, Lilibet Hagel; two children

EDUCATION
U. of Nebraska, Omaha, B.A. 1971 (history)

MILITARY SERVICE
Army, 1967-68

CAREER
Investment bank executive; cellular telephone company founder; lobbyist; congressional aide; radio talk show host

POLITICAL HIGHLIGHTS
Veterans Administration deputy administrator, 1981-82

ELECTION RESULTS

2002 GENERAL		
Chuck Hagel (R)	397,438	82.8%
Charlie A. Matulka (D)	70,290	14.6%
John J. Graziano (LIBERT)	7,423	1.6%
Phil Chase (I)	5,066	1.1%
2002 PRIMARY		
Chuck Hagel (R)		unopposed

PREVIOUS WINNING PERCENTAGES
1996 (56%)

Elected 1996; 2nd term

Hagel shares many qualities with John McCain, the maverick Arizona Republican and presidential candidate with whom he is often compared. The two senators have much in common: heroic service in Vietnam, blunt-spoken candor and impatience with the status quo. Hagel has been called "McCain without the attitude."

But one overriding issue separates the two: the Iraq War, which both voted to authorize back in 2002. Although McCain has sharply criticized President Bush's conduct of the war, he endorsed the president's determination to keep fighting for a stable outcome and supported Bush's early 2007 decision to deploy more than 21,000 additional U.S. combat troops to Iraq. Hagel has turned against the war, saying that only a "political accommodation" among Iraqis can bring stability to that nation, not a stepped-up military campaign.

In the teeth of a White House veto threat, Hagel was one of two Senate Republicans who voted in March 2007 for a war funding bill that set a March 31, 2008, goal for withdrawal of troops. (Gordon H. Smith of Oregon was the other.) "Now in our fifth year of the war in Iraq, the Congress must assert itself in a very real and responsible way to fulfill our constitutional responsibilities in matters of war as a co-equal branch of our government," Hagel told the Senate the day before the vote.

His high-profile split with Bush and most Senate Republicans came at a point when Hagel — often mentioned as a possible 2008 presidential contender — was still deliberating his own political future. After months of suspense, he held a March 2007 news conference in Omaha to announce that he had nothing to announce. He said he would decide later in the year whether to run for president, run for re-election or retire. "In making this announcement, I believe there will still be political options open to me at a later date," Hagel said, adding that the "political currents in America are more unpredictable today than at any time in modern history."

In contrast to McCain, Hagel has been highly supportive of Bush on issues other than Iraq. On roll call votes in the 109th Congress (2005-06), he supported the president's position 93 percent of the time, more often than all but two other Republicans — Wayne Allard of Colorado and John Cornyn of Texas. McCain, on the other hand, backed Bush on 84 percent of the votes — only six GOP senators backed Bush less often.

Hagel is a more traditional conservative than McCain, who has displayed a populist streak on health care, environmental and budget issues. The Nebraskan embraces GOP tenets of tax cuts and reductions in federal spending. With a perspective rooted in his business background, he stresses the importance of internationalism, and of "dynamic, global, interconnected" markets. In 2002, he supported fast-track authority for the president to negotiate trade deals that cannot be amended by Congress, and he voted for the string of trade agreements that followed, including the controversial 2005 Central America Free Trade Agreement.

He is a social conservative, voting against a 2006 bill to ease limits on federally funded stem cell research and backing proposed constitutional amendments in 2004 and 2006 to outlaw same-sex marriage. (McCain voted the other way on both issues.)

Hagel works across party lines when he finds common ground with Democrats. To address the problem of the overburdened armed forces, he cosponsored legislation in 2004 with Democrat Jack Reed of Rhode Island to expand the Army permanently by adding 30,000 active-duty soldiers.

An affable, articulate self-made millionaire and decorated Vietnam veteran, Hagel had never held elective office before his successful 1996 long-shot bid for the Senate against popular Democratic Gov. Ben Nelson. (Nelson won the state's other Senate seat when it came open in 2000.) Hagel got off to a fast start in Washington. He made a fortuitous early decision to accept a request from Indiana Republican Richard G. Lugar, then the No. 2 Republican on the Foreign Relations Committee, to join the panel at a time few lawmakers were interested in foreign affairs. A series of retirements and election losses allowed Hagel to rise quickly in the committee hierarchy, putting him in an influential position to affect policy after the Sept. 11 terrorist attacks placed a premium on foreign policy expertise. Among panel Republicans, he is second only to Lugar in seniority.

Hagel expanded his knowledge by traveling extensively overseas, meeting with top foreign leaders and slogging through tedious hours of committee hearings. That commitment, and his affinity for Lugar's "realist" brand of foreign policy, helped the two forge a close working relationship. Hagel also can usually find common ground with Democrat Joseph R. Biden Jr. of Delaware, who chairs the committee in the 110th Congress (2007-08). His Capitol Hill office features a painting of Sir Winston Churchill, with nearby busts of Presidents Dwight D. Eisenhower and Theodore Roosevelt.

Hagel's compelling personal story contributed to his rapid political rise. He grew up in a small town in Nebraska, where he started working as a carhop at a drive-in restaurant when he was 9 years old. After his father died, Hagel, age 16 and the oldest child, helped supervise his younger siblings. In high school, he successfully ran for student council president, attracting attention by tying a live chicken to the hood of his car and driving around blaring out his positions.

Later, Hagel enlisted in the Army and spent a year as an infantryman in Vietnam, serving side by side with his brother, Tom. Hagel was seriously wounded twice and received two Purple Hearts. He suffered burns, which required a decade to heal completely, when an enemy mine exploded underneath his armored personnel carrier. His brother was in the same carrier and was knocked unconscious. Hagel pulled him to safety.

After graduating from college in 1971, he landed a job with Republican Rep. John Y. McCollister of Nebraska and rose to become his top aide. Hagel then became a lobbyist for the Firestone Tire and Rubber Company and campaigned heavily in 1980 for Ronald Reagan, who rewarded him with a top job at the Veterans Administration. But Hagel's family life suffered. His 1979 marriage to Patricia Lloyd ended in divorce in 1982.

Hagel left government that year to start a business on a financial shoestring, selling his seven-year-old Buick and two insurance bonds and investing his net worth of $5,000 in a cellular phone company that he began with two partners. That company, Vanguard Cellular Systems Inc., became the country's second-largest independent cell phone company and made Hagel a multimillionaire. Hagel was a recipient of the 2001 Horatio Alger Award, which recognizes self-made business leaders who have overcome adversity.

He entered the 1996 Senate primary as the underdog against state Attorney General Don Stenberg but spent lavishly from his personal funds and won the nomination with more than 60 percent of the vote. In the fall, Hagel made his centerpiece issue tax cuts as a stimulant of economic growth, which he said would do more to address societal problems than any government program. Helped by GOP criticism that Nelson was breaking an earlier pledge to serve out his term as governor, Hagel won by 14 percentage points. In 2002, Hagel's victory margin of 68 points over Democrat Charlie A. Matulka was the largest in Nebraska Senate election history.

KEY VOTES

2006

- Yes Confirm Samuel A. Alito Jr. to the Supreme Court
- Yes Allow consideration of a bill to establish a $140 billion trust fund to compensate victims of asbestos exposure
- Yes Extend tax cuts for two years at a cost of $70 billion over five years
- Yes Overhaul immigration policy with border security, enforcement and guest worker program
- Yes Allow consideration of a bill to permanently repeal the estate tax
- No Urge President Bush to begin troop withdrawals from Iraq in 2006
- No Lift President Bush's restrictions on stem cell research funding
- Yes Authorize military tribunals for suspected terrorists

2005

- Yes Curb class action lawsuits by shifting them from state to federal courts
- Yes Allow confirmation vote on Priscilla R. Owen to the U.S. Court of Appeals for the 5th Circuit
- Yes Oppose mandatory emissions limits and block recognition of global warming as a threat
- Yes Approve free-trade pact with five Central American countries
- Yes Pass energy policy overhaul favored by President Bush emphasizing domestic oil and gas production
- Yes Shield gunmakers from lawsuits when their products are used in crimes
- Yes Ban torture of prisoners in U.S. custody
- No Renew 16 provisions of the Patriot Act
- Yes Allow final vote on opening the Arctic National Wildlife Refuge to oil and gas exploration

CQ VOTE STUDIES

	PARTY UNITY		PRESIDENTIAL SUPPORT	
	Support	Oppose	Support	Oppose
2006	84%	16%	96%	4%
2005	94%	6%	89%	11%
2004	93%	7%	94%	6%
2003	96%	4%	98%	2%
2002	94%	6%	98%	2%
2001	92%	8%	96%	4%
2000	94%	6%	49%	51%
1999	92%	8%	36%	64%
1998	89%	11%	42%	58%
1997	92%	8%	59%	41%

INTEREST GROUPS

	AFL-CIO	ADA	CCUS	ACU
2006	13%	5%	100%	75%
2005	21%	10%	94%	96%
2004	9%	20%	93%	87%
2003	8%	15%	87%	100%
2002	23%	10%	95%	95%
2001	25%	25%	100%	84%
2000	0%	0%	100%	88%
1999	0%	5%	100%	88%
1998	0%	0%	94%	72%
1997	0%	5%	100%	80%

Sen. Ben Nelson (D)

CAPITOL OFFICE
224-6551
senator@bennelson.senate.gov
bennelson.senate.gov
720 Hart 20510-2706; fax 228-0012

COMMITTEES
Agriculture, Nutrition & Forestry
Appropriations
Armed Services
(Personnel - chairman)
Rules & Administration

RESIDENCE
Omaha

BORN
May 17, 1941, McCook, Neb.

RELIGION
Methodist

FAMILY
Wife, Diane Nelson; four children

EDUCATION
U. of Nebraska, B.A. 1963 (philosophy), M.A. 1965 (philosophy), J.D. 1970

CAREER
Lawyer; insurance company executive

POLITICAL HIGHLIGHTS
Neb. director of insurance, 1975-76; governor, 1991-99; Democratic nominee for U.S. Senate, 1996

ELECTION RESULTS

2006 GENERAL		
Ben Nelson (D)	378,388	63.9%
Pete Ricketts (R)	213,928	36.1%
2006 PRIMARY		
Ben Nelson (D)		unopposed

PREVIOUS WINNING PERCENTAGES
2000 (51%)

Elected 2000; 2nd term

Fresh from a comfortable win in an unambiguously "red" state, Nelson began his second term fully validated by his constituents as one of the Senate's most unpredictable voters. His propensity for voting in opposition to his party peaked in 2006 — his re-election year — and Nelson says he has no plans to let go of the maverick streak that helped win him his job.

While party-line-crossing senators can sometimes find themselves on the outs with their own party, Nelson has carefully leveraged his lack of predictability to secure the full attention of both President Bush and Majority Leader Harry Reid, a Nevada Democrat.

Bush, who is known for bestowing nicknames, first called Nelson "Nelly" and then "Benny," but the senator, saying he preferred a more "macho" moniker, convinced the president to call him "Benator." Nelson says he is in constant contact with the White House and that the president's advisers frequently consult him as they try to find ways to get Bush's agenda through Congress. "The policy people work with me, the political people work on me," Nelson says of the executive branch.

Early in the 110th Congress (2007-08), Nelson's influence within his own chamber allowed him to put his mark on the first Senate-passed piece of legislation to call for a withdrawal of U.S. troops from Iraq. In the Democratic struggle to come up with the votes to defeat a GOP effort to gut the withdrawal provisions in a 2007 supplemental spending bill, Nelson insisted on adding benchmarks of progress for the Iraqi government and reporting requirements for the commander of the coalition forces. "When they put the benchmarks in, the game changed," he said after the vote.

Nelson had solidified his credentials as a negotiator in 2005, when he helped lead a bipartisan group of senators who wanted to avert a potentially damaging Senate showdown over judicial nominees. Nelson and 13 colleagues — mostly mavericks and moderates — spent weeks in private meetings hammering out a deal that would stop then Majority Leader Bill Frist, a Tennessee Republican, from using a parliamentary maneuver to do away with filibusters of nominees to the federal bench. The group agreed to allow some previously filibustered nominees through and to block future nominees only under "extraordinary circumstances." The deal left the definition of that phrase up to each senator in the group, which was dubbed the Gang of 14.

Nelson is one of a small but growing number of Senate Democrats who oppose abortion rights in most cases. In the 109th Congress (2005-06), he supported a bill that would criminalize the transport of a minor across state lines to get an abortion, and he voted in 2003 to ban a medical procedure opponents call "partial birth" abortion, unless it is necessary to save the woman's life. He also was the only Senate Democrat to vote against expanding federal funding for embryonic stem cell research in 2006.

Nelson shows his Democratic stripes, though, when the Senate considers changes to Social Security, Medicare or farm programs. He has said he is a strong supporter of federal entitlement programs for the elderly. And he was an avid proponent of the Democrats' plan to boost agriculture incomes in the 2002 farm bill, though he lamented that wealthy farmers would reap financial benefits from a number of its programs.

In 2006, on votes in which Democrats and Republicans were opposed along party lines, Nelson voted against his party 64 percent of the time. That was the highest incidence of party opposition among all other members of

Congress that year as well as in Nelson's Senate career. Also in 2006, Nelson voted in favor of Bush's position 76 percent of the time — more than any other Senate Democrat.

Nelson's support for many conservative proposals has led some in the Republican Party to view him as a possible convert. Efforts to persuade Nelson to switch became more frequent after Vermont's James M. Jeffords left the GOP in 2001 to become an independent. Nelson has given no sign that he is any more interested in changing parties than he was when approached by the Nebraska GOP. "I've had people talking to me about that for a decade or more," he says.

As a Republican, Nelson would not enjoy the leverage he has now, which guarantees his ability to affect public policy. If that were not reason enough, his longstanding political rivalry with Nebraska's senior senator, Republican Chuck Hagel, provides additional insurance to Democratic leaders that Nelson will never switch. Though Nelson and Hagel both attest to a fine and ever-improving working relationship, the two have one of the most famously bad relationships in the Senate. It started in 1996, when Hagel defeated Nelson in his bid for the Senate. "I got over losing. He never got over winning," Nelson is fond of saying to explain the rift.

Nelson prides himself on being a practical joker. As governor, he participated in a segment of the TV show "Candid Camera" in which he told visitors to his office that he was planning to change the state's name to "something much more modern . . . something like Zenmar or Quentron." He also held a party for others named Ben Nelson. Twelve people from Nebraska, 10 from other states and one dog attended.

In 2002, he testified in his state's behalf in a lawsuit filed by a company denied a license for a low-level radioactive waste facility. The company alleged that Nelson improperly used his political power to ensure the license would not be granted. Nebraska has agreed to pay $141 million to settle the issue, but Nelson still defends the state regulators' decision.

Nelson's rise to the Senate is mostly the product of perseverance. Since age 17, when he was elected governor of a model Nebraska high school legislature, Nelson has yearned for statewide office. The election of his high school superintendent and debate coach, Ralph Brooks, to be Nebraska's governor convinced Nelson that "you didn't have to be from a big city to have an opportunity in politics."

He grew up in McCook, a small town in south-central Nebraska where his mother started a taxpayers' watchdog group. Her attention to how tax revenue was spent was not lost on her son. "Watching the purse strings is the most important basic thing you can do in government," he says.

He considered joining the ministry while at the University of Nebraska, but opted instead for law school and, upon graduation, began a long career in insurance law. He ran an insurance company, headed a national association of insurance regulators and directed his state's insurance department. In 1990, he launched his first statewide bid for office, surviving the Democratic primary for governor by just 42 votes. He went on to defeat the incumbent, Republican Kay Orr, by 4,000 votes.

After eight years as governor, he returned in 1999 to his law firm, Kaufman-Nelson-Pattee. There he helped states develop Washington lobbying strategies, though he is careful to note that he was never a lobbyist himself. When Democratic Sen. Bob Kerrey announced he would retire the next year, Nelson was a shoo-in for the Democratic nomination to be his successor. He then defeated the Republican candidate, Attorney General Don Stenberg, by 2 percentage points — the closest Senate election in Nebraska history. His second win — against a self-funded candidate who dramatically outspent Nelson — was by 28 percentage points.

KEY VOTES

2006

- Yes Confirm Samuel A. Alito Jr. to the Supreme Court
- No Allow consideration of a bill to establish a $140 billion trust fund to compensate victims of asbestos exposure
- Yes Extend tax cuts for two years at a cost of $70 billion over five years
- No Overhaul immigration policy with border security, enforcement and guest worker program
- Yes Allow consideration of a bill to permanently repeal the estate tax
- No Urge President Bush to begin troop withdrawals from Iraq in 2006
- No Lift President Bush's restrictions on stem cell research funding
- Yes Authorize military tribunals for suspected terrorists

2005

- Yes Curb class action lawsuits by shifting them from state to federal courts
- Yes Allow confirmation vote on Priscilla R. Owen to the U.S. Court of Appeals for the 5th Circuit
- Yes Oppose mandatory emissions limits and block recognition of global warming as a threat
- Yes Approve free-trade pact with five Central American countries
- Yes Pass energy policy overhaul favored by President Bush emphasizing domestic oil and gas production
- Yes Shield gunmakers from lawsuits when their products are used in crimes
- Yes Ban torture of prisoners in U.S. custody
- Yes Renew 16 provisions of the Patriot Act
- Yes Allow final vote on opening the Arctic National Wildlife Refuge to oil and gas exploration

CQ VOTE STUDIES

	PARTY UNITY		PRESIDENTIAL SUPPORT	
	Support	Oppose	Support	Oppose
2006	36%	64%	76%	24%
2005	46%	54%	76%	24%
2004	52%	48%	82%	18%
2003	57%	43%	80%	20%
2002	51%	49%	91%	9%
2001	58%	42%	74%	26%

INTEREST GROUPS

	AFL-CIO	ADA	CCUS	ACU
2006	47%	35%	83%	64%
2005	71%	55%	94%	60%
2004	82%	65%	81%	52%
2003	62%	45%	86%	42%
2002	62%	50%	63%	55%
2001	81%	70%	71%	56%

Rep. Jeff Fortenberry (R)

CAPITOL OFFICE
225-4806
fortenberry.house.gov
1517 Longworth 20515-2701; fax 225-5686

COMMITTEES
Agriculture
Foreign Affairs
Small Business

RESIDENCE
Lincoln

BORN
Dec. 27, 1960, Baton Rouge, La.

RELIGION
Roman Catholic

FAMILY
Wife, Celeste Fortenberry; five children

EDUCATION
Louisiana State U., B.A. 1982 (economics); Georgetown U., M.P.P. 1986; Franciscan U. of Steubenville, M.Div. 1996 (theology)

CAREER
Publishing firm public relations manager and sales representative; economist; congressional aide

POLITICAL HIGHLIGHTS
Lincoln City Council, 1997-2001

ELECTION RESULTS

2006 GENERAL		
Jeff Fortenberry (R)	121,015	58.4%
Maxine Moul (D)	86,360	41.6%
2006 PRIMARY		
Jeff Fortenberry (R)		unopposed
2004 GENERAL		
Jeff Fortenberry (R)	143,756	54.2%
Matt Connealy (D)	113,971	43.0%
Steven R. Larrick (GREEN)	7,345	2.8%

Elected 2004; 2nd term

Fortenberry didn't start out as a Republican, or even a Nebraskan. Born and raised in Louisiana, he changed both his residence and his party affiliation as an adult. But he never lost the interest in politics and foreign affairs that he developed as a child. He was in the fifth grade when he wrote a letter to President Richard Nixon about Nixon's historic 1972 trip to China.

Given that early start, it is no surprise that Fortenberry followed his Republican predecessor in the 1st District seat, Doug Bereuter, onto what is now called the House Foreign Affairs Committee. But Fortenberry is a considerably more conservative Republican than Bereuter, a prominent moderate who stepped down in 2004 after nearly 26 years in the House.

Fortenberry has generally backed President Bush's policy on the Iraq War and joined the administration in opposition to a fixed target date for the withdrawal of forces. He voted against the March 2007 war supplemental funding bill passed in the House because it set a deadline of August 2008 for U.S. troop withdrawal. "We can all agree the goal is to end the war," he said afterward, "but I believe it must be done in a thoughtful and strategic manner. Establishing a fixed arbitrary deadline for withdrawal is not the appropriate course of action. It may undermine the goal of stabilization."

He serves on the Middle East and South Asia Subcommittee of Foreign Affairs, and his views of the region are more nuanced than those of the typical U.S. lawmaker. They were influenced, he says, by his travels to Egypt as a college student years ago, when he immersed himself in Arab history, culture and religion. He says many of his colleagues fail to consider those underlying elements. "We make assumptions about what steps these countries can actually make toward rapid revitalization without taking into account cultural and religious factors," he says.

Fortenberry has a more conventional assignment — for a Nebraska lawmaker — on the Agriculture panel, where he will have a hand in the rewrite of farm policy scheduled for the 110th Congress (2007-08). He wants to limit commodity payments and restructure them, noting that 10 percent of farmers receive 70 percent of all payments.

Like other Midwesterners, he wants to promote additional incentives for production of renewable fuels such as corn-based ethanol. His enthusiasm is tempered, however, by his concern about the impact of higher corn prices on cattlemen, who are seeing feed costs climb as the demand for corn increases. In addition, he worries that farmers in his state and elsewhere will invest heavily in ethanol production plants, only to see deep-pocketed outside investors step in later and undercut them, driving them out of business.

With oil prices high, Fortenberry is reconsidering his opposition to increased fuel efficiency standards for motor vehicles. "Fuel standards help us conserve," he told the Lincoln Journal Star in 2006. "It may be time to increase fuel standards, though I would always prefer incentives."

A Roman Catholic, Fortenberry is a social conservative. The father of five daughters, he opposes abortion and voted in 2006 for a proposed constitutional amendment to ban same-sex marriage.

Fortenberry was born and raised in Baton Rouge, La., and his parents divorced when he was about 10. His father, an insurance salesman, died in a car accident when Fortenberry was 12 and he says the loss instilled a feeling of responsibility at an early age and taught him the importance of fatherhood.

His interest in Nixon's trip to China was just the start of his fascination with world events. He followed current events closely as a high school student and at 17 served as a page to a Democratic Louisiana state senator. Fortenberry was a registered Democrat until 1982, the year he graduated from college. President Ronald Reagan, he says, "was a key political figure in my formative years." The Republican president better reflected his own emerging conservative values than did Democrats, he concluded.

He moved to Washington, D.C., for graduate study in public policy at Georgetown University and got an internship at the U.S. Department of Agriculture. He then worked for a Senate subcommittee on intergovernmental relations, where he focused on why land prices were falling in Nebraska — the state he later would call home.

As much as he enjoyed the secular world of Washington, Fortenberry felt something was missing. "I had a real deep nagging of the heart to really go into the deeper questions of life," he told the Lincoln Journal Star in 2006. In 1993, with one advanced degree under his belt, Fortenberry enrolled in the Franciscan University of Steubenville, in Ohio, where he earned a master's in theology. It was there he met his wife, Celeste.

After he got his degree, the couple packed up their belongings and headed west to Lincoln, Neb., where he became public relations director for what is now Sandhill Publishing. He plunged into civic life and quickly landed a seat on the Lincoln City Council, serving from 1997 to 2001.

Bereuter's decision to retire from the House — he actually resigned his seat early, in late August 2004 — created a free-for-all in the Republican primary, the first such competitive intraparty contest in more than a quarter-century. Bereuter backed Curt Bromm, the Speaker of Nebraska's unicameral legislature. But Bromm's voting record was hammered by the Club for Growth, a conservative anti-tax organization. Fortenberry campaigned hard, shaking every hand he could find. Once, only two people showed up to hear him; he spent 90 minutes with them. In the seven-candidate field, he won with 39 percent of the vote, leading Bromm by just more than 6 percentage points.

In the solidly Republican 1st District, Fortenberry won by 11 percentage points in November against Democratic state Sen. Matt Connealy, who played down his party affiliation and touted his background as a farmer. Although Democrats hoped that former Lt. Gov. Maxine Moul could do better in 2006, the Lincoln Journal Star endorsed Fortenberry and he defeated Moul by almost 17 points.

KEY VOTES

2006

No Stop broadband companies from favoring select Internet traffic

Yes Affirm U.S. commitment to war in Iraq and reject setting a withdrawal date for troops

Yes Repeal requirement for bilingual ballots at the polls

Yes Permit U.S. sale of civilian nuclear technology to India

Yes Build a 700-mile fence on the U.S.-Mexico border to curb illegal crossings

Yes Permit warrantless wiretaps of suspected terrorists

2005

Yes Intervene in the life-support case of Terri Schiavo

No Lift President Bush's restrictions on stem cell research funding

No Prohibit FBI access to library and bookstore records

Yes Approve free-trade pact with five Central American countries

Yes Pass energy policy overhaul favored by President Bush emphasizing domestic oil and gas production

Yes End mandatory preservation of habitat of endangered animal and plant species

Yes Ban torture of prisoners in U.S. custody

CQ VOTE STUDIES

	PARTY UNITY		PRESIDENTIAL SUPPORT	
	Support	Oppose	Support	Oppose
2006	89%	11%	87%	13%
2005	95%	5%	87%	13%

INTEREST GROUPS

	AFL-CIO	ADA	CCUS	ACU
2006	21%	5%	93%	84%
2005	20%	5%	93%	92%

NEBRASKA 1
East — Lincoln, Fremont

The 1st takes in eastern Nebraska, excluding Omaha and its suburbs. The district includes the state's capital, Lincoln, and the University of Nebraska's Memorial Stadium, which could qualify as the state's third-largest city when filled to its 74,000-seat capacity. Despite the small-town, rural feel, economic diversification in Lincoln, Norfolk and South Sioux City is helping to make the eastern part of the state more urban.

Lincoln's economy has experienced significant growth, led by expanding state and city governments and the university. Residents enjoy a low cost of living, combined with better-than-average earnings increases as compared with the national average. The University of Nebraska Technology Park, a joint venture between the university and private investors, has boosted the university's research activities and brought several companies to the area since it opened in 1997. The park is located in a northwestern section of the city that has been declared blighted, and local officials hope that the park's expansion will boost redevelopment efforts. Hospitals and the presence of banking and insurance industries also help sustain the city's economy.

The region is still heavily dependent on agriculture, but with a modern twist. Traditional crop and hog farming is supplemented by other agribusiness, such as meat processing, food packaging and fertilizer production. Polling and telemarketing call centers add to the white-collar job opportunities in the area.

Although the district was home to populist William Jennings Bryan and many of his supporters at the turn of the 20th century, the 1st now votes consistently Republican at all levels. The University of Nebraska makes Lincoln more liberal, but voter registration favors the GOP in both the city and surrounding Lancaster County. The strongest Democratic areas are in the northeast, especially in Thurston County, which is made up entirely by the Omaha and Winnebago American Indian reservations.

MAJOR INDUSTRY

Agriculture, higher education, technology, health care, government

CITIES

Lincoln, 225,581; Fremont, 25,174; Norfolk, 23,516

NOTABLE

Johnny Carson, former host of "The Tonight Show," grew up in Norfolk; Lincoln Airport is one of the designated emergency landing locations for the space shuttle.

Rep. Lee Terry (R)

CAPITOL OFFICE
225-4155
leeterry.house.gov
1524 Longworth 20515-2702; fax 226-5452

COMMITTEES
Energy & Commerce

RESIDENCE
Omaha

BORN
Jan. 29, 1962, Omaha, Neb.

RELIGION
Methodist

FAMILY
Wife, Robyn Terry; three children

EDUCATION
U. of Nebraska, B.S. 1984 (political science); Creighton U., J.D. 1987

CAREER
Lawyer

POLITICAL HIGHLIGHTS
Omaha City Council, 1991-99 (president, 1994-95)

ELECTION RESULTS

2006 GENERAL		
Lee Terry (R)	99,475	54.7%
Jim Esch (D)	82,504	45.3%
2006 PRIMARY		
Lee Terry (R)	52,890	83.6%
Steven Laird (R)	10,380	16.4%
2004 GENERAL		
Lee Terry (R)	152,608	61.1%
Nancy Thompson (D)	90,292	36.2%
John J. Graziano (LIBERT)	4,656	1.9%

PREVIOUS WINNING PERCENTAGES
2002 (63%); 2000 (66%); 1998 (66%)

Elected 1998; 5th term

Terry is trying to raise his profile in Congress, starting with enormous pictures of himself on 17 billboards in and around Omaha. He put them up shortly after the 2006 election gave him his narrowest win in five races. "Thank you for your trust," the signs said, next to a cheerful portrait of Terry.

Indeed, the Nebraska Republican was happy to return to Congress, given the miserable year the GOP had in general and the sort of campaign attacks he endured in particular. His Democratic opponent, political newcomer Jim Esch, portrayed Terry as a backbencher without much to show for four terms in the House. Terry himself acknowledged his perception problem. "People feel I haven't done a lot out here, but I really have," he told the Omaha World-Herald just before the November election.

Ultimately, Terry, his campaign treasury almost $1 million lighter, won re-election with an underwhelming 55 percent of the vote against an underfunded Esch, a 30-year-old lawyer and Chamber of Commerce official. That was a drop-off from earlier contests when he garnered more than 60 percent. Nevertheless relieved, Terry rented the billboard space throughout his Omaha-based district, the most urban of the three Nebraska districts. "I felt very moved to thank the people that stuck with me," he says.

Raising his profile won't be easy with Democrats in the majority. It's the first time Terry has had to navigate in the minority, plus the Nebraska delegation as a whole has lost clout. It is all Republican, except for Democratic Sen. Ben Nelson.

As a member of the Energy and Commerce Committee, Terry's signature issue is federal funding for the development of alternative fuels, particularly corn-based ethanol, as a way of easing dependence on foreign oil — and as a way of finding new markets for a crop his district produces in abundance. An increase in demand for ethanol would be a boon for both Nebraska's corn farms and its small towns with ethanol plants.

In addition to its current use in gasoline, ethanol shows promise of someday being used to make hydrogen for fuel cells, which produce electricity cleanly, emitting only water and heat. Terry and Democrat Mike Doyle of Pennsylvania have sponsored legislation providing tax credits to promote the commercialization of hydrogen fuel cells and requiring that all new federal government buildings use fuel cells to generate backup power. He also won inclusion of hydrogen fuel cell incentives in the 2005 energy bill enacted into law.

Another big priority for Terry is getting broadband Internet service to rural areas, a key issue for many farm-state lawmakers. "Competitiveness in the 21st century is about moving data and information," he says.

In 2003, Terry was the subject of a spurt of media attention as one of just eight lawmakers to vote against creation of a federal "do not call" list for telemarketers. His vote prompted calls from angry constituents fed up with constant sales calls. "It's about jobs, jobs, jobs, jobs," Terry told National Public Radio, explaining that 39,000 people in his district are employed, directly or indirectly, by telemarketers.

Terry looks out for the interests of Offutt Air Force Base, located just south of Omaha. Employing more than 11,000 military and civilian personnel, it is as much a part of the community as the Mutual of Omaha insurance company. Offutt is the home of the U.S. Strategic Command, where any nuclear war would be planned, and President Bush went there for part of the day following the Sept. 11 terrorist attacks.

The Union Pacific Railroad has its headquarters in Omaha, making rail issues a concern of Terry's. He sponsored a law enacted in 2001, at the behest of both labor and management, to restructure the federal railroad pension system to allow some funds to be invested in stocks and bonds.

Terry is a loyal partisan who votes consistently with the House Republican leadership. Unlike more-combative conservatives who came to the House earlier in the 1990s, Terry has positioned himself as a pragmatist. "I want to fight the good fight on abortion, but that doesn't mean I drag down an appropriations bill," he told the World-Herald.

Yet Terry casts a conservative vote on most social issues. He opposed federal funding for embryonic stem cell research, which uses cells from surplus embryos at in vitro fertilization clinics. And he supported a constitutional amendment to ban same-sex marriage. But as a former trial lawyer, he does not always vote with Republicans in favor of changing tort laws.

Terry was raised in Omaha, where his father was a news anchor with a political talk show. Young Terry would sometimes go to work with him to watch interviews with congressmen, senators and other local celebrities. He had two autographs on his bedroom wall: one from Evel Knievel and the other from conservative Nebraska Sen. Roman Hruska.

When he was in 8th grade, Terry handed out pamphlets for his father's unsuccessful run for the House in 1976 — the seat Terry himself won two decades later. In college, Terry planned a career in politics. After getting his law degree, he was elected to the Omaha City Council, where he served for eight years.

In 1998, his position on the city council made him the front-runner for the House seat that Republican Jon Christensen vacated to make a failed run for governor. Terry won the four-way primary by 10 percentage points and then triumphed by 31 points in November over an underfunded Democrat, newscaster Mike Scott. Democrats in 2002 held out some hope for victory in Jim Simon, a wealthy former AOL executive. But Terry won with 63 percent of the vote and almost matched that in 2004, earning 61 percent to defeat Democratic state Sen. Nancy Thompson.

When he first ran for Congress, Terry pledged to serve no more than three terms, but he has since backed away from that promise. He said he quickly realized when he got to Washington the benefits that come with seniority.

Terry belongs to a small group of lawmakers who save money by living in their offices during the workweek. He sleeps on an air mattress and uses the House gym to shave and shower, commuting home on weekends.

KEY VOTES

2006

- No Stop broadband companies from favoring select Internet traffic
- Yes Affirm U.S. commitment to war in Iraq and reject setting a withdrawal date for troops
- Yes Repeal requirement for bilingual ballots at the polls
- Yes Permit U.S. sale of civilian nuclear technology to India
- Yes Build a 700-mile fence on the U.S.-Mexico border to curb illegal crossings
- Yes Permit warrantless wiretaps of suspected terrorists

2005

- Yes Intervene in the life-support case of Terri Schiavo
- No Lift President Bush's restrictions on stem cell research funding
- No Prohibit FBI access to library and bookstore records
- Yes Approve free-trade pact with five Central American countries
- Yes Pass energy policy overhaul favored by President Bush emphasizing domestic oil and gas production
- Yes End mandatory preservation of habitat of endangered animal and plant species
- No Ban torture of prisoners in U.S. custody

CQ VOTE STUDIES

	PARTY UNITY		PRESIDENTIAL SUPPORT	
	Support	Oppose	Support	Oppose
2006	97%	3%	97%	3%
2005	94%	6%	85%	15%
2004	93%	7%	88%	12%
2003	96%	4%	89%	11%
2002	92%	8%	84%	16%

INTEREST GROUPS

	AFL-CIO	ADA	CCUS	ACU
2006	14%	0%	100%	92%
2005	13%	0%	89%	92%
2004	29%	0%	90%	92%
2003	0%	5%	97%	76%
2002	11%	5%	85%	88%

NEBRASKA 2

East — Omaha and suburbs

Formerly the eastern terminus of the Union Pacific Railroad, Omaha is the heart of the 2nd District. Omaha grew up as a blue-collar city: a railroad junction, a Missouri River port and a place where cattle became steaks. To outsiders, this broad-shouldered, gritty image remains. But the city has become mainly a place of downtown office buildings and white-collar jobs in agriculture and insurance businesses. It also is known as the nation's 1-800 capital, thanks to a glut of call centers for telemarketing, customer service and credit processing operations.

Omaha's economy has grown at nearly the same rate as the national economy since 2002, and residents of Omaha enjoy a relatively low cost of living. Local officials are continuing economic diversification efforts, and the city is home to five Fortune 500 companies. Offutt Air Force Base, the district's largest employer, contributes billions of dollars into the local economy annually. Building on the success of an earlier downtown redevelopment plan, the city has implemented a new plan to guide revitalization of the northern section of downtown. Omaha continues to expand outward, and officials from the city and surrounding Douglas County have considered merging into a single municipality.

The 2nd is a reliably Republican district, although Omaha's dwindling blue-collar base still supports some Democrats. Douglas County, home to more than 80 percent of district residents, has voted for the GOP presidential candidate every time but once since Harry S Truman. George W. Bush took 61 percent of the 2nd's vote in the 2004 presidential election, his lowest tally in the Republican state.

MAJOR INDUSTRY

Phone service centers, military, agriculture, insurance

MILITARY BASES

Offutt Air Force Base, 8,427 military, 2,055 civilian (2005)

CITIES

Omaha, 390,007; Bellevue, 44,382; Papillion, 16,363

NOTABLE

Omaha's Florence neighborhood was the site of the first white settlement in Nebraska, founded in 1846 by a group of Mormons led by Brigham Young fleeing religious persecution in Iowa; Billionaire investor Warren Buffett lives in Omaha — his father, Republican Howard Buffett, represented Omaha in the House from 1943-49 and 1951-53.

Rep. Adrian Smith (R)

CAPITOL OFFICE
225-6435
adriansmith.house.gov
503 Cannon 20515-2703; fax 225-0207

COMMITTEES
Agriculture
Budget
Science & Technology

RESIDENCE
Gering

BORN
Dec. 19, 1970, Scottsbluff, Neb.

RELIGION
Christian

FAMILY
Single

EDUCATION
Liberty U., attended 1989-90; U. of Nebraska, B.S. 1993 (secondary education)

CAREER
Storage company owner; realtor; education workshop coordinator; substitute teacher

POLITICAL HIGHLIGHTS
Gering City Council, 1994-98; Neb. Legislature, 1999-2007

ELECTION RESULTS

2006 GENERAL		
Adrian Smith (R)	113,687	55.0%
Scott Kleeb (D)	93,046	45.0%
2006 PRIMARY		
Adrian Smith (R)	42,218	39.5%
John Hanson (R)	30,501	28.5%
Jay Vavricek (R)	29,224	27.3%
David Harris (R)	2,934	2.7%
Douglas Polk (R)	2,020	1.9%

Elected 2006; 1st term

Smith came to Washington on a locally focused pledge to look out for the ranchers and farmers in Nebraska's vast 3rd District, which has three-quarters of the state's land area and is the inspiration for Pulitzer Prize-winning author Willa Cather's novels about life in rural America.

Smith immediately landed his top-choice assignment, a seat on the Agriculture Committee. Each of his three predecessors served on that panel, including the most recent, Republican Tom Osborne, who left the House in a failed bid for governor.

The committee appointment by GOP leaders allows Smith to have a hand in a major overhaul of farm policy scheduled for the 110th Congress (2007-08). His district is composed predominately of cattle ranchers and sugar beet and wheat farmers. He is particularly interested in boosting incentives for ethanol and biodiesel fuels and in reducing the capital gains tax for landowners who sell to new farmers. Smith generally supports farm subsidies, though he would cap them for the largest producers.

There is no contesting Smith's devotion to conservative causes and to Ronald Reagan, his political hero in honor of whom he kept a "Reagan Shrine" in his real estate office. In his mid-30s, Smith has been in politics all his adult life. His father chaired the county GOP, and his mother was secretary of the state Republican Party. Smith was elected to the Gering City Council at age 23, then served in the Nebraska Legislature for eight years.

In the 2006 race for the House, Smith survived a divisive GOP primary but took flak for the aggressive intervention in his behalf by the Club for Growth, a conservative anti-tax organization whose positions on rural issues — including opposing farm subsidies — are highly unpopular in the 3rd District. Democrat Scott Kleeb, a political novice who had spent only his summers in Nebraska, kept the issue alive during the fall campaign by highlighting $400,000 in campaign contributions Smith got from the group. Smith said he accepted the help based on the club's anti-tax views. He managed a 10 percentage point win in a district where registered Republicans outnumber Democrats 3-to-1.

NEBRASKA 3

West — Grand Island, North Platte, Scottsbluff

Scouting what would later become the Oregon Trail, early 19th century explorers described this section of the country as the "Great American Desert." Most of the 3rd's land is arid, and most of the district's population lives along the Platte River.

Grand Island, North Platte and Scottsbluff each serve as regional centers for the retail and health care needs of the surrounding counties. Industry and manufacturing also locate around these areas, as well as in Columbus, Hastings and Kearney. The rest of the land in the district's 69 counties is left to cattle ranchers and sugar beet, soybean and wheat farmers. The extensive Union Pacific (UP) railroad network brings crops from isolated areas to larger markets.

The 3rd's agrarian economy is susceptible to changes in the region's weather, and water is a precious commodity here. Drought conditions since 1999 have hurt grazing operations and caused poor crop yields. Every county in the 3rd was designated as a drought disaster area in 2006, but the westernmost areas have been hit hardest. In addition to securing federal aid, state and local officials are working to increase conservation, and water-use restrictions are commonplace. The 1st and 2nd districts dominate state politics, while the 3rd has several of the nation's poorest counties.

Although Democratic pockets exist in Greeley, Sherman and Saline counties, the 3rd overall is conservative and strongly favors GOP candidates. George W. Bush took 75 percent of the 3rd's 2004 presidential vote, his highest showing in the state.

MAJOR INDUSTRY
Agriculture, food processing, transportation

CITIES
Grand Island, 42,940; Kearney, 27,431

NOTABLE
UP's Bailey Yard in North Platte is the world's largest railroad classification yard.

NEVADA

Gov. Jim Gibbons (R)

First elected: 2006
Length of term: 4 years
Term expires: 1/11
Salary: $117,000
Phone: (775) 684-5670

Residence: Reno
Born: Dec. 16, 1944; Sparks, Nev.
Religion: Mormon
Family: Wife, Dawn Gibbons; three children
Education: U. of Nevada, Reno, B.S. 1967 (geology), M.S. 1973 (mining geology); Southwestern U., J.D. 1979
Military service: Air Force, 1967-71; Nev. Air National Guard, 1975-95
Career: Airline pilot; lawyer; geologist
Political highlights: Nev. Assembly, 1989-94 (minority whip, 1993); Republican nominee for governor, 1994, U.S. House, 1997-2007

Election results:

2006 GENERAL		
Jim Gibbons (R)	279,003	47.9%
Dina Titus (D)	255,684	43.9%
None of these candidates	20,699	3.6%
Christopher H. Hansen (IA)	20,019	3.4%
Craig Bergland (GREEN)	6,753	1.2%

Lt. Gov. Brian R. Krolicki (R)

First elected: 2006
Length of term: 4 years
Term expires: 1/11
Salary: $110,000
Phone: (775) 684-5637

LEGISLATURE

Legislature: February-June in odd-numbered years, limit of 120 days

Senate: 21 members, 4-year terms
2007 ratios: 11 R, 10 D; 15 men, 6 women
Salary: $138/day in session; $91/day allowance
Phone: (775) 684-1402

Assembly: 42 members, 2-year terms
2007 ratios: 27 D, 15 R; 29 men, 13 women
Salary: $138/day in session; $91/day allowance
Phone: (775) 684-8555

TERM LIMITS

Governor: 2 terms
Senate: 3 terms
Assembly: 6 terms

URBAN STATISTICS

CITY	POPULATION
Las Vegas	478,434
Reno	180,480
Henderson	175,381
North Las Vegas	115,488

REGISTERED VOTERS

Democrat	40%
Republican	39%
Nonpartisan/others	21%

POPULATION

2006 population (est.)	2,495,529
2000 population	1,998,257
1990 population	1,201,833
Percent change (1990-2000)	+66.3%
Rank among states (2006)	35
Median age	35
Born in state	21.3%
Foreign born	15.8%
Violent crime rate	524/100,000
Poverty level	10.5%
Federal workers	14,701
Military	11,932

ELECTIONS

STATE ELECTION OFFICIAL
(775) 684-5705
DEMOCRATIC PARTY
(702) 737-8683
REPUBLICAN PARTY
(702) 258-9182

MISCELLANEOUS

Web: www.nv.gov
Capital: Carson City

U.S. CONGRESS

Senate: 1 Democrat, 1 Republican
House: 2 Republicans, 1 Democrat

2000 Census Statistics by District

DIST.	2004 VOTE FOR PRESIDENT		WHITE	BLACK	ASIAN	HISP	MEDIAN INCOME	WHITE COLLAR	BLUE COLLAR	SERVICE INDUSTRY	OVER 64	UNDER 18	COLLEGE EDUCATION	RURAL	SQ. MILES
	BUSH	KERRY													
1	42%	57%	52%	12%	5%	28%	$39,480	48%	23%	29%	10%	27%	15%	0%	177
2	57	41	75	2	3	15	$43,879	55	25	20	11	26	19	21	105,079
3	50	49	69	5	6	16	$50,749	57	18	25	12	24	20	4	4,570
STATE	50	48	65	7	4	20	$44,581	53	22	25	11	26	18	8	109,826
U.S.	50.7	48.3	69	12	4	13	$41,994	60	25	15	12	26	24	21	3,537,438

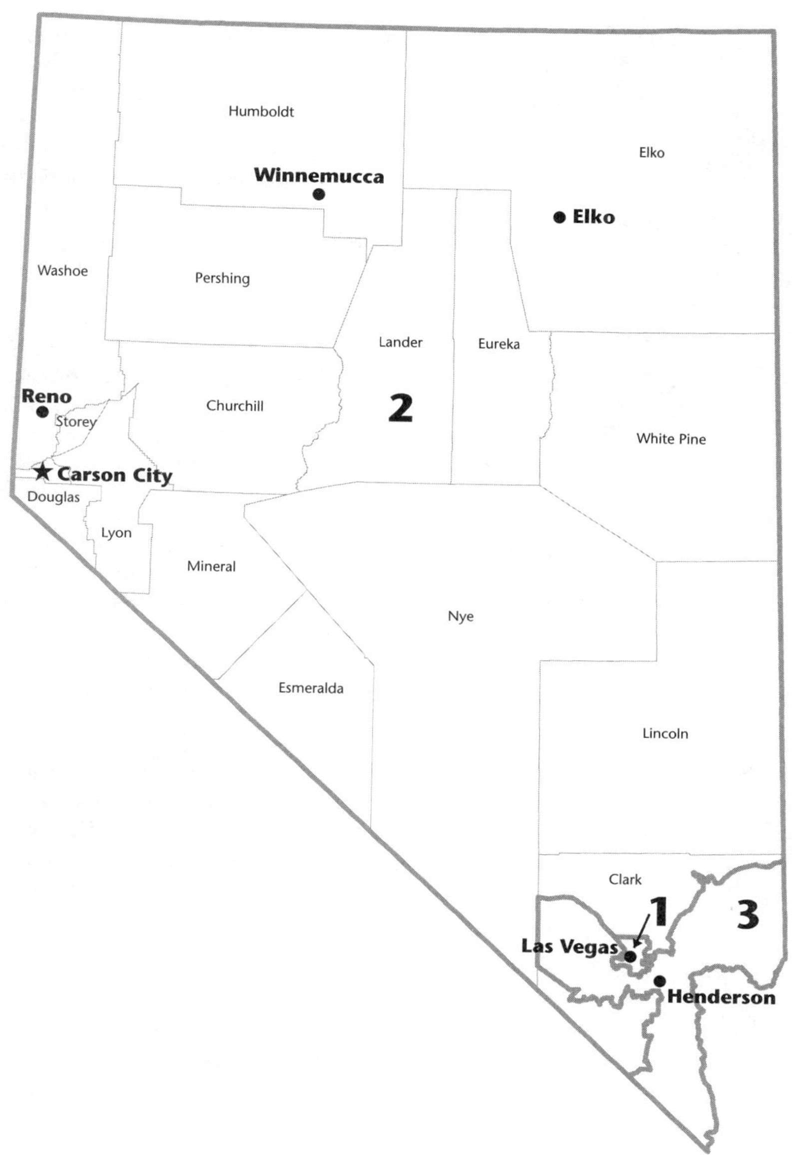
Humboldt
Winnemucca
Elko
Elko
Washoe
Pershing
Lander
Eureka
Reno
Storey
Churchill
2
White Pine
Carson City
Douglas
Lyon
Mineral
Nye
Esmeralda
Lincoln
Clark
1
3
Las Vegas
Henderson

Sen. Harry Reid (D)

CAPITOL OFFICE
224-3542
reid.senate.gov
528 Hart 20510-2803; fax 224-7327

COMMITTEES
Rules & Administration

RESIDENCE
Searchlight

BORN
Dec. 2, 1939, Searchlight, Nev.

RELIGION
Mormon

FAMILY
Wife, Landra Reid; five children

EDUCATION
Southern Utah State College, A.S. 1959; Utah State U., B.A. 1961 (history & political science); George Washington U., J.D. 1964; U. of Nevada, Las Vegas, attended 1969-70

CAREER
Lawyer

POLITICAL HIGHLIGHTS
Nev. Assembly, 1969-71; lieutenant governor, 1971-75; Democratic nominee for U.S. Senate, 1974; candidate for mayor of Las Vegas, 1975; Nevada Gaming Commission chairman, 1977-81; U.S. House, 1983-87

ELECTION RESULTS

2004 GENERAL		
Harry Reid (D)	494,805	61.1%
Richard Ziser (R)	284,640	35.1%
None of these candidates	12,968	1.6%
Thomas L. Hurst (LIBERT)	9,559	1.2%
2004 PRIMARY		
Harry Reid (D)		unopposed

PREVIOUS WINNING PERCENTAGES
1998 (48%); 1992 (51%); 1986 (50%); 1984 House Election (56%); 1982 House Election (58%)

Elected 1986; 4th term

As the new majority leader, Reid is the most powerful member of the Senate. But that doesn't mean he always gets what he wants. The historic 2006 election that transferred power from the GOP to the Democrats gave Reid just a one-vote majority. Not only does he have to contend with a still sizable bloc of Senate Republicans, Reid has to satisfy the excitable liberal core in his own party that is as susceptible to overreaching as conservatives were during more than a dozen years of Republican rule.

Outwardly, Reid lacks modern political panache. He can be taciturn, even dour on television, without the personal charisma of the presidential hopefuls in his caucus. He prefers reading books to hosting fundraising dinners, and he shuns the nonstop self-promotion that consumes many lawmakers. He spends his free time with his grandchildren. "I'm not much for yelling and screaming. That's just not who I am," Reid says.

But the Democratic colleagues who put him on the leadership track know the side of Reid that is a scrappy former amateur boxer, a wily parliamentarian and an effective behind-the-scenes operator who can count votes. Eric Herzik, a University of Nevada political scientist and longtime Reid watcher, said, "He likes to say he'd rather dance than fight, but a lot of people have gotten bruised dancing with him."

When Reid ascended to majority leader in the 110th Congress (2007-08), he was quick to lay out an agenda tracking the issues Democrats used to oust Republican incumbents in the election. He led the Senate to pass a spending bill setting a timetable for the withdrawal of troops from Iraq, and he called for expanding government health programs for millions of uninsured Americans. He also hinted at a tax increase for the top 1 percent of income-earners to offset spending on Democratic priorities.

But Reid's most daunting task is managing expectations and egos in a place where a small group of senators, or even just one, can filibuster bills into an early retirement, and where a handful of lawmakers harbor presidential ambitions. And if Reid has a match as a savvy tactician, it is Mitch McConnell, the thick-skinned, four-term GOP minority leader from Kentucky. Moreover, President Bush made it clear that he got his veto pen out at the start of the 110th Congress and was not afraid to use it liberally with the congressional Democrats' agenda.

As legislation roared out of the House under the guidance of Speaker Nancy Pelosi, Reid had to temper the excitement. In 2007, the House sent over a controversial plan to allow the government to use its buying power to negotiate lower drug prices with the private sector, but it was blocked by Senate Republicans after heavy lobbying by the pharmaceutical industry. In another instance, Reid got through the Senate an expansion of embryonic stem cell research, but without the votes to overcome a veto.

Though he promotes bedrock Democratic values, Reid, more than many in his caucus, is apt to consult with conservatives with whom he shares some beliefs on social issues. A practicing Mormon, Reid often votes with Republicans in favor of restrictions on abortion. A defender of his state's economically important mining industry, he can be skeptical of new environmental controls.

Reid is a stickler for Senate rules and is more likely than his GOP predecessor as majority leader, Tennessee's Bill Frist, to let committees work their will. He told McConnell in a phone call shortly before the 2006 election that he favored "real" conference committees to hammer out differences between the House and Senate versions of bills. They should include members of both parties and be open, Reid said, in a departure from the GOP-only conferences held out of the public eye during Republican rule.

Reid has a sharp edge that sometimes gets him into trouble. In May 2005, he had to apologize for calling Bush a "loser" in remarks to Las Vegas high school students. And in 2007, he declared that the war in Iraq "is lost," a pronouncement some Democrats thought went too far. Ethical concerns are another potential weakness for Reid. In 2006, he amended his Senate financial statements to reflect a previously undisclosed $700,000 profit on a land deal with a businessman friend in 1998.

Before being elected leader, Reid was the party's second-in-command as the whip for six years under Tom Daschle, the former Senate minority leader. When Daschle was defeated for re-election in 2004, Reid in a matter of hours lined up the votes he needed to move up.

When Democrats won control in 2006, there was no question Reid would make the transition from minority to majority leader. In the previous two years, he had held Democrats together to prevent Frist from passing a reduction in the estate tax and rallied his troops to stop Frist from taking away the minority's power to filibuster judicial nominations. A bipartisan group of senators, the Gang of 14, struck a deal to keep the GOP leadership from permanently altering Senate tradition.

Reid grew up in a cabin without indoor plumbing in the tiny mining town of Searchlight, Nev., on the edge of the Mojave Desert. His mother was a high school dropout who took in laundry to support the family; his father was an alcoholic miner who killed himself at 58. As a young man, Reid was an amateur middleweight who sometimes sparred with pros in exhibition fights. But he wanted out of Searchlight and a boxer's hardscrabble life.

Reid applied himself to his studies, boarding with families 40 miles away in Henderson to attend high school, where he became student body president. History teacher Donal O'Callaghan, also the local Democratic chairman, took notice and helped arrange a scholarship for Reid at Utah State University. He earned a law degree at George Washington University in Washington, D.C., while moonlighting as a U.S. Capitol police officer.

Reid returned to Henderson and, at age 28, won election to the Nevada Assembly. When his mentor, O'Callaghan, became governor in 1970, Reid was elected the youngest lieutenant governor in state history. He made a bid for the U.S. Senate in 1974 but lost to Republican Paul Laxalt. O'Callaghan rescued Reid after a few years with an appointment as chairman of the Nevada Gaming Commission, giving him oversight of the state's top industry at a time it was tainted by organized crime. Reid later told the Las Vegas Review-Journal, "They put bombs on my car, there were threatening phone calls at night, people tried to bribe me and went to jail."

In 1982, Reid won the first of two terms in the U.S. House. But he still had his heart set on the Senate, and in 1986 tried again. Though he carried only two of Nevada's 16 counties against Republican Rep. Jim Santini, one of them was Clark County, Reid's Las Vegas political base where a majority of the state's voters live. He won with 50 percent of the vote.

In 1992, Democrat Charles Woods, a wealthy broadcast executive, held Reid to 53 percent in the primary. In the general election, Reid outspent GOP rancher Demar Dahl 5-to-1 to prevail with 51 percent.

In his 1998 campaign, Reid won by only 428 votes over Republican John Ensign, a House member from Las Vegas, in a bitter contest. Reid called Ensign "an embarrassment to the state," and Ensign described Reid as an "old card shark." After Ensign was elected in 2000 to the state's other Senate seat, the two reconciled. In 2004, Reid easily defeated Republican Richard Ziser, an activist against same-sex marriage, for a fourth term.

KEY VOTES

2006

- No Confirm Samuel A. Alito Jr. to the Supreme Court
- No Allow consideration of a bill to establish a $140 billion trust fund to compensate victims of asbestos exposure
- No Extend tax cuts for two years at a cost of $70 billion over five years
- Yes Overhaul immigration policy with border security, enforcement and guest worker program
- No Allow consideration of a bill to permanently repeal the estate tax
- Yes Urge President Bush to begin troop withdrawals from Iraq in 2006
- Yes Lift President Bush's restrictions on stem cell research funding
- No Authorize military tribunals for suspected terrorists

2005

- No Curb class action lawsuits by shifting them from state to federal courts
- Yes Allow confirmation vote on Priscilla R. Owen to the U.S. Court of Appeals for the 5th Circuit
- No Oppose mandatory emissions limits and block recognition of global warming as a threat
- No Approve free-trade pact with five Central American countries
- No Pass energy policy overhaul favored by President Bush emphasizing domestic oil and gas production
- Yes Shield gunmakers from lawsuits when their products are used in crimes
- Yes Ban torture of prisoners in U.S. custody
- No Renew 16 provisions of the Patriot Act
- No Allow final vote on opening the Arctic National Wildlife Refuge to oil and gas exploration

CQ VOTE STUDIES

	PARTY UNITY		PRESIDENTIAL SUPPORT	
	Support	Oppose	Support	Oppose
2006	93%	7%	57%	43%
2005	92%	8%	38%	62%
2004	83%	17%	61%	39%
2003	95%	5%	53%	47%
2002	94%	6%	71%	29%
2001	96%	4%	65%	35%
2000	94%	6%	92%	8%
1999	92%	8%	82%	18%
1998	81%	19%	79%	21%
1997	83%	17%	84%	16%

INTEREST GROUPS

	AFL-CIO	ADA	CCUS	ACU
2006	93%	90%	50%	12%
2005	93%	100%	50%	4%
2004	100%	90%	53%	21%
2003	100%	70%	35%	21%
2002	100%	85%	45%	10%
2001	100%	100%	43%	20%
2000	88%	90%	40%	12%
1999	100%	90%	35%	12%
1998	75%	90%	56%	20%
1997	86%	85%	50%	8%

Sen. John Ensign (R)

CAPITOL OFFICE
224-6244
ensign.senate.gov
119 Russell 20510-2805; fax 228-2193

COMMITTEES
Armed Services
Budget
Commerce, Science & Transportation
Veterans' Affairs

RESIDENCE
Las Vegas

BORN
March 25, 1958, Roseville, Calif.

RELIGION
Christian

FAMILY
Wife, Darlene Ensign; three children

EDUCATION
U. of Nevada, Las Vegas, attended 1976-79; Oregon State U., B.S. 1981; Colorado State U., D.V.M. 1985

CAREER
Veterinarian; casino manager

POLITICAL HIGHLIGHTS
U.S. House, 1995-99; sought Republican nomination for U.S. Senate, 1998

ELECTION RESULTS

2006 GENERAL		
John Ensign (R)	322,501	55.4%
Jack Carter (D)	238,796	41.0%
None of these candidates	8,232	1.4%
David K. Schumann (IA)	7,774	1.3%
2006 PRIMARY		
John Ensign (R)	127,023	90.5%
None of these candidates	6,754	4.8%
Ed Hamilton (R)	6,649	4.7%

PREVIOUS WINNING PERCENTAGES
2000 (55%); 1996 House Election (50%); 1994 House Election (48%)

Elected 2000; 2nd term

A rising star in Republican circles, Ensign is a ferocious competitor, whether he's on the golf course, running track or working Capitol Hill. Friends say he turns everyday tasks into head-to-head contests. "If you walk with him in the airport, he wants to beat you and be first at the gate," said Pete Ernaut, a Republican political consultant and former Ensign campaign manager.

That attitude will serve Ensign well in the leadership position he assumed at the start of the 110th Congress (2007-08) — chairman of the National Republican Senatorial Committee, the campaign arm of Senate Republicans. Helping the GOP reclaim the majority will be a formidable task: In 2008, the party will have to defend 21 Senate seats, compared with 12 for the Democrats. The challenge is compounded by the fact that most of those Democrats hold safe seats, and the presidential race is expected to consume the bulk of the political money available.

But those who know Ensign say he shouldn't be underestimated. In addition to his strong competitive streak, he has a reputation as an effective fundraiser with numerous contacts in the real estate and high-tech industries. Colleagues say the silver-haired, perpetually tan veterinarian also can articulate a conservative message effectively.

Ensign first came to Congress as part of the Republican takeover in 1995, and he adheres to the strain of fiscal conservatism that distinguished many of the newcomers in that watershed political year. He disdains government spending and is more likely to cast his lot with maverick Arizona Republican Sen. John McCain and his campaign against wasteful spending than he is with party-backed spending bills laden with home-state projects.

In February 2006, Ensign raised a budget point of order against comprehensive legislation that would have created a trust fund to compensate victims of asbestos exposure. He based his motion on a prohibition against legislation that would authorize more than $5 billion in spending during any 10-year period, starting in 2016. His move helped doom the bill; the test vote fell one vote short of the 60 required to waive the point of order.

Ensign usually supports President Bush and the GOP leadership, defending the president's unpopular Iraq War strategy even in 2007, when many of his colleagues had turned against it. "From what I see, the president has the only plan on the table that does not ensure defeat," he said.

But Ensign opposed the 2006 Senate immigration bill, which tracked Bush's proposals for a guest worker program and a path to citizenship for the estimated 12 million illegal immigrants living in the United States. And he voted against Bush's 2003 Medicare prescription drug law.

He opposes embryonic stem cell research and sponsored a 2006 initiative, passed by the Senate but stalled in conference, to make it a federal crime to help a minor circumvent parental notification laws by crossing state lines to obtain an abortion.

Ensign has emerged as a leader on technology issues. He is the top-ranking Republican on the Commerce Committee's panel on Science, Technology and Innovation, which he chaired in the 109th Congress (2005-06) when GOP leaders also made him chairman of their High Tech Task Force. He has received generous political contributions from high-tech interests, and has taken a lead role in trying to build a Republican bridge to Silicon Valley by championing an extension of the research and development tax credit.

On some issues, Ensign has shown an inclination to work with Democrats. In a commentary published in the Wall Street Journal in December 2006, he and Democratic Sen. Hillary Rodham Clinton of New York urged the Bush administration to press Iraq to apportion its oil revenues so that "every individual Iraqi would share in the country's oil wealth."

And Ensign has forged an unusually close relationship with Nevada's senior senator, Democrat Harry Reid, now the Senate's majority leader. The two work together so closely on Nevada-specific legislation that Nevada political commentator Jon Ralston refers to them as "Harry Ensign." Their relationship is remarkable given the fact that Reid defeated Ensign in an acrimonious 1998 race. But neither man let the wounds fester, and Ensign won the other Senate seat in 2000. "I wish other people had the same non-aggression pact we have," Reid told reporters in November 2006.

Ensign and Reid consistently fight to stop the establishment of a nuclear waste storage facility at Yucca Mountain, 90 miles northwest of Las Vegas. Opposition to the repository has long been a unifying force for Nevada lawmakers, regardless of party.

Ensign so far has fared better in his efforts to protect Nevada's gaming industry, an economic mainstay. From his seat on the Commerce panel, he has fought against legislation outlawing gambling on college sports, which is legal in Nevada. And he has worked to limit Internet gambling, which can cut into casinos' revenues.

Ensign got an early glimpse of the gambling world, though it was hardly a glamorous one. His mother, who raised Ensign and his two siblings by herself, worked a $12-a-day job at Harrah's casino as a "change girl," doling out quarters to slot-machine players. During the 1995 debate on welfare overhaul, Ensign pointed to his mother's refusal to accept government assistance as an example for others. "We were brought up in a family where you just don't take things," he said. "Welfare was for people who couldn't work, not for people who wouldn't work."

His mother eventually remarried, to a man who rose to become chairman and CEO of Mandalay Resort Group. Ensign worked in casinos and even became a general manager at two of them in Las Vegas, but he decided to follow his interest in animals and became a veterinarian. He opened Las Vegas' first 24-hour animal hospital.

Both the casino and veterinary jobs gave him experience in dealing with people and solving problems, so it was hardly a stretch for Ensign to enter politics. GOP leaders urged him to run for the House in 1994 and, though he was a political novice, he assembled an impressive organization of volunteers and embarked on an energetic precinct-walking effort. In the Republican sweep that year, he overcame a large Democratic registration advantage to squeeze past four-term Democrat James Bilbray in the Las Vegas-based 1st District by just 1,436 votes.

As a freshman, he landed a prized seat on the Ways and Means Committee, where he took an active part in the overhaul of the nation's welfare system. He left the House to challenge Reid in 1998, losing by just 428 votes. Then, in early 1999, Democrat Richard H. Bryan announced he wouldn't seek a third Senate term. Though Democrat Ed Bernstein, an attorney, was an aggressive foe, Ensign spent twice as much money and won with 55 percent of the vote in 2000.

In 2006, he drew opposition from Jack Carter, eldest son of former President Jimmy Carter, who campaigned on a platform critical of Republicans on the Iraq War. Although one poll in late August showed the two men virtually neck and neck, Carter was subsequently hospitalized with colitis, taking him off the campaign trail for several weeks. Ensign, meanwhile, outspent Carter heavily in ads that stressed his legislative accomplishments, and he won again with 55 percent.

KEY VOTES

2006

- Yes Confirm Samuel A. Alito Jr. to the Supreme Court
- No Allow consideration of a bill to establish a $140 billion trust fund to compensate victims of asbestos exposure
- Yes Extend tax cuts for two years at a cost of $70 billion over five years
- No Overhaul immigration policy with border security, enforcement and guest worker program
- Yes Allow consideration of a bill to permanently repeal the estate tax
- No Urge President Bush to begin troop withdrawals from Iraq in 2006
- No Lift President Bush's restrictions on stem cell research funding
- Yes Authorize military tribunals for suspected terrorists

2005

- Yes Curb class action lawsuits by shifting them from state to federal courts
- Yes Allow confirmation vote on Priscilla R. Owen to the U.S. Court of Appeals for the 5th Circuit
- Yes Oppose mandatory emissions limits and block recognition of global warming as a threat
- Yes Approve free-trade pact with five Central American countries
- Yes Pass energy policy overhaul favored by President Bush emphasizing domestic oil and gas production
- Yes Shield gunmakers from lawsuits when their products are used in crimes
- Yes Ban torture of prisoners in U.S. custody
- Yes Renew 16 provisions of the Patriot Act
- Yes Allow final vote on opening the Arctic National Wildlife Refuge to oil and gas exploration

CQ VOTE STUDIES

	PARTY UNITY		PRESIDENTIAL SUPPORT	
	Support	Oppose	Support	Oppose
2006	91%	9%	90%	10%
2005	94%	6%	89%	11%
2004	90%	10%	100%	0%
2003	95%	5%	98%	2%
2002	90%	10%	96%	4%
2001	88%	12%	97%	3%
House Service:				
1998	82%	18%	27%	73%
1997	87%	13%	30%	70%
1996	80%	20%	40%	60%
1995	89%	11%	18%	82%

INTEREST GROUPS

	AFL-CIO	ADA	CCUS	ACU
2006	20%	5%	92%	100%
2005	15%	5%	88%	100%
2004	9%	15%	75%	92%
2003	0%	10%	91%	100%
2002	15%	15%	95%	85%
2001	19%	20%	93%	84%
House Service:				
1998	20%	25%	83%	88%
1997	0%	5%	80%	100%
1996	18%	5%	88%	85%
1995	0%	0%	100%	96%

Rep. Shelley Berkley (D)

CAPITOL OFFICE
225-5965
www.berkley.house.gov
405 Cannon 20515-2801; fax 225-3119

COMMITTEES
Veterans' Affairs
Ways & Means

RESIDENCE
Las Vegas

BORN
Jan. 20, 1951, Manhattan, N.Y.

RELIGION
Jewish

FAMILY
Husband, Larry Lehrner; two children, two stepchildren

EDUCATION
U. of Nevada, Las Vegas, B.A. 1972 (political science); U. of San Diego, J.D. 1976

CAREER
Lawyer

POLITICAL HIGHLIGHTS
Nev. Assembly, 1983-85; University and Community College System of Nevada Board of Regents, 1990-98

ELECTION RESULTS

2006 GENERAL		
Shelley Berkley (D)	85,025	64.8%
Kenneth Wegner (R)	40,917	31.2%
Jim Duensing (LIBERT)	2,843	2.2%
Darnell Roberts (IA)	2,339	1.8%
2006 PRIMARY		
Shelley Berkley (D)	29,655	90.1%
Asimo Sondra Lawlor (D)	3,267	9.9%
2004 GENERAL		
Shelley Berkley (D)	133,569	66.0%
Russ Mickelson (R)	63,005	31.1%
Jim Duensing (LIBERT)	5,862	2.9%

PREVIOUS WINNING PERCENTAGES
2002 (54%); 2000 (52%); 1998 (49%)

Elected 1998; 5th term

Berkley may be in her fifth term in Congress, but she's still more Las Vegas neon than Washington button-down. In 2005, she told her local newspaper she was still "black and blue" after cosmetic surgery. Shortly after her election in 1998, she appeared at a news conference in high-heeled tennis shoes. And in 1999, she was married at Bally's casino with 19 bridesmaids to attend her.

Her lack of inhibition has helped her fight for plum committee assignments and defend Nevada's interests on Capitol Hill.

After the Democrats won control of Congress in the 2006 elections, Berkley snagged the seat on the powerful Ways and Means Committee that she had pursued for years. From that spot, she'll be able to influence legislation affecting industries vital to Nevada's economy — gaming and tourism.

Many thought Berkley would not get the Ways and Means post because in late 2006 she had backed Steny H. Hoyer of Maryland in the contest for majority leader over Speaker Nancy Pelosi's choice for the post, John P. Murtha of Pennsylvania. Berkley also had supported Hoyer when he ran against Pelosi in 2001 for Democratic whip. "I have been a Steny person since I came here, so I suspect I will continue that," Berkley told the Las Vegas Review-Journal. But Berkley also fretted that her loyalty to Hoyer, who won the leadership post, would jeopardize her chance for a seat on the tax-writing panel. "This is hardball up here, I can tell you," Berkley said. She expressed hope that an influential fellow Nevadan, Senate Majority Leader Harry Reid, would put in a good word for her with Pelosi.

Pelosi apparently held no grudge. Berkley got the assignment to Ways and Means.

Berkley is the lone Democrat in the three-member Nevada House delegation. Although Republican Jon Porter also serves on Ways and Means, Berkley may be in a better position to benefit the state now that Democrats are in control. She vows to work with both Porter and Republican Dean Heller, the other member of the delegation, to help Nevada.

Helping Nevada means helping the gaming industry. And Nevada companies want to get into Internet gambling, which is now controlled by offshore companies. Congress in 2006 barred online gambling businesses from accepting credit cards or electronic transfers for the purpose of betting, except for wagers made on horse races. In an attempt to stave off the Republican bill, the Nevada delegation pushed for an 18-month study of online gaming. They failed, but Berkley intends to make another run at the issue in the 110th Congress (2007-08).

Nevada's biggest political battle is against the proposed nuclear waste repository at Yucca Mountain, about 100 miles northwest of Las Vegas. In March 2007, the Department of Energy unveiled a plan to speed construction of the Yucca Mountain dump, and the Bush administration included $500 million in its fiscal 2008 budget to proceed with the plan. The Nevada Senate delegation — Reid and Republican John Ensign — countered with legislation mandating that nuclear waste stay where it is produced. Berkley will push that bill on the House side and will work with Porter and Heller to clip Yucca Mountain funding.

In the 109th Congress (2005-06), Berkley was the top-ranking Democrat on the Veterans' Affairs panel's Disability Assistance and Memorial Affairs Subcommittee, with jurisdiction ranging from veterans' disability benefits to burial benefits, life insurance and veterans' cemeteries. On the International Relations Committee (now Foreign Affairs), Berkley served on the Middle East and Central Asia Subcommittee, allowing her to pursue her interest in Israel. In the summer of 2006, Berkley supported a House resolution backing Israel in its war with the militant group Hezbollah in Lebanon.

She gave up her seat on Foreign Affairs in the 110th Congress to serve on Ways and Means. She retains her assignment on the Veterans' Affairs Committee, but does not chair a subcommittee.

Berkley's parents came to the United States from Eastern Europe and moved to Las Vegas when she was 6 years old. She attended the University of Nevada at Las Vegas, where she served as student body president before graduating with a political science degree. After earning a law degree from the University of San Diego, Berkley returned to Las Vegas to start a career. She served two years in the state Assembly in the mid-1980s, but became better known as a state university regent. She served as vice president of government and legal affairs for the Sands Hotel, and as board chairwoman of the Nevada Hotel and Motel Association.

Although Berkley was known as a Democratic Party activist in her home state, she bills herself as a moderate who can work with Republicans. A member of the centrist New Democrat Coalition, a group that tends to be receptive to business concerns, Berkley describes herself as an opponent of gun control, a position echoed by many Western politicians. But she voted against a House bill in 2004 that would have lifted a ban on the private possession of handguns in the District of Columbia. And in 2003, she opposed a measure that would have nullified lawsuits by dozens of cities against gun manufacturers for crimes related to firearms. She has said in the past that votes in favor of gun safety do not conflict with her belief that the federal government must not prevent citizens from owning guns.

Berkley first won election to the House in 1998 when Ensign gave up his 1st District seat to run for the Senate — unsuccessfully, that year, when he was narrowly defeated by Reid. (Ensign won election to the other Senate seat in 2000.) Berkley squeaked by Republican Don Chairez, a former county judge, by just 3 percentage points after battling ethics questions involving memos she had written several years before advising a legal client to make campaign contributions to judges as a way to curry favor.

In 2000, fending off the same ethics questions, Berkley defeated then state Sen. Jon Porter (now her 3rd District colleague) by 8 percentage points. Redistricting following the 2000 census left her with a more urban, Democratic constituency, and Berkley won in 2002 and 2004 by ever-wider margins. In 2006, she won with 65 percent of the vote.

KEY VOTES

2006

Yes Stop broadband companies from favoring select Internet traffic
No Affirm U.S. commitment to war in Iraq and reject setting a withdrawal date for troops
No Repeal requirement for bilingual ballots at the polls
Yes Permit U.S. sale of civilian nuclear technology to India
Yes Build a 700-mile fence on the U.S.-Mexico border to curb illegal crossings
No Permit warrantless wiretaps of suspected terrorists

2005

No Intervene in the life-support case of Terri Schiavo
Yes Lift President Bush's restrictions on stem cell research funding
Yes Prohibit FBI access to library and bookstore records
No Approve free-trade pact with five Central American countries
No Pass energy policy overhaul favored by President Bush emphasizing domestic oil and gas production
No End mandatory preservation of habitat of endangered animal and plant species
Yes Ban torture of prisoners in U.S. custody

CQ VOTE STUDIES

	PARTY UNITY		PRESIDENTIAL SUPPORT	
	Support	Oppose	Support	Oppose
2006	90%	10%	32%	68%
2005	92%	8%	28%	72%
2004	93%	7%	41%	59%
2003	93%	7%	27%	73%
2002	87%	13%	42%	58%

INTEREST GROUPS

	AFL-CIO	ADA	CCUS	ACU
2006	100%	80%	54%	13%
2005	93%	90%	54%	13%
2004	93%	95%	60%	8%
2003	100%	85%	36%	27%
2002	89%	85%	50%	16%

NEVADA 1

Las Vegas

Neon lights and the chance of easy money continue to reel pleasure seekers into the 1st, which includes Las Vegas and its immediate environs. Gambling and tourism drive economic and population growth in this increasingly urbanized district.

The area has enjoyed generally healthy economic expansion over the past two decades, and large and small gaming companies have continued to thrive and fuel the region's explosive growth. The local economic downturn after the Sept. 11, 2001, terrorist attacks cost many workers their jobs as visitors stayed away; while it took years for the number of visitors to match 2000 levels, more than 39 million people visited Las Vegas in 2006, with an economic impact of $39.4 billion.

Downtown Las Vegas is no longer the focal point of the gambling industry, as large, newer luxury resorts on Las Vegas Boulevard lure visitors to the newest part of the "Strip," located south of downtown and beyond the Las Vegas city limits. Traffic congestion, a byproduct of the growing population and healthy economy, has become a major problem.

Discussion in California about opening more casinos on American Indian reservations worries the industry here, but city leaders are excited about local public-private tourism projects. More than a decade ago, a consortium of downtown-based casino owners and the city began an ongoing renewal project designed to bring visitors back to historic downtown Las Vegas. The Fremont Street Experience has succeeded in attracting some visitors, but it has not been able to challenge the Strip's dominance.

Although some pockets of Republicans live in the district, the urban 1st has a strong Democratic base in unionized service workers and does not include most of the fast-growing GOP-leaning suburbs. The 1st was the only Nevada district that John Kerry won in the 2004 presidential race.

MAJOR INDUSTRY

Tourism, gambling, conventions

CITIES

Las Vegas (pt.), 362,908; North Las Vegas, 115,488; Paradise (unincorporated) (pt.), 77,893; Sunrise Manor (unincorp.) (pt.), 68,288

NOTABLE

The Little White Wedding Chapel on Las Vegas Boulevard has a drive-through window for weddings.

Rep. Dean Heller (R)

CAPITOL OFFICE
225-6155
heller.house.gov
1023 Longworth 20515-2802; fax 225-5679

COMMITTEES
Education & Labor
Natural Resources
Small Business

RESIDENCE
Carson City

BORN
May 10, 1960, Castro Valley, Calif.

RELIGION
Mormon

FAMILY
Wife, Lynne Heller; four children

EDUCATION
U. of Southern California, B.S. 1985 (business administration)

CAREER
Commercial banker; chief deputy state treasurer; stockbroker

POLITICAL HIGHLIGHTS
Nev. Assembly, 1990-94; Nev. secretary of state, 1995-2007

ELECTION RESULTS

2006 GENERAL		
Dean Heller (R)	117,168	50.3%
Jill Derby (D)	104,593	44.9%
Daniel Rosen (I)	5,524	2.4%
James C. Kroshus (IA)	5,439	2.3%
2006 PRIMARY		
Dean Heller (R)	24,770	35.9%
Sharron E. Angle (R)	24,349	35.3%
Dawn Gibbons (R)	17,317	25.1%
Thomas Glenn (R)	1,835	2.7%
Richard Gilster (R)	721	1.0%

Elected 2006; 1st term

Heller, a former stockbroker, aligns himself with Republicans who focus on fiscal conservatism and limited government rather than those who are most concerned with social issues such as abortion.

During his second week in office, he was the only one of the 13 GOP freshmen elected in 2006 to vote for a bill expanding federal funding for medical research on stem cells taken from surplus embryos at in vitro fertilization clinics. He also voted with the Democrats on their 2007 bill to implement more recommendations of the independent Sept. 11 commission.

A former state legislator and Nevada secretary of state, he wants to build on his work on Nevada's public employees' retirement system — which he says was going bankrupt until he wrote a ballot initiative that shielded it from legislators. That may have to wait, however. His seat on the Natural Resources Committee gives him a stronger voice on public lands, water rights and mining issues that are critical to his Western state.

He also serves on the Small Business panel, where he was named ranking Republican of the Finance and Tax Subcommittee. As secretary of state in Nevada, he was responsible for registering thousands of businesses a year.

The urge to seek political office has been with Heller since a boyhood newspaper route took him to the Nevada Capitol building. Heller says his "supply side" economic views were shaped by a conversation he had with former Republican Rep. Jack F. Kemp of New York (1971-89) at the wedding of Kemp's nephew, with whom Heller worked as a stockbroker.

In 2006, as five-term Republican Rep. Jim Gibbons launched his successful campaign for governor, Heller hit his term limit as secretary of state. He went after the open House seat, but so did four others, including Gibbons' wife, a state legislator. Heller edged state Assemblywoman Sharron E. Angle by a scant 421 votes in the primary. A state district court rejected her attempt to have the results nullified and a new primary ordered.

Democrats put up state university regent Jill Derby, who matched him in campaign spending, but Heller prevailed by 5 percentage points in the GOP-leaning district.

NEVADA 2

Reno, Carson City and the 'Cow Counties'

The conservative-leaning 2nd takes in everything outside of Las Vegas and its suburbs — almost all of the state's vast rural areas. Reno and the capital, Carson City, anchor the 2nd in the west, and in the district's "Cow Counties," agriculture, mining and ranching dominate. Nearly 90 percent of the district's land is federally owned.

In the 1800s, the gold rush attracted fortune hunters to Reno. Fortune hunters now are more inclined to try their luck in the city's casinos or head to Lake Tahoe. Although five million tourists visited Reno in 2005, officials in the gambling industry are concerned that new Indian reservation casinos in California will lure visitors away. Yucca Mountain, the proposed national nuclear waste storage site located in Nye County, is a contentious issue among residents. The 2nd also dips into two areas of Clark County in the southern part of the state, taking in Nellis Air Force Base and much of the northern part of Clark, as well as a few suburban communities in the county's southwest.

The 2nd has sent Republicans to Congress since its creation in 1982. It votes mostly Republican in local elections and is becoming increasingly conservative. In 2004, George W. Bush garnered 57 percent of the district's presidential vote, which was his highest total in the state.

MAJOR INDUSTRY
Gambling, mining, manufacturing

MILITARY BASES
Nellis Air Force Base, 8,100 military, 4,000 civilian (2006); Naval Air Station Fallon, 1,129 military, 1,400 civilian (2007)

CITIES
Reno, 180,480; Sparks, 66,346; Carson City, 52,457; Pahrump (unincorporated), 24,631

NOTABLE
White King, a deceased polar bear on display in Elko, may be the world's largest.

Rep. Jon Porter (R)

CAPITOL OFFICE
225-3252
www.porter.house.gov
218 Cannon 20515-2803; fax 225-2185

COMMITTEES
Budget
Ways & Means

RESIDENCE
Henderson

BORN
May 16, 1955, Fort Dodge, Iowa

RELIGION
Roman Catholic

FAMILY
Divorced; two children

EDUCATION
Briar Cliff College, attended 1973-77 (theology)

CAREER
Farm insurance company branch manager and agent; electronics repairman and distributor

POLITICAL HIGHLIGHTS
City Council of Boulder City, 1983-93 (mayor, 1987-1991); Nev. Senate, 1995-2002; Republican nominee for U.S. House, 2000

ELECTION RESULTS

2006 GENERAL		
Jon Porter (R)	102,232	48.5%
Tessa Hafen (D)	98,261	46.6%
Joshua Hansen (IA)	5,329	2.5%
Joseph P. Silvestri (LIBERT)	5,157	2.4%
2006 PRIMARY		
Jon Porter (R)		unopposed
2004 GENERAL		
Jon Porter (R)	162,240	54.5%
Tom Gallagher (D)	120,365	40.4%
Joseph P. Silvestri (LIBERT)	9,260	3.1%
Richard O'Dell (X)	6,053	2.0%

PREVIOUS WINNING PERCENTAGES
2002 (56%)

Elected 2002; 3rd term

Jon Porter is a country and rock Republican who can reach across the aisle — to play keyboards with a Democratic lead singer, Collin C. Peterson of Minnesota. Together with three other GOP lawmakers they make up a band called "The Second Amendments" that plays in Iraq at Christmas and bridges partisan differences while making music together.

Porter harmonized well enough with 3rd District voters to win a third term in 2006 despite a powerful national anti-Republican wave that almost carried him out with the tide. His suburban Las Vegas district is evenly split between the parties, but Republican turnout was higher, which proved critical for Porter.

Future challengers might bear in mind that Porter is literally a long-distance runner. After taking up the sport in 2000, Porter in 2003 completed the 26-mile Marine Corps Marathon and, more recently, a number of shorter races.

Porter knows how to make strategic alliances. In the January 2006 race to replace former Majority Leader Tom DeLay, who was forced to step down after his 2005 indictment in Texas on campaign finance charges, Porter backed underdog John A. Boehner of Ohio over Whip Roy Blunt of Missouri. Porter had worked with Boehner on the Education and the Workforce Committee. Boehner prevailed, and in early 2007 Porter was rewarded with a seat on the Ways and Means Committee.

Nevada Democrat Shelley Berkley also nabbed a Ways and Means seat in the 110th Congress (2007-08), affording the state's small delegation an outsize opportunity to influence revenue legislation affecting the gaming and tourism industries that are crucial to Nevada's economy.

Porter is eager to raise the national profile of the tourism industry. He says the $90 billion-a-year industry is vital to the U.S. economy but draws too little attention from policy makers. Las Vegas alone gets 42 million visitors per year, he says. He would like to encourage even more to come by beefing up funds for baggage screening personnel and by easing visa hassles for overseas visitors, especially those from Asia, so they'll visit Las Vegas rather than the closer Macau, a former Portuguese territory in China that is giving Las Vegas a run for its money as a gamblers' paradise.

Porter, like other Nevada lawmakers, will continue to fight construction of a nuclear waste repository at Yucca Mountain, about 100 miles northwest of Las Vegas. In the 109th Congress (2005-06), when he chaired the Government Reform Federal Work Force and Agency Subcommittee, he investigated possible fraud by federal researchers working on the project.

The Department of Energy is planning to open Yucca Mountain in 2017, nearly 20 years later than the original 1998 target date. While Senate Majority Leader Harry Reid is the leader of the state effort to block the project, Porter is also working to cut the Bush administration's proposed funding for the project and to pass legislation mandating that nuclear waste be stored where it is produced. From his seat of the Budget Committee, Porter sought in early 2007 to zero-out funding for the project in the non-binding congressional budget resolution. He lost, 12-22.

Education also is an important issue to Porter, the one-time mayor of Boulder City, Nevada. He says fast-growing Nevada ran into a disturbing problem when hiring out-of-state teachers: Not all states require criminal background checks for teachers, which means a Nevada school could inadvertently hire a teacher with a criminal past. Working with child advocate John Walsh, whose son Adam was abducted and murdered in 1981, Porter introduced legislation mandating criminal background checks for teachers in states that had not required them before. The House passed the bill, which was subsequently enacted in July 2006 as part of the larger Adam Walsh Child Protection Act aimed at shielding children from sexual exploitation and violent crime.

Porter likes a road trip for a cause. As Hurricane Katrina churned through the Gulf of Mexico in 2005, he drove to the Gulf Coast with a group that included his campaign finance director, who had family in Mississippi. They hauled generators, fresh water and Gatorade down to Mississippi and then helped to clean damaged houses in the storm's wake.

He has been to Iraq three times, including Christmas season trips in 2005 and 2006, when The Second Amendments played for U.S. troops in Iraq, Afghanistan, Kuwait and elsewhere. Along with Porter and Peterson, the band includes GOP Reps. Dave Weldon of Florida, Kenny Hulshof of Missouri and Thaddeus McCotter of Michigan. Porter spent his spare time talking with the soldiers he encountered. "It may be a cliché," Porter says, "but these troops are so committed and believe in the course of action we are taking." He backs President Bush's 2007 troop escalation.

Born in Iowa, Porter attended Briar Cliff College in Sioux City but left before earning a degree. He married an elementary school teacher and settled in Henderson, Nev., where he worked as a farm insurance agent, eventually managing 40 agents. He won a seat on the Boulder City Council in 1983, serving for a decade, including a stint as mayor. In 1994, he was elected to the state Senate.

In 2000, Porter took on Berkley, then completing her freshman term in the Las Vegas-based 1st District. He lost, but drew a respectable 44 percent of the vote. In 2002, after reapportionment had given Nevada a third House seat, Porter went after the new 3rd District seat. Democrats hoped the low-key Porter would be eclipsed by their energetic candidate, Clark County Commissioner Dario Herrera. But Herrera was hurt by ethics questions, and Porter won by 19 percentage points.

In 2006, Porter faced Tessa Hafen, a 29-year-old former aide to Reid. Porter amassed more than twice as much campaign cash as Hafen, stressed his independence from the GOP party line (he split with his fellow Republicans about 13 percent of the time in the 109th Congress) and touted the benefits of his seat on the Transportation Committee. He also took a tough stand on immigration. Democratic turnout in Clark County was anemic, and he edged Hafen by less than 2 percentage points.

KEY VOTES

2006

No Stop broadband companies from favoring select Internet traffic

Yes Affirm U.S. commitment to war in Iraq and reject setting a withdrawal date for troops

Yes Repeal requirement for bilingual ballots at the polls

Yes Permit U.S. sale of civilian nuclear technology to India

Yes Build a 700-mile fence on the U.S.-Mexico border to curb illegal crossings

Yes Permit warrantless wiretaps of suspected terrorists

2005

Yes Intervene in the life-support case of Terri Schiavo

Yes Lift President Bush's restrictions on stem cell research funding

Yes Prohibit FBI access to library and bookstore records

Yes Approve free-trade pact with five Central American countries

Yes Pass energy policy overhaul favored by President Bush emphasizing domestic oil and gas production

Yes End mandatory preservation of habitat of endangered animal and plant species

Yes Ban torture of prisoners in U.S. custody

CQ VOTE STUDIES

	PARTY UNITY		PRESIDENTIAL SUPPORT	
	Support	Oppose	Support	Oppose
2006	84%	16%	93%	7%
2005	90%	10%	80%	20%
2004	83%	17%	82%	18%
2003	94%	6%	98%	2%

INTEREST GROUPS

	AFL-CIO	ADA	CCUS	ACU
2006	36%	10%	100%	80%
2005	20%	5%	93%	84%
2004	27%	15%	100%	76%
2003	13%	5%	100%	88%

NEVADA 3

Las Vegas suburbs

The roughly pinwheel-shaped 3rd is located in Clark County, which has absorbed most of the explosive population growth that has made Nevada one of the nation's fastest-growing states. The district includes a chunk of Las Vegas, but is mainly composed of the city's suburbs.

Most of the district's population lives in suburbs such as Henderson, Spring Valley and Paradise. Summerlin, to the west, is a massive planned community along the western rim of Las Vegas Valley. These areas are populated with many conservative-leaning new arrivals to the state, as well as one of the fastest-growing elderly populations in the country. This rapid population growth and suburban expansion has brought an influx of white-collar workers and created many new construction jobs in the 3rd. Another byproduct of growth has been increasing demand on the Colorado River for fresh water, a valuable commodity in these hot, desert communities, and water-use restrictions have become common.

Although most of the area's casinos are in the urban 1st District, the expansion of the Las Vegas "Strip" southward has brought some of the large, newer resorts into the 3rd. The district is home to many who work in the gambling industry and are part of the area's strong union structure. The busy McCarran International Airport also is located here.

To the east, along the Arizona border near Utah, the population is largely Mormon, an influence that has spread into suburbs such as Henderson. In the south, the 3rd contains lightly populated mining communities around Laughlin. Small ranching communities and the scenic Red Rock Canyon National Conservation Area are in the district's western reaches.

The 3rd is politically competitive. George W. Bush edged John Kerry here with only 50 percent of the 2004 presidential vote. As suburban areas expand, Republicans may have more of an advantage in the future.

MAJOR INDUSTRY

Gambling, mining, ranching

CITIES

Henderson, 175,381; Spring Valley (unincorporated), 117,390; Las Vegas (pt.), 115,526; Paradise (unincorporated) (pt.), 108,177

NOTABLE

Hoover Dam, about 30 miles southeast of Las Vegas, often is called one of the greatest engineering works in history.

NEW HAMPSHIRE

Gov. John Lynch (D)

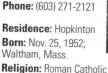

First elected: 2004
Length of term: 2 years
Term expires: 1/09
Salary: $103,000
Phone: (603) 271-2121

Residence: Hopkinton
Born: Nov. 25, 1952; Waltham, Mass.
Religion: Roman Catholic
Family: Wife, Susan Lynch; three children
Education: U. of New Hampshire, B.A. 1974 (English); Harvard U., M.B.A. 1979; Georgetown U., J.D. 1984
Career: Business consulting firm owner; furniture manufacturing company president; college admissions director; state party executive director
Political highlights: No previous office

Election results:

2006 GENERAL		
John Lynch (D)	298,761	74.0%
Jim Coburn (R)	104,288	25.8%

Senate President Sylvia B. Larsen (D)

(no lieutenant governor)
Phone: (603) 271-2111

LEGISLATURE

General Court: January-June

Senate: 24 members, 2-year terms
2007 ratios: 14 D, 10 R; 14 men, 10 women
Salary: $200/2-year term
Phone: (603) 271-2111

House: 400 members, 2-year terms
2007 ratios: 236 D, 160 R, 1 I, 3 vacancies; 255 men, 142 women
Salary: $200/2-year term
Phone: (603) 271-3661

TERM LIMITS

Governor: No
Senate: No
House: No

URBAN STATISTICS

CITY	POPULATION
Manchester	107,006
Nashua	86,605
Concord	40,687
Derry	34,021
Rochester	28,461

REGISTERED VOTERS

Unaffiliated	44%
Republican	30%
Democrat	26%

POPULATION

2006 population (est.)	1,314,895
2000 population	1,235,786
1990 population	1,109,252
Percent change (1990-2000)	+11.4%
Rank among states (2006)	41
Median age	37.1
Born in state	43.3%
Foreign born	4.4%
Violent crime rate	175/100,000
Poverty level	6.5%
Federal workers	7,933
Military	4,435

ELECTIONS

STATE ELECTION OFFICIAL
(603) 271-3242
DEMOCRATIC PARTY
(603) 225-6899
REPUBLICAN PARTY
(603) 225-9341

MISCELLANEOUS

Web: www.nh.gov
Capital: Concord

U.S. CONGRESS

Senate: 2 Republicans
House: 2 Democrats

2000 Census Statistics by District

DIST.	2004 VOTE FOR PRESIDENT BUSH	KERRY	WHITE	BLACK	ASIAN	HISP	MEDIAN INCOME	WHITE COLLAR	BLUE COLLAR	SERVICE INDUSTRY	OVER 64	UNDER 18	COLLEGE EDUCATION	RURAL	SQ. MILES
1	51%	48%	95%	1%	1%	2%	$50,135	63%	24%	13%	12%	25%	29%	33%	2,449
2	47	52	95	1	1	2	$48,762	62	25	13	12	25	29	48	6,519
STATE	49	50	95	1	1	2	$49,467	62	25	13	12	25	29	41	8,968
U.S.	50.7	48.3	69	12	4	13	$41,994	60	25	15	12	26	24	21	3,537,438

Coos
Grafton
Carroll
2
1
Belknap
Strafford
Sullivan
Merrimack
Rochester
Concord ★
Dover
Portsmouth
Manchester
Rockingham
Cheshire
Hillsborough
Nashua

Sen. Judd Gregg (R)

CAPITOL OFFICE
224-3324
gregg.senate.gov
393 Russell 20510-2904; fax 224-4952

COMMITTEES
Appropriations
Budget - ranking member
Health, Education, Labor & Pensions

RESIDENCE
Rye Beach

BORN
Feb. 14, 1947, Nashua, N.H.

RELIGION
Congregationalist

FAMILY
Wife, Kathleen Gregg; three children

EDUCATION
Columbia U., A.B. 1969; Boston U., J.D. 1972, LL.M. 1975

CAREER
Lawyer

POLITICAL HIGHLIGHTS
N.H. Governor's Executive Council, 1979-81; U.S. House, 1981-89; governor, 1989-93

ELECTION RESULTS

2004 GENERAL		
Judd Gregg (R)	434,847	66.2%
Doris "Granny D" Haddock (D)	221,549	33.7%
2004 PRIMARY		
Judd Gregg (R)	60,597	91.6%
Tom Alciere (R)	2,682	4.1%
Michael Tipa (R)	2,563	3.9%

PREVIOUS WINNING PERCENTAGES
1998 (68%); 1992 (48%); 1986 House Election (74%); 1984 House Election (76%); 1982 House Election (71%); 1980 House Election (64%)

Elected 1992; 3rd term

When the Republicans lost control of the Senate in the 110th Congress, Gregg had to give up his Budget chairmanship after just two years and before he had a chance to take a leadership role in the future of Social Security, Medicare, Medicaid and the tax code.

Now the panel's ranking member, Gregg proved in the first few months of the 110th Congress (2007-08) that he does not intend to sit on the sidelines. He played the foil to Democrats on several of the new majority's priorities, including proposals opposing President Bush's plan to send more troops to Iraq. Gregg sponsored what became the GOP's primary retort to Democratic plans — a resolution pledging to maintain funding for troops. Democrats, led by Majority Leader Harry Reid of Nevada, put together several compromise proposals, but Minority Leader Mitch McConnell of Kentucky refused to allow votes on them unless Reid allowed a vote on Gregg's proposal.

It was a vote many Democrats were keen to avoid. At one point, Reid accused Gregg of behaving like a basketball player who comes onto the court "not to score points but to rough people up." But in the end, McConnell and Gregg won: The Senate approved Gregg's resolution 82-16, and rejected one by Reid that outlined a deadline for troop withdrawal.

Gregg, usually a stalwart Bush supporter, admitted he had doubts about the troop increase but said he believed Congress needed to signal its support for those in the field. He said he originally thought his resolution "was going to be a non-event and it became a cause célèbre."

Gregg gave up the chairmanship of the Health, Education, Labor and Pensions Committee, and sought the Budget Committee post after his reelection in 2004. He saw it as a chance to tackle a federal deficit he says was far too large and to make the difficult cuts in politically sacrosanct entitlement programs that he viewed as the only way to bring long-term budget deficits under control.

But his two years as Budget chairman provided mixed results. In 2005, he pushed a budget resolution through his committee that called for $32 billion in spending cuts over five years but lost a floor fight over reductions in Medicaid and other mandatory programs, and the savings called for by the budget were pared to $17 billion when moderate Republicans deserted Gregg and the GOP leadership.

In March 2006, Gregg pushed a budget resolution through the Senate that was very different from the House version and the two chambers never negotiated a compromise. It was the third time in five years Congress did not produce an annual budget blueprint, as required by the 1974 Budget Act to guide appropriations and other fiscal policy decisions.

Another Gregg effort to enact a package of deficit controls never made it to the Senate floor. He then tried to push a stripped-down measure allowing the president to propose packages of cuts in recently enacted spending bills and receive an up-or-down vote — with no opportunity for amendments or right to filibuster in the Senate. But stiff opposition from senior GOP appropriators and Democrats stalled that bill as well.

In 2007, Gregg worked with new Budget Chairman Kent Conrad of North Dakota to devise a proposal for a bipartisan commission that would examine ways to slow the growth of entitlement programs and overhaul tax policy. But he and Conrad were unable to find a middle ground on which to base a budget resolution.

In general, Gregg is one of Congress' few consistent spending hawks. He joined a handful of other fiscal conservatives in voting against the Medicare prescription drug benefit bill in 2003, and has bucked some in the GOP by proposing strict spending caps. At one time, he had been a supporter of pay-as-you-go budget rules that require offsets for tax cuts and new entitlement programs, but Gregg abandoned that view in 2004 and says he views PAYGO "as no more than a stalking horse for tax increases."

Gregg is also a senior member of the Budget Committee's traditional rival — the Appropriations Committee. In the 110th Congress, he took the top-ranking Republican spot at the State-Foreign Operations Subcommittee after chairing the Homeland Security Subcommittee in the 109th Congress (2005-06) and the Commerce-Justice-State Subcommittee in the 108th Congress (2003-04).

A conservative on social issues, Gregg has battled legislation designed to ban job discrimination against homosexuals, saying a federal law should not overturn state rulings. He has also been a longtime ally of anti-abortion forces. As governor from 1989-93, he vetoed bills that would have bolstered abortion rights provisions in New Hampshire law. In the Senate, he has voted to ban a procedure opponents call "partial birth" abortion.

But Gregg made an about-face on gay marriage in the 109th Congress, voting against a constitutional ban on same-sex marriage after supporting it in 2004. Gregg credited his change of heart to the fact that the 2003 Massachusetts Supreme Court ruling declaring such bans unconstitutional did not lead to judicial imposition of gay marriage across the country as he feared. "The past two years have shown that federalism, not more federal laws, is a viable and preferable approach," he told the Associated Press.

In summer 2005, Gregg saw the end of a disturbing personal chapter when two men who had kidnapped his wife in 2003 were sentenced to long jail terms. The men broke into Gregg's home in McLean, Va., held Kathleen Gregg down and threatened to rape and kill her while they ransacked the house. She persuaded the men to take her to the bank, which they did at knifepoint. She managed to escape after giving them the money.

The son of a former GOP governor of New Hampshire — Hugh Gregg, who served from 1953-55 — Gregg has spent most of his life in public service. He practiced law only a short time before launching his political career in 1978, when he unseated a Republican incumbent to join the five-member state executive council. Two years later, he won the House seat of retiring Republican James C. Cleveland. His training as a tax attorney helped win him a seat on the Ways and Means Committee, but he manifested a strait-laced Yankee distaste for deal-cutting and had little role in the tax code overhaul of 1986.

Two years later, he left Congress for a pair of two-year terms as governor. In each race, he took at least 60 percent of the vote.

When Gregg sought to return to Washington in 1992, he ran into stiff opposition. New Hampshire's economic woes fired up an angry electorate, putting pro-business Democrat John Rauh in a position to give Gregg his toughest electoral fight. Bill Clinton captured the state in the presidential race and Gregg lost most of the counties in his old congressional district on the western side of New Hampshire. But Gregg carried the populous southeast corner and the GOP "North Country" and prevailed by 3 percentage points.

Gregg won an easy re-election to the Senate in 1998, even after his opponent, George Condodemetraky, accused him of draft-dodging. Gregg vehemently denied the accusations — he received a valid medical deferment, he said — and refused to debate his opponent on television. Gregg walked away with 68 percent of the vote. In 2004, Gregg defeated Democrat Doris "Granny D" Haddock with 66 percent.

KEY VOTES

2006

Yes Confirm Samuel A. Alito Jr. to the Supreme Court
No Allow consideration of a bill to establish a $140 billion trust fund to compensate victims of asbestos exposure
Yes Extend tax cuts for two years at a cost of $70 billion over five years
Yes Overhaul immigration policy with border security, enforcement and guest worker program
Yes Allow consideration of a bill to permanently repeal the estate tax
No Urge President Bush to begin troop withdrawals from Iraq in 2006
Yes Lift President Bush's restrictions on stem cell research funding
Yes Authorize military tribunals for suspected terrorists

2005

Yes Curb class action lawsuits by shifting them from state to federal courts
Yes Allow confirmation vote on Priscilla R. Owen to the U.S. Court of Appeals for the 5th Circuit
No Oppose mandatory emissions limits and block recognition of global warming as a threat
Yes Approve free-trade pact with five Central American countries
No Pass energy policy overhaul favored by President Bush emphasizing domestic oil and gas production
Yes Shield gunmakers from lawsuits when their products are used in crimes
Yes Ban torture of prisoners in U.S. custody
Yes Renew 16 provisions of the Patriot Act
Yes Allow final vote on opening the Arctic National Wildlife Refuge to oil and gas exploration

CQ VOTE STUDIES

	PARTY UNITY		PRESIDENTIAL SUPPORT	
	Support	Oppose	Support	Oppose
2006	90%	10%	93%	7%
2005	91%	9%	82%	18%
2004	94%	6%	98%	2%
2003	92%	8%	93%	7%
2002	81%	19%	96%	4%
2001	96%	4%	100%	0%
2000	98%	2%	38%	62%
1999	94%	6%	33%	67%
1998	91%	9%	43%	57%
1997	87%	13%	63%	37%

INTEREST GROUPS

	AFL-CIO	ADA	CCUS	ACU
2006	7%	15%	100%	72%
2005	7%	5%	72%	72%
2004	0%	15%	88%	88%
2003	0%	15%	78%	85%
2002	15%	10%	100%	85%
2001	13%	0%	100%	88%
2000	0%	0%	86%	100%
1999	0%	0%	76%	91%
1998	0%	5%	89%	76%
1997	0%	10%	100%	76%

Sen. John E. Sununu (R)

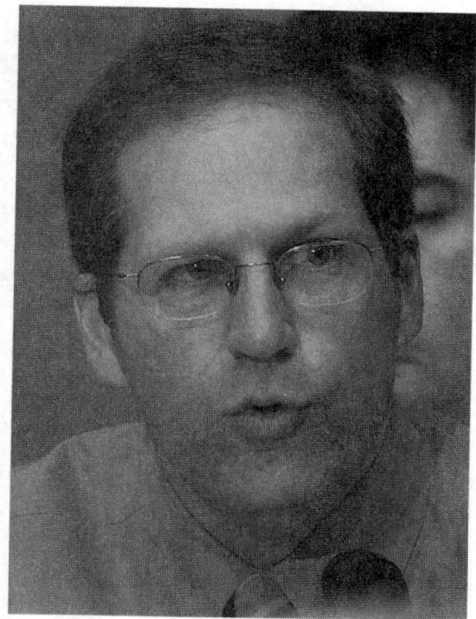

CAPITOL OFFICE
224-2841
sununu.senate.gov
111 Russell 20510-2903; fax 228-4131

COMMITTEES
Banking, Housing & Urban Affairs
Commerce, Science & Transportation
Foreign Relations
Homeland Security & Governmental Affairs
Joint Economic

RESIDENCE
Waterville Valley

BORN
Sept. 10, 1964, Boston, Mass.

RELIGION
Roman Catholic

FAMILY
Wife, Kitty Sununu; three children

EDUCATION
Massachusetts Institute of Technology, B.S. 1987 (mechanical engineering), M.S. 1987 (mechanical engineering); Harvard U., M.B.A. 1991

CAREER
Corporate financial officer; management consultant; mechanical engineer

POLITICAL HIGHLIGHTS
U.S. House, 1997-2003

ELECTION RESULTS

2002 GENERAL		
John E. Sununu (R)	227,229	50.8%
Jeanne Shaheen (D)	207,478	46.4%
Clarence G. Blevens (LIBERT)	9,835	2.2%
2002 PRIMARY		
John E. Sununu (R)	81,920	53.5%
Robert C. Smith (R)	68,608	44.8%
Kenneth Scot Stremsky (R)	2,694	1.8%

PREVIOUS WINNING PERCENTAGES
2000 House Election (52%); 1998 House Election (67%); 1996 House Election (50%)

Elected 2002; 1st term

Soft-spoken and approachable, Sununu has been mistaken during his time in Congress for an aide. He's been known to stop in Senate hallways to talk baseball with reporters — a subject he is passionate about. (He's an avid Red Sox fan.) But Sununu's manner belies his deep family connections within conservative Republican politics, and his own drive and independent-minded approach to a number of issues important to him and his state — from taxes to air quality.

The name Sununu (suh-NU-nu) is to New Hampshire what Bush is to Texas. Sununu is the son of a famous political father, John H. Sununu, the state's governor from 1983 to 1989 and then chief of staff to President George H. W. Bush for three years. Like the Bushes, the Sununus are conservative-leaning Republicans. In the Senate, Sununu votes mostly the party line, but he will buck the GOP at times, particularly on fiscal matters.

The Senate's youngest member, he went against his party leadership in 2006 on the practice of earmarking spending for home-state projects. He also called for cuts in the budget to offset the cost of rebuilding after Hurricane Katrina. And in 2003, he was one of a small group of conservative Republicans who voted against the administration's Medicare prescription drug plan, fearing its costs would escalate over time. He also favors a flat tax, saying the government uses the tax code to "engineer the way we live."

In the 109th Congress (2005-06), with a characteristic lack of flash and posturing, Sununu helped force the Bush administration to accept new restrictions addressing civil liberties concerns on a 2001 anti-terrorism law, brokering a bipartisan deal that opened the way for renewing the law. "New Hampshire has always had a certain independence and respect for civil liberties — and a libertarian lean in the people," Sununu says. "Maybe that colors my interest in these issues."

As a member of the Sununu clan, he may come to politics naturally, but he is not a natural politician. Sununu credits his background in mechanical engineering and business for giving him an analytical, common-sense approach to problem solving that he says separates him from other politicians. And unlike some of his harder-line conservative colleagues, Sununu does not regard compromise as capitulation. "There's nothing contradictory about being fiscally conservative and pragmatic," he says.

Reserved in public settings, Sununu nonchalantly strolled the halls of the House during his six years there, usually with his hands in his pockets. He did not make incendiary floor speeches and he rarely attended news conferences. Passersby took him for a 30-something congressional aide. But his measured approach made him a bridge-builder between the conflicting worlds of his two committees: Budget, where Republicans try to hold down spending, and Appropriations, where members of both parties like to spend on projects for the folks back home.

Sununu says he enjoys the greater freedom he has in the Senate to shape policy. Though low in seniority on the Commerce, Science and Transportation Committee, Sununu has drawn on his engineering and business background to carve out a specialty in telecommunications. Congress has been trying to update the law governing the rapidly changing industry and Sununu has demonstrated an ability to keep up with new technologies and the corresponding need to alter regulatory schemes.

He has focused on such issues as keeping Internet phone service free of state regulation to nurture its development, maintaining Internet privacy and improving telecommunications service to rural areas.

With a seat on the Foreign Relations Committee, Sununu and Vermont Democratic Sen. Patrick J. Leahy were the congressional members of the U.S. delegation to the 59th General Assembly of the United Nations in 2004. Sununu, the only Palestinian-American in the Senate — he is the grandson of Lebanese-Palestinian immigrants — also helped lead a team that observed the 2005 Palestinian elections.

Sununu also sits on the Banking, Housing and Urban Affairs Committee, and he has helped write legislation to tighten oversight over mortgage finance giants Fannie Mae and Freddie Mac, which have been roiled by accounting scandals.

He has been out front on an environmental issue that is particularly sensitive in New Hampshire — air quality. There's anger back home that the Northeastern states have become the "tailpipe of America," with some of the worst air pollution in the country. Air currents carry emissions from Midwestern power plants and cause acid rain to fall in the East. He worked against the White House by joining other Northeastern Republicans and most Democrats early in 2003 in an unsuccessful bid to delay a Bush administration rule that weakened air pollution regulations. Yet on other key environmental issues without a specific impact on New England, such as oil drilling in Alaska or global warming, Republican leaders have been able to count on Sununu's support of the GOP line.

Sununu was elected to the Senate at age 38, defeating incumbent Republican Sen. Robert C. Smith in the primary and incumbent Democratic Gov. Jeanne Shaheen in the general election.

While in junior high school, Sununu says he observed firsthand his mother's work as a school board member; her experiences taught him the importance and difficulties of public service. During his father's campaign for governor in 1982, when Sununu was 17, he watched statewide politicking as he drove his father to campaign appearances around the state.

In school, he had an aptitude for science and math, which he turned into engineering degrees from the Massachusetts Institute of Technology and a business degree from Harvard. He landed a job as chief financial officer for Teletrol Systems Inc., an innovative heating and cooling equipment maker in New Hampshire owned by Dean Kamen, inventor of the Segway Human Transporter, a motorized two-wheel scooter.

Sununu's opportunity to enter the family business came in 1996, when after three terms Republican Bill Zeliff gave up the 1st District House seat to run unsuccessfully for the GOP gubernatorial nomination. Sununu benefited from his name and won a seven-person GOP primary by 476 votes. In the general election, Sununu edged Joseph F. Keefe, the state Democratic chairman, by 3 percentage points. Sununu cruised to a second term in 1998 with 67 percent of the vote. But in 2000, he won by only 8 percentage points against Democratic state Rep. Martha Fuller Clark, who outspent him.

Though that modest win raised some eyebrows, GOP operatives turned to Sununu soon afterward, sensing incumbent Smith's vulnerability could hamper the party's ability to win back control of the Senate in 2002. Sununu jumped into the Senate race in the fall of 2001. Smith attacked him for waging a battle that would leave Republicans divided after the primary. Sununu countered that Republicans needed to put forward their strongest candidate to take on Shaheen, who had been a popular governor.

Sununu won the GOP nomination in September by 9 percentage points — the first person to unseat an elected senator in a primary since 1992. His high-profile victory eight weeks before the general election gave him a bounce in public opinion polls. Shaheen closed the gap in October, but a strong turnout of Republican voters helped propel Sununu to a 4-point victory.

KEY VOTES

2006

Yes Confirm Samuel A. Alito Jr. to the Supreme Court

No Allow consideration of a bill to establish a $140 billion trust fund to compensate victims of asbestos exposure

Yes Extend tax cuts for two years at a cost of $70 billion over five years

No Overhaul immigration policy with border security, enforcement and guest worker program

Yes Allow consideration of a bill to permanently repeal the estate tax

No Urge President Bush to begin troop withdrawals from Iraq in 2006

No Lift President Bush's restrictions on stem cell research funding

Yes Authorize military tribunals for suspected terrorists

2005

? Curb class action lawsuits by shifting them from state to federal courts

Yes Allow confirmation vote on Priscilla R. Owen to the U.S. Court of Appeals for the 5th Circuit

Yes Oppose mandatory emissions limits and block recognition of global warming as a threat

Yes Approve free-trade pact with five Central American countries

No Pass energy policy overhaul favored by President Bush emphasizing domestic oil and gas production

? Shield gunmakers from lawsuits when their products are used in crimes

Yes Ban torture of prisoners in U.S. custody

No Renew 16 provisions of the Patriot Act

Yes Allow final vote on opening the Arctic National Wildlife Refuge to oil and gas exploration

CQ VOTE STUDIES

	PARTY UNITY		PRESIDENTIAL SUPPORT	
	Support	Oppose	Support	Oppose
2006	91%	9%	90%	10%
2005	87%	13%	81%	19%
2004	94%	6%	96%	4%
2003	96%	4%	95%	5%
House Service:				
2002	93%	7%	92%	8%
2001	93%	7%	95%	5%
2000	95%	5%	28%	72%
1999	95%	5%	18%	82%
1998	91%	9%	25%	75%
1997	95%	5%	29%	71%

INTEREST GROUPS

	AFL-CIO	ADA	CCUS	ACU
2006	13%	20%	91%	88%
2005	8%	10%	64%	83%
2004	0%	10%	93%	100%
2003	0%	15%	83%	95%
House Service:				
2002	13%	0%	90%	92%
2001	0%	0%	100%	92%
2000	10%	10%	85%	96%
1999	0%	0%	88%	100%
1998	0%	0%	94%	92%
1997	0%	5%	100%	92%

Rep. Carol Shea-Porter (D)

CAPITOL OFFICE
225-5456
shea-porter.house.gov
1508 Longworth 20515-2901; fax 225-5822

COMMITTEES
Armed Services
Education & Labor

RESIDENCE
Rochester

BORN
Dec. 1952, Brooklyn, N.Y.

RELIGION
Roman Catholic

FAMILY
Husband, Gene Porter; two children

EDUCATION
U. of New Hampshire, B.A. 1975 (social services), M.P.A. 1979

CAREER
Community college instructor; social worker

POLITICAL HIGHLIGHTS
No previous office

ELECTION RESULTS

2006 GENERAL		
Carol Shea-Porter (D)	100,691	51.3%
Jeb Bradley (R)	95,527	48.6%
2006 PRIMARY		
Carol Shea-Porter (D)	12,497	54.0%
Jim Craig (D)	7,944	34.3%
Gary Dodds (D)	1,125	4.9%
Peter M. Sullivan (D)	1,021	4.4%
David Jarvis (D)	422	1.8%

Elected 2006; 1st term

The first woman from New Hampshire to be elected to Congress, Shea-Porter surprised many in the Granite State when she defeated two-term Republican incumbent Jeb Bradley.

A social worker and community college instructor, Shea-Porter had been an activist on a number of liberal causes, most prominently in opposition to the Iraq War. But she was known to few voters when she started her race. She also had a modest campaign treasury and relied mostly on the efforts of a network of grass-roots supporters. The day after the election, Democratic National Committee Chairman Howard Dean stumbled to recall Shea-Porter's hyphenated last name.

She said her decision to move from outside activism to a run for elective office was clinched by two visits she paid to New Orleans after it was hit hard in August 2005 by Hurricane Katrina. Shea-Porter said she saw a lack of federal response to the needs of those who were devastated by the flooding, stating that the "government had abandoned people."

Upon her return to New Hampshire, Shea-Porter started her campaign and "never looked back." She ran on a platform of increasing the minimum wage, advocating universal health care and denouncing the Bush administration's decision to go to war in Iraq and its handling of the conflict. She was given a seat on the Armed Services Committee. She also sits on the Education and Labor Committee, where she said she will speak up for the middle class and for the poor. Her background as a social worker means "I understand the gaps between the intent and delivery," she said.

Shea-Porter grew up in Durham in a house that included her six brothers and sisters, her parents, a great-uncle, and her grandmother. She said her family also often provided a temporary home to area children who were facing difficult times in their lives.

Shea-Porter easily won the September primary, trouncing state House Democratic leader Jim Craig, the choice of the party establishment. The low primary turnout left many skeptical that Shea-Porter could repeat the feat in November. Yet she beat Bradley by almost 3 percentage points.

NEW HAMPSHIRE 1

East — Manchester, Rochester

The 1st covers about one-fourth of New Hampshire's land, mainly in the southeast, yet contains most of its larger communities, including the most populous, Manchester. Many residents of southeastern towns in the 1st, especially Dover, Portsmouth, Hampton and Exeter, commute to Boston.

Manchester, which boasts technology and manufacturing companies and a profitable health care industry, grew slowly in the 1990s, but fears of recession have abated as the city's economy has diversified. Upper-income Bedford to the southwest and Hooksett to the north are growing rapidly.

The Portsmouth Naval Shipyard, across the state line in Kittery, Maine, employs many district residents and serves as an economic anchor in the eastern part of the district. Portsmouth has lost population since 1990, partly due to the closing of Pease Air Force Base in 1991.

Despite strong GOP roots and a slight Republican lean, the 1st has become increasingly competitive in recent years. Democratic-leaning Strafford County, which includes Durham (home to the University of New Hampshire) and Dover, gives Democrats healthy margins at the polls. Carroll County, in the northern end of the district, thrives primarily on tourism and farming, and the rural areas still barely favor the GOP. Republicans do well in medium- and smaller-size towns, but the GOP no longer reliably dominates population centers such as Manchester, although voters there did oust their Democratic mayor in 2005. George W. Bush narrowly won the 1st's 2004 presidential vote with 51 percent.

MAJOR INDUSTRY
Health care, computer manufacturing

CITIES
Manchester, 107,006; Rochester, 28,461; Dover, 26,884; Derry (unincorporated), 22,661

NOTABLE
Robert Frost operated a farm in Derry that is now a state historic site.

Rep. Paul W. Hodes (D)

CAPITOL OFFICE
225-5206
hodes.house.gov
506 Cannon 20515-2902; fax 225-2946

COMMITTEES
Financial Services
Oversight & Government Reform

RESIDENCE
Concord

BORN
March 21, 1951, Manhattan, N.Y.

RELIGION
Jewish

FAMILY
Wife, Peggo Horstmann Hodes; two children

EDUCATION
Dartmouth College, A.B. 1972 (French & drama); Boston College, J.D. 1978

CAREER
Lawyer; musician; state prosecutor

POLITICAL HIGHLIGHTS
Democratic nominee for U.S. House, 2004

ELECTION RESULTS

2006 GENERAL		
Paul W. Hodes (D)	108,743	52.7%
Charles Bass (R)	94,088	45.6%
Ken Blevens (LIBERT)	3,305	1.6%
2006 PRIMARY		
Paul W. Hodes (D)	18,002	98.5%
write-ins (D)	276	1.5%

Elected 2006; 1st term

Hodes is an interesting mix of the legal and the theatrical. As a New Hampshire assistant attorney general, Hodes prosecuted homicides and white-collar crimes and won the state's first criminal case against an environmental polluter. But his first love is music and theater. He and his wife, Peggo, founded a musical group called "Peggosus." They have recorded six children's albums, which have earned several Parents' Choice awards.

After graduating from Dartmouth College and before attending law school, Hodes (rhymes with "roads") returned to New York City where he was raised and spent three years working in the entertainment business as a stage actor, playwright, film producer and musical director. He also developed a radio show. But Hodes' grandmother told him he should go to law school so he would have a career to fall back on if the theater didn't work out.

Hodes said his music background makes him particularly interested in issues related to intellectual property rights. He also wants to speed up the development of alternative fuels to eliminate U.S. dependence on foreign oil. He says the 2001 No Child Left Behind education law needs either to be fixed or to be better funded. But the issue that tops his legislative agenda is the Iraq War, and he wants to hold the Bush administration accountable for what he says is its failed policy.

Hodes sits on the Financial Services and Oversight and Government Reform committees. He says he is a reflection of his constituents, whom he describes as having "a strong tradition for practical problem-solving."

Hodes first ran against the 2nd District's GOP incumbent Charles Bass in 2004, losing by 20 percentage points. Although the district had over time developed a slight Democratic lean — it narrowly favored Sen. John Kerry for president in 2004 — Bass had prevailed for six terms by projecting an image of a moderate who disagreed with Republican leaders on some key issues. But in 2006, Hodes was much better organized and better funded than in his first run. And Bass was much more burdened by a political atmosphere working against Republicans in his home state. Hodes garnered 53 percent of the vote to Bass' 46 percent.

NEW HAMPSHIRE 2

West — Nashua, Concord

The 2nd encompasses the entire western half of New Hampshire and most of the state's southern border with Massachusetts, extending from white-collar territory in the southern tier to the mountains and forests of the sparsely populated "North Country."

The district has an economy as varied as its population. Many former Massachusetts residents who fled higher tax rates live along the populous southern tier of the district in towns such as Salem, Windham and Atkinson, but still work across the state line. Nashua, the 2nd's most populous city, remains deeply involved in the computer and defense electronics industries.

The economy of the heavily forested North Country is closely tied to paper manufacturing and wood products. In the far northern reaches of the state, about 20 miles from the border with Quebec, is tiny Dixville Notch, where residents cast the nation's first votes at the stroke of midnight on Election Day. In between Nashua and the North Country lie smaller blue-collar towns, many of which depend on tourism revenue from lake visitors and skiers.

Once rock-ribbed Republican, the 2nd has become highly competitive in recent years. Democrat John Kerry won the district's 2004 presidential vote, thanks in part to the Democratic lean of Nashua and the liberalism of Concord, the state capital, and the college towns of Hanover and Keene. Other population centers are politically competitive, and the northern counties tend to lean Republican.

MAJOR INDUSTRY
Electronics, computers, manufacturing

CITIES
Nashua, 86,605; Concord, 40,687; Keene, 22,563; Claremont, 13,151

NOTABLE
The State House in Concord is the oldest U.S. legislative building in which both houses continue to sit in their original chambers.

NEW JERSEY

Gov. Jon Corzine (D)

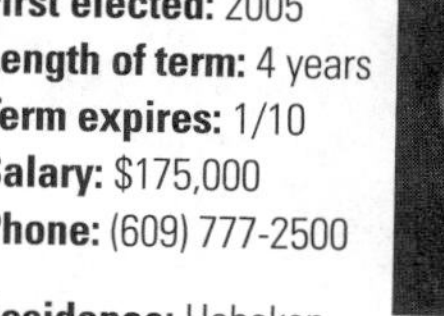

Pronounced: COR-zyne
First elected: 2005
Length of term: 4 years
Term expires: 1/10
Salary: $175,000
Phone: (609) 777-2500

Residence: Hoboken
Born: Jan. 1, 1947; Taylorville, Ill.
Religion: Christian non-denominational
Family: Divorced; three children
Education: U. of Illinois, B.A. 1969; U. of Chicago, M.B.A. 1973
Military service: Marine Corps Reserve, 1969-75
Career: Investment bank CEO, manager; bond trader
Political highlights: U.S. Senate, 2001-06

Election results:

2005 GENERAL		
Jon Corzine (D)	1,224,551	53.5%
Doug Forrester (R)	985,271	43.0%
Hector L. Castillo (ENC)	29,452	1.3%

Senate President Richard J. Codey (D)

(no lieutenant governor)
Phone: (609) 292-5213

LEGISLATURE

Legislature: Year-round with recess

Senate: 40 members, 4-year terms
2007 ratios: 22 D, 18 R; 33 men, 7 women
Salary: $49,000
Phone: (609) 292-4840

Assembly: 80 members, 2-year terms
2007 ratios: 50 D, 30 R; 64 men, 16 women
Salary: $49,000
Phone: (609) 292-4840

TERM LIMITS

Governor: 2 consecutive terms
Senate: No
Assembly: No

URBAN STATISTICS

CITY	POPULATION
Newark	273,546
Jersey City	240,055
Paterson	149,222
Elizabeth	120,568
Edison	97,687

REGISTERED VOTERS

Unaffiliated	58%
Democrat	24%
Republican	18%

POPULATION

2006 population (est.)	8,724,560
2000 population	8,414,350
1990 population	7,730,188
Percent change (1990-2000)	+8.9%
Rank among states (2006)	10
Median age	36.7
Born in state	53.4%
Foreign born	17.5%
Violent crime rate	384/100,000
Poverty level	8.5%
Federal workers	64,174
Military	27,982

ELECTIONS

STATE ELECTION OFFICIAL
(609) 292-3760
DEMOCRATIC PARTY
(609) 392-3367
REPUBLICAN PARTY
(609) 989-7300

MISCELLANEOUS

Web: www.state.nj.us
Capital: Trenton

U.S. CONGRESS

Senate: 2 Democrats
House: 7 Democrats, 6 Republicans

2000 Census Statistics by District

DIST.	2004 VOTE FOR PRESIDENT BUSH	KERRY	WHITE	BLACK	ASIAN	HISP	MEDIAN INCOME	WHITE COLLAR	BLUE COLLAR	SERVICE INDUSTRY	OVER 64	UNDER 18	COLLEGE EDUCATION	RURAL	SQ. MILES
1	39%	60%	71%	16%	3%	8%	$47,473	62%	23%	15%	12%	27%	21%	1%	335
2	50	49	72	14	2	10	$44,173	54	24	23	14	25	18	21	1,982
3	51	48	83	9	3	4	$55,282	68	19	14	17	24	27	4	926
4	56	43	81	8	2	8	$54,073	65	20	14	16	25	25	7	719
5	57	42	86	1	7	4	$72,781	73	16	11	13	26	39	17	1,099
6	43	56	62	16	8	12	$55,681	66	20	14	12	24	30	0	196
7	53	46	79	4	8	7	$74,823	74	16	10	13	25	42	10	595
8	41	58	54	13	5	26	$51,954	64	23	13	13	25	28	0	107
9	41	58	61	7	11	19	$52,437	67	20	13	15	21	30	0	93
10	18	81	21	57	4	15	$38,177	58	24	18	11	27	18	0	66
11	57	42	83	3	6	7	$79,009	76	14	10	12	25	45	7	610
12	45	54	72	11	9	5	$69,668	76	14	10	13	25	42	7	633
13	31	68	32	11	6	48	$37,129	56	28	16	11	23	21	0	57
STATE	46	53	66	13	6	13	$55,146	66	20	14	13	25	30	6	7,417
U.S.	50.7	48.3	69	12	4	13	$41,994	60	25	15	12	26	24	21	3,537,438

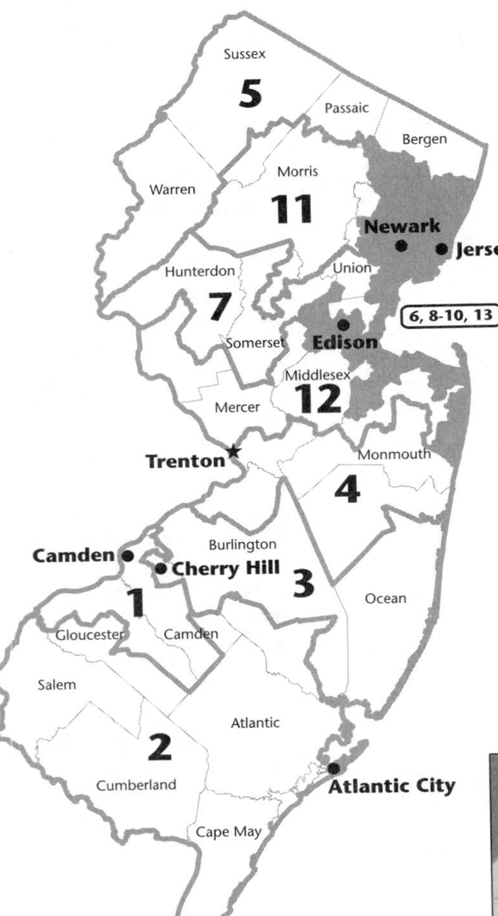
Sussex
5
Passaic
Bergen
Warren
Morris
11
Newark
Jersey City
Hunterdon
Union
7
6, 8-10, 13
Somerset
Edison
Middlesex
12
Mercer
Trenton
Monmouth
4
Camden
Burlington
Cherry Hill
3
1
Ocean
Gloucester
Camden
Salem
Atlantic
2
Cumberland
Atlantic City
Cape May

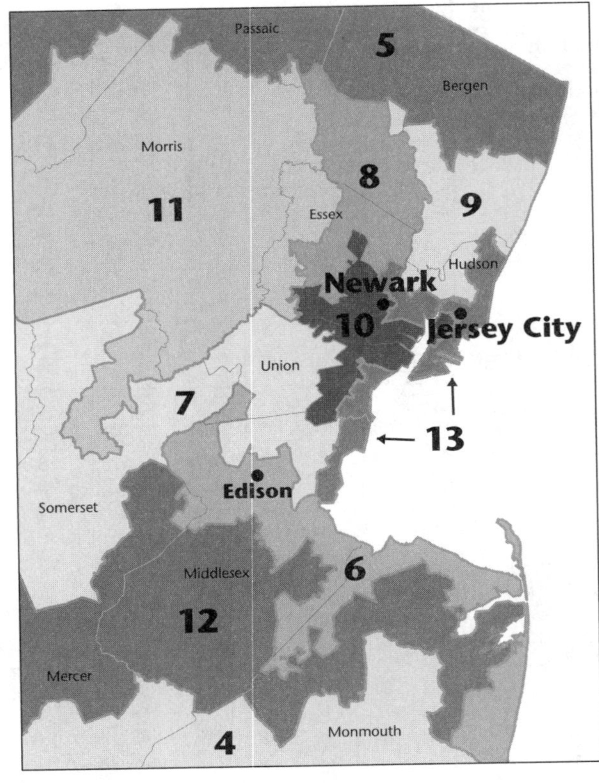
Passaic
5
Bergen
Morris
8
11
Essex
9
Hudson
Newark
10
Jersey City
Union
7
13
Edison
Somerset
Middlesex
6
12
Mercer
4
Monmouth

Sen. Frank R. Lautenberg (D)

CAPITOL OFFICE
224-3224
lautenberg.senate.gov
324 Hart 20510-3003; fax 228-4054

COMMITTEES
Appropriations
Budget
Commerce, Science & Transportation
(Surface Transportation and Merchant Marine - chairman)
Environment & Public Works
(Transportation Safety, Infrastructure Security & Water Quality - chairman)

RESIDENCE
Cliffside Park

BORN
Jan. 23, 1924, Paterson, N.J.

RELIGION
Jewish

FAMILY
Wife, Bonnie Lautenberg; four children

EDUCATION
Columbia U., B.S. 1949 (economics)

MILITARY SERVICE
Army, 1942-46

CAREER
Paycheck processing firm founder

POLITICAL HIGHLIGHTS
No previous office

ELECTION RESULTS

2002 GENERAL		
Frank R. Lautenberg (D)	1,138,193	53.9%
Doug Forrester (R)	928,439	44.0%
Ted Glick (GREEN)	24,308	1.2%
1994 GENERAL		
Frank R. Lautenberg (D)	1,033,487	50.3%
Garabed "Chuck" Haytaian (R)	966,244	47.0%

PREVIOUS WINNING PERCENTAGES
1988 (54%); 1982 (51%)

Elected 1982; 4th term

Did not serve 2001-2003

Lautenberg has the potent combination of years of experience and few political concerns, freeing him to speak his mind about the Bush administration. An unabashed liberal, he often prefers stinging sound bites to statesmanship.

In March 2006, he condemned the administration's proposed takeover of U.S. port operations by a United Arab Emirates-owned company. "We wouldn't transfer the title to the devil; we're not going to transfer it to Dubai," said Lautenberg, whose comments drew protests from an Arab-American civil rights group. He denied that he intended the remark as an insult to Arabs. In 2004, he stunned some colleagues after publicly mocking Vice President Dick Cheney as a "chicken hawk," saying the vice president — who did not serve in Vietnam — was among the Republicans who had no business questioning Democratic presidential candidate John Kerry's military record.

With Democrats in the majority, however, Lautenberg is trying to adjust to his new responsibilities instead of simply being a critic. "You hate to spend your time muscle-flexing when there's work to be done," he said in December 2006.

Lautenberg will have ample opportunities for work. He has returned to the Appropriations Committee, where he served for 15 years before his brief retirement from the Senate from 2001 to 2003. Lautenberg accepted the plum post after hinting that he would seek the top Democratic spot on the Homeland Security and Governmental Affairs Committee — a move that would have angered Connecticut independent Joseph I. Lieberman, who was in line to become its chairman. Democrats want Lieberman to remain happy as they need to keep him in their caucus to maintain their majority.

Lautenberg also continues to serve on the Environment and Public Works and Commerce, Science and Transportation committees. On Public Works, he chairs the panel on Transportation Safety, Infrastructure Security and Water Quality. He plans to delve into such issues as security at chemical plants, a leading anti-terrorism concern in New Jersey's industrial corridor, and protecting the state's rivers, lakes and wetlands.

On Commerce, Lautenberg chairs the Surface Transportation Subcommittee. He has teamed with Senate Republican Whip Trent Lott of Mississippi on a renewed effort to revive Amtrak, long one of Lautenberg's pet causes. In January 2007, the senators introduced a bill that would authorize $11.4 billion for the struggling national passenger railroad for six years as part of a strategic overhaul plan that would provide states with grants to improve rail infrastructure. The GOP-controlled House blocked a similar measure in 2005, after the Senate had endorsed it, but Lautenberg was optimistic about its chances in a Democratic Congress. "After several gloomy years, the future of America's passenger railroad is bright," he said.

At 83, Lautenberg is the Senate's third-oldest member, behind 89-year-old Democrat Robert C. Byrd of West Virginia and a few months shy of Alaska Republican Ted Stevens. But he said he's enjoying himself so much that he plans to run again in 2008. He said he's in excellent health, citing frequent trips to the gym and skiing as often as he can. Colleagues note younger staff members struggle to keep up as he briskly walks the halls of the Capitol.

Although Lautenberg is candid about his distaste for raising the vast sums of money required for a statewide New Jersey election, New York Sen. Charles E. Schumer, chairman of the Democratic Senatorial Campaign

Committee, has pledged to help. Given New Jersey's Democratic tilt and the apparent lack of a primary challenge from any of the state's House members, Lautenberg would appear to have little trouble.

Lautenberg had retired from public life at the end of 2000, bringing down the curtain on an 18-year Senate career. He was summoned back when New Jersey Democratic Sen. Robert G. Torricelli was forced to abandon his bid for re-election amid revelations of improper dealings with a campaign donor. It was just five weeks before the election. The party furiously courted replacement candidates but they all declined the race, and Democrats feared losing the seat to wealthy Republican businessman Doug Forrester.

Age 78 at the time, Lautenberg was perhaps an older candidate than party leaders would have preferred, but he was well-known and still popular in New Jersey. The race ended in a rout, with Lautenberg winning by 10 percentage points. He later said that leaving the Senate was among the worst decisions of his life. With characteristic bluntness, he told the Newark Star-Ledger, "I missed it like hell."

Democrats were grateful for his return, but not so much that they restored the seniority he had accrued during his first stint in the Senate. Lautenberg lost the perquisites and authority over policy decisions afforded more-senior members. He was as low in rank on his committees as any other freshman, though he did land a seat on the Commerce committee.

During his first Senate tenure, Lautenberg was known for taking on two of Washington's most influential forces — the tobacco and gun lobbies. A former two-pack-a-day smoker, he was the driving force in the Senate behind the 1989 law that banned smoking on domestic airline flights. And he led the crusade to restrict smoking in most federal buildings. In 1997, he pushed through language barring anyone convicted of domestic violence from possessing a firearm. And he won a Senate vote in 1999 to require background checks on all people who buy firearms at gun shows.

He takes a more conservative stand on fiscal matters. From his then senior seat on the Budget Committee, Lautenberg gave crucial Democratic congressional backing to the 1997 budget-balancing deal that had been struck mainly between President Bill Clinton and the GOP.

Born in Paterson, Lautenberg is the son of Polish and Russian immigrants. His parents moved their family a dozen times in their constant search for work. His father, Sam, worked in silk mills, sold coal and once ran a tavern. When his father died of cancer, Lautenberg, then a teenager, worked nights and weekends to help the family stay afloat.

After high school, Lautenberg enlisted and served in the Army Signal Corps in Europe during World War II. When he returned, he enrolled in Columbia University on the GI Bill, graduating with an economics degree in 1949. With two boyhood friends from his old neighborhood, he started a payroll services company, Automatic Data Processing, and turned it into one of the world's largest computing services companies.

While the business grew, Lautenberg dabbled in politics as a Democratic activist and fundraiser. His $90,000 contribution to George McGovern's 1972 campaign earned him a place on President Richard Nixon's enemies list.

In 1982, he decided to run for the open New Jersey Senate seat after veteran Democratic incumbent Harrison A. Williams Jr. was convicted in the Abscam corruption probe. Spending $4 million of his own money, an unusually large sum in that era, Lautenberg took 51 percent of the vote to defeat Republican Rep. Millicent Fenwick.

In 1988, he won with 54 percent against an aggressive challenge from Republican Pete Dawkins, once the Army's youngest brigadier general. Lautenberg survived the 1994 GOP tide with a 3 percentage point victory over conservative state Assembly Speaker Garabed "Chuck" Haytaian.

KEY VOTES

2006

- No Confirm Samuel A. Alito Jr. to the Supreme Court
- No Allow consideration of a bill to establish a $140 billion trust fund to compensate victims of asbestos exposure
- No Extend tax cuts for two years at a cost of $70 billion over five years
- Yes Overhaul immigration policy with border security, enforcement and guest worker program
- No Allow consideration of a bill to permanently repeal the estate tax
- Yes Urge President Bush to begin troop withdrawals from Iraq in 2006
- Yes Lift President Bush's restrictions on stem cell research funding
- Yes Authorize military tribunals for suspected terrorists

2005

- No Curb class action lawsuits by shifting them from state to federal courts
- No Allow confirmation vote on Priscilla R. Owen to the U.S. Court of Appeals for the 5th Circuit
- No Oppose mandatory emissions limits and block recognition of global warming as a threat
- No Approve free-trade pact with five Central American countries
- No Pass energy policy overhaul favored by President Bush emphasizing domestic oil and gas production
- No Shield gunmakers from lawsuits when their products are used in crimes
- Yes Ban torture of prisoners in U.S. custody
- No Renew 16 provisions of the Patriot Act
- No Allow final vote on opening the Arctic National Wildlife Refuge to oil and gas exploration

CQ VOTE STUDIES

	PARTY UNITY		PRESIDENTIAL SUPPORT	
	Support	Oppose	Support	Oppose
2006	97%	3%	46%	54%
2005	98%	2%	27%	73%
2004	96%	4%	57%	43%
2003	97%	3%	44%	56%
2000	98%	2%	98%	2%
1999	96%	4%	93%	7%
1998	97%	3%	90%	10%
1997	94%	6%	87%	13%
1996	93%	7%	90%	10%
1995	94%	6%	87%	13%

INTEREST GROUPS

	AFL-CIO	ADA	CCUS	ACU
2006	93%	100%	42%	0%
2005	93%	100%	29%	0%
2004	100%	100%	38%	0%
2003	100%	95%	26%	15%
2000	75%	90%	46%	4%
1999	78%	100%	44%	0%
1998	88%	95%	50%	4%
1997	71%	95%	60%	0%
1996	100%	95%	15%	0%
1995	100%	100%	16%	0%

Sen. Robert Menendez (D)

CAPITOL OFFICE
224-4744
menendez.senate.gov
317 Hart 20510-3004; fax 228-2197

COMMITTEES
Banking, Housing & Urban Affairs
Budget
Energy & Natural Resources
Foreign Relations
(International Development - chairman)

RESIDENCE
Hoboken

BORN
Jan. 1, 1954, Manhattan, N.Y.

RELIGION
Roman Catholic

FAMILY
Divorced; two children

EDUCATION
Saint Peter's College, B.A. 1976 (political science & urban studies); Rutgers U., J.D. 1979

CAREER
Lawyer

POLITICAL HIGHLIGHTS
Union City Board of Education, 1974-82; mayor of Union City, 1986-92; N.J. Assembly, 1987-91; N.J. Senate, 1991-93; U.S. House, 1993-2006

ELECTION RESULTS

2006 GENERAL		
Robert Menendez (D)	1,200,843	53.4%
Thomas H. Kean Jr. (R)	997,775	44.3%
2006 PRIMARY		
Robert Menendez (D)	159,604	84.0%
James D. Kelly Jr. (D)	30,340	16.0%

PREVIOUS WINNING PERCENTAGES
2004 House Election (76%); 2002 House Election (78%); 2000 House Election (79%); 1998 House Election (80%); 1996 House Election (79%); 1994 House Election (71%); 1992 House Election (64%)

Elected 2006; 1st full term

Appointed January 2006

After winning an appointment to the Senate in early 2006 and cementing his position in a narrow November election, Menendez is fulfilling a childhood dream and settling into a job he has wanted for years. In his battles for the seat, he brought to bear a formidable set of skills honed in the rough-and-tumble world of New Jersey politics and the internal machinations of the U.S. House, where he served as the No. 3 Democratic leader.

Menendez was by no means the only applicant for the Senate appointment when Democrat Jon Corzine won election as New Jersey governor in November 2005. The competition to fill out the remaining year of Corzine's Senate term began almost the moment Corzine entered the governor's race. All but one of New Jersey's seven House Democrats were considered contenders, and two of them — Frank Pallone Jr. and Robert E. Andrews — competed vigorously with Menendez for Corzine's favor. But no one could outmaneuver or outwork Menendez. Despite some concerns about ethics issues, Corzine picked him for the seat.

One of only two Cuban-American Democrats in Congress (there are four Republicans of Cuban heritage on Capitol Hill), Menendez served as House Democratic Caucus chairman from late 2002 until his move up to the Senate early in 2006. He was the first Hispanic of either party elected to a top leadership post in Congress, and is one of three now serving in the Senate.

Like the GOP Cuban-Americans, Menendez is a hard-liner on U.S. relations with the Castro regime. But on most issues, he's a liberal Democrat, fighting for labor's causes, a balanced immigration policy, health coverage for the uninsured and an end to U.S. involvement in the Iraq War. He voted against the 2002 resolution authorizing President Bush to use force in Iraq, and credited his consistent opposition to the war as the biggest contributor to his Senate election. In 2007, he voted for a war supplemental funding bill that sets a goal of March 31, 2008, for most U.S. troops to be out of Iraq.

He also aggressively pursues more-parochial goals, such as increased funds for pollution cleanup, protection of his state's ocean beaches, renewal of federal terrorism risk insurance and tighter chemical plant security — New Jersey has more than 110 chemical facilities.

His tenacity pays dividends. With the other three Senate Democrats from New Jersey and New York, Menendez in 2006 dug in against a Republican-drafted bill to renew the popular 1990 Ryan White CARE Act, which governs about $2 billion in federally subsidized AIDS drugs and other services. Republicans sought to change the funding distribution, shifting millions from New York and New Jersey to smaller states. The four Democrats stood fast, forcing a compromise that provided a cushion for their states.

In a July 2006 protest against Bush administration plans to ease standards for reporting the release of toxic pollutants, Menendez and fellow New Jersey Democrat Frank R. Lautenberg blocked Senate action on Bush's nominee to head the Environmental Protection Agency office in charge of monitoring toxic releases. At the end of November, EPA Administrator Stephen L. Johnson said the agency was scrapping its plans to relax the rules. The senators then lifted their "hold" on the stalled nomination.

Getting the Democratic Caucus chairmanship was no easy trick in the 108th Congress (2003-04). Menendez beat veteran Rosa DeLauro of Connecticut by a single vote, when a confluence of circumstances helped him in the final stretch. Menendez and DeLauro agreed to permit Colorado Democrat Mike Feeley to vote, though his election results were in doubt.

(After a lengthy recount, he lost to Republican Bob Beauprez.) Feeley backed Menendez while one of DeLauro's supporters, Darlene Hooley of Oregon, missed the vote because of knee surgery.

In the House, Menendez served as the top-ranking Democrat on the International Relations Western Hemisphere Subcommittee, where he was an important voice in shaping Latin American policy. During the 110th Congress (2007-08), he continues to exert influence over that policy, having won an assignment to the Senate Foreign Relations Committee and the chairmanship of the Subcommittee on International Development. He has charged Bush with neglecting the United States' neighbors to the south while spending billions on the Iraq War.

A native New Yorker and the son of Cuban immigrants, Menendez won election to the Union City school board in 1974 while still in college. He was elected mayor of Union City in 1986 and to the state legislature in 1987, serving in both offices simultaneously. He was named to fill a state Senate vacancy in early 1991 and that November won the seat.

Redistricting for the 1990s nearly doubled the Hispanic population in the 13th District. In 1992, when Democratic Rep. Frank J. Guarini decided to retire after 14 years, Menendez won the primary with 68 percent of the vote and the general election with 64 percent. His re-election vote shares thereafter approached 80 percent.

While making his mark in the House, Menendez kept an eye on the Senate, raising millions of dollars for a future campaign. He planned to run for an open seat in 2000, but dropped out when Democratic Sen. Robert G. Torricelli instead backed Corzine, who went on to win. After Torricelli was rebuked by the Senate Ethics Committee and dropped his bid for a second term in September 2002, state party leaders approached Menendez about becoming the replacement nominee, but he turned them down.

When Corzine ran for governor, Menendez liked his chances. National Hispanic groups rallied behind him, lobbying Corzine relentlessly in his behalf. All of the Senate aspirants shared Corzine's liberal philosophy, but Menendez boasted formidable fundraising skills — an asset heading into a tough 2006 general-election race against Republican state Sen. Thomas H. Kean Jr., son of a popular former governor and chairman of the independent Sept. 11 commission. Menendez by late 2005 had amassed a huge campaign treasury to prepare for a Senate race, far outpacing his rivals.

"Is he aggressive? Yeah," Corzine told The Bergen Record with a laugh, after deciding Menendez was best suited to hold the seat for Democrats. "But I believe in competency and people who get things done, and Bob is one of those people."

Menendez is a longtime political kingmaker in Hudson County, a Democratic bastion with a history of corruption. As the election campaign heated up, Kean repeatedly called him a "Hudson County political boss" and reminded voters of past reports, including allegations that Menendez had steered lobbying contracts to a woman with whom he had a personal relationship. Menendez denied the accusation, but Kean had plenty of others. He charged that Menendez was still engaged in questionable dealings, and federal investigators subpoenaed records regarding a Union City rental property deal Menendez had with a nonprofit organization that receives federal funds. Critics said he unethically steered contracts to the group while they paid him rent. Menendez denied wrongdoing, and struck back hard, accusing Kean of dirty campaign tactics and ethical lapses of his own.

The campaign was noisy, bitter and expensive. Republicans saw it as their best chance for a take-away in the November elections, and the national party poured money into the race in October. But Menendez comfortably outgunned Kean in fundraising, and he prevailed by 9 percentage points.

KEY VOTES

2006

No Confirm Samuel A. Alito Jr. to the Supreme Court
No Allow consideration of a bill to establish a $140 billion trust fund to compensate victims of asbestos exposure
No Extend tax cuts for two years at a cost of $70 billion over five years
Yes Overhaul immigration policy with border security, enforcement and guest worker program
No Allow consideration of a bill to permanently repeal the estate tax
Yes Urge President Bush to begin troop withdrawals from Iraq in 2006
Yes Lift President Bush's restrictions on stem cell research funding
Yes Authorize military tribunals for suspected terrorists

House Service:
2005

? Intervene in the life-support case of Terri Schiavo
Yes Lift President Bush's restrictions on stem cell research funding
Yes Prohibit FBI access to library and bookstore records
No Approve free-trade pact with five Central American countries
No Pass energy policy overhaul favored by President Bush emphasizing domestic oil and gas production
No End mandatory preservation of habitat of endangered animal and plant species
Yes Ban torture of prisoners in U.S. custody

CQ VOTE STUDIES

	PARTY UNITY		PRESIDENTIAL SUPPORT	
	Support	Oppose	Support	Oppose
2006	95%	5%	50%	50%
House Service:				
2005	93%	7%	24%	76%
2004	93%	8%	34%	66%
2003	93%	7%	24%	76%
2002	87%	13%	28%	72%
2001	89%	11%	30%	70%
2000	91%	9%	78%	22%
1999	91%	9%	81%	19%
1998	90%	10%	78%	22%
1997	90%	10%	76%	24%

INTEREST GROUPS

	AFL-CIO	ADA	CCUS	ACU
2006	93%	90%	55%	4%
House Service:				
2005	93%	100%	40%	4%
2004	93%	85%	35%	8%
2003	93%	90%	37%	20%
2002	89%	95%	42%	8%
2001	100%	95%	35%	16%
2000	100%	95%	38%	8%
1999	100%	100%	24%	4%
1998	100%	95%	33%	12%
1997	100%	90%	40%	13%

Rep. Robert E. Andrews (D)

CAPITOL OFFICE
225-6501
www.house.gov/andrews
2439 Rayburn 20515-3001; fax 225-6583

COMMITTEES
Armed Services
Budget
Education & Labor
(Health, Employment, Labor & Pensions - chairman)

RESIDENCE
Haddon Heights

BORN
Aug. 4, 1957, Camden, N.J.

RELIGION
Episcopalian

FAMILY
Wife, Camille Spinello Andrews; two children

EDUCATION
Bucknell U., B.A. 1979 (political science); Cornell U., J.D. 1982

CAREER
Lawyer; professor

POLITICAL HIGHLIGHTS
Camden County Board of Freeholders, 1987-90 (director, 1988-90); sought Democratic nomination for governor, 1997

ELECTION RESULTS

2006 GENERAL		
Robert E. Andrews (D)		unopposed
2006 PRIMARY		
Robert E. Andrews (D)		unopposed
2004 GENERAL		
Robert E. Andrews (D)	201,163	75.0%
S. Daniel Hutchison (R)	66,109	24.7%

PREVIOUS WINNING PERCENTAGES
2002 (93%); 2000 (76%); 1998 (73%); 1996 (76%); 1994 (72%); 1992 (67%); 1990 (54%); 1990 Special Election (55%)

Elected 1990; 9th full term

Andrews has his feet in the House but his eyes on the Senate. Like other hopefuls passed over in 2005, he was disappointed when newly elected Democratic Gov. Jon Corzine chose another House Democrat, Robert Menendez, for the Senate seat that Corzine gave up when he was elected governor. But Andrews came away with Corzine's endorsement for a 2008 race if senior senator Frank R. Lautenberg chooses to retire then.

That does not guarantee him a free ride to the Democratic nomination. Others in the House delegation intend to compete for the next available Senate seat, and Andrews is not particularly well-known statewide. He comes from the southern part of New Jersey, which has not been a good springboard for statewide office for Democrats. Also, Andrews has already lost one statewide bid. He was narrowly defeated for the gubernatorial nomination in 1997 by Democrat James E. McGreevey, who later was forced to resign following a personal scandal.

After wavering for months, Andrews bypassed a second gubernatorial bid in 2005, instead endorsing Corzine. But Rep. Frank Pallone Jr. had lined up behind Corzine weeks earlier, and like Andrews, Pallone is interested in moving to the Senate.

Andrews' willingness to defer to Corzine, and his rising standing in the party on Capitol Hill, contrast with his early reputation as a talented but power-hungry lone wolf with his own agenda. After his 1997 loss to McGreevey, he largely withdrew from party politics and had harsh words not only for some party leaders but for the political system, saying that "people who control vast sums of money have undue leverage." But since then, he has worked with Democrats on some of their core issues and become more vocal in the party's caucus meetings, where he is credited with insightful arguments that have helped fine-tune party positions.

With the Democrats regaining the majority in the 110th Congress (2007-08), Andrews took over the gavel of the Education and Labor Committee's Health, Employment, Labor and Pensions Subcommittee.

During the 109th Congress (2005-06), he was deeply involved in writing legislation to overhaul federal regulation of the private pension system. Andrews served on the House-Senate conference committee charged with drafting the final bill. He fought to protect worker benefits while also giving corporations relief from excessive paperwork. He also worked to ensure that older workers were not harmed when their employers switched from a traditional defined-benefit pension plan to a "cash-balance" plan.

In the end, however, GOP congressional leaders abandoned the conference process and brought another pension bill up for a vote. Andrews voted against that measure, objecting to the tactic and to the final bill's treatment of Continental Airlines, which is a major employer in New Jersey.

Earlier in his career, Andrews also was a member of the conference committee that in 2001 wrote the final version of the sweeping No Child Left Behind public education overhaul.

He has the minor distinction of introducing more bills each Congress than any other member, on topics ranging from veterans' benefits to the incineration of solid wastes. Andrews says it's more than a publicity gimmick; he likes to have bills ready so that when companionable legislation with a strong likelihood of passing comes along, he's ready. "Most major bills that get enacted are the omnibus type," Andrews said. "We go into our files and see if [our] bills can become provisions in bigger legislation."

He was an early advocate of the creation of a House committee to oversee the Department of Homeland Security, and when it was formed in 2003 Andrews took a leave of absence from the Armed Services Committee to serve on it. He gave up the seat in 2005 to return to Armed Services. He is somewhat hawkish on foreign policy, and supported the U.S. invasion of Iraq.

But in early 2007, Andrews came out against President Bush's plan to send thousands of additional combat troops to Iraq and also voted for a measure that would require to United States to begin pulling its troops out by March 2008. He was named to serve on the Armed Services Oversight Subcommittee, re-established by the Democrats at the start of the 110th Congress.

Andrews is not a schmoozer, but he is pleasant and approachable and has a dry sense of humor. "I guess they want to build a mud castle," he once said of a Delaware River dredging project that would have deposited most of the sludge in his district.

At night, he usually takes the train home to Haddon Heights, south of Camden, to be with his wife and two school-age daughters, whom he credits with making him less of a workaholic.

The son and grandson of shipyard workers, Andrews generally takes the side of organized labor, opposing free-trade agreements he says could cost U.S. workers their jobs. He is a fairly conventional Northeastern Democrat, supporting environmental protection, abortion rights and gun control.

When Andrews was 14, he went to work for the Suburban Newspaper Group, a local newspaper chain, hoping to cover basketball and football. Instead, he was assigned to report on local government, for $6 an article. "The experience covering government and what went on in the local scene made me want to be a part of it," he says. The first in his family to go to college, Andrews was a teaching assistant in his senior year at Bucknell University and wrote this question to serve as the entire final exam for an introductory political science class: "Politics is everything. Explain."

After a half-dozen years practicing law, Andrews at age 29 won a seat on the Camden County governing board. He became known as a young reformer, and two years later was chosen to head the board.

He was a protégé of liberal Democratic Rep. James J. Florio. After Florio was elected governor in 1989, Andrews took his place in the House, winning a 1990 special election (and a full term the same day) despite voter anger at Florio over a big state tax increase that year. Andrews did not directly repudiate the governor but took a "no new taxes" pledge for his first term.

Andrews has easily won re-election ever since, and in 2006 the Republicans declined to field a candidate.

KEY VOTES

2006

Yes Stop broadband companies from favoring select Internet traffic

No Affirm U.S. commitment to war in Iraq and reject setting a withdrawal date for troops

No Repeal requirement for bilingual ballots at the polls

Yes Permit U.S. sale of civilian nuclear technology to India

Yes Build a 700-mile fence on the U.S.-Mexico border to curb illegal crossings

No Permit warrantless wiretaps of suspected terrorists

2005

? Intervene in the life-support case of Terri Schiavo

Yes Lift President Bush's restrictions on stem cell research funding

Yes Prohibit FBI access to library and bookstore records

No Approve free-trade pact with five Central American countries

No Pass energy policy overhaul favored by President Bush emphasizing domestic oil and gas production

No End mandatory preservation of habitat of endangered animal and plant species

Yes Ban torture of prisoners in U.S. custody

CQ VOTE STUDIES

	PARTY UNITY		PRESIDENTIAL SUPPORT	
	Support	Oppose	Support	Oppose
2006	94%	6%	35%	65%
2005	92%	8%	23%	77%
2004	94%	6%	26%	74%
2003	93%	7%	26%	74%
2002	88%	12%	41%	59%

INTEREST GROUPS

	AFL-CIO	ADA	CCUS	ACU
2006	86%	85%	40%	16%
2005	92%	95%	42%	8%
2004	93%	95%	24%	0%
2003	100%	75%	38%	16%
2002	89%	90%	32%	8%

NEW JERSEY 1

Southwest – Camden, Pennsauken

The 1st is a Democratic stronghold in southwestern New Jersey across the Delaware River from Philadelphia. Its largest concentration of residents lives in the troubled city of Camden, one of the poorest in the nation. Almost two-thirds of the district's population lives in Camden County, with most of the rest in Gloucester County and a handful on the western edge of Burlington County.

For decades, Camden has been plagued by the departure of residents and businesses, a shrinking tax base, surging unemployment and crime, particularly drug trafficking. A research firm named Camden the most dangerous city in the United States in 2005. The state government assumed control of the city's finances and in 2002 approved a $175 million plan to redevelop and revitalize the area.

There are some good signs for the city. An aquarium and a 25,000-seat outdoor amphitheater have attracted more tourists to the waterfront, which is starting to generate interest from corporations, thanks in part to tax incentives set up by the state. The city also joined its port facilities with Philadelphia's to create one of the largest on the Eastern Seaboard, and the EPA launched a redevelopment initiative to clean up industrial waste. Camden also is home to the Campbell Soup Company.

As distressed as the city is, some of its suburbs are developing, and Bridgeport, in northern Gloucester County, is home to a large industrial park, while Paulsboro, a refinery town on the Delaware River, is to be the site of a new cargo port scheduled for 2009. The district also takes in the Rutgers University-Camden campus and Glassboro's Rowan University.

Blacks and Hispanics form an overwhelming majority of the population in Camden, while many whites live in the surrounding suburbs. Overall, blacks and Hispanics combined total one-fourth of the population. The 1st has a large working-class contingent, and John Kerry took 60 percent of the vote here in the 2004 presidential election.

MAJOR INDUSTRY

Shipping, manufacturing, health care, education

CITIES

Camden, 79,904; Pennsauken (unincorporated), 35,737; Glassboro, 19,068

NOTABLE

Poet Walt Whitman lived in Camden at the time of his death.

Rep. Frank A. LoBiondo (R)

CAPITOL OFFICE
225-6572
www.house.gov/lobiondo
2427 Rayburn 20515-3002; fax 225-3318

COMMITTEES
Armed Services
Transportation & Infrastructure

RESIDENCE
Ventnor

BORN
May 12, 1946, Bridgeton, N.J.

RELIGION
Roman Catholic

FAMILY
Wife, Tina Ercole; two children

EDUCATION
Saint Joseph's U., B.S. 1968 (business administration)

CAREER
Trucking company operations manager

POLITICAL HIGHLIGHTS
Cumberland County Board of Freeholders, 1985-87; N.J. Assembly, 1988-94; Republican nominee for U.S. House, 1992

ELECTION RESULTS

2006 GENERAL		
Frank A. LoBiondo (R)	111,245	61.6%
Viola Thomas-Hughes (D)	64,279	35.6%
Robert E. Mullock (PGS)	3,071	1.7%
2006 PRIMARY		
Frank A. LoBiondo (R)		unopposed
2004 GENERAL		
Frank A. LoBiondo (R)	172,779	65.1%
Timothy J. Robb (D)	86,792	32.7%

PREVIOUS WINNING PERCENTAGES
2002 (69%); 2000 (66%); 1998 (66%); 1996 (60%); 1994 (65%)

Elected 1994; 7th term

LoBiondo has been an example of how a moderate Republican survives in a conservative-led House, and his act is not likely to change now that the Democrats are in charge.

His style is low-key; he prefers to work behind the scenes, and reporters who cover him regularly say he can come across as aloof. LoBiondo (lo-bee-ON-dough) is rarely quoted in the media, and his views come to light most clearly on his votes. Like many in the GOP Class of '94, he hews to the right on fiscal policy, gun control and abortion. But he is more than willing to buck the party leadership when it comes to labor issues. LoBiondo says he is not seeking to be a maverick, but that his votes represent the views of his district.

His personal background also plays a role. The son of a small trucking company owner, he helped run the business for years, often acting as the family's chief labor negotiator, working out union disputes with dock workers, drivers and mechanics. He carried a union card and says he still has a commercial driver's license.

GOP conservatives can typically count on LoBiondo when it comes to votes on fiscal policy and gun control. He is a strong advocate of spending restraint and has voted against a number of programs that many Republicans support, including the National Aeronautics and Space Administration's International Space Station. He has supported President Bush's tax cuts. The National Rifle Association has backed all of his House races.

In 2002, he supported the resolution authorizing the war in Iraq, and in early 2007 he voted against a House war supplemental funding bill that included a timeline for withdrawal of U.S. troops from Iraq.

But he often strays from the party line on labor issues. He joined other moderates opposing the White House in 2005 on a wage protection law known as Davis-Bacon. The administration had suspended the law in areas devastated by Hurricane Katrina, hoping to encourage cheaper, faster rebuilding. LoBiondo's group successfully petitioned the White House to reinstate the law, which requires federal construction contractors to pay workers the prevailing local wage. Then, in 2007, he voted for a wastewater treatment bill that included language to expand the scope of the wage law — language that drew a veto threat from Bush. In 2006, he led a group of GOP moderates who pressured their leaders to permit a vote on increasing the minimum wage.

As a result, LoBiondo has received substantial support from labor unions, who like his record not only on increasing the minimum wage, but also on opposing foreign trade agreements and protecting wages. He gets raves from environmentalists. He was one of only 11 House Republicans endorsed by the Sierra Club in the 2004 election and one of only eight in 2006.

His deviations from the party line are a response to district interests, he says. An economically diverse area, the district includes small farms and the beach towns of Cape May and Atlantic City, with its large hotels and casinos and its crime-ridden poorer sections. LoBiondo's legislative efforts include coastal protection, tourism, gambling and agriculture. He has worked quietly to bring in funds to his district. For the town of Wildwood, he has helped secure millions of dollars in loans and grants through the Rural Development Program for projects ranging from sewer repairs to a parking study.

When the Democrats took over Congress in 2007, LoBiondo lost his top-ranking slot on Transportation and Infrastructure's Coast Guard and Maritime Transportation Subcommittee (he remained on the panel), but picked up a seat on the Aviation Subcommittee. Among the first issues to arise was a proposed aviation treaty with the European Union known as Open Skies. LoBiondo joined the full committee's chairman, Minnesota Democrat James L. Oberstar , in demanding more clarity on the issue of foreign control over U.S. carriers.

As Coast Guard and Maritime Transportation Subcommittee chairman from 2001-06, LoBiondo unabashedly pushed for more money for the Coast Guard, including its long-term funding plan, Deepwater. In 2006, the subcommittee was jolted into the spotlight with the furor over a United Arab Emirates company, Dubai Ports World, that was to take control of operations at major U.S. ports in a business arrangement approved by the Bush administration. The deal fell apart under congressional pressure.

GOP leaders in 2003 gave LoBiondo a seat on the Armed Services Committee — where he still serves — as a reward for forgoing a 2002 Senate run, a move that would have left his district vulnerable to a Democratic takeover.

As he reaped the benefits of seniority in Congress, LoBiondo backed off the 12-year term limit pledge that he and many other 1994 GOP candidates took. "I didn't fully understand what personal relationships and seniority could mean to the district," he told The Associated Press in 2003. New Jersey Democrats criticized his decision, but voters re-elected him in 2004 by a wide margin. If he had kept his pledge, he would have left Congress in 2006.

His grandparents came to southern New Jersey from Sicily and established a vegetable farm, on which LoBiondo grew up. In the 1920s, when Atlantic City's hospitality industry was booming, his father bought a used truck to take his produce to market himself. He was soon doing the same for the neighbors, and the family farm became LoBiondo Brothers Motor Express Inc., where LoBiondo worked for 26 years.

He credits his father with kick-starting his political career. His father was mayor of rural Deerfield Township, president of the school board, an active member of the Kiwanis and founder of the local fire department. "He would say it was a tremendous opportunity for him to be able to come to this country," LoBiondo recalls. "Basically the philosophy was, 'You give back.' "

The younger LoBiondo was elected to a county office in 1984, not intending to go further. But the state assemblyman from the district told LoBiondo he had cancer and would be retiring. He encouraged LoBiondo to run for the seat. He won, and served in the statehouse for almost seven years.

In 1992, he challenged Democratic Rep. William J. Hughes and lost. Two years later, Hughes retired and LoBiondo tried again, winning with 65 percent of the vote. He has won with ease ever since.

KEY VOTES

2006

No Stop broadband companies from favoring select Internet traffic
Yes Affirm U.S. commitment to war in Iraq and reject setting a withdrawal date for troops
No Repeal requirement for bilingual ballots at the polls
Yes Permit U.S. sale of civilian nuclear technology to India
Yes Build a 700-mile fence on the U.S.-Mexico border to curb illegal crossings
Yes Permit warrantless wiretaps of suspected terrorists

2005

Yes Intervene in the life-support case of Terri Schiavo
No Lift President Bush's restrictions on stem cell research funding
No Prohibit FBI access to library and bookstore records
No Approve free-trade pact with five Central American countries
No Pass energy policy overhaul favored by President Bush emphasizing domestic oil and gas production
No End mandatory preservation of habitat of endangered animal and plant species
Yes Ban torture of prisoners in U.S. custody

CQ VOTE STUDIES

	PARTY UNITY		PRESIDENTIAL SUPPORT	
	Support	Oppose	Support	Oppose
2006	73%	27%	73%	27%
2005	81%	19%	70%	30%
2004	82%	18%	68%	32%
2003	84%	16%	76%	24%
2002	84%	16%	80%	20%

INTEREST GROUPS

	AFL-CIO	ADA	CCUS	ACU
2006	50%	25%	73%	68%
2005	47%	30%	70%	60%
2004	60%	30%	76%	60%
2003	53%	25%	70%	64%
2002	22%	15%	75%	80%

NEW JERSEY 2
South — Atlantic City, Vineland

One of the state's most politically and economically diverse districts, the 2nd stretches from the Philadelphia suburbs in Gloucester County to the beach communities of Ocean City and Cape May, taking in much of the southern tier of the state.

The western corner of the 2nd is largely rural Salem County, home to a nuclear energy plant run by PSEG. The district's center includes Cumberland and Atlantic counties, where farmers' markets and small agrarian communities grow peaches, blueberries, cranberries, tomatoes and soybeans. South Cumberland County is the 2nd's most industrial area, although the economy is shifting from glass and plastics manufacturing to service. Cumberland County houses one federal and three state prisons.

The 2nd includes one of the nation's most well-known gambling resort destinations, Atlantic City, where hotels and casinos create huge numbers of jobs, but where the poorer parts of the city are ravaged by crime and urban blight.

Tourism is the cash crop in shore communities on the eastern side of the district. Boating and commercial and sport fishing thrive on the Delaware Bay and on the Atlantic Ocean along the Cape May County coastline. The area is a leading state producer of clams, and the bay is the focus of a major oyster revitalization project. The Delaware River's busy port also contributes to the economy.

This is a Republican-leaning district, and locals generally support smaller government and oppose gun control. Democrats do fare well in statewide elections, in parts of Atlantic and Cumberland counties, and in some of the district's more industrial towns. Of New Jersey's congressional districts, the 2nd handed George W. Bush his smallest victory margin — 1 percentage point — in the 2004 presidential election.

MAJOR INDUSTRY
Gambling, tourism, agriculture, petroleum, manufacturing

CITIES
Vineland, 56,271; Atlantic City, 40,517; Millville, 26,847; Bridgeton, 22,771

NOTABLE
The main federal air marshal training facility is in Pomona at Atlantic City International Airport; The U.S. Coast Guard Training Center in Cape May is the nation's only Coast Guard recruit training center.

Rep. H. James Saxton (R)

CAPITOL OFFICE
225-4765
www.house.gov/saxton
2217 Rayburn 20515-3003; fax 225-0778

COMMITTEES
Armed Services
Natural Resources
Joint Economic - ranking member

RESIDENCE
Mount Holly

BORN
Jan. 22, 1943, Nicholson, Pa.

RELIGION
Methodist

FAMILY
Divorced; two children

EDUCATION
East Stroudsburg State College, B.A. 1965 (education); Temple U., attended 1967-68 (education)

CAREER
Real estate broker; teacher

POLITICAL HIGHLIGHTS
N.J. Assembly, 1976-82; N.J. Senate, 1982-84

ELECTION RESULTS

2006 GENERAL		
H. James Saxton (R)	122,559	58.4%
Rich Sexton (D)	86,113	41.0%
2006 PRIMARY		
H. James Saxton (R)		unopposed
2004 GENERAL		
H. James Saxton (R)	195,938	63.4%
Herb Conaway (D)	107,034	34.7%
Edward "Rob" Forchion (LMP)	4,914	1.6%

PREVIOUS WINNING PERCENTAGES
2002 (65%); 2000 (57%); 1998 (62%); 1996 (64%); 1994 (66%); 1992 (59%); 1990 (58%); 1988 (69%); 1986 (65%); 1984 (61%); 1984 Special Election (62%)

Elected 1984; 12th full term

Nearing the quarter-century mark in Congress, Saxton is an expert in three big policy areas that dovetail well with the concerns of his district — environmental protection, defense and economics. While his influence has dwindled with the Democratic takeover, it is by no means depleted.

He is a leader in efforts to protect the world's oceans and is one of the House's strongest environmentalists. In January 2007, Saxton was one of seven House Republicans calling on President Bush and GOP leaders to "face climate change head-on and develop concrete solutions." Co-chairman of the House Oceans Caucus and of the Congressional Wildlife Refuge Caucus, he was one of just eight House Republicans endorsed by the Sierra Club in 2006, winning its support for his election for the fourth time in a row.

Seniority put Saxton in line to chair what is now the Natural Resources Committee at the start of the 108th Congress (2003-04). But he had two strikes against him: He is an Easterner on a committee long led by Westerners, and he is a pro-environment moderate in a party of conservative property rights advocates. He decided against waging what likely would have been a futile fight for the chairmanship after GOP leaders tapped him to lead a newly created Armed Services Subcommittee on Terrorism, Unconventional Threats and Capabilities — something he had advocated since 1994.

Now the No. 2 Republican on the full Armed Services Committee, Saxton will have a shot at the top GOP slot in the next Congress because ranking Republican Duncan Hunter of California is retiring at the end of the 110th Congress (2007-08). It remains to be seen whether Saxton's frequent departures from the party line on domestic issues will be held against him in the very different Armed Services arena. For now, he is serving as top Republican on the Air and Land Forces Subcommittee and has moved down the list on the terrorism panel.

Saxton frequently grills the Pentagon's decision makers about their strategic choices and prods the military brass to provide better equipment to U.S. forces in Iraq and elsewhere. But he agrees with Bush that Iraq is a critical battleground in a larger war on terrorism. He opposes Democratic demands for a timetable for U.S. withdrawal. "This is a war where it will be years and perhaps decades to bring to a conclusion. And the worst thing we can do is to send messages that we are not serious about carrying out our duties in defense of this generation and . . . future generations of Americans," he told the House in February 2007.

Saxton has long urged greater awareness of the worldwide terrorism threat and pressed for preparations to counter it. He helped pass legislation in 1998 creating five National Guard Weapons of Mass Destruction Civil Support Teams — one of which gave New York an operational team that responded to the attacks on the World Trade Center. In the 107th Congress (2001-02), he served as chairman of a special oversight panel on terrorism.

As chairman of Armed Services' Military Installations Subcommittee in the 107th Congress, Saxton championed more defense spending and advocated expanded roles for the 3rd District's Fort Dix and McGuire Air Force Base. Through four rounds of base closures — 1989, 1991, 1993 and 1995 — he fought successfully to shield those facilities and nearby Lakehurst Naval station from closure. In the 2005 round, he persuaded the Pentagon to combine the three into the nation's first joint Army, Air Force, Navy base — a "mega-base" that was awarded dozens more aircraft, more than 1,500 additional personnel and millions of dollars in new construction funds. It was a huge win for Saxton and his district.

Saxton may find life on the Natural Resources panel — where he serves on the Fisheries, Wildlife and Oceans Subcommittee — more congenial with Democrats in charge. For years, he has fought his Republican colleagues on the panel who favor mining, logging, grazing, and oil and gas drilling on public lands over environmental protection.

Saxton champions coastal interests important to a district that stretches from the Philadelphia suburbs to the Jersey Shore. A friend of the late marine biologist Jacques Cousteau and his son, Jean-Michel Cousteau, Saxton in 2000 won passage of a law directing the Environmental Protection Agency to develop new standards for pollutants in coastal waters.

Saxton "adopted" a striped bass several years ago to promote research and conservation of the ocean's waters. The fish, tagged with an electronic device, can be tracked on his Web site. In 2007, the U.S. Fish and Wildlife Service honored him as "Fisheries and Habitat Conservation Legislator of the Year" for his success the year before in winning enactment of legislation promoting volunteerism at the nation's fish hatcheries.

He also is the ranking Republican on the Joint Economic Committee, a House-Senate panel that he chaired three times during the dozen years Republicans controlled the House before the 110th Congress. A fiscal conservative who advocates increased tax incentives for savings, he has reintroduced proposals to allow investors to defer taxes on some of their mutual fund capital gains distributions and to eliminate a requirement that retirees start withdrawing funds from their Individual Retirement Accounts, 401(k) plans and other retirement savings at age 70½.

A former real estate broker and elementary school teacher, Saxton served in the state legislature for eight years before making a bid for the House seat left open in 1984 by the death of another environmentally friendly Republican, Edwin B. Forsythe. Saxton had support from the strong GOP organization in Burlington County, but he faced two rivals from Ocean and Camden counties. Saxton ran ads on Philadelphia TV stations to attract voters in Camden County and drew support from his large state Senate constituency. After surviving the primary, he had little trouble winning the special election to complete Forsythe's term and the general election on the same day.

Saxton had tough re-election races in 1990, when he took 58 percent of the vote against former Cherry Hill City Council member John H. Adler, and in 2000, when longtime Cherry Hill Mayor Susan Bass Levin held him to 57 percent. But he has tightened his grip on the seat since then.

KEY VOTES

2006

- No Stop broadband companies from favoring select Internet traffic
- Yes Affirm U.S. commitment to war in Iraq and reject setting a withdrawal date for troops
- No Repeal requirement for bilingual ballots at the polls
- Yes Permit U.S. sale of civilian nuclear technology to India
- Yes Build a 700-mile fence on the U.S.-Mexico border to curb illegal crossings
- Yes Permit warrantless wiretaps of suspected terrorists

2005

- Yes Intervene in the life-support case of Terri Schiavo
- No Lift President Bush's restrictions on stem cell research funding
- No Prohibit FBI access to library and bookstore records
- Yes Approve free-trade pact with five Central American countries
- No Pass energy policy overhaul favored by President Bush emphasizing domestic oil and gas production
- No End mandatory preservation of habitat of endangered animal and plant species
- Yes Ban torture of prisoners in U.S. custody

CQ VOTE STUDIES

	PARTY UNITY		PRESIDENTIAL SUPPORT	
	Support	Oppose	Support	Oppose
2006	81%	19%	80%	20%
2005	85%	15%	80%	20%
2004	84%	16%	76%	24%
2003	88%	12%	84%	16%
2002	91%	9%	87%	13%

INTEREST GROUPS

	AFL-CIO	ADA	CCUS	ACU
2006	43%	20%	67%	68%
2005	27%	20%	81%	60%
2004	50%	35%	81%	64%
2003	38%	20%	79%	72%
2002	13%	0%	90%	92%

NEW JERSEY 3

South central – Cherry Hill, Toms River

The 3rd crosses New Jersey's south-central section and takes in its entire political spectrum, from the solidly Republican shores of Ocean County to the staunchly Democratic Cherry Hill area in Camden County.

The presence of Fort Dix (shared with the 4th District) and McGuire Air Force Base make national defense a salient issue in the 3rd. The 2005 BRAC round dictated that the two bases, along with the Lakehurst Naval station (in the 4th), be combined into a "mega-base" by 2011, and BRAC also directed that aircraft and additional jobs go to the new joint base.

Communities around Toms River are concerned that offshore waste disposal and other environmental issues may affect their beach tourist industry. Local officials, who mostly are Republicans, emphasize their "green" credentials. Burlington County, most of which is in the 3rd, is one of the largest cranberry-producing counties in the nation.

The district has a lot of wealthy elderly voters, many living in retirement communities along Route 70. Municipal and school budgets, as well as tax rates, are among the lowest in the state — due in part to the high voter turnout by these residents.

Residential and commercial growth dominates the short strip of land in Burlington County that abuts the Delaware River. While part of the county, such as Cinnaminson and Moorestown, is Republican-leaning, other sections support Democrats on the statewide level and can combine with the district's small share of Camden County to make elections competitive. Heavily Republican Ocean County, however, gives the district its GOP lean. George W. Bush won the district by less than 3 percentage points in the 2004 presidential election.

MAJOR INDUSTRY

Retail, health care, agriculture, tourism, defense

MILITARY BASES

Fort Dix (Army), 8,870 military, 1,119 civilian (2007) (shared with the 4th); McGuire Air Force Base, 5,189 military, 1,636 civilian (2007)

CITIES

Toms River (unincorporated), 86,327; Springdale (unincorporated), 14,409

NOTABLE

NFL Films, home to the world's largest sports film library, is based in Mt. Laurel.

Rep. Christopher H. Smith (R)

CAPITOL OFFICE
225-3765
www.house.gov/chrissmith
2373 Rayburn 20515-3004; fax 225-7768

COMMITTEES
Foreign Affairs

RESIDENCE
Hamilton

BORN
March 4, 1953, Rahway, N.J.

RELIGION
Roman Catholic

FAMILY
Wife, Marie Smith; four children

EDUCATION
Trenton State College, B.A. 1975 (business)

CAREER
Sporting goods executive; state anti-abortion group director

POLITICAL HIGHLIGHTS
Republican nominee for U.S. House, 1978

ELECTION RESULTS

2006 GENERAL		
Christopher H. Smith (R)	124,482	65.7%
Carol E. Gay (D)	62,905	33.2%
2006 PRIMARY		
Christopher H. Smith (R)		unopposed
2004 GENERAL		
Christopher H. Smith (R)	192,671	67.0%
Amy Vasquez (D)	92,826	32.3%

PREVIOUS WINNING PERCENTAGES
2002 (66%); 2000 (63%); 1998 (62%); 1996 (64%); 1994 (68%); 1992 (62%); 1990 (63%); 1988 (66%); 1986 (61%); 1984 (61%); 1982 (53%); 1980 (57%)

Elected 1980; 14th term

While Smith may be best known as a leader of the anti-abortion forces in Congress, he has devoted at least as much energy to other priorities, including international human rights, veterans' health care and the global battle against AIDS. He says they are all related.

"It's my faith that motivates me," Smith explains. "I am very involved with right-to-life issues. It's all interconnected. It's all working for the disenfranchised, one big continuum."

Abortion recurs as an issue every Congress, and every time, Smith can be found manning the barricades, whether to prevent federal funds from paying for the abortions of poor women, or to stop foreign aid to agencies that counsel women about abortion, or to protect the legal rights of abortion protesters. In the 108th Congress (2003-04), Smith spearheaded the drive that led to enactment of a ban on a procedure that anti-abortion groups call "partial birth" abortion.

Smith's latest crusade is a bill requiring that women seeking abortions be told that a fetus feels pain. But in 2006, Smith failed to muster the two-thirds majority needed when GOP leaders tried to rush the measure through under expedited procedures in the closing days of the session. With Democrats in control, he will find it harder to advance such proposals.

Smith was unceremoniously stripped of the Veterans' Affairs Committee chairmanship at the start of the 109th Congress (2005-06) and left the panel he had served on for 24 years. Speaker J. Dennis Hastert took away his gavel after Smith battled to increase veterans' health care funding in the face of demands by President Bush and GOP leaders for leaner budgets. Smith says the 2007 disclosures of severe problems at Walter Reed Army Medical Center in Washington and veterans' hospitals around the country vindicated his stance. "Health care cannot be provided on the cheap. If you do not invest in modern facilities, adequate staffing levels and necessary equipment, you end up with inadequate care," he wrote in an op-ed piece for the Asbury Park Press.

Henry J. Hyde of Illinois, a popular Republican and a fellow anti-abortion crusader, softened Smith's fall in 2005 by giving him the gavel of the International Relations subcommittee dealing with Africa and human rights. Hyde, the full committee chairman at the time, created the panel with Smith's interests in mind. Smith is the top-ranking Republican on the panel in the 110th Congress (2007-08).

The New Jersey lawmaker has long championed human rights. He is a member of the Commission on Security and Cooperation in Europe, also known as the Helsinki Commission, set up to monitor human rights in Europe after the signing of the 1975 Helsinki accords between the United States and the Soviet Union. In 1998, he won enactment of a law establishing a federal program to help victims of torture both in the United States and abroad. He steered a renewal through Congress in 2006.

Smith has a special interest in the rights of children and has sponsored legislation to monitor child labor conditions abroad and crack down on abuses. He often refers in conversation to his own four children, whose photographs are prominently displayed in his congressional office. In 2000, he won enactment of a law to combat trafficking in women and children, who are often forced into prostitution; in 2006, Bush signed Smith's bill toughening anti-trafficking measures and calling for $361 million in funding over two years.

Smith says he has held more than 300 hearings on human rights over the years, including 26 hearings on China alone. "I get front-page coverage on the pro-life issue but get stories buried inside the papers on other issues," he notes.

Smith parted with his fellow Republicans and with Bush more often than all but seven other GOP House members in the 109th Congress. He was one of 27 Republicans voting against the Central American Free Trade Agreement, one of eight voting against a measure making it harder to win asylum in the United States, and one of 34 opposing legislation to limit the scope of the Endangered Species Act. He also was one of 24 Republicans who wrote to House GOP leaders opposing a 2005 budget bill provision to open the Arctic National Wildlife Refuge to oil drilling. In 1989, long before the climate change issue rose to public prominence, Smith won House adoption of an amendment to the State Department authorization bill calling for creation of an "information network" to track and disseminate information about global warming. The measure died in the Senate.

In the 110th Congress, as Democrats pushed their "first 100 hours" agenda of top-priority bills through the House, Smith was one of 17 Republicans who backed five of the six measures; three other GOP lawmakers supported all six. Smith voted to raise the minimum wage, to require Medicare officials to negotiate for lower prescription drug prices, to recoup oil royalties from faulty leases, to adopt more recommendations of the independent Sept. 11 commission and to tighten House ethics rules. His lone no vote came on a bill to expand federal funding for stem cell research using cells harvested from surplus embryos at in vitro fertilization clinics.

Shaken by the Sept. 11 terrorist attacks and by anthrax-laced letters to Congress believed to have originated in Trenton, in his district, Smith sponsored and worked hard to pass legislation giving the Department of Veterans Affairs a role in the war on terrorism. The measure established four centers at veterans' hospitals to research and develop responses to biological, chemical or radiological attacks.

Smith has always been able to count on support from veterans when opponents tried to paint him as obsessed with abortion to the exclusion of other societal issues. He also has developed one of the most effective constituent service operations in the House, which never hurts at election time.

Smith was executive director of the New Jersey Right to Life Committee before winning election to Congress at age 27. He defeated 13-term Democrat Frank Thompson Jr., who had been tainted by a bribery scandal. He faced a stiff challenge in his first re-election battle, taking just 53 percent of the vote, but hasn't fallen below 60 percent since.

KEY VOTES

2006

No Stop broadband companies from favoring select Internet traffic

Yes Affirm U.S. commitment to war in Iraq and reject setting a withdrawal date for troops

No Repeal requirement for bilingual ballots at the polls

No Permit U.S. sale of civilian nuclear technology to India

Yes Build a 700-mile fence on the U.S.-Mexico border to curb illegal crossings

Yes Permit warrantless wiretaps of suspected terrorists

2005

Yes Intervene in the life-support case of Terri Schiavo

No Lift President Bush's restrictions on stem cell research funding

No Prohibit FBI access to library and bookstore records

No Approve free-trade pact with five Central American countries

No Pass energy policy overhaul favored by President Bush emphasizing domestic oil and gas production

No End mandatory preservation of habitat of endangered animal and plant species

Yes Ban torture of prisoners in U.S. custody

CQ VOTE STUDIES

	PARTY UNITY		PRESIDENTIAL SUPPORT	
	Support	Oppose	Support	Oppose
2006	72%	28%	67%	33%
2005	79%	21%	60%	40%
2004	77%	23%	67%	33%
2003	85%	15%	78%	22%
2002	89%	11%	80%	20%

INTEREST GROUPS

	AFL-CIO	ADA	CCUS	ACU
2006	50%	30%	67%	68%
2005	60%	30%	70%	60%
2004	67%	40%	76%	54%
2003	33%	30%	69%	71%
2002	22%	10%	80%	80%

NEW JERSEY 4
Central — part of Trenton, Lakewood

The 4th spreads across the center of the state, where the Garden State begins its transition from South to North Jersey, extending from Trenton and the Delaware River to the Jersey Shore and coastal communities such as Point Pleasant and Spring Lake.

The district includes much of the southern and eastern portions of Trenton, the state capital. While these areas vote Democratic, they do not lean quite as strongly as other parts of the city, which are contained in the 12th District to the north. Most of Trenton's white residents live in the 4th, which includes the historically Italian neighborhood of Chambersburg. But the area is not without diversity — more than 25 percent of the 4th's portion of Trenton is black and 30 percent is Hispanic.

The area's military bases are important to the economy, but the district does not rely solely on defense. Trenton and its suburbs have a diverse range of businesses, and the towns along the Jersey Shore in Ocean and Monmouth counties depend heavily on tourism. The 4th also includes rural territory dotted with horse and agricultural farms, in areas such as Colts Neck. Like many areas in central and southern New Jersey, the 4th is loaded with small towns, such as Hightstown in Mercer and Manasquan in Monmouth counties, and the district takes in a chunk of Burlington County, a growing area outside of Philadelphia. Burlington Coat Factory, a clothing retail chain, is headquartered in Burlington.

Ocean and Monmouth counties dominate the 4th's geography and give the district its GOP lean. George W. Bush did 10 percentage points better in the 4th (56 percent) than he did statewide in the 2004 presidential election. Lakewood Township, with its large Jewish population, gave Democrat Jon Corzine a majority of its 2005 gubernatorial vote.

MAJOR INDUSTRY
State government, tourism, manufacturing, defense

MILITARY BASES
Fort Dix (Army), 8,870 military, 7,806 civilian (2006) (shared with the 3rd); Naval Air Engineering Station Lakehurst, 425 military, 2,072 civilian (2006)

CITIES
Trenton (pt.), 37,745; Lakewood (unincorporated), 36,065

NOTABLE
Trenton, a Revolutionary War battleground, was temporarily the U.S. capital; Bruce Springsteen hails from Freehold.

Rep. Scott Garrett (R)

CAPITOL OFFICE
225-4465
garrett.house.gov
1318 Longworth 20515-3005; fax 225-9048

COMMITTEES
Budget
Financial Services

RESIDENCE
Wantage

BORN
July 9, 1959, Englewood, N.J.

RELIGION
Protestant

FAMILY
Wife, Mary Ellen Garrett; two children

EDUCATION
Montclair State College, B.A. 1981 (political science); Rutgers U., J.D. 1984

CAREER
Lawyer

POLITICAL HIGHLIGHTS
N.J. Assembly, 1990-2003; sought Republican nomination for U.S. House, 1998, 2000

ELECTION RESULTS

2006 GENERAL		
Scott Garrett (R)	112,142	54.9%
Paul Aronsohn (D)	89,503	43.8%
R. Matthew Fretz (AIV)	2,597	1.3%
2006 PRIMARY		
Scott Garrett (R)	23,760	86.4%
Michael J. Cino (R)	3,747	13.6%
2004 GENERAL		
Scott Garrett (R)	171,220	57.6%
Anne Wolfe (D)	122,259	41.1%

PREVIOUS WINNING PERCENTAGES
2002 (59%)

Elected 2002; 3rd term

Garrett's adherence to conservative ideals can make even like-minded GOP leaders nostalgic for the days when his suburban New Jersey district routinely sent a moderate to the House every two years.

Appeals for party loyalty at critical times are wasted on Garrett. As a brand-new member of the Budget Committee, he was one of just seven House Republicans to vote in 2003 against the final GOP-drafted budget resolution. That same year, he voted against the Medicare prescription drug bill, one of the biggest initiatives of President Bush's first term. He voted against federal aid for victims of Hurricane Katrina in 2005, and against the Bush administration's free-trade agreement with Central America the same year.

He was a leader in a push by GOP conservatives to rein in specific earmarks on spending or tax bills, and is a frequent sponsor of floor amendments to trim appropriations bills. One of his favorites, an amendment limiting the number of federal workers who could attend the same out-of-town conference, was attached to two bills in 2005 and four in 2006.

With equally strong views on social issues, Garrett is at home in the "traditional values" wing of the GOP. He favors prohibitions on same-sex marriage, stem cell research and abortion. In 2005, he helped push through Congress a law barring the use of federal funds to enforce a Supreme Court decision that upheld the right of local governments to seize private property for economic development.

Unlike many other House GOP conservatives, Garrett cannot afford to dismiss differing viewpoints out of hand. His North Jersey district is in the heart of the urban Northeast. Socially moderate suburbanites of Bergen County offset his core constituency — conservative voters in farming villages and new exurban developments in the western portion of the district.

Though he can't often bring himself to vote with moderates, he has inched away from some of the positions he held back in the years when he was unsuccessfully challenging his moderate predecessor, Republican Marge Roukema, in primary contests. He once advocated government tuition vouchers for private school students but now says a tax credit for tuition would suffice. "I think I'm sort of in the middle," he told The Bergen Record in 2002.

Still, in 2006 he was the only New Jersey Republican to vote against continuing a ban on offshore drilling. And he was the only New Jersey lawmaker to receive an "A" in 2006 from the National Taxpayers Union.

On most issues, Garrett votes with his compatriots in the Republican Study Committee, the most conservative group of House members. He is a tax-cutting diehard who believes higher taxes pose the biggest threat to the economy. He says the government's red ink can be wiped out by controlling the spending side of the ledger.

An evangelical Christian, Garrett opposes abortion even in cases of rape and incest, favoring an exception only to save the life of the woman. Garrett, who with his wife, Mary Ellen, has two teenage daughters, is outspoken in the campaign to amend the Constitution to ban same-sex marriage. "Our kids need strong families, and strong families work best when kids have a mom and a dad at home, engaged in their lives," he says.

Garrett does not pursue funds for many parochial projects, preferring to focus on selected priorities that he deems appropriate for the federal government. He helped target $50 million in homeland security spending for New Jersey, which, with its proximity to Manhattan, is especially sensitive to the terrorism threat. And he cosponsored with GOP Rep. Rodney Frelinghuysen of New Jersey a $25 million bill to preserve open space in the Highlands, a region of hills and mountains in northern New Jersey that is an important source of drinking water threatened by exurban sprawl. He otherwise gets low scores from environmental groups who don't like his support for energy exploration in Alaska's Arctic National Wildlife Refuge or his opposition to stringent clean air regulations.

State Democrats initially mocked Garrett for his fealty to Bush, but those critics were silenced temporarily after his vote against the president's Medicare prescription drug bill, which he cast in spite of tremendous pressure from House GOP leaders and from the president himself.

Garrett is the youngest of four children of an executive salesman for Uniroyal and a stay-at-home mother who, in search of a more bucolic life, moved from Bergen County's rapidly building suburbs to a 100-acre farm in Wantage, where they grew greenhouse tomatoes, Yorkshire pigs and Christmas trees. Garrett's older brother still raises Christmas trees there.

He took an early interest in civics, publishing an alternative high school newspaper that questioned the school administration's spending practices and getting elected student government treasurer. Garrett kept a picture of Reagan-era budget guru David A. Stockman over his desk. After getting his law degree, he worked in insurance and jumped into politics. He served more than a decade in the New Jersey legislature, where he belonged to a group of maverick, very conservative Republicans called the "mountain men."

In 1998, he took on the moderate Roukema. He lost the primary but got the attention of national conservative groups, including the Club for Growth, an influential anti-tax group that spent more than $250,000 in his behalf two years later. Again, he lost, but by only 2,000 votes. By 2002, pressure from the right and battles with the conservative House GOP leadership had taken their toll on Roukema and she retired, paving the way for Garrett.

Luckily for him, two Republican moderates wanted the seat as well, and they split the large moderate vote in Bergen County. Garrett swept two more-rural, conservative counties, including Sussex County, a place that "with its muddy pickup trucks, rolling pastures and brick evangelical churches, is as red-state as New Jersey gets. It's rural, it's white and it's Republican," according to The Bergen Record. Garrett prevailed.

He had a tough Democratic opponent in ophthalmologist Anne Sumers. But GOP leaders came to his aid, with the National Republican Congressional Committee spending heavily on issue ads attacking Sumers. Garrett won with 59 percent of the vote. In 2006, he garnered 55 percent.

KEY VOTES

2006

- No Stop broadband companies from favoring select Internet traffic
- Yes Affirm U.S. commitment to war in Iraq and reject setting a withdrawal date for troops
- Yes Repeal requirement for bilingual ballots at the polls
- Yes Permit U.S. sale of civilian nuclear technology to India
- Yes Build a 700-mile fence on the U.S.-Mexico border to curb illegal crossings
- No Permit warrantless wiretaps of suspected terrorists

2005

- Yes Intervene in the life-support case of Terri Schiavo
- No Lift President Bush's restrictions on stem cell research funding
- \- Prohibit FBI access to library and bookstore records
- No Approve free-trade pact with five Central American countries
- Yes Pass energy policy overhaul favored by President Bush emphasizing domestic oil and gas production
- Yes End mandatory preservation of habitat of endangered animal and plant species
- No Ban torture of prisoners in U.S. custody

CQ VOTE STUDIES

	PARTY UNITY		PRESIDENTIAL SUPPORT	
	Support	Oppose	Support	Oppose
2006	89%	11%	83%	17%
2005	98%	2%	84%	16%
2004	98%	2%	88%	12%
2003	97%	3%	89%	11%

INTEREST GROUPS

	AFL-CIO	ADA	CCUS	ACU
2006	14%	20%	87%	100%
2005	20%	5%	85%	100%
2004	7%	5%	95%	100%
2003	13%	15%	93%	96%

NEW JERSEY 5

North and west — Bergenfield, Paramus

Although the 5th stretches across northern New Jersey, three-fifths of its population is packed into northern Bergen County, which is home to affluent, Republican-leaning voters, many of whom commute into New York City. The rest of the district is scenic and hilly, and includes the state's small portion of the Appalachian Trail.

The 5th's property values and income levels are among the highest in the state, and no municipality here has more than 30,000 residents. The 5th also has the smallest minority population of any New Jersey district.

Saddle River, in wealthy Bergen County, is home to multimillion-dollar homes, but Bergen County's tony suburbs contrast with a more rural feel in the 5th's portion of Passaic County to the west, which includes attractions dating back to the colonial era.

The scenic back country of Sussex and Warren counties traditionally has been a mix of farmland and small towns, but both counties have started to change as young professionals from New York City move into the area. Warren County's population has increased by more than 20 percent since 1990, and the county continues to experience significant housing development.

The 5th tends to vote Republican, but Democrats remain successful in some pockets, including Tenafly in Bergen County and Phillipsburg in south Warren County, the only county to lie entirely within the district's boundaries. George W. Bush captured 57 percent of the 5th's vote in the 2004 presidential election — his second-best showing in the state. The Bergen County portion of the district favored Bush by 8 percentage points, and his margin was even more lopsided in the 5th's part of the three outlying counties. Despite the GOP strength, most voters continue to register as independents.

MAJOR INDUSTRY

Pharmaceuticals, electronics, shipping, agriculture

CITIES

West Milford (unincorporated), 26,410; Bergenfield, 26,247; Paramus, 25,737; Ridgewood, 24,936

NOTABLE

Mars US, manufacturer of the M&M's brand, has a national office in Hackettstown; The New Jersey Botanical Garden is in Ringwood.

Rep. Frank Pallone Jr. (D)

CAPITOL OFFICE
225-4671
www.house.gov/pallone
237 Cannon 20515-3006; fax 225-9665

COMMITTEES
Energy & Commerce
(Health - chairman)
Natural Resources

RESIDENCE
Long Branch

BORN
Oct. 30, 1951, Long Branch, N.J.

RELIGION
Roman Catholic

FAMILY
Wife, Sarah Pallone; three children

EDUCATION
Middlebury College, B.A. 1973 (history & French); Tufts U., M.A. 1974 (international relations); Rutgers U., J.D. 1978

CAREER
Lawyer

POLITICAL HIGHLIGHTS
Long Branch City Council, 1982-88; N.J. Senate, 1984-88

ELECTION RESULTS

2006 GENERAL		
Frank Pallone Jr. (D)	98,615	68.6%
Leigh-Ann Bellew (R)	43,539	30.3%
Herbert L. Tarbous (DIS)	1,619	1.1%
2006 PRIMARY		
Frank Pallone Jr. (D)	unopposed	
2004 GENERAL		
Frank Pallone Jr. (D)	153,981	66.9%
Sylvester Fernandez (R)	70,942	30.8%
Virginia A. Flynn (LIBERT)	2,829	1.2%
Mac Dara Francis X. Lyden (X)	2,399	1.0%

PREVIOUS WINNING PERCENTAGES
2002 (66%); 2000 (68%); 1998 (57%); 1996 (61%); 1994 (60%); 1992 (52%); 1990 (49%); 1988 (52%); 1988 Special Election (52%)

Elected 1988; 10th full term

After nearly two decades in the House, the hard-charging and ambitious Pallone has yet to achieve his long-sought goal of moving to the Senate. Instead, he remains at the forefront of House Democratic efforts to shape health and environmental policy, as well as his party's message.

Pallone (puh-LOAN) vigorously promotes his liberal views on health care and environmental issues from his seats on the Energy and Commerce and Natural Resources committees. In 110th Congress (2007-08), he chairs the Energy panel's Health Subcommittee, where his overarching concern is reducing health care costs.

Other priorities include strengthening Medicaid, renewing the State Children's Health Insurance Program — a decade-old experiment in providing health insurance to children of the working poor — and closing gaps in the Medicare prescription drug program. In the 109th Congress (2005-06), Pallone sponsored a measure signed into law that provides grants to states to establish and improve electronic programs for monitoring controlled substances, primarily to combat the overuse and abuse of prescription drugs.

A native of the Jersey shore town of Long Branch, he represents a swath of the coastline, and coastal environmental issues have always been a major concern. As a member of the state Senate, he pushed legislation to limit ocean dumping of garbage and sewage sludge. In the 109th Congress, he sponsored an amendment to a spending bill that would have the National Academy of Sciences study which coastal population centers are most at risk from the impact of rising sea levels due to global warming.

He has promoted continuation of the federal program to bulk up beaches with additional sand. But he has opposed plans to mine sand and gravel in the Atlantic, arguing that it would hurt marine life. He and others in the New Jersey delegation have opposed a Bush administration proposal to study the economic and environmental impact of allowing oil drilling off the Jersey coast, and in the 110th Congress he offered a bill that would permanently prohibit drilling off the coast from Maine to North Carolina.

Pallone has called for an end to the use of the gasoline additive MTBE, which has contaminated drinking water supplies. In part because of his concerns about the potential environmental damage from expanded global trade, he has opposed all major trade liberalization laws enacted since his arrival in Congress.

With energy issues prominent on the Democratic agenda, Pallone figures to be a player in that area as well. He has been a leading backer of a national requirement for electricity suppliers to step up production from wind, solar and other renewable sources. More than 20 states, including New Jersey, already have such a requirement, which Pallone describes as "a market-driven, effective way of weaning ourselves off our national addiction to foreign oil."

Pallone tends to the interests of the sizable Indian-American community in the 6th District; he is one of the founders of the House Caucus on India and Indian-Americans. He supported the 2006 U.S.-India nuclear pact allowing U.S. shipments of civilian nuclear fuel to India, saying it would help keep the country as a strategic ally in the increasingly unstable region. He has also taken a special interest in Armenian issues because of a large district presence and a longstanding curiosity about the area.

Pallone serves on several leadership committees, including as communications chairman of the Democratic Policy Committee, coordinating the party's message on the House floor. He is a dependable Democratic vote, siding with his party 97 percent of the time in the 109th Congress.

Pallone had hoped to switch chambers after New Jersey Democratic Sen. Jon Corzine announced he was running for governor in 2005. He promptly endorsed Corzine and made known his interest in being appointed to the Senate vacancy if Corzine won the gubernatorial election. But the nod went to fellow House Democrat Robert Menendez, a tough competitor in New Jersey's rough-and-tumble political landscape.

Both Pallone and Menendez had weighed Senate races in 2002, when Sen. Robert G. Torricelli dropped his re-election bid that September after he was rebuked by colleagues for ethical lapses. But they demurred, and party leaders instead lured Senate veteran Frank R. Lautenberg out of retirement for a new term. Pallone also considered a Senate bid in 2000 but backed off as party leaders urged him to seek re-election as part of their push to regain control of the House. He is likely to be among the first in line for Lautenberg's seat when the senator retires.

Pallone inherited his interest in politics from his father, who was a police officer in Long Branch and a longtime activist in local Democratic affairs, including the campaigns of Democratic Rep. James J. Howard. From the time he was 7 years old, Pallone remembers his father taking him to rallies and political dinners. After graduating from Middlebury College, he enrolled at Tufts University's prestigious Fletcher School of Diplomacy. He was accepted into an exchange program that would have allowed him to spend a year studying in Switzerland, a common track to a State Department job. But Pallone says he realized he was more interested in Jersey politics, and instead went to law school at Rutgers University, where he later ended up teaching.

Howard eventually urged Pallone to run for the Long Branch City Council in 1982. One year later, Pallone won a state Senate seat. In March 1988, Howard died of a heart attack and many Democratic insiders, including Howard's widow, lined up behind Pallone. In November, he won two elections on the same day — a special election to fill the vacancy and a full term in his own right — each by only 5 percentage points. He has faced several other electoral challenges since then, the closest of which came in 1990 when he squeaked by with a margin of just 4,258 votes.

New Jersey lost a House seat in reapportionment for the 1990s, and Pallone had to scramble again to hold his redrawn district. But redistricting after the 2000 census protected all the state's incumbents, and he has coasted to re-election since then.

KEY VOTES

2006

- Yes Stop broadband companies from favoring select Internet traffic
- No Affirm U.S. commitment to war in Iraq and reject setting a withdrawal date for troops
- No Repeal requirement for bilingual ballots at the polls
- Yes Permit U.S. sale of civilian nuclear technology to India
- No Build a 700-mile fence on the U.S.-Mexico border to curb illegal crossings
- No Permit warrantless wiretaps of suspected terrorists

2005

- No Intervene in the life-support case of Terri Schiavo
- Yes Lift President Bush's restrictions on stem cell research funding
- Yes Prohibit FBI access to library and bookstore records
- No Approve free-trade pact with five Central American countries
- No Pass energy policy overhaul favored by President Bush emphasizing domestic oil and gas production
- No End mandatory preservation of habitat of endangered animal and plant species
- Yes Ban torture of prisoners in U.S. custody

CQ VOTE STUDIES

	PARTY UNITY		PRESIDENTIAL SUPPORT	
	Support	Oppose	Support	Oppose
2006	97%	3%	23%	77%
2005	97%	3%	17%	83%
2004	96%	4%	18%	82%
2003	97%	3%	22%	78%
2002	95%	5%	30%	70%

INTEREST GROUPS

	AFL-CIO	ADA	CCUS	ACU
2006	100%	100%	27%	4%
2005	93%	100%	30%	4%
2004	93%	95%	24%	4%
2003	100%	95%	30%	20%
2002	89%	100%	35%	4%

NEW JERSEY 6

East central — New Brunswick, Plainfield, part of Edison

Wedged in the heart of suburbs south of New York and Newark, the 6th combines industrial communities in Middlesex County with a long, thin stretch that incorporates beach towns in Monmouth County.

Like much of the state, the 6th previously was politically competitive, but has leaned toward Democrats in recent years. Democratic Plainfield in Union County and part of Somerset in Somerset County were added in the last redistricting in an attempt to pull the 6th even further to the left. John Kerry took 56 percent of the district's presidential vote in 2004.

East of Somerset, New Brunswick consolidates two Democratic voting blocs — students from Rutgers University and African-Americans. Nearby Piscataway, Highland Park and the wealthier suburb of Metuchen also favor Democrats. Middle-class and independent-voting residents cluster around Edison (shared with the 7th), which is home to some corporate offices and manufacturing. The 6th includes residents with various ethnic backgrounds, ranging from the Irish and Polish who populate South Amboy in Middlesex County to the Italians who are prevalent in Long Branch in Monmouth County. Edison has an established Indian community.

In Monmouth County, the problems of Asbury Park, a vacation site made famous by rocker Bruce Springsteen, are an exception to the area's generally sunny outlook. Yet hope exists here, thanks to a 10-year, $1.25 billion waterfront redevelopment plan that broke ground in 2004, and some success in reducing the city's narcotics trade. Other shore communities in the district include Deal, a summer enclave for Syrian Jews, and Atlantic Highlands, where many area residents catch a ferry to jobs in New York City.

MAJOR INDUSTRY

Higher education, technology, pharmaceuticals, manufacturing

CITIES

Edison (unincorporated) (pt.), 65,782; New Brunswick, 48,573; Plainfield, 47,829; Sayreville, 40,377; Long Branch, 31,340

NOTABLE

The Sandy Hook Light, opened in 1764, is the nation's oldest standing lighthouse.

Rep. Mike Ferguson (R)

CAPITOL OFFICE
225-5361
www.house.gov/ferguson
214 Cannon 20515-3007; fax 225-9460

COMMITTEES
Energy & Commerce

RESIDENCE
Warren

BORN
July 22, 1970, Ridgewood, N.J.

RELIGION
Roman Catholic

FAMILY
Wife, Maureen Ferguson; four children

EDUCATION
U. of Notre Dame, B.A. 1992 (government); Georgetown U., M.P.P. 1995 (education policy)

CAREER
College instructor; education consulting firm owner

POLITICAL HIGHLIGHTS
Republican nominee for U.S. House, 1998

ELECTION RESULTS

2006 GENERAL		
Mike Ferguson (R)	98,399	49.4%
Linda Stender (D)	95,454	48.0%
Thomas D. Abrams (WTN)	3,176	1.6%
Darren Young (LIBERT)	2,046	1.0%
2006 PRIMARY		
Mike Ferguson (R)		unopposed
2004 GENERAL		
Mike Ferguson (R)	162,597	56.9%
Steve Brozak (D)	119,081	41.7%

PREVIOUS WINNING PERCENTAGES
2002 (58%); 2000 (52%)

Elected 2000; 4th term

Ferguson represents a district in north-central New Jersey where the electorate is split almost down the middle, but he steers a legislative course right of center. He splits with most Republicans on environmental issues and occasionally on education and labor, but he is generally a dependable vote for the leadership and the White House.

House GOP leaders give Ferguson plenty of leeway when he does go his own way in the interest of keeping his seat in the Republican column. To bolster his standing at home, the leadership put him on the powerful Energy and Commerce Committee in 2003.

He was the vice chairman of its Health Subcommittee in the 109th Congress (2005-06), and late in 2006 he won approval of his bill to establish a federal respite care program — to give temporary relief to principal caregivers of ill family members. He has become increasingly involved in telecommunications issues as well, in part because some big names in the field, including Verizon Wireless and Lucent Technologies Inc., are headquartered in his district. In the 110th Congress (2007-08), he serves on the Health and Telecommunications subcommittees.

His constituents were greatly affected by the Sept. 11 terrorist attacks. Eighty-one people from the 7th District died, and Ferguson and his wife visited all of their families. Ferguson has pressed to adjust the funding formula for homeland security grants to steer more money to areas facing the highest risk of future attacks. And as the Energy panel assembled its portion of the deficit reduction law in 2005, Ferguson won inclusion of a provision that called on the Federal Communications Commission to set aside spectrum for broadband communications among first-responders. Although the provision was later dropped from the final bill, the FCC in 2006 moved on its own to address the issue."It doesn't make sense that my 7-year-old son can e-mail his grandfather a photograph on a cell phone, but first-responders are using walkie-talkies," Ferguson said in support of the FCC's review.

Ferguson is a social conservative, strongly opposed to abortion, even in cases of rape or incest. In 2005, he voted against federal funding of embryonic stem cell research, saying he could not endorse "the destruction of a human embryo" for any purpose. The year before, and again in 2006, he voted for a constitutional amendment to ban same-sex marriage, and in 2003 he supported creation of private school vouchers in the District of Columbia.

Ferguson favors more federal aid for education and strong environmental regulation, stands that can put him at odds with his party. The first legislation he ever introduced sought increased federal funding of the Individuals with Disabilities Education Act. He also has urged more funding for Pell Grants for college students and for teacher training and reading programs.

He has voted to block oil drilling in the Arctic National Wildlife Refuge, and was one of 24 House Republicans who signed a letter to GOP leaders warning them to keep an ANWR provision out of the deficit reduction bill in 2005. The resistance from so many GOP members ultimately forced negotiators to drop a Senate-passed drilling provision from the final version.

Ferguson also has voted to bar new energy leases within national monuments, prohibit the Interior Department from changing regulations on hard-rock mining and increase funding for alternative energy sources. He was one of 34 House Republicans to vote against a 2005 bill that environmentalists said would have severely weakened the Endangered Species Act.

On labor issues, Ferguson supports an increase in the minimum wage and approves of the Davis-Bacon prevailing wage standards that apply to workers on federally funded construction projects.

Ferguson has secured millions of dollars for improvements to Route 22, an important highway in his district. And in 2005, he got $5 million tucked into the annual energy and water appropriations bill for the Green Brook flood control project, an important local priority. In 2006, after years of lobbying, Ferguson won agreement from the Pentagon to remove toxic mercury from a military depot in Hillsborough, N.J., where it had been stored for years.

Major drug companies such as Merck & Co., Pfizer Inc. and Bristol-Myers Squibb Co. maintain facilities in the 7th District, and Ferguson has been careful not to upset them. In 2003, he voted against legislation allowing importation of prescription drugs from 25 industrial countries. Pharmaceutical companies said those products might not be safe.

Ferguson, who learned golf from his father, is a member of the famed Baltusrol Golf Club in Springfield, N.J. He plays a better-than-respectable game, with a 5 handicap. But most of his spare time is spent watching sports on TV, playing with his children and riding his bike.

His first taste of political life in the nation's capital came as a high school senior, in the Washington Workshops seminar program. That led him to major in government at Notre Dame, where he lost a race for student body president. As a senior, he became a mentor to a second-grade child of poor Polish immigrants, an experience that guided him toward public service.

After getting his master's degree in public policy, specializing in education policy, he eventually decided he was "more interested in making policy than analyzing it." He ran for the House in 1998, in the neighboring 6th District, where he was helped by the fundraising prowess of his father, a politically well-connected public relations executive. Although he spent more than $1 million, he lost to incumbent Democrat Frank Pallone Jr.

Undeterred, Ferguson moved to the 7th District, where Republican Bob Franks was abandoning the seat to run for the Senate in 2000. Ferguson confronted the carpetbagger label directly. "It's because I want to go to Congress, because I want to serve," he said when asked why he moved.

He beat out three rivals — including Thomas H. Kean Jr., son of the former New Jersey governor — for the GOP nomination. In November, he defeated the former mayor of Fanwood, Maryanne S. Connelly. Redistricting after the 2000 census helped all of New Jersey's House incumbents, but Ferguson may have benefited the most. His winning margins grew in 2002 and 2004. In 2006, bucking a strong national Democratic tide, he squeaked past Democratic state Rep. Linda Stender by less than 3,000 votes.

KEY VOTES

2006

- No Stop broadband companies from favoring select Internet traffic
- Yes Affirm U.S. commitment to war in Iraq and reject setting a withdrawal date for troops
- No Repeal requirement for bilingual ballots at the polls
- Yes Permit U.S. sale of civilian nuclear technology to India
- Yes Build a 700-mile fence on the U.S.-Mexico border to curb illegal crossings
- Yes Permit warrantless wiretaps of suspected terrorists

2005

- Yes Intervene in the life-support case of Terri Schiavo
- No Lift President Bush's restrictions on stem cell research funding
- No Prohibit FBI access to library and bookstore records
- Yes Approve free-trade pact with five Central American countries
- Yes Pass energy policy overhaul favored by President Bush emphasizing domestic oil and gas production
- No End mandatory preservation of habitat of endangered animal and plant species
- Yes Ban torture of prisoners in U.S. custody

CQ VOTE STUDIES

	PARTY UNITY		PRESIDENTIAL SUPPORT	
	Support	Oppose	Support	Oppose
2006	77%	23%	87%	13%
2005	89%	11%	87%	13%
2004	85%	15%	71%	29%
2003	93%	7%	90%	10%
2002	87%	13%	88%	12%

INTEREST GROUPS

	AFL-CIO	ADA	CCUS	ACU
2006	43%	20%	80%	64%
2005	13%	5%	89%	76%
2004	36%	30%	95%	67%
2003	20%	0%	90%	75%
2002	11%	5%	85%	84%

NEW JERSEY 7

North central — Woodbridge Township

The 7th, which zigzags across north-central New Jersey from the Delaware River to Woodbridge, is centered in bedroom communities that serve as a starting point for those commuting to Newark and New York City. It is a competitive district where moderate Republicans hold sway.

All four of the 7th's counties boast long histories, with charters dating back centuries. In New Providence, for example, residents dumped the town's supply of salt into a brook during the Revolutionary War to prevent the British from taking it.

Although the western areas of the district are less densely populated, the entire 7th has experienced some corporate and industrial growth. Parts of Somerset and Hunterdon counties, once dotted by horse farms, have been developed into office parks and shopping malls. Both counties, particularly Hunterdon, have remained safely Republican.

Drug manufacturers fuel the economy, led by Merck & Co. in Whitehouse Station. Insurance giant Chubb is based in Warren (Somerset County). Roche Molecular Systems in Branchburg and Alcatel-Lucent in Murray Hill (Union County) are major employers.

The district has several of New Jersey's superfund toxic waste sites, and residents tend to be environmentally conscious. Other important local issues include aircraft noise from nearby Newark Liberty International Airport (in the 10th and 13th districts) and money for infrastructure. Amtrak's Metropark station, the only stop in the 7th for north-central New Jersey residents headed up or down the East Coast, is in Iselin.

The district contains a number of wealthy, heavily Republican areas in Somerset and Hunterdon counties, and George W. Bush captured 53 percent of the 7th's 2004 presidential vote. It also contains a large chunk of Democratic Union County, but the 7th's portion is highly competitive.

MAJOR INDUSTRY

Pharmaceuticals, manufacturing, telecommunications

CITIES

Edison (unincorporated) (pt.), 31,905; Westfield, 29,644; Union (unincorporated) (pt.), 27,066; Scotch Plains (unincorporated), 22,732

NOTABLE

The U.S. equestrian team's headquarters is in Gladstone.

Rep. Bill Pascrell Jr. (D)

CAPITOL OFFICE
225-5751
pascrell.house.gov
2464 Rayburn 20515-3008; fax 225-5782

COMMITTEES
Ways & Means

RESIDENCE
Paterson

BORN
Jan. 25, 1937, Paterson, N.J.

RELIGION
Roman Catholic

FAMILY
Wife, Elsie Marie Pascrell; three children

EDUCATION
Fordham U., B.A. 1959 (journalism), M.A. 1961 (philosophy)

MILITARY SERVICE
Army, 1961; Army Reserve, 1962-67

CAREER
City official; teacher

POLITICAL HIGHLIGHTS
Paterson Board of Education, 1977-81 (president, 1981); N.J. Assembly, 1988-97; mayor of Paterson, 1990-97

ELECTION RESULTS

2006 GENERAL		
Bill Pascrell Jr. (D)	97,568	70.9%
Jose M. Sandoval (R)	39,053	28.4%
2006 PRIMARY		
Bill Pascrell Jr. (D)		unopposed
2004 GENERAL		
Bill Pascrell Jr. (D)	152,001	69.5%
George Ajjan (R)	62,747	28.7%
Joseph A. Fortunato (GREEN)	4,072	1.9%

PREVIOUS WINNING PERCENTAGES
2002 (67%); 2000 (67%); 1998 (62%); 1996 (51%)

Elected 1996; 6th term

To some of his colleagues, Pascrell is known as "Silky." Though that affectionate nickname is partially an homage to his hometown of Paterson, which was known as "Silk City" in the late 19th and early 20th centuries for its production of silk fabrics, he notes that his Damon Runyonesque personality might have something to do with it. "I'm a neighborhood guy," he says.

Indeed, Pascrell's focus in Congress remains right where it has been from the day he arrived: on his district. The working-class town of Paterson, the heart of the territory he represents, is where his Italian immigrant grandparents settled. It is where he served as head of the school board, mayor and a state legislator. And it is where he still has his home, a modest house in a middle-class neighborhood.

As mayor and in the state Assembly, Pascrell (pass-KRELL) devoted his attention to jobs, public safety and education.

In Congress, his legislative priorities include highways and other transportation projects, assistance for firefighters, prescription drug coverage for the elderly, and shoring up Social Security and Medicare. Early in the 110th Congress (2007-08), the House passed his bill to authorize almost $2 billion to help municipalities repair and replace sewer systems.

He generally backs Democratic Party positions on matters such as gun control and education funding. But he has voted for tougher penalties for juvenile offenders, a Republican-written overhaul of the nation's public housing system and a ban on the medical procedure described by its opponents as "partial birth" abortion.

At the start of the 110th Congress, House Democratic leaders gave Pascrell a prized seat on the Ways and Means Committee. The assignment reflected Pascrell's longstanding interests in Medicare and trade issues, but it also was due to his outspoken backing of Pennsylvania Democrat John P. Murtha for majority leader. Murtha had been House Speaker Nancy Pelosi's candidate over Maryland Democrat Steny H. Hoyer, who won the job.

Pascrell is a close friend of Murtha, the chairman of the House Defense Appropriations Subcommittee and one of the most vocal opponents of the war in Iraq. Although Pascrell voted in 2002 to authorize the use of force in Iraq, he supported Murtha's 2005 resolution calling for the withdrawal and redeployment of all U.S. forces stationed there. "We can't be the police dog there for the next 10 years," he said.

To join Ways and Means, Pascrell had to relinquish his seat on the Transportation and Infrastructure Committee. While a member of that panel, he made sure the six-year surface transportation bill passed by the House in the 109th Congress (2005-06) contained funding for road and bridge projects in his district. And he won adoption of a House floor amendment allowing New Jersey and other states to bar companies that have donated to political candidates or parties from participating in federal highway contracts. New Jersey, fighting corruption allegations, had enacted legislation banning the awarding of state contracts worth more than $17,500 to those who had donated to state or county political parties in the previous 18 months.

Pascrell also had to give up a seat on the Homeland Security Committee. He had been the top-ranking Democrat on the panel's Emergency Preparedness Subcommittee, where he championed more funding for firefighters and other emergency personnel. He successfully shepherded through Congress in 2000 a bill creating a federal program to direct hundreds of millions of dollars to hire, train and equip local firefighters. He won reauthorization of the program in 2004.

He has been an outspoken opponent of efforts by businesses to open the door wider for highly skilled foreign workers. In the 110th Congress, he introduced a bill to impose stiffer limits on H-1B visa holders and insist on stronger efforts to recruit U.S. workers first for those jobs.

Pascrell is extremely proud of his Italian heritage and has cosponsored legislation seeking to end what he and others regard as offensive portrayals of Italian-Americans on "The Sopranos" and in other media.

Pascrell, whose father worked for the railroad, was the first member of his family to go to high school, and his neighborhood pals razzed him when he went off to college. He worked his way through Fordham University, earning a bachelor's degree in journalism and a master's in philosophy. He then embarked on a 12-year career as a high school teacher in neighboring Paramus, and along the way did a stint in the Army. In 1974, he began working for the city of Paterson, first as director of the public works department and then heading up the planning and development office. At the same time, he got involved in local politics, as a campaign volunteer for Democratic Rep. Robert A. Roe and others. He was appointed to the Paterson Board of Education and was eventually elected its president.

Pascrell won a seat in the state Assembly in 1987 and simultaneously served as mayor of Paterson beginning in 1990. As mayor, he promoted tough law enforcement measures, particularly in drug trafficking. To make it more difficult for dealers to communicate with their customers, he personally ripped out the lines and receivers of pay telephones that had not been issued a city permit. In 1996, his New Jersey mayoral colleagues of both parties elected him "mayor of the year."

Pascrell was his party's choice to take on Rep. Bill Martini in 1996, two years after the freshman Republican's narrow victory had ended 34 years of Democratic hegemony in the 8th District. The national party gave Pascrell a boost, inviting him to speak at the 1996 Democratic National Convention. The AFL-CIO targeted the race as a key labor battlefield. Pascrell needed every bit of help he could get: He toppled Martini by just 6,200 votes. In acknowledgment of his tenuous hold on the seat, Pascrell immediately began amassing a war chest for 1998, which dissuaded Martini from running. Since then, Pascrell's re-election contests have been routine.

Like numerous other Democrats in New Jersey's House delegation, Pascrell is interested in ascending to the Senate if and when incumbent Frank R. Lautenberg steps down. "Some people may think I'm too old," says Pascrell, who turned 70 at the start of the 110th Congress, "but I'm ready."

KEY VOTES

2006

- Yes Stop broadband companies from favoring select Internet traffic
- No Affirm U.S. commitment to war in Iraq and reject setting a withdrawal date for troops
- No Repeal requirement for bilingual ballots at the polls
- No Permit U.S. sale of civilian nuclear technology to India
- Yes Build a 700-mile fence on the U.S.-Mexico border to curb illegal crossings
- No Permit warrantless wiretaps of suspected terrorists

2005

- No Intervene in the life-support case of Terri Schiavo
- Yes Lift President Bush's restrictions on stem cell research funding
- Yes Prohibit FBI access to library and bookstore records
- No Approve free-trade pact with five Central American countries
- No Pass energy policy overhaul favored by President Bush emphasizing domestic oil and gas production
- No End mandatory preservation of habitat of endangered animal and plant species
- Yes Ban torture of prisoners in U.S. custody

CQ VOTE STUDIES

	PARTY UNITY		PRESIDENTIAL SUPPORT	
	Support	Oppose	Support	Oppose
2006	95%	5%	25%	75%
2005	93%	7%	15%	85%
2004	94%	6%	31%	69%
2003	92%	8%	30%	70%
2002	89%	11%	48%	52%

INTEREST GROUPS

	AFL-CIO	ADA	CCUS	ACU
2006	100%	95%	27%	12%
2005	93%	100%	37%	0%
2004	100%	90%	40%	4%
2003	100%	80%	33%	24%
2002	100%	90%	50%	12%

NEW JERSEY 8

Northeast – Paterson, Clifton, Passaic

The 8th is a diverse combination of urban centers and suburban towns that begins in Pompton Lakes and moves south through the southern portion of Passaic County into northern Essex County, extending into parts of Livingston, West Orange and South Orange, just to the west of Newark. It includes Paterson, the state's third-largest city, as well as Clifton and Passaic.

Paterson was once known for silk mills that made it a leading textile producer in the late 19th century. But after labor strife and the introduction of rayon and other materials, the city experienced a serious economic downturn from which it never fully recovered. Yet there may be some light at the end of the tunnel: Center City, a major development project in downtown Paterson, is expected to be completed by late 2008.

The 8th also includes some less populated areas, which have more of a small town feel but still have to deal with a frequent nemesis of North Jersey residents — traffic. Wayne is mostly residential, but is perhaps best known as the home of a retail power center: Willowbrook Mall. The district is a melting pot of cultures with dozens of ethnic groups, from a large Peruvian community in Paterson to an enclave of Polish and Turkish residents in Clifton.

The 8th's slice of Passaic County gives Democrats a solid base in recent years — especially Paterson, with its deep-seated labor tradition. Overall, the district is more than one-fourth Hispanic and 13 percent black. John Kerry received 58 percent of the presidential vote in 2004.

Republicans fare better in the district's Essex County portion, which is mostly suburban and includes wealthy Livingston (shared with the 11th) and the middle-class towns of Nutley and Belleville. Many residents here commute to Newark or New York.

MAJOR INDUSTRY

Pharmaceuticals, manufacturing, communications, education

CITIES

Paterson, 149,222; Clifton, 78,672; Passaic, 67,861; Wayne (unincorporated), 54,069; Bloomfield (unincorporated), 47,683

NOTABLE

Cooking expert Martha Stewart and Sen. Frank R. Lautenberg graduated from Nutley High School; Toys "R" Us is headquartered in Wayne.

Rep. Steven R. Rothman (D)

CAPITOL OFFICE
225-5061
www.house.gov/rothman
2303 Rayburn 20515-3009; fax 225-5851

COMMITTEES
Appropriations
Science & Technology

RESIDENCE
Fair Lawn

BORN
Oct. 14, 1952, Englewood, N.J.

RELIGION
Jewish

FAMILY
Wife, Jennifer Rothman; five children

EDUCATION
Syracuse U., B.A. 1974 (political philosophy); Washington U., J.D. 1977

CAREER
Lawyer

POLITICAL HIGHLIGHTS
Mayor of Englewood, 1983-89; Democratic nominee for Bergen County Board of Freeholders, 1989; Bergen County Surrogate Court judge, 1993-96

ELECTION RESULTS

2006 GENERAL		
Steven R. Rothman (D)	105,853	71.5%
Vincent Micco (R)	40,879	27.6%
2006 PRIMARY		
Steven R. Rothman (D)		unopposed
2004 GENERAL		
Steven R. Rothman (D)	146,038	67.5%
Edward Trawinski (R)	68,564	31.7%

PREVIOUS WINNING PERCENTAGES
2002 (70%); 2000 (68%); 1998 (65%); 1996 (56%)

Elected 1996; 6th term

Starting out with a small law practice over a barbershop in Englewood, Rothman cut his teeth on local Democratic politics in a congested, noisy suburb in New Jersey, and he has kept his focus in Congress on quality-of-life issues there.

As an appropriator, he has secured federal money for highway and mass transit projects for his densely populated district, made up of commuter suburbs of New York City. Rothman is the Washington point man for an intensely local battle over bustling Teterboro Airport. Because it is convenient to Manhattan, there have been repeated efforts to increase traffic there from corporate and small chartered jets, and Rothman generally takes up the cause of noise-weary neighborhoods.

That's not to say he wouldn't mind having a broader portfolio of national policy issues one day. Rothman has his eye on the Senate and intends to run upon the retirement of Sen. Frank R. Lautenberg, who is in his 80s. Rothman wanted to run when Democrat Jon Corzine ran successfully for New Jersey governor in 2005, but, like other Democrats with designs on the seat, had to step aside for Rep. Robert Menendez, whom Corzine appointed to fill out the rest of his Senate term, giving Menendez incumbent status in the 2006 election. Menendez was elected to a full term.

Rothman is generally a dependable vote for the Democratic leadership. In the 109th Congress (2005-06), he stuck with his party 95 percent of the time when Democrats and Republicans squared off on an issue.

He sides with his party on abortion rights, environmental protection, gun control and health care. He does, however, make an occasional foray into Republican territory, such as his support for a proposed constitutional amendment to ban desecration of the U.S. flag. "People can find plenty of ways to denigrate this country and still maintain their freedom of speech, but they can do it without desecrating the flag," Rothman once said.

A former Bergen County Surrogate Court judge, he sometimes votes with the GOP for tougher punishments for violent offenders, and he supports the death penalty.

Although Rothman voted in 2002 to authorize the war in Iraq, he has since joined House Democrats in calling for a withdrawal of U.S. troops. He has more sway on the issue in the 110th Congress (2007-08) than before. His party is now in the majority, and in 2007 Rothman moved from Appropriations' Transportation Subcommittee to the Defense spending panel, at the center of the battle between Congress and President Bush over war funding.

In March 2006, Rothman opposed a $91.8 billion supplemental spending bill for the war, and in 2007 he voted to condemn Bush's decision to send in thousands of additional combat troops. Shortly after his first trip to Iraq in 2007, he said, "If we ever had any moral obligations to stabilize that region after we botched the post-Saddam era, I believe after four years, half a trillion dollars, 3,100 American service men and women's lives, 25,000 wounded, we've met that moral obligation and it is time to withdraw all of our combat troops from Iraq."

In the 109th Congress, Rothman was preoccupied with airplanes and commuter trains. In 2006, he secured $3.6 million in federal funding for construction of New Jersey Transit's Northern Branch Line commuter rail project. A transportation spending bill also contained his provision to continue a ban on large jets at Teterboro. He has sponsored the ban since 2003, when the Federal Aviation Administration announced plans to overturn the airport's long-established weight limit.

Rothman has worked over several years to preserve the remaining 8,400 acres of undeveloped land in the Meadowlands, where the stadium for the Giants and the Jets football teams is located. He would like to see the land become a park, with bird-watching platforms and nature trails.

In the 110th Congress, he added a seat on the Science panel, from which he looks out for federal research projects important to northern New Jersey.

Rothman was born in Englewood. His grandparents came through Ellis Island as Jewish immigrants from Russia, Poland and Austria. His father was a tool and dye maker, until a moonlighting venture building houses with a friend evolved into a good business developing industrial real estate.

His family was not active in politics, but he said, "I was always taught that I should be interested in justice, and not just for me or my family but for everyone, and that it was my obligation as a human being to pursue justice and fight for it."

After graduating from high school, Rothman landed a summer internship with a local state senator, Democrat Matthew Feldman. As mayor of Teaneck in the early 1960s, Feldman led that city's racial integration of neighborhoods and public schools and was a strong supporter of the creation of the state of Israel. Feldman became Rothman's role model and galvanized his interest in law and politics.

At Syracuse University, Rothman majored in political philosophy, then got a law degree from Washington University in St. Louis. He opened his practice in 1978 and got involved in local Democratic Party politics. In 1983, he was elected Englewood mayor. He later made an unsuccessful bid for Bergen County freeholder, or councilman, but won his next campaign, for the court judgeship, in 1993.

In 1996, Rothman ran for the House, when Robert G. Torricelli gave up his seat to run successfully for the Senate. Rothman took 80 percent of the primary vote and 56 percent in the general election. He has won re-election easily ever since.

His personal life took a happy turn in the last Congress. As a divorced father of two, Rothman followed the path of modern romance and employed an online dating service for Jewish singles called JDate.com. He advertised himself as Steve3366, a Libra, and a lawyer working in the U.S. Congress. In 2005, Rothman met Jennifer Anne Beckenstein; she was living in Suffern, N.Y., and did not know Rothman was actually a member of Congress until they met in person. "We fell in love and got married," Rothman says. The couple has five children between them.

KEY VOTES

2006

Yes Stop broadband companies from favoring select Internet traffic

No Affirm U.S. commitment to war in Iraq and reject setting a withdrawal date for troops

No Repeal requirement for bilingual ballots at the polls

No Permit U.S. sale of civilian nuclear technology to India

No Build a 700-mile fence on the U.S.-Mexico border to curb illegal crossings

No Permit warrantless wiretaps of suspected terrorists

2005

No Intervene in the life-support case of Terri Schiavo

Yes Lift President Bush's restrictions on stem cell research funding

Yes Prohibit FBI access to library and bookstore records

No Approve free-trade pact with five Central American countries

No Pass energy policy overhaul favored by President Bush emphasizing domestic oil and gas production

No End mandatory preservation of habitat of endangered animal and plant species

Yes Ban torture of prisoners in U.S. custody

CQ VOTE STUDIES

	PARTY UNITY		PRESIDENTIAL SUPPORT	
	Support	Oppose	Support	Oppose
2006	98%	2%	9%	91%
2005	93%	7%	29%	71%
2004	94%	6%	31%	69%
2003	90%	10%	25%	75%
2002	87%	13%	32%	68%

INTEREST GROUPS

	AFL-CIO	ADA	CCUS	ACU
2006	100%	90%	27%	8%
2005	87%	95%	48%	5%
2004	93%	95%	30%	5%
2003	100%	80%	38%	20%
2002	89%	95%	42%	12%

NEW JERSEY 9

Northeast – Hackensack, part of Jersey City

Across the Hudson from northern Manhattan, the 9th is a predominately wealthy but overwhelmingly Democratic district that takes in southeast Bergen County before dipping into parts of Hudson County and suburbs adjacent to Newark. Prestigious areas lie in the north, including Englewood Cliffs and Fort Lee; the district becomes more blue-collar and middle-class as it runs south into Lyndhurst and parts of Jersey City.

The district is a mix of tightly packed neighborhoods in areas such as Leonia and Ridgefield and more commercial parts such as Secaucus. As New York City apartment prices have climbed, many commuters have moved to the 9th's Hudson River towns, like Edgewater, in new housing. In its northwestern sliver, the district's small section of Passaic County consists entirely of Hawthorne, an older bedroom community.

Redevelopment has strengthened the 9th's already solid economy. Anchored by East Rutherford's Meadowlands Sports Complex, the southern part of the 9th has seen increased commercial and residential development. Construction has begun on the $2 billion retail and entertainment portion of the Meadowlands Xanadu project, and football's Jets and Giants are hoping to break ground on a new joint stadium in 2007. But the news is not all good for the complex, as hockey's Devils and soccer's Red Bulls move south to Newark and Harrison, respectively, and basketball's Nets likely move to Brooklyn.

The 9th's part of Bergen is Democratic, as the county's Republican areas are in the 5th District. Englewood and Hackensack both gave John Kerry more than 70 percent of the 2004 presidential vote, with Teaneck close behind. The strong Hispanic population around Jersey City (shared with the 10th and 13th) and sizable proportions of black, Jewish and Asian voters also contribute to the Democrats' strength here. Kerry took 58 percent of the 9th's vote in 2004.

MAJOR INDUSTRY

Manufacturing, health care, shipping, stadium events

CITIES

Jersey City (pt.), 58,129; Hackensack, 42,677; Teaneck (unincorporated), 39,260; Kearny (pt.), 38,250; Fort Lee, 35,461; Fair Lawn, 31,637

NOTABLE

Teterboro Airport is home to the Aviation Hall of Fame and Museum of New Jersey.

Rep. Donald M. Payne (D)

CAPITOL OFFICE
225-3436
www.house.gov/payne
2209 Rayburn 20515-3010; fax 225-4160

COMMITTEES
Education & Labor
Foreign Affairs
(Africa & Global Health - chairman)

RESIDENCE
Newark

BORN
July 16, 1934, Newark, N.J.

RELIGION
Baptist

FAMILY
Widowed; three children

EDUCATION
Seton Hall U., B.A. 1957 (social studies)

CAREER
Computer forms company executive; company community affairs director; teacher

POLITICAL HIGHLIGHTS
Essex County Board of Freeholders, 1972-78; sought Democratic nomination for Essex County executive, 1978; sought Democratic nomination for U.S. House, 1980; Newark Municipal Council, 1982-88; sought Democratic nomination for U.S. House, 1986

ELECTION RESULTS

2006 GENERAL		
Donald M. Payne (D)		unopposed
2006 PRIMARY		
Donald M. Payne (D)		unopposed
2004 GENERAL		
Donald M. Payne (D)	155,697	96.9%
Toy-Ling Washington (GREEN)	2,927	1.8%
Sara J. Lobman (S)	2,089	1.3%

PREVIOUS WINNING PERCENTAGES
2002 (84%); 2000 (88%); 1998 (84%); 1996 (84%); 1994 (76%); 1992 (78%); 1990 (81%); 1988 (77%)

Elected 1988; 10th term

Payne's career has been marked by an unwavering commitment to addressing the problems of Africa, which he first visited more than 30 years ago. While other lawmakers pursue more popular causes, he fights for U.S. attention and aid to the world's poorest continent.

Payne has led congressional efforts to sanction the government of Sudan for the murder, rape and plunder of black Africans in Darfur, the country's western region. The atrocities have been attributed to mostly Arab militias backed by the government. In 2006, Payne helped win House passage of a bill to deny U.S. visas to Sudanese officials and militia commanders and to block access to their assets in the United States. He wanted even more stringent sanctions, but he called the bill "a first step in the right direction."

Payne is the chairman of the Foreign Relations Committee's Africa Subcommittee. He travels regularly to the continent, and his office is filled with African sculptures, masks and artifacts he's collected over the years. He has pushed each administration since 1989 to provide more aid to Africa, saying the U.S. effort there is "very, very underfunded." One of his favorite arguing points is to note that the United States gave more money to Western Europe in a single year after World War II than it has given to all of Africa over a 10-year period, a comparison rooted in his memory of reading about the Marshall Plan as a young newspaper delivery boy.

With his seniority in the House, Payne has been in line for several years to take a top Democratic spot on a subcommittee of the Education panel, but he has chosen to stick with the Africa Subcommittee, where he was the ranking minority member from 1999-2007 when the Republicans were in control. During the committee downsizing and consolidation of the 1990s, he fought successfully to maintain the Africa panel as a distinct entity.

Payne's behind-the-scenes influence reached a high point during the Clinton administration. He persuaded President Bill Clinton to travel to Africa and joined him on a 1998 visit. In 2000, he helped in the negotiations that led to enactment of a law expanding trade with sub-Saharan Africa.

As a Democrat, Payne has had less clout with the White House in recent years. But President Bush appointed him as a congressional delegate to the United Nations in 2003 and again in 2005.

Payne sees parallels between the U.S. civil rights movement and the African independence drive, both of which unfolded in the 1960s. He says Africa's problems continued after the colonial era because its nations were liberated politically but not economically. He says that in many U.S. cities, black mayors have won election but their cities have struggled because businesses were still owned by "the same people" as before.

One of the most liberal members, Payne in the 109th Congress (2005-06) opposed Bush more often than any other House member — 94 percent of the time. He is a defender of traditional Democratic priorities and has applied his concern for human rights abroad to problems closer to home, deploring police brutality, racial profiling and the burning of black churches.

From his seat on the Education Committee, Payne has fought to target federal funds to low-income school districts. He says it is time to "stop the apartheid we see in education — one side is black or Hispanic and poor, the other side is affluent and predominately white."

Payne is generally a low-key operator. "I would not call myself electrifying," he once said. "But I think there is a lot of dignity in being able to achieve things without having to create rapture."

Payne served a term as chairman of the Congressional Black Caucus starting in 1995, just as the GOP took control of the House and cut off congressional funding for such groups. He helped raise money privately to maintain caucus operations. He served from 2003-07 on the Democratic Steering Committee, which determines Democratic committee assignments.

Payne grew up poor in Newark during the Depression. His mother died when he was 7, and he went to live with his grandmother because his father worked long hours on the docks. He took his first job at age 9, delivering the Newark Star-Ledger, which he read along his route.

Payne credits much of his rise in life to an organization called The Leaguers, and to its founders, Reynold and Mary Burch, both leaders of Newark's black community. Burch used her contacts with Seton Hall University to help Payne win a four-year scholarship. Payne was the first president of The Leaguers, which is more than 50 years old and works to provide Newark inner-city teenagers with encouragement, education and work opportunities, and social outlets.

A high school history teacher and football coach after college, Payne also headed a "storefront YMCA" in Newark in the late 1950s and was the first black president of the National Council of YMCAs in 1970. He later served as chairman of the YMCA's International Committee on Refugees. He still serves on the board of the Newark YMCA.

In 1963, Payne moved into business as community affairs director for the Newark-based Prudential Insurance Co. Later, he was vice president of a computer forms company founded by his brother. At the same time, the widowed Payne was raising his three children and building his political career. He served six years as an Essex County freeholder, akin to a county councilman, and another six on the Newark Municipal Council.

It took him three tries to win election in the black-majority 10th District, where his path was blocked by legendary Democrat Peter W. Rodino Jr., who had held the seat since 1949. As chairman of the Judiciary Committee, Rodino led the 1974 impeachment proceedings against President Richard Nixon, but it was Rodino's steadfast advocacy of civil rights legislation that earned him the votes of the district's blacks.

In 1980 and 1986, Payne tried unsuccessfully to unseat Rodino, arguing that a black person could better represent the district. When Rodino decided to retire in 1988, party officials got behind Payne. He easily defeated city council colleague Ralph T. Grant Jr. in the primary, and his November victory was a formality in the overwhelmingly Democratic district. He became the first black representative from New Jersey and has won easily ever since.

KEY VOTES

2006

Yes Stop broadband companies from favoring select Internet traffic
No Affirm U.S. commitment to war in Iraq and reject setting a withdrawal date for troops
No Repeal requirement for bilingual ballots at the polls
No Permit U.S. sale of civilian nuclear technology to India
No Build a 700-mile fence on the U.S.-Mexico border to curb illegal crossings
No Permit warrantless wiretaps of suspected terrorists

2005

No Intervene in the life-support case of Terri Schiavo
Yes Lift President Bush's restrictions on stem cell research funding
Yes Prohibit FBI access to library and bookstore records
No Approve free-trade pact with five Central American countries
? Pass energy policy overhaul favored by President Bush emphasizing domestic oil and gas production
? End mandatory preservation of habitat of endangered animal and plant species
Yes Ban torture of prisoners in U.S. custody

CQ VOTE STUDIES

	PARTY UNITY		PRESIDENTIAL SUPPORT	
	Support	Oppose	Support	Oppose
2006	99%	1%	5%	95%
2005	99%	1%	7%	93%
2004	99%	1%	9%	91%
2003	98%	2%	20%	80%
2002	98%	2%	16%	84%

INTEREST GROUPS

	AFL-CIO	ADA	CCUS	ACU
2006	100%	85%	14%	4%
2005	100%	85%	29%	0%
2004	100%	95%	5%	0%
2003	100%	80%	25%	17%
2002	100%	90%	30%	0%

NEW JERSEY 10
Northeast – parts of Newark and Jersey City

Covering a multiracial, urban region centered in Newark, the black-majority 10th provides a solid base for Democrats. Outside Newark (which is shared with the 13th), the district extends into Essex County's working-class suburbs of Irvington, East Orange and Orange. It also takes in portions of Jersey City (shared with the 9th and 13th districts) and Elizabeth (shared with the 13th).

The 10th's portion of Newark is made up of the largely black central, south and west wards of the city. The central ward was decimated in the 1967 riots and has been slow to recover. Although deep poverty continues to be a problem in some spots, efforts to revitalize the area have had some success. The area is home to University Heights Science Park, a collaboration between three universities and start-up technology companies. The New Jersey Institute of Technology has completed an $83.5 million plan to make over its Newark campus to convince students to live on what has been regarded as a commuter campus. A performing arts center and new retail outlets in Essex County also are helping.

Newark Liberty International Airport (some of which is in the 13th) is a transportation center for travelers to New York City, as well as a hub for Continental Airlines. Newark Penn Station is the state's busiest transit location with connections to Amtrak, PATH and New Jersey Transit rail and Bus service. Port Newark-Elizabeth (partly in the 13th) also provides jobs for the region.

The district votes consistently Democratic at all levels, although Millburn, a wealthy enclave shared with the 11th, and Rahway include some Republicans. John Kerry posted his highest percentage in the state here in the 2004 presidential election, winning 81 percent of the district's vote.

MAJOR INDUSTRY

Aviation, shipping, insurance, higher education, pharmaceuticals

CITIES

Newark (pt.), 155,413; Elizabeth (pt.), 74,984; East Orange, 69,824; Jersey City (pt.), 63,725; Irvington (unincorporated), 60,695; Orange (unincorporated), 32,868; Linden (pt.), 30,356

NOTABLE

Economist Milton Friedman grew up in Rahway; The University of Medicine and Dentistry of New Jersey, headquartered in Newark, is the nation's largest public university of the health sciences.

Rep. Rodney Frelinghuysen (R)

CAPITOL OFFICE
225-5034
frelinghuysen.house.gov
2442 Rayburn 20515-3011; fax 225-3186

COMMITTEES
Appropriations

RESIDENCE
Harding

BORN
April 29, 1946, Manhattan, N.Y.

RELIGION
Episcopalian

FAMILY
Wife, Virginia T. Frelinghuysen; two children

EDUCATION
Hobart College, B.A. 1969; Trinity College (Conn.), attended 1971 (American history)

MILITARY SERVICE
Army, 1969-71

CAREER
County board aide

POLITICAL HIGHLIGHTS
Morris County Board of Freeholders, 1974-83 (director, 1980); sought Republican nomination for U.S. House, 1982; N.J. Assembly, 1983-94; sought Republican nomination for U.S. House, 1990

ELECTION RESULTS

2006 GENERAL		
Rodney Frelinghuysen (R)	126,085	71.6%
Tom Wyka (D)	47,414	26.9%
2006 PRIMARY		
Rodney Frelinghuysen (R)		unopposed
2004 GENERAL		
Rodney Frelinghuysen (R)	200,915	67.9%
James W. Buell (D)	91,811	31.0%

PREVIOUS WINNING PERCENTAGES
2002 (72%); 2000 (68%); 1998 (68%); 1996 (66%); 1994 (71%)

Elected 1994; 7th term

There's nothing flashy about Frelinghuysen, a wealthy New Jersey blueblood from a long line of public servants dating to the Revolutionary War. The sixth member of his family to serve in Congress, he seldom makes waves — or news, for that matter. But he gets his job done.

In 2002, Frelinghuysen (FREE-ling-high-zen) led the fight to preserve one of the oldest trees on the Capitol grounds, an English elm that was endangered by construction work on the underground Capitol Visitor Center. Some of his ancestors may well have enjoyed the shade of that ancient English elm: The first Frelinghuysen served in the Continental Congress; another was a senator and also secretary of State; one ran for vice president on a ticket with Henry Clay; and Frelinghuysen's father, Peter H. Frelinghuysen, served in the House for 22 years, until 1975.

Noting that he was 6 years old when his father first ran for Congress, Frelinghuysen observed in a newspaper interview, "A lot of what you do in life is the direct result of those who bring you up. It either drives you toward this life or drives you away."

One of 23 Republicans remaining in the House from the 73-member Class of '94, Frelinghuysen looks out for the interests of New Jersey in general and his district in particular as the state's lone Republican and most senior member on the Appropriations Committee. During the dozen years of GOP rule that ended in 2007, Frelinghuysen's position on the committee was crucial for his constituents and his state. Even now, it is a major asset.

Outside of the Appropriations panel, he picks his way carefully through the thicket of issues that divide the two parties. He splits with the GOP's conservative majority on environmental matters, civil rights and selected social issues. But he is a supporter of the Bush-era tax cuts, has backed the president's decisions on the Iraq War and has sided with Republican conservatives on immigration.

After inching patiently up the seniority ladder on the Appropriations Committee, Frelinghuysen finally laid claim to a subcommittee gavel at the start of the 108th Congress (2003-04). In the 109th Congress (2005-06), he saw it taken away. There was nothing personal about the grab-back. Frelinghuysen just suffered collateral damage from Majority Leader Tom DeLay insisting that the Appropriations Committee be restructured and its subcommittees reduced from 13 to 10. As the most junior of the subcommittee chairmen, Frelinghuysen was a loser in the scramble, along with two other "cardinals," as the panel leaders are called.

In the 110th Congress (2007-08), Democrats restructured the Appropriations Committee again. Frelinghuysen wound up as the top-ranking Republican on the Commerce-Justice-Science Subcommittee. He also serves on the Defense Subcommittee, and on the new Select Intelligence Oversight Panel within the Appropriations Committee.

Frelinghuysen is a moderate on environmental issues, backing land conservation efforts and anti-pollution regulations, positions that sit well with his upscale, suburban constituents. In the 109th Congress, he opposed opening Alaska's Arctic National Wildlife Refuge to oil drilling. He voted in 2005 against limiting the scope of the Endangered Species Act, and in 2006 was one of 25 House Republicans opposing a measure to make it easier for private landowners to challenge a state or local government's "taking" of their property. Critics said the bill went beyond eminent domain seizures and could jeopardize zoning and other land-use regulation.

While his voting record on abortion-related issues is mixed, Frelinghuysen often sides with Democrats on other social issues. In 2004 and 2006, he voted against a proposed constitutional amendment to outlaw same-sex marriage. In 2006, he was one of 44 Republicans voting to preserve a requirement for bilingual ballots in the landmark Voting Rights Act. And in 2007, when Democrats launched a new effort to pass a constitutional Equal Rights Amendment for women, Frelinghuysen was one of nine original GOP cosponsors.

Frelinghuysen has worked hard to preserve the Highlands, areas of mountainous and scenic watershed lands in northern New Jersey, New York, Pennsylvania and Connecticut. The federal purchase of lands in the Sterling Forest in 1996 was due to his efforts, and in the years that followed, Frelinghuysen has won additional funds to set aside more of the Highlands. In 2004, he won enactment of the Highlands Conservation Act authorizing federal funds for land conservation partnerships in the four-state region.

Frelinghuysen also continues to secure millions for the expansion of the Morristown National Historical Park and the Great Swamp Wildlife Refuge, cleanups of toxic waste at superfund sites, flood protection, wetlands purchases and protection of the state's 127 miles of shoreline.

He has pursued federal dollars for local mass transit projects, New York Harbor dredging and the Picatinny Arsenal, as well as changes in Veterans Affairs Department funding formulas to direct more health care spending to New Jersey. Since the Sept. 11 terrorist attacks, he has been at the forefront of steering federal money to New York and New Jersey.

Frelinghuysen began his political career after college and an Army stint in Vietnam, going to work for Dean Gallo, then a Morris County freeholder and later a member of the House. Frelinghuysen became a freeholder himself in 1974. In 1982, he lost a GOP primary for the 12th District seat, but in 1983 he won a state Assembly seat. In 1990, he failed again in a contest for the 12th District, running third in the Republican primary won by Dick Zimmer, who went on to serve three terms in the House.

When Frelinghuysen won election to the House in 1994, the victory was bittersweet because it followed the death of his friend and mentor Gallo. Ill health had forced Gallo in August of that year to abandon his campaign for a sixth term. Gallo anointed Frelinghuysen, who had been managing the re-election bid, as his successor. Frelinghuysen sailed to victory in the Republican-dominated district, but Gallo died two days before the November election. Frelinghuysen has easily won re-election since then.

KEY VOTES

2006

- No — Stop broadband companies from favoring select Internet traffic
- Yes — Affirm U.S. commitment to war in Iraq and reject setting a withdrawal date for troops
- No — Repeal requirement for bilingual ballots at the polls
- Yes — Permit U.S. sale of civilian nuclear technology to India
- Yes — Build a 700-mile fence on the U.S.-Mexico border to curb illegal crossings
- Yes — Permit warrantless wiretaps of suspected terrorists

2005

- ? — Intervene in the life-support case of Terri Schiavo
- Yes — Lift President Bush's restrictions on stem cell research funding
- No — Prohibit FBI access to library and bookstore records
- Yes — Approve free-trade pact with five Central American countries
- Yes — Pass energy policy overhaul favored by President Bush emphasizing domestic oil and gas production
- No — End mandatory preservation of habitat of endangered animal and plant species
- No — Ban torture of prisoners in U.S. custody

CQ VOTE STUDIES

	PARTY UNITY		PRESIDENTIAL SUPPORT	
	Support	Oppose	Support	Oppose
2006	87%	13%	83%	17%
2005	89%	11%	83%	17%
2004	88%	12%	79%	21%
2003	91%	9%	85%	15%
2002	84%	16%	85%	15%

INTEREST GROUPS

	AFL-CIO	ADA	CCUS	ACU
2006	29%	25%	80%	60%
2005	13%	15%	89%	60%
2004	20%	25%	100%	67%
2003	13%	10%	93%	64%
2002	11%	15%	95%	80%

NEW JERSEY 11

North central — Morris County

Exclusive, pastoral estates and Fortune 500 firms make the 11th one of the most privileged districts in the nation. Located in northern New Jersey and centered in Morris County, the district has the nation's second-highest median income. Residents here live mainly in small to midsize bedroom communities connected by a number of interstate highways and state routes. The district has experienced some population growth as couples and families move here to get away from large cities, and suburban sprawl has become a major issue.

While the 11th is loaded with commuters making trips to New York, it also is a hotbed for corporate activity. Time-Warner moved some jobs to Morris County in 2005, joining an already strong corporate presence in the district that includes giants like Nabisco (Kraft Foods) in East Hanover and Honeywell's headquarters in Morristown. Pharmaceutical companies have found the area attractive, with Pfizer, in Morris Plains, and Novartis, in East Hanover, basing major operations in the district and Wyeth headquartered in Madison. Attempts are under way to diversify the area's economy, which was hurt by corporate layoffs. Morris County officials hope to lure tourists to historic parks, dwellings and other sites.

In addition to all of Morris County, the district takes in chunks of Essex County in the east, Somerset County in the south, Sussex County in the northwest and a sliver of Passaic County in the northeast.

The area's voters have been economically conservative for some time, but the district now appears to be shifting to the right on social issues as well. The 11th is one of the most solidly Republican districts in the northeast, and George W. Bush captured 57 percent of the vote here in the 2004 presidential election, his highest total in New Jersey.

MAJOR INDUSTRY
Pharmaceuticals, finance, telecommunications, manufacturing

MILITARY BASES
Picatinny Arsenal (Army), 73 military, 3,000 civilian (2007)

CITIES
Morristown, 18,544; Dover, 18,188; Madison, 16,530

NOTABLE
Florham Park is expected to be the new home of the New York Jets football team's headquarters and training facility by mid-2008.

Rep. Rush D. Holt (D)

CAPITOL OFFICE
225-5801
holt.house.gov
1019 Longworth 20515-3012; fax 225-6025

COMMITTEES
Appropriations Select Intelligence Oversight Panel - chairman
Education & Labor
Natural Resources
Select Intelligence

RESIDENCE
Hopewell

BORN
Oct. 15, 1948, Weston, W.Va.

RELIGION
Quaker

FAMILY
Wife, Margaret Lancefield; three children

EDUCATION
Carleton College, B.A. 1970 (physics); New York U., M.S. 1980 (physics), Ph.D. 1981 (physics)

CAREER
University research assistant director; physics professor

POLITICAL HIGHLIGHTS
Sought Democratic nomination for U.S. House, 1996

ELECTION RESULTS

2006 GENERAL		
Rush D. Holt (D)	125,468	65.7%
Joseph S. Sinagra (R)	65,509	34.3%
2006 PRIMARY		
Rush D. Holt (D)		unopposed
2004 GENERAL		
Rush D. Holt (D)	171,691	59.3%
Bill Spadea (R)	115,014	39.7%

PREVIOUS WINNING PERCENTAGES
2002 (61%); 2000 (49%); 1998 (50%)

Elected 1998; 5th term

Brainy Holt is a physicist and five-time "Jeopardy" champion who gave out bumper stickers one election year that read, "My congressman *is* a rocket scientist." These days, he uses his smarts on the Intelligence Committee, as one of House Speaker Nancy Pelosi's hand-picked watchdogs for the nation's spy agencies.

Holt also has a strong interest in keeping Congress smart and has made it his quest to resurrect the former Office of Technology Assessment, a bipartisan office that used to analyze scientific research and compile reports for lawmakers. It was shuttered in the mid-1990s as part of GOP cost-cutting measures. Scientific American magazine named Holt one of its "50 visionaries" for his efforts to restore funding for the OTA.

In the 110th Congress (2007-08), Holt heads a new Appropriations subcommittee charged with overseeing spending on intelligence programs, which dovetails with his work on the regular House Intelligence Committee, where he's had a seat since 2003. Called the Select Intelligence Oversight Panel, its mission is to scrutinize the 16 intelligence agencies' budgets. Holt's new panel was established in response to a recommendation by the independent Sept. 11 commission, which studied problems in intelligence gathering before the attacks on New York and Washington.

Widely respected for his intellect, Holt is among the Intelligence Committee's most liberal members. In recent years, he has focused on the impact on civil liberties of the Bush administration's intelligence policies. Holt in 2006 criticized the National Security Agency's practice of conducting domestic wiretapping without first obtaining a warrant as "a presidential power grab." He later argued against a GOP bill to allow warrantless electronic surveillance, saying, "The president wants to turn a vacuum cleaner on the communications of innocent Americans, with no checks and balances, trampling the rights of many in the search for a few." Holt has also called for taping interviews with terrorism suspects, who are detained under less stringent rules than other criminal suspects.

Holt has complained about the intelligence community's lack of foreign language speakers in the field. A shortage of agents with foreign language skills is often cited as one of the biggest problems in U.S. intelligence gathering in an age of terrorist threats from abroad. Holt has pushed proposals to increase funds for universities to establish programs in critical languages such as Arabic, Farsi and Pashto and to provide scholarships to language students in exchange for federal service.

Another of Holt's priorities is election reform. He has pressed for legislation to upgrade the electronic voting machines introduced in many states after the hotly contested 2000 presidential election uncovered serious voting irregularities in Florida. Holt wants all of the new electronic machines to have the capability to produce backup paper records. "These new machines are vulnerable to massive fraud," he wrote in an op-ed article.

On the Education and Labor Committee, Holt's focus is promoting math and science education. He believes people have confused his understanding of science with intelligence, which, he says, points to a perception problem: "We have this strange attitude toward science, like you have to be a member of a special fraternity to understand science." In one of the rare instances that he agrees with President Bush, Holt supports the president's proposal to hold public schools accountable for science test scores in the same way they are held responsible for reading and math achievement under the No Child

Left Behind law enacted in 2002.

Holt says he developed his interest in science at an early age from his mother, who earned a master's degree in zoology and taught science at a junior college. He also learned politics at home. His mother was a West Virginia state legislator and secretary of state. His father, Rush Dew Holt, was elected to the U.S. Senate from West Virginia at age 29. He had to wait six months to take office because under the Constitution senators must be at least 30 years old. Holt's father died when Holt was in first grade, and he and his mother later moved to Washington, D.C., where he went to high school and she worked for the Department of Housing and Urban Development.

Holt eventually earned a Ph.D. in physics, doing his doctoral dissertation on the outer layer of the sun. He holds a patent for improving the efficiency of solar ponds, a source of thermal energy, though he says he has yet to earn "a dime" from it. "It didn't provide more than intellectual satisfaction, I'm sorry to say."

After school, he worked at the State Department on arms control and space activities, then became the assistant director of Princeton University's Plasma Physics Laboratory. While living in Princeton, N.J., he became interested in running for office. He told the Newark Star-Ledger that his motivation was a distaste for the "shortsightedness and mean-spiritedness of the Gingrich Congress."

Holt first ran for the House in 1996, losing in the Democratic primary to David N. Del Vecchio, who in turn lost a close race to Republican Michael Pappas. Two years later, Holt portrayed socially conservative Pappas as too far to the right for the district and won.

His 5,000-vote victory made Holt one of the GOP's most-targeted incumbents in 2000. His campaign against moderate Republican Dick Zimmer, who had held the House seat for three terms ending in 1996, was bitter, and the outcome was in doubt for three weeks after Election Day. Holt was eventually declared the victor by 651 votes.

The GOP kept the 12th District on its target list for 2002 and offered up an attractive candidate, DeForest "Buster" Soaries, an African-American Baptist minister who had served as New Jersey's secretary of state. Benefiting slightly from redistricting, Holt won with 61 percent of the vote. His subsequent victories have been by comfortable margins.

Holt is a five-time winner on the TV quiz show "Jeopardy" and is amused by the attention that it brings. Given the reaction he gets from journalists covering his campaigns, he says, "it must be the most significant thing I've done."

KEY VOTES

2006

Yes Stop broadband companies from favoring select Internet traffic
No Affirm U.S. commitment to war in Iraq and reject setting a withdrawal date for troops
No Repeal requirement for bilingual ballots at the polls
No Permit U.S. sale of civilian nuclear technology to India
No Build a 700-mile fence on the U.S.-Mexico border to curb illegal crossings
No Permit warrantless wiretaps of suspected terrorists

2005

No Intervene in the life-support case of Terri Schiavo
Yes Lift President Bush's restrictions on stem cell research funding
Yes Prohibit FBI access to library and bookstore records
No Approve free-trade pact with five Central American countries
No Pass energy policy overhaul favored by President Bush emphasizing domestic oil and gas production
No End mandatory preservation of habitat of endangered animal and plant species
Yes Ban torture of prisoners in U.S. custody

CQ VOTE STUDIES

	PARTY UNITY		PRESIDENTIAL SUPPORT	
	Support	Oppose	Support	Oppose
2006	97%	3%	15%	85%
2005	97%	3%	11%	89%
2004	98%	2%	26%	74%
2003	97%	3%	22%	78%
2002	94%	6%	30%	70%

INTEREST GROUPS

	AFL-CIO	ADA	CCUS	ACU
2006	100%	95%	20%	5%
2005	93%	100%	33%	0%
2004	93%	95%	19%	4%
2003	93%	95%	23%	8%
2002	100%	90%	40%	8%

NEW JERSEY 12

Central — part of Trenton, East Brunswick, Princeton

Set in the middle of the state, the 12th begins in Hunterdon County, slides south to hit ethnically diverse Trenton (shared with the 4th) and then picks up East Brunswick as it winds east to Monmouth County. It ends just short of the Atlantic Ocean in shore communities such as Rumson.

Despite its jagged shape, many of the district's towns are similar. Office parks dominate the landscape in these affluent and white communities. But there are pockets of blue-collar diversity, such as in the state capital, Trenton, with its black-majority population. Plainsboro in Middlesex County is among the areas with large Asian populations.

The 12th has benefited from economic growth, although midsize communities such as Ewing in Mercer County contend with the side effects of suburban sprawl. In addition to the Capitol, the district also boasts the governor's official residence, the stately and imposing Drumthwacket in Princeton. Delaware River towns, such as Frenchtown and Lambertville in Hunterdon County, offer quaint antiques shops and bed-and-breakfasts. The 2005 BRAC round dealt the 12th a blow, as Fort Monmouth made the closure list and must be shut down by late 2011.

Old money and suburban affluence made the area historically Republican, except for a small Democratic constituency anchored by Princeton's academic community. An influx of independents and the northeast's rising Democratic wave in national elections have shifted the district's politics, but it remains competitive. John Kerry took 54 percent of the 12th's vote in the 2004 presidential election, but George W. Bush did carry the district's portions of Hunterdon and Monmouth counties.

MAJOR INDUSTRY

Higher education, military, pharmaceuticals

MILITARY BASES

Fort Monmouth (Army), 467 military, 5,088 civilian (2007)

CITIES

Trenton (pt.), 47,658; East Brunswick (unincorporated), 46,756; North Brunswick (unincorporated), 36,287; Ewing (unincorporated), 35,707

NOTABLE

The New Jersey Vietnam Veterans' Memorial is on the grounds of the PNC Bank Arts Center, a 17,500-seat concert venue in Holmdel.

Rep. Albio Sires (D)

CAPITOL OFFICE
225-7919
www.house.gov/sires
1024 Longworth 20515-3013; fax 226-0792

COMMITTEES
Financial Services
Foreign Affairs

RESIDENCE
West New York

BORN
Jan. 26, 1951, Bejucal, Cuba

RELIGION
Roman Catholic

FAMILY
Wife, Adrienne Sires; one stepchild

EDUCATION
Saint Peter's College, B.A. 1974 (Spanish & marketing); Middlebury College, M.A. 1985 (Spanish)

CAREER
Property title insurance firm owner; state community affairs agency aide; teacher

POLITICAL HIGHLIGHTS
Candidate for West New York Town Commission, 1983; Republican nominee for U.S. House, 1986; Republican nominee for Hudson County Board of Chosen Freeholders, 1987; candidate for West New York Town Commission, 1991; candidate for West New York Town Commission (recall election), 1993; West New York Town Commission, 1995-2006 (mayor, 1995-2006); N.J. Assembly, 2000-06 (Speaker, 2002-06)

ELECTION RESULTS

2006 GENERAL		
Albio Sires (D)	77,238	77.5%
John J. Guarini (R)	19,284	19.4%
Brian Williams (SW)	1,049	1.1%
2006 PRIMARY		
Albio Sires (D)	24,661	72.2%
Joseph Vas (D)	9,486	27.8%
2006 SPECIAL		
Albio Sires (D)	75,403	96.7%
Dick Hester (PLC)	2,592	3.3%
2006 PRIMARY SPECIAL		
Albio Sires (D)	24,216	90.1%
James Geron (D)	2,647	9.9%

Elected 2006; 1st full term

In 1986, an ambitious young New Jersey Republican named Sires gambled on a long-shot bid for the House. The result was a trouncing at the hands of veteran Democratic Rep. Frank J. Guarini, but it was only the beginning of what turned out to be a bright political career for Sires. It culminated, 20 years later, with his election to the House — as a Democrat.

Sires (SEAR-eez — like "series"), a former high school Spanish teacher, has evolved from a Republican to an independent to a loyal member of the powerful Democratic machine in Hudson County.

Sires replaced Democrat Robert Menendez, who was tapped by newly elected Gov. Jon Corzine to fill his Senate seat starting in January 2006. Menendez's 13th District seat remained vacant until November 2006 when Sires won both the special election to serve out Menendez's unexpired term and the general election for a full term in his own right.

He was sworn into office Nov. 13, 2006, and joked that the two-month head start not only helped him "get a better office" but allowed him to begin work on major issues such as funding stem cell research and implementing recommendations by the panel that investigated the Sept. 11 terrorist attacks. Homeland security matters are of particular concern to the district, which lies across the Hudson River from Manhattan and includes port facilities, several bridges and two major tunnels into New York City.

Sires got the seat he sought on the Foreign Affairs Committee. The first bill he sponsored called for the Iraqi government to match funding provided by the United States for reconstruction. "This whole war in Iraq has just been a waste of manpower . . . a waste of money," he said in 2007.

Born in Bejucal, Cuba, Sires became New Jersey's first Hispanic House Speaker in 2002, and his congressional win to replace fellow Cuban-American Menendez continued the 13th District's Hispanic representation. Benefiting from his Hudson County ties, Sires posted a landslide victory in the 2006 Democratic primary against state Rep. Joseph Vas. That win in the Democratic stronghold sewed up his election in November against Republican John J. Guarini, a second cousin to Frank J. Guarini.

NEW JERSEY 13

Northeast — parts of Jersey City and Newark

Within sight of some of the nation's best-known landmarks, including the Statue of Liberty and Manhattan's skyscrapers, the 13th covers a long, thin swath from part of North Bergen to Perth Amboy along the Hudson River, Newark Bay and Arthur Kill. The 13th takes in parts of Jersey City and Newark, linking together Hispanic areas to create a Hispanic plurality (48 percent).

A transportation hub, the 13th includes parts of Port Newark-Elizabeth and Newark Liberty International Airport, both of which are shared with the 10th. Several lines carry commuters across the district, and PATH trains, ferries and tunnels bring passengers to and from New York. There is a sizable manufacturing sector in areas such as Kearny (shared with 9th) and Carteret.

Hoboken has seen gentrification, as young professionals and financial companies have moved across the river from Manhattan. Officials are hoping to turn long-suffering Jersey City, which is shared with the 9th and 10th districts, into "Wall Street West." In Harrison, a new 25,000-seat stadium for the region's soccer team, the Red Bulls, is expected by summer 2008 and is part of a billion-dollar redevelopment plan to build cafes, bars, apartments and parking.

Portuguese, Indian, Irish and Puerto Rican communities add to the district's diversity and its overwhelming Democratic vote. A Middle Eastern community is growing, and much of the Cuban population is based in West New York and Union City. John Kerry won 68 percent of the 13th's 2004 presidential vote.

MAJOR INDUSTRY
Transportation, health care, retail, finance

CITIES
Jersey City (pt.), 118,201; Newark (pt.), 118,133; Union City, 67,088

NOTABLE
Frank Sinatra was born in Hoboken.

NEW MEXICO

Gov. Bill Richardson (D)

First elected: 2002
Length of term: 4 years
Term expires: 1/11
Salary: $110,000
Phone: (505) 476-2200

Residence: Santa Fe
Born: Nov. 15, 1947; Pasadena, Calif.
Religion: Roman Catholic
Family: Wife, Barbara Richardson
Education: Tufts U., B.A. 1970 (political science & French), M.A. 1971 (international relations)
Career: International trade consultant; state party official; congressional aide
Political highlights: Democratic nominee for U.S. House, 1980; U.S. House, 1983-97; United Nations ambassador, 1997-98; Energy secretary, 1998-2001

Election results:

2006 GENERAL		
Bill Richardson (D)	384,806	68.8%
John Dendahl (R)	174,364	31.2%

Lt. Gov. Diane Denish (D)

First elected: 2002
Length of term: 4 years
Term expires: 1/11
Salary: $85,000
Phone: (505) 476-2250

LEGISLATURE

Legislature: 60 days January-March in odd-numbered years; 30 days January-February in even-numbered years

Senate: 42 members, 4-year terms
2007 ratios: 24 D, 18 R; 31 men, 11 women
Salary: $142/day per diem
Phone: (505) 986-4714

House: 70 members, 2-year terms
2007 ratios: 42 D, 28 R; 48 men, 22 women
Salary: $142/day per diem
Phone: (505) 986-4751

TERM LIMITS

Governor: 2 consecutive terms
Senate: No
House: No

URBAN STATISTICS

CITY	POPULATION
Albuquerque	448,607
Las Cruces	74,267
Santa Fe	62,203
Rio Rancho	51,765
Roswell	45,293

REGISTERED VOTERS

Democrat	49%
Republican	33%
Unaffiliated/others	18%

POPULATION

2006 population (est.)	1,954,599
2000 population	1,819,046
1990 population	1,515,069
Percent change (1990-2000)	+20.1%
Rank among states (2006)	36
Median age	34.6
Born in state	51.5%
Foreign born	8.2%
Violent crime rate	758/100,000
Poverty level	18.4%
Federal workers	28,772
Military	17,163

ELECTIONS

STATE ELECTION OFFICIAL
(505) 827-3620
DEMOCRATIC PARTY
(505) 830-3650
REPUBLICAN PARTY
(505) 298-3662

MISCELLANEOUS

Web: www.state.nm.us
Capital: Santa Fe

U.S. CONGRESS

Senate: 1 Democrat, 1 Republican
House: 2 Republicans, 1 Democrats

2000 Census Statistics by District

DIST.	2004 VOTE FOR PRESIDENT BUSH	KERRY	WHITE	BLACK	ASIAN	HISP	MEDIAN INCOME	WHITE COLLAR	BLUE COLLAR	SERVICE INDUSTRY	OVER 64	UNDER 18	COLLEGE EDUCATION	RURAL	SQ. MILES
1	48%	51%	49%	2%	2%	43%	$38,413	65%	19%	16%	11%	26%	30%	9%	4,717
2	58	41	44	2	1	47	$29,269	53	29	18	13	29	17	29	69,493
3	45	54	41	1	1	36	$35,058	60	23	17	11	29	24	37	47,146
STATE	50	49	45	2	1	42	$34,133	60	23	17	12	28	24	25	121,356
U.S.	50.7	48.3	69	12	4	13	$41,994	60	25	15	12	26	24	21	3,537,438

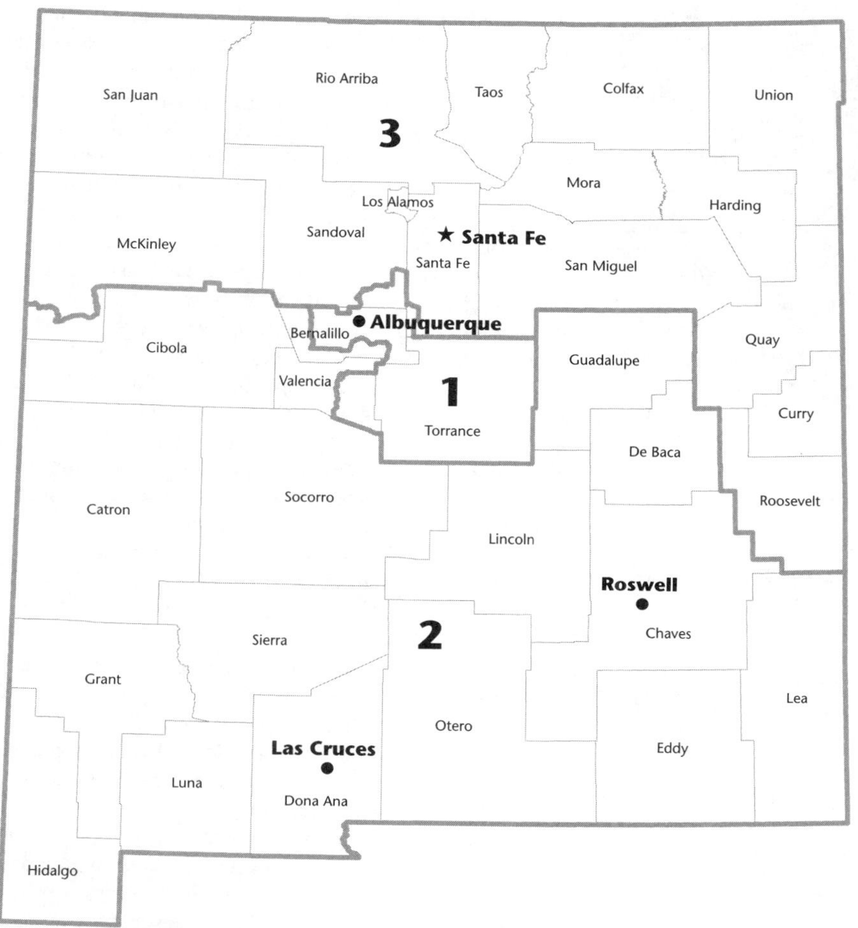
San Juan
Rio Arriba
Taos
Colfax
Union
3
Mora
Harding
Los Alamos
McKinley
Sandoval
★ Santa Fe
Santa Fe
San Miguel
Albuquerque
Bernalillo
Cibola
Quay
Guadalupe
Valencia
1
Torrance
Curry
De Baca
Catron
Socorro
Roosevelt
Lincoln
Roswell
Chaves
Sierra
2
Grant
Lea
Otero
Las Cruces
Eddy
Luna
Dona Ana
Hidalgo

Sen. Pete V. Domenici (R)

Elected 1972; 6th term

CAPITOL OFFICE
224-6621
domenici.senate.gov
328 Hart 20510-3101; fax 228-0900

COMMITTEES
Appropriations
Budget
Energy & Natural Resources - ranking member
Homeland Security & Governmental Affairs
Indian Affairs

RESIDENCE
Albuquerque

BORN
May 7, 1932, Albuquerque, N.M.

RELIGION
Roman Catholic

FAMILY
Wife, Nancy Domenici; eight children

EDUCATION
U. of Albuquerque, attended 1950-52;
U. of New Mexico, B.S. 1954 (education);
U. of Denver, LL.B. 1958

CAREER
Lawyer

POLITICAL HIGHLIGHTS
Albuquerque City Commission, 1966-70 (chairman and exofficio mayor, 1967-70);
Republican nominee for governor, 1970

ELECTION RESULTS

2002 GENERAL		
Pete V. Domenici (R)	314,193	65.0%
Gloria Tristani (D)	168,863	35.0%
2002 PRIMARY		
Pete V. Domenici (R)		unopposed

PREVIOUS WINNING PERCENTAGES
1996 (65%); 1990 (73%); 1984 (72%); 1978 (53%); 1972 (54%)

A member of one of the Senate's dwindling stable of proud old bulls, Domenici found himself in 2007 in an unfamiliar and uncomfortable position — as a central figure in a scandal that threatened to overshadow his distinguished career shaping budget and energy policy.

At issue was whether Domenici (doe-MEN-ih-chee) pressured David Iglesias, the Republican U.S. attorney for New Mexico, to investigate allegations of voter fraud among Democrats before the critical November 2006 elections and then played a role in Iglesias' departure. Iglesias was among a group of prosecutors fired in December, touching off a wave of allegations that the dismissals were politically motivated.

Iglesias said Domenici telephoned him at home to ask whether the politically charged voter fraud investigations would be done before the elections. When Iglesias told him no, he said the senator responded, "'I'm very sorry to hear that," and hung up — a move the prosecutor viewed as intimidation.

Domenici denied pressuring Iglesias, as did his colleague in the House, Republican Heather A. Wilson, a protégé of Domenici who also had contacted Iglesias. But the Senate Ethics Committee signaled in March 2007 the beginning of a preliminary inquiry into the senator's actions. The matter stunned colleagues on both sides of the aisle, who regard Domenici with tremendous affection, and raised questions about whether he would seek a seventh term. Aides and colleagues described Domenici as deeply embarrassed by the matter.

Prior to the scandal, Domenici had repeatedly told reporters he would run again in 2008, when he will be 76. "The thought of not being here and doing what I do as a senator is just as hard, if not harder" than running another election campaign, he said later.

Nevertheless, the years have begun to catch up with Domenici. He suffers from painful elbow and shoulder injuries and from chronic arthritis in his hip and back. He occasionally rides around in a motorized scooter and awkwardly shakes hands with his left hand.

Domenici's committee assignments reflect years of high regard and influence in the GOP. He is a former chairman of the Budget Committee and was its top-ranking Republican for 22 years. He has been the top Republican on the Energy and Natural Resources Committee since 2003. He also has the same role on the Energy and Water Subcommittee of the Appropriations Committee, giving him double clout on nuclear policy issues of vital importance to his state.

Domenici steers prodigious amounts of money to New Mexico, and he has taken special care of the Energy Department's Sandia and Los Alamos nuclear weapons laboratories. He is such an ardent protector of their funding that some employees refer to him as "St. Pete."

Domenici is the second-most-senior Republican in the Senate, trailing only Ted Stevens of Alaska. On Sept. 7, 2006, he joined an elite group of eight senators in all of U.S. history who had cast at least 13,000 roll call votes over their careers.

If Republicans regain control of the Senate in 2008, Domenici could wind up chairing the Appropriations Committee. Because of GOP term limits, Thad Cochran of Mississippi would have to relinquish the gavel then, and only Arlen Specter of Pennsylvania, also well into his 70s, would be ahead of Domenici in committee seniority.

Domenici, however, dismisses speculation about Appropriations as premature. For the 110th Congress (2007-08), his focus is on his duties on the Energy and Natural Resources panel, where as chairman in the 109th Congress (2005-06), he worked with home-state colleague Jeff Bingaman, then the panel's top-ranking Democrat and now chairman, to steer a long-stalled national energy overhaul to enactment in 2005. He still has a lengthy list of follow-up goals, including a big one that has eluded the GOP repeatedly: opening up Alaska's Arctic National Wildlife Refuge to oil and gas drilling.

Although the 2005 energy law was aimed mainly at encouraging greater supply over the coming decades, skyrocketing gas prices led to pressure on Congress to develop short-term fixes. Domenici obliged by cutting a deal in July 2006 on a bill that would rapidly expand Gulf Coast offshore oil and gas drilling by millions of acres while protecting Florida's beaches.

Domenici is an unflagging promoter of nuclear power. He argues that it has been unjustly labeled as unsafe and that it can help meet future energy demands in an economical manner that does not threaten health or the environment. "In the 21st century, nuclear power will be a major contributor to global peace and a better quality of life for both the developed and undeveloped world," he predicted in a 2004 book he wrote on the topic.

For all his clout on policy, Domenici has never been able to translate his stature into a GOP leadership post. Less of a conservative firebrand than others in his party, he was left behind as Senate Republicans moved to the right to pick their leaders. He watched his close ally Bob Dole of Kansas overtake him in a 1984 bid for majority leader and later lost two races for the chairmanship of the Republican Policy Committee, in 1990 and 2000.

Domenici can work with a broad spectrum of lawmakers. In years past, he teamed with conservative Phil Gramm, a Texas Republican, on Social Security legislation and worked with liberal Paul Wellstone, a Minnesota Democrat, on mental health issues. He has a daughter who suffers from schizophrenia, and her struggles caused him to lead a push to make health insurers treat mental illness like any other ailment. He intends to make such legislation a major goal in his remaining time as a senator.

Domenici first was thrust into the limelight on budget issues in the 1980s, when the GOP controlled the Senate and he served his first stint as Budget Committee chairman, leading the panel in its three-way battles with the Reagan administration and the Democratically controlled House. He was more interested in balancing the budget than in providing the fiscal stimulus sought by "supply side" conservatives. President Ronald Reagan's budget director, David A. Stockman, called him a "Hooverite."

During the Clinton administration, Domenici helped produce a 1997 deal to balance the budget by fiscal 2002. The sprawling pact offered tax cuts that had long been sought by Republicans plus limited new money for selected Democratic priorities such as health care for children.

One of five children, Domenici worked in his immigrant Italian father's wholesale grocery business as a youth, learning fiscal restraint. When Domenici was accepted to law school, his father agreed to finance his education but demanded to be repaid if his son brought home an "F."

Domenici was a good enough pitcher in college to receive a contract from a Brooklyn Dodgers farm team in 1954. But he gave up baseball after a season, taught math for a year and then went to law school.

After four years in Albuquerque city government in the late 1960s, he ran for governor in 1970, losing by 5 percentage points. Undeterred, Domenici sought the Senate seat being vacated by Democrat Clinton P. Anderson in 1972. He linked his Democratic foe, banker and former state Rep. Jack Daniels, to the unpopular presidential candidacy of George McGovern and won with 54 percent of the vote. He struggled to win re-election in 1978, but has had little trouble holding the seat since then.

KEY VOTES

2006

- Yes Confirm Samuel A. Alito Jr. to the Supreme Court
- Yes Allow consideration of a bill to establish a $140 billion trust fund to compensate victims of asbestos exposure
- Yes Extend tax cuts for two years at a cost of $70 billion over five years
- Yes Overhaul immigration policy with border security, enforcement and guest worker program
- Yes Allow consideration of a bill to permanently repeal the estate tax
- No Urge President Bush to begin troop withdrawals from Iraq in 2006
- No Lift President Bush's restrictions on stem cell research funding
- Yes Authorize military tribunals for suspected terrorists

2005

- Yes Curb class action lawsuits by shifting them from state to federal courts
- Yes Allow confirmation vote on Priscilla R. Owen to the U.S. Court of Appeals for the 5th Circuit
- No Oppose mandatory emissions limits and block recognition of global warming as a threat
- Yes Approve free-trade pact with five Central American countries
- Yes Pass energy policy overhaul favored by President Bush emphasizing domestic oil and gas production
- Yes Shield gunmakers from lawsuits when their products are used in crimes
- Yes Ban torture of prisoners in U.S. custody
- Yes Renew 16 provisions of the Patriot Act
- Yes Allow final vote on opening the Arctic National Wildlife Refuge to oil and gas exploration

CQ VOTE STUDIES

	PARTY UNITY		PRESIDENTIAL SUPPORT	
	Support	Oppose	Support	Oppose
2006	85%	15%	91%	9%
2005	93%	7%	89%	11%
2004	97%	3%	94%	6%
2003	96%	4%	97%	3%
2002	89%	11%	96%	4%
2001	89%	11%	96%	4%
2000	94%	6%	51%	49%
1999	93%	7%	33%	67%
1998	83%	17%	57%	43%
1997	85%	15%	67%	33%

INTEREST GROUPS

	AFL-CIO	ADA	CCUS	ACU
2006	20%	0%	100%	75%
2005	29%	15%	94%	91%
2004	17%	15%	100%	95%
2003	0%	5%	100%	85%
2002	25%	15%	100%	88%
2001	21%	10%	100%	90%
2000	0%	0%	100%	95%
1999	11%	5%	94%	88%
1998	13%	5%	100%	70%
1997	0%	25%	100%	60%

Sen. Jeff Bingaman (D)

CAPITOL OFFICE
224-5521
senator_bingaman@bingaman.senate.gov
bingaman.senate.gov
703 Hart 20510-3102; fax 224-2852

COMMITTEES
Energy & Natural Resources - chairman
Finance
(Energy, Natural Resources & Infrastructure - chairman)
Health, Education, Labor & Pensions
Joint Economic

RESIDENCE
Sante Fe

BORN
Oct. 3, 1943, El Paso, Texas

RELIGION
Methodist

FAMILY
Wife, Anne Bingaman; one child

EDUCATION
Harvard U., A.B. 1965 (government);
Stanford U., J.D. 1968

MILITARY SERVICE
Army Reserve, 1968-74

CAREER
Lawyer

POLITICAL HIGHLIGHTS
N.M. attorney general, 1979-83

ELECTION RESULTS

2006 GENERAL		
Jeff Bingaman (D)	394,365	70.6%
Allen W. McCulloch (R)	163,826	29.3%
2006 PRIMARY		
Jeff Bingaman (D)		unopposed

PREVIOUS WINNING PERCENTAGES
2000 (62%); 1994 (54%); 1988 (63%); 1982 (54%)

Elected 1982; 5th term

As chairman of the Energy and Natural Resources Committee, Bingaman is a good follow-up to his home-state colleague Pete V. Domenici, the panel's former chairman and now top-ranking Republican. The two have served together longer than any other Senate pair, and they share many goals on energy matters. The low-key Bingaman has always put the intricacies of policy above the fervor of politics; Domenici describes him as "agreeable and sensible."

Bingaman regularly defers to other lawmakers when it comes to taking credit for legislative accomplishments. He avoids the television talk-show circuit and seldom takes part in news conferences. One of his former press secretaries often joked that she had to "bribe" the senator with candy to motivate him to do media interviews. His tendency to let others grab the spotlight led one New Mexico political writer to label him as "Mr. Spock in a Senate of Captain Kirks," a reference to the "Star Trek" television show's cerebral, logical and ego-free character. Indeed, Bingaman is so self-effacing that the "About Jeff Bingaman" page of his Senate Web site includes just two paragraphs of biography. The rest of the page is given over to a civics tutorial on how the Senate and its committees operate.

The strong working relationship between Domenici and Bingaman was among the reasons Congress was able to pass a comprehensive energy bill in 2005, capping a three-year effort. In the 108th Congress (2003-04), Bingaman uncharacteristically rebuked Domenici, accusing him of shutting out Democrats from negotiations on the bill. When the 109th Congress began in 2005, Domenici worked more closely with Bingaman on the effort.

With Democrats now in control, Bingaman will be setting the priorities, not Domenici. He has argued for a greater emphasis on conservation, energy efficiency and renewable resources. And he will not continue the Republican push to open up Alaska's Arctic National Wildlife Refuge to oil drilling. In 2006, Bingaman and Domenici brokered a bill to allow offshore drilling in the Gulf Coast region, but when Domenici subsequently rewrote the bill to woo Florida's senators and other Gulf Coast lawmakers, Bingaman withdrew his support. He objected that the Senate-passed measure would bar drilling in hundreds of miles of area off the Florida coast — at a time when Cuba can drill within 50 miles of the state — and would give away too much revenue to Gulf states.

Bingaman, like most Democrats, wants the 110th Congress (2007-08) to tackle the controversial subject of global warming, saying it must become a leading national priority. He backs legislation to create a modified cap-and-trade system to limit greenhouse gas emissions, but he agreed in early 2007 that the Environment and Public Works Committee has lead jurisdiction on the issue. With liberal Barbara Boxer of California in charge of that panel, its bill could go further than his in mandating reductions of emissions thought to contribute to warming. But Bingaman will be waiting with floor amendments designed to garner broader support.

Bingaman is a pragmatist who concentrates his energies on what is achievable. He often writes amendments designed to win broad bipartisan support. In June 2006, he added language to a tax bill that would require the Treasury Department to regulate and monitor income tax preparers. He was able to get several education provisions into the huge catchall spending measure passed at the end of 2004, including funds for dropout prevention, Advanced Placement classes and a program that gives grants to large high schools that want to create "smaller learning communities" on their campuses.

From his seat on the Health, Education, Labor and Pensions Committee, Bingaman teamed with then Majority Leader Bill Frist to introduce legislation aimed at reducing obesity among children and adolescents. He added a provision to the 2004 child nutrition law that tripled funding for a program to promote healthful eating and physical activity in public schools. "We ought to be making a major push to support nutrition education in schools," he said.

When Democrats lost seats on committees in 2003 after Republicans regained control of the Senate, Bingaman was forced to give up his slot on the Armed Services Committee. His workmanlike devotion to detail on that panel had earned him comparisons with its venerated retired chairman, Democrat Sam Nunn of Georgia. Bingaman looked out for New Mexico's military bases and was a strong proponent of putting defense technologies to use in the private sector. That position is popular in New Mexico — home to two of the Energy Department's national laboratories, Sandia and Los Alamos, which have sought new missions since the end of the Cold War.

A member of the powerful Finance Committee, Bingaman has supported some Bush administration free-trade agreements that other Democrats assailed on grounds that they lacked adequate labor and environmental protections. He was one of just 10 Senate Democrats to support the 2005 Central American Free Trade Agreement, and also voted for legislation in 2002 giving the president fast-track trade negotiating authority.

Bingaman has taken on a variety of unglamorous but important assignments in the Senate. In the late 1990s he served on task forces studying Social Security, and the settlement between tobacco companies and the states. At the request of then Minority Leader Harry Reid, Bingaman helped lead a 2005 effort to ensure that ranking committee members worked together smoothly. And he sits on the Democratic Steering Committee, which helps make committee assignments.

Bingaman grew up in the mining town of Silver City, where his father was a science professor at Western New Mexico University and his mother taught elementary school. As a boy, he had a paper route and was active in the Boy Scouts, earning the rank of Eagle Scout. His uncle John Bingaman was a confidant of the state's 24-year Democratic senator, Clinton Anderson. While at Stanford University Law School, Bingaman worked for Democratic Sen. Robert F. Kennedy's 1968 presidential campaign. He also met a fellow law student, Anne Kovacovich, whom he married after graduation. Returning to New Mexico, he served as counsel to the 1969 state constitutional convention, joined a politically connected law firm and was elected attorney general in 1978. (Bingaman's wife served as assistant attorney general for antitrust law in the Clinton administration.)

When Bingaman ran for the Senate in 1982, he was little known outside the political and legal communities but politically unscarred. He won 54 percent of the vote to topple incumbent GOP Sen. Harrison H. Schmitt, a former Apollo astronaut, who appeared more interested in pet subjects such as 21st century technology than in the state's struggling economy.

Only one re-election race since has featured a serious challenger — Colin McMillan, a former Pentagon official who used much of his own money in 1994 to aggressively criticize Bingaman for his stance on fees for grazing on public lands and his support for President Bill Clinton's budget policy. But McMillan could not make sufficient inroads in Democratic counties, and Bingaman won with 54 percent. In 2006, he coasted to re-election with 71 percent of the vote.

KEY VOTES

2006

No Confirm Samuel A. Alito Jr. to the Supreme Court

No Allow consideration of a bill to establish a $140 billion trust fund to compensate victims of asbestos exposure

No Extend tax cuts for two years at a cost of $70 billion over five years

Yes Overhaul immigration policy with border security, enforcement and guest worker program

No Allow consideration of a bill to permanently repeal the estate tax

Yes Urge President Bush to begin troop withdrawals from Iraq in 2006

Yes Lift President Bush's restrictions on stem cell research funding

No Authorize military tribunals for suspected terrorists

2005

Yes Curb class action lawsuits by shifting them from state to federal courts

Yes Allow confirmation vote on Priscilla R. Owen to the U.S. Court of Appeals for the 5th Circuit

No Oppose mandatory emissions limits and block recognition of global warming as a threat

Yes Approve free-trade pact with five Central American countries

Yes Pass energy policy overhaul favored by President Bush emphasizing domestic oil and gas production

No Shield gunmakers from lawsuits when their products are used in crimes

Yes Ban torture of prisoners in U.S. custody

No Renew 16 provisions of the Patriot Act

No Allow final vote on opening the Arctic National Wildlife Refuge to oil and gas exploration

CQ VOTE STUDIES

	PARTY UNITY		PRESIDENTIAL SUPPORT	
	Support	Oppose	Support	Oppose
2006	94%	6%	51%	49%
2005	85%	15%	43%	57%
2004	90%	10%	64%	36%
2003	91%	9%	50%	50%
2002	78%	22%	79%	21%
2001	91%	9%	68%	32%
2000	87%	13%	95%	5%
1999	88%	12%	84%	16%
1998	87%	13%	87%	13%
1997	88%	12%	92%	8%

INTEREST GROUPS

	AFL-CIO	ADA	CCUS	ACU
2006	93%	100%	36%	8%
2005	86%	95%	72%	13%
2004	92%	90%	71%	12%
2003	85%	95%	48%	10%
2002	92%	90%	60%	17%
2001	100%	90%	50%	29%
2000	75%	85%	64%	16%
1999	78%	100%	59%	4%
1998	75%	85%	56%	0%
1997	57%	90%	60%	0%

Rep. Heather A. Wilson (R)

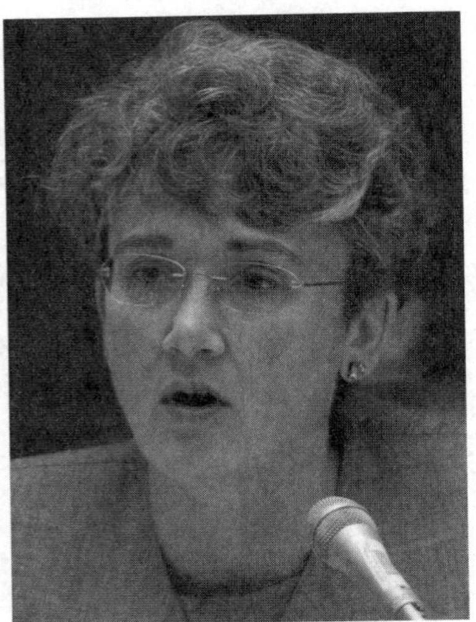

CAPITOL OFFICE
225-6316
wilson.house.gov
442 Cannon 20515-3101; fax 225-4975

COMMITTEES
Energy & Commerce
Select Intelligence

RESIDENCE
Albuquerque

BORN
Dec. 30, 1960, Keene, N.H.

RELIGION
Methodist

FAMILY
Husband, Jay Hone; three children

EDUCATION
U.S. Air Force Academy, B.S. 1982 (international politics); Oxford U., M.Phil. 1984 (Rhodes scholar), D.Phil. 1985 (international relations)

MILITARY SERVICE
Air Force, 1978-89

CAREER
Management consultant; National Security Council staff member

POLITICAL HIGHLIGHTS
N.M. Children, Youth and Families secretary, 1995-98

ELECTION RESULTS

2006 GENERAL		
Heather A. Wilson (R)	105,986	50.2%
Patricia Madrid (D)	105,125	49.8%
2006 PRIMARY		
Heather A. Wilson (R)		unopposed
2004 GENERAL		
Heather A. Wilson (R)	147,372	54.4%
Richard Romero (D)	123,339	45.5%

PREVIOUS WINNING PERCENTAGES
2002 (55%); 2000 (50%); 1998 (48%); 1998 Special Election (45%)

Elected June 1998; 5th full term

Wilson's political future looked promising. She had continually fended off Democratic election challenges in her left-leaning district. She was seen as a potential successor to Republican Sen. Pete V. Domenici, her political mentor. The House passed several major bills on which she served as chief sponsor, and she was one of the most prominent Republican women on national security matters.

But in early 2007, Wilson found herself in a scandal that threw her career into uncertainty. She and Domenici faced allegations that they tried to strong-arm the Republican U.S. attorney for New Mexico, David Iglesias, in an effort to boost Wilson's chances in her tough 2006 re-election battle. Both Domenici and Wilson acknowledged contacting Iglesias before the election to ask about the status of investigations of corruption involving Democrats. Iglesias subsequently testified to Congress that he believed both lawmakers were seeking to apply pressure on him to return indictments, though neither had said anything so explicit. He was later fired, and said he believed the two lawmakers were behind it.

Wilson, along with Domenici, denied pressuring Iglesias, saying her intent was to relay complaints that the prosecutor was intentionally delaying corruption prosecutions. But she became the target of a watchdog group, Citizens for Responsibility and Ethics in Washington, which called for a House ethics committee investigation. The group argued that Wilson might have violated House rules governing members' communications with executive branch officials and independent agencies.

A former Air Force officer who is the only female military veteran currently serving in Congress, Wilson is ordinarily a reliable ally of the White House and the GOP leadership. But in her own quiet way, she has demonstrated she will buck them both when her own convictions or the interests of her district conflict with the party line.

One area in which Wilson appeared to distance herself from President Bush in the 109th Congress (2005-06) was the administration's use of wiretaps without warrants to gather information on terrorist activity. She was the first Republican to raise concerns about it publicly, and she sponsored the leading House bill on the matter. Her measure would have required greater congressional notification about surveillance programs.

The bill never made it to the president's desk because the Senate never voted on legislation regarding the program. Democrats were critical of the Wilson proposal, claiming it was a sop to Bush. Privately, they alleged it had been shoved to the front of the agenda to benefit Wilson and make her appear independent of the president.

Wilson had legislative successes in other areas, including a bill she sponsored making oil and gasoline price gouging a federal crime. The House passed it in May 2006 amid soaring gas prices. A month later, the Judiciary Committee approved another of her bills to create a claims process for veterans affected by the theft of personal data from a laptop computer. The bill was in response to reports that a laptop stolen from a Veterans Affairs Department employee contained information on an estimated 26.5 million veterans.

Despite her legislative victories, Wilson still had problems with her leadership. She said the House Republican leadership revoked her waiver to serve on both the Energy and Commerce and Armed Services panels in the 109th Congress, removing her from the latter because, as she told the Albuquerque Tribune, Speaker J. Dennis Hastert "told me I was too independent."

She said she has always regarded herself as an iconoclast who makes up her own mind. "Nobody's ever been able to tell me what to do," she said.

Wilson serves on the Intelligence Committee, where she is the top-ranking Republican on the Technical and Tactical Intelligence Subcommittee. She has both defended and criticized Bush on the Iraq War. She opposed his troop increase plan in early 2007, saying the Iraqis "have to stand up and take the lead with respect to sectarian violence." Yet she refused to vote for a House resolution condemning the president's plan.

Wilson was a high school junior in New Hampshire when the Air Force Academy opened its doors to women, and she decided she wanted to be a pilot, like her father and grandfather. She graduated from the academy in 1982, the third class that included women. But she never got a pilot's license; instead, she went to Oxford as a Rhodes scholar. There, she earned master's and doctoral degrees in international relations.

After serving in the Air Force in Europe, Wilson took a job in 1989 with the National Security Council under President George H.W. Bush. In 1991, she married and moved to New Mexico. She started a consulting firm and joined GOP Gov. Gary E. Johnson's Cabinet in 1995.

She resigned that post early in 1998 to run for the House when Republican Steven H. Schiff, who had skin cancer, said he would retire. When Schiff died in March, Wilson became the GOP nominee for the special election to finish his term. She prevailed by 5 percentage points against multimillionaire businessman and Democratic state Sen. Phillip J. Maloof. She won election to a full term by 7 percentage points.

In 2002, in territory that retained its Democratic lean after redistricting, Wilson won by 11 points over state Sen. Richard Romero. She bested him again in their 2004 rematch, this time by 9 percentage points.

In 2006, Wilson drew her strongest opponent in New Mexico Attorney General Patricia Madrid, and their race became one of the most hostile — and closest — in the national campaign for control of the House. Madrid sought to capitalize on anti-GOP sentiment by arguing that Wilson was too beholden to Bush. Madrid also tried to link Wilson to the late-breaking scandal concerning Florida GOP Rep. Mark Foley, who resigned after revelations that he had written sexually suggestive e-mails to underage House pages. Wilson was a member of the House Page Board from 2001 to 2004.

But Wilson questioned Madrid's performance as attorney general amid allegations of corruption by two former state treasurers. Wilson's long-standing efforts on district issues, including its defense-oriented industries, helped her pull out a win by just 861 votes, the fourth-closest House election.

KEY VOTES

2006

Yes Stop broadband companies from favoring select Internet traffic
? Affirm U.S. commitment to war in Iraq and reject setting a withdrawal date for troops
No Repeal requirement for bilingual ballots at the polls
Yes Permit U.S. sale of civilian nuclear technology to India
Yes Build a 700-mile fence on the U.S.-Mexico border to curb illegal crossings
Yes Permit warrantless wiretaps of suspected terrorists

2005

? Intervene in the life-support case of Terri Schiavo
Yes Lift President Bush's restrictions on stem cell research funding
No Prohibit FBI access to library and bookstore records
Yes Approve free-trade pact with five Central American countries
Yes Pass energy policy overhaul favored by President Bush emphasizing domestic oil and gas production
Yes End mandatory preservation of habitat of endangered animal and plant species
Yes Ban torture of prisoners in U.S. custody

CQ VOTE STUDIES

	PARTY UNITY		PRESIDENTIAL SUPPORT	
	Support	Oppose	Support	Oppose
2006	83%	17%	87%	13%
2005	82%	18%	70%	30%
2004	79%	21%	88%	12%
2003	91%	9%	89%	11%
2002	90%	10%	90%	10%

INTEREST GROUPS

	AFL-CIO	ADA	CCUS	ACU
2006	50%	25%	93%	67%
2005	46%	25%	96%	75%
2004	33%	25%	95%	84%
2003	13%	20%	93%	72%
2002	11%	5%	100%	84%

NEW MEXICO 1

Central — Albuquerque

Built around Albuquerque, the 1st is the only urban district in a sparsely populated, desert state. Since the Manhattan Project set the region on a technology-driven course in the 1940s, Albuquerque has grown from 35,000 people before WWII to more than 440,000 in 2000. Albuquerque continues to be the driving force behind New Mexico's growth.

Sandia National Laboratories is the basis for a steady defense industry, and its success has contributed to a surge in computer, laser and other technology firms in the area, including Emcore and nearby Intel (located in the 3rd). Sandia, which employs 8,600 people, coordinates with two other major employers in the district, the University of New Mexico and the Air Force Research Laboratory at Kirtland Air Force Base, to conduct energy and defense research. The technology industry draws high numbers of PhDs to Albuquerque.

New Mexico has made strong investments in clean, renewable and alternative energy research. A 2004 law, revised in 2007, requires utility companies to invest in alternative energy, and some local companies, such as Albuquerque-based Advent Solar, are taking advantage.

Democrats hold most local offices, but Republicans are competitive at all levels. The GOP has held the U.S. House seat since its creation in 1968, with the area traditionally sending fiscally conservative, defense-oriented moderate Republicans to Congress. Much of the GOP vote comes from the mainly white, upper-middle-class Northeast Heights section of Albuquerque, but the large government workforce and predominately Hispanic South Valley provide Democrats with an overall edge in voter registration.

MAJOR INDUSTRY

Higher education, scientific research, defense, government

MILITARY BASES

Kirtland Air Force Base, 5,200 military, 17,800 civilian (2006)

CITIES

Albuquerque (pt.), 442,365; South Valley (unincorporated), 39,060; North Valley (unincorporated), 11,923

NOTABLE

Albuquerque's annual International Balloon Fiesta is the world's largest hot air balloon event; The National Atomic Museum, soon to become the National Museum of Nuclear Science and History, is in Albuquerque.

Rep. Steve Pearce (R)

CAPITOL OFFICE
225-2365
pearce.house.gov
1607 Longworth 20515-3102; fax 225-9599

COMMITTEES
Financial Services
Natural Resources

RESIDENCE
Hobbs

BORN
Aug. 24, 1947, Lamesa, Texas

RELIGION
Baptist

FAMILY
Wife, Cynthia Pearce; one child

EDUCATION
New Mexico State U., B.B.A. 1970 (economics); Eastern New Mexico U., M.B.A. 1991

MILITARY SERVICE
Air Force, 1971-76

CAREER
Oil well services company owner; corporate pilot

POLITICAL HIGHLIGHTS
N.M. House, 1997-2001; sought Republican nomination for U.S. Senate, 2000

ELECTION RESULTS

2006 GENERAL		
Steve Pearce (R)	92,620	59.4%
Albert D. Kissling (D)	63,119	40.5%
2006 PRIMARY		
Steve Pearce (R)		unopposed
2004 GENERAL		
Steve Pearce (R)	130,498	60.2%
Gary King (D)	86,292	39.8%

PREVIOUS WINNING PERCENTAGES
2002 (56%)

Elected 2002; 3rd term

The bad news for two of Pearce's New Mexico colleagues may prove to be good news for him. When Republican Sen. Pete V. Domenici and his protégé, 1st District Rep. Heather A. Wilson, became enmeshed in a 2007 scandal over whether they played a role in the firing of U.S. Attorney David Iglesias, Pearce quickly made it clear he had never contacted Iglesias over his investigation of Democratic voting irregularities. The scandal may well hurt Wilson's quest to move to the Senate, and Pearce could reap the benefits.

Pearce has been a faithful party regular, and state Republican leaders may look to him to run for statewide office. It has also been Pearce's good fortune that his rural district abuts the West Texas oil-patch area where President Bush got his political start. Pearce's loyalty to Bush and his agenda helped him win his seat in 2002 and keep it since then. In the 109th Congress (2005-06), he supported Bush's position 92 percent of the time and voted with his party 97 percent of the time on votes that pitted most Republicans against most Democrats.

A self-described "very conservative" politician, Pearce has been a strong supporter of Bush's economic program and his pre-emptive action against Iraq. Once an oil well parts business owner, he believes public lands should be open to more oil and gas exploration along with other commercial uses.

Pearce spends much of his time attending to constituent needs in the sprawling district, something that has boosted his re-election efforts. He also frequently deals with public lands issues from his seat on the Natural Resources Committee. In the 109th Congress, then committee Chairman Richard W. Pombo, another Western conservative, appointed Pearce head of the Subcommittee on National Parks, vaulting him over other more senior Republicans. Pearce had the panel examine whether too much emphasis was placed on preserving parks at the expense of recreation. "Too often," he said in December 2005, "parks have been managed as if a snapshot had been taken and nothing should change."

Pearce also introduced controversial legislation aimed at resolving disputes over road rights of way, often a heated topic in rural areas with a large federal presence. His bill would have enabled states and counties to claim ownership of roads across federal land that existed before 1986 and give them authority without seeking approval of federal agencies or the military. Critics said the bill would impose a standard so low that it could open public lands to virtually any type of use.

After Democrats won control of the House in the 2006 elections, Pearce left the top spot on the parks panel and became ranking Republican on the Energy and Mineral Resources Subcommittee.

Pearce can differ from many in his party on immigration. As a border-state congressman, he disagrees with lawmakers seeking to cut the flow of immigrants from Mexico and other nations. "I've got good conservative friends of mine who say we should lock the borders down and that we should stop all immigration," he said in early 2005. "My response to them is, 'You don't understand that we don't have enough workers.' " Still, Pearce believes that securing the border is the first step toward comprehensive immigration reform. He has called for adding border guards as well as putting money into advanced surveillance technologies. He voted in 2006 in favor of building a fence along the U.S.-Mexico border, despite doubts about such a barrier's effectiveness in his district.

Pearce would like to serve eventually on the Appropriations Committee, where his GOP predecessor, Joe Skeen, was able to steer millions of federal dollars for farming, ranching and energy projects to the district each year. But with the Democratic takeover, Pearce had to abandon that goal as well as give up his seat on the Homeland Security Committee. He continues to serve on the Financial Services Committee.

In November 2006, Pearce challenged Texas Rep. Kay Granger for the vice chairmanship of the GOP conference, the fourth-ranking position in the leadership. He said in a letter to colleagues that the elections had demonstrated that the public voted against Republicans rather than for Democrats and that his party "talked too much about things in the wrong way." Despite such efforts, Granger defeated him easily, 124-63.

Pearce shares with many in his party his conservative views on social issues. He opposes more gun control and expanded abortion rights, and he wants to amend the Constitution to prohibit same-sex marriage. He says he rises at 4:30 a.m. daily to read the Bible.

Pearce jumped into the 2nd District race after Skeen's failing health led to his retirement in 2002. Although conservative-leaning, the district has a large Hispanic population that helps yield a Democratic voter registration edge. And the socially conservative views of the Democratic nominee, state Sen. John Arthur Smith, gave the party hope that he might have crossover appeal. But Pearce had a money advantage and help from the Bush administration, and he won by 12 percentage points.

In 2004, Pearce squared off against an even better-known Democrat — Gary King, a businessman, lawyer and state legislator for 12 years who had deep New Mexico political roots. His father, Bruce King, was the longest-serving governor in state history. The year before the election, King moved into a rented house in Carlsbad, and began putting what he said was more than 100,000 miles on his car traveling around the vast 69,493-square-mile district, which includes part of 18 New Mexico counties. He campaigned on improving health care and the economy.

Pearce sought to portray King as a carpetbagger and — taking a well-worn page from the GOP campaign playbook — a tax-and-spend liberal. King was unable to gain much traction in a swing state that the Bush campaign desperately sought to add to the presidential victory column after barely losing it in 2000. With Bush and Vice President Dick Cheney making numerous campaign stops in New Mexico, Pearce won with 60 percent.

In 2006, he drew a far less politically seasoned opponent in Democrat Albert D. Kissling, a minister and activist for affordable housing. He again won easily, with 59 percent of the vote.

KEY VOTES

2006

- No Stop broadband companies from favoring select Internet traffic
- Yes Affirm U.S. commitment to war in Iraq and reject setting a withdrawal date for troops
- No Repeal requirement for bilingual ballots at the polls
- Yes Permit U.S. sale of civilian nuclear technology to India
- Yes Build a 700-mile fence on the U.S.-Mexico border to curb illegal crossings
- Yes Permit warrantless wiretaps of suspected terrorists

2005

- Yes Intervene in the life-support case of Terri Schiavo
- No Lift President Bush's restrictions on stem cell research funding
- No Prohibit FBI access to library and bookstore records
- Yes Approve free-trade pact with five Central American countries
- Yes Pass energy policy overhaul favored by President Bush emphasizing domestic oil and gas production
- Yes End mandatory preservation of habitat of endangered animal and plant species
- No Ban torture of prisoners in U.S. custody

CQ VOTE STUDIES

	PARTY UNITY		PRESIDENTIAL SUPPORT	
	Support	Oppose	Support	Oppose
2006	98%	2%	97%	3%
2005	96%	4%	87%	13%
2004	94%	6%	91%	9%
2003	98%	2%	98%	2%

INTEREST GROUPS

	AFL-CIO	ADA	CCUS	ACU
2006	14%	5%	100%	92%
2005	27%	0%	96%	96%
2004	13%	0%	95%	96%
2003	0%	5%	97%	88%

NEW MEXICO 2
South – Las Cruces, Roswell, Little Texas

Before hosting the first atomic bomb explosion in 1945, the mostly rural 2nd, covering the southern half of the state, looked like the old American West. Since then, the area has attracted nuclear research and waste facilities to the Chihuahua Desert's deep salt beds and remote location.

Towns in the 2nd have built a stable economy on traditional Western industries: copper and lead mining in the Mexican Highlands along the Arizona border; and oil and gas, as well as cattle and sheep ranching, in the southeastern corner of the state, dubbed Little Texas after the Texans who settled the region in the early 20th century. Severe water shortages prevent large-scale industrial development and larger corporate farming, although the northern part of the 2nd is a major producer of pistachios. New Mexico's strong military presence is evident in the 2nd, home of Holloman Air Force Base and White Sands Missile Range.

New Mexico State University, based in Las Cruces and known for its agricultural research, is increasing its role in the technology industry. The university uses a 64,000-acre section of its ranch as a proving ground for new border security technologies developed by government contractors.

Democrats hold the vast majority of local offices, but the 2nd leans to the GOP at the federal level. Republicans have made gains with Hispanic residents here, who make up 47 percent of the population, especially with the many Hispanics who trace their local ancestry back several generations. In the 2004 presidential election, the 2nd was the state's only district won by George W. Bush, who captured 58 percent here.

MAJOR INDUSTRY
Agriculture, mining, oil and gas production, defense

MILITARY BASES
Holloman Air Force Base, 4,148 military, 21,966 civilian (2005); White Sands Missile Range, 434 military, 6,158 civilian (2006)

CITIES
Las Cruces, 74,267; Roswell, 45,293; Alamogordo, 35,582; Hobbs, 28,657; Carlsbad, 25,625

NOTABLE
White Sands National Monument is the world's largest gypsum dune field; Roswell hosts an annual UFO festival near the site where a UFO allegedly crashed in 1947.

Rep. Tom Udall (D)

CAPITOL OFFICE
225-6190
www.tomudall.house.gov
1410 Longworth 20515-3103; fax 226-1331

COMMITTEES
Appropriations

RESIDENCE
Santa Fe

BORN
May 18, 1948, Tuscon, Ariz.

RELIGION
Mormon

FAMILY
Wife, Jill Z. Cooper; one stepchild

EDUCATION
Prescott College, B.A. 1970 (government & political science); Cambridge U., B.L.L. 1975; U. of New Mexico, J.D. 1977

CAREER
Lawyer

POLITICAL HIGHLIGHTS
Assistant U.S. attorney, 1978-81; sought Democratic nomination for U.S. House, 1982; Democratic nominee for U.S. House, 1988; N.M. attorney general, 1991-99

ELECTION RESULTS

2006 GENERAL		
Tom Udall (D)	144,880	74.6%
Ronald L. Dolin (R)	49,219	25.4%
2006 PRIMARY		
Tom Udall (D)		unopposed
2004 GENERAL		
Tom Udall (D)	175,269	68.7%
Gregory M. Tucker (R)	79,935	31.3%

PREVIOUS WINNING PERCENTAGES
2002 (100%); 2000 (67%); 1998 (53%)

Elected 1998; 5th term

Udall has a political bloodline beyond almost that of any lawmaker whose last name isn't Kennedy. His father was a congressman and secretary of Interior; his uncle was a congressman and a candidate for president; and his cousin is a congressman from Colorado. With the Democrats' ascension to the majority and his appointment to a key committee post in the 110th Congress (2007-08), Udall has the chance to distinguish himself and build on his family's notable legacy.

Udall and his cousin, Democrat Mark Udall, were elected to the House on the same day in 1998, bringing to Congress a second generation of the Udall family. Tom's father, Stewart L. Udall, represented Arizona in the House in the late 1950s before serving as secretary of Interior in the Kennedy and Johnson administrations. Tom's uncle, Morris K. Udall, succeeded his brother, Stewart, in the House in 1961 and was a prominent force there for the next 30 years, well-known for his advocacy of environmental protection. He is perhaps best remembered for his 1976 presidential bid as a liberal alternative to Georgia Gov. Jimmy Carter. "From the time I was 6, I heard my father and uncle talk about public service," Tom recalls.

In the 110th Congress, Udall won a coveted slot on the Appropriations Committee, after toiling for eight years in the minority in mostly low-key fashion on the Resources, Veterans' Affairs and Small Business committees. He is expected to use the post to try to generously fund technologies that promote alternative energy sources such as solar and wind. He and Republican Sen. Pete V. Domenici, also of New Mexico, hope to steer energy-related work to Los Alamos National Laboratory, which sits in Udall's district and has sought to expand its mission beyond developing nuclear weapons.

Like many progressive Democrats, Udall is eager to focus attention on energy and environmental issues, especially through a comprehensive energy policy that puts global warming front and center. He also would like to do more to address the production declines in relatively inexpensive and easy-to-obtain petroleum; he founded the Congressional Peak Oil Caucus with Maryland Republican Rep. Roscoe G. Bartlett.

Despite his solidly liberal voting record, Udall points to his alliance with Bartlett, a conservative on most issues, as evidence of his interest in working in concert with Republicans. "If you look at the history of bold environmental legislation, it's taken significant bipartisanship to take those actions," Udall says. He introduced global warming legislation in March 2006, but spent years before that seeking a GOP cosponsor until Wisconsin Republican Tom Petri signed on.

Udall's biggest bipartisan victory was persuading the Republican-controlled Congress late in 2006 to pass a bill to protect the environmentally fragile Valle Vidal in his state's northeast region — known to its admirers as "the Yellowstone of New Mexico" — from energy and mineral development. Environmentalists argued that the area's natural beauty and pristine land could be lost forever if drilling were allowed. Udall also won passage of a measure that would help American Indian veterans be buried in veterans' cemeteries on tribal land. In 2007, the House passed his bill aimed at combating methamphetamine abuse by American Indians.

Affable and well-liked among his colleagues, Udall has been a longtime ally of House Speaker Nancy Pelosi. At the start of the 108th Congress (2003-04), he was elected by regional colleagues to the Steering and Policy Committee, which makes Democratic committee assignments.

Udall, who speaks Spanish, takes pains to stay in touch with his constituents, who range from the nuclear scientists at Los Alamos National Laboratory and wealthy liberals in Santa Fe to rural Hispanics and American Indians living in areas where unemployment remains fixed at more than 40 percent. He maintains six offices across his sprawling district, which encompasses northern New Mexico and is roughly the size of Pennsylvania. "I believe very much in access," he says.

Udall was born in Tucson, Ariz., the state where the Udall clan is centered. After earning degrees from both Prescott College and Cambridge University in England, he entered law school at the University of New Mexico, graduating in 1977. After that, he stayed on in the state as an appeals court law clerk. He then worked as an assistant U.S. attorney and chief counsel to the state Department of Health and Environment before going into private practice.

He also worked with his father in behalf of two groups of radiation victims: Navajo Indians who had been exposed while mining uranium for use in weapons work and southern Utah residents living downwind of bomb fallout from the Nevada Test Site. Before health researchers documented excessive cancer levels among those Utahns, the federal government had dismissed their claims. Udall said the experience underscored the importance of having government officials engage and listen to the public: "I saw that [the agencies involved] had a penchant for secrecy, saying, 'Because we're the ones who know the most about it, we know what's best.'"

During this period, Udall ran for Congress twice unsuccessfully: He lost the 1982 primary to Democratic Rep. Bill Richardson and the 1988 general election to Republican Rep. Steven H. Schiff before capturing the attorney general's post in 1990. He spent eight years there involved in a range of issues, from challenging the opening of a planned nuclear waste dump to investigating high gasoline prices. "I'm a much better congressman having served eight years as AG," he says. "To come here [to Washington] with no state experience would have been a big void."

In 1998, Udall made a third try for the House. Local Democrats were eager to oust incumbent Bill Redmond, a conservative Republican minister who had won a three-way special election in May 1997 to replace Richardson when he left to become President Bill Clinton's U.N. ambassador. Udall won an eight-candidate Democratic primary, then handily beat Redmond in November. Since then, he has carved out a comfortable political niche in the district, winning with three-quarters of the vote in 2006.

KEY VOTES

2006

Yes Stop broadband companies from favoring select Internet traffic
No Affirm U.S. commitment to war in Iraq and reject setting a withdrawal date for troops
No Repeal requirement for bilingual ballots at the polls
No Permit U.S. sale of civilian nuclear technology to India
No Build a 700-mile fence on the U.S.-Mexico border to curb illegal crossings
No Permit warrantless wiretaps of suspected terrorists

2005

? Intervene in the life-support case of Terri Schiavo
Yes Lift President Bush's restrictions on stem cell research funding
Yes Prohibit FBI access to library and bookstore records
No Approve free-trade pact with five Central American countries
Yes Pass energy policy overhaul favored by President Bush emphasizing domestic oil and gas production
No End mandatory preservation of habitat of endangered animal and plant species
Yes Ban torture of prisoners in U.S. custody

CQ VOTE STUDIES

	PARTY UNITY		PRESIDENTIAL SUPPORT	
	Support	Oppose	Support	Oppose
2006	96%	4%	10%	90%
2005	97%	3%	11%	89%
2004	95%	5%	21%	79%
2003	97%	3%	18%	82%
2002	98%	2%	20%	80%

INTEREST GROUPS

	AFL-CIO	ADA	CCUS	ACU
2006	100%	95%	29%	4%
2005	100%	95%	41%	0%
2004	93%	100%	29%	8%
2003	100%	100%	23%	12%
2002	89%	100%	35%	0%

NEW MEXICO 3
North — Santa Fe, Rio Rancho, Farmington

Since artist Georgia O'Keeffe first painted northern New Mexico in 1929, the 3rd's breathtaking scenery and unique Spanish and American Indian heritage have attracted thousands of artists and tourists. Today, galleries and ski resorts still attract visitors from around the world, while an influx of retirees has made the area one of the fastest-growing parts of the state.

But the 3rd is a district of extremes. Alongside luxury resorts and the bountiful art trade is extraordinary poverty. Gallup, in McKinley County, boasts millionaires, while the county itself remains one of the poorest in the nation. Large American Indian populations in the northwest struggle with modest farming and ranching ventures, while the same area provides lofty incomes for oil and gas producers. Many western reservations are plagued with alcoholism and drug abuse, and Rio Arriba County in the north has one of the nation's highest drug mortality rates.

The Defense Department's 2005 BRAC recommendation to close Cannon Air Force Base, near Clovis in the 3rd's east, would have devastated the surrounding rural community, which depends on the base to support its economy. But the BRAC Commission voted to move the base's F-16 squadrons elsewhere, while still keeping the base open.

Hispanics, American Indians and Santa Fe's wealthy, liberal base give Democrats a 2-to-1 edge in voter registration. Conservative pockets exist in areas such as Rio Rancho, where Intel employs 5,200 workers; Los Alamos National Laboratory, where the atomic bomb was developed; and among energy producers in San Juan County in the 3rd's northwest.

MAJOR INDUSTRY
State government, ranching, farming, tourism, defense

MILITARY BASES
Cannon Air Force Base, 3,471 military, 614 civilian (2007)

CITIES
Santa Fe, 62,203; Rio Rancho (pt.), 46,701; Farmington, 37,844; Clovis, 32,667; Gallup, 20,209

NOTABLE
Santa Fe, the nation's second-oldest city, was founded in 1607; Roughly 100 tribes show their work at the Santa Fe Indian Market each August; The Aztec Ruins National Monument in Aztec features structures and artifacts from the 1100s and 1200s.

NEW YORK

Gov. Eliot Spitzer (D)

First elected: 2006
Length of term: 4 years
Term expires: 1/11
Salary: $179,000
Phone: (518) 474-8390

Residence: Manhattan
Born: June 10, 1959; Bronx, N.Y.
Religion: Jewish
Family: Wife, Silda Wall Spitzer; three children
Education: Princeton U., A.B. 1981 (public & international affairs); Harvard U., J.D. 1984
Career: Lawyer; city prosecutor
Political highlights: Sought Democratic nomination for N.Y. attorney general, 1994; N.Y. attorney general, 1999-2007

Election results:

2006 GENERAL		
Eliot Spitzer (D)	3,086,709	69.6%
John J. Faso (R)	1,274,335	28.7%
Malachy McCourt (GREEN)	42,166	1.0%

Lt. Gov. David A. Paterson (D)

First elected: 2006
Length of term: 4 years
Term expires: 1/11
Salary: $151,500
Phone: (518) 474-4623

LEGISLATURE

Legislature: Officially year-round; main session January-June

Senate: 62 members, 2-year terms
2007 ratios: 33 R, 29 D; 52 men, 10 women
Salary: $79,500
Phone: (518) 455-3216

Assembly: 150 members, 2-year terms
2007 ratios: 107 D, 42 R, 1 vacancies; 110 men, 39 women
Salary: $79,500
Phone: (518) 455-4218

TERM LIMITS

Governor: No
Senate: No
Assembly: No

URBAN STATISTICS

CITY	POPULATION
New York City	8,008,278
Buffalo	292,648
Rochester	219,773
Yonkers	196,086
Syracuse	147,306

REGISTERED VOTERS

Democrat	47%
Republican	27%
Unaffiliated/others	26%

POPULATION

2006 population (est.)	19,306,183
2000 population	18,976,457
1990 population	17,990,455
Percent change (1990-2000)	+5.5%
Rank among states (2006)	3
Median age	35.9
Born in state	65.3%
Foreign born	20.4%
Violent crime rate	554/100,000
Poverty level	14.6%
Federal workers	133,980
Military	57,987

ELECTIONS

STATE ELECTION OFFICIAL
(518) 474-6220
DEMOCRATIC PARTY
(212) 725-8825
REPUBLICAN PARTY
(518) 462-2601

MISCELLANEOUS

Web: www.state.ny.us
Capital: Albany

U.S. CONGRESS

Senate: 2 Democrats
House: 23 Democrats, 6 Republicans

2000 Census Statistics by District

DIST.	2004 VOTE FOR PRESIDENT BUSH	KERRY	WHITE	BLACK	ASIAN	HISP	MEDIAN INCOME	WHITE COLLAR	BLUE COLLAR	SERVICE INDUSTRY	OVER 64	UNDER 18	COLLEGE EDUCATION	RURAL	SQ. MILES
1	49.4%	48.7%	84%	4%	2%	8%	$61,884	64%	21%	15%	12%	26%	27%	6%	646
2	45	53	72	10	3	14	$71,147	66	20	14	12	27	31	0	239
3	52	47	87	2	3	7	$70,561	69	17	14	15	24	31	0	183
4	44	55	62	18	4	14	$66,799	68	17	15	14	25	31	0	90
5	36	63	44	5	24	23	$51,156	65	18	17	15	22	34	0	66
6	15	84	13	52	9	17	$43,546	57	21	22	11	27	18	0	40
7	25	74	28	17	13	40	$36,990	57	21	22	13	24	20	0	26
8	27	72	69	5	11	12	$47,061	79	10	11	14	18	48	0	15
9	44	56	64	4	15	14	$45,426	68	18	14	17	21	31	0	37
10	13	86	16	60	3	17	$30,212	60	18	22	10	30	18	0	18
11	13	86	21	59	4	12	$34,082	61	16	23	9	27	25	0	12
12	19	80	23	9	16	49	$29,195	51	28	21	9	26	17	0	19
13	55	45	71	6	9	11	$50,092	65	18	17	13	24	24	0	65
14	24	74	66	5	11	14	$57,152	82	8	10	13	13	57	0	13
	9	90	16	31	3	48	$27,934	64	15	21	11	24	25	0	10

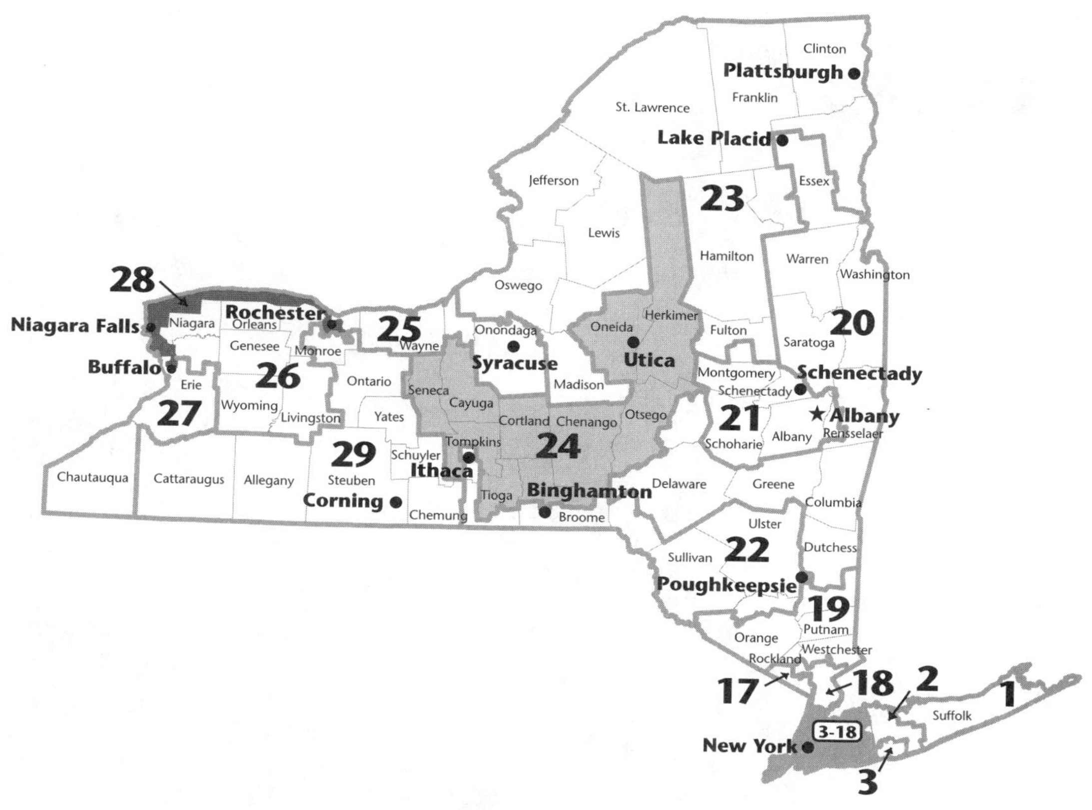

2000 Census Statistics by District

DIST.	2004 VOTE FOR PRESIDENT BUSH	KERRY	WHITE	BLACK	ASIAN	HISP	MEDIAN INCOME	WHITE COLLAR	BLUE COLLAR	SERVICE INDUSTRY	OVER 64	UNDER 18	COLLEGE EDUCATION	RURAL	SQ. MILES
16	10%	89%	3%	30%	2%	63%	$19,311	46%	24%	30%	7%	35%	8%	0%	12
17	33	66	41	30	5	20	$44,868	65	16	19	13	27	29	0	127
18	42	57	67	9	5	16	$68,887	73	13	14	14	25	44	1	222
19	53	45	84	5	2	8	$64,337	67	19	14	11	27	32	21	1,401
20	53	45	93	2	1	2	$44,239	61	24	15	14	24	25	55	7,018
21	43	55	85	7	2	3	$40,254	66	19	15	15	23	27	16	1,935
22	45	53	80	8	3	8	$38,586	61	22	17	14	24	24	32	3,246
23	51	47	93	3	1	2	$35,434	52	29	19	12	25	16	65	13,235
24	52	46	92	3	1	2	$36,082	57	25	17	15	24	19	49	6,164
25	48	50	87	7	2	2	$43,188	65	21	14	14	26	28	21	1,620
26	55	43	92	3	2	2	$46,653	62	24	14	14	25	26	29	2,731
27	44	53	89	4	1	5	$36,884	58	26	16	16	24	20	18	1,830
28	36	62	62	29	1	6	$31,751	58	23	18	14	26	21	7	534
29	56	42	93	3	2	1	$41,875	61	24	15	14	25	26	42	5,660
STATE	40	58	62	15	5	15	$43,393	64	20	17	13	25	27	13	47,214
U.S.	50.7	48.3	69	12	4	13	$41,994	60	25	15	12	26	24	21	3,537,438

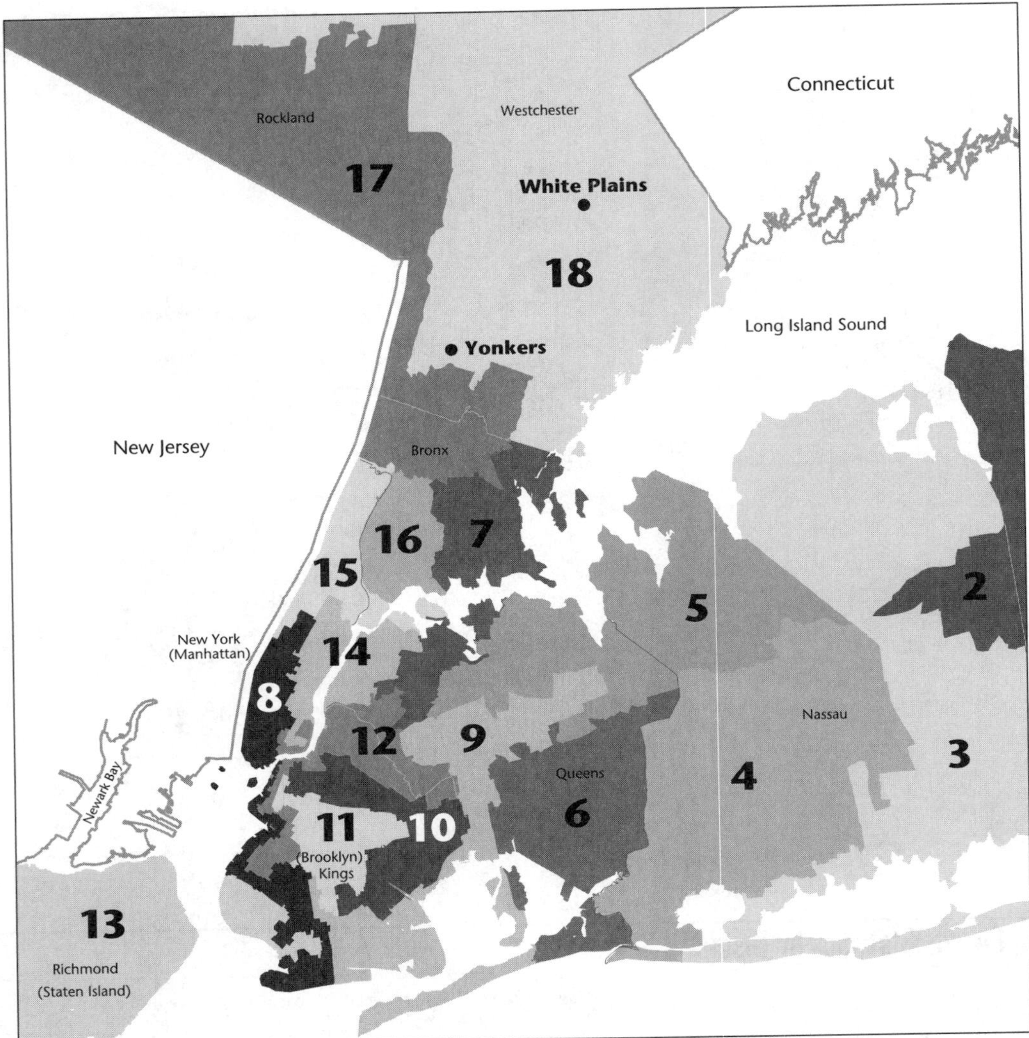

Connecticut
Rockland
Westchester
17
White Plains
18
Long Island Sound
Yonkers
New Jersey
Bronx
16
7
15
2
5
New York
(Manhattan)
14
8
Nassau
12
9
3
Newark Bay
Queens
4
11
10
6
(Brooklyn)
Kings
13
Richmond
(Staten Island)

Sen. Charles E. Schumer (D)

CAPITOL OFFICE
224-6542
schumer.senate.gov
313 Hart 20510-3203; fax 228-1218

COMMITTEES
Banking, Housing & Urban Affairs
(Housing, Transportation & Community Development - chairman)
Finance
Judiciary
(Administrative Oversight & the Courts - chairman)
Rules & Administration
Joint Economic - chairman
Joint Library

RESIDENCE
Brooklyn

BORN
Nov. 23, 1950, Brooklyn, N.Y.

RELIGION
Jewish

FAMILY
Wife, Iris Weinshall; two children

EDUCATION
Harvard U., A.B. 1971, J.D. 1974

CAREER
Lawyer

POLITICAL HIGHLIGHTS
N.Y. Assembly, 1975-81; U.S. House, 1981-99

ELECTION RESULTS

2004 GENERAL

Schumer (D, INDC, WFM)	4,769,824	71.2%
Howard Mills (R)	1,625,069	24.2%
Marilyn F. O'Grady (C)	220,960	3.3%

2004 PRIMARY

Charles E. Schumer (D)	unopposed

PREVIOUS WINNING PERCENTAGES
1998 (55%); 1996 House Election (75%); 1994 House Election (73%); 1992 House Election (89%); 1990 House Election (80%); 1988 House Election (78%); 1986 House Election (93%); 1984 House Election (72%); 1982 House Election (79%); 1980 House Election (77%)

Elected 1998; 2nd term

Schumer is an articulate ambassador for his party who speaks with authority on a wide range of issues via frequent television appearances, reliably clever quotes and an incessant stream of news releases. Also one of the party's top fundraisers, Schumer raked in record amounts of money for Democrats in their successful takeover of the Senate in 2006, and was promptly rewarded with the newly created post of vice chairman of the Democratic Caucus, the No. 3 leadership job.

Majority Leader Harry Reid of Nevada created the post for Schumer as a reward for his wildly successful two-year stint as chairman of the Democratic Senatorial Campaign Committee. The brash New Yorker raised $121 million in the 2005-06 cycle, leaving his Republican counterpart in the dust in the race for dollars to fuel races around the country. The GOP committee, led by Sen. Elizabeth Dole of North Carolina, took in $89 million.

In his leadership post, Schumer ranks just behind Reid and Majority Whip Richard J. Durbin of Illinois. Schumer is finally enjoying a level of clout compatible with his ambition and appetite for attention. He has a large role in shaping policy and strategy for the Democratic Caucus and a more explicit role in shaping the party's message.

Though overshadowed on the national stage by New York's junior senator, Democratic presidential candidate Hillary Rodham Clinton, Schumer is no wallflower. He jumps into any issue that strikes his fancy without concern for stepping on the toes of other senators. One of his favorite strategies is calling press conferences on slow-news Sundays and getting on the evening news. Among his friends, Schumer counts that other New York virtuoso of media manipulation, real estate developer Donald Trump.

His campaign committee assignment in the pivotal 2006 election made the most of Schumer's competitive personality and boundless energy. He aggressively courted donors and left nothing to chance with the candidates. His message? "We'll give you money, but you have to hire a campaign manager, a finance director and a communications director who we approve. They have to toe the line," Schumer told the New York Times in early 2006.

He recruited moderate Democrats to compete against Republican incumbents, and rebuffed protests from abortion rights groups, a traditional Democratic ally, in recruiting popular Pennsylvania Treasurer Bob Casey, who opposes abortion, to challenge GOP Sen. Rick Santorum. Casey defeated Santorum. "He projects strength," former Sen. Bob Kerrey, a Nebraska Democrat, said of Schumer. "If you get in the ring with him, you'd better be prepared to go the distance, because he is."

Schumer had been mulling a 2006 run for New York governor when Reid offered him the campaign committee job. Reid sweetened the deal by giving him a coveted spot on the powerful Finance Committee. Schumer accepted, and avoided what could have been a bruising gubernatorial primary against state Attorney General Eliot Spitzer, who is now governor.

A veteran Judiciary Committee member, Schumer weighs in on high-profile issues ranging from abortion to the war on terrorism. In 2007, he played a leading role in investigating the motivations of the Bush administration in the firings of eight federal prosecutors. He demanded the resignation of Attorney General Alberto R. Gonzales for approving the dismissals and misleading the committee about his role.

In the 109th Congress (2005-06), Schumer was out front in the party's opposition to President Bush's conservative judicial nominees. He was one of 21 Democrats who voted against both John G. Roberts Jr. and Samuel A. Alito Jr. for the Supreme Court.

Schumer was deeply involved in efforts to curb the administration's use of expanded police powers to pursue terrorists after revelations that the National Security Agency was doing surveillance without court review.

In 1994, while still in the House, Schumer was a main sponsor of the anti-crime law that put 100,000 new police officers on the beat, banned 19 assault weapons and created a "three strikes" mandatory life sentence for repeat violent offenders. An advocate for crime victims, Schumer in 2002 lambasted the Justice Department for requiring rape victims to help pay for the collection of forensic evidence against their attackers, which he likened to "asking the family of a homicide victim to pay for the autopsy."

An ardent gun control advocate, he was the chief sponsor of the 1993 Brady law requiring background checks for handgun purchases, and a 2006 bill requiring that stolen guns be reported in every state. When the National Rifle Association called him "the criminal's best friend," Schumer shot back, "I wear this like a badge of honor."

On the Banking, Housing and Urban Affairs Committee, Schumer has pressed to reduce transaction fees paid by the securities industry while also seeking more protection for consumers with bad credit, prompting the American Banker newsletter to describe Schumer as "one of the few members of the often polarized Senate Banking and Judiciary committees that can make both industry and community groups happy."

Schumer was born and raised in the Kings Highway section of Brooklyn. His father, Abe, owned a pest extermination business and his mother, Selma, stayed at home with Schumer and his two siblings.

He says he "didn't have a political bone" in his body until his freshman year at Harvard. The Young Democrats chapter asked him to work on Eugene McCarthy's presidential campaign. Schumer had been rejected from the basketball team and had yet to make a friend at Harvard. So he accepted and went to New Hampshire to campaign for McCarthy, an experience he describes in his 2007 book, "Positively American," as "exhilarating," especially after McCarthy did well. Schumer gave up organic chemistry and decided to become a lawyer with the goal of getting into politics.

As his parents were driving him home after law school, Schumer announced that he would decline a job at a prominent law firm and run for the state Assembly. They argued all the way to Brooklyn, but he was steadfast. Schumer won the seat at age 23. "My first election night, in September 1974, was probably the hardest of my career," he wrote. "When the polls closed, I had no idea what was going to happen, in part because my mother had told all her friends to vote against me!"

Six years later, Schumer easily won the Brooklyn-based U.S. House seat of Democrat Elizabeth Holtzman, who was running for the Senate.

In 1998, after 18 years in the House, Schumer took on Republican Sen. Alfonse D'Amato, winning the Democratic nomination with 51 percent of the vote against former Rep. Geraldine A. Ferraro, the 1984 vice presidential nominee, and New York City Public Advocate Mark Green.

In the fall, D'Amato branded Schumer as too liberal and attacked him for missing floor votes while campaigning. Schumer pointed to his anti-crime and gun control efforts in the House, and recounted D'Amato's ethics problems. Though D'Amato spent $24 million to Schumer's $17 million, Schumer won with 55 percent of the vote.

In 2004, he carried 61 of New York's 62 counties, losing only in sparsely populated Hamilton County in the northern part of the state — despite repeated visits to the area. "One staffer joked that the problem in Hamilton was that I had met each of the voters personally," Schumer says.

KEY VOTES

2006

No Confirm Samuel A. Alito Jr. to the Supreme Court
No Allow consideration of a bill to establish a $140 billion trust fund to compensate victims of asbestos exposure
No Extend tax cuts for two years at a cost of $70 billion over five years
Yes Overhaul immigration policy with border security, enforcement and guest worker program
? Allow consideration of a bill to permanently repeal the estate tax
Yes Urge President Bush to begin troop withdrawals from Iraq in 2006
Yes Lift President Bush's restrictions on stem cell research funding
No Authorize military tribunals for suspected terrorists

2005

Yes Curb class action lawsuits by shifting them from state to federal courts
Yes Allow confirmation vote on Priscilla R. Owen to the U.S. Court of Appeals for the 5th Circuit
No Oppose mandatory emissions limits and block recognition of global warming as a threat
No Approve free-trade pact with five Central American countries
No Pass energy policy overhaul favored by President Bush emphasizing domestic oil and gas production
No Shield gunmakers from lawsuits when their products are used in crimes
Yes Ban torture of prisoners in U.S. custody
No Renew 16 provisions of the Patriot Act
No Allow final vote on opening the Arctic National Wildlife Refuge to oil and gas exploration

CQ VOTE STUDIES

	PARTY UNITY		PRESIDENTIAL SUPPORT	
	Support	Oppose	Support	Oppose
2006	93%	7%	52%	48%
2005	93%	7%	31%	69%
2004	91%	9%	62%	38%
2003	96%	4%	47%	53%
2002	95%	5%	68%	32%
2001	92%	8%	65%	35%
2000	97%	3%	98%	2%
1999	94%	6%	91%	9%
House Service:				
1998	94%	6%	85%	15%
1997	90%	10%	83%	17%

INTEREST GROUPS

	AFL-CIO	ADA	CCUS	ACU
2006	100%	100%	64%	4%
2005	86%	100%	39%	8%
2004	100%	100%	65%	12%
2003	85%	95%	39%	10%
2002	92%	85%	50%	10%
2001	100%	95%	43%	16%
2000	75%	95%	53%	12%
1999	89%	100%	53%	4%
House Service:				
1998	100%	100%	36%	9%
1997	100%	85%	40%	19%

Sen. Hillary Rodham Clinton (D)

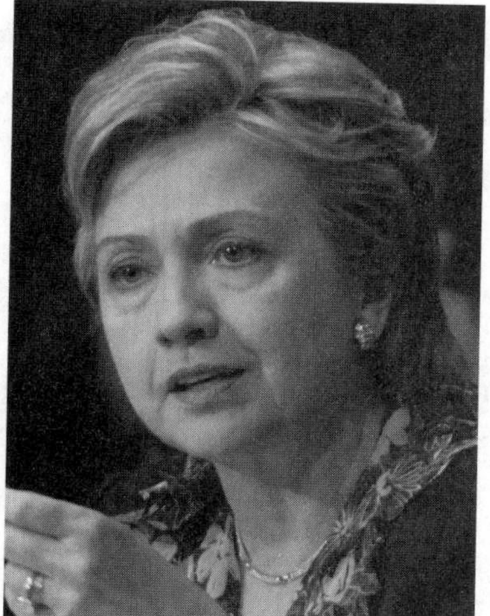

CAPITOL OFFICE
224-4451
clinton.senate.gov
476 Russell 20510-3204; fax 228-0282

COMMITTEES
Armed Services
Environment & Public Works
(Superfund & Environmental Health - chairwoman)
Health, Education, Labor & Pensions
Special Aging

RESIDENCE
Chappaqua

BORN
Oct. 26, 1947, Chicago, Ill.

RELIGION
Methodist

FAMILY
Husband, Bill Clinton; one child

EDUCATION
Wellesley College, B.A. 1969; Yale U., J.D. 1973

CAREER
First lady; lawyer; law school professor; congressional aide

POLITICAL HIGHLIGHTS
No previous office

ELECTION RESULTS

2006 GENERAL		
Clinton (D, INDC, WFM)	3,008,428	67.0%
John Spencer (R, C)	1,392,189	31.0%
Howie Hawkins (GREEN)	55,469	1.2%
2006 PRIMARY		
Hillary Rodham Clinton (D)	640,955	83.7%
Jonathan B. Tasini (D)	124,999	16.3%

PREVIOUS WINNING PERCENTAGES
2000 (55%)

Elected 2000; 2nd term

In one term as the junior senator from New York, Clinton transformed herself into a more appealing national figure, silencing the critics who doubted she could shed the baggage from her past as the love-her-or-hate-her former first lady. She made a point of reaching across party lines on selected issues and she inched toward the political center, talking more about faith and prayer, and counseling tolerance of people opposed to abortion and same-sex marriage.

As 2008 drew closer, Clinton also dropped many of the New York-centric topics that had preoccupied her first Senate term in favor of national themes that defined her as a potential Democratic nominee for president. She set out to dominate the field of emerging White House pretenders, setting a sizzling first-quarter fundraising pace in 2007 of more than $26 million.

As a woman, she gave the early presidential posturing a new look. And paired with the other potential nominee coming on strong for the Democrats, Illinois Sen. Barack Obama, an African-American, the fight for the nomination was shaping up to be historic, raising the questions: Is the country ready for the first woman president? Can she be beaten by the first black presidential candidate?

During the initial years of her first term in the Senate, Clinton stayed almost totally focused on New York issues, proving herself as a public servant to a state where she hadn't spent much time. Clinton grew up in the well-heeled Chicago suburb of Park Ridge, and spent much of her early adulthood in Arkansas, as the political spouse of then Gov. Bill Clinton.

By the time she stood for re-election in 2006, Clinton had invested significant time cultivating upstate moderates and Republicans to lessen her dependence on New York City's liberal voters. She also intentionally focused on parochial issues in her first term, working to secure funding for the city's subway system and economic development projects for upstate New York. She was instrumental in saving the Niagara Air Base from closure, keeping 800 New York state jobs in the process.

To avoid stoking speculation about her presidential ambition, she declined to answer reporters' questions about a candidacy; her stock answer was that she was focused solely on being the best senator from New York. She dutifully attended every committee meeting and in 2006 participated in 99 percent of all Senate roll call votes.

Her colleagues grew to know her as an extremely well-prepared legislator who asked specific, serious policy questions at hearings and kept the political rhetoric to a minimum. Despite her lack of seniority on the Armed Services Committee, she won the admiration of its senior members. Sen. John W. Warner of Virginia, then chairman, described Clinton as "very industrious. She does her homework very carefully."

Her seat on Armed Services, a plum she secured in 2003, allowed her to fill a gap in her portfolio — military and foreign affairs. But she went into the 110th Congress (2007-08) facing deepening questions about her position on the war in Iraq. Clinton voted for the 2002 resolution sanctioning the invasion, and although she has been a vocal critic of the president's handling of the conflict, she must now contend with Obama, who was not in the Senate at the time but spoke against the war.

Clinton has made a point of reaching across the aisle for political partnerships, often with her husband's former critics. She partnered with Sen. Lindsey Graham, a South Carolina Republican, on military issues and traveled with him to Iraq, setting aside hard feelings over Graham's role in the 1998 impeachment proceedings against President Clinton. She supported President Bush's nomination of Michael Chertoff to be Homeland Security secretary, despite his role leading the Whitewater investigation into the Clintons' real estate dealings.

Such bipartisan partnerships belie a generally liberal voting record. Clinton voted with her party 94 percent of the time in the 109th Congress (2005-06) on votes that pitted Democrats against Republicans.

Despite her efforts to be a model freshman senator, she has never been far from the limelight. Her 2003 memoir, "Living History," for which she received an advance of $8 million, became the fastest-selling non-fiction book of that time. And Democratic officials got a blunt reminder that Clinton was not just another senator when they passed her over for a speaking role at the 2004 party convention in Boston. Democratic women objected loudly and she was given a prime-time role introducing her husband.

By the end of six years in the Senate, she was ready to move back onto the national stage. In the first half of 2006, Clinton launched a series of major policy speeches on energy, privacy rights and the economy. Later that year, she held private meetings with top New York Democratic officials to ask for their support, including House Ways and Means Chairman Charles B. Rangel, the dean of the New York congressional delegation.

She began spending more time in early primary and caucus states, where Obama and other serious contenders, such as former Sen. John Edwards of North Carolina, had already paid several visits. She had no worries about name recognition, but she needed to reach out to anti-war liberals who dominate the early primaries.

The daughter of a furniture company executive, Hillary Rodham was ambitious, with the smarts to back it up. She went to Yale University, a fateful choice that resulted in her meeting fellow student Bill Clinton, her equal in intelligence and ambition. After graduation, they went to Texas to work in the 1972 George McGovern campaign. Bill Clinton then returned to his native Arkansas to teach law and lay the foundation to run for office, while she went to Washington to work for the House Judiciary Committee special counsel on the impeachment of President Richard Nixon. The two married in 1975 and she joined him in Arkansas, working for the Rose Law Firm in Little Rock and for the Legal Services Corp.

Their first attempt to get Bill Clinton elected to office failed, when he lost a 1974 House race. But as a political unit, they were a disciplined and savvy team, even though as a couple they famously fought and Clinton's career was shadowed by chronic rumors of his dalliances with other women.

He went on to become Arkansas governor and a leader of the centrist movement in the Democratic Party; she was his top adviser and activist first lady. They brought that operating mode to the White House in 1993. Hillary Clinton had an enormous impact on Oval Office decisions in her husband's two terms, including an ill-fated attempt in 1993 to revamp the health care system. She stood by him publicly in his darkest hour, impeachment proceedings in 1998 stemming from his attempt to cover up an affair with a White House intern.

Once her husband finished his second term, Clinton was free to pursue a political career of her own. Though she had never lived in New York, she announced that she would move there and run for the Senate. As a former first lady, she had tremendous advantages in the Democratic-leaning state, but Republicans pounced on the fact that she had never lived there and accused her of sheer political ambition. They had a strong and seasoned candidate in Rep. Rick Lazio, but Clinton won handily by 12 percentage points. In 2006, she romped to re-election with two-thirds of the vote.

KEY VOTES

2006

- No Confirm Samuel A. Alito Jr. to the Supreme Court
- No Allow consideration of a bill to establish a $140 billion trust fund to compensate victims of asbestos exposure
- No Extend tax cuts for two years at a cost of $70 billion over five years
- Yes Overhaul immigration policy with border security, enforcement and guest worker program
- No Allow consideration of a bill to permanently repeal the estate tax
- Yes Urge President Bush to begin troop withdrawals from Iraq in 2006
- Yes Lift President Bush's restrictions on stem cell research funding
- No Authorize military tribunals for suspected terrorists

2005

- No Curb class action lawsuits by shifting them from state to federal courts
- Yes Allow confirmation vote on Priscilla R. Owen to the U.S. Court of Appeals for the 5th Circuit
- No Oppose mandatory emissions limits and block recognition of global warming as a threat
- No Approve free-trade pact with five Central American countries
- No Pass energy policy overhaul favored by President Bush emphasizing domestic oil and gas production
- No Shield gunmakers from lawsuits when their products are used in crimes
- Yes Ban torture of prisoners in U.S. custody
- No Renew 16 provisions of the Patriot Act
- No Allow final vote on opening the Arctic National Wildlife Refuge to oil and gas exploration

CQ VOTE STUDIES

	PARTY UNITY		PRESIDENTIAL SUPPORT	
	Support	Oppose	Support	Oppose
2006	93%	7%	50%	50%
2005	96%	4%	31%	69%
2004	96%	4%	61%	39%
2003	98%	2%	47%	53%
2002	93%	7%	67%	33%
2001	97%	3%	61%	39%

INTEREST GROUPS

	AFL-CIO	ADA	CCUS	ACU
2006	93%	95%	67%	8%
2005	86%	100%	35%	12%
2004	100%	95%	50%	0%
2003	85%	95%	35%	10%
2002	92%	95%	45%	10%
2001	100%	95%	43%	12%

Rep. Timothy H. Bishop (D)

CAPITOL OFFICE
225-3826
www.house.gov/timbishop
225 Cannon 20515-3201; fax 225-3143

COMMITTEES
Budget
Education & Labor
Transportation & Infrastructure

RESIDENCE
Southampton

BORN
June 1, 1950, Southampton, N.Y.

RELIGION
Roman Catholic

FAMILY
Wife, Kathryn Bishop; two children

EDUCATION
College of the Holy Cross, A.B. 1972; Long Island U., M.P.A. 1981

CAREER
College provost and administrator

POLITICAL HIGHLIGHTS
No previous office

ELECTION RESULTS

2006 GENERAL		
Bishop (D, INDC, WFM)	104,360	62.2%
Italo A. Zanzi (R, C)	63,328	37.8%
2006 PRIMARY		
Timothy H. Bishop (D)		unopposed
2004 GENERAL		
Bishop (D, INDC, WFM)	156,354	56.2%
Bill Manger (R, C)	121,855	43.8%

PREVIOUS WINNING PERCENTAGES
2002 (50%)

Elected 2002; 3rd term

As a liberal from a Republican-leaning district on eastern Long Island, Bishop makes sure he appeals to middle-of-the-road voters and puts elbow grease into constituent service. And he has shown he can raise money like a political veteran, in amounts that scare away the hard competition.

Bishop's focus in the House is education. He spent nearly 30 years as an administrator at a small college on Long Island, half of those as provost. He jumped into politics relatively late in life and without much of a political résumé. He was 52 when he challenged incumbent Republican Felix J. Grucci Jr. and won in 2002, largely because Grucci bungled his campaign.

Bishop pursues his education priorities from his seat on the Education and Labor Committee, a second-choice assignment for some but not for a lawmaker with a strong interest in both subjects. He is a crusader for more federal funds to help schools adapt to the 2001 No Child Left Behind law, the Bush administration initiative imposing new testing requirements and sink-or-swim standards on public schools. He also wants the government to pay its promised 40 percent share of the tab for programs for disabled students under the Individuals with Disabilities Education Act.

In 2005, Bishop tried unsuccessfully to amend a Republican bill making cuts in student aid. His amendment would have offered rebates to students whose Pell grants had recently been reduced or eliminated because of eligibility changes made by the Education Department.

He was a forceful advocate in 2007 for the new Democratic majority's bill cutting interest rates on college loans. "Protecting and supporting education has long been one of the core principles of the Democratic Party, and now I think that we are acting on that," Bishop said. He also secured a seat on the Budget Committee in the 110th Congress (2007-08).

The son of a telephone lineman, Bishop is also a friend of organized labor. In his first term in the House, he pushed a proposal in the Education Committee to increase the minimum wage from $5.15 to $7 an hour and another to require company pension boards to have employee representation. He actively opposed the Bush administration's plan to scale back worker protections for overtime pay. During debate, Bishop described how his father worked more than 80 hours a week, and depended on overtime wages to put five children through college.

Bishop's top-priority fiscal issue is the repeal of the alternative minimum tax, which was designed to ensure that wealthy taxpayers pay at least some taxes but in effect has forced middle-class taxpayers to pay more. His constituents are disproportionately affected, principally because the law does not allow deductions for property taxes, which are sky-high in the New York City area.

The 1st District covers the eastern half of Long Island's "fishtail," a place of economic extremes that has working-class suburbs like Smithtown but also the tony Hamptons, where the city's business elite spend summers. The area also includes coastal villages where fishing is a mainstay and concentrations of artists are attracted by the light and cliffs overlooking the sea.

Bishop has deep roots in the district. His father's family came to Southampton from Southampton, England, in 1643, and his great-great-grandfather was mayor of the town. He still lives a block from the house where he grew up. His mother's family were potato farmers, and Bishop has warm memories of weekends helping out during harvest time.

After getting a master's degree in public administration, Bishop in 1973 took a job as an admissions counselor at Southampton College, and worked his way up with jobs as dean of enrollment and director of financial aid. He eventually became provost of the school, where half the students are the first member of their family to get a college degree, like Bishop.

When he decided to take on Grucci in 2002, Bishop's only political experience was a stint as chairman of the Southampton Town Board of Ethics. It seemed a quixotic campaign against an incumbent who had all the advantages. Grucci, former president of Fireworks by Grucci, was well-known, well-financed and a Republican in a district where the GOP enjoyed a 3-2 edge over Democrats.

But Bishop had some things going for him, especially a 30-year friendship with entertainment mogul Robert F.X. Sillerman, who had a home in the Hamptons. Sillerman, who became chancellor at Southampton College in 1993, was Bishop's campaign chairman and tapped Hollywood and Hamptons money circles to help him.

Then Grucci made a serious misstep. He ran an ad wrongly accusing Bishop of covering up a student rape while he was provost, a charge based on an old, discredited article in a student newspaper. Bishop won public sympathy as a result. He also was able to hurt Grucci on an important local issue, environmental protection, by publicizing a county health department report identifying the Grucci fireworks factory in Yaphank as a likely source of pollution in local drinking water wells.

Once in office, Bishop worked to make himself less dispensable to voters, who have a history of trading in congressmen like cars. Since 1999, the seat has changed hands three times. Bishop doubled the aides doing constituent service and won a coveted seat on the Transportation and Infrastructure Committee, where he has been able to lobby for grants for his district.

He was also able to secure $240 million for Brookhaven National Laboratory, a major physics research facility in the 1st District. He raised an impressive $2 million in campaign funds. The one blemish on his first term was a media revelation that he had accepted a gift from Sillerman of $21,000 for college costs for his daughter, Meghan. Bishop said his friend has never asked for a legislative favor.

His 2004 re-election was secured when the Republicans' best candidate, John Jay LaVelle, supervisor of Brookhaven, stayed out of the race. Bishop was able to easily defeat Bill Manger, a former federal transportation official. In 2006, he handily defeated Republican Italo A. Zanzi, a vice president for Major League Baseball, by more than 20 percentage points.

KEY VOTES

2006

- Yes Stop broadband companies from favoring select Internet traffic
- \- Affirm U.S. commitment to war in Iraq and reject setting a withdrawal date for troops
- No Repeal requirement for bilingual ballots at the polls
- Yes Permit U.S. sale of civilian nuclear technology to India
- Yes Build a 700-mile fence on the U.S.-Mexico border to curb illegal crossings
- No Permit warrantless wiretaps of suspected terrorists

2005

- No Intervene in the life-support case of Terri Schiavo
- Yes Lift President Bush's restrictions on stem cell research funding
- Yes Prohibit FBI access to library and bookstore records
- No Approve free-trade pact with five Central American countries
- No Pass energy policy overhaul favored by President Bush emphasizing domestic oil and gas production
- No End mandatory preservation of habitat of endangered animal and plant species
- Yes Ban torture of prisoners in U.S. custody

CQ VOTE STUDIES

	PARTY UNITY		PRESIDENTIAL SUPPORT	
	Support	Oppose	Support	Oppose
2006	97%	3%	31%	69%
2005	95%	5%	15%	85%
2004	95%	5%	32%	68%
2003	96%	4%	18%	82%

INTEREST GROUPS

	AFL-CIO	ADA	CCUS	ACU
2006	100%	85%	40%	16%
2005	93%	95%	41%	0%
2004	100%	100%	48%	4%
2003	100%	90%	30%	16%

NEW YORK 1

Eastern Suffolk County – Hamptons, Smithtown, Brookhaven

Covering the eastern two-thirds of Long Island's Suffolk County, the 1st reaches out into the Atlantic Ocean. Its western edge is home to small communities that have grown alongside the district's research facilities, while its eastern end takes in the elite estates of some of New York's wealthiest in the Hamptons and Shelter Island. The rural end of the island retains its pastoral character, with fishing villages and farms scattered throughout.

Scientific research, attracted by local colleges and Brookhaven National Laboratory, dominates the district's economy. Stony Brook University ...dical Center ranks among the top 15 U.S. teaching hospitals, while ...haven has produced six Nobel Prize recipients. On a smaller ...c scale, the 1st's portion of Long Island's wine industry also has ... presence. In three decades, the industry has grown from ... 30 wineries and more than 3,000 acres.

The 1st takes in some blue-collar towns and areas that depend on fishing and tourism, where environmental issues rank high. Coastal towns, such as Montauk, are second homes for the region's elite.

The 1st's lingering rural temperament and small-town feel make it more likely to lean to the right than many other districts near New York City. Voter registration favors Republicans, but the district's brand of conservatism remains moderate, with many residents supporting more-liberal views on abortion and gun control. Republicans dominate at the local level, but Democrats make the 1st competitive in federal elections. George W. Bush and John Kerry each took 49 percent of the 1st's 2004 presidential vote, with Bush winning narrowly.

MAJOR INDUSTRY

Higher education, research, health care, tourism

CITIES

Coram (unincorporated), 34,923; Centereach (unincorporated), 27,285; Shirley (unincorporated), 25,395; Medford (unincorporated), 21,985

NOTABLE

The Montauk Point Lighthouse, built in 1796, was the first lighthouse in New York State; The Big Duck, a duck-shaped structure and shop built in 1931 that stands 20 feet tall, graces Route 24 in Flanders.

Rep. Steve Israel (D)

CAPITOL OFFICE
225-3335
www.house.gov/israel
432 Cannon 20515-3202; fax 225-4669

COMMITTEES
Appropriations

RESIDENCE
Huntington

BORN
May 30, 1958, Brooklyn, N.Y.

RELIGION
Jewish

FAMILY
Wife, Marlene Budd; two children

EDUCATION
Nassau Community College, A.A. 1978 (liberal arts); Syracuse U., attended 1978-79; George Washington U., B.A. 1982 (political science)

CAREER
Public relations and marketing firm manager; assistant county executive; university fundraising director; Jewish advocacy group county director; congressional aide

POLITICAL HIGHLIGHTS
Democratic nominee for Suffolk County Legislature, 1987; Huntington Town Board, 1993-2001 (majority leader, 1997-2001)

ELECTION RESULTS

2006 GENERAL		
Steve Israel (D, INDC, WFM)	105,276	70.4%
John W. Bugler (R, C)	44,212	29.6%
2006 PRIMARY		
Steve Israel (D)	unopposed	
2004 GENERAL		
Steve Israel (D, INDC, WFM)	161,593	66.6%
Richard Hoffmann (R, C)	80,950	33.4%

PREVIOUS WINNING PERCENTAGES
2002 (58%); 2000 (48%)

Elected 2000; 4th term

A pragmatic deal maker, Israel looks for opportunities to open doors — even after he hits people with them. On a busy day in the House in 2005, Israel was racing to catch a flight home and flung open a door with such force it struck the guy in front of him, Rep. Timothy V. Johnson, an Illinois Republican. The two had not met before, so Israel introduced himself and he and Johnson went on to form the Center Aisle Caucus, which tries to find agreement between Democrats and Republicans on legislation.

Bipartisan groups come and go with a varying degree of success on Capitol Hill, but Israel calculates his caucus' chances this way: "Republicans and Democrats are going to disagree on 60 percent of the issues, which gives us a fundamental obligation to try and pass the 40 percent we can agree on. And that would make America 100 percent better off."

Although he has a liberal bent, the Long Island Democrat is a member of the Blue Dog Coalition of conservative Democrats, one of only three New Yorkers in the group. He also joined the moderate New Democrat Coalition.

His tendency to reach for the center is an asset in his new assignment to the powerful Appropriations Committee, which controls the federal purse strings. Appropriations is one of the rare places where the two parties work together; they are responsible for 12 mandatory annual spending bills. To take the sought-after seat under party rules, Israel had to give up the Armed Services Committee, which had been an important posting in his early years in Congress. The Sept. 11 terrorist attacks took place nine months into his first term in the House, and 112 of his constituents perished, thrusting Israel into the thick of the national security debate that followed.

He has since broadened his notion of national security to include energy independence, calling U.S. dependence on foreign oil "as much a threat to our survival as the Cold War [was]." He has pressed Defense Department contractors in his district to study ways to reduce the country's foreign oil dependency.

Israel is the champion of legislation to require airlines to equip planes with anti-missile technology. The flight paths of John F. Kennedy International Airport are above his district, and he became concerned about the proliferation of shoulder-fired missiles after one was launched at, but missed, an Israeli airplane as it took off from a Kenyan airport in 2002.

Israel's measure stalled because of the cost to the airline industry — an estimated $10 billion. He is also pushing a more modest bill requiring anti-missile technology on commercial airplanes transporting U.S. troops to the Middle East. The government would foot the bill for installing the systems on civil reserve aircraft, which he says would cost less than in-flight entertainment systems.

One of Israel's top concerns is health care. He has pushed to beef up the Food and Drug Administration's ability to crack down on counterfeit drugs. And he once buttonholed President Bush to talk about prescription drug coverage for seniors under Medicare when the president stopped by the Capitol to pass along holiday greetings to lawmakers in December. "I just planted myself at the exit of the room. He was going to have to knock me down to get past," Israel later told The New York Times.

Israel has also worked for the availability of affordable housing, an issue of concern to his suburban constituents. On the Armed Services panel, he has focused on the issue of professional military education, encouraging more training of mid-career officers.

Israel became interested in politics at an early age. He started reading newspapers in elementary school, after hearing the news in school one day that Sen. Robert F. Kennedy, a New York Democrat and the late president's brother, had been assassinated. "I was thinking, at fourth grade, 'Why would someone get killed for what they believed in?' " he said.

In high school, Israel rode his bicycle after school to the campaign headquarters of Democrat Franklin Ornstein, who in 1974 waged an unsuccessful challenge to GOP Rep. Norman F. Lent. As a political science student at George Washington University, Israel worked part time for California Democratic Rep. Robert T. Matsui and then spent three years with Rep. Richard L. Ottinger, a New York Democrat.

Israel returned to Long Island in 1983, where he worked as a fundraiser for Touro College, a Jewish-sponsored institution. In 1987, he lost a bid for the Suffolk County Legislature.

Israel formed his own fundraising and public relations firm, and was also the director of the Institute on the Holocaust and the Law, which is affiliated with Touro and the American Jewish Congress. He stayed active in local politics, winning a seat on the Huntington Town Board in a 1993 special election. During his seven years on the board, Israel worked with Republicans to put the town on a sound financial footing. He was the first local official to offer information about his activities on the Internet, establishing his own Web page.

During his years in Long Island politics, Israel said, he always had in mind a return to Washington.

His chance came in 2000 when New York Mayor Rudolph W. Giuliani announced that he had prostate cancer and was giving up his bid for the Senate. The 2nd District's four-term congressman, Republican Rick A. Lazio, stepped in to take the GOP Senate nomination and Israel, by then a prominent municipal official on Long Island, immediately launched a campaign for the open seat.

Israel narrowly beat out Suffolk County legislator David Bishop for the Democratic nod and went on to win in the general election.

His hold on the seat seemed tenuous in 2002. There was talk that redistricting might put him and Republican Rep. Felix Grucci Jr. in the same district. There was also the specter of a challenge from the popular Lazio, whom GOP strategists were urging to make a comeback. Neither event came to pass and Israel won re-election comfortably with just more than 58 percent of the vote. He won with nearly 67 percent in 2004 and with 70 percent in 2006.

KEY VOTES

2006

Yes Stop broadband companies from favoring select Internet traffic
No Affirm U.S. commitment to war in Iraq and reject setting a withdrawal date for troops
No Repeal requirement for bilingual ballots at the polls
Yes Permit U.S. sale of civilian nuclear technology to India
Yes Build a 700-mile fence on the U.S.-Mexico border to curb illegal crossings
No Permit warrantless wiretaps of suspected terrorists

2005

No Intervene in the life-support case of Terri Schiavo
Yes Lift President Bush's restrictions on stem cell research funding
Yes Prohibit FBI access to library and bookstore records
No Approve free-trade pact with five Central American countries
No Pass energy policy overhaul favored by President Bush emphasizing domestic oil and gas production
No End mandatory preservation of habitat of endangered animal and plant species
Yes Ban torture of prisoners in U.S. custody

CQ VOTE STUDIES

	PARTY UNITY		PRESIDENTIAL SUPPORT	
	Support	Oppose	Support	Oppose
2006	93%	7%	28%	72%
2005	94%	6%	24%	76%
2004	92%	8%	30%	70%
2003	90%	10%	31%	69%
2002	83%	17%	41%	59%

INTEREST GROUPS

	AFL-CIO	ADA	CCUS	ACU
2006	100%	90%	50%	12%
2005	87%	90%	52%	8%
2004	93%	100%	47%	13%
2003	80%	90%	47%	20%
2002	67%	75%	58%	32%

NEW YORK 2

Long Island – Brentwood, Commack

Covering most of western Suffolk County and a small part of east-central Nassau County on Long Island, the 2nd is full of suburban communities that combine to give the district New York's highest median income. Many residents who do not commute to New York City also contribute to the district's large white-collar workforce by working at computer and electronics firms in the 2nd.

The district, once dependent on the defense industry, now hosts many computer and technology companies. The 2nd's portion of Nassau County, which includes Jericho, Old Bethpage, Plainview and Woodbury, has a burgeoning computer sector that provides thousands of jobs for ...rict residents. Aeroflex, which manufactures microelectronic ...ts, is based in Plainview.

...ses a relatively diverse population, mixing well-to-do ...uch as the district's Nassau County portion and Dix Hills ...- and working-class neighborhoods. During the ...Yorkers flock to the district's communities along the Atlantic Ocean in the south. Some residents in the coastal areas still make modest incomes in the fishing industry, but Fire Island (shared with the 3rd) relies on tourism.

With a nearly 30 percent minority population, a significant Jewish community and a blue-collar base, the 2nd has a substantial, but not overwhelming, Democratic vote. Moderate Republicans tend to do well in local races, but the district favors Democratic candidates in federal elections, and John Kerry captured 53 percent of the vote here in the 2004 presidential election.

MAJOR INDUSTRY

Computers, electronics, service

CITIES

Brentwood (unincorporated), 53,917; Commack (unincorporated), 36,363; Central Islip (unincorporated), 31,950; Huntington Station (unincorporated), 29,910

NOTABLE

The Walt Whitman Birthplace State Historic Site and Interpretive Center is in West Hills (South Huntington); Ocean Beach, a village on the Fire Island National Seashore, prohibits eating and drinking on the beach; Islip Long Island MacArthur Airport is near Ronkonkoma.

Rep. Peter T. King (R)

CAPITOL OFFICE
225-7896
pete.king@mail.house.gov
www.house.gov/king
339 Cannon 20515-3203; fax 226-2279

COMMITTEES
Financial Services
Homeland Security - ranking member

RESIDENCE
Seaford

BORN
April 5, 1944, Manhattan, N.Y.

RELIGION
Roman Catholic

FAMILY
Wife, Rosemary King; two children

EDUCATION
St. Francis College, B.A. 1965 (history);
U. of Notre Dame, J.D. 1968

MILITARY SERVICE
N.Y. National Guard, 1968-73

CAREER
Lawyer

POLITICAL HIGHLIGHTS
Hempstead Town Council, 1978-81; Nassau County comptroller, 1981-93; Republican nominee for N.Y. attorney general, 1986

ELECTION RESULTS

2006 GENERAL		
Peter T. King (R, INDC, C)	101,787	56.0%
David L. Mejias (D, WFM)	79,843	44.0%
2006 PRIMARY		
Peter T. King (R)	11,077	84.0%
Robert Previdi (R)	2,110	16.0%
2004 GENERAL		
Peter T. King (R, INDC, C)	171,259	63.0%
Blair H. Mathies Jr. (D)	100,737	37.0%

PREVIOUS WINNING PERCENTAGES
2002 (72%); 2000 (60%); 1998 (64%); 1996 (55%); 1994 (59%); 1992 (50%)

Elected 1992; 8th term

Republicans lost the majority and King lost his chairman's gavel just as he was completing a transformation from colorful wise guy to policy whiz. He's as quotable as ever, though he has a greater appreciation for life in the majority now that his short run at the helm of the Homeland Security Committee is over.

King, who is the senior Republican on Homeland Security for the 110th Congress (2007-08), guided the committee to a series of impressive legislative accomplishments after taking over the gavel in September 2005. A $2 billion port security bill passed and was signed into law, and the committee's legislation calling for more border patrol agents and surveillance equipment was adopted as part of the House immigration overhaul. King also had a hand in the restructuring of the Federal Emergency Management Agency after its bungling of the Hurricane Katrina crisis.

Through it all, King was still King — outspoken, and at times persuasive, but at times insensitive to the fallout from his blunt talk. Reflecting on his affinity for controversy, King said in an interview, "Sometimes I don't know whether I'm a great leader or Forrest Gump." He was referring to the misfit film character's unwitting involvement in current events, but he might as well have been talking about Gump's propensity for saying exactly what he's thinking.

King took on what he viewed as hypocrisy in his own party on a guest worker bill for illegal immigrants, saying, "Republicans are caving in to corporate America and big businesses that want cheap labor." But he came under fire for suggesting that airport screeners single out people who looked Middle Eastern or South Asian.

Still, King moved some significant bills through the politically polarized House. Just before the 2006 election, Congress passed his legislation to screen millions of containers that enter the United States each year, which some maritime security experts called a "Trojan Horse" for the smuggling of humans, drugs or weapons.

The bill was the finale to a debate over port security that King dominated. It began with revelations that a United Arab Emirates company was to purchase operations at six U.S. port terminals. King was the first Republican to denounce the deal publicly, and became a sought-after source for reporters covering the story. "We're not going to let Democrats get to the right of us on homeland security," King proclaimed. Under congressional pressure, the company decided to sell its interest in the ports.

King was made Homeland Security chairman after campaigning hard for the job. When Republican Christopher Cox of California left the House in August 2005 to head the Securities and Exchange Commission, King lobbied to be his replacement though more-senior members were ahead of him. He waged what leadership insiders rated as an impressive bid centered on his passion for homeland security, his personal connection to Sept. 11 — King lost several friends at the World Trade Center — and a history of vigorously backing the party on national security issues.

King is just enough of a GOP maverick to get his name into the newspapers and on the air frequently, and just enough of a conservative to keep himself in the good graces of the Republican leadership. He's one of the few members of Congress to have pictures of himself with both Bill Clinton and George W. Bush on his wall. Bush's nickname for him is "Pedro."

King votes with his party on most fiscal and social issues, supportin expanded trade opportunities and private school vouchers, while opposing abortion. But he also supports labor unions' efforts to raise the minimum wage and expand worker protections.

The son of a New York City police officer, King supports law enforcement and has a strong interest in coordination between the federal government and local police and firefighters in combating terrorism.

King has had an important role promoting peace efforts in Northern Ireland. He has made several trips to Northern Ireland and has a close relationship with Gerry Adams, the leader of Sinn Fein, the political wing of the Irish Republican Army. Nevertheless, in 2005, frustrated with increasing criminal behavior in the IRA, King called for it to disband, a major step for one of Sinn Fein's biggest backers in Congress.

King draws on his experiences to fuel his pastime — fiction writing. In his 2004 book "Vale of Tears," the congressman protagonist faces radical Islamists in cahoots with the IRA.

His interest in Irish affairs — three of his grandparents are from Ireland — brought King close to New York Democratic Sen. Hillary Rodham Clinton. King worked closely with the Clinton White House on the 1998 peace accord and flew to Ireland on Air Force One for the celebration. The same year, King argued against President Clinton's impeachment by the House, one of only four Republicans to vote against all four impeachment articles.

A veteran of the rough-and-tumble politics of Nassau County, King grew up in a blue-collar Queens neighborhood where kids were as likely to be boxing fans as baseball fans. "This is the one sport where you are out there on your own," King, who boxes for exercise, once told Newsday. "There are other individual sports like tennis, but if you lose in boxing you get your head split open, you lose your teeth and the whole world sees."

He borrowed money to attend Notre Dame's law school. Afterward, he interned (along with Rudolph Giuliani) at Richard Nixon's New York law firm. He entered public life in 1972 as a deputy Nassau County attorney and eventually became the county comptroller, serving three terms. During his tenure, King lost a 1986 run for New York attorney general.

When veteran GOP Rep. Norman F. Lent stepped down in 1992, King moved quickly to establish himself as Lent's successor. After coasting through the primary, he narrowly survived a contest against the better-funded Democrat, Steve A. Orlins.

He routinely won re-election every two years — until 2006, when the anti-GOP tide put him at risk from a strong Democratic challenger. It was a closer match than usual, but he prevailed with 56 percent of the vote.

KEY VOTES

2006

- No Stop broadband companies from favoring select Internet traffic
- Yes Affirm U.S. commitment to war in Iraq and reject setting a withdrawal date for troops
- Yes Repeal requirement for bilingual ballots at the polls
- Yes Permit U.S. sale of civilian nuclear technology to India
- Yes Build a 700-mile fence on the U.S.-Mexico border to curb illegal crossings
- Yes Permit warrantless wiretaps of suspected terrorists

2005

- ? Intervene in the life-support case of Terri Schiavo
- No Lift President Bush's restrictions on stem cell research funding
- No Prohibit FBI access to library and bookstore records
- Yes Approve free-trade pact with five Central American countries
- Yes Pass energy policy overhaul favored by President Bush emphasizing domestic oil and gas production
- Yes End mandatory preservation of habitat of endangered animal and plant species
- No Ban torture of prisoners in U.S. custody

CQ VOTE STUDIES

	PARTY UNITY		PRESIDENTIAL SUPPORT	
	Support	Oppose	Support	Oppose
2006	89%	11%	95%	5%
2005	89%	11%	83%	17%
2004	83%	17%	77%	23%
2003	93%	7%	89%	11%
2002	92%	8%	84%	16%

INTEREST GROUPS

	AFL-CIO	ADA	CCUS	ACU
2006	36%	5%	100%	76%
2005	20%	0%	89%	83%
2004	50%	25%	80%	71%
2003	27%	15%	83%	72%
2002	0%	10%	85%	83%

NEW YORK 3

Long Island – Levittown, Hicksville, Long Beach

Most of Long Island's eastern Nassau County and the south shore of western Suffolk County make up the 3rd, where extravagant estates mingle with some of the nation's oldest middle-class suburbs. The district boasts New York State's second-highest median income and is overwhelmingly white, with the lowest percentage of black residents (2 percent) in the state and the lowest percentage of Hispanics (7 percent) in the New York City area.

Once a major local presence, aircraft manufacturing giant Northrop Grumman still plays a reduced role in the 3rd's economy. Information -hnology companies, such as those in Farmingdale's Broad Hollow -ience Park, have spread throughout the 3rd and neighboring Long -tricts, diversifying the local economy. The district also enjoys an -ent rate that remains below state and national averages.

-sts the district's economy. Thousands of visitors flock to -ke Freeport's "Nautical Mile" and to beautiful golf -page State Park, which will host the 2009 U.S. Open Championship. The 3rd is home to a variety of beautiful south shore beaches, including Long Beach and Jones Beach, which hosts an outdoor summer concert series. Other visitors travel to President Theodore Roosevelt's Sagamore Hill estate in Oyster Bay and his nearby grave in Youngs Memorial Cemetery.

The district tends to favor Republican candidates, but a significant labor presence from construction and professional unions gives Democrats some areas of strength. Democrats also have made gains in Nassau County overall, but George W. Bush won the 3rd in 2004 with 52 percent of the presidential vote.

MAJOR INDUSTRY
Information technology, higher education, service

CITIES
Levittown (unincorporated), 53,067; Hicksville (unincorporated) (pt.), 39,670; Long Beach, 35,462; West Islip (unincorporated) (pt.), 27,171; Lindenhurst (pt.), 27,162; Glen Cove, 26,622

NOTABLE
The C.W. Post Campus of Long Island University, named for the breakfast cereal and food company founder, is located on the grounds of the former Brookville estate of the magnate's daughter.

Rep. Carolyn McCarthy (D)

CAPITOL OFFICE
225-5516
www.house.gov/carolynmccarthy
106 Cannon 20515-3204; fax 225-5758

COMMITTEES
Education & Labor
(Healthy Families & Communities - chairwoman)
Financial Services

RESIDENCE
Mineola

BORN
Jan. 5, 1944, Brooklyn, N.Y.

RELIGION
Roman Catholic

FAMILY
Widowed; one child

EDUCATION
Glen Cove Nursing School, L.P.N. 1964

CAREER
Nurse

POLITICAL HIGHLIGHTS
No previous office

ELECTION RESULTS

2006 GENERAL		
McCarthy (D, INDC, WFM)	101,861	64.9%
Martin W. Blessinger (R, C)	55,050	35.1%
2006 PRIMARY		
Carolyn McCarthy (D)		unopposed
2004 GENERAL		
McCarthy (D, INDC, WFM)	159,969	63.0%
James A. Garner (R, C)	94,141	37.1%

PREVIOUS WINNING PERCENTAGES
2002 (56%); 2000 (61%); 1998 (53%); 1996 (57%)

Elected 1996; 6th term

More than most people, McCarthy has lived a life marked by tragedy. A strong and resolute woman, she has used her misfortunes to change the direction of her life.

As a high school student, McCarthy said she planned on being a gym teacher. Then her boyfriend was involved in a serious car accident. She watched as a private-duty nurse cared for him and as he died of his injuries a few days later. "I came home that day and applied to nursing school," she told Good Housekeeping magazine. She worked as a nurse for more than 30 years, caring for patients who were hopelessly burned and terminal — the kind "nobody else would touch," she said.

After McCarthy married, she and her stockbroker husband lived in Mineola, Long Island, where they raised their son. In December 1993, a deranged gunman opened fire on a Long Island Rail Road commuter train, killing McCarthy's husband, Dennis, and seriously wounding her adult son, Kevin. Her son was paralyzed and not expected to walk again, but with McCarthy's determination and care, he was able to resume his commute to Manhattan to work.

Three years after the shootings, a vote by her congressman against gun control got her into politics. McCarthy was incensed when freshman Republican Daniel Frisa voted in 1996 to eliminate a ban on semiautomatic weapons. A Republican, she contacted local party officials about mounting a challenge to Frisa. They tried to discourage her, so she quit the GOP and launched a campaign as a Democrat to unseat him.

McCarthy raised more than $1 million, outspent Frisa and campaigned on gun control and health policy. She said Frisa was out of the mainstream and in the mold of conservative House Speaker Newt Gingrich. Frisa seemed at a loss for an effective response, and she won the election by 17 percentage points.

Her efforts on gun control have had somewhat limited success in the Republican-controlled House, but with her party now setting the agenda she is in a better position. She does not expect, however, to have enough votes to finally reinstate the assault weapons ban — even though she again offered such legislation in early 2007 — but says she plans to still focus on improving gun safety and enforcing current laws.

In the 108th Congress (2003-04), she suffered a major setback when House Republicans blocked an extension of an assault weapons ban that had been in place for 10 years. "I know I get very emotional about it," she said as the ban neared an end. "The problem is I know the effect it's going to have in this country as it comes down the road. I know there are going to be a lot more families, they're going to be, unfortunately, in the same position that I was in. And we're going to see a lot more of our police officers, unfortunately, gunned down."

In the 109th Congress (2005-06), she pushed a proposal to ban gun purchases by anyone on the government's "do not fly" list, but it was turned back. She also failed to gain support for a measure in 2006 to authorize funding to help states enter their records on felony criminal convictions and domestic violence incidents into the FBI's National Instant Criminal Background Check System (NICS). Gun dealers use NICS to search for information that would disqualify a person from buying a firearm.

But she has had some success. In 2005, she persuaded the Judiciary Committee to eliminate a provision in an anti-gang measure that would ha allowed children in grade school to carry a firearm anywhere as long as they were in the company of a parent. "Today was a good day because we got rid of something bad in the bill," McCarthy told Newsday. "Personally, I don't know why a 9-year-old should ever have a gun."

Having struggled with dyslexia, McCarthy has a special interest in education and has been active on the Education and Labor Committee. For the 110th Congress (2007-08), she was given the gavel of the Healthy Families and Communities Subcommittee. During her tenure on the committee, she has pressed for more federal aid to school districts to help cope with the costs of educating learning-disabled children. And she has backed multibillion-dollar Democratic plans to pay for new teachers and renovate aging schools, but she has opposed GOP proposals for school vouchers.

She played an active role in the 107th Congress (2001-02) as the Education panel drafted President Bush's No Child Left Behind overhaul of federal elementary and secondary education programs. McCarthy joined forces with Dale E. Kildee, a Michigan Democrat, and Mark Souder, an Indiana Republican, to defeat an attempt to consolidate drug-abuse prevention and after-school programs into a single block grant.

McCarthy is a steady friend of labor and supports legislation to promote abortion rights and environmental protection. But she can sometimes tilt toward conservatism: She has backed constitutional amendments to ban desecration of the U.S. flag and to require a two-thirds congressional majority to raise federal taxes. She also has voted to repeal the estate tax, although she opposed Bush's 2003 tax cuts and the 2003 Medicare bill.

McCarthy was born in Brooklyn and her family moved to Mineola when she was 8. She said the house they bought was across a dirt road from a dairy farm. She and her husband had their wedding reception at the house, which they later bought from her parents. Twenty-seven years later, McCarthy held his funeral reception there. Her kitchen is full of plates with Norman Rockwell paintings on them; she estimates she owns about 40 of the collectibles.

She always will be first and foremost identified with the tragedy that propelled her into public life and inspired her continuing crusade for tougher gun control laws. "I've come to peace with the fact that that will be in my obituary," she told The Associated Press.

Since her initial race in 1996, McCarthy has won re-election each term by a healthy margin, with the exception of her second contest, in 1998, when eight-term state Rep. Gregory R. Becker held her to a 6 percentage point margin.

KEY VOTES

2006

Yes Stop broadband companies from favoring select Internet traffic
Yes Affirm U.S. commitment to war in Iraq and reject setting a withdrawal date for troops
No Repeal requirement for bilingual ballots at the polls
Yes Permit U.S. sale of civilian nuclear technology to India
Yes Build a 700-mile fence on the U.S.-Mexico border to curb illegal crossings
No Permit warrantless wiretaps of suspected terrorists

2005

? Intervene in the life-support case of Terri Schiavo
Yes Lift President Bush's restrictions on stem cell research funding
Yes Prohibit FBI access to library and bookstore records
No Approve free-trade pact with five Central American countries
No Pass energy policy overhaul favored by President Bush emphasizing domestic oil and gas production
No End mandatory preservation of habitat of endangered animal and plant species
Yes Ban torture of prisoners in U.S. custody

CQ VOTE STUDIES

	PARTY UNITY		PRESIDENTIAL SUPPORT	
	Support	Oppose	Support	Oppose
2006	92%	8%	30%	70%
2005	93%	7%	22%	78%
2004	94%	6%	32%	68%
2003	91%	9%	28%	72%
2002	84%	16%	45%	55%

INTEREST GROUPS

	AFL-CIO	ADA	CCUS	ACU
2006	100%	90%	47%	20%
2005	93%	90%	50%	8%
2004	93%	100%	45%	12%
2003	93%	85%	40%	24%
2002	67%	80%	60%	32%

NEW YORK 4

Southwest Nassau County — Hempstead

The Long Island-based 4th extends east from the Queens border to take in southwest and west-central Nassau County. The district combines wealthy white-collar suburbanites, some of whom commute to Wall Street, with low- and middle-income residents.

Bordered roughly by Interstate 495 in the north, the 4th picks up numerous medium-size communities and includes a small portion of Long Island's Atlantic Ocean coastline in Atlantic Beach. Hempstead is home to Hofstra University's 240-acre campus, which continues to be the catalyst for Hempstead's economy. Local businesses in nearby [illegible]ondale and surrounding areas benefit from people who visit Nassau [illegible]m to see hockey's New York Islanders or other arena events.

[illegible]cline in the defense industry that began two decades ago, [illegible]logy companies still provide jobs here. A number of [illegible]dents are employed by John F. Kennedy International [illegible] in the 6th District), Belmont Park race track or [illegible]uch as Garden City's Roosevelt Field Mall. Hospitals and health care facilities throughout the district also employ many area residents.

The 4th has the largest minority population of Long Island's four congressional districts, and has a Democratic base, particularly in Hempstead and Uniondale, which include large black and Hispanic communities. The largely Jewish "Five Towns" (Inwood, Lawrence, Cedarhurst, Woodmere and Hewlett), in the 4th's southwestern corner, also lean Democratic. In local elections, the 4th favors some moderate Republicans, but Democrats win in federal and statewide races, and John Kerry took 55 percent of the district's vote in the 2004 presidential election.

MAJOR INDUSTRY

Health care, technology, higher education

CITIES

Hempstead, 56,554; East Meadow (unincorporated), 37,461; Valley Stream, 36,368; Freeport (pt.), 34,958; Elmont (unincorporated), 32,657

NOTABLE

Drinkmaker Snapple was founded in Valley Stream; In 1957, Adelphi University hosted the first National Wheelchair Games; Garden City's Cradle of Aviation Museum celebrates Long Island's aviation heritage.

Rep. Gary L. Ackerman (D)

CAPITOL OFFICE
225-2601
gary_ackerman@mail.house.gov
www.house.gov/ackerman
2243 Rayburn 20515-3205; fax 225-1589

COMMITTEES
Financial Services
Foreign Affairs
(Middle East & South Asia - chairman)

RESIDENCE
Queens

BORN
Nov. 19, 1942, Brooklyn, N.Y.

RELIGION
Jewish

FAMILY
Wife, Rita Ackerman; three children

EDUCATION
Queens College, B.A. 1965

CAREER
Teacher; newspaper publisher and editor; advertising executive

POLITICAL HIGHLIGHTS
Sought Democratic nomination for New York City Council at large, 1977; N.Y. Senate, 1979-83

ELECTION RESULTS

2006 GENERAL		
Gary L. Ackerman (D, INDC, WFM)	unopposed	
2006 PRIMARY		
Gary L. Ackerman (D)	unopposed	
2004 GENERAL		
Gary L. Ackerman (D, INDC, WFM)	119,726	71.3%
Stephen Graves (R, C)	46,867	27.9%

PREVIOUS WINNING PERCENTAGES
2002 (92%); 2000 (68%); 1998 (65%); 1996 (64%); 1994 (55%); 1992 (52%); 1990 (100%); 1988 (100%); 1986 (77%); 1984 (69%); 1983 Special Election (50%)

Elected March 1983; 12th full term

As the new chairman of the House subcommittee on U.S. policy in the Middle East, Ackerman is pushing the Bush administration for more aggressive involvement in brokering peace in the region. And with his acid wit and fresh carnation tucked into his suit coat daily, he is hard to ignore.

The son of a New York cab driver, Ackerman is Jewish, strongly pro-Israel and given to straight talk, not diplomatic grandiloquence. "I think the Bush administration has been completely detached," he told Newsday soon after taking the gavel of the Foreign Affairs panel's Subcommittee on Middle East and South Asia in 2007. "And what they have done has been botched completely."

Ackerman says the administration lost an opportunity to reach out to Palestinian Authority President Mahmoud Abbas in his power struggle with the terrorist group Hamas, to prevent the formation of a coalition government. Ackerman favors a two-state solution that gives the Palestinians their own state if they recognize Israel's right to exist.

Ackerman also wants President Bush to put conditions on aid to Pakistan to encourage it to step up measures against terrorists on its soil. At one of the first hearings called by Ackerman, he said, "It is long past time for the Congress to add benchmarks on aid to Pakistan to ensure that progress against terrorism and towards restoring democracy is actually made."

A respected voice on foreign policy who often travels overseas, Ackerman is not hostile to bipartisan endeavors with Republicans. After the Sept. 11 terrorist attacks, Ackerman forged an unlikely alliance with GOP Reps. Tom DeLay of Texas and Roy Blunt of Missouri, both Christian conservatives, on a bill that would have severed ties between the United States and Yasser Arafat's Palestinian Authority.

To promote global security, Ackerman says, the United States must stay engaged in dialogue with nations such as China and North Korea that are allegedly involved in weapons proliferation. Breaking with his allies in labor, he voted in 2000 to grant China permanent normal trade status. He also has successfully battled efforts by conservatives to cut aid to India.

In spite of the seriousness of his subject matter, Ackerman is quirky and colorful, funny and unorthodox. He is a sometimes guest of shock radio jock Howard Stern. In Washington, he lives on a houseboat on the Potomac called the Unsinkable II. He says the original Unsinkable wasn't.

At a hearing in February 2007 with Secretary of State Condoleezza Rice, Ackerman criticized the Pentagon for firing linguists fluent in Arabic and Farsi because they are homosexual. "For some reason, the military seems more afraid of gay people than they are of terrorists," he said. "And if the terrorists ever got a hold of this information, they would get a platoon of lesbians to chase us out of Baghdad."

When the House in 1999 took up a constitutional amendment to ban desecration of the U.S. flag, Ackerman came to the floor wearing a tie depicting the flag as an illustration of what would be banned under the amendment. In a radio interview with Stern, Ackerman described himself as "naked and draped in the flag."

Ackerman holds liberal views on education, health care and the environment. As a senior Democrat on the Financial Services panel, he sponsored a bill in 2007 to stop some credit card companies from charging customers fees to pay their bills online or by phone even when they are paying on time.

Ackerman tends to the parochial concerns of his sprawling, diverse 5th

District. He saved the U.S. Coast Guard station at Eatons Neck from threatened closure; he pushed for resolution of the 1994 Long Island Rail Road strike; and he lobbies relentlessly for funds to clean up Long Island Sound. When Newsday rated 10 Long Island and Queens members of Congress in 2004, Ackerman drew the top score.

He sports a white carnation boutonniere daily, a habit he picked up 30 years ago as a New York public school teacher. One morning, he stopped at a florist, added a flower to his lapel, and told his students, who assumed incorrectly that it was his birthday, "Every day is special."

Ackerman was born in Brooklyn and grew up in a Queens housing project with his parents and a brother. His mother was a Polish immigrant. When she died, Ackerman found a shoebox with a copy of her father's naturalization papers, with the place of birth listed as "Warsaw, Russia."

He trusted his father, a cab driver, for a sense of what people in New York were thinking, later calling him his "pollster" and "always right on the money."

After college, Ackerman was a social studies teacher. In 1969, as a new father, he successfully sued the New York City Board of Education for the right of a father to receive unpaid leave to care for newborns, at a time when the benefit was offered only to women.

He later left teaching to launch his own community newspaper in Queens, and subsequently had run-ins with the local Democratic machine. He is still on the board of managers of Tribco LLC, publisher of the Queens Tribune and nine other weekly newspapers.

Ackerman's political career began in 1978 with a state Senate seat. After Democratic Rep. Benjamin S. Rosenthal died in 1983, Ackerman persuaded Democratic leaders to support him in the special-election race against a wealthy independent, pollster Douglas Schoen, and a less competitive GOP candidate. Ackerman won with 50 percent of the vote and then cruised through four re-elections in the then 7th District.

In redistricting for the 1992 election, some of Ackerman's base in Queens was replaced with conservative, suburban areas in Nassau and Suffolk counties, throwing him into Long Island's 5th District. He was also hurt by revelations that he had 111 overdrafts at the House members' bank during the scandal over special checking privileges for lawmakers. But he prevailed by 7 percentage points over GOP Suffolk County Legislator Allan E. Binder, rolling up a big margin in what remained of his Queens district. Further changes to the boundaries before the 2002 election made the 5th more Democratic. Ackerman was unopposed in the 2006 election.

KEY VOTES

2006

No Stop broadband companies from favoring select Internet traffic

No Affirm U.S. commitment to war in Iraq and reject setting a withdrawal date for troops

No Repeal requirement for bilingual ballots at the polls

Yes Permit U.S. sale of civilian nuclear technology to India

No Build a 700-mile fence on the U.S.-Mexico border to curb illegal crossings

No Permit warrantless wiretaps of suspected terrorists

2005

? Intervene in the life-support case of Terri Schiavo

Yes Lift President Bush's restrictions on stem cell research funding

Yes Prohibit FBI access to library and bookstore records

No Approve free-trade pact with five Central American countries

No Pass energy policy overhaul favored by President Bush emphasizing domestic oil and gas production

No End mandatory preservation of habitat of endangered animal and plant species

Yes Ban torture of prisoners in U.S. custody

CQ VOTE STUDIES

	PARTY UNITY		PRESIDENTIAL SUPPORT	
	Support	Oppose	Support	Oppose
2006	95%	5%	33%	67%
2005	98%	3%	24%	76%
2004	99%	1%	30%	70%
2003	95%	5%	23%	77%
2002	93%	7%	32%	68%

INTEREST GROUPS

	AFL-CIO	ADA	CCUS	ACU
2006	93%	95%	47%	8%
2005	93%	95%	37%	4%
2004	93%	95%	41%	4%
2003	100%	95%	26%	17%
2002	100%	95%	37%	4%

NEW YORK 5

Northeast Queens; northwest Nassau County

The 5th stretches east from south of LaGuardia Airport in Queens into northwestern Nassau County, reaching Roslyn and East Hills. Almost 80 percent of the Democratic-leaning 5th's residents live in Queens.

Half of New York City's Asians live in Queens, especially in downtown Flushing, which has the second-largest Chinatown in New York. The district has the largest Asian population of any congressional district outside Hawaii or California. The neighborhoods of North Corona and South Corona have a strong Hispanic influence.

Flushing is currently experiencing residential and retail development, focused particularly on its waterfront, and the 5th's economy, especially in Flushing, is supported by successful small businesses as well as national chains. The economy here also is heavily driven by white-collar jobs located outside the district, and is boosted by the U.S. Merchant Marine Academy at Kings Point and major sporting venues — Shea Stadium and the soon-to-be-built CitiField (respectively, the current and future homes of baseball's Mets) in Flushing and the USTA National Tennis Center in Flushing Meadows-Corona Park, where the U.S. Open tennis tournament is held each year.

Although pockets of low-income neighborhoods exist in the 5th, northeastern Queens has affluent areas such as the Douglaston and Little Neck neighborhoods near the Nassau County line. Before fanning eastward into Nassau, the district buttonhooks to the south and west along the Grand Central Parkway to take in some communities in north Jamaica. In Nassau County along Long Island's "Gold Coast," the 5th's residents enjoy a rich lifestyle.

Nassau tends to be politically competitive, but the strong Democratic tilt of Queens helped John Kerry take 63 percent of the district's vote during the 2004 presidential election.

MAJOR INDUSTRY

Higher education, health care, small business

CITIES

New York (pt.), 517,889; Port Washington (unincorporated), 15,215; Great Neck, 9,538

NOTABLE

Trumpet virtuoso Louis Armstrong is buried at Flushing Cemetery.

Rep. Gregory W. Meeks (D)

CAPITOL OFFICE
225-3461
www.house.gov/meeks
2342 Rayburn 20515-3206; fax 226-4169

COMMITTEES
Financial Services
Foreign Affairs

RESIDENCE
Queens

BORN
Sept. 25, 1953, Harlem, N.Y.

RELIGION
Baptist

FAMILY
Wife, Simone-Marie Meeks; three children

EDUCATION
Adelphi U., B.A. 1975; Howard U., J.D. 1978

CAREER
Workers' compensation board judge; lawyer; city prosecutor

POLITICAL HIGHLIGHTS
N.Y. Assembly, 1993-98

ELECTION RESULTS

2006 GENERAL	
Gregory W. Meeks (D)	unopposed
2006 PRIMARY	
Gregory W. Meeks (D)	unopposed
2004 GENERAL	
Gregory W. Meeks (D, WFM)	unopposed

PREVIOUS WINNING PERCENTAGES
2002 (97%); 2000 (100%); 1998 (100%); 1998 Special Election (56%)

Elected February 1998; 5th full term

Meeks can see the jets thundering off from John F. Kennedy International Airport from his Queens congressional district, a daily reminder that the airport is the main economic driver for the largely black, solidly middle-class constituency he represents. In the House, he is an advocate for airlines and airline workers, and a major booster on the Financial Services panel for New York City's financial industry.

Meeks typifies the new breed of pro-business black politician that has emerged since the civil rights movement. Much of his work in Congress takes place in Financial Services, where his focus is modernizing the rules for Wall Street. He is a member of both the New Democrat Coalition and the Democratic Leadership Council, which advance politically moderate policies. The New York Daily News once said Meeks represents "a generational shift in the city's black political leadership."

One of Meeks' current projects is trying to set new ground rules for money market funds, which are now 30 years old and still subject to rules of that era. Meeks uses his committee seat as a forum for promoting affordable housing. He opposes plans to tighten regulation of Fannie Mae and Freddie Mac, the government-chartered mortgage giants, and in 2004 introduced legislation to repeal a controversial community service requirement for public housing residents.

Bills affecting airlines get Meeks' attention. In 1999, he helped start-up airline JetBlue get regulatory approval to operate at JFK, and later pushed through legislation to increase air service from both New York City airports to cities in upstate New York, including Syracuse, Buffalo and Albany. In the 108th Congress (2003-04), Meeks helped secure $22 million to help soundproof schools in the Queens neighborhoods surrounding the airport.

Meeks generally sticks with his party in battles with Republicans. He voted with his party 91 percent of the time in the 109th Congress (2005-06) on issues that polarized the two major parties.

He opposed building 700 miles of fence and providing electronic surveillance along the U.S.-Mexico border to stem the flow of illegal immigration and he voted against legislation getting rid of requirements for bilingual voting assistance at the polls.

But Meeks voted for President Bush's Central American Free Trade Agreement, though House Democratic leaders viewed the vote as a test of party unity as well as a stand against what they termed a lack of labor protections in the accord. Organized labor also regarded defeat of CAFTA as a priority. Meeks caught flak from labor leaders in his district, but said the agreement would boost cargo traffic at JFK.

Meeks engages in more-traditional efforts in the civil rights realm. He was once arrested for protesting the under-representation of minority law clerks at the Supreme Court. And after four New York City police officers shot and killed Guinean immigrant Amadou Diallo in 1999, he joined other black leaders in protesting police violence against minorities.

In 2006, Diallo's name was invoked again after another sensational shooting incident, this time in Queens. Three police officers were charged in the fatal shooting of Sean Bell — an unarmed African-American who was killed in a hail of 50 bullets in the early morning hours of his wedding day. "If this is yet another case of excessive force, then the police officers must be held accountable to the fullest extent allowed by the law," Meeks said. The first officer to shoot at Bell's car has claimed he believed there was a gun in the car.

Raised in public housing in East Harlem, Meeks says affordable child care and education are essential to helping people improve their lot. His district was hit hard by the economic aftershocks of the Sept. 11 terrorist attacks. Though Democrats were unable to obtain help for the thousands of airline workers who were laid off, Meeks backed the law providing up to $15 billion in aid for the airlines. He and other New York lawmakers also championed US Airways' successful effort to obtain a $900 million federal loan guarantee.

Meeks traces his interest in public affairs to his mother, who resumed her education when her four children were in their teens and frequently got her kids involved in community improvement projects. As a youth, his idol was legendary civil rights attorney and Supreme Court Justice Thurgood Marshall. "From the time that I could remember, I wanted to be a lawyer," Meeks told Newsday newspaper. "I always admired Thurgood Marshall and I learned from my parents what he was doing to make life better for people of color."

After graduating from Howard University Law School, Meeks began his career as a Queens County assistant district attorney and narcotics crime prosecutor. After a brief stint on the state Commission of Investigation, which probes wrongdoing by state officials and organized crime, Meeks was appointed as a state workers' compensation judge. During those years, Meeks became involved in a variety of community projects — neighborhood cleanups, street repairs, traffic problems and street safety — in the working-class neighborhood of Far Rockaway, where his parents eventually moved.

Meeks says he always thought his involvement in politics would be behind the scenes, but in 1992 he ran for and won the first of three terms to the state Assembly. In his years in Albany, he had seats on committees that oversaw state codes, the judiciary, insurance, small business and government operations.

When Democrat Floyd H. Flake resigned his 6th District seat in the House in late 1997 to lead an influential African Methodist Episcopal church in Jamaica, Queens, he endorsed Meeks as his successor.

Meeks also got the backing of local Democratic leaders in the February 1998 special election. He captured 56 percent of the vote in a five-way contest. He was unopposed in the election for a full term in November and has not drawn Republican opposition in subsequent elections.

Meeks was national co-chairman of the Kerry-Edwards campaign in 2004, and took part in a 20-person Democratic "truth squad" that crisscrossed the battleground states denouncing Bush administration policies.

KEY VOTES

2006

No Stop broadband companies from favoring select Internet traffic

No Affirm U.S. commitment to war in Iraq and reject setting a withdrawal date for troops

No Repeal requirement for bilingual ballots at the polls

Yes Permit U.S. sale of civilian nuclear technology to India

No Build a 700-mile fence on the U.S.-Mexico border to curb illegal crossings

No Permit warrantless wiretaps of suspected terrorists

2005

? Intervene in the life-support case of Terri Schiavo

Yes Lift President Bush's restrictions on stem cell research funding

Yes Prohibit FBI access to library and bookstore records

Yes Approve free-trade pact with five Central American countries

Yes Pass energy policy overhaul favored by President Bush emphasizing domestic oil and gas production

No End mandatory preservation of habitat of endangered animal and plant species

Yes Ban torture of prisoners in U.S. custody

CQ VOTE STUDIES

	PARTY UNITY		PRESIDENTIAL SUPPORT	
	Support	Oppose	Support	Oppose
2006	88%	12%	41%	59%
2005	93%	7%	32%	68%
2004	94%	6%	37%	63%
2003	93%	7%	25%	75%
2002	94%	6%	26%	74%

INTEREST GROUPS

	AFL-CIO	ADA	CCUS	ACU
2006	86%	90%	57%	8%
2005	92%	90%	59%	12%
2004	93%	75%	55%	9%
2003	87%	95%	45%	16%
2002	89%	85%	45%	4%

NEW YORK 6

Southeast Queens – Jamaica, St. Albans

The black-majority, mostly middle-class 6th is economically focused around John F. Kennedy International Airport on Jamaica Bay in southeastern Queens. It is the only district wholly within the 2.2 million-resident borough of Queens.

The 6th is bound roughly by Cross Bay Boulevard to the west, Grand Central Parkway to the north and the Nassau County line to the east. South of the airport, across Jamaica Bay, the 6th takes in part of Rockaway, including Edgemere and Far Rockaway. Included in the 6th's boundaries are St. John's University, located in the far north, and Aqueduct Racetrack, in the far west.

More than a generation ago, communities such as Springfield Gardens and St. Albans were settled by an Irish and Italian Catholic middle class. The demographics have completely changed today, and the district's strong health care and education industries have made it one of the nation's most economically sound black-majority districts. Nevertheless, some areas, such as South Jamaica, suffer from high unemployment and urban ills. JFK Airport, the 6th's largest employer, provides a steady job base. Nicknamed "Where America Greets the World," JFK is New York City's busiest and largest airport. Airport-based jobs, complemented by employment in health care, municipal government and residential construction, give the 6th a strong union constituency. According to the 2000 census, district residents have the nation's longest average travel time to work — more than 47 minutes.

With a sizable Hispanic constituency to go along with its black majority, the district is overwhelmingly Democratic. John Kerry won 84 percent of the 6th's vote in the 2004 presidential election, and Democrats outnumber Republicans 8-to-1 in voter registration.

MAJOR INDUSTRY

Airport, health care, education

CITIES

New York (pt.), 654,361

NOTABLE

On Feb. 7, 1964, what would become known as "Beatlemania" began at JFK Airport as the Beatles held their first U.S. press conference; King Park in Jamaica was the farm of Rufus King, a delegate to the Constitutional Convention and later a Federalist senator from New York.

Rep. Joseph Crowley (D)

CAPITOL OFFICE
225-3965
write2joecrowley@mail.house.gov
crowley.house.gov
2404 Rayburn 20515-3207; fax 225-1909

COMMITTEES
Foreign Affairs
Ways & Means

RESIDENCE
Queens

BORN
March 16, 1962, Queens, N.Y.

RELIGION
Roman Catholic

FAMILY
Wife, Kasey Crowley; three children

EDUCATION
Queens College, B.A. 1985 (communications & political science)

CAREER
State legislator

POLITICAL HIGHLIGHTS
N.Y. Assembly, 1987-99

ELECTION RESULTS

2006 GENERAL		
Joseph Crowley (D, WFM)	63,997	84.0%
Kevin Brawley (R, C)	12,220	16.0%
2006 PRIMARY		
Joseph Crowley (D)		unopposed
2004 GENERAL		
Joseph Crowley (D, WFM)	104,275	80.9%
Joseph Cinquemain (R, C)	24,548	19.1%

PREVIOUS WINNING PERCENTAGES
2002 (73%); 2000 (72%); 1998 (69%)

Elected 1998; 5th term

A burly 6-foot, 4-inch Irishman with the gift of gab, Crowley is the son of a New York cop and has been in politics for much of his life. He is a people-person and though he's lost two bids for leadership posts in the Democratic Party, he cannot be counted out as a serious contender in the future.

Crowley (KRAU-lee) kicked off his fifth term by winning a prized spot on the House Ways and Means Committee, an exclusive posting that forced him to give up his seat on the Financial Services Committee though he got a waiver from the leadership to stay on Foreign Affairs.

Among his goals on Ways and Means, Crowley wants to address soaring health care costs and the anxiety among senior citizens about their Social Security and Medicare benefits. He is not a fan of overhauling Social Security, as the Bush administration proposed, even though the government retirement fund is projected to run short of meeting its obligations in coming years. "I don't look at the issue of Social Security as a crisis," says Crowley, who favors creating government incentives for private savings to supplement Social Security.

Assigned to the Trade Subcommittee on Ways and Means, Crowley says he wants to be a voice "for reasonable, fair trade agreements" that incorporate labor and environmental standards. In the 109th Congress (2005-06), he joined a bipartisan group of lawmakers who called on the administration to renegotiate the Central American Free Trade Agreement. In 2002, he voted against presidential fast-track trade negotiating authority.

He is not categorically opposed to global trade deals, however. He split with his party to back free-trade pacts with Chile and Singapore in the 108th Congress (2003-04), and in 2006 he cosponsored legislation to establish permanent normal trade relations with Vietnam.

Crowley wants to get on the leadership track, but he's been on the wrong side of House Speaker Nancy Pelosi in recent contests. In February 2006, he made a bid for the vice chairmanship of the Democratic Caucus, the lowest rung on the elected leadership ladder, but lost to John B. Larson of Connecticut, a Pelosi ally. Crowley was aligned with Steny H. Hoyer of Maryland, a Pelosi rival. On a first ballot, Crowley got 79 votes to Larson's 66, and a third candidate, Jan Schakowsky of Illinois (also a Pelosi ally), got 56. In the runoff between Crowley and Larson, most of Schakowsky's supporters moved to Larson, who beat Crowley, 116-87.

In 2005, Crowley was on the shortlist to chair the Democratic Congressional Campaign Committee, an appointive post, but the job went to another rising star in the party, Rahm Emanuel of Illinois, the former top Clinton aide. "Do I still have leadership ambitions? Ah, it's tough to get this bug out of ya, no matter what," Crowley says.

He retains some important roles in the caucus, however. He is an impressive fundraiser for the DCCC, he is one of nine chief deputy whips who help round up votes and enforce party discipline, and he sits on the leadership-run Steering Committee, which makes committee assignments.

He is among the Democratic moderates who call themselves New Democrats. In 2002, Crowley voted to authorize President Bush to use force against Iraq, but he has since joined the majority of Democrats in castigating Bush's handling of the war. Although Crowley personally opposes abortion, he has voted with abortion rights forces, including opposing GOP attempts in 2003 to tie foreign aid to a nation's abortion policies.

Like other New Yorkers, Crowley has spent substantial time on issues stemming from the Sept. 11 terrorist attacks, including working to ensure compensation for victims' families. An estimated 105 families in his district lost a family member in the collapse of the World Trade Center towers. Crowley was personally affected: His cousin, firefighter John Moran, was killed.

Crowley comes from a close-knit family. Today he, his siblings and his mother all live within three miles of one another in Queens, where Crowley was born and raised. His mother emigrated from County Armagh in Northern Ireland as a young girl. His father, a first-generation Irish-American, was a city police officer who earned a law degree at night. As a youth, Crowley rode the subway every day into Manhattan to attend Power Memorial Academy, an all-boys Catholic high school.

Crowley inherited his political thirst from his father and even more from his uncle, Walter Crowley, a well-known local politician who served on the New York City Council. But Crowley truly flourished under the mentorship of Democrat Thomas J. Manton, his predecessor in the 7th District, whom he once considered an enemy.

In 1984, Manton beat Crowley's beloved uncle in a four-way primary for the House seat. Then in 1986, Manton tapped him on the shoulder at an Irish dinner dance and asked whether he'd thought about running for the local assembly seat, which had unexpectedly opened up. "Inside I was saying, 'Are you talking to me? I hate you. You beat my uncle,' " Crowley recalls.

Crowley went on to win the seat at the age of 24, just a year out of college. He spent 12 years in Albany, and developed a close friendship with Manton. In 1998, Manton picked Crowley as his successor in the U.S. House by announcing his retirement several days after the filing deadline and then joining with other party officials in nominating him. Crowley swamped the Republican candidate, corporate security manager James J. Dillon, in the general election. While Manton's tactics angered other Democrats, Crowley successfully defended his seat in 2000. His work in Washington has satisfied former critics, and he has won his last three elections with ease.

In 2006, Manton's mentorship helped secure Crowley one last political victory. When Manton died in July 2006, Crowley was unanimously elected to take over the helm of the Queens Democratic Party, the most powerful political machine in New York.

A guitar player, Crowley does a decent imitation of rocker Van Morrison singing "Wild Nights." He occasionally sings in public, and once belted out the national anthem before a New York Knicks basketball game.

KEY VOTES

2006

No Stop broadband companies from favoring select Internet traffic
No Affirm U.S. commitment to war in Iraq and reject setting a withdrawal date for troops
No Repeal requirement for bilingual ballots at the polls
Yes Permit U.S. sale of civilian nuclear technology to India
No Build a 700-mile fence on the U.S.-Mexico border to curb illegal crossings
No Permit warrantless wiretaps of suspected terrorists

2005

? Intervene in the life-support case of Terri Schiavo
Yes Lift President Bush's restrictions on stem cell research funding
Yes Prohibit FBI access to library and bookstore records
No Approve free-trade pact with five Central American countries
No Pass energy policy overhaul favored by President Bush emphasizing domestic oil and gas production
No End mandatory preservation of habitat of endangered animal and plant species
Yes Ban torture of prisoners in U.S. custody

CQ VOTE STUDIES

	PARTY UNITY		PRESIDENTIAL SUPPORT	
	Support	Oppose	Support	Oppose
2006	89%	11%	35%	65%
2005	97%	3%	15%	85%
2004	93%	7%	30%	70%
2003	92%	8%	27%	73%
2002	93%	7%	39%	61%

INTEREST GROUPS

	AFL-CIO	ADA	CCUS	ACU
2006	93%	95%	57%	8%
2005	93%	95%	44%	8%
2004	93%	90%	55%	9%
2003	80%	95%	37%	20%
2002	78%	95%	50%	8%

NEW YORK 7
Part of Queens and the Bronx

Few districts in the nation are as ethnically and racially diverse as the 7th, which takes in part of northern Queens and the eastern part of the Bronx. Blacks, Hispanics and Asians each make up more than 10 percent of the population, with Hispanics a clear plurality at 40 percent.

A majority of residents live in the 7th's northern tier in the Bronx. This area reaches as far west as the Bronx Zoo and the New York Botanical Garden and as far north as Co-op City, which houses more than 15,000 apartments, and the Westchester County line. The Bronx portion also includes Morris Park, Pelham Bay and Throgs Neck, and takes in both sides of the Whitestone Bridge. While portions of the Bronx struggle economically, the areas around Eastchester Bay have some of the borough's highest incomes. The health care industry is a major employer in the Bronx.

In the district's southern portion, the 7th climbs north from near the intersection of the Brooklyn-Queens and Long Island expressways (in the neighboring 12th), to take in Woodside, Jackson Heights, East Elmhurst and LaGuardia Airport. This fast-growing area is heavily Hispanic and spurred much of Queens' 14 percent population growth rate in the 1990s. LaGuardia provides thousands of jobs and makes the Queens area a transportation hub. Northeast of the airport, the district also includes most of Flushing Bay, College Point and a small part of Flushing.

Like most New York City districts, the 7th strongly supports Democrats, although a bit less uniformly. It is mostly middle-class and residential, but steady growth tied to the city has spurred new businesses. John Kerry easily carried the 7th with 74 percent of the vote in the 2004 presidential election.

MAJOR INDUSTRY
Airport, health care, service

CITIES
New York (pt.), 654,360

NOTABLE
The Maritime Industry Museum and SUNY Maritime College are at Fort Schuyler in Throgs Neck, where the East River meets Long Island Sound; The Bronx Zoo is the largest urban wildlife conservation facility in the nation.

Rep. Jerrold Nadler (D)

CAPITOL OFFICE
225-5635
www.house.gov/nadler
2334 Rayburn 20515-3208; fax 225-6923

COMMITTEES
Judiciary
(Constitution, Civil Rights & Civil Liberties - chairman)
Transportation & Infrastructure

RESIDENCE
Manhattan

BORN
June 13, 1947, Brooklyn, N.Y.

RELIGION
Jewish

FAMILY
Wife, Joyce L. Miller; one child

EDUCATION
Columbia U., A.B. 1969 (government);
Fordham U., J.D. 1978

CAREER
Lawyer; state legislative aide

POLITICAL HIGHLIGHTS
N.Y. Assembly, 1976-92; candidate for Manhattan borough president, 1985; candidate for New York City comptroller, 1989

ELECTION RESULTS

2006 GENERAL		
Jerrold Nadler (D, WFM)	108,536	85.0%
Eleanor Friedman (R)	17,413	13.6%
Dennis E. Adornato (C)	1,673	1.3%
2006 PRIMARY		
Jerrold Nadler (D)		unopposed
2004 GENERAL		
Jerrold Nadler (D, WFM)	162,082	80.5%
Peter Hort (R, C, INDC)	39,240	19.5%

PREVIOUS WINNING PERCENTAGES
2002 (76%); 2000 (81%); 1998 (86%); 1996 (82%); 1994 (82%); 1992 (81%); 1992 Special Election (100%)

Elected 1992; 8th full term

The 8th District of lower Manhattan has yet to recover fully from the Sept. 11 terrorist attacks, which destroyed its most visible landmark — the Twin Towers of the World Trade Center. Nadler has spent the past five years trying to help his constituents heal from the tragedy.

He is particularly angry at the federal government. He considers it "malfeasance" that the Environmental Protection Agency has not responded to district concerns about air contaminants and other environmental degradation resulting from the collapse of the two skyscrapers.

He says the federal government has failed to clean up homes, workplaces and schools near the site and that contaminants have seeped into the buildings' interiors. "People are slowly being poisoned to this day," Nadler says, adding that he fears there will be decades' worth of lung cancer and asbestos poisoning cases as a consequence of the contaminants.

Nadler (NAD-ler) also complains that the Bush administration has done little to provide medical care for the tens of thousands of first-responders — police officers, firefighters and iron workers — who were at the site during or after the fall of the towers, and who now show symptoms of various pulmonary ailments. "These people were permitted to work on the pile for 50 days without proper protection, and they're getting sick now," Nadler says.

In 2007, he reintroduced a measure that would provide Medicare benefits for people suffering from Sept. 11-related illnesses. It would also establish screening, testing and research facilities for health conditions stemming from the terrorist attacks.

The 8th stretches from Manhattan's Upper West Side through Greenwich Village and into Brooklyn, and it is home to one of the largest concentrations of liberal Jewish voters and gay and lesbian political activists in the country. Nadler's politics match those of his constituents. When there is legislation to restrict abortion, prohibit same-sex marriage or ban flag burning, Nadler is in the thick of the fray arguing for civil liberties and individual rights.

In 2006, he was a vocal opponent of a constitutional amendment — ultimately rejected by the House — barring same-sex marriage, which he said was motivated by political expediency. "What's a Constitution between friends when there's an election coming up?" Nadler said. Also in 2006, he led the opposition to a Republican-sponsored measure making it difficult and more expensive to sue government officials over public expressions of religion. "We will be telling government officials everywhere that Congress thinks it's OK to violate religious liberties with impunity," he said, adding that the bill would result in "gutting the ability of the courts to enforce the First Amendment."

Nadler was quick to promote his views in the 110th Congress (2007-08), as chairman of the Judiciary Committee's Constitution, Civil Rights and Civil Liberties Subcommittee. He introduced legislation aimed at ensuring habeas corpus and due process for suspected terrorists. He also has conducted hearings on ethics reform changes to the Lobby Disclosure Act and on charges of lax enforcement at the Justice Department's Civil Rights Division.

Nadler has criticized the administration's funding for national security programs, saying it is "disastrously out of whack." When press reports in July 2006 revealed that the Homeland Security Department was providing anti-terrorism grants to a bean festival and an insect zoo but not to areas of Manhattan, Nadler said Homeland Security officials were using the grants as a "slush fund."

During debate on port security legislation in 2006, he pressed for an amendment that would have required all cargo to be screened before leaving foreign ports for the United States. The proposal failed but Nadler vowed not to give up. And a few month later, in 2007, the House voted to require screening of cargo at ports, to be phased in over three years. Nadler noted that he had been pushing for such a requirement for four years.

From his seat on the Transportation and Infrastructure Committee, Nadler in 2006 secured $100 million for the engineering and design phase of a freight rail tunnel under New York Harbor to connect Brooklyn with Bayonne, N.J. The Brooklyn terminus of the proposed tunnel would be in the 8th District. Nadler says the tunnel will foster economic development, reduce air pollution and lower consumer costs in the city.

Nadler took on a more personal struggle in 2002 when he decided to undergo gastric bypass surgery to tackle obesity issues that had the 5-foot-4 lawmaker weighing in at 338 pounds. Five years later, the weight loss is still "significant" as are the health benefits, according his staff.

Born in Brooklyn, Nadler spent his early years on a New Jersey poultry farm. His family moved back to New York City after the farm failed. He stayed in the city to pursue his education, earning a degree in government from Columbia University and a law degree from Fordham, which he attended at night while working at an off-track betting office during the day.

Politics has been a lifelong passion for Nadler. In high school, he became friends with Dick Morris — who was later to gain fame and then notoriety as a political consultant to President Bill Clinton — and roomed with Morris at Columbia. Nadler organized students against the Vietnam War to campaign for Eugene McCarthy in the 1968 New Hampshire Democratic presidential primary. He was an aide to a New York state senator, and he campaigned for liberal Democrat Ted Weiss' election to Congress. In 1976, Nadler won a seat in the state Assembly. He served there for 16 years.

When Weiss died on the eve of the 1992 Democratic primary, voters renominated him nonetheless, giving party officials the right to pick a successor. That set off a scramble among the ample cadre of Democratic activists, with six candidates jumping into the frenetic nine-day race for the nomination. While others, such as former Rep. Bella S. Abzug, were better known to the public, Nadler had longstanding ties to the insiders who would cast the votes. He got the nomination and went on to win the special election as well as the general election for a full term on the same day. In the overwhelmingly Democratic district, Nadler has won re-election with ease.

KEY VOTES

2006

Yes Stop broadband companies from favoring select Internet traffic
No Affirm U.S. commitment to war in Iraq and reject setting a withdrawal date for troops
No Repeal requirement for bilingual ballots at the polls
No Permit U.S. sale of civilian nuclear technology to India
No Build a 700-mile fence on the U.S.-Mexico border to curb illegal crossings
No Permit warrantless wiretaps of suspected terrorists

2005

No Intervene in the life-support case of Terri Schiavo
Yes Lift President Bush's restrictions on stem cell research funding
Yes Prohibit FBI access to library and bookstore records
No Approve free-trade pact with five Central American countries
No Pass energy policy overhaul favored by President Bush emphasizing domestic oil and gas production
No End mandatory preservation of habitat of endangered animal and plant species
Yes Ban torture of prisoners in U.S. custody

CQ VOTE STUDIES

	PARTY UNITY		PRESIDENTIAL SUPPORT	
	Support	Oppose	Support	Oppose
2006	99%	1%	15%	85%
2005	98%	2%	13%	87%
2004	99%	1%	18%	82%
2003	99%	1%	13%	87%
2002	97%	3%	18%	82%

INTEREST GROUPS

	AFL-CIO	ADA	CCUS	ACU
2006	100%	100%	27%	4%
2005	93%	100%	35%	0%
2004	100%	100%	29%	0%
2003	100%	100%	21%	12%
2002	100%	95%	26%	0%

NEW YORK 8

West Side Manhattan; Borough Park; Coney Island

Starting just west of Central Park, the 8th travels south through Manhattan's West Side, taking in part of the Theater District and Times Square, then Chelsea, Greenwich Village, SoHo and Wall Street. It skips across the East River to skim Brooklyn's western waterfront, followed by some working-class areas, much of Brighton Beach and some of Brooklyn's southern coastline, including Coney Island.

The Sept. 11, 2001, terrorist attacks on the World Trade Center occurred in the 8th. After some debate over the rehabilitation of the area, reconstruction of lower Manhattan has begun in full force, bringing with it government grants to create new businesses, job opportunities and major construction projects.

In Brooklyn, the past decade produced dramatic increases in the retail sector, with a rise in the number of quirky local shops and eclectic restaurants, and a newly vibrant night life. New residential and commercial building projects are expected to breathe life into the area's recently declining construction sector. Meanwhile, Manhattan's thriving financial industry continues to be the district's economic stronghold.

Manhattan's heavily Democratic West Side has sent liberal representatives to Congress for decades. The 8th's active civic communities — gay, Jewish, minority, artistic and academic — have supported Democratic presidential candidates overwhelmingly for years. There are some GOP voters in Brooklyn's middle-class neighborhoods, such as Borough Park and Bensonhurst, who back candidates with more conservative views. George W. Bush actually won the 8th's portion of Brooklyn with 53 percent of the 2004 presidential vote, but overall John Kerry took 72 percent of the 8th's vote. Bush did not carry a single precinct in the 8th's part of Manhattan.

MAJOR INDUSTRY

Finance, retail, tourism, manufacturing, small business

CITIES

New York (pt.), 654,360

NOTABLE

Home of the future Freedom Tower and World Trade Center Memorial, Statue of Liberty, Empire State Building, Governors Island, South Street Seaport, American Museum of Natural History, Lincoln Center, Penn Station, Madison Square Garden, City Hall and New York University.

Rep. Anthony Weiner (D)

CAPITOL OFFICE
225-6616
weiner@mail.house.gov
www.house.gov/weiner
1122 Longworth 20515-3209; fax 226-7253

COMMITTEES
Energy & Commerce
Judiciary

RESIDENCE
Queens

BORN
Sept. 4, 1964, Brooklyn, N.Y.

RELIGION
Jewish

FAMILY
Single

EDUCATION
State U. of New York, Plattsburgh, B.A. 1985 (political science)

CAREER
Congressional aide

POLITICAL HIGHLIGHTS
New York City Council, 1992-99; sought Democratic nomination for mayor of New York, 2005

ELECTION RESULTS

2006 GENERAL		
Anthony Weiner (D, WFM)		unopposed
2006 PRIMARY		
Anthony Weiner (D)		unopposed
2004 GENERAL		
Anthony Weiner (D, WFM)	113,025	71.3%
Gerard J. Cronin (R, C, INDC)	45,451	28.7%

PREVIOUS WINNING PERCENTAGES
2002 (66%); 2000 (68%); 1998 (66%)

Elected 1998; 5th term

A quintessential New Yorker, Weiner is a brash, close-in brawler who relishes the city's intensely personal politics. Although he fell short in his 2005 bid for mayor of the Big Apple, he appears to have burnished his reputation by turning in a respectable performance and then making a graceful exit from the contest.

Weiner (WEE-ner) was defeated in the Democratic primary by Fernando Ferrer, the better-known former Bronx borough president who initially appeared to fall just shy of the 40 percent vote share needed to claim victory. Weiner withdrew in order to avert a bitter runoff, and urged his backers to unify behind Ferrer, earning the gratitude of party leaders. After Republican Mayor Michael Bloomberg defeated Ferrer, Weiner became the early front-runner for the Democratic nod in 2009, when term limits will prevent Bloomberg from running again.

The scrappy congressman regularly dives into local disputes. That can mean battling a new stadium site one day, objecting to the closing of the gym at his old high school on another, and trying on a third to resolve a fight over whether a local restaurant should be forced to remove flower-filled planters. (Weiner issued a press release siding with the flowers.)

The city's raucous tabloids delight in describing Weiner as a "political hot dog" and pronouncing, "Weiner on a roll!" He not only doesn't mind the wordplay, he uses it himself. Among the slogans in his political debut, a run for student government in college, was "Vote for Weiner. He'll be frank."

Weiner never misses a chance to tout the federal funds he has steered to his Brooklyn and Queens district. Soon after losing the mayoral primary, Weiner trumpeted a $5.75 million initiative for a local nonprofit to employ homeless New Yorkers to clean up graffiti around the city. A few months later he joined a city councilman in urging the Ford Motor Co. to build hybrid Crown Victorias, the vehicle most often used for New York taxicabs. A fleet of hybrid cabs would save gasoline and reduce air pollution, he argued.

A Judiciary Committee member, he has worked furiously since the Sept. 11 terrorist attacks to enhance security. He added a provision to the 2002 law creating the Department of Homeland Security to permit federal authorities to share security intelligence with local police. He fought to reserve a larger share of funds for New York and other major cities considered the likeliest targets of future attacks. "If we are at the point where the terrorists are targeting the Charlotte [N.C.] Raptor Museum, or whatever it is they have down there, then we are in big trouble," he told The New York Times.

In January 2007, he blamed rising violent crime rates on "years of neglect for local law enforcement by the Bush administration" and pledged to provide "the resources [police] need to keep our communities safe."

Always ready to take on President Bush's policies, Weiner is a favorite of the cable news shows. As Democrats in general shied from challenging Bush on national security in 2002, Weiner on Fox News questioned the effectiveness of the war on terrorism: "Show me a victory," he said.

The terrorist attacks also deepened Weiner's activism on issues relating to the Middle East. His district is heavily Jewish, and he is a persistent advocate of Israel. When Hamas, a militant Islamic party that has called for the destruction of Israel, won a majority of seats in 2006 Palestinian parliamentary elections, Weiner called for an immediate halt to U.S. aid. Weiner is Jewish, and while he describes himself as "not overtly" religious, his faith lends "a moral component to my work for justice in the Middle East and for the homeless in New York City."

Young, energetic and ambitious, Weiner found his footing quickly in the House. A solid Democratic liberal, he was often frustrated under GOP control. During the 109th Congress (2005-06), Republicans on the Judiciary panel rejected his attempt to amend a gun control bill to strip provisions that eased penalties on gun dealers. "You're not trying to reform the ATF, you're trying to gut handgun laws," he told the panel.

In the 110th Congress (2007-08), Weiner won a seat on the influential Energy and Commerce Committee. He set forth on a number of issues, cosponsoring a bill calling for the online registration of addresses of convicted sex offenders and pressing for a congressional probe of long-term care insurers.

Weiner is a champion of consumer interests. Mindful of the substantial elderly population in his district, he has proposed giving bigger annual cost-of-living increases to Social Security beneficiaries in the most expensive cities. And he wants to require the New York City subway system to be equipped so that cell phone users can make a 911 call in any of its underground stations.

Weiner previously sat on the Transportation and Infrastructure Committee, where as a freshman he won approval of $30 million over three years to encourage aircraft builders to design quieter engines, a big concern for his constituents who live beneath the takeoff and final approach paths of both LaGuardia and Kennedy airports.

The middle son of a lawyer father and a schoolteacher mother, Weiner grew up on a tree-lined street in the Park Slope section of Brooklyn, going to public schools. He attended the State University of New York at Plattsburgh because of its prowess in his sport, ice hockey. It was there that his professors noticed his gift for debate, a knack for making a cogent argument for any position and a tenacity for driving it home. Comfortable in his political science major, Weiner decided he wanted to be in Congress someday.

After graduation, he spent six years as an aide to Democrat Charles E. Schumer, then in the House. In 1991, at age 27, Weiner became the youngest person at the time ever elected to the New York City Council. Seven years later, he was elected to Congress and was chosen by his freshman class to represent them in the Democratic whip organization.

After Schumer vacated the seat in 1998 for a successful Senate run, Weiner won a tight four-way primary by 489 votes. He coasted in the strongly Democratic district in November and in every election since.

He now lives in Queens, playing goalie on an amateur hockey team, the Falcons, when he's in town. In Washington, he shares a Capitol Hill apartment with Massachusetts Democratic Rep. Michael E. Capuano.

KEY VOTES

2006

Yes Stop broadband companies from favoring select Internet traffic

No Affirm U.S. commitment to war in Iraq and reject setting a withdrawal date for troops

No Repeal requirement for bilingual ballots at the polls

Yes Permit U.S. sale of civilian nuclear technology to India

Yes Build a 700-mile fence on the U.S.-Mexico border to curb illegal crossings

No Permit warrantless wiretaps of suspected terrorists

2005

No Intervene in the life-support case of Terri Schiavo

Yes Lift President Bush's restrictions on stem cell research funding

Yes Prohibit FBI access to library and bookstore records

No Approve free-trade pact with five Central American countries

No Pass energy policy overhaul favored by President Bush emphasizing domestic oil and gas production

No End mandatory preservation of habitat of endangered animal and plant species

Yes Ban torture of prisoners in U.S. custody

CQ VOTE STUDIES

	PARTY UNITY		PRESIDENTIAL SUPPORT	
	Support	Oppose	Support	Oppose
2006	96%	4%	23%	77%
2005	99%	1%	15%	85%
2004	99%	1%	30%	70%
2003	97%	3%	22%	78%
2002	95%	5%	24%	76%

INTEREST GROUPS

	AFL-CIO	ADA	CCUS	ACU
2006	100%	95%	40%	8%
2005	93%	95%	37%	0%
2004	100%	100%	38%	4%
2003	87%	100%	30%	17%
2002	100%	100%	32%	8%

NEW YORK 9

Parts of Brooklyn and Queens – Forest Hills, Rockaway, Sheepshead Bay

The Democratic-leaning, predominately white 9th takes in north-central and western Queens and slides along the Jamaica Bay coastline into southeastern Brooklyn. Almost 70 percent of residents live in Queens.

The district extends westward from near Nassau County at the edge of Oakland Gardens through Fresh Meadows and Hillcrest to Forest Hills. Many of Queens' wealthiest communities are in the northern part of the 9th, and median household incomes in this area top $100,000.

The 9th narrows and runs south from Forest Park — the third-largest park in Queens and home to free Queens Symphony Orchestra concerts each summer — to take in part of the Woodhaven, Ozone Park and Lindenwood neighborhoods. In these areas, Hispanics now outnumber whites, and the Asian population is rapidly expanding.

The district also takes in much of the Rockaway area in far southwestern Queens along the Atlantic Ocean. Breezy Point, an exclusive community at the tip of the Rockaways, has the nation's highest concentration of Irish-Americans (60 percent) according to the 2000 census. In Brooklyn, the district includes Floyd Bennett Field, which was New York City's first municipal airport, and much of the Gateway National Recreation Area on Jamaica Bay. Farther west, Sheepshead Bay, a popular area fishing spot, has seen an influx of Russian immigrants.

Previously a Democratic stronghold, the 9th, particularly its Brooklyn portion, moved right in the aftermath of the Sept. 11, 2001, terrorist attacks. George W. Bush carried the Brooklyn part with 53 percent of the vote in the 2004 presidential election, and overall John Kerry was held to his second-lowest percentage (56 percent) of any New York City district.

MAJOR INDUSTRY

Service, finance, insurance, manufacturing

CITIES

New York (pt.), 654,360

NOTABLE

Howard Hughes' historic 1938 around-the-world flight started and ended at Floyd Bennett Field; Kings Plaza Shopping Center, billed as the first indoor mall in New York City, opened in 1970 near Mill Basin.

Rep. Edolphus Towns (D)

CAPITOL OFFICE
225-5936
www.house.gov/towns
2232 Rayburn 20515-3210; fax 225-1018

COMMITTEES
Energy & Commerce
Oversight & Government Reform
(Government Management, Organization & Procurement - chairman)

RESIDENCE
Brooklyn

BORN
July 21, 1934, Chadbourn, N.C.

RELIGION
Baptist

FAMILY
Wife, Gwendolyn Towns; two children

EDUCATION
North Carolina A&T State U., B.S. 1956;
Adelphi U., M.S.W. 1973

MILITARY SERVICE
Army, 1956-58

CAREER
Professor; hospital administrator

POLITICAL HIGHLIGHTS
Brooklyn Borough deputy president, 1976-82

ELECTION RESULTS

2006 GENERAL		
Edolphus Towns (D)	72,171	92.2%
Jonathan H. Anderson (R)	4,666	6.0%
Ernest Johnson (C)	1,470	1.9%
2006 PRIMARY		
Edolphus Towns (D)	19,469	47.4%
Charles Barron (D)	15,345	37.4%
Roger L. Green (D)	6,237	15.2%
2004 GENERAL		
Edolphus Towns (D, WFM)	136,113	91.5%
Harvey R. Clarke (R)	11,099	7.5%
Mariana Blume (C)	1,554	1.1%

PREVIOUS WINNING PERCENTAGES
2002 (98%); 2000 (90%); 1998 (92%); 1996 (91%); 1994 (89%); 1992 (96%); 1990 (93%); 1988 (89%); 1986 (89%); 1984 (85%); 1982 (84%)

Elected 1982; 13th term

Towns has had a tough couple of years. Democratic Leader Nancy Pelosi threatened to boot him off the Energy and Commerce Committee in 2005 for not voting often enough with his party. His vote for the Central American Free Trade Agreement angered key constituencies back in New York. And while he came out on top in the September 2006 Democratic primary, it was by a narrower margin than would be expected of a 12-term veteran from New York City.

Two candidates smelling opportunity, a city councilman and a state assemblyman, jumped into the Democratic primary against Towns. (He had no primary competition in 2002 and 2004.) They emphasized his CAFTA vote, what they called his lackluster record over a lengthy tenure in Congress, a larger-than-average number of missed votes and a history of support for the tobacco industry. Towns also has a strained relationship with Assemblyman Vito J. Lopez, the new chairman of the Brooklyn Democratic Party. Towns prevailed, but with just 47 percent of the vote.

Yet Towns, in his early 70s, can look back on a career with a few notable successes. He helped bring considerable largess to his Brooklyn district and built a political base that could someday be useful to his son, New York Assemblyman Darryl Towns, if he decides to run for Congress.

His successes in the House are rarely news in a town full of more-prominent and self-promoting lawmakers. "I should jump out and push and get in front of the cameras, but that's just not my nature," he says.

He won inclusion of a provision in the 1996 Telecommunications Act that allowed small businesses, minorities and women in business to put money from a new Telecommunications Development Fund into interest-bearing accounts with the fund. More recently, he won approval in 2006 of a proposal authorizing $30 million to expand the use of electronic medical records to better coordinate care for low-income and uninsured patients.

Towns' major legislative accomplishment was the 1990 passage of the Student Right to Know Act requiring colleges to report the graduation rates of their scholarship athletes.

The last couple of years have not been so good. In December 2005, Pelosi called a private meeting with Towns and told him to stick with the party on important votes or lose his seat on the Energy panel. Pelosi, who became Speaker of the House in early 2007, was angry about the Central American Free Trade Agreement vote in 2005 and that Towns missed a key vote that year on a budget bill that Republicans only narrowly got through the House, 217-215. Towns was one of two absent Democrats.

Towns later said he and Pelosi worked out their differences and that in his view the missed vote was not a big deal. "People miss budget votes all the time," he said. Of his vote for CAFTA, which gave the GOP a 217-215 win, he said, "I can't always vote the way certain people vote. I respect leadership. But if I feel something is not in the best interest of the people I represent, I have to deviate from the normal pattern."

The CAFTA vote also caused headaches for Towns with the leaders of New York's powerful labor unions. Towns said he didn't anticipate the extent of the negative reaction. He said international trade helps his district, which includes employees of nearby John F. Kennedy Airport in Queens. "I've been in Congress for a long time, and I've voted with labor probably 99 percent of the time," he said. "If there is one vote that I cast that they don't like, I don't understand why there would be a problem with my entire record."

Towns' district is home to many low-income and working-class people who are trying to get onto the ladder of economic success. He wants the federal government to increase educational opportunities, improve health services and spur economic development.

From his seat on the Energy panel's Telecommunications and the Internet Subcommittee, Towns has tried to bridge the "digital divide," supporting a measure in the 109th Congress (2005-06) to foster the use of technology at colleges that predominately serve blacks, Hispanics and other minorities. Over the years, he has helped secure federal funding for numerous projects in Brooklyn, including $153 million for a federal courthouse and a $150 million reconstruction bond for the borough's Interfaith Hospital. In 2007, he voted for an energy bill that would require oil and gas companies to renegotiate faulty drilling leases with the Interior Department or pay a new fee on production if they want to bid on future leases.

In the 110th Congress (2007-08), Towns opted not to seek the gavel of one of the Energy subcommittees, instead going for the chair of the Oversight and Government Reform Subcommittee on Government Management. He said he planned to investigate the Defense Department's "no-bid contracts," particularly those related to the war in Iraq. Towns has been an opponent of the Iraq War and says the billions spent on it should have been invested in education and health care.

Although Towns gained some notice — and peeved some Democrats — when he endorsed Republican Rudolph Giuliani for re-election as mayor of New York City in 1997, he usually votes a liberal line in the House.

Towns was born in southeastern North Carolina and graduated from historically black North Carolina A&T in Greensboro. After a two-year stint in the Army, he worked as a teacher and hospital administrator and earned a master's degree in social work from Adelphi University, on Long Island. In 1976, he was appointed Brooklyn Borough deputy president.

His chance to run for the House came in 1982 after redistricting gave the 11th District an almost even split of blacks and Hispanics. The new district included some Brooklyn territory that had been represented by white Democratic Rep. Frederick W. Richmond, but an indictment on charges of income tax evasion and possession of marijuana led him to resign.

Towns drew support from party regulars and from a rival faction calling for change. He fended off two Hispanic primary contenders to win nomination with 50 percent of the vote, then won easily in November. Redistricting in 1992 put him in a newly drawn but just as Democratic 10th District, where he faced tough primary battles several times.

KEY VOTES

2006

- No — Stop broadband companies from favoring select Internet traffic
- No — Affirm U.S. commitment to war in Iraq and reject setting a withdrawal date for troops
- No — Repeal requirement for bilingual ballots at the polls
- Yes — Permit U.S. sale of civilian nuclear technology to India
- No — Build a 700-mile fence on the U.S.-Mexico border to curb illegal crossings
- No — Permit warrantless wiretaps of suspected terrorists

2005

- ? — Intervene in the life-support case of Terri Schiavo
- Yes — Lift President Bush's restrictions on stem cell research funding
- Yes — Prohibit FBI access to library and bookstore records
- Yes — Approve free-trade pact with five Central American countries
- Yes — Pass energy policy overhaul favored by President Bush emphasizing domestic oil and gas production
- ? — End mandatory preservation of habitat of endangered animal and plant species
- Yes — Ban torture of prisoners in U.S. custody

CQ VOTE STUDIES

	PARTY UNITY		PRESIDENTIAL SUPPORT	
	Support	Oppose	Support	Oppose
2006	94%	6%	30%	70%
2005	93%	7%	33%	67%
2004	96%	4%	15%	85%
2003	96%	4%	20%	80%
2002	94%	6%	32%	68%

INTEREST GROUPS

	AFL-CIO	ADA	CCUS	ACU
2006	100%	95%	53%	8%
2005	86%	70%	60%	14%
2004	100%	90%	33%	0%
2003	100%	80%	33%	18%
2002	100%	80%	40%	4%

NEW YORK 10

Part of Brooklyn — Bedford-Stuyvesant, Canarsie, Downtown Brooklyn, East New York

The boomerang-shaped 10th begins just inland of Brooklyn's industrial waterfront and heads east, bounding back southwest after reaching the Queens border. The Democratic district is one of New York's most economically and ethnically diverse.

The black-majority 10th scoops up a chunk west of Flatbush Avenue that includes part of Midwood in south-central Brooklyn. East of this area, the 10th takes in Georgetown and Canarsie. Canarsie's racial composition has changed dramatically, as neighborhoods that were once largely white now host many blacks of Caribbean descent. Many families here are solidly middle-class, an exception for most of the 10th. Northeast of Canarsie, East New York is home to Gateway Center, a large suburban-style retail project that has spurred affordable housing in the area.

Farther north and west, the 10th includes Bedford-Stuyvesant, which was once beset by crime and poverty but has benefited from an ongoing rebirth led by black residents refurbishing brownstone houses. Old factories have become new office and residential buildings, and "Bed-Stuy" is now the 10th's cultural center. In its northwestern corner, the 10th cups the Brooklyn Navy Yard (in the 12th) to take in Fort Greene and part of Williamsburg — diverse areas with large minority populations.

The 10th's declining manufacturing base has caused unemployment, and a landmark Pfizer plant is set to close before 2009. Government jobs in Downtown Brooklyn and education jobs at the 10th's colleges, such as Brooklyn College and Long Island University-Brooklyn, aid the economy.

GOP candidates have found some small pockets of support from Jewish voters in Williamsburg and Midwood, but they pale in comparison with the overwhelming Democratic voting patterns of the rest of the 10th.

MAJOR INDUSTRY

Government, higher education, small business, retail

CITIES

New York (pt.), 654,361

NOTABLE

A Spike Lee film, "Do the Right Thing," was set in Bedford-Stuyvesant.

Rep. Yvette D. Clarke (D)

CAPITOL OFFICE
225-6231
clarke.house.gov
1029 Longworth 20515-3211; fax 226-0112

COMMITTEES
Education & Labor
Homeland Security
Small Business

RESIDENCE
Brooklyn

BORN
Nov. 21, 1964, Brooklyn, N.Y.

RELIGION
Christian

FAMILY
Single

EDUCATION
Oberlin College, attended 1982-86 (Black studies)

CAREER
Local economic development director; day care and youth program coordinator; state agency aide; state legislative aide

POLITICAL HIGHLIGHTS
New York City Council, 2002-06; sought Democratic nomination for U.S. House, 2004

ELECTION RESULTS

2006 GENERAL		
Yvette D. Clarke (D, WFM)	88,334	90.0%
Stephen Finger (R, LIBERT)	7,447	7.6%
Mariana Blume (C)	1,325	1.4%
Ollie M. McClean (FDM)	996	1.0%
2006 PRIMARY		
Yvette D. Clarke (D)	15,711	30.6%
David S. Yassky (D)	13,928	27.2%
Carl Andrews (D)	11,685	22.8%
Chris Owens (D)	9,971	19.4%

Elected 2006; 1st term

A passion for public service and a healthy dose of ambition seem to characterize both Clarke and her mother, Una. Both served on the New York City Council. And both tried to oust longtime Democratic Rep. Major R. Owens from his seat in the 11th District. The younger Clarke finally captured the prize, but only after Owens retired at the end of 12 terms.

Clarke took over her mother's seat on the city council after a term limit forced Una Clarke to step down in 2001. Clarke chaired the committee charged with rebuilding the New York City Fire Department after the Sept. 11 terrorist attacks and continues to promote the city's interests as a Homeland Security Committee member. When the panel drafted a rail security bill in 2007, Clarke won adoption of an amendment requiring labor organizations to provide security training for rail and transit workers.

Before serving on the city council, Clarke directed business development through the Bronx Empowerment Zone and the Bronx branch of the New York City Empowerment Zone. She will put that experience to use as a member of the Small Business Committee.

While on the council, Clarke won adoption of an ordinance requiring city government buildings to have twice as many restroom stalls for women as for men. She is cosponsoring a bill by her New York Democratic colleague Edolphus Towns that would apply the same requirement to bathrooms in federal buildings.

Clarke is an outspoken opponent of the Iraq War and a member of the Out of Iraq Caucus. Party leaders had to struggle to secure her vote for a war funding bill in March 2007 that set an August 2008 deadline for withdrawal of U.S. troops from Iraq; she wanted a faster withdrawal. She continues to press for an end to the war, arguing that, "Americans want our troops home."

Una Clarke lost a primary contest against Owens in 2000, and Yvette Clarke took her turn and lost in 2004. In 2006, the younger Clarke beat out a trio of other hopefuls, including the congressman's son, political activist Chris Owens, to claim the nomination. That was tantamount to election in the heavily Democratic district; the November race was a formality.

NEW YORK 11

Part of Brooklyn — Flatbush, Crown Heights, Park Slope

The predominately working-class 11th, nestled in central Brooklyn, is home to a large black population (59 percent); minorities overall make up almost four-fifths of the district's population.

At the heart of the 11th is Flatbush, a working-class black and Hispanic neighborhood that is home to many Caribbean immigrants. The area's West Indian Carnival Parade attracts hundreds of thousands of visitors each year, and local economic development officials hope some of them will return to Brooklyn at other times.

The 11th is home to the headquarters of the Chabad-Lubavitch Hasidic Jews in diverse Crown Heights. To the east, Brownsville is heavily black. The district also extends northwest through Prospect Park, Park Slope and Carroll Gardens into parts of Cobble Hill and Brooklyn Heights. Prospect Park attracts more than 7 million visitors each year, and residents and visitors also head to the nearby Brooklyn Museum of Art and Brooklyn Botanic Garden.

Many district residents work at area medical facilities, including Kings County Hospital Center, and small businesses here support the area's retail industry. Parts of Brooklyn's richest neighborhoods, including Park Slope and Brooklyn Heights, are in the 11th, although GOP pockets there have a minimal effect on elections: George W. Bush finished with only 13 percent of the vote here in the 2004 presidential election.

MAJOR INDUSTRY
Health care, retail

CITIES
New York (pt.), 654,361

NOTABLE
A housing complex is on the site of Ebbets Field, once home to the Brooklyn Dodgers.

Rep. Nydia M. Velázquez (D)

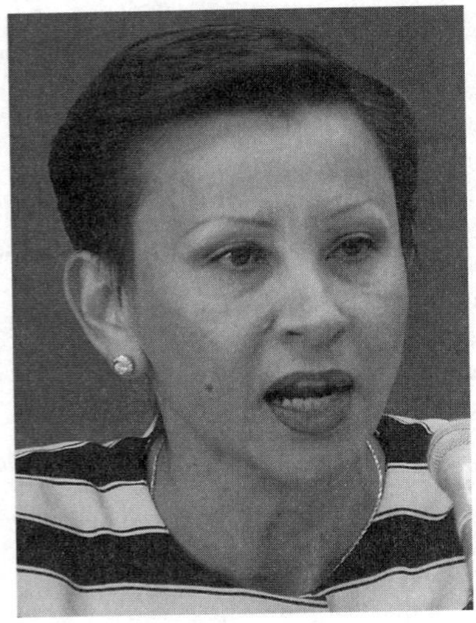

CAPITOL OFFICE
225-2361
www.house.gov/velazquez
2466 Rayburn 20515-3212; fax 226-0327

COMMITTEES
Financial Services
Small Business - chairwoman

RESIDENCE
Brooklyn

BORN
March 28, 1953, Yabucoa, P.R.

RELIGION
Roman Catholic

FAMILY
Husband, Paul Bader

EDUCATION
U. of Puerto Rico, B.A. 1974 (political science); New York U., M.A. 1976 (political science)

CAREER
Puerto Rican Community Affairs Department director; professor; congressional aide

POLITICAL HIGHLIGHTS
New York City Council, 1984-85; defeated for election to New York City Council, 1984

ELECTION RESULTS

2006 GENERAL		
Nydia M. Velázquez (D, WFM)	62,847	89.7%
Allan Romaguera (R, C)	7,182	10.3%
2006 PRIMARY		
Nydia M. Velázquez (D)		unopposed
2004 GENERAL		
Nydia M. Velázquez (D, WFM)	107,796	86.3%
Paul A. Rodriguez (R, C)	17,166	13.7%

PREVIOUS WINNING PERCENTAGES
2002 (96%); 2000 (86%); 1998 (84%); 1996 (85%); 1994 (92%); 1992 (77%)

Elected 1992; 8th term

Velázquez is the first Hispanic woman to chair a committee in Congress — the House Small Business Committee. Earlier, she broke another barrier by becoming the first Hispanic woman to hold the top-ranking minority slot on a committee, also on Small Business.

From her new perch, Velázquez (full name: NID-ee–uh veh-LASS-kez) says modernizing the Small Business Administration is her primary objective. "This is an agency that used to be Cabinet level, but has seen its budget cut nearly in half over the past five years, and has fallen victim to mismanagement," Velázquez says. "It is vital that we restore the SBA to the economic powerhouse that it once was."

Health insurance for small businesses is another priority, and one on which the liberal New Yorker has been willing to buck her party in the past. Velázquez in 2003 endorsed the Bush administration's association health plan proposal, which streamlined regulations for small businesses that pool their money to buy health insurance through the new associations. Most other Democrats opposed the bill because it allowed the groups to sidestep state mandates for insurers to cover certain diseases and screenings.

Velázquez also wants to reduce the regulations faced by small business, permit venture capital investment in firms with grants from the SBA's Innovation Research Program and increase the number of federal contracts going to entrepreneurs.

The committee tends to be a bipartisan haven. Its top leaders usually agree on the goal of helping small business, and Velázquez usually worked well with former Republican Chairman Donald Manzullo of Illinois. But in May 2006, Manzullo abruptly canceled a markup on legislation to renew the SBA's authorization after Velázquez and other Democrats derailed the measure by offering a flood of amendments. They said the bill didn't go far enough to force change at the SBA. The House then passed a temporary authorization to extend all programs through February 2007.

Led by Velázquez, Democrats sharply criticized the SBA for being slow to process disaster loans in areas hard-hit by Hurricane Katrina in 2005. She called on Administrator Hector V. Barreto to resign, which he ultimately did in April 2006. She wasn't happy when the White House replaced him with Steven C. Preston, an executive with the ServiceMaster Corporation, which Velázquez described as "a Fortune 500 company whose issues are nothing like those faced by the average small-business owner."

In 2006, Velázquez released the seventh annual report compiled by committee Democrats rating the performance of 22 federal agencies in ensuring that smaller firms receive their share of government contracts. The report found that large businesses, such as Rolls Royce and Microsoft, had received up to $12 billion in small-business contracts.

In addition to chairing Small Business, Velázquez remains on the Financial Services Committee, where she pushes for more-affordable housing in her district and across the nation. In 2007, she introduced a bill to enable local governments to purchase buildings owned by the Housing and Urban Development Department, and slated for foreclosure, to preserve for use as affordable housing for low-income families.

The first woman of Puerto Rican descent to be elected to Congress, Velázquez represents more than 100,000 Puerto Rican constituents and focuses on matters affecting the island commonwealth. She backed a 2006 resolution to allow its citizens to call a constitutional convention to "exercise their right to self-determination," and in 2007 she sponsored a similar measure.

She also has a keen interest in immigration issues, the focus of her district casework. In 2006, she participated in demonstrations protesting Republican proposals to criminalize undocumented immigrants. From 1986 until her election to the House, she had worked as a liaison between the Puerto Rican government and Latino communities in the United States. During that time, she also joined other Puerto Rican lawmakers in demanding that the Navy stop using the island of Vieques, just off Puerto Rico, for bombing practice.

Velázquez was raised in the sugar cane region in southeastern Puerto Rico with her twin sister and seven other siblings. Her father cut cane and her mother helped make ends meet by selling food to other cane workers. Her father also ran a small business that made cinder blocks. He was a community leader, founding a political party in their hometown of Yabucoa. Her father, with just a third-grade education, sparked her interest in politics.

"When I was only 5 years old, I used to watch my father stand on a flatbed truck and campaign for his political party," she says. "I watched him work hard to support our family as a small-business owner, and I saw firsthand the importance of giving people a voice. My father instilled in me a sense of justice and perseverance that I carry with me to this day."

Velázquez graduated from the University of Puerto Rico with a degree in political science, the first in her family to receive a college diploma. She went to New York City for graduate school. She taught Puerto Rican studies at Hunter College, worked as a special assistant to Democratic Rep. Edolphus Towns, served on the New York City Council and then became liaison between the Puerto Rican government and U.S. Latino communities.

Her local name recognition increased significantly before her 1992 House race, when she ran a Hispanic voter registration drive financed by the Puerto Rican government. Critics said she targeted the Brooklyn sections that later became part of a redrawn, Hispanic-majority district.

Her biggest obstacle in the Democratic primary was nine-term incumbent Stephen J. Solarz, whose district had been dismantled in redistricting. Solarz hired Hispanic advisers and learned a few Spanish phrases, but he was unknown to many in the new district. Velázquez beat him by a 5 percentage point margin, then won the general election with 77 percent of the vote.

Velázquez has won seven more times with at least 84 percent of the vote, even though the Hispanic population in the 12th District was cut from a majority to a strong plurality during 1997 court-ordered redistricting. The New York Post reported in 2005 that Velázquez was exploring a run for New York City mayor in 2009. Velázquez has offered no comment on the speculation.

KEY VOTES

2006

- Yes Stop broadband companies from favoring select Internet traffic
- No Affirm U.S. commitment to war in Iraq and reject setting a withdrawal date for troops
- No Repeal requirement for bilingual ballots at the polls
- No Permit U.S. sale of civilian nuclear technology to India
- No Build a 700-mile fence on the U.S.-Mexico border to curb illegal crossings
- No Permit warrantless wiretaps of suspected terrorists

2005

- ? Intervene in the life-support case of Terri Schiavo
- Yes Lift President Bush's restrictions on stem cell research funding
- Yes Prohibit FBI access to library and bookstore records
- No Approve free-trade pact with five Central American countries
- No Pass energy policy overhaul favored by President Bush emphasizing domestic oil and gas production
- No End mandatory preservation of habitat of endangered animal and plant species
- Yes Ban torture of prisoners in U.S. custody

CQ VOTE STUDIES

	PARTY UNITY		PRESIDENTIAL SUPPORT	
	Support	Oppose	Support	Oppose
2006	99%	1%	10%	90%
2005	98%	2%	18%	82%
2004	96%	4%	15%	85%
2003	97%	3%	22%	78%
2002	99%	1%	24%	76%

INTEREST GROUPS

	AFL-CIO	ADA	CCUS	ACU
2006	93%	100%	27%	4%
2005	80%	100%	48%	0%
2004	87%	100%	32%	8%
2003	100%	90%	25%	14%
2002	89%	95%	35%	0%

NEW YORK 12

Lower East Side of Manhattan; parts of Brooklyn and Queens

The 12th combines part of Manhattan's Lower East Side with portions of Brooklyn and Queens. Minorities make up more than three-fourths of the population of this working-class Democratic bastion, which has a Hispanic plurality (49 percent).

Two-thirds of the 12th's registered voters live in Brooklyn. In its southwestern corner, the district begins in Sunset Park, which has large Hispanic and Chinese populations. The district narrows while running north near Brooklyn's waterfront before taking in the Brooklyn Navy Yard, part of Williamsburg, and Greenpoint, which has a large Polish population. The Greenpoint and Williamsburg waterfront areas are undergoing zoning changes that will include more than 50 acres of new parkland and may spur new affordable housing. The 12th then moves southeast, along the Brooklyn-Queens border, to the heavily Hispanic neighborhoods of East Williamsburg, Bushwick and Cypress Hills.

On the Queens side of the border, the 12th takes in parts of the Sunnyside and Woodside neighborhoods. Originally a heavily Irish area, the 12th's part of Queens now includes residents with a diverse mix of ethnic backgrounds, including a growing Hispanic immigrant population from many different countries. The district also includes the Brooklyn, Manhattan and Williamsburg bridges, and it crosses the East River into Manhattan to take in Chinatown, part of Little Italy and the Lower East Side. Nearly one in five registered voters lives in Manhattan.

The 12th's economy, anchored by the region's numerous health care facilities, also has a significant blue-collar workforce affiliated with industries along the East River. John Kerry defeated George W. Bush by more than 60 percentage points in the 12th's 2004 presidential vote.

MAJOR INDUSTRY

Health care, manufacturing, service

CITIES

New York (pt.), 654,360

NOTABLE

Brooklyn's Green-Wood Cemetery, where the more than 560,000 interred include Leonard Bernstein, Horace Greeley and notorious 19th century New York politician William M. "Boss" Tweed.

Rep. Vito J. Fossella (R)

CAPITOL OFFICE
225-3371
www.house.gov/fossella
2453 Rayburn 20515-3213; fax 226-1272

COMMITTEES
Energy & Commerce

RESIDENCE
Staten Island

BORN
March 9, 1965, South Beach, N.Y.

RELIGION
Roman Catholic

FAMILY
Wife, Mary Pat Fossella; three children

EDUCATION
U. of Pennsylvania, B.S. 1987;
Fordham U., J.D. 1993

CAREER
Management consultant; lawyer

POLITICAL HIGHLIGHTS
New York City Council, 1994-97

ELECTION RESULTS

2006 GENERAL		
Vito J. Fossella (R, C, INDC)	59,334	56.8%
Stephen A. Harrison (D, WFM)	45,131	43.2%
2006 PRIMARY		
Vito J. Fossella (R)		unopposed
2004 GENERAL		
Vito J. Fossella (R, C)	112,934	59.0%
Frank J. Barbaro (D, INDC, WFM)	78,500	41.0%

PREVIOUS WINNING PERCENTAGES
2002 (70%); 2000 (65%); 1998 (65%); 1997 Special Election (61%)

Elected 1997; 5th full term

Fossella is the only Republican in the House who represents a significant chunk of largely Democratic New York City. It's the part that would secede if it had its druthers, and that helps explain how two powerful Italian-American families — the Molinaris and the Fossellas — have kept Staten Island securely in the GOP column in recent elections.

The district's mostly white, upper-middle-class voters sometimes feel alienated from the metropolis that supports their comfortable suburban lifestyle. So disenchanted were they with New York City's Democratic leaders that in an early 1990s referendum, they overwhelmingly voted to secede from the city and would have done so if the state legislature hadn't blocked the move. They tend to prefer Republicans to Democrats and conservatives like Fossella to the Rockefeller moderates common elsewhere in the Northeast. Local politics was long dominated by former GOP borough president Guy Molinari, who once called Fossella "my son."

Fossella (full name: VEE-toe Fuh-SELL-ah) opposes abortion and gets a B-plus rating from the National Rifle Association for his pro-gun ownership positions. He backed all of President Bush's tax cuts, supported a constitutional amendment to ban same-sex marriage and advocated oil drilling in Alaska's Arctic National Wildlife Refuge. In 2005, he voted with his party 90 percent of the time on key votes that broke along party lines.

His loyalties are sometimes torn on labor issues, which is one area where he finds common ground with Northeastern GOP moderates. He broke with conservatives in 2004 to support an extension of unemployment benefits for an additional 13 weeks, one of only 39 Republicans to do so. The same year, Fossella stuck with the GOP and voted against a Democratic amendment that sought to protect overtime pay for workers after the Bush administration changed eligibility requirements for some workers.

Fossella has departed from the GOP line on a handful of other issues lately. He opposed the president's plan for partially privatizing Social Security, and he supported using federal funds for research on embryonic stem cell lines.

For parochial and personal reasons, the White House also cannot count on Fossella to go along with any effort to scale back federal aid to New York City in the era of terrorist threats. He vigorously challenged the administration's 2006 decision to cut funding for anti-terrorism programs for New York by 40 percent. And in 2007, he lashed out at Bush for proposing a reduction in funds targeted to help the city cope with bioterrorism. "The more you take away, the less the city's capable of doing and this is the fact," he fumed.

He lost several friends and high school classmates on Sept. 11, 2001, as well as 30 fellow parishioners from St. Clare's Roman Catholic Church on Staten Island. Before he came to Congress, Fossella worked as a consultant for three years at the World Trade Center. "I can relate to the horror of being trapped on the 98th floor," he says. "It hits home more for me than for most people."

His seat on the Energy and Commerce Committee has put him in the right position to help those directly affected by the attacks. Fossella was successful in lobbying to protect $125 million in worker compensation for emergency personnel who responded to the terrorist attacks after the administration tried to rescind the money. In 2007, he cosponsored a bill with New York Democratic colleague Carolyn B. Maloney that would extend long-term medical monitoring to anyone exposed to Ground Zero toxins and federally funded health care to those who are sick as a result.

In 2006, Fossella sponsored a successful amendment to the intelligence authorization bill setting aside $18 million to improve information sharing among federal, state and local agencies investigating terrorists.

When the House was under GOP rule, Speaker J. Dennis Hastert gave Fossella special permission to also serve on the Financial Services Committee. Energy and Commerce members typically are not allowed to serve on other committees. But after Republicans lost the majority for the 110th Congress (2007-08), he was back to just the Energy Committee.

On Financial Services, he built a portfolio on issues important to Wall Street. In 2001, he won enactment of a law that slashed federal fees on stock trades, a move Fossella said would help spur market activity. The bill also increased salaries for employees of the Securities and Exchange Commission as the agency was investigating corporate accounting scandals.

Brash, quick with a sound bite and telegenic, Fossella was once described by the New York Daily News as possessing a "self-deprecating, smart-aleck" style. "I am a simple guy," he says. "My job every day is defined by how I can best serve the people of Brooklyn and Staten Island."

Fossella likes to mix it up in the Big Apple's raucous politics. He co-chaired Republican Mayor Michael Bloomberg's re-election campaign in 2005. And though he hails from a long line of Democrats, Fossella switched parties in 1990, a move he attributes to his rightward philosophic leanings and to the rise of popular former Mayor Rudolph W. Giuliani, who made being a conservative from New York City respectable.

Fossella comes from a well-known Italian-American political family on Staten Island. His father, Vito Sr., served in Mayor Ed Koch's administration; an uncle, Frank Fossella, was a city council member. From 1935 until his death in 1944, his great-grandfather James O'Leary was a Democratic House member from New York. When Rep. Susan Molinari announced in 1997 that she was resigning from the House for a career in television, her father, Guy, a former House member who was borough president at the time, tapped Fossella as the heir apparent.

Fossella already had a solid political résumé. A Fordham University-trained lawyer and a graduate of the University of Pennsylvania, he was on the city council, occupying the same seat once held by his uncle. He led an effort to build new public schools on Staten Island.

During his 1997 special-election campaign for the House, which coincided with the New York mayoral race, Giuliani's landslide re-election margins in the 13th helped propel Fossella to easy victory. He won his next three races with more than 60 percent of the vote. In the past two elections, he has faced lively Democratic challenges, but has held on with better than 56 percent.

KEY VOTES

2006

No Stop broadband companies from favoring select Internet traffic

Yes Affirm U.S. commitment to war in Iraq and reject setting a withdrawal date for troops

Yes Repeal requirement for bilingual ballots at the polls

Yes Permit U.S. sale of civilian nuclear technology to India

Yes Build a 700-mile fence on the U.S.-Mexico border to curb illegal crossings

Yes Permit warrantless wiretaps of suspected terrorists

2005

Yes Intervene in the life-support case of Terri Schiavo

Yes Lift President Bush's restrictions on stem cell research funding

No Prohibit FBI access to library and bookstore records

Yes Approve free-trade pact with five Central American countries

Yes Pass energy policy overhaul favored by President Bush emphasizing domestic oil and gas production

Yes End mandatory preservation of habitat of endangered animal and plant species

No Ban torture of prisoners in U.S. custody

CQ VOTE STUDIES

	PARTY UNITY		PRESIDENTIAL SUPPORT	
	Support	Oppose	Support	Oppose
2006	87%	13%	93%	7%
2005	90%	10%	83%	17%
2004	88%	12%	84%	16%
2003	95%	5%	98%	2%
2002	94%	6%	87%	13%

INTEREST GROUPS

	AFL-CIO	ADA	CCUS	ACU
2006	29%	10%	100%	75%
2005	20%	5%	93%	84%
2004	43%	20%	90%	78%
2003	20%	15%	96%	82%
2002	11%	0%	95%	92%

NEW YORK 13

Staten Island; part of southwest Brooklyn

New York City's only Republican district, the 13th includes all of Staten Island (Richmond County) and a small portion of southwestern Brooklyn across the Verrazano Narrows Bridge. Nearly three-fourths of the district's population lives on Staten Island.

A large Italian-American, predominately Catholic population on both sides of the Verrazano gives the 13th a socially conservative edge, and its large retired population and white, upper-middle-class suburban residents have sent Republicans to the House since 1982. The 13th gave George W. Bush 55 percent of its 2004 presidential vote, making it the only New York City district Bush carried.

One of the district's largest employers is Staten Island University Hospital, and retail and construction jobs also provide work for residents. Once New York City's primary landfill, the now-closed Fresh Kills landfill temporarily reopened following the Sept. 11, 2001, terrorist attacks to receive and process most of the debris. Staten Island lost more than 250 residents in the attacks, and a memorial to the local victims is on the north waterfront near the Staten Island Ferry terminal, where the ferry departs to bring Island residents into lower Manhattan.

The least diverse borough, Staten Island is the only one in which whites make up a majority of the residents (71 percent). Hispanic and black populations live mostly in the borough's northeast. There is an Asian presence in some of the borough's north-central neighborhoods, and the 13th has the second-most residents of Arab descent in the nation.

The Brooklyn portion of the district extends from the Verrazano into Bay Ridge, Dyker Heights and part of Bensonhurst, before buttonhooking south of Cropsey Avenue and moving east to Ocean Parkway, taking in the Gravesend neighborhood.

MAJOR INDUSTRY

Health care, retail, communications, construction

MILITARY BASES

Fort Hamilton (Army), 970 military, 925 civilian (2007)

CITIES

New York (pt.), 654,631

NOTABLE

The 1977 disco movie "Saturday Night Fever" was set in Bay Ridge.

Rep. Carolyn B. Maloney (D)

CAPITOL OFFICE
225-7944
rep.carolyn.maloney@mail.house.gov
www.house.gov/maloney
2331 Rayburn 20515-3214; fax 225-4709

COMMITTEES
Financial Services
(Financial Institutions & Consumer Credit - chairwoman)
Oversight & Government Reform
Joint Economic

RESIDENCE
Manhattan

BORN
Feb. 19, 1948, Greensboro, N.C.

RELIGION
Presbyterian

FAMILY
Husband, Clifton H.W. Maloney; two children

EDUCATION
Greensboro College, A.B. 1968

CAREER
State legislative aide; teacher

POLITICAL HIGHLIGHTS
New York City Council, 1982-93

ELECTION RESULTS

2006 GENERAL		
Maloney (D, INDC, WFM)	119,582	84.5%
Danniel Maio (R)	21,969	15.5%
2006 PRIMARY		
Carolyn B. Maloney (D)		unopposed
2004 GENERAL		
Maloney (D, INDC, WFM)	186,688	81.1%
Anton Srdanovic (R, C)	43,623	18.9%

PREVIOUS WINNING PERCENTAGES
2002 (75%); 2000 (74%); 1998 (77%); 1996 (72%); 1994 (64%); 1992 (50%)

Elected 1992; 8th term

Maloney has been a member on a mission since the Sept. 11 terrorist attacks that transformed her city, her nation and her goals in Congress. She is tireless in her efforts to help rebuild New York City and to aid survivors of the World Trade Center disaster and the first-responders who fought to save them. She isn't likely to lose that focus; she wears a silver bracelet with 9-11-01 engraved on it.

Maloney, who represents western Queens and a good portion of the east side of Manhattan, was in her Capitol Hill office when she got a call from a friend in New York telling her a plane had crashed into the World Trade Center. She turned on the television and watched in horror as the second plane struck and the Twin Towers collapsed. From her office window, she saw smoke billowing from the Pentagon, the third target hit that day. She rented a car and drove straight to New York. Her congressional ID card got her past the barricades, and she went to a makeshift fire and police headquarters. "What can I do?" she asked. "We need phones." She racked her brain, then called Florida Republican C.W. Bill Young, at the time chairman of the House Appropriations Committee. The next morning, the phones arrived.

In 2004, Maloney helped win enactment of a sweeping bill to reorganize U.S. intelligence operations. The measure followed many of the recommendations of the independent commission that reviewed intelligence failures surrounding the Sept. 11 attacks and created a national intelligence director with authority over the budgets of all U.S. spy agencies. She calls it the "most important work I've done in Congress."

Maloney and Connecticut Republican Christopher Shays, a colleague on the Oversight and Government Reform Committee, sponsored an intelligence overhaul bill in the 108th Congress (2003-04) that mirrored Senate-passed legislation but drew opposition from House GOP leaders. It went nowhere at first in the House. But their efforts paid off when a House-Senate conference produced a bill largely resembling their approach.

In the 109th Congress (2005-06), she turned her attention to long-term health effects on first-responders and others who worked near Ground Zero. She and New York Republican Peter T. King secured $75 million in 2005 for the Centers for Disease Control and Prevention to screen, monitor and treat those injured or sickened by the Sept. 11 attacks and their aftermath. A separate law enacted in early 2006 carried a provision from one of Maloney's bills granting federal military retirement credit to all National Guard soldiers who toiled on state active duty in the affected areas of New York and Virginia in the year after the attacks. In 2007, she sponsored a bill that would extend long-term medical monitoring to everyone exposed to Ground Zero toxins and federally funded health care to anyone who is sick as a result.

Maloney has long been an advocate of abortion rights and the causes of women worldwide, and she's not media-shy in her efforts. In October 2001, she sought to demonstrate the plight of Afghan women under the Taliban by coming to the House floor in a head-to-toe blue burqa.

She condemned President Bush over his decision to cut U.S. contributions to the U.N. Population Fund, which helps to deliver birth control information and services to women in Third World nations. Maloney said the funding cut "sends a message that when push comes to shove, the administration's right-wing base comes first."

Maloney introduces scores of bills, many representing priorities for the Caucus for Women's Issues, which she used to co-chair. In each of the past five Congresses, as well as the 110th Congress (2007-08), she has introduced an equal rights constitutional amendment, though without much success. Her high mark for cosponsors was 211 in the 107th Congress (2001-02), short of the two-thirds needed for approval of a constitutional amendment.

In 2007, she introduced a bill that would require employers to allow their workers 24 hours of unpaid leave a year for school activities. It also would create pilot programs to help states provide paid family leave.

Maloney's legislation to permit breast-feeding on federal property, which she introduced after women nursing their babies were asked to leave the Capitol, federal museums and parks, became law in 1999. In 2006, a bill to address sex trafficking that she cosponsored with Republican Deborah Pryce of Ohio was enacted as part of a broader measure. Maloney and Republican Michael N. Castle of Delaware authored a 2005 law authorizing the minting of a series of $1 coins that will feature each of the U.S. presidents. The first coin, displaying George Washington, was issued in early 2007.

On the Oversight and Government Reform Committee, Maloney puts her New York City Council expertise on procurement and government contracting policies to use. She was the city government's top watchdog against government waste, chairing the Committee on Contracts.

Maloney also serves on the Financial Services Committee, where she has worked to hold down credit card interest rates, protect the elderly from fraud and give senior citizens in public housing the right to own pets. She became chairwoman of the Financial Institutions and Consumer Credit Subcommittee in the 110th Congress and claimed an early victory when the House passed her bill to revamp the government's process for scrutinizing the national security risks posed by foreign investments.

She hails from Greensboro, N.C. "Growing up, my role models were nurses and schoolteachers," she says. She went to New York City for a visit in her early 20s and stayed, eventually teaching adult education in East Harlem and joining the city's vast educational bureaucracy. Maloney says she realized government had a greater impact than any teacher on the education of the city's youth, and she moved to Albany to work for the state legislature. Five years later, she was elected to the New York City Council, where she served about 10 years.

When Maloney ran against seven-term GOP Rep. Bill Green in 1992, media hype about the "Year of the Woman" lent momentum to her underdog challenge. She also benefited from redistricting, which forced Green to campaign on some unfamiliar turf. She beat him narrowly with 50 percent of the vote. Her election victories since then have been runaways.

KEY VOTES

2006

Yes Stop broadband companies from favoring select Internet traffic

No Affirm U.S. commitment to war in Iraq and reject setting a withdrawal date for troops

No Repeal requirement for bilingual ballots at the polls

Yes Permit U.S. sale of civilian nuclear technology to India

Yes Build a 700-mile fence on the U.S.-Mexico border to curb illegal crossings

No Permit warrantless wiretaps of suspected terrorists

2005

? Intervene in the life-support case of Terri Schiavo

Yes Lift President Bush's restrictions on stem cell research funding

Yes Prohibit FBI access to library and bookstore records

No Approve free-trade pact with five Central American countries

No Pass energy policy overhaul favored by President Bush emphasizing domestic oil and gas production

No End mandatory preservation of habitat of endangered animal and plant species

Yes Ban torture of prisoners in U.S. custody

CQ VOTE STUDIES

	PARTY UNITY		PRESIDENTIAL SUPPORT	
	Support	Oppose	Support	Oppose
2006	94%	6%	33%	67%
2005	98%	2%	17%	83%
2004	97%	3%	28%	72%
2003	96%	4%	25%	75%
2002	93%	7%	34%	66%

INTEREST GROUPS

	AFL-CIO	ADA	CCUS	ACU
2006	93%	85%	43%	8%
2005	93%	100%	37%	0%
2004	100%	100%	45%	4%
2003	80%	95%	33%	16%
2002	89%	100%	53%	4%

NEW YORK 14

East Side of Manhattan; western Queens

Home to New York City's wealthy high-society, the 14th's traditional old-money elite have been supplanted by "limousine liberals" — highly educated young professionals devoted to the arts. The 14th has the nation's highest percentage of residents with at least a bachelor's degree (57 percent) and the country's highest percentage of people who walk to work (22 percent).

Taking in all of Central Park in the district's northwestern corner, the 14th's western edge then roughly follows Broadway south toward Union Square before narrowing to reach the Lower East Side. Landmarks include Carnegie Hall, Rockefeller Center, Grand Central Terminal, the United Nations, the Chrysler Building and Fifth Avenue's Museum Mile, which includes the Metropolitan Museum of Art.

But the tony neighborhoods of Manhattan's East Side do not tell the whole story of a district that crosses Roosevelt Island to pick up ethnic working-class sections of Queens, such as Astoria, and some poorer sections. Long Island City, once an industrial powerhouse, experienced decline but is seeing a resurgence through commercial development and the construction of waterfront luxury apartments, and a burgeoning arts community has taken advantage of affordable housing in the area.

The 14th is both economically and ethnically diverse. In the 1980s and 1990s, immigrants moved to the region and still call the district home. In fact, 40 percent of the district's population speaks a language other than English at home.

Republicans generally are unable to compete against the overwhelming Democratic presence in this district: Democrat John Kerry won 74 percent of the 14th's presidential vote in 2004. Extremely active politically, residents of the 14th are known for making some of the largest campaign contributions in the nation.

MAJOR INDUSTRY

Finance, publishing, communications, advertising, health care, tourism

CITIES

New York (pt.), 654,361

NOTABLE

Gracie Mansion, in Carl Schurz Park, is the official residence of New York's mayor; The American Museum of the Moving Image is in Astoria.

Rep. Charles B. Rangel (D)

CAPITOL OFFICE
225-4365
www.house.gov/rangel
2354 Rayburn 20515-3215; fax 225-0816

COMMITTEES
Ways & Means - chairman
Joint Taxation - chairman

RESIDENCE
Manhattan

BORN
June 11, 1930, Manhattan, N.Y.

RELIGION
Roman Catholic

FAMILY
Wife, Alma Rangel; two children

EDUCATION
New York U., B.S. 1957; St. John's U., LL.B. 1960

MILITARY SERVICE
Army, 1948-52

CAREER
Lawyer

POLITICAL HIGHLIGHTS
Assistant U.S. attorney, 1961-62; N.Y. Assembly, 1967-71; sought Democratic nomination for N.Y. City Council president, 1969

ELECTION RESULTS

2006 GENERAL		
Charles B. Rangel (D, WFM)	103,916	94.0%
Edward Daniels (R)	6,592	6.0%
2006 PRIMARY		
Charles B. Rangel (D)		unopposed
2004 GENERAL		
Charles B. Rangel (D, WFM)	161,351	91.1%
Kenneth P. Jefferson Jr. (R)	12,355	7.0%
Jessie Fields (INDC)	3,345	1.9%

PREVIOUS WINNING PERCENTAGES
2002 (88%); 2000 (92%); 1998 (93%); 1996 (91%); 1994 (97%); 1992 (95%); 1990 (97%); 1988 (97%); 1986 (96%); 1984 (97%); 1982 (97%); 1980 (96%); 1978 (96%); 1976 (97%); 1974 (97%); 1972 (96%); 1970 (87%)

Elected 1970; 19th term

Rangel's Capitol Hill office is littered with memorabilia — a portrait of the Rev. Martin Luther King Jr., a framed Purple Heart from his Korean War service, a collection of statues from official trips to Africa and a basketball from St. John's University, where he went to law school. The 2006 elections handed him the one prize that had eluded him for more than three decades — the gavel of the powerful Ways and Means Committee.

Fed up with iron-fisted GOP control, the old-school liberal was on the verge of retirement when Democrats swept back into power. Rangel immediately rethought his career plans, and happily ascended to a job giving him sway over everything from tax and trade policy to Social Security and Medicare. While his policy options are constrained by a Republican White House, he has wasted no time changing the tone within the committee, which had soured dramatically under abrasive Republican Bill Thomas of California, who had just retired after six years as chairman.

At the start of the two-year 110th Congress in January 2007, Rangel called an informal committee session that quickly became known as the "Kumbaya meeting," because both sides expressed remorse at the deterioration of civility in recent years. He then worked hand in glove with the new top Republican, Jim McCrery of Louisiana, to advance bipartisan legislation providing small-business tax breaks, added relief for Hurricane Katrina victims, taxpayer identity protections and a ban on genetic discrimination by health insurers — all before the 2007 spring recess.

One of Rangel's top priorities is a restructuring of the alternative minimum income tax, which has hit an increasing number of middle-class taxpayers each year. But repeal of the tax is estimated to cost the government about $1 trillion over 10 years. Replacing that revenue is a problem for Rangel; he has started taking a hard look at the roughly $340 billion annual gap between money owed to the IRS and taxes collected.

With Rangel at Ways and Means, President Bush has had to shelve his idea of creating private accounts within Social Security. But Rangel and McCrery opened negotiations with the administration early in 2007 on an overhaul of trade policy that could ultimately lead to renewal of fast-track trade authority allowing the administration to negotiate trade agreements that Congress cannot amend. A bill giving Bush expanded powers over trade deals passed in 2002, with Rangel opposing it. With the law set to expire in 2007, Democrats have said they would not renew it without significant new labor and environmental standards and a greater say for Congress.

Business lobbyists know Rangel as a deal-cutting pragmatist. They set out to work with him, where possible, rather than against him. In 2002, he helped engineer an economic stimulus bill that paired GOP tax breaks for business with a Democratic extension of unemployment benefits for laid-off workers. In 2000, he bucked labor unions to endorse permanent normalized trade relations with China. And in 2007, he began talks with the White House on trade deals in the face of opposition from many in his own party.

The Harlem-based lawmaker has had his greatest success legislatively with efforts to spur economic development in underserved neighborhoods. He wrote the 1993 "empowerment zones" law providing tax credits to businesses that move into blighted areas and also the 1986 tax credit for developers of low-income housing.

A founder of the Congressional Black Caucus, Rangel champions gun control, affirmative action and abortion rights, and he was a passionate critic of the 1996 law ending welfare's status as an entitlement.

After the U.S. invasion of Iraq in 2003, Rangel spoke out against it and proposed legislation to reinstate the military draft. He argued that the all-volunteer military relied too heavily on poor and working-class enlistees who needed jobs and education benefits. GOP leaders called his bluff, bringing the politically unpopular bill to the floor just before the 2004 election. Rangel voted against it. But he renewed his call for a draft after the 2006 elections, only to see Democratic leaders dismiss the notion.

Rangel laments the partisanship of today's House. "You could have friends in 1970, you could have mentors. There was an opportunity to talk with people on your committee, from your delegation. [Now] it takes years to build friendships, but it only takes one election to shatter them."

In the 109th Congress (2005-06), Rangel clashed repeatedly with Republican Chairman Thomas; each viewed the other as intransigent. In 2003, Rangel gathered committee Democrats in a library near the Ways and Means hearing room to protest having little time to review a complicated bill. Thomas called in the Capitol Police to evict Rangel's rebels, but later apologized, tearfully, on the House floor.

A natural wit, quick with a rejoinder or a pun, the raspy-voiced Rangel is often sought out by television reporters. Interviewed by a New York television station in 2005, Rangel was asked his view of Bush. "Well," he said. "I really think that he shatters the myth of white supremacy once and for all. It shows that, in this great country, anybody can become president."

His long tenure has not been without setbacks. He was among the lawmakers swept up in the House bank scandal in the early 1990s, and in 1999 he was entangled in a financial scandal at Harlem's historic Apollo Theater. The state of New York later dropped a lawsuit against Rangel and others on the theater board, saying they acted in good faith.

Raised by his seamstress mother and her family in Harlem, Rangel dropped out of high school at 16, joined the Army and won a Purple Heart and Bronze Star in the Korean War after surviving firefights that claimed much of his unit. Once back home, he finished high school and college, then landed an internship in the local district attorney's office.

After four years in the state Assembly, he ran for the U.S. House in 1970, ousting Rep. Adam Clayton Powell Jr. in the Democratic primary. He won his first general election with 87 percent of the vote and has amassed even larger wins ever since. His only significant challenger after that first race was Powell's son and namesake who unsuccessfully took him on in the 1994 primary.

KEY VOTES

2006

Yes Stop broadband companies from favoring select Internet traffic

No Affirm U.S. commitment to war in Iraq and reject setting a withdrawal date for troops

No Repeal requirement for bilingual ballots at the polls

Yes Permit U.S. sale of civilian nuclear technology to India

No Build a 700-mile fence on the U.S.-Mexico border to curb illegal crossings

No Permit warrantless wiretaps of suspected terrorists

2005

? Intervene in the life-support case of Terri Schiavo

Yes Lift President Bush's restrictions on stem cell research funding

Yes Prohibit FBI access to library and bookstore records

No Approve free-trade pact with five Central American countries

No Pass energy policy overhaul favored by President Bush emphasizing domestic oil and gas production

No End mandatory preservation of habitat of endangered animal and plant species

Yes Ban torture of prisoners in U.S. custody

CQ VOTE STUDIES

	PARTY UNITY		PRESIDENTIAL SUPPORT	
	Support	Oppose	Support	Oppose
2006	96%	4%	27%	73%
2005	98%	2%	16%	84%
2004	98%	2%	19%	81%
2003	96%	4%	21%	79%
2002	98%	2%	24%	76%

INTEREST GROUPS

	AFL-CIO	ADA	CCUS	ACU
2006	100%	95%	40%	4%
2005	93%	100%	38%	0%
2004	93%	95%	30%	0%
2003	83%	85%	25%	19%
2002	100%	95%	32%	0%

NEW YORK 15

Northern Manhattan – Harlem, Washington Heights

The 15th takes in Upper Manhattan's Harlem and Washington Heights and picks up a few blocks of the Bronx to its north. East of Harlem, it includes Randalls, Wards and Rikers islands. At only 10 square miles in size, the 15th is the nation's smallest district in area.

The past two decades have brought substantial change to the district, with Puerto Rican and Dominican immigrants supplanting the district's African-American majority. Hispanics now far outnumber non-Hispanic blacks, but low voter participation among Hispanics means the smaller black population (31 percent of residents) continues to dominate the district's politics.

Harlem's 1996 designation as a federal empowerment zone resulted in an economic resurgence. Refurbished brownstones, new restaurants, national retail chains and prominent corporations have moved into the area. Washington Heights is experiencing similar revitalization.

The district's hospitals and colleges, along with many small businesses, provide much of the employment, although many jobs are out of reach to less-educated residents. Among the 15th's universities are Columbia in Morningside Heights, and the area's thriving health care industry hosts major research and teaching hospitals, including New York Presbyterian Hospital. Many residents also are employed on Rikers Island, the roughly 15,000-inmate New York City correctional facility in the East River that is officially part of the Bronx, but is connected to Queens by a bridge.

Since its creation in 1944, the decidedly liberal 15th District seat has been held by one of two black Democrats: Adam Clayton Powell Jr. or Rep. Rangel. The district gave Democrat John Kerry 89.7 percent of its 2004 presidential vote, making the 15th his best district in the country.

MAJOR INDUSTRY

Health care, higher education, retail, city government

CITIES

New York (pt.), 654,361

NOTABLE

Legendary venues such as the Cotton Club and the Apollo Theater drew jazz greats and comedians; Former President Bill Clinton opened the New York office of his foundation on 125th Street in Harlem.

Rep. José E. Serrano (D)

Elected March 1990; 9th full term

Serrano is always mindful that he represents one of the poorest districts in the country. As a new member of the college of cardinals, as the 12 Appropriations subcommittee chairmen are known, he will be attentive to social welfare spending for the inhabitants of the Bronx.

When Democrats ascended to the majority in 2007, Serrano, in his ninth full term, got the gavel of the Financial Services Appropriations Subcommittee, making him one of the brokers for the spending bills that run the federal government. Serrano (full name: ho-ZAY sa-RAH-no, with a rolled 'R') says his principal legislative priority "is ensuring that the South Bronx gets its fair share for education, jobs, housing and economic development."

"This is my 33rd year in public office," Serrano, a former New York assemblyman, said in 2007. "When I came here, I spoke no English. I grew up in the projects. Now I am a member of Congress. I try not to forget that. I try to remember it every day."

As a senior Democrat on Appropriations in 2005, Serrano secured $5 million for restoration of the High Bridge, a historic, 1848 structure that connects Manhattan to neighborhoods north of Yankee Stadium in the Bronx. It had been closed for decades after falling into disrepair but a civic movement was born with the mission of saving it.

In the past, Serrano has obtained federal money to clean up the Bronx River, plant trees in the borough and reduce air pollution from trucks, believed to be a contributing factor in the high incidence of asthma among his constituents. He proudly notes that a beaver was spotted living in the Bronx River in 2007, for the first time in two centuries. Biologists named it José, in Serrano's honor.

In 2006, Serrano got the attention of the White House when he cut a deal with Venezuelan leader Hugo Chávez for cheap oil for the poverty-plagued South Bronx as winter set in. The Bush administration opposes the socialist Chávez government, which is highly critical of U.S. foreign policy. Serrano helped broker a deal in which Citgo Petroleum Corp., which is controlled by the Venezuelan government, sold 5 million gallons of heating oil at 45 percent below the market rate to nonprofit housing organizations in the Bronx.

Serrano also raised eyebrows in the administration in 2007 when he signed on to a bill by Democratic Rep. Jim McGovern of Massachusetts that would require the withdrawal of U.S. troops within six months and cut off funding for the war thereafter. Serrano was among three appropriators, including Barbara Lee of California and John W. Olver of Massachusetts, to join in the measure, which went further in calling for an end to the war than other Democratic resolutions that year.

"We have created a mess in Iraq," he said. "And the sooner we admit that and pull out, the fewer American soldiers will be needlessly lost."

Serrano's voting record is solidly Democratic. In the 109th Congress (2005-06), he stuck with his party 96 percent of the time on issues that polarized the two parties. He wins high marks from the liberal Americans for Democratic Action and typically gets a zero rating from the American Conservative Union.

The Puerto Rican-born Serrano weighs in on issues of importance to the island commonwealth, whose delegate to Congress has no vote on the House floor. Close to 200,000 of Serrano's constituents are of Puerto Rican descent, and he says citizens of the island should be allowed to decide whether Puerto Rico is granted statehood or independence. In 2007, he

CAPITOL OFFICE
225-4361
jserrano@mail.house.gov
www.house.gov/serrano
2227 Rayburn 20515-3216; fax 225-6001

COMMITTEES
Appropriations
(Financial Services - chairman)

RESIDENCE
Bronx

BORN
Oct. 24, 1943, Mayaguez, P.R.

RELIGION
Roman Catholic

FAMILY
Wife, Mary Staucet; five children

EDUCATION
Dodge Vocational H.S., graduated 1961;
Lehman College, attended 1979-80

MILITARY SERVICE
Army Medical Corps, 1964-66

CAREER
School district administrator; banker

POLITICAL HIGHLIGHTS
N.Y. Assembly, 1975-90; sought Democratic nomination for Bronx borough president, 1985

ELECTION RESULTS

2006 GENERAL		
José E. Serrano (D, WFM)	56,124	95.3%
Ali Mohamed (R, C)	2,759	4.7%
2006 PRIMARY		
José E. Serrano (D)		unopposed
2004 GENERAL		
José E. Serrano (D, WFM)	111,638	95.2%
Ali Mohamed (R, C)	5,610	4.8%

PREVIOUS WINNING PERCENTAGES
2002 (92%); 2000 (96%); 1998 (95%); 1996 (96%); 1994 (96%); 1992 (91%); 1990 (93%); 1990 Special Election (92%)

sponsored a bill calling for a plebiscite for Puerto Ricans to choose between the status quo or a change in status, either to statehood or to independence.

In 2000, Serrano was arrested outside the White House for protesting the Navy's continued use of the island of Vieques, off the coast of Puerto Rico, for training exercises using live bombs. On the Vieques issue and others, Serrano has aligned with black activist Al Sharpton, and he endorsed Sharpton's 2004 presidential bid in the Democratic primaries that year.

Serrano is a strong advocate of liberalized immigration laws, backing extension of a program that allows some immigrants to apply for residency even if they are in the country illegally. He is also the sponsor of legislation that would consider the rights of children born in the United States if their parents are being deported. It would require a federal judge to consider the welfare of a child before an alien parent is deported.

In 2001, he won approval of a measure granting posthumous citizenship to victims of the Sept. 11 terrorist attacks who had been in the process of becoming citizens.

Since the mid-1990s, Serrano has offered "English-plus" legislation, which encourages all residents of the United States not only to become proficient in English but also to preserve or gain skills in other languages as well. The measure began as a response to conservative proposals to make English the official language. "Multilingualism is an asset, not a liability," he says.

Serrano grew up in the Millbrook Houses, a public housing project in the Bronx. His parents had emigrated from Puerto Rico when he was 7, and Serrano says he learned English by listening to the Frank Sinatra records his father brought back from the Army. Serrano became a big fan, amassing a large collection of Sinatra records and sponsoring the 1997 measure that awarded Sinatra a congressional gold medal.

Serrano graduated from a vocational high school, served in the Army, and then took a job in a New York City bank and began making political contacts, which helped him win a state Assembly seat in 1974. His tenure in Albany, including a stint as chairman of the Assembly Education Committee, made him a fixture in New York Hispanic politics. His son, José Marco Serrano, was elected to the New York City Council in 2001 and to the state Senate in 2004.

When U.S. Democratic Rep. Robert Garcia resigned his seat in 1990 after he was convicted of defense contract extortion, Serrano moved quickly to stake his claim. He breezed to victory with 92 percent of the vote in the special election and won a full term with 93 percent that November.

He has won all his subsequent re-elections with at least 91 percent.

KEY VOTES

2006

- Yes Stop broadband companies from favoring select Internet traffic
- No Affirm U.S. commitment to war in Iraq and reject setting a withdrawal date for troops
- No Repeal requirement for bilingual ballots at the polls
- No Permit U.S. sale of civilian nuclear technology to India
- No Build a 700-mile fence on the U.S.-Mexico border to curb illegal crossings
- No Permit warrantless wiretaps of suspected terrorists

2005

- Yes Intervene in the life-support case of Terri Schiavo
- Yes Lift President Bush's restrictions on stem cell research funding
- Yes Prohibit FBI access to library and bookstore records
- No Approve free-trade pact with five Central American countries
- No Pass energy policy overhaul favored by President Bush emphasizing domestic oil and gas production
- No End mandatory preservation of habitat of endangered animal and plant species
- Yes Ban torture of prisoners in U.S. custody

CQ VOTE STUDIES

	PARTY UNITY		PRESIDENTIAL SUPPORT	
	Support	Oppose	Support	Oppose
2006	96%	4%	16%	84%
2005	96%	4%	9%	91%
2004	98%	2%	12%	88%
2003	96%	4%	22%	78%
2002	96%	4%	26%	74%

INTEREST GROUPS

	AFL-CIO	ADA	CCUS	ACU
2006	100%	90%	15%	4%
2005	93%	100%	33%	4%
2004	100%	100%	30%	0%
2003	100%	90%	21%	23%
2002	100%	90%	37%	0%

NEW YORK 16

South Bronx

The 16th, which covers the distressed neighborhoods of the South Bronx, is the nation's poorest district in terms of median income and is one of the least educated. One-third of families live on a household income of less than $10,000, and the area is plagued by urban ills and low rates of home ownership. Some South Bronx neighborhoods have begun to turn around, thanks to grass-roots community work and federal empowerment zone money.

The South Bronx, overtaken by a post-World War II influx of Hispanics to New York City, has elected men of Puerto Rican origin to the House since 1970. The 16th's strong Puerto Rican influence is complemented by African and South and Central American immigrant communities. The district's 3 percent non-Hispanic white population is the nation's lowest.

Subsidized economic development organizations have built several downtown developments of single-family and low-rise housing on vacant lots. These buildings are being occupied by people who grew up in the district, worked their way out, and are now returning to help rebuild their old neighborhoods. Light manufacturing firms also have set up shop, replacing some of the heavy industry that moved out decades ago. The Fulton Fish Market, which recently moved from lower Manhattan to Hunts Point, houses more than 35 wholesalers, making it the nation's largest grouping of seafood wholesalers.

The district is home to one of New York City's iconic landmarks: Yankee Stadium. Local businesses rely on the economic benefit of hosting the oft-visited "Bronx Bombers." Fordham University also is in the 16th.

The 16th is one of the most strongly Democratic districts in the nation — it was John Kerry's second-best in the 2004 presidential election, behind only the neighboring 15th — but like many districts with large minority and immigrant populations, voter turnout is low.

MAJOR INDUSTRY

Health care, light manufacturing, seafood distribution

CITIES

New York (pt.), 654,360

NOTABLE

The Edgar Allan Poe Cottage in the Bronx (the writer's last home) is owned by New York City.

Rep. Eliot L. Engel (D)

CAPITOL OFFICE
225-2464
www.house.gov/engel
2161 Rayburn 20515-3217; fax 225-5513

COMMITTEES
Energy & Commerce
Foreign Affairs
(Western Hemisphere - chairman)

RESIDENCE
Bronx

BORN
Feb. 18, 1947, Bronx, N.Y.

RELIGION
Jewish

FAMILY
Wife, Patricia Ennis Engel; three children

EDUCATION
Hunter-Lehman College, B.A. 1969 (history); City U. of New York, Lehman College, M.A. 1973 (guidance & counseling); New York Law School, J.D. 1987

CAREER
Teacher; guidance counselor

POLITICAL HIGHLIGHTS
Bronx Democratic district leader, 1974-77; N.Y. Assembly, 1977-88

ELECTION RESULTS

2006 GENERAL		
Eliot L. Engel (D, WFM)	93,614	76.4%
Jim Faulkner (R, INDC, C)	28,842	23.6%
2006 PRIMARY		
Eliot L. Engel (D)	26,564	83.0%
Jessica Flagg (D)	5,430	17.0%
2004 GENERAL		
Eliot L. Engel (D, WFM)	140,530	76.2%
Matthew I. Brennan (R)	40,524	22.0%
Kevin Brawley (C)	3,482	1.9%

PREVIOUS WINNING PERCENTAGES
2002 (63%); 2000 (90%); 1998 (88%); 1996 (85%); 1994 (78%); 1992 (80%); 1990 (61%); 1988 (56%)

Elected 1988; 10th term

An ardent defender of Israel, Engel has spent his years on the House Foreign Affairs Committee focused largely on the Middle East. But in a challenging shift of emphasis, he finds himself chairing the Western Hemisphere Subcommittee.

"It's not a field in which I've done a lot," he acknowledged after taking the gavel for the 110th Congress (2007-08). "But being a representative from New York, where there are a lot of immigrant communities from Latin America and the Caribbean, it was a natural thing for me." Engel relishes his new subcommittee duties and says he hopes the post will give him a footing to be a leader on immigration issues.

If there's one thing Engel finds natural, it's serving his constituents — immigrant and otherwise. A lifelong resident of the Bronx and a product of its Democratic clubs, he keeps more staff in New York than in Washington and makes sure they help all comers. A 1996 Wall Street Journal article dubbed him "The Mayor" of his district, a tribute to his attention to voters' everyday concerns such as overcrowded subways or broken traffic lights. "Even if someone disagrees with how I vote, if they know I am hardworking and available to them, they're going to vote for me," Engel says.

In one area of foreign policy, Engel has had a change of heart. He says if he had known how "incompetent" the Bush administration would be in prosecuting the war in Iraq, he wouldn't have voted to authorize it in 2002 — even if the intelligence about weapons of mass destruction had turned out to be right. The fact that the United States has become bogged down in Iraq has hurt its ability to combat other urgent problems, including global terrorism, he says.

Despite his criticism of President Bush's conduct of the Iraq War, Engel was among the pro-Israel lawmakers who persuaded House Democratic leaders to drop a provision from a March 2007 war funding bill that would have barred the president from taking military action against Iran without congressional authorization. He argued that Bush needed maximum flexibility to pressure Iran to end its nuclear program and its support of radical Islamic groups that foment violence against Israel. He warned at a House Democratic Caucus meeting that he would vote against the bill unless the provision was deleted. "Iran is the biggest culprit in aiding and abetting terrorism, not only in the Middle East but around the world," Engel argues.

He also sees Syria as a deadly threat to Israel and the broader Middle East. During the 108th Congress (2003-04), Engel teamed with Republican Ileana Ros-Lehtinen of Florida to win passage of a sanctions bill targeting Syria, battling the persistent misgivings of the State Department. He calls the measure "my most important accomplishment." Five months after signing the bill into law, Bush used it to impose tough sanctions on Syria. The president labeled Syrian government activities "an extraordinary threat to the national security of the United States."

Engel was an early proponent of U.S. intervention in the civil war in Yugoslavia. In 1993, he joined a bipartisan group of lawmakers who urged the Clinton administration to take sides in Bosnia against the Serbs, who were being accused of "ethnic cleansing," the forced removal of Muslims.

He opposed granting China normal trade status in 2000 because of the country's human rights abuses. "Are we only for the almighty dollar or are we for morality and doing what's right?" he asked. In 2005, he voted for a bill to sanction countries that sell arms or defense technology to China.

In keeping with his district's leanings, Engel votes a liberal line on domestic issues, siding with labor unions, rejecting punitive immigration measures and opposing limits on civil liberties in the name of fighting terrorism. In his career, he has supported the Democratic Party position more than 90 percent of the time.

In addition to serving on Foreign Affairs, Engel sits on the Energy and Commerce Committee, where he is active on legislation related to health care, illegal drugs, consumer protection and telecommunications.

For much of his tenure, Engel has been content to attend to constituent service and the nuts and bolts of legislation. But on one day every year, he has a brief moment on the national stage: He arrives early in the House chamber for the annual State of the Union address to grab an aisle seat so he can greet the president and renew acquaintances with a number of ambassadors. He began the practice as a freshman with President George H. W. Bush and has continued it ever since. "The constituents love it," he said in 2003. "And as long as they love it, I love it."

Engel grew up in the Bronx and earned his political spurs in local Democratic clubs. Engel's father was a welder and active in his local union. "He had a very strong sense of social justice and doing what was right for working people," Engel says. Father and son walked picket lines together.

Engel says he has always been a political junkie and adds that as a boy he memorized the names of all 100 senators then serving. He attended New York City public schools, where he later worked as a teacher and guidance counselor. He was elected to the state Assembly in 1977, when he defeated the candidate endorsed by the Democratic Party.

In the Assembly, he worked on housing and substance abuse issues and established his credentials in the "reform" wing of the Bronx Democratic organization. In 1988, he challenged Democratic Rep. Mario Biaggi, who was on trial for bribery, conspiracy and extortion. In August, Biaggi was convicted and resigned, but his name remained on the ballot for both the primary and the general election (the latter because he regularly received the endorsement of district Republicans). Engel won both contests.

He easily rebuffed a Biaggi comeback attempt in 1992, and has faced only nominal opposition since. Engel is one of the few non-minority lawmakers who represent a district in which a majority of the population belongs to a racial or ethnic minority. But the only race that has afforded Engel a competitive minority challenger was the 2000 primary against state Sen. Larry E. Seabrook. Engel won that contest by more than 9 percentage points.

KEY VOTES

2006

- Yes Stop broadband companies from favoring select Internet traffic
- No Affirm U.S. commitment to war in Iraq and reject setting a withdrawal date for troops
- No Repeal requirement for bilingual ballots at the polls
- Yes Permit U.S. sale of civilian nuclear technology to India
- No Build a 700-mile fence on the U.S.-Mexico border to curb illegal crossings
- No Permit warrantless wiretaps of suspected terrorists

2005

- Yes Intervene in the life-support case of Terri Schiavo
- Yes Lift President Bush's restrictions on stem cell research funding
- Yes Prohibit FBI access to library and bookstore records
- No Approve free-trade pact with five Central American countries
- No Pass energy policy overhaul favored by President Bush emphasizing domestic oil and gas production
- No End mandatory preservation of habitat of endangered animal and plant species
- Yes Ban torture of prisoners in U.S. custody

CQ VOTE STUDIES

	PARTY UNITY		PRESIDENTIAL SUPPORT	
	Support	Oppose	Support	Oppose
2006	95%	5%	34%	66%
2005	93%	7%	26%	74%
2004	96%	4%	36%	64%
2003	94%	6%	24%	76%
2002	89%	11%	44%	56%

INTEREST GROUPS

	AFL-CIO	ADA	CCUS	ACU
2006	100%	95%	36%	4%
2005	93%	95%	41%	0%
2004	93%	90%	35%	4%
2003	100%	95%	30%	20%
2002	100%	90%	50%	12%

NEW YORK 17

North Bronx; part of Westchester and Rockland counties — Mount Vernon, part of Yonkers

The 17th takes in the northwestern part of the Bronx and parts of Westchester and Rockland counties northwest of New York City. Blacks and Hispanics together constitute a majority of residents in the district, which is ethnically, racially and economically diverse territory.

Riverdale, a heavily Jewish neighborhood, sits at the western edge of the Bronx and is one of New York's most affluent areas. It is home to numerous college preparatory schools, medical facilities and upper-class residential neighborhoods. East of Riverdale, on the other side of Van Cortlandt Park and Woodlawn Cemetery, there is a large black population. The 17th reaches almost as far east as the mammoth Co-op City apartment complex (in the 7th). About 45 percent of district residents live in the Bronx.

In Westchester County, home to one-fourth of the 17th's residents, the district takes in all of heavily black Mount Vernon, which hosts commercial industries and some notable health care facilities, including Mount Vernon Hospital. Other black and Hispanic communities are found in western Yonkers, and there are predominately white areas, many with residents of Italian and Irish descent, in southeastern Yonkers. Yonkers' portion of Hudson River waterfront is expected to become a terminus for water taxis moving commuters to and from Manhattan beginning in 2007. The 17th narrows significantly in northern Yonkers, meandering north along Route 9 and the Hudson River to cross the Tappan Zee Bridge into Rockland County, where the rest of the district's population lives.

John Kerry took 66 percent of the 17th's 2004 presidential vote — tallying 81 percent of the vote in the district's portion of the Bronx.

MAJOR INDUSTRY

Health care, higher education, city government

CITIES

New York (pt.), 292,423; Yonkers (pt.), 87,617; Mount Vernon, 68,381; Spring Valley, 25,464

NOTABLE

Duke Ellington, Elizabeth Cady Stanton, F.W. Woolworth, Nellie Bly and "Bat" Masterson are among those buried in Woodlawn Cemetery.

Rep. Nita M. Lowey (D)

CAPITOL OFFICE
225-6506
www.house.gov/lowey
2329 Rayburn 20515-3218; fax 225-0546

COMMITTEES
Appropriations
(State-Foreign Operations - chairwoman)
Homeland Security

RESIDENCE
Harrison

BORN
July 5, 1937, Bronx, N.Y.

RELIGION
Jewish

FAMILY
Husband, Stephen Lowey; three children

EDUCATION
Mount Holyoke College, B.A. 1959 (marketing)

CAREER
State government aide; homemaker

POLITICAL HIGHLIGHTS
N.Y. assistant secretary of state, 1985-87

ELECTION RESULTS

2006 GENERAL		
Nita M. Lowey (D, WFM)	124,256	70.7%
Richard A. Hoffman (R, C)	51,450	29.3%
2006 PRIMARY		
Nita M. Lowey (D)	unopposed	
2004 GENERAL		
Nita M. Lowey (D, INDC, WFM)	170,715	69.8%
Richard A. Hoffman (R)	73,975	30.2%

PREVIOUS WINNING PERCENTAGES
2002 (92%); 2000 (67%); 1998 (83%); 1996 (64%); 1994 (57%); 1992 (56%); 1990 (63%); 1988 (50%)

Elected 1988; 10th term

After nearly two decades in the Congress, the high-energy Lowey got the gavel of the House subcommittee that doles out foreign aid, joining the elite "college of cardinals," as the 12 appropriations chairmen are known. She is a big fan of increasing foreign aid funding and can be counted on to block those trying to prevent international family planning programs from getting a share of that money.

Her outward appearance as a doting grandmother belies her inner steel and political savvy. Lowey (LO-ee) parcels out federal funding with toughness and political finesse, and at election time, she is one of the House Democrats' best fundraisers.

Two of her constituents are more well-known than she is — Bill and Hillary Rodham Clinton, who have their official residence in Chappaqua. Overshadowed by the pair politically, Lowey has handled the situation with grace, say fellow Democrats. Her hopes of advancing to the Senate in 2000 were dashed when Clinton moved to New York for her successful run for the seat of retiring Democratic Sen. Daniel Patrick Moynihan. Lowey has since developed strong ties with the Clintons, helping Hillary with her presidential fundraising. They also teamed up in 2004 and again in 2006 on a bill to make basic education for children worldwide a goal of U.S. foreign policy.

"I stepped aside for her, and that's it," Lowey says, adding that she was confident at the time that she would someday be the top-ranking Democrat or chairwoman of a House committee. But Lowey still harbors ambitions for the Senate and would be among the likely candidates for Clinton's seat if her quest for the presidency in 2008 is successful.

On Appropriations, Lowey pushes for bigger aid packages to both Israel and the Arab world. In the past, she has helped Israel in securing aid, but she also has supported increases for basic education in Muslim countries, from $98 million in 2001 to $520 million in 2006, in the hope of providing alternatives to *madrasahs*, Islamic religious schools.

A defender of abortion rights, Lowey also has her sights set on reversing President Bush's executive order barring the use of U.S. foreign aid funds for family planning programs abroad that perform or counsel about abortion. Bush imposed the ban in 2001, and Congress has the power to revoke it, although any attempt to do so would likely provoke a presidential veto. "But I think it will make a very strong statement," Lowey says.

In 2007, Lowey won appointment to a new Appropriations Committee panel that will oversee spending on intelligence matters.

Issues affecting women and health care also are important to Lowey. She introduced legislation in 2006 to require the National Institutes of Health to study possible environmental causes of breast cancer. And in 1998, she got the government to agree to cover contraception for federal workers along with other pharmaceuticals. One of her major achievements in recent years was a law passed in 2004 requiring the food industry to more clearly label products that contain the eight most common allergens: milk, eggs, fish, shellfish, tree nuts, peanuts, wheat and soybeans.

While Lowey proudly wears her liberal credentials, she also is an inside player who maneuvers skillfully through the appropriations process. She won the coveted seat on Appropriations in 1993 by aggressively lobbying the Democratic leadership. In recent years, she brought home millions of dollars for a ferry system to run from Rockland County through Yonkers, in her Westchester County district, to lower Manhattan; the ferry was to begin operation in 2007.

From her seat on the Homeland Security Committee, Lowey has pushed for establishing a threat-based formula for localities getting federal homeland security grants, which in effect would help New York get a larger share of the funds. In 2007, Lowey introduced a bill requiring the Transportation Security Agency to screen all airport workers. "Meticulously screening passengers but giving workers open access is like installing an expensive home security system but leaving your back door wide open," said Lowey.

She also went after the TSA in the 109th Congress (2005-06), with legislation that would grant collective bargaining rights to the nation's federal airport screeners. The measure became a provision in the 2007 House-passed bill implementing the recommendations of the Sept. 11 commission.

A dutiful fundraiser, Lowey in 2000 helped raise $6 million for House Democrats' effort to recruit and elect women candidates. Two years later, picked by the party leadership to head the Democratic Congressional Campaign Committee, she set fundraising records. For the 2006 elections, Lowey gave $375,000 of her war chest to Democratic candidates.

Lowey got her start in politics more than 30 years ago. She was a homemaker in Queens when she volunteered in a neighbor's 1974 campaign for lieutenant governor. The neighbor was Mario Cuomo. Though Cuomo lost the primary race, new Democratic Gov. Hugh L. Carey appointed him secretary of state, and he hired Lowey to work in the anti-poverty division.

By the mid-1980s, Cuomo was governor and Lowey was the top aide to new Secretary of State Gail Shaffer. Lowey made an impressive debut in electoral politics in 1988 when she unseated two-term GOP Rep. Joseph J. DioGuardi in the then 20th District. Lowey survived a primary against Hamilton Fish III, publisher of The Nation magazine and son of a GOP House member, and against businessman Dennis Mehiel. She raised $1.3 million, a huge sum for a challenger at the time.

In the general election, DioGuardi outspent her. But his campaign was damaged by a newspaper account of a scheme involving a New Rochelle auto dealer funneling $57,000 in corporate contributions to DioGuardi's campaign. Lowey won narrowly.

DioGuardi returned for a rematch in 1990, but Lowey won decisively. Since then, she has outdistanced all competition. Lowey's first campaign benefited from her personal wealth, including more than $650,000 of her own money, largely derived from her husband's law firm of Lowey Dannenberg Bemporad & Selinger. The GOP declined to field a candidate in 2002, and she won handily in 2004 and 2006.

KEY VOTES

2006

Yes Stop broadband companies from favoring select Internet traffic
No Affirm U.S. commitment to war in Iraq and reject setting a withdrawal date for troops
No Repeal requirement for bilingual ballots at the polls
Yes Permit U.S. sale of civilian nuclear technology to India
No Build a 700-mile fence on the U.S.-Mexico border to curb illegal crossings
No Permit warrantless wiretaps of suspected terrorists

2005

? Intervene in the life-support case of Terri Schiavo
Yes Lift President Bush's restrictions on stem cell research funding
Yes Prohibit FBI access to library and bookstore records
No Approve free-trade pact with five Central American countries
No Pass energy policy overhaul favored by President Bush emphasizing domestic oil and gas production
No End mandatory preservation of habitat of endangered animal and plant species
Yes Ban torture of prisoners in U.S. custody

CQ VOTE STUDIES

	PARTY UNITY		PRESIDENTIAL SUPPORT	
	Support	Oppose	Support	Oppose
2006	98%	2%	23%	77%
2005	98%	2%	13%	87%
2004	95%	5%	35%	65%
2003	94%	6%	24%	76%
2002	94%	6%	26%	74%

INTEREST GROUPS

	AFL-CIO	ADA	CCUS	ACU
2006	100%	95%	40%	4%
2005	93%	95%	41%	0%
2004	100%	100%	47%	4%
2003	87%	95%	33%	16%
2002	100%	90%	40%	4%

NEW YORK 18

Most of Westchester County — New Rochelle, most of Yonkers

The 18th takes in large portions of southern and central Westchester County before hopping the Hudson River to pick up most of New City and Congers and all of Haverstraw in Rockland County. Mostly white-collar, the district is home to wealthy and educated suburbanites who are employed in the health care, higher education and technology industries.

Many of the 18th's residents enjoy an easy commute to white-collar jobs in Manhattan. The district takes in the northern portion of Yonkers and also includes Ossining, site of Sing Sing prison — its location north of the city on the Hudson River led New Yorkers to refer to prison-bound criminals as being "sent up the river."

Working-class areas in the 18th include Port Chester and urban sections of White Plains and New Rochelle. White Plains is home to Westchester County's largest concentration of retail activity, and the city's centerpiece includes Renaissance Square — a hotel, office and condominium complex under construction downtown. Both White Plains and New Rochelle are home to several college campuses, including Iona College. The district also hosts several corporate headquarters: PepsiCo in Purchase; IBM in Armonk; ITT in White Plains; and Reader's Digest in Pleasantville.

The 18th is a well-to-do residential district that leans Democratic, but not overwhelmingly. Westchester County has a Republican base, and wealthy New York suburbs such as Scarsdale are the district's hallmark. But Westchester's working-class communities, coupled with some affluent Democratic areas, are more than enough to offset the GOP base. John Kerry carried the district with 57 percent of the vote in the 2004 presidential election.

MAJOR INDUSTRY

Health care, higher education, retail

CITIES

Yonkers (pt.), 108,469; New Rochelle, 72,182; White Plains, 53,077

NOTABLE

North Tarrytown was renamed Sleepy Hollow in honor of the Washington Irving story set there; Thomas Paine Cottage and Museum is in New Rochelle.

Rep. John Hall (D)

CAPITOL OFFICE
225-5441
johnhall.house.gov
1217 Longworth 20515-3219; fax 225-3289

COMMITTEES
Select Energy Independence & Global Warming
Transportation & Infrastructure
Veterans' Affairs
(Disability Assistance & Memorial Affairs - chairman)

RESIDENCE
Dover Plains

BORN
July 23, 1948, Baltimore, Md.

RELIGION
Christian

FAMILY
Wife, Pamela Bingham Hall; one child

EDUCATION
Notre Dame U., attended 1964-65 (physics); Loyola U. (Md.), attended 1965-66 (English)

CAREER
Songwriter and musician; ski instructor

POLITICAL HIGHLIGHTS
Ulster County Legislature, 1990-91; Saugerties Central School District Board of Education, 1996-98 (president, 1998)

ELECTION RESULTS

2006 GENERAL		
John Hall (D)	100,119	51.2%
Sue W. Kelly (R, INDC, C)	95,359	48.8%
2006 PRIMARY		
John Hall (D)	11,231	49.5%
Judith Aydelott (D)	6,110	26.9%
Ben Shuldiner (D)	3,568	15.7%
Darren J. Rigger (D)	1,799	7.9%

Elected 2006; 1st term

Hall was the lead singer of the pop band Orleans in the 1970s when he wrote the song "Still the One." Thirty years later, President Bush used it as the theme song for his 2004 re-election campaign. Hall told The New York Times he had a lawyer draft a formal letter of complaint.

Using his song is just one among many things that Hall dislikes about the Bush administration. He decided to run for office out of concern for the administration's energy policy. Opposed to nuclear energy, he helped found a group in the 1980s called Musicians United for Safe Energy, which raised more than $1 million for renewable energy projects.

Though he is a veteran liberal activist who has long been involved in Democratic politics in the Hudson River Valley area, he admits that he gained extra attention because of his rock-and-roll past. "Being a musician and songwriter in the political world didn't hurt," Hall said. He also penned the pop standard "Dance with Me." Hall was recruited by longtime Democratic Rep. Maurice D. Hinchey, whose district also runs along the Hudson River. Hall had helped raise money for Hinchey's campaigns.

Democratic leaders rewarded Hall for upsetting GOP incumbent Sue W. Kelly, and made him the chairman of the Veterans' Affairs Subcommittee on Disability Assistance and Memorial Affairs, which provides oversight of veterans' benefits. He said he plans to address the "scandalous" backlog of 600,000 veterans' benefit claims. "Regardless of what one thinks of a party policy or a particular war, once an individual puts on the uniform of our country and goes to fight for us, they deserve the best care," Hall said.

He also sits on the Transportation and Infrastructure Committee, where his focus is on addressing traffic congestion and water-quality issues in his district. Many of the residents commute to New York City.

In deciding to take on Kelly, Hall built a strong grass-roots campaign and ended up dominating the four-candidate primary field. Kelly, who had served six terms, was a centrist who had won with more than 60 percent of the vote in her past four re-elections. But Hall surprised her, winning 51 percent of the vote to Kelly's 49 percent.

NEW YORK 19

Hudson Valley — Peekskill

Wedged between Connecticut and New Jersey, the 19th connects the New York City suburbs to upstate New York. The Hudson River flows through the center of the district, along which lie some of the state's richest communities in the south and technology and research firms in the north. East and west of the river are rural towns and farms where onions, lettuce and celery are grown.

The southeastern, Westchester County portion of the district is known for its elegant exurban homes that attract celebrities and wealthy commuters from Manhattan. The median family income approaches $200,000 in some places. Growing Peekskill, with a working- and middle-class base, is in the midst of a waterfront redevelopment project and has an expanding technology sector.

The area north of Peekskill is called the Hudson Highlands, where the river has steep embankments on both sides. The U.S. Military Academy is here, and just north of West Point in Dutchess County is Beacon, which faces Newburgh (in the 22nd) and New Windsor across the Hudson River. Technology and research firms continue to move into the mid-Hudson region, which includes areas just south of Poughkeepsie.

The wealth in the 19th's southern parts and the rural character of its western reaches — which extend to the foothills of the Catskill Mountains — help give the district a GOP lean. But Democrats can ride national trends to victory here, as they did in 2006 when the 19th changed party hands.

MAJOR INDUSTRY
Computers, telecommunications, agriculture

MILITARY BASES
U.S. Military Academy, 1,200 military, 2,300 civilian (2007)

CITIES
Peekskill, 22,441; Jefferson Valley-Yorktown (unincorporated), 14,891; Beacon, 13,808

NOTABLE
The home and farm of John Jay, first chief justice of the United States, is in Katonah.

Rep. Kirsten Gillibrand (D)

CAPITOL OFFICE
225-5614
gillibrand.house.gov
120 Cannon 20515-3220; fax 225-6234

COMMITTEES
Agriculture
Armed Services

RESIDENCE
Greenport

BORN
Dec. 9, 1966, Albany, N.Y.

RELIGION
Roman Catholic

FAMILY
Husband, Jonathan Gillibrand; one child

EDUCATION
Darmouth College, A.B. 1988 (Asian studies); U. of California, Los Angeles, J.D. 1991

CAREER
Lawyer; U.S. Housing and Urban Development Department aide

POLITICAL HIGHLIGHTS
No previous office

ELECTION RESULTS

2006 GENERAL

Kirsten Gillibrand (D, WFM)	125,168	53.1%
John E. Sweeney (R, INDC, C)	110,554	46.9%

2006 PRIMARY

Kirsten Gillibrand (D)	unopposed

Elected 2006; 1st term

As a young girl, Gillibrand canvassed door-to-door with her grandmother, a pioneer for women's rights who founded the first women's Democratic club in Albany. While campaigning for the House, Gillibrand pledged to honor her grandmother's legacy as a reformer.

Upon her arrival in Congress, Gillibrand (full name: KEER-sten JILL-uh-brand) immediately set about trying to make governing more transparent, starting with her own congressional office. She posts her daily schedule on the Web so her constituents can see which lobbyists she's meeting with and which fundraisers she's attending each day.

Gillibrand is a member of the Blue Dogs, a coalition of conservative House Democrats. She joined, she says, because the group's mission of fiscal restraint matches her own. She supports tax reduction measures for middle-class families, including a $10 billion plan to allow parents to deduct up to $10,000 a year in college tuition.

A fierce critic of the Iraq War, Gillibrand says she'll use her assignment to the Armed Services Committee to ask "tough questions" about U.S. policy. She also plans to look out for her district's veterans and active-duty members.

From her seat on the Agriculture Committee, Gillibrand focuses on working to preserve farmland, helping dairy farmers and stabilizing commodity prices. She would like to see tax breaks for manufacturers that make more fuel-efficient farm equipment or develop biofuels.

As an attorney, Gillibrand concentrated on securities litigation. During the Clinton administration, she served as special counsel to the secretary of Housing and Urban Development, Andrew Cuomo.

A first-time candidate, Gillibrand was unrelenting in attacking four-term GOP Rep. John E. Sweeney on ethics issues, including ties to lobbying groups. Republicans attempted to turn the tables on Gillibrand over her husband's investments, but she capitalized on allegations that Sweeney tried to gloss over a past drunken driving incident. She also proved to be one of the year's strongest non-incumbent fundraisers. Her libertarian viewpoints and her own ethics pledge helped her win by about 6 percentage points.

NEW YORK 20

North Hudson Valley — Saratoga Springs, Glens Falls

Running along the state's eastern border, the politically competitive 20th starts just outside Poughkeepsie and roughly follows Interstate 87 north into the scenic Adirondack Mountains and the resort areas of Lake George and Essex County. Lake Placid, site of the 1932 and 1980 Winter Olympics, is in Essex County at the district's northern tip.

The 20th covers much of the primarily residential Hudson River Valley, where apple farms are the core of its agriculture industry. The district's population hub is in its center, in the Albany-Schenectady-Troy area. Although those three cities are all in the 21st, the 20th claims much of their GOP-leaning suburbia, and they have helped fuel a suburban boom in southern Saratoga County. Saratoga Springs attracts tourists during the summer months for its world-class horse racing, and Malta's Saratoga Technology-Energy Park will add hundreds of technology manufacturing and alternate energy research jobs to the district.

The 20th's southern end is made up of mainly rural and rugged land, and it extends west from the Hudson River through Greene County to pick up rural territory in Delaware and Otsego counties.

The presence of many unionized state workers outside Albany makes labor an important constituency, but dairy farmers and small-town voters give the GOP a slight edge. The 20th, which has the state's lowest minority percentage, gave George W. Bush 53 percent of its 2004 presidential vote, but elected a Democrat to its House seat in 2006.

MAJOR INDUSTRY
Agriculture, tourism, manufacturing

CITIES
Saratoga Springs, 26,186; Glens Falls, 14,354

NOTABLE
The National Bottle Museum in Ballston Spa celebrates the history of glass bottle-making.

Rep. Michael R. McNulty (D)

CAPITOL OFFICE
225-5076
mike.mcnulty@mail.house.gov
www.house.gov/mcnulty
2210 Rayburn 20515-3221; fax 225-5077

COMMITTEES
Ways & Means
(Social Security - chairman)

RESIDENCE
Green Island

BORN
Sept. 16, 1947, Troy, N.Y.

RELIGION
Roman Catholic

FAMILY
Wife, Nancy Ann McNulty; four children

EDUCATION
College of the Holy Cross, A.B. 1969 (political science)

CAREER
Public official

POLITICAL HIGHLIGHTS
Green Island supervisor, 1970-77; Democratic nominee for N.Y. Assembly, 1976; mayor of Green Island, 1977-83; N.Y. Assembly, 1983-89

ELECTION RESULTS

2006 GENERAL		
McNulty (D, INDC, C, WFM)	167,604	78.2%
Warren Redlich (R)	46,752	21.8%
2006 PRIMARY		
Michael R. McNulty (D)	26,246	85.8%
Thomas J. Raleigh (D)	4,341	14.2%
2004 GENERAL		
McNulty (D, INDC, C, WFM)	194,033	70.8%
Warren Redlich (R)	80,121	29.2%

PREVIOUS WINNING PERCENTAGES
2002 (75%); 2000 (74%); 1998 (74%); 1996 (66%); 1994 (67%); 1992 (63%); 1990 (64%); 1988 (62%)

Elected 1988; 10th term

For a political "lifer," McNulty is an anomaly. Modest in manner and aspirations, he harbors no ambitions for higher office. He looks out for his district, attends his committee meetings and casts his votes. But he flies so far under the radar on Capitol Hill that he is all but undetectable.

"I'm a workhorse rather than a show horse," he says. "I don't put out a lot of press releases, and I don't make a lot of speeches. I come in early every morning and work hard." He has been a House member for almost two decades but says, "Especially at night, when the Capitol's lit up, I still pinch myself. It is such an honor to serve here."

McNulty sits on the powerful Ways and Means Committee, where there are plenty of outsize egos prepared to grab the limelight that he shuns. He became chairman of the Social Security Subcommittee in 2007, and his goal in that role is typically modest: "My first priority is to do no harm." He opposes President Bush's proposal for individual investment accounts within Social Security and says talk of a looming fiscal crisis is overblown. "As of right now," he says, "the system is solvent for the next 30 years, though we will probably face problems down the line."

McNulty won his seat on Ways and Means after his first two terms in the House, during which he served as a vote-counter in the Democratic whip organization. He has always been an organization man. He is the scion of a Democratic dynasty in the gritty blue-collar town of Green Island and has spent his entire adult life in politics. At 22, he was elected town supervisor, a post his grandfather and father had held. After six years as mayor and six more in the state Assembly, he was hand-picked by the Albany area's Democratic bosses in 1988 to take the state capital's seat in Congress. He has never been seriously challenged in an election.

As a child, he spent a lot of time with his father, then mayor of Green Island. "I liked the interaction when I watched my father help people," McNulty recalls. Inspired by his father's example, he has devoted his career to helping his constituents. "Some call it pork, but I'm very, very proud of the things that I take back to my district," he says.

A reliable Democratic vote on most issues, McNulty broke with his party and was one of only 14 Democrats to vote against a 2007 supplemental spending bill providing additional funding for the Iraq War. The measure also set a deadline of August 2008 for U.S. troop withdrawal. Like half the Democratic naysayers, McNulty wants a more expeditious U.S. exit.

McNulty is rock-solid in his backing of organized labor's causes. He has repeatedly voted against the major trade liberalization laws of the past dozen or so years, from the North American Free Trade Agreement in 1993 to the Central American Free Trade Agreement in 2005.

He was a vocal opponent of the 2001 law allowing the president to extend normal trade status to Vietnam, and he voted against 2006 legislation that normalized relations permanently. McNulty, whose brother Bill was killed in the Vietnam War, argued that the country should not be rewarded with that economic benefit because it had insufficiently accounted for U.S. military personnel still missing since the conflict.

He sometimes differs with his party on social issues, especially those involving abortion. He voted to outlaw a procedure termed "partial birth" abortion by its opponents. He would prohibit federal workers' health plans from paying for abortions and would prevent public funding of the procedure except in cases of rape, incest or danger to the life of the woman. He voted for the 1996 law barring federal recognition of same-sex marriages but against proposed constitutional amendments in 2004 and 2006 that sought to outlaw gay unions.

The McNulty name has been a force in local upstate New York politics since 1914, when the congressman's grandfather, John J. McNulty, was elected Green Island tax collector. He went on to serve as town supervisor, county board chairman and county sheriff. The congressman's father, Jack McNulty Jr., served as town supervisor starting in 1949 and was later mayor. The congressman's sister, Ellen McNulty-Ryan, is the current Green Island mayor. So deep is the family tie to the town that McNulty, in his infrequent press releases, is identified as "Congressman Michael R. McNulty, D-Green Island."

In his long political career, McNulty has waged only one unsuccessful campaign, a 1976 challenge to a GOP assemblyman. But he bounced back in 1982 to win the first of his three terms in the legislature. While an assemblyman, McNulty once introduced legislation to make Uncle Sam the official state patriot. The icon is believed to have been modeled after Samuel Wilson, a meatpacker from Troy, which is in McNulty's district.

McNulty likes to spotlight such historical tidbits. In 2005, he sponsored a resolution to recognize Dr. Richard Shuckburgh, a British Army surgeon, as the primary author of the lyrics to "Yankee Doodle." Shuckburgh is said to have written the ditty in the 1750s after viewing provincial forces near Fort Crailo, in the city of Rensselaer, N.Y.

McNulty's opening to move to Washington came with the sudden retirement in 1988 of 30-year Democratic incumbent Samuel S. Stratton, whose health was failing. Within hours of the announcement, the district's Democratic leaders met and chose McNulty to replace him on the ballot. McNulty defeated local GOP official Peter Bakal with 62 percent of the vote.

Following the 2000 census, the 21st District was enlarged slightly because of reapportionment, in which New York gave up two House seats. But the district's solid Democratic cast was not altered. McNulty grabbed three-quarters of the vote in 2002, up a shade from his 2000 total.

In 2004, his Republican opponent, Warren Redlich, questioned McNulty's decision to pay his brother close to $35,000 over two years to serve as his campaign treasurer. That was McNulty's second-largest campaign expense, after a $50,000 contribution to the Democratic Congressional Campaign Committee. Voters didn't seem to mind, however; he still garnered 71 percent of the vote. In 2006, once again facing Redlich, he scored his biggest victory ever, taking 78 percent of the vote.

KEY VOTES

2006

- Yes Stop broadband companies from favoring select Internet traffic
- No Affirm U.S. commitment to war in Iraq and reject setting a withdrawal date for troops
- ? Repeal requirement for bilingual ballots at the polls
- No Permit U.S. sale of civilian nuclear technology to India
- No Build a 700-mile fence on the U.S.-Mexico border to curb illegal crossings
- No Permit warrantless wiretaps of suspected terrorists

2005

- Yes Intervene in the life-support case of Terri Schiavo
- Yes Lift President Bush's restrictions on stem cell research funding
- Yes Prohibit FBI access to library and bookstore records
- No Approve free-trade pact with five Central American countries
- No Pass energy policy overhaul favored by President Bush emphasizing domestic oil and gas production
- No End mandatory preservation of habitat of endangered animal and plant species
- Yes Ban torture of prisoners in U.S. custody

CQ VOTE STUDIES

	PARTY UNITY		PRESIDENTIAL SUPPORT	
	Support	Oppose	Support	Oppose
2006	96%	4%	18%	82%
2005	93%	7%	26%	74%
2004	91%	9%	29%	71%
2003	92%	8%	30%	70%
2002	90%	10%	28%	72%

INTEREST GROUPS

	AFL-CIO	ADA	CCUS	ACU
2006	100%	75%	27%	20%
2005	93%	95%	41%	12%
2004	100%	90%	33%	16%
2003	100%	90%	24%	28%
2002	100%	85%	30%	12%

NEW YORK 21

Capital District — Albany, Schenectady, Troy

As the terminus of the Erie Canal, which connects the Great Lakes to the Hudson River, New York's Capital District was one of the state's earliest industrial centers. Blue-collar workers and state employees give the Albany-Schenectady-Troy area a substantial union population and a solidly Democratic vote.

Government workers abound in Albany, home to the state capital. The state university at Albany's College of Nanoscale Science and Engineering is devoted exclusively to nanotechnology research and development. The university, along with other local colleges, has spurred the district's economy and helped make it a regional center for New York's technology industry. The Egg, a performing arts complex located downtown at Empire State Plaza, is a centerpiece of Albany's skyline.

Despite large-scale, decades-long industrial losses, manufacturing remains a force in the district. Retail and wholesale jobs saw a boom during the 1990s, and service jobs now account for about one-third of non-agricultural employment. Already shaped by their Victorian architecture and industrial history, Schenectady and Troy are each constructing industrial parks that should attract technology and alternative energy businesses. The rest of the 21st includes rolling farm fields in the west and a gateway to the Adirondack Mountains in its north.

The 21st is Democratic, but most local Democrats would not be described as liberal. As local officials attempt to lure a larger white-collar workforce to the district, the number of Republicans may increase. Overall, John Kerry carried the district with 55 percent of the vote during the 2004 presidential election.

MAJOR INDUSTRY

Government, service, manufacturing, technology

MILITARY BASES

Watervliet Arsenal (Army), 1 military, 1,100 civilian (2007)

CITIES

Albany, 95,658; Schenectady, 61,821; Troy, 49,170

NOTABLE

One of Schenectady's zip codes is 12345; Samuel Wilson, a meatpacker who provided the Army with much of its rations during the War of 1812, is believed to be the inspiration for "Uncle Sam" and is buried in Troy.

Rep. Maurice D. Hinchey (D)

CAPITOL OFFICE
225-6335
www.house.gov/hinchey
2431 Rayburn 20515-3222; fax 226-0774

COMMITTEES
Appropriations
Natural Resources
Joint Economic

RESIDENCE
Hurley

BORN
Oct. 27, 1938, Manhattan, N.Y.

RELIGION
Roman Catholic

FAMILY
Wife, Allison Lee; three children

EDUCATION
State U. of New York, New Paltz, B.S. 1968 (political science & English), M.A. 1970 (English)

MILITARY SERVICE
Navy, 1956-59

CAREER
State education department aide; state highway toll collector; cement and paper mill equipment operator

POLITICAL HIGHLIGHTS
Democratic nominee for N.Y. Assembly, 1972; N.Y. Assembly, 1975-93

ELECTION RESULTS

2006 GENERAL		
Maurice D. Hinchey (D, INDC, WFM)	unopposed	
2006 PRIMARY		
Maurice D. Hinchey (D)	unopposed	
2004 GENERAL		
Hinchey (D, C, INDC, WFM)	167,489	67.2%
William A. Brenner (R)	81,881	32.8%

PREVIOUS WINNING PERCENTAGES
2002 (64%); 2000 (62%); 1998 (62%); 1996 (55%); 1994 (49%); 1992 (50%)

Elected 1992; 8th term

A populist with a street-fighting style, Hinchey is one of the president's harshest critics in Congress, on issues ranging from the war in Iraq to the regulation of food and drugs. His job in Congress, as he sees it, is to fight for the "little guy" against large drug companies, media conglomerates or a White House too tightly linked to such powerful special interests.

As a member of the Appropriations subcommittee that funds the Food and Drug Administration, Hinchey has repeatedly assailed the management of that agency under President Bush. He has excoriated the FDA for what he considers its lax reviews of prescription drugs, including the painkiller Vioxx, which was removed from the market in 2004 because of potentially lethal side effects. He also blamed the flu vaccine shortage of 2004-05 on FDA missteps.

When the agency tried to stem criticism by creating a new drug safety review board in February 2005, Hinchey angrily dismissed it as "a farce." "The real problem with the FDA is that it remains far too closely tied to the pharmaceutical industry," he said. He says the FDA has been "completely corrupted" by this administration and is rampant with conflicts of interest. He won a small victory in 2005 with enactment of a requirement for disclosure of potential conflicts of interest among members of FDA advisory groups that recommend whether new drugs and medical devices should be approved for marketing. But it was watered down from a version that passed the House.

If the FDA draws his ire on occasion, Bush's Iraq policy infuriates Hinchey almost daily. He has repeatedly suggested that powerful economic interests were behind the decision to go to war in Iraq, and that top U.S. officials, beginning with the president and Vice President Dick Cheney, a former Halliburton CEO, distorted intelligence reports to justify the war. "One of the major responsibilities of the next Congress will be a very focused and comprehensive examination of this administration, particularly regarding its rationale for the attack and subsequent disastrous occupation of Iraq," he said in October 2006. He was one of 38 House members who cosponsored a resolution introduced late in 2005 by Michigan Democrat John Conyers Jr. calling for a preliminary impeachment inquiry.

Hinchey was at the forefront of efforts in the 108th Congress (2003-04) to overturn a Federal Communications Commission rule loosening ownership restrictions and allowing greater concentration of media holdings by large corporations. He said the FCC was producing "a new censorship in America" that meant "a select few will determine what information and entertainment the public will have access to."

In 2005, he suggested, without evidence, that Bush adviser Karl Rove had a role in misleading CBS News when it used apparently forged documents in a story about the president's National Guard service during the Vietnam War.

Environmental policies are Hinchey's passion. A fight in the 1970s over the development of a huge power plant on the Hudson River was the primary reason for his entry into electoral politics. In the state Assembly, he chaired the Environmental Conservation Committee investigating the "Love Canal" contamination scandal and drafting bills to combat acid rain and create the Hudson River Valley Greenway. In Congress, Hinchey won passage of a bill to designate much of the Greenway region as a National Heritage Area. He also has been involved in a long-running effort to require General Electric to clean up toxic polychlorinated biphenyls, or PCBs, discharged into the Hudson River from its plant north of Albany.

In the 110th Congress (2007-08), he was able to rejoin the Natural Resources Committee, where he had served in his first three terms. In 1995, he had angered Utah lawmakers by proposing to designate 5.7 million acres of Utah as wilderness. In 2007, he asked the Interior Department to declare a moratorium on oil or gas leasing of "wilderness quality" land in Utah.

Hinchey can deviate from the majority of his party on gun issues. In 1996, he was the only New York Democrat to vote to repeal a ban on certain semi-automatic assault-style weapons. Yet he supported the 1993 Brady bill, which calls for a five-day waiting period for handgun purchases; and in 2004, he voted against repealing the District of Columbia's gun control law. Hinchey drew unwelcome attention during his first House term when he was charged with carrying a loaded handgun in his baggage at Ronald Reagan Washington National Airport. He eventually pleaded no contest and was given a suspended sentence.

Despite his pinstriped suits and elegant silk ties, Hinchey comes from a working-class background. Born in Manhattan, he spent most of his childhood in Greenwich Village. His family moved upstate, to Saugerties, when he was a teenager; he split his time between his new home and his old haunts in Manhattan. His father worked at a cement plant. Hinchey joined the Navy right after high school, serving aboard a destroyer in the Pacific. After his discharge, he returned home and worked in a local cement plant for five years. Then he enrolled in college and worked his way through collecting tolls on the New York State Thruway on the 11 p.m. to 7 a.m. "graveyard" shift. He asked for that shift so that he could do his studying during quiet periods. "I never got an awful lot of sleep," he admits, but the English major worked full time and earned his degree in four years.

Hinchey's parents had been active in local party politics, and after college he was encouraged to get involved in behind-the-scenes political activities while starting a career in education. He lost his first bid for the state Assembly, in 1972, but won two years later to begin an 18-year tenure in Albany.

In 1992, when nine-term Democratic Rep. Matthew F. McHugh retired, Hinchey went after the seat. He started as the Democratic primary underdog, facing Binghamton Mayor Juanita M. Crabb. He prevailed by pushing a plan to revitalize the economy of the recession-hit region. In November, he edged Republican Bob Moppert, a six-year county legislator, by 8,819 votes. He survived a 1994 rematch by an even closer margin of slightly more than 1,200 votes. Since then, however, he has rolled up more-comfortable margins. In 2006, for the only time in his career, he had no opposition in November.

KEY VOTES

2006

- Yes Stop broadband companies from favoring select Internet traffic
- No Affirm U.S. commitment to war in Iraq and reject setting a withdrawal date for troops
- No Repeal requirement for bilingual ballots at the polls
- No Permit U.S. sale of civilian nuclear technology to India
- No Build a 700-mile fence on the U.S.-Mexico border to curb illegal crossings
- No Permit warrantless wiretaps of suspected terrorists

2005

- ? Intervene in the life-support case of Terri Schiavo
- Yes Lift President Bush's restrictions on stem cell research funding
- Yes Prohibit FBI access to library and bookstore records
- No Approve free-trade pact with five Central American countries
- No Pass energy policy overhaul favored by President Bush emphasizing domestic oil and gas production
- No End mandatory preservation of habitat of endangered animal and plant species
- Yes Ban torture of prisoners in U.S. custody

CQ VOTE STUDIES

	PARTY UNITY		PRESIDENTIAL SUPPORT	
	Support	Oppose	Support	Oppose
2006	98%	2%	7%	93%
2005	98%	2%	11%	89%
2004	99%	1%	20%	80%
2003	98%	2%	16%	84%
2002	99%	1%	20%	80%

INTEREST GROUPS

	AFL-CIO	ADA	CCUS	ACU
2006	100%	100%	27%	4%
2005	93%	100%	30%	4%
2004	100%	95%	25%	0%
2003	100%	95%	28%	12%
2002	100%	100%	30%	4%

NEW YORK 22

South central — Binghamton, Poughkeepsie, Ithaca

The scenic 22nd reaches from the hills above Cayuga Lake to the east bank of the Hudson River. Most residents are found at those extremes: Ithaca and Binghamton in the west and the Hudson Valley region, including Poughkeepsie, Newburgh and Kingston, in the east.

Ithaca, at the district's northwestern tip, is home to Cornell University, Ithaca College and a corps of liberal activists, and the city remains one of the few expanding economies in the 22nd. The district then extends south from Ithaca to the Pennsylvania border, before turning east and stretching along the border from Tioga County to Sullivan County, taking in Broome County's Tri-Cities — Binghamton, Johnson City and Endicott. The 22nd then widens in Sullivan to head for Hudson River population centers in Orange, Ulster and Duchess counties.

Manufacturing jobs in the 22nd have declined, and many local officials are working to recruit more technology companies to the area. Defense companies, such as Lockheed Martin and BAE Systems, are still major local employers, although IBM, which was headquartered in Endicott, has significantly reduced operations in the area. Officials hope to use the state university in Binghamton as an anchor for economic development.

In general, the 22nd is rural, with a large portion of the Catskill Mountains in the center and many apple and dairy farms throughout. The Catskills' Borscht Belt, a prominent Jewish resort area, declined as tourists began vacationing in more exotic locales, but officials are hoping to reinvigorate the hospitality industry here.

The district's mixture of cities and farmland creates a politically competitive environment, although the region's blue-collar history and the liberal areas surrounding the 22nd's universities give Democrats an edge. John Kerry took 53 percent of the district's 2004 presidential vote.

MAJOR INDUSTRY

Higher education, agriculture, technology

CITIES

Binghamton, 47,380; Poughkeepsie, 29,871; Ithaca, 29,287

NOTABLE

A State Historic Site in Newburgh marks where Gen. George Washington had his headquarters and residence from 1782 to 1783; Bethel was the site of the marathon Woodstock rock concert in 1969.

Rep. John M. McHugh (R)

CAPITOL OFFICE
225-4611
www.house.gov/mchugh
2366 Rayburn 20515-3223; fax 226-0621

COMMITTEES
Armed Services
Oversight & Government Reform
Select Intelligence

RESIDENCE
Pierrepont Manor

BORN
Sept. 29, 1948, Watertown, N.Y.

RELIGION
Roman Catholic

FAMILY
Divorced

EDUCATION
Utica College of Syracuse U., B.A. 1970 (political science); State U. of New York, Albany, M.P.A. 1977

CAREER
State legislative aide; city official; insurance broker

POLITICAL HIGHLIGHTS
N.Y. Senate, 1985-93

ELECTION RESULTS

2006 GENERAL		
John M. McHugh (R, INDC, C)	106,781	63.1%
Robert J. Johnson (D, WFM)	62,318	36.9%
2006 PRIMARY		
John M. McHugh (R)		unopposed
2004 GENERAL		
McHugh (R, C, INDC, WFM)	160,079	70.7%
Robert J. Johnson (D)	66,448	29.3%

PREVIOUS WINNING PERCENTAGES
2002 (100%); 2000 (74%); 1998 (79%); 1996 (71%); 1994 (79%); 1992 (61%)

Elected 1992; 8th term

McHugh won a glamorless, decade-long battle to restructure the Postal Service in the 109th Congress (2005-06), perhaps most impressive for its success in keeping the government's mail-delivery system solvent and competitive in an era of instant communication. He brought together a diverse array of stakeholders, including unions, Postal Service competitors such as FedEx and UPS, and postal-dependent businesses. "I think I'm most proud of that," he says.

But McHugh's main legislative arena is the Armed Services Committee, where ranking Republican Duncan Hunter's expected retirement at the end of the 110th Congress in 2008 would leave McHugh second on the GOP seniority list. He spent six years as chairman of the panel's personnel subcommittee and is now the subcommittee's ranking Republican.

McHugh couples sharp focus and quiet determination on policy with a down-to-earth collegiality that endears him to fellow lawmakers and to the journalists and Capitol support staff who hover just outside the House chamber. Before Speaker Nancy Pelosi banned smoking there, McHugh could often be spotted sitting just off the House floor relaxing with a smoke and a legislative briefing book.

His political skills, put to use in Capitol committee rooms and hallways rather than in front of television cameras, have earned him the confidence of colleagues who elected him to the Republican Steering Committee, a group that makes the all-important committee assignments.

But on the war in Iraq, McHugh was not in sync with his party.

Early in 2007, he demonstrated his displeasure with the president's seemingly open-ended commitment to the war by introducing his own version of a supplemental spending bill that provided about half the funding requested by the president and would have required new requests for the rest of the money. McHugh's plan also asserted that future spending requests be predicated on the achievement of a series of benchmarks for handing control of Iraq to Iraqis.

However, he would not sanction a timeline, formulated by Democrats, calling for a withdrawal of troops if similar benchmarks were not met and a later withdrawal if they were met. "It's a terrible message for our troops. We've already admitted we're outta there. 'You go over there and maybe die.' That's not what you say to troops. Even though that may be how the field plays out. If the Iraqis fail this time, if they do, you take the vote and get those people out now," he said in 2007.

In the 108th Congress (2003-04), McHugh was in the spotlight as a defender of the Bush administration when some Democrats raised the possibility that the military draft might be reinstated. To quash such suggestions, House GOP leaders forced a floor vote on a bill sponsored by Democrat Charles B. Rangel of New York that called for a renewed draft. McHugh led the Republican side of the debate, emphasizing that the White House had no intention of abandoning the all-volunteer force, and the bill was overwhelmingly defeated.

(McHugh says a childhood bout with rheumatic fever made him ineligible when he tried to enlist in the Air Force and later when he was called to submit to a draft-required physical.)

As one of the few remaining Republicans from the increasingly Democratic Northeastern region of the country, McHugh strays from the party line more often than most of his colleagues. He supports labor on a number of issues and has won the AFL-CIO's endorsement several times.

But on fiscal policy and most social issues, he casts a dependably Republican vote. One exception came in the 109th Congress, when he voted against a $50 billion package of spending cuts because of a $3 copay for Medicaid recipients that he said would result in poor people forgoing medical treatment. His vast upstate district, one of New York's poorest, is heavily dependent on defense spending at Fort Drum and on agriculture, particularly dairy farming and apple growing.

The 10th Mountain Division, based at Fort Drum, was one of the first Army units deployed in Afghanistan in 2001. McHugh has been able to direct funding to maintain Fort Drum's standing as one of the Army's most modern bases on the East Coast, and, as a result of base closings elsewhere in the country, it is in line to get more personnel and more money.

McHugh is one of the defenders of dairy interests in the House. Throughout his career, McHugh has voted against giving the president more powers in negotiating trade agreements, saying that he does not think the dairy industry would be adequately protected in the resulting trade liberalization pacts. He and his dairy industry allies were satisfied with the farm bill written in 2002. While it did not include an interstate compact for Northeast dairy farmers to help them compete with Midwest milk producers, it did add a national income-support program for dairy farmers.

After graduating from college, McHugh abandoned plans to earn a law degree and worked for his father's insurance business. He didn't like the work, and he eventually landed a job as the assistant city manager in his hometown of Watertown, N.Y.

When he decided he needed a graduate degree after five years, he enrolled in the public affairs school at Albany State University, which required him to become an intern in a government office. That, in turn, led him to state Sen. H. Douglas Barclay. Barclay paid him for the internship and offered him a job when he graduated. When Barclay retired nearly a decade later, he cleared the field for McHugh to succeed him.

In 1992, Republican Rep. David O'B. Martin decided to retire after 12 years in the House, and McHugh jumped into the race. He won the primary over a more conservative opponent, Morrison J. Hosley Jr., a local business owner and Hamilton town supervisor. That was tantamount to winning election in the historically Republican North Country; he won his first term with 61 percent of the vote and has done better than that ever since, and even when his party lost control of the neighboring 20th and 24th districts in 2006, McHugh cruised to re-election with 63 percent of the vote.

KEY VOTES

2006

- ? Stop broadband companies from favoring select Internet traffic
- Yes Affirm U.S. commitment to war in Iraq and reject setting a withdrawal date for troops
- Yes Repeal requirement for bilingual ballots at the polls
- Yes Permit U.S. sale of civilian nuclear technology to India
- Yes Build a 700-mile fence on the U.S.-Mexico border to curb illegal crossings
- Yes Permit warrantless wiretaps of suspected terrorists

2005

- Yes Intervene in the life-support case of Terri Schiavo
- No Lift President Bush's restrictions on stem cell research funding
- No Prohibit FBI access to library and bookstore records
- No Approve free-trade pact with five Central American countries
- Yes Pass energy policy overhaul favored by President Bush emphasizing domestic oil and gas production
- Yes End mandatory preservation of habitat of endangered animal and plant species
- Yes Ban torture of prisoners in U.S. custody

CQ VOTE STUDIES

	PARTY UNITY		PRESIDENTIAL SUPPORT	
	Support	Oppose	Support	Oppose
2006	84%	16%	85%	15%
2005	89%	11%	78%	22%
2004	87%	13%	76%	24%
2003	88%	12%	83%	17%
2002	90%	10%	85%	15%

INTEREST GROUPS

	AFL-CIO	ADA	CCUS	ACU
2006	57%	15%	86%	75%
2005	47%	20%	81%	80%
2004	50%	20%	90%	64%
2003	67%	35%	68%	67%
2002	22%	15%	85%	79%

NEW YORK 23

North — Watertown, Plattsburgh, Oswego

The vast 23rd covers more than one-fourth of the state, bordering Lake Champlain, the St. Lawrence Seaway and Lake Ontario. The waterways provide an inexpensive source of electricity, which has lured some heavy industry to the district. But most of the district is rural, full of small towns, dairy farms, maple syrup producers and colleges. It reaches south to Oneida Lake and Madison County.

Fort Drum (near Watertown, the district's largest city) is one of the largest and most modern Army facilities on the East Coast. It thus far has been safe from post-Cold War base closures, and consists of 107,000 acres and trains almost 80,000 troops annually. Roughly 30 miles from Ontario, Watertown's economy relies on Canadian visitors. The proximity to waterways and forests made paper production a major industry in the district, but many mills have been forced to close their doors, although Georgia Pacific retains its presence in Plattsburgh.

Unemployment remains a problem throughout the 23rd, as harsh winters and high transportation costs make attracting jobs difficult. Bright spots include seasonal tourism — the 23rd covers much of the Adirondack Mountains, where winter weather caters to snowmobile riders and ice fishers, and long summers attract visitors to seasonal-use cottages.

The northeastern corner of the state has sent Republicans to the U.S. House since the 1872 election. Republicans hold a registration edge and George W. Bush took 51 percent of the vote here in the 2004 presidential election, but Democrats have had increasing success at the local level in recent years.

MAJOR INDUSTRY

Agriculture, manufacturing, tourism, defense

MILITARY BASES

Fort Drum, 15,082 military, 3,626 civilian (2006)

CITIES

Watertown, 26,705; Plattsburgh, 18,816; Oswego, 17,954

NOTABLE

In 1775, Ethan Allen led the Green Mountain Boys — and Benedict Arnold — in seizing Fort Ticonderoga from the British; Little Trees air fresheners were invented in Watertown, which is home to the headquarters and a manufacturing plant of Car-Freshener Corporation.

Rep. Michael Arcuri (D)

CAPITOL OFFICE
225-3665
arcuri.house.gov
327 Cannon 20515-3224; fax 225-1891

COMMITTEES
Rules
Transportation & Infrastructure

RESIDENCE
Utica

BORN
June 11, 1959, Utica, N.Y.

RELIGION
Roman Catholic

FAMILY
Divorced; two children

EDUCATION
State U. of New York, Albany, B.A. 1981 (history); New York Law School, J.D. 1984

CAREER
Lawyer; college instructor

POLITICAL HIGHLIGHTS
Oneida County district attorney, 1994-2007

ELECTION RESULTS

2006 GENERAL

Michael Arcuri (D, INDC, WFM)	109,686	53.9%
Ray Meier (R, C)	91,504	45.0%
Michael J. Sylvia III (LIBERT)	2,134	1.0%

2006 PRIMARY

Michael Arcuri (D)	unopposed

Elected 2006; 1st term

Arcuri is the first Democrat to represent the 24th District in nearly 60 years. But he is not too far removed in his politics from the Republican who held the seat for 24 years — Sherwood Boehlert. Boehlert was a moderate known for his strong support of the environment.

Arcuri (are-CURE-ee) is content to be compared with his predecessor, saying Boehlert "was liberal on many of the social issues, and he was fiscally conservative, and I think that really defines my position on issues better than anything else." An Oneida County district attorney for 12 years, Arcuri is a member of the Blue Dog Coalition, a group of fiscally conservative Democrats. He said he decided to run for Congress after watching lawmakers debate the federal budget and then vote to cut student loan programs. "I thought, there they go again balancing the budget on the shoulders of the people that need it the most."

An opponent of the war in Iraq, Arcuri said he was at first hesitant to call for a troop withdrawal deadline. But he ended up supporting a 2007 supplemental spending bill for the war that included a withdrawal timetable.

Arcuri was given his first choice in committee assignments with a seat on the Transportation and Infrastructure Committee. "In our district, roads — or lack thereof — are a critical issue," he said. He also sits on the Rules Committee, a prestigious assignment for a freshman legislator.

Democrats had predicted for years that they would have a strong shot to win the 24th once Boehlert retired. The Republican nominee, state Sen. Ray Meier, sought to brand Arcuri as just another tax-and-spend Democrat.

But Meier's efforts to gain traction were hindered when the National Republican Congressional Committee (NRCC), which runs the national House campaigns, announced that it had produced an ad, independently of Meier's campaign, accusing Arcuri of seeking taxpayer reimbursement for a phone-sex call. Arcuri's swift response to the charges — including evidence that the number was called accidentally when an aide misdialed — led to charges that the NRCC was distorting the truth, even though the ad never aired. Arcuri beat Meier easily by almost 9 percentage points.

NEW YORK 24

Central — Utica, Rome, Auburn

The J-shaped 24th starts at the western edge of the Adirondack Mountains, sweeps through the central part of the state — south of Syracuse and north of Binghamton — and extends into the Finger Lakes region. In the heart of the Leatherstocking Region made famous by James Fenimore Cooper, the area is known for its rich history and depends on dairy farming and local colleges.

Much of the 24th's central region is full of small-size towns that are influenced by the farming seasons. These areas become crowded each fall, as visitors embark on foliage tours and trips to the region's cider mills. The district is home to the Oneida Indian Nation's Turning Stone Casino in Verona, and also to several halls of fame, including the National Baseball Hall of Fame in Cooperstown, the National Soccer Hall of Fame in Oneonta and the National Distance Running Hall of Fame in Utica.

In the west, the 24th is home to other historical gems, including the Women's Rights Convention and the National Women's Hall of Fame in Seneca Falls. This area serves as the gateway to the Finger Lakes, which, among other things, attracts wine connoisseurs to dozens of wineries. The 24th's main population center is in Oneida County. Oneida's Utica and Rome are aging industrial cities on the Mohawk River that suffered as manufacturing jobs left the state.

Although the 24th's natural beauty makes earth-friendly policies important here, these are Yankee Republicans, and they gave George W. Bush 52 percent of their 2004 presidential vote. But Democratic pockets in Utica and along college campuses can sway outcomes, as they did for Rep. Arcuri in 2006.

MAJOR INDUSTRY
Agriculture, tourism, manufacturing

CITIES
Utica, 60,651; Rome, 34,950; Auburn, 28,574

NOTABLE
Francis Bellamy, author of the Pledge of Allegiance, is buried in Rome.

Rep. James T. Walsh (R)

CAPITOL OFFICE
225-3701
rep.james.walsh@mail.house.gov
www.house.gov/walsh
2372 Rayburn 20515-3225; fax 225-4042

COMMITTEES
Appropriations

RESIDENCE
Onondaga

BORN
June 19, 1947, Syracuse, N.Y.

RELIGION
Roman Catholic

FAMILY
Wife, DeDe Ryan Walsh; three children

EDUCATION
St. Bonaventure U., B.A. 1970 (history)

CAREER
Marketing executive; social worker; Peace Corps volunteer

POLITICAL HIGHLIGHTS
Syracuse Common Council, 1978-88 (president, 1986-88); sought nomination for Onondaga County executive, 1987

ELECTION RESULTS

2006 GENERAL		
James T. Walsh (R, INDC, C)	110,525	50.8%
Dan Maffei (D, WFM)	107,108	49.2%
2006 PRIMARY		
James T. Walsh (R)		unopposed
2004 GENERAL		
James T. Walsh (R, INDC, C)	189,063	90.4%
Howie Hawkins (GREEN)	20,106	9.6%

PREVIOUS WINNING PERCENTAGES
2002 (72%); 2000 (69%); 1998 (69%); 1996 (55%); 1994 (58%); 1992 (56%); 1990 (63%); 1988 (57%)

Elected 1988; 10th term

After 18 years in the House, Walsh barely survived the last election, nearly sunk by the anti-Republican surge that swept the country. His seniority allowed him to claim the top minority seat on a powerful Appropriations subcommittee, making for a happy ending to a rough two-year spell for Walsh.

He is the ranking Republican on the subcommittee that controls spending for the Labor, Health and Human Services and Education departments, a sizable chunk of the federal government. That returns him to a position of prominence in the world of appropriators. Two years earlier, he had fallen into disfavor with GOP Majority Leader Tom DeLay of Texas, who then gutted the subcommittee he chaired and reassigned him to a military quality-of-life panel with a much diminished bailiwick.

DeLay was driven from power by an ethics scandal, and John A. Boehner of Ohio ascended to Republican leader. After Walsh's close call in the 2006 election, Boehner did not stand in his way to be the lead Republican on the labor and health subcommittee, a posting that will help raise his visibility at home. "It's a tremendous step up for me in terms of my legislative responsibilities," Walsh told the Syracuse Post-Standard.

Walsh is a political moderate who was often at odds with the party's conservative leaders. In the 109th Congress (2005-06), he voted with his party 88 percent of the time on issues that divided the two major parties, putting him in the bottom 25 percent in party unity among House Republicans. Early in 2007, he was one of just 16 Republicans who voted for five of the six bills on the newly-in-power Democrats' "first 100 hours" agenda.

An appropriator at heart, he is a defender of earmarks, the parochial projects that lawmakers tuck into appropriations bills to help curry favor with voters. Budget conservatives want to end earmarks as wasteful spending, but Walsh says the practice has a long congressional tradition and though earmarks are sometimes abused, they give lawmakers the ability to solve problems unique to their districts.

In the 108th Congress (2003-04), Walsh bucked GOP leaders as they tried to rein in spending by subcommittee chairmen, dubbed the college of cardinals. Constrained by a budget cap he felt was unfair, Walsh wrote a bill that increased spending for veterans' programs but cut $1 billion from the National Aeronautics and Space Administration. That did not sit well with DeLay, who represented a space-dependent district around the Johnson Space Center. Walsh's bill also included generous funding for veterans, housing and environmental programs in his district and New York. DeLay blocked the bill from getting to the floor.

Early the next year, in 2005, GOP leaders moved against Walsh and the other cardinals, forcing a reorganization of the Appropriations Committee. The subcommittee Walsh had chaired for six years — which funded programs for space, veterans' affairs, and housing and urban development as well as the Environmental Protection Agency — was dismantled, and he wound up with the gavel at a reconstituted panel with far less authority.

In the 110th Congress (2007-08), Walsh wants to raise his visibility on environmental issues with the aim of filling the shoes of former New York GOP Rep. Sherwood Boehlert, who led a moderate faction in battles with anti-regulation conservatives until he retired in 2006. "The advantage I have, that maybe Sherry didn't, is that there's no real animosity within our [Republican] conference toward me," he told the Post-Standard. "There was toward him. I have a reputation for being able to work with both sides of the aisle."

His colleagues on Appropriations view Walsh as a fair and effective legislator open to bipartisan cooperation. Appropriations Chairman David R. Obey, a Wisconsin Democrat, calls Walsh "a first-class legislator."

Another of Walsh's interests is funding for AmeriCorps, the national service program modeled after the Peace Corps, where Walsh spent two years teaching rice-growing techniques in Nepal. Whenever the House voted to cut the program because conservatives didn't like it, Walsh worked behind the scenes to restore it.

Still, Walsh considers bringing home the bacon his proudest achievement, citing federal funds he secured for neighborhood renewal in Syracuse and for cleaning up the polluted Onondaga Lake, adjacent to the city. So he was bitter when the city's voters gave him tepid support in 2006.

Walsh beat former congressional aide Democrat Dan Maffei by only 3,417 votes. Maffei outpolled him in parts of the city, prompting Walsh to tell the Post-Standard, "I've worked harder in the city of Syracuse than I have in any other part of the district. I have given my heart and soul to that city. And I'll continue to do that, but I've got a little hole in my heart."

Walsh, who supported the invasion of Iraq in 2003, was hurt by the strong sentiment against the war. He held a series of town-hall meetings in the Syracuse area after the election and said later, "The war was more important [to voters] than all the work I'd done for them. That surprised me. But I got the message." In early 2007, Walsh opposed President Bush's plan to send more combat troops into Iraq.

Walsh got a close view of politics at an early age. His father was mayor of Syracuse and served in the U.S. House. He attended Christian Brothers Academy and grew up surrounded by cousins and members of his extended family on Tipperary Hill, an Irish-American neighborhood known for its traffic light — the green light is on top. (Walsh brings dignitaries to the neighborhood to see the light and to quaff a pint of Guinness at nearby Coleman's bar, among them Ireland's prime minister, Bartholomew "Bertie" Ahern.)

Being the son of the mayor had its perks. "We had great seats for the [Rolling] Stones when they came through Syracuse," Walsh recalls. On the other hand, "Not only was I his son, but I look like him, so I couldn't get away with anything." Walsh says the political lesson he took from his father was, "Treat all people with respect."

Walsh served more than a decade on the Syracuse city council, including roughly three years as council president. He got into Congress on his first try in 1988, with the retirement of four-term GOP incumbent George C. Wortley. And he won re-election handily, until 2006.

KEY VOTES

2006

- No Stop broadband companies from favoring select Internet traffic
- Yes Affirm U.S. commitment to war in Iraq and reject setting a withdrawal date for troops
- No Repeal requirement for bilingual ballots at the polls
- Yes Permit U.S. sale of civilian nuclear technology to India
- Yes Build a 700-mile fence on the U.S.-Mexico border to curb illegal crossings
- Yes Permit warrantless wiretaps of suspected terrorists

2005

- Yes Intervene in the life-support case of Terri Schiavo
- No Lift President Bush's restrictions on stem cell research funding
- No Prohibit FBI access to library and bookstore records
- Yes Approve free-trade pact with five Central American countries
- Yes Pass energy policy overhaul favored by President Bush emphasizing domestic oil and gas production
- No End mandatory preservation of habitat of endangered animal and plant species
- Yes Ban torture of prisoners in U.S. custody

CQ VOTE STUDIES

	PARTY UNITY		PRESIDENTIAL SUPPORT	
	Support	Oppose	Support	Oppose
2006	84%	16%	79%	21%
2005	92%	8%	86%	14%
2004	87%	13%	85%	15%
2003	94%	6%	93%	7%
2002	88%	12%	87%	13%

INTEREST GROUPS

	AFL-CIO	ADA	CCUS	ACU
2006	57%	25%	79%	63%
2005	13%	0%	89%	64%
2004	40%	20%	90%	67%
2003	14%	5%	93%	75%
2002	22%	15%	84%	75%

NEW YORK 25

North central – Syracuse, most of Irondequoit

Syracuse, in the district's east, is the 25th's only major city and is its economic hub. The district stretches west, roughly along Lake Ontario in the north and the Erie Canal in the south, from Onondaga County to reach most of Irondequoit in the Rochester suburbs. Syracuse and the Rochester area are home to diverse economies that rely on educational institutions to spur other industries, and small towns and farms fill most of the land between the two cities.

More than two-thirds of the 25th's residents live in Onondaga County, which is home to Syracuse. Past layoffs in manufacturing are now being offset by job increases in higher education, health care and service professions. Syracuse University is the district's economic mainstay and is located in the city on University Hill, which is a fast-growing area that also includes the State University of New York Upstate Medical University. Proposed development along the Onondaga Lake includes controversial plans to expand the city's Carousel Center shopping mall into "Destiny USA," a shopping and entertainment mega-venue, which supporters hope would provide thousands of local jobs and attract millions of visitors to Syracuse annually.

South of Syracuse, small towns rely on dairy and fruit farms.The district also includes coastal and inland farming-based towns stretching from Fair Haven in the east to the banks of the Genesee River in the west. Many Rochester-area residents work in white-collar industries.

Minorities and blue-collar workers contribute to the Democratic vote in Syracuse, while GOP candidates get votes from social conservatives scattered throughout the 25th and fiscal conservatives located in rural and suburban clusters. The politically diverse 25th gave a slight majority of its vote to John Kerry in the 2004 presidential election.

MAJOR INDUSTRY

Agriculture, service, manufacturing, higher education, health care

CITIES

Syracuse, 147,306; Irondequoit (unincorporated) (pt.), 32,661

NOTABLE

Syracuse native Charles F. Brannock invented the Brannock Device, used to measure feet for shoe size; Syracuse University's Carrier Dome is the largest on-campus domed stadium in the country.

Rep. Thomas M. Reynolds (R)

CAPITOL OFFICE
225-5265
www.house.gov/reynolds
332 Cannon 20515-3226; fax 225-5910

COMMITTEES
Ways & Means

RESIDENCE
Clarence

BORN
Sept. 3, 1950, Belfonte, Pa.

RELIGION
Presbyterian

FAMILY
Wife, Donna Reynolds; four children

EDUCATION
Griffith Institute H.S., graduated 1968;
Kent State U., attended 1968-69 (business)

MILITARY SERVICE
N.Y. Air National Guard, 1970-76

CAREER
Real estate and insurance broker;
state legislative aide

POLITICAL HIGHLIGHTS
Concord Town Council, 1974-82; Erie County Legislature, 1982-88 (Republican leader, 1987-88); N.Y. Assembly, 1989-99 (minority leader, 1995-98)

ELECTION RESULTS

2006 GENERAL		
Thomas M. Reynolds (R, C)	109,257	52.0%
Jack Davis (D, WFM, INDC)	100,914	48.0%
2006 PRIMARY		
Thomas M. Reynolds (R)	unopposed	
2004 GENERAL		
Thomas M. Reynolds (R, INDC, C)	157,466	55.6%
Jack Davis (D, WFM)	125,613	44.4%

PREVIOUS WINNING PERCENTAGES
2002 (74%); 2000 (69%); 1998 (57%)

Elected 1998; 5th term

Reynolds' favorite adage is "All politics is local." But he may want to add another bromide to his lessons to live by: "Quit while you're ahead."

A tough and gruff strategist for Republicans in the House, Reynolds chaired the National Republican Congressional Committee (NRCC), the party's campaign arm, when it was successful in holding the GOP majority in 2004, but also chaired it in 2006, when it was not. In fact, he barely hung on to his own seat, getting re-elected with just 52 percent of the vote after he came under criticism for his handling of information about Florida Republican Rep. Mark Foley's inappropriate behavior with House pages.

When Republicans lost the House, he was roundly second-guessed by newly disenfranchised Republicans. Once on the shortlist of possible House speakers, he was no longer so well-positioned to move up.

During the campaign, Reynolds kept GOP candidates trained on local issues as the Democrats focused on the war in Iraq, immigration, and public corruption, leaving Reynolds open to criticism that Republicans lacked a coherent response. He stuck to a "block and tackle" strategy of knocking on doors and turning out Republican voters.

Even after the party lost both chambers of Congress, Reynolds said it was the right approach. "I would not change the strategy of 'All politics is local.' I'm a perfect example," he said, referring to his own re-election.

Moreover, Reynolds did well in one important aspect of the NRCC job. He raised substantially more money — $179 million — than his Democratic counterpart, the chairman of the Democratic Congressional Campaign Committee, Rahm Emanuel of Illinois, who raised less than $140 million.

The burly Reynolds is happy to play the role of partisan attack dog when necessary. But he also works across party lines for New York's interests. He teamed with Democratic Sen. Hillary Rodham Clinton in 2005 to remove the Niagara Falls Air Reserve Station from the list of military bases to be shuttered. He even cosponsored a bill with Emanuel to restore and clean up the Great Lakes.

Given his advice to his peers about focusing on local problems, he ironically took heat at home for getting too involved in national affairs. The Buffalo News groused in a 2006 editorial, "Reynolds needs to twist arms and attract money to the region he represents, especially for a new federal courthouse, with as much energy" as he puts into the NRCC.

In 2001, Reynolds angered some at home when he helped the GOP leadership pass an anti-terrorism spending bill that contained less money than New Yorkers said they had been promised for Sept. 11 recovery. But his loyalty pleased the White House. And Reynolds lobbied for New York in other ways, including tax breaks for redevelopment in lower Manhattan.

Reynolds gave up his seat on the leadership-driven Rules Committee in 2005 to take a seat on the Ways and Means Committee. His bill providing a one-year exemption from the alternative minimum tax for many middle-income taxpayers was rolled into a larger package of tax breaks that became law in 2006. He introduced a similar bill in the 110th Congress (2007-08) providing AMT relief for the 2007 tax year.

A former minority leader in the New York Assembly, Reynolds showed fundraising and organizational acumen as a party leader in western New York and in the state Assembly, which is why then GOP Speaker J. Dennis Hastert tapped him to co-chair Battleground 2000, an unprecedented effort by the NRCC to raise money to help embattled incumbents, challengers and open-seat candidates. Reynolds pressed lawmakers who had large cash reserves and safe seats to write checks; he talked others into conducting special fundraisers — all strategies the party uses today. Later, as NRCC chairman, he raised $185 million during the 2004 campaign season despite a new ban on unregulated "soft money" contributions.

Reynolds grew up in southern Erie County. He entered Kent State University as a business major, but left when his mother became ill. He returned home to help his traveling salesman father raise his younger siblings and never went back to college. He worked in the real estate and insurance businesses before becoming an aide to a state assemblyman. At age 23, he was elected to the Concord Town Council.

After eight years, he moved up to the Erie County Legislature, following in the footsteps of GOP Rep. Bill Paxon, whom he had met when they were Young Republicans. In 1988, when Paxon ran for Congress, Reynolds won election to Paxon's seat in the state Assembly; he became minority leader in 1995. In that role, Reynolds sharpened his negotiating skills, and helped build a Republican political infrastructure in Erie County, long a Democratic stronghold.

In the meantime, he remained close with Paxon, whose influence in the House was growing. Reynolds was Paxon's campaign manager, and Paxon returned the favor by managing Reynolds' campaign in 1998 to replace him in the House after he retired. Reynolds easily won a 15 percentage point victory over history professor Bill Cook.

Despite significant redistricting due to the loss of two House seats after the 2000 census, Reynolds found himself in a solid, albeit renumbered, GOP district. In 2004, Democratic industrialist Jack Davis held him to 56 percent of the vote and was back for a rematch two years later.

Reynolds' 2006 campaign took a tumble with the Foley affair. He was among the House leaders who knew Foley sent questionable e-mails to former pages but did not press for an investigation. The House ethics committee, in a report in December 2006, said Reynolds showed little "curiosity regarding why a young former page would have been made uncomfortable by e-mails from Foley."

Considered a shoo-in before the Foley scandal broke, Reynolds suddenly found himself trailing Davis in polls. But he benefited from the district's general Republican leanings, and by an event just as unexpected as the Foley eruption — a freak mid-October snowstorm in western New York that enabled Reynolds to take the spotlight in pursuing disaster aid for constituents.

KEY VOTES

2006

- No — Stop broadband companies from favoring select Internet traffic
- Yes — Affirm U.S. commitment to war in Iraq and reject setting a withdrawal date for troops
- Yes — Repeal requirement for bilingual ballots at the polls
- Yes — Permit U.S. sale of civilian nuclear technology to India
- Yes — Build a 700-mile fence on the U.S.-Mexico border to curb illegal crossings
- Yes — Permit warrantless wiretaps of suspected terrorists

2005

- ? — Intervene in the life-support case of Terri Schiavo
- No — Lift President Bush's restrictions on stem cell research funding
- No — Prohibit FBI access to library and bookstore records
- Yes — Approve free-trade pact with five Central American countries
- Yes — Pass energy policy overhaul favored by President Bush emphasizing domestic oil and gas production
- Yes — End mandatory preservation of habitat of endangered animal and plant species
- Yes — Ban torture of prisoners in U.S. custody

CQ VOTE STUDIES

	PARTY UNITY		PRESIDENTIAL SUPPORT	
	Support	Oppose	Support	Oppose
2006	93%	7%	95%	5%
2005	94%	6%	80%	20%
2004	96%	4%	88%	12%
2003	97%	3%	100%	0%
2002	96%	4%	92%	8%

INTEREST GROUPS

	AFL-CIO	ADA	CCUS	ACU
2006	29%	5%	100%	87%
2005	13%	0%	93%	83%
2004	20%	5%	100%	92%
2003	7%	5%	100%	80%
2002	11%	0%	100%	92%

NEW YORK 26

Suburban Buffalo and Rochester; rural west

Moving east from suburban Buffalo to the Rochester suburbs, the Republican-leaning 26th scoops up miles of farmland in between and to the south. Slightly less than half the district's residents live in Niagara and Erie counties, and manufacturing drives their local economies. Abundant dairy farms and apple orchards shape the rural regions.

The population is anchored in the district's portion of Erie County, particularly in Amherst, a white-collar suburb northeast of Buffalo that has been ranked as one of the safest suburbs in the nation. The north campus of the state university at Buffalo, which houses all of the university's programs apart from architecture, planning and medicine, and corporate office parks are Amherst mainstays. The town favored John Kerry in the 2004 presidential election.

North of Amherst, the 26th's share of Niagara County includes Lockport and North Tonawanda, which becomes a tourist hotspot each summer. Visitors are attracted to North Tonawanda's Gateway Harbor Park, the last spot before the Erie Canal joins the Niagara River and part of major development along the waterfront. As in Erie, the Niagara portion of the 26th is politically competitive, with registered Republicans only slightly outnumbering Democrats.

Moving east, the New York State Thruway links Erie County to the Republican-leaning Rochester suburbs of western Monroe County. Between Buffalo and Rochester are numerous vegetable and grain farms of rural western New York. Wyoming County is solidly Republican and heavily agricultural. Livingston County includes Conesus Lake, which is at the western edge of New York's Finger Lakes region, and part of the Genesee River, which flows north into Rochester. Overall, the 26th gave George W. Bush 55 percent of its 2004 presidential vote.

MAJOR INDUSTRY

Manufacturing, agriculture, service

CITIES

North Tonawanda, 33,262; Lockport, 22,279; Batavia, 16,256

NOTABLE

Batavia was home to the first Union soldier to enlist in the Civil War: Medal of Honor winner Charles Rand; The Herschell Carrousel Factory Museum is in North Tonawanda; The Jell-O museum in LeRoy celebrates the beginnings of the famous gelatin dessert.

Rep. Brian Higgins (D)

CAPITOL OFFICE
225-3306
brian.higgins@mail.house.gov
www.house.gov/higgins
431 Cannon 20515-3227; fax 226-0347

COMMITTEES
Oversight & Government Reform
Transportation & Infrastructure

RESIDENCE
Buffalo

BORN
Oct. 6, 1959, Buffalo, N.Y.

RELIGION
Roman Catholic

FAMILY
Wife, Mary Jane Hannon; two children

EDUCATION
State U. of New York, Buffalo State, B.A. 1984 (political science), M.A. 1985 (history); Harvard U., M.P.A. 1996 (public policy & administration)

CAREER
County council chief of staff; state legislative aide

POLITICAL HIGHLIGHTS
Buffalo Common Council, 1988-94; Democratic nominee for Erie County comptroller, 1993; N.Y. Assembly, 1999-2004

ELECTION RESULTS

2006 GENERAL		
Brian Higgins (D, INDC, WFM)	140,027	79.3%
Michael J. McHale (R)	36,614	20.7%
2006 PRIMARY		
Brian Higgins (D)		unopposed
2004 GENERAL		
Brian Higgins (D, INDC, WFM)	143,332	50.7%
Nancy Naples (R, C)	139,558	49.3%

Elected 2004; 2nd term

Higgins' intense focus on parochial issues such as redeveloping Buffalo's waterfront and eliminating tolls on the Niagara Thruway prompted one local newspaper to describe him as "the best state legislator" in Washington, D.C. Higgins took the jab in stride, and laughed all the way to the polls.

Higgins' immersion in local economic development in his freshman term in Congress got him re-elected in 2006 with more than 79 percent of the vote, a trouncing for the Republican Party and its candidate, prosecutor Michael J. McHale. Just two years earlier, the district had been competitive; Higgins won then with just 51 percent of the vote.

Higgins' quest is to improve the image and economy of his faded Rust Belt hometown of Buffalo, situated on the shore of Lake Erie. He wants to redevelop the city from "an old industrial environment to an exciting vibrant waterfront city in the tradition of Baltimore and Chicago."

As a freshman lawmaker in 2005, Higgins took the lead in negotiations with the State Power Authority, demanding it help finance waterfront development in exchange for the right to operate the Niagara Power Project for 50 years. He wound up helping engineer a deal for $279 million for city improvements.

Launching that effort without consulting more-senior lawmakers — including New York's two Democratic senators and fellow western New York House Democrat Louise M. Slaughter — bruised egos and led to complaints that he took more than his fair share of the credit. But he won the affection of the local press. "Higgins separated himself from the docile political herd and stepped into the leadership vacuum that sucks life out of this community," the Buffalo News said.

In the 110th Congress (2007-08), Higgins moved on to advocating for a local corporation to take over control of the harbor development from the state, which he says hasn't moved fast enough.

His seat on the Transportation and Infrastructure Committee, one of the most parochial committees, has helped him get federal help for a region that lies at the juncture of major highways and Great Lakes waterways, and that is a major portal for trade with Canada. In 2005, Higgins helped steer $42 million to his district in a major surface transportation bill that year. He also threatened to withhold federal aid from the Niagara Thruway Authority unless it removed 75-cent tolls from the road.

His district's proximity to Canada contributes to Higgins' belief that senior citizens should be allowed to buy U.S.-made prescription drugs across the border, where they are often cheaper. He voted for the new Democratic majority's "first 100 hours" bill to let the federal government negotiate volume discounts of drugs for Medicare beneficiaries.

He also opposed a Bush administration proposal to require passports for U.S.-Canada border crossings. Congress, he said, should stall implementation "until a new administration comes in and takes a more thoughtful approach to border security."

In his first term in the House, Higgins developed a conservative voting record for a Democrat, favoring a constitutional amendment banning flag burning and opposing a deadline for U.S. troop withdrawal from Iraq. He argued it would be irresponsible to withdraw and allow the country to stay mired in civil war. "No one wants the American troops to come home more than I do," he told the Buffalo News. "But to set an arbitrary deadline, that plays right into the hands of the enemy."

Those votes help explain why Higgins got booed at a live taping of comedian Al Franken's liberal talk-radio program in Buffalo.

Higgins says his votes reflect the beliefs of his blue-collar district. "The voting behavior of that district is very conservative and I'm a product of that neighborhood and a product of that community," he says.

But he is not conservative enough to satisfy all constituents. His support for federal funding of embryonic stem cell research, which uses surplus embryos from in vitro fertilization, prompted a rebuke in 2007 from a lay deacon during a Sunday Mass in the church where he was baptized and married. Higgins walked out of the service, and later got an apology from the pastor, who said he felt "horrible" about the incident.

The Higgins family has been in Buffalo since his grandfather emigrated from Ireland as a 12-year-old orphan. His grandfather was a bricklayer, a trade he handed down to Higgins' father and uncles. Higgins and all four siblings, including his sister, helped their father lay bricks growing up in South Buffalo. One of his uncles was president of the Buffalo Federation of Labor. Another was president of the Bricklayers local. His father served on the Buffalo Common Council and was later a commissioner of the state workers' compensation board.

Higgins broke the family tradition in bricklaying and got into politics as a career. He got his undergraduate degree in political science from Buffalo State in 1984, followed by a master's in history a year later. He was elected to the Buffalo Common Council in 1987 at the age of 28.

After losing a 1993 bid for Erie County comptroller, he left upstate New York to get a master's degree at Harvard's Kennedy School of Government. He came home, continued working as a legislative aide and gave lectures at his alma mater, where he focused on the rise and fall of Buffalo as what he calls "one of the great industrial centers" of the United States. He was elected to the New York State Assembly in 1998, where he focused on local economic development.

When Republican U.S. Rep. Jack Quinn ended his 12-year run in Washington in 2004, Higgins jumped into the race and emerged the winner in a five-way Democratic primary.

In the general election, he won by only 3,774 votes, ending years of frustration for Democrats during the long tenure of Quinn, a moderate who satisfied the Democratic-leaning constituency with a pro-labor voting record. Higgins had a pro-labor record in the state Assembly during his three terms. The decision by most unions to back him over his Republican rival, Erie County Comptroller Nancy Naples, was a key factor in the race.

KEY VOTES

2006

Yes Stop broadband companies from favoring select Internet traffic

Yes Affirm U.S. commitment to war in Iraq and reject setting a withdrawal date for troops

No Repeal requirement for bilingual ballots at the polls

Yes Permit U.S. sale of civilian nuclear technology to India

No Build a 700-mile fence on the U.S.-Mexico border to curb illegal crossings

No Permit warrantless wiretaps of suspected terrorists

2005

Yes Intervene in the life-support case of Terri Schiavo

Yes Lift President Bush's restrictions on stem cell research funding

Yes Prohibit FBI access to library and bookstore records

No Approve free-trade pact with five Central American countries

No Pass energy policy overhaul favored by President Bush emphasizing domestic oil and gas production

No End mandatory preservation of habitat of endangered animal and plant species

Yes Ban torture of prisoners in U.S. custody

CQ VOTE STUDIES

	PARTY UNITY		PRESIDENTIAL SUPPORT	
	Support	Oppose	Support	Oppose
2006	89%	11%	33%	67%
2005	89%	11%	29%	71%

INTEREST GROUPS

	AFL-CIO	ADA	CCUS	ACU
2006	100%	85%	43%	20%
2005	87%	95%	52%	16%

NEW YORK 27
West – most of Buffalo, south and east suburbs

Tucked along the shores of Lake Erie in western New York, the 27th contains all of Erie County south of Buffalo and all but the northeastern corner of the city itself (which is in the 28th). Most of Buffalo's minority residents live in the 28th's portion of the city.

Urban revitalization has helped Buffalo reduce its high unemployment and shed its Rust Belt image. Auto manufacturing remains important in the area, and the city still has a large blue-collar workforce. Shipping and manufacturing remain vital to the city, but its economy has diversified to include white-collar jobs in the finance, insurance and real estate industries — growth driven mostly by two banks: HSBC and M&T, which provide thousands of area jobs. Health research facilities also are expanding in the Buffalo area.

Local leaders continue to see the waterfront as the core of Buffalo's renaissance effort. Development along the inner harbor is ongoing, and many officials believe the outer harbor presents a valuable opportunity to create both public space and commercial developments. The local professional sports teams, particularly football's Bills and hockey's Sabers, are a source of pride in the city.

South of Buffalo, the 27th follows the New York State Thruway to the southwest to take in all of Chautauqua County, which borders Lake Erie on the north and Pennsylvania on the south and west. This area is mainly made up of small communities that depend on agriculture and a robust grape-growing industry.

While these mostly rural areas south of Buffalo in both Erie and Chautauqua counties give Republicans strong support, they cannot match the city's strong union ties: Buffalo helped John Kerry win 53 percent of the 27th's 2004 presidential vote.

MAJOR INDUSTRY

Auto manufacturing, government, agriculture, tourism

CITIES

Buffalo (pt.), 163,179; Cheektowaga (unincorporated), 79,988; West Seneca (unincorporated), 45,943; Jamestown, 31,730

NOTABLE

Westfield, home to a Welch's plant, calls itself the "Grape Juice Capital of the World."

Rep. Louise M. Slaughter (D)

CAPITOL OFFICE
225-3615
www.slaughter.house.gov
2469 Rayburn 20515-3228; fax 225-7822

COMMITTEES
Rules - chairwoman

RESIDENCE
Fairport

BORN
Aug. 14, 1929, Harlan County, Ky.

RELIGION
Episcopalian

FAMILY
Husband, Robert Slaughter; three children

EDUCATION
U. of Kentucky, B.S. 1951 (microbiology), M.P.H. 1953

CAREER
State government aide; market researcher; microbiologist

POLITICAL HIGHLIGHTS
Monroe County Legislature, 1975-79; N.Y. Assembly, 1983-87

ELECTION RESULTS

2006 GENERAL		
Slaughter (D, INDC, WFM)	111,386	73.2%
John E. Donnelly (R, C)	40,844	26.8%
2006 PRIMARY		
Louise M. Slaughter (D)		unopposed
2004 GENERAL		
Slaughter (D, WFM)	159,655	72.6%
Michael D. Laba (R, C)	54,543	24.8%
Francina J. Cartonia (INDC)	5,678	2.6%

PREVIOUS WINNING PERCENTAGES
2002 (62%); 2000 (66%); 1998 (65%); 1996 (57%); 1994 (57%); 1992 (55%); 1990 (59%); 1988 (57%); 1986 (51%)

Elected 1986; 11th term

Slaughter went from being the powerless top-ranking Democrat on the Rules Committee to becoming one of the most powerful women in the House when her party took control in 2007. Speaker Nancy Pelosi appointed Slaughter to chair Rules, which is used by the majority party to control the legislation reaching the House floor and has great influence over the outcome.

Relishing the role reversal, Slaughter took the lead in writing an ethics reform bill, speaking out against the war in Iraq and pushing her long-stalled legislation to bar discrimination in health care coverage based on a person's genetic makeup. "I'm a Kentucky mountain woman with more energy than 10 people," she told the Rochester Democrat and Chronicle newspaper. "I just absolutely thrive on this."

Only weeks after pledging to "restore civility, responsibility and accountability to the political process," as head of the Rules Committee, Slaughter brushed off complaints that Democrats were using the same heavy-handed methods that they themselves once objected to by ramming through their "first 100 hours" legislative agenda without permitting amendments from the GOP minority.

Though Slaughter does the bidding of the Democratic leadership, she jumped out ahead of Pelosi on ethics changes. She proposed the hiring of an inspector general to monitor Congress and an independent board to investigate ethics complaints. Currently, lawmakers police themselves through the Committee on Standards of Official Conduct, and most members of the House prefer it that way. Slaughter's proposal got a cool reception from Pelosi.

Slaughter is an expert on medical issues, reflecting her background as a bacteriologist with a master's degree in public health. She doesn't mince words when she thinks complex issues are being given short shrift. During consideration of the Medicare prescription drug bill in the 108th Congress (2003-04), Slaughter sarcastically noted that the House was to discuss the issue for only three hours — compared with two weeks of Senate debate. "We are not naming a post office here. We are considering . . . the most important change to Medicare since its creation," she said.

The Democratic takeover improved the odds for Slaughter's long battle to bar employers and health insurers from discriminating against people based on their genetic profiles. The House was expected to pass the measure in 2007.

Slaughter is a strong advocate of the arts and co-chairs the Congressional Arts Caucus. In 2004, she won adoption of an amendment boosting funds for the National Endowment for the Arts by $10 million and for the National Endowment for the Humanities by $3.5 million.

Slaughter lives in a suburb of Rochester where she has spent most of her adult life, but she was brought up in the mountains of Kentucky's Harlan County. She is genuinely a coal miner's daughter. When she came to Congress in 1987, Democratic leaders took a liking to her warmth, grit and liberal views. They gave her a seat on the Rules Committee in 1989 and on the Budget Committee in 1991.

But her rise through the party then slowed. She lost a bid to be vice chairwoman of the Democratic Caucus in the 104th Congress (1995-96). And she was edged out in the 105th Congress (1997-98) for the top-ranking Democratic slot on the Budget Committee.

In 2002, while Pelosi was still the Democratic whip, she named Slaughter her point person on "issues that concern women," from abortion rights to health care and education; in the 108th Congress, Slaughter was the Democratic co-chairwoman of the Congressional Caucus for Women's Issues.

Her legislative successes include the establishment of a national task force to ensure that children get proper care in the event of a terrorist attack, and a bill to increase education about the health risks of the anti-miscarriage drug DES, which has caused cancer and abnormalities in the children of some women who took the drug.

While working on national issues, Slaughter also tends to the interests of major employers in her district, among them Eastman Kodak and Xerox. She fought against the Western Hemisphere Travel Initiative that would require Canadians entering the United States to show national identification. Slaughter said it would harm her border district's economy by slowing traffic. She also remains involved in the district's fight to win more-frequent and less-expensive airline service. She helped lure to Rochester low-cost carriers JetBlue, in 2000, and AirTran Airways, in 2002.

Slaughter moved with her husband to New York in the 1950s. Her first brush with public policy came in 1971 when she joined neighbors to try to save a stand of trees from development. "I thought in my best Kentucky fashion that if I would put on my best dress and go and be very nice and polite and ask them to save this forest that they would say, 'Well, why not?' " she later told the Associated Press. "And they just handed me my hat."

The episode sparked an interest in politics. She served as a Monroe County legislator and as an assistant to Mario Cuomo, then New York's secretary of state. In 1982, she ousted a Republican incumbent to move to the state Assembly, where she served four years before winning her seat in the House with 51 percent of the vote against conservative first-term Republican Fred J. Eckert. Actor Richard Gere, with whom she shared an interest in Central American issues, campaigned door-to-door with her.

Not until 1998, in her seventh House election, did Slaughter begin to draw better than 60 percent.

Reapportionment after the 2000 census cost New York two House seats, and the state legislature placed Slaughter in the same district as 14-term Democrat John J. LaFalce. When efforts to alter the remap failed, LaFalce retired rather than face Slaughter in a primary. She won by 25 percentage points in November 2002 and quickly began cultivating new parts of her district in Buffalo and Niagara Falls. She has won handily ever since, including in 2006 when a bout of shingles kept her sidelined during most of the race.

KEY VOTES

2006

Yes Stop broadband companies from favoring select Internet traffic
No Affirm U.S. commitment to war in Iraq and reject setting a withdrawal date for troops
? Repeal requirement for bilingual ballots at the polls
No Permit U.S. sale of civilian nuclear technology to India
No Build a 700-mile fence on the U.S.-Mexico border to curb illegal crossings
No Permit warrantless wiretaps of suspected terrorists

2005

? Intervene in the life-support case of Terri Schiavo
Yes Lift President Bush's restrictions on stem cell research funding
Yes Prohibit FBI access to library and bookstore records
No Approve free-trade pact with five Central American countries
Yes Pass energy policy overhaul favored by President Bush emphasizing domestic oil and gas production
No End mandatory preservation of habitat of endangered animal and plant species
Yes Ban torture of prisoners in U.S. custody

CQ VOTE STUDIES

	PARTY UNITY		PRESIDENTIAL SUPPORT	
	Support	Oppose	Support	Oppose
2006	99%	1%	14%	86%
2005	97%	3%	14%	86%
2004	98%	2%	24%	76%
2003	98%	2%	11%	89%
2002	98%	2%	16%	84%

INTEREST GROUPS

	AFL-CIO	ADA	CCUS	ACU
2006	100%	85%	29%	9%
2005	100%	100%	41%	4%
2004	100%	95%	44%	0%
2003	100%	100%	27%	12%
2002	100%	100%	22%	0%

NEW YORK 28

Northwest — Rochester, part of Buffalo

A small strip of land along the shore of Lake Ontario serves as a connector for the ends — Buffalo and Rochester — of the telephone receiver-shaped 28th. The district encompasses the northeastern portion of Buffalo, all of Niagara Falls and almost all of Rochester, giving the 28th most of the Democratic-rich voting areas in western New York.

Both Buffalo and Rochester are trying to recover from economic decline last decade. Job losses in the manufacturing sector largely have been offset by service industries, but the lower salaries have exacerbated the problems of Rochester's low-income residents.

Optic and imaging manufacturing firms drive Rochester's economy, joined by technology companies that benefit from proximity to the area's major corporations, Eastman Kodak and Xerox, and academic institutions. The University of Rochester is a top employer, and its optics institute is top-ranked, while the Rochester Institute of Technology has one of the nation's best imaging science departments. Also, research at the State University of New York at Buffalo, the Roswell Park Cancer Institute and the Hauptman-Woodward Medical Research Institute is helping to transform the Buffalo region into a major health care hub.

Niagara Falls attracts millions of tourists from around the world, although many of those visitors travel to the Canadian side of the border rather than the 28th's side. Local officials are hoping revitalization efforts, which include the Seneca Niagara Casino, will draw visitors to the U.S. shore.

Between Rochester and Buffalo, the 28th is home to rural communities that farm fruit and favor GOP candidates. Minorities total 38 percent of the 28th's population, giving it a far higher proportion of minority residents than any other New York district north of Westchester County. Combined with a blue-collar workforce, minorities helped John Kerry win 62 percent of the district's vote in the 2004 presidential election.

MAJOR INDUSTRY

Service, manufacturing, tourism, higher education, research

CITIES

Rochester (pt.), 219,729; Buffalo (pt.), 129,469; Niagara Falls, 55,593

NOTABLE

Women's rights activist Susan B. Anthony and abolitionist Frederick Douglass are both buried in Rochester's Mount Hope Cemetery.

Rep. John R. "Randy" Kuhl Jr. (R)

CAPITOL OFFICE
225-3161
kuhl.house.gov
1505 Longworth 20515-3229; fax 226-6599

COMMITTEES
Agriculture
Education & Labor
Transportation & Infrastructure

RESIDENCE
Hammondsport

BORN
April 19, 1943, Bath, N.Y.

RELIGION
Episcopalian

FAMILY
Divorced; three children

EDUCATION
Union College, B.S. 1966 (civil engineering); Syracuse U., J.D. 1969

CAREER
Lawyer

POLITICAL HIGHLIGHTS
N.Y. Assembly, 1981-87; N.Y. Senate, 1987-2004

ELECTION RESULTS

2006 GENERAL		
Kuhl (R, INDC, C)	106,077	51.4%
Eric Massa (D, WFM)	100,044	48.5%
2006 PRIMARY		
John R. "Randy" Kuhl Jr. (R)		unopposed
2004 GENERAL		
John R. "Randy" Kuhl Jr. (R)	136,883	50.7%
Samara Barend (D, WFM)	110,241	40.8%
Mark W. Assini (C)	17,272	6.4%
John Ciampoli (INDC)	5,819	2.2%

Elected 2004; 2nd term

Kuhl has yet to lock down his upstate New York district though it is predominately Republican and though he represented the area for nearly a quarter century in Albany.

In his first re-election bid in 2006, Kuhl (COOL) prevailed by nearly 3 percentage points over Eric Massa, a former Navy officer and congressional aide who immediately began preparing for a rematch in 2008. The district was represented for nine terms by Republican Amo Houghton, a moderate more typical of the GOP's liberal bent in the Northeast. Kuhl's voting record is decidedly to the right of Houghton's; plus, 2006 in general was a bad year for the Grand Old Party.

Kuhl also has been a booster for President Bush in the war in Iraq, speaking out against Democratic demands to curb the military buildup there and to bring U.S. troops home. He called a 2007 Democratic spending bill that included benchmarks for withdrawing troops a "plan for retreat and defeat in Iraq." Kuhl said in 2006, "I firmly believe this is a war on terror, against terrorists, and we need to fight this on their shores rather than ours."

Kuhl came to the House as a 61-year-old freshman in 2005, and is well-known in the southwestern New York district for his 24 years in the state legislature. Continuing a tradition started nearly three decades ago as a member of the state Assembly, Kuhl in his first term held 290 town meetings in the small towns and farm communities that dot his bucolic 5,660-square-mile district.

Though Kuhl says, "I never saw a tax I liked," he does like to spend tax dollars in his district. In Albany, his knack for securing local transportation grants earned him the nickname "Kuhl Aid" among local officials. In Washington, he requested and got a seat on the Transportation and Infrastructure Committee, among the most parochial of committees, and he has kept the dollars flowing. During his re-election campaign, Kuhl often presented oversize checks representing federal aid for which he took credit. "Find me another freshman that had the kind of money coming back to the district that I did," Kuhl said to the Elmira Star-Gazette newspaper on launching his re-election bid in May 2006.

At the start of the 110th Congress (2007-08), Kuhl, from his seat on the Agriculture Committee, signed on as a sponsor of legislation aimed at helping growers of specialty crops, including apples and grapes, which are plentiful in his district. He was also looking out for the interests of dairy farmers and wineries in a rewrite of farm policy that got under way in 2007.

Kuhl's first legislative initiative was legislation renaming a three-mile stretch of highway around Elmira after Houghton, who co-founded the centrist Republican Main Street Partnership.

Kuhl, by contrast, established a conservative voting record in the 109th Congress (2005-06). He opposed federal funding of embryonic stem cell research, supported the administration's controversial use of warrantless wiretaps in terrorism investigations and favored repealing bilingual language assistance provided for under the Voting Rights Act. In 2005, Kuhl favored congressional intervention in the case of Terri Schiavo, a brain-damaged Florida woman who became a rallying point for social conservatives when her husband obtained court permission to remove her from life support, over the objections of her parents.

Overall, Kuhl voted with Bush 90 percent of the time in the 109th Congress on issues on which the White House staked out a position. Bush, Vice

President Dick Cheney and first lady Laura Bush all made appearances for him in his district in the 2006 campaign.

Kuhl has found some common ground with Democrats on labor issues. He voted in favor of an increase in the federal minimum wage in both 2006 and 2007. He also broke with the White House by opposing proposed cuts in the Medicare medical program for senior citizens.

Kuhl grew up in the district's Finger Lakes region of central New York. His father moved there in 1933, becoming one of the first doctors in the tiny village of Hammondsport. His mother was a local school nurse. Kuhl spent his boyhood sailing and swimming on Keuka Lake. In his teens, he was a tour guide for the Gold Seat Winery in Hammondsport. He still lives in his parents' former cottage on the west side of the lake, a few miles from his boyhood home.

Kuhl's father wanted him to follow in his footsteps, but realized that that probably was not going to happen after Kuhl passed out watching him perform an appendectomy at the local hospital. Kuhl studied civil engineering at Union College in Schenectady, but halfway through decided he didn't like the solitary life of a scientist. He went to law school at Syracuse University, got his degree and opened a small law firm in his hometown.

Kuhl was elected to the New York Assembly in 1980, serving six years before moving to the state Senate. His public career survived a well-publicized 1997 arrest and subsequent drunken driving conviction. Police in Corning, N.Y., found him asleep in a parked car with the motor running. His blood-alcohol level was twice the legal limit.

When Houghton decided to retire after nine terms in 2004, Kuhl established himself early on as the front-runner, thanks to an endorsement from Houghton that provided a centrist sheen. Organized labor also helped him, viewing him as one of the friendlier Republicans in the state Senate, and believing there was little chance for a Democrat to win.

Kuhl fended off a challenge from the right in the GOP primary and did not look at first to be seriously threatened in the general election. But the outcome was closer than expected. He defeated first-time Democratic candidate Samara Barend by 10 percentage points, after he was bruised by the release of information from previously sealed divorce records. The records, obtained by a volunteer for the Barend campaign, revealed that Kuhl had threatened his wife with a shotgun at a 1994 dinner party. Kuhl called the revelation "political sabotage," but did not dispute its accuracy.

Two years later, he defeated Massa, who once worked for the House Armed Services Committee, with 51 percent of the vote.

KEY VOTES

2006

- No Stop broadband companies from favoring select Internet traffic
- Yes Affirm U.S. commitment to war in Iraq and reject setting a withdrawal date for troops
- Yes Repeal requirement for bilingual ballots at the polls
- Yes Permit U.S. sale of civilian nuclear technology to India
- Yes Build a 700-mile fence on the U.S.-Mexico border to curb illegal crossings
- Yes Permit warrantless wiretaps of suspected terrorists

2005

- Yes Intervene in the life-support case of Terri Schiavo
- No Lift President Bush's restrictions on stem cell research funding
- No Prohibit FBI access to library and bookstore records
- Yes Approve free-trade pact with five Central American countries
- Yes Pass energy policy overhaul favored by President Bush emphasizing domestic oil and gas production
- Yes End mandatory preservation of habitat of endangered animal and plant species
- Yes Ban torture of prisoners in U.S. custody

CQ VOTE STUDIES

	PARTY UNITY		PRESIDENTIAL SUPPORT	
	Support	Oppose	Support	Oppose
2006	89%	11%	95%	5%
2005	93%	7%	85%	15%

INTEREST GROUPS

	AFL-CIO	ADA	CCUS	ACU
2006	43%	5%	100%	83%
2005	33%	15%	89%	92%

NEW YORK 29

Southern Tier — Elmira, Corning; Rochester suburbs

The 29th blankets much of the southwestern portion of New York known as the Southern Tier, encompassing a mix of forests, lakes, farms and small towns. It also reaches north to take in the western half of the Finger Lakes region and some of Rochester's suburbs.

Agriculture helps drive the economy, mostly through dairy farms and wineries. The Finger Lakes and surrounding parks draw thousands of visitors annually, and the Finger Lakes region is the largest wine-producing area by volume outside of California.

In the north, the 29th takes in southern parts of Monroe County outside Rochester, where a plurality of the district's residents live. It wraps around the west, south and east sides of the city, taking in mostly GOP-leaning towns such as Chili and Pittsford.

The 29th's westernmost point is Cattaraugus County, a rural area that includes Allegany State Park and St. Bonaventure University. To the east, Republicans hold a better than 2-1 registration advantage over Democrats in Allegany, Steuben and Yates counties. Steuben County contains Corning, one of the better-known U.S. company towns due to its glass products and costly crystal pieces. Neighboring Elmira, located in Chemung, is home to aircraft construction, fire hydrant and bottle manufacturing plants. Olean, in Cattaraugus, hosts the headquarters of kitchen cutlery maker CUTCO.

Republicans hold an edge over Democrats in voter registration here, and despite the district's large presence of blue-collar workers, George W. Bush had his best showing in the state in the 29th in both the 2000 and 2004 presidential elections. The 29th also has the lowest percentage of Hispanic residents (1 percent) in any New York district.

MAJOR INDUSTRY
Agriculture, manufacturing, tourism

CITIES
Elmira, 30,940; Brighton (unincorporated) (pt.), 25,869

NOTABLE
Watkins Glen International race track ("The Glen") is just south of Seneca Lake outside the village of Watkins Glen in Schuyler County.

NORTH CAROLINA

Gov. Michael F. Easley (D)

First elected: 2000
Length of term: 4 years
Term expires: 1/09
Salary: $130,629
Phone: (919) 733-4240

Residence: Rocky Mount
Born: March 23, 1950; Nash County, N.C.
Religion: Roman Catholic
Family: Wife, Mary Easley; one child
Education: U. of North Carolina, B.A. 1972 (political science); North Carolina Central U., J.D. 1976
Career: Lawyer
Political highlights: Brunswick, Bladen and Columbus County district attorney, 1982-92; sought Democratic nomination for U.S. Senate, 1990; N.C. attorney general, 1993-2001

Election results:

2004 GENERAL		
Michael F. Easley (D)	1,939,154	55.6%
Patrick J. Ballantine (R)	1,495,021	42.9%
Barbara J. Howe (LIBERT)	52,513	1.5%

Lt. Gov. Beverly Perdue (D)

First elected: 2000
Length of term: 4 years
Term expires: 1/09
Salary: $115,289
Phone: (919) 733-7350

LEGISLATURE

General Assembly: January-June

Senate: 50 members, 2-year terms
2007 ratios: 29 D, 21 R; 43 men, 7 women
Salary: $13,951
Phone: (919) 733-4111

House: 120 members, 2-year terms
2007 ratios: 68 D, 52 R; 83 men, 37 women
Salary: $13,951
Phone: (919) 733-4111

TERM LIMITS

Governor: 2 consecutive terms
Senate: No
House: No

URBAN STATISTICS

CITY	POPULATION
Charlotte	540,828
Raleigh	276,093
Greensboro	223,891
Durham	187,035
Winston-Salem	185,776

REGISTERED VOTERS

Democrat	45%
Republican	35%
Unaffiliated	20%

POPULATION

2006 population (est.)	8,856,505
2000 population	8,049,313
1990 population	6,628,637
Percent change (1990-2000)	+21.4%
Rank among states (2006)	11
Median age	35.3
Born in state	63%
Foreign born	5.3%
Violent crime rate	498/100,000
Poverty level	12.3%
Federal workers	60,331
Military	118,281

ELECTIONS

STATE ELECTION OFFICIAL
(919) 733-7173
DEMOCRATIC PARTY
(919) 821-2777
REPUBLICAN PARTY
(919) 828-6423

MISCELLANEOUS

Web: www.ncgov.com
Capital: Raleigh

U.S. CONGRESS

Senate: 2 Republicans
House: 7 Democrats, 6 Republicans

2000 Census Statistics by District

DIST.	2004 VOTE FOR PRESIDENT BUSH	KERRY	WHITE	BLACK	ASIAN	HISP	MEDIAN INCOME	WHITE COLLAR	BLUE COLLAR	SERVICE INDUSTRY	OVER 64	UNDER 18	COLLEGE EDUCATION	RURAL	SQ. MILES
1	43%	57%	44%	50%	0%	3%	$28,410	46%	37%	18%	14%	26%	12%	52%	7,199
2	55	45	59	30	1	8	$36,510	52	34	14	10	26	16	50	3,956
3	68	32	76	17	1	4	$37,510	56	29	15	12	24	20	47	6,192
4	44	55	69	21	4	5	$53,847	75	14	11	8	25	48	17	1,253
5	67	33	88	7	1	4	$39,710	54	34	12	13	23	20	57	4,402
6	69	30	85	9	1	4	$43,503	56	33	11	14	24	23	48	2,944
7	56	44	63	23	0	4	$33,998	50	34	16	13	25	18	55	6,087
8	54	45	62	27	2	7	$38,390	53	33	14	11	26	18	31	3,283
9	63	36	83	10	2	4	$55,059	69	20	10	10	25	36	16	991
10	67	33	85	9	1	3	$37,649	45	42	12	13	24	14	50	3,302
11	57	43	90	5	0	3	$34,720	52	32	16	18	21	21	56	6,025
12	37	63	45	45	2	7	$35,775	52	32	16	11	26	19	11	821
13	47	53	63	27	2	6	$41,060	60	26	13	11	23	27	26	2,256
STATE	56	44	70	21	1	5	$39,184	56	31	14	12	24	23	40	48,711
U.S.	50.7	48.3	69	12	4	13	$41,994	60	25	15	12	26	24	21	3,537,438

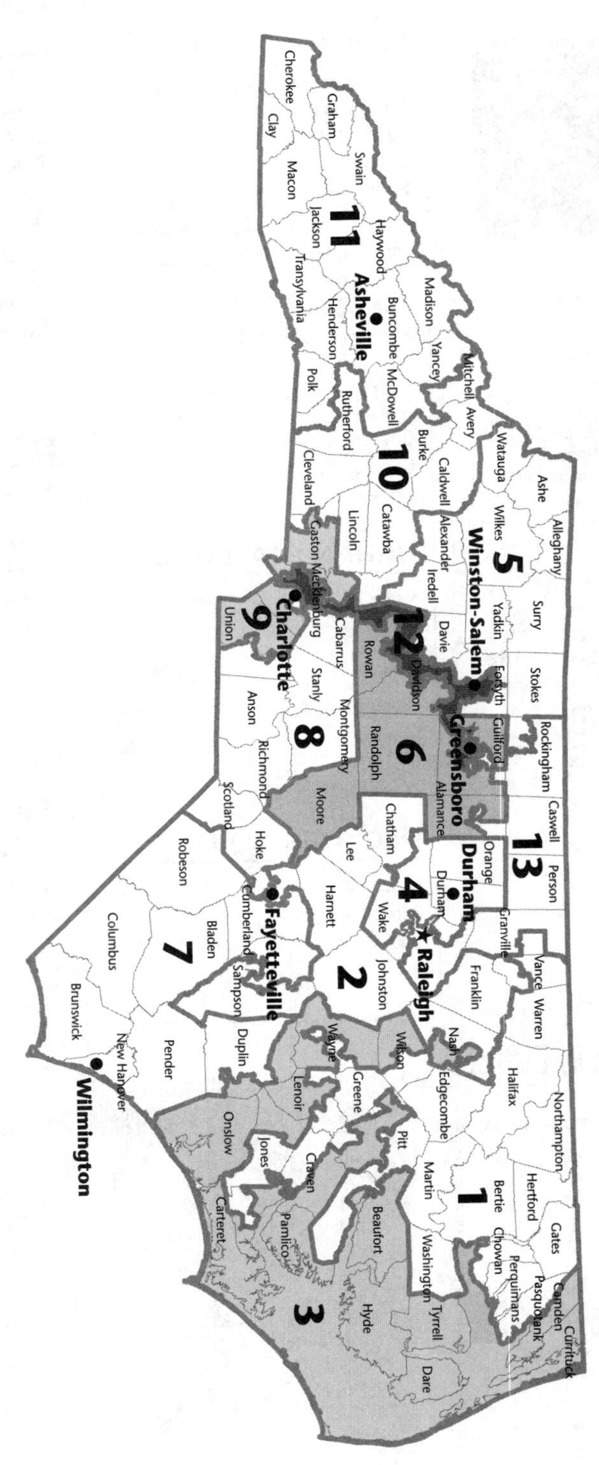
Cherokee
Clay
Graham
Swain
Macon
Jackson
Haywood
11
Transylvania
Madison
Asheville
Buncombe
Henderson
Yancey
Polk
Rutherford
McDowell
Mitchell
Avery
Burke
10
Cleveland
Caldwell
Watauga
Ashe
Alleghany
Wilkes
Lincoln
Catawba
Alexander
5
Winston-Salem
Gaston
Mecklenburg
Iredell
Surry
Charlotte
9
Union
Cabarrus
12
Davie
Yadkin
Forsyth
Stokes
Rowan
Davidson
Stanly
Anson
Montgomery
8
Randolph
6
Greensboro
Guilford
Rockingham
Richmond
Scotland
Moore
Chatham
Alamance
Caswell
13
Orange
Durham
Person
Robeson
Hoke
Lee
4
Fayetteville
Cumberland
Harnett
Wake
Raleigh
Granville
Vance
Warren
Columbus
Bladen
7
Sampson
2
Johnston
Franklin
Brunswick
New Hanover
Wilmington
Pender
Duplin
Wayne
Wilson
Nash
Halifax
Northampton
Lenoir
Greene
Edgecombe
Onslow
Jones
Craven
Pitt
Martin
1
Bertie
Hertford
Gates
Carteret
Pamlico
Beaufort
Washington
Chowan
Perquimans
Pasquotank
Camden
Currituck
3
Hyde
Tyrrell
Dare

Sen. Elizabeth Dole (R)

CAPITOL OFFICE
224-6342
dole.senate.gov
555 Dirksen 20510-3301; fax 224-1100

COMMITTEES
Armed Services
Banking, Housing & Urban Affairs
Small Business & Entrepreneurship
Special Aging

RESIDENCE
Salisbury

BORN
July 29, 1936, Salisbury, N.C.

RELIGION
Presbyterian

FAMILY
Husband, Bob Dole

EDUCATION
Duke U., B.A. 1958 (political science);
Harvard U., M.A. 1960 (education & government), J.D. 1965

CAREER
American Red Cross president; lawyer;
White House aide

POLITICAL HIGHLIGHTS
Federal Trade Commission, 1973-79; Transportation secretary, 1983-87; Labor secretary, 1989-90; sought Republican nomination for president, 2000

ELECTION RESULTS

2002 GENERAL		
Elizabeth Dole (R)	1,248,664	53.6%
Erskine Bowles (D)	1,047,983	45.0%
Sean Haugh (LIBERT)	33,807	1.5%
2002 PRIMARY		
Elizabeth Dole (R)	342,631	80.4%
Jim Snyder (R)	60,477	14.2%
Jim Parker (R)	8,752	2.1%
Ada M. Fisher (R)	6,045	1.4%

Elected 2002; 1st term

National politics consumed much of Dole's time and energy in the past two years while she was chairwoman of her party's main fundraising arm in the Senate, the National Republican Senatorial Committee (NRSC). But after a bruising election year in 2006 for both the GOP and her personally, Dole is back to being a freshman senator from North Carolina, with a re-election campaign ahead and the changing, often struggling economy of her home state as the most pressing issue at hand.

Dole doesn't promote herself as a feminist but she's a pioneer among women in politics. She worked in the administrations of five presidents and was once talked about as a potential Republican nominee for president. The wife of former Senate Majority Leader Bob Dole of Kansas, the 1996 Republican nominee for president, Dole knew the ways of the Senate well before her election.

She beat a strong Democratic opponent to win her seat in 2002, and she won her position as NRSC chairwoman, the first rung on the Senate leadership ladder, by just one vote in a hard-fought campaign against Norm Coleman of Minnesota.

As it turned out, the job proved more a liability to her career than an asset. Insiders questioned her political savvy as what appeared to be a plum job left her at the scene of a party debacle in which Democrats scored a net gain of six seats and took control of the chamber. Although President Bush's unpopularity, the Iraq War and a series of congressional ethics scandals had far more impact on the outcome in November 2006, Dole's perceived shortcomings in recruiting and fundraising left her bruised after the election. The committee raised $89 million, considerably less than the $121 million raked in by the Democratic senatorial committee.

Her party woes have now become personal. In the first quarter of 2007, Senate GOP leaders included Dole in a select group of five vulnerable Republican incumbents for whom they are soliciting early and extra financial support. And some prominent Democrats in North Carolina were thinking of taking her on.

Reflecting on the 2006 election, Dole singled out one issue. "It was, let's face it, Iraq, Iraq, Iraq," she said. "It was a steady rain for two years."

In the 110th Congress (2007-08), her focus is on shoring up her standing at home. As in previous congresses, she casts many of the issues she has taken on — such as a proposal to strengthen community colleges to train workers for higher-skill work — as ways of helping families and businesses in North Carolina to make the transition from traditional manufacturing and to thrive in the new global economy.

On the Senate floor, Dole is methodical and chooses her words carefully, but she seems to have relaxed enough to stray sometimes from her prepared remarks. On her visits home, she uses a warmer, more folksy tone.

She has done her duty as a freshman to familiarize herself with parochial issues and defend her state's interests when necessary. As soon as she got to Congress, Dole secured a seat on the Armed Services Committee, a pivotal position for a state with several military bases. She has promised to continue to work to bring more defense spending to the state.

Her seat on the Banking Committee is a good match with Charlotte's interests as a regional financial center. She has been working for tougher regulation of the government-sponsored mortgage finance giants Fannie Mae and Freddie Mac, both of which have been connected to multibillion-dollar accounting scandals. She has also been involved in efforts to fight "predatory lending," with a focus first on helping men and women in the armed services.

Dole has also proposed legislation that would help provide grants for small-business owners to get short-term postsecondary training to help them compete in the new economy. The measure would allow second- and third-year students to borrow more for tuition if they are pursuing high-wage, high-growth occupations.

Though she has backed the Bush administration's pro-trade agenda, she has bashed China for denying workers a "level playing field" in international trade. "Many of North Carolina's economic woes related to manufacturing can be summed up in one word," Dole says in her speeches back home. "One word. And I know you know what it is: China."

She favors making the president's tax cuts permanent, saying that cutting taxes and reducing regulation on business will help lower the state's higher-than-average unemployment and the decline of the once-thriving textile industry. On most issues, Dole toes the Republican line.

Despite her reliably Republican rhetoric, Dole often has to walk a fine line between emphasizing her GOP credentials and trying not to alienate her state's middle-of-the-road voters and conservative Democrats. One case in point was her position on the Family and Medical Leave Act, which guarantees workers time off to attend to major personal matters. Though she opposed the measure when Clinton signed it into law in 1993 and when running for president in 1999, she said in 2002 that it had proved itself over 10 years and that she would like to see it expanded.

A Harvard Law School graduate, Dole began her Washington career as a consumer affairs aide to President Lyndon B. Johnson and later to President Richard Nixon. She then served as a member of the Federal Trade Commission under Presidents Gerald R. Ford and Jimmy Carter and as assistant for public liaison in the Reagan administration. Originally a Democrat, she switched party affiliation when she married Dole.

In February 1983, she became the first woman to serve as secretary of the Transportation Department. In January 1989, she was sworn in as secretary of the Labor Department under President George H.W. Bush. She did not enter the private sector until 1991, when she became president of the American Red Cross.

Though she was regarded in the run-up to 2000 as the first woman to make a serious bid for the presidency, critics derided her campaign appearances as overly controlled and said she was unable to connect well with voters. She abandoned her campaign in October 1999, before a single primary or caucus was held, citing the overwhelming fundraising advantage that party front-runner George W. Bush had established.

Dole had not lived in North Carolina since she graduated from Duke University in 1958, and in the 2002 Senate campaign some opponents tried to portray her as a Washington insider and a carpetbagger. But this criticism was blunted by the fact that her competition, Democrat Erskine Bowles, was the former chief of staff to President Bill Clinton and had spent many years inside the Beltway himself.

Dole benefited from having only minor opposition in the September 2002 Republican primary, while Bowles had serious opposition for the Democratic nomination. That allowed Dole to spend the summer touring the state and accruing almost universally positive publicity.

Rural voters had much to do with her impressive 9 percentage point win over Bowles, as did the strong early endorsement she received from former political rival Bush. Her 54 percent vote tally was the highest percentage any North Carolina Senate candidate had received since 1978.

KEY VOTES

2006

- Yes Confirm Samuel A. Alito Jr. to the Supreme Court
- Yes Allow consideration of a bill to establish a $140 billion trust fund to compensate victims of asbestos exposure
- Yes Extend tax cuts for two years at a cost of $70 billion over five years
- No Overhaul immigration policy with border security, enforcement and guest worker program
- Yes Allow consideration of a bill to permanently repeal the estate tax
- No Urge President Bush to begin troop withdrawals from Iraq in 2006
- No Lift President Bush's restrictions on stem cell research funding
- Yes Authorize military tribunals for suspected terrorists

2005

- Yes Curb class action lawsuits by shifting them from state to federal courts
- Yes Allow confirmation vote on Priscilla R. Owen to the U.S. Court of Appeals for the 5th Circuit
- Yes Oppose mandatory emissions limits and block recognition of global warming as a threat
- Yes Approve free-trade pact with five Central American countries
- Yes Pass energy policy overhaul favored by President Bush emphasizing domestic oil and gas production
- Yes Shield gunmakers from lawsuits when their products are used in crimes
- Yes Ban torture of prisoners in U.S. custody
- Yes Renew 16 provisions of the Patriot Act
- Yes Allow final vote on opening the Arctic National Wildlife Refuge to oil and gas exploration

CQ VOTE STUDIES

	PARTY UNITY		PRESIDENTIAL SUPPORT	
	Support	Oppose	Support	Oppose
2006	94%	6%	90%	10%
2005	93%	7%	93%	7%
2004	94%	6%	92%	8%
2003	96%	4%	98%	2%

INTEREST GROUPS

	AFL-CIO	ADA	CCUS	ACU
2006	33%	5%	83%	96%
2005	14%	5%	94%	96%
2004	33%	25%	100%	92%
2003	8%	15%	91%	80%

Sen. Richard M. Burr (R)

CAPITOL OFFICE
224-3154
burr.senate.gov
217 Russell 20510-3306; fax 228-2981

COMMITTEES
Energy & Natural Resources
Health, Education, Labor & Pensions
Indian Affairs
Veterans' Affairs
Select Intelligence

RESIDENCE
Winston-Salem

BORN
Nov. 30, 1955, Charlottesville, Va.

RELIGION
Methodist

FAMILY
Wife, Brooke Burr; two children

EDUCATION
Wake Forest U., B.A. 1978 (communications)

CAREER
Marketing manager; kitchen appliance salesman

POLITICAL HIGHLIGHTS
Republican nominee for U.S. House, 1992; U.S. House, 1995-2005

ELECTION RESULTS

2004 GENERAL		
Richard M. Burr (R)	1,791,450	51.6%
Erskine Bowles (D)	1,632,527	47.0%
Tom Bailey (LIBERT)	47,743	1.4%
2004 PRIMARY		
Richard M. Burr (R)	302,319	87.9%
John Ross Hendrix (R)	25,971	7.6%
Albert Lee Wiley Jr. (R)	15,585	4.5%

PREVIOUS WINNING PERCENTAGES
2002 House Election (70%); 2000 House Election (93%); 1998 House Election (68%); 1996 House Election (62%); 1994 House Election (57%)

Elected 2004; 1st term

The easygoing Burr, who spent a decade in the House, is not hard to spot in the formal, tradition-bound Senate. He's the man in shirt sleeves, sauntering with his suit jacket flung over one shoulder. Some senators prefer drivers, but Burr likes to chauffeur himself and has been known to roll up those sleeves to scoop ice cream on the campaign trail. When he ran for the seat in 2004, he was criticized for appearing too relaxed, too devil-may-care, about what was expected to be a close race.

Appearances can be deceiving. Since he won the election, Burr has quickly applied the expertise gained in the House on biological terrorism and other health care issues to carve out a niche in the Senate. A member of the Health, Education, Labor and Pensions Committee, he chaired its Bioterrorism and Public Health Preparedness Subcommittee in the 109th Congress (2005-06), where he championed broad changes to the nation's public health system to protect against terrorism and other disasters. Just before Congress adjourned in 2006, he was able to win congressional approval of his bill aimed at boosting the nation's bioterror and disease outbreak preparedness. President Bush signed the bill.

That success was the culmination of Burr's two-year effort in the Senate to renew and update a 2002 law that strengthened national defenses against biological or chemical attacks in the aftermath of the Sept. 11 terrorist attacks. Burr, when he was in the House, had been a chief negotiator on the legislation that led to that original law.

In 2005, the must-pass defense spending bill included his provision to shield drug manufacturers from lawsuits involving vaccines and drugs designated for use treating or preventing disease outbreaks or bioterror attacks. Burr took some flak for it from Democrats, who said it offered blanket protection to the big, profitable drug companies that are major political contributors of Burr's. The senator noted that those large firms, known collectively as "Big Pharma," are not involved in vaccine production, though he hopes that they will be in the future because the public stands to benefit.

The former appliance salesman has a flair for translating complex policy issues into easy-to-understand terms. His interest in health care issues is driven in part by a desire to watch out for his state's medical technology, medical education and pharmaceutical industries. North Carolina's economic base has been transitioning from the old mainstays of tobacco, textiles and furniture to the technology, research and financial industries now clustered around the state's two metropolises, Raleigh and Charlotte. Burr's hometown of Winston-Salem is home to the R.J. Reynolds Tobacco Co., but it has been working to nurture health care and biomedical research sectors, anchored by local colleges and universities.

Yet he still must look out for the traditional industries that remain politically important in North Carolina, including cigarette manufacturers and farmers who depend on tobacco. His 2004 campaign for the Senate against a strong Democratic candidate, former Clinton chief of staff Erskine Bowles, got a big boost from the passage that year of a tobacco buyout bill he helped write. It steered $3.8 billion to the state's tobacco farmers, while fighting off Federal Drug Administration (FDA) regulation opposed by the industry, and was hugely popular in the state. Personally, Burr is anti-tobacco; he quit smoking cigarettes in 1998 after making a televised vow to do so.

Burr also watches out for the textile industry, a vital part of his state's economy. He has consistently opposed expanding trade with China. And though he said at the time of its approval that he supported the North American Free Trade Agreement — which passed before he came to Congress — Burr reversed his stance the day he filed to run for the Senate, saying the trade pact had been a mistake. He voted for the Central American Free Trade Agreement in 2005, despite fears among many in his home state that it could harm U.S. textile workers. In 2006, those concerns led him to vote against a trade pact with Oman.

Also in 2006, Burr won enactment of a law extending the Ed-Flex program, which allows states such as North Carolina that are deemed to have strong accountability standards to waive some federal regulations for local school districts.

Born in Virginia, the son of a Presbyterian minister, Burr is descended from Aaron Burr, the New York senator and vice president. His father moved the family to Winston-Salem when Burr was 6, and became locally prominent as the head of the city's 3,000-member First Presbyterian Church. His father was often gone, ministering to his large flock, and Burr, a standout football player at R.J. Reynolds High School, said many years later that he remembers looking up into the stands and seeing only his mother, according to the Charlotte Observer.

After college, Burr took a job with Carswell Distributing selling appliances and teaching housewives how to cook with their newfangled microwave ovens. He rose to national sales manager, and also became active politically in the growing conservative anti-tax movement, co-chairing North Carolina Taxpayers United.

Burr came home from his job one day in 1991 and surprised his wife by announcing he wanted to run for Congress, even though he had no political experience and no clue what a congressman earned. He lost his first bid, in 1992, got back in the fray two years later and won with 57 percent of the vote against state Sen. A.P. "Sandy" Sands.

He arrived in Congress as part of the GOP's ideals-driven Class of '94, and soon proved to be more pragmatic than many of the newcomers. He played a large role in winning passage in 1997 of legislation to speed FDA approval of new drugs and medical devices. The powerful then chairman of the Energy and Commerce Committee, Republican Billy Tauzin of Louisiana, took notice and elevated Burr to vice chairman of the committee though there were more-senior Republicans in line ahead of him.

That same year, during the GOP's fight with the Clinton administration over a major bill that balanced the budget in part with steep spending cuts, Burr was among the small group of Republicans who voted against the legislation. He said he worried that the bill cut too much from government health care programs.

Later, he worked with other Republicans to develop a plan to curb the high cost of prescription drugs for Medicare beneficiaries, declaring that younger generations had an obligation to help seniors finance their medical needs.

Encouraged by state party officials to run for governor in 2000, Burr declined, saying the job was too administrative for him. Burr had his eye on the Senate. He wanted to run for an open seat in 2002, but deferred to Elizabeth Dole, the former Cabinet secretary who was the Bush administration's choice. He began preparing to run for Democrat John Edwards' Senate seat more than a year in advance of the 2004 election — a departure from his usual spur-of-the-moment style — even before Edwards announced he would not seek re-election. Burr weathered criticism for an initially lackluster campaign against Bowles, who was running a second time after being defeated by Dole two years earlier.

Aided by Bush's strong showing, Burr won with 52 percent of the vote to Bowles' 47 percent.

KEY VOTES

2006

Yes Confirm Samuel A. Alito Jr. to the Supreme Court
Yes Allow consideration of a bill to establish a $140 billion trust fund to compensate victims of asbestos exposure
Yes Extend tax cuts for two years at a cost of $70 billion over five years
No Overhaul immigration policy with border security, enforcement and guest worker program
Yes Allow consideration of a bill to permanently repeal the estate tax
No Urge President Bush to begin troop withdrawals from Iraq in 2006
Yes Lift President Bush's restrictions on stem cell research funding
Yes Authorize military tribunals for suspected terrorists

2005

Yes Curb class action lawsuits by shifting them from state to federal courts
Yes Allow confirmation vote on Priscilla R. Owen to the U.S. Court of Appeals for the 5th Circuit
Yes Oppose mandatory emissions limits and block recognition of global warming as a threat
Yes Approve free-trade pact with five Central American countries
Yes Pass energy policy overhaul favored by President Bush emphasizing domestic oil and gas production
Yes Shield gunmakers from lawsuits when their products are used in crimes
Yes Ban torture of prisoners in U.S. custody
Yes Renew 16 provisions of the Patriot Act
Yes Allow final vote on opening the Arctic National Wildlife Refuge to oil and gas exploration

CQ VOTE STUDIES

	PARTY UNITY		PRESIDENTIAL SUPPORT	
	Support	Oppose	Support	Oppose
2006	94%	6%	88%	12%
2005	95%	5%	89%	11%
House Service:				
2004	92%	8%	79%	21%
2003	94%	6%	96%	4%
2002	95%	5%	92%	8%
2001	95%	5%	93%	7%
2000	92%	8%	22%	78%
1999	93%	7%	17%	83%
1998	92%	8%	24%	76%
1997	94%	6%	28%	72%

INTEREST GROUPS

	AFL-CIO	ADA	CCUS	ACU
2006	20%	10%	67%	92%
2005	29%	5%	94%	92%
House Service:				
2004	33%	10%	94%	87%
2003	27%	15%	93%	84%
2002	11%	0%	100%	96%
2001	17%	10%	96%	88%
2000	10%	5%	80%	88%
1999	33%	5%	84%	87%
1998	10%	5%	82%	92%
1997	13%	10%	90%	92%

Rep. G.K. Butterfield (D)

CAPITOL OFFICE
225-3101
www.house.gov/butterfield
413 Cannon 20515-3301; fax 225-3354

COMMITTEES
Energy & Commerce

RESIDENCE
Wilson

BORN
April 27, 1947, Wilson, N.C.

RELIGION
Baptist

FAMILY
Divorced; two children

EDUCATION
North Carolina Central U., B.A. 1971 (political science & sociology), J.D. 1974

MILITARY SERVICE
Army, 1968-70

CAREER
Lawyer; child care center owner

POLITICAL HIGHLIGHTS
Candidate for Wilson City Council, 1976; N.C. Superior Court judge, 1989-2001; N.C. Supreme Court, 2001-02; defeated for election to N.C. Supreme Court, 2002; N.C. Superior Court judge, 2003-04

ELECTION RESULTS

2006 GENERAL		
G.K. Butterfield (D)		unopposed
2006 PRIMARY		
G.K. Butterfield (D)		unopposed
2004 GENERAL		
G.K. Butterfield (D)	137,667	64.0%
Greg Dority (R)	77,508	36.0%

PREVIOUS WINNING PERCENTAGES
2004 Special Election (71%)

Elected July 2004; 2nd full term

A descendant of slaves, Butterfield is a former state judge who maintains a relatively low profile on Capitol Hill and focuses on his role as advocate for the poorest and most heavily black district in rural North Carolina. In the 110th Congress (2007-08), he secured a seat on the sought-after Energy and Commerce Committee.

He no doubt was helped by the fact that he sits on the leadership-run Steering and Policy Committee. Under Democratic Caucus rules, Butterfield had to give up his seats on the Armed Services and Agriculture committees to take the Energy and Commerce slot.

In another measure of his upward movement in the caucus, in 2007 he was named one of the nine chief deputy whips.

On the Energy panel, Butterfield is in a better position now to press his ideas for making technology accessible in rural areas. In 2005, he urged the Federal Communications Commission to move more slowly toward an all-digital cable television system. Although a huge advance technologically, such a system requires a change in cable equipment that could cost customers $250 each. "Unfortunately, in poor rural places like eastern North Carolina, this could leave a lot of people in the dark when it comes to watching television," he said.

Butterfield has worked to get minority farmers a larger slice of the federal pie, winning approval of an amendment adding an additional $1.9 million to the agriculture spending bill in 2005. He also worked to get $5 million in 2006 for the Rural Community Advancement program, which pays for infrastructure in poor, rural areas.

The district claims more tobacco farmers than any other in the country, and Butterfield supported the 2004 measure that let farmers cash out of the federal tobacco quota system, a method of keeping prices stable by limiting how much tobacco can be sold from each acre each year. He then set up a service to help constituents figure out how to apply for the aid.

Since his arrival in Congress, Butterfield has tried to stop the Navy from building an airstrip in his district. He has gone toe-to-toe with the Pentagon on a plan called the "Outlying Landing Field," where the Navy would conduct 32,000 practice flights a year for pilots of F/A-18 Super Hornet jets. District residents opposed to the plan have sought to challenge the project in court on environmental grounds. The proposed site would be near a large bird sanctuary, the Pocosin Lakes National Wildlife Refuge, which is a winter home to migratory birds. Several small towns also are nearby, and construction of the airfield would force the removal of some homes.

Butterfield succeeded in zeroing out money for the airstrip in the House version of the 2005 defense authorization bill. But he ultimately had to settle for a compromise. The final version of the bill set aside $30 million, a third of what the Pentagon had sought. Still, he has continued his efforts: "I have done all I can to persuade the Navy. So far it has fallen on deaf ears," Butterfield said in December 2006. At the start of the 110th Congress, the project stalled while the Navy conducted an environmental impact study.

Butterfield grew up in Wilson, N.C. His great-grandfather was a white slave owner who conceived a child with one of his slaves. The child, Butterfield's grandfather, was born in the final days of slavery and became a minister. Butterfield's mother was a schoolteacher. His father, George Kenneth Butterfield, for whom Butterfield is named, was a native of Bermuda who came to the United States at age 16. A decade later, he opened a dental office and practiced for 50 years.

He became a civic leader, and the all-white political establishment granted him the right to vote as a "favor," says Butterfield. The elder Butterfield began encouraging other African-Americans to register to vote but stopped under pressure from white leaders. He resumed the effort after the Depression. When literacy tests were introduced to discourage blacks from voting, Butterfield's father began teaching people to read. He then ran for the city council, winning narrowly in 1953.

In 1957, while the family was vacationing in New York, town officials replaced ward-by-ward elections — which had allowed the elder Butterfield to win among a black-majority constituency — with at-large elections. That eliminated chances for any black candidate to succeed. "I saw how the political system was manipulated to obtain an unfair result," Butterfield says. "Having seen that injustice has made me want to be involved politically."

Those childhood events convinced Butterfield to go into law. Ultimately, he got the last word in his father's long fight by handling several voting rights lawsuits in eastern North Carolina counties that resulted in the court-ordered implementation of district elections for local officials.

Butterfield failed in his own city council bid in 1976. But he won election as a Superior Court judge in 1988 and held that job until Democratic Gov. Michael F. Easley elevated him to the state Supreme Court in 2001. After Butterfield lost a bid in 2002 for election to that seat in his own right, Easley reinstated him on the lower court.

In 2004, when Democratic Rep. Frank W. Ballance Jr. gave up his seat midterm due to illness, party officials tapped Butterfield, a friend of Ballance, to succeed him. He defeated Republican security consultant Greg Dority in the July 20 special election by 44 percentage points in the decidedly Democratic district. In a repeat matchup for a full term that November, when more than three times as many people voted because of the presidential race, Butterfield won by 28 points. In 2006, he was unopposed.

Within months of arriving in Congress, Butterfield got involved in a parochial battle in the nation's capital — what to name the new Major League team that brought baseball back to Washington in 2005 after a 35-year absence. Some favored the old name, the Senators, but Democratic Mayor Anthony A. Williams suggested the Grays, after the Homestead Grays, a Negro League team in the 1940s. The Grays' star slugger, Buck Leonard, grew up in Butterfield's district, in Rocky Mount. Butterfield fired off letters to fellow House members and to baseball officials urging them to adopt the name. The team ended up being called the Nationals.

KEY VOTES

2006

No Stop broadband companies from favoring select Internet traffic
No Affirm U.S. commitment to war in Iraq and reject setting a withdrawal date for troops
No Repeal requirement for bilingual ballots at the polls
Yes Permit U.S. sale of civilian nuclear technology to India
No Build a 700-mile fence on the U.S.-Mexico border to curb illegal crossings
No Permit warrantless wiretaps of suspected terrorists

2005

No Intervene in the life-support case of Terri Schiavo
Yes Lift President Bush's restrictions on stem cell research funding
Yes Prohibit FBI access to library and bookstore records
No Approve free-trade pact with five Central American countries
Yes Pass energy policy overhaul favored by President Bush emphasizing domestic oil and gas production
No End mandatory preservation of habitat of endangered animal and plant species
Yes Ban torture of prisoners in U.S. custody

CQ VOTE STUDIES

	PARTY UNITY		PRESIDENTIAL SUPPORT	
	Support	Oppose	Support	Oppose
2006	89%	11%	37%	63%
2005	93%	7%	30%	70%
2004	87%	13%	27%	73%

INTEREST GROUPS

	AFL-CIO	ADA	CCUS	ACU
2006	93%	95%	47%	16%
2005	93%	85%	56%	12%
2004	—	35%	57%	0%

NORTH CAROLINA 1

Northeast — parts of Goldsboro, Rocky Mount and Greenville

Situated among eastern North Carolina tobacco fields and Baptist churches, the 1st is a poor, rural Democratic stronghold. It has the lowest education and income levels of any congressional district in the state.

The 1st, which takes in all of 13 counties and parts of 10 others, is the only black-majority district in the state — 50 percent of residents are black. The main body of the district sits along the Virginia border, with appendages winding south to take in parts of several of the region's commercial centers — Goldsboro, Kinston and Greenville, which shares East Carolina University with the adjacent 3rd.

The area's economy is based overwhelmingly on manufacturing and agriculture. Cotton and peanut fields prevail in the northern counties, while tobacco, hogs and poultry dominate farther south. Manufacturing, primarily of textiles and lumber products, is scattered throughout.

Registered Democrats outnumber Republicans by more than 4-to-1 in the 1st, and Democrats generally dominate. Although many white voters claim the Democratic roots of their forefathers, they often support GOP candidates at the state and national levels. Republicans also find support in coastal areas such as Perquimans and Chowan counties. In the 2004 gubernatorial race, Edgecombe County was Democratic Gov. Michael F. Easley's best county, and the other four counties in Easley's top five also are in the 1st, north of Edgecombe. The 1st supported Democrat John Kerry by a 14 percentage point margin in the 2004 presidential election.

MAJOR INDUSTRY
Agriculture, manufacturing, health care

MILITARY BASES
Marine Corps Air Station Cherry Point, 10,700 military, 5,500 civilian (2007); Seymour Johnson Air Force Base, 4,633 military, 1,029 civilian (2006)

CITIES
Goldsboro (pt.), 36,187; Rocky Mount (pt.), 32,062; Wilson (pt.), 25,068; Greenville (pt.), 22,028

NOTABLE
Caleb Bradham started selling "Brad's Drink" in 1898 at his New Bern drug store — the beverage is now known as Pepsi-Cola.

Rep. Bob Etheridge (D)

CAPITOL OFFICE
225-4531
www.house.gov/etheridge
1533 Longworth 20515-3302; fax 225-5662

COMMITTEES
Agriculture
(General Farm Commodities & Risk Management - chairman)
Budget
Homeland Security

RESIDENCE
Lillington

BORN
Aug. 7, 1941, Sampson County, N.C.

RELIGION
Presbyterian

FAMILY
Wife, Faye Cameron Etheridge; three children

EDUCATION
Campbell College, B.S. 1965 (business administration)

MILITARY SERVICE
Army, 1965-67

CAREER
Hardware store owner; tobacco farmer

POLITICAL HIGHLIGHTS
Harnett County Commission, 1973-77 (chairman, 1975-77); N.C. House, 1979-87; N.C. superintendent of Public Instruction, 1989-96

ELECTION RESULTS

2006 GENERAL		
Bob Etheridge (D)	85,993	66.5%
Dan Mansell (R)	43,271	33.5%
2006 PRIMARY		
Bob Etheridge (D)		unopposed
2004 GENERAL		
Bob Etheridge (D)	145,079	62.3%
Billy J. Creech (R)	87,811	37.7%

PREVIOUS WINNING PERCENTAGES
2002 (65%); 2000 (58%); 1998 (57%); 1996 (53%)

Elected 1996; 6th term

North Carolina's 2nd District is home to many who work in the state capital of Raleigh or nearby Research Triangle Park. But it also takes in rural areas dotted with family farms, and Etheridge comes from one of those. He has been a hardware store owner, a part-time farmer, a Sunday school teacher and a Boy Scout leader. And for more than three decades, he has been a politician too, holding local, state and federal office.

The 2nd District voted Republican in each of the past three presidential elections, and Etheridge is well aware of that fact. A member of the moderate, pro-business New Democrat Coalition, he typically splits with the more liberal majority of House Democrats about 15 percent of the time. The Raleigh News & Observer, which endorsed his 2006 re-election bid, called him "a canny middle-of-the-roader with proven appeal across party lines."

Etheridge supports President Bush's position more often than the average House Democrat, but his backing is selective, varying from year to year depending on the specific positions the president has embraced. In 2006, for example, Etheridge sided with Bush on 50 percent of the roll call votes on which the president staked out a position. But the year before, he backed Bush only 24 percent of the time.

Etheridge was the only Democrat in the North Carolina delegation voting in 2002 to give Bush fast-track trade negotiating authority, which limits Congress' role in trade agreements. North Carolina's powerful textile lobby, which fears job losses from free-trade pacts, vowed retribution at the voting booth.

But the 2nd District is not so concerned with textiles. Etheridge has a strong base among his district's farmers, and the Raleigh area is focused on attracting technology firms. Etheridge has voted accordingly, and in the 108th Congress (2003-04) he continued his support for free-trade agreements, backing pacts with Chile, Singapore and Australia. He was one of just 22 House Democrats backing a trade deal with Oman in 2006; but the year before, he sided with a majority of his party in voting against the Central American Free Trade Agreement.

He watches out for farmers from his perch on the Agriculture Committee, where he now chairs the commodities subcommittee. That means he will play a major role in the rewrite of the 2002 farm law scheduled for the 110th Congress (2007-08). Despite his support for some degree of free trade, he is not about to slash payments to farmers to please negotiators in the so-called Doha round of world trade talks. "We're writing the farm bill," he says, "and Doha won't dictate it. Unless we see a major breakthrough in negotiations, we're not going to reduce payments."

Etheridge was pleased when Congress in 2004 enacted a buyout for tobacco farmers as part of a corporate tax cut bill. The measure meant $3.9 billion for farmers in North Carolina. Etheridge, a part-time tobacco farmer at the time, was one of eight members of Congress benefiting from the deal. He grows soybeans and grains and raises cattle. His greatest pleasure on weekends, he says, is to "get on the tractor. It takes me back."

Part of Fort Bragg is in his district, and Etheridge has been a supporter of U.S. troops fighting in Iraq. But he no longer backs the president's war policy. "After nearly four years of the Iraq War with thousands of lives lost, it is long past time for the president and the Congress to change course," he wrote in a Dec. 17, 2006, op-ed piece for the News & Observer. Earlier that year, he voted to oppose any move to set a timetable for withdrawal of

U.S. troops. But in early 2007, he voted against the president's decision to deploy thousands more troops to Iraq and in favor of a war funding bill that set an August 2008 target for a troop withdrawal.

Before coming to Congress, Etheridge was the head of North Carolina's public school system for almost eight years. He has spoken at length in the House of his desire to "build on what is working well in our public schools, rather than scapegoating public school principals, teachers, parents and children." He supported the No Child Left Behind Act in 2001, but says its mandatory testing and standards should not be enforced until the federal government provides all the funds authorized by the law — which it has never done. He believes the federal government should aid in school construction.

A member of the Homeland Security Committee, he proudly touts the 2006 implementation of legislation he introduced in 2002 to grant federal survivor benefits to the families of firefighters, police and emergency personnel who die in the line of duty from heart attacks or strokes. He credits one of his constituents for inspiring the law.

Born, raised and educated in east-central North Carolina, Etheridge spent his childhood on the family farm. When he went off to nearby Campbell College (now university), he spent most of his time on the basketball court. He got a full basketball scholarship and became team captain.

He first entered politics in 1972. He won election to the Harnett County Commission, serving for four years, the last two as chairman. In 1978, he won the first of four terms in the state House, where he rose to chair the Appropriations Committee. Then he moved to statewide office, holding the school superintendency for about eight years.

During his years as state school superintendent, Etheridge came under pressure to run for Congress. He says Democratic Party officials urged him to run in both 1988 and in 1994. He turned them down.

But in 1996, he finally said yes. Freshman Republican David Funderburk had been a zealous supporter of the House GOP's conservative agenda in the 104th Congress (1995-96). Following the national Democratic script, Etheridge called Funderburk a threat to entitlement programs such as Social Security, Medicare and Medicaid. Etheridge's deep local roots helped him win with 53 percent of the vote.

In 1998, conservative state Sen. Dan Page and the national GOP went after Etheridge aggressively, seeking to tie him to President Bill Clinton and his White House sex scandal. But Etheridge had given Republicans little opportunity to tag him as a liberal, and he won by 16 percentage points.

He has coasted ever since. He captured two-thirds of the vote in 2006.

KEY VOTES

2006

- No Stop broadband companies from favoring select Internet traffic
- Yes Affirm U.S. commitment to war in Iraq and reject setting a withdrawal date for troops
- No Repeal requirement for bilingual ballots at the polls
- Yes Permit U.S. sale of civilian nuclear technology to India
- Yes Build a 700-mile fence on the U.S.-Mexico border to curb illegal crossings
- No Permit warrantless wiretaps of suspected terrorists

2005

- Yes Intervene in the life-support case of Terri Schiavo
- Yes Lift President Bush's restrictions on stem cell research funding
- Yes Prohibit FBI access to library and bookstore records
- No Approve free-trade pact with five Central American countries
- Yes Pass energy policy overhaul favored by President Bush emphasizing domestic oil and gas production
- No End mandatory preservation of habitat of endangered animal and plant species
- Yes Ban torture of prisoners in U.S. custody

CQ VOTE STUDIES

	PARTY UNITY		PRESIDENTIAL SUPPORT	
	Support	Oppose	Support	Oppose
2006	84%	16%	50%	50%
2005	88%	12%	24%	76%
2004	85%	15%	47%	53%
2003	90%	10%	33%	67%
2002	87%	13%	50%	50%

INTEREST GROUPS

	AFL-CIO	ADA	CCUS	ACU
2006	93%	80%	60%	44%
2005	100%	95%	52%	16%
2004	87%	85%	52%	20%
2003	87%	90%	47%	32%
2002	78%	80%	60%	24%

NORTH CAROLINA 2

Central — parts of Raleigh and Fayetteville

From the thriving state capital of Raleigh, the 2nd pinwheels east, north and south to take in several surrounding rural counties and part of Fayetteville. While the high-tech Research Triangle Park, the area's economic hub, lies in the neighboring 4th, its influence radiates through the low hills of this eastern Piedmont district.

Research Triangle techies, university academics and government employees live in Raleigh (shared with the 4th and 13th districts) and form the basis of the district's Democratic tilt. Much of the region consists of booming and increasingly urban bedroom communities such as Garner. Sprawl has begun to infiltrate surrounding counties as well, but they still rely primarily on tobacco farming (especially in Johnston and Harnett counties) and blue-collar manufacturing jobs. The district has a strong military presence, as it includes Pope Air Force Base and part of Fort Bragg (shared with the 7th and 8th), located at the southwestern edge of the district.

Although a 24-point district registration advantage exaggerates the Democratic party's strength — Republicans run well in areas such as Johnston County despite the Democratic edge — the GOP has a tough time here in local races. The 2nd's Democratic lean is aided by the presence of a black-majority section of Fayetteville, and the district also contains the mostly black and strongly Democratic southeastern part of Raleigh. The 2nd has a higher percentage of Hispanic residents (8 percent) than any other district in the state.

MAJOR INDUSTRY

Technology, government, military, agriculture, manufacturing

MILITARY BASES

Fort Bragg (Army), 43,003 military, 9,954 civilian (2006) (shared with the 7th and 8th); Pope Air Force Base, 6,381 military, 774 civilian (2004)

CITIES

Fayetteville (pt.), 49,899; Raleigh (pt.), 45,368; Fort Bragg (unincorporated), 29,183; Sanford, 23,220

NOTABLE

A highway sign — made of brick — outside Sanford claims that it is the brick capital of the United States; The Harnett County town of Erwin grew up around a denim plant, formerly called itself the "denim capital of the world," and still holds a fall festival called "Denim Days."

Rep. Walter B. Jones (R)

CAPITOL OFFICE
225-3415
congjones@mail.house.gov
www.house.gov/jones
2333 Rayburn 20515-3303; fax 225-3286

COMMITTEES
Armed Services
Financial Services

RESIDENCE
Farmville

BORN
Feb. 10, 1943, Farmville, N.C.

RELIGION
Roman Catholic

FAMILY
Wife, Joe Anne Jones; one child

EDUCATION
North Carolina State U., attended 1962-65 (history); Atlantic Christian College, B.A. 1968 (history)

MILITARY SERVICE
N.C. National Guard, 1967-71

CAREER
Lighting company executive; insurance benefits company executive; office supply company executive

POLITICAL HIGHLIGHTS
N.C. House, 1983-93 (served as a Democrat); sought Democratic nomination for U.S. House, 1992

ELECTION RESULTS

2006 GENERAL		
Walter B. Jones (R)	99,519	68.6%
Craig Weber (D)	45,458	31.4%
2006 PRIMARY		
Walter B. Jones (R)		unopposed
2004 GENERAL		
Walter B. Jones (R)	171,863	70.7%
Roger A. Eaton (D)	71,227	29.3%

PREVIOUS WINNING PERCENTAGES
2002 (91%); 2000 (61%); 1998 (62%); 1996 (63%); 1994 (53%)

Elected 1994; 7th term

Jones was the Bush administration's early warning signal in the House of cracks in Republican support for the war in Iraq. A conservative from a pro-military district who voted for going to war, Jones turned against the White House in June 2005, joining House Democrats in a resolution calling on the president to develop a plan to withdraw U.S. troops.

His change of heart was not without risk for Jones politically. It met with hostility from soldiers stationed at Camp Lejeune, the East Coast headquarters for the Marine Corps, located in his district. When President Bush made a public appearance in Fayetteville, not far from Jones' district, Jones was not invited to share the stage with the president.

Some local Republicans also disapproved, and there was talk of a primary challenge to Jones in the 2006 election. But Jones acted aggressively to head one off, making repeated trips home and holding town hall meetings at which he explained his position. Ultimately, there was no challenge from within his party and Jones was returned to the House with nearly 70 percent of the vote.

Jones is now as vocal in opposing the war as he was in supporting it initially. It was Jones who in 2003 coined the phrase "freedom fries" as an alternative to French fries, to protest France's refusal to support the U.S. invasion of Iraq. But as more became known about the buildup to the war, Jones felt betrayed by the administration's reliance on faulty intelligence. He took to the House floor, quoting English poet and author Rudyard Kipling: "If any question why we died, tell them because our fathers lied."

After reading investigative reporter James Bamford's "A Pretext for War," an indictment of the administration's prewar intelligence, Jones arranged briefings with Bamford for several House members. Later in 2006, he accepted an offer from Democratic Leader Harry Reid of Nevada to attend a Senate Democratic Policy Committee meeting to hear testimony from retired generals and former administration officials. Jones said later, "When you send kids to die for a country, you need to make it nonpartisan."

In February 2007, he was among 17 Republicans to vote for the Democrats' resolution disapproving of Bush's plan to send more than 21,000 additional combat troops to Iraq. The following month, he was one of just two Republicans who voted for the House's war funding bill that set an August 2008 deadline for withdrawal of U.S. troops from Iraq.

Jones also wants to be sure Congress has a say in any engagement with Iran. In January 2007, he introduced a non-binding bipartisan resolution stating that unless Iran attacked the United States, the president would have to get "specific authorization pursuant to law from Congress, prior to initiating any use of military force against Iran."

With the exception of the Iraq War, Jones is usually to the right of Bush. In the 109th Congress (2005-06), he supported the president's positions only 57 percent of the time, about the same rate as the most liberal Republicans who oppose Bush from the left.

He remains one of the few unreconstructed "true believers" of the GOP takeover Class of '94. He still sees little virtue in compromise. In July 2006, Jones quit the Republican Study Committee, a group of the most conservative House members, after RSC chairman Mike Pence of Indiana announced a compromise position on illegal immigration. Jones favored a harder line calling for deporting illegal aliens and more border security.

His signature issue is a so-far unsuccessful effort to allow churches to take part in political activity without fear of losing their tax-exempt status. He also wants to mandate that local school boards create parents' committees to review library books in elementary schools, a move spurred by his discovery of a Norwegian children's book, entitled "King and King," about two kings who fall in love.

Jones has backed measures to make English the nation's official language, to provide vouchers to help parents pay for private school tuition and to outlaw same-sex marriage. He advocates phasing out the tax code.

He is especially frustrated by his party's spending habits and has joined a minority of Republicans in voting against GOP-written budgets. In 2004, he urged fellow conservatives to form a "suicide squad" to vote no on spending increases under any circumstances — an example he had set a year earlier by refusing to vote for the GOP's Medicare prescription drug bill despite a long night of arm-twisting by Bush and party leaders. Regardless of his calls for belt-tightening, he rarely fails to get behind federal programs popular in his district, such as the price-support program for peanut growers.

On the Armed Services Committee, Jones looks out for the military installations in the 3rd District, and has written a number of bills aimed at improving pay, benefits and housing for military personnel and veterans.

He was one of 27 Republicans to vote against the Central American Free Trade Agreement in 2005, a highly sensitive issue in his textile-producing state. And he usually joins Democrats to oppose offshore oil and gas drilling due to its potential impact on tourism at Outer Banks beaches in his district.

Jones grew up around politics and government. His father was Democratic Rep. Walter B. Jones Sr., a pragmatist who was a bit more liberal than his son. Jones attended Virginia's Hargrave Military Academy, which emphasized Christian values and where he became a standout basketball player. He graduated from Atlantic Christian College in 1968. Jones did a stint in the National Guard and then took a job as a wine broker with a region covering North Carolina and Virginia. Raised a Baptist, he converted to Catholicism when he was 29.

Jones was almost 40 when he followed his father into politics. In 1982, the local Democratic Party asked him to finish the term of a state assemblyman who had died in office. Jones wound up staying for a decade.

In 1992, the senior Jones fell ill and retired from the House. Jones ran for his father's 1st District seat as a Democrat, but lost a primary runoff. The next year, he registered as a Republican, feeling he had more in common with the GOP philosophically, including his opposition to abortion. He ran in the 3rd District in 1994, and was swept into office by the strong GOP tide that year.

KEY VOTES

2006

Yes Stop broadband companies from favoring select Internet traffic
P Affirm U.S. commitment to war in Iraq and reject setting a withdrawal date for troops
Yes Repeal requirement for bilingual ballots at the polls
No Permit U.S. sale of civilian nuclear technology to India
Yes Build a 700-mile fence on the U.S.-Mexico border to curb illegal crossings
No Permit warrantless wiretaps of suspected terrorists

2005

Yes Intervene in the life-support case of Terri Schiavo
No Lift President Bush's restrictions on stem cell research funding
Yes Prohibit FBI access to library and bookstore records
No Approve free-trade pact with five Central American countries
No Pass energy policy overhaul favored by President Bush emphasizing domestic oil and gas production
Yes End mandatory preservation of habitat of endangered animal and plant species
Yes Ban torture of prisoners in U.S. custody

CQ VOTE STUDIES

	PARTY UNITY		PRESIDENTIAL SUPPORT	
	Support	Oppose	Support	Oppose
2006	64%	36%	53%	47%
2005	81%	19%	61%	39%
2004	86%	14%	75%	25%
2003	86%	14%	73%	27%
2002	89%	11%	72%	28%

INTEREST GROUPS

	AFL-CIO	ADA	CCUS	ACU
2006	62%	45%	50%	79%
2005	17%	45%	58%	80%
2004	36%	30%	70%	79%
2003	33%	25%	70%	92%
2002	22%	10%	63%	96%

NORTH CAROLINA 3

East — Jacksonville, part of Greenville, Outer Banks

The 3rd runs along the eastern shore from the Virginia border to north of Wilmington, sweeping from the fragile barrier islands of the Outer Banks to the tobacco and peanut fields of the coastal plain. It is a large swath of rural land inlaid with waterways, affluent vacation towns and military facilities; the closest thing to skyscrapers here are historic lighthouses that dot the shoreline.

Many residents earn their living through fishing, farming and tourism. The 3rd's military bases have a large impact on the economy, particularly Camp Lejeune, which deployed a high percentage of its Marines abroad following the Sept. 11, 2001, terrorist attacks. From the southernmost coast, two fingers of land reach northwest, taking in turkey, hog and wheat farms.

The western leg of the 3rd stretches from Onslow County in the south, where Jacksonville and Camp Lejeune are located, all the way north to Nash County, including western Rocky Mount. Another leg stretches northwest to Greenville in Pitt County, where the main part of the East Carolina University campus is located (shared with the 1st).

Although registered Democrats still outnumber Republicans here, the 3rd has a conservative bent and supports GOP candidates on the federal level. George W. Bush took 68 percent of the 2004 presidential vote here, and the district's portions of Lenoir and Jones counties were Bush's second- and third-best counties in the state.

MAJOR INDUSTRY

Military, agriculture, tourism

MILITARY BASES

Camp Lejeune Marine Corps Base, 43,000 military, 4,861 civilian (2005); New River Marine Corps Air Station, 6,000 military, 600 civilian (2007)

CITIES

Jacksonville, 66,715; Greenville (pt.), 38,448; Wilson (pt.), 19,337

NOTABLE

Dare County is named for Virginia Dare, the first child born of English parents in America (1587); Kitty Hawk is where Wilbur and Orville Wright made their first flight; The infamous pirate Edward Teach, better known as Blackbeard, lived in Hammock House in Beaufort.

Rep. David E. Price (D)

CAPITOL OFFICE
225-1784
price.house.gov
2162 Rayburn 20515-3304; fax 225-2014

COMMITTEES
Appropriations
(Homeland Security - chairman)

RESIDENCE
Chapel Hill

BORN
Aug. 17, 1940, Erwin, Tenn.

RELIGION
Baptist

FAMILY
Wife, Lisa Price; two children

EDUCATION
Mars Hill College, attended 1957-59; U. of North Carolina, B.A. 1961 (American history & math); Yale U., B.D. 1964 (theology), Ph.D. 1969 (political science)

CAREER
Professor

POLITICAL HIGHLIGHTS
N.C. Democratic Party chairman, 1983-84; U.S. House, 1987-95; defeated for re-election to U.S. House, 1994

ELECTION RESULTS

2006 GENERAL		
David E. Price (D)	127,340	65.0%
Steve Acuff (R)	68,599	35.0%
2006 PRIMARY		
David E. Price (D)	39,637	89.5%
Kent Kanoy (D)	2,768	6.2%
Oscar Lewis (D)	1,886	4.3%
2004 GENERAL		
David E. Price (D)	217,441	64.1%
Todd A. Batchelor (R)	121,717	35.9%

PREVIOUS WINNING PERCENTAGES
2002 (61%); 2000 (62%); 1998 (57%); 1996 (54%); 1992 (65%); 1990 (58%); 1988 (58%); 1986 (56%)

Elected 1986; 10th term
Did not serve 1995-97

After almost two decades in Congress, Price has his first position of real power as the chairman of the House Appropriations Homeland Security Subcommittee. He intended to use the post to help Democrats refocus federal funds to combat the most urgent terrorism threats.

He also wanted to beef up the Federal Emergency Management Agency, a part of the Department of Homeland Security that was universally assailed for its botched response to Hurricane Katrina in 2005. "The reason I'm so concerned about FEMA is because North Carolina is in hurricane alley," Price says. "We need to press on improvements."

Price is not shy about using his Appropriations seat to funnel money to North Carolina and his district. With the defeat of Republican Charles H. Taylor, who chaired the Interior Subcommittee in the 109th Congress (2005-06), Price is the Tar Heel state's only representative on the spending panel. Even during his years in the minority, he snagged millions of dollars annually for the 4th District's many research facilities, both private and public, and for more mundane needs such as refurbishing Chapel Hill's buses and helping build a new wastewater treatment facility in Efland.

The 4th is home to Raleigh-Durham-Chapel Hill Research Triangle Park, where many academics and Northern transplants have come to work. Price is a perfect fit for a district that is home to 11 colleges and universities, including Duke, where he once taught political science. The son of a high school principal father and an English teacher mother, he uses his years on Capitol Hill to promote learning at every level. Price also is the author of four books on Congress and the U.S. political system.

With its highly educated constituency, the 4th is one of the South's more politically progressive districts — a fact that has allowed Price to indulge himself with a more liberal voting record than the typical Southern Democrat. But he tempers his liberalism with the occasional vote in support of tobacco growers and other traditional local interests. In 2004, for example, he was among the minority of Democrats who voted for a corporate tax bill that carried a $10 billion buyout for tobacco farmers.

Given his personal background and district makeup, Price cites education as a top priority. In 2004, the House passed a bill containing much of his Teaching Fellows Act, a measure to provide college scholarships to students who agree to become public school teachers. He considers it his proudest legislative achievement. In the 110th Congress (2007-08), he intended to press for additional measures aimed at improving teacher quality and retention.

In 2002, he sought to improve technical education and training programs at community colleges in a reauthorization of the Advanced Technology Education program at the National Science Foundation, which in 1993 was established by a Price-authored bill. Price scored a victory when Congress in 1997 passed legislation he had been advocating for several years that made interest on student loans tax deductible and permitted penalty-free withdrawals from IRAs for education expenses.

As the Bush administration seeks to restrain the growth of many domestic research enterprises and shift additional funds toward defense, Price fights to maintain research funding for non-defense purposes.

He voted for legislation in 2000 granting China permanent normal trade status, contending the measure would bolster U.S. jobs through increased exports. But since then, he — like the majority of his party — has become increasingly skeptical of the free-trade deals negotiated by the Bush administration. He opposed 2002 legislation granting the president fast-track trade negotiating authority, and he voted against the Central America Free Trade Agreement in 2005 and the Oman trade agreement in 2006.

He has also been a critic of the Iraq War, voting against the 2002 resolution authorizing President Bush to use force against the regime of Saddam Hussein and introducing a bill in October 2005 calling for a timetable for the withdrawal of U.S. troops.

Democratic leaders called on Price's political science background in 2001, naming him to an ad hoc committee to recommend improvements in election procedures. He also gets credit for helping to shape the truth-in-advertising provisions of the 2002 campaign finance law. In the 108th Congress (2003-04), he led an effort to increase cooperation between Congress and legislative bodies in developing nations, including such areas as staff training, information and technology access, and general promotion of legislative transparency and accountability.

On a more partisan level, national Democratic Party leaders in December 2004 tapped Price and former Labor Secretary Alexis Herman to lead a review of the party's nominating system, including its reliance on initial Iowa and New Hampshire contests dominated by rural, white voters.

Born in East Tennessee, Price got his undergraduate degree at the University of North Carolina and then went to Yale for graduate study, earning political science and divinity degrees. While teaching political science at Duke University in the 1970s, he became heavily involved in state Democratic politics. He served as chairman of the state party in 1983 and 1984, and in 1985 became a founding member of the national Democratic Leadership Council, which sought to expand the influence of party moderates.

The contacts Price made in his party work helped him raise money and attract supporters for a successful House race in 1986. After beating out three opponents for the Democratic nomination, he ousted freshman GOP Rep. Bill Cobey by 12 percentage points. He won re-election three times by comfortable margins but lost to former Raleigh Police Chief Fred Heineman by 1,215 votes in the GOP takeover landslide of 1994.

Price avenged that defeat in the next election, waging an aggressive campaign that emphasized door-to-door canvassing and plenty of personal contact with voters. He won by almost 11 percentage points in 1996 and has prevailed easily in subsequent elections. In a district made more comfortably Democratic after the last reapportionment, Price has not dipped below 60 percent in the past four elections.

KEY VOTES

2006

- Yes Stop broadband companies from favoring select Internet traffic
- No Affirm U.S. commitment to war in Iraq and reject setting a withdrawal date for troops
- No Repeal requirement for bilingual ballots at the polls
- Yes Permit U.S. sale of civilian nuclear technology to India
- No Build a 700-mile fence on the U.S.-Mexico border to curb illegal crossings
- No Permit warrantless wiretaps of suspected terrorists

2005

- No Intervene in the life-support case of Terri Schiavo
- Yes Lift President Bush's restrictions on stem cell research funding
- Yes Prohibit FBI access to library and bookstore records
- No Approve free-trade pact with five Central American countries
- No Pass energy policy overhaul favored by President Bush emphasizing domestic oil and gas production
- No End mandatory preservation of habitat of endangered animal and plant species
- Yes Ban torture of prisoners in U.S. custody

CQ VOTE STUDIES

	PARTY UNITY		PRESIDENTIAL SUPPORT	
	Support	Oppose	Support	Oppose
2006	92%	8%	33%	67%
2005	96%	4%	16%	84%
2004	90%	10%	41%	59%
2003	92%	8%	25%	75%
2002	92%	8%	38%	62%

INTEREST GROUPS

	AFL-CIO	ADA	CCUS	ACU
2006	100%	95%	47%	4%
2005	93%	100%	48%	4%
2004	87%	95%	52%	12%
2003	80%	90%	43%	24%
2002	78%	95%	55%	0%

NORTH CAROLINA 4

Central – Durham, Chapel Hill, part of Raleigh

The 4th revolves around Research Triangle Park and the three major universities at the vertices of the triangle. The medical and technological research park was created in the 1950s by a group of academics, politicians and businessmen who saw a need to diversify the state's economy beyond the traditional tobacco and textile industries. While based primarily in the Triangle, the 4th also passes through the rolling hills and evergreen forests of the piedmont region.

Duke University in Durham represents the northern point of the triangle, while the University of North Carolina at Chapel Hill takes up the western point and North Carolina State University in Raleigh (shared with the 2nd and 13th districts) is the southeastern point. A strong university and research presence gives the 4th the state's highest education rate, with nearly half of residents age 25 and older holding a college degree.

As the Research Triangle grew, especially in the 1980s, the Durham of James B. Duke's Lucky Strike cigarettes largely disappeared, and developers began converting tobacco warehouses into apartment buildings. The region's educational and technological strengths have helped the Raleigh-Durham area land a spot on the Forbes top 10 best places for business and career for four years in a row, peaking at number 2 in 2006. The district has North Carolina's second-highest median income.

The 4th is a Democratic stronghold, with the party drawing support not only from the large black population in Durham but also from the liberal atmosphere surrounding the university in Chapel Hill. A Democrat has held the district's House seat for all but four years since 1969, but the area's highly educated voters — one in five holds a postgraduate or professional degree — can be independent-minded.

MAJOR INDUSTRY

Technology research, higher education

CITIES

Durham, 187,035; Cary (pt.), 83,478; Chapel Hill, 48,715; Raleigh (pt.), 38,149

NOTABLE

Universities in the 4th have won seven of the last 26 NCAA Division I men's basketball championships; Home to the Durham Bulls baseball team; The University of North Carolina at Chapel Hill, the nation's first state university, was chartered in 1789 and opened to students in 1795.

Rep. Virginia Foxx (R)

CAPITOL OFFICE
225-2071
www.foxx.house.gov
430 Cannon 20515-3305; fax 225-2995

COMMITTEES
Agriculture
Education & Labor
Oversight & Government Reform

RESIDENCE
Watauga County

BORN
June 29, 1943, Bronx, N.Y.

RELIGION
Roman Catholic

FAMILY
Husband, Tom Foxx; one child

EDUCATION
Lees-McRae College, attended 1961; Appalachian State Teachers' College, attended 1962-63; U. of North Carolina, B.A. 1968 (English), M.A.C.T. 1972 (sociology); U. of North Carolina, Greensboro, Ed.D. 1985 (curriculum and teaching/higher education)

CAREER
Community college president; nursery and landscaping company owner; state government official; professor; secretary

POLITICAL HIGHLIGHTS
Candidate for Watauga County Board of Education, 1974; Watauga County Board of Education, 1977-89; N.C. Senate, 1995-2004

ELECTION RESULTS

2006 GENERAL		
Virginia Foxx (R)	96,138	57.2%
Roger Sharpe (D)	72,061	42.8%
2006 PRIMARY		
Virginia Foxx (R)		unopposed
2004 GENERAL		
Virginia Foxx (R)	167,546	58.8%
Jim A. Harrell Jr. (D)	117,271	41.2%

Elected 2004; 2nd term

Foxx came to the House with a deep reserve of life experiences and a stubborn streak that have led her to defy her party's leaders from time to time, transforming her periodically from backbencher to swing voter.

Elected at age 61, she was one of the oldest members of the freshman class of 2004. She quickly drew on her decade in the North Carolina State Legislature as she maneuvered her way through Congress. "Having been in the legislature for 10 years, I have some sense of decorum and process," she said.

She also drew on her personal experiences growing up in the mountains of North Carolina. "I'm the eldest child of a very poor family, and I take everything I do seriously."

She was the first freshman to get a bill passed by the House in 2005, a measure allowing military personnel to put their combat pay into tax-deferred Individual Retirement Accounts. Previously, contributions to IRAs were limited to either $4,000 or the individual's taxable income, whichever was less. Foxx introduced the bill after hearing from a constituent whose son, while serving in Iraq, tried to contribute some combat pay to an IRA but was told he could not do so. Because combat pay is tax-exempt, many military personnel serving in Iraq and Afghanistan did not have any taxable earnings available for investment in IRAs.

Colleagues warned Foxx that as a new member, she would never get her bill through the House Ways and Means Committee unscathed. But she not only steered it through the committee and the full House, she saw it signed into law by President Bush in 2006.

Foxx is usually a party loyalist and dependable conservative vote. But she can dig in and refuse to compromise on occasion. In a GOP caucus where freshmen normally are eager to show party unity and stay in the good graces of their leaders, Foxx stood out like a sore thumb in 2005 when she opposed a popular bill funding the emergency spending needed after Hurricane Katrina, one of just 11 House members to do so. She also was one of 27 Republicans to vote against the Central American Free Trade Agreement, a major administration priority that passed the House by just two votes in 2005.

While GOP leaders dragooned a number of Republicans from states hit hard by manufacturing job losses into voting for CAFTA, Foxx was immovable. She told Bush in person she was not going to vote for the bill, and she fielded calls from Vice President Dick Cheney, Secretary of State Condoleezza Rice and U.S. Trade Representative Rob Portman during the CAFTA debate. When she took the floor and voted against the trade bill, then Speaker J. Dennis Hastert told her to wait around in the cloakroom, perhaps hoping she could be cajoled into changing her vote.

She couldn't be. "I made a promise during the campaign," Foxx said. "It was pivotal in terms of testing whether or not I would do what I promised."

In 2007, Hanesbrands Inc. announced the closing of its fabrics plant in Winston-Salem as its pursued lower-cost production in the Caribbean and Central America. Foxx told constituents that was why she voted against CAFTA.

But she has displeased many of her constituents on the issue of Iraq. In 2006, after a visit to Iraq, she reportedly gave a glowing report about the progress of the war. Letters from her critics flowed into the local Winston-Salem Journal. And in early 2007, she backed Bush's plan to increase troop levels. Criticizing the Democrats' resolution disapproving of the plan, she stated on the House floor, "This is the decisive battle of our generation, and this is a defining moment of our time. We cannot afford to lose."

Foxx had a hardscrabble upbringing in the mountain hollows of western North Carolina. She is the granddaughter of Italian immigrants, and the family struggled to get by. She grew up in a house that did not have running water or electricity until she was 14 years old.

"There's no reason why somebody with my background should make it to Congress," she says. "I believe I've lived the American dream."

In her teens, she was the janitor at her high school as part of an after-school job. As she was sweeping floors one day, a teacher told her she was smart and needed to go to college, marry a college man and get out of town.

She did all three. She got her bachelor's and advanced degrees from the University of North Carolina. A small-town girl, she briefly tried out New York City in the mid-1960s, where she worked as a typist on Wall Street. But she returned to the mountains of North Carolina and married Tom Foxx, who came from similarly humble beginnings. (He lived out of a school bus his final years in high school.) They settled in Watauga County and started a successful nursery and landscaping business.

She says her husband influenced her political views. She became a strong backer of the Republican Party, even though her parents were Democrats.

Foxx serves on the Agriculture Committee, a key assignment for a member whose district has both tobacco farms and a thriving Christmas tree industry. She will be working to protect both as Congress tackles a scheduled rewrite of the 2002 farm bill in the 110th Congress (2007-08).

A former member of the county school board and a college professor, Foxx also sits on the Education and Labor Committee. In 2005, she won adoption of a committee amendment to the higher education reauthorization bill that prohibited the Education Department from creating a database to compile the personal information of college students.

Foxx lives on the western edge of the sprawling 5th District, whose population center of Winston-Salem and surrounding Forsyth County is a good 90-minute drive from her mountain home.

She got her start in politics during a dozen years on the Watauga County Board of Education, and then served for a decade in the state Senate. When 5th District Republican Rep. Richard M. Burr decided to run for the Senate in 2004, Foxx joined the race to succeed him — as did seven other Republicans. In the primary, she narrowly trailed Vernon Robinson, a conservative African-American on the Winston-Salem City Council. She defeated him in a runoff, and went on to best Democrat Jim A. Harrell Jr. in November.

In 2006, she was unopposed in the primary and prevailed against Democrat Roger Sharpe, taking 57 percent of the vote.

KEY VOTES

2006

- No Stop broadband companies from favoring select Internet traffic
- Yes Affirm U.S. commitment to war in Iraq and reject setting a withdrawal date for troops
- Yes Repeal requirement for bilingual ballots at the polls
- Yes Permit U.S. sale of civilian nuclear technology to India
- Yes Build a 700-mile fence on the U.S.-Mexico border to curb illegal crossings
- Yes Permit warrantless wiretaps of suspected terrorists

2005

- Yes Intervene in the life-support case of Terri Schiavo
- No Lift President Bush's restrictions on stem cell research funding
- No Prohibit FBI access to library and bookstore records
- No Approve free-trade pact with five Central American countries
- Yes Pass energy policy overhaul favored by President Bush emphasizing domestic oil and gas production
- Yes End mandatory preservation of habitat of endangered animal and plant species
- No Ban torture of prisoners in U.S. custody

CQ VOTE STUDIES

	PARTY UNITY		PRESIDENTIAL SUPPORT	
	Support	Oppose	Support	Oppose
2006	97%	3%	83%	17%
2005	99%	1%	87%	13%

INTEREST GROUPS

	AFL-CIO	ADA	CCUS	ACU
2006	14%	5%	93%	96%
2005	20%	5%	78%	100%

NORTH CAROLINA 5

Northwest – part of Winston-Salem

This northern Piedmont district stretches west from Winston-Salem through rolling hills and rural towns to the Tennessee border. Its northern counties, which run along the Virginia border, are filled with small rural towns such as Mount Airy, the childhood home of Andy Griffith and the inspiration for the fictional setting of his 1960s television series.

The district's major population center is in Winston-Salem and surrounding Forsyth County, home to R.J. Reynolds Tobacco. The company's corporate headquarters is in the 12th District (which has most of Winston-Salem), but its largest plant is in the 5th, in the appropriately named town of Tobaccoville. The economy of Forsyth County has veered away from its one-time mainstays, tobacco and textiles. Tobacco production still employs many people, but it now ranks second to health care, partly because of Wake Forest University's medical center.

With the decline of the tobacco industry, many tobacco farmers have converted their farms into vineyards and wineries. The 1.4 million acre Yadkin Valley wine region, most of which is in the district, has become a tourist destination. The 5th also is home to the Krispy Kreme Doughnuts headquarters, a BB&T division headquarters and a Tyson Foods division. A Dell manufacturing site on the edge of Winston-Salem opened in 2005, creating hundreds of jobs and aiming to eventually employ thousands.

Textile and blue-collar work still prevails in other counties, and grazing cattle wander over Surry County's low, rolling hills. The 5th is the state's most rural district and is solid GOP territory. The party dominates Davie and Yadkin counties, west of Winston-Salem, with Yadkin serving as the state's best county for George W. Bush in the 2004 presidential race. The 5th's share of the largely Democratic Forsyth County leans Republican, as most of Winston-Salem's sizable black population is in the 12th.

MAJOR INDUSTRY

Health care, tobacco, textiles, agriculture

CITIES

Winston-Salem (pt.), 69,790; Statesville (pt.), 23,280; Kernersville, 17,126

NOTABLE

First organized in 1924, the Old Time Fiddlers Convention (now called the Ole Time Fiddler's and Bluegrass Festival) in Union Grove is the longest-running bluegrass festival in the nation and has been recognized with a Local Legacy award from the Library of Congress.

Rep. Howard Coble (R)

CAPITOL OFFICE
225-3065
howard.coble@mail.house.gov
coble.house.gov
2468 Rayburn 20515-3306; fax 225-8611

COMMITTEES
Judiciary
Transportation & Infrastructure

RESIDENCE
Greensboro

BORN
March 18, 1931, Greensboro, N.C.

RELIGION
Presbyterian

FAMILY
Single

EDUCATION
Appalachian State Teachers' College, attended 1949-50 (history); Guilford College, A.B. 1958 (history); U. of North Carolina, J.D. 1962

MILITARY SERVICE
Coast Guard, 1952-56; Coast Guard Reserve, 1960-82; Coast Guard, 1977-78

CAREER
Lawyer; insurance claims supervisor

POLITICAL HIGHLIGHTS
N.C. House, 1969; assistant U.S. attorney, 1969-73; N.C. Department of Revenue secretary, 1973-77; Republican nominee for N.C. treasurer, 1976; N.C. House, 1979-83

ELECTION RESULTS

2006 GENERAL		
Howard Coble (R)	108,433	70.8%
Rory Blake (D)	44,661	29.2%
2006 PRIMARY		
Howard Coble (R)		unopposed
2004 GENERAL		
Howard Coble (R)	207,470	73.2%
William W. Jordan (D)	76,153	26.9%

PREVIOUS WINNING PERCENTAGES
2002 (90%); 2000 (91%); 1998 (89%); 1996 (73%); 1994 (100%); 1992 (71%); 1990 (67%); 1988 (62%); 1986 (50%); 1984 (51%)

Elected 1984; 12th term

A cigar-smoking, tough-talking former prosecutor, Coble was in line to become the top-ranking Republican on the House Judiciary Committee in the 110th Congress (2007-08), but seniority alone was not enough to get him the promotion to the most powerful job for the minority party on the committee.

Coble proved too independent for GOP leaders and the job instead went to Lamar Smith of Texas. Coble has tangled with his party and the Bush administration on several high-profile issues, most notably the war in Iraq and the Central America Free Trade Agreement (CAFTA). In 2007, after the Democrats took control of the House, Coble was one of only 17 Republicans who backed a Democratic resolution opposing President Bush's call for additional troops. "I've never been a real good rubber stamp," Coble says.

Coble has long been skeptical of Bush's Iraq policy. He was one of the first House Republicans to openly question the continued U.S. military deployment, saying in 2005, "I am not convinced that maintaining a presence there is going to serve our national interest measurably."

Then in 2006, Coble criticized the administration's planning for a new Iraqi government post-invasion. The White House either had "no strategy or it was a badly flawed strategy," he said. "If I knew about the imperfect or inept preparations, I probably would have voted against dispatching troops."

He has consistently voted against the administration's requests to Congress to fund the war, opposing a $94.5 billion war and hurricane supplemental spending bill in 2006 and an $82 billion supplemental bill in 2005. He also was among a small group of Republicans in early 2007 who voted in opposition to Bush's plan to send more combat troops into Iraq.

Coble was at odds with his party on other big issues in the 109th Congress (2005-06). He supported federal funding of embryonic stem cell research, which many conservatives oppose on grounds it is a form of abortion. He voted against the free-trade agreement with Central America and also against free-trade pacts with Oman and Bahrain, and he opposed Republican efforts to cap monetary damages in lawsuits.

Coble had to withstand pressure from GOP leaders and the president on the trade pacts, particularly CAFTA, which he considered an important personal issue, as well as a sensitive one for his home state, where many of the nation's remaining textile factories are located. His mother sewed pockets onto overalls in a North Carolina textile factory in the days before air conditioning. Textile workers in his district viewed the trade agreement as a threat to their jobs. Coble told Bush during a White House visit, "When I go into these plants and have employees plead with me to vote no, that's my mama talking to me." When the president offered to make an appearance in his district, Coble declined, saying he had a prior commitment that day. He was one of only 27 Republicans to vote against CAFTA in 2005.

He was also one of the very few to earn the support of the Association of Trial Lawyers of America, a trade group closely associated with Democrats that has fought GOP attempts to cap damages in lawsuits. Coble says the issue "ought to be resolved by jurors."

On most fiscal and social matters, Coble remains a reliable Southern conservative vote. In his opposition to the 2006 spending bill, he said it pushed the nation closer to financial crisis. "We're hemorrhaging," Coble told the Greensboro News & Record newspaper, and he called the Iraq War a financial "albatross hanging around our neck."

He regularly attacks wasteful government spending, and has called for extending the service requirement for graduates of military academies from five years to eight years, saying the current payback for their education is inadequate. He is one of the few lawmakers who declines to participate in the congressional pension program, calling it "a taxpayer ripoff." He has tried without success to scale it back.

Coble is less concerned about the spending the government does in his home state. From his seat on the Transportation and Infrastructure Committee, he unapologetically helped secure $50 million for his district in the 2005 surface transportation bill. "Those of us on the Transportation Committee usually do pretty well, and I have no problem with that," he said. "I think your own committee should take care of you."

As chairman of the Judiciary panel's Crime, Terrorism and Homeland Security Subcommittee during the 109th Congress, he found little fault with the Bush administration's policy of indefinite detention, without trial, of suspected terrorists at the U.S. naval base in Guantánamo Bay, Cuba. And he once told a reporter he agreed with the detention of Japanese-Americans during World War II, but after a flurry of criticism, retracted the statement.

The Homeland Security Subcommittee chairmanship put him in the middle of the fight over renewing the Patriot Act, the 2001 anti-terrorism law. He backed giving law enforcement the power to seize library and bookstore records. A Coast Guard veteran, he knows security issues and has pushed for more federal money for port security. "I have a deep feeling the messengers of evil will come next time through a port or harbor," Coble says.

In 2007, he became top-ranking member of the subcommittee dealing with courts and intellectual property — a panel he chaired in 1997-2002.

Coble was a federal prosecutor and then North Carolina's chief tax collector in the mid-1970s. After four years as a state representative, he considered running for governor in 1984, but instead became the GOP's candidate against freshman Democratic Rep. Robin Britt after winning the primary by 164 votes. Coble stressed his fiscal conservatism while painting Britt as an extravagant liberal who had voted against President Ronald Reagan on two of every three votes in 1983. Tapping into the votes of conservative Democrats who crossed party lines in Reagan's re-election landslide that year, Coble won by 2,662 votes.

Britt plotted a comeback, and in 1986 only 79 votes separated him from Coble. Britt challenged the election results, but was unsuccessful. Coble has had little to worry about since. He garnered more than 70 percent of the vote in 2004 and 2006.

KEY VOTES

2006

No Stop broadband companies from favoring select Internet traffic
Yes Affirm U.S. commitment to war in Iraq and reject setting a withdrawal date for troops
Yes Repeal requirement for bilingual ballots at the polls
Yes Permit U.S. sale of civilian nuclear technology to India
Yes Build a 700-mile fence on the U.S.-Mexico border to curb illegal crossings
Yes Permit warrantless wiretaps of suspected terrorists

2005

\+ Intervene in the life-support case of Terri Schiavo
Yes Lift President Bush's restrictions on stem cell research funding
No Prohibit FBI access to library and bookstore records
No Approve free-trade pact with five Central American countries
Yes Pass energy policy overhaul favored by President Bush emphasizing domestic oil and gas production
Yes End mandatory preservation of habitat of endangered animal and plant species
No Ban torture of prisoners in U.S. custody

CQ VOTE STUDIES

	PARTY UNITY		PRESIDENTIAL SUPPORT	
	Support	Oppose	Support	Oppose
2006	94%	6%	73%	27%
2005	94%	6%	78%	22%
2004	94%	6%	71%	29%
2003	96%	4%	87%	13%
2002	95%	5%	82%	18%

INTEREST GROUPS

	AFL-CIO	ADA	CCUS	ACU
2006	15%	10%	93%	92%
2005	20%	10%	78%	84%
2004	13%	5%	95%	88%
2003	13%	50%	86%	80%
2002	11%	10%	75%	92%

NORTH CAROLINA 6
Central — parts of Greensboro and High Point

Located in the heart of the state, the 6th takes in part of the city of Greensboro and surrounding Guilford County, then spreads south to Moore County to pick up the upscale golf and retirement centers of Southern Pines and Pinehurst — host to two men's U.S. Open Championships in the last decade — near Fort Bragg. Solid GOP turf, the district gave George W. Bush his best showing in the state (69 percent) in the 2004 presidential race.

The 6th takes in two large chunks of Guilford County that are connected at a single point, on the Reedy Fork Creek in the northern part of the county. The Guilford portions surround Greensboro, although most of the city's more diverse and Democratic-leaning population resides in the 12th or 13th district. The rural part of the 6th is tobacco country: 2,000 residents are employed in factories for two brands owned by Lorillard Tobacco Company, which is based in the 13th.

Greensboro is home to a blend of manufacturing and service companies, particularly in the textile, furniture and insurance industries. It also hosts the North American headquarters of Volvo Trucks, and boasts a major office of the VF Corp. (Wrangler Jeans). An American Express regional credit card service center and six colleges and universities have helped to diversify Greensboro's economy. By 2009, FedEx expects to operate out of a new regional hub at Greensboro's Piedmont-Triad International Airport.

As in much of the state, trade issues loom large here, particularly in the textile and furniture industries. Nearby High Point is a national furniture manufacturing hub, and its market draws 75,000 people annually. Foreign competition from Asia and elsewhere, as well as attempts by Las Vegas officials to lure furniture trade shows to their new convention center, threaten High Point's dominance.

MAJOR INDUSTRY
Tobacco, textiles, furniture manufacturing

CITIES
Greensboro (pt.), 59,010; High Point (pt.), 33,404; Asheboro, 21,672

NOTABLE
The Richard Petty Museum in Randleman honors the NASCAR legend, who voiced the character "The King," based on Petty's #43 car, in Pixar's 2006 movie "Cars."

Rep. Mike McIntyre (D)

CAPITOL OFFICE
225-2731
congmcintyre@mail.house.gov
www.house.gov/mcintyre
2437 Rayburn 20515-3307; fax 225-5773

COMMITTEES
Agriculture
(Specialty Crops, Rural Development & Foreign Agriculture - chairman)
Armed Services

RESIDENCE
Lumberton

BORN
Aug. 6, 1956, Lumberton, N.C.

RELIGION
Presbyterian

FAMILY
Wife, Dee McIntyre; two children

EDUCATION
U. of North Carolina, B.A. 1978 (political science), J.D. 1981

CAREER
Lawyer

POLITICAL HIGHLIGHTS
No previous office

ELECTION RESULTS

2006 GENERAL		
Mike McIntyre (D)	101,787	72.8%
Shirley Davis (R)	38,033	27.2%
2006 PRIMARY		
Mike McIntyre (D)		unopposed
2004 GENERAL		
Mike McIntyre (D)	180,382	73.2%
Ken Plonk (R)	66,084	26.8%

PREVIOUS WINNING PERCENTAGES
2002 (71%); 2000 (70%); 1998 (91%); 1996 (53%)

Elected 1996; 6th term

When McIntyre's father, a city councilman in Lumberton, N.C., took his 16-year-old son to a 1972 victory party for newly elected Democratic Rep. Charlie Rose, the young McIntyre precociously declared that he wanted to be the congressman from the 7th District when he grew up. When Rose retired 24 years later, McIntyre replaced him.

McIntyre is among the most conservative of Democrats in the House, even by the standards of the Blue Dog Coalition, a group of the chamber's most conservative Democrats of which he is a member. But his politics fit his constituency, which is made up of tobacco farmers, military employees, gun aficionados, and religious conservatives who advocate prayer in public schools and oppose abortion.

While he splits with his party on social issues and the occasional fiscal policy vote, McIntyre joins with labor unions and most House Democrats in opposing legislation to liberalize international commerce. "Free trade has been anything but free," McIntyre says. "It's been very costly" to North Carolina's textile and apparel industries. In 2005, he voted against the Central American Free Trade Agreement with five countries.

Republicans sounded him out about switching parties when he first arrived on Capitol Hill. But McIntyre says he feels tied to the Democratic Party by family and regional roots and prefers to try to move it toward the center. Organized and earnest, he now appears to have a lock on his seat, re-elected in 2006 by more than 72 percent of the vote.

Rural economic development tops his legislative priorities. He pushed for legislation to provide tax breaks and other aid to communities hard-hit by job losses stemming from the North American Free Trade Agreement. And for several years, he has sponsored a bill to create a seven-state Southeast Crescent Authority, modeled after the Appalachian Regional Council, to assist economically distressed counties in the southeastern United States.

McIntyre tries to boost tourism in his region and has pushed for federal funding to help restore storm-damaged beaches along the North Carolina coast. Six hurricanes hit the 7th District in McIntyre's first four years in office, harming tourism in the coastal areas.

He also has sought to help the Lumbee Indians in North Carolina get federal recognition as a tribe, which they need in order to open a casino. The Cherokee Nation, which has its own casino and hotel in the state, fears such a facility would bring unwanted competition and has been fighting the Lumbee bill in Congress.

McIntyre has seats on the Agriculture and Armed Services committees, useful assignments for representing a district where farming is big business and the military is a major influence. Fort Bragg employs many of his constituents, while Camp Lejeune is just over the 3rd District line to the east.

For years, McIntyre was a stout defender of the federal tobacco program, which he said was essential to preserving small family farms in North Carolina. But in the early 2000s, declaring "it is time for a new approach," he developed a controversial plan to buy out tobacco growers. From 2003 through 2006, he was the top-ranking Democrat on the Agriculture subcommittee with jurisdiction over tobacco programs and helped push a $10 billion tobacco buyout bill to passage in 2004 as part of a corporate tax measure. In the 110th Congress (2007-08), he became chairman of that subcommittee.

McIntyre was raised in Lumberton, an inland town in the southern half of the state where he still lives with his wife and where he raised his two sons. His father was an optometrist and his mother a bank branch manager.

McIntyre showed an early interest in politics. He was chairman of the Teen Democrats in high school and spent the summer after his junior year in high school in Washington, participating in a congressional seminar program. There, his ambition to be in Congress was cemented.

He was standing at the back of the room the day White House lawyer John Dean testified before the Senate Watergate Committee, which was chaired by North Carolina's Sam J. Ervin Jr. McIntyre followed the Watergate scandal closely and, instead of being turned off from politics, decided more people should get involved in the process.

The next summer, he returned to Capitol Hill as an intern in Rose's office. At the University of North Carolina, he majored in political science and was vice president of the campus chapter of college Democrats. He later was an organizer of the Robeson County Young Democrats.

"When I was a student at Carolina, both in college and law school," he recalls, "I had a poster up on the wall of my room that I kept there those seven years that said, 'The secret of success is constancy of purpose.' " He points to Bill McArthur, another native of southeast North Carolina, who became an astronaut despite being rejected by the National Aeronautics and Space Administration six times. (McIntyre, who remembers being fascinated by space as a youth, is a staunch advocate of NASA.)

After law school, McIntyre got involved in dozens of community, church, civic and professional activities as he built a law practice in Lumberton. All the while, he kept alive his childhood dream of succeeding Rose.

When Rose announced his retirement in 1996, McIntyre was one of seven Democratic primary entrants. He took 23 percent of the vote, 7 percentage points behind Rose Marie Lowry-Townsend, a well-known American Indian and teachers union president. McIntyre got the backing of influential leaders in the district's African-American community, and their support helped him win the runoff and secure the Democratic nomination with 52 percent.

McIntyre's Republican opponent was Bill Caster, a New Hanover County commissioner and retired Coast Guard officer. McIntyre's conservative stance on most issues helped blunt the GOP attacks, and he won with 53 percent. That was his last contest of any note.

The political makeup of the 7th District was altered only slightly by the latest remapping, and McIntyre has won with more than 70 percent in each of the past three elections.

KEY VOTES

2006

- No Stop broadband companies from favoring select Internet traffic
- Yes Affirm U.S. commitment to war in Iraq and reject setting a withdrawal date for troops
- No Repeal requirement for bilingual ballots at the polls
- Yes Permit U.S. sale of civilian nuclear technology to India
- Yes Build a 700-mile fence on the U.S.-Mexico border to curb illegal crossings
- No Permit warrantless wiretaps of suspected terrorists

2005

- Yes Intervene in the life-support case of Terri Schiavo
- No Lift President Bush's restrictions on stem cell research funding
- Yes Prohibit FBI access to library and bookstore records
- No Approve free-trade pact with five Central American countries
- Yes Pass energy policy overhaul favored by President Bush emphasizing domestic oil and gas production
- Yes End mandatory preservation of habitat of endangered animal and plant species
- Yes Ban torture of prisoners in U.S. custody

CQ VOTE STUDIES

	PARTY UNITY		PRESIDENTIAL SUPPORT	
	Support	Oppose	Support	Oppose
2006	74%	26%	63%	37%
2005	71%	29%	57%	43%
2004	74%	26%	59%	41%
2003	78%	22%	48%	52%
2002	72%	28%	54%	46%

INTEREST GROUPS

	AFL-CIO	ADA	CCUS	ACU
2006	79%	50%	73%	64%
2005	80%	70%	62%	48%
2004	80%	60%	60%	60%
2003	93%	70%	52%	48%
2002	67%	55%	53%	48%

NORTH CAROLINA 7
Southeast – Wilmington, part of Fayetteville

The 7th stretches from the well-off historic port city of Wilmington in the southeast to the military-fueled commercial hub of Fayetteville in the north. In between lie tobacco fields, hog farms and manufacturing plants.

Fort Bragg — a sliver of the huge military base is on the edge of the 7th's portion of Fayetteville — is integral to the area. Tobacco, textiles and agriculture also drive the local economy, although textile declines have led to high unemployment in some counties. Free-trade agreements are viewed with suspicion here.

Like Fayetteville (shared with the 2nd and 8th), Wilmington grew significantly in the 1990s, its growth reflected in its expanding medical center and emerging biotechnology industry. The city also has become a desirable retirement community, and the area's Atlantic beaches have made the district a tourist spot, aiding the 7th's economy.

Wealthy condo-dwellers in Wilmington and surrounding New Hanover County exert a rightward influence. But the region's poor farmers, Lumbee Indians (mainly in Robeson County), and cohesive black community in Fayetteville and rural Bladen and Columbus counties provide a slight Democratic lean. The 7th voted for George W. Bush in the 2000 and 2004 presidential elections, but both times also supported Democrat Michael F. Easley in the governor's race.

Due in part to Robeson County, the 7th has the fifth-largest percentage of American Indians of any district in the nation, and the largest percentage of any district east of the Mississippi River. Almost 19 percent of Duplin County (shared with the 3rd) is Hispanic, and 15 percent of the population there speaks a language other than English at home.

MAJOR INDUSTRY
Agriculture, military, manufacturing, tourism

MILITARY BASES
Fort Bragg (Army), 43,003 military, 9,954 civilian (2006) (shared with the 2nd and 8th)

CITIES
Wilmington, 75,838; Lumberton, 20,795; Fayetteville (pt.), 19,418

NOTABLE
Wilmington has a strong film and television production industry, with movies like "Sleeping with the Enemy" and "Blue Velvet" filmed there.

Rep. Robin Hayes (R)

CAPITOL OFFICE
225-3715
www.hayes.house.gov
130 Cannon 20515-3308; fax 225-4036

COMMITTEES
Agriculture
Armed Services
Transportation & Infrastructure

RESIDENCE
Concord

BORN
Aug. 14, 1945, Concord, N.C.

RELIGION
Presbyterian

FAMILY
Wife, Barbara Hayes; two children

EDUCATION
Duke U., B.A. 1967 (history)

CAREER
Hosiery mill owner; air transport company owner; highway construction company owner

POLITICAL HIGHLIGHTS
Concord Board of Aldermen, 1975-78 (served as a Democrat); N.C. House, 1993-97; Republican nominee for governor, 1996

ELECTION RESULTS

2006 GENERAL		
Robin Hayes (R)	60,926	50.1%
Larry Kissell (D)	60,597	49.9%
2006 PRIMARY		
Robin Hayes (R)		unopposed
2004 GENERAL		
Robin Hayes (R)	125,070	55.5%
Beth Troutman (D)	100,101	44.5%

PREVIOUS WINNING PERCENTAGES
2002 (54%); 2000 (55%); 1998 (51%)

Elected 1998; 5th term

North Carolina's textile industry has been of central importance to Hayes' family and the district he represents. His great-grandfather, J.W. Cannon, founded the mill town of Kannapolis, and his grandfather made a fortune in textiles. With the industry in decline and thousands of jobs moved overseas, protecting the livelihood of the workers who remain is vital for Hayes.

Yet in trying to be loyal to President Bush, Hayes has cast tough votes in support of trade bills that were extremely unpopular in his district. Twice since Bush took office, the textile company heir has bowed to pressure from GOP leaders and cast pivotal votes to rescue trade legislation. And he almost paid the price with his seat in Congress.

In 2006, a political unknown, schoolteacher Larry Kissell, almost pulled off a huge electoral upset, losing by just 329 votes in a race that was not made official until more than three weeks after Election Day. It was the second-closest congressional race of the year, and Kissell quickly announced he would be back for a rematch in 2008.

Hayes cast one of the deciding votes in 2001 in favor of fast-track legislation giving the president the authority to negotiate trade agreements that Congress must approve or reject without alteration. He was accused of nothing short of treachery by textile workers back home. But then in 2005, he again switched his no vote to yes to help deliver the Central America Free Trade Agreement for Bush. He had declared he was "flat-out, completely, horizontally opposed to CAFTA," but reversed himself after a midnight cloakroom meeting with then Speaker J. Dennis Hastert.

Hayes says he received important concessions for his votes, including a pledge from the administration to protect domestic textilemakers by ensuring that China would not be allowed to exploit CAFTA. Hayes and other lawmakers wanted U.S.-made fabric, not fabric from China, to be used in duty-free apparel assembled in Central America. Hayes said his fast-track vote helped secure protections for textile dyeing and finishing operations.

Both votes forced him to spend a great deal of time reassuring his constituents that he could be trusted to defend their interests. "Obviously, it comes up everywhere we go," Hayes' spokeswoman said after the CAFTA vote. Once Hayes explains his votes, she said, "usually the response is pretty good. People say, 'OK, I get it now.' "

But in 2006, Hayes put his foot down and helped derail a trade bill providing preferential treatment for apparel from developing countries that he said would be "devastating" to the U.S. textile industry.

Hayes has earned a reputation at home and on Capitol Hill as one of Congress' staunchest defenders of tobacco, another industry that has been important to his state's economy for generations. He has lobbied the Bush White House to include tobacco companies and farmers in trade deals, despite pressure to keep the industry from the table.

His committee assignments help him tend to the needs of his politically competitive district, which had elected a Democrat, W. G. "Bill" Hefner, for a dozen terms until Hefner's retirement in 1998. Hayes serves on the Agriculture panel, where tobacco tends to get a sympathetic hearing, and on the Transportation and Infrastructure Committee, where he works to spur economic growth in his district by securing funds for improvements at small airports.

From his seat on the Armed Services Committee, Hayes pursues better equipment, higher pay and improved housing for military personnel. He says he would like to see the Pentagon streamline its bidding process and adopt cost-saving innovations developed in the business world.

With an eye toward parochial industries, he won a provision in the 2002 defense authorization law requiring that the Defense Department look first to U.S. producers and suppliers when buying textiles, specialty metals or agriculture products. In 2006, he introduced legislation to require the Homeland Security Department to buy only U.S.-made textiles, including such items as uniforms, tents and cots.

Unpretentious and affable, Hayes is the scion of North Carolina's most prominent families. His grandfather, Charles Cannon, was a major influence in his life, and owned Cannon Mills, famous for its towels. The family donated large sums to schools and hospitals in the region. Hayes worked at the mill through college and, as an only child, was groomed to take over the business. But wanting to strike out on his own, he left Concord, a small city northeast of Charlotte, to try different ventures, even moving his family to Alaska to run a company that flew freight and passengers in and out of the bush. Hayes told the Charlotte Observer that he and his wife, Barbara, lived without electricity for a year and home-schooled their two young children. He later bought a small air charter business back in Concord, and with his inheritance from the family textile fortune, also purchased a hosiery mill.

Hayes says he was "a typical Southern conservative Democrat," but switched to become a Republican in 1991 after the party grew too liberal for him. In the House, he typically casts a reliably conservative vote.

His first taste of politics was serving for three years as a Concord alderman in the 1970s. After switching parties, Hayes ran successfully for a seat in the state House and later was elected GOP whip.

He made a 1996 bid for governor, trouncing the establishment's choice for the GOP nomination, former Charlotte Mayor Richard Vinroot. But Hayes lost the general election to Democratic incumbent James B. Hunt.

Running for Congress two years later, Hayes outspent Democratic lawyer Mike Taylor by a 3-1 margin and won with 51 percent of the vote. He took 55 percent in a rematch with Taylor in 2000. Remapping for this decade added Democrats to the 8th District, and the new demographics, combined with his trade votes, have made Hayes vulnerable, as evidenced in the 2006 election.

Hayes is a hunting and fishing enthusiast, and has been a leader in the Congressional Sportsmen's Caucus. He is a strong supporter of gun owners' rights. A NASCAR racing fan, he once was part-owner of a racing team, and in 2001 helped arrange an Air Force flyover honoring the late driver Dale Earnhardt before a race at North Carolina Speedway.

KEY VOTES

2006

- No — Stop broadband companies from favoring select Internet traffic
- Yes — Affirm U.S. commitment to war in Iraq and reject setting a withdrawal date for troops
- Yes — Repeal requirement for bilingual ballots at the polls
- Yes — Permit U.S. sale of civilian nuclear technology to India
- Yes — Build a 700-mile fence on the U.S.-Mexico border to curb illegal crossings
- Yes — Permit warrantless wiretaps of suspected terrorists

2005

- Yes — Intervene in the life-support case of Terri Schiavo
- No — Lift President Bush's restrictions on stem cell research funding
- No — Prohibit FBI access to library and bookstore records
- Yes — Approve free-trade pact with five Central American countries
- Yes — Pass energy policy overhaul favored by President Bush emphasizing domestic oil and gas production
- Yes — End mandatory preservation of habitat of endangered animal and plant species
- No — Ban torture of prisoners in U.S. custody

CQ VOTE STUDIES

	PARTY UNITY		PRESIDENTIAL SUPPORT	
	Support	Oppose	Support	Oppose
2006	94%	6%	85%	15%
2005	99%	1%	89%	11%
2004	94%	6%	76%	24%
2003	99%	1%	91%	9%
2002	97%	3%	82%	18%

INTEREST GROUPS

	AFL-CIO	ADA	CCUS	ACU
2006	43%	5%	93%	88%
2005	13%	0%	89%	92%
2004	21%	5%	95%	88%
2003	20%	5%	93%	84%
2002	22%	5%	75%	96%

NORTH CAROLINA 8

South central — parts of Charlotte, Fayetteville, Concord and Kannapolis

The 8th connects the worlds of eastern and western North Carolina, spanning from Charlotte in the west to military-dominated Fayetteville in the east. This is a district split along geographic, economic and political lines. Charlotte adds a distinctly urban component to an otherwise predominately suburban and rural district.

Cabarrus, a fast-growing county north of Charlotte, and Cumberland, which includes the 8th's share of Fayetteville, are the district's most-populous counties. Cabarrus is largely white and heavily Republican. Cumberland is more politically competitive.

In Mecklenburg County, which includes Charlotte and is the 8th's third major population center, the district reaches as far west as Memorial Stadium and Independence Park, nearly reaching downtown Charlotte. The 8th's share of Charlotte is more than one-third black, giving the district's portion of Mecklenburg a decidedly Democratic lean.

Textile-based economies in the cities along Interstate 85, notably Concord and Kannapolis, have suffered major losses over the past few years as manufacturing jobs have headed overseas. In the east, the 8th becomes poorer and more rural as it reaches into the Sandhills region. This part of the district has a strong military flavor — Fort Bragg (shared with the 2nd and 7th) takes up land in Hoke and Cumberland counties.

The 8th is politically competitive. In 2000 and 2004, George W. Bush took 53 percent and 54 percent of the district's presidential vote, respectively, while Democrat Michael F. Easley won the district's gubernatorial vote.

MAJOR INDUSTRY
Military, manufacturing, agriculture, livestock

MILITARY BASES
Fort Bragg (Army), 43,003 military, 9,954 civilian (2006) (shared with the 2nd and 7th)

CITIES
Charlotte (pt.), 100,756; Concord (pt.), 55,938; Fayetteville (pt.), 51,698

NOTABLE
North Carolina Speedway and Rockingham Dragway, known collectively as "The Rock," can draw 250,000 people to NASCAR races; Fayetteville was home to the original Putt-Putt miniature golf course.

Rep. Sue Myrick (R)

CAPITOL OFFICE
225-1976
myrick@mail.house.gov
myrick.house.gov
230 Cannon 20515-3309; fax 225-3389

COMMITTEES
Energy & Commerce

RESIDENCE
Charlotte

BORN
Aug. 1, 1941, Tiffin, Ohio

RELIGION
Evangelical Methodist

FAMILY
Husband, Ed Myrick; two children, three stepchildren

EDUCATION
Heidelberg College, attended 1959-60 (elementary education)

CAREER
Advertising executive; secretary

POLITICAL HIGHLIGHTS
Candidate for Charlotte City Council, 1981; Charlotte City Council, 1983-85; sought Republican nomination for mayor of Charlotte, 1985; mayor of Charlotte, 1987-91; sought Republican nomination for U.S. Senate, 1992

ELECTION RESULTS

2006 GENERAL		
Sue Myrick (R)	106,206	66.5%
Bill Glass (D)	53,437	33.5%
2006 PRIMARY		
Sue Myrick (R)		unopposed
2004 GENERAL		
Sue Myrick (R)	210,783	70.2%
Jack Flynn (D)	89,318	29.8%

PREVIOUS WINNING PERCENTAGES
2002 (72%); 2000 (69%); 1998 (69%); 1996 (63%); 1994 (65%)

Elected 1994; 7th term

Myrick's biggest legislative victories have come not from her conservative causes but from a personal battle that turned her into a leading advocate of expanded cancer research and health care coverage for cancer treatment. A breast cancer survivor, Myrick shepherded into law a measure that provides treatment for low-income women diagnosed with breast or cervical cancer. In 2006, she steered through the House a bill reauthorizing early detection programs, though it stalled short of enactment.

Myrick underwent surgery for cancer in 1999 and received treatments for about six months, keeping up with floor votes by wearing a pink surgical mask to reduce the risk of infection. She won passage of her cancer diagnosis legislation a year later, and said her experience has helped her keep things in perspective. She says it persuaded her to work "very hard not to get back in the same rat race."

In 2003, she relinquished her seat on the leadership-controlled Rules Committee for a slot on the Energy and Commerce Committee, where she could focus on her work in the Health Subcommittee.

Since she came to Congress with the conservative vanguard of 1994, Myrick has been outspoken on budget issues. During the 108th Congress (2003-04), Myrick chaired the Republican Study Committee (RSC), a group of about 100 of the most conservative members of the House. During the 2004 election campaign, Myrick and the committee produced pocket checklists of "six commandments" for conservatives. Slashing the size and cost of government figured high on the list. "A lot of our base around the country is very disturbed about spending," she told The Washington Times. "We hear about it when we go home."

In 2005, she and other members of the RSC threatened to hold up the budget resolution unless GOP leaders agreed to a new mechanism for enforcing spending caps. The group eventually relented under pressure from Republican leaders, settling for a relatively weak enforcement scheme. "I felt like I had my hands tied behind my back all the time," Myrick said.

Despite her rhetoric about federal spending, Myrick has worked to secure millions of dollars for projects in her home district, and is quick to announce the award of federal grants ranging from homeless aid to parkway improvements.

Myrick joined with other conservatives pushing for a crackdown on illegal immigration in 2005 and 2006, sponsoring a bill to deny highway aid to states that accept taxpayer identification numbers in lieu of Social Security numbers in issuing driver's licenses. Her state, Myrick said, had become a destination for illegal aliens who discovered that the taxpayer ID numbers were easier to obtain.

Myrick drew criticism from Arab-Americans in early 2003 for a comment during a speech on domestic security threats. As the United States prepared for war in Iraq, she said, "Look at who runs all the convenience stores across the country."

From a textile-producing state that has suffered significant trade-related job losses, Myrick has been a sharp critic of the Bush administration's free-trade policies. She has taken particular aim at China with a bill authorizing "appropriate action" if the Asian giant does not revamp its trade practices.

She was one of a group of North Carolina House Republicans who in 2006 opposed House Ways and Means Chairman Bill Thomas' proposal to extend some trade preferences to Haiti. They forced Republican leaders to pull the bill from the floor, but it passed later that year. "We want to help Haiti, but we feel that this is not the way to do it," Myrick said. "What happens is Haiti becomes a trans-shipment point for China."

But Myrick voted in 2000 to give China permanent normal trade status, and was one of several Republicans who cast deciding votes in 2002 granting President Bush fast-track trade negotiating authority, backing the bill after Bush pledged to help the textile industry. She also voted for the 2005 Central American Free Trade Agreement, which passed, 217-215.

Her ardent conservatism and her distinct status as the only Southern Republican woman in the Class of '94 caught the attention of party leaders when she first arrived in Congress. She got a seat on the Budget Committee in her first term and a post on Rules in her second.

But in 1997, she joined a small group of disgruntled conservatives who, impatient with the pace of the "Republican revolution," plotted to depose Newt Gingrich as Speaker. The coup was foiled, and Myrick's influence in the House waned. She lost a race for secretary of the Republican Conference to Deborah Pryce of Ohio.

Born in Tiffin, Ohio, Myrick was reared on a farm. Her parents grew peaches but later switched to nursery stock used in landscaping. As a child, she got 50 cents an hour for staffing the family's take-out snack stand, which sold sandwiches and drinks.

She attended Heidelberg College in her hometown for just a year before her parents decided that their limited financial resources should be used for her three brothers' higher education. They figured "I'd just get married," Myrick said. She took a secretarial job at an army depot.

Myrick had no political aspirations until the early 1980s, when she and her husband sparred with the Charlotte City Council over the purchase of a property for use as a combination home and business. She ran for the city council in 1981 and lost, but was victorious two years later. In 1985, she lost a bid to become mayor of Charlotte; but in 1987, she won the office, ousting Harvey B. Gantt. She was re-elected in 1989.

After five-term GOP Rep. Alex McMillan announced his retirement in 1994, Myrick's political experience gave her wide name recognition in a five-way Republican primary. Still, she struggled to win the nomination, prevailing only when news broke that her principal opponent, state House Minority Leader David Balmer, had falsified his résumé. That November, she met only modest Democratic resistance. She has easily won re-election since then.

KEY VOTES

2006

- No Stop broadband companies from favoring select Internet traffic
- Yes Affirm U.S. commitment to war in Iraq and reject setting a withdrawal date for troops
- Yes Repeal requirement for bilingual ballots at the polls
- Yes Permit U.S. sale of civilian nuclear technology to India
- Yes Build a 700-mile fence on the U.S.-Mexico border to curb illegal crossings
- Yes Permit warrantless wiretaps of suspected terrorists

2005

- Yes Intervene in the life-support case of Terri Schiavo
- No Lift President Bush's restrictions on stem cell research funding
- No Prohibit FBI access to library and bookstore records
- Yes Approve free-trade pact with five Central American countries
- Yes Pass energy policy overhaul favored by President Bush emphasizing domestic oil and gas production
- Yes End mandatory preservation of habitat of endangered animal and plant species
- No Ban torture of prisoners in U.S. custody

CQ VOTE STUDIES

	PARTY UNITY		PRESIDENTIAL SUPPORT	
	Support	Oppose	Support	Oppose
2006	96%	4%	92%	8%
2005	97%	3%	89%	11%
2004	99%	1%	91%	9%
2003	98%	2%	96%	4%
2002	97%	3%	88%	12%

INTEREST GROUPS

	AFL-CIO	ADA	CCUS	ACU
2006	14%	0%	100%	92%
2005	17%	0%	87%	96%
2004	0%	0%	95%	100%
2003	0%	10%	96%	88%
2002	11%	0%	100%	96%

NORTH CAROLINA 9
South central — parts of Charlotte and Gastonia

The predominately Republican 9th centers around Charlotte, the largest metropolitan area in the state. Nearly 40 percent of district residents live within the city's limits, and nearly 60 percent live in Mecklenburg County, which includes Charlotte.

The primarily white suburbs on the southern side of Charlotte provide the city with many of its bankers, brokers, accountants, health care professionals and other white-collar workers. Most of Charlotte's black residents live in the 8th or 12th districts. The 9th has the highest median household income in North Carolina, due to upper-middle-class areas such as Huntersville, in northern Mecklenburg County.

The region's tremendous growth over the last two decades, following 1990s banking-industry consolidation, has brought the traffic congestion, shopping malls and higher home values that usually accompany suburban sprawl. Charlotte is now the nation's biggest banking center after New York.

To the west, Gastonia and the surrounding towns have been hurt by continuing declines in the textile industry. The 9th, however, decreased its dependence on manufacturing and textiles, and the population of Gastonia still grew by 20 percent in the 1990s.

Republicans hold a 34 percent registration advantage in the district, and dominate elections in the 9th. Union County, a suburban bedroom community located southeast of Charlotte, is the fastest-growing county in the state, and the 9th's portion of the county gave George W. Bush 73 percent of its presidential vote in 2004. Overall, Bush captured 63 percent of the 9th's 2004 vote. Since the 9th became a Charlotte-based district prior to the 1968 election, it has only been represented in the U.S. House by Republicans.

MAJOR INDUSTRY

Finance, service, retail, manufacturing

CITIES

Charlotte (pt.), 243,947; Gastonia (pt.), 60,498; Huntersville, 24,960

NOTABLE

After six years of planning, a Gaston County veterans' group in 1998 succeeded in hoisting the largest flying American flag in the nation — 114 feet by 65 feet; Pineville hosts the James K. Polk State Historic Site.

Rep. Patrick T. McHenry (R)

CAPITOL OFFICE
225-2576
patrick.mchenry@mail.house.gov
www.house.gov/mchenry
224 Cannon 20515-3310; fax 225-0316

COMMITTEES
Budget
Financial Services
Oversight & Government Reform

RESIDENCE
Cherryville

BORN
Oct. 22, 1975, Charlotte, N.C.

RELIGION
Roman Catholic

FAMILY
Single

EDUCATION
North Carolina State U., attended 1994-97; Belmont Abbey College, B.A. 2000 (history)

CAREER
Real estate broker; U.S. Labor Department special assistant; campaign aide

POLITICAL HIGHLIGHTS
Republican nominee for N.C. House, 1998; N.C. House, 2003-05

ELECTION RESULTS

2006 GENERAL		
Patrick T. McHenry (R)	94,179	61.8%
Richard Carsner (D)	58,214	38.2%
2006 PRIMARY		
Patrick T. McHenry (R)		unopposed
2004 GENERAL		
Patrick T. McHenry (R)	157,884	64.2%
Anne N. Fischer (D)	88,233	35.9%

Elected 2004; 2nd term

McHenry is the newest darling of the Republican leadership for his habit of mischievously agitating the opposition. He frequently jabs at Democratic leaders on the floor of the House and on the television talk-show circuit, using his quick wit and sense of humor to blunt his sharp attacks.

The youngest member of the House, McHenry in some ways is not far removed from his days as a College Republican. Just months into his first year in the House, his appetite for hardball politics put him at the center of a khakis-and-blazer electoral controversy. During a particularly nasty fight in 2005 for the presidency of the College Republican National Committee — the electoral battleground where GOP political strategists such as Lee Atwater, Karl Rove and Ralph Reed cut their teeth — McHenry made phone calls to North Carolina College Republicans urging them to change their votes and help elect his friend Paul Gourley, who won. McHenry was accused of threatening retribution, a charge he denied.

When Democratic House Speaker Nancy Pelosi's hand-picked candidate for majority leader, John P. Murtha of Pennsylvania, was trounced by Steny H. Hoyer of Maryland in late 2006, McHenry gleefully reproved her. "Pelosi's ultimate Machiavellian move didn't work," he said. "This is a direct affront to her leadership, which of course puts a smile on my face."

His partisanship occasionally draws comparisons to former Majority Leader Tom DeLay, the Texas Republican famous for his no-holds-barred style, and there is no reason to think McHenry will abandon his bomb-throwing ways now that Republicans are in the minority.

"I think my combative style is what we need more of as a minority party," he says. "I've been willing to step up and fight when it comes to core conservative issues."

He is fearless on the House floor, even engaging in repartee with legendary debater Barney Frank, when the Massachusetts Democrat sat in the Speaker's chair during consideration of embryonic stem cell research legislation in 2007. Frank shot down McHenry's repeated "parliamentary inquiries" as political statements not inquiries, prompting Republican Joe L. Barton of Texas to object that Frank had engaged in the same tactics as McHenry when he was in the minority.

In the 110th Congress (2007-08), McHenry was in the vanguard of an effort to use a House procedure called the "motion to recommit" to win last-minute adoption of GOP-favored amendments to Democratic-written bills.

Despite his relative youth — when McHenry told President Bush that he had been a youth organizer for Bush-Cheney 2000, Bush replied, "Boy, looks like you still could be" — the legislative process is nothing new to McHenry. He came to Congress at age 29 with a term in the North Carolina House under his belt.

When he is not trying to get under the skin of Democratic adversaries, McHenry, who won a coveted appointment to the Financial Services Committee as a freshman, has focused on legislation to help nearby Charlotte's prosperous financial services industry.

Like most junior members, his legislative record is fairly short. But at the end of the 109th Congress (2005-06), he won enactment of a measure that allows banks and other financial institutions involved in multiple transactions to combine the agreements in a single contract. The legislation was sought by banks and similar entities as a way to save money by simplifying the large number of transactions they conduct daily.

Another McHenry bill, designed to make it easier for nonprofit credit unions to become for-profit banks, never made it out of committee. In a less-than-flattering profile of McHenry, the liberal Washington Monthly magazine said the legislation would have pleased Republican leaders at the expense of many of McHenry's constituents, who get lower interest rates from their credit unions than they would from banks.

McHenry rarely departs from the GOP line, siding with Republicans 99 percent of the time in the 109th Congress on votes that split along party lines. His most notable deviation came on the Central America Free Trade Agreement in 2005. McHenry, whose district is home to textile and furniture manufacturers, was one of 27 Republicans to vote against the pact. Many western North Carolina residents blame trade liberalization laws for job losses.

He nearly broke with the GOP again during a Budget Committee vote on the budget for 2006, at first backing a Democratic amendment that incorporated budget rules favored by his colleagues on the conservative Republican Study Committee. But he switched his vote to no after discussing the matter with senior Republicans on the Budget panel, helping to defeat the amendment by a single vote.

"I wasn't being squeezed," McHenry said later. "In the two minutes that it took to see who was voting for and against the bill, I decided that [Budget Chairman Jim] Nussle and the leaders had worked hard to produce a budget, the leanest budget since [President Ronald] Reagan, and I wanted to support him on that."

McHenry had already compiled a lengthy résumé when veteran GOP Rep. Cass Ballenger announced in 2004 that he would retire from the seat he had held since 1986. McHenry had served as chairman of the state College Republicans and as treasurer for the national College Republicans organization in the late 1990s. He also had worked on several campaigns, including fellow North Carolina Republican Rep. Robin Hayes' failed 1996 gubernatorial bid and Bush's successful 2000 presidential race, as well as his own contests for the state legislature.

In the 2004 race for the 10th District seat, McHenry had to battle through a four-way Republican primary. His second place finish put him in a runoff against David Huffman, a well-known local sheriff. With a financial boost from the Club for Growth, a Washington-based group that supports fiscally conservative candidates, he won by a scant 85 votes.

In November, he defeated little-known party activist Anne N. Fischer by more than 28 percentage points in the overwhelmingly Republican district.

He cruised to re-election in 2006 with 62 percent of the vote.

KEY VOTES

2006

- No — Stop broadband companies from favoring select Internet traffic
- Yes — Affirm U.S. commitment to war in Iraq and reject setting a withdrawal date for troops
- Yes — Repeal requirement for bilingual ballots at the polls
- Yes — Permit U.S. sale of civilian nuclear technology to India
- Yes — Build a 700-mile fence on the U.S.-Mexico border to curb illegal crossings
- Yes — Permit warrantless wiretaps of suspected terrorists

2005

- Yes — Intervene in the life-support case of Terri Schiavo
- No — Lift President Bush's restrictions on stem cell research funding
- No — Prohibit FBI access to library and bookstore records
- No — Approve free-trade pact with five Central American countries
- Yes — Pass energy policy overhaul favored by President Bush emphasizing domestic oil and gas production
- Yes — End mandatory preservation of habitat of endangered animal and plant species
- No — Ban torture of prisoners in U.S. custody

CQ VOTE STUDIES

	PARTY UNITY		PRESIDENTIAL SUPPORT	
	Support	Oppose	Support	Oppose
2006	98%	2%	83%	17%
2005	99%	1%	87%	13%

INTEREST GROUPS

	AFL-CIO	ADA	CCUS	ACU
2006	7%	10%	93%	92%
2005	20%	5%	89%	100%

NORTH CAROLINA 10
West — Hickory

Set among the small towns of the western part of the state, the 10th has a rustic, small-business and conservative flavor. A solidly Republican district, the 10th has sent a GOP lawmaker to the U.S. House for almost 40 years, and many residents who consider themselves conservative Democrats will support Republicans in federal races.

While the 10th includes some suburban communities near Charlotte, it is mostly rural — only one town, Hickory, has a population of more than 20,000. Suburban sprawl has reached the eastern and southern edges of the 10th, especially in Hickory, where the furniture industry employs a large part of the workforce. Historically, the economy of the southern counties was based largely on textile and furniture manufacturing, with cotton-growing areas in Cleveland County. In the north, there are Christmas tree growers, and tourists visit the mountains near the Tennessee border and ski in areas like Banner Elk. Iredell County (shared with the 5th) is mostly rural and agricultural, with some manufacturing.

Technology manufacturing is on the upswing here, filling in some of the employment gaps created by downturns in textile and furniture manufacturing. Fiber-optic cable manufacturing also is important, and the 10th has the state's highest percentage of blue-collar workers. Google announced in 2007 that it plans to build a data center in Lenoir.

The 10th's political preference is set by Catawba County (Hickory), the district's most populous, which gave George W. Bush 67 percent of its 2004 presidential vote. Democrats run better in Cleveland and Burke counties, but Caldwell and Lincoln counties are heavily Republican. Avery and Mitchell counties, on the Tennessee border, are strongly Republican and were GOP gubernatorial nominee Patrick J. Ballantine's best counties in 2004.

MAJOR INDUSTRY
Manufacturing, agriculture

CITIES
Hickory, 37,222; Shelby, 19,477; Mooresville (pt.), 18,782

NOTABLE
The Elliott-Carnegie Public Library in Hickory was the last U.S. public library to receive a grant from the Carnegie Foundation (in 1917); Despite the 10th's Republican slant, the longest-serving congressman from North Carolina, Democrat Bob Doughton, represented the 10th for 42 years.

Rep. Heath Shuler (D)

CAPITOL OFFICE
225-6401
shuler.house.gov
512 Cannon 20515-3311; fax 226-6422

COMMITTEES
Natural Resources
Small Business
(Rural & Urban Entrepreneurship - chairman)
Transportation & Infrastructure

RESIDENCE
Waynesville

BORN
Dec. 31, 1971, Bryson City, N.C.

RELIGION
Baptist

FAMILY
Wife, Nikol Shuler; two children

EDUCATION
U. of Tennessee, B.A. 2001 (psychology)

CAREER
Real estate company owner; medical record smart card company president; professional football player

POLITICAL HIGHLIGHTS
No previous office

ELECTION RESULTS

2006 GENERAL		
Heath Shuler (D)	124,972	53.8%
Charles H. Taylor (R)	107,342	46.2%
2006 PRIMARY		
Heath Shuler (D)	29,921	74.6%
Michael Morgan (D)	10,180	25.4%

Elected 2006; 1st term

Hopes were high the first time Shuler came to the nation's capital as a first-round draft pick for the Washington Redskins. The quarterback's five years in the National Football League didn't match the expectations from his University of Tennessee standout career, but with an equally auspicious beginning as a politician, he has a chance to do better the second time around.

Shuler (SHOO-lur), a devout Christian, is more conservative than the average Democrat. He opposes abortion rights and gun control, and plans to seek balanced budgets as part of the Blue Dog Coalition, a group of conservative House Democrats that backed his campaign. Despite some policy differences, Shuler says he chose his party because of family lessons about helping those in need. "If you look at one reason why I am a Democrat, it's because the party helps those who can't help themselves. It's a moral obligation," he said.

In his first week, Shuler broke from his party to vote against expanding funding for embryonic stem cell research, which uses surplus embryos from in vitro fertilization. But the leadership did not hold a grudge. Shuler was named chairman of the Small Business Committee's Subcommittee on Rural and Urban Entrepreneurship and was chosen to serve as one of several deputy whips, one of the first rungs on the party leadership ladder.

Much of his district's western edge is public land, so his two additional appointments to the Transportation and Infrastructure and Natural Resources committees were good fits.

He won his seat by defeating GOP Rep. Charles H. Taylor. Though Shuler was Taylor's toughest challenger in several elections, it was an uphill battle to unseat the eight-term congressman until the Wall Street Journal in October 2006 published a front-page story questioning whether Taylor used his seat on the powerful Appropriations Committee to benefit himself and business partners. The story came on top of other questions raised about Taylor's ethics over the years and also at a time when voters were fed up with corruption scandals in Congress.

NORTH CAROLINA 11
West — Asheville

Based in the Great Smoky Mountains of Appalachia, the 11th is a largely rural district dotted with tree farms, wood mills and campgrounds. While agriculture and forestry long have played a key role in the region's economy, retail trade and health care are becoming major employers, and residential development is now mirroring retail growth.

People flock to the area's ski slopes, as well as to hiking trails in parks, forests and on Mount Mitchell (the highest peak east of the Mississippi River). Tourists also enjoy the Biltmore Estate, the nation's largest privately owned home, where 900,000 visit each year.

Local economic engine Asheville and surrounding Buncombe County take in one-third of the 11th's residents. Real estate developers are showing increasing interest in Asheville's blend of urban amenities, such as health care services and art galleries, and mountain remoteness. Retail growth and hospitality services have expanded the job base, but declines in manufacturing continue to restrict economic opportunity here.

Attractive to retirees, the 11th has the highest median age and the smallest black population of any North Carolina district. The Cherokee Reservation gives it a larger than average American Indian population. The district leans Republican, but Democrats lead in voter registration. Buncombe barely favored George W. Bush in the 2004 presidential race, giving him a slim 600-vote win, but every other county here gave Bush a higher percentage. Henderson County votes solidly Republican.

MAJOR INDUSTRY
Retail, forest products, health care, tourism

CITIES
Asheville, 68,889; Hendersonville, 10,420

NOTABLE
Many of the state's Cherokee Indians are descendants of the Cherokees who hid to avoid forced migration to Oklahoma.

Rep. Melvin Watt (D)

CAPITOL OFFICE
225-1510
nc12@mail.house.gov
www.house.gov/watt
2236 Rayburn 20515-3312; fax 225-1512

COMMITTEES
Financial Services
(Oversight & Investigations - chairman)
Judiciary

RESIDENCE
Charlotte

BORN
Aug. 26, 1945, Charlotte, N.C.

RELIGION
Presbyterian

FAMILY
Wife, Eulada Watt; two children

EDUCATION
U. of North Carolina, B.S. 1967 (business administration); Yale U., J.D. 1970

CAREER
Nursing home owner; campaign manager; lawyer

POLITICAL HIGHLIGHTS
N.C. Senate, 1985-86

ELECTION RESULTS

2006 GENERAL		
Melvin Watt (D)	71,345	67.0%
Ada M. Fisher (R)	35,127	33.0%
2006 PRIMARY		
Melvin Watt (D)		unopposed
2004 GENERAL		
Melvin Watt (D)	154,908	66.8%
Ada M. Fisher (R)	76,898	33.2%

PREVIOUS WINNING PERCENTAGES
2002 (65%); 2000 (65%); 1998 (56%); 1996 (71%); 1994 (66%); 1992 (70%)

Elected 1992; 8th term

With one of the sharpest minds on the Judiciary Committee, Watt is an important player on the panel. He's also a standout leader among African-American lawmakers, having served in the 109th Congress (2005-06) as chairman of the Congressional Black Caucus, one of the most influential unofficial groups that help shape policy for Democrats in Washington.

Watt faced three high-profile issues during his term as the caucus' chairman. The first was the case of Georgia Democrat Cynthia A. McKinney, who struck a Capitol police officer when he tried to stop her for identification as she walked past a security checkpoint without a congressional lapel pin. Watt chose not to involve the caucus, skipping a press conference where McKinney implied that she had been singled out by the police because she is a black woman.

Watt did weigh in when another case attracted widespread attention, objecting to his party's treatment of Louisiana Democrat William J. Jefferson, the target of a federal corruption probe. When the House voted in 2006 to remove Jefferson from his seat on the Ways and Means Committee, Watt argued that the House, and specifically the Democratic Caucus, used a double standard because Jefferson is black. There is no House rule calling for removal of a rank-and-file member not charged with a crime.

Watt and the caucus also were at odds with the Democratic leadership over the chairmanship of the Intelligence Committee. Despite his having the unanimous support of the Congressional Black Caucus, Speaker Nancy Pelosi skipped over caucus member Alcee L. Hastings of Florida, whose impeachment as a federal judge a generation ago still raises eyebrows. (Also passed over was Californian Jane Harman, with whom Pelosi does not get along.) Instead, she installed Texan Silvestre Reyes at the panel's helm.

On the Judiciary Committee, Watt was the chief Democratic negotiator in 2006 on a measure to extend the 1965 Voting Rights Act. He was able to produce a bipartisan bill that was praised by both GOP Chairman F. James Sensenbrenner Jr. of Wisconsin and senior panel Democrat John Conyers Jr. of Michigan. Watt and Sensenbrenner are usually at opposite poles on issues. Watt said he got heavily involved because the bill dealt with redistricting, and "I've been the poster child of redistricting. My district was changed five times in a 10-year period so people knew that I understood that issue."

He had less success in his effort to stop the renewal of the Patriot Act, a law passed after the Sept. 11 terrorist attacks giving law enforcement broad powers to investigate terrorism suspects. Watt has been among a faction in Congress that says the law tramples on civil liberties and gives police too much power to monitor the activities of the innocent. He voted against renewing the Patriot Act in 2005, and failed in his efforts to attach an amendment requiring the government to disclose information about library record searches. "Some of us who have a different history in America with delegation of authority to the government and the abuse of that authority proceed a lot differently than others," he said.

A Yale-trained lawyer, Watt is usually a fierce partisan on the Judiciary Committee. He shows a more bipartisan style on the Financial Services panel, where the battles between the parties are usually not as emotional. Watt frequently seeks out Republicans in search of a deal, often scribbling amendments in the margins of the legislation under discussion.

Although Watt sees his role as an advocate for the little guy, he is on cordial terms with the business community. Charlotte's big financial services companies, including Wachovia and Bank of America, credit Watt with giving their views a fair hearing, and he occasionally agrees with them, opposing, for example, proposals to raise the $100,000 ceiling on federally insured deposits. "Trying to walk the balance between the banker interests and the consumer interests is very difficult," he says.

Watt and his Democratic colleagues on Financial Services are now in a position to advance legislation they've been advocating for years to end abusive lending practices and racial and ethnic disparities in mortgage lending. In the 110th Congress, Watt was given the gavel of the committee's Oversight and Investigations Subcommittee, where he launched an investigation into Hurricane Katrina-related insurance claims.

Underpinning Watt's success is the determination he developed during a difficult early life. Raised in a fatherless household, he grew up in rural Mecklenburg County in a tin-roofed shack that lacked running water and electricity. After attending a segregated high school, he went on to graduate Phi Beta Kappa from the University of North Carolina, posting the highest academic average in the business school. He then earned his law degree from Yale.

Watt worked for several years as an attorney for a firm specializing in civil rights law. He interrupted his practice for a brief stint as an appointed state senator and to manage the 1990 Senate campaign of Democrat Harvey Gantt, who nearly upset GOP incumbent Jesse Helms that year.

In 1992, when a widely meandering black-majority district was created, Watt won it with relative ease and became one of the first African-Americans to represent North Carolina in Congress. But the boundaries of Watt's district were challenged in court throughout the 1990s, and the 12th District's lines were redrawn twice during the decade in response to lawsuits alleging unconstitutional racial gerrymandering.

In 2001, the state's map was redrawn yet again, when North Carolina received an additional House seat because of population gains. The Democrats in charge of the process made sure to give Watt electorally safe territory. But the changing shape of his district has proved more of a distraction than a political threat: He consistently wins with at least 65 percent of the vote.

Watt, a good athlete, runs, plays tennis and is the Democrats' pitcher in the annual charity baseball game with GOP lawmakers. He also is a fan of NASCAR racing, and promotes the hiring of more minorities for management and marketing jobs in the industry, as well as for drivers and pit crews.

KEY VOTES

2006

- Yes Stop broadband companies from favoring select Internet traffic
- No Affirm U.S. commitment to war in Iraq and reject setting a withdrawal date for troops
- No Repeal requirement for bilingual ballots at the polls
- Yes Permit U.S. sale of civilian nuclear technology to India
- No Build a 700-mile fence on the U.S.-Mexico border to curb illegal crossings
- No Permit warrantless wiretaps of suspected terrorists

2005

- No Intervene in the life-support case of Terri Schiavo
- Yes Lift President Bush's restrictions on stem cell research funding
- Yes Prohibit FBI access to library and bookstore records
- No Approve free-trade pact with five Central American countries
- No Pass energy policy overhaul favored by President Bush emphasizing domestic oil and gas production
- No End mandatory preservation of habitat of endangered animal and plant species
- Yes Ban torture of prisoners in U.S. custody

CQ VOTE STUDIES

	PARTY UNITY		PRESIDENTIAL SUPPORT	
	Support	Oppose	Support	Oppose
2006	97%	3%	17%	83%
2005	98%	2%	16%	84%
2004	97%	3%	26%	74%
2003	99%	1%	13%	87%
2002	97%	3%	25%	75%

INTEREST GROUPS

	AFL-CIO	ADA	CCUS	ACU
2006	100%	95%	47%	4%
2005	93%	100%	35%	0%
2004	93%	95%	29%	0%
2003	100%	100%	21%	12%
2002	88%	90%	40%	4%

NORTH CAROLINA 12

Central — parts of Charlotte, Winston-Salem and Greensboro

The Democratic 12th, North Carolina's smallest district in geographic size, winds north from Charlotte to the Triad area of Greensboro, Winston-Salem and High Point. The district became known as the mother of all racial gerrymanders when it was originally drawn for the 1992 elections. Struck down by the courts and widely ridiculed for a serpentine shape that aimed to maximize the black population, the 12th was redrawn twice in the 1990s. The current 12th is 45 percent black and has a massive Democratic tilt. In both 2000 and 2004, the district gave the Democratic presidential nominee his best showing in the state.

While not as contorted as its 1990s predecessors, the current 12th zigzags from Charlotte along Interstate 85 north and east to take in part of Salisbury, and then scoops up large black populations in Winston-Salem, High Point and Greensboro. The district takes in about one-third of Charlotte's population but two-thirds of its black residents, and 60 percent of Winston-Salem's population but nearly 90 percent of its black residents. Most of the 12th's black residents are lower- to middle-class.

Nearly one-third of the 12th's residents live in Charlotte, with its booming economy. Home to Bank of America, the city is now the nation's biggest banking center outside of New York. The Biddleville neighborhood, west of the business district, hosts the predominately black Johnson C. Smith University and is a hub of the black community. But the city's downtown — known as "uptown" — has its share of poverty and crime.

Highway infrastructure in the Triad area, including the junction of three interstates, couples with the Charlotte airport to create a good base for trade. Furniture manufacturing is vital to High Point's local economy.

MAJOR INDUSTRY

Finance, transportation, health care

CITIES

Charlotte (pt.), 196,125; Winston-Salem (pt.), 115,986; Greensboro (pt.), 62,075; High Point (pt.), 52,429; Salisbury (pt.), 26,399

NOTABLE

A Woolworth's lunch counter in Greensboro was the site of the first major civil rights sit-in in 1960.

Rep. Brad Miller (D)

CAPITOL OFFICE
225-3032
www.house.gov/bradmiller
1722 Longworth 20515-3313; fax 225-0181

COMMITTEES
Financial Services
Foreign Affairs
Science & Technology
(Investigations & Oversight - chairman)

RESIDENCE
Raleigh

BORN
May 19, 1953, Fayetteville, N.C.

RELIGION
Episcopalian

FAMILY
Wife, Esther Hall

EDUCATION
U. of North Carolina, B.A. 1975 (political science); London School of Economics, M.S.C. 1978 (comparative government); Columbia U., J.D. 1979

CAREER
Lawyer

POLITICAL HIGHLIGHTS
Sought Democratic nomination for N.C. secretary of state, 1988; N.C. House, 1993-95; defeated for re-election to N.C. House, 1994; N.C. Senate, 1997-2002

ELECTION RESULTS

2006 GENERAL		
Brad Miller (D)	98,540	63.7%
Vernon L. Robinson (R)	56,120	36.3%
2006 PRIMARY		
Brad Miller (D)		unopposed
2004 GENERAL		
Brad Miller (D)	160,896	58.8%
Virginia Johnson (R)	112,788	41.2%

PREVIOUS WINNING PERCENTAGES
2002 (55%)

Elected 2002; 3rd term

Miller is among a small group of white Southern Democrats left in Congress, but that doesn't make him a conservative of the old school. He frequently speaks out in favor of increased funding for public education, stepped-up environmental protection and a more equal distribution of tax benefits among income groups.

His liberal streak reflects the political makeup of North Carolina's northern tier. It is more urban than many Southern districts, and the technology and biotechnology firms in the Research Triangle around Raleigh have drawn thousands of well-educated transplants. The district also takes in sizable black neighborhoods, students and faculty at the University of North Carolina's Greensboro campus and blue-collar textile workers, all Democratic-leaning constituencies.

Miller serves on the Financial Services Committee, where he will resume his push for a bill to curb predatory mortgage lending. Modeled after a North Carolina law he wrote in the state legislature, Miller's legislation curbs interest rates, points and fees. Among those hardest hit by such loans are members of minority groups, the elderly and the working poor.

He chairs the Science and Technology Committee's Investigations and Oversight Subcommittee and is probing allegations that the Bush administration has manipulated science to support its policies. "It is not good government when agency action is based on economic or political backroom deals rather than environmental or public health consequences," said Miller.

A member of the Foreign Affairs Committee, he has called for an end to U.S. involvement in the Iraq War. Speaking on the House floor in early 2007, he said a resolution disapproving of Bush's plan to increase troop levels in Iraq was "a first step toward doing our duty by looking realistically at events in Iraq." He also introduced a bill, with North Carolina colleague David E. Price, to terminate President Bush's war authority by the end of 2007.

Now that he has a couple of terms under his belt, Miller hopes to play a larger role in Congress. But he will pick his shots. A cautious and mild-tempered politician, Miller describes his approach: "I have tried to spot issues that I care about that do not already have someone who is an established, recognized champion and expert from the point of view that I would come at that issue on."

Among Miller's varied constituents are tobacco farmers who live in the rural stretch between the two population centers of Raleigh and Greensboro. He was an avid supporter in 2004 of the $10 billion government buyout of tobacco farmers, whose product was a staple of the state's economy until the market for tobacco collapsed in recent years.

In his first year in office, Miller earned a perfect 100 percent score from the nation's leading union federation, the AFL-CIO. In December 2005, he used Bush's visit to a John Deere-Hitachi manufacturing plant in Kernersville, N.C., to criticize the president's economic policies, blaming them for the loss of 173,000 manufacturing jobs in the state since 2001.

Miller got the political bug early in life. He often cites an inspirational visit to the U.S. Capitol as a 9-year-old. Yet reaching his goal of working under the great white dome wasn't easy. His father, the manager of the local post office in Fayetteville, N.C., died of a heart attack when Miller was 12. He and his siblings were raised by their mother, a school cafeteria bookkeeper.

She pushed her children to go to college — something she and her husband had aspired to but never had the financial means to do themselves.

"If what I did in my life was determined by what my parents did, I'd be in Fayetteville working at a post office," Miller says. "But I had a different opportunity because we are an open, meritocratic society."

Miller graduated from the University of North Carolina and later got a law degree from Columbia University in New York City. Never having set foot outside the United States, in between those degrees he decided to broaden his experience by getting a master's degree in comparative government at the London School of Economics and Political Science.

He clerked for a year for now-retired federal appellate Judge J. Dickson Phillips Jr. in Chapel Hill, then moved to Raleigh to work as a litigator at private firms. He became chairman of the Wake County Democratic Party, and waited for an opportunity to run for office.

In 1988, he narrowly lost a Democratic primary for secretary of state. He was primed to run for the state legislature in 1992 after redistricting created a new House district that included his neighborhood. He won the seat, but lost it two years later in the GOP surge of 1994. He got even two years later by unseating a Republican in the state Senate, where he served three terms.

While in the legislature, Miller wrote North Carolina's safe gun-storage law, one of the first of its kind; cosponsored a law ending the state sales tax on food; and pushed for higher teacher salaries and smaller class sizes.

When reapportionment after the 2000 census gave North Carolina a new U.S. House seat, Miller, as chairman of the state Senate redistricting committee, helped draw the new 13th District for himself, giving it a Democratic voter registration advantage and including much of his political base.

In a fierce general-election race, Miller defeated GOP businesswoman Carolyn W. Grant by 12 percentage points. He outspent Grant 2-to-1, and benefited from endorsements from labor unions, teachers and environmentalists. Grant charged Miller with voting for $1 billion in new taxes and giving state lawmakers a big pay raise. Miller's ads claimed that Grant used her son's college fund to buy a car, an assertion made in a civil lawsuit by Grant's former husband and one she steadfastly denied.

His generally liberal voting record prompted serious challenges in the past two elections. In 2004, then GOP Speaker J. Dennis Hastert and North Carolina Republican Sen. Elizabeth Dole campaigned for his opponent, lawyer and former Hill aide Virginia Johnson, but Miller won easily with 59 percent of the vote. In 2006, Republican Vernon L. Robinson, calling himself the "black Jesse Helms," after the state's notoriously conservative former senator, ran a sharply negative campaign, dubbing Miller a "San Francisco liberal." Miller beat Robinson by a nearly 2-1 margin.

KEY VOTES

2006

Yes Stop broadband companies from favoring select Internet traffic
P Affirm U.S. commitment to war in Iraq and reject setting a withdrawal date for troops
No Repeal requirement for bilingual ballots at the polls
Yes Permit U.S. sale of civilian nuclear technology to India
Yes Build a 700-mile fence on the U.S.-Mexico border to curb illegal crossings
No Permit warrantless wiretaps of suspected terrorists

2005

No Intervene in the life-support case of Terri Schiavo
Yes Lift President Bush's restrictions on stem cell research funding
Yes Prohibit FBI access to library and bookstore records
No Approve free-trade pact with five Central American countries
No Pass energy policy overhaul favored by President Bush emphasizing domestic oil and gas production
No End mandatory preservation of habitat of endangered animal and plant species
Yes Ban torture of prisoners in U.S. custody

CQ VOTE STUDIES

	PARTY UNITY		PRESIDENTIAL SUPPORT	
	Support	Oppose	Support	Oppose
2006	90%	10%	38%	62%
2005	93%	7%	26%	74%
2004	89%	11%	38%	62%
2003	96%	4%	17%	83%

INTEREST GROUPS

	AFL-CIO	ADA	CCUS	ACU
2006	100%	90%	47%	17%
2005	93%	100%	41%	0%
2004	87%	90%	43%	8%
2003	100%	95%	34%	12%

NORTH CAROLINA 13

North central – parts of Raleigh and Greensboro

The 13th is defined by its urban anchors of Greensboro and Raleigh, which are connected by several rural counties along the Virginia border. Almost half of the district's population lives in Wake County (Raleigh), including a large number of government employees and recent arrivals from out of state.

The district encompasses northern and central Raleigh, an area that falls into the Research Triangle and is built around an economy of technology, biotechnology and financial services. The 13th takes in about 70 percent of Raleigh's residents (the city is shared with the 2nd and 4th), and its slice of the city includes most of downtown and the state Capitol. In Greensboro, the state's third-most-populous city, tobacco processing long was the city's economic backbone, and Lorillard Tobacco, the nation's third-largest tobacco company, is still important to the region. Tobacco's influence on the economy, however, has decreased.

While Raleigh and Greensboro have grown rapidly and feature diverse economies, the northern, rural areas of Rockingham, Caswell, Person and Granville counties, on the Virginia border, and Alamance County, south of Caswell and shared with the 6th, still rely heavily on farming and manufacturing, particularly tobacco and textiles. The 13th dips into Alamance to reach Burlington.

The 13th has an overall Democratic lean, in part because of a sizable black population and a number of white moderates and liberals in the urban areas. Registered Democrats outnumber Republicans by nearly 2-to-1, but the actual Democratic advantage at the polls is smaller.

The potential for swing voting exists in both the cities and suburbs, and the 13th had the state's closest vote in the last two presidential elections, with the Democratic candidate winning both times. In 2004, John Kerry won solidly in the district's portion of Guilford and Alamance counties but lost heavily in Person County and the 13th's part of Rockingham County.

MAJOR INDUSTRY

Technology, financial services, state government, textiles, agriculture

CITIES

Raleigh (pt.), 192,576; Greensboro (pt.), 102,806; Burlington (pt.), 23,836

NOTABLE

Caswell County has one of the largest Amish communities in the South.

NORTH DAKOTA

Gov. John Hoeven (R)

Residence: HO-ven
First elected: 2000
Length of term: 4 years
Term expires: 12/08
Salary: $92,483
Phone: (701) 328-2200

Residence: Bismarck
Born: March 13, 1957; Bismarck, N.D.
Religion: Roman Catholic
Family: Wife, Mikey Hoeven; two children
Education: Dartmouth College, B.A. 1979 (history & economics); Northwestern U., M.B.A. 1981
Career: Bank CEO
Political highlights: No previous office

Election results:

2004 GENERAL		
John Hoeven (R)	220,803	71.3%
Joseph A. Satrom (D)	84,877	27.4%
Roland Riemers (I)	4,193	1.4%

Lt. Gov. Jack Dalrymple (R)

First elected: 2000
Length of term: 4 years
Term expires: 12/08
Salary: $71,797
Phone: (701) 328-2200

LEGISLATURE

Legislative Assembly: January-April in odd-numbered years

Senate: 47 members, 4-year terms
2007 ratios: 26 R, 21 D; 41 men, 6 women
Salary: $125/day in session
Phone: (701) 328-2916

House: 94 members, 4-year terms
2007 ratios: 60 R, 34 D; 76 men, 18 women
Salary: $125/day in session
Phone: (701) 328-2916

TERM LIMITS

Governor: No
Senate: No
House: No

URBAN STATISTICS

CITY	POPULATION
Fargo	90,599
Bismarck	55,532
Grand Forks	49,321
Minot	36,567
Mandan	16,718

REGISTERED VOTERS

Voters do not register by party.

POPULATION

2006 population (est.)	635,867
2000 population	642,200
1990 population	638,800
Percent change (1990-2000)	+0.5%
Rank among states (2006)	48
Median age	36.2
Born in state	72.5%
Foreign born	1.9%
Violent crime rate	81/100,000
Poverty level	11.9%
Federal workers	9,656
Military	12,479

ELECTIONS

STATE ELECTION OFFICIAL
(701) 328-4146
DEMOCRATIC PARTY
(701) 255-0460
REPUBLICAN PARTY
(701) 255-0030

MISCELLANEOUS

Web: www.discoverend.com
Capital: Bismarck

U.S. CONGRESS

Senate: 2 Democrats
House: 1 Democrat

2000 Census Statistics by District

DIST.	2004 VOTE FOR PRESIDENT BUSH	KERRY	WHITE	BLACK	ASIAN	HISP	MEDIAN INCOME	WHITE COLLAR	BLUE COLLAR	SERVICE INDUSTRY	OVER 64	UNDER 18	COLLEGE EDUCATION	RURAL	SQ. MILES
AL	63%	35%	92%	1%	1%	1%	$34,604	59%	24%	17%	15%	25%	22%	44%	68,976
STATE	63	35	92	1	1	1	$34,604	59	24	17	15	25	22	44	68,976
U.S.	50.7	48.3	69	12	4	13	$41,994	60	25	15	12	26	24	21	3,537,438

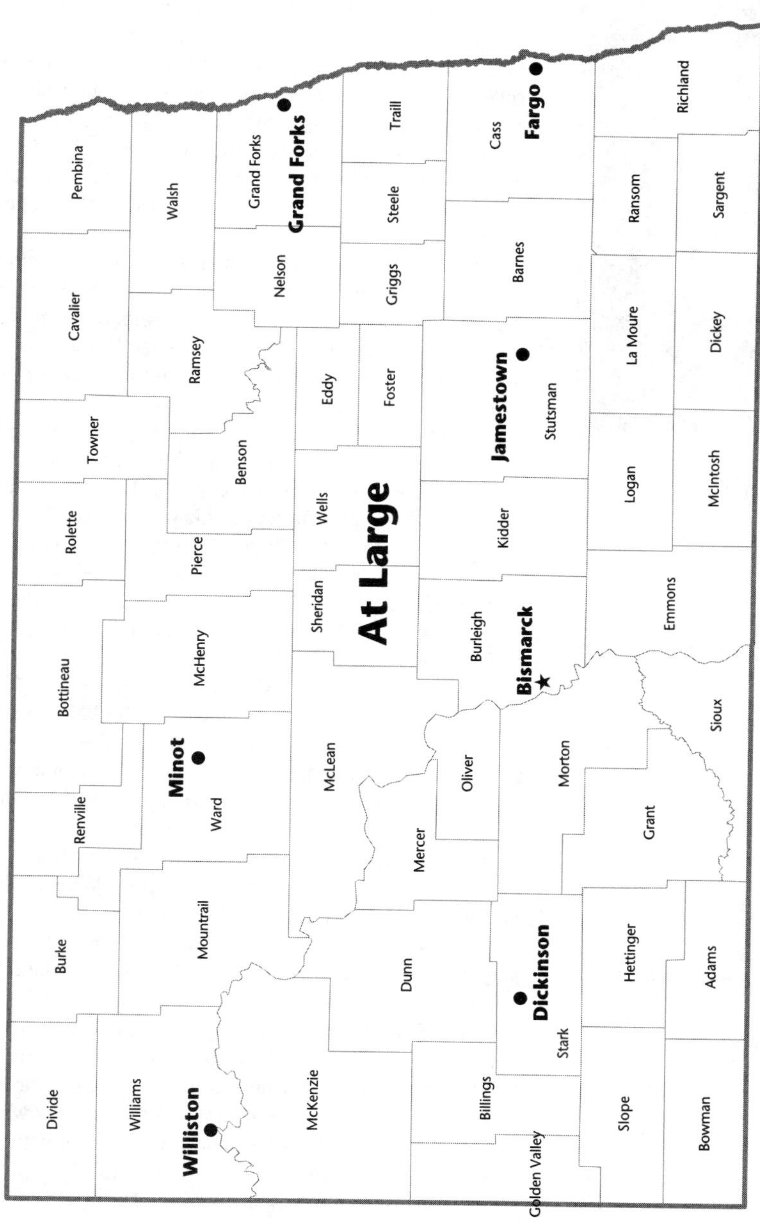
At Large
Fargo
Grand Forks
Jamestown
Bismarck
Minot
Dickinson
Williston
Pembina
Walsh
Grand Forks
Traill
Cass
Richland
Steele
Ransom
Sargent
Cavalier
Nelson
Griggs
Barnes
Ramsey
Eddy
Foster
Stutsman
La Moure
Dickey
Towner
Benson
Wells
Logan
McIntosh
Rolette
Pierce
Kidder
Sheridan
Emmons
Bottineau
McHenry
Burleigh
Sioux
Renville
Ward
McLean
Oliver
Morton
Grant
Mercer
Burke
Mountrail
Dunn
Hettinger
Adams
Stark
Divide
Williams
McKenzie
Billings
Slope
Bowman
Golden Valley

Sen. Kent Conrad (D)

CAPITOL OFFICE
224-2043
senator@conrad.senate.gov
conrad.senate.gov
530 Hart 20510-3403; fax 224-7776

COMMITTEES
Agriculture, Nutrition & Forestry
(Energy, Science & Technology - chairman)
Budget - chairman
Finance
(Taxation, IRS Oversight & Long-Term Growth - chairman)
Indian Affairs
Joint Taxation

RESIDENCE
Bismarck

BORN
March 12, 1948, Bismarck, N.D.

RELIGION
Unitarian

FAMILY
Wife, Lucy Calautti; one child

EDUCATION
U. of Missouri, attended 1967; Stanford U., A.B. 1971 (government & political science); George Washington U., M.B.A. 1975

CAREER
Management and personnel director

POLITICAL HIGHLIGHTS
Candidate for N.D. auditor, 1976; N.D. tax commissioner, 1981-87

ELECTION RESULTS

2006 GENERAL

Kent Conrad (D)	150,146	68.8%
Dwight Grotberg (R)	64,417	29.5%
Roland Riemers (I)	2,194	1.0%

2006 PRIMARY

Kent Conrad (D)	unopposed

PREVIOUS WINNING PERCENTAGES
2000 (62%); 1994 (58%); 1992 Special Election (63%); 1986 (50%)

Elected 1986; 4th full term

A certified deficit hawk with a visceral aversion to debt, Conrad is now in a position to stem the tide of red ink that he sees as endangering the nation. As chairman of the Budget Committee in a Senate narrowly controlled by Democrats, he is determined to put a stop to the cascade of spending and tax cuts enacted without offsets under President Bush.

Conrad was at the forefront of Democrats calling for a return to pay-as-you-go budget rules requiring spending increases and tax cuts to be matched by comparable reductions elsewhere. Republicans let those rules lapse in 2002 and reinstating them will make it tougher for Democrats to increase funding for some of their top priorities, such as beefing up the Medicare prescription drug benefit. But Conrad is adamant.

This is Conrad's second stint at the helm of the Budget Committee; he led the panel from mid-2001 to 2003 when Democrats controlled the Senate by a single vote. He managed to get a budget out of committee on a party-line vote in 2002, but it never came to the floor due to a lack of votes. That was the first time since the advent of the modern budget process in 1974 that the Senate did not adopt a budget resolution, a fact Republicans noted with glee. Given the equally tight Democratic margin in the 110th Congress (2007-08), Conrad has his work cut out for him again.

He has repeatedly condemned the Bush administration for piling up debt, displaying a chart in 2006 showing 42 small heads stacked next to one huge George W. Bush head. His point: It took 42 presidents 224 years to run up $1 trillion in U.S. debt held abroad, while "this president more than doubled that amount in five years."

The chart was vintage Conrad. He was labeled "The Statistician" by Time magazine, which named him one of the 10 best senators in April 2006. He is well-known for his use of charts to make his case. He carts them to the Senate floor for debates on the budget, on spending bills, on agriculture policy, on almost anything. In 2001, the Rules and Administration Committee gave Conrad his own chart-printing equipment because he was running off more than all his colleagues combined. "Never get between Conrad and his charts," quipped Democratic Whip Richard J. Durbin of Illinois during a budget debate in December 2005.

Conrad does not fit the stereotype of a rugged Westerner; he looks more like a bookish "Jeopardy" contestant. But he is a relentless advocate for farmers and the communities built around them, even when his efforts to help them conflict with his fiscal sensibilities. He has been a leader of Western lawmakers' often thwarted efforts throughout the Bush presidency to provide emergency aid to farmers and ranchers hit by drought.

A constant critic of the GOP-drafted 1996 farm law, which sought to phase out traditional crop subsidies and replace them with fixed but declining annual payments, Conrad played a central role in writing the 2002 reversal of that policy that substantially expanded farm subsidies. A member of the Agriculture Committee, he will be involved in a rewrite of that law during the 110th Congress, with a focus on promoting renewable energy sources such as corn-based ethanol and other biofuels. "It's time to look to the Midwest rather than the Mideast for our energy," he says.

Conrad also has not been bashful about pressing for millions of dollars in improvements to the Air Force bases in Grand Forks and Minot. He is a defender of funding for the state National Guard's 119th Fighter Wing, nicknamed the Happy Hooligans, and in 2005 he was able to help protect all of the state's major military bases from closure during the latest BRAC round.

Conrad has disappointed conservatives at times by signaling that he might side with them, then voting against them at the last minute. In the 106th Congress (1999-2000), he decided after much deliberation to oppose a constitutional amendment barring flag desecration. In the 104th (1995-96), Conrad made a late decision to oppose a constitutional amendment mandating a balanced federal budget, which he said could threaten Social Security.

On most social issues, Conrad's positions reflect the more conservative side of the prairie populist tradition from which he hails. In 2004, he voted to make it a criminal offense to injure or kill a fetus during the commission of a violent crime. Before that, he opposed allowing federal employees' health care plans to cover abortion. But he sides with most Democrats in objecting to a constitutional amendment to ban same-sex marriage.

Although he fought Bush's proposal to create private accounts within Social Security, Conrad expressed his willingness to search for ways to shore up the long-term solvency of Social Security. "I'm willing to work with anyone on the problems facing this country, but they've got to be willing to work with me too," he said. "When you work together, both sides have to give, both sides have to make accommodations, and this administration has shown no willingness to give on anything."

Conrad's early years were marked by the deaths of his parents, who were killed in an automobile accident when he was 5. He and his brothers were raised by his grandparents, who moved into the family home in Bismarck. He was surrounded by uncles, aunts and cousins who included him in their vacations and other activities. "I was sort of a group project in many ways," he says fondly.

He went to high school at a U.S. military base in Libya, where he lived with family friends, an experience that shaped his later views on Iraq and the Middle East. "Anybody who knows the history of that part of the world knows that whoever has gone in there, whatever their intentions, have quickly been seen as occupiers rather than liberators, and almost without exception it has ended badly," he said in 2006.

Upon his return to North Dakota, he headed a statewide campaign — while still a teenager — to grant voting rights to 19-year-olds. The effort failed, but his engagement in politics continued. He was elected state tax commissioner in 1980, and he gained widespread popularity by vigorously auditing out-of-state corporations.

Then, in 1986, the troubles besetting North Dakota's farms and small towns gave Conrad an opening against Republican Sen. Mark Andrews. By linking the incumbent to the Reagan administration's unpopular farm policy, Conrad defeated Andrews by 2,000 votes. Conrad carried only one of the state's four major population centers; his victory was built in the countryside.

During that first Senate campaign, Conrad pledged that he would not seek re-election unless the trade and budget deficits were significantly reduced during his term in office. In April 1992, he kept his promise by announcing his retirement.

But in September of that year, North Dakota's senior senator, Democrat Quentin N. Burdick, died at age 84. Democrats persuaded Conrad to run in a special election the following December, and he won with 63 percent of the vote against Republican state Rep. Jack Dalrymple. He has sailed to re-election since then.

On the wall in Conrad's office in Bismarck hangs a prized gift from the state's Standing Rock American Indian Tribe — a framed resolution bearing his honorary Sioux name, "Namni Sni," which means, "Never Turns Back."

Both Conrad and his wife, Lucy Calautti, are avid baseball fans. She has been a lobbyist for Major League Baseball since 2000.

KEY VOTES

2006

Yes Confirm Samuel A. Alito Jr. to the Supreme Court
No Allow consideration of a bill to establish a $140 billion trust fund to compensate victims of asbestos exposure
No Extend tax cuts for two years at a cost of $70 billion over five years
Yes Overhaul immigration policy with border security, enforcement and guest worker program
No Allow consideration of a bill to permanently repeal the estate tax
Yes Urge President Bush to begin troop withdrawals from Iraq in 2006
Yes Lift President Bush's restrictions on stem cell research funding
No Authorize military tribunals for suspected terrorists

2005

Yes Curb class action lawsuits by shifting them from state to federal courts
Yes Allow confirmation vote on Priscilla R. Owen to the U.S. Court of Appeals for the 5th Circuit
? Oppose mandatory emissions limits and block recognition of global warming as a threat
No Approve free-trade pact with five Central American countries
Yes Pass energy policy overhaul favored by President Bush emphasizing domestic oil and gas production
Yes Shield gunmakers from lawsuits when their products are used in crimes
Yes Ban torture of prisoners in U.S. custody
No Renew 16 provisions of the Patriot Act
No Allow final vote on opening the Arctic National Wildlife Refuge to oil and gas exploration

CQ VOTE STUDIES

	PARTY UNITY		PRESIDENTIAL SUPPORT	
	Support	Oppose	Support	Oppose
2006	78%	22%	52%	48%
2005	76%	24%	48%	52%
2004	81%	19%	62%	38%
2003	85%	15%	58%	42%
2002	86%	14%	66%	34%
2001	90%	10%	66%	34%
2000	87%	13%	90%	10%
1999	87%	13%	73%	27%
1998	87%	13%	75%	25%
1997	82%	18%	81%	19%

INTEREST GROUPS

	AFL-CIO	ADA	CCUS	ACU
2006	93%	85%	45%	33%
2005	85%	85%	69%	21%
2004	100%	90%	53%	20%
2003	77%	80%	70%	15%
2002	100%	95%	45%	10%
2001	94%	85%	50%	36%
2000	71%	85%	42%	29%
1999	89%	90%	53%	16%
1998	88%	90%	61%	16%
1997	57%	65%	50%	16%

Sen. Byron L. Dorgan (D)

CAPITOL OFFICE
224-2551
senator@dorgan.senate.gov
dorgan.senate.gov
322 Hart 20510-3405; fax 224-1193

COMMITTEES
Appropriations
(Energy-Water - chairman)
Commerce, Science & Transportation
(Interstate Commerce, Trade & Tourism - chairman)
Energy & Natural Resources
(Energy - chairman)
Indian Affairs - chairman

RESIDENCE
Bismarck

BORN
May 14, 1942, Dickinson, N.D.

RELIGION
Lutheran

FAMILY
Wife, Kim Dorgan; four children (one deceased)

EDUCATION
U. of North Dakota, B.S. 1965; U. of Denver, M.B.A. 1966

CAREER
Aerospace company management trainer

POLITICAL HIGHLIGHTS
N.D. tax commissioner, 1969-80; Democratic nominee for U.S. House, 1974; U.S. House, 1981-92

ELECTION RESULTS

2004 GENERAL

Byron L. Dorgan (D)	211,843	68.3%
Mike Liffrig (R)	98,553	31.8%

2004 PRIMARY

Byron L. Dorgan (D)	unopposed

PREVIOUS WINNING PERCENTAGES
1998 (63%); 1992 (59%); 1990 House Election (65%); 1988 House Election (71%); 1986 House Election (76%); 1984 House Election (79%); 1982 House Election (72%); 1980 House Election (57%)

Elected 1992; 3rd term

Dorgan is the personification of prairie populism, railing against the large and distant forces — multinational corporations, foreign governments, drug companies — that, he says, don't give a whit about ordinary Americans like the hardworking people scattered across his state's windswept plains.

No senator is quicker to defend the family farmer, excoriate multinationals and denounce abuses of power by big government and big business. His pithy pronouncements, on the floor and at news conferences, regularly capture in vivid, plain English what some senators fail to convey in entire speeches. In 2006, as gasoline prices were soaring and oil companies racked up record earnings, Dorgan fought in vain to enact a windfall profits tax.

With the Democrats in control in the 110th Congress (2007-08), Dorgan is well positioned to act on his list of perennial legislative initiatives; he secured the chairmanship of the Indian Affairs Committee as well as three subcommittees — only three other senators hold as many gavels.

He wasted no time pushing his agenda, reintroducing measures allowing for the import of prescription drugs from Canada, prohibiting the import of goods made with sweatshop labor, addressing fraud in federal contracting, promoting alternative fuels research and improving the restitution for victims of crime.

Dorgan also occupies a middle rung on the Democratic leadership ladder as the chairman of the Democratic Policy Committee. He has yearned to move up to the top tier but has been stymied by other ambitious Democrats. In 2004, after Minority Leader Tom Daschle of South Dakota was defeated for re-election, prompting a leadership reshuffling, Dorgan considered running for the No. 2 job of party whip. He bowed out days later when Richard J. Durbin of Illinois claimed enough votes to prevail.

At the outset of the 110th Congress, his colleagues chose Dorgan for a fifth, two-year term as policy chairman, the engine for new ideas for Senate Democrats. He was credited with expanding the committee's mission to include aggressive oversight of the executive branch when few of the Republican-controlled regular committees were doing any. His hearings, even without benefit of subpoena power, exposed disillusionment with the war in Iraq among top military brass and failures of private contractors there to deliver on promised services.

After the Democratic sweep in 2006, Dorgan claimed the gavel of the Indian Affairs Committee. While in the minority as the panel's senior Democrat, he built a working relationship with Republican Chairman John McCain of Arizona. The two ran the high-profile investigation into the activities of convicted lobbyist Jack Abramoff, suspected of bilking American Indian tribes with casino operations. In 2006, they teamed up on legislation to tighten federal regulation of Indian gaming and worked to develop a legislative settlement for a decade-old lawsuit seeking damages in the billions for federal mismanagement of Indian trust fund accounts.

Dorgan parted company with McCain, and with a majority of his fellow Democrats, on another issue that generated far more heat in 2006 — immigration. He was among a handful of Democrats who opposed the legalization of millions of immigrant workers already in the United States illegally.

Dorgan was raised in the wheat-growing and ranching community of Regent, where, he likes to say, he graduated in the top five of his high school class of nine. Farm issues often dominate his agenda. In late 2006, he held up a routine agriculture spending bill by adding $4 billion in aid to farmers who lost crops and livestock to drought and fire in 2005 and 2006. Budget conservatives objected, halting progress on the bill. Although he generally opposed the Bush administration's efforts to scale back the 2002 farm law, he strongly supported its proposal to put a $250,000 limit on federal farm payments. Dorgan believes federal payments should go to family farms, not agribusiness.

Hopes for a huge new market for U.S. farm commodities led Dorgan to support a 2000 law granting permanent normal trade relations to China. By 2006, however, he was ready to reverse course, charging that unchecked product counterfeiting, artificially low wages for China's workers and other abuses had created an uneven playing field for U.S. farmers. Dorgan joined Republican Lindsey Graham of South Carolina in seeking to revoke China's permanent normal trade status, declaring there was "nothing normal" about a relationship that had led to huge trade deficits.

He also has been a leader in a bipartisan effort to end the embargo on trade with Cuba, and has hailed the limited agricultural sales permitted under current law. As chairman of the Senate Commerce panel's trade subcommittee, Dorgan is holding a series of hearings in 2007 to spotlight flaws in U.S. trade policy.

Although Dorgan is a shade to the left of Democrat Kent Conrad, his North Dakota partner in the Senate, the two are very much in harmony both politically and personally. When Dorgan first ran for Congress in 1974, Conrad was his campaign manager. When Dorgan won a House seat six years later, his successor as state tax commissioner was Conrad. Lucy Calautti, Conrad's wife, was Dorgan's chief of staff for 10 years.

As a Democrat representing a state that twice voted solidly for President Bush, Dorgan takes care not to stray too far to the left of his constituents. He joined Republicans, for example, in supporting the 1996 welfare overhaul. He was in the minority of Democrats who voted in 2002 to authorize the use of force in Iraq. In 2003, he supported a ban on a procedure that opponents call "partial birth" abortion. In 2005, he voted to confirm Chief Justice John G. Roberts Jr., but in 2006 he voted against Justice Samuel A. Alito Jr.

Other than a brief stint with a Denver-based aerospace firm, Dorgan has spent virtually his entire career in government. Back home in Regent, population 211, his father was in the petroleum business. His parents also raised horses and were active in the Farmers Union, providing Dorgan his earliest exposure to civic involvement.

While Dorgan was still in graduate school, Gov. William Guy recruited him to be deputy tax commissioner. In 1969, when the commissioner died, Dorgan took his place, becoming, at 26, the youngest constitutional officer in North Dakota's history. He made a name for himself by speaking out on an array of issues and suing out-of-state corporations for unpaid taxes.

Dorgan took on GOP Rep. Mark Andrews in 1974, holding him to 56 percent of the vote. When Andrews ran for the Senate in 1980, Dorgan captured the at-large House seat in a campaign in which he tempered his liberal reputation by supporting an anti-abortion constitutional amendment and decrying government waste. He won five re-elections with ease and became a leading opponent on the Ways and Means Committee of the tax cuts proposed by Presidents Ronald Reagan and George H.W. Bush.

He won election to the Senate with 59 percent of the vote in 1992, after Conrad announced he was retiring to fulfill a campaign pledge to leave the Senate that year unless the deficit was reduced. (Conrad won a Senate seat that year anyway, after Sen. Quentin N. Burdick died.) Dorgan was re-elected in 1998 with 63 percent and widened that edge to 68 percent in 2004.

KEY VOTES

2006

- No Confirm Samuel A. Alito Jr. to the Supreme Court
- No Allow consideration of a bill to establish a $140 billion trust fund to compensate victims of asbestos exposure
- No Extend tax cuts for two years at a cost of $70 billion over five years
- No Overhaul immigration policy with border security, enforcement and guest worker program
- No Allow consideration of a bill to permanently repeal the estate tax
- Yes Urge President Bush to begin troop withdrawals from Iraq in 2006
- Yes Lift President Bush's restrictions on stem cell research funding
- No Authorize military tribunals for suspected terrorists

2005

- No Curb class action lawsuits by shifting them from state to federal courts
- No Allow confirmation vote on Priscilla R. Owen to the U.S. Court of Appeals for the 5th Circuit
- ? Oppose mandatory emissions limits and block recognition of global warming as a threat
- No Approve free-trade pact with five Central American countries
- Yes Pass energy policy overhaul favored by President Bush emphasizing domestic oil and gas production
- Yes Shield gunmakers from lawsuits when their products are used in crimes
- Yes Ban torture of prisoners in U.S. custody
- No Renew 16 provisions of the Patriot Act
- No Allow final vote on opening the Arctic National Wildlife Refuge to oil and gas exploration

CQ VOTE STUDIES

	PARTY UNITY		PRESIDENTIAL SUPPORT	
	Support	Oppose	Support	Oppose
2006	80%	20%	46%	54%
2005	88%	12%	40%	60%
2004	84%	16%	62%	38%
2003	90%	10%	55%	45%
2002	88%	12%	70%	30%
2001	91%	9%	68%	32%
2000	90%	10%	90%	10%
1999	88%	12%	73%	27%
1998	87%	13%	76%	24%
1997	87%	13%	81%	19%

INTEREST GROUPS

	AFL-CIO	ADA	CCUS	ACU
2006	93%	95%	33%	12%
2005	86%	100%	33%	17%
2004	100%	95%	50%	20%
2003	92%	80%	61%	10%
2002	100%	90%	50%	20%
2001	94%	85%	50%	36%
2000	75%	90%	46%	16%
1999	100%	95%	35%	12%
1998	88%	90%	61%	12%
1997	86%	80%	50%	16%

Rep. Earl Pomeroy (D)

CAPITOL OFFICE
225-2611
rep.earl.pomeroy@mail.house.gov
www.pomeroy.house.gov
1501 Longworth 20515-3401; fax 226-0893

COMMITTEES
Agriculture
Ways & Means

RESIDENCE
Mandan

BORN
Sept. 2, 1952, Valley City, N.D.

RELIGION
Presbyterian

FAMILY
Divorced; two children

EDUCATION
Valley City State U., attended 1970-71; U. of North Dakota, B.A. 1974 (political science); U. of Durham (United Kingdom), attended 1975 (legal history); U. of North Dakota, J.D. 1979

CAREER
Lawyer

POLITICAL HIGHLIGHTS
N.D. House, 1981-85; N.D. insurance commissioner, 1985-93

ELECTION RESULTS

2006 GENERAL		
Earl Pomeroy (D)	142,934	65.7%
Matt Mechtel (R)	74,687	34.3%
2006 PRIMARY		
Earl Pomeroy (D)		unopposed
2004 GENERAL		
Earl Pomeroy (D)	185,130	59.6%
Duane Sand (R)	125,684	40.4%

PREVIOUS WINNING PERCENTAGES
2002 (52%); 2000 (53%); 1998 (56%); 1996 (55%); 1994 (52%); 1992 (57%)

Elected 1992; 8th term

On the surface, Pomeroy is the very picture of a Midwesterner, friendly and relaxed with a schoolboy grin, the product of an upbringing that he describes as "pretty much Ozzie and Harriet." But his politics are more complex, and he can be torn between his international interests and social welfare bent and the agricultural and conservative foundations of his state.

Pomeroy and his now ex-wife adopted two Korean children, and he helped re-unite a family torn apart in the Kosovo war. In 2005, he helped an Iraqi family immigrate to North Dakota after the father was killed assisting North Dakota National Guard soldiers. But he is a strong supporter of government subsidies for U.S. farmers and an opponent of free-trade deals, positions that amount to closing U.S. markets to foreign farmers.

He has voted to limit access to abortion and says tax dollars should not be used to pay for the procedure. In 2006, he voted for a bill that would have criminalized the transport of minors across state lines to get an abortion. His vote represents North Dakota values, Pomeroy says. "There's a strong consensus there that taxpayer funding of abortion is not a good use of money." But Pomeroy supports federal funding of embryonic stem cell research because North Dakota has a high incidence of type 1 juvenile diabetes and Parkinson's disease. "Their hope for a cure is in stem cell research," he said in an interview. "I think we'll look back on this administration and shake our heads at its disregard for science."

Keeping to the center is wise politics in a state that has strongly supported President Bush, giving him 63 percent of the vote in 2004. Pomeroy has had his own share of close elections.

Pomeroy is well-known in the House for his expertise on complex financial issues, particularly insurance and pension law. He honed his knowledge of pension law during eight years as North Dakota's insurance commissioner. He has worked with members of both parties on private pension issues, and once added a proposal to pension overhaul legislation to make it easier for workers to transfer their retirement savings to a new job.

In 2001, he won appointment to the Ways and Means Committee, where he sits on the Social Security panel. He is no fan of Bush's proposal to divert some of Social Security's payroll taxes into individual investment accounts. After Pomeroy's father died in 1971, his family relied on Social Security survivor benefits to put him through college.

He also sits on the Agriculture Committee, where he does his best to protect his state's farmers. He fought Bush's attempts to re-open the border to Canadian beef cattle imports and to pass a free-trade agreement with Australia. Pomeroy says the free-trade pact could harm North Dakota wheat growers. He's skeptical of the reputed benefits of free-trade deals in general. "Those deals haven't opened up markets," he says.

In the 110th Congress (2007-08), Pomeroy plans to continue to focus on issues important to rural America. He wants to examine a provision of the tax code that he believes has helped inflate the price of farmland, and he plans to continue to press for higher Medicare reimbursement rates for rural hospitals. Early in 2007, he and South Dakota Democrat Stephanie Herseth-Sandlin made the case for including emergency agriculture spending in a supplemental spending bill for the war on Iraq. Pomeroy said the funds were necessary and there was a precedent for "making sure our farmers aren't wiped out by natural disasters."

Pomeroy had initially supported Bush on the invasion of Iraq, and in

October 2005, he told the Grand Forks Herald that withdrawing troops wouldn't be a good idea. But by 2007, he said he has "completely lost confidence" in the war, and that he feels he was duped into supporting it. "I feel very badly about that vote and this war that was launched under circumstances that did not exist," he says.

Pomeroy has been close to North Dakota's two Democratic senators, Kent Conrad and Byron L. Dorgan, since the 1970s. Just a year out of college, Pomeroy drove Dorgan around the state in an unsuccessful campaign for the House. Conrad was Dorgan's campaign manager. "They're like brothers to me," he says. "We trust each other, we see the world the same way." The three friends work closely on state-specific issues such as getting disaster aid to farmers who have lost crops due to flood and fire.

Pomeroy grew up in a small North Dakota town where his father ran a feed and fertilizer store. He and his brother raised chickens on the family's small farm to make a few extra dollars. As a young man, he traveled with his church to Mississippi to work in the civil rights battle and helped mentally disabled people in his hometown. By "immersion in issues that represented real areas of neglect, I came to see politics as a way to advance social change," he said.

During college, Pomeroy won a Rotary Foundation award to study legal history at the University of Durham in the United Kingdom. When he returned to the states, he was inspired to enter law school, a result of his overseas studies and television. "All my life, I loved watching those lawyer shows on TV," he said. "The lawyers on those shows were always fighting for great causes." While in law school, he managed his brother Glenn's campaign for the state legislature. In 1980, Pomeroy won his own seat. "In North Dakota, there are no waiting lines for political participation," he said. "You don't have to be wealthy and you don't have to be a third- or fourth-generation politician."

In 1992, Pomeroy and his wife decided to join the Peace Corps and move to Russia, but at that year's state Democratic convention Conrad announced his retirement due to a campaign promise not to seek re-election unless the deficit was reduced. A political scramble ensued. Then-Rep. Dorgan went after Conrad's Senate seat, while a party delegate urged Pomeroy to consider a run for the House. Hours before the nominations were to begin, Pomeroy agreed to the campaign, which he won by 17 percentage points.

In all of his subsequent re-elections, he has been held to less than 60 percent of the vote. But in 2006, he won easily with 66 percent against little-known GOP opponent Matt Mechtel, a 37-year-old soybean farmer.

KEY VOTES

2006

- Yes Stop broadband companies from favoring select Internet traffic
- No Affirm U.S. commitment to war in Iraq and reject setting a withdrawal date for troops
- No Repeal requirement for bilingual ballots at the polls
- Yes Permit U.S. sale of civilian nuclear technology to India
- Yes Build a 700-mile fence on the U.S.-Mexico border to curb illegal crossings
- No Permit warrantless wiretaps of suspected terrorists

2005

- Yes Intervene in the life-support case of Terri Schiavo
- Yes Lift President Bush's restrictions on stem cell research funding
- Yes Prohibit FBI access to library and bookstore records
- No Approve free-trade pact with five Central American countries
- Yes Pass energy policy overhaul favored by President Bush emphasizing domestic oil and gas production
- Yes End mandatory preservation of habitat of endangered animal and plant species
- Yes Ban torture of prisoners in U.S. custody

CQ VOTE STUDIES

	PARTY UNITY		PRESIDENTIAL SUPPORT	
	Support	Oppose	Support	Oppose
2006	81%	19%	47%	53%
2005	80%	20%	41%	59%
2004	82%	18%	47%	53%
2003	76%	24%	51%	49%
2002	78%	22%	58%	42%

INTEREST GROUPS

	AFL-CIO	ADA	CCUS	ACU
2006	100%	80%	50%	38%
2005	93%	90%	67%	36%
2004	93%	85%	67%	28%
2003	73%	65%	57%	36%
2002	78%	70%	60%	32%

NORTH DAKOTA

At large

North Dakota includes fertile eastern Red River farmlands, wheat-covered plains, arid grasslands farther west and Teddy Roosevelt's beloved ranches near the western border.

The state's agriculture-based economy must withstand extreme weather conditions, most recently severe droughts in the northwestern and southwestern corners. The climate, foreign competition and a reduction in federal support systems have shaken the state's agricultural foundation. The energy industry — biofuel, coal, gas and oil — is growing in the western part of the state, helping to offset the agricultural downturn. Technology has emerged as a significant economic contributor in the eastern part of the state, with Fargo hosting a Microsoft campus.

Economic trends have intensified migration of the state's young people away from rural farming communities and into the cities of Fargo and Grand Forks, where a diversified economy, health care facilities and several universities provide greater job choice. Local lawmakers have supported legislation that would encourage people, through tax breaks and other incentives, to live and work in scarcely populated, rural areas.

North Dakota's entire congressional delegation has been Democratic for two decades. Republicans are more numerous and unwavering in the western part of the state, while eastern communities and American Indian reservations are more supportive of Democrats. But Republican roots are strong throughout the state — the state legislature and governorship are GOP-controlled and George W. Bush handily carried the state in the 2004 presidential election.

MAJOR INDUSTRY
Agriculture, energy, technology, health care, higher education

MILITARY BASES
Minot Air Force Base, 4,590 military, 1,237 civilian (2006); Grand Forks Air Force Base, 2,310 military, 1,112 civilian (2006)

CITIES
Fargo, 90,599; Bismarck, 55,532; Grand Forks, 49,321; Minot, 36,567

NOTABLE
Lewis and Clark met Sacagawea, the Shoshone Indian woman who guided them to the Pacific Ocean, near the Mandan Indian village; The National Buffalo Museum is in Jamestown.

OHIO

Gov. Ted Strickland (D)

First elected: 2006
Length of term: 4 years
Term expires: 1/11
Salary: $144,830
Phone: (614) 466-3555

Residence: Bexley
Born: Aug. 4, 1941; Lucasville, Ohio
Religion: Methodist
Family: Wife, Frances Smith Strickland
Education: Asbury College, B.A. 1963 (history); U. of Kentucky, M.A. 1966 (guidance counseling); Asbury Theological Seminary, M.A. 1967 (divinity); U. of Kentucky, Ph.D. 1980 (counseling psychology)
Career: Professor; psychologist; minister
Political highlights: Democratic nominee for U.S. House, 1976, 1978, 1980; U.S. House, 1993-95; defeated for re-election to U.S. House, 1994; U.S. House, 1997-2007

Election results:

2006 GENERAL		
Ted Strickland (D)	2,435,384	60.5%
J. Kenneth Blackwell (R)	1,474,285	36.6%
William S. Peirce (X)	71,468	1.8%
Robert Fitrakis (X)	40,965	1.0%

Lt. Gov. Lee Fisher (D)

First Elected: 2006
Length of term: 4 years
Term expires: 1/11
Salary: Does not receive salary as lieutenant governor; earns $142,500 as the director of the Department of Development
Phone: (614) 466-3379

LEGISLATURE

General Assembly: January-June in odd-numbered years; January-July in even-numbered years

Senate: 33 members, 4-year terms
2007 ratios: 21 R, 12 D; 27 men, 6 women
Salary: $58,934
Phone: (614) 466-4900

House: 99 members, 2-year terms
2007 ratios: 53 R, 46 D; 83 men, 16 women
Salary: $58,934
Phone: (614) 466-3357

TERM LIMITS

Governor: 2 terms
Senate: 2 consecutive terms
House: 4 consecutive terms

URBAN STATISTICS

CITY	POPULATION
Columbus	711,470
Cleveland	478,403
Cincinnati	331,285
Toledo	313,619
Akron	217,074

REGISTERED VOTERS

Democrat	47%
Republican	47%
Unaffiliated	7%

POPULATION

2006 population (est.)	11,478,006
2000 population	11,353,140
1990 population	10,847,115
Percent change (1990-2000)	+4.7%
Rank among states (2006)	7
Median age	36.2
Born in state	74.7%
Foreign born	3%
Violent crime rate	334/100,000
Poverty level	10.6%
Federal workers	80,445
Military	36,713

ELECTIONS

STATE ELECTION OFFICIAL
(614) 466-2585
DEMOCRATIC PARTY
(614) 221-6563
REPUBLICAN PARTY
(614) 228-2481

MISCELLANEOUS

Web: www.ohio.gov
Capital: Columbus

U.S. CONGRESS

Senate: 1 Democrat, 1 Republican
House: 11 Republicans, 7 Democrats

2000 Census Statistics by District

DIST.	2004 VOTE FOR PRESIDENT BUSH	KERRY	WHITE	BLACK	ASIAN	HISP	MEDIAN INCOME	WHITE COLLAR	BLUE COLLAR	SERVICE INDUSTRY	OVER 64	UNDER 18	COLLEGE EDUCATION	RURAL	SQ. MILES
1	50%	49%	69%	27%	1%	1%	$37,414	60%	23%	16%	13%	26%	22%	5%	416
2	64	36	92	5	1	1	$46,813	64	23	13	12	26	29	27	2,612
3	54	45	79	17	1	1	$41,591	60	26	14	14	25	23	15	1,595
4	65	34	92	5	1	1	$40,100	47	38	15	14	26	13	41	4,620
5	61	38	94	1	0	4	$41,701	46	40	14	13	26	15	51	6,128
6	50	49	95	2	0	1	$32,888	52	32	16	15	23	14	50	5,198
7	57	42	89	7	1	1	$43,248	57	28	14	12	25	19	29	2,848
8	64	35	92	4	1	1	$43,753	56	30	14	12	26	19	22	2,014
9	42	58	80	14	1	4	$40,265	55	29	16	14	26	20	14	1,102
10	41	58	87	4	2	5	$41,841	63	23	14	16	23	23	1	195
11	18	81	39	56	2	2	$31,998	61	21	17	15	26	23	0	135
12	51	49	72	22	2	2	$47,289	68	18	13	10	27	32	12	1,016
13	44	56	82	12	1	4	$44,524	59	27	14	14	26	22	7	531
14	52	47	94	2	1	1	$51,304	62	25	12	13	26	27	26	1,797
15	50	49	85	7	3	2	$43,885	66	20	14	10	23	32	9	1,178

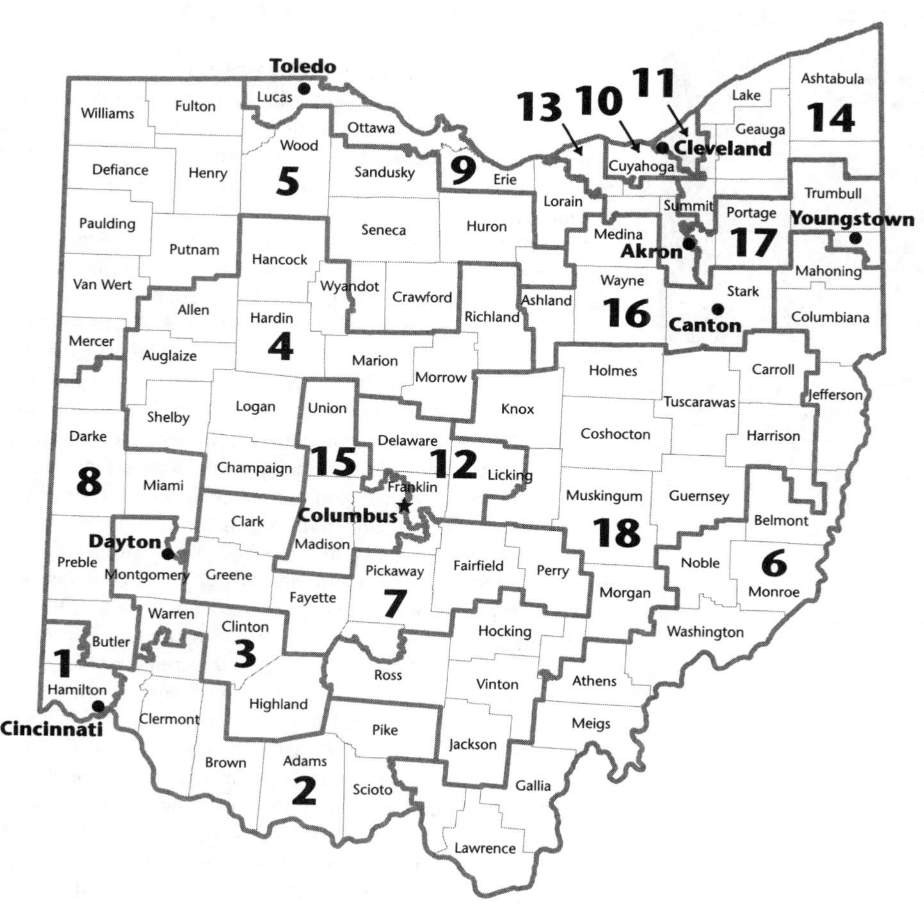

2000 Census Statistics by District

DIST.	2004 VOTE FOR PRESIDENT BUSH	KERRY	WHITE	BLACK	ASIAN	HISP	MEDIAN INCOME	WHITE COLLAR	BLUE COLLAR	SERVICE INDUSTRY	OVER 64	UNDER 18	COLLEGE EDUCATION	RURAL	SQ. MILES
16	54%	46%	92%	5%	1%	1%	$41,801	55%	31%	14%	14%	26%	19%	26%	1,732
17	37	63	85	12	1	2	$36,705	52	32	16	15	24	16	16	1,006
18	57	42	96	2	0	1	$34,462	46	38	16	14	26	11	57	6,826
STATE	51	49	84	11	1	2	$40,956	57	28	15	13	25	21	23	40,948
U.S.	50.7	48.3	69	12	4	13	$41,994	60	25	15	12	26	24	21	3,537,438

Sen. George V. Voinovich (R)

CAPITOL OFFICE
224-3353
voinovich.senate.gov
524 Hart 20510-3504; fax 228-1382

COMMITTEES
Environment & Public Works
Foreign Relations
Homeland Security & Governmental Affairs

RESIDENCE
Cleveland

BORN
July 15, 1936, Cleveland, Ohio

RELIGION
Roman Catholic

FAMILY
Wife, Janet Voinovich; four children (one deceased)

EDUCATION
Ohio U., B.A. 1958 (government); Ohio State U., J.D. 1961

CAREER
Lawyer; state prosecutor

POLITICAL HIGHLIGHTS
Ohio House, 1967-71; Cuyahoga County auditor, 1971-76; Cuyahoga County Commission, 1977-78; lieutenant governor, 1979; mayor of Cleveland, 1979-89; Republican nominee for U.S. Senate, 1988; governor, 1991-99

ELECTION RESULTS

2004 GENERAL		
George V. Voinovich (R)	3,464,356	63.9%
Eric D. Fingerhut (D)	1,961,171	36.2%
2004 PRIMARY		
George V. Voinovich (R)	640,082	76.6%
John R. Mitchel (R)	195,476	23.4%

PREVIOUS WINNING PERCENTAGES
1998 (56%)

Elected 1998; 2nd term

After voting for President Bush's massive tax cuts in 2001 and 2003, Voinovich is one of the few congressional Republicans to express buyer's remorse. As huge annual budget deficits have returned and the cumulative national debt has soared, he has voiced strong reservations about further tax cuts. He has even suggested that a temporary tax increase might be warranted.

In 2006, Voinovich was one of three Senate Republicans voting against an extension of the reduced tax rates for capital gains and dividends enacted in 2003. When Republicans tried to permanently repeal the federal estate tax, Voinovich was one of two Senate Republicans to vote against the effort, which failed. "I don't like the estate tax," he explained, "but I think doing away with it is bad. We've got to raise revenue to pay for expenses."

Early in the 110th Congress (2007-08), as the Democratically controlled Senate debated the federal budget, Voinovich was one of two Republicans to vote against an amendment making room for an extension of all the 2001 tax cuts. He was the sole Republican voting against a separate GOP amendment calling for a reduction in the alternative minimum tax rate.

Voinovich sees fiscal disaster in the combined strains of Iraq War funding, soaring Social Security and Medicare costs, and reduced tax revenues. A fierce proponent of pay-as-you-go budgeting, he says, "I think everybody is playing games. If we were responsible right now, we would have a temporary tax. We're putting everything on the credit card for our children."

The Ohio Republican isn't afraid to go it alone on other issues. In 2005, he balked at confirming Bush's controversial choice to be U.S. representative to the United Nations. Voinovich, a member of the Foreign Relations Committee, cited John R. Bolton's confrontational personality and uncompromising approach to foreign policy in refusing to support the nomination. Bush sent Bolton to the United Nations anyway, with a temporary appointment that circumvented Senate confirmation. By 2006, Voinovich was willing to vote for Bolton, having watched him perform in the job. But Democratic critics remained adamant, and Bolton resigned in December.

Voinovich (VOY-no-vitch) is friendlier to labor and its causes than many Republicans. As mayor of Cleveland in the 1980s, he worked closely with public employee unions to rescue the city from insolvency. He says he weighs labor issues one by one: "Some I support, others I don't."

In 2002, as the Senate worked on legislation to create the Department of Homeland Security, Voinovich's colleagues often called on his knowledge of government personnel issues. Though he was actively engaged in the congressional debate, Voinovich was not included in the inner circle of GOP negotiators. His historically good working relations with government employee unions gave other Republicans pause.

In the 109th Congress (2005-06), on votes that pitted one party against the other, Voinovich sided with his fellow Republicans 81 percent of the time. Only a half-dozen other Republicans split with their party more often.

His independent and unassuming ways appear to sit well back home. Voinovich was re-elected to a second term in 2004 with 64 percent of the vote, when Bush, at the top of the ticket, was just squeaking by in Ohio. Voinovich is well-known in the state. In addition to his 10 years as Cleveland's mayor, he was Ohio's governor for eight years.

As a result of this past experience, Voinovich frequently argues for more local control in deciding how to spend federal funds. He applauded the 1999

"Ed-Flex" law that gave states the flexibility to spend federal education money with fewer strings attached. But in 2001, he cast one of only three Republican no votes in the Senate against Bush's No Child Left Behind legislation, a major rewrite of education policy that was signed into law in 2002 and that tied federal aid to performance on student achievement tests. Voinovich called it an "all-out assault on local control."

Of Serbian and Slovenian ancestry, Voinovich in his first year as a senator took a politically risky stance as a vocal opponent of the NATO military action in Kosovo, which involved U.S. forces. He advocated continued diplomatic negotiations with Serb leader Slobodan Milosevic, but refused to go to Serbia as long as Milosevic was in control. He also played a leading Senate role in the 2002 expansion of NATO that brought in Slovenia, Romania and the Baltic states, and still hopes to see Balkan nations such as Macedonia, Croatia and Albania join the alliance in the future. He traveled to the region in 2006 for high-level meetings.

Voinovich chaired the Senate Ethics Committee in the 108th Congress (2003-04) and the 109th Congress, an often thankless task that few senators enjoy. He had to investigate allegations that fellow Republican Richard C. Shelby of Alabama had passed classified national security information to the media. The committee cleared Shelby in 2005.

As the Senate debated tighter ethics and lobbying rules in 2007, Voinovich, like most of his colleagues, opposed creation of an outside office to investigate complaints against senators. He argued that it could create conflicts between the investigative body and the committee members who would have to decide what action to take after an investigation was completed.

To his dismay, he got the most public attention in his first term for boycotting a Capitol Hill hearing on coal mining regulations at which a member of the teen idol band Backstreet Boys was to testify. Voinovich, who had worked to bring the Rock and Roll Hall of Fame to Cleveland, said he objected to the growing use of celebrities to get media attention for issues on which they have no expertise. "This isn't about music, it's about substance," he said. "Even if this guy was a polka musician, I would still object to him."

The grandson of immigrants reared on Cleveland's east side, where he still lives, Voinovich is the oldest of six children. His father was an architect, his mother a schoolteacher. Until Voinovich was 16, he wanted to be a doctor. But, he said, "sciences and I didn't get along, and I like other stuff better — like Boy Scouts." He became president of his high school class and was voted most likely to succeed. Friends from that era tell him he predicted even then that he would someday be mayor and governor.

He made it, and then some. After an early political career that included four years in the state House and four more as Cuyahoga County auditor, he was elected lieutenant governor in 1978. The next year, he unseated Cleveland Mayor Dennis J. Kucinich, now a Democratic Ohio congressman, after the city went into financial default on Kucinich's watch. With the help of a financial control board, Voinovich reversed some of the city's problems.

He lost a 1988 race against Democratic Sen. Howard M. Metzenbaum, by 14 percentage points. "I was damaged goods," he says. "But we have a tradition in Ohio. You can't win statewide until you run and lose."

Voinovich rebounded two years later, winning the governorship. During his two terms, he won acclaim for putting the state on solid financial footing. In 1998, when Democratic Sen. John Glenn retired after four terms, Voinovich was instantly his presumptive successor. He was not seriously challenged for the GOP nomination and won the general election easily over Democrat Mary O. Boyle, a former Cuyahoga County commissioner. His 2004 re-election was a breeze; he won by almost 28 percentage points.

KEY VOTES

2006

Yes Confirm Samuel A. Alito Jr. to the Supreme Court
Yes Allow consideration of a bill to establish a $140 billion trust fund to compensate victims of asbestos exposure
No Extend tax cuts for two years at a cost of $70 billion over five years
Yes Overhaul immigration policy with border security, enforcement and guest worker program
No Allow consideration of a bill to permanently repeal the estate tax
No Urge President Bush to begin troop withdrawals from Iraq in 2006
No Lift President Bush's restrictions on stem cell research funding
Yes Authorize military tribunals for suspected terrorists

2005

Yes Curb class action lawsuits by shifting them from state to federal courts
Yes Allow confirmation vote on Priscilla R. Owen to the U.S. Court of Appeals for the 5th Circuit
Yes Oppose mandatory emissions limits and block recognition of global warming as a threat
Yes Approve free-trade pact with five Central American countries
Yes Pass energy policy overhaul favored by President Bush emphasizing domestic oil and gas production
Yes Shield gunmakers from lawsuits when their products are used in crimes
Yes Ban torture of prisoners in U.S. custody
Yes Renew 16 provisions of the Patriot Act
Yes Allow final vote on opening the Arctic National Wildlife Refuge to oil and gas exploration

CQ VOTE STUDIES

	PARTY UNITY		PRESIDENTIAL SUPPORT	
	Support	Oppose	Support	Oppose
2006	77%	23%	89%	11%
2005	84%	16%	87%	13%
2004	88%	12%	90%	10%
2003	93%	7%	95%	5%
2002	88%	12%	96%	4%
2001	92%	8%	95%	5%
2000	78%	22%	59%	41%
1999	87%	13%	45%	55%

INTEREST GROUPS

	AFL-CIO	ADA	CCUS	ACU
2006	40%	20%	75%	56%
2005	29%	15%	100%	68%
2004	42%	30%	94%	76%
2003	15%	15%	100%	83%
2002	33%	5%	95%	90%
2001	13%	15%	93%	83%
2000	13%	10%	80%	64%
1999	33%	20%	82%	88%

Sen. Sherrod Brown (D)

CAPITOL OFFICE
224-2315
brown.senate.gov
455 Russell 20510-3503; fax 228-6321

COMMITTEES
Agriculture, Nutrition & Forestry
Banking, Housing & Urban Affairs
Health, Education, Labor & Pensions
Veterans' Affairs

RESIDENCE
Avon

BORN
Nov. 9, 1952, Mansfield, Ohio

RELIGION
Lutheran

FAMILY
Wife, Connie Schultz; two children, two stepchildren

EDUCATION
Yale U., B.A. 1974 (Russian & East European studies); Ohio State U., M.A. 1979 (education), M.A. 1981 (public administration)

CAREER
College instructor

POLITICAL HIGHLIGHTS
Ohio House, 1975-83; Ohio secretary of state, 1983-91; defeated for re-election as Ohio secretary of state, 1990; U.S. House, 1993-2007

ELECTION RESULTS

2006 GENERAL		
Sherrod Brown (D)	2,257,369	56.2%
Mike DeWine (R)	1,761,037	43.8%
2006 PRIMARY		
Sherrod Brown (D)	583,776	78.1%
Merrill Samuel Keiser (D)	163,628	21.9%

PREVIOUS WINNING PERCENTAGES
2004 House Election (67%); 2002 House Election (69%); 2000 House Election (65%); 1998 House Election (62%); 1996 House Election (60%); 1994 House Election (49%); 1992 House Election (53%)

Elected 2006; 1st term

Brown espouses a liberal populism that is a sharp departure from the moderately conservative views of Republican Mike DeWine, whom he defeated in 2006, and much more like those of DeWine's Democratic predecessor, Howard M. Metzenbaum (1974, 1976-95).

A self-described progressive with acute political instincts, Brown counsels Democrats and liberals to take definite stands rather than blurring differences with Republican opponents on policy issues. Brown dismisses that as "Republican lite," and instead exhorts liberals to highlight differences with their opponents. "Make the sharp contrast between what they have done and a bold, progressive version of what progressives can do," Brown told a conference of liberals in 2006.

Brown made a mark during his 14-year tenure in the House with his vigorous opposition to treaties such as the North American and Central American free-trade agreements, which he says have harmed the manufacturing industry in his state and across the nation and exacerbated the nation's trade deficit. The author of a 2004 book, "The Myths of Free Trade," he says he would revamp trade pacts with incentives for corporations to create jobs in this country rather than outsource them.

"We need a trade policy that rewards companies that keep production, and headquarters, in the United States, investing at home as well as in opportunities abroad," Brown said in March 2007 — a month after he became a chief sponsor of legislation to rescind permanent normal trade relations with China.

A vigorous advocate of increasing the federal minimum wage, Brown's vote at the start of the 110th Congress (2007-08) to increase that wage floor to $7.25 per hour over two years reflected his virtual unanimity with the positions of labor unions. In 10 of his 14 years in the House, Brown received a 100 percent score from the AFL-CIO.

He wears his allegiance on his chest — literally: A lapel pin depicting a canary in a cage serves as a reminder that miners a century ago brought canaries into shafts to determine whether there were toxic gases present. People are living longer and have a better quality of life, Brown said in 2006, because of "what progressives have fought for" over the past century — including programs such as Social Security, Medicare, workers' compensation, pension guarantees, and clean air and water.

Brown entered the Senate as a strong opponent of the Bush administration's strategy in Iraq; during the 2006 campaign, he advocated a plan to withdraw troops over the next 18 to 24 months. "Voters and people across the country want to see a very different Iraq policy," Brown said that month. "Most people, overwhelming numbers in this country, do not want American soldiers in the midst of a civil war. And it's time for a very different direction in Iraq."

Brown opposed many other Bush administration initiatives — including the 2003 Medicare prescription drug law and a 2005 overhaul of energy laws, which Brown says were boons to industry. He would revoke tax cuts for the wealthy but use them to help middle-class families, including providing breaks for college tuition.

His liberalism also extends to social issues, and infuses both his public life and his private life. Long divorced, Brown had become an enthusiastic reader of columns about Cleveland's neglected and needy written by a liberal local newspaper woman. Brown sent an admiring e-mail to the writer, future Pulitzer-prize winner Connie Schultz. E-mailing led to a meeting and quickly to romance; less than a year after their first date in 2003, they were married. To avoid a conflict of interest, Schultz gave up her column once Brown's Senate campaign got under way.

Raised in Mansfield, in the north-central part of the state, Brown's first taste of elective office came as student council president in high school, where he also found time to become an Eagle Scout. He spent summers working on the family dairy farm in nearby Lexington.

Brown is the first Ohio senator in more than 40 years to sit on the Agriculture Committee, where his priorities for the 2007 farm bill reauthorization include expanded conservation and renewable energy initiatives, greater assistance for beginning farmers and nutrition programs that make fruits and vegetables more affordable.

His interest in politics was sparked by the Vietnam War, the civil rights movement and the 1968 presidential candidacy of Robert F. Kennedy.

Brown was 21 when he was elected to the Ohio House in 1974 — the same year he earned a degree in Russian studies from Yale. He served in the state legislature for eight years, followed by an eight-year stint as Ohio secretary of state. He was defeated for re-election in 1990 by Republican Bob Taft, who would later serve two terms as governor.

In 1992, Brown won the open seat in the 13th District — which lies west of Cleveland — overcoming criticism that he moved into the district to run for Congress. He won a coveted seat on the Energy and Commerce Committee and spent much of his time focusing on trade issues and his strong opposition to the North American Free Trade Agreement, which President Bill Clinton supported.

Brown was nearly defeated for re-election in 1994, a strong Republican year. But he won subsequent elections with ease and in the process amassed a huge campaign treasury to prepare for a long-anticipated bid for governor or senator. Brown originally said that he would not challenge DeWine, citing professional and personal obligations. But he reversed himself in October 2005, saying, "After consulting with my family, fellow Ohioans, and state and national leaders in the Democratic Party, I was honored to accept the call to run statewide."

Early in the campaign, Brown was running even with DeWine, if not a little ahead of him, in public opinion polls — more a reflection of the difficult political environment facing Republicans in 2006 than a sign of DeWine's vulnerabilities. DeWine was hurt by strong public disapproval of Ohio Republicans — including Taft, who had pleaded guilty to misdemeanor campaign finance violations.

DeWine's low-key, moderate style and stance carried some risks in the 2006 campaign. Many conservatives were not pleased with his votes for some gun control measures and his role in helping broker a compromise on federal judicial nominees. But DeWine's voting record was not independent-minded enough — at least not in the anti-Republican climate prevailing in 2006 — to placate Democrats and independents.

DeWine hammered Brown's voting record, particularly his positions on tax policy and national security issues. But Brown won by nearly a half-million votes and a 12 percentage point margin, racking up large percentages in the counties around Cleveland and the state's Mahoning Valley — traditionally the most unionized part of Ohio.

The Ohio Senate race was one of the most expensive in the country. Total spending for the race, by the candidates and the parties, approached $41 million, according to the Federal Election Commission. Of that, DeWine's campaign had expenditures in excess of $14 million, while Brown's spent close to $11 million.

KEY VOTES

House Service:

2006

- Yes Stop broadband companies from favoring select Internet traffic
- No Affirm U.S. commitment to war in Iraq and reject setting a withdrawal date for troops
- No Repeal requirement for bilingual ballots at the polls
- Yes Permit U.S. sale of civilian nuclear technology to India
- Yes Build a 700-mile fence on the U.S.-Mexico border to curb illegal crossings
- No Permit warrantless wiretaps of suspected terrorists

2005

- ? Intervene in the life-support case of Terri Schiavo
- Yes Lift President Bush's restrictions on stem cell research funding
- Yes Prohibit FBI access to library and bookstore records
- No Approve free-trade pact with five Central American countries
- No Pass energy policy overhaul favored by President Bush emphasizing domestic oil and gas production
- No End mandatory preservation of habitat of endangered animal and plant species
- Yes Ban torture of prisoners in U.S. custody

CQ VOTE STUDIES

House Service:

	PARTY UNITY		PRESIDENTIAL SUPPORT	
	Support	Oppose	Support	Oppose
2006	92%	8%	36%	64%
2005	97%	3%	7%	93%
2004	98%	2%	26%	74%
2003	99%	1%	11%	89%
2002	98%	2%	22%	78%
2001	98%	2%	12%	88%
2000	97%	3%	81%	19%
1999	95%	5%	80%	20%
1998	97%	3%	83%	17%
1997	96%	4%	82%	18%

INTEREST GROUPS

House Service:

	AFL-CIO	ADA	CCUS	ACU
2006	93%	75%	40%	25%
2005	93%	100%	33%	4%
2004	100%	95%	24%	4%
2003	100%	100%	25%	16%
2002	100%	95%	25%	4%
2001	100%	95%	22%	4%
2000	100%	90%	25%	4%
1999	100%	100%	0%	0%
1998	100%	100%	17%	4%
1997	100%	100%	22%	12%

Rep. Steve Chabot (R)

CAPITOL OFFICE
225-2216
www.house.gov/chabot
129 Cannon 20515-3501; fax 225-3012

COMMITTEES
Foreign Affairs
Judiciary
Small Business - ranking member

RESIDENCE
Cincinnati

BORN
Jan. 22, 1953, Cincinnati, Ohio

RELIGION
Roman Catholic

FAMILY
Wife, Donna Chabot; two children

EDUCATION
College of William & Mary, B.A. 1975 (history); Northern Kentucky U., J.D. 1978

CAREER
Lawyer; teacher

POLITICAL HIGHLIGHTS
Independent candidate for Cincinnati City Council, 1979; Republican candidate for Cincinnati City Council, 1983; Cincinnati City Council, 1985-90; Republican nominee for U.S. House, 1988; Hamilton County County Board of Commissioner, 1990-95

ELECTION RESULTS

2006 GENERAL		
Steve Chabot (R)	105,680	52.2%
John Cranley (D)	96,584	47.8%
2006 PRIMARY		
Steve Chabot (R)		unopposed
2004 GENERAL		
Steve Chabot (R)	173,430	59.8%
Greg Harris (D)	116,235	40.1%

PREVIOUS WINNING PERCENTAGES
2002 (65%); 2000 (53%); 1998 (53%); 1996 (54%); 1994 (56%)

Elected 1994; 7th term

A diehard from the Republican Class of '94, Chabot is a fierce defender of conservative social positions on the Judiciary Committee. He keeps a framed copy of the House GOP's "Contract with America" on a wall in his congressional office. He won't let his party forget that the GOP came to power in 1994 by promising a balanced budget and then presided over several years of large deficits. Chabot often voted no on Republican-written spending bills when his party was in control.

In 2006, Chabot (SHAB-it) defied Don Young, the GOP chairman of the Transportation and Infrastructure Committee, by seeking to bar the use of federal money to build logging roads for timber companies. Young, of Alaska, wanted the Forest Service to construct roads in the Tongass National Forest in his home state. Chabot said later, "Taxpayers are being ripped off when they have to pay millions of dollars to build roads that are going to benefit the timber industry. To me, that's corporate welfare at its worst."

Chabot usually fails when he takes on the Republican establishment on budget issues, but he gets high praise from conservative groups such as the National Taxpayers Union and Citizens Against Government Waste, one of the harshest critics of the government's spending habits.

In 2007, Chabot became the top Republican on the Small Business panel, where a chief priority is to continue GOP efforts aimed at permitting small businesses to band together to obtain affordable health insurance for their workers.

The Judiciary Committee gives him a forum for expressing his view that the nation is being brought low by "rogue" federal judges. As the chairman of the Judiciary Subcommittee on the Constitution from 2001 to 2006, he advocated numerous, ultimately unsuccessful, proposals to amend the Constitution to ban flag desecration, outlaw same-sex marriage, require a balanced budget, protect crime victims' rights and allow people to pray and display religious symbols on public property.

One of his anti-abortion bills did become law but was struck down in federal court and sent to the Supreme Court to be settled. The legislation outlaws a controversial procedure its opponents call "partial birth" abortion.

Chabot's views on social problems are an even tougher sell in a Democratic Congress. He has his best opportunity to legislate when he finds common ground across the aisle. For example, Chabot joined with liberal Democrat Jerrold Nadler of New York in 2007 on a bill aimed at protecting individual privacy. The measure requires government agencies to prepare privacy impact statements before issuing new regulations.

Chabot also had some success with legislation to empower people challenging government seizures of their property. The House passed the bill on the second try in September 2006 but the Senate did not take up the measure. Chabot was taking aim at recent Supreme Court decisions supporting state and local governments in eminent domain cases.

Though not shy about voicing his conservative beliefs, Chabot often does so with a soft touch, rarely raising his voice or pounding the podium. But his rhetoric has a bite. In 1999, as one of the 13 impeachment "managers" who presented the House's case for removing President Bill Clinton from office, Chabot said of Clinton, "He raised his right hand and swore to tell the truth, the whole truth and nothing but the truth. Then he lied."

Chabot was born and raised in Cincinnati. His father was an optician, and Chabot lived in a trailer for the first few years of his life, working part-time jobs to help with tuition at his parochial high school. In college, he majored in history, then taught elementary school in Cincinnati while attending law school at night across the river at Northern Kentucky University. A few years after earning his law degree, he opened a neighborhood law practice.

Chabot remembers his disappointment at the Watergate scandal and the subsequent pardoning of President Richard Nixon, whom he had voted for in 1972. He supported Democrat Jimmy Carter in the 1976 presidential election over President Gerald Ford after Ford pardoned Nixon.

Chabot's political career began on the Cincinnati City Council. After two failed bids for a seat, the first at age 26, Chabot was elected to the city council in 1985. He lost a congressional bid against Democrat Thomas A. Luken in 1988, then won election in 1990 to Hamilton County's board of commissioners.

Chabot launched his second congressional campaign in 1994 against first-term Democrat David Mann. Emphasizing his blue-collar beginnings and Catholic roots, Chabot campaigned on a platform of lower taxes, less government and change in Washington. With national trends strongly favoring the GOP, he won with 56 percent of the vote.

In the next three elections, Chabot had to fend off charges of being too far to the right for his constituents, who voted for Clinton twice and for Al Gore in 2000. He never topped 54 percent of the vote. But redistricting after the 2000 census made the 1st District more Republican, and in 2002 Chabot cruised to a fifth term with 65 percent and a sixth with 60 percent.

Chabot was among the Republicans who drew strong Democratic challengers in 2006, but he — along with the other nine GOP House members from Ohio on the November ballot — ultimately prevailed. The national wave that toppled the GOP from Congress was still keenly felt in Ohio as Republican Sen. Mike DeWine lost his seat that year.

Chabot's challenger was Democrat John Cranley, a Cincinnati city councilor. In response to Cranley's attacks that Washington had changed him, Chabot ran an ad saying he had lived in the same house for 21 years, been married to the same woman for 33 years, still cut his own grass and drove "the same old '93 Buick." The car had more than 154,000 miles on it, Chabot said.

The local newspaper, the Cincinnati Enquirer, endorsed Cranley in an editorial that read, "Chabot has served with honor, but his effectiveness seems to have peaked. It is time for him to come home." Nevertheless, he was reelected with 52 percent of the vote. By early 2007, the Democrats had targeted Chabot's seat and signed up state Rep. Steve Driehaus to run against him.

KEY VOTES

2006

No Stop broadband companies from favoring select Internet traffic
Yes Affirm U.S. commitment to war in Iraq and reject setting a withdrawal date for troops
No Repeal requirement for bilingual ballots at the polls
Yes Permit U.S. sale of civilian nuclear technology to India
Yes Build a 700-mile fence on the U.S.-Mexico border to curb illegal crossings
? Permit warrantless wiretaps of suspected terrorists

2005

Yes Intervene in the life-support case of Terri Schiavo
No Lift President Bush's restrictions on stem cell research funding
No Prohibit FBI access to library and bookstore records
Yes Approve free-trade pact with five Central American countries
Yes Pass energy policy overhaul favored by President Bush emphasizing domestic oil and gas production
Yes End mandatory preservation of habitat of endangered animal and plant species
No Ban torture of prisoners in U.S. custody

CQ VOTE STUDIES

	PARTY UNITY		PRESIDENTIAL SUPPORT	
	Support	Oppose	Support	Oppose
2006	89%	11%	95%	5%
2005	95%	5%	89%	11%
2004	95%	5%	79%	21%
2003	95%	5%	91%	9%
2002	96%	4%	85%	15%

INTEREST GROUPS

	AFL-CIO	ADA	CCUS	ACU
2006	21%	10%	93%	96%
2005	13%	0%	89%	96%
2004	20%	10%	95%	96%
2003	7%	10%	90%	96%
2002	11%	0%	90%	96%

OHIO 1

Western Cincinnati and suburbs

Nestled in Ohio's southwestern corner, the 1st takes in more than three-fourths of Cincinnati's residents. Traditional German Catholic conservatives in the city and a growing suburban base are crucial to Republicans, while Cincinnati's 43 percent black population is key to Democrats. The politically competitive district has one of the largest black populations overall among Republican-held districts.

The city's diverse economy, which boasts research firms, corporate headquarters and a manufacturing base, has fortified Cincinnati against periodic economic downturns. Access to the Ohio River to the south has helped the city earn a reputation as a regional commercial center. Manufacturing accounts for many blue-collar jobs in the district, and General Electric's aircraft engine branch has headquarters in Cincinnati.

Corporate headquarters in the city, including Procter & Gamble, Federated Department Stores, and Kroger, one of the nation's largest grocery retailers, fuel the district's retail industry and make the city a magnet for consumer market research and development firms.

Cincinnati also has built a reputation as a regional cultural and entertainment hub. Among other attractions, the 1st is home to the Museum Center at Union Terminal, Carew Tower (the tallest building in the city), and Paul Brown Stadium — or "The Jungle," as the home field of football's Bengals is known locally.

Cincinnati's heavily black neighborhoods, including Over-the-Rhine, Avondale and Bond Hill, vote dependably Democratic. Outside of Cincinnati, Hamilton County is becoming slightly more Democratic as the county's GOP base moves farther north. The 1st's heavily Republican share of Butler County (shared with the 8th) and remaining GOP-friendly suburbs in Hamilton County offset the Democratic vote in Cincinnati. In the 2004 presidential election, George W. Bush narrowly lost the 1st's share of Hamilton, but his margin in southwestern Butler County enabled him to eke out a win districtwide.

MAJOR INDUSTRY

Consumer products development and manufacturing, service

CITIES

Cincinnati (pt.), 257,122; Norwood, 21,675; Forest Park, 19,463

NOTABLE

The National Underground Railroad Freedom Center is in Cincinnati.

Rep. Jean Schmidt (R)

CAPITOL OFFICE
225-3164
www.house.gov/schmidt
238 Cannon 20515-3502; fax 225-1992

COMMITTEES
Agriculture
Transportation & Infrastructure

RESIDENCE
Loveland

BORN
Nov. 29, 1951, Cincinnati, Ohio

RELIGION
Roman Catholic

FAMILY
Husband, Peter Schmidt; one child

EDUCATION
U. of Cincinnati, B.A. 1974 (political science)

CAREER
Homemaker; teacher

POLITICAL HIGHLIGHTS
Miami Township trustee, 1990-2000; Clermont County Republican Party chairwoman, 1996-98; Ohio House, 2001-04; sought Republican nomination for Ohio Senate, 2004

ELECTION RESULTS

2006 GENERAL		
Jean Schmidt (R)	120,112	50.5%
Victoria Wulsin (D)	117,595	49.4%
2006 PRIMARY		
Jean Schmidt (R)	33,938	47.7%
Bob McEwen (R)	30,297	42.6%
Deborah A. Kraus (R)	4,433	6.2%
James E. Constable (R)	2,526	3.5%
2005 SPECIAL		
Jean Schmidt (R)	59,671	51.6%
Paul Hackett (D)	55,886	48.4%

Elected August 2005; 1st full term

Schmidt's House career got off to a rough start with a blooper on the floor that saddled her with the label of lightweight. Since then, she has worked at damage control by expressing regret and getting down to work.

In November 2005, after less than three months in office, Schmidt described a prominent Democrat and decorated Marine veteran as a "coward." While defending President Bush and the Iraq War, she recounted a phone call from a constituent in the military and said, "He asked me to send Congress a message: Stay the course. He also asked me to send Congressman Murtha a message: Cowards cut and run, Marines never do."

Her comments sparked boos from lawmakers in the chamber, and Schmidt withdrew her words immediately. She later told reporters that she did not know that Pennsylvania Democrat John P. Murtha was a Marine and a war veteran. She wrote him a note of apology, which he accepted, but that did not end the fallout for Schmidt. The Cincinnati Enquirer called her remarks "way out of line" and she was ridiculed in a TV skit.

The incident reinforced her reputation among critics back in Ohio as "Mean Jean." While Schmidt doesn't care for the nickname, she is proud of her toughness. "You have to be in this environment," Schmidt says. "Politics is not for the faint of heart."

By and large, there is little difference in voting behavior between Schmidt and her predecessor, Republican Rob Portman, who resigned the seat in April 2005 to be Bush's trade envoy. But the two differ markedly in the array of issues for which they are known.

While Portman principally made his mark in economic policy on the tax-writing Ways and Means Committee, Schmidt is a former state legislator with an anti-abortion activist history who is more closely identified with social conservatism.

Before being elected to the House, she was president of the Cincinnati-area Right to Life organization and campaigned on a promise to "uphold the moral values that this district holds so dear." She opposes abortion in all cases and also opposes the death penalty. She supports a constitutional amendment banning same-sex marriage. Schmidt sometimes carries a Bersa semiautomatic handgun that her stockbroker husband gave her as a present.

Schmidt mostly matches her views on social issues with right-of-center economic policy positions. She supports making Bush's tax cuts permanent and favors a flat rate rather than the existing income-based graduated system. Unlike Portman, she is skeptical about some free-trade pacts.

Her legislative achievement in her first term was an amendment making it easier for the public to access the disclosure information of foreign lobbyists. It passed in the House but was not taken up in the Senate.

Those activities won her praise from The Enquirer, which endorsed her in 2006 and said that, though "her comments still can be distressingly simplistic on topics such as North Korea," she had "quietly been establishing herself as a working congresswoman."

In the 110th Congress (2007-08), Schmidt planned to push legislation requiring abortion providers to discuss fetal pain. And, from her seat on the Transportation and Infrastructure Committee, Schmidt says she wants to investigate the causes of airplane delays.

Schmidt grew up around auto racing in Clermont County in southern Ohio. Her father, Gus Hoffman, was a race car driver and founder of Hoffman Auto Racing. She says the "best day of my life" was May 8, 1974, when her father's car qualified for the Indianapolis 500. By the late 1970s, she and her twin sister had jobs at the track. "All of us got the racing bug," she says.

She may be a conservative Republican, but Schmidt has a feminist streak that budded in her early years. She remembers feeling left out when the boys got to go out to the racing pits and the girls "were never allowed to cross that fence." Later, she says, after years of loyal political work, a local Republican Party leader passed her over to run for township trustee and told her the job would require she deal with two labor unions and "women just can't handle unions." Schmidt ran anyway, and won.

She got interested in politics in her youth. She remembers watching the Kennedy-Nixon debate as an 8-year-old with her parents. Her mother was for John F. Kennedy because, she says, "he was Catholic and cute." Her dad favored Richard Nixon.

After graduating from the University of Cincinnati in 1974 with a degree in political science, Schmidt worked as a bank manager and fitness instructor. Also in the 1970s, she took up running after giving birth to her daughter and suffering postpartum depression. She began with a half-mile run. Today, Schmidt says she has run in more than 60 marathons, including many Boston marathons.

After her stint as township trustee, she went on to serve four years in the Ohio House. Following a loss for the state Senate, Schmidt became president of the anti-abortion group.

When Portman left Congress, Schmidt entered a crowded field of better-known Republicans, including former Rep. Bob McEwen and Pat DeWine, a county commissioner and son of Ohio's then Sen. Mike DeWine. She won, and then beat Democrat Paul Hackett by just more than 3 percentage points, the closest election in her Republican-leaning district since 1974.

National security contributed to her surprisingly narrow victory over Democratic lawyer and Iraq War veteran Hackett. Though Schmidt supported Bush's Iraq policy, political newcomer Hackett accused the administration of misleading the nation into war and failing to secure the peace. Schmidt kept her campaign focused on social issues.

Up for re-election for the first time in 2006, Schmidt had to stave off a primary challenge by McEwen before eking out a narrow 2,517-vote victory over Democratic challenger Victoria Wulsin, a physician who ran a non-profit AIDS prevention organization. The race was so close that Wulsin didn't concede until late November. Wulsin said she would try again in 2008.

Schmidt has said she will voluntarily limit her House service to no more than six terms.

KEY VOTES

2006

- No Stop broadband companies from favoring select Internet traffic
- Yes Affirm U.S. commitment to war in Iraq and reject setting a withdrawal date for troops
- Yes Repeal requirement for bilingual ballots at the polls
- Yes Permit U.S. sale of civilian nuclear technology to India
- Yes Build a 700-mile fence on the U.S.-Mexico border to curb illegal crossings
- Yes Permit warrantless wiretaps of suspected terrorists

2005

- Yes End mandatory preservation of habitat of endangered animal and plant species
- No Ban torture of prisoners in U.S. custody

CQ VOTE STUDIES

	PARTY UNITY		PRESIDENTIAL SUPPORT	
	Support	Oppose	Support	Oppose
2006	96%	4%	97%	3%
2005	98%	2%	87%	13%

INTEREST GROUPS

	AFL-CIO	ADA	CCUS	ACU
2006	14%	0%	100%	88%
2005	0%	0%	82%	88%

OHIO 2

Eastern Cincinnati and suburbs; Portsmouth

The 2nd stretches from some of Ohio's wealthiest areas in eastern Cincinnati and Hamilton County in the state's southwest to struggling rural communities in southern Ohio. One of the state's most solidly GOP districts, it has a distinct split between its suburban and rural elements.

The district's economy revolves around light manufacturing and the retail and service industries, and the 2nd's economic health has been boosted by construction around Cincinnati's downtown. The 2nd takes in less than one-fourth of the city's residents, including upscale neighborhoods of Hyde Park and Mount Lookout. Nearly 40 percent of the population lives in Hamilton County, including the well-to-do areas of Madeira, Mariemont, Blue Ash and the Village of Indian Hill.

To the east, fast-growing and once-undeveloped Clermont County has attracted significant business growth and residential development, in large part due to the county's low taxes. To the north, Warren County has experienced sizable residential growth as well-off families migrate to southern Warren from Hamilton County.

Farther east, Brown, Adams, Pike and Scioto counties are all struggling economically. Pike and Scioto on the 2nd's eastern edge have some of the state's highest unemployment rates. The counties depend mainly on agriculture — corn and soybeans are the major crops grown in the region, while tobacco is still grown in Brown and Adams counties.

The 2nd is reliably Republican. While rural and sparsely populated Pike and Scioto counties lean Democratic, they have considerably less political pull than Cincinnati's wealthy Republican establishment. The remaining five counties all have a strong GOP influence. George W. Bush won more than 70 percent of the vote in Clermont and Warren in the 2004 presidential election and took the 2nd overall with 64 percent of its vote.

MAJOR INDUSTRY

Manufacturing, service, retail, agriculture

CITIES

Cincinnati (pt.), 74,163; Portsmouth, 20,909

NOTABLE

The John P. Parker House in Ripley is now a museum dedicated to Parker, who helped hundreds of slaves escape along the well-traveled Underground Railroad route across the Ohio River from Kentucky; Ulysses S. Grant's birthplace in Point Pleasant is a state historical site.

Rep. Michael R. Turner (R)

CAPITOL OFFICE
225-6465
oh03.wyr@mail.house.gov
www.house.gov/miketurner
1740 Longworth 20515-3503; fax 225-6754

COMMITTEES
Armed Services
Oversight & Government Reform
Veterans' Affairs

RESIDENCE
Centerville

BORN
Jan. 11, 1960, Dayton, Ohio

RELIGION
Protestant

FAMILY
Wife, Lori Turner; two children

EDUCATION
Ohio Northern U., B.A. 1982 (political science); Case Western Reserve U., J.D. 1985; U. of Dayton, M.B.A. 1992

CAREER
Real estate developer; lawyer

POLITICAL HIGHLIGHTS
Mayor of Dayton, 1994-2002; defeated for re-election as mayor of Dayton, 2001

ELECTION RESULTS

2006 GENERAL		
Michael R. Turner (R)	127,978	58.5%
Richard Chema (D)	90,650	41.5%
2006 PRIMARY		
Michael R. Turner (R)		unopposed
2004 GENERAL		
Michael R. Turner (R)	197,290	62.3%
Jane Mitakides (D)	119,448	37.7%

PREVIOUS WINNING PERCENTAGES
2002 (59%)

Elected 2002; 3rd term

Turner is creating a niche for himself as one of the Republicans' go-to guys on urban issues, using his experience as a former two-term Dayton mayor to press for federal initiatives to promote public-private partnerships, regulatory relief for cities and tax incentives for development.

On arriving in Congress in 2003, he approached then Speaker J. Dennis Hastert to urge that the party get more involved in solving urban problems, traditionally the realm of Democrats. Hastert made Turner chairman of a 24-member working group called Saving America's Cities, which focuses on economic development for cities, tracks promising bills and works with the committee chairmen to advance legislation.

In 2005, Government Reform Committee Chairman Thomas M. Davis III, a Virginia Republican, gave Turner the chairmanship of the new Federalism and the Census Subcommittee to handle oversight of federal mandates on states and localities, a post that suited his interests nicely. In the 110th Congress (2007-08), Turner continued his membership on the renamed Oversight and Government Reform panel, and became the top Republican on a reconfigured subcommittee with jurisdiction over federal information policy and the census.

As Dayton's mayor from 1994 to 2002, Turner reversed the city's downtown decline with programs that built a new arts center, a minor league baseball stadium and a restored riverfront. A project he dubbed "Rehabarama," a public-private partnership to restore historic houses, was recognized by the National Trust for Historic Preservation. He also promoted redevelopment of contaminated sites known as brownfields. "From being a Republican mayor for a 10 percent Republican city, I have a great deal of experience working in a nonpartisan way...to pull together a broad coalition," he says.

Turner is a booster of administration proposals to provide federal incentives for charitable and religious groups to treat social ills, such as homelessness and drug addiction. He cosponsored a bill making it easier for people to deduct charitable contributions from their income taxes. He also has supported government-paid vouchers for private or parochial school tuition.

A party loyalist, he has backed President Bush on most issues, including the war in Iraq (although he expressed misgivings about the administration's conduct of the war beginning late in 2006) and controversial trade deals such as the Central American Free Trade Agreement. Despite big losses of manufacturing jobs in his district, Turner said CAFTA was good for Dayton because many of its products sold in those countries were subject to tariffs, while competing imported goods are not.

But he fought the administration in 2005 on its plans to dismantle the Community Development Block Grant program, which is popular with mayors. As chairman of the subcommittee with jurisdiction over aid to states and localities, Turner was a leader in the fight to save the program. In the end, Congress kept CDBG and its 2006 funding intact.

With blue-collar roots, Turner splits with Bush and most of his fellow Republicans on issues affecting workers. He was one of only 39 Republicans to vote for a Democratic amendment in 2004 to give workers who had exhausted their state unemployment an additional 13 weeks of benefits.

Turner's father, Ray, worked for more than 40 years at a General Motors plant and was a member of the electrical workers union. His mother, Vivian, was an elementary schoolteacher. He was raised in Dayton and attended public schools.

His father had dropped out of school at age 16 to work at the plant. But after putting his wife through school and pushing Turner toward college, his father decided he did not want to be the only one in the family without a high school diploma, so he belatedly got one. Today, Turner considers educational opportunity an American prerogative. The two greatest freedoms in this country, he says, are "our opportunities to pursue economic and educational growth."

Like many working-class Americans, Turner is also a social conservative. He is outspoken in his opposition to same-sex marriage and abortion, and was especially involved in pushing a GOP bill recognizing a fetus as a legal victim when the fetus is injured or killed in an attack on the mother.

One of Turner's major parochial preoccupations is looking out for Wright-Patterson Air Force Base. He was involved in efforts to secure nearly $700 million in federal money for research and development at the base in 2005, getting help from David L. Hobson of Ohio, a senior GOP member of the Appropriations Defense Subcommittee.

Turner practiced law before winning his first term as mayor in 1993. He had become involved in nonprofit groups in Dayton dealing with low-income housing, homelessness and community development and decided to try to tackle those problems from city hall. He lost his bid for a third term to a popular Democratic state senator. But Turner's bipartisan appeal caught the eye of GOP recruiters scouring the country for House candidates.

When Bush tapped 12-term Democratic Rep. Tony P. Hall to serve as ambassador to a trio of world hunger relief organizations, Turner was a party favorite to run for the seat. With Ohio forced to give up one House seat after the 2000 reapportionment, the GOP-dominated state General Assembly had redrawn the 3rd District to make it more Republican.

Turner first beat back a big-spending primary challenge from newspaper publisher Roy Brown, whose father and grandfather had served in the House. He then took 59 percent of the vote to defeat Democrat Rick Carne, Hall's former chief of staff. Turner was easily re-elected in 2004.

In 2006, after the first Democratic nominee, Stephanie Studebaker, had to drop out over her involvement in a domestic violence case, Turner faced a serious challenger in former federal prosecutor Richard Chema. But Turner prevailed by 17 percentage points.

The seemingly mild-mannered congressman stays trim with an interest in martial arts. He and his wife, his two daughters, and his late-70s father all are Tae Kwan Do martial arts students. Turner, who got into the sport at age 12, has a 2nd degree black belt.

KEY VOTES

2006

- No Stop broadband companies from favoring select Internet traffic
- Yes Affirm U.S. commitment to war in Iraq and reject setting a withdrawal date for troops
- Yes Repeal requirement for bilingual ballots at the polls
- Yes Permit U.S. sale of civilian nuclear technology to India
- Yes Build a 700-mile fence on the U.S.-Mexico border to curb illegal crossings
- Yes Permit warrantless wiretaps of suspected terrorists

2005

- Yes Intervene in the life-support case of Terri Schiavo
- No Lift President Bush's restrictions on stem cell research funding
- No Prohibit FBI access to library and bookstore records
- Yes Approve free-trade pact with five Central American countries
- Yes Pass energy policy overhaul favored by President Bush emphasizing domestic oil and gas production
- Yes End mandatory preservation of habitat of endangered animal and plant species
- No Ban torture of prisoners in U.S. custody

CQ VOTE STUDIES

	PARTY UNITY		PRESIDENTIAL SUPPORT	
	Support	Oppose	Support	Oppose
2006	91%	9%	90%	10%
2005	92%	8%	85%	15%
2004	92%	8%	88%	12%
2003	98%	2%	96%	4%

INTEREST GROUPS

	AFL-CIO	ADA	CCUS	ACU
2006	29%	5%	93%	80%
2005	27%	5%	96%	80%
2004	33%	5%	100%	88%
2003	7%	5%	100%	88%

OHIO 3

Southwest – most of Dayton, Kettering

Dayton, once one of the state's most successful manufacturing centers, has suffered economic setbacks and a torrent of departures that displaced its manufacturing base. The city has struggled to diversify what has become an increasingly service-oriented economy.

Montgomery County, which surrounds Dayton, is the 3rd's dominant jurisdiction. Midway between Cincinnati and Dayton, fast-growing Warren County (shared with the 2nd) has bedroom communities for both cities, while Clinton and Highland counties to the east are more rural but increasingly developed. Although Warren is booming, Montgomery, which accounts for nearly three-fourths of the district's residents, has lost population over the past decade.

Despite general economic setbacks, the area's defense industry has had some success in attracting aerospace, medical research and information technology companies to the area around Wright-Patterson Air Force Base (shared with the 7th). A new "Tech Town" district in eastern Dayton (shared with the 8th), envisioned as a robust technology corridor and business center, is under construction on a former industrial site along interstate and rail distribution routes.

The urban vote — driven by Dayton's ample black population and large blue-collar workforce — makes Montgomery slightly Democratic. Dayton's southern suburbs include GOP-inclined, white-collar areas such as Kettering and Centerville. The counties outside of Montgomery give the 3rd its GOP lean. Warren County gave George W. Bush 72 percent of its 2004 presidential vote, and he nearly reached that mark in both Clinton and Highland counties.

MAJOR INDUSTRY

Manufacturing, defense, service

MILITARY BASES

Wright-Patterson Air Force Base, 10,166 military, 10,332 civilian (2005) (shared with the 7th District)

CITIES

Dayton (pt.), 137,180; Kettering, 57,502; Trotwood, 27,420

NOTABLE

The National Museum of the U.S. Air Force (at Wright-Patterson) is the world's largest and oldest military aviation museum; The Highland County Courthouse in Hillsboro is Ohio's oldest courthouse still in use.

Rep. Jim Jordan (R)

CAPITOL OFFICE
225-2676
jordan.house.gov
515 Cannon 20515-3504; fax 226-0577

COMMITTEES
Judiciary
Oversight & Government Reform
Small Business

RESIDENCE
Urbana

BORN
Feb. 17, 1964, Troy, Ohio

RELIGION
Christian non-denominational

FAMILY
Wife, Polly Jordan; four children

EDUCATION
U. of Wisconsin, B.S. 1986 (economics); Ohio State U., M.A. 1991 (education); Capital U., J.D. 2001

CAREER
College wrestling coach

POLITICAL HIGHLIGHTS
Ohio House, 1995-2000; Ohio Senate, 2001-06

ELECTION RESULTS

2006 GENERAL		
Jim Jordan (R)	129,958	60.0%
Richard E. Siferd (D)	86,678	40.0%
2006 PRIMARY		
Jim Jordan (R)	38,017	50.6%
Frank A. Guglielmi (R)	22,504	29.9%
Kevin Nestor (R)	8,460	11.3%
James R. Stahl (R)	2,596	3.5%
Nathan J. Martin (R)	2,358	3.1%
Charles W. Weasel (R)	1,239	1.6%

Elected 2006; 1st term

Entering Congress after a tenure in the Ohio legislature in which he was among the most conservative legislators, Jordan immediately began charting a rightward course in Congress on both social and economic policy.

When evaluating legislation, Jordan says he asks himself, "Will this decision benefit families?" Bills that prompt a yes answer include those that reduce government spending, taxes and regulations and those that limit abortion. Jordan introduced numerous anti-abortion bills as an Ohio legislator and supports federal efforts to ban same-sex marriage.

Jordan brandished his conservatism early in the 110th Congress (2007-08); he was one of 50 House Republicans who voted against all six signature pieces of legislation Democrats promoted during the 2006 campaign and then steered to passage in January 2007. The following month he sponsored an amendment, rejected by the Judiciary Committee, that would have added an abortion rider to a bill intended to expand access to a program that provides money to combat the drug methamphetamine.

Jordan will also use his seat on Judiciary to oppose illegal immigration. He supports strengthening border security measures and cracking down on businesses that knowingly employ illegal immigrants.

He likely will join Republicans in opposing Democratic budget and tax proposals. And he will not shy away from criticizing his own party when he feels it is not doing enough to fight for tax and spending reductions.

But partisan enmity is not Jordan's style. He said he is a "happy warrior . . . the guy who is fighting for the things I believe in and the things that I think make this country special — but do it with a smile."

A champion wrestler in high school and college, Jordan was a college wrestling coach. He pursued a career in politics to help "empower families." By 2006, he was a 12-year veteran of the Ohio legislature when Republican Rep. Michael G. Oxley retired, paving the way for Jordan to prevail in the strongly conservative-leaning 4th District — first in the primary election over wealthy businessman Frank A. Guglielmi, and then in the general election over Democratic lawyer Richard E. Siferd.

OHIO 4

West central — Mansfield, Lima, Findlay

The 4th, a solid block of Ohio Corn Belt counties, supports soybeans, corn, livestock and Republicans. Not one of the 11 counties in the 4th has backed a Democratic presidential candidate since 1964, and George W. Bush swept the counties again in 2004. Two of the three most populous, Allen and Hancock counties, last voted Democratic in the Roosevelt-Landon contest of 1936.

Corn and soybeans are integral to the 4th's economy, and new ethanol plants and a strong agricultural base have stabilized the 4th's economy after years of decline in the auto and defense sectors. Recently, an army tank plant in Lima that builds the Abrams tank has increased production after emerging safely from the 2005 BRAC round.

Manufacturing remains important as the 4th tries to maintain its roots: Small industrial companies and large auto plants continue to spur the economy. There is a Ford engine plant in Lima and a General Motors plant in Mansfield, while Honda expands facilities in East Liberty. Ada is home to a Wilson Sporting Goods facility, and Cooper Tire & Rubber and Marathon Ashland Petroleum are both based in Findlay.

Democrats have few pockets of support, but they can normally count on votes in Mansfield, which is one-fifth black. While those votes help Democrats locally, they barely make a dent in the district's underlying Republican lean. Bush won 65 percent of the 4th's 2004 presidential vote, his best showing in Ohio.

MAJOR INDUSTRY
Agriculture, auto manufacturing, oil

CITIES
Mansfield, 49,346; Lima, 40,081; Findlay, 38,967; Marion, 35,318

NOTABLE
Astronaut Neil Armstrong's hometown of Wapakoneta has a museum in his honor.

Rep. Paul E. Gillmor (R)

CAPITOL OFFICE
225-6405
paul.gillmor@mail.house.gov
gillmor.house.gov
1203 Longworth 20515-3505; fax 225-1985

COMMITTEES
Financial Services

RESIDENCE
Tiffin

BORN
Feb. 1, 1939, Tiffin, Ohio

RELIGION
Methodist

FAMILY
Wife, Karen L. Gillmor; five children

EDUCATION
Miami U. (Ohio), attended 1958-59;
Ohio Wesleyan U., B.A. 1961; U. of Michigan, J.D. 1964

MILITARY SERVICE
Air Force, 1965-66

CAREER
Lawyer

POLITICAL HIGHLIGHTS
Ohio Senate, 1967-89 (minority leader, 1978-80, 1983-84; president, 1981-82, 1985-88); sought Republican nomination for governor, 1986

ELECTION RESULTS

2006 GENERAL		
Paul E. Gillmor (R)	129,813	56.8%
Robin Weirauch (D)	98,544	43.2%
2006 PRIMARY		
Paul E. Gillmor (R)		unopposed
2004 GENERAL		
Paul E. Gillmor (R)	196,649	67.1%
Robin Weirauch (D)	96,656	33.0%

PREVIOUS WINNING PERCENTAGES
2002 (67%); 2000 (70%); 1998 (67%); 1996 (61%); 1994 (73%); 1992 (100%); 1990 (68%); 1988 (61%)

Elected 1988; 10th term

The son of a banker from a small town in Ohio, Gillmor is a low-profile conservative who looks out for the banking industry on the House Financial Services Committee. He is also a pragmatist who has joined on legislation with some of the most liberal members of the House.

When Republicans had the majority, Gillmor had seats on the sought-after Energy and Commerce Committee and the Financial Services Committee, a committee with a smaller portfolio. With the changeover to Democratic control, Republican representation was reduced on committees and Gillmor had to give up one of his assignments. He opted to stay on Financial Services, where he could have more impact as the top-ranking Republican on the Financial Institutions and Consumer Credit Subcommittee. He also has a history of being able to set ideology aside to work with Democrats. "I don't have the reputation of being a strident partisan, which sometimes makes a difference," Gillmor told The Columbus Dispatch newspaper. "I found it just works better that way whether you are in the majority or the minority."

In the 110th Congress (2007-08), Gillmor teamed up with Rep. Barney Frank of Massachusetts, the liberal chairman of the full Financial Services panel, on a bill keeping Wal-Mart and other big retailers out of the banking business. Their legislation closed a loophole in banking laws that allowed bank-like entities to engage in limited financial operations, such as providing credit cards or loans. The giant Wal-Mart, based in Bentonville, Ark., wanted a charter to process the approximately 140 million credit, debit and check transactions made in its stores each month, causing alarm in the banking industry. Wal-Mart subsequently withdrew its application. Gillmor has also worked with Democrat Edward J. Markey of Massachusetts to restrict sales of a customer's financial and medical information.

Gillmor is a loyal member of the GOP rank and file. In the 109th Congress (2005-06), he voted with his party 94 percent of the time on issues that divided the two parties. He is also a deputy whip, helping to round up votes for the Republican leadership.

He has backed the Bush administration's tax cuts and most of the legislation advanced by the conservative wing of the party. He supported the administration's use of warrantless wiretaps in terrorism investigations, he favored putting limits on the Endangered Species Act and he voted against federal funding for embryonic stem cell research, which uses surplus embryos from in vitro fertilization clinics.

Gillmor achieved a legislative success in 2005 when Congress passed his measure to create a national sex-offender database. The law established a national registry of sex criminals on the Internet, and makes it easier for law enforcement officials to track sex offenders across state lines.

On education, Gillmor has taken a different tack from other policymakers in Washington — most of whom rallied behind President Bush's No Child Left Behind law that focuses federal aid on children failing academically. Gillmor has said Congress also must look out for children who are ahead. In 2005, he sponsored a bill to subsidize training for teachers of intellectually gifted children. "The education of the gifted is sometimes given short shrift. We want to have everybody educated," he says. "Frankly, the cure for cancer and the next technological advance are going to come out of the gifted child."

In earlier years in the House, Gillmor was heavily involved in environmental legislation as the chairman of the Energy panel's Environment and Hazardous Materials Subcommittee. In the 107th Congress (2001-02), he shepherded to enactment a law to help clean up and develop contaminated industrial sites known as brownfields, mainly by giving states more control over the process and shielding small businesses from liability.

Gillmor grew up in tiny Old Fort, Ohio, which had a population of 300 at the time. Everyone knew everyone else, and people didn't lock their doors unless they were going out of town, he says. He now lives in Tiffin, with around 18,000 people, only 10 miles away.

Gillmor's father, Paul Marshall Gillmor, started a trucking company beginning with one truck he drove himself and eventually building a fleet of 200. His mother kept the company's books, and as a high-schooler Gillmor spent Saturdays cleaning the oil tankers. He was active in the Boy Scouts and a member of the honor society. The Gillmors also raised show horses. "We did pretty good," he recalls. "We never went to a horse show that we didn't come back from with at least one ribbon."

The family's wealth grew, as did its community activism. The Gillmors gave to the local hospital, theater and schools, and donated land for sports fields. His father became president of the local bank and was active in the Republican Party, though he never ran for office. Gillmor's mother, a Democrat, backed a Republican for the first time when she voted for her son.

Gillmor went to Miami University in Ohio, then transferred to Ohio Wesleyan to be with his girlfriend, whom he later married. After graduating from law school, he served in the Air Force as a judge advocate in 1965-66. Returning to civilian life, Gillmor won a seat in the state Senate. Thirteen years later, after the GOP took over the chamber with a one-vote majority, Gillmor won the Senate presidency over a fiery conservative by stressing the need for negotiation within the GOP as well as with the Democrats, who controlled the state House and the governorship.

In 1986, he lost a bid for the gubernatorial nomination. Two years later, Gillmor ran to replace Republican Delbert L. Latta, who was retiring after 30 years in the U.S. House. Gillmor's principal primary opponent was Latta's son, Robert, a 32-year-old lawyer. In a bitter contest, Gillmor towered over the newcomer in personal recognition, stressing his fiscal conservatism and successes in the legislature. Latta campaigned aggressively, aided by his father's ready-made organization.

Gillmor won the primary by just 27 votes, the smallest margin in any 1988 House contest, but garnered 61 percent of the vote in the general election. He has won handily ever since.

KEY VOTES

2006

- No Stop broadband companies from favoring select Internet traffic
- Yes Affirm U.S. commitment to war in Iraq and reject setting a withdrawal date for troops
- Yes Repeal requirement for bilingual ballots at the polls
- Yes Permit U.S. sale of civilian nuclear technology to India
- Yes Build a 700-mile fence on the U.S.-Mexico border to curb illegal crossings
- Yes Permit warrantless wiretaps of suspected terrorists

2005

- Yes Intervene in the life-support case of Terri Schiavo
- No Lift President Bush's restrictions on stem cell research funding
- Yes Prohibit FBI access to library and bookstore records
- Yes Approve free-trade pact with five Central American countries
- Yes Pass energy policy overhaul favored by President Bush emphasizing domestic oil and gas production
- Yes End mandatory preservation of habitat of endangered animal and plant species
- No Ban torture of prisoners in U.S. custody

CQ VOTE STUDIES

	PARTY UNITY		PRESIDENTIAL SUPPORT	
	Support	Oppose	Support	Oppose
2006	94%	6%	91%	9%
2005	94%	6%	88%	12%
2004	93%	7%	91%	9%
2003	94%	6%	94%	6%
2002	93%	7%	92%	8%

INTEREST GROUPS

	AFL-CIO	ADA	CCUS	ACU
2006	21%	0%	100%	84%
2005	14%	0%	92%	82%
2004	27%	5%	100%	84%
2003	20%	5%	93%	72%
2002	13%	5%	100%	88%

OHIO 5

Northwest – Bowling Green, Tiffin, Fremont

Bordering Indiana and Michigan in the northwestern corner of the state, the 5th cuts south of Toledo into the north-central portion of Ohio. Flat farmland born out of the once-impervious Great Black Swamp covers the middle of the state's second-largest district in land area. The district's largest jurisdiction is centrally located Wood County, with the rest of the population spread evenly between counties east and west of Wood.

The largest city in Wood County, and in the district, is Bowling Green. The city is heavily dependent on Bowling Green State University, but local officials hope the city's new Innovative Technology Park will help diversify its economy. North of Wood, across the Maumee River, the district picks up Republican-leaning southern suburbs in Toledo-dominated Lucas County (most of which is in the 9th District). Wheat, tomatoes, soybeans and corn dominate most of Wood's land area.

Many of the remaining counties form the heart of Ohio's wheat-growing country, and are devoted almost exclusively to agriculture and food packaging. The 5th leads Ohio in wheat, soybean and corn production. East and west of Wood, the areas host migrant-worker Hispanic populations during harvesting months, which helps boost the district's Hispanic population to 4 percent, double the state's average. Manufacturing also is important here, with a Heinz Ketchup plant in Fremont, an Arm & Hammer Baking Soda site in Old Fort and a large Whirlpool washing machine production facility in Clyde.

The 5th is strong GOP territory. Fifteen of the 16 counties that lie wholly or partly within the 5th voted for George W. Bush in the 2004 presidential election — the lone exception was Lucas County, although the 5th's small share of that county also backed Bush. Putnam County, located southwest of Wood, gave Bush his best showing in Ohio (76 percent). Overall, Bush took the district with 61 percent of the vote.

MAJOR INDUSTRY
Agriculture, manufacturing

CITIES
Bowling Green, 29,636; Tiffin, 18,135; Fremont, 17,345

NOTABLE
Perrysburg, named to honor Commodore Oliver Perry's victory over the British in the 1813 Battle of Lake Erie, is one of only a handful of U.S. cities to have been planned by the federal government.

Rep. Charlie Wilson (D)

CAPITOL OFFICE
225-5705
charliewilson.house.gov
226 Cannon 20515-3506; fax 225-5907

COMMITTEES
Financial Services
Science & Technology

RESIDENCE
St. Clairsville

BORN
Jan. 18, 1943, Martins Ferry, Ohio

RELIGION
Roman Catholic

FAMILY
Divorced; four children

EDUCATION
Ohio U., B.G.S. 1980 (general studies)

CAREER
Real estate company owner; funeral home and furniture company owner; auto worker

POLITICAL HIGHLIGHTS
Ohio House, 1997-2004 (assistant minority leader, 2000-04); Ohio Senate, 2005-06

ELECTION RESULTS

2006 GENERAL		
Charlie Wilson (D)	135,628	62.1%
Chuck Blasdel (R)	82,848	37.9%
2006 PRIMARY		
Charlie Wilson (D) - write-in	43,687	66.1%
Bob Carr (D)	14,900	22.6%
John S. Luchansky (D)	7,459	11.3%

Elected 2006; 1st term

Wilson came to Washington with the single goal of increasing employment for his southeastern Ohio district, which straddles Appalachia. "My focus in the Congress will be jobs, jobs and, of course, jobs," he said.

To help the region's steelworkers, he is pushing for changes in trade policy. "Free trade is not really fair trade," he says. "We need to keep our steel mills functional in the event we need them, rather than be dependent on offshore steel."

Wilson once worked as a welder and painter on an auto assembly line in Lorraine, Ohio, building Ford Falcons and Comets. He ran his family's funeral parlor and furniture store and then went into business for himself by opening a real estate firm. His family roots in eastern Ohio date back more than 108 years, and he says his views on social issues are a product of the largely rural region. Wilson opposes abortion; and, raised in an area where hunting and fishing are popular pursuits, he is a member of the National Rifle Association.

Upon his arrival in Congress, he won a coveted spot on the Financial Services Committee. "I can use what I've done my whole life as a businessman," said Wilson, who was also chairman of a local bank.

Wilson served eight years in the Ohio House, including four years as assistant minority leader, before moving to the state Senate. In 2006, he was the presumed favorite for the 6th District seat being vacated by Democratic Rep. Ted Strickland, who ran successfully for governor.

But in an embarrassing error, Wilson's campaign failed to collect the 50 valid signatures needed to qualify for the primary, requiring him to run as a write-in candidate. To overcome that hurdle, Wilson ran a tireless primary campaign against two opponents, using his own money to hire door-to-door canvassers armed with hand-held computers. He also won the support of the national Democratic Party, which usually stays out of primaries but saw him as the most electable of the three Democrats.

He won nearly two-thirds of the votes cast in the primary before breezing to victory over Republican state Rep. Chuck Blasdel in the general election.

OHIO 6

South and east — Boardman, Athens, Steubenville

The 6th parallels the Ohio River for nearly 300 miles, bordering three states and taking in hardscrabble areas from Ohio's Appalachia to the Mahoning Valley near Youngstown.

Many counties in the 6th's old coal mining areas have high unemployment rates and difficulty retaining younger residents. Meigs County has Ohio's lowest median household income, and Scioto (shared with the 2nd) and Lawrence counties also struggle.

Athens, in Athens County, is home to Ohio University and has a liberal slant. Farther north, Monroe County has Ohio's highest unemployment rate (13 percent). Jefferson County has lost population in each of the past four censuses and has Ohio's highest proportion of elderly residents. One-third of residents live in Mahoning and Columbiana counties, in the district's north, which rely on steel, retail and manufacturing.

The 6th has a Democratic orientation, but it leans conservative on social issues and is highly competitive in presidential elections. Meigs and the southern counties tend to blend populist fiscal policy with social conservatism. Washington County is one of the 6th's few solidly GOP areas, but north of Washington, the 6th tilts Democratic, with Monroe, Belmont and Jefferson counties strongly Democratic, especially in local races. The 6th's share of Mahoning takes in Boardman and Poland and is more competitive than the solidly Democratic part of Mahoning in the 17th. George W. Bush won seven of the district's 12 counties en route to narrow wins here in 2000 and 2004.

MAJOR INDUSTRY
Service, manufacturing

CITIES
Boardman (unincorporated), 37,215; Athens, 21,342; Steubenville, 19,015

NOTABLE
Gallipolis, in Gallia County, was founded in 1790 by a group of 500 French immigrants.

Rep. David L. Hobson (R)

CAPITOL OFFICE
225-4324
www.house.gov/hobson
2346 Rayburn 20515-3507; fax 225-1984

COMMITTEES
Appropriations

RESIDENCE
Springfield

BORN
Oct. 17, 1936, Cincinnati, Ohio

RELIGION
Methodist

FAMILY
Wife, Carolyn Hobson; three children

EDUCATION
Ohio Wesleyan U., B.A. 1958;
Ohio State U., J.D. 1963

MILITARY SERVICE
Ohio Air National Guard, 1958-63

CAREER
Financial executive

POLITICAL HIGHLIGHTS
Candidate for Ohio House, 1982;
Ohio Senate, 1982-90 (majority whip, 1986-88; president pro tempore, 1988-90)

ELECTION RESULTS

2006 GENERAL		
David L. Hobson (R)	137,899	60.6%
William R. Conner (D)	89,579	39.4%
2006 PRIMARY		
David L. Hobson (R)		unopposed
2004 GENERAL		
David L. Hobson (R)	186,534	65.0%
Kara Anastasio (D)	100,617	35.0%

PREVIOUS WINNING PERCENTAGES
2002 (68%); 2000 (68%); 1998 (67%); 1996 (68%); 1994 (100%); 1992 (71%); 1990 (62%)

Elected 1990; 9th term

An easygoing legislator who enjoys the trust and respect of members on both sides of the aisle, Hobson is not one to toot his own horn. He doesn't have to. His congressional résumé shows how much the GOP leadership has relied on him since his arrival in 1991.

He was appointed to the Rules Committee as a freshman, a rare honor. He was named to the Appropriations Committee as a sophomore, and he has chaired two of its subcommittees. He gained a broad grasp of fiscal policy as Speaker Newt Gingrich's appointee to the Budget Committee in the late 1990s. And he was one of the earliest backers of John A. Boehner's successful 2006 bid for House majority leader. The two Ohio Republicans entered Congress together, represent adjoining districts and are close political allies. Hobson campaigned for Boehner in the majority leader's race, and Boehner earlier had helped him land the Budget post. Hobson often is called on by the conservative-dominated leadership to act as an informal conduit to GOP moderates.

With the Democrats in control in the 110th Congress (2007-08), Speaker Nancy Pelosi is also turning to the 16-year veteran. In early 2007, Hobson was the lone Republican on a couple of Pelosi-sponsored trips to the Middle East, including one in April that brought him flak from his party. President Bush and Boehner sharply criticized the delegation's stop in Syria, which included a meeting with President Bashar Assad. But Hobson told the Columbus Dispatch that the trip "served a good purpose," with the group delivering the message that, despite disagreement on Iraq War funding, Republicans and Democrats are unified in their opposition to countries that aid terrorists.

In his 50s when he arrived on Capitol Hill, Hobson already had years of experience in politics and business. Not only had he risen to a leadership position in the Ohio Senate, he also had served as chairman of a financial services company and on the boards of a bank, an oil company and a restaurant concern. He had a broader perspective than younger, more ambitious and less patient colleagues and is still called "Uncle Dave" by some. He typically urges new aides to "call me Dave."

Hobson can be direct. "I think I'm fairly blunt," he says. But he treats others respectfully and expects the same in return. In 2006, Hobson voiced his displeasure at receiving budget justifications from the Army Corps of Engineers only 42 hours before a subcommittee hearing, and the documents were incomplete. "If the administration wants the Congress to give respectful considerations to the president's budget request, it's time to start showing some respect to Congress," he said.

Hobson became chairman of the Energy and Water Development Appropriations Subcommittee in 2003 after four years at the helm of the Military Construction Subcommittee. He says the only other subcommittee he would want to chair is Defense, where he is the second-ranking Republican. In the 110th Congress, Hobson is the top Republican on the Energy and Water panel.

As chairman, Hobson delved deeply into both parts of his panel's jurisdiction, pressing for modernization of the nation's nuclear weapons program and for more efficient water transportation. He also pushed subcommittee members to exercise more oversight, and lamented that most of them tend to be interested in only one area, energy or water.

Nuclear weapons policy is one area where he tends to be more liberal than most House Republicans. He blocked funding for Bush's plan to convert some existing nuclear warheads into "bunker buster" models that could penetrate hardened, underground facilities. "With all the proliferation threats we now face with countries like Iran, Pakistan and North Korea, are we really sending the right signal to those countries and the rest of the world when we embark on nuclear weapons initiatives?" Hobson asked Defense Secretary Donald H. Rumsfeld at a 2004 hearing. He also clashed with Senate appropriators over his support for a nuclear waste repository at Yucca Mountain in Nevada and his proposals to cut spending on nuclear weapons labs.

Hobson has used his considerable influence on Appropriations to safeguard key local interests, including Wright-Patterson Air Force Base, the largest single-site employer in Ohio. A street at the base is named for him.

Another parochial concern is the Rickenbacker intermodal facility, a new distribution facility near Rickenbacker International Airport southeast of Columbus that will increase the amount of freight that can be delivered by air, rail and truck throughout the Midwest. Hobson, along with fellow GOP Ohioans Deborah Pryce and Pat Tiberi, secured $30 million for the project in the 2005 transportation authorization bill.

Hobson has a strong interest in health care. During the Gingrich speakership, he helped draft the GOP version of patients' rights legislation that died in a standoff with the Senate. In 1996, he helped win passage of legislation to protect the health insurance of workers who lose or change jobs. At the state level, he was chairman of the Ohio Senate's health committee.

It's not unusual for Hobson to break with GOP hard-liners on select issues. In 1996, for example, he expressed a willingness to negotiate with President Bill Clinton on a balanced-budget plan, rather than risk a government shutdown as many House Republicans were willing to do. When Congress and the White House struck a balanced-budget deal the next year, he fought to keep it on course. He voted against a massive highway bill that authorized more spending than the agreement called for, and he counseled against tax cuts that might endanger the deficit-reduction plan.

Hobson started in politics with an appointment to the state Senate seat that Republican Mike DeWine gave up in a successful bid for the U.S. House. After four years in Columbus, Hobson's GOP colleagues chose him to be majority whip. In 1990, he was elected to Congress with 62 percent of the vote after DeWine gave up his House seat to run for lieutenant governor. Hobson has won with 65 percent or better ever since, and he has no plans to call it quits. Married since 1959, he says, "My kids are worried I'll retire and drive my wife crazy."

KEY VOTES

2006

No Stop broadband companies from favoring select Internet traffic
Yes Affirm U.S. commitment to war in Iraq and reject setting a withdrawal date for troops
Yes Repeal requirement for bilingual ballots at the polls
Yes Permit U.S. sale of civilian nuclear technology to India
Yes Build a 700-mile fence on the U.S.-Mexico border to curb illegal crossings
Yes Permit warrantless wiretaps of suspected terrorists

2005

Yes Intervene in the life-support case of Terri Schiavo
No Lift President Bush's restrictions on stem cell research funding
No Prohibit FBI access to library and bookstore records
Yes Approve free-trade pact with five Central American countries
Yes Pass energy policy overhaul favored by President Bush emphasizing domestic oil and gas production
? End mandatory preservation of habitat of endangered animal and plant species
No Ban torture of prisoners in U.S. custody

CQ VOTE STUDIES

	PARTY UNITY		PRESIDENTIAL SUPPORT	
	Support	Oppose	Support	Oppose
2006	94%	6%	87%	13%
2005	94%	6%	87%	13%
2004	92%	8%	82%	18%
2003	95%	5%	96%	4%
2002	94%	6%	90%	10%

INTEREST GROUPS

	AFL-CIO	ADA	CCUS	ACU
2006	29%	10%	93%	76%
2005	20%	0%	96%	83%
2004	20%	5%	100%	88%
2003	7%	5%	100%	88%
2002	11%	0%	100%	88%

OHIO 7

Central – Springfield, Lancaster, part of Columbus

The Republican-leaning 7th, based south of Columbus, is a diverse swath of land across south-central Ohio that includes urban, suburban and rural areas.

The district's two most-populous counties — Greene and Clark — form the western arm of the 7th. Wright-Patterson Air Force Base, most of which is in Greene, is the largest single-site employer in Ohio. The base is the economic anchor of the county, which also has several colleges and universities. Clark and its county seat, Springfield, are home to auto manufacturing plants, distribution firms and technology companies. Nextedge, a new research and high-technology park, is in Springfield.

Residential growth around Columbus, a small part of which is in the 7th, has especially affected Fairfield County, which is a bedroom community filling up with white-collar commuters. Pickaway County has suffered from the loss of television manufacturing jobs, but expansion at the Rickenbacker International Airport, a major cargo hub in Franklin County just north of Pickaway's northern border, should help offset economic losses. Fayette, the least-populous county wholly within the 7th, is a major horse-breeding area. Much of Perry County, the easternmost county in the 7th, relies on manufacturing and agriculture. Overall, the district supports corn, wheat and soybean production.

The 7th leans Republican, but the district is somewhat disparate. Clark and Perry counties are competitive, with both parties garnering support. Pickaway, traditionally Republican-leaning, has recently become more competitive. Fairfield, Fayette and Green counties are solidly Republican. George W. Bush captured 57 percent of the 7th's 2004 presidential vote.

MAJOR INDUSTRY
Manufacturing, military, technology research, agriculture

MILITARY BASES
Wright-Patterson Air Force Base, 10,166 military, 10,332 civilian (2005) (shared with the 3rd District)

CITIES
Springfield, 65,358; Columbus (pt.), 51,097; Beavercreek, 37,984; Lancaster, 35,335; Fairborn, 32,052

NOTABLE
The modern combine, invented in Springfield, helped revolutionize harvesting and the agriculture industry.

Rep. John A. Boehner (R)

CAPITOL OFFICE
225-6205
john.boehner@mail.house.gov
johnboehner.house.gov
1011 Longworth 20515-3508; fax 225-0704

COMMITTEES
No committee assignments

RESIDENCE
West Chester Township

BORN
Nov. 17, 1949, Cincinnati, Ohio

RELIGION
Roman Catholic

FAMILY
Wife, Debbie Boehner; two children

EDUCATION
Xavier U., B.S. 1977

MILITARY SERVICE
Navy, 1968

CAREER
Plastics and packaging executive

POLITICAL HIGHLIGHTS
Union Township Board of Trustees, 1982-84; Ohio House, 1985-91

ELECTION RESULTS

2006 GENERAL		
John A. Boehner (R)	136,863	63.8%
Mort Meier (D)	77,640	36.2%
2006 PRIMARY		
John A. Boehner (R)		unopposed
2004 GENERAL		
John A. Boehner (R)	201,675	69.0%
Jeff Hardenbrook (D)	90,574	31.0%

PREVIOUS WINNING PERCENTAGES
2002 (71%); 2000 (71%); 1998 (71%); 1996 (70%); 1994 (100%); 1992 (74%); 1990 (61%)

Elected 1990; 9th term

Boehner is one of Capitol Hill's most impressive second acts. Booted from the leadership in the 1990s, the Ohio Republican remade his image from has-been power broker to savvy legislator and triumphed when he was chosen leader of the House Republicans in 2006, his political rehabilitation complete. Had his party managed to hang on to the majority that year, Boehner would have been on his way to becoming Speaker of the House.

A crafty strategist who looks and sounds good on television, Boehner (BAY-ner) holds the top leadership post in the minority. His colleagues chose him over conservative Mike Pence of Indiana 10 days after a disastrous midterm election in which Republicans lost the majority in both the House and the Senate. "The rebuilding begins now," Boehner said after his 168-27 win over Pence, the outgoing chairman of the conservative Republican Study Committee who had called for a leadership housecleaning. J. Dennis Hastert of Illinois, the House Speaker during the 109th Congress (2005-06), absorbed the blame for the party's loss. Boehner had served under Hastert as majority leader for less than a year and was spared the backlash.

In choosing Boehner, Republicans got an inside organization man who started life as a barkeeper's son and went on to get rich in the packaging business. He is known as a results-oriented strategist and tireless worker. After Republicans suffered losses in the 1998 elections, Boehner was upset in his bid for re-election as GOP Conference chairman. He swallowed the loss and began transforming himself into a legislative workhorse. He also kept up his prolific fundraising for his party and quietly cultivated goodwill with his colleagues by throwing frequent after-hours parties where members and their staff could kick back after a late night of work on the floor.

He adapted quickly to life in the minority party when the 110th Congress opened in 2007. Despite the growing unpopularity of the war in Iraq, Boehner held the party together on several key votes. On a Democratic resolution opposing President Bush's call for more troops, he lost only 17 Republicans though predictions had been for as many as 60 defections. When Democratic House Speaker Nancy Pelosi created a special committee on global warming, Boehner filled the GOP seats on the panel with known foes of mandated reductions in greenhouse gas emissions.

Boehner is one of the most distinctive personalities in the House. Always tanned, usually chain-smoking Barclay cigarettes, he delivers his statements in a booming baritone voice that resonates throughout a hearing room. When a fellow member or a reporter asks a difficult question, he responds with the "Boehner shrug," a stiff, unquotable raising of the shoulders that encourages the questioner to drop the subject.

If he has a weakness, it is his fondness for socializing with lobbyists, especially on the golf course, where he likes to unwind. Republicans were sullied by multiple influence-peddling scandals in 2005 and 2006. Part of Boehner's job is helping to restore the party's credibility. He got back into the leadership as a result of one of those scandals. Tom DeLay of Texas, one of the most powerful politicians of his time, stepped down in 2005 as majority leader to fight charges of improper fundraising. Whip Roy Blunt of Missouri, the third-ranking leader, sought to move up, but he was considered too close to DeLay. After a spirited race, Boehner defeated Blunt in early 2006 by 122-109 on a second-ballot vote. John Shadegg of Arizona dropped out after trailing on the first ballot.

Before that, Boehner was the chairman of the Education and the Workforce Committee from 2001 to 2006. His bipartisan negotiations on Bush's signature education bill, the No Child Left Behind Act, set the tone for his transformation from leadership loser to accomplished committee chairman. When he met with President-elect Bush in Austin in late 2000 to discuss the bill, Boehner insisted that transition team officials also invite George Miller of California, soon to become the top-ranking committee Democrat. The unlikely partnership forged that day helped get Bush's initiative past many obstacles put up by opponents in both parties.

Boehner came to Congress in 1991 as a young Republican bent on changing the congressional culture at a time his party was frozen out of power. He was one of the Gang of Seven freshmen who railed against the excesses of incumbents and pushed for full disclosure during the House bank check-kiting scandal. Boehner's zeal made him a favorite of the new breed of confrontational Republicans led by Newt Gingrich of Georgia. After the GOP claimed the majority in 1995, Boehner became GOP Conference chairman, the No. 4 leader who handled message and communications.

But three years later, he was dumped after being suspected of participating in a secret, failed effort among a handful of leaders to oust Gingrich, whose popularity had tumbled. When Republicans lost seats in the 1998 election, they cleaned house, getting rid of Gingrich and Boehner.

Boehner's crisp, expensive suits and patrician bearing belie his blue-collar upbringing in western Ohio's Rust Belt, where he was the second of 12 children. As a kid, he rose at 5 a.m. to help his father, Earl Boehner, sort bottles and mop floors at Andy's Cafe restaurant and bar. He worked his way through Xavier College as a janitor, one of only two in his family to earn a college degree. "I just decided I had to go to college," Boehner recalls. "It was never talked about in our house because, I think, my parents never saw it as a possibility, and there was no reason to raise false expectations."

After school, he and a partner bought a small plastics and packaging firm, Nucite Sales Inc., and built it into a multimillion-dollar business. His first political race brought him a seat on the sleepy township board. "He was good-looking and sharp as a tack, and that doesn't hurt in politics," recalls Patricia William, the longtime township treasurer.

Boehner went on to serve six years in the Ohio House, and then in 1990 jumped into the primary against Rep. Donald E. "Buz" Lukens, who had been convicted of having sex with a teenage girl. Boehner outspent the front-runner, former Rep. Thomas N. Kindness, and won the primary with 49 percent of the vote. In November, he bested former Democratic Mayor Gregory V. Jolivette of Hamilton and has had easy re-elections ever since.

KEY VOTES

2006

No Stop broadband companies from favoring select Internet traffic
Yes Affirm U.S. commitment to war in Iraq and reject setting a withdrawal date for troops
No Repeal requirement for bilingual ballots at the polls
Yes Permit U.S. sale of civilian nuclear technology to India
Yes Build a 700-mile fence on the U.S.-Mexico border to curb illegal crossings
Yes Permit warrantless wiretaps of suspected terrorists

2005

Yes Intervene in the life-support case of Terri Schiavo
No Lift President Bush's restrictions on stem cell research funding
No Prohibit FBI access to library and bookstore records
Yes Approve free-trade pact with five Central American countries
Yes Pass energy policy overhaul favored by President Bush emphasizing domestic oil and gas production
Yes End mandatory preservation of habitat of endangered animal and plant species
No Ban torture of prisoners in U.S. custody

CQ VOTE STUDIES

	PARTY UNITY		PRESIDENTIAL SUPPORT	
	Support	Oppose	Support	Oppose
2006	96%	4%	100%	0%
2005	97%	3%	91%	9%
2004	97%	3%	100%	0%
2003	97%	3%	100%	0%
2002	97%	3%	92%	8%

INTEREST GROUPS

	AFL-CIO	ADA	CCUS	ACU
2006	14%	5%	100%	88%
2005	13%	0%	88%	100%
2004	7%	0%	100%	100%
2003	7%	5%	100%	84%
2002	11%	0%	100%	88%

OHIO 8

Southwest – Hamilton, most of Middletown

Hugging the state's western border, the 8th is fertile GOP ground that is steered economically and politically by Butler County, home to the district's two largest cities, Hamilton and Middletown. The district's solid Republican tilt is anchored in Butler, which has long voted Republican, and its expanding suburbs have escalated the rightward trend — the county is known for electing some of Ohio's more conservative state and congressional legislators.

Butler and Miami counties have propelled the district's rapid growth through residential construction and commercial development. West Chester Township, in Butler, is one of the state's fastest-growing suburbs, and many residents commute to Cincinnati or Dayton. The 8th's strong manufacturing base, grounded in the steel industry, and a healthy agricultural sector have helped keep the district's economy strong. The 8th also encompasses a slice of Montgomery County, including parts of northeast Dayton near Wright-Patterson Air Force Base, which is in the 3rd and 7th districts.

About half of the 8th's residents live outside Butler in a string of fertile Corn Belt counties — Mercer (shared with the 5th), Darke and Preble. Corn and soybeans are the major cash crops here, and poultry and livestock also are moneymakers. All three counties are among the most productive in the state, and Darke ranks first in Ohio in total agricultural productivity. The district is tops in the state in raising turkeys.

George W. Bush defeated John Kerry in Butler by more than 30 percentage points in the 2004 presidential election. Mercer and Darke backed Bush with 75 percent and 70 percent of the vote, respectively, in 2004. Miami County, the district's second-most-populous, gave Bush 66 percent in 2004. Exceptions to the GOP dominance are Oxford — which includes Miami University and backed Kerry in 2004 — and the urban portion of Montgomery in the 8th.

MAJOR INDUSTRY

Agriculture, manufacturing, higher education

CITIES

Hamilton (pt.), 60,675; Middletown (pt.), 49,574; Fairfield, 42,097

NOTABLE

The Voice of America Park and VOA Museum, a planned center to document the radio service's history, is in West Chester Township.

Rep. Marcy Kaptur (D)

CAPITOL OFFICE
225-4146
rep.kaptur@mail.house.gov
www.house.gov/kaptur
2186 Rayburn 20515-3509; fax 225-7711

COMMITTEES
Appropriations
Budget

RESIDENCE
Toledo

BORN
June 17, 1946, Toledo, Ohio

RELIGION
Roman Catholic

FAMILY
Single

EDUCATION
U. of Wisconsin, B.A. 1968 (history);
U. of Michigan, M.U.P. 1974 (urban planning);
Massachusetts Institute of Technology, attended 1981 (urban planning)

CAREER
White House aide; urban planner

POLITICAL HIGHLIGHTS
No previous office

ELECTION RESULTS

2006 GENERAL		
Marcy Kaptur (D)	153,880	73.6%
Bradley S. Leavitt (R)	55,119	26.4%
2006 PRIMARY		
Marcy Kaptur (D)		unopposed
2004 GENERAL		
Marcy Kaptur (D)	205,149	68.1%
Larry A. Kaczala (R)	95,983	31.9%

PREVIOUS WINNING PERCENTAGES
2002 (74%); 2000 (75%); 1998 (81%); 1996 (77%); 1994 (75%); 1992 (74%); 1990 (78%); 1988 (81%); 1986 (78%); 1984 (55%); 1982 (58%)

Elected 1982; 13th term

Kaptur is the antithesis of the modern blown-dry, soundbite politician. She still lives with her brother, Stephen, in the same small house where they grew up, and she attends Mass at the same church where she was baptized. She grows a vegetable garden and cans some of the produce; she bakes Polish coffee cakes and makes Polish sausages at the holidays; she paints watercolors; she sews her own curtains. She dislikes fundraising.

She represents an ethnic, blue-collar district and is a supporter of labor. She once worked as an autoworker to help pay for college.

Kaptur is in her 13th term in the House, and she is the most senior Democratic woman. But her longevity has not translated into increased political power, and she does not seem dismayed by that fact.

She now ranks fifth in seniority on the Appropriations Committee but does not chair a subcommittee even though she was the top Democrat on the Agriculture panel from 1997-2005. In fact, she is the most senior Democrat in the House without a gavel or elected leadership post of some sort, a fact that sparked criticism from the hometown Toledo Blade newspaper. She explained that she gave up the top spot on Agriculture Appropriations in 2005 in order to grab a seat on the Defense spending subcommittee.

Kaptur opposes U.S. involvement in Iraq, and voted in 2002 against authorizing the war. She has demanded that the Pentagon account for its contracting practices there. During a March 2007 hearing on that issue, Kaptur said that despite repeated inquiries to the Pentagon, she has never learned what four military contractors were doing in Fallujah, Iraq, before they were killed by Iraqi insurgents. "I am a member who does not support the privatization of our military," Kaptur said in an interview. "It is in America's national interest to have people in the military pledged to the time-tested values of duty, honor and country — not bounty and mercenary."

Agriculture is Ohio's biggest industry, and Kaptur has always looked out for the interests of the farmers in her district (she still serves on the Agriculture Appropriations Subcommittee). The agricultural mix in the 9th District is quite diverse and includes corn, beans, beef, dairy and wheat. She backs most agricultural subsidies, saying it is only fair to help U.S. industries survive when they have to comply with labor, environmental and health standards that are higher than in other nations.

Kaptur says she believes the country needs to gain energy independence and find new power sources, particularly renewable energy sources. In a 2005 agriculture bill, she wrote a section providing $25 million a year to support the development of renewable energy. She told the Cleveland Plain Dealer she would like to see Ohio develop an "Ohio car," an energy-efficient vehicle built in the state. She also sees ethanol as a future alternative fuel to imported oil. Kaptur and other farm-state lawmakers want the government to allocate more funding for start-up grants for ethanol production.

True to her labor roots, Kaptur has opposed all the major trade expansion initiatives of President Bush and those of President Bill Clinton. She voted against free-trade agreements with Australia, Chile and Singapore in the 108th Congress (2003-04) and against the Central American Free Trade Agreement in the 109th Congress (2005-06). In 2007, she introduced a bill to revoke China's normal trade status with the United States.

She capped a 17-year political and legislative effort in 2004 when she presided over the opening of the World War II Memorial on the National Mall. The project was sparked by the request of a constituent, who wondered why there was no monument in Washington to World War II soldiers. That was the beginning of a long and complex fight over the $182 million memorial's location and design.

A supporter of campaign financing reform, Kaptur says the Democratic Party's emphasis on fundraising has caused it to lose its historical focus on the needs of the working class. In 2002, she challenged Californian Nancy Pelosi for the position of minority leader simply to make that point. Once she gave her speech, she withdrew her name.

Kaptur is more socially conservative than many in her party, but her views match those of her ethnic blue-collar constituents — Germans, Irish, Poles, Hungarians and Hispanics — who share the Roman Catholic Church's opposition to abortion. Kaptur herself is of the same stock. Her father's parents were from western Poland; her mother's from eastern Poland, in an area now part of Ukraine.

Her father ran a grocery store in Rossford, just south of Toledo, where he was known for giving credit to people who couldn't afford food for the week. Kaptur says when she first ran for office, people came up to her and said his generosity had saved their family. But her father had to sell the store after suffering two heart attacks. He took a job with the Jeep automaker in order to gain health insurance. The experience left her with a lifelong interest in the plight of the uninsured, she says.

After the 1997 death of her mother, Anastasia, Kaptur and her brother founded the nonprofit Anastasia Fund, which has helped support democracy movements in Ukraine, China and Mexico. Kaptur also has established the Kaptur Community Fund, which makes charitable donations in Toledo; she regularly contributes her congressional pay raise to the fund.

Kaptur was studying for her doctorate in urban planning at the Massachusetts Institute of Technology when she was recruited to challenge first-term GOP Rep. Ed Weber in 1982. With northwest Ohio in a deep recession, Weber's support for President Ronald Reagan's economic policies proved politically fatal; Kaptur won by 19 percentage points.

She was held to 55 percent of the vote in 1984 but has won by overwhelming margins since. In 2004, she annoyed her 12 Republican colleagues in the Ohio delegation by helping to recruit Democratic candidates to run against them — a breach of longstanding political protocol. The Republicans retaliated by raising significant funds for her opponent, Lucas County Auditor Larry A. Kaczala, who held her to a mere 68 percent. In 2006, she bounced back to her norm, winning close to 75 percent of the vote against Republican Bradley S. Leavitt, a 32-year-old electrician and Navy veteran.

KEY VOTES

2006

Yes Stop broadband companies from favoring select Internet traffic
No Affirm U.S. commitment to war in Iraq and reject setting a withdrawal date for troops
No Repeal requirement for bilingual ballots at the polls
No Permit U.S. sale of civilian nuclear technology to India
P Build a 700-mile fence on the U.S.-Mexico border to curb illegal crossings
No Permit warrantless wiretaps of suspected terrorists

2005

No Intervene in the life-support case of Terri Schiavo
No Lift President Bush's restrictions on stem cell research funding
Yes Prohibit FBI access to library and bookstore records
No Approve free-trade pact with five Central American countries
No Pass energy policy overhaul favored by President Bush emphasizing domestic oil and gas production
No End mandatory preservation of habitat of endangered animal and plant species
Yes Ban torture of prisoners in U.S. custody

CQ VOTE STUDIES

	PARTY UNITY		PRESIDENTIAL SUPPORT	
	Support	Oppose	Support	Oppose
2006	88%	12%	27%	73%
2005	93%	7%	23%	77%
2004	97%	3%	33%	67%
2003	95%	5%	25%	75%
2002	96%	4%	24%	76%

INTEREST GROUPS

	AFL-CIO	ADA	CCUS	ACU
2006	100%	85%	33%	21%
2005	93%	95%	41%	21%
2004	100%	95%	33%	8%
2003	100%	95%	24%	28%
2002	100%	95%	30%	18%

OHIO 9

North — Toledo, Sandusky

Along nearly 80 miles of Lake Erie's shoreline, the strongly Democratic 9th moves east from Lucas County and Toledo into Cleveland's orbit in Lorain County. More than two-thirds of the district's population resides in Lucas. Outside of Lucas, farmland and vacation spots contribute to the local economy.

At the mouth of Maumee River, the largest river flowing into the Great Lakes, Toledo accounts for about half of the 9th's residents. The city's blue-collar industries struggle to provide enough jobs. Once nicknamed the "Glass City" because of its history in that industry, Toledo has relied on auto manufacturing for decades. DaimlerChrysler and General Motors continue to employ many district residents; Toledo is home to Jeep and GM production plants. The city's health care sector has experienced growth, especially with the merger of the University of Toledo and the Medical University of Ohio, which resulted in Ohio's third-largest public university operating budget.

Agriculture is important to the 9th, with greenhouse and fruit production leading the way, but tourism is another key secondary economy. Sandusky's Cedar Point attracts more than 3 million visitors annually to its 364-acre amusement park and resort: Cedar Point claims the most rides (69) and roller coasters (17) of any park in the world. In addition, millions of visitors travel to Lake Erie's Bass Islands each year.

Toledo's large concentrations of ethnic blue-collar workers — Germans, Irish, Poles and Hungarians — make it a lonely Democratic outpost in rural, Republican northwestern Ohio. John Kerry took 61 percent of the 2004 presidential vote in the 9th's share of Lucas and 58 percent overall in the district. The 9th's easternmost county of Lorain (shared with the 13th) leans Democratic and includes the strongly liberal area around Oberlin College. The district's Republicans are concentrated in the more affluent suburbs on Toledo's west side.

MAJOR INDUSTRY

Auto manufacturing, agriculture, health care, tourism

CITIES

Toledo, 313,619; Sandusky, 27,844; Oregon, 19,355; Sylvania, 18,670

NOTABLE

Oberlin College, founded in 1833, was the first coeducational institution of higher learning in the United States.

Rep. Dennis J. Kucinich (D)

Elected 1996; 6th term

CAPITOL OFFICE
225-5871
www.house.gov/kucinich
2445 Rayburn 20515-3510; fax 225-5745

COMMITTEES
Education & Labor
Oversight & Government Reform
(Domestic Policy - chairman)

RESIDENCE
Cleveland

BORN
Oct. 8, 1946, Cleveland, Ohio

RELIGION
Roman Catholic

FAMILY
Wife, Elizabeth Kucinich; one child

EDUCATION
Case Western Reserve U., B.A., M.A. 1973 (speech communications)

CAREER
Video producer; public power consultant; sportswriter

POLITICAL HIGHLIGHTS
Cleveland City Council, 1969-75; Democratic nominee for U.S. House, 1972; independent candidate for U.S. House, 1974; mayor of Cleveland, 1977-79; defeated for re-election as mayor of Cleveland, 1979; Cleveland City Council, 1983-85; sought Democratic nomination for U.S. House, 1988, 1992; Ohio Senate, 1995-97; sought Democratic nomination for president, 2004

ELECTION RESULTS

2006 GENERAL		
Dennis J. Kucinich (D)	138,393	66.4%
Michael D. Dovilla (R)	69,996	33.6%
2006 PRIMARY		
Dennis J. Kucinich (D)	51,485	76.4%
Barbara Anne Ferris (D)	15,890	23.6%
2004 GENERAL		
Dennis J. Kucinich (D)	172,406	60.0%
Edward Fitzpatrick Herman (R)	96,463	33.6%
Barbara Anne Ferris (I)	18,343	6.4%

PREVIOUS WINNING PERCENTAGES
2002 (74%); 2000 (75%); 1998 (67%); 1996 (49%)

Decades after his days as the boy wonder of Cleveland politics, Kucinich is a man rejuvenated. His quixotic quest for the presidency in 2004 and a new marriage have broadened his fan base and intensified his enjoyment of life. He continues to pursue the anti-war and pro-labor goals that have animated his career on Capitol Hill, and he cheerfully shrugs off his inability to actually win enactment of major items on his agenda.

An anti-war anchor for his party in the House, Kucinich (ku-SIN-itch) failed spectacularly in his 2004 bid for the Democratic presidential nomination, but that didn't deter him from jumping into the 2008 race as well. His 2004 campaign drew public attention to his longstanding proposals to create a Cabinet-level Department of Peace, enact a single-payer national health care plan and force a U.S. withdrawal from the World Trade Organization. He thinks his colleagues in Congress will pay attention eventually. "A lot of these ideas are pretty new to members, so you keep working on it year after year," he said. "I mean, I'm pretty persistent."

Kucinich, a self-described pacifist, fought the 2002 law authorizing President Bush to launch a pre-emptive military strike on Iraq. While his attempt to build support for a longer course of diplomacy came up short, Kucinich's proposal for a delay received 101 votes on the House floor.

He and five other Democrats then sued to bar Bush from attacking without a specific congressional declaration of war. A federal appeals court tossed out the suit in March 2003. Similarly, in 1999 he joined two dozen other lawmakers in an unsuccessful suit maintaining that President Bill Clinton had illegally committed U.S. troops to a NATO bombing campaign without congressional approval.

Kucinich opposed both the 2001 anti-terrorism law known as the Patriot Act and its 2005 reauthorization, calling it an assault on civil liberties. In a 2002 speech that generated thousands of mostly supportive e-mail responses, Kucinich railed against Bush's conduct of the campaign against terrorism as a "war without end." In 2005, when Republicans championed a resolution expressing the House's commitment to achieving victory in Iraq, Kucinich countered with one saying that Iraq's Council of Representatives should decide whether the U.S. military remained in the country.

Kucinich distinguishes himself not only by his perseverance but also by his rhetorical flourishes and self-deprecating wit. When he arrived in Congress, he handed out trading cards featuring himself as a 4-foot-9-inch, 97-pound backup high school quarterback in 1960. Speaking at a journalists' black-tie awards dinner a few months later, he brought down the house when he promised to civilize Washington by introducing it to three Cleveland staples: kielbasa, polka and bowling.

In his 2004 campaign for president, a highly publicized contest run by a political Web site to get the candidate a dinner date brought more recognition than any of his political positions. He actually went on a date with the winner of the Web contest, but nothing more came of it, except perhaps a renewed interest in romance.

In August 2005, after 18 years of bachelorhood, Kucinich married a consultant for a monetary think tank who is 30 years his junior and several inches taller than he. His new wife is British, raised in a picturesque town not far from London, and she is intimately familiar with that very cosmopolitan city. Kucinich had a hardscrabble childhood on the streets of Cleveland. Yet for all their superficial differences, the congressman says they are a perfect match in worldview. Kucinich, who is twice divorced, said, "I'm happier than I've ever been. I have a real partnership."

The son of a truck driver who was often out of work, Kucinich and his six siblings moved frequently and sometimes slept in the family car for weeks at a time. His mother would send Kucinich, the oldest, to the corner store to get milk bottles heated for the little ones, according to a Boston Globe profile, and when he was 12, Kucinich shined shoes to bring in extra money even as his own cheap ones were falling apart.

He worked two jobs to put himself through college, getting a master's degree in speech communications, and launching a career as a copy editor, sportswriter and political commentator, jobs that taught him to reduce complicated public policy disagreements to easily understood terms.

Elected mayor of Cleveland at 31, he served a single controversial term. The city fell into financial default and his popularity sank so low he wore a bulletproof vest to throw out the first pitch of the Cleveland Indians' 1978 season. Later that year, he barely survived a recall vote, and the next year he lost to Republican George V. Voinovich, now Ohio's senior senator.

But then both Cleveland and its former mayor rebounded. Bucking the GOP tide, Kucinich seized a state Senate seat from a Republican incumbent in 1994. Two years later, he toppled two-term Republican Rep. Martin R. Hoke on his fifth try for Congress, a quest he began as an anti-Vietnam War candidate in 1972. Kucinich put together a strong grass-roots effort in a Democratic-leaning district and won by 3 percentage points after linking Hoke to Speaker Newt Gingrich of Georgia, a polarizing figure in 1996. His subsequent elections have been cakewalks.

In six terms in the House, he has won enactment of only one law, a 1998 measure to make a television program, "Window on America," available to the Ukrainian Museum and Archives in Cleveland.

One of Kucinich's passions is warning Americans about genetically modified food, which would carry government labels under legislation he has proposed since 1999. "If we are what we eat, shouldn't we know what is in our food, so we know what we will become?" he asked.

Kucinich meditates and is comfortable with a New Age crowd of supporters that includes actress Shirley MacLaine, who is his daughter's godmother. Practicing what he preaches, Kucinich made a radical change in his own diet in 1995, becoming a vegan after almost five decades eating rich Eastern European food. Now his meals include rice, tofu and green tea. "Once I was able to make the transition, I've had enormous amounts of energy, I sleep better, and I don't get tired as much," he said.

KEY VOTES

2006

- Yes Stop broadband companies from favoring select Internet traffic
- No Affirm U.S. commitment to war in Iraq and reject setting a withdrawal date for troops
- No Repeal requirement for bilingual ballots at the polls
- No Permit U.S. sale of civilian nuclear technology to India
- No Build a 700-mile fence on the U.S.-Mexico border to curb illegal crossings
- No Permit warrantless wiretaps of suspected terrorists

2005

- ? Intervene in the life-support case of Terri Schiavo
- Yes Lift President Bush's restrictions on stem cell research funding
- Yes Prohibit FBI access to library and bookstore records
- No Approve free-trade pact with five Central American countries
- No Pass energy policy overhaul favored by President Bush emphasizing domestic oil and gas production
- No End mandatory preservation of habitat of endangered animal and plant species
- Yes Ban torture of prisoners in U.S. custody

CQ VOTE STUDIES

	PARTY UNITY		PRESIDENTIAL SUPPORT	
	Support	Oppose	Support	Oppose
2006	97%	3%	13%	87%
2005	98%	2%	11%	89%
2004	96%	4%	22%	78%
2003	96%	4%	22%	78%
2002	96%	4%	26%	74%

INTEREST GROUPS

	AFL-CIO	ADA	CCUS	ACU
2006	93%	100%	20%	4%
2005	93%	100%	30%	0%
2004	100%	90%	6%	0%
2003	100%	90%	15%	24%
2002	100%	80%	20%	0%

OHIO 10

Cleveland — West Side and suburbs

Taking in the western portion of Cleveland, the 10th follows the migration of its ethnic residents into the western and southern suburbs. The line between the 10th and 11th districts generally divides Cleveland's white and black neighborhoods. The 10th contains large concentrations of ethnic voters, including Poles, Turks and African immigrants, especially in areas such as Parma.

Once solely dependent on manufacturing, this Democratic district has gradually made the transition to a service economy, with growth in the banking and financial services sectors as well. Although manufacturing is still the backbone of the city's economy, the 10th has attracted smaller technology companies and Cleveland has undergone a decades-long downtown restoration. The 10th also is home to Cleveland Hopkins International Airport, a hub for Continental Airlines that provides many jobs in the region.

The immediate suburbs have a strong union presence and a Democratic lean. Traditionally Democratic-leaning, middle-income communities that abut western Cleveland, such as Brooklyn and Lakewood, are losing population. Blue-collar workers at a local Ford plant in Brook Park make that city decidedly Democratic. Farther west, incomes rise, as does the level of Republicanism: Bay Village, Westlake and Rocky River residents have above-average incomes and voted solidly for George W. Bush in the 2004 presidential election.

The strong Democratic tendencies of Cleveland — the 10th's share of the city gave John Kerry 70 percent of its 2004 presidential vote — coupled with the GOP lean of some of the city's western and southern suburbs, give the 10th a decided but not overwhelming Democratic tilt. Overall, Kerry took 58 percent of the district's presidential vote in 2004.

MAJOR INDUSTRY

Manufacturing, banking, technology, auto parts

CITIES

Cleveland (pt.), 190,224; Parma, 85,655; Lakewood, 56,646; North Olmsted, 34,113; Westlake, 31,719

NOTABLE

Cleveland is home to NASA's John H. Glenn Research Center; North Olmsted was the first city in the United States to prohibit municipal purchases of materials or goods made under sweatshop conditions.

Rep. Stephanie Tubbs Jones (D)

CAPITOL OFFICE
225-7032
www.house.gov/tubbsjones
1009 Longworth 20515-3511; fax 225-1339

COMMITTEES
Standards of Official Conduct - chairwoman
Ways & Means

RESIDENCE
Cleveland

BORN
Sept. 10, 1949, Cleveland, Ohio

RELIGION
Baptist

FAMILY
Widowed; one child

EDUCATION
Case Western Reserve U., B.A. 1971 (sociology), J.D. 1974

CAREER
Lawyer; municipal judge

POLITICAL HIGHLIGHTS
Cleveland Municipal Court judge, 1982-83; Cuyahoga County Common Pleas Court judge, 1983-91; Cuyahoga County prosecutor, 1991-99

ELECTION RESULTS

2006 GENERAL		
Stephanie Tubbs Jones (D)	146,799	83.4%
Lindsey N. String (R)	29,125	16.6%
2006 PRIMARY		
Stephanie Tubbs Jones (D)		unopposed
2004 GENERAL		
Stephanie Tubbs Jones (D)		unopposed

PREVIOUS WINNING PERCENTAGES
2002 (76%); 2000 (85%); 1998 (80%)

Elected 1998; 5th term

As the new chairwoman of the House ethics committee, Jones is on the front line of the debate over Congress' ability to police itself in the wake of several influence-peddling scandals in the last Congress. House Speaker Nancy Pelosi, who considers her an ally, chose her for the spot though Jones herself had come under scrutiny for accepting a large number of vacation-destination trips paid for by private interests.

Such trips figured in some career-breaking controversies in the 109th Congress (2005-06), including one that forced powerful Republican Majority Leader Tom DeLay from office. A barrage of media reports about members of Congress traveling on the dime of lobbyists or lobbying organizations followed. Jones was one of the most frequent travelers, logging 75 trips at a cost of more than $100,000, according to a study of congressional travel from 2000 to 2006 by the group PoliticalMoneyLine.

Among her destinations were Las Vegas, where she attended a 2005 conference paid for by the United Steelworkers, and Barbados, paid for by the National Bar Association. She said she had "no apologies for the trips that I have taken during my tenure in Congress" and that she traveled for speaking engagements as "the only African-American woman and only Democratic woman on the Ways and Means Committee."

It was not Jones' first brush with ethics questions. In 2004, she was forced to reimburse thousands of dollars to her campaign treasury when a Federal Election Commission audit said she might have spent the money for personal reasons.

A longtime ally of Pelosi and a robust fundraiser for the party, Jones was tapped for the ethics chairmanship instead of Alan B. Mollohan of West Virginia, who was the senior Democrat on the panel but had come under fire for questionable personal financial dealings. Pelosi called Jones, a former municipal judge, "tough and smart."

She will have to be, for one of the House's toughest jobs. The Committee on Standards of Official Conduct, as the ethics committee is formally known, is supposed to police the behavior of fellow lawmakers but often fails to investigate its own until after the press or law enforcement agencies have acted. The committee has been criticized as toothless, and after a season of scandal there were calls by watchdog groups and others for an independent commission to take over.

Jones was among the five African-Americans who claimed committee chairmanships when the Democrats ascended to the majority in 2007. Before that, she grabbed the spotlight by launching a protest of George W. Bush's electoral victory in her home state, throwing a wrench into the normally routine approval by Congress of Electoral College results. In January 2005, Jones rose in a half-empty chamber to register the protest and was joined by the requisite one senator, Democrat Barbara Boxer of California. That met the legal threshold for forcing debate.

The actual outcome was never in doubt, and Bush was certified as the winner. Jones said the point was to call attention to problems with voting machines and voter registration in the state, where Bush beat Democratic Sen. John Kerry of Massachusetts by 119,000 votes. The move put Jones, who was co-chairwoman of Kerry's 2004 presidential campaign, in the history books. The official tally of electoral votes had last been challenged in 1969, when the vote of one elector for Gov. George Wallace was contested. Congress certified Richard Nixon as the winner.

Another locus of activity for Jones is the powerful Ways and Means Committee, which writes tax, trade and health care policy. She has considerably more impact there now that Democrats have the majority.

She got the seat in 2003 by publicly protesting that the panel had no African-American woman. Republicans at the time were trying to shrink the committee, which would have shut out Jones. To avoid embarrassment, they left the number of seats the same, and Democratic leaders appointed Jones. Since then, she has been active in efforts to protect American workers from the effects of global trade. In 2005, she proposed doubling — to $519 million — funding for Trade Adjustment Assistance, which helps workers who lose jobs as a result of free-trade pacts. Her plan was voted down.

Jones voted with House Democrats 96 percent of the time on votes pitting the two parties against each other in the 109th Congress. Before getting on Ways and Means, she used her seats on the Financial Services and Small Business committees to boost economic development in her district, attack predatory lending practices and champion laid-off workers who lose pensions when their employers go bankrupt.

Jones and her two sisters were raised in the Glenville neighborhood of Cleveland. Her father, Andrew Tubbs, was a United Airlines skycap for 40 years and her mother, Mary Tubbs, worked at an American Greeting Cards factory. Both were active in the Bethany Baptist Church, where her mother was a deaconess and where Jones is still a member.

Jones got involved in politics as a college student when she joined a group of Vietnam War demonstrators who forced Case Western Reserve University in Cleveland to shut down in the spring of 1970.

After planning for a career in social work, Jones changed her mind and went to law school. Her first job was litigating for the Equal Employment Opportunity Commission. Seven years later, in 1981, she was elected to a Cleveland municipal judgeship. Two years after that, she was appointed by the governor to a judgeship handling felony cases. Jones was elected in 1991 as the Cuyahoga County prosecutor, overseeing a staff of about 300.

In 1998, she ran for the House seat of retiring Rep. Louis Stokes, a 15-term Democrat who was Ohio's first black member of Congress and a mentor to Jones. He endorsed her as his successor. Jones' convincing victory in the Democratic primary — her two closest rivals were the Rev. Marvin A. McMickle and state Sen. Jeffrey Johnson — all but sealed her election in the overwhelmingly Democratic district.

Jones briefly considered entreaties that she run in 2001 for mayor of Cleveland and she thought about a bid for governor in 2002.

KEY VOTES

2006

Yes Stop broadband companies from favoring select Internet traffic

No Affirm U.S. commitment to war in Iraq and reject setting a withdrawal date for troops

No Repeal requirement for bilingual ballots at the polls

Yes Permit U.S. sale of civilian nuclear technology to India

No Build a 700-mile fence on the U.S.-Mexico border to curb illegal crossings

No Permit warrantless wiretaps of suspected terrorists

2005

? Intervene in the life-support case of Terri Schiavo

Yes Lift President Bush's restrictions on stem cell research funding

Yes Prohibit FBI access to library and bookstore records

No Approve free-trade pact with five Central American countries

No Pass energy policy overhaul favored by President Bush emphasizing domestic oil and gas production

No End mandatory preservation of habitat of endangered animal and plant species

Yes Ban torture of prisoners in U.S. custody

CQ VOTE STUDIES

	PARTY UNITY		PRESIDENTIAL SUPPORT	
	Support	Oppose	Support	Oppose
2006	95%	5%	27%	73%
2005	96%	4%	20%	80%
2004	97%	3%	29%	71%
2003	98%	2%	16%	84%
2002	98%	2%	24%	76%

INTEREST GROUPS

	AFL-CIO	ADA	CCUS	ACU
2006	100%	90%	40%	4%
2005	92%	100%	38%	4%
2004	100%	85%	38%	5%
2003	100%	90%	22%	16%
2002	100%	85%	39%	0%

OHIO 11

Cleveland — East Side and suburbs

The 11th includes the poor, inner-city areas of Cleveland's East Side, as well as many of the city's notable tourist and spectator destinations, and extends out to the east to take in upper-middle-class suburbs. The district's black majority and liberal suburbanites combine to make it very Democratic, and the 2006 Democratic gubernatorial and U.S. Senate nominees each captured more than 80 percent of the 11th's vote.

Driving the district's staunch Democratic bent is its 60 percent share of Cleveland, which gave John Kerry 92 percent of its presidential vote in 2004. Much of the 11th's black majority lives in inner-city neighborhoods, often below the poverty line, and the district has Ohio's lowest median income. There are some middle-class neighborhoods toward Lake Erie, inhabited mostly by Italian-Americans and Eastern Europeans.

Although suburban growth has lured many businesses and residents outside the city, the 11th is gradually making itself a medical, biotechnology and banking hub. Cleveland's cultural center, located in University Circle, is home to Case Western Reserve University. The Circle also is the face of Cleveland's health care industry; the University Hospitals of Cleveland, Cleveland Clinic and Louis Stokes Veteran Affairs Medical Center all are located here. Driving west from the circle along historic Euclid Avenue, the city's geographic center includes the Rock and Roll Hall of Fame, the city's sports stadiums and Public Square. Midwest banking giant National City also is based in the district.

The upper-middle-class suburbs of Cleveland Heights, Shaker Heights and University Heights to the east of Cleveland are home to large communities of Jews and young professionals, forming some of Ohio's most liberal and racially integrated areas. Farther east, the 11th takes in areas such as Mayfield Heights, Richmond Heights, Lyndhurst and Pepper Pike, which has one of the highest incomes in the state.

MAJOR INDUSTRY

Health care, manufacturing, utilities, education

CITIES

Cleveland (pt.), 288,179; Euclid, 52,717; Cleveland Heights, 49,958; Shaker Heights, 29,405; East Cleveland, 27,217; Maple Heights, 26,156

NOTABLE

A landmark 1926 case brought by the city of Euclid was the first U.S. Supreme Court decision to uphold city zoning ordinances.

Rep. Pat Tiberi (R)

CAPITOL OFFICE
225-5355
www.house.gov/tiberi
113 Cannon 20515-3512; fax 226-4523

COMMITTEES
Budget
Ways & Means

RESIDENCE
Genoa Township

BORN
Oct. 21, 1962, Columbus, Ohio

RELIGION
Roman Catholic

FAMILY
Wife, Denice Tiberi; one child

EDUCATION
Ohio State U., B.A. 1985 (journalism)

CAREER
Realtor; congressional district aide

POLITICAL HIGHLIGHTS
Ohio House, 1993-2001 (majority leader, 1999-2001)

ELECTION RESULTS

2006 GENERAL		
Pat Tiberi (R)	145,943	57.3%
Bob Shamansky (D)	108,746	42.7%
2006 PRIMARY		
Pat Tiberi (R)		unopposed
2004 GENERAL		
Pat Tiberi (R)	198,912	62.0%
Edward S. Brown (D)	122,109	38.0%

PREVIOUS WINNING PERCENTAGES
2002 (64%); 2000 (53%)

Elected 2000; 4th term

A close ally of Minority Leader John A. Boehner, a fellow Buckeye State lawmaker, Tiberi is a behind-the-scenes force working to boost GOP fortunes at the polls. With friends in high places, Tiberi in the 110th Congress (2007-08) got the seat on the House Ways and Means Committee that he'd had his eye on for a few years.

In addition to hailing from the same state, Tiberi (TEA-berry) and Boehner also worked hand in glove on the Education Committee, which Boehner chaired until 2006. Tiberi, one of the GOP leader's most trusted allies, worked on Boehner's campaign to defeat Missouri Republican Roy Blunt in a tense intraparty fight for Republican leader in the 109th Congress (2005-06). Tiberi is also close to Deborah Pryce of Ohio, the former chairwoman of the Republican Conference.

Tiberi did the party's bidding in 2005 in helping to defeat a ballot initiative in Ohio that would have changed the state's redistricting process in a way that could have cost Republicans seats in the next election. He was the point person between Ohio Republicans in Congress and the opposition effort in the state. As a token of gratitude, Rep. Thomas M. Reynolds of New York, then chairman of the National Republican Congressional Committee, gave Tiberi a framed map of the state signed by Ohio's GOP lawmakers. Every Ohio Republican incumbent on the November ballot won re-election.

Tiberi was one of the endangered Republicans who survived in the 2006 elections, albeit with just 57 percent of the vote. His Democratic opponent was 79-year-old Bob Shamansky, a wealthy attorney and real estate investor who had served one term in the House in the early 1980s. Shamansky increasingly became a threat as the election neared and public confidence in the Bush administration and the Republican-controlled Congress plummeted.

Tiberi's main legislative focus in the last Congress was a bipartisan effort that renewed the law governing social services for senior citizens through fiscal 2011. Called the Older Americans Act, the law was part of President Lyndon B. Johnson's 1965 Great Society agenda and calls for about $1.8 billion in annual spending. It is probably best known for the venerable Meals on Wheels program, which provides millions of low-income seniors with nutrition and also health screenings, counseling and employment. Rubén Hinojosa, a Texas Democrat who worked with Tiberi on the legislation, said he's "fair and is willing to find a way to make things work."

Another bill Tiberi was heavily involved with extended hiring preferences for federal jobs to veterans with more than 180 days on active duty. Under previous law, veterans had to serve 30 consecutive days in combat to qualify for the benefit.

Tiberi was no stranger to the ways of Congress when he won his seat in the 2000 election. He had spent eight years handling constituent casework for Republican Rep. John R. Kasich and another eight years as a member of the state House. When Kasich decided to step out of public life, Tiberi leapt at the chance to run for the seat, and Kasich quickly endorsed his former aide. Some of Kasich's staff, who had been Tiberi's supervisors and co-workers in the 1980s, now work for him — an unusual display of both staff longevity and loyalty. Tiberi's time as a congressional aide was spent at Kasich's district office in Columbus, not on Capitol Hill, and he has made constituent service a high priority.

A lifelong resident of his district, Tiberi is still most comfortable, he says, in the Columbus neighborhood of Northland where he grew up and spent most of his life. As a local newspaper columnist once said, "Every groundbreaking, every parade, every ribbon-cutting with a pair of scissors to spare . . . is likely to find Pat Tiberi," and "that's bad news for the Democrats, who now stand about 4,000 chicken lunches behind Tiberi."

In his first two terms, Tiberi was a dependable supporter of President Bush and the GOP leadership. In the 109th Congress, however, he began to distance himself from the president, expressing skepticism about his proposal to allow workers to divert some Social Security payroll taxes into private accounts. He supported the president's positions only 79 percent of the time in the 109th Congress, compared with scores in the 80s and 90s for most other House Republicans.

Tiberi is the eldest of three children of Italian immigrants who arrived in the United States three years before he was born. His father was a machinist, his mother a seamstress. Tiberi told The Columbus Dispatch that his first political allegiance, given his working-class background, came when he and some school friends "looked at each other and said, 'I guess we're Democrats.' " Tiberi was the first in his family to go to college.

He met his wife, Denice, at a Northlands High School marching band alumni gathering. He played trumpet; she played flute. Tiberi, who was senior class president, says he had no interest in politics as a career until a political science class at Ohio State University led to an internship in Kasich's office — and a change of party. He became a Republican.

In 1992, state legislative district remapping created an open seat in his neighborhood. He ran and spent four terms in the state House, rising to majority leader in 1999 and earning a reputation as a conservative willing to work with Democrats. He established a DNA database to track violent criminals and was a prime mover behind a state law that for a time limited large jury awards but later was ruled unconstitutional. Tiberi also wrote legislation requiring performance audits for schools.

Barred by an Ohio term limit law from seeking re-election to the General Assembly in 2000, Tiberi was considering a career change when Kasich announced he was leaving the House. Kasich's support helped Tiberi cruise to an easy primary victory over three rivals. Democrats put up a formidable opponent, Columbus City Councilwoman Maryellen O'Shaughnessy. Tiberi racked up big margins in the suburban GOP strongholds of Delaware and Licking counties and won by 9 percentage points. He won re-election comfortably until his scare in 2006.

KEY VOTES

2006

No	Stop broadband companies from favoring select Internet traffic
Yes	Affirm U.S. commitment to war in Iraq and reject setting a withdrawal date for troops
Yes	Repeal requirement for bilingual ballots at the polls
Yes	Permit U.S. sale of civilian nuclear technology to India
Yes	Build a 700-mile fence on the U.S.-Mexico border to curb illegal crossings
Yes	Permit warrantless wiretaps of suspected terrorists

2005

Yes	Intervene in the life-support case of Terri Schiavo
No	Lift President Bush's restrictions on stem cell research funding
No	Prohibit FBI access to library and bookstore records
Yes	Approve free-trade pact with five Central American countries
Yes	Pass energy policy overhaul favored by President Bush emphasizing domestic oil and gas production
Yes	End mandatory preservation of habitat of endangered animal and plant species
Yes	Ban torture of prisoners in U.S. custody

CQ VOTE STUDIES

	PARTY UNITY		PRESIDENTIAL SUPPORT	
	Support	Oppose	Support	Oppose
2006	92%	8%	87%	13%
2005	95%	5%	71%	29%
2004	92%	8%	82%	18%
2003	95%	5%	91%	9%
2002	95%	5%	88%	12%

INTEREST GROUPS

	AFL-CIO	ADA	CCUS	ACU
2006	36%	0%	100%	84%
2005	27%	5%	96%	88%
2004	13%	10%	100%	96%
2003	7%	5%	100%	84%
2002	11%	0%	100%	96%

OHIO 12

Central – Eastern Columbus and suburbs

The 12th includes the eastern half of Columbus in Franklin County and suburban counties to the north and east of the city. The district has a slight Republican lean, with a strong GOP influence in the 12th's suburbs balancing a Democratic tilt in Columbus.

The 12th's economy relies heavily on Columbus' business sector, and the city's expanding financial services and strong retail sectors — Limited Brands, which includes Victoria's Secret and Express, is headquartered in Columbus — have helped spur the district's economy. Columbus has become primarily white-collar, and its thriving service economy has led to significant growth in both the city and its adjacent areas.

Democrats find support in the urban, predominately black part of the district in Franklin County. Within Franklin County, but outside Columbus, the 12th includes Dublin, an upscale, solidly GOP suburb in the northwest part of the county known to many as the headquarters of Wendy's. Dublin also is home to health care manufacturer Cardinal Health, which is among the top 20 in the Fortune 500. Westerville, Gahanna and Reynoldsburg — traditionally Republican areas outside Columbus — show signs of increasing Democratic support, and John Kerry carried the 12th's share of Franklin by a double-digit margin in the 2004 presidential election.

North of Franklin, Delaware County has experienced explosive growth — its population more than doubled over the past 15 years — and it has the state's lowest unemployment and highest household income. Offsetting the Democrats in Franklin County are Republicans in Delaware and western Licking County, whose numbers are swelling due to the overall growth. George W. Bush took 66 percent of the 2004 presidential vote in Delaware County and 63 percent in Licking (shared with the 18th), a margin large enough to give him 51 percent of the 12th's overall vote.

MAJOR INDUSTRY

Financial services, manufacturing, service, government

CITIES

Columbus (pt.), 275,882; Westerville, 35,318; Gahanna, 32,636; Reynoldsburg, 32,069; Dublin (pt.), 31,370; Delaware, 25,243

NOTABLE

The Anti-Saloon League, which lobbied successfully for Prohibition, was based in Westerville beginning in 1909.

Rep. Betty Sutton (D)

Elected 2006; 1st term

Sutton has spent her career pressing for accountability and honesty in government, and she capitalized on the Capitol Hill corruption scandals that contributed to the 2006 Democratic election sweep. Now, as a member of the House Rules Committee, she's in a position to help clean up the mess.

Although Rules Committee Chairwoman Louise M. Slaughter, a New York Democrat, had trouble recruiting lawmakers to serve on the panel in the 110th Congress (2007-08), Sutton was an eager volunteer. She had campaigned for the House on a six-point anti-corruption platform, and she proudly took the House floor on the opening day of the Congress to champion a package of toughened ethics rules that Democrats made their first order of business. "Today, we sever the links between those who would buy influence on Capitol Hill and those who would willingly sell it," Sutton said.

On other issues, Sutton's views closely resemble those of her predecessor, Democratic Rep. Sherrod Brown, who is now Ohio's junior senator. A labor lawyer, she is pro-union. She spoke out in early 2007 to help win House passage of a bill making it easier for workers to unionize.

The youngest of six children, Sutton was born and raised in Barberton, in northeastern Ohio. Her mother was clerk-treasurer for the city library, while her father worked in a boilermaker factory. She was still in law school at the University of Akron when she won election to the Barberton City Council. The next year, she moved onto the Summit County Council, then ran successfully for the Ohio state House. During her time in the legislature, she pushed to curb lobbyists' influence and to limit campaign spending.

In the 2006 open seat race, Sutton got the Democratic nod by defeating former Rep. Tom Sawyer and shopping mall heiress Capri S. Cafaro. Sutton's win was a major victory for EMILY's List, the group that backs Democratic women candidates who support abortion rights. The political action committee had staged an intensive publicity effort in Sutton's behalf. Sutton then posted a 22 percentage point victory over her Republican opponent, Lorain Mayor Craig Foltin, who had a record of winning on Democratic turf but who could not overcome the poor environment for the GOP nationwide.

CAPITOL OFFICE
225-3401
sutton.house.gov
1721 Longworth 20515-3513; fax 225-2266

COMMITTEES
Budget
Rules

RESIDENCE
Copley Township

BORN
July 31, 1963, Barberton, Ohio

RELIGION
Methodist

FAMILY
Husband, Doug Corwon; two stepchildren

EDUCATION
Kent State U., B.A. 1985 (political science); U. of Akron, J.D. 1990

CAREER
Lawyer; campaign aide; modeling school administrator

POLITICAL HIGHLIGHTS
Barberton City Council, 1990-91; Summit County Council, 1991-92 (vice president, 1992); Ohio House, 1993-2000

ELECTION RESULTS

2006 GENERAL		
Betty Sutton (D)	135,639	61.2%
Craig Foltin (R)	85,922	38.8%
2006 PRIMARY		
Betty Sutton (D)	21,268	30.9%
Capri S. Cafaro (D)	16,915	24.5%
Tom Sawyer (D)	14,837	21.5%
Gary J. Kucinich (D)	9,891	14.4%
Bill Grace (D)	3,537	5.1%
Michael Lyons (D)	1,030	1.5%
John L. Wolfe (D)	949	1.4%

OHIO 13

Northeast – part of Akron and suburbs, Cleveland suburbs

The lightning bolt-shaped 13th runs from the shores of Lake Erie west of Cleveland, southeast through the city's mostly middle-class suburbs to Akron (shared with 17th). Summit is the most populous county in the 13th, making up 44 percent of the population.

Many tire factories have left Akron, once known as the world's rubber capital, but auto plants and corporate headquarters still keep the city rolling. Akron also is a scientific research hub, and the University of Akron's College of Polymer Science and Polymer Engineering is here. The city also hosts some of Ohio's leading health care providers, such as the Akron Children's Hospital.

The 13th includes 60 percent of Akron's residents, including much of its black population. Blue-collar workers, together with blacks, ethnic whites and the University of Akron community, help the city retain its Democratic character.

Bordering Lake Erie at the 13th's other end is Lorain County, which has large steel and medical device plants. The 13th's portions of Lorain County include staunchly Democratic Lorain and Sheffield Lake and Democratic-leaning Elyria. Avon and Avon Lake are upper-middle-class and GOP-friendly.

In the district's middle are some GOP-leaning communities in southern Cuyahoga County and northern Medina County. But Summit and Lorain's dominance gives the 13th a Democratic tilt. John Kerry won 56 percent of the district's presidential vote in 2004.

MAJOR INDUSTRY
Polymer research, steel, auto parts, health

CITIES
Akron (pt.), 129,298; Lorain, 68,652; Elyria, 55,953; Cuyahoga Falls (pt.), 39,051

NOTABLE
National Inventors Hall of Fame is in Akron.

Rep. Steven C. LaTourette (R)

Elected 1994; 7th term

LaTourette is a moderate Republican who plays up his independence from the GOP leadership, a popular stance back home. In 2006, when Republicans elsewhere in Ohio succumbed to the Democratic tidal wave, he won re-election by a comfortable margin.

He wasted no time cementing his reputation in the opening weeks of the 110th Congress (2007-08). LaTourette (la-tuh-RETT) voted for five of the six measures on the Democratic leadership's "first 100 hours" priority agenda, including a minimum wage increase and a reduction in student loan interest rates. (He voted against a bill to repeal some oil industry tax breaks and shift the funds into alternative energy development.) By the 2007 spring break, LaTourette had split with his party more often than all but 11 other House Republicans on votes pitting the two parties against each other that year.

It is important not to overstate LaTourette's moderate stance, however, or his independence. In the 109th Congress (2005-06), he went against his fellow Republicans on 16 percent of the votes pitting the two parties against each other. Still, almost two dozen other GOP members surpassed him.

LaTourette voted for President Bush's tax cuts in 2001 and 2003, and for subsequent legislation extending them. He voted for oil drilling in Alaska's Arctic National Wildlife Refuge, and he supported a controversial 2005 bill to streamline environmental reviews of new or expanded oil refineries. The House passed the measure, 212-210, but it died in the Senate.

LaTourette voted in 2002 to authorize the war in Iraq, but he was one of 17 Republicans to vote with Democrats in early 2007 against Bush's decision to deploy additional troops there. He refused, however, to support a war funding bill that set a timetable for withdrawal. "It's the biggest piece of crap I've ever seen in my life," he said.

A social conservative, LaTourette opposes abortion and voted in 2004 and 2006 to amend the Constitution to outlaw same-sex marriage. But he backs expanded research on stem cells from discarded embryos created for in vitro fertilization, voting in 2006 to override Bush's veto of that legislation and in 2007 in support of another stem cell bill.

LaTourette has been skeptical of free-trade deals. He voted against normalizing trade relations with China in 2000 and opposed the 2002 renewal of fast-track trade authority that permits expedited action on trade pacts with no amendments. He pledged to vote against 2005 legislation implementing the Central American Free Trade Agreement, but wound up voting for it as GOP leaders scrounged for votes to salvage the pact. It passed, 217-215.

When LaTourette was first elected, he hoped to win a seat on the Judiciary Committee, given his background as a private attorney, public defender and prosecutor. (He still says his long-range aspiration is to be a judge.) But Ralph Regula, dean of the Ohio GOP delegation, told him he would be more useful to the state on the Transportation and Infrastructure Committee. And indeed, the assignment has allowed him to funnel substantial highway and infrastructure funds to his district and state.

Now in his seventh term, he has twice broken a term limit pledge. But his seniority proved useful during the 2005 round of military base closings, when he helped stave off closure of Cleveland's Defense Finance and Accounting Service office, saving 1,100 jobs.

Despite his best efforts to highlight the federal monies he has directed home, LaTourette found media attention focused elsewhere in his nasty 2004 re-election battle. The Akron Beacon Journal summed things up in an

CAPITOL OFFICE
225-5731
www.house.gov/latourette
2371 Rayburn 20515-3514; fax 225-3307

COMMITTEES
Financial Services
Transportation & Infrastructure

RESIDENCE
Concord

BORN
July 22, 1954, Cleveland, Ohio

RELIGION
Methodist

FAMILY
Wife, Jennifer LaTourette; five children

EDUCATION
U. of Michigan, B.A. 1976 (history);
Cleveland State U., J.D. 1979

CAREER
Lawyer

POLITICAL HIGHLIGHTS
Candidate for Lake County prosecutor, 1984;
Lake County prosecutor, 1989-94

ELECTION RESULTS

2006 GENERAL		
Steven C. LaTourette (R)	144,069	57.6%
Lewis R. Katz (D)	97,753	39.1%
Werner J. Lange (X)	8,500	3.4%
2006 PRIMARY		
Steven C. LaTourette (R)		unopposed
2004 GENERAL		
Steven C. LaTourette (R)	201,652	62.8%
Capri S. Cafaro (D)	119,714	37.3%

PREVIOUS WINNING PERCENTAGES
2002 (72%); 2000 (65%); 1998 (66%); 1996 (55%); 1994 (48%)

October story by saying he had "reneged on a pledge not to seek a sixth term; cheated on and left his wife for a woman who now lobbies one of his committees; taken money from the tainted campaign war chest of House Majority Leader Tom DeLay, R-Texas, then refused to recuse himself from the ethics committee hearings that eventually rebuked DeLay."

LaTourette's ex-wife posted lawn signs supporting his Democratic opponent, shopping mall heiress Capri S. Cafaro. The state Democratic Party asked the Justice Department to investigate LaTourette's relationship with the lobbyist, Jennifer Laptook, his former chief of staff. The congressman fought back, telling the Cleveland Plain Dealer he had broken no laws or ethics rules. "I am a divorced person who has stayed overnight at her home," he said of his former aide. "I am involved in a serious personal relationship." (LaTourette and Laptook married in February 2005.)

The whole brouhaha was only part of what wound up as the most expensive House race in Ohio, with total spending of $4.3 million, according to campaign finance reports. LaTourette won with 63 percent of the vote.

The race indirectly kept attention on LaTourette's links to former Democratic Rep. James A. Traficant Jr., whom the House expelled in 2002 following his conviction on corruption charges. Cafaro's father, J.J. Cafaro, was sentenced to probation for bribing Traficant to help his company. Traficant was a friend of LaTourette's, so the ethics case was especially painful for him, though he ultimately voted to expel Traficant.

In early 2005, LaTourette was removed from his seat on the House ethics committee by GOP leaders who felt he and other Republican members had been too quick to vote to admonish DeLay for ethical lapses.

LaTourette was raised in a politically active home. His mother and grandmother volunteered for the Cleveland area's longtime GOP congresswoman, Frances Payne Bolton. His grandmother inspired one of his legislative efforts, a bill requiring sweepstakes mailers to disclose the slim odds of winning. In her mid-80s, she had subscribed to Field and Stream magazine thinking it would boost her chances of winning.

Even as a youth, LaTourette was not afraid to rock the boat a bit. In high school, he led a petition drive to permit students to wear jeans and grow facial hair. He has sported a beard since he was 18 "because I've always thought my face looked better that way."

LaTourette was in his second term as Lake County prosecutor when he decided to run for Congress in 1994. Dubbing Democratic freshman Eric Fingerhut an out-of-touch liberal, LaTourette won by 5 percentage points. He has been re-elected by comfortable margins since then.

KEY VOTES

2006

No Stop broadband companies from favoring select Internet traffic
Yes Affirm U.S. commitment to war in Iraq and reject setting a withdrawal date for troops
Yes Repeal requirement for bilingual ballots at the polls
Yes Permit U.S. sale of civilian nuclear technology to India
Yes Build a 700-mile fence on the U.S.-Mexico border to curb illegal crossings
Yes Permit warrantless wiretaps of suspected terrorists

2005

? Intervene in the life-support case of Terri Schiavo
Yes Lift President Bush's restrictions on stem cell research funding
Yes Prohibit FBI access to library and bookstore records
Yes Approve free-trade pact with five Central American countries
Yes Pass energy policy overhaul favored by President Bush emphasizing domestic oil and gas production
No End mandatory preservation of habitat of endangered animal and plant species
Yes Ban torture of prisoners in U.S. custody

CQ VOTE STUDIES

	PARTY UNITY		PRESIDENTIAL SUPPORT	
	Support	Oppose	Support	Oppose
2006	82%	18%	73%	27%
2005	86%	14%	71%	29%
2004	86%	14%	82%	18%
2003	88%	12%	85%	15%
2002	89%	11%	82%	18%

INTEREST GROUPS

	AFL-CIO	ADA	CCUS	ACU
2006	50%	20%	93%	72%
2005	50%	15%	78%	71%
2004	47%	15%	86%	71%
2003	33%	25%	87%	72%
2002	22%	15%	85%	76%

OHIO 14
Northeast – Cleveland and Akron suburbs

The Republican-leaning 14th moves eastward along the Lake Erie shoreline from just outside Cleveland to the Pennsylvania border in the state's northeastern corner. The depressed far northeastern communities remain reliant on the ailing steel, chemical and auto manufacturing industries, but have seen some new life from an influx of former Cleveland residents moving here from the city. Wealthy suburban residents help give the district the state's highest median income.

The 14th's portion of Cuyahoga County includes the upscale villages of Bentleyville and Moreland Hills in the east, while Progressive Insurance is based in Mayfield Village. The district's lakeshore region, which takes in Lake and Ashtabula counties, is home to fruit farms and much of Ohio's wine grape acreage. South of Lake, the district takes in all of Geauga County — a Republican-leaning, affluent, well-educated area — and northern Portage County. The 14th also includes northern Trumbull County and northeastern Summit County, taking in Stow and Twinsburg.

Despite being Ohio's smallest county in land area, more than one-third of the district's residents live in Lake County. Chemical company Lubrizol has headquarters in Wickliffe, which also is a manufacturing site for ABB, a power and automation technologies company. In Geauga County, the KraftMaid Cabinetry corporate headquarters in Middlefield is one of the top employers in the county.

In Lake, Republicans generally perform well in areas south of Mentor, such as Kirtland. Democrats do well in Painesville, where more than half of Lake's blacks and Hispanics live. Lake narrowly backed George W. Bush in the 2004 presidential election. Ashtabula County, the state's largest in land area, backed John Kerry in 2004, but overall, Bush carried the district's vote with 52 percent. Although Cuyahoga County generally favors Democrats, Bentleyville, Chagrin Falls, Gates Mills and Hunting Valley all supported the Republican U.S. Senate nominee in 2006, four of the only five areas in the county to do so.

MAJOR INDUSTRY
Manufacturing, health care, chemicals

CITIES
Mentor, 50,278; Stow, 32,139; Willoughby, 22,621; Hudson, 22,439

NOTABLE
Twinsburg calls its annual August gathering of twins the world's largest.

Rep. Deborah Pryce (R)

CAPITOL OFFICE
225-2015
www.house.gov/pryce
320 Cannon 20515-3515; fax 225-3529

COMMITTEES
Financial Services

RESIDENCE
Upper Arlington

BORN
July 29, 1951, Warren, Ohio

RELIGION
Presbyterian

FAMILY
Divorced; two children (one deceased)

EDUCATION
Ohio State U., B.A. 1973; Capital U., J.D. 1976

CAREER
City prosecutor

POLITICAL HIGHLIGHTS
Franklin County Municipal Court judge, 1985-92

ELECTION RESULTS

2006 GENERAL		
Deborah Pryce (R)	110,739	50.1%
Mary Jo Kilroy (D)	109,677	49.6%
2006 PRIMARY		
Deborah Pryce (R)		unopposed
2004 GENERAL		
Deborah Pryce (R)	166,520	60.0%
Mark P. Brown (D)	110,915	40.0%

PREVIOUS WINNING PERCENTAGES
2002 (67%); 2000 (68%); 1998 (66%); 1996 (71%); 1994 (71%); 1992 (44%)

Elected 1992; 8th term

A lot has changed for Pryce in the current Congress. She has been transformed from the highest-ranking woman ever to serve in the House Republican leadership to a chastened survivor of the 2006 Democratic tidal wave, which very nearly swept her out of office.

When Republicans controlled the House, Pryce chaired the Republican Conference, the No. 4 rung on the leadership ladder. That gave her a seat at the table when important strategic decisions were made. More moderate than the rest of the GOP leadership, at least in tone and temperament, she became an invaluable communicator for her party.

Voters in her Columbus-based district were not impressed by her leadership activities; indeed, her absorption with national issues and her association with the scandal-scarred GOP leadership team clearly hurt her in 2006. She won by only 1,062 votes, less than half a percentage point.

"I got a message loud and clear in my campaign," Pryce says. "My constituents wanted to see more of me. I wasn't able to do that in the leadership."

She did not seek a leadership post in the 110th Congress (2007-08). Instead, she became the top-ranking Republican on a Financial Services subcommittee. She had planted the seeds of change in 2005, when she gave up her seat on the leadership-dominated Rules Committee to reclaim a spot on Financial Services. She had been on leave from that panel since 1995, when she was first named to the committee, but had retained her seniority.

"My focus has totally changed," she says, from "process and politics and communications" to substantive legislation. She now can address issues important to Columbus, one of the country's financial services centers, including the subprime mortgage crisis, implementation of the 2002 Sarbanes-Oxley corporate accountability law and the security of financial data.

Even if Republicans had maintained control of the House, Pryce likely could not have gone higher in the GOP hierarchy. When she switched from the Rules Committee to Financial Services in 2005, the Columbus Dispatch said the move represented "a recognition that she has advanced as far as anyone who believes in abortion rights can in the Republican leadership." Pryce's commitment to abortion rights is qualified, however. She voted in 2003 to outlaw a procedure opponents call "partial birth" abortion, and in 2006 she backed a measure to criminalize transport of a minor across state lines to circumvent parental notification laws.

One of just three Republican women elected to the House in 1992, Pryce was a star from the start. Her first-term colleagues named her their "interim leader" in the early weeks of 1993, and Speaker Newt Gingrich put her on the Rules Committee in 1995. In the 105th Congress (1997-98), Pryce was elected Republican Conference secretary, a low-level elected leadership post.

Her votes on fiscal policy are reliably Republican, but she parts company with conservatives on selected social issues. In 2004 and 2006, she voted against a proposed constitutional amendment to ban same-sex marriage. And in 2006, she voted to override President Bush's veto of a bill to permit federal funding of medical research on stem cells harvested from surplus embryos at in vitro fertilization clinics.

Earlier, in 1998, Pryce opposed two impeachment articles brought against President Bill Clinton. She was the only elected GOP leader who did not vote yes on all four charges.

Freed from requirements to toe the party line, Pryce may edge closer to the center in the 110th Congress. When Democrats put forward their "first

100 hours" agenda in the opening days of the 2007 session, Pryce voted for four of the six bills, including an increase in the federal minimum wage.

Pryce voted against a 2007 resolution opposing Bush's decision to deploy additional U.S. troops to Iraq, and against a war funding bill that set a timetable for a U.S. withdrawal. But she remained cautious about the U.S. role in Iraq. "I would say my district is probably 50-50 in wanting a withdrawal. My view is that this is our last best chance for success," Pryce said in March 2007.

Her political success has been clouded by personal tragedy. She became a champion of legislation to improve cancer care, particularly for children, after her 9-year-old daughter, Caroline, died of cancer in 1999. Two years later, she and her husband, Randy Walker, began divorce proceedings, ending a 21-year marriage. Even as their marriage foundered, Pryce and Walker formed Hope Street Kids, a program to support cancer research.

In 2002, Pryce adopted an infant daughter, Mia, after realizing, she said, that she missed being a mother. It has helped her understand the challenges that all single parents face. "Being a single mom is tough, no matter what your occupation," she said.

Pryce introduced legislation early in the 109th Congress (2005-06), cosponsored by moderate Pennsylvania Democrat John P. Murtha, that would provide grants to promote pain management and end-of-life care for children with life-threatening conditions such as cancer. She sponsored a 2000 law to boost funding to prevent child abuse and to investigate such crimes. She also has worked to make adoption easier for qualified applicants, and cosponsored the 1996 law that streamlined adoption procedures for children in foster care. A co-founder of the House Cancer Caucus, Pryce says, "Sometimes life gives you a reason to do your job. It sure happened to me."

Having studied, worked and lived in the Columbus area for three decades, Pryce is well-versed in the nuances of her district. After getting her law degree from Capital University, she was a city prosecutor. In 1985, she was elected judge on the Franklin County Municipal Court.

She resigned in 1992 to enter the crowded GOP field for the House seat of retiring Republican Chalmers P. Wylie. She won the nomination and prevailed in a tight, three-way general-election race. She had no troubles thereafter until 2006, when Mary Jo Kilroy, a Franklin County commissioner, gave her the scare of her political career.

Pryce was declared the winner only after a recount, squeaking by with a half-point margin. Kilroy already has vowed to run against Pryce again in 2008, though she may not be alone in that endeavor. GOP campaign units have rushed to help Pryce restore her grip on the district.

KEY VOTES

2006

- No Stop broadband companies from favoring select Internet traffic
- Yes Affirm U.S. commitment to war in Iraq and reject setting a withdrawal date for troops
- Yes Repeal requirement for bilingual ballots at the polls
- Yes Permit U.S. sale of civilian nuclear technology to India
- Yes Build a 700-mile fence on the U.S.-Mexico border to curb illegal crossings
- Yes Permit warrantless wiretaps of suspected terrorists

2005

- Yes Intervene in the life-support case of Terri Schiavo
- Yes Lift President Bush's restrictions on stem cell research funding
- No Prohibit FBI access to library and bookstore records
- Yes Approve free-trade pact with five Central American countries
- Yes Pass energy policy overhaul favored by President Bush emphasizing domestic oil and gas production
- Yes End mandatory preservation of habitat of endangered animal and plant species
- Yes Ban torture of prisoners in U.S. custody

CQ VOTE STUDIES

	PARTY UNITY		PRESIDENTIAL SUPPORT	
	Support	Oppose	Support	Oppose
2006	90%	10%	90%	10%
2005	94%	6%	84%	16%
2004	91%	9%	85%	15%
2003	94%	6%	93%	7%
2002	95%	5%	92%	8%

INTEREST GROUPS

	AFL-CIO	ADA	CCUS	ACU
2006	36%	20%	100%	72%
2005	13%	15%	88%	83%
2004	14%	15%	100%	83%
2003	7%	0%	100%	72%
2002	13%	5%	100%	88%

OHIO 15

Western Columbus and suburbs

The 15th is centered in Franklin County and on Columbus, the state's centrally located capital. It takes in most of Columbus, including all of the city that lies west of High Street, a major north-south thoroughfare. Ohio State University, one of the nation's largest universities and a major regional employer and research hub, is located in the 15th's portion of Columbus, as is the State Capitol, City Hall, the stadium for soccer's Crew and the arena for hockey's Blue Jackets.

Columbus, Ohio's most populous city, has continued to grow, and Franklin County's expanding service sector, which includes several large technology and research centers, has aided the district's economy. Columbus serves as the home for the headquarters of many corporations, including Nationwide Mutual Insurance and American Electric Power. Columbus is not known as a tourist destination, but large crowds descend on the city for Ohio State home football games.

Outside of Franklin County, Madison County to the west is a major corn- and soybean-producing area. Marysville, in Union County north of Madison, is home to soybean fields, livestock and Honda auto and motorcycle plants.

The politically competitive 15th's portion of Franklin County, where nearly 90 percent of district residents live, leans slightly Democratic. Ohio State's academic community and neighborhoods in the West Side of Columbus support Democrats, but Republicans are strong in suburbs west of the Olentangy and Scioto rivers, such as Hilliard and Grove City. In 2004, John Kerry carried the 15th's share of Franklin County, but George W. Bush achieved a razor-thin victory districtwide by dominating the vote in rural, and dependably Republican, Madison and Union counties. Union County last voted for a Democratic presidential candidate in 1932.

MAJOR INDUSTRY

Retail trade, government, health care, research, higher education

CITIES

Columbus (pt.), 384,491; Upper Arlington, 33,686; Grove City, 27,075

NOTABLE

A full-scale replica of Christopher Columbus' ship, the Santa Maria, is in Columbus; Ohio State hosts the annual Farm Science Review, one of the largest farm exhibitions in the world, in Madison County near London.

Rep. Ralph Regula (R)

CAPITOL OFFICE
225-3876
www.house.gov/regula
2306 Rayburn 20515-3516; fax 225-3059

COMMITTEES
Appropriations

RESIDENCE
Navarre

BORN
Dec. 3, 1924, Beach City, Ohio

RELIGION
Episcopalian

FAMILY
Wife, Mary Regula; three children

EDUCATION
Mount Union College, B.A. 1948 (business administration); William McKinley School of Law, LL.B. 1952

MILITARY SERVICE
Navy, 1944-46

CAREER
Lawyer; teacher; principal

POLITICAL HIGHLIGHTS
Ohio Board of Education, 1960-64;
Ohio House, 1965-67; Ohio Senate, 1967-73

ELECTION RESULTS

2006 GENERAL		
Ralph Regula (R)	137,167	58.3%
Thomas Shaw (D)	97,955	41.7%
2006 PRIMARY		
Ralph Regula (R)	32,526	58.4%
Matt Miller (R)	23,170	41.6%
2004 GENERAL		
Ralph Regula (R)	202,544	66.6%
Jeff Seemann (D)	101,817	33.5%

PREVIOUS WINNING PERCENTAGES
2002 (69%); 2000 (69%); 1998 (64%); 1996 (69%); 1994 (75%); 1992 (64%); 1990 (59%); 1988 (79%); 1986 (76%); 1984 (72%); 1982 (66%); 1980 (79%); 1978 (78%); 1976 (67%); 1974 (66%); 1972 (57%)

Elected 1972; 18th term

Gerald Ford made Regula an appropriator and he has been a member of that powerful club ever since. He is a master of the arcane rules and mores that govern passage of the annual spending bills. But he is more a practitioner than a partisan, as appropriators tend to be. The late Democratic Speaker Thomas P. "Tip" O'Neill Jr. was a friend, as is David R. Obey, the feisty Democratic Appropriations chairman who says Regula is "as sweet a man as you can find" and one of the House's "most laid-back members."

In his first House term, then Minority Leader Ford supported him for a slot on Appropriations, shortly before Ford was sworn in as president. The seat went to a more senior member, but Ford's backing catapulted Regula to the head of the line and he got on the panel in his second term. Now the second most senior Republican in the House, he is as seasoned a lawmaker as they come, maneuvering deftly among GOP factions and across party lines.

But Regula (REG-you-luh), in his early 80s, has been hurt at times by his moderation on some spending and policy issues and his aversion to the round-the-clock fundraising that defines leadership politics. In the 109th Congress (2005-06), his seniority should have put him in line to chair the committee. But then House Majority Leader Tom DeLay in 2005 passed him over in favor of Jerry Lewis of California, who had less seniority but was a superior party fundraiser and was viewed as more of a team player by conservatives intent on making deep cuts in federal domestic spending in President Bush's second term. In the 110th Congress (2007-08), with his party in the minority, he was named ranking Republican on the Appropriations Financial Services and General Government Subcommittee.

Some conservatives have pegged Regula, who lives on a farm in Ohio and calls himself a "tree hugger," as too liberal. Among them are Westerners concerned about private property rights, whom he spent a lot of time courting when he chaired the Interior Appropriations Subcommittee from 1994-2000.

Regula splits with the party's right on a handful of other issues as well: He has supported a minimum wage increase and family planning programs and resisted proposals for taxpayer-financed private school vouchers. He voted in 2002 against a measure granting the president expanded fast-track negotiating authority for trade agreements — a vote that some Republicans invoked later, during the 2005 discussions about choosing a new Appropriations chairman. In 2006, he voted to override Bush's veto of a stem cell research bill.

But Regula will play hardball against Democrats when his party has a lot at stake. In 2003, after Democrats on the committee voted unanimously against the Labor-HHS spending bill to press their point that it allocated too little for domestic programs, Regula — then chairman of the subcommittee — slashed all of their earmarks, the special projects tucked into spending bills that members request for their districts and then tout at election time. The following year, most committee Democrats voted for Regula's bill.

A big parks booster, Regula considers his role in creating and funding Cuyahoga Valley National Park in Ohio his greatest legislative achievement. During his 30 years on the Interior subcommittee, he made national parks his priority, particularly a maintenance backlog at park buildings. One of his initiatives was an entry fee that has raised more than $1 billion for maintaining campsites, lodges and bathrooms. The effort was inspired in part by his wife's visit to an unkempt restroom in Yellowstone National

Park. Mary Regula pronounced it "awful," and her husband was chagrined by conditions at the flagship national park.

Regula is dean of the Ohio Republican delegation, and his popularity among House colleagues is useful in pressing his state's parochial concerns. He defends federal support of clean-coal technology research, a program of particular interest in his area, where most electricity is produced by coal-fired plants.

Regula also has championed aggressive moves to support the domestic steel industry, which remains a potent economic force in northeastern Ohio, and was a proponent of Bush's tariffs on steel imports.

His hometown causes include preserving the memory of President William McKinley, Canton's most famous son. Regula, who graduated from a now-defunct law school named after the 25th president, helped engineer the purchase of a house McKinley lived in, which since 1998 has housed the National First Ladies' Library, founded by Regula's wife.

At the beginning of each Congress, Regula introduces a bill that has the effect of preventing Alaskans from changing the name of Mount McKinley — the nation's tallest peak — to Denali, its Native Alaskan name.

Regula, son of an Ohio farmer, returns home every weekend to the cattle farm in Navarre that once was his father's. He calls it his "Garden of Eden." His brother lives on a nearby farm also once run by his father, and Regula's three grown children and their children "live about two minutes" away. In Washington, Regula drives around in a pickup truck.

Serving in the Navy was a turning point in his life. "My dad said I ought to be a farmer. And I probably would have, except I got to the Navy and the Navy saw something in me and decided to send me to officers' training. I have to say, it gave me a shot of self-confidence." He went to college on the GI Bill, then got his law degree at night.

A schoolteacher and principal for seven years, he got his first experience in politics as a member of the Ohio Board of Education for four years. The state Republican Party then recruited him to run for the General Assembly. As a state House member and later a state senator, he represented a large swath of Stark County — the heart of the 16th District.

When Republican Frank Bow retired in 1972 after 22 years in the House, Regula was viewed as the logical successor. He won with 57 percent of the vote. Over the past several contests, he has been re-elected with roughly 68 percent of the vote, until 2006 when he won with 58 percent. That drop — and his age — spurred rumors of Regula's possible retirement and piqued Democrats' interest in the seat for 2008.

KEY VOTES

2006

Yes Stop broadband companies from favoring select Internet traffic
Yes Affirm U.S. commitment to war in Iraq and reject setting a withdrawal date for troops
Yes Repeal requirement for bilingual ballots at the polls
Yes Permit U.S. sale of civilian nuclear technology to India
Yes Build a 700-mile fence on the U.S.-Mexico border to curb illegal crossings
Yes Permit warrantless wiretaps of suspected terrorists

2005

Yes Intervene in the life-support case of Terri Schiavo
Yes Lift President Bush's restrictions on stem cell research funding
No Prohibit FBI access to library and bookstore records
Yes Approve free-trade pact with five Central American countries
Yes Pass energy policy overhaul favored by President Bush emphasizing domestic oil and gas production
Yes End mandatory preservation of habitat of endangered animal and plant species
Yes Ban torture of prisoners in U.S. custody

CQ VOTE STUDIES

	PARTY UNITY		PRESIDENTIAL SUPPORT	
	Support	Oppose	Support	Oppose
2006	89%	11%	85%	15%
2005	92%	8%	85%	15%
2004	93%	7%	85%	15%
2003	95%	5%	96%	4%
2002	94%	6%	90%	10%

INTEREST GROUPS

	AFL-CIO	ADA	CCUS	ACU
2006	38%	15%	80%	71%
2005	20%	5%	93%	76%
2004	20%	0%	100%	88%
2003	7%	5%	97%	88%
2002	22%	5%	95%	88%

OHIO 16
Northeast — Canton

Settled in the northeast quadrant of Ohio, the 16th features a contrast between rural areas, which make up roughly one-quarter of the district's land, and urban Canton. The left-leaning and blue-collar city is known in historical circles as William McKinley's home base; McKinley ran much of his 1896 presidential campaign from a front porch on North Market Street.

Canton, with a manufacturing and steel-producing history, has retained a high-skill manufacturing base despite previous industry employment declines. To overcome manufacturing job losses, the city has supported a transition to retail and service-based employment, resulting in more than 1,000 new jobs. Major employers include Aultman Hospital, Timken, which manufactures bearings, and vacuum cleaner maker Hoover.

Canton is a working-class city that votes solidly Democratic. In 2004, presidential candidate John Kerry defeated George W. Bush by a better than 2-1 ratio in the city, which also has a black population that exceeds 20 percent.

As Canton's population continues its nearly 60-year decline — it now accounts for just one-fifth of Stark County's population — the city's Democratic base has become less important to the 16th's overall political picture. Massillon and Alliance, the county's next-most-populous cities, however, also lean Democratic.

As a whole, the 16th leans Republican primarily because of rural conservative areas west of Stark County, although northern Stark County is upper-middle-class and GOP-leaning as well. Wayne County is a top state producer of oats, hay and dairy products. The 16th also takes in most of Ashland County, which also leans conservative. While Canton's political role has dimmed, the GOP margin in the 16th is not overwhelming. Bush only won 54 percent of the district's vote in 2004.

MAJOR INDUSTRY

Steel, manufacturing, health care

CITIES

Canton, 80,806; Massillon, 31,325; Medina, 25,139; Wooster, 24,811

NOTABLE

The Professional Football Hall of Fame and William McKinley's burial site are in Canton; Jacob Coxey, whose "army" of unemployed men marched to Washington, D.C., after the Panic of 1893, was from Massillon.

Rep. Tim Ryan (D)

CAPITOL OFFICE
225-5261
timryan.house.gov
1421 Longworth 20515-3517; fax 225-3719

COMMITTEES
Appropriations

RESIDENCE
Niles

BORN
July 16, 1973, Niles, Ohio

RELIGION
Roman Catholic

FAMILY
Divorced

EDUCATION
Bowling Green State U., B.A. 1995 (political science); Franklin Pierce Law Center, J.D. 2000

CAREER
Congressional aide

POLITICAL HIGHLIGHTS
Ohio Senate, 2001-02

ELECTION RESULTS

2006 GENERAL		
Tim Ryan (D)	170,369	80.3%
Don Manning II (R)	41,925	19.7%
2006 PRIMARY		
Tim Ryan (D)		unopposed
2004 GENERAL		
Tim Ryan (D)	212,800	77.2%
Frank V. Cusimano (R)	62,871	22.8%

PREVIOUS WINNING PERCENTAGES
2002 (51%)

Elected 2002; 3rd term

Although he is one of the youngest Democrats in Congress, Ryan has become a leading party messenger on the economic double whammy of cheap imports and outsourcing of jobs overseas. It is a subject he knows all too well, as the representative from one of the most depressed industrial regions in the country.

In just his third term, he not only has a seat on the Democratic Steering Committee, which makes committee assignments, but he won an appointment to the Appropriations Committee. (He had to give up seats on the Armed Services and Education panels.)

Ryan co-chairs both the Manufacturing Caucus, which he founded in his first term with Republican Donald Manzullo of Illinois, and the 30-Something Working Group, a collection of youthful Democrats who take the floor for after-hours speeches aimed at engaging younger C-SPAN viewers.

Like most House Democrats, Ryan is highly skeptical of free-trade deals with countries that lack strong labor laws, and he is especially critical of the trade and monetary practices of China. He is at the forefront of House efforts to punish the Asian giant if it does not take steps to revalue its currency and improve its balance of trade with the United States.

"When dealing with China, I think it is immensely important to state the obvious — while the United States might be playing by the rules, China is playing to win," Ryan told the U.S.-China Economic and Security Review Commission in 2005.

On the Armed Services Committee, Ryan devoted much of his energy in 2005 to a successful campaign to spare Youngstown Air Reserve Station during the latest round of military base closings. He then secured more than $3 million in federal funds for improvements there.

Ryan also used his seat on the Education and the Workforce Committee to score a politically popular victory for soldiers in Iraq. A bill he introduced, later included in the 2006 deficit reduction law, gives active-duty military personnel interest-free deferments of their student loan payments.

Though he is a reliably liberal vote on most issues, Ryan, like many of his colleagues from socially conservative working-class districts, opposes abortion and supports gun ownership rights. After Democratic losses in 2004, Ryan said the party suffered from unreasonable absolutism on social issues.

In 2006 and again in 2007, he teamed with liberal Democratic Rep. Rosa DeLauro of Connecticut to sponsor a bill that sought to reduce abortions. It included provisions aimed at preventing unintended pregnancies as well as strengthening alternatives to abortion, such as adoption tax credits and help — such as food stamps and child care subsidies — for poor mothers.

In what he regards as the toughest vote of his first term, Ryan bucked strong sentiment in his district and voted in 2003 against a constitutional amendment to ban flag burning. He said he feared civil liberties were under assault, and voted against the flag amendment again in 2005. He twice has voted against amending the Constitution to ban same-sex marriage.

Ryan works to find creative ways to get federal help to bring jobs and business to his district. In 2004, he secured $300,000 to study the potential gains of building the first indoor motor speedway near Youngstown as a tourist attraction. He also got $16 million for projects in a transportation bill, including $3 million to expand the National Packard Museum in Warren, Ohio, where the first Packard car was built. When that project was singled out by budget watchdog groups as an example of pork barrel spending,

Ryan said, "I make no apologies for getting federal money for one of the most economically depressed areas of the country. Sixty years ago, no one complained when the citizens of my district were funding the war effort and the interstate highway system and the GI bill."

Like many cities in the Rust Belt, Youngstown hopes to retain its young people. With a concentration of students at Youngstown's three colleges and medical school, Ryan sees youth as key to economic turnaround. On the Education panel, he pushed legislation to provide a tax credit for the purchase of textbooks. And on Appropriations in the 110th Congress (2007-08), he has a seat on the subcommittee that funds federal education programs.

After his parents divorced when Ryan was in grade school, he and his older brother were raised by their mother and grandparents. His mother, then and now, was a chief deputy clerk of Trumbull County. His grandmother worked for the county clerk of courts, while his grandfather was a steelworker. Both were union members. Ryan was a star football player in high school and at Youngstown State University until he ruined his knee.

He says one of the major influences in his life was Joseph Campbell, a seminal American writer on mythology and comparative religion. "Joseph Campbell teaches all of us to follow our bliss and embrace the wonder and mystery of nature, religion and spirituality," he says. "His teachings enrich my faith and inspire my work as a public servant. I also believe his message of tolerance, inclusion and respect for other religions is exactly what our society needs at this time." Futurist Alvin Toffler has also influenced him. On the other hand, his office features a prominently displayed autographed Rolling Stone magazine cover photo of musician Dave Matthews.

Ryan got his first taste of Capitol Hill in the mid-1990s as an aide to the area's longtime House member, James A. Traficant Jr. In 2000, the year he completed law school, Ryan won election to the Ohio Senate.

In 2002, with Traficant facing jail on bribery and racketeering charges (he was eventually expelled from the House), Ryan entered a highly competitive primary for Traficant's seat. He faced eight-term Rep. Tom Sawyer, who was thrown into the district by reapportionment. Sawyer outspent him 10-to-1, but had lost much of his old political base in redistricting and had alienated labor by his vote for the 1993 North American Free Trade Agreement. Ryan prevailed, and went on to easily defeat GOP state Sen. Ann Womer Benjamin.

In 2006, Ryan was on a shortlist of Democrats weighing a bid to unseat GOP Sen. Mike DeWine. But, concerned about the fundraising challenges involved and the "brutal" campaign he expected, he decided to seek another House term. He cruised to victory with 80 percent of the vote.

KEY VOTES

2006

Yes Stop broadband companies from favoring select Internet traffic

No Affirm U.S. commitment to war in Iraq and reject setting a withdrawal date for troops

No Repeal requirement for bilingual ballots at the polls

Yes Permit U.S. sale of civilian nuclear technology to India

Yes Build a 700-mile fence on the U.S.-Mexico border to curb illegal crossings

No Permit warrantless wiretaps of suspected terrorists

2005

? Intervene in the life-support case of Terri Schiavo

Yes Lift President Bush's restrictions on stem cell research funding

Yes Prohibit FBI access to library and bookstore records

No Approve free-trade pact with five Central American countries

Yes Pass energy policy overhaul favored by President Bush emphasizing domestic oil and gas production

No End mandatory preservation of habitat of endangered animal and plant species

Yes Ban torture of prisoners in U.S. custody

CQ VOTE STUDIES

	PARTY UNITY		PRESIDENTIAL SUPPORT	
	Support	Oppose	Support	Oppose
2006	90%	10%	37%	63%
2005	91%	9%	30%	70%
2004	95%	5%	30%	70%
2003	95%	5%	29%	71%

INTEREST GROUPS

	AFL-CIO	ADA	CCUS	ACU
2006	92%	80%	47%	28%
2005	100%	95%	48%	25%
2004	100%	80%	35%	17%
2003	100%	95%	30%	32%

OHIO 17

Northeast — Youngstown, Warren, part of Akron

Bordering Pennsylvania in part of northeastern Ohio's Mahoning Valley, including Youngstown, the 17th is a Democratic bastion. Once a leading steel producer, the valley now symbolizes industrial decline; most of the mills that have not been torn down are either silent or abandoned.

A sustained economic downturn hit the area hard, but manufacturing still employs one-fourth of Trumbull County's workforce, and there are several auto plants and distribution centers in the Mahoning Valley. The regional airport in Vienna houses a large Air Force Reserve base, and downtown revitalization in Youngstown has led new restaurants and retail and office buildings, with their service and white-collar jobs, to pop up around town.

Despite some economic diversification, young people searching for jobs often look elsewhere — the district's median age (37) is above the national median — and the population of most cities has declined. Youngstown's population hovered around 170,000 from the 1930s to the 1960s; the 2000 census found just 82,000 people living in the city.

The 17th's share of Mahoning County, which includes Youngstown, gave 71 percent of its vote to John Kerry in the 2004 presidential election; the county overall last voted for a GOP presidential candidate in 1972. Some of the cities that propel Trumbull County's staunch Democratic lean are Warren, the county's most populous city, Niles and Girard. A plurality of district residents live in Trumbull, which is shared with the 14th District.

Parts of Summit and Portage counties to the west are less solidly Democratic, although they still supported Kerry by a double-digit margin in 2004. The Summit portion includes the eastern half of Akron, a city that once produced 90 percent of the nation's tires and is still home to Goodyear Tire & Rubber. The Portage portion includes Kent, where Kent State University is located. Overall, Kerry took 63 percent of the vote districtwide, which made the 17th his second-best district in Ohio.

MAJOR INDUSTRY

Automobile assembly, manufacturing

CITIES

Akron (pt.), 87,776; Youngstown, 82,026; Warren, 46,832

NOTABLE

The Butler Institute of American Art, dedicated in 1919, was one of the first museums to display only American art.

Rep. Zack Space (D)

CAPITOL OFFICE
225-6265
space.house.gov
315 Cannon 20515-3518; fax 225-3394

COMMITTEES
Agriculture
Transportation & Infrastructure
Veterans' Affairs

RESIDENCE
Dover

BORN
Jan. 27, 1961, Dover, Ohio

RELIGION
Greek Orthodox

FAMILY
Wife, Mary Space; two children

EDUCATION
Kenyon College, B.A. 1983 (political science); Ohio State U., J.D. 1986

CAREER
Lawyer; county public defender

POLITICAL HIGHLIGHTS
Sought Democratic nomination for Ohio House, 1990; Dover law director, 2000-06

ELECTION RESULTS

2006 GENERAL		
Zack Space (D)	129,646	62.1%
Joy Padgett (R)	79,259	37.9%
2006 PRIMARY		
Zack Space (D)	18,251	38.7%
Jennifer Stewart (D)	12,071	25.6%
Joseph P. Sulzer (D)	11,340	24.0%
Ralph A. Applegate (D)	5,514	11.7%

Elected 2006; 1st term

No one in the 110th Congress (2007-08) is more closely identified with the issue of congressional ethics than Space — and not just because his father's first name is Socrates. Space succeeded Republican Rep. Bob Ney, who pleaded guilty in 2006 to federal corruption charges stemming from his association with convicted lobbyist Jack Abramoff.

"Coming from a district whose previous congressman became mired, and then consumed, by scandal, my fellow district residents and I understand all too intimately the perils associated with weak and loosely monitored ethics regulations," Space said in a Jan. 4, 2007, floor speech as the Democratic House prepared to pass an ethics and lobbying overhaul.

Space bemoans his district's loss of manufacturing jobs, which he attributes in part to trade pacts he says have not required or enforced adequate labor standards. He would punish countries that do not abide by strong labor standards and provide incentives for those that do.

Skyrocketing health care costs also make it hard for companies to stay open in a district that Space says has not reaped the fruits of the surging national economy. "Drive around my district," Space said during the campaign, and "you'll see all kinds of abandoned factories — or if they're not abandoned, they're not being used as warehouses."

The local economy has long been reliant on coal, and Space says promoting clean-coal technologies would boost employment and help wean the nation from foreign energy sources. He also plans to use his Agriculture Committee seat to advance ethanol and other alternative fuels.

After law school, his only time away from Dover, Space joined his father's law firm. In 2000, he was appointed the top law officer for his hometown.

In 2006, Space came from behind to win the four-candidate Democratic primary, buoyed by a strong showing in his home county. In the summer, Ney relinquished the GOP nomination and was replaced on the ballot by state Sen. Joy Padgett, who was burdened by her ties to unpopular Republican Gov. Bob Taft and to Ney, who pleaded guilty in October and resigned just four days before the November election. Space coasted with 62 percent of the vote.

OHIO 18

East — Zanesville, Chillicothe

Ohio's most geographically vast district, the 18th envelops 12 whole counties and parts of four others in eastern and southern Ohio. Beginning in the north, the 18th takes in the rolling hills south of Canton and runs southwest to rugged areas of Appalachia. The socially conservative district, which roughly parallels but does not touch the Ohio River, depends on steel and coal jobs and includes a large Catholic population of ethnic Eastern Europeans and Greeks.

The 18th's most-populous county is Tuscarawas, which relies on agriculture and has some manufacturing. Newark (shared with the 12th) in Licking County is slowly becoming a research and manufacturing center. South of Muskingum County (Zanesville), the district narrows as it takes in Morgan County and northwestern Athens County, although Ohio University and Athens are in the 6th. Moving westward, the 18th remains rural as it crosses forests to take in most of Ross County, including Chillicothe.

The blue-collar 18th leans Republican, although Tuscarawas tends to be more Democratic and can push a Democrat to victory here, as it did in 2006 by giving Rep. Space 73 percent of its vote. Holmes County, to Tuscarawas' west, is Amish country and is heavily Republican; George W. Bush took 75 percent of the county's 2004 presidential vote. Coshocton County, south of Holmes, also generally supports Republicans. Bush took 57 percent of the 18th's presidential vote in 2004 and won all of the counties that lie entirely within the district.

MAJOR INDUSTRY
Steel, manufacturing, agriculture, coal

CITIES
Zanesville, 25,586; Chillicothe, 21,796

NOTABLE
Aviator Amelia Earhart called Zanesville "the most recognizable city in the country" from the air because of its Y-shaped bridge across the Muskingum and Licking rivers.

OKLAHOMA

Gov. Brad Henry (D)

First elected: 2002
Length of term: 4 years
Term expires: 1/11
Salary: $140,000
Phone: (405) 521-2342

Residence: Shawnee
Born: July 10, 1963; Shawnee, Okla.
Religion: Baptist
Family: Wife, Kim Henry; three children
Education: U. of Oklahoma, B.A. 1985 (economics), J.D. 1988
Career: Lawyer
Political highlights: Okla. Senate, 1993-2002

Election results:

2006 GENERAL		
Brad Henry (D)	616,135	66.5%
Ernest Istook (D)	310,327	33.5%

Lt. Gov. Jari Askins (D)

First elected: 2006
Length of term: 4 years
Term expires: 1/11
Salary: $109,250
Phone: (405) 521-2161

LEGISLATURE

Legislature: February-May

Senate: 48 members, 4-year terms
2007 ratios: 24 D, 24 R; 41 men, 7 women
Salary: $38,400
Phone: (405) 524-0126

House: 101 members, 2-year terms
2007 ratios: 57 R, 44 D; 89 men, 12 women
Salary: $38,400
Phone: (405) 521-2711

TERM LIMITS

Governor: 2 terms
Senate: No more than 12 years combined
House: No more than 12 years combined

URBAN STATISTICS

CITY	POPULATION
Oklahoma City	506,132
Tulsa	393,049
Norman	95,694
Lawton	92,757
Broken Arrow	74,859

REGISTERED VOTERS

Democrat	50%
Republican	39%
Unaffiliated	11%

POPULATION

2006 population (est.)	3,579,212
2000 population	3,450,654
1990 population	3,145,585
Percent change (1990-2000)	+9.7%
Rank among states (2006)	28
Median age	35.5
Born in state	62.6%
Foreign born	3.8%
Violent crime rate	498/100,000
Poverty level	14.7%
Federal workers	44,984
Military	41,575

ELECTIONS

STATE ELECTION OFFICIAL
(405) 521-2391
DEMOCRATIC PARTY
(405) 427-3366
REPUBLICAN PARTY
(405) 528-3501

MISCELLANEOUS

Web: www.ok.gov
Capital: Oklahoma City

U.S. CONGRESS

Senate: 2 Republican
House: 4 Republicans, 1 Democrat

2000 Census Statistics by District

DIST.	2004 VOTE FOR PRESIDENT BUSH	KERRY	WHITE	BLACK	ASIAN	HISP	MEDIAN INCOME	WHITE COLLAR	BLUE COLLAR	SERVICE INDUSTRY	OVER 64	UNDER 18	COLLEGE EDUCATION	RURAL	SQ. MILES
1	65%	35%	74%	9%	1%	5%	$38,610	63%	23%	14%	12%	26%	26%	10%	1,737
2	59	41	70	4	0	2	$27,885	48	35	17	15	26	13	64	20,563
3	72	28	81	4	1	5	$32,098	54	30	16	14	26	18	49	34,089
4	67	33	78	7	2	5	$35,510	57	27	16	12	26	20	37	10,212
5	64	36	68	14	3	8	$33,893	61	24	15	13	26	25	12	2,067
STATE	66	34	74	7	1	5	$33,400	57	28	16	13	26	20	35	68,667
U.S.	50.7	48.3	69	12	4	13	$41,994	60	25	15	12	26	24	21	3,537,438

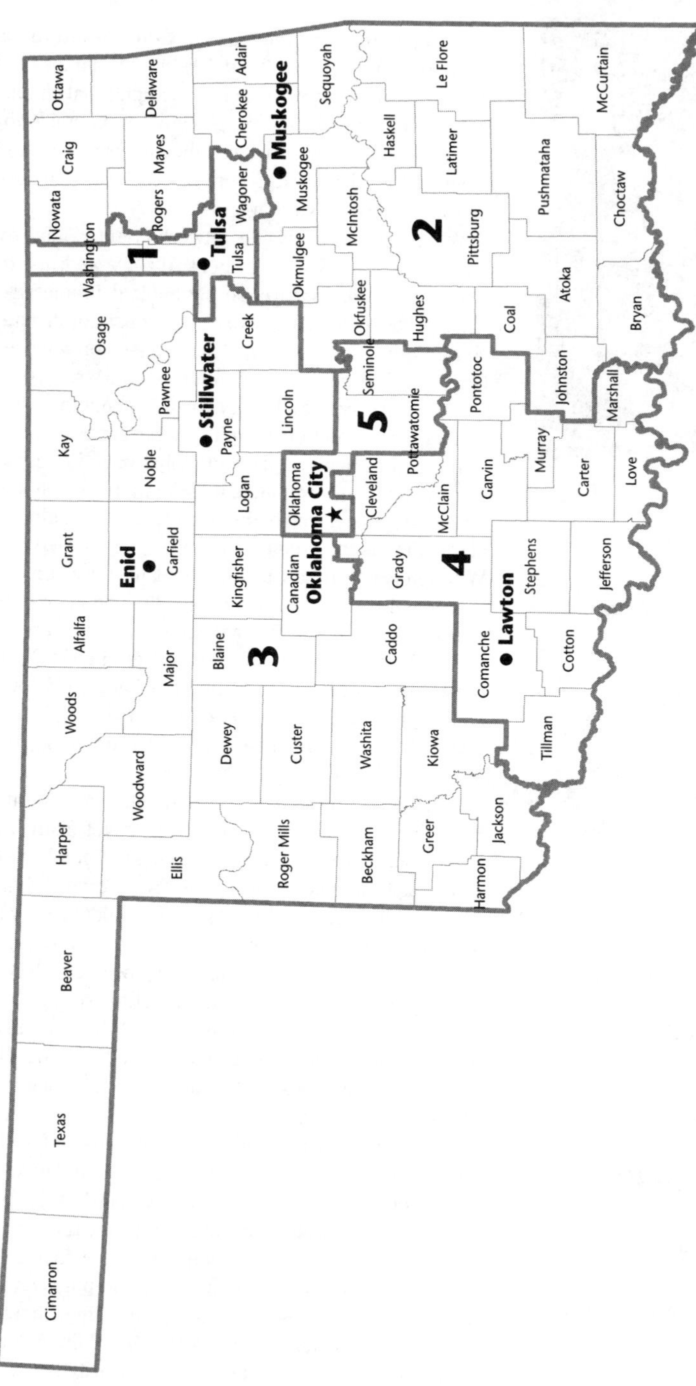

1
2
3
4
5
Tulsa
Muskogee
Stillwater
Enid
Oklahoma City
Lawton
Ottawa
Delaware
Adair
Sequoyah
Le Flore
McCurtain
Craig
Mayes
Cherokee
Haskell
Latimer
Pushmataha
Nowata
Rogers
Wagoner
Muskogee
McIntosh
Pittsburg
Choctaw
Washington
Tulsa
Okmulgee
Atoka
Osage
Creek
Okfuskee
Hughes
Coal
Bryan
Pawnee
Seminole
Pontotoc
Johnston
Marshall
Kay
Noble
Payne
Lincoln
Pottawatomie
Murray
Logan
Oklahoma
Cleveland
McClain
Garvin
Carter
Love
Grant
Garfield
Kingfisher
Canadian
Grady
Stephens
Jefferson
Alfalfa
Major
Blaine
Caddo
Comanche
Cotton
Woods
Dewey
Custer
Washita
Kiowa
Tillman
Woodward
Harper
Ellis
Roger Mills
Beckham
Greer
Jackson
Harmon
Beaver
Texas
Cimarron

Sen. James M. Inhofe (R)

CAPITOL OFFICE
224-4721
inhofe.senate.gov
453 Russell 20510-3603; fax 228-0380

COMMITTEES
Armed Services
Environment & Public Works - ranking member

RESIDENCE
Tulsa

BORN
Nov. 17, 1934, Des Moines, Iowa

RELIGION
Presbyterian

FAMILY
Wife, Kay Inhofe; four children

EDUCATION
U. of Tulsa, B.A. 1973

MILITARY SERVICE
Army, 1957-58

CAREER
Real estate developer; insurance executive

POLITICAL HIGHLIGHTS
Okla. House, 1967-69; Okla. Senate, 1969-77; Republican nominee for governor, 1974; Republican nominee for U.S. House, 1976; mayor of Tulsa, 1978-84; defeated for re-election as mayor of Tulsa, 1984; U.S. House, 1987-94

ELECTION RESULTS

2002 GENERAL		
James M. Inhofe (R)	583,579	57.3%
David L. Walters (D)	369,789	36.3%
James Germalic (I)	65,056	6.4%
2002 PRIMARY		
James M. Inhofe (R)		unopposed

PREVIOUS WINNING PERCENTAGES
1996 (57%); 1994 Special Election (55%); 1992 House Election (53%); 1990 House Election (56%); 1988 House Election (53%); 1986 House Election (55%)

Elected 1994; 2nd full term

Inhofe is the chief obstacle in Congress to the global warming movement, which he calls a "hoax." While President Bush has edged closer to the center on the issue by acknowledging that climate change is a problem, Inhofe has refused to blink. The environmental lobby will have a tough job getting a clampdown on "greenhouse gases" through the Senate Environment and Public Work Committee as long as he is the senior Republican on the narrowly divided panel.

When national television networks went looking for a counterpoint to former Democratic Vice President Al Gore and his movie "An Inconvenient Truth" in 2006, they frequently booked Inhofe (IN-hoff) on their shows. "The political agenda of extremists must not dictate our efforts to provide common-sense protections that are based on science," he likes to say. When Gore testified before the committee in March 2007, Inhofe called him an "alarmist" who would damage the U.S. economy and he suggested Gore was hypocritical for not pledging to cut energy use in his own home.

Inhofe has been the face of global warming denial since 2003, when, as chairman of the committee, he said on the Senate floor, "With all of the hysteria, all of the fear, all of the phony science, could it be that man-made global warming is the greatest hoax ever perpetrated on the American people?" When he went to Italy six months later for a conference on the topic, environmentalists distributed posters of his photo and the statement.

Most of his views on environmental issues are right of center, not at all unusual for someone whose first experience in Washington was as a young Oklahoma legislator protesting the Lady Bird Johnson highway beautification project. Early in his chairmanship, Inhofe met a few times with some of the influential national environmental groups, but doesn't bother anymore. "They hate me," he says.

The committee is among the most polarized on Capitol Hill. California Sen. Barbara Boxer, who took the gavel from Inhofe when Democrats won majorities in Congress in 2006, is as liberal on energy and environment issues as Inhofe is conservative. "You would be hard-pressed to imagine a bigger philosophical change," said Frank O'Donnell, head of the Clean Air Watch environmental group. Moreover, the panel has 10 Democrats and nine Republicans, giving Inhofe the power to stall Boxer's legislation by convincing just one moderate Democrat to cross party lines.

Inhofe is familiar with this strategy. When he ran the panel, his preferred legislation often died on tie votes. In 2005, the panel stalled on the administration's "Clear Skies" bill, which would replace a regulatory approach to industrial air pollution with a market-driven system. Environmentalists and many Democrats opposed the plan because it failed to reduce emissions of carbon dioxide, the chemical most associated with global warming.

Earlier, in the 108th Congress (2003-04), Inhofe focused the committee on a sweeping, multi-year bill to authorize highways, public transportation systems and road safety. Lawmakers were unable to complete work on the bill because of disagreements among Republicans and between Congress and the White House over the generosity of new funding and the way it should be apportioned to the states. The bill's failure was a disappointment for Inhofe, who had made it his top priority for that Congress.

But in early 2007, Inhofe, a fierce opponent of a mandatory cap on greenhouse gas emissions, and Boxer showed an ability to work together — pairing up to send to the House floor a bill to require federal buildings to reduce their energy use. It was believed to be a rare alliance.

Brash and blunt, Inhofe has little patience for bridge-building in the Senate, where any individual or group can tie up a bill forever. He gets top ratings from the National Taxpayers' Union and has a lifetime "A+" grade from the National Rifle Association.

Tulsa's generally conservative voters, including its many religious fundamentalists, love him. Inhofe predicted in a 1999 speech that President Bill Clinton's affair with White House intern Monica Lewinsky would trigger a moral revolution and end the "age of perversion." In 2001, he told the Senate that Israel had a right to take harsh measures with the Palestinians because God had promised the land to the Jews.

A pro-defense lawmaker whose state has several military installations, Inhofe sits on the Armed Services Committee, where he has strongly supported a national missile defense system and increased spending to improve the military's readiness for combat. Drafted into the Army in 1957, he credits the service with teaching him discipline and an appreciation for getting an education. Inhofe was stationed in Fort Chaffee, Ark., and Fort Lee, Va.

Born in Des Moines, Iowa, Inhofe's parents moved in 1942 to Tulsa in search of jobs in the insurance industry. Inhofe inherited their penchant for business, hiring his American Indian neighbors to pick blackberries for him and then selling the berries in the neighborhood. At 15, he worked as a door-to-door salesman. He still lives in a house just three houses away from the one in which he was raised.

Inhofe has about 50 years of experience as a pilot. He's never lost his love of flying though he has nearly lost his life. In September 2006, his TV-8 single-engine stunt plane spun out of control on landing in Tulsa, an incident he attributed to a malfunctioning rudder. While flying to Oklahoma City in 1999, his private plane lost a propeller, forcing him to make an emergency high-speed landing. He likes daredevil aerobatics, and only one aide in his office will fly with him. Inhofe taught his four children to fly and had wedding rehearsal dinners for both his daughters in his hangar.

After his stint in the service, Inhofe followed his parents' career path into insurance, then became a real estate developer. As a businessman, Inhofe became frustrated with an "over-regulated society," which launched him into a 10-year career in the Oklahoma legislature. On his first trip to the nation's capital in 1967, he testified before what was then called the Senate Public Work Committee in opposition to the Lady Bird Johnson Highway Beautification Act because he disliked its property rights provisions.

While a state senator, Inhofe lost a 1974 campaign for governor to Democrat David L. Boren. Elected mayor of Tulsa in 1978, he was defeated for re-election in 1984. He bounced back two years later and picked up a House seat for the GOP, taking 55 percent of the vote to succeed Democrat James R. Jones. He never cracked 56 percent in four elections in the state's most Republican district. In 1988, his campaign was complicated when he sued his brother over a stock sale involving the family insurance business.

In 1994, when Sen. Boren decided to leave midterm, Inhofe made a run for the seat, facing Rep. Dave McCurdy, a conservative and pro-business Democrat favored to win. But McCurdy became closely associated with Clinton, whom he introduced at the 1992 Democratic National Convention. Inhofe won by 15 percentage points.

When he stood for election to a full term in 1996, Democrats were deterred by Inhofe's lopsided victory two years earlier and did not mount a significant challenge. Inhofe defeated Jim Boren, a cousin of the former senator, by 17 percentage points. In 2002, Inhofe won by 21 points against former Democratic Gov. David L. Walters, who was hobbled by past campaign finance improprieties.

KEY VOTES

2006

- Yes Confirm Samuel A. Alito Jr. to the Supreme Court
- No Allow consideration of a bill to establish a $140 billion trust fund to compensate victims of asbestos exposure
- Yes Extend tax cuts for two years at a cost of $70 billion over five years
- No Overhaul immigration policy with border security, enforcement and guest worker program
- Yes Allow consideration of a bill to permanently repeal the estate tax
- No Urge President Bush to begin troop withdrawals from Iraq in 2006
- No Lift President Bush's restrictions on stem cell research funding
- Yes Authorize military tribunals for suspected terrorists

2005

- Yes Curb class action lawsuits by shifting them from state to federal courts
- Yes Allow confirmation vote on Priscilla R. Owen to the U.S. Court of Appeals for the 5th Circuit
- Yes Oppose mandatory emissions limits and block recognition of global warming as a threat
- Yes Approve free-trade pact with five Central American countries
- Yes Pass energy policy overhaul favored by President Bush emphasizing domestic oil and gas production
- Yes Shield gunmakers from lawsuits when their products are used in crimes
- No Ban torture of prisoners in U.S. custody
- Yes Renew 16 provisions of the Patriot Act
- Yes Allow final vote on opening the Arctic National Wildlife Refuge to oil and gas exploration

CQ VOTE STUDIES

	PARTY UNITY		PRESIDENTIAL SUPPORT	
	Support	Oppose	Support	Oppose
2006	94%	6%	88%	12%
2005	94%	6%	91%	9%
2004	98%	2%	92%	8%
2003	98%	2%	97%	3%
2002	96%	4%	96%	4%
2001	96%	4%	95%	5%
2000	100%	0%	30%	70%
1999	95%	5%	23%	77%
1998	97%	3%	14%	86%
1997	99%	1%	49%	51%

INTEREST GROUPS

	AFL-CIO	ADA	CCUS	ACU
2006	20%	0%	91%	100%
2005	21%	5%	83%	100%
2004	17%	10%	100%	100%
2003	0%	5%	100%	84%
2002	17%	10%	100%	100%
2001	25%	10%	93%	96%
2000	13%	5%	85%	100%
1999	11%	0%	94%	100%
1998	0%	5%	76%	100%
1997	14%	5%	50%	100%

Sen. Tom Coburn (R)

CAPITOL OFFICE
224-5754
www.coburn.senate.gov
172 Russell 20510-3602; fax 224-6008

COMMITTEES
Homeland Security & Governmental Affairs
Health, Education, Labor & Pensions
Indian Affairs
Judiciary

RESIDENCE
Muskogee

BORN
March 14, 1948, Casper, Wyo.

RELIGION
Baptist

FAMILY
Wife, Carolyn Coburn; three children

EDUCATION
Oklahoma State U., B.S. 1970 (accounting); U. of Oklahoma, M.D. 1983

CAREER
Physician; optical firm manager

POLITICAL HIGHLIGHTS
U.S. House, 1995-2001

ELECTION RESULTS

2004 GENERAL		
Tom Coburn (R)	763,433	52.8%
Brad Carson (D)	596,750	41.3%
Sheila Bilyeu (I)	86,663	6.0%
2004 PRIMARY		
Tom Coburn (R)	145,974	61.2%
Kirk Humphreys (R)	59,877	25.1%
Bob Anthony (R)	29,596	12.4%
Jay Richard Hunt (R)	2,944	1.2%

PREVIOUS WINNING PERCENTAGES
1998 House Election (58%); 1996 House Election (55%); 1994 House Election (52%)

Elected 2004; 1st term

The Senate has not mellowed Coburn, who first came to Congress as a member of the zealous House Republican Class of '94. He is as blunt and brash as he was in the other chamber, with similar results. He shakes things up but is rarely a sponsor on major legislation. "He's the same Tom Coburn," The Oklahoman newspaper editorialized in 2005. "Alienating some folks, inspiring others, inviting praise and scorn, prompting questions about whether he's the taxpayers' best friend and his own worst enemy."

An obstetrician and self-styled citizen-legislator, he rails against an incumbency mindset in Congress that he says puts staying in power ahead of passing conservative legislation. "We have a deficit of moral courage in the United States Congress," Coburn likes to say.

Coburn suffers no such deficit. As a freshman senator, he took on the sensitive subject of members' earmarks, funding for pet projects that lawmakers frequently slip into spending bills. Coburn highlighted a $223 million earmark for a proposed bridge to connect the Alaskan mainland and the 50 residents of Gravina Island, a project lampooned in the national press as the bridge to nowhere. Though most of his amendments to end earmarks did not pass, they galvanized budget conservatives. (Coburn does not lobby for earmarks for his state.)

It also made him some powerful enemies. Veteran GOP Sen. Ted Stevens of Alaska threatened to resign if Coburn prevailed. And Christopher S. Bond of Missouri, another senior GOP appropriator, sniffed, "I don't need a senator from Oklahoma telling me what's good for the state of Missouri." Coburn earlier alienated House Speaker J. Dennis Hastert by suggesting he needed a "spinal transplant" to rein in spending and ought to resign.

His one victory against earmarks came in late 2006, when he teamed with Democrat Barack Obama of Illinois on a bill establishing a searchable online database listing the recipients of all federal spending. Their bill passed after bloggers on the Internet publicized the names of two senators — Stevens and fellow appropriator Robert C. Byrd, a West Virginia Democrat — who had put a secret "hold" on it, which any senator has the power to do without revealing his or her identity.

After the 2006 election, fearing a last-minute spending spree by Congress, Coburn and a band of conservatives halted the last-minute passage of a large bill likely to be laden with pork barrel spending. That had the effect of forcing the government to continue to run at the previous year's level. Conservative columnist George Will wrote, "Coburn is the most dangerous creature that can come to the Senate, someone simply uninterested in being popular."

His indifference on that score probably helps explain why he wound up nine votes short of the 60 votes he needed to overrule the Senate Ethics Committee in 2005 when it refused to modify a longstanding ban on outside payment for professional services. Coburn wanted to keep collecting just enough fees from his obstetrics practice in Muskogee to cover his costs. The House had allowed him to do so; the Senate did not. He said he would keep on seeing patients anyway whenever he was home.

Coburn is not entirely immune to the political pressures of everyday Senate life. After heavy lobbying by GOP leaders, he cast the deciding vote in 2006 against a tough budget rule that would have forced Congress to find offsetting cuts or tax increases when it wanted to spend more money. A few months earlier, Coburn had voted in favor of the pay-as-you-go rule.

Coburn is one of the rare non-lawyers on the Senate Judiciary Committee. He tends to be more deferential to senior colleagues there, though he was the first on the panel in April 2007 to call for the resignation of Attorney General Alberto R. Gonzales over the firings of eight U.S. attorneys that had political overtones.

As in the House, he is a champion of anti-abortion measures and other conservative social policies. One of the first Senate bills he cosponsored was the Unborn Child Pain Awareness Act of 2005 requiring physicians to tell women that after the 20th week of a pregnancy an abortion would likely cause the fetus to feel pain. During his six-year House tenure he often led the charge to tack conservative social policies onto must-pass spending bills.

Blunt talk is not new to Coburn, who once called state legislators "a bunch of crapheads." He got into hot water in 1997 with remarks about NBC's broadcast of "Schindler's List," a dramatic film about the Holocaust that Coburn said contained too much nudity, violence and profanity. He was castigated by some prominent Republicans for not recognizing the historical accuracy of the film; a contrite Coburn responded with an apology.

Coburn was born in Casper, Wyo., but grew up in Muskogee, which is still his hometown. He had a strained relationship with his father, an alcoholic with an eighth-grade education who founded a successful optical business. (They reconciled six months before his father's death.) His father's company made equipment to process optical lenses, and eventually became Muskogee's biggest employer. After his junior year at Oklahoma State, Coburn married Carolyn Denton, a former Miss Oklahoma he'd had a crush on since elementary school. He went to work for his father at age 22 and for several years managed a branch of the business in Virginia, Coburn Optical Products. He built it into a $40 million venture, which Revlon bought in 1975.

Coburn moved back to Oklahoma, and at age 31, decided to go to medical school, earning the nickname "Gramps" from his classmates. He credits his career change to his experience with cancer. When he was just 23, Coburn's mother noticed a change in a birthmark behind his left ear. A doctor diagnosed a malignant melanoma, a deadly form of skin cancer, and Coburn spent the next two years in treatment. He still has a pronounced scar on his neck. He fought a second battle against cancer, this time colon cancer, shortly before he decided to run for the Senate in 2004.

Coburn was a first-time candidate for public office when he ran for the House in 1994, a year of voter disgruntlement with incumbents and a favorable one for neophytes. One day, he read in the Muskogee Phoenix a comment about nationalizing health care by Rep. Mike Synar, the incumbent Democrat, whose views were more to the left than those of his district. "I said to myself, 'Somebody has got to run against this guy,' " Coburn recalls. Synar in fact lost in the primary, and Coburn went on to beat his Democratic replacement, a 71-year-old retired middle school teacher.

Unlike many lawmakers elected in the GOP takeover, Coburn stuck to his term limits pledge, serving three terms in the House and then leaving. But he missed the fray, and in 2004 ran for the seat of retiring GOP Sen. Don Nickles. He had a hard fight against Democrat Brad Carson, a moderate House member who seemed suited for the historically Democratic yet conservative state. Despite a gaffe-prone campaign, Coburn won by more than 11 percentage points. Carson was hurt by sharing the ballot with a successful measure to add a same-sex marriage ban to the Oklahoma Constitution, which increased turnout among Coburn's base, the Christian right.

Coburn promises to serve no more than two Senate terms. "Washington tends to change people," he once said. "What makes me valuable to my district is [that] there's nothing in Washington that I want."

KEY VOTES

2006

- Yes Confirm Samuel A. Alito Jr. to the Supreme Court
- Yes Allow consideration of a bill to establish a $140 billion trust fund to compensate victims of asbestos exposure
- Yes Extend tax cuts for two years at a cost of $70 billion over five years
- No Overhaul immigration policy with border security, enforcement and guest worker program
- Yes Allow consideration of a bill to permanently repeal the estate tax
- No Urge President Bush to begin troop withdrawals from Iraq in 2006
- No Lift President Bush's restrictions on stem cell research funding
- Yes Authorize military tribunals for suspected terrorists

2005

- Yes Curb class action lawsuits by shifting them from state to federal courts
- Yes Allow confirmation vote on Priscilla R. Owen to the U.S. Court of Appeals for the 5th Circuit
- Yes Oppose mandatory emissions limits and block recognition of global warming as a threat
- Yes Approve free-trade pact with five Central American countries
- Yes Pass energy policy overhaul favored by President Bush emphasizing domestic oil and gas production
- Yes Shield gunmakers from lawsuits when their products are used in crimes
- No Ban torture of prisoners in U.S. custody
- Yes Renew 16 provisions of the Patriot Act
- Yes Allow final vote on opening the Arctic National Wildlife Refuge to oil and gas exploration

CQ VOTE STUDIES

	PARTY UNITY		PRESIDENTIAL SUPPORT	
	Support	Oppose	Support	Oppose
2006	92%	8%	88%	12%
2005	93%	7%	91%	9%
House Service:				
2000	91%	9%	23%	77%
1999	90%	10%	14%	86%
1998	94%	6%	16%	84%
1997	93%	7%	24%	76%
1996	91%	9%	29%	71%
1995	93%	7%	18%	82%

INTEREST GROUPS

	AFL-CIO	ADA	CCUS	ACU
2006	27%	5%	64%	100%
2005	21%	5%	89%	100%
House Service:				
2000	20%	15%	63%	95%
1999	38%	10%	67%	100%
1998	22%	5%	71%	100%
1997	0%	5%	78%	95%
1996	9%	10%	80%	89%
1995	0%	0%	96%	100%

Rep. John Sullivan (R)

CAPITOL OFFICE
225-2211
sullivan.house.gov
114 Cannon 20515-3601; fax 225-9187

COMMITTEES
Energy & Commerce
Select Energy Independence & Global Warming

RESIDENCE
Tulsa

BORN
Jan. 1, 1965, Tulsa, Okla.

RELIGION
Roman Catholic

FAMILY
Wife, Judy Sullivan; five children (one deceased)

EDUCATION
Northeastern State U., B.B.A 1992 (marketing)

CAREER
Real estate broker; petroleum marketing executive

POLITICAL HIGHLIGHTS
Okla. House, 1995-2002

ELECTION RESULTS

2006 GENERAL		
John Sullivan (R)	116,920	63.6%
Alan Gentges (D)	56,724	30.9%
Bill Wortman (I)	10,085	5.5%
2006 PRIMARY		
John Sullivan (R)	38,279	83.2%
Evelyn L. Rogers (R)	5,826	12.7%
Fran Moghaddam (R)	1,895	4.1%
2004 GENERAL		
John Sullivan (R)	187,145	60.2%
Doug Dodd (D)	116,731	37.5%
John Krymski (I)	7,058	2.3%

PREVIOUS WINNING PERCENTAGES
2002 (56%); 2002 Special Election (54%)

Elected January 2002; 3rd full term

There's no mistaking where Sullivan stands along the spectrum of GOP politics. He's on the far right, among the conservatives who believe in a very limited role for the federal government. He sums up his political philosophy this way: "If it's in the Yellow Pages, government shouldn't be doing it."

Sullivan was a vociferous critic of President Bush's proposal to allow some illegal immigrants to remain in the country as guest workers. In 2005, Sullivan voted for a punitive House bill that would have made it a federal crime to live in the United States illegally. He tried to toughen it even further, offering an unsuccessful amendment to require mandatory deportation of all illegal immigrants who could not prove they had been in the United States a year or more. His proposal also would have allowed state and local police to jail illegal immigrants until they could be deported. "In my district, residents complain as truckloads of illegal aliens are released into their neighborhoods rather than being detained," Sullivan said of his Tulsa constituents.

He has fought to beef up immigration enforcement in Oklahoma, introducing legislation to establish a field office in his home base of Tulsa. The only Immigration and Customs Enforcement office in the state is in Oklahoma City, more than 100 miles away. He was instrumental in increasing that office's staffing from four to 12.

While Sullivan loves to trumpet his success snagging special projects for his district — among his biggest catches have been $21 million for the Oklahoma National Guard and more than $13 million in defense contracts — he is a fierce critic of other kinds of federal spending. A member of the Republican Study Committee, the most conservative Republicans, he aggressively challenges spending he considers excessive and was among those urging spending cuts in other programs to offset the billions of dollars Congress appropriated in 2005 and 2006 to help the Gulf Coast recover from a devastating hurricane season.

Sullivan's party loyalty — he sided with a majority of Republicans 97 percent of the time on party-line votes in the 109th Congress (2005-06) — and his background as a petroleum marketing executive helped secure him a coveted seat on the Energy and Commerce Committee, an important perch for his energy-producing part of the world. He supported the 2005 energy policy overhaul and legislation to streamline regulatory reviews of new or expanded refineries. He has said he believes the United States is too dependent on foreign oil and should expand domestic production and develop alternative fuel sources — and that Tulsa could play a key role.

A supporter of offshore oil drilling, he voted against Democratic legislation in 2007 that aimed to recoup royalties lost due to faulty drilling leases issued by the government and to roll back several oil industry tax breaks. He also was appointed in the 110th Congress (2007-08) to a new House select panel on global warming and energy independence.

A member of the Energy and Commerce panel's Health Subcommittee, he pushed legislation in 2007 mandating that private insurance companies provide equal coverage for mental and physical illnesses.

His first turn at stardom came in July 2003 when he defied a doctor's orders to stay in bed and went to the House floor in a wheelchair to cast the deciding vote on a bill to significantly change the Head Start early education program. He had been injured two days before when a security barrier at a Capitol parking lot malfunctioned and hit the car in which he was riding, setting off the air bag. "The people of the 1st District of Oklahoma trust me to do my job," he said. "That's exactly what I'm going to do in Washington, no matter how hard it may be at times." The bill ultimately died in the Senate.

Sullivan got his first taste of politics when, as a kid walking to kindergarten, he saw yard signs in his neighborhood for presidential contestants Richard Nixon and George McGovern. Not knowing what they meant, he asked his parents if they could get one. That touched off a battle royal between his Democratic mother and Republican father that ended with his mother flinging a glass of orange juice at his dad. Sullivan still remembers the pulp dripping down the wall.

Ultimately, it was his father's political leanings that swayed the boy. He trailed along as his father worked to elect Henry Bellmon, Oklahoma's first Republican governor, and when he went to college, Sullivan initially majored in political science. After his father died he switched to marketing, thinking that in practical terms that degree might make it easier to land a job later and pay off his student loans.

He worked as a real estate broker and a petroleum marketing executive, but he continued to be fascinated by politics and ran a political memorabilia business. He also worked on several GOP campaigns. In 1994, when a local state House seat opened up, Sullivan ran and won. During seven years in the legislature, he battled to reduce sales and estate taxes, and championed an annual one-day sales tax "holiday" on school-related purchases.

In 2001, Republican Rep. Steve Largent left his House seat to run for governor. In the five-way primary, Sullivan bested Cathy Keating, wife of GOP Gov. Frank Keating and the expected front-runner. In the special election, he defeated Democrat and former Tulsa School Board member Doug Dodd. By the time he ran for his first full term in the fall of 2002, the district had been redrawn to make it more safely Republican and he beat Dodd in a rematch.

His re-election in 2004 came after a tough campaign. Past supporters, including an earlier political consultant to Sullivan who accused his former boss of cheating him out of nearly $20,000 in fees, backed GOP businessman Bill Wortman in the primary. Sullivan's office later acknowledged his aides used phony names to telephone call-in radio shows and pose easy questions to their boss. Wortman seized on that and on two cases in which he said Sullivan lied about his police record.

Sullivan has long acknowledged a rocky youth in which careless drinking led to several arrests, including one for assault. He has often spoken about the dangers of alcohol consumption for high school students. But voters evidently are untroubled by his past. In 2006, he won with nearly 64 percent of the vote.

KEY VOTES

2006

No	Stop broadband companies from favoring select Internet traffic
Yes	Affirm U.S. commitment to war in Iraq and reject setting a withdrawal date for troops
Yes	Repeal requirement for bilingual ballots at the polls
Yes	Permit U.S. sale of civilian nuclear technology to India
Yes	Build a 700-mile fence on the U.S.-Mexico border to curb illegal crossings
Yes	Permit warrantless wiretaps of suspected terrorists

2005

Yes	Intervene in the life-support case of Terri Schiavo
No	Lift President Bush's restrictions on stem cell research funding
?	Prohibit FBI access to library and bookstore records
Yes	Approve free-trade pact with five Central American countries
Yes	Pass energy policy overhaul favored by President Bush emphasizing domestic oil and gas production
Yes	End mandatory preservation of habitat of endangered animal and plant species
No	Ban torture of prisoners in U.S. custody

CQ VOTE STUDIES

	PARTY UNITY		PRESIDENTIAL SUPPORT	
	Support	Oppose	Support	Oppose
2006	97%	3%	95%	5%
2005	97%	3%	89%	11%
2004	97%	3%	85%	15%
2003	98%	2%	100%	0%
2002	99%	1%	88%	12%

INTEREST GROUPS

	AFL-CIO	ADA	CCUS	ACU
2006	15%	5%	100%	92%
2005	13%	5%	85%	100%
2004	7%	0%	100%	100%
2003	0%	0%	100%	88%
2002	13%	0%	89%	—

OKLAHOMA 1

Tulsa; Wagoner and Washington counties

Wooden homes on small plots of land in the city's outskirts contrast with the skyscrapers of downtown Tulsa, the heart of the 1st and one of the most solidly Republican enclaves in Oklahoma. Tulsa and Oklahoma City, the two main metropolitan areas in the state, have a friendly rivalry. Tulsa is more insular and tied to old money than Oklahoma City and the rest of the state, and Tulsans like to distinguish themselves from the "dust-on-their-boots" stereotype of the rest of Oklahoma.

Once the "oil capital of the world," Tulsa thrived on drilling for oil until the market dried up in the 1980s. The dramatic rise in both demand and price for oil beginning in late 2005, however, has breathed new life into the industry, which remains one of the top enterprises in the region. Despite the resurgence, the city is still actively seeking to diversify its economic identity, and efforts that began two decades ago are now paying off. Tulsa has become a manufacturing hub for flight simulators, and while aviation and aerospace production remains profitable, the financial services and telecommunications sectors have helped prolong growth.

Real estate prices are beginning to rise as the economy expands and Tulsa and its neighboring cities continue to annex land. Young professionals are moving into the city's center. South Tulsa is sprinkled with luxury homes, and subdivisions are springing up in the fast-growing suburbs of Broken Arrow, Jenks and Owasso, which has more than doubled in population since 1990.

Democrats split the votes in the 1st's local elections, but Republicans dominate at the federal level. The region has voted for a Democratic presidential candidate only twice since 1920. Socially conservative issues play well in the district, which is the home of Oral Roberts University.

MAJOR INDUSTRY

Oil, aerospace, telecommunications, financial services, defense manufacturing

CITIES

Tulsa (pt.), 387,419; Broken Arrow, 74,859; Bartlesville, 34,746; Owasso, 18,502; Sand Springs (pt.), 17,172

NOTABLE

Oral Roberts University is known for its 200-foot Prayer Tower and the "Praying Hands" sculpture at the campus' main entrance.

Rep. Dan Boren (D)

CAPITOL OFFICE
225-2701
www.house.gov/boren
216 Cannon 20515-3602; fax 225-3038

COMMITTEES
Armed Services
Financial Services
Natural Resources

RESIDENCE
Muskogee

BORN
Aug. 2, 1973, Shawnee, Okla.

RELIGION
Methodist

FAMILY
Wife, Andrea Boren

EDUCATION
Texas Christian U., B.A. 1997 (economics); U. of Oklahoma, M.B.A. 2001

CAREER
College fundraiser; congressional district aide; bank teller; state utility regulation commission aide

POLITICAL HIGHLIGHTS
Okla. House, 2002-04

ELECTION RESULTS

2006 GENERAL		
Dan Boren (D)	122,347	72.7%
Patrick K. Miller (R)	45,861	27.3%
2006 PRIMARY		
Dan Boren (D)		unopposed
2004 GENERAL		
Dan Boren (D)	179,579	65.9%
Wayland Smalley (R)	92,963	34.1%

Elected 2004; 2nd term

Boren is a Democrat who behaves like one only about half the time. His voting record in the 109th Congress (2005-06) showed him to be the most conservative House Democrat. He once co-hosted an event in his district with uber-conservative Sen. Tom Coburn because he couldn't think of many members of his own party who would be welcome there. "It would kill me to bring in a liberal to Oklahoma," he told The Weekly Standard magazine.

Just after the 2006 election, when Democrats were celebrating the historic rise of Nancy Pelosi as the incoming House Speaker, Boren declined to endorse the California liberal until he met her to ask for assurances she was willing to include Republicans and conservative Democrats in legislative deal-making. "My district will not re-elect me if I go to the left," Boren told the Tulsa World newspaper.

Boren is a member of the Blue Dog Coalition, a group of more than 40 House Democrats whose influence grew after the 2006 election swept in a large freshman class of centrists. Its centerpiece issue is eliminating deficit spending.

A fiscal conservative, he was one of 12 Democrats to vote against the leadership's budget resolution for the 2008 budget year, stating he could not "support a budget that includes not a single spending cut." But he has not repudiated earmarks — special-interest projects added to spending bills to help members curry favor with voters. "I've asked for money for roads and for our universities and I'm proud of it," Boren told the Tulsa World in 2006. And, with the sort of reasoning that fiscally conservative defenders of earmarks have used for years, he says, "If the money is not spent here, it's going to be spent somewhere else."

He says he fundamentally agrees with the Democratic goal of "giving opportunity to all" on issues such as education and health care, but he has come out against his party on a number of other issues. In his first term, he broke with his party to support the Republican energy policy overhaul and the GOP's immigration plan cracking down on illegal aliens. He was the only Democrat to side with Republicans by voting in favor of giving the Federal Bureau of Investigation access to records about books that people take out of libraries and buy in bookstores.

Boren angered party leaders for joining seven other Democrats in voting for a GOP-crafted lobbying and ethics bill in 2006. And he was one of only two Democrats in 2007 to vote against a bill that would make it easier for unions to establish themselves in the workplace.

Boren drew the line against cooperating with Republicans on Social Security, however, opposing President Bush's plan to partially privatize the program by letting individuals invest part of their savings on their own.

Boren also says he's a "pro-business, pro-gun Democrat." As testimonial, his office walls are covered with the fruits of his hunting trips: stuffed deer heads, a wild turkey and a bear skin.

He is the third generation of Boren to serve in Congress from Oklahoma. His father was Democrat David L. Boren, a U.S. senator who resigned his seat in 1994 to become president of the University of Oklahoma. His grandfather, Lyle Boren, served in the House from 1937 to 1947. The 2nd District of today includes about half of the area Boren's grandfather once represented.

During the 110th Congress (2007-08), he was granted a seat on the Financial Services Committee. That panel is generally an "exclusive committee" — meaning members cannot serve on any other committee. But leaders granted him a waiver to retain his seats on the Natural Resources and Armed Services committees.

Boren's seat on Natural Resources — with jurisdiction over American Indian lands — is important in a district with the nation's third-highest percentage of American Indians. His seat on Armed Services helps him burnish his pro-military credentials in a state that includes such major facilities as Tinker Air Force Base and the Army's Fort Sill.

In 2007, Boren spoke out against Bush's plan to send additional combat troops into the Iraq War and voted for a Democratic resolution disapproving of the strategy. But he was one of 14 Democrats to vote against a war funding bill that set a deadline for withdrawal of U.S. forces from Iraq.

Boren was born two years before his father became governor of Oklahoma, and it's been total immersion in politics since. He was 5 when his father was elected to the Senate. His parents divorced when he was young, and he split his time between living in Oklahoma with his mother, the late Janna L. Robbins, and in Washington with his father.

After college, he worked as an aide to Denise Bode, who headed the Oklahoma utility regulatory agency and once worked in Sen. Boren's office. In 2002, at the age of 29, he beat an incumbent for an Oklahoma House seat.

In his brief tenure in the legislature, Boren built a centrist-right record as a proponent of tax cuts and of efforts to make it more difficult for trial lawyers to press what he termed frivolous lawsuits. Just a year into his term, a U.S. House seat opened when Oklahoma Democrat Brad Carson left for an ultimately unsuccessful Senate bid. Boren didn't hesitate to go for it.

His name recognition helped him beat local District Attorney Kalyn Free, a member of the Cherokee Nation, in the primary. He had been portrayed as not Democratic enough after reports that he had once registered as a Republican. Boren said he once registered as an independent when he was working for a Republican on the utility commission, but that he was never a registered Republican. Although Democrats outnumber Republicans in the district, they tend to be of a conservative variety, the philosophical heirs to what were known as Yellow Dog Democrats. He sprinted past Republican Wayland Smalley, a horse breeder, in the general election.

Afterward, he married a woman whose family also has great cachet in Oklahoma; his wife, Andrea, is the sister of Josh Heupel, who led the University of Oklahoma's football team to a 2000 national championship.

Boren's conservative credentials and nearly 3-1 re-election margin over Republican Patrick K. Miller in 2006 has led to speculation that he could be a serious challenger to Republican Senator James Inhofe in 2008.

KEY VOTES

2006

- No Stop broadband companies from favoring select Internet traffic
- Yes Affirm U.S. commitment to war in Iraq and reject setting a withdrawal date for troops
- No Repeal requirement for bilingual ballots at the polls
- Yes Permit U.S. sale of civilian nuclear technology to India
- Yes Build a 700-mile fence on the U.S.-Mexico border to curb illegal crossings
- Yes Permit warrantless wiretaps of suspected terrorists

2005

- Yes Intervene in the life-support case of Terri Schiavo
- Yes Lift President Bush's restrictions on stem cell research funding
- No Prohibit FBI access to library and bookstore records
- No Approve free-trade pact with five Central American countries
- Yes Pass energy policy overhaul favored by President Bush emphasizing domestic oil and gas production
- Yes End mandatory preservation of habitat of endangered animal and plant species
- Yes Ban torture of prisoners in U.S. custody

CQ VOTE STUDIES

	PARTY UNITY		PRESIDENTIAL SUPPORT	
	Support	Oppose	Support	Oppose
2006	54%	46%	85%	15%
2005	59%	41%	65%	35%

INTEREST GROUPS

	AFL-CIO	ADA	CCUS	ACU
2006	57%	25%	100%	72%
2005	60%	55%	81%	64%

OKLAHOMA 2

East – Muskogee, 'Little Dixie'

The 2nd's overall Democratic lean does not disguise a cultural split between the district's regions. Running from Kansas to Texas in eastern Oklahoma, the 2nd takes in outlying areas of Tulsa to the north and the "Little Dixie" region in the south. Farming and die-hard "Yellow Dog" Democrats typify southeastern Oklahoma, while northeastern residents are more liberal, at least by Oklahoma's standards. Still, both areas support Republicans in presidential races — in 2004, George W. Bush won every county in the 2nd.

The district, especially Little Dixie, suffers from a high susceptibility to severe drought conditions. Southeast Oklahoma was particularly hard-hit by long-term drought conditions that escalated in 2005. The threat of fire, crop failures and reduced grazing options for livestock is a concern for farmers in a district that relies on ranching and agriculture. In addition to raising beef and poultry, farmers here cultivate peanuts and wheat.

Other natural resources also bolster the region's economy. The number of small oil and natural gas wells has grown to meet recent increased industry demands. The timber industry in rocky southeastern McCurtain County supports paper mills, saw mills and other secondary industries. Pittsburg County hosts McAlester Army Ammunition Plant, a high-capacity ordnance storage facility.

Farther north, the forested section in the foothills of the Ozark Mountains is a poor rural area with Democratic sympathies. Lakes and waterways — including Lake Eufaula, the state's largest lake — attract tourists. The remote locations here also appeal to the elderly: The 2nd has Oklahoma's greatest proportion of people age 65 or older. The 2nd also has the nation's third-largest district share of American Indians (17 percent), and includes Tahlequah, the Cherokee Nation's capital.

MAJOR INDUSTRY

Ranching, timber, oil and gas, agriculture

MILITARY BASES

McAlester Army Ammunition Plant, 1 military, 1,200 civilian (2007)

CITIES

Muskogee, 38,310; McAlester, 17,783; Claremore, 15,873

NOTABLE

The American Indian "Trail of Tears" of 1838-39 ended in Tahlequah — nearly 20 percent of the Cherokee Nation died en route.

Rep. Frank D. Lucas (R)

CAPITOL OFFICE
225-5565
www.house.gov/lucas
2311 Rayburn 20515-3603; fax 225-8698

COMMITTEES
Agriculture
Financial Services
Science & Technology

RESIDENCE
Cheyenne

BORN
Jan. 6, 1960, Cheyenne, Okla.

RELIGION
Baptist

FAMILY
Wife, Lynda Lucas; three children

EDUCATION
Oklahoma State U., B.S. 1982
(agricultural economics)

CAREER
Farmer; rancher

POLITICAL HIGHLIGHTS
Republican nominee for Okla. House, 1984, 1986;
Okla. House, 1989-94

ELECTION RESULTS

2006 GENERAL		
Frank D. Lucas (R)	128,042	67.5%
Sue Barton (D)	61,749	32.5%
2006 PRIMARY		
Frank D. Lucas (R)		unopposed
2004 GENERAL		
Frank D. Lucas (R)	215,510	82.2%
Gregory M. Wilson (I)	46,621	17.8%

PREVIOUS WINNING PERCENTAGES
2002 (76%); 2000 (59%); 1998 (65%); 1996 (64%);
1994 (70%); 1994 Special Election (54%)

Elected May 1994; 7th full term

Lucas was born and raised on a farm in Cheyenne, Okla., which the Lucas family has owned since the turn of the 20th century. Even though he grew up in such a rural area — Cheyenne has a population of 2,400 — Lucas had no trouble finding his inner politician.

As a child, he accompanied his Republican father (his mother was a Texas Democrat) to local political events. In the 1960s, Lucas distinctly remembers meeting Oklahoma Republican Rep. John N. Happy Camp, who served in the House from 1969 to 1975. "I was impressed by people involved in politics, and I felt like it was my responsibility to be involved and make a difference," he said. At Oklahoma State University, Lucas was a student senator and president of the College Republicans; he also volunteered in local campaigns. But he majored in agricultural economics and he always came home to the family farm.

Lucas has held on to the farm while many of his neighbors moved to towns and cities. The population of Roger Mills County, where the Lucas farm is located, has dropped significantly since 1980. In fact, the population drain throughout rural Oklahoma led to the state losing one of its House seats in reapportionment after the 2000 census, leaving it with five.

That steady emptying of rural Oklahoma is an underlying factor in much of Lucas' legislative agenda and his close attention to constituent service. The 3rd District encompasses almost half the geographic area of the state, and though many of his constituents are suburbanites living near Oklahoma City and Tulsa, Lucas' main focus is on rural life. When he is in Washington, his wife runs their beef cattle and wheat operation.

Lucas is the top Republican on the Agriculture Committee's Conservation, Credit, Energy and Research Subcommittee. He had previously chaired the panel and played a major role in developing the farm bill that Congress enacted in 2002. That measure is up for renewal in 2007, and he will no doubt be just as involved.

Agriculturally, Lucas represents one of the most diverse regions in the Midwest. Farmers in his district grow everything from wheat and rye to peanuts and cotton. Representing the various interests on Capitol Hill is perhaps Lucas' biggest challenge. "It's a balancing act," he says. "It's just like I have three children. I try not to pick my favorites." At the same time, Lucas plays up the similarities among his farming constituents. "They all want to use property as they see fit; they all want cyclical payments," he says, referring to subsidies given to farmers when crop prices drop.

He wants the 2007 farm bill to continue providing direct support payments to farmers, a provision that is likely to be controversial given the budget deficit and reports that some payments are going to people who don't farm. He also wants a permanent disaster relief title that would compensate farmers for crops and livestock they lose to fire, flood and drought.

On most other issues, Lucas is a party loyalist and a reliable supporter of the president's agenda. In 2006, he voted in agreement with a majority of his party 98 percent of the time, and he supported President Bush's position 95 percent of the time.

When it comes to social policy, Lucas falls right in line with his party's conservatives. He supports efforts to ban abortion and prohibit same-sex marriage and stem cell research. He helped to pass a bill in 2006 that would keep the words "Under God" in the Pledge of Allegiance, and in 2002 and 2003 he offered legislation to create a constitutional amendment protecting the right to say the pledge in American schools.

But he also listens when constituents demand a departure from the GOP agenda. Lucas voted against the 2006 renewal of the Patriot Act, an anti-terrorism law that gives the government more powers to investigate suspected terrorists. Lucas said that, in town meeting after town meeting, he heard his constituents say, "This should be over with. We want a return to normalcy," which he said to them means less government involvement in their lives.

When he was first elected, Lucas spent a lot of time working on legislation stemming from the April 1995 bombing in downtown Oklahoma City that destroyed the Alfred P. Murrah Federal Building and killed 168 people. The federal building used to be in Lucas' old district, the 6th. In the years after the bombing, Lucas helped secure more than $100 million in federal funds for relief, recovery and rebuilding of the area. He also won passage of a measure to establish a national memorial on the bombing site.

In 2006, Lucas, an avid coin collector who sits on the Financial Services Committee, introduced the Numismatic Rarities Certainty Act, a bill that would keep the government from claiming possession of any coin minted before 1933. He says his favorite coin is a 1971 Eisenhower dollar. When he was 11 years old, he says he spent the year saving his pennies to buy the coin. He had no idea his grandmother was planning to give him the coveted coin for Christmas. She died shortly before the holiday, so it was his grandfather who gave it to him. Lucas says he would take "no amount of money in the world for that coin."

After graduating from Oklahoma State University, Lucas returned home to Cheyenne and made two unsuccessful bids for a state House seat in what was then a mostly Democratic area. He then captured a state House seat in a sprawling rural district in 1988.

When 10-term Democratic Rep. Glenn English resigned the 6th District seat in early 1994 to head a rural electric lobbying association, Lucas made his run for the House. He outpolled four other Republicans to win the nomination. Stressing his work in agriculture and his lifelong residency in the district, he won 54 percent of the vote in the special election against Democrat Dan Webber Jr., who had spent years in Washington as an aide to Oklahoma Democratic Sen. David L. Boren.

That was Lucas' closest election. In 2002, he racked up a big victory in the new 3rd District, redrawn in decennial redistricting to be favorable to the GOP. In 2006, even though it was a tough year nationally for Republicans, Lucas captured more than 67 percent of the vote.

KEY VOTES

2006

- No Stop broadband companies from favoring select Internet traffic
- Yes Affirm U.S. commitment to war in Iraq and reject setting a withdrawal date for troops
- Yes Repeal requirement for bilingual ballots at the polls
- Yes Permit U.S. sale of civilian nuclear technology to India
- Yes Build a 700-mile fence on the U.S.-Mexico border to curb illegal crossings
- Yes Permit warrantless wiretaps of suspected terrorists

2005

- Yes Intervene in the life-support case of Terri Schiavo
- No Lift President Bush's restrictions on stem cell research funding
- No Prohibit FBI access to library and bookstore records
- Yes Approve free-trade pact with five Central American countries
- Yes Pass energy policy overhaul favored by President Bush emphasizing domestic oil and gas production
- Yes End mandatory preservation of habitat of endangered animal and plant species
- No Ban torture of prisoners in U.S. custody

CQ VOTE STUDIES

	PARTY UNITY		PRESIDENTIAL SUPPORT	
	Support	Oppose	Support	Oppose
2006	98%	2%	95%	5%
2005	97%	3%	87%	13%
2004	94%	6%	87%	13%
2003	97%	3%	94%	6%
2002	98%	2%	88%	12%

INTEREST GROUPS

	AFL-CIO	ADA	CCUS	ACU
2006	7%	5%	93%	88%
2005	13%	0%	92%	92%
2004	17%	0%	95%	96%
2003	7%	10%	97%	92%
2002	0%	0%	100%	96%

OKLAHOMA 3

Panhandle; west and north-central Oklahoma

Nothing stops the constant wind that forces its way across the 3rd's flat plains in western and north-central Oklahoma, an area that was devastated by the Dust Bowl in the 1930s. Few areas have suffered the vacillations of the oil industry more than the 3rd, and oil busts chased residents from the area over the years. But since 2005, skyrocketing oil prices have made the small drilling operations that dot the 3rd's landscape profitable, giving people a reason to stay or even move back.

Demand for domestic petroleum has revived oil exploration, and industry demand for workers has exceeded local supply. The growth of high-paying jobs, along with royalties for landowners who allow drilling, has boosted the 3rd's economy. Other area energy interests are renewable energy sources, such as grains for biofuel processing, and wind farms.

The 3rd also depends on crops and livestock, and the district, the state's largest, leads Oklahoma in hogs, cattle, wheat, sorghum and sunflower seeds. The average farm and ranch size here has grown markedly, as agricultural sustainability now requires larger operations than in the past. Always thriving Stillwater, home to Oklahoma State University, brings droves to Boone Pickens Stadium to watch Big 12 football.

Bible Belt conservatism typifies the eastern plains areas north and west of Oklahoma City, while the southern part of the district is home to conservative Democrats who support Democrats for state office. Cimarron, Texas and Beaver counties on the panhandle are the most heavily Republican-voting counties in the state, and George W. Bush topped 80 percent in each of these in the 2004 presidential election. Overall, the 3rd gave Bush 72 percent of its 2004 vote, tops in the state.

MAJOR INDUSTRY
Oil, agriculture, military, higher education

MILITARY BASES
Altus Air Force Base, 2,200 military, 2,384 civilian (2005); Vance Air Force Base, 1,100 military, 150 civilian (2007)

CITIES
Enid, 47,045; Stillwater, 39,065; Ponca City, 25,919; Altus, 21,447

NOTABLE
Roger Mills County on the western border, named in 1892 by referendum, honors U.S. Rep. and later Sen. Roger Q. Mills, who represented neighboring Texas in Congress from 1873 until 1899.

Rep. Tom Cole (R)

CAPITOL OFFICE
225-6165
www.house.gov/cole
236 Cannon 20515-3604; fax 225-3512

COMMITTEES
Armed Services
Natural Resources

RESIDENCE
Moore

BORN
April 28, 1949, Shreveport, La.

RELIGION
Methodist

FAMILY
Wife, Ellen Cole; one child

EDUCATION
Grinnell College, B.A. 1971 (history); Yale U., M.A. 1974 (British history); U. of Oklahoma, Ph.D. 1984 (19th Century British history)

CAREER
Political consultant; party official; congressional district director; professor

POLITICAL HIGHLIGHTS
Okla. Republican Party chairman, 1985-89; Okla. Senate, 1989-91; Okla. secretary of state, 1995-99

ELECTION RESULTS

2006 GENERAL		
Tom Cole (R)	118,266	64.6%
Hal Spake (D)	64,775	35.4%
2006 PRIMARY		
Tom Cole (R)		unopposed
2004 GENERAL		
Tom Cole (R)	198,985	77.8%
Charlene K. Bradshaw (I)	56,869	22.2%

PREVIOUS WINNING PERCENTAGES
2002 (54%)

Elected 2002; 3rd term

Cole is a political being to his core, and his deep party loyalty and prolific fundraising helped earn him the rank-and-file votes to become chairman of the National Republican Congressional Committee (NRCC), the House Republicans' main fundraising arm. His task: help the GOP regain control of Congress in 2008.

An affable, chatty man with a wry sense of humor, Cole has long had his eye on the leadership post, doing what it usually takes to get there: raising money for colleagues in tough races. Between his personal campaign and political action committee Cole shelled out some $800,000 to fellow Republicans for their 2006 races, an impressive sum for a relatively junior lawmaker. Among those who regularly donate to Cole are American Indian tribes, including the 40,000-member Chickasaw Nation, of which he is a member and which operates 12 casinos in Oklahoma.

Cole won the NRCC position in November 2006 on the second ballot of a three-way race with Pete Sessions of Texas and Phil English of Pennsylvania. Focused on ensuring Republicans have enough money for a 2008 comeback effort, he quickly called on House GOP incumbents to pay up and help whittle down the substantial debt the NRCC incurred from the 2006 elections.

His earliest political experiences were with the campaigns of his late mother, Helen Cole, a state legislator. He says he got hooked on the thrill of winning a political race, a feeling akin to being in a locker room after a football victory. He worked as district director for former GOP Rep. Mickey Edwards of Oklahoma, served in the state Senate and was the executive director for the NRCC. In the run-up to the 2000 election, he was chief of staff for the Republican National Committee.

By the time he got to the House as a freshman in 2003, Cole was well acquainted with the top GOP leaders, including then Speaker J. Dennis Hastert. It didn't take long for Hastert to give the savvy former Fulbright scholar a seat on the Armed Services Committee. Cole also was made a deputy whip, helping GOP leaders round up votes for important bills.

In the 109th Congress (2005-06), Cole was given a spot on the Rules Committee, an arm of the leadership that sets the ground rules for debate on legislation. And when Hastert decided to clean house at the ethics committee in 2005 after the panel admonished his close ally, former Majority Leader Tom DeLay, he tapped Cole as one of his replacements for Republicans who had been punished for their independence.

With his move to the NRCC chairmanship, he is off the Rules and ethics panels, but has returned to the seats that he left on the Armed Services and Natural Resources committees at the end of the 108th Congress (2003-04).

Cole is the only American Indian in Congress and his place on Natural Resources has put him in the right spot to look out for tribal rights and land. Cole, whose office is chock-full of tribal masks, books and rugs, has long been a major booster of American Indians, taking up their causes in their disagreements with the federal government. He opposed the Bush administration's proposal to cut Indian programs to pay some $7 million in legal fees as part of a 1996 lawsuit seeking to force the Interior Department to account for funds in individual Indian trust accounts.

One of his first legislative accomplishments was a 2004 law that allowed the city of Sulphur to swap land with the government to allow the Chickasaws to build a cultural center at the edge of a federally protected area. When the Interior Department tried late in the process to ban gaming on the land, Cole said, "It was pretty insulting to the Chickasaws, to spring something on us like that at the last minute — what a microcosm of Indian history."

He also was a defender of tribes in the aftermath of the scandal involving GOP lobbyist Jack Abramoff, who pleaded guilty in January 2006 to bilking tribes of millions of dollars for work he never did. The scandal focused attention on the influx of Indian casino money into congressional lobbying and fundraising in recent years. "This is not the time in my view for tribes to back out of the [political] process," Cole said. "For the first time in 500 years, opportunity is moving toward us, not away from us."

On Armed Services, he applauded President Bush's 2007 plan to send additional troops into Iraq — "Sometimes you just have to suck it up and get it done," he told The Tulsa World newspaper — although he called for benchmarks to ensure the Iraqis were doing their part. He voted against a war funding bill that would have set a deadline for withdrawal of U.S. troops from Iraq.

But in April 2007, as public dismay over the war continued to mount, he criticized the administration for not beefing up the number of troops years ago rather than straining soldiers with extended tours. "It reflects poor planning several years ago," he said.

He grilled Defense Secretary Donald H. Rumsfeld during a 2004 Armed Services hearing into the abuses of Iraqi inmates at the Abu Ghraib prison. He told Rumsfeld the Defense Department was "extraordinarily slow in understanding the implications of what was going on," and asked, "When were you planning to let us know?" Cole says he was motivated partly by memories of an uncle who was abused as a prisoner of war in Japan during World War II. "He weighed 92 pounds when he got out," he recalls. "It scarred him for his whole life."

He also departed from the party line in 2003 when he voted to block a provision of the anti-terrorism law known as the Patriot Act that allows search warrants to be used without warning the subjects in advance.

Cole, whose father was a civilian Air Force employee, was the first in his family to finish college. He earned a master's degree from Yale University and a doctorate from the University of Oklahoma, both in British history. He was a Fulbright fellow at the University of London.

He was a founding partner of Cole, Hargrave, Snodgrass & Associates, a political consulting firm. In 1994, he ran the campaign of friend J.C. Watts Jr. for the 4th District. When Watts retired in 2002, Cole jumped into the race for the seat and defeated former Democratic state Sen. Darryl Roberts with 54 percent of the vote. In 2004, he faced no Democratic opposition and won re-election with 78 percent. He was reelected in 2006 with 65 percent.

KEY VOTES

2006

- No Stop broadband companies from favoring select Internet traffic
- Yes Affirm U.S. commitment to war in Iraq and reject setting a withdrawal date for troops
- Yes Repeal requirement for bilingual ballots at the polls
- Yes Permit U.S. sale of civilian nuclear technology to India
- Yes Build a 700-mile fence on the U.S.-Mexico border to curb illegal crossings
- Yes Permit warrantless wiretaps of suspected terrorists

2005

- Yes Intervene in the life-support case of Terri Schiavo
- No Lift President Bush's restrictions on stem cell research funding
- No Prohibit FBI access to library and bookstore records
- Yes Approve free-trade pact with five Central American countries
- Yes Pass energy policy overhaul favored by President Bush emphasizing domestic oil and gas production
- Yes End mandatory preservation of habitat of endangered animal and plant species
- No Ban torture of prisoners in U.S. custody

CQ VOTE STUDIES

	PARTY UNITY		PRESIDENTIAL SUPPORT	
	Support	Oppose	Support	Oppose
2006	96%	4%	95%	5%
2005	98%	2%	91%	9%
2004	97%	3%	91%	9%
2003	96%	4%	98%	2%

INTEREST GROUPS

	AFL-CIO	ADA	CCUS	ACU
2006	21%	0%	100%	84%
2005	14%	0%	96%	100%
2004	20%	0%	100%	96%
2003	7%	5%	100%	84%

OKLAHOMA 4

South central – Norman, Lawton, part of Oklahoma City

Home to the state's largest university and two military bases, the 4th covers part of Oklahoma City, its southern suburbs, and the western edges of "Little Dixie," so named for its southern influence. Oklahomans flock to Norman for Sooner football games at the University of Oklahoma, whose stadium can hold nearly every resident who lives in Norman.

Military jobs in the 4th expanded during the 1990s, increasing the area's population and enhancing its defense presence. The 2002 Crusader artillery system cancellation hurt Fort Sill and the city of Lawton, which is heavily dependent on the base, but the 2005 BRAC round eased worries about the base's future. The fort is now scheduled to gain thousands of jobs, and the area expects 10,000 new residents by 2011.

The 4th's economy suffered from low oil prices a decade ago, and long-term drought conditions have decimated the region. Still, the oil industry has enjoyed recent price increases, and agriculture remains an essential economic cog. Farms here grow soybeans, cotton, peanuts and wheat.

The 4th echoes the state's GOP preference in national elections. Although once confined to presidential races, the tendency now extends to congressional candidates and state legislators. Democrats remain competitive, especially in the district's rural, southern areas and around the university, although Republicans find strength in other parts of Norman. Overall, George W. Bush received 67 percent of the 4th's vote in the 2004 presidential election.

MAJOR INDUSTRY

Military, higher education, oil, agriculture

MILITARY BASES

Tinker Air Force Base, 6,000 military, 14,000 civilian (2007); Fort Sill (Army), 9,205 military, 6,214 civilian (2007)

CITIES

Norman, 95,694; Lawton, 92,757; Oklahoma City (pt.), 70,896; Midwest City (pt.), 45,044; Moore, 41,138

NOTABLE

The National Oceanic and Atmospheric Administration's National Weather Service Storm Prediction Center is located in Norman; Apache warrior Geronimo was imprisoned at the Fort Sill Military Reservation.

Rep. Mary Fallin (R)

CAPITOL OFFICE
225-2132
fallin.house.gov
1432 Longworth 20515-3605; fax 226-1463

COMMITTEES
Natural Resources
Small Business
Transportation & Infrastructure

RESIDENCE
Oklahoma City

BORN
Dec. 9, 1954, Warrensburg, Mo.

RELIGION
Christian non-denominational

FAMILY
Divorced; two children

EDUCATION
Oklahoma Baptist U., attended 1973-75; Oklahoma State U., B.S. 1977 (family relations and child development); U. of Central Oklahoma, attended 1979-81 (business administration)

CAREER
Real estate broker; hotel properties manager; state tourism agency official

POLITICAL HIGHLIGHTS
Okla. House, 1990-94; lieutenant governor, 1995-2007

ELECTION RESULTS

2006 GENERAL		
Mary Fallin (R)	108,936	60.4%
David Hunter (D)	67,293	37.3%
Matthew Horton Woodson (I)	4,196	2.3%
2006 PRIMARY RUNOFF		
Mary Fallin (R)	26,748	63.1%
Mick Cornett (R)	15,669	36.9%
2006 PRIMARY		
Mary Fallin (R)	16,691	34.6%
Mick Cornett (R)	11,718	24.3%
Denise Bode (R)	9,139	18.9%
Kevin Calvey (R)	4,870	10.1%
Fred Morgan (R)	4,493	9.3%
Johnny B. Roy (R)	1,376	2.9%

Elected 2006; 1st term

Fallin entered the 110th Congress (2007-2008) as one of the most politically seasoned freshmen. After four years in the state House and 12 years as Oklahoma's lieutenant governor, she knows how public policy gets developed and implemented.

Fallin (FAL-in — rhymes with "Allen") can be expected to line up with GOP conservatives on most issues, as she did during her service in Oklahoma and along the campaign trail. She ran under the slogan "Faith, Family, Freedom." She wants to make the Bush-era tax cuts permanent and eliminate earmarks as part of a drive to cut spending and shrink the size of government. She also wants to curb the rising costs of health care and education. During the initial months of the 110th Congress leading up to the spring break, she was one of a dozen Republicans who sided with her party 100 percent of the time on votes pitting the two parties against each other.

Fallin serves on the Small Business Committee, where she has a chance to continue the work she began at the state level pressing for regulatory relief and other help for small-business owners.

Fallin is only the second woman from Oklahoma to serve in Congress; the other was Republican Alice Mary Robertson, who served a single term from 1921-23. No stranger to trailblazing, Fallin was Oklahoma's first female lieutenant governor and the first Republican elected to the position.

Fallin's interest in public service was piqued by her father and mother. Both served as mayor of Tecumseh, a small city about 25 miles southeast of Oklahoma City. "Public service was a family tradition," she says. Her parents were Democrats, but her mother and grandmother switched their party registrations in order to vote for her.

Fallin had planned to run for re-election as lieutenant governor until seven-term Republican Ernest Istook announced he would run for governor in 2006, leaving open his 5th District seat. She finished first in a six-way primary but fell below the threshold necessary to win outright. She easily clinched the nomination in a runoff after winning the backing of four of her primary rivals, and handily defeated Democratic surgeon David Hunter.

OKLAHOMA 5

Most of Oklahoma City

The 5th contains all of downtown Oklahoma City, including the governor's mansion and state Capitol, and is home to several colleges and universities. Oil and gas, along with some agriculture, make up a large chunk of the district's economy. An oil price collapse roughly 20 years ago caused residents to leave the area and forced the city to diversify, but a recent spike in oil prices has brought new growth to the industry.

Local manufacturing has taken hits recently — Bridgestone/Firestone and General Motors closed plants in 2006. But job growth exists in the science and technology fields. Dell Computers opened a customer service center in 2004, and the biosciences sector now employs tens of thousands in the region. The 5th shares some of those jobs with the 3rd and 4th districts, as it does with jobs associated with Tinker Air Force Base, which is in the 4th.

A new arena, restaurants and apartments are revitalizing downtown Oklahoma City. The Bricktown neighborhood, once filled with abandoned warehouses, is now a staple of the city's nightlife. A federal campus opened in 2003 just north of the site of the 1995 bombing of the Alfred P. Murrah Federal Building.

Republicans dominate the 5th. The towns of Shawnee and Seminole, both home to large American Indian populations, and the largely black northeastern portion of Oklahoma City, are not enough to threaten the GOP's hold. George W. Bush took 64 percent of district's vote in the 2004 presidential election.

MAJOR INDUSTRY
Oil, technology, bioscience, government, higher education, agriculture

CITIES
Oklahoma City (pt.), 420,387; Edmond, 68,315

NOTABLE
Seminole County is the historic Seminole Nation territory, accepted by the tribes in exchange for their departure from the Florida Territory.

OREGON

Gov. Theodore R. Kulongoski (D)

Pronounced: koo-long-GOSS-ski
First elected: 2002
Length of term: 4 years
Term expires: 1/11
Salary: $93,600
Phone: (503) 378-3111

Residence: Portland
Born: Nov. 5, 1940; Missouri
Religion: Roman Catholic
Family: Wife, Mary Oberst; three children
Education: U. of Missouri, B.A. 1967 (political science & public administration), J.D. 1970
Military service: Marine Corps, 1960-63
Career: Lawyer
Political highlights: Ore. House, 1975-79; Ore. Senate, 1979-81; Democratic nominee for U.S. Senate, 1980; Democratic nominee for governor, 1982; Ore. insurance commissioner, 1987-91; Ore. attorney general, 1993-97; Ore. Supreme Court, 1997-2001

Election results:

2006 GENERAL		
Theodore R. Kulongoski (D)	699,786	50.7%
Ron Saxton (R)	589,748	42.8%
Mary Starrette (CNSTP)	50,229	3.6%
Joe Keating (GREEN)	20,030	1.5%
Richard Morley (LIBERT)	16,798	1.2%

Secretary of State Bill Bradbury (D)

(no lieutenant governor)
Phone: (503) 986-1523

LEGISLATURE

Legislative Assembly: January-June in odd-numbered years

Senate: 30 members, 4-year terms
2007 ratios: 18 D, 11 R, 1 I; 21 men, 9 women
Salary: $18,408
Phone: (503) 986-1187

House: 60 members, 2-year terms
2007 ratios: 31 D, 29 R; 35 men, 25 women
Salary: $18,408
Phone: (503) 986-1187

TERM LIMITS

Governor: 2 terms
Senate: No
House: No

URBAN STATISTICS

CITY	POPULATION
Portland	529,121
Eugene	137,893
Salem	136,924
Gresham	90,205

REGISTERED VOTERS

Democrat	39%
Republican	36%
Unaffiliated	22%
Others	3%

POPULATION

2006 population (est.)	3,700,758
2000 population	3,421,399
1990 population	2,842,321
Percent change (1990-2000)	+20.4
Rank among states (2006)	27
Median age	36.3
Born in state	45.3%
Foreign born	8.5%
Violent crime rate	351/100,000
Poverty level	11.6%
Federal workers	29,090
Military	12,984

ELECTIONS

STATE ELECTION OFFICIAL
(503) 986-1518
DEMOCRATIC PARTY
(503) 224-8200
REPUBLICAN PARTY
(503) 587-9233

MISCELLANEOUS

Web: www.oregon.gov
Capital: Salem

U.S. CONGRESS

Senate: 1 Democrat, 1 Republican
House: 4 Democrats, 1 Republican

2000 Census Statistics by District

DIST.	2004 VOTE FOR PRESIDENT BUSH	KERRY	WHITE	BLACK	ASIAN	HISP	MEDIAN INCOME	WHITE COLLAR	BLUE COLLAR	SERVICE INDUSTRY	OVER 64	UNDER 18	COLLEGE EDUCATION	RURAL	SQ. MILES
1	44%	55%	81%	1%	5%	9%	$48,464	65%	22%	13%	10%	25%	33%	13%	2,941
2	61	38	86	0	1	9	$35,600	54	29	17	15	26	19	36	69,491
3	32	66	77	5	5	8	$42,063	59	25	16	11	24	25	7	1,021
4	49.0	49.3	90	1	2	4	$35,796	55	28	17	15	23	21	31	17,181
5	50	49	84	1	2	10	$44,409	61	25	15	13	26	27	20	5,362
STATE	47	51	84	2	3	8	$40,916	59	26	15	13	25	25	21	95,997
U.S.	50.7	48.3	69	12	4	13	$41,994	60	25	15	12	26	24	21	3,537,438

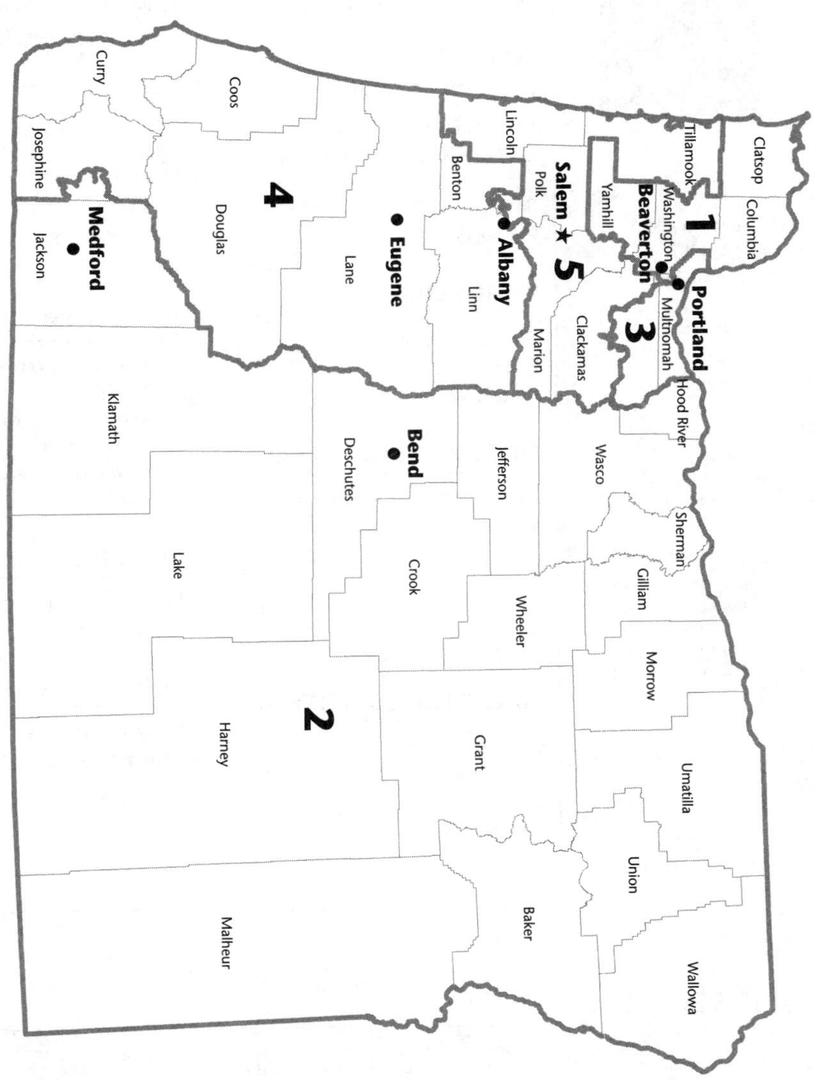
Curry
Coos
Josephine
Jackson
Medford
Douglas
4
Lane
Eugene
Benton
Lincoln
Linn
Albany
Polk
Salem
5
Marion
Yamhill
Clackamas
Tillamook
Washington
Beaverton
1
Clatsop
Columbia
Portland
Multnomah
3
Hood River
Klamath
Deschutes
Bend
Jefferson
Wasco
Sherman
Lake
Crook
Gilliam
Wheeler
Morrow
2
Harney
Grant
Umatilla
Union
Baker
Malheur
Wallowa

Sen. Ron Wyden (D)

CAPITOL OFFICE
224-5244
wyden.senate.gov
223 Dirksen 20510-3703; fax 228-2717

COMMITTEES
Budget
Energy & Natural Resources
(Public Lands & Forests - chairman)
Finance
Select Intelligence
Special Aging

RESIDENCE
Portland

BORN
May 3, 1949, Wichita, Kan.

RELIGION
Jewish

FAMILY
Wife, Nancy Bass-Wyden; two children

EDUCATION
U. of California, Santa Barbara, attended 1967-69; Stanford U., A.B. 1971 (political science); U. of Oregon, J.D. 1974

CAREER
Senior citizen advocacy group state director; lawyer; professor

POLITICAL HIGHLIGHTS
U.S. House, 1981-96

ELECTION RESULTS

2004 GENERAL		
Ron Wyden (D)	1,128,728	63.4%
Al King (R)	565,254	31.8%
Teresa Keane (I)	43,053	2.4%
Dan Fitzgerald (LIBERT)	29,582	1.7%
2004 PRIMARY		
Ron Wyden (D)		unopposed

PREVIOUS WINNING PERCENTAGES
1998 (61%); 1996 Special Election (48%); 1994 House Election (73%); 1992 House Election (77%); 1990 House Election (81%); 1988 House Election (99%); 1986 House Election (86%); 1984 House Election (72%); 1982 House Election (78%); 1980 House Election (72%)

Elected January 1996; 2nd full term

Wyden sides with his party on floor votes, but in his day-to-day work away from the chamber, he likes to find a path around the partisan divide that swallows so much legislation in the Senate. While some of his colleagues cling to their ideological moorings, he cultivates allies from both ends of the political spectrum to advance bills on matters great and small.

For years, he has teamed with conservative Republican Charles E. Grassley of Iowa to force senators who place secret "holds" to block legislation to identify themselves. In 2003, he helped negotiate a compromise version of President Bush's so-called Healthy Forests legislation to combat wildfires. The following year, Wyden worked with Republican George Allen of Virginia to extend a ban on state taxation of Internet access through October 2007. Wyden wrote the original moratorium in 1998, and at the start of the 110th Congress (2007-08), he introduced a bill to make the ban permanent. Eight Republicans and one Democrat were original cosponsors.

Wyden was the keynote speaker at the Consumer Electronics Association's Washington forum in 2007. He has become an acknowledged expert on technology issues, which he enjoys precisely because they do not break along ideological lines. "If ever there were issues that are truly bipartisan," he says, "technology really illustrates the point."

Democratic leaders gave him a coveted seat on the Finance Committee in the 109th Congress (2005-06), and added him to the party's leadership team as a deputy whip in 2007. But he professes no interest in stepping onto the national stage. "I'm not running for president," Wyden said. "I'll be the Senate's designated driver, so that if everybody's out running and folks get a little intoxicated, I can take them home."

The son of a librarian, Wyden approaches issues as a student, mastering some of the most complex issues to come before Congress. While in the House, he was a senior member of the Energy and Commerce Committee, where he developed significant expertise on health care.

He was an advocate of expanding Medicare to cover seniors' prescription drug costs well before the 2003 law was passed. In the 109th Congress, he fought GOP proposals to make deep cuts in Medicaid, the joint federal-state health program for the poor, and championed both the importation of cheaper prescription drugs from abroad and legislation to allow Medicare officials to negotiate lower drug prices for seniors.

In 2007, he worked with business leaders and well-known Republicans to draft a health plan designed to cover all Americans. "I happen to think that the Republicans are right in terms of stressing personal responsibility. The Democrats are absolutely right in saying we've got to get everybody covered," Wyden said in explaining his proposal, which would make individuals responsible for buying health insurance, rather than employers.

He is a foe of the tobacco industry, garnering wide television coverage in 1994 when he asked a panel of tobacco executive witnesses whether they considered tobacco addictive. Under oath, they all denied that it is. He repeated the question in 1998 during Senate Commerce hearings, and four of the five CEOs recanted.

There is one health-related issue unique to Oregon: It is the only state in the country with a law permitting physician-assisted suicide. Wyden considers his vigorous defense of that law his finest hour. He faced an uphill fight in the 106th Congress (1999-2000) after House conservatives easily passed a bill prohibiting doctors from prescribing drugs designed to cause a patient's death, and many senators signaled their support for the measure. But Wyden waged a furious battle to run out the legislative clock in 2000, threatening to filibuster the bill, enlisting the support of influential groups such as the American Cancer Society, and combing through other bills to ensure that no one slipped the House plan into them.

In the 109th Congress, Wyden was again front and center on a right-to-die issue. As a grueling court battle over a severely brain-damaged Florida woman named Terri Schiavo was ending, GOP conservatives pushed a bill through the House designed to restore a feeding tube that had been taken out at her husband's request. The measure authorized the removal to federal courts — after all state remedies were exhausted — of cases such as Schiavo's involving incapacitated people who had not executed an advance directive authorizing the withholding of sustenance. Wyden twice blocked Senate consideration of that measure, relenting only when a compromise was crafted allowing but not requiring federal courts to intervene in the Schiavo case only. They did not, and the 41-year-old woman soon died.

Oregon is the only state in the nation to conduct all its elections by mail. Wyden successfully protected Oregon's unique mail-ballot system from changes when a federal law overhauling voting procedures was enacted at the end of 2002. He introduced a bill in 2007 to create an $18 million grant program to help other states transition to a vote-by-mail system.

During his 15 years in the House, Wyden developed a reputation as something of a media hound. His style has since mellowed, however. "He gets his share of publicity, but he does more than his share of work," said Republican Gordon H. Smith, Oregon's junior senator.

Wyden has forged an unusually close working relationship with Smith, whom he edged in a bitter 1996 Senate special-election contest. (Smith won the state's other Senate seat later that year.) The two senators have a nonaggression pact; they refuse to comment on one another's positions to avoid conflict. They have a standing lunch date on Thursdays, and they serve together on the Finance Committee, making Oregon the only state with two senators on that powerful panel. "We just decided that out of this crucible we had learned a lot about each other," Wyden said. "If anything, we respected each other more for what we had been through."

Their friendship put Wyden in a difficult position in the 2002 election, when Democrats mounted a strong challenge to Smith. Wyden made clear he was happy to campaign for the Democratic candidate, Bill Bradbury, but would not say anything negative about Smith. He'll face the same challenge in 2008, when Smith will again be up for re-election.

Wyden was Oregon executive director for the Gray Panthers, an organization promoting senior citizens' interests, when he first ran for the House in 1980. He ousted Democratic Rep. Robert Duncan in the primary and won with 72 percent in November in a Democratic Portland-based district.

When GOP Sen. Bob Packwood resigned in 1995 rather than face expulsion for personal misconduct, Wyden jumped into the special-election race. Despite some stumbles — most notably on a televised quiz show in which he failed to quote the price of common grocery items — he edged fellow Democratic Rep. Peter A. DeFazio in the primary.

In the general election, the gangly, rumpled Wyden refused to trade in his wrinkled sweaters for natty suits on the campaign trail, despite the urging of his staff. He narrowly defeated Smith by portraying himself as a reasonable-minded alternative to the conservative state Senate president on such issues as education, the environment, revamping Medicare and balancing the budget. He won re-election in 1998 with 61 percent of the vote and in 2004 with 63 percent.

KEY VOTES

2006

No Confirm Samuel A. Alito Jr. to the Supreme Court

No Allow consideration of a bill to establish a $140 billion trust fund to compensate victims of asbestos exposure

No Extend tax cuts for two years at a cost of $70 billion over five years

Yes Overhaul immigration policy with border security, enforcement and guest worker program

No Allow consideration of a bill to permanently repeal the estate tax

Yes Urge President Bush to begin troop withdrawals from Iraq in 2006

Yes Lift President Bush's restrictions on stem cell research funding

No Authorize military tribunals for suspected terrorists

2005

No Curb class action lawsuits by shifting them from state to federal courts

Yes Allow confirmation vote on Priscilla R. Owen to the U.S. Court of Appeals for the 5th Circuit

No Oppose mandatory emissions limits and block recognition of global warming as a threat

Yes Approve free-trade pact with five Central American countries

No Pass energy policy overhaul favored by President Bush emphasizing domestic oil and gas production

No Shield gunmakers from lawsuits when their products are used in crimes

Yes Ban torture of prisoners in U.S. custody

No Renew 16 provisions of the Patriot Act

No Allow final vote on opening the Arctic National Wildlife Refuge to oil and gas exploration

CQ VOTE STUDIES

	PARTY UNITY		PRESIDENTIAL SUPPORT	
	Support	Oppose	Support	Oppose
2006	94%	6%	51%	49%
2005	94%	6%	26%	74%
2004	93%	7%	62%	38%
2003	93%	7%	47%	53%
2002	87%	13%	74%	26%
2001	90%	10%	64%	36%
2000	97%	3%	95%	5%
1999	91%	9%	91%	9%
1998	88%	12%	85%	15%
1997	83%	17%	86%	14%

INTEREST GROUPS

	AFL-CIO	ADA	CCUS	ACU
2006	100%	100%	42%	8%
2005	79%	95%	33%	4%
2004	100%	100%	59%	4%
2003	92%	90%	43%	15%
2002	85%	85%	60%	15%
2001	100%	95%	43%	8%
2000	63%	90%	60%	8%
1999	78%	100%	59%	4%
1998	75%	100%	56%	4%
1997	71%	80%	70%	8%

Sen. Gordon H. Smith (R)

CAPITOL OFFICE
224-3753
gsmith.senate.gov
404 Russell 20510-3704; fax 228-3997

COMMITTEES
Commerce, Science & Transportation
Energy & Natural Resources
Finance
Indian Affairs
Special Aging - ranking member

RESIDENCE
Pendleton

BORN
May 25, 1952, Pendleton, Ore.

RELIGION
Mormon

FAMILY
Wife, Sharon Smith; three children (one deceased)

EDUCATION
Brigham Young U., B.A. 1976 (history); Southwestern U., J.D. 1979

CAREER
Frozen food company owner; lawyer

POLITICAL HIGHLIGHTS
Ore. Senate, 1993-97 (president, 1995-97); Republican nominee for U.S. Senate, 1996 (special election)

ELECTION RESULTS

2002 GENERAL		
Gordon H. Smith (R)	712,287	56.2%
Bill Bradbury (D)	501,898	39.6%
Dan Fitzgerald (LIBERT)	29,979	2.4%
Lon Mabon (CNSTP)	21,703	1.7%
2002 PRIMARY		
Gordon H. Smith (R)	306,504	98.9%
write-ins	3,439	1.1%

PREVIOUS WINNING PERCENTAGES
1996 (50%)

Elected 1996; 2nd term

Smith is moderate, personable and independent, traits that serve him well in his liberal-leaning state. A self-made millionaire who transformed his family's unprofitable frozen vegetable processing company into one of the largest in the country, Smith is also telegenic and fashionable in his tailored double-breasted suits. He's a proud member of the Frozen Food Industry Hall of Fame.

A former Mormon bishop with deep moral convictions, Smith works to ensure that the poor can obtain health care, that homosexuals are treated with respect and that promising medical research is supported by the government. He has broken with most in his party over the Iraq War.

Smith took aim at the problem of uninsured children by offering a successful amendment to the budget resolution in 2007 to allow for an increase in federal cigarette taxes to fund a program to cover some 6 million uninsured children eligible for but not enrolled in a state health insurance program or in Medicaid. "There is nothing more important than providing health care for our nation's children," Smith said in March 2007. "Raising the tobacco tax provides real dollars to get this done. Even if it takes a fight, I think it's one worth fighting."

Smith is one of the few Senate Republicans to vocally oppose the war in Iraq. He and Chuck Hagel of Nebraska were the only two Republicans who voted in March 2007 to keep a provision in a $123 billion supplemental spending bill telling the president when he should start withdrawing U.S. combat troops from Iraq. The bill set a non-binding "goal" of removing most U.S. troops from Iraq by March 31, 2008. Two days later, the Senate passed the spending bill, 51-47, with Hagel and Smith joining all 48 Democrats present and independent Bernard Sanders of Vermont in supporting it.

Smith announced his opposition to the war in December 2006. "I, for one, am at the end of my rope when it comes to supporting a policy that has our soldiers patrolling the same streets in the same way, being blown up by the same bombs day after day. That is absurd. It may even be criminal. I cannot support that anymore," Smith said on the Senate floor. Smith faces a tough re-election fight in 2008: National Democratic Party officials have already announced they are targeting his seat, and he knows well that public support for the war has continued to fade.

On some social issues, Smith will vote with the majority of his party. He is personally opposed to abortion and homosexuality. But he weighs carefully when and how his personal values should shape his policy decisions.

Unlike his party's president, he supports expanding federal funding for medical research on stem cells taken from surplus embryos at in vitro fertilization clinics. Smith has sponsored legislation to expand such research, saying it has remarkable potential for treating deadly genetic diseases, including Parkinson's disease, which runs in his family. "A true 'ethic of life' includes caring for the living," Smith said.

Smith has also confounded some conservatives in his party by joining with Massachusetts Democrat Edward M. Kennedy on a measure to make attacks perpetrated against homosexuals because of their sexual orientation a federal crime. "As a nation founded on the ideals of tolerance and justice, we simply cannot accept violence that is motivated by bias and hate," Smith said in April 2007 when introducing the measure. But in 2004 and again in 2006, he voted in favor of amending the Constitution to prohibit same-sex marriage.

Smith voted in agreement with his party 81 percent of the time on votes that pitted the two parties against each other in the 109th Congress (2005-06). He was among 10 Republicans to have voted most often against their party's majority. He also voted in agreement with President Bush only 81 percent of the time.

Smith sits on the Finance Committee, where his business background has helped him master often obscure but essential details of tax and business policy. During the writing of a corporate tax bill that passed in late 2004, Smith was the chief champion of giving U.S.-based multinationals like Oregon's own Nike a huge one-time tax break if they invest foreign profits back home. Skeptics feared the incentive to "repatriate" foreign profits amounts to a corporate giveaway, but Smith argued the move would create thousands of new U.S. jobs. With a seat on the Commerce, Science and Transportation Committee, he looks out for his state's high-tech industry. And he is the top-ranking Republican on the Special Aging Committee.

Smith's bouts of independence continue a political tradition in Oregon. Voters there sent moderate Republican Sens. Mark Hatfield and Bob Packwood to Washington to give party leaders fits for decades. While Smith can do the same, he does not always bow to the views of his constituents. Torn between representing the will of Oregon voters, who passed a referendum legalizing physician-assisted suicide, and his own belief that human life should not be cut short, Smith announced in 2000 that he would back a bill forbidding doctors to prescribe drugs designed to cause a patient's death.

Smith has faced his own personal tragedy with a death that came too soon. On Sept. 8, 2003, Smith's son Garrett, who suffered from depression, committed suicide one day before his 22nd birthday. Smith has written a book about his son called "Remembering Garrett." And he was the force behind the Garrett Lee Smith Memorial Act passed by Congress to help set up screening programs to identify teenagers who are susceptible to suicide.

On July 8, 2004, Smith took the Senate floor seeking support for the suicide prevention bill. "He was a beautiful child, a handsome baby boy," Smith said, choking back sobs. "His exuberance for life, however, began to dim in his elementary years. . . . There are simply no parental preparations adequate to this crisis in one's child's life, no owner's manual to help you bury a child, especially when the cause is suicide. So I've committed myself to trying to find meaning in Garrett's life." The bill passed unanimously that night and Bush signed the $82 million, three-year Garrett Lee Smith Memorial Act in October 2004.

Smith entered politics in 1992, winning a state Senate seat and then becoming Senate president in just two years. In a bid to move to the U.S. Senate, he battled veteran Democratic Rep. Ron Wyden in a January 1996 special election to replace Republican Bob Packwood, who had to resign because of personal and financial transgressions. Wyden won after attacking Smith for receiving support from groups opposed to abortion and gay rights, for environmental violations at his food processing plant, and for his lavish personal spending.

When Hatfield announced his retirement later that year, Smith initially said he would not run again. But national Republicans urged him into the fray. Easily winning the GOP nod, he managed a 4 percentage point win over Democratic businessman Tom Bruggere. In 2002, Smith beat Oregon Secretary of State Bill Bradbury by more than 16 percentage points.

The bitterness of their 1996 contest faded relatively quickly, and Smith and Wyden now enjoy a good working relationship. The two crisscross Oregon together at the start of each new Congress. "Our natures are to find solutions, not just confrontations," Smith said. "He simply starts from the left. I start from the right."

KEY VOTES

2006

Yes Confirm Samuel A. Alito Jr. to the Supreme Court
Yes Allow consideration of a bill to establish a $140 billion trust fund to compensate victims of asbestos exposure
Yes Extend tax cuts for two years at a cost of $70 billion over five years
Yes Overhaul immigration policy with border security, enforcement and guest worker program
Yes Allow consideration of a bill to permanently repeal the estate tax
No Urge President Bush to begin troop withdrawals from Iraq in 2006
Yes Lift President Bush's restrictions on stem cell research funding
Yes Authorize military tribunals for suspected terrorists

2005

Yes Curb class action lawsuits by shifting them from state to federal courts
Yes Allow confirmation vote on Priscilla R. Owen to the U.S. Court of Appeals for the 5th Circuit
Yes Oppose mandatory emissions limits and block recognition of global warming as a threat
Yes Approve free-trade pact with five Central American countries
Yes Pass energy policy overhaul favored by President Bush emphasizing domestic oil and gas production
\+ Shield gunmakers from lawsuits when their products are used in crimes
Yes Ban torture of prisoners in U.S. custody
Yes Renew 16 provisions of the Patriot Act
Yes Allow final vote on opening the Arctic National Wildlife Refuge to oil and gas exploration

CQ VOTE STUDIES

	PARTY UNITY		PRESIDENTIAL SUPPORT	
	Support	Oppose	Support	Oppose
2006	80%	20%	83%	17%
2005	82%	18%	79%	21%
2004	89%	11%	94%	6%
2003	92%	8%	97%	3%
2002	66%	34%	91%	9%
2001	82%	18%	93%	7%
2000	89%	11%	62%	38%
1999	86%	14%	43%	57%
1998	85%	15%	55%	45%
1997	83%	17%	65%	35%

INTEREST GROUPS

	AFL-CIO	ADA	CCUS	ACU
2006	13%	15%	100%	72%
2005	31%	20%	88%	58%
2004	33%	40%	100%	76%
2003	0%	20%	86%	78%
2002	38%	35%	85%	75%
2001	44%	25%	79%	80%
2000	0%	10%	100%	84%
1999	11%	15%	94%	76%
1998	0%	5%	94%	72%
1997	0%	25%	100%	72%

Rep. David Wu (D)

CAPITOL OFFICE
225-0855
www.house.gov/wu
2338 Rayburn 20515-3701; fax 225-9497

COMMITTEES
Education & Labor
Foreign Affairs
Science & Technology
(Technology & Innovation - chairman)

RESIDENCE
Portland

BORN
April 8, 1955, Hsinchu, Taiwan

RELIGION
Presbyterian

FAMILY
Wife, Michelle Wu; two children

EDUCATION
Stanford U., B.S. 1977; Harvard Medical School, attended 1978; Yale U., J.D. 1982

CAREER
Lawyer

POLITICAL HIGHLIGHTS
No previous office

ELECTION RESULTS

2006 GENERAL		
David Wu (D)	169,409	62.8%
Derrick Kitts (R)	90,904	33.7%
Drake Davis (LIBERT)	4,497	1.7%
Dean Wolf (CNSTP)	4,370	1.6%
2006 PRIMARY		
David Wu (D)	55,188	87.1%
Alexa J. Lewis (D)	4,795	7.6%
Shantu Shah (D)	1,595	2.5%
Pavel Goberman (D)	1,582	2.5%
2004 GENERAL		
David Wu (D)	203,771	57.5%
Goli Ameri (R)	135,164	38.2%
Dean Wolf (I)	13,882	3.9%

PREVIOUS WINNING PERCENTAGES
2002 (63%); 2000 (58%); 1998 (50%)

Elected 1998; 5th term

Born in Taiwan and the first person of full Chinese ancestry to serve in the House, Wu has spent most of his five terms in the House as a quiet backbencher who works tenaciously for his district. He tries to shun the spotlight, but he is not always successful.

He gained statewide publicity in 2005 as the only member of the Oregon delegation to oppose plans for an American Indian gaming casino to be built in the Columbia River Gorge. Wu said he was concerned about the environmental impacts of the casino on the gorge, but others wondered whether he was worried that the proposed casino would be just 45 miles east of Portland and could take business away from a competing one located in Wu's district. But Wu contended that "somebody had to speak up for the gorge." He said on the House floor, "We should not sacrifice our national treasures, our communities or our souls upon the altar of Indian casino gambling."

He also generated some unwelcome headlines when he apologized for intervening in a case of an imprisoned Portland executive. Wu wrote a letter to officials at the U.S. Bureau of Prisons in 2005 asking them to hold off on a plan to transfer inmate Andrew Wiederhorn, whom he called a "friend and constituent," to a Minnesota prison hospital. Wu said Wiederhorn needs special treatment for diabetes and should be sent to a Portland halfway house. Wiederhorn, who had donated thousands of dollars to Wu's campaign, had pleaded guilty to being part of a scheme to conceal massive investment losses from clients and to filing a false tax return.

And Wu got unusual publicity in 2007 by comparing the Bush administration to Star Trek characters. Wu's one-minute speech on the House floor opposing President Bush's plans for a troop increase in Iraq referred to "Rise of the Vulcans," a book about the influence of neoconservatives on Bush's war policy. Wu said the White House advisers are ideologues, unlike Star Trek's Vulcans, "who made their decisions based on logic and fact." Wu then said there are Klingons in the White House. But unlike real Klingons, Wu said, those in the White House "have never fought a battle of their own."

Rush Limbaugh blasted Wu as an "idiot Democrat," and conservative bloggers also called him names. "What's been said of me is that I've always had the lowest profile in the Oregon delegation," Wu told the Oregonian in January 2007. "You know what? This is not the way that I would have chosen to raise my profile."

Wu describes his politics as fiscally conservative and socially liberal. He is a member of the centrist, pro-business New Democrat Coalition, and he will occasionally support GOP measures that favor the business community. He attracted a great deal of attention in 2003, when he cast the last vote during the nearly three-hour roll call in which the House passed the final version of the GOP-drafted bill to add a prescription drug benefit to Medicare. Only after Republican leaders had engineered a victory by switching four GOP votes did Wu cast his ballot in favor of the measure. He was one of just 16 Democrats to vote for the bill. Yet in early 2007, he voted with his entire party in favor of a measure requiring the federal government to negotiate with drug companies the prices of drugs covered under Medicare.

In the 110th Congress (2007-08), Wu sits on the Foreign Affairs Committee where he can continue to address issues involved in U.S. relations with mainland China, including its record on human rights. In the 109th Congress (2005-06), he supported a Republican-sponsored resolution that sanctioned countries that sell arms or defense-related technology to China.

In his 1998 campaign, Wu said he would vote against permanently granting China the same low tariff rates that most other nations enjoy unless its human rights record improved. When the issue came to a vote in 2000, however, many doubted Wu would stick to that position.

He represents part of Oregon's "Silicon Forest," which is heavily dependent on the success of Pacific Rim trade. And he is a former partner in a law firm that represented high-tech businesses on issues including trade. But Wu stuck by his campaign promise. Not only did he vote against the legislation, but he also helped opponents try to defeat it. Wu's decision so angered the computer-chip behemoth Intel Corp. and the athletic shoe giant Nike Inc. that both gave money to his 2000 opponent.

Wu also sits on the Science and Technology Committee, where he is the chairman of the Technology and Innovation Subcommittee. He says he wants to update the nation's technology transfer laws.

Wu arrived in the United States with his mother and sisters in 1961, when he was 6 years old. The family joined Wu's father, who had come to this country to study when Wu was four months old.

Addressing the 2000 Democratic National Convention, Wu said he became involved in public life because of the difference government decisions had made to his family. He said that his family had been able to move to the United States because President John F. Kennedy had expanded quotas previously used to limit the number of Chinese immigrants.

Wu had never held public office when Democrat Elizabeth Furse's retirement opened up a House seat in 1998. He was well-known in the Portland legal and business communities and was able to edge past Washington County Commission Chairman Linda Peters in the Democratic primary. In the general election, the district's Democratic leanings lifted Wu to a 3 percentage point victory over public relations consultant Molly Bordonaro.

In 2004, three weeks before the Nov. 2 election, the Portland Oregonian published a story saying that as a Stanford University student in 1976, Wu "was brought to the campus police annex after his ex-girlfriend said he tried to force her to have sex." The woman did not seek criminal prosecution nor file a formal disciplinary complaint, the newspaper said.

Wu issued an apology the same day. Portland-area voters apparently viewed the story as a cheap shot. Wu won re-election comfortably over Iranian immigrant and local businesswoman Goli Ameri.

His 2006 opponent, state GOP Rep. Derrick Kitts, claimed Wu's positions on trade and other issues were out of sync with the district. But Wu won easily with 63 percent of the vote.

KEY VOTES

2006

- Yes Stop broadband companies from favoring select Internet traffic
- No Affirm U.S. commitment to war in Iraq and reject setting a withdrawal date for troops
- No Repeal requirement for bilingual ballots at the polls
- No Permit U.S. sale of civilian nuclear technology to India
- No Build a 700-mile fence on the U.S.-Mexico border to curb illegal crossings
- No Permit warrantless wiretaps of suspected terrorists

2005

- No Intervene in the life-support case of Terri Schiavo
- Yes Lift President Bush's restrictions on stem cell research funding
- Yes Prohibit FBI access to library and bookstore records
- No Approve free-trade pact with five Central American countries
- No Pass energy policy overhaul favored by President Bush emphasizing domestic oil and gas production
- No End mandatory preservation of habitat of endangered animal and plant species
- Yes Ban torture of prisoners in U.S. custody

CQ VOTE STUDIES

	PARTY UNITY		PRESIDENTIAL SUPPORT	
	Support	Oppose	Support	Oppose
2006	92%	8%	23%	77%
2005	92%	8%	29%	71%
2004	90%	10%	38%	62%
2003	90%	10%	33%	67%
2002	88%	12%	42%	58%

INTEREST GROUPS

	AFL-CIO	ADA	CCUS	ACU
2006	100%	90%	33%	12%
2005	93%	100%	50%	8%
2004	87%	90%	55%	12%
2003	80%	90%	37%	16%
2002	89%	95%	45%	16%

OREGON 1

Western Portland and suburbs; Beaverton

Nestled on the western bank of the Willamette River, Portland's "Silicon Forest" hums with companies assembling computer components. The 1st District combines three distinct parts: The booming western Portland suburbs; a northern section that follows the Columbia River to the Pacific Ocean and relies on traditional outdoor industries; and a southern portion that extends to take in all of Yamhill County and its part of the Willamette Valley's wine region.

Washington County, which accounts for 65 percent of the district's population, has a highly educated workforce and is the economic engine for the 1st. Aided by a light-rail line that stretches to Hillsboro, towns that were once bedroom communities have turned into satellite cities with their own streams of commuters. The populations of Hillsboro, Beaverton and suburbs farther west have exploded since 1990, with Hillsboro more than doubling in residents. East of Washington, the 1st's portion of Portland includes the historic and bustling Pearl District neighborhood.

Outside the Portland metro area, the 1st is struggling to keep its traditional logging and fishing industries intact. The constant battle between loggers and environmentalists has dampened forestry, and salmon stocks are dwindling due to excessive harvests and hydroelectric dams. State officials are working to transition workers in both fields to emerging industries in the area. Electronics, vineyards and nurseries now lead the 1st's economy, and tourism and the remnants of the timber industry round out much of the job market. With a number of large businesses in the district, international trade is a hot issue.

Washington County epitomizes the 1st's competitiveness — John Kerry won the county with 52 percent of the vote in the 2004 presidential election. Democrats do well in Multnomah and in the far northern counties of Clatsop and Columbia, while the GOP has the edge in Yamhill. Overall, Kerry took the 1st with 55 percent of the vote.

MAJOR INDUSTRY
Electronics, computer manufacturing, wine production, nurseries

CITIES
Beaverton, 76,129; Portland (pt.), 74,097; Hillsboro, 70,186; Aloha (unincorporated), 41,741; Tigard, 41,223

NOTABLE
Nike is headquartered in Beaverton.

Rep. Greg Walden (R)

CAPITOL OFFICE
225-6730
www.walden.house.gov
1210 Longworth 20515-3702; fax 225-5774

COMMITTEES
Energy & Commerce
Select Energy Independence & Global Warming

RESIDENCE
Hood River

BORN
Jan. 10, 1957, The Dalles, Ore.

RELIGION
Episcopalian

FAMILY
Wife, Mylene Walden; two children (one deceased)

EDUCATION
U. of Alaska, Fairbanks, attended 1974-75;
U. of Oregon, B.S. 1981 (journalism)

CAREER
Radio station owner; congressional aide

POLITICAL HIGHLIGHTS
Ore. House, 1989-95 (majority leader, 1991-93);
Ore. Senate, 1995-97 (assistant majority leader, 1995-97)

ELECTION RESULTS

2006 GENERAL		
Greg Walden (R)	181,529	66.8%
Carol Voisin (D)	82,484	30.4%
Jack Alan Brown (CNSTP)	7,193	2.6%
2006 PRIMARY		
Greg Walden (R)	70,519	90.2%
Paul A. Daghlian (R)	7,401	9.5%
2004 GENERAL		
Greg Walden (R)	248,461	71.6%
John C. McColgan (D)	88,914	25.6%
Jim Lindsay (LIBERT)	4,792	1.4%
Jack Alan Brown (I)	4,060	1.2%

PREVIOUS WINNING PERCENTAGES
2002 (72%); 2000 (74%); 1998 (61%)

Elected 1998; 5th term

The 2nd District includes more forests than any other district in the nation, and Walden has made forest management a focal point of his congressional career. He is also willing and able to work with Democrats to pass measures that benefit his sprawling district, which includes at least part of 10 national forests.

In 2003, he coordinated a bipartisan push to get what he called a Healthy Forests measure through Congress, which authorized logging and other steps to thin forests on public lands to reduce wildfires.

Yet as chairman of the Resources Subcommittee on Forests and Forest Health in the 109th Congress (2005-06), Walden was stymied in his efforts to pass another forestry bill to accelerate salvage logging and cleanup of federal lands hit by wildfires, hurricanes and natural disasters. The measure also would have allowed agencies to bypass standard environmental review procedures by pre-approving cleanup plans. Walden reasoned that well-managed forests help combat global warming because wildfires, which release carbon and other greenhouse gases, are less likely. The provisions drew criticism from some Democrats and environmentalists who said it would allow agencies to offer approvals for salvage logging before proper evaluations were completed. Although the bill passed in the House in May 2006, "it just went into the dumpster in the Senate," Walden said.

The federal government also owns more than half the land in the 2nd, and Walden's constituents are not happy when the government restricts how they can use the land. Walden has called the area he represents "a district under siege by federal policies." He has repeatedly pushed legislation to require reviews by outside scientists before the government makes decisions about endangered animals and plants and to encourage federal agencies to consider input from affected landowners before adding new species to those protected by the Endangered Species Act.

But the district is also gaining jobs because of recreational tourism, and Walden and his Oregon Democratic colleague Earl Blumenauer have sponsored a bill to declare 77,000 acres of the Mount Hood National Forest as wilderness, making it off-limits to timber companies and developers. "Most of my party doesn't get up every morning and say, 'How do I add to the wilderness?'" Walden told the Portland Oregonian in August 2006.

In the 110th Congress (2007-08), Walden will spend his time trying to renew a 2000 law that provides a formula for rural counties that receive revenue-sharing payments for being home to U.S. Forest Service and Bureau of Land Management lands. The federal government compensates those counties that lose tax money because the government owns large portions of land. The payments are used to help finance schools and roads.

In the 1990s, the principal source of those revenues, federal timber sales, declined by more than 70 percent nationwide. Oregon's county budgets were hit particularly hard. The 2000 law established a six-year payment formula for counties that receive the revenue-sharing payments. The act expired in September 2006, and without reauthorization Oregon would lose nearly $280 million a year from the funding. Walden and Oregon Democrat Peter A. DeFazio teamed up in 2005 to sponsor a measure to reauthorize the act for seven years. The bill never moved in the 109th Congress, and the two reintroduced it on the first day of the new Congress. Walden has called the measure his No. 1 priority in the 110th Congress.

Walden also has made it a priority to rid his district and state of the manufactured drug called methamphetamine. He said that in 2004 his district had 20 percent of Oregon's population but 35 percent of meth lab seizures. He joined with President Bush in 2006 as the president signed legislation that included new controls on cold-medicine ingredients that are used to brew methamphetamine and new penalties for people who run meth labs.

Like most Westerners, Walden opposes gun control laws, but he has adopted a middle-ground position on abortion. He opposes federal funding for abortions and voted to outlaw a procedure its opponents call "partial birth" abortion. But he does not support a reversal of the Supreme Court's *Roe v. Wade* decision establishing the right to abortion, saying the decision of whether to have an abortion should be left to the individual. He says his views on that question were shaped after 1993, when he and his wife, Mylene, considered but rejected aborting a fetus diagnosed with a congenital heart defect. The baby boy was born prematurely and died.

Raised on an 80-acre cherry orchard property, Walden worked at his father's radio station in Hood River. He developed his own broadcast voice as a disc jockey and talk-show host, and later bought the business with his wife. Their company, Columbia Gorge Broadcasters Inc., operated five radio stations before he sold the enterprise in January 2007. Walden's father served in the Oregon legislature and his mother volunteered for the Red Cross. "Watching what they did instilled in me pretty early that you have an obligation to your community as well as your family," he says.

Walden was introduced to politics working as an aide to GOP Rep. Denny Smith of Oregon for about five years in the 1980s. But his own low-key, consensus-seeking style developed during eight years in the state legislature, including three years as House majority leader and two as assistant Senate majority leader. In temperament, he more closely resembles another Republican from Oregon named Smith: his predecessor, Bob Smith.

Walden threatened to run for the House as an independent in 1996 against Republican Rep. Wes Cooley, who had been accused of lying about his military record in a voter pamphlet after winning the GOP primary two years earlier. But Bob Smith was lured out of retirement with the promise of the Agriculture Committee chairmanship. When he agreed to run, both Walden and Cooley bowed out.

Smith again decided to retire in 1998, and Walden became the front-runner. He won the primary handily, then easily bested Democrat Kevin M. Campbell, a former county judge, in the heavily GOP district. His closest race since was the most recent, in 2006, when he took 67 percent of the vote to defeat Democrat Carol Voisin, a Southern Oregon University instructor.

KEY VOTES

2006

No Stop broadband companies from favoring select Internet traffic
Yes Affirm U.S. commitment to war in Iraq and reject setting a withdrawal date for troops
Yes Repeal requirement for bilingual ballots at the polls
Yes Permit U.S. sale of civilian nuclear technology to India
Yes Build a 700-mile fence on the U.S.-Mexico border to curb illegal crossings
Yes Permit warrantless wiretaps of suspected terrorists

2005

? Intervene in the life-support case of Terri Schiavo
Yes Lift President Bush's restrictions on stem cell research funding
Yes Prohibit FBI access to library and bookstore records
Yes Approve free-trade pact with five Central American countries
Yes Pass energy policy overhaul favored by President Bush emphasizing domestic oil and gas production
Yes End mandatory preservation of habitat of endangered animal and plant species
Yes Ban torture of prisoners in U.S. custody

CQ VOTE STUDIES

	PARTY UNITY		PRESIDENTIAL SUPPORT	
	Support	Oppose	Support	Oppose
2006	93%	7%	87%	13%
2005	92%	8%	80%	20%
2004	93%	7%	82%	18%
2003	92%	8%	94%	6%
2002	95%	5%	90%	10%

INTEREST GROUPS

	AFL-CIO	ADA	CCUS	ACU
2006	31%	15%	100%	80%
2005	20%	20%	93%	76%
2004	27%	15%	100%	80%
2003	13%	15%	96%	76%
2002	11%	5%	100%	96%

OREGON 2

East and Southwest – Medford, Bend

Hostility toward the federal government makes the rural and sometimes rugged 2nd Oregon's most reliably Republican district. It covers the eastern two-thirds of the state — bordering Washington, Idaho, Nevada and California. The federal government owns most of the land, which has fertile fields, towering mountains and protected forests.

The strength of the local agriculture industry lies in its diversity. The district's southeast is home to the state's heartiest livestock region, while its north harvests more bushels of wheat than anywhere else in Oregon. From the district's northwest near Mount Hood to the Rogue River Valley in southern Oregon is a rich fruit belt: almost all of the state's pears are grown either in Jackson County or Hood River County, which leads the nation in pear production. Cherries and apples are grown here as well.

The 2nd's timber and fishing industries have been hindered for decades by federal habitat and species protections. The economic difficulties caused by these restrictions drove people away from the region in the 1980s, but an influx of retirees and a growing tourism industry have attracted newcomers. The 2nd's part of Hells Canyon in the northeast (shared with Idaho) is a magnet for tourists. Crater Lake National Park and Upper Klamath Lake, both in Klamath County, also attract visitors.

Medford, in Jackson County, is the 2nd's largest city and is a health care hub for southern Oregon. Health facilities here employ thousands of residents. Less than 20 miles southeast of Medford is Ashland, which has hosted the Oregon Shakespeare Festival since 1935.

In the 2004 presidential election, George W. Bush won 19 of the 20 counties wholly or partly within the 2nd — Hood River County was the exception — and Bush's top five Oregon counties were here. Democrats are scattered in parts of Ashland and Bend, and are too few to swing the 2nd. Overall, Bush took 61 percent of the district's 2004 presidential vote.

MAJOR INDUSTRY

Agriculture, forestry, tourism

CITIES

Medford, 63,154; Bend, 52,029; Grants Pass, 23,003; Altamont (unincorporated), 19,603; Ashland, 19,522; Klamath Falls, 19,462

NOTABLE

Crater Lake is the deepest lake in the United States.

Rep. Earl Blumenauer (D)

CAPITOL OFFICE
225-4811
blumenauer.house.gov
2267 Rayburn 20515-3703; fax 225-8941

COMMITTEES
Budget
Select Energy Independence & Global Warming
Ways & Means

RESIDENCE
Portland

BORN
Aug. 16, 1948, Portland, Ore.

RELIGION
Unspecified

FAMILY
Wife, Margaret Kirkpatrick; two children

EDUCATION
Lewis and Clark College, B.A. 1970 (political science), J.D. 1976

CAREER
Public official

POLITICAL HIGHLIGHTS
Ore. House, 1973-77; Multnomah County Commission, 1978-86; candidate for Portland City Council, 1980; Portland City Council, 1986-96; candidate for mayor of Portland, 1992

ELECTION RESULTS

2006 GENERAL		
Earl Blumenauer (D)	186,380	73.5%
Bruce Broussard (R)	59,529	23.5%
David Brownlow (CNSTP)	7,003	2.8%
2006 PRIMARY		
Earl Blumenauer (D)	63,350	90.7%
John Sweeney (D)	6,338	9.1%
2004 GENERAL		
Earl Blumenauer (D)	245,559	70.9%
Tami Mars (R)	82,045	23.7%
Walter F. "Walt" Brown (S)	10,678	3.1%
Dale Winegarden (I)	7,119	2.1%

PREVIOUS WINNING PERCENTAGES
2002 (67%); 2000 (67%); 1998 (84%); 1996 (67%); 1996 Special Election (70%)

Elected May 1996; 6th full term

An ardent longtime supporter of the environmental movement, Blumenauer has shown a canny ability to work with Republicans to steer legislative proposals through Congress even under GOP rule. In the 110th Congress (2007-08), with his party in the majority, he is in an even better position to influence the growing debate on global warming — an issue he takes on personally every day — and to protect the interests of his port-city district.

Blumenauer (BLUE-men-hour) gained a coveted seat on the Ways and Means Committee in 2007, where he has a greater voice in tax and trade issues, including those related to environmental policy. House Speaker Nancy Pelosi of California picked Blumenauer to serve on a new committee charged with investigating global warming issues and making recommendations for legislation.

Blumenauer, the second-ranking Democrat on the Select Committee on Energy Independence and Global Warming, has long advocated reducing greenhouse gases that contribute to global warming. He is an avid runner and cyclist who refuses to own a car in Washington. Wearing his trademark bow ties, he bikes to his Capitol Hill office from his nearby apartment and cycles to meetings at the White House on a burnt-orange Trek-brand mountain bike called the Portland.

One of the first things he did when he entered Congress in 1996 was create a bike caucus, encouraging the use of bicycles rather than cars as a way to exercise as well as to reduce fossil fuel emissions. He used the caucus, and his seat on the Transportation and Infrastructure Committee from 1997 to 2006, to shepherd billions of dollars for bicycle trails, pedestrian facilities, mass transit systems and historic preservation. Also looking out for his district, he secured federal money for Portland to build a 5.8-mile Interstate Max light-rail line extension between downtown and the Columbia River, which opened in 2004.

Early in 2007, he voted for passage of a bill that would raise taxes on the oil industry and recoup offshore drilling royalties lost due to faulty government leases. He also proposed legislation providing an investment tax credit to individuals to offset the upfront cost of installing a wind turbine to create clean, renewable energy. He has reintroduced a bill to amend the tax code to allow employers to offer their employees a bicycle commuting allowance. And he said he would push for the creation of a panel of experts to review the tax code and identify activities that impact carbon emissions.

Under GOP rule, Blumenauer showed a willingness to avoid the shrill partisanship that typically stymies legislative consensus — and he saw some successes. In 2006, he and conservative Oregon Republican Greg Walden produced a bill adding 77,500 acres to protected wilderness areas around Mount Hood after the two took a 41-mile hike together on the Timberline Trail circumnavigating the mountain. They also met with experts in geology, forestry, wilderness and climatology, prompting an admiring editorial in the Portland Oregonian newspaper.

In 2004, Blumenauer saw years of bipartisan persistence pay off when President Bush signed his "Two Floods and You're Out" bill, which discourages homeowners from rebuilding in flood-ravaged areas to avert repeated claims on the federal flood insurance program.

In 2005, he teamed with Arizona Republican Jeff Flake in a fruitless attempt to put economic strictures on a $3.4 billion locks and dams project on the Upper Mississippi and Illinois rivers. Blumenauer said the project showed poor priorities in water projects. "Now, after Katrina, it kind of drives that point home, where we spend hundreds of millions of dollars on the wrong stuff and leave communities at risk," he said.

Blumenauer also found common ground with the GOP on trade issues. In 2005, he was one of 21 Democrats who voted against blocking the sale of U.S. oil giant Unocal to a company owned by the Chinese government. In both cases, the companies backed out of the transactions. In 2006, he was one of only eight Democrats to vote against barring the sale of facilities at six major U.S. ports to a company owned by the United Arab Emirates.

On more-traditional trade issues, Blumenauer chooses his path carefully. He voted for the 2000 law making permanent normal U.S. trade relations with China, noting that one in five jobs in his district was tied to trade with the Pacific Rim. But in 2002, he opposed the revival of fast-track trade negotiating authority for the president. By 2003, he was helping round up House votes for a free-trade agreement with Chile and voting for trade pacts with Singapore, Australia and Morocco. In 2005 and 2006, he lined up with his fellow Democrats against the Central American Free Trade Agreement and a pact with Oman, but voted for an agreement with Bahrain.

When it comes to the war in Iraq, he sticks close with his party. He voted against going to war and in remarks at the World Affairs Council in Portland just weeks after the 2002 vote, he predicted the United States would become bogged down in Iraq by outbreaks of violence, recrimination and revenge that "could unleash a chain of events which would make Iraq's neighbors and the United States long for the relative stability of the last 15 years." He said in 2006, "I have never felt so bad about being right about something."

An activist since his teens, Blumenauer was just one year out of college in 1971 when he testified before Congress in support of a constitutional amendment to lower the voting age to 18. Elected to the state House at 24, in four years he rose to chair the Revenue Committee. He then spent eight years on the Multnomah County Commission, followed by 10 years on the Portland City Council, where he was instrumental in establishing Portland's ambitious land-use planning procedures to control metropolitan sprawl.

He ran unsuccessfully for mayor of Portland in 1992, but won a 1996 special election to the House. The 3rd District seat was vacant after Democrat Ron Wyden won a special Senate election to replace Republican Bob Packwood, who had resigned the previous fall. Blumenauer easily took the primary and cruised through the general election. He has won easily ever since. Blumenauer briefly contemplated challenging GOP Sen. Gordon H. Smith in the 2008 election but opted against it.

KEY VOTES

2006

Yes Stop broadband companies from favoring select Internet traffic

No Affirm U.S. commitment to war in Iraq and reject setting a withdrawal date for troops

No Repeal requirement for bilingual ballots at the polls

No Permit U.S. sale of civilian nuclear technology to India

No Build a 700-mile fence on the U.S.-Mexico border to curb illegal crossings

No Permit warrantless wiretaps of suspected terrorists

2005

? Intervene in the life-support case of Terri Schiavo

Yes Lift President Bush's restrictions on stem cell research funding

Yes Prohibit FBI access to library and bookstore records

No Approve free-trade pact with five Central American countries

No Pass energy policy overhaul favored by President Bush emphasizing domestic oil and gas production

No End mandatory preservation of habitat of endangered animal and plant species

Yes Ban torture of prisoners in U.S. custody

CQ VOTE STUDIES

	PARTY UNITY		PRESIDENTIAL SUPPORT	
	Support	Oppose	Support	Oppose
2006	97%	3%	8%	92%
2005	97%	3%	11%	89%
2004	93%	7%	23%	77%
2003	95%	5%	20%	80%
2002	96%	4%	25%	75%

INTEREST GROUPS

	AFL-CIO	ADA	CCUS	ACU
2006	93%	90%	27%	8%
2005	93%	100%	37%	4%
2004	93%	95%	26%	9%
2003	87%	100%	27%	16%
2002	100%	100%	35%	4%

OREGON 3

North and east Portland; eastern suburbs

Split by the Willamette River, the city of Portland has two personalities. The eastern portion, covered by the 3rd, still depends on the blue-collar economy that made the city a thriving international port for lumber and fruit. The Port of Portland and Portland International Airport make the city a leading center of trade and distribution. Computer chips and cappuccino drive the city's western side (in the 1st and 5th districts).

Area sports fans watch basketball's Trailblazers at the riverfront Rose Garden arena, and the city's many breweries are well-known havens for beer enthusiasts. The 3rd's portion of Portland takes in the University of Portland and several hospitals that drive the local health care industry.

The 3rd's second-largest city, Gresham, was once a thriving farm community. It is now the easternmost stop on Portland's light-rail system and is growing. Beyond the Portland metropolitan area, the district quickly turns rural. Its far eastern border reaches Mount Hood — Oregon's highest peak at 11,239 feet — and the Mount Hood National Forest in the western part of the Cascade Range.

Compared with the rest of Portland, the 3rd is a multicultural haven. There is a large black population in precincts just east of the Willamette River, near Interstate 5 and Martin Luther King Jr. Blvd. A sizable Hispanic population resides in northeastern Portland and in Gresham and Wood Village east of the city. Asians are numerous in east-central Portland, near 82nd Avenue and Interstate 205.

Portland's liberal leanings make the 3rd Oregon's most staunchly Democratic district. John Kerry won 71 percent of the 3rd's share of Multnomah County in the 2004 presidential election. George W. Bush narrowly won the district's portion of Clackamas County, which is more rural and politically competitive, but any Republican strength there is not large enough to weaken Portland's strong Democratic slant. Overall, Kerry took 66 percent of the 3rd's vote.

MAJOR INDUSTRY

Wholesale trade and distribution, health care, education, manufacturing

CITIES

Portland (pt.), 432,388; Gresham, 90,205; Milwaukie, 20,490

NOTABLE

"The Simpsons" creator Matt Groening grew up in Portland — perhaps coincidentally, many of his characters share the names of local streets.

Rep. Peter A. DeFazio (D)

CAPITOL OFFICE
225-6416
www.house.gov/defazio
2134 Rayburn 20515-3704; fax 225-0032

COMMITTEES
Homeland Security
Natural Resources
Transportation & Infrastructure
(Highways & Transit - chairman)

RESIDENCE
Springfield

BORN
May 27, 1947, Needham, Mass.

RELIGION
Roman Catholic

FAMILY
Wife, Myrnie L. Daut

EDUCATION
Tufts U., B.A. 1969 (economics & political science); U. of Oregon, attended 1969-71 (international studies), M.S. 1977 (public administration & gerontology)

MILITARY SERVICE
Air Force, 1967-71

CAREER
Congressional aide

POLITICAL HIGHLIGHTS
Lane County Commission, 1982-86; sought Democratic nomination for U.S. Senate (special election), 1996

ELECTION RESULTS

2006 GENERAL		
Peter A. DeFazio (D)	180,607	62.2%
Jim Feldkamp (R)	109,105	37.6%
2006 PRIMARY		
Peter A. DeFazio (D)		unopposed
2004 GENERAL		
Peter A. DeFazio (D)	228,611	61.0%
Jim Feldkamp (R)	140,882	37.6%

PREVIOUS WINNING PERCENTAGES
2002 (64%); 2000 (68%); 1998 (70%); 1996 (66%); 1994 (67%); 1992 (71%); 1990 (86%); 1988 (72%); 1986 (54%)

Elected 1986; 11th term

One of the House's most liberal members, DeFazio loves to taunt Republicans about easy re-elections from a district that twice this decade split its presidential vote evenly between the two parties. His durability also led to a prized subcommittee gavel when his party won a House majority in the past election. He is the new chairman of the Highways and Transit Subcommittee of the Transportation and Infrastructure Committee.

"Twenty years in Congress and I finally get to wield a gavel," DeFazio (da-FAH-zee-o) told the Portland Oregonian newspaper.

The subcommittee may not have much sex appeal, but it is the perfect spot for fulfilling the bringing-home-the-bacon aspect of a congressman's job. It drafts the multibillion-dollar highway bills that Congress enacts every few years; the next one is scheduled for 2009. DeFazio secured $200 million to fix bridges along Interstate 5 in Oregon in the last major highway bill in 2005. "I got the single largest allocation for a Democrat," he says of the subcommittee then controlled by the GOP.

DeFazio has pushed a liberal, populist agenda since the day he arrived in Congress in 1987. He is loud, persistent and viewed by his critics as a smart aleck — characteristics that earned him a reputation as "long on straight talk and short on political rhetoric," according to The World newspaper of Coos Bay.

A member of the Progressive Caucus, a group of about 70 of the most liberal House members, DeFazio seems to connect not only with the liberals in the urban parts of his district but also with more-conservative voters in the 4th District's rural reaches. He hasn't polled less than 60 percent of the vote since his first race. He drives a 1968 Plymouth Barracuda convertible around Oregon and wears jeans and khakis when he meets with constituents.

He has been especially outspoken in opposing free-trade agreements. He opposed normalizing trade relations with China in 2000 and a free-trade pact in 2005 with five Central American countries, asserting that they lead to shuttered factories and jobless workers. "Our trade policy's a disaster, plain and simple," DeFazio says. "How are you going to be a great nation if you don't make things anymore?"

He was an early opponent of the war in Iraq, and also an ardent advocate for National Guard troops called up to serve in Iraq. After hearing disturbing stories about the housing conditions and shortages of supplies at Fort Hood in Texas, where many Oregon National Guard units trained before going abroad, DeFazio and Democrat Darlene Hooley of Oregon's 5th District visited the base. They found health-threatening molds in barracks, unreliable food service and supply shortages so severe that troops were using their own money to buy radios, computers and cleaning supplies.

"The attitude that the National Guard is inferior to the regular Army and can make do with second-rate equipment has to change. . . . They serve in the same hostile environments and must have the training, equipment and support they need to accomplish their mission and return home safe and sound," DeFazio and Hooley wrote in a 2003 letter to then Defense Secretary Donald H. Rumsfeld. DeFazio said most of the problems were remedied after their complaints.

He is also engaged on the Natural Resources Committee, where DeFazio often faces a juggling act on forest issues. His constituency includes two groups with conflicting interests on those issues — loggers, who oppose curbs on timber cutting, and environmentalists who want restrictions. The competing pressures were evident in 2003, when DeFazio first opposed a sweeping forest-thinning bill championed by Oregon Republican Greg Walden, then voted for a final version that was significantly altered in the Senate at Oregon Democrat Ron Wyden's insistence.

DeFazio often teams up with Walden to protect Oregon's interests on public lands issues. The two represent most of the state outside of the populated northwest corner and, even though Walden is the sole Republican in Oregon's House delegation, they work well together. DeFazio and Walden fought efforts by the Bush administration to force the federally owned Bonneville Power Administration, headquartered in Portland, to charge higher rates for its electricity as a deficit-trimming step.

DeFazio is active on security issues from his seat on the Homeland Security Committee. After the Sept. 11 terrorist attacks, he led the House Democrats' campaign against GOP efforts to retain private contract workers as airport screeners. The aviation security law ultimately enacted not only federalized the baggage screeners but also made a number of other security changes that DeFazio had been urging for years.

DeFazio grew up in Massachusetts. His first taste of politics came as a boy at the knee of his great-uncle, Jerimiah Crowley, a classic Boston pol who followed the word "Republican" with the Boston-accented epithet "bastuhd" so often that for a long time young DeFazio thought it was one word — "Republicanbastuhd."

His father was a teacher and a coach who also ran a camp on Cape Cod, where DeFazio spent summers working as a golf caddy.

DeFazio first moved to Oregon to attend the University of Oregon. While a student there, he established a seniors employment program still in existence. After earning a graduate degree in gerontology, he ran a senior citizens' program for a time, then landed a job as a specialist on elder issues with Democratic U.S. Rep. James Weaver, a hot-tempered populist.

In 1982, DeFazio struck out on his own, getting elected to the Lane County Commission. He earned a reputation for aggressiveness by suing to nullify contracts between Oregon utilities and the Washington Public Power Supply System, whose failed nuclear projects resulted in rate increases.

When Weaver announced he would not seek re-election in 1986, DeFazio stepped in. Casting himself as heir to Weaver's populist mantle, he squeaked by in the primary, won the seat with 54 percent and has held it safely since. In 2004 and 2006, DeFazio faced Republican Jim Feldkamp, a U.S. Navy veteran and former FBI agent. DeFazio won each race with more than 60 percent of the vote.

KEY VOTES

2006

Yes Stop broadband companies from favoring select Internet traffic

No Affirm U.S. commitment to war in Iraq and reject setting a withdrawal date for troops

No Repeal requirement for bilingual ballots at the polls

No Permit U.S. sale of civilian nuclear technology to India

Yes Build a 700-mile fence on the U.S.-Mexico border to curb illegal crossings

No Permit warrantless wiretaps of suspected terrorists

2005

? Intervene in the life-support case of Terri Schiavo

Yes Lift President Bush's restrictions on stem cell research funding

Yes Prohibit FBI access to library and bookstore records

No Approve free-trade pact with five Central American countries

No Pass energy policy overhaul favored by President Bush emphasizing domestic oil and gas production

No End mandatory preservation of habitat of endangered animal and plant species

Yes Ban torture of prisoners in U.S. custody

CQ VOTE STUDIES

	PARTY UNITY		PRESIDENTIAL SUPPORT	
	Support	Oppose	Support	Oppose
2006	91%	9%	17%	83%
2005	91%	9%	17%	83%
2004	90%	10%	27%	73%
2003	94%	6%	17%	83%
2002	94%	6%	24%	76%

INTEREST GROUPS

	AFL-CIO	ADA	CCUS	ACU
2006	93%	90%	47%	28%
2005	87%	100%	37%	12%
2004	100%	95%	43%	16%
2003	100%	100%	14%	25%
2002	100%	95%	30%	12%

OREGON 4

Southwest – Eugene, Springfield, part of Corvallis

Taking in the southern half of Oregon's Pacific coast and parts of the Cascade Mountains, the 4th's economy is dependent on the district's natural resources. Environmentalists, loggers and fishermen combine to give the 4th a potentially combustible political mix.

Federal government regulations imposed by the courts and the Clinton administration caused numerous layoffs in the district's forestry and fishing industries in the 1990s. During that time, the 4th endured the slowest population growth of any Oregon district. Blue-collar areas that once thrived on these industries, such as in fishing towns in Coos and Curry counties, continue to experience unemployment rates higher than the state average. Local salmon fishers, like other industry workers along the nation's West Coast, experienced low 2005 and 2006 harvests.

Agriculture in the 4th is based in the fertile valley between the Cascade and Coast mountain ranges. The Umpqua Valley provides rich soil for the region's strong wine grape industry and for a variety of field crops. Beyond agriculture, the 5th has come to rely on tourism and expanding retirement communities. These new elderly residents are establishing second homes near the district's coastal areas or mountain ranges.

Eugene and Springfield, the district's most populous cities, have fared better, and are growing rapidly. Research at the University of Oregon in Eugene, still a hotbed of environmentalism, has lured technology companies. Computer manufacturers, software developers, retailers and the service industry now drive this area's economy.

The electoral success of liberal Rep. DeFazio belies the 4th's political competitiveness. Eugene and Springfield make Lane County reliably Democratic. Linn and Douglas counties vote solidly Republican, and Coos and Curry counties lean toward the GOP. Democrat John Kerry won a 49 percent plurality here in the 2004 presidential vote.

MAJOR INDUSTRY

Forestry, agriculture, fishing, technology, tourism

CITIES

Eugene, 137,893; Springfield, 52,864; Albany (pt.), 36,950; Corvallis (pt.), 32,076; Roseburg, 20,017; Coos Bay, 15,374

NOTABLE

Much of the movie "Stand by Me" was filmed in Lane County.

Rep. Darlene Hooley (D)

CAPITOL OFFICE
225-5711
www.house.gov/hooley
2430 Rayburn 20515-3705; fax 225-5699

COMMITTEES
Budget
Energy & Commerce
Science & Technology

RESIDENCE
West Linn

BORN
April 4, 1939, Williston, N.D.

RELIGION
Lutheran

FAMILY
Divorced; two children

EDUCATION
Pasadena Nazarene College, attended 1957-59 (psychology); Oregon State U., B.S. 1961 (education)

CAREER
Teacher

POLITICAL HIGHLIGHTS
West Linn City Council, 1977-81; Ore. House, 1981-87; Clackamas County Commission, 1987-97

ELECTION RESULTS

2006 GENERAL		
Darlene Hooley (D)	146,973	54.0%
Mike Erickson (R)	116,424	42.8%
Paul Aranas (PACGRN)	4,194	1.5%
Douglas Patterson (CNSTP)	4,160	1.5%
2006 PRIMARY		
Darlene Hooley (D)	54,649	98.9%
write-ins	606	1.1%
2004 GENERAL		
Darlene Hooley (D)	184,833	52.9%
Jim Zupancic (R)	154,993	44.3%
Jerry Defoe (LIBERT)	6,463	1.9%

PREVIOUS WINNING PERCENTAGES
2002 (55%); 2000 (57%); 1998 (55%); 1996 (51%)

Elected 1996; 6th term

Most of Hooley's legislative efforts are directed toward her Willamette Valley district. Pragmatic and hardworking, she understands that achieving success with legislation most often involves some compromise, and she will cross the aisle to get her initiatives passed.

She gained a seat on the Energy and Commerce Committee for the 110th Congress (2007-08) and, more important, a slot on its Health Subcommittee. Hooley has long tried to end the production of the chemically manufactured drug methamphetamine, which has particularly afflicted rural areas.

She worked with other rural lawmakers to add provisions to a 2006 measure reauthorizing the Office of National Drug Control Policy to focus more federal effort on controlling meth. Hooley added an amendment to require the drug czar's office to send Congress a comprehensive strategy to address the growing meth problem, including plans to curb access to chemicals used to produce the drug and ways to reduce demand and treat those addicted to it. "In my three decades of public service, I do not think I have ever seen a problem as pervasive or as damaging as the methamphetamine epidemic that is sweeping our country," Hooley said.

Hooley also helped create a grant program to help children living in homes where meth or other drugs are manufactured. When funding for the program fell through, Hooley cosponsored a bill early in 2007 to authorize $20 million in grants for the program over two years.

Hooley opposes the war in Iraq and voted against authorizing it in 2002. When voting in February 2007 for a Democratic resolution opposing President Bush's decision to send thousands more troops to Iraq, Hooley said, "It is beyond comprehension to view the proposal as anything other than an expansion of the war; it is beyond comprehension to view this as anything other than a step backward instead of forward."

She takes a close interest in the treatment of military personnel and their families, as a high percentage of National Guard soldiers from her district are serving in Iraq. In March 2007, she won a three-year battle with the Pentagon when the House passed her amendment giving National Guard and reserve soldiers returning from combat the option of seeking medical treatment at the military facility closest to their home. "My goal is to try to do the best we can do with the mess that the president made out of [Iraq]," she says. "And I want to make sure that our soldiers are taken care of."

Hooley is a member of the centrist New Democrat Coalition and like many in her state, she tends to be liberal on social issues but fiscally conservative. She supports abortion rights and has voted against amending the Constitution to prohibit same-sex marriage.

She supported Bush's $1.35 trillion tax cut in 2001 and voted for corporate tax cuts and extensions of existing tax breaks in 2004. But she opposed the president's $330 billion tax cut in 2003, saying it would not benefit a broad segment of the population. That same year, Hooley was one of 41 Democrats who voted to repeal the estate tax permanently. Her first bill in the House was a joint effort with Republican John Cooksey of Louisiana to reduce estate taxes on family-owned small businesses and farms.

Environmental issues can be tricky in Oregon, as many residents of the state make their living by logging, farming or fishing. In the 109th Congress (2005-06), Hooley opposed Republican-led attempts to reduce clean air and clean water regulations.

In June 2006, she joined other West Coast lawmakers in obstructing floor action until the House gave salmon fishermen in those states $2 million in disaster relief after new federal regulations curtailed their catch. She asked for $60 million in disaster relief for commercial salmon fishermen and American Indian tribes to be included in the fiscal 2007 supplemental spending bill.

Hooley spent the first eight years of her life on her family's wheat farm in Williston, N.D., which lacked running water or electricity. When the local school closed, Hooley went to live with an aunt to attend first and second grades. Her family then moved to Salem, Ore., where Hooley worked summers picking fruit and beans.

She earned a degree in education from Oregon State University and went on to become a reading, music and physical education teacher. "I want people to have opportunities to succeed," she says. "I mean, I lived the American Dream. I grew up on a farm, my dad had a fourth-grade education, and I'm in Congress."

She launched her second career in 1977 after the West Linn City Council rejected her proposal to make safety improvements to a public playground where her son had been injured in a fall. Council members said replacing the cement under the equipment would be too expensive, so she decided to run for the council and won. The council replaced the cement and eventually bought new playground equipment as well.

After four years on the city council, Hooley served in the Oregon House and 10 years on the Clackamas County Commission. Deciding to serve in Washington was not her idea, Hooley says. "I really frankly got talked into doing this job by a lot of different people," she said, including then Vice President Al Gore.

In her 1996 House race, she easily outpaced two lesser-known Democrats to claim the party's nomination and the right to take on conservative GOP freshman Rep. Jim Bunn, who had won narrowly in 1994. Hooley quickly gained the support of national Democrats, who helped with a barrage of negative ads portraying Bunn as too conservative for the district. Bunn, who depended on support from religious conservatives, was also hurt by his divorce and subsequent marriage to his 31-year-old chief of staff.

Hooley prevailed with 51 percent of the vote. Her re-election contests have been competitive — the 5th is a swing district that narrowly favored Bush in 2004. In 2006, she faced off against wealthy transportation services company executive Mike Erickson, a first-time candidate recruited by Republican officials. Erickson backed his bid with $1.6 million of his own money, but Hooley prevailed with 54 percent.

KEY VOTES

2006

Yes Stop broadband companies from favoring select Internet traffic

No Affirm U.S. commitment to war in Iraq and reject setting a withdrawal date for troops

No Repeal requirement for bilingual ballots at the polls

No Permit U.S. sale of civilian nuclear technology to India

Yes Build a 700-mile fence on the U.S.-Mexico border to curb illegal crossings

No Permit warrantless wiretaps of suspected terrorists

2005

? Intervene in the life-support case of Terri Schiavo

Yes Lift President Bush's restrictions on stem cell research funding

Yes Prohibit FBI access to library and bookstore records

No Approve free-trade pact with five Central American countries

No Pass energy policy overhaul favored by President Bush emphasizing domestic oil and gas production

No End mandatory preservation of habitat of endangered animal and plant species

Yes Ban torture of prisoners in U.S. custody

CQ VOTE STUDIES

	PARTY UNITY		PRESIDENTIAL SUPPORT	
	Support	Oppose	Support	Oppose
2006	91%	9%	25%	75%
2005	93%	7%	18%	82%
2004	87%	13%	35%	65%
2003	91%	9%	24%	76%
2002	87%	13%	37%	63%

INTEREST GROUPS

	AFL-CIO	ADA	CCUS	ACU
2006	93%	90%	53%	24%
2005	93%	95%	52%	13%
2004	87%	95%	60%	16%
2003	87%	95%	38%	25%
2002	88%	90%	50%	12%

OREGON 5

Willamette Valley — Salem, part of Portland

Oregon City, the western terminus of the 2,000-mile Oregon Trail, in 1844 became the first incorporated city west of the Mississippi River. For settlers who made the five-month journey from Independence, Mo., the area marked the end of an arduous trek to Oregon's fertile Willamette Valley. The 5th takes in the northern part of that valley and the state capital of Salem, then spills over the Coast Range to cover two Pacific counties, Tillamook and Lincoln. It also includes a small part of Portland (shared with the 1st and 3rd districts).

Clackamas, Marion and Polk counties are at the heart of the Willamette Valley, Oregon's most fertile farmland. The valley is the center of the state's profitable trade in greenhouse crops, seeds and berries. Hops from Marion and Clackamas counties go into some of the nation's finest beers. Polk County grows cherries and wine grapes; wineries dot Polk and Marion counties.

Once exclusively dependent on agriculture and timber, the district's economy has diversified and now supports environmental research and technology manufacturing. Salem and surrounding Marion County are home to many government workers and have a robust food processing industry. Portland's residential suburbs have begun expanding south into Clackamas County, into places such as Oregon City and Lake Oswego. Many residents here work in Portland, but others work in the 5th's manufacturing sectors, particularly in technology and metals.

The 5th is highly competitive, thanks largely to independent voters in Marion and Clackamas counties. Marion, the district's most populous jurisdiction, tends to vote narrowly Republican in close statewide races. Strong Democratic areas include Corvallis (shared with the 4th), which is home to Oregon State University, and southwestern Multnomah County, which hosts some affluent liberals around Lewis & Clark College. Overall, George W. Bush won 50 percent of the 5th's 2004 presidential vote.

MAJOR INDUSTRY
Agriculture, timber, food processing, manufacturing, state government

CITIES
Salem, 136,924; Lake Oswego (pt.), 35,263; Keizer, 32,203

NOTABLE
Salem's Willamette University, established in 1842, was the first university in the west.

PENNSYLVANIA

Gov. Edward G. Rendell (D)

First elected: 2002
Length of term: 4 years
Term expires: 1/11
Salary: $164,396
Phone: (717) 787-2500

Residence: Philadelphia
Born: Jan. 5, 1944; New York, N.Y.
Religion: Jewish
Family: Wife, Marjorie O. Rendell; one child
Education: U. of Pennsylvania, B.A. 1965 (political science); Villanova U., J.D. 1968
Military service: Army Reserve, 1968-74
Career: Lawyer; city prosecutor
Political highlights: Philadelphia district attorney, 1978-86; sought Democratic nomination for governor, 1986; sought Democratic nomination for mayor of Philadelphia, 1987; mayor of Philadelphia, 1992-2000; Democratic National Committee chairman, 1999-2001

Election results:

2006 GENERAL		
Edward G. Rendell (D)	2,470,517	60.4%
Lynn Swann (R)	1,622,135	39.6%

Lt. Gov. Catherine Baker Knoll (D)

First elected: 2002
Length of term: 4 years
Term expires: 1/11
Salary: $138,242
Phone: (717) 787-3300

LEGISLATURE

General Assembly: Year-round with recess

Senate: 50 members, 4-year terms
2007 ratios: 29 R, 21 D; 44 men, 6 women
Salary: $73,613
Phone: (717) 787-5920

House: 203 members, 2-year terms
2007 ratios: 102 D, 101 R; 176 men, 27 women
Salary: $73,613
Phone: (717) 787-2372

TERM LIMITS

Governor: 2 consecutive terms
Senate: No
House: No

URBAN STATISTICS

CITY	POPULATION
Philadelphia	1,517,550
Pittsburgh	334,563
Allentown	106,632
Erie	103,717
Upper Darby	81,821

REGISTERED VOTERS

Democrat	48%
Republican	40%
Others	12%

POPULATION

2006 population (est.)	12,440,621
2000 population	12,281,054
1990 population	11,881,643
Percent change (1990-2000)	+3.4%
Rank among states (2006)	6
Median age	38
Born in state	77.7%
Foreign born	4.1%
Violent crime rate	420/100,000
Poverty level	11%
Federal workers	105,903
Military	43,271

ELECTIONS

STATE ELECTION OFFICIAL
(717) 787-5280
DEMOCRATIC PARTY
(717) 920-8470
REPUBLICAN PARTY
(717) 234-4901

MISCELLANEOUS

Web: www.state.pa.us
Capital: Harrisburg

U.S. CONGRESS

Senate: 1 Democrat, 1 Republican
House: 11 Democrats, 8 Republican

2000 Census Statistics by District

DIST.	2004 VOTE FOR PRESIDENT		WHITE	BLACK	ASIAN	HISP	MEDIAN INCOME	WHITE COLLAR	BLUE COLLAR	SERVICE INDUSTRY	OVER 64	UNDER 18	COLLEGE EDUCATION	RURAL	SQ. MILES
	BUSH	KERRY													
1	15%	84%	33%	45%	5%	15%	$28,261	57%	21%	22%	12%	28%	14%	0%	59
2	12	87	30	61	4	3	$30,646	66	15	19	14	24	24	0	59
3	53	46	94	3	0	1	$35,884	52	31	16	15	24	18	42	3,969
4	54	45	94	3	1	1	$43,547	64	23	14	17	24	27	22	1,302
5	61	39	96	1	1	1	$33,254	51	33	15	15	22	17	54	11,042
6	48	51	86	7	2	4	$55,611	68	20	12	14	25	34	14	813
7	47	53	88	5	4	1	$56,126	73	16	11	15	24	36	1	290
8	48	51	91	3	2	2	$59,207	68	21	11	13	26	31	9	619
9	67	33	96	2	0	1	$34,910	49	36	16	16	24	13	59	7,160
10	60	40	95	2	0	1	$35,996	53	32	15	17	23	17	55	6,558
11	47	52	93	2	1	3	$34,979	54	30	16	18	22	16	27	2,218
12	48	51	95	3	0	1	$30,612	51	31	18	19	21	14	38	2,752
13	43	56	86	6	4	3	$49,319	68	19	12	17	23	29	2	255
14	30	69	73	23	2	1	$30,139	62	19	20	18	21	21	0	162
15	49	50	86	3	2	8	$45,330	59	27	14	16	24	22	13	845

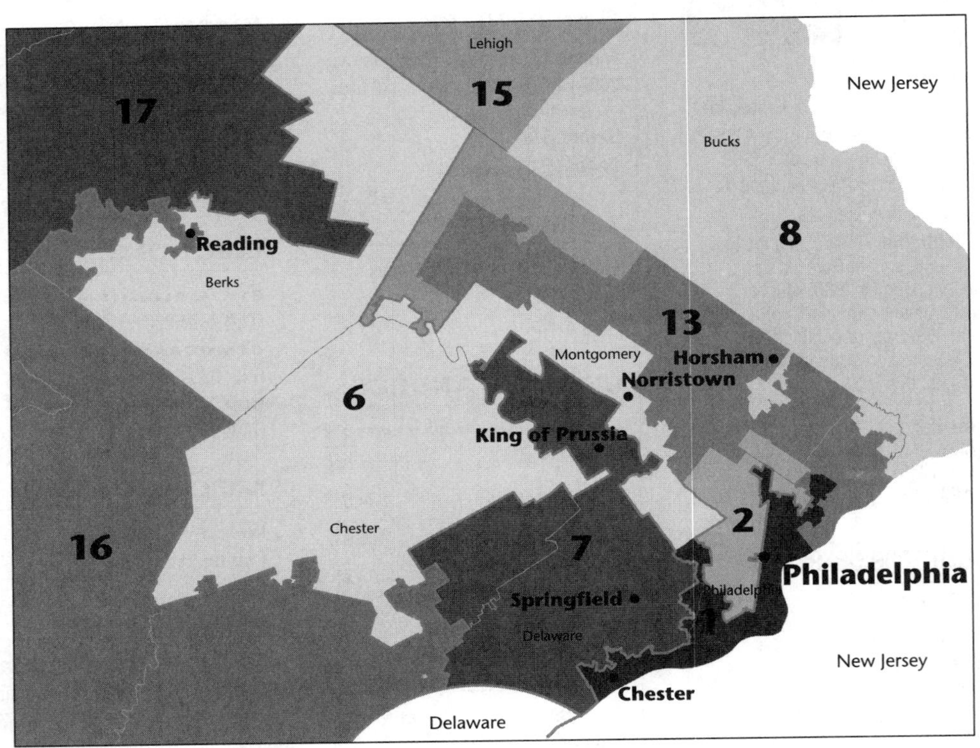

2000 Census Statistics by District

DIST.	2004 VOTE FOR PRESIDENT BUSH	KERRY	WHITE	BLACK	ASIAN	HISP	MEDIAN INCOME	WHITE COLLAR	BLUE COLLAR	SERVICE INDUSTRY	OVER 64	UNDER 18	COLLEGE EDUCATION	RURAL	SQ. MILES
16	61%	38%	85%	4%	1%	9%	$45,934	54%	31%	14%	13%	27%	23%	24%	1,290
17	58	42	87	7	1	3	$40,473	55	31	14	16	23	17	31	2,335
18	54	45	95	2	1	1	$44,938	66	20	14	18	22	29	16	1,432
19	64	36	92	3	1	3	$45,345	57	30	13	14	24	21	29	1,658
STATE	48	51	84	10	2	3	$40,106	60	26	15	16	24	22	23	44,817
U.S.	50.7	48.3	69	12	4	13	$41,994	60	25	15	12	26	24	21	3,537,438

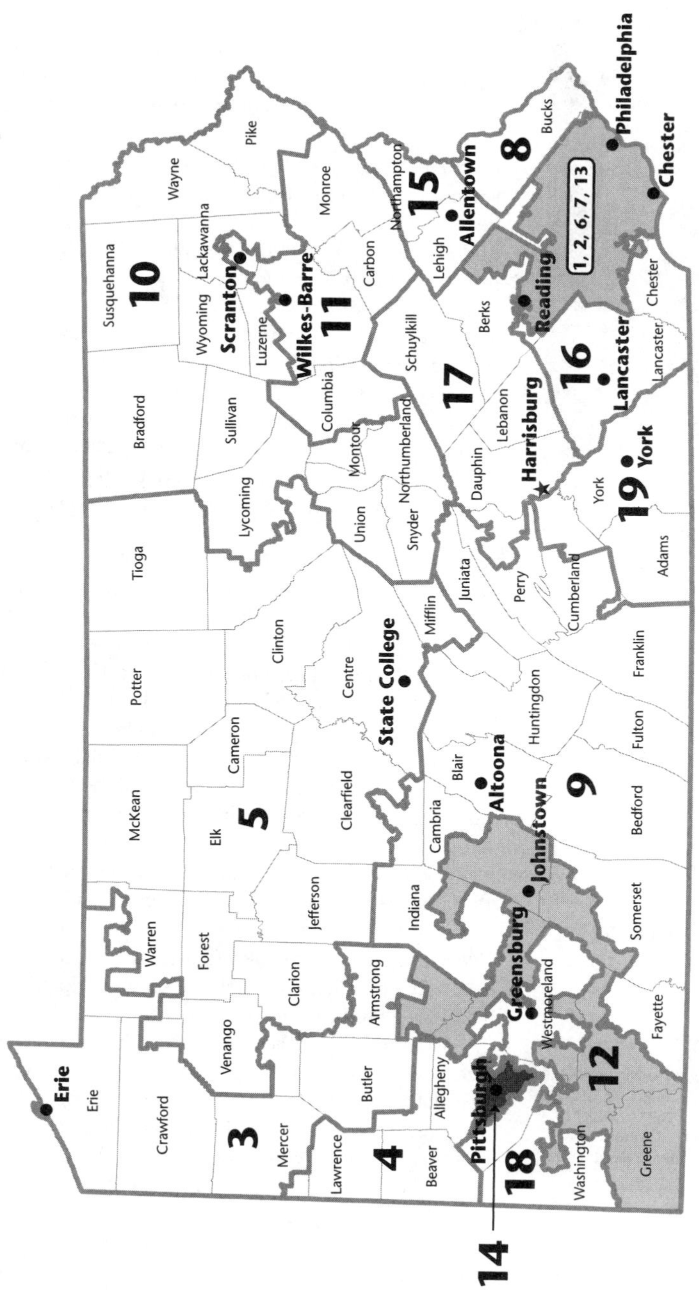

Erie
Erie
Crawford
Mercer
Lawrence
Beaver
Butler
Venango
Warren
Forest
Clarion
Armstrong
Allegheny
Pittsburgh
Washington
Greene
Fayette
Westmoreland
Greensburg
Indiana
Jefferson
Elk
McKean
Cameron
Potter
Clearfield
Cambria
Johnstown
Somerset
Bedford
Blair
Altoona
Huntingdon
Fulton
Franklin
Centre
State College
Clinton
Tioga
Lycoming
Mifflin
Juniata
Perry
Cumberland
Adams
York
Snyder
Union
Northumberland
Montour
Columbia
Dauphin
Harrisburg
Lebanon
Lancaster
Chester
Berks
Reading
Schuylkill
Carbon
Lehigh
Allentown
Northampton
Monroe
Pike
Wayne
Susquehanna
Lackawanna
Wyoming
Scranton
Luzerne
Wilkes-Barre
Bradford
Sullivan
Bucks
Philadelphia
Chester
1, 2, 6, 7, 13
3
4
5
8
9
10
11
12
14
15
16
17
18
19

Sen. Arlen Specter (R)

CAPITOL OFFICE
224-4254
arlen_specter@specter.senate.gov
specter.senate.gov
711 Hart 20510-3802; fax 228-1229

COMMITTEES
Appropriations
Judiciary - ranking member
Veterans' Affairs
Special Aging

RESIDENCE
Philadelphia

BORN
Feb. 12, 1930, Wichita, Kan.

RELIGION
Jewish

FAMILY
Wife, Joan Specter; two children

EDUCATION
U. of Pennsylvania, B.A. 1951 (international relations); Yale U., LL.B. 1956

MILITARY SERVICE
Air Force, 1951-53

CAREER
Lawyer; professor

POLITICAL HIGHLIGHTS
Philadelphia district attorney, 1966-74; Republican nominee for mayor of Philadelphia, 1967; defeated for re-election as Philadelphia district attorney, 1973; sought Republican nomination for U.S. Senate, 1976; sought Republican nomination for governor, 1978

ELECTION RESULTS

2004 GENERAL		
Arlen Specter (R)	2,925,080	52.6%
Joseph M. Hoeffel (D)	2,334,126	42.0%
James N. Clymer (CNSTP)	220,056	4.0%
Betsy Summers (LIBERT)	79,263	1.4%
2004 PRIMARY		
Arlen Specter (R)	530,839	50.8%
Patrick J. Toomey (R)	513,693	49.2%

PREVIOUS WINNING PERCENTAGES
1998 (61%); 1992 (49%); 1986 (56%); 1980 (50%)

Elected 1980; 5th term

Freed from the responsibility of moving controversial bills and nominations through the Senate Judiciary Committee, Specter may find life in the minority a bit of a relief after two years as the panel's chairman.

Although the Pennsylvania moderate fought hard to claim the gavel for the 109th Congress (2005-06), he was forced to operate on a very short leash once he got it. GOP conservatives distrust him, and they let him become chairman only after extracting a pledge that he would advance all of President Bush's judicial nominees to the full Senate, regardless of his own views of the selections.

Specter kept his word. Although he reserved the right to vote against nominees on the floor, he did not do so, even when other GOP moderates did. He shepherded Bush's two Supreme Court nominees to confirmation in 2005 and 2006, as well as several controversial appeals court nominees.

As Judiciary's ranking minority member in the 110th Congress (2007-08), Specter has more room to roam. In early 2007, he teamed with Democratic Chairman Patrick J. Leahy of Vermont in pressing for documents and testimony from top Justice Department officials involved in the firings of eight U.S. attorneys.

Notoriously blunt and sure of himself to the point of cockiness, he is a constant irritant to the conservatives who dominate the GOP. But liberals don't have much use for him either; they don't like it that they can't predict where he'll be in do-or-die battles. Specter enraged conservatives when he opposed the nomination of Robert H. Bork to the high court in 1987, and similarly angered liberals four years later by defending conservative nominee Clarence Thomas against sexual harassment charges by Anita Hill.

Specter inadvertently provoked conservatives again in late 2004 when he declared that he thought it unlikely that the Senate would confirm judicial nominees who favored ending the legal right to abortion. "When you talk about judges who would change the right of a woman to choose, overturn *Roe v. Wade*, I think that is unlikely," Specter said, shortly after the election that year, as he was jockeying to become Judiciary chairman.

Conservative groups mounted a furious campaign to deny him the gavel. Specter launched a counteroffensive of contrition in the media and among fellow Republicans. Ultimately, he survived the firestorm, but he remained on notice that his every move was being watched.

Specter managed the grueling confirmation proceedings for Chief Justice John G. Roberts Jr. and Justice Samuel A. Alito Jr. while battling the debilitating effects of cancer treatment. In February 2005, he was diagnosed with advanced Hodgkin's disease, a cancer of the lymphatic system. He made a point of scheduling his biweekly chemotherapy sessions on Fridays so that he could be ready for work on Mondays.

The treatments, which were just ending as the Roberts hearings began, left him gaunt and completely bald. During committee sessions, he kept a handkerchief ready for constant sniffles and watery eyes, and gulped Gatorade to combat dehydration. He continued to arrive for meetings precisely on time, chiding tardy colleagues. His doctor said he had a good chance of overcoming the disease. In the 1990s, Specter survived both a brain tumor and heart problems that led to bypass surgery.

Like other Mid-Atlantic states, Pennsylvania tilts Democratic, which is one reason Specter departs so often from the GOP line. In the 109th Congress, he sided with fellow Republicans on just 66 percent of roll call votes pitting the two parties against each other. Only three GOP senators scored lower.

But he is less likely to stray when his vote is decisive. In 2005, Specter backed a budget-cutting bill even as five other GOP moderates sided with Democrats. That created a 50-50 tie, allowing Vice President Dick Cheney to step in to cast the deciding GOP vote.

When the administration's use of warrantless surveillance of Americans in terrorism investigations became public in 2006, Specter was sharply critical. He sponsored a bill compelling the president to get approval from a special court created for that purpose in the 1978 Foreign Intelligence Surveillance Act. But most Republicans sided with Bush, who insisted he had constitutional authority for the wiretaps. Specter was so eager to be a central player that he rewrote his bill, capitulating on his demand for court review.

Specter is most likely to join Democrats to increase spending for domestic priorities. As top Republican on the Appropriations subcommittee that funds the departments of Labor, Health and Human Services, and Education, he has fought to boost spending on education and health care.

He also supports labor on occasion. He held up a fiscal 2004 spending bill because he disagreed with a Bush administration decision curtailing overtime pay for some federal workers. Specter offered a compromise creating a commission to study the issue, but GOP leaders rejected it and he ultimately relented. Specter also gave in to party leaders in 2002, when he voted for repeal of the Clinton-era federal ergonomics rule even though he had long sided with labor on the issue of repetitive stress injuries.

Specter strongly supports expanded embryonic stem cell research, though in 2006 he joined fellow Pennsylvania Republican Rick Santorum, an anti-abortion leader, on legislation encouraging research into obtaining stem cells without destroying embryos. That was partly political payback for Santorum's support in Specter's 2004 primary race against conservative challenger Patrick J. Toomey.

The son of a Jewish peddler who immigrated from Ukraine, Specter grew up mostly in Kansas, though Harry Specter moved the family from place to place, selling blankets to farmers in Nebraska during the winter and melons to Midwestern housewives in the summer. The family later settled in Philadelphia, and Specter launched his career there.

He was elected district attorney in Philadelphia twice, in 1965 and 1969, but suffered political setbacks, including losing a race for mayor. But in the 1960s, he also made a name for himself as a top aide to the Warren Commission, helping to devise the "single bullet" theory that a lone gunman was responsible for the 1963 assassination of President John F. Kennedy.

His political luck changed when he ran for the Senate in 1980, defeating Pittsburgh Mayor Pete Flaherty for an open seat.

In the Senate, Specter became known for occasional quirkiness. During the1999 impeachment trial of President Bill Clinton, he invoked Scottish law by voting "Not proven, therefore not guilty," while everyone else voted "guilty" or "not guilty," according to U.S. law. Specter said he wanted to make the point that the trial had been superficial in his view.

Specter's aggressive grilling of Hill during the Thomas confirmation hearings — he called her testimony "flat-out perjury" — infuriated many women. In the 1992 election, Democratic challenger Lynn Yeakel, head of a Philadelphia women's fundraising organization, made an issue of his treatment of Hill, and held Specter to a 3 percentage point win.

He had another close call in 2004, when conservative Toomey challenged him in the primary. With the White House on his side and Santorum vouching for him with conservatives, Specter won with 51 percent of the vote, and went on to defeat Democratic Rep. Joseph M. Hoeffel in November with 53 percent.

KEY VOTES

2006

Yes Confirm Samuel A. Alito Jr. to the Supreme Court
Yes Allow consideration of a bill to establish a $140 billion trust fund to compensate victims of asbestos exposure
? Extend tax cuts for two years at a cost of $70 billion over five years
Yes Overhaul immigration policy with border security, enforcement and guest worker program
Yes Allow consideration of a bill to permanently repeal the estate tax
No Urge President Bush to begin troop withdrawals from Iraq in 2006
Yes Lift President Bush's restrictions on stem cell research funding
Yes Authorize military tribunals for suspected terrorists

2005

Yes Curb class action lawsuits by shifting them from state to federal courts
Yes Allow confirmation vote on Priscilla R. Owen to the U.S. Court of Appeals for the 5th Circuit
No Oppose mandatory emissions limits and block recognition of global warming as a threat
No Approve free-trade pact with five Central American countries
Yes Pass energy policy overhaul favored by President Bush emphasizing domestic oil and gas production
Yes Shield gunmakers from lawsuits when their products are used in crimes
Yes Ban torture of prisoners in U.S. custody
Yes Renew 16 provisions of the Patriot Act
Yes Allow final vote on opening the Arctic National Wildlife Refuge to oil and gas exploration

CQ VOTE STUDIES

	PARTY UNITY		PRESIDENTIAL SUPPORT	
	Support	Oppose	Support	Oppose
2006	61%	39%	76%	24%
2005	69%	31%	85%	15%
2004	70%	30%	88%	12%
2003	84%	16%	89%	11%
2002	60%	40%	89%	11%
2001	60%	40%	87%	13%
2000	67%	33%	59%	41%
1999	64%	36%	53%	47%
1998	49%	51%	60%	40%
1997	50%	50%	71%	29%

INTEREST GROUPS

	AFL-CIO	ADA	CCUS	ACU
2006	31%	30%	100%	43%
2005	54%	45%	88%	63%
2004	64%	45%	87%	75%
2003	16%	25%	87%	65%
2002	46%	35%	85%	50%
2001	63%	40%	79%	56%
2000	50%	40%	53%	62%
1999	44%	40%	47%	48%
1998	83%	45%	60%	33%
1997	57%	70%	50%	32%

Sen. Bob Casey (D)

CAPITOL OFFICE
224-6324
casey.senate.gov
383 Russell 20510-3804; fax 228-0604

COMMITTEES
Agriculture, Nutrition & Forestry
Banking, Housing & Urban Affairs
Foreign Relations
Special Aging
Joint Economic

RESIDENCE
Scranton

BORN
April 13, 1960, Scranton, Pa.

RELIGION
Roman Catholic

FAMILY
Wife, Terese Casey; four children

EDUCATION
College of the Holy Cross, A.B. 1982 (English); Catholic U. of America, J.D. 1988

CAREER
Lawyer; campaign aide

POLITICAL HIGHLIGHTS
Pa. auditor general, 1997-2005; sought Democratic nomination for governor, 2002; Pa. treasurer, 2005-07

ELECTION RESULTS

2006 GENERAL		
Bob Casey (D)	2,392,984	58.7%
Rick Santorum (R)	1,684,778	41.3%
2006 PRIMARY		
Bob Casey (D)	629,271	84.6%
Chuck Pennacchio (D)	66,364	8.9%
Alan Sandals (D)	48,113	6.5%

Elected 2006; 1st term

As the son of the popular late governor, Casey carries both his father's name and his legacy in politics. The Caseys of Pennsylvania are Catholic, anti-abortion Democrats, liberal on almost every score except abortion rights and gun control and unlikely to be persuaded otherwise.

On one of his first votes in the Senate, the 46-year-old Casey was true to family form when he voted against a bill to expand federal funding for embryonic stem cell research, though the measure was part of the much touted agenda of the Democratic majority in the 110th Congress (2007-08).

Like other anti-abortion lawmakers, Casey opposes the research because it uses cells from surplus embryos from in vitro fertilization clinics. On stem cell research, his position is the same as that of Sen. Rick Santorum, the No. 3 Republican Senate leader he ousted in one of the biggest Democratic triumphs of the 2006 election. But on other major bills in the party's inaugural agenda, like setting a date for troop withdrawals from Iraq and increasing the federal minimum wage, Casey toed the party line.

Casey's father, Robert Patrick Casey (also known as Bob Casey), was governor from 1987 to 1995 and led the anti-abortion wing of the Democratic Party in that era. He famously was denied a speaking role by Bill Clinton at the 1992 Democratic National Convention; he then snubbed Clinton when Clinton stumped in Pennsylvania, a swing state in that year's presidential contest. The Caseys' conservatism on abortion rights and gun control is part of their appeal to the state's crossover voters.

Casey Jr. is a chip off the block in other ways. He still lives with his wife and four daughters in Scranton, where the Caseys have their political base. His career in state politics tracked his father's. He was elected state auditor, and both father and son lost elections for governor, though his father ultimately prevailed. "It took him 20 years to be elected governor, so he lost when I was 6 years old, 10 years old, 18 years old, and he won when I was 26," says Casey, who has the same distinguishing bushy eyebrows. His chief of staff in the Senate, James W. Brown, was his father's former top aide in Harrisburg.

Another thing he shares with his father is a genetic history, one that puts him at risk of the same disease that took the elder Casey's life in 2000 at age 68. Bob Casey was stricken with amyloidosis, a genetic condition in which proteins turn against the body and destroy internal organs; he underwent a heart-liver transplant in 1993. His son has a 50 percent chance of possessing the same gene but has chosen not to have the simple blood test that can determine whether he does. "I'm not real anxious to find out, but I probably should," Casey says. "I would think maybe in my 50s, to be sure. I'm lucky in the sense that, by the time somebody like me would have trouble, there probably would be a pharmaceutical remedy."

Casey says he stays fit by running a couple days a week, "but not real far." He says, "I live in a section in Scranton called 'The Hills,' and they are mighty hills — very, very steep hills."

His main quest as a freshman senator is expansion of a Clinton-era program that provides low-income children access to health care services under Medicaid, called the State Children's Health Insurance Program. Casey would like to cover all uninsured children, but he's bound to be somewhat overshadowed on the issue by political heavyweights who have also made it a priority, including Sen. Hillary Rodham Clinton of New York.

Casey also must compete for attention with the state's senior senator,

Arlen Specter, a moderate who is the top-ranking Republican on the Judiciary Committee. Ironically, Casey and Specter have more in common ideologically than did Specter and his GOP predecessor; Santorum belonged to a faction of far-right conservatives that often tried to curb Specter's authority. One of Casey's first moves in 2007 was teaming with Specter to successfully persuade the Bush administration to restore $100 million in the budget for a Schuylkill County facility to turn coal into fuel.

Casey snagged committee assignments reflective of the state's urban-rural mix. He sits on both the Agriculture and the Banking, Housing and Urban Affairs committees. He also got a spot on the Foreign Relations Committee, which will help to expand his policy expertise on international issues. Casey wants a "clear exit strategy" in Iraq but does not support a timetable for U.S. troop withdrawals, as many Democrats do.

He hews closely to the party line on tax and budget issues. Liberal and pro-labor, he favors repeal of President Bush's tax cuts for people making more than $200,000 a year, and he would retain a tax on very large estates. He also opposes recent free-trade pacts, which organized labor fought against, including the Central American Free Trade Agreement.

Growing up in working-class Scranton, he was the fourth of eight children, and the first boy in a devoutly Catholic family. His grandfather worked in the coal mines; his father became a lawyer.

The family's finances were sometimes volatile, given his father's numerous campaigns and the vicissitudes of his employment, but Casey recalls a happy upbringing. "With that many children, it's hard to convey a sense that everyone's equal, and that each parent loves each child as much as the other. And they did that," he says. "If you add up all the hours that my mother spent just doing the wash and just doing everything it takes to run that big a household, it would be half her life, doing just basic things. She had a great ability to handle it all." All of the Casey children except two brothers who practice law in Philadelphia still live within 10 miles of each other.

Casey graduated from the College of the Holy Cross in 1982, then spent a year teaching fifth grade in Philadelphia with the Jesuits. Like his father, he got his law degree, then practiced in Scranton until he won his first election as state auditor general in 1996. During two terms, Casey conducted a hard-hitting audit of nursing homes that led to the resignation of the state's top health official.

In 2004, he ran for state treasurer and won, attracting the attention of national Democrats in Washington, who were gearing up for a challenge to Santorum. The conservative senator was viewed as vulnerable in a state that had voted Democratic in four previous presidential elections. Sen. Charles E. Schumer of New York, the chairman of the Senate Democrats' campaign organization, recruited Casey to take on Santorum.

Casey blew by two lesser-known candidates to secure the Democratic nomination, then prepared for what was widely anticipated to be a titanic and close contest. Santorum and fellow Republicans ridiculed the low-key Casey as noncommittal on important issues, weak on fighting terrorism and dealing with illegal immigration, and unwilling to meet the energetic Santorum in a long series of debates. But the fact that Santorum was so eager to debate was a sign of his underdog status. Plus, Casey's conservative social positions took away a typical line of GOP attack. Casey raised plenty of money, and the political wind was in the Democrats' direction.

As it turned out, the race wasn't close. Casey defeated Santorum by a landslide 17 percentage points, reflecting the controversial nature of the incumbent's positioning and the unpopularity of Bush. Casey led Santorum even outside the state's traditional Democratic bastions of Philadelphia and Allegheny County, which includes Pittsburgh.

Rep. Robert A. Brady (D)

CAPITOL OFFICE
225-4731
www.house.gov/robertbrady
206 Cannon 20515-3801; fax 225-0088

COMMITTEES
Armed Services
House Administration - chairman
(Capitol Security - chairman)
Joint Printing - chairman

RESIDENCE
Philadelphia

BORN
April 7, 1945, Philadelphia, Pa.

RELIGION
Roman Catholic

FAMILY
Wife, Debra Brady; two children

EDUCATION
St. Thomas More H.S., graduated 1963

CAREER
Union lobbyist; local government official; carpenter

POLITICAL HIGHLIGHTS
34th Ward Democratic Executive Committee, 1967-present (leader, 1980-present); candidate for Philadelphia City Council, 1983; Philadelphia Democratic Party chairman, 1986-present; sought Democratic nomination for mayor of Philadelphia, 2007

ELECTION RESULTS

2006 GENERAL		
Robert A. Brady (D)		unopposed
2006 PRIMARY		
Robert A. Brady (D)		unopposed
2004 GENERAL		
Robert A. Brady (D)	214,462	86.3%
Deborah L. Williams (R)	33,266	13.4%

PREVIOUS WINNING PERCENTAGES
2002 (86%); 2000 (88%); 1998 (81%); 1998 Special Election (74%)

Elected May 1998; 5th full term

Brady has been a major player in Philadelphia's machine politics for nearly 20 years. He's not a particularly active legislator in Washington, but he has been effective enough in tending to his constituents that he has a commanding grip on his district, which has a mostly black constituency.

He is also a good soldier for the House Democratic leadership, and in 2007 Speaker Nancy Pelosi made him chairman of the House Administration Committee, which controls office space and member privileges, and also oversees federal elections. Brady replaced Juanita Millender-McDonald, a California Democrat who died of cancer in April 2007. The following month, Brady lost a bid for Philadelphia mayor; he was defeated in the Democratic primary by City Council Member Michael Nutter.

Running for mayor was a relatively low-risk decision for Brady. There was no requirement for him to give up his congressional seat to make the attempt. The same was true for one of his opponents, House Democrat Chaka Fattah, who also lost the Democratic primary.

The colorful Brady is known as a fixer who settles tribal feuds among Democrats over lunch at the Palm in Philadelphia. He negotiated a treaty between state Sen. Vincent Fumo and electricians union business manager John "Johnny Doc" Dougherty, and then worked in 2006 to ease bad blood between Mayor John Street and City Councilman James Kenney.

In mid-2006, closed-door arguments over choosing the leader of North Philadelphia's 43rd Ward got so loud that other building occupants called the police. Brady was unfazed. "Nobody got beat up and nobody got locked up," he told the Philadelphia Inquirer. "People say the Democratic Party is dead, but I say it's alive and kickin'."

Brady also is known for his mediation of labor disputes. In 2005, he dropped in at 11 p.m. to see whether he could lend a hand on transit strike negotiations that had become so tense that Mayor Street and Gov. Edward G. Rendell stayed on the sidelines. In 2005, Brady literally talked Councilman Rick Mariano off the brink, after he had gone to the top of City Hall in a highly publicized suicide scare just before he was to be indicted.

Life in Congress could be positively dull in comparison, but Brady has been putting his skills to use as the interim chairman of House Administration. The committee functions a bit like a city council for the House. The ultimate insider's panel, its members handle election challenges and federal election laws. They also oversee the day-to-day functions, large and small, of the institution — including the all-important allocation of lawmakers' parking spots and office space.

His new job, and his deep connections to Philadelphia, keep him shuttling constantly between the two cities. But he says he goes only by train, not by plane. "I don't fly no more," Brady once told the Inquirer. "I'm not afraid of flying, I'm afraid of crashing."

While Brady has a strong party allegiance — in the 109th Congress (2005-06), he voted with his party 92 percent of the time — he has even stronger ties to Appropriations powerhouse John P. Murtha of Pennsylvania. Brady works with the committee veteran to bring federal projects to his district. "I'm Murtha's guy. I say to him, 'What do you need me to do,' " Brady said in 2003, and Murtha returns the loyalty. "I have no idea about the politics of Philadelphia, but Brady is a master," Murtha told the Inquirer. "He pays close attention. He listens to suggestions, and he's well-liked." Brady has honored his mentor by having one of the nation's biggest cranes at the Philadelphia Naval Shipyard named for him.

Brady also worked with Murtha, and with Republican Sen. Arlen Specter of Pennsylvania, to secure $4.5 million for the struggling Wills Eye Hospital, but future attempts to send money home may be hamstrung by conservative efforts to rein in earmarks for individual lawmakers.

Brady's loyalty to organized labor is unassailable, reflecting his working-class roots. In 2001, Brady infuriated some longtime allies in the environmental lobby by supporting President Bush's proposal to allow oil drilling in Alaska's Arctic National Wildlife Refuge, an idea backed by the Teamsters Union and the AFL-CIO's building trades division as part of a push for domestic energy jobs. Five years later, he voted to lift the ban on new drilling for oil and natural gas in all U.S. coastal waters.

An athlete in his younger days, Brady once teamed up with Wilt Chamberlain in a neighborhood pickup game. Though he had scholarship offers for college, Brady went right to work as a carpenter to help support his family. After 12 years in the trade, he moved into a full-time post with the carpenters union. Brady still carries a union card and has a lifetime score of 100 percent in the AFL-CIO's rating of congressional voting records.

Just 22 years old when he was elected to the 34th Ward Democratic Executive Committee, Brady has been in the local party organization ever since. He held a variety of posts at City Hall, the city's redevelopment agency and the Pennsylvania Turnpike Authority. Many of those positions enabled him to find jobs for people, and he once dubbed himself "the largest employment agency in Pennsylvania."

Brady's close attention to constituent needs reflects a lesson he learned years ago. He remembers deciding to become politically involved when his mother concluded that the local party boss was being insufficiently attentive to her request for a new bulb in a street lamp.

Before he ran for the U.S. House, Brady had sought elective office just once, losing his bid for a seat on the City Council in 1983. But his grasp of city politics — as well as nominating rules that favored the candidate with the backing of the party machinery — made him a formidable candidate in the 1998 special election. The seat came open when Democratic Rep. Thomas M. Foglietta resigned to become ambassador to Italy.

Brady received the Democratic nomination, which practically ensured his victory in the strongly Democratic district. He won the special election with 74 percent of the vote, and has rolled up even bigger tallies since.

KEY VOTES

2006

No Stop broadband companies from favoring select Internet traffic
No Affirm U.S. commitment to war in Iraq and reject setting a withdrawal date for troops
No Repeal requirement for bilingual ballots at the polls
Yes Permit U.S. sale of civilian nuclear technology to India
No Build a 700-mile fence on the U.S.-Mexico border to curb illegal crossings
No Permit warrantless wiretaps of suspected terrorists

2005

Yes Intervene in the life-support case of Terri Schiavo
Yes Lift President Bush's restrictions on stem cell research funding
Yes Prohibit FBI access to library and bookstore records
No Approve free-trade pact with five Central American countries
? Pass energy policy overhaul favored by President Bush emphasizing domestic oil and gas production
No End mandatory preservation of habitat of endangered animal and plant species
Yes Ban torture of prisoners in U.S. custody

CQ VOTE STUDIES

	PARTY UNITY		PRESIDENTIAL SUPPORT	
	Support	Oppose	Support	Oppose
2006	92%	8%	30%	70%
2005	93%	7%	18%	82%
2004	96%	4%	18%	82%
2003	91%	9%	21%	79%
2002	94%	6%	31%	69%

INTEREST GROUPS

	AFL-CIO	ADA	CCUS	ACU
2006	100%	95%	53%	16%
2005	100%	100%	35%	4%
2004	100%	95%	19%	4%
2003	100%	100%	31%	21%
2002	100%	95%	45%	4%

PENNSYLVANIA 1

South and central Philadelphia; Chester

Birthplace of the Constitution, the 1st boasts many recognizable icons, such as the Liberty Bell and the Philly cheesesteak. With 90 percent of its population in Philadelphia, the W-shaped 1st is the state's most racially and ethnically diverse district. The rest of the 1st falls in a working-class slice of Delaware County.

Beyond the historical streets, much of the 1st has a bleak economic landscape. The district has the state's lowest median income and only 14 percent of its residents have a college education. Cutbacks to the factory-employed workforce continue to give the district high unemployment. Construction jobs have increased, and the Booming Kvaerner Philadelphia shipyards have helped, but neither has replaced earlier industry losses, and the 1st is increasingly dependent on government and health care jobs. Philadelphia International Airport's rapid growth provides jobs and a large annual contribution to the local economy.

Football's Eagles, baseball's Phillies, basketball's 76ers and hockey's Flyers play in arenas and stadiums on Broad Street in South Philadelphia. Local officials hope the sports complex can revitalize nearby neighborhoods, which are still recovering from past economic loss, and developers are hoping to build two casinos in the city.

Blacks represent the largest population bloc in the 1st, at 45 percent, and whites make up one-third of the district's population. The district also has a large Asian presence, concentrated in Philadelphia's Chinatown, and nearly three-fourths of Philadelphia's Hispanic population resides in the 1st. The district's Italian-American population supports a famous food market, which is the oldest and largest outdoor market in the United States. The 1st's strong union presence and substantial minority population make it a slam-dunk for Democratic candidates. John Kerry took 84 percent of the vote here in the 2004 presidential election.

MAJOR INDUSTRY

Government, service, health care, shipbuilding, airport

CITIES

Philadelphia (pt.), 571,130; Chester, 36,854

NOTABLE

Eastern State Penitentiary, the most expensive upon its opening in 1829, held gangster Al Capone.

Rep. Chaka Fattah (D)

CAPITOL OFFICE
225-4001
www.house.gov/fattah
2301 Rayburn 20515-3802; fax 225-5392

COMMITTEES
Appropriations

RESIDENCE
Philadelphia

BORN
Nov. 21, 1956, Philadelphia, Pa.

RELIGION
Baptist

FAMILY
Wife, Renee Chenault-Fattah; four children

EDUCATION
Community College of Philadelphia, attended 1976 (political science); U. of Pennsylvania, M.A. 1986 (government administration)

CAREER
Public official

POLITICAL HIGHLIGHTS
Democratic candidate for Philadelphia City Commission, 1978; Pa. House, 1983-89; Pa. Senate, 1989-95; Consumer Party nominee for U.S. House (special election), 1991; sought Democratic nomination for mayor of Philadelphia, 2007

ELECTION RESULTS

2006 GENERAL		
Chaka Fattah (D)	165,867	88.6%
Michael Gessner (R)	17,291	9.2%
David G. Baker (GREEN)	4,125	2.2%
2006 PRIMARY		
Chaka Fattah (D)		unopposed
2004 GENERAL		
Chaka Fattah (D)	253,226	88.0%
Stewart Bolno (R)	34,411	12.0%

PREVIOUS WINNING PERCENTAGES
2002 (88%); 2000 (98%); 1998 (87%); 1996 (88%); 1994 (86%)

Elected 1994; 7th term

Fattah has gradually climbed the rungs of political power during 12 years in a Republican-dominated world and can boast some legislative accomplishments largely due to his willingness to work with conservatives on the other side of the aisle. His opportunities for success broadened in the 110th Congress (2007-08) with the Democratic takeover and his ascension in the ranks of the Appropriations Committee.

In the first part of 2007, Fattah (full name: SHOCK-ah fa-TAH) waged an unsuccessful battle for Philadelphia mayor to succeed Democrat John Street. He got into the race in the fall of 2006, saying the job offered more opportunity to affect outcomes and to make a difference. Fattah emphasized his ideas for overhauling the public schools and for slashing the city's poverty rate. His high profile locally gave him a lead in a crowded Democratic primary in the early polls.

But political analysts said Fattah ran an unfocused campaign, and he lost the May mayoral primary to Michael Nutter, a Philadelphia city councilman who was endorsed by both of the city's major newspapers. Democratic Rep. Robert A. Brady, who represents the 1st District, also based in Philadelphia, was another losing candidate in the race. Neither had to give up his House seat to run.

Fattah got his seat on the powerful Appropriations Committee in 2001. Two years later, then Minority Leader Nancy Pelosi forced Fattah to choose between his seat on Appropriations and his ranking member slot on the House Administration Committee. He picked Appropriations.

Even though he has long since left his seat on the Education panel, he still views education as his top legislative priority. His primary mission is to end poverty in Philly, and he sees education as "a way out," he told The Philadelphia Inquirer in January 2007.

He considers his most significant legislative achievement to be the Gear Up program, which encourages low-income youths to set their sights on college. The grant program became law in 1998 after Fattah joined with conservative Republican Mark Souder of Indiana and won key support from the Clinton administration. The program underwrites tutoring, mentoring and counseling for students as early as sixth or seventh grade, and gives schools incentives to offer college-preparatory classes.

The Bush administration has twice sought to eliminate funding for Gear Up, but Fattah and other program supporters have kept money flowing to it.

Fattah continues to press a second major education initiative: a student bill of rights that would require states to ensure that students in urban areas have the same access to quality education as their suburban counterparts. He also promotes education outside of Congress, as a founder and active fundraiser for CORE Philly, a nonprofit program that provides scholarships to help Philadelphia high school graduates attend select Pennsylvania colleges.

Fattah's own academic career is decidedly unconventional. Fattah dropped out of high school in early 1974, but got a General Equivalency Diploma (GED) later that year. He took undergraduate classes at a Philadelphia community college, but never graduated. Later, as a state lawmaker, he obtained a master's degree in 1986 from the University of Pennsylvania.

On the Appropriations Committee, Fattah has sought to address problems of blood supply contamination in AIDS-ravaged Africa. In 2005, he secured $2 million in the annual foreign aid bill to provide blood that was free of HIV, malaria and other diseases. A year later, he won House approval of a provision calling for a strategic plan to ensure a safe blood supply for Africa. His efforts drew letters of praise from U.N. Secretary General Kofi Annan and British Prime Minister Tony Blair.

Fattah arrived in Congress in 1995, just as Republicans assumed control. He became whip for the Congressional Black Caucus and wasted no time denouncing the new majority's ideas. During a debate early in the 104th Congress (1995-96) on a GOP proposal to overhaul the welfare system, he said, "We have some tough cowboys here on the floor of the House. This is a new, interesting kind of wagon train in which the cowboys have decided to throw the women and infants and the children and the senior citizens out of the wagon train so they can get where they are going faster. It is cruel."

Born Arthur Davenport, one of six boys in an inner-city household headed by his widowed mother, his name changed when his mother married community activist David Fattah. According to an Inquirer profile hung on his office wall, Fattah's mother named him "Chaka" in honor of a Zulu warrior. Fattah's parents produced a magazine for the black community and established their home as House of UMOJA, a neighborhood gathering spot and foster care haven for city youths trying to work their way out of gang life.

He met Democratic Rep. William H. Gray III and worked on one of his campaigns, and then, at age 22, finished fourth in a run for a municipal office. Four years later, he took on a Democratic Party-backed incumbent and won a state House seat and became, at 25, the youngest person ever elected to the state legislature. It was the first time — but by no means the last — that he challenged the party establishment and won.

After six years in the state House and six in the state Senate, Fattah entered the 1991 special-election race to succeed Gray, who had resigned to become president of the United Negro College Fund. The Democratic Party backed longtime City Councilman Lucien E. Blackwell, and Fattah temporarily quit the party to run on the Consumer Party ticket, but lost.

Redistricting for the 1990s — in which Fattah had a hand as a member of the state Senate — reduced the percentage of African-Americans in the 2nd District from 80 percent to 62 percent. That put Blackwell at risk because his appeal was strongest among West Philly's poor and working-class blacks, and in 1994 Fattah challenged his renomination. The incumbent had the backing of Mayor Edward G. Rendell and then City Council President Street.

But Fattah outworked Blackwell, claiming the primary victory. In the overwhelmingly Democratic 2nd, which changed only marginally in redistricting following the 2000 census, Fattah has not been seriously challenged.

KEY VOTES

2006

No Stop broadband companies from favoring select Internet traffic
No Affirm U.S. commitment to war in Iraq and reject setting a withdrawal date for troops
No Repeal requirement for bilingual ballots at the polls
Yes Permit U.S. sale of civilian nuclear technology to India
No Build a 700-mile fence on the U.S.-Mexico border to curb illegal crossings
No Permit warrantless wiretaps of suspected terrorists

2005

Yes Intervene in the life-support case of Terri Schiavo
Yes Lift President Bush's restrictions on stem cell research funding
Yes Prohibit FBI access to library and bookstore records
No Approve free-trade pact with five Central American countries
No Pass energy policy overhaul favored by President Bush emphasizing domestic oil and gas production
- End mandatory preservation of habitat of endangered animal and plant species
Yes Ban torture of prisoners in U.S. custody

CQ VOTE STUDIES

	PARTY UNITY		PRESIDENTIAL SUPPORT	
	Support	Oppose	Support	Oppose
2006	96%	4%	28%	72%
2005	96%	4%	11%	89%
2004	99%	1%	20%	80%
2003	95%	5%	17%	83%
2002	97%	3%	28%	72%

INTEREST GROUPS

	AFL-CIO	ADA	CCUS	ACU
2006	100%	100%	40%	8%
2005	92%	95%	40%	4%
2004	100%	85%	22%	0%
2003	100%	95%	21%	20%
2002	100%	95%	37%	0%

PENNSYLVANIA 2

West Philadelphia; Chestnut Hill; Cheltenham

From the vantage point of the William Penn statue atop City Hall, one can see the 2nd stretching west and north over some of Philadelphia's long-established neighborhoods. The district encompasses Center City skyscrapers, then moves west across the Schuylkill River past the University of Pennsylvania. West Philadelphia, once Irish, Greek and Jewish, is now nearly all black and features pockets of middle-class and poor communities. Overall, African-Americans represent more than three-fifths of the 2nd's residents.

Except for the Montgomery County township of Cheltenham, the 2nd is wholly within Philadelphia. The district includes the affluent city neighborhoods of Rittenhouse Square, one of five squares Penn designed in his original plan of the city, and Chestnut Hill, in the city's northwest corner. Fairmount Park, which flanks the Schuylkill River, houses the city's art museum, zoo and "Boathouse Row," and runs north along diverse, middle-class neighborhoods, some of which have seen some recent gentrification, and ends in Chestnut Hill.

Some of the city's lowest family incomes are found in neighborhoods just north of downtown. Partnerships with thriving area businesses have provided some relief to poor areas of the city. As part of the University of Pennsylvania's "Penn Compact," which was launched in 2004, the school collaborates with local communities on initiatives aimed at improving public education, public health, economic development, employment opportunities, quality of life and the physical landscape of West Philadelphia and Philadelphia. In addition, the institution's acclaimed medical school complements the 2nd's health care industry.

The 2nd's blue-collar workforce and large minority population give it an overwhelming Democratic majority. In the 2004 presidential election, John Kerry had his best showing in the state here, taking 87 percent of the district's vote.

MAJOR INDUSTRY
Higher education, health care, tourism

CITIES
Philadelphia (pt.), 609,480; Glenside (unincorporated) (pt.), 3,093

NOTABLE
The steps of the Philadelphia Museum of Art were immortalized in the movie, "Rocky"; The 30th Street Station is in West Philadelphia.

Rep. Phil English (R)

CAPITOL OFFICE
225-5406
www.house.gov/english
2332 Rayburn 20515-3803; fax 225-3103

COMMITTEES
Ways & Means
Joint Economic

RESIDENCE
Erie

BORN
June 20, 1956, Erie, Pa.

RELIGION
Roman Catholic

FAMILY
Wife, Christiane English

EDUCATION
U. of Pennsylvania, B.A. 1979 (political science)

CAREER
State legislative aide

POLITICAL HIGHLIGHTS
Erie City controller, 1986-89; Republican nominee for Pa. treasurer, 1988

ELECTION RESULTS

2006 GENERAL		
Phil English (R)	108,525	53.6%
Steven Porter (D)	85,110	42.1%
Timothy J. Hagberg (CNSTP)	8,706	4.3%
2006 PRIMARY		
Phil English (R)		unopposed
2004 GENERAL		
Phil English (R)	166,580	60.1%
Steven Porter (D)	110,684	39.9%

PREVIOUS WINNING PERCENTAGES
2002 (78%); 2000 (61%); 1998 (63%); 1996 (51%); 1994 (49%)

Elected 1994; 7th term

Sometimes losing isn't altogether bad. English expressed relief in late 2006 after losing a three-way race to lead the National Republican Congressional Committee, the campaign arm of the House GOP, which is charged with helping his party retake the House.

"Being in the leadership is a real challenge where there's a full-blown reaction against your party," English said. Although he placed third in the election contest for NRCC chairman, he agreed to lead an effort to retire the campaign committee's debt in 2007.

Moderate stands on trade, the Iraq War and union priorities helped English survive what he called a "real regional wipeout" for Northeastern Republicans in 2006. But the midterm election ended the congressional careers of his closest home-state GOP allies, Rep. Melissa A. Hart and Sen. Rick Santorum, both of whom once employed English.

English continued to plot an independent course early in the 110th Congress (2007-08). He was one of only 17 Republicans to back a resolution denouncing President Bush's decision to deploy thousands more U.S. troops to Iraq. He also voted for Democratic bills to increase the minimum wage and to reduce student loan interest rates.

"I am a social conservative who is also an economic populist, who is also pro-business," English says.

His expertise on tax issues has made him an important player in that arena ever since GOP leaders in 1995 made him the first Republican freshman in decades to serve on the Ways and Means Committee. In the 110th Congress, English became the ranking Republican on the Select Revenue Measures Subcommittee. From that post, he is positioned to lead his party's defense of Bush-era tax cuts set to expire in 2010.

Like Democrats, English wants to repeal the alternative minimum tax, which was created in 1969 to ensure that the wealthiest Americans could not avoid paying income tax. Now, the AMT hits more and more taxpayers each year because it is not indexed for inflation. "The AMT is terrible tax policy," English said, estimating that some 20 million taxpayers will be affected by it in 2008.

In 2007, he introduced legislation to repeal both the individual AMT and the corporate AMT, which hits capital-intensive industries including manufacturing, mining and construction. "The AMT is correctly called the anti-manufacturing tax," said English.

He also partnered with his Ways and Means colleague, Democrat Stephanie Tubbs Jones of Ohio to introduce a bill amending the tax code to spur the rehabilitation of historic buildings and create more affordable rental housing. Neighborhoods can be revitalized, he said, "by creating incentives to renovate our forgotten warehouses, homes, factories and hotels and re-use them as places to work and live."

English often works with business groups on favorable tax proposals. He helped win a "homeland investment" provision in the 2004 corporate tax law that provided a reduced tax rate for one year on foreign profits brought home by multinational companies.

He once tried to saw through the 5,000-page U.S. tax code in his hometown of Erie to illustrate how huge it has become. But the chain saw knocked the book off the table twice. Even after putting the code on the sidewalk, he was only able to nick it with the chain saw. Tax reform, English joked, will be difficult indeed.

English is not afraid to buck his party on trade or labor issues. In 2005, he voted against the Central American Free Trade Agreement in committee — the only Republican to do so. English then switched sides and helped the leadership pass the measure on the House floor after they agreed to allow a vote on his proposal to tax Chinese imports produced with government subsidies. His China bill passed the House but died in the Senate.

In 2002, English sided with steel workers by leading an effort to persuade Bush to impose tariffs on imported steel to help domestic steel companies, at the expense of U.S. manufacturers that wanted low-cost steel imports. The tariffs were repealed in 2003.

English was one of 22 Republicans who voted in 2004 to prevent the Labor Department from taking away eligibility of workers for overtime pay. (He had backed his party on a similar vote in 2003.) He also voted in favor of providing an additional 13 weeks of unemployment benefits for people who had exhausted their state benefits. But he does not always side with labor. He voted against a 2007 Democratic proposal that would have allowed union organizers to bypass secret-ballot elections at a company if a majority of its workers sign cards authorizing a union.

English's interest in politics began at an early age. The son of an Erie lawyer who was active in community affairs, English was a political science major in college and an alternate delegate, at age 20, to the 1976 Republican National Convention.

After college, English specialized in tax and social welfare issues for eight years as a legislative aide in a closely divided Pennsylvania State Legislature. In 1985, he was elected city controller of Erie, on a pledge to be a watchdog over the Democratically dominated government. He was the first Republican elected to citywide office in 20 years. In 1988, at the midpoint of his four-year term, he ran for state treasurer. He lost by nearly 500,000 votes.

When his term as controller was over, he moved from candidate to strategist. He helped Santorum, then a little-known underdog, organize his 1990 upset of Democratic Rep. Doug Walgren. English then returned to Harrisburg as a legislative staffer, including a stint as chief of staff to then state Senator Hart. He jumped at the chance to run for an open House seat in 1994, when GOP Rep. Tom Ridge ran, successfully, for governor.

The 3rd District still lies within a partisan battleground, and English's winning percentages in his first two races hovered near 50 percent of the vote. His evolving ideology helped him crack 60 percent of the vote in each election since 1998. However, in 2006, the strong anti-GOP tide tempered his winning vote share to 54 percent.

KEY VOTES

2006

No Stop broadband companies from favoring select Internet traffic
Yes Affirm U.S. commitment to war in Iraq and reject setting a withdrawal date for troops
No Repeal requirement for bilingual ballots at the polls
Yes Permit U.S. sale of civilian nuclear technology to India
Yes Build a 700-mile fence on the U.S.-Mexico border to curb illegal crossings
Yes Permit warrantless wiretaps of suspected terrorists

2005

Yes Intervene in the life-support case of Terri Schiavo
No Lift President Bush's restrictions on stem cell research funding
No Prohibit FBI access to library and bookstore records
Yes Approve free-trade pact with five Central American countries
Yes Pass energy policy overhaul favored by President Bush emphasizing domestic oil and gas production
Yes End mandatory preservation of habitat of endangered animal and plant species
Yes Ban torture of prisoners in U.S. custody

CQ VOTE STUDIES

	PARTY UNITY		PRESIDENTIAL SUPPORT	
	Support	Oppose	Support	Oppose
2006	90%	10%	95%	5%
2005	93%	7%	85%	15%
2004	88%	12%	76%	24%
2003	93%	7%	91%	9%
2002	93%	7%	87%	13%

INTEREST GROUPS

	AFL-CIO	ADA	CCUS	ACU
2006	43%	15%	100%	80%
2005	20%	5%	93%	88%
2004	40%	25%	90%	68%
2003	21%	20%	93%	68%
2002	11%	0%	95%	92%

PENNSYLVANIA 3

Northwest – Erie

Nestled in the northwestern corner of the state, the 3rd takes in all of Erie County — Pennsylvania's only Lake Erie coastline — and includes parts of six other counties. The economy of this Rust Belt, historically blue-collar area centers around the city of Erie's port and industrial sector.

Erie County, where roughly 45 percent of the district's residents live, has retained an industrial presence despite many years of industry decline. Overall, manufacturing makes up nearly a quarter of the county's workforce and the number of jobs in the service sector has increased by more than 20 percent since 1990. General Electric is the city's largest employer, and the health care industry here continues to grow. There are several high precision technology companies in the area, and the city also attracts nearly 4 million visitors each year, especially during the warmer months, to the public beaches and Presque Isle State Park.

Outside of Erie, no city has more than 17,000 residents. These communities are dominated by small business and scores of tooling and machine shops, especially in Crawford County. Mercer County (a small portion of which is in the 4th) still has some steel mills and boasts the largest concentration of pipe and tube production companies in the nation. Like most of the district, Butler County in the south is dominated by manufacturing, although Butler also benefits from the presence of Slippery Rock University.

The city of Erie's median household income is well below the state or national averages, while townships in surrounding areas are above the median. Pockets of black residents in northern and central Erie help give the county a Democratic lean, and Mercer also has a Democratic lean. These Democratic tendencies are offset by the Republican leanings in Butler and Crawford counties. Overall, the district gave George W. Bush 53 percent of its presidential vote in 2004.

MAJOR INDUSTRY

Manufacturing, service

CITIES

Erie, 103,717; Sharon, 16,328; Butler, 15,121

NOTABLE

The reconstructed U.S. Brig Niagara, a fighting ship from the War of 1812, is docked in Erie; In 1941, the Bantam Car Company of Butler developed the Bantam Reconnaissance Car, the prototype of the Jeep.

Rep. Jason Altmire (D)

Elected 2006; 1st term

Altmire upset three-term GOP incumbent Melissa A. Hart by running as a conservative Democrat, which he says is in line with his politically "down-the-middle" constituents of western Pennsylvania.

Though this is Altmire's first time in a public office, it isn't his first time in Washington. He worked nearly seven years as a congressional aide to former Florida Democratic Rep. Pete Peterson in the 1990s. Altmire was part of a congressional task force on health care during the 1993 push by President Bill Clinton for a new national health care policy. He said the experience led him to consider a career in health care services.

He went to school at night and earned a master's degree in health services administration. And he ended up working for the Federation of American Hospitals and then the University of Pittsburgh Medical Center. He wants to allow the importation of prescription drugs from Canada and Western Europe, and says the government should negotiate prescription drug prices for Medicare directly with manufacturers.

A social conservative, Altmire backs gun owners' rights and opposes abortion. But he supports federal funding for embryonic stem cell research because, he said, he saw the benefits of it at the Pittsburgh medical center.

Altmire was given a seat on the Education and Labor Committee, where he hopes to help revise the No Child Left Behind national education law. He said he regularly heard complaints from teachers and administrators in his district that the 2002 law is too cumbersome.

Altmire grew up as the only child of a single parent in a working-class neighborhood of Lower Burrell. His mother was a schoolteacher. He lettered in two sports in high school and was a walk-on football player at Florida State, which won its first Sugar Bowl while he was on the team.

Altmire said he decided to run against Hart because he couldn't understand how the 4th District could be represented by someone with "such a right-of-center voting record." After besting local businesswoman Georgia Berner in the primary, he linked Hart to President Bush and the GOP congressional leadership. Altmire won with 52 percent of the vote.

CAPITOL OFFICE
225-2565
altmire.house.gov
1419 Longworth 20515-3804; fax 226-2274

COMMITTEES
Education & Labor
Small Business
(Investigations & Oversight - chairman)
Transportation & Infrastructure

RESIDENCE
McCandless

BORN
March 7, 1968, Kittanning, Pa.

RELIGION
Roman Catholic

FAMILY
Wife, Kelly Altmire; two children

EDUCATION
Florida State U., B.S. 1990 (political science); George Washington U., M.H.S.A. 1998 (health services administration)

CAREER
Hospital association executive; lobbyist; congressional aide

POLITICAL HIGHLIGHTS
No previous office

ELECTION RESULTS

2006 GENERAL		
Jason Altmire (D)	131,847	51.9%
Melissa A. Hart (R)	122,049	48.1%
2006 PRIMARY		
Jason Altmire (D)	32,322	54.9%
Georgia Berner (D)	26,596	45.1%

PENNSYLVANIA 4

West — Pittsburgh suburbs

The 4th begins in the southwest corner of Mercer County and runs down the state's western border before heading east to wrap around the northern and eastern sides of Pittsburgh. Once a top steel producer, this traditionally blue-collar district has yet to fully recover from economic hardships.

The area's major highways and proximity to Pittsburgh make the 4th attractive to commuters as well as new or expanding companies. Although abandoned steel mills still line the rivers here, other sectors are beginning to prosper. The 4th's health care industry is a major employer, as are a growing number of computer firms. Larger companies, such as Respironics in Murrysville, TRACO in Cranberry Township and USG in Aliquippa, bring jobs to the area.

The district has yet to regain the population it had during its booming steel days, but some areas, including parts of southern Butler County, are experiencing rapid residential growth. These areas are becoming home to a growing white-collar, well-educated workforce, much of which is employed in the health care industry. Outside of Pittsburgh's exurbs, smaller communities produce numerous agricultural products, including corn, soybeans, dairy and winter wheat.

Although union tradition usually has kept the district's area Democratic from the township level to the presidency, Republicans can break the Democratic grip. The 4th's GOP base is found in small farming communities and wealthy Pittsburgh suburbs such as Franklin Park, Fox Chapel and Marshall Township. In 2006, Democrats recaptured the 4th after six years of GOP control.

MAJOR INDUSTRY
Health care, steel, manufacturing

CITIES
Ross Township, 32,551; Shaler Township, 29,757; McCandless Township, 29,022

NOTABLE
New Castle calls itself the fireworks capital of the United States.

Rep. John E. Peterson (R)

CAPITOL OFFICE
225-5121
www.house.gov/johnpeterson
123 Cannon 20515-3805; fax 225-5796

COMMITTEES
Appropriations

RESIDENCE
Pleasantville

BORN
Dec. 25, 1938, Titusville, Pa.

RELIGION
Methodist

FAMILY
Wife, Saundra Peterson; one child

EDUCATION
Titusville H.S., graduated 1956

MILITARY SERVICE
Army Reserve, 1957-63

CAREER
Supermarket owner

POLITICAL HIGHLIGHTS
Pleasantville Borough Council, 1969-77; Pa. House, 1977-85; Pa. Senate, 1985-97

ELECTION RESULTS

2006 GENERAL		
John E. Peterson (R)	115,126	60.1%
Donald L. Hilliard (D)	76,456	39.9%
2006 PRIMARY		
John E. Peterson (R)		unopposed
2004 GENERAL		
John E. Peterson (R)	192,852	88.0%
Thomas A. Martin (LIBERT)	26,239	12.0%

PREVIOUS WINNING PERCENTAGES
2002 (87%); 2000 (83%); 1998 (85%); 1996 (60%)

Elected 1996; 6th term

Peterson, who grew up five miles from the nation's first successful oil well, is a staunch and consistent protector of the oil and gas industry — even when it comes to issues well beyond the borders of his sprawling district in northern Pennsylvania. But while his overwhelming re-election victories may allow him to stray a bit, he still tailors his legislative portfolio to fit the district's rural needs, focusing on rural health care and economic development, particularly from his position on the Appropriations Committee.

Peterson is as conservative as they come on most issues. He opposes abortion, supports gun owners' rights and wants to give parents taxpayer-financed vouchers to pay tuition at private schools. In the 109th Congress, he voted with his party 96 percent of the time. With a strong work ethic developed at a young age when his family struggled to make ends meet, he doesn't give up on his pursuits — particularly when it comes to offshore drilling.

In the 109th Congress (2005-06), Peterson — whose district is the birthplace of America's oil industry — waged a determined battle for legislation to lift longstanding moratoriums on offshore drilling along the nation's coastlines. While the House did pass a broad measure, the bill that made it into law only opened a patch of ocean south of the Florida panhandle.

Peterson argues that high natural gas prices are pushing jobs overseas, and he thinks President Bush is behind the curve in recognizing the crisis. "I'm going to tell you, if the president doesn't step forward on this, it's going to be on his time, on his watch, that major industries leave this country," Peterson warned in a 2006 Web telecast.

In a fierce fight for his bill in the 109th Congress, Peterson sought to play on anti-Castro sentiment in hopes of winning the votes of skeptical Florida lawmakers who wanted to keep drilling rigs far from their beaches. Since Cuba, which lies about 100 miles from Florida, already had begun developing oil resources off its own shores, the United States should lift its decades-old drilling moratorium, he said. "It's astounding we're going to sit here and say, 'We're not going to produce,' and, meanwhile, our good friend [Cuban President] Fidel Castro is going to suck it up under our noses," Peterson told The Miami Herald.

Peterson wasted no time renewing his attack in the 110th Congress (2007-08). In January, he again paired up with Democratic Senator Mary L. Landrieu of Louisiana to call for expanded drilling opportunities along the nation's Outer Continental Shelf. Peterson railed against the Bush administration at a March 2007 Appropriations subcommittee hearing, saying, "It makes absolutely no sense to continue a moratorium, which is having such negative effects on our economy and the daily lives of our citizens."

Peterson also has spent considerable time focusing on issues closer to home. His district covers almost one-quarter of the state, sprawling across more than 10,000 square miles of mountains, valleys, hamlets and a sizable national forest. It is the home of Punxsutawney Phil, the famous groundhog who every February determines whether spring is on its way. The largest urban area is a college town — State College, home of Pennsylvania State University.

Peterson has pushed for legislation to improve health care access in rural areas. In 2003, he and other members of the Congressional Rural Caucus, which he co-chairs, convinced congressional leaders to include increased payments to rural hospitals and health care providers in a Medicare overhaul plan — which became law — that also provided a prescription drug benefit. In January 2007, he voted against a Democratic bill that would require the government to negotiate drug prices on behalf of Medicare drug beneficiaries, saying it would allow bureaucrats to set the price for prescriptions and reduce seniors' access to essential medications.

From his seat on the Appropriations subcommittee with jurisdiction over the National Institutes of Health budget, Peterson has helped Penn State and Pennsylvania's five other medical schools win a hefty share of federal research money.

Peterson was born and raised in the small town of Titusville near the spot where Edwin Drake drilled the country's first oil well. His father was a steelworker who never went to high school and who was a recovering alcoholic. The four children went to work to help with family expenses, and college was never an option for Peterson.

He emerged from this childhood with a strong work ethic, as well as an aversion to alcohol that led to his work combating substance abuse among rural youths. He is among the most vocal advocates of legislation mandating random drug testing for all high school students, saying it could reduce overall drug use and school violence. "Schools that use random drug testing not only provide young people with a good reason to say no to drugs, but also give parents a report card that may help save their child's life," he says.

A year after completing high school, Peterson joined the Army Reserve and then opened a small grocery store in nearby Pleasantville with his brother and a family friend, who put up the money. Peterson eventually bought out his partners and expanded the store, which he sold in 1984.

He entered politics in 1969, at the urging of businessmen in Pleasantville, winning a seat on the borough council. After eight years, he was elected to the state House in a special election. Eight years after that, he moved to the state Senate, where he chaired the Public Health and Welfare Committee and the Republican Policy Committee.

When Republican Rep. William F. Clinger did not seek re-election in 1996, Peterson made a run for it and won with 60 percent of the vote. But his victory did not come easily; he had to fight off three opponents in the Republican primary, including Bob Shuster, a son of Bud Shuster, then the veteran congressman from a neighboring district.

His Republican base secure, Peterson has had no re-election difficulty. From 1998 to 2004, Democrats declined to field a candidate, and in 2006 Peterson routed his Democratic opponent, winning by 20 percentage points despite the anti-Republican mood nationwide.

KEY VOTES

2006

- ? Stop broadband companies from favoring select Internet traffic
- Yes Affirm U.S. commitment to war in Iraq and reject setting a withdrawal date for troops
- Yes Repeal requirement for bilingual ballots at the polls
- Yes Permit U.S. sale of civilian nuclear technology to India
- Yes Build a 700-mile fence on the U.S.-Mexico border to curb illegal crossings
- Yes Permit warrantless wiretaps of suspected terrorists

2005

- Yes Intervene in the life-support case of Terri Schiavo
- No Lift President Bush's restrictions on stem cell research funding
- Yes Prohibit FBI access to library and bookstore records
- Yes Approve free-trade pact with five Central American countries
- Yes Pass energy policy overhaul favored by President Bush emphasizing domestic oil and gas production
- Yes End mandatory preservation of habitat of endangered animal and plant species
- No Ban torture of prisoners in U.S. custody

CQ VOTE STUDIES

	PARTY UNITY		PRESIDENTIAL SUPPORT	
	Support	Oppose	Support	Oppose
2006	97%	3%	92%	8%
2005	95%	5%	83%	17%
2004	92%	8%	79%	21%
2003	96%	4%	91%	9%
2002	94%	6%	84%	16%

INTEREST GROUPS

	AFL-CIO	ADA	CCUS	ACU
2006	14%	0%	93%	88%
2005	15%	0%	92%	92%
2004	33%	15%	100%	83%
2003	13%	10%	90%	83%
2002	13%	0%	100%	100%

PENNSYLVANIA 5

North central — State College

The sprawling 5th covers one-fourth of the state's land area and takes in all or part of 17 counties in north-central Pennsylvania. Bordering New York to its north, the district extends as far south as Mifflin County and Centre County, where the state's largest university, Pennsylvania State University, is in State College. Decidedly conservative, the district's small towns, which are spread among state and national parks and forests, depend on small businesses and an ailing manufacturing industry.

State College, known by locals as "Happy Valley," is the district's most populated city. The city and the university, a research institution, have attracted manufacturing firms that specialize in electronics and computer products. Both AccuWeather and C-COR, a communications network company, have their global headquarters here.

While State College's workforce is technologically advanced, the 5th's other counties remain tied to timber production, manufacturing, oil refining and tourism. In 2004, parts of the district's western region were designated as the Oil Region National Heritage Area. Thousands of tourists visit the district, many of them traveling through the heart of the Allegheny National Forest on the 5th's portion of scenic and meandering Route 6, which stretches more than 400 miles across northern Pennsylvania and passes scores of hamlets that dot the landscape. Punxsutawney, home of Punxsutawney Phil, draws national attention each Groundhog Day.

Much of the 5th — particularly the northern counties — votes Republican, and George W. Bush won all of its counties in the 2004 presidential election en route to garnering 61 percent of the overall district vote. Some exceptions exist: Penn State keeps Centre County competitive for Democrats.

MAJOR INDUSTRY
Manufacturing, higher education, timber, tourism

CITIES
State College, 38,420; St. Marys, 14,502; Oil City, 11,504

NOTABLE
The Grand Canyon of Pennsylvania lies amid the roughly 160,000 acres of the Tioga State Forest; Drake's Well, the birthplace of the modern petroleum industry, is located along the banks of Oil Creek near Titusville; South Williamsport hosts the Little League World Series each summer.

Rep. Jim Gerlach (R)

CAPITOL OFFICE
225-4315
www.house.gov/gerlach
308 Cannon 20515-3806; fax 225-8440

COMMITTEES
Financial Services
Transportation & Infrastructure

RESIDENCE
West Pikeland Township

BORN
Feb. 25, 1955, Ellwood City, Pa.

RELIGION
Protestant

FAMILY
Wife, Karen Gerlach; three children, three stepchildren

EDUCATION
Dickinson College, B.A. 1977 (political science); Dickinson School of Law, J.D. 1980

CAREER
Lawyer

POLITICAL HIGHLIGHTS
Republican nominee for Pa. House, 1986; Pa. House, 1991-95; Pa. Senate, 1995-2003

ELECTION RESULTS

2006 GENERAL		
Jim Gerlach (R)	121,047	50.7%
Lois Murphy (D)	117,892	49.3%
2006 PRIMARY		
Jim Gerlach (R)		unopposed
2004 GENERAL		
Jim Gerlach (R)	160,348	51.0%
Lois Murphy (D)	153,977	49.0%

PREVIOUS WINNING PERCENTAGES
2002 (51%)

Elected 2002; 3rd term

By steadily moving away from President Bush over two terms in the House, Gerlach managed to stave off an aggressive Democratic challenger in 2006. He could be a model for Republican moderates hoping to hang onto their seats in 2008.

Gerlach's (GUR-lock) voting record is peppered with a number of high-profile stands against Bush and the House GOP leadership on issues ranging from same-sex marriage to oil drilling in wilderness areas. Under pressure from labor unions, he publicly disavowed Bush's proposal to overhaul Social Security with private savings accounts. So when his opponent in 2006, lawyer Lois Murphy, tried to tie him to Bush, Gerlach replied, "When I think he's wrong, I let him know."

On the biggest issue of the election, the war in Iraq, Gerlach expressed doubts about Bush's policies though he ultimately opposed a Democratic effort in 2007 to tie war spending to troop withdrawal deadlines.

Gerlach represents a classic swing suburban district that was redrawn after the 2000 census with a slight Republican edge. He has won all of his elections by less than 3 percentage points. The GOP leadership is understanding, therefore, when he drifts from party positions. The leaders have also helped him raise his visibility, giving him a seat on the Transportation and Infrastructure Committee, from which he can direct highway money to his district, and on the Financial Services Committee, a magnet for campaign contributions from banking and insurance firms.

Over his career, Gerlach's voting record practically mirrored the decline in Bush's approval ratings. In 2003, Gerlach backed the president's position 91 percent of the time. In 2004, that rate fell to 76 percent, and in both 2005 and 2006, it dropped to 69 percent.

In the 110th Congress (2007-08), Gerlach backed several initiatives of the new Democratic majority, including votes to increase the federal minimum wage and to fund embryonic stem cell research, which uses surplus embryos from in vitro fertilization.

Gerlach has used his environmental record to prove his independence from the White House. He opposed drilling in the Arctic National Wildlife Refuge, though in 2005 he switched his vote under pressure from GOP leaders to help pass a major energy bill. In 2006, he pushed legislation that created tax incentives for purchases of hybrid vehicles. He succeeded in moving legislation through the House in September 2006 giving federal cash incentives to cities that take steps to maintain open space, a longtime issue for Gerlach dating to his days in the Pennsylvania General Assembly.

In 2007, Gerlach and two Democrats, Rep. Ron Kind of Wisconsin and Sen. Robert Menendez of New Jersey, introduced sweeping legislation to increase renewable energy production, expand access to locally grown foods and protect drinking water supplies. "Through his years of representation, Jim Gerlach had developed a brand image as independent, compassionate and likeable," Republican strategist John Brabender wrote in Campaigns and Elections magazine.

Before coming to Congress, Gerlach spent 12 years as a well-regarded state legislator. He was the prime sponsor of Pennsylvania's 1996 welfare law overhaul. He also championed legislation to combat suburban sprawl and mediated disputes between local authorities.

Though Pennsylvania lost two seats in post-2000 reapportionment, Gerlach's colleagues in the Republican-dominated General Assembly redrew the congressional map for this decade with him in mind. No House incumbent chose to run in the redrawn 6th District — which had a close partisan split, but overlapped with much of Gerlach's state Senate territory — and he was unopposed for the GOP nod in 2002. In November, he won by 5,520 votes over Democratic lawyer Dan Wofford, the son of former U.S. Sen. Harris Wofford. His two subsequent re-elections were also difficult.

Calling herself a "fiscally disciplined Democrat," Murphy in her first challenge to Gerlach in 2004 collected endorsements from the Sierra Club and other national issue groups, such as MoveOn.org and Emily's List, a fundraising group that supports women candidates. She also was able to keep pace with Gerlach in the size of her war chest, thanks in no small measure to retaining Pennsylvania Democratic Gov. Edward G. Rendell as one of her campaign co-chairmen.

Gerlach painted Murphy as too liberal for the district, helped by national GOP attack ads, one of which had a picture of Murphy next to the phrase, "Negotiating with Taliban." It was based on an opinion piece by a board member of the Council for a Livable World, a group that had endorsed Murphy. She accused Gerlach of "an outrageous smear," but he won with 51 percent.

Gerlach spent much of the 109th Congress (2005-06) preparing for a rematch after being named one of the GOP's most vulnerable incumbents by political prognosticators. In the 2006 race, Murphy outdid him raising campaign funds, $4.1 million to $3.4 million. Fundraising committees for the two major parties also spent about $6.8 million in independent expenditures on the race.

The campaigns again were marked by considerable negative advertising, with Gerlach calling his opponent "Liberal Lois," and painting her as a tax-and-spend Democrat. Murphy went by the playbook of the national Democrats and tried to tie Gerlach to Bush's policies and the war in Iraq.

In one high-impact television ad shortly before Election Day, Gerlach addressed the camera clad in a bright orange sweater and methodically denied Murphy's accusations point by point. He also won endorsements from some traditionally Democratic constituencies, such as the National Education Association and local teachers' unions.

Gerlach defied the national trend and defeated the Democrat by slightly more than 3,000 votes, even while political giants fell around him.

Early in 2007, the Federal Election Commission fined his campaign $120,000 — one of the largest fines ever — for inaccurate campaign finance reports in 2004 and 2005. Gerlach said a clerical error was to blame: "The wrong number was put on the wrong line."

KEY VOTES

2006

- No Stop broadband companies from favoring select Internet traffic
- Yes Affirm U.S. commitment to war in Iraq and reject setting a withdrawal date for troops
- No Repeal requirement for bilingual ballots at the polls
- Yes Permit U.S. sale of civilian nuclear technology to India
- Yes Build a 700-mile fence on the U.S.-Mexico border to curb illegal crossings
- Yes Permit warrantless wiretaps of suspected terrorists

2005

- ? Intervene in the life-support case of Terri Schiavo
- Yes Lift President Bush's restrictions on stem cell research funding
- No Prohibit FBI access to library and bookstore records
- Yes Approve free-trade pact with five Central American countries
- Yes Pass energy policy overhaul favored by President Bush emphasizing domestic oil and gas production
- No End mandatory preservation of habitat of endangered animal and plant species
- Yes Ban torture of prisoners in U.S. custody

CQ VOTE STUDIES

	PARTY UNITY		PRESIDENTIAL SUPPORT	
	Support	Oppose	Support	Oppose
2006	70%	30%	69%	31%
2005	82%	18%	69%	31%
2004	84%	16%	76%	24%
2003	91%	9%	91%	9%

INTEREST GROUPS

	AFL-CIO	ADA	CCUS	ACU
2006	57%	45%	79%	62%
2005	40%	35%	81%	56%
2004	14%	20%	100%	68%
2003	7%	5%	97%	72%

PENNSYLVANIA 6

Southeast – part of Berks and Chester counties, Philadelphia suburbs

The 6th takes in urban, suburban and rural communities stretching from a slice of Montgomery County in the Philadelphia area, including the county seat of Norristown, through northern Chester County and southern and eastern portions of Berks County, including part of Reading and all of Kutztown. Most of the district's land is spread through sparsely populated towns.

Manufacturing remains the 6th's largest industry, and factories are found throughout, especially in areas such as Coatesville. Vanguard, an investment management company, is based in the district, and a growing food processing sector should help further diversify the 6th's economy. Once known for its railroads and industrial prowess, the economy of Berks County has branched out to include service and retail jobs. Reading has moved away from its industrial image, becoming an entertainment and shopping hub outside of Philadelphia.

With its share of historical sites and untouched land, the 6th enjoys a modest tourism industry. The district is home to numerous covered bridges, old mill towns and Pennsylvania Dutch communities. It also is home to both the Hopewell Furnace National Historic Site in Elverson and Valley Forge National Historical Park (shared with the 7th), where George Washington trained the soldiers of the Continental Army during the Revolutionary War.

The 6th makes the nation's dwindling list of competitive districts: John Kerry bested Republican George W. Bush here in the 2004 presidential election by 3 percentage points, while GOP Rep. Gerlach won by just over 1 percentage point in 2006. Growth and water-use issues dominate much of the political discussion in the region, which is mostly situated in the area triangulated by Philadelphia, Reading and Lancaster.

MAJOR INDUSTRY

Manufacturing, tourism, retail

CITIES

Reading (pt.), 36,911; Norristown, 31,282; Pottstown, 21,859

NOTABLE

The largest quilt sale in the United States takes places each year at the Kutztown Pennsylvania German Festival.

Rep. Joe Sestak (D)

CAPITOL OFFICE
225-2011
sestak.house.gov
1022 Longworth 20515-3807; fax 225-8137

COMMITTEES
Armed Services
Education & Labor
Small Business

RESIDENCE
Edgmont

BORN
Dec. 12, 1951, Secane, Pa.

RELIGION
Roman Catholic

FAMILY
Wife, Susan Clark-Sestak; one child

EDUCATION
U.S. Naval Academy, B.S. 1974 (American political systems); Harvard U., M.P.A. 1980, Ph.D. 1984 (political economy & government)

MILITARY SERVICE
Navy, 1974-2005

CAREER
Navy officer

POLITICAL HIGHLIGHTS
No previous office

ELECTION RESULTS

2006 GENERAL		
Joe Sestak (D)	147,898	56.4%
Curt Weldon (R)	114,426	43.6%
2006 PRIMARY		
Joe Sestak (D)		unopposed

Elected 2006; 1st term

A retired Navy vice admiral, Sestak is the highest-ranking former military officer ever to serve in the U.S. House of Representatives. His appointment to the Armed Services Committee is a textbook fit for a man who served as Director of Defense Policy on the National Security Council in the Clinton administration.

Described by colleagues as a brilliant and exceptionally demanding leader with a solid grasp of national security issues, Sestak (SESS-tack) has the perspective of a career military man with three decades in the Navy. He considers the Iraq War a "tragic misadventure" and planned to use his committee slot to push for the redeployment of troops beginning in 2007.

He campaigned on the Naval Academy's tenet of, "Don't lie, don't steal, don't cheat" — a theme that helped him topple 10-term Republican Curt Weldon after Weldon was accused of using his post to get contracts for his daughter's lobbying firm. Sestak also ran on his vehement opposition to the Bush administration's handling of the war on terrorism.

Sestak says government should emulate how the military treats its members by supporting universal health care, significant education benefits and equal rights for women and minorities.

When Sestak's daughter was in the hospital fighting brain cancer, the parents of a boy with leukemia in the neighboring bed were tormented over how to pay for their son's care without health insurance. That experience led Sestak to adopt health care as a priority and to propose a nine-step approach in which government takes a more active role in the areas of accountability, benefits and insurance plan choices without seizing control of the entire system. However, Sestak in his freshman term did not win appointment to any of the committees handling health care policy. His second major assignment is to the Education and Labor Committee.

Though he considers the 7th District his home, prior to the election Sestak hadn't lived there since 1970, when he left for the academy and began his Navy career. Since winning his seat, he has bought a home in the district, and has met with businesses, unions and schools in search of ways to create jobs.

PENNSYLVANIA 7

Suburban Philadelphia — most of Delaware County

Anchored in the suburbs south and west of Philadelphia, the politically competitive 7th takes in vast tracts of middle-class suburbia, including most of Delaware County, the district's population center, as well as southwestern Montgomery and eastern Chester counties.

Older suburbs in Delaware County such as Norwood, Ridley Park, Media and Upper Darby are mostly white and working-class. Oil refineries and chemical facilities continue to drive the economy around the Delaware River communities of Marcus Hook and Trainer. Upper Merion Township in Montgomery County has been expanding rapidly since the 1990s opening of the Blue Route (Interstate 476), which links Interstate 95 along the Delaware River with the Schuylkill Expressway near King of Prussia.

A Boeing helicopter facility in Ridley Park and Lockheed Martin's plant in King of Prussia provide many jobs, as do the district's pharmaceutical and technology sectors. The rapid growth of white-collar jobs has given the district the state's most educated workforce. New developments, many of which are springing up in the less-populated areas of Chester County, are attracting city residents.

Either major party can win here, with Democrats making inroads in previously Republican Delaware County. John Kerry took 53 percent of the district's vote in the 2004 presidential election, and voters here replaced their GOP House member with a Democrat in 2006.

MAJOR INDUSTRY
Pharmaceuticals, defense, health care

CITIES
Radnor Township, 30,878; Drexel Hill (unincorporated), 29,364

NOTABLE
Villanova University hosts the largest student-organized Special Olympics festival.

Rep. Patrick J. Murphy (D)

CAPITOL OFFICE
225-4276
patrickmurphy.house.gov
1007 Longworth 20515-3808; fax 225-9511

COMMITTEES
Armed Services
Select Intelligence

RESIDENCE
Bristol Township

BORN
Oct. 19, 1973, Philadelphia, Pa.

RELIGION
Roman Catholic

FAMILY
Wife, Jennifer Murphy; one child

EDUCATION
Bucks County Community College, attended 1991-92; King's College (Pa.), B.S. 1996 (psychology & human resources); Widener U., Harrisburg, J.D. 1999

MILITARY SERVICE
Army, 1996-2004; Army Reserve, 2004-present

CAREER
Lawyer; military prosecutor; college instructor

POLITICAL HIGHLIGHTS
No previous office

ELECTION RESULTS

2006 GENERAL		
Patrick J. Murphy (D)	125,656	50.3%
Michael G. Fitzpatrick (R)	124,138	49.7%
2006 PRIMARY		
Patrick J. Murphy (D)	17,889	64.6%
Andrew L. Warren (D)	9,812	35.4%

Elected 2006; 1st term

Murphy has the kind of credibility few can match when he calls for a new direction in Iraq and a withdrawal of U.S. combat forces. He has been there, done that, and he is the only member of Congress who has.

The former Army paratrooper served in Iraq from June 2003 to January 2004 as a captain in the 82nd Airborne Division. He lost 19 members of his unit in combat. "Walking in my own combat boots, I saw firsthand this administration's failed policy in Iraq," he told the House on Feb. 13, 2007, as he urged members to oppose President Bush's decision to deploy thousands more troops to the battlefront. Murphy also cosponsored legislation mandating a withdrawal of combat forces from Iraq. "Our troops have done their job — now it's time to start bringing them home," he said in February 2007.

Democratic leaders gave him seats on two high-profile committees: Armed Services and Select Intelligence. He introduced a resolution that would require quarterly reports on the expenditures of military and reconstruction funds in Iraq, including efforts to obtain assistance from other countries and an assessment of future funding needs. And he cosponsored numerous measures to improve benefits for returning war veterans.

Murphy is allied with the fiscally conservative Blue Dog Coalition. In 2007, he joined 11 other Democrats who broke with their party and voted against the budget resolution. He said it failed to protect middle-class tax breaks enacted under Republicans or to rein in government spending.

Murphy is the youngest of three children. His father was a Philadelphia police officer and his mother was a legal secretary. He first put on an Army uniform in 1993 as an ROTC cadet in college. After graduating from law school at Widener University, he taught at West Point, served as a military prosecutor and was deployed to Bosnia in 2002.

Murphy edged incumbent Republican Rep. Michael G. Fitzpatrick by a mere 1,518 votes in one of the tightest races of the 2006 elections. It was a busy few months for Murphy, who got married in June, was elected in November and became a father a few weeks later.

PENNSYLVANIA 8

Northern Philadelphia suburbs — Bucks County

North of Philadelphia, the 8th takes in all of Bucks County, a small part of Montgomery County and a slice of Northeast Philadelphia. Founded in 1682 as one of the state's three original counties, Bucks' stately mansions, scenery and charm still attract wealthy new residents. Development began in the 1950s with the opening of Levittown, one of the earliest planned U.S. suburbs. The area's healthy, white-collar economy now claims to support more than 20,000 small businesses.

Steel, once a major employer in Bucks, saw cutbacks for blue-collar workers. A deep-water port makes the 8th something of a distribution and warehouse center, and the district also is home to several hospitals. One of the state's first racetrack/casino enterprises opened in the county in 2006.

Voters in the 8th tend to be fiscally conservative but support environmentalism and hold moderate stances on some social issues. Upper Bucks leans Republican, and the GOP also does well in wealthy Upper and Lower Makefield townships.

Although the GOP dominates local elections in the 8th, Democrats compete in statewide and federal elections and are strong in southeastern Bucks and in the Pennsylvania suburbs of Trenton, N.J. Democratic Gov. Edward G. Rendell took 70 percent of the Bucks County vote in 2006. Democratic Rep. Murphy narrowly lost Bucks in 2006, but he secured 62 percent of the vote in the 8th's portion of Montgomery County, enough for him to win the district.

MAJOR INDUSTRY
Health care, wholesale and retail trade

CITIES
Levittown (unincorporated), 53,966; Philadelphia (pt.), 30,938

NOTABLE
George Washington's Delaware River crossing is re-enacted in Washington Crossing each Christmas Day.

Rep. Bill Shuster (R)

CAPITOL OFFICE
225-2431
www.house.gov/shuster
204 Cannon 20515-3809; fax 225-2486

COMMITTEES
Armed Services
Natural Resources
Small Business
Transportation & Infrastructure

RESIDENCE
Hollidaysburg

BORN
Jan. 10, 1961, McKeesport, Pa.

RELIGION
Lutheran

FAMILY
Wife, Rebecca Shuster; two children

EDUCATION
Dickinson College, B.A. 1983 (political science & history); American U., M.B.A. 1987

CAREER
Car dealer; tire company manager

POLITICAL HIGHLIGHTS
No previous office

ELECTION RESULTS

2006 GENERAL		
Bill Shuster (R)	121,069	60.3%
Tony Barr (D)	79,610	39.7%
2006 PRIMARY		
Bill Shuster (R)		unopposed
2004 GENERAL		
Bill Shuster (R)	184,320	69.5%
Paul I. Politis (D)	80,787	30.5%

PREVIOUS WINNING PERCENTAGES
2002 (71%); 2001 Special Election (52%)

Elected May 2001; 3rd full term

Now in his third full term, Shuster appears to have cemented his grip on the House seat his father held for more than 28 years. He has done so by shunning the national spotlight and concentrating on steering federal funds home for economic development and public works improvements.

Known as the "king of asphalt," GOP Rep. Bud Shuster was chairman of the Transportation and Infrastructure Committee for six years before he resigned in January 2001 citing health concerns, though he also had been reprimanded by the House ethics committee in 2000 for his relationship with a longtime former aide-turned-lobbyist.

By waiting until after he was sworn in for a 15th term to resign, the elder Shuster paved the way for his son to be anointed to run for his seat in an abbreviated special election. Bill Shuster not only won, he also followed his father onto the Transportation and Infrastructure Committee, where House GOP leaders held a seat open for him. He swiftly set to work getting federal help for his economically distressed district, and by the end of his freshman year, he boasted of winning funding for 18 district projects.

He had some big shoes to fill. His father was famed for bringing home the bacon. He has numerous Pennsylvania roadways named after him as a thank-you from grateful constituents — including a "Bud Shuster Highway" and a separate "Bud Shuster Byway."

In the 110th Congress (2007-08), Bill Shuster is the top-ranking Republican on the Railroads, Pipelines and Hazardous Materials Subcommittee. His father now lobbies for the railroads, which historically have played a significant role in the 9th District.

Shuster also serves on the Natural Resources Committee and its Energy and Mineral Resources Subcommittee. It's a good fit for his district as wind energy is becoming increasingly important to the 9th and coal mining remains relevant to western Pennsylvania.

In the 109th Congress (2005-06), Shuster chaired the Transportation Committee's Economic Development, Public Buildings and Emergency Management Subcommittee. He was front and center in the effort to defend the panel's jurisdiction over the Federal Emergency Management Agency, and he supported legislation to restore FEMA to its pre-Sept. 11 status as an independent, Cabinet-level agency. But Congress eventually chose to keep FEMA in its new home at the Department of Homeland Security, while granting it elevated standing there.

Shuster's subcommittee also approved legislation designed to strengthen dam safety, as well as a measure intended to ensure that religious schools, like other nonprofits, are eligible to receive disaster assistance from FEMA.

Shuster's district includes the Shanksville, Pa., site where United Airlines Flight 93 crashed after passengers heroically fought hijackers trying to fly the plane to Washington, D.C., on Sept. 11, 2001. In 2007, Shuster introduced legislation to posthumously award a Congressional Gold Medal to the passengers and crew members of Flight 93.

Shuster was a member of the Armed Services Committee in the 109th Congress but had to go on leave from the panel in the 110th Congress (2007-08) after the Democratic takeover cost Republicans seats on every panel.

A loyal Republican and devout conservative on both fiscal and social policy, Shuster rarely opposes his party's leaders. During the 109th Congress, he sided with his fellow Republicans on 97 percent of the votes pitting the two parties against each other. He backed President Bush on

90 percent of the votes on which the president took a position. His loyalty was rewarded when he was elevated to the post of deputy Republican whip for the 110th Congress after serving as one of several dozen assistant whips.

Shuster had to deal with an ethical issue during his first full House term. As his hard-fought 2004 primary campaign was under way, one of his congressional aides was accused of spying on his political opponent at his home and at fundraising events. Shuster said the aide was acting independently, but the aide said Shuster had ordered the spying.

Bill Shuster was not the first of Bud Shuster's sons to seek a House seat. Bill's brother, Bob, ran in 1996 to succeed retiring nine-term GOP Rep. William F. Clinger in the 5th District, which borders the 9th District. He lost the Republican primary to John E. Peterson, who went on to win and hold the seat. Bob Shuster was mentioned as a possible 9th District candidate after his father's resignation, but Bill emerged as the Shuster of choice.

An automobile dealer, Bill Shuster had no prior experience in elective office. "This is about Bill Shuster, and Bill Shuster standing on his own two feet," he told the Chambersburg (Pa.) Public Opinion. "I run my own show." But he acknowledged his father would be a tough act to follow, saying, "He set very high standards that I have to live up to."

Despite his family ties, Shuster's special-election victory in May 2001 was closer than expected. Although seriously outspent, conservative Democrat Scott Conklin ran a tireless campaign, driving throughout the expansive district in his own car. Shuster appeared to be hindered by the hard feelings among some Republicans who felt he had been given the nomination unfairly. About a dozen Republicans had emerged as contenders, but GOP officials in the district tapped Shuster at a special convention in February. Shuster ultimately defeated Conklin, a Centre County commissioner, with 52 percent of the vote to Conklin's 44 percent.

After an easy re-election in 2002, Shuster had another tough campaign in 2004. But this time the challenge came during the primary, not in the general election. Republican Michael DelGrosso, a financial consultant who also enjoyed a high degree of name recognition as his family name is found on pasta sauces, went after him in the primary. Though DelGrosso came within 2 percentage points of defeating him, Shuster went on to win in November with almost 70 percent of the vote.

In 2006, he was unopposed in the GOP primary and won re-election with 60 percent of the vote in a year when Democrats ousted four other House Republicans from Pennsylvania.

KEY VOTES

2006

No Stop broadband companies from favoring select Internet traffic

Yes Affirm U.S. commitment to war in Iraq and reject setting a withdrawal date for troops

Yes Repeal requirement for bilingual ballots at the polls

Yes Permit U.S. sale of civilian nuclear technology to India

Yes Build a 700-mile fence on the U.S.-Mexico border to curb illegal crossings

Yes Permit warrantless wiretaps of suspected terrorists

2005

? Intervene in the life-support case of Terri Schiavo

No Lift President Bush's restrictions on stem cell research funding

No Prohibit FBI access to library and bookstore records

Yes Approve free-trade pact with five Central American countries

Yes Pass energy policy overhaul favored by President Bush emphasizing domestic oil and gas production

Yes End mandatory preservation of habitat of endangered animal and plant species

No Ban torture of prisoners in U.S. custody

CQ VOTE STUDIES

	PARTY UNITY		PRESIDENTIAL SUPPORT	
	Support	Oppose	Support	Oppose
2006	97%	3%	93%	7%
2005	98%	2%	87%	13%
2004	96%	4%	82%	18%
2003	97%	3%	91%	9%
2002	98%	2%	88%	12%

INTEREST GROUPS

	AFL-CIO	ADA	CCUS	ACU
2006	14%	0%	100%	84%
2005	20%	5%	93%	100%
2004	15%	5%	100%	96%
2003	20%	10%	93%	88%
2002	11%	0%	95%	96%

PENNSYLVANIA 9
South central — Altoona

Situated in the south-central part of Pennsylvania, the 9th contains no booming metropolis — Altoona, the largest city, is tucked into the Allegheny Mountains and maintains a small-town feel. Most of the 9th's towns have populations under 5,000, making this one of the nation's 20 most rural districts.

Altoona's early growth was due to the Pennsylvania Railroad; its Horseshoe Curve permitted completion of a trans-Pennsylvania rail line. Dependent on transportation industries for centuries — first rail and later interstate highway — to drive the local economy, Altoona has initiated redevelopment plans to bolster its manufacturing and agriculture sectors. South of Altoona, Breezewood, the self-proclaimed "Traveler's Oasis," continues to lure road-weary travelers to hotels and fast-food restaurants with its garish display of signs at the Pennsylvania Turnpike interchange with Interstate 70.

Still, the bulk of the district's land is rural and depends on agriculture. But that rural land is producing more than crops. Since 2001, there are more of the towering windmills that rise above farms in Somerset and Fayette counties (shared with 12th), and the output capacity of these utility- and small-scale windmills is increasing as the area supports further wind-fueled renewable energy projects.

Most voters in the 9th oppose gun control and "big government" policies. Its small-business owners and farmers also tend to be fiscally conservative. The district solidly backs Republicans at all levels, and the 9th includes George W. Bush's top three Pennsylvania counties from the 2004 presidential election: Fulton (76 percent), Bedford (73 percent) and the district's part of Perry County (72 percent). Overall, the 9th gave Bush 67 percent of the vote — his best showing in the state.

MAJOR INDUSTRY
Agriculture, manufacturing, service

MILITARY BASES
Letterkenny Army Depot, 3 military, 2,875 civilian (2007)

CITIES
Altoona, 49,523; Chambersburg, 17,862; Waynesboro, 9,614

NOTABLE
A memorial to United Airlines Flight 93 is in Shanksville, where the hijacked airplane crashed in a field Sept. 11, 2001.

Rep. Christopher Carney (D)

CAPITOL OFFICE
225-3731
carney.house.gov
416 Cannon 20515-3810; fax 225-9594

COMMITTEES
Homeland Security
(Management & Oversight - chairman)
Transportation & Infrastructure

RESIDENCE
Dimock Township

BORN
March 2, 1959, Cedar Rapids, Iowa

RELIGION
Roman Catholic

FAMILY
Wife, Jennifer Carney; five children

EDUCATION
Cornell College, B.S.S. 1981 (environmental studies & history); U. of Wyoming, M.A. 1983 (international relations); U. of Nebraska, Ph.D. 1993 (political science)

MILITARY SERVICE
Naval Reserve, 1995-present

CAREER
U.S. Defense Department counterterrorism consultant; professor

POLITICAL HIGHLIGHTS
No previous office

ELECTION RESULTS

2006 GENERAL		
Christopher Carney (D)	110,115	52.9%
Don Sherwood (R)	97,862	47.1%
2006 PRIMARY		
Christopher Carney (D)		unopposed

Elected 2006; 1st term

Carney says he won his seat in the traditionally Republican 10th District because of three things: his centrist policy stands, his strong grass-roots campaign and a national mood that had soured on Republicans. It also didn't hurt that the GOP incumbent, Don Sherwood, was involved in a sex scandal with a younger woman who claimed Sherwood had tried to strangle her. Sherwood later admitted to a lengthy extramarital affair.

Carney is well aware that his constituents are not used to being represented by a Democrat. He paints himself as an independent thinker who won't just vote along party lines. "If there is a good Democratic ideal I will support it and if there is a good Republican ideal I will support it," Carney says. "That is what I can promise my constituents."

Carney is a Naval Reserve veteran who served as a Pentagon adviser on counterterrorism prior to becoming a political science professor at Pennsylvania State University. He briefed key intelligence officials on a possible relationship between Iraq and al Qaeda in the months before the Iraq War began.

While that background is certain to put him at odds with many of his Democratic colleagues, Carney says his extensive experience in national security issues will allow him to ask the "right questions" of the Bush administration. His expertise made him a perfect fit for the Homeland Security Committee, where he wants to secure resources for first-responders, protect U.S. borders and provide oversight on sensitive nuclear materials. Carney was made chairman of the Management and Oversight Subcommittee.

He also got a seat on the Transportation and Infrastructure panel, which he hopes to parlay into funding for roads and bridges damaged by floods that washed over northeastern Pennsylvania in the summer of 2006.

True to his centrist claims, Carney is socially conservative. He opposes same-sex marriage and supports gun owners' rights. Yet as a cancer survivor, Carney backs federal funding of embryonic stem cell research.

In his first run for public office, Carney managed to unseat Sherwood with a 6 percentage point margin.

PENNSYLVANIA 10

Northeast — Central Susquehanna Valley

Situated in the upper northeastern corner of Pennsylvania, the 10th is home to a portion of the Pocono Mountains region, a retreat known for its skiing, fishing and golfing.

The four Central Susquehanna Valley counties of Northumberland, Union, Snyder and Montour account for 30 percent of the population and contribute to the 10th's manufacturing, retail and service industries. Northumberland has many manufacturers, while Snyder includes the Susquehanna Valley Mall. Montour is home to the Geisinger Health System and Danville State Hospital, which employ many residents.

The 10th includes some of the state's best areas for lumber and agriculture. The latter is particularly prominent in Bradford County, which is among the state and national leaders in dairy production, and in Northumberland and Snyder counties, known for their poultry. Tourism remains strong, especially during summer, when visitors come for the scenery in the district's east and for the Little League World Series, played annually in South Williamsport (in the neighboring 5th), in its western reaches. Fast-growing Pike County includes many commuters to New Jersey and New York City who prefer its small-town setting, cheaper land and access to main highways.

The 10th has large swaths of rural, socially conservative heartland and is predominately Republican. Democrats crop up in Carbondale and Archbald in Lackawanna County and in parts of Northumberland County, but most voters are heavily inclined to support the GOP.

MAJOR INDUSTRY
Agriculture, manufacturing, tourism, timber

CITIES
Williamsport, 30,706

NOTABLE
The mammoth Starrucca Viaduct has carried trains across Lanesboro since 1848.

Rep. Paul E. Kanjorski (D)

CAPITOL OFFICE
225-6511
kanjorski.house.gov
2188 Rayburn 20515-3811; fax 225-0764

COMMITTEES
Financial Services
(Capital Markets, Insurance & GSEs - chairman)
Oversight & Government Reform
Science & Technology

RESIDENCE
Nanticoke

BORN
April 2, 1937, Nanticoke, Pa.

RELIGION
Roman Catholic

FAMILY
Wife, Nancy Kanjorski; one child

EDUCATION
Temple U., attended 1957-62; Dickinson School of Law, attended 1962-65

MILITARY SERVICE
Army, 1960-61

CAREER
Lawyer

POLITICAL HIGHLIGHTS
Sought Democratic nomination for U.S. House (special election), 1980; sought Democratic nomination for U.S. House, 1980

ELECTION RESULTS

2006 GENERAL		
Paul E. Kanjorski (D)	134,340	72.5%
Joseph F. Leonardi (R)	51,033	27.5%
2006 PRIMARY		
Paul E. Kanjorski (D)		unopposed
2004 GENERAL		
Paul E. Kanjorski (D)	171,147	94.4%
Kenneth C. Brenneman (CNSTP)	10,105	5.6%

PREVIOUS WINNING PERCENTAGES
2002 (56%); 2000 (66%); 1998 (67%); 1996 (68%); 1994 (67%); 1992 (67%); 1990 (100%); 1988 (100%); 1986 (71%); 1984 (59%)

Elected 1984; 12th term

Kanjorski was first elected to the House when Pennsylvania freshman Patrick J. Murphy of the 8th District had just celebrated his 11th birthday. Now serving his 12th term, Kanjorski knows a good deal about House practices and procedures. Serving as a House page in 1954, he narrowly missed becoming a casualty when Puerto Rican terrorists sprayed gunfire on the House chamber from the visitor's gallery. In the aftermath, he helped carry three wounded congressmen from the floor.

A longtime member of the Financial Services Committee — he is now the second-ranking Democrat — Kanjorski serves as chairman of the Capital Markets, Insurance, and Government Sponsored Enterprises Subcommittee. In the 110th Congress (2007-08), he will need to work with the Senate on overhauling mortgage finance giants Freddie Mac and Fannie Mae, the two financial behemoths that are the foundation of the U.S. housing market.

Kanjorski supports an overhaul measure that Chairman Barney Frank of Massachusetts brokered with the Treasury Department in early 2007. The two lawmakers also want to use the overhaul measure to help provide funding for affordable housing.

Kanjorski's panel also will oversee the effort to extend the Terrorism Risk Insurance Act, which provides a federal insurance backstop for results of terrorist acts. Enacted as a temporary fix following the Sept. 11 attacks and reauthorized in a scaled-back version in 2005, the program expires Dec. 31, 2007. Insurance and corporate real estate companies and other business groups want Congress to make the terrorism insurance permanent — a position Frank supports. Kanjorski's support doesn't extend that far. He favors a six- to 16-year extension and hopes a private market for terrorism insurance will develop.

As Kanjorski moves into the national spotlight on these high-profile financial issues, he will still look after the people of the 11th District, the main focus of most of his legislative career. In the 109th Congress (2005-06), he surprised 13 communities back home with $160,000 in grants he inserted into the 2005 federal surface transportation law in their behalf. He was also happy to announce in late 2004 that he had obtained $1.4 million for the city of Wilkes-Barre in the catchall spending bill that passed at the end of the session. Kanjorski also touts the work he has done to resurrect the Wyoming Valley Levee Raising Project, a roughly $200 million flood control project on the Susquehanna River that had languished for years after its authorization.

His close friendship with Pennsylvania Democrat John P. Murtha, an Appropriations subcommittee chairman and dean of the Pennsylvania delegation, has helped him secure federal funds.

Kanjorski underwent triple-bypass heart surgery in March 2007, just before his 70th birthday, after doctors discovered that coronary heart disease had significantly constricted three arteries. He made a speedy recovery, returning to work in late April.

A Polish-American Catholic, Kanjorski reflects the concerns of the white, ethnic, working-class people who still dominate politics in his part of Pennsylvania. He holds a conservative social view, opposing abortion and gun control and supporting school prayer. But in 2004 and 2006, he voted against a constitutional amendment to ban same-sex marriage. A supporter of organized labor and a loyal Democrat on fiscal matters, he repeatedly has weighed in against President Bush's proposed tax cuts.

In 2002, Kanjorski sided with most of his colleagues in authorizing military action against Iraq. The following year, however, he voted against appropriating $87.5 billion for the Iraq War effort, saying he supported the troops but worried that the administration lacked a "clear objective and well-reasoned plan" in Iraq.

In 2007, he supported a Democratic resolution disapproving of Bush's decision to deploy more than 21,000 additional U.S. combat troops to Iraq. Kanjorski declared the president's plan was "too little to make a difference in a city of 6 million who are unwilling to see beyond their sectarian differences, and too much burden to place on an American military already stretched to the breaking point."

Kanjorski was the subject of news reports in 2002 that the FBI was looking into allegations that he had steered federal grants to businesses connected to his family. The FBI never confirmed or denied the reports.

Kanjorski was born and raised in Nanticoke, just southwest of Wilkes-Barre. He attended Temple University and the Dickinson College School of Law, but did not graduate from either. He became a lawyer and worked as an attorney in Northeast Pennsylvania for almost 20 years. He was an administrative law judge for workers' compensation cases, and served as the unpaid assistant city solicitor for Nanticoke for more than a decade.

After two unsuccessful House campaigns in 1980 (one in a special election), Kanjorski owed his 1984 House victory to an intestinal parasite and a sunny beach. The outcome of his primary challenge to Democratic Rep. Frank Harrison might have been different if not for the discovery that water supplies in parts of the 11th District were contaminated with the Giardia parasite. As people boiled their water to make it drinkable, Kanjorski noted that his opponent had flown off on a congressional excursion to Costa Rica, and ran an ad that included a shot of Harrison on the beach.

Harrison tried to ignore Kanjorski and stressed his experience in Washington, but Kanjorski leapt from long shot to victor. In November, he defeated Republican Robert P. Hudock with 59 percent of the vote.

That was his closest election — he has been unopposed twice — until 2002. The national GOP, taking note of the unfavorable publicity stemming from the FBI investigation, invested heavily in that year's race. Their candidate, Hazleton Mayor Louis J. Barletta, pursued the ethics attack aggressively. But Kanjorski prevailed by 13 percentage points, thanks to a big margin in the Lackawanna County portion of the district. In 2004, he did not have a GOP challenger, and in 2006 he coasted to victory with more than 72 percent of the vote.

KEY VOTES

2006

- Yes Stop broadband companies from favoring select Internet traffic
- No Affirm U.S. commitment to war in Iraq and reject setting a withdrawal date for troops
- No Repeal requirement for bilingual ballots at the polls
- Yes Permit U.S. sale of civilian nuclear technology to India
- Yes Build a 700-mile fence on the U.S.-Mexico border to curb illegal crossings
- No Permit warrantless wiretaps of suspected terrorists

2005

- Yes Intervene in the life-support case of Terri Schiavo
- Yes Lift President Bush's restrictions on stem cell research funding
- Yes Prohibit FBI access to library and bookstore records
- No Approve free-trade pact with five Central American countries
- Yes Pass energy policy overhaul favored by President Bush emphasizing domestic oil and gas production
- No End mandatory preservation of habitat of endangered animal and plant species
- Yes Ban torture of prisoners in U.S. custody

CQ VOTE STUDIES

	PARTY UNITY		PRESIDENTIAL SUPPORT	
	Support	Oppose	Support	Oppose
2006	83%	17%	36%	64%
2005	80%	20%	39%	61%
2004	88%	12%	27%	73%
2003	84%	16%	31%	69%
2002	79%	21%	42%	58%

INTEREST GROUPS

	AFL-CIO	ADA	CCUS	ACU
2006	100%	70%	43%	29%
2005	93%	80%	48%	24%
2004	100%	80%	30%	21%
2003	100%	85%	27%	36%
2002	100%	75%	50%	24%

PENNSYLVANIA 11

Northeast – Scranton, Wilkes-Barre

In the 20th century, the health of northeastern Pennsylvania's 11th was inextricably linked to the production, manufacturing and sale of coal. The industry virtually disappeared in the 1960s, and the loss significantly altered the economy of the Wyoming Valley.

Revitalization efforts are ongoing, including projects earlier this decade to build a new terminal at the Wilkes-Barre/Scranton International Airport and complete a $48 million renovation of the Wilkes-Barre VA Medical Center. There also are long-term proposals to restore passenger and freight rail service from Scranton to New York City.

The Susquehanna River has been both a blessing and a curse to the 11th. The Wyoming Valley Levee Raising Project still receives millions of dollars to repair levees originally damaged by Hurricane Agnes in 1972 and to prevent future damage. Despite the ongoing possibility of flooding, the river's presence also has advantages: A portion of the levee funds were allocated for a riverfront project to create a new landing area, fishing and boating pier, performance amphitheater and walking trails.

The 11th has a decided but not absolute Democratic lean, the result of a large Irish population and a strong union tradition. Democrats do well in Scranton and Luzerne County, with strong showings in Wilkes-Barre and in smaller cities to the north and east. Democrat John Kerry won the 11th by 5 percentage points in the 2004 presidential election.

The decline of coal and an investment in technology-driven businesses have helped Republicans, who do well in Columbia County. George W. Bush won both Carbon and Monroe counties, fast-growing areas in the Poconos where many newcomers commute via Interstate 80 to their jobs in New Jersey and New York.

MAJOR INDUSTRY
Manufacturing, retail trade, tourism

MILITARY BASES
Tobyhanna Army Depot, 47 military, 4,300 civilian (2007)

CITIES
Scranton, 76,415; Wilkes-Barre, 43,123; Hazleton, 23,329

NOTABLE
Scranton's Houdini Museum and Psychic Theater honors the magician's legacy and explores elements of the paranormal, such as séances, in stage performances.

Rep. John P. Murtha (D)

Elected February 1974; 17th full term

An ex-Marine and the House Democrats' leading defense hawk, Murtha transformed the debate over the war in Iraq when he called for the withdrawal of U.S. troops in 2005, marking a turning point in congressional support for the war. He is Speaker Nancy Pelosi's point man on anti-war legislation, though his alliance with her was not enough to catapult him into the top ranks of the leadership in the 110th Congress (2007-08).

After Democrats won control of the House in the past election, Murtha challenged Maryland's Steny H. Hoyer for the job of majority leader, the No. 2 position in the House leadership. Pelosi pushed Murtha's candidacy with the rank and file, but the aggressive campaigning backfired. In secret balloting, Democrats chose Hoyer, the party whip who had been quietly lobbying for the job for months and who had raised thousands of dollars for their re-election campaigns. The vote was 149-86 for Hoyer.

Murtha chaired Pelosi's campaign for minority leader in 2002, and she can often be seen consulting with him in the "Pennsylvania corner," the last row of the chamber immediately right of the center aisle.

As the chairman of the Defense Appropriations Subcommittee, Murtha in 2007 guided through the House a hotly debated set of conditions for continued funding for the war, including withdrawal of troops from Iraq by August 2008. Republicans and the White House wanted no strings attached to the spending bill.

But it was Murtha's November 2005 announcement that caused a political earthquake. He called for a speedy but controlled withdrawal from Iraq, making him the first prominent congressional hawk to turn publicly against the war. A decorated Vietnam combat veteran, he retired in 1990 as a colonel in the reserves after 37 years. He has been either the chairman or the top-ranking minority member of the defense panel since 1989.

He was a strong supporter of the 2002 measure authorizing President Bush to use force against Iraq. Over time, he fought in vain for more troops and money, and by late 2005 concluded the operation was headed in the wrong direction. "You can't sustain a war with the small force that we have," he said, urging that 160,000 U.S. troops be replaced by a far smaller "quick reaction" force that could destroy terrorist camps in the region.

Republicans called Murtha unpatriotic, but had a tough time making it stick. When then GOP Majority Leader Tom DeLay of Texas in 2004 called his demands for more troops and money a "craven political stunt," Murtha was furious, having helped DeLay for years round up Democratic votes for appropriations bills. The next time he saw DeLay, a former insect exterminator, on the floor, Murtha said, "After all the goddamn deals we've done. When I was in Vietnam, you were killing bugs."

Murtha likes to work the Pentagon the way he works the House — face to face. Impatient with the PowerPoint presentations favored by the brass, Murtha travels without fanfare to deployments in far-off regions to assess U.S. progress. His Iraq decision was informed by frequent visits to injured soldiers at military hospitals in the Washington area. "Generals, they have to talk the party line, but the troops . . . give me a lot of information about what's going on that I can't get almost anyplace else," he says.

Murtha is attentive to military quality-of-life issues. He was a leader in the successful drive by the Pentagon in the late 1990s to increase pay, improve military pensions and expand retirees' health benefits.

Despite formidable vote-counting skills and a wide network of allies in

CAPITOL OFFICE
225-2065
www.house.gov/murtha
2423 Rayburn 20515-3812; fax 225-5709

COMMITTEES
Appropriations
(Defense - chairman)

RESIDENCE
Johnstown

BORN
June 17, 1932, New Martinsville, W.Va.

RELIGION
Roman Catholic

FAMILY
Wife, Joyce Murtha; three children

EDUCATION
U. of Pittsburgh, B.A. 1962 (economics)

MILITARY SERVICE
Marine Corps, 1952-55, 1966-67;
Marine Corps Reserve, 1967-90

CAREER
Car wash owner and operator

POLITICAL HIGHLIGHTS
Democratic nominee for U.S. House, 1968;
Pa. House, 1969-74

ELECTION RESULTS

2006 GENERAL		
John P. Murtha (D)	123,472	60.8%
Diana Irey (R)	79,612	39.2%
2006 PRIMARY		
John P. Murtha (D)		unopposed
2004 GENERAL		
John P. Murtha (D)		unopposed

PREVIOUS WINNING PERCENTAGES
2002 (73%); 2000 (71%); 1998 (68%); 1996 (70%); 1994 (69%); 1992 (100%); 1990 (62%); 1988 (100%); 1986 (67%); 1984 (69%); 1982 (61%); 1980 (59%); 1978 (69%); 1976 (68%); 1974 (58%); 1974 Special Election (50%)

the Democratic Caucus, Murtha's reputation was tainted in the early 1980s when he was an unprosecuted co-conspirator and witness for prosecutors in the FBI bribery probe known as Abscam, which resulted in convictions of one senator and several House members. More recently, government watchdog groups have questioned federal funds he got for clients of KSA Consulting, a firm that employs his brother, Robert.

On Appropriations, Murtha believes in keeping the wheels of government turning through compromise and judicious applications of legislative lubricant, such as earmarks, the hometown projects requested by individual members that budget conservatives decry as wasteful spending. "Members come to us all the time," he says. "We listen to them . . . and we take care of the ones we think are important."

Murtha grew up in Mt. Pleasant, Pa., in a family with a long tradition of military service. His mother's ancestors fought in the Revolutionary War. His father, who ran a gas station and car wash, served in World War II. In high school, Murtha was athletic, playing football and basketball. At the urging of his schoolteacher mother, he acted in school plays, until a fateful turn in the role of a professor in "Little Women." During a graceful bow, his trousers split. "So I could never turn my back to the audience," he recalls.

Murtha entered college after high school, but left to join the Marines in 1952. His mother, he said, "cried for a week." (He eventually earned a college degree, but it took him until 1962.) Returning home after a three-year hitch, he helped run his family's gas station, but remained in the Marine Reserves. In 1966, with the Vietnam conflict under way, Murtha voluntarily returned to active duty, ultimately earning a Bronze Star and two Purple Hearts.

His political career began with a stint in the statehouse. When longtime GOP Rep. John P. Saylor died in 1973, Cambria County (Johnstown) Democrats found an attractive candidate in Murtha. He won narrowly over Harry M. Fox, a former Saylor aide, in a 1974 special election that focused on the Republicans' Watergate problems.

After Pennsylvania lost two House seats in the 2000 census, the GOP-dominated legislature drew a map that pitted Murtha against four-term Democratic Rep. Frank R. Mascara in the primary. Murtha's fundraising, boosted by defense contractors and labor unions, overwhelmed Mascara. Murtha won the primary by nearly 2-to-1 and was re-elected with 73 percent of the vote. In 2004, he ran unopposed, but in 2006 the GOP fielded Washington County Commissioner Diana Irey, who took on Murtha after he called for U.S. troops to be pulled from Iraq. Murtha won with almost 61 percent of the vote.

KEY VOTES

2006

- Yes Stop broadband companies from favoring select Internet traffic
- No Affirm U.S. commitment to war in Iraq and reject setting a withdrawal date for troops
- No Repeal requirement for bilingual ballots at the polls
- Yes Permit U.S. sale of civilian nuclear technology to India
- No Build a 700-mile fence on the U.S.-Mexico border to curb illegal crossings
- No Permit warrantless wiretaps of suspected terrorists

2005

- No Intervene in the life-support case of Terri Schiavo
- Yes Lift President Bush's restrictions on stem cell research funding
- Yes Prohibit FBI access to library and bookstore records
- No Approve free-trade pact with five Central American countries
- Yes Pass energy policy overhaul favored by President Bush emphasizing domestic oil and gas production
- Yes End mandatory preservation of habitat of endangered animal and plant species
- Yes Ban torture of prisoners in U.S. custody

CQ VOTE STUDIES

	PARTY UNITY		PRESIDENTIAL SUPPORT	
	Support	Oppose	Support	Oppose
2006	76%	24%	43%	57%
2005	76%	24%	38%	62%
2004	80%	20%	34%	66%
2003	73%	27%	51%	49%
2002	75%	25%	55%	45%

INTEREST GROUPS

	AFL-CIO	ADA	CCUS	ACU
2006	100%	65%	50%	28%
2005	100%	75%	62%	40%
2004	93%	50%	48%	30%
2003	100%	85%	43%	56%
2002	100%	55%	61%	32%

PENNSYLVANIA 12

Southwest – Johnstown

The strangely contorted 12th hopscotches in southwestern Pennsylvania across nine counties, eight of which are shared with other districts. Once a booming center of coal, steel and iron production, this area is diversifying to escape economic distress and industrial loss.

Johnstown, the district's most populous city, was once a center of industry, but floods, recession, coal and steel industry decline and scarce opportunities in manufacturing left the region with skyrocketing unemployment by the late 1980s. More recently, the city and district have bounced back, in part by attracting new biomedical research and health care companies, such as specialized care provider Conemaugh Health System, and a number of defense and research firms, such as KDH Defense Systems. Capitalizing on past hardships, the Johnstown Flood Museum also draws tourists to the area, and tourism now contributes nearly $150 million to the region each year.

On the other side of the district in the state's southwestern corner, Greene County — which borders West Virginia to its west and south and is the only county solely within the 12th — has an unemployment rate that continuously ranks above the state's average. Just north of Greene, Washington County's city of Washington is in the midst of a $100 million downtown revitalization project. The project includes a new seven-story Nationwide Centre, which will consolidate some offices of Nationwide Appraisal Services (part of LandAmerica), and includes a new amphitheater, hotel and parking garage. The district also has a small agriculture industry, which produces corn, wheat and cattle.

The 12th has been a Democratic stronghold since the New Deal. Like other Pennsylvania towns with an industrial past and aging residents, Johnstown wants federal help, but many voters are more socially conservative than the national Democratic Party. George W. Bush won both Cambria and Greene counties in the 2004 presidential election. Overall, Democrat John Kerry won the 12th's 2004 vote with 51 percent.

MAJOR INDUSTRY

Manufacturing, service, health care, tourism

CITIES

Johnstown, 23,906; Washington, 15,268; New Kensington, 14,701

NOTABLE

The National Drug Intelligence Center in Johnstown tracks illegal drugs.

Rep. Allyson Y. Schwartz (D)

CAPITOL OFFICE
225-6111
schwartz.house.gov
423 Cannon 20515-3813; fax 226-0611

COMMITTEES
Budget
Ways & Means

RESIDENCE
Jenkintown

BORN
Oct. 3, 1948, Queens, N.Y.

RELIGION
Jewish

FAMILY
Husband, David Schwartz; two children

EDUCATION
Simmons College, B.A. 1970 (sociology); Bryn Mawr College, M.S.W. 1972

CAREER
Municipal child and elderly welfare official; women's health center founder; nonprofit health plan assistant director

POLITICAL HIGHLIGHTS
Pa. Senate, 1991-2004; sought Democratic nomination for U.S. Senate, 2000

ELECTION RESULTS

2006 GENERAL		
Allyson Y. Schwartz (D)	147,368	66.1%
Raj Peter Bhakta (R)	75,492	33.9%
2006 PRIMARY		
Allyson Y. Schwartz (D)		unopposed
2004 GENERAL		
Allyson Y. Schwartz (D)	171,763	55.8%
Melissa Brown (R)	127,205	41.3%
John P. McDermott (CNSTP)	5,291	1.7%
Chuck Moulton (LIBERT)	3,865	1.3%

Elected 2004; 2nd term

Schwartz is on her way up in the House, and fast. In her second term, she won a coveted seat on the Ways and Means Committee, the only sophomore to secure such a plum assignment. A formidable fundraiser, she also was chosen to help Democrats develop more donors among women across the country. And she is mentioned as a potential future Senate contender.

Even as a freshman, Schwartz got a taste of the tax, Social Security and Medicare issues she will now address on Ways and Means. She was given a seat on the Budget Committee, the only Democratic newcomer assigned to the panel in the 109th Congress (2005-06).

In 2006, Schwartz repeatedly spoke out for improved homeland security policies and the more effective use of federal funds for U.S. security. The suburban Philadelphia lawmaker criticized government spending being redirected from cities to small communities. "Homeland security funding should be based on risk not politics," she said. Schwartz also pushed for the screening of all cargo coming into the country by ship or airplane.

Health care is her specialty. A Pennsylvania state senator for 14 years before her election to Congress, she calls her state's Children's Health Insurance Program "one of my proudest accomplishments," and wants to expand the joint federal-state version to cover most American children who do not have health care coverage. She also wants to tackle broader problems of health care coverage and affordability, but says "the health care agenda is something that I hope to get done in my next term and in future terms. It's not all going to happen in one fell swoop."

Schwartz first entered the public eye in 1975 as the co-founder and first director of a women's health clinic. She had spent a year at the Philadelphia Health Department as a graduate student, then worked for a fledgling HMO for three years before helping to start the Elizabeth Blackwell women's clinic, which offered a full range of health services, including abortions. She and her partners took out a bank loan to launch the clinic, and she says her work there helped her understand the challenges facing small businesses. "I've had experience not just as a legislator but as a health care provider," she notes.

In 1983, Schwartz wrote health care position papers for Wilson Goode, who was in the midst of a successful campaign for mayor. During Goode's second term, she became commissioner of Health and Human Services, serving until she won election to the state Senate in 1990. She defeated a 12-year incumbent to claim that seat.

During her first term in Congress, Schwartz served not only on the Budget Committee but also on the Transportation and Infrastructure Committee. She sought assignment to the latter because she knew it would give her a chance to direct funds to her district in a concrete fashion as the committee wrote a new surface transportation law. But her first challenge came on water, not land, with an oil spill from a vessel traveling up the Delaware River. Just weeks after arriving on Capitol Hill, Schwartz worked with the Republican leaders of the Coast Guard Subcommittee to write legislation to protect navigable waterways from oil spills.

As work on the big surface transportation law progressed, she helped secure $16 million for a 10-mile greenway bike path, walkway and road along the Delaware River in an underutilized industrial area that is now redeveloping with high-end condos and homes.

As a freshman, her first speech on the House floor was not on legislative initiatives or policy goals as is often the case. Instead, Schwartz, who is Jewish, chose to speak during a commemoration of the 60th anniversary of the liberation of the Nazis' Auschwitz death camp in Poland. She described her mother's escape from Austria to America as a teenager in the early days of World War II. "Those who survived the Holocaust could not hide their gratitude and love for this country, relishing the opportunity and freedom granted to them as new Americans," Schwartz said. "My own love and respect for our country and my belief in our responsibility to each other stems in great part from this strong sense of patriotism."

Although Schwartz was born and raised in Flushing, in Queens, N.Y., her parents met in Philadelphia, where her father was in dental school and her mother had been sent by a group helping Jewish refugees. Her maternal grandmother committed suicide shortly before Schwartz's mother as a teenager escaped to the United States, and she spoke of her painful past only in "fits and starts," Schwartz says. "My mother was very clear that painful experiences in childhood don't necessarily make you stronger, which is maybe where my interest in children and family comes from."

Schwartz's mother could not overcome the pain; she committed suicide herself when Schwartz was 26. "These experiences stay with you. You just don't get past them by saying so," Schwartz says of her mother's traumas. She worries about helping soldiers returning from Iraq and their families avoid the sense of isolation her mother felt. "Our troops come home with experiences separate from their families — some good and some very difficult," she told a National Prayer Breakfast in 2007.

Schwartz moved to Philadelphia in the 1970s so her husband David, now a cardiologist, could attend Jefferson Medical School. She earned her graduate degree in social work at Bryn Mawr, and the couple stayed in the city.

After building her career in Philadelphia and at the state legislature in Harrisburg, Schwartz jumped into the primary race for the Democratic nomination to run against GOP Sen. Rick Santorum in 2000. While she demonstrated impressive fundraising skills, she came in second in a six-way primary, behind Rep. Ron Klink, who lost to Santorum that November.

A long-shot bid by 13th District Democrat Joseph M. Hoeffel to unseat GOP Sen. Arlen Specter in 2004 gave Schwartz a chance for a second try at Congress. She won a hard-fought primary. Then, calling on her solid political base and campaign bankroll, she won by more than 14 percentage points — trouncing ophthalmologist Melissa Brown, a three-time GOP candidate for the House. She was re-elected in 2006 with almost two-thirds of the vote.

KEY VOTES

2006

- No Stop broadband companies from favoring select Internet traffic
- No Affirm U.S. commitment to war in Iraq and reject setting a withdrawal date for troops
- No Repeal requirement for bilingual ballots at the polls
- No Permit U.S. sale of civilian nuclear technology to India
- No Build a 700-mile fence on the U.S.-Mexico border to curb illegal crossings
- No Permit warrantless wiretaps of suspected terrorists

2005

- No Intervene in the life-support case of Terri Schiavo
- Yes Lift President Bush's restrictions on stem cell research funding
- Yes Prohibit FBI access to library and bookstore records
- No Approve free-trade pact with five Central American countries
- No Pass energy policy overhaul favored by President Bush emphasizing domestic oil and gas production
- No End mandatory preservation of habitat of endangered animal and plant species
- Yes Ban torture of prisoners in U.S. custody

CQ VOTE STUDIES

	PARTY UNITY		PRESIDENTIAL SUPPORT	
	Support	Oppose	Support	Oppose
2006	91%	9%	27%	73%
2005	92%	8%	17%	83%

INTEREST GROUPS

	AFL-CIO	ADA	CCUS	ACU
2006	100%	85%	47%	16%
2005	93%	90%	44%	4%

PENNSYLVANIA 13

East — Northeast Philadelphia, part of Montgomery County

With its residents nearly evenly divided between Montgomery County and Northeast Philadelphia, the 13th combines white-collar suburbia with a portion of the city known for its blue-collar grit. The district extends northwest from the Delaware River in the city into northern Montgomery County suburbs and eventually out into rural areas near the county's western border.

Prescription drugs and health care are prevalent issues in the district, thanks to a large senior citizen population in Northeast Philadelphia. Education also draws attention, as Philadelphia public schools are in worse shape than Montgomery County schools. Public housing and energy issues also are of concern to residents.

Many shopping centers, strip malls, health care and pharmaceutical facilities and small businesses are found throughout Northeast Philadelphia. Planned redevelopment along the Delaware River would add new housing, a greenway trail and public access to the north riverfront. The 2005 BRAC round ordered Naval Air Station Willow Grove closed by 2011, but the state hopes to take over the base and reduce estimated job losses. The 13th also includes Philadelphia Northeast Airport, a general aviation airport.

Democrats have enjoyed an advantage in recent statewide and federal races, while local races in Montgomery County tend to be more competitive. Since 1988, Montgomery has gone from voting Republican for president by 22 percentage points to backing Democrat John Kerry by 12 points in 2004. Overall, Kerry took 56 percent of the 13th's 2004 vote.

MAJOR INDUSTRY
Health and business services, chemicals

MILITARY BASES
Naval Air Station Willow Grove, 1,569 military, 754 civilian (2007)

CITIES
Philadelphia (pt.), 306,002; Lansdale, 16,071

NOTABLE
Pennypack Park, which is known as the green heart of Northeast Philadelphia, is home to the Pennypack Bridge — a stone bridge that has been in use since 1697.

Rep. Mike Doyle (D)

CAPITOL OFFICE
225-2135
www.house.gov/doyle
401 Cannon 20515-3814; fax 225-3084

COMMITTEES
Energy & Commerce
Standards of Official Conduct
Veterans' Affairs

RESIDENCE
Forest Hills

BORN
Aug. 5, 1953, Pittsburgh, Pa.

RELIGION
Roman Catholic

FAMILY
Wife, Susan Doyle; four children

EDUCATION
Pennsylvania State U., B.S. 1975 (community development)

CAREER
Insurance company executive; state legislative aide

POLITICAL HIGHLIGHTS
Swissvale Borough Council, 1977-81 (served as a Republican)

ELECTION RESULTS

2006 GENERAL		
Mike Doyle (D)	161,075	90.1%
Titus North (GREEN)	17,720	9.9%
2006 PRIMARY		
Mike Doyle (D)	54,213	75.9%
Mike Isaac (D)	17,193	24.1%
2004 GENERAL		
Mike Doyle (D)		unopposed

PREVIOUS WINNING PERCENTAGES
2002 (100%); 2000 (69%); 1998 (68%); 1996 (56%); 1994 (55%)

Elected 1994; 7th term

In his seven terms in office, Doyle has pursued an agenda aimed at transforming western Pennsylvania into a more diverse modern economy that melds Pittsburgh's traditional manufacturing base with high-technology industries. "Steel is no longer king," Doyle says. "We see Pittsburgh's niche in high-tech manufacturing."

His grandfather and father were steelworkers, and Doyle himself worked summers in the steel mills, where he learned he wanted to do something else. That something else turned out to be politics, an arena where he has fought to help revitalize Pennsylvania's troubled steel towns.

One priority for Doyle is legislation establishing a national park outside Pittsburgh that would highlight the historic role of the steel industry. Under his bill, the national historic site would include the location of a steelworker uprising in 1892, known as the Battle of Homestead, as well as the Carrie Furnace Complex and the Hot Metal Bridge connecting the two. Doyle's grandfather worked at the Carrie Furnace. Doyle reintroduced his bill in 2007, while his Pennsylvanian colleagues, Republican Sen. Arlen Specter and Democratic Sen. Bob Casey, sponsored similar legislation in their chamber.

Doyle continues to look out for the interests of the steel industry. He has urged the federal government to take steps to protect domestic firms from what he regards as unfair foreign competition. In 2005, he voted against the GOP-backed Central American Free Trade Agreement. "I'm not going to vote for these agreements when there's not a level playing field," he says, arguing that the other countries in CAFTA are not hampered by labor and environmental laws as stringent as those in the United States. Doyle says he's not against all trade agreements, pointing to his support for pacts with Australia, Canada and European countries whose labor and environmental standards he says are more in line with those of the United States.

He has become more of a party loyalist over time. In his first term, he sided with Democrats on only 70 percent of the votes pitting the two parties against each other. In the 109th Congress (2005-06), he backed his party 90 percent of the time. He also has supported his party leadership by agreeing to sit on the House ethics committee, generally regarded as a thankless assignment.

Doyle has been a reliable ally of organized labor and generally has toed the party line on issues such as access to health care, background checks for gun purchases and opposition to a constitutional amendment banning same-sex marriage. But Doyle parts with many Democrats on environmental issues. He opposes stricter clean air standards because of the additional requirements on the steel, coal and auto industries.

Doyle uses his seat on the Energy and Commerce Committee to promote legislation aimed at moving the country toward energy independence. In 2007, he co-authored a measure with California Republican Mary Bono to require that new federal buildings meet higher standards of energy efficiency. In the 109th Congress, Doyle and his committee colleague, Republican Lee Terry of Nebraska, attached an amendment to the GOP energy bill to double federal funding for research on hydrogen fuel cells from $2 billion to $4 billion over five years.

Doyle earned a degree in community development from Penn State in 1975, then returned to his hometown of Swissvale, just east of Pittsburgh. He entered the insurance business, became involved in community affairs as executive director of the Turtle Creek Valley Citizens Union, and was elected to the Swissvale Borough Council, serving as finance and recreation chairman.

For many years, he worked for Republican state Sen. Frank A. Pecora, and it was out of deference to his boss that Doyle switched his party registration to the GOP. But in 1992, Pecora changed his affiliation to the Democrats to challenge Republican Rick Santorum, then seeking election to a second House term. Pecora lost decisively. Doyle jumped back to the Democratic Party that same year.

In 1994, when Santorum first ran for the Senate, Doyle took up where his old boss had left off and ran in the open 18th District, surviving a seven-person primary and winning the Democratic nomination with 20 percent of the vote. In the general election, Doyle was not well-known across the district, but neither was GOP nominee John McCarty, a former aide to Pennsylvania Sen. John Heinz. Using some of the "time for a change" rhetoric popularized by GOP conservatives, Doyle capitalized on the district's Democratic leanings to win by 10 percentage points. He was one of just four Democrats who swam against the national GOP tide that year to capture a House seat that had been in Republican hands. Doyle won the next three elections by substantial margins.

Heading into redistricting after the 2000 census, Doyle was regarded as one of the more vulnerable incumbents in the nation, given Pennsylvania's loss of two House seats and the GOP's control of the redistricting process. But Doyle caught a series of breaks.

The remapping at first seemed to have dealt him a tough hand, shoving him into the 14th District of fellow Democrat William J. Coyne. But Coyne decided to retire after 11 terms, and none of a number of potentially tough Democratic challengers ended up running in 2002. State Republicans, who had made the new 14th heavily Democratic in order to put more Republicans in surrounding districts, declined to field a candidate against Doyle in November. He also was unopposed in 2004. In 2006, he easily defeated Green Party candidate Titus North.

Doyle's love of baseball has propelled him to manager of the Democrats' team for the annual congressional charity baseball game, held at Washington, D.C.'s RFK Stadium. Doyle's nickname is "Mad Dog" and he won't let lawmakers cut practice, which is held from 7-9 a.m. most weekday mornings in the spring. Rank doesn't get anyone a spot in his starting lineup. "I'm not a believer in seniority when it comes to baseball. We only play the best," he says.

KEY VOTES

2006

Yes Stop broadband companies from favoring select Internet traffic

No Affirm U.S. commitment to war in Iraq and reject setting a withdrawal date for troops

No Repeal requirement for bilingual ballots at the polls

Yes Permit U.S. sale of civilian nuclear technology to India

No Build a 700-mile fence on the U.S.-Mexico border to curb illegal crossings

No Permit warrantless wiretaps of suspected terrorists

2005

No Intervene in the life-support case of Terri Schiavo

Yes Lift President Bush's restrictions on stem cell research funding

Yes Prohibit FBI access to library and bookstore records

No Approve free-trade pact with five Central American countries

Yes Pass energy policy overhaul favored by President Bush emphasizing domestic oil and gas production

No End mandatory preservation of habitat of endangered animal and plant species

Yes Ban torture of prisoners in U.S. custody

CQ VOTE STUDIES

	PARTY UNITY		PRESIDENTIAL SUPPORT	
	Support	Oppose	Support	Oppose
2006	91%	9%	35%	65%
2005	90%	10%	28%	72%
2004	93%	7%	29%	71%
2003	88%	12%	37%	63%
2002	90%	10%	38%	62%

INTEREST GROUPS

	AFL-CIO	ADA	CCUS	ACU
2006	100%	85%	47%	12%
2005	100%	95%	44%	16%
2004	100%	80%	48%	12%
2003	100%	85%	34%	42%
2002	100%	80%	45%	8%

PENNSYLVANIA 14
Pittsburgh and some close-in suburbs

The 14th includes all of Pittsburgh and some of its close-in suburbs. The city's economic transformation from "steel capital" into the region's banking and health care hub has made it a great success story in an otherwise suffering Rust Belt.

Medical centers and universities, parks, skyscrapers and technology firms have replaced the steel industry's smokestacks that once rose between and along the Allegheny, Monongahela and Ohio rivers. A thriving, corporate downtown has grown up in the "Golden Triangle," where the Allegheny and Monongahela rivers meet to form the Ohio. Baseball's Pirates, at PNC Park, and football's Steelers, at Heinz Field, both play in modern stadiums just across the Allegheny from downtown. Local officials are working to clean up, or "redd up" in Pittsburgheese, the city, which now has one of the lowest crime rates among the nation's top 25 metropolitan areas. Health care and technology companies here are establishing relationships with the many local colleges.

Areas such as Monroeville and Penn Hills (both shared with the 18th) have attracted commercial development and some technology jobs, while others have languished. Many of Pittsburgh's neighborhoods, such as Bloomfield and Lawrenceville, retain their ethnic roots — mainly German, Italian, Irish and Polish. Squirrel Hill long has been the center of the city's Jewish population.

Even with the diversification of the 14th's economy, the district retains strong Democratic roots. Union strength translates into lopsided margins, and Democrats far outnumber Republicans, whose outposts in the region are found mostly in the neighboring 4th and 18th districts. Pittsburgh's staunch Democratic support is rivaled only by cross-state districts in Philadelphia. John Kerry took 75 percent of the Pittsburgh vote and 69 percent of the 14th's vote in the 2004 presidential election.

MAJOR INDUSTRY

Banking, government, health care, higher education

CITIES

Pittsburgh, 334,563; Penn Hills (unincorporated) (pt.), 35,864; McKeesport, 24,040; West Mifflin, 22,464; Wilkinsburg, 19,196

NOTABLE

The Andy Warhol Museum, as well as the bridge over the Allegheny River renamed for the artist in 2005, celebrates Pittsburgh's native son.

Rep. Charlie Dent (R)

CAPITOL OFFICE
225-6411
dent.house.gov
116 Cannon 20515-3815; fax 226-0778

COMMITTEES
Homeland Security
Transportation & Infrastructure

RESIDENCE
Allentown

BORN
May 24, 1960, Allentown, Pa.

RELIGION
Presbyterian

FAMILY
Wife, Pamela Dent; three children

EDUCATION
Pennsylvania State U., B.A. 1982
(foreign service & international politics);
Lehigh U., M.P.A. 1993

CAREER
College fundraiser; electronics salesman;
hotel clerk; congressional aide

POLITICAL HIGHLIGHTS
Pa. House, 1991-99; Pa. Senate, 1999-2005

ELECTION RESULTS

2006 GENERAL		
Charlie Dent (R)	106,153	53.6%
Charles Dertinger (D)	86,186	43.5%
Greta Browne (GREEN)	5,802	2.9%
2006 PRIMARY		
Charlie Dent (R)	unopposed	
2004 GENERAL		
Charlie Dent (R)	170,634	58.6%
Joe Driscoll (D)	114,646	39.4%
Richard J. Piotrowski (LIBERT)	3,660	1.3%

Elected 2004; 2nd term

Dent is one of a dwindling band of moderate House Republicans from the Northeast. After a tough re-election victory in 2006, he returned to Washington for his sophomore term with a renewed commitment to political independence.

"When I first ran for Congress, my Republican primary opponents were trying to connect me to Ted Kennedy and Hillary Clinton, and the Democrats were trying to say I'm a Tom DeLay, George Bush rubber stamp, so I guess I'm positioned right where I need to be," he says.

Prior to the 2007 spring recess, he voted with the GOP just 77 percent of the time in the first three months of the 110th Congress (2007-08). Only 13 House Republicans split with their party more often. That marked a continuing move away from party orthodoxy for Dent, who sided with his fellow Republicans on 89 percent of the votes pitting the parties against each other in 2005, but on only 81 percent in 2006.

Moderation, especially on social issues, runs in Dent's family. He supports abortion rights just like his aunt, Mary Dent Crisp, his father's sister and a longtime GOP activist in Arizona. She famously resigned her post as co-chairwoman of the Republican National Convention in 1980 to protest the party's anti-abortion platform.

In the 109th Congress (2005-06), Dent was one of 22 Republicans who voted to allow female soldiers at overseas bases to have privately funded abortions. He was one of just five voting against a bill to allow the parents of Terri Schiavo, a severely brain-damaged Florida woman, to ask federal courts to order her feeding tube kept in place against the wishes of her husband.

Before coming to Congress in 2005, Dent had staked out moderate positions on issues from abortion to gay rights during 14 years in the Pennsylvania General Assembly and Senate. Among other things, he helped pass legislation adding sexual orientation to the state's hate crimes law.

Dent broke with President Bush over federal funding for expanded medical research on stem cells drawn from surplus embryos at in vitro fertilization clinics, voting to override Bush's veto of the legislation in 2006. He voted for a similar stem cell bill in 2007, along with four of the other five bills on the newly-in-charge Democrats' "first 100 hours" agenda.

And at the beginning of the 110th Congress, Dent's centrist bona fides were further bolstered when his colleagues elected him co-chairman of the Tuesday Group, an alliance of 40 moderate Republicans.

Dent reflects the political centrism of his Lehigh Valley district, which went for Massachusetts Sen. John Kerry in the 2004 presidential election by a mere 726 votes out of more than 300,000 cast. A lifelong resident of Allentown, Dent has deep roots in the district. His family has been in Pennsylvania since colonial times. His great-grandfather started a well-known hardware business in the district; his father worked at Bethlehem Steel in the human resources department, and his mother was a high school teacher.

Dent says his political awakening came in high school, when he took a class on the Cold War. He majored in foreign service and international politics at Penn State, then interned with one of his predecessors in Congress, former GOP Rep. Don Ritter. He went on to work as a salesman in the electronics industry and as a development officer for Lehigh University.

Dent says his experience at the university, where he helped win state funding for the school, sparked his interest in running for office. In 1990, he ran for the Pennsylvania General Assembly, defeating a Democratic incumbent. He credits his upset win to knocking "on over 20,000 doors" and running a "door-to-door, grass-roots, shoe-leather campaign." Eight years later, he won an open state Senate seat, serving there for six years.

He decided to run for Congress in 2004 when Republican Rep. Patrick J. Toomey retired and launched an unsuccessful primary challenge to moderate GOP Sen. Arlen Specter. Unlike Toomey, a conservative who decried federal spending, Dent has eagerly sought his share. He boasts of bringing home more than $50 million in the 2005 highway legislation.

He also drew notice at home for efforts to pass legislation aimed at barring the Delaware American Indian tribe of Oklahoma from reclaiming long-lost tribal land in Pennsylvania for a casino.

From his post on the Homeland Security Committee, Dent succeeded in amending a 2007 rail security bill with a provision calling for deployment of radiographic imaging of railroad cars for weapons of mass destruction, illegal immigrants or contraband. He is a leader in efforts to improve screening of rail cargo and passengers on trains and buses entering the United States.

Early in 110th Congress, Dent won adoption of a floor amendment to an alternative energy research bill that requires federal agencies to research the infrastructure challenges posed by hydrogen fuels, which he hopes might benefit a local company engaged in hydrogen research. He is a co-founder of a congressional caucus devoted to developing hydrogen and fuel cell technologies.

And, true to form, Dent has continued to weigh his votes on every issue carefully, siding with Democrats in supporting a minimum wage increase, but joining Republican colleagues in opposing Democratic efforts to condemn Bush's Iraq policy.

Dent has reason to be careful. His bid for a second term in 2006 was expected to be a cakewalk, but it didn't turn out that way. No Democrat met the filing deadline for a ballot line in the Democratic primary, but a month later Northampton County Councilman Charles Dertinger announced he would run as a write-in candidate. He won a spot on the November ballot.

Despite a severe fundraising deficit — Dertinger raised $90,000 to Dent's $1.3 million — and little support from national Democrats, Dertinger made a race of it. Playing off the party's national themes, Dertinger attempted to link Dent to Bush and the war in Iraq. Dent pulled out a victory in the end, but his 54 percent share of the vote was a relatively close call, especially compared with the 59 percent he drew in 2004 against a far better-funded Democrat, Joe Driscoll. As a result, Dent figures to be a big Democratic target in 2008.

KEY VOTES

2006

- No Stop broadband companies from favoring select Internet traffic
- Yes Affirm U.S. commitment to war in Iraq and reject setting a withdrawal date for troops
- No Repeal requirement for bilingual ballots at the polls
- Yes Permit U.S. sale of civilian nuclear technology to India
- Yes Build a 700-mile fence on the U.S.-Mexico border to curb illegal crossings
- Yes Permit warrantless wiretaps of suspected terrorists

2005

- No Intervene in the life-support case of Terri Schiavo
- Yes Lift President Bush's restrictions on stem cell research funding
- No Prohibit FBI access to library and bookstore records
- Yes Approve free-trade pact with five Central American countries
- Yes Pass energy policy overhaul favored by President Bush emphasizing domestic oil and gas production
- Yes End mandatory preservation of habitat of endangered animal and plant species
- Yes Ban torture of prisoners in U.S. custody

CQ VOTE STUDIES

	PARTY UNITY		PRESIDENTIAL SUPPORT	
	Support	Oppose	Support	Oppose
2006	81%	19%	80%	20%
2005	89%	11%	78%	22%

INTEREST GROUPS

	AFL-CIO	ADA	CCUS	ACU
2006	43%	30%	93%	72%
2005	27%	25%	89%	76%

PENNSYLVANIA 15

East — Allentown, Bethlehem

Centered in the Lehigh Valley about 60 miles north of Philadelphia and abutting the Delaware River, the 15th takes in Allentown, Bethlehem and Easton — historically known as steel and coal industry strongholds.

The region once suffered from the Rust Belt blues that singer Billy Joel enshrined in his 1982 song, "Allentown." Bethlehem Steel, at one time the Lehigh Valley's largest employer and one of the world's largest manufacturers of steel, filed for bankruptcy in 2001 and was bought by International Steel Group in 2003. Over the last decade, the area has reinvented its economy as a distribution center, and warehouses now dot a landscape where factories and small farms once were mainstays.

Olympus America moved its headquarters to the 15th in 2006. Other major employers include the Lehigh Valley Hospital complex, Air Products and Chemicals, electric utility PPL, Mack Trucks and technology company Agere Systems. Rodale Press, a large publisher of health- and fitness-related books and magazines, including Prevention Magazine and "The South Beach Diet," is located in Emmaus.

Many of the district's towns date to colonial times, some with well-established Pennsylvania Dutch heritages. But the 250-year-old German influence has been diluted by a century of immigration and steady migration from New Jersey and New York commuters. Those commuters have brought higher incomes to the area, and the migration has made the region the fastest-growing in Pennsylvania.

Blue-collar, ethnic workers provide a dwindling yet still powerful base for Democrats, and John Kerry narrowly won the 15th's 2004 presidential vote. But the increasing white-collar constituency and a socially conservative streak among blue-collar voters have helped Republicans win House contests here. Voters re-elected GOP Rep. Dent in 2006, but overwhelmingly supported Democrats for governor and the U.S. Senate.

MAJOR INDUSTRY

Manufacturing, technology, warehousing, health care

CITIES

Allentown, 106,632; Bethlehem, 71,329; Easton, 26,263

NOTABLE

The Lehigh Valley Velodrome — a premier site for track racing — has hosted an annual Bike Swap Meet in October since its first full season in 1976; Easton is home to the Crayola crayon factory.

Rep. Joe Pitts (R)

CAPITOL OFFICE
225-2411
www.house.gov/pitts
420 Cannon 20515-3816; fax 225-2013

COMMITTEES
Energy & Commerce

RESIDENCE
Kennett Square

BORN
Oct. 10, 1939, Lexington, Ky.

RELIGION
Protestant

FAMILY
Wife, Virginia M. "Ginny" Pitts; three children

EDUCATION
Asbury College, A.B. 1961 (philosophy & religion); West Chester State College, M.Ed. 1972 (comprehensive sciences)

MILITARY SERVICE
Air Force, 1963-69

CAREER
Nursery and landscaping business owner; teacher

POLITICAL HIGHLIGHTS
Pa. House, 1973-97

ELECTION RESULTS

2006 GENERAL		
Joe Pitts (R)	115,741	56.6%
Lois K. Herr (D)	80,915	39.5%
John A. Murphy (I)	7,958	3.9%
2006 PRIMARY		
Joe Pitts (R)		unopposed
2004 GENERAL		
Joe Pitts (R)	183,620	64.4%
Lois K. Herr (D)	98,410	34.5%
William R. Hagen (GREEN)	3,269	1.2%

PREVIOUS WINNING PERCENTAGES
2002 (88%); 2000 (67%); 1998 (71%); 1996 (59%)

Elected 1996; 6th term

In Congress, Pitts resolutely follows the same road he traveled during 24 years in the Pennsylvania legislature — one with few left turns. He is a strong proponent of cutting taxes and limiting the scope of the federal government, and a fervent opponent of abortion.

He serves on the Energy and Commerce Committee, which he joined in 2005 because he felt he could best serve his district from that panel. With his district's agricultural areas constantly pressured by development, he has pushed a bill that would exempt farmers from paying federal capital gains taxes on profits made from selling off development rights. The bill is intended to provide an incentive to farmers to preserve their land permanently.

To accept the assignment to the Energy panel, Pitts had to relinquish his seat on the House's international affairs committee. But he still devotes significant time and energy to humanitarian work and personal diplomacy.

His interest in foreign policy is far deeper and more personal than most House members. The son of missionaries who worked for many years in the Philippines, he has grown increasingly concerned about the Bush administration's handling of the Iraq War. He is especially critical of the president's refusal to negotiate with Iraq's neighbors, Iran and Syria. "Dialogue is not a sign of weakness; it's a sign of confidence," Pitts said in early 2007. He said the United States should be more willing to learn from those who have a different culture or religion. "Don't teach. Don't go and preach." Instead, he said, "treat them with dignity and respect" and ask for advice. "They will help you; many of them will help you."

But in early 2007, he voted against a Democratic resolution disapproving of President Bush's plan to send more than 21,000 additional combat troops into Iraq, saying it was only an attempt to score political points and would damage soldiers' morale. He also opposed a war funding bill that set a troop withdrawal deadline.

Pitts practices his own diplomacy, inviting ambassadors from 195 countries to his district every year. "We have host families pick them up, and we take them for three and a half days to businesses, cultural historic sites, show them a good time at dinner theater," he said. One diplomat told him that he had been in the United States for four years but had never before met a "real American family" or stayed in a "real American home." The ambassador said the experience "changed our view of America." That is the point, Pitts says. He personally hosts a monthly luncheon for ambassadors. "I believe in relational politics. I believe in that type of engagement and diplomacy."

In the aftermath of the Sept. 11 terrorist attacks, Pitts and a handful of other lawmakers formed the Silk Road Caucus to promote greater contact between the United States and Central Asia. He has organized equipment drives for hospitals in Pakistan and he is active in a number of human rights organizations, including the U.S. Commission on Security and Cooperation in Europe, better known as the Helsinki Commission.

As the House member representing Lancaster County, the best-known Amish community in the nation, Pitts has become the chief defender of their simple, rural lifestyle. He fought to win the Amish an exemption from child labor laws to ensure that Amish teenagers can enter apprenticeships once their formal education is complete. The proposal was included in a catchall spending bill Bush signed in 2004.

Pitts is at the center of most battles on social issues. When Congress rewrote the federal bankruptcy law in 2005, Pitts and other conservatives objected to an amendment aimed at preventing demonstrators — particularly protesters at abortion clinics — from filing for bankruptcy to avoid paying court-ordered fines. Pitts was pleased when the Senate rejected the amendment. "This is a victory for free speech," he said.

Pitts leads the Values Action Team, a group of about 70 social conservatives. Members of that group and other social conservatives showed their muscle in 2005 when the House voted to clear Senate-passed legislation bringing the federal courts into the Florida dispute over whether to reconnect a feeding tube that had been sustaining the life of Terri Schiavo, a severely brain-damaged woman. "We played a role in that, in urging the leadership to act," Pitts said after the vote. The following year, Pitts and Republican Marilyn Musgrave of Colorado led an unsuccessful effort to win House adoption of a constitutional amendment to ban same-sex marriage.

Many of Pitts' goals stem from his experiences as a child of missionaries and as a young father. He spent most of his youth in the back country of the Philippines, where his parents were engaged in missionary work. He says he witnessed poverty and devastation close up, but also saw the personal satisfaction that a life in public service can bring.

After returning to his native Kentucky, marrying and earning a college degree in philosophy and religion, Pitts and his wife embarked on teaching careers. When she became pregnant, Pitts discovered that the family could not live on just one teaching salary. So he joined the Air Force for five and a half years, including three tours of duty in Southeast Asia in which he flew 116 combat missions as the navigator and electronic warfare officer of a B-52. He considered an Air Force career but rejected the idea when his 14-month-old son didn't recognize him once he returned home from active duty.

After the Air Force stint, the family moved to Pennsylvania, and Pitts returned to teaching high school math and science. He eventually joined his wife's family's landscape and nursery business, then started his own landscaping firm. Though he was active on local campaigns, Pitts did not think of running for office himself until colleagues persuaded him to make a bid for an open state House seat in 1972. He upset the party-endorsed candidate and served there for 24 years, including eight years as chairman of the Appropriations Committee.

When Robert S. Walker, a leading figure in the GOP's 1994 takeover of the U.S. House, decided to retire in 1996, Pitts won a hard-fought five-way primary race and — boosted by the Republican Party's more than 2-1 edge in registered voters in the district — won easily in November. In 2006, he was re-elected with 57 percent of the vote, his lowest total ever.

KEY VOTES

2006

No Stop broadband companies from favoring select Internet traffic
Yes Affirm U.S. commitment to war in Iraq and reject setting a withdrawal date for troops
Yes Repeal requirement for bilingual ballots at the polls
Yes Permit U.S. sale of civilian nuclear technology to India
Yes Build a 700-mile fence on the U.S.-Mexico border to curb illegal crossings
Yes Permit warrantless wiretaps of suspected terrorists

2005

Yes Intervene in the life-support case of Terri Schiavo
No Lift President Bush's restrictions on stem cell research funding
No Prohibit FBI access to library and bookstore records
Yes Approve free-trade pact with five Central American countries
Yes Pass energy policy overhaul favored by President Bush emphasizing domestic oil and gas production
Yes End mandatory preservation of habitat of endangered animal and plant species
Yes Ban torture of prisoners in U.S. custody

CQ VOTE STUDIES

	PARTY UNITY		PRESIDENTIAL SUPPORT	
	Support	Oppose	Support	Oppose
2006	95%	5%	84%	16%
2005	97%	3%	85%	15%
2004	97%	3%	91%	9%
2003	98%	2%	98%	2%
2002	97%	3%	88%	12%

INTEREST GROUPS

	AFL-CIO	ADA	CCUS	ACU
2006	8%	5%	92%	86%
2005	7%	0%	88%	100%
2004	13%	5%	95%	100%
2003	7%	5%	100%	88%
2002	0%	0%	94%	100%

PENNSYLVANIA 16

Southeast – Lancaster, part of Reading

Located in southeastern Pennsylvania and bordering Delaware and Maryland, the 16th includes all of Lancaster County, the southern half of Chester County and portions of southwest Berks County, including part of Reading. Containing much of the so-called Pennsylvania Dutch Country, the 16th is a Republican bastion.

The strong work ethic of the local labor force and the district's proximity to major roadways attract companies to the area, which is central to the mid-Atlantic's major markets. Economic expansion has attracted new residents, and some of the area's farmland has been built over with tract housing. Rolling and pastoral Chester County (shared with the 6th and 7th) has grown by more than 28 percent since the 1990s. The Kennett Square area produces one of the nation's largest mushroom crops.

Although the 16th welcomes the development, farm preservation remains a major concern, especially in Lancaster County, a national leader in agricultural product sales and poultry and livestock raising.

Tourism also enhances the 16th's robust economy. An estimated 7 million visitors annually flock to Dutch Country to gaze at Amish horse-drawn carriages, browse at quilt shops and dine in family-style restaurants.

Since the dawn of the Civil War, the areas in the 16th have favored the GOP at all levels. Lancaster County, which accounts for more than 70 percent of the district population, sets the district's conservative political tone with its Amish heritage. George W. Bush won 66 percent of the county's vote in the 2004 presidential election. Chester County is more socially moderate, but Bush still won the 16th's share of the county by 4 percentage points in 2004. The only real Democratic strength is in Reading (shared with the 6th District), which is heavily Democratic as a result of its large Hispanic and black populations. Overall, Bush won the 16th with 61 percent of the vote in 2004.

MAJOR INDUSTRY

Agriculture, tourism, manufacturing

CITIES

Lancaster, 56,348; Reading (pt.), 44,296; West Chester, 17,861

NOTABLE

The original five-and-dime store that started the Woolworth chain opened in Lancaster in 1879.

Rep. Tim Holden (D)

CAPITOL OFFICE
225-5546
www.holden.house.gov
2417 Rayburn 20515-3817; fax 226-0996

COMMITTEES
Agriculture
(Conservation, Credit, Energy & Research - chairman)
Transportation & Infrastructure

RESIDENCE
St. Clair

BORN
March 5, 1957, St. Clair, Pa.

RELIGION
Roman Catholic

FAMILY
Wife, Gwen Holden

EDUCATION
U. of Richmond, attended 1976-77;
Bloomsburg U., B.A. 1980 (sociology)

CAREER
Probation officer; insurance broker; realtor

POLITICAL HIGHLIGHTS
Schuylkill County sheriff, 1985-93

ELECTION RESULTS

2006 GENERAL		
Tim Holden (D)	137,253	64.5%
Matthew A. Wertz (R)	75,455	35.5%
2006 PRIMARY		
Tim Holden (D)		unopposed
2004 GENERAL		
Tim Holden (D)	172,412	59.1%
Scott Paterno (R)	113,592	38.9%
Russ Diamond (LIBERT)	5,782	2.0%

PREVIOUS WINNING PERCENTAGES
2002 (51%); 2000 (66%); 1998 (61%); 1996 (59%); 1994 (57%); 1992 (52%)

Elected 1992; 8th term

Holden may be out of step with his party at times, but the former sheriff is right in sync with his working-class constituents in central Pennsylvania, who are worried about holding onto their jobs and their guns. He has proved to be more resilient than state Republicans had expected.

An easygoing and affable man whom his constituents call Timmy, Holden rarely speaks on the House floor. He makes little effort to seek the limelight, on the floor or elsewhere. "The last thing Congress needs is another prima donna looking for C-SPAN time," he says. "I like to work behind the scenes to get stuff done."

But after 15 years as a member of the House Agriculture Committee, the low-key lawmaker is seeing his profile rise. In the 110th Congress (2007-08), a major rewrite of farm policy is getting under way and Holden wields the gavel of Agriculture's Subcommittee on Conservation, Credit, Energy and Research. With the panel's jurisdiction expanded by Democrats to include energy issues, Holden has wasted no time laying claim to a piece of the debate. The topic for his first hearing as chairman was renewable energy financing options.

Conservation programs — especially ones that provide funds for the purchase of development rights to farm lands — are another major concern for the lawmaker. Holden fought in vain to block cuts to these programs in 2005, when the Agriculture Committee cut more than $1 billion from farm programs as part of a Republican deficit reduction package. His district is home to a mix of dairy farmers, vegetable growers, orchard owners and other types of farmers who don't necessarily benefit from the big farm subsidy programs for crops such as wheat and corn.

Holden also sits on the Transportation and Infrastructure Committee, where he has touted his successes in securing funding for local highway and transit projects in the 1998 and 2005 surface transportation laws. His pet project is working to make the 17th District's large reserves of coal more marketable by spurring researchers to develop technology to burn the fuel more cleanly.

Holden is a member of the Blue Dog Coalition, a group of more than 40 of the most conservative House Democrats. In the 109th Congress (2005-06), he agreed with President Bush's position 54 percent of the time; only 13 Democrats voted with the president more frequently. He breaks with his party on social issues like abortion and same-sex marriage, and also on a range of other topics. Holden observes that "most Democrats in Pennsylvania are conservative, rural, not pro-choice, not gun control, the exception being the Philadelphia guys."

He voted in 2005 for the GOP energy policy overhaul, and for Republican bills to limit class action lawsuits and to cap damages in medical malpractice cases. The following year, he supported a tough border security bill that most House Democrats opposed. "I am for the wall up against Mexico and penalties for employers," Holden says. "I think conservatives are right on the immigration issue." He also was one of only four Democrats to oppose the requirement for mandatory bilingual assistance at the polls on Election Day when the Voting Rights Act came up for renewal in 2006.

But Holden often sides with Democrats and organized labor on issues such as the minimum wage and an extension of unemployment benefits. He also has taken labor's side by opposing most trade agreements during his tenure in Congress, despite the fact that his state includes many export-minded businesses in industries such as communications and steel, as well as a number of firms that import chemicals for use in their manufacturing processes.

His mentor in politics is fellow Democratic Keystone State lawmaker John P. Murtha, a former Marine who created a national uproar in 2005 by calling for withdrawal of U.S. troops from Iraq. Holden calls Murtha his mentor and "a great friend."

Holden won some short-lived television fame in 2006. On the quiz show "Jeopardy," contestants were asked to identify the home state of "Murtha, Dent and Holden." The correct answer: "What is Pennsylvania?"

Holden's family has a tradition of public service. "I was taught it was a noble profession," he says. His great-grandfather, John Siney, founded the Miner's Benevolent Association, the forerunner of the United Mine Workers. His father, Joseph "Sox" Holden, was a Schuylkill County commissioner for almost two decades and also was a catcher for the Philadelphia Phillies from 1934-36. Holden keeps his dad's #10 jersey framed in his office and takes the field in the same position at the annual congressional charity baseball game.

He exercises religiously at the gym and enjoys watching Notre Dame play football. "As an Irish Catholic, you were raised to like Notre Dame," Holden says. "No offense to Penn State, but that's how it is." He has made three trips to Northern Ireland as part of the bipartisan congressional Friends of Ireland group, which promotes peace and power-sharing in Northern Ireland.

Holden started college in Virginia on a football scholarship but returned home after a year to recuperate from a bout of tuberculosis and then stayed close by to finish school. He earned an insurance license while in college and a real estate broker's license soon afterward. He worked in both fields part time for years afterward to make ends meet while he served as a probation officer; sergeant-at-arms in the Pennsylvania House; and Schuylkill County sheriff, a post he won for the first time at age 28.

When 12-term Democratic Rep. Gus Yatron retired in 1992, Holden won by 4 percentage points in what was then the 6th District, waging an effective "man-of-the-people" campaign. He won re-election with increasing margins until 2002, when Republicans figured that 20-year veteran GOP incumbent Rep. George W. Gekas could defeat Holden in the newly drawn 17th District. But Holden hung on to the seat.

In 2004, Scott Paterno, son of legendary Penn State football coach Joe Paterno, raised more than $1 million to try to unseat Holden. To no avail: Holden clobbered Paterno by more than 20 percentage points. In 2006, his GOP foe, Matthew A. Wertz, citing health and personal reasons, suspended his campaign in September and Holden won by 29 percentage points.

KEY VOTES

2006

- No Stop broadband companies from favoring select Internet traffic
- Yes Affirm U.S. commitment to war in Iraq and reject setting a withdrawal date for troops
- Yes Repeal requirement for bilingual ballots at the polls
- Yes Permit U.S. sale of civilian nuclear technology to India
- Yes Build a 700-mile fence on the U.S.-Mexico border to curb illegal crossings
- No Permit warrantless wiretaps of suspected terrorists

2005

- Yes Intervene in the life-support case of Terri Schiavo
- No Lift President Bush's restrictions on stem cell research funding
- Yes Prohibit FBI access to library and bookstore records
- No Approve free-trade pact with five Central American countries
- Yes Pass energy policy overhaul favored by President Bush emphasizing domestic oil and gas production
- Yes End mandatory preservation of habitat of endangered animal and plant species
- Yes Ban torture of prisoners in U.S. custody

CQ VOTE STUDIES

	PARTY UNITY		PRESIDENTIAL SUPPORT	
	Support	Oppose	Support	Oppose
2006	79%	21%	56%	44%
2005	75%	25%	52%	48%
2004	76%	24%	48%	52%
2003	78%	22%	49%	51%
2002	67%	33%	60%	40%

INTEREST GROUPS

	AFL-CIO	ADA	CCUS	ACU
2006	100%	60%	53%	64%
2005	93%	80%	63%	40%
2004	93%	70%	67%	48%
2003	93%	70%	40%	60%
2002	89%	65%	60%	40%

PENNSYLVANIA 17

East central – Harrisburg, Lebanon, Pottsville

Anchored in the eastern part of south-central Pennsylvania, the 17th is home to Harrisburg, the state capital, which sits 100 miles west of Philadelphia and 200 miles east of Pittsburgh. The 17th has two distinct zones: a stretch of agricultural lands along the Susquehanna River in the west, and industrial areas in Schuylkill and Berks counties in the east. Here, in GOP-minded central Pennsylvania, state government and manufacturing remain key sources of employment.

Harrisburg's skyline is dominated by the Capitol, with a dome inspired by St. Peter's Basilica in Rome. With many government employees and a black majority, the city typically votes Democratic. Visitors wanting a real taste of Dauphin County skip Harrisburg and go to Hershey, also known as "the sweetest place on Earth," where even the streetlights are shaped like Hershey Kisses. The chocolate factory stands in the center of town, emitting the most pleasant of industrial odors.

Computer and electrical components manufacturing drive the economy in Dauphin and Lebanon counties. Harrisburg, in Dauphin, is a major distribution hub for metropolitan markets in the mid-Atlantic region, and it hosts the Penn State Hershey Medical Center. The proliferation of service jobs has helped mitigate the impact of other losses. Officials look to balance the needs of agricultural producers with those of industrial workers, making trade a potent issue in the 17th.

The 17th has a distinct Republican lean, but moderate Democrats can play here due to the district's mix of agrarian and industrial communities. The GOP is strong in Lebanon County and in the areas of Dauphin outside of Harrisburg. Democrats are competitive in Schuylkill County, long a coal mining powerhouse, with comfortable margins in Shenandoah, Pottsville and Mahanoy. Republican gubernatorial nominee Lynn Swann won both Dauphin and Lebanon counties in his unsuccessful 2006 campaign. George W. Bush took 58 percent of the district's vote in the 2004 presidential election.

MAJOR INDUSTRY

Government, service, manufacturing, tourism, agriculture, biotechnology

CITIES

Harrisburg, 48,950; Lebanon, 24,461; Pottsville, 15,549

NOTABLE

Pottsville is home to Yuengling, America's oldest active brewery.

Rep. Tim Murphy (R)

CAPITOL OFFICE
225-2301
murphy.house.gov
322 Cannon 20515-3818; fax 225-1844

COMMITTEES
Energy & Commerce

RESIDENCE
Upper St. Clair

BORN
Sept. 11, 1952, Cleveland, Ohio

RELIGION
Roman Catholic

FAMILY
Wife, Nan Murphy; one child

EDUCATION
Wheeling College, B.S. 1974 (psychology); Cleveland State U., M.A. 1976 (psychology); U. of Pittsburgh, Ph.D. 1979 (psychology)

CAREER
Psychologist; professor

POLITICAL HIGHLIGHTS
Pa. Senate, 1997-2003

ELECTION RESULTS

2006 GENERAL		
Tim Murphy (R)	144,632	57.8%
Chad Kluko (D)	105,419	42.2%
2006 PRIMARY		
Tim Murphy (R)		unopposed
2004 GENERAL		
Tim Murphy (R)	197,894	62.8%
Mark G. Boles (D)	117,420	37.2%

PREVIOUS WINNING PERCENTAGES
2002 (60%)

Elected 2002; 3rd term

Murphy, who gave medical advice as "Dr. Tim" on Pittsburgh radio and television, has struggled to make himself heard on Capitol Hill.

A psychologist and former professor, Murphy has been striving to make health care his signature issue in Congress. But he was not able to move a health bill out of committee in the 109th Congress (2005-06). His efforts included what turned out to be a bad bargain. In the neck-and-neck race for House majority leader in 2006, Murphy cut a deal with Roy Blunt of Missouri: Murphy would vote for Blunt in the leadership race if Blunt agreed to help advance Murphy's health legislation.

Blunt lost.

Prospects for Murphy's bills are even more difficult with the Democrats in charge in the 110th Congress (2007-08), even though Murphy did get the spot he sought on the Energy and Commerce Committee's Health Subcommittee.

The Pittsburgh Post-Gazette, which endorsed him in 2004, changed its mind in 2006. The paper said Murphy's health care proposals, "although sensible, don't go to the heart of the problem." It added, "He polishes a broken machine, one that leaves millions uninsured," and it criticized him further for being too "bullish" on the deteriorating Iraq War.

Nonetheless, Murphy drubbed Democrat Chad Kluko by nearly 16 percentage points in his suburban Pittsburgh district, defying an anti-Republican tide that swept Democrats into control of Congress.

The legislation for which Murphy sought Blunt's help would provide liability protection to doctors volunteering at community health centers, which often serve uninsured patients. He also introduced a measure to promote the use of electronic prescriptions and medical record-keeping to track every aspect of a patient's care. "There's nobody who works harder in Congress on reforming the health care system," Murphy told the Pittsburgh Tribune-Review in 2006.

Murphy had more success in the 109th Congress with his effort to keep the Defense Department from closing a military installation in his district. In 2005, the Pentagon proposed closing the Pittsburgh International Airport Air Reserve Station, at a cost of 322 jobs. The installation was spared after Murphy and Pennsylvania Democrat John P. Murtha fought for it before the Base Realignment and Closure Commission.

Perhaps Murphy's biggest legislative success in the 109th Congress was House passage of his bill making it illegal for callers to "spoof" caller-ID devices. The bill was prompted by election-season phone calls critical of Murphy that had been rigged to appear as though they originated in his own offices. "People thought we were making the calls," he told The Associated Press in 2006. The bill died in the Senate, but the House Democrats passed a similar measure early in the 110th Congress with Murphy as a cosponsor.

In 2005, Murphy provided a much-needed vote to deliver a victory to President Bush on the Central American Free Trade Agreement (CAFTA). Opponents argued that the trade pact would give a boost to unfair foreign competition in U.S. markets, and that votes were traded in exchange for favorable consideration of certain proposals, including for highway funding. Murphy said that he voted yes on CAFTA based on its merits.

"The real enemy is China, and I can't say that in any stronger terms," he said. Still, Murphy acknowledged that he was aware of a possible connection between his CAFTA vote and his bid to secure $3 million for Pittsburgh's proposed Southern Beltway in the conference report on the surface transportation bill. "I'm trying to keep my highways in here," he said.

Murphy has consistently supported the Bush administration's Iraq War strategy. Even an injury in a road accident there in November 2005 did little to dull his enthusiasm for the president's efforts. He said at the time that violence in parts of Iraq did not reflect conditions across the country and that the more than 2,100 U.S. troops that had been killed up to that point should be viewed in the context of "hundreds of thousands" Iraqi deaths.

Murphy modified his stance on the war in 2007 to sound a more conditional note on the administration's war policies, but he voted against the Democrats' resolution criticizing Bush's escalation of troop levels and against a war-spending measure setting a troop withdrawal deadline.

Motivated to run for elective office by a desire to address problems in managed care, Murphy won a state Senate seat in 1996. Within two years, he had pushed through the legislature a "Patients' Bill of Rights." In 2001, Murphy co-wrote a book titled "The Angry Child: Regaining Control When Your Child Is Out of Control." The book explored the sources of anger in children and recommended ways parents could respond.

Growing up as one of 11 children, Murphy paid his way through school by cleaning out horse stalls and digging graves. He supports vouchers and other programs that could allow low-income families to send their children to private or parochial schools.

Murphy, who taught himself to play guitar, performed in acoustic bands in high school, college and graduate school. The bands played coffeehouses where, he said, he would earn enough to buy an expensive hamburger — but he also once opened in Cleveland for banjo legend Earl Scruggs.

Pennsylvania lost a pair of House seats in reapportionment after the 2000 census. But the Republican-controlled General Assembly was able to draw a congressional map with an 18th District south of Pittsburgh configured to favor a Republican — Murphy, in particular. He had become the presumptive heir to the seat when the incumbent House member living in the new 18th, four-term Democrat Frank R. Mascara, decided to mount what proved to be an unsuccessful primary challenge to Murtha.

Murphy took 60 percent of the vote to defeat Democrat Jack M. Machek in 2002, and two years later won with 63 percent over political newcomer Mark G. Boles, a physician, after having raised almost 10 times more money than his opponent.

KEY VOTES

2006

- No Stop broadband companies from favoring select Internet traffic
- Yes Affirm U.S. commitment to war in Iraq and reject setting a withdrawal date for troops
- Yes Repeal requirement for bilingual ballots at the polls
- Yes Permit U.S. sale of civilian nuclear technology to India
- Yes Build a 700-mile fence on the U.S.-Mexico border to curb illegal crossings
- Yes Permit warrantless wiretaps of suspected terrorists

2005

- Yes Intervene in the life-support case of Terri Schiavo
- No Lift President Bush's restrictions on stem cell research funding
- No Prohibit FBI access to library and bookstore records
- Yes Approve free-trade pact with five Central American countries
- Yes Pass energy policy overhaul favored by President Bush emphasizing domestic oil and gas production
- Yes End mandatory preservation of habitat of endangered animal and plant species
- Yes Ban torture of prisoners in U.S. custody

CQ VOTE STUDIES

	PARTY UNITY		PRESIDENTIAL SUPPORT	
	Support	Oppose	Support	Oppose
2006	91%	9%	87%	13%
2005	91%	9%	80%	20%
2004	92%	8%	84%	16%
2003	97%	3%	98%	2%

INTEREST GROUPS

	AFL-CIO	ADA	CCUS	ACU
2006	43%	10%	93%	80%
2005	21%	15%	92%	84%
2004	36%	20%	95%	92%
2003	27%	10%	97%	88%

PENNSYLVANIA 18

West – Pittsburgh suburbs, part of Washington and Westmoreland counties

Taking in suburbs of Pittsburgh on three sides of the city, the socially conservative 18th moves east from Washington County through parts of southern Allegheny County into Westmoreland County. Access to major waterways made the first half of the 20th century prosperous for parts of the 18th, which was once a prodigious producer of steel. Now, many areas outside the Pittsburgh suburbs, especially in southwestern Washington and southeastern Westmoreland, are struggling economically.

Roughly 55 percent of the 18th's residents live in Allegheny County, which is dominated by Pittsburgh. The Democratic-leaning city is in the 14th District, and most of Allegheny's wealthy Republican suburbs are in the 4th. The 18th's share of the suburbs includes well-off areas in southwestern Allegheny such as Upper St. Clair and Mount Lebanon, as well as middle- and working-class Democratic enclaves like Carnegie and Dormont, which are just southwest of Pittsburgh.

The district's universities and hospitals have lured some technology companies to the area, as has the 18th's high percentage of residents with a college degree, at 29 percent. Located in the district's northwest, Pittsburgh International Airport provides thousands of jobs for the 18th and is one of U.S. Airways' hubs.

The 18th includes most of Westmoreland County, which is a former Democratic bastion that has moved to the right, supporting George W. Bush by 12 percentage points in the 2004 presidential election. Overall, Bush captured 54 percent of the 18th's vote in 2004.

MAJOR INDUSTRY

Health care, technology, manufacturing, air cargo, steel

CITIES

Bethel Park, 33,556; Mount Lebanon (unincorporated), 33,017; Monroeville (pt.), 24,294

NOTABLE

Andy Warhol is buried in Bethel Park; The Meadowcroft Museum of Rural Life, near Avella in Washington County, preserves the history of 19th century rural life in western Pennsylvania.

Rep. Todd R. Platts (R)

CAPITOL OFFICE
225-5836
www.house.gov/platts
1032 Longworth 20515-3819; fax 226-1000

COMMITTEES
Education & Labor
Oversight & Government Reform
Transportation & Infrastructure

RESIDENCE
York

BORN
March 5, 1962, York, Pa.

RELIGION
Episcopalian

FAMILY
Wife, Leslie Platts; two children

EDUCATION
Shippensburg U., B.S. 1984 (public administration); Pepperdine U., J.D. 1991

CAREER
Lawyer; gubernatorial and state legislative aide

POLITICAL HIGHLIGHTS
Pa. House, 1993-2000; sought Republican nomination for York County Commission, 1995

ELECTION RESULTS

2006 GENERAL		
Todd R. Platts (R)	142,512	64.0%
Philip J. Avillo Jr. (D)	74,625	33.5%
Derf W. Maitland (GREEN)	5,640	2.5%
2006 PRIMARY		
Todd R. Platts (R)		unopposed
2004 GENERAL		
Todd R. Platts (R)	224,274	91.5%
Charles J. Steel (GREEN)	8,890	3.6%
Michael L. Paoletta (LIBERT)	8,456	3.5%
Lester B. Searer (CNSTP)	3,474	1.4%

PREVIOUS WINNING PERCENTAGES
2002 (91%); 2000 (73%)

Elected 2000; 4th term

While Platts' Democratic opponents at election time have tried to portray him as a rubber stamp for his party, it's a charge that bounces right off — sometimes to the chagrin of Republican leaders.

In the 110th Congress (2007-08), Platts was one of only three Republicans to vote for all six bills that the Democratic majority brought to the floor as part of its "first 100 hours" agenda. The legislation increased the federal minimum wage, expanded funding for embryonic stem cell research and gave the government the ability to use its bulk purchasing power to negotiate lower prices for prescription drugs in the Medicare program. "I've regularly been willing to go my own way," Platts says.

His goals for the 110th Congress are similarly at odds with the GOP's party line. He wants to reauthorize the National and Community Service Trust Act, which includes the Americorps program, a Clinton-era program patterned after the Peace Corps. Platts' niece is an alumna.

He also wants to reauthorize the Community Service Block Grant, a program that President Bush has proposed eliminating. He is the lead Republican cosponsor of a bill that would force automakers to raise their fuel efficiency and another that would require electric utilities to use more renewable energy sources.

Political apostasy is a hallmark of Platts' career. In his first term, in 2001-02, he was one of 20 Republicans who signed a discharge petition that forced the GOP leadership to bring campaign finance legislation to a vote. And then he was one of the 41 Republicans to vote for the bill that became law in 2002.

Platts supported his party on 79 percent of the party-line votes in the 109th Congress (2005-06), placing him among the 20 most disloyal Republicans. He says there have been few repercussions. Eleven months after the campaign finance vote, he got the chairmanship of a Government Reform subcommittee. In the 110th Congress, he has retained three committee assignments, including a seat on the desirable Transportation and Infrastructure panel, which decides how federal highway dollars are spent.

Good government is an obsession for Platts, down to the "Mr. Smith Goes to Washington" poster hanging in his office. He takes no political action committee money, writes bills on government management practices and wonders why the government's books are not as tidy as his own finances. "If my checkbook is off by 10 cents, I'll stay up all night until I find that 10 cents. Your checkbook is off by $2 billion," Platts once lectured a National Aeronautics and Space Administration official appearing before his subcommittee.

Platts was the lead Republican cosponsor on three of four bills the House passed in March 2007, including one strengthening whistleblower protections for federal workers and another making it easier to get information from the government through the Freedom of Information Act. Bush has said he would veto that one, as well as another Platts sponsored that would deny presidents and vice presidents the authority to unilaterally shield their records from public view.

In the 109th Congress, Platts was one of a handful of Republicans to vote with Democrats for a tough House ethics bill — and against a less restrictive, rival bill supported by his party's leaders. That put him at odds with his leadership and, in an odd twist, won him some unfavorable press. In a fall 2006 issue of Esquire, the magazine made endorsements in every congressional race and endorsed Platts' opponent based on Platts' vote against the GOP measure. The magazine overlooked his vote for the stronger, Democratic alternative. Esquire issued an apology and a correction after the magazine hit newsstands. "It's probably the only way I'm ever going to get into Esquire," Platts joked.

His reputation for trying to keep government on the straight and narrow dates to his days as a member of the Pennsylvania House, where he aggravated colleagues by being unbending and going after their perquisites of office. The York Daily Record newspaper once dubbed him the "King of Clean."

Platts says he may have picked up his stubborn tendencies from his father, who bucked the local Little League establishment with his belief that every child who showed up at practice should play.

Education is another area where Platts has tried to work across the aisle. He once wrote an early childhood education bill with Rep. George Miller of California, the liberal Democrat who is now chairman of the Education and Labor Committee, that sought to boost the pay and improve the training of child care workers. Unlike many Republicans, Platts opposes vouchers for private schools, and says the federal government should keep its longstanding promise to pay its full share of the costs of educating disabled students under the Individuals with Disabilities Education Act.

Platts says being a member of Congress has been his ambition since he was a teenager. He won election to the state legislature at the age of 30 after paying his dues in local politics and civic organizations.

He worked for Republican Gov. Dick Thornburgh and served as a legislative committee staff member and assistant finance director for the state Republican Party. Then in 1992, Platts made his first bid for elective office — a seat in the state House. He campaigned on a reform platform, assembled a large band of volunteers and won comfortably.

He made an unsuccessful run for the York County Commission in 1995, but then went on to win two more state House terms.

In early 1999, when former Republican Rep. William F. Goodling announced his plan to retire in 2000, Platts was the first candidate to jump into the race. Though greatly outspent in the GOP primary, Platts won with 33 percent of the vote. The district's Republican leanings ensured his victory against a nominal Democrat.

He didn't face another Democratic opponent until the 2006 election, when history professor Phillip J. Avillo Jr. took barely 34 percent of the vote — despite Esquire's misinformed endorsement.

KEY VOTES

2006

- No — Stop broadband companies from favoring select Internet traffic
- Yes — Affirm U.S. commitment to war in Iraq and reject setting a withdrawal date for troops
- Yes — Repeal requirement for bilingual ballots at the polls
- Yes — Permit U.S. sale of civilian nuclear technology to India
- Yes — Build a 700-mile fence on the U.S.-Mexico border to curb illegal crossings
- Yes — Permit warrantless wiretaps of suspected terrorists

2005

- Yes — Intervene in the life-support case of Terri Schiavo
- Yes — Lift President Bush's restrictions on stem cell research funding
- No — Prohibit FBI access to library and bookstore records
- Yes — Approve free-trade pact with five Central American countries
- Yes — Pass energy policy overhaul favored by President Bush emphasizing domestic oil and gas production
- No — End mandatory preservation of habitat of endangered animal and plant species
- Yes — Ban torture of prisoners in U.S. custody

CQ VOTE STUDIES

	PARTY UNITY		PRESIDENTIAL SUPPORT	
	Support	Oppose	Support	Oppose
2006	72%	28%	80%	20%
2005	84%	16%	80%	20%
2004	88%	12%	85%	15%
2003	91%	9%	89%	11%
2002	85%	15%	82%	18%

INTEREST GROUPS

	AFL-CIO	ADA	CCUS	ACU
2006	50%	25%	93%	72%
2005	33%	25%	85%	67%
2004	33%	20%	95%	84%
2003	27%	20%	90%	76%
2002	11%	5%	85%	88%

PENNSYLVANIA 19

South central – York, Gettysburg

Situated west of the Susquehanna River, mostly east of the South Mountain ridge and mostly south of Harrisburg (in the neighboring 17th), the 19th's historic landscape has a reliably Republican constituency and flourishing agricultural and manufacturing industries.

Located along several major highways, the district is a prime location for manufacturing and distribution centers, including depots and logistical support facilities for the Defense Department, and York County serves as the 19th's industrial hub. Residential growth, a more recent trend, also can be attributed to the district's location — many Marylanders have moved here for lower taxes and affordable real estate. Adams and York counties both have grown by more than 20 percent since 1990, with Cumberland having grown 16 percent over the same time period.

Tourism also plays a major role in the district's economy. Nearly 2 million visitors each year come to see the site of the 1863 Battle of Gettysburg in Adams County, now a largely fruit-growing area. Many come for the annual re-enactment of one of the Civil War's most significant battles and to see monuments, military grave sites, historic markers and the site of Abraham Lincoln's Gettysburg Address.

George W. Bush won 64 percent of the 19th's vote in the 2004 presidential election. Cumberland County (shared with the 9th) is strongly Republican, with Bush winning 63 percent of the district's portion of the county. York and Adams also have strong GOP leans, with Democrats only finding strength in the city of York, where blacks and Hispanics combined make up more than 40 percent of the population, and Gettysburg, which has a large college-age population.

MAJOR INDUSTRY

Agriculture, manufacturing, distribution, defense, tourism

MILITARY BASES

Defense Distribution Depot Susquehanna, 296 military, 1,047 civilian (2004); Carlisle Barracks, 602 military, 1,065 civilian (2007)

CITIES

York, 40,862; Carlisle, 17,970; Hanover, 14,535

NOTABLE

York served as the first U.S. Capital from 1777-78 while the British occupied Philadelphia; Tours are available of the York Harley-Davidson manufacturing facility, which covers 230 acres and employs 3,200.

RHODE ISLAND

Gov. Donald L. Carcieri (R)

Pronounced: CAR-cheery
First elected: 2002
Length of term: 4 years
Term expires: 1/11
Salary: $117,118
Phone: (401) 222-2080

Residence: East Greenwich
Born: Dec. 16, 1942; East Greenwich, R.I.
Religion: Roman Catholic
Family: Wife, Sue Carcieri; four children
Education: Brown U., A.B. 1965 (international relations)
Career: Manufacturing company executive; aid relief worker; bank executive; teacher
Political highlights: No previous office

Election results:

2006 GENERAL		
Donald L. Carcieri (R)	197,306	51.0%
Charles J. Fogarty (D)	189,503	49.0%

Lt. Gov. Elizabeth Roberts (D)

First elected: 2006
Length of term: 4 years
Term expires: 1/11
Salary: $99,214
Phone: (401) 222-2371

LEGISLATURE

General Assembly: January-June

Senate: 38 members, 2-year terms
2007 ratios: 33 D, 5 R; 31 men, 7 women
Salary: $13,089
Phone: (401) 222-6655

House: 75 members, 2-year terms
2007 ratios: 62 D, 13 R; 60 men, 15 women
Salary: $13,089
Phone: (401) 222-2466

TERM LIMITS

Governor: 2 terms
Senate: No
House: No

URBAN STATISTICS

CITY	POPULATION
Providence	173,618
Warwick	85,808
Cranston	79,269
Pawtucket	72,958
East Providence	48,688

REGISTERED VOTERS

Unaffiliated	52%
Democrat	36%
Republican	11%

POPULATION

2006 population (est.)	1,067,610
2000 population	1,048,319
1990 population	1,003,464
Percent change (1990-2000)	+4.5%
Rank among states (2006)	43
Median age	36.7
Born in state	61.4%
Foreign born	11.4%
Violent crime rate	298/100,000
Poverty level	11.9%
Federal workers	10,207
Military	9,161

ELECTIONS

STATE ELECTION OFFICIAL
(401) 222-2345
DEMOCRATIC PARTY
(401) 721-9900
REPUBLICAN PARTY
(401) 732-8282

MISCELLANEOUS

Web: www.ri.gov
Capital: Providence

U.S. CONGRESS

Senate: 2 Democrats
House: 2 Democrats

2000 Census Statistics by District

DIST.	2004 VOTE FOR PRESIDENT BUSH	KERRY	WHITE	BLACK	ASIAN	HISP	MEDIAN INCOME	WHITE COLLAR	BLUE COLLAR	SERVICE INDUSTRY	OVER 64	UNDER 18	COLLEGE EDUCATION	RURAL	SQ. MILES
1	36%	62%	83%	4%	2%	7%	$40,616	61%	23%	15%	15%	23%	26%	4%	325
2	41	57	81	4	3	10	$44,129	61	23	16	14	25	25	14	720
STATE	39	59	82	4	2	9	$42,090	61	23	16	15	24	26	9	1,045
U.S.	50.7	48.3	69	12	4	13	$41,994	60	25	15	12	26	24	21	3,537,438

Woonsocket
1
Providence
Pawtucket
Providence
Cranston
Bristol
Warwick
Bristol
2
Kent
Newport
Newport
1
Newport
Washington
2

Sen. Jack Reed (D)

CAPITOL OFFICE
224-4642
reed.senate.gov
728 Hart 20510-3903; fax 224-4680

COMMITTEES
Appropriations
(Military Construction-VA - acting chairman)
Armed Services
(Emerging Threats & Capabilities - chairman)
Banking, Housing & Urban Affairs
(Securities, Insurance & Investment - chairman)
Health, Education, Labor & Pensions

RESIDENCE
Cranston

BORN
Nov. 12, 1949, Providence, R.I.

RELIGION
Roman Catholic

FAMILY
Wife, Julia Reed; one child

EDUCATION
U.S. Military Academy, B.S. 1971 (engineering); Harvard U., M.P.P. 1973, J.D. 1982

MILITARY SERVICE
Army, 1971-79; Army Reserve, 1979-91

CAREER
Lawyer

POLITICAL HIGHLIGHTS
R.I. Senate, 1985-91; U.S. House, 1991-97

ELECTION RESULTS

2002 GENERAL		
Jack Reed (D)	253,774	78.4%
Robert G. Tingle (R)	69,808	21.6%
2002 PRIMARY		
Jack Reed (D)		unopposed

PREVIOUS WINNING PERCENTAGES
1996 (63%); 1994 House Election (68%); 1992 House Election (71%); 1990 House Election (59%)

Elected 1996; 2nd term

As a West Point graduate and former Army paratrooper, Reed's credentials make him a leading voice of the opposition to the war in Iraq. Several of the top military commanders in Iraq and Afghanistan were his contemporaries at West Point, and he is particularly well informed about U.S. progress in the war zones.

He was among the first prominent national figures to lose confidence in Defense Secretary Donald H. Rumsfeld, calling for his resignation in late 2004. Reed, known for his careful analysis of issues, had concluded that the administration had significantly underestimated the insurgency in Iraq, inadequately supplied U.S. troops and then ignored pleas for armored vehicles. Rumsfeld was in a state of denial, he said, and the defense secretary's "corrosive" management style had eroded the ability of military leaders to offer informed advice. Rumsfeld was ultimately forced to resign but not until much later, in late 2006.

Reed was one of 21 Democrats to vote against authorizing the war in Iraq in 2002. But once the invasion was under way, Reed supported extra funding for the war and pushed to expand the Army in order to lessen the burden on reservists pressed into repeated tours of duty. The reserves, which by mid-2004 accounted for 40 percent of U.S. forces in Iraq, "are stretched to the limit and beyond," Reed said. "We can't sustain the reserve force if they're being called up every other year." Congress ultimately agreed in 2004 to add 20,000 soldiers and take the Army's active duty roster beyond 500,000.

Early in 2007, when President Bush announced he was sending thousands more troops to Baghdad, Reed's reaction was typically analytical. His bottom line: "Most people I spoke to, particularly military people, doubt seriously that simply adding 20,000 troops to a city with a population, roughly, of 6 million can make a difference."

Reed has visited Iraq nine times. He and Gen. John P. Abizaid, the former commander of the United States Central Command, were in the same parachute brigade in the 82nd Airborne Division. While Reed never served in combat, he says his training and service give him an appreciation for the military's power — and its limits. "It's very impressive when you're lighting up the night sky pretty quickly. But decisive action usually involves political, economic, social and cultural action as well. In many respects, military power buys you time to do everything else right. I don't think in Iraq, and in Afghanistan for that matter, we have used that military power effectively."

The new Democratic Senate majority in the 110th Congress (2007-08) enabled Reed to reclaim the coveted seat on the Appropriations Committee that he held briefly for 18 months in 2001 and 2002. Early in 2007, as South Dakota Democrat Tim Johnson recuperated from a serious brain injury, Reed stood in for him as chairman of the spending panel's Military Construction-VA Subcommittee.

His seat on the Armed Services Committee allows Reed to push for continued support for the Rhode Island-based Naval Undersea Warfare Center and the Naval Education Training Center. He also works to protect federal contracts for the building of attack submarines at the General Dynamics Electric Boat Corp., which employs roughly 10,000 workers in its Rhode Island and nearby Groton, Conn., facilities.

Reed has a reputation for a serious-minded approach described by a Providence Journal columnist as "exhaustive, respectful, heavy on the factual findings, light on the polemics." In the 109th Congress (2005-06),

Reed took on a larger role when Democratic Leader Harry Reid restructured the Democratic Senatorial Campaign Committee by creating regional chairmen; he made Reed responsible for the Northeast.

Reed is a dependable liberal on most social issues. In 2004, he voted to extend the assault weapons ban for another 10 years. In recent years, he voted against banning a procedure its opponents call "partial birth" abortion, and he opposed amending the Constitution to prohibit same-sex marriage.

He took to the Senate floor in 2005 to rail against Bush's plan to create private investment accounts within Social Security. And when the administration and congressional Republicans looked for places to cut in the domestic portion of the budget, Reed used his post as the top-ranking Democrat on the Banking panel's Housing and Transportation Subcommittee to protect vulnerable federal housing programs. He has taken the lead in securing increased funding for the Low-Income Home Energy Assistance Program to help low-income residents pay energy bills.

Reed has helped several thousand Liberian refugees who have settled in Rhode Island stay in the United States to escape a long-running civil war. They do not have permanent residency, and until they do, Reed annually asks the White House to permit them to stay another year.

Reed grew up in a working-class family in Cranston, where his father, Joseph Reed, was a school custodian and his mother, Mary Monahan, a factory worker. The senator remembers his parents as smart and capable, and his father eventually became a custodial supervisor of the city's school system. When he died in 1982, a conference room at the administrative building was named for him; Reed announced his first Senate run in that room.

Reed's mother grew up in a mixed Irish and Portuguese neighborhood and spoke fluent Portuguese. Coming out of high school at a time when financial aid for college did not exist, her disappointment at being unable to continue her education fueled a determination that all three of her children would go to college, and they did.

At age 12, Reed told his parents he wanted to go to a military service academy. He finished second in his class at his Catholic prep school, where he was an overachieving, 124-pound defensive back. His parents had his teeth straightened after learning he needed good teeth to qualify for West Point. Reed was admitted, barely meeting the minimum height requirement. After graduation, the Army put him through a master's program at the John F. Kennedy School of Government at Harvard University. Reed then commanded a company of the Army's 82nd Airborne Division and taught at West Point.

After attaining the rank of captain, he left the Army at age 29 to attend Harvard Law School. He returned home to a job in Rhode Island's biggest corporate law firm. In 1984, he won a seat in the state Senate.

Six years later, Reed took 59 percent of the vote to win the 2nd District House seat, which Republican Rep. Claudine Schneider gave up to run, unsuccessfully, for the Senate.

When Democratic Sen. Claiborne Pell decided to retire in 1996 after 36 years in office, Reed was well prepared to run. He overcame a vigorous negative advertising campaign paid for by the National Republican Senatorial Committee, which portrayed him as a tax-and-spend liberal. He won with 63 percent of the vote against Republican state Treasurer Nancy J. Mayer. In 2002, he won handily with 78 percent.

In 2005, Reed married at age 55. He and Julia Hart, then 39, an employee of the Senate office that arranges international travel for senators, wed in West Point's Catholic chapel, a first marriage for both. The two met during an official trip to Afghanistan in 2002. In January 2007, their daughter was born. "I'm told that's probably a more demanding job than most of the things I have done in my life," Reed said of fatherhood.

KEY VOTES

2006

No Confirm Samuel A. Alito Jr. to the Supreme Court
No Allow consideration of a bill to establish a $140 billion trust fund to compensate victims of asbestos exposure
No Extend tax cuts for two years at a cost of $70 billion over five years
Yes Overhaul immigration policy with border security, enforcement and guest worker program
No Allow consideration of a bill to permanently repeal the estate tax
Yes Urge President Bush to begin troop withdrawals from Iraq in 2006
Yes Lift President Bush's restrictions on stem cell research funding
No Authorize military tribunals for suspected terrorists

2005

Yes Curb class action lawsuits by shifting them from state to federal courts
No Allow confirmation vote on Priscilla R. Owen to the U.S. Court of Appeals for the 5th Circuit
No Oppose mandatory emissions limits and block recognition of global warming as a threat
No Approve free-trade pact with five Central American countries
No Pass energy policy overhaul favored by President Bush emphasizing domestic oil and gas production
No Shield gunmakers from lawsuits when their products are used in crimes
Yes Ban torture of prisoners in U.S. custody
No Renew 16 provisions of the Patriot Act
No Allow final vote on opening the Arctic National Wildlife Refuge to oil and gas exploration

CQ VOTE STUDIES

	PARTY UNITY		PRESIDENTIAL SUPPORT	
	Support	Oppose	Support	Oppose
2006	96%	4%	53%	47%
2005	98%	2%	29%	71%
2004	98%	2%	60%	40%
2003	98%	2%	45%	55%
2002	98%	2%	66%	34%
2001	99%	1%	64%	36%
2000	97%	3%	95%	5%
1999	96%	4%	89%	11%
1998	98%	2%	90%	10%
1997	99%	1%	86%	14%

INTEREST GROUPS

	AFL-CIO	ADA	CCUS	ACU
2006	100%	100%	42%	4%
2005	93%	100%	33%	0%
2004	100%	100%	35%	0%
2003	100%	100%	26%	20%
2002	100%	100%	40%	0%
2001	100%	100%	36%	4%
2000	75%	95%	46%	12%
1999	100%	100%	47%	4%
1998	88%	95%	56%	0%
1997	100%	100%	44%	0%

Sen. Sheldon Whitehouse (D)

CAPITOL OFFICE
224-2921
whitehouse.senate.gov
502 Hart 20510-3904; fax 228-6362

COMMITTEES
Budget
Environment & Public Works
Judiciary
Select Intelligence
Special Aging

RESIDENCE
Providence

BORN
Oct. 20, 1955, Manhattan, N.Y.

RELIGION
Episcopalian

FAMILY
Wife, Sandra Whitehouse; two children

EDUCATION
Yale U., B.A. 1978 (architecture);
U. of Virginia, J.D. 1982

CAREER
Lawyer; gubernatorial aide

POLITICAL HIGHLIGHTS
R.I. Department of Business Regulation director, 1992-94; U.S. attorney, 1994-98; R.I. attorney general, 1999-2003; sought Democratic nomination for governor, 2002

ELECTION RESULTS

2006 GENERAL		
Sheldon Whitehouse (D)	206,043	53.5%
Lincoln Chafee (R)	178,950	46.5%
2006 PRIMARY		
Sheldon Whitehouse (D)	69,290	81.5%
Christopher F. Young (D)	8,939	10.5%
Carl L. Sheeler (D)	6,755	7.9%

Elected 2006; 1st term

Whitehouse once lost a race for the Democratic nomination for Rhode Island governor because his opponent was better organized and better financed. He described the aftermath of that 2002 contest to a local news broadcast: "It combined elements of losing a loved one, getting dumped by your girlfriend, having your house broken into and losing the big game."

That was not going to happen to Whitehouse again. Four years later, he joined the small, esteemed class of Democrats who unseated Republican incumbents in 2006 to put the party just over the top of majority control of the Senate. He was rewarded with choice committee assignments and lots of camera time on front-burner issues ranging from the war in Iraq to global warming to the Bush administration firings of eight U.S. attorneys.

In one of the most closely watched races of the midterm election, White-House, the son of a career diplomat, beat Republican moderate Lincoln Chafee, the son of a senator, who was well-liked in Rhode Island because of his liberal politics but tarred by Whitehouse as beholden to an unpopular president. For Republicans, Whitehouse's victory ended the Chafee family legacy in the Senate; Lincoln and his father, John H. Chafee, had held the seat for a total of 30 years. For Democrats, winning meant control of the Senate by just one seat.

Whitehouse says overhauling the troubled U.S. health care delivery system is the "No. 1 priority" of his first term. He wants to scrap the Medicare prescription drug plan Republicans wrote in 2003, and he favors giving the federal government the power to bargain down prescription drug prices with pharmaceutical companies.

"I want to be a loyal progressive Democrat and there are, I think, battles that need to be fought to restore the balance in this country, the political balance in this country," Whitehouse says.

As a former U.S. attorney and Rhode Island attorney general, Whitehouse was assigned to the Judiciary Committee just as Democrats were beginning an investigation into the possibly politically motivated firings of U.S. attorneys around the country. That gave him a visible role in the grilling of Attorney General Alberto R. Gonzales. He also got on the Environment and Public Works Committee, just as the new majority kicked off work on legislation to curb global warming, sharing the limelight with former Sen. Al Gore, the 2000 Democratic presidential candidate who was lobbying on Capitol Hill for curbs on greenhouse gas emissions.

To round things out, Whitehouse got a seat on the Intelligence Committee, where he can build on an interest in national security issues that grew out of a youth spent largely abroad. It also gives him a voice on the war in Iraq, the single biggest issue of the election in a state where Democrats outnumber Republicans 2-to-1.

When he had been in office for just two months, Whitehouse made a trip to Iraq to talk to U.S. military and diplomatic leaders. He says he was reminded of the lessons from the Vietnam War, a subject he has more than passing familiarity with, having spent part of his boyhood in Southeast Asia when his father was the ambassador to Laos and Thailand.

"Having seen it up close, I think about how difficult it was, and ultimately unsuccessful, to try to impose America's will on a country by military presence, and I can't help but think of the comparisons to Iraq," Whitehouse says. "As doctrinaire as the Vietnamese communists were . . . the degree of the cultural chasm between the Vietnamese communists and America was considerably less than the cultural chasm between the Islamic fundamentalist terrorists and America. They had a very different view of the future, but they were really looking toward a future, whereas my impression is a lot of the terrorists are looking back to a 14th century past, with women as property and infidels driven out and power in the hands of the clerics."

Whitehouse is the son of a wealthy ambassador, Charles S. Whitehouse, who worked first for the Central Intelligence Agency and then for the State Department. Whitehouse's grandfather was also a career diplomat.

He was educated at St. Paul's, a boarding school in New Hampshire, and lived part of the time with his parents in France, South Africa, Cambodia, Laos and Vietnam. As a young man, he taught for a while in Vietnam.

"I taught English at the Vietnamese-English Association; [my father] was the deputy ambassador," Whitehouse recalls. "We'd have breakfast in the morning; he'd get in the big car with the flags and he'd head out of the gates of the house we were in and off to the embassy compound. I'd get on my bicycle and head out the other way, and pedal across town to the little school where I taught."

Whitehouse did his undergraduate work at Yale, where his father had gone and coincidentally roomed with John H. Chafee, Lincoln's father. He earned his law degree from the prestigious University of Virginia. In 1986, he married Sandra Thornton, trained as a marine biologist and the daughter of a First Jersey National Bank vice president.

Fellow Democrats often rib Whitehouse about his blueblood upbringing and his button-down ways. At a roast for Whitehouse in 2002, then Lt. Gov. Charles J. Fogarty offered him a can of "Stiff Begone," as a cure for "the uptight WASP."

After law school, Whitehouse clerked for the Virginia Supreme Court, then worked briefly as a private attorney. "I decided I wanted to be a public service lawyer and that's what I really spent most of my career doing," Whitehouse says. "I came into politics very incrementally."

He was a lawyer for the state attorney general's office for five years in the 1980s; then in 1994, he was appointed by President Bill Clinton as a U.S. attorney. In that role, he secured the largest fine in state history for an oil spill off the coast that wiped out millions of lobsters, fish and birds. He also launched a public corruption investigation of Buddy Cianci, the Providence mayor who wound up going to jail. Whitehouse was elected Rhode Island attorney general in 1998, and in 2002 made his ill-fated bid for governor.

With Republicans vulnerable leading up to the 2006 midterm election, and with the president's popularity sinking to a spectacularly low 22 percent in liberal-leaning Rhode Island, Whitehouse challenged an already weakened Chafee, who had survived a tough primary staged by conservatives unhappy with his moderate voting record. Chafee had been appointed to the seat when his father died in office in 1999, and had been elected to a six-year term. It was his first re-election campaign.

Whitehouse spent a year and half preparing and raising money. His strategy was to attack Republicans at large, and their hold on power in Congress, rather than Chafee's record, which many voters had no problem with. He accused the party of selling out to pharmaceutical companies with their 2003 prescription drug plan and of trying to privatize Social Security, though the latter proposal died in Congress in 2005. His message on Iraq, calling for a pullout of U.S. forces, especially resonated. Chafee didn't help his cause when he said candidly that he sometimes felt obliged to vote with his party.

Whitehouse won with 54 percent of the vote, becoming one of six Democratic challengers to unseat Republican senators in 2006.

Rep. Patrick J. Kennedy (D)

CAPITOL OFFICE
225-4911
www.patrickkennedy.house.gov
407 Cannon 20515-3901; fax 225-3290

COMMITTEES
Appropriations
Natural Resources

RESIDENCE
Portsmouth

BORN
July 14, 1967, Brighton, Mass.

RELIGION
Roman Catholic

FAMILY
Single

EDUCATION
Providence College, B.A. 1991 (social science)

CAREER
Public official

POLITICAL HIGHLIGHTS
R.I. House, 1989-95

ELECTION RESULTS

2006 GENERAL		
Patrick J. Kennedy (D)	124,634	69.2%
Jonathan P. Scott (R)	41,836	23.2%
Kenneth A. Capalbo (I)	13,634	7.6%
2006 PRIMARY		
Patrick J. Kennedy (D)		unopposed
2004 GENERAL		
Patrick J. Kennedy (D)	124,923	64.1%
David W. Rogers (R)	69,819	35.8%

PREVIOUS WINNING PERCENTAGES
2002 (60%); 2000 (67%); 1998 (67%); 1996 (69%); 1994 (54%)

Elected 1994; 7th term

Kennedy is a tireless champion of improved treatment for mental health problems. He has promoted legislation to require health insurers to cover the care of mental illness as fully as they cover other ailments. And he has used his seat on the Appropriations Committee to press for improved screening and treatment of post-traumatic stress syndrome and other mental disorders among soldiers returning from the war in Iraq.

Kennedy is more conservative than his famous father, Sen. Edward M. Kennedy of Massachusetts. In his biggest political split with the liberal senator, the younger Kennedy voted in 2002 to authorize President Bush to wage war in Iraq; he was the only member of the Rhode Island delegation to do so. His father, from the start, was one of the sharpest opponents of the war. By 2007, the congressman also had turned against the conflict, joining other House Democrats in voting to set a deadline for U.S. troop withdrawal.

Both Kennedys have worked to advance so-called mental health parity legislation, often citing the experience of the elder Kennedy's sister, Rosemary, as the inspiration for their interest in the issue. No mental health coverage measure has ever made it all the way through the legislative process, but with Democrats in charge in both chambers, supporters are bullish about the bill's prospects this time around. For his part, Patrick J. Kennedy is doing what he can to advance the legislation. He and a Republican backer of the bill, Jim Ramstad of Minnesota, are touring the country to build popular support. Unlike previous mental health measures, this year's version includes substance abuse as a mental illness covered under the bill.

Kennedy also has sponsored legislation to change the name of the National Institute on Drug Abuse to the National Institute on Diseases of Addiction. The legislation would also change the National Institute on Alcohol Abuse and Alcoholism to the National Institute on Alcohol Disorders and Health. Kennedy says the name changes would reflect the fact that addictions are medical disorders.

Kennedy himself has struggled with drug abuse, depression and bipolar disorder since he was a teenager. A member of one of America's most famous political dynasties, he often has talked of the burdens of the family name and the stresses that come with it.

In 2006, he continued to battle the addiction demons that have haunted him much of his life. Just when it seemed he had surmounted the kind of embarrassing incidents that marked his earlier years in the House, he was back in the headlines after crashing his car into a Capitol security barrier.

The accident was his second within a month. The first, a two-car crash back home, drew less attention; local police said he was at fault, but they found no evidence of intoxication or impairment. The early morning May 4 incident at the Capitol was a different matter. The congressman told Capitol Police he was on his way to a House vote, but the House was not in session. The police report said Kennedy was unsteady on his feet and had slurred speech and red, watery eyes. Kennedy blamed a mix of prescription drugs; he later said he was addicted to the painkiller OxyContin.

He entered a monthlong rehabilitation program at the Mayo Clinic, then pleaded guilty to driving under the influence of prescription drugs and was sentenced to drug treatment, a year's probation and a $350 fine. The day after the accident, The New York Times later reported, Kennedy got a phone call — and a lifeline — from Republican Rep. Ramstad, a recovering alcoholic whom he did not know well. The older man, who had long advocated 12-step recovery programs and treatment for substance abuse, became Kennedy's Alcoholics Anonymous sponsor.

Kennedy started attending daily AA meetings. He still relies heavily on Ramstad, who watches over the younger man carefully, offering advice and support. They talk every day and gather regularly for dinner with other recovering alcoholics and addicts, many of them prominent Washingtonians.

The most memorable moment of Kennedy's legislative career may have been a 1996 floor speech in which he urged Congress to retain a ban on certain semiautomatic assault-style weapons. "Families like mine know all too well what the damage of weapons can do," said a choked-up Kennedy, who lost two famous uncles to assassinations with guns. "You will never know what it's like because you don't have someone in your family killed. It's not the person who's killed; it's the whole family that's affected."

No one else in Congress can boast of such a legendary political lineage, which still counts for something in New England. His late uncles were President John F. Kennedy and Sen. Robert F. Kennedy of New York. A grandfather, Joseph P. Kennedy, was the first Securities and Exchange Commission chairman and ambassador to Great Britain. A great-grandfather, John Francis Fitzgerald, represented Boston in the House at the end of the 19th century. A cousin, Joseph P. Kennedy II, represented Boston in the House a century later, from 1987 to 1999.

Patrick J. Kennedy's political ascent began early, like that of most Kennedys. As a 21-year-old student at Providence College, he won election to the state House in 1988. Six years later, he was sent to Washington, one of just 13 Democrats elected to the House during the 1994 Republican tide that year. Kennedy was the youngest person in the 104th Congress (1995-96).

At the start of his third term, Kennedy was appointed chairman of the Democratic Congressional Campaign Committee, a leadership role that put him in charge of raising money for Democratic House candidates. He pulled in almost $100 million for the 2000 campaigns, a record that was more than double what had been raised by the committee in 1998.

Kennedy was unabashed about the value of the Kennedy name, saying, "When we're going around the country, it helps get your calls returned." He rewarded major donors with visits to the family's fabled compound in Hyannis Port, Mass.

Over the years, Republicans have tried to capitalize on Kennedy's personal troubles, but his re-election bids have never drawn less than 60 percent of the vote.

KEY VOTES

2006

- Yes Stop broadband companies from favoring select Internet traffic
- No Affirm U.S. commitment to war in Iraq and reject setting a withdrawal date for troops
- No Repeal requirement for bilingual ballots at the polls
- No Permit U.S. sale of civilian nuclear technology to India
- No Build a 700-mile fence on the U.S.-Mexico border to curb illegal crossings
- No Permit warrantless wiretaps of suspected terrorists

2005

- No Intervene in the life-support case of Terri Schiavo
- Yes Lift President Bush's restrictions on stem cell research funding
- Yes Prohibit FBI access to library and bookstore records
- No Approve free-trade pact with five Central American countries
- No Pass energy policy overhaul favored by President Bush emphasizing domestic oil and gas production
- No End mandatory preservation of habitat of endangered animal and plant species
- Yes Ban torture of prisoners in U.S. custody

CQ VOTE STUDIES

	PARTY UNITY		PRESIDENTIAL SUPPORT	
	Support	Oppose	Support	Oppose
2006	96%	4%	21%	79%
2005	96%	4%	22%	78%
2004	95%	5%	35%	65%
2003	96%	4%	27%	73%
2002	89%	11%	40%	60%

INTEREST GROUPS

	AFL-CIO	ADA	CCUS	ACU
2006	100%	85%	31%	10%
2005	93%	95%	37%	4%
2004	93%	95%	40%	8%
2003	100%	95%	27%	25%
2002	100%	90%	40%	8%

RHODE ISLAND 1

East – Pawtucket, part of Providence, Newport

The Democratic 1st includes Rhode Island's entire border with Massachusetts, both to the north and east. It takes in northern Providence County, including Woonsocket and the other industrial towns in the Blackstone Valley, before narrowing as it moves south to scoop up Pawtucket and the northeastern part of Providence, the state capital. It then runs south along the east bank of Narragansett Bay to pick up the scenic coastal town of Newport and the southeast island communities.

The nation's first successful textile mill was in Pawtucket, and the 1st is still dominated by its historic manufacturing cities. Over the past two decades, however, employment in the north has transitioned away from manufacturing, with growth in banking, biotechnology and health care. Woonsocket is home to CVS, one of the nation's largest drugstore chains, while toy and game manufacturer Hasbro is based in Pawtucket.

The coastal economy south of Providence relies largely on maritime defense. Companies such as Raytheon, which makes components for Navy submarines in Portsmouth, as well as a large naval base and training center in Newport, fuel the industry. Visitors to Newport, as well as Providence, make tourism an important economic component.

The 1st's share of Providence includes the state Capitol, the affluent and picturesque East Side neighborhood and several colleges, including Brown University and Providence College. Democrats dominate the district, bolstered by students, government workers and minority voters. Some small, wealthy coastal towns support the GOP, but larger towns lean Democratic. In past statewide elections, however, the district has supported some moderate Republicans for governor and U.S. Senate.

MAJOR INDUSTRY

Health care, government, education, tourism, defense, manufacturing

MILITARY BASES

Naval Station Newport, 1,622 military, 3,845 civilian (2007)

CITIES

Pawtucket, 72,958; Providence (pt.), 72,102; East Providence, 48,688; Woonsocket, 43,224; North Providence (unincorporated), 32,411

NOTABLE

Touro Synagogue in Newport, designed by colonial architect Peter Harrison and dedicated in 1762, is the oldest U.S. synagogue; The International Tennis Hall of Fame is in Newport.

Rep. Jim Langevin (D)

CAPITOL OFFICE
225-2735
www.house.gov/langevin
109 Cannon 20515-3902; fax 225-5976

COMMITTEES
Homeland Security
(Emerging Threats - chairman)
Select Intelligence

RESIDENCE
Warwick

BORN
April 22, 1964, Warwick, R.I.

RELIGION
Roman Catholic

FAMILY
Single

EDUCATION
Rhode Island College, B.A. 1990
(political science & public administration);
Harvard U., M.P.A. 1994

CAREER
Public official

POLITICAL HIGHLIGHTS
R.I. House, 1989-95; R.I. secretary of state, 1995-2001

ELECTION RESULTS

2006 GENERAL		
Jim Langevin (D)	140,315	72.7%
Rodney D. Driver (I)	52,729	27.3%
2006 PRIMARY		
Jim Langevin (D)	24,985	61.8%
Jennifer L. Lawless (D)	15,456	38.2%
2004 GENERAL		
Jim Langevin (D)	154,392	74.5%
Arthur "Chuck" Barton III (R)	43,139	20.8%
Edward M. Morabito (I)	6,196	3.0%
Dorman J. Hayes Jr. (I)	3,303	1.6%

PREVIOUS WINNING PERCENTAGES
2002 (76%); 2000 (62%)

Elected 2000; 4th term

When House Democrats mustered their forces in early 2007 for a renewed attempt to expand federal funding for embryonic stem cell research, they enlisted Langevin as their ambassador to anti-abortion members of their freshman class.

Langevin (LAN-juh-vin) told the new lawmakers about his personal struggle with the issue. He opposes abortion except in cases of rape, incest or to save a woman's life. But he supports expanded research on stem cells extracted from surplus embryos at in vitro fertilization clinics that otherwise would be discarded. "Being pro-life isn't just about protecting life in the womb," he told the freshmen. "It has to be about protecting and extending the quality of life for people who are living among us." He didn't need to mention his direct interest in the research: an accidental shooting that left him a quadriplegic as a teenager.

"I recognize that I can be a visible symbol of the promise of stem cell research," Langevin says. "But it goes far beyond Jim Langevin and spinal cord injuries. It's also about the millions of other people whose lives could be extended or improved as a result of stem cell research." The research is thought to hold promise for treatment of a wide range of diseases such as Parkinson's, Alzheimer's and diabetes.

Langevin is the first quadriplegic to serve in the House. At age 16, he was accidentally shot while working with the Warwick, R.I., police as part of a Boy Scout Explorer program. He says he is convinced he will walk again one day, but meanwhile he will continue to promote legislation to help the disabled through research and improved treatment and services.

In the 109th Congress (2005-06), he helped win enactment of a bill authorizing federal grants to agencies that recruit and train people to provide a respite to families caring for disabled patients at home. Langevin had pushed the legislation since 2002; it finally passed after he deferred to a Republican to serve as chief sponsor in the GOP-controlled House. He also has pressed for legislation to enhance research on paralysis. The measure — named for the late actor Christopher Reeve, who was paralyzed in an equestrian accident — was first introduced in 2003, and Langevin again is a cosponsor in 2007.

There is another issue Langevin also continues to champion: fire safety. In 2007, he reintroduced a bill he has sought ever since a deadly fire at a West Warwick, R.I., nightclub killed 100 people in 2003. The measure would let businesses take accelerated depreciation on their tax returns for the costs of retrofitting their property with automatic sprinkler systems.

He also has introduced several bills on gun safety, including requirements for trigger locks. Although his Roman Catholic faith informs his stance against abortion, he takes a liberal view on most other social issues. He voted in 2004 and 2006 against amending the Constitution to prohibit same-sex marriage, and he opposed an effort in 2003 to create a private school voucher program in Washington, D.C.

Langevin serves on the Homeland Security Committee, where in the 110th Congress (2007-08) he is chairman of the Emerging Threats Subcommittee. Early in 2007, he advanced legislation to impose new restrictions on sales of ammonium nitrate, a chemical compound that has been used by terrorists to make bombs. He also introduced a bill to create a center within the Department of Homeland Security to consolidate and monitor data from biological surveillance systems to help detect and respond quickly to a biological attack or an outbreak of disease.

In 2007, he joined the Select Intelligence Committee at the behest of Speaker Nancy Pelosi. To do so, he took a leave of absence from the Armed Services Committee, where he had served from 2001 through 2006.

Langevin originally hoped to enforce laws, not write them. As a boy, he dreamed of being a police officer or an FBI agent. He enrolled in a police department cadet program in his hometown of Warwick, riding along with police officers and getting to know the daily police routine. On Aug. 22, 1980, his life and ambitions changed forever.

He was in the police locker room with two members of the SWAT team when one of them inadvertently pulled the trigger of a loaded gun. The bullet ricocheted off a locker and hit Langevin in the neck, severing his spinal cord and leaving him paralyzed. He has no use of his legs and only minimal use of his hands and arms. An aide helps him with domestic chores, and he uses a motorized wheelchair. Congressional leaders gave him a ground-floor office and renovated access to the House chamber to ensure that he could move around there readily.

After Langevin's injury, he and his family were amazed at the hundreds of strangers who pitched in to help. He resolved to somehow repay them and soon decided that public service and politics was the way he could do that. He volunteered in Frank Flaherty's 1984 campaign for mayor of Warwick, and Flaherty recalls being amazed at Langevin's tenacity, making phone calls and stuffing envelopes even with limited use of his hands. Later, when Flaherty was still mayor and Langevin was in the legislature, "he'd come in looking for something for his area of the city, and he'd drive me crazy, chase me around. I used to threaten to unplug the battery on his wheelchair so I wouldn't have to listen," Flaherty told The Providence Journal.

At age 21, while still a college student, Langevin was elected as a delegate to the Rhode Island Constitutional Convention. In 1988, he won the first of three terms in the Rhode Island House, where he played a key role in drafting a ballot issue that resulted in a reduction in the size of the state legislature. In 1994, he was elected secretary of state, a position in which he built a reputation as an advocate of greater access to government. He also was a force behind the state's upgrading of its voting machines.

In 2000, when 2nd District Democratic Rep. Bob Weygand decided to run for the Senate, Langevin was ready to make a bid for the U.S. House. In the solidly Democratic district, Langevin's 62 percent of the vote greatly outpaced the Republican and a third-party candidate, who actually came in second. He has won re-election easily since then.

KEY VOTES

2006

- Yes Stop broadband companies from favoring select Internet traffic
- No Affirm U.S. commitment to war in Iraq and reject setting a withdrawal date for troops
- No Repeal requirement for bilingual ballots at the polls
- No Permit U.S. sale of civilian nuclear technology to India
- No Build a 700-mile fence on the U.S.-Mexico border to curb illegal crossings
- No Permit warrantless wiretaps of suspected terrorists

2005

- Yes Intervene in the life-support case of Terri Schiavo
- Yes Lift President Bush's restrictions on stem cell research funding
- Yes Prohibit FBI access to library and bookstore records
- No Approve free-trade pact with five Central American countries
- No Pass energy policy overhaul favored by President Bush emphasizing domestic oil and gas production
- No End mandatory preservation of habitat of endangered animal and plant species
- Yes Ban torture of prisoners in U.S. custody

CQ VOTE STUDIES

	PARTY UNITY		PRESIDENTIAL SUPPORT	
	Support	Oppose	Support	Oppose
2006	94%	6%	30%	70%
2005	92%	8%	20%	80%
2004	91%	9%	42%	58%
2003	95%	5%	28%	72%
2002	91%	9%	35%	65%

INTEREST GROUPS

	AFL-CIO	ADA	CCUS	ACU
2006	93%	75%	33%	16%
2005	93%	85%	44%	8%
2004	93%	85%	45%	25%
2003	100%	85%	27%	24%
2002	100%	85%	45%	8%

RHODE ISLAND 2

West — part of Providence, Warwick, Cranston

Bordering Connecticut on one side and the Narragansett Bay on the other, the 2nd occupies the western two-thirds of Rhode Island. It covers rolling hills in the north, as well as most of the metropolitan area around Providence (shared with the 1st). In the south, Washington County's beaches and lakes attract tourists and residents alike.

The 2nd is experiencing a lengthy transition from a blue-collar to a white-collar economy, as manufacturing continues a decline that began more than a decade ago. Maritime defense contractors here, including General Dynamics' Electric Boat submarine facility at Quonset Point, are feeling the pinch of declining demand and have cut thousands of jobs. Former textile mills in Providence remain abandoned or are being converted into condos or offices, and Aviation company Textron is based in the 2nd's part of the city.

The heavy statewide investment in developing the area's service sector appears to be paying off. The 2nd has enjoyed significant growth in the technology, health care and financial services industries. The changes are causing population shifts, with residents leaving Providence for Washington County, attracted by the growing number of businesses centered in the county's idyllic landscape. As white residents have departed the Providence area, more blacks and Hispanics have moved in, increasing the city's already Democratic tendency. The 2nd is home to several major colleges, including Johnson & Wales University, Rhode Island College and the University of Rhode Island.

The 2nd is home to many working- and middle-class towns, such as Warwick, that have a substantial union presence that votes Democratic. No Republican presidential candidate has carried the district since Ronald Reagan in 1984. Despite the Democratic dominance, the district's large Catholic population makes abortion a key issue that can impact electoral outcomes here.

MAJOR INDUSTRY

Service, defense, banking, higher education, tourism

CITIES

Providence (pt.), 101,516; Warwick, 85,808; Cranston, 79,269

NOTABLE

Block Island, 12 miles off the southern coast, is a scenic vacation spot that has 17 miles of beaches and 365 fresh water ponds.

SOUTH CAROLINA

Gov. Mark Sanford (R)

First elected: 2002
Length of term: 4 years
Term expires: 1/11
Salary: $106,078
Phone: (803) 734-2100

Residence: Sullivan's Island
Born: May 28, 1960; Fort Lauderdale, Fla.
Religion: Episcopalian
Family: Wife, Jenny Sanford; four children
Education: Furman U., B.A. 1983 (business administration); U. of Virginia, M.B.A. 1988
Military service: Air Force Reserve, 2002-present
Career: Real estate investor; investment banker
Political highlights: U.S. House, 1995-2001

Election results:

2006 GENERAL		
Mark Sanford (R)	601,868	55.1%
Tommy Moore (D)	489,076	44.8%

Lt. Gov. André Bauer (R)

First elected: 2002
Length of term: 4 years
Term expires: 1/11
Salary: $46,545
Phone: (803) 734-2080

LEGISLATURE

General Assembly: January-June

Senate: 46 members, 4-year terms
2007 ratios: 26 R, 20 D; 45 men, 1 woman
Salary: $10,400
Phone: (803) 212-6200

House: 124 members, 2-year terms
2007 ratios: 73 R, 51 D; 111 men, 13 women
Salary: $10,400
Phone: (803) 734-2010

TERM LIMITS

Governor: 2 consecutive terms
Senate: No
House: No

URBAN STATISTICS

CITY	POPULATION
Columbia	116,278
Charleston	96,650
North Charleston	79,641
Greenville	56,002
Rock Hill	49,765

REGISTERED VOTERS

Voters do not register by party.

POPULATION

2006 population (est.)	4,321,249
2000 population	4,012,012
1990 population	3,486,703
Percent change (1990-2000)	+15.1%
Rank among states (2006)	25
Median age	35.4
Born in state	64%
Foreign born	2.9%
Violent crime rate	805/100,000
Poverty level	14.1%
Federal workers	27,923
Military	57,585

ELECTIONS

STATE ELECTION OFFICIAL
(803) 734-9060
DEMOCRATIC PARTY
(803) 799-7798
REPUBLICAN PARTY
(803) 988-8440

MISCELLANEOUS

Web: www.mysc.gov
Capital: Columbia

U.S. CONGRESS

Senate: 2 Republicans
House: 4 Republicans, 2 Democrats

2000 Census Statistics by District

DIST.	2004 VOTE FOR PRESIDENT BUSH	KERRY	WHITE	BLACK	ASIAN	HISP	MEDIAN INCOME	WHITE COLLAR	BLUE COLLAR	SERVICE INDUSTRY	OVER 64	UNDER 18	COLLEGE EDUCATION	RURAL	SQ. MILES
1	61%	38%	74%	21%	1%	3%	$40,713	60%	23%	17%	12%	24%	25%	22%	2,645
2	60	40	68	26	1	3	$42,915	63	23	14	11	25	29	34	4,767
3	65	34	76	21	1	2	$36,092	49	37	14	13	24	17	50	5,392
4	65	34	75	20	1	3	$39,417	56	31	13	12	25	22	26	2,151
5	57	42	64	32	1	2	$35,416	48	38	13	12	26	15	53	7,035
6	39	61	40	57	1	1	$28,967	48	34	18	12	26	14	52	8,120
STATE	58	41	66	29	1	2	$37,082	54	31	15	12	25	20	40	30,109
U.S.	50.7	48.3	69	12	4	13	$41,994	60	25	15	12	26	24	21	3,537,438

Greenville
Pickens
Oconee
Spartanburg
Greenville
Spartanburg
Anderson
Anderson
Cherokee
York
Rock Hill
Union
Chester
Lancaster
Chesterfield
Marlboro
Dillon
Laurens
Newberry
Fairfield
Abbeville
Greenwood
McCormick
Saluda
Edgefield
Columbia
Richland
Lexington
Aiken
Kershaw
Lee
Darlington
Florence
Marion
Florence
Horry
Sumter
Sumter
Clarendon
Williamsburg
Calhoun
Orangeburg
Georgetown
Barnwell
Bamberg
Dorchester
Berkeley
Allendale
Hampton
Colleton
Charleston
Charleston
Jasper
Beaufort
1
2
3
4
5
6
1

Sen. Lindsey Graham (R)

CAPITOL OFFICE
224-5972
lgraham.senate.gov
290 Russell 20510-4001; fax 224-3808

COMMITTEES
Agriculture, Nutrition & Forestry
Armed Services
Budget
Judiciary
Veterans' Affairs

RESIDENCE
Seneca

BORN
July 9, 1955, Seneca, S.C.

RELIGION
Southern Baptist

FAMILY
Single

EDUCATION
U. of South Carolina, B.A. 1977 (psychology), attended 1977-78 (public administration), J.D. 1981

MILITARY SERVICE
Air Force, 1982-88; S.C. Air National Guard, 1989-94; Air Force, 1990; Air Force Reserve, 1995-present

CAREER
Lawyer; military prosecutor

POLITICAL HIGHLIGHTS
S.C. House, 1993-95; U.S. House, 1995-2003

ELECTION RESULTS

2002 GENERAL		
Lindsey Graham (R)	595,218	54.4%
Alex Sanders (D)	484,422	44.2%
2002 PRIMARY		
Lindsey Graham (R)		unopposed

PREVIOUS WINNING PERCENTAGES
2000 House Election (68%); 1998 House Election (100%); 1996 House Election (60%); 1994 House Election (60%)

Elected 2002; 1st term

Graham is a senator to watch, no matter which party controls the White House or Congress. By dint of his intellectual gifts and sharp political instinct, the South Carolina lawyer with the folksy demeanor usually has a significant impact on the major battles in Congress. At the White House, his name comes up in discussions of future Supreme Court justices.

Graham is a more genteel version of his role model, the more prominent and earthier Sen. John McCain of Arizona. Like McCain, he has a knack for bucking his party leaders and going his own way, often ultimately staking out positions with widespread popular appeal. With the words "long story short," he launches into a lawyerly summary of the state of play on a piece of legislation or a constitutional conundrum before cutting to the heart of politically sensitive issues. "Some big problems, whether it be the war on terror or Social Security, are going to require bipartisanship," Graham says. "And I know the only way we're going to get that bipartisanship is for somebody to break away from the pack. And I don't mind doing that."

In the 109th Congress (2005-06), Graham was a dealmaker on several major issues, including the battle over judicial nominations and the debate over the government's treatment of terrorism suspects.

He was part of a GOP troika, with McCain and Sen. John W. Warner of Virginia, that forced President Bush to back down on tough measures for the treatment of suspected terrorists. A former military prosecutor, Graham had credibility on the issue, as did McCain, a former prisoner of war. The White House thought it best to engage the three in private talks, and eventually it had to give up on redefining U.S. obligations under the Geneva Conventions, which might have allowed investigators more leeway to use harsh coercion tactics with suspects. Graham made the case that backing away from the international treaty would give other countries an excuse to mistreat U.S. troops in future wars. "When I tell my constituents that what we do today may come back to haunt us tomorrow, people listen," he said.

From his seat on the Judiciary Committee, Graham was at the center of a partisan war in 2005 over several of Bush's appellate court nominations, which were targeted for filibuster, a common Senate delaying tactic. As the Senate neared a climactic showdown over blocking the use of the filibuster, Graham joined six other Republicans and seven Democrats in a renegade Gang of 14 that brokered an eleventh-hour compromise: Democrats agreed to allow up-or-down votes on conservative nominees while still reserving the filibuster option for extreme cases.

Conservative activists in South Carolina and prominent evangelical Christians took Graham to the woodshed for his willingness to compromise. "We were about to walk off the edge of a cliff as a body, the Senate," Graham said in an interview months later. "Over time, people have understood it was a very smart thing to do."

In 2007, as the Judiciary Committee investigated whether the White House and Attorney General Alberto R. Gonzales had fired eight federal prosecutors for political reasons, Graham gave voice to growing GOP skepticism about the various explanations Gonzales gave for the firings. "Mr. Attorney General, most of this is a stretch," Graham told Gonzales pointedly at one public hearing. He stopped short of urging the attorney general to resign, but said he had "a lot of damage to repair."

Graham's search for the productive middle in politics marks an evolution from his early days on Capitol Hill. He arrived with the rambunctious

House GOP Class of 1994, a large bloc of conservatives who vowed to transform the federal government. He was one of the leaders of a 1997 effort by conservatives to oust GOP Speaker Newt Gingrich of Georgia because they felt he was increasingly ineffective and too willing to compromise with President Bill Clinton. Gingrich put down the insurrection and the plotters wound up looking like ambitious bunglers.

Later in 1998, Graham redeemed himself as one of the 13 House managers in the impeachment case against Clinton. He was more restrained stylistically than other conservatives condemning the president for a sexual affair with a White House intern. "Is this Watergate or Peyton Place?" he said.

In the 2000 GOP presidential primary, Graham made waves by backing McCain over then Texas Gov. George W. Bush, becoming an ardent, articulate and often quoted McCain advocate, even though Bush had the support of South Carolina's party establishment. Bush won the state's primary, effectively ending McCain's campaign. Two years later, Graham was among only 41 House Republicans who voted for the campaign finance overhaul that was at the core of McCain's candidacy.

Once elected to the Senate in 2002, Graham continued his contrarian ways, breaking with most Republicans to oppose the president's Medicare overhaul creating a prescription drug benefit, which he called costly and ineffective.

But for all his headline-grabbing defections from the fold, Graham is a conservative at heart. He has been an unwavering backer of the Iraq War, insisting in March 2007 that "I'm willing to lose my job over this."

He once joined an effort to shut down the National Endowment for the Arts and typically favors limiting the scope of the federal government. He is an opponent of gun control, and he has voted to amend the Constitution to outlaw flag desecration and ban same-sex marriage. Graham has backed legislation making it a federal crime to harm a fetus in the course of committing any one of 68 federal offenses.

Born in July 1955, six months after his predecessor, Sen. Strom Thurmond, was first sworn in to the Senate, Graham is the son of a tavern owner and grew up racking billiards in his parents' bar in the textile town of Central, S.C. The premature death of both parents when he was not yet out of college left him to care for his 13-year-old sister, Darlene, whom he legally adopted. "It changes your world and you have to grow up a lot quicker," Graham said. There wasn't sufficient health insurance to cover his mother's care for cancer, he recalls, and the bills piled up.

After law school, he joined the Air Force and later transferred to Germany as a prosecutor. His most celebrated case was defending a demoted Air Force pilot on a drug charge, which exposed flaws in the service's drug-testing system and led to an overhaul of the program. The case landed young Graham an appearance on the television news show "60 Minutes."

In 1992, Graham won a state House seat, but his stay was brief. He saw an opportunity for advancement early in 1994, when 10-term Democratic Rep. Butler Derrick decided to retire. With the 3rd District, like South Carolina as a whole, trending Republican, Graham won easily that fall, beating Democratic state Sen. James Bryan with 60 percent of the vote.

He won three more terms with relative ease and began planning for a Senate run after Thurmond made it clear his seventh full term would be his last. By 2002, Graham had become the senior Republican in the state's congressional delegation, and he was unopposed for his party's nomination. Democrats put up Alex Sanders, a quick-witted former president of the College of Charleston who stressed his conservative credentials. But Graham repeatedly portrayed him as a party loyalist who would vote with "Washington liberals." Graham won by 10 percentage points.

KEY VOTES

2006

- Yes Confirm Samuel A. Alito Jr. to the Supreme Court
- No Allow consideration of a bill to establish a $140 billion trust fund to compensate victims of asbestos exposure
- Yes Extend tax cuts for two years at a cost of $70 billion over five years
- Yes Overhaul immigration policy with border security, enforcement and guest worker program
- Yes Allow consideration of a bill to permanently repeal the estate tax
- No Urge President Bush to begin troop withdrawals from Iraq in 2006
- No Lift President Bush's restrictions on stem cell research funding
- Yes Authorize military tribunals for suspected terrorists

2005

- Yes Curb class action lawsuits by shifting them from state to federal courts
- Yes Allow confirmation vote on Priscilla R. Owen to the U.S. Court of Appeals for the 5th Circuit
- No Oppose mandatory emissions limits and block recognition of global warming as a threat
- No Approve free-trade pact with five Central American countries
- Yes Pass energy policy overhaul favored by President Bush emphasizing domestic oil and gas production
- Yes Shield gunmakers from lawsuits when their products are used in crimes
- Yes Ban torture of prisoners in U.S. custody
- Yes Renew 16 provisions of the Patriot Act
- Yes Allow final vote on opening the Arctic National Wildlife Refuge to oil and gas exploration

CQ VOTE STUDIES

	PARTY UNITY		PRESIDENTIAL SUPPORT	
	Support	Oppose	Support	Oppose
2006	82%	18%	91%	9%
2005	92%	8%	89%	11%
2004	92%	8%	92%	8%
2003	96%	4%	95%	5%
House Service:				
2002	89%	11%	82%	18%
2001	93%	7%	84%	16%
2000	98%	2%	17%	83%
1999	89%	11%	18%	82%
1998	92%	8%	22%	78%
1997	95%	5%	25%	75%

INTEREST GROUPS

	AFL-CIO	ADA	CCUS	ACU
2006	7%	0%	92%	83%
2005	29%	20%	83%	96%
2004	8%	25%	88%	92%
2003	17%	15%	83%	90%
House Service:				
2002	22%	15%	70%	83%
2001	17%	15%	78%	88%
2000	10%	5%	70%	100%
1999	56%	20%	50%	88%
1998	10%	15%	76%	88%
1997	0%	5%	90%	92%

Sen. Jim DeMint (R)

CAPITOL OFFICE
224-6121
demint.senate.gov
340 Russell 20510-4002; fax 228-5143

COMMITTEES
Commerce, Science & Transportation
Energy & Natural Resources
Foreign Relations
Joint Economic

RESIDENCE
Greenville

BORN
Sept. 2, 1951, Greenville, S.C.

RELIGION
Presbyterian

FAMILY
Wife, Debbie DeMint; four children

EDUCATION
U. of Tennessee, B.S. 1973 (communications); Clemson U., M.B.A. 1981

CAREER
Market research company owner; advertising and sales representative

POLITICAL HIGHLIGHTS
U.S. House, 1999-2005

ELECTION RESULTS

2004 GENERAL		
Jim DeMint (R)	857,167	53.7%
Inez Tenenbaum (D)	704,384	44.1%
2004 PRIMARY RUNOFF		
Jim DeMint (R)	154,644	59.2%
David Beasley (R)	106,480	40.8%
2004 PRIMARY		
David Beasley (R)	107,847	36.6%
Jim DeMint (R)	77,567	26.3%
Thomas Ravenel (R)	73,167	24.8%
Charlie Condon (R)	27,694	9.4%
Mark McBride (R)	6,479	2.2%

PREVIOUS WINNING PERCENTAGES
2002 House Election (69%); 2000 House Election (80%); 1998 House Election (58%)

Elected 2004; 1st term

When Senate leaders unveiled new disclosure rules in the name of paring pork in 2007, DeMint saw the same old pig meandering around the Capitol with a new shade of lipstick and a designer veil. Its "reform" label, he feared, would allow the Senate's old guard to keep the existing system largely intact while claiming to have cleaned it up — a death sentence for the stringent rules DeMint sought.

DeMint's genial but determined commitment to social and fiscal conservatism landed him the chairmanship of the Republican Steering Committee, the Senate's caucus of conservative lawmakers. As the newly installed chairman he forced a floor showdown. Majority Whip Richard J. Durbin of Illinois moved to table DeMint's amendment — requiring the identification of the sponsor and recipient for any earmark — and avert a vote on the substance. But some first-term Democrats, fresh off the campaign trail, opted for the stronger assault on an earmarking culture that some blame for profligate spending and congressional scandals. They were joined by a handful of more senior Democrats.

By the time the dust had settled, the ethics and lobbying overhaul bill — with DeMint's amendment — was passed by the Senate. DeMint had not only beaten Democratic leaders on the policy but also had forced them into an embarrassing tactical pirouette. The secret to his success: He borrowed his earmark disclosure language from House Speaker Nancy Pelosi. "We've got to be kind of scrappy," says DeMint.

With a broad ethics overhaul bill stalled in 2007, DeMint continued his assault on earmarks by offering amendments to strip specific earmarks from a number of bills. In the first four months of 2007, DeMint had offered 54 floor amendments, the most of any senator. He lost almost every time, sometimes accomplishing little except annoying his colleagues.

DeMint's attack on earmarks could have caused headaches for senior members of his own party had Republicans been in the majority. "In the majority, you don't want to hurt your own guys," he concedes. But it's easier now to rally the troops against Democratic bills and motions.

With a background in advertising and market research, DeMint likes making bold proposals that spark debate, such as his call to scrap the tax code, which he illustrated in 2000 by scattering all 17,000 pages of the Internal Revenue Code from a hot air balloon over his hometown of Greenville.

DeMint has been a loyal ally to President Bush on many issues, but he sometimes finds himself standing a bit to the president's right, as the last conservative line of defense. That distinguishes him from the state's senior senator and DeMint's occasional tennis partner, Lindsey Graham, whose independent streak runs in the other direction. DeMint was far more likely than Graham to stay in line with his fellow Republicans on votes pitting the two parties against each other. His 97 percent party unity score tied for third among Senate Republicans in the 109th Congress (2005-06), while Graham's 88 percent score was less than that of all but a dozen of his colleagues.

A political neophyte when he was first elected to the House in 1998, DeMint was elected freshman class president and quickly distinguished himself as a leader among the ultra-conservative lawmakers. DeMint fiercely opposed the Medicare drug law in 2003 because of its hefty price tag.

In the Senate, he broke with Bush on an immigration overhaul in the 109th Congress, banding together with House and Senate conservatives to ensure that legislation creating a guest worker program and a "path to citizenship" for illegal immigrants did not reach Bush's desk. In 2007, he seized on bipartisan opposition to Bush's proposal to provide a standard tax deduction for family health care by offering his own vision for extending private insurance to the uninsured: $4,000 tax credits to encourage families to buy high-deductible health plans and put money in health savings accounts.

"That's my No. 1 mission: to save the country from socialized health care," he told the Greenville News.

As a market researcher, DeMint became an expert at positioning a product in a crowded marketplace, be it Homelite chainsaws or St. Pauli Girl beer. He uses that background in Washington to tout his ideas. He likes to emphasize his work on bipartisan legislation, not just conservative initiatives. His press releases often trumpet his work with Democrats such as Sen. Barack Obama of Illinois and Rep. Louise M. Slaughter of New York.

DeMint gathered more than 280 cosponsorships in 2001 on legislation to double the adoption tax credit to $10,000. "When I present something to the chairman of Ways and Means, I need to show there is overwhelming support, because I am not a member of the committee," DeMint said. His work led to the credit being included in the $1.35 trillion, 10-year tax cut enacted that year. Like other conservatives, DeMint is no fan of the federal income tax system and would like to see it replaced by a tax on the consumption of goods and services.

He knows some of his positions make him a punching bag for the opposition. "That's the painful part. You make yourself very vulnerable in a campaign," he says. "But the only way to get something done is to stake out an idea and stand outside the box. To come up with a better solution, you have to understand what your choices are and get a debate going."

His loyalty to a pro-business agenda has gotten DeMint into trouble at home on occasion, especially for his pro-trade stances. In the House, he was derided in 2002 for joining the razor-thin majority that helped enact the law reviving fast-track trade authority, which allows the president to negotiate treaties that Congress must approve or reject without amendment.

His vote infuriated the state's powerful textile interests, which see themselves as losers when trade is liberalized, and it became the key issue when DeMint sought re-election to the House in 2002. But he won with 62 percent of the vote in the primary and 69 percent in the general election.

Raised by a single mother who operated a dance school out of the home, DeMint and his three siblings grew up quickly, vacuuming the house and handling adult household chores at a young age. Yet DeMint sparked controversy during his Senate campaign when he asserted during a debate that unwed mothers with live-in boyfriends should not teach in public schools. He also said a "practicing homosexual" should be similarly barred. He later apologized, saying it was up to states to decide who is fit to teach.

DeMint entered politics in 1992 as an unpaid adviser to his predecessor in the House, Republican Bob Inglis. Six years later, when Inglis gave up the seat for an unsuccessful Senate bid, DeMint won the GOP nomination against state Sen. Mike Fair, who had the backing of the Christian Coalition. DeMint went on to win the general election by 18 percentage points.

Facing a self-imposed six-year term limit in the House in 2004, DeMint ran for the Senate. Veteran Sen. Ernest F. Hollings announced his retirement that year, and DeMint easily defeated former Gov. David Beasley in a GOP primary runoff before beating Inez Tenenbaum, the state education superintendent, in the general election. His victory gave South Carolina two Republican senators for the first time since Reconstruction. And Inglis won back his old House seat in the same election.

KEY VOTES

2006

Yes Confirm Samuel A. Alito Jr. to the Supreme Court
No Allow consideration of a bill to establish a $140 billion trust fund to compensate victims of asbestos exposure
Yes Extend tax cuts for two years at a cost of $70 billion over five years
No Overhaul immigration policy with border security, enforcement and guest worker program
Yes Allow consideration of a bill to permanently repeal the estate tax
No Urge President Bush to begin troop withdrawals from Iraq in 2006
No Lift President Bush's restrictions on stem cell research funding
Yes Authorize military tribunals for suspected terrorists

2005

Yes Curb class action lawsuits by shifting them from state to federal courts
Yes Allow confirmation vote on Priscilla R. Owen to the U.S. Court of Appeals for the 5th Circuit
Yes Oppose mandatory emissions limits and block recognition of global warming as a threat
Yes Approve free-trade pact with five Central American countries
Yes Pass energy policy overhaul favored by President Bush emphasizing domestic oil and gas production
Yes Shield gunmakers from lawsuits when their products are used in crimes
Yes Ban torture of prisoners in U.S. custody
Yes Renew 16 provisions of the Patriot Act
Yes Allow final vote on opening the Arctic National Wildlife Refuge to oil and gas exploration

CQ VOTE STUDIES

	PARTY UNITY		PRESIDENTIAL SUPPORT	
	Support	Oppose	Support	Oppose
2006	97%	3%	90%	10%
2005	96%	4%	91%	9%
House Service:				
2004	98%	2%	92%	8%
2003	98%	2%	89%	11%
2002	97%	3%	85%	15%
2001	98%	2%	95%	5%
2000	98%	2%	22%	78%
1999	97%	3%	11%	89%

INTEREST GROUPS

	AFL-CIO	ADA	CCUS	ACU
2006	13%	0%	92%	100%
2005	21%	5%	89%	96%
House Service:				
2004	0%	0%	92%	100%
2003	7%	20%	93%	96%
2002	11%	0%	90%	100%
2001	0%	0%	96%	100%
2000	0%	0%	90%	100%
1999	11%	0%	92%	91%

Rep. Henry E. Brown Jr. (R)

CAPITOL OFFICE
225-3176
brown.house.gov
1124 Longworth 20515-4001; fax 225-3407

COMMITTEES
Natural Resources
Transportation & Infrastructure
Veterans' Affairs

RESIDENCE
Hanahan

BORN
Dec. 20, 1935, Bishopville, S.C.

RELIGION
Baptist

FAMILY
Wife, Billye Brown; three children (one deceased)

EDUCATION
Berkeley H.S., graduated 1953

MILITARY SERVICE
S.C. National Guard, 1953-62

CAREER
Grocery chain executive; grocery store data processor; shipyard worker

POLITICAL HIGHLIGHTS
Hanahan City Council, 1981-85;
S.C. House, 1985-2000

ELECTION RESULTS

2006 GENERAL		
Henry E. Brown Jr. (R)	115,766	59.7%
Randy Maatta (D, WFM)	73,218	37.7%
James E. Dunn (GREEN)	4,875	2.5%
2006 PRIMARY		
Henry E. Brown Jr. (R)		unopposed
2004 GENERAL		
Henry E. Brown Jr. (R)	186,448	87.8%
James E. Dunn (GREEN)	25,674	12.1%

PREVIOUS WINNING PERCENTAGES
2002 (89%); 2000 (60%)

Elected 2000; 4th term

Brown is a fiscal conservative — except when it comes to sending federal tax dollars to his district. Along with his efforts to fund home-state projects, he also works to boost benefits for veterans.

A top priority for Brown is finding federal money to finish an extension of Interstate 73 leading to Myrtle Beach, the vacation hotspot in the 1st District. "Here is a community with more than 14 million visitors coming in a year," he says. The interstate "is a big issue because it is going to take a lot of money."

He has pressed for federal funds to deepen Charleston Harbor, replace an aging bridge across the Cooper River, and pump sand onto South Carolina's eroded beaches. He also advocates funding for Charleston-area military bases and contractors.

From his seat on the Veterans' Affairs Committee, Brown has sought to expand veterans' benefits. He has pushed for legislation to allow retired members of the military who have service-connected disabilities to receive both their military retirement pay and disability compensation. He also has worked to increase the funding that veterans can receive for on-the-job training and to permit spouses of deceased veterans to remarry without losing benefits.

Brown has backed efforts to require military hospitals and VA facilities that are near each other to share equipment and operating rooms, staff and patients. In the 109th Congress (2005-06), he lobbied for a $70 million VA hospital to be built next to a Medical University of South Carolina building, but the proposal was slowed by leaders of the Senate Veterans' Affairs Committee, who thought it would set a bad precedent of using VA construction money for projects not directly serving veterans. Eventually, Brown got $37 million for the Charleston facility.

The congressman has backed President Bush's tax cuts and is conservative on social issues as well, opposing abortion and same-sex marriage. He cites the Bible to explain his views on the Iraq War, which he supports. "The hostility has been documented in the Bible," he says of Iraq — a nation he prefers to call by the name of its Biblical ancestor, Babylon. "I tell you, if we weren't over there, we would be having car bombs here."

Brown's faith-based conservatism was evident from his first term, when he introduced a resolution backing the right of public schools to display the words "God Bless America." He was angry that the American Civil Liberties Union objected to a "God Bless America" display mounted at a California public school in response to the Sept. 11 terrorist attacks. The resolution passed the House unanimously.

Brown's district, which includes nearly three-quarters of the South Carolina coast, has become increasingly attractive to northern snowbirds, including some from Canada. That led Brown to help start the Congressional Friends of Canada Caucus in the 109th Congress; David Wilkins, the U.S. ambassador to Canada, has been a close Brown ally since their days together in the South Carolina legislature. A priority for the caucus is adjusting new security rules that will make it more difficult for Canadians to cross into the United States.

Brown gained some national notoriety in March 2004, when he lost control of a fire he set on his property, burning 20 acres of the Francis Marion National Forest. The matter became controversial after a pair of Forest Service whistleblowers claimed the agency delayed ticketing Brown because he threatened a congressional review of its work. The agency issued Brown a $250 ticket in September of that year, but officials did not bill the congressman the additional $4,000 or more for the cost of fighting the fire, saying their policy of charging those responsible for accidental fires was under review at the time. Brown, who denied any wrongdoing, paid the $250 fine reluctantly and contended the spread of the fire had not been his fault.

In 2005, Brown joined the Natural Resources Committee, giving him a role in oversight of the Forest Service, as well as South Carolina's coastal resources. He supports drilling for oil and gas off all of the nation's coasts, including South Carolina. "If it's okay for Alabama, Louisiana and Texas, it should be okay for other states," he told the Ft. Lauderdale Sun-Sentinel.

Brown grew up on a farm about 25 miles north of Charleston. After high school, he entered the National Guard and got a job in North Charleston with the local electric company, where he was among the early workers in the emerging information technology field. Later, he went to work at the Charleston Naval Shipyard, where his father had worked. He then began a long career with Piggly Wiggly Carolina Co., the South Carolina franchisee of the Southern grocery chain, eventually becoming a vice president of the firm's computer operations.

Brown was active in civic affairs in the town of Hanahan, north of Charleston; he served first on the planning board and then, in 1981, won a seat on the nonpartisan city council. By 1985, he was serving in the state legislature. He topped his nearly 16 years in the South Carolina House by becoming the first Republican in more than 100 years to chair the Ways and Means Committee, in 1995.

His predecessor in Congress, Republican Mark Sanford, had announced at the start of his tenure that he would serve only six years. So in 1998, just a few days after Brown won re-election to the state House and Sanford won the last of his three terms, Brown filed documents stating his intent to run for Congress in two years.

Brown distinguished himself in a crowd of five Republicans by mailing 20,000 Oh Henry! candy bars to voters. He finished first in the primary and took 55 percent of the vote against former state transportation official Buck Limehouse in a runoff election. In November, he easily outpaced Internet entrepreneur Andy Brack, a longtime aide to South Carolina Sen. Ernest F. Hollings.

He didn't face another Democratic opponent until 2006, when he was challenged by accountant and real estate investor Randy Maatta. In a poor political climate for Republicans, Brown won with just less than 60 percent.

KEY VOTES

2006

- No Stop broadband companies from favoring select Internet traffic
- Yes Affirm U.S. commitment to war in Iraq and reject setting a withdrawal date for troops
- Yes Repeal requirement for bilingual ballots at the polls
- Yes Permit U.S. sale of civilian nuclear technology to India
- Yes Build a 700-mile fence on the U.S.-Mexico border to curb illegal crossings
- Yes Permit warrantless wiretaps of suspected terrorists

2005

- ? Intervene in the life-support case of Terri Schiavo
- No Lift President Bush's restrictions on stem cell research funding
- No Prohibit FBI access to library and bookstore records
- Yes Approve free-trade pact with five Central American countries
- Yes Pass energy policy overhaul favored by President Bush emphasizing domestic oil and gas production
- Yes End mandatory preservation of habitat of endangered animal and plant species
- No Ban torture of prisoners in U.S. custody

CQ VOTE STUDIES

	PARTY UNITY		PRESIDENTIAL SUPPORT	
	Support	Oppose	Support	Oppose
2006	97%	3%	95%	5%
2005	96%	4%	83%	17%
2004	97%	3%	91%	9%
2003	97%	3%	96%	4%
2002	95%	5%	82%	18%

INTEREST GROUPS

	AFL-CIO	ADA	CCUS	ACU
2006	7%	0%	100%	84%
2005	13%	0%	93%	96%
2004	20%	0%	100%	96%
2003	7%	10%	97%	88%
2002	11%	0%	95%	96%

SOUTH CAROLINA 1

East – part of Charleston, Myrtle Beach

Taking in most of the state's coastline, the 1st is marked by two of South Carolina's landmark tourist destinations: Charleston and Myrtle Beach. Horry County, which includes Myrtle Beach, still has plenty of farmland but is one of the state's fastest-growing areas.

Charleston, 80 percent of whose residents live in the 1st, is one of the nation's busiest ports, and shipping long has been a staple of the local economy. The military also maintains a strong presence here: Charleston Air Force Base provides airlift operations for troops, military equipment and medical supplies, and Naval Weapons Station Charleston is a training, engineering and logistics center. The city is an icon of the New South, but retains its traditional culture. Surrounded by reminders of antebellum history, it is nicknamed the "Holy City" due to the church steeples marking its skyline. The homes and boulevards of the city's large historic district attract hordes of visitors.

Moving north, tourism and agriculture dominate. Tobacco farming is prominent in the inland areas, and Myrtle Beach, a popular destination for vacations and conventions, welcomes millions of visitors annually. The area is known as much for its championship golf courses as for its beaches. Conservation efforts have become increasingly popular in response to rapid residential and commercial development that has brought congestion, pollution, wetlands destruction and beach erosion.

The area's wealth has kept the area reliably Republican. Horry County gave George W. Bush 62 percent of the vote in the 2004 presidential election, and Bush took 61 percent of the 1st's overall vote.

MAJOR INDUSTRY

Tourism, shipping, agriculture, military, tobacco

MILITARY BASES

Charleston Air Force Base, 3,900 military, 1,021 civilian (2007); Naval Weapons Station Charleston, 195 military, 411 civilian (2006)

CITIES

Charleston (pt.), 77,434; Mount Pleasant, 47,609; North Charleston (pt.), 45,530; Goose Creek, 29,208; Summerville, 27,752; Myrtle Beach, 22,759

NOTABLE

Charleston Harbor is home to Fort Sumter, where the first battle of the Civil War took place in 1861; Fort Moultrie on nearby Sullivan's Island marks the first decisive victory in the American Revolution.

Rep. Joe Wilson (R)

CAPITOL OFFICE
225-2452
www.joewilson.house.gov
212 Cannon 20515-4002; fax 225-2455

COMMITTEES
Armed Services
Education & Labor
Foreign Affairs

RESIDENCE
Springdale

BORN
July 31, 1947, Charleston, S.C.

RELIGION
Presbyterian

FAMILY
Wife, Roxanne Wilson; four children

EDUCATION
Washington and Lee U., B.A. 1969 (political science); U. of South Carolina, J.D. 1972

MILITARY SERVICE
Army Reserve, 1972-75;
S.C. National Guard, 1975-2003

CAREER
Lawyer; campaign aide;
U.S. Energy Department official

POLITICAL HIGHLIGHTS
Pine Ridge town judge, 1974-76; Republican nominee for S.C. Senate, 1976; Springdale town judge, 1977-80; S.C. Senate, 1985-2001

ELECTION RESULTS

2006 GENERAL		
Joe Wilson (R)	127,811	62.6%
Michael Ray Ellisor (D)	76,090	37.3%
2006 PRIMARY		
Joe Wilson (R)		unopposed
2004 GENERAL		
Joe Wilson (R)	181,862	65.0%
Michael Ray Ellisor (D)	93,249	33.3%
Steve Lefemine (CNSTP)	4,447	1.6%

PREVIOUS WINNING PERCENTAGES
2002 (84%); 2001 Special Election (73%)

Elected December 2001; 3rd full term

Wilson speaks with a certain authority on defense issues. He was in the South Carolina National Guard for close to three decades, retiring as a colonel, and served in the Army Reserve for three years. His family is also well connected to the military. One of his sons served a one-year tour of duty as an intelligence officer in Iraq, a second son graduated from the U.S. Naval Academy, a third is in the National Guard, and his youngest son is a member of his college ROTC program.

Wilson sits on the Armed Services Committee, where his mentor and predecessor in the 2nd District, Floyd D. Spence, was once chairman. Wilson remains a strong voice of support for the war in Iraq. As the co-founder of the Victory in Iraq Caucus, he has firmly denounced the idea that leaving Iraq before liberating it is an option. Although he at first expressed reluctance to send more troops to the beleaguered country, once President Bush asked for thousands more soldiers, Wilson was right behind him. He said Bush made it clear that the Iraqi government will also have to increase its military role in liberating the country. "I have always said troop strength should be a determination of the military leaders. Period," he said. "I don't believe in micromanaging a war."

Later in 2007, Wilson adamantly opposed a Democratically sponsored resolution denouncing Bush's decision to send more troops to Iraq and suggesting a timeline for U.S. troop withdrawal. "For me, a timeline is determined by both sides," he said in an interview. "And since the other side has determined that this is the center front for the global war on terror, timetables can't be established."

Wilson is also a firm supporter of the military presence in his state. He was pleased when the military bases in his district and the rest of South Carolina not only survived the 2005 round of base closures but also were expanded as facilities elsewhere were consolidated.

Wilson voted with his party 97 percent of the time in the 109th Congress (2005-06) on votes that pitted a majority of each party against the other, and he voted with the president 92 percent of the time. The only high-profile measure where he veered away from his party's position was a 2005 vote to implement the Central American Free Trade Agreement. Wilson, like many others in his state delegation, had concerns about CAFTA's impact on the state's textile industry. But when the votes were cast, Wilson ended up voting yes, helping to ensure its narrow 217 to 215 passage. He said later, "I was assured that this would be beneficial to the textile industry."

A member of the Education and Labor Committee, Wilson has expressed concerns about the reauthorization of the No Child Left Behind education law that mandates national testing standards. Wilson said he has doubts about how much involvement the federal government should have in local school decisions. "I represent some of the wealthiest communities in North America and some of the poorest communities in North America," Wilson said. "So what works in one community won't work in another." In the 110th Congress (2007-08), he is the top-ranking Republican on the committee's Workforce Protections Subcommittee.

One of Wilson's greatest legislative successes came when his bill to expand a loan forgiveness program for teachers in poverty-stricken public schools was made part of a bill signed by Bush at the end of 2004. All qualifying teachers in poor public schools can be forgiven up to $5,000, but Wilson's provision raised the amount to $17,500 for math, science and special education teachers.

Wilson's sharp and careless remarks sometimes land him in hot water. He endlessly criticized Sen. John Kerry, the 2004 Democratic presidential candidate, who had served in Vietnam with distinction. His criticism angered former Democratic Sen. Max Cleland of Georgia, a Kerry supporter who lost an arm and both legs in Vietnam. Cleland denounced Wilson and similar critics as "a bunch of chicken hawks who never went to war, never felt a wound, but are so quick to criticize a man who went to war and got wounded doing it." Wilson had a student deferment during Vietnam.

And a few months after the June 2003 death of South Carolina GOP Sen. Strom Thurmond, a South Carolina icon and former segregationist, a black woman named Essie Mae Washington-Williams acknowledged that she was Thurmond's illegitimate daughter. Despite compelling evidence and quick acceptance by Thurmond's family, Wilson told The State newspaper of Columbia, "It's a smear on the image that [Thurmond] has as a person of high integrity who has been so loyal to the people of South Carolina." Wilson, his wife and three of his sons had all interned in Thurmond's office. He later apologized for his remark.

Wilson said his first recollection of politics was when he was a "pop runner" — fetching soft drinks for poll workers. His mother was a Democrat, but Wilson, recalling his admiration for President Dwight Eisenhower, always thought he might be a Republican. He made the transition from working on Democratic races to Republican ones in 1960. He met his wife at a camp for Republican teenagers where she was a camper and he was a counselor.

In addition to working for Thurmond while in college, Wilson joined Spence's office while in law school. He managed five of Spence's re-election campaigns, as well as being involved in numerous statewide GOP campaigns in the 1980s and 1990s while working as a real estate lawyer.

Wilson came up short in a contest for the state Senate in 1976, losing after a recount. After a two-year stint with the Department of Energy in Washington, Wilson successfully challenged a GOP incumbent in 1984 for the first of four terms in the state Senate. After Spence died in 2001, Wilson said he had his deathbed endorsement. He jumped into the special-election race just one day after Spence's funeral. While Wilson's claim rankled some of his rivals, it was backed up by Spence's widow. He won the five-way GOP primary with 76 percent of the vote and cruised to a 48 percentage point win.

Democrats did not even come up with a challenger in 2002. In 2004, Wilson won with 65 percent of the vote against Democratic attorney Michael Ray Ellisor. He faced Ellisor again in 2006, winning with 63 percent.

KEY VOTES

2006

- No Stop broadband companies from favoring select Internet traffic
- Yes Affirm U.S. commitment to war in Iraq and reject setting a withdrawal date for troops
- Yes Repeal requirement for bilingual ballots at the polls
- Yes Permit U.S. sale of civilian nuclear technology to India
- Yes Build a 700-mile fence on the U.S.-Mexico border to curb illegal crossings
- Yes Permit warrantless wiretaps of suspected terrorists

2005

- Yes Intervene in the life-support case of Terri Schiavo
- No Lift President Bush's restrictions on stem cell research funding
- No Prohibit FBI access to library and bookstore records
- Yes Approve free-trade pact with five Central American countries
- Yes Pass energy policy overhaul favored by President Bush emphasizing domestic oil and gas production
- Yes End mandatory preservation of habitat of endangered animal and plant species
- No Ban torture of prisoners in U.S. custody

CQ VOTE STUDIES

	PARTY UNITY		PRESIDENTIAL SUPPORT	
	Support	Oppose	Support	Oppose
2006	97%	3%	92%	8%
2005	97%	3%	91%	9%
2004	99%	1%	91%	9%
2003	98%	2%	94%	6%
2002	97%	3%	82%	18%

INTEREST GROUPS

	AFL-CIO	ADA	CCUS	ACU
2006	7%	5%	91%	91%
2005	13%	0%	93%	100%
2004	13%	0%	100%	96%
2003	13%	5%	93%	84%
2002	22%	10%	80%	92%

SOUTH CAROLINA 2

Central and south — part of Columbia and suburbs, Hilton Head Island

The 2nd runs from the coast up the Georgia border and into central South Carolina, button-hooking north around Columbia and scooping up some of the capital city. The district's two ends take in some of the state's wealthiest areas — steadily growing Columbia suburbs in Richland and Lexington counties, and Beaufort and Hilton Head Island in the south.

State and local government are the Columbia area's largest employers, but the private sector is growing, and health care also is an important industry in the 2nd. On the Georgia border, the Department of Energy's Savannah River Site nuclear complex, which is shared with the 3rd, provides many area jobs. Considerably poorer smaller towns and rural areas dot the land between Columbia and Hilton Head, which is a hot destination for retirees and tourists. Many families in black-majority Allendale, Hampton and Jasper counties live below the poverty line, relying on tenant farming and sharecropping.

Military issues are important here. Just up the shore from swank resorts, recruits sweat at the Parris Island Marine Corps Recruitment camp. Fort Jackson in Richland County in the north and Beaufort Marine Corps Air Station also contribute to the district's heavy military presence.

Despite Democratic support in rural areas, wealthy white-collar professionals in the north and south push the district firmly into the Republican column. George W. Bush won 72 percent of the 2004 presidential vote in Lexington County, the 2nd's most-populous, and he took 60 percent of the overall district vote.

MAJOR INDUSTRY

Tourism, government, military, health care, agriculture

MILITARY BASES

Fort Jackson (Army), 5,200 military, 3,900 civilian (2006); Beaufort Marine Corps Air Station, 3,885 military, 918 civilian (2007); Marine Corps Recruitment Depot (Parris Island), 1,500 military, 865 civilian (2007)

CITIES

Columbia (pt.), 59,771; Hilton Head Island, 33,862

NOTABLE

Mitchelville, established on Hilton Head Island during the Civil War, was the first U.S. town founded specifically for freed black slaves.

Rep. J. Gresham Barrett (R)

CAPITOL OFFICE
225-5301
www.house.gov/barrett
439 Cannon 20515-4003; fax 225-3216

COMMITTEES
Budget
Financial Services
Foreign Affairs
Standards of Official Conduct

RESIDENCE
Westminster

BORN
Feb. 14, 1961, Westminster, S.C.

RELIGION
Baptist

FAMILY
Wife, Natalie Barrett; three children

EDUCATION
The Citadel, B.S. 1983 (business administration)

MILITARY SERVICE
Army, 1983-87

CAREER
Furniture store owner

POLITICAL HIGHLIGHTS
S.C. House, 1997-2002

ELECTION RESULTS

2006 GENERAL		
J. Gresham Barrett (R)	111,882	62.9%
Lee Ballenger (D, WFM)	66,039	37.1%
2006 PRIMARY		
J. Gresham Barrett (R)		unopposed
2004 GENERAL		
J. Gresham Barrett (R)		unopposed

PREVIOUS WINNING PERCENTAGES
2002 (67%)

Elected 2002; 3rd term

A graduate of The Citadel military academy in South Carolina, Barrett remains one of President Bush's staunchest supporters on the war in Iraq. Even as Congress passed legislation in 2007 calling for the withdrawal of U.S. forces, Barrett defended the president's plan to send thousands of additional combat troops to the battlefront. "You can boil it down to something very simple," he said. "The surge is the last best chance that we have in saving Iraq."

He is equally loyal when it comes to his party, siding with fellow Republicans 98 percent of the time in the 109th Congress (2005-06) on votes that split the two parties. As fiscally and socially conservative as they come, Barrett will break with his party leaders when they take positions he doesn't consider conservative enough.

He was one of only 33 House members, and the only South Carolina Republican, to vote against a renewal of the landmark 1965 Voting Rights Act in 2006. He objected to the provision in the law requiring states with a history of discrimination to get approval from the Justice Department before making changes to their voting procedures. South Carolina is one of nine states affected.

In his first year in Congress in 2003, he voted against the GOP bill to add a prescription drug benefit to Medicare, a top priority for Bush and so important to Republican leaders that they kept the House in session all night until they had the votes to pass the measure. Barrett said the bill would do more harm than good, telling the Columbia State newspaper, "What we did today was take a 30-year loan out on an old broken-down boat, slapped some patches on it and stuck it back in the water."

On the Budget Committee, Barrett frequently calls for more fiscal discipline. He has received a 94 percent lifetime score from Citizens Against Government Waste, a Washington-based group that fights pork barrel spending.

A committed social conservative, he was critical of judges in Massachusetts who authorized same-sex marriages, saying, "The decision we are now left with is not whether the Constitution will be amended, but who will amend it — activist judges or the American people?"

Barrett has formed a friendship with another ambitious young conservative, Indiana's Mike Pence, who challenged John A. Boehner of Ohio for the post of GOP leader in the 110th Congress (2007-08). Barrett and Pence met at a prayer breakfast, and Barrett says that on the topics of religion, politics and family, the two think alike.

Since entering Congress, Barrett has devoted much of his time to looking out for the Energy Department's Savannah River Site, a sprawling nuclear weapons complex located mostly in his district that has been seeking new missions since the end of the Cold War to stabilize its shrinking workforce. A champion of nuclear power, he has promoted the idea of building a new reactor at the site and called for expanding the use of nuclear power nationwide.

Barrett is undeterred by criticism from environmentalists and others who say nuclear power is unsafe and not economical when factoring in the start-up costs. After visiting France, which derives more than three-quarters of its energy from nuclear plants, he said he believes nuclear power is the only way to keep up with demand in the United States. "Critics often use this issue to scare the American public," Barrett wrote in a

2005 column in The State newspaper. "Having spent all but eight years of my life less than 20 miles from three reactors, I can attest to their safety."

Like other South Carolina lawmakers, Barrett tries to help the state's beleaguered textile industry. He has opposed granting the president fast-track authority to negotiate trade agreements that Congress cannot amend, even though many business-oriented Republicans support fast-track procedures. He agreed to vote for the Central American Free Trade Agreement in 2005 only after provisions were added to address the concerns of his state's textile manufacturers. "It took a lot of wheeling and dealing," Barrett said. "At the end, our textile guys said this is something we can live with and this is something we honestly think will make our industry stronger."

Barrett describes himself as "a real country boy." He boasts that he had never visited Washington, D.C., until he was running for Congress and never had flown on an airplane before jumping out of one during his Army training. He entered the Army after graduating from The Citadel, where his brother and two nephews also went. "Imagine a world where people will do what they say they will do . . . where you can give your word as a contract," said Barrett, in explaining the enduring hold the school has on him when he spoke at The Citadel's 2005 commencement.

After four years as an Army field artillery officer, Barrett left the military with the rank of captain to join the family furniture business, which closed in 2004. Barrett's conservative credentials were forged in the state House, where he served three terms. He led the fight there to ban late-term abortion. He also sponsored a 1998 education measure that established statewide standards for all subjects and grades.

His involvement in George W. Bush's 2000 South Carolina presidential primary campaign helped him build a strong organization for his first House bid, which came in 2002 when Republican Lindsey Graham gave up the 3rd District seat to run for the Senate. Barrett won the Republican nod over five rivals and then claimed the general-election win by better than 2-to-1 over George Brighthарp, a high school guidance counselor.

Barrett's and Graham's homes are about 10 miles apart, and Barrett was often compared with Graham during the campaign. After his election, Barrett told the Greenville News that he considered his predecessor "a wonderful mentor and a wonderful friend."

In 2004, bowing to the district's strong conservative leanings, Democrats did not field a candidate. Barrett won by almost 26 percentage points in 2006. Like Graham, Barrett is now talked about as a potential candidate for higher office, including a possible run for governor in 2010.

KEY VOTES

2006

No Stop broadband companies from favoring select Internet traffic
Yes Affirm U.S. commitment to war in Iraq and reject setting a withdrawal date for troops
Yes Repeal requirement for bilingual ballots at the polls
Yes Permit U.S. sale of civilian nuclear technology to India
Yes Build a 700-mile fence on the U.S.-Mexico border to curb illegal crossings
Yes Permit warrantless wiretaps of suspected terrorists

2005

Yes Intervene in the life-support case of Terri Schiavo
No Lift President Bush's restrictions on stem cell research funding
No Prohibit FBI access to library and bookstore records
Yes Approve free-trade pact with five Central American countries
Yes Pass energy policy overhaul favored by President Bush emphasizing domestic oil and gas production
Yes End mandatory preservation of habitat of endangered animal and plant species
No Ban torture of prisoners in U.S. custody

CQ VOTE STUDIES

	PARTY UNITY		PRESIDENTIAL SUPPORT	
	Support	Oppose	Support	Oppose
2006	96%	4%	90%	10%
2005	99%	1%	93%	7%
2004	99%	1%	85%	15%
2003	98%	2%	91%	9%

INTEREST GROUPS

	AFL-CIO	ADA	CCUS	ACU
2006	7%	10%	93%	96%
2005	14%	0%	85%	100%
2004	0%	0%	100%	100%
2003	20%	10%	87%	92%

SOUTH CAROLINA 3

West – Anderson, Aiken, Greenwood

Encompassing the northwestern corner of the state, the 3rd is a predominately rural, conservative district. Many voters here are converts to the Republican Party, having shifted over from a "Yellow Dog" Democratic past. When former Representative, and now Senator, Lindsey Graham won this seat in 1994, he was the first Republican to do so since Reconstruction.

Residents of the 3rd enjoy the fruits of a vibrant, diversified economy. The base of engineers surrounding the Energy Department's Savannah River Site nuclear complex, which is shared with the neighboring 2nd District, has helped attract Fortune 500 firms and several U.S. divisions of foreign companies to the area. Fujifilm's medical products plant in Greenwood was the first built outside of Japan.

To the northwest, Anderson has built an industrial economy, relying on appliance and automotive parts manufacturing. Many textile operations have shifted to high-technology fiber manufacturing, although textile mills still employ many residents. Clemson University provides the economic and social nexus for Pickens County at the 3rd's northern tip.

Agriculture is a significant part of the 3rd's economy, especially in southern areas: Edgefield and Saluda counties are two of the top peach-producing counties in the state. Aiken County (shared with the 2nd) also ranks high in peach production. Cotton is another important crop here.

The district votes solidly Republican in federal and statewide races. The 3rd's most populous voting jurisdictions — Anderson, Aiken and Pickens counties — are heavily Republican. The counties in the 3rd's midsection are more rural and less Republican-leaning, but also less populous. This area includes McCormick County, which has a black majority. The 3rd gave George W. Bush 65 percent of its presidential vote in 2004.

MAJOR INDUSTRY

Nuclear research, manufacturing, textiles, agriculture

CITIES

Anderson, 25,514; Aiken (pt.), 22,810; Greenwood, 22,071; Easley, 17,754

NOTABLE

The 70,000-acre Lake Thurmond, previously known as Clarks Hill Lake, was renamed for former GOP Sen. Strom Thurmond, the oldest person ever to serve in the Senate.

Rep. Bob Inglis (R)

CAPITOL OFFICE
225-6030
inglis.house.gov
330 Cannon 20515-4004; fax 226-1177

COMMITTEES
Foreign Affairs
Science & Technology

RESIDENCE
Travelers Rest

BORN
Oct. 11, 1959, Savannah, Ga.

RELIGION
Presbyterian

FAMILY
Wife, Mary Anne Inglis; five children

EDUCATION
Duke U., B.A. 1981 (political science);
U. of Virginia, J.D. 1984

CAREER
Lawyer

POLITICAL HIGHLIGHTS
U.S. House, 1993-99; Republican nominee for U.S. Senate, 1998

ELECTION RESULTS

2006 GENERAL		
Bob Inglis (R)	115,553	64.2%
William Griff Griffith (D)	57,490	32.0%
John Cobin (LIBERT)	4,467	2.5%
C. Faye Walters (GREEN)	2,336	1.3%
2006 PRIMARY		
Bob Inglis (R)		unopposed
2004 GENERAL		
Bob Inglis (R)	188,795	69.8%
Brandon P. Brown (D)	78,376	29.0%
C. Faye Walters (NL)	3,273	1.2%

PREVIOUS WINNING PERCENTAGES
1996 (71%); 1994 (73%); 1992 (50%)

Elected 2004; 5th term

Also served 1993-99

Inglis returned to Congress in 2005 after a six-year hiatus, chastened by a failed Senate bid. He has tempered his self-righteousness — gone is the white sign on his office door: "Notice to all PACs: Remember, you didn't give me a dime and I don't owe you a thing." But he is more willing than ever to vote his own mind.

He also has abandoned the self-imposed term limit that ended his first stretch in Congress in 1998. Term limits, he says now, are a form of "unilateral disarmament." After once labeling members of the Appropriations spending panels "big hogs," he is not so adamant about pork as he was, saying federal money earmarked for the districts of certain lawmakers has its merits. "One of the things I would change from Inglis 1.0 was a sense of being pure as the driven snow and everyone was a lesser creature," says Inglis, who returned to Congress with more grey speckles in his close-cropped hair. "Inglis 2.0 is the new and improved version."

This time around, Inglis is proving far more willing to buck party leaders, too, with his votes on the environment, social policy and national security issues. That independent streak got Inglis (ING-lis) in trouble at the start of the 110th Congress (2007-08) when he joined 16 other Republicans in voting in favor of a non-binding Democratically sponsored resolution against President Bush's plan to send more than 21,000 additional combat troops to Iraq.

His decision shocked constituents in his solidly conservative district. Local Republican Party leaders said the vote might even cost Inglis his job and considered a resolution rebuking him for his vote. His predecessor and friend, Sen. Jim DeMint, likened Inglis' decision to voting against the invasion of Normandy during World War II "after our troops have hit the beach," according to the Charleston Post and Courier.

Inglis was unapologetic about the vote, but scrambled to minimize the damage with multiple mailings to constituents and an explanation of the vote on his Web site. He said he fears the troop increase would "send the wrong message to the Iraqi leadership," who, he believes, must "start taking responsibility for their country." The Web message also touts his support for more funds for the troops and his opposition to a troop withdrawal timetable.

Since returning to Congress, Inglis has split with his party on a number of key initiatives. He voted in 2005 against drilling in the Arctic National Wildlife Refuge. He also opposed an attempt by conservatives to strip federal courts of jurisdiction over the Pledge of Allegiance, a move aimed at preventing federal judges from ruling the phrase "under God" unconstitutional. In 2006, Inglis voted against a GOP-drafted bill dealing with electronic anti-terrorism surveillance and bucked his party when the Judiciary Committee considered a bill on the treatment of detained accused terrorists.

In deference to Bush, Inglis agreed to support the Central American Free Trade Agreement in 2005 after obtaining assurances that it would close loopholes that might threaten textile workers in South Carolina. Inglis voted against the North American Free Trade Agreement in 1994.

His votes and more-moderate positions are a far cry from the self-described revolutionary who came to Congress in 1993 after ambushing a popular Democratic incumbent. The first-term Inglis voted to impeach President Bill Clinton and declared himself a soldier in a "culture war to determine whose set of values rule." He took the bold political step of opposing federal money for a major local highway project. "We are quick to criticize Democrats for being tax-and-spend liberals," he said then. "But that may be more honest than being no-tax and spend Republicans."

With his three-term limit approaching, Inglis decided to challenge Democratic Sen. Ernest F. Hollings in 1998. Having rejected political action committee donations, he was outspent more than 2-to-1 by Hollings and lost the race 53 percent to 46 percent.

Inglis returned to his Greenville law firm, toyed with running for lieutenant governor and never lost his yen for the Senate. But when Hollings retired in 2004, GOP Rep. Jim DeMint decided to run for the seat, sidelining Inglis. He then opted to run for DeMint's seat — the one he had held before.

Republican leaders, happy to have the seat safely in the GOP column, welcomed Inglis back by giving him partial credit for past service and put him back on Judiciary, where he had previously served. (He left Judiciary in the 110th Congress for a spot on the Foreign Affairs Committee.)

As the top-ranking Republican on the Science and Technology Subcommittee on Energy and the Environment in 2007, Inglis says his priority is fostering the development of alternative energy sources. He wants the Energy Department to offer cash prizes for new developments in hydrogen energy.

On other science issues, he remains loyal to conservative ideas. He supports teaching the concept of intelligent design along with evolution in public schools, and he participated in a panel discussion at a conference titled, "Uncommon Dissent: Scientists Who Find Darwinism Unconvincing."

Inglis was born in Savannah, Ga., and grew up in the small town of Bluffton, S.C., population 825. His father, an industrial engineer, commuted to Savannah from the family's home on 14 acres outside of town.

Inglis first got interested in politics during high school, with the 1976 presidential campaign. His father supported Southern Democrat Jimmy Carter. Relatives of Jody Powell, Carter's press secretary, attended the Inglis' church. But Inglis was inspired by Republican candidate Ronald Reagan, after hearing him give a speech in Charleston.

He was a straight arrow at Duke University, a fraternity boy who regularly attended Bible study. After graduating from the University of Virginia's law school, he went on to become the youngest partner in one of Greenville's most prestigious law firms at the age of 31.

In 1992, he saw a chance to defeat incumbent Democratic Rep. Liz J. Patterson. He advertised himself as a Washington outsider — "un-bought and not for sale." He won 50 percent of the vote in a district that George H.W. Bush dominated that year. His still-familiar name and the district's overwhelming GOP leanings enabled Inglis to cruise through a comeback campaign in 2004. He won handily again in 2006.

KEY VOTES

2006

- No — Stop broadband companies from favoring select Internet traffic
- Yes — Affirm U.S. commitment to war in Iraq and reject setting a withdrawal date for troops
- Yes — Repeal requirement for bilingual ballots at the polls
- Yes — Permit U.S. sale of civilian nuclear technology to India
- Yes — Build a 700-mile fence on the U.S.-Mexico border to curb illegal crossings
- No — Permit warrantless wiretaps of suspected terrorists

2005

- Yes — Intervene in the life-support case of Terri Schiavo
- No — Lift President Bush's restrictions on stem cell research funding
- No — Prohibit FBI access to library and bookstore records
- Yes — Approve free-trade pact with five Central American countries
- Yes — Pass energy policy overhaul favored by President Bush emphasizing domestic oil and gas production
- Yes — End mandatory preservation of habitat of endangered animal and plant species
- Yes — Ban torture of prisoners in U.S. custody

CQ VOTE STUDIES

	PARTY UNITY		PRESIDENTIAL SUPPORT	
	Support	Oppose	Support	Oppose
2006	89%	11%	90%	10%
2005	93%	7%	76%	24%

INTEREST GROUPS

	AFL-CIO	ADA	CCUS	ACU
2006	7%	15%	87%	84%
2005	13%	5%	85%	80%
1998	10%	—	—	—

SOUTH CAROLINA 4

Northwest – Greenville, Spartanburg

The 4th is South Carolina's most compact district and is centered on Greenville County, the state's most-populous. Greenville and Spartanburg counties together account for 95 percent of the district population. The 4th also takes in Union County, a heavily forested and lightly populated area, and the northernmost tip of Laurens County.

Once known only for its textile mills, the area is now home to diversified manufacturing and warehousing industries. The cities of Greenville and Spartanburg are leaders in per capita investment by foreign companies. Michelin's North American base is in Greenville, and Spartanburg's BMW plant is the exclusive producer of the Z4 and X5 models.

Greenville has become a research hub and is building the 250-acre International Center for Automotive Research, a public-private venture with Clemson University. The adjacent Millennium Campus is a 150-acre office park that is recruiting corporate headquarters.

While no longer the textile capital of the world, the 4th retains a strong textile presence. Industry giant Milliken & Co. is headquartered in Spartanburg. Although textile companies have less political influence than they once did, trade issues are important here. Agriculture still plays a role in the Spartanburg area despite a strong manufacturing industry, and the county's orchards yield one of the South's biggest peach crops.

The combination of business-oriented conservatives and social conservatives focused around Greenville-based Bob Jones University keeps the 4th solidly Republican. With its rank-and-file textile workers and farm laborers, Spartanburg County is less heavily Republican than Greenville County. Nonetheless, in key 2004 races both counties voted for GOP candidates by landslide margins, and Republican Gov. Mark Sanford won both counties with at least 60 percent of the vote in 2006.

MAJOR INDUSTRY

Manufacturing, textiles, agriculture

CITIES

Greenville, 56,002; Spartanburg, 39,673; Wade Hampton (unincorporated), 20,458; Taylors (unincorporated), 20,125; Greer, 16,843

NOTABLE

Spartanburg was named for the local "Spartan Rifles" militia unit of the Revolutionary War.

Rep. John M. Spratt Jr. (D)

CAPITOL OFFICE
225-5501
www.house.gov/spratt
1401 Longworth 20515-4005; fax 225-0464

COMMITTEES
Armed Services
Budget - chairman

RESIDENCE
York

BORN
Nov. 1, 1942, Charlotte, N.C.

RELIGION
Presbyterian

FAMILY
Wife, Jane Spratt; three children

EDUCATION
Davidson College, A.B. 1964 (history); Oxford U., M.A. 1966 (philosophy, politics & economics; Marshall scholar); Yale U., LL.B. 1969

MILITARY SERVICE
Army, 1969-71

CAREER
Lawyer; insurance agency owner

POLITICAL HIGHLIGHTS
No previous office

ELECTION RESULTS

2006 GENERAL		
John M. Spratt Jr. (D)	99,669	56.9%
Ralph Norman (R)	75,422	43.1%
2006 PRIMARY		
John M. Spratt Jr. (D)		unopposed
2004 GENERAL		
John M. Spratt Jr. (D)	152,867	63.0%
Albert F. Spencer (R)	89,568	36.9%

PREVIOUS WINNING PERCENTAGES
2002 (86%); 2000 (59%); 1998 (58%); 1996 (54%); 1994 (52%); 1992 (61%); 1990 (100%); 1988 (70%); 1986 (100%); 1984 (92%); 1982 (68%)

Elected 1982; 13th term

In an era of partisan venom and political showboating, Spratt stands apart. His office walls are lined with books, not self-important photographs of himself. He does not indulge in snappy sound bites or cheap shots. He is a policy wonk and exudes gravitas, but he is no stuffed shirt.

During almost a quarter-century in office, he has become one of the leading experts in Congress on both the federal budget and defense, which consumes the lion's share of that budget. The top-ranking Democrat on the Budget Committee since 1997, he stepped confidently into the chairmanship after his party took control in the 110th Congress (2007-08).

In January 2007, he led Democrats in the speedy adoption of pay-as-you-go budget rules requiring all new tax cuts or entitlement program spending to be offset. Republicans had allowed such rules to lapse so they could push through tax cuts without regard to their impact on the deficit.

Spratt then set to work building a consensus within the Democratic Caucus on a plan to balance the budget within five years, which he steered through the House in March 2007. Erasing the deficit, he says, is essential in order to stop the expansion of the national debt. Interest payments on that debt are eating up a growing share of the annual budget. "As long as that wedge in the budget is widening each year, it's squeezing out other priorities and our ability to address Social Security and Medicare," he says.

Spratt has repeatedly called on President Bush to convene a budget summit like the one in 1997 that led to the balanced-budget deal between President Bill Clinton and the GOP-run Congress. Spratt was a lead negotiator on that legislation, which he calls "the biggest achievement that I can lay any claim to." The pact turned big deficits into a budget surplus by the time Bush replaced Clinton in 2001. But once Republicans allowed the pay-as-you-go rules to lapse, deficits returned as security spending arising from the Sept. 11 terrorist attacks and the war in Iraq drove up spending and tax cuts drained revenue.

Spratt and Senate Budget Committee Chairman Kent Conrad of North Dakota, another deficit "hawk," began meeting early in 2007 with Treasury Secretary Henry M. Paulson Jr. and White House budget director Rob Portman, a former Ohio GOP House member, in a preliminary quest for a broad agreement. But Democrats were awaiting signs that Bush was prepared to put tax increases, as well as spending cuts, on the table.

Meanwhile, Spratt continued to worry about the strain on the military and the drain on the budget from the war in Iraq. He is the No. 2 Democrat on the Armed Services Committee, where he has served since he arrived in the House in 1983. He is pro-defense but with an eye toward fiscal consequences. In 2002, when Bush asked Congress for the authority to invade Iraq, Spratt backed him, but also commissioned the Congressional Budget Office to study the costs. As the costs of the war escalated, Spratt in 2004 called on the administration to request additional money to cover them before the November election that year. Bush waited until after he won his second term to send Congress an $82 billion supplemental spending request to finance military operations in Iraq and Afghanistan, and to provide aid to the victims of the 2004 Asian tsunami.

Spratt is more conservative than the typical House Democrat, and not just on fiscal policy. In 2006, he was one of just 18 Democrats voting to authorize warrantless electronic surveillance of communications involving terrorist suspects. In both 2004 and 2006, he supported a constitutional amendment to ban same-sex marriage, and he voted in 2003 to outlaw a procedure that opponents call "partial birth" abortion.

Spratt has been a leading advocate for the textile industry, which helps fuel the 5th District's economy. He voted for the North American Free Trade Agreement in 1993 after Clinton got the Philippines and some other developing countries to accept a longer phaseout of U.S. quotas limiting textile imports. He voted against the 2002 law giving the president authority to negotiate fast-track trade deals that would be subject to a vote by Congress, but not open to amendment. And he opposed the 2005 Central American Free Trade Agreement.

Besides textiles, the 5th District used to depend heavily on tobacco farming, especially in the eastern counties, which tend to slightly favor Republican candidates. Spratt's fiscal discipline took a back seat to supporting tobacco farmers in 2004, when he voted for a $137 billion corporate tax bill that included a $10 billion buyout of tobacco farmers.

Spratt has often had to work to convince his conservative-leaning constituents that he understands and defends their interests. With his lofty academic credentials — he holds degrees from Davidson, Oxford and Yale — and his background as a lawyer, banker and insurance agency owner, Spratt is not the obvious choice to represent voters from poor textile towns.

He grew up in York, where he still lives. His father was a lawyer who owned a small community bank. His older sister married Hugh L. McColl Jr., who later became chairman and CEO of Bank of America. Spratt views McColl, who retired from the bank in 2001, as a mentor.

After law school, Spratt served two years in the Army, working in the comptroller's office at the Pentagon. The job gave him insights into how the Defense Department operates, which he draws upon to this day. When he left, his place was taken by Paulson — now Bush's Treasury secretary.

Spratt returned to South Carolina, joined his father's law firm and became president of the bank. "It's not hard to become president when your family owns 89 percent and your brother-in-law [McColl] has a better job," he jokes.

Spratt won his first House race in 1982 by arguing that his work with small-town law clients and bank depositors gave him an understanding of their circumstances. He trounced a longtime friend and legal client, Republican John Wilkerson, by 36 percentage points, and he won re-election with ease throughout the 1980s. But in the 1990s, he was targeted by the national GOP. He survived the GOP sweep of 1994 by just 4 percentage points and did not win more than 60 percent of the vote in the next three elections. After an easier ride in 2002 and 2004, he won with just 57 percent in 2006.

KEY VOTES

2006

No Stop broadband companies from favoring select Internet traffic

Yes Affirm U.S. commitment to war in Iraq and reject setting a withdrawal date for troops

No Repeal requirement for bilingual ballots at the polls

Yes Permit U.S. sale of civilian nuclear technology to India

Yes Build a 700-mile fence on the U.S.-Mexico border to curb illegal crossings

Yes Permit warrantless wiretaps of suspected terrorists

2005

No Intervene in the life-support case of Terri Schiavo

Yes Lift President Bush's restrictions on stem cell research funding

Yes Prohibit FBI access to library and bookstore records

No Approve free-trade pact with five Central American countries

Yes Pass energy policy overhaul favored by President Bush emphasizing domestic oil and gas production

No End mandatory preservation of habitat of endangered animal and plant species

Yes Ban torture of prisoners in U.S. custody

CQ VOTE STUDIES

	PARTY UNITY		PRESIDENTIAL SUPPORT	
	Support	Oppose	Support	Oppose
2006	84%	16%	44%	56%
2005	88%	12%	27%	73%
2004	86%	14%	41%	59%
2003	90%	10%	25%	75%
2002	88%	12%	42%	58%

INTEREST GROUPS

	AFL-CIO	ADA	CCUS	ACU
2006	100%	75%	50%	44%
2005	100%	90%	52%	12%
2004	93%	80%	48%	20%
2003	100%	95%	32%	33%
2002	100%	80%	55%	16%

SOUTH CAROLINA 5

North central — Rock Hill

The expansive 5th covers all or part of 14 mostly rural counties in the north-central part of the state, stretching from near Charlotte, N.C., to the Columbia suburbs, while also spreading west to Newberry County and east to Dillon County. Tobacco farmers, white-collar Charlotte commuters and textile workers make this a conservative district, although it still clings to traditional Southern Democrat roots.

Lee, Darlington, Marlboro and Dillon counties grow wheat, as well as cotton for the textile mills that historically have dominated the region's economy. Labor costs have forced many companies to downsize or close textile plants in the area, which struggles with unemployment rates above the national average. Local officials face the challenge of retaining existing textile mills while also diversifying the local economy. Darlington and Dillon also depend heavily on tobacco farming.

Rock Hill, although still dependent on textiles, now serves as a home for white-collar commuters and Winthrop University. Rock Hill's plan to attract diversified business interests and lure new residents is based in the 250-acre redesigned downtown area known as the "Textile Corridor."

The city of Sumter, once the center of a large agricultural area, is shifting toward industry. Seven miles west, Shaw Air Force Base supports a large portion of the area's economy, and more than 800 new jobs are expected to move to the base by 2011 as part of the 2005 BRAC round.

The 5th tends to favor Republicans slightly in federal races, but conservative Democratic candidates who appeal to the district's numerous poor and rural residents can win here. Democrats also are helped by the district's 32 percent black population, the largest of any South Carolina district except the black-majority 6th.

MAJOR INDUSTRY

Agriculture, textiles, military, tobacco

MILITARY BASES

Shaw Air Force Base, 6,114 military, 766 civilian (2006)

CITIES

Rock Hill, 49,765; Sumter (pt.), 20,518; Gaffney, 12,968

NOTABLE

The Lee County Cotton Festival, held every October, celebrates the agricultural history of "King Cotton."

Rep. James E. Clyburn (D)

CAPITOL OFFICE
225-3315
jclyburn@mail.house.gov
clyburn.house.gov
2135 Rayburn 20515-4006; fax 225-2313

COMMITTEES
No committee assignments

RESIDENCE
Columbia

BORN
July 21, 1940, Sumter, S.C.

RELIGION
African Methodist Episcopal

FAMILY
Wife, Emily Clyburn; three children

EDUCATION
South Carolina State College, B.A. 1962 (social studies)

CAREER
State official; teacher

POLITICAL HIGHLIGHTS
Candidate for S.C. House, 1970; S.C. human affairs commissioner, 1974-92; sought Democratic nomination for S.C. secretary of state, 1978, 1986

ELECTION RESULTS

2006 GENERAL		
James E. Clyburn (D)	100,213	64.4%
Gary McLeod (R)	53,181	34.2%
Antonio Williams (GREEN)	2,224	1.4%
2006 PRIMARY		
James E. Clyburn (D)		unopposed
2004 GENERAL		
James E. Clyburn (D)	161,987	67.0%
Gary McLeod (R, C)	79,600	32.9%

PREVIOUS WINNING PERCENTAGES
2002 (67%); 2000 (72%); 1998 (73%); 1996 (69%); 1994 (64%); 1992 (65%)

Elected 1992; 8th term

Like Harry S Truman, the man he considers his political inspiration, Clyburn was not a young man when he got to Congress. Elected at 52, he seemed unworried about cutting a dynamic public figure in Washington. Clyburn, like Truman, proved easy to underestimate. He is a skilled inside operator, and his leadership abilities have carried him into the upper echelons of the House Democratic hierarchy.

When Democrats won control of the House in 2006, Clyburn was unanimously chosen majority whip, the third-ranking leadership post. He is only the second African-American in history to have the job; the first was Bill Gray, a Pennsylvania Democrat (1979-91). Clyburn is the highest-ranking African-American legislator currently serving in Congress. No black lawmaker has attained a higher leadership office than whip.

Illinois Democrat Rahm Emanuel, who as chairman of the Democrats' campaign committee was instrumental in the party's victory, considered challenging Clyburn, but opted out after it became clear that the Congressional Black Caucus preferred Clyburn. Emanuel, who had ruffled feathers at the CBC with his aggressive fundraising, still wound up with a leadership post — succeeding Clyburn as Democratic Caucus chairman. Clyburn had been Caucus chairman since late 2005.

One of his tasks as whip was putting together sufficient votes for a bill that tied spending on the Iraq War to a timeline for withdrawing troops, a measure that ultimately was successful in Congress.

Clyburn's ascent through the ranks began as soon as he arrived in the House in 1993. Quietly and methodically, he advanced, winning a seat on the Appropriations Committee in 1999 and getting elected CBC chairman that year. In 2003, he was chosen vice chairman of the Democratic Caucus, which positioned him to move up to chairman when Robert Menendez of New Jersey left the House for the Senate.

Worried that Democrats were losing "values" voters after they failed to gain ground in the 2004 elections, party leaders turned to Clyburn, a minister's son, to head a task force charged with reaching out to religious leaders and helping the party frame issues in faith-based terms. Often invoking Bible passages, Clyburn advanced the notion, "Faith without works is dead. A school lunch program is a faith program."

Clyburn sides with the liberal party leadership on most issues, but casts an occasional conservative vote. He has voted for constitutional amendments to require a balanced federal budget, to set congressional term limits and to allow Congress to ban desecration of the flag. But he has opposed a GOP effort to outlaw same-sex marriage.

He routes as much federal money as he can to his district, which is among the poorest in the nation. Clyburn touts $7 million he says he helped secure in the fiscal 2007 transportation spending bill, and he has been at the forefront of efforts to obtain federal funding for historically black colleges, including his alma mater, South Carolina State.

His knack for earmarking dollars for the folks back home brought him some unwanted attention in 2005, when the Myrtle Beach Sun News reported that his nephew's architecture firm got $70,000 in design work for a project sought by the congressman. Clyburn shrugged it off, saying he has a "bushel of family members" working in local and state government and some are bound to benefit from federal money.

Politics is a Clyburn family tradition. He is the first African-American elected to Congress from South Carolina since his great-uncle, George Washington Murray, served in the U.S. House during Reconstruction. An uncle is in the state legislature and a cousin was a U.S. attorney.

Clyburn was born in 1940 in Sumter, S.C., the son of the minister for Sumter's 100-member Church of God. His mother was a beautician, and he recalls his childhood as "happy and comfortable" and "poor."

Clyburn attended segregated public schools as legal challenges to segregation were making their way to the Supreme Court. One of those cases originated in nearby Summerton, and each morning Clyburn's father would cap the family's recitation of Bible verses with a special prayer for "the people over there in Summerton." His mother eventually sent Clyburn to a private all-black boarding school called Mather Academy, her alma mater. In college, Clyburn studied history and got a degree in social studies.

The family was Republican, a legacy of several generations that embraced the party of Abraham Lincoln. Clyburn stuck with the GOP until the mid-1960s, when he became disillusioned with the racial politics of Dixiecrats-turned-Republicans such as South Carolina Sen. Strom Thurmond. He also jumped into the civil rights movement, becoming an early member of the Student Nonviolent Coordinating Committee, affiliated with the Rev. Martin Luther King Jr.'s Southern Leadership Conference. He was arrested several times and once spent four days in jail. The U.S. Supreme Court overturned a state court that convicted him and others of "breach of peace" for demonstrating against segregation.

From boyhood, Clyburn wanted to run for public office and read every book he could find about Truman, whom he admired for his grit in defeating wealthy New York Gov. Thomas Dewey in 1948.

A few years after college, Clyburn was hired by the state employment commission, its only black employee even though the agency was charged with ensuring federal money went to non-segregated programs. In 1971, Democratic Gov. John West named him a special assistant for human resources, and three years later he became Human Affairs commissioner.

In 1978 and 1986, he unsuccessfully sought the Democratic nomination for secretary of state. When 1992 redistricting created the black-majority 6th District, he saw his opening. White Democratic Rep. Robin Tallon at first said he would seek re-election but then backed out. Clyburn and four other black Democrats entered the primary; all had some political experience, but none was able to match Clyburn's name recognition in the black community or his connections in the white Democratic Party establishment. Clyburn took 56 percent of the primary vote and won with 65 percent in November.

KEY VOTES

2006

- No Stop broadband companies from favoring select Internet traffic
- No Affirm U.S. commitment to war in Iraq and reject setting a withdrawal date for troops
- No Repeal requirement for bilingual ballots at the polls
- Yes Permit U.S. sale of civilian nuclear technology to India
- No Build a 700-mile fence on the U.S.-Mexico border to curb illegal crossings
- No Permit warrantless wiretaps of suspected terrorists

2005

- No Intervene in the life-support case of Terri Schiavo
- Yes Lift President Bush's restrictions on stem cell research funding
- Yes Prohibit FBI access to library and bookstore records
- No Approve free-trade pact with five Central American countries
- Yes Pass energy policy overhaul favored by President Bush emphasizing domestic oil and gas production
- No End mandatory preservation of habitat of endangered animal and plant species
- Yes Ban torture of prisoners in U.S. custody

CQ VOTE STUDIES

	PARTY UNITY		PRESIDENTIAL SUPPORT	
	Support	Oppose	Support	Oppose
2006	94%	6%	35%	65%
2005	92%	8%	25%	75%
2004	93%	7%	30%	70%
2003	95%	5%	25%	75%
2002	97%	3%	31%	69%

INTEREST GROUPS

	AFL-CIO	ADA	CCUS	ACU
2006	100%	95%	50%	12%
2005	93%	85%	48%	9%
2004	86%	90%	45%	13%
2003	100%	90%	39%	25%
2002	100%	95%	50%	0%

SOUTH CAROLINA 6

Central and east – parts of Columbia, Florence and Charleston

A black-majority district designed to take in African-American areas in Columbia, Charleston and elsewhere in the state, the 6th includes all or part of 15 counties in the eastern half of the state, starting near the North Carolina border and reaching the southeastern coast. With five of the state's six poorest counties, the 6th has the state's lowest median household income, although it also includes historically black South Carolina State University and other institutions of higher learning.

In the rural portions of the district, many families depend on tobacco, corn, cotton and related agribusiness for their incomes. Many areas of the district continue to experience double-digit unemployment rates, caused in part by the loss of textile jobs as the industry struggles to compete with less-expensive imports.

Other sectors of the district's economy have fared better. Plastics, pharmaceuticals, textiles and paperboard manufacturing sustain many in the city of Florence (shared with the 5th), which is more middle-class than most of the rest of the 6th. Honda has two plants in Timmonsville, near Florence, that manufacture all-terrain vehicles and personal watercraft. In the coastal parts of the 6th, maritime industries and tourism support the economy. The 6th's portion of Columbia includes the state Capitol complex, and state and local government agencies provide many area jobs. Private sector employment in the Columbia area is growing, and health care now is a major source of employment.

The 6th gives solid and consistent support to Democrats at all levels. The district's black-majority areas — including the 6th's shares of Columbia and North Charleston, which are more than two-thirds black — make this district a Democratic lock.

MAJOR INDUSTRY

Agriculture, government, textiles, higher education, tourism

CITIES

Columbia (pt.), 56,507; North Charleston (pt.), 34,111; Florence (pt.), 26,623; Charleston (pt.), 19,216; Sumter (pt.), 19,125

NOTABLE

Clarendon County (pop. 32,502) can claim five South Carolina governors, all related to each other.

SOUTH DAKOTA

Gov. Michael Rounds (R)

First elected: 2002
Length of term: 4 years
Term expires: 1/11
Salary: $108,711
Phone: (605) 773-3212

Residence: Pierre
Born: Oct. 24, 1954; Pierre, S.D.
Religion: Roman Catholic
Family: Wife, Jean Rounds; four children
Education: South Dakota State U., B.S. 1977 (political science)
Career: Insurance and real estate executive; insurance agent; campaign aide
Political highlights: S.D. Senate, 1991-2000 (majority leader, 1995-2000)

Election results:

2006 GENERAL		
Michael Rounds (R)	206,990	61.7%
Jack Billion (D)	121,226	36.1%
Steve Willis (CNSTP)	4,010	1.2%
Tom Gerber (LIBERT)	3,282	1.0%

Lt. Gov. Dennis Daugaard (R)

First elected: 2002
Length of term: 4 years
Term expires: 1/11
Salary: $16,343
Phone: (605) 773-3661

LEGISLATURE

Legislature: 40 days in odd-numbered years starting in January; 35 days in even-numbered years, starting in January

Senate: 35 members, 2-year terms
2007 ratios: 20 R, 15 D; 30 men, 5 women
Salary: $12,000/2-year-term
Phone: (605) 773-3821

House: 70 members, 2-year terms
2007 ratios: 50 R, 20 D; 57 men, 13 women
Salary: $12,000/2-year-term
Phone: (605) 773-3851

TERM LIMITS

Governor: 2 consecutive terms
Senate: 2 consecutive terms
House: 4 consecutive terms

URBAN STATISTICS

CITY	POPULATION
Sioux Falls	123,975
Rapid City	59,607
Aberdeen	24,658

REGISTERED VOTERS

Republican	47%
Democrat	38%
Others	15%

POPULATION

2006 population (est.)	781,919
2000 population	754,844
1990 population	696,004
Percent change (1990-2000)	+8.5%
Rank among states (2006)	46
Median age	35.6
Born in state	68.1%
Foreign born	1.8%
Violent crime rate	167/100,000
Poverty level	13.2%
Federal workers	10,803
Military	8,489

ELECTIONS

STATE ELECTION OFFICIAL
(605) 773-3537
DEMOCRATIC PARTY
(605) 271-5405
REPUBLICAN PARTY
(605) 224-7347

MISCELLANEOUS

Web: www.state.sd.us
Capital: Pierre

U.S. CONGRESS

Senate: 1 Democrat, 1 Republican
House: 1 Democrat

2000 Census Statistics by District

DIST.	2004 VOTE FOR PRESIDENT BUSH	KERRY	WHITE	BLACK	ASIAN	HISP	MEDIAN INCOME	WHITE COLLAR	BLUE COLLAR	SERVICE INDUSTRY	OVER 64	UNDER 18	COLLEGE EDUCATION	RURAL	SQ. MILES
AL	60%	38%	88%	1%	1%	1%	$35,282	59%	25%	16%	14%	27%	22%	48%	75,885
STATE	60	38	88	1	1	1	$35,282	59	25	16	14	27	22	48	75,885
U.S.	50.7	48.3	69	12	4	13	$41,994	60	25	15	12	26	24	21	3,537,438

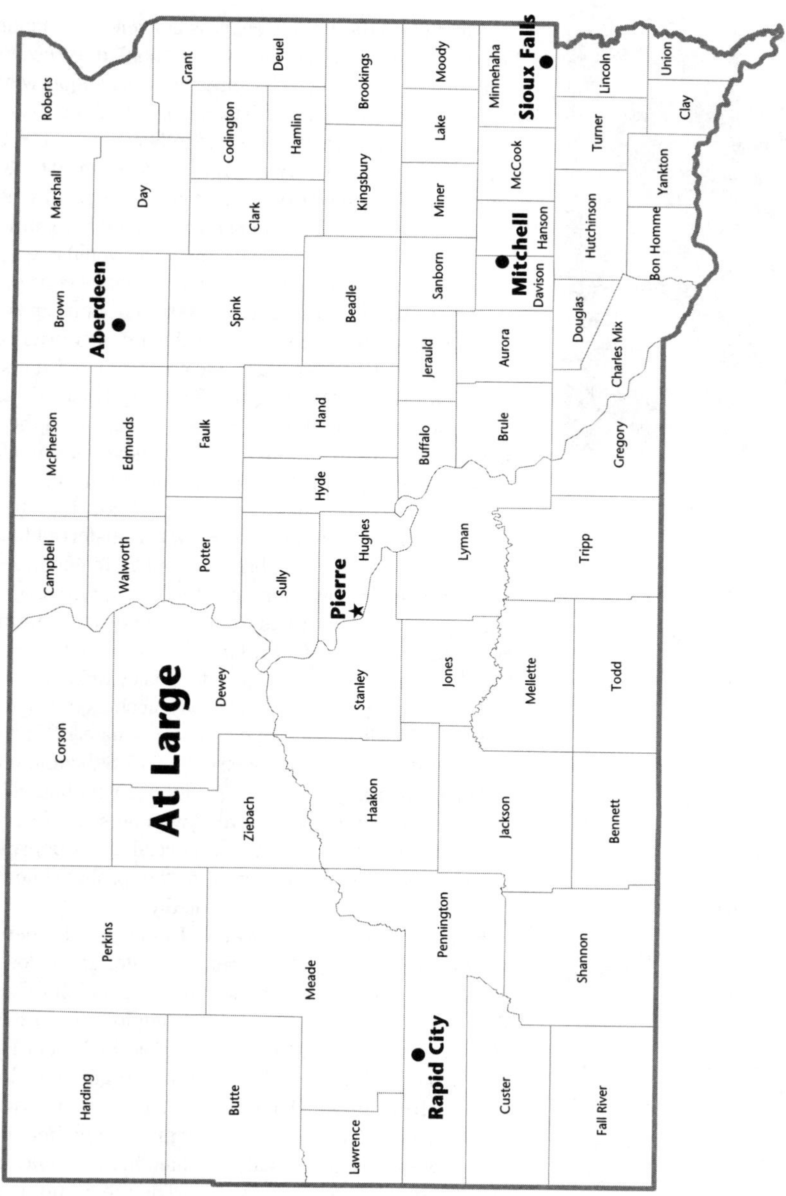
At Large
Aberdeen
Sioux Falls
Mitchell
Pierre
Rapid City
Roberts
Grant
Deuel
Codington
Hamlin
Brookings
Moody
Minnehaha
Lincoln
Union
Clay
Marshall
Day
Clark
Kingsbury
Lake
McCook
Turner
Yankton
Brown
Spink
Beadle
Miner
Hanson
Hutchinson
Bon Homme
Sanborn
Davison
Douglas
Charles Mix
Jerauld
Aurora
McPherson
Edmunds
Faulk
Hand
Buffalo
Brule
Gregory
Hyde
Campbell
Walworth
Potter
Sully
Hughes
Lyman
Tripp
Corson
Dewey
Stanley
Jones
Mellette
Todd
Ziebach
Haakon
Jackson
Bennett
Perkins
Meade
Pennington
Shannon
Harding
Butte
Lawrence
Custer
Fall River

Sen. Tim Johnson (D)

CAPITOL OFFICE
224-5842
johnson.senate.gov
136 Hart 20510-4104; fax 228-5765

COMMITTEES
Appropriations
(Military Construction-VA - chairman)
Banking, Housing & Urban Affairs
(Financial Institutions - chairman)
Energy & Natural Resources
(Water & Power - chairman)
Indian Affairs
Select Ethics - chairman

RESIDENCE
Vermillion

BORN
Dec. 28, 1946, Canton, S.D.

RELIGION
Lutheran

FAMILY
Wife, Barbara Johnson; three children

EDUCATION
U. of South Dakota, B.A. 1969 (political science), M.A. 1970 (political science); Michigan State U., attended 1970-71 (political science); U. of South Dakota, J.D. 1975

CAREER
Lawyer; county prosecutor; state legislative aide

POLITICAL HIGHLIGHTS
S.D. House, 1979-83; S.D. Senate, 1983-87; U.S. House, 1987-97

ELECTION RESULTS

2002 GENERAL		
Tim Johnson (D)	167,481	49.6%
John Thune (R)	166,957	49.5%
2002 PRIMARY		
Tim Johnson (D)	65,438	94.8%
Herman Eilers (D)	3,558	5.2%

PREVIOUS WINNING PERCENTAGES
1996 (51%); 1994 House Election (60%); 1992 House Election (69%); 1990 House Election (68%); 1988 House Election (72%); 1986 House Election (59%)

Elected 1996; 2nd term

Even before the 110th Congress convened in January 2007, the Senate held its collective breath as Johnson battled to recover from emergency brain surgery to correct a life-threatening condition. More was at stake than one senator's survival. The balance of power was also on the line.

Democrats had won the Senate in November 2006 by the narrowest of margins, gaining effective control of 51 seats to 49 for Republicans. If Johnson died or was forced to resign, an interim replacement — almost certainly a Republican — would have been appointed by South Dakota Republican Gov. Mike Rounds. The resulting 50-50 tie would have given Vice President Dick Cheney a tie-breaking vote and returned control to the GOP.

Johnson was stricken Dec. 13, 2006. It became apparent that something was wrong when he stuttered and slurred his words inexplicably during a conference call with reporters. He was examined at his Capitol office, then rushed to George Washington University Hospital. Admiral John Eisold, attending physician of the U.S. Capitol, explained the next day that Johnson suffered from a congenital arteriovenous malformation that had caused bleeding in his brain and produced the stroke-like symptoms.

The senator remained hospitalized for months, slowly regaining strength, speech and mobility. He was transferred to a rehabilitation center in February, then discharged April 27 to continue his recovery at his home in Washington's northern Virginia suburbs.

His colleagues first rushed to his bedside, offering prayers, support and comfort to his wife, Barbara, and his family. Then they stepped up to fill in for him, with Majority Leader Harry Reid of Nevada assigning other senators to temporarily occupy chairmanships Johnson had been scheduled to hold. That list was topped by the Senate Ethics Committee and the Appropriations Military Construction-VA Subcommittee.

The outpouring of concern for Johnson continued long after he was on the mend. In a chamber crowded with outsize egos, he is an unassuming and well-liked anomaly. After two decades in Congress, he can still move through the Capitol unrecognized. "I'm probably not the most colorful in the Senate," he says quite contentedly.

Since the 2004 defeat of former Democratic Leader Tom Daschle, Johnson has been South Dakota's senior senator. He is close to Daschle and was apprehensive about working with Republican John Thune, who had toppled Daschle two years after almost unseating Johnson in 2002. But two other senators who serve with former rivals, Majority Leader Harry Reid of Nevada and Republican Gordon H. Smith of Oregon, told Johnson what he has found to be true — making friends of former adversaries can be useful.

Johnson and Thune now charter planes together for the long trips home and share a table at the state fair, handing out information to constituents about their work on Capitol Hill. They team up on issues important to their largely rural state, and Johnson says their working relationship is very good. "It was time for us to move on," he said.

Johnson also votes with Thune, and most Senate Republicans, on selected other issues, part of the balancing act required of a Democrat from a Republican-leaning state. In 2005, he was one of just two Democrats voting to cut off a filibuster against renewing the 2001 anti-terrorism law known as the Patriot Act. Earlier that year, he helped Republicans to victories on laws to shield gun manufacturers, dealers and importers from lawsuits and to transfer many class action suits from state to federal courts.

Johnson also voted to confirm both of President Bush's successful Supreme Court nominees, Chief Justice John G. Roberts Jr. and Justice Samuel A. Alito Jr. He was one of only four Democrats to vote for Alito.

Johnson is often engaged in less contentious work, with a focus on issues of interest to his constituencies. He was a strong proponent of the 2002 farm bill that gave producers a sturdier federal safety net. Johnson inserted a provision into that law to require mandatory country-of-origin labels on fruit, vegetables and meat — helpful to the ranchers in his state. He has fought ever since to get the provision implemented. From his seat on the Appropriations Committee, he has directed funds to an array of South Dakota projects, particularly those aimed at helping veterans and American Indians, many of whom live in poverty on reservations.

At the start of the 109th Congress (2005-06), Reid chose Johnson to succeed him as the top Democrat on the Ethics Committee, a thankless assignment. In 2005, Johnson joined GOP Chairman George V. Voinovich of Ohio to enforce a ban on outside compensation, ordering Oklahoma Republican Tom Coburn to stop earning income from his medical practice. Coburn fought the ruling. "I simply do not believe that the Senate should vote in favor of any proposal that would loosen our ethical boundaries and increase the opportunities for ethical violations," Johnson said in a floor speech at the time.

When Johnson was elected to the House in 1986, his wife gave up her tenured position as a University of South Dakota social work professor to move the family to Washington, where she became a public school social worker. All three Johnson children went to school in Virginia but returned to South Dakota for college. Johnson introduced legislation in the 108th Congress (2003-04) to bar telemarketers from calling between 5:30 p.m. and 7:30 p.m. as a way of keeping family dinner hours "sacred." He says he regularly advises new senators to bring their families to Washington, so that they can attend school meetings and their children's athletic activities, as he did.

Family issues almost stopped Johnson from running for the Senate though he had a good shot at unseating GOP incumbent Larry Pressler in 1996. In the middle of the campaign, Johnson's wife learned she had breast cancer, the first of two bouts with the disease she has suffered. He offered to drop out, but she encouraged him to stay in and he went on to win the race.

Johnson himself is a cancer survivor, having had successful surgery for prostate cancer in 2004. He also is deaf in his left ear as a result of surgery to remove a benign tumor discovered on his eardrum when he underwent a physical for and was refused admission to the U.S. military during the Vietnam War.

A fourth-generation South Dakotan, Johnson won a seat in the state legislature in 1978, then ran for Congress in 1986 when Daschle gave up the state House seat for a Senate race. After a narrow primary win, Johnson easily won the general election. When he took on Pressler in 1996, he won by just 8,600 votes, the only challenger to defeat a sitting senator that year.

Six years later, his re-election bid sparked a titanic showdown between the two political parties. Thune was personally recruited by Bush to take on Johnson, while Daschle jumped in full throttle to defend Johnson. The state's 760,000 inhabitants were bombarded with television ads, and both candidates broke all previous records for spending. Throughout the campaign, Johnson's quiet style was compared with that of the more gregarious, and handsome, Thune. In the end, it was Johnson who prevailed by 524 votes.

Johnson is up for re-election again in 2008, but his health problems have cast a cloud over his plans. His colleagues, concerned about holding the seat in the narrowly divided Senate, jumped in to raise campaign funds while he was still hospitalized. Republicans stewed, uncertain whether they would face Johnson or another Democratic candidate.

KEY VOTES

2006

Yes Confirm Samuel A. Alito Jr. to the Supreme Court
No Allow consideration of a bill to establish a $140 billion trust fund to compensate victims of asbestos exposure
No Extend tax cuts for two years at a cost of $70 billion over five years
Yes Overhaul immigration policy with border security, enforcement and guest worker program
No Allow consideration of a bill to permanently repeal the estate tax
Yes Urge President Bush to begin troop withdrawals from Iraq in 2006
Yes Lift President Bush's restrictions on stem cell research funding
Yes Authorize military tribunals for suspected terrorists

2005

Yes Curb class action lawsuits by shifting them from state to federal courts
Yes Allow confirmation vote on Priscilla R. Owen to the U.S. Court of Appeals for the 5th Circuit
No Oppose mandatory emissions limits and block recognition of global warming as a threat
No Approve free-trade pact with five Central American countries
Yes Pass energy policy overhaul favored by President Bush emphasizing domestic oil and gas production
Yes Shield gunmakers from lawsuits when their products are used in crimes
Yes Ban torture of prisoners in U.S. custody
Yes Renew 16 provisions of the Patriot Act
No Allow final vote on opening the Arctic National Wildlife Refuge to oil and gas exploration

CQ VOTE STUDIES

	PARTY UNITY		PRESIDENTIAL SUPPORT	
	Support	Oppose	Support	Oppose
2006	83%	17%	57%	43%
2005	83%	17%	45%	55%
2004	90%	10%	60%	40%
2003	93%	7%	50%	50%
2002	85%	15%	68%	32%
2001	87%	13%	71%	29%
2000	91%	9%	98%	2%
1999	93%	7%	78%	22%
1998	93%	7%	89%	11%
1997	86%	14%	87%	13%

INTEREST GROUPS

	AFL-CIO	ADA	CCUS	ACU
2006	87%	85%	50%	12%
2005	86%	95%	60%	13%
2004	100%	85%	59%	11%
2003	100%	80%	39%	15%
2002	100%	90%	53%	15%
2001	94%	85%	64%	32%
2000	75%	80%	60%	16%
1999	89%	95%	47%	8%
1998	88%	90%	56%	4%
1997	71%	80%	70%	12%

Sen. John Thune (R)

CAPITOL OFFICE
224-2321
thune.senate.gov
493 Russell 20510-4103; fax 228-5429

COMMITTEES
Agriculture, Nutrition & Forestry
Armed Services
Commerce, Science & Transportation
Small Business & Entrepreneurship

RESIDENCE
Sioux Falls

BORN
Jan. 7, 1961, Pierre, S.D.

RELIGION
Protestant

FAMILY
Wife, Kimberley Thune; two children

EDUCATION
Biola U., B.S. 1983 (business administration); U. of South Dakota, M.B.A. 1984

CAREER
Lobbyist; local governments association executive; U. S. Small Business Administration official; congressional aide

POLITICAL HIGHLIGHTS
S.D. Republican Party executive director, 1989-91; S.D. railroad director, 1991-93; U.S. House, 1997-2003; Republican nominee for U.S. Senate, 2002

ELECTION RESULTS

2004 GENERAL		
John Thune (R)	197,848	50.6%
Tom Daschle (D)	193,340	49.4%
2004 PRIMARY		
John Thune (R)		unopposed

PREVIOUS WINNING PERCENTAGES
2000 House Election (73%); 1998 House Election (75%); 1996 House Election (58%)

Elected 2004; 1st term

After an eventful election to the Senate came an equally eventful freshman term for Thune. On a fast track in the GOP, he was appointed to the Republican leadership in 2007 and given a seat on his top-choice committee — Agriculture — just as Congress was preparing for a major rewrite of farm policy, the No. 1 issue in his breadbasket state.

Thune was tapped by maverick conservative Republican Whip Trent Lott of Mississippi to join the leadership as chief deputy whip. That gives him a role in building support for GOP positions as well as in the formulation of the minority party's opposition strategy in the Democratically controlled Senate. It also positions him to run for one of the more prominent elected positions in the leadership in the future. Thune has been a party favorite since his spectacular 2004 defeat of Democratic Leader Tom Daschle in one of the year's most-watched congressional races.

Tall and lean, the former college star athlete is also attractive and telegenic, which helps in snaring coveted invitations from the Sunday political talk shows. He calls himself a "right-of-center conservative," and says South Dakota's populist tradition keeps him from drifting to the hard right of the political spectrum. But his strong religious faith, which he says guides his actions in Congress, keeps Thune (THOON) rooted in the conservative wing. He favors a constitutional amendment to ban same-sex marriage and opposes embryonic stem cell research, which uses surplus embryos from in vitro fertilization. He is also a loyal GOP soldier in the areas of cutting taxes, limiting spending and restricting abortion.

For Thune, most national issues pale in importance compared with agriculture. Upon arriving in the Senate in 2005, he tried unsuccessfully to get on the Agriculture Committee. Because of his giant-slaying performance the November before, Republican leaders promised he'd be on the committee by the time the farm bill was up for renewal in 2007. True to their word, he got a seat on the panel for the 110th Congress (2007-08).

Thune is an advocate for the renewable energy provisions in the president's annual budgets, and he has considered cuts in farm subsidies for operations with more than $200,000 in annual income: "I like the direction [of] acknowledging that these program payments ought to be targeted to full-time family farm operations and not to the really huge conglomerate operations."

Thune says trade deals that are opening overseas markets for South Dakota's farmers are a solution to the shaky farm economy and are preferable to increasing federal farm supports. In 2000, Thune voted in the House for permanent normal trade relations with China. But on the campaign trail in 2004, he took a stand against a free-trade deal with Australia, citing concerns about tariff reductions on imported beef and wheat. Thune expressed concern in 2007 about a deal with Brazil to promote ethanol production there. Noting that one reason for using ethanol for fuel is to reduce dependence on foreign sources, Thune told The Associated Press, "It makes no sense to replace one source of foreign energy with another."

Thune, whose office is decorated with a mounted pheasant and buffalo to remind him of what sets his state apart, is an avid hunter. "There's no place I'm happier than out in a field of CRP," he says of the federal Conservation Reserve Program, which pays farmers to set aside acreage for wildlife habitat.

Although he is loyal to his party by and large, voting with the Republican leadership 90 percent of the time in the 109th Congress (2005-06), he will play hardball when he wants something badly enough.

Five months into his first year in the Senate, Ellsworth Air Force Base in South Dakota was slated to be closed by the Base Realignment and Closure Commission. Thune's fierce response surprised even an administration used to angry members of Congress with endangered military bases back home. Thune declared he would oppose the confirmation of President Bush's embattled nominee for ambassador to the United Nations, John R. Bolton. He refused to budge for three months, and his protest also held up Senate floor consideration of the fiscal 2006 defense authorization bill. Ultimately, the commission announced that Ellsworth would be removed from the base closing list.

The low point of Thune's first term was criticism from government waste watchdog groups and editorial pages around the country after he engineered a change in the 2005 surface transportation bill that made a South Dakota railroad company he once worked for as a lobbyist uniquely qualified for a federal loan. The criticism, plus a "Porker of the Month" award from the Washington-based Citizens Against Government Waste, resulted in the multimillion-dollar loan being withdrawn. Thune, who added the provision as a member of the Commerce, Science and Transportation Committee, complained the loan was brought down by mischaracterizations.

The son of a high school teacher and a librarian, Thune stresses support for the little towns and small businesses that dot South Dakota.

He grew up in the small town of Murdo, about 40 miles south of the capital city of Pierre. He was a star athlete in both high school and college, and his basketball prowess set him on his course to the Senate. The perpetually tan senator is still a fitness buff, and frequently can be spotted running on the national Mall in shorts and a T-shirt after the Senate's last vote of the day.

Impressed with Thune's performance in a basketball game during his freshman year in high school, South Dakota Rep. James Abdnor struck up a conversation with the young man and they stayed in touch over the years. After Thune completed graduate school, he moved to Washington to work for then Sen. Abdnor, specializing in tax and small-business issues. After Abdnor was defeated for re-election in 1986, Thune followed him to the Small Business Administration, where Abdnor served as administrator.

In 1989, Thune served a few months as deputy staff director of the Senate Small Business Committee and then returned to South Dakota, where he was executive director of the state Republican Party and then state railroad director. In 1993, he was named executive director of the South Dakota Municipal League, an association of local governments.

Thune considered passing up the run that landed him in the Senate, after a painful, and very close, loss in 2002 to Democratic Sen. Tim Johnson.

"It hurt for a while," Thune told the Argus Leader in Sioux Falls, of his 524-vote defeat. "But then I got up and got going again."

Ironically, it was Johnson who first gave Thune the opportunity to run for Congress, when he left South Dakota's lone House seat in 1996 to mount a successful challenge to Republican Sen. Larry Pressler.

Thune made a bid for the House seat, winning the primary over Lt. Gov. Carole Hillard to get the GOP nod. In November, Thune handily defeated Rick Weiland, a longtime Daschle aide, by 21 percentage points and was re-elected by impressive margins in 1998 and 2000. Eight years after trouncing his aide, Thune eked out a victory over Daschle, by more than 1 percentage point.

Despite an awkward period after the election, he and Johnson said they would work together. "We are here to get things done for South Dakota, and sharing that cause actually gives us a great deal in common," Thune said.

KEY VOTES

2006

- Yes Confirm Samuel A. Alito Jr. to the Supreme Court
- No Allow consideration of a bill to establish a $140 billion trust fund to compensate victims of asbestos exposure
- Yes Extend tax cuts for two years at a cost of $70 billion over five years
- No Overhaul immigration policy with border security, enforcement and guest worker program
- Yes Allow consideration of a bill to permanently repeal the estate tax
- No Urge President Bush to begin troop withdrawals from Iraq in 2006
- No Lift President Bush's restrictions on stem cell research funding
- Yes Authorize military tribunals for suspected terrorists

2005

- Yes Curb class action lawsuits by shifting them from state to federal courts
- Yes Allow confirmation vote on Priscilla R. Owen to the U.S. Court of Appeals for the 5th Circuit
- Yes Oppose mandatory emissions limits and block recognition of global warming as a threat
- No Approve free-trade pact with five Central American countries
- Yes Pass energy policy overhaul favored by President Bush emphasizing domestic oil and gas production
- Yes Shield gunmakers from lawsuits when their products are used in crimes
- Yes Ban torture of prisoners in U.S. custody
- Yes Renew 16 provisions of the Patriot Act
- Yes Allow final vote on opening the Arctic National Wildlife Refuge to oil and gas exploration

CQ VOTE STUDIES

	PARTY UNITY		PRESIDENTIAL SUPPORT	
	Support	Oppose	Support	Oppose
2006	95%	5%	87%	13%
2005	87%	13%	86%	14%
House Service:				
2002	83%	17%	82%	18%
2001	92%	8%	81%	19%
2000	91%	9%	29%	71%
1999	91%	9%	22%	78%
1998	95%	5%	23%	77%
1997	95%	5%	27%	73%

INTEREST GROUPS

	AFL-CIO	ADA	CCUS	ACU
2006	20%	0%	92%	100%
2005	21%	10%	93%	92%
House Service:				
2002	13%	10%	90%	88%
2001	33%	10%	91%	80%
2000	10%	5%	85%	76%
1999	11%	10%	92%	80%
1998	0%	5%	100%	92%
1997	13%	5%	90%	88%

Rep. Stephanie Herseth-Sandlin (D)

Elected June 2004; 2nd full term

CAPITOL OFFICE
225-2801
stephanie.herseth@mail.house.gov
hersethsandlin.house.gov
331 Cannon 20515-4101; fax 225-5823

COMMITTEES
Agriculture
Natural Resources
Select Energy Independence & Global Warming
Veterans' Affairs
(Economic Opportunity - chairwoman)

RESIDENCE
Brookings

BORN
Dec. 3, 1970, Aberdeen, S.D.

RELIGION
Lutheran

FAMILY
Husband, Max Sandlin

EDUCATION
Georgetown U., B.A. 1993 (government), M.A. 1996 (government), J.D. 1996

CAREER
Farm union official; lawyer; professor

POLITICAL HIGHLIGHTS
Democratic nominee for U.S. House, 2002

ELECTION RESULTS

2006 GENERAL		
Stephanie Herseth-Sandlin (D)	230,468	69.1%
Bruce W. Whalen (R)	97,864	29.3%
Larry Rudebusch (LIBERT)	5,230	1.6%
2006 PRIMARY		
Stephanie Herseth-Sandlin (D)		unopposed
2004 GENERAL		
Stephanie Herseth-Sandlin (D)	207,837	53.4%
Larry Diedrich (R)	178,823	45.9%

PREVIOUS WINNING PERCENTAGES
2004 Special Election (51%)

Still in her 30s, Herseth-Sandlin has had a promising start in Congress. In 2006, Esquire magazine called her "South Dakota's golden girl."

Her easy 2006 re-election with almost 70 percent of the vote and Democratic Sen. Tim Johnson's subsequent brain surgery and long recovery prompted speculation about her future. She would be on the shortlist of Democratic candidates for a Senate race.

Herseth-Sandlin is one of just two women in the House to represent an entire state; Republican Barbara Cubin of Wyoming is the other. She already has most of the responsibility — though not the power — of a senator. The small size of South Dakota's delegation and the conservative leanings of the state make her less partisan than other Democrats. "Herseth is not a rabid partisan," the Aberdeen American News said in an editorial endorsing her 2006 re-election. "This is incredibly important as South Dakota's lone voice in the House."

Herseth-Sandlin's special-election win in 2004 was the only bright moment for South Dakota Democrats in a year that saw the dramatic upset of her home-state colleague — Senate Minority Leader Tom Daschle.

House Democratic leaders helped Herseth-Sandlin gain a secure grip on the seat with some key committee assignments for the rest of the 108th Congress (2003-04). Then-Minority Leader Nancy Pelosi of California arranged for Democratic Rep. Mike Thompson of California to resign from the Agriculture Committee to open a seat for Herseth-Sandlin. She also was given an assignment to what is now called the Natural Resources Committee, which handles American Indian affairs, and a post on the Veterans' Affairs Committee. Both panels are good fits for issues and constituencies in her state.

On the Agriculture panel, she is an advocate for alternative energy. In 2006, she introduced legislation to double the share of renewable fuels sold in the United States, expand the number of vehicles that run on ethanol and provide incentives for the development of biofuel plants. At the start of the 110th Congress (2007-08), she was hoping to get the bill included in a major rewrite of federal farm policy that was getting under way.

Herseth-Sandlin says growing up on a South Dakota farm gave her a unique perspective that convinced her that "rural" means more than agriculture. It also means energy, housing, health care policy and economic development.

Like many rural Democrats, Herseth-Sandlin is a member of the Blue Dog Coalition, a group of more than 40 conservative House Democrats. She was one of 36 Democrats to support a stringent border security and immigration enforcement bill in 2005. She also split with a majority of her party to support the GOP-crafted energy policy overhaul that year. And in 2006, Herseth-Sandlin was one of just 18 Democrats voting to authorize warrantless electronic surveillance of terrorism suspects. She backs a proposed constitutional amendment to ban same-sex marriage, but supports abortion rights and embryonic stem cell research.

Herseth-Sandlin's political roots in the state run deep. Her grandfather, Ralph E. Herseth, was the Democratic governor from 1959 to 1961. Her grandmother, Lorna B. Herseth, was South Dakota secretary of state from 1973 to 1979. And her father, Lars Herseth, spent 20 years in the legislature and was the unsuccessful gubernatorial nominee in 1986. After that campaign, her parents divorced.

Herseth-Sandlin grew up on her family's farm and ranch near Houghton, in the northeast part of the state. She graduated summa cum laude from Georgetown University in Washington, D.C., with a bachelor's degree in government. She went on to get her law degree from Georgetown as well.

After law school, Herseth-Sandlin worked on energy and telecommunications issues for the South Dakota Public Utilities Commission in Pierre, organizing meetings with tribal leaders on utility regulation. She was also executive director of the South Dakota Farmers Union Foundation.

Herseth-Sandlin first ran for the U.S. House in 2002, but lost in a contest for the seat vacated by Republican John Thune, who was running for the Senate. She received 46 percent of the vote but was defeated by Republican Gov. Bill Janklow. But Janklow's career was effectively ended when he killed a motorcyclist with his car in August 2003 after running a stop sign at high speed. Convicted of second-degree manslaughter, Janklow resigned in January 2004.

In the June special election, Herseth-Sandlin won with 51 percent of the vote over former Republican state Sen. Larry Diedrich, a victory of just 3,005 votes out of some 262,000 cast. She made note of the unusual circumstances in a speech on the House floor two days later: "My standing here was born from tragedy," she said. "But from great sorrows come new beginnings."

She used her first five months in the House to cement her standing back home. In the general race that November, Herseth-Sandlin, then 33, won her first full term by a margin of more than 7 percentage points.

Herseth-Sandlin is the first woman from South Dakota to win a general election to Congress, though two Republican women briefly served in the Senate — Gladys Pyle, who came to Washington for two months after winning a special election in 1938, and Vera C. Bushfield, who was appointed in 1948 to complete the term of her husband when he died in office.

Herseth-Sandlin's 2004 general election was aided by the focus on the nationally watched Senate race, in which Daschle ultimately was toppled by Thune. National Republican organizations and GOP-leaning independent groups poured money into the Senate race, but the House contest was largely unimpeded by national political forces. Herseth-Sandlin's moderate voting record and roots in the state helped her to beat Diedrich, who was back for a rematch.

At her 36th birthday party in December 2006, Herseth-Sandlin announced her engagement to former Rep. Max Sandlin, a Texas Democrat 18 years her senior whom she met during her failed 2002 campaign against Janklow. They married in March 2007.

KEY VOTES

2006

Yes Stop broadband companies from favoring select Internet traffic

Yes Affirm U.S. commitment to war in Iraq and reject setting a withdrawal date for troops

No Repeal requirement for bilingual ballots at the polls

Yes Permit U.S. sale of civilian nuclear technology to India

Yes Build a 700-mile fence on the U.S.-Mexico border to curb illegal crossings

Yes Permit warrantless wiretaps of suspected terrorists

2005

Yes Intervene in the life-support case of Terri Schiavo

Yes Lift President Bush's restrictions on stem cell research funding

Yes Prohibit FBI access to library and bookstore records

No Approve free-trade pact with five Central American countries

Yes Pass energy policy overhaul favored by President Bush emphasizing domestic oil and gas production

Yes End mandatory preservation of habitat of endangered animal and plant species

Yes Ban torture of prisoners in U.S. custody

CQ VOTE STUDIES

	PARTY UNITY		PRESIDENTIAL SUPPORT	
	Support	Oppose	Support	Oppose
2006	76%	24%	50%	50%
2005	79%	21%	39%	61%
2004	76%	24%	45%	55%

INTEREST GROUPS

	AFL-CIO	ADA	CCUS	ACU
2006	86%	65%	80%	60%
2005	87%	85%	63%	33%
2004	63%	55%	50%	31%

SOUTH DAKOTA

At large

South Dakota's agriculture-based economy has largely recovered from low crop prices a decade ago, with farmers in the eastern part of the state now selling corn for new ethanol plants.

Uncertainty in the agriculture industry has contributed to a steady migration into the state's cities, where finance, computers and health care have gradually become primary industries. Corporations such as Citibank and Wells Fargo have set up some operations here in order to take advantage of lower taxes and wages. In the west, away from the most populated areas, the arid, hilly portion of the state relies on ranching, mining and tourism. The Badlands, along with Mount Rushmore and other Black Hills attractions, are here.

South Dakota has one of the nation's highest percentages of American Indians, at just more than 8 percent of the population. All nine of the state's Indian reservations grew in population over the decade, and eight of the nine operate casinos. While gaming has been an economic bright spot, it has failed to eliminate the poverty conditions on reservations.

Shannon County, home to the Pine Ridge Indian Reservation, is one of the nation's poorest counties.

The Missouri River, which splits the state, sometimes is considered a political divide as well — western ranching Republicans edge out eastern urban and farming Democrats at the polls. Overall, a 10-point voter registration advantage to the GOP helped George W. Bush take 60 percent of the state's 2004 presidential vote. Although South Dakotans often vote Republican at the local level, they will support Democrats in some federal races: Democrats have won elections to Congress, but the state has not supported a Democratic presidential candidate since 1964.

MAJOR INDUSTRY

Agriculture, finance, tourism

MILITARY BASES

Ellsworth Air Force Base, 3,664 military, 1,011 civilian (2006)

CITIES

Sioux Falls, 123,975; Rapid City, 59,607; Aberdeen, 24,658

NOTABLE

More than 200 Sioux were massacred in one day at Wounded Knee in 1890; The largest and most complete fossil of a Tyrannosaurus Rex ever found was uncovered near Faith in 1990.

TENNESSEE

Gov. Phil Bredesen (D)

Pronounced: BREAD-eh-sen
First elected: 2002
Length of term: 4 years
Term expires: 1/11
Salary: $155,000
Phone: (615) 741-2001

Residence: Nashville
Born: Nov. 21, 1943; Oceanport, N.J.
Religion: Presbyterian
Family: Wife, Andrea Conte; one child
Education: Harvard U., S.B. 1967 (physics)
Career: Health insurance company founder; health care executive; computer programmer
Political highlights: Candidate for Mass. Senate, 1970; candidate for mayor of Nashville, 1987; sought Democratic nomination for U.S. House, 1987; mayor of Nashville, 1991-99

Election results:

2006 GENERAL		
Phil Bredesen (D)	1,247,491	68.6%
Jim Bryson (R)	540,853	29.7%

Lt. Gov. Ronald L. Ramsey (R)

First elected: 2007*
Length of term: 2 years
Term expires: 1/09
Salary: $54,369
Phone: (615) 741-2368
*Elected by the Senate

LEGISLATURE

General Assembly: 90 days over 2 years starting in January

Senate: 33 members, 4-year terms
2007 ratios: 16 R, 16 D, 1 I; 26 men, 7 women
Salary: $18,123
Phone: (615) 741-2730

House: 99 members, 2-year terms
2007 ratios: 53 D, 46 R; 85 men, 14 women
Salary: $18,123
Phone: (615) 741-2901

TERM LIMITS

Governor: 2 terms
Senate: No
House: No

URBAN STATISTICS

CITY	POPULATION
Memphis	650,100
Nashville-Davidson	569,891
Knoxville	173,890
Chattanooga	155,554
Clarksville	103,455

REGISTERED VOTERS

Voters do not register by party.

POPULATION

2006 population (est.)	6,038,803
2000 population	5,689,283
1990 population	4,877,185
Percent change (1990-2000)	+16.7%
Rank among states (2006)	16
Median age	35.9
Born in state	64.7%
Foreign born	2.8%
Violent crime rate	707/100,000
Poverty level	13.5%
Federal workers	50,140
Military	25,585

ELECTIONS

STATE ELECTION OFFICIAL
(615) 741-7956
DEMOCRATIC PARTY
(615) 327-9779
REPUBLICAN PARTY
(615) 269-4260

MISCELLANEOUS

Web: www.state.tn.us
Capital: Nashville

U.S. CONGRESS

Senate: 2 Republicans
House: 5 Democrats, 4 Republicans

2000 Census Statistics by District

	2004 VOTE FOR PRESIDENT														
DIST.	BUSH	KERRY	WHITE	BLACK	ASIAN	HISP	MEDIAN INCOME	WHITE COLLAR	BLUE COLLAR	SERVICE INDUSTRY	OVER 64	UNDER 18	COLLEGE EDUCATION	RURAL	SQ. MILES
1	68%	32%	95%	2%	0%	1%	$31,228	50%	35%	15%	15%	22%	15%	45%	4,093
2	65	35	90	6	1	1	$36,796	60	26	14	13	23	23	29	2,427
3	61	38	85	11	1	2	$35,434	54	32	14	14	23	19	36	3,411
4	58	41	93	4	0	2	$31,645	45	42	13	14	24	11	68	10,038
5	47	52	68	23	2	4	$40,419	64	22	14	11	23	28	11	894
6	60	40	89	6	1	3	$39,721	53	35	12	11	25	16	47	5,480
7	68	32	83	11	1	2	$50,090	64	24	12	10	27	29	39	6,292
8	53	46	74	22	0	2	$33,001	48	38	15	13	26	13	53	8,262
9	29	70	35	59	2	3	$33,806	60	24	15	11	27	22	0	321
STATE	57	43	79	16	1	2	$36,360	56	31	14	12	25	20	36	41,217
U.S.	50.7	48.3	69	12	4	13	$41,994	60	25	15	12	26	24	21	3,537,438

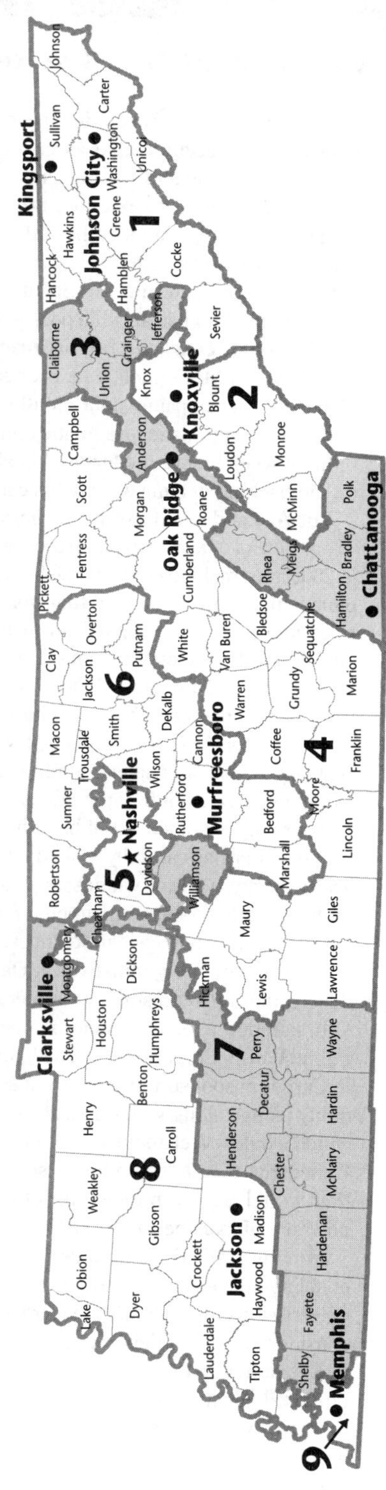
Kingsport
Johnson City
Knoxville
Oak Ridge
Chattanooga
Nashville
Murfreesboro
Clarksville
Jackson
Memphis
1
2
3
4
5
6
7
8
9
Johnson
Carter
Sullivan
Washington
Unicoi
Hawkins
Greene
Hancock
Hamblen
Cocke
Claiborne
Grainger
Jefferson
Sevier
Union
Knox
Blount
Campbell
Anderson
Loudon
Monroe
Scott
Morgan
Roane
McMinn
Polk
Fentress
Cumberland
Rhea
Meigs
Bradley
Pickett
Hamilton
Overton
Bledsoe
Sequatchie
Clay
Putnam
White
Van Buren
Jackson
Marion
Grundy
Warren
DeKalb
Macon
Smith
Trousdale
Cannon
Coffee
Franklin
Wilson
Sumner
Rutherford
Bedford
Moore
Robertson
Davidson
Lincoln
Marshall
Williamson
Cheatham
Maury
Giles
Montgomery
Dickson
Hickman
Lewis
Lawrence
Stewart
Houston
Humphreys
Perry
Wayne
Benton
Decatur
Hardin
Henry
Carroll
Henderson
Chester
McNairy
Weakley
Gibson
Madison
Hardeman
Obion
Crockett
Haywood
Fayette
Lake
Dyer
Lauderdale
Tipton
Shelby

Sen. Lamar Alexander (R)

CAPITOL OFFICE
224-4944
alexander.senate.gov
455 Dirksen 20510-4204; fax 228-3398

COMMITTEES
Appropriations
Environment & Public Works
Health, Education, Labor & Pensions
Rules & Administration

RESIDENCE
Walland

BORN
July 3, 1940, Maryville, Tenn.

RELIGION
Presbyterian

FAMILY
Wife, Honey Alexander; four children

EDUCATION
Vanderbilt U., B.A. 1962 (Latin American history); New York U., J.D. 1965

CAREER
Education consulting firm chairman; lobbyist; university president; White House aide; congressional aide; lawyer

POLITICAL HIGHLIGHTS
Republican nominee for governor, 1974; governor, 1979-87; Education secretary, 1991-93; sought Republican nomination for president, 1996, 2000

ELECTION RESULTS

2002 GENERAL		
Lamar Alexander (R)	891,420	54.3%
Bob Clement (D)	728,295	44.3%
2002 PRIMARY		
Lamar Alexander (R)	295,052	53.8%
Ed Bryant (R)	233,678	42.6%
Mary Taylor Shelby (R)	5,589	1.0%

Elected 2002; 1st term

In his first term, Alexander has adeptly applied the experience and knowledge he accumulated as governor of Tennessee and as a former secretary of education to the policy-making arena of Capitol Hill. Yet despite his impressive résumé, he had as much difficulty cracking the Senate leadership ranks as he did sparking voters' interest during two campaigns for president.

Shortly after entering the Senate in 2003, Alexander made clear his desire for the Republican whip post — the No. 2 leadership position — once his Tennessee colleague Bill Frist retired and the incumbent whip, Kentucky's Mitch McConnell, took over as GOP leader in the 110th Congress (2007-08). He campaigned for months, presenting himself to fellow Republicans as an optimistic, pragmatic conservative who could work well with them. A week before the leadership elections, he announced he had lined up the backing of a majority of his caucus.

But Alexander did not count on a strong last-minute challenge from Trent Lott of Mississippi, a former whip who resigned as majority leader in 2002 after making controversial statements in support of then South Carolina Sen. Strom Thurmond that were characterized as racist. Lott, a practiced and aggressively partisan deal-maker, jumped into the whip race after Republicans lost the Senate majority. Lott pulled off a stunning one-vote victory in November 2006. "I learned that senators, like most Americans, like a good comeback," a chastened Alexander said.

As a consolation prize of sorts, McConnell named Alexander to a coveted seat on the Appropriations Committee. The assignment enables him to have a direct say over funding the education, energy and environmental issues on which he spends most of his time.

Alexander has carefully looked after the interests of the Tennessee Valley Authority, a power wholesaler, and his state's Oak Ridge National Laboratory, while pushing an agenda that would greatly boost the amount of money spent on physical sciences. He has tried to build support for advanced computing initiatives at Oak Ridge, which has been involved in developing high-end supercomputers.

In addition to Appropriations, Alexander sits on the Environment and Public Works Committee. In 2006, he joined Delaware Democrat Thomas R. Carper in sponsoring a bill to cut carbon dioxide emissions from electric utility plants, along with other gases. Alexander portrayed the legislation, which would affect about 40 percent of the carbon dioxide produced in the United States, as a "common-sense next step" alternative to other initiatives that would have a bigger impact on the economy. The measure went nowhere, in part because of a lack of industry consensus.

In early 2007, the lawmakers split over how to structure a system for enabling utilities to buy and sell pollution allowances to meet an overall cap on emissions. Alexander's measure is one of several that Senate leaders are considering as they develop their climate agenda for the 110th Congress.

Alexander, who served two terms as Tennessee's governor, has emerged as one of the most ardent advocates for state and local governments in Washington, working to protect their interests on issues from immigration to Internet taxation. He backed a provision in the fiscal 2006 budget resolution designed to make it tougher for Congress to pass the cost of new federal programs down to states or localities.

But education remains Alexander's main area of expertise. It is unusual for two senators from the same state and party to serve on the same committee, but Alexander received special permission upon arriving in Congress to join Frist on the Health, Education, Labor and Pensions Committee.

Alexander, whose education credentials also include a stint as president of the University of Tennessee, set out to improve the teaching of history and civics in schools. In the 108th Congress (2003-04), he pushed into law a measure to create summer academies for outstanding teachers and students to teach and learn about those subjects.

In March 2007, Alexander reintroduced a bipartisan bill aimed at maintaining U.S. leadership in science and technology. The measure was in response to a National Academies report that warned of a decline in U.S. competitiveness. He said the bill would strengthen students' educational opportunities in science and math fields, and called it "the most important piece of legislation in this session for our country's future."

Alexander also has focused on strengthening Head Start, an education and nutrition program that provides services to almost 1 million children annually. He has called for the creation of 200 centers of excellence and governors' councils to identify good teaching practices.

Alexander generally concentrates on legislation that can attract Democratic support, noting that Senate rules all but demand consensus. He went a step further in 2007, reaching across the aisle by forming an ad hoc bipartisan breakfast group with Connecticut independent Joseph I. Lieberman. The group averages a couple dozen senators at its weekly gatherings.

A seventh-generation Tennessean, Alexander was born and raised in the state's mountainous east. He worked his way through Vanderbilt University, where, as a student newspaper editor, he led a campaign to desegregate the school. After graduating with a degree in Latin American history, he earned a law degree at New York University.

His first run for office, at age 34, was an unsuccessful 1974 bid for governor against Democrat Roy Blanton. Four years later, with the help and advice of his mentor and friend, Senate GOP leader Howard H. Baker Jr. of Tennessee, Alexander ran again. This time, he gained national attention by traversing the state on foot — he is a lifelong hiker — in what would become his trademark red-and-black plaid shirt. The voters loved it, electing him with 56 percent of the vote over financier Jake Butcher, whom the Democrats nominated when the scandal-scarred Blanton stepped aside.

During eight years as governor, Alexander built a reputation as a pragmatist who lured businesses to Tennessee and pushed a major education package through a Democratically controlled General Assembly. He then spent more than three years as the chief executive of Tennessee's state university system. He joined President George H.W. Bush's Cabinet in 1991, serving as secretary of Education for two years.

Alexander geared up for the 1996 presidential election, but his campaign foundered when he had a hard time coming up with memorable campaign themes. He dropped out soon after finishing third behind Bob Dole and Patrick J. Buchanan in the New Hampshire primary. He set his sights on the 2000 nomination but stopped campaigning in the summer of 1999, when George W. Bush had become the clear front-runner.

Two years later, when Fred Thompson announced he was retiring after eight years in the Senate, Republicans looked to Alexander to take his place. The Democrats nominated then Rep. Bob Clement, a Nashville-area lawmaker since 1998. With both national parties pumping money into the race, it turned ugly; the candidates dredged up decades-old allegations about each other's business dealings and political history. But Alexander won by 10 percentage points. Alexander remains popular in Tennessee and may have less trouble winning re-election in 2008.

KEY VOTES

2006

Yes Confirm Samuel A. Alito Jr. to the Supreme Court
Yes Allow consideration of a bill to establish a $140 billion trust fund to compensate victims of asbestos exposure
Yes Extend tax cuts for two years at a cost of $70 billion over five years
No Overhaul immigration policy with border security, enforcement and guest worker program
Yes Allow consideration of a bill to permanently repeal the estate tax
No Urge President Bush to begin troop withdrawals from Iraq in 2006
Yes Lift President Bush's restrictions on stem cell research funding
Yes Authorize military tribunals for suspected terrorists

2005

Yes Curb class action lawsuits by shifting them from state to federal courts
Yes Allow confirmation vote on Priscilla R. Owen to the U.S. Court of Appeals for the 5th Circuit
No Oppose mandatory emissions limits and block recognition of global warming as a threat
Yes Approve free-trade pact with five Central American countries
Yes Pass energy policy overhaul favored by President Bush emphasizing domestic oil and gas production
Yes Shield gunmakers from lawsuits when their products are used in crimes
Yes Ban torture of prisoners in U.S. custody
Yes Renew 16 provisions of the Patriot Act
Yes Allow final vote on opening the Arctic National Wildlife Refuge to oil and gas exploration

CQ VOTE STUDIES

	PARTY UNITY		PRESIDENTIAL SUPPORT	
	Support	Oppose	Support	Oppose
2006	94%	6%	93%	7%
2005	92%	8%	88%	12%
2004	95%	5%	98%	2%
2003	98%	2%	98%	2%

INTEREST GROUPS

	AFL-CIO	ADA	CCUS	ACU
2006	20%	5%	92%	72%
2005	21%	5%	100%	88%
2004	0%	15%	94%	92%
2003	0%	10%	100%	85%

Sen. Bob Corker (R)

CAPITOL OFFICE
224-3344
corker.senate.gov
185 Dirksen 20510-4205; fax 228-0566

COMMITTEES
Energy & Natural Resources
Foreign Relations
Small Business & Entrepreneurship
Special Aging

RESIDENCE
Chattanooga

BORN
Aug. 24, 1952, Orangeburg, S.C.

RELIGION
Protestant

FAMILY
Wife, Elizabeth Corker; two children

EDUCATION
U. of Tennessee, B.S. 1974 (industrial management)

CAREER
Commercial real estate developer; construction company owner

POLITICAL HIGHLIGHTS
Sought Republican nomination for U.S. Senate, 1994; Tenn. Finance and Administration Department commissioner, 1995-96; mayor of Chattanooga, 2001-05

ELECTION RESULTS

2006 GENERAL		
Bob Corker (R)	929,911	50.7%
Harold E. Ford Jr. (D)	879,976	48.0%
2006 PRIMARY		
Bob Corker (R)	231,541	48.1%
Ed Bryant (R)	161,189	33.5%
Van Hilleary (R)	83,078	17.3%
Tate Harrison (R)	5,309	1.1%

Elected 2006; 1st term

Corker was an incurable workaholic even before he began his climb from construction worker to wealthy real estate developer to U.S. senator. He got his first job, picking up trash, as a 13-year-old and has been working at one thing or another ever since.

When he served as Tennessee's commissioner of finance in the mid-1990s, he sometimes went to work at 4 a.m. He worked such long hours that his wife, Elizabeth, would bring their two young daughters and the family dog to visit him at the state Capitol, where they would rollerblade and chase each other around the first floor of the building.

In 2006, Corker worked his way from underdog to top dog in a Senate race that gave Republicans their only new senator in the 110th Congress (2007-08). He bested three other Republicans to win the nomination, then defeated Democratic Rep. Harold E. Ford Jr. to capture the seat vacated by Majority Leader Bill Frist, who retired. Corker had lost to Frist in the 1994 Senate Republican primary, the only defeat of his career.

Corker is at least as conservative as Frist, whether on fiscal policy, the war in Iraq or social issues. While Frist, a former heart surgeon, reversed his initial stand against medical research on stem cells extracted from surplus embryos from in vitro fertilization clinics, Corker in 2007 voted against legislation to lift restrictions on federal funding of such research. Frist had voted for a similar bill in 2006. Corker's opposition left Senate supporters of the bill one vote short of the two-thirds majority that would be needed to override a presidential veto.

The Tennessean acknowledges that his constituents, like other Americans, are frustrated by the war in Iraq. But he said he was willing to give President Bush's 2007 troop increase a chance to work. In characteristic, hands-on fashion, he made a trip to the war zone in February, to observe the situation for himself. He met with U.S. generals and troops, and with Iraqi officials as well. When he came back, he refused to support any of the resolutions about the war, Democratic or Republican, that were popping up on the Senate floor. "To me all of this, from Day One, has been about political posturing and not about dealing with the realities of the war," he told an MSNBC interviewer. "The way we deal with the war is either fund it or not fund it."

Senate Democratic leaders did not address the issue in quite that way. They put forth a bill that provided billions of dollars for the war but required Bush to begin withdrawing U.S. combat forces within 120 days, with a goal of completing the pullout by March 31, 2008. Corker voted no.

After losing control of the Senate, GOP leaders didn't have many plums available to award Corker in the 110th. But they gave him a seat on the Energy and Natural Resources panel, where he intends to promote the development of alternative energy sources such as ethanol and biodiesel. He previously worked on the issue as mayor of Chattanooga, where a building in the city's downtown now runs on hydrogen fuel cell technology.

Corker was born in Orangeburg, S.C., but his family moved to Chattanooga when he was 11. His father, a DuPont engineer, was transferred there. Corker adjusted quickly and was president of his senior class in high school. He worked a variety of jobs as a teenager, earned a college degree in industrial management, then took a job as a construction superintendent. He loved being outdoors and working with his hands. College friends with coat-and-tie jobs were shocked when they would visit him on a job site. "I might not have shaved. I was drinking day-old coffee. I had mud all over me." His friends could not understand why a college graduate would relish such work. But he not only relished the work, he thrived on it.

After four years, he started his own construction company with a pickup truck and $8,000 he had saved. By the time he sold the company in 1990, it was operating in 18 states, with projects ranging from strip malls to apartments. He also owned Corker Group, a successful real estate development company, which he sold in 2006, retaining just two properties.

Corker's views on public policy were shaped by his work experience and his religion. In business, he decided, a light hand from government was best when it came to taxes and regulation. A church mission to Haiti in the 1980s opened his eyes to poverty and led him to public service. He began working weekends back home to revitalize inner city neighborhoods, and then started a nonprofit organization that he proudly says has helped more than 10,000 families secure affordable housing.

Corker initially planned to run for governor in 1994 but deferred to GOP Rep. Don Sundquist, who won the election. After Corker lost to Frist in the Senate primary, Sundquist made him state finance commissioner.

During his 1995-96 stint as finance commissioner, Corker spent about 80 percent of his time on health care issues, developing expertise that he is likely to build on in the Senate. It is a topic of considerable concern to small businesses, and the freshman Republican was given a seat on the Small Business and Entrepreneurship Committee.

Elected mayor of Chattanooga in 2001, Corker launched a successful $120 million effort to transform the city's waterfront with a new park, a Riverwalk, museum expansions and other features. He was, as usual, a hands-on executive. "I loved being mayor more than anything I've ever been in my life," he recalled in a March 2007 interview. "You could create a bold vision and just make it happen."

Three years into his mayoral service, he was invited to join Frist and the senator's two young sons on their annual hike. Along the way, the GOP leader convinced Corker he should consider running for the Senate, as Frist was retiring after his second term.

Corker entered the primary as something of an underdog, up against two former GOP congressmen — Van Hilleary and Ed Bryant. They painted him as a moderate who had been inconsistent on abortion, which they strongly opposed. But Corker poured his own money into the race, and his branding as the only "non-career politician" in the field helped him. In the three-way contest, Corker won handily.

Ford was waiting. Democrats had cleared a path for the five-term Memphis congressman, a centrist who was seeking to become the first popularly elected African-American senator from the South. Corker emphasized his faith and his conservative values and made a pitch for votes from ordinary Tennesseans, including Democrats, by talking about his days "pouring concrete" as a construction laborer.

The race turned nasty with a late October television ad by the Republican National Committee satirizing Ford's supposed attendance at a Super Bowl party sponsored by Playboy. The ad closed with a white woman winking and saying, "Harold, call me." Democrats and civil rights groups erupted in anger, calling the ad racist. Corker's campaign denounced the ad as "over the top, tacky and . . . not reflective of the kind of campaign we are running." They asked the RNC to yank the commercial, but had no authority to do anything.

The election contest went down to the wire, with late polls often in conflict about who was ahead and by how much. When the votes were counted, Corker had won by just less than 3 percentage points. The first bill Corker introduced in the Senate was a measure that would, among other things, give the candidate control over campaign ads in his behalf.

Rep. David Davis (R)

Elected 2006; 1st term

A respiratory therapist and owner of two health care businesses, Davis says his career in the medical field gives him a unique understanding of the health care issues facing the country.

One way the country can pare back health care costs is by expanding home and community-based care, he says, adding that "with the graying of America," health costs are an issue that will affect everyone. Davis gained a seat on the Small Business Committee, where the experience of running his own companies should come in handy.

A conservative Republican from a conservative district, Davis should be a solid vote for his party. He opposes abortion and same-sex marriage. He said he decided to run for Congress because of his "strong faith and belief in God. . . . I felt like our country was drifting away from the country I grew up in." He voted no on five of the six bills on the Democrats' "first 100 hours" legislative agenda. Davis' lone yes came on a bill to reduce federal interest rates for college students whose families qualify for subsidized loans.

Davis also sits on the Homeland Security Committee, and stands by his party's president on the Iraq War. In March 2007, he voted against a $124 billion supplemental spending bill for the war that included language outlining a plan to remove all but a vestige of the current U.S. troops in Iraq. "This legislation had many harmful components," Davis said in a statement. "It includes a timeline for withdrawal of our men and women in uniform. We do not need to have a timeline handed to the terrorists. The terrorists are watching. They will wait us out and prevail."

Davis was assured of a seat in the House once he won the GOP primary, as 1st District voters have sent a Republican to Congress since 1880. But Davis' path to Washington was far from smooth in running to replace retiring five-term GOP Rep. Bill Jenkins. He won his party's nomination with a meager 22 percent of the vote, emerging from a crowded field of 13 candidates just about 600 votes ahead of his second-place competitor. Davis went on to win easily in the general election over Democrat Rick Trent, a Morristown city councilman, taking 61 percent of the vote.

CAPITOL OFFICE
225-6356
daviddavis.house.gov
514 Cannon 20515-4201; fax 225-5714

COMMITTEES
Education & Labor
Homeland Security
Small Business

RESIDENCE
Johnson City

BORN
Nov. 6, 1959, Johnson City, Tenn.

RELIGION
Baptist

FAMILY
Wife, Joyce Davis, two children

EDUCATION
California College for Health Sciences, A.S. 1983 (respiratory therapy); Milligan College, B.S. 1991 (organizational management)

CAREER
Oxygen therapy clinic owner; medical equipment company owner; respiratory therapist

POLITICAL HIGHLIGHTS
Unicoi County Republican Party chairman, 1995-96; sought Republican nomination for U.S. House, 1996; Tenn. House, 1999-2006

ELECTION RESULTS

2006 GENERAL		
David Davis (R)	108,336	61.1%
Rick Trent (D)	65,538	37.0%
2006 PRIMARY		
David Davis (R)	16,583	22.2%
Richard S. Venable (R)	16,010	21.4%
Richard H. Roberts (R)	13,580	18.2%
Phil Roe (R)	12,864	17.2%
Larry Waters (R)	7,885	10.5%
Vance W. Cheek (R)	3,334	4.5%
Peggy Parker Barnett (R)	1,709	2.3%
Dan Smith (R)	1,087	1.5%
Bill F. Breeding (R)	818	1.1%

TENNESSEE 1

Northeast — Tri-Cities, Morristown

Rolling hills and mountains cover the 1st, which combines a manufacturing sector to the east with smaller agricultural and tourism centers to the west and south.

Near Virginia, the Tri-Cities of Kingsport, Johnson City and Bristol anchor the district's economy. They focus their energies on drug manufacturing, chemicals and auto parts. East Tennessee State University in Johnson City is a major employer and a medical hub for much of this part of Appalachia. In the 1st's northwest, Hancock and Hawkins are severely impoverished. Farmers in Cocke, Sevier and Greene counties raise livestock, tobacco and fruits, providing one of the only sources of economic stability here.

Hamblen County offers outdoor recreation, and Morristown, which is known for its Civil War heritage, also has popular watersports sites. Farther south, tourists take in the Great Smoky Mountains National Park and the excursion circuit of outlet shopping malls and neon-lit amusement parks. Gatlinburg's Star Cars Museum houses famous cars from movies, and Dolly Parton's theme park Dollywood in Pigeon Forge brings in millions of dollars each year.

East Tennessee's strong Republican lean dates to the Civil War. Nine of George W. Bush's top 13 Tennessee counties in the 2004 presidential election were wholly or partly in the 1st, and he did not take less than 60 percent of the vote in any of the 1st's dozen counties.

MAJOR INDUSTRY
Tourism, health care, manufacturing, farming

CITIES
Johnson City, 55,469; Kingsport, 44,905; Morristown, 24,965; Bristol, 24,821

NOTABLE
Jonesborough, the state's oldest settlement, is home to the National Storytelling Festival.

Rep. John J. "Jimmy" Duncan Jr. (R)

CAPITOL OFFICE
225-5435
www.house.gov/duncan
2207 Rayburn 20515-4202; fax 225-6440

COMMITTEES
Natural Resources
Oversight & Government Reform
Transportation & Infrastructure

RESIDENCE
Knoxville

BORN
July 21, 1947, Lebanon, Tenn.

RELIGION
Presbyterian

FAMILY
Wife, Lynn Duncan; four children

EDUCATION
U. of Tennessee, B.S. 1969 (journalism);
George Washington U., J.D. 1973

MILITARY SERVICE
Tenn. National Guard and Army Reserve, 1970-87

CAREER
Judge; lawyer

POLITICAL HIGHLIGHTS
Knox County Criminal Court judge, 1981-88

ELECTION RESULTS

2006 GENERAL		
John J. "Jimmy" Duncan Jr. (R)	157,095	77.7%
John Greene (D)	45,025	22.3%
2006 PRIMARY		
John J. "Jimmy" Duncan Jr. (R)	55,295	87.4%
Ralph McGill (R)	7,994	12.6%
2004 GENERAL		
John J. "Jimmy" Duncan Jr. (R)	215,575	79.1%
John Greene (D)	52,155	19.1%
Charles E. Howard (X)	4,978	1.8%

PREVIOUS WINNING PERCENTAGES
2002 (79%); 2000 (89%); 1998 (89%); 1996 (71%); 1994 (90%); 1992 (72%); 1990 (81%); 1988 (56%); 1988 Special Election (56%)

Elected 1988; 10th full term

An unassuming, hard-working legislator who likes to concentrate on local issues, Duncan keeps getting crosswise with President Bush and the House Republican leadership — especially on the war in Iraq. He isn't about to follow anyone he thinks is headed in the wrong direction, but his independence has exacted a price.

At the start of the 110th Congress (2007-08), Duncan sought to become the top-ranking Republican on the Transportation and Infrastructure Committee. But GOP leaders reached below him and three others on the seniority ladder to anoint John L. Mica of Florida, a dependable party loyalist. In the 109th Congress (2005-06), Mica sided with Bush on 93 percent of the votes on which the president had staked out a position; Duncan, just 73 percent. Mica went along with his fellow Republicans on 98 percent of the votes pitting the two parties against each other, to Duncan's 91 percent.

It wasn't the first time Duncan's independence cost him a top committee post. He was among three senior members of the Resources Committee to be passed over for the chairmanship at the start of the 108th Congress (2003-04).

This time around, it probably didn't help that Duncan had publicly supported GOP Whip Roy Blunt of Missouri for the party's top leadership post in 2006 — only to see the prize go to John A. Boehner of Ohio. Whatever the cause, Duncan had to settle for a lesser plum, the top-ranking Republican slot on the big Highways and Transit Subcommittee.

Duncan emulates his father, John J. Duncan, who held the eastern Tennessee seat before him for more than 23 years, by tending to local concerns and eschewing the national spotlight. Still, the national spotlight has fallen on him more than once in recent years.

He was one of just six Republicans to vote in 2002 against authorizing Bush to go to war against Iraq and one of 17 in his party voting in 2007 to oppose the president's decision to send thousands more U.S. troops to the battlefront. Ron Paul of Texas is the only Republican still in the House who voted the same way on both occasions. In 2002, Duncan said he was not convinced that Iraqi leader Saddam Hussein was an imminent threat. A year later, angry that the administration was not pushing Iraq to pick up some of the reconstruction tab, Duncan was one of five GOP House members to vote against a war funding bill.

He is a conservative on fiscal policy and social issues. He says the first thing he asks his staff when they discuss a proposal is, "How much does it cost?" He often votes against appropriations bills he regards as bloated. He voted no on a catchall fiscal 2004 spending bill even though it included $10.8 million for projects and programs he sought for his district. And in 1997, he voted to abolish crop insurance subsidies for tobacco, even though it was the largest cash crop grown by East Tennessee farmers.

There's something else Duncan won't be spending money on, not his own nor the taxpayers': communications technology. He does not carry a cell phone or a BlackBerry, according to the Chattanooga Times Free Press. He told the newspaper he doesn't even know how to turn on a computer. "I am a low-tech person living in a high-tech world," he declared.

He served in the 109th Congress as chairman of the Transportation Subcommittee on Water Resources and Environment, which has jurisdiction over water quality, development of dams, ports, and the locally crucial Tennessee Valley Authority. But he was unable to win enactment of a huge water resources bill, which stalled in conference with the Senate. The committee's new Democratic leaders quickly pushed a revised version through the House in April 2007, adding $45 million in projects in Duncan's district that had not been in the previous measure.

Duncan earlier chaired the Aviation Subcommittee, where he helped write the aviation security law enacted two months after the Sept. 11 terrorist attacks. The measure required tighter screening at airports, better equipment to detect explosives and stronger cockpit doors.

Although Duncan voted for the North American Free Trade Agreement in 1993, he says he has become increasingly concerned about domestic job losses to overseas manufacturers. He was one of only 27 Republicans who voted against enacting the 2002 law giving the president fast-track authority to negotiate trade agreements that Congress cannot amend.

From his Natural Resources panel seat, Duncan contends that out-of-control conservationists "will absolutely destroy our standard of living. Unfortunately, we cannot turn our entire nation into a giant tourist attraction." In 2006, he voted to open Alaska's Arctic National Wildlife Refuge to oil drilling and to end a moratorium on most offshore oil and gas exploration.

Duncan also serves on the Oversight and Government Reform Committee, and in early 2007 he cheered committee approval and House passage of legislation requiring public disclosure of big-dollar donors to presidential libraries. He had been trying to win passage of similar legislation since the 106th Congress (1999-2000), inspired by what he considered questionable contributions to the library of President Bill Clinton.

The congressman occasionally wonders what his life would have been like if the senior Duncan had chosen another career. His father was part of a business group that brought minor league baseball to Knoxville in 1956; young Duncan spent five and a half happy seasons as the Smokies bat boy and was the public address announcer during his first year in college. Then his father switched to politics, and Jimmy Duncan followed in his footsteps.

The younger Duncan served seven years as a criminal court judge in Knox County, helping build a reputation to run for office in his own right when his father, in failing health, announced that the 100th Congress (1987-88) would be his last. (His father died in 1988, shortly after that announcement.)

In his first House race, Duncan campaigned primarily as his father's successor, even appearing on the ballot as John J. Duncan though he goes by Jimmy. He won 56 percent of the vote in both the special and general elections that year and has not been seriously challenged since.

KEY VOTES

2006

No Stop broadband companies from favoring select Internet traffic
No Affirm U.S. commitment to war in Iraq and reject setting a withdrawal date for troops
Yes Repeal requirement for bilingual ballots at the polls
Yes Permit U.S. sale of civilian nuclear technology to India
Yes Build a 700-mile fence on the U.S.-Mexico border to curb illegal crossings
Yes Permit warrantless wiretaps of suspected terrorists

2005

Yes Intervene in the life-support case of Terri Schiavo
No Lift President Bush's restrictions on stem cell research funding
Yes Prohibit FBI access to library and bookstore records
Yes Approve free-trade pact with five Central American countries
Yes Pass energy policy overhaul favored by President Bush emphasizing domestic oil and gas production
Yes End mandatory preservation of habitat of endangered animal and plant species
Yes Ban torture of prisoners in U.S. custody

CQ VOTE STUDIES

	PARTY UNITY		PRESIDENTIAL SUPPORT	
	Support	Oppose	Support	Oppose
2006	89%	11%	74%	26%
2005	93%	7%	72%	28%
2004	92%	8%	82%	18%
2003	89%	11%	76%	24%
2002	91%	9%	62%	38%

INTEREST GROUPS

	AFL-CIO	ADA	CCUS	ACU
2006	14%	10%	87%	88%
2005	20%	5%	81%	92%
2004	20%	5%	90%	88%
2003	13%	15%	83%	80%
2002	11%	5%	75%	92%

TENNESSEE 2

East – Knoxville

Nestled in the valley of the Great Smoky Mountains at the mouth of the Tennessee River, the 2nd envelopes Knoxville and stretches south and west to include several conservative, rural counties. The district's economy is almost solely determined by the success of Knoxville, while surrounding areas are full of small towns and forests, lakes and parks.

State and federal jobs in the district are abundant for residents despite their criticisms of big government year after year. Restaurants, hotels and other businesses in the district, however, depend on revenue from the influx of people who attend sporting events at the University of Tennessee, which is located in Knoxville. In fact, on football game days, the University's Neyland Stadium surpasses the state's fifth-largest city, holding more than 104,000 orange-and-white clad fans. The university's basketball arena and the Women's Basketball Hall of Fame also draw significant crowds.

Knoxville had struggled for years to revitalize its downtown, but state and private medical facilities have spurred recent economic growth. Rejuvenated areas of the city, such as historic Market Street, now attract many tourists. The district's less-populated rural regions provide a tourist destination outside of Knoxville's orbit and continue to lure visitors to mountain locales.

Like all of East Tennessee, the 2nd has a long history of voting Republican, and the district has not sent a Democrat to the U.S. House since before the Civil War. Downtown Knoxville, which includes much of the city's black population and is the only real Democratic pocket, could not prevent George W. Bush from taking surrounding Knox County by 25 percentage points in the 2004 presidential election. He exceeded his Knox County percentage in each of the 2nd's other counties.

MAJOR INDUSTRY

Higher education, medical services, tourism, government

CITIES

Knoxville, 173,890; Maryville, 23,120; Farragut, 17,720; Athens, 13,220

NOTABLE

A statue in Haley Heritage Square honors "Roots" author Alex Haley, who made his home in Knoxville; The town of Alcoa is named after the company whose manufacturing plant there produces enough aluminum sheet every minute to make 75,000 beverage cans.

Rep. Zach Wamp (R)

CAPITOL OFFICE
225-3271
www.house.gov/wamp
1436 Longworth 20515-4203; fax 225-3494

COMMITTEES
Appropriations

RESIDENCE
Chattanooga

BORN
Oct. 28, 1957, Fort Benning, Ga.

RELIGION
Baptist

FAMILY
Wife, Kim Wamp; two children

EDUCATION
U. of North Carolina, attended 1977-78 (industrial relations); U. of Tennessee, attended 1978-79; U. of North Carolina, attended 1979-80 (political science)

CAREER
Real estate broker

POLITICAL HIGHLIGHTS
Republican nominee for U.S. House, 1992

ELECTION RESULTS

2006 GENERAL		
Zach Wamp (R)	130,791	65.7%
Brent Benedict (D)	68,324	34.3%
2006 PRIMARY		
Zach Wamp (R)	57,569	87.3%
June Griffin (R)	3,579	5.4%
Doug Vandagriff (R)	3,112	4.7%
Charles E. Howard (R)	1,702	2.6%
2004 GENERAL		
Zach Wamp (R)	166,154	64.7%
John Wolfe Jr. (D)	84,295	32.9%
June Griffin (X)	3,018	1.2%

PREVIOUS WINNING PERCENTAGES
2002 (65%); 2000 (64%); 1998 (66%); 1996 (56%); 1994 (52%)

Elected 1994; 7th term

In 1984, Wamp was addicted to cocaine and alcohol. He had passed time at a pair of prestigious universities, North Carolina and Tennessee, without earning a degree, and he appeared to be headed nowhere.

"I knew I was losing control," he told the Knoxville News-Sentinel. But the rebel gained religion after going to a rehabilitation clinic, and a decade later he was part of Newt Gingrich's "Republican Revolution." Wamp sees himself as a "spiritual man," and he uses the word often to describe both his personal life and his career. He is devoted to the House Prayer Breakfast, where several dozen members from both parties meet weekly to sing hymns, discuss their problems and pray.

But if Wamp has learned temperance, he hasn't entirely suppressed his intensity or his rebellious nature. He abandoned ambitions for elected leadership in the House and for a 2006 U.S. Senate run but now plans to run for governor in 2010. "It is likely that I will run for governor in 2010," he said. "I feel the pull of Tennessee on me again, and I can see the need."

Wamp broke a term limit pledge to run again for the 110th Congress (2007-08), telling the Chattanooga Times Free Press in early 2006, "I still don't plan on staying forever but after Sept. 11, I felt like I should renew my commitment to public service." His zeal for cutting federal spending has been softened by his service on the Appropriations Committee, where he gladly earmarks money for the 3rd District.

While few would question his conservative credentials, he has not been shy about challenging GOP leaders on campaign finance, ethics and other high-profile issues. After House Republicans voted in November 2004 to change their ethics rules in a way that could have allowed Majority Leader Tom DeLay to retain his leadership post if indicted in his home state of Texas, Wamp drew the line. He warned that he and other Republicans might break ranks on one of the first votes of the 109th Congress (2005-06) if the leadership brought the proposed change to the floor. DeLay and other GOP leaders backed off. Wamp briefly weighed a challenge to DeLay.

He also broke ranks with GOP leaders in 2003, when he tried to convert part of President Bush's funding request for Iraq from a grant to a loan, and he turned heads and rankled party leaders in 2002, when he joined Democrats in pushing for an overhaul of campaign finance laws. Only later in his career did Wamp begin accepting political action committee donations.

But he has been a firm supporter of the administration on the war in Iraq. In early 2007, he publicly backed the president's call to send thousands more troops to Iraq, and he told the Times Free Press that the Democrats' proposed timeline for troop withdrawal was a "bad precedent for Congress." He often links the current conflict in Iraq to the nation's role in World War II. "Hitler did not attack us, but he was a real threat to the world," he told the Chattanooga newspaper in March 2007. "We're in Iraq not because we want to be, but because we're taking on a threat."

His interests and voting record generally put him in the heart of the conservative mainstream. He belongs to the House Pro-Life Caucus and is a reliable vote for tax cuts. He voted in both 2004 and 2006 in favor of a constitutional amendment to prohibit same-sex marriage.

His legislative work in recent years has focused on renewable energy issues important to the Tennessee Valley Authority and the Oak Ridge National Laboratory, which is located in his district.

Despite a campaign pledge to cut spending and balance the budget,

Wamp continued a Tennessee tradition in his first term by fighting GOP efforts to abolish agencies that are the economic lifeblood of his state — the Tennessee Valley Authority and the Appalachian Regional Commission. At the start of his second term, he became the first Republican from Tennessee since 1910 to sit on the Appropriations Committee. "You can't be a strident ideologue on Appropriations," Wamp has said. In the 110th Congress, he is the top Republican on the Legislative Branch Appropriations Subcommittee. Wamp is no stranger to the Capitol Hill grounds. For years, he has personally led tour groups through the Capitol — more than 1,700 of them.

He is an avid believer in physical fitness. With workout video star Richard Simmons at his side, he unveiled legislation in 2007 that would include physical education among those subjects for which states must establish academic testing standards. "An innocent victim of 'No Child Left Behind' has been physical education in the schools," he told the Times Free Press. Another Wamp initiative would give tax breaks to employers who pay for their workers to work out.

A self-described "gym rat," Wamp is the co-founder, along with Colorado's Mark Udall, of the Congressional Fitness Caucus, which aims to encourage their time-strapped colleagues to make time for fitness activities. He organizes pickup basketball games in the House gym and off campus.

Wamp was raised in a Democratic family with deep roots in Southern politics. His great-great-great-grandfather spent 40 years in the Alabama legislature, and his great-uncle was a leader in the Alabama General Assembly. Wamp himself voted for Jimmy Carter in 1976 but entered the GOP fold four years later, concluding that Ronald Reagan offered a "breath of hope and optimism for America" in the depths of the Iran hostage crisis. He was so taken with Reagan's campaign that he drove with several University of North Carolina fraternity brothers from Chapel Hill to Washington, D.C., on election night to celebrate the GOP victory.

Wamp won his first election in high school, as student body president. At 26, he became the youth coordinator for a victorious Chattanooga mayoral candidate. Four years later, he chaired his local GOP organization. Community leaders urged him to run for public office, but he demurred, saying he had "been through too many mud puddles in my life." But when his wife joined in, Wamp, a real estate broker, decided to run. He came within 3,000 votes of unseating Democratic Rep. Marilyn Lloyd in 1992. He tried again in 1994, when Lloyd retired after 10 terms, and won with 52 percent of the vote. He has won his past five re-elections with 64 percent or better.

KEY VOTES

2006

- No Stop broadband companies from favoring select Internet traffic
- Yes Affirm U.S. commitment to war in Iraq and reject setting a withdrawal date for troops
- Yes Repeal requirement for bilingual ballots at the polls
- Yes Permit U.S. sale of civilian nuclear technology to India
- Yes Build a 700-mile fence on the U.S.-Mexico border to curb illegal crossings
- Yes Permit warrantless wiretaps of suspected terrorists

2005

- Yes Intervene in the life-support case of Terri Schiavo
- No Lift President Bush's restrictions on stem cell research funding
- No Prohibit FBI access to library and bookstore records
- Yes Approve free-trade pact with five Central American countries
- Yes Pass energy policy overhaul favored by President Bush emphasizing domestic oil and gas production
- Yes End mandatory preservation of habitat of endangered animal and plant species
- Yes Ban torture of prisoners in U.S. custody

CQ VOTE STUDIES

	PARTY UNITY		PRESIDENTIAL SUPPORT	
	Support	Oppose	Support	Oppose
2006	95%	5%	87%	13%
2005	94%	6%	87%	13%
2004	93%	7%	79%	21%
2003	93%	7%	89%	11%
2002	90%	10%	82%	18%

INTEREST GROUPS

	AFL-CIO	ADA	CCUS	ACU
2006	14%	5%	87%	88%
2005	20%	0%	88%	88%
2004	13%	0%	100%	88%
2003	7%	15%	90%	100%
2002	0%	5%	80%	96%

TENNESSEE 3

East – Chattanooga, Oak Ridge

From the borders of Kentucky and Virginia to its north and Georgia and North Carolina to its south, the 3rd spans the height of Tennessee. Chattanooga, the district's largest city, continues to attract technology jobs to the growing community.

The 3rd's geographic center falls near Oak Ridge, where multidisciplinary high-technology national research facilities sprawl over parts of Anderson and Roane counties. Once solely dependent on federal dollars, Oak Ridge has begun to promote its "Secret City" history and selection as one site of the Manhattan Project.

Half of the 3rd's population resides in Hamilton County, which includes Chattanooga and abuts Georgia. With the city as its anchor, the 3rd is becoming the "Technology Corridor" of the state, modeling its growth on Research Triangle Park in North Carolina. The highway system out of Chattanooga encourages collaboration among local technology companies with those in Oak Ridge and Knoxville (in the 2nd District), as well as partnerships in both Virginia and Alabama.

Complementing Chattanooga's beautiful scenery, the city has injected life into its downtown over the past several decades through renewal projects such as the Tennessee Aquarium, a rejuvenated waterfront and a growing local University of Tennessee campus. Just east of Chattanooga, Bradley — including the city of Cleveland — and Polk counties offer tours of the Cherokee National Forest and a rich history of the Cherokee Indians.

District residents support low-tax fiscal policies and hold conservative views on social issues, making the 3rd a Republican-leaning district. In 2004, George W. Bush took 57 percent of Hamilton County's presidential vote, but he did even better in the district overall (61 percent) and took 73 percent of the vote in Bradley County.

MAJOR INDUSTRY

Nuclear and high-technology research, technology, higher education

CITIES

Chattanooga, 155,554; Cleveland, 37,192; Oak Ridge, 27,387

NOTABLE

Ruby Falls in Chattanooga is the nation's largest underground waterfall; The 1925 Scopes "Monkey" Trial in Dayton (Rhea County) upheld a law making it illegal to teach evolution.

Rep. Lincoln Davis (D)

CAPITOL OFFICE
225-6831
www.house.gov/lincolndavis
410 Cannon 20515-4204; fax 226-5172

COMMITTEES
Agriculture
Financial Services

RESIDENCE
Pall Mall

BORN
Sept. 13, 1943, Pall Mall, Tenn.

RELIGION
Baptist

FAMILY
Wife, Lynda Davis; three children

EDUCATION
Tennessee Technological U., B.S. 1966 (agronomy)

CAREER
Farmer; construction company owner; U.S. Agriculture Department official

POLITICAL HIGHLIGHTS
Mayor of Byrdstown, 1979-83; Tenn. House, 1981-85; sought Democratic nomination for U.S. House, 1984, 1994; Tenn. Senate, 1997-2003

ELECTION RESULTS

2006 GENERAL		
Lincoln Davis (D)	123,666	66.4%
Kenneth Martin (R)	62,449	33.6%
2006 PRIMARY		
Lincoln Davis (D)	56,618	86.2%
Norma Cartwright (D)	6,564	10.0%
Harvey Howard (D)	2,511	3.8%
2004 GENERAL		
Lincoln Davis (D)	138,459	54.8%
Janice H. Bowling (R)	109,993	43.5%
Ken Martin (X)	4,194	1.7%

PREVIOUS WINNING PERCENTAGES
2002 (52%)

Elected 2002; 3rd term

Davis is a down-to-earth lawmaker who combines social conservatism with a populist championship of the little guy. One of a shrinking band of white Southern Democrats, he is considered a potential candidate for the governorship of the Volunteer State in 2010.

He got a look at what's involved in a statewide race in 2006, when he served as chairman of the unsuccessful Senate campaign of former Democratic Rep. Harold E. Ford Jr. In the 110th Congress (2007-08), Davis won appointment to the Financial Services Committee, a panel Ford served on and used to develop a deeper fundraising base. Davis should be able to do the same in anticipation of his own possible statewide run.

A devout Baptist who delivered the closing prayer at the National Prayer Breakfast in early 2005, Davis vowed in his successful 2002 campaign that no candidate would "outgun me, outpray me or outdaddy me." National Democratic Party types did not understand the potency of the "values" issue. "We were told by the [Democratic Congressional Campaign Committee]: 'You're running this election wrong. You're running it on values, and you're going to lose,' " Davis told The New York Times in September 2002. "When I heard that, I just giggled at them."

During the 109th Congress (2005-06), Davis sided with President Bush on 67 percent of the votes on which the president staked out a position. Only three other House Democrats supported Bush more often, and only four others split with their own party more often than Davis on votes that pitted Democrats against Republicans.

Davis is a member of the Blue Dog Coalition, a group of the most conservative House Democrats. While social and environmental issues account for many of his departures from the party line, he also has refused to join his colleagues in setting a date certain for a U.S. withdrawal from Iraq. In 2007, he voted against an Iraq War funding bill that set a timetable for a U.S. redeployment, citing the "heartburn" he got from the measure's withdrawal deadline. He did, however, join fellow Democrats in denouncing Bush's January 2007 decision to send thousands more troops to Iraq.

The bulk of Davis' legislative work has been focused on finding an economic engine for his poor, rural district. In addition to Financial Services, he serves on the Agriculture Committee, where he will work to protect the interests of farmers in his region as the committee in 2007 drafts a new farm bill.

He is the sponsor of a 2007 bill to add five counties in his district — Giles, Hickman, Lawrence, Lewis and Lincoln — to the area officially designated as the Appalachian Region, making them eligible for federal economic development assistance from the Appalachian Regional Commission. And he is a defender of Social Security, introducing legislation to ensure that benefits for those eligible for Old Age, Survivor and Disability support through that program are paid through the end of the month in which they die.

Davis was one of about three-dozen Democrats who voted in 2004 and 2006 for a proposed constitutional amendment to ban same-sex marriage, saying he and most of his constituents "insist that our nation define marriage as a union between a man and a woman." He also voted for the 2003 law that banned a procedure opponents call "partial birth" abortion. That was no surprise, since one of the highlights of his career in the state Senate, where he spent six years before being elected to Congress, was his sponsorship of the Tennessee law that banned the procedure at the state level. In 2004, he was the only Democratic congressman to win the endorsement of the anti-abortion group Tennessee Right to Life. Early in 2007, he was working on legislation to encourage more women to carry pregnancies to term, with grants to states for the support of teens and college students who are pregnant or have children, health coverage for pregnant women and an expansion of the adoption tax credit.

Davis also parts ways with most Democrats on environmental issues. In the 109th Congress, he voted to open Alaska's Arctic National Wildlife Refuge to oil and gas drilling, lift a moratorium on most offshore oil drilling, ease environmental reviews in order to speed construction of new refineries and limit the scope of the Endangered Species Act.

Still, Davis votes with Democrats on many high-profile domestic issues. In 2003, he voted to allow prescription drugs to be imported from Canada, arguing that "it's so unfair for Americans to be paying for research and development" that adds to the costs of the same medications Canadians get for less money. He opposed a GOP bill that year to give states more control over the Head Start program for poor children. In 2006, he opposed GOP efforts to repeal bilingual ballot requirements in the Voting Rights Act.

But Davis angered some members of his party when he voted for the 2003 Medicare prescription drug benefit bill, written mostly by Republicans, after opposing the original House version. He struggled with his vote for the final bill but decided reduced drug costs for Medicare beneficiaries and increased payments to rural hospitals were too valuable to pass up.

Davis says he ran for Congress to give people in his district "a voice of understanding from someone who grew up the same way they did." A farmer who started a construction business before launching his political career, Davis says he dug the water lines for his house himself and identifies with people in his district who still don't have access to water utilities. For them, the most immediate needs are economic development and personal needs such as health care, he says.

Davis lost Democratic primaries for open House seats in 1984 and 1994 before winning on his third try in 2002. He worked with the General Assembly in the redistricting process to increase Democratic strength in the 4th District before running for the seat left open by Republican Van Hilleary's gubernatorial bid.

He won the primary with 57 percent of the vote against Fran Marchum, a well-funded opponent running to his left, and then defeated Republican Janice H. Bowling, a former top aide to Hilleary, by 6 percentage points in the general election. He won a 2004 rematch against Bowling, increasing his margin to 11 percentage points, and took 66 percent of the vote in 2006.

KEY VOTES

2006

No Stop broadband companies from favoring select Internet traffic
Yes Affirm U.S. commitment to war in Iraq and reject setting a withdrawal date for troops
No Repeal requirement for bilingual ballots at the polls
Yes Permit U.S. sale of civilian nuclear technology to India
Yes Build a 700-mile fence on the U.S.-Mexico border to curb illegal crossings
Yes Permit warrantless wiretaps of suspected terrorists

2005

Yes Intervene in the life-support case of Terri Schiavo
No Lift President Bush's restrictions on stem cell research funding
Yes Prohibit FBI access to library and bookstore records
No Approve free-trade pact with five Central American countries
Yes Pass energy policy overhaul favored by President Bush emphasizing domestic oil and gas production
Yes End mandatory preservation of habitat of endangered animal and plant species
Yes Ban torture of prisoners in U.S. custody

CQ VOTE STUDIES

	PARTY UNITY		PRESIDENTIAL SUPPORT	
	Support	Oppose	Support	Oppose
2006	67%	33%	70%	30%
2005	67%	33%	65%	35%
2004	68%	32%	59%	41%
2003	74%	26%	56%	44%

INTEREST GROUPS

	AFL-CIO	ADA	CCUS	ACU
2006	79%	35%	93%	80%
2005	67%	70%	78%	64%
2004	67%	60%	86%	56%
2003	79%	75%	70%	61%

TENNESSEE 4

Middle Tennessee – northeast and south

Stretching across more than 10,000 square miles and touching Tennessee's borders with Kentucky in the north and Alabama and Georgia in the south, the 4th is the state's most geographically vast district. It is a melting pot of Tennessee's three regions, as plains turn east into rolling hills that merge with the Cumberland Plateau and eventually the Appalachian Mountains.

While the 4th falls in the orbit of Oak Ridge and Chattanooga in the east and Nashville in the west, it is overwhelmingly rural. Columbia, with just 33,000 residents, is the district's most populous city. No one major media market serves all of the 4th, forcing coverage to be shared with larger ones from Oak Ridge, Chattanooga, Nashville and Huntsville, Ala. The district's median income is below that of the state, and its constituency has the lowest level of formal education of any Tennessee district.

The 4th includes tobacco farms and light manufacturing in the south. Spring Hill, in Maury County, is experiencing some economic uncertainty as General Motors has closed its original Saturn plant and is determining the future of its operations in the city. Proximity to Nashville is one reason the populations of Maury and next-door Williamson County (shared with the 7th) continue to grow. Although tourism plays only a small role in the district's economy overall, the northern region of the 4th does attract visitors to the Big South Fork National River and Recreation Area in Fentress, Pickett and Scott counties.

Although the 4th has an ancestrally Democratic lean, underlying social conservatism — manifested in opposition to abortion and gun control measures — gives the 4th a Republican edge in federal contests. In 2004, Republican George W. Bush won the 4th by 17 percentage points, taking 22 of the 24 counties that are wholly or partly in the district.

MAJOR INDUSTRY
Agriculture, auto parts, manufacturing, tobacco

MILITARY BASES
Arnold Air Force Base, 75 military, 2,500 civilian (2007)

CITIES
Columbia, 33,055; Tullahoma, 17,994

NOTABLE
The Jack Daniel's sour mash whiskey distillery in Lynchburg is located in dry Moore County.

Rep. Jim Cooper (D)

CAPITOL OFFICE
225-4311
cooper.house.gov
1536 Longworth 20515-4205; fax 226-1035

COMMITTEES
Armed Services
Budget
Oversight & Government Reform

RESIDENCE
Nashville

BORN
June 19, 1954, Nashville, Tenn.

RELIGION
Episcopalian

FAMILY
Wife, Martha Hayes Cooper; three children

EDUCATION
U. of North Carolina, B.A. 1975 (history & economics); Oxford U., B.A., M.A. 1977 (Rhodes scholar); Harvard U., J.D. 1980

CAREER
Investment firm owner; investment bank managing director; lawyer

POLITICAL HIGHLIGHTS
U.S. House, 1983-95; Democratic nominee for U.S. Senate, 1994

ELECTION RESULTS

2006 GENERAL		
Jim Cooper (D)	122,919	69.0%
Thomas F. Kovach (R)	49,702	27.9%
Ginny Welsch (I)	3,766	2.1%
2006 PRIMARY		
Jim Cooper (D)	38,148	91.6%
Jason Pullias (D)	3,518	8.4%
2004 GENERAL		
Jim Cooper (D)	168,970	69.3%
Scott Knapp (R)	74,978	30.7%

PREVIOUS WINNING PERCENTAGES
2002 (64%); 1992 (66%); 1990 (69%); 1988 (100%); 1986 (100%); 1984 (75%); 1982 (66%)

Elected 2002; 9th term

Also served 1983-95

A self-described "nerd," Cooper has become an increasingly outspoken Democratic advocate of deficit reduction and a budget process overhaul. He is among his party's most experienced fiscal experts, having logged more than a decade in Congress and then eight years in the financial world before he returned to Capitol Hill for a whole new round in 2003.

Cooper has used his seat on the Budget Committee to spotlight one of his biggest gripes — the calculation of the federal budget on a cash accounting basis that reflects current expenditures and revenues only.

Cooper argues that only accrual accounting that recognizes statutory commitments to future spending, such as Social Security and Medicare obligations, can show the true condition of the federal budget. In fiscal 2005, he noted, the reported deficit was $319 billion on a cash basis, but it was $760 billion if calculated by the accrual method. Calling the use of cash accounting "misleading," Cooper succeeded in persuading the Budget Committee in 2006 to adopt an amendment requiring use of accrual accounting. He wrote the foreword for a subsequent book, "The Financial Report of the United States," that explained the differences in the numbers.

Cooper has championed what he regards as other common-sense budget approaches, including an unsuccessful push to require congressional earmarks to be included in the text of legislation instead of buried in accompanying committee reports. (When it comes to earmarks for his own district, Cooper reveals in advance the list of projects for which he wants funding.)

He also called for a return to pay-as-you-go budget rules requiring both tax cuts and spending increases to be offset. House Democrats adopted the budget rules when they gained power in the 110th Congress (2007-08). Earlier, he broke with his party to support a White House-backed measure that would have allowed the president to rescind a package of spending items, or tax provisions affecting a single person or entity, and receive an expedited up-or-down vote in both chambers without amendments.

Cooper, a member of the Blue Dog Coalition of conservative House Democrats, splits with his party on a variety of issues ranging from trade to gun control. He served as the coalition's policy co-chairman in the 109th Congress (2005-06).

Early in 2007, he even split with most Blue Dogs when he was unable to get their backing for a budget plan that called for the extension of some soon-to-expire tax breaks and cuts in some entitlement programs. He wound up casting the lone Democratic vote for a competing GOP budget plan to cut entitlements and freeze other domestic spending.

"I'm not a very ideological person. Practicality is the hallmark," Cooper said when he returned to Capitol Hill in 2003. He found a much-altered Congress, one in which bitter partisanship had replaced cooperation across party lines. He told The Tennessean newspaper how shocked he was at the chilly reception he got from Budget Committee Republicans during a break in a hearing in 2003. "A lot of Republicans wouldn't even say hello, and here you are eating pizza right next to them," he said.

On the Armed Services Committee, Cooper has regularly joined other Democrats in rebuking the Bush administration for what they consider poor planning to rebuild postwar Iraq. He has called the Pentagon's endeavors there "a stunning case of mismanagement."

Republicans aren't the only ones to draw criticism from Cooper. He caused a stir among Democrats in a candid assessment to the Washington Post of his party's struggles to win over disgruntled voters. "The comment I hear is, 'I'd really like to vote for you guys, but I can't stand the folks I see on TV,'" he told the newspaper. He later explained in an interview that the party needs to better identify its best messengers and let them speak for the party: "The public can't understand 208 voices. We need [lawmakers] who look and act the part."

Cooper said his frustration with current conditions on Capitol Hill grows out of his longtime affection for government. His father, Prentice, was Tennessee's governor in the 1960s, and Cooper grew up with an eye toward public service. He made it through the University of North Carolina in just three years, attended Oxford as a Rhodes Scholar, then picked up a law degree from Harvard. After practicing law for two years, he ran for an open House seat in 1982 against Sen. Howard Baker's daughter Cissy and won easily, becoming at age 28 the youngest member of the House.

Despite his youthfulness, Cooper developed a reputation as a skilled dealmaker. From his seat on the Energy and Commerce Committee, he was a key player on issues ranging from health care to telecommunications policy to clean air. But when he ran for the Senate in 1994, he was trounced by actor and attorney Fred Thompson.

Cooper then took a break from politics. He entered the investment banking world and taught business at the Owen Graduate School of Management at Vanderbilt University. He says all lawmakers ought to be more knowledgeable about financial issues, noting that even members of the Armed Services panel need to understand the business world in looking at procurement. "The private sector experience is the best thing to happen to me," he said. "I'm so much better informed on issues than I was before."

When a House seat in Tennessee opened up in 2002 after Democrat Bob Clement decided to run for the Senate, Cooper jumped at the chance for a comeback. Despite surgery in June 2002 to remove a tumor from his colon — doctors said the cancer had not spread — Cooper won the August primary with 47 percent of the vote to 24 percent for his closest competitor. He captured 64 percent that November against businessman Robert Duvall, and has had no trouble holding the seat since then.

Although white-majority urban Democratic districts are located mainly in Democratic "blue" states, Cooper's district, based in the state capital of Nashville, is an exception. The area has historic ties to a founder of the Democratic Party: "In Tennessee, the district is often called the Andrew Jackson district," Cooper notes.

KEY VOTES

2006

- Yes Stop broadband companies from favoring select Internet traffic
- Yes Affirm U.S. commitment to war in Iraq and reject setting a withdrawal date for troops
- No Repeal requirement for bilingual ballots at the polls
- Yes Permit U.S. sale of civilian nuclear technology to India
- Yes Build a 700-mile fence on the U.S.-Mexico border to curb illegal crossings
- No Permit warrantless wiretaps of suspected terrorists

2005

- ? Intervene in the life-support case of Terri Schiavo
- Yes Lift President Bush's restrictions on stem cell research funding
- Yes Prohibit FBI access to library and bookstore records
- Yes Approve free-trade pact with five Central American countries
- No Pass energy policy overhaul favored by President Bush emphasizing domestic oil and gas production
- No End mandatory preservation of habitat of endangered animal and plant species
- Yes Ban torture of prisoners in U.S. custody

CQ VOTE STUDIES

	PARTY UNITY		PRESIDENTIAL SUPPORT	
	Support	Oppose	Support	Oppose
2006	82%	18%	37%	63%
2005	80%	20%	38%	62%
2004	82%	18%	35%	65%
2003	85%	15%	33%	67%
1994	50%	40%	69%	28%

INTEREST GROUPS

	AFL-CIO	ADA	CCUS	ACU
2006	79%	70%	53%	40%
2005	67%	80%	59%	24%
2004	79%	85%	57%	13%
2003	87%	80%	53%	36%
1994	33%	40%	92%	67%

TENNESSEE 5

Nashville

Home of the Grand Ole Opry and the Country Music Hall of Fame and Museum, the 5th's Nashville long has been known for its place in country music history. The state capital, however, has left behind that one-dimensional image to become a cosmopolitan mecca for tourism, culture and higher education. With many buildings in the classical style, Nashville proclaims itself the "Athens of the South."

Although the district is most famous for its rich music tradition, state government is the top employer and Nashville is a higher education hub for the Volunteer State. The 5th also is a health care center, and the city hosts several research facilities, including the Vanderbilt University Medical Center. Nashville's Printers Alley is now an entertainment district, but the name gives credence to the district's still-thriving publishing sector.

Two large sports arenas — the home of football's Titans and hockey's Predators — enhance the district's already strong entertainment sector. Events at auto racing's Nashville Superspeedway, which is located just outside of the district in the neighboring 6th's portion of Lebanon, also are major draws. Meanwhile, bargain retail stores and other attractions lure tourists and locals to suburban areas.

The Nashville area's economic boom, which has spread across most of the 5th, attracted young, Republican-leaning, upper-class couples to the neighborhoods of Bellevue and Hermitage. The strongly Democratic city core of government employees, academics and unions, however, negates almost any chance that the district could fall into Republican hands. No Republican won Nashville's congressional seat during the 20th century, and Democrat John Kerry took 55 percent of the Davidson County vote and 52 percent of the districtwide vote in the 2004 presidential election.

MAJOR INDUSTRY

Government, music, higher education, publishing, health care, tourism

CITIES

Nashville-Davidson (pt.), 524,339; Lebanon (pt.), 12,718

NOTABLE

"The Hermitage" was the home of Andrew Jackson; A full-scale reproduction of the Parthenon was built in 1897 and stands in Nashville's Centennial Park.

Rep. Bart Gordon (D)

CAPITOL OFFICE
225-4231
gordon.house.gov
2310 Rayburn 20515-4206; fax 225-6887

COMMITTEES
Energy & Commerce
Science & Technology - chairman

RESIDENCE
Murfreesboro

BORN
Jan. 24, 1949, Murfreesboro, Tenn.

RELIGION
Methodist

FAMILY
Wife, Leslie Gordon; one child

EDUCATION
Middle Tennessee State U., B.S. 1971;
U. of Tennessee, J.D. 1973

MILITARY SERVICE
Army Reserve, 1971-72

CAREER
Lawyer; state party official

POLITICAL HIGHLIGHTS
Tenn. Democratic Party chairman, 1981-83

ELECTION RESULTS

2006 GENERAL		
Bart Gordon (D)	129,069	67.1%
David R. Davis (R)	60,392	31.4%
Robert L. Garrison (I)	2,035	1.1%
2006 PRIMARY		
Bart Gordon (D)	53,916	92.3%
J. Patrick Lyons (D)	4,490	7.7%
2004 GENERAL		
Bart Gordon (D)	167,448	64.2%
Nick Demas (R)	87,523	33.6%
J. Patrick Lyons (X)	3,869	1.5%

PREVIOUS WINNING PERCENTAGES
2002 (66%); 2000 (62%); 1998 (55%); 1996 (54%); 1994 (51%); 1992 (57%); 1990 (67%); 1988 (76%); 1986 (77%); 1984 (63%)

Elected 1984; 12th term

As chairman of the Science and Technology Committee, Gordon will prod the Bush administration for a stronger financial commitment to science and space exploration initiatives. And although he may disagree with the president's science priorities, on social issues he is not as far removed from the White House as many of his fellow Democratic chairmen.

Tennessee has grown more Republican over the years and Gordon, who is now in his second decade in the House, has grown more conservative along with it. He supports tax cuts and gun owners' rights, and he takes a hard line on immigration. In 2006, he was one of 15 Democrats voting in favor of extending Bush's tax cuts for another five years, and he was one of 18 Democrats who voted for a measure authorizing electronic surveillance of suspected terrorists without first obtaining approval from a government court. In 2004, he sided with other social conservatives in supporting a constitutional ban on same-sex marriage.

Gordon voted in agreement with President Bush 63 percent of the time in 2006, and sided with a majority of his party 74 percent of the time on party-line votes, in both instances ranking among the least loyal Democrats.

Under his chairmanship, the Science panel wasted no time in the 110th Congress (2007-08) churning out bills on matters that had been languishing for years. Gordon acknowledged to the Nashville Tennessean newspaper that he benefits from Democratic leadership interest in technology and competitiveness.

The committee approved legislation in 2007 to greatly expand funding for the National Science Foundation and the National Institute of Standards and Technology beyond what the Bush administration proposed.

Gordon also is concerned that U.S. technical jobs are being lost to overseas employers. "If the United States fails to reverse the slide of falling math and science scores in our schools, our leadership in the world economy will be lost," Gordon said. Early in 2007, the House passed his bill to recruit 10,000 math and science teachers annually by providing scholarships to science, math and engineering students who commit to becoming teachers when they finish their degrees.

Under Gordon's leadership, the Science panel is looking into the problem of climate change. This is an issue that also falls under the purview of the Energy and Commerce Committee, on which Gordon sits. "I really think there is a problem in scientific integrity in this administration. There has not been enough oversight," Gordon said. "The Science committee needs to be a vehicle for a better understanding of global warming and climate change." Gordon is also interested in promoting alternative fuels and energy efficiency.

Gordon has been generally supportive of administration plans to return humans to the moon in preparation for a future mission to Mars. But he has criticized the administration's spending blueprint, which so far has consisted of shifting money from NASA's aeronautics and science research programs to fund human exploration.

The spread of methamphetamine production is also an issue that concerns him. In 2007, the House passed legislation sponsored by Gordon that would require the Environmental Protection Agency to create guidelines for the cleanup of illegal methamphetamine labs. The measure would give the EPA a year to come up with the guidelines, which state and local governments could use voluntarily. Meth lab sites are notoriously toxic to people and the surrounding environment, Gordon said. One pound of the drug's production results in as many as five pounds of waste chemicals.

Like many in his party, Gordon is a firm believer in protecting the rights of workers. He has sided with organized labor for an increase in the minimum wage, and in the 108th Congress (2003-04) he opposed Bush administration efforts to change overtime rules for some federal workers.

Gordon is known in the House for being fast on his feet. He annually finishes first among lawmakers in the three-mile Capital Challenge road race, beating out such athletes as former GOP Rep. Jim Ryun of Kansas, the first high school miler to break the four-minute mark.

Gordon grew up in Murfreesboro, Tenn., where his father was a farmer and his mother a schoolteacher. Gordon says he first became interested in politics through his grandfather, who was a county commissioner, and his father, who started the local farm bureau. He spent four years in the Army ROTC and was commissioned for the Vietnam War, but he suffered from an ulcer and was honorably discharged. He then opened a law practice in Murfreesboro. "My first jury trial was a dog bite case," he said. "I had murders and dog bites — everything a small-town lawyer does."

Gordon had firsthand experience with politics as a college student, when he went to work in the 1968 congressional campaign of Democratic state Rep. John Bragg, who lost the race. Fresh out of law school, Gordon won a seat on the state Democratic Executive Committee, and in 1979 he parlayed his contacts into a position as the party's executive director. Two years later, he won the party chairmanship, attracting notice with his computerized mailing lists and fundraising efforts.

When Al Gore gave up his House seat in 1984 to run for the Senate, Gordon was ready. He won a six-way primary with 28 percent of the vote. Despite the potentially explosive issue of a paternity suit that had been brought against him and later was dismissed, he won all but two counties on Election Day. Gordon generally won re-election by comfortable margins until 1994, the year the Republicans took over Congress, when he was held to 51 percent by lawyer Steve Gill. His next three re-election victories were also comparatively close.

But the Democratic state legislature helped Gordon substantially in redistricting for this decade, adding two Democratic-leaning counties and taking away some heavily GOP territory in suburban Nashville.

As a result, he trounced Robert L. Garrison, a libertarian GOP gadfly, by 34 percentage points in 2002. He defeated his Republican opponents in 2004 and 2006 by a 2-1 margin.

KEY VOTES

2006

Yes Stop broadband companies from favoring select Internet traffic
Yes Affirm U.S. commitment to war in Iraq and reject setting a withdrawal date for troops
No Repeal requirement for bilingual ballots at the polls
Yes Permit U.S. sale of civilian nuclear technology to India
Yes Build a 700-mile fence on the U.S.-Mexico border to curb illegal crossings
Yes Permit warrantless wiretaps of suspected terrorists

2005

? Intervene in the life-support case of Terri Schiavo
Yes Lift President Bush's restrictions on stem cell research funding
Yes Prohibit FBI access to library and bookstore records
No Approve free-trade pact with five Central American countries
Yes Pass energy policy overhaul favored by President Bush emphasizing domestic oil and gas production
No End mandatory preservation of habitat of endangered animal and plant species
Yes Ban torture of prisoners in U.S. custody

CQ VOTE STUDIES

	PARTY UNITY		PRESIDENTIAL SUPPORT	
	Support	Oppose	Support	Oppose
2006	74%	26%	63%	37%
2005	74%	26%	46%	54%
2004	72%	28%	55%	45%
2003	81%	19%	37%	63%
2002	74%	26%	54%	46%

INTEREST GROUPS

	AFL-CIO	ADA	CCUS	ACU
2006	79%	50%	80%	60%
2005	80%	90%	74%	40%
2004	87%	75%	75%	42%
2003	100%	75%	53%	52%
2002	75%	70%	68%	40%

TENNESSEE 6
Middle Tennessee - Murfreesboro

Nashville's population boom continues to spill into much of the 6th, which forms a sideways V-shape around Tennessee's capital city clockwise from the north to the south. The hilly countryside includes two notable college communities — Middle Tennessee State University in Murfreesboro, and Tennessee Tech University in Cookeville — establishing a top-tier industry for the district's economy.

A well-developed highway system eases the commute into the neighboring 5th District's Nashville from Murfreesboro for those 6th District residents who have state government jobs in the capital. Most residents, however, rely more on automobile manufacturing jobs in the 6th itself, spurred by a major Nissan plant in Smyrna, and local parts suppliers feed other plants located around the state. Although the recent tobacco quota buyout hurt some of the 6th's farming communities, Robertson County still is the state's top producer of tobacco. The distribution of books, videos and music also is big business in the district.

Rutherford County, which surrounds Murfreesboro, grew by more than 50 percent in the 1990s and has been targeted as a center for retail-sector revitalization. The planned commercial sites are expected to complement the already preserved areas commemorating the Civil War.

In recent presidential elections, Republican candidates have benefited from the presence of newly arrived suburbanites in the historically Democratic 6th. In fact, George W. Bush thrashed John Kerry by 20 percentage points in 2004 and took more than 60 percent of the vote in the district's most populous counties of Rutherford and Sumner. Unionized conservative Democrats are losing their clout as socially conservative tendencies launch local Republicans into public office.

MAJOR INDUSTRY

Auto manufacturing, distribution, tobacco, higher education

CITIES

Murfreesboro, 68,816; Hendersonville, 40,620; Smyrna, 25,569; Cookeville, 23,923; Gallatin, 23,230

NOTABLE

Former Rep. Joe L. Evins' idea for a fiddler jamboree in Smithville succeeded, and the event now attracts hundreds of thousands of visitors annually; Shelbyville is the heart of Tennessee Walking Horse country; Carthage is the hometown of former Vice President Al Gore.

Rep. Marsha Blackburn (R)

CAPITOL OFFICE
225-2811
www.house.gov/blackburn
509 Cannon 20515-4207; fax 225-3004

COMMITTEES
Energy & Commerce
Select Energy Independence & Global Warming

RESIDENCE
Brentwood

BORN
June 6, 1952, Laurel, Miss.

RELIGION
Presbyterian

FAMILY
Husband, Chuck Blackburn; two children

EDUCATION
Mississippi State U., B.S. 1973 (home economics)

CAREER
Retail marketing company owner; state economic development official; sales manager

POLITICAL HIGHLIGHTS
Williamson County Republican Party chairwoman, 1989-91; Republican nominee for U.S. House, 1992; Tenn. Senate, 1999-2002

ELECTION RESULTS

2006 GENERAL		
Marsha Blackburn (R)	152,288	66.0%
Bill Morrison (D)	73,369	31.8%
2006 PRIMARY		
Marsha Blackburn (R)		unopposed
2004 GENERAL		
Marsha Blackburn (R)		unopposed

PREVIOUS WINNING PERCENTAGES
2002 (71%)

Elected 2002; 3rd term

Regarded as a rising star among House Republicans almost from the moment she arrived, Blackburn was tripped up at the end of 2006 when she lost a bid for the No. 3 post in the GOP leadership. Her chances to shine were further diminished by the Democratic takeover of the House.

Blackburn was one of four Republicans (and the lone woman) vying to chair the GOP Conference in the 110th Congress (2007-08). She and two other contenders were members of the Republican Study Committee, the more than 100 strong group that forms the vanguard of conservatives in the House. But the winner, on the third ballot, was establishment candidate Adam H. Putnam of Florida, who led all the way. Blackburn was knocked out on the second ballot, trailing far behind Putnam and Jack Kingston of Georgia. Instead, she was named communications chairwoman of the National Republican Congressional Committee.

Before taking aim at a House leadership post, Blackburn had looked hard at the race to succeed Bill Frist, the Senate GOP leader who retired at the end of the 109th Congress (2005-06). But in early 2005, she decided against a bid just a week after filing papers with the Federal Election Commission to start a new political action committee, called Wedge PAC. The name reflects her maiden name, Wedgeworth, as well as "wedge issues," such as same-sex marriage, abortion and gun rights, about which she feels strongly.

Her backing of gun rights is so enthusiastic that in one of her 2002 campaign ads, she cited not just her avid support of the right to bear arms, but her perfect score on a marksmanship test with her Smith & Wesson .38.

Blackburn became known early in her House career for speaking her mind in GOP caucus meetings. It is a pattern she established previously as a Tennessee state senator. "One of the things I learned while I was in the statehouse is that it's very easy to just keep your mouth shut and vote no," she said in 2003. "But that's not fair to everyone who's involved. It's much more honest to get involved in how the legislation is shaped."

Blackburn was known as a firebrand at the Tennessee Senate, particularly for her relentless and ultimately successful crusade against a state income tax. She was so outspoken on the tax issue that a Memphis newspaper headline asked, "Can Rabble-Rouser Become Team Player?" as she arrived on Capitol Hill. She displays a gold-plated ax, with the words "Ax the Tax," in her House office as a reminder of that crusade.

Blackburn has continued her zealous campaign against taxes in the House. She cosponsored legislation to allow residents of Tennessee and the eight other states without broadly based income taxes to deduct state sales taxes when calculating their federal tax liability, a provision that became law in 2004 and was renewed in 2006. She also has fought any and all suggestions for tax increases, instead urging cuts in domestic spending to offset even emergency outlays such as disaster relief following Hurricane Katrina in 2005. Blackburn and 20 other RSC members wrote President Bush on Sept. 15 that year, calling for offsetting cuts in other domestic spending.

A party loyalist, Blackburn is a reliable supporter of Bush and her leadership. In 2006, she supported the president 89 percent of the time, and she voted in agreement with her party 98 percent of the time.

Republican leaders in 2005 rewarded Blackburn for her loyalty with a coveted assignment to the Energy and Commerce Committee. She was bumped from the panel briefly when the GOP lost its majority in the 110th

Congress, but was soon reassigned after the death of Republican Charlie Norwood of Georgia created a vacancy. She also was given a seat on the Select Committee on Energy Independence and Global Warming.

One business-related issue on which Blackburn scored success as a member of Energy and Commerce was a 2006 law gradually removing long-standing federal restrictions preventing Southwest Airlines from flying nonstop between Dallas' Love Field and most states. Southwest flies more than five times more passengers through Nashville than the next-busiest carrier. Blackburn told The Associated Press that she introduced legislation on the issue in 2004 as a way to get more-affordable airfares between cities such as Dallas and Nashville that share "a lot of business synergy."

Born in rural Mississippi, Blackburn learned civic involvement from her family. Her mother was active in the local 4-H clubs and Blackburn went to college on a 4-H scholarship. Her father instilled a sense of frugality. "It really has an impact watching your parents and uncles and seeing how frugal they are and how hard they work," she says.

Blackburn worked in a series of business and government jobs before coming to Congress. She paid her way through college selling books door-to-door for the Nashville-based Southwestern Company, and worked there after college as well. She said the experience helped develop her confidence.

She got her start in politics as Republican Party chairwoman in Williamson County. She ran for Congress in 1992 against Democratic Rep. Bart Gordon, drawing 41 percent of the vote. In the mid-1990s, she served a stint as executive director of Tennessee's Film, Entertainment, and Music Commission, and then won election to the state Senate in 1998.

In 2002, she leveraged the income tax issue and her base in the Nashville suburbs to prevail in a crowded primary field after four-term Republican Rep. Ed Bryant left his 7th District seat open for what would prove an unsuccessful Senate bid. The nomination ensured her victory in the Republican stronghold. She was the first woman from Tennessee to be elected in her own right and remains the lone woman in the state's delegation.

After Blackburn's first term, Democrats declined to field a candidate against her — an acknowledgment of her popularity in the district. The situation did not prevent her from raising more than $800,000, much of it from health care, legal and business services groups. During her 2006 campaign, she was unscathed by a Memphis Commercial-Appeal article reporting that her campaign committee and PAC had given $123,000 to a company run by her lobbyist son-in-law. Blackburn sailed to re-election with roughly two-thirds of the vote.

KEY VOTES

2006

- No Stop broadband companies from favoring select Internet traffic
- Yes Affirm U.S. commitment to war in Iraq and reject setting a withdrawal date for troops
- Yes Repeal requirement for bilingual ballots at the polls
- Yes Permit U.S. sale of civilian nuclear technology to India
- Yes Build a 700-mile fence on the U.S.-Mexico border to curb illegal crossings
- Yes Permit warrantless wiretaps of suspected terrorists

2005

- Yes Intervene in the life-support case of Terri Schiavo
- No Lift President Bush's restrictions on stem cell research funding
- No Prohibit FBI access to library and bookstore records
- Yes Approve free-trade pact with five Central American countries
- Yes Pass energy policy overhaul favored by President Bush emphasizing domestic oil and gas production
- Yes End mandatory preservation of habitat of endangered animal and plant species
- No Ban torture of prisoners in U.S. custody

CQ VOTE STUDIES

	PARTY UNITY		PRESIDENTIAL SUPPORT	
	Support	Oppose	Support	Oppose
2006	98%	2%	89%	11%
2005	99%	1%	93%	7%
2004	99%	1%	91%	9%
2003	98%	2%	96%	4%

INTEREST GROUPS

	AFL-CIO	ADA	CCUS	ACU
2006	14%	0%	100%	96%
2005	13%	0%	89%	100%
2004	7%	0%	100%	100%
2003	0%	5%	97%	88%

TENNESSEE 7

Eastern Memphis suburbs; southern Nashville suburbs; most of Clarksville

A tailor-made, meandering district, the 7th touches five other Tennessee districts and borders Kentucky to the north and Mississippi and Alabama to the south. The 7th's population centers fall at both ends of the district, near Memphis in the southwest and near Nashville in the east.

Almost one-third of district voters live in Shelby County suburbs outside Memphis, giving the 7th a strongly anti-tax and socially conservative bent despite a Democratic past. Shelby has experienced growth as middle-class residents migrate from downtown Memphis (in the 9th) to the outskirts of the county, a trend that helps explain the 7th's GOP shift.

Williamson County, outside of Nashville, mirrors Shelby in its growth and Republican leanings — Bush took more than 70 percent of the 7th's share of Williamson. Economically, the region is thriving. The recent relocation of Nissan's North American regional headquarters to Franklin near the company's primary North American manufacturing plant in Smyrna (in the 6th) included construction of a $100 million facility and a boost of thousands of jobs.

The bulk of the area between Shelby and Williamson sweeps over vast farming regions that produce corn, tobacco and hogs. Northwest of Williamson, the district ambles northward along the Cumberland River to take in most of Clarksville. The Clarksville area has benefited from diverse manufacturing, a robust education sector around Austin Peay State University (nearby in the 8th) and expansions at Fort Campbell — which straddles the Tennessee-Kentucky line. In 2004, George W. Bush won every county here except Hardeman and Perry.

MAJOR INDUSTRY

Agriculture, manufacturing

MILITARY BASES

Fort Campbell, 30,334 military, 4,388 civilian (2006) (shared with Kentucky's 1st District)

CITIES

Clarksville (pt.), 83,680; Bartlett (pt.), 40,409; Germantown (pt.), 34,200

NOTABLE

Shiloh National Military Park memorializes the soldiers who died in one of the bloodiest battles of the Civil War.

Rep. John Tanner (D)

CAPITOL OFFICE
225-4714
www.house.gov/tanner
1226 Longworth 20515-4208; fax 225-1765

COMMITTEES
Foreign Affairs
Ways & Means

RESIDENCE
Union City

BORN
Sept. 22, 1944, Halls, Tenn.

RELIGION
Disciples of Christ

FAMILY
Wife, Betty Ann Tanner; two children

EDUCATION
U. of Tennessee, B.S. 1966 (business), J.D. 1968

MILITARY SERVICE
Navy, 1968-72; Tenn. National Guard, 1974-2000

CAREER
Lawyer; insurance company owner

POLITICAL HIGHLIGHTS
Tenn. House, 1977-89

ELECTION RESULTS

2006 GENERAL		
John Tanner (D)	129,610	73.2%
John Farmer (R)	47,492	26.8%
2006 PRIMARY		
John Tanner (D)		unopposed
2004 GENERAL		
John Tanner (D)	173,623	74.3%
James L. Hart (R)	59,853	25.6%

PREVIOUS WINNING PERCENTAGES
2002 (70%); 2000 (72%); 1998 (100%); 1996 (67%); 1994 (64%); 1992 (84%); 1990 (100%); 1988 (62%)

Elected 1988; 10th term

Tanner is a founder of the Blue Dog Coalition, a group of the most fiscally conservative Democrats and a significant force in the liberal-dominated House Democratic Caucus. Tanner has been a leader in drafting the group's alternative budget proposals, which sometimes have served as a basis for compromises between Democrats and Republicans. The historic 1997 balanced-budget deal was what Tanner calls a "constructive middle ground" that borrowed heavily from the Blue Dogs' idea bank.

Tanner's main issue is the national debt and the grave threat he believes it poses to the country. He keeps a running tally of the debt on his Web site, along with a "your share" calculation for each American. He rarely misses an opportunity to preach about the perils of fiscal profligacy.

"Foreigners are financing our deficit spending, and if you do not think that is dangerous, then you have not studied history," Tanner told the House in 2004. He says the financial vulnerability created by foreign ownership of U.S. debt is a national security issue.

Tanner opposes tax cuts that are not offset by comparable reductions in spending. He voted against President Bush's $1.35 trillion tax cut in 2001 and the $350 billion tax bill in 2003. But he did support a 2006 bill linking a permanent reduction in the estate tax to an increase in the minimum wage.

Growing spending on entitlement programs also concerns Tanner. In both 2005 and 2007, he offered legislation establishing a commission to recommend changes to Social Security and Medicare to keep them solvent.

He also has a conservative tilt on many social issues. He supports the drive for a constitutional amendment banning same-sex marriage and voted to outlaw a procedure that opponents call "partial birth" abortion. Tanner was among the 52 Democrats who voted in 2004 for a bill that would have repealed the municipal gun control laws of Washington, D.C.

He has supported Bush more often than the typical Democrat and splits with his party's majority more frequently than all but a smattering of other Democrats. Since helping to form the Blue Dog Coalition in 1995, he has continually tried to pull his party to the political center, ground that is preferred by his rural and small-town constituents. The coalition numbers more than 40 members and Tanner thinks the group represents the "common sense" center where most Americans are ideologically.

Though the coalition often agrees with the Republicans, Tanner's philosophy of government is in keeping with his party's. Government has a basic obligation to invest in both "infrastructure and human capital," he says. "When one looks at ideology, there is more tolerance of differing opinions in the Democratic Party than there seems to be in the Republican Party."

Although his departures from the Democratic pack sometimes irk party leaders, Tanner was named a chief deputy whip at the start of the 109th Congress (2005-06), giving him a seat at the table at leadership meetings. Early in the 110th Congress (2007-08), fulfilling his whip duties, he spent considerable time working with his fellow Blue Dogs on an emergency spending bill that contained a timetable for U.S. withdrawal of its troops from Iraq.

Unlike most others in his party, Tanner is a free-trade advocate, both as a member of the influential Ways and Means Committee and on the House floor. In 2005, he was one of just 15 Democrats who voted for the Central America Free Trade Agreement. He also voted for the 2002 bill giving the president fast-track negotiating authority to enter into trade agreements that can't be amended by Congress. Tanner had a parochial interest in the fast-track legislation as well. He inserted a provision limiting the Customs fees charged for inspection of packages from overseas, a modification sought by Memphis-based FedEx Corp. and other delivery companies.

After Republicans took control of the majority in Congress in 1995, Tanner worked with moderate Delaware Republican Michael N. Castle on a bipartisan bill overhauling the welfare system. President Bill Clinton endorsed the Tanner-Castle measure, and elements of their bill eventually became part of the landmark law enacted in 1996.

Tanner voted in favor of giving Bush the authority to wage war in Iraq, and in the 2004 anti-war documentary "Fahrenheit 9/11," filmmaker Michael Moore included a brief clip featuring Tanner. Moore stopped Tanner and several other lawmakers on the street outside the Capitol to ask whether they would like to enlist their own kids to serve in Iraq. Tanner gave Moore a friendly greeting, accepted a military recruitment brochure from him and exchanged a few polite words.

His pet project is a bill, endorsed by the Blue Dogs, overhauling the redistricting process, which he sees as largely responsible for the political polarization of Congress. It would put congressional mapmaking in the hands of commissions appointed by state legislatures, taking it away from politicians. His idea has attracted favorable newspaper editorials but little attention from party leaders.

Tanner's father was a farmer who also worked in the insurance business. His mother ran a dress shop. After earning his undergraduate and law degrees at the University of Tennessee, Tanner spent four years prosecuting courts-martial in the Navy. He then joined a private practice in his hometown of Union City. In 1976, he ran for the state House at the urging of colleagues in the American Legion, where he was a state officer. Tanner served in the General Assembly for 12 years.

In 1988, when Democratic Rep. Ed Jones, a longtime family friend, retired after nearly two decades in the House, Tanner was fast out of the blocks. He assembled a solid organization and financial base, boosted by his relationships with Jones and state House Speaker Ned Ray McWherter. His relaxed, good-old-boy style helped him win over rural and small-town voters. He took 62 percent of the vote against Republican Ed Bryant, a Jackson lawyer, and has rolled to re-election ever since.

After Al Gore was elected vice president in 1992, the Tennessee governor — then McWherter — was in the position of appointing an interim replacement to fill Gore's seat in the Senate. The job was said to be Tanner's for the asking, but he told McWherter he preferred to stay on in the House.

KEY VOTES

2006

- No Stop broadband companies from favoring select Internet traffic
- No Affirm U.S. commitment to war in Iraq and reject setting a withdrawal date for troops
- No Repeal requirement for bilingual ballots at the polls
- Yes Permit U.S. sale of civilian nuclear technology to India
- Yes Build a 700-mile fence on the U.S.-Mexico border to curb illegal crossings
- No Permit warrantless wiretaps of suspected terrorists

2005

- Yes Intervene in the life-support case of Terri Schiavo
- Yes Lift President Bush's restrictions on stem cell research funding
- Yes Prohibit FBI access to library and bookstore records
- Yes Approve free-trade pact with five Central American countries
- Yes Pass energy policy overhaul favored by President Bush emphasizing domestic oil and gas production
- Yes End mandatory preservation of habitat of endangered animal and plant species
- Yes Ban torture of prisoners in U.S. custody

CQ VOTE STUDIES

	PARTY UNITY		PRESIDENTIAL SUPPORT	
	Support	Oppose	Support	Oppose
2006	74%	26%	66%	34%
2005	74%	26%	38%	62%
2004	74%	26%	39%	61%
2003	77%	23%	44%	56%
2002	70%	30%	56%	44%

INTEREST GROUPS

	AFL-CIO	ADA	CCUS	ACU
2006	71%	55%	86%	58%
2005	73%	75%	70%	50%
2004	69%	60%	56%	43%
2003	80%	90%	70%	48%
2002	67%	70%	80%	39%

TENNESSEE 8

West - Jackson, parts of Memphis and Clarksville

The mighty Mississippi to the west and the Tennessee and Cumberland rivers to the east frame the rolling hills and flat farmland that make up the predominately rural 8th. As residents flood to Memphis' northern suburbs and Nashville's western outposts, this once Democratic-leaning district shows growing Republican ties.

In the 2004 presidential election, suburban areas outside of the state's two most populous cities helped Republican George W. Bush defeat Democrat John Kerry by 7 percentage points in the 8th. Large black populations in Lake, Lauderdale and Haywood, however, helped Kerry win those counties. Conservative-leaning Democrats have held the area's House seat since Reconstruction.

The 8th is poor, but stable manufacturing in the Jackson area protects the economy from further decline. A Pringles potato chip facility in Jackson employs many district residents, and tire, auto and textile plants dot less-populated areas. Mechanization hurt factory employment, but it improved productivity on the district's many small cotton and soybean farms and chicken-processing plants. Two state prisons provide much-needed government jobs, and a naval air station has rebounded after previous downsizing. In the north, Clarksville's population has risen due to military growth and the expansion of Austin Peay State University.

The Tennessee River feeds into Kentucky Lake in the northeast, where conservationists journey each summer. The waterways of the Tennessee Valley Authority dams and power plants attract many avid hunters and fishermen to the district. Thousands of birdwatchers flock to Reelfoot Lake in the northwest each winter to view bald eagle migration.

MAJOR INDUSTRY

Manufacturing, agriculture, government

MILITARY BASES

Naval Support Activity Mid-South, 1,800 military, 200 civilian (2004)

CITIES

Jackson, 59,643; Memphis (pt.), 53,080; Clarksville (pt.), 19,775

NOTABLE

A 60-foot tall replica of the Eiffel Tower is in Paris, which is also home to the World's Biggest Fish Fry.

Rep. Steve Cohen (D)

CAPITOL OFFICE
225-3265
cohen.house.gov
1004 Longworth 20515-4209; fax 225-5663

COMMITTEES
Judiciary
Transportation & Infrastructure

RESIDENCE
Memphis

BORN
May 24, 1949, Memphis, Tenn.

RELIGION
Jewish

FAMILY
Single

EDUCATION
Vanderbilt U., B.A. 1971 (history); Memphis State U., J.D. 1973

CAREER
Lawyer

POLITICAL HIGHLIGHTS
Democratic nominee for Tenn. House, 1970; Tenn. Constitutional Convention, 1977-78 (vice president, 1977-78); Shelby County Commission, 1978-80; Shelby County General Sessions Court, 1980-80; defeated for election to Shelby County General Sessions Court, 1981; Tenn. Senate, 1983-2006; sought Democratic nomination for governor, 1994; sought Democratic nomination for U.S. House, 1996

ELECTION RESULTS

2006 GENERAL		
Steve Cohen (D)	103,341	59.9%
Jake Ford (I)	38,243	22.2%
Mark White (R)	31,002	18.0%
2006 PRIMARY		
Steve Cohen (D)	23,629	30.9%
Nikki Tinker (D)	19,164	25.1%
Joseph S. Ford Jr. (D)	9,334	12.2%
Julian T. Bolton (D)	8,055	10.6%
Ed Stanton (D)	6,927	9.1%
Ron Redwing (D)	2,169	2.8%
Marvell R. Mitchell (D)	1,804	2.4%
Ralph White (D)	1,700	2.2%
Joseph B. Kyles (D)	1,336	1.7%

Elected 2006; 1st term

Cohen represents a Memphis-based black-majority district that had sent a member of the Ford family to the House for the previous 32 years. Cohen won the seat of Harold E. Ford Jr., who ran unsuccessfully for the U.S. Senate seat vacated by Republican Bill Frist. Ford's father had represented the district for 22 years.

Cohen served for 24 years as a state senator, and maintained a good relationship with African-American voters. He also is the self-proclaimed "father of Tennessee's lottery," which raises money for state education and scholarships programs.

When he arrived in Washington, Cohen joined the Progressive Caucus, a group of the most liberal House members. He also got a seat on the Transportation and Infrastructure Committee, and didn't waste time pushing his own proposals. He saw early success when the House adopted, as an amendment to a transit security bill, his proposal establishing a program to minimize rail transportation of hazardous materials that are toxic when inhaled.

He opposes U.S. involvement in Iraq, and he voted for a 2007 supplemental spending bill that included a timetable for U.S. troop withdrawal. Cohen said he wavered about voting for the bill because "it's difficult for me to give another dollar and another life to the care and custody of this administration."

Cohen is from a family with deep roots, four generations' worth, in Memphis. He contracted polio as a child and had to give up his love of sports, he says, so he turned to his other passion — politics. On the day he registered to vote, he also filed for office. When he decided to go after Ford's seat in 2006, he first had to survive a 15-candidate primary race. The only white candidate, Cohen won with barely 31 percent of the vote.

His general-election campaign became complicated when Jake Ford, Harold Ford's brother, unexpectedly filed to run as an independent. A pharmaceutical company representative, Jake Ford had little political experience. Local party leaders coalesced behind Cohen, and he won with 60 percent of the vote over both Ford and GOP businessman Mark White.

TENNESSEE 9

Memphis

The 9th takes in most of the state's largest city, Memphis, which sits atop the bluffs of the Mississippi River. Memphis is 60 percent African-American, and counts more black residents than any Southern city outside of Texas. Traditional GOP voters gravitated out of the district to the outskirts of Shelby County, making the 9th the most comfortable Democratic district in Tennessee.

The area first sent an African-American to Congress in 1974, initiating a reign of Democratic black political power in Memphis. Local elections tend to be decided along racial lines, but residents historically vote for Democrats in federal races. The 9th has favored Democratic candidates with at least 60 percent of the vote for decades.

Memphis is the most populated city along the Mississippi and uses its central location between St. Louis and New Orleans, as well as Memphis International Airport, to thrive as a distribution center. FedEx and AutoZone, the nation's largest auto parts retailer, have headquarters in the 9th. The district also depends on St. Jude Children's Research Hospital and a local health care industry.

Renewal efforts have paved the way for inner-city economic development and new residential communities downtown. Tourism is a mainstay for the 9th, and both the FedExForum and Liberty Bowl Memorial Stadium draw audiences. Music-minded Memphis visitors take in Beale Street, and tourists flock here to honor two icons — Elvis Presley and Martin Luther King Jr. In 1968, King was assassinated at the Lorraine Motel, which is now a civil rights museum.

MAJOR INDUSTRY
Distribution, health care, tourism

CITIES
Memphis (pt.), 571,661

NOTABLE
Graceland was the home of Elvis Presley.

TEXAS

Gov. Rick Perry (R)

First elected: 2002; assumed office Dec. 21, 2000, following the resignation of George W. Bush, R, to become president

Length of term: 4 years

Term expires: 1/11

Salary: $115,345

Phone: (512) 463-2000

Residence: Austin

Born: March 4, 1950; Paint Creek, Texas

Religion: Methodist

Family: Wife, Anita Perry; two children

Education: Texas A&M U., B.S. 1972 (animal science)

Military service: Air Force, 1972-77

Career: Farmer; rancher

Political highlights: Texas House, 1984-90; Texas department of Agriculture commissioner, 1990-98; lieutenant governor, 1999-2000

Election results:

2006 GENERAL		
Rick Perry (R)	1,716,792	39.0%
Chris Bell (D)	1,310,337	29.8%
Carole Keeton Strayhorn (I)	796,851	18.1%
Richard S. "Kinky" Friedman (I)	547,674	12.4%

Lt. Gov. David Dewhurst (R)

First elected: 2002

Length of term: 4 years

Term expires: 1/11

Salary: $7,200

Phone: (512) 463-0001

LEGISLATURE

Legislature: January-May in odd-numbered years

Senate: 31 members, 4-year terms

2007 ratios: 20 R, 11D; 27 men, 4 women

Salary: $7,200

Phone: (512) 463-0001

House: 150 members, 2-year terms

2007 ratios: 81R, 69 D; 117 men, 33 women

Salary: $7,200

Phone: (512) 463-0845

TERM LIMITS

Governor: No

Senate: No

House: No

URBAN STATISTICS

CITY	POPULATION
Houston	1,953,631
Dallas	1,188,580
San Antonio	1,144,646
Austin	656,562
El Paso	563,662

REGISTERED VOTERS

Voters do not register by party.

MISCELLANEOUS

Web: www.state.tx.us

Capital: Austin

POPULATION

2006 population (est.)	23,507,783
2000 population	20,851,820
1990 population	16,986,510
Percent change (1990-2000)	+22.8%
Rank among states (2006)	2
Median age	32.3
Born in state	62.2%
Foreign born	13.9%
Violent crime rate	545/100,000
Poverty level	15.4%
Federal workers	173,367
Military	170,659

REDISTRICTING

The U.S. Supreme Court on June 28, 2006, invalidated part of the map that was used in the 2004 election. The U.S. District Court for the Eastern District of Texas on August 4, 2006, issued a new map that reconfigured five of Texas' 32 districts.

ELECTIONS

STATE ELECTION OFFICIAL
(512) 463-5650

DEMOCRATIC PARTY
(512) 478-9800

REPUBLICAN PARTY
(512) 477-9821

U.S. CONGRESS

Senate: 2 Republicans

House: 19 Republicans, 13 Democrats

2000 Census Statistics by District

DIST.	2004 VOTE FOR PRESIDENT BUSH	KERRY	WHITE	BLACK	ASIAN	HISP	MEDIAN INCOME	WHITE COLLAR	BLUE COLLAR	SERVICE INDUSTRY	OVER 64	UNDER 18	COLLEGE EDUCATION	RURAL	SQ. MILES
1	69%	30%	71%	18%	1%	9%	$33,461	53%	31%	15%	14%	26%	18%	49%	8,508
2	63	36	64	19	3	13	$47,029	63	24	13	10	27	23	11	1,937
3	66	33	63	9	8	17	$60,878	75	15	10	5	29	41	1	265
4	70	29	79	10	1	8	$38,276	56	29	14	13	27	18	50	9,534
5	67	33	72	12	2	13	$41,007	60	27	14	12	27	19	32	5,429
6	66	33	66	13	3	16	$45,857	62	24	13	9	28	24	20	6,198
7	64	35	67	6	7	18	$57,846	79	11	9	9	24	50	0	198
8	72	27	80	9	1	9	$40,459	56	30	15	11	27	18	50	8,150
9	30	70	17	37	11	33	$34,870	58	23	19	6	30	24	0	154
10	61	38	66	9	4	19	$52,465	70	19	11	8	28	35	19	3,803
11	78	22	65	4	1	30	$32,711	55	28	17	15	27	17	29	34,995
12	67	33	67	6	2	24	$41,735	58	28	14	10	28	21	17	2,168
13	77	22	74	6	1	18	$33,501	53	29	18	14	26	17	30	40,197
14	67	33	62	10	2	25	$41,335	56	29	15	11	28	19	29	7,095
15	51	49	20	2	1	78	$26,840	52	28	19	11	32	13	18	10,717

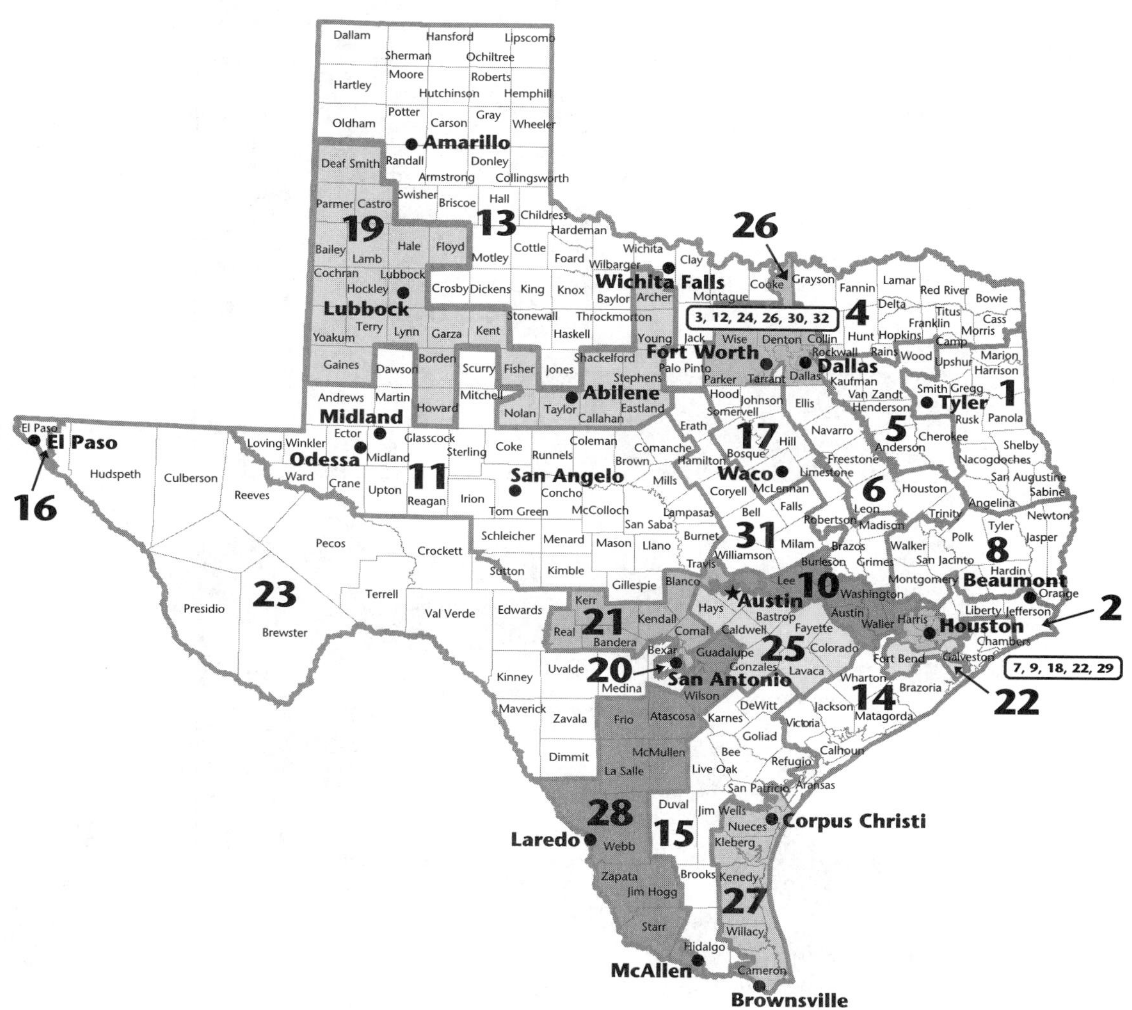

2000 Census Statistics by District

DIST.	2004 VOTE FOR PRESIDENT BUSH	KERRY	WHITE	BLACK	ASIAN	HISP	MEDIAN INCOME	WHITE COLLAR	BLUE COLLAR	SERVICE INDUSTRY	OVER 64	UNDER 18	COLLEGE EDUCATION	RURAL	SQ. MILES
16	43%	56%	17%	3%	1%	78%	$31,245	58%	25%	17%	10%	32%	17%	2%	581
17	69	30	71	10	1	15	$35,253	57	27	16	12	25	20	36	7,691
18	28	72	20	40	3	36	$31,291	52	30	18	8	29	14	0	227
19	77	22	64	5	1	29	$31,575	57	26	17	13	27	19	26	25,268
20	44	55	23	7	1	67	$31,937	57	24	19	10	29	15	0	184
21	66	34	68	6	3	21	$49,036	73	15	12	12	24	37	19	5,130
22	64	35	61	9	8	20	$57,932	69	20	11	7	29	32	5	971
23	57	43	30	3	1	65	$33,574	56	27	17	10	31	18	24	48,456
24	65	35	64	10	6	18	$56,098	73	17	10	6	27	36	1	334
25	46	54	53	10	2	34	$39,794	61	23	15	9	25	28	25	6,146

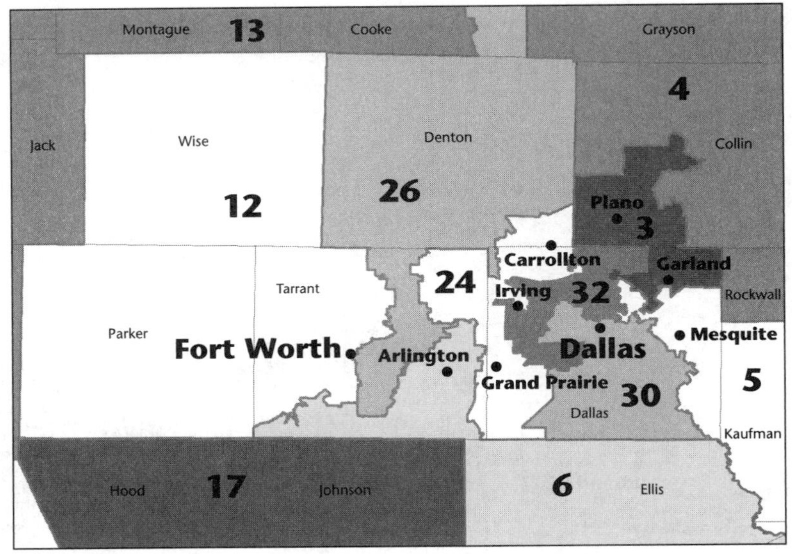

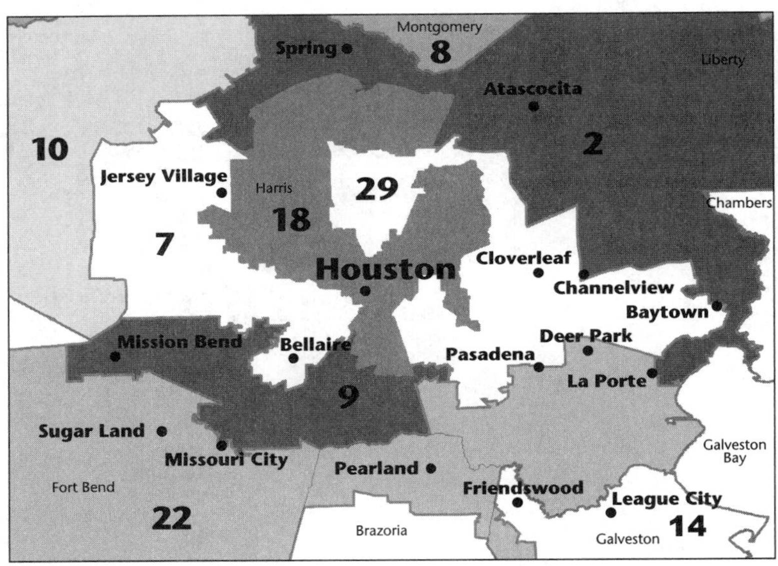

2000 Census Statistics by District

DIST.	2004 VOTE FOR PRESIDENT BUSH	KERRY	WHITE	BLACK	ASIAN	HISP	MEDIAN INCOME	WHITE COLLAR	BLUE COLLAR	SERVICE INDUSTRY	OVER 64	UNDER 18	COLLEGE EDUCATION	RURAL	SQ. MILES
26	64%	35%	66%	15%	2%	14%	$48,714	64%	22%	13%	8%	29%	27%	9%	1,292
27	55	45	28	2	1	68	$31,327	55	26	18	11	31	16	11	4,720
28	54	46	20	1	0	78	$28,866	51	31	18	9	34	13	21	13,600
29	44	55	22	10	1	66	$31,751	40	43	16	7	33	6	1	236
30	25	75	22	41	1	34	$33,505	52	31	17	8	30	16	1	317
31	66	33	66	13	2	16	$43,381	63	23	14	9	29	24	22	7,134
32	59	40	50	8	4	36	$45,725	66	21	13	9	25	36	0	160
STATE	61	38	52	11	3	32	$39,927	61	25	15	10	28	23	17	261,797
U.S.	50.7	48.3	69	12	4	13	$41,994	60	25	15	12	26	24	21	3,537,438

Sen. Kay Bailey Hutchison (R)

CAPITOL OFFICE
224-5922
hutchison.senate.gov
284 Russell 20510-4304; fax 224-0776

COMMITTEES
Appropriations
Commerce, Science & Transportation
Rules & Administration
Veterans' Affairs

RESIDENCE
Dallas

BORN
July 22, 1943, Galveston, Texas

RELIGION
Episcopalian

FAMILY
Husband, Ray Hutchison; two children

EDUCATION
U. of Texas, J.D. 1967, B.A. 1992

CAREER
Broadcast journalist; lawyer; banking executive; candy company owner

POLITICAL HIGHLIGHTS
Texas House, 1973-76; National Transportation Safety Board, 1976-78; sought Republican nomination for U.S. House, 1982; Texas treasurer, 1991-93

ELECTION RESULTS

2006 GENERAL

Kay Bailey Hutchison (R)	2,661,789	61.7%
Barbara Ann Radnofsky (D)	1,555,202	36.0%
Scott Lanier Jameson (LIBERT)	97,672	2.3%

2006 PRIMARY

Kay Bailey Hutchison (R)	unopposed

PREVIOUS WINNING PERCENTAGES
2000 (65%); 1994 (61%); 1993 Special Runoff Election (67%)

Elected June 1993; 3rd full term

Hutchison, once dismissed by critics as "the Breck Girl," has become a powerful force in Texas politics and in the Senate, where she is a member of the Republican leadership. Even with Congress under Democratic control, her ability to reach across the aisle and build consensus lets her continue to push through legislation important to her.

The one-time Texas cheerleader doesn't play to the galleries; she prefers to work behind the scenes on issues important to her state. This has contributed in no small measure to the success she has achieved and to the overwhelming support she receives at the ballot box. She breezed to a third term in 2006 with 62 percent of the vote.

Hutchison has allowed her state's junior senator, Republican John Cornyn, to step out in front on most national issues, just as she deferred to his talkative predecessor, Republican Phil Gramm. But in 2005, it was Hutchison, not Cornyn, who publicly entertained a challenge to incumbent Texas Republican Gov. Rick Perry — the second time she had considered such a race. As she had four years earlier, she ultimately decided against taking him on. But she said in early 2007 that she would consider running for vice president if the 2008 GOP presidential nominee should ask her.

That is not a far-fetched notion, especially if there's a woman on the Democratic ticket. As head of the Republican Policy Committee, Hutchison is one of the highest-ranking GOP women in the nation. She has years of experience in state and federal office, both executive and legislative, and the polish of a former broadcast journalist. She is known for putting "a friendly face" on the GOP view of the world.

More moderate than Cornyn, who is a leader of the GOP right in the Senate, Hutchison supports basic abortion rights and federal funding for expanded embryonic stem cell research, which many in her party oppose, including Cornyn. In the 109th Congress (2005-06), Cornyn supported President Bush on 94 percent of votes on which the president took a position, tying him with Wayne Allard of Colorado as the Senate's most loyal Bush supporter. Hutchison backed Bush's position 88 percent of the time, putting her in the middle ranks of GOP senators.

A member of the Appropriations Committee, Hutchison chaired the Military Construction-VA Subcommittee from 2001 to 2006, and is the panel's ranking Republican in the 110th Congress (2007-08). She has used her seat to funnel millions of dollars to Texas for a wide array of projects and to look out for its many military installations.

Hutchison also serves on the Commerce, Science and Transportation Committee, where she is the ranking Republican on the Space and Aeronautics Subcommittee, a boon for NASA's Johnson Space Center in Houston. She is on the Aviation Subcommittee as well, and has worked hard to help airlines based in her state. In 2004, Hutchison included a proposal in the intelligence bill to tighten security at air cargo facilities.

She was instrumental in helping to resolve a dispute that raged for decades between American Airlines and Southwest Airlines over the use of Dallas' Love Field, which is Southwest's headquarters. Hutchison in 2006 steered to enactment a bill implementing a complex local agreement settling the fight. "It was one of my most significant victories," she says.

In her first Senate term, Hutchison was the lead sponsor on a bill to repeal the "marriage penalty," which resulted in some two-income married couples paying higher income taxes than if each were single. It was incorporated into the 2001 tax cut law.

Hutchison first won election to the Senate Republican leadership at the end of 2000, breaking into the ranks of what used to be an all-male team following the death of Georgia Republican Paul Coverdell. She began at No. 4 on the leadership ladder, and held that rank until 2006, when Republicans chose their leaders for the 110th Congress. Without fuss, Hutchison dropped down a notch to the No. 5 position to let Cornyn take her old job. She has made no attempt to move up to the top leadership posts.

Her solid career and leadership experience have quieted the critics who used to portray her as superficial. When she was Texas state treasurer, the late liberal Texas newspaper columnist Molly Ivins dubbed her "the Breck Girl," after an old shampoo commercial featuring a woman tossing her long tresses. Hutchison jokes that she was happy to hand off the moniker to Democrat John Edwards, a 2008 presidential contender whose $400 haircuts drew waves of ridicule in 2007. "I was really glad to see finally that news reporters started talking about men's hair," Hutchison said.

She is also aware of her role as a model for younger women, and in 2004 published a book, "American Heroines," about women pioneers. Hutchison was the first, and so far only, woman elected to the Senate from Texas.

She graduated in 1967 from the University of Texas School of Law, one of only five women in a class of 500. But she found law firms were not willing to hire women, assuming they would get married and quit or move away. "From the day I walked into law school, I started hitting brick walls," she says. Instead, Hutchison took a job as a legal correspondent for a television station, where she was able to put her training to use.

From an old Texas family, she grew up in La Marque, a small town on the Gulf Coast. Her great-great-grandfather, Charles S. Taylor, was a signer of the Texas Declaration of Independence. In an elementary school diary, Hutchison once penciled, "I want to be president of the United States." But she says she never had any real political ambitions until a local GOP leader urged Hutchison, a TV reporter, to run for the state legislature. She did and was elected in 1972, a time when most women in Texas politics were Democrats.

In Austin, Hutchison teamed on legislation with Democrat Sarah Weddington, the lawyer who filed the case that led to the *Roe v. Wade* decision establishing a woman's right to have an abortion. The two sponsored bills protecting victims of sex offenses, including a ban on publishing the names of rape victims. Hutchison herself has been the victim of a stalker.

In 1976, President Gerald Ford appointed her to the National Transportation Safety Board. Hutchison moved to Dallas in 1978 and married for a second time, to attorney Ray Hutchison, a former colleague in the state House. She unsuccessfully sought the Republican nomination for an open U.S. House seat in 1982. Hutchison spent a good chunk of the 1980s in the business world, as a banking executive and owner of a candy manufacturing company. Returning to politics in 1990, she was elected state treasurer.

In 1993, she won a special Senate election called after President Bill Clinton chose longtime Democratic Sen. Lloyd Bentsen to be his Treasury secretary. Democratic Gov. Ann Richards appointed Bob Krueger, a former House member, to the seat. Hutchison challenged him in the state's open primary, also competing against Republican Reps. Joe L. Barton and Jack Fields. Krueger and Hutchison tied with 29 percent of the vote; she won the runoff with 67 percent. She has won easily ever since.

In 2001, Hutchison and her husband adopted an infant girl, whom they named Kathryn Bailey Hutchison, and an infant boy, whom they named Houston Taylor Hutchison. "We have, for many years, been trying to add to our wonderful family, and this is truly a dream come true," the Hutchisons said after the adoptions.

KEY VOTES

2006

Yes Confirm Samuel A. Alito Jr. to the Supreme Court
Yes Allow consideration of a bill to establish a $140 billion trust fund to compensate victims of asbestos exposure
Yes Extend tax cuts for two years at a cost of $70 billion over five years
No Overhaul immigration policy with border security, enforcement and guest worker program
Yes Allow consideration of a bill to permanently repeal the estate tax
No Urge President Bush to begin troop withdrawals from Iraq in 2006
Yes Lift President Bush's restrictions on stem cell research funding
Yes Authorize military tribunals for suspected terrorists

2005

Yes Curb class action lawsuits by shifting them from state to federal courts
Yes Allow confirmation vote on Priscilla R. Owen to the U.S. Court of Appeals for the 5th Circuit
Yes Oppose mandatory emissions limits and block recognition of global warming as a threat
Yes Approve free-trade pact with five Central American countries
Yes Pass energy policy overhaul favored by President Bush emphasizing domestic oil and gas production
Yes Shield gunmakers from lawsuits when their products are used in crimes
Yes Ban torture of prisoners in U.S. custody
Yes Renew 16 provisions of the Patriot Act
Yes Allow final vote on opening the Arctic National Wildlife Refuge to oil and gas exploration

CQ VOTE STUDIES

	PARTY UNITY		PRESIDENTIAL SUPPORT	
	Support	Oppose	Support	Oppose
2006	91%	9%	84%	16%
2005	90%	10%	96%	4%
2004	89%	11%	94%	6%
2003	94%	6%	96%	4%
2002	92%	8%	96%	4%
2001	90%	10%	96%	4%
2000	96%	4%	45%	55%
1999	90%	10%	29%	71%
1998	92%	8%	37%	63%
1997	95%	5%	63%	37%

INTEREST GROUPS

	AFL-CIO	ADA	CCUS	ACU
2006	20%	5%	92%	84%
2005	14%	15%	94%	92%
2004	8%	25%	94%	84%
2003	0%	10%	100%	75%
2002	23%	5%	95%	100%
2001	19%	10%	85%	96%
2000	0%	0%	93%	96%
1999	0%	0%	94%	88%
1998	0%	0%	100%	88%
1997	0%	5%	100%	92%

Sen. John Cornyn (R)

CAPITOL OFFICE
224-2934
cornyn.senate.gov
517 Hart 20510-4302; fax 228-2856

COMMITTEES
Armed Services
Budget
Judiciary
Select Ethics - vice chairman

RESIDENCE
San Antonio

BORN
Feb. 2, 1952, Houston, Texas

RELIGION
Church of Christ

FAMILY
Wife, Sandy Cornyn; two children

EDUCATION
Trinity U., B.A. 1973 (journalism); St. Mary's U. (Texas), J.D. 1977; U. of Virginia, LL.M. 1995

CAREER
Lawyer; real estate agent

POLITICAL HIGHLIGHTS
Texas District Court judge, 1985-91; Texas Supreme Court, 1991-97; Texas attorney general, 1999-2002

ELECTION RESULTS

2002 GENERAL		
John Cornyn (R)	2,496,243	55.3%
Ron Kirk (D)	1,955,758	43.3%
2002 PRIMARY		
John Cornyn (R)	478,825	77.3%
Bruce Rusty Lang (R)	46,907	7.6%
Douglas G. Deffenbaugh (R)	43,611	7.0%
Dudley F. Mooney (R)	32,202	5.2%
Lawrence Cranberg (R)	17,757	2.9%

Elected 2002; 1st term

As he moves through the final years of his first Senate term, Cornyn has become one of the GOP's most ardent and vocal defenders of the Bush administration on topics ranging from U.S. treatment of enemy combatants to the virtues of President Bush's judicial nominees.

Cornyn was elected vice chairman of the Senate Republican Conference, the No. 4 rung on the leadership ladder, for the 110th Congress (2007-08). He already had been viewed as a spokesman for the conservative point of view on some hot-button issues, including same-sex marriage and warrantless surveillance of electronic communications between individuals in the United States and terrorism suspects abroad. And he was literally a one-man rapid response team to critics of Bush's Supreme Court selections.

Cornyn (CORE-nin) was parked in the Senate Press Gallery ready to rebut Democratic critics the night of July 19, 2005, when Bush announced his nomination of John G. Roberts Jr. to the high court. (Roberts later was nominated and confirmed as chief justice.) And he stood by White House counsel Harriet Miers, a fellow Texan, to the bitter end as other conservatives assailed her as an unknown who might stray toward moderation. He accused conservative pundits of creating a "poisonous atmosphere" that doomed her high court nomination.

Cornyn, who wears cowboy boots emblazoned "United States Senate Texas" with his business suits, has close ties to both Bush and Karl Rove, the president's senior political strategist. Cornyn rose to prominence in Texas a few years ahead of Bush, a former governor, but the two became friends during their time together in Austin. Bush, who is fond of giving his friends nicknames, telephoned Cornyn on election night in 2002 to say, "Congratulations, Johnny Boy."

About the only major issue on which he has split with the president is immigration. Cornyn rejected the comprehensive approach favored by Bush and passed by the Senate in 2006 because it included a path to eventual U.S. citizenship for most illegal immigrants now in the United States. Instead, he offered his own bill, with Republican Jon Kyl of Arizona, to require immigrants to return home before they could apply for temporary guest worker status that did not include eventual citizenship. Hispanics protested his bill outside his offices in Dallas and Houston, but Cornyn told The Dallas Morning News, "I didn't get into this debate to score political points." In the 110th Congress, he was granted the ranking member seat on the Judiciary Subcommittee on Immigration, and early in 2007 he and Kyl entered discussions with the White House with the aim of finding a resolution on the issue.

In the wake of revelations that dismissals of eight U.S. attorneys were the result of a coordinated campaign between White House and Justice Department officials, Cornyn's support of the White House wavered. With Attorney General Alberto R. Gonzales in the hot seat, Cornyn said, "Appearances are troubling. This has not been handled well. But in Texas we believe in having a fair trial and then the hanging."

As chairman of the Judiciary Subcommittee on the Constitution in the 108th Congress (2003-04), Cornyn had spearheaded efforts to pass proposed constitutional amendments banning same-sex marriage and flag burning. He also sponsored a constitutional amendment to allow Congress to pass a law establishing a mechanism for replacing lawmakers in the event that a quarter of the House or Senate are killed or incapacitated. None of the proposals made it through the Senate.

A former Texas attorney general, district court judge and state Supreme Court judge, Cornyn chafes at many judicial rulings on social issues. "If the judiciary gets into the business of making blatantly political decisions, it pretty much does away with the need for a Congress," he said. In 2005, he raised some eyebrows with a Senate floor speech in which he suggested that public anger over politically charged decisions might be responsible for several instances of violence against judges. He returned to the floor a day later to say, "There is no possible justification for courthouse violence."

From his seat on the Armed Services Committee, Cornyn also backed without reservation Bush's decision to wage war in Iraq and the president's effort to deploy a national missile defense system. In 2007, he stood behind Bush's plan to send more than 21,000 additional combat troops into Iraq.

Cornyn was among a number of Republicans who urged former Armed Services Chairman John W. Warner of Virginia to back off from investigating allegations of prisoner abuse by the U.S. military at Iraq's Abu Ghraib prison. And in 2005, he was one of just nine senators — all Republicans — to vote against an amendment by John McCain of Arizona banning cruel, inhumane or degrading treatment of prisoners captured in the war on terror.

Cornyn, who once considered a career in journalism, is a strong proponent of more openness in government. He is a forceful advocate of the Freedom of Information Act, steering a bill through the Senate in 2005 that would require Congress to tell the public when it exempts information from FOIA disclosures. In 2006, and again in 2007, he helped guide legislation through the Judiciary Committee to permit applicants to track the progress of their requests for information. The bill, approved in April 2007, also would require agencies to respond to FOIA requests within 20 days.

Elected state attorney general in 1998, Cornyn was the first Republican to hold the post since Reconstruction. Like Bush's, his career in state government was characterized primarily by a pro-business, limited-government philosophy. He favored strict restrictions on medical malpractice lawsuits, and while on the state Supreme Court, he joined a ruling allowing cigarette companies to partially escape responsibility for smoking-related health claims.

Cornyn is the son of a World War II B-17 pilot. His family eventually settled in San Antonio, where his father became an Air Force pathologist. A wrestler in high school and college, Cornyn majored in journalism at Texas' Trinity University. He was eventually turned off by reporters' low salaries and waited tables at a Steak and Ale restaurant while earning his real estate license. When that career faltered in a sagging economy, Cornyn went to law school. He later practiced law in San Antonio, specializing in defending doctors against medical malpractice lawsuits.

In 1984, some Republican friends of his — looking to crack the Democrats' longstanding hold on Texas' judicial elections — approached him at a Super Bowl party and asked him to run for a state district court seat. He did, and he won. Six years later, he was elected to the state Supreme Court. In 1998, he won a bruising attorney general's race against Democrat Jim Mattox.

As attorney general, Cornyn chaired a commission tasked with proposing new political boundaries to the state legislature after the 2000 census. He presented a redistricting plan that could have resulted in major Republican gains. The courts eventually imposed a less partisan map, but his efforts raised his standing with Rove.

When Texas GOP Sen. Phil Gramm decided to retire in 2002, Cornyn ran for the seat and won a GOP primary against four little-known opponents with 77 percent of the vote. In the November race against Dallas' former mayor, Ron Kirk, Cornyn ran on his loyalty to Bush — an overwhelmingly popular figure in the state — and won with 55 percent.

KEY VOTES

2006

Yes Confirm Samuel A. Alito Jr. to the Supreme Court
Yes Allow consideration of a bill to establish a $140 billion trust fund to compensate victims of asbestos exposure
Yes Extend tax cuts for two years at a cost of $70 billion over five years
No Overhaul immigration policy with border security, enforcement and guest worker program
Yes Allow consideration of a bill to permanently repeal the estate tax
No Urge President Bush to begin troop withdrawals from Iraq in 2006
No Lift President Bush's restrictions on stem cell research funding
Yes Authorize military tribunals for suspected terrorists

2005

Yes Curb class action lawsuits by shifting them from state to federal courts
Yes Allow confirmation vote on Priscilla R. Owen to the U.S. Court of Appeals for the 5th Circuit
Yes Oppose mandatory emissions limits and block recognition of global warming as a threat
Yes Approve free-trade pact with five Central American countries
Yes Pass energy policy overhaul favored by President Bush emphasizing domestic oil and gas production
Yes Shield gunmakers from lawsuits when their products are used in crimes
No Ban torture of prisoners in U.S. custody
Yes Renew 16 provisions of the Patriot Act
Yes Allow final vote on opening the Arctic National Wildlife Refuge to oil and gas exploration

CQ VOTE STUDIES

	PARTY UNITY		PRESIDENTIAL SUPPORT	
	Support	Oppose	Support	Oppose
2006	97%	3%	91%	9%
2005	95%	5%	98%	2%
2004	97%	3%	96%	4%
2003	99%	1%	98%	2%

INTEREST GROUPS

	AFL-CIO	ADA	CCUS	ACU
2006	13%	0%	83%	96%
2005	14%	10%	89%	96%
2004	8%	5%	100%	100%
2003	0%	10%	100%	85%

Rep. Louie Gohmert (R)

CAPITOL OFFICE
225-3035
www.house.gov/gohmert
510 Cannon 20515-4301; fax 226-1230

COMMITTEES
Judiciary
Natural Resources
Small Business

RESIDENCE
Tyler

BORN
Aug. 18, 1953, Pittsburg, Texas

RELIGION
Baptist

FAMILY
Wife, Kathy Gohmert; three children

EDUCATION
Texas A&M U., B.A. 1975 (history);
Baylor U., J.D. 1977

MILITARY SERVICE
Army, 1978-82

CAREER
Lawyer; state prosecutor

POLITICAL HIGHLIGHTS
Smith County District Court judge, 1993-2002;
Texas Court of Appeals chief justice, 2002-03

ELECTION RESULTS

2006 GENERAL		
Louie Gohmert (R)	104,099	68.0%
Roger L. Owen (D)	46,303	30.2%
Donald Perkison (LIBERT)	2,668	1.7%
2006 PRIMARY		
Louie Gohmert (R)		unopposed
2004 GENERAL		
Louie Gohmert (R)	157,068	61.5%
Max Sandlin (D)	96,281	37.7%

Elected 2004; 2nd term

Gohmert has a slow, soft East Texas drawl that is a strange contrast to his unapologetically sharp tongue. He says he is comfortable speaking his mind after serving for 10 years as a trial judge for the Smith County District Court. "As a judge, you have to look people in the eye and make decisions," he says. "Former judges don't seem to have a problem having the courage to stand up and say what we believe is right."

Conservative on both social and economic issues, Gohmert owes his seat to former House Majority Leader Tom DeLay, a fellow Texan, who orchestrated the highly partisan Texas redistricting plan that produced a net gain of seven Republican seats at the start of the 109th Congress (2005-06).

Gohmert's experience as a judge is reflected in the legislation he introduced in his first term to increase criminal penalties against people who threaten or attack judges and prosecutors. He said it was prompted by the 2005 murder in Chicago of U.S. District Judge Joan Lefkow's husband and mother by a litigant she ruled against in a medical malpractice suit. Another incident occurred in Gohmert's hometown of Tyler. In February 2005, an armed man killed his ex-wife and wounded his son and several police officers right outside the Smith County courthouse where Gohmert had presided.

Gohmert says he has been threatened many times by defendants and people he put in jail, including in a letter from an inmate who threatened his family and mentioned the church they attend. The court security bill passed in the House in 2005 but didn't advance through the Senate. Gohmert says he's hopeful a new version of the measure will win enactment in the 110th Congress (2007-08).

Despite his background as a judge, Gohmert can be a harsh critic of the U.S. Supreme Court. He particularly disliked a 2005 decision that allowed local governments to invoke eminent domain to take over private development projects. In a July 2005 op-ed piece for The Washington Times, Gohmert and fellow Texas GOP Reps. John Carter and Ted Poe wrote that the high court almost makes "it sound 'fair' that private property can be taken from one legitimate owner and forcibly transferred to one who offers greater financial rewards to the ruler."

Gohmert was given a seat on the Judiciary Committee during his first term, where he proved to be a dogged conservative voice. He strained the patience of both Democrats and Republicans during a July 2006 committee markup on a measure aimed at reducing recidivism rates of newly released prisoners. Gohmert tried nine times over three hours to add language expressly stating that faith-based organizations would be eligible for funds under the bill. All of his attempts to add the language were rejected.

He was similarly persistent during a March 2007 debate on a bill to help former inmates adjust to life after imprisonment. In two separate Judiciary meetings, he tried to strike the phrase "creed and religion" from an amendment prohibiting religious groups from discriminating against employees. Gohmert angered Jewish Democrats when he suggested that not allowing religious groups to only hire employees of like faith could force Jewish organizations to hire Nazis.

Gohmert also raised eyebrows during committee debate that month on a bill that would give the District of Columbia a voting House member — a plan he opposes. He called for the creation of congressional districts made up of military installations with 10,000 or more personnel, and he threatened to offer at least 40 amendments, one for each base. He sounded serious, but quit after offering two proposals. "If we really support our troops and think it's constitutional to create new congressional districts, then let's really support our troops and give them a vote," Gohmert said before throwing in the towel.

A fiscal hawk, Gohmert opposes annual automatic raises in federal spending to compensate for inflation. But when Hurricane Rita hit his district in 2005, he said the federal government wasn't doing enough to reimburse "the many communities, faith-based entities and the state of Texas," which had "drained [their] assets to save lives," The Washington Post reported.

A strong supporter of the Iraq War, Gohmert called Iraqi dictator Saddam Hussein "a murderin', bloodsuckin' thief" in The Dallas Morning News. But he met his match in 2006 facing off with John P. Murtha, a former Marine and combat veteran, on the House floor. Gohmert suggested that if Iraq War critics like Murtha had "prevailed after the bloodbaths in Normandy and in the Pacific . . . we would be here speaking Japanese or German." Murtha shot back, asking if Gohmert had served in Normandy or Vietnam as a combat soldier. Gohmert replied quietly that he hadn't and then thanked the Pennsylvania Democrat for "all that he has done with the wounded."

Gohmert grew up in Mount Pleasant, an East Texas town of 8,000 where his father worked as an architect and his mother taught eighth-grade English. He worked a variety of jobs while growing up, including hauling hay, pumping gas and working at a construction site. He first won elected office as class president of his junior high school. He followed his father in attending Texas A&M University, where he was given an ROTC scholarship and rose to the rank of brigade commander in the school's Corps of Cadets.

Gohmert attended law school, then worked as an assistant district attorney for three east Texas counties while waiting for his call to active military duty. He served four years as an Army lawyer at Ft. Benning, Ga.

Returning to Texas in 1982, he worked as a civil litigator on mostly contract and insurance cases. His mother's death in 1992 prompted him to think over her advice to become a judge. He ran in 1993 after he was unable to find anyone willing to challenge the Smith County District Court incumbent, who had called Gohmert asking to be set up romantically with a client of Gohmert's who had a case pending in his courtroom. He served for the next 10 years, then was appointed by the governor to the Texas Court of Appeals.

After DeLay's success in pushing through the Texas redistricting plan, Gohmert unseated four-term Democratic Rep. Max Sandlin in 2004 by almost 24 percentage points. In 2006, Gohmert again won easily with 68 percent of the vote.

KEY VOTES

2006

- No Stop broadband companies from favoring select Internet traffic
- Yes Affirm U.S. commitment to war in Iraq and reject setting a withdrawal date for troops
- Yes Repeal requirement for bilingual ballots at the polls
- Yes Permit U.S. sale of civilian nuclear technology to India
- Yes Build a 700-mile fence on the U.S.-Mexico border to curb illegal crossings
- Yes Permit warrantless wiretaps of suspected terrorists

2005

- Yes Intervene in the life-support case of Terri Schiavo
- No Lift President Bush's restrictions on stem cell research funding
- No Prohibit FBI access to library and bookstore records
- Yes Approve free-trade pact with five Central American countries
- Yes Pass energy policy overhaul favored by President Bush emphasizing domestic oil and gas production
- Yes End mandatory preservation of habitat of endangered animal and plant species
- No Ban torture of prisoners in U.S. custody

CQ VOTE STUDIES

	PARTY UNITY		PRESIDENTIAL SUPPORT	
	Support	Oppose	Support	Oppose
2006	93%	7%	78%	22%
2005	95%	5%	88%	12%

INTEREST GROUPS

	AFL-CIO	ADA	CCUS	ACU
2006	18%	5%	100%	96%
2005	15%	0%	85%	96%

TEXAS 1
Northeast — Tyler, Longview

In this lush portion of East Texas, tree-covered hills and cypress swamps share space with what remains of the once-prominent oil centers in Longview and Tyler. Slow population growth and miles of forests and farmland are hallmarks of the 1st, which runs roughly 140 miles along the Louisiana border and takes in the Toledo Bend Reservoir. The district shares more traits with its traditionally laid-back Cajun neighbors than with the fast-paced urban life of nearby Dallas and its suburbs.

Timber is still central to the economy of the southern part of the 1st, complemented by poultry, dairy and beef cattle operations. But timber has faced stiff competition from companies in China and South America, where wage and energy costs are lower. Further, in 2005 Hurricane Rita caused severe wind damage to the local timber crop, while manufacturing and oil sustained only minor interruptions. Heavy rains in parts of the district, and power loss throughout most counties, disrupted residents' ability to occupy their homes and operate businesses.

In Smith County, the 1st's western edge, Tyler's economy is growing rapidly. It has healthy timber, natural gas and health care industries, with some hospital systems based in the city. Tyler and Longview, in neighboring Gregg County, have healthy manufacturing sectors, with Eastman Chemical, Carrier and Trane facilities here, and SYSCO building a distribution center scheduled to begin operations in mid-2008.

Residents tend to be conservative, even among Democrats, and the region associates itself with the Bible Belt that stretches through much of the South. Many of the largest and most-populated counties in the district — Nacogdoches, Rusk, Gregg and Smith — vote reliably Republican. George W. Bush won 69 percent of the district's 2004 presidential vote, but conservative Democrats historically can win pockets in the 1st, especially in rural Marion County. The district has one of the largest percentages of elderly residents in Texas, which makes access to health care an important issue in rural areas.

MAJOR INDUSTRY

Timber, agriculture, manufacturing, steel, oil and gas

CITIES

Tyler, 83,650; Longview, 73,344; Lufkin, 32,709; Nacogdoches, 29,914

NOTABLE

Tyler boasts the nation's largest public rose garden, with 30,000 roses.

Rep. Ted Poe (R)

CAPITOL OFFICE
225-6565
www.house.gov/poe
1605 Longworth 20515-4302; fax 225-5547

COMMITTEES
Foreign Affairs
Transportation & Infrastructure

RESIDENCE
Humble

BORN
Sept. 10, 1948, Temple, Texas

RELIGION
United Church of Christ

FAMILY
Wife, Carol Poe; four children

EDUCATION
Abilene Christian College, B.A. 1970 (political science); U. of Houston, J.D. 1973

MILITARY SERVICE
Air Force Reserve, 1970-76

CAREER
County prosecutor; college instructor

POLITICAL HIGHLIGHTS
Harris County District Court judge, 1981-2003

ELECTION RESULTS

2006 GENERAL		
Ted Poe (R)	90,490	65.6%
Gary E. Binderim (D)	45,080	32.7%
Justo J. Perez (LIBERT)	2,295	1.7%
2006 PRIMARY		
Ted Poe (R)		unopposed
2004 GENERAL		
Ted Poe (R)	139,951	55.5%
Nick Lampson (D)	108,156	42.9%
Sandra Leigh Saulsbury (LIBERT)	3,931	1.6%

Elected 2004; 2nd term

Poe first gained notoriety for his unorthodox and tough sentencing of criminals as a Texas criminal court judge. He still prefers to be called "judge" over "congressman," favoring his 22-year judicial career in Harris County, where he would publicly shame convicts in what became known as "Poe-etic justice."

Although he says he was shy as a child, he is now regularly found on the House floor when the daily business is done, espousing his conservative views before the C-SPAN cameras. "I'm still shy," he says. "But when it comes to getting down in the mud and the blood and the beer with people, I usually have a position and I tell them what I think."

Poe says he is a "conservative" first and a "Republican" second, and he proclaimed to The Beaumont Enterprise that he does not "drink the party Kool-Aid." In the 109th Congress (2005-06), Poe voted with his party 92 percent of the time on votes that pitted a majority of the two parties against each other. He supported President Bush 83 percent of the time.

True to his conservative views, Poe has zero tolerance for illegal immigrants, whom he casts as a critical threat to national security. He took on an uphill campaign in 2006 to win a presidential pardon for two Texas Border Patrol agents, who he said were wrongly imprisoned for shooting an illegal immigrant bringing drugs across the border.

Although he has not been able to get a seat on the Judiciary Committee, as he hoped, Poe has not abandoned the law enforcement and judicial issues that were his focus before his election to Congress.

A key concern for Poe is border enforcement. He is irritated by Bush's support of an immigration bill that would let illegal immigrants earn a path to citizenship. Poe also has denounced a one-year pilot project under the North American Free Trade Agreement that would let 100 Mexican trucking companies carry cargo within the United States.

"Our federal government wants to give out blanket amnesty to all those illegally in our country, our banks are blatantly targeting the illegal cash economy, our Justice Department prosecutes border agents over illegals committing crimes in our country, and now our Transportation Department has opened our borders to untold trouble," Poe said. "It is time our government starts doing what is best for the United States and stop working for Mexico."

Poe does back the president on the war in Iraq, however. He says the military generals should be left alone to "finish the job." When he learned there were complaints of abuse of terrorism suspects held at Guantánamo Bay, he called it "annoying."

As a member of the Transportation and Infrastructure Committee, Poe looks out for the economic interests of his suburban Houston district, such as energy production and Gulf Coast shipping. Topping his priorities is a project to widen and deepen the Sabine Neches Waterway, where 20 percent to 30 percent of the nation's commercial jet fuel is produced and shipped. Poe was the lead sponsor of a 2006 measure to block the Department of Transportation from allowing foreign control of U.S. airlines. "American airlines should be just that, owned by Americans," Poe said.

Poe sat on the Small Business Committee in the 109th Congress, where he supported a plan to allow small businesses to join together under one health care plan. He said he was disappointed when the proposal was omitted from a bill to increase the minimum wage passed by the House in early

2007. He said he voted for the Democratic measure because his constituents demanded it.

Another key issue for Poe is the protection of abused and neglected children. He wants to create a national registry for convicted pedophiles and other sex offenders. Judges who do not meet his own tough sentencing standards, particularly in cases involving children, earn a mention in Poe's "Judges Hall of Shame" during his regular floor speeches. The speeches always end with, "That's just the way it is." He has introduced legislation that would allow U.S. Supreme Court proceedings to be televised.

The boot-wearing lawmaker is a proud Texan. Born in Temple and raised in Houston, Poe has filled his Capitol Hill office with photographs of the Texas countryside that he has personally snapped.

He said a major turning point in his life came in the ninth grade. "I was shy so my daddy made me take speech class so that I would talk more. I've been talking ever since, I guess," he said. He often delivers motivational speeches to law enforcement groups.

Poe was deeply influenced by his grandmother, a "Yellow Dog Democrat," who died at the age of 99. "She never forgave me for being a Republican. She told me once, 'I'm not sure you can go to Heaven being a Republican.' She might have meant it too," Poe chuckled.

He said he was also affected by the story of William Barrett Travis, the Texas commander at the Battle of the Alamo. Posted at the door of Poe's personal office is a framed copy of Travis' Letter from the Alamo, which Poe often quotes in his speeches.

Poe earned a political science degree from Abilene Christian College and a law degree from the University of Houston Law Center. He served in the U.S. Air Force Reserve. He was an assistant district attorney and chief felony prosecutor for eight years and never lost a jury trial.

He says he became a Republican when Gov. William Clements named him to the bench. One of Poe's more famous punishments required an auto thief to serve jail time — and to hand over the keys of his Trans Am to his victim, a 75-year-old grandmother, who drove the car until the stolen vehicle was recovered and repaired. He also once made a burglar stand on a sidewalk wearing a sign that read, "I stole from this store."

In 2004, Poe entered the race for the 2nd District, which had been redrawn by then GOP Majority Leader Tom DeLay to favor his own party. The district included almost half the former 9th District constituent base represented by four-term Democrat Nick Lampson. Poe ousted Lampson with 56 percent of the vote. He won again easily in 2006 by 33 percentage points.

KEY VOTES

2006

- No Stop broadband companies from favoring select Internet traffic
- Yes Affirm U.S. commitment to war in Iraq and reject setting a withdrawal date for troops
- Yes Repeal requirement for bilingual ballots at the polls
- Yes Permit U.S. sale of civilian nuclear technology to India
- Yes Build a 700-mile fence on the U.S.-Mexico border to curb illegal crossings
- Yes Permit warrantless wiretaps of suspected terrorists

2005

- Yes Intervene in the life-support case of Terri Schiavo
- No Lift President Bush's restrictions on stem cell research funding
- Yes Prohibit FBI access to library and bookstore records
- Yes Approve free-trade pact with five Central American countries
- Yes Pass energy policy overhaul favored by President Bush emphasizing domestic oil and gas production
- Yes End mandatory preservation of habitat of endangered animal and plant species
- No Ban torture of prisoners in U.S. custody

CQ VOTE STUDIES

	PARTY UNITY		PRESIDENTIAL SUPPORT	
	Support	Oppose	Support	Oppose
2006	90%	10%	85%	15%
2005	94%	6%	81%	19%

INTEREST GROUPS

	AFL-CIO	ADA	CCUS	ACU
2006	21%	10%	87%	84%
2005	20%	0%	89%	92%

TEXAS 2

East – Beaumont, Port Arthur, part of Houston and northern and eastern suburbs

The 2nd stretches 100 miles from Louisiana and the Gulf of Mexico west to some of Houston's more affluent northern suburbs. In the east are Beaumont, an oil city on the Neches River, and Port Arthur, 15 miles away on Sabine Lake, and the two cities anchor the 2nd's robust shipping-based economy. In late 2005, Hurricane Rita made landfall along the Sabine River, the border between Texas and Louisiana, halting refinery and shipping for several days, downing power lines and trees across the district and damaging rice and soybean crops.

Petrochemical manufacturing dominates the area between Beaumont and Port Arthur. Major manufacturing sites here include an ExxonMobil Chemical plant in Beaumont and Huntsman facilities in Port Arthur and Port Neches. The 2nd has a large rural portion, with unpopulated areas in Jefferson and Liberty counties. Liberty County's population continues to grow, and many residents make the long commute into Houston.

A southern branch dips into Houston's eastern suburbs and takes in part of Baytown, a petrochemical city. The rest of the 2nd's portion of Harris County, near Lake Houston and to its west, is suburban. Many residents work at George Bush Intercontinental Airport (in the adjacent 18th). The district hosts several large companies in traditional blue-collar industries and a growing white-collar employment sector, but a lack of economic diversification has hurt the 2nd, and unemployment rates remain high.

The 2nd tends to vote like Texas overall — mostly conservative and Republican — but not overwhelmingly enough to shut out Democrats. Harris County provides candidates with a solid Republican base, but the Beaumont area tends to favor moderate to conservative Democrats.

MAJOR INDUSTRY

Petrochemicals, shipping, service

CITIES

Beaumont, 113,866; Port Arthur, 57,755; Houston (pt.), 57,580

NOTABLE

South of Beaumont, the Spindletop-Gladys City Boomtown Museum is located on the site of the 1901 gusher that began Texas' oil boom; The Babe Didrikson Zaharias Museum in Beaumont honors the woman who is considered by many to be the nation's best female athlete of all time.

Rep. Sam Johnson (R)

CAPITOL OFFICE
225-4201
samjohnson.house.gov
1211 Longworth 20515-4303; fax 225-1485

COMMITTEES
Ways & Means

RESIDENCE
Plano

BORN
Oct. 11, 1930, San Antonio, Texas

RELIGION
Methodist

FAMILY
Wife, Shirley Johnson; three children

EDUCATION
Southern Methodist U., B.B.A. 1951; George Washington U., M.S.I.A. 1974 (international affairs)

MILITARY SERVICE
Air Force, 1951-79

CAREER
Home builder; Top Gun flight school director; Air Force pilot

POLITICAL HIGHLIGHTS
Texas House, 1985-91

ELECTION RESULTS

2006 GENERAL		
Sam Johnson (R)	88,690	62.5%
Dan Dodd (D)	49,529	34.9%
Christopher J. Claytor (LIBERT)	3,662	2.6%
2006 PRIMARY		
Sam Johnson (R)	13,348	85.3%
Bob Johnson (R)	2,292	14.7%
2004 GENERAL		
Sam Johnson (R)	180,099	85.6%
Paul Jenkins (I)	16,966	8.1%
James Vessels (LIBERT)	13,287	6.3%

PREVIOUS WINNING PERCENTAGES
2002 (74%); 2000 (72%); 1998 (91%); 1996 (73%); 1994 (91%); 1992 (86%); 1991 Special Runoff Election (53%)

Elected May 1991; 8th full term

Johnson once roomed with Sen. John McCain of Arizona when they were both held at a prison camp in Hanoi during the Vietnam War. Johnson spent seven years as a POW, and half the time he was held in solitary confinement. He says he decided to become active in politics while being held in the prison camp. "You can sit there and shoot bullets at the government all day, but unless you get personally involved, you can't get a lot done," he says in his slow Texas drawl.

A career Air Force pilot — he once was the director of the Air Force's "Top Gun" fighter pilot school — Johnson is a stalwart defender of the U.S. military and its involvement in Iraq. When the House narrowly passed a $124.2 billion war supplemental in March 2007 that would set a timetable for the withdrawal of U.S. troops from Iraq, Johnson brought a hush to the House when he described the last days of the war in Vietnam. "Just think back to the dark day in history when we saw visions of American Marines airlifting Vietnamese out of the U.S. Embassy," he said on the floor. "Do you remember that? That's what happens when America makes a commitment, Congress cuts the funding, and we go home with our tails between our legs." Johnson added, "Frankly, we all want our troops to come home . . . when the job is done." He voted against the bill.

Johnson has worked hard to help the military. He pressed legislation to increase the "death gratuity" paid to the families of military personnel killed while on duty and to make the sum tax-exempt. "It's unconscionable to me that the knock on the door by the military chaplain is followed by a knock on the door from the tax man," he said in 2003 when the House passed a modest increase in the benefit. A far more generous boost was included in the Iraq War supplemental spending bill passed early in 2005.

National security and military matters have been a top Johnson priority during his congressional career. The day after the Sept. 11 terrorist attacks, Johnson told his colleagues in a House floor speech that the devastation in New York and Virginia was worse than the B-52 bombing raids he lived through while a prisoner in Hanoi.

A quiet lawmaker, Johnson is well liked by everyone, even those members with whom he disagrees. He is a faithful member of the conservative branch of his party, and he represents a solidly Republican district. He is one of the four founders of the conservative Republican Study Committee, originally known as the Conservative Action Team. On votes pitting most Democrats against most Republicans, he stuck with his party 98 percent of the time in the 109th Congress (2005-06), while voting in agreement with President Bush 88 percent of the time.

He did vote against Bush's position on a 2006 measure to grant permanent normal trade relations to Vietnam. The bill, which failed to pass in the House, would have meant Congress no longer would have to vote every year on whether to renew normal trade relations with the fast-growing Asian nation. Johnson had returned to Vietnam in January 2006 and laid a wreath at the former U.S. embassy in Saigon. Calling the trip "an eye opener," Johnson said, "I still think Vietnam is communist, and they don't have a government of the people, by the people and for the people."

A longtime member of the Ways and Means Committee, Johnson is now the ranking Republican on the Social Security Subcommittee. He not only supported the president's effort to allow for personal accounts within the Social Security system, he went beyond it. He introduced a bill in 2005 to allow workers to divert their entire Social Security payroll tax into a private account. He said that it is crucial to deal now with the high Medicare and Social Security costs that are swelling the nation's budget deficit. "I think we've got to address them," he said. "It is silly to ignore them."

Johnson has long pushed for legislation to make it easier for small business to band together to purchase health insurance. The House passed his measure in July 2005, which would exempt association health plans from state laws that mandate insurance coverage for specific treatments and procedures. Johnson says that by eliminating the need to comply with a tangle of state regulations, small businesses would be more likely to band together and better able to negotiate lower health insurance prices.

Johnson is concerned about illegal immigration, which he says is "the most serious issue we face in Texas right now." Although his district, which includes parts of Dallas and its suburbs, is 400 miles from Mexico, he wants the federal government to strengthen control of the borders.

One of his proudest achievements, he says, is the creation of the Congressional Youth Advisory Council in his district. The council selects about four dozen high school students whom he meets with four times a year to talk about current events. He says the program gives him a window on those issues that are important to young people.

Johnson did not plan on a military career. He says participation in the ROTC was mandatory when he went to high school. He was aiming at a career in business and law when the Korean War intervened, and his entire ROTC class at Southern Methodist University was called to duty. Accepted into flight training school, he soon fell in love with flying and was sold on a career in the Air Force. In addition to his combat missions over Korea and Vietnam, Johnson was a member of the Thunderbirds precision flying team for two years.

Johnson does not talk much about his days as a POW, but he did write a book about his experience, "Captive Warriors." Upon his release in 1973, he had three operations on his right hand, including a tendon transplant, and then he resumed flying.

After retiring from the Air Force in 1979 as a colonel, Johnson went into the home building business in Dallas. He got into local Republican Party affairs and, in 1984, won a seat in the Texas House. When GOP Rep. Steve Bartlett resigned in March 1991 to run for mayor of Dallas, Johnson overcame a tough scramble to win his party's nomination. He's had no trouble since then in the wealthy, solidly Republican district. He was re-elected with nearly 63 percent of the vote in 2006.

KEY VOTES

2006

No Stop broadband companies from favoring select Internet traffic

? Affirm U.S. commitment to war in Iraq and reject setting a withdrawal date for troops

Yes Repeal requirement for bilingual ballots at the polls

Yes Permit U.S. sale of civilian nuclear technology to India

? Build a 700-mile fence on the U.S.-Mexico border to curb illegal crossings

Yes Permit warrantless wiretaps of suspected terrorists

2005

? Intervene in the life-support case of Terri Schiavo

No Lift President Bush's restrictions on stem cell research funding

No Prohibit FBI access to library and bookstore records

Yes Approve free-trade pact with five Central American countries

Yes Pass energy policy overhaul favored by President Bush emphasizing domestic oil and gas production

Yes End mandatory preservation of habitat of endangered animal and plant species

No Ban torture of prisoners in U.S. custody

CQ VOTE STUDIES

	PARTY UNITY		PRESIDENTIAL SUPPORT	
	Support	Oppose	Support	Oppose
2006	98%	2%	82%	18%
2005	98%	2%	93%	7%
2004	99%	1%	93%	7%
2003	99%	1%	96%	4%
2002	98%	2%	89%	11%

INTEREST GROUPS

	AFL-CIO	ADA	CCUS	ACU
2006	17%	5%	91%	90%
2005	8%	0%	88%	96%
2004	0%	0%	100%	100%
2003	0%	5%	100%	88%
2002	13%	0%	90%	100%

TEXAS 3

Part of Dallas and northeast suburbs – Plano, most of Garland and McKinney

The rapidly expanding Dallas suburbs of Plano, McKinley, Frisco and Allen in Collin County form the heart of the 3rd, which also takes in part of Dallas itself and most of Garland and Rowlett in northeastern Dallas County. The 3rd's residents are overwhelmingly white and Republican, and they have the state's highest median income. Growing banking, telecommunications and defense industries employ many residents.

Many corporate headquarters have moved into the Plano area, and wealthy executives have built expensive homes in Frisco and the surrounding areas. The concentration of telecommunications and electronics firms along U.S. Highway 75 has earned that area the name "Telecom Corridor." Electronic Data Systems and Texas Instruments, which recently built a new plant in the 3rd's portion of Richardson (shared with the 32nd), have major presences along the corridor. Richardson has benefited greatly from technology firms and expanding banking and financial services industries. Frisco also is undergoing a population and development boom. Downtown Dallas is in the 30th, but many white-collar workers commute from the 3rd.

Redistricting prior to the 2004 election made the 3rd more compact, removing part of Richardson and many of the Collin County exurbs on the edge of the old district, while adding a few pockets closer to downtown Dallas. Forty percent of the new district's residents live in Dallas County.

Collin County, the state's fastest-growing county in the 1990s, is filled with upwardly mobile professionals and is strongly Republican. In 2004, George W. Bush won 70 percent of the presidential vote in the 3rd's share of Collin and 57 percent of the district's Dallas County portion. During his successful 2006 re-election, Republican Gov. Rick Perry did 8 percentage points better in the 3rd than he did statewide.

MAJOR INDUSTRY
Telecommunications, transportation, banking, defense

CITIES
Plano, 219,890; Garland (pt.), 142,379; Dallas (pt.), 128,651

NOTABLE
Seven-time Tour de France winner Lance Armstrong grew up in Plano.

Rep. Ralph M. Hall (R)

CAPITOL OFFICE
225-6673
www.house.gov/ralphhall
2405 Rayburn 20515-4304; fax 225-3332

COMMITTEES
Energy & Commerce
Science & Technology - ranking member

RESIDENCE
Rockwall

BORN
May 3, 1923, Fate, Texas

RELIGION
Methodist

FAMILY
Wife, Mary Ellen Hall; three children

EDUCATION
Texas Christian U., attended 1943 (pre-law); U. of Texas, attended 1946-47 (pre-law); Southern Methodist U., LL.B. 1951

MILITARY SERVICE
Navy, 1942-45

CAREER
Lawyer; aluminum company president

POLITICAL HIGHLIGHTS
Rockwall County judge, 1951-63; Texas Senate, 1963-73 (president pro tempore, 1968-69; served as a Democrat); sought Democratic nomination for lieutenant governor, 1972

ELECTION RESULTS

2006 GENERAL		
Ralph M. Hall (R)	106,495	64.4%
Glenn Melancon (D)	55,278	33.4%
Kurt G. Helm (LIBERT)	3,496	2.1%
2006 PRIMARY		
Ralph M. Hall (R)		unopposed
2004 GENERAL		
Ralph M. Hall (R)	182,866	68.3%
Jim Nickerson (D)	81,585	30.5%
Kevin D. Anderson (LIBERT)	3,491	1.3%

PREVIOUS WINNING PERCENTAGES *
2002 (58%); 2000 (60%); 1998 (58%); 1996 (64%); 1994 (59%); 1992 (58%); 1990 (100%); 1988 (66%); 1986 (72%); 1984 (58%); 1982 (74%); 1980 (52%)
* Elected as a Democrat 1980-2002

Elected 1980; 14th term

The oldest member of the House, Hall lost the chance to cap his long career in Congress with a committee chairmanship when the Republicans lost power in 2007. He had been in line to take the helm at the Science Committee, but instead became its ranking Republican.

The irony for Hall, in his mid-80s, is that he might well have become a committee chairman had he remained a Democrat rather than switching parties in 2004. Democrats appoint chairmen according to seniority, of which Hall has plenty.

One of Hall's top priorities on the Science and Technology Committee is the Bush administration's plan to send a man to Mars, with its potential to bring new missions to the Johnson Space Center in Houston. Committee Chairman Bart Gordon of Tennessee also supports the mission, but disagrees with plans to pay for it by shifting money from NASA's aeronautics and research programs.

As a booster of NASA, Hall has championed the space agency's biomedical and basic science programs. After the 2003 loss of the space shuttle *Columbia*, Hall pressed for a greater focus on safety, adding an amendment to the annual NASA funding bill directing the agency to conduct studies on improving space shuttle crew survivability.

Hall also believes that cutting-edge research should be a integral part of U.S. counterterrorism efforts. In the wake of the Sept. 11 terrorist attacks, Hall lobbied for designating an undersecretary of science and technology in the new Homeland Security Department. In April 2007, the House passed a bill Hall cosponsored that would authorize federal grants through 2012 for early-career scientists and engineers at universities and other organizations.

From a rural East Texas district, Hall has been involved in developing an early-warning system for droughts, sponsoring a successful bill in 2006 with Democrat Mark Udall of Colorado that authorized $81 million for such a system.

In 2005, Hall introduced a bill to exempt large animal feedlot operations from a 1980 law creating the government's Superfund for environmental cleanups. The effort came after a federal judge ruled that phosphorous in cow manure can be defined as a hazardous substance under the Superfund law. Though it garnered 191 cosponsors, the bill went nowhere. But the Environmental Protection Agency in 2007 said it would develop a rule to exempt farms from such cleanup requirements. And Hall said he would still push in 2007 for legislation specifying that manure cannot be treated as a "pollutant or contaminant" or "hazardous substance" under the Superfund law.

Despite his work in behalf of the state of Texas and his long service in the House, Hall failed in 2006 to get the endorsement of the most influential newspaper that covers his district — The Dallas Morning News. "A fiscal conservative, he wisely favors entitlement reform and free trade, but he doesn't offer the district the energetic, progressive leadership it deserves," the newspaper said. However, the paper also declined to endorse his young Democratic challenger, Glenn Melancon, a college history professor, and Hall won re-election with more than 64 percent of the vote.

Stylistically, Hall is anything but a firebrand. An infrequent sponsor of legislation, he prefers to look after the interests of Texas' oil and gas industry quietly from his seat on the Energy and Commerce Committee.

A fiscal conservative, Hall favors scrapping most of the existing tax code and replacing it with a flat tax or a national sales tax. In 2001, he was one of only nine House Democrats to support an indefinite extension of President Bush's $1.35 trillion tax cut of 2001, set to expire in 2010. Hall stands with the right on social issues as well, opposing abortion and same-sex marriage.

His flagging allegiance to House Democrats was evident for years before he switched parties. In 1985, he voted "present" rather than support the re-election of liberal Democrat Thomas P. "Tip" O'Neill Jr. of Massachusetts as Speaker. In 1998, he was one of only five Democrats to support the impeachment of President Bill Clinton on the critical first charge of lying to a federal grand jury. In 2000, he publicly championed the presidential candidacy of Republican Texas Gov. George W. Bush. After the 2002 election, Hall told GOP leaders he would consider backing Republican J. Dennis Hastert of Illinois for Speaker if his vote were the deciding one.

He consistently strayed from the party line more often than any other House member in the early 2000s. An old friend of the Bush family, Hall celebrated his 80th birthday at the White House. Some speculated he would leave the Democratic Party after Republicans gained control of Congress in 1994. Instead, he helped start the Blue Dog Coalition, a group of conservative House Democrats that sought to pull the party to the right.

He seemed content with his role as party maverick until the Republicans gave him a yank in their direction. In 2003, the GOP-controlled Texas Legislature drew a new congressional map that left Hall vulnerable. The new 4th District, Republican-leaning and conservative, contained only about a third of Hall's constituents, which meant he could face a tough re-election battle. Five minutes before the state candidate filing deadline in January 2004, Hall registered as a Republican.

Hall's folksy humor and boundless supply of rural Texas stories can defuse tension, and his political acumen gives him influence when he decides to weigh in. He generally eschews quick legislative fixes. He says he places more of a premium on "doing it right, rather than doing it now."

Hall got an early start in politics. He was elected as county judge, or chief executive, of tiny Rockwall County in 1950 while still attending law school in nearby Dallas. Twelve years later, he moved up to the state Senate and spent a decade there, rising to become president pro tempore.

After finishing fourth in the Democratic primary for lieutenant governor in 1972, he left public life for a time. But when 4th District Democrat Ray Roberts announced his retirement in 1980, Hall took the seat with 52 percent of the vote. He won by comfortable margins as a Democrat through 2002. In 2004, Hall won the general election with more than two-thirds of the vote. He won with similar ease in 2006.

KEY VOTES

2006

- No Stop broadband companies from favoring select Internet traffic
- Yes Affirm U.S. commitment to war in Iraq and reject setting a withdrawal date for troops
- Yes Repeal requirement for bilingual ballots at the polls
- Yes Permit U.S. sale of civilian nuclear technology to India
- Yes Build a 700-mile fence on the U.S.-Mexico border to curb illegal crossings
- Yes Permit warrantless wiretaps of suspected terrorists

2005

- Yes Intervene in the life-support case of Terri Schiavo
- No Lift President Bush's restrictions on stem cell research funding
- No Prohibit FBI access to library and bookstore records
- Yes Approve free-trade pact with five Central American countries
- Yes Pass energy policy overhaul favored by President Bush emphasizing domestic oil and gas production
- Yes End mandatory preservation of habitat of endangered animal and plant species
- No Ban torture of prisoners in U.S. custody

CQ VOTE STUDIES

	PARTY UNITY		PRESIDENTIAL SUPPORT	
	Support	Oppose	Support	Oppose
2006	93%	7%	85%	15%
2005	96%	4%	84%	16%
2004	92%	8%	82%	18%
2003	51%	49%	85%	15%
2002	40%	60%	70%	30%

INTEREST GROUPS

	AFL-CIO	ADA	CCUS	ACU
2006	21%	5%	93%	84%
2005	20%	5%	92%	92%
2004	13%	5%	100%	84%
2003	33%	15%	93%	72%
2002	22%	15%	85%	88%

TEXAS 4

Northeast – Sherman, Texarkana, Paris

The 4th begins in Dallas' eastern and northern suburbs before moving east to sparsely populated and rural areas in the northeastern corner of the state. The district extends along the Oklahoma and Arkansas borders, taking in Texarkana, but its four western counties contain about half of the population. It has Texas' second-highest percentage of white residents (79 percent) and lowest percentage of Hispanics (8 percent).

The district includes a mix of suburban and rural communities, with no city having more than 40,000 residents. In the east, timber, oil and natural gas remain prominent, but this portion of the 4th faces economic challenges from foreign timber companies and cattle ranchers. Dallas commuters and other white-collar workers populate the burgeoning western counties, especially Collin. This area hosts soccer's FC Dallas at Pizza Hut Park—a regional sports complex in Frisco that also is used as a retail center and entertainment venue.

The district's growing health care sector helps the district's rural areas from slipping further, and a steady manufacturing presence now drives economic growth. Pilgrim's Pride chicken is headquartered in Pittsburg, and a Tyson Foods meat production plant in Sherman also employs many district residents. The Texarkana-area economy narrowly avoided taking a hit when members of the BRAC commission reversed a 2005 Defense Department recommendation to close the Red River Army Depot.

Associated with the Bible Belt that stretches through much of the South, the 4th is fertile territory for the GOP. Even Democrats, who can win local races in the east, tend to be conservative here. Republican candidates generally dominate overall, and in the 2004 presidential election, George W. Bush won every county in the 4th and took 70 percent of the vote.

MAJOR INDUSTRY
Manufacturing, agriculture, retail, health care

MILITARY BASES
Red River Army Depot, 3 military, 2,500 civilian (2006)

CITIES
Sherman, 35,082; Texarkana, 34,782; Paris, 25,898; Greenville, 23,960

NOTABLE
Former House Speaker Sam Rayburn hailed from Bonham, now home of the Sam Rayburn Library and Museum; Paris hosts the annual Uncle Jesse's Memorial Big Bass Classic, inspired by TV's "Dukes of Hazzard."

Rep. Jeb Hensarling (R)

CAPITOL OFFICE
225-3484
www.house.gov/hensarling
132 Cannon 20515-4305; fax 226-4888

COMMITTEES
Budget
Financial Services

RESIDENCE
Dallas

BORN
May 29, 1957, Stephenville, Texas

RELIGION
Episcopalian

FAMILY
Wife, Melissa Hensarling; two children

EDUCATION
Texas A&M U., B.A. 1979 (economics);
U. of Texas, J.D. 1982

CAREER
Child support collection software firm owner; corporate communications executive; senatorial campaign committee executive director; congressional district and campaign aide; lawyer

POLITICAL HIGHLIGHTS
No previous office

ELECTION RESULTS

2006 GENERAL		
Jeb Hensarling (R)	88,478	61.8%
Charlie Thompson (D)	50,983	35.6%
Mike Nelson (LIBERT)	3,791	2.6%
2006 PRIMARY		
Jeb Hensarling (R)		unopposed
2004 GENERAL		
Jeb Hensarling (R)	148,816	64.5%
Bill Bernstein (D)	75,911	32.9%
John Gonzalez (LIBERT)	6,118	2.7%

PREVIOUS WINNING PERCENTAGES
2002 (58%)

Elected 2002; 3rd term

Hensarling was the surprise choice of the conservative wing of the Republican Party when he was selected to chair the Republican Study Committee for the 110th Congress (2007-08).

A true fiscal conservative, he says tax cuts can stimulate the economy and spending cuts can curb the deficit. He has sometimes gone against both his party and the White House in his quest for fiscal restraint. He also would like to outlaw the funding "emergencies" often used by lawmakers to go over budget caps and would require a two-thirds majority vote in both the House and the Senate to approve any spending over the budget.

But he struck a conciliatory note after his election to head the RSC, a group of about 100 conservative Republicans. "The RSC is the keeper of the conservative flame," Hensarling (HENN-sur-ling) said after the election results were announced. "We need to do a better job of advocacy for our party."

Hensarling says his goal is to unify the party and make sure the group becomes known less for opposing its own party on spending issues and more for pushing conservative principles in House policy debates. By a vote of 57-42, Hensarling beat out Todd Tiahrt of Kansas.

As chairman of the RSC's budget committee in the 109th Congress (2005-06), Hensarling was an outspoken budget hawk, often clashing with his party's appropriators over spending increases. Tiahrt, in contrast, sits on the Appropriations Committee, which sometimes put him at odds with the RSC's budget restraint crusade. "I may have had an advantage that my record was a little clearer in this organization" on budget issues, Hensarling said.

Hensarling and outgoing RSC Chairman Mike Pence of Indiana had attacked some of the appropriators' practices in the 109th Congress, such as anonymous earmarks in spending bills. Hensarling had cautioned in the fall of 2006 that the U.S. electorate was growing critical of Republican efforts to load spending bills with projects benefiting their home districts and favored a proposal to identify earmark sponsors in Appropriations' committee reports. Identifying the sponsors would lead to a decrease in earmark requests, he said. "I am pretty sure that many members will think twice before requesting that hundreds and thousands of federal taxpayer dollars be spent on the Museum of Glass or on water-free urinals," he said.

Hensarling believes that his party's free-spending ways contributed to its defeat in the 2006 elections. He says he sees a chastened party emerging after losing the majority. "Frankly, there is nothing like a two-by-four slapped across one's head to get one's attention," he says.

Hensarling's mentor is former Texas Sen. Phil Gramm, who also made a career of trying to hold down federal spending. Hensarling was a student of Gramm's at Texas A&M University, where Gramm taught economics. He later ran one of the senator's re-election campaigns and then the National Republican Senatorial Committee, the Senate Republicans' electioneering arm, when Gramm chaired the organization.

Hensarling sits on the Budget and Financial Services committees. From the Budget panel, he has been a strong advocate for President Bush's economic policies, including the administration's tax cuts. When he has broken from his party, it has usually been on issues where he is further to the right.

But in most cases, he is a firm believer in the policies put forth by his party and its president. On votes pitting most Democrats against most Republicans, he stuck with his party 97 percent of the time in the 109th Congress, while voting in agreement with Bush 90 percent of the time.

Hensarling is also socially conservative. He voted in both 2004 and 2006 for a constitutional amendment to ban same-sex marriage, and he opposes abortion, voting in 2006 to make it a felony to take a minor across state lines for an abortion. "I believe that faith and family are the genius of America," he says. "The government does a lot in a poor or mediocre fashion."

In the 109th Congress, Hensarling helped negotiate a solution to a decades-old conflict over statutory restrictions imposed on Southwest Airlines' flights out of its Dallas Love Field headquarters. A law enacted in 1980 had limited Southwest to short-haul flights to neighboring states out of Love Field, and the airline wanted the restriction removed so it could fly national routes to and from the Dallas airport. Though Hensarling helped negotiate a complex agreement between Southwest, American Airlines, the Dallas-Fort Worth Airport and the two cities to give Southwest the ability to fly nationally, he ultimately voted against the final agreement because it reduced the number of gates at Love Field from 32 to 20. The bill became law, which Hensarling says is fine. "It didn't get reformed quite the way I would have wanted to reform it," he said.

Hensarling was born in Stephenville, Texas. His father and grandfather were poultry farmers but Hensarling decided early that he would not enter the family business. He says his first taste of politics came in 1964, when his Republican parents had him knocking on doors for Barry Goldwater. He started a Republican Club at his high school, and acted as a GOP precinct captain at Texas A&M University.

Three years out of law school, Hensarling was hired in 1985 to oversee Gramm's field offices in Texas. When Gramm was promoted to the Senate leadership as chairman of the National Republican Senatorial Committee in the run-up to the 1992 election, he made Hensarling his executive director. Running the committee helped Hensarling build a network of political friends on Capitol Hill.

He took a break from government to go home to Texas to start his own business, a firm that made computer software to help single parents collect child support payments. Hensarling's chance to run for Congress came in 2002, when Texas gained two seats in reapportionment after the 2000 census and the 5th District was reconfigured.

Republican Pete Sessions, who had represented the 5th for three terms, decided to run in the new 32nd District. Hensarling won a five-way primary. In the general election, he faced Democrat Ron Chapman, a Dallas-area judge. Hensarling won easily by 18 percentage points. In his last two elections, he has won with more than 60 percent of the vote.

KEY VOTES

2006

No Stop broadband companies from favoring select Internet traffic
Yes Affirm U.S. commitment to war in Iraq and reject setting a withdrawal date for troops
Yes Repeal requirement for bilingual ballots at the polls
Yes Permit U.S. sale of civilian nuclear technology to India
Yes Build a 700-mile fence on the U.S.-Mexico border to curb illegal crossings
Yes Permit warrantless wiretaps of suspected terrorists

2005

Yes Intervene in the life-support case of Terri Schiavo
No Lift President Bush's restrictions on stem cell research funding
No Prohibit FBI access to library and bookstore records
Yes Approve free-trade pact with five Central American countries
Yes Pass energy policy overhaul favored by President Bush emphasizing domestic oil and gas production
Yes End mandatory preservation of habitat of endangered animal and plant species
No Ban torture of prisoners in U.S. custody

CQ VOTE STUDIES

	PARTY UNITY		PRESIDENTIAL SUPPORT	
	Support	Oppose	Support	Oppose
2006	96%	4%	85%	15%
2005	98%	2%	93%	7%
2004	98%	2%	100%	0%
2003	97%	3%	98%	2%

INTEREST GROUPS

	AFL-CIO	ADA	CCUS	ACU
2006	7%	10%	93%	100%
2005	13%	0%	81%	100%
2004	8%	0%	95%	100%
2003	0%	5%	90%	88%

TEXAS 5

Part of Dallas and east suburbs — Mesquite, part of Garland; Palestine

Beginning in eastern Dallas, the 5th winds east and southeast through Dallas County suburbs and six other counties. Although only 14 percent of Dallas County's population is in the 5th, the county is home to almost half of the district's residents.

The 5th's part of Dallas differs from the glitz that characterizes the portion in the neighboring 32nd. The district takes in eastern and northeastern Dallas, which have more of a working-class flavor and are home to many small businesses. Areas surrounding White Rock Lake, such as Old Lake Highlands, however, are upper-middle-class. Mesquite, a suburb east of the city, also is a major voting base. Located in far eastern Dallas County, its economic landscape continues to diversify. Union Pacific Railroad operates a distribution facility in the city's Skyline Industrial Park, a regional industrial center east of the Dallas-Fort Worth Metroplex.

Many of the district's suburbs have growing populations and provide easy access to a bustling metropolis while supplying the benefits of small-town life. Southeast of Dallas, the district moves from flat prairies into the forest region of East Texas. Prisons are large employers in rural parts of the district, and cattle, natural gas and coal are important industries as well.

The 5th generally favors Republicans. GOP areas abound in northeastern Dallas and in Anderson and Henderson counties well southeast of the city. Some heavily Hispanic areas in Dallas County's southeastern precincts tend to vote more Democratic, and Mesquite often is politically competitive. But George W. Bush still took two-thirds of the 5th's 2004 presidential vote, carrying all seven of the 5th's counties in the process.

MAJOR INDUSTRY

Small business, technology, prisons, ranching

CITIES

Mesquite, 124,523; Dallas (pt.), 95,286; Garland (pt.), 73,389

NOTABLE

Resistol Arena is home to the Mesquite Championship Rodeo; In 2006, the National Scientific Balloon Facility in Palestine was renamed the Columbia Scientific Balloon Facility to honor the NASA crew that was lost over East Texas in 2003.

Rep. Joe L. Barton (R)

CAPITOL OFFICE
225-2002
joebarton.house.gov
2109 Rayburn 20515-4306; fax 225-3052

COMMITTEES
Energy & Commerce - ranking member

RESIDENCE
Ennis

BORN
Sept. 15, 1949, Waco, Texas

RELIGION
Methodist

FAMILY
Wife, Terri Barton; four children

EDUCATION
Texas A&M U., B.S. 1972 (industrial engineering); Purdue U., M.S. 1973 (industrial administration)

CAREER
Engineering consultant

POLITICAL HIGHLIGHTS
Sought Republican nomination for U.S. Senate (special election), 1993

ELECTION RESULTS

2006 GENERAL		
Joe L. Barton (R)	91,927	60.5%
David T. Harris (D)	56,369	37.1%
Carl Nulsen (LIBERT)	3,740	2.5%
2006 PRIMARY		
Joe L. Barton (R)		unopposed
2004 GENERAL		
Joe L. Barton (R)	168,767	66.0%
Morris Meyer (D)	83,609	32.7%
Stephen Schrader (LIBERT)	3,251	1.3%

PREVIOUS WINNING PERCENTAGES
2002 (70%); 2000 (88%); 1998 (73%); 1996 (77%); 1994 (76%); 1992 (72%); 1990 (66%); 1988 (68%); 1986 (56%); 1984 (57%)

Elected 1984; 12th term

Barton has been around long enough to be savvy about the political complexities of passing major legislation, but he hasn't always been able to close the deal. With a guiding faith in free markets, he's often reluctant to compromise if it means creating more government regulation. His take-it-or-leave-it approach generally worked fine while Republicans controlled the House, but he may need to modify it under Democratic rule.

He can do that when it suits his purposes. The conservative Texan chaired the powerful Energy and Commerce Committee from early 2004 until the start of the 110th Congress in 2007, and he helped win enactment in 2005 of the first major energy policy overhaul in decades. To strike a deal with the Senate, Barton had to drop items he had pushed for years, including oil drilling in Alaska's Arctic National Wildlife Refuge and legal protections for manufacturers of the gasoline additive MTBE, which had contaminated groundwater supplies. He also included his committee's Democrats in the final negotiations, earning the trust of the formidable ranking minority member, John D. Dingell of Michigan, who succeeded him as chairman in the 110th Congress (2007-08).

The turning point came in a closed-door meeting among Barton, Dingell and Sens. Pete V. Domenici and Jeff Bingaman of New Mexico. Barton pledged to allow input from the Democrats, if they in turn agreed not to stall the deliberations. The pledges of cooperation played out in a conference of intense, late-night trade-offs. Barton later reflected, "It's hard to sit there and negotiate when you know you have the votes" to win without Democrats. "But if you do that, at the end when it comes to the floor, everybody has a stake in it," he said.

After Democrats captured the House in the 2006 elections, Barton made a bid for the minority leader's job, joining Mike Pence of Indiana in challenging John A. Boehner of Ohio. But unlike Pence, Barton withdrew before the balloting began and threw his support to Boehner, who won.

A former oil company engineer, Barton is the go-to guy in the House for the oil and gas industries, keystones of the Texas economy. They trust him to shield them from what they see as potentially drastic new rules, and he relies on them for political cash; they are among his top contributors.

When gasoline prices surged after hurricanes Katrina and Rita in 2005, Barton and his allies renewed their push for drilling in the Alaskan wilderness, for lifting a longstanding moratorium on most offshore oil and gas exploration, and for loosening environmental regulations on new or expanded oil refineries. Most of their proposals passed the House but fell short of enactment, blocked by Democrats and moderate Republicans.

Barton is the House's chief global warming skeptic, resisting calls for a reduction in emissions of greenhouse gases and questioning the claims of scientists analyzing climate research. A longtime advocate of nuclear power, he is a force behind efforts to build a permanent nuclear waste dump at Yucca Mountain in Nevada.

An important player on telecommunications policy as well, Barton in 2005 pushed through a requirement that broadcasters switch from analog to digital transmission signals by early 2009. Two years before the deadline, concerns were mounting that consumers might be caught off guard by the change, which will necessitate use of set-top converter boxes for households that do not have digital-ready televisions. In 2007, Barton introduced a bill to require retailers and broadcasters to step up efforts to warn consumers about the switch.

On the campaign trail, Barton portrays himself as a churchgoing, bone-deep conservative. A reliable anti-abortion vote in his two decades in Congress, he nonetheless supported legislation in 2005 and 2007 to expand federally supported stem cell research, which uses surplus embryos from in vitro fertilization clinics. He says he was influenced by his father's death from complications of diabetes and by the death of his brother, Texas District Judge Jon Barton, who succumbed to liver cancer in 2000 at age 44.

Gay rights groups dislike Barton for his efforts to keep homosexuals out of the military and to amend the Constitution to prohibit same-sex marriage. Barton says homosexuality is "abnormal" and "immoral" in his view.

In recent years, Barton has had to modify his pro-family campaign literature, which used to tout his marriage to his "high school sweetheart." Barton divorced his wife, Janet, in 2003. He remarried and had a child in 2005; he has three grown children from his first marriage.

Born in Waco, Barton is the son of an agribusiness salesman and a schoolteacher. His father in his later years was a plant geneticist, breeding new strains of cotton. Barton studied industrial engineering at Texas A&M University, his dad's alma mater, then got a master's degree from Purdue University. He returned to Ennis, and became an engineering consultant for Atlantic Richfield Co.

In 1981, Barton was a White House fellow at the Department of Energy when he got the government bug. His first run for public office was a successful 1984 race for the House seat of Republican Phil Gramm, who moved to the Senate. Barton squeaked through the primary, then faced Democrat Dan Kubiak, a former state representative. Barton managed to link Kubiak to liberal Democratic presidential nominee Walter F. Mondale, whose positions were unpopular in the 6th District. He also masterminded a registration drive that added thousands of new Republicans to the rolls in his district. Aided by Ronald Reagan's coattails, Barton won.

When Democrat Lloyd Bentsen left the Senate in 1993 to be President Bill Clinton's Treasury secretary, Barton jumped into the special-election contest, but he finished a distant third. He mulled a second bid for the Senate when Gramm retired in 2002, but pulled back when the Bush White House endorsed Republican John Cornyn, the former Texas attorney general who had been appointed to fill out the remainder of Gramm's term. Barton has had no trouble winning re-election to the House.

A respectable amateur baseball player, Barton coached the GOP congressional baseball team in 2006, and was once its star pitcher.

KEY VOTES

2006

- No Stop broadband companies from favoring select Internet traffic
- Yes Affirm U.S. commitment to war in Iraq and reject setting a withdrawal date for troops
- Yes Repeal requirement for bilingual ballots at the polls
- Yes Permit U.S. sale of civilian nuclear technology to India
- Yes Build a 700-mile fence on the U.S.-Mexico border to curb illegal crossings
- Yes Permit warrantless wiretaps of suspected terrorists

2005

- ? Intervene in the life-support case of Terri Schiavo
- Yes Lift President Bush's restrictions on stem cell research funding
- No Prohibit FBI access to library and bookstore records
- Yes Approve free-trade pact with five Central American countries
- Yes Pass energy policy overhaul favored by President Bush emphasizing domestic oil and gas production
- Yes End mandatory preservation of habitat of endangered animal and plant species
- No Ban torture of prisoners in U.S. custody

CQ VOTE STUDIES

	PARTY UNITY		PRESIDENTIAL SUPPORT	
	Support	Oppose	Support	Oppose
2006	95%	5%	87%	13%
2005	96%	4%	87%	13%
2004	97%	3%	94%	6%
2003	98%	2%	96%	4%
2002	98%	2%	90%	10%

INTEREST GROUPS

	AFL-CIO	ADA	CCUS	ACU
2006	7%	15%	93%	88%
2005	14%	0%	92%	92%
2004	7%	0%	100%	96%
2003	7%	5%	97%	88%
2002	13%	0%	100%	96%

TEXAS 6

Suburban Dallas — Arlington; parts of Fort Worth and Mansfield; Corsicana

The overwhelming majority of the 6th's land area is a boot-shaped band of counties that extends southeast from Ellis County, but nearly two-thirds of the district's population lives just north of Ellis in eastern or southern Tarrant County. This suburban-rural district takes in a sliver of Fort Worth and all of Arlington in the Dallas-Fort Worth Metroplex before stretching southeast along Interstate 45, where it becomes more rural and its economy more reliant on agriculture.

Despite a local General Motors plant that employs more than 2,500 area workers, Arlington has mainly shed its blue-collar image. Today, the University of Texas at Arlington is among the city's top employers, and the school has been an incubator for the city's growing technology sector. In addition, hundreds of thousands of people travel to Arlington each summer to visit the Six Flags Over Texas amusement park, while others head to the Rangers ballpark for baseball. The new Cowboys football stadium is scheduled to open here in 2009.

South of Tarrant, most of the rest of the district's residents live in Ellis and Navarro counties. Ellis, which includes Waxahachie and Ennis, used to be dependent on cotton farming, but the cement industry has taken hold here. Farther south, Freestone and Leon counties are rural, less-populated and sustained by oil, ranching and farming. Houston and northern Trinity counties, east of Leon, have a fairly large timber industry.

The 6th is heavily Republican. Most of the Tarrant precincts are aligned with the GOP, although there is some Democratic strength in southern Fort Worth and eastern Arlington, where the population is more diverse. Ellis' overwhelming Republican support makes the 6th a safe haven for GOP candidates.

MAJOR INDUSTRY

Transportation, home building, technology, agriculture

CITIES

Arlington, 332,968; Mansfield (pt.), 27,409; Fort Worth (pt.), 26,709

NOTABLE

Squeeze-box melodies and traditional Czech culture on display at the National Polka Festival have lured visitors to Ennis for over 40 years.

Rep. John Culberson (R)

CAPITOL OFFICE
225-2571
www.culberson.house.gov
428 Cannon 20515-4307; fax 225-4381

COMMITTEES
Appropriations

RESIDENCE
Houston

BORN
Aug. 24, 1956, Houston, Texas

RELIGION
Methodist

FAMILY
Wife, Belinda Culberson; one child

EDUCATION
Southern Methodist U., B.A. 1981 (history); South Texas College of Law, J.D. 1988

CAREER
Lawyer; political advertising agency employee; oil rig mud logger

POLITICAL HIGHLIGHTS
Texas House, 1987-2001

ELECTION RESULTS

2006 GENERAL		
John Culberson (R)	99,318	59.2%
Jim Henley (D)	64,514	38.5%
Drew Parks (LIBERT)	3,953	2.4%
2006 PRIMARY		
John Culberson (R)		unopposed
2004 GENERAL		
John Culberson (R)	175,440	64.1%
John Martinez (D)	91,126	33.3%
Paul Staton (I)	3,713	1.4%
Drew Parks (LIBERT)	3,372	1.2%

PREVIOUS WINNING PERCENTAGES
2002 (89%); 2000 (74%)

Elected 2000; 4th term

Culberson is one of the unheralded conservative foot soldiers who support GOP leaders and keep the party on a rightward tack. He may not agree with President Bush on the issue most important to him — curbing illegal immigration — but Culberson is above all a team player.

He sticks with his fellow Republicans almost all of the time on votes that break along partisan lines — just less than 98 percent of the time in the 109th Congress (2005-06). The numbers even understate Culberson's loyalty. In 2003, he voted for a major expansion of the Medicare program with a prescription drug benefit despite being opposed to it. He switched his vote from yes to no only after it was clear Speaker J. Dennis Hastert had the votes he needed to pass the bill. When then GOP Majority Leader Tom DeLay came under fire for questionable ethics in 2005, Culberson was among his staunchest defenders. He and DeLay had both come from Houston-area districts and had worked together on local issues.

Now in his fourth term, Culberson stays largely behind the scenes on most issues, but uses his power as an appropriator to make changes in immigration law. They may be not be earthshaking, but little by little he has had an impact. He carries in his suit pocket a machine gun bullet he says he found on a tour at the International Bridge in Laredo, which he uses to illustrate his oft-repeated point: "We will either have law and order on the border or plata o plomo," which translates to "silver or lead."

From his seat on the powerful Appropriations Committee, he placed a provision in a 2006 spending bill preventing the Homeland Security Department from processing nearly all new immigration applications. Culberson maintained that a huge backlog of old applications prevented the agency from conducting thorough background checks. He sponsored another measure to give $100 million to Southern border county sheriffs to hire, train and equip new deputies for border security.

The Bush administration, which has charted a more moderate course on immigration, thinks Culberson goes too far. Culberson outlined a plan in 2005 to create armed civilian militias to help local police along the Mexican border, but Homeland Security Secretary Michael Chertoff dismissed it saying, "The border is a very dangerous place. This is not a place for people to play as amateurs."

If the administration doesn't like his views on the subject, then the feeling is passionately mutual. Immigration is one area where Culberson feels no obligation to march with Bush. "Our borders are open. Our laws are not being enforced because the chief executive officer of the United States is deliberately not enforcing them," he once said. "I'm fed up with the refusal to protect the border and to enforce immigration law."

Culberson has championed the cause of two Border Patrol agents who were sentenced to prison in 2006 for shooting a fleeing Mexican drug trafficker and hiding evidence, saying that it was an "unjust criminal prosecution of two officers who were protecting our borders from criminals and terrorists." Some lawmakers are calling on Bush to pardon the agents.

Culberson's political hero is Thomas Jefferson. Several portraits of the third president hang on his office walls, one set at precisely Jefferson's 6-foot, 2-1/2-inch height. One wall is lined with volumes of his writings. Culberson calls himself a "Jeffersonian Republican" for the shared view that governmental power should reside chiefly with the states.

Culberson lives by the old adage that all politics is local. As an appropriator, he keeps his district stocked with federal money for new highways and flood control projects and for the Houston-based space program.

In his first term, Culberson was put on the Republican Steering Committee, and won over colleagues by selflessly focusing on securing good appointments for other freshmen, which meant he lost out on his top committee choice, Transportation and Infrastructure. But the 13 other freshmen who got slots on the panel pledged to support funding for Culberson's No. 1 priority — expansion of the Katy Freeway, a 22-mile stretch of Interstate 10 in the Houston area that is among the most congested highways in the country. In 2005, party leaders rewarded him with appointment to Appropriations. In the 110th Congress (2007-08), he serves on the subcommittee responsible for NASA funding.

The third of four children, Culberson was born in Houston and is a lifelong resident of the district. His father was a political consultant and graphic designer who worked on Republican Sen. John Tower's re-election campaign in 1966, when Culberson was 10. "From the time I was literally big enough to drag my dad's camera bag around, I would go with him on all of those [campaign] trips," he recalls.

At Southern Methodist University, he was campus chairman for the 1980 presidential campaign of George H.W. Bush. (Culberson represents Bush's old House district.) After college, Culberson worked with his father while getting his law degree. At age 30, he won a seat in the Texas House and stayed for 14 years while also practicing civil defense law.

In the state House, Culberson waged an ultimately successful 11-year campaign to return control of the troubled Texas prison system to the state from the supervision of federal Judge William Wayne Justice. On his desk in Washington, Culberson keeps a framed miniature version of the court order. One of his goals is a constitutional amendment to give state legislators the right to approve federal judges every 10 years.

Also in his office is a refurbished mahogany roll-top desk that he bought at an antiques store when he discovered that it had once belonged to his great-great-uncle, Charles Culberson, who was governor of Texas from 1895 to 1899 and a U.S. senator from 1899 to 1923.

Culberson won his seat in the House after Rep. Bill Archer, a Republican who rose to become chairman of the House Ways and Means Committee, retired after 30 years in 2000. Several Republicans got into the race, but Culberson finished first in a seven-way primary and survived an expensive runoff, which ensured his election in the solidly Republican district. In 2006, Culberson was re-elected with 59 percent of the vote.

KEY VOTES

2006

No Stop broadband companies from favoring select Internet traffic
Yes Affirm U.S. commitment to war in Iraq and reject setting a withdrawal date for troops
Yes Repeal requirement for bilingual ballots at the polls
Yes Permit U.S. sale of civilian nuclear technology to India
? Build a 700-mile fence on the U.S.-Mexico border to curb illegal crossings
Yes Permit warrantless wiretaps of suspected terrorists

2005

Yes Intervene in the life-support case of Terri Schiavo
No Lift President Bush's restrictions on stem cell research funding
No Prohibit FBI access to library and bookstore records
Yes Approve free-trade pact with five Central American countries
Yes Pass energy policy overhaul favored by President Bush emphasizing domestic oil and gas production
? End mandatory preservation of habitat of endangered animal and plant species
No Ban torture of prisoners in U.S. custody

CQ VOTE STUDIES

	PARTY UNITY		PRESIDENTIAL SUPPORT	
	Support	Oppose	Support	Oppose
2006	97%	3%	95%	5%
2005	98%	2%	93%	7%
2004	97%	3%	90%	10%
2003	97%	3%	91%	9%
2002	99%	1%	85%	15%

INTEREST GROUPS

	AFL-CIO	ADA	CCUS	ACU
2006	14%	10%	93%	88%
2005	14%	0%	88%	92%
2004	0%	0%	100%	96%
2003	7%	15%	93%	96%
2002	11%	0%	90%	100%

TEXAS 7

Western Houston and suburbs — Bellaire, West University Place, Jersey Village

Situated in western Houston, the 7th starts inside the Interstate 610 loop at Main Street south of downtown before moving through the city's western outposts and into the suburbs. White-collar executives, good schools and religious conservatism characterize much of the 7th, and George W. Bush took 64 percent of the 2004 presidential vote here.

The 7th includes some of Houston's oil and gas industry, as well as much of the Texas Medical Center, Houston's museum district (both of which are shared with the 9th and 18th districts), and the Galleria shopping and corporate complex.

The medical center, which collaborates with area universities, employs tens of thousands of area residents. Rice University, which is adjacent to the medical center, focuses on nanotechnology and other applied sciences. An emphasis on attracting technology firms and corporate headquarters has enabled the 7th to enjoy decades of economic growth.

Three-fifths of district residents live in Houston, and the 7th's share of the city is mostly middle-class. Minorities, mainly Hispanics, make up one-third of the 7th's population. Northwest Houston has a large Hispanic population, and there are sizable black and Asian populations in southwest Houston. As with other Houston districts, the 7th was a temporary home to evacuees in 2005 after hurricanes Katrina and Rita.

Close ties to the oil and gas and health care industries make the 7th one of the state's wealthiest districts. Tony villages Piney Point, Bunker Hill and Hunters Creek, which are near Interstate 10 and surrounded on all sides by Houston, bring up the median income. The 7th also is one of the nation's top 10 most-educated districts, with half of its residents age 25 years or older having a bachelor's degree.

MAJOR INDUSTRY
Energy, health care, education and research, retail

CITIES
Houston (pt.), 390,922; Bellaire, 15,642; West University Place, 14,211

NOTABLE
On Sept. 12, 1962, during a speech at Rice University Stadium, President John F. Kennedy famously proclaimed that an American would reach the moon before the end of that decade.

Rep. Kevin Brady (R)

CAPITOL OFFICE
225-4901
rep.brady@mail.house.gov
www.house.gov/brady
301 Cannon 20515-4308; fax 225-5524

COMMITTEES
Ways & Means
Joint Economic

RESIDENCE
The Woodlands

BORN
April 11, 1955, Vermillion, S.D.

RELIGION
Roman Catholic

FAMILY
Wife, Cathy Brady; two children

EDUCATION
U. of South Dakota, B.S. 1990
(mass communication)

CAREER
Chamber of commerce executive

POLITICAL HIGHLIGHTS
Texas House, 1991-96

ELECTION RESULTS

2006 GENERAL		
Kevin Brady (R)	105,665	67.3%
James "Jim" Wright (D)	51,393	32.7%
2006 PRIMARY		
Kevin Brady (R)		unopposed
2004 GENERAL		
Kevin Brady (R)	179,599	68.9%
James "Jim" Wright (D)	77,324	29.7%
Paul Hansen (LIBERT)	3,705	1.4%

PREVIOUS WINNING PERCENTAGES
2002 (93%); 2000 (92%); 1998 (93%); 1996 General Runoff Election (59%)

Elected December 1996; 6th term

No one questions Brady's unwavering loyalty to the Republican Party, but visitors to his Capitol Hill office sometimes do a double-take when they see a photograph of the late Ann Richards, the famously tart-tongued former Democratic governor of Texas. What they do not realize is that it is a snapshot of his roots.

Pictured with Richards is Brady's mother, Nancy, a big fan of the salty Texan. "They look like they could be sisters. . . . They both have big white hair," Brady notes. The two women had something else in common, too: unswerving allegiance to the Democratic Party. "That ain't changing," he says, with a laugh. It's Brady who changed parties, not his family. His uncle was a Democratic state senator, his father a county party official in South Dakota, where the congressman was born. Brady moved to Texas at age 26 to take a job with the Chamber of Commerce in Beaumont; his parents earlier had eloped to San Antonio to be married just before his father, then a staff sergeant in the Air Force, shipped out to the Korean War.

Brady credits his experience as a Chamber of Commerce executive, first in South Dakota and later in Texas, for drawing him to the business-friendly Republican Party. With the ardor of a convert, he has been a staunch GOP loyalist ever since. He is a member of the Republican Study Committee, the most conservative wing of the party, and an ally of its new chairman, Jeb Hensarling of Texas.

Brady comes across as a regular guy, a dad who sometimes brings his two young sons to his congressional office, a baseball devotee who relishes the annual charity ballgame against the Democrats. (He was named the Republican team's MVP in 2005.) With his ready smile and easy laughter, he can be fiercely partisan without seeming confrontational.

In a decade on Capitol Hill, Brady has worked his way into key posts. His membership on the Ways and Means Committee made him a player on tax and trade issues during the GOP reign, and he scored some major victories on both. In 2004, he won enactment of a tax provision allowing residents of Texas and other states that have no state income tax to take a federal deduction for sales taxes instead. The deduction was extended in 2006. In 2004, Republican leaders tapped Brady to take the lead on Ways and Means in steering the controversial Central American Free Trade Agreement to enactment. He helped keep the administration up to date on the latest vote count, and he counseled trade officials on the timing of sending the legislation to Congress. The bill squeaked through in 2005.

Brady was absorbed through much of the 109th Congress (2005-06) in securing disaster relief for his part of Texas in the wake of the devastating Gulf Coast hurricanes of 2005. His district, close to the Louisiana border, was among the first to take in Katrina evacuees. Hurricane Rita later damaged 70,000 homes in the area and destroyed $1 billion in timber. "It was very frustrating. FEMA was stretched very thin," Brady said. He pushed to replace the agency's "top-down" bureaucratic model with regional offices that could work more closely with state and local first-responders.

Transforming government has been a theme for Brady almost since the moment he arrived in Congress. He routinely sponsors legislation — similar to a law he won in Texas that has eliminated 52 agencies — to set expiration dates for each federal agency, department and program unless they are affirmatively renewed. In 2006, the Government Reform Committee approved his bill, but it stalled short of the House floor.

Brady for a while split with his party on the issue of gun rights. When he was 12 years old, his father, a lawyer, was shot and killed in a South Dakota courtroom by the deranged spouse of a client, and the incident shaped his outlook on the politically volatile topic of gun control. As a state representative, Brady was one of just two Republicans to oppose a bill allowing Texans to carry concealed weapons. But he has softened his view since, saying the law has not been abused and has protected many individuals and small businesses "in tough areas."

Although he generally shuns the spotlight, Brady momentarily became associated with one of the more unseemly partisan disputes in recent years. When Republicans and Democrats on Ways and Means squared off over the handling of a pension bill in 2003, the situation escalated to the point of Chairman Bill Thomas of California calling the Capitol Police and members exchanging vicious verbal taunts and possibly physical threats. Putting much of the blame on California Democrat Pete Stark, Brady said on the House floor, "I did not know whether this gentleman could control either his emotions or his bodily functions." Following Democratic protests, Brady apologized and agreed to withdraw his comments.

Brady attended the University of South Dakota. He left college in 1978 without graduating because he had neglected to complete the paperwork for a work-study class. After an opponent in his first Texas House race in 1990 unearthed Brady's lack of a degree, Brady dug out the old course work and cleared up the incomplete grade. He went on to serve six years as a state representative in Austin.

When Republican Jack Fields announced he would not seek re-election in the 8th District in 1996, it took Brady an arduous four races to become his successor. Wealthy Republican physician Gene Fontenot emerged on top in the March GOP primary, but did not win a majority of the vote. Brady had much stronger ties to the district and defeated Fontenot in the April runoff.

Later in the year, however, a panel of three federal judges redrew the 8th as well as 12 other Texas congressional districts in response to a Supreme Court ruling that found illegal "racial gerrymandering" in the Texas map. The court ordered new elections. In November, Fontenot forced Brady into a December runoff. Brady finally prevailed with 59 percent of the vote.

He has been safely ensconced in Congress ever since. His district changed dramatically when the Texas Legislature redrew the state's congressional map in 2003, stretching the 8th District more than 150 miles from Houston to Louisiana. But it remained solidly Republican, and Brady won re-election easily in 2004 and 2006.

KEY VOTES

2006

- No Stop broadband companies from favoring select Internet traffic
- Yes Affirm U.S. commitment to war in Iraq and reject setting a withdrawal date for troops
- Yes Repeal requirement for bilingual ballots at the polls
- Yes Permit U.S. sale of civilian nuclear technology to India
- Yes Build a 700-mile fence on the U.S.-Mexico border to curb illegal crossings
- Yes Permit warrantless wiretaps of suspected terrorists

2005

- ? Intervene in the life-support case of Terri Schiavo
- No Lift President Bush's restrictions on stem cell research funding
- No Prohibit FBI access to library and bookstore records
- Yes Approve free-trade pact with five Central American countries
- Yes Pass energy policy overhaul favored by President Bush emphasizing domestic oil and gas production
- Yes End mandatory preservation of habitat of endangered animal and plant species
- No Ban torture of prisoners in U.S. custody

CQ VOTE STUDIES

	PARTY UNITY		PRESIDENTIAL SUPPORT	
	Support	Oppose	Support	Oppose
2006	96%	4%	97%	3%
2005	98%	2%	91%	9%
2004	98%	2%	94%	6%
2003	98%	2%	92%	8%
2002	97%	3%	85%	15%

INTEREST GROUPS

	AFL-CIO	ADA	CCUS	ACU
2006	7%	5%	100%	88%
2005	13%	0%	89%	96%
2004	7%	0%	100%	100%
2003	0%	10%	97%	84%
2002	13%	0%	100%	100%

TEXAS 8
East central — The Woodlands, Conroe

A Republican stronghold, the 8th begins in Houston's rapidly growing Montgomery County suburbs north of the city and moves east through rural areas to the Louisiana border. Four-fifths of district residents are white, the highest percentage of white residents in any Texas district.

Located about 30 miles north of downtown Houston, The Woodlands — a large planned community that gets its name from its proximity to Sam Houston National Forest — is an exclusive area filled with large houses and some of the state's highest-rated schools. The area is a corporate and business center, and several petroleum and biotechnology companies have made their homes here.

The timber industry and some cattle ranches populate the northern part of Montgomery County, although much of the county is turning into suburbanized bedroom communities for Houston. Conroe has one of the largest lakes in the area and is home to many wealthy lakefront homeowners. Lake Conroe also offers golf courses, resorts and marinas, and some of the 8th's lakes provide drinking water to Houston and are a magnet for retirees. High winds during Hurricane Rita, and the subsequent loss of electricity and running water, damaged residential areas in the 8th, as well as the forests and cattle ranches. Farther north are Huntsville and Livingston, where a Texas State Penitentiary, which houses the state's death row, is a major employer.

In the southeastern part of the 8th, the economy relies on petrochemical production, and relies on ship repair in Orange County and nearby Beaumont and Port Arthur (both in the 2nd District). Abundant pine forests in the district's east spur a thriving timber industry. Slow population growth and a high percentage of blue-collar workers have made it difficult to attract higher-paying service jobs here.

MAJOR INDUSTRY

Petrochemicals, shipping, timber, education, prisons

CITIES

The Woodlands (unincorporated), 55,649; Conroe, 36,811; Huntsville, 35,078

NOTABLE

Texas' Lone Star flag was designed in Montgomery County in 1839; Huntsville honors Sam Houston, the first president of the Republic of Texas, with a 67-foot-tall statue of him.

Rep. Al Green (D)

CAPITOL OFFICE
225-7508
al.green@mail.house.gov
www.house.gov/algreen
425 Cannon 20515-4309; fax 225-2947

COMMITTEES
Financial Services
Homeland Security

RESIDENCE
Houston

BORN
Sept. 1, 1947, New Orleans, La.

RELIGION
Christian

FAMILY
Divorced

EDUCATION
Florida A&M U., attended 1966-71; Tuskegee Institute of Technology, attended; Texas Southern U., J.D. 1973

CAREER
Lawyer; NAACP chapter president

POLITICAL HIGHLIGHTS
Harris County Justice of the Peace Court judge, 1977-2004; candidate for mayor of Houston, 1981

ELECTION RESULTS

2006 GENERAL		
Al Green (D)		unopposed
2006 PRIMARY		
Al Green (D)		unopposed
2004 GENERAL		
Al Green (D)	114,462	72.2%
Arlette Molina (R)	42,132	26.6%
Stacey Lynn Bourland (LIBERT)	1,972	1.2%

Elected 2004; 2nd term

Green speaks softly and deliberately, but his voice resonates with a passion rooted in a desire for civil rights and economic justice that comes from being the son of an auto mechanic and a maid. He walks the halls of Congress looking more like a social worker than a politician. He always wears a lapel badge that reads, "God Is Good All the Time."

During his first term in the House, Green's legislative priorities were largely put on hold as he tended to the thousands of evacuees who came to Houston in the aftermath of hurricanes Katrina and Rita — more than 20,000 hurricane victims came to his district alone. He spent much of his time dealing with the post-hurricane chaos, including meeting demands for increased police protection, education, housing and social services. "In every adversity, I have found that there is opportunity," he says.

Green's Houston district is one of the country's most diverse and poor. Green sits on the Financial Services Committee, where he pays particular attention to insurance, housing and lender practices that hurt low- to moderate-income neighborhoods. He has focused his efforts on extending housing vouchers for hurricane victims, trying to create more-affordable housing and watching for housing discrimination.

In 2007, the House backed his proposal to extend a temporary housing voucher program run by the Federal Emergency Management Agency until the end of the year. Eligible families would then be allowed to transfer to the Section 8 housing program that subsidizes rent payments for low-income families. During a hearing to study FEMA's slow response to provide housing, Green said the families of Sept. 11 victims received an average of $3.1 million in financial compensation, while FEMA continually misses deadlines to provide even basic housing assistance for the hurricane evacuees. "We cannot treat the people of New York better than we treat people in New Orleans," said Green, who was born in the Crescent City.

Like others in the liberal wing of his party, Green calls for a national affordable health care system, and calls the current system a "sickness care system" that leaves the uninsured and unemployed seeking help in expensive emergency rooms. "I don't think people ought to receive good health care by virtue of their station in life," Green said. All children should receive health care without question, he believes.

He also wants to give everyone the opportunity to attend college, and he would like to see the No Child Left Behind education law include pay raises for teachers.

Green, a longtime advocate of a minimum wage increase, was pleased when measures boosting the rate passed both chambers in early 2007. However, he called it "an important first step." If he had his way, minimum wage would be indexed to ensure that someone working full-time remained above the federal poverty line. "No one should work full-time and still stand in the welfare line," he told the Houston Chronicle in late 2006.

Green gained a seat on the Homeland Security Committee in the 110th Congress (2007-08), where he is watchful of issues critical to Houston such as rail and cargo security and border enforcement. As is true for many in the Texas delegation, immigration issues are important to Green. Yet while many Texas politicians focus on closing America's borders, Green is more intent on helping those immigrants who are already here.

A longtime civil rights activist, he was arrested in 2006 along with other members of the Congressional Black Caucus at the Embassy of Sudan, where they were protesting the genocide in Darfur. The lawmakers were charged with trespassing, fined $50 and released.

Green wants the American people to have a "better sense of goodwill toward each other." He often recites the eight-verse poem "The Cold Within" by James Patrick Kenny, which tells the story of six people who died in the cold because greed and spite kept each from contributing to a fire that would have kept them all warm. "The point is this," Green says. "If we don't learn to live together as brothers and sisters…we will perish as fools."

Born in New Orleans, Green grew up in Florida where his maternal grandfather was a Methodist minister. Green says he required the children in his church to recite poetry or Bible verses on holidays. Green attended Florida A&M University and the Tuskegee Institute of Technology through work-study and grant programs. He did not earn an undergraduate degree but eventually gained a law degree from the Thurgood Marshall School of Law at Texas Southern University. "I like to remind people that if Al Green — without a bachelor's degree, who barely made it through law school — can make it, I would hope that would inspire others to believe that they can make it too."

After law school, he co-founded the law firm of Green, Wilson, Dewberry and Fitch, where his practice included criminal defense. One of his adversaries in the courtroom, who became a good friend, was then prosecutor Ted Poe. Poe, a Republican, was elected to represent Texas' 2nd District in 2004.

Green served for 26 years as a Justice of the Peace. During the 1980s and early 1990s, he was president of the local chapter of the National Association for the Advancement of Colored People. He cites as a major accomplishment a sevenfold increase in the chapter's membership and the purchase of a permanent headquarters.

Green took advantage of the GOP-inspired remapping of Texas congressional districts prior to the 2004 election, which significantly altered the demographics of the 9th District. The redistricting map took the former 25th District in suburban Houston represented by Democrat Chris Bell and shifted it to include more of Houston's urban areas.

Green scored a crushing 2-1 victory over Bell in the new 9th, then won his general election with even greater ease in one of the few remaining Democratic strongholds in Texas. He faced no opposition in 2006.

He shares the same name as the famous soul singer, which he says can be a disadvantage because "people often ask me to sing." But he likes to point out that the name "Alexander," picked by his mother, means "helper of humankind."

KEY VOTES

2006

- No Stop broadband companies from favoring select Internet traffic
- No Affirm U.S. commitment to war in Iraq and reject setting a withdrawal date for troops
- No Repeal requirement for bilingual ballots at the polls
- Yes Permit U.S. sale of civilian nuclear technology to India
- No Build a 700-mile fence on the U.S.-Mexico border to curb illegal crossings
- No Permit warrantless wiretaps of suspected terrorists

2005

- Yes Intervene in the life-support case of Terri Schiavo
- Yes Lift President Bush's restrictions on stem cell research funding
- Yes Prohibit FBI access to library and bookstore records
- No Approve free-trade pact with five Central American countries
- Yes Pass energy policy overhaul favored by President Bush emphasizing domestic oil and gas production
- No End mandatory preservation of habitat of endangered animal and plant species
- Yes Ban torture of prisoners in U.S. custody

CQ VOTE STUDIES

	PARTY UNITY		PRESIDENTIAL SUPPORT	
	Support	Oppose	Support	Oppose
2006	94%	6%	30%	70%
2005	93%	7%	20%	80%

INTEREST GROUPS

	AFL-CIO	ADA	CCUS	ACU
2006	100%	95%	60%	20%
2005	100%	100%	48%	16%

TEXAS 9

Southern Houston and suburbs — Mission Bend

The 9th, which takes in southern Houston and a few suburban communities to the west, is Texas' smallest district in land area but is its most ethnically diverse — black residents make up 37 percent of residents, with one-third of the population Hispanic, 17 percent white and 11 percent Asian.

The district's eastern edge takes in largely black communities such as Sunnyside, which is one of the oldest black communities in Houston. As the 9th stretches west, it picks up the entertainment complex Reliant Park. Among other venues, the park is home to Reliant Stadium, which is the home field for football's Texans, and the historic Astrodome. Local officials have discussed turning the multi-use Astrodome into a convention hotel, but final decisions have not been made.

The western portion of the 9th takes in much of Houston's Asian community, with Chinese, Korean and Japanese enclaves in addition to several South Asian immigrant communities. Almost one-third of district residents are foreign-born, the highest percentage in the state. In this growing area, retail dominates and businesses spring up with signs in both English and Asian languages. The Chinatown area boasts one of the nation's largest Asian-themed malls, the Hong Kong City Mall, which attracts not only local ethnic-Chinese crowds but also visiting tourists.

Leading the local health care sector, part of the Texas Medical Center falls in the 9th in the Hermann Park area (shared with the 7th and 18th districts). The 9th's portion of the medical center includes the Houston Academy of Medicine and the Michael E. Debakey VA Medical Center. Job creation is a high priority among the area's many poor residents.

The 9th strongly supports Democrats, and former Rep. Chris Bell took 59 percent of the district's 2006 gubernatorial vote here. Only the 30th and 18th districts gave Bell higher percentages of the vote.

MAJOR INDUSTRY

Retail, health care, entertainment

CITIES

Houston (pt.), 551,793; Mission Bend (unincorporated), 30,831

NOTABLE

Tens of thousands of evacuees from Louisiana arrived at the Astrodome following landfall of Hurricane Katrina in 2005.

Rep. Michael McCaul (R)

CAPITOL OFFICE
225-2401
www.house.gov/mccaul
131 Cannon 20515-4310; fax 225-5955

COMMITTEES
Foreign Affairs
Homeland Security
Science & Technology
Standards of Official Conduct

RESIDENCE
Austin

BORN
Jan. 14, 1962, Dallas, Texas

RELIGION
Roman Catholic

FAMILY
Wife, Linda McCaul; five children

EDUCATION
Trinity U., B.A. 1984 (business & history); St. Mary's U. (Texas), J.D. 1987

CAREER
U.S. Justice Department official; state and federal prosecutor; lawyer

POLITICAL HIGHLIGHTS
No previous office

ELECTION RESULTS

2006 GENERAL		
Michael McCaul (R)	97,726	55.3%
Ted Ankrum (D)	71,415	40.4%
Michael Badnarik (LIBERT)	7,614	4.3%
2006 PRIMARY		
Michael McCaul (R)		unopposed
2004 GENERAL		
Michael McCaul (R)	182,113	78.6%
Robert Fritsche (LIBERT)	35,569	15.4%
Lorenzo Sadun (I) - write-in	13,961	6.0%

Elected 2004; 2nd term

McCaul attributes his long career in public service to the example set by his father, a B-17 pilot during World War II, and his education at the Jesuit College Preparatory Academy of Dallas, where he was taught to be "a man for others."

The call of the private sector might also be faint because McCaul is one of the wealthiest members of Congress. His wife, Linda, is the daughter of Clear Channel broadcasting CEO Lowry Mays, and McCaul opened the family checkbook to the tune of nearly $2 million to win his first campaign.

A former prosecutor and counterterrorism official, McCaul has been pegged by his peers and Republican leaders as a possible standout. He was elected freshman class liaison to the leadership in the 109th Congress (2005-06), and is in his second term as a member of Minority Whip Roy Blunt's vote-counting operation.

That sense of service to his colleagues led him in 2007 to accept one of the most thankless jobs in Congress: an assignment to the Committee on Standards of Official Conduct, better known as the ethics committee. Few lawmakers want to be responsible for passing judgment on the behavior of their peers. The post has its upside, however, because smooth handling of the undesirable duties can be rewarded with future plums.

And the role of ethics investigator is a familiar one for McCaul, who was a prosecutor in the U.S. Justice Department's public integrity section before becoming deputy to current Sen. John Cornyn, who was then the Texas attorney general. Once McCaul was elected to Congress, his experience in counterterrorism — he served as chief of terrorism and national security for the U.S. attorney in Austin — made him a natural selection for the Homeland Security Committee, where he is the top Republican on the Subcommittee on Emerging Threats.

Most of McCaul's legislative efforts have been aimed at cracking down on illegal immigration, which he says is a national security issue. He backed the House version of an immigration overhaul focused primarily on border-enforcement measures, and he derided as "amnesty" a three-pronged Senate approach that would have established a guest-worker program and given illegal immigrants currently in the country a path to citizenship. It was a rare instance in his first term that he found himself opposing President Bush, who backed the Senate version of the legislation.

McCaul says citizens should be able to volunteer to serve in counterterrorism and border-enforcement programs. He introduced a bill in the 109th Congress that would have created a Citizen Corps for homeland security issues and a Border Corps. The latter group would be authorized to engage in activities such as surveillance, communications, transportation, administrative support, "line watch" operations to prevent illegal border crossings and smuggling, and air, water, horse and bike patrols.

"We've seen volunteers with the United States Coast Guard Auxiliary succeed in helping to defend our country, and I now think it's time the Department of Homeland Security make use of all the people who want to volunteer to help keep America safe along our nation's borders," he said. The bill did not move in the 109th Congress, however.

In his first two years in Congress, McCaul was nearly always a loyal vote for the GOP: In the 109th Congress, he voted with his party 95 percent of the time on votes that pitted most Republicans against most Democrats.

McCaul proved to be conservative on both fiscal and social issues, supporting his party's tax cuts, voting to make it a felony to take a minor across state lines for an abortion, and agreeing to eliminate requirements that states provide bilingual voting assistance. He voted in 2006 in favor of a constitutional amendment that would define marriage as a union of a man and a woman. He is a member of the Republican Study Committee, a group of about 100 of the most conservative members of the House.

He did part ways with the GOP early in the 110th Congress (2007-08), voting with 67 other House Republicans to support a bill, written by the Democrats, to implement the remaining recommendations of the Sept. 11 commission, including enhancing port security.

McCaul's focus on terrorism has led him to try to legislate in the international arena. The House adopted his amendment prohibiting the use of funds to support the United Nations' Human Rights Council as long as its membership includes nations designated as state sponsors of terrorism. The provision did not become law, however.

He has an opportunity to keep an eye on international security issues from his seat on the Foreign Affairs Committee. McCaul has repeatedly expressed an interest in the concept of the U.S. government fomenting internal resistance to the Iranian government, particularly through the MEK — a group listed by the State Department as a foreign terrorist organization. At a hearing in January 2007, he asked Secretary of State Condoleezza Rice what the U.S. government is doing to assist any internal resistance in Iran and whether the MEK could be removed from the list of terrorist groups.

McCaul also sits on the Science and Technology Committee, which oversees the space policies important to those of his constituents involved in the work of the Johnson Space Flight Center in Houston. Yet he does not sit on the subcommittee with jurisdiction over space programs. He introduced bills in the 109th Congress to promote high-risk, high-reward research and to integrate education and research.

The 2004 GOP primary that marked McCaul's political debut was an eight-candidate free-for-all. McCaul, who amassed key support from Republican insiders, won the runoff with 63 percent of the vote. Democrats did not field a candidate in November, and McCaul took 79 percent of the vote, thanks to new district lines that split his hometown of Austin and brought in many more GOP-leaning voters to counter Austin's Democratic bent.

In 2006, a bad year for Republicans, McCaul won at the polls against former NASA official Ted Ankrum with just 55 percent of the vote.

KEY VOTES

2006

- No Stop broadband companies from favoring select Internet traffic
- Yes Affirm U.S. commitment to war in Iraq and reject setting a withdrawal date for troops
- Yes Repeal requirement for bilingual ballots at the polls
- Yes Permit U.S. sale of civilian nuclear technology to India
- Yes Build a 700-mile fence on the U.S.-Mexico border to curb illegal crossings
- Yes Permit warrantless wiretaps of suspected terrorists

2005

- Yes Intervene in the life-support case of Terri Schiavo
- No Lift President Bush's restrictions on stem cell research funding
- No Prohibit FBI access to library and bookstore records
- Yes Approve free-trade pact with five Central American countries
- Yes Pass energy policy overhaul favored by President Bush emphasizing domestic oil and gas production
- Yes End mandatory preservation of habitat of endangered animal and plant species
- Yes Ban torture of prisoners in U.S. custody

CQ VOTE STUDIES

	PARTY UNITY		PRESIDENTIAL SUPPORT	
	Support	Oppose	Support	Oppose
2006	94%	6%	90%	10%
2005	96%	4%	85%	15%

INTEREST GROUPS

	AFL-CIO	ADA	CCUS	ACU
2006	21%	0%	100%	83%
2005	20%	5%	93%	96%

TEXAS 10

East central – eastern Austin and western Houston suburbs

The 10th mimics a drive that many University of Texas students from the Houston area know well as they travel back and forth to school in Austin. The district stretches west from the northern Houston suburbs and follows U.S. Highway 290 to Austin, where it hugs downtown as it wraps around the city's northwestern edge. Along its 150-mile journey, the 10th picks up affluent suburbs, a technology belt and a chunk of farmland.

Narrowly missing the Democratic stronghold of Hyde Park and the University of Texas in Austin, the 10th instead takes in the more upscale areas of the Arboretum, Far West and the neighborhood of West Lake, part of Austin's hill country. The district also reaches up to Pflugerville and the northern suburbs, which host many of Austin's technology companies. Both IBM and Samsung have plants in the city, and Dell is based in Round Rock, just across the district line in the 31st. Although the majority of the University of Texas flagship campus is in the adjacent 21st, the 10th takes in the university's J.J. Pickle Research Campus.

As the district moves east from Austin, it becomes increasingly rural, and takes in the towns of Elgin, Giddings, Hempstead and Prairie View. This area also includes Brenham, which is home to ice cream maker Blue Bell Creameries. The district then dips back into more-urban areas as it takes in suburbs in northwestern Harris County, including Tomball and part of Spring, which continue to experience population growth as people move farther from downtown Houston. Most residents here commute, which makes transportation policy an important issue.

Although the 10th includes vastly different urban, suburban and rural areas, it is reliably Republican. George W. Bush captured 61 percent of the district's 2004 presidential vote.

MAJOR INDUSTRY
Software, technology, agriculture

CITIES
Austin (pt.), 209,200; Pflugerville, 16,335

NOTABLE
Serbin's "Wendish Fest," held every September, celebrates the region's link to Slavic community and culture.

Rep. K. Michael Conaway (R)

CAPITOL OFFICE
225-3605
conaway.house.gov
511 Cannon 20515-4311; fax 225-1783

COMMITTEES
Agriculture
Armed Services
Budget

RESIDENCE
Midland

BORN
June 11, 1948, Borger, Texas

RELIGION
Baptist

FAMILY
Wife, Suzanne Conaway; four children

EDUCATION
East Texas State U., B.B.A. 1970 (accounting)

MILITARY SERVICE
Army, 1970-72

CAREER
Accountant; bank chief financial officer; oil and gas exploration company chief financial officer

POLITICAL HIGHLIGHTS
Midland school board, 1985-88; candidate for U.S. House (special election), 2003

ELECTION RESULTS

2006 GENERAL		
K. Michael Conaway (R)		unopposed
2006 PRIMARY		
K. Michael Conaway (R)		unopposed
2004 GENERAL		
K. Michael Conaway (R)	177,291	76.8%
Wayne Raasch (D)	50,339	21.8%
Jeffrey C. Blunt (LIBERT)	3,347	1.5%

Elected 2004; 2nd term

It is a good bet that no one in Congress knows President Bush as well as Conaway. As Bush's friend and former business partner during the 1980s, they struggled together to meet payroll at their Midland-based energy company. In Bush's first year as governor in 1995, he appointed Conaway to the state Board of Public Accountancy, where Conaway served for seven years, including five years as the agency's chairman.

Now in his second term in Congress, Conaway is an ally of the president's on his often-questioned strategy for the Iraq War. And he used his background as a certified public accountant to argue for Bush's ultimately failed 2005 campaign to revamp Social Security by creating personal savings accounts. In the 109th Congress (2005-06), he sided with Bush on 90 percent of the votes on which the president took a public position.

But on two issues that are important to his district — agriculture and immigration — Conaway has firmly disagreed with the administration.

Conaway sits on the House Agriculture Committee, representing a district in Central and West Texas that includes vast farmland and cotton fields. He began the 110th Congress (2007-08) opposed to the administration's proposed new farm bill that would cap commodity payments based on income. Conaway was intent on having Congress write extensions to current law, but the administration was facing pressure to limit commodity payments to large farming operations in order to increase conservation subsidies to small farms.

On immigration, Conaway was the most outspoken Texas Republican advocate of a comprehensive overhaul of immigration law, similar to what Bush called for in 2006. Other party conservatives wanted to limit legislation to securing the border. However, Conaway differed with Bush on the definition of "comprehensive." Conaway was willing to combine more border enforcement with a limited, temporary worker program for immigrants, not the broader earned citizenship program for illegal immigrants favored by Bush. Any plan containing a path to citizenship would be considered "a disaster" by voters in his district, Conaway maintained.

His immigration stance reflects the political realities in his district — an area conservative in philosophy, yet with an agricultural economy that traditionally has relied on immigrant laborers. "Much of our casework in the district is with folks who are trying to dot all the i's and cross all the t's and abide by the rules, and they have a very difficult time working with immigration [agencies]," Conaway said.

Another priority of Conaway's is to increase oil and gas production, which also is important in his district. In 2007, he was working to have Odessa picked as the site for the FutureGen Initiative, a $1 billion government-industry partnership to build and operate an emissions-free, coal-fired electric and hydrogen production plant.

The committee assignment that plays to his professional background is the House Budget Committee, where he tries to keep a watch on government spending. His goal is to reduce the national debt by forcing Congress to make choices in spending priorities. On the first day of the 110th Congress, he proposed "No New Programs" legislation, which would change House rules to require that the creation of any new federal program be combined with the elimination of an existing program of equal or greater cost.

One of his personal goals, however, did not get a hearing in his freshman term, when his party controlled Congress. House Judiciary Committee

Chairman F. James Sensenbrenner Jr. of Wisconsin refused to consider a bill by Conaway that would have required all members of Congress and senior staff to "read and understand" the U.S. Constitution and submit "written proof" that they had fulfilled the requirement once every two-year congressional session.

"Just as lawyers and doctors understand the law and human anatomy, it is imperative for serving legislators in Congress to understand the Constitution," Conaway said. He keeps a pocket version himself and writes in the cover the dates he reads it; he also compels his aides to provide documentation that they have read the Constitution during the previous year.

From the time he was in elementary school, Conaway told his parents he would go to college on a football scholarship, even though he thought he had limited ability. He played on Odessa Permian High School's first state championship football team as defensive end and offensive tackle. (The school's football program was the basis for the book, "Friday Night Lights," which spawned a film and television series.) Conaway in fact won a football scholarship, after graduating from Permian in 1966. Of his limited college football career, he says, "I didn't play a lot on Saturdays."

He was a pre-law major in college, but a professor persuaded him to switch to accounting. He received his degree from East Texas State University (now Texas A&M University-Commerce) in 1970. He was a military police officer at the Army's Fort Hood in Texas from 1970 to 1972, then went to work for Price Waterhouse & Co., settling in Midland.

From 1981 to 1986, Conaway was chief financial officer of and an investor in Arbusto Energy Inc. (later Bush Exploration), which Bush owned. In the company's toughest times, Conaway said he learned that Bush "has a great heart and he's pretty quick to make a decision, doesn't spend a lot of time looking backwards, looking in the rearview mirror. He's focused mainly on going forward."

In 1993, Conaway began his own accounting firm. He also is an ordained deacon in the Baptist Church.

His first elective office was on the Midland school board. In 2003, he lost a House special-election race in the 19th District by just 587 votes to fellow Republican Randy Neugebauer. Shortly after that, a GOP-inspired mid-decade congressional redistricting deliberately put Neugebauer and Conaway in different districts, and Conaway breezed to victory in 2004 in the new Midland-based 11th District. He won both his primary and general-election contests by ratios of roughly 3-to-1. In 2006, he was unopposed for re-election.

KEY VOTES

2006

- No Stop broadband companies from favoring select Internet traffic
- Yes Affirm U.S. commitment to war in Iraq and reject setting a withdrawal date for troops
- Yes Repeal requirement for bilingual ballots at the polls
- Yes Permit U.S. sale of civilian nuclear technology to India
- No Build a 700-mile fence on the U.S.-Mexico border to curb illegal crossings
- Yes Permit warrantless wiretaps of suspected terrorists

2005

- Yes Intervene in the life-support case of Terri Schiavo
- No Lift President Bush's restrictions on stem cell research funding
- No Prohibit FBI access to library and bookstore records
- Yes Approve free-trade pact with five Central American countries
- Yes Pass energy policy overhaul favored by President Bush emphasizing domestic oil and gas production
- Yes End mandatory preservation of habitat of endangered animal and plant species
- No Ban torture of prisoners in U.S. custody

CQ VOTE STUDIES

	PARTY UNITY		PRESIDENTIAL SUPPORT	
	Support	Oppose	Support	Oppose
2006	98%	2%	93%	7%
2005	96%	4%	87%	13%

INTEREST GROUPS

	AFL-CIO	ADA	CCUS	ACU
2006	7%	0%	100%	88%
2005	13%	0%	93%	96%

TEXAS 11

West central – Midland, Odessa, San Angelo

Starting in Burnet County in the center of the state, the 11th is characterized by stark plains, mesas and oil rigs. It slices from west of Austin to the New Mexico border, taking in San Angelo, Midland, Odessa and vast stretches of rural land. The population here is overwhelmingly white and Republican.

In the west lies oil country and the Permian Basin, home to Midland and Odessa. The economy of Odessa is still based heavily on petroleum — a crude oil boom in the early part of the decade gave the area some of the lowest unemployment numbers in the state — but the city also has become a regional telecommunications and distribution center.

While the western portion of the 11th is mostly high desert plains, the southeastern section moves into the highland lakes region, taking in part of the state's hill country. Here, agriculture dominates, with cotton, row crops, cattle, sheep, goats and small grains key to the economy. This region also has grown in popularity with hunters, and tourism has boomed at the area's resorts and lakes.

Thirty percent of the district's residents are Hispanic, and immigration continues to be an issue throughout the region as illegal workers play a heavy role in the oil and agricultural industries. The 11th also has the state's highest percentage of residents over age 65 (15 percent) due to a relatively inexpensive cost of living and good area health care.

The immense 11th gave Republican George W. Bush 78 percent of its 2004 presidential vote, the highest percentage Bush received in any Texas congressional district. In 2006, Democrat Chris Bell received 17 percent of the 11th's gubernatorial vote, his statewide low.

MAJOR INDUSTRY
Oil and gas, agriculture, cattle, tourism

MILITARY BASES
Goodfellow Air Force Base, 1,389 military, 769 civilian (2007)

CITIES
Midland, 94,996; Odessa, 90,943; San Angelo, 88,439; Brownwood, 18,813

NOTABLE
The novel, movie and television drama, "Friday Night Lights," is based on the Odessa Permian High School football team; The Globe of the Great Southwest in Odessa is a replica of the famous Elizabethan-era theater used by William Shakespeare.

Rep. Kay Granger (R)

CAPITOL OFFICE
225-5071
texas.granger@mail.house.gov
kaygranger.house.gov
440 Cannon 20515-4312; fax 225-5683

COMMITTEES
Appropriations

RESIDENCE
Fort Worth

BORN
Jan. 18, 1943, Greenville, Texas

RELIGION
Methodist

FAMILY
Divorced; three children

EDUCATION
Texas Wesleyan U., B.S. 1965

CAREER
Insurance agency owner; teacher

POLITICAL HIGHLIGHTS
Fort Worth Zoning Commission, 1981-89; Fort Worth City Council, 1989-91; mayor of Fort Worth, 1991-95

ELECTION RESULTS

2006 GENERAL		
Kay Granger (R)	98,371	66.9%
John R. Morris (D)	45,676	31.1%
Gardner Osborne (LIBERT)	2,888	2.0%
2006 PRIMARY		
Kay Granger (R)		unopposed
2004 GENERAL		
Kay Granger (R)	173,222	72.3%
Felix Alvarado (D)	66,316	27.7%

PREVIOUS WINNING PERCENTAGES
2002 (92%); 2000 (63%); 1998 (62%); 1996 (58%)

Elected 1996; 6th term

Granger, the only woman in the House Republican leadership, is a solid supporter of President Bush and a dependable team player. A former teacher, businesswoman and mayor of Fort Worth, she has paid her dues and worked her way into the top ranks of her party.

Granger set her sights on the leadership in her freshman term, when she was given a position as assistant GOP whip. She finally made it to the elected leadership in late 2006, when Republicans chose their leaders for the 110th Congress (2007-08). She defeated Steve Pearce of New Mexico by 124-63 to become vice chairwoman of the Republican Conference, the No. 4 leadership post.

The post opened up when Jack Kingston of Georgia ran unsuccessfully for the conference chairmanship after Deborah Pryce of Ohio stepped down. Granger, like Pryce, is on the rolls of the moderate Republican Main Street Partnership. But unlike Pryce, she is sheepish to be identified with the group. "I'm really unaligned," she said. "And I'm conservative."

Granger considered a run for a low-level leadership position in the 107th Congress (2001-02), but backed off. Two years later, then Majority Whip Roy Blunt of Missouri passed her over for chief deputy whip in favor of Eric Cantor of Virginia. But Granger kept her head up and continued to serve as a leader for her party on a range of issues, including Iraq.

She was part of the first congressional delegation to visit Iraq after the war began in 2003, and she co-chairs the bipartisan Iraqi Women's Caucus, traveling to Iraq before the country's January 2006 elections to meet with women candidates seeking a role in the new Iraq government. "I learned more probably than they learned from me," she said. "I learned what real courage is."

In 2005, House GOP leaders made her co-chairwoman of a 21-member Congressional War on Terror team assigned to promote an upbeat message about progress in Iraq. "We're aware of the declining support shown in the polls, and we are very concerned that message is hurting morale, particularly of families" of soldiers serving in Iraq, Granger said.

As the war dragged on and public support waned further, Granger continued to back Bush's policy. She took the House floor in early 2007 to urge patience. "Failing to secure Iraq will result in massive instability in the Middle East, which will undoubtedly spill over to the rest of the world," she said.

Named to the Appropriations Committee in her second term, she was assigned to its Defense Subcommittee in the 109th Congress (2005-06), a major plus for someone who represents an area tied to defense manufacturers such as Lockheed Martin Corp. and Bell Helicopter Textron. She used her post to keep federal dollars flowing to those defense manufacturers and other local interests. She supports continued funding of the F-35 Joint Strike Fighter, the F-22 and the V-22 Osprey aircraft. When the House in June 2006 passed a $427.6 billion fiscal 2007 Defense appropriations bill, she won adoption of a floor amendment stripping out a prohibition on the sale of Lockheed Martin's F-22A Raptor aircraft to foreign governments.

The Democratic takeover in the 110th Congress bumped Granger off the Defense Subcommittee. She now serves on the Military Construction-VA, Homeland Security and Energy-Water panels.

Early in 2000, her district office in a Fort Worth office building was destroyed by a tornado, presaging another uncomfortably close brush with disaster: Granger had just left a meeting at the Pentagon on Sept. 11,

2001, when hijacked American Airlines Flight 77 slammed into the building. She reunited with those present at the meeting on the third anniversary of the terrorist attacks to discuss progress on the war against terrorism. Defense Secretary Donald H. Rumsfeld presented all in attendance with the first honorary Global War on Terrorism coins.

Granger's legislative priorities are shaped by her background. Her interest in championing tax-free education savings accounts for college can be traced to her own experience working her way through school and to the difficulties a favorite niece of hers had in saving enough money to pay for her daughter's education. Having raised three children as a single mother, she also has supported GOP efforts to allow compensatory time off in place of premium pay for overtime worked.

Granger was born in Greenville, Texas, to two public school teachers who divorced when she was 13. After completing college, she became a teacher in the same Birdville school district that named an elementary school after her mother. She taught literature and journalism for 10 years.

In 1978, she went into the insurance business, eventually founding her own agency. In 1981, she was appointed to the Fort Worth Zoning Commission, where she served until she won a seat on the city council in 1989. Two years later, she won a nonpartisan election to become mayor.

During her mayoral tenure, citizen patrol initiatives and other anti-gang efforts helped cut city crime by 50 percent. She lured new businesses to the city, and she was able to reduce property taxes for the first time in 11 years. Her pro-business stands endeared her to the Fort Worth business community, which in 1999 made her the first woman chosen as outstanding business executive of the year. Both parties courted her when Democratic Rep. Pete Geren decided not to seek re-election in 1996.

After choosing to run under the Republican banner and resigning as mayor, Granger heard grumbling from some on the GOP right. She was attacked by two primary opponents as a liberal and was opposed by the Tarrant County Republican chairman. But she won nomination with a whopping 69 percent of the GOP primary vote. That November, she defeated another former Fort Worth mayor, Hugh Parmer, by 17 percentage points, becoming the first Republican woman elected to the House from Texas.

Granger has not faced a real contest since then, though she narrowly escaped a redistricting-inspired face-off against Democratic Rep. Martin Frost in 2004. Instead, he ran against Pete Sessions, and Granger coasted against Democrat Felix Alvarado. In 2006, she easily won a sixth term, taking two-thirds of the vote against Democrat John R. Morris.

KEY VOTES

2006

- No Stop broadband companies from favoring select Internet traffic
- Yes Affirm U.S. commitment to war in Iraq and reject setting a withdrawal date for troops
- Yes Repeal requirement for bilingual ballots at the polls
- Yes Permit U.S. sale of civilian nuclear technology to India
- Yes Build a 700-mile fence on the U.S.-Mexico border to curb illegal crossings
- Yes Permit warrantless wiretaps of suspected terrorists

2005

- ? Intervene in the life-support case of Terri Schiavo
- Yes Lift President Bush's restrictions on stem cell research funding
- No Prohibit FBI access to library and bookstore records
- Yes Approve free-trade pact with five Central American countries
- Yes Pass energy policy overhaul favored by President Bush emphasizing domestic oil and gas production
- Yes End mandatory preservation of habitat of endangered animal and plant species
- No Ban torture of prisoners in U.S. custody

CQ VOTE STUDIES

	PARTY UNITY		PRESIDENTIAL SUPPORT	
	Support	Oppose	Support	Oppose
2006	97%	3%	95%	5%
2005	97%	3%	91%	9%
2004	96%	4%	94%	6%
2003	96%	4%	96%	4%
2002	96%	4%	85%	15%

INTEREST GROUPS

	AFL-CIO	ADA	CCUS	ACU
2006	8%	5%	100%	76%
2005	13%	0%	89%	80%
2004	15%	0%	100%	91%
2003	13%	5%	100%	80%
2002	0%	0%	95%	96%

TEXAS 12

Part of Fort Worth and suburbs; Parker and Wise counties

The Republican-leaning 12th takes in most of western Tarrant County, including two-thirds of Fort Worth, and all of rural Parker and Wise counties. The mostly white, middle-class district contains downtown Fort Worth, but also takes in a mix of suburban and rural areas.

The 12th's solid economy is built around transportation. A major airport, a Naval air base, several main railroad lines and interstate highways are in or adjacent to the district, supporting aerospace, distribution services and retail sectors. The Burlington Northern Santa Fe Railroad has its headquarters in the 12th, and Union Pacific is active here.

Fort Worth's economy continues to grow and diversify. The University of North Texas Health Science Center headlines the local medical services industry. Electronics retailer Radio Shack and homebuilder D.R. Horton are based in the district, and defense contractors such as Lockheed Martin create jobs and fuel economic growth. The Stockyards district, once a stop on the cattle trails north into Oklahoma, is now a national historic district celebrating Fort Worth's role in the American West. The city's Sundance Square, named after the infamous outlaw, has become a downtown retail and entertainment destination.

Redistricting prior to the 2004 election did not diminish the district's GOP strength. There are still some Democratic areas in downtown Fort Worth, but areas in Tarrant County outside the city are overwhelmingly Republican, as are Parker and Wise counties. Parker includes Weatherford, which has become more Republican as it undergoes a transition from rural town into part of the Fort Worth suburbs. George W. Bush won two-thirds of the 2004 presidential vote here.

MAJOR INDUSTRY

Defense technology, transportation, health care

MILITARY BASES

Naval Air Station Fort Worth, 1,958 military, 1,800 civilian (2007)

CITIES

Fort Worth (pt.), 349,997; Haltom City, 39,018; Watauga, 21,908

NOTABLE

The National Cowgirl Museum is in Fort Worth, as is Billy Bob's Texas, a 127,000-square-foot honky tonk and rodeo.

Rep. William M. "Mac" Thornberry (R)

CAPITOL OFFICE
225-3706
www.house.gov/thornberry
2457 Rayburn 20515-4313; fax 225-3486

COMMITTEES
Armed Services
Select Intelligence

RESIDENCE
Clarendon

BORN
July 15, 1958, Clarendon, Texas

RELIGION
Presbyterian

FAMILY
Wife, Sally Thornberry; two children

EDUCATION
Texas Tech U., B.A. 1980 (history);
U. of Texas, J.D. 1983

CAREER
Lawyer; cattleman; U.S. State Department official; congressional aide

POLITICAL HIGHLIGHTS
No previous office

ELECTION RESULTS

2006 GENERAL		
Thornberry (R)	108,107	74.4%
Roger J. Waun (D)	33,460	23.0%
Jim Thompson (LIBERT)	3,829	2.6%
2006 PRIMARY		
William M. "Mac" Thornberry (R)		unopposed
2004 GENERAL		
Thornberry (R)	189,448	92.3%
M.J. "Smitty" Smith (LIBERT)	15,793	7.7%

PREVIOUS WINNING PERCENTAGES
2002 (79%); 2000 (68%); 1998 (68%); 1996 (67%); 1994 (55%)

Elected 1994; 7th term

Thornberry has always had an intense interest in national security. "It's what the federal government was created to do," he says. A member of both the Armed Services and Intelligence committees, he has played a major role in reviewing how well the U.S. intelligence community is operating in this era of global terrorism.

Thornberry says that in the 110th Congress (2007-08) he will focus on developing what he calls "metrics" that can be used to measure progress on improving intelligence capabilities. He uses as an example being able to quantify the increase of Arabic language experts in the intelligence community. He says that at almost every Intelligence panel hearing someone asks whether there are now more Arabic speakers working in the intelligence agencies. "We get these verbal assurances that you could replay year after year without the kind of hard measures we need," he said. He is working with intelligence officials "to try to put quantitative measures on whether we're getting better, and it's hard," he says.

Thornberry had drafted a bill to create a new department to oversee homeland security almost six months before the terrorist attacks of Sept. 11, 2001. After that day, creating such a department suddenly topped everyone's to-do list, and Thornberry's bill became the foundation for the legislation the House passed in 2002. GOP leaders in 2003 rewarded him with a seat on the new Homeland Security Committee, giving him oversight of the new department as it was built from the ground up.

Long an advocate for creating an assistant secretary for "cybersecurity" — that is, elevating the issue's importance within the department — Thornberry saw that idea become reality during an internal department reorganization in 2005, a year after he left the Homeland Security Committee to move to Intelligence.

During the 109th Congress (2005-06), Thornberry was chairman of Intelligence's new oversight panel. The subcommittee was established to monitor effectiveness of the law uniting U.S. intelligence functions under one director, and in 2006 it issued a report concluding the law's implementation had been a "mixed bag," in Thornberry's words. It found fault with the Office of the Director of National Intelligence's approach to implementing the overhaul, and concluded the DNI should be focusing on high priorities such as information sharing rather than taking a more scattershot approach.

A longtime member of Armed Services, he has been a firm supporter of the Iraq War, lecturing reporters in 2005 that they were "missing a big story" about progress being made in the war-torn nation. But he also understands the concerns of those who want the troops to come home. "In our area, we have lost soldiers. It's very real. You know all of their families," he said in November 2005. "And they ask, 'Are we winning? Are we making progress? And are we going to stand by the Iraqis, or leave, the way we did in Vietnam?' "

But he continued to stand behind the Bush administration even as much of the public turned against the White House approach to the war. In 2007, he voted against a Democratic resolution disapproving of President Bush's plan to send more than 21,000 additional combat troops into Iraq, saying the resolution was a political ploy and would damage troop morale. He also opposed a Democratic war funding bill setting a timeline for withdrawal of troops from Iraq.

From his Armed Services seat, he has been a steady protector of the military plants and bases in his district. In a September 2006 defense authorization bill, he announced that he secured $2.3 billion for the V-22 Osprey tilt-rotor aircraft, $523 million to upgrade 18 helicopters for the Marines' H-1 program, and $683 million for continued research and development of the new presidential helicopter, Marine One. All of these aircraft are built at the district's Bell-Boeing helicopter plant. He also said he gained $480 million for Amarillo's Pantex weapons assembly and disassembly plant.

Thornberry is a reliable vote for his party. On votes pitting most Democrats against most Republicans, he stuck with his party 97 percent of the time in the 109th Congress, and he voted in agreement with Bush 94 percent of the time on votes on which the president took a public stand. When asked to describe his political philosophy, he states bluntly, "conservative."

He traces his conservatism to his upbringing on the cattle ranch that has been in his family for more than 70 years. "Someone in the federal government was telling us what to do on a farm 7 miles down a dirt road outside a town of 2,000 people," he said.

He's still in the ranching business with his brothers and owns a one-third stake in the Thornberry Brothers Cattle Partnership. He is a proponent of property owners' rights and says federal laws and regulations impinge unduly on farmers' land-use decisions.

Thornberry's district is among the nation's leading producers of cotton, wheat and peanuts, so he also has a keen interest in federal subsidies for those crops despite the ideological leanings that prompted him to support the Republican Party's 1996 Freedom to Farm law, which sought to replace New Deal-era crop subsidies with a system based on the free market.

Thornberry worked for five years as an aide on Capitol Hill after graduating from the University of Texas law school in 1983. He was a legislative aide to Texas GOP Rep. Tom Loeffler, then was chief of staff for Rep. Larry Combest, another Texas Republican. In 1988, he was deputy assistant secretary of State for legislative affairs in the Reagan administration, where he got to know the inner workings of the House.

Thornberry took a break from politics in 1989 and went to work in an Amarillo law firm while helping run his family's cattle ranch. Then in 1994, he challenged Democratic incumbent Bill Sarpalius, who had become vulnerable in the conservative district because of his support for raising taxes as part of President Bill Clinton's 1993 budget plan. Thornberry played up his family's close ties to the land and beat Sarpalius with 55 percent of the vote. He has won re-election easily since. In 2006, he took more than 74 percent of the vote.

KEY VOTES

2006

- No — Stop broadband companies from favoring select Internet traffic
- Yes — Affirm U.S. commitment to war in Iraq and reject setting a withdrawal date for troops
- Yes — Repeal requirement for bilingual ballots at the polls
- Yes — Permit U.S. sale of civilian nuclear technology to India
- Yes — Build a 700-mile fence on the U.S.-Mexico border to curb illegal crossings
- Yes — Permit warrantless wiretaps of suspected terrorists

2005

- Yes — Intervene in the life-support case of Terri Schiavo
- No — Lift President Bush's restrictions on stem cell research funding
- No — Prohibit FBI access to library and bookstore records
- Yes — Approve free-trade pact with five Central American countries
- Yes — Pass energy policy overhaul favored by President Bush emphasizing domestic oil and gas production
- Yes — End mandatory preservation of habitat of endangered animal and plant species
- No — Ban torture of prisoners in U.S. custody

CQ VOTE STUDIES

	PARTY UNITY		PRESIDENTIAL SUPPORT	
	Support	Oppose	Support	Oppose
2006	97%	3%	95%	5%
2005	98%	2%	93%	7%
2004	98%	2%	97%	3%
2003	98%	2%	96%	4%
2002	94%	6%	92%	8%

INTEREST GROUPS

	AFL-CIO	ADA	CCUS	ACU
2006	7%	5%	100%	88%
2005	7%	0%	85%	100%
2004	7%	0%	100%	100%
2003	0%	10%	97%	88%
2002	0%	0%	95%	92%

TEXAS 13
Panhandle — Amarillo; Wichita Falls

The conservative 13th encompasses much of the Texas Panhandle, including the city of Amarillo, then extends east along the Oklahoma border to take in the South Plains and much of the Red River Valley. It juts south twice to add more agricultural territory as well as pick up Jones County's small portion of Abilene. The district takes in Wichita Falls and reaches east to haul in the western half of Cooke County, about 50 miles north of Fort Worth. Monstrous and mainly rural, the 13th includes all or part of 44 counties, 40 of which have a population of under 25,000.

Once a main stop on Route 66, Amarillo, the 13th's most populous city, continues to be the Panhandle's economic center despite declines in the once-dominant oil industry. Pantex employs thousands at the nation's only nuclear weapons assembly and disassembly plant. The city also contributes to the military's V-22 Osprey tilt-rotor aircraft. It also has a significant food processing sector, and Tyson Foods is a major employer.

Wichita Falls also was heavily dependent on the oil and gas industries, but today factories are numerous. Sheppard Air Force Base is a major employer, but the base will lose thousands of jobs in the 2005 BRAC round. The city is a medical hub and its local prison provides stable jobs. The Ogalla Aquifer supports many district farmers, who are among the nation's top producers of cotton, sorghum, peanuts and wheat.

The 13th is one of the most Republican districts in Texas. The GOP excels in many of the rural small towns that dot the area, particularly around Amarillo. Ochiltree County, in the Panhandle, gave 92 percent of the vote to George W. Bush in the 2004 presidential election. Closer to blue-collar Wichita Falls, voters have traditionally favored Democrats at the local level, but even this area votes solidly Republican in state and national elections. Overall, Bush captured 77 percent of the district's 2004 vote.

MAJOR INDUSTRY
Agriculture, oil, defense

MILITARY BASES
Sheppard Air Force Base, 3,125 military, 4,023 civilian (2006)

CITIES
Amarillo, 173,627; Wichita Falls, 104,197; Pampa, 17,887

NOTABLE
Mineral Wells was a popular destination for people seeking to drink the water and soak themselves in specially constructed bathhouses.

Rep. Ron Paul (R)

CAPITOL OFFICE
225-2831
rep.paul@mail.house.gov
www.house.gov/paul
203 Cannon 20515-4314; fax 225-1655

COMMITTEES
Financial Services
Foreign Affairs
Joint Economic

RESIDENCE
Lake Jackson

BORN
Aug. 20, 1935, Pittsburgh, Pa.

RELIGION
Protestant

FAMILY
Wife, Carol Wells Paul; five children

EDUCATION
Gettysburg College, B.S. 1957 (pre-med); Duke U., M.D. 1961

MILITARY SERVICE
Air Force, 1963-65; Pa. Air National Guard, 1965-68

CAREER
Physician

POLITICAL HIGHLIGHTS
Republican nominee for U.S. House, 1974; U.S. House, 1976-77; defeated for re-election to U.S. House, 1976; U.S. House, 1979-85; sought Republican nomination for U.S. Senate, 1984; Libertarian nominee for president, 1988

ELECTION RESULTS

2006 GENERAL		
Ron Paul (R)	94,380	60.2%
Shane Sklar (D)	62,429	39.8%
2006 PRIMARY		
Ron Paul (R)	24,086	77.6%
Cynthia Sinatra (R)	6,935	22.4%
2004 GENERAL		
Ron Paul (R)		unopposed

PREVIOUS WINNING PERCENTAGES
2002 (68%); 2000 (60%); 1998 (55%); 1996 (51%); 1982 (99%); 1980 (51%); 1978 (51%); 1976 Special Runoff Election (56%)

Elected 1996; 9th full term

Also served 1976-77, 1979-85

Paul is willing to stand alone. Whenever there is a roll call vote in the House with one vote in the no column, it is usually Paul's. It is not that he dislikes the process of legislating, he just believes the government has no right to take any action not specifically authorized by the Constitution. But his absolutist view limits his effectiveness as a lawmaker.

Still, he makes his point and he has gathered a small but loyal national following. He is also running as a GOP candidate for the presidency in 2008. He last ran for the presidency in 1988, as a Libertarian, and received about 432,000 votes or 0.5 percent of the total. As the Libertarian candidate, he renounced the GOP, spoke out against "corporate welfare" — certain tax breaks and subsidies for big business — and advocated drug legalization.

Paul disagrees with his party on many things, but most visibly on the U.S. involvement in Iraq. He was among just six Republicans who voted in 2002 against giving President Bush authority to wage war there. He says the resolution was unconstitutional because it transferred the right to declare war from Congress to the executive branch. He also was one of 17 Republicans who supported a February 2007 Democratic resolution that disapproved of Bush's plan to send more troops to Iraq.

Paul says the United States should not fight wars that are undeclared. "We should mind our own business and take the advice of the Founders," he told MSNBC in March 2007. "And that is, stay out of entangling alliances; don't get involved in nation building; and don't get involved in the internal affairs of other nations." However, that same month he voted against a war funding bill that set a timeline for withdrawal of U.S. troops from Iraq.

In an April 30 column on his Web site, he criticized Democrats on war issues for "giving the president all the money he asked for and more to keep fighting it, while demanding that he fight it in the manner they see fit." Paul said it would make more sense to repeal the authority Congress gave the president and "disavow presidential discretion in starting wars. Then we should start bringing our troops home in the safest manner possible."

On other issues as well, Paul has long cultivated a reputation as a Republican contrarian. He voted against the 2003 Medicare prescription drug law, which most Republicans backed and Bush signed into law, on grounds that it was a vast expansion of the federal government. "I would introduce this novel idea, that we ought to follow the Constitution," he said in the MSNBC interview. "And that means the government should be very limited and the power of the presidency should be limited."

In the 109th Congress (2005-06), Paul had the lowest presidential support score among House Republicans, backing Bush only 37 percent of the time on votes on which the president took a public position. On votes pitting Republicans against Democrats, Paul backed his party just 70 percent of the time. Only two House Republicans had lower party unity scores.

Paul has voted repeatedly to cut taxes, a position shared by most libertarians. "I think our economic system is in a lot worse shape than most people believe," Paul said. "One of these days the country will wake up and realize how far in debt we are."

His Libertarian beliefs also make him an erratic ally of other GOP causes. He says he believes marriage is the union of one man and one woman, yet he voted in 2004 and 2006 against a proposed constitutional amendment to ban same-sex marriage, saying "everyone is an individual and ought to be treated equally." He also opposes a constitutional amendment to ban flag burning. But he parts company with many in the Libertarian Party, most of whom believe in maximizing individual freedoms, and opposes abortion. Before his congressional service, Paul worked as an obstetrician for 30 years, and he has said he delivered more than 4,000 babies during his medical career. Some on Capitol Hill call him Dr. No because of his medical degree and his penchant for voting no on routine, non-binding legislation.

A member of the Foreign Affairs panel, Paul has decried U.S. foreign policy as "worldwide imperialism" that spurred the Sept. 11 attacks. "A growing number of Americans are concluding that the threat we now face comes more as a consequence of our foreign policy than because the bad guys envy our freedoms and prosperity," he said nine months afterward.

He also was the lone Republican dissenter on a July 2006 resolution backing Israel and its bombardment of Lebanese targets in retaliation for attacks by the terrorist group Hezbollah. It slammed the Islamists for launching "unprovoked and reprehensible armed attacks" on "undisputed Israeli territory." During floor debate, Paul said foreign interventions do not work and the resolution would only help expand Middle East violence.

Paul also takes a dim view of U.S. aid to foreign countries, and he opposes U.S. support for the International Monetary Fund and the World Trade Organization. He has sponsored legislation requiring the United States to withdraw from the United Nations.

Although he has in the past voted for trade liberalization, Paul voted against the 2002 bill renewing presidential fast-track trade negotiating authority. Paul and independent Bernard Sanders of Vermont introduced a bill in 2004 to block federal assistance to companies that outsource U.S. jobs to foreign countries. He was one of only 27 Republicans to vote against the Central American Free Trade Agreement in 2005.

Paul's years in the House tally a little more than 17 years over three separate tenures. He first won a seat in an April 1976 special election to replace Democrat Bob Casey, defeating former Democratic state Rep. Bob Gammage. But in November's general election, Gammage felled Paul by 268 votes. In 1978, Paul won back the seat by 1,200 votes.

In 1984, Paul left his House seat for an unsuccessful Senate bid. He won election 12 years later in the 14th District, which included areas he had represented in his earlier House career. In the primary, he ousted Greg Laughlin, who had held the seat since 1989 but had switched from the Democratic Party in 1995. He won the general election by just 3 percentage points, despite criticism that he supported the legalization of drugs. He was unopposed in 2004 and won by 20 percentage points in 2006.

KEY VOTES

2006

- No Stop broadband companies from favoring select Internet traffic
- No Affirm U.S. commitment to war in Iraq and reject setting a withdrawal date for troops
- Yes Repeal requirement for bilingual ballots at the polls
- No Permit U.S. sale of civilian nuclear technology to India
- Yes Build a 700-mile fence on the U.S.-Mexico border to curb illegal crossings
- No Permit warrantless wiretaps of suspected terrorists

2005

- ? Intervene in the life-support case of Terri Schiavo
- No Lift President Bush's restrictions on stem cell research funding
- Yes Prohibit FBI access to library and bookstore records
- No Approve free-trade pact with five Central American countries
- No Pass energy policy overhaul favored by President Bush emphasizing domestic oil and gas production
- ? End mandatory preservation of habitat of endangered animal and plant species
- Yes Ban torture of prisoners in U.S. custody

CQ VOTE STUDIES

	PARTY UNITY		PRESIDENTIAL SUPPORT	
	Support	Oppose	Support	Oppose
2006	68%	32%	36%	64%
2005	72%	28%	38%	62%
2004	82%	18%	44%	56%
2003	74%	26%	43%	57%
2002	76%	24%	51%	49%

INTEREST GROUPS

	AFL-CIO	ADA	CCUS	ACU
2006	31%	45%	60%	76%
2005	50%	40%	33%	76%
2004	20%	50%	56%	78%
2003	47%	60%	46%	75%
2002	29%	30%	50%	76%

TEXAS 14

Northern Gulf Coast – Victoria, Galveston

Taking in a 200-mile stretch of the Gulf Coast, the 14th extends from north of Galveston to Rockport, which is just north of Corpus Christi. Dominated by farms and petrochemical plants, the district leans Republican and is overwhelmingly dependent on its coastal and agricultural industries.

The district's population center is located in its northeast. More than half of its residents live in Galveston and Brazoria counties (both shared with the 22nd). Chemical companies, such as Dow and Sterling, have facilities in Texas City, Freeport and North Seadrift. The city of Galveston continues to diversify economically, with a solid service sector and a growing tourism industry. The Port of Galveston is a high-volume Gulf Coast cruise-ship port, and the University of Texas Medical Branch at Galveston is the city's largest employer.

Victoria, the district's only city outside of Galveston County that has more than 30,000 residents, is a leading oil and chemical center. Farther south, the district also draws nature lovers to Goose Island State Park, the Aransas National Wildlife Refuge and several bird sanctuaries.

Economic mainstays such as commercial shrimping along the coast and inland farming provide secure employment for many district residents. Farmers here grow rice, sorghum and corn, and raise cattle. Hurricane Rita forced evacuations from Galveston and surrounding areas in 2005, but the storm did not cause lasting damage to local farms or homes.

Now mostly Republican, the 14th has Democratic roots and a sizable minority population (38 percent) that is mostly Hispanic (25 percent overall). The 14th elects Republicans, but generally not by the large margins the more solidly Republican suburban Houston districts rack up. Locally, Republicans tend to do very well in rural counties here, but the large number of factory jobs in the Galveston area allows unions to wield some political power. Residents also tend to be socially conservative.

MAJOR INDUSTRY

Petrochemicals, agriculture, shrimping

CITIES

Victoria, 60,603; Galveston, 57,247; League City (pt.), 45,279; Texas City (pt.), 31,979; Lake Jackson, 26,386

NOTABLE

Galveston claims to be the site of many Texas firsts, including the first telephone (1878), first medical college (1886) and first golf course (1898).

Rep. Rubén Hinojosa (D)

CAPITOL OFFICE
225-2531
rep.hinojosa@mail.house.gov
hinojosa.house.gov
2463 Rayburn 20515-4315; fax 225-5688

COMMITTEES
Education & Labor
(Higher Education, Lifelong Learning & Competitiveness - chairman)
Financial Services
Foreign Affairs

RESIDENCE
Mercedes

BORN
Aug. 20, 1940, Edcouch, Texas

RELIGION
Roman Catholic

FAMILY
Wife, Martha Hinojosa; five children

EDUCATION
U. of Texas, B.B.A. 1962; U. of Texas, Pan American, M.B.A. 1980

CAREER
Food processing executive

POLITICAL HIGHLIGHTS
Texas State Board of Education, 1974-84 (chairman of special populations)

ELECTION RESULTS

2006 GENERAL		
Rubén Hinojosa (D)	43,236	61.8%
Paul B. Haring (R)	16,601	23.7%
Eddie Zamora (R)	10,150	14.5%
2006 PRIMARY		
Rubén Hinojosa (D)		unopposed
2004 GENERAL		
Rubén Hinojosa (D)	96,089	57.8%
Michael D. Thamm (R)	67,917	40.8%
William R. Cady (LIBERT)	2,352	1.4%

PREVIOUS WINNING PERCENTAGES
2002 (100%); 2000 (88%); 1998 (58%); 1996 (62%)

Elected 1996; 6th term

At the South Texas elementary school Hinojosa attended as a child, Mexican-American children were segregated from white students and he spoke only Spanish, as he did at home. So it is hardly surprising that improving the lot of minority students always has been a major priority for the son of Mexican immigrants.

In 2007, Hinojosa (full name: ru-BEN ee-na-HO-suh) became chairman of the House Education and Labor Committee's panel on higher education. During 1997 debate on reauthorization of the Higher Education Act, he was the driving force behind an effort to redirect existing programs to target resources to the neediest students, including Hispanics and American Indians. Since then, he has helped win substantial increases in federal aid to colleges that serve large numbers of Hispanic students, with funding ballooning from $12 million in 1998 to $95 million in 2006. He also has worked to increase funding for bilingual and migrant education and for Head Start.

Hinojosa used education to better his own life — he entered Congress as a wealthy executive in a family-owned business that employed 400 people — and he intends to do all he can to help others have the same opportunity. He has served as chairman of the Congressional Hispanic Caucus education task force since his first term, and he plans to use his powerful new platform to craft policies that will strengthen education for minority students and English learners. "We need to increase the college know-how in the communities that have not had access to college opportunities," he said at a subcommittee hearing in 2007.

He is a staunch advocate of the Education Department's TRIO programs of outreach and support for disadvantaged students. And he introduced legislation in 2007 to authorize $300 million to improve classrooms, equipment and faculty development in universities that serve Hispanic students in post-graduate programs.

Hinojosa views education, trade and transportation as the most powerful ways to improve life in his Texas border district. Combating the tough economic situation has guided his agenda. When he took office in 1997, unemployment was 25 percent in some areas. Poverty is pervasive in much of his district. "According to the 2000 census, the median income for persons living in the 15th district was $26,840. There are more than 7,500 households that lack complete plumbing facilities," he told his colleagues during a 2007 debate on clean water programs.

Like many Democrats, he opposed legislation in 2006 that authorized the construction of 700 miles of fencing along the U.S.-Mexico border. "While a physical fence may work for certain parts of the border, at others it would choke off economic prosperity," Hinojosa said. He supports comprehensive immigration reform that not only secures U.S. borders but also addresses the plight of illegal immigrants already in the country and gives their children college access and financial aid eligibility. Education, he says, is the surest way to turn those young people into productive, tax-paying Americans.

Hinojosa was one of four Texas Democrats who broke ranks with their party in 2002 to authorize the Bush administration to negotiate trade agreements that Congress can approve or reject, but cannot amend. He also supported the Central American Free Trade Agreement in 2005, one of just 15 Democrats to do so. While that agreement and most other Bush-era trade pacts were anathema to labor unions, a bedrock Democratic constituency, Hinojosa sees increased trade as offering the hope of improved highways, commerce and jobs for his constituents.

He breaks with the liberal majority of his fellow Democrats fairly often. He backed a 2003 law banning a procedure that opponents call "partial birth" abortion, supported a 2005 GOP effort to limit the scope of the Endangered Species Act and voted for a 2006 bill to lift a moratorium on most offshore oil leasing nationwide. His background in the business world has made him more sympathetic than the average Democrat to the concerns of business owners; in 2006, he was one of just 10 House Democrats to be recognized with the U.S. Chamber of Commerce's "Spirit of Enterprise" award.

He also focuses on issues of specific interest to his district. He has been at odds with the administration over water conservation — an important matter in his district. Mexico owes Texas a considerable amount of water that is badly needed by South Texas irrigators, and Hinojosa says the administration "literally sold South Texas down the river" in a 2002 agreement. He has lobbied for new highway funding to help the 15th District serve as a trade route from Mexico. But Hinojosa was unsuccessful in his bid for a spot on the Appropriations panel in the 110th Congress (2007-08).

Hinojosa is the eighth of 11 children born to Mexican immigrant parents who put a high premium on education, even though they had little themselves. His parents even moved the family when they saw their children falling behind in inferior, segregated schools.

After completing his own education, Hinojosa joined the family food-processing business, H & H Foods, serving 20 years as its president and chief financial officer. He got his start in electoral politics in the early 1970s, when he was elected to his local school board. He went on to serve for a decade on the Texas State Board of Education. He was instrumental in creating the South Texas Community College system in the upper Rio Grande Valley. In recognition of his lifelong support of education, two Texas school districts in 2002 named schools after him.

The Hinojosa family's prominence and his own community involvement helped Hinojosa win his House seat in 1996. He succeeded Democrat E. "Kika" de la Garza, who retired after 32 years. Given the 15th's strong one-party voting tradition — it is a Democratic bulwark in the Lone Star State — Hinojosa's biggest challenge was winning his party's nomination. In a hotly contested five-way battle, he edged out lawyer Jim Selman.

Against Republican minister Tom Haughey, Hinojosa won by 26 percentage points in 1996 and by 17 points in a 1998 rematch. He has won comfortably ever since, unscathed by two redistrictings.

KEY VOTES

2006

- No Stop broadband companies from favoring select Internet traffic
- No Affirm U.S. commitment to war in Iraq and reject setting a withdrawal date for troops
- No Repeal requirement for bilingual ballots at the polls
- Yes Permit U.S. sale of civilian nuclear technology to India
- No Build a 700-mile fence on the U.S.-Mexico border to curb illegal crossings
- No Permit warrantless wiretaps of suspected terrorists

2005

- ? Intervene in the life-support case of Terri Schiavo
- Yes Lift President Bush's restrictions on stem cell research funding
- Yes Prohibit FBI access to library and bookstore records
- Yes Approve free-trade pact with five Central American countries
- Yes Pass energy policy overhaul favored by President Bush emphasizing domestic oil and gas production
- Yes End mandatory preservation of habitat of endangered animal and plant species
- Yes Ban torture of prisoners in U.S. custody

CQ VOTE STUDIES

	PARTY UNITY		PRESIDENTIAL SUPPORT	
	Support	Oppose	Support	Oppose
2006	78%	22%	49%	51%
2005	84%	16%	37%	63%
2004	90%	10%	36%	64%
2003	85%	15%	38%	62%
2002	89%	11%	41%	59%

INTEREST GROUPS

	AFL-CIO	ADA	CCUS	ACU
2006	93%	60%	87%	36%
2005	93%	80%	74%	44%
2004	93%	90%	63%	13%
2003	87%	80%	53%	36%
2002	71%	80%	61%	20%

TEXAS 15

South central – Harlingen, Edinburg, part of McAllen

Based in southern Texas, the 15th takes in agricultural and cattle areas southeast of San Antonio and then dips down to the state's border with Mexico. A federal court redrew the 15th's lines in August 2006 and somewhat truncated its convoluted boundaries, restoring its Hispanic population to 77.6 percent, the second-highest of any district. The large minority presence contributes to the district's overall Democratic lean.

While the district reaches more than 225 miles north to south, its population is skewed to the south. Nearly 60 percent of the 15th's residents live in Hidalgo County (shared with the 28th), and nearly nine in 10 of Hidalgo's residents are Hispanic. This is one of the nation's poorest areas, and community leaders struggle to establish jobs and provide job training. Hidalgo is by far the most populous and fastest-growing county in the district, but it continues to struggle with high unemployment and poverty. Along the Mexican border, *maquiladoras* — assembly or manufacturing plants that use low-cost labor and import many parts from the United States — are the mainstay. NAFTA has helped the economy, and trade with Mexican border cities adds jobs.

Burgeoning international trade has prompted local leaders to push for improvements in transportation infrastructure — the region claims to be the largest populated area without easy access to an interstate highway.

The 2006 remapping enhanced the 15th's Democratic lean, although Republicans run well in some sparsely populated northern counties like DeWitt and Refugio. Chris Bell, the 2006 Democratic nominee for governor, carried the 15th by 5 points. The 15th would have backed President George W. Bush's presidential re-election by 2 points had it existed in 2004, when its antecedent backed Bush by 10 points.

MAJOR INDUSTRY
Trade, manufacturing, agriculture, health care

CITIES
McAllen (pt.), 61,658; Harlingen, 57,564; Edinburg, 48,465; Weslaco, 26,935

NOTABLE
Caro Brown, the first woman to win a Pulitzer Prize for journalism, worked at the Alice Daily News during the 1940s and 1950s.

Rep. Silvestre Reyes (D)

CAPITOL OFFICE
225-4831
www.house.gov/reyes
2433 Rayburn 20515-4316; fax 225-2016

COMMITTEES
Appropriations Select Intelligence Oversight Panel
Armed Services
Select Intelligence - chairman

RESIDENCE
El Paso

BORN
Nov. 10, 1944, Canutillo, Texas

RELIGION
Roman Catholic

FAMILY
Wife, Carolina Reyes; three children

EDUCATION
U. of Texas, attended 1964-65; Texas Western College, attended 1965-66 (criminal justice); El Paso Community College, A.A. 1977 (criminal justice)

MILITARY SERVICE
Army, 1966-68

CAREER
U.S. Border Patrol assistant regional official and agent

POLITICAL HIGHLIGHTS
Canutillo School Board, 1968-70

ELECTION RESULTS

2006 GENERAL		
Silvestre Reyes (D)	61,116	78.7%
Gordon R. Strickland (LIBERT)	16,572	21.3%
2006 PRIMARY		
Silvestre Reyes (D)		unopposed
2004 GENERAL		
Silvestre Reyes (D)	108,577	67.5%
David Brigham (R)	49,972	31.1%
Brad Clardy (LIBERT)	2,224	1.4%

PREVIOUS WINNING PERCENTAGES
2002 (100%); 2000 (68%); 1998 (88%); 1996 (71%)

Elected 1996; 6th term

With Democrats poised to try to make a pivotal turn in the war in Iraq, Reyes emerged from a messy process in the House to become Speaker Nancy Pelosi's pick for chairman of the Intelligence Committee in the 110th Congress (2007-08).

Pelosi passed over Jane Harman of California, a political rival and the panel's senior Democrat, who had campaigned openly for the gavel. Also rejected was Florida's Alcee L. Hastings, whose federal judgeship in Florida had ended in scandal when Congress impeached and removed him in 1989.

Third in line was Reyes (full name: sil-VES-treh RAY-ess, with rolled R), a thoughtful, pragmatic legislator. Like Pelosi, Reyes had voted against the war in Iraq. Instead of publicly seeking the job, he emphasized the oversight responsibilities facing Democrats as voters demanded an exit from Iraq.

But controversy dogged his selection. He told Newsweek that "20,000 to 30,000" more troops were needed in Iraq to "dismantle the militias," a view opposite Pelosi's. Then, in an interview with Congressional Quarterly that received worldwide attention, Reyes failed a pop quiz. Asked whether al Qaeda was Sunni or Shiite, Reyes replied, "Al Qaeda, they have both." He added, "Predominately — probably Shiite." (In fact, the terrorist organization's Sunni roots are key to its founding.)

Reyes first said he was tired but later admitted he had stumbled. "When you screw up, you admit it, then you move on," he told the Washington Post.

He moved on. During the Democratic House's first floor debate on Iraq, Reyes said there was a time when more boots on the ground might have made a difference, but that time had passed. "Sending more troops to Iraq now just gives our enemies more targets and puts more soldiers at risk."

Reyes sees the 110th Congress as an opportunity for much needed "oversight, oversight, oversight." He bristled at Vice President Dick Cheney's threat to ignore congressional subpoenas. "I think the president and his administration have forgotten there are three branches of government with equal importance," he said.

Reyes helped lead an effort that forced Attorney General Alberto R. Gonzales to turn over documents detailing the National Security Agency's eavesdropping program. He also began reviewing the FBI's use of "national security letters" to secretly collect information from third parties, such as telephone companies and banks, without a warrant.

Reyes strongly opposed a 2006 GOP bill authorizing the NSA's warrantless surveillance program, arguing it would gut a 1978 law requiring a warrant to monitor communications between U.S. citizens and terrorist suspects abroad. "After the past few years, 'Just trust us,' just doesn't work for me anymore," Reyes said.

Reyes has advocated more diversity in the intelligence community and information-sharing among federal agencies. He has vowed to watch the administration's handling of Iran to avoid a repeat of the mistakes made before the war in Iraq.

Looking out for hometown interests, Reyes has protected funding for El Paso's regional military facilities at Fort Bliss, White Sands Missile Range and Holloman Air Force Base. As a result of the 2005 base realignment process and the military's overseas re-basing initiative, Fort Bliss could more than double, growing by as many as 20,000 soldiers in the next four years, to become a major testing and training facility for equipment and tactics.

A 26-year veteran of the U.S. Border Patrol, Reyes in 2005 and 2007 joined

California Republican David Dreier on a bill that would stiffen penalties for employers who hire illegal immigrants and would create new Social Security cards with digital pictures and encrypted identification codes that could be checked against an electronic database.

Though he previously backed a border fence near San Diego, he opposed a 2006 law authorizing a 700-mile fence along the Mexico border, calling it neither smart nor effective. He continues to press for comprehensive legislation to secure the border, legalize undocumented immigrants already in the country and offer a guest worker program for future immigrants.

Reyes' law enforcement background complicates his immigration stance. At one time, this former chairman of the Congressional Hispanic Caucus came under fire for appearing to adhere more to immigration laws than to his Hispanic roots.

On Capitol Hill, as in El Paso, Reyes is known as "Silver," a nickname first given to him by his high school football coach who called him the "silver lining," based on his first name, Silvestre, and his linebacker position.

He was born and raised on a farm in Canutillo, Texas, five miles outside El Paso. The oldest of 10 children, he and his two brothers next in line were delivered by a midwife. His father, grandfather and uncle grew cotton and alfalfa on two farms totaling 2,000 acres. "It was the only life I knew until I was drafted by the Army," he says.

He briefly attended the University of Texas at Austin on a small debate scholarship. Working while attending classes proved difficult, and after a year, he returned home and enrolled in what was then Texas Western College (now the University of Texas at El Paso). When he took a break from the spring semester in 1966, he was drafted.

Reyes spent two and a half years in the Army, 13 months of that in Vietnam as a helicopter crew chief and gunner. "I came out surviving," he said of his combat experience.

In 1969, he joined the Border Patrol. He rose through the ranks to become sector chief in McAllen and El Paso, and won national recognition for beginning "Operation Hold the Line" in El Paso, stationing more officers at the border to prevent unauthorized crossings of the Rio Grande. The program is still part of the government's strategy for the Southwest border.

El Paso community leaders persuaded Reyes to run for Congress when Democrat Ronald D. Coleman announced his retirement. Reyes became the district's first Hispanic representative after defeating a former Coleman aide in the party primary and runoff, and then winning the general election in 1996. Since then, Reyes has easily won re-election.

KEY VOTES

2006

- ? Stop broadband companies from favoring select Internet traffic
- No Affirm U.S. commitment to war in Iraq and reject setting a withdrawal date for troops
- No Repeal requirement for bilingual ballots at the polls
- Yes Permit U.S. sale of civilian nuclear technology to India
- No Build a 700-mile fence on the U.S.-Mexico border to curb illegal crossings
- No Permit warrantless wiretaps of suspected terrorists

2005

- ? Intervene in the life-support case of Terri Schiavo
- Yes Lift President Bush's restrictions on stem cell research funding
- Yes Prohibit FBI access to library and bookstore records
- No Approve free-trade pact with five Central American countries
- Yes Pass energy policy overhaul favored by President Bush emphasizing domestic oil and gas production
- No End mandatory preservation of habitat of endangered animal and plant species
- Yes Ban torture of prisoners in U.S. custody

CQ VOTE STUDIES

	PARTY UNITY		PRESIDENTIAL SUPPORT	
	Support	Oppose	Support	Oppose
2006	85%	15%	47%	53%
2005	81%	19%	39%	61%
2004	86%	14%	38%	62%
2003	82%	18%	38%	62%
2002	85%	15%	41%	59%

INTEREST GROUPS

	AFL-CIO	ADA	CCUS	ACU
2006	100%	80%	57%	36%
2005	100%	80%	60%	41%
2004	92%	70%	62%	26%
2003	87%	80%	50%	36%
2002	100%	75%	39%	19%

TEXAS 16

West – El Paso and suburbs

Situated along the Rio Grande in the desert landscape that characterizes the western reaches of Texas, the 16th takes in El Paso and some of its suburbs. The district, joined to Mexico and El Paso's sister city, Ciudad Juarez, by the Bridge of the Americas, has a 77.7 percent Hispanic population, more than any other district in the nation.

Mexico has had a deep effect on the area's economy and demographics, and growth in El Paso was fueled by trade with Mexico long before free-trade zones and global markets flourished. Companies on the U.S. side of the border provide supplies and services to plants in Mexico, and residents from Ciudad Juarez regularly cross the border to shop in El Paso. NAFTA contributed to an explosion of *maquiladoras,* twin plants in which Mexican workers do the bulk of the manufacturing labor and U.S. workers complete the products with final details, although local leaders now worry about increased competition from China.

While Fort Bliss already is important to the district's economy, the base is slated to grow dramatically as a result of the 2005 BRAC round. The area's growing population threatened to overwhelm its water supply, but conservation efforts largely have succeeded here, and a desalination plant is set to meet the needs of the larger Fort Bliss community.

Not only did the redistricting prior to the 2004 election and the 2006 court-ordered redrawing of the neighboring 23rd District not affect the 16th's borders, the 16th was the only Texas district that kept the same district lines in the wake of the 2004 remapping. Democrats held the 16th's U.S. House seat for all but two years in the 20th century, often unchallenged by Republicans since the 1960s. In 2004, John Kerry won 56 percent of the 16th's presidential vote, his fifth-highest showing in the state. Illegal immigration and associated drug smuggling, along with rising levels of gang violence, are major concerns in this border region.

MAJOR INDUSTRY

Trade, defense, manufacturing

MILITARY BASES

Fort Bliss (Army), 17,000 military, 7,500 civilian (2006)

CITIES

El Paso, 563,662; Socorro, 27,152

NOTABLE

The National Border Patrol Museum boasts aircraft, vehicles and boats.

Rep. Chet Edwards (D)

CAPITOL OFFICE
225-6105
edwards.house.gov
2369 Rayburn 20515-4317; fax 225-0350

COMMITTEES
Appropriations
(Military Construction-VA - chairman)
Budget

RESIDENCE
Waco

BORN
Nov. 24, 1951, Corpus Christi, Texas

RELIGION
Methodist

FAMILY
Wife, Lea Ann Edwards; two children

EDUCATION
Texas A&M U., B.A. 1974 (economics); Harvard U., M.B.A. 1981

CAREER
Radio station executive; congressional aide

POLITICAL HIGHLIGHTS
Sought Democratic nomination for U.S. House, 1978; Texas Senate, 1983-91

ELECTION RESULTS

2006 GENERAL		
Chet Edwards (D)	92,478	58.1%
Van Taylor (R)	64,142	40.3%
Guillermo Acosta (LIBERT)	2,504	1.6%
2006 PRIMARY		
Chet Edwards (D)		unopposed
2004 GENERAL		
Chet Edwards (D)	125,309	51.2%
Arlene Wohlgemuth (R)	116,049	47.4%
Clyde Garland (LIBERT)	3,390	1.4%

PREVIOUS WINNING PERCENTAGES
2002 (52%); 2000 (55%); 1998 (82%); 1996 (57%); 1994 (59%); 1992 (67%); 1990 (53%)

Elected 1990; 9th term

Democrat Edwards is President Bush's congressman, and he says he considers it "an honor to have the president as a constituent." In 2004, Bush swept Edwards' district with 69 percent of the vote, but Edwards happily notes that he carried Crawford, the town nearest Bush's Texas ranch, both that year and in 2006.

A moderate-to-conservative lawmaker with a knack for deal-making, Edwards in 2004 was the sole Lone Star state survivor among a group of Democrats targeted by a 2003 redistricting plan engineered by then House Majority Leader Tom DeLay and other Texas Republicans. Six others lost and one retired.

"He was very good one-on-one," David Kent, a Republican county chairman, told the Waco Tribune-Herald after the 2004 election. "His personality helped him win the race."

Edwards is a veteran member of the Appropriations Committee and chairman of its Military Construction-VA Subcommittee in the 110th Congress (2007-08). Having repeatedly accused Republicans of neglecting veterans' needs as thousands of troops return from Iraq, he moved swiftly to address the problem. In early 2007, when appropriators drafted a $124.2 billion war funding bill, they added billions more than Bush had sought for military construction, veterans' health programs and military health care.

Edwards is also a senior member of the Budget Committee, where he helped write a fiscal 2008 budget resolution that made room for $3.5 billion more in veterans' spending that Bush requested. "With this budget, we say that supporting our veterans is a real cost of war, just as real as the cost of guns, tanks and bullets," Edwards told the House.

He is proud of the role he played earlier in his career in helping to modernize military housing through a federal-private partnership that began in the mid-1990s; the government has put up $1.5 billion for the program and the private sector has contributed $20 billion. "Ninety percent of all new military housing is being built through this program. In the old way, we funded 100 percent through federal money and some colonel would design a box house for people to live in," Edwards told the House.

He also has been a leader in combating nuclear proliferation, using his seat on the Appropriations subcommittee with jurisdiction over nuclear weapons to protect programs designed to prevent nuclear materials from falling into the wrong hands.

Like other Democrats, Edwards has grown disillusioned with the Iraq War. He voted in 2002 to authorize Bush to use force against Saddam Hussein's regime, but by 2007 he had turned against the president's conduct of the war. He opposed Bush's deployment of thousands more troops to Iraq and supported a war funding bill that set a timetable for withdrawing U.S. combat forces. "I want U.S. forces fighting terrorists, not standing on street corners in Baghdad as target practice for Sunnis and Shiites locked in deep-rooted sectarian violence," he said in February 2007.

Energy is another issue important to Edwards, whose district includes part of the Barnett shale, the largest natural gas field in the United States. The House in 2007 passed a bill he cosponsored with Colorado Democrat Mark Udall to set up pilot plants to test ways to treat water extracted during energy production in order to make it usable for irrigation and other purposes. He also worked behind the scenes on the energy bill that Democrats passed as part of their top-priority agenda at the start of the 110th Congress in order to ensure that it did not harm independent gas and oil producers.

In 2003, Edwards gave up his post as chief deputy whip for House Democrats. But he remains an important link between conservative Democrats and the more liberal majority of his party.

In the 109th Congress (2005-06), Edwards backed Bush on 56 percent of the votes on which the president took a position, which was more often than all but nine other Democrats. He voted to authorize warrantless electronic surveillance of terrorism suspects, and he supported oil drilling in Alaska's Arctic National Wildlife Refuge. He also backed a proposed constitutional amendment to outlaw same-sex marriage.

However, Edwards has opposed Bush's "charitable choice" initiative because it would allow religious organizations to discriminate in hiring. Nor does he support government-funded vouchers for private-school education. Finessing the potential conflict between his views and those of the many religious conservatives in his district, Edwards argues that religion is too important to be entangled in the corporeal world of politics.

In 1994, Edwards voted for a ban on 19 types of assault-style weapons in the wake of two mass killings in his district. In 1991, a man with an automatic pistol killed 22 people and wounded 20 in a Killeen cafeteria. Two years later, guns were involved in some of the deaths in a violent confrontation between federal agents and members of the Branch Davidian religious sect in Waco. In 2004, however, Edwards reversed his position on the assault weapons ban, saying it had not reduced crime.

As a student at Texas A&M University, he was a leader in the Student Conference on National Affairs, where he got to know the local congressman, Democrat Olin E. "Tiger" Teague. As he was finishing college, Edwards accepted a job on Teague's congressional staff, intending to stay a year and then attend Harvard Business School. One year stretched into three. Teague told Edwards he planned to retire and that Edwards should run for his seat. The crowded Democratic primary in 1978 included a young Texas A&M economics professor, Phil Gramm, who edged past Edwards by fewer than 200 votes and went on to win election to the House and later the Senate.

Edwards earned a master's degree at Harvard, then returned to Texas, where he worked in real estate and owned a rural radio station. He was elected to the state Senate in 1982, and when Democratic Rep. Marvin Leath announced he would step down in 1990, Edwards moved to the 11th District to run for the House. He won with 53 percent of the vote. Having survived the 2004 remap, he had an easier time in 2006, winning with 58 percent. But given the GOP tilt of his district, he can't ever really relax.

KEY VOTES

2006

No Stop broadband companies from favoring select Internet traffic

Yes Affirm U.S. commitment to war in Iraq and reject setting a withdrawal date for troops

No Repeal requirement for bilingual ballots at the polls

Yes Permit U.S. sale of civilian nuclear technology to India

Yes Build a 700-mile fence on the U.S.-Mexico border to curb illegal crossings

Yes Permit warrantless wiretaps of suspected terrorists

2005

Yes Intervene in the life-support case of Terri Schiavo

Yes Lift President Bush's restrictions on stem cell research funding

Yes Prohibit FBI access to library and bookstore records

No Approve free-trade pact with five Central American countries

Yes Pass energy policy overhaul favored by President Bush emphasizing domestic oil and gas production

Yes End mandatory preservation of habitat of endangered animal and plant species

Yes Ban torture of prisoners in U.S. custody

CQ VOTE STUDIES

	PARTY UNITY		PRESIDENTIAL SUPPORT	
	Support	Oppose	Support	Oppose
2006	66%	34%	60%	40%
2005	75%	25%	52%	48%
2004	73%	27%	50%	50%
2003	76%	24%	46%	54%
2002	76%	24%	47%	53%

INTEREST GROUPS

	AFL-CIO	ADA	CCUS	ACU
2006	71%	55%	87%	68%
2005	80%	85%	74%	36%
2004	73%	65%	81%	48%
2003	80%	80%	64%	40%
2002	89%	75%	65%	36%

TEXAS 17

East central – Waco, College Station, Bryan

The 17th begins south of Fort Worth and moves southeast mainly through fertile farmland to reach Bryan and College Station in Brazos County. On the way, it picks up Waco and George W. Bush's "Western White House" in Crawford, both in centrally located McLennan County.

One-third of district residents live in Waco or surrounding McLennan County. Waco, which is the 17th's largest city and the largest population center between Austin and Dallas, hosts Baylor University and a strong education sector. Defense-related firm L-3 Communications provides additional jobs in Waco.

The district jogs east and then southeast from Waco, meandering through sparsely populated counties and into Brazos, where the district's southern portion is centered. College Station is home to Texas A&M University, which includes the George Bush Presidential Library and Museum and is a major employer here. Unlike the more-liberal University of Texas at Austin, Texas A&M has a conservative agricultural and military tradition that favors GOP candidates.

Rapidly growing Johnson County, in the 17th's northeastern corner, has become a bedroom community for Fort Worth and is home to some of the city's southern suburbs. The county's most populous city, Cleburne, and its neighboring communities rely on light manufacturing. Along the Squaw Creek Reservoir west of Johnson, a nuclear plant in Somervell County employs many district residents. Other energy concerns also are important to the district, especially in the northern counties that cover parts of the Barnett shale natural gas reservoir.

Bush's connection to the area as well as redistricting prior to 2004 has given the district a distinct GOP lean; Bush took 69 percent of the 17th's presidential vote in 2004. But Rep. Edwards' comfortable 2006 re-election shows that conservative "Yellow Dog" Democrats and ticket splitters can still provide a winning margin for Democrats.

MAJOR INDUSTRY

Agriculture, higher education, light manufacturing, defense

CITIES

Waco, 113,726; College Station, 67,890; Bryan, 65,660; Cleburne, 26,005

NOTABLE

A complex near Waco was the site of a deadly standoff in 1993 between federal agents and members of the Branch Davidian religious group.

Rep. Sheila Jackson-Lee (D)

CAPITOL OFFICE
225-3816
www.jacksonlee.house.gov
2435 Rayburn 20515-4318; fax 225-3317

COMMITTEES
Foreign Affairs
Homeland Security
(Transportation Security and Infrastructure Protection - chairwoman)
Judiciary

RESIDENCE
Houston

BORN
Jan. 12, 1950, Queens, N.Y.

RELIGION
Seventh-day Adventist

FAMILY
Husband, Elwyn Lee; two children

EDUCATION
Yale U., B.A. 1972 (political science);
U. of Virginia, J.D. 1975

CAREER
Lawyer; congressional aide

POLITICAL HIGHLIGHTS
Democratic nominee for Texas District Court judge, 1984; Democratic nominee for Harris County Probate Court judge, 1986; Houston municipal judge, 1987-89; Democratic nominee for Texas District Court judge, 1988; Houston City Council, 1990-95

ELECTION RESULTS

2006 GENERAL		
Sheila Jackson-Lee (D)	65,936	76.6%
Ahmad R. Hassan (R)	16,448	19.1%
Patrick Warren (LIBERT)	3,667	4.3%
2006 PRIMARY		
Sheila Jackson-Lee (D)		unopposed
2004 GENERAL		
Sheila Jackson-Lee (D)	136,018	88.9%
Thomas Andrew Bazan (I)	9,787	6.4%
Brent Sullivan (LIBERT)	7,183	4.7%

PREVIOUS WINNING PERCENTAGES
2002 (77%); 2000 (76%); 1998 (90%); 1996 (77%); 1994 (73%)

Elected 1994; 7th term

One of the House's most outspoken members, the loquacious Jackson-Lee is making a transition to a larger, national role on homeland security issues after several years of focusing on immigration, civil rights and other issues of interest to her majority black and Hispanic district in Houston.

She is the chairwoman of the House Homeland Security Subcommittee on Transportation Security and Infrastructure Protection. The panel is responsible for overseeing and bolstering the government's efforts to protect airports, seaports, railroads and highways, as well as hospitals and power plants. "As we all know, terrorists don't signal or call ahead before they attack. We saw this in Madrid and London, amongst other horrible incidents," she said in March 2007, referring to deadly train bombings in 2004 and 2005, respectively.

Elected in 1994, Jackson-Lee is getting her first taste in the House of life in the majority. Although she was the top-ranking Democrat on the Judiciary Committee's immigration panel in the 109th Congress (2005-06), a more senior Democrat, Zoe Lofgren of California, claimed the gavel of that panel in the 110th Congress (2007-08). Still, Jackson-Lee remains on the immigration panel and has ample opportunity to help shape policy there.

Jackson-Lee also serves on the Foreign Affairs Committee. She caused consternation at the White House in February 2007 by being the first member of Congress to visit leftist leader Hugo Chávez of Venezuela after Chávez won re-election. He had just announced that his government would seize majority control of oil operations in Venezuela from foreign companies, including Houston-based ConocoPhillips. Jackson-Lee defended her trip as an effort to protect Houston's oil industry jobs, telling The Houston Chronicle, "We've made a serious mistake in not engaging with President Chávez. I came to break the tension, to warm up a chilled relationship."

When Democrats were in the minority, Jackson-Lee was known mainly for her tendency to talk at length on a universe of topics. Her verbal marathons in front of the C-SPAN cameras prompted some to dismiss her as a publicity hound, but her outspokenness ensured her liberal views got an airing in the conservative-dominated House. She typically assessed the latest move by the Bush administration as "shameless" or "outrageous," and she was particularly critical of the war in Iraq, advocating an immediate troop withdrawal. Her constant presence on the House floor raised the bar on political long-windedness. Her colleagues defended their own talkativeness by declaring, ". . . but I'm no Sheila Jackson-Lee."

Like Democratic Rep. Barbara Jordan, the noted black liberal from Houston who served from 1973 to 1979 and was Jackson-Lee's role model, she has used her seat on the Judiciary Committee to focus on civil rights, abortion rights and other liberal causes. "I had the privilege of being part of the generation of people who were moved by movements and moved by the voices and messages of Medgar Evers, Martin Luther King and Fannie Lou Hamer," she says. "I always viewed my charge from their history and stories to be a change-maker."

She was highly critical of the administration's response to the minority victims of Hurricane Katrina. As soon as her party took control of the House in January 2007, Jackson-Lee introduced a bill creating a commission with subpoena power to chronicle the responses to the 2005 hurricane by the federal, state and local governments and to recommend corrective action.

She also has been active in the human rights campaign to call attention to genocide in Sudan. In April 2006, Jackson-Lee was among five members of Congress arrested for disorderly conduct at the Sudanese Embassy in Washington for protesting the killings in the Darfur region by government-backed militias. They were released after paying a $50 fine.

In early 2007, as the Bush administration issued regulations governing chemical plant security, Jackson-Lee introduced legislation barring the use of federal funds for chemical plant security unless a facility met or exceeded security standards imposed by the state or local government. She had a powerful ally in Sen. Joseph I. Lieberman, the Connecticut independent who chairs the Senate's Homeland Security Committee.

Two topics leave Jackson-Lee with little to say: the notoriously high turnover rate in her congressional office and her past political ties to the late Enron Corp. Chairman Kenneth L. Lay, who was convicted of securities fraud. Enron's financial collapse in 2001 had a major economic impact on Jackson-Lee's district, but she let other Democrats rail against alleged corporate abuses. Lay was one of her chief fundraisers and backers in 1994 when she won a hotly contested Democratic primary.

Several news organizations have reported that she abuses her aides by having them chauffeur her between her office and nearby apartment and by berating them for minor failures. The Texas Monthly magazine once dubbed her "a royal pain" for breaching protocol by arriving 50 minutes late and in business attire for a formal dinner for the queen of Thailand.

Born in Queens, New York, and educated at Yale and the University of Virginia law school, where she was one of three African-Americans in her class, Jackson-Lee moved to Texas when her husband took a job with the University of Houston. She made two unsuccessful bids for local judgeships before winning appointment as a municipal judge in 1987. After another failed election campaign for a judgeship, in 1990 she won an at-large seat on the city council, where her initiatives included a gun safety law imposing penalties on gun owners who fail to keep guns away from children. She also pushed for expanded summer hours at city parks and recreation centers as a way to reduce gang activity.

Jackson-Lee came to Congress after knocking off incumbent Democrat Craig Washington in the 1994 primary election. Washington had lost the support of the Houston business establishment and several other important constituencies, and Jackson-Lee garnered 63 percent of the vote in the primary. In the heavily Democratic district, that win was tantamount to election. She hasn't faced a primary challenger since 2002, and in her 2006 general election she outpaced her opponent by nearly 58 percentage points.

KEY VOTES

2006

- No Stop broadband companies from favoring select Internet traffic
- No Affirm U.S. commitment to war in Iraq and reject setting a withdrawal date for troops
- No Repeal requirement for bilingual ballots at the polls
- Yes Permit U.S. sale of civilian nuclear technology to India
- No Build a 700-mile fence on the U.S.-Mexico border to curb illegal crossings
- No Permit warrantless wiretaps of suspected terrorists

2005

- ? Intervene in the life-support case of Terri Schiavo
- Yes Lift President Bush's restrictions on stem cell research funding
- Yes Prohibit FBI access to library and bookstore records
- No Approve free-trade pact with five Central American countries
- Yes Pass energy policy overhaul favored by President Bush emphasizing domestic oil and gas production
- No End mandatory preservation of habitat of endangered animal and plant species
- Yes Ban torture of prisoners in U.S. custody

CQ VOTE STUDIES

	PARTY UNITY		PRESIDENTIAL SUPPORT	
	Support	Oppose	Support	Oppose
2006	93%	7%	34%	66%
2005	93%	7%	28%	72%
2004	96%	4%	21%	79%
2003	96%	4%	17%	83%
2002	97%	3%	21%	79%

INTEREST GROUPS

	AFL-CIO	ADA	CCUS	ACU
2006	100%	100%	53%	16%
2005	93%	100%	56%	14%
2004	93%	95%	53%	4%
2003	100%	95%	31%	12%
2002	100%	100%	26%	4%

TEXAS 18

Downtown Houston

The 18th takes in the central part of Houston, with appendages spreading to the south and northeast, as well as a C-shaped swath out to the northwest and north. Downtown's older black neighborhoods and more-progressive residents make up the 18th, which includes some of the city's poorest areas. Downtown Houston has seen revitalization, with an ongoing resurgence in residential, retail and corporate construction.

The district is diverse: 40 percent of residents are black and 36 percent are Hispanic, and a large portion of the city's gay and lesbian residents live in the 18th. Some of the district's most heavily black areas are just south of downtown, and heavily Hispanic neighborhoods can be found just north of downtown, between Interstate 45 and the Eastex Freeway. While the district is mainly inner-city urban, it does includes the Heights, a trendier neighborhood populated with some young professionals. The northern arm of the 18th picks up George Bush Intercontinental Airport.

Downtown office buildings are filled with oil and gas employees and other white-collar businesses and service workers, but most commute here from outside the district. Downtown also hosts some corporate giants, such as Halliburton and CenterPoint Energy, whose headquarters are housed in its iconic — and well-lit — skyscraper. Downtown workers can avoid high daytime temperatures by using the miles of underground tunnels that connect many of Houston's buildings. The 18th also takes in the Theater District, with the Hobby Center for the Performing Arts, and the district is home to baseball's Astros, basketball's Rockets and Comets and soccer's Dynamo.

The large black and Hispanic populations make the 18th one of the most strongly Democratic districts in Texas, and Texas Southern University and the University of Houston add to the area's liberal bent. Democrat John Kerry won 72 percent of the district's 2004 presidential vote, his second-best showing in the state, and Gov. Rick Perry took his second-lowest percentage here in the 2006 gubernatorial race.

MAJOR INDUSTRY

Energy, government, business services, entertainment

CITIES

Houston (pt.), 507,631

NOTABLE

Houston's KUHT became the nation's first public TV station in May 1953.

Rep. Randy Neugebauer (R)

CAPITOL OFFICE
225-4005
www.randy.house.gov
429 Cannon 20515-4319; fax 225-9615

COMMITTEES
Agriculture
Financial Services
Science & Technology

RESIDENCE
Lubbock

BORN
Dec. 24, 1949, St. Louis, Mo.

RELIGION
Baptist

FAMILY
Wife, Dana Neugebauer; two children

EDUCATION
Texas Tech U., B.B.A. 1972 (accounting)

CAREER
Land developer; homebuilding company executive; bank executive

POLITICAL HIGHLIGHTS
Lubbock City Council, 1992-98

ELECTION RESULTS

2006 GENERAL		
Randy Neugebauer (R)	94,785	67.7%
Robert Ricketts (D)	41,676	29.8%
Fred Jones (LIBERT)	3,349	2.4%
2006 PRIMARY		
Randy Neugebauer (R)		unopposed
2004 GENERAL		
Randy Neugebauer (R)	136,459	58.4%
Charles W. Stenholm (D)	93,531	40.1%
Richard Peterson (LIBERT)	3,524	1.5%

PREVIOUS WINNING PERCENTAGES
2003 Special Runoff Election (51%)

Elected June 2003; 2nd full term

Neugebauer is a conservative Republican stalwart, an unwavering advocate of lower taxes, less federal spending and smaller government. He won his House seat in a 2003 special election through equal measures of luck and labor, and he has kept it because his record and his affable personality have proved a good match for his district.

Neugebauer (NAW-geh-bow-er) was one of 10 House Republicans singled out in March 2007 for recognition as a "defender of economic freedom" by the Club for Growth, a conservative political action organization, and he is a member of the Republican Study Committee, a group of about 100 of the most conservative House members.

Neugebauer has supported all of the tax cuts advanced since he arrived in Congress and he is an avid advocate of repealing the federal estate tax. "It's one of the most egregious taxes we have on the books today," he says. He opposes abortion and same-sex marriage, voting in both 2004 and 2006 in favor of a constitutional amendment to outlaw such unions. He supports opening the Arctic National Wildlife Refuge to oil drilling, and in 2006 voted to lift a moratorium on most offshore oil and gas drilling.

"He's a very conservative Republican who is very much in the mold of Larry Combest and other Texas Republicans," said Dan Isett, former chairman of the Lubbock County GOP, referring to the retired congressman from West Texas whom Neugebauer succeeded.

With a seat on the Agriculture Committee, once chaired by Combest, Neugebauer will work in the 110th Congress (2007-08) to protect his district's many cotton, wheat, and peanut producers, along with its cattle ranchers. He is the top-ranking Republican on the new Horticulture and Organic Agriculture Subcommittee, which has jurisdiction over fruits and vegetables, honey, marketing and promotion orders, pesticides, and organic agriculture. He also serves on the commodities subcommittee, which is especially important to his district's growers.

Although farm policy disputes often break along crop lines, not party divides, Neugebauer's conservatism is evident on the Financial Services Committee. In 2007, he opposed legislation requiring mortgage finance giants Fannie Mae and Freddie Mac to set aside money to create an affordable housing fund, decrying what he called a "Robin Hood" approach. In 2006, when the House passed an Iraq War supplemental spending bill that also provided $19.2 billion in hurricane relief, on top of the $51.8 billion appropriated soon after Hurricane Katrina in 2005, Neugebauer tried but failed to split off the hurricane money and require that it be offset. In 2007, he objected to legislation the committee steered through the House that called for rebuilding public housing destroyed by Katrina. That, he said, would create "the second-worst disaster in the history of New Orleans."

He has backed President Bush on the war in Iraq, which he sees as inextricably linked to the fight against terrorism. "My family was in New York on 9/11," he told the House in March 2007. "My daughter-in-law and her mother were supposed to be at the World Trade Center. . . . America was attacked. We have been attacked before. We know this enemy is going to come back and attack us again."

Neugebauer was born in St. Louis, Mo., where his parents had met in college, but was raised in Lubbock, Texas, his mother's hometown. His father sold insurance, and his mother worked as a real estate agent and interior designer. They divorced when Neugebauer was 9, and his father died soon thereafter.

A family down the street owned a trampoline, and Neugebauer often bounced away his afternoons instead of doing his homework. He became so skilled at back flips, twists and other moves that when he was in college, he joined The Flying Matadors, a trampoline group that toured the state doing demonstrations. He suffered his share of injuries, but says they taught him a good life lesson: "If you fly off, you have to get right back up there. Otherwise, you'll never bounce again."

He graduated from Texas Tech University with a degree in accounting, and became a commercial real estate developer and homebuilder. His business experiences left him wary of government. "I've lived under the consequences of government policy," he says. "The government should empower people, not take their money."

He was elected to the Lubbock City Council in 1992 and served until 1998. A deacon in his Baptist church, he is married to his high school sweetheart. Though no longer the lithe trampoline artist of yesteryear, he still enjoys skiing trips with his grandsons and is an avid fly fisherman.

Neugebauer arrived in the House in June 2003 after winning a special election to replace Combest, who resigned that year for personal reasons. He faced 13 Republicans and two Democrats in the 2003 special election. In an initial round of balloting, he and accountant K. Michael Conaway finished first and second, respectively. Conaway had close ties to the president. He was a partner in the oil business with Bush in the 1980s and hailed from Midland, the district's second-largest city and Bush's former home.

Neugebauer's home and political base was in Lubbock, the district's largest city, which helped him considerably in the runoff. He won in June 2003 by just 587 votes. (Conaway got a second chance after a Texas remap engineered by former House Majority Leader Tom DeLay and other state Republicans took effect, and won a seat of his own in 2004.)

By the time Neugebauer ran for re-election in 2004, the remap had matched him against 26-year Democratic Rep. Charles W. Stenholm, who found himself running in places where people didn't know him well, and where his party label was a liability, even though he was among the most conservative of congressional Democrats.

Neugebauer campaigned vigorously, greeting voters anywhere he could find them and pumping hands at Friday night high school football games. He defeated Stenholm by 18 percentage points in one of the most expensive races of the year, with Neugebauer alone spending $3 million. In 2006, he romped to re-election with more than two-thirds of the vote.

KEY VOTES

2006

No Stop broadband companies from favoring select Internet traffic
Yes Affirm U.S. commitment to war in Iraq and reject setting a withdrawal date for troops
Yes Repeal requirement for bilingual ballots at the polls
Yes Permit U.S. sale of civilian nuclear technology to India
Yes Build a 700-mile fence on the U.S.-Mexico border to curb illegal crossings
Yes Permit warrantless wiretaps of suspected terrorists

2005

Yes Intervene in the life-support case of Terri Schiavo
No Lift President Bush's restrictions on stem cell research funding
No Prohibit FBI access to library and bookstore records
Yes Approve free-trade pact with five Central American countries
Yes Pass energy policy overhaul favored by President Bush emphasizing domestic oil and gas production
Yes End mandatory preservation of habitat of endangered animal and plant species
No Ban torture of prisoners in U.S. custody

CQ VOTE STUDIES

	PARTY UNITY		PRESIDENTIAL SUPPORT	
	Support	Oppose	Support	Oppose
2006	97%	3%	87%	13%
2005	99%	1%	87%	13%
2004	98%	2%	85%	15%
2003	98%	2%	97%	3%

INTEREST GROUPS

	AFL-CIO	ADA	CCUS	ACU
2006	7%	5%	100%	100%
2005	13%	0%	93%	100%
2004	20%	5%	100%	96%
2003	0%	10%	95%	83%

TEXAS 19
West central – Lubbock, Abilene, Big Spring

The conservative 19th begins in the Panhandle, then extends south and east through cattle and cotton country around Lubbock to Abilene. It then turns north, almost reaching Wichita Falls. With ranches, cattle and remnants of the cowboy lifestyle, the 19th offers a taste of the Wild West.

The western part of the district, which includes Lubbock, is heavily agricultural, although that industry extends east through most of the district. Lubbock, the district's largest city, thrives on the surrounding acres of cotton and calls itself the world's largest cottonseed-processing center. Home to Texas Tech University, the city has become an educational and medical hub for the southwest Panhandle. Lubbock's Depot District has brought development and revenue to its downtown, and a growing wine industry outside the city provides a little boost to an already steady economy. Lubbock County accounts for more than one-third of the district's population.

Abilene also has made an effort to revitalize its downtown. Local officials are seeing results as a burgeoning telecommunications sector develops there. A nearby Air Force base is a stable part of the economy, and the prison industry has done well, with several state and contract facilities around the district. Peanut farms are found throughout the 19th, and Gaines County is one of the largest industry producers in the state. Famine and drought have hurt cattle and cotton over the past decade.

As in much of the South, conservative Democrats used to dominate the area: As recently as 1978, George W. Bush lost a race for the Lubbock-area House seat to a Democrat. But the 19th has become a Republican stronghold in all races. George W. Bush received more than 70 percent of the 2004 presidential vote in 24 of the 25 counties wholly included in the 19th. Overall, he took 77 percent of the district's vote.

MAJOR INDUSTRY
Cattle, agriculture, oil and gas, defense

MILITARY BASES
Dyess Air Force Base, 5,009 military, 407 civilian (2006)

CITIES
Lubbock, 199,564; Abilene (pt.), 110,442; Big Spring, 25,233

NOTABLE
Lubbock's Buddy Holly Center honors the native musician, who died in a February 1959 plane crash in Iowa.

Rep. Charlie Gonzalez (D)

CAPITOL OFFICE
225-3236
www.house.gov/gonzalez
303 Cannon 20515-4320; fax 225-1915

COMMITTEES
Energy & Commerce
House Administration
(Contested Election (Fla. 13th) - chairman)
Small Business
(Regulations, Healthcare & Trade - chairman)

RESIDENCE
San Antonio

BORN
May 5, 1945, San Antonio, Texas

RELIGION
Roman Catholic

FAMILY
Wife, Belinda Trevino; one child

EDUCATION
U. of Texas, B.A. 1969 (government);
St. Mary's U. (Texas), J.D. 1972

MILITARY SERVICE
Texas Air National Guard, 1969-75

CAREER
Lawyer; teacher

POLITICAL HIGHLIGHTS
Bexar County judge, 1982-87; Texas District Court judge, 1988-97

ELECTION RESULTS

2006 GENERAL		
Charlie Gonzalez (D)	68,348	87.4%
Michael Idrogo (LIBERT)	9,897	12.6%
2006 PRIMARY		
Charlie Gonzalez (D)		unopposed
2004 GENERAL		
Charlie Gonzalez (D)	112,480	65.5%
Roger Scott (R)	54,976	32.0%
Jessie Bouley (LIBERT)	2,377	1.4%
Michael Idrogo (I)	1,971	1.2%

PREVIOUS WINNING PERCENTAGES
2002 (100%); 2000 (88%); 1998 (63%)

Elected 1998; 5th term

The deep affection in the 20th District for the Gonzalez name, coupled with its two-thirds Hispanic population, make this one of the country's safest Democratic seats. Gonzalez is the son of the famously independent Henry B. Gonzalez, who served in the House for 37 years and was known in the region simply as "Henry B."

The son's pragmatic, New Democrat brand of politics contrasts with his father's passionate and stubborn populism. A self-described moderate, Gonzalez voted with his party 88 percent of the time on votes pitting most Democrats against most Republicans in the 109th Congress (2005-06). But he shares his father's zeal for ensuring civil rights.

Gonzalez in 2006 supported President Bush's plan calling for stiffer penalties for employers who hire illegal immigrants coupled with establishment of a legal path to citizenship for those currently in the United States. Yet as the chairman of the civil rights task force for the Congressional Hispanic Caucus, Gonzalez has been outspoken on Bush's controversial nominees for Cabinet posts and judgeships. He voiced strong opposition in 2005 to the appointment of Alberto R. Gonzales as attorney general after the nominee declined to seek the caucus' endorsement.

Gonzalez led the Hispanic Caucus' successful campaign in 2002 and 2003 against the confirmation of Miguel A. Estrada as the first Latino on the Court of Appeals for the District of Columbia Circuit, the most influential federal bench after the Supreme Court. Gonzalez said Estrada failed the caucus' minimum standards for protecting the legal rights of minorities and victims of discrimination. Estrada met fierce opposition from other Democrats as well and withdrew from consideration.

Gonzalez was a member of the election task force that Democrats formed in the aftermath of Florida's contested ballot recounts after the 2000 presidential election. As a member of the House Administration Committee, he chairs the task force established to investigate allegations that voting machine errors contributed to the razor-thin 2006 victory by Republican Vern Buchanan in Florida's 13th District. Democrat Christine Jennings, who was declared the loser to Buchanan by 369 votes, has contested the results. The task force is to examine what Jennings contends is a glitch in touchscreen voting machines that resulted in the disappearance of 18,000 votes in the congressional race.

In 2004, Gonzalez received a plum seat on the Energy and Commerce Committee after being passed over once before. The Hispanic Caucus had backed him for a seat that instead went to California Democrat Hilda L. Solis, who was closer to Democratic Leader Nancy Pelosi of California. Gonzalez was given one of the next seats to come open, when Texas Rep. Ralph M. Hall defected to the GOP.

On Energy and Commerce, he watches over the interests of AT&T, the San Antonio-based telecommunications giant and a major political campaign donor. He opposed a change in telecommunications law pushed in 2006 by other committee Democrats that would have established so-called network neutrality by requiring major operators such as SBC to provide equal access over their broadband networks to rivals and small, independent Web site operators.

As the newly installed chairman of the Small Business Committee's Regulation, Healthcare and Trade Subcommittee in the Democratically controlled 110th Congress (2007-08), Gonzalez reintroduced legislation he sponsored in the previous Congress that provides tax incentives, grants and subsidized loans to help small health care providers install and maintain health information technology. Gonzalez says health care IT could improve the quality of medical care delivered and save the health care system billions of dollars. Without these incentives, he said, "small physician practices will be left behind the technological curve and as a result, patients will fail to benefit from the quality of care electronic health records provide."

A supporter of trade liberalization, Gonzalez enthusiastically touted the benefits of the 1993 North American Free Trade Agreement, which his father had virulently opposed. But, siding with labor unions, which had promoted his first congressional bid, he reversed course to vote against the 2002 law giving the president authority to negotiate trade deals that cannot be amended by Congress. And in 2005, when it came to implementing a free-trade agreement with most Central American countries, Gonzalez joined the majority of his party in voting no.

Gonzalez is the third of eight children and the only one who followed his father into public life. He was a teenager when his father was first elected to Congress. After graduating from a public high school, Gonzalez earned a bachelor's degree in government from the University of Texas at Austin and a law degree from St. Mary's School of Law in San Antonio. He taught fifth grade for a year and then went into private law practice. In 1982, he was elected to the county bench and spent the next 15 years as a local and state trial judge. In that time, he helped speed the resolution of domestic violence cases and promoted mediation as an alternative to litigation.

When his father announced his retirement, Gonzalez jumped into a seven-way Democratic primary to succeed him in 1998. To let his son stand on his own, the elder Gonzalez declined to endorse him until just before the primary. "He raised us all to be independent," Gonzalez says. "He would say, 'Look at the arguments, look at the issue from all sides, then weigh it carefully. Make your arguments, and if you have to, acknowledge your mistakes.' "

Gonzalez won the nomination with 62 percent of the vote in a runoff against former San Antonio council member Maria A. Berriozabal. In the general election, he won with 63 percent. In both 2000 and 2002, Gonzalez faced no major-party opposition.

He escaped the fate of six other Texas Democratic incumbents who lost seats after the 2003 remap of the state's congressional districts. Gonzalez's GOP opponent in 2004 was a political novice and he won with a little more than 65 percent. In 2006, the Republicans chose not to field a candidate.

KEY VOTES

2006

- No — Stop broadband companies from favoring select Internet traffic
- No — Affirm U.S. commitment to war in Iraq and reject setting a withdrawal date for troops
- No — Repeal requirement for bilingual ballots at the polls
- Yes — Permit U.S. sale of civilian nuclear technology to India
- No — Build a 700-mile fence on the U.S.-Mexico border to curb illegal crossings
- No — Permit warrantless wiretaps of suspected terrorists

2005

- ? — Intervene in the life-support case of Terri Schiavo
- Yes — Lift President Bush's restrictions on stem cell research funding
- Yes — Prohibit FBI access to library and bookstore records
- No — Approve free-trade pact with five Central American countries
- Yes — Pass energy policy overhaul favored by President Bush emphasizing domestic oil and gas production
- No — End mandatory preservation of habitat of endangered animal and plant species
- Yes — Ban torture of prisoners in U.S. custody

CQ VOTE STUDIES

	PARTY UNITY		PRESIDENTIAL SUPPORT	
	Support	Oppose	Support	Oppose
2006	89%	11%	33%	67%
2005	86%	14%	26%	74%
2004	88%	12%	35%	65%
2003	90%	10%	27%	73%
2002	94%	6%	28%	72%

INTEREST GROUPS

	AFL-CIO	ADA	CCUS	ACU
2006	100%	95%	57%	16%
2005	80%	90%	63%	16%
2004	87%	95%	62%	20%
2003	80%	95%	50%	20%
2002	100%	100%	45%	0%

TEXAS 20

Downtown San Antonio

A city rich in history, San Antonio witnessed the death of Davy Crockett and the fall of the Alamo. Since those rugged days in the early 1800s, San Antonio has grown into one of the nation's largest cities. The strongly Democratic 20th takes in much of the city, including the heavily Hispanic West Side, downtown San Antonio and some close-in communities.

A huge military presence in San Antonio once fueled the economy here, but mid-1990s downsizing diminished its importance. Local leaders redeveloped the former Kelly Air Force Base, and the KellyUSA business park on the site is currently supervised by Port San Antonio. The park's tenants include technology, aeronautics and manufacturing firms. Hospitals such as the Baptist Medical Center and several Christus Santa Rosa facilities help make the district a regional health care hub. AT&T and Clear Channel (located in the neighboring 21st) play major roles in the area's thriving telecommunications sector.

Tourism and convention business have boosted the city's economy and contributed to a revitalization of the urban center. The Alamo, site of the 1836 battle with Mexico, is in the heart of downtown. The city's scenic Paseo del Rio, or Riverwalk, also draws visitors with its shops, hotels and restaurants that wind along the San Antonio River. Events at the Alamodome — less than one mile from the river — also draw crowds.

Mid-decade redistricting added several predominately black neighborhoods to the 20th along its southeastern edge near downtown, increasing Democratic strength in this Hispanic-majority district that Democrats have long dominated. The only significant Republican presence in the district is in the largely white, higher-income areas northwest and northeast of downtown San Antonio.

MAJOR INDUSTRY
Health care, tourism, military, telecommunications, trade

MILITARY BASES
Lackland Air Force Base, 27,123 military, 6,726 civilian (2005)

CITIES
San Antonio (pt.), 590,575

NOTABLE
Future President Theodore Roosevelt recruited for the "Rough Riders," the first volunteer cavalry in the Spanish-American War, at the bar in the Menger Hotel (built 1859), which is adjacent to the Alamo and still open.

Rep. Lamar Smith (R)

CAPITOL OFFICE
225-4236
lamarsmith.house.gov
2409 Rayburn 20515-4321; fax 225-8628

COMMITTEES
Homeland Security
Judiciary - ranking member
Science & Technology

RESIDENCE
San Antonio

BORN
Nov. 19, 1947, San Antonio, Texas

RELIGION
Christian Scientist

FAMILY
Wife, Beth Smith; two children

EDUCATION
Yale U., B.A. 1969 (American studies); Southern Methodist U., J.D. 1975

CAREER
Lawyer; rancher; reporter

POLITICAL HIGHLIGHTS
Texas House, 1981-82; Bexar County Commissioners Court, 1983-85

ELECTION RESULTS

2006 GENERAL		
Lamar Smith (R)	122,486	60.1%
John Courage (D)	49,957	24.5%
Gene Kelly (D)	18,355	9.0%
Tommy Calvert (I)	5,280	2.6%
James Arthur Strohm (LIBERT)	4,076	2.0%
James Lyle Peterson (I)	2,189	1.1%
2006 PRIMARY		
Lamar Smith (R)		unopposed
2004 GENERAL		
Lamar Smith (R)	209,774	61.5%
Rhett R. Smith (D)	121,129	35.5%
Jason Pratt (LIBERT)	10,216	3.0%

PREVIOUS WINNING PERCENTAGES
2002 (73%); 2000 (76%); 1998 (91%); 1996 (76%); 1994 (90%); 1992 (72%); 1990 (75%); 1988 (93%); 1986 (61%)

Elected 1986; 11th term

Smith is a faithful conservative and party loyalist, who is the top Republican on the Judiciary Committee in the 110th Congress (2007-08). He cherishes his seat on Judiciary, where his genial personality softens his hard-line conservative politics.

His style is quite different from the Republican who chaired the committee in the 109th Congress (2005-06), F. James Sensenbrenner Jr. of Wisconsin, who could be prickly and blunt. But the two are on the same page legislatively as Smith is an equally solid social conservative who has pushed for get-tough approaches to illegal immigration and to "frivolous" lawsuits against businesses. His bill imposing mandatory sanctions on attorneys who file such lawsuits passed the House in the 108th Congress (2003-04) but the Senate ignored it.

Smith and Sensenbrenner differed on civil rights, however. When the House agreed in 2006 to renew for 25 years expiring provisions of the 1965 Voting Rights Act, Smith toed the party line, supporting four Republican amendments aimed at scaling back parts of the landmark law. All four were opposed by Sensenbrenner, who usually sides with Democrats on civil rights issues.

On immigration policy, Smith says that lax enforcement of immigration laws contributed to the 2001 terrorist attacks, and he wants beefed up border security. The bill he helped write in 2005 took a much different approach than the one preferred by President Bush and the Senate, which called for a legalization plan for most of the country's illegal immigrants and a new guest worker program. The gap proved impossible to bridge that year, and Republicans failed to get a compromise bill to conference. Smith said, "It's hard to justify legislation that would reward millions of lawbreakers, attract more illegal immigrants and depress American workers' wages."

Smith's hard line on immigration is not new. The signature legislation of his House career is the 1996 law that cracked down on illegal immigration by increasing penalties for document fraud and the smuggling of aliens. It also made it easier for illegal immigrants to be detained at the border or deported. In 2004, he butted heads with GOP leaders and the technology industry by refusing to move a bill making more visas available to foreign technology industry workers. Smith said businesses should first have to demonstrate they had tried without success to hire U.S. workers, but the leaders overruled him and the visa expansion passed.

Smith pursued an ambitious agenda as chairman of Judiciary's Subcommittee on Courts, the Internet and Intellectual Property. His attempt to overhaul patent law faltered, however, because of disagreements among the technology, pharmaceutical and biotechnology industries. He reintroduced a patent law overhaul bill in early 2007 that had bipartisan support.

His panel did produce a bill, which passed in the House, to establish criminal penalties for the fraudulent acquisition or unauthorized disclosure of confidential phone records. The panel also attempted to solve the problem of "orphan works," copyrighted material that is so old or that has changed ownership so frequently, users can't locate owners to get permission.

He surprised the Democrats early in 2007 when he managed to delay passage of a measure to give the delegate for the District of Columbia full voting rights on the House floor. Near the end of the debate, Smith offered a motion that called for adding language to repeal the District's ban on handguns and other local gun control laws. His motion caused the sponsors to pull the bill from the floor, but it later passed the House, without the gun control language, in April 2007.

On the Science and Technology Committee, Smith, an occasional stargazer, joined with Democrat Nick Lampson of Texas in 2002 to press legislation to lay out clear goals for NASA's human space flight program after completion of the International Space Station. Among the goals is developing a reusable vehicle by 2022 that can travel to Mars and back.

Smith served on the House ethics committee in the 109th Congress at the request of then House Speaker J. Dennis Hastert. Hastert asked him to return to the panel, although Smith already had done a stint, even chairing the committee in 1999 and 2000. The Speaker and his powerful sidekick, Majority Leader Tom DeLay, wanted to send a message to the GOP committee members who voted in the previous Congress to admonish DeLay for ethical lapses. Hastert replaced them with Smith and other loyalists. Smith also had close ties to DeLay and had given to his legal defense fund.

But Smith is not unwilling to render a harsh judgment against a fellow Republican: During his earlier tenure as chairman, the ethics panel issued a formal Letter of Reproval against Transportation Committee Chairman Bud Shuster of Pennsylvania, saying Shuster had "engaged in serious official misconduct" and "committed substantial violations of House rules."

Smith is a fifth- or sixth-generation Texan, depending on whom you ask in his family. The family arrived in Texas around 1850, just five years after statehood, and its political involvement stretches back almost that long. His grandfather was district attorney in San Antonio and an unsuccessful House candidate. His great-grandfather was a San Antonio judge, and his great-great-grandfather was mayor of Galveston.

After graduating from Yale, Smith worked as a business reporter for the Christian Science Monitor in Boston. He then went back to school, got a law degree, and returned home to San Antonio. He was first elected to a seat in the state legislature in Austin and then served on the Bexar County Commission. He won election to Congress in 1986 when Republican Tom Loeffler left to run, unsuccessfully, for governor. After George W. Bush — then a Midland oilman with one losing congressional race under his belt — decided not to seek the seat, Smith won a six-way contest for the GOP nod.

Smith won the general election over former Democratic state Sen. Pete Snelson, with the help of Texas political consultant Karl Rove, later a top Bush aide. Smith garnered at least 70 percent of the vote in subsequent elections until 2004 and 2006, when he won with just more than 60 percent.

KEY VOTES

2006

No Stop broadband companies from favoring select Internet traffic
Yes Affirm U.S. commitment to war in Iraq and reject setting a withdrawal date for troops
Yes Repeal requirement for bilingual ballots at the polls
Yes Permit U.S. sale of civilian nuclear technology to India
Yes Build a 700-mile fence on the U.S.-Mexico border to curb illegal crossings
Yes Permit warrantless wiretaps of suspected terrorists

2005

Yes Intervene in the life-support case of Terri Schiavo
No Lift President Bush's restrictions on stem cell research funding
No Prohibit FBI access to library and bookstore records
Yes Approve free-trade pact with five Central American countries
Yes Pass energy policy overhaul favored by President Bush emphasizing domestic oil and gas production
Yes End mandatory preservation of habitat of endangered animal and plant species
No Ban torture of prisoners in U.S. custody

CQ VOTE STUDIES

	PARTY UNITY		PRESIDENTIAL SUPPORT	
	Support	Oppose	Support	Oppose
2006	97%	3%	97%	3%
2005	98%	2%	89%	11%
2004	97%	3%	88%	12%
2003	99%	1%	100%	0%
2002	97%	3%	89%	11%

INTEREST GROUPS

	AFL-CIO	ADA	CCUS	ACU
2006	7%	0%	100%	84%
2005	13%	0%	93%	96%
2004	7%	0%	100%	92%
2003	0%	5%	100%	88%
2002	13%	0%	100%	96%

TEXAS 21

Central – northeast San Antonio and suburbs, part of Austin and suburbs

The 21st is a heavily Republican, mostly urban and suburban district that takes in most of San Antonio and part of Austin and also extends westward to scoop up some of Texas' rugged Hill Country.

As it existed during the 2004 election, the 21st was nearly equally divided between Bexar County (San Antonio) and Travis County (Austin). But a court-ordered 2006 remap skewed the district's population toward Bexar, where a slight majority of district residents now live. The 21st's share of Bexar (pronounced BEAR) takes in the mostly comfortable north and northeastern parts of San Antonio and its suburbs, which have a strong Republican lean. The district also includes employment anchors San Antonio International Airport and Fort Sam Houston.

Roughly one-in-five district residents live in Austin's Travis County. The 21st's share of the county encompasses the main University of Texas campus and parts of downtown Austin, including the Capitol and governor's mansion. The 21st also takes in some wealthy suburbs and rural areas in the western part of Travis County.

Comal County, located northeast of San Antonio, makes up only one-eighth of the district's population, but it adds to the district's strong Republican tilt. The 21st's share of the Texas Hill County includes the Bandera County home of musician Richard S. "Kinky" Friedman, who took 28 percent of the county vote (a statewide high) in his independent campaign for governor in 2006. Overall, however, the district's GOP lean was on display in Republican Gov. Rick Perry's defeat of Democratic former Rep. Chris Bell by 16 percentage points here.

MAJOR INDUSTRY
Technology, government, higher education, defense

MILITARY BASES
Fort Sam Houston (Army), 13,935 military, 8,594 civilian (2007)

CITIES
San Antonio (pt.), 259,488; Austin (pt.), 77,118; New Braunfels (pt.), 35,328

NOTABLE
Lyndon B. Johnson was born in Blanco County; Bandera bills itself as the cowboy capital of the world; Austin is home to North America's largest urban colony of Mexican free-tailed bats.

Rep. Nick Lampson (D)

CAPITOL OFFICE
225-5951
lampson.house.gov
436 Cannon 20515-4322; fax 225-5241

COMMITTEES
Agriculture
Science & Technology
(Energy & Environment - chairman)
Transportation & Infrastructure

RESIDENCE
Stafford

BORN
Feb. 14, 1945, Beaumont, Texas

RELIGION
Roman Catholic

FAMILY
Wife, Susan Lampson; two children

EDUCATION
Lamar U., B.S. 1968 (biology), M.Ed. 1971 (school administration)

CAREER
Home health care business owner; teacher; college instructor

POLITICAL HIGHLIGHTS
Sought Democratic nomination for Texas House, 1970; Jefferson County Democratic Party chairman, 1972-74; Jefferson County tax assessor-collector, 1977-95; Texas Board of Tax Professional Examiners, 1977-83 (chairman, 1981-83); U.S. House, 1997-2005; defeated for re-election to U.S. House, 2004

ELECTION RESULTS

2006 GENERAL		
Nick Lampson (D)	76,775	51.8%
Shelley Sekula-Gibbs (R) - write-in	61,938	41.8%
M. Bob Smither (LIBERT)	9,009	6.1%
2006 PRIMARY		
Nick Lampson (D)		unopposed

PREVIOUS WINNING PERCENTAGES
2002 (59%); 2000 (59%); 1998 (64%); 1996 General Runoff Election (53%)

Elected December 1996; 5th term

Did not serve 2005-07

Lampson is not your typical freshman lawmaker. He had served four terms in the House before losing in 2004 when his district was redrawn. The irony is that he now represents the district once held by the man who orchestrated his loss — former GOP Majority Leader Tom DeLay.

Plagued by ethics controversies in the 109th Congress (2005-06), DeLay still won his March 2006 primary. A few weeks later, he announced his resignation — and his intention to declare legal residency in Virginia, which he hoped would disqualify him from running in Texas and allow GOP officials to substitute a different candidate on the ballot. But Democrats contested the maneuver in court and won.

Faced with the choice of running for re-election or leaving the Republican ballot slot vacant, DeLay chose the latter option. That forced the GOP's substitute candidate, Houston City Councilwoman Shelley Sekula-Gibbs, to wage a write-in campaign that failed Nov. 7. She lost to Lampson by 10 percentage points. Adding to the oddity of the race was the unusual consolation prize obtained by Sekula-Gibbs. She won a special election, also held Nov. 7, to fill the few remaining weeks of DeLay's unexpired term — Lampson opted not to compete in that contest.

Lampson now finds himself representing a district that typically votes Republican. In 2004, district voters backed President Bush with 64 percent of the vote. Republicans immediately began lining up potential candidates to take on Lampson in 2008. The Houston Chronicle reported in April 2007 that Lampson was weighing the idea of challenging Republican Sen. John Cornyn in 2008 instead of battling for re-election in the 22nd District.

But he brushes aside suggestions that he is too liberal for his new district, pointing to endorsements from the National Rifle Association, and he plays down the idea that his new district is significantly different from his old one. "The people are very much alike," Lampson says.

He was placed on two committees that should help him help his district — Transportation and Infrastructure, and Science and Technology. The Johnson Space Center is located in his new district, and he will use his Science seat to help keep NASA and the space center viable. He was also made chairman of the Energy and Environment Subcommittee. "Science is a really big deal for me," Lampson said. He also gained a seat on the Agriculture Committee, which might help him protect sugar cane growers in his district as the committee begins a renewal of the huge farm bill in 2007.

Lampson campaigned on issues of fiscal responsibility. But when it comes to earmarks in appropriations bills — funding for special projects in members' districts — Lampson says earmarks can be vital to a region's progress. He also says, though, that they should be vetted by the committee before being added to the spending bills.

In his first speech on the House floor in the 110th Congress (2007-08), Lampson urged the House to tighten rules on lobbying and lawmakers' receipt of travel and gifts — issues that generated ethics questions for Republicans during the 109th Congress. Of the six items leading off the Democratic agenda in the 110th Congress, he supported five. He voted against a measure ending tax breaks for oil companies.

After his return to Congress, Lampson stepped into an old role, becoming co-chairman of the Missing and Exploited Children's Caucus, which he helped found after a girl from his district was abducted and murdered in 1997. The caucus received unwanted attention in the 2006 scandal involving former GOP Rep. Mark Foley of Florida, who resigned after disclosures that he had sent sexually explicit e-mails to young male House pages. Foley was serving as caucus co-chairman when he left Congress.

Lampson is keenly aware of his new district's Muslim residents, who viewed DeLay as hostile to their interests. He has made sure to court their votes, and he has spoken to the Muslim American Society and Islamic Circle of North America's annual conference in Houston. He has also visited local mosques and spoken with local Muslim religious leaders.

On the Iraq War, Lampson in the 110th Congress expressed concern about Bush's decision to send more than 21,000 additional combat troops to the battlefield, but said he would not support cutting off funding for the troops. He voted in favor of a $124 billion supplemental spending bill in 2007 that included a timetable for the withdrawal of U.S. troops.

Lampson's grandparents came to Texas from Sicily. He has five brothers and sisters, and says his childhood was filled with hand-me-down clothes. His mother taught him the value of community. "Even as little as we had, my mother always had something for a family that lived not too far from us that had less than we did," Lampson says.

His father died when Lampson was 12, and his mother worked hard to care for the children, including a sister stricken with polio. "We were a struggling family, to put it nicely," Lampson says. They got by with help from Social Security and the March of Dimes, which donated a wheelchair for his sister. He says he is continually inspired by his older sister, who has served as his campaign manager in several of his election outings.

He worked sweeping floors at a local school and delivering groceries to help with the family's expenses. He also earned some money playing the saxophone professionally for six years, gigs that included stints with a number of local bands.

But Lampson says his mother, who had only a fifth-grade education, emphasized schooling above all else, and eventually he and all of his siblings earned college degrees. His mother earned her high school equivalency degree at the age of 80.

A conversation with John Connally, a former governor of Texas, inspired him to seek political office, Lampson says. While in college at Lamar University, Lampson met Connally and asked him how he knew that he wanted to be a politician. "He told me that for him, public service could be best accomplished through elected office," Lampson recalls.

Like other male family members, Lampson has a history of heart disease. He underwent quadruple bypass surgery in March 2007.

CQ VOTE STUDIES>

	PARTY UNITY		PRESIDENTIAL SUPPORT	
	Support	Oppose	Support	Oppose
2004	85%	15%	41%	59%
2003	88%	12%	33%	67%
2002	87%	13%	36%	64%
2001	83%	17%	34%	66%
2000	82%	18%	69%	31%

INTEREST GROUPS

	AFL-CIO	ADA	CCUS	ACU
2004	87%	80%	62%	21%
2003	100%	85%	37%	28%
2002	89%	75%	55%	21%
2001	100%	85%	48%	21%
2000	90%	75%	57%	24%

TEXAS 22

Southeast Houston and southern suburbs — Sugar Land, Pearland, part of Pasadena

Generally wealthy, white-collar and Republican, the 22nd includes a majority of Fort Bend County and a chunk of northern Brazoria County, as well as a piece of Galveston County south of Houston and a slice of the city itself. Although George W. Bush took 64 percent of the district's 2004 presidential vote and Gov. Rick Perry won a plurality here in the 2006 gubernatorial race, Democrats captured the 22nd's House seat in 2006.

The 22nd takes in the booming communities of Sugar Land and Pearland, as well as affluent areas surrounding the Lyndon B. Johnson Space Center. Wealthy NASA scientists and astronauts who live nearby in Clear Lake help give the 22nd the state's second-highest median income.

Slightly less than two-fifths of the population resides in Fort Bend County, which includes Sugar Land. Since the 1960s, the area has changed from a sugar-growing center into suburbia. Imperial Sugar, which maintains its headquarters in the city, closed its local sugar refinery in 2003. The closure did not stall economic growth, and local officials plan to redevelop the industrial site. The city has welcomed other new development, such as a town square retail center, and in 2006, Money Magazine ranked Sugar Land as one of the nation's best places to live.

On its northeastern edge, the 22nd takes in part of southeastern Harris County, where 45 percent of district residents live. This area trends toward the upscale: Some of the wealthiest areas in the county are in southeastern Houston, near Ellington Field, a former Air Force base that now houses the space center's aircraft operations and hopes to attract commercial operations. The district also sneaks north to grab Houston Hobby Airport, making transportation a key issue.

MAJOR INDUSTRY

Aerospace, transportation, retail, agriculture

CITIES

Houston (pt.), 109,880; Sugar Land, 63,328; Pasadena (pt.), 57,020; Pearland (pt.), 37,628; Missouri City (pt.), 32,855; Deer Park (pt.), 28,493

NOTABLE

The annual "Texian Market Days" in Fort Bend County include re-enactments of 1830s pioneer life, when the area was settled by some of the "Old 300" families led by Stephen F. Austin.

Rep. Ciro D. Rodriguez (D)

CAPITOL OFFICE
225-4511
rodriguez.house.gov
2458 Rayburn 20515-4323; fax 225-2237

COMMITTEES
Appropriations
Veterans' Affairs

RESIDENCE
San Antonio

BORN
Dec. 9, 1946, Piedras Negras, Mexico

RELIGION
Roman Catholic

FAMILY
Wife, Carolina Pena Rodriguez; one child

EDUCATION
St. Mary's U. (Texas), B.A. 1973 (political science); Our Lady of the Lake U., M.S.W. 1978

CAREER
Lobbyist; social worker; college instructor

POLITICAL HIGHLIGHTS
Harlandale Independent School District Board of Trustees, 1975-87; Texas House, 1987-97; U.S. House, 1997-2005; defeated in primary for re-election to U.S. House, 2004; sought Democratic nomination for U.S. House, 2006

ELECTION RESULTS

2006 GENERAL RUNOFF		
Ciro D. Rodriguez (D)	38,256	54.3%
Henry Bonilla (R)	32,217	45.7%
2006 GENERAL		
Henry Bonilla (R)	60,175	48.6%
Ciro D. Rodriguez (D)	24,594	19.9%
Albert Uresti (D)	14,552	11.8%
Lukin Gilliland (D)	13,728	11.1%
Craig T. Stephens (I)	3,341	2.7%
August G. "Augie" Beltran (D)	2,647	2.1%
Rick Bolanos (D)	2,564	2.1%
Adrian DeLeon (D)	2,198	1.8%

PREVIOUS WINNING PERCENTAGES
2002 (71%); 2000 (89%); 1998 (91%); 1997 Special Runoff Election (67%)

Elected April 1997; 4th full term
Did not serve 2005-07

One of a handful of members serving in Congress for the second time around, Rodriguez clings to the liberal views that characterized his initial tenure in the House from 1997 to 2005. But this time, he has a better chance of translating those views into legislative action.

Rodriguez is now in the majority for the first time, and that helped him win a seat on the Appropriations Committee. He had sought the assignment without success twice before; Democratic seats were difficult to come by during the dozen years of GOP control. He is eager to direct federal dollars to his struggling district to improve infrastructure and alleviate chronic unemployment along the Mexico border. "We need to help small communities with roads, bridges and sewage plants," he said in 2006. "Throughout this country, our local communities are having a rough time with our infrastructure."

Rodriguez also serves on the Veterans' Affairs Committee, as he did during his earlier service in the House. He has long been a voluble advocate of improving veterans' health care. Early in the 110th Congress (2007-08), he backed bills to increase compensation for disabled veterans.

During his earlier tenure in the House, Rodriguez served on the Armed Services Committee. He worked to preserve jobs at defense installations and for contractors in the San Antonio area. But he is no hawk on military matters. He voted against authorizing the war in Iraq in 2002, and he supported both a February 2007 resolution opposing President Bush's decision to deploy more than 21,000 additional combat troops to Iraq and a March 2007 war funding bill that set a timeline for troop withdrawals from Iraq.

Rodriguez almost always sides with the positions advocated by labor unions — in five of his seven full years in the House, Rodriguez received a perfect 100 score from the AFL-CIO. He is among the most enthusiastic backers of a higher federal minimum wage.

Rodriguez voted against the 2003 Medicare prescription drug law — supported by most Republicans and opposed by most Democrats — on the grounds that it "begins to dismantle Medicare as we know it." He opposes creating private investment accounts within the Social Security system, financed by a diversion of payroll taxes. Rodriguez sees the guaranteed benefits of the current system as a lifeline for many poor Americans who have no pensions or other secure source of retirement income.

Rodriguez's stunning victory over Republican Rep. Henry Bonilla in 2006 proved that there can be second acts in American politics — even in the same election year. Rodriguez seemed doomed to defeat after he lost a March 2006 primary in the adjacent 28th District to Democratic Rep. Henry Cuellar, who had narrowly unseated him in a 2004 primary.

But in August 2006, a federal court redrew Bonilla's 23rd District to include more Hispanics, as the Supreme Court had mandated in a June decision that otherwise upheld most of a 2003 redistricting map enacted by Texas Republicans. With his political base in southern San Antonio appended to the redrawn 23rd District, Rodriguez pivoted to take on Bonilla, who was the only Mexican-American Republican in Congress.

Rodriguez's campaign did not start well. He struggled to raise money and there were indications he might even drop out of the race. But the first indicator that Rodriguez might pull off the upset came in the Nov. 7 "blanket" primary, in which Bonilla wound up with 49 percent of the vote, just short of the majority needed for an outright victory. That forced him into a

December runoff with Rodriguez, whose 20 percent vote share was good enough to best the other five Democrats in the race.

In the runoff campaign, the cash-rich Democratic Congressional Campaign Committee spent heavily on a television advertising campaign to attack Bonilla and promote Rodriguez, who took a surprisingly large 54 percent of the vote in the low-turnout December contest. Rodriguez said after his victory that he has come to appreciate the "window of opportunity" that serving in Congress provides — but also to understand that it opens for just two years at a time. "I don't take it for granted anymore," he said.

Rodriguez was born on the Mexican side of the Rio Grande. His family often moved back and forth across the border as his father took a series of jobs working on large industrial refrigeration units. They settled in the San Antonio area when Rodriguez was 3 years old. He became a U.S. citizen when he was 18. Of the six children in the family, he is the only one who attended college. He began his college studies intending to be a pharmacist but soon turned to social work. He has held jobs helping heroin addicts and patients in mental health clinics.

"My experience as a social worker had a profound influence on my decision to enter public life," Rodriguez said in March 2007. "I could see that many of the challenges facing my clients and those that I worked with had stemmed from the decisions being made at the public policy level. Serving in Congress allows me to be able to continue to help my clients in a broader capacity."

Rodriguez served for a dozen years on a local school board and for 10 years in the Texas House; in both capacities, he endeavored to boost funding for schools in poor areas.

In 1997, when Democratic Rep. Frank Tejeda died after a battle with brain cancer, Rodriguez decided to run for the seat. Out of a field of 15 candidates, Rodriguez finished first in the March special election, but his 46 percent share of the vote fell short of the majority required to win the seat outright. In the April runoff, he easily defeated another Democrat, former San Antonio City Councilman Juan Solis.

Rodriguez easily won his primary and general elections until 2004, when Cuellar surprised him in the Democratic primary, which was certified after a series of recounts, lawsuits and accusations of voting fraud lodged by Rodriguez and his supporters.

He lost his 2006 primary rematch with Cuellar by almost 13 percentage points, but the court-ordered redistricting gave him a second chance — and a new lease on a House seat.

CQ VOTE STUDIES

	PARTY UNITY		PRESIDENTIAL SUPPORT	
	Support	Oppose	Support	Oppose
2004	92%	8%	35%	65%
2003	92%	8%	20%	80%
2002	96%	4%	25%	75%
2001	88%	12%	31%	69%
2000	94%	6%	84%	16%

INTEREST GROUPS

	AFL-CIO	ADA	CCUS	ACU
2004	93%	90%	53%	13%
2003	100%	85%	40%	21%
2002	100%	95%	40%	0%
2001	100%	85%	39%	12%
2000	100%	85%	50%	12%

TEXAS 23

Southwest – south and northwest San Antonio and suburbs, Del Rio

Larger than most states east of the Mississippi River, the 23rd takes in more than 700 miles of border with Mexico along the Rio Grande River, skimming El Paso in the west and reaching as far east as San Antonio, the district's population center. Nearly 60 percent of residents live in San Antonio or in surrounding Bexar County.

The 23rd was the focal point of a legal challenge to a 2004 Republican-drawn congressional map. The Supreme Court in June 2006 upheld nearly all of the 2004 map, but invalidated the 23rd on the grounds that its 55 percent Hispanic population was insufficient to meet federal Voting Rights Act protections for racial and ethnic minorities.

A federal court in August 2006 restored the 23rd's Hispanic population to 65 percent by moving the heavily Hispanic south side of San Antonio into the 23rd from the adjacent 28th. These alterations lessened the 23rd's GOP tilt: where Republican Gov. Rick Perry in 2006 would have won by 15 points under the 23rd's 2004 configuration, he carried the redrawn 23rd by just 3.5 points. South San Antonio's Democratic lean contrasts with the Republican, mostly white areas in the city's north and in its suburbs.

Maverick and Val Verde counties are overwhelmingly Hispanic areas on the 23rd's southern border, which includes some of the nation's poorest areas. Seasonal employment, an influx of immigrants and an abundance of cheaper Mexican labor contribute to high unemployment, although an increase in trade and manufacturing has benefited the area. In San Antonio, a $1.2 billion Toyota Tundra plant that opened in 2006 employs nearly 2,000 people, but the area economy took a hit from the 2005 BRAC round, which ordered the Air Force's Brooks City-Base closed by 2011.

MAJOR INDUSTRY

Agriculture, trade, tourism, defense

MILITARY BASES

Laughlin Air Force Base, 1,420 military, 1,800 civilian (2007); Brooks City-Base (Air Force), 1,297 military, 1,268 civilian (2005)

CITIES

San Antonio (pt.), 294,335; Del Rio, 33,867; Eagle Pass, 22,413

NOTABLE

Texas' largest county, Brewster, is roughly 6,200 square miles.

Rep. Kenny Marchant (R)

CAPITOL OFFICE
225-6605
www.marchant.house.gov
1037 Longworth 20515-4324; fax 225-0074

COMMITTEES
Education & Labor
Financial Services
Oversight & Government Reform

RESIDENCE
Coppell

BORN
Feb. 23, 1951, Bonham, Texas

RELIGION
Nazarene

FAMILY
Wife, Donna Marchant; four children

EDUCATION
Southern Nazarene U., B.A. 1974 (religion); Nazarene Theological Seminary, attended 1975-76

CAREER
Real estate developer; homebuilding company owner

POLITICAL HIGHLIGHTS
Carrollton City Council, 1980-84 (mayor pro tempore, 1983-84); mayor of Carrollton, 1984-86; Texas House, 1987-2005

ELECTION RESULTS

2006 GENERAL		
Kenny Marchant (R)	83,835	59.8%
Gary R. Page (D)	52,075	37.2%
Mark Frohman (LIBERT)	4,228	3.0%
2006 PRIMARY		
Kenny Marchant (R)	unopposed	
2004 GENERAL		
Kenny Marchant (R)	154,435	64.0%
Gary R. Page (D)	82,599	34.2%
James H. Lawrence (LIBERT)	4,340	1.8%

Elected 2004; 2nd term

Marchant isn't likely to turn up much on C-SPAN. He prefers to work quietly in the background and leave the speechmaking to others. And he has had his fill of being a legislative leader.

During his time in the Texas House, Marchant (MARCH-unt) chaired major committees, including Financial Institutions, and he was the state House Republican Chairman in 2002 when his party won control of the House, for the first time since Reconstruction. He effectively was the caucus chairman, the whip and policy chairman all in one, preferring to work behind the scenes and in committees. "I've never been much of an orator. Probably, in 18 years in the Texas House, I gave eight speeches," Marchant said.

So when Congress debated a 2007 resolution in opposition to President Bush's plan to send thousands more U.S. troops to Iraq, Marchant went to the House floor a couple of times, with speech in hand, but arrived too late and missed his chance. No big deal; he had his remarks in support of Bush's strategy entered into the Congressional Record. "Here, it's a little more wordy," he said with a laugh, also noting that freshmen do not call themselves "freshmen," but "new members."

Once in Washington, Marchant became a reliable Republican vote, siding with his party 98 percent of the time on votes that divided the two parties in the 109th Congress (2005-06).

He'd like to move up the ladder in the House, but not necessarily run for a leadership position. "I've had a lot of that. It's a lot of fun, but you make a lot of enemies," Marchant said.

Now in his second term, Marchant strives to be productive without being showy. He will have his chance, taking a seat in the 110th Congress (2007-08) on the prominent Financial Services Committee, which will match an interest he had in Austin. Such assignments are often doled out to party loyalists, and Marchant arrived with a party-building record. He helped draw the redistricting map that was planned by former House Majority Leader Tom DeLay of Texas to create more GOP seats, including the one Marchant now represents.

A longstanding dispute involving the cities of Fort Worth and Dallas, Dallas-Fort Worth Airport, American Airlines and Southwest Airlines over the use of Dallas Love Field quieted down in 2006 when Congress passed legislation to phase out flight restrictions at Love Field. Texas Republican Sen. Kay Bailey Hutchison led the settlement talks, but Marchant was a critical player since much of the Dallas-Fort Worth Airport is in the 24th District and American Airlines makes its headquarters there.

In early 2007, as momentum built for a "Passenger Bill of Rights," after weather delays caused passengers to be stranded for hours on airplanes, Marchant opposed the idea. "I think it's fair to give industry a chance to self-regulate. If we come back a year from now and that same thing is beginning to happen again, I'll be the first one to get on."

Such is the thinking of a homebuilder-turned-politician who wants less government intrusion, lower government spending, lower taxes, and protection of property rights. In 2007, he voted for the Democrats' bill to raise the minimum wage, but expressed concern that it did not have measures to mollify small businesses.

He is a familiar face to Bush, who was governor of Texas for six of the years that Marchant was in the state House. He supports the president's strategy in Iraq but opposes his call for comprehensive immigration reform. In the

109th Congress, he offered a bill to prevent children born in the United States to illegal alien parents from automatically obtaining U.S. citizenship.

As a member of the Education and Labor Committee, Marchant backs extension of Bush's No Child Left Behind education plan. But he arranged a meeting in his district between Education Secretary Margaret Spellings and local business and school leaders so that she could hear firsthand their demands for local flexibility on matters that cannot be managed from Washington, such as the hiring of tutors for students.

He also sits on the Oversight and Government Reform Committee, where he serves as the ranking Republican on the Federal Workforce, Post Office and District of Columbia Subcommittee.

Marchant is one of the wealthiest lawmakers from Texas, with $14 million in three cattle ranches and investments. He assists area churches through the Marchant Family Foundation.

He grew up in Farmers Branch, where his father and two uncles owned a four-chair barbershop. "We went to church three or four times a week and I went to church camps," Marchant remembers. "All of my activities basically revolved around the church." He received a degree in religion from Southern Nazarene University in Bethany, Okla., and attended the Nazarene Theological Seminary in Kansas City, Mo.

But after a year of study, as he and his wife, Donna, were expecting their first child, Marchant says he found that, "I was not very happy, and began to doubt that was really, really what I should plan to do." The couple returned to Texas.

Marchant became a roofing contractor, work he had done to pay his way through college. From there, he began importing and installing wooden shingles, then building new homes and developing lots to sell to builders. By 1989, his business was developing 400 houses a year, he says.

He chaired the local homebuilders association, which suspected city inspectors of soliciting bribes. That spurred him to run for and win a seat on the Carrollton City Council in 1980.

Four years later, he became mayor. In 1987, he moved to the state House, and won his first congressional race in 2004 with 64 percent of the vote. He won re-election comfortably with 60 percent of the vote against Democrat Gary R. Page, who received 37 percent.

During his time in the state legislature, Marchant had to deal with hardship. In 1998, his wife and two youngest children were in a car accident while on a church trip to Mexico. Though his wife and daughter have recovered, Marchant's son remains paralyzed from the waist down.

KEY VOTES

2006

No Stop broadband companies from favoring select Internet traffic
Yes Affirm U.S. commitment to war in Iraq and reject setting a withdrawal date for troops
Yes Repeal requirement for bilingual ballots at the polls
Yes Permit U.S. sale of civilian nuclear technology to India
Yes Build a 700-mile fence on the U.S.-Mexico border to curb illegal crossings
Yes Permit warrantless wiretaps of suspected terrorists

2005

Yes Intervene in the life-support case of Terri Schiavo
No Lift President Bush's restrictions on stem cell research funding
No Prohibit FBI access to library and bookstore records
Yes Approve free-trade pact with five Central American countries
Yes Pass energy policy overhaul favored by President Bush emphasizing domestic oil and gas production
Yes End mandatory preservation of habitat of endangered animal and plant species
No Ban torture of prisoners in U.S. custody

CQ VOTE STUDIES

	PARTY UNITY		PRESIDENTIAL SUPPORT	
	Support	Oppose	Support	Oppose
2006	98%	2%	97%	3%
2005	98%	2%	89%	11%

INTEREST GROUPS

	AFL-CIO	ADA	CCUS	ACU
2006	7%	0%	100%	92%
2005	13%	0%	93%	92%

TEXAS 24

Part of Dallas and western suburbs — Grand Prairie, Carrollton, part of Irving

Taking in most of the more affluent suburbs sandwiched between Dallas and Fort Worth, the 24th was designed in redistricting prior to 2004 to be a Republican stronghold. The district is heavily white (64 percent), gave George W. Bush 65 percent of its 2004 presidential vote, and was among Gov. Rick Perry's top seven districts during his 2006 re-election.

The district's economy revolves around Dallas-Fort Worth International Airport and the businesses the airport has attracted to the area. The airport, a small part of which is in the neighboring 26th, is the largest employer in the district. American Airlines makes its headquarters in the district and uses the airport as its primary hub.

East of the airport, a corporate hub in Irving's Las Colinas financial district, which is shared with the 32nd, also fuels the district's economy. The area combines financial stability with low tax rates, high quality of life and good transportation — all of which contribute to its reputation as a prime destination for domestic and international corporate relocation. The 12,000-acre planned business and residential community at the doorstep of the high-traffic airport boasts thousands of companies, including global headquarters for Kimberly-Clark and Celanese. Other large businesses, such as Citigroup, provide the district with additional revenue and jobs.

Although most of the region's attractions and entertainment venues are in neighboring districts, the 24th hosts the Lone Star Park and the Nokia Theatre, both of which are located in Grand Prairie, and the Gaylord Texan resort and convention center in Grapevine.

Many residents from the wealthy suburbs commute into either Fort Worth or Dallas, making transportation policy a major issue in the district.

MAJOR INDUSTRY

Transportation, manufacturing, corporate headquarters

CITIES

Grand Prairie (pt.), 122,502; Carrollton, 109,576; Irving (pt.), 59,755; Bedford; 47,152; Euless, 46,005; Grapevine (pt.), 42,057; Dallas (pt.), 37,512

NOTABLE

Grand Prairie is home to the National Championship Indian Powwow.

Rep. Lloyd Doggett (D)

CAPITOL OFFICE
225-4865
lloyd.doggett@mail.house.gov
www.house.gov/doggett
201 Cannon 20515-4325; fax 225-3073

COMMITTEES
Budget
Ways & Means
Joint Economic

RESIDENCE
Austin

BORN
Oct. 6, 1946, Austin, Texas

RELIGION
Methodist

FAMILY
Wife, Libby Belk Doggett; two children

EDUCATION
U. of Texas, B.B.A. 1967, J.D. 1970

CAREER
Lawyer

POLITICAL HIGHLIGHTS
Texas Senate, 1973-85; Democratic nominee for U.S. Senate, 1984; Texas Supreme Court, 1989-94

ELECTION RESULTS

2006 GENERAL		
Lloyd Doggett (D)	109,911	67.3%
Grant Rostig (R)	42,975	26.3%
Barbara Cunningham (LIBERT)	6,942	4.2%
Brian Parrett (I)	3,596	2.2%
2006 PRIMARY		
Lloyd Doggett (D)		unopposed
2004 GENERAL		
Lloyd Doggett (D)	108,309	67.6%
Rebecca Armendariz Klein (R)	49,252	30.7%
James Warner (LIBERT)	2,656	1.7%

PREVIOUS WINNING PERCENTAGES
2002 (84%); 2000 (85%); 1998 (85%); 1996 (56%); 1994 (56%)

Elected 1994; 7th term

Doggett has evidenced a political staying power by getting re-elected in a district that keeps changing underneath him. And after years of being in the minority, with relatively little power to effect change, he is in a good position to make his voice heard in the 110th Congress (2007-08). He is a strong backer of House Speaker Nancy Pelosi, a member of the powerful Ways and Means Committee and the panel's liaison with the Budget Committee.

A liberal former Texas Supreme Court justice, Doggett seldom missed an opportunity as a member of the minority to upbraid, outmaneuver or otherwise confound Republican conservatives, particularly fellow Texan Tom DeLay, the House majority leader. Doggett even led a parliamentary group that used various delaying tactics to hold up the GOP agenda. Now in the majority, he says, "It's just such a change from knowing each day when you walk across the street that you will be on the losing end of a vote."

He has fought to close tax loopholes that favor wealthy individuals and corporations and to ensure that no senior citizens are left behind by the Medicare program or by a Social Security program that is seeing its trust fund receipts borrowed by successive administrations.

In 2005, he opposed President Bush's plan to allow workers to divert a portion of their Social Security taxes into personal investment accounts. At a Ways and Means Committee hearing in May of that year, Doggett argued that Bush and Ways and Means Chairman Bill Thomas of California were not seeking to strengthen Social Security but to destroy it. He noted that Thomas had said he wanted to make Social Security solvent "for all time." "We've got some steers down in Texas that have been fixed for all time, and my fear is the same thing is about to happen to Social Security," Doggett said.

On Medicare, Doggett says he wants to make sure that "the prescription drug program reaches the people who need it the most." To that end, he reintroduced legislation in 2007 designed to help low-income seniors and people with disabilities enroll in a drug plan.

Doggett has a passion for protecting the environment, and he says the House should lead by example by being more energy efficient. (He is diligent about recycling in his own Capitol Hill office.) On environmental policy, he wants to direct more funding to renewable energy initiatives and clean energy research. He also advocates tax incentives aimed at conservation. In 2007, he sponsored legislation to provide a tax credit for new plug-in hybrid motor vehicles.

Doggett has consistently opposed the Iraq War, and it is an issue that has occupied much of his time outside of the Ways and Means Committee. During House consideration in late 2002 of a resolution authorizing the president to take military action against Iraq, Doggett led an ad hoc whip organization to round up votes in opposition. In 2007, he argued for a "phased redeployment" that would pull U.S. troops out of Iraq and refocus U.S. military power on Afghanistan. He also maintains that all war expenditures should be on budget, and clearly visible. "Ten billion dollars a month spent in Iraq is an expenditure we can ill afford," he says.

Doggett, whose scathing words about DeLay and the Republican majority in general often turned up in the Texas media, was a top target when DeLay led a drive to redraw Texas' congressional districts in 2003 in a successful bid to enlarge the Republican majority in the House. DeLay engineered a redistricting plan that dismantled the 10th District that Doggett represented, splintering it into three districts. Doggett quickly decided to run in the new 25th District, which stretched 350 miles from Austin to the Texas-Mexico border and was drawn to elect a Hispanic candidate. He gave up his hillside West Austin home and moved to the heavily Hispanic east side, where he still lives in an old house he and his wife restored.

In June 2006, the U.S. Supreme Court ruled that the GOP-drawn map was unconstitutional because it diluted the political influence of Hispanic voters in Texas' 23rd District. Subsequently, a three-judge panel redrew the 23rd and four nearby districts, including Doggett's 25th. The judges' map made Doggett's new district more compact and less Hispanic. The district also gained three rural counties to the southeast of Austin, requiring Doggett to keep up with agricultural concerns and issues related to the economic development of small communities. (But the core set of issues that he has worked on will remain the same in the 110th Congress, he says.) With the redistricting decision behind him, in November 2006 Doggett won with 67 percent of the vote.

Born and raised in Austin, Doggett went to the University of Texas, where he was elected student body president. Within two years of earning his law degree in 1970, he won election to the state Senate. He served until 1985, compiling a record of support for consumers and for civil rights while backing the death penalty and tough criminal sanctions against drug traffickers and violent criminals. Fellow state senators knew he was ready to filibuster when he donned white leather tennis shoes, which kept him comfortable during long stints on his feet. The shoes now hang in his congressional office.

In 1984, he ran for the U.S. Senate, beating two veteran House members, Bob Krueger and Kent Hance, in the Democratic primary. But in November, he was crushed by GOP Rep. Phil Gramm. Four years later, Doggett won a seat on the Texas Supreme Court, which handles only civil cases. He was on the bench when 81-year-old Democratic Rep. J.J. Pickle announced his retirement in 1994.

Doggett was the first Democrat to announce his candidacy, and his quick start spared him a tough primary. Raising $1.2 million, he surmounted that year's GOP takeover tide and won by 16 percentage points over real estate consultant A. Jo Baylor, who had hoped to become the first black Republican woman elected to Congress.

He has consistently won re-election by significant margins, even with his shifting districts.

KEY VOTES

2006

Yes Stop broadband companies from favoring select Internet traffic

No Affirm U.S. commitment to war in Iraq and reject setting a withdrawal date for troops

No Repeal requirement for bilingual ballots at the polls

No Permit U.S. sale of civilian nuclear technology to India

No Build a 700-mile fence on the U.S.-Mexico border to curb illegal crossings

No Permit warrantless wiretaps of suspected terrorists

2005

? Intervene in the life-support case of Terri Schiavo

Yes Lift President Bush's restrictions on stem cell research funding

Yes Prohibit FBI access to library and bookstore records

No Approve free-trade pact with five Central American countries

No Pass energy policy overhaul favored by President Bush emphasizing domestic oil and gas production

No End mandatory preservation of habitat of endangered animal and plant species

Yes Ban torture of prisoners in U.S. custody

CQ VOTE STUDIES

	PARTY UNITY		PRESIDENTIAL SUPPORT	
	Support	Oppose	Support	Oppose
2006	97%	3%	21%	79%
2005	97%	3%	13%	87%
2004	95%	5%	27%	73%
2003	97%	3%	18%	82%
2002	95%	5%	22%	78%

INTEREST GROUPS

	AFL-CIO	ADA	CCUS	ACU
2006	92%	90%	23%	8%
2005	93%	90%	38%	4%
2004	93%	95%	39%	4%
2003	93%	90%	30%	12%
2002	100%	100%	30%	4%

TEXAS 25

South central – most of Austin

One of five Texas districts redrawn in 2006 by a federal court, the 25th is an Austin-dominated district that is much more compact than its 2004 antecedent, which stretched south in a narrow band from Austin to the Rio Grande River on the Mexican border.

More than 60 percent of district residents live in Travis County (Austin), nearly all of whom live within the city limits. The district takes in the southern portion of Travis, including Austin-Bergstrom International Airport. The economy here revolves around the University of Texas (located in the 21st), state government and the technology industry.

Austin's ties to the academic community and the public sector, coupled with its racial and ethnic diversity, give Travis, and thus the 25th District, a decidedly liberal tilt. Travis was the only one of Texas' 254 counties that voted against a state constitutional amendment banning same-sex marriage in November 2005.

Southwest of Travis lies Hays County, which was appended to the 25th in the 2006 remapping. Hays is growing rapidly: Its population increased by more than one-third between 2000 and 2006. Many of these new residents came from Travis County.

From Travis and Hays, the 25th fans southeast to scoop up less-populated areas. Bastrop County, located east of Austin, was added to the 25th in the 2006 remapping and is experiencing robust population growth. Fayette, Gonzales, Lavaca and Colorado counties, which form the eastern half of the 25th, usually vote Republican — Democrat Chris Bell finished in third place in each of these counties in the 2006 governor's race, behind Republican Gov. Rick Perry and independent Carole Keeton Strayhorn, a former Republican. But these conservative-leaning areas do not have the population to dislodge the 25th from its Democratic moorings.

MAJOR INDUSTRY

Technology, higher education, state government, ranching, agriculture

CITIES

Austin (pt.), 358,434; San Marcos, 34,733; Lockhart, 11,615

NOTABLE

The Texas Legislature deemed Lockhart the barbecue capital of Texas in 1999.

Rep. Michael C. Burgess (R)

Elected 2002; 3rd term

CAPITOL OFFICE
225-7772
burgess.house.gov
1224 Longworth 20515-4326; fax 225-2919

COMMITTEES
Energy & Commerce

RESIDENCE
Flower Mound

BORN
Dec. 23, 1950, Rochester, Minn.

RELIGION
Episcopalian

FAMILY
Wife, Laura Lee Burgess; three children

EDUCATION
North Texas State U., B.S. 1972 (biology), M.S. 1976 (physiology); U. of Texas Health Science Center, Houston, M.D. 1977; U. of Texas Southwestern Medical Center, Dallas, M.S. 2000 (medical management)

CAREER
Physician

POLITICAL HIGHLIGHTS
No previous office

ELECTION RESULTS

2006 GENERAL		
Michael C. Burgess (R)	94,219	60.2%
Tim Barnwell (D)	58,271	37.2%
Rich Haas (LIBERT)	3,993	2.6%
2006 PRIMARY		
Michael C. Burgess (R)		unopposed
2004 GENERAL		
Michael C. Burgess (R)	180,519	65.8%
Lico Reyes (D)	89,809	32.7%
James Gholston (LIBERT)	4,211	1.5%

PREVIOUS WINNING PERCENTAGES
2002 (75%)

An obstetrician-gynecologist from the conservative flank of the Republican Party, Burgess is hoping to parlay his seat on the Energy and Commerce panel's Health Subcommittee into a place at the table for Capitol Hill's health care debates.

He wants to promote Republican health policy mainstays: curbing medical malpractice lawsuits, expanding the private sector role in Medicare and tightening income eligibility for poor children covered by the State Children's Health Insurance Program (SCHIP).

While he's likely to struggle to get traction on his proposals in a Democratic-controlled House, Burgess showed early in the 110th Congress (2007-08) that he's capable of reaching across the aisle. He joined Texas Democrat Gene Green to pass a bill that would authorize $46 million over five years in matching grants to help develop state trauma networks. Most states have trauma care coordinators to direct the most seriously injured patients to proper hospitals, but the networks' quality and sophistication vary. Green called Burgess "a good partner on the trauma care."

Burgess tried without success in the 109th Congress (2005-06) to pass a bill to undo scheduled Medicare payment cuts to doctors and to arm Medicare beneficiaries with more information on the quality of physician care. "I am really worried about the physician workforce," he says. The Medicare payment formula has annual cuts of about 5 percent lined up for nine years. Replacing the cuts with a modest yearly payment increase to reflect the rising expense of delivering care would cost the government $218 billion over 10 years, according to the Congressional Budget Office. There's bipartisan agreement that the sustainable growth rate formula must be scrapped but nobody has figured out yet how to pay for doing so. Burgess says he will again try to change the Medicare payment system in the 110th Congress.

Burgess says patient care ultimately suffers if doctors get squeezed by shrinking Medicare payments and by the costs of malpractice lawsuits. He adds that middle-aged doctors are quitting and it may become harder to recruit young doctors.

One of Burgess' top priorities is reining in medical malpractice suits, which for him is "an issue of fundamental fairness."

A second-generation doctor who says he has delivered more than 3,000 babies, Burgess was sued in the late 1980s by a family whose baby died during a difficult C-section. He was not in charge of the delivery, he says, but was called in to assist another obstetrician. He says the incident helped convince him that the medical liability system needed to be overhauled. He says even though Texas and other states are taking steps such as caps on damage awards, "we need more than just a piece-by-piece, state-by-state solution." Frivolous lawsuits and the costs of defensive medicine are a national problem, he says.

Early in the 110th Congress, the Energy and Commerce Committee began working on reauthorizing the children's health insurance program. Burgess lined up with the Bush administration's proposal to scale back eligibility for SCHIP to children from families who earn less than 200 percent of the federal poverty level, or $27,380 for a family of two. Many states have expanded eligibility for the program to children from families earning up to 350 percent of the poverty level, and to some adults. In 2007, Burgess introduced legislation barring SCHIP coverage to adults except pregnant women. "We lost our way as far as who should be covered," he says of SCHIP.

Burgess, who usually votes with his party more than 95 percent of the time, opposes abortion and expansion of embryonic stem cell research. In 2005, he voted against legislation that would have increased the number of embryonic stem cell lines available for federally funded research. In a bid for votes on the House floor, Burgess played an audio clip of a fetal heartbeat. "This is what the debate is all about," he told the chamber.

On immigration, Burgess says Congress' top priority should be bolstering border enforcement. He voted in favor of immigration legislation favored by House GOP leaders that the House passed in late 2005. The measure would have increased border controls, made it a felony to be in the United States illegally, and punished anyone caught aiding illegal immigrants — including humanitarian workers and clergy. The legislation died after the House and Senate were unable to agree on an approach to immigration overhaul. But late in 2006, Congress did pass a measure — which President Bush signed — authorizing construction of about 700 miles of fencing on the U.S.-Mexico border. Burgess voted for that bill as well.

There have been exceptions to Burgess' support for leadership priorities. In 2004, he voted against the intelligence overhaul legislation that had been recommended by the independent, bipartisan commission that investigated the Sept. 11 terrorist attacks. Burgess sided with Judiciary Committee Chairman F. James Sensenbrenner Jr., who said the final bill did not do enough to improve border security. Burgess also opposed a Bush administration rule requiring banks to accept Mexican identification cards; he said such measures show too little respect for the importance of earning U.S. citizenship.

Burgess replaced Dick Armey, who held the 26th District seat for 18 years, including eight as House majority leader. He has taken up the cause of the flat tax, the issue Armey championed for many years.

To take Armey's place in Congress, Burgess had to defeat the nine-term lawmaker's son, Scott Armey, in the 2002 primary to fill the retiring majority leader's seat. The 26th District had just been redrawn to favor Scott Armey, who finished first in the six-way primary. But he only won 45 percent of the vote, not enough to prevent a runoff. Burgess campaigned against him by handing out literature declaring, "My dad is not Dick Armey," and prevailed in the runoff with 55 percent of the vote. He won easily in November in the solidly Republican district.

In 2004, Burgess cruised to a second-term victory with 66 percent of the vote against Democrat Lico Reyes, a local political activist and owner of a disc jockey business. In 2006, Burgess won with 60 percent.

KEY VOTES

2006

- No Stop broadband companies from favoring select Internet traffic
- Yes Affirm U.S. commitment to war in Iraq and reject setting a withdrawal date for troops
- Yes Repeal requirement for bilingual ballots at the polls
- Yes Permit U.S. sale of civilian nuclear technology to India
- Yes Build a 700-mile fence on the U.S.-Mexico border to curb illegal crossings
- Yes Permit warrantless wiretaps of suspected terrorists

2005

- Yes Intervene in the life-support case of Terri Schiavo
- No Lift President Bush's restrictions on stem cell research funding
- Yes Prohibit FBI access to library and bookstore records
- Yes Approve free-trade pact with five Central American countries
- Yes Pass energy policy overhaul favored by President Bush emphasizing domestic oil and gas production
- Yes End mandatory preservation of habitat of endangered animal and plant species
- No Ban torture of prisoners in U.S. custody

CQ VOTE STUDIES

	PARTY UNITY		PRESIDENTIAL SUPPORT	
	Support	Oppose	Support	Oppose
2006	93%	7%	87%	13%
2005	97%	3%	89%	11%
2004	96%	4%	88%	12%
2003	98%	2%	93%	7%

INTEREST GROUPS

	AFL-CIO	ADA	CCUS	ACU
2006	21%	5%	92%	83%
2005	13%	0%	88%	96%
2004	20%	5%	100%	96%
2003	7%	5%	100%	88%

TEXAS 26

Eastern Fort Worth and suburbs; most of Denton County

The 26th stretches north from southeastern Fort Worth and its surrounding suburbs to take in almost all of Denton County and the eastern part of rural Cooke County. The district's strong economy depends mainly on transportation, with abundant white-collar industries.

The heart of the district is fast-growing Denton County, the southern part of which is filled with burgeoning upper-middle-class Dallas-Fort Worth suburbs. Time Warner Cable has large facilities here, and education and technology are important: The University of North Texas engineering program emphasizes nanotechnology research and applications. Parts of the expansive Barnett shale natural gas reservoir are located in Denton, and drilling provides thousands of jobs.

Roughly 45 percent of residents live in Fort Worth and its Tarrant County suburbs, mainly in middle-class areas such as North Richland Hills. The 26th also grabs Forest Hill and Everman, areas south of downtown with large black populations. Much of Cooke County is agricultural, relying mostly on cattle and dairy farms, with oat and wheat farms as well.

A small part of Dallas-Fort Worth International Airport lies in the 26th, and the airport is a major employer. Fort Worth Alliance Airport (shared with the 12th) was the nation's first airport to be built specifically to serve business needs. Bell Helicopter Textron's headquarters is in Hurst.

Voters here support Republicans. The district's portion of Denton County gave George W. Bush 71 percent of its 2004 presidential vote, while the district's part of Tarrant County gave him 53 percent of the vote. Overall, Bush garnered 64 percent of the 26th's vote.

MAJOR INDUSTRY
Transportation, telecommunications

CITIES
Fort Worth (pt.), 153,549; Denton, 80,537; Lewisville (pt.), 58,106; North Richland Hills (pt.), 55,445; Flower Mound, 50,702; Hurst (pt.), 30,832

NOTABLE
The Texas Motor Speedway is in Denton County; The town council in Clark changed the town's name to DISH in 2005 to win 10 years of free basic satellite television from DISH Network for all 125 residents.

Rep. Solomon P. Ortiz (D)

CAPITOL OFFICE
225-7742
www.house.gov/ortiz
2110 Rayburn 20515-4327; fax 226-1134

COMMITTEES
Armed Services
(Readiness - chairman)
Natural Resources

RESIDENCE
Corpus Christi

BORN
June 3, 1937, Robstown, Texas

RELIGION
Methodist

FAMILY
Divorced; two children

EDUCATION
Institute of Applied Science, attended 1962;
Del Mar College, attended 1965-67

MILITARY SERVICE
Army, 1960-62

CAREER
Law enforcement official

POLITICAL HIGHLIGHTS
Nueces County constable, 1965-69; Nueces County Commission, 1969-77; Nueces County sheriff, 1977-83

ELECTION RESULTS

2006 GENERAL		
Solomon P. Ortiz (D)	62,058	56.8%
William "Willie" Vaden (R)	42,538	38.9%
Robert Powell (LIBERT)	4,718	4.3%
2006 PRIMARY		
Solomon P. Ortiz (D)		unopposed
2004 GENERAL		
Solomon P. Ortiz (D)	112,081	63.1%
William "Willie" Vaden (R)	61,955	34.9%
Christopher J. Claytor (LIBERT)	3,500	2.0%

PREVIOUS WINNING PERCENTAGES
2002 (61%); 2000 (63%); 1998 (63%); 1996 (65%); 1994 (59%); 1992 (55%); 1990 (100%); 1988 (100%); 1986 (100%); 1984 (64%); 1982 (64%)

Elected 1982; 13th term

Ortiz might be called a "readiness hawk." And as the Iraq War grinds into its fifth year, he says his top priority in the 110th Congress (2007-08) will be to fix what he calls "a broken military," whose troops are staggering from multiple deployments, training difficulties and equipment bottlenecks.

The chairman of the Armed Services panel's Readiness Subcommittee and the most senior Democrat in the Texas House delegation, Ortiz is in a prime position to influence these issues, which are critical to the Army helicopter maintenance depot and other military facilities in his district, which stretches wide along the Gulf of Mexico from Corpus Christi to Brownsville. Ortiz also is on the Natural Resources Committee, which handles fisheries policy, water issues along the U.S.-Mexico border and other matters important to his constituents.

The largely Hispanic 27th District leans Democratic, but it favored President Bush in the 2004 election. Ortiz, likewise, is not a straight-party vote on Capitol Hill. He broke with his party on 23 percent of votes in the 109th Congress (2005-06). And in 2005, he was one of only 15 Democrats to side with Republicans in approving the Central American Free Trade Agreement with Costa Rica, El Salvador, Guatemala, Honduras and Nicaragua.

In general, Ortiz says he's comfortable working with Republicans. "I've been able to gain the trust of members on both sides of the aisle," he says. He calls himself conservative on social issues, opposing same-sex marriage, for instance, but says he is progressive on economic ones. This mirrors attitudes in his district, which is home to many people in need of better educational and employment opportunities and health care services.

In 2005, he teamed with Republican Sen. Trent Lott of Mississippi to fight the Pentagon's recommended closure of two Gulf Coast bases, one of which, the Naval Station Ingleside, employs nearly 3,000 military and civilian personnel in Ortiz's district. He also worked with Texas Republican Sen. Kay Bailey Hutchison in an ultimately unsuccessful effort to save Ingleside.

Many of Ortiz's constituents earn their living at military bases, including Naval Air Station Corpus Christi, Naval Air Station Kingsville and the Corpus Christi Army Depot. Roughly 3,000 civilian depot employees service Army helicopters such as the Apache. So Ortiz also is a fierce foe of Pentagon proposals to privatize repairs at large military maintenance depots.

Ortiz says when it comes to critical repair work it is dangerous to rely on private companies that might have labor problems or use their monopoly as leverage to boost costs. Taking note in early 2005 of the continued fighting in Iraq, Ortiz said, "One only needs to watch the evening news to know how much wear and tear we are putting on our helicopters and how much rapid, reliable maintenance we need on those birds."

The depots are critical to readiness because they keep equipment up to standard. But Ortiz says Corpus Christi and other military facilities are struggling to keep pace with the volume of helicopters returning from Iraq for servicing.

Ortiz is also concerned about caring for soldiers returning to Texas from Iraq and Afghanistan and for the families of those soldiers. In 2005, the Census Bureau ranked Texas third in the number of its military veterans, 1.7 million. By early 2007, 48 soldiers from Ortiz's district and the Rio Grande Valley area had been killed in the Iraq War.

Ortiz has made a point of visiting the families of killed and wounded soldiers from his district. He says many of those families are too poor to travel to the VA hospital in San Antonio, which is a two-and-a-half-hour drive from Corpus Christi and six or more hours from the Rio Grande Valley. So Ortiz is working to get a VA hospital in South Texas, a cause for him for 20 years. Iraq casualties and the 2007 scandal over poor conditions at Walter Reed Army Hospital and VA hospitals nationwide, combined with Democratic control of Congress, could improve the chances for Ortiz's efforts. In early 2007, he introduced legislation that would mandate that the VA provide for the health care needs of veterans in South Texas.

In 2007, he also backed legislation aimed at preventing suicides among veterans. And he cosponsored a bill to prevent the Pentagon from raising health care costs for military retirees.

As a young man, Ortiz served in the Army's military police, gaining experience that helped put him on his path to a career in law enforcement and government. He shows a special interest in troop quality of life and in seeing that military personnel are given a chance at upward mobility.

On the Natural Resources Committee, water is a major concern of Ortiz — specifically, the lack of water that plagues farmers and municipalities in the Rio Grande Valley.

In dealing with the panoply of homeland defense issues facing Congress since the Sept. 11 terrorist attacks, Ortiz has had to balance three priorities: his conservative instinct on questions of national security; the economic dependence of many of his constituents on easy access for day-trippers crossing the Rio Grande; and his determination to protect Hispanics against discrimination.

The child of a migrant family, Ortiz grew up poor near Corpus Christi, working a variety of odd jobs to help his family. When he was 16, his father died. He dropped out of high school and later joined the Army. "It was the one place that would give me free room and board and let me send my check back home to my mother," he recalls.

He left the Army in 1962 and two years later waged his first political campaign, defeating the incumbent Nueces County constable. In 1968, he became the first Hispanic elected to the county commission; in 1976, he was the first Hispanic to win election as county sheriff, his springboard to the House in 1982. That year, the three-judge federal panel in charge of redistricting created the 27th District with a 60 percent Hispanic majority. He won the seat with 64 percent of the vote. His district's boundaries have not changed much since, and in his recent re-elections he has cruised to victory with vote totals near 60 percent. In 2006, he struggled a bit, getting just 57 percent, his lowest percentage since 1992.

KEY VOTES

2006

No Stop broadband companies from favoring select Internet traffic
No Affirm U.S. commitment to war in Iraq and reject setting a withdrawal date for troops
No Repeal requirement for bilingual ballots at the polls
Yes Permit U.S. sale of civilian nuclear technology to India
No Build a 700-mile fence on the U.S.-Mexico border to curb illegal crossings
No Permit warrantless wiretaps of suspected terrorists

2005

? Intervene in the life-support case of Terri Schiavo
Yes Lift President Bush's restrictions on stem cell research funding
Yes Prohibit FBI access to library and bookstore records
Yes Approve free-trade pact with five Central American countries
Yes Pass energy policy overhaul favored by President Bush emphasizing domestic oil and gas production
Yes End mandatory preservation of habitat of endangered animal and plant species
Yes Ban torture of prisoners in U.S. custody

CQ VOTE STUDIES

	PARTY UNITY		PRESIDENTIAL SUPPORT	
	Support	Oppose	Support	Oppose
2006	76%	24%	57%	43%
2005	78%	22%	45%	55%
2004	83%	17%	47%	53%
2003	79%	21%	44%	56%
2002	82%	18%	42%	58%

INTEREST GROUPS

	AFL-CIO	ADA	CCUS	ACU
2006	100%	65%	80%	40%
2005	87%	70%	70%	40%
2004	93%	55%	47%	28%
2003	87%	80%	54%	56%
2002	78%	85%	42%	25%

TEXAS 27

Southern Gulf Coast – Corpus Christi, Brownsville

Anchored by Corpus Christi in the north, the 27th runs south to the Rio Grande River, with the Gulf of Mexico on its eastern coast. Ranches, as well as industries tied to the coast, are the mainstays between the two largest cities, Corpus Christi and Brownsville, which together take in nearly two-thirds of the 27th's population.

Corpus Christi relies on tourism, with oil and gas remaining among its biggest industries. Petrochemical refining, also found up and down the coast, is becoming more common here as well. The area's military facilities are key to the region's economic health, and the 2005 BRAC round dealt the area a blow by ordering the Ingleside Naval Station closed by 2010 and by reducing forces at the Corpus Christi air station. At its northern tip, just north of Corpus Christi, the 27th also includes more than half of San Patricio County's population.

Farther south, in the Rio Grande Valley, the port city of Brownsville struggles with an influx of illegal immigrants and high poverty, but new manufacturing plants and *maquiladoras* — plants that use low-cost labor and import many parts from the United States — have helped. Visitors from Mexico boost Brownsville's retail industry, and ecotourism also adds to the economy by drawing bird and turtle watchers to the area's wetlands.

The Hispanic-majority district (68 percent) generally supports Democrats, and has elected the same Democrat to the U.S. House since its creation prior to the 1982 election. But the 27th's Democratic lean is not overwhelming. George W. Bush took 55 percent of the district's 2004 presidential vote.

MAJOR INDUSTRY
Manufacturing, trade, tourism, military, petrochemicals

MILITARY BASES
Naval Air Station Corpus Christi, 1,800 military, 2,700 civilian; Corpus Christi Army Depot, 12 military, 3,315 civilian (2004); Naval Station Ingleside, 2,559 military, 224 civilian (2006); Naval Air Station Kingsville, 754 military, 1,210 civilian (2004)

CITIES
Corpus Christi, 277,454; Brownsville, 139,722; Kingsville, 25,575

NOTABLE
Padre Island National Seashore runs most of the district's length.

Rep. Henry Cuellar (D)

CAPITOL OFFICE
225-1640
henry.cuellar@mail.house.gov
www.house.gov/cuellar
336 Cannon 20515-4328; fax 225-1641

COMMITTEES
Agriculture
Homeland Security
(Emergency Communications - chairman)
Small Business

RESIDENCE
Laredo

BORN
Sept. 19, 1955, Laredo, Texas

RELIGION
Roman Catholic

FAMILY
Wife, Imelda Cuellar; two children

EDUCATION
Laredo Community College, A.A. 1976 (political science); Georgetown U., B.S.F.S. 1978; U. of Texas, J.D. 1981; Laredo State U., M.B.A. 1982 (international trade); U. of Texas, Ph.D. 1998 (government)

CAREER
Lawyer; international trade firm owner

POLITICAL HIGHLIGHTS
Texas House, 1987-2001; Texas secretary of state, 2001; Democratic nominee for U.S. House, 2002

ELECTION RESULTS

2006 GENERAL		
Henry Cuellar (D)	52,574	67.6%
Frank Enriquez (D)	15,798	20.3%
Ron Avery (C)	9,383	12.1%
2006 PRIMARY		
Henry Cuellar (D)	24,256	53.1%
Ciro D. Rodriguez (D)	18,484	40.5%
Victor M. Morales (D)	2,943	6.4%
2004 GENERAL		
Henry Cuellar (D)	106,323	59.0%
James F. "Jim" Hopson (R)	69,538	38.6%
Ken Ashby (LIBERT)	4,305	2.4%

Elected 2004; 2nd term

A self-described "moderate conservative" Democrat, Cuellar has been a vote the president can count on. In the 109th Congress (2005-06), he sided more often with President Bush on votes where the president took a stand than all but one other Democratic member of the House.

Cuellar (KWAY-are) voted 71 percent of the time with Bush; only Oklahoma Democrat Dan Boren sided more often with the president. Cuellar also stuck with his party only 67 percent of the time, putting him among the 10 House Democrats who disagreed most often with their own party on votes that pitted Democrats against Republicans in the 109th Congress.

Cuellar's voting record may not be that surprising: He endorsed George W. Bush, then governor of Texas, for the presidency in 2000; the next year, he took a plum job as Texas secretary of state under Bush's successor, Republican Gov. Rick Perry.

On specific key votes in 2006, his fiscal and social conservatism was clearly evident. He was one of 15 Democrats voting to extend reduced tax rates on capital gains and dividend income through 2010, and one of just eight to support a GOP lobbying and ethics bill that targeted funds earmarked in spending bills for members' pet projects. He also was one of 34 Democrats backing a constitutional amendment to prohibit same-sex marriage, and one of 49 voting to make it a felony to take a minor across state lines with the intent of circumventing state parental abortion notification laws.

The Hispanic-majority 28th District backed Bush in the 2004 presidential election, so Cuellar's political views seem fairly well aligned with those of his constituents. His socially conservative bent also can be explained in part by the influence of his Roman Catholic religion. But Cuellar says he has no interest in joining the GOP. "The best way to produce results is to set labels aside and work in a bipartisan manner," he says.

At the start of the 110th Congress (2007-08), there were signs that Cuellar was trying to improve relations with his own party. He voted for all six signature bills the House Democrats steered to passage in the "first 100 hours" agenda of their new majority rule. This is not to say that Cuellar will start to tack to the left. In fact, he says, "We are now the Democratic Party that believes in legislating and governing from the center."

He has the distinction of being the first Democrat ever to gain the endorsement of the Club for Growth, a conservative political organization that supports cutting taxes and spending. The group praised Cuellar for amassing a "pro-growth" voting record in his first term that included supporting the Central American Free Trade Agreement in 2005 and a permanent repeal of estate taxes. Cuellar was among the 15 Democrats who sided with nearly every Republican to pass CAFTA, which the Democratic leadership and labor unions vigorously opposed. Cuellar notes that his hometown of Laredo is the busiest inland trade port in the nation.

Cuellar sits on the Agriculture Committee, from which he can assist the many farmers in his district who grow peanuts, cotton and sorghum. He also sits on Homeland Security, where he chairs a subcommittee that has jurisdiction over emergency preparedness and response — a useful post for a congressman from a district on the U.S.-Mexico border.

Cuellar likes to emphasize his constituent service and accessibility. He tries to help local communities secure federal grants for their programs. So it was perhaps fitting that Cuellar introduced a bill in 2007 that calls for higher customer service standards within the federal government.

Cuellar was born in Laredo, the eldest of eight children born to migrant workers who had an elementary school education. He went on to earn an array of academic degrees, including law and business degrees, and a doctorate in government.

Cuellar was first elected to the Texas House in 1986, at age 31, and served there 14 years. In the state House, he wrote legislation that provided hundreds of millions of dollars in college financial aid.

Cuellar was appointed Texas secretary of state in early 2001, but he resigned later that year to prepare for a 2002 campaign against Republican Rep. Henry Bonilla in Texas' 23rd District. Cuellar lost by just more than 4 percentage points in a closer-than-expected race.

A Republican-drawn congressional map implemented for the 2004 elections moved part of Webb County (Laredo), Cuellar's political base, to the 28th District, a heavily Hispanic and primarily San Antonio-based district that had been represented since 1997 by Democrat Ciro D. Rodriguez. Cuellar challenged Rodriguez in the 2004 primary, even though Rodriguez had backed Cuellar's 2002 campaign against Bonilla. A huge turnout in the Laredo area helped Cuellar eke out a narrow win that was certified only after a series of recounts, lawsuits and accusations of voting fraud lodged by Rodriguez and his supporters.

Rodriguez was back to challenge Cuellar in 2006. Angered by Cuellar's frequent votes with Republicans, liberal activists and labor unions sided with Rodriguez and circulated a photograph of Bush affectionately taking Cuellar's face in his hands as the president waded through a crowd of well-wishers after his 2006 State of the Union address.

But Cuellar was well prepared for the anticipated rematch and touted his accessibility and ability to bring federal funds to the district. He again dominated Rodriguez in Webb County and won the primary by almost 13 percentage points.

No Republican opposed Cuellar in the 2006 general election, but he had to wage another campaign after a federal court in August redrew his district and four others to comply with a Supreme Court decision in June that partially invalidated the Texas congressional map. The federal panel's new map strengthened Cuellar by including all of Webb County in the 28th District. He won 68 percent of the vote in a special November election against two minor opponents.

Rodriguez, meanwhile, took advantage of the second chance and unseated Bonilla in the adjacent 23rd District — where Cuellar was nearly elected in 2002 — so Rodriguez and Cuellar are now House colleagues.

KEY VOTES

2006

No Stop broadband companies from favoring select Internet traffic
Yes Affirm U.S. commitment to war in Iraq and reject setting a withdrawal date for troops
No Repeal requirement for bilingual ballots at the polls
Yes Permit U.S. sale of civilian nuclear technology to India
No Build a 700-mile fence on the U.S.-Mexico border to curb illegal crossings
Yes Permit warrantless wiretaps of suspected terrorists

2005

Yes Intervene in the life-support case of Terri Schiavo
Yes Lift President Bush's restrictions on stem cell research funding
? Prohibit FBI access to library and bookstore records
Yes Approve free-trade pact with five Central American countries
Yes Pass energy policy overhaul favored by President Bush emphasizing domestic oil and gas production
Yes End mandatory preservation of habitat of endangered animal and plant species
Yes Ban torture of prisoners in U.S. custody

CQ VOTE STUDIES

	PARTY UNITY		PRESIDENTIAL SUPPORT	
	Support	Oppose	Support	Oppose
2006	63%	37%	85%	15%
2005	70%	30%	57%	43%

INTEREST GROUPS

	AFL-CIO	ADA	CCUS	ACU
2006	64%	35%	100%	68%
2005	60%	70%	89%	52%

TEXAS 28

South central – Laredo; part of McAllen

Webb and Hidalgo counties on the Mexican border are the two major population centers in the 28th, a heavily Hispanic and Democratic-leaning district. One of five districts redrawn by a federal court in 2006, the 28th also stretches northward along Interstate 35 to absorb territory northeast of San Antonio.

Under the old 2004 map, Laredo and surrounding Webb County were split between the 23rd and 28th districts, but the 2006 map placed the county wholly within the 28th. About 30 percent of district residents live in Webb, where international trade is crucial for Laredo, the nation's largest inland port of entry. Agriculture also is important to this area, with peanuts, cotton, sorghum, carrots and beef dominating the market.

Another 30 percent of the 28th's population lives in Hidalgo County, a fast-growing area where the district takes in nearly half of McAllen and almost all of Mission. Like Webb, the 28th's share of Hidalgo (shared with the 15th District) is overwhelmingly Hispanic. West of Hidalgo, Starr County is the nation's most heavily Hispanic county (97.5 percent). At 77.5 percent, the 28th is the third-most heavily Hispanic district in the nation, just behind Texas' 16th and 15th districts.

Hidalgo and Starr also are among the most economically depressed counties in the nation. In Starr, nearly half of all families live below the poverty line, and the 28th overall has a greater share of families below the poverty line than any other Texas district. But the economy is starting to show improvement as the number of small businesses rise.

Under its 2004 configuration, the 28th's dominant population center was Bexar County in and around San Antonio. But the 2006 court map excised nearly all of Bexar from the 28th, save for an eastern sliver of the county that includes Randolph Air Force Base.

MAJOR INDUSTRY
Agriculture, international trade, defense

MILITARY BASES
Randolph Air Force Base, 4,178 military, 4,000 civilian (2006)

CITIES
Laredo, 176,576; McAllen (pt.), 44,756; Mission (pt.), 42,721; Seguin, 22,011

NOTABLE
The "streets of Laredo" inspired titles for a cowboy ballad and a novel.

Rep. Gene Green (D)

CAPITOL OFFICE
225-1688
www.house.gov/green
2335 Rayburn 20515-4329; fax 225-9903

COMMITTEES
Energy & Commerce
Foreign Affairs
Standards of Official Conduct

RESIDENCE
Houston

BORN
Oct. 17, 1947, Houston, Texas

RELIGION
Methodist

FAMILY
Wife, Helen Albers Green; two children

EDUCATION
U. of Houston, B.B.A. 1971; Bates College of Law, attended 1971-77

CAREER
Lawyer

POLITICAL HIGHLIGHTS
Texas House, 1973-85; Texas Senate, 1985-92

ELECTION RESULTS

2006 GENERAL		
Gene Green (D)	37,174	73.5%
Eric Story (R)	12,347	24.4%
Clifford Lee Messina (LIBERT)	1,029	2.0%
2006 PRIMARY		
Gene Green (D)		unopposed
2004 GENERAL		
Gene Green (D)	78,256	94.1%
Clifford Lee Messina (LIBERT)	4,868	5.9%

PREVIOUS WINNING PERCENTAGES
2002 (95%); 2000 (73%); 1998 (93%); 1996 (68%); 1994 (73%); 1992 (65%)

Elected 1992; 8th term

Green is a classic liberal on some issues, a business advocate on others, and a Texan to the bone. His hybrid politics embody the sometimes contradictory nature of his working-class, largely Hispanic district in oil country.

Energy issues and health care are Green's priorities. And while he operated effectively in the minority, he wasted no time in 2007 taking advantage of his newfound majority status, introducing a plethora of bills — 19 on the first day alone. Elected in 1992, two years before the Republicans took control of Congress, he knows that majority status can be fleeting. As he puts it, "Just as I found out where the restrooms were, I found that we had Newt Gingrich as a Speaker."

Although the folksy Green strays from his party on the environment, gun control, juvenile crime and selected other issues important to his constituents, he enjoys good relations with Democratic leaders, in part because he doesn't trumpet his disagreements. But that doesn't mean he doesn't feel the pull of party loyalty. Despite the presence of Shell and Exxon Mobil refineries in his district, Green voted with Democrats in early 2007 to rescind some petroleum industry tax breaks, some of which he had voted to include in a GOP energy bill in 2005.

Green said he cast his vote only after House Speaker Nancy Pelosi agreed to give him and other lawmakers from petroleum-producing districts a seat at the table as the Democrats crafted the energy legislation. Passed as part of House Democrats' "first 100 hours" agenda in the new Congress, the legislation would roll back approximately $14 billion in tax breaks and other subsidies for oil and gas companies and put the cash into a fund to promote alternatives to fossil fuels. The sum includes about $4.4 billion in royalties that Democrats are pushing the Interior Department to recover from flawed offshore drilling leases issued in 1998 and 1999.

In the 110th Congress (2007-08), Green got a special waiver to add a seat on the Foreign Affairs Committee to his committee portfolio, along with his continued service on the ethics panel.

In the 109th Congress (2005-06), Green cosponsored legislation that would have opened all U.S. offshore areas to drilling, but the measure was thwarted by Florida lawmakers. A more limited measure promoted by GOP Sen. Pete V. Domenici of New Mexico that opens only 8.3 million acres to drilling in the eastern Gulf of Mexico was enacted. Nevertheless, Green was happy to dent the two-decade old moratorium on new offshore drilling areas. "It's the best thing we've had in 20 years," he said.

Green says he likes working with Republicans, and he does so not only on energy, but also on health care. Early in 2007, he teamed up with Republican and fellow Texan Michael C. Burgess, a physician, to pass a bill to upgrade states' trauma care systems. It was a victory Green had sought for years, ever since he heard about a man, seriously injured in a car accident, who could not get treatment at an overcrowded Houston trauma center. The man had to be taken to Austin, where he died the next day.

The congressman also wants to make health care more accessible by expanding community clinics. His district, he said, does not have enough health care facilities or doctors. In the 110th Congress, as a member of the Energy and Commerce Committee, Green said he wants to reauthorize and expand the State Children's Health Insurance Program. Some states want to include families in the program — which is fine with Green — but he says he wants to make sure children are covered first.

Green introduced legislation in 2007 to attack the spread of tuberculosis. Usually, the disease appears in port cities like Houston, he says, carried from overseas. "We can actually stop TB in the country if we provide federal assistance to our local community health centers to treat it and monitor people," he says.

Green also tends to constituent needs through his annual Immunization Day, which provides free vaccinations to children, and Citizenship Day, which helps residents obtain citizenship.

Unlike some conservative Democrats, Green has opposed most GOP tax-cutting efforts. He voted against a popular bill in 2000 to cut taxes on married couples, saying it "only benefits the wealthiest of Americans and does nothing to help the working folks in my district." In 2001 and 2003, he opposed President Bush's signature tax cuts for much the same reason, although he did support the 2004 corporate tax cut package.

Green has opposed most trade bills, reflecting the views of workers in his blue-collar district. He voted against the North American Free Trade Agreement in 1993, despite support for it from Houston's business community, and he opposed the Central American Free Trade Agreement in 2005.

Although he votes with his party more often than most white Southern Democrats, party leaders cannot take Green for granted. He voted for Republican-sponsored legislation to toughen criminal penalties for violent juvenile offenders and to overhaul public housing policies. He joins with Republicans in opposing new Environmental Protection Agency clean air standards that would affect Houston. He generally opposes gun control proposals, and he has sided with social conservatives to support the display of the Ten Commandments in public schools and government buildings.

On abortion, Green's current view differs from his earlier position. In February 1992, a month before his first House primary, he dropped his opposition to abortion when he came under attack for having sponsored anti-abortion bills in the state legislature. Green said he had gradually changed his views on abortion, but critics said he changed his mind to enhance his prospects of winning the congressional seat. In 2002 and 2003, he voted against banning a procedure critics call "partial birth" abortion.

Green won a hard-fought five-way primary in 1992, besting Houston City Council member Ben Reyes in two runoffs — the first was voided after election officials found some Republicans had illegally crossed over and cast ballots. Green won the general election with 65 percent of the vote in the largely Democratic 29th District. Although it is a Hispanic-majority district, Green has not faced a serious primary or general-election challenge since then.

KEY VOTES

2006

- No — Stop broadband companies from favoring select Internet traffic
- Yes — Affirm U.S. commitment to war in Iraq and reject setting a withdrawal date for troops
- No — Repeal requirement for bilingual ballots at the polls
- Yes — Permit U.S. sale of civilian nuclear technology to India
- No — Build a 700-mile fence on the U.S.-Mexico border to curb illegal crossings
- No — Permit warrantless wiretaps of suspected terrorists

2005

- ? — Intervene in the life-support case of Terri Schiavo
- Yes — Lift President Bush's restrictions on stem cell research funding
- Yes — Prohibit FBI access to library and bookstore records
- No — Approve free-trade pact with five Central American countries
- Yes — Pass energy policy overhaul favored by President Bush emphasizing domestic oil and gas production
- No — End mandatory preservation of habitat of endangered animal and plant species
- Yes — Ban torture of prisoners in U.S. custody

CQ VOTE STUDIES

	PARTY UNITY		PRESIDENTIAL SUPPORT	
	Support	Oppose	Support	Oppose
2006	84%	16%	43%	57%
2005	82%	18%	35%	65%
2004	87%	13%	27%	73%
2003	85%	15%	28%	72%
2002	86%	14%	31%	69%

INTEREST GROUPS

	AFL-CIO	ADA	CCUS	ACU
2006	100%	85%	50%	33%
2005	100%	100%	48%	28%
2004	93%	85%	45%	20%
2003	93%	85%	43%	36%
2002	100%	90%	35%	16%

TEXAS 29

Part of Houston and eastern suburbs — most of Pasadena and Baytown

The blue-collar, Hispanic-majority 29th arcs from northern to southeastern Houston, with an eastern tail that extends to Baytown. The district is full of refineries and factories that employ many union workers, who contribute to making the 29th solidly Democratic, despite traditionally poor voter turnout in the Hispanic community.

The 29th includes one-fifth of Harris County's population, and slightly more than half of the district's residents live in Houston. It takes in most of the Houston Ship Channel, which handles high levels of both foreign and domestic traffic, and picks up most of middle-class Channelview. The heart of Houston's $15 billion petrochemical complex is along the channel, which has caused concern among residents about possible health effects of living so close to such a thriving industrial corridor.

The 29th also includes working-class areas outside of the Interstate 610 loop such as Jacinto City, Galena Park, South Houston and much of Pasadena (shared with the 22nd) and Baytown (shared with the 2nd).

The Hispanic majority increased here in redistricting prior to the 2004 election, and Hispanics now make up two-thirds of the district's population. The heaviest concentrations of Hispanics are in South Houston, Jacinto City, Houston and Pasadena. According to 2000 census data, nearly one-quarter of district residents are not U.S. citizens, the highest percentage in Texas, and 60 percent speak a language other than English at home.

The 29th has the largest blue-collar workforce and the lowest high school graduation rate (50 percent of the over-25 population) in Texas. One-third of district residents are age 17 or under, the highest percentage in the state.

MAJOR INDUSTRY

Petrochemicals, energy, construction, shipping

CITIES

Houston (pt.), 334,766; Pasadena (pt.), 84,654; Baytown (pt.), 35,003

NOTABLE

The Battleship Texas, docked at the San Jacinto Battleground state park, became the nation's first battleship memorial museum in 1948.

Rep. Eddie Bernice Johnson (D)

CAPITOL OFFICE
225-8885
rep.e.b.johnson@mail.house.gov
www.house.gov/ebjohnson
1511 Longworth 20515-4330; fax 226-1477

COMMITTEES
Science & Technology
Transportation & Infrastructure
(Water Resources & Environment - chairwoman)

RESIDENCE
Dallas

BORN
Dec. 3, 1935, Waco, Texas

RELIGION
Baptist

FAMILY
Divorced; one child

EDUCATION
Texas Christian U., B.S. 1967 (nursing); Southern Methodist U., M.P.A. 1976

CAREER
Business relocation company owner; nurse; U.S. Health, Education & Welfare Department official

POLITICAL HIGHLIGHTS
Texas House, 1973-77; Texas Senate, 1987-93

ELECTION RESULTS

2006 GENERAL		
Eddie Bernice Johnson (D)	81,348	80.2%
Wilson Aurbach (R)	17,850	17.6%
Ken Ashby (LIBERT)	2,250	2.2%
2006 PRIMARY		
Eddie Bernice Johnson (D)		unopposed
2004 GENERAL		
Eddie Bernice Johnson (D)	144,513	93.0%
John Davis (LIBERT)	10,821	7.0%

PREVIOUS WINNING PERCENTAGES
2002 (74%); 2000 (92%); 1998 (72%); 1996 (55%); 1994 (73%); 1992 (72%)

Elected 1992; 8th term

As a young girl attending segregated schools in Waco, Johnson's goal was to go to medical school and become a doctor. But she was encouraged by her high school counselor to become a nurse because "nurses were more feminine." Although she never fulfilled her dream of getting a medical degree, Johnson has been a trailblazer for women and minorities in politics. The first African-American elected to represent Dallas in Congress, Johnson has a strong commitment to liberal social causes. Yet she is pragmatic enough to compromise with Republicans to get bills passed and to reach out to business interests that can help her district.

Johnson has yet to make it to a top committee, and she has made known her interest in serving on Ways and Means.

In 2007, Johnson became chairwoman of the Transportation panel's Water Resources and Environment Subcommittee. The subcommittee quickly produced a number of clean water and water development measures, including a massive $14 billion bill that passed the House to authorize hundreds of water projects. Included was $298 million for a project on the Trinity River in the Dallas area.

In spite of her liberal profile, Johnson casts some pro-business votes. Breaking ranks with organized labor, she supported legislation in 2000 granting China permanent normal trade status. "Trade with China means jobs for North Texas, growth for Dallas-Fort Worth and the export of American values to the world's most populous nation," she said.

Johnson hopes her legacy in Congress will include steering the liberal Congressional Black Caucus toward effective coalitions with business groups rather than relying exclusively on its traditional allies in labor, the clergy and civil rights. As its chairwoman in 2001 and 2002, she hosted the caucus' first technology and energy summits to bridge the digital divide in poor communities and to encourage minority students to study science.

On the Science and Technology Committee, she emphasizes the importance of federal investment in scientific research. Johnson has lobbied for a federal grant program to encourage children to study math and science, and for the expansion of minority participation in science research.

Yet she retains an allegiance to the caucus' core civil rights mission. Johnson fought changes proposed by some Southern Republicans to the Voting Rights Act, which the House considered in 2006. GOP leaders had been expecting a routine vote to extend the act for 25 years when a coalition of Republicans from Georgia and Texas raised an uproar over a section renewing the requirement that certain states get permission from the Justice Department to make changes in their election laws or procedures. The objectors said it was unfair to impose pre-clearance requirements on select states. Johnson disagreed, and told the Dallas Morning News, "Unfortunately, we still have people who'd rather not have minorities vote."

Also in 2006, Johnson was arrested for disorderly conduct with six other caucus members at the Sudanese embassy in Washington while protesting the genocide in Darfur by Janjaweed militias under the control of the Sudanese government.

From her seat on Transportation, Johnson has been instrumental in bringing federal dollars to the nearby Dallas-Fort Worth International Airport. She has played a key role in the longstanding battle over additional flights in and out of Dallas Love Field. The airport is the headquarters for Southwest Airlines and the company has long sought repeal of the law prohibiting long-haul flights from the airport. Johnson had backed the law, known as the Wright amendment, after its author, former Speaker Jim Wright of Texas, arguing that Congress should not get involved without a local agreement. In 2006, after key players, including Southwest and American airlines, reached a compromise to phase out the restrictions, Johnson backed legislation to implement the deal and helped round up votes on Capitol Hill.

During the 108th Congress (2003-04), Johnson generated some controversy when a former aide accused her of discrimination. After failing to get the federal lawsuit dismissed on technical grounds, Johnson employed an unusual legal strategy, invoking Congress' constitutional protection from being questioned about "speech or debate" and asserting that the former aide's duties were "directly related to the due functioning of the legislative process." An appeals court ruled that lawmakers can mount a defense by claiming that employment decisions were based on legislative concerns.

When Johnson finished high school, her father, a government worker, insisted she go to college. She completed an undergraduate degree in nursing, and went on to get a master's in public administration from Southern Methodist University. Eventually, she rose to be chief psychiatric nurse at the Veterans Administration Hospital in Dallas.

She won her election to the state House in 1972 — the first black woman from Dallas to achieve the distinction — and began getting invitations to places she would otherwise not be welcome in a city where government and business were dominated by white men. "I'd get these invitations that would be from the insurance club or stuff like that where women didn't go, and I'd show up," she said. "They couldn't turn me away, [and] I didn't back down."

In the late 1970s, she turned to private business, setting up Eddie Bernice Johnson and Associates, which helped businesses expand or relocate in the Dallas-Fort Worth area. She continued to run the business after her 1986 election to the state Senate, and expanded the company's reach in 1988 to include airport concessions management. She was so adept at wielding power in the state legislature that she ran for the U.S. House in 1992 by drawing a district preordained to elect her.

Johnson generally has won re-election with ease. Initially, her electoral fate was caught up in the judicial and legislative wrangling over minority-majority House districts, including the 30th. After the U.S. Supreme Court in 1996 threw out some House districts in Texas as "racial gerrymanders," Johnson landed in a substantially redrawn district that was 42 percent new to her. But she captured a 55 percent majority in an eight-person contest, and has won by wide margins since.

KEY VOTES

2006

No Stop broadband companies from favoring select Internet traffic

No Affirm U.S. commitment to war in Iraq and reject setting a withdrawal date for troops

No Repeal requirement for bilingual ballots at the polls

Yes Permit U.S. sale of civilian nuclear technology to India

No Build a 700-mile fence on the U.S.-Mexico border to curb illegal crossings

No Permit warrantless wiretaps of suspected terrorists

2005

? Intervene in the life-support case of Terri Schiavo

Yes Lift President Bush's restrictions on stem cell research funding

Yes Prohibit FBI access to library and bookstore records

No Approve free-trade pact with five Central American countries

Yes Pass energy policy overhaul favored by President Bush emphasizing domestic oil and gas production

No End mandatory preservation of habitat of endangered animal and plant species

Yes Ban torture of prisoners in U.S. custody

CQ VOTE STUDIES

	PARTY UNITY		PRESIDENTIAL SUPPORT	
	Support	Oppose	Support	Oppose
2006	94%	6%	35%	65%
2005	96%	4%	14%	86%
2004	93%	7%	34%	66%
2003	96%	4%	20%	80%
2002	95%	5%	22%	78%

INTEREST GROUPS

	AFL-CIO	ADA	CCUS	ACU
2006	100%	95%	60%	16%
2005	100%	100%	37%	0%
2004	87%	100%	63%	17%
2003	100%	95%	34%	20%
2002	89%	95%	45%	0%

TEXAS 30

Downtown Dallas and southern suburbs

Confined to Dallas County, the 30th stretches from Dallas Love Field southeast into downtown Dallas. It then dips south to take in some suburbs, such as Lancaster, where many black families have relocated after leaving the city. Black residents account for 41 percent of the population — the highest percentage in any Texas district — and, combined with the 34 percent of residents who are Hispanic, minorities make up more than three-fourths of the 30th's population.

Love Field, an alternative to the large Dallas-Fort Worth International Airport (in the 24th and 26th), is a hub for Southwest Airlines, a low-cost airline whose headquarters are in the 30th. The airport will be introducing new service over the next several years as federal restrictions on flight patterns and regional-only service are phased out. Some local officials expect these changes to accommodate increased air travel demand from a growing population. As the population has swelled, road congestion and air pollution have become concerns.

Although only a slight majority of district residents hold white-collar jobs, the Dallas-Fort Worth Metroplex is a banking, high-tech and transportation center. The district is home to several Fortune 500 firms, including Southwest, home-building company Centex and energy provider TXU. Downtown Dallas attracts visitors to the American Airlines Center, which is home to basketball's Mavericks and hockey's Stars, and the historic Cotton Bowl continues to host college football games.

The only Democratic district in the Dallas-Fort Worth area, the 30th gave Democratic challenger Chris Bell 63 percent of the vote in the 2006 gubernatorial race, his highest percentage in the state. The 30th also was John Kerry's best Texas district (75 percent) in the 2004 presidential election. Democrats run strongly in the heavily black precincts just south of Illinois Avenue, and in largely Hispanic precincts near Love Field.

MAJOR INDUSTRY

Transportation, banking, technology

CITIES

Dallas (pt.), 533,878; DeSoto, 37,646; Lancaster, 25,894

NOTABLE

Dealey Plaza and the Texas School Book Depository, where John F. Kennedy was assassinated in 1963; The flagship Neiman Marcus store still operates at the downtown Dallas location where it opened in 1914.

Rep. John Carter (R)

CAPITOL OFFICE
225-3864
www.house.gov/carter
408 Cannon 20515-4331; fax 225-5886

COMMITTEES
Appropriations

RESIDENCE
Round Rock

BORN
Nov. 6, 1941, Houston, Texas

RELIGION
Lutheran

FAMILY
Wife, Erika Carter; four children

EDUCATION
Texas Technological College, B.A. 1964 (history); U. of Texas, J.D. 1969

CAREER
Lawyer; state legislative aide

POLITICAL HIGHLIGHTS
Candidate for Texas House, 1980; Texas District Court judge, 1981-2001

ELECTION RESULTS

2006 GENERAL		
John Carter (R)	90,869	58.5%
Mary Beth Harrell (D)	60,293	38.8%
Matt McAdoo (LIBERT)	4,221	2.7%
2006 PRIMARY		
John Carter (R)		unopposed
2004 GENERAL		
John Carter (R)	160,247	64.8%
Jon Porter (D)	80,292	32.5%
Celeste Adams (LIBERT)	6,888	2.8%

PREVIOUS WINNING PERCENTAGES
2002 (69%)

Elected 2002; 3rd term

A true party loyalist, Carter ascended to a leadership spot in the 110th Congress (2007-08) with election by his peers as GOP Conference secretary. Carter had been a close ally of the powerful former Majority Leader Tom DeLay of Texas, and his entry into the leadership shows his ability to stand on his own after DeLay's departure amid an ethics scandal in 2006.

Carter belongs to the Republican Study Committee, a group of the most conservative members of the House. Though the group bucks the leadership on a regular basis to promote conservative principles, Carter usually sticks with his party; in the 109th Congress (2005-06), he voted the GOP line 98 percent of the time on votes that pitted the majority of his party against the majority of Democrats. He is also a staunch supporter of the Bush administration on the war in Iraq.

A district court judge for many years before he came to the House, Carter is a law-and-order conservative who is called "Judge," a nickname given to him by former House Speaker J. Dennis Hastert. He successfully lobbied for an amendment to apply the death penalty for an act of terrorism that results in deaths. It was passed as part of the 2005 reauthorization of the Patriot Act, the nation's cornerstone anti-terrorism law. In 2004, the president signed into law his bill creating a felony crime of "aggravated identity theft" for bank, wire or mail fraud involving identity theft.

He calls border security his top priority, and he actively opposes President Bush's proposal to allow some illegal immigrants to remain in the United States under a new guest worker program. He also opposed renewing parts of the 1965 Voting Rights Act requiring foreign language assistance at the polls. "I simply believe you should be able to read, write and speak English to be a voter in the United States," Carter said. That stance brought him a rebuke from the Austin American-Statesman, which editorialized that voting rights should be determined by citizenship, not literacy.

Carter has been an appropriator since 2005, and despite his conservatism, he joined other appropriators in resisting calls for reform of earmarks, the special projects tucked into the government spending bills to help individual lawmakers. He was one of only 24 Republicans who voted against a 2006 resolution requiring the Appropriations subcommittees to identify earmarks and their sponsors.

Carter holds one of two seats Texas was given as a result of population gains in the 1990s, and he came to the House as an ally of DeLay, who, like him, is from Houston. When DeLay ran into trouble with a campaign fundraising investigation in Texas, Carter was one of only 20 Republicans to vote in 2005 to retain Republican-written rules that allowed leaders to keep their jobs if indicted. The rules were later withdrawn. Interviewed on the CBS television program "60 Minutes," Carter said the fundraising probe was politically motivated. "A good district attorney can indict a ham sandwich if he wants to, and Mr. [Ronnie] Earle understands that," Carter said. "The accusations harm, as much as the convictions."

His association with DeLay brought him some negative press. Carter was among eight lawmakers, including DeLay, who accepted trips to South Korea from a registered foreign agent, despite House rules prohibiting the practice. The lawmakers said they were unaware that the organization that paid for the trip was an agent of the South Korean government.

Carter arrived on Capitol Hill in 2003 at age 61, older than many newcomers and more politically seasoned as an elected state judge for two decades. While he was a trial court judge, Carter helped found the Williamson County Juvenile Academy, which he calls a "quasi-military boot camp and alternative education program."

He grew up comfortably as the son of John J. Carter, the general manager of Humble Oil and Refining Co., the precursor to Exxon. His father, from Kentucky, started at the company as a bookkeeper, rose to manager of the natural gas division and married his secretary, Carter's mother.

Carter's first job was at age 14, working in a laundry on Saturdays. Later in high school, he worked summers on oil and gas pipelines. After graduating from Bellaire High School in Houston, Carter and a bunch of his friends chose to attend Texas Tech University in Lubbock.

He says he developed his conservative philosophy through his studies and friendships in college. As a law student at the University of Texas at Austin, Carter says, he was one of a handful of conservatives. "I think I had the only Goldwater button in law school. I got criticized by several professors," Carter notes, and they weren't all just teasing.

During a summer in Holland, working on a pipeline project for Bechtel Corp., Carter rented a flat and fell in love with the landlady's sister, Erika, and married her in 1968. He took a job as a counsel for the Texas legislature, and "kind of got bit by the bug," he says. He moved his family to the small town of Round Rock, set up a law practice, and in 1980 ran unsuccessfully for a seat in the Texas House. He had given up his law practice for a year and the family lived off their savings. After the loss, Carter resumed his practice, but it didn't take long for fortune to swing in his favor.

In 1981, he was appointed district court judge of Williamson County, and he then won election to the position in 1982. "I was the first Republican to win in Williamson County. And now there are no Democrats in our county," Carter says. "I was very active in building the Republican Party. Some call me the Godfather of the Republican Party in Williamson County."

He left the bench after 20 years to run for Congress, Carter says, because of the terrorist attacks of Sept. 11, 2001. "They blew up the World Trade Center. It's that simple," he said.

In his first House race in 2002, Carter competed in an eight-person field in the Republican primary. He finished second behind Houston oil executive Peter Wareing, then prevailed in the runoff election with 57 percent of the vote. In the general election, Carter easily defeated Democratic computer consultant David Bagley with 69 percent. He won in 2004 with nearly 65 percent of the vote, and in 2006 he took more than 58 percent.

KEY VOTES

2006

- No Stop broadband companies from favoring select Internet traffic
- \+ Affirm U.S. commitment to war in Iraq and reject setting a withdrawal date for troops
- Yes Repeal requirement for bilingual ballots at the polls
- Yes Permit U.S. sale of civilian nuclear technology to India
- Yes Build a 700-mile fence on the U.S.-Mexico border to curb illegal crossings
- Yes Permit warrantless wiretaps of suspected terrorists

2005

- Yes Intervene in the life-support case of Terri Schiavo
- No Lift President Bush's restrictions on stem cell research funding
- No Prohibit FBI access to library and bookstore records
- Yes Approve free-trade pact with five Central American countries
- Yes Pass energy policy overhaul favored by President Bush emphasizing domestic oil and gas production
- Yes End mandatory preservation of habitat of endangered animal and plant species
- No Ban torture of prisoners in U.S. custody

CQ VOTE STUDIES

	PARTY UNITY		PRESIDENTIAL SUPPORT	
	Support	Oppose	Support	Oppose
2006	97%	3%	95%	5%
2005	98%	2%	93%	7%
2004	98%	2%	94%	6%
2003	99%	1%	94%	6%

INTEREST GROUPS

	AFL-CIO	ADA	CCUS	ACU
2006	15%	0%	100%	88%
2005	13%	0%	89%	92%
2004	7%	0%	100%	96%
2003	0%	5%	100%	88%

TEXAS 31

East central – north Austin suburbs, Killeen

The solidly Republican 31st is made up of suburbs and rural areas extending from the northern Austin suburbs through fertile agricultural land in central Texas to Erath County, located about 60 miles southwest of Fort Worth.

In the south, the district takes in Williamson County, its largest population base and one of Texas' fastest-growing areas. A flourishing suburban enclave north of Austin, the county enjoys a growing, diversified economy that continues to attract new residents. Computer giant Dell and TECO-Westinghouse Motor Company are based in Round Rock and propel the thriving local technology and manufacturing sectors.

The 31st's other main population center is Bell County, located just north of Williamson. Fort Hood, a massive Army base near Killeen that is split with Coryell County, is a crucial part of the area economy. The base is slated to lose a few thousand jobs as part of the 2005 BRAC round, but it still will retain about 40,000 personnel. Six state correctional facilities in Coryell County also create area jobs.

Agriculture, especially dairy and grains, is an economic staple in rural Erath and Hamilton counties in the district's north. Cattle and poultry ranches and farms growing corn and sorghum dot the landscape of eastern counties. The discovery of a large deposit of lignite in southern Milam County led Aluminum Company of America (ALCOA) to locate its largest U.S. smelting plant near Rockdale a half-century ago; the plant is still churning out raw aluminum and employs more than 1,000 people.

The 31st strongly favors Republicans in both its rural and suburban areas. Rural Erath County, the northernmost county in the district, gave George W. Bush 77 percent of its 2004 presidential vote, and Bush took 65 percent in Williamson County and 66 percent of the 31st's vote overall.

MAJOR INDUSTRY

Technology, manufacturing, military, agriculture

MILITARY BASES

Fort Hood (Army), 45,000 military, 4,000 civilian (2006)

CITIES

Killeen, 86,911; Round Rock (pt.), 60,060; Temple, 54,514

NOTABLE

Former baseball pitcher Nolan Ryan owns the Round Rock Express, a minor-league affiliate of the Houston Astros.

Rep. Pete Sessions (R)

CAPITOL OFFICE
225-2231
petes@mail.house.gov
sessions.house.gov
1514 Longworth 20515-4332; fax 225-5878

COMMITTEES
Rules

RESIDENCE
Dallas

BORN
March 22, 1955, Waco, Texas

RELIGION
United Methodist

FAMILY
Wife, Nete Sessions; two children

EDUCATION
Southwest Texas State U., attended 1973-74; Southwestern U., B.S. 1978 (political science)

CAREER
Public policy analyst; telephone company executive

POLITICAL HIGHLIGHTS
Sought Republican nomination for U.S. House (special election), 1991; Republican nominee for U.S. House, 1994

ELECTION RESULTS

2006 GENERAL		
Pete Sessions (R)	71,461	56.4%
Will Pryor (D)	52,269	41.3%
John B. Hawley (LIBERT)	2,922	2.3%
2006 PRIMARY		
Pete Sessions (R)		unopposed
2004 GENERAL		
Pete Sessions (R)	109,859	54.3%
Martin Frost (D)	89,030	44.0%
Michael D. Needleman (LIBERT)	3,347	1.7%

PREVIOUS WINNING PERCENTAGES
2002 (68%); 2000 (54%); 1998 (56%); 1996 (53%)

Elected 1996; 6th term

Sessions is all conservative and all Texan. He chairs a group called the House Results Caucus, whose motto is, "Give the government the money it needs, but not a penny more." He favors "outsourcing" some government functions to take advantage of lower costs and private sector innovation. He wants a crackdown on illegal immigration.

His speech is pure Texas drawl. He sometimes greets visitors to his office wearing a cowboy hat and offering a cup of hot chocolate, his favorite drink, while a photographer snaps a picture of Sessions and his guest for his growing wall collection.

Sessions' wife, Nete, and their two sons live in Dallas. He pulls out a photo of his wife, who is Mexican, when asked about his political appeal to the 36 percent of his constituents who are Hispanic and vote mainly Democratic. "I am very aware of Hispanic needs and am in tune with their needs as parents on the issues of jobs, health care, and education," he says.

Although he is a fierce partisan on most matters, there is one issue on which Sessions regularly reaches across the aisle. The father of a son who has Down syndrome, Sessions since 2000 has joined with liberal Democratic Rep. Henry A. Waxman of California in an effort to help families with incomes above the poverty line buy into Medicaid coverage for children with special needs. "I know firsthand why families with disabled children are turning down jobs, turning down overtime and are unable to earn enough money to adequately provide for their family — just so their child can qualify for Medicaid," Sessions said.

The bill passed in 2006 and was signed into law. It had come close to passing in the previous Congress but hit a snag when GOP leaders balked at its $900 million price tag and insisted on compensating cuts in other social programs. Reducing ongoing programs for other disabled patients or foster care was an unacceptable choice to many cosponsors, and the bill died.

Sessions has been a reliable vote for his party and has survived several tough elections, but he was unable to break into the Republican leadership in the 110th Congress (2007-08). He ran for chairman of the National Republican Congressional Committee, the campaign arm of the House GOP that raises money and recruits candidates. The post instead went to Tom Cole of Oklahoma, who had more experience in organizing campaigns as a former NRCC executive director and chief of staff of the Republican National Committee. But Sessions made a respectable showing, attracting 81 votes to 102 for Cole on a second ballot. Both are members of the conservative Republican Study Committee; they beat out moderate Rep. Phil English of Pennsylvania on the first ballot.

Although Sessions lost that contest, he retained his seat on the Rules Committee, giving him a role in the minority party's legislative strategy. The leadership-driven panel determines which bills get to the floor and the ground rules for debating them. Sessions was awarded a seat on the panel in his second term; he remains on leave from the Financial Services Committee, where he had served as freshman.

If Cole has more experience running campaigns, Sessions has had more experience surviving them. The son of former FBI Director William S. Sessions, it took him three tries to win election to the House. And once he got there, he changed districts.

In his first attempt, in 1991, he came in sixth in a special election to succeed 3rd District GOP Rep. Steve Bartlett, who left to run for mayor of Dallas. On his second try, in 1994, Sessions quit his job as a Bell telephone executive to run in the 5th District against incumbent Democrat John Bryant. He lost, 50 percent to 47 percent. After that, Sessions spent some time as vice president for public policy at the National Center for Policy Analysis, a Dallas-based conservative think tank.

His third try came in 1996, when Bryant left his 5th District seat to run for the Senate. This time, Sessions won with 53 percent of the vote against John Pouland, a former Dallas County Democratic chairman.

Following the 2000 census, Texas districts were redrawn to reflect population shifts. Although fellow Republicans were not pleased, Sessions abandoned the 5th District seat to run in the new 32nd District, which had more Republican voters. He said at the time that it was more compact and would require less campaign travel, which was important to his family life. Sessions cruised to victory in the new district with 68 percent of the vote, a career high for him. (Jeb Hensarling kept the 5th in the GOP column.)

Things didn't remain static for long. In 2003, state Republicans, led by then House Majority Leader Tom DeLay, redrew the map again, with the aim of expanding the GOP majority in Congress. The new boundaries eliminated 13-term Democrat Martin Frost's Dallas/Fort Worth-based district, and threw him in direct competition with Sessions in the 32nd.

That touched off the costliest election of 2004. The Sessions-Frost matchup provoked a media frenzy, and money poured in from around the country. Expenditures reached the $9 million mark, with Sessions spending $4.4 million, and Frost a little more than that at $4.6 million. Sessions prevailed with 54 percent to Frost's 44 percent.

The map was challenged as unconstitutionally diluting minority voting strength, in part for the way it broke up Frost's heavily minority district and appended pieces of it to five other districts, including Sessions', that leaned Republican and were mostly white. But the U.S. Supreme Court ultimately rejected those claims in July 2006, leaving most of the GOP map intact.

As in the 2004 primary, Sessions did not face a challenger in the 2006 primary. He took the general election with more than 56 percent of the vote.

Born in Waco, the son of a former federal judge and FBI director, Sessions was educated at Southwestern University in Georgetown, Texas. After college, he went to work at Southwestern Bell Telephone Co. and Bell Communications Research.

KEY VOTES

2006

- No Stop broadband companies from favoring select Internet traffic
- ? Affirm U.S. commitment to war in Iraq and reject setting a withdrawal date for troops
- ? Repeal requirement for bilingual ballots at the polls
- Yes Permit U.S. sale of civilian nuclear technology to India
- Yes Build a 700-mile fence on the U.S.-Mexico border to curb illegal crossings
- Yes Permit warrantless wiretaps of suspected terrorists

2005

- ? Intervene in the life-support case of Terri Schiavo
- No Lift President Bush's restrictions on stem cell research funding
- ? Prohibit FBI access to library and bookstore records
- Yes Approve free-trade pact with five Central American countries
- Yes Pass energy policy overhaul favored by President Bush emphasizing domestic oil and gas production
- Yes End mandatory preservation of habitat of endangered animal and plant species
- No Ban torture of prisoners in U.S. custody

CQ VOTE STUDIES

	PARTY UNITY		PRESIDENTIAL SUPPORT	
	Support	Oppose	Support	Oppose
2006	98%	2%	100%	0%
2005	99%	1%	90%	10%
2004	99%	1%	94%	6%
2003	99%	1%	98%	2%
2002	99%	1%	87%	13%

INTEREST GROUPS

	AFL-CIO	ADA	CCUS	ACU
2006	10%	0%	100%	96%
2005	13%	0%	93%	100%
2004	13%	0%	100%	100%
2003	0%	5%	100%	88%
2002	13%	0%	100%	100%

TEXAS 32
Northern Dallas; most of Irving and Richardson

The hook-shaped 32nd is located in northern and western Dallas County and essentially encircles downtown Dallas. It includes a chunk of the city and part of Dallas' northern and western suburbs. Although it does not include downtown, the 32nd is home to much of the Dallas business community. Many district residents work downtown, and several Fortune 500 companies are located off the Lyndon B. Johnson Freeway, which runs as the northwestern border of the district.

Beginning southwest of downtown, in the Hispanic area of Oak Cliff, the district moves west through heavily Hispanic areas in Cockrell Hill and a section of Grand Prairie into the southern part of Irving (shared with the 24th). South Irving has a vibrant Hispanic population, while central Irving is becoming increasingly white with a blue-collar middle class. North Irving is home to high-income, technology-oriented professionals in Las Colinas, where many large companies, such as ExxonMobil, are based.

The district then curves east to re-enter Dallas and also take in the exclusive "Park Cities," made up of Highland Park and University Park. This area, almost entirely white, has its own school system and local government and is home to Southern Methodist University (SMU).

The 32nd continues north to the county line, through less exclusive neighborhoods. The metropolitan area's "telecom corridor" also is in northern Dallas, with Texas Instruments, the standard-bearer, based just outside the district in the 3rd. Many TI employees reside in the 32nd, and Richardson (shared with the 3rd) is an emerging technology and finance community. Many residents work at Dallas-Forth Worth International Airport or Dallas Love Field airport, both of which border the 32nd.

The 32nd is solidly Republican. George W. Bush took 59 percent of the presidential vote here in 2004. The GOP is particularly strong in the wealthy communities near SMU, while Democrats do well in the far southern reaches of the district near downtown Dallas.

MAJOR INDUSTRY
Telecommunications, oil, retail, higher education

CITIES
Dallas (pt.), 393,211; Irving (pt.), 131,860; Richardson (pt.), 70,890

NOTABLE
Texas Stadium, the Dallas Cowboys' current home, is in Irving.

UTAH

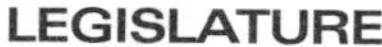

Gov. Jon Huntsman Jr. (R)

First elected: 2004
Length of term: 4 years
Term expires: 1/09
Salary: $126,000
Phone: (801) 538-1000

Residence: Salt Lake City

Born: March 26, 1960; Palo Alto, Calif.

Religion: Mormon

Family: Wife, Mary Kaye Huntsman; seven children

Education: U. of Utah, attended 1981-84; U. of Pennsylvania, B.A. 1987 (international politics)

Career: Chemical company CEO; U.S. Commerce Department official

Political highlights: U.S. ambassador to Singapore, 1992-93; deputy U.S. trade representative, 2001-03

Election results:

2004 GENERAL		
Jon Huntsman Jr. (R)	531,190	57.7%
Scott M. Matheson Jr. (D)	380,359	41.3%

Lt. Gov. Gary R. Herbert (R)

First elected: 2004
Length of term: 4 years
Term expires: 1/09
Salary: $98,900
Phone: (801) 538-1000

LEGISLATURE

Legislature: 45 days yearly January-March

Senate: 29 members, 4-year terms
2007 ratios: 21 R, 8 D; 26 men, 3 women
Salary: $130/day in session
Phone: (801) 538-1035

House: 75 members, 2-year terms
2007 ratios: 55 R, 20 D; 60 men, 15 women
Salary: $130/day in session
Phone: (801) 538-1029

TERM LIMITS

Governor: No
Senate: No
House: No

URBAN STATISTICS

CITY	POPULATION
Salt Lake City	181,743
West Valley City	108,896
Provo	105,166
Sandy	88,418
Orem	84,324

REGISTERED VOTERS

Registration by party began in May 1999, however, not all voters have declared an affiliation and the numbers are kept on a county basis.

POPULATION

2006 population (est.)	2,550,063
2000 population	2,233,169
1990 population	1,722,850
Percent change (1990-2000)	+29.6%
Rank among states (2006)	34
Median age	27.1
Born in state	62.9%
Foreign born	7.1%
Violent crime rate	256/100,000
Poverty level	9.4%
Federal workers	32,961
Military	16,621

ELECTIONS

STATE ELECTION OFFICIAL
(801) 538-1041

DEMOCRATIC PARTY
(801) 328-1212

REPUBLICAN PARTY
(801) 533-9777

MISCELLANEOUS

Web: www.utah.gov
Capital: Salt Lake City

U.S. CONGRESS

Senate: 2 Republicans
House: 2 Republicans, 1 Democrat

2000 Census Statistics by District

DIST.	2004 VOTE FOR PRESIDENT BUSH	KERRY	WHITE	BLACK	ASIAN	HISP	MEDIAN INCOME	WHITE COLLAR	BLUE COLLAR	SERVICE INDUSTRY	OVER 64	UNDER 18	COLLEGE EDUCATION	RURAL	SQ. MILES
1	73%	25%	83%	1%	2%	11%	$45,058	59%	27%	14%	9%	32%	25%	11%	20,768
2	66	31	88	1	2	6	$45,583	66	21	14	11	30	31	15	45,624
3	77	20	85	0	2	10	$46,568	60	27	14	6	35	22	9	15,751
STATE	72	26	85	1	2	9	$45,726	61	25	14	9	32	26	12	82,144
U.S.	50.7	48.3	69	12	4	13	$41,994	60	25	15	12	26	24	21	3,537,438

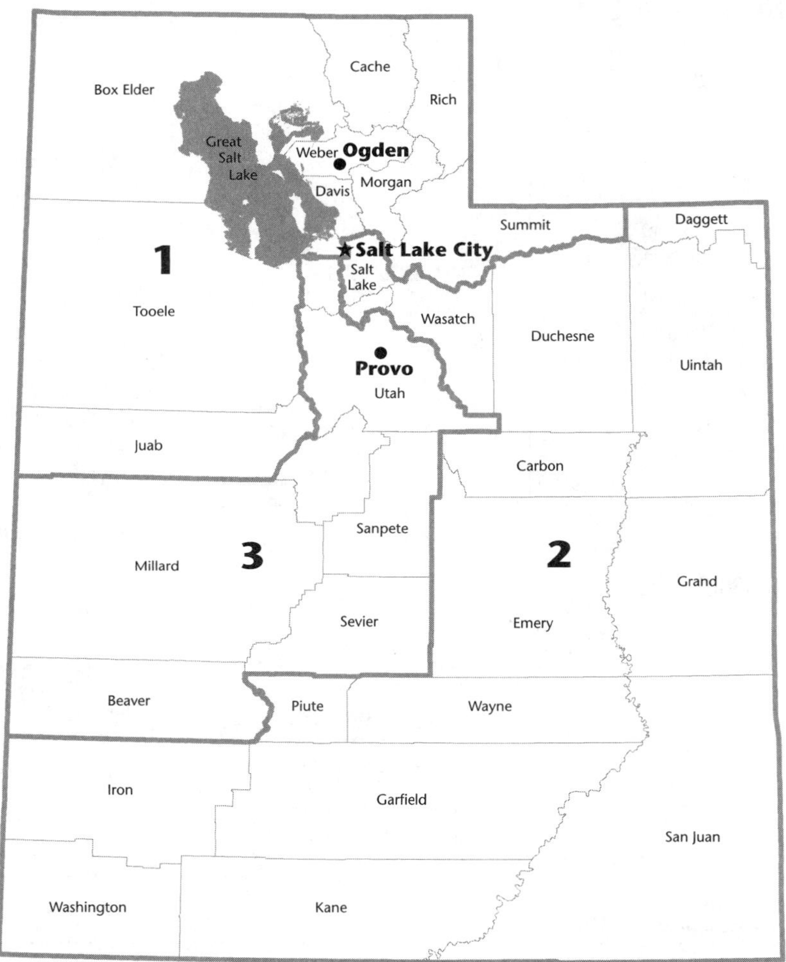
Cache
Box Elder
Rich
Great Salt Lake
Weber
Ogden
Morgan
Davis
Summit
Daggett
1
Salt Lake City
Salt Lake
Tooele
Wasatch
Duchesne
Provo
Utah
Uintah
Juab
Carbon
Sanpete
3
2
Millard
Grand
Sevier
Emery
Beaver
Piute
Wayne
Iron
Garfield
San Juan
Washington
Kane

Sen. Orrin G. Hatch (R)

CAPITOL OFFICE
224-5251
hatch.senate.gov
104 Hart 20510-4402; fax 224-6331

COMMITTEES
Finance
Health, Education, Labor & Pensions
Judiciary
Select Intelligence
Joint Taxation

RESIDENCE
Salt Lake City

BORN
March 22, 1934, Pittsburgh, Pa.

RELIGION
Mormon

FAMILY
Wife, Elaine Hatch; six children

EDUCATION
Brigham Young U., B.S. 1959 (history);
U. of Pittsburgh, J.D. 1962

CAREER
Lawyer

POLITICAL HIGHLIGHTS
Sought Republican nomination for president, 2000

ELECTION RESULTS

2006 GENERAL		
Orrin G. Hatch (R)	356,238	62.4%
Pete Ashdown (D)	177,459	31.1%
Scott N. Bradley (CNSTP)	21,526	3.8%
Roger I. Price (PC)	9,089	1.6%
2006 PRIMARY		
Orrin G. Hatch (R)		unopposed

PREVIOUS WINNING PERCENTAGES
2000 (66%); 1994 (69%); 1988 (67%); 1982 (58%); 1976 (54%)

Elected 1976; 6th term

Nothing more aptly characterizes Hatch than the title of his autobiography, "The Square Peg." A conservative Republican, he is a close friend of liberal Senate icon Edward M. Kennedy of Massachusetts. A frugal workaholic, he is a clotheshorse, art lover and successful songwriter.

Hatch, who had no political experience when he first ran for the Senate, now has spent more than half his life there. He is the chamber's fourth-longest-serving Republican. And he is the second-highest-ranking Republican on the Finance Committee, where he had chaired the Subcommittee on Health Care until Republicans lost control of Congress in 2006.

Hatch has chaired two full committees — the panel now known as Health, Education, Labor and Pensions, which he headed in the early 1980s, and the Judiciary Committee, which he chaired earlier this decade.

At Judiciary, Hatch has been in the middle of some of Congress' hottest fights, over issues such as tort reform, the expansion of law enforcement's powers to fight terrorism and the confirmation of President Bush's controversial judicial picks. Just as he supported conservatives Clarence Thomas and Robert Bork for Supreme Court appointments in an earlier era, Hatch backed Bush's nominees to the hilt. His 2006 questioning of Samuel A. Alito Jr., Bush's second successful Supreme Court nominee, was so uncritical that the Salt Lake City Tribune observed that Hatch "isn't just a member of the Samuel Alito fan club. He is also the president." And Hatch was among the most enthusiastic backers of Bush's nomination of Vice Adm. J. Michael McConnell as director of national intelligence in 2007.

During Congress' investigation of the administration's 2006 firings of eight U.S. attorneys, he declined to pose tough questions to Attorney General Alberto R. Gonzales. But Hatch did support California Democrat Dianne Feinstein's bill to take away the attorney general's ability to appoint interim U.S. attorneys who could serve indefinitely without Senate confirmation.

In 2005, as chairman of the Judiciary Subcommittee on Intellectual Property, Hatch won enactment of bipartisan legislation that outlawed the use of camcorders in movie theaters and punished the distribution of pirated movies or songs prior to their release. The successful measure also legalized movie-filtering technology that lets viewers skip over objectionable material. For two years before that, he had tried in vain to make it illegal for companies to intentionally induce customers to infringe copyrights via digital file sharing. His efforts landed him on the cover of Billboard Magazine in 2003.

Much of Hatch's interest in copyright stems from his avocation as a songwriter whose work has been performed by the Osmonds and pop singer Gladys Knight. Hooked on music since he started taking piano lessons at age 6, he started writing poetry in college. In 1996, singer-songwriter Janice Kapp Perry asked him to write some hymns with her. He wrote 10 songs in a weekend, the core of the "My God Is Love" album. Since then, he's written more than 700 songs and produced several discs of religious, romantic and patriotic songs, earning $39,092 in royalties in 2005. He is still often spotted scribbling song lyrics between Senate votes.

His friendship with Kennedy reaches back decades, despite their clashing political philosophies. They both serve on the Judiciary and the Health, Education and Labor panels, and have worked together to advance numerous bills. Kennedy once crossed the Senate aisle to give Hatch a hug.

Hatch also collaborates with other Democrats on occasion. In 2007, he and Judiciary Chairman Patrick J. Leahy of Vermont pushed a bill to overhaul patent laws. He worked with Judiciary member Feinstein in the 109th Congress (2005-06) on a bill to crack down on gangs, and with several Finance Committee Democrats to combat elder abuse.

Hatch is more willing than many GOP conservatives to back government programs for the poor. He has supported federal programs to immunize children and to offer job training. His 1997 partnership with Kennedy produced a program to provide health insurance to children whose low-income parents do not qualify for Medicaid. His political philosophy on social issues is influenced by his membership in the Church of Jesus Christ of Latter-day Saints, the dominant religion in Utah that encourages helping the disadvantaged and prohibits consumption of alcohol, tobacco and caffeine. It also encourages large families; Hatch is the father of six.

But in 2007, he opposed a Democratic proposal to allow the government to negotiate prescription drug prices for Medicare, and he cast one of only two votes in the Senate against the Democrats' broad ethics reform bill.

A GOP loyalist and Bush supporter on most issues — including the Iraq War — Hatch splits with the president on embryonic stem cell research, which he considers the "most important biomedical research in the history of the planet." He is a strong abortion foe but says he doesn't think research on embryos discarded by fertility clinics is tantamount to taking a life. "I believe being pro-life is not only about caring for the unborn but about caring for the living as well," Hatch told the Salt Lake City Deseret Morning News in 2006. In vain, he pleaded with Bush not to veto a stem cell bill passed by Congress in 2006.

In 2007, the Senate passed another stem cell bill, but it was still one vote shy of the two-thirds majority needed to overturn a veto. "Every year, we go up more," Hatch said. "It's just a matter of time until we win."

Hatch has been thwarted repeatedly on another objective — a constitutional amendment to allow Congress to outlaw flag burning. In 2006, he came just one vote short in the Senate of the two-thirds majority needed.

Born in Pittsburgh, Hatch grew up in poverty. The family lost its home during the Depression, so Hatch's father, a lather, borrowed $100 to buy an acre of land in the hills above Pittsburgh, where he built a home of blackened lumber salvaged from a fire. A Meadow Gold Dairy sign constituted one wall of the house, which lacked indoor plumbing. The family grew their own food; Hatch tended the chickens and sold their eggs.

During World War II, when Hatch was 11 years old, his older brother and beloved hero, Jesse, a B-24 nose gunner, died in a bombing raid over Italy. Just weeks afterward, a lock of hair over Hatch's forehead turned white. It has stayed that way ever since, though it is now buried in gray. When it came time for Hatch to serve his mission as a young Mormon, he chose to serve two, one for himself, and one for his brother, Jesse.

He worked his way through college and law school as a janitor, an all-night desk clerk in a girls' dormitory and a metal lather. As a lather, he joined an AFL-CIO union. To house a growing family that included three of his six children by the time he finished law school, he plastered the inside of his family's old chicken coop.

In his first Senate campaign, in 1976, he made Washington's burdensome regulatory role a campaign theme. He won the GOP nomination over Jack W. Carlson, a former assistant secretary of interior, and then defeated incumbent Democrat Frank E. Moss with 54 percent of the vote. He was re-elected in 1982 with 58 percent. In 1988, he defeated Brian Moss, the son of the senator he had ousted, by a 2-1 ratio, and his past three re-elections have been by similarly impressive margins. In 1999, Hatch launched a quixotic bid for president. Lacking money and broad political support, he finished last in Iowa's GOP caucuses and dropped out.

KEY VOTES

2006

- Yes Confirm Samuel A. Alito Jr. to the Supreme Court
- Yes Allow consideration of a bill to establish a $140 billion trust fund to compensate victims of asbestos exposure
- Yes Extend tax cuts for two years at a cost of $70 billion over five years
- No Overhaul immigration policy with border security, enforcement and guest worker program
- Yes Allow consideration of a bill to permanently repeal the estate tax
- No Urge President Bush to begin troop withdrawals from Iraq in 2006
- Yes Lift President Bush's restrictions on stem cell research funding
- Yes Authorize military tribunals for suspected terrorists

2005

- Yes Curb class action lawsuits by shifting them from state to federal courts
- Yes Allow confirmation vote on Priscilla R. Owen to the U.S. Court of Appeals for the 5th Circuit
- Yes Oppose mandatory emissions limits and block recognition of global warming as a threat
- Yes Approve free-trade pact with five Central American countries
- Yes Pass energy policy overhaul favored by President Bush emphasizing domestic oil and gas production
- Yes Shield gunmakers from lawsuits when their products are used in crimes
- Yes Ban torture of prisoners in U.S. custody
- Yes Renew 16 provisions of the Patriot Act
- Yes Allow final vote on opening the Arctic National Wildlife Refuge to oil and gas exploration

CQ VOTE STUDIES

	PARTY UNITY		PRESIDENTIAL SUPPORT	
	Support	Oppose	Support	Oppose
2006	93%	7%	88%	12%
2005	96%	4%	93%	7%
2004	98%	2%	94%	6%
2003	98%	2%	99%	1%
2002	93%	7%	98%	2%
2001	95%	5%	97%	3%
2000	94%	6%	55%	45%
1999	92%	8%	30%	70%
1998	87%	13%	48%	52%
1997	87%	13%	63%	37%

INTEREST GROUPS

	AFL-CIO	ADA	CCUS	ACU
2006	20%	5%	92%	84%
2005	14%	5%	100%	92%
2004	8%	10%	100%	96%
2003	0%	10%	100%	80%
2002	23%	5%	100%	95%
2001	6%	5%	86%	96%
2000	0%	0%	100%	95%
1999	11%	0%	88%	84%
1998	0%	5%	94%	80%
1997	0%	15%	100%	68%

Sen. Robert F. Bennett (R)

CAPITOL OFFICE
224-5444
bennett.senate.gov
431 Dirksen 20510-4403; fax 228-1168

COMMITTEES
Appropriations
Banking, Housing & Urban Affairs
Rules & Administration - ranking member
Joint Economic
Joint Library
Joint Printing

RESIDENCE
Salt Lake City

BORN
Sept. 18, 1933, Salt Lake City, Utah

RELIGION
Mormon

FAMILY
Wife, Joyce Bennett; six children

EDUCATION
U. of Utah, B.S. 1957 (political science)

MILITARY SERVICE
Utah National Guard, 1957-60

CAREER
Time management company CEO; management consultant; public relations and marketing executive; U.S. Transportation Department official; congressional aide

POLITICAL HIGHLIGHTS
No previous office

ELECTION RESULTS

2004 GENERAL		
Robert F. Bennett (R)	626,640	68.7%
R. Paul Van Dam (D)	258,955	28.4%
Gary R. Van Horn (C)	17,289	1.9%
2004 PRIMARY		
Robert F. Bennett (R)		unopposed

PREVIOUS WINNING PERCENTAGES
1998 (64%); 1992 (55%)

Elected 1992; 3rd term

Bennett isn't officially part of the Senate Republican leadership, but he might as well be. As counsel to Minority Leader Mitch McConnell, Bennett is among his party's most influential behind-the-scenes figures, with a seat at the table in leadership meetings and orders to reach out to Republicans as well as Democrats at the minority leader's behest. "I do whatever McConnell needs done," he said.

Bennett had a similar role when his close friend McConnell served as Senate Republican whip. As the Kentucky Republican waited his turn to lead his caucus in the 110th Congress (2007-08), he relied on Bennett as his hand-picked adviser and de facto campaign manager. Others have noted Bennett's effectiveness in the job: When former Massachusetts Gov. Mitt Romney launched his presidential campaign in early 2007, he named Idaho Republican Larry E. Craig and Bennett as his Senate liaisons to help him corral more supporters.

Such backroom assignments are a good fit for Bennett. Steady and thoughtful, with more substance than flash, he measures his words carefully, doesn't get publicly ruffled and generally leaves the television podium to others. Reporters seek him out not for pithy sound bites but for reasoned explanations of business-friendly conservative positions and insights about the Senate's inner workings.

Bennett was the founding chairman of the Senate GOP's High Technology Task Force in 1999, and takes an avid interest in technology issues as top-ranking Republican on the Agriculture Appropriations Subcommittee. In particular, he believes the Food and Drug Administration needs to modernize its operations to increase and improve research and development, which he said will eventually lead to lower health care costs.

He believes his colleagues don't fully understand the information age. "Through industrial-age eyes, you say...'These drug companies are making huge profits! They're manufacturing a dinky little pill — it's obscene!' he said in February 2007. "Through the eyes of the information age, you say the more R&D that can be done here, the more little pills that can be created — that means you don't have to have an operation for prostate cancer."

Bennett also has a penchant for gadgets: In 2000, he was the first senator to drive a high-mileage, low-emissions gasoline-electric hybrid car. (He's now on his second model, a Ford Escape SUV.) Along with Democrat Ron Wyden of Oregon, he proposed a plan in September 2006 to reward drivers for buying fuel-efficient cars. He said he likes the concept because it does not seek to raise Corporate Average Fuel Economy standards, something the auto industry has fought.

A member of the Joint Economic Committee, Bennett hopes to educate colleagues about finding solutions to complex problems, such as those surrounding Social Security. After President Bush came out with a much-criticized proposal in 2005 to move some Social Security funds to personal savings accounts, Bennett unveiled an alternative that would raise the retirement age and index payments based on need. He also pitched a separate plan to create private retirement accounts. He continues to talk quietly with Democrats about finding common ground on the issue.

As the No. 2 Republican on the Banking, Housing and Urban Affairs Committee, Bennett is a plainspoken consensus builder. He learned how to achieve bipartisan compromise from his father, Wallace F. Bennett, who preceded him as a senator from Utah. The senior Bennett served from 1951 to 1974, and people who knew both men say that though the son is taller, he is otherwise the image of his father in looks and mannerisms.

Bennett often takes the side of business interests who regard some Democratic proposals as overreaching. In January 2007, as Democrats proposed legislation to require credit card companies to provide more details to consumers and to correct marketing practices they portrayed as predatory, Bennett urged lawmakers to avoid imposing requirements or sanctions that would amount to price controls over the industry. Early in the 110th Congress, he also opposed legislation that would block Wal-Mart Stores Inc. and other retailers from owning their own banks, as such charters are prevalent in his home state.

Although a solid conservative on regulatory and fiscal issues, Bennett breaks party ranks on occasion. He backs efforts to curb tobacco sales to youths and opposes a constitutional amendment to ban desecration of the U.S. flag. He also supports funding for the National Endowment for the Arts, citing his passion for preserving American culture.

In March 2007, before the Senate Rules and Administration Committee voted to expedite the Senate campaign finance disclosure process, he drew wide criticism when he floated an amendment to eliminate campaign expenditure limits on party-coordinated spending. He withdrew his amendment after Rules Chairwoman Dianne Feinstein of California promised to hold a hearing on his proposal.

Bennett has joined other Western Republicans who oppose environmental restraints on public lands. He was outraged when President Bill Clinton used his executive authority to create national monuments in Utah and other states in the West after 1999, blocking mining and ranching on the lands. In the 109th Congress (2005-06), he proposed a controversial wilderness bill for one area of Utah that environmentalists criticized as a giveaway to private developers in the nation's fifth-fastest-growing county. Bennett said that the criticism was misguided, but the measure failed to pass.

Bennett's rangy physique is hard to miss around the Capitol. The 6-foot, 6-inch Utahn often bypasses the elevators to get his exercise on the stairs. And his homespun sense of humor can be endearing. In 2004, his campaign billboards carried the slogan: "Big Heart. Big Ideas. Big Ears."

Originally a businessman, Bennett decided to run for office after taking his company — makers of the Franklin Day Planner schedule organizer — from a four-person shop in 1984 to an $82 million company in 1991 with more than 700 on staff, according to Inc. magazine.

His successful 1992 bid for the Senate at age 59 was his first involvement in a campaign of his own; he had managed his father's 1962 Senate run and had worked for him as an aide. In the 1970s, he was an adviser to Richard Nixon and owned a public relations firm that employed E. Howard Hunt, who was indicted in the Watergate burglary that ultimately led to Nixon's resignation. He left Washington in 1974 to go to work for Howard Hughes at Summa Corporation and then at Hughes Airwest.

In his first Senate bid, Bennett faced competition in the primary but edged past steel company executive Joe Cannon, the brother of Rep. Chris Cannon, who now represents the 3rd District. He went on to beat Democratic Rep. Wayne Owens in the general election. Bennett raised $4.5 million and outspent Owens by more than 2-to-1 en route to victory.

In 1996, Bennett paid a $55,000 fine to the Federal Election Commission for what he called "unintentional violations" during the 1992 campaign. That seemed to have little effect on his re-election campaign in 1998, when he handily defeated Democratic surgeon Scott Leckman. In 2004, he easily beat former Utah Attorney General R. Paul Van Dam with 69 percent of the vote.

KEY VOTES

2006

Yes Confirm Samuel A. Alito Jr. to the Supreme Court

Yes Allow consideration of a bill to establish a $140 billion trust fund to compensate victims of asbestos exposure

Yes Extend tax cuts for two years at a cost of $70 billion over five years

Yes Overhaul immigration policy with border security, enforcement and guest worker program

Yes Allow consideration of a bill to permanently repeal the estate tax

No Urge President Bush to begin troop withdrawals from Iraq in 2006

Yes Lift President Bush's restrictions on stem cell research funding

Yes Authorize military tribunals for suspected terrorists

2005

Yes Curb class action lawsuits by shifting them from state to federal courts

Yes Allow confirmation vote on Priscilla R. Owen to the U.S. Court of Appeals for the 5th Circuit

Yes Oppose mandatory emissions limits and block recognition of global warming as a threat

Yes Approve free-trade pact with five Central American countries

Yes Pass energy policy overhaul favored by President Bush emphasizing domestic oil and gas production

Yes Shield gunmakers from lawsuits when their products are used in crimes

Yes Ban torture of prisoners in U.S. custody

Yes Renew 16 provisions of the Patriot Act

Yes Allow final vote on opening the Arctic National Wildlife Refuge to oil and gas exploration

CQ VOTE STUDIES

	PARTY UNITY		PRESIDENTIAL SUPPORT	
	Support	Oppose	Support	Oppose
2006	87%	13%	90%	10%
2005	96%	4%	93%	7%
2004	97%	3%	94%	6%
2003	97%	3%	97%	3%
2002	94%	6%	98%	2%
2001	96%	4%	96%	4%
2000	92%	8%	52%	48%
1999	93%	7%	31%	69%
1998	84%	16%	53%	47%
1997	87%	13%	62%	38%

INTEREST GROUPS

	AFL-CIO	ADA	CCUS	ACU
2006	20%	15%	100%	72%
2005	14%	5%	100%	92%
2004	8%	20%	100%	88%
2003	0%	10%	100%	80%
2002	23%	5%	100%	100%
2001	13%	5%	100%	100%
2000	0%	5%	100%	95%
1999	11%	0%	94%	84%
1998	0%	10%	89%	64%
1997	0%	10%	100%	68%

Rep. Rob Bishop (R)

CAPITOL OFFICE
225-0453
www.house.gov/robbishop
124 Cannon 20515-4401; fax 225-5857

COMMITTEES
Armed Services
Education & Labor
Natural Resources

RESIDENCE
Brigham City

BORN
July 13, 1951, Salt Lake City, Utah

RELIGION
Mormon

FAMILY
Wife, Jeralynn Bishop; five children

EDUCATION
U. of Utah, B.A. 1974 (political science)

CAREER
Teacher; lobbyist

POLITICAL HIGHLIGHTS
Utah House, 1979-95 (Speaker, 1993-95); Utah Republican Party chairman, 1997-2001

ELECTION RESULTS

2006 GENERAL		
Rob Bishop (R)	112,546	63.1%
Steven Olsen (D)	57,922	32.5%
Mark Hudson (CNSTP)	5,539	3.1%
Lynn Badler (LIBERT)	2,467	1.4%
2006 PRIMARY		
Rob Bishop (R)		unopposed
2004 GENERAL		
Rob Bishop (R)	199,615	67.9%
Steve Thompson (D)	85,630	29.1%
Charles Johnston (C)	4,510	1.5%
Richard W. Soderberg (PC)	4,206	1.4%

PREVIOUS WINNING PERCENTAGES
2002 (61%)

Elected 2002; 3rd term

Serving in the House has been an eye-opener for Bishop, a former high school history instructor. Textbooks, he says, "aren't even close to reality about how Congress works." The actual process is "very sloppy."

Bishop describes himself as a "classic conservative," and he fits the mold of other Western Republicans. He is an ardent advocate of states' rights, property rights and gun owners' rights. His experience in Congress has merely solidified his belief in all of the above. "I want to leave this office with less power to do things than when I came here," he says.

He pushed a bill in the 109th Congress (2005-06) that would have required the federal government to pay property taxes on land it owns, and another that would have allowed Western states to take over 5 percent of the federal land within their borders, including the mineral rights — free of charge.

Bishop is a member of the Republican Study Committee, the most conservative wing of the House GOP, and for the most part is a loyal foot soldier for his leadership. But he does stray occasionally. He was one of 13 Republicans to vote in 2006 against a reauthorization of the 2001 Patriot Act anti-terrorism law, arguing it did not provide sufficient protection for civil liberties. The year before, he was one of 38 Republicans voting to bar the use of federal funds to go after a person's library or bookstore records.

Bishop served on the Rules Committee in the 109th Congress, which required him to give up assignments on the Armed Services, Resources and Science committees. After Democrats took control in the 110th Congress (2007-08), he lost his seat on Rules and returned to Armed Services and the renamed Natural Resources Committee. He also was given a seat on Education and Labor, a good fit for the former teacher but something of a risk for Republican leaders since Bishop heartily dislikes President Bush's 2001 No Child Left Behind education law, which is due for a rewrite.

During his tenure in the House, Bishop has worked to protect various interests in his district. His return to Armed Services has given him a chance to promote the F-35A Lightning II stealth fighter plane that is intended to replace the F-16 and A-10. Some of the planes would be stationed at Hill Air Force Base in Bishop's district, a facility he was able to protect during the 2005 round of military base closures.

Bishop won enactment in early 2006 of a provision establishing a wilderness area in Utah's western desert near the Air Force's Utah Test and Training Range, thereby blocking a proposed nuclear waste dump on the Skull Valley Goshute Indian Reservation. In 2007, he got the top-ranking Republican slot on the Natural Resources Subcommittee overseeing parks and public lands. One of the first bills he put before the panel would raise the height of a 14-mile-long dam to increase water capacity and potentially solve some of Utah's future water problems.

For several years, Bishop worked to add a fourth congressional seat to his state's delegation. Utah barely missed gaining another district during reapportionment that followed the 2000 census. Virginia Republican Thomas M. Davis III and Bishop devised a bill that would increase the size of the House to 437 members, giving one seat to Republican Utah and the other to Democratic Washington, D.C. Republican leaders refused to put the bill on the floor. The Democratically controlled House in 2007 approved a similar measure, but this time around Bishop chose to vote "present" instead of voting for or against the bill. He said the process had dragged on too long and Utah had been pushed around too much. He said he'd just as soon wait until after the

2010 Census, when Utah likely would get a new member anyway.

Sometimes Bishop's efforts in behalf of his district's interests have cost him some unfavorable news coverage. Bishop went to bat for Perry City in a 2004 battle with the Army Corps of Engineers over the city's plan to replace a portion of a seasonal wetlands near the Great Salt Lake with a sewage lagoon. The Salt Lake Tribune called the city's proposal "indefensible." The newspaper also wrote that Bishop's "boorish" criticism of a Corps official led to the employee's transfer.

The Tribune also criticized Bishop in his first term for seeking favors for a local company. In 2003, he wrote to the authors of a measure on national energy policy asking them to reclassify waste at the Energy Department's defunct Fernald nuclear bomb plant in Ohio so that a Utah company, Envirocare, could compete for a federal contract to dispose of the waste. Envirocare withdrew its application after two months of intense public opposition. Bishop, who had done lobbying work for the company before coming to Congress, declined interview requests from The Tribune for more than a month to demonstrate his displeasure with its coverage.

Bishop was exposed to politics at an early age. When he was a boy, his father, an accountant, served as mayor of his hometown of Kaysville, and as a GOP delegate and a campaign volunteer. "I remember him vividly, sitting at the telephone at the kitchen table, calling delegates. I thought that everybody did that. I thought that all families were involved politically," Bishop said. He works the phones himself every night.

After graduating from college, Bishop taught high school English, debate and history in Brigham City. He later added German and Advanced Placement government courses. He spent two years in Germany as part of his Mormon mission experience.

He continued teaching even after he won election to the Utah legislature, where he served 16 years in the state House, the last two as Speaker. In Washington, he loves to play tour guide for Capitol visitors, telling one group that the Rayburn House Office Building has "the warmth of a mental institution" and later explaining that the House's electronic voting system works as follows: "Green is yes, red is no and yellow is 'I don't know what I'm doing.' "

After a stint as state Republican Party chairman, Bishop jumped into the 2002 race to succeed Republican James V. Hansen, who retired. He easily defeated state House Majority Leader Kevin Garn for the GOP nomination, then won the general election with 61 percent of the vote. In 2004, his Democratic opponent attacked Bishop on the Envirocare issue but had trouble raising money. Bishop cruised to victory both then and in 2006.

KEY VOTES

2006

- No Stop broadband companies from favoring select Internet traffic
- ? Affirm U.S. commitment to war in Iraq and reject setting a withdrawal date for troops
- Yes Repeal requirement for bilingual ballots at the polls
- Yes Permit U.S. sale of civilian nuclear technology to India
- Yes Build a 700-mile fence on the U.S.-Mexico border to curb illegal crossings
- Yes Permit warrantless wiretaps of suspected terrorists

2005

- ? Intervene in the life-support case of Terri Schiavo
- No Lift President Bush's restrictions on stem cell research funding
- Yes Prohibit FBI access to library and bookstore records
- Yes Approve free-trade pact with five Central American countries
- Yes Pass energy policy overhaul favored by President Bush emphasizing domestic oil and gas production
- Yes End mandatory preservation of habitat of endangered animal and plant species
- No Ban torture of prisoners in U.S. custody

CQ VOTE STUDIES

	PARTY UNITY		PRESIDENTIAL SUPPORT	
	Support	Oppose	Support	Oppose
2006	97%	3%	89%	11%
2005	97%	3%	78%	22%
2004	97%	3%	85%	15%
2003	97%	3%	92%	8%

INTEREST GROUPS

	AFL-CIO	ADA	CCUS	ACU
2006	15%	10%	93%	87%
2005	20%	10%	81%	100%
2004	14%	5%	95%	100%
2003	0%	0%	100%	88%

UTAH 1

North – part of Salt Lake City, Ogden

In the 1840s, Mormon pioneers journeyed into the mountainous terrain of northern Utah. Today, the 1st — covering the northernmost part of the state — retains that Mormon influence. The district contains more than half of Salt Lake City, bringing in most of downtown and Temple Square, which includes the Tabernacle and the headquarters of the Church of Jesus Christ of Latter-day Saints. Salt Lake City International Airport also is in the 1st District.

Ogden, the district's second-largest city, was once a lively railroad town but today includes facilities for such major employers as Autoliv, a car safety systems producer, and the IRS, which recently opened a new call center downtown. Defense is important to the 1st. The 2005 BRAC round saved Hill Air Force Base, one of the state's largest employers, but scheduled the closure of the Deseret Chemical Depot.

The 1st contains much of Utah's ski country in the north-central part of the state, including Park City, a wealthy resort town. In rural areas, agriculture is king. Utah State University is in Logan in Cache County.

Despite the district's overall GOP tilt, many of the areas in Salt Lake City lean Democratic. The 1st combines some of Utah's poorest urban areas with some of its most wealthy, including the heavily populated Davis County, a solidly Republican suburb. Most of the rural areas favor Republicans, although Democrats pick up some votes in Park City and in Weber County. Overall, George W. Bush took 73 percent of the district's 2004 presidential vote.

MAJOR INDUSTRY

Manufacturing, defense, technology, tourism, agriculture

MILITARY BASES

Hill Air Force Base, 4,500 military, 11,854 civilian (2007); Dugway Proving Ground, 28 military, 754 civilian (2007); Tooele Army Depot, 2 military, 425 civilian (2007); Deseret Chemical Depot, 2 military, 150 civilian (2007)

CITIES

Salt Lake City (pt.), 94,049; Ogden, 77,226; Layton, 58,474; Logan, 42,670; Bountiful, 41,301; Roy, 32,885; Clearfield, 25,974; Tooele, 22,502

NOTABLE

Great Salt Lake is the world's second-largest saltwater lake; Park City has been the home of the U.S. Ski and Snowboard Team since 1974 and home of the U.S. Ski Association since 1988.

Rep. Jim Matheson (D)

CAPITOL OFFICE
225-3011
www.house.gov/matheson
1323 Longworth 20515-4402; fax 225-5638

COMMITTEES
Energy & Commerce
Science & Technology

RESIDENCE
Salt Lake City

BORN
March 21, 1960, Salt Lake City, Utah

RELIGION
Mormon

FAMILY
Wife, Amy Matheson; two children

EDUCATION
Harvard U., A.B. 1982 (government);
U. of California, Los Angeles, M.B.A. 1987

CAREER
Energy consulting firm owner; energy company project manager; environmental policy think tank advocate

POLITICAL HIGHLIGHTS
No previous office

ELECTION RESULTS

2006 GENERAL		
Jim Matheson (D)	133,231	59.0%
LaVar Christensen (R)	84,234	37.3%
W. David Perry (CNSTP)	3,395	1.5%
Bob Brister (GREEN)	3,338	1.5%
2006 PRIMARY		
Jim Matheson (D)		unopposed
2004 GENERAL		
Jim Matheson (D)	187,250	54.8%
John Swallow (R)	147,778	43.2%
Jeremy Paul Petersen (C)	3,541	1.0%

PREVIOUS WINNING PERCENTAGES
2002 (49%); 2000 (56%)

Elected 2000; 4th term

Matheson has found the secret to survival in one of the most Republican of states. With a voting record that often looks more "red" than "blue," he has tightened his grip on his House seat and gained a say on some of the most important domestic issues facing the country.

During his election campaigns, he has downplayed his party affiliation and instead called attention to his independence. The strategy seems to be working: He rolled up a 22 percentage point margin in 2006, the biggest of his congressional career. "I try to take each issue and vote how to represent my constituents," Matheson told the Deseret Morning News.

At the start of the 110th Congress (2007-08), Matheson won a coveted assignment to the Energy and Commerce Committee, whose sweeping jurisdiction stretches from energy issues to health care to telecommunications. To take the prize, he had to relinquish seats on the Financial Services and Transportation and Infrastructure committees, but he was able to retain his seat on the Science and Technology panel.

Matheson's record reflects the conservative views of his constituents and the independent outlook of his late father, Scott Matheson, a well-liked two-term governor. In the 109th Congress (2005-06), only seven other Democrats split with their party more often on floor votes pitting Democrats against Republicans. Only 10 sided more often with President Bush on issues on which he had staked out a position.

In early 2007, Matheson was one of just 13 House Democrats who voted against the final version of an Iraq War funding bill that set a timetable for the withdrawal of U.S. troops, although he said, "We are all frustrated by the lack of progress in Iraq." Earlier, however, he voted for a non-binding resolution opposing Bush's decision to send thousands more troops to the battlefront.

Matheson affiliates with the Blue Dog Coalition of conservative House Democrats. He was a co-chairman of the group in the 109th Congress. He has repeatedly called for an up or down vote on the automatic 1.7 percent pay increase members of Congress receive, which he says is not appropriate "in a time of staggering debt."

Despite his concern about the national debt, he supported the Bush tax cuts of 2001 and 2003, as well as the 2004 corporate tax cut. He also joined Republicans in backing a 2005 bill to repeal the federal estate tax.

Matheson is mostly likely to stick with Democrats on issues related to education, health and labor. In the opening days of the 110th Congress, he supported the Democratic leadership's entire "first 100 hours" priority agenda, which included an increase in the federal minimum wage and a reduction of interest rates on student loans.

Party leaders give him plenty of leeway, knowing the nature of his constituency. In 2007, when the House passed a bill to grant voting rights to the Democratic delegate from the District of Columbia and add another House seat for Republican-dominated Utah, Democratic leaders held up the bill until they were sure nothing in it could jeopardize Matheson's seat.

During his tenure on the Transportation Committee, Matheson took the lead in the authorization of a number of pilot projects at airports around the country to test new security technologies that use biometric identifiers, such as retinal scans, photographs, fingerprints and voice prints. He also worked to gain highway and transit funding, including a massive overhaul of Interstate 15 and a new light-rail commuter line in Salt Lake County.

Matheson joined with Utah Republicans in an effort to win resumption of federal compensation to people who had become ill as a result of exposure to radiation from Cold War-era atomic bomb testing in Nevada, including 185 Utahns. Compensation for those "downwinders" was authorized in 1990, but funding had halted in 2000.

The issue resonates with Matheson, whose father died in 1990 of bone marrow cancer, a disease linked to radiation exposure. Scott Matheson had lived in an area of southern Utah affected by the nuclear tests. When legislation to advance construction of a nuclear waste dump at Nevada's Yucca Mountain came before the 107th Congress (2001-02), Matheson voted no, saying that Westerners had been exposed to enough nuclear dangers.

He successfully fought the Defense Threat Reduction Agency's proposed detonation of a 700-ton conventional explosive in June 2006 at the Nevada Test Site. He said, "The prospect of even a non-nuclear 'mushroom cloud' over the Nevada Test Site brings back bitter memories of how the government lied when it said that there was no danger." In the 110th Congress, Matheson was considering introducing legislation banning all nuclear weapons testing. He vowed to keep a careful eye on any steps the government might take toward a resumption of tests.

Although his father was the governor, Matheson says that his mother, Norma, who involved herself in all sorts of civic projects, was actually more responsible for his own interest in public service.

He also credits his Mormon upbringing, which he says infuses him with a sense of moral purpose. He says that sense of morality and commitment to family and community are what draw him to the Democratic Party, and Matheson often cites moral responsibility as a rationale for his votes on issues ranging from congressional pay raises to veterans' benefits.

During his college days as a government major at Harvard, Matheson served a summer internship in the office of House Speaker Thomas P. "Tip" O'Neill Jr., a Massachusetts Democrat. After college, he worked at an environmental policy think tank in Washington for three years. He returned to Utah after graduate school and worked in a number of private sector energy jobs. He also started his own energy consulting firm.

Matheson decided to run for Congress in 2000 after Merrill Cook, a mercurial two-term GOP incumbent, lost the GOP primary to Internet executive Derek W. Smith. Smith received a dose of bad press over his past business practices, and Matheson sailed to victory by 15 percentage points.

In post-2000 census redistricting, Republicans redrew the 2nd District to guarantee a GOP victory. It didn't work. Matheson squeaked to victory in 2002 by 1,641 votes. He has solidified his grip each election since then.

KEY VOTES

2006

- Yes Stop broadband companies from favoring select Internet traffic
- Yes Affirm U.S. commitment to war in Iraq and reject setting a withdrawal date for troops
- No Repeal requirement for bilingual ballots at the polls
- Yes Permit U.S. sale of civilian nuclear technology to India
- Yes Build a 700-mile fence on the U.S.-Mexico border to curb illegal crossings
- Yes Permit warrantless wiretaps of suspected terrorists

2005

- Yes Intervene in the life-support case of Terri Schiavo
- Yes Lift President Bush's restrictions on stem cell research funding
- Yes Prohibit FBI access to library and bookstore records
- Yes Approve free-trade pact with five Central American countries
- Yes Pass energy policy overhaul favored by President Bush emphasizing domestic oil and gas production
- Yes End mandatory preservation of habitat of endangered animal and plant species
- Yes Ban torture of prisoners in U.S. custody

CQ VOTE STUDIES

	PARTY UNITY		PRESIDENTIAL SUPPORT	
	Support	Oppose	Support	Oppose
2006	66%	34%	67%	33%
2005	69%	31%	43%	57%
2004	64%	36%	50%	50%
2003	75%	25%	56%	44%
2002	76%	24%	48%	52%

INTEREST GROUPS

	AFL-CIO	ADA	CCUS	ACU
2006	57%	45%	87%	64%
2005	60%	75%	78%	40%
2004	60%	70%	86%	48%
2003	73%	70%	70%	36%
2002	56%	80%	65%	40%

UTAH 2

South and east — part of Salt Lake City, rural Utah

The 2nd forms a reverse "L" shape, moving south from eastern Salt Lake City to take in the eastern half of Utah before moving westward to scoop up the state's southwestern corner, a ranching center and growing retirement hub.

Much of eastern Salt Lake County consists of bedroom communities such as Murray. The area also is home to the University of Utah, the state's largest public university. The university's Rice-Eccles Stadium is currently home to soccer's Real Salt Lake, although club and local officials are trying to overcome opposition and build the team a new stadium in Sandy. The 2nd also hosts a number of health care companies, including a large, and growing, BD Medical plant in Sandy.

Decades after sharp population declines, some of the 2nd's rural eastern communities have begun to rebound: Grand County has seen new life with telecommuter and artist communities in Moab. The area has not yet fully recovered, however, and unemployment is high. In the southwestern portion of the district, St. George in Washington County has more than doubled in population since 1990 with its many retirees.

Land-use issues are important in the 2nd, which includes all five of the state's national parks — Arches, Bryce Canyon, Canyonlands, Capitol Reef and Zion. Much of the district is federal land.

Although Salt Lake City has Democratic areas, the 2nd's portion of the city is the generally Republican eastern side. The district's part of Salt Lake County, where almost 60 percent of the 2nd's residents live, does provide some Democratic votes, as does Carbon County, a mining center in the middle of the state. Washington and Iron counties, in the southwest, are the district's most Republican. George W. Bush took 66 percent of the 2nd's presidential vote in 2004.

MAJOR INDUSTRY

Manufacturing, tourism, ranching, financial services

CITIES

Sandy, 88,418; Salt Lake City (pt.), 87,694; St. George, 49,663; Murray, 34,024; Millcreek (unincorporated), 30,377

NOTABLE

Moab, located just south of Arches National Park, hosts the Fat Tire Festival for mountain-biking enthusiasts every October.

Rep. Chris Cannon (R)

CAPITOL OFFICE
225-7751
cannon.ut03@mail.house.gov
www.house.gov/cannon
2436 Rayburn 20515-4403; fax 225-5629

COMMITTEES
Judiciary
Natural Resources
Oversight & Government Reform

RESIDENCE
Mapleton

BORN
Oct. 20, 1950, Salt Lake City, Utah

RELIGION
Mormon

FAMILY
Wife, Claudia Fox Cannon; eight children (one deceased)

EDUCATION
Brigham Young U., B.S. 1974 (economics); Harvard U., attended 1975-76 (business); Brigham Young U., J.D. 1980

CAREER
Venture capital executive; steel company executive; Cabinet department lawyer

POLITICAL HIGHLIGHTS
Utah Republican Party finance chairman, 1992-94

ELECTION RESULTS

2006 GENERAL		
Chris Cannon (R)	95,455	57.7%
Christian Burridge (D)	53,330	32.2%
Jim Noorlander (CNSTP)	14,533	8.8%
Philip Lear Hallman (LIBERT)	2,080	1.3%
2006 PRIMARY		
Chris Cannon (R)	32,881	55.7%
John D. Jacob (R)	26,143	44.3%
2004 GENERAL		
Chris Cannon (R)	173,010	63.4%
Beau Babka (D)	88,748	32.5%
Ronald Winfield (C)	5,089	1.9%
Jim Dexter (LIBERT)	3,691	1.4%

PREVIOUS WINNING PERCENTAGES
2002 (67%); 2000 (59%); 1998 (77%); 1996 (51%)

Elected 1996; 6th term

After a decade in the House, Cannon has evolved into a thoughtful, pragmatic legislator who will reach across the aisle on issues that matter to him. His current conciliatory manner contrasts sharply with his early years in the House when he was a vocal advocate for the impeachment of President Bill Clinton. He calls himself a principled conservative who says he gets along fine with similarly principled liberals.

Cannon was one of a minority of conservative House Republicans who supported President Bush's proposal to allow for a guest worker program and path to citizenship for illegal immigrants. The GOP measure, which passed the House in February 2005, emphasized border security and tougher workplace enforcement of immigration laws.

Cannon says he favors strengthened border security and denies opponents' charges that he favors amnesty for illegal immigrants. But he shares a view held by many in the business community that the nation's economy requires the labor of large numbers of immigrants, who should be provided the legal opportunity to seek jobs under a guest worker program. He also portrays allowing immigrants to seek freedom and economic opportunity in this country as a human rights concern.

His more moderate view of immigration policy became an issue in his 2006 primary election. After he won the primary, Cannon said, "I'm very pleased people in my district said they want thoughtfulness, not harshness, on immigration." He was one of 44 Republicans in July 2006 to side with a majority of Democrats opposing a GOP move to strike provisions from a renewal of the Voting Rights Act that require bilingual ballots and voting assistance in areas with a significant number of voters with limited English.

He may take a more centrist view on immigration, but he is not by any means a moderate Republican. In the 109th Congress (2005-06), he voted with his party 97 percent of the time on votes that pitted the two parties against each other. His presidential support rate was 89 percent. He insists he's no less partisan than he was before. "I'm very partisan, and very philosophically clear," he says.

At the start of his second term, Cannon was one of the 13 Republican "managers" from the Judiciary Committee who presented the House's case for impeaching Clinton in the Senate trial. Cannon continued to call for Clinton's resignation after he was acquitted. In 2007, however, he complained that Democrats were being too partisan in their inquiry about the firings of eight United States attorneys.

From his seat on Judiciary, Cannon has sided with panel Democrats to insist on a phaseout of some of the provisions in the anti-terrorism law known as the Patriot Act. Cannon says Congress needs to consider carefully how to balance liberty and security. He is the top Republican on the Commercial and Administrative Law Subcommittee.

Cannon is also smart enough to pay attention to the home fires. Land use is an important issue in Utah, where the government owns much of the land. Cannon was first elected to the House after beating the incumbent Democrat in 1996 by riding a wave of anger over Clinton's 1996 unilateral designation of 1.7 million acres of Utah as a national monument. The act closed the area, called Grand Staircase-Escalante, to mining companies.

He sits on the Natural Resources Committee, and in the 109th Congress he won enactment of a law that conveyed 207 acres of federal land in southwest Utah to Beaver County, which planned to sell part of it.

Cannon says that if he weren't a politician he would be a technology entrepreneur. "There are huge opportunities to apply technology to serve" industry and society, he says. His district is home to a flourishing computer industry, including the Novell company. He wants Congress to pass a permanent ban on taxing Internet access. He also says that schools don't make enough use of technology. "We ought to adapt our education system to the technology we have today, and get away from the industrial model of a bell rings and everyone goes home," he said.

A member of the Republican Study Committee, a group of the most conservative House Republicans, Cannon keeps to the right on most social issues. He opposes abortion and voted in favor of a 2006 measure proposing a constitutional amendment to ban same-sex marriage.

Cannon's family has a long history in Utah politics. His great-grandfather, George Q. Cannon, was a territorial delegate in the House from 1873 to 1881.

The second of seven children, Cannon and his family moved to California when he was 8 years old. He returned to Utah to attend Brigham Young University, where he met his wife. He took time out from school to serve on a Mormon mission to Guatemala and El Salvador, which he said has influenced his views on immigration. After flunking out of Harvard Business School in 1976, he returned to BYU for a law degree. After three years as an associate solicitor in the Interior Department under President Ronald Reagan and a stint as a Commerce Department lawyer, he returned to Utah to start a business.

He teamed up with his brother, Joe, to buy and reopen Geneva Steel Co. in 1987. After a falling out with Joe, Cannon started his own venture capital firm, Cannon Industries. Active in state party politics, Cannon headed up Tennessee Republican Lamar Alexander's 1996 presidential campaign in Utah. Cannon's financial statements put his worth at more than $10 million — some of which funded his 8,000-vote 1996 victory over Democrat Bill Orton.

In the strongly Republican 3rd, Cannon usually has easy general elections, but he can face stiff competition in the primary. In 2004, he went up against Republican Matt Throckmorton, who held him to 58 percent of the vote and forced him to spend almost a half-million dollars to defend his seat.

In 2006, former GOP Rep. Merrill Cook and developer John D. Jacob challenged Cannon. Cannon needed 60 percent of the party convention vote to avoid a primary election, but he couldn't get there. After Cook was eliminated, Jacob came out on top on the second ballot, 52 percent to 48 percent. Cannon went on to win the June primary with 56 percent of the vote, and in November he easily beat Democrat Christian Burridge with 58 percent.

KEY VOTES

2006

- No Stop broadband companies from favoring select Internet traffic
- ? Affirm U.S. commitment to war in Iraq and reject setting a withdrawal date for troops
- No Repeal requirement for bilingual ballots at the polls
- Yes Permit U.S. sale of civilian nuclear technology to India
- Yes Build a 700-mile fence on the U.S.-Mexico border to curb illegal crossings
- Yes Permit warrantless wiretaps of suspected terrorists

2005

- Yes Intervene in the life-support case of Terri Schiavo
- No Lift President Bush's restrictions on stem cell research funding
- No Prohibit FBI access to library and bookstore records
- Yes Approve free-trade pact with five Central American countries
- Yes Pass energy policy overhaul favored by President Bush emphasizing domestic oil and gas production
- Yes End mandatory preservation of habitat of endangered animal and plant species
- No Ban torture of prisoners in U.S. custody

CQ VOTE STUDIES

	PARTY UNITY		PRESIDENTIAL SUPPORT	
	Support	Oppose	Support	Oppose
2006	98%	2%	92%	8%
2005	96%	4%	87%	13%
2004	98%	2%	87%	13%
2003	98%	2%	98%	2%
2002	96%	4%	87%	13%

INTEREST GROUPS

	AFL-CIO	ADA	CCUS	ACU
2006	14%	5%	100%	90%
2005	13%	0%	93%	100%
2004	18%	0%	100%	100%
2003	0%	5%	97%	88%
2002	0%	0%	94%	95%

UTAH 3
Central — part of Salt Lake County, Provo

Utah's centrally located 3rd takes in some Salt Lake City suburbs and then follows Interstate 15 south to Provo and Orem, the district's economic centers. It also stretches west to pick up rural Millard and Beaver counties on the state's western border. A heavily Mormon-influenced district, the 3rd has one of the highest concentrations of married couples and has the lowest median age (24.5) of any district in the nation. The district has a heavy GOP tilt, and George W. Bush received 77 percent of the 3rd's vote in the 2004 presidential election.

Salt Lake County's residents make up slightly less than half of the 3rd's population. These southwestern suburbs have grown rapidly since 1990, and the southern suburbs here have attracted younger married couples. Many are lower-income, socially conservative areas that tend to vote Republican, but small Democratic pockets exist in places such as suburban West Valley City, the 3rd's largest city. Most of the state's Asian population is located here and in nearby Taylorsville.

The Provo-Orem area has a flourishing computer industry. Newly minted graduates from the 3rd's colleges have helped make the area attractive to businesses, and some of the industry's big-name companies, such as Novell, maintain key facilities here. Many companies in the dietary supplement industry are also headquartered here. Brigham Young University, located in Provo, is one of the state's largest employers.

Outside Utah and Salt Lake counties, cattle ranching, farming, mining and tourism sustain small-town life. Ranchers in Millard County and hog farmers in Beaver County tend to vote Republican, but the mining community of Magna and the railroad town of Milford will support Democratic candidates.

MAJOR INDUSTRY

Technology, mining, higher education, ranching

CITIES

West Valley City, 108,896; Provo, 105,166; Orem, 84,324; West Jordan, 68,336; Taylorsville, 57,439; Kearns (unincorporated), 33,659

NOTABLE

Philo T. Farnsworth, credited with inventing television, lived in Provo; Brigham Young University was founded on an acre of land on Oct. 16, 1875; Millard County and its county seat, Fillmore, are named after President Millard Fillmore.

VERMONT

Gov. Jim Douglas (R)

First elected: 2002
Length of term: 2 years
Term expires: 1/09
Salary: $143,977
Phone: (802) 828-3333

Residence: Middlebury
Born: June 21, 1951; East Longmeadow, Mass.
Religion: United Church of Christ
Family: Wife, Dorothy Douglas; two children
Education: Middlebury College, A.B. 1972 (Russian)
Career: Gubernatorial aide
Political highlights: Vt. House, 1973-79 (majority leader, 1977-79); Vt. secretary of state, 1981-93; Republican nominee for U.S. Senate, 1992; Vt. treasurer, 1995-2003

Election results:

2006 GENERAL		
Jim Douglas (R)	148,014	56.4%
Scudder Parker (D)	108,090	41.2%

Lt. Gov. Brian Dubie (R)

First elected: 2002
Length of term: 2 years
Term expires: 1/09
Salary: $61,116
Phone: (802) 828-2226

LEGISLATURE

General Assembly: January-April

Senate: 30 members, 2-year terms
2007 ratios: 23 D, 7 R; 20 men, 10 women
Salary: $601/week
Phone: (802) 828-2241

House: 150 members, 2-year terms
2007 ratios: 93 D, 49 R, 6 PRO, 2 I; 93 men, 57 women
Salary: $601/week
Phone: (802) 828-2247

TERM LIMITS

Governor: No
Senate: No
House: No

URBAN STATISTICS

CITY	POPULATION
Burlington	38,889
Essex	18,626
Rutland	17,292
Colchester	16,986
South Burlington	15,814

REGISTERED VOTERS

Voters do not register by party.

POPULATION

2006 population (est.)	623,908
2000 population	608,827
1990 population	562,758
Percent change (1990-2000)	+8.2%
Rank among states (2006)	49
Median age	37.7
Born in state	54.3%
Foreign born	3.8%
Violent crime rate	114/100,000
Poverty level	9.4%
Federal workers	5,630
Military	4,605

ELECTIONS

STATE ELECTION OFFICIAL
(802) 828-2304
DEMOCRATIC PARTY
(802) 229-1783
REPUBLICAN PARTY
(802) 223-3411

MISCELLANEOUS

Web: www.vermont.gov
Capital: Montpelier

U.S. CONGRESS

Senate: 1 Democrat, 1 independent
House: 1 Democrat

2000 Census Statistics by District

DIST.	2004 VOTE FOR PRESIDENT BUSH	KERRY	WHITE	BLACK	ASIAN	HISP	MEDIAN INCOME	WHITE COLLAR	BLUE COLLAR	SERVICE INDUSTRY	OVER 64	UNDER 18	COLLEGE EDUCATION	RURAL	SQ. MILES
AL	39%	59%	96%	0%	1%	1%	$40,856	61%	25%	15%	13%	24%	29%	62%	9,250
STATE	39	59	96	0	1	1	$40,856	61	25	15	13	24	29	62	9,250
U.S.	50.7	48.3	69	12	4	13	$41,994	60	25	15	12	26	24	21	3,537,438

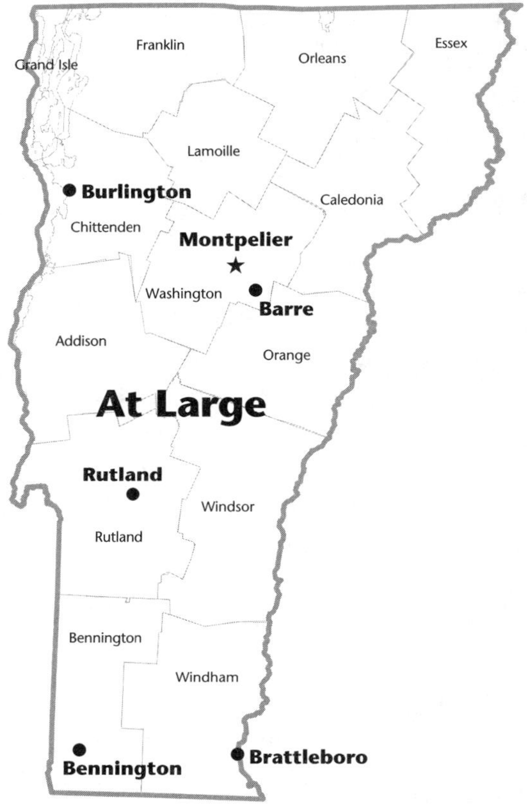
Franklin
Grand Isle
Orleans
Essex
Lamoille
Burlington
Caledonia
Chittenden
Montpelier
Washington
Barre
Addison
Orange
At Large
Rutland
Windsor
Rutland
Bennington
Windham
Bennington
Brattleboro

Sen. Patrick J. Leahy (D)

CAPITOL OFFICE
224-4242
leahy.senate.gov
433 Russell 20510-4502; fax 224-3479

COMMITTEES
Agriculture, Nutrition & Forestry
(Nutrition & Food Assistance - chairman)
Appropriations
(State-Foreign Operations - chairman)
Judiciary - chairman

RESIDENCE
Middlesex

BORN
March 31, 1940, Montpelier, Vt.

RELIGION
Roman Catholic

FAMILY
Wife, Marcelle Leahy; three children

EDUCATION
St. Michael's College, B.A. 1961 (political science); Georgetown U., J.D. 1964

CAREER
Lawyer

POLITICAL HIGHLIGHTS
Chittenden County state's attorney, 1966-75

ELECTION RESULTS

2004 GENERAL		
Patrick J. Leahy (D)	216,972	70.6%
John "Jack" McMullen (R)	75,398	24.5%
Cris Ericson (M)	6,486	2.1%
Craig Hill (GREEN)	3,999	1.3%
Keith Stern (I)	3,300	1.1%
2004 PRIMARY		
Patrick J. Leahy (D)	27,459	94.3%
Craig Hill (D)	1,573	5.4%

PREVIOUS WINNING PERCENTAGES
1998 (72%); 1992 (54%); 1986 (63%); 1980 (50%); 1974 (50%)

Elected 1974; 6th term

Leahy is chairman of the Senate Judiciary Committee, scene of some of the most brutal battles in Congress. And during the Republican reign, he lost more battles than he won. But he wasted no time taking on the Bush administration after Democrats regained control in the 2006 elections.

On issues ranging from warrantless surveillance of communications involving suspected terrorists to the firings of eight federal prosecutors for reasons that appeared suspiciously political, the Vermont Democrat launched a vigorous oversight effort that produced both headlines and push-back from the Justice Department and White House.

Despite some heated partisan skirmishes, Leahy's warm relationship with top-ranking Republican Arlen Specter of Pennsylvania has improved the panel's atmosphere. Leahy works much more comfortably with Specter than he did with conservative Republican Orrin G. Hatch of Utah, who preceded Specter as chairman when the GOP was in the majority. "We wanted to lower the rancor," Leahy told the Philadelphia Inquirer in 2006. "We wanted people to look at us and say, 'This is the way the Senate should be run.' "

At the start of the 110th Congress (2007-08), Leahy restored a pair of bipartisan committee traditions that Republicans had scrapped. In keeping with the first, the "blue slip" process, he said no judicial nomination would advance unless both senators from a state agreed. The second tradition, he said, requires the consent of both parties before a judicial nomination can advance in the second half of a presidential election year such as 2008.

Leahy occasionally has drawn criticism from Democratic allies who say he is too accommodating. He caught a lot of flak from liberal groups in 2005 for his support of John G. Roberts Jr., President Bush's nominee for chief justice of the United States. Leahy later opposed conservative Supreme Court nominee Samuel A. Alito Jr., joining a quixotic filibuster attempt by Massachusetts Democrats John Kerry and Edward M. Kennedy.

Some Democrats on the committee groused when Leahy worked hand in hand with Specter in 2005 on a bill to create a $140 billion trust fund to compensate people sickened by asbestos exposure, a bill that two key Democratic constituencies, consumer groups and trial lawyers, opposed.

Leahy and Specter first met in 1970 when both were young district attorneys attending a conference. They renewed their friendship after Specter was elected to the Senate a decade later. When Specter lost his hair during cancer treatment in 2005, the nearly bald Leahy sent him a photograph of the two of them, calling it the "bald brothers." Specter hung it in his office.

Still, over the years, Leahy has joined other Democrats in some pitched battles, including the confirmation of Supreme Court Justice Clarence Thomas. The lawmaker also has been a leading critic of Bush's conservative appeals court nominees. When Republicans raged about Democratic judicial filibusters in the 108th Congress (2003-04), Leahy shot back that they had earlier blocked dozens of President Bill Clinton's nominees to the bench. Now that Democrats are in charge of the Senate, they can kill nominations in committee without resorting to filibusters.

A frequent critic of Bush's conduct of the war in Iraq, Leahy in 2004 called for a congressional investigation of reconstruction contracts awarded to Halliburton, the energy services company formerly headed by Vice President Dick Cheney. That's when Cheney hurled the f-word at him during a famously angry clash on the Senate floor.

Leahy is fifth in seniority among Senate Democrats. He frequently reminds his fellow senators of his lengthy tenure, his Vermont roots and his experience as a prosecutor. In his speeches, he often mentions his 218-acre maple and pine tree farm in Middlesex, Vt., where his favorite spot is a rocking chair in his 1850 white clapboard farmhouse, with its view of Camel's Hump Mountain. The farm was purchased in 1957 by his father, an Irish-American who ran a printing business in Montpelier, the state capital. His mother's family, Italian immigrants, worked in Vermont's granite quarries. Leahy is well-known in the small state, where politics tends to be intimate. Constituents greet him as he grocery shops at the local food co-op.

Leahy's political longevity allows him to pursue multiple policy interests. He considers his long campaign against the use of land mines the most important. He has pushed for a worldwide ban, frequently clashing on the issue with both the Bush and Clinton administrations.

He has made more headway on other objectives, winning access for federal inmates to post-conviction DNA testing, continued funding of school lunch programs, and enactment of a 1996 law that made many of the government's electronic records public.

Leahy was Judiciary chairman on Sept. 11, 2001. The first major legislation enacted in response to the terrorist attacks was the administration's Patriot Act greatly expanding law enforcement powers to investigate terrorists. Leahy worked to modify the measure, warning that it infringed on civil liberties. "As draconian as it was, the terrorism bill was far more constitutional than it would have been had I not been chairman," Leahy says. When the law came up for renewal in the 109th Congress (2005-06), he opposed extending several expiring provisions of the law, but the White House and congressional Republicans prevailed.

In November 2001, federal authorities intercepted an anonymous letter addressed to Leahy that was laced with deadly anthrax spores. But unlike an earlier letter to then Democratic Leader Tom Daschle of South Dakota that created a bioterrorism scare in Congress, this one caused no harm.

Now in his 60s, Leahy is plugged into pop culture and technology. A fan of the Batman comic character, he and his son had cameos in the 1997 film "Batman and Robin." He's also a "Deadhead," who created a stir in 1994 when he took Jerry Garcia and others of The Grateful Dead to lunch in the Senate dining room. Surviving band members play at his fundraisers. A skilled amateur photographer, Leahy took a picture of President Ronald Reagan's second inaugural that was featured in U.S. News and World Report.

In 1996, he was one of the first in Congress to launch a Web site, and was dubbed the "Cyber Senator." He dives into technology-related issues on Judiciary, especially efforts to update copyright law with privacy protections for medical and financial records.

Leahy generally supports abortion rights, but he voted in 2003 for the law banning a procedure that opponents call "partial birth" abortion.

Leahy is quick to protect the interests of his rural state. On the Agriculture Committee, he is a defender of Northeastern dairy farmers during conflicts with other dairy-producing regions. In 1998, Leahy quietly got a bill passed designating Lake Champlain as a Great Lake, making it eligible for federal anti-pollution grants. He had the law rescinded after complaints from senators from actual Great Lake states in the Midwest.

Leahy was just 34 when he was first elected to the Senate in 1974 in the Watergate-fueled voter backlash that helped him beat a favored Republican. He overcame the GOP landslide of 1980 to win his first re-election by just 2,500 votes. That close call lured former GOP Gov. Richard A. Snelling out of retirement to challenge him six years later. But by then Leahy was well-financed and comfortably entrenched. He won with 63 percent of the vote, and has all but coasted to re-election ever since.

KEY VOTES

2006

No Confirm Samuel A. Alito Jr. to the Supreme Court
Yes Allow consideration of a bill to establish a $140 billion trust fund to compensate victims of asbestos exposure
No Extend tax cuts for two years at a cost of $70 billion over five years
Yes Overhaul immigration policy with border security, enforcement and guest worker program
No Allow consideration of a bill to permanently repeal the estate tax
Yes Urge President Bush to begin troop withdrawals from Iraq in 2006
Yes Lift President Bush's restrictions on stem cell research funding
No Authorize military tribunals for suspected terrorists

2005

No Curb class action lawsuits by shifting them from state to federal courts
Yes Allow confirmation vote on Priscilla R. Owen to the U.S. Court of Appeals for the 5th Circuit
No Oppose mandatory emissions limits and block recognition of global warming as a threat
No Approve free-trade pact with five Central American countries
No Pass energy policy overhaul favored by President Bush emphasizing domestic oil and gas production
No Shield gunmakers from lawsuits when their products are used in crimes
Yes Ban torture of prisoners in U.S. custody
No Renew 16 provisions of the Patriot Act
No Allow final vote on opening the Arctic National Wildlife Refuge to oil and gas exploration

CQ VOTE STUDIES

	PARTY UNITY		PRESIDENTIAL SUPPORT	
	Support	Oppose	Support	Oppose
2006	97%	3%	46%	54%
2005	97%	3%	36%	64%
2004	94%	6%	58%	42%
2003	97%	3%	51%	49%
2002	98%	2%	67%	33%
2001	98%	2%	62%	38%
2000	94%	6%	89%	11%
1999	94%	6%	82%	18%
1998	87%	13%	83%	17%
1997	89%	11%	87%	13%

INTEREST GROUPS

	AFL-CIO	ADA	CCUS	ACU
2006	93%	95%	33%	0%
2005	86%	100%	28%	0%
2004	100%	100%	50%	8%
2003	85%	85%	35%	16%
2002	100%	95%	55%	0%
2001	100%	100%	38%	8%
2000	75%	85%	58%	8%
1999	100%	95%	41%	4%
1998	88%	90%	56%	12%
1997	67%	80%	60%	13%

Sen. Bernard Sanders (I)

CAPITOL OFFICE
224-5141
sanders.senate.gov
332 Dirksen 20510-4503; fax 228-0776

COMMITTEES
Budget
Energy & Natural Resources
Environment & Public Works
Health, Education, Labor & Pensions
Veterans' Affairs

RESIDENCE
Burlington

BORN
Sept. 8, 1941, Brooklyn, N.Y.

RELIGION
Jewish

FAMILY
Wife, Jane O'Meara Sanders; four children

EDUCATION
Brooklyn College, attended 1959-60;
U. of Chicago, B.A. 1964 (political science)

CAREER
College instructor; freelance writer; documentary filmmaker; carpenter

POLITICAL HIGHLIGHTS
Liberty Union candidate for U.S. Senate, 1972; Liberty Union candidate for governor, 1972; Liberty Union candidate for U.S. Senate, 1974; Liberty Union candidate for governor, 1976; mayor of Burlington, 1981-89; independent candidate for governor, 1986; independent candidate for U.S. House, 1988; U.S. House, 1991-2007

ELECTION RESULTS

2006 GENERAL		
Bernard Sanders (I)	171,638	65.4%
Rich Tarrant (R)	84,924	32.4%
2006 PRIMARY		
Bernard Sanders (D)	35,954	94.2%
others	2,232	5.8%

PREVIOUS WINNING PERCENTAGES
2004 House Election (67%); 2002 House Election (64%); 2000 House Election (69%); 1998 House Election (63%); 1996 House Election (55%); 1994 House Election (50%); 1992 House Election (58%); 1990 House Election (56%)

Elected 2006; 1st term

Sanders has taken his brand of "Democratic socialism" to the Senate after 16 years as the most prominent left-wing member of the House. He brings to the Senate his provocative style and strong views on a host of issues, including the concerns of the poor and the middle class, the threat of global warming and the care and protection of civil liberties.

Sanders succeeds James M. Jeffords, who also served in the Senate as an independent, though he left the Republican Party to do so. Sanders has never been a member of either established political party. He caucuses with the Democrats, however, just as he did in the House.

Sanders has always been a free spirit. After college, he lived on a kibbutz in Israel and then briefly in New York — he had grown up in Brooklyn. He moved to Vermont in 1968 as part of a wave of liberals abandoning urban life for Vermont's green acres. He held a variety of jobs from free-lance writer to carpenter as his involvement in progressive politics increased.

While other transplants flocked to the Democratic Party, Sanders helped found Vermont's anti-capitalist, anti-Vietnam War Liberty Union Party, from which he ran for statewide office four times in the early 1970s. He keeps a plaque on his office wall honoring Eugene V. Debs, founder of the American Socialist Party. Sanders was the first identifiable socialist in the House since Wisconsin's Victor L. Berger, who served four terms in the 1910s and 1920s.

An untiring advocate for the poor and middle class, he blasted President Bush's budget proposal in 2007 for overlooking those who are struggling economically. Sanders told the Burlington Free Press, "Congress should not continue to worry about millionaires and billionaires while we're losing good-paying jobs and families can't afford health care and college tuition. We've got to recreate the great American middle class." During floor debate in March on the Senate's budget blueprint for the next fiscal year, senators rejected his proposal to repeal tax breaks for those earning more than $1 million a year and direct the increased revenue to special education.

Sanders has opposed the war in Iraq since its inception. He wants to withdraw U.S. troops as soon as it's feasible, he says. "Let me be very clear in giving you my perspective on this war," Sanders said on the Senate floor in February 2007. "In my view, President Bush's war in Iraq has been a disaster. It is a war we were misled into and a war many of us believed we never should have gotten into in the first place." In early 2007, as concerns intensified about Iran's nuclear program, and the potential for confrontation with the country rose, Sanders offered a resolution that would require the president to ask Congress' permission before using force against Iran.

Sanders sits on the Environment and Public Works Committee, where he can further his strong views on how to protect the environment. The committee's chairwoman, Barbara Boxer of California, has joined with him on a bill that aims to reduce U.S. greenhouse gas emissions to 80 percent below 1990 levels by the year 2050. The bill sets some of the most stringent greenhouse gas reduction levels of any congressional measure.

As a member of the Health, Education, Labor and Pensions Committee, Sanders will join with its chairman, Massachusetts Sen. Edward M. Kennedy, to advocate for a national health care system. He has long railed against "corporate greed," and has singled out the pharmaceutical industry for its huge profits. He has led constituents across the Canadian border to buy prescription drugs at lower prices than they can find in the United States.

In 2006, Sanders brokered a deal to gain access to cheaper Venezuelan home heating oil, despite the Bush administration's criticism of the anti-American views of that country's leader, Hugo Chávez. Having low heating costs is important in Vermont where the winters are long, and Sanders was particularly critical of Bush's 2007 budget cuts to a federal program that provides heating assistance for poor people. A member of the Budget Committee, he gained Senate approval of an amendment to a war funding bill to restore $25 million for the program.

Sanders has long opposed foreign-trade agreements that he says put U.S. workers at a disadvantage. He introduced legislation in the House, along with libertarian Republican Ron Paul of Texas, to block federal financial assistance to companies that outsource U.S. jobs to overseas labor markets. "I think Congress has got to tell these guys, who've received billions of dollars in corporate welfare from the American taxpayer, enough is enough," he said on CNN in 2005. The House rejected a resolution he cosponsored with Paul in 2005 to end U.S. participation in the World Trade Organization.

Sanders had more success finding common ground with libertarian Republicans who share his concern about civil liberties. He and Paul were successful in the House in 2005 with a provision to repeal a part of the Patriot Act anti-terrorism law that gave federal investigators access to the shopping and reading habits of bookstore and library patrons.

And like more-mainstream politicians, he has made no apologies for directing money home to Vermont, getting $7.3 million included in the 2005 surface transportation bill to improve a 93-mile-long railroad track that was being converted for use by snowmobilers. Sanders said snowmobiling promotes economic development in the state and helps people stay fit.

Sanders was born and reared in Brooklyn, where his father, a Jewish immigrant from Poland whose family was killed in the Holocaust, was a paint salesman. His mother died at age 46 when Sanders was 19.

His political philosophy was largely influenced by his older brother and later by his experiences as a student at the University of Chicago. After his four failed bids for statewide office, he made a move for local office and in 1981 unseated the Democratic incumbent by 10 votes to become Burlington's first socialist mayor. He won three more two-year terms by pursuing populist goals while presiding over the revitalization of the city's downtown.

Sanders was seen as a spoiler when he ran in 1988 for Vermont's lone House seat, vacated when Republican Jeffords left to run for the Senate. Still, Sanders lost to Republican Peter Smith by only 4 percentage points. When the two squared off in 1990, Smith's efforts to portray Sanders as an admirer of Communist Cuban dictator Fidel Castro backfired, and Sanders won with 56 percent of the vote.

In 1992, Democrats went out of their way not to field a strong candidate and Sanders won re-election against Tim Philbin, a favorite of the state GOP's conservative wing, but he barely held on in 1994, a banner year for Republicans nationwide. After another anemic showing in 1996, his vote share rose to more than 60 percent in 1998 and stayed there. In 2004, he captured his highest percentage yet with more than two-thirds of the vote.

When Jeffords announced plans to retire, Sanders jumped into the Senate race. Running as a Democrat, he had no trouble beating four political unknowns in the primary. With his Democratic rivals licked, he reverted to form, running as an independent in the general. Sanders was quite a contrast to his GOP foe, Richard Tarrant, a software magnate who spent $7 million of his own money to blanket the state with negative ads. Tarrant tried to paint Sanders as a radical, but Sanders won easily with 65 percent of the vote. The Democratic Senatorial campaign arm, chaired by New York Sen. Charles E. Schumer, backed his bid financially. (The two attended the same schools in Brooklyn.)

KEY VOTES

House Service:

2006

- Yes Stop broadband companies from favoring select Internet traffic
- No Affirm U.S. commitment to war in Iraq and reject setting a withdrawal date for troops
- No Repeal requirement for bilingual ballots at the polls
- No Permit U.S. sale of civilian nuclear technology to India
- No Build a 700-mile fence on the U.S.-Mexico border to curb illegal crossings
- No Permit warrantless wiretaps of suspected terrorists

2005

- ? Intervene in the life-support case of Terri Schiavo
- Yes Lift President Bush's restrictions on stem cell research funding
- Yes Prohibit FBI access to library and bookstore records
- No Approve free-trade pact with five Central American countries
- No Pass energy policy overhaul favored by President Bush emphasizing domestic oil and gas production
- No End mandatory preservation of habitat of endangered animal and plant species
- Yes Ban torture of prisoners in U.S. custody

CQ VOTE STUDIES

House Service:

	PARTY UNITY		PRESIDENTIAL SUPPORT	
	Support	Oppose	Support	Oppose
2006	98%	2%	15%	85%
2005	97%	3%	15%	85%
2004	98%	2%	29%	71%
2003	95%	5%	15%	85%
2002	98%	2%	18%	82%
2001	97%	3%	16%	84%
2000	96%	4%	78%	22%
1999	96%	4%	76%	24%
1998	95%	5%	85%	15%
1997	94%	6%	73%	27%

INTEREST GROUPS

House Service:

	AFL-CIO	ADA	CCUS	ACU
2006	100%	100%	27%	8%
2005	93%	100%	33%	8%
2004	100%	95%	30%	4%
2003	100%	100%	14%	20%
2002	100%	95%	16%	0%
2001	100%	100%	22%	8%
2000	100%	95%	23%	4%
1999	100%	100%	8%	12%
1998	100%	100%	18%	8%
1997	100%	100%	20%	12%

Rep. Peter Welch (D)

CAPITOL OFFICE
225-4115
welch.house.gov
1404 Longworth 20515-4501; fax 225-6790

COMMITTEES
Oversight & Government Reform
Rules

RESIDENCE
Hartland

BORN
May 2, 1947, Springfield, Mass.

RELIGION
Roman Catholic

FAMILY
Widowed; five children

EDUCATION
College of the Holy Cross, A.B. 1969 (history); U. of California, Berkeley, J.D. 1973

CAREER
Lawyer; county public defender

POLITICAL HIGHLIGHTS
Vt. Senate, 1981-89 (minority leader, 1983-85; president pro tempore, 1985-89); sought Democratic nomination for U.S. House, 1988; Democratic nominee for governor, 1990; Vt. Senate, 2002-07 (president pro tempore, 2003-07)

ELECTION RESULTS

2006 GENERAL		
Peter Welch (D)	139,815	53.2%
Martha Rainville (R)	117,023	44.5%
2006 PRIMARY		
Peter Welch (D)	34,706	97.1%
write-ins	1,033	2.9%

Elected 2006; 1st term

Welch won the seat of independent Bernard Sanders, one of the most liberal members of the House. Although not a democratic socialist like Sanders, who went on to the U.S. Senate, Welch shares many of the same liberal views. He wants to bring the U.S. troops home from Iraq, roll back tax breaks given to the wealthy and allow the federal government to negotiate directly with drug companies for lower prescription prices under Medicare.

Welch served as president pro tempore of the Vermont Senate for the past four years, where he said "fiscal responsibility" was one of his guiding principles. He says the Bush administration's tax cuts have contributed to the nation's large deficit and have done little to help the middle class.

Welch says he was opposed to the war in Iraq from the start. After voting in March 2007 for a supplemental spending bill for the war that includes a troop withdrawal timetable, Welch said, "Congress today is finally revoking the president's blank check for the war in Iraq. With this vote, we are at long last holding this president accountable, replacing presidential lip service with the congressional force of law."

He will be watching closely in 2007 as the House takes up a renewal of the massive farm bill. Vermont's economy is heavily dependent on agriculture, and Welch says he wants the farm bill to help small family farms compete against the larger corporate operations.

He sits on the Rules Committee, a prestigious assignment for a freshman, as well as the Oversight and Government Reform Committee.

Welch has been active in Vermont politics for years. He served in the state Senate in the 1980s and made an unsuccessful bid for governor in 1990. In 2001, Gov. Howard Dean appointed him to fill a state Senate vacancy within Welch's home district. In the 1990s, Welch all but disappeared from the Vermont political world when his wife was diagnosed with cancer. She died in September 2004.

In 2006, Welch defeated first-time GOP candidate Martha Rainville, the state's adjutant general. Although she was moderate on many issues, the political tide was against her, and Welch won with 53 percent of the vote.

VERMONT

At large

Resting on the shores of Lake Champlain and rolling through the rustic Green Mountains, the nation's second-least-populous state feels like a good, small-town neighbor.

Small businesses mix with dairy farms, manufacturing plants and electronics companies. The technology boom died down in the early 1990s, but the state has tried to re-ignite it. Officials also are hoping to convince tourists, so prevalent on the ski slopes in winter, to visit the state year-round. In addition, urban dwellers from other states — flatlanders, as they are called in Vermont — are continuing to buy summer homes here, especially in the scenic northeast.

Once a remote rural bastion of Yankee Republicanism, Vermont moved solidly to the left 20 years ago as an influx of young liberal urbanites joined the remnants of the late-1960s counterculture settlers. In state and federal races, the strong progressive contingency in Burlington and surrounding Chittenden County usually out votes Yankee libertarian conservatives, based mostly in East Montpelier and some of the Burlington suburbs. Still, Republicans can still win here, as Gov. Jim Douglas has done since 2002.

In recent years, the state's liberal Progressive Party and other left-leaning independents have split Democratic voters, occasionally aiding GOP victories. The state's rural areas, including the Northeast Kingdom, hold some GOP votes, but Democrats dominate central Vermont and the southeastern corner. Many small urban centers, such as Montpelier and Rutland, now support Democrats.

MAJOR INDUSTRY
Manufacturing, tourism, dairy farming

CITIES
Burlington, 38,889; Rutland, 17,292

NOTABLE
Ben & Jerry's ice cream began in Burlington in a renovated former gas station.

VIRGINIA

Gov. Tim Kaine (D)

First elected: 2005
Length of term: 4 years
Term expires: 1/10
Salary: $175,000
Phone: (804) 786-2211

Residence: Richmond
Born: Feb. 26, 1958; St. Paul, Minn.
Religion: Roman Catholic
Family: Wife, Anne Holton; three children
Education: U. of Missouri, A.B. 1979 (economics); Harvard U., J.D. 1983
Career: Lawyer
Political highlights: Richmond City Council, 1994-2001 (mayor, 1998-2001); lieutenant governor, 2002-06

Election results:

2005 GENERAL		
Tim Kaine (D)	1,025,942	51.7%
Jerry W. Kilgore (R)	912,327	46.0%
H. Russ Potts Jr. (I)	43,953	2.2%

Lt. Gov. Bill Bolling (R)

First elected: 2005
Length of term: 4 years
Term expires: 1/10
Salary: $36,321
Phone: (804) 786-2078

LEGISLATURE

General Assembly: 60 days January-March in even-numbered years; 40 days January-February in odd-numbered years

Senate: 40 members, 4-year terms
2007 ratios: 23 R, 17 D; 32 men, 8 women
Salary: $18,000
Phone: (804) 698-7410

House: 100 members, 2-year terms
2007 ratios: 57 R, 40 D, 3 I; 84 men, 16 women
Salary: $17,640
Phone: (804) 698-1500

TERM LIMITS

Governor: No consecutive terms
Senate: No
House: No

URBAN STATISTICS

CITY	POPULATION
Virginia Beach	425,257
Norfolk	234,403
Chesapeake	199,184
Richmond	197,790
Newport News	180,150

REGISTERED VOTERS

Voters do not register by party.

POPULATION

2006 population (est.)	7,642,884
2000 population	7,078,515
1990 population	6,187,358
Percent change (1990-2000)	+14.4%
Rank among states (2006)	12
Median age	35.7
Born in state	51.9%
Foreign born	8.1%
Violent crime rate	282/100,000
Poverty level	9.6%
Federal workers	156,871
Military	170,046

ELECTIONS

STATE ELECTION OFFICIAL
(804) 864-8901
DEMOCRATIC PARTY
(804) 644-1966
REPUBLICAN PARTY
(804) 780-0111

MISCELLANEOUS

Web: www.virginia.gov
Capital: Richmond

U.S. CONGRESS

Senate: 1 Democrat, 1 Republican
House: 8 Republicans, 3 Democrats

2000 Census Statistics by District

DIST.	2004 VOTE FOR PRESIDENT BUSH	KERRY	WHITE	BLACK	ASIAN	HISP	MEDIAN INCOME	WHITE COLLAR	BLUE COLLAR	SERVICE INDUSTRY	OVER 64	UNDER 18	COLLEGE EDUCATION	RURAL	SQ. MILES
1	60%	39%	75%	18%	2%	3%	$50,257	63%	23%	14%	11%	26%	27%	36%	3,773
2	58	42	67	21	4	4	$44,193	63	22	15	9	26	26	8	961
3	33	66	38	56	1	3	$32,238	55	26	19	12	26	17	8	1,118
4	57	43	62	33	1	2	$45,249	58	28	14	11	27	20	29	4,489
5	56	43	72	24	1	2	$35,739	53	33	14	15	23	19	64	8,922
6	63	36	85	11	1	2	$37,773	56	29	15	15	22	21	35	5,647
7	61	38	78	16	2	2	$50,990	68	20	12	12	25	33	30	3,514
8	35	64	57	13	9	16	$63,430	77	11	12	9	20	54	0	123
9	59	39	93	4	1	1	$29,783	49	36	15	15	21	14	66	8,803
10	55	44	77	7	7	7	$71,560	72	16	11	7	28	43	17	1,856
11	50	49	67	10	11	9	$80,397	77	12	12	8	27	49	4	388
STATE	54	45	70	19	4	5	$46,677	64	23	14	11	25	30	27	39,594
U.S.	50.7	48.3	69	12	4	13	$41,994	60	25	15	12	26	24	21	3,537,438

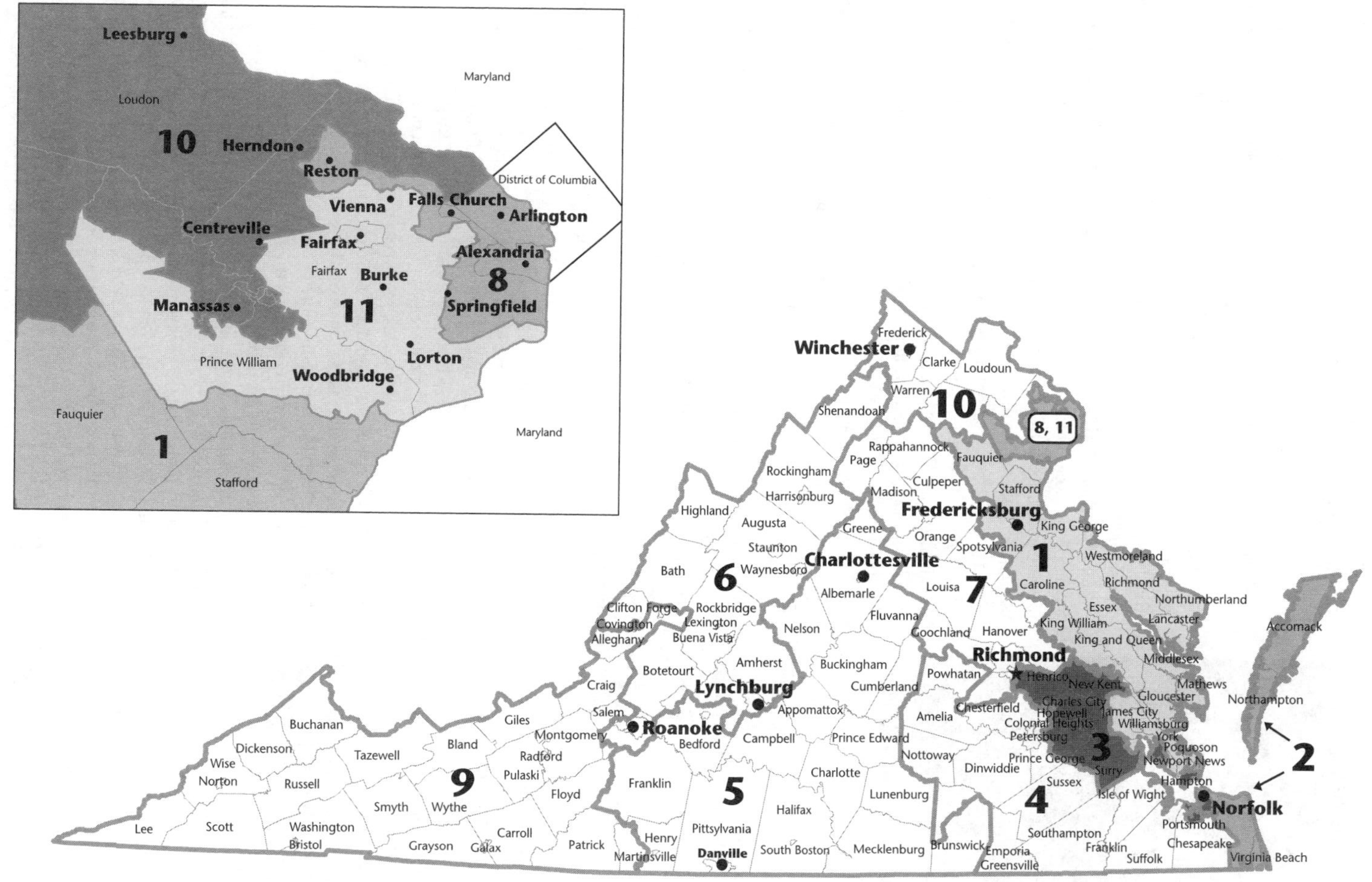
Leesburg
Loudon
Maryland
10
Herndon
Reston
District of Columbia
Vienna
Falls Church
Arlington
Centreville
Fairfax
Alexandria
Fairfax
Burke
8
Manassas
11
Springfield
Prince William
Lorton
Woodbridge
Fauquier
Maryland
1
Stafford
Winchester
Frederick
Clarke
Loudoun
Warren
10
Shenandoah
8, 11
Rappahannock
Page
Fauquier
Rockingham
Culpeper
Madison
Stafford
Harrisonburg
Fredericksburg
Highland
Augusta
Greene
King George
Orange
Staunton
Spotsylvania
1
Westmoreland
Charlottesville
Bath
6
Waynesboro
Louisa
7
Caroline
Richmond
Albemarle
Northumberland
Essex
Clifton Forge
Rockbridge
Fluvanna
Covington
Lexington
King William
Lancaster
Nelson
Alleghany
Buena Vista
Goochland
Hanover
King and Queen
Accomack
Middlesex
Amherst
Buckingham
Richmond
Botetourt
Powhatan
Henrico
Craig
Lynchburg
Cumberland
New Kent
Mathews
Gloucester
Charles City
Northampton
Salem
Appomattox
Chesterfield
James City
Hopewell
Buchanan
Roanoke
Amelia
Colonial Heights
Williamsburg
Giles
Montgomery
Petersburg
York
Bland
Bedford
Campbell
Prince Edward
3
Poquoson
Dickenson
Tazewell
Radford
Nottoway
2
Prince George
Newport News
Wise
Pulaski
Dinwiddie
Surry
9
Charlotte
Norton
Russell
Franklin
5
Sussex
Hampton
Floyd
Lunenburg
Isle of Wight
Smyth
Wythe
Halifax
4
Norfolk
Lee
Scott
Washington
Carroll
Pittsylvania
Southampton
Portsmouth
Henry
Patrick
Mecklenburg
Brunswick
Franklin
Chesapeake
Bristol
Grayson
Galax
Martinsville
Danville
South Boston
Emporia
Suffolk
Virginia Beach
Greensville

Sen. John W. Warner (R)

CAPITOL OFFICE
224-2023
warner.senate.gov
225 Russell 20510-4601; fax 224-6295

COMMITTEES
Armed Services
Environment & Public Works
Homeland Security & Governmental Affairs
Select Intelligence

RESIDENCE
Alexandria

BORN
Feb. 18, 1927, Washington, D.C.

RELIGION
Episcopalian

FAMILY
Wife, Jeanne Warner; three children

EDUCATION
Washington and Lee U., B.S. 1949 (engineering); U. of Virginia, LL.B. 1953

MILITARY SERVICE
Navy, 1944-46; Marine Corps, 1950-52; Marine Corps Reserve, 1952-64

CAREER
Lawyer; farmer

POLITICAL HIGHLIGHTS
Assistant U.S. attorney, 1956-60; under secretary of the Navy, 1969-72; secretary of the Navy, 1972-74

ELECTION RESULTS

2002 GENERAL		
John W. Warner (R)	1,229,894	82.6%
Nancy Spannaus (I)	145,102	9.7%
Jacob G. Hornberger Jr. (I)	106,055	7.1%
2002 PRIMARY		
John W. Warner (R)		unopposed

PREVIOUS WINNING PERCENTAGES
1996 (52%); 1990 (81%); 1984 (70%); 1978 (50%)

Elected 1978; 5th term

Warner is the senator from Central Casting. He looks and talks like the Hollywood image of a patrician elder statesman, which he is. His grandiloquent speaking style, fine suits and celebrity circle of friends from his former marriage to actress Elizabeth Taylor once led to his being dismissed as a wealthy dilettante, but Warner is more complex and thoughtful than that, and, with nearly three decades of service in the Senate, has no need to establish his bona fides.

As chairman of the Armed Services Committee during the last four years of the Republican majority, Warner was at the center of events as the Senate acted out in microcosm the nation's conflicts over the Iraq War, the struggle against the al Qaeda terrorist network and the merits of higher defense spending. To all of those arguments, Warner brought his personal zest for the issues, his instinct for developing consensus solutions and his aptitude for Senate politics.

When the Democrats gained the Senate majority in 2007, Warner yielded the panel's gavel to Carl Levin of Michigan, the committee's longtime ranking member. Levin and Warner worked together like an old married couple, even though they often were not on the same page politically. That relationship is still a friendly one though Warner is no longer the top Republican on the panel and may be more visible on other committees. He was forced by Republican caucus rules to relinquish the top-ranking spot to John McCain of Arizona. Warner remained a member of Armed Services.

Although he had the seniority to claim the top minority seat on the Environment and Public Works Committee, Warner declined to do so, saying he would devote his time to national security issues and to prepare for re-election to a sixth, six-year term in 2008, when he will be 81.

But Warner nonetheless emerged as a key player on the Energy panel in the debate over global warming when he said he would consider Democratic proposals to impose limits on greenhouse gas emissions. "I love the outdoors, and I cherish the moments I'm with my grandchildren now, sharing the simple joys of fishing and hunting that I had with my wonderful father and others," he said. "So I feel an obligation to make this work."

Warner also had a high-profile role in the debate that unfolded in the 110th Congress (2007-08) over the war. In a breach of party solidarity, Warner in January 2007 came out against President Bush's proposed buildup of troops. Because of his prominence on the issue, Warner's move was a setback for Bush on the eve of his State of the Union address, and it bolstered Democratic efforts to put conditions on spending for the war.

Warner's leadership on Armed Services during the 109th Congress (2005-06) once again showed him to be one of the more interesting, and conflicted, figures in the Senate. He tries to be a good Republican by hewing to the administration's policies, but his tendency to reach across the aisle to build consensus, and his independent streak, at times make that impossible. Still, when he breaks ranks, he tends to do it with understatement and courtliness; he is never brash or strident.

Warner played the role of a moderate during hearings on the most controversial of Bush's judicial nominations, that of Harriet Miers to the Supreme Court. Her name was eventually withdrawn in October 2005 less than a month after Bush had sent it to Capitol Hill. During Senate debate, Warner was one of seven Republicans who joined with seven Democrats to form the Gang of 14, a coalition that helped keep either party from using parliamentary procedures to win Senate battles over judicial nominees. Democrats in the group agreed not to filibuster judicial nominations except in "extraordinary" circumstances, while Republicans agreed not to employ a parliamentary force play to end judicial filibusters altogether.

But Warner was stung by his experience in defending the president's controversial nomination. He said he had staked his reputation on standing by the White House and defending Miers, only to see many of his GOP colleagues defect from the cause.

The whole incident made him cautious in May 2006, when a wave of retired generals and many Democrats were calling for Defense Secretary Donald H. Rumsfeld to resign. While many Republicans robustly defended Rumsfeld, Warner was noticeably tepid. In a Senate floor speech that month, the best he could say about Rumsfeld was that the two had a "satisfactory, hardworking relationship." Rumsfeld resigned late that year.

On the treatment of suspected terrorists detained in U.S. prisons abroad, Warner also bucked the White House without grandstanding. In 2005, Warner stood side-by-side with two fellow Armed Services Republicans, McCain and Lindsey Graham of South Carolina, to force through Congress legislation banning the torture of suspected terrorists. But he allowed McCain to be the public face of their position. In 2006, Warner again allied himself with McCain and Graham in seeking major changes to the military commissions that the administration had set up to try alleged war criminals at the U.S. naval base in Guantánamo Bay, Cuba.

On Iraq, Warner's support had been crucial to the White House, and he provided it, except on the occasions when he called into question the Pentagon's prosecution of the war. He continually called on the administration to improve the non-military aspects of Iraq's war and economic recovery.

But until early 2007, Warner also staunchly defended the decision to invade and the need to push on despite mounting casualties. When the Senate in June 2006 debated a Democratic amendment to a defense bill calling for a withdrawal from Iraq in 2007, Warner led the opposition, saying, "What we have on the line is the credibility of the United States of America."

Warner marched to his own beat when the committee wrote a bill authorizing defense spending for fiscal 2007. The bill was at odds with the White House on several issues, including authorizing troop strength levels above the president's recommendation.

Born and raised in Washington, D.C., Warner's father was a surgeon who schooled his children in everything from linguistics to Latin to mathematics. Warner joined the Navy at 17 to fight in World War II, and then became a Marine in 1950 to fight in the Korean War. Despite his exemplary military record and government service as Navy secretary, Warner has never been the choice of conservatives among Virginia's Republicans. Some saw him as a socialite and fortune-hunter. Before his marriage to Taylor, he was married to heiress Catherine Mellon and received a reported $7 million from her in their divorce settlement.

He became the party's Senate nominee in 1978 only after their pick, Richard Obenshain, died in a plane crash two months after defeating Warner at the state GOP convention. On the campaign trail, Taylor's celebrity guaranteed large crowds, and Warner held on to win by fewer than 5,000 votes in the closest Senate election in Virginia history.

He won re-election handily in 1984 and 1990.

But in 1996, after fending off an intraparty challenge, he was held to 52 percent of the vote by Democrat Mark Warner (no relation), a cellular telephone entrepreneur and later, governor of Virginia, who spent more than $10 million of his own money. In 2002, Warner drew no Democratic opponent, but there was talk of mounting a challenge to him in 2008.

KEY VOTES

2006

- Yes Confirm Samuel A. Alito Jr. to the Supreme Court
- Yes Allow consideration of a bill to establish a $140 billion trust fund to compensate victims of asbestos exposure
- Yes Extend tax cuts for two years at a cost of $70 billion over five years
- Yes Overhaul immigration policy with border security, enforcement and guest worker program
- Yes Allow consideration of a bill to permanently repeal the estate tax
- No Urge President Bush to begin troop withdrawals from Iraq in 2006
- Yes Lift President Bush's restrictions on stem cell research funding
- Yes Authorize military tribunals for suspected terrorists

2005

- Yes Curb class action lawsuits by shifting them from state to federal courts
- Yes Allow confirmation vote on Priscilla R. Owen to the U.S. Court of Appeals for the 5th Circuit
- No Oppose mandatory emissions limits and block recognition of global warming as a threat
- Yes Approve free-trade pact with five Central American countries
- Yes Pass energy policy overhaul favored by President Bush emphasizing domestic oil and gas production
- Yes Shield gunmakers from lawsuits when their products are used in crimes
- Yes Ban torture of prisoners in U.S. custody
- Yes Renew 16 provisions of the Patriot Act
- Yes Allow final vote on opening the Arctic National Wildlife Refuge to oil and gas exploration

CQ VOTE STUDIES

	PARTY UNITY		PRESIDENTIAL SUPPORT	
	Support	Oppose	Support	Oppose
2006	81%	19%	91%	9%
2005	86%	14%	89%	11%
2004	88%	12%	90%	10%
2003	95%	5%	97%	3%
2002	82%	18%	91%	9%
2001	85%	15%	96%	4%
2000	92%	8%	52%	48%
1999	87%	13%	39%	61%
1998	85%	15%	39%	61%
1997	89%	11%	67%	33%

INTEREST GROUPS

	AFL-CIO	ADA	CCUS	ACU
2006	27%	10%	100%	64%
2005	21%	10%	100%	88%
2004	17%	25%	100%	72%
2003	0%	10%	100%	80%
2002	31%	15%	95%	79%
2001	25%	20%	86%	96%
2000	0%	0%	100%	92%
1999	0%	10%	100%	84%
1998	13%	20%	100%	79%
1997	0%	10%	100%	80%

Sen. Jim Webb (D)

CAPITOL OFFICE
224-4024
webb.senate.gov
144 Russell 20510-4604; fax 228-6363

COMMITTEES
Armed Services
Foreign Relations
Veterans' Affairs
Joint Economic

RESIDENCE
Falls Church

BORN
Feb. 9, 1946, St. Joseph, Mo.

RELIGION
Protestant

FAMILY
Wife, Hong Le Webb; five children

EDUCATION
U. of Southern California, attended 1963-64; U.S. Naval Academy, B.S. 1968; Georgetown U., J.D. 1975

MILITARY SERVICE
Marine Corps, 1968-72

CAREER
Author; screenwriter; journalist; U.S. Defense Department official; congressional aide; lawyer

POLITICAL HIGHLIGHTS
Navy secretary, 1987-88

ELECTION RESULTS

2006 GENERAL		
Jim Webb (D)	1,175,606	49.6%
George Allen (R)	1,166,277	49.2%
Glenda Gail Parker (IGREEN)	26,102	1.1%
2006 PRIMARY		
Jim Webb (D)	83,298	53.5%
Harris Miller (D)	72,486	46.5%

Elected 2006; 1st term

Webb is unquestionably the star of the Senate Democratic freshman Class of 2006, a group not lacking for luster. His narrow victory over incumbent Sen. George Allen clinched a majority for the Democrats in the Senate, and they hailed the Vietnam-era Marine Corps veteran as a newcomer who could speak with authority on defense and foreign policy, areas where the party traditionally has been weaker than Republicans.

It hardly bore mentioning that Webb, the former Navy secretary in the Reagan White House, is a former Republican. He emerged in the 110th Congress (2007-08) as a leading Democratic critic of the Bush administration's policies in Iraq. In January 2007, party leaders tapped Webb to give the response to President Bush's annual State of the Union address, a rare privilege for a freshman.

During the Senate campaign, Webb described the invasion of Iraq as a "strategic blunder" that has exacerbated terrorism, and advocated a diplomatic solution involving countries near Iraq that are historically and culturally invested in that country. Webb in fact shed his longtime GOP affiliation over the administration's Iraq policy, and was an early dissenter of the decision in 2002 to conduct military operations in Iraq. "Those who are pushing for a unilateral war in Iraq know full well that there is no exit strategy if we invade and stay," he wrote in a newspaper column shortly before the Senate voted to give Bush authority to invade Iraq.

But Webb does not seem destined to be a one-issue senator; he's certainly not a one-career senator. His professional roles have ranged from congressional committee counsel to award-winning journalist. Of his eight books, his 1978 Vietnam War novel "Fields of Fire" is his best-known.

With his ramrod posture, brusque manner and unadorned candor, Webb comes off as more ex-Marine than lawyer or writer. Majority Leader Harry Reid described Webb as "impish" and compared him with former Nebraska Democratic Sen. Bob Kerrey, another former Vietnam veteran who freely spoke his mind.

His frankness earned Webb some attention even before he was sworn in. At a post-election reception at the White House, the president asked Webb about the senator-elect's son Jimmy, a Marine who was serving in Iraq. Webb tersely responded, "That's between me and my boy, Mr. President."

In March 2007, Webb was again in the news after an aide was arrested for carrying a loaded handgun into a Senate office building. The gun belonged to Webb, who described the incident as a mix-up. But he also used it to highlight his support for gun owners' rights and his legal right to carry a concealed weapon in Virginia.

That position puts Webb at odds with most members of his party. But Webb was an allegiant Democrat in the first three months of 2007, siding with his new party about nine out of 10 times on Senate votes that pitted most Republicans against most Democrats.

Webb espouses a populist economic platform that highlights what he views as the perils of globalization and of corporate excess — including the growing divide between the affluent and the lower income stratas, and stagnating wages at a time other economic indicators are strong. One week after he was sworn in as senator, Webb said that he wanted to "work on strong legislative proposals and intellectual approaches so that we can actually bring some true changes, rather than simply remonstrate about these issues." He planned to try to work with North Dakota Sen. Byron L. Dorgan, a respected farm-state populist and a critic of corporate abuses, and fellow freshmen Sens. Sherrod Brown of Ohio and Jon Tester of Montana, who also evinced populist themes in their winning 2006 campaigns.

The Webb family has its roots in Virginia's mountainous southwestern region, where his great-great-grandparents are buried just outside of Gate City. The son of an Air Force pilot who fought in World War II, Webb grew up in a military family that hopscotched the country during his youth. The Webbs were Democratic by and large, but he became a Republican because he agreed with the party's positions on national security.

Webb attended the University of Southern California for one year on an ROTC scholarship, then transferred to the U.S. Naval Academy, where he was a boxer. In 1967, he lost an Academy boxing championship to Oliver L. North, who would later become a household name for his role in the Iran-Contra affair. "Both were popular and disliked each other," a Navy boxing coach told The Associated Press in 1991.

Webb graduated from the Marine officers' school in Quantico, Virginia, finishing first in his class of 243. As an infantryman during the Vietnam War, he was awarded the Navy Cross, the Silver Star Medal, two Bronze Star Medals and two Purple Hearts. Webb's third wife, whom he met long after his service, is Vietnamese, and he speaks the language fluently.

Webb earned a law degree in 1975, then served as counsel to the House Veterans' Affairs Committee during the Carter administration. He also did screenwriting and was an executive producer of the 2000 movie "Rules of Engagement," which was based on a story by Webb and starred Tommy Lee Jones.

Less than a year before the November 2006 election, it seemed unlikely that the Democrats could defeat Allen, much less capture the Senate — or that Webb, a longtime Republican who had never sought elective office, would be an integral part of helping Democrats accomplish both. Webb in fact had endorsed Allen's election to the Senate in 2000.

Webb joined the Senate race only in February 2006, just four months before a Democratic primary election in which technology industry lobbyist Harris Miller, a longtime party activist, was already competing. But Democratic leaders eventually came to view Webb, despite his longtime GOP affiliation, as a stronger general-election candidate than Miller. The Democratic Senatorial Campaign Committee (DSCC), which traditionally stays neutral in contested primaries, endorsed Webb just before the June primary, which Webb won by 7 percentage points.

Webb began the fall campaign against Allen as a distinct underdog. He was substantially underfunded against the well-heeled Allen, who also was recognized as a potential 2008 presidential candidate. But balance in the Senate race shifted sharply in August, when Allen used the word "macaca" to mock an Indian-American volunteer for Webb who had been videotaping him at a campaign appearance. Critics skewered Allen for using an epithet that refers to a monkey, though Allen denied knowing it was a racial slur. But the video streaked across the Internet and effectively doomed Allen's presidential ambitions and his Senate re-election.

As Webb closed the gap in the polls, Allen's campaign went on the offensive, brandishing a 1979 article Webb wrote for Washingtonian magazine in which he expressed opposition to combat roles for women and also referred to the Naval Academy dormitory as "a horny woman's dream."

But Webb was buoyed substantially by a favorable political environment for Democrats and a DSCC television advertising campaign attacking Allen. On Election Day, Webb pulled out a 9,329 vote victory — a margin of four-tenths of one percentage point — on the strength of a dominant showing in the northern Virginia suburbs of Washington, D.C.

Rep. Jo Ann Davis (R)

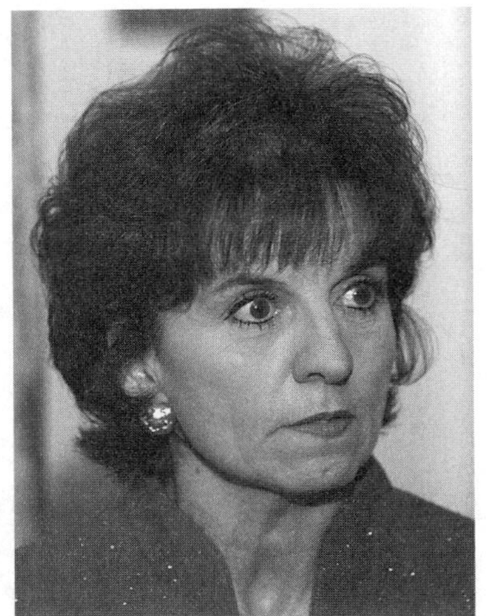

CAPITOL OFFICE
225-4261
www.house.gov/joanndavis
1123 Longworth 20515-4601; fax 225-4382

COMMITTEES
Armed Services
Foreign Affairs

RESIDENCE
Gloucester

BORN
June 29, 1950, Rowan, N.C.

RELIGION
Assemblies of God

FAMILY
Husband, Chuck Davis; two children

EDUCATION
Kecoughtan H.S., graduated 1968

CAREER
Realtor; administrative assistant

POLITICAL HIGHLIGHTS
Va. House, 1998-2001

ELECTION RESULTS

2006 GENERAL		
Jo Ann Davis (R)	143,889	63.0%
Shawn M. O'Donnell (D)	81,083	35.5%
Marvin F. Pixton III (I)	3,236	1.4%
2006 PRIMARY		
Jo Ann Davis (R)		unopposed
2004 GENERAL		
Jo Ann Davis (R)	225,071	78.6%
William A. Lee (I)	57,434	20.0%
write-ins	4,029	1.4%

PREVIOUS WINNING PERCENTAGES
2002 (96%); 2000 (58%)

Elected 2000; 4th term

In a Congress full of up-from-nothing stories, Davis stands out. The daughter of a bus driver from Virginia's Tidewater region, she quit college after one day because she was homesick. But she went on to build a successful real estate business, land a seat in the House and pick up a series of committee assignments critical to the interests of the military families and veterans in her district.

"I am not your typical politician," she likes to say. "I'm a country girl who believes in straight talk and common sense, conservative ideas."

Davis started 110th Congress (2007-08) with greater battles than trying to steer legislation through a Democratically controlled Congress; in early February 2007, she was diagnosed for the second time with breast cancer while being treated for an unrelated medical problem. She was away from Capitol Hill for more than two months, but in late April she vowed to resume work while receiving chemotherapy treatments every three weeks. She was first diagnosed with breast cancer in September 2005 and underwent a mastectomy and chemo treatments in 2006.

Her plate was already quite full at work when the second diagnosis came. On the first day of the new Congress, she introduced a whopping 23 bills, including one calling for a reduction in drug prices for Medicare patients and another seeking federal recognition for the Rappahannock Tribe of Virginia. She also offered a bill that would require group health plans to include coverage for post-mastectomy reconstructive surgery.

She lost her seat on the Intelligence Committee when the Democrats took over in 2007, but retained her place on Armed Services and became the ranking Republican of the Readiness Subcommittee — a crucial appointment for her district, which stretches from Washington's exurbs to Newport News and is crammed with military bases and shipbuilding facilities, including the world's largest, Norfolk Naval Base.

Among the first issues the Armed Services panel had to address were the revelations about poor patient care at Walter Reed Army Medical Center. Davis immediately cosponsored a bill — which the House easily passed — to increase the ranks of caseworkers and counselors in the military health system, and to force the Pentagon and Veterans Affairs Department to make their medical information systems interoperable.

In February 2007, Davis criticized President Bush's plan to send more than 21,000 additional combat troops into the Iraq War: "I'm almost of the opinion that it's too little, too late," she told the Newport News Daily Press. But she opposed the Democrats' war funding bill that included a timeline for withdrawal of U.S. troops from Iraq. She missed the vote on the bill, but said she believed enacting the bill "would have dangerous consequences."

One of her early legislative victories in her first term was approval of her bill to expand the Servicemembers' Group Life Insurance program to include spouses and children of veterans. The changes were retroactive to cover service members killed in the terrorist attack on the *USS Cole* in Yemen in 2000 as well as National Guardsmen, including 18 from Virginia, killed in an airplane crash in March 2001.

Davis has pushed to reduce the number of years that the Department of Defense can lease foreign-built ships, a practice that discourages domestic shipbuilding. She also seeks to authorize the Navy to contract for the first CVN-21 aircraft carrier, to be built at Newport News in her district. In 2005, the House passed her bill to keep work on the *USS Carl Vinson* — an important home district project — on schedule for delivery in 2008.

Davis affiliates with the conservative Republican Study Committee. She opposes abortion, including in cases of rape or incest, gets an "A" from the National Rifle Association and wants to ban same-sex marriage. A Christian outspoken about her faith, she raised a minor ruckus in late 2005 when she introduced a non-binding resolution — which the House passed — giving sanction to the traditions and symbols of Christmas. Davis said she wanted to stop the political correctness that prompted some retail chains to ban their employees from wishing customers a "Merry Christmas."

With a large pool of elderly military retirees in her district, she departs from Republicans on issues related to Medicare and Medicaid, two government health programs serving the elderly and the poor. In 2005, she joined 42 other Republicans in protesting proposed Medicaid funding cuts. The following year, she introduced a bill that would have let the government negotiate prices for Medicare prescription drugs. The Democratic House passed a similar bill in January 2007.

Davis also has split with her party to vote against drilling for oil in national monument areas, against cutting sugar subsidies and against mandatory school testing. In 2002, she was one of only 27 House Republicans who voted against the law that gave Bush fast-track authority to negotiate trade deals that Congress cannot amend.

She grew up in a trailer in Hampton, where the James River empties into the Chesapeake Bay in the flat Tidewater region of eastern Virginia. Her father, who died in 1987, held a number of blue-collar jobs; he and his wife, "Shorty," played in a bluegrass band. Sunday morning in the Davis household was like a scene from "Coal Miner's Daughter," with the guitars, fiddles and mandolins going.

Davis was a secretary for a real estate company for 10 years before getting a real estate license and starting her own company. She was one of the founding partners of a worldwide network of real estate firms that specialize in helping military families relocate from one base to another. Active in professional and civic organizations, she did not consider entering politics until a friend suggested it. She won a close election to the Virginia House in 1997, capitalizing on grass-roots support from conservatives.

Early in 2000, she was the first Republican to jump into the race when Republican Rep. Herbert H. Bateman announced his retirement. She won a narrow victory in a five-way contest, and took the November election by more than 20 percentage points. The first Republican woman ever to represent Virginia in Congress, Davis has coasted to re-election since.

KEY VOTES

2006

No Stop broadband companies from favoring select Internet traffic
Yes Affirm U.S. commitment to war in Iraq and reject setting a withdrawal date for troops
? Repeal requirement for bilingual ballots at the polls
? Permit U.S. sale of civilian nuclear technology to India
Yes Build a 700-mile fence on the U.S.-Mexico border to curb illegal crossings
Yes Permit warrantless wiretaps of suspected terrorists

2005

Yes Intervene in the life-support case of Terri Schiavo
No Lift President Bush's restrictions on stem cell research funding
No Prohibit FBI access to library and bookstore records
- Approve free-trade pact with five Central American countries
Yes Pass energy policy overhaul favored by President Bush emphasizing domestic oil and gas production
Yes End mandatory preservation of habitat of endangered animal and plant species
Yes Ban torture of prisoners in U.S. custody

CQ VOTE STUDIES

	PARTY UNITY		PRESIDENTIAL SUPPORT	
	Support	Oppose	Support	Oppose
2006	87%	13%	87%	13%
2005	93%	7%	79%	21%
2004	91%	9%	76%	24%
2003	93%	7%	82%	18%
2002	96%	4%	82%	18%

INTEREST GROUPS

	AFL-CIO	ADA	CCUS	ACU
2006	40%	5%	83%	80%
2005	33%	15%	78%	84%
2004	33%	10%	90%	88%
2003	27%	15%	80%	80%
2002	25%	5%	75%	96%

VIRGINIA 1

East – parts of Newport News and Hampton, Fredericksburg

The Republican-friendly 1st lies along the Potomac River and Chesapeake Bay, stretching from the Northern Virginia suburbs and exurbs of Washington, D.C., all the way south to the shipbuilding cities of Hampton and Newport News. Along the way, popular tourist destinations, such as Williamsburg, Jamestown and Yorktown, recall Virginia's colonial past.

Industry in the 1st revolves around military installations and NASA sites, which have attracted a growing technology private sector. Colleges and universities contribute to diversifying the district's economic base, as do shipbuilding and tourism. Inland, agriculture and poultry help drive the economy.

The 1st's northern counties are expanding rapidly as Washington commuters continue to move farther from the city. Spotsylvania County (one-fifth of which is in the 7th District) has more than doubled in population since 1990 as a result of its proximity to both Richmond and Washington and its location on the Interstate 95 corridor. Stafford County, just north of Fredericksburg, also has seen rapid growth and is the 1st's most populous county. Despite fairly high housing prices, Fauquier (shared with the 10th) also has seen steady growth.

The 1st is solidly Republican, and the party controls local offices here. George W. Bush took 60 percent of the district's 2004 presidential vote.

MAJOR INDUSTRY

Defense, technology, agriculture, tourism, higher education

MILITARY BASES

Marine Corps Base Quantico, 6,114 military, 7,177 civilian (2006); Naval Surface Warfare Center, Dahlgren Division, 542 military, 7,000 civilian (2007); Naval Weapons Station Yorktown, 164 military, 1,357 civilian (2007); Fort A.P. Hill (Army), 378 military, 493 civilian (2006)

CITIES

Newport News (pt.), 71,800; Hampton (pt.), 31,755; Fredericksburg, 19,279

NOTABLE

George Washington and Robert E. Lee both were born in Westmoreland County, and their birth sites attract visitors; Jamestown, settled in 1607, was the first permanent English settlement in North America.

Rep. Thelma Drake (R)

CAPITOL OFFICE
225-4215
drake.house.gov
1208 Longworth 20515-4602; fax 225-4218

COMMITTEES
Armed Services
Transportation & Infrastructure

RESIDENCE
Norfolk

BORN
Nov. 20, 1949, Elyria, Ohio

RELIGION
United Church of Christ

FAMILY
Husband, Thomas E. "Ted" Drake; two children

EDUCATION
Elyria H.S., graduated 1967

CAREER
Realtor; siding company owner

POLITICAL HIGHLIGHTS
Republican nominee for Va. House, 1993; Va. House, 1996-2004

ELECTION RESULTS

2006 GENERAL		
Thelma Drake (R)	88,777	51.3%
Phil Kellam (D)	83,901	48.5%
2006 PRIMARY		
Thelma Drake (R)		unopposed
2004 GENERAL		
Thelma Drake (R)	132,946	55.1%
David Ashe (D)	108,180	44.8%

Elected 2004; 2nd term

Drake's primary focus in Congress is all things military as she represents a district that historically has had the greatest number of active-duty military personnel.

It was axiomatic that, when she first came to the House in 2004, she would be appointed to the Armed Services panel — a post that has become expected for lawmakers from Virginia's Tidewater area, which is home to so many military families and a number of key military installations.

Drake, who continues to serve on Armed Services, says she wants to make sure the military "has the most modern weapons systems, that they've got the armaments and the tools that they need to be on the front line." Shipyards employ thousands of district residents, and Drake supports the Navy's next-generation aircraft carrier, CVN-21. "I think that people here are concerned about the number of ships in our military." Drake also sees the military as an instrument of job creation through partnerships with local colleges and universities.

Drake opposed Democratic efforts in early 2007 to set deadlines for the withdrawal of U.S. troops from Iraq. "A retreat at this point in time could, down the road, necessitate our troops returning to an Iraq that is much more dangerous than the one they left," Drake said in February 2007.

Her support for a strong military, coupled with her social conservatism and anti-tax views, makes her a dependable vote for President Bush and House Republican leaders. In the 109th Congress (2005-06), she sided with Bush on 92 percent of the votes on which he took a position and with her party on 97 percent of votes pitting Democrats against Republicans.

In early 2007, Drake voted against five of the six top-priority measures promoted by the new House Democratic majority, including a federal minimum wage increase and a mandate that the federal government negotiate with pharmaceutical companies to reduce prices of drugs covered under a 2003 Medicare prescription drug law. The only bill of the six she supported was designed to cut interest rates on student loans.

Drake was not in Congress when Bush signed major tax cut measures in 2001 and 2003, but she has consistently defended them and opposed efforts to rescind or dilute them. Her background as a realtor informs her views. "As a realtor, before coming to Congress, I can't tell you how many times I would hear from people, 'I can't sell that rental property because I can't pay that capital gains tax,' " Drake said in February 2007.

A shift to minority political status in the 110th Congress (2007-08) bumped Drake from the Education and Resources committees. She kept her seat on Armed Services and was named to the Transportation and Infrastructure Committee. That assignment is a good fit for Drake, whose coastal district abuts the Chesapeake Bay and is influenced by maritime, highway and railroad transportation.

In March 2007, Drake introduced legislation to allow Virginia officials to remove High Occupancy Vehicle (HOV) designations along area interstates without having to repay federal-aid highway funds. The HOV lanes are not being used, she says.

On other issues, Drake was supportive during her first term of Republican efforts to overhaul liability laws. In July 2006, the House passed a Drake-sponsored bill to grant a liability shield to "good Samaritan" pilots who fly public benefit missions, such as transporting patients or organ donations. But the Senate did not take up the legislation.

Drake grew up in Elyria, Ohio, near Cleveland, and left Catholic school her senior year of high school after she became pregnant. She married her boyfriend, graduated from a public high school and soon thereafter the young family relocated to Norfolk. A divorce left Drake a young single mother, but she refused public aid. "I always felt I was the only person responsible for myself," Drake told The Virginian Pilot newspaper in 2004. "You don't turn to other people to help you."

Drake, who has remarried twice, most recently in 1990, pursued a career selling real estate. She lost her first bid for political office — a 1993 campaign for the Virginia House of Delegates — but she defeated the Democratic incumbent in a rematch two years later. In the state House, she worked on housing issues and promoted tax cuts and legislation to require parental notification prior to a minor's having an abortion.

Until late August 2004, Drake fully expected to return to Richmond in 2005 for her 10th year in the state House. But she quickly switched gears when she was hand-picked by local party officials as an emergency replacement nominee for the 2nd District seat after two-term GOP incumbent Ed Schrock unexpectedly decided to retire on the eve of the 2004 Republican convention.

Though she had to jump-start her campaign, Drake capitalized on the Republicans' slight edge in the conservative-leaning district. She benefited from name recognition she had developed in her legislative career, the strong district showing by Bush, and aid from the state and national Republican parties. Although Democrat David Ashe, a Marine Corps veteran who served in Iraq, ran aggressively, Drake won by a comfortable 10 percentage point margin.

Drake faced a tougher challenge in 2006 from Phil Kellam, the elected revenue commissioner in Virginia Beach and a member of a prominent political family. It was an interesting matchup: Kellam has a political base in Virginia Beach, which is more populous and Republican-leaning than Drake's hometown of Norfolk, which leans Democratic.

With Bush's popularity waning, even in the normally Republican-leaning 2nd District, Kellam criticized Drake for siding so consistently with the administration and her party. Drake and her Republican allies — namely, the National Republican Congressional Committee — portrayed Kellam as weak on national security issues.

Drake won by 4,876 votes — less than 3 percentage points; her significant 5,429-vote margin in Virginia Beach overcame her small vote deficits to Kellam elsewhere in the district.

KEY VOTES

2006

No Stop broadband companies from favoring select Internet traffic
Yes Affirm U.S. commitment to war in Iraq and reject setting a withdrawal date for troops
Yes Repeal requirement for bilingual ballots at the polls
Yes Permit U.S. sale of civilian nuclear technology to India
Yes Build a 700-mile fence on the U.S.-Mexico border to curb illegal crossings
Yes Permit warrantless wiretaps of suspected terrorists

2005

Yes Intervene in the life-support case of Terri Schiavo
No Lift President Bush's restrictions on stem cell research funding
No Prohibit FBI access to library and bookstore records
Yes Approve free-trade pact with five Central American countries
Yes Pass energy policy overhaul favored by President Bush emphasizing domestic oil and gas production
Yes End mandatory preservation of habitat of endangered animal and plant species
No Ban torture of prisoners in U.S. custody

CQ VOTE STUDIES

	PARTY UNITY		PRESIDENTIAL SUPPORT	
	Support	Oppose	Support	Oppose
2006	97%	3%	95%	5%
2005	98%	2%	89%	11%

INTEREST GROUPS

	AFL-CIO	ADA	CCUS	ACU
2006	21%	0%	100%	88%
2005	20%	5%	93%	92%

VIRGINIA 2

Southeast – Virginia Beach, parts of Norfolk and Hampton

Taking in the state's Atlantic coastline, the 2nd is dominated by Virginia Beach, a center for white-collar military families and retirees. The district includes parts of Norfolk and Hampton and crosses the Chesapeake Bay inlet to reach Virginia's portion of the Delmarva Peninsula.

Two-thirds of the 2nd's population lives in the state's largest city, Virginia Beach, but growth has slowed in recent years in the wake of military base closings and land scarcity in the city's urban northern section. The 2005 BRAC round ordered Fort Monroe, in nearby Hampton, closed by 2011, but scheduled personnel increases at the district's other installations may mean the 2nd will avoid job losses.

The 2nd includes half of Norfolk (shared with the 3rd), a largely blue-collar and Democratic-leaning area with a sizable Filipino population and a history as an important port city. The naval base here still dominates the district's economy, which is bolstered by shipbuilding and shipping companies. On the peninsula, Accomack and Northampton counties attract beach-related tourism.

The 2nd's conservatism derives more from military and economic issues than social questions. Voters favor the GOP, but Democrats did well here in 2005, winning most state legislative seats outside of Virginia Beach. Democratic Gov. Tim Kaine even won Virginia Beach's vote in 2005.

MAJOR INDUSTRY

Military, tourism, shipbuilding

MILITARY BASES

Naval Station Norfolk, 54,000 military, 11,000 civilian (2007); Naval Air Station Oceana, 12,000 military, 2,500 civilian; Langley Air Force Base, 8,722 military, 2,370 civilian (2007); Naval Amphibious Base Little Creek, 7,700 military, 1,815 civilian; Naval Air Station Oceana Dam Neck Annex, 3,600 military, 1,300 civilian (2005); Fort Monroe (Army), 1,393 military, 1,948 civilian (2005); Fort Story (Army), 987 military, 205 civilian (2004)

CITIES

Virginia Beach, 425,257; Norfolk (pt.), 112,102; Hampton (pt.), 54,753

NOTABLE

The Chesapeake Bay Bridge-Tunnel, just north of Virginia Beach, is the longest bridge-tunnel in the world at 17.6 miles.

Rep. Robert C. Scott (D)

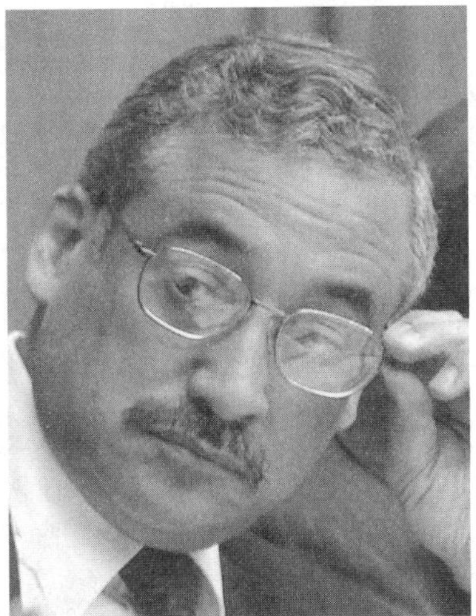

CAPITOL OFFICE
225-8351
bobby.scott@mail.house.gov
www.house.gov/scott
1201 Longworth 20515-4603; fax 225-8354

COMMITTEES
Budget
Education & Labor
Judiciary
(Crime, Terrorism & Homeland Security - chairman)

RESIDENCE
Newport News

BORN
April 30, 1947, Washington, D.C.

RELIGION
Episcopalian

FAMILY
Divorced

EDUCATION
Harvard U., A.B. 1969; Boston College, J.D. 1973

MILITARY SERVICE
Army Reserve, 1970-74; Mass. National Guard, 1974-76

CAREER
Lawyer

POLITICAL HIGHLIGHTS
Va. House, 1979-83; Va. Senate, 1983-93; Democratic nominee for U.S. House, 1986

ELECTION RESULTS

2006 GENERAL		
Robert C. Scott (D)	133,546	96.1%
write-ins	5,448	3.9%
2006 PRIMARY		
Robert C. Scott (D)		unopposed
2004 GENERAL		
Robert C. Scott (D)	159,373	69.3%
Winsome Sears (R)	70,194	30.5%

PREVIOUS WINNING PERCENTAGES
2002 (96%); 2000 (98%); 1998 (76%); 1996 (82%); 1994 (79%); 1992 (79%)

Elected 1992; 8th term

For all but the first two of his 14 years in the House, Scott was playing defense — fighting a rearguard action against a conservative Republican majority bent on cutting social programs and expanding the government's powers to eavesdrop.

He was one of the stalwart liberal voices on the Judiciary Committee, but without the votes to back up his ideas. In committee and on the floor, he battled Republican efforts to stiffen prison sentences, crack down on illegal immigration, amend the Constitution to promote conservative social positions, and exempt faith-based organizations from anti-discrimination laws.

Now, with Democrats running the House, Scott is the chairman of the Judiciary panel's Crime, Terrorism and Homeland Security Subcommittee, and he is on offense — moving quickly to advance bills that would expand federal grants to hire more police officers, increase penalties for hate crimes, reduce criminal recidivism and encourage law students to choose public service jobs.

Scott says that while the GOP, when it ran the House, passed bills that were "politically popular," his own focus is on policies that have been shown by research to be effective in reducing crime.

The first African-American to represent Virginia since 1891, Scott's political philosophy has a strong civil libertarian strain, which sometimes puts him at odds with his own party. In 2002, he was one of only 12 House Democrats who voted against a campaign finance law revision. He viewed one of its core provisions — prohibiting advocacy groups from mentioning specific candidates in their broadcast advertisements close to an election — as an unconstitutional restriction on free speech.

He is a persistent foe of proposals to expand law enforcement authority, fearing violations of individual rights. He often points out that federal wiretapping rules were created as "a tool of last resort" for investigations of organized crime, but says the Bush administration inappropriately relies on wiretapping to probe a broad array of crimes and possible terrorism links.

Scott was a vocal opponent of the 2001 anti-terrorism law known as the Patriot Act, which was enacted with overwhelming support by Congress six weeks after the attacks of Sept. 11. He said the new intelligence-gathering provisions in the statute trampled on individual liberties. In the 109th Congress (2005-06), he voted against a reauthorization of the law, along with most other House Democrats.

Scott has long argued that the "tough on crime" approach does not work. He says education, jobs and family-support programs are a better answer. "It makes no sense, waiting for the children to mess up and then lock them up, when it is cheaper to invest in crime prevention programs and prevent them from getting in trouble in the first place," he said.

In 2004, he helped lead Democratic opposition to a balanced-budget constitutional amendment, saying it was an act of hypocrisy for Republicans to champion the amendment while voting for tax cuts that added to record budget deficits. He is not a big fan of proposed constitutional amendments; in opposing many such GOP proposals to protect the flag, promote school prayer, limit taxation or extend rights to crime victims, Scott's trademark response was that he took an oath to "support and defend" the Constitution, not "support and amend" it.

In 2007, he led a Congressional Black Caucus task force that developed an alternative budget plan. It called for the immediate repeal of tax cuts for upper-income taxpayers and for increased spending on domestic programs, including health care, education and job training. The plan was rejected, with all Republicans and half of the Democrats voting no.

From his seat on the Education and Labor Committee, Scott argues that standardized test scores place low-income school districts and their students at a disadvantage. In 2001, he voted against House passage of the No Child Left Behind Act requiring annual math and reading testing of students, although he did support the final version of the law.

Scott drops his liberal mantle when it comes to looking out for southeast Virginia's military and tobacco interests. A former member of the Army Reserve and the National Guard, Scott is one of the stronger pro-Pentagon voices in the Congressional Black Caucus. He promotes the interests of his district's shipbuilders and military bases; Northrop Grumman Newport News and the Army's Fort Eustis are major employers. The district is also home to one of the nation's largest cigarette plants, a south Richmond facility operated by Philip Morris USA. In 2006, his interest in ports led Scott to propose that all cargo entering U.S. ports be subject to inspection.

Scott is the son of a surgeon and a teacher. When local white officials resisted court-ordered integration of the public schools, the Scotts, along with other well-to-do black families, sent their son to Groton, the prestigious Massachusetts prep school. He graduated from Harvard University and earned his law degree from Boston College. He returned home to Newport News after law school and became active in local civic groups, which eventually led him into politics. "I just didn't think enough was getting done," he says.

Scott won a seat in the state House in 1978 and in five years moved up to the state Senate. In his first run for Congress, in 1986, he failed to unseat Republican Herbert H. Bateman, capturing 44 percent of the vote. Six years later, after redistricting resulted in a 3rd District that was 64 percent black, Scott tried again. With no incumbent running, he took two-thirds of the vote in a three-way Democratic primary and breezed to victory in November. He became the second black Virginian to serve in the House after John Mercer Langston, a Republican who served a few months in 1890 and 1891.

Scott won by lopsided margins again in 1994 and 1996, but when a federal panel struck down the 3rd District's boundaries in 1997, his political future seemed in jeopardy. The new lines drawn by the General Assembly kept the black population at 54 percent, but Scott won handily in 1998, with 76 percent of the vote, and has ever since. In 2006, he was unopposed.

KEY VOTES

2006

- Yes Stop broadband companies from favoring select Internet traffic
- No Affirm U.S. commitment to war in Iraq and reject setting a withdrawal date for troops
- No Repeal requirement for bilingual ballots at the polls
- Yes Permit U.S. sale of civilian nuclear technology to India
- No Build a 700-mile fence on the U.S.-Mexico border to curb illegal crossings
- No Permit warrantless wiretaps of suspected terrorists

2005

- No Intervene in the life-support case of Terri Schiavo
- Yes Lift President Bush's restrictions on stem cell research funding
- Yes Prohibit FBI access to library and bookstore records
- No Approve free-trade pact with five Central American countries
- Yes Pass energy policy overhaul favored by President Bush emphasizing domestic oil and gas production
- No End mandatory preservation of habitat of endangered animal and plant species
- Yes Ban torture of prisoners in U.S. custody

CQ VOTE STUDIES

	PARTY UNITY		PRESIDENTIAL SUPPORT	
	Support	Oppose	Support	Oppose
2006	95%	5%	27%	73%
2005	95%	5%	13%	87%
2004	98%	2%	12%	88%
2003	97%	3%	9%	91%
2002	96%	4%	23%	77%

INTEREST GROUPS

	AFL-CIO	ADA	CCUS	ACU
2006	100%	100%	27%	4%
2005	100%	100%	41%	4%
2004	100%	100%	29%	4%
2003	100%	100%	23%	12%
2002	100%	95%	42%	4%

VIRGINIA 3

Southeast – parts of Richmond, Norfolk and Newport News, Portsmouth

The black-majority 3rd begins in the state capital of Richmond and reaches southeast into military and shipbuilding territory, including parts of Newport News, Hampton and Norfolk, and the entire city of Portsmouth. The 3rd is the strongest Democratic district in Virginia.

The 3rd long has benefited from hosting one of the nation's largest ports, at Hampton Roads, and from Richmond's financial sector. State government also drives the economy of Richmond and its environs, as does manufacturing. Richmond is home to one of the largest cigarette plants in the nation, a Philip Morris USA facility.

The Hampton Roads area has a heavy concentration of naval installations as well as associated shipbuilding and ship repair companies. Among these is the nation's largest privately owned shipyard — Northrop Grumman Newport News — which builds naval aircraft carriers and submarines. The 3rd's military installations received mixed results from the 2005 BRAC round, with all three facilities affected by the shuffling of personnel, but none scheduled for closure.

Richmond, Portsmouth and Norfolk, which have substantial black populations, all gave John Kerry more than 60 percent of their vote in the 2004 presidential election. Overall, Kerry took 66 percent of the 3rd's vote, his best showing in any Virginia congressional district. Despite Democrats' dominance of the 3rd, Republicans are strong in some areas, particularly in New Kent County and Prince George County, which is shared with the 4th District.

MAJOR INDUSTRY

Defense, shipbuilding and repair, shipping, tobacco, government

MILITARY BASES

Norfolk Naval Shipyard at Portsmouth, 50 military, 7,800 civilian (2007); Fort Eustis (Army), 4,777 military, 2,715 civilian (2006); Naval Medical Center Portsmouth, 3,026 military, 1,547 civilian (2005)

CITIES

Richmond (pt.), 144,520; Norfolk (pt.), 122,301; Newport News (pt.), 108,350; Portsmouth, 100,565; Hampton (pt.), 59,929

NOTABLE

The Edgar Allan Poe Museum is in Richmond, where Poe lived.

Rep. J. Randy Forbes (R)

CAPITOL OFFICE
225-6365
www.house.gov/forbes
307 Cannon 20515-4604; fax 226-1170

COMMITTEES
Armed Services
Judiciary

RESIDENCE
Chesapeake

BORN
Feb. 17, 1952, Chesapeake, Va.

RELIGION
Baptist

FAMILY
Wife, Shirley Forbes; four children

EDUCATION
Randolph-Macon College, B.A. 1974 (political science); U. of Virginia, J.D. 1977

CAREER
Lawyer; state legislative aide

POLITICAL HIGHLIGHTS
Va. House, 1990-97 (Republican floor leader, 1994-97); Va. Republican Party chairman, 1996-2000; Va. Senate, 1997-2001 (Republican floor leader, 1998-2000)

ELECTION RESULTS

2006 GENERAL		
J. Randy Forbes (R)	150,967	76.1%
Albert P. Burckard Jr. (IGREEN)	46,487	23.4%
2006 PRIMARY		
J. Randy Forbes (R)	unopposed	
2004 GENERAL		
J. Randy Forbes (R)	182,444	64.5%
Jonathan Menefee (D)	100,413	35.5%

PREVIOUS WINNING PERCENTAGES
2002 (98%); 2001 Special Election (52%)

Elected June 2001; 3rd full term

Forbes has long been a force in Virginia state politics, though he has yet to achieve the national status of his two law school classmates, former Republican Gov. James S. Gilmore III and former GOP Sen. George Allen.

A well-regarded state lawmaker before coming to Congress, Forbes has spent most of his career immersed in the politics of the Tidewater region of coastal Virginia. Indeed, in his initial years in the House, he concentrated on local issues, which paid off for him in a big way in 2005 when Fort Lee Army Base in his district not only got a reprieve from the base closing commission, but was slated to double in size with the addition of more than 7,000 personnel. That was welcome news in an area with one of the largest concentrations of military bases in the nation.

With moves like that, Forbes has been able to solidify his claim on what had been a swing district; it was previously represented by Democrat Norman Sisisky for 18 years. Now Forbes is free to branch out, and in the 109th Congress (2005-06) he delved into foreign policy, particularly U.S. policy with China. On an official visit there in 2005, Forbes observed Chinese shipbuilding and military modernization, and came away believing that the U.S. government knows too little about a potential rival. "This is going to be a major, major superpower on the world scene in very short order. The frightening thing is they know much about us and we know very little about them," he says. "Our trade deficit is financing the purchase of weapons that are pointed at us. We are not connecting the dots."

Forbes has pressed for legislation to discourage foreign companies from selling sensitive military technology to China. And in the 109th Congress, he led efforts to block the purchase of the U.S. oil firm Unocal by a company owned by the Chinese government.

Forbes is usually a reliable vote for his party. On votes pitting most Democrats against most Republicans, he stuck with his party 94 percent of the time in the 109th Congress, while voting in agreement with President Bush 91 percent of the time. A notable exception was his opposition in 2004 to the intelligence overhaul bill backed by the GOP leadership and the White House. He was unhappy that the final legislation dropped border security measures he favored, including stricter regulations of driver's licenses.

A Sunday school teacher at his Baptist church, Forbes opposes abortion and in 2006 pressed for a ban on a procedure critics call "partial birth" abortion. He is also against gun control. His conservative credentials, combined with a business law background, led House leaders to appoint Forbes to a seat on the Judiciary Committee. He has pursued a tough law-and-order agenda, backing a bill that increased prison terms and fines for corporate wrongdoing and another to arm airline pilots with handguns in cockpits for a two-year trial period. In 2004, he supported a bill to exempt off-duty and retired law enforcement officers from concealed weapons laws. And in 2006, he won House passage of a bill targeting illegal aliens who belong to criminal gangs.

Forbes also serves on the Armed Services Committee, where, in addition to Fort Lee, he looks out for the Norfolk Naval Shipyard.

Forbes grew up in what was then rural Chesapeake, a city that since his boyhood has almost tripled in size to 200,000 people. His grandparents farmed, and Forbes rode horses around town. (He still has a passion for horses and owns three.)

After getting a law degree from the University of Virginia in 1977, Forbes returned to Chesapeake and practiced law for several years, becoming a partner in the firm Kaufman and Canoles. Inspired by his popular civic booster father, Malcolm, he got involved in politics in 1989, running successfully for a seat in the Virginia House of Delegates. He spent almost a dozen years in the legislature, becoming Republican floor leader in the House and later achieving the same position in the state Senate. His name was attached to several significant bills, including one that abolished parole for felony convictions and another to return lottery profits to local governments. Forbes was also known for leading a campaign to boost funding for school construction.

When former law school chum George Allen became governor, he made Forbes the chairman of the state Republican Party. Under Forbes' watch from 1996 to 2000, the party won several state offices and became the dominant power in Virginia politics. Forbes also stayed involved in the affairs of his hometown of Chesapeake, where he sometimes got under the skin of other Republicans, who complained he tried to play kingmaker.

The soft-spoken but fiercely competitive Forbes hungered for his own move into statewide politics. Early in 2001, he geared up to run for lieutenant governor, facing a tough primary contest against state House Delegate Jay K. Katzen. But when 4th District Rep. Sisisky, a conservative Democrat, died that March after lung cancer surgery, Forbes switched to the special election to succeed him, encouraged by party leaders.

Forbes won the nomination in April at a contentious convention, and went on to face state Sen. Louise Lucas, a black Democrat and former shipyard worker popular with African-American and working-class voters. Lucas was bidding to become the first black woman elected to Congress from Virginia. The race got national attention, turning into the first referendum on the Bush presidency and Republican efforts to boost their slim majority in the House. The candidates and national parties spent more than $7 million during the 32-day campaign, or about $52 for every vote.

Forbes won in balloting that broke along racial lines. His hold on the competitive district improved dramatically in the 2002 election, following a controversial redistricting that moved a number of African-American neighborhoods into the neighboring 3rd District, where blacks already constituted the majority of voters. Democrats objected that the move packed minority votes into a single district, while boosting the white population in the 4th District from 57 percent to more than 60 percent. A federal appeals court upheld the plan in September 2004.

Two months later, in November 2004, Forbes easily beat 26-year-old Democratic challenger Jonathan Menefee, a novice and former aide to presidential candidate John Kerry. In 2006, Democrats did not field a candidate.

KEY VOTES

2006

- No Stop broadband companies from favoring select Internet traffic
- Yes Affirm U.S. commitment to war in Iraq and reject setting a withdrawal date for troops
- Yes Repeal requirement for bilingual ballots at the polls
- Yes Permit U.S. sale of civilian nuclear technology to India
- \+ Build a 700-mile fence on the U.S.-Mexico border to curb illegal crossings
- Yes Permit warrantless wiretaps of suspected terrorists

2005

- Yes Intervene in the life-support case of Terri Schiavo
- No Lift President Bush's restrictions on stem cell research funding
- No Prohibit FBI access to library and bookstore records
- Yes Approve free-trade pact with five Central American countries
- Yes Pass energy policy overhaul favored by President Bush emphasizing domestic oil and gas production
- Yes End mandatory preservation of habitat of endangered animal and plant species
- Yes Ban torture of prisoners in U.S. custody

CQ VOTE STUDIES

	PARTY UNITY		PRESIDENTIAL SUPPORT	
	Support	Oppose	Support	Oppose
2006	93%	7%	93%	7%
2005	95%	5%	89%	11%
2004	96%	4%	82%	18%
2003	97%	3%	93%	7%
2002	98%	2%	85%	15%

INTEREST GROUPS

	AFL-CIO	ADA	CCUS	ACU
2006	29%	10%	100%	92%
2005	20%	5%	89%	92%
2004	14%	5%	100%	100%
2003	7%	10%	97%	88%
2002	11%	0%	85%	100%

VIRGINIA 4

Southeast – Chesapeake, Petersburg

Located among the rivers and swamps of southeastern and south-central Virginia, the 4th begins in Hampton Roads in the growing city of Chesapeake before heading west into rural tobacco- and peanut-producing areas. It then bends north to reach the Tri-Cities area — Petersburg, Hopewell and Colonial Heights — south of Richmond.

Chesapeake, by far the 4th's most-populous city, has grown by nearly 45 percent since 1990 as manufacturing and other industries moved in alongside residents who commute to nearby Norfolk or Virginia Beach. The city has a varied business community that features steel, textiles and mutual funds, and it continues to attract new companies.

Farther north, the Tri-Cities area received a boost from the 2005 BRAC round, which ordered a near doubling of personnel at Fort Lee by the end of 2011. Outside of the 4th's population centers, tobacco and peanut farming play a central role in the economy. There also are pork-producing facilities here in sparsely populated counties such as Isle of Wight and Sussex.

The 4th votes comfortably Republican at the national and statewide levels. Democrats fare better in areas with sizable black voting blocs — the district has the state's second-largest black population (33 percent) — and Democrats can win local elections across the 4th. Petersburg, which is four-fifths black, gave presidential candidate John Kerry 81 percent of the vote in 2004, his best showing in the state. Overall, the district gave George W. Bush 57 percent of its 2004 presidential vote.

MAJOR INDUSTRY

Military, agriculture, tobacco, health care, manufacturing

MILITARY BASES

Fort Lee (Army), 3,400 military, 3,200 civilian (2007); U.S. Joint Forces Command Joint Warfighting Center, 1,359 military, 1,218 civilian (2007); Defense Supply Center, Richmond, 44 military, 2,430 civilian (2004); Naval Support Activity Norfolk, Northwest Annex, 937 military, 775 civilian (2007)

CITIES

Chesapeake, 199,184; Suffolk, 63,677; Petersburg, 33,740; Hopewell, 22,354

NOTABLE

Suffolk, which calls itself the peanut capital of the world, is the birthplace of Planters' Mr. Peanut and hosts an annual Suffolk Peanut Festival.

Rep. Virgil H. Goode Jr. (R)

CAPITOL OFFICE
225-4711
www.house.gov/goode
1520 Longworth 20515-4605; fax 225-5681

COMMITTEES
Appropriations

RESIDENCE
Rocky Mount

BORN
Oct. 17, 1946, Richmond, Va.

RELIGION
Baptist

FAMILY
Wife, Lucy D. Goode; one child

EDUCATION
U. of Richmond, B.A. 1969; U. of Virginia, J.D. 1973

MILITARY SERVICE
Va. National Guard, 1969-75

CAREER
Lawyer

POLITICAL HIGHLIGHTS
Va. Senate, 1973-97 (served as a Democrat); sought Democratic nomination for U.S. Senate, 1982, 1994

ELECTION RESULTS

2006 GENERAL		
Virgil H. Goode Jr. (R)	125,370	59.1%
Al Weed (D)	84,682	39.9%
2006 PRIMARY		
Virgil H. Goode Jr. (R)		unopposed
2004 GENERAL		
Virgil H. Goode Jr. (R)	172,431	63.7%
Al Weed (D)	98,237	36.3%

PREVIOUS WINNING PERCENTAGES *
2002 (63%); 2000 (67%); 1998 (99%); 1996 (60%)
* Elected as a Democrat 1996-98; elected as an independent 2000

Elected 1996; 6th term

Goode rode out a storm of negative press in the last Congress to be re-elected by a comfortable margin, and he is trying these days to lower his profile a notch. First his name surfaced in a federal public corruption investigation in 2005, then he stirred a tempest with remarks about the Koran and Muslims in the United States.

Nonetheless, Goode (GUDE — rhymes with "food") remains popular in his conservative district, a swath of rural southern Virginia, which returned him to Washington with 59 percent of the vote in spite of a very tough year for Republicans, especially those tainted by scandal.

Though never accused of wrongdoing, Goode was connected in federal documents to an influence peddling scandal that sent former Rep. Randy "Duke" Cunningham, a California Republican, to jail for accepting $2.4 million in bribes from MZM Corp., a defense contractor. In a plea bargain, Mitchell Wade, the former MZM chairman, named Goode as "Representative A," the recipient of almost $90,000 in campaign contributions from the company from 2003 to 2005. Wade admitted that he had directed MZM employees to donate to Goode and to former GOP Rep. Katherine Harris of Florida. He also said he believed Goode helped slip a $3.6 million earmark for the company into an appropriations bill for a project in Martinsville, in Goode's district. Goode later gave the MZM money to several charities.

Just as that controversy was receding, Goode told constituents in a 2006 newsletter that "diversity visas" of the Clinton era had admitted too many Muslims from the Middle East, posing a threat to "the values and beliefs traditional to the United States of America." He also objected to the House's first Muslim member, Keith Ellison, a Minnesota Democrat, taking a symbolic oath of office on a Koran. "If American citizens don't wake up and adopt the Virgil Goode position on immigration there will likely be many more Muslims elected to office and demanding the use of the Koran," he said.

The Council on American-Islamic Relations called on Goode to apologize, and he declined. But in early 2007, Goode sent an olive branch to Muslims by meeting a delegation of religious leaders, including three Muslims, and saying he planned on attending a Muslim gathering later in the year.

Still, Goode retains a tough stance on illegal immigration. In the 109th Congress (2005-06), he strongly opposed President Bush's guest worker proposal and with Rep. Duncan Hunter, a California Republican, co-authored a bill calling for construction of a security fence along the U.S. border with Mexico, at a cost of $5 billion to $7 billion. Their legislation also denied citizenship to children born in the United States to undocumented parents and stiffened the penalties for companies hiring illegal immigrants. It attracted nearly 50 cosponsors but was not taken up by the House.

Goode is also the sponsor of a measure making English the official national language. "In countries where there is a lack of common unifying language, there is more discord and often efforts to split up the country," he said. "I am fearful that we will have efforts in the country in a few years to split up part of the United States."

Health care is another current theme for Goode. In 2007, he introduced legislation that would allow U.S. taxpayers who have overpaid their federal taxes to voluntarily contribute the extra money to a fund providing coverage for uninsured Americans diagnosed with catastrophic illnesses.

A solid conservative on most issues, Goode opposes abortion and same-sex marriage. In 2004, he helped found the Second Amendment Caucus, a forum for lawmakers who oppose gun control laws.

When it comes to free trade, though, he sides with liberal Democrats and organized labor. He blames economic problems in his district — particularly past manufacturing job losses — on free-trade agreements. He has voted against free-trade pacts with Australia, Morocco, Singapore and Chile, and in 2005 he opposed Bush's Central American Free Trade Agreement.

Although first elected to Congress as a Democrat in 1996, Goode has been a Republican since 2000. That year, he declared himself an independent, and the GOP leadership rewarded him with a prized seat on Appropriations. In 2002, he sought re-election as a Republican.

For many years, Goode had resisted entreaties to switch to the GOP, explaining that "Daddy was a Democrat" who had instilled in his son an appreciation for New Deal programs that aided rural areas. Virgil Sr. was in the state legislature and also served as a state prosecutor; a stretch of highway in Rocky Mount is named after him. Virgil Jr. recalls tagging along as his father attended gatherings around the wood stoves at the general stores that were the prime small-town meeting places. "If you could get the country store vote, you had it made," Goode recalls.

After graduation from law school, Goode got into politics when an opening developed in the state Senate. He made no secret about his ambitions for higher office, and twice unsuccessfully pursued the Democratic nomination for the U.S. Senate.

After the 1995 election yielded partisan deadlock in the state Senate, Democrats retained effective control because the Democratic lieutenant governor held a tie-breaking vote. Goode became a pivotal power broker between the Democrats and the Republicans, and the two parties established a power-sharing arrangement.

In 1996, the day after Democrat L. F. Payne Jr. announced he would not seek another term, Goode launched his bid for Congress. He campaigned in a down-home style reminiscent of his father's, driving to small-town events where he spoke off the cuff and handed out emery boards and pencils embossed with his name. (His father used to give out small kitchen implements.) He won by 24 percentage points. In 1998, he drew no Republican foe.

While the 2006 election was one of his more competitive races, he still handily defeated Democrat Al Weed, a former World Bank official who was endorsed by the local paper, The Roanoke Times.

KEY VOTES

2006

No Stop broadband companies from favoring select Internet traffic
Yes Affirm U.S. commitment to war in Iraq and reject setting a withdrawal date for troops
Yes Repeal requirement for bilingual ballots at the polls
No Permit U.S. sale of civilian nuclear technology to India
Yes Build a 700-mile fence on the U.S.-Mexico border to curb illegal crossings
Yes Permit warrantless wiretaps of suspected terrorists

2005

Yes Intervene in the life-support case of Terri Schiavo
No Lift President Bush's restrictions on stem cell research funding
No Prohibit FBI access to library and bookstore records
No Approve free-trade pact with five Central American countries
Yes Pass energy policy overhaul favored by President Bush emphasizing domestic oil and gas production
Yes End mandatory preservation of habitat of endangered animal and plant species
No Ban torture of prisoners in U.S. custody

CQ VOTE STUDIES

	PARTY UNITY		PRESIDENTIAL SUPPORT	
	Support	Oppose	Support	Oppose
2006	93%	7%	82%	18%
2005	93%	7%	84%	16%
2004	91%	9%	76%	24%
2003	93%	7%	87%	13%
2002	93%	7%	74%	26%

INTEREST GROUPS

	AFL-CIO	ADA	CCUS	ACU
2006	36%	0%	93%	88%
2005	36%	15%	81%	88%
2004	33%	10%	90%	96%
2003	20%	10%	87%	84%
2002	11%	5%	75%	96%

VIRGINIA 5

South central – Danville, Charlottesville

Rich in Civil War landmarks, the 5th extends from the central part of Virginia just north of Charlottesville to the south-central border with North Carolina, an area known as Southside.

The mostly rural 5th is relatively poor, and the district relies heavily on agriculture and textiles. Known as the heart of tobacco country, the 5th has suffered a decline in the industry, which led to above-average unemployment in the district's southwestern corner. Recently, manufacturing has taken a more prominent role, and the 5th has seen new industries move in and existing operations expand. Danville, the district's largest city, is a tobacco and textile center on the North Carolina border, and just to the west is Martinsville, a textile and furniture town. Charlottesville, in the northern part of the district, has seen a higher rate of job growth than the state average, due in part to a growing public sector there. The district's northern tip also has several wineries.

While the district is reliably conservative, party labels hold little meaning here, as evidenced by Rep. Goode's ability to switch parties and maintain his 5th District dominance. Democrats as well as independents hold some state House seats, and while Democrat Tim Kaine was unable to replicate his predecessor Mark Warner's success in the district, he was able to capture several counties here in the 2005 gubernatorial race.

One notable exception to the 5th's conservative posture is the city of Charlottesville, home to the University of Virginia, which almost always backs Democrats. Charlottesville gave John Kerry 72 percent of its vote in the 2004 presidential election — his second-best showing in the state. Overall, George W. Bush took 56 percent of the 5th's 2004 presidential vote, slightly ahead of his statewide percentage.

MAJOR INDUSTRY

Agriculture, tobacco, manufacturing, textiles, service

CITIES

Danville, 48,411; Charlottesville, 45,049; Martinsville, 15,416

NOTABLE

Appomattox Court House, now a National Park Service site, was where Confederate Gen. Robert E. Lee surrendered to end the Civil War; Thomas Jefferson's Monticello estate is south of Charlottesville; The National D-Day Memorial is in Bedford, which had more residents killed per capita during the Normandy invasion than any other U.S. locality.

Rep. Robert W. Goodlatte (R)

CAPITOL OFFICE
225-5431
talk2bob@mail.house.gov
www.house.gov/goodlatte
2240 Rayburn 20515-4606; fax 225-9681

COMMITTEES
Agriculture - ranking member
Judiciary

RESIDENCE
Roanoke

BORN
Sept. 22, 1952, Holyoke, Mass.

RELIGION
Christian Scientist

FAMILY
Wife, Maryellen Goodlatte; two children

EDUCATION
Bates College, B.A. 1974 (government); Washington and Lee U., J.D. 1977

CAREER
Lawyer; congressional aide

POLITICAL HIGHLIGHTS
Roanoke City Republican Committee chairman, 1980-83; 6th Congressional District Republican Party chairman, 1983-88

ELECTION RESULTS

2006 GENERAL		
Robert W. Goodlatte (R)	153,187	75.1%
Barbara Jean Pryor (I)	25,129	12.3%
Andre D. Peery (I)	24,731	12.1%
2006 PRIMARY		
Robert W. Goodlatte (R)		unopposed
2004 GENERAL		
Robert W. Goodlatte (R)	206,560	96.7%
write-ins	7,088	3.3%

PREVIOUS WINNING PERCENTAGES
2002 (97%); 2000 (99%); 1998 (69%); 1996 (67%); 1994 (100%); 1992 (60%)

Elected 1992; 8th term

As the top-ranking Republican on the Agriculture Committee, Goodlatte is sure to play a significant role in the renewal of the massive, multi-year farm bill, which is due to expire in 2007. His challenge is to remain faithful to his conservative fiscal beliefs while also responding to the nation's farmers who worry that Congress will target crop subsidies as it tries to reduce the federal budget deficit. Goodlatte also continues his vigilant watch over technology issues being debated at all levels in the House.

Goodlatte (GOOD-lat) was chairman of the Agriculture Committee for four years before the Democrats regained the majority in the House with the 2006 elections. He had some early successes — helping to pass President Bush's so-called Healthy Forests initiative and a long-sought buyout program for tobacco farmers. But farm-state lawmakers were disappointed in 2006 that a $4.9 billion agriculture disaster aid bill did not move in either chamber. The measure would have helped farmers whose crops and livestock were devastated by drought, flood or fire in 2005 and 2006. Goodlatte did not press for the bill, saying GOP leaders gave him no signal they would provide the extra funding.

When he was chairman, Goodlatte said that all the programs under the panel's jurisdiction would get close scrutiny during the rewrite of the farm bill, including crop subsidies, nutrition programs, food stamps and conservation programs. But now that he is in the minority, his 2005 proposal to cut the food stamp program by $844 million over five years is likely to be scaled back. His measure went well beyond the $630 million cut the White House wanted. True to his fiscally conservative nature, Goodlatte also sought to trim $1 billion from commodity programs; part of that total would have eliminated a federal cotton marketing subsidy in 2006.

Goodlatte has a special interest in technology policy as it affects rural areas. He says rural areas of the United States will be economically competitive in the future only if they keep pace in the computer age. He sees communications technology today as comparable to the railroad in the 19th century. "If the railroad came through your town and connected you with the rest of the country, you'd boom. If it didn't, you'd go bust," he says.

As a lawyer in Roanoke, Goodlatte took advantage of the latest communications and information technology to build a competitive practice that included a specialty in immigration law. "Using technology, I was able to compete with lawyers from Washington and New York," he recalls.

During his 15 years in the House, Goodlatte has been a player on almost every major computer-related bill before Congress, including those aimed at protecting users' privacy, preserving intellectual copyright protections for artists and creators of software, shielding children from indecent material, and safeguarding consumers from fraud. In 2004, the House overwhelmingly passed his measure setting criminal penalties for using privacy-invading "spyware" to tap into personal computers to steal information or damage hardware.

As a member of the Judiciary Committee, Goodlatte weighs in on such technology concerns as cyber-security and Internet gambling. In 2006, the House passed his bill to curb Internet gambling by prohibiting gambling businesses from accepting credit cards and electronic transfers for online betting. The measure also modified the 1961 Wire Act to clarify that its prohibitions also apply to Internet gambling, not just sports bets placed over telephone wires. "We feel this type of gambling is particularly pernicious,"

Goodlatte told The Washington Times.

When discussing the measure, Goodlatte points to the fact that a similar bill was killed in 2000 after heavy lobbying by the now disgraced lobbyist Jack Abramoff. Abramoff was representing the Connecticut-based gambling company eLottery, which helps state and international governments and American Indian tribes market lottery tickets online. The company hired Abramoff to lobby against the 2000 bill, which would have established criminal penalties for Web sites offering Internet gambling.

Goodlatte's positions on technology are driven by the philosophy that government generally should stay out of the way of innovators and entrepreneurs. That is a conservative's perspective, but Goodlatte notes that many Internet-related issues lend themselves to bipartisanship. A frequent Goodlatte partner on technology matters is Democrat Rick Boucher, of the neighboring 9th District and who also sits on the Judiciary Committee.

Boucher and Goodlatte paired up to promote a bill making it easier for parties involved in some class action lawsuits to transfer cases from state to federal court. Proponents of the legislation said it would prevent "venue shopping" by trial lawyers who deliberately bring cases in jurisdictions friendly to plaintiffs. The measure was signed into law by Bush in 2005.

Goodlatte had a middle-class upbringing in western Massachusetts. His father managed a Friendly's ice cream store, and his mother worked part-time in a department store. His parents liked to visit places with historical significance, feeding in particular a lifelong interest in presidential history. Vacations for the lawmaker often include a stop at the home of a U.S. president. His favorite stop was President Ronald Reagan's California ranch. With clothes in the closet and a jar of jelly beans on the counter, "it looks like Ronald and Nancy Reagan just went out on a trail ride and they'll be back any minute," he said. In 2006, the House passed Goodlatte's bill providing funds for a Woodrow Wilson presidential library in his district. (The 28th president was born in Staunton, Virginia.)

Goodlatte was president of the College Republicans at Bates College in Maine. After getting a law degree at Washington and Lee University in Lexington, Va., Goodlatte entered private practice and also worked for the area's Republican congressman, M. Caldwell Butler.

Goodlatte considered running for Congress in 1986, but the birth of his second child at the start of the campaign season kept him out of the race. In 1992, however, when Democratic Rep. Jim Olin retired after five terms, Goodlatte decided the time was right. He won easily, and has faced no formidable opponent in the seven elections since.

KEY VOTES

2006

- No Stop broadband companies from favoring select Internet traffic
- Yes Affirm U.S. commitment to war in Iraq and reject setting a withdrawal date for troops
- Yes Repeal requirement for bilingual ballots at the polls
- Yes Permit U.S. sale of civilian nuclear technology to India
- Yes Build a 700-mile fence on the U.S.-Mexico border to curb illegal crossings
- Yes Permit warrantless wiretaps of suspected terrorists

2005

- Yes Intervene in the life-support case of Terri Schiavo
- No Lift President Bush's restrictions on stem cell research funding
- No Prohibit FBI access to library and bookstore records
- Yes Approve free-trade pact with five Central American countries
- Yes Pass energy policy overhaul favored by President Bush emphasizing domestic oil and gas production
- Yes End mandatory preservation of habitat of endangered animal and plant species
- Yes Ban torture of prisoners in U.S. custody

CQ VOTE STUDIES

	PARTY UNITY		PRESIDENTIAL SUPPORT	
	Support	Oppose	Support	Oppose
2006	99%	1%	95%	5%
2005	96%	4%	85%	15%
2004	98%	2%	88%	12%
2003	96%	4%	95%	5%
2002	99%	1%	88%	12%

INTEREST GROUPS

	AFL-CIO	ADA	CCUS	ACU
2006	14%	0%	100%	92%
2005	20%	5%	93%	96%
2004	13%	0%	100%	100%
2003	7%	10%	97%	84%
2002	0%	0%	95%	100%

VIRGINIA 6

Northwest – Roanoke, Lynchburg

Running along the Shenandoah Valley, the conservative 6th stretches down much of Virginia's western border with West Virginia, combining mountainous terrain, small towns, medium-size cities and natural beauty.

Roanoke, the 6th's most populous city, hosts several industries, including furniture and electrical products manufacturing. In recent years, some manufacturing and technology companies have either opened or expanded facilities in the region. Roanoke also has begun attracting biomedical and biotechnology companies by creating business parks in redeveloped areas of the city.

Outside metropolitan Roanoke and Lynchburg, the 6th depends mainly on dairy farming, livestock and poultry. Rockingham County in the north leads the state in livestock and hay production, and the district has a sizable Mennonite population. The district also attracts tourists, who come to see the scenic Blue Ridge Mountains and natural caverns, as well as students. The 6th has many colleges and universities, including James Madison University in Harrisonburg. The Harrisonburg area led the state in job growth in 2006, largely from service sector expansion fueled by businesses providing support to James Madison and other schools in the surrounding community.

The 6th has a large population of senior citizens, a mostly white-collar workforce and a generous dose of Republicans, although the rural valley's brand of Republicanism has traditionally been a moderate one, and Democrats and independents still win some local elections. Roanoke has a strong Democratic base with union ties, but Republicans have done well in Roanoke's suburbs, in Lynchburg and in most rural areas. Overall, George W. Bush captured 63 percent of the vote here in the 2004 presidential election, his best showing in the state.

MAJOR INDUSTRY

Agriculture, livestock, manufacturing, tourism

CITIES

Roanoke, 94,911; Lynchburg, 65,269; Harrisonburg, 40,468; Cave Spring (unincorporated), 24,941; Salem, 24,747; Staunton, 23,853

NOTABLE

Natural Bridge is in Rockbridge County; Thomas Jefferson's Poplar Forest in Bedford County features tours of Jefferson's octagonal "other" home; A greenhouse in Harrisonburg boasts a 3.5 acre corn maze.

Rep. Eric Cantor (R)

CAPITOL OFFICE
225-2815
cantor.house.gov
329 Cannon 20515-4607; fax 225-0011

COMMITTEES
Ways & Means

RESIDENCE
Glen Allen

BORN
June 6, 1963, Richmond, Va.

RELIGION
Jewish

FAMILY
Wife, Diana Cantor; three children

EDUCATION
George Washington U., B.A. 1985 (political science); College of William & Mary, J.D. 1988; Columbia U., M.S. 1989 (real estate development)

CAREER
Lawyer; real estate developer; campaign aide

POLITICAL HIGHLIGHTS
Va. House, 1992-2001

ELECTION RESULTS

2006 GENERAL		
Eric Cantor (R)	163,706	63.9%
James M. Nachman (D)	88,206	34.4%
W. Brad Blanton (I)	4,213	1.6%
2006 PRIMARY		
Eric Cantor (R)		unopposed
2004 GENERAL		
Eric Cantor (R)	230,765	75.5%
W. Brad Blanton (I)	74,325	24.3%

PREVIOUS WINNING PERCENTAGES
2002 (69%); 2000 (67%)

Elected 2000; 4th term

Cantor has a bright future in the Republican leadership in the House. An estimable vote-counter and fundraiser, he is the able assistant to Whip Roy Blunt of Missouri. If things continue to go well for him, he should be able to move up to a top elected leadership job in the future.

Though Republicans had a dismal showing in the 2006 elections, Cantor was credited with helping raise enough money to keep them competitive. As chairman of the House GOP's "Battleground" fundraising committee, Cantor helped bring in $25 million for fellow Republicans in tight races, exceeding the previous record of $21.5 million in 2004.

Cantor has performed with distinction since 2002 in the chief deputy whip's job, an appointive post seen as a launching pad for higher elected leadership posts. After Republican Majority Leader Tom DeLay stepped down following his indictment in 2005 on campaign finance-related charges in Texas, Blunt temporarily assumed the leader's duties. Blunt retained the whip's title, but Cantor took over many of his duties, which included knowing how more than 200 Republicans plan to vote on a given issue, working to resolve the problems of those who don't want to side with the leadership and convincing others it's in their best interest to toe the line.

When the party held leadership elections in early 2006, Blunt was hoping to become majority leader and Cantor was favored to replace him as whip. But Blunt lost to John A. Boehner of Ohio, then stayed on in the whip's job, leaving Cantor no way to move up. Even after losing their majority in November 2006, Republicans decided to stick with the Boehner-Blunt leadership combo.

The low point for Cantor was getting wrapped up in the Jack Abramoff influence-peddling scandal. Cantor was among the leaders who in 2003 signed a letter that helped an American Indian tribe represented by lobbyist Abramoff. That year, Cantor also held a fundraiser at an Abramoff-owned restaurant, and received $12,000 in campaign donations from him, though Cantor claimed to know the lobbyist on only a "casual" basis. He later gave $10,000 of the money to a Richmond-area charity.

Overall, Cantor draws high marks from his colleagues. In early 2007, he worked to keep the majority of the party united against a Democratic war funding bill that exceeded President Bush's request and included a timeline for withdrawal of U.S. troops from Iraq; only two Republicans voted for the resolution. It was a marked improvement from the month before, when 17 Republicans voted for a resolution expressing disapproval for Bush's plan to send more than 21,000 additional combat troops into Iraq.

When the leadership put a campaign reform bill targeting so-called 527 groups on the floor in spring 2006, Cantor persuaded several Republican fence-sitters to vote for it. Also in 2006, he helped drum up votes to pass an important leadership initiative requiring greater disclosure of earmarks, additions to spending bills that benefit members' districts or special interests. Powerful appropriators had opposed the changes. In the 108th Congress (2003-04), Cantor worked to ensure House passage of a corporate tax cut by helping affix tobacco buyout legislation to the package.

Cantor's own legislative focus tends to be on tax issues handled by the Ways and Means Committee, on which he serves. In 2006, he introduced a bill to create tax incentives for premium payments and contributions to high-deductible health savings accounts. He also was the lead sponsor of a bill to make permanent the 15 percent tax cut on dividend income.

As the sole Jewish Republican in the House, Cantor is a natural nexus between the party's Christian conservatives and traditionally Democratic Jewish campaign donors that they court with their hawkish support for Israel. Despite his short congressional tenure, Cantor ranks among the top beneficiaries of pro-Israel campaign dollars and is a spokesman for the party on Israel. As chairman of a task force on terrorism, which briefs Republicans and makes legislative recommendations, he has urged a tougher U.S. stance against Syria, Iran and Iraq. When Palestinian leader Yasser Arafat died in 2004, Cantor called him "the father of the modern terrorist state."

Though he is becoming recognizable on political talk shows and on the Republican fundraising circuit, particularly among pro-Israel donors, Cantor is in just his fourth term in the House. He was named chief deputy whip after his first term, when DeLay ascended to majority leader and Blunt, DeLay's chief deputy, became whip. Blunt bypassed several senior members of DeLay's operation to make Cantor his chief lieutenant. Tension developed between the hard-boiled DeLay and the softer-edged Blunt, but Cantor managed to stay out of the conflict.

Cantor grew up in a well-to-do, politically active Richmond family. His father, Eddie, was on the board of the Virginia Housing Development Authority, and his mother, Mary Lee, was a board member of the Family and Children's Trust Fund and the Science Museum of Virginia.

While in college, Cantor interned for then Rep. Thomas J. Bliley Jr. of Virginia, driving the lawmaker's 1982 campaign car around the district he would one day represent. He also worked as an aide to Walter A. Stosch, a member of the Virginia House of Delegates.

When Stosch ran for the state Senate in 1991, Cantor made a bid for the open seat. The 28-year-old out-organized and outspent two more-experienced rivals and won, becoming the youngest member of the state House. Cantor was seen as a pro-business state legislator. He sponsored a bill limiting how much Philip Morris USA, based in Richmond, had to pay in punitive damages to smokers, and he killed a bill to reduce telemarketing calls.

Bliley's campaign machinery stood behind Cantor when needed, and Cantor frequently served as Bliley's campaign chairman. When Bliley announced his retirement, Cantor joined the race to replace him. He won the primary by a scant 263 votes. But in November, he sailed to victory in the heavily Republican district with two-thirds of the vote.

His re-elections have been easy, including a 2002 pasting of Ben L. "Cooter" Jones, who served in the Georgia House more than a decade ago but is best-known from the television series "The Dukes of Hazzard."

KEY VOTES

2006

- No — Stop broadband companies from favoring select Internet traffic
- Yes — Affirm U.S. commitment to war in Iraq and reject setting a withdrawal date for troops
- Yes — Repeal requirement for bilingual ballots at the polls
- Yes — Permit U.S. sale of civilian nuclear technology to India
- Yes — Build a 700-mile fence on the U.S.-Mexico border to curb illegal crossings
- Yes — Permit warrantless wiretaps of suspected terrorists

2005

- Yes — Intervene in the life-support case of Terri Schiavo
- No — Lift President Bush's restrictions on stem cell research funding
- No — Prohibit FBI access to library and bookstore records
- Yes — Approve free-trade pact with five Central American countries
- Yes — Pass energy policy overhaul favored by President Bush emphasizing domestic oil and gas production
- Yes — End mandatory preservation of habitat of endangered animal and plant species
- No — Ban torture of prisoners in U.S. custody

CQ VOTE STUDIES

	PARTY UNITY		PRESIDENTIAL SUPPORT	
	Support	Oppose	Support	Oppose
2006	98%	2%	95%	5%
2005	98%	2%	89%	11%
2004	98%	2%	97%	3%
2003	99%	1%	100%	0%
2002	99%	1%	90%	10%

INTEREST GROUPS

	AFL-CIO	ADA	CCUS	ACU
2006	7%	5%	100%	92%
2005	13%	0%	93%	96%
2004	7%	0%	100%	100%
2003	0%	50%	100%	88%
2002	11%	0%	100%	100%

VIRGINIA 7

Central — part of Richmond and suburbs

The solidly Republican 7th begins in part of Richmond and its affluent old-money suburbs, then reaches northwest to the Shenandoah Valley through farmland and new Washington, D.C., exurbs.

Many of the 7th's residents work in Richmond, a longtime center of state government and commerce. Richmond also was one of the South's early manufacturing centers, concentrating on tobacco processing. Richmond-based Philip Morris USA continues to employ thousands of district residents.

The northeastern stretch of the 7th is changing, with declining traditional farming communities being transformed into exurban areas by new residents with long commutes to Washington or its close-in suburbs. Elsewhere, the northern 7th has a local wine industry, and durable goods manufacturing serves as a major employer in Page County.

A plurality of district residents live in Henrico County (shared with the 3rd), which cups Richmond in a backward C-shape. Henrico generally leans Republican, although it backed Democrat Tim Kaine in the 2005 gubernatorial election. Chesterfield County, which is shared with the 4th, borders Richmond to the south and west and has a stronger GOP lean. The 7th's portion of Richmond includes some strong Republican voters who live in the city's western end.

As a whole, the 7th is reliably Republican, and it is difficult for any Democratic candidate to stitch together a victory here. In the 2004 presidential election, John Kerry carried only the district's portions of Caroline County and Richmond from within the 7th's territory, and overall George W. Bush took 61 percent of the 7th's vote, his second-best effort in the state. Sparsely populated Rappahannock, the 7th's northernmost county, did vote a Democratic ticket in the 2005 statewide elections.

MAJOR INDUSTRY

Agriculture, government, manufacturing

CITIES

Richmond (pt.), 53,270; Tuckahoe (unincorporated), 43,242; Mechanicsville (unincorporated), 30,464

NOTABLE

Luray Caverns, in Page County, features a pipe organ made of stalactites; James Madison's Montpelier estate is in Orange County.

Rep. James P. Moran (D)

CAPITOL OFFICE
225-4376
moran.house.gov
2239 Rayburn 20515-4608; fax 225-0017

COMMITTEES
Appropriations

RESIDENCE
Arlington

BORN
May 16, 1945, Buffalo, N.Y.

RELIGION
Roman Catholic

FAMILY
Wife LuAnn Bennett; four children

EDUCATION
College of the Holy Cross, B.A. 1967 (economics); City U. of New York, Bernard M. Baruch School of Finance, attended 1967-68; U. of Pittsburgh, M.P.A. 1970

CAREER
Investment broker; congressional aide

POLITICAL HIGHLIGHTS
Alexandria City Council, 1979-84 (vice mayor, 1982-84); mayor of Alexandria, 1985-90 (served as an independent 1985-88)

ELECTION RESULTS

2006 GENERAL		
James P. Moran (D)	144,700	66.4%
Tom M. O'Donoghue (R)	66,639	30.6%
James T. Hurysz (I)	6,094	2.8%
2006 PRIMARY		
James P. Moran (D)		unopposed
2004 GENERAL		
James P. Moran (D)	171,986	59.7%
Lisa Marie Cheney (R)	106,231	36.9%
James T. Hurysz (I)	9,004	3.1%

PREVIOUS WINNING PERCENTAGES
2002 (60%); 2000 (63%); 1998 (67%); 1996 (66%); 1994 (59%); 1992 (56%); 1990 (52%)

Elected 1990; 9th term

One of the more colorful personalities in the House, Moran's temper and his personal finances often have detracted from his work as a member of Congress, though he has tried to clean up his act in recent years. He even poked fun at his reputation as a hothead by cooperating with a stunt on a popular late-night comedy show in 2006 in which he pretended to throw a punch at host Stephen Colbert.

His only controversial move of late was of the sort that's appreciated by his Democratic-leaning district in the Virginia suburbs just outside of Washington, D.C. In April 2006, Moran and a group of Democrats were arrested by the U.S. Secret Service in front of the Embassy of Sudan for protesting the violence in Darfur. It was an effort, Moran said, to "bring the atrocities sanctioned by the Sudanese government against their own people to their own embassy's doorstep."

Moran has shored himself up politically by being an energetic advocate for more pay and better health and retirement benefits for federal workers, a significant presence in the patchwork of suburbs just across the Potomac River that he represents. From his seat on the Appropriations Committee, Moran has cut deals across party lines to bring in millions of dollars for local roads, education programs, law enforcement and low-income housing.

Moran's district includes the Pentagon, but he is an anti-war Democrat who displays photographs of Virginians killed in the conflict in the hallway outside his office. "I don't think the loss of their lives is worth anything that we can achieve by this war," Moran said.

Based on his feelings about the war, Moran found himself on the wrong side of the contest for majority leader in 2006. He sided with Pennsylvania Democrat John P. Murtha, a decorated Marine veteran who has led Democratic opposition to the war, in his challenge to Rep. Steny H. Hoyer of Maryland. If Murtha had won, Moran would have had a shot at the chairmanship of the Interior and Environment Appropriations Subcommittee. Instead, Moran holds his party's No. 2 slot on that panel — behind Chairman Norm Dicks of Washington.

It's not the first time he's lost out on a key leadership post. He has had a penchant for saying and doing things that spawn campaign challenges and anger party leaders. Once, in a committee dispute, Moran told Indiana Republican Dan Burton, "You pull that again and I'll break your nose."

In 2002, the Washington Post ran a front-page story about Moran borrowing $50,000 from an America Online executive and using the money to trade in stocks before repaying it months later. The following year, he received a hailstorm of criticism with a remark suggesting that Jewish influence was a major factor in the White House's push to wage war in Iraq. Moran apologized, but Democratic Leader Pelosi stripped him of his post in the whip organization.

Two years later, Moran saw his top-ranking seat on Appropriations' Legislative Branch Subcommittee evaporate when the GOP leadership abolished the panel, folding its work into the full committee.

Despite his sometimes confrontational manner, Moran has earned a reputation as an able negotiator. He often collaborates with GOP Rep. Thomas M. Davis III from the neighboring 11th District. The two were instrumental in getting the District of Columbia to close its prison in Lorton, Virginia, and in securing federal funds to replace the Woodrow Wilson Bridge.

Moran joined with two House colleagues in 1997 to found the moderate New Democrat Coalition. While he normally votes with the majority of his party, he sometimes goes against the grain. For example, he has voted for trade liberalization measures, and he supported a 2005 bill backed by President Bush to rein in class action lawsuits.

But he sticks with his party on every vote opposing the Iraq War. Speaking in April 2007 on a Democratic war funding bill that would have set a timeline for withdrawal of U.S. troops from Iraq, Moran said the main point of the legislation was to send a message to the White House. "This is the last train out of the station to send a message on the surge," he said, speaking of Bush's plan to send more than 21,000 additional combat troops into Iraq.

The son of a professional boxer and Washington Redskins football player, Moran takes pride in his prowess as an amateur heavyweight, including college bouts at Holy Cross and an exhibition match with former heavyweight champion Joe Frazier. He comes by his pugilism honestly. Once, when he was a boy, someone came to the family's door with a petition to prevent an African-American family from moving into the neighborhood. "My father not only refused to sign it, he actually punched him in the nose," Moran said. "He leveled him. My father was a very powerful man."

Moran grew up in a Boston suburb, one of seven siblings, all of whom have been involved in politics. His father, a conservative Irish Catholic, "was a big supporter of the Kennedys and loved [Thomas P.] 'Tip' O'Neill," says Moran.

First elected to the Alexandria City Council in 1979, Moran saw his career derailed briefly in 1984 when, after pleading no contest to a misdemeanor conflict-of-interest charge, he resigned as vice mayor. Running as an independent the next year, he unseated the incumbent mayor. He was serving as mayor in 1990 when he ran for Congress, upsetting six-term Republican Stan Parris. Moran focused on his support for abortion rights and Parris' anti-abortion views, winning with 52 percent of the vote.

Republicans tested Moran in 1992 and 1994 with a quality challenger in Kyle E. McSlarrow, but Moran prevailed by solid margins. In 2002 and 2004, Moran slipped to about 60 percent, a sign voters were tiring of his family problems and financial dealings. Moran's wife of 11 years, Mary, filed for divorce in 1999, a day after calling police during a domestic argument. In court filings, she blamed the couple's poor finances on $120,000 in bad stock trades Moran had made. He married for a third time in 2004 to LuAnn Bennett, a successful commercial real estate developer.

In the 2006 election, Moran bounced back, winning with better than 65 percent of the vote.

KEY VOTES

2006

- Yes Stop broadband companies from favoring select Internet traffic
- No Affirm U.S. commitment to war in Iraq and reject setting a withdrawal date for troops
- No Repeal requirement for bilingual ballots at the polls
- Yes Permit U.S. sale of civilian nuclear technology to India
- Yes Build a 700-mile fence on the U.S.-Mexico border to curb illegal crossings
- No Permit warrantless wiretaps of suspected terrorists

2005

- No Intervene in the life-support case of Terri Schiavo
- Yes Lift President Bush's restrictions on stem cell research funding
- Yes Prohibit FBI access to library and bookstore records
- Yes Approve free-trade pact with five Central American countries
- No Pass energy policy overhaul favored by President Bush emphasizing domestic oil and gas production
- No End mandatory preservation of habitat of endangered animal and plant species
- Yes Ban torture of prisoners in U.S. custody

CQ VOTE STUDIES

	PARTY UNITY		PRESIDENTIAL SUPPORT	
	Support	Oppose	Support	Oppose
2006	90%	10%	33%	67%
2005	92%	8%	24%	76%
2004	89%	11%	41%	59%
2003	89%	11%	26%	74%
2002	84%	16%	42%	58%

INTEREST GROUPS

	AFL-CIO	ADA	CCUS	ACU
2006	93%	95%	53%	16%
2005	80%	90%	65%	4%
2004	87%	95%	67%	24%
2003	86%	95%	54%	88%
2002	67%	70%	68%	21%

VIRGINIA 8

Washington suburbs — Arlington, Alexandria, part of Fairfax County

Taking in the close-in Northern Virginia suburbs of Washington, D.C., the 8th is mostly upper-income and strongly Democratic — in no small part because of a racially and ethnically diverse population of blacks, Asians and Hispanics, who together total about 40 percent of residents. The 8th also has the nation's fourth-largest number of residents of Arab ancestry.

The 8th bustles with technology businesses and defense contractors, drawn to the district's substantial military presence, including the Pentagon and Fort Belvoir, which will receive more than 10,000 new personnel as a result of the 2005 BRAC round. While government and defense-related jobs are important here, technology has become a hot industry again after federal procurement contracts helped the area recover from the national "dot-com" downturn. These fields rely on well-educated employees, so it is no surprise that 54 percent of the district's residents have a college degree, the second-highest mark in the nation.

Roughly half of the 8th's residents live in an elongated swath of Fairfax County that reaches from the Potomac River, near Mount Vernon (shared with the 11th), past Falls Church and Tysons Corner to Reston. Alexandria and Arlington typically give Democratic statewide candidates their highest vote percentages in the state. A GOP presidential candidate has not won a majority in either jurisdiction since 1972, and the 8th was one of George W. Bush's worst Virginia districts in the 2004 presidential vote.

MAJOR INDUSTRY

Government, technology, defense, service

MILITARY BASES

Pentagon, 11,000 military, 13,000 civilian (2005); Fort Belvoir (Army), 7,249 military, 10,326 civilian (2007); Fort Myer (Army), 2,843 military, 1,330 civilian (2004); Naval Sea Systems Command, 379 military, 2,364 civilian (2005); Henderson Hall, 2,156 military, 54 civilian (2007)

CITIES

Arlington (unincorporated), 189,453; Alexandria, 128,283; Reston (unincorporated) (pt.), 56,275; Franconia (unincorporated), 31,907

NOTABLE

The Torpedo Factory Art Center, in Alexandria, was a World War II munitions factory that has been converted into an art school and gallery.

Rep. Rick Boucher (D)

CAPITOL OFFICE
225-3861
ninthnet@mail.house.gov
www.house.gov/boucher
2187 Rayburn 20515-4609; fax 225-0442

COMMITTEES
Energy & Commerce
(Energy & Air Quality - chairman)
Judiciary

RESIDENCE
Abingdon

BORN
Aug. 1, 1946, Abingdon, Va.

RELIGION
Methodist

FAMILY
Wife, Amy Boucher

EDUCATION
Roanoke College, B.A. 1968 (political science);
U. of Virginia, J.D. 1971

CAREER
Lawyer

POLITICAL HIGHLIGHTS
Va. Senate, 1976-82

ELECTION RESULTS

2006 GENERAL		
Rick Boucher (D)	129,705	67.8%
C.W. "Bill" Carrico (R)	61,574	32.2%
2006 PRIMARY		
Rick Boucher (D)		unopposed
2004 GENERAL		
Rick Boucher (D)	150,039	59.3%
Kevin Triplett (R)	98,499	38.9%
Seth Davis (I)	4,341	1.7%

PREVIOUS WINNING PERCENTAGES
2002 (66%); 2000 (70%); 1998 (61%); 1996 (65%); 1994 (59%); 1992 (63%); 1990 (97%); 1988 (63%); 1986 (99%); 1984 (52%); 1982 (50%)

Elected 1982; 13th term

A techno-geek of long standing, Boucher prides himself on mastering the latest gadgets before others have even heard of them. In 2002, he bragged about having satellite radio in his Jeep and wiring his home gazebo so he could be online while sitting out in his yard. He is seldom caught these days without the latest BlackBerry wireless device and his laptop computer.

His obsession with technology drives his work in Congress, where he serves on both the Energy and Commerce Telecommunications Subcommittee and the Judiciary subcommittee that handles digital copyright and other intellectual property rights. Technology matters have engrossed Boucher (BOW — rhymes with "now" — chur) since he tried to improve satellite TV service for his constituents in the 1980s.

In 2007, he added another high-profile issue to his portfolio when he was given the gavel of the Energy and Commerce Subcommittee on Energy and Air Quality. The panel is charged with writing legislation to curb emissions of carbon dioxide and other greenhouse gases that scientists say contribute to global warming. It is a critical role, as Democrats intend to make climate change a signature issue. And it was a role for which Boucher required some different thinking. "To date I have been a skeptic about the need for a mandatory U.S. program for greenhouse gas control. But my view is changing," he said in March 2007.

Boucher launched a series of hearings on the issue. Leading proposals would establish a nationwide emissions limit and create a market-style system in which manufacturers and utilities could swap pollution credits. But he intends to look out for his coal-mining district, which could be economically vulnerable to tough new emissions controls. He is likely to insist that any caps on coal-burning power plant emissions be conditioned on the availability of new technology to capture and store the carbon dioxide. He also is looking into "coal-to-liquids technology" — a way to use coal to offset petroleum imports.

Although some describe him as bland, he has another, livelier side — one that manifested itself in 2006 when he married longtime girlfriend Amy Hauslohner, a Virginia journalist and guitarist with a local band. Their wedding ceremony was held on a former railroad bridge overlooking Damascus, Va., that is now part of the Virginia Creeper Trail. Boucher had secured $750,000 in federal funds in 2003 to repair the trestles and trail. They bicycled to the ceremony more than a dozen miles from his hometown of Abingdon and back again afterward. Their wedding meal consisted of a chicken and bean burrito at a local Mexican restaurant, topped off by a slice of coconut cake from the counter at the Alvarado Train Station restaurant.

Co-founder of the Congressional Internet Caucus, Boucher has convinced voters in his rural district that high-speed Internet connections and other digital age trappings will grow local job opportunities beyond the old pillars of coal mining, livestock raising and tobacco farming. By 2002, the 9th District had more telemedicine sites than any other district in the country. Communities throughout the area were wired with fiber optics and Abingdon was dubbed "the most wired small town in America" by Yahoo Life Magazine.

Boucher in 2007 introduced legislation to revamp the Universal Service Fund, which was created to ensure access to affordable phone service across the country. He also planned to resume efforts to overhaul telecom policy affecting wireless, cable and Internet industries.

Boucher likes the fact that technology issues typically do not break along party lines. Boucher's father was a Republican commonwealth's attorney in Washington County, while his mother was the county's Democratic Party chairwoman. Her father was a Democratic state representative. "I understood at an early age that partisanship is not important," Boucher says. "Bipartisanship is the best way to accomplish anything."

His votes reflect his pick-and-choose approach to public policy. Boucher parts ways with most Democrats on gun control and gay rights, siding with the overwhelming sentiment in his district, where gun owners' rights are sacred and same-sex marriage is considered an alien concept.

On Judiciary, he often is the rare Democrat siding with Republicans. One of his committee partners on intellectual property legislation is Republican Robert W. Goodlatte, his neighbor in Virginia's 6th District. The two also joined forces on legislation enacted in 2005 making it easier to transfer class action lawsuits from state to federal court.

With the music and motion picture industries lobbying to tighten piracy laws, Boucher continues to push legislation to protect the right of consumers to copy films and music at home for personal use.

Tobacco farmers are another important Boucher constituency; he voted in the 108th Congress (2003-04) for legislation to abolish the federal quota system for tobacco and reimburse farmers for their losses. The buyout was approved as part of the corporate tax overhaul enacted in 2004.

Boucher has said that by the age of 12, he had decided to become a lawyer and be a part of public life. He recalls a couple years later attending a John F. Kennedy rally in Abingdon at which Harry S Truman spoke. After graduating from the University of Virginia Law School, he joined a Wall Street firm, worked as an advance man for George McGovern's 1972 presidential campaign, and joined the family law firm in 1978.

He won a seat in the state Senate before he turned 30, then took on GOP Rep. William C. Wampler in 1982. With high unemployment plaguing the district's coal fields, Boucher won by just 1,123 votes. Two years later, he edged to a 4 percentage point victory over state Rep. Jefferson Stafford. Solid re-election victories then became Boucher's norm for a while.

But 2004 began to look different when former NASCAR executive Kevin Triplett stepped forward and said too many local jobs had been lost on Boucher's watch. Boucher said he had "an agenda for progress" that was offsetting job losses in textiles and manufacturing and boosting the district's economy. He served as the grand marshal for NASCAR's Food City 500 at the Bristol Motor Speedway. On Election Day, he crossed the finish line far ahead of Triplett. Two years later in 2006, he faced only minimal opposition.

KEY VOTES

2006

- Yes Stop broadband companies from favoring select Internet traffic
- Yes Affirm U.S. commitment to war in Iraq and reject setting a withdrawal date for troops
- No Repeal requirement for bilingual ballots at the polls
- Yes Permit U.S. sale of civilian nuclear technology to India
- Yes Build a 700-mile fence on the U.S.-Mexico border to curb illegal crossings
- No Permit warrantless wiretaps of suspected terrorists

2005

- ? Intervene in the life-support case of Terri Schiavo
- Yes Lift President Bush's restrictions on stem cell research funding
- Yes Prohibit FBI access to library and bookstore records
- No Approve free-trade pact with five Central American countries
- Yes Pass energy policy overhaul favored by President Bush emphasizing domestic oil and gas production
- No End mandatory preservation of habitat of endangered animal and plant species
- Yes Ban torture of prisoners in U.S. custody

CQ VOTE STUDIES

	PARTY UNITY		PRESIDENTIAL SUPPORT	
	Support	Oppose	Support	Oppose
2006	79%	21%	33%	67%
2005	83%	17%	33%	67%
2004	81%	19%	38%	62%
2003	83%	17%	31%	69%
2002	81%	19%	49%	51%

INTEREST GROUPS

	AFL-CIO	ADA	CCUS	ACU
2006	93%	75%	60%	36%
2005	93%	90%	59%	25%
2004	73%	75%	67%	32%
2003	93%	90%	53%	28%
2002	89%	80%	70%	21%

VIRGINIA 9

Southwest – Blacksburg, Bristol

Encompassing the mountains and forests of Virginia's southwestern corner, the rural 9th accommodates the college towns of Blacksburg and Radford, as well as the smaller coal and factory towns nestled close to neighboring West Virginia, North Carolina, Tennessee and Kentucky.

The district has struggled with high poverty rates and a weak economic base, and the 9th is Virginia's poorest congressional district, with a median income of less than $30,000. It also has the state's highest percentage of blue-collar workers, as coal mining and manufacturing provide most of the area's jobs. Despite the presence of one of the state's largest universities — Virginia Tech in Blacksburg — the 9th has Virginia's lowest percentage of college-educated residents (14 percent).

Even with resources available from the district's colleges and universities, some counties perpetually struggle to provide residents with clean drinking water, and the district's local population has remained stagnant since the 1990s. State and local leaders have worked to improve district residents' quality of life by promoting the scenic Blue Ridge Parkway to attract tourism revenue, and by using federal wireless Internet-access grants in several counties to increase learning opportunities for residents.

Known as the Fighting 9th due to its fiercely competitive politics and ornery isolation from the political establishment in Richmond, the 9th supports Republicans in presidential elections. Four years after carrying the 9th by a dozen percentage points, George W. Bush dominated Democrat John Kerry by 20 percentage points in 2004, marking Bush's biggest four-year improvement in any Virginia district. But the 9th has elected a Democrat to Congress for more than two decades, and the party also fares well in local races.

MAJOR INDUSTRY

Manufacturing, coal mining, agriculture

CITIES

Blacksburg, 39,573; Bristol, 17,367; Christiansburg, 16,947; Radford, 15,859

NOTABLE

The Blue Ridge Parkway's oft-photographed Mabry Mill (1910), restored as a fully operational grist mill, is now used for mountain craft exhibits; Abingdon's still-thriving Barter Theatre allowed local residents to trade excess produce and livestock for admission during the Depression.

Rep. Frank R. Wolf (R)

CAPITOL OFFICE
225-5136
www.house.gov/wolf
241 Cannon 20515-4610; fax 225-0437

COMMITTEES
Appropriations

RESIDENCE
Vienna

BORN
Jan. 30, 1939, Philadelphia, Pa.

RELIGION
Presbyterian

FAMILY
Wife, Carolyn Wolf; five children

EDUCATION
Pennsylvania State U., B.A. 1961 (political science); Georgetown U., LL.B. 1965

MILITARY SERVICE
Army Reserve, 1962-63

CAREER
Lawyer; U.S. Interior Department official; congressional aide; lobbyist

POLITICAL HIGHLIGHTS
Sought Republican nomination for U.S. House, 1976; Republican nominee for U.S. House, 1978

ELECTION RESULTS

2006 GENERAL		
Frank R. Wolf (R)	138,213	57.3%
Judy M. Feder (D)	98,769	41.0%
2006 PRIMARY		
Frank R. Wolf (R)		unopposed
2004 GENERAL		
Frank R. Wolf (R)	205,982	63.8%
James Socas (D)	116,654	36.1%

PREVIOUS WINNING PERCENTAGES
2002 (72%); 2000 (84%); 1998 (72%); 1996 (72%); 1994 (87%); 1992 (64%); 1990 (61%); 1988 (68%); 1986 (60%); 1984 (63%); 1982 (53%); 1980 (51%)

Elected 1980; 14th term

After many years of supplying his district with new roads and bridges, veteran appropriator Wolf has increasingly turned to foreign affairs as a focus in the House. In the 110th Congress (2007-08), he is the top-ranking Republican on the Appropriations subcommittee overseeing spending for the State Department and foreign operations.

The 26-year House veteran is particularly interested in U.S. policy in the Middle East. He was a force behind the creation of the Iraq Study Group, an independent panel made up of policy experts that recommended a new course in Iraq. Wolf was miffed that President Bush chose to ignore many of its recommendations for diplomatic solutions, and introduced a resolution in the 110th Congress calling for the recommendations of the ISG to become U.S. strategy. The bill gained only 11 cosponsors.

Wolf proposed the study group in 2005 after returning from his third trip to Iraq and concluding that "fresh eyes" were needed to conduct a critical review of the U.S. mission in Iraq. The group was co-chaired by former Secretary of State James A. Baker, a Republican, and former Rep. Lee Hamilton, a Democrat.

Wolf continues to travel extensively in the Middle East. While Democratic House Speaker Nancy Pelosi's trip to Syria in March 2007 drew ire from the White House, Wolf defended engaging Syria diplomatically and planned a visit to Syria himself. "Being willing to talk to Syria is not a sign of weakness, but of self-confidence," he said.

With an interest in global human rights, Wolf also has joined many liberal Democrats in trying to focus attention on genocide in the Darfur region of Sudan, where government-backed militias have conducted wanton killing sprees. After five trips to the region, Wolf said, "I drove past dozens of pillaged villages and walked through what was left of four burned to the ground. I heard countless stories about rape, murder and plunder."

In 2006, Wolf and Democratic Rep. Donald M. Payne of New Jersey circulated a letter to state governors urging them to cease dealings with companies doing business with the governing regime in Sudan.

Wolf's other major interest is federal policy that affects the lives of government workers, many of whom live in his Northern Virginia district and its many suburbs of Washington, D.C. He is a leading congressional proponent of telecommuting and its potential to relieve the area's clogged roads. Wolf says the federal government should be leading the trend, and added a provision to a fiscal 2006 spending bill requiring some federal agencies to increase the number of telecommuting employees in order to receive $5 million in funding.

He also uses his seat on the powerful Appropriations Committee to send home millions of dollars in transportation projects and for first-responder programs, given his district's proximity to the nation's capital. Wolf was one of 25 House Republicans who went against their party to support creation of an independent probe of the Sept. 11 terrorist attacks.

A history buff, Wolf is heavily involved in efforts to preserve the many historic sites and battlefields in his district. His pet project is winning designation of a 175-mile corridor from Gettysburg, Pennsylvania, to Charlottesville, Virginia, as a National Heritage Area. It is modeled after the Shenandoah Valley Battlefields National Historic District, which Wolf helped create in the late 1990s.

Wolf is a devout Christian and strong opponent of legalized gambling. In

2006, he asked Bush to halt the opening of new casinos owned and operated by American Indian tribes, some of which were at the center of a corruption scandal involving lobbyist Jack Abramoff.

Wolf says he can't remember a time he wasn't interested in politics and government. He was born and raised in Philadelphia, the son of a police officer and a cafeteria worker. His interest grew out of a boyhood fascination with history. He read biographies of George Washington, Thomas Jefferson and Abraham Lincoln.

In third grade, Wolf remembers, he had a stutter that some classmates made fun of. He dreamed of winning respect by becoming a political leader like the people he read about. (Many politicians paper their walls with pictures of themselves and famous political figures; Wolf keeps only two pictures on his, one of Lincoln and one of Washington.)

In college Wolf majored in political science and then earned his law degree from Georgetown University in Washington. He became an aide to Pennsylvania GOP Rep. Edward G. Biester. He later served as a deputy assistant in the Interior Department during the Nixon and Ford administrations, and also was a lobbyist for baby food and farm implement manufacturers.

Though most members of his family were Democrats, Wolf says he became a Republican because he believed in lower taxes, a strong national defense and a tough approach to fighting communism during the Cold War. He credits Ronald Reagan with getting him into office.

Wolf was unsuccessful in his first two attempts to win a House seat, but edged closer each time. In 1976, he failed to get the GOP nomination; in 1978, he lost the general election. But he remembered his history and knew that George Washington lost his first election to the Virginia House of Delegates, and thus was not discouraged from trying again in 1980, the year of the Reagan Revolution in national politics. In a rematch that year with Rep. Joseph L. Fisher, the Democrat who had beaten him in 1978, Wolf was hoisted by the Reagan surge to a narrow victory over Fisher.

He had a tough re-election race in 1982, but then enjoyed smooth rides until 2006. With the 10th District becoming incrementally more Democratic, Wolf had more of a struggle in a year many factors were working against Republicans, including an unpopular president and several scandals involving Republican members of Congress. His Democratic opponent, Judy M. Feder, an architect of President Bill Clinton's health care plan, attacked Wolf's initial support for the war in Iraq.

Wolf prevailed with 57 percent of the vote, 16 percentage points better than Feder, but much less than the 30 percentage points he was used to.

KEY VOTES

2006

- Yes Stop broadband companies from favoring select Internet traffic
- Yes Affirm U.S. commitment to war in Iraq and reject setting a withdrawal date for troops
- Yes Repeal requirement for bilingual ballots at the polls
- Yes Permit U.S. sale of civilian nuclear technology to India
- Yes Build a 700-mile fence on the U.S.-Mexico border to curb illegal crossings
- Yes Permit warrantless wiretaps of suspected terrorists

2005

- ? Intervene in the life-support case of Terri Schiavo
- No Lift President Bush's restrictions on stem cell research funding
- No Prohibit FBI access to library and bookstore records
- Yes Approve free-trade pact with five Central American countries
- Yes Pass energy policy overhaul favored by President Bush emphasizing domestic oil and gas production
- No End mandatory preservation of habitat of endangered animal and plant species
- Yes Ban torture of prisoners in U.S. custody

CQ VOTE STUDIES

	PARTY UNITY		PRESIDENTIAL SUPPORT	
	Support	Oppose	Support	Oppose
2006	85%	15%	80%	20%
2005	90%	10%	84%	16%
2004	85%	15%	85%	15%
2003	93%	7%	93%	7%
2002	89%	11%	82%	18%

INTEREST GROUPS

	AFL-CIO	ADA	CCUS	ACU
2006	50%	10%	67%	64%
2005	20%	5%	89%	60%
2004	40%	25%	90%	76%
2003	27%	15%	83%	80%
2002	11%	5%	80%	92%

VIRGINIA 10

North — part of Fairfax County, Loudoun County

Located in the northern part of Virginia, the GOP-friendly 10th bridges a dizzying range of economies and lifestyles, with mountains and farmland at one end and congested Washington, D.C., suburbs at the other. A hotbed of economic activity in the 1990s that continued into this decade, the 10th is a mostly white-collar area that includes some of the state's wealthiest counties — Loudoun and parts of Fauquier and Fairfax.

Most of the district's population resides in suburban Northern Virginia, and many residents commute to jobs in Washington or the inner suburbs just outside the nation's capital. Technology-magnet Loudoun County, which includes Leesburg and Washington Dulles International Airport, has tripled in population since 1990. About one-third of district residents live in Fairfax County (shared with the 8th and 11th), which includes Chantilly.

Agriculture and manufacturing fuel the economy in the rest of the 10th, which is solidly Republican and less densely populated. Clarke and Frederick counties produce about half of Virginia's apples and peaches. Winchester, in Frederick County, is the center of the state's apple-growing industry. Recently, outer areas such as Winchester and Manassas have seen an increase in methamphetamine use and distribution. The 10th also has seen a rise in violent gang activity in Northern Virginia, and slow-growth advocates have fared well in some recent elections here as the region grapples with its rapid expansion.

In presidential and state legislative races, Loudoun continues to vote decidedly Republican, although not as overwhelmingly as in the past. Democrat John Kerry narrowly carried the 10th's share of Fairfax County, a more politically competitive area, in the 2004 presidential election, although George W. Bush won the 10th with 55 percent of the vote.

MAJOR INDUSTRY

Technology, government, manufacturing, agriculture

CITIES

Chantilly (unincorporated), 41,041; McLean (unincorporated) (pt.), 37,427; Manassas, 35,135; Centreville (unincorporated) (pt.), 33,053; Leesburg, 28,311; Winchester, 23,585

NOTABLE

The "Enola Gay," which dropped an atomic bomb in World War II, is at the National Air and Space Museum's Udvar-Hazy Center near Dulles.

Rep. Thomas M. Davis III (R)

CAPITOL OFFICE
225-1492
tomdavis.house.gov
2348 Rayburn 20515-4611; fax 225-3071

COMMITTEES
Homeland Security
Oversight & Government Reform - ranking member

RESIDENCE
Vienna

BORN
Jan. 5, 1949, Minot, N.D.

RELIGION
Christian Scientist

FAMILY
Wife, Jeannemarie A. Devolites-Davis; three children

EDUCATION
Amherst College, B.A. 1971 (political science); U. of Virginia, J.D. 1975

MILITARY SERVICE
Army, 1971-72; Va. National Guard, 1972-79; Army Reserve, 1972-79

CAREER
Lawyer; professional services firm executive; state legislative aide

POLITICAL HIGHLIGHTS
Fairfax County Board of Supervisors, 1980-94 (chairman, 1991-94)

ELECTION RESULTS

2006 GENERAL		
Thomas M. Davis III (R)	130,468	55.5%
Andrew L. Hurst (D)	102,511	43.6%
2006 PRIMARY		
Thomas M. Davis III (R)		unopposed
2004 GENERAL		
Thomas M. Davis III (R)	186,299	60.3%
Ken Longmyer (D)	118,305	38.3%
Joseph Oddo (I)	4,338	1.4%

PREVIOUS WINNING PERCENTAGES
2002 (83%); 2000 (62%); 1998 (82%); 1996 (64%); 1994 (53%)

Elected 1994; 7th term

Davis is one of the most savvy politicians in the House, and he has positioned himself prominently to make a run for the U.S. Senate should his home-state colleague, Republican John W. Warner, decide to retire.

But it is from his seat on the Oversight and Government Reform Committee — first as chairman, now as ranking member — that he has indulged his passion for overhauling the way the federal bureaucracy does business.

Whether it's the Federal Emergency Management Agency's failings after Hurricane Katrina or scandals in the veterans health care system, government is "dysfunctional," he says. "Somebody has got to start paying attention to governance issues," rather than the wedge issues that absorb the attention of both parties, he says. Davis also puts special focus on issues important to the District of Columbia, whose good health he views as crucial to the entire metropolitan region, including his chunk of northern Virginia.

A political junkie since childhood, Davis cemented his reputation as one of his party's most adept operatives — and built himself a constituency among colleagues — by guiding House Republicans to a larger majority in the 2002 election. As chairman of the National Republican Congressional Committee (NRCC), he helped defend incumbents, he raised money for them, and he recruited candidates for open seats. He is now serving as a senior adviser to the committee's current chairman, Tom Cole of Oklahoma.

As chairman of the Government Reform panel in the 109th Congress (2005-06), Davis put himself into the thick of high-profile debates. In early 2005, he became familiar to viewers of the ESPN cable sports network with his hearings on steroid use in baseball. Some of the sport's biggest stars testified, a few under subpoena. The witnesses included sluggers Sammy Sosa and Rafael Palmeiro and former players Jose Canseco and Mark McGwire. The subject matter was dear to Davis. As a kid, he used to memorize Washington Senators box scores and now recites district-by-district political data with the same amazing recall. Davis is a season ticket holder of the Nationals, the Washington, D.C., baseball team.

As chairman, Davis won the cooperation of the committee's senior Democrat, Henry A. Waxman of California, who had fought bitterly with past chairmen whom he considered too partisan. Although their committee roles have flipped and Waxman wields the gavel, Davis is looking to work with him on issues such as strengthening the security of the federal government's data. He's been focusing on the issue since the Sept. 11 terrorist attacks, but it took on new urgency after a string of data security breaches in 2006 that compromised the personal information of millions of Americans.

Davis' often rumpled appearance and intemperance with Diet Coke belie the sharp organizational skills he possesses, including a keen sense of the legislative and political playing fields. A Senate page in the mid-1960s, he wrote a college paper titled "The Political Realignment of the Outer South."

Davis applies to the legislative process the same considerable strategic and tactical skills that made him a star at the NRCC. He has delved into federal employment and purchasing practices, which are important issues for the government workers and contractors in Northern Virginia and the suburbs just outside of Washington.

He spends time working on initiatives to help the capital city. His 2007 bill to reauthorize the D.C. College Access Act, which allows graduates of Washington, D.C., high schools to attend colleges around the nation at in-state tuition rates — is making its way through Congress. Another 2007 measure he is pushing would provide $1.5 billion in federal money to the D.C.-area Metro public transit system, if D.C., Virginia and Maryland agree to provide dedicated sources of state money for the system. "It's a Democratic Congress; I'm not going to make any big policy advances," he said. "I can still focus on the region and make a difference for the region."

But the most important effort Davis has made in behalf of the District is to seek for its residents a full vote in the House. For years, Davis has tirelessly backed a measure, which the House passed in April 2007, to give the D.C. delegate full floor voting privileges. The legislation would also add one more House seat for Utah. The bill's mostly Democratic supporters cast the issue as one of fairness to the more than half-million District residents who do not have full representation in Congress. The D.C. delegate can vote in committee but not on bills brought to the House floor.

The White House and some Republicans have argued that the proposal would violate a section of the Constitution stating that House members shall be elected by "people of the several states." To give D.C. a vote in Congress, they say, would require a constitutional amendment. But Davis says, "Those of us who are supporting this bill are not nervous about its constitutionality." The debate, Davis said, is not about "what Congress can do. It is a debate about what Congress is willing to do."

After becoming actively involved in the 2002 debate over creating the Department of Homeland Security — his proposals on procurement and contracting policies were included in the law — Davis has tried to implement the president's management agenda, which includes efforts to boost competition between the government and private companies to provide public services.

Davis is often mentioned as a contender to succeed his state's senior senator, Warner. He argues that his strong track record and political base in northern Virginia would be important assets in a statewide race. But even as Davis has cultivated his base of support among all Republicans, he also has tried to improve his relations with conservatives, who are key to his statewide ambitions. Still, he voted 87 percent of the time with his party in the 109th Congress on votes that pitted the two parties against each other, placing him among the more moderate members of the caucus.

Davis built his career in government. He had been on the board of supervisors in Fairfax County for about 15 years when he took on one-term Democratic Rep. Leslie L. Byrne, a member of her party's leadership and an aggressive partisan. He won by 8 percentage points and has been easily re-elected ever since. The 55 percent share of the vote he won in 2006 was his lowest since his first election.

KEY VOTES

2006

Yes Stop broadband companies from favoring select Internet traffic
Yes Affirm U.S. commitment to war in Iraq and reject setting a withdrawal date for troops
No Repeal requirement for bilingual ballots at the polls
Yes Permit U.S. sale of civilian nuclear technology to India
Yes Build a 700-mile fence on the U.S.-Mexico border to curb illegal crossings
Yes Permit warrantless wiretaps of suspected terrorists

2005

Yes Intervene in the life-support case of Terri Schiavo
Yes Lift President Bush's restrictions on stem cell research funding
No Prohibit FBI access to library and bookstore records
Yes Approve free-trade pact with five Central American countries
Yes Pass energy policy overhaul favored by President Bush emphasizing domestic oil and gas production
No End mandatory preservation of habitat of endangered animal and plant species
Yes Ban torture of prisoners in U.S. custody

CQ VOTE STUDIES

	PARTY UNITY		PRESIDENTIAL SUPPORT	
	Support	Oppose	Support	Oppose
2006	86%	14%	85%	15%
2005	88%	12%	80%	20%
2004	88%	12%	91%	9%
2003	90%	10%	96%	4%
2002	90%	10%	82%	18%

INTEREST GROUPS

	AFL-CIO	ADA	CCUS	ACU
2006	29%	15%	80%	56%
2005	15%	5%	85%	57%
2004	20%	10%	100%	80%
2003	15%	5%	93%	68%
2002	11%	10%	84%	88%

VIRGINIA 11

Washington suburbs – parts of Fairfax and Prince William counties

Anchored in the suburbs of Washington, D.C., the 11th is home to a well-educated, professional and upper-income workforce that boasts the nation's highest median income (more than $80,000). Like other nearby suburban areas, the 11th has become more racially and ethnically diverse: It has the largest Asian population (11 percent of residents) in Virginia, as well as a robust Hispanic population.

Two-thirds of the population lives in Fairfax County (shared with the 8th and 10th districts). The balance lives in Prince William County, a burgeoning area south and west of Fairfax, or in Fairfax city, a separate jurisdiction within Fairfax County. Many residents work in Washington, either for the federal government or for private companies linked to the government. Technology contributes to local economic growth, and Fairfax County's office parks are home to dozens of firms. The technology-sector growth — and related traffic woes — have made telecommuting an increasingly attractive option for area workers.

Tailor-made for a centrist Republican, the 11th tends to lean left on social issues, although Prince William County is generally more conservative, and to lean right on fiscal issues. But traffic congestion is so rampant that many residents are willing to accept tax increases to pay for transportation improvements.

The 11th's growth has made it highly competitive and politically indecisive. George W. Bush carried Fairfax County and city in the 2000 presidential race, but lost to Democrat John Kerry in 2004. Similarly, Prince William County favored Democratic gubernatorial nominee Tim Kaine in 2005, after supporting Republican Mark Earley in 2001.

MAJOR INDUSTRY

Government, technology, service

CITIES

Burke (unincorporated), 57,737; Dale City (unincorporated), 55,971; Annandale (unincorporated) (pt.), 51,350

NOTABLE

Fairfax County has a larger population than seven states: Montana, Delaware, South Dakota, North Dakota, Alaska, Vermont and Wyoming.

WASHINGTON

Gov. Christine Gregoire (D)

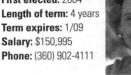

Pronounced: GREG-wahr
First elected: 2004
Length of term: 4 years
Term expires: 1/09
Salary: $150,995
Phone: (360) 902-4111

Residence: Olympia
Born: March 24, 1947; Adrian, Mich.
Religion: Roman Catholic
Family: Husband, Mike Gregoire; two children
Education: U. of Washington, B.A. 1969 (speech & sociology); Gonzaga U., J.D. 1977
Career: Lawyer; state social services department caseworker; clerk typist
Political highlights: Wash. Department of Ecology director, 1988-92; Wash. attorney general, 1993-2004

Election results:

2004 GENERAL		
Christine Gregoire (D)	1,373,361	48.87%
Dino Rossi (R)	1,373,232	48.86%
Ruth Bennett (LIBERT)	63,465	2.3%

Lt. Gov. Brad Owen (D)

First elected: 1996
Length of term: 4 years
Term expires: 1/09
Salary: $78,930
Phone: (360) 786-7700

LEGISLATURE

Legislature: 105 days January-May in odd-numbered years; 60 days January-March in even-numbered years

Senate: 49 members, 4-year terms
2007 ratios: 32 D, 17 R; 31 men, 18 women
Salary: $36,311
Phone: (360) 786-7550

House: 98 members, 2-year terms
2007 ratios: 62 D, 36 R; 70 men, 28 women
Salary: $36,311
Phone: (360) 786-7750

TERM LIMITS

Governor: 2 terms
Senate: No
House: No

URBAN STATISTICS

CITY	POPULATION
Seattle	563,374
Spokane	195,629
Tacoma	193,556
Vancouver	143,560
Bellevue	109,569

REGISTERED VOTERS

Voters do not register by party.

POPULATION

2006 population (est.)	6,395,798
2000 population	5,894,121
1990 population	4,866,692
Percent change (1990-2000)	+21.1%
Rank among states (2006)	14
Median age	35.3
Born in state	47.2%
Foreign born	10.4%
Violent crime rate	370/100,000
Poverty level	10.6%
Federal workers	66,061
Military	74,250

ELECTIONS

STATE ELECTION OFFICIAL
(360) 902-4151
DEMOCRATIC PARTY
(206) 583-0664
REPUBLICAN PARTY
(206) 575-2900

MISCELLANEOUS

Web: www.access.wa.gov
Capital: Olympia

U.S. CONGRESS

Senate: 2 Democrats
House: 6 Democrats, 3 Republicans

2000 Census Statistics by District

DIST.	2004 VOTE FOR PRESIDENT BUSH	KERRY	WHITE	BLACK	ASIAN	HISP	MEDIAN INCOME	WHITE COLLAR	BLUE COLLAR	SERVICE INDUSTRY	OVER 64	UNDER 18	COLLEGE EDUCATION	RURAL	SQ. MILES
1	42%	56%	82%	2%	8%	4%	$58,565	69%	18%	12%	10%	26%	36%	5%	439
2	47	51	86	1	3	6	$45,441	55	29	16	12	26	22	31	6,564
3	50	48	88	1	3	5	$44,426	57	28	15	11	27	21	29	7,515
4	63	35	68	1	1	26	$37,764	53	31	16	11	30	19	29	19,051
5	57	41	88	1	2	5	$35,720	60	23	17	13	25	24	28	22,864
6	45	53	78	6	4	5	$39,205	55	27	18	14	25	20	21	6,781
7	19	79	67	8	13	6	$45,864	71	15	14	12	17	44	2	141
8	48	51	82	2	8	4	$63,854	69	20	11	9	28	37	12	2,579
9	46	53	73	6	7	7	$46,495	59	25	15	10	26	22	5	608
STATE	46	53	79	3	5	7	$45,776	61	24	15	11	26	28	18	66,544
U.S.	50.7	48.3	69	12	4	13	$41,994	60	25	15	12	26	24	21	3,537,438

Bellingham
Whatcom
San Juan
Skagit
2
Island
Snohomish
Clallam
Everett
1, 7
Jefferson
Seattle
King
Kitsap
6
Mason
Tacoma
Grays Harbor
8
Olympia
9
Pierce
Thurston
Pacific
3
Lewis
Wahkiakum
Cowlitz
Skamania
Clark
Vancouver
Okanogan
Ferry
Stevens
Pend Oreille
5
Chelan
Douglas
Lincoln
Spokane
Spokane
Kittitas
4
Grant
Adams
Whitman
Yakima
Franklin
Garfield
Yakima
Columbia
Benton
Walla Walla
Asotin
Klickitat

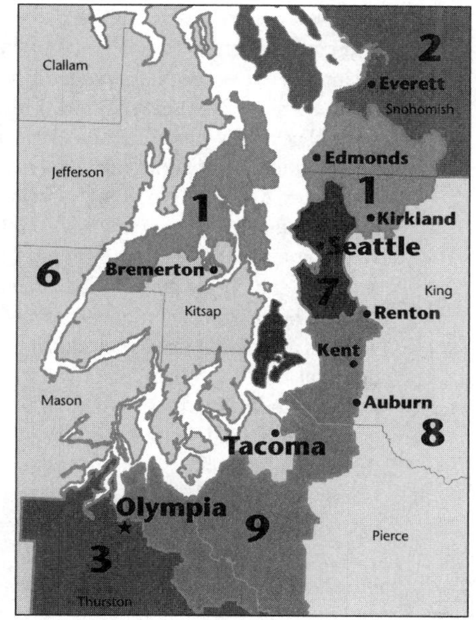
2
Clallam
Everett
Snohomish
Edmonds
Jefferson
1
1
Kirkland
Seattle
6
Bremerton
7
King
Kitsap
Renton
Kent
Mason
Auburn
8
Tacoma
Olympia
9
Pierce
3
Thurston

Sen. Patty Murray (D)

CAPITOL OFFICE
224-2621
murray.senate.gov
173 Russell 20510-4704; fax 224-0238

COMMITTEES
Appropriations
(Transportation-HUD - chairwoman)
Budget
Health, Education, Labor & Pensions
(Employment & Workplace Safety - chairwoman)
Rules & Administration
Veterans' Affairs
Joint Printing

RESIDENCE
Seattle

BORN
Oct. 11, 1950, Bothell, Wash.

RELIGION
Roman Catholic

FAMILY
Husband, Rob Murray; two children

EDUCATION
Washington State U., B.A. 1972

CAREER
Parenting class instructor

POLITICAL HIGHLIGHTS
Candidate for Shoreline School Board, 1983; Shoreline School Board, 1983-89; Wash. Senate, 1989-93

ELECTION RESULTS

2004 GENERAL		
Patty Murray (D)	1,549,708	55.0%
George Nethercutt (R)	1,204,584	42.7%
J. Mills (LIBERT)	34,055	1.2%
Mark B. Wilson (GREEN)	30,304	1.1%
2004 PRIMARY		
Patty Murray (D)	709,497	92.2%
Warren E. Hanson (D)	46,490	6.0%
Mohammad H. Said (D)	13,527	1.8%

PREVIOUS WINNING PERCENTAGES
1998 (58%); 1992 (54%)

Elected 1992; 3rd term

Patty Murray has made a career of being underestimated. Once famously dismissed as a "mom in tennis shoes," today she chairs the Appropriations Transportation Subcommittee. She also serves on the spending panel's health and labor subcommittee, is the second-ranking Democrat on the Budget Committee and occupies a spot in the Senate Democratic leadership.

A tenacious politician, Murray has a hand in national issues ranging from Amtrak policy to education. But she says her political lodestar is ensuring that Congress stays focused on things affecting everyday Americans. "Your head can get so wrapped up in D.C. and the latest Karl Rove scandal that you forget that there are people who can't get to work, or they've come home from a war and can't get a job," Murray says.

She describes herself as a "grass roots" senator who prefers to hold town meetings to gather information and mobilize people, a reflection of how she got involved in politics in the first place.

In the early 1980s, angered that the state legislature planned to eliminate a preschool program in which her children were enrolled, Murray packed the two youngsters into the car and drove to the state capital to complain. She was dismissed by a legislator there who told her, "You can't make a difference. You're just a mom in tennis shoes." Murray says of the incident, "I drove home as angry as I could be, saying he has no right to tell me I can't make a difference." She organized a statewide parents' campaign to revive the program, an effort that succeeded in just three months. That led Murray to six years on her local school board and four years in the state Senate.

In her 1992 U.S. Senate quest, she bested two better-known moderates with years of congressional experience in the primary and general races. In 1998, she was re-elected with 58 percent of the vote. In 2004, the head of the Repupblican Senate campaign committee said she would be no match for "giant killer" George Nethercutt, a House member who had beaten Democratic Speaker Tom Foley in 1994. Murray won by 12 percentage points.

Her backing of government social programs and her work ethic stem from her childhood. Her father managed a dime store, where she and her six siblings often put in long hours. They had to fend off ailments without health care because it was too expensive, and often they made their own clothes. When she was a teenager, Murray's father was diagnosed with multiple sclerosis and had to stop working. The family briefly went on welfare until her mother completed a government-funded program that enabled her to work as a bookkeeper. She credits the program with saving the family from financial ruin.

"Despite the fact that we had no money, each one of us was expected to go to college and work to pay for it," Murray says. She worked her way through college, taking any job she could find: in a glass shop, as a secretary taking shorthand and, one summer, cleaning bathrooms in a state park. All of her siblings, including her twin sister, earned college degrees.

Murray has had a hand in a wide range of consumer issues. She has introduced legislation to protect employees from exposure to asbestos and hosted a town hall meeting on Wal-Mart's employment practices.

A member of the Veterans' Affairs Committee, Murray has called regularly for more funding for veterans' health care, particularly for those returning from war with traumatic brain injuries that often require long-term care. She blasted the administration over how much the ongoing war was increasing veterans' health care costs and creating administrative and patient care problems at military veterans' medical facilities and the Veterans Affairs Department.

Though Murray voted against the 2002 resolution granting President Bush the authority to go to war, she took some flak in 2006 from anti-war activists who claim she has not taken a strong enough stance against the war. In June of that year, she had supported an amendment to the fiscal 2007 defense authorization bill urging the president to begin withdrawing troops by the end of the year, but voted against a different amendment that would have set a firm deadline. She switched her vote again in March 2007, voting for a war funding bill that called for most troops to be pulled out by 2008.

With Republicans charging that Democrats were putting troops at risk with their bill, the Senate earlier in the month had adopted her resolution stating that the president and Congress should not do anything to endanger troops and should provide any funds the troops need for training and equipment.

In 2005, the mom in tennis shoes became assistant floor leader, responsible for helping coordinate activity during floor debates. It is no accident that Murray arrived at this point. Her career is the result of a long series of small steps, carefully planned and executed. She is also willing to take chances. Murray personally intervened in late 2000 to end a strike affecting the state's two largest newspapers, the Seattle Post-Intelligencer and The Seattle Times. Political analysts said her involvement carried many political risks and few benefits, but was instrumental in ending the strike.

Mindful of the price Speaker Foley paid when he was tarred as a national political figure neglectful of the folks back home, she attends to her state's needs. Her Appropriations post gives her a say over the allocation of $90 billion in transportation spending each year, and she makes sure her state gets a healthy share. Her prowess has prompted some to call her "Patty Magnuson," a reference to Washington's legendary Democratic Sen. Warren Magnuson, who was famed for securing billions of federal dollars for the state.

Murray's penchant for directing tax dollars back home has not gone unnoticed. She was taken to task by Arizona Republican Sen. John McCain, a frequent critic of lawmakers' earmarked spending, when she attached $3 million for a maritime museum to the transportation spending bill in 2001. Murray sat stone-faced in the chamber as McCain blasted her project as an example of "pork barrel spending."

She is a fierce promoter of Washington's two mega employers, Microsoft and Boeing. She repeatedly denounced the long-running federal antitrust case against Microsoft even though it was triggered by Democratic President Bill Clinton. And she was one of the prime movers behind a $23 billion deal to lease 100 Boeing 767 airplanes for the Air Force to use as aerial tankers. Criticized by McCain, the deal fell apart amid corruption allegations. She also regularly presses the Bush administration to take action against Boeing chief nemesis Airbus, a French conglomerate that has supplanted Boeing as the world's biggest maker of commercial jetliners.

Murray has won some fights with the administration, including funding for her Operation Safe Commerce, a pilot project that tracks U.S.-bound cargo containers in foreign ports to prevent them from being used to smuggle terrorists or weapons into the United States.

Though she eschews such labels as "feminist," Murray is nonetheless concerned with women's issues. She once vowed to hold up the nomination of the head of the Food and Drug Administration until the agency made a decision on approving over-the-counter sales of morning-after birth control pills.

Through it all, Murray has used her trademark tennis shoes to remind voters of her humble roots. She passes out "Golden Tennis Shoe" awards to constituents who, like her, have been community activists.

KEY VOTES

2006

- No Confirm Samuel A. Alito Jr. to the Supreme Court
- No Allow consideration of a bill to establish a $140 billion trust fund to compensate victims of asbestos exposure
- No Extend tax cuts for two years at a cost of $70 billion over five years
- Yes Overhaul immigration policy with border security, enforcement and guest worker program
- No Allow consideration of a bill to permanently repeal the estate tax
- Yes Urge President Bush to begin troop withdrawals from Iraq in 2006
- Yes Lift President Bush's restrictions on stem cell research funding
- No Authorize military tribunals for suspected terrorists

2005

- No Curb class action lawsuits by shifting them from state to federal courts
- No Allow confirmation vote on Priscilla R. Owen to the U.S. Court of Appeals for the 5th Circuit
- No Oppose mandatory emissions limits and block recognition of global warming as a threat
- Yes Approve free-trade pact with five Central American countries
- No Pass energy policy overhaul favored by President Bush emphasizing domestic oil and gas production
- No Shield gunmakers from lawsuits when their products are used in crimes
- Yes Ban torture of prisoners in U.S. custody
- No Renew 16 provisions of the Patriot Act
- No Allow final vote on opening the Arctic National Wildlife Refuge to oil and gas exploration

CQ VOTE STUDIES

	PARTY UNITY		PRESIDENTIAL SUPPORT	
	Support	Oppose	Support	Oppose
2006	92%	8%	59%	41%
2005	95%	5%	33%	67%
2004	91%	9%	63%	37%
2003	97%	3%	49%	51%
2002	86%	14%	75%	25%
2001	96%	4%	65%	35%
2000	94%	6%	87%	13%
1999	93%	7%	88%	12%
1998	91%	9%	82%	18%
1997	93%	7%	87%	13%

INTEREST GROUPS

	AFL-CIO	ADA	CCUS	ACU
2006	93%	95%	50%	4%
2005	79%	95%	44%	0%
2004	92%	90%	75%	8%
2003	85%	90%	43%	10%
2002	92%	90%	55%	10%
2001	100%	85%	64%	4%
2000	63%	90%	64%	8%
1999	88%	100%	59%	4%
1998	88%	90%	56%	4%
1997	71%	90%	70%	0%

Sen. Maria Cantwell (D)

CAPITOL OFFICE
224-3441
cantwell.senate.gov
511 Dirksen 20510-4705; fax 228-0514

COMMITTEES
Commerce, Science & Transportation
(Oceans, Atmosphere, Fisheries & Coast Guard - chairwoman)
Energy & Natural Resources
Finance
Indian Affairs
Small Business & Entrepreneurship

RESIDENCE
Edmonds

BORN
Oct. 13, 1958, Indianapolis, Ind.

RELIGION
Roman Catholic

FAMILY
Single

EDUCATION
Miami U. (Ohio), B.A. 1980 (public policy)

CAREER
Internet audio company executive; public relations consultant

POLITICAL HIGHLIGHTS
Wash. House, 1987-92; U.S. House, 1993-95; defeated for re-election to U.S. House, 1994

ELECTION RESULTS

2006 GENERAL		
Maria Cantwell (D)	1,184,659	56.9%
Mike McGavick (R)	832,106	39.9%
Bruce Guthrie (LIBERT)	29,331	1.4%
Aaron Dixon (GREEN)	21,254	1.0%
2006 PRIMARY		
Maria Cantwell (D)	570,677	90.8%
Hong Tran (D)	33,124	5.3%
Mike the Mover (D)	11,274	1.8%
Michael Goodspaceguy Nelson (D)	9,454	1.5%

PREVIOUS WINNING PERCENTAGES
2000 (49%); 1992 House Election (55%)

Elected 2000; 2nd term

Cantwell is smart, attractive in front of the TV cameras, and tenacious on the political battlefield. Her main drawback is an often-mentioned aloofness that makes her seem more like the dot-com executive she once was than the public figure she is today. She is almost wholly unequipped with a politician's gift of gab, and has difficulty articulating her not inconsiderable legislative activities in a way that ensures she accrues the credit. During the 2006 campaign, Republicans mocked her as Senator Can't-speak-well.

But Cantwell got the last word, defeating the well-financed Republican, Mike McGavick, a former chief executive officer of the Safeco Insurance Company. She had headed into that first re-election campaign overshadowed by her state's senior senator, liberal firebrand Patty Murray, but won with 57 percent of the vote. She had even cracked the "Cascade Curtain," the mountain range separating the Republican rural east from the Democratic urban west portions of the state. Her win affirmed her energetic work on several local issues and her success stepping out in a couple of national debates.

Senate Democratic leaders rewarded her in the 110th Congress (2007-08) with a seat on the Finance Committee, one of the most powerful and prestigious panels. They were pleased not just with Cantwell's win, but also with her loyalty to the party on crucial votes.

Cantwell in her first term was the main Democratic opponent of a controversial plan to open the Arctic National Wildlife Refuge in Alaska to energy exploration, a move that won her the enmity of a powerful fellow senator, Republican Ted Stevens of Alaska, a chamber elder and main backer of opening ANWR.

In December 2005, Cantwell won passage of a resolution stripping the ANWR provision from a defense spending bill. Furious, Stevens vowed to retaliate against her in her election. "I will go to every state and tell them what you've done," he fumed on the floor, glaring in Cantwell's direction. "I will go to Washington state many, many times."

Cantwell also was among the first members of Congress to pick up on the significance of Enron Corp.'s manipulation of the West Coast energy market, which cost Washington state utility customers more than $1 billion in unnecessary charges and foreshadowed the company's downfall. And she waged campaigns against price-gouging by oil companies when gas prices topped $3 a gallon and succeeded in adding a provision to the 2005 energy bill for federal funding for the development of biofuels.

Her role in energy and environmental issues won her a perfect score from the League of Conservation Voters, whose opinion counted among Washington state's many pro-regulation liberals. "I am tenacious. I never let go," Cantwell told The Seattle Times in 2006.

Cantwell combines a pro-business stance with support for traditional Democratic views on core social issues such as abortion rights. She voted with fellow Democrats 92 percent of the time on votes that broke along party lines in the 109th Congress (2005-06). But she disappointed some liberals with her tepid criticism of the war in Iraq, and her refusal to repudiate her 2002 vote in favor of President Bush's request to invade.

By 2007, her views on the Iraq War were more in line with the public's. She said in February that she did not support Bush's plan to send more than 21,000 additional combat troops into Iraq. The following month she voted for a war funding bill that set a goal for U.S. troop withdrawals.

On local issues, Cantwell worked to gain federal benefits for former workers at the Hanford Nuclear Reservation in her state, some of whom became ill when they worked with plutonium used in the production of nuclear weapons. And she traveled to Cuba, Mexico and China to try to drum up interest for Washington state's apples, potatoes and lentils.

In the 110th Congress, Cantwell retained her seat on the Commerce, Science and Transportation Committee, a position important for her state's international trade- and technology-dependent economy. She chairs its fisheries and Coast Guard subcommittee, where she began an investigation into a troubled $24 billion, 25-year plan to upgrade the Coast Guard's fleet. Called Deepwater, the effort has been plagued by errors, delays and cost overruns. In April 2007, the full committee approved her bill to overhaul the program and mandate stricter oversight.

Cantwell, a native of Indiana, is the second of five children and the first person in her family to graduate from college. She was exposed early to politics by her father, Paul Cantwell, who brought the family to the nation's capital in 1965 when he took a job working for home-state Democratic Rep. Andrew Jacobs. After a year, he moved the family back to Indiana and took a seat as a county commissioner.

After earning a degree in public policy, Cantwell worked on the unsuccessful gubernatorial campaign of Jerry Springer, who went on to talk show fame. In 1983, she moved to the Seattle area to be a political organizer for Democratic presidential candidate Alan Cranston. She worked in public relations, then was elected to the state legislature at age 28, serving from 1987 to 1992. Cantwell was elected to the U.S. House in 1992, the same year her father was elected to the Indiana House. She served only one term before getting knocked out in the Republican tide of 1994.

Cantwell put politics aside for a few years, joining a Seattle Internet start-up, RealNetworks, the software company that invented RealPlayer and other Internet audio and video products. She rose to be senior vice president of consumer products, becoming a multimillionaire.

"She's very product-driven, very strategic in her approach. She's not a back-slapping pol. She's like a chess player thinking 20 moves ahead," said Michael Meehan, a political consultant and Cantwell's former chief of staff. "Some people mistake that for aloofness. If anybody gets a chance to be in a room with Maria Cantwell, they quickly find out she's very smart, is willing to take risks, and she's very focused."

She tapped into her personal wealth in 2000 to run for the Senate, spending $10 million to unseat Republican incumbent Sen. Slade Gorton. She blew past the favored Democratic opponent, state Insurance Commissioner Deborah Senn, in Washington's open primary. But Cantwell carried only five of the state's 39 counties, all around Puget Sound, in her narrow general-election victory over Gorton. With just more than 2,000 votes separating the candidates, the results were so close that her victory was not declared official until nearly a month after the election.

Sen. Stevens loomed large in the 2006 race, making good on this threat to campaign against her. But the senator's support for McGavick backfired when the candidate had to return $14,000 Stevens helped him raise from an Alaska oil company that figured into an FBI criminal investigation of members of the Alaska State Legislature.

McGavick tried to run a relatively clean race against Cantwell, even criticizing national Republicans for running ads questioning her relationship with Ron Dotzauer, a former boyfriend and campaign manager turned lobbyist. McGavick tried to make an issue of Cantwell's effectiveness in the Senate, and she criticized him for laying off thousands of employees at Safeco and another company, then pocketing millions when he left the firms. Cantwell won the race by 17 percentage points.

KEY VOTES

2006

No Confirm Samuel A. Alito Jr. to the Supreme Court
No Allow consideration of a bill to establish a $140 billion trust fund to compensate victims of asbestos exposure
No Extend tax cuts for two years at a cost of $70 billion over five years
Yes Overhaul immigration policy with border security, enforcement and guest worker program
No Allow consideration of a bill to permanently repeal the estate tax
Yes Urge President Bush to begin troop withdrawals from Iraq in 2006
Yes Lift President Bush's restrictions on stem cell research funding
No Authorize military tribunals for suspected terrorists

2005

Yes Curb class action lawsuits by shifting them from state to federal courts
No Allow confirmation vote on Priscilla R. Owen to the U.S. Court of Appeals for the 5th Circuit
No Oppose mandatory emissions limits and block recognition of global warming as a threat
Yes Approve free-trade pact with five Central American countries
Yes Pass energy policy overhaul favored by President Bush emphasizing domestic oil and gas production
No Shield gunmakers from lawsuits when their products are used in crimes
Yes Ban torture of prisoners in U.S. custody
No Renew 16 provisions of the Patriot Act
No Allow final vote on opening the Arctic National Wildlife Refuge to oil and gas exploration

CQ VOTE STUDIES

	PARTY UNITY		PRESIDENTIAL SUPPORT	
	Support	Oppose	Support	Oppose
2006	92%	8%	54%	46%
2005	92%	8%	36%	64%
2004	90%	10%	66%	34%
2003	96%	4%	52%	48%
2002	82%	18%	81%	19%
2001	98%	2%	64%	36%
House Service:				
1994	92%	8%	86%	14%
1993	92%	8%	80%	20%

INTEREST GROUPS

	AFL-CIO	ADA	CCUS	ACU
2006	87%	95%	58%	12%
2005	86%	95%	56%	8%
2004	83%	95%	65%	8%
2003	85%	90%	39%	15%
2002	85%	80%	55%	25%
2001	100%	100%	50%	12%
House Service:				
1994	67%	70%	83%	14%
1993	83%	80%	36%	17%

Rep. Jay Inslee (D)

CAPITOL OFFICE
225-6311
jay.inslee@mail.house.gov
www.house.gov/inslee
403 Cannon 20515-4701; fax 226-1606

COMMITTEES
Energy & Commerce
Natural Resources
Select Energy Independence & Global Warming

RESIDENCE
Bainbridge Island

BORN
Feb. 9, 1951, Seattle, Wash.

RELIGION
Protestant

FAMILY
Wife, Trudi Inslee; three children

EDUCATION
Stanford U., attended 1969-70;
U. of Washington, B.A. 1973 (economics);
Willamette U., J.D. 1976

CAREER
Lawyer

POLITICAL HIGHLIGHTS
Wash. House, 1989-93; U.S. House, 1993-95; defeated for re-election to U.S. House, 1994; sought Democratic nomination for governor, 1996

ELECTION RESULTS

2006 GENERAL		
Jay Inslee (D)	163,832	67.7%
Larry W. Ishmael (R)	78,105	32.3%
2006 PRIMARY		
Jay Inslee (D)		unopposed
2004 GENERAL		
Jay Inslee (D)	204,121	62.3%
Randy Eastwood (R)	117,850	36.0%
Charles Moore (LIBERT)	5,798	1.8%

PREVIOUS WINNING PERCENTAGES
2002 (56%); 2000 (55%); 1998 (50%); 1992 (51%)

Elected 1998; 6th term

Also served 1993-95

With a seat on the powerful Energy and Commerce Committee, along with posts on the Natural Resources panel and the new committee on global warming, Inslee is finally where he wants to be. He has a hand in the issues his suburban Seattle constituency cares about — environmental protection and technological innovation. It's a long way from his humbling rejection by voters in the mid-1990s, when he lost a re-election bid in a far more conservative district in the rural eastern part of the state.

After his defeat, Inslee moved to the Seattle suburbs, and in 1998 ran for the House again, this time successfully in a more liberal and politically compatible district. He won appointment to the Energy Committee in 2005, enabling him to move from the fringe of policy making to the thick of things.

He has a pocketful of ideas for developing clean, alternative sources of fuel and cutting down on pollution: legislation to encourage the development of technology to harness water power in the Puget Sound and other coastal areas; to design and build more energy-efficient buildings; and to encourage individuals and small businesses to generate some of their own electricity. "I'm in the catbird seat on dealing with energy policy," he told the Medill News Service early in 2007. When President Bush met with House Democrats at a party retreat in February 2007, it was Inslee who challenged the president on global warming.

Not surprisingly, a month later when the House voted to create a special committee to study global warming issues, Speaker Nancy Pelosi named Inslee to the panel.

In the 109th Congress (2005-06), Inslee was a leader in the House in a pro-consumer fight to keep big telecommunications companies from favoring certain content providers. He tried but failed to attach an amendment to a major telecommunications bill that would have banned phone and cable companies from charging Web sites for faster data transmission and from blocking their online competitors' content and services.

A member of the Natural Resources Committee, Inslee is a longtime foe of easing environmental rules for timber harvesting. He helped lead the Democratic charge against a GOP proposal to resume logging on public lands after forest fires, which proponents argued would hasten forest recovery. Inslee and a coalition that included the Natural Resources Defense Council and the World Wildlife Fund contended that the measure, which passed, would circumvent environmental reviews and result in the construction of roads in pristine areas. "Here we go again," Inslee said during debate. "First we had a clean-skies bill that allowed more pollution, then we saw a deficit-reduction bill that increased our national debt. Now we have a forest-recovery bill that assures we'll use less science and less common sense . . . to make decisions on where and how to do forest-recovery plans."

On the Natural Resources panel in the 110th Congress (2007-08), he won House passage of his bill to give national park status to the site on Bainbridge Island that saw the transfer of the first Japanese-Americans to internment camps during World War II. Inslee, who lives on Bainbridge, first introduced the legislation in 2006.

Inslee grew up in Seattle, where his father was a high school biology teacher and a coach. A star football and basketball player, Inslee is still athletically active and plays in the annual congressional baseball game and in an annual geezer basketball tournament. He and a group of middle-aged friends who call themselves the Hoopaholics play basketball for three days straight to raise money for children's charities.

Inslee was accepted to Stanford but left after only a year for the University of Washington because his savings from summer jobs during high school ran out. (Today, he is a big backer of increasing federal Pell grants for college students.) As a young man, Inslee wasn't particularly interested in politics. He earned a law degree, married his high school sweetheart and settled in tiny Selah in south-central Washington, where he was in private practice for 18 years.

His experiences with a local school bond issue changed his mind about politics. The Inslees co-chaired a campaign to raise money for a new high school after Selah failed to pass a bond five times. As a result, the school was about to go to double classroom shifts, meaning some students would have had to get to the overcrowded building at 6 a.m. The Inslees' bond drive was successful, but the victory party was short. The state legislature cut funding for the school in half. Inslee went to the state capital in Olympia to raise "holy heck," which ultimately led him to run successfully for his own seat in the legislature in 1988.

When 4th District Republican Rep. Sid Morrison announced he was giving up his seat in the House to run for governor in 1992, Inslee got into the race. His folksy style and tireless campaigning lifted him to a narrow primary victory and to an equally narrow win in November over Republican Doc Hastings.

Once in the House, Inslee bucked his party on some high-visibility votes. He voted against President Bill Clinton's deficit-reduction package that raised taxes, and he opposed a five-day waiting period for handgun purchases. But he also voted to ban some types of assault-style weapons, which provoked the powerful National Rifle Association. With the group pouring resources into defeating him, Inslee lost a rematch with Hastings by almost 7 percentage points.

Inslee moved back to the Seattle area, settled on Bainbridge and returned to legal work. He waged an unsuccessful primary bid for governor in 1996. Then in 1998, he unseated two-term Republican Rep. Rick White in the suburban Seattle 1st District. His victory was partly thanks to the third-party candidacy of Bruce Craswell, whose 6 percent tally was seen as coming largely from White's GOP base.

In 2003, Inslee considered a run for governor to replace retiring Democrat Gary Locke. He decided against it, however, and won re-election in 2004. He has steadily increased his victory margins, from 6 percentage points in 1998 to 26 percentage points in 2004, to a high of 35 points in 2006.

KEY VOTES

2006

- Yes Stop broadband companies from favoring select Internet traffic
- No Affirm U.S. commitment to war in Iraq and reject setting a withdrawal date for troops
- No Repeal requirement for bilingual ballots at the polls
- Yes Permit U.S. sale of civilian nuclear technology to India
- No Build a 700-mile fence on the U.S.-Mexico border to curb illegal crossings
- No Permit warrantless wiretaps of suspected terrorists

2005

- ? Intervene in the life-support case of Terri Schiavo
- Yes Lift President Bush's restrictions on stem cell research funding
- Yes Prohibit FBI access to library and bookstore records
- No Approve free-trade pact with five Central American countries
- No Pass energy policy overhaul favored by President Bush emphasizing domestic oil and gas production
- No End mandatory preservation of habitat of endangered animal and plant species
- Yes Ban torture of prisoners in U.S. custody

CQ VOTE STUDIES

	PARTY UNITY		PRESIDENTIAL SUPPORT	
	Support	Oppose	Support	Oppose
2006	93%	7%	28%	72%
2005	97%	3%	17%	83%
2004	94%	6%	26%	74%
2003	96%	4%	22%	78%
2002	96%	4%	28%	72%

INTEREST GROUPS

	AFL-CIO	ADA	CCUS	ACU
2006	93%	90%	47%	12%
2005	93%	95%	37%	0%
2004	93%	100%	43%	4%
2003	87%	100%	37%	20%
2002	89%	95%	45%	4%

WASHINGTON 1

Puget Sound (west and east) – north Seattle suburbs

Nestled on Washington's Puget Sound between mountain ranges to the east and west, the 1st has become a suburban haven. The district is home to wealthy residents who work at technology giants and biotechnology companies located throughout the greater Seattle area.

Naval bases spur the economy on the west side of the Sound. The eastern portion of the 1st, which includes the northern borders of Lake Washington and runs along the eastern coast of the Sound, accounts for more than 80 percent of the district's population. Aviation and technology companies located here continue to drive the district's population growth. Bothell, in southern Snohomish, hosts many biotechnology, biomedical and technology firms' headquarters and manufacturing sites.

Tourism also is important to the 1st. Travelers can take a 35-minute ferry ride from downtown Seattle to Bainbridge Island or drive north on Interstate 5 to one of the casinos in the 2nd District. In the Sammamish River Valley, the 1st is home to leading Washington state wineries — Chateau Ste. Michelle and Columbia — and outdoor recreation sites, while the Future of Flight Aviation Center and Boeing Tour attracts visitors to Mukilteo.

Democrats have the edge in the district, with its well-educated, socially liberal professionals. The Snohomish portion is the most politically competitive of the three counties; the King and Kitsap county portions are slightly more Democratic.

MAJOR INDUSTRY

Software, military, aviation, tourism

MILITARY BASES

Naval Base Kitsap (Bangor), 5,743 military, 2,779 civilian (2004); Naval Undersea Warfare Center Keyport, 33 military, 1,417 civilian (2005)

CITIES

Kirkland (pt.), 44,406; Edmonds, 39,515; Shoreline (pt.), 35,694; Seattle Hill-Silver Firs (unincorporated), 35,311; Redmond (pt.), 34,759

NOTABLE

Poulsbo is home to the annual Scandinavian celebration Viking Fest; The Junior Softball World Series is played each summer in Kirkland.

Rep. Rick Larsen (D)

CAPITOL OFFICE
225-2605
rick.larsen@mail.house.gov
www.house.gov/larsen
107 Cannon 20515-4702; fax 225-4420

COMMITTEES
Armed Services
Small Business
Transportation & Infrastructure

RESIDENCE
Everett

BORN
June 15, 1965, Arlington, Wash.

RELIGION
Methodist

FAMILY
Wife, Tiia Karlen; two children

EDUCATION
Pacific Lutheran U., B.A. 1987 (political science); U. of Minnesota, M.P.A. 1990 (public affairs)

CAREER
Dental association lobbyist; port economic development official

POLITICAL HIGHLIGHTS
Snohomish County Council, 1998-2000 (chairman, 1999)

ELECTION RESULTS

2006 GENERAL		
Rick Larsen (D)	157,064	64.2%
Doug Roulstone (R)	87,730	35.8%
2006 PRIMARY		
Rick Larsen (D)		unopposed
2004 GENERAL		
Rick Larsen (D)	202,383	63.9%
Suzanne Sinclair (R)	106,333	33.6%
Bruce Guthrie (LIBERT)	7,966	2.5%

PREVIOUS WINNING PERCENTAGES
2002 (50%); 2000 (50%)

Elected 2000; 4th term

A father of two who rides the subway to work on Capitol Hill every day, Larsen is among the unsung lawmakers who focus on their districts rather than striving to make a splash nationally. "I'm in no position to change the world," he told the Seattle Times newspaper. "I am in a position to help the people I represent."

A moderate Democrat in a politically competitive district, Larsen takes a pragmatic and bipartisan approach to his work in Congress. He affiliates with the moderate New Democrat Coalition and has a middle-of-the-road voting record. He supported President Bush about a third of the time in the 109th Congress (2005-06) on issues that drew a White House position.

Having spent most of his tenure in the minority, Larsen has not made much of a mark on legislation. But once Democrats took over in 2007, he redoubled efforts on his signature bill to designate more than 106,000 acres of land about 60 miles northeast of Seattle as a protected wilderness area. The targeted land is in the Mt. Baker-Snoqualmie National Forest.

He has sponsored the bill in each of the past four Congresses, and though it had bipartisan support in the state's congressional delegation and passed the Senate with the help of Washington Democratic Sen. Patty Murray, it never got through the House. Resources Committee Chairman Richard W. Pombo, a conservative California Republican often at war with the environmental lobby, refused to accept it.

With Pombo and his party vanquished in the 110th Congress (2007-08), Larsen's bill won swift approval from the renamed Natural Resources Committee and the House promptly passed it.

Larsen counts among his legislative successes a law he helped pass in his freshman term to improve pipeline safety after a 1999 explosion in Bellingham killed three people. In 2005, he won enactment of provisions designed to provide safeguards to mail-order brides from abroad.

He is involved with a growing effort in Congress to combat methamphetamine use and the so-called meth labs that have plagued communities nationwide. He is co-chairman of the House Meth Caucus, which is focused on prevention, treatment and education. And in 2007, he was pressing for a crackdown on bulk sales of dextromethorphan (DXM), alarmed by the number of teenagers using cough syrup and pure DXM to get high.

Larsen is the co-founder, with Illinois Republican Mark Steven Kirk, of the U.S.-China Working Group. "Washington state is just across the ocean from the world's fastest-growing economy and a modernizing, growing military," he says. Larsen and Kirk in the 109th Congress introduced a bill to provide funding for the Department of Commerce to place 17 additional commercial service officers in China. The proposal also would pay for increased participation of U.S. students in Chinese language programs.

Larsen has supported some major Republican initiatives in recent years. He was among the minority of House Democrats who supported a 2005 bankruptcy overhaul making it harder for consumers to erase their debts. In 2002, he was one of only 25 Democrats who voted to give the president fast-track authority to negotiate trade agreements that Congress cannot amend — although he joined most of his party in opposing the 2005 Central American Free Trade Agreement. He has backed a permanent repeal of the estate tax. And he voted for Bush's 2001 tax cut package, although not for the 2003 follow-on or the 2004 extension of the earlier cuts.

Larsen has opposed other Bush priorities, including the 2003 bill creating a prescription drug benefit for senior citizens under the Medicare program, and a medical malpractice bill that set limits on damage awards.

As a member of the Armed Services Committee, he opposed the 2002 resolution authorizing the invasion of Iraq and has since been consistent in his opposition to the war. In 2006, Larsen voted to reject any "arbitrary deadlines" for the withdrawal of U.S. forces, but in 2007 he declined to support the president's call for additional troops and backed legislation to establish a timetable for withdrawal.

Larsen was born and raised in Snohomish County, just north of Seattle. One of eight children of a utility company power line worker, he says he was influenced to enter public service by his family. His parents were involved in community activities, and his father was a city councilman.

After earning a bachelor's degree in political science and a master's in public affairs, Larsen worked for the Port of Everett helping businesses comply with clean water requirements. He then became the director of public affairs for the Washington Dental Association.

His first foray into electoral politics was in 1997, when he waged a successful door-to-door campaign for the Snohomish County Council. He chaired the council in 1999.

When three-term Republican Rep. Jack Metcalf retired in 2000, local Democratic Party strategists saw promise in Larsen, and persuaded a potential rival, state Rep. Jeff Morris, to stay out of the open-seat contest for the 2nd District, thus averting a divisive primary. Running as a moderate, Larsen scored a coup by returning the politically split district to Democratic hands.

Though he backs some expansion of international trade, which the AFL-CIO has fought, Larsen received campaign help from organized labor, as well as from other traditionally Democratic organizations, such as abortion rights and environmental groups; all mounted campaigns in Larsen's behalf in the final weeks of the race. Larsen prevailed by 12,000 votes against GOP state Rep. John Koster, who had run on a strongly conservative platform.

Redistricting following the 2000 census did little to change the competitive nature of the 2nd District, and the 2002 race between Larsen and Norma Smith, a former aide to Metcalf, was hard-fought.

Larsen was vigorous in bringing in campaign donations during his freshman term and was able to spend $1.8 million, triple the amount Smith spent. As he had done in his first race for the House, Larsen won with just 50 percent of the vote, but this time his margin was less than 9,000 votes.

He had a much easier time in 2004 and 2006, each time defeating Republican challengers with 64 percent of the vote.

KEY VOTES

2006

- No Stop broadband companies from favoring select Internet traffic
- Yes Affirm U.S. commitment to war in Iraq and reject setting a withdrawal date for troops
- No Repeal requirement for bilingual ballots at the polls
- Yes Permit U.S. sale of civilian nuclear technology to India
- No Build a 700-mile fence on the U.S.-Mexico border to curb illegal crossings
- No Permit warrantless wiretaps of suspected terrorists

2005

- ? Intervene in the life-support case of Terri Schiavo
- Yes Lift President Bush's restrictions on stem cell research funding
- Yes Prohibit FBI access to library and bookstore records
- No Approve free-trade pact with five Central American countries
- Yes Pass energy policy overhaul favored by President Bush emphasizing domestic oil and gas production
- No End mandatory preservation of habitat of endangered animal and plant species
- Yes Ban torture of prisoners in U.S. custody

CQ VOTE STUDIES

	PARTY UNITY		PRESIDENTIAL SUPPORT	
	Support	Oppose	Support	Oppose
2006	89%	11%	35%	65%
2005	93%	7%	28%	72%
2004	92%	8%	29%	71%
2003	90%	10%	36%	64%
2002	88%	12%	38%	62%

INTEREST GROUPS

	AFL-CIO	ADA	CCUS	ACU
2006	86%	85%	67%	20%
2005	93%	90%	59%	16%
2004	93%	90%	48%	8%
2003	87%	95%	50%	32%
2002	67%	85%	60%	24%

WASHINGTON 2

Puget Sound – Bellingham, most of Everett

Extending from the Cascade Mountains to San Juan Island in the northwestern corner of the state, the 2nd covers an area that is mostly rural in its topography and moderate in its politics. Most residents live along Interstate 5, a technology corridor that runs up the state's coast, while rural areas just west of the mountains provide open expanses of land, much of it national forest. Between lies a fertile agricultural plain.

Everett, the district's most populous city, is home to Boeing's largest aerospace facility, which employs thousands of district residents. Other manufacturing companies linked to Seattle's technology industries are located in the 2nd, and these white-collar jobs drive the local economy.

Although no longer dominant, the 2nd's natural resources industries continue to provide some jobs in the rural east, and agriculture workers produce everything from raspberries to dairy products. Tourists and conservationists travel to the state and national forests that line the western slope of the Cascade Range in eastern Whatcom, Skagit and Snohomish counties.

West of the mountains and north of Mount Vernon, residents are closer to Vancouver, British Columbia, than to Seattle. These areas are popular havens for retirees seeking a slower pace not too far from big city amenities. San Juan County, a collection of islands southwest of Bellingham, has the highest median age in the state (47 years).

The 2nd is highly competitive politically and tends to be represented by centrists. The urban centers of Everett in the south and Bellingham in the north are liberal, while rural areas lean conservative. San Juan County was John Kerry's best Washington county in the 2004 presidential election and helped him win the 2nd with 51 percent of its overall vote.

MAJOR INDUSTRY

Aviation, computer software, shipping

MILITARY BASES

Naval Air Station Whidbey Island, 7,914 military, 1,286 civilian (2001); Naval Station Everett, 5,657 military, 653 civilian (2004)

CITIES

Everett (pt.), 87,329; Bellingham, 67,171; Mount Vernon, 26,232

NOTABLE

Skagit County, home to the world's largest tulip fields, hosts a tulip festival every April; There are no stop lights on the San Juan Islands.

Rep. Brian Baird (D)

CAPITOL OFFICE
225-3536
www.house.gov/baird
2443 Rayburn 20515-4703; fax 225-3478

COMMITTEES
Budget
Science & Technology
(Research & Science Education - chairman)
Transportation & Infrastructure

RESIDENCE
Vancouver

BORN
March 7, 1956, Chama, N.M.

RELIGION
Protestant

FAMILY
Wife, Rachel Nugent; two children

EDUCATION
U. of Utah, B.S. 1977 (psychology);
U. of Wyoming, M.S. 1980 (clinical psychology), Ph.D. 1984 (clinical psychology)

CAREER
Professor; psychologist

POLITICAL HIGHLIGHTS
Democratic nominee for U.S. House, 1996

ELECTION RESULTS

2006 GENERAL		
Brian Baird (D)	147,065	63.1%
Michael Messmore (R)	85,915	36.9%
2006 PRIMARY		
Brian Baird (D)		unopposed
2004 GENERAL		
Brian Baird (D)	193,626	61.9%
Thomas Crowson (R)	119,027	38.1%

PREVIOUS WINNING PERCENTAGES
2002 (62%); 2000 (56%); 1998 (55%)

Elected 1998; 5th term

Baird might be Congress' funniest backbencher. A moderate-to-liberal Democrat elected in 1998, he has spent his career toiling at local issues. Well-known at home thanks to frequent meet-and-greets in his Vancouver district and a "Ski with Your Congressman Day," he is also recognized around Capitol Hill for his keen sense of political humor and dead-on impersonation of the president.

Baird-as-Bush once announced a new Operation Solar Landing initiative: "It's gonna put a man on the sun. Now, I know, I know, you pointy-headed academics and you liberal judges, you don't think we can do that. [Pause.] Heh. We're going at night!"

Comedically bipartisan, Baird also is said to do a pretty good impression of Rep. Barney Frank, the liberal, gay Massachusetts Democrat who frequently excoriates conservatives from the well of the House. Baird in 2005 won the annual "Funniest Celebrity in Washington" contest run by an anti-poverty group.

With all the shtick, it's hard to tell whether Baird is kidding when, for example, he tells his local newspaper, The Columbian of Vancouver, that he is thrilled to be the best local congressman he can be. "I love being able to say we got the water system in Pe Ell [Wash.]," Baird told a reporter.

But if diligence is a marker, Baird is serious. He assiduously attends to his district, securing $2 million to fight methamphetamine abuse and sponsoring legislation to protect the White Salmon River. He is a town hall warrior who has held constituent events in schools, community centers and railroad stations. When the Columbia River flooded a few years back, he helped with the sandbagging.

Baird won a big victory in the 108th Congress (2003-04) when President Bush signed into law his bill to allow residents of seven states without an income tax to deduct state sales taxes instead when calculating their federal tax liability for 2004 and 2005. Washington is one of the seven states. The deduction was extended in 2006, and with Democrats in the majority in the 110th Congress (2007-08), Baird has a better shot at success in his ongoing effort to make it permanent.

In 2007, he became chairman of the Science and Technology Committee's Research and Science Education Subcommittee. He swiftly began advancing legislation to beef up research funding and boost scholarships for science and math education, which he sees as crucial to the nation's future.

Though Baird sided with his fellow Democrats on 90 percent of the votes pitting the two parties against each other in the 109th Congress (2005-06), he sometimes goes his own way. In 2005, most Democrats opposed a GOP bill to intervene in the case of Terri Schiavo, a brain-damaged Florida woman whose husband wanted to remove her from life support, but whose parents did not. Baird voted with conservatives to let a federal judge review the decision, as Schiavo's parents wanted.

He also voted with Republicans in 2006 to authorize construction of 700 miles of fencing along the U.S.-Mexico border, but opposed GOP legislation to make it a felony to be in the United States without legal papers and to tighten standards for winning asylum here.

"I've always worked on a bipartisan basis because there are good ideas and good people on both sides," says Baird, with the reasoning that has made him appealing to the district's independent-minded voters. "I think that's why people say, 'I'll vote for you even though I'm a Republican' —

because they know that I respect people from all sides."

Like other Democrats from the Pacific Northwest, he struggles to balance protection of the environment with the need to help the timber industry, which is vital to his state's economy. In 2005, he and Oregon Republican Rep. Greg Walden sponsored a bill that allowed more salvage logging in national forests where trees had been damaged by fire or storms.

Baird's broader interests tend to fall in the "good government" category. He supports direct popular election of presidents, calling the Electoral College system "a cockamamie, undemocratic process." He also espouses a constitutional amendment to allow each House member to choose two potential successors to serve temporarily in the event that a majority of House members are killed. The appointed members would serve until a special election is held. Baird's proposal drew only 63 votes in 2004. Instead, the House passed legislation requiring special elections to fill House seats within 45 days of a catastrophe killing 100 or more members.

A clinical psychologist, Baird grew up in a small town in Colorado, where his father was a civics teacher and school principal, and served on the city council. His mother owned a small business and was a community volunteer.

During his professional career, he worked with troubled war veterans, juvenile delinquents and drug addicts. He also taught at a community college and was a professor at Pacific Lutheran University in Tacoma.

When no Democrat chose to run against conservative GOP Rep. Linda Smith in 1996, Baird decided he would do so and put together an underfunded grass-roots campaign. "People quite literally laughed," he recalls. But he lost by just 887 votes — and caught the political bug. He immediately set about preparing for a run in the next congressional election in two years.

In 1998, Smith gave up her House seat for an unsuccessful Senate bid. Baird was well-organized and better-financed this time around. He got support from organized labor, environmentalists and other liberal groups, and won by nearly 10 percentage points over GOP state Sen. Don Benton.

Baird divorced after the election, and in April 2000 he married Rachel Nugent, an economist with the Center for Global Development. They live close to the Capitol and share duties looking after their twin boys, born in March 2005. Baird takes the early morning shift as his wife heads to work. She picks them up from day care in the afternoons, while he's tending to legislative business. "My boys know what my beeper is," he says.

Baird has won re-election with increasing ease. In 2006, he beat political newcomer Michael Messmore, a retired airline captain, with 63 percent.

KEY VOTES

2006

Yes Stop broadband companies from favoring select Internet traffic
No Affirm U.S. commitment to war in Iraq and reject setting a withdrawal date for troops
No Repeal requirement for bilingual ballots at the polls
Yes Permit U.S. sale of civilian nuclear technology to India
Yes Build a 700-mile fence on the U.S.-Mexico border to curb illegal crossings
No Permit warrantless wiretaps of suspected terrorists

2005

Yes Intervene in the life-support case of Terri Schiavo
Yes Lift President Bush's restrictions on stem cell research funding
Yes Prohibit FBI access to library and bookstore records
No Approve free-trade pact with five Central American countries
No Pass energy policy overhaul favored by President Bush emphasizing domestic oil and gas production
No End mandatory preservation of habitat of endangered animal and plant species
Yes Ban torture of prisoners in U.S. custody

CQ VOTE STUDIES

	PARTY UNITY		PRESIDENTIAL SUPPORT	
	Support	Oppose	Support	Oppose
2006	89%	11%	37%	63%
2005	92%	8%	18%	82%
2004	89%	11%	37%	63%
2003	94%	6%	24%	76%
2002	92%	8%	32%	68%

INTEREST GROUPS

	AFL-CIO	ADA	CCUS	ACU
2006	86%	80%	53%	20%
2005	87%	95%	56%	9%
2004	92%	90%	53%	17%
2003	93%	95%	33%	16%
2002	100%	90%	58%	12%

WASHINGTON 3

Southwest – Vancouver, most of Olympia

Located in Washington's southwestern corner, the 3rd is a politically competitive district that includes liberals in the state capital of Olympia and suburbanites in the Vancouver area. The cities are connected by Interstate 5, west and east of which lies considerable open rural territory.

The district's population center is Clark County (Vancouver), where slightly more than half of the 3rd's residents live. The county experienced considerable population growth in the 1990s that is continuing. Nearly one-third of county residents cross the Columbia River each day to jobs in Oregon, almost all of them to Portland. These commuters tend to work in manufacturing or in the rebounding technology sector. Traffic problems have prompted local officials to expand roads and add new bridges along the interstate. Vancouver's local economy is developing rapidly, especially in health care, and there are new residential and commercial developments planned for downtown.

The district's other population pocket, the capital city of Olympia — where government jobs dominate the workforce — is at the 3rd's northern tip. Southeast of Olympia, the district includes vast stretches of woodlands in the Cascade Mountains. West of capital city are forests and beaches along the Pacific Ocean. The western part of the 3rd has a hearty logging industry, leaving the district's timber trade robust despite declines in the Cascade Range to the east. Manufacturing along Interstate 5 plays a large role in Lewis County's economy.

Clark, like the district at large, is politically competitive. The Democratic vote in Vancouver is offset by Republican strength in the suburbs outside of the city. Olympia, in Thurston County, also offers a Democratic vote, while the smaller communities elsewhere in the district tend to favor Republicans. Overall, George W. Bush took 50 percent of the 3rd's vote in the 2004 presidential election.

MAJOR INDUSTRY

Timber, computer hardware, manufacturing, mining

CITIES

Vancouver, 143,560; Olympia (pt.), 35,230; Longview 34,660

NOTABLE

Mount St. Helens erupted May 18, 1980, killing 57 people and destroying enough lumber for 300,000 two-bedroom homes; The World Kite Museum and Hall of Fame is located in Long Beach.

Rep. Doc Hastings (R)

CAPITOL OFFICE
225-5816
www.house.gov/hastings
1214 Longworth 20515-4704; fax 225-3251

COMMITTEES
Rules
Standards of Official Conduct - ranking member

RESIDENCE
Pasco

BORN
Feb. 7, 1941, Spokane, Wash.

RELIGION
Protestant

FAMILY
Wife, Claire Hastings; three children

EDUCATION
Columbia Basin College, attended 1959-61; Central Washington U., attended 1964

MILITARY SERVICE
Army Reserve, 1964-69

CAREER
Paper supply business owner

POLITICAL HIGHLIGHTS
Wash. House, 1979-87; Republican nominee for U.S. House, 1992

ELECTION RESULTS

2006 GENERAL		
Doc Hastings (R)	115,246	59.9%
Richard Wright (D)	77,054	40.1%
2006 PRIMARY		
Doc Hastings (R)	54,968	76.7%
Claude L. Oliver (R)	16,661	23.3%
2004 GENERAL		
Doc Hastings (R)	154,627	62.6%
Sandy Matheson (D)	92,486	37.4%

PREVIOUS WINNING PERCENTAGES
2002 (67%); 2000 (61%); 1998 (69%); 1996 (53%); 1994 (53%)

Elected 1994; 7th term

The Democratic takeover of Congress cost Hastings the chairmanship of the House ethics committee, but that was one gavel he was happy to put down. There is no more onerous job in Congress.

His leadership of the Committee on Standards of Official Conduct, as the ethics panel is formally titled, got off to a rocky start in 2005 with a 16-month partisan standoff over staffing and rules that paralyzed the panel's operations. It drew to a close in 2006 with an investigation into the way top GOP leaders had handled warnings about Florida Republican Rep. Mark Foley's improper contacts with underage congressional pages. Foley resigned in September after the disclosure of sexually explicit e-mail messages to former male pages. The ethics committee found that Republican leaders and their aides had been negligent, but recommended no sanctions.

Hastings' conduct of the investigation clearly didn't hurt his standing with Republican leaders. In the 110th Congress (2007-08), he is the only GOP holdover on the ethics panel and one of just three on the Rules Committee. Top party leaders appoint the members of both panels.

Hastings, an uber party loyalist who is subdued and quiet by nature, has served on the ethics committee since 2001. He knew that chairing the panel would be a thankless task when then Speaker J. Dennis Hastert tapped him for the job. Hastert had ousted the former chairman, Joel Hefley of Colorado, and two other Republicans who were deemed disloyal, after the ethics committee in 2004 admonished then House Majority Leader Tom DeLay of Texas for repeated breaches of the rules. The leaders also pushed through changes in the ethics rules that favored DeLay.

Hastings stirred furious criticism from Democrats and the media when he fired the committee's director and put in place his own chief of staff, who was not an attorney. Top staff, usually lawyers, had traditionally been chosen jointly by the chairman and the senior Democrat. Changes in the rules, too, had usually been bipartisan.

Democrats on the panel refused to allow the committee to conduct even routine business. Hastings and GOP leaders were forced to back down, and the rules changes were revoked. The stalemate ended when Howard L. Berman of California replaced Alan B. Mollohan of West Virginia as ranking Democrat in 2006. The committee got back to work.

The potential taint of scandal touched Hastings' own office early in 2007. John McKay, one of eight U.S. attorneys whose firings prompted congressional investigations, said Hastings' then chief of staff called him in 2004 to ask whether he was investigating potential fraud in the disputed Washington state gubernatorial election. McKay told the aide it would be improper to answer, and that was the end of the matter. Hastings told the Lewiston, Idaho, Morning Tribune the call was "entirely appropriate," but several groups pressed for an investigation of the affair.

Hastings is not among the GOP's rhetorical stars, but he was a particular favorite of Hastert, who reportedly included him on a list of potential successors as Speaker of the House in the event of a disaster. Party leaders chose him to preside over the House during the historic November 2003 vote on President Bush's Medicare prescription drug bill. At the leaders' direction, Hastings held open the vote for an extraordinary three hours while the Speaker and the GOP whip team furiously struggled to round up the final votes they needed to push the legislation to passage.

His loyalty has not gone unrewarded. In addition to his seat on the

Rules Committee, which puts him at the center of most legislative battles, he served from 2001 to 2005 on the Budget Committee, which writes the annual federal spending blueprint.

First elected in the GOP sweep of 1994, Hastings is from a heavily Republican district and has a safe seat, which is one of the reasons he is often chosen for the tough jobs. Even in the Democratic tidal wave of 2006, he stayed relatively high and dry, taking 60 percent of the vote. It was his lowest percentage since 1996.

He is known as "Doc," a family nickname he's had since childhood, and he mindfully tends to business at home. As founder and chairman of the House Nuclear Cleanup Caucus, he has led congressional efforts to speed up environmental restoration of radioactive waste sites. His district is home to the Hanford Nuclear Reservation, once a major employer. It now stands idle as the nation's most toxic relic of the Cold War, and Hastings has secured hundreds of millions of dollars to clean it up.

In 2004, he backed a law to get the federal government to study the potential for adding historic Manhattan Project sites, including the Hanford reactor, to the national park system. For years, former nuclear workers and residents have sought to preserve Hanford's B Reactor as a museum. The world's first full-scale plutonium production reactor, it was built as part of the top-secret Manhattan Project to produce the atomic bomb.

Hastings aggressively watches over his district's agriculture interests, funneling federal dollars to support farmers and protesting what he sees as unfair foreign competition to Washington's lucrative apple industry. He also looks out for other state resources. In 2006, Hastings introduced legislation to make it easier to kill protected California sea lions who threaten migrating Washington state salmon.

Before coming to Congress, Hastings ran his family's paper supply business in Pasco and was active in local GOP politics. He was elected to the Washington House in 1978 and served eight years, winning leadership posts as assistant majority leader and chairman of the GOP caucus.

In 1992, Hastings drew solid backing from GOP religious activists and was considered the most conservative of the four Republicans running to succeed GOP Rep. Sid Morrison, a moderate who ran unsuccessfully for governor that year. Though Hastings won his party's nomination handily, he narrowly lost to Democrat Jay Inslee. In a 1994 rematch, Hastings cast the campaign as a referendum on Inslee's support for President Bill Clinton, unpopular in the GOP-leaning district. Hastings ousted Inslee. He has won handily ever since.

KEY VOTES

2006

- No — Stop broadband companies from favoring select Internet traffic
- Yes — Affirm U.S. commitment to war in Iraq and reject setting a withdrawal date for troops
- Yes — Repeal requirement for bilingual ballots at the polls
- Yes — Permit U.S. sale of civilian nuclear technology to India
- Yes — Build a 700-mile fence on the U.S.-Mexico border to curb illegal crossings
- Yes — Permit warrantless wiretaps of suspected terrorists

2005

- Yes — Intervene in the life-support case of Terri Schiavo
- ? — Lift President Bush's restrictions on stem cell research funding
- No — Prohibit FBI access to library and bookstore records
- Yes — Approve free-trade pact with five Central American countries
- Yes — Pass energy policy overhaul favored by President Bush emphasizing domestic oil and gas production
- Yes — End mandatory preservation of habitat of endangered animal and plant species
- No — Ban torture of prisoners in U.S. custody

CQ VOTE STUDIES

	PARTY UNITY		PRESIDENTIAL SUPPORT	
	Support	Oppose	Support	Oppose
2006	97%	3%	95%	5%
2005	96%	4%	87%	13%
2004	96%	4%	97%	3%
2003	97%	3%	96%	4%
2002	98%	2%	92%	8%

INTEREST GROUPS

	AFL-CIO	ADA	CCUS	ACU
2006	7%	0%	100%	88%
2005	29%	5%	96%	92%
2004	13%	0%	100%	100%
2003	0%	10%	97%	88%
2002	11%	0%	100%	92%

WASHINGTON 4
Central — Yakima and Tri-Cities

Lying just east of the Cascade Mountains, the 4th includes some of the state's most fertile land as well as large stretches of the Columbia River (shared with the 3rd and 5th), which works its way down the middle of the district before turning west to form the state's border with Oregon.

Yakima County is the 4th's largest, both in land area and population, and is home to the Yakima Valley, known as the fruit bowl of the Northwest. It includes Yakama Indian Reservation and part of the U.S. Army's Yakima Training Center, which spreads into Kittitas County. Heavily irrigated agriculture drives the valley, which is full of apple orchards and fields of hops. In fact, the valley produces more than 75 percent of the total U.S. hops crop and hosts the Hop Growers of America.

Benton County to the east takes in the 4th's other population center. The Tri-Cities of Kennewick, Richland and Pasco on the Columbia River are a hotbed for scientific research. This area also is home to the Energy Department's Hanford nuclear site and Pacific Northwest National Laboratory, which is the district's primary employer and takes up nearly 600 square miles on the Columbia. Hanford is the most contaminated nuclear site in the nation, and negotiations are ongoing to build — and transport Hanford waste to — a national waste repository in Nevada.

The Wenatchee National Forest sustains some timber jobs despite recent cutbacks. The Columbia Basin project delivers water to the area's wineries and potato, corn and fruit farms. Many of these agrarian areas have attracted populations that are more than 75 percent Hispanic.

The 4th is the state's most conservative district. George W. Bush won every county in the district in the 2004 presidential election and took the district with 63 percent of the vote.

MAJOR INDUSTRY

Scientific research, fruit orchards and other agriculture, timber

CITIES

Yakima, 71,845; Kennewick, 54,693; Richland, 38,708; Pasco, 32,066

NOTABLE

The oldest skeleton ever found in North America was discovered on the banks of the Columbia River in Richland in 1996; Maryhill's Stonehenge Memorial, a full-scale replica of England's famous neolithic henge, was the first monument in the United States dedicated to the dead of WWI.

Rep. Cathy McMorris Rodgers (R)

CAPITOL OFFICE
225-2006
cathy.mcmorris@mail.house.gov
www.mcmorris.house.gov
1708 Longworth 20515-4705; fax 225-3392

COMMITTEES
Armed Services
Education & Labor
Natural Resources

RESIDENCE
Loon Lake

BORN
May 22, 1969, Salem, Ore.

RELIGION
Christian non-denominational

FAMILY
Husband, Brian Rodgers; one child

EDUCATION
Pensacola Christian College, B.A. 1990 (pre-law); U. of Washington, M.B.A. 2002

CAREER
Fruit orchard worker; state legislative aide

POLITICAL HIGHLIGHTS
Wash. House, 1994-2004 (minority leader, 2002-03)

ELECTION RESULTS

2006 GENERAL		
Cathy McMorris Rodgers (R)	134,967	56.4%
Peter J. Goldmark (D)	104,357	43.6%
2006 PRIMARY		
Cathy McMorris Rodgers (R)		unopposed
2004 GENERAL		
Cathy McMorris Rodgers (R)	179,600	59.7%
Don Barbieri (D)	121,333	40.3%

Elected 2004; 2nd term

Rare among Republicans, Rodgers enjoys fond memories of the 109th Congress (2005-06). While her party was besieged by scandal, policy blunders and catastrophic election losses, Rodgers succeeded at both politics and romance. She helped write popular bipartisan education legislation and won a tough re-election campaign. Along the way she met a guy, got married and had a son.

A wunderkind in the GOP who became a member of the Washington House at age 24, served as the chamber's minority leader and within a decade was elected to Congress, Rodgers now must balance life as a legislator and new mother. "I don't want to take on too much until it becomes more routine," says Rodgers, who gave birth to her son in April 2007.

Nonetheless, she is co-chairing the Congressional Women's Caucus with Democrat Lois Capps of California, and she serves on three committees — Natural Resources, Education and Labor, and Armed Services. Her goal is appointment to the powerful Energy and Commerce or Ways and Means panel.

Rodgers credits her political ambition to her father, Wayne, who owned an orchard and was active in civic affairs. The family is descended from the first settlers to travel the Oregon Trail to the Pacific Northwest, and for a time lived in British Columbia. They moved to Kettle Falls, Washington, on the Columbia River 30 miles south of the Canadian border, as Rodgers and her brother, Jeff, were preparing to enter high school.

Wayne McMorris bought an orchard and opened a fruit stand, The Peachcrest Fruit Basket, growing and selling cherries, peaches, apricots, pears, apples, strawberries and raspberries. She and her brother did every job on the farm, including the pruning, the thinning, the picking, and the selling at the stand. "It was just a great way for me to learn about small business issues and what's involved in making a living from the land," Rodgers says. Her father also chaired the Stevens County GOP and was president of the local Chamber of Commerce.

When she graduated from college, a family friend, Bob Morton, asked Rodgers to manage his campaign for the state House. After he won, she became a legislative assistant in his office. When Morton was appointed to the state Senate in 1993, Rodgers was appointed to replace him in the state House. She won the seat outright the next year and was elected minority leader in 2002.

Two years later, when former GOP Rep. George Nethercutt unsuccessfully attempted to unseat Democratic Sen. Patty Murray, Rodgers won a three-way Republican primary for Nethercutt's seat. She then bested the Democratic candidate, Spokane businessman Don Barbieri, by 19 percentage points.

In Congress, Rodgers was immediately popular, chosen by freshman Republicans to represent them on the Steering Committee, which makes committee assignments. She bonded with another fast-rising Republican freshman, Patrick T. McHenry of North Carolina, though the conservative and combative McHenry is different in style than Rodgers. "He's a little more antagonistic than I am," she said, laughing.

In her first term, she focused on issues traditionally important to her district such as fending off environmentalists intent on dismantling dams along the Snake and Columbia rivers, which Rodgers contends would harm farmers. She lobbied the Pentagon to spare Spokane's biggest employer, Fairchild Air Force Base, from the latest round of base closures, and also fought to keep the Walla Walla veterans' hospital open.

In 2006, Rodgers also sponsored a meaty piece of legislation intended to increase the ranks of scientists and engineers, in part by recruiting them to teach in schools. Reflecting President Bush's goals, her provision was adopted by the House as part of legislation to renew the Higher Education Act. But it failed to become law when the HEA reauthorization stalled in the Senate.

Now in the minority, Rodgers' legislative goals are modest. She continues to press for her science education bill. Her work with Capps on the women's caucus includes backing legislation that would ban discrimination based on genetic information. On the Natural Resources Committee, she hopes to convince Chairman Nick J. Rahall II, a West Virginia Democrat, to take up an overhaul of the National Environmental Policy Act.

Rodgers met her husband in the summer of 2005 at an annual barbecue hosted by the lawmaker. A campaign volunteer brought her brother, Brian Rodgers, to the event. She only briefly met the retired Naval officer and son of John Rodgers, who served as mayor of Spokane from 1967 to 1977. But the lawmaker, who is tall and pretty, made an impact. "His sister called my brother the next day and asked my brother if I ever go out on dates," Rodgers recalled. "Brian followed up with a letter."

John Rodgers, who was working at a church and living in San Diego at the time, invited her to a football game at his alma mater, the Naval Academy in Annapolis. "It was a great first date," she said, though Navy fell to Stanford, 41-38. Rodgers contributed $250 to her campaign. He proposed on Valentine's Day 2006 and the two married in August, just as Rodgers faced a tough re-election challenge.

Her opponent was Peter J. Goldmark, a molecular biologist and rancher who had served on the Okanogan School Board. Lightly regarded when he announced his candidacy, Goldmark proved tenacious in a bad climate for Republicans, attacking Rodgers as a Washington insider subservient to the Bush administration.

He criticized her for conditions at Spokane's veterans' hospital after the death of an 83-year-old who had been refused treatment at the hospital's urgent care center because it had closed shortly before his arrival. Put on the defensive despite voting for increases in spending for the Department of Veterans Affairs, Rodgers made campaign appearances with veterans, including her husband. Ultimately, she beat Goldmark by 13 percentage points.

KEY VOTES

2006

- No Stop broadband companies from favoring select Internet traffic
- Yes Affirm U.S. commitment to war in Iraq and reject setting a withdrawal date for troops
- Yes Repeal requirement for bilingual ballots at the polls
- Yes Permit U.S. sale of civilian nuclear technology to India
- Yes Build a 700-mile fence on the U.S.-Mexico border to curb illegal crossings
- Yes Permit warrantless wiretaps of suspected terrorists

2005

- ? Intervene in the life-support case of Terri Schiavo
- No Lift President Bush's restrictions on stem cell research funding
- No Prohibit FBI access to library and bookstore records
- Yes Approve free-trade pact with five Central American countries
- Yes Pass energy policy overhaul favored by President Bush emphasizing domestic oil and gas production
- Yes End mandatory preservation of habitat of endangered animal and plant species
- Yes Ban torture of prisoners in U.S. custody

CQ VOTE STUDIES

	PARTY UNITY		PRESIDENTIAL SUPPORT	
	Support	Oppose	Support	Oppose
2006	98%	2%	92%	8%
2005	98%	2%	89%	11%

INTEREST GROUPS

	AFL-CIO	ADA	CCUS	ACU
2006	15%	5%	100%	96%
2005	20%	5%	93%	100%

WASHINGTON 5

East – Spokane

With beautiful forests and lush fields, the 5th is anchored by the greater Spokane region, which takes in slightly less than two-thirds of the district's population and is a trade hub for the inland Northwest.

Spokane used to rely on manufacturing, but growth in the electronics sector and the health care industry have offered new opportunities for workers. It also serves as a hub for retail and telecommunications businesses. The largest city between Minneapolis and Seattle, Spokane also has the nation's largest municipal wireless Internet-access zone.

North of Spokane, no city surpasses the 6,000-resident mark. This region is home to numerous national and state forests, and it once relied on logging and mining, but both industries have been hard-hit by recent productivity decreases and employment losses. Okanogan County grows apples and pears, and ranchers there raise sheep and goats.

The fertile soil of the district's south produces some of the most desired wheat in the world. The Walla Walla Sweet Onion is another well-known product grown in the district. Nestled at the foot of the Blue Mountains near Oregon, Walla Walla is the district's second-most-populous city, has a thriving arts community and attracts tourists to its dozens of local vineyards and wineries.

Spokane County can be politically competitive, but the natural resource-dependent economy in rural communities make for voters who eschew federal interference and support private property rights. George W. Bush won all 12 of the 5th's counties in the 2004 presidential election, and the 5th included his four best Washington counties.

MAJOR INDUSTRY

Agriculture, manufacturing, health care

MILITARY BASES

Fairchild Air Force Base, 4,534 military, 1,267 civilian (2004)

CITIES

Spokane, 195,629; Walla Walla, 29,686

NOTABLE

Ranald MacDonald, the first person to teach the English language in Japan — he taught the samurai who later interpreted trade negotiations between Commodore Perry and the Tokugawa Shogunate — is buried in a Ferry County cemetery.

Rep. Norm Dicks (D)

CAPITOL OFFICE
225-5916
www.house.gov/dicks
2467 Rayburn 20515-4706; fax 226-1176

COMMITTEES
Appropriations
(Interior-Environment - chairman)
Homeland Security

RESIDENCE
Belfair

BORN
Dec. 16, 1940, Bremerton, Wash.

RELIGION
Lutheran

FAMILY
Wife, Suzanne Dicks; two children

EDUCATION
U. of Washington, B.A. 1963 (political science), J.D. 1968

CAREER
Congressional aide

POLITICAL HIGHLIGHTS
No previous office

ELECTION RESULTS

2006 GENERAL		
Norm Dicks (D)	158,202	70.6%
Doug Cloud (R)	65,883	29.4%
2006 PRIMARY		
Norm Dicks (D)		unopposed
2004 GENERAL		
Norm Dicks (D)	202,919	69.0%
Doug Cloud (R)	91,228	31.0%

PREVIOUS WINNING PERCENTAGES
2002 (64%); 2000 (65%); 1998 (68%); 1996 (66%); 1994 (58%); 1992 (64%); 1990 (61%); 1988 (68%); 1986 (71%); 1984 (66%); 1982 (63%); 1980 (54%); 1978 (61%); 1976 (74%)

Elected 1976; 16th term

A master of Capitol Hill's inside game, Dicks has long been a player on national security and natural resource issues, though until recently he had never been a member of the Democratic leadership nor a committee chairman. When his party took control of the House in the 110th Congress (2007-08), Dicks finally secured a gavel, after 30 years in the House, becoming chairman of the Interior and Environment Appropriations Subcommittee.

Dicks also is the second-ranking Democrat on the Defense Appropriations Subcommittee — just behind his longtime friend, Chairman John P. Murtha of Pennsylvania. Given that Dicks is one of the House's top authorities on national security policy, it is unlikely the leadership will shape positions on Iraq or in the war on terrorism without his input.

In 2002, Dicks was among a bipartisan group of nine House members hand-picked by the Bush administration to help secure votes on the resolution authorizing the president to use force against Iraq. But by 2006, Dicks' views on the war and his support for the administration's strategy had changed. That year, he joined his party's ranks by voting no on a resolution that rejected setting an "arbitrary" date for troop withdrawals.

And less than a year later, he voted for a resolution opposing the White House plan to send more than 21,000 additional U.S. combat troops into Iraq. Speaking on the House floor in February, he said, "I . . . deplore the mistakes by this administration: failing to deploy enough troops to stabilize Iraq, disbanding the Iraqi Army, failing to provide jobs and economic restoration. Those are but a few." In March, speaking in support of a war funding bill that set a timeline for withdrawal, he demanded a "greater accountability for both the policy and funding of the Iraq War."

Dicks is an environmentalist at heart and his priorities for the Interior Appropriations panel in the 110th Congress reflect this interest. Like the Democratic leadership, he is looking to force global warming onto the national agenda. He also wants to boost maintenance and staffing at national parks, which he says were neglected in a dozen years of GOP budgets.

His district, in Washington's Olympic peninsula, takes in such scenic areas as Olympic national park and forest, Puget Sound and mountain-rimmed coastlines along the Pacific. In 2000, Dicks sponsored a law adding vast tracts of wilderness to the federal conservation trust. He's secured billions of dollars for the Pacific Northwest, including millions for salmon protection and for the rehabilitation of the city of Tacoma.

His subcommittee's wide-ranging jurisdiction includes the U.S. Forest Service, which is important to the state's timber industry, and a number of agencies serving American Indians — another important constituency for him.

Dicks is attentive to the state's substantial military economy. The Navy has a major nuclear submarine base in Bremerton, Dicks' hometown, and Fort Lewis in the neighboring 9th District is the largest Army base on the West Coast. Chicago-based aerospace giant Boeing Co. has substantial operations in the state, and Dicks is sometimes called "Mr. Boeing." He was among the staunchest backers of the development of the B-2 stealth bomber, which Boeing helped build. A model of the B-2, used in raids in Iraq and Afghanistan, is on display in the congressman's office.

Boeing also figures in one of Dicks' biggest setbacks in recent years. He pushed a $21 billion no-bid contract that called for the government to lease 100 tanker planes from Boeing, until Sen. John McCain of Arizona criticized it as a sweet deal for Boeing and an Air Force procurement official admitted to illegally helping the company while negotiating a lucrative job offer.

Dicks believes in large military budgets and is among a small group of pro-defense Democrats who say President Bush's defense budgets have underfunded weapons modernization and quality of life for the troops.

An internationalist who wants to assert U.S. leadership around the world, Dicks was at the center of nuclear arms reduction talks between the United States and the Soviet Union in the 1980s. He teamed with friend and then Sen. Albert Gore of Tennessee and then Rep. Les Aspin of Wisconsin to negotiate a deal allowing the Reagan administration to develop the MX missile, which many Democrats opposed, as a bargaining chip with the Soviet Union.

In the 1990s, as the senior Democrat on the House Committee on Intelligence, Dicks was at the fore of early efforts to bring efficiencies to the nation's many-layered intelligence operations. In 1998, he co-led, with GOP Rep. Christopher Cox of California, a bipartisan investigation of China's efforts to obtain sensitive U.S. technology — a probe that also revealed security lapses at U.S. nuclear weapons laboratories.

With his booming bass voice, Dicks is a blend of boisterous bonhomie, irrepressible humor, bullheaded tenacity and years of political training. He learned from a past master, Washington Democrat Warren G. Magnuson, an influential Senate appropriator for whom Dicks worked after law school.

Dicks grew up in Bremerton, population 37,000, the son of an electrician at Puget Sound Naval Shipyard. He excelled at sports and became a linebacker at the University of Washington, where his game name was "Dizzy Dicks." He wasn't good enough to go pro, so after graduating with a degree in political science, he went to law school with an eye on a career in politics.

He got his first taste of campaigning by pouring drinks aboard the campaign plane for the Democratic candidate for governor in 1968. In need of a job when his candidate lost, Dicks was quickly hired by Magnuson.

When 6th District incumbent Rep. Floyd Hicks was named to the state Supreme Court in 1976, Dicks went home to run for the seat. He tapped the resources of organized labor and other special interests to beat three competitors in the Democratic primary, including the Tacoma mayor. He easily won that November and has carried his district with at least 60 percent of the vote in all but two elections.

At one time, Dicks wanted to move up to the Senate. He considered running in 1988, but decided some of his pro-defense positions made him unmarketable statewide, especially with Seattle's liberals. As consolation, Dicks figured it was only a matter of time before he would become a committee chairman in the House.

KEY VOTES

2006

- Yes Stop broadband companies from favoring select Internet traffic
- No Affirm U.S. commitment to war in Iraq and reject setting a withdrawal date for troops
- No Repeal requirement for bilingual ballots at the polls
- Yes Permit U.S. sale of civilian nuclear technology to India
- No Build a 700-mile fence on the U.S.-Mexico border to curb illegal crossings
- No Permit warrantless wiretaps of suspected terrorists

2005

- No Intervene in the life-support case of Terri Schiavo
- Yes Lift President Bush's restrictions on stem cell research funding
- Yes Prohibit FBI access to library and bookstore records
- Yes Approve free-trade pact with five Central American countries
- Yes Pass energy policy overhaul favored by President Bush emphasizing domestic oil and gas production
- No End mandatory preservation of habitat of endangered animal and plant species
- Yes Ban torture of prisoners in U.S. custody

CQ VOTE STUDIES

	PARTY UNITY		PRESIDENTIAL SUPPORT	
	Support	Oppose	Support	Oppose
2006	86%	14%	33%	67%
2005	92%	8%	24%	76%
2004	90%	10%	31%	69%
2003	89%	11%	31%	69%
2002	85%	15%	36%	64%

INTEREST GROUPS

	AFL-CIO	ADA	CCUS	ACU
2006	93%	85%	50%	8%
2005	93%	85%	52%	0%
2004	93%	85%	48%	13%
2003	87%	90%	38%	20%
2002	88%	80%	60%	13%

WASHINGTON 6

West — Bremerton, Tacoma, Olympic Peninsula

The 6th includes the Olympic Mountains, which drop to the coast of the Pacific Ocean in the district's west. The lush Olympic National Park and Olympic National Forest constitute more than one-third of the 6th's land — about 1.6 million protected acres — making the area a very popular tourist destination.

Surrounding the mountainous region, small towns strive to move beyond a reliance on the lumber and fishing industries, which have suffered from mill closures and industry downturns. Hoquiam, located in the district's southwest, seems to be succeeding: Imperium Renewables plans to build the largest biodiesel plant in the nation there by 2008. Port Angeles and Sequim in the northeast have become havens for retirees.

More than half of the 6th's residents live in its eastern portion, near Tacoma and its suburbs. Once a main railroad terminus, the city's economy continues to be driven by the manufacturing and shipping industries. Recent revitalization plans have lured residents back downtown, especially near the University of Washington-Tacoma campus and the waterfront. The eastern portion of the 6th near the Puget Sound also depends heavily on the military. Bremerton, located north of Tacoma, is home to the Puget Sound Naval Shipyard and the Bremerton Navy base, and the 6th has a substantial local Coast Guard presence.

Tacoma's blue-collar, heavily unionized electorate generally gives Democrats the edge in the district's populated Pierce County portion. But independent voters, who can be socially moderate, prevent the district from moving out of the reach of Republicans. The 6th gave John Kerry 53 percent of its vote in the 2004 presidential election.

MAJOR INDUSTRY

Lumber, fishing, shipping, health care, tourism

MILITARY BASES

Puget Sound Naval Shipyard and Intermediate Maintenance Facility, 927 military, 9,386 civilian (2005); Naval Base Kitsap (Bremerton), 320 military (5,740 military on home-ported ships), 16 civilian (2002)

CITIES

Tacoma (pt.), 176,853; Bremerton, 37,259; University Place, 29,933; Lakewood (pt.), 26,878; Port Angeles, 18,397

NOTABLE

Port Townsend celebrates the rhododendron bloom with "Rhodyfest."

Rep. Jim McDermott (D)

CAPITOL OFFICE
225-3106
www.house.gov/mcdermott
1035 Longworth 20515-4707; fax 225-6197

COMMITTEES
Ways & Means
(Income Security & Family Support - chairman)

RESIDENCE
Seattle

BORN
Dec. 28, 1936, Chicago, Ill.

RELIGION
Episcopalian

FAMILY
Wife, Therese Hansen; two children

EDUCATION
Wheaton College (Ill.), B.S. 1958;
U. of Illinois, M.D. 1963

MILITARY SERVICE
Navy Medical Service Corps, 1968-70

CAREER
Psychiatrist

POLITICAL HIGHLIGHTS
Wash. House, 1971-73; sought Democratic nomination for governor, 1972; Wash. Senate, 1975-87; Democratic nominee for governor, 1980; sought Democratic nomination for governor, 1984

ELECTION RESULTS

2006 GENERAL		
Jim McDermott (D)	195,462	79.4%
Steve Beren (R)	38,715	15.7%
Linnea S. Noreen (I)	11,956	4.9%
2006 PRIMARY		
Jim McDermott (D)	95,065	91.0%
Donovan Rivers (D)	4,837	4.6%
Joshua Smith (D)	4,526	4.3%
2004 GENERAL		
Jim McDermott (D)	272,302	80.7%
Carol Thorne Cassady (R)	65,226	19.3%

PREVIOUS WINNING PERCENTAGES
2002 (74%); 2000 (73%); 1998 (88%); 1996 (81%); 1994 (75%); 1992 (78%); 1990 (72%); 1988 (76%)

Elected 1988; 10th term

The outgoing, intense McDermott is a steadfast liberal in a House that has moved to the right over the course of his career. He acknowledges the trend, but refuses to bend to it. He is not one to go with the flow.

A senior member of the Ways and Means Committee, he has fought every tax cut bill of the Bush era. During a floor speech in December 2005, McDermott waved two red Christmas stockings to illustrate the impact of Republican fiscal policies. From the "poor" stocking, he transferred small presents representing benefits for the elderly and disabled, loans for college students, food stamp funds and so on. "What's left for poor people?" he asked with a flourish. "Look at that! A lump of coal!"

The only psychiatrist in Congress, McDermott is to the left of most Democrats on health care, favoring a universal government-run system. He is a sharp critic of the 2003 Medicare prescription drug law, which he says offers inadequate benefits and is "just way beyond the complexity that any 96-year-old can figure out."

McDermott was deeply frustrated by the way Republican Chairman Bill Thomas of California ran the Ways and Means Committee in the 109th Congress (2005-06), saying Thomas shunned compromise and shut Democrats out. It was "a very controlling majority," he complained. In the 110th Congress (2007-08), he runs his own Ways and Means panel — the Subcommittee on Income Security and Family Support.

Yet McDermott doesn't always go along with his own party. In 1993, President Bill Clinton's first year in office, McDermott proposed, and pushed vigorously for, a single-payer health care plan to give Americans insurance through a taxpayer-financed system. He ignored his own leadership's requests that members delay introducing health care bills in deference to Clinton, who was drafting a White House proposal as one of his first undertakings. The complex Clinton plan failed, but McDermott helped hasten its demise by rallying support among House liberals for his own bill.

In recent years, McDermott has returned to his roots in the 1960s antiwar movement. He voted against the 2002 resolution authorizing President Bush to use force in Iraq. And he swallowed his misgivings in March 2007 and voted for a supplemental spending bill for the war in Iraq that included a timetable for U.S. troop withdrawal. McDermott ended up casting the final vote that gave Speaker Nancy Pelosi the 218 votes she needed to guarantee passage of the legislation. He said the vote was hard for him and other liberals because the measure did not outline a hasty end to the war nor cut off funding for deployments. "It was terrible," McDermott said, but he added that he saw the vote as "the first test" of whether the Democrats will be able to hold their majority together on important issues.

During the Vietnam War, McDermott was stationed in Long Beach, Calif., where, as a Navy psychiatrist, his job was to decide whether to return sailors and Marines to battle. McDermott says one of his heroes from that period is Ernest Gruening, an Alaska Democrat who cast one of the two Senate votes against the 1964 Gulf of Tonkin resolution, which led to U.S. involvement in Vietnam. A third of a century later, McDermott urged a go-slow approach in attacking Afghanistan to root out terrorists and counseled against the war with Iraq.

McDermott doesn't give up easily. He spent years warning of the potential health risks that depleted uranium posed to U.S. soldiers and their families. He said that the substance, which is used in bullets and armor-penetrating artillery shells, can cause birth defects and leukemia. Calling for a study of the health threat, he teamed up with the punk rock group Anti-Flag, which in early 2006 released a song, "Depleted Uranium Is a War Crime," and asked its fans to sign a petition supporting McDermott's measure. In 2006, the annual defense authorization bill contained his language on a study of the material's health effects on U.S. servicemembers.

For the past decade, McDermott has been embroiled in a long-running lawsuit filed against him by Republican Rep. John A. Boehner of Ohio, now the House minority leader, over the release of an illegally taped cellular telephone call in late 1996. A conference call among GOP leaders was recorded by a couple in Florida, who heard them discussing the ethical questions being raised about Republican Speaker Newt Gingrich. The tape wound up in McDermott's hands and excerpts appeared in newspaper stories.

McDermott, then a member of the ethics committee, resigned from the panel amid allegations that he had leaked the tape. Boehner, one of the participants in the call, sued in 1998, alleging his privacy had been violated. In May 2007, in a 5-4 opinion, the U.S. Court of Appeals for the D.C. Circuit reaffirmed an earlier decision that McDermott is liable for damages in the case. The judges ruled that McDermott was not protected by the First Amendment when he passed the tape along to The New York Times. The judges ordered an award to Boehner of $10,000 in statutory damages, $50,000 in punitive damages, as well as attorney costs, which Boehner said have exceeded $600,000. Boehner had offered to drop his lawsuit if McDermott would admit his mistake, apologize to the House and donate $10,000 to charity. McDermott chose to appeal the award.

Born and raised in Illinois, McDermott was the first member of his family to go to college. After medical school at the University of Illinois, his residency training took him to Seattle. Following a two-year stint in the Navy Medical Service Corps, he returned to Seattle to launch a career in medicine. He quickly was attracted to local politics, winning a seat in the state House in 1970 and starting a lengthy legislative career punctuated by three losing bids for governor — in 1972, 1980 and 1984. After two years in the state House and a two-year break, he won four state Senate elections.

McDermott left the state Senate in 1987 to go to the Congo, then known as Zaire, as a Foreign Service medical officer. Less than a year later, when Democratic Rep. Mike Lowry announced his plans to run for the U.S. Senate, McDermott arranged to be released from his Foreign Service commitment to return to Washington to run for Lowry's seat in 1988. Since then, his re-election races have been runaways.

KEY VOTES

2006

Yes Stop broadband companies from favoring select Internet traffic
No Affirm U.S. commitment to war in Iraq and reject setting a withdrawal date for troops
No Repeal requirement for bilingual ballots at the polls
No Permit U.S. sale of civilian nuclear technology to India
No Build a 700-mile fence on the U.S.-Mexico border to curb illegal crossings
No Permit warrantless wiretaps of suspected terrorists

2005

No Intervene in the life-support case of Terri Schiavo
Yes Lift President Bush's restrictions on stem cell research funding
Yes Prohibit FBI access to library and bookstore records
No Approve free-trade pact with five Central American countries
No Pass energy policy overhaul favored by President Bush emphasizing domestic oil and gas production
No End mandatory preservation of habitat of endangered animal and plant species
Yes Ban torture of prisoners in U.S. custody

CQ VOTE STUDIES

	PARTY UNITY		PRESIDENTIAL SUPPORT	
	Support	Oppose	Support	Oppose
2006	97%	3%	15%	85%
2005	99%	1%	14%	86%
2004	99%	1%	21%	79%
2003	98%	2%	13%	87%
2002	97%	3%	14%	86%

INTEREST GROUPS

	AFL-CIO	ADA	CCUS	ACU
2006	93%	95%	20%	4%
2005	93%	100%	37%	0%
2004	100%	95%	15%	0%
2003	100%	100%	21%	13%
2002	100%	95%	28%	0%

WASHINGTON 7

Seattle and suburbs

The most populous city in the Pacific Northwest, Seattle is nicknamed the "Emerald City," and it remains the gem of the Evergreen State. The city anchors the 7th, which is diverse, liberal and well educated. From the top of the iconic Space Needle, tourists can see the Seattle skyline and both the Cascade and Olympic mountain ranges.

The 7th is home to technology-based companies and industry leaders, including retailer Amazon.com and software manufacturer Adobe. The aviation and biotechnology industries also are big employers. The University of Washington is a major research university. The Bill and Melinda Gates Foundation, which is building a new headquarters complex in downtown Seattle, donates billions of dollars annually to global health and development projects and to national education and technology projects. The Port of Seattle is one of the nation's major international gateway terminals.

Congestion remains a huge problem throughout the region, but the Sounder commuter train between Tacoma and Seattle alleviates some pressure. Local Seattle officials plan to extend current light rail lines to the region's major airport (in the adjacent 9th) by the end of 2009, before Vancouver, British Columbia, located 3 hours away, hosts the 2010 Winter Olympics; the city hopes to attract tourists arriving for the event.

The percentage of Seattle residents who describe themselves as members of two races is nearly twice the national average. At 13 percent, Asians make up Seattle's largest minority population and have influenced the International District. The Capitol Hill and University District neighborhoods are destinations for both residents and tourists.

The 7th's urban setting and large population of minorities and singles make it a liberal bastion. Democratic candidates regularly dominate the district in all races. In 2004, John Kerry captured 79 percent of the 7th's presidential vote — easily Kerry's best showing in the state.

MAJOR INDUSTRY
Computer software, trade, aviation, health care

CITIES
Seattle (pt.), 552,834; White Center (unincorporated), 20,975

NOTABLE
The Fraternal Order of Eagles was founded in 1898 at a Seattle shipyard.

Rep. Dave Reichert (R)

CAPITOL OFFICE
225-7761
representative.reichert@mail.house.gov
www.house.gov/reichert
1223 Longworth 20515-4708; fax 225-4282

COMMITTEES
Homeland Security
Science & Technology
Transportation & Infrastructure

RESIDENCE
Auburn

BORN
Aug. 29, 1950, Detroit Lakes, Minn.

RELIGION
Lutheran - Missouri Synod

FAMILY
Wife, Julie Reichert; three children

EDUCATION
Concordia College (Ore.), A.A. 1970

MILITARY SERVICE
Air Force Reserve, 1971-76; Air Force, 1976

CAREER
Police officer; grocery warehouse worker

POLITICAL HIGHLIGHTS
King County sheriff, 1997-2005

ELECTION RESULTS

2006 GENERAL		
Dave Reichert (R)	129,362	51.5%
Darcy Burner (D)	122,021	48.5%
2006 PRIMARY		
Dave Reichert (R)		unopposed
2004 GENERAL		
Dave Reichert (R)	173,298	51.5%
Dave Ross (D)	157,148	46.7%
Spencer Garrett (LIBERT)	6,053	1.8%

Elected 2004; 2nd term

Thirty years as a cop gave Reichert skills that easily translate to his work in Congress. Trying to placate opposing sides on hot-button social issues and ducking verbal punches from political opponents is not terribly different than keeping the peace as the local sheriff he once was.

Reichert (RIKE-ert) walked a fine line on such divisive issues as abortion and the environment in his first term, keeping both sides happy enough that he was re-elected in 2006 in his politically competitive, suburban Seattle district, albeit narrowly. Democrats attacked him as a smooth-talking Republican Party mouthpiece and environmental groups criticized his lukewarm stance on fighting global warming. But Reichert had established a moderate record that resisted labeling as extreme.

His positions on environmental issues — key for his green-leaning Pacific Northwest constituents — have been mixed. He voted against oil and gas exploration in the Arctic National Wildlife Refuge in Alaska and helped kill a plan that would have allowed more oil tanker traffic in Puget Sound. But he caught flak during the campaign for telling the Sierra Club that he was not convinced that human activity caused global warming. The mention made the news, circulated in the blogosphere and was criticized by former Democratic presidential candidate Al Gore. The Sierra Club endorsed Reichert's opponent.

He says he fervently opposes abortion, but he does not always vote with conservatives on their litmus-test bills. In 2006, he reversed his position and supported federal funding for stem cell research, which uses surplus embryos from in vitro fertilization. Reichert voted to override President Bush's veto of the bill.

His change of heart on the issue was "the most difficult I have encountered as a member of Congress," he said, and came about after he visited a cancer research center and consulted with women in his life, including a daughter who underwent in vitro fertilization as well as six female aides in his office. He says he decided research using embryonic stem cells is different from taking a life in an abortion.

In his first term, Reichert got his top-choice committee assignment — Homeland Security — and parlayed his law enforcement background into the chairmanship of the Emergency Communications, Preparedness, and Response Subcommittee. He drafted high-profile bills to improve communication between first-responders and to restructure the Federal Emergency Management Agency within the Department of Homeland Security.

He also burnished his credentials as a go-to man on security issues, and in the 110th Congress (2007-08) he is the top-ranking Republican on the Homeland Security Subcommittee on Intelligence, Information-Sharing and Terrorism Risk Assessment. He also has seats on the Science and Technology Committee and the Transportation and Infrastructure panel.

In 2007, Reichert joined Washington state Democrats to lobby for federal fixes to an Army medical center. And he weighed in against the Bush administration when it fired a U.S. attorney in his state, arguing that the man was treated unfairly. The attorney was among eight U.S. attorneys across the country whose firings caused a controversy because of their political overtones. In 2006, he fought to add $7 billion to the annual budget to fund spending for education, health and low-income energy subsidy programs.

Being on good terms with the state's Democrats is bound to help him with his legislative efforts now that they are in the majority. "We might have different opinions, but you have to work together," Reichert says.

The oldest of seven children with an abusive father, Reichert's childhood was far from ideal. While sharing a two-bedroom duplex with the growing family in a rough neighborhood (the boys slept in the garage), Reichert took on the role of protector. It stuck, and he began thinking about a career in police work. "Even at 6 years old, I wanted to help people," he says.

But school was never his strong suit, and he assumed he would end up in a factory like his father. "When you grow up in a chaotic home life, [school] wasn't really a priority," said Reichert, who once ran away and lived in a car for three months. A tuition waiver at a two-year college in Oregon got him on track, and spots as the pitcher on the baseball team and as the football quarterback brought out his leadership skills.

Reichert tried six times before he passed the test required to get hired by the King County sheriff's office, but once there he advanced through the ranks. He started as a patrol officer in 1972, became an undercover agent and then made sergeant in 1990. Seven years later, he was elected sheriff. "I never had the vision of being promoted above sergeant," he said. "But for each position I had, I looked at the next step and thought, 'I can do it.' "

In a twist of fate, Reichert became sheriff just before the office in 2001 caught Green River serial killer Gary Ridgway, a case Reichert had supervised earlier in his career. Ridgway confessed to killing at least 48 women in the early 1980s in the Seattle area. The story made Reichert a media star, but scuttled his first plan for political office; he decided to see that case to its conclusion rather than run for governor in 2004 as he was being urged to do.

Reichert's name naturally came up when six-term Republican Rep. Jennifer Dunn decided not to run for re-election in 2004. His name recognition gave him a huge advantage in the GOP primary. But in the general election, he faced another local celebrity, radio commentator Dave Ross.

The national parties' campaign committees spent more on the contest than on any other House race in 2004, and it turned out to be one of the closest of the year, with Reichert nabbing a 5 percentage point win.

In his 2006 bid for re-election, he faced Microsoft executive Darcy Burner. The campaign was expensive and each candidate spent more than $3 million, not including the millions their respective parties put toward the race. After an arduous, weeks-long vote count, Reichert eked out a 3 point victory.

KEY VOTES

2006

- Yes Stop broadband companies from favoring select Internet traffic
- \+ Affirm U.S. commitment to war in Iraq and reject setting a withdrawal date for troops
- No Repeal requirement for bilingual ballots at the polls
- Yes Permit U.S. sale of civilian nuclear technology to India
- Yes Build a 700-mile fence on the U.S.-Mexico border to curb illegal crossings
- Yes Permit warrantless wiretaps of suspected terrorists

2005

- No Intervene in the life-support case of Terri Schiavo
- No Lift President Bush's restrictions on stem cell research funding
- No Prohibit FBI access to library and bookstore records
- Yes Approve free-trade pact with five Central American countries
- Yes Pass energy policy overhaul favored by President Bush emphasizing domestic oil and gas production
- No End mandatory preservation of habitat of endangered animal and plant species
- Yes Ban torture of prisoners in U.S. custody

CQ VOTE STUDIES

	PARTY UNITY		PRESIDENTIAL SUPPORT	
	Support	Oppose	Support	Oppose
2006	80%	20%	82%	18%
2005	88%	12%	86%	14%

INTEREST GROUPS

	AFL-CIO	ADA	CCUS	ACU
2006	23%	25%	73%	56%
2005	20%	10%	88%	64%

WASHINGTON 8

Eastside Seattle suburbs – Bellevue

The 8th is Washington's wealthiest district, and it takes in the prosperous King County suburbs outside Seattle in its west and beautiful farmland in its east and south. Seattle's Eastside suburbs have become fertile ground for the Pacific Northwest's technology businesses, and the fast growth has caused traffic congestion and fueled debates over infrastructure upgrades and smart growth.

The 8th's largest population center is Bellevue, which is one of the most diverse areas in the state — nearly 20 percent of its population is Asian and one-fourth is foreign born. Some of Bellevue's largest employers are Boeing, Expedia and T-Mobile USA. Lincoln Square in Bellevue's financial and retail district is expanding in order to meet the needs of regional giant Microsoft, among other companies. The city's Bellevue Square is a resort and shopping center that attracts visitors from throughout the Pacific Northwest.

South of Bellevue, in one of the most private areas in an otherwise bustling region, tony Gold Coast hamlets such as Hunts Point, Clyde Hill, Yarrow Point and Medina host million dollar homes on Lake Washington.

In addition to its near-in Seattle suburbs, the 8th continues east to the border of King County and heads south to take in a mostly rural part of Pierce County, which includes a portion of the Cascade Range and Mt. Rainier National Park, Washington's highest point.

Once a stronghold for Republican politics, the 8th's population boom has created an urban and Democratic-minded constituency. Generally fiscally conservative and socially moderate, residents of the politically competitive district gave John Kerry 51 percent of the vote in the 2004 presidential election. The area's growing number of minority votes will continue to influence elections.

MAJOR INDUSTRY

Aviation manufacturing, software, logging

CITIES

Bellevue, 109,569; Kent (pt.), 35,620; Sammamish, 34,104

NOTABLE

Mount Rainier, an active volcano, is the most heavily glaciated peak in the lower 48 states — it is covered by more than 35 square miles of snow and glacial ice.

Rep. Adam Smith (D)

CAPITOL OFFICE
225-8901
www.house.gov/adamsmith
2402 Rayburn 20515-4709; fax 225-5893

COMMITTEES
Armed Services
(Terrorism, Unconventional Threats & Capabilities - chairman)
Foreign Affairs

RESIDENCE
Tacoma

BORN
June 15, 1965, Washington, D.C.

RELIGION
Episcopalian

FAMILY
Wife, Sara Smith; two children

EDUCATION
Fordham U., B.A. 1987 (political science);
U. of Washington, J.D. 1990

CAREER
City prosecutor; lawyer

POLITICAL HIGHLIGHTS
Wash. Senate, 1991-97

ELECTION RESULTS

2006 GENERAL		
Adam Smith (D)	119,038	65.7%
Steven C. Cofchin (R)	62,082	34.3%
2006 PRIMARY		
Adam Smith (D)		unopposed
2004 GENERAL		
Adam Smith (D)	162,433	63.3%
Paul J. Lord (R)	88,304	34.4%
Robert F. Losey (GREEN)	5,934	2.3%

PREVIOUS WINNING PERCENTAGES
2002 (59%); 2000 (62%); 1998 (65%); 1996 (50%)

Elected 1996; 6th term

No one illustrates better than Smith the disillusionment many members of Congress feel about the war in Iraq. The centrist Democrat voted in 2002 to authorize President Bush to use force against Saddam Hussein's regime, and he sided with Republicans in 2006 against setting a troop withdrawal deadline. But by 2007, Smith had had enough.

As Bush moved to deploy more than 21,000 additional U.S. troops to the war-torn country, Smith balked. "We are going the wrong way," he said. "We are adding troops and not bringing peace and stability to Iraq." In February 2007, he voted for a Democratic resolution opposing the increase, telling the House that Bush and his administration had "failed to an almost incomprehensible level to learn from past errors." In March, he backed a war funding bill that required a withdrawal of U.S. combat forces by the end of August 2008. He also introduced his own bill that month to terminate congressional authorization of the war effort.

The Washington Democrat now has a direct say on defense and foreign policy as a member of both the Armed Services and Foreign Affairs committees. He chairs the Armed Services Subcommittee on Terrorism, Unconventional Threats and Capabilities. His membership on Armed Services allows him to look out for the interests of defense contractor Boeing and his district's two military installations — Fort Lewis, the Army's largest training base on the West Coast, and McChord Air Force Base.

Smith considers himself a man of the middle. A leader of the pro-business New Democrat Coalition, he has repeatedly sought to nudge his more liberal colleagues closer to the ideological center. And as a lawmaker from a politically competitive, largely suburban district, he has found that embracing positions near the middle has paid off at election time.

He sides with his fellow Democrats on social issues, but he sometimes bucks his party's liberal majority on fiscal policy, crime and national security. In 2004, Smith was one of only four Democrats to oppose an amendment to the 2001 anti-terrorism law, known as the Patriot Act, to prohibit federal agents from searching library records and bookstore customer lists to aid terrorism investigations. The amendment died on a tie vote, and Washington state liberals excoriated Smith. He later told civil libertarians that he should have voted the other way. "It is quite possible that I looked at it incorrectly," he said.

By the 109th Congress (2005-06), Smith had indeed changed his mind, alarmed by what he saw as the Bush administration's growing disregard for civil liberties. He voted in 2005 with other Democrats to prohibit the FBI from gaining access to library and bookstore records. The following year, he voted against authorizing warrantless wiretaps of terrorism suspects communicating with individuals within the United States.

Though timber giant Weyerhaeuser Co. is headquartered in the 9th District, Smith usually sides with urban Democrats against more logging on public lands. But in 2003, he voted for the final version of the GOP's "Healthy Forests" act, which allows thinning of many forest areas for wildfire prevention. He opposed a more sweeping House version of the bill.

Smith is a free-trade advocate, but he has opposed some Bush-era trade deals because he felt they did not protect labor standards. After voting against similar bills in 1998 and 2001, Smith in 2002 split with his party leaders and backed legislation giving the president fast-track authority to negotiate trade agreements that Congress cannot amend. In the 108th Congress

(2003-04), he voted for trade accords with Australia, Chile, Morocco and Singapore. By the 109th Congress, however, he was growing skeptical. He voted against the Central American Free Trade Agreement in 2005, pleasing unions that had criticized his earlier pro-trade votes but antagonizing many businesses in his trade-friendly district. "All I am looking for in trade is getting some reasonable labor protections," Smith says. "We want to make sure economic growth is properly spread out."

On tax cuts, Smith in 2001 voted for Republican bills to reduce taxes for married couples, phase out the estate tax and boost incentives for retirement savings, measures that became part of the $1.35 trillion, 10-year tax cut enacted later that year. He voted against the overall package, however. In 2005, Smith voted for a GOP bill to permanently repeal estate taxes.

Smith's success in positioning himself as a pragmatic centrist has helped him cement his political standing among his mainly white-collar constituents. He is the only person ever re-elected to Congress from Washington's 9th District, which was created in 1992 when the state gained another seat in that decade's reapportionment. His two predecessors — one a Democrat, the other a Republican — each lost after one term.

Smith's father, who worked as a baggage handler at the Seattle-Tacoma International Airport, died of a heart attack when the congressman was just 19. The family went on welfare, and Smith worked his way through college loading trucks for the United Parcel Service. He was a Teamsters union member, and still supports organized labor on most issues other than trade.

Smith likes to say that he is a lifelong resident of the area he represents in Congress. Technically, though, he is an "inside-the-Beltway" native, having been born in the District of Columbia one week before the Smiths adopted him and took him to the "other Washington."

The fall after he earned his law degree in 1990, he won a state Senate seat in an upset and, at 25, became the youngest state senator in the country. Four years later, when many Democratic officeholders in the state were swept away by the 1994 Republican tide, he won a second term.

By 1996, at age 31, Smith was well-known as a tireless campaigner who had made repeat visits to many of the 40,000 homes in his legislative district. He challenged GOP Rep. Randy Tate, a favorite of social conservatives, who had ridden into office on the big GOP wave of 1994. Smith triumphed by 3 percentage points and has won fairly comfortably since then.

But he never gets too comfortable in Washington, D.C. Smith sleeps in his office in the Rayburn Building, bedding down in a storeroom.

KEY VOTES

2006

- Yes Stop broadband companies from favoring select Internet traffic
- Yes Affirm U.S. commitment to war in Iraq and reject setting a withdrawal date for troops
- No Repeal requirement for bilingual ballots at the polls
- Yes Permit U.S. sale of civilian nuclear technology to India
- Yes Build a 700-mile fence on the U.S.-Mexico border to curb illegal crossings
- No Permit warrantless wiretaps of suspected terrorists

2005

- ? Intervene in the life-support case of Terri Schiavo
- Yes Lift President Bush's restrictions on stem cell research funding
- Yes Prohibit FBI access to library and bookstore records
- No Approve free-trade pact with five Central American countries
- No Pass energy policy overhaul favored by President Bush emphasizing domestic oil and gas production
- No End mandatory preservation of habitat of endangered animal and plant species
- Yes Ban torture of prisoners in U.S. custody

CQ VOTE STUDIES

	PARTY UNITY		PRESIDENTIAL SUPPORT	
	Support	Oppose	Support	Oppose
2006	88%	12%	45%	55%
2005	90%	10%	24%	76%
2004	84%	16%	38%	62%
2003	85%	15%	40%	60%
2002	81%	19%	38%	62%

INTEREST GROUPS

	AFL-CIO	ADA	CCUS	ACU
2006	85%	75%	57%	21%
2005	87%	85%	50%	12%
2004	86%	90%	55%	17%
2003	80%	85%	50%	24%
2002	63%	85%	63%	23%

WASHINGTON 9

South Seattle suburbs; small part of Tacoma

Taking in numerous cities in the south Puget Sound region, the 9th runs south of Seattle along Interstate 5 before picking up small parts of Tacoma and Olympia, the state capital, en route to rural areas that offer spectacular views of Mount Rainier's 14,410-foot peak (in the 8th).

Just south of the Seattle city line, the 9th's northern end takes in predominantly middle-class King County suburbs, where half of its population lives. This area includes most of Burien, SeaTac and Tukwila (shared with the 7th) and Renton (shared with the 8th). SeaTac, named after the area's major cities, includes the region's major airport and is home to Alaska Airlines' corporate headquarters. Boeing has a commercial airplane production facility in Renton, where the 737 jet plane is built. The wealthiest areas are in southern King, including Federal Way, where timber giant Weyerhaeuser is headquartered.

South of King, Pierce County's suburbs account for 40 percent of the 9th's population and Thurston County makes up the rest. Pierce County also includes the deep-water Port of Tacoma, which has diversified the area's economy and helped it become a magnet for technology companies looking for fast distribution opportunities. Thurston includes part of Olympia (shared with the 3rd) as well as the most rural portion of the district.

The 9th is politically ambivalent, giving John Kerry 53 percent of the vote in the 2004 presidential election. Democrats fare better in the King and Thurston portions of the district than they fare in Pierce. The blue-collar workers from Boeing and Tacoma's port form a Democratic base throughout the district, while fiscally conservative suburbanites tend to vote Republican.

MAJOR INDUSTRY

Aviation manufacturing, computer software, hardware

MILITARY BASES

Fort Lewis (Army), 20,484 military, 4,500 civilian (2001); McChord Air Force Base, 6,524 military, 2,086 civilian (2004)

CITIES

Federal Way, 83,259; Kent (pt.), 43,904; Puyallup, 33,011

NOTABLE

The 17-day Western Washington Fair in Puyallup is the largest annual event in the state.

WEST VIRGINIA

Gov. Joe Manchin III (D)

First elected: 2004
Length of term: 4 years
Term expires: 1/09
Salary: $95,000
Phone: (304) 558-2000

Residence: Fairmont
Born: August 24, 1947; Fairmont, W.Va.
Religion: Roman Catholic
Family: Wife, Gayle Manchin; three children
Education: West Virginia U., B.A. 1970 (business administration)
Career: Coal brokerage company owner; carpet store owner
Political highlights: W.Va. House, 1983-85; W.Va. Senate, 1987-97; sought Democratic nomination for governor, 1996; W.Va. secretary of state, 2001-05

Election results:

2004 GENERAL		
Joe Manchin III (D)	472,758	63.5%
Monty Warner (R)	253,131	34.0%
Jesse Johnson (MOUNT)	18,430	2.5%

Senate President Earl Ray Tomblin (D)

(no lieutenant governor)
Phone: (304) 855-7270

LEGISLATURE

General Assembly: January-March, limit of 60 days

Senate: 34 members, 4-year terms
2007 ratios: 23 D, 11 R; 32 men, 2 women
Salary: $15,000
Phone: (304) 357-7800

House: 100 members, 2-year terms
2007 ratios: 72 D, 28 R; 83 men, 17 women
Salary: $15,000
Phone: (304) 340-3200

TERM LIMITS

Governor: 2 consecutive terms
Senate: No
House: No

URBAN STATISTICS

CITY	POPULATION
Charleston	53,421
Huntington	51,475
Parkersburg	33,099
Wheeling	31,419

REGISTERED VOTERS

Democrat	57%
Republican	30%
Unaffiliated	12%
Others	1%

POPULATION

2006 population (est.)	1,818,470
2000 population	1,808,344
1990 population	1,793,477
Percent change (1990-2000)	+0.8%
Rank among states (2006)	37
Median age	38.9
Born in state	74.2%
Foreign born	1.1%
Violent crime rate	317/100,000
Poverty level	17.9%
Federal workers	21,235
Military	10,203

ELECTIONS

STATE ELECTION OFFICIAL
(304) 558-6000
DEMOCRATIC PARTY
(304) 342-8121
REPUBLICAN PARTY
(304) 768-0493

MISCELLANEOUS

Web: www.wv.gov
Capital: Charleston

U.S. CONGRESS

Senate: 2 Democrats
House: 2 Democrats, 1 Republican

2000 Census Statistics by District

DIST.	2004 VOTE FOR PRESIDENT BUSH	KERRY	WHITE	BLACK	ASIAN	HISP	MEDIAN INCOME	WHITE COLLAR	BLUE COLLAR	SERVICE INDUSTRY	OVER 64	UNDER 18	COLLEGE EDUCATION	RURAL	SQ. MILES
1	58%	41%	96%	2%	1%	1%	$30,303	54%	29%	17%	16%	22%	16%	46%	6,286
2	57	42	94	4	1	1	$33,198	55	30	15	15	23	16	54	8,459
3	53	46	94	4	0	1	$25,630	53	30	18	16	22	12	62	9,332
STATE	56	43	95	3	1	1	$29,696	54	29	17	15	22	15	54	24,078
U.S.	50.7	48.3	69	12	4	13	$41,994	60	25	15	12	26	24	21	3,537,438

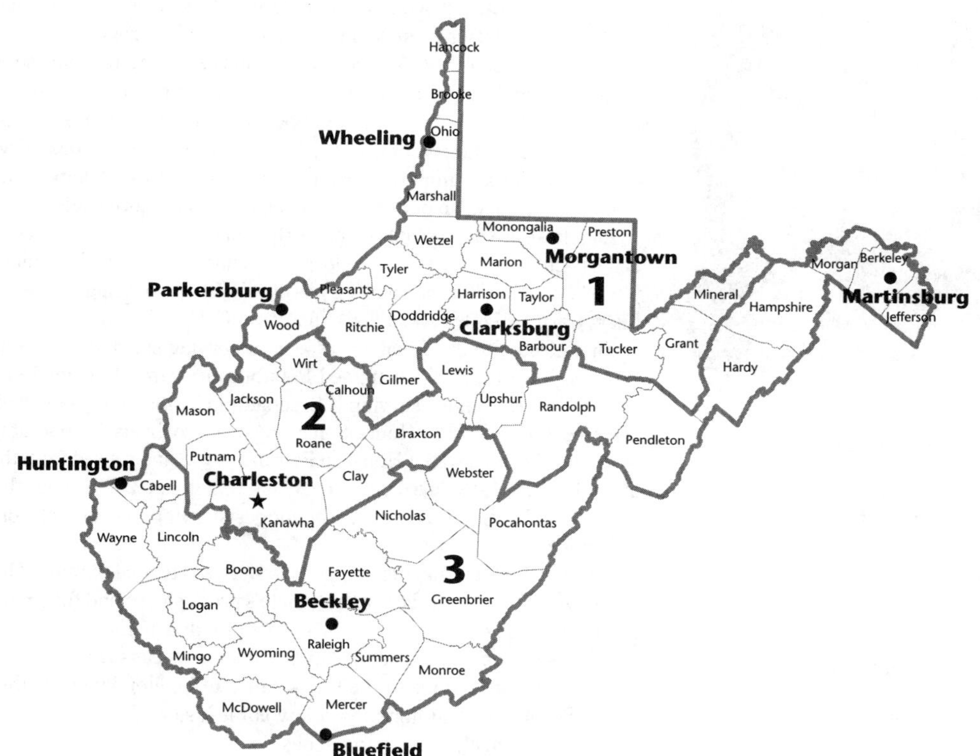

Hancock
Brooke
Ohio
Wheeling
Marshall
Wetzel
Monongalia
Preston
Morgantown
Tyler
Marion
Parkersburg
Pleasants
Harrison
Taylor
1
Wood
Ritchie
Doddridge
Clarksburg
Barbour
Tucker
Mineral
Grant
Hampshire
Morgan
Berkeley
Martinsburg
Jefferson
Hardy
Wirt
Calhoun
Gilmer
Lewis
Upshur
Randolph
Mason
Jackson
2
Roane
Braxton
Pendleton
Huntington
Cabell
Putnam
Charleston
Clay
Webster
Kanawha
Nicholas
Pocahontas
Wayne
Lincoln
Boone
Fayette
3
Greenbrier
Logan
Beckley
Raleigh
Mingo
Wyoming
Summers
Monroe
McDowell
Mercer
Bluefield

Sen. Robert C. Byrd (D)

CAPITOL OFFICE
224-3954
byrd.senate.gov
311 Hart 20510-4801; fax 228-0002

COMMITTEES
Appropriations - chairman
(Homeland Security - chairman)
Armed Services
Budget
Rules & Administration

RESIDENCE
Shepherdstown

BORN
Nov. 20, 1917, North Wilkesboro, N.C.

RELIGION
Baptist

FAMILY
Widowed; two children

EDUCATION
American U., J.D. 1963; Marshall U., B.A. 1994 (political science)

CAREER
Butcher

POLITICAL HIGHLIGHTS
W.Va. House, 1947-51; W.Va. Senate, 1951-53; U.S. House, 1953-59

ELECTION RESULTS

2006 GENERAL		
Robert C. Byrd (D)	296,276	64.4%
John R. Raese (R)	155,043	33.7%
Jesse Johnson (MOUNT)	8,565	1.9%
2006 PRIMARY		
Robert C. Byrd (D)	159,154	85.7%
Billy Hendricks Jr. (D)	26,609	14.3%

PREVIOUS WINNING PERCENTAGES
2000 (78%); 1994 (69%); 1988 (65%); 1982 (69%); 1976 (100%); 1970 (78%); 1964 (68%); 1958 (59%); 1956 House Election (57%); 1954 House Election (63%); 1952 House Election (56%)

Elected 1958; 9th term

The longest-serving senator in U.S. history, Byrd long ago took on the aura of living legend. Though the years have exacted a toll, he remains at his post, day in and day out, on guard against those who would trifle with the Senate's rules or trample on its constitutional prerogatives.

There is no peak left for Byrd to scale in the Senate he loves so dearly. He is the president pro tempore, third in the line of succession to the presidency after the vice president and Speaker of the House. He is chairman of the Appropriations Committee, for the third time. He has served as majority leader and minority leader, as majority whip and Democratic conference secretary. No one has ever been elected to more leadership posts.

And those are not the only contests Byrd has won. In a political career that dates back to 1946, he has never lost an election. "There are four things people believe in in West Virginia," he has often said. "God Almighty; Sears, Roebuck; Carter's Little Liver Pills; and Robert C. Byrd."

First elected to the Senate in 1958 after serving six years in the House, Byrd on June 12, 2006, surpassed Republican Strom Thurmond of South Carolina as the longest-serving U.S. senator in history. Only one challenge remains: the combined House-Senate record of Arizona Democrat Carl T. Hayden, who entered the House in February 1912 and retired from the Senate in January 1969. Byrd could overtake that in late 2009, about the time of his 92nd birthday, to become the longest-serving member of Congress in history.

More important than his longevity is Byrd's vigorous pursuit of his self-appointed roles as guardian of the Senate's prerogatives and the grand master of its rules and procedures. He can be prickly and imperious, and he is notoriously long-winded, tying up the floor and causing headaches for whoever is trying to make the trains run. But he literally wrote the book on the Senate — an authoritative four-volume history that began as a series of characteristically flowery speeches.

In 2004, he published a very different book that articulated his distress at the emergence of a political culture of deep polarization and expanding executive power. During the 2004 presidential contest between President Bush and Democratic Sen. John Kerry of Massachusetts, Byrd went on tour to promote "Losing America," a book in which he asserts that the Sept. 11 terrorist attacks transformed "a lackluster, inarticulate, visionless president into a national and international leader, nearly unquestioned by the media or by members of either party."

He has tried without much success to curb what he views as executive branch encroachment during the Bush years, leading the opposition to initiatives such as presidential authority to enter trade pacts that Congress cannot amend.

Byrd reveres the Constitution; he keeps a copy close at hand and can recite much of it from memory. Among his favorite passages is Article 1, Section 9, clause 7 — "No money shall be drawn from the Treasury, but in consequence of appropriations made by law."

In 1989, Byrd stepped down after 12 years as the Senate's top Democratic leader in order to claim the Appropriations Committee gavel. He vowed to steer $1 billion back home to West Virginia within five years, and met that goal in less than three. Byrd served a second stint as chairman for 18 months starting in June 2001, when Democrats briefly regained control of the Senate. He took the gavel a third time when Democrats took over in 2007.

Whether as chairman or as ranking minority member, he has ensured that the stream of federal dollars to West Virginia continues unabated. The Charleston Gazette has called him a "one-man economic development program," and the Mountain State is dotted with highways, dams and other federal projects named for him. In 1997, his grateful state installed a 10-foot bronze statue of the senator in the state Capitol rotunda.

Conservatives have assailed the special-project earmarks Byrd loves to insert for his state and for those of allies such as Democrat Daniel K. Inouye of Hawaii and Republican Ted Stevens of Alaska. The Senate voted in early 2007 to require disclosure of earmark sponsors, but that is unlikely to bother Byrd, who happily takes credit for every dime he directs to his state.

No one has been a sharper Iraq War critic than Byrd. He voted against authorizing the conflict and tried in vain to persuade his colleagues it was folly. The day before the war began in 2003, Byrd told the Senate that Bush had chosen to channel the country's rage over the Sept. 11 terrorist attacks toward Iraqi dictator Saddam Hussein. "And villain he is," he said. "But he is the wrong villain. And this is the wrong war." In May 2007, he and Hillary Rodham Clinton, New York Democratic senator and presidential candidate, introduced a resolution that would require Bush to ask Congress to renew authorization for the war before he could extend military operations beyond Oct. 11, 2007. He said, "the president's rationale for going to war — toppling Saddam Hussein and eliminating the threat of the late Iraqi leader getting a hold of weapons of mass destruction — is no longer relevant."

Byrd was born Cornelius Calvin Sale Jr. When he was 1, his mother died and his father gave him to an aunt and uncle, Vlurma and Titus Byrd. The couple reared him in the hardscrabble coal country of southern West Virginia. Byrd graduated first in his high school class and married his high school sweetheart, Erma Ora. The very next day, he wrote in his 2005 autobiography, he handed her his wallet and said, "Here is the pocketbook. You keep it." Her death in March 2006 ended a partnership of almost 69 years. "She was God's greatest gift to me," Byrd told his Senate colleagues.

He worked as a gas station attendant, grocery store clerk, shipyard welder and butcher. It took him 12 years to save enough money to go to college. He learned to play the fiddle as a boy, and his talents helped him win a seat in the state legislature in 1946. Friends drove Byrd around the hills and hollows, where he brought the voters out by playing "Cripple Creek" and "Rye Whiskey." A picture of him as a boy, fiddle and bow in hand, is on the cover of his autobiography, "Child of the Appalachian Coalfields."

Byrd's political career has featured its share of mistakes, some quite spectacular. As a young man, he joined the Ku Klux Klan because, he said, of his alarm over communism. It was a decision he came to publicly regret. In 1964, he filibustered the landmark Civil Rights Act, at one point holding the floor with a 14-hour speech that is among the longest on record. He also has lamented that chapter of his career.

Byrd first started up the Senate leadership ladder in 1967, winning election as Democratic conference secretary. In 1971, he stunned outsiders when he ousted Sen. Edward M. Kennedy of Massachusetts as majority whip, the No. 2 post. Today, the two old adversaries usually can be found side by side, fighting to advance Democratic programs and thwart Bush's priorities.

In 2007, Stevens passed Thurmond as the longest-serving Republican senator. (Thurmond began his career as a Democrat.) Byrd took the floor to pay tribute to his old friend, reciting from memory a Ralph Waldo Emerson poem: "Not gold, but only men can make a nation great and strong; men who for truth and honor's sake stand fast and labor long. Real men who work while others sleep, who dare while others fly. They build a nation's pillars deep and lift them to the sky."

KEY VOTES

2006

Yes	Confirm Samuel A. Alito Jr. to the Supreme Court
No	Allow consideration of a bill to establish a $140 billion trust fund to compensate victims of asbestos exposure
No	Extend tax cuts for two years at a cost of $70 billion over five years
No	Overhaul immigration policy with border security, enforcement and guest worker program
No	Allow consideration of a bill to permanently repeal the estate tax
Yes	Urge President Bush to begin troop withdrawals from Iraq in 2006
Yes	Lift President Bush's restrictions on stem cell research funding
No	Authorize military tribunals for suspected terrorists

2005

No	Curb class action lawsuits by shifting them from state to federal courts
Yes	Allow confirmation vote on Priscilla R. Owen to the U.S. Court of Appeals for the 5th Circuit
No	Oppose mandatory emissions limits and block recognition of global warming as a threat
No	Approve free-trade pact with five Central American countries
Yes	Pass energy policy overhaul favored by President Bush emphasizing domestic oil and gas production
Yes	Shield gunmakers from lawsuits when their products are used in crimes
Yes	Ban torture of prisoners in U.S. custody
No	Renew 16 provisions of the Patriot Act
No	Allow final vote on opening the Arctic National Wildlife Refuge to oil and gas exploration

CQ VOTE STUDIES

	PARTY UNITY		PRESIDENTIAL SUPPORT	
	Support	Oppose	Support	Oppose
2006	74%	26%	49%	51%
2005	84%	16%	44%	56%
2004	90%	10%	63%	37%
2003	93%	7%	54%	46%
2002	82%	18%	70%	30%
2001	86%	14%	71%	29%
2000	72%	28%	75%	25%
1999	80%	20%	70%	30%
1998	72%	28%	74%	26%
1997	81%	19%	81%	19%

INTEREST GROUPS

	AFL-CIO	ADA	CCUS	ACU
2006	80%	80%	25%	21%
2005	86%	95%	44%	20%
2004	100%	90%	38%	8%
2003	100%	95%	29%	30%
2002	85%	75%	40%	15%
2001	75%	85%	21%	40%
2000	63%	75%	40%	28%
1999	100%	80%	47%	20%
1998	88%	80%	44%	16%
1997	100%	70%	40%	16%

Sen. John D. Rockefeller IV (D)

CAPITOL OFFICE
224-6472
rockefeller.senate.gov
531 Hart 20510-4802; fax 224-7665

COMMITTEES
Commerce, Science & Transportation
(Aviation Operations, Safety & Security - chairman)
Finance
(Health Care - chairman)
Veterans' Affairs
Select Intelligence - chairman
Joint Taxation

RESIDENCE
Charleston

BORN
June 18, 1937, Manhattan, N.Y.

RELIGION
Presbyterian

FAMILY
Wife, Sharon Percy; four children

EDUCATION
International Christian U. (Tokyo), attended 1957-60; Harvard U., A.B. 1961 (Asian languages & history)

CAREER
College president; VISTA volunteer

POLITICAL HIGHLIGHTS
W.Va. House, 1967-69; W.Va. secretary of state, 1969-73; Democratic nominee for governor, 1972; governor, 1977-85

ELECTION RESULTS

2002 GENERAL		
John D. Rockefeller IV (D)	275,281	63.1%
Jay Wolfe (R)	160,902	36.9%
2002 PRIMARY		
John D. Rockefeller IV (D)	198,327	89.9%
Bruce Barilla (D)	11,178	5.1%
William "Bill" Galloway (D)	11,173	5.1%

PREVIOUS WINNING PERCENTAGES
1996 (77%); 1990 (68%); 1984 (52%)

Elected 1984; 4th term

The great-grandson and namesake of the founder of Standard Oil Co., Rockefeller went to West Virginia as a young anti-poverty volunteer in the 1960s and never left. His surname may be a symbol of American wealth, but Rockefeller represents one of the nation's poorest states and he has devoted his career to helping those less fortunate than he is.

Rockefeller cannot hope to match the influence of his senior colleague, Robert C. Byrd, who as the chairman or top-ranking Democrat on the Appropriations Committee has funneled billions of dollars to the state. But Rockefeller is a fierce defender of the local steel industry, doing what he can to help it battle foreign competition. In West Virginia, he is called the "Senator of Steel." And he uses his Finance Committee position to advance his state's interests and improve health coverage.

Rockefeller is at the fore of national security issues as chairman of the Intelligence Committee in the 110th Congress (2007-08). During the 109th Congress (2005-06), he was among those clashing with the Bush administration over the National Security Agency's warrantless electronic surveillance of communications between Americans and terrorism suspects abroad. The administration eventually gave in, returning to a special court set up under a 1978 law to review such wiretaps. But in 2007, Bush officials asked Congress for explicit authorization to resume the snooping without court reviews. Rockefeller was decidedly cool to the request.

After the 2003 invasion of Iraq failed to produce any sign of the weapons of mass destruction that President Bush had cited as a reason for war, the Intelligence Committee undertook an exhaustive review of prewar intelligence. In 2004, Rockefeller partnered with then Chairman Pat Roberts, a Kansas Republican, to issue a scathing report on the CIA's information-gathering prior to the invasion. The détente did not last long. The two soon fought over a second phase of the probe examining the way top administration policy makers had used the prewar intelligence. Rockefeller said in 2006 that "administration officials cherry-picked, exaggerated or ignored intelligence to justify the decision they had already made." The investigation stalled, but after Democrats gained control of the Senate in the 2006 elections, Rockefeller vowed the committee would finish it.

When the White House began saber-rattling about Iran's nuclear program early in 2007, Rockefeller formed a study group to examine U.S. intelligence about Iran. His initial assessment: The analysis was better than it had been on Iraq, but intelligence collection was slower than it should be.

Tall and bookish, Rockefeller has worked hard to gain the confidence of West Virginians from the day he arrived in 1964 as a 27-year-old volunteer with VISTA's Action for Appalachia Youth program. He was an unlikely transplant. He had been reared on Manhattan's Upper East Side, schooled at Exeter prep and Harvard University, and had just come from three years abroad studying Japanese. But Rockefeller loved the state. He got involved in West Virginia politics, winning a seat in the state legislature, and he has lived there ever since.

In a way, his wealth insulates him from suspicion back home. With no need to curry favor or solicit campaign cash in heavy doses from special interests, Rockefeller can devote all of his energy to the Senate. He uses self-deprecating humor to urge his constituents to see him as just plain "Jay." And he passionately takes on the causes of the working class and the poor.

He refused to vote for Bush's Medicare prescription drug bill in 2003 because he felt it gave private insurers too big a role in the program. Like most Democrats, Rockefeller wants to give the Department of Health and Human Services — rather than private insurance companies — the power to negotiate drug prices on behalf of Medicare beneficiaries, anticipating that would result in lower prices.

Rockefeller was supposed to be on the House-Senate negotiating team that drafted the final version of the drug bill. But he and several other Democratic conferees were shut out of the talks by House Ways and Means Chairman Bill Thomas, a California Republican, even though Rockefeller had a long record of working on Medicare issues, including service on a blue-ribbon panel in the 1990s that studied the long-term solvency of the program.

Rockefeller also has fought the Bush administration over funding for a joint federal-state health insurance program for poor children. When the administration decided to redistribute more than $1 billion in unspent money in the State Children's Health Insurance Program, which covers children from families not poor enough to qualify for Medicaid, Rockefeller sponsored legislation that would have allowed states to tap into the money beyond the deadline. Republicans opposed it and it foundered.

During debate on an overhaul of welfare programs in the 107th Congress (2001-02), Rockefeller called for an additional $8 billion for child care services over five years. Also during that period, Rockefeller had a hand in writing the airline industry bailout and aviation security laws enacted soon after the Sept. 11 terrorist attacks. In the 110th Congress, the Senate Commerce, Science and Transportation Subcommittee on Aviation, which he chairs, was seeking ways to finance upgrades to the nation's overburdened air traffic control system. He warned that a "food fight" between competing aviation interests could make the task difficult, if not impossible.

Rockefeller considers the future of the domestic steel industry a "life or death" issue, and has waged knock-down fights with administrations of both parties to protect it when it has been threatened by low-cost imports. He also engages on policy affecting mining, another important local industry. After 12 miners died at West Virginia's Sago Mine in 2006, Rockefeller and Byrd successfully pushed a bill through the Senate that set stiff minimum penalties for negligent mine owners.

Rockefeller's ascent in West Virginia politics had some bumps. After serving in the state House and as secretary of state, he lost a race for governor in 1972. He strengthened his ties to the state by taking a job as president of West Virginia Wesleyan College, then went on to win the governorship on his second try, in 1976, and serve two terms.

In the early 1980s, his popularity slid as the state's economy resisted his attempts to fulfill a campaign promise to fix it. He ran for the Senate in 1984, going after the seat of retiring Democrat Jennings Randolph. He won with just 52 percent of the vote despite spending $12 million against political neophyte John Raese. He has won more easily since, and was elected to a fourth term in 2002, besting former GOP state Sen. Jay Wolfe.

In the first half of 2006, Rockefeller was slowed considerably by back surgery that was more extensive than expected and required several months of recovery. In 2005, his wife, Sharon, was diagnosed and treated for colorectal cancer.

Given his name recognition, wealth and political experience, Rockefeller was sometimes mentioned as a potential presidential candidate, and he considered and declined a race in 1992. Asked about his interest in the 2004 campaign, Rockefeller told The Charleston Daily Mail in 2001, "I am sufficiently private to not want to do this. There's a point where I've decided to say, 'You can't have all of me.'"

KEY VOTES

2006

- No Confirm Samuel A. Alito Jr. to the Supreme Court
- No Allow consideration of a bill to establish a $140 billion trust fund to compensate victims of asbestos exposure
- ? Extend tax cuts for two years at a cost of $70 billion over five years
- ? Overhaul immigration policy with border security, enforcement and guest worker program
- ? Allow consideration of a bill to permanently repeal the estate tax
- ? Urge President Bush to begin troop withdrawals from Iraq in 2006
- Yes Lift President Bush's restrictions on stem cell research funding
- Yes Authorize military tribunals for suspected terrorists

2005

- Yes Curb class action lawsuits by shifting them from state to federal courts
- Yes Allow confirmation vote on Priscilla R. Owen to the U.S. Court of Appeals for the 5th Circuit
- No Oppose mandatory emissions limits and block recognition of global warming as a threat
- No Approve free-trade pact with five Central American countries
- Yes Pass energy policy overhaul favored by President Bush emphasizing domestic oil and gas production
- Yes Shield gunmakers from lawsuits when their products are used in crimes
- Yes Ban torture of prisoners in U.S. custody
- No Renew 16 provisions of the Patriot Act
- No Allow final vote on opening the Arctic National Wildlife Refuge to oil and gas exploration

CQ VOTE STUDIES

	PARTY UNITY		PRESIDENTIAL SUPPORT	
	Support	Oppose	Support	Oppose
2006	84%	16%	55%	45%
2005	93%	7%	40%	60%
2004	88%	12%	64%	36%
2003	96%	4%	50%	50%
2002	90%	10%	71%	29%
2001	97%	3%	66%	34%
2000	96%	4%	97%	3%
1999	94%	6%	89%	11%
1998	93%	7%	94%	6%
1997	88%	12%	86%	14%

INTEREST GROUPS

	AFL-CIO	ADA	CCUS	ACU
2006	100%	60%	83%	10%
2005	86%	100%	50%	4%
2004	100%	90%	41%	12%
2003	92%	100%	30%	15%
2002	100%	90%	45%	15%
2001	100%	100%	43%	12%
2000	75%	85%	60%	4%
1999	89%	100%	41%	4%
1998	100%	90%	56%	0%
1997	71%	70%	67%	8%

Rep. Alan B. Mollohan (D)

CAPITOL OFFICE
225-4172
www.house.gov/mollohan
2302 Rayburn 20515-4801; fax 225-7564

COMMITTEES
Appropriations
(Commerce-Justice-Science - chairman)

RESIDENCE
Fairmont

BORN
May 14, 1943, Fairmont, W.Va.

RELIGION
Baptist

FAMILY
Wife, Barbara Mollohan; five children

EDUCATION
College of William & Mary, A.B. 1966 (political science); West Virginia U., J.D. 1970

MILITARY SERVICE
Army Reserve, 1970-83

CAREER
Lawyer

POLITICAL HIGHLIGHTS
No previous office

ELECTION RESULTS

2006 GENERAL		
Alan B. Mollohan (D)	100,939	64.3%
Chris Wakim (R)	55,963	35.6%
2006 PRIMARY		
Alan B. Mollohan (D)		unopposed
2004 GENERAL		
Alan B. Mollohan (D)	166,583	67.8%
Alan Lee Parks (R)	79,196	32.2%

PREVIOUS WINNING PERCENTAGES
2002 (100%); 2000 (88%); 1998 (85%); 1996 (100%); 1994 (70%); 1992 (100%); 1990 (67%); 1988 (75%); 1986 (100%); 1984 (54%); 1982 (53%)

Elected 1982; 13th term

Mollohan is now in his 25th year in the House. Most of those years he flew under the national radar as he worked diligently to direct federal money home to his economically depressed state. But the spotlight found him in 2006 when he became embroiled in a partisan dispute and then was the target of ethics questions.

Mollohan was the top-ranking Democrat on the Committee on Standards of Official Conduct, or House ethics committee, from 2003 to 2006. It is an unwelcome assignment for most lawmakers as the committee, composed equally of Republicans and Democrats, enforces House rules. In 2004, the committee looked into two ethics complaints lodged against GOP Majority Leader Tom DeLay of Texas and voted unanimously to admonish the lawmaker for three instances of inappropriate conduct.

Republican leaders, angered by the panel's action against DeLay, retaliated, removing the committee's Republican chairman and two other GOP members and replacing them with party loyalists. The GOP also pushed new ethics rules through the House that Democrats said gutted the committee's powers. In response, Mollohan refused to allow the committee to organize or to function, while other Democrats used procedural maneuvers to tie up activity on the floor. GOP leaders eventually relented and rescinded the rules changes.

But then Mollohan himself became the subject of an ethics complaint. A conservative watchdog group in Virginia, the National Legal and Policy Center, reported that Mollohan, a senior member of the Appropriations Committee, had directed numerous earmarks to nonprofit organizations he set up in his district. The group also said he had failed to properly disclose various loans and assets, including interests in companies, on his financial reports over an eight-year period. In July 2006, he responded only that he had misstated more than a dozen transactions on his financial disclosure forms.

The Justice Department subpoenaed documents from the three West Virginia nonprofit organizations. But Mollohan said the allegations were unfounded and noted that the Justice Department had never contacted him about the matter. "I welcome any review of my efforts to diversify the economy of West Virginia, as well as any of our financial investments," Mollohan told the Charleston Daily Mail in April 2006. "All of them are above board, and we operate transparently."

Nevertheless, he resigned from the ethics committee. "When you are charged with reviewing questions raised about other members and somebody's raising questions about you, you are not in a position to review questions raised by other people," he said. "That is just a credibility issue."

He then recused himself from all matters concerning the Justice Department in his position as chairman of the Appropriations Commerce-Justice-Science Subcommittee in the 110th Congress (2007-08).

Mollohan also was among several lawmakers who had received campaign donations from defense contractor MZM Inc. or its former owner, Mitchell Wade. Wade had pleaded guilty to bribing former California Republican Rep. Randy "Duke" Cunningham, who resigned his seat in the wake of the scandal. Mollohan donated to charity the contributions he had received from MZM Inc. and Wade.

He first gained a seat on the Appropriations Committee in mid-1986 and has used it to win federal dollars for new prisons, health clinics, research centers, industrial parks, roads and water projects for his mostly rural district.

He regularly combines forces with his state's most revered politician, Robert C. Byrd, chairman of the Senate Appropriations Committee.

Mollohan largely reflects the values of his state's residents. Like most Democrats, he opposes free-trade agreements that he believes threaten his constituents' jobs. He voted against the 2005 Central American Free Trade Agreement. He also voted against President Bush's tax cuts and authorizing the war in Iraq.

But he maintains a more conservative stance on social issues. Mollohan strongly opposes abortion and chaired the House Pro-Life Caucus for many years. In 2006, he voted in favor of a measure making it a federal crime to take a minor across state lines for an abortion. "On this issue, I am aligned with my constituents and with my beliefs," Mollohan said.

Mollohan also has sided with conservatives on some issues of environmental regulation, a stance that grows out of his state's dependence on coal mining, steelmaking and other heavy industries.

The son of a congressman, Mollohan worked as a lawyer in Washington before succeeding his father. When he was 9 years old, his father, Robert H. Mollohan, was elected to Congress. He was on the House floor for his father's swearing-in ceremony and, as he told the Charleston Daily Mail, "I remember it like yesterday. I think it was kind of a biological imprinting on my brain. I said, 'This is what I want to do.' That's when I knew."

Mollohan struggled to claim his father's House seat. Some voters questioned his career as a D.C.-based corporate attorney. But the elder Mollohan had close connections with party officials, as well as with business and labor leaders; their support proved crucial to the son's narrow primary win in 1982. Mollohan won with just 53 percent of the vote that fall. In 1984, he was held to 54 percent. His general elections since have been easy.

Redistricting after the 1990 census threw him into a primary against colleague Harley O. Staggers Jr. Both men had followed their fathers to Congress, but Staggers portrayed himself as the "outsider," criticizing Mollohan for writing overdrafts at the private bank for House members. Mollohan highlighted the importance of his seat on Appropriations. He won the 1992 primary by 24 percentage points and was unopposed in the general election.

In 2004, Mollohan faced GOP competition for the first time since 1994, defeating Republican Alan Lee Parks with 68 percent. He faced a tougher challenge in 2006 from Republican state Rep. Chris Wakim. But Mollohan was helped by Wakim's admissions that he exaggerated his academic and military credentials and made illegal payouts to patrons who played on video poker machines. Mollohan won with better than 64 percent.

KEY VOTES

2006

No Stop broadband companies from favoring select Internet traffic

No Affirm U.S. commitment to war in Iraq and reject setting a withdrawal date for troops

No Repeal requirement for bilingual ballots at the polls

Yes Permit U.S. sale of civilian nuclear technology to India

Yes Build a 700-mile fence on the U.S.-Mexico border to curb illegal crossings

No Permit warrantless wiretaps of suspected terrorists

2005

Yes Intervene in the life-support case of Terri Schiavo

No Lift President Bush's restrictions on stem cell research funding

Yes Prohibit FBI access to library and bookstore records

No Approve free-trade pact with five Central American countries

Yes Pass energy policy overhaul favored by President Bush emphasizing domestic oil and gas production

Yes End mandatory preservation of habitat of endangered animal and plant species

Yes Ban torture of prisoners in U.S. custody

CQ VOTE STUDIES

	PARTY UNITY		PRESIDENTIAL SUPPORT	
	Support	Oppose	Support	Oppose
2006	77%	23%	54%	46%
2005	78%	22%	36%	64%
2004	81%	19%	29%	71%
2003	77%	23%	42%	58%
2002	78%	22%	34%	66%

INTEREST GROUPS

	AFL-CIO	ADA	CCUS	ACU
2006	93%	60%	50%	46%
2005	93%	75%	56%	52%
2004	92%	65%	37%	24%
2003	100%	80%	41%	50%
2002	89%	75%	40%	24%

WEST VIRGINIA 1

North — Parkersburg, Wheeling, Morgantown

Located in the northernmost part of the state, the Democratic-leaning 1st has a large rural component, but is the most urban of West Virginia's three districts. It contains six of the state's 10 largest cities and West Virginia University (WVU), the state's largest school. Wheeling, an industrial town and commercial center in the north, and Parkersburg, a regional trade center in the west, are two of the main urban areas.

As factories shut down and coal mines began mechanizing operations in the 1980s, unemployment swept through the district and most counties experienced a population decrease. Since 2000, the 1st has seen its unemployment rate peak at more than 7 percent, although the rate has slowly declined since 2003.

Coal and steel are still among the district's biggest employers, but a budding technology sector has brightened economic prospects. The FBI, Energy Department and NASA have facilities in the district. The Institute for Scientific Research, a joint venture between WVU and the West Virginia High Technology Consortium Foundation, recently opened a software engineering research and development facility in Fairmont, which boasts that it is now one of the largest such centers in the country.

The 1st long has elected Democrats to Congress, but Republicans fare better in statewide and local elections, particularly in Doddridge County. Wheeling, in the Northern Panhandle, is often a target of national political campaigns because its media market reaches into neighboring Ohio and Pennsylvania. The 1st gave George W. Bush 54 percent of the vote in the 2000 presidential election, and Bush expanded on that in 2004, garnering 58 percent of the vote. Only two of the district's 20 counties, Brooke and Marion, favored Democrat John Kerry in 2004, and both counties only gave Kerry 51 percent of their presidential vote.

MAJOR INDUSTRY

Coal, steel, technology, chemicals

CITIES

Parkersburg, 33,099; Wheeling, 31,419; Morgantown, 26,809; Weirton, 20,411; Fairmont, 19,097; Clarksburg, 16,743

NOTABLE

The Wheeling Suspension Bridge, opened in 1849, is the oldest operating suspension bridge in the world; Confederate General Thomas "Stonewall" Jackson was born in Clarksburg.

Rep. Shelley Moore Capito (R)

CAPITOL OFFICE
225-2711
capito.house.gov
1431 Longworth 20515-4802; fax 225-7856

COMMITTEES
Financial Services
Transportation & Infrastructure

RESIDENCE
Charleston

BORN
Nov. 26, 1953, Glen Dale, W.Va.

RELIGION
Presbyterian

FAMILY
Husband, Charles L. Capito Jr.; three children

EDUCATION
Duke U., B.S. 1975 (zoology); U. of Virginia, M.Ed. 1976 (counselor education)

CAREER
University system information center director; college career counselor

POLITICAL HIGHLIGHTS
W.Va. House, 1997-2001

ELECTION RESULTS

2006 GENERAL		
Shelley Moore Capito (R)	94,110	57.2%
Mike Callaghan (D)	70,470	42.8%
2006 PRIMARY		
Shelley Moore Capito (R)		unopposed
2004 GENERAL		
Shelley Moore Capito (R)	147,676	57.5%
Erik Wells (D)	106,131	41.3%
Julian Martin (I)	3,218	1.3%

PREVIOUS WINNING PERCENTAGES
2002 (60%); 2000 (48%)

Elected 2000; 4th term

Capito had a tough time in the fall of 2006. A member of the House Page Board, she was drawn into the controversy when news reports broke that Florida GOP Rep. Mark Foley had sent sexually suggestive e-mails to male House pages.

Then her party lost control of the House, and she lost her seat on the powerful Rules Committee. Yet, affable and cheery, she prefers to look on the bright side. Capito (CAP-ih-toe) was happy to be re-elected in a year that was difficult for many GOP incumbents. Her ability to "weather the storm...certainly gives me a good feeling in terms of spreading my wings and going statewide," she said. Capito has made it known she has statewide ambitions, and political insiders consider a 2008 Senate run likely if Democrat John D. Rockefeller IV opts to retire.

The Foley scandal broke a few weeks before Election Day. Capito said that the House Republican leadership, including the GOP chairman of the Page Board who had known about Foley's behavior, had kept her in the dark. "I am very upset about it and I think it is disgusting, quite frankly," she said at the time. She worked with the Democratic leadership on a measure that overhauled the Page Board, requiring equal representation by both parties and more frequent meetings.

Capito has a moderate voting record, which helps her in a state where she is the only Republican in the congressional delegation. She is a member of the moderate Republican Main Street Partnership, and while she usually votes with her party on matters involving taxes, defense and energy, she will break away on some labor, trade and health issues.

Capito was one of just 17 Republicans to vote for five of the six bills in the Democrats' "first 100 hours" agenda at the beginning of the 110th Congress (2007-08), including a measure to raise the minimum wage. Like most of her GOP colleagues, she voted against a bill that would require the government to negotiate drug prices for Medicare.

Her moderate views extend to the war in Iraq. When the House in February 2007 considered a resolution opposing President Bush's request for additional combat troops for Iraq, Capito said she would vote against the resolution because of her concern that it would lay "the foundation to begin cutting funding for our troops." But she also spoke out against the troop increase. "When the president announced his plan for a troop surge last month, I expressed my disagreement," she said. "And as we debate this resolution today, I still harbor those grave concerns."

After losing her seat on Rules, Capito returned in 2007 to seats on the Financial Services and Transportation and Infrastructure committees. Every lawmaker likes to bring home dollars for district roads and Capito is no exception. Even without the seat on the Transportation panel in the 109th Congress (2005-06), she won $87 million in a highway funding bill for U.S. 35, an important road in the western part of her district that she says is plagued by floods and congestion.

Remaining a moderate in today's more partisan political world can be tricky, and Capito's politics are accordingly complex. Like her Democratic predecessor, Rep. Bob Wise, Capito backs gun owners' and abortion rights. But she has supported numerous limits to abortion, voting to ban a procedure opponents call "partial birth" abortion and to require that parents be notified before a minor can obtain an abortion.

When Bush sought to overhaul Medicare by creating a prescription drug benefit for seniors, Capito was a close ally. Appointed vice chairman of a GOP prescription drug task force, Capito campaigned for the plan before its enactment in 2003.

But when Bush sought to overhaul Social Security in 2005, Capito balked. She called the administration's proposal to create individual investment accounts — which would partially privatize Social Security — a "tough sell." Capito says she told Bush privately that she had reservations.

Capito votes more closely with her party when it comes to energy issues — particularly concerning the coal industry, "If it's good for coal mining, it's good for West Virginia," she says. Industry profits are not her only concern. In January 2006, a fire at the Sago Mine in Capito's district killed 12 miners. In response, she joined with Democrats to push into law more-stringent safety rules for coal mine operators, including increased fines for safety violations.

When she is not legislating, Capito can be found on the court. A tennis player in college, she still plays regularly. She also runs and plays in the annual congressional charity baseball game.

The daughter of former Gov. Arch A. Moore Jr., Capito was 2 when her father won his first House election. He was governor when she went to college. He served 12 years before his career ended when he pled guilty to federal charges that included taking illegal campaign contributions for his gubernatorial campaign. He served three years in prison and paid $750,000 to settle a lawsuit against him.

Capito went to college planning to become a doctor. But she decided that it would be tougher to balance motherhood with a career in medicine than with one in politics. Capito waited until her youngest child was 11 to enter politics, winning a seat in the West Virginia House of Delegates in 1996. There, she was recognized for her work on children's health issues. After four years in the state House, she ran for the 2nd District seat, which opened up when Wise ran successfully for governor.

Capito survived two of the most expensive House election campaigns of the decade to win and keep her seat. In 2000, she narrowly beat wealthy class action attorney Jim Humphreys, who plowed almost $7 million into the race. In their 2002 rematch, the most expensive House campaign that year, Capito won by 20 percentage points. After her re-election, she voted for a campaign finance overhaul bill opposed by her party's leaders, which included her amendment to increase fundraising limits and to permit extra help from political parties for candidates who face wealthy, self-funded opponents. She has won her last two elections easily.

KEY VOTES

2006

No Stop broadband companies from favoring select Internet traffic
Yes Affirm U.S. commitment to war in Iraq and reject setting a withdrawal date for troops
Yes Repeal requirement for bilingual ballots at the polls
Yes Permit U.S. sale of civilian nuclear technology to India
Yes Build a 700-mile fence on the U.S.-Mexico border to curb illegal crossings
Yes Permit warrantless wiretaps of suspected terrorists

2005

Yes Intervene in the life-support case of Terri Schiavo
Yes Lift President Bush's restrictions on stem cell research funding
No Prohibit FBI access to library and bookstore records
No Approve free-trade pact with five Central American countries
Yes Pass energy policy overhaul favored by President Bush emphasizing domestic oil and gas production
Yes End mandatory preservation of habitat of endangered animal and plant species
Yes Ban torture of prisoners in U.S. custody

CQ VOTE STUDIES

	PARTY UNITY		PRESIDENTIAL SUPPORT	
	Support	Oppose	Support	Oppose
2006	88%	12%	87%	13%
2005	90%	10%	75%	25%
2004	89%	11%	79%	21%
2003	90%	10%	85%	15%
2002	89%	11%	80%	20%

INTEREST GROUPS

	AFL-CIO	ADA	CCUS	ACU
2006	43%	15%	100%	80%
2005	38%	25%	85%	76%
2004	47%	30%	90%	72%
2003	33%	15%	87%	68%
2002	22%	15%	85%	76%

WEST VIRGINIA 2

Center — Charleston, Eastern Panhandle

The economically diverse 2nd stretches across the mountainous state from the Ohio border to the Eastern Panhandle at Harpers Ferry. It is home to poor coal mining areas and isolated towns, as well as the more-prosperous capital city of Charleston and its commuters in the east.

Charleston, the district's pre-eminent city, is a center for chemical plants, state employees and retail shopping. Chemical plants cut back in the late 1990s and a sluggish economy hit manufacturers hard, but there has been an upswing in state chemical exports. Overall, much of the recent job growth has come from a boom in telemarketing firms moving to the state and from retail expansion around Charleston, although overseas competition has slowed telemarketing growth since 2000.

The mountainous regions north and east of Kanawha County remain dependent on coal, although production has dropped, particularly in Clay County, due in part to companies declaring bankruptcy and to declining demand. Putnam County takes in Buffalo, which is the site of a Toyota plant that expanded operations in 2006 for the fourth time since opening.

Economic depression in the 1980s drove residents from the 2nd. But beginning in the 1990s, the district's eastern counties began filling with Washington, D.C., commuters, causing rapid growth. The district has the highest median income in the state, at just over $33,000.

The 2nd was loyal to Democrats in House elections for 18 years before electing a Republican in 2000. Expanding GOP territories dot the district, particularly in the Panhandle, where Republicans have made gains in party registration. Berkeley County, which includes Martinsburg, voted a straight GOP ticket in 2004, from the presidential and gubernatorial races down to state legislative contests. Overall, George W. Bush carried the district with 57 percent in the 2004 presidential election, after winning 54 percent here in 2000. Braxton County was the only county to favor Democrat John Kerry in 2004, although with just 50 percent of the vote.

MAJOR INDUSTRY

Chemicals, lumber, manufacturing, retail, coal, telephone call centers

CITIES

Charleston, 53,421; Martinsburg, 14,972; South Charleston, 13,390

NOTABLE

The Toyota plant in Buffalo was the company's first automatic transmission production facility outside of Japan.

Rep. Nick J. Rahall II (D)

CAPITOL OFFICE
225-3452
nrahall@mail.house.gov
www.rahall.house.gov
2307 Rayburn 20515-4803; fax 225-9061

COMMITTEES
Natural Resources - chairman
Transportation & Infrastructure

RESIDENCE
Beckley

BORN
May 20, 1949, Beckley, W.Va.

RELIGION
Presbyterian

FAMILY
Wife, Melinda Rahall; three children

EDUCATION
Duke U., B.A. 1971 (political science); George Washington U., attended 1972 (graduate studies)

CAREER
Broadcasting executive; travel agent; congressional aide

POLITICAL HIGHLIGHTS
No previous office

ELECTION RESULTS

2006 GENERAL		
Nick J. Rahall II (D)	92,413	69.4%
Kim Wolfe (R)	40,820	30.6%
2006 PRIMARY		
Nick J. Rahall II (D)		unopposed
2004 GENERAL		
Nick J. Rahall II (D)	142,682	65.2%
Rick Snuffer (R)	76,170	34.8%

PREVIOUS WINNING PERCENTAGES
2002 (70%); 2000 (91%); 1998 (87%); 1996 (100%); 1994 (64%); 1992 (66%); 1990 (52%); 1988 (61%); 1986 (71%); 1984 (67%); 1982 (81%); 1980 (77%); 1978 (100%); 1976 (46%)

Elected 1976; 16th term

Rahall was 27 when he first came to the House, and he has served for more than 30 years. His longevity has made him the chairman of one committee, and the second-ranking Democrat on another. He learned early that to stay in Congress he needs to meet the needs of his rural, coal-country constituents, and this he has done with steady commitment.

Rahall is out of step with many in his party. His voting record reflects his 3rd District residents; he and they are culturally conservative but strongly pro-labor and welcoming of government services and economic development. He opposes gun control, abortion and same-sex marriage.

Rahall has defined his congressional role for decades by his posts on the Natural Resources and the Transportation and Infrastructure committees. He is now chairman of Natural Resources and the No. 2 Democrat on Transportation. He said the committees give him "an oar in two streams: on one hand, building West Virginia's public works infrastructure; and on the other, preserving West Virginia's nature and most-abundant resources."

But he also has broader interests. The grandson of Lebanese immigrants, Rahall (RAY-haul) is a vocal opponent of both the Iraq War and U.S. policy toward Israel. He encourages closer ties with Arab countries, and early in the 110th Congress (2007-08) he joined Speaker Nancy Pelosi on a trip to Syria that was sharply criticized by the Bush administration because the group met with President Bashar Assad.

Rahall voted against the 2002 resolution authorizing the war in Iraq, and he continues to be critical of the White House's Middle East strategy. He supports a timetable for withdrawal from Iraq, saying "our troops will not be there forever to babysit a civil war." But Rahall has found few in the House who will join with him in his position on Israel and Lebanon. He was one of only eight lawmakers who opposed a resolution expressing unconditional support for Israel in its 2006 conflict with the Lebanese Hezbollah group. "Israel is our ally," he told The Associated Press. "Where I have a problem is when we give an ally an unconditional blank check."

Rahall also opposes most free-trade legislation, inspired by his interest in protecting jobs in his economically hard-pressed district. He voted against the 2005 Central American Free Trade Agreement, and said he wants to be sure that the rights of labor are protected under future trade agreements.

In 2006, Rahall and the rest of the state delegation grew concerned about labor conditions in West Virginia's own mines after accidents in the Sago and Aracoma mines killed 14 miners. Rahall supported mine safety legislation that cleared in the 109th Congress (2005-06), which included raised fines for safety violations, required wireless communications equipment and tracking devices in all underground mines, and established grants for new mine safety technology. He blamed budget and personnel cuts at the Mine Safety and Health Administration during President Bush's first term for lax enforcement of mine safety laws. "The entire history of mine laws has been written in the blood of coal miners — it always takes a disaster to wake us up," he said.

Rahall not only wants to keep coal mines safe, he wants to keep them open. He has championed the development of large-scale coal-to-liquid fuel technology, which he says could help the country move toward energy independence. While some environmentalists argue against investing in a fuel that would continue to produce carbon emissions, Rahall contends that a cleaner, more efficient technology is possible with more investment. "Coal is our most abundant natural resource, enough to last for several hundred years," Rahall said. "The wind doesn't always blow, the sun doesn't always shine. While I support those as well, they can't do it alone. Coal will always be with us."

Inspired in part by ever-increasing oil prices in 2006, Rahall has fought against subsidies given to the oil industry. He won an early victory in the 110th Congress when the House passed a measure he sponsored to rescind billions of dollars in tax breaks for oil companies. The recouped funds would be directed toward alternative energy programs.

He also has opposed Republican and Bush administration efforts to overhaul the Endangered Species Act by making it harder to add new species to the list of endangered animals and plants. As chairman of Natural Resources, he said in early 2007 that he would support adding a provision to the Interior-Environment appropriations bill to block regulatory changes. "That type of dismantling of the [Endangered Species Act], that was attempted in the past and sounds like is being attempted in a backdoor fashion by this administration, needs to stop," Rahall said.

Rahall continues to be successful in securing federal largess for his state, particularly from his spot on the Transportation panel. He has been involved in drafting every highway bill for the past 30 years, and in the 2004 reauthorization, he procured more than $2 billion in infrastructure projects for his state. He also helped land $189 million in federal funding for a medium-security prison to be built in his district.

Rahall comes from an affluent West Virginia family that owns broadcasting properties. After graduating from Duke University, he was an aide to Democratic Sen. Robert C. Byrd of West Virginia before going home to work in the family businesses.

His chance to run for office came in 1976, when Democratic Rep. Ken Hechler ran for governor. Rahall, then 27, spent family money on a media campaign none of his foes could match, and won the nomination with 37 percent of the vote. After the primary, Hechler, who lost the governor's race, mounted an unsuccessful write-in drive to keep his House seat.

Rahall's only re-election difficulties have come at times his personal behavior was an issue. He racked up gambling debts in the mid-1980s, got divorced (he remarried in 2005), took many trips financed by taxpayers or lobbyists and pleaded guilty to alcohol-related reckless driving charges. The closest call of his entire congressional career came in 1990, when he won by just 4 percentage points against a state representative he had trounced two years earlier. In 2006, his opponent tried to make his pro-Arab stance an issue, but he still won by nearly 40 points.

KEY VOTES

2006

- No Stop broadband companies from favoring select Internet traffic
- No Affirm U.S. commitment to war in Iraq and reject setting a withdrawal date for troops
- No Repeal requirement for bilingual ballots at the polls
- Yes Permit U.S. sale of civilian nuclear technology to India
- Yes Build a 700-mile fence on the U.S.-Mexico border to curb illegal crossings
- No Permit warrantless wiretaps of suspected terrorists

2005

- ? Intervene in the life-support case of Terri Schiavo
- No Lift President Bush's restrictions on stem cell research funding
- Yes Prohibit FBI access to library and bookstore records
- No Approve free-trade pact with five Central American countries
- Yes Pass energy policy overhaul favored by President Bush emphasizing domestic oil and gas production
- No End mandatory preservation of habitat of endangered animal and plant species
- Yes Ban torture of prisoners in U.S. custody

CQ VOTE STUDIES

	PARTY UNITY		PRESIDENTIAL SUPPORT	
	Support	Oppose	Support	Oppose
2006	82%	18%	47%	53%
2005	87%	13%	33%	67%
2004	87%	13%	45%	55%
2003	89%	11%	35%	65%
2002	88%	12%	28%	72%

INTEREST GROUPS

	AFL-CIO	ADA	CCUS	ACU
2006	93%	65%	47%	48%
2005	93%	90%	56%	44%
2004	86%	75%	52%	28%
2003	100%	85%	30%	44%
2002	100%	80%	40%	24%

WEST VIRGINIA 3

South — Huntington, Beckley

The 3rd is a largely rural region that takes in the state's southern counties, sharing borders with Virginia, Kentucky and Ohio. Known as the "coal district," it is home to five of the state's 10 leading coal-producing counties, including the top producer, Boone County.

The last 20 years have been hard on the 3rd. As the coal industry mechanized production, the need for manpower was sharply reduced. Unemployment rates have declined since 1996, but remain higher than the national average. These struggles combined with persistent pockets of Appalachian poverty to give the district the third-lowest median income in the nation as of the last census, at slightly more than $25,600.

The 3rd attracts visitors with its ski resorts, whitewater rafting and The Greenbrier, a luxury resort hotel in White Sulphur Springs that hosts congressional party retreats. Raleigh County is home to Tamarack, a state and private cultural center featuring in-house artisans, live music, regional cuisine and retail shopping.

Huntington, by far the district's largest city and home to Marshall University, is cushioned by its location on the Ohio River and a diversified economy of tobacco growers as well as oil and steel companies.

Despite a continued Democratic lead in party registration and an overall district-wide preference for Democrats elsewhere on the ballot, George W. Bush made major inroads here in the last two presidential elections. He lost the 3rd by just 4 percentage points in 2000, but won the district in 2004 with 53 percent of the vote. Raleigh County is one of the the most Republican parts of the 3rd, but voters, especially those in the city of Beckley, elect a fair number of Democrats, often because many run unopposed. Still, Raleigh was Bush's best 2004 county in the 3rd, giving him 61 percent of the vote.

MAJOR INDUSTRY

Coal, wood products, tourism

CITIES

Huntington, 51,475; Beckley, 17,254; Bluefield, 11,451

NOTABLE

The New River Gorge Bridge, north of Fayetteville in Fayette County, is the second-longest steel-arch bridge in the world and the second-highest bridge in the United States.

WISCONSIN

Gov. James E. Doyle (D)

First elected: 2002
Length of term: 4 years
Term expires: 1/11
Salary: $137,094
Phone: (608) 266-1212

Residence: Madison
Born: Nov. 23, 1945; Washington, D.C.
Religion: Roman Catholic
Family: Wife, Jessica Laird Doyle; two children
Education: Stanford U., attended 1963-66; U. of Wisconsin, B.A. 1967 (history); Harvard U., J.D. 1972
Career: Lawyer; Peace Corps volunteer
Political highlights: Dane County district attorney, 1977-82; Wis. attorney general, 1991-2003

Election results:

2006 GENERAL		
James E. Doyle (D)	1,139,115	52.7%
Mark Green (R)	979,427	45.3%
Nelson Eisman (WG)	40,709	1.9%

Lt. Gov. Barbara Lawton (D)

First elected: 2002
Length of term: 4 years
Term expires: 1/11
Salary: $72,394
Phone: (608) 266-3516

LEGISLATURE

General Assembly: 10 floor periods of varying lengths over a 2-year session

Senate: 33 members, 4-year terms
2007 ratios: 18 D, 15 R; 25 men, 8 women
Salary: $47,413
Phone: (608) 266-2517

Assembly: 99 members, 2-year terms
2007 ratios: 52 R, 47 D; 77 men, 22 women
Salary: $47,413
Phone: (608) 266-1501

TERM LIMITS

Governor: No
Senate: No
Assembly: No

URBAN STATISTICS

CITY	POPULATION
Milwaukee	596,974
Madison	208,054
Green Bay	102,313
Kenosha	90,352
Racine	81,855

REGISTERED VOTERS

Voters do not register by party.

POPULATION

2006 population (est.)	5,556,506
2000 population	5,363,675
1990 population	4,891,769
Percent change (1990-2000)	+9.6%
Rank among states (2006)	20
Median age	36
Born in state	73.4%
Foreign born	3.6%
Violent crime rate	237/100,000
Poverty level	8.7%
Federal workers	29,286
Military	18,937

ELECTIONS

STATE ELECTION OFFICIAL
(608) 266-8005
DEMOCRATIC PARTY
(608) 255-5172
REPUBLICAN PARTY
(608) 257-4765

MISCELLANEOUS

Web: www.wisconsin.gov
Capital: Madison

U.S. CONGRESS

Senate: 2 Democrats
House: 5 Democrats, 3 Republicans

2000 Census Statistics by District

DIST.	2004 VOTE FOR PRESIDENT BUSH	KERRY	WHITE	BLACK	ASIAN	HISP	MEDIAN INCOME	WHITE COLLAR	BLUE COLLAR	SERVICE INDUSTRY	OVER 64	UNDER 18	COLLEGE EDUCATION	RURAL	SQ. MILES
1	53%	46%	87%	5%	1%	6%	$50,372	57%	30%	13%	12%	26%	22%	16%	1,680
2	37	62	89	4	2	3	$46,979	64	23	14	11	23	32	24	3,511
3	48	51	96	0	1	1	$40,006	53	31	16	13	25	20	57	13,565
4	30	69	50	33	3	11	$33,121	54	28	18	11	28	18	0	112
5	63	36	94	1	2	2	$58,594	68	22	10	14	25	35	15	1,273
6	56	42	94	1	1	2	$44,242	49	37	14	14	25	17	39	5,641
7	49	50	95	0	1	1	$39,026	52	34	15	15	25	17	58	18,787
8	55	44	92	1	1	2	$43,274	54	33	14	13	26	19	44	9,740
STATE	49	50	87	6	2	4	$43,791	57	29	14	13	26	22	32	54,310
U.S.	50.7	48.3	69	12	4	13	$41,994	60	25	15	12	26	24	21	3,537,438

Douglas
Bayfield
Iron
Ashland
Vilas
Burnett
Washburn
Sawyer
Price
Oneida
Florence
Forest
Polk
Barron
Rusk
7
Marinette
Lincoln
Langlade
8
Taylor
St. Croix
Chippewa
Menominee
Oconto
Dunn
Marathon
Eau Claire
Shawano
Pierce
Door
Pepin
Eau Claire
Clark
Kewaunee
Green Bay
Wood
Portage
Waupaca
Buffalo
3
Outagamie
Brown
Jackson
Trempealeau
Manitowoc
Waushara
Winnebago
Calumet
Adams
Oshkosh
Lake Winnebago
La Crosse
Monroe
Juneau
Marquette
Green Lake
Fond du Lac
Sheboygan
6
Vernon
Columbia
Dodge
Ozaukee
Sauk
Washington
Richland
Crawford
5
4
Madison
Waukesha
Milwaukee
Waukesha
Iowa
2
Grant
Dane
Jefferson
Milwaukee
Racine
1
Racine
Lafayette
Green
Rock
Walworth
Kenosha
Kenosha

Sen. Herb Kohl (D)

CAPITOL OFFICE
224-5653
kohl.senate.gov
330 Hart 20510-4903; fax 224-9787

COMMITTEES
Appropriations
(Agriculture - chairman)
Judiciary
(Antitrust, Competition Policy & Consumer Rights - chairman)
Special Aging - chairman

RESIDENCE
Milwaukee

BORN
Feb. 7, 1935, Milwaukee, Wis.

RELIGION
Jewish

FAMILY
Single

EDUCATION
U. of Wisconsin, B.A. 1956; Harvard U., M.B.A. 1958

MILITARY SERVICE
Army Reserve, 1958-64

CAREER
Professional basketball team owner; department and grocery store owner

POLITICAL HIGHLIGHTS
Wis. Democratic Party chairman, 1975-77

ELECTION RESULTS

2006 GENERAL		
Herb Kohl (D)	1,439,214	67.3%
Robert Gerald Lorge (R)	630,299	29.5%
Rae Vogeler (WG)	42,434	2.0%
Ben J. Glatzel (I)	25,096	1.2%
2006 PRIMARY		
Herb Kohl (D)	308,178	85.7%
Ben Masel (D)	51,245	14.2%

PREVIOUS WINNING PERCENTAGES
2000 (62%); 1994 (58%); 1988 (52%)

Elected 1988; 4th term

A quiet, unassuming multimillionaire with little interest in the limelight, Kohl is a rare beast in the political arena. Paradoxically, his massive personal wealth helps him maintain the support of Wisconsin's liberal-trending voters. He finances his own campaigns and doesn't take money from special interests; his slogan in every campaign has been the same — "Nobody's senator but yours."

In his fourth term, Kohl is a fixture in his state and in the Senate, where he chairs the Special Aging Committee in the 110th Congress (2007-08), as well as an Appropriations subcommittee and a Judiciary subcommittee. He uses his posts and his experience to look after his state's interests. He has learned how to campaign and how to deal with the media. The self-made man, whose name is on department stores across the nation, says his initial run for office was a strange experience for a businessman unaccustomed to making public appearances.

"That was a difficult step for me to take, becoming a public figure," Kohl said in a 2007 interview. It turned out his discomfort helped him connect with Wisconsin voters "because they saw that I wasn't a cold politician. . . . People still see me as a non-politician who's in public service."

Kohl displayed his independence from corporate influence early in 2007, taking on the pharmaceutical industry. The Judiciary Committee approved a bill he sponsored to stop makers of brand-name drugs from making deals with would-be competitors to delay the market entrance of cheaper generic versions of their products. He tucked a provision into a war funding bill to extend Wisconsin's special SeniorCare prescription drug program, which the Bush administration wanted to roll into Medicare. And he was seeking more money to help the Food and Drug Administration review and approve generic drugs faster. "We can have a huge impact on the cost of drugs in this country . . . and it does not reduce the quality of health care one iota," Kohl said.

A moderate who sees partisanship as the biggest obstacle to legislating, Kohl is not afraid to cross the party aisle. Concerned about the explosion of civil litigation, in 2005 he supported a Republican bill making it harder to bring class action lawsuits. He was one of 14 Democrats backing another measure that year to shield gun manufacturers and dealers from liability for gun violence. In 2006, he was one of 13 Democrats voting to waive Budget Act objections to a GOP-sponsored bill creating a trust fund to compensate victims of asbestos exposure. Democrats and labor unions considered the fund too small to compensate victims adequately.

Kohl was one of only a dozen Democrats to vote for President Bush's $1.35 trillion tax cut in 2001 and one of 15 Democrats to back the initial version of the GOP's spending blueprint for the year. But in 2003, he voted against slashing tax rates on dividends and capital gains. And in 2006, he opposed Republican efforts to repeal the federal estate tax.

A senior member of the Appropriations Committee, Kohl is chairman of its Agriculture Subcommittee. He has leveraged his position on that panel to help his state's dairy farmers, who are both influential politically and dependent on federal spending. Early in the 110th Congress, Kohl attached a one-month extension of the Milk Income Loss Contract to a supplemental spending bill. The extension was designed to ensure that the costs of the dairy subsidies were built into the budget baseline for the rewrite of the farm bill due by September 2007. Kohl helped create the MILC program in 2002 to replace an even more controversial payment system, and he knows it faces considerable peril.

Kohl also has a personal tie to agriculture. Since the mid-1970s, he has owned a horse and cattle ranch near Jackson, Wyo. "I get a lot of renewal out there, spiritual and physical," Kohl told the Milwaukee Journal Sentinel in 2006. "It's a beautiful place, and I built it, so I have the feeling of creating something very special."

Unlike many in Congress, Kohl doesn't yearn for higher office or worry about a personal legacy. "It's not something that I spend a lot of time thinking about," he said. "I hope when I'm finished people say, 'he was always there for us, he was always accessible.'" He has routinely rejected pay raises since he entered the Senate.

On the Judiciary panel, Kohl carefully assessed Bush's two Supreme Court nominees. He voted in 2005 to confirm Chief Justice John G. Roberts Jr., but opposed confirmation of Justice Samuel A. Alito Jr in 2006.

As chairman of Judiciary's Competition, Antitrust Policy and Consumer Rights Subcommittee, Kohl labored in 2007 to block what he viewed as anti-competitive airline, satellite radio and oil industry mergers.

Kohl is aligned with most other Democrats on issues such as health care and education. He is a strong supporter of child nutrition programs and a champion of measures to encourage private companies to provide child care for their workers.

Kohl not only looks to direct federal dollars to education, he also allocates a portion of his considerable personal wealth to education-related endeavors. Kohl gave the University of Wisconsin, his alma mater, $25 million in 1995 to build a sports arena. And each year, his Herb Kohl Educational Foundation has awarded $1,000 grants to 100 teachers and their schools, and to high school seniors across Wisconsin. Started in 1990, the fund had awarded some $6 million by 2007.

Kohl's parents immigrated to the United States in the 1920s — his mother from Russia, his father from Poland. They opened a small food store in Milwaukee, where Kohl worked after school and on weekends. One of his childhood friends (and later his college roommate) was Bud Selig, who went on to become a wealthy car dealer, owner of the Milwaukee Brewers baseball team and commissioner of Major League Baseball.

After earning a master's degree in business from Harvard, Kohl returned home and, with his two brothers, set about expanding the family grocery business into a department store chain. There were more than 100 stores when the chain was sold in 1979.

Kohl, who has never married, decided in 1985 to buy the Milwaukee Bucks National Basketball Association franchise, primarily to keep the team in Milwaukee. "I thought it was a stupid investment," he later admitted, but he was a fan, and he saw the deal as "a combination of my own personal interest and public need." Kohl, the sole owner, purchased the team for $19 million. By 2007, Forbes magazine valued the team at $260 million.

Kohl's first public involvement in politics came in 1975 when Democratic Gov. Patrick Lucey asked him to chair the state Democratic Party. He did the job for two years, despite his discomfort with some of its public aspects.

In 1988, when Democrat William O. Proxmire stepped down after 31 years in the Senate, Democrats pressed an initially ambivalent Kohl to run. He had plenty of name recognition, and he spent nearly $7.5 million (most of it his own money) on the campaign. Kohl's total outlay was double the previous state record.

He won a three-way Democratic primary with 47 percent of the vote and defeated GOP state Sen. Susan Engeleiter by 4 percentage points in the fall. Kohl has won with comfortable margins ever since.

KEY VOTES

2006

- No Confirm Samuel A. Alito Jr. to the Supreme Court
- Yes Allow consideration of a bill to establish a $140 billion trust fund to compensate victims of asbestos exposure
- No Extend tax cuts for two years at a cost of $70 billion over five years
- Yes Overhaul immigration policy with border security, enforcement and guest worker program
- No Allow consideration of a bill to permanently repeal the estate tax
- Yes Urge President Bush to begin troop withdrawals from Iraq in 2006
- Yes Lift President Bush's restrictions on stem cell research funding
- No Authorize military tribunals for suspected terrorists

2005

- Yes Curb class action lawsuits by shifting them from state to federal courts
- Yes Allow confirmation vote on Priscilla R. Owen to the U.S. Court of Appeals for the 5th Circuit
- No Oppose mandatory emissions limits and block recognition of global warming as a threat
- No Approve free-trade pact with five Central American countries
- Yes Pass energy policy overhaul favored by President Bush emphasizing domestic oil and gas production
- Yes Shield gunmakers from lawsuits when their products are used in crimes
- Yes Ban torture of prisoners in U.S. custody
- No Renew 16 provisions of the Patriot Act
- No Allow final vote on opening the Arctic National Wildlife Refuge to oil and gas exploration

CQ VOTE STUDIES

	PARTY UNITY		PRESIDENTIAL SUPPORT	
	Support	Oppose	Support	Oppose
2006	91%	9%	57%	43%
2005	89%	11%	45%	55%
2004	95%	5%	66%	34%
2003	94%	6%	50%	50%
2002	84%	16%	79%	21%
2001	89%	11%	69%	31%
2000	87%	13%	79%	21%
1999	90%	10%	91%	9%
1998	87%	13%	86%	14%
1997	74%	26%	90%	10%

INTEREST GROUPS

	AFL-CIO	ADA	CCUS	ACU
2006	87%	90%	50%	16%
2005	86%	100%	67%	13%
2004	92%	100%	44%	4%
2003	100%	95%	35%	25%
2002	92%	85%	60%	15%
2001	88%	90%	54%	16%
2000	63%	85%	60%	20%
1999	78%	100%	41%	4%
1998	88%	85%	44%	4%
1997	29%	70%	80%	20%

Sen. Russ Feingold (D)

CAPITOL OFFICE
224-5323
feingold.senate.gov
506 Hart 20510-4904; fax 224-2725

COMMITTEES
Budget
Foreign Relations
(African Affairs - chairman)
Judiciary
(Constitution - chairman)
Select Intelligence

RESIDENCE
Middleton

BORN
March 2, 1953, Janesville, Wis.

RELIGION
Jewish

FAMILY
Divorced; two children

EDUCATION
U. of Wisconsin, B.A. 1975 (history & political science); Oxford U., B.A. 1977 (Rhodes scholar); Harvard U., J.D. 1979

CAREER
Lawyer

POLITICAL HIGHLIGHTS
Wis. Senate, 1983-93

ELECTION RESULTS

2004 GENERAL

Russ Feingold (D)	1,632,697	55.4%
Tim Michels (R)	1,301,183	44.1%

2004 PRIMARY

Russ Feingold (D)	unopposed

PREVIOUS WINNING PERCENTAGES
1998 (51%); 1992 (53%)

Elected 1992; 3rd term

Feingold finally has both company and clout in his once-lonely campaigns to rein in the Bush administration's war in Iraq and to combat what he sees as dangerous incursions on civil liberties undertaken in the name of fighting terrorism.

In 2002, Feingold (FINE-gold) voted against authorizing President Bush to use force in Iraq. Only 20 other Democrats and one independent joined him then, and even fewer supported his subsequent calls for a deadline for withdrawing U.S. troops. In mid-2006, just 13 senators, including Feingold, voted for an amendment by Massachusetts Democrat John Kerry mandating the withdrawal of U.S. troops from Iraq by the following summer.

By April 2007, the political climate had changed dramatically. Feingold's demand for a withdrawal timetable was included in a war funding bill that passed Congress. Bush vetoed the bill because of the deadline provision.

Six weeks after the Sept. 11 terrorist attacks, legislation giving the Bush administration sweeping new powers to investigate, detain and prosecute suspected terrorists sailed through Congress. Many Democrats believed, as Feingold did, that the Patriot Act threatened civil liberties of everyday Americans. But they voted for it anyway for the sake of national unity in a time of crisis. Feingold cast the only no vote in the Senate.

In 2005, Feingold was no longer alone. Four GOP senators joined almost all of the chamber's Democrats in a filibuster that stalled a reauthorization of the Patriot Act; they insisted on a rewrite to better protect civil liberties. The revised bill eventually passed in 2006, but it still didn't satisfy Feingold. He called the changes a "fig leaf" and again voted no, joined this time by nine other senators.

In the 110th Congress (2007-08), Feingold chairs the Senate Judiciary Committee's Constitution Subcommittee, which gives him a strong say on civil liberties issues. He quickly moved to strengthen privacy protections, advancing a bill he sponsored to safeguard personal information collected and stored in government databases.

Encouraged by liberal party activists, the Wisconsin senator considered running for president in 2008, but he announced in late 2006 that he would not join the crowded Democratic field.

In his third term, Feingold is perhaps best known for a 2002 campaign finance overhaul that informally bears his name, along with that of Republican Sen. John McCain of Arizona. The two won enactment of the law after years of effort, overcoming the strenuous objections of leaders of both parties. The Supreme Court subsequently upheld the law's major provisions, which set a number of new rules and banned "soft money," unregulated big-dollar donations to parties that were swamping political contests.

Feingold continues to press for added campaign finance and lobbying restrictions. He and McCain introduced a bill to curb so-called 527 groups, which they say have become a channel for the kind of large contributions political parties can no longer accept. In 2006 and again in 2007, the two also pushed to crack down on lobbyists and toughen Senate ethics rules.

Feingold is not particularly popular with his colleagues. Other senators tend to see him as sanctimonious and resent the media attention he attracts. Judiciary Committee Chairman Arlen Specter of Pennsylvania exploded when Feingold walked out of a 2006 meeting at which senators were voting on a proposed constitutional amendment to ban same-sex marriage. Feingold objected to holding the meeting in a room off the Senate chamber that was open to the press but not to the general public. "I do not need to be lectured by you," Specter snapped. "We have a quorum here and if you want to leave, good riddance." Feingold retorted, "I enjoyed your lecture, too. See ya, Mr. Chairman."

His stubbornness can tie up the Senate, a source of aggravation for his colleagues. In the final hours before Congress adjourned in 1999, Feingold and a handful of other Midwesterners fought provisions in a session-ending catchall spending measure that they claimed were unfair to home-state dairy interests. Feingold stalked the Senate floor with books of cheese recipes, among other potential filibuster reading materials, threatening a days-long delay in adjournment. He gave up only after overwhelmingly losing a test vote.

Feingold is a longtime proponent of a balanced federal budget. A member of the Budget Committee, he resolutely works to stop deficit spending. He supported the ill-fated line-item veto, and in 1998 he voted to sustain President Bill Clinton's veto of a list of military construction projects even though a $4 million training facility in Milwaukee was on the list. He has fought to restore pay-as-you-go budget rules requiring offsets for tax cuts or new spending. And he regularly joins McCain and Republican Tom Coburn of Oklahoma in voting to delete earmarks, funding for members' pet home-state projects.

Although he is liberal on most issues, he is not always predictable. When most Democrats in 2001 opposed the nomination of Missouri Sen. John Ashcroft for attorney general because of his ultra-conservative views, Feingold voted yes in committee and on the floor. His most famous break with his party came in 1999, when he was the only Democratic senator to vote against a proposal to dismiss the impeachment charges against Clinton. Feingold did, however, vote to acquit Clinton, saying the charges were not important enough to warrant removal from office.

Feingold's paternal grandfather came from Russia, landing at Ellis Island and moving to Janesville, Wis., in 1917, when the senator's father was 5 years old. Feingold says there were only 12 Jewish students in his high school, "and most of those were my relatives." His father, Leon, was an attorney; his mother, Sylvia, worked at a title company. Their family, he once told C-SPAN, regularly violated the old dinner-table dictum about avoiding discussions about religion and politics. "I'm a senator, and my little sister is the first woman rabbi in Wisconsin history," he said. "That's what happens when you talk about religion and politics at the table."

Elected to the state Senate in 1982, he entered the U.S. Senate primary a decade later. He scored a long-shot victory over better-known rivals and then knocked off incumbent GOP Sen. Bob Kasten. In the course of the campaign, he ran a series of humorous, offbeat television ads. One showed him using the back of his left hand as a map of his travels across Wisconsin, boasting he knew the state like the back of his hand. Another showed him opening an empty closet, assuring viewers, "No skeletons."

Six years later, Feingold's tendency to buck the system nearly cost him his seat. He began his 1998 re-election campaign favored to beat GOP Rep. Mark W. Neumann. The McCain-Feingold restrictions were not yet law, but Feingold decided to play by the bill's rules anyway. He declined most forms of outside money, and asked national Democrats not to run ads in his behalf paid for with the kind of money his bill would limit. Feingold barely held on, beating the well-financed Neumann by just 2 percentage points.

In 2004, however, Feingold faced a weaker opponent, construction executive Tim Michels, and had none of the fundraising troubles of his first two campaigns. This time, Feingold won easily, defeating Michels by 11 points.

KEY VOTES

2006

No Confirm Samuel A. Alito Jr. to the Supreme Court

No Allow consideration of a bill to establish a $140 billion trust fund to compensate victims of asbestos exposure

No Extend tax cuts for two years at a cost of $70 billion over five years

Yes Overhaul immigration policy with border security, enforcement and guest worker program

No Allow consideration of a bill to permanently repeal the estate tax

Yes Urge President Bush to begin troop withdrawals from Iraq in 2006

Yes Lift President Bush's restrictions on stem cell research funding

No Authorize military tribunals for suspected terrorists

2005

No Curb class action lawsuits by shifting them from state to federal courts

No Allow confirmation vote on Priscilla R. Owen to the U.S. Court of Appeals for the 5th Circuit

No Oppose mandatory emissions limits and block recognition of global warming as a threat

No Approve free-trade pact with five Central American countries

No Pass energy policy overhaul favored by President Bush emphasizing domestic oil and gas production

No Shield gunmakers from lawsuits when their products are used in crimes

Yes Ban torture of prisoners in U.S. custody

No Renew 16 provisions of the Patriot Act

No Allow final vote on opening the Arctic National Wildlife Refuge to oil and gas exploration

CQ VOTE STUDIES

	PARTY UNITY		PRESIDENTIAL SUPPORT	
	Support	Oppose	Support	Oppose
2006	92%	8%	47%	53%
2005	95%	5%	37%	63%
2004	95%	5%	66%	34%
2003	93%	7%	53%	47%
2002	84%	16%	67%	33%
2001	89%	11%	61%	39%
2000	92%	8%	90%	10%
1999	88%	12%	82%	18%
1998	86%	14%	83%	17%
1997	86%	14%	86%	14%

INTEREST GROUPS

	AFL-CIO	ADA	CCUS	ACU
2006	93%	100%	25%	8%
2005	86%	100%	17%	13%
2004	92%	100%	35%	8%
2003	100%	95%	26%	25%
2002	92%	90%	20%	5%
2001	94%	95%	29%	20%
2000	88%	100%	20%	8%
1999	100%	100%	24%	8%
1998	100%	90%	28%	12%
1997	86%	95%	20%	8%

Rep. Paul D. Ryan (R)

CAPITOL OFFICE
225-3031
www.house.gov/ryan
1113 Longworth 20515-4901; fax 225-3393

COMMITTEES
Budget - ranking member
Ways & Means

RESIDENCE
Janesville

BORN
Jan. 29, 1970, Janesville, Wis.

RELIGION
Roman Catholic

FAMILY
Wife, Janna Ryan; three children

EDUCATION
Miami U. (Ohio), B.A. 1992 (political science & economics)

CAREER
Congressional aide; economic policy analyst

POLITICAL HIGHLIGHTS
No previous office

ELECTION RESULTS

2006 GENERAL		
Paul D. Ryan (R)	161,320	62.6%
Jeffrey C. Thomas (D)	95,761	37.2%
2006 PRIMARY		
Paul D. Ryan (R)		unopposed
2004 GENERAL		
Paul D. Ryan (R)	233,372	65.4%
Jeffrey C. Thomas (D)	116,250	32.6%
Norman Aulabaugh (I)	4,252	1.2%

PREVIOUS WINNING PERCENTAGES
2002 (67%); 2000 (67%); 1998 (57%)

Elected 1998; 5th term

Ryan is a leader in an emerging group of GOP lawmakers known as "growth hawks," advocates of the supply-side theory that lower taxes help spur economic activity, producing greater prosperity for individuals and more revenue for the government.

Ryan is both articulate and partisan. A former legislative aide, he has a direct speaking style similar to that of his two mentors, Jack F. Kemp and William J. Bennett, former Republican Cabinet secretaries and co-founders of Empower America, a conservative think tank.

He gained a seat on the Budget Committee in 2005 and in the 110th Congress (2007-08) he became the panel's ranking Republican. He also sits on the tax-writing Ways and Means Committee and its Social Security Subcommittee. As the top Budget Republican, he offered the GOP alternative to the Democrats' fiscal 2008 budget resolution. Ryan called the Democrats' budget irresponsible for failing to acknowledge a "spending tidal wave" from entitlement programs for the baby boom generation.

The Republican plan targeted a $99 billion surplus in fiscal 2012 largely by counting unchecked revenue from the alternative minimum tax, which was originally created to prevent wealthy taxpayers from using deductions and credits to eliminate tax liability. The AMT was not indexed for inflation and gradually has expanded to include more middle-class taxpayers.

Ryan wanted to change the budget rules in 2004, when the House considered but defeated legislation to require Congress to stick to its budget or risk across-the-board spending cuts. The measure would have revived statutory caps on appropriations and imposed pay-as-you-go rules requiring offsets for any increases in mandatory spending. "Right now, the budget process is broken," Ryan said. The House rejected an amendment to the bill offered by Ryan and Texas Democrat Charles W. Stenholm to allow the president to force Congress to vote on his recommendations to eliminate earmarked projects from appropriations bills.

But Ryan was back in 2006, sponsoring a measure he helped steer through the House to permit the president to target individual spending items in appropriations bills that reached his desk. The proposed cuts would have to go to Congress for an up-or-down vote, without amendment, within 14 legislative days. The measure was backed by nearly three dozen Democrats in addition to 212 Republicans, but it stalled in the Senate.

Like other members of the conservative Republican Study Committee, Ryan is a sharp critic of member earmarks. In March 2007, he voted against a $124.3 billion supplemental spending bill to pay for military operations in Iraq and Afghanistan. Ryan said that the bill became a vehicle for billions of dollars in pork barrel projects, such as money for spinach farmers and citrus producers. The bill passed the House, 218-212.

He also voted in 2004 against a $283.2 billion, six-year highway and mass transit bill, criticizing the number of earmarked projects it contained. But he has used his seat on Ways and Means to take care of some home-state interests, such as protecting Wisconsin's welfare system. An avid bow hunter, he helped get a provision into the 2004 corporate tax law simplifying excise taxes on youth bows and arrow accessories. He said it equalized tax treatment by closing a loophole that had allowed arrows assembled outside the United States to avoid the excise tax imposed on wholly domestic products.

Ryan was a vocal proponent of President Bush's plan to overhaul the

Social Security system by allowing creation of private investment accounts. "If we stick to the status quo, down the road we will face the awful choice between cutting benefits, raising taxes or boundless borrowing," he said. He has offered his own version, allowing workers to choose whether to invest part of their payroll taxes in personal accounts or remain in the traditional Social Security system. Those sticking with the traditional system would not face benefit cuts, as they would under Bush's plan.

Ryan, the youngest of four children, was just 16 and the only child still at home when his lawyer father died. His mother used Social Security survivor's benefits to help pay for his college education. "At a very, very difficult time in our lives, Social Security was there for us," Ryan said.

Bush's proposals for Social Security are not intended to change benefits paid to the disabled and children whose parents have died. But Democrats contend that money needed to finance the transition to a system of private accounts would drain the pool of funds available to pay those benefits.

Ryan is strongly interested in health care, advocating a consumer-driven system built on competition among providers. But first, he says, improved health information technology and more transparency are needed to give consumers clear, accurate information about costs and quality of doctors, hospitals and other health care providers.

Ryan says he "wasn't one of these guys who thought from second grade on that he wanted to run for Congress." But after college, he took a job as an aide to Wisconsin GOP Sen. Bob Kasten, in his personal office and on the Small Business Committee. After a stint at Empower America, Ryan was a top aide for Kansas Republican Sam Brownback in the House and Senate. "I got really addicted to public service," he said.

After five years in Washington, he "got very homesick" and returned to Wisconsin to work in his family's earth-moving and construction business. When GOP Rep. Mark W. Neumann decided in late 1997 to run for the Senate, Ryan was persuaded to run for the open seat. His opponent in November was Democrat Lydia Spottswood, a former Kenosha City Council president who nearly beat Neumann in 1996. Ryan proved a superior campaigner — he earned the nickname "robocandidate" — and won by more than 27,000 votes, a surprisingly large margin given that the previous three races in the district had been won by margins of 4,000 votes or fewer.

In 2000, he won with more than 66 percent of the vote. Redistricting after the 2000 census gave him a GOP-leaning district. He won with better than 65 percent in both 2002 and 2004, and by 63 percent in 2006. He beat the same opponent, Democratic doctor Jeffrey C. Thomas, in all four re-elections.

KEY VOTES

2006

No Stop broadband companies from favoring select Internet traffic
Yes Affirm U.S. commitment to war in Iraq and reject setting a withdrawal date for troops
Yes Repeal requirement for bilingual ballots at the polls
Yes Permit U.S. sale of civilian nuclear technology to India
Yes Build a 700-mile fence on the U.S.-Mexico border to curb illegal crossings
Yes Permit warrantless wiretaps of suspected terrorists

2005

Yes Intervene in the life-support case of Terri Schiavo
No Lift President Bush's restrictions on stem cell research funding
No Prohibit FBI access to library and bookstore records
Yes Approve free-trade pact with five Central American countries
Yes Pass energy policy overhaul favored by President Bush emphasizing domestic oil and gas production
Yes End mandatory preservation of habitat of endangered animal and plant species
Yes Ban torture of prisoners in U.S. custody

CQ VOTE STUDIES

	PARTY UNITY		PRESIDENTIAL SUPPORT	
	Support	Oppose	Support	Oppose
2006	94%	6%	93%	7%
2005	94%	6%	80%	20%
2004	94%	6%	79%	21%
2003	94%	6%	90%	10%
2002	92%	8%	82%	18%

INTEREST GROUPS

	AFL-CIO	ADA	CCUS	ACU
2006	14%	0%	100%	92%
2005	13%	0%	89%	96%
2004	20%	20%	90%	92%
2003	7%	20%	93%	84%
2002	13%	0%	100%	96%

WISCONSIN 1
Southeast – Kenosha, Racine

From the wealthy Milwaukee suburbs on the coast of Lake Michigan to the center of Rock County, the 1st blends rural communities with some of the state's largest industrial areas. The district's two largest cities are sandwiched between Milwaukee and Chicago along the lake: Racine, originally settled by Danish immigrants; and Kenosha, with a large Italian-American community.

Kenosha and Walworth counties, which are major manufacturing areas, are experiencing faster population growth than the state's average. Much of this expansion is due to new residents who commute to Milwaukee or Chicago, both less than an hour's drive away, who are attracted by lower housing prices and cheaper living. Abbott, an Illinois-based pharmaceutical company, is the biggest employer in the area.

Racine, still recovering from the manufacturing recession that began in 2000, has some of the state's highest unemployment rates. But SC Johnson, the consumer products manufacturer, has continued to have a major presence in the area. On the other side of the district, the General Motors plant in Janesville was spared recent downsizing, and the company has invested millions of dollars to upgrade the 1st's plant for production of newer SUV models.

Resorts catering to wealthy vacationers from nearby Chicago ring Lake Geneva and Lake Delavan in Walworth County, while Kenosha lures gamblers with Dairyland Greyhound Park, a large dog-racing track.

The district has a slight Republican lean, but is about evenly split between the two parties: Of the six counties wholly or partly in the 1st, two are strongly Democratic (Kenosha and Rock), two are strongly Republican (Walworth and Waukesha) and two are highly competitive (Racine and Milwaukee). Overall, George W. Bush captured 53 percent of the 1st's presidential vote in 2004.

MAJOR INDUSTRY

Automotive manufacturing, heavy machine manufacturing, agriculture

CITIES

Kenosha, 90,352; Racine, 81,855; Janesville (pt.), 59,474; Greenfield, 35,476

NOTABLE

Racine hosts the Salmon-A-Rama annual fishing contest; C. Latham Sholes invented the typewriter in Kenosha.

Rep. Tammy Baldwin (D)

CAPITOL OFFICE
225-2906
tammybaldwin.house.gov
2446 Rayburn 20515-4902; fax 225-6942

COMMITTEES
Energy & Commerce
Judiciary

RESIDENCE
Madison

BORN
Feb. 11, 1962, Madison, Wis.

RELIGION
Unspecified

FAMILY
Partner, Lauren Azar

EDUCATION
Smith College, A.B. 1984 (math & government); U. of Wisconsin, J.D. 1989

CAREER
Lawyer; public policy analyst

POLITICAL HIGHLIGHTS
Madison City Council, 1986; Dane County Board of Supervisors, 1986-94; Wis. Assembly, 1993-99

ELECTION RESULTS

2006 GENERAL		
Tammy Baldwin (D)	191,414	62.8%
Dave Magnum (R)	113,015	37.1%
2006 PRIMARY		
Tammy Baldwin (D)		unopposed
2004 GENERAL		
Tammy Baldwin (D)	251,637	63.3%
Dave Magnum (R)	145,810	36.7%

PREVIOUS WINNING PERCENTAGES
2002 (66%); 2000 (51%); 1998 (52%)

Elected 1998; 5th term

Born and reared in Madison, the hotbed of liberalism that dominates her district, Baldwin reflects the progressive views of her constituency and the passion for politics of her upbringing.

Her outlook was deeply influenced by her maternal grandparents, who raised her while her mother attended the University of Wisconsin and participated in various civil rights and anti-war demonstrations in the 1960s. Her grandfather, a biochemist, and grandmother, who worked at the costume lab at the university, lived through two world wars, the Depression and the attainment of women's suffrage. "Those experiences also informed their style of parenting — how important it was to be self-sufficient, to get a good education and to give back to one's community," Baldwin recalls.

She keeps a framed quote in her office from anthropologist Margaret Mead: "Never doubt that a small group of thoughtful, committed citizens can change the world. Indeed, it is the only thing that ever has."

Baldwin's commitment to elective office got off to a dubious start. In her official biography, under the heading, "If at First You Don't Succeed," she recalls: "In 1975, I ran for Student Council President at my middle school . . . AND LOST. In 1980, I competed for a chance to be my high school graduation speaker . . . AND LOST. And in 1983, I ran for class president at my college . . . AND LOST!"

Nevertheless, she became a political trailblazer. She was still in law school when she won her first election at age 24. She is the first woman elected to Congress from Wisconsin, and the first openly gay woman to be elected to Congress. She exchanged marriage vows in 1998 with Lauren Azar, a lawyer, though same-sex unions are not legal in Wisconsin.

In the 109th Congress (2005-06), she was granted a coveted seat on the Energy and Commerce Committee, an assignment she had long sought. In exchange, Baldwin gave up posts on the Judiciary and Budget committees. (She was able to regain the Judiciary seat in 2007.)

Health care issues, which fall under Energy and Commerce's broad jurisdiction, are Baldwin's top concern, although she is frustrated that the panel has failed to tackle the plight of roughly 46 million uninsured Americans. That and soaring health care costs are "staggering problems" that cry out for action, she says. She pushes Congress to provide universal health care coverage, and fights every GOP effort to reduce Medicare or Medicaid benefits.

Early in 2007, Baldwin watched President Bush sign into law her bill to reauthorize funding for a breast and cervical cancer screening program, as well as a bill that would expand benefits for veterans with impaired vision.

In the 110th Congress (2007-08), Baldwin is joining three House colleagues — Democrat Barney Frank of Massachusetts and Republicans Deborah Pryce of Ohio and Christopher Shays of Connecticut — in legislation to outlaw bias against homosexuals in most U.S. workplaces.

Baldwin's self-deprecating humor helps her connect on a personal level, especially with conservatives who frown on her lifestyle. She was a hit with her speech in 1999 at the annual congressional dinner in Washington. "I'm one of the first elected officials who represents a group historically discriminated against," Baldwin said. "A group that has been kept out of jobs, harassed at the workplace. A group that's been unfairly stereotyped and made the object of rude and base humor. Of course, I'm talking about blondes . . . especially blondes named Tammy."

A member of the Progressive Caucus, the most liberal faction in the House, Baldwin supports a minimum wage increase, expansion of Head Start and the Family and Medical Leave Act, and more social service spending. She opposed the Bush administration tax cuts, and she has been a vocal critic of what she sees as "an unprecedented amount of meddling in science" by administration political appointees in agencies ranging from NASA to the Centers for Disease Control and Prevention.

Baldwin typically sides with her party on defense and foreign policy issues. She was one of the first House Democrats to publicly oppose Bush's moves toward war with Iraq, nearly 10 months before Congress began debating a resolution sanctioning the use of military force. The administration, she said, was preparing to invade Iraq without having shown a clear link to the Sept. 11 terrorist attacks. She was one of 37 House members who cosponsored a resolution calling for an impeachment inquiry of Bush. In March 2007, she voted for a war funding bill that set a timeline for withdrawal of U.S. troops from Iraq.

But in 2006, she was one of just seven Democrats to vote for a bill — which narrowly passed — to require so-called 527 groups to comply with the same disclosure requirements and campaign finance laws that apply to political parties and political action committees.

She tends to parochial concerns, pressing for more federal funds for her district. She says that, in principle, she opposes earmarking, in which lawmakers slip special projects into spending bills for pet home-state projects. But as long as the practice continues, she says she wants Wisconsin to get its fair share. She opposed a 2004 free-trade agreement with Australia that could have hurt Wisconsin's dairy farmers. And when asked in 2004 what her toughest vote was, she quipped, "Any telecommunications bill that might deny my constituents access to Packer games."

While studying law at the University of Wisconsin, Baldwin in 1986 was appointed to the Madison City Council to fill a vacancy. Later that year, she won the first of four terms as a Dane County supervisor. In 1992, she was elected to the Wisconsin Assembly, where she served six years.

With her own impressive fundraising and help from EMILY's List, a political action committee that supports Democratic women candidates, Baldwin edged out two well-known opponents in the 1998 primary. She then beat former state Insurance Commissioner Josephine Musser by 6 percentage points. In 2000, she eked out a 3 percentage point victory over moderate Republican John Sharpless, a history professor. She won handily in the next three elections.

KEY VOTES

2006

Yes Stop broadband companies from favoring select Internet traffic

No Affirm U.S. commitment to war in Iraq and reject setting a withdrawal date for troops

No Repeal requirement for bilingual ballots at the polls

No Permit U.S. sale of civilian nuclear technology to India

No Build a 700-mile fence on the U.S.-Mexico border to curb illegal crossings

No Permit warrantless wiretaps of suspected terrorists

2005

No Intervene in the life-support case of Terri Schiavo

Yes Lift President Bush's restrictions on stem cell research funding

Yes Prohibit FBI access to library and bookstore records

No Approve free-trade pact with five Central American countries

No Pass energy policy overhaul favored by President Bush emphasizing domestic oil and gas production

No End mandatory preservation of habitat of endangered animal and plant species

Yes Ban torture of prisoners in U.S. custody

CQ VOTE STUDIES

	PARTY UNITY		PRESIDENTIAL SUPPORT	
	Support	Oppose	Support	Oppose
2006	99%	1%	13%	87%
2005	99%	1%	13%	87%
2004	98%	2%	32%	68%
2003	99%	1%	18%	82%
2002	99%	1%	23%	77%

INTEREST GROUPS

	AFL-CIO	ADA	CCUS	ACU
2006	100%	95%	20%	0%
2005	93%	100%	30%	0%
2004	100%	100%	29%	4%
2003	100%	100%	23%	12%
2002	100%	100%	25%	0%

WISCONSIN 2

South — Madison

Once described by former GOP Gov. Lee Dreyfus as "23 square miles surrounded by reality," Madison long has been Wisconsin's liberal centerpiece. Madison, Wisconsin's capital city, is the 2nd's political heart, although growing numbers of socially liberal, fiscally conservative young professionals in the suburbs may have a future impact.

Located on an isthmus between two of the five area lakes, Madison is known as one of the nation's most liveable cities, diminished only by its biting winters. The state university system's flagship campus has a major influence on the city, and an educated, white-collar population fuels the stable economy. University resources and expertise have boosted associated industries, such as biotechnology, and have kept unemployment levels low. Other large employers include state government, technology firms and light manufacturing companies.

Outside of Madison, the 2nd resembles most of the rest of Wisconsin. Dane County's dairy and beef farms have declined, but this is still the state's top agricultural region. Beloit, near the Illinois border, is a struggling blue-collar manufacturing city. Tourists are lured to the district by New Glarus, touted as America's "Little Switzerland," in Green County in the district's southwest. The Wisconsin Dells — ancient natural limestone formations along the Wisconsin River — attract visitors to the district's north, which features many commercial waterparks.

The 2nd generally is divided politically into Madison versus everywhere else, with residents of the university- and government-dominated capital standing in contrast to social conservatives and residents of the district's farming communities. Overall, the 2nd is strongly Democratic, and only the Milwaukee-based 4th District exceeds the 2nd in its Democratic tendencies. John Kerry won 66 percent of the 2004 presidential vote in Dane County, which surrounds Madison, while carrying the 2nd overall with 62 percent of the vote.

MAJOR INDUSTRY

Higher education, agriculture, government

CITIES

Madison, 208,054; Beloit, 35,775; Fitchburg, 20,501; Sun Prairie, 20,369

NOTABLE

The Ringling Brothers started their circus — which later merged with Barnum and Bailey's "Greatest Show on Earth" — in Baraboo in 1884.

Rep. Ron Kind (D)

CAPITOL OFFICE
225-5506
www.house.gov/kind
1406 Longworth 20515-4903; fax 225-5739

COMMITTEES
Natural Resources
Ways & Means

RESIDENCE
La Crosse

BORN
March 16, 1963, La Crosse, Wis.

RELIGION
Lutheran

FAMILY
Wife, Tawni Kind; two children

EDUCATION
Harvard U., A.B. 1985; London School of Economics, M.A. 1986; U. of Minnesota, J.D. 1990

CAREER
County prosecutor; lawyer

POLITICAL HIGHLIGHTS
No previous office

ELECTION RESULTS

2006 GENERAL		
Ron Kind (D)	163,322	64.8%
Paul R. Nelson (R)	88,523	35.1%
2006 PRIMARY		
Ron Kind (D)	39,765	83.7%
Chip De Nure (D)	7,744	16.3%
2004 GENERAL		
Ron Kind (D)	204,856	56.4%
Dale W. Schultz (R)	157,866	43.5%

PREVIOUS WINNING PERCENTAGES
2002 (63%); 2000 (64%); 1998 (71%); 1996 (52%)

Elected 1996; 6th term

Inspired by the career of Sen. William O. Proxmire, Kind is a product of Wisconsin's good-government tradition who says he strives to carry on Proxmire's legacy of frugality. He donates his congressional pay raises to charity, and he returns about 10 percent of his office allotment to the federal treasury each year. "Fiscal responsibility starts at home, the things you control. And for me, that's this office," he says.

In the 110th Congress (2007-08), Kind gave up his post as a chief deputy whip and gained a coveted seat on the Ways and Means panel, giving him a chance to expand his lessons on fiscal restraint far beyond his office.

Kind had to give up his posts on the Budget and Education committees, but education remains a priority. He was able to keep his seat on the Natural Resources Committee, important both for his rural western Wisconsin district along the upper Mississippi River and for Kind personally: He is a co-chairman of the Congressional Sportsmen's Caucus.

One area where he'd like to see more federal spending, not less, however, is on public education. Kind, who worked his way through Harvard as a janitor on campus, calls education "the great equalizer." During his tenure on the Education panel, he fought, in vain, to stave off provisions in the fiscal 2006 deficit reduction act that boosted borrowing costs for college students and their parents, calling the proposals "a raid on student aid." Earlier in his Capitol Hill career, his amendments to boost professional development for teachers and to help recruit teachers and principals were included in the 2001 No Child Left Behind Act.

Only the third Democrat to represent his western, dairy-producing district in the past 90 years, Kind believes that bipartisanship is essential to legislative success. Generally more cooperative than combative in his dealings with Republicans, Kind has supported President Bush's positions somewhat more often than the average House Democrat. He is one of four co-chairmen of the moderate New Democrat Coalition.

Kind and Bush bantered as the president arrived in the House chamber for his 2007 State of the Union Message, according to the Wisconsin State Journal, and Kind later got Bush to autograph a program for an injured National Guardsman whom Kind had invited to witness the speech.

In both 2006 and 2007, Kind offered legislation combining his interests in agriculture and conservation. In 2007, along with Republican Jim Gerlach of Pennsylvania, he drafted sweeping legislation, which they called the Healthy Farms, Foods and Fuels Act, to increase renewable energy production, expand access to locally grown foods and protect drinking water supplies.

In 2006, he was named "Fisheries and Habitat Conservation Legislator of the Year" by the U.S. Fish and Wildlife Service. Raised in La Crosse on the banks of the Mississippi river, Kind grew up hunting, fishing, camping and biking. "I am a river rat," he says. The outdoor life fostered "a greater appreciation of the importance of preserving and protecting our resources." Kind is teaching his two young sons to hunt and fish.

Perhaps his most lasting legislative legacy so far is the Veterans History Project at the Library of Congress. The volunteer-driven operation has collected more than 45,000 video and audio tapes, letters and cards, photographs, drawings and other mementos from soldiers in the wars of the 20th and 21st centuries. Kind introduced the bill creating the project in September 2000, and it whizzed through Congress in less than a month. The collection of oral histories is now the nation's largest. In 2007, he enlisted film-maker Ken Burns to help with the project in conjunction with a Burns documentary on World War II.

The idea for the oral history project came to him on a Father's Day weekend as Kind was sitting in the yard with his father and uncle — veterans of the Korean conflict and of World War II, respectively — listening to them talk. He had never heard the stories before, and he grabbed a video camera to capture them for his boys.

Like other New Democrats, Kind was the focus of heavy lobbying when the House voted in 2002 to grant the president expedited trade negotiating authority, known as fast-track. In the end, Kind, the son of a union leader who lost his phone company job after a strike, voted with labor and against the bill. He said it did not adequately address environmental concerns or the needs of displaced U.S. workers. In subsequent votes on individual trade agreements negotiated under fast-track authority, Kind's position has varied — he voted for pacts with Singapore, Chile, Morocco and Bahrain and against the Central American Free Trade Agreement and a pact with Oman.

Federal protection for the dairy industry is the top parochial issue for a district that includes Eau Claire, the historic center of the U.S. dairy industry. In a political advertisement in 2000, Kind and his family sported milk mustaches and the industry's "Got Milk?" message. In 2004, Kind successfully proposed several provisions aimed at encouraging increased milk consumption in public schools.

Kind is an up-by-the-bootstraps success story. Reared in a blue-collar neighborhood, he was a high school football and basketball star, and won an academic scholarship to Harvard University, where he quarterbacked on the football team before suffering a career-ending shoulder injury. As a summer intern for Proxmire in 1984, Kind did research for the senator's annual "Golden Fleece" awards, which showcased wasteful federal spending.

In addition to Proxmire's strong influence, Kind also was inspired to try politics by an experience he had backpacking through Eastern Europe just as communism was crumbling. In Berlin in 1990, Kind took a sledgehammer to the recently opened Berlin Wall and shook hands with new Czechoslovakian President Vaclav Havel. He still has a chunk of the wall, shaped like Wisconsin, on his desk. He earned a master's degree at the London School of Economics, a law degree in Minnesota, worked two years at a Milwaukee law firm, then returned home to La Crosse to become a county prosecutor.

When GOP Rep. Steve Gunderson announced his retirement, Kind entered the 1996 race. With little money, he waged a grass-roots campaign, beat Jim Harsdorf with 52 percent of the vote, and has won easily since.

KEY VOTES

2006

Yes Stop broadband companies from favoring select Internet traffic

Yes Affirm U.S. commitment to war in Iraq and reject setting a withdrawal date for troops

No Repeal requirement for bilingual ballots at the polls

Yes Permit U.S. sale of civilian nuclear technology to India

Yes Build a 700-mile fence on the U.S.-Mexico border to curb illegal crossings

No Permit warrantless wiretaps of suspected terrorists

2005

? Intervene in the life-support case of Terri Schiavo

Yes Lift President Bush's restrictions on stem cell research funding

Yes Prohibit FBI access to library and bookstore records

No Approve free-trade pact with five Central American countries

No Pass energy policy overhaul favored by President Bush emphasizing domestic oil and gas production

No End mandatory preservation of habitat of endangered animal and plant species

Yes Ban torture of prisoners in U.S. custody

CQ VOTE STUDIES

	PARTY UNITY		PRESIDENTIAL SUPPORT	
	Support	Oppose	Support	Oppose
2006	88%	12%	34%	66%
2005	89%	11%	23%	77%
2004	87%	13%	41%	59%
2003	89%	11%	26%	74%
2002	86%	14%	29%	71%

INTEREST GROUPS

	AFL-CIO	ADA	CCUS	ACU
2006	100%	85%	53%	25%
2005	87%	75%	59%	20%
2004	93%	90%	47%	24%
2003	80%	95%	38%	20%
2002	78%	90%	47%	8%

WISCONSIN 3

West – Eau Claire, La Crosse

Regarded as the nation's dairy capital, the 3rd boasts hundreds of thousands of cows. While fewer family farms are succeeding here, the district still leads the state in dairy production as corporate farming takes over.

Eau Claire and La Crosse have seen declines in their manufacturing industries, but their hospital systems are the biggest employers in the district and the local service industry is on the rise. The five branches of Wisconsin's state university system in the 3rd have placed an emphasis on computer and technology education, and both Eau Claire and La Crosse have experienced growth in their technology sectors. Meanwhile, bedroom communities in St. Croix County — inhabited by commuters to Minneapolis-St. Paul, just across the Minnesota state line — are experiencing the fastest population growth in the state.

Recreational tourism also contributes to the 3rd's economy. The Mississippi River provides a 250-mile natural western border to the district, snaking from near Minnesota's Twin Cities to the Illinois border along rolling prairies and nutrient-rich soil. Birdwatchers flock to the river to spot bald eagles perched on the steep bluffs, and lakes in the north attract sportsmen and retirees.

The 3rd has a slight Democratic lean and voted narrowly for John Kerry in the 2004 presidential election. Most of the 19 counties wholly or partly in the district are politically competitive, and in the 2004 presidential contest, all but three gave the winner a margin of victory of less than 10 percentage points.

MAJOR INDUSTRY

Dairy farming, manufacturing, tourism, technology, health care

MILITARY BASES

Fort McCoy (Army), 602 military, 1,366 civilian (2005)

CITIES

Eau Claire (pt.), 59,794; La Crosse, 51,818; Menomonie, 14,937

NOTABLE

Taliesin, Frank Lloyd Wright's estate, is in Spring Green; Pepin hosts the annual "Laura Ingalls Wilder Days," honoring the native-born author of the "Little House" books and holding demonstrations of the crafts, music and daily life of 1870s Wisconsin.

Rep. Gwen Moore (D)

CAPITOL OFFICE
225-4572
www.house.gov/gwenmoore
1239 Longworth 20515-4904; fax 225-8135

COMMITTEES
Budget
Financial Services
Small Business

RESIDENCE
Milwaukee

BORN
April 18, 1951, Racine, Wis.

RELIGION
Baptist

FAMILY
Single; three children

EDUCATION
Marquette U., B.A. 1978 (political science)

CAREER
State agency legislative analyst; city development specialist; VISTA volunteer

POLITICAL HIGHLIGHTS
Wis. Assembly, 1989-92; Wis. Senate, 1993-2004 (president pro tempore, 1997-98)

ELECTION RESULTS

2006 GENERAL		
Gwen Moore (D)	136,735	71.3%
Perfecto Rivera (R)	54,486	28.4%
2006 PRIMARY		
Gwen Moore (D)	31,042	97.4%
write-ins	823	2.6%
2004 GENERAL		
Gwen Moore (D)	212,382	69.6%
Gerald H. Boyle (R)	85,928	28.2%
Tim Johnson (I)	3,733	1.2%

Elected 2004; 2nd term

Combating urban poverty is a top priority for Moore, who knows the issue firsthand as a former teenage single mother on welfare. She remembers once talking a grocery store clerk into accepting an IOU for $30 worth of groceries. "I am really in sync with people who struggle on a day-to-day basis," says Moore, who represents the city of Milwaukee and a few of its working-class suburbs. "You don't have to have a 'D' after your name to understand that people have to eat."

She has attacked the Bush administration for spending billions of dollars on the war in Iraq and tax cuts for well-off Americans while cutting programs that provide food to the poor. Moore was the only House member to vote against a bill in 2005 that allowed for-profit foster care agencies to receive federal funds for placing youths needing specialized care. Moore said she's wary of creating profit incentives to place foster children.

In her first term in Congress, Moore could claim some modest victories from her seat on the Financial Services Committee. She won approval of her legislation to protect the identity of domestic violence victims who receive homeless assistance. And she successfully pressed for an amendment to help public housing assistance recipients become homeowners by allowing them to improve their creditworthiness with prompt rent payments.

A seasoned politician before coming to Congress, Moore has made boosting appropriations for her hometown a priority. She boasts of having steered millions of dollars in transportation improvements and funds for a new medical center to Milwaukee. She is sometimes mentioned in the Milwaukee media as a potential challenger in 2008 to Mayor Tom Barrett, who is not universally liked by the city's black residents.

Moore was the first member of the Wisconsin congressional delegation to cosponsor a proposal to begin bringing troops home from Iraq. She also joined fellow Democratic Rep. Tammy Baldwin in calling for impeachment proceedings against President Bush for invading Iraq based on faulty intelligence data.

In 2006, she made a publicized foray into foreign policy when she was arrested, with other members of the Congressional Black Caucus, for protesting outside the Sudanese Embassy to call attention to genocide in Darfur.

Moore was born in Racine, the eighth of nine children of a factory worker father and a teacher. She got into politics as a student in Milwaukee's public schools in the late 1960s, inspired by the Rev. Martin Luther King Jr. and the civil rights movement. She was student council president of North Division High School, where she pushed city officials to replace an aging building that lacked science labs and showers for athletes. Moore also organized a school walk-out over a lack of textbooks describing black American history after slavery. A picture of a young Moore leading the protest is on display today inside America's Black Holocaust Museum in Milwaukee.

At age 18, Moore got pregnant during her freshman year at Marquette University. She went on government assistance, but continued her studies in political science, taking eight years to finally earn her bachelor's degree.

In that period, she recalls being so destitute that one December day she walked into a grocery store, filled a wagon with $30 of groceries, and asked the cashier to let her sign the receipt as a promise of payment later. Moore's washer and dryer were repossessed not long before she would have owned them because she couldn't make the last few payments.

Still, Moore graduated from Marquette in 1978. She went to work as a VISTA volunteer and organized a community credit union in her North Milwaukee neighborhood, where traditional banks wouldn't lend money. She later worked in a variety of government jobs, including as a neighborhood development specialist for Milwaukee's city government.

In 1988, she was elected to the state Assembly and later won a seat in the Senate. She became a leader on urban issues on the legislature's joint finance committee and earned bipartisan praise for her work on Wisconsin's welfare reform program in the mid-1990s, one of the first to pioneer transition-to-work requirements.

In 2004, when pro-labor Democrat Gerald D. Kleczka decided to retire after 20 years, Moore entered a highly competitive primary for his 4th District seat. She faced state Sen. Tim Carpenter, the only openly gay member of the Senate, and former state party chairman Matt Flynn. The three shared similar philosophies, favoring abortion rights and reductions in the Bush tax cuts for the top income groups. But Moore benefited from the recent mayoral race in which Barrett, who is white, narrowly defeated acting Mayor Marvin Pratt, who is black, in a contest that divided the city's neighborhoods by race.

In the general-election contest with Republican Gerald H. Boyle, an Iraq War veteran, Moore downplayed race as an issue. "It's a novelty to other people," she told The Associated Press. "But I've been black for 53 years."

Moore became the first African-American member of Congress from Wisconsin and took a symbolic oath of office from Wisconsin state Supreme Court justice Lois Butler, who is also an African-American.

Her victory was marred by the arrest in January 2005 of her then 25-year-old son, Sowande Omukunde, one of five workers for the Kerry-Edwards presidential campaign charged with slashing the tires of Republican get-out-the-vote vehicles on Election Day. Prosecutors recommended probation, but the judge sentenced Omokunde and three co-defendants to several months in jail. He has since completed his sentence and returned to school. "I've loved him. I've supported him," said Moore

Moore got more unwanted press in 2005 when the Milwaukee Sentinel reported that her election campaign had paid her sister $44,000 for work on the campaign, though she lives in Georgia. Moore's campaign treasurer said her sister had helped Moore cultivate relationships in Washington. Voters seemed unperturbed. In 2006, Moore easily beat Republican challenger Perfecto Rivera with 71 percent of the vote.

KEY VOTES

2006

- Yes Stop broadband companies from favoring select Internet traffic
- No Affirm U.S. commitment to war in Iraq and reject setting a withdrawal date for troops
- No Repeal requirement for bilingual ballots at the polls
- No Permit U.S. sale of civilian nuclear technology to India
- No Build a 700-mile fence on the U.S.-Mexico border to curb illegal crossings
- No Permit warrantless wiretaps of suspected terrorists

2005

- ? Intervene in the life-support case of Terri Schiavo
- Yes Lift President Bush's restrictions on stem cell research funding
- Yes Prohibit FBI access to library and bookstore records
- No Approve free-trade pact with five Central American countries
- No Pass energy policy overhaul favored by President Bush emphasizing domestic oil and gas production
- No End mandatory preservation of habitat of endangered animal and plant species
- Yes Ban torture of prisoners in U.S. custody

CQ VOTE STUDIES

	PARTY UNITY		PRESIDENTIAL SUPPORT	
	Support	Oppose	Support	Oppose
2006	98%	2%	13%	87%
2005	97%	3%	11%	89%

INTEREST GROUPS

	AFL-CIO	ADA	CCUS	ACU
2006	93%	100%	20%	4%
2005	93%	100%	38%	0%

WISCONSIN 4

Milwaukee

On the shores of Lake Michigan, the 4th takes in all of Milwaukee, Wisconsin's largest city. Once rooted in manufacturing, the city now has cosmopolitan rhythm. It has a major art museum, a large summer music festival and professional sports teams: basketball's Bucks, baseball's Brewers and minor league hockey's Admirals. It also continues to serve as the tap of Miller Brewing and the home of Harley-Davidson.

Milwaukee has lost population since the 1960s, mainly due to a shrinking blue-collar manufacturing base. Nevertheless, downtown revitalization efforts have lured new businesses and young professionals.

The Milwaukee area also includes the headquarters for several Fortune 500 firms, such as auto parts manufacturer Johnson Controls and global staffing company Manpower. Manpower recently chose a site adjacent to northern Milwaukee for its new corporate headquarters, creating a multi-million dollar development project and thousands of construction jobs for city residents. A large student population is spread among the city's colleges, including the local University of Wisconsin campus.

Once known for the stark racial, cultural and economic differences in formerly segregated parts of the city, Milwaukee is minority-majority, with blacks (37 percent) and Hispanics (12 percent) together outnumbering whites. City officials say Milwaukee is becoming more integrated, but it is not uncommon to find almost completely black areas in the north-central part of the city and exclusively white and Hispanic areas in the south, where communities of Polish and German immigrants once settled.

Milwaukee once was the socialist hub of the country, and this history, combined with the city's remaining blue-collar enclaves, large minority population and strong union presence, make the 4th the most Democratic district in the state. Milwaukee overwhelmingly supported Democratic Gov. James E. Doyle's re-election in 2006, with only four of the city's wards supporting Doyle's Republican challenger.

MAJOR INDUSTRY

Machinery manufacturing, service

CITIES

Milwaukee, 596,974; South Milwaukee, 21,256; West Allis (pt.), 20,936

NOTABLE

The world's largest four-sided clock is on the Allen-Bradley building.

Rep. F. James Sensenbrenner Jr. (R)

CAPITOL OFFICE
225-5101
sensenbrenner@mail.house.gov
www.house.gov/sensenbrenner
2449 Rayburn 20515-4905; fax 225-3190

COMMITTEES
Judiciary
Science & Technology
Select Energy Independence & Global Warming - ranking member

RESIDENCE
Menomonee Falls

BORN
June 14, 1943, Chicago, Ill.

RELIGION
Episcopalian

FAMILY
Wife, Cheryl Sensenbrenner; two children

EDUCATION
Stanford U., A.B. 1965 (political science); U. of Wisconsin, J.D. 1968

CAREER
Lawyer

POLITICAL HIGHLIGHTS
Wis. Assembly, 1969-75; Wis. Senate, 1975-79

ELECTION RESULTS

2006 GENERAL		
F. James Sensenbrenner Jr. (R)	194,669	61.8%
Bryan Kennedy (D)	112,451	35.7%
Bob Levis (WG)	4,432	1.4%
Robert R. Raymond (I)	3,525	1.1%
2006 PRIMARY		
F. James Sensenbrenner Jr. (R)		unopposed
2004 GENERAL		
F. James Sensenbrenner Jr. (R)	271,153	66.6%
Bryan Kennedy (D)	129,384	31.8%
Tim Peterson (LIBERT)	6,549	1.6%

PREVIOUS WINNING PERCENTAGES
2002 (86%); 2000 (74%); 1998 (91%); 1996 (74%); 1994 (100%); 1992 (70%); 1990 (100%); 1988 (75%); 1986 (78%); 1984 (73%); 1982 (100%); 1980 (78%); 1978 (61%)

Elected 1978; 15th term

Versed on the issues and ahead of the pack in seniority, Sensenbrenner doesn't suffer fools lightly. Known as much for his prickliness as his smarts, he can be downright ornery to colleagues, journalists, unprepared witnesses and even constituents. He breaks ranks with the Republican White House when he wants to, and in spite of himself manages to leave a deep imprint on major legislation.

An heir to the Kimberly Clark fortune, Sensenbrenner has spent his entire career in politics and government, rising from the statehouse to the U.S. House and ultimately to his dream job of chairing the House Judiciary Committee. He enjoyed considerable power during his six-year reign, but his influence waned in 2007. Sensenbrenner had to give up the gavel after Republicans lost control of the House. He then tried to leverage his seniority to be named the senior Republican on the Science and Technology Committee. But GOP leaders rejected that idea and gave the post to Ralph M. Hall of Texas.

He was given the ranking member slot on a new Select Committee on Energy Independence and Global Warming. Like four of the other five Republicans given spots on the panel, he voted against its creation in the first place — and pledged to push for a gradual approach to tackling climate change that would not harm the economy. In his way, he had already made his opinion known on the issue. When Speaker Nancy Pelosi appeared before the Science panel in February to testify on her quest for caps on greenhouse gas emissions, he refused to let her leave without taking questions. He then took issue with her ideas, saying they "could wreck our economy."

His final months as Judiciary chairman were pure Sensenbrenner theater. He defied President Bush on immigration policy, abruptly ended a hearing that displeased him by turning off the lights, and chastised a federal judge for his sentencing judgment — all par for the course for the gruff Midwesterner, who likes to relax with imported cigars aboard his pontoon boat on a Wisconsin lake.

The battle over immigration policy in 2006 was a study in his independence from party leaders. Sensenbrenner led a hard-line group that rejected the president's proposed guest worker program in favor of a bill emphasizing border security and punishing illegal immigrants and the employers who hire them. When the Senate passed a bill closer to Bush's ideal, Congress bogged down on the issue.

A few of his ideas made it into law, however, including legislation to build 700 miles of fence on the U.S.-Mexico border, along with a "virtual fence" of cameras and other surveillance technology. In 2005, Congress cleared his bill compelling states to demand proof of citizenship when issuing driver's licenses. But responding to states' complaints about exorbitant costs to comply with the mandate, several lawmakers in early 2007 made moves to remove or delay the requirement.

Sensenbrenner is usually in the middle of fights conservatives pick with the federal judiciary. He caught flak from the legal community in 2005 for a letter to the 7th U.S. Circuit Court of Appeals complaining that a sentence given a drug courier was too lenient. The same year, he led the debate in favor of congressional intervention in the case of Terri Schiavo, a severely brain-damaged Florida woman being kept alive by a feeding tube. He has since backed off a bit from confrontation with the courts, especially after his proposal to take away the federal courts' jurisdiction in cases involving the Pledge of Allegiance failed on a tie vote in committee in 2006.

He has been prone to tantrums. He adjourned a 2005 hearing on the Patriot Act when the questions irked him. Carrying his gavel, he stalked off after shutting off the microphone and lights while a Democratic witness was speaking. The next year, a GOP colleague told The New York Times that Sensenbrenner treats everyone equally — "like dogs." The following day, the chairman circulated a basket of dog biscuits at a committee meeting.

But Sensenbrenner has had a significant impact on legislation. He helped write the original Patriot Act of 2001 after the terrorist attacks on New York and Washington. He was a force behind changes in bankruptcy law in 2005 making it harder for people to escape their debts. And he was one of the House managers of the impeachment case against President Bill Clinton in 1998. He is often credited with clever use of parliamentary rules to advance his bills and with mastering a wide array of subjects. A former aide told Milwaukee Magazine in 2006, "He's like Congressman Google."

On most issues, he is an ardent conservative, opposing abortion, gun control and same-sex marriage. He was the only member of the Wisconsin delegation to support Bush's plan for a troop "surge" in Iraq. But he has a liberal's soft spot for voting rights for minorities. In his final year as chairman, he focused on winning an extension of the 1965 Voting Rights Act, and was riled that committee Republicans threw up roadblocks by trying to eliminate requirements for bilingual assistance at polling places.

Among the wealthiest lawmakers, Sensenbrenner is heir to a paper and cellulose manufacturing fortune that began with his great-grandfather's invention of the Kotex sanitary napkin after World War I. As a teenager, he was drawn to politics, once helping his math teacher win a race for county surveyor. He studied political science at Stanford University, earned a law degree from the University of Wisconsin at Madison in 1968, then was elected to the state Assembly. He spent a decade in the legislature, part of it as assistant Senate minority leader.

When Republican Bob Kasten left the 9th District seat to run for governor in 1978, Sensenbrenner, with a solid political base in the affluent suburbs bordering Lake Michigan, was the obvious successor. He had to dip into family wealth to overcome a strong primary challenge from Susan Engeleiter, a state legislator, but he won the general election with 61 percent of the vote.

Sensenbrenner told the Milwaukee Journal Sentinel that he has no plans to retire from Congress. He lost the paper's support in 2006 when it found fault with his immigration stance and his acceptance of $200,000 in world travel paid for by lobbyists and think tanks. He still won with 62 percent.

KEY VOTES

2006

Yes Stop broadband companies from favoring select Internet traffic
? Affirm U.S. commitment to war in Iraq and reject setting a withdrawal date for troops
No Repeal requirement for bilingual ballots at the polls
Yes Permit U.S. sale of civilian nuclear technology to India
Yes Build a 700-mile fence on the U.S.-Mexico border to curb illegal crossings
Yes Permit warrantless wiretaps of suspected terrorists

2005

Yes Intervene in the life-support case of Terri Schiavo
No Lift President Bush's restrictions on stem cell research funding
No Prohibit FBI access to library and bookstore records
Yes Approve free-trade pact with five Central American countries
Yes Pass energy policy overhaul favored by President Bush emphasizing domestic oil and gas production
Yes End mandatory preservation of habitat of endangered animal and plant species
Yes Ban torture of prisoners in U.S. custody

CQ VOTE STUDIES

	PARTY UNITY		PRESIDENTIAL SUPPORT	
	Support	Oppose	Support	Oppose
2006	92%	8%	84%	16%
2005	93%	7%	81%	19%
2004	94%	6%	79%	21%
2003	91%	9%	82%	18%
2002	94%	6%	85%	15%

INTEREST GROUPS

	AFL-CIO	ADA	CCUS	ACU
2006	21%	10%	87%	83%
2005	20%	0%	77%	96%
2004	27%	20%	86%	92%
2003	0%	25%	80%	80%
2002	13%	0%	95%	92%

WISCONSIN 5
Southeast – Milwaukee suburbs

A mix of suburbs, glacier-carved landscape and Lake Michigan shoreline, the 5th is experiencing rapid job and population growth. Washington and Waukesha counties have become destinations for Milwaukee-area white-collar workers who are leaving downtown and settling their families in the city's affluent suburbs.

These expanding communities offer employment in all sectors and no longer rely on Milwaukee's economy for jobs, although some residents still make the daily trip into the city. Waukesha County's population has grown by 25 percent since 1990, while Washington County has grown by one-third over the same period. Most residents in Ozaukee County, north of Milwaukee, commute out of the county to service or office jobs.

Many of the district's manufacturing jobs are found in Waukesha County. The county's major employers are Kohl's Department Store, which has its headquarters in Menomonee Falls; Quad Graphics, a printing company based in Sussex; and engine manufacturer Briggs and Stratton, located in Wauwatosa. The northern and western outskirts of the 5th are still mostly rural and populated with dairy farms and cattle ranches, although strip malls and housing developments have started to encroach.

Many residents of the 5th still proudly celebrate their diverse European heritages — German, Belgian, Dutch and Eastern European folk festivals attract tourists almost every weekend of the summer. Vacationers travel to the Port Washington area in Ozaukee County for the recreational fishing and boating opportunities along Lake Michigan.

The strong GOP lean in Ozaukee, Washington and Waukesha makes the 5th the state's most heavily Republican district: It gave 63 percent of its vote to George W. Bush in the 2004 presidential election. Democrats are competitive only in the district's portion of Milwaukee County.

MAJOR INDUSTRY
Service, manufacturing, retail

CITIES
Waukesha, 64,825; Wauwatosa, 47,271; West Allis (pt.), 40,318

NOTABLE
The Schurz Family in Watertown started the first kindergarten in America in 1856; The last covered bridge in Wisconsin is found in Cedarburg over Cedar Creek.

Rep. Tom Petri (R)

CAPITOL OFFICE
225-2476
www.house.gov/petri
2462 Rayburn 20515-4906; fax 225-2356

COMMITTEES
Education & Labor
Transportation & Infrastructure

RESIDENCE
Fond du Lac

BORN
May 28, 1940, Marinette, Wis.

RELIGION
Lutheran

FAMILY
Wife, Anne Neal Petri; one child

EDUCATION
Harvard U., A.B. 1962 (government), J.D. 1965

CAREER
Lawyer; White House aide; Peace Corps volunteer

POLITICAL HIGHLIGHTS
Wis. Senate, 1973-79; Republican nominee for U.S. Senate, 1974

ELECTION RESULTS

2006 GENERAL		
Tom Petri (R)	201,367	98.9%
write-ins	2,190	1.1%
2006 PRIMARY		
Tom Petri (R)		unopposed
2004 GENERAL		
Tom Petri (R)	238,620	67.0%
Jef Hall (D)	107,209	30.1%
Carol Ann Rittenhouse (WG)	10,081	2.8%

PREVIOUS WINNING PERCENTAGES
2002 (99%); 2000 (65%); 1998 (93%); 1996 (73%); 1994 (100%); 1992 (53%); 1990 (100%); 1988 (74%); 1986 (97%); 1984 (76%); 1982 (65%); 1980 (59%); 1979 Special Election (50%)

Elected April 1979; 14th full term

Petri doesn't really fit well with the firebrand conservatives who have come to dominate the House GOP in recent years. Understated and collegial, he sides with fiscal conservatives on most issues but splits with his party on issues such as campaign finance law, education and federal spending on transportation and infrastructure projects.

Now No. 6 in overall seniority among House Republicans, he has pursued his goals through thick and thin. He wasn't unduly upset about the Democrats' return to power following the 2006 elections. "I've been in the minority more than I have been in the majority," he said. "I keep telling my colleagues, who are making demands, that we are no longer in the majority and to be respectful. . . . I've always tried to do legislation by building coalitions and reaching out to people from both parties."

His willingness to deal with all comers has cost him clout in the past with the GOP leadership. Despite his seniority, Petri (PEA-try) was passed over for the chairmanship of a full committee at one point, and more recently for a ranking Republican committee slot. But that hasn't discouraged him from taking his own path when he deems it necessary — and his wide re-election margins allow him to do so. In February 2007, Petri was one of 17 Republicans to vote for the Democrats' resolution opposing President Bush's plan to send more than 21,000 additional combat troops into the Iraq War.

GOP leaders first skipped over Petri in 2001, when — despite his being next in line in seniority for the post — they gave the chairmanship of the Education Committee to John A. Boehner of Ohio, a party loyalist and prolific fundraiser who is now House minority leader.

Petri has a longstanding interest in education policy and will cross party lines to create bipartisan legislation. In the 109th Congress (2005-06), Petri, with Massachusetts Democratic Sen. Edward M. Kennedy and other Democrats, held a news conference touting his bill to give colleges an incentive to use a program that provides student loans directly from the U.S. Treasury rather than a guaranteed private-lender program favored by many Republicans. Under his bill, the money colleges saved from bank fees could be used to issue more student loans or provide Pell grants — with a portion also marked for deficit reduction. He is pressing his proposal again in the 110th Congress (2007-08).

Petri is a longtime leader on the Transportation and Infrastructure Committee, where he had hoped to become ranking member in 2007, when term limits forced Republican Don Young of Alaska to step down. But even though Petri ranked directly below Young in seniority, GOP leaders passed him over once again, reaching several rungs down the seniority ladder to elevate Florida's John L. Mica.

But he did get the ranking Republican slot on the Aviation Subcommittee, which in the 110th Congress will consider such issues as the Aviation Trust Fund, air traffic control modernization, FAA personnel management, and baggage and checkpoint screening technology. His district is home to the Experimental Aircraft Association, Basler Turbo Conversions and Oshkosh Truck, a manufacturer of aircraft rescue and fire fighting vehicles.

Petri had chaired the Highways, Transit and Pipelines Subcommittee from 2001 to 2006. He played a critical role in writing the six-year, $218 billion 1998 surface transportation bill, then the most expensive highway measure in U.S. history. When work on reauthorizing the law began in 2003, Petri supported a $375 billion bill sponsored by Young. But Bush denounced the bill as too costly and rejected its proposed increase in the federal gasoline tax. After repeated veto threats and a dozen temporary extensions of the 1998 law, Petri and other advocates of higher spending were forced to yield. After Bush signed the $286.5 billion reauthorization measure in 2005, Petri, with characteristic bluntness, said, "Is this a bill? Compared to what?"

Changes to campaign finance law have drawn Petri's attention. He supported the 2002 overhaul, which most House Republicans opposed. He introduced legislation in the past three Congresses aimed at encouraging more participation in election campaigns by citizens making small contributions. In 2007, he reintroduced his bill to curb "push polls" — Petri calls them "smear polls" — in which pollsters ask prospective voters leading questions intended to convey negative information about a candidate in the form of an ostensibly objective survey.

Petri has been a staunch free-trade supporter, backing the 2002 restoration of fast-track authority allowing the president to negotiate trade deals that Congress cannot amend. He also supported the 2005 Central American Free Trade Agreement.

Born in northern Wisconsin, Petri spent his early childhood in San Juan, Puerto Rico, where his father, a Navy pilot, was stationed. World War II changed his life forever — his father was killed in the conflict.

As a teenager, Petri got his first job by marching down to the local radio station and asking to become a disc jockey. He soon became the host of "Teen Time," a weekly show that made him the Badger State's youngest on-air personality. He worked his way through college as a teller at a local bank, then earned a law degree at Harvard. He clerked for Judge James E. Doyle Sr., the father of Wisconsin's current Democratic governor, before joining the Peace Corps for a stint in Somalia. Once home, Petri started a law practice in Fond du Lac. He won a state Senate seat in 1972 at age 32.

Petri was chosen to be the GOP Senate nominee against Democrat Gaylord Nelson in 1974, but he lost in the aftermath of the Watergate scandal and what turned out to be a terrible year for Republicans. The exposure and increased name recognition from that race, however, helped him win a close contest for the House in a 1979 special election to replace Republican William A. Steiger, who had died in office.

Petri easily won election to a full term in 1980. He coasted until his 1992 re-election campaign, when he was hit by negative publicity about 77 overdrafts at the private bank for House members. He pulled through with 53 percent of the vote, his worst re-election total ever. He has won easily ever since, taking 67 percent in 2004 and running unopposed in 2006.

KEY VOTES

2006

- No — Stop broadband companies from favoring select Internet traffic
- Yes — Affirm U.S. commitment to war in Iraq and reject setting a withdrawal date for troops
- Yes — Repeal requirement for bilingual ballots at the polls
- Yes — Permit U.S. sale of civilian nuclear technology to India
- Yes — Build a 700-mile fence on the U.S.-Mexico border to curb illegal crossings
- Yes — Permit warrantless wiretaps of suspected terrorists

2005

- ? — Intervene in the life-support case of Terri Schiavo
- No — Lift President Bush's restrictions on stem cell research funding
- Yes — Prohibit FBI access to library and bookstore records
- Yes — Approve free-trade pact with five Central American countries
- Yes — Pass energy policy overhaul favored by President Bush emphasizing domestic oil and gas production
- Yes — End mandatory preservation of habitat of endangered animal and plant species
- Yes — Ban torture of prisoners in U.S. custody

CQ VOTE STUDIES

	PARTY UNITY		PRESIDENTIAL SUPPORT	
	Support	Oppose	Support	Oppose
2006	90%	10%	85%	15%
2005	88%	12%	80%	20%
2004	89%	11%	85%	15%
2003	87%	13%	84%	16%
2002	86%	14%	82%	18%

INTEREST GROUPS

	AFL-CIO	ADA	CCUS	ACU
2006	14%	5%	87%	76%
2005	13%	5%	85%	72%
2004	33%	20%	95%	80%
2003	0%	20%	77%	80%
2002	0%	10%	85%	80%

WISCONSIN 6

East central – Oshkosh, Sheboygan, Fond du Lac

In 1854, a group of dissatisfied Whigs, Free Soilers and Democrats met in a Ripon schoolhouse in Fond du Lac County to dream up the Republican Party. Today, the 6th District's inland farms and small towns hold enough socially conservative Lutherans and Catholics to provide a distinct Republican lean despite having the largest population of blue-collar workers in the state. In the 2004 presidential election, every county in the 6th except Adams supported George W. Bush.

Manitowoc County, on Lake Michigan, has a longstanding reputation as a shipbuilding center. South along the lake, Sheboygan County is famed for its meat processing, calling itself the "bratwurst capital of the world." The county also is known for manufacturing, including plumbing company Kohler. Near the inland Lake Winnebago, Oshkosh — where the "B'Gosh" overalls originated more than a century ago — is one of the largest producers of military and specialty trucks in the world. And the paper industry, based mainly in Neenah and Menasha, is a leading employer for the district.

Although family dairy farms in the district have struggled, the 6th's west remains farming territory. Large corporate farms have acquired some small farms, making them more profitable, and others have turned away from dairy to new crops such as beans, peas and corn. Fruits and vegetables thrive in Adams County, and Marquette and Waushara counties grow Christmas trees.

Many of the 6th's residents are descendants of German immigrants who settled the area in the 1850s, and the district still claims more people of German ancestry (60 percent) than any other in the nation. In more recent waves of immigration, the Hmong population continues to grow in Sheboygan, Manitowoc and Winnebago counties.

MAJOR INDUSTRY

Paper, agriculture, tourism, manufacturing

CITIES

Oshkosh, 62,916; Sheboygan, 50,792; Fond du Lac, 42,203

NOTABLE

The Wisconsin Maritime Museum is in Manitowoc; Oshkosh's annual Experimental Aircraft Association AirVenture convention draws hundreds of thousands of people and exhibits 10,000 airplanes.

Rep. David R. Obey (D)

CAPITOL OFFICE
225-3365
www.house.gov/obey
2314 Rayburn 20515-4907; fax 225-3240

COMMITTEES
Appropriations - chairman
(Labor-HHS-Education - chairman)

RESIDENCE
Wausau

BORN
Oct. 3, 1938, Okmulgee, Okla.

RELIGION
Roman Catholic

FAMILY
Wife, Joan Obey; two children

EDUCATION
U. of Wisconsin, B.S. 1960 (political science), M.A. 1962 (political science)

CAREER
Real estate broker

POLITICAL HIGHLIGHTS
Wis. Assembly, 1963-69

ELECTION RESULTS

2006 GENERAL		
David R. Obey (D)	161,903	62.2%
Nick Reid (R)	91,069	35.0%
Mike Miles (WG)	7,391	2.8%
2006 PRIMARY		
David R. Obey (D)		unopposed
2004 GENERAL		
David R. Obey (D)	241,306	85.7%
Mike Miles (WG)	26,518	9.4%
Larry Oftedahl (CNSTP)	12,841	4.6%

PREVIOUS WINNING PERCENTAGES
2002 (64%); 2000 (63%); 1998 (61%); 1996 (57%); 1994 (54%); 1992 (64%); 1990 (62%); 1988 (62%); 1986 (62%); 1984 (61%); 1982 (68%); 1980 (65%); 1978 (62%); 1976 (73%); 1974 (71%); 1972 (63%); 1970 (68%); 1969 Special Election (52%)

Elected April 1969; 19th full term

After a dozen years leading a guerrilla war against the GOP's fiscal policies, Obey is back in command at the Appropriations Committee and itching to put a Democratic stamp on the annual spending bills. But his maneuvering room is severely circumscribed by President Bush's determination to maintain tight limits on domestic spending.

An old-style liberal who has held his seat for nearly 40 years, Obey (OH-bee) is a complex man of indisputable intelligence and legislative prowess. His combustible personality and brutal candor on the House floor are matched by a deep understanding of the policy preferences and politics at work behind the scenes. He is dismayed by the partisanship infecting committee deliberations in recent years and has vowed to go back to an older model of operations. "I don't think politics works unless you define your differences. But resolving them is what's missing now," Obey says. "I believe in fighting out your differences before five and having a drink after five."

Unlike the majority of House Democrats, Obey remembers what it was like to have real power. He rose to Appropriations chairman in 1994, though he kept the job for just nine months before Republicans captured control of the House. As chairman, Obey worked to resolve problems with the GOP minority before they could delay the bills. As a result, Congress cleared all of its annual spending bills individually by the Oct. 1 start of the fiscal year, which hasn't happened since. Republicans used catchall spending bills, rather than individual bills, to keep the government running, maximizing control for GOP leaders and Bush. Ironically, the first spending bill Obey tackled in 2007 was a similar omnibus measure. Republicans, stung by their November defeat, had dumped a pile of unfinished bills on the new Democratic majority when Congress adjourned in late 2006.

During the dozen years of GOP control, Obey maintained working relationships with three Republican chairmen. He describes his immediate predecessor, Jerry Lewis of California, as "civil and decent." He was closer to Lewis' predecessor, C.W. Bill Young of Florida, and considers former chairman Robert L. Livingston of Louisiana a good friend. Obey also has high regard for Ralph Regula of Ohio, a senior GOP appropriator who has sometimes sided with him in fighting administration cuts in domestic spending.

As chairman, Obey wants to increase spending for education, medical research, community development block grants, veterans' medical care and other domestic priorities. His first thorny challenge in the 110th Congress (2007-08) was a massive supplemental spending bill to fund the Iraq War. Democrats tied the funds to a deadline for the withdrawal of U.S. troops. But they had to back off after Bush vetoed the measure.

Stopping Obey from getting his way on spending bills is a priority for the Bush White House, but the wily legislator is masterful at finding ways to lay bare divisions in the Republican Party. In 2006, he succeeded in attaching to a committee-approved spending bill the Democrats' proposed increase in the minimum wage from $5.15 an hour to $7.25, though Republicans still controlled Congress. Another Obey amendment, to prevent the creation of permanent military bases in Iraq, made it into another spending bill.

Obey's parochial projects find their way into the spending bills as well. He tried to amend one of them to compensate farmers for losses when milk prices fall, a popular idea in his dairy state. Though it was defeated in the House, Wisconsin Sen. Herb Kohl took up the cause when the Senate drafted its version of the agriculture appropriations bill.

In the minority, Obey regularly pressed to boost spending for health and education programs by raising taxes for millionaires, a plan Republicans routinely killed. He sometimes flushed out GOP moderates uncomfortable with cutting social programs. In drafting the education spending bill in 2006, Regula added back money for college preparation for low-income students, funds that were under the knife.

Obey, who "came here as a rebel," considers himself an institutionalist with respect for the ideals of civilized debate and collegiality. He directed a rewrite of the House ethics code after a series of scandals in the 1970s, when Democrats controlled the chamber. And after Republicans were ensnared by lobbying and influence-peddling scandals in the 109th Congress (2005-06), Obey sponsored a Democratic bill that sought to restrict privately paid travel for lawmakers.

His pugnacity is legendary. Sometimes he seems close to boiling over, the array of pencils in his shirt pocket threatening to topple out as he wags his finger at the Republican side of the aisle. But it's not just Republicans who draw his ire. Early in his career, when fellow Democrat John J. Rooney of New York tried to cut him off during committee debate, Obey replied, "Kiss my fanny, you senile old bastard. What do you know?"

Although he lists his occupation as real estate broker, Obey has been a politician almost all his adult life. At the University of Wisconsin, he majored in political science and was the campus coordinator for 1960 presidential candidate Hubert H. Humphrey. At 24, he was elected to the state House. At 30, he won his seat in Congress in a 1969 special election to succeed Melvin R. Laird, President Richard Nixon's first defense secretary.

Obey was the first Democrat to represent the 7th District, and he has won at least three-fifths of the vote in all but two re-election races. A liberal nonetheless mindful of sentiment in his largely rural and small-town district, he supports gun owners' rights and votes for some restrictions on abortion.

Obey grew up in a Republican family in Wausau. When he was a boy, his father, who ran a local floor-covering business, had surgery that threatened his ability to work. "We were scared," Obey recalls. "That experience taught me that working families are just one paycheck away from economic disaster. And it showed me firsthand the importance of every family having access to good health care."

Obey shows no sign of retiring anytime soon. "I came here because I wanted to see equal access to education, tax fairness and I thought it was a mortal sin that everyone didn't have health care," he says. "I don't do this because it's so much fun — not that I don't have some fun."

KEY VOTES

2006

Yes	Stop broadband companies from favoring select Internet traffic
No	Affirm U.S. commitment to war in Iraq and reject setting a withdrawal date for troops
No	Repeal requirement for bilingual ballots at the polls
No	Permit U.S. sale of civilian nuclear technology to India
No	Build a 700-mile fence on the U.S.-Mexico border to curb illegal crossings
No	Permit warrantless wiretaps of suspected terrorists

2005

?	Intervene in the life-support case of Terri Schiavo
Yes	Lift President Bush's restrictions on stem cell research funding
Yes	Prohibit FBI access to library and bookstore records
No	Approve free-trade pact with five Central American countries
No	Pass energy policy overhaul favored by President Bush emphasizing domestic oil and gas production
No	End mandatory preservation of habitat of endangered animal and plant species
Yes	Ban torture of prisoners in U.S. custody

CQ VOTE STUDIES

	PARTY UNITY		PRESIDENTIAL SUPPORT	
	Support	Oppose	Support	Oppose
2006	94%	6%	22%	78%
2005	95%	5%	18%	82%
2004	93%	7%	26%	74%
2003	93%	7%	20%	80%
2002	94%	6%	32%	68%

INTEREST GROUPS

	AFL-CIO	ADA	CCUS	ACU
2006	100%	90%	20%	20%
2005	93%	100%	35%	16%
2004	100%	90%	25%	4%
2003	100%	100%	13%	24%
2002	100%	90%	26%	8%

WISCONSIN 7

Northwest – Wausau, Superior, Stevens Point

Wisconsin's largest and most rural district, the 7th stretches north and west from the state's central counties to the Apostle Islands in the waters of southern Lake Superior. Small towns and family farms checker the district, carrying a populist flavor and retaining threads of mid-twentieth century LaFollette progressivism.

Farming sustains the district's economy, although cold weather in the north shaves a full month off the growing season. The dairy industry is in decline, but small, 60-cow farms still populate the northern half of the 7th. Centrally located Marathon County leads Wisconsin in dairy production. The nutrient-rich soil in the Central Sands country in the state's midsection produces seed potatoes, cranberries, vegetables and ginseng. Some small metalworking and paper factories — the industries that attracted immigrants to the 7th in the 19th century — still produce their goods. Stevens Point and Wausau continue to be local insurance hubs, despite one large takeover by an out-of-state company.

The tranquil lifestyle in the small towns appeals to senior citizens, and the 7th's hundreds of lakes in the north are a natural draw for tourists. The University of Wisconsin campuses at Stevens Point and Superior attract young people to the area. A large number of Hmong immigrants from Asia's eastern coast have settled in Marathon County. One fast-growing area of the district is Polk County, which capitalizes on its proximity to the Minneapolis-St. Paul metropolitan area.

Blue-collar regions around Stevens Point and Wausau, and along Lake Superior in the north, consistently vote Democratic, while descendants of Scandinavian immigrants in north-central Wisconsin and a Christian Right contingent keep the region politically competitive. John Kerry narrowly won the district with 50 percent of its 2004 presidential vote.

MAJOR INDUSTRY

Agriculture, paper, manufacturing

CITIES

Wausau, 38,426; Superior, 27,368; Stevens Point, 24,551

NOTABLE

The American Birkebeiner, from Cable to Hayward, is North America's largest cross-country ski marathon; Poniatowski is the center of the western hemisphere's northern half; Colby cheese is named after a town here; Hayward is home to the National Fresh Water Fishing Hall of Fame.

Rep. Steve Kagen (D)

Elected 2006; 1st term

A physician who founded a string of allergy clinics in Wisconsin, Kagen is promoting a plan to ensure guaranteed access to health coverage through a standard policy that every insurer would have to offer to every American — "a single risk pool, 300 million strong."

He may have to find others to advance his "No Patient Left Behind" plan. His committee assignments focus on agriculture and transportation, not health care. With the Agriculture panel working on a major rewrite of farm policy in the 110th Congress (2007-08), Kagen is well positioned to help his state's dairy industry. "I used to work in a dairy, and some of my best friends have cheese companies," Kagen says. "I understand the needs of agriculture."

Kagen, who turned over his clinic business to his brother in January 2007, got in hot water the same month with the Food and Drug Administration, which told him to stop making and selling allergy vaccines across state lines without the required "biologics" license.

He also drew unwelcome publicity for telling a small group of hometown peace activists that during a White House reception for freshman lawmakers, he had bragged to President Bush's political adviser Karl Rove that, "I kicked your ass." There was more, all of it decidedly over the top. The White House dismissed Kagen's account as "ridiculous," and Kagen was peppered with editorial criticism back home. The Appleton Post-Crescent reported that he apologized in a letter to constituents, calling his remarks a "mishandled attempt at humor."

In addition to running his allergy clinics prior to his election to Congress, Kagen served as an assistant clinical professor of allergy/immunology at the Medical College of Wisconsin and as an allergy consultant for CNN.

The 8th District seat came open when Republican Mark Green left to make an unsuccessful bid for governor. Kagen ran as an outsider, while John Gard, his GOP foe, was the state's Assembly Speaker and had been a lawmaker since 1987. Kagen raised nearly $3.2 million, $2.5 million of it from his own pockets, in what became the costliest House race in state history. He won by 2 percentage points. Both parties immediately targeted the seat for 2008.

CAPITOL OFFICE
225-5665
kagen.house.gov
1232 Longworth 20515-4908; fax 225-5729

COMMITTEES
Agriculture
Transportation & Infrastructure

RESIDENCE
Appleton

BORN
Dec. 12, 1949, Neenah, Wis.

RELIGION
Jewish

FAMILY
Wife, Gayle Kagen; four children

EDUCATION
U. of Wisconsin, B.S. 1972 (molecular biology), M.D. 1976

CAREER
Allergy clinic owner; physician

POLITICAL HIGHLIGHTS
No previous office

ELECTION RESULTS

2006 GENERAL		
Steve Kagen (D)	141,570	50.9%
John Gard (R)	135,622	48.8%
2006 PRIMARY		
Steve Kagen (D)	25,623	47.6%
Jamie Wall (D)	15,427	28.7%
Nancy Nusbaum (D)	12,731	23.7%

WISCONSIN 8
Northeast — Green Bay, Appleton

On autumn Sundays, all eyes in Wisconsin turn to the 8th to watch football's Green Bay Packers. Regardless of the team's fortunes, the Packers represent the emotional heart of the state, and they pull in millions of dollars. But the district's blue-collar feel stems from the Fox River Valley's paper industry, which stretches southwest from Green Bay.

The 8th's mostly stable economy depends on natural resources. The sparsely populated north contains the state's largest tracts of forests, supplying the local paper industry. Fertile soil in the district's south supports grain, and the open land hosts ranches. Appleton and Green Bay have some high-skill manufacturing.

The area draws many tourists, especially from Milwaukee and Chicago, during the more temperate seasons. Forests and lakes in Vilas County, near the Michigan border, lure outdoorsmen and nature lovers. The Door County peninsula jutting into Lake Michigan has 250 miles of shore and attracts wealthier vacationers to upscale second homes, vineyards, apple and cherry orchards, and artists' colonies. The 8th also is home to six American Indian tribes, each of which boasts a reservation-based casino.

The largely Catholic 8th has a long history of social conservatism. Although the district has a slight GOP lean, Brown County (Green Bay) has competitive areas and Democrats dominate Menominee County. George W. Bush won the 8th's 2004 presidential vote, but district voters elected a Democrat to the House in 2006 with 51 percent of the vote.

MAJOR INDUSTRY
Paper products, casinos, agriculture, tourism

CITIES
Green Bay, 102,313; Appleton (pt.) 69,270

NOTABLE
The snowmobile was invented in Sayner.

WYOMING

Gov. Dave Freudenthal (D)

Pronounced: FREED-en-thal
First elected: 2002
Length of term: 4 years
Term expires: 1/11
Salary: $120,000
Phone: (307) 777-7434
Residence: Cheyenne
Born: Oct. 12, 1950; Thermopolis, Wyo.
Religion: Episcopalian
Family: Wife, Nancy Freudenthal; four children
Education: Amherst College, B.A. 1973 (economics); U. of Wyoming, J.D. 1980
Career: Lawyer; gubernatorial aide; state economic development official
Political highlights: Wyo. State Planning Coordinator, 1975-77; U.S. attorney, 1994-2001

Election results:

2006 GENERAL		
Dave Freudenthal (D)	135,516	70.0%
Ray Hunkins (R)	58,100	30.0%

Secretary of State Max Maxfield (R)

(no lieutenant governor)
First elected: 2006
Length of term: 4 years
Term expires: 1/11
Salary: $92,000
Phone: (307) 777-5333

LEGISLATURE

General Assembly: 40 days January-March in odd-numbered years; 20 days February-March in even-numbered years

Senate: 30 members, 4-year terms
2007 ratios: 23 R, 7 D; 26 men, 4 women
Salary: $150/day in session
Phone: (307) 777-7711

House: 60 members, 2-year terms
2007 ratios: 43 R, 17 D; 43 men, 17 women
Salary: $150/day in session
Phone: (307) 777-7852

TERM LIMITS

Governor: 2 terms
Senate: 3 terms
House: 6 terms

URBAN STATISTICS

CITY	POPULATION
Cheyenne	53,011
Casper	49,644
Laramie	27,204
Gillette	19,646

REGISTERED VOTERS

Republican	62%
Democrat	26%
Others/unaffiliated	12%

POPULATION

2006 population (est.)	515,004
2000 population	493,782
1990 population	453,588
Percent change (1990-2000)	+8.9%
Rank among states (2006)	50
Median age	36.2
Born in state	42.5%
Foreign born	2.3%
Violent crime rate	267/100,000
Poverty level	11.4%
Federal workers	7,186
Military	6,224

ELECTIONS

STATE ELECTION OFFICIAL
(307) 777-7186
DEMOCRATIC PARTY
(307) 473-1457
REPUBLICAN PARTY
(307) 234-9166

MISCELLANEOUS

Web: www.wyoming.gov
Capital: Cheyenne

U.S. CONGRESS

Senate: 2 Republicans
House: 1 Republican

2000 Census Statistics by District

DIST.	2004 VOTE FOR PRESIDENT BUSH	KERRY	WHITE	BLACK	ASIAN	HISP	MEDIAN INCOME	WHITE COLLAR	BLUE COLLAR	SERVICE INDUSTRY	OVER 64	UNDER 18	COLLEGE EDUCATION	RURAL	SQ. MILES
AL	69%	29%	89%	1%	1%	6%	$37,892	54%	29%	17%	12%	26%	22%	35%	97,100
STATE	69	29	89	1	1	6	$37,892	54	29	17	12	26	22	35	97,100
U.S.	50.7	48.3	69	12	4	13	$41,994	60	25	15	12	26	24	21	3,537,438

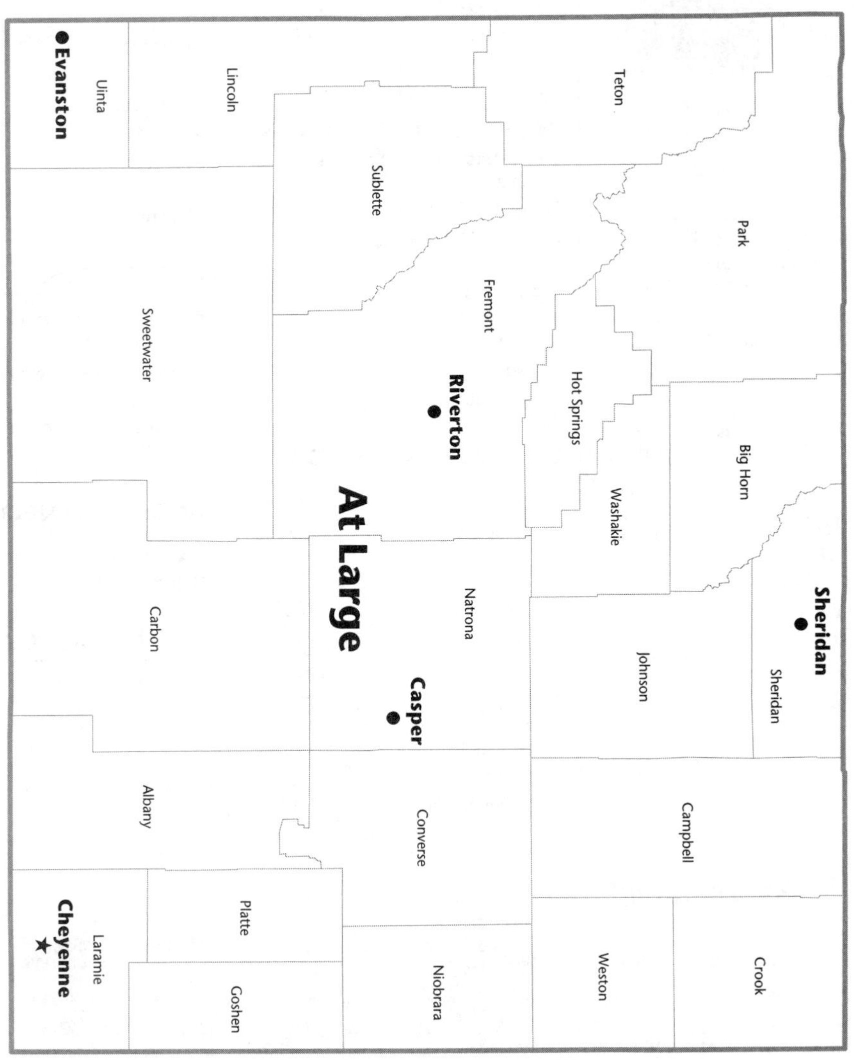
Evanston
Uinta
Lincoln
Teton
Sublette
Park
Fremont
Sweetwater
Riverton
Hot Springs
Big Horn
Washakie
At Large
Sheridan
Sheridan
Natrona
Carbon
Johnson
Casper
Albany
Converse
Campbell
Cheyenne
Laramie
Platte
Goshen
Niobrara
Weston
Crook

Sen. Craig Thomas (R)

CAPITOL OFFICE
224-6441
thomas.senate.gov
307 Dirksen 20510-5003; fax 224-1724

COMMITTEES
Energy & Natural Resources
Environment & Public Works
Finance
Indian Affairs - vice chairman
Select Ethics

RESIDENCE
Casper

BORN
Feb. 17, 1933, Cody, Wyo.

RELIGION
Methodist

FAMILY
Wife, Susan Thomas; four children

EDUCATION
U. of Wyoming, B.A. 1955; La Salle U., LL.B. 1963

MILITARY SERVICE
Marine Corps, 1955-59

CAREER
Power company trade association executive; agricultural association executive

POLITICAL HIGHLIGHTS
Sought Republican nomination for Wyo. treasurer, 1978; sought Republican nomination for Wyo. treasurer, 1982; Wyo. House, 1985-89; U.S. House, 1989-95

ELECTION RESULTS

2006 GENERAL

Craig Thomas (R)	135,174	70.1%
Dale Groutage (D)	57,671	29.9%

2006 PRIMARY

Craig Thomas (R)	unopposed

PREVIOUS WINNING PERCENTAGES
2000 (74%); 1994 (59%); 1992 House Election (58%); 1990 House Election (55%); 1989 Special House Election (52%)

Elected 1994; 3rd term

Sen. Thomas died June 4, 2007, of acute myeloid leukemia. He was 74. Politics in America had gone to press by the time of his death. Under Wyoming law, Democratic Gov. Dave Freudenthal was required to appoint a Republican to fill the seat until a special election could take place in 2008.

Almost two decades in Washington have done little to dull Thomas' Western sensibilities. From his rodeo letterhead to his plainspoken style and reliably conservative votes, Thomas isn't one for an identity crisis. "If anything, I have become more comfortable as a Republican as time has gone on. We have figured out who we are over the years," he says.

Like most Western Republicans, Thomas is a fiscal conservative, an advocate of multiple uses of public lands, a defender of private property rights and a supporter of his state's farmers and ranchers.

Thomas is a popular presence in the famously clubby Senate. He is quick with humor, as is his wife Susan, who is seen laughing with members outside the chamber so frequently that she is sometimes mistaken for a lobbyist or Hill staffer by those who don't know better.

He finds the caustic partisanship of today's political climate disturbing. But he does his part to sweeten matters. When the Senate's "candy desk" became available at the beginning of the 110th Congress (2007-08), Thomas grabbed it. Located at the rear of the chamber adjacent to the aisle, it is stocked with treats and serves as a bipartisan magnet during floor votes and debate. (Pennsylvania Republican Rick Santorum, defeated in 2006, was the last occupant of the desk.)

Thomas pursues his state's interests in a quiet, methodical way that has made him remarkably few enemies. He is known for his courtesy and diplomacy even on bitterly contested issues, but he is no pushover. He is a former Marine Corps captain.

His committee assignments position him well to address issues his constituents care about. In the 110th Congress, he claimed the top Republican position on the Indian Affairs Committee, from which he hopes to help fuel economic development on his state's 2.2 million-acre Wind River reservation east of Jackson, which is home to the Eastern Shoshone and Northern Arapaho tribes.

He also serves on the Energy and Natural Resources, Environment and Public Works, and Finance committees. On the latter, he won an intramural battle with Utah's Orrin G. Hatch to serve as top Republican on the new energy subcommittee. Thomas planned to use the position in part to promote advanced coal technology.

By the numbers, Thomas is indistinguishable from his Wyoming GOP colleagues, Sen. Michael B. Enzi and Rep. Barbara Cubin. Their presidential support and party unity scores in the 109th Congress (2005-06) are nearly identical. But Thomas is more open than the other two to the concerns of environmentalists, hunters, fishermen, outfitters and ranchers about the impact that Wyoming's current oil and gas boom is having on the state's wildlife habitat, rivers and ranches.

As ranking Republican on the Energy and Natural Resources National Parks Subcommittee, Thomas looks out for Grand Teton and Yellowstone national parks in northwestern Wyoming, which are major tourist draws and economic engines. In 2004, Thomas pushed a provision to a catchall spending bill allowing snowmobiles continued access to Yellowstone and Grand

Teton parks. President Bill Clinton tried to phase out snowmobile use, but the Bush administration reversed that regulation. "We needed to provide certainty for visitors and those providing services in our parks," Thomas said.

Thomas says there should be multiple uses for federal lands, including wilderness preservation. He says he enjoys nothing more than a horseback ride through Wyoming's spectacular wilderness areas, and has criticized Bush administration proposals to trim spending on national parks. In 2001 and 2002, Thomas sided with environmentalists by proposing a ban on tours by air over the parks, winning praise from the same "green" groups that often fight him tooth and nail. "It's kind of scary," Thomas mused. "I bet they are asking themselves, 'What the hell are we doing?' "

Thomas really riled environmental groups in 104th Congress (1995-96), when he took the lead on a bill allowing 12 Western states to take control of 270 million acres of federal land, including wilderness areas that were among the nation's few remaining pristine ecosystems. Thomas said the states could do a better job overseeing the lands than the federal Bureau of Land Management. The proposal got a lot of media attention at a time Republicans were under pressure to prove they cared about the environment. Thomas reluctantly delayed his bill.

As a member of the Finance Committee, Thomas has backed President Bush's efforts to cut taxes and trim spending. Like other senators from rural states, Thomas is acutely aware that many of his constituents lack access to even basic medical services. He shares the chairmanship of the Senate Rural Health Caucus with Iowa Democrat Tom Harkin, and the two have pressed for legislation to increase physician recruitment incentives, equalize Medicare payments to rural and urban health care providers, and help fund telemedicine programs.

Before he came to Congress, Thomas was vice president of the Wyoming Farm Bureau and once headed the rural electric trade association in Wyoming. Raised on a ranch near Wapiti, just east of Yellowstone, he is a defender of the state's cattle industry. Thomas and 10 other senators urged the White House to push Japan to reopen its border to U.S. beef after the country banned imports of the beef in 2003, when a cow infected with mad cow disease was found at a slaughterhouse in Washington state.

Thomas suffered a health scare in 2006, when he was diagnosed with leukemia two days after his re-election to a third term. He was away from work only about a month to undergo treatment and maintained his normal routine of morning calisthenics and light running throughout his ordeal.

Wyoming is also the home state of Thomas' friend Vice President Dick Cheney. It was Cheney who floated Thomas' name to become secretary of the Interior in 2001 and again in 2006, but Thomas says he is content with his role in the Senate.

Thomas had difficulty breaking into politics. He twice sought the GOP nomination for state treasurer, losing both times. Then in 1984, at age 51, he was elected to the Wyoming House. In 1989, when Cheney was nominated by President George H.W. Bush to be secretary of Defense, Thomas got the nod from the party's state central committee. He won the special election to succeed Cheney in the House with 52 percent of the vote.

Five years later, GOP Sen. Malcolm Wallop retired and Thomas ran for his seat with history weighing heavily on his side — Democrats have not won a U.S. Senate election in Wyoming since 1970. Democrats nominated popular Gov. Mike Sullivan, who, though hardly a liberal, had ties to Clinton dating to their service together in the National Governors Association. He also was the first sitting governor to endorse Clinton for president. Thomas won handily by almost 20 percentage points. In 2000 and 2006, he did even better, swamping his Democratic foes by wide margins.

KEY VOTES

2006

- Yes Confirm Samuel A. Alito Jr. to the Supreme Court
- Yes Allow consideration of a bill to establish a $140 billion trust fund to compensate victims of asbestos exposure
- Yes Extend tax cuts for two years at a cost of $70 billion over five years
- No Overhaul immigration policy with border security, enforcement and guest worker program
- Yes Allow consideration of a bill to permanently repeal the estate tax
- No Urge President Bush to begin troop withdrawals from Iraq in 2006
- No Lift President Bush's restrictions on stem cell research funding
- Yes Authorize military tribunals for suspected terrorists

2005

- Yes Curb class action lawsuits by shifting them from state to federal courts
- Yes Allow confirmation vote on Priscilla R. Owen to the U.S. Court of Appeals for the 5th Circuit
- Yes Oppose mandatory emissions limits and block recognition of global warming as a threat
- No Approve free-trade pact with five Central American countries
- Yes Pass energy policy overhaul favored by President Bush emphasizing domestic oil and gas production
- Yes Shield gunmakers from lawsuits when their products are used in crimes
- Yes Ban torture of prisoners in U.S. custody
- Yes Renew 16 provisions of the Patriot Act
- Yes Allow final vote on opening the Arctic National Wildlife Refuge to oil and gas exploration

CQ VOTE STUDIES

	PARTY UNITY		PRESIDENTIAL SUPPORT	
	Support	Oppose	Support	Oppose
2006	97%	3%	91%	9%
2005	94%	6%	84%	16%
2004	99%	1%	96%	4%
2003	99%	1%	98%	2%
2002	96%	4%	94%	6%
2001	97%	3%	97%	3%
2000	97%	3%	40%	60%
1999	96%	4%	31%	69%
1998	95%	5%	39%	61%
1997	98%	2%	57%	43%

INTEREST GROUPS

	AFL-CIO	ADA	CCUS	ACU
2006	13%	5%	90%	96%
2005	21%	10%	89%	92%
2004	8%	5%	100%	100%
2003	0%	0%	100%	85%
2002	15%	10%	90%	100%
2001	13%	5%	100%	96%
2000	0%	0%	92%	92%
1999	0%	0%	100%	87%
1998	13%	5%	89%	84%
1997	0%	10%	90%	84%

Sen. Michael B. Enzi (R)

CAPITOL OFFICE
224-3424
enzi.senate.gov
379A Russell 20510-5004; fax 228-0359

COMMITTEES
Banking, Housing & Urban Affairs
Budget
Health, Education, Labor & Pensions - ranking member
Small Business & Entrepreneurship

RESIDENCE
Gillette

BORN
Feb. 1, 1944, Bremerton, Wash.

RELIGION
Presbyterian

FAMILY
Wife, Diana Enzi; three children

EDUCATION
George Washington U., B.A. 1966 (accounting); U. of Denver, M.S. 1968 (retail marketing)

MILITARY SERVICE
Wyo. Air National Guard, 1967-73

CAREER
Accountant; computer programmer; shoe store owner

POLITICAL HIGHLIGHTS
Mayor of Gillette, 1975-83; Wyo. House, 1987-91; Wyo. Senate, 1991-96

ELECTION RESULTS

2002 GENERAL		
Michael B. Enzi (R)	133,710	73.0%
Joyce Jansa Corcoran (D)	49,570	27.1%
2002 PRIMARY		
Michael B. Enzi (R)	78,612	85.9%
Crosby "Cros" Allen (R)	12,931	14.1%

PREVIOUS WINNING PERCENTAGES
1996 (54%)

Elected 1996; 2nd term

The Senate's only accountant, Enzi has a knack for numbers that came in handy in 2006 as he led congressional negotiations on a complex overhaul of the federal law governing the nation's private pension system. The final result was the crowning achievement of Enzi's career to date and one of the most significant bills enacted in the 109th Congress (2005-06).

Enzi was then the chairman of the Senate Health, Education, Labor and Pensions Committee, where he worked closely with the liberal Edward M. Kennedy to draft the pension bill in 2005 and steer it through the Senate with only two dissenting votes. The next year, Enzi (EN-zee) chaired the conference committee that spent five months writing the final version, which required companies to fully fund their pension obligations and provided incentives for workers to boost their own retirement savings. Again, Kennedy was his partner.

The two are still paired on the committee in the 110th Congress (2007-08), only now Kennedy is the chairman and Enzi the ranking Republican. Early in 2007, the two worked in tandem on legislation to overhaul the Food and Drug Administration's drug approval program, in which drug companies pay fees to the FDA to review and approve new pharmaceutical products. The fees are essential to FDA operations.

Representing the "Cowboy State," with its trademark bucking bronco on its license tags, the quiet, conservative Enzi displays the typical Westerner's aversion to government regulation and taxation. But he is a pragmatist with a bent for getting things done. In his two years as chairman of the HELP Committee, he accomplished more than some of his predecessors did over a far longer span. In addition to the landmark pension law, he steered to enactment the first major mine safety legislation in nearly three decades and a reauthorization of the primary vocational education law.

In taking the HELP gavel in 2005, Enzi had to give up chairmanship of the Banking Committee's Securities and Investment Subcommittee, which he had held the previous four years. From that perch, he worked in 2002 with Maryland Democrat Paul S. Sarbanes, then chairman of the full Banking panel, to pass new federal standards for accounting and corporate governance of companies whose stock is sold to the public. The legislation is known throughout the corporate world by the shorthand term Sarbanes-Oxley.

Enzi vigorously opposes regulations that affect public lands and water. As tourism becomes ever more important to Wyoming, his senior colleague, Republican Craig Thomas, has occasionally sided with conservationists and environmentalists fighting to protect the state's wide open spaces. Enzi usually opts to give the oil and gas industry, mining companies, loggers and ranchers free rein.

Enzi generally favors liberalized foreign trade, including agricultural trade with Cuba and expanded ties with China, which could help the farmers and ranchers in his state. But he and Thomas both voted against the Central American Free Trade Agreement in 2005.

Enzi regularly goes to bat for small businesses and says that many lawmakers have no notion of the problems faced by such firms. While some in Congress refer to companies with 100 to 500 workers as small businesses, he says, "To me, a small business is when the person who writes the checks also sweeps the front walk, cleans the toilets and waits on the customers." Once, faced with a proposal by the Clinton administration to protect mine workers from noise, Enzi commented, "I seriously question whether those who wrote this rule have ever actually been to a mine."

He did not, however, question the need for stronger mine safety regulations after a series of accidents in early 2006 killed dozens of coal miners. Instead, he worked with Kennedy and other Democratic senators to draft a bipartisan bill that sailed through both chambers within weeks. Six years earlier, in 2000, Enzi worked with Kennedy to pass a bill designed to protect hospital workers against potentially deadly needle pricks. That won him the endorsement of one of the nation's largest unions, the Service Employees International Union, in 2002. "I really am concerned about worker safety," Enzi says. "I just want to be sure it's done in a way that actually promotes safety and doesn't just beat up on companies."

He opposed the ergonomics regulations imposed in the final days of the Clinton administration and helped orchestrate their repeal in 2001. He has tried repeatedly to advance legislation that would allow small businesses to band together to buy health insurance for their owners and workers, circumventing state coverage mandates. So far, his efforts have been thwarted by a coalition of consumer groups, major insurance companies, labor unions, doctors and others.

He had more success with another longstanding effort. In 2005, as part of a broad energy policy overhaul, Enzi won an extension of Daylight Savings Time. He promoted the change at the request of a second-grade teacher and her class in Sheridan, Wyo., who wanted more daylight for trick-or-treating on Halloween. Enzi, whose daughter Amy is a teacher, was following in the footsteps of his predecessor, Republican Sen. Alan K. Simpson, who also tried several times to pass the bill.

A former computer programmer, Enzi created a stir in his first year in office by announcing his intention to bring his laptop computer onto the Senate floor, where there is a ban on mechanical devices that might be distracting. The Rules Committee refused to grant his request. Enzi continues to press for a rules change, but he's also found a way around it — the BlackBerry, which allows him to send and receive e-mail messages while he's on the floor. Although the little communications devices are also theoretically banned, Enzi says, "you'll find people using them all the time." He doesn't confess directly, but says, "I find them a very useful tool. I don't know how we got along without them."

Enzi was born in Bremerton, Wash., where his father was working in the naval shipyards during World War II. The family moved to Wyoming soon after his birth. After graduating from high school in Sheridan, Enzi headed east to George Washington University in Washington, D.C., where he earned an accounting degree.

He returned west to the University of Denver, where he collected a master's in retail marketing in 1968. The following year, he married and moved back to Wyoming with his wife, Diana, settling in Gillette, where they started their own small business, NZ Shoes. They later added stores in Sheridan and Miles City, Mont.

Enzi began his political career by winning election as mayor of Gillette in 1974, when he was 30. In 1986, he won a seat in the state House, and by 1991 he was serving in the state Senate.

When Simpson retired after 18 years, Enzi went after his Senate seat. In the 1996 primary, he faced several well-known Republican opponents. By building a network of supporters drawn in part from the Wyoming Christian Coalition and stressing his opposition to abortion, he narrowly won the primary. He took the general election by 12 percentage points over Kathy Karpan, a former two-term Wyoming secretary of state.

In 2002, he won re-election with 73 percent of the vote over Democrat Joyce Jansa Corcoran, the former mayor of Lander.

KEY VOTES

2006

Yes Confirm Samuel A. Alito Jr. to the Supreme Court
Yes Allow consideration of a bill to establish a $140 billion trust fund to compensate victims of asbestos exposure
Yes Extend tax cuts for two years at a cost of $70 billion over five years
No Overhaul immigration policy with border security, enforcement and guest worker program
Yes Allow consideration of a bill to permanently repeal the estate tax
No Urge President Bush to begin troop withdrawals from Iraq in 2006
No Lift President Bush's restrictions on stem cell research funding
Yes Authorize military tribunals for suspected terrorists

2005

Yes Curb class action lawsuits by shifting them from state to federal courts
Yes Allow confirmation vote on Priscilla R. Owen to the U.S. Court of Appeals for the 5th Circuit
Yes Oppose mandatory emissions limits and block recognition of global warming as a threat
No Approve free-trade pact with five Central American countries
Yes Pass energy policy overhaul favored by President Bush emphasizing domestic oil and gas production
Yes Shield gunmakers from lawsuits when their products are used in crimes
Yes Ban torture of prisoners in U.S. custody
Yes Renew 16 provisions of the Patriot Act
Yes Allow final vote on opening the Arctic National Wildlife Refuge to oil and gas exploration

CQ VOTE STUDIES

	PARTY UNITY		PRESIDENTIAL SUPPORT	
	Support	Oppose	Support	Oppose
2006	98%	2%	91%	9%
2005	94%	6%	84%	16%
2004	97%	3%	98%	2%
2003	99%	1%	97%	3%
2002	95%	5%	93%	7%
2001	95%	5%	99%	1%
2000	97%	3%	35%	65%
1999	95%	5%	24%	76%
1998	96%	4%	31%	69%
1997	98%	2%	51%	49%

INTEREST GROUPS

	AFL-CIO	ADA	CCUS	ACU
2006	8%	5%	91%	96%
2005	21%	10%	78%	96%
2004	9%	5%	100%	96%
2003	0%	5%	100%	80%
2002	17%	10%	89%	100%
2001	20%	10%	100%	92%
2000	0%	0%	100%	92%
1999	0%	0%	94%	92%
1998	0%	0%	94%	92%
1997	14%	10%	70%	88%

Rep. Barbara Cubin (R)

CAPITOL OFFICE
225-2311
www.house.gov/cubin
1114 Longworth 20515-5001; fax 225-3057

COMMITTEES
Energy & Commerce

RESIDENCE
Casper

BORN
Nov. 30, 1946, Salinas, Calif.

RELIGION
Episcopalian

FAMILY
Husband, Frederick William Cubin; two children

EDUCATION
Creighton U., B.S. 1969 (chemistry); Casper College, attended 1993 (business administration)

CAREER
Medical office manager; realtor; chemist

POLITICAL HIGHLIGHTS
Wyo. House, 1987-93; Wyo. Senate, 1993-95

ELECTION RESULTS

2006 GENERAL		
Barbara Cubin (R)	93,336	48.3%
Gary Trauner (D)	92,324	47.8%
Thomas R. Rankin (LIBERT)	7,481	3.9%
2006 PRIMARY		
Barbara Cubin (R)	50,004	60.0%
Bill Winney (R)	33,287	40.0%
2004 GENERAL		
Barbara Cubin (R)	132,107	55.3%
Ted Ladd (D)	99,989	41.8%
Lewis Stock (LIBERT)	6,581	2.8%

PREVIOUS WINNING PERCENTAGES
2002 (61%); 2000 (67%); 1998 (58%); 1996 (55%); 1994 (53%)

Elected 1994; 7th term

Wyoming, like the rest of the Mountain West, is changing as a trickle of new residents and a flood of tourists seek out its wide open spaces and spectacular scenery. But Cubin remains anchored in the old way of life, fiercely defending the right of individuals and industries to mine, log, graze and drill the land to extract the bountiful natural resources of the nation's least populous state.

Her uncompromising approach and sometimes prickly personality may be wearing a bit thin back home. Although Wyoming is one of the most heavily Republican states, Cubin (CUE-bin) nearly lost her seat in 2006. Her 48 percent vote share was the second-lowest of any winning House candidate that year. Although it had supported her in 2004, the Casper Star-Tribune, the state's largest newspaper, this time endorsed Democrat Gary Trauner, saying Cubin "delivers more rancor than achievement."

Nearly half of Wyoming's 97,100 square miles are under the federal government's jurisdiction, an important factor in a state whose economy — though tilting more toward tourism each year — still relies heavily on extractive industries and ranching. The Bush era has brought an enormous boom in oil and gas production, from coalbed methane in the Powder River Basin in the northeast to natural gas development in the Pinedale region in the southwest. But the energy development has come at a price, threatening water quality and wildlife migration corridors. Ranchers, hunters, fishermen, outfitters and others who once scorned environmentalists now are joining forces with them to lobby for curbs on new drilling leases and protection of the natural resources they all depend upon.

Cubin's lifetime rating from the League of Conservation Voters is just 3 percent. She regularly battles efforts to shield more land from development, arguing in 2000, "The last thing we need in Wyoming is more federal land when the government can't adequately manage the property it has now." She made a small exception in 2007, sponsoring a bill to expand Grand Teton National Park by about 50 acres that local landowners wanted to donate.

Wyoming is the nation's leading coal producer, and Cubin has tried since the 108th Congress (2003-04) to rewrite a portion of the 1977 Surface Mining Control and Reclamation Act that finances mine cleanups nationwide — she wants to recoup more of the fees her state's coal companies pay into an abandoned mine cleanup fund based on the amount of coal they mine. Western states, such as Wyoming, have accumulated substantial balances in the fund because they have few waste sites to clean up. Eastern states with declining amounts of coal, such as Pennsylvania, have large reclamation projects and less revenue to fund them. "Wyoming money is being used to clean up Eastern problems," Cubin said. In 2006, the House included her provision addressing the funding issue in a broad, year-end bill covering a number of issues, but the Senate refused to go along.

As Democrats took control of the House at the start of the 110th Congress (2007-08), Cubin had to give up her seat on the Natural Resources Committee, where she had focused much of her efforts in the past. She will continue to promote energy development from her seat on the Energy and Commerce Committee, while also championing measures to improve access to health care and expand telecommunications in rural areas, important issues in sparsely populated Wyoming.

Cubin also has become an advocate of increased screening of women for heart disease, along with improved education and research. She cosponsored bipartisan legislation in 2007 to promote such efforts after suffering a mild heart attack in the summer of 2005 while waiting at Virginia's Dulles International Airport to board a plane home to Wyoming.

An ardent advocate of gun owners' rights who was elected to a three-year term on the board of the National Rifle Association in 2003, Cubin found herself in hot water in the 108th Congress for her rhetoric. During debate on a gun bill, she said one amendment would have barred the sale of guns "to anybody under drug treatment. So does that mean if you go into a black community, you cannot sell a gun to any black person?" That remark, perceived by some of her colleagues as racist, sparked outrage, but not an official reprimand. Cubin apologized.

She drew more adverse press coverage for remarks she made after a debate in the final days of her 2006 campaign. Libertarian Party candidate Thomas R. Rankin, who was confined to a wheelchair with multiple sclerosis, told local reporters that Cubin became irritated by something he had said and snapped at him, "If you weren't sitting in that chair, I'd slap you across the face." Her remark was widely denounced, and she later apologized.

Reared in Casper, Cubin earned a degree in chemistry and had a variety of jobs, including work as a chemist and real estate agent. She also served as manager of her husband's medical practice. She was active in local party politics and various civic groups, including the Wyoming State Choir, the PTA, a suicide prevention organization and a homeless shelter.

Over the years, her community activities led her to enter elective politics. Cubin served six years in the Wyoming House and two years in the state Senate, specializing in energy-related matters.

Her opening to Congress came in 1994, when Republican Craig Thomas left the state's lone House seat to run for the Senate. Drawing on her base in Casper and benefiting from the fact that she was the only woman in the race, Cubin prevailed in a five-way primary and went on to defeat Democratic lawyer Bob Schuster by 12 percentage points.

She initially won re-election comfortably. But in the 2004 primary, she faced multiple challengers after missing 12 percent of all House roll call votes in the 108th Congress and 27 percent in the 107th to care for her husband, Frederick, who has been hospitalized several times for non-malignant tumors, pancreatic problems and surgical complications. Cubin prevailed again, but her 55 percent vote shares in both the primary and the general election were below her norm.

In 2006, facing Internet executive Trauner, she had the closest call of her House career, prevailing by a scant 1,012 votes, a margin of .5 percent.

KEY VOTES

2006

No Stop broadband companies from favoring select Internet traffic
Yes Affirm U.S. commitment to war in Iraq and reject setting a withdrawal date for troops
Yes Repeal requirement for bilingual ballots at the polls
Yes Permit U.S. sale of civilian nuclear technology to India
Yes Build a 700-mile fence on the U.S.-Mexico border to curb illegal crossings
Yes Permit warrantless wiretaps of suspected terrorists

2005

? Intervene in the life-support case of Terri Schiavo
No Lift President Bush's restrictions on stem cell research funding
Yes Prohibit FBI access to library and bookstore records
No Approve free-trade pact with five Central American countries
Yes Pass energy policy overhaul favored by President Bush emphasizing domestic oil and gas production
Yes End mandatory preservation of habitat of endangered animal and plant species
No Ban torture of prisoners in U.S. custody

CQ VOTE STUDIES

	PARTY UNITY		PRESIDENTIAL SUPPORT	
	Support	Oppose	Support	Oppose
2006	98%	2%	94%	6%
2005	94%	6%	80%	20%
2004	97%	3%	82%	18%
2003	97%	3%	94%	6%
2002	97%	3%	85%	15%

INTEREST GROUPS

	AFL-CIO	ADA	CCUS	ACU
2006	15%	0%	100%	91%
2005	20%	5%	88%	96%
2004	13%	0%	100%	100%
2003	0%	5%	96%	91%
2002	0%	0%	88%	100%

WYOMING

At large

Wyoming, the least populated state, basks in its wide-open spaces, which define its libertarian politics and natural resource-based economy. The Grand Tetons' jagged peaks rise more than 5,000 feet from the floor of the Jackson Hole Valley to their 13,000-foot apex, less than 10 miles from the nation's steepest ski slopes at Jackson Hole Mountain. Tourist attractions, which include Yellowstone National Park — the first national park and one of the most visited in the nation — are economic staples.

The state also relies on mining and commodities sales, so booms and busts coincide with market prices for those goods. After several years of budget shortfalls, the state has been experiencing surpluses due to rising oil and natural gas prices and increased coal-bed methane mining. The minerals industry is expanding due to increased access to attainable natural gas reserves and a growing number of drilling rigs. The state lacks a diversified employment base, however, and many skilled workers and college graduates have left the state for better-paying jobs.

Residents savor their land and resources and reject government intrusion of any kind, especially in dictating how land may be used. In most regions, residents are happy with the state's relative seclusion and tranquil lifestyle and do not particularly favor population growth. The state's lawmakers are loath to raise taxes and dare not entertain a dreaded income tax. Wyoming has no corporate or personal income taxes and has a statewide 4 percent sales tax.

Wyoming voters are predominately Republican, but they will sometimes allow personality to triumph over party if a Democratic candidate is moderate and unaffiliated with the national party. Wyoming has not elected a Democrat to Congress since 1976, but has elected a Democratic governor in seven of the last nine elections.

MAJOR INDUSTRY
Mining, tourism, agriculture

MILITARY BASES
Francis E. Warren Air Force Base, 3,764 military, 956 civilian (2004)

CITIES
Cheyenne, 53,011; Casper, 49,644; Laramie, 27,204; Gillette, 19,646

NOTABLE
Jackson was the first U.S. town ever to elect an all-female slate — mayor, council and marshal — in 1920.

Del. Eni F.H. Faleomavaega (D)

Elected 1988; 10th term

Faleomavaega has served in the House for 20 years, his longevity earning him a subcommittee chair in the 110th Congress (2007-08). He is the fourth-highest-ranking Democrat on Foreign Affairs and chairman of its Asia, the Pacific and the Global Environment panel. Faleomavaega (full name: EN-ee FOL-ee-oh-mav-ah-ENG-uh) is also a senior member of Natural Resources.

His committee spots are a good match for his island territory. Faleomavaega is intent on improving American Samoa's economy, which is dominated by tuna fishing and processing. It took two tries, but in the 109th Congress (2005-06), he won a provision to extend an important tax credit that Faleomavaega says will help American Samoa's tuna industry "remain competitive," especially against low-wage Thailand. StarKist and Chicken of the Sea operate canneries that generate 80 percent of American Samoa's private sector economy, and Faleomavaega wants to keep the companies there. The two tuna companies employ 5,000 of his constituents in their canneries.

Faleomavaega also hopes to gain a tsunami monitoring and early warning system for the islands to avoid a disaster on the scale of the deadly 2004 tsunami in Southeast Asia that killed more than 186,000 people. He also presses for Congress to remove the limit on federal Medicaid dollars that territories can receive, as many Samoans are dependent on public health care.

Faleomavaega went to high school in Hawaii when his father was stationed there in the Navy. He earned a bachelor's from Brigham Young University, joined the Army and served in Vietnam, then returned to the mainland for law school. He worked for eight years in Washington, first as an executive assistant to American Samoa's first elected representative to the Capitol, A.U. Fuimaono, then for California Democratic Rep. Phillip Burton, the Interior Committee chairman, whom he credits for much of his success.

Faleomavaega returned to Pago Pago in 1981, serving as a deputy attorney general and then as lieutenant governor. He is a "matai" — a Samoan chief — a title he has held since 1988. Faleomavaega is actually his title; his family name is Hunkin. He has had tough re-election battles since first winning in 1988; in 2006, he won with a plurality of 47 percent of the vote.

CAPITOL OFFICE
225-8577
faleomavaega@mail.house.gov
www.house.gov/faleomavaega
2422 Rayburn 20515-5201; fax 225-8757

COMMITTEES
Foreign Affairs
(Asia, the Pacific & the Global Environment - chairman)
Natural Resources

RESIDENCE
Pago Pago

BORN
Aug. 15, 1943, Vailoatai, Am. Samoa

RELIGION
Mormon

FAMILY
Wife, Hinanui Bambridge Hunkin; five children

EDUCATION
Brigham Young U., A.A. 1964, B.A. 1966 (political science); Texas Southern U., attended 1969 (law); U. of Houston, J.D. 1972; U. of California, Berkeley, LL.M. 1973

MILITARY SERVICE
Army, 1966-69; Army Reserve, 1983-2001

CAREER
Lawyer; territorial prosecutor; congressional aide

POLITICAL HIGHLIGHTS
Democratic candidate for U.S. House, 1984; lieutenant governor, 1985-89

ELECTION RESULTS

2006 GENERAL		
Eni F.H. Faleomavaega (D)	5,195	47.1%
Amata Aumua (R)	4,493	40.7%
Ae Ae Muavaefaatasi Jr (I)	1,345	12.2%
2004 GENERAL		
Eni F.H. Faleomavaega (D)	12,108	64.6%
Aumua Amata Coleman (R)	6,646	35.4%

PREVIOUS WINNING PERCENTAGES
2002 General Runoff Election (55%); 2000 General Runoff Election (61%); 1998 (86%); 1996 General Runoff Election (56%); 1994 (64%); 1992 (65%); 1990 (55%); 1988 (51%)

AMERICAN SAMOA

In the heart of Polynesia, American Samoa is the nation's southernmost territory and the least populated entity represented in the U.S. House. Located about 2,500 miles southwest of Hawaii, it is composed of five volcanic islands and two outlying coral atolls (total land area, 76 square miles, slightly more than the District of Columbia). Tourists venture here for snorkeling, fishing and hiking.

An 1899 treaty gave the United States control over the islands in the eastern portion of the Samoan archipelago. During World War II, the U.S. Marine Corps, attracted by the deep-water harbor at Pago Pago, made the island an advanced training and staging center. Today it is an unincorporated territory of the United States, administered by the Interior Department. Residents are U.S. nationals, not citizens, and the territory has had a non-voting delegate since 1981.

Most land here is communally owned. Per capita income is very low, and federal aid, including welfare and food stamps, is vital. Economic growth, even in the promising tourism sector, is hindered by American Samoa's isolation, limited transportation and susceptibility to hurricanes.

Tuna fishing and processing plants are the key elements of the private sector economy, but the islands' tuna processing now is threatened by lower-wage competition from South America and Southeast Asia. In recent years, there has been a concerted government effort to cope with the islands' limited resources of fresh water.

MAJOR INDUSTRY
Tuna processing, government, handicrafts, tourism

VILLAGES
Tafuna, 8,409; Nu'uuli, 5,154; Pago Pago, 4,278

NOTABLE
Anthropologist Margaret Mead studied on Ta'u and wrote "Coming of Age in Samoa."

Del. Eleanor Holmes Norton (D)

Elected 1990; 9th term

The takeover of Congress by the Democrats after the 2006 election brought Norton closer to her top political goal, which is to give Washington residents full representation in the House and thereby change her own title from Delegate to Representative.

In April 2007, the House passed a measure to give the D.C. delegate full floor voting privileges while also adding one more House seat for Utah. The bill's mostly Democratic supporters cast the issue as one of fairness to the more than half-million District residents who pay taxes but do not have full representation in Congress. The D.C. delegate can vote in committees and in the House when it is sitting as the Committee of the Whole. Delegates were given similar voting privileges in 1993, only to lose them in 1995, when Republicans were in control of the House.

Norton said she "made baby steps" under the Republicans, but she was waiting for the Democrats to retake the majority "in order to get these very important structural changes for the District's self-governing rights."

Norton is highly regarded in both the city and on Capitol Hill. She serves on the Oversight and Government Reform Committee, an important assignment as the panel has jurisdiction over matters involving the District. She won a key victory in the 109th Congress (2005-06) with passage of a bill giving the city government mid-year budget autonomy, allowing it to spend locally raised funds without returning to secure congressional approval.

Norton also serves on the Homeland Security Committee and the Transportation panel, where she chairs the Economic Development, Public Buildings and Emergency Management Subcommittee.

A native Washingtonian, Norton graduated in the last segregated class at Dunbar High School. Her father was a city employee, and her mother a teacher. After earning a law degree at Yale and working in Mississippi with civil rights groups, she took a job with the American Civil Liberties Union. She was teaching law at Georgetown University in 1990 when D.C. Delegate Walter E. Fauntroy stepped down to run for mayor. She routinely wins with better than 90 percent of the vote.

CAPITOL OFFICE
225-8050
www.norton.house.gov
2136 Rayburn 20515-5101; fax 225-3002

COMMITTEES
Homeland Security
Oversight & Government Reform
Transportation & Infrastructure
(Economic Development, Public Buildings & Emergency Management - chairwoman)

RESIDENCE
Washington

BORN
June 13, 1937, Washington, D.C.

RELIGION
Episcopalian

FAMILY
Divorced; two children

EDUCATION
Antioch College, B.A. 1960 (history); Yale U., M.A. 1963 (American studies), LL.B. 1964

CAREER
Professor; lawyer

POLITICAL HIGHLIGHTS
New York City Human Rights Commission, 1971-77; Equal Employment Opportunity Commission chairwoman, 1977-81

ELECTION RESULTS

2006 GENERAL		
Eleanor Holmes Norton (D)	111,726	97.3%
write-ins	3,051	2.7%
2006 PRIMARY		
Eleanor Holmes Norton (D)	95,419	92.8%
Andy Miscuk (D)	6,681	6.5%
2004 GENERAL		
Eleanor Holmes Norton (D)	202,027	91.3%
Michael Monroe (R)	18,296	8.3%

PREVIOUS WINNING PERCENTAGES
2002 (93%); 2000 (90%); 1998 (90%); 1996 (90%); 1994 (89%); 1992 (85%); 1990 (62%)

DISTRICT OF COLUMBIA

"Taxation Without Representation." That slogan on the District's license plates sums up succinctly residents' displeasure at not being able to participate fully in a democracy that they host. The city's budget and laws are subject to review and veto by Congress, a body in which the residents have no vote.

Although residents have a vote for president, a non-voting delegate in the House (since 1971), and an elected mayor (since 1974), efforts to gain full participation in the U.S. government — including bids for statehood — have not yet succeeded.

It is no surprise that the main business of the nation's capital is government. Hundreds of thousands work for the federal or local governments or in related work in the private sector, such as lobbying, law and journalism. It also is no surprise that the District draws hordes of tourists who come to see the Smithsonian museums, national monuments and other well-known sites.

Although the city has one of the wealthier and most-educated populations in the nation, that wealth is not spread evenly throughout the District, with the wealthiest areas in the northwest quadrant. Some revitalized enclaves, such as just east of the U.S. Capitol, attract national chains and young professionals. Local officials hope planned development along both sides of the Anacostia River — including new stadiums for baseball's Nationals and soccer's United — will spur further economic growth.

MAJOR INDUSTRY
Government, professional services

MILITARY BASES
Walter Reed Army Medical Center, 1,679 military, 2,206 civilian; Bolling Air Force Base, 1,961 military, 1,007 civilian; Fort McNair (Army), 1,017 military, 1,033 civilian (2004)

2006 POPULATION (EST.)
Washington, 581,530

NOTABLE
Since residents began casting votes for president in 1964, the Republican candidate's share has ranged from a high of 22 percent in 1972 to a low of 9 percent in 2000 and 2004.

Del. Madeleine Z. Bordallo (D)

CAPITOL OFFICE
225-1188
madeleine.bordallo@mail.house.gov
www.house.gov/bordallo
427 Cannon 20515-5301; fax 226-0341

COMMITTEES
Armed Services
Natural Resources
(Fisheries, Wildlife & Oceans - chairwoman)

RESIDENCE
Tumuning

BORN
May 31, 1933, Graceville, Minn.

RELIGION
Roman Catholic

FAMILY
Widowed; one child

EDUCATION
Saint Mary's College (Ind.), attended 1952-53; The College of St. Catherine, A.A. 1953 (music & voice)

CAREER
Guam first lady; shoe company founder; radio show host

POLITICAL HIGHLIGHTS
Guam Senate, 1981-83, 1987-95; Democratic nominee for governor, 1990; lieutenant governor, 1995-2003

ELECTION RESULTS

2006 GENERAL		
Madeleine Z. Bordallo (D)	32,677	96.5%
write-ins	1,201	3.5%
2006 PRIMARY		
Madeleine Z. Bordallo (D)	20,194	98.7%
write-ins	269	1.3%
2004 GENERAL		
Madeleine Z. Bordallo (D)	31,051	97.4%
write-ins	837	2.6%

PREVIOUS WINNING PERCENTAGES
2002 (65%)

Elected 2002; 3rd term

Bordallo moved from Minnesota to Guam when she was 15 and her father took a job there as a high school principal. She fell in love with the Pacific island and has lived there for nearly 60 years, more than 40 of which she has spent in public life.

Bordallo's top legislative focus is protecting Guam's military bases, which feed the island's economy. Guam is in a strategically significant location near Asia, and after North Korea's unsuccessful test of a long-range ballistic missile in 2006, Bordallo (bore-DAA-yo) raised concerns about the threat posed by her territory's proximity to the rogue state. She sits on the Armed Services Committee, where she does her best to bring home defense and homeland security funds. She also is a member of the Natural Resources Committee, and in the 110th Congress (2007-08) moved up to chair the Fisheries, Wildlife and Oceans Subcommittee.

She has long prodded the U.S. government to provide restitution for islanders who spent 32 months under Japanese occupation during World War II. Her bill would set aside up to $25,000 for reparations, but limit eligibility to Chamorros, the indigenous people, who survived the occupation and were still alive in 1990, and to their direct survivors. Bordallo said, "we have waited 62 years" for reparations. She reintroduced the bill in early 2007.

After attending college in the Midwest to study music, Bordallo returned to Guam and married Ricardo J. Bordallo, the son of a wealthy island family. Ricardo served as the island's governor and Bordallo won a seat in the island's legislature. But in 1990, caught up in a corruption case, Ricardo wrapped himself in the Guam flag, chained himself to a statue of Chief Kepuha on the island's main thoroughfare and shot himself in the head.

"It was probably the most difficult time of my life," Bordallo said, but she credits the Guam custom of mourning with helping her recover. "You are never left alone; you are always surrounded by family and friends."

In 2002, when five-term Democratic Del. Robert A. Underwood ran unsuccessfully for governor of Guam, Bordallo sought the delegate post. She won with 65 percent of the vote, and has been unopposed since.

GUAM

"Where America's day starts," Guam is the largest and most southerly island in the Marianas archipelago. At 212 square miles, it is about three times the size of the District of Columbia. More than 3,800 miles west of Hawaii and across the International Date Line from the U.S. mainland, Guam is closer to Tokyo than Honolulu.

The indigenous people, the Chamorros, first had contact with Europeans in 1521 with the visit of Ferdinand Magellan. Spain ceded Guam to the United States in 1898, and the U.S. Navy administered Guam until 1950, when residents were granted U.S. citizenship and elected a local government. Guam has had a non-voting delegate in the House since 1973. Although residents are citizens, they may not vote in presidential elections.

Guam's economy is heavily dependent on the U.S. military presence, which is expected to increase here by 2014, when thousands of U.S. Marines will be relocated to Guam from bases in Japan. Tropical climate, pristine beaches and a picturesque countryside make the island an ideal vacation spot, and tourism is vital to the local economy. Per capita income in 2001 was $10,872.

Most food and other consumer goods are imported. In recent years, Guam has had to cope with large influxes of illegal immigrants, mostly from China and Burma, who pay smugglers to sneak them onto the island, where they seek asylum in the United States.

MAJOR INDUSTRY
Military, tourism, construction, shipping

MILITARY BASES
Naval Station Guam, 4,050 military, 1,806 civilian; Andersen Air Force Base, 2,170 military, 400 civilian (2004)

DISTRICTS
Dededo, 42,980; Yigo, 19,474; Tamuning, 18,012

NOTABLE
If measured from its base at the bottom of the undersea Marianas Trench, Mount Humuyong Manglo in southern Guam would be the highest mountain in the world.

Res. Cmmsr. Luis Fortuño (R)

CAPITOL OFFICE
225-2615
luis.fortuno@mail.house.gov
www.house.gov/fortuno
126 Cannon 20515-5401; fax 225-2154

COMMITTEES
Education & Labor
Foreign Affairs
Natural Resources

RESIDENCE
Guaynabo

BORN
Oct. 31, 1960, San Juan, P.R.

RELIGION
Roman Catholic

FAMILY
Wife, Luce Fortuno; three children

EDUCATION
Georgetown U., B.S.F.S. 1982; U. of Virginia, J.D. 1985

CAREER
Lawyer

POLITICAL HIGHLIGHTS
P.R. Tourism Company executive director, 1993-96; P.R. Economic Development and Commerce secretary, 1994-96

ELECTION RESULTS

2004 GENERAL		
Luis Fortuño (NP)	947,098	48.5%
Roberto Prats-Palerm (POPDEM)	937,572	48.0%
Edwin Irizarry (PRI)	55,503	2.8%
2003 PRIMARY		
Luis Fortuño (NP)	363,217	61.4%
Carlos A. Romeró-Barcelo (NP)	151,898	25.7%
Charlie Rodriquez (NP)	37,828	6.4%
Miriam Ramirez (NP)	25,075	4.2%
write-ins	13,931	2.4%

Elected 2004; 1st term

The only House member with a four-year term, Fortuño is Puerto Rico's first resident commissioner aligned with the GOP in Congress.

Since his arrival on Capitol Hill, Republican leaders have involved Fortuño (loo-EES four-TOON-yo) in outreach efforts to Hispanic communities across the country. He was elected chairman of the GOP's Congressional Hispanic Conference for the 110th Congress (2007-08). He also was selected as the top Republican on Natural Resources' new Insular Affairs Subcommittee, becoming the first Puerto Rican Republican to hold a leadership position in Congress. The panel's jurisdiction is the political relations between the United States and its territories, including Puerto Rico.

No political issue absorbs Puerto Ricans more than the island's status. Fortuño sponsored a bill in the 109th Congress (2005-06) that would have triggered two plebiscites allowing residents to choose between their current status as a U.S. territory or a "permanent nonterritorial status" and, depending on that vote's outcome, between independence or statehood. Fortuño favors statehood and says Puerto Ricans who have fought and died in U.S. wars, including Iraq, should be able to vote for their commander in chief. In the 110th Congress, he sponsored a similar measure with New York Democrat José E. Serrano.

Democrats instituted new rules in the 110th Congress granting limited voting rights to the delegates, but Fortuño's most notable vote so far occurred within the Republican Conference in 2006. When ballots were counted in the election for a new majority leader, the tally was larger than thought possible. It took several minutes to realize that the extra vote was Fortuño's. (He voted for Roy Blunt of Missouri, who lost to John A. Boehner of Ohio.)

An attorney with a law degree from the University of Virginia, Fortuño was a Georgetown University student when he volunteered in Ronald Reagan's 1980 presidential campaign. Guidance from former Puerto Rican Gov. Luis A. Ferré, a statehood advocate and influential Republican leader, cemented Fortuño's GOP ideals. The island had long been a Democratic stronghold, but in 2004 Fortuño eked out a razor-thin victory.

PUERTO RICO

Puerto Rico, the largest and most populated (3.8 million) of the territories, has been a self-governing commonwealth of the United States since 1952. Median household income here in 2005 was about $17,000 — high by Caribbean standards, but still only about half that of the poorest state.

Christopher Columbus arrived in Puerto Rico in 1493, and the Spanish arrived 15 years later. The Spanish brought slaves to work in the sugar cane fields, and slavery was not abolished on the island until 1873. Spain ceded the territory to the United States in 1898 following the Spanish-American War. Its residents became U.S. citizens in 1917, but they cannot vote for president. Since 1901, Puerto Ricans have been represented in the House by a resident commissioner.

The island's political status has been a longstanding issue, with various factions favoring continued commonwealth status, statehood or independence. In 2004, Puerto Ricans made it clear that public opinion is still closely split between statehood and commonwealth status, as voters sent Res. Cmmsr. Fortuño, who favors statehood, to Congress while Anibal Acevedo-Vilá, a strong proponent of commonwealth status, was elected governor.

Puerto Rico's economy, one of the most stable in the Caribbean, thrives off its tourism industry and industrial sector. Nearly 5 million tourists visit Puerto Rico each year; El Yunque tropical forest and local beaches are popular destinations. U.S. firms also invest heavily here, encouraged by tax incentives and by duty-free access to the United States.

MAJOR INDUSTRY
Manufacturing, service, tourism

MILITARY BASES
Fort Buchanan, 190 military, 699 civilian (2004)

CITIES
San Juan (unincorporated), 434,374; Bayamón (unincorporated), 224,044

NOTABLE
Coliseo Roberto Clemente was named after the baseball star and Puerto Rico native.

Del. Donna M.C. Christensen (D)

CAPITOL OFFICE
225-1790
donna.christensen@mail.house.gov
www.house.gov/christian-christensen
1510 Longworth 20515-5501; fax 225-5517

COMMITTEES
Homeland Security
Natural Resources
(Insular Affairs - chairwoman)

RESIDENCE
St. Croix

BORN
Sept. 19, 1945, Teaneck, N.J.

RELIGION
Moravian

FAMILY
Husband, Chris Christensen; two children, four stepchildren

EDUCATION
Saint Mary's College (Ind.), B.S. 1966 (biology); George Washington U., M.D. 1970

CAREER
Physician; health official

POLITICAL HIGHLIGHTS
Virgin Is. Democratic Territorial Committee, 1980-97 (chairwoman, 1980-82); Virgin Is. Board of Education, 1984-86; Virgin Is. acting commissioner of health, 1993-94; sought Democratic nomination for U.S. House, 1994

ELECTION RESULTS

2006 GENERAL		
Donna M.C. Christensen (D)	18,322	62.9%
Warren B. Mosler (I)	10,800	37.1%
2004 GENERAL		
Donna M.C. Christensen (D)	17,379	65.8%
Warren B. Mosler (I)	7,522	28.5%
Krim M. Ballentine (R)	1,512	5.7%
2002 GENERAL		
Donna M.C. Christensen (D)	20,414	67.7%
Virdin C. Brown (ICM)	4,456	14.8%
Lilliana Belardo de O'Neal (R)	4,286	14.2%
Garry A. Sprauve (I)	996	3.3%

PREVIOUS WINNING PERCENTAGES
2000 (78%); 1998 (80%); 1996 General Runoff Election (52%)

Elected 1996; 6th term

Two good things have happened for Christensen with the Democrats assuming the majority in the 110th Congress (2007-08). First, she took the chair of Natural Resources' Insular Affairs Subcommittee, a panel that had been abolished by the Republicans in 1997. The subcommittee oversees all the U.S. territories, the Marshall Islands, Micronesia and Palau.

Second, the House reaffirmed the right of the delegates from the territories and the District of Columbia to vote in the Committee of the Whole, providing them with limited floor voting rights. When the rule change was debated, Christensen mentioned the sacrifice made by members of the Virgin Islands National Guard in the Iraq War: "I am forced to ask on their behalf and on behalf of all of the people of the Virgin Islands who have sent our loved ones to every war from the Revolutionary to this . . . why is it that some would seek to deny us an even limited vote in the Committee of the Whole?"

The daughter of a St. Croix judge, Christensen is a physician by training, and focuses on the health and economic well-being of her constituents. She wants to ensure that they get their share of dollars from federal programs, such as Supplemental Security Income. She has sponsored a bill to lift the cap on the amount of funding the territory can receive for Medicaid.

Christensen also sits on the Homeland Security Committee, where she has succeeded in winning funds for local port defense. To attract business and industry, Christensen has worked for tax and tariff laws favorable to the V.I., as it is known locally.

Inspired by a booklet encouraging African-American students to consider careers in medicine, Christensen went to medical school at George Washington University. After postgraduate training in San Francisco and Washington, D.C., she returned to the Virgin Islands, where, during the course of a 20-year medical career, she worked in clinics and hospitals on St. Croix. She moved into administrative posts, including acting commissioner of health.

She unsuccessfully sought the delegate post in 1994. But in 1996 she was back, edging Del. Victor O. Frazer, who ran as an independent, and Republican Kenneth Mapp, in a three-way battle. She has won easily since.

VIRGIN ISLANDS

The Virgin Islands, just east of Puerto Rico, are known for their subtropical climate, beautiful beaches, duty-free shopping and — far too often — for being in the path of tropical storms. The first three attributes have helped build a thriving tourism industry, while the storms have made economic development an uneven and difficult process.

Spain asserted its authority over the islands after Christopher Columbus arrived in 1493, and over the next century Spanish settlers killed or drove out the native Indians. Spain showed no real interest in establishing a colony on the Virgin Islands, however. Denmark established a colony on St. Thomas in the latter half of the 17th century, and sugar plantations drove the islands' economy until slavery was abolished in 1848. The U.S. government bought the islands from Denmark for $25 million in 1917.

The Virgin Islands is an unincorporated territory and is under the jurisdiction of the Interior Department. The territory is composed of 68 islands and cays, but only four are inhabited. It had a population in 2000 of 108,612, a 7 percent increase over 1990. Residents are U.S. citizens but may not vote for president. The Virgin Islands has had a non-voting House delegate since 1973.

Cruise ships make regular stops at the islands, principally at the capital of Charlotte Amalie on St. Thomas. Passengers stream ashore to take advantage of duty-free shopping, and most of the Virgin Islands' tourists leave without spending a night. A large petroleum refinery and a rum distillery on St. Croix, as well as light industry on other islands, provide other bases of economic stability.

MAJOR INDUSTRY
Tourism, petroleum refining, rum distilling, watch assembly

CITIES
Charlotte Amalie, 11,004; Christiansted, 2,637

NOTABLE
The Virgin Islands is the only U.S. territory where traffic travels on the left.

Member Statistics

The 2006 election produced a political realignment on Capitol Hill that culminated with a historic first — the elevation of Democrat Nancy Pelosi of California as the first female Speaker of the House.

Over time, Congress has gained a few more women and a little more diversity, but a demographic analysis shows that the 110th Congress, like those before it, is still dominated by white, middle-aged men.

These pages offer unique facts and figures about the men and women of the 110th Congress, their backgrounds and their ties to others who came before them.

The 110th Congress by the Numbers

535 The **total membership** of Congress, not including the five delegates.

153 The number of Roman Catholics in Congress. Protestants make up the largest religious group, but **Catholics** are the largest single denomination.

89 The number of **women** in Congress, including delegates. They represent 17 percent of the total membership.

85 The number of House **Democrats** (37 percent) who served **in the House before Republicans began their 12-year reign in 1995**. There are 63 House Republicans (31 percent) that have experience in the minority prior to that takeover.

71 The percentage of white constituents in Minnesota's 5th District, represented by African-American freshman Democrat Keith Ellison. He has the **largest share of white residents represented by a black House member**.

59 The percentage of black constituents in Tennessee's 9th District, represented by freshman Democrat Steve Cohen. It's the **highest share of black residents represented by a white House member**.

57 The **average age** in Congress; it's 56 for House members and 62 for senators.

42 The age of New Hampshire Republican Sen. **John E. Sununu**, who has been the youngest senator since his 2003 arrival.

4 The number of senators in the 110th Congress who are among the longest-serving in history. West Virginia Democrat **Robert C. Byrd** holds the all-time tenure record. The others, and their ranking on the list, are Democrats **Edward M. Kennedy** of Massachusetts (3rd) and **Daniel K. Inouye** of Hawaii (4th) and Republican **Ted Stevens** of Alaska (7th).

2 The number of Buddhists in Congress. Freshman Democrats **Hank Johnson** of Georgia and **Mazie K. Hirono** of Hawaii are the first **Buddhists** ever to serve in Congress. Also, freshman Democrat **Keith Ellison** of Minnesota is the first **Muslim** to serve in Congress.

1 The number of women ever elected to Congress from the state of New Hampshire. Freshman Democratic Rep. **Carol Shea-Porter** is the first.

Get to know the 110th Congress with these fact files, charts, statistics and other handy reference guides. Immerse yourself in campaign finance numbers. Check out who's in which caucus, scope out who's a doctor, Rhodes scholar or pilot. Plus, you can test your congressional IQ with Did You Know?

Senate Seniority

Senate rank is first determined by the length of consecutive service in the Senate. For senators who entered the Senate on the same day, several tie-breaking procedures determine seniority.

In order of precedence, these factors are: previous Senate service, service as the vice president, previous House service, service in the Cabinet, service as a state governor. If a tie still exists, senators are ranked according to their state's population at the time of swearing in.

Note: Sen. Richard C. Shelby began his service as a Democrat and the Republican Conference credited his service as a Democrat toward his seniority ranking. Sen. Joseph I. Lieberman previously served in the Senate as a Democrat from Jan. 3, 1989 until Jan. 4, 2007.

DEMOCRATS

1.	Robert C. Byrd, W.Va.	Jan. 7, 1959
2.	Edward M. Kennedy, Mass.	Nov. 7, 1962
3.	Daniel K. Inouye, Hawaii	Jan. 9, 1963
4.	Joseph R. Biden Jr., Del.	Jan. 3, 1973
5.	Patrick J. Leahy, Vt.	Jan. 14, 1975
6.	Max Baucus, Mont.	Dec. 15, 1978
7.	Carl Levin, Mich.	Jan. 15, 1979
8.	Christopher J. Dodd, Conn.	Jan. 5, 1981
9.	Jeff Bingaman, N.M.	Jan. 3, 1983
10.	John Kerry, Mass.	Jan. 2, 1985
11.	Tom Harkin, Iowa	Jan. 3, 1985
12.	John D. Rockefeller IV, W.Va.	Jan. 15, 1985
13.	Barbara A. Mikulski, Md.	Jan. 6, 1987
14.	Harry Reid, Nev.	Jan. 6, 1987
15.	Kent Conrad, N.D.	Jan. 6, 1987
16.	Herb Kohl, Wis.	Jan. 3, 1989
17.	Daniel K. Akaka, Hawaii	April 28, 1990
18.	Dianne Feinstein, Calif.	Nov. 4, 1992
19.	Byron L. Dorgan, N.D.	Dec. 15, 1992
20.	Barbara Boxer, Calif.	Jan. 5, 1993
21.	Russ Feingold, Wis.	Jan. 5, 1993
22.	Patty Murray, Wash.	Jan. 5, 1993
23.	Ron Wyden, Ore.	Feb. 6, 1996
24.	Richard J. Durbin, Ill.	Jan. 7, 1997
25.	Tim Johnson, S.D.	Jan. 7, 1997
26.	Jack Reed, R.I.	Jan. 7, 1997
27.	Mary L. Landrieu, La.	Jan. 7, 1997
28.	Charles E. Schumer, N.Y.	Jan. 6, 1999
29.	Blanche Lincoln, Ark.	Jan. 6, 1999
30.	Evan Bayh, Ind.	Jan. 6, 1999
31.	Bill Nelson, Fla.	Jan. 3, 2001
32.	Thomas R. Carper, Del.	Jan. 3, 2001
33.	Debbie Stabenow, Mich.	Jan. 3, 2001
34.	Maria Cantwell, Wash.	Jan. 3, 2001
35.	Ben Nelson, Neb.	Jan. 3, 2001
36.	Hillary Rodham Clinton, N.Y.	Jan. 3, 2001
37.	Frank R. Lautenberg, N.J.	Jan. 7, 2003
		Also served 1983-2001
38.	Mark Pryor, Ark.	Jan. 7, 2003
39.	Barack Obama, Ill.	Jan. 3, 2005
40.	Ken Salazar, Colo.	Jan. 3, 2005
41.	Robert Menendez, N.J.	Jan. 18, 2006
42.	Benjamin L. Cardin, Md.	Jan. 4, 2007
43.	Sherrod Brown, Ohio	Jan. 4, 2007
44.	Bob Casey, Pa.	Jan. 4, 2007
45.	Jim Webb, Va.	Jan. 4, 2007
46.	Claire McCaskill, Mo.	Jan. 4, 2007
47.	Amy Klobuchar, Minn.	Jan. 4, 2007
48.	Sheldon Whitehouse, R.I.	Jan. 4, 2007
49.	Jon Tester, Mont.	Jan. 4, 2007

REPUBLICANS

1.	Ted Stevens, Alaska	Dec. 24, 1968
2.	Pete V. Domenici, N.M.	Jan. 3, 1973
3.	Richard G. Lugar, Ind.	Jan. 4, 1977
4.	Orrin G. Hatch, Utah	Jan. 4, 1977
5.	Thad Cochran, Miss.	Dec. 27, 1978
6.	John W. Warner, Va.	Jan. 2, 1979
7.	Charles E. Grassley, Iowa	Jan. 5, 1981
8.	Arlen Specter, Pa.	Jan. 5, 1981
9.	Mitch McConnell, Ky.	Jan. 3, 1985
10.	Richard C. Shelby, Ala.	Jan. 6, 1987
11.	John McCain, Ariz.	Jan. 6, 1987
12.	Christopher S. Bond, Mo.	Jan. 6, 1987
13.	Trent Lott, Miss.	Jan. 3, 1989
14.	Larry E. Craig, Idaho	Jan. 3, 1991
15.	Judd Gregg, N.H.	Jan. 5, 1993
16.	Robert F. Bennett, Utah	Jan. 5, 1993
17.	Kay Bailey Hutchison, Texas	June 14, 1993
18.	James M. Inhofe, Okla.	Nov. 30, 1994
19.	Olympia J. Snowe, Maine	Jan. 4, 1995
20.	Jon Kyl, Ariz.	Jan. 4, 1995
21.	Craig Thomas, Wyo.	Jan. 4, 1995
22.	Sam Brownback, Kan.	Nov. 27, 1996
23.	Pat Roberts, Kan.	Jan. 7, 1997
24.	Wayne Allard, Colo.	Jan. 7, 1997
25.	Jeff Sessions, Ala.	Jan. 7, 1997
26.	Gordon H. Smith, Ore.	Jan. 7, 1997
27.	Chuck Hagel, Neb.	Jan. 7, 1997
28.	Susan Collins, Maine	Jan. 7, 1997
29.	Michael B. Enzi, Wyo.	Jan. 7, 1997
30.	Jim Bunning, Ky.	Jan. 6, 1999
31.	Michael D. Crapo, Idaho	Jan. 6, 1999
32.	George V. Voinovich, Ohio	Jan. 6, 1999
33.	John Ensign, Nev.	Jan. 3, 2001
34.	Lisa Murkowski, Alaska	Dec. 20, 2002
35.	Saxby Chambliss, Ga.	Jan. 7, 2003
36.	Lindsey Graham, S.C.	Jan. 7, 2003
37.	John E. Sununu, N.H.	Jan. 7, 2003
38.	Elizabeth Dole, N.C.	Jan. 7, 2003
39.	Lamar Alexander, Tenn.	Jan. 7, 2003
40.	John Cornyn, Texas	Jan. 7, 2003
41.	Norm Coleman, Minn.	Jan. 7, 2003
42.	Richard M. Burr, N.C.	Jan. 3, 2005
43.	Jim DeMint, S.C.	Jan. 3, 2005
44.	Tom Coburn, Okla.	Jan. 3, 2005
45.	John Thune, S.D.	Jan. 3, 2005
46.	Johnny Isakson, Ga.	Jan. 3, 2005
47.	David Vitter, La.	Jan. 3, 2005
48.	Mel Martinez, Fla.	Jan. 3, 2005
49.	Bob Corker, Tenn.	Jan. 4, 2007

INDEPENDENTS

1.	Joseph I. Lieberman, Conn.	Jan. 3, 1989
2.	Bernard Sanders, Vt.	Jan. 4, 2007

House Seniority

DEMOCRATS

House Democrats determine seniority by length of service. Members who previously served in the House are given some credit for that service — when they return they are ranked above other members of that entering class.

For members who joined at the beginning of a Congress, service is credited from the session's first day. Seniority for members who won special elections is credited from the election's date. No credit is given for other prior service, such as serving as a senator or governor.

1.	John D. Dingell, Mich.	Dec. 13, 1955
2.	John Conyers Jr., Mich.	Jan. 4, 1965
3.	David R. Obey, Wis.	April 1, 1969
4.	Charles B. Rangel, N.Y.	Jan. 21, 1971
5.	Pete Stark, Calif.	Jan. 3, 1973
6.	John P. Murtha, Pa.	Feb. 5, 1974
7.	George Miller, Calif.	Jan. 14, 1975
8.	James L. Oberstar, Minn.	Jan. 14, 1975
9.	Henry A. Waxman, Calif.	Jan. 14, 1975
10.	Edward J. Markey, Mass.	Nov. 2, 1976
11.	Norm Dicks, Wash.	Jan. 4, 1977
12.	Dale E. Kildee, Mich.	Jan. 4, 1977
13.	Nick J. Rahall II, W.Va.	Jan. 4, 1977
14.	Ike Skelton, Mo.	Jan. 4, 1977
15.	Barney Frank, Mass.	Jan. 5, 1981
16.	Tom Lantos, Calif.	Jan. 5, 1981
17.	Steny H. Hoyer, Md.	May 19, 1981
18.	Howard L. Berman, Calif.	Jan. 3, 1983
19.	Rick Boucher, Va.	Jan. 3, 1983
20.	Marcy Kaptur, Ohio	Jan. 3, 1983
21.	Sander M. Levin, Mich.	Jan. 3, 1983
22.	Alan B. Mollohan, W.Va.	Jan. 3, 1983
23.	Solomon P. Ortiz, Texas	Jan. 3, 1983
24.	John M. Spratt Jr., S.C.	Jan. 3, 1983
25.	Edolphus Towns, N.Y.	Jan. 3, 1983
26.	Gary L. Ackerman, N.Y.	March 1, 1983
27.	Bart Gordon, Tenn.	Jan. 3, 1985
28.	Paul E. Kanjorski, Pa.	Jan. 3, 1985
29.	Peter J. Visclosky, Ind.	Jan. 3, 1985
30.	Peter A. DeFazio, Ore.	Jan. 6, 1987
31.	John Lewis, Ga.	Jan. 6, 1987
32.	Louise M. Slaughter, N.Y.	Jan. 6, 1987
33.	Nancy Pelosi, Calif.	June 2, 1987
34.	Jerry F. Costello, Ill.	Aug. 9, 1988
35.	Frank Pallone Jr., N.J.	Nov. 8, 1988
36.	Eliot L. Engel, N.Y.	Jan. 3, 1989
37.	Nita M. Lowey, N.Y.	Jan. 3, 1989
38.	Jim McDermott, Wash.	Jan. 3, 1989
39.	Michael R. McNulty, N.Y.	Jan. 3, 1989
40.	Richard E. Neal, Mass.	Jan. 3, 1989
41.	Donald M. Payne, N.J.	Jan. 3, 1989
42.	John Tanner, Tenn.	Jan. 3, 1989
43.	Gene Taylor, Miss.	Oct. 17, 1989
44.	José E. Serrano, N.Y.	March 20, 1990
45.	Robert E. Andrews, N.J.	Nov. 6, 1990
46.	Neil Abercrombie, Hawaii	Jan. 3, 1991
		Also served Sept. 1986-Jan. 1987
47.	Robert E. "Bud" Cramer, Ala.	Jan. 3, 1991
48.	Rosa DeLauro, Conn.	Jan. 3, 1991
49.	Chet Edwards, Texas	Jan. 3, 1991
50.	William J. Jefferson, La.	Jan. 3, 1991
51.	James P. Moran, Va.	Jan. 3, 1991
52.	Collin C. Peterson, Minn.	Jan. 3, 1991
53.	Maxine Waters, Calif.	Jan. 3, 1991
54.	John W. Olver, Mass.	June 4, 1991
55.	Ed Pastor, Ariz.	Sept. 24, 1991
56.	Jerrold Nadler, N.Y.	Nov. 3, 1992
57.	Xavier Becerra, Calif.	Jan. 5, 1993
58.	Sanford D. Bishop Jr., Ga.	Jan. 5, 1993
59.	Corrine Brown, Fla.	Jan. 5, 1993
60.	James E. Clyburn, S.C.	Jan. 5, 1993
61.	Anna G. Eshoo, Calif.	Jan. 5, 1993
62.	Bob Filner, Calif.	Jan. 5, 1993
63.	Gene Green, Texas	Jan. 5, 1993
64.	Luis V. Gutierrez, Ill.	Jan. 5, 1993
65.	Alcee L. Hastings, Fla.	Jan. 5, 1993
66.	Maurice D. Hinchey, N.Y.	Jan. 5, 1993
67.	Tim Holden, Pa.	Jan. 5, 1993
68.	Eddie Bernice Johnson, Texas	Jan. 5, 1993
69.	Carolyn B. Maloney, N.Y.	Jan. 5, 1993
70.	Martin T. Meehan, Mass.	Jan. 5, 1993
71.	Earl Pomeroy, N.D.	Jan. 5, 1993
72.	Lucille Roybal-Allard, Calif.	Jan. 5, 1993
73.	Bobby L. Rush, Ill.	Jan. 5, 1993
74.	Robert C. Scott, Va.	Jan. 5, 1993
75.	Bart Stupak, Mich.	Jan. 5, 1993
76.	Nydia M. Velázquez, N.Y.	Jan. 5, 1993
77.	Melvin Watt, N.C.	Jan. 5, 1993
78.	Lynn Woolsey, Calif.	Jan. 5, 1993
79.	Albert R. Wynn, Md.	Jan. 5, 1993
80.	Bennie Thompson, Miss.	April 13, 1993
81.	Sam Farr, Calif.	June 8, 1993
82.	Lloyd Doggett, Texas	Jan. 4, 1995
83.	Mike Doyle, Pa.	Jan. 4, 1995
84.	Chaka Fattah, Pa.	Jan. 4, 1995
85.	Sheila Jackson-Lee, Texas	Jan. 4, 1995
86.	Patrick J. Kennedy, R.I.	Jan. 4, 1995
87.	Zoe Lofgren, Calif.	Jan. 4, 1995
88.	Jesse L. Jackson Jr., Ill.	Dec. 12, 1995
89.	Elijah E. Cummings, Md.	April 16, 1996
90.	Earl Blumenauer, Ore.	May 21, 1996
91.	David E. Price, N.C.	Jan. 6, 1997
		Also served 1987-95
92.	Tom Allen, Maine	Jan. 6, 1997
93.	Marion Berry, Ark.	Jan. 6, 1997
94.	Leonard L. Boswell, Iowa	Jan. 6, 1997
95.	Allen Boyd, Fla.	Jan. 6, 1997
96.	Julia Carson, Ind.	Jan. 6, 1997
97.	Danny K. Davis, Ill.	Jan. 6, 1997
98	Diana DeGette, Colo.	Jan. 6, 1997
99.	Bill Delahunt, Mass.	Jan. 6, 1997
100.	Bob Etheridge, N.C.	Jan. 6, 1997
101.	Rubén Hinojosa, Texas	Jan. 6, 1997
102.	Darlene Hooley, Ore.	Jan. 6, 1997
103.	Carolyn Cheeks Kilpatrick, Mich.	Jan. 6, 1997
104.	Ron Kind, Wis.	Jan. 6, 1997
105.	Dennis J. Kucinich, Ohio	Jan. 6, 1997
106.	Carolyn McCarthy, N.Y.	Jan. 6, 1997
107.	Jim McGovern, Mass.	Jan. 6, 1997
108.	Mike McIntyre, N.C.	Jan. 6, 1997

109. Bill Pascrell Jr., N.J. — Jan. 6, 1997
110. Silvestre Reyes, Texas — Jan. 6, 1997
111. Steven R. Rothman, N.J. — Jan. 6, 1997
112. Loretta Sanchez, Calif. — Jan. 6, 1997
113. Brad Sherman, Calif. — Jan. 6, 1997
114. Adam Smith, Wash. — Jan. 6, 1997
115. Vic Snyder, Ark. — Jan. 6, 1997
116. Ellen O. Tauscher, Calif. — Jan. 6, 1997
117. John F. Tierney, Mass. — Jan. 6, 1997
118. Robert Wexler, Fla. — Jan. 6, 1997
119. Gregory W. Meeks, N.Y. — Feb. 3, 1998
120. Lois Capps, Calif. — March 10, 1998
121. Barbara Lee, Calif. — April 7, 1998
122. Robert A. Brady, Pa. — May 19, 1998
123. Jay Inslee, Wash. — Jan. 6, 1999 *Also served 1993-95*
124. Brian Baird, Wash. — Jan. 6, 1999
125. Tammy Baldwin, Wis. — Jan. 6, 1999
126. Shelley Berkley, Nev. — Jan. 6, 1999
127. Michael E. Capuano, Mass. — Jan. 6, 1999
128. Joseph Crowley, N.Y. — Jan. 6, 1999
129. Charlie Gonzalez, Texas — Jan. 6, 1999
130. Rush D. Holt, N.J. — Jan. 6, 1999
131. Stephanie Tubbs Jones, Ohio — Jan. 6, 1999
132. John B. Larson, Conn. — Jan. 6, 1999
133. Dennis Moore, Kan. — Jan. 6, 1999
134. Grace F. Napolitano, Calif. — Jan. 6, 1999
135. Jan Schakowsky, Ill. — Jan. 6, 1999
136. Mike Thompson, Calif. — Jan. 6, 1999
137. Mark Udall, Colo. — Jan. 6, 1999
138. Tom Udall, N.M. — Jan. 6, 1999
139. Anthony Weiner, N.Y. — Jan. 6, 1999
140. David Wu, Ore. — Jan. 6, 1999
141. Joe Baca, Calif. — Nov. 16, 1999
142. Jane Harman, Calif. — Jan. 3, 2001 *Also served 1993-99*
143. William Lacy Clay, Mo. — Jan. 3, 2001
144. Susan A. Davis, Calif. — Jan. 3, 2001
145. Michael M. Honda, Calif. — Jan. 3, 2001
146. Steve Israel, N.Y. — Jan. 3, 2001
147. Jim Langevin, R.I. — Jan. 3, 2001
148. Rick Larsen, Wash. — Jan. 3, 2001
149. Jim Matheson, Utah — Jan. 3, 2001
150. Betty McCollum, Minn. — Jan. 3, 2001
151. Mike Ross, Ark. — Jan. 3, 2001
152. Adam B. Schiff, Calif. — Jan. 3, 2001
153. Hilda L. Solis, Calif. — Jan. 3, 2001
154. Diane Watson, Calif. — June 5, 2001
155. Stephen F. Lynch, Mass. — Oct. 16, 2001
156. Jim Cooper, Tenn. — Jan. 7, 2003 *Also served 1983-95*
157. Timothy H. Bishop, N.Y. — Jan. 7, 2003
158. Dennis Cardoza, Calif. — Jan. 7, 2003
159. Artur Davis, Ala. — Jan. 7, 2003
160. Lincoln Davis, Tenn. — Jan. 7, 2003
161. Rahm Emanuel, Ill. — Jan. 7, 2003
162. Raúl M. Grijalva, Ariz. — Jan. 7, 2003
163. Jim Marshall, Ga. — Jan. 7, 2003
164. Kendrick B. Meek, Fla. — Jan. 7, 2003
165. Michael H. Michaud, Maine — Jan. 7, 2003
166. Brad Miller, N.C. — Jan. 7, 2003
167. C.A. Dutch Ruppersberger, Md. — Jan. 7, 2003
168. Tim Ryan, Ohio — Jan. 7, 2003
169. Linda T. Sánchez, Calif. — Jan. 7, 2003
170. David Scott, Ga. — Jan. 7, 2003
171. Chris Van Hollen, Md. — Jan. 7, 2003
172. Ben Chandler, Ky. — Feb. 17, 2004
173. Stephanie Herseth-Sandlin, S.D. — June 1, 2004
174. G.K. Butterfield, N.C. — July 20, 2004
175. John Barrow, Ga. — Jan. 4, 2005
176. Melissa Bean, Ill. — Jan. 4, 2005
177. Dan Boren, Okla. — Jan. 4, 2005
178. Russ Carnahan, Mo. — Jan. 4, 2005
179. Emanuel Cleaver II, Mo. — Jan. 4, 2005
180. Jim Costa, Calif. — Jan. 4, 2005
181. Henry Cuellar, Texas — Jan. 4, 2005
182. Al Green, Texas — Jan. 4, 2005
183. Brian Higgins, N.Y. — Jan. 4, 2005
184. Daniel Lipinski, Ill. — Jan. 4, 2005
185. Charlie Melancon, La. — Jan. 4, 2005
186. Gwen Moore, Wis. — Jan. 4, 2005
187. John Salazar, Colo. — Jan. 4, 2005
188. Allyson Y. Schwartz, Pa. — Jan. 4, 2005
189. Debbie Wasserman-Schultz, Fla. — Jan. 4, 2005
190. Doris Matsui, Calif. — March 10, 2005
191. Albio Sires, N.J. — Nov. 13, 2006
192. Nick Lampson, Texas — Jan. 4, 2007 *Also served 1997-2005*
193. Ciro D. Rodriguez, Texas — Jan. 4, 2007 *Also served 1997-2005*
194. Baron P. Hill, Ind. — Jan. 4, 2007 *Also served 1999-2005*
195. Jason Altmire, Pa. — Jan. 4, 2007
196. Michael Arcuri, N.Y. — Jan. 4, 2007
197. Nancy Boyda, Kan. — Jan. 4, 2007
198. Bruce Braley, Iowa — Jan. 4, 2007
199. Christopher Carney, Pa. — Jan. 4, 2007
200. Kathy Castor, Fla. — Jan. 4, 2007
201. Yvette D. Clarke, N.Y. — Jan. 4, 2007
202. Steve Cohen, Tenn. — Jan. 4, 2007
203. Joe Courtney, Conn. — Jan. 4, 2007
204. Joe Donnelly, Ind. — Jan. 4, 2007
205. Keith Ellison, Minn. — Jan. 4, 2007
206. Brad Ellsworth, Ind. — Jan. 4, 2007
207. Gabrielle Giffords, Ariz. — Jan. 4, 2007
208. Kirsten Gillibrand, N.Y. — Jan. 4, 2007
209. John Hall, N.Y. — Jan. 4, 2007
210. Phil Hare, Ill. — Jan. 4, 2007
211. Mazie K. Hirono, Hawaii — Jan. 4, 2007
212. Paul W. Hodes, N.H. — Jan. 4, 2007
213. Hank Johnson, Ga. — Jan. 4, 2007
214. Steve Kagen, Wis. — Jan. 4, 2007
215. Ron Klein, Fla. — Jan. 4, 2007
216. Dave Loebsack, Iowa — Jan. 4, 2007
217. Tim Mahoney, Fla. — Jan. 4, 2007
218. Jerry McNerney, Calif. — Jan. 4, 2007
219. Harry E. Mitchell, Ariz. — Jan. 4, 2007
220. Christopher S. Murphy, Conn. — Jan. 4, 2007
221. Patrick J. Murphy, Pa. — Jan. 4, 2007
222. Ed Perlmutter, Colo. — Jan. 4, 2007
223. John Sarbanes, Md. — Jan. 4, 2007
224. Joe Sestak, Pa. — Jan. 4, 2007
225. Heath Shuler, N.C. — Jan. 4, 2007
226. Carol Shea-Porter, N.H. — Jan. 4, 2007
227. Zack Space, Ohio — Jan. 4, 2007
228. Betty Sutton, Ohio — Jan. 4, 2007
229. Tim Walz, Minn. — Jan. 4, 2007
230. Peter Welch, Vt. — Jan. 4, 2007
231. Charlie Wilson, Ohio — Jan. 4, 2007
232. John Yarmuth, Ky. — Jan. 4, 2007

REPUBLICANS

House Republicans determine seniority by length of service. Members who previously served in the House are usually given credit for most of that service.

For members who joined at the beginning of a Congress, service is credited from the first day of the session. Seniority for members who won special elections is credited from the date of the election.

Reps. Rodney Alexander, Nathan Deal, Virgil H. Goode Jr., and Ralph M. Hall began their tenure as Democrats. The GOP Conference credited their service as Democrats toward their seniority. No credit is given for other prior service, such as serving as a governor.

1. C.W. Bill Young, Fla. — Jan. 21, 1971
2. Ralph Regula, Ohio — Jan. 3, 1973
3. Don Young, Alaska — March 6, 1973
4. Jerry Lewis, Calif. — Jan. 15, 1979
5. F. James Sensenbrenner Jr., Wis. — Jan. 15, 1979
6. Tom Petri, Wis. — April 3, 1979
7. David Dreier, Calif. — Jan. 5, 1981
8. Ralph M. Hall, Texas — Jan. 5, 1981
9. Duncan Hunter, Calif. — Jan. 5, 1981
10. Harold Rogers, Ky. — Jan. 5, 1981
11. Christopher H. Smith, N.J. — Jan. 5, 1981
12. Frank R. Wolf, Va. — Jan. 5, 1981
13. Dan Burton, Ind. — Jan. 3, 1983
14. H. James Saxton, N.J. — Nov. 6, 1984
15. Joe L. Barton, Texas — Jan. 3, 1985
16. Howard Coble, N.C. — Jan. 3, 1985
17. Richard H. Baker, La. — Jan. 6, 1987
18. Elton Gallegly, Calif. — Jan. 6, 1987
19. J. Dennis Hastert, Ill. — Jan. 6, 1987
20. Wally Herger, Calif. — Jan. 6, 1987
21. Lamar Smith, Texas — Jan. 6, 1987
22. Fred Upton, Mich. — Jan. 6, 1987
23. Christopher Shays, Conn. — Aug. 18, 1987
24. Jim McCrery, La. — April 16, 1988
25. John J. "Jimmy" Duncan Jr., Tenn. — Nov. 8, 1988
26. Paul E. Gillmor, Ohio — Jan. 3, 1989
27. Dana Rohrabacher, Calif. — Jan. 3, 1989
28. Cliff Stearns, Fla. — Jan. 3, 1989
29. James T. Walsh, N.Y. — Jan. 3, 1989
30. Ileana Ros-Lehtinen, Fla. — Aug. 29, 1989
31. Ron Paul, Texas — Jan. 6, 1997 *Also served 1976-77, 79-85*
32. John A. Boehner, Ohio — Jan. 3, 1991
33. Dave Camp, Mich. — Jan. 3, 1991
34. John T. Doolittle, Calif. — Jan. 3, 1991
35. Wayne T. Gilchrest, Md. — Jan. 3, 1991
36. David L. Hobson, Ohio — Jan. 3, 1991
37. Jim Ramstad, Minn. — Jan. 3, 1991
38. Sam Johnson, Texas — May 18, 1991
39. Spencer Bachus, Ala. — Jan. 5, 1993
40. Roscoe G. Bartlett, Md. — Jan. 5, 1993
41. Steve Buyer, Ind. — Jan. 5, 1993
42. Ken Calvert, Calif. — Jan. 5, 1993
43. Michael N. Castle, Del. — Jan. 5, 1993
44. Nathan Deal, Ga. — Jan. 5, 1993
45. Lincoln Diaz-Balart, Fla. — Jan. 5, 1993
46. Terry Everett, Ala. — Jan. 5, 1993
47. Robert W. Goodlatte, Va. — Jan. 5, 1993
48. Peter Hoekstra, Mich. — Jan. 5, 1993
49. Peter T. King, N.Y. — Jan. 5, 1993
50. Jack Kingston, Ga. — Jan. 5, 1993
51. Joe Knollenberg, Mich. — Jan. 5, 1993
52. John Linder, Ga. — Jan. 5, 1993
53. Donald Manzullo, Ill. — Jan. 5, 1993
54. John M. McHugh, N.Y. — Jan. 5, 1993
55. Howard P. "Buck" McKeon, Calif. — Jan. 5, 1993
56. John L. Mica, Fla. — Jan. 5, 1993
57. Deborah Pryce, Ohio — Jan. 5, 1993
58. Ed Royce, Calif. — Jan. 5, 1993
59. Vernon J. Ehlers, Mich. — Dec. 7, 1993
60. Frank D. Lucas, Okla. — May 10, 1994
61. Ron Lewis, Ky. — May 24, 1994
62. Steve Chabot, Ohio — Jan. 4, 1995
63. Barbara Cubin, Wyo. — Jan. 4, 1995
64. Thomas M. Davis III, Va. — Jan. 4, 1995
65. Phil English, Pa. — Jan. 4, 1995
66. Rodney Frelinghuysen, N.J. — Jan. 4, 1995
67. Doc Hastings, Wash. — Jan. 4, 1995
68. Walter B. Jones, N.C. — Jan. 4, 1995
69. Ray LaHood, Ill. — Jan. 4, 1995
70. Tom Latham, Iowa — Jan. 4, 1995
71. Steven C. LaTourette, Ohio — Jan. 4, 1995
72. Frank A. LoBiondo, N.J. — Jan. 4, 1995
73. Dan Lungren, Calif. — Jan. 4, 2005 *Also served 1979-89*
74. Sue Myrick, N.C. — Jan. 4, 1995
75. George Radanovich, Calif. — Jan. 4, 1995
76. John Shadegg, Ariz. — Jan. 4, 1995
77. Mark Souder, Ind. — Jan. 4, 1995
78. William M. "Mac" Thornberry, Texas — Jan. 4, 1995
79. Todd Tiahrt, Kan. — Jan. 4, 1995
80. Zach Wamp, Tenn. — Jan. 4, 1995
81. Dave Weldon, Fla. — Jan. 4, 1995
82. Jerry Weller, Ill. — Jan. 4, 1995
83. Edward Whitfield, Ky. — Jan. 4, 1995
84. Roger Wicker, Miss. — Jan. 4, 1995
85. Jo Ann Emerson, Mo. — Nov. 5, 1996
86. Robert B. Aderholt, Ala. — Jan. 6, 1997
87. Roy Blunt, Mo. — Jan. 6, 1997
88. Kevin Brady, Texas — Jan. 6, 1997
89. Chris Cannon, Utah — Jan. 6, 1997
90. Virgil H. Goode Jr., Va. — Jan. 6, 1997
91. Kay Granger, Texas — Jan. 6, 1997
92. Kenny Hulshof, Mo. — Jan. 6, 1997
93. Jerry Moran, Kan. — Jan. 6, 1997
94. John E. Peterson, Pa. — Jan. 6, 1997
95. Charles W. "Chip" Pickering Jr., Miss. — Jan. 6, 1997
96. Joe Pitts, Pa. — Jan. 6, 1997
97. Pete Sessions, Texas — Jan. 6, 1997
98. John Shimkus, Ill. — Jan. 6, 1997
99. Vito J. Fossella, N.Y. — Nov. 4, 1997
100. Mary Bono, Calif. — April 7, 1998
101. Heather A. Wilson, N.M. — June 23, 1998
102. Judy Biggert, Ill. — Jan. 6, 1999
103. Robin Hayes, N.C. — Jan. 6, 1999
104. Bob Inglis, S.C. — Jan. 4, 2005 *Also served 1993-99*
105. Gary G. Miller, Calif. — Jan. 6, 1999

106. Thomas M. Reynolds, N.Y. Jan. 6, 1999
107. Paul D. Ryan, Wis. Jan. 6, 1999
108. Mike Simpson, Idaho Jan. 6, 1999
109. Tom Tancredo, Colo. Jan. 6, 1999
110. Lee Terry, Neb. Jan. 6, 1999
111. Greg Walden, Ore. Jan. 6, 1999
112. Brian P. Bilbray, Calif. June 13, 2006
Also served 1995-2001
113. Todd Akin, Mo. Jan. 3, 2001
114. Henry E. Brown Jr., S.C. Jan. 3, 2001
115. Eric Cantor, Va. Jan. 3, 2001
116. Shelley Moore Capito, W.Va. Jan. 3, 2001
117. Ander Crenshaw, Fla. Jan. 3, 2001
118. John Culberson, Texas Jan. 3, 2001
119. Jo Ann Davis, Va. Jan. 3, 2001
120. Mike Ferguson, N.J. Jan. 3, 2001
121. Jeff Flake, Ariz. Jan. 3, 2001
122. Sam Graves, Mo. Jan. 3, 2001
123. Darrell Issa, Calif. Jan. 3, 2001
124. Timothy V. Johnson, Ill. Jan. 3, 2001
125. Ric Keller, Fla. Jan. 3, 2001
126. Mark Steven Kirk, Ill. Jan. 3, 2001
127. Mike Pence, Ind. Jan. 3, 2001
128. Todd R. Platts, Pa. Jan. 3, 2001
129. Adam H. Putnam, Fla. Jan. 3, 2001
130. Denny Rehberg, Mont. Jan. 3, 2001
131. Mike Rogers, Mich. Jan. 3, 2001
132. Pat Tiberi, Ohio Jan. 3, 2001
133. Bill Shuster, Pa. May 15, 2001
134. J. Randy Forbes, Va. June 19, 2001
135. Jeff Miller, Fla. Oct. 16, 2001
136. John Boozman, Ark. Nov. 20, 2001
137. Joe Wilson, S.C. Dec. 18, 2001
138. John Sullivan, Okla. Feb. 15, 2002
139. Rodney Alexander, La. Jan. 7, 2003
140. J. Gresham Barrett, S.C. Jan. 7, 2003
141. Rob Bishop, Utah Jan. 7, 2003
142. Marsha Blackburn, Tenn. Jan. 7, 2003
143. Jo Bonner, Ala. Jan. 7, 2003
144. Ginny Brown-Waite, Fla. Jan. 7, 2003
145. Michael C. Burgess, Texas Jan. 7, 2003
146. John Carter, Texas Jan. 7, 2003
147. Tom Cole, Okla. Jan. 7, 2003
148. Mario Diaz-Balart, Fla. Jan. 7, 2003
149. Tom Feeney, Fla. Jan. 7, 2003
150. Trent Franks, Ariz. Jan. 7, 2003
151. Scott Garrett, N.J. Jan. 7, 2003
152. Jim Gerlach, Pa. Jan. 7, 2003
153. Phil Gingrey, Ga. Jan. 7, 2003
154. Jeb Hensarling, Texas Jan. 7, 2003
155. Steve King, Iowa Jan. 7, 2003
156. John Kline, Minn. Jan. 7, 2003
157. Thaddeus McCotter, Mich. Jan. 7, 2003
158. Candice S. Miller, Mich. Jan. 7, 2003
159. Tim Murphy, Pa. Jan. 7, 2003
160. Marilyn Musgrave, Colo. Jan. 7, 2003
161. Devin Nunes, Calif. Jan. 7, 2003
162. Steve Pearce, N.M. Jan. 7, 2003
163. Jon Porter, Nev. Jan. 7, 2003
164. Rick Renzi, Ariz. Jan. 7, 2003
165. Mike D. Rogers, Ala. Jan. 7, 2003
166. Michael R. Turner, Ohio Jan. 7, 2003
167. Randy Neugebauer, Texas June 3, 2003
168. Charles Boustany Jr., La. Jan. 4, 2005
169. K. Michael Conaway, Texas Jan. 4, 2005
170. Geoff Davis, Ky. Jan. 4, 2005
171. Charlie Dent, Pa. Jan. 4, 2005
172. Thelma Drake, Va. Jan. 4, 2005
173. Jeff Fortenberry, Neb. Jan. 4, 2005
174. Virginia Foxx, N.C. Jan. 4, 2005
175. Louis Gohmert, Texas Jan. 4, 2005
176. Bobby Jindal, La. Jan. 4, 2005
177. John R. "Randy" Kuhl Jr., N.Y. Jan. 4, 2005
178. Connie Mack, Fla. Jan. 4, 2005
179. Kenny Marchant, Texas Jan. 4, 2005
180. Michael McCaul, Texas Jan. 4, 2005
181. Patrick T. McHenry, N.C. Jan. 4, 2005
182. Ted Poe, Texas Jan. 4, 2005
183. Tom Price, Ga. Jan. 4, 2005
184. Dave Reichert, Wash. Jan. 4, 2005
185. Cathy McMorris Rogers, Wash. Jan. 4, 2005
186. Lynn Westmoreland, Ga. Jan. 4, 2005
187. Jean Schmidt, Ohio Aug. 3, 2005
188. John Campbell, Calif. Dec. 7, 2005
189. Michele Bachmann, Minn. Jan. 4, 2007
190. Gus Bilirakis, Fla. Jan. 4, 2007
191. Vern Buchanan, Fla. Jan. 4, 2007
192. David Davis, Tenn. Jan. 4, 2007
193. Mary Fallin, Okla. Jan. 4, 2007
194. Dean Heller, Nev. Jan. 4, 2007
195. Jim Jordan, Ohio Jan. 4, 2007
196. Doug Lamborn, Colo. Jan. 4, 2007
197. Kevin McCarthy, Calif. Jan. 4, 2007
198. Peter Roskam, Ill. Jan. 4, 2007
199. Bill Sali, Idaho Jan. 4, 2007
200. Adrian Smith, Neb. Jan. 4, 2007
201. Tim Walberg, Mich. Jan. 4, 2007

Pronunciation Guide for Congress

Some members of Congress whose names are frequently mispronounced:

SENATE

Daniel K. Akaka, D-Hawaii – uh-KAH-kuh
Evan Bayh, D-Ind. – BY
Saxby Chambliss, R-Ga. – SAX-bee CHAM-bliss
John Cornyn, R-Texas – CORE-nin
Michael D. Crapo, R-Idaho – CRAY-poe
Pete V. Domenici, R-N.M. – doe-MEN-ih-chee
Michael B. Enzi, R-Wyo. – EN-zee
Russ Feingold, D-Wis. – FINE-gold
Dianne Feinstein, D-Calif. – FINE-stine
James M. Inhofe, R-Okla. – IN-hoff
Daniel K. Inouye, D-Hawaii – in-NO-ay
Amy Klobuchar, D-Minn. – KLO-buh-shar
Jon Kyl, R-Ariz. – KILE
Mary L. Landrieu, D-La. – LAN-drew
Barack Obama, D-Ill. – buh-ROCK oh-BAH-mah
Debbie Stabenow, D-Mich. – STAB-uh-now
John E. Sununu, R-N.H. – suh-NU-nu
John Thune, R-S.D. – THOON
George V. Voinovich, R-Ohio – VOY-no-vitch

HOUSE

Robert B. Aderholt, R-Ala. – ADD-er-holt
Michael Arcuri, D-N.Y. – are-CURE-ee
Michele Bachmann, R-Minn. – BOCK-man
Spencer Bachus, R-Ala. – BACK-us
John Barrow, D-Ga. – BEAR-oh (rhymes with "arrow")
Xavier Becerra, D-Calif. – HAH-vee-air beh-SEH-ra
Gus Bilirakis, R-Fla. – bil-uh-RACK-iss
Earl Blumenauer, D-Ore. – BLUE-men-hour
John A. Boehner, R-Ohio – BAY-ner
John Boozman, R-Ark. – BOZE-man
Madeleine Z. Bordallo, D-Guam – bore-DAA-yo
Rick Boucher, D-Va. – BOW (rhymes with "now")-chur
Charles Boustany Jr., R-La. – boo-STAN-knee
Nancy Boyda, D-Kan. – BOY-duh
Steve Buyer, R-Ind. – BOO-yer
Shelley Moore Capito, R-W.Va. – CAP-ih-toe
Michael E. Capuano, D-Mass. – KAP-you-AH-no
Steve Chabot, R-Ohio – SHAB-it
Joseph Crowley, D-N.Y. – KRAU-lee
Barbara Cubin, R-Wyo. – CUE-bin
Henry Cuellar, D-Texas – KWAY-are
Artur Davis, D-Ala. – ar-TOUR
Peter A. DeFazio, D-Ore. – da-FAH-zee-o
Diana DeGette, D-Colo. – de-GET
Bill Delahunt, D-Mass. – DELL-a-hunt
Rosa DeLauro, D-Conn. – da-LAUR-o
Lincoln Diaz-Balart, R-Fla. – DEE-az ba-LART
Mario Diaz-Balart, R-Fla. – DEE-az ba-LART
Vernon J. Ehlers, R-Mich. – AY-lurz
Anna G. Eshoo, D-Calif. – EH-shoo
Eni F.H. Faleomavaega, D-Am. Samoa – EN-ee FOL-ee-oh-mav-ah-ENG-uh
Mary Fallin, R-Okla. – FAL-in (rhymes with "Allen")
Chaka Fattah, D-Pa. – SHOCK-ah fa-TAH
Luis Fortuño, R-P.R. – loo-EES four-TOON-yo
Vito J. Fossella, R-N.Y. – VEE-toe Fuh-SELL-ah
Rodney Frelinghuysen, R-N.J. – FREE-ling-high-zen
Elton Gallegly, R-Calif. – GAL-uh-glee
Jim Gerlach, R-Pa. – GUR-lock
Kirsten Gillibrand, D-N.Y. – KEER-sten JILL-uh-brand
Virgil H. Goode Jr., R-Va. – GUDE (rhymes with "food")
Robert W. Goodlatte, R-Va. – GOOD-lat
Luis V. Gutierrez, D-Ill. – loo-EES goo-tee-AIR-ez
Jeb Hensarling, R-Texas – HENN-sur-ling
Rubén Hinojosa, D-Texas – ru-BEN ee-na-HO-suh
Mazie K. Hirono, D-Hawaii – may-ZEE hee-RO-no
Paul W. Hodes, D-N.H. – rhymes with "roads"
Peter Hoekstra, R-Mich. – HOOK-struh
Kenny Hulshof, R-Mo. – HULLZ-hoff
Bob Inglis, R-S.C. – ING-lis
Darrell Issa, R-Calif. – EYE-sah
Bobby Jindal, R-La. – JIN-dle
Dennis J. Kucinich, D-Ohio – ku-SIN-itch
John R. "Randy" Kuhl Jr., R-N.Y. – COOL
Doug Lamborn, R-Colo. – LAMB-born
Jim Langevin, D-R.I. – LAN-juh-vin
Steven C. LaTourette, R-Ohio – la-tuh-RETT
Frank A. LoBiondo, R-N.J. – lo-bee-ON-dough
Dave Loebsack, D-Iowa – LOBE-sack
Zoe Lofgren, D-Calif. – ZO LOFF-gren
Nita M. Lowey, D-N.Y. – LO-ee
Donald Manzullo, R-Ill. – man-ZOO-low
Kenny Marchant, R-Texas – MARCH-unt
Charlie Melancon, D-La. – meh-LAW-sawn
John L. Mica, R-Fla. – MY-cah
Michael H. Michaud, D-Maine – ME-shoo
Jerrold Nadler, D-N.Y. – NAD-ler
Randy Neugebauer, R-Texas – NAW-geh-bow-er
Devin Nunes, R-Calif. – NEW-ness
David R. Obey, D-Wis. – OH-bee
Frank Pallone Jr., D-N.J. – puh-LOAN
Bill Pascrell Jr., D-N.J. – pass-KRELL
Ed Pastor, D-Ariz. – pas-TORE
Nancy Pelosi, D-Calif. – pa-LO-see
Tom Petri, R-Wis. – PEA-try
George Radanovich, R-Calif. – ruh-DON-o-vitch
Nick J. Rahall II, D-W.Va. – RAY-haul
Ralph Regula, R-Ohio – REG-you-luh
Denny Rehberg, R-Mont. – REE-berg
Dave Reichert, R-Wash. – RIKE-ert
Silvestre Reyes, D-Texas – sil-VES-treh RAY-ess (rolled "R")
Dana Rohrabacher, R-Calif. – ROAR-ah-BAH-ker
Ileana Ros-Lehtinen, R-Fla. – il-ee-AH-na ross-LAY-tin-nen
Bill Sali, R-Idaho – Like "Sally"
Jan Schakowsky, D-Ill. – shuh-KOW-ski
José E. Serrano, D-N.Y. – ho-ZAY sa-RAH-no (rolled "R")
Joe Sestak, D-Pa. – SESS-tack
John Shadegg, R-Ariz. – SHAD-egg
John Shimkus, R-Ill. – SHIM-kus
Heath Shuler, D-N.C. – SHOO-lur
Albio Sires, D-N.J. – SEAR-eez (like "series")
Hilda L. Solis, D-Calif. – soh-LEEZ
Mark Souder, R-Ind. – SOW (rhymes with "now")-dur
Bart Stupak, D-Mich. – STU-pack
Tom Tancredo, R-Colo. – tan-CRAY-doe
Ellen O. Tauscher, D-Calif. – TAU (rhymes with "now")-sher
Todd Tiahrt, R-Kan. – TEE-hart
Pat Tiberi, R-Ohio – TEA-berry
Nydia M. Velázquez, D-N.Y. – NID-ee-uh veh-LASS-kez
Peter J. Visclosky, D-Ind. – vis-KLOSS-key
Tim Walz, D-Minn. – WALLS
Anthony Weiner, D-N.Y. – WEE-ner
Lynn Woolsey, D-Calif. – WOOL-zee

Fastest Members of Congress

Each year a number of members of Congress participate in a three-mile footrace in Washington, D.C. Here are the times posted by the 35 members of Congress who ran in the 2007 race:

Member	Time
Rep. Bart Gordon, D-Tenn.	18:24
Sen. John Thune, R-S.D.	19:10
Rep. Daniel Lipinski, D-Ill.	19:56
Rep. Bob Inglis, R-S.C.	20:32
Sen. John E. Sununu, R-N.H.	20:34
Sen. John Ensign, R-Nev.	20:35
Rep. Jim Marshall, D-Ga.	21:14
Rep. Zach Wamp, R-Tenn.	21:16
Rep. Tom Feeney, R-Fla.	21:36
Rep. Earl Pomeroy, D-N.D.	22:14
Rep. Jean Schmidt, R-Ohio	22:41
Rep. Jim Matheson, D-Utah	22:52
Rep. Baron P. Hill, D-Ind.	22:57
Rep. Charlie Dent, R-Pa.	23:11
Rep. J. Gresham Barrett, R-S.C.	23:38
Sen. Jim DeMint, R-S.C.	23:57
Sen. Bob Corker, R-Tenn.	24:47
Rep. Earl Blumenauer, D-Ore.	25:19

Member	Time
Rep. Peter A. DeFazio, D-Ore.	25:39
Rep. Kenny Hulshof, R-Mo.	26:00
Rep. Todd Akin, R-Mo.	26:06
Sen. Jack Reed, D-R.I.	26:15
Rep. Shelley Moore Capito, R-W.Va.	26:18
Rep. Mark Udall, D-Colo.	26:49
Rep. Pete Sessions, R-Texas	27:34
Rep. José Serrano, D-N.Y.	28:14
Rep. Russ Carnahan, D-Mo.	28:18
Sen. Jeff Bingaman, D-N.M.	28:58
Rep. Jane Harman, D-Calif.	29:07
Sen. John Cornyn, R-Texas	29:08
Sen. Charles E. Grassley, R-Iowa	29:16
Rep. Mike Pence, R-Ind.	30:25
Sen. Kay Bailey Hutchison, R-Texas	36:14
Sen. Lisa Murkowski, R-Alaska	38:29
Sen. Richard G. Lugar, R-Ind.	39:39

Born in D.C.

Member
Rep. Jo Ann Emerson, R-Mo.
Rep. Hank Johnson, D-Ga.
Del. Eleanor Holmes Norton, D-D.C.
Rep. Robert C. Scott, D-Va.
Rep. Adam Smith, D-Wash.
Rep. Cliff Stearns, R-Fla.
Sen. John W. Warner, R-Va.

M.D.'s

Member	Field
Sen. Tom Coburn, R-Okla.	Obstetrician
Rep. Charles Boustany Jr., R-La.	Heart surgeon
Rep. Michael C. Burgess, R-Texas	Obstetrician
Del. Donna M.C. Christensen, D-Virgin Is.	Physician
Rep. Phil Gingrey, R-Ga.	Obstetrician
Rep. Steve Kagen, D-Wis.	Allergy/Immunology
Rep. Jim McDermott, D-Wash.	Psychiatrist
Rep. Ron Paul, R-Texas	Obstetrician
Rep. Tom Price, R-Ga.	Orthopedic surgeon
Rep. Vic Snyder, D-Ark.	Family practice
Rep. Dave Weldon, R-Fla.	Internal medicine

Born Abroad

There are 15 members of Congress and two delegates who were born outside the 50 states and the District of Columbia:

Member	Country
Rep. Geoff Davis, R-Ky.	Canada
Rep. Diana DeGette, D-Colo.	Japan
Rep. Lincoln Diaz-Balart, R-Fla.	Cuba
Del. Eni F.H. Faleomavaega, D-Am. Samoa	Am. Samoa
Res. Cmmsr. Luis Fortuño, R-P.R.	Puerto Rico
Rep. Mazie K. Hirono, D-Hawaii	Japan
Rep. Peter Hoekstra, R-Mich.	Netherlands
Rep. Tom Lantos, D-Calif.	Hungary
Sen. Mel Martinez, R-Fla.	Cuba
Sen. John McCain, R-Ariz.	Panama Canal Zone
Rep. Ciro D. Rodriguez, D-Texas	Mexico
Rep. Ileana Ros-Lehtinen, R-Fla.	Cuba
Rep. José Serrano, D-N.Y.	Puerto Rico
Rep. Albio Sires, D-N.J.	Cuba
Rep. Chris Van Hollen, D-Md.	Pakistan
Rep. Nydia M. Velázquez, D-N.Y.	Puerto Rico
Rep. David Wu, D-Ore.	Taiwan

Former Congressional Staffers

Below are the 75 members who previously worked as paid, full-time congressional aides. Internships and campaign work are not included.

Member	Congressional Office	Years
Sen. Lamar Alexander, R-Tenn.	Sen. Howard H. Baker Jr., R-Tenn.	1967-68
Rep. Jason Altmire, D-Pa.	Rep. Pete Peterson, D-Fla.	1991-96
Rep. Tom Allen, D-Maine	Sen. Edmund S. Muskie, D-Maine	1970-71
Sen. Robert F. Bennett, R-Utah	Rep. Sherman P. Lloyd, R-Utah	1963
	Sen. Wallace Bennett, R-Utah	1963-64
Rep. Jo Bonner, R-Ala.	Rep. Sonny Callahan, R-Ala.	1985-2002
Rep. Dan Boren, D-Okla.	Rep. Wes Watkins, R-Okla.	2000-01
Sen. Barbara Boxer, D-Calif.	Rep. John L. Burton, D-Calif.	1974-76
Rep. Dave Camp, R-Mich.	Rep. Bill Schuette, R-Mich.	1984-87
Rep. Dennis Cardoza, D-Calif.	Rep. Gary A. Condit, D-Calif.	1989
Rep. Julia Carson, D-Ind.	Rep. Andrew Jacobs Jr., D-Ind.	1965-72
Rep. William Lacy Clay, D-Mo.	House Clerk	1977-83
Sen. Hillary Rodham Clinton, D-N.Y.	House Judiciary Committee	c. 1974
Rep. Tom Cole, R-Okla.	Rep. Mickey Edwards, R-Okla.	1982-84
Sen. Susan Collins, R-Maine	Rep./Sen. William S. Cohen, R-Maine	1975-87
Rep. John Conyers Jr., D-Mich.	Rep. John D. Dingell, D-Mich.	1958-61
Rep. Jim Costa, D-Calif.	Rep. John Krebs, D-Calif.	1975-76
Rep. Peter A. DeFazio, D-Ore.	Rep. James Weaver, D-Ore.	1977-82
Rep. Rosa DeLauro, D-Conn.	Sen. Christopher J. Dodd, D-Conn.	1981-87
Rep. Charlie Dent, R-Pa.	Rep. Don Ritter, R-Pa.	1982
Rep. Norm Dicks, D-Wash.	Sen. Warren G. Magnuson, D-Wash.	1968-76
Rep. Chet Edwards, D-Texas	Rep. Olin E. Teague, D-Texas	1974-77
Del. Eni F.H. Faleomavaega, D-Am. Samoa	Del. A.U. Fuimaono, D-Am. Samoa	1973-75
	House Interior and Insular Affairs Committee	1975-81
Rep. Bob Filner, D-Calif.	Sen. Hubert H. Humphrey, D-Minn.	1975
	Rep. Donald M. Fraser, D-Minn.	1976
	Rep. Jim Bates, D-Calif.	1984
Rep. Jeff Fortenberry, R-Neb.	Senate Governmental Affairs subcommittee	1985-86
Rep. Barney Frank, D-Mass.	Rep. Michael Harrington, D-Mass.	1971-72
Rep. Robert W. Goodlatte, R-Va.	Rep. M. Caldwell Butler, R-Va.	1977-79
Sen. Chuck Hagel, R-Neb.	Rep. John Y. McCollister, R-Neb.	1971-77
Rep. Phil Hare, D-Ill.	Rep. Lane Evans, D-Ill.	1983-2006
Sen. Tom Harkin, D-Iowa	Rep. Neal Smith, D-Iowa	1969-70
Rep. Jane Harman, D-Calif.	Sen. John V. Tunney, D-Calif.	1972-73
	Senate Judiciary Committee	1975-77
Rep. Jeb Hensarling, R-Texas	Sen. Phil Gramm, R-Texas	1985-89
Rep. Steve Israel, D-N.Y.	Rep. Richard L. Ottinger, D-N.Y.	1980-83
Rep. Sheila Jackson-Lee, D-Texas	House Select Committee on Assassinations	1977-78
Rep. William J. Jefferson, D-La.	Sen. J. Bennett Johnston Jr., D-La.	1973-75
Rep. Mark Steven Kirk, R-Ill.	Rep. John Edward Porter, R-Ill.	1984-89
	House International Relations Committee	1995-2000
Rep. Ray LaHood, R-Ill.	Rep. Tom Railsback, R-Ill.	1977-82
	Rep. Robert H. Michel, R-Ill.	1983-94
Rep. Tom Lantos, D-Calif.	Sen. Joseph R. Biden Jr., D-Del.	1980
Rep. Barbara Lee, D-Calif.	Rep. Ronald V. Dellums, D-Calif.	1975-86
Rep. Jerry Lewis, R-Calif.	Rep. Jerry L. Pettis, R-Calif.	1967
Sen. Blanche Lincoln, D-Ark.	Rep. Bill Alexander, D-Ark.	1982-84
Rep. Daniel Lipinski, D-Ill.	Rep. Rod R. Blagojevich, D-Ill.	1999-2000
Rep. Zoe Lofgren, D-Calif.	Rep. Don Edwards, D-Calif.	1970-79
Sen. Trent Lott, R-Miss.	Rep. William M. Colmer, D-Miss.	1968-72
Rep. Kevin McCarthy, R-Calif.	Rep. Bill Thomas, R-Calif.	1987-2002
Sen. Mitch McConnell, R-Ky.	Sen. Marlow W. Cook, R-Ky.	1969-70
Rep. Jim McCrery, R-La.	Rep. Buddy Roemer, D-La.	1981-84
Rep. Jim McGovern, D-Mass.	Rep. Joe Moakley, D-Mass.	1981-93
Rep. Martin T. Meehan, D-Mass.	Rep. James M. Shannon, D-Mass.	1979-81
Rep. John L. Mica, R-Fla.	Sen. Paula Hawkins, R-Fla.	1981-85

Rep. James P. Moran, D-Va.	Senate Appropriations Committee	1976-79
Rep. James L. Oberstar, D-Minn.	Rep. John A. Blatnik, D-Minn.	1964-74
Rep. Charles W. "Chip" Pickering Jr., R-Miss.	Sen. Trent Lott, R-Miss.	1991-95
Rep. Nick J. Rahall II, D-W.Va.	Sen. Robert C. Byrd, D-W.Va.	1971-74
Rep. Jim Ramstad, R-Minn.	Rep. Tom Kleppe, R-N.D.	1970
Rep. Denny Rehberg, R-Mont.	Rep. Ron Marlenee, R-Mont.	1979-82
	Sen. Conrad Burns, R-Mont.	1989-91
Sen. Pat Roberts, R-Kan.	Sen. Frank Carlson, R-Kan.	1967-68
	Rep. Keith G. Sebelius, R-Kan.	1968-80
Rep. Peter Roskam, R-Ill.	Rep. Tom DeLay, R-Texas	1985-86
	Rep. Henry J. Hyde, R-Ill.	1986-87
Rep. Paul D. Ryan, R-Wis.	Sen. Bob Kasten, R-Wis.	1992
	Rep./Sen. Sam Brownback, R-Kan.	1995-97
Rep. Tim Ryan, D-Ohio	Rep. James A. Traficant Jr., D-Ohio	1995-97
Sen. Olympia J. Snowe, R-Maine	Rep. William S. Cohen, R-Maine	1973
Rep. Mark Souder, R-Ind.	Rep./Sen. Daniel R. Coats, R-Ind.	1983-85, 89-93
	House Select Committee on Children, Youth & Families	1985-89
Rep. William M. "Mac" Thornberry, R-Texas	Rep. Tom Loeffler, R-Texas	1983-85
	Rep. Larry Combest, R-Texas	1985-88
Sen. John Thune, R-S.D.	Sen. James Abdnor, R-S.D.	1985-86
	Senate Small Business Committee	1989
Rep. Pat Tiberi, R-Ohio	Rep. John R. Kasich, R-Ohio	1983-91
Rep. Fred Upton, R-Mich.	Rep. David A. Stockman, R-Mich.	1977-81
Rep. Chris Van Hollen, D-Md.	Sen. Charles McC. Mathias Jr., R-Md.	1985-87
	Senate Foreign Relations Committee	1987-89
Rep. Nydia M. Velázquez, D-N.Y.	Rep. Edolphus Towns, D-N.Y.	1983
Rep. Peter J. Visclosky, D-Ind.	Rep. Adam Benjamin Jr., D-Ind.	1977-82
Rep. Greg Walden, R-Ore.	Rep. Denny Smith, R-Ore.	1981-86
Sen. Jim Webb, D-Va.	House Veterans' Affairs Committee	1977-81
Rep. Anthony Weiner, D-N.Y.	Rep. Charles E. Schumer, D-N.Y.	1985-91
Rep. Jerry Weller, R-Ill.	Rep. Tom Corcoran, R-Ill.	1980-81
Rep. Roger Wicker, R-Miss.	Rep. Trent Lott, R-Miss.	1980-82
Rep. Frank R. Wolf, R-Va.	Rep. Edward G. Biester, R-Pa.	1968-71
Rep. John Yarmuth, D-Ky.	Sen. Marlow W. Cook, R-Ky.	1971-74

Former Pages

Members of Congress who once served as congressional pages:

Member	**Years**
Rep. Dan Boren, D-Okla.	1989
Rep. Jim Cooper, D-Tenn.	1970
Rep. Ander Crenshaw, R-Fla.	1961
Rep. Thomas M. Davis III, R-Va.	1963-67
Rep. John D. Dingell, D-Mich.	1938-42
Sen. Christopher J. Dodd, D-Conn.	c. 1960
Rep. Rush D. Holt, D-N.J.	1963-64
Rep. Paul E. Kanjorski, D-Pa.	1953-54
Sen. Mark Pryor, D-Ark.	1982
Rep. Roger Wicker, R-Miss.	1967

Rhodes Scholars

Members of Congress who have been Rhodes scholars:

Rep. Tom Allen, D-Maine
Rep. Jim Cooper, D-Tenn.
Sen. Russ Feingold, D-Wis.
Rep. Bobby Jindal, R-La.
Sen. Richard G. Lugar, R-Ind.
Sen. David Vitter, R-La.
Rep. Heather A. Wilson, R-N.M.

Women in Congress

Senate (11 D, 5 R)

Barbara Boxer, D-Calif.
Maria Cantwell, D-Wash.
Hillary Rodham Clinton, D-N.Y.
Susan Collins, R-Maine
Elizabeth Dole, R-N.C.
Dianne Feinstein, D-Calif.
Kay Bailey Hutchison, R-Texas
Amy Klobuchar, D-Minn.
Mary L. Landrieu, D-La.
Blanche Lincoln, D-Ark.
Claire McCaskill, D-Mo.
Barbara A. Mikulski, D-Md.
Lisa Murkowski, R-Alaska
Patty Murray, D-Wash.
Olympia J. Snowe, R-Maine
Debbie Stabenow, D-Mich.

House (52 D, 21 R)

Michele Bachmann, R-Minn.
Tammy Baldwin, D-Wis.
Melissa Bean, D-Ill.
Shelley Berkley, D-Nev.
Judy Biggert, R-Ill.
Marsha Blackburn, R-Tenn.
Mary Bono, R-Calif.
Del. Madeleine Z. Bordallo, D-Guam
Nancy Boyda, D-Kan.
Corrine Brown, D-Fla.
Ginny Brown-Waite, R-Fla.
Shelley Moore Capito, R-W.Va.
Lois Capps, D-Calif.
Julia Carson, D-Ind.
Kathy Castor, D-Fla.
Del. Donna M.C. Christensen, D-V.I.
Yvette D. Clarke, D-N.Y.
Barbara Cubin, R-Wyo.
Jo Ann Davis, R-Va.
Susan A. Davis, D-Calif.
Diana DeGette, D-Colo.
Rosa DeLauro, D-Conn.
Thelma Drake, R-Va.
Jo Ann Emerson, R-Mo.
Anna G. Eshoo, D-Calif.
Mary Fallin, R-Okla.
Virginia Foxx, R-N.C.
Gabrielle Giffords, D-Ariz.
Kirsten Gillibrand, D-N.Y.
Kay Granger, R-Texas
Jane Harman, D-Calif.
Stephanie Herseth-Sandlin, D-S.D.
Mazie K. Hirono, D-Hawaii
Darlene Hooley, D-Ore.
Sheila Jackson-Lee, D-Texas
Eddie Bernice Johnson, D-Texas
Stephanie Tubbs Jones, D-Ohio
Marcy Kaptur, D-Ohio
Carolyn Cheeks Kilpatrick, D-Mich.
Barbara Lee, D-Calif.
Zoe Lofgren, D-Calif.
Nita M. Lowey, D-N.Y.
Carolyn B. Maloney, D-N.Y.
Doris Matsui, D-Calif.
Carolyn McCarthy, D-N.Y.
Betty McCollum, D-Minn.
Candice S. Miller, R-Mich.
Gwen Moore, D-Wis.
Marilyn Musgrave, R-Colo.
Sue Myrick, R-N.C.
Grace F. Napolitano, D-Calif.
Del. Eleanor Holmes Norton, D-D.C.
Nancy Pelosi, D-Calif.
Deborah Pryce, R-Ohio
Cathy McMorris Rodgers, R-Wash.
Ileana Ros-Lehtinen, R-Fla.
Lucille Roybal-Allard, D-Calif.
Linda T. Sánchez, D-Calif.
Loretta Sanchez, D-Calif.
Jan Schakowsky, D-Ill.
Jean Schmidt, R-Ohio
Allyson Y. Schwartz, D-Pa.
Carol Shea-Porter, D-N.H.
Louise M. Slaughter, D-N.Y.
Hilda L. Solis, D-Calif.
Betty Sutton, D-Ohio
Ellen O. Tauscher, D-Calif.
Nydia M. Velázquez, D-N.Y.
Debbie Wasserman-Schultz, D-Fla.
Maxine Waters, D-Calif.
Diane Watson, D-Calif.
Heather A. Wilson, R-N.M.
Lynn Woolsey, D-Calif.

10 Oldest Members of Congress

Member	Birthdate
Sen. Robert C. Byrd, D-W.Va.	Nov. 20, 1917
Rep. Ralph M. Hall, R-Texas	May 3, 1923
Sen. Ted Stevens, R-Alaska	Nov. 18, 1923
Sen. Frank R. Lautenberg, D-N.J.	Jan. 23, 1924
Sen. Daniel K. Inouye, D-Hawaii	Sept. 7, 1924
Sen. Daniel K. Akaka, D-Hawaii	Sept. 11, 1924
Rep. Ralph Regula, R-Ohio	Dec. 3, 1924
Rep. Roscoe G. Bartlett, R-Md.	June 3, 1926
Rep. John D. Dingell, D-Mich.	July 8, 1926
Sen. John W. Warner, R-Va.	Feb. 18, 1927

10 Youngest Members of Congress

Member	Birthdate
Rep. Patrick T. McHenry, R-N.C.	Oct. 22, 1975
Rep. Adam H. Putnam, R-Fla.	July 31, 1974
Rep. Patrick J. Murphy, D-Pa.	Oct. 19, 1973
Rep. Devin Nunes, R-Calif.	Oct. 1, 1973
Rep. Christopher S. Murphy, D-Conn.	Aug. 3, 1973
Rep. Dan Boren, D-Okla.	Aug. 2, 1973
Rep. Tim Ryan, D-Ohio	July 16, 1973
Rep. Heath Shuler, D-N.C.	Dec. 31, 1971
Rep. Bobby Jindal, R-La.	June 10, 1971
Rep. Adrian Smith, R-Neb.	Dec. 19, 1970

Minorities in Congress

American Indian

House (1 R)

Tom Cole, R-Okla.

Asian Indian

House (1 R)

Bobby Jindal, R-La.

Asian

Senate (2 D)

Daniel K. Akaka, D-Hawaii
Daniel K. Inouye, D-Hawaii

House (5 D)

Del. Eni F.H. Faleomavaega, D-Am. Samoa
Mazie K. Hirono, D-Hawaii
Michael M. Honda, D-Calif.
Doris Matsui, D-Calif.
David Wu, D-Ore.

Hispanic

Senate (2 D, 1 R)

Mel Martinez, R-Fla.
Robert Menendez, D-N.J.
Ken Salazar, D-Colo.

House (20 D, 4 R)

Joe Baca, D-Calif.
Xavier Becerra, D-Calif.
Henry Cuellar, D-Texas
Lincoln Diaz-Balart, R-Fla.
Mario Diaz-Balart, R-Fla.
Res. Cmmsr. Luis Fortuño, R-P.R.
Charlie Gonzalez, D-Texas
Raúl M. Grijalva, D-Ariz.
Luis V. Gutierrez, D-Ill.
Rubén Hinojosa, D-Texas
Grace F. Napolitano, D-Calif.
Solomon P. Ortiz, D-Texas
Ed Pastor, D-Ariz.
Silvestre Reyes, D-Texas
Ciro D. Rodriguez, D-Texas
Ileana Ros-Lehtinen, R-Fla.
Lucille Roybal-Allard, D-Calif.
John Salazar, D-Colo.
Linda T. Sánchez, D-Calif.
Loretta Sanchez, D-Calif.
José E. Serrano, D-N.Y.
Albio Sires, D-N.J.
Hilda L. Solis, D-Calif.
Nydia M. Velázquez, D-N.Y.

Black

Senate (1 D)

Barack Obama, D-Ill.

House (41 D)

Sanford D. Bishop Jr., D-Ga.
Corrine Brown, D-Fla.
G.K. Butterfield, D-N.C.
Julia Carson, D-Ind.
Del. Donna M.C. Christensen, D-Virgin Is.
Yvette D. Clarke, D-N.Y.
William Lacy Clay, D-Mo.
Emanuel Cleaver II, D-Mo.
James E. Clyburn, D-S.C.
John Conyers Jr., D-Mich.
Elijah E. Cummings, D-Md.
Artur Davis, D-Ala.
Danny K. Davis, D-Ill.
Keith Ellison, D-Minn.
Chaka Fattah, D-Pa.
Al Green, D-Texas
Alcee L. Hastings, D-Fla.
Jesse L. Jackson Jr., D-Ill.
Sheila Jackson-Lee, D-Texas
William J. Jefferson, D-La.
Eddie Bernice Johnson, D-Texas
Hank Johnson, D-Ga.
Stephanie Tubbs Jones, D-Ohio
Carolyn Cheeks Kilpatrick, D-Mich.
Barbara Lee, D-Calif.
John Lewis, D-Ga.
Kendrick B. Meek, D-Fla.
Gregory W. Meeks, D-N.Y.
Gwen Moore, D-Wis.
Del. Eleanor Holmes Norton, D-D.C.
Donald M. Payne, D-N.J.
Charles B. Rangel, D-N.Y.
Bobby L. Rush, D-Ill.
David Scott, D-Ga.
Robert C. Scott, D-Va.
Bennie Thompson, D-Miss.
Edolphus Towns, D-N.Y.
Maxine Waters, D-Calif.
Diane Watson, D-Calif.
Melvin Watt, D-N.C.
Albert R. Wynn, D-Md.

Class of 2006

Senate (8 D, 1 R, 1 I)
Sherrod Brown, D-Ohio
Benjamin L. Cardin, D-Md.
Bob Casey, D-Pa.
Bob Corker, R-Tenn.
Amy Klobuchar, D-Minn.
Claire McCaskill, D-Mo.
Bernard Sanders, I-Vt.
Jon Tester, D-Mont.
Jim Webb, D-Va.
Sheldon Whitehouse, D-R.I

House (39 D, 13 R)
Jason Altmire, D-Pa.
Michael Arcuri, D-N.Y.
Michele Bachmann, R-Minn.
Gus Bilirakis, R-Fla.
Nancy Boyda, D-Kan.
Bruce Braley, D-Iowa
Vern Buchanan, R-Fla.
Christopher Carney, D-Pa.
Kathy Castor, D-Fla.
Yvette D. Clarke, D-N.Y.
Steve Cohen, D-Tenn.
Joe Courtney, D-Conn.
David Davis, R-Tenn.
Joe Donnelly, D-Ind.
Keith Ellison, D-Minn.
Brad Ellsworth, D-Ind.
Mary Fallin, R-Okla.
Gabrielle Giffords, D-Ariz.
Kirsten Gillibrand, D-N.Y.
John Hall, D-N.Y.
Phil Hare, D-Ill.
Dean Heller, R-Nev.
Mazie K. Hirono, D-Hawaii
Paul W. Hodes, D-N.H.
Hank Johnson, D-Ga.
Jim Jordan, R-Ohio
Steve Kagen, D-Wis.
Ron Klein, D-Fla.
Doug Lamborn, R-Colo.
Dave Loebsack, D-Iowa
Tim Mahoney, D-Fla.
Kevin McCarthy, R-Calif.
Jerry McNerney, D-Calif.
Harry E. Mitchell, D-Ariz.
Patrick J. Murphy, D-Pa.
Christopher S. Murphy, D-Conn.
Ed Perlmutter, D-Colo.
Peter Roskam, R-Ill.
Bill Sali, R-Idaho
John Sarbanes, D-Md.
Joe Sestak, D-Pa.
Carol Shea-Porter, D-N.H.
Heath Shuler, D-N.C.
Albio Sires, D-N.J.
Adrian Smith, R-Neb.
Zack Space, D-Ohio
Betty Sutton, D-Ohio
Tim Walberg, R-Mich.
Tim Walz, D-Minn.
Peter Welch, D-Vt.
Charlie Wilson, D-Ohio
John Yarmuth, D-Ky.

Former Governors

Nine members have served as a governor.

Member	Years
Sen. Lamar Alexander, R-Tenn.	1979-87
Sen. Evan Bayh, D-Ind.	1989-97
Sen. Christopher S. Bond, R-Mo.	1973-77, 1981-85
Sen. Thomas R. Carper, D-Del.	1993-2001
Rep. Michael N. Castle, R-Del.	1985-93
Sen. Judd Gregg, R-N.H.	1989-93
Sen. Ben Nelson, D-Neb.	1991-99
Sen. John D. Rockefeller IV, D-W.Va.	1977-85
Sen. George V. Voinovich, R-Ohio	1991-99

Party Switchers

Six members changed party affiliation after their election to Congress. Several other members switched parties before coming to Congress; they are not listed below.

Member	Old Party	New Party	Date Switched
Rep. Rodney Alexander, La.	D	R	Sept. 7, 2004
Rep. Nathan Deal, Ga.	D	R	April 10, 1995
Rep. Virgil H. Goode Jr., Va.	D	I	Jan. 24, 2000
Rep. Virgil H. Goode Jr., Va.	I	R	Aug. 1, 2002
Rep. Ralph M. Hall, Texas	D	R	Jan. 5, 2004
Sen. Joseph I. Lieberman, Conn.	D	I	Jan. 4, 2007
Sen. Richard C. Shelby, Ala.	D	R	Nov. 9, 1994

Congressional Half-Life

Members who have served more than half of their lives in Congress. Length of service is as of Jan. 4, 2007.

Member	Age at Swearing-in	Length of Service	Percent of Life in Congress
Rep. John D. Dingell, D-Mich.	29 years, 158 days	51 years, 22 days	64
Sen. Robert C. Byrd, D-W.Va.	35 years, 44 days	54 years	61
Sen. Edward M. Kennedy, D-Mass.	30 years, 258 days	44 years, 58 days	59
Sen. Daniel K. Inouye, D-Hawaii	34 years, 348 days	47 years, 136 days	58
Rep. David R. Obey, D-Wis.	30 years, 180 days	37 years, 278 days	56
Rep. John Conyers Jr., D-Mich.	35 years, 233 days	42 years	54
Sen. Joseph R. Biden Jr., D-Del.	30 years, 44 days	34 years	53
Sen. Trent Lott, R-Miss.	31 years, 86 days	34 years	52
Rep. Nick J. Rahall II, D-W.Va.	27 years, 229 days	30 years	52
Rep. George Miller, D-Calif.	29 years, 242 days	32 years	52
Sen. Christopher J. Dodd, D-Conn.	30 years, 233 days	32 years	51
Rep. Edward J. Markey, D-Mass.	30 years, 114 days	30 years, 63 days	50

Note: Markey joined the congressional half-life club Feb. 24, 2007. Sen. Thad Cochran, R-Miss., will reach the half-life mark on Jan. 30, 2008, and Sen. Max Baucus, D-Mont., will join him on Feb. 17, 2008. Reps. David Dreier, R-Calif., and Christopher H. Smith, R-N.J., will make the list on July 7, 2008, and Nov. 7, 2008, respectively.

Former Representatives in Senate

26 Republicans, 23 Democrats, 1 Independent

Member	Party, State	Served in House
Daniel K. Akaka	D-Hawaii	1977-90
Wayne Allard	R-Colo.	1991-97
Max Baucus	D-Mont.	1975-78
Barbara Boxer	D-Calif.	1983-93
Sherrod Brown	D-Ohio	1993-2007
Sam Brownback	R-Kan.	1995-96
Jim Bunning	R-Ky.	1987-99
Richard M. Burr	R-N.C.	1995-2005
Robert C. Byrd	D-W.Va.	1953-59
Maria Cantwell	D-Wash.	1993-95
Benjamin L. Cardin	D-Md.	1987-2007
Thomas R. Carper	D-Del.	1983-93
Saxby Chambliss	R-Ga.	1995-2003
Tom Coburn	R-Okla.	1995-2001
Thad Cochran	R-Miss.	1973-78
Larry E. Craig	R-Idaho	1981-91
Michael D. Crapo	R-Idaho	1993-99
Jim DeMint	R-S.C.	1999-2005
Christopher J. Dodd	D-Conn.	1975-81
Byron L. Dorgan	D-N.D.	1981-92
Richard J. Durbin	D-Ill.	1983-97
John Ensign	R-Nev.	1995-99
Lindsey Graham	R-S.C.	1995-2003
Charles E. Grassley	R-Iowa	1975-81
Judd Gregg	R-N.H.	1981-89
Tom Harkin	D-Iowa	1975-85
James M. Inhofe	R-Okla.	1987-94
Daniel K. Inouye	D-Hawaii	1959-63
Johnny Isakson	R-Ga.	1999-2005
Tim Johnson	D-S.D.	1987-97
Jon Kyl	R-Ariz.	1987-95
Blanche Lincoln	D-Ark.	1993-97
Trent Lott	R-Miss.	1973-89
John McCain	R-Ariz.	1983-87
Robert Menendez	D-N.J.	1993-2006
Barbara A. Mikulski	D-Md.	1977-87
Bill Nelson	D-Fla.	1979-91
Jack Reed	D-R.I.	1991-97
Harry Reid	D-Nev.	1983-87
Pat Roberts	R-Kan.	1981-97
Bernard Sanders	I-Vt.	1991-2007
Charles E. Schumer	D-N.Y.	1981-99
Richard C. Shelby	R-Ala.	1979-87
Olympia J. Snowe	R-Maine	1979-95
Debbie Stabenow	D-Mich.	1997-2001
John E. Sununu	R-N.H.	1997-2003
Craig Thomas	R-Wyo.	1989-95
John Thune	R-S.D.	1997-2003
David Vitter	R-La.	1999-2005
Ron Wyden	D-Ore.	1981-96

Senators Up for Election in 2008

21 Republicans, 12 Democrats

Lamar Alexander	R-Tenn.
Wayne Allard*	R-Colo.
Max Baucus	D-Mont.
Joseph R. Biden Jr.†	D-Del.
Saxby Chambliss	R-Ga.
Thad Cochran	R-Miss.
Norm Coleman	R-Minn.
Susan Collins	R-Maine
John Cornyn	R-Texas
Larry E. Craig	R-Idaho
Elizabeth Dole	R-N.C.
Pete V. Domenici	R-N.M.
Richard J. Durbin	D-Ill.
Michael B. Enzi	R-Wyo.
Lindsey Graham	R-S.C.
Chuck Hagel	R-Neb.
Tom Harkin	D-Iowa
James M. Inhofe	R-Okla.
Tim Johnson	D-S.D.
John Kerry	D-Mass.
Mary L. Landrieu	D-La.
Frank R. Lautenberg	D-N.J.
Carl Levin	D-Mich.
Mitch McConnell	R-Ky.
Mark Pryor	D-Ark.
Jack Reed	D-R.I.
Pat Roberts	R-Kan.
John D. Rockefeller IV	D-W.Va
Jeff Sessions	R-Ala.
Gordon H. Smith	R-Ore.
Ted Stevens	R-Alaska
John E. Sununu	R-N.H.
John W. Warner	R-Va.

* Not running for re-election.

† Running for president doesn't preclude running for re-election.

Most and Least Legislation

These current members introduced the most and the least legislation in the 109th Congress (2005-06).

Most — Senate

Dianne Feinstein, D-Calif. *	129
Charles E. Schumer, D-N.Y. *	98
Sam Brownback, R-Kan.	97
Gordon H. Smith, R-Ore.	94
Hillary Rodham Clinton, D-N.Y. *	90
Olympia J. Snowe, R-Maine *	89
Richard J. Durbin, D-Ill.	85
Arlen Specter, R-Pa.	85
Richard M. Burr, R-N.C.	81
Frank R. Lautenberg, D-N.J.	79

Least — Senate

Mark Pryor, D-Ark. †	12
Richard C. Shelby, R-Ala.	12
Robert C. Byrd, D-W.Va. †	13
Mitch McConnell, R-Ky.	14
Thad Cochran, R-Miss.	15
Pat Roberts, R-Kan.†	15
Tom Coburn, R-Okla.	16
John E. Sununu, R-N.H. †	16
Robert F. Bennett, R-Utah †	17
Herb Kohl, D-Wis. †	20

Most — House

Robert E. Andrews, D-N.J.*	128
Phil English, R-Pa. *	82
Carolyn B. Maloney, D-N.Y. *	78
Ron Paul, R-Texas *	71
F. James Sensenbrenner Jr., R-Wis.	68
Don Young, R-Alaska *	63
Charles B. Rangel, D-N.Y. *	60
Steve Buyer, R-Ind.	58
Nita M. Lowey, D-N.Y.	55
Michael N. Castle, R-Del.	52

Least — House

Lynn Westmoreland, R-Ga.	1
Melvin Watt, D-N.C. †	2
Henry Cuellar, D-Texas	2
Grace F. Napolitano, D-Calif.	2
Mike Doyle, D-Pa. †	3
Anna G. Eshoo, D-Calif.	3
Trent Franks, R-Ariz.	3
Connie Mack, R-Fla.	3
John P. Murtha, D-Pa.	3
Harold Rogers, R-Ky. †	3
John Tanner, D-Tenn. †	3
Gene Taylor, D-Miss.	3
C.W. Bill Young, R-Fla.	3

* Also in the top 10 in the 108th Congress.

† Also in the bottom 10 in the 108th Congress.

All told, 8,152 House measures were introduced in the 109th Congress – an average of 15.1 per member.

Members With a Parent Who Served in Congress

There are 29 members of Congress with a parent who served in Congress. Walter B. Jones is the only one on the list who belongs to a different political party than his parent. * Directly succeeded their parent in the same seat.

Member	Parent	Years Parent Served
Sen. Evan Bayh, D-Ind.	Sen. Birch Bayh, D-Ind.	1963-81
Sen. Robert F. Bennett, R-Utah	Sen. Wallace F. Bennett, R-Utah	1951-74
Rep. Gus Bilirakis, R-Fla. *	Rep. Michael Bilirakis, R-Fla	1983-2007
Rep. Dan Boren, D-Okla.	Sen. David L. Boren, D-Okla.	1979-94
Rep. Shelley Moore Capito, R-W.Va.	Rep. Arch A. Moore Jr., R-W.Va.	1957-69
Rep. Russ Carnahan, D-Mo.	Sen. Jean Carnahan, D-Mo.	2001-02
Rep. William Lacy Clay, D-Mo. *	Rep. William L. Clay, D-Mo.	1969-2001
Rep. John D. Dingell, D-Mich. *	Rep. John D. Dingell Sr., D-Mich.	1933-55
Sen. Christopher J. Dodd, D-Conn.	Rep./Sen. Thomas J. Dodd, D-Conn.	1953-57, 1959-71
Rep. John J. "Jimmy" Duncan Jr., R-Tenn. *	Rep. John J. Duncan, R-Tenn.	1965-88
Rep. Rodney Frelinghuysen, R-N.J.	Rep. Peter H. Frelinguysen, R-N.J.	1953-75
Rep. Charlie Gonzalez, D-Texas *	Rep. Henry B. Gonzalez, D-Texas	1961-99
Rep. Rush D. Holt, D-N.J.	Sen. Rush Dew Holt, D-W.Va.	1935-41
Rep. Walter B. Jones, R-N.C.	Rep. Walter B. Jones Sr., D-N.C.	1966-92
Rep. Patrick J. Kennedy, D-R.I.	Sen. Edward M. Kennedy, D-Mass.	1962-present
Sen. Jon Kyl, R-Ariz.	Rep. John H. Kyl, R-Iowa	1959-65, 1967-73
Rep. Daniel Lipinski, D-Ill. *	Rep. William O. Lipinski, D-Ill.	1983-2005
Rep. Connie Mack, R-Fla.	Rep./Sen. Connie Mack, R-Fla.	1983-2001
Rep. Kendrick B. Meek, D-Fla. *	Rep. Carrie P. Meek, D-Fla.	1993-2003
Rep. Alan B. Mollohan, D-W.Va. *	Rep. Robert H. Mollohan, D-W.Va.	1953-57, 1969-83
Sen. Lisa Murkowski, R-Alaska *	Sen. Frank H. Murkowski, R-Alaska	1981-2002
Rep. Nancy Pelosi, D-Calif.	Rep. Thomas D'Alesandro Jr., D-Md.	1939-47
Sen. Mark Pryor, D-Ark.	Rep./Sen. David Pryor, D-Ark.	1966-73, 1979-97
Rep. Lucille Roybal-Allard, D-Calif.	Rep. Edward R. Roybal, D-Calif.	1963-93
Rep. John Sarbanes, D-Md.	Rep./Sen. Paul S. Sarbanes, D-Md.	1971-2007
Rep. Bill Shuster, R-Pa. *	Rep. Bud Shuster, R-Pa.	1973-2001
Rep. Mark Udall, D-Colo.	Rep. Morris K. Udall, D-Ariz.	1961-91
Rep. Tom Udall, D-N.M.	Rep. Stewart L. Udall, D-Ariz.	1955-61
Rep. James T. Walsh, R-N.Y.	Rep. William F. Walsh, R-N.Y.	1973-79

Members Whose Spouse Served in Congress

Member	Spouse	Spouse's Service
Rep. Mary Bono, R-Calif.	Rep. Sonny Bono, R-Calif.	1995-98
Rep. Lois Capps, D-Calif.	Rep. Walter Capps, D-Calif.	1997
Sen. Elizabeth Dole, R-N.C.	Rep./Sen. Bob Dole, R-Kan.	1961-96
Rep. Jo Ann Emerson, R-Mo.	Rep. Bill Emerson, R-Mo.	1981-96
Rep. Stephanie Herseth-Sandlin, D-S.D.	Rep. Max Sandlin, D-Texas	1997-2005
Rep. Doris Matsui, D-Calif.	Rep. Robert T. Matsui, D-Calif.	1979-2005
Sen. Olympia J. Snowe, R-Maine	Rep. John R. McKernan Jr., R-Maine	1983-87

Siblings in Congress

Rep. Lincoln Diaz-Balart, R-Fla.	Rep. Mario Diaz-Balart, R-Fla.
Rep. John Salazar, D-Colo.	Sen. Ken Salazar, D-Colo.
Rep. Sander M. Levin, D-Mich.	Sen. Carl Levin, D-Mich.
Rep. Loretta Sanchez, D-Calif.	Rep. Linda T. Sánchez, D-Calif.

First Cousins in Congress

Rep. Mark Udall, D-Colo.
Rep. Tom Udall, D-N.M.

Members Who Served in the Military

There are 130 members with military service. Included is service in the National Guard and reserves. The years of service includes both active and inactive duty, and an asterisk denotes a combat veteran.

Senate (16 R, 13D)	Years
Daniel K. Akaka, D-Hawaii *	1945-47
Robert F. Bennett, R-Utah	1957-60
Jeff Bingaman, D-N.M.	1968-74
Thomas R. Carper, D-Del. *	1968-91
Thad Cochran, R-Miss.	1959-61
Larry E. Craig, R-Idaho	1970-72
Christopher J. Dodd, D-Conn.	1969-75
Michael B. Enzi, R-Wyo.	1967-73
Lindsey Graham, R-S.C.	1982-present
Chuck Hagel, R-Neb. *	1967-68
Tom Harkin, D-Iowa	1962-74
James M. Inhofe, R-Okla.	1957-58
Daniel K. Inouye, D-Hawaii *	1943-47
Johnny Isakson, R-Ga.	1966-72
Edward M. Kennedy, D-Mass.	1951-53
John Kerry, D-Mass. *	1966-70
Herb Kohl, D-Wis.	1958-64
Frank R. Lautenberg, D-N.J.	1942-46
Richard G. Lugar, R-Ind.	1957-60
John McCain, R-Ariz. *	1958-81
Bill Nelson, D-Fla.	1965-71
Jack Reed, D-R.I.	1971-91
Pat Roberts, R-Kan.	1958-62
Jeff Sessions, R-Ala.	1973-86
Arlen Specter, R-Pa.	1951-53
Ted Stevens, R-Alaska *	1943-46
Craig Thomas, R-Wyo.	1955-59
John W. Warner, R-Va. *	1944-46, 1950-64
Jim Webb, D-Va. *	1968-72

House (57 R, 44D)	Years
Todd Akin, R-Mo.	1972-80
Rodney Alexander, R-La.	1965-71
Joe Baca, D-Calif.	1966-68
Spencer Bachus, R-Ala.	1969-71
J. Gresham Barrett, R-S.C.	1983-87
Sanford D. Bishop Jr., D-Ga.	1971
John A. Boehner, R-Ohio	1968
Leonard L. Boswell, D-Iowa *	1956-76
Allen Boyd, D-Fla. *	1969-71
Henry E. Brown Jr., R-S.C.	1953-62
Vern Buchanan, R-Fla.	1970-76
Dan Burton, R-Ind.	1956-62
G.K. Butterfield, D-N.C.	1968-70
Steve Buyer, R-Ind. *	1980-present
Christopher Carney, D-Pa.	1995-present
Howard Coble, R-N.C. *	1952-56, 1960-82
K. Michael Conaway, R-Texas	1970-72
John Conyers Jr., D-Mich. *	1948-57
Robert E. "Bud" Cramer, D-Ala.	1972, 1976-78
Geoff Davis, R-Ky.	1976-87
Thomas M. Davis III, R-Va.	1971-79
Nathan Deal, R-Ga.	1966-68
Peter A. DeFazio, D-Ore.	1967-71
Bill Delahunt, D-Mass.	1963-71
John D. Dingell, D-Mich. *	1944-46
John J. "Jimmy" Duncan Jr., R-Tenn.	1970-87
Bob Etheridge, D-N.C.	1965-67
Terry Everett, R-Ala.	1955-59
Eni F.H. Faleomavaega, D-Am. Samoa	1966-69, 1983-2001
Rodney Frelinghuysen, R-N.J. *	1969-71
Wayne T. Gilchrest, R-Md. *	1964-68
Paul E. Gillmor, R-Ohio	1965-66
Louie Gohmert, R-Texas	1978-82
Charlie Gonzalez, D-Texas	1969-75
Virgil H. Goode Jr., R-Va.	1969-75
Bart Gordon, D-Tenn.	1971-72
Ralph M. Hall, R-Texas *	1942-45
Phil Hare, D-Ill.	1969-75
Doc Hastings, R-Wash.	1964-69
Maurice D. Hinchey, D-N.Y.	1956-59
David L. Hobson, R-Ohio	1958-63
Duncan Hunter, R-Calif. *	1969-71
Darrell Issa, R-Calif.	1970-72, 1976-88
William J. Jefferson, D-La.	1969-75
Sam Johnson, R-Texas *	1951-79
Walter B. Jones, R-N.C.	1967-71
Paul E. Kanjorski, D-Pa.	1960-61
Peter T. King, R-N.Y.	1968-73
Mark Steven Kirk, R-Ill. *	1989-present
John Kline, R-Minn. *	1969-94
Joe Knollenberg, R-Mich.	1955-57
Ron Lewis, R-Ky.	1972
John Linder, R-Ga.	1967-69
Edward J. Markey, D-Mass.	1968-73
Jim Marshall, D-Ga. *	1968-70
Jim McDermott, D-Wash.	1968-70
Gary G. Miller, R-Calif.	1967-68
Alan B. Mollohan, D-W.Va.	1970-83
Dennis Moore, D-Kan.	1970-73
Patrick J. Murphy, D-Pa. *	1996-present
John P. Murtha, D-Pa. *	1952-55, 1966-90
Solomon P. Ortiz, D-Texas	1960-62
Bill Pascrell Jr., D-N.J.	1961-67
Ron Paul, R-Texas	1963-68
Steve Pearce, R-N.M. *	1971-76
Collin C. Peterson, D-Minn.	1963-69
John E. Peterson, R-Pa.	1957-63
Joe Pitts, R-Pa. *	1963-69
Ted Poe, R-Texas	1970-76
Jim Ramstad, R-Minn.	1968-74

Charles B. Rangel, D-N.Y. *	1948-52	Pete Stark, D-Calif.	1955-57
Ralph Regula, R-Ohio	1944-46	Cliff Stearns, R-Fla.	1963-67
Dave Reichert, R-Wash.	1971-76	John Tanner, D-Tenn.	1968-72, 1974-2000
Silvestre Reyes, D-Texas *	1966-68	Gene Taylor, D-Miss.	1971-84
Thomas M. Reynolds, R-N.Y.	1970-76	Mike Thompson, D-Calif. *	1969-73
Harold Rogers, R-Ky.	1956-63	Edolphus Towns, D-N.Y.	1956-58
Mike Rogers, R-Mich.	1985-88	Tim Walz, D-Minn.	1981-2005
Bobby L. Rush, D-Ill.	1963-68	Dave Weldon, R-Fla.	1981-92
John Salazar, D-Colo.	1973-76	Edward Whitfield, R-Ky.	1967-73
Robert C. Scott, D-Va.	1970-76	Roger Wicker, R-Miss.	1976-2004
José E. Serrano, D-N.Y.	1964-66	Heather A. Wilson, R-N.M.	1978-89
Joe Sestak, D-Pa. *	1974-2005	Joe Wilson, R-S.C.	1972-2003
John Shadegg, R-Ariz.	1969-75	Frank R. Wolf, R-Va.	1962-63
John Shimkus, R-Ill.	1980-present	C.W. Bill Young, R-Fla.	1948-57
Vic Snyder, D-Ark.	1967-69	Don Young, R-Alaska	1955-57
John M. Spratt Jr., D-S.C.	1969-71		

Members' Children Who Served in Iraq War

Member	Child's Name	Relationship	Branch
Rep. Todd Akin, R-Mo.	Perry Akin	son	Marine Corps
Sen. Christopher S. Bond, R-Mo.	Sam Bond	son	Marine Corps
Rep. Jo Ann Emerson, R-Mo.	Jessica Gladney	stepchild	Army
Rep. Duncan Hunter, R-Calif.	Duncan Duane Hunter	son	Marine Corps
Sen. Tim Johnson, D-S.D.	Brooks Johnson	son	Army
Rep. John Kline, R-Minn.	John Daniel Kline	son	Army
Rep. Ileana Ros-Lehtinen, R-Fla.	Douglas Lehtinen	stepchild	Marine Corps
	Lindsey Nelson Lehtinen	daughter-in-law	Marine Corps
Rep. Lucille Roybal-Allard, D-Calif.	Guy Mark Allard	stepchild	Army
Sen. Jim Webb, D-Va.	Jimmy Webb	son	Marine Corps
Rep. Joe Wilson, R-S.C.	Alan Wilson	son	S.C. National Guard

High Fliers

Members of Congress who have a current pilot's license:

Rep. Leonard L. Boswell, D-Iowa
Rep. Allen Boyd, D-Fla.
Rep. Chet Edwards, D-Texas
Rep. Sam Graves, R-Mo.
Sen. Tom Harkin, D-Iowa
Rep. Robin Hayes, R-N.C.
Sen. James M. Inhofe, R-Okla.
Rep. Collin C. Peterson, D-Minn.
Rep. John Salazar, D-Colo.
Sen. Ted Stevens, R-Alaska

Peace Corps Volunteers

Members of Congress who have served in the Peace Corps:

Member	Country	Years
Sen. Christopher J. Dodd, D-Conn.	Dominican Republic	1966-68
Rep. Sam Farr, D-Calif.	Colombia	1964-66
Rep. Michael M. Honda, D-Calif.	El Salvador	1965-67
Rep. Tom Petri, R-Wis.	Somalia	1966-67
Rep. Christopher Shays, R-Conn.	Fiji	1968-70
Rep. James T. Walsh, R-N.Y.	Nepal	1970-72

Member Occupations

	House			Senate			Congress
	Democrat	Republican	Total	Democrat	Republican	Total	Total
Actor/Entertainment	3		3	1		1	4
Aeronautics		2	2				2
Agriculture	10	15	25	2	4	6	31
Artistic/Creative		1	1	2 *		2	3
Business	91	123	214	11	28	39	253
Clergy	1	2	3				3
Education	58	36	94	8 *	7	15	109
Engineering	3	1	4		1	1	5
Health Care	6	3	9				9
Homemaker/Domestic	5	4	9				9
Journalism	4	4	8	4 *	3	7	15
Labor/Blue Collar	7	6	13	2 *	1	3	16
Law	109	76	185	36 *	31	67	252
Law Enforcement	7	3	10				10
Medicine/Doctor	3	9	12		3	3	15
Military	2	3	5		1	1	6
Professional Sports	1		1		1	1	2
Public Service/Politics	143	89	232	24	21	45	277
Real Estate	4	33	37	1	2	3	40
Science	3	3	6				6
Secretarial/Clerical	4	5	9				9
Technical	1	1	2				2
Miscellaneous	2		2				2

Some members have had more than one occupation; delegates are not included.

* Total includes independents Joseph I. Lieberman, Conn., and Bernard Sanders, Vt.

Member Religious Affiliations

	House			Senate			Congress
	Democrat	Republican	Total	Democrat	Republican	Total	Total
African Methodist Episcopal	3		3				3
Baptist	27	32	59	1	6	7	66
Buddhist	2		2				2
Christian Church	1		1				1
Christian Reformed Church		2	2				2
Christian Scientist		5	5				5
Community of Christ	1		1				1
Disciples of Christ	1		1				1
Eastern Orthodox	3	2	5		1	1	6
Episcopalian	9	20	29	4	6	10	39
Jewish	29	1	30	11*	2	13	43
Lutheran	9	7	16	3		3	19
Methodist	23	27	50	5	7	12	62
Mormon	2	8	10	1	4	5	15
Muslim	1		1				1
Pentecostal		4	4				4
Presbyterian	13	21	34	2	8	10	44
Protestant - Unspecified	12	27	39	3	4	7	46
Quaker	1		1				1
Roman Catholic	87	41	128	16	9	25	153
Seventh-day Adventist	1	1	2				2
Unitarian	1		1	1		1	2
United Church of Christ/ Congregationalist		3	3	4	2	6	9
Unspecified	6		6				6

Delegates are not included.

* Includes independents Joseph I. Lieberman, Conn., and Bernard Sanders, Vt.

Senate Presidential Support and Opposition

Support scores represent how often a senator sided with President Bush on roll call votes on which the president took a clear position beforehand. Opposition scores represent how often a senator voted against the president's position. During the 109th Congress (2005-06), there were 115 such votes in the Senate. Only members of the 110th Congress who voted more than half the time in 2005 and 2006 are listed.

109th Congress: Top Scorers

Support — Democrats	
Ben Nelson, Neb.	75.7%
Mary L. Landrieu, La.	68.2
Mark Pryor, Ark.	61.7
Blanche Lincoln, Ark.	55.8
Joseph I. Lieberman, Conn.*	55.7
Max Baucus, Mont.	55.0
Bill Nelson, Fla.	55.0
Ken Salazar, Colo.	54.5
Thomas R. Carper, Del.	53.9
Tim Johnson, S.D.	52.25
Herb Kohl, Wis.	52.25
Daniel K. Inouye, Hawaii	51.5
Kent Conrad, N.D.	50.0
Carl Levin, Mich.	50.0
Harry Reid, Nev.	49.12
Evan Bayh, Ind.	49.09
Patty Murray, Wash.	48.7
Dianne Feinstein, Calif.	48.6
Jeff Bingaman, N.M.	47.7
John D. Rockefeller IV, W.Va.	47.5

Support — Republicans	
John Cornyn, Texas	93.91%
Wayne Allard, Colo.	93.86
Chuck Hagel, Neb.	92.9
Ted Stevens, Alaska	92.8
Sam Brownback, Kan.	92.5
Mitch McConnell, Ky.	92.2
Johnny Isakson, Ga.	92.1
Saxby Chambliss, Ga.	92.0
Thad Cochran, Miss.	91.9
Mel Martinez, Fla.	91.8
Lamar Alexander, Tenn.	91.15
Robert F. Bennett, Utah	91.15
Elizabeth Dole, N.C.	91.1
Jeff Sessions, Ala.	91.0
Christopher S. Bond, Mo.	90.43
Orrin G. Hatch, Utah	90.38
Jim DeMint, S.C.	90.35
Jim Bunning, Ky.	90.18
Pete V. Domenici, N.M.	90.18
Pat Roberts, Kan.	90.18

Opposition — Democrats	
Tom Harkin, Iowa	61.6%
Edward M. Kennedy, Mass.	60.6
Frank R. Lautenberg, N.J.	60.4
Barbara Boxer, Calif.	60.2
Richard J. Durbin, Ill.	58.41
Ron Wyden, Ore.	58.41
Patrick J. Leahy, Vt.	58.3
Hillary Rodham Clinton, N.Y.	57.5
Barack Obama, Ill.	57.3
Christopher J. Dodd, Conn.	57.01
Joseph R. Biden Jr., Del.	56.99
Barbara A. Mikulski, Md.	56.76
Charles E. Schumer, N.Y.	56.76
Russ Feingold, Wis.	56.6
Jack Reed, R.I.	56.5
Byron L. Dorgan, N.D.	56.3
John Kerry, Mass.	56.0
Debbie Stabenow, Mich.	55.8
Daniel K. Akaka, Hawaii	55.0
Maria Cantwell, Wash.	53.5
Robert C. Byrd, W.Va.	52.6

Opposition — Republicans	
Olympia J. Snowe, Maine	28.6%
Susan Collins, Maine	27.8
Arlen Specter, Pa.	20.6
Gordon H. Smith, Ore.	18.9
John McCain, Ariz.	15.6
Norm Coleman, Minn.	13.8
John Thune, S.D.	13.5
John E. Sununu, N.H.	13.4
Michael D. Crapo, Idaho	13.3
Richard C. Shelby, Ala.	13.0
David Vitter, La.	12.5
Charles E. Grassley, Iowa	12.17
George V. Voinovich, Ohio	12.17
Craig Thomas, Wyo.	11.9
Michael B. Enzi, Wyo.	11.8
Judd Gregg, N.H.	11.7
Lisa Murkowski, Alaska	11.54
Kay Bailey Hutchison, Texas	11.5
Richard M. Burr, N.C.	11.4
Richard G. Lugar, Ind.	11.3
James M. Inhofe, Okla.	10.9

* An independent in the 110th Congress, Lieberman caucuses with the Democrats.

Senate Party Unity and Opposition

Support scores represent how often a senator voted with his or her party's majority against a majority of the other party. Opposition scores represent how often a senator voted against his or her party's majority. In the 109th Congress (2005-06), there were 389 such "party unity" votes in the Senate. Only members of the 110th Congress who voted more than half the time in 2005 and 2006 are listed.

109th Congress: Top Scorers

Support — Democrats

Edward M. Kennedy, Mass.	99.5%
Richard J. Durbin, Ill.	98.4
Barbara Boxer, Calif.	98.1
Barbara A. Mikulski, Md.	97.3
Jack Reed, R.I.	97.2
Patrick J. Leahy, Vt.	96.9
Frank R. Lautenberg, N.J.	96.7
Tom Harkin, Iowa	96.62
Barack Obama, Ill.	96.62
John Kerry, Mass.	96.0
Carl Levin, Mich.	95.9
Daniel K. Akaka, Hawaii	95.8
Hillary Rodham Clinton, N.Y.	94.5
Christopher J. Dodd, Conn.	94.2
Ron Wyden, Ore.	94.1
Russ Feingold, Wis.	94.0
Patty Murray, Wash.	93.8
Charles E. Schumer, N.Y.	93.3
Harry Reid, Nev.	92.5
Debbie Stabenow, Mich.	91.9

Support — Republicans

Jim Bunning, Ky.	97.9%
Mitch McConnell, Ky.	97.7
Jon Kyl, Ariz.	96.65
Jeff Sessions, Ala.	96.65
Jim DeMint, S.C.	96.63
Wayne Allard, Colo.	96.13
John Cornyn, Texas	96.1
Michael B. Enzi, Wyo.	95.7
Johnny Isakson, Ga.	95.6
Craig Thomas, Wyo.	94.9
Michael D. Crapo, Idaho	94.8
Trent Lott, Miss.	94.65
Charles E. Grassley, Iowa	94.6
Richard M. Burr, N.C.	94.57
Saxby Chambliss, Ga.	94.52
Orrin G. Hatch, Utah	94.5
James M. Inhofe, Okla.	94.3
Pat Roberts, Kan.	94.0
David Vitter, La.	93.7
Elizabeth Dole, N.C.	93.6

Opposition — Democrats

Ben Nelson, Neb.	58.0%
Mary L. Landrieu, La.	24.3
Max Baucus, Mont.	23.9
Kent Conrad, N.D.	22.9
Thomas R. Carper, Del.	22.2
Mark Pryor, Ark.	21.4
Robert C. Byrd, W.Va.	20.1
Bill Nelson, Fla.	19.6
Blanche Lincoln, Ark.	18.8
Tim Johnson, S.D.	16.9
Byron L. Dorgan, N.D.	15.3
Ken Salazar, Colo.	13.6
Joseph I. Lieberman, Conn.*	12.0
Jeff Bingaman, N.M.	11.1
Evan Bayh, Ind.	10.62
Herb Kohl, Wis.	10.62
John D. Rockefeller IV, W.Va.	10.1
Daniel K. Inouye, Hawaii	10.03
Joseph R. Biden Jr., Del.	10.0
Dianne Feinstein, Calif.	8.6
Maria Cantwell, Wash.	8.3

Opposition — Republicans

Olympia J. Snowe, Maine	44.0%
Susan Collins, Maine	38.0
Arlen Specter, Pa.	34.5
Norm Coleman, Minn.	22.9
John McCain, Ariz.	19.2
Gordon H. Smith, Ore.	18.7
George V. Voinovich, Ohio	18.65
Richard G. Lugar, Ind.	16.6
John W. Warner, Va.	15.8
Lindsey Graham, S.C.	11.8
Lisa Murkowski, Alaska	11.7
John E. Sununu, N.H.	11.4
Ted Stevens, Alaska	11.2
Pete V. Domenici, N.M.	10.5
Chuck Hagel, Neb.	9.84
Kay Bailey Hutchison, Texas	9.79
John Thune, S.D.	9.7
Judd Gregg, N.H.	9.6
Mel Martinez, Fla.	9.5
Sam Brownback, Kan.	9.1
Richard C. Shelby, Ala.	8.1

* An independent in the 110th Congress, Lieberman caucuses with the Democrats.

House Presidential Support and Opposition

Support scores represent how often a House member sided with President Bush on roll call votes on which the president took a clear position beforehand. Opposition scores represent how often a member voted against the president's position. During the 109th Congress (2005-06), there were 86 such votes in the House. Only members of the 110th Congress who voted more than half the time in 2005 and 2006 are listed.

109th Congress: Top Scorers

Support — Democrats

Dan Boren, Okla.	74.1%
Henry Cuellar, Texas	70.7
Robert E. "Bud" Cramer, Ala.	68.8
Lincoln Davis, Tenn.	67.4
Jim Marshall, Ga.	61.6
Charlie Melancon, La.	61.2
Ike Skelton, Mo.	60.7
Mike McIntyre, N.C.	59.5
Collin C. Peterson, Minn.	57.0
Chet Edwards, Texas	55.8
John Barrow, Ga.	55.3
Sanford D. Bishop Jr., Ga.	55.0
Jim Matheson, Utah	54.7
Tim Holden, Pa.	54.1
Bart Gordon, Tenn.	53.5
Ben Chandler, Ky.	52.9
Gene Taylor, Miss.	52.4
Solomon P. Ortiz, Texas	51.3
Allen Boyd, Fla.	51.19
John Salazar, Colo.	51.16
Mike Ross, Ark	50.63
John Tanner, Tenn.	50.6

Support — Republicans

John A. Boehner, Ohio	95.2%
Pete Sessions, Texas	94.7
Roy Blunt, Mo.	94.12
John Culberson, Texas	94.12
William M. "Mac" Thornberry, Texas	94.12
Jim McCrery, La.	94.05
Kevin Brady, Texas	93.98
John Carter, Texas	93.98
Todd Akin, Mo.	93.02
Ander Crenshaw, Fla.	93.02
Kay Granger, Texas	93.02
Adam H. Putnam, Fla.	93.02
Kenny Marchant, Texas	92.94
John L. Mica, Fla.	92.94
John Shadegg, Ariz.	92.94
Tom Cole, Okla.	92.86
Lamar Smith, Texas	92.86
Richard H. Baker, La.	92.5
Spencer Bachus, Ala.	92.3
12 members tied	91.9

Opposition — Democrats

Donald M. Payne, N.J.	93.9%
Pete Stark, Calif.	91.8
Diane Watson, Calif.	91.1
Maurice D. Hinchey, N.Y.	90.6
Earl Blumenauer, Ore.	90.1
Barbara Lee, Calif.	89.53
Lynn Woolsey, Calif.	89.53
Rosa DeLauro, Conn.	89.4
Tom Udall, N.M.	89.3
John Lewis, Ga.	88.5
Raúl M. Grijalva, Ariz.	88.37
Dennis J. Kucinich, Ohio	88.37
Edward J. Markey, Mass.	88.37
John Conyers Jr., Mich.	88.24
Gwen Moore, Wis.	88.24
José E. Serrano, N.Y.	88.1
Jan Schakowsky, Ill.	88.0
Henry A. Waxman, Calif.	87.7
Four members tied	87.2

Opposition — Republicans

Ron Paul, Texas	63.0%
Christopher Shays, Conn.	45.2
Walter B. Jones, N.C.	42.5
Timothy V. Johnson, Ill.	36.9
Christopher H. Smith, N.J.	36.5
Wayne T. Gilchrest, Md.	34.9
Jim Ramstad, Minn.	31.4
Jim Gerlach, Pa.	31.0
Roscoe G. Bartlett, Md.	29.4
Michael N. Castle, Del.	29.3
Frank A. LoBiondo, N.J.	29.1
Jo Ann Emerson, Mo.	28.9
Steven C. LaTourette, Ohio	28.2
John J. "Jimmy" Duncan Jr., Tenn.	27.06
Jeff Flake, Ariz.	27.06
Jerry Moran, Kan.	26.74
Mark Steven Kirk, Ill.	26.74
Judy Biggert, Ill.	24.42
Howard Coble, N.C.	24.42
Fred Upton, Mich.	22.1
Heather A. Wilson, N.M.	21.7

House Party Unity and Opposition

Support scores represent how often a House member voted with his or her party's majority against a majority of the other party. Opposition scores represent how often a member voted against his or her party's majority on such party unity tests. In the 109th Congress (2005-06) there were 623 such "party unity" votes in the House. Only members of the 110th Congress who voted more than half the time in 2005 and 2006 are listed.

109th Congress: Top Scorers

Support — Democrats

Donald M. Payne, N.J.	99.5%
Jan Schakowsky, Ill.	99.3
John Lewis, Ga.	99.22
Xavier Becerra, Calif.	99.16
Tammy Baldwin, Wis.	99.0
Barbara Lee, Calif.	98.86
Jerrold Nadler, N.Y	98.85
George Miller, Calif.	98.85
Raúl M. Grijalva, Ariz.	98.7
Hilda L. Solis, Calif.	98.68
Jim McGovern, Mass.	98.55
Nancy Pelosi, Calif.	98.52
Lynn Woolsey, Calif.	98.52
Pete Stark, Calif.	98.47
Martin T. Meehan, Mass.	98.45
Diane Watson, Calif.	98.44
Rosa DeLauro, Conn.	98.38
Linda T. Sánchez, Calif.	98.38
Nydia M. Velázquez, N.Y.	98.37
Maurice D. Hinchey, N.Y.	98.17
Henry A. Waxman, Calif.	98.17

Support — Republicans

Pete Sessions, Texas	98.8%
Marsha Blackburn, Tenn.	98.7
Wally Herger, Calif.	98.54
Todd Akin, Mo.	98.53
Patrick T. McHenry, N.C.	98.53
Randy Neugebauer, Texas	98.4
Marilyn Musgrave, Colo.	98.3
Eric Cantor, Va.	98.1
Roy Blunt, Mo.	98.0
Virginia Foxx, N.C.	97.91
Sam Johnson, Texas	97.89
Richard H. Baker, La.	97.83
John Carter, Texas	97.83
Gary G. Miller, Calif.	97.83
John L. Mica, Fla.	97.73
J. Gresham Barrett, S.C.	97.7
Kenny Marchant, Texas	97.7
Lamar Smith, Texas	97.67
John Culberson, Texas	97.65
Frank D. Lucas, Okla.	97.55

Opposition — Democrats

Dan Boren, Okla.	43.3%
Robert E. "Bud" Cramer, Ala.	40.1
Collin C. Peterson, Minn.	36.3
Jim Marshall, Ga.	34.0
Charlie Melancon, La.	33.4
Lincoln Davis, Tenn.	33.1
Henry Cuellar, Texas	33.0
Jim Matheson, Utah	32.1
Gene Taylor, Miss.	31.1
Chet Edwards, Texas	29.6
Allen Boyd, Fla.	28.8
John Barrow, Ga.	28.4
Mike McIntyre, N.C.	27.7
John Tanner, Tenn.	26.4
Bart Gordon, Tenn.	26.0
Sanford D. Bishop Jr., Ga.	25.4
Ike Skelton, Mo.	24.5
Marion Berry, Ark.	24.4
John P. Murtha, Pa.	24.2
Mike Ross, Ark.	24.1
Tim Holden, Pa.	23.4
Solomon P. Ortiz, Texas	23.2

Opposition — Republicans

Christopher Shays, Conn.	37.4%
Ron Paul, Texas	30.3
Walter B. Jones, N.C.	27.2
Jim Ramstad, Minn.	24.8
Christopher H. Smith, N.J.	24.5
Jim Gerlach, Pa.	23.4
Michael N. Castle, Del.	23.1
Frank A. LoBiondo, N.J.	22.47
Wayne T. Gilchrest, Md.	22.46
Timothy V. Johnson, Ill.	22.1
Todd R. Platts, Pa.	21.3
Mark Steven Kirk, Ill.	20.1
Vernon J. Ehlers, Mich.	19.1
Heather A. Wilson, N.M.	17.1
H. James Saxton, N.J.	16.9
Mike Ferguson, N.J.	16.6
Steven C. LaTourette, Ohio	15.95
Fred Upton, Mich.	15.89
Dave Reichert, Wash.	15.8
Charlie Dent, Pa.	14.8
John M. McHugh, N.Y.	13.3
Thomas M. Davis III, Va.	13.2

New Democrat Coalition

All 58 members are House Democrats.

Chairwoman: Ellen O. Tauscher, Calif.

Jason Altmire, Pa.
Michael Arcuri, N.Y.
Brian Baird, Wash.
John Barrow, Ga.
Melissa Bean, Ill.
Shelley Berkley, Nev.
Bruce Braley, Iowa
Lois Capps, Calif.
Russ Carnahan, Mo.
Christopher Carney, Pa.
Ben Chandler, Ky.
Joe Courtney, Conn.
Joseph Crowley, N.Y.
Henry Cuellar, Texas
Artur Davis, Ala.
Susan A. Davis, Calif.
Rahm Emanuel, Ill.
Eliot L. Engel, N.Y.
Bob Etheridge, N.C.
Gabrielle Giffords, Ariz.
Kirsten Gillibrand, N.Y.
Charlie Gonzalez, Texas
Jane Harman, Calif.
Stephanie Herseth-Sandlin, S.D.
Brian Higgins, N.Y.
Baron P. Hill, Ind.
Rush D. Holt, N.J.
Darlene Hooley, Ore.
Jay Inslee, Wash.
Steve Israel, N.Y.
Ron Kind, Wis.
Ron Klein, Fla.
Nick Lampson, Texas
Rick Larsen, Wash.
John B. Larson, Conn.
Tim Mahoney, Fla.
Carolyn McCarthy, N.Y.
Mike McIntyre, N.C.
Kendrick B. Meek, Fla.
Gregory W. Meeks, N.Y.
Charlie Melancon, La.
Dennis Moore, Kan.
James P. Moran, Va.
Christopher S. Murphy, Conn.
Patrick J. Murphy, Pa.
Ed Perlmutter, Colo.
David E. Price, N.C.
Loretta Sanchez, Calif.
Adam B. Schiff, Calif.
Allyson Y. Schwartz, Pa.
David Scott, Ga.
Joe Sestak, Pa.
Adam Smith, Wash.
Vic Snyder, Ark.
Tom Udall, N.M.
Debbie Wasserman-Schultz, Fla.
David Wu, Ore.

Republican Main Street Partnership

The partnership also includes several governors and former elected officials. All members are Republicans.

Rep. Judy Biggert, Ill.
Rep. Mary Bono, Calif.
Rep. Ginny Brown-Waite, Fla.
Rep. Ken Calvert, Calif.
Rep. Dave Camp, Mich.
Rep. Shelley Moore Capito, W.Va.
Rep. Michael N. Castle, Del., president
Sen. Norm Coleman, Minn.
Sen. Susan Collins, Maine, board member
Rep. Thomas M. Davis III, Va., board member
Rep. Charlie Dent, Pa.
Rep. David Dreier, Calif.
Rep. Vernon J. Ehlers, Mich.
Rep. Jo Ann Emerson, Mo.
Rep. Phil English, Pa.
Rep. Rodney Frelinghuysen, N.J.
Rep. Jim Gerlach, Pa.
Rep. Wayne T. Gilchrest, Md.
Rep. Paul E. Gillmor, Ohio
Rep. Kay Granger, Texas
Rep. David L. Hobson, Ohio
Rep. Timothy V. Johnson, Ill.
Rep. Mark Steven Kirk, Ill.
Rep. John R. "Randy" Kuhl Jr., N.Y.
Rep. Ray LaHood, Ill.
Rep. Steven C. LaTourette, Ohio
Rep. Jerry Lewis, Calif.
Rep. Frank A. LoBiondo, N.J.
Sen. John McCain, Ariz.
Rep. Jim McCrery, La.
Sen. Lisa Murkowski, Alaska
Rep. Tom Petri, Wis.
Rep. Todd R. Platts, Pa.
Rep. Jon Porter, Nev.
Rep. Deborah Pryce, Ohio
Rep. Jim Ramstad, Minn.
Rep. Ralph Regula, Ohio
Rep. H. James Saxton, N.J.
Rep. Christopher Shays, Conn.
Sen. Gordon H. Smith, Ore.
Sen. Olympia J. Snowe, Maine, board member
Sen. Arlen Specter, Pa.
Rep. Michael R. Turner, Ohio
Rep. Fred Upton, Mich., board member
Rep. Greg Walden, Ore.
Rep. James T. Walsh, N.Y.
Rep. Jerry Weller, Ill.
Rep. Heather A. Wilson, N.M.

Blue Dog Coalition

All 43 members are House Democrats.

Co-Chairmen: Allen Boyd, Fla., Mike Ross, Ark., Dennis Moore, Kan.

Michael Arcuri, N.Y.
Joe Baca, Calif.
John Barrow, Ga.
Melissa Bean, Ill.
Marion Berry, Ark.
Sanford D. Bishop Jr., Ga.
Dan Boren, Okla.
Leonard L. Boswell, Iowa
Dennis Cardoza, Calif.
Ben Chandler, Ky.
Jim Cooper, Tenn.
Jim Costa, Calif.
Robert E. "Bud" Cramer, Ala.
Lincoln Davis, Tenn.
Joe Donnelly, Ind.
Brad Ellsworth, Ind.
Kirsten Gillibrand, N.Y.
Jane Harman, Calif.
Stephanie Herseth-Sandlin, S.D.
Baron P. Hill, Ind.
Tim Holden, Pa.
Steve Israel, N.Y.
Tim Mahoney, Fla.
Jim Marshall, Ga.
Jim Matheson, Utah
Mike McIntyre, N.C.
Charlie Melancon, La.
Michael H. Michaud, Maine
Patrick J. Murphy, Pa.
Collin C. Peterson, Minn.
Earl Pomeroy, N.D.
John Salazar, Colo.
Loretta Sanchez, Calif.
Adam B. Schiff, Calif.
David Scott, Ga.
Heath Shuler, N.C.
John Tanner, Tenn.
Gene Taylor, Miss.
Mike Thompson, Calif.
Charlie Wilson, Ohio

Congressional Hispanic Caucus

There are 21 members, all of whom are House Democrats, except Democratic Sen. Menendez.

Chairman: Joe Baca, Calif.

Xavier Becerra, Calif.
Dennis Cardoza, Calif
Jim Costa, Calif.
Henry Cuellar, Texas
Charlie Gonzalez, Texas
Raúl M. Grijalva, Ariz.
Luis V. Gutierrez, Ill.
Rubén Hinojosa, Texas
Robert Menendez, N.J.
Grace F. Napolitano, Calif.
Solomon P. Ortiz, Texas
Ed Pastor, Ariz.
Silvestre Reyes, Texas
Ciro D. Rodriguez, Texas
Lucille Roybal-Allard, Calif.
John Salazar, Colo.
José E. Serrano, N.Y.
Albio Sires, N.J.
Hilda L. Solis, Calif.
Nydia M. Velázquez, N.Y.

Congressional Black Caucus

There are 42 members, all of whom are House Democrats, except Democratic Sen. Obama.

Chairwoman: Carolyn Cheeks Kilpatrick, Mich.

Sanford D. Bishop Jr., Ga.
Corrine Brown, Fla.
G.K. Butterfield, N.C.
Julia Carson, Ind.
Del. Donna M.C. Christensen, Virgin Is.
Yvette D. Clarke, N.Y.
William Lacy Clay, Mo.
Emanuel Cleaver II, Mo.
James E. Clyburn, S.C.
John Conyers Jr., Mich.
Elijah E. Cummings, Md.
Artur Davis, Ala.
Danny K. Davis, Ill.
Keith Ellison, Minn.
Chaka Fattah, Pa.
Al Green, Texas
Alcee L. Hastings, Fla.
Jesse L. Jackson Jr., Ill.
Sheila Jackson-Lee, Texas
William J. Jefferson, La.
Eddie Bernice Johnson, Texas
Hank Johnson, Ga.
Stephanie Tubbs Jones, Ohio
Barbara Lee, Calif.
John Lewis, Ga.
Kendrick B. Meek, Fla.
Gregory W. Meeks, N.Y.
Gwen Moore, Wis.
Del. Eleanor Holmes Norton, D.C.
Barack Obama, Ill.
Donald M. Payne, N.J.
Charles B. Rangel, N.Y.
Bobby L. Rush, Ill.
David Scott, Ga.
Robert C. Scott, Va.
Bennie Thompson, Miss.
Edolphus Towns, N.Y.
Maxine Waters, Calif.
Diane Watson, Calif.
Melvin Watt, N.C.
Albert R. Wynn, Md.

Republican Study Committee

The list is not comprehensive, as the caucus permits individual members to decide whether to publicize their membership. All members are House Republicans.

Chairman: Jeb Hensarling, Texas

Robert B. Aderholt, Ala.
Todd Akin, Mo.
Rodney Alexander, La.
Michele Bachmann, Minn.
Spencer Bachus, Ala.
J. Gresham Barrett, S.C.
Roscoe G. Bartlett, Md.
Joe L. Barton, Texas
Brian P. Bilbray, Calif.
Rob Bishop, Utah
Marsha Blackburn, Tenn.
John Boozman, Ark.
Kevin Brady, Texas
Henry E. Brown Jr., S.C.
Vern Buchanan, Fla.
Michael C. Burgess, Texas
Dan Burton, Ind.
Dave Camp, Mich.
John Campbell, Calif.
Chris Cannon, Utah
Eric Cantor, Va.
John Carter, Texas
Steve Chabot, Ohio
Tom Cole, Okla.
K. Michael Conaway, Texas
Barbara Cubin, Wyo.
John Culberson, Texas
David Davis, Tenn.
Geoff Davis, Ky.
Jo Ann Davis, Va.
Mario Diaz-Balart, Fla.
John T. Doolittle, Calif.
Thelma Drake, Va.
Mary Fallin, Okla.
Tom Feeney, Fla.
Jeff Flake, Ariz.
J. Randy Forbes, Va.
Jeff Fortenberry, Neb.
Res. Cmmsr. Luis Fortuño, P.R.
Virginia Foxx, N.C.
Trent Franks, Ariz.
Scott Garrett, N.J.
Phil Gingrey, Ga.
Louie Gohmert, Texas
Virgil H. Goode Jr., Va.
Robert W. Goodlatte, Va.
Wally Herger, Calif.
Peter Hoekstra, Mich.
Duncan Hunter, Calif.
Bob Inglis, S.C.
Darrell Issa, Calif.
Bobby Jindal, La.
Sam Johnson, Texas
Jim Jordan, Ohio
Steve King, Iowa
Jack Kingston, Ga.
John Kline, Minn.
Doug Lamborn, Colo.
Ron Lewis, Ky.
John Linder, Ga.
Dan Lungren, Calif.
Donald Manzullo, Ill.
Michael McCaul, Texas
Patrick T. McHenry, N.C.
Howard P. "Buck" McKeon, Calif.
Gary G. Miller, Calif.
Jeff Miller, Fla.
Jerry Moran, Kan.
Marilyn Musgrave, Colo.
Sue Myrick, N.C.
Randy Neugebauer, Texas
Mike Pence, Ind.
Joe Pitts, Pa.
Ted Poe, Texas
Tom Price, Ga.
George Radanovich, Calif.
Denny Rehberg, Mont.
Thomas M. Reynolds, N.Y.
Cathy McMorris Rodgers, Wash.
Peter Roskam, Ill.
Ed Royce, Calif.
Paul D. Ryan, Wis.
Bill Sali, Idaho
Pete Sessions, Texas
John Shadegg, Ariz.
Adrian Smith, Neb.
Lamar Smith, Texas
Mark Souder, Ind.
Cliff Stearns, Fla.
John Sullivan, Okla.
Tom Tancredo, Colo.
William M. "Mac" Thornberry, Texas
Michael R. Turner, Ohio
Tim Walberg, Mich.
Zach Wamp, Tenn.
Dave Weldon, Fla.
Lynn Westmoreland, Ga.
Joe Wilson, S.C.

Senate Common Ground Coalition

Co-Chairwomen: Mary L. Landrieu, D-La.*, Olympia J. Snowe, R-Maine *

Robert F. Bennett, R-Utah
Thomas R. Carper, D-Del.
Norm Coleman, R-Minn.
Susan Collins, R-Maine *
Charles E. Grassley, R-Iowa
Joseph I. Lieberman, I-Conn.*
Blanche Lincoln, D-Ark.
Lisa Murkowski, R-Alaska
Ben Nelson, D-Neb.*
Bill Nelson, D-Fla.
Mark Pryor, D-Ark.*
Ken Salazar, D-Colo.*
Gordon H. Smith, R-Ore.
John W. Warner, R-Va.*

* Member of ad hoc Gang of 14 in the 109th Congress, which also included John McCain, R-Ariz., Lindsey Graham, R-S.C., Mike DeWine, R-Ohio, Lincoln Chafee, R-R.I., Robert C. Byrd, D-W.Va., and Daniel K. Inouye, D-Hawaii.

Progressive Caucus

There are 73 members, all of whom are Democrats, except Sanders, who is an independent.

Co-Chairwomen: Reps. Barbara Lee, Calif., and Lynn Woolsey, Calif.

Rep. Neil Abercrombie, Hawaii
Rep. Tammy Baldwin, Wis.
Rep. Xavier Becerra, Calif.
Del. Madeleine Z. Bordallo, Guam
Rep. Robert A. Brady, Pa.
Rep. Corrine Brown, Fla.
Sen. Sherrod Brown, Ohio
Rep. Michael E. Capuano, Mass.
Rep. Julia Carson, Ind.
Del. Donna M.C. Christensen, V.I.
Rep. Yvette D. Clarke, N.Y.
Rep. William Lacy Clay, Mo.
Rep. Emanuel Cleaver II, Mo.
Rep. Steve Cohen, Tenn.
Rep. John Conyers Jr., Mich.
Rep. Elijah E. Cummings, Md.
Rep. Danny K. Davis, Ill.
Rep. Peter A. DeFazio, Ore.
Rep. Rosa DeLauro, Conn.
Rep. Keith Ellison, Minn.
Rep. Sam Farr, Calif.
Rep. Chaka Fattah, Pa.
Rep. Bob Filner, Calif.
Rep. Barney Frank, Mass.
Rep. Raúl M. Grijalva, Ariz.
Rep. Luis V. Gutierrez, Ill.
Rep. John Hall, N.Y.
Rep. Phil Hare, Ill.
Rep. Maurice D. Hinchey, N.Y.
Rep. Mazie K. Hirono, Hawaii
Rep. Michael M. Honda, Calif.
Rep. Jesse L. Jackson Jr., Ill.
Rep. Sheila Jackson-Lee, Texas
Rep. Eddie Bernice Johnson, Texas
Rep. Hank Johnson, Ga.
Rep. Stephanie Tubbs Jones, Ohio
Rep. Marcy Kaptur, Ohio
Rep. Carolyn Cheeks Kilpatrick, Mich.
Rep. Dennis J. Kucinich, Ohio
Rep. Tom Lantos, Calif.
Rep. John Lewis, Ga.
Rep. Dave Loebsack, Iowa
Rep. Carolyn B. Maloney, N.Y.
Rep. Edward J. Markey, Mass.
Rep. Jim McDermott, Wash.
Rep. Jim McGovern, Mass.
Rep. George Miller, Calif.
Rep. Gwen Moore, Wis.
Rep. Jerrold Nadler, N.Y.
Del. Eleanor Holmes Norton, D.C.
Rep. John W. Olver, Mass.
Rep. Ed Pastor, Ariz.
Rep. Donald M. Payne, N.J.
Rep. Charles B. Rangel, N.Y.
Rep. Bobby L. Rush, Ill.
Rep. Linda T. Sánchez, Calif.
Sen. Bernard Sanders, Vt.
Rep. Jan Schakowsky, Ill.
Rep. Jose E. Serrano, N.Y.
Rep. Louise M. Slaughter, N.Y.
Rep. Hilda L. Solis, Calif.
Rep. Pete Stark, Calif.
Rep. Bennie Thompson, Miss.
Rep. John F. Tierney, Mass.
Rep. Tom Udall, N.M.
Rep. Nydia M. Velázquez, N.Y.
Rep. Maxine Waters, Calif.
Rep. Diane Watson, Calif.
Rep. Melvin Watt, N.C.
Rep. Henry A. Waxman, Calif.
Rep. Peter Welch, Vt.

Other Caucus Leadership

All are House members.

Congressional Caucus for Women's Issues
Lois Capps, D-Calif., co-chairwoman
Cathy McMorris Rodgers, R-Wash., co-chairwoman

Congressional Hispanic Conference
Res. Cmmsr. Luis Fortuño, P.R., chairman

Hispanic Districts

Congressional districts with the largest percentage of Hispanics: (Hispanics may be of any race)

District	Hispanic	Member
Texas 16	77.7%	Reyes, D
Texas 15	77.6%	Hinojosa, D
Texas 28	77.5%	Cuellar, D
California 34	77.2%	Roybal-Allard, D
Illinois 4	74.5%	Gutierrez, D
California 38	70.6%	Napolitano, D
California 31	70.2%	Becerra, D
Florida 21	69.7%	Diaz-Balart, R
Texas 27	68.1%	Ortiz, D
Texas 20	67.1%	Gonzalez, D

Black Districts

Congressional districts with the largest percentage of African-Americans:

District	Black	Member
Illinois 1	65.2%	Rush, D
Louisiana 2	63.7%	Jefferson, D
Mississippi 2	63.2%	Thompson, D
Illinois 2	62.0%	Jackson, D
Alabama 7	61.7%	Davis, D
Illinois 7	61.6%	Davis, D
Michigan 14	61.1%	Conyers, D
Pennsylvania 2	60.7%	Fattah, D
Michigan 13	60.5%	Kilpatrick, D
New York 10	60.2%	Towns, D

Asian Districts

Congressional districts with the largest percentage of Asians:

District	Asian	Member
Hawaii 1	53.6%	Abercrombie, D
California 15	29.2%	Honda, D
California 8	28.7%	Pelosi, D
California 12	28.5%	Lantos, D
California 13	28.2%	Stark, D
Hawaii 2	28.0%	Hirono, D
New York 5	24.5%	Ackerman, D
California 29	23.7%	Schiff, D
California 16	23.4%	Lofgren, D
California 32	18.4%	Solis, D

American Indian Districts

Congressional districts with the largest percentage of American Indians:

District	Indian	Member
Arizona 1	22.1%	Renzi, R
New Mexico 3	18.9%	Udall, D
Oklahoma 2	16.8%	Boren, D
Alaska AL	15.4%	Young, R
North Carolina 7	8.5%	McIntyre, D
South Dakota AL	8.1%	Herseth-Sandlin, D
Montana AL	6.0%	Rehberg, R
Oklahoma 3	6.0%	Lucas, R
Oklahoma 1	5.8%	Sullivan, R
Oklahoma 4	5.5%	Cole, R

Oldest Districts

Congressional districts with the highest median age:

District	Median Age	Member
Florida 13	47.4	Buchanan, R
Florida 14	47.4	Mack, R
Florida 5	45.5	Brown-Waite, R
Florida 19	45.1	Wexler, D
Florida 16	44.5	Mahoney, D
Florida 10	43.9	Young, R
Florida 22	43.0	Klein, D
Florida 9	41.1	Bilirakis, R
Florida 15	41.0	Weldon, R
Pennsylvania 18	41.0	Murphy, R

Youngest Districts

Congressional districts with the lowest median age:

District	Median Age	Member
Utah 3	24.5	Cannon, R
California 43	26.7	Baca, D
California 20	26.9	Costa, D
Arizona 4	27.1	Pastor, D
Illinois 4	27.2	Gutierrez, D
Texas 29	27.4	Green, D
New York 16	27.5	Serrano, D
California 47	27.6	Sanchez, D
Utah 1	27.6	Bishop, R
California 34	27.9	Roybal-Allard, D

Statistics in the boxes appearing on pp. 1160-1161 are from the U.S. Census Bureau.

Richest Districts

Congressional districts with the highest median household income in 1999:

District	Income	Member
Virginia 11	$80,397	Davis, R
New Jersey 11	$79,009	Frelinghuysen, R
California 14	$77,985	Eshoo, D
Georgia 6	$75,611	Price, R
California 15	$74,947	Honda, D
New Jersey 7	$74,823	Ferguson, R
Colorado 6	$73,393	Tancredo, R
New Jersey 5	$72,781	Garrett, R
Illinois 13	$71,686	Biggert, R
Illinois 10	$71,663	Kirk, R

Poorest Districts

Congressional districts with the lowest median household income in 1999:

District	Income	Member
New York 16	$19,311	Serrano, D
Kentucky 5	$21,915	Rogers, R
Texas 15	$26,840	Hinojosa, D
California 31	$26,093	Becerra, D
Alabama 7	$26,672	Davis, D
California 20	$26,800	Costa, D
West Virginia 3	$25,630	Rahall, D
Mississippi 2	$26,894	Thompson, D
Louisiana 5	$27,453	Alexander, R
Louisiana 2	$27,514	Jefferson, D

Districts With Most Government Workers

Congressional districts with the largest percentage of workers employed by local, state, federal or international government organizations:

District	Workers	Member
Maryland 4	29.0%	Wynn, D
Maryland 5	28.8%	Hoyer, D
Florida 2	28.5%	Boyd, D
Alaska AL	26.8%	Young, R
New Mexico 3	25.8%	Udall, D
California 5	24.8%	Matsui, D
New York 10	24.6%	Towns, D
Arizona 1	24.4%	Renzi, R
Maryland 7	24.3%	Cummings, D
Virginia 11	24.2%	Davis, R

Most Educated Districts

Congressional districts with the largest percentage of people, aged 25 and older, with at least a bachelor's degree:

District	Degree	Member
New York 14	56.9%	Maloney, D
Virginia 8	53.8%	Moran, D
Maryland 8	53.7%	Van Hollen, D
California 30	53.5%	Waxman, D
California 14	52.2%	Eshoo, D
Georgia 6	50.7%	Price, R
Texas 7	50.0%	Culberson, R
Virginia 11	48.9%	Davis, R
North Carolina 4	48.0%	Price, D
New York 8	47.8%	Nadler, D

Least Educated Districts

Congressional districts with the largest percentage of people, 25 and older, without a high school diploma:

District	No Diploma	Member
California 34	53.7%	Roybal-Allard, D
California 31	52.5%	Becerra, D
California 20	49.8%	Costa, D
Texas 29	49.8%	Green, D
California 47	49.6%	Sanchez, D
New York 16	49.5%	Serrano, D
Illinois 4	48.3%	Gutierrez, D
Texas 28	44.0%	Cuellar, D
New York 12	43.6%	Velázquez, D
California 38	41.6%	Napolitano, D

Districts With Most Foreign Born

Congressional districts with the largest percentage of residents born outside the United States (Americans born abroad are not included):

District	Foreign Born	Member
Florida 21	56.6%	Diaz-Balart, R
California 31	56.2%	Becerra, D
Florida 18	54.0%	Ros-Lehtinen, R
California 47	50.7%	Sanchez, D
California 34	47.2%	Roybal-Allard, D
Florida 25	46.6%	Diaz-Balart, R
New York 5	45.6%	Ackerman, D
California 28	44.0%	Berman, D
California 29	43.8%	Schiff, D
California 32	41.7%	Solis, D

Closest Elections of 2006

Race	Winner	Votes	Loser	Votes	Margin
Connecticut 2	Joe Courtney, D	121,248	Rob Simmons, R	121,165	83
North Carolina 8	Robin Hayes, R	60,926	Larry Kissell, D	60,597	329
Florida 13	Vern Buchanan, R	119,309	Christine Jennings, D	118,940	369
New Mexico 1	Heather A. Wilson, R	105,986	Patricia Madrid, D	105,125	861
Georgia 12 *	John Barrow, D	71,651	Max Burns, R	70,787	864
Wyoming AL	Barbara Cubin, R	93,336	Gary Trauner, D	92,324	1,012
Ohio 15	Deborah Pryce, R	110,739	Mary Jo Kilroy, D	109,677	1,062
Pennsylvania 8	Patrick J. Murphy, D	125,656	Michael G. Fitzpatrick, R	124,138	1,518
Georgia 8	Jim Marshall, D	80,660	Mac Collins, R	78,908	1,752
Ohio 2	Jean Schmidt, R	120,112	Victoria Wulsin, D	117,595	2,517

* Also finished in the top 10 in the 2004 election.

Fewest Votes Received

Winning House candidates in contested elections who received the fewest votes in 2006:

Member	Votes Received
William J. Jefferson, D-La. (2) *	35,153
Gene Green, D-Texas (29)	37,174
Ciro D. Rodriguez, D-Texas (23) *	38,256
Rubén Hinojosa, D-Texas (15)	43,236
Loretta Sanchez, D-Calif. (47)	47,134
Henry Cuellar, D-Texas (28)	52,574
Joe Baca, D-Calif. (43)	52,791
José E. Serrano, D-N.Y. (16)	56,124
Ed Pastor, D-Ariz. (4)	56,464
Lucille Roybal-Allard, D-Calif. (34)	57,459
Vito J. Fossella, R-N.Y. (13)	59,334

* runoff

Most Votes Received

Winning House candidates who received the most votes in 2006:

Member	Votes Received
Denny Rehberg, R-Mont. (AL)	239,124
Stephanie Herseth-Sandlin, D-S.D. (AL)	230,468
Tom Petri, R-Wis. (6)	201,367
Jim McDermott, D-Wash. (7)	195,462
F. James Sensenbrenner Jr., R-Wis. (5)	194,669
Tammy Baldwin, D-Wis. (2)	191,414
Earl Blumenauer, D-Ore. (3)	186,380
Wayne T. Gilchrest, R-Md. (1)	185,177
Jim Ramstad, R-Minn. (3)	184,333
Peter Hoekstra, R-Mich. (2)	183,006

Most Votes Cast

The 10 congressional districts in which the most votes were cast in 2006:

District	Votes Cast
Montana AL	406,134
South Dakota AL	333,562
Wisconsin 5	315,180
Wisconsin 2	304,688
Minnesota 6	302,188
Minnesota 2	290,540
Oregon 4	290,244
Missouri 2	287,617
Michigan 8	284,471
Minnesota 3	284,244

Fewest Votes Cast

The 10 districts in which the fewest votes were cast in 2006 in contested elections:

District	Votes Cast
Texas 29	50,550
New York 16	58,883
Louisiana 2 *	62,164
Texas 15	69,987
New York 12	70,029
Texas 23 *	70,473
California 34	74,819
California 47	75,619
New York 7	76,217
Texas 16	77,688

* runoff

Under 50 Percent

Winners of 2006 elections who received less than half the votes cast:

Member	Percent
Marilyn Musgrave, R-Colo.	45.6
Barbara Cubin, R-Wyo.	48.3
Jon Porter, R-Nev.	48.5
John T. Doolittle, R-Calif.	49.1
Jon Tester, D-Mont.	49.2
Mike Ferguson, R-N.J.	49.4
Tim Mahoney, D-Fla.	49.5
Claire McCaskill, D-Mo.	49.6
Jim Webb, D-Va.	49.6
Joseph I. Lieberman, I-Conn.	49.7
Tim Walberg, R-Mich.	49.9
Bill Sali, R-Idaho	49.9

Narrow Democratic Wins in Bush Districts

These 19 Democrats won by less than 10 percentage points in 2006 in House districts whose voters preferred George W. Bush for president in 2004:

Member	Percentage Point Victory Margin
Jim Marshall, Ga. (8)	1.1
Tim Mahoney, Fla. (16)	1.9
Steve Kagen, Wis. (8)	2.1
John Hall, N.Y. (19)	2.4
Carol Shea-Porter, N.H. (1)	2.6
Nancy Boyda, Kan. (2)	3.5
Jason Altmire, Pa. (4)	3.9
Harry E. Mitchell, Ariz. (5)	4.0
Baron P. Hill, Ind. (9)	4.5
Leonard L. Boswell, Iowa (3)	5.2
Tim Walz, Minn. (1)	5.6
Christopher Carney, Pa. (10)	5.9
Kirsten Gillibrand, N.Y. (20)	6.2
Jerry McNerney, Calif. (11)	6.5
Melissa Bean, Ill. (8)	6.9
Heath Shuler, N.C. (11)	7.6
Joe Donnelly, Ind. (2)	8.0
Ciro D. Rodriguez, Tex. (23) *	8.6
Michael Arcuri, N.Y. (24)	8.9

* runoff

Narrow Democratic Wins in Kerry Districts

These nine Democrats won by less than 10 percentage points in 2006 in House districts whose voters preferred John Kerry for president in 2004:

Member	Percentage Point Victory Margin
Joe Courtney, Conn. (2)	0.03
John Barrow, Ga. (12)	0.607
Patrick J. Murphy, Pa. (8)	0.608
John Yarmuth, Ky. (3)	2.4
Dave Loebsack, Iowa (2)	2.8
Ron Klein, Fla. (22)	3.8
Paul W. Hodes, N.H. (2)	7.1
Julia Carson, Ind. (7)	7.5
Peter Welch, Vt. (AL)	8.7

Narrow Republican Wins in Bush Districts

These 26 Republicans won by less than 10 percentage points in 2006 in House districts whose voters preferred George W. Bush for president in 2004:

Member	Percentage Point Victory Margin
Vern Buchanan, Fla. (13)	0.2
Robin Hayes, N.C. (8)	0.3
Deborah Pryce, Ohio (15)	0.48
Barbara Cubin, Wyo. (AL)	0.52
Jean Schmidt, Ohio (2)	1.1
Mike Ferguson, N.J. (7)	1.5
Jon Porter, Nev. (2)	1.9
Marilyn Musgrave, Colo. (4)	2.5
Peter Roskam, Ill. (6)	2.7
Thelma Drake, Va. (2)	2.8
John R. "Randy" Kuhl Jr., N.Y. (29)	2.9
John T. Doolittle, Calif. (4)	3.2
Tim Walberg, Mich. (7)	3.95
Thomas M. Reynolds, N.Y. (26)	3.97
Steve Chabot, Ohio (1)	4.5
Bill Sali, Idaho (1)	5.1
Joe Knollenberg, Mich. (9)	5.3
Dean Heller, Nev. (2)	5.4
Ric Keller, Fla. (8)	7.1
Michele Bachmann, Minn. (6)	8.0
Rick Renzi, Ariz. (1)	8.306
Geoff Davis, Ky. (4)	8.313
Mark Souder, Ind. (3)	8.6
Lee Terry, Neb. (2)	9.3
Brian P. Bilbray, Calif. (50)	9.6
Adrian Smith, Neb. (3)	9.98

Narrow Republican Wins in Kerry Districts

These six Republicans won by less than 10 percentage points in 2006 in House districts whose voters preferred John Kerry for president in 2004:

Member	Percentage Point Victory Margin
Heather A. Wilson, N.M. (1)	0.4
Jim Gerlach, Pa. (6)	1.3
James T. Walsh, N.Y. (25)	1.6
Dave Reichert, Wash. (8)	2.9
Christopher Shays, Conn. (4)	3.4
Mark Steven Kirk, Ill. (10)	6.8

CAMPAIGN FINANCE

Top 10 Senate Spenders in 2006

The chart is based on Federal Election Commission reports of expenditures from Jan. 1, 2005, through Dec. 31, 2006. The first column lists the top spenders who were elected or re-elected in the 2006 election.

Name, Party, State	Expenditures	Opponent	Expenditures
Hillary Rodham Clinton, D-N.Y.	$34,358,255	John Spencer, R	$5,660,688
Bob Corker, R-Tenn.	$18,565,935	Harold E. Ford Jr., D	$15,302,455
Bob Casey, D-Pa.	$17,592,212	Rick Santorum, R	$25,832,567
Joseph I. Lieberman, I-Conn.	$17,210,710	Ned Lamont, D	$20,614,353
Bill Nelson, D-Fla.	$16,116,224	Katherine Harris, R	$9,334,232
Jon Kyl, R-Ariz.	$15,571,727	Jim Pederson, D	$14,703,074
Maria Cantwell, D-Wash.	$14,013,932	Mike McGavick, R	$10,842,132
Bob Menendez, D-N.J.	$13,328,665	Tom H. Kean Jr., R	$7,762,370
Claire McCaskill, D-Mo.	$11,705,967	Jim Talent, R	$14,340,762
Debbie Stabenow, D-Mich.	$11,220,506	Mike Bouchard, R	$6,050,148

CAMPAIGN FINANCE

Top 10 House Spenders in 2006

The chart is based on Federal Election Commission reports of expenditures from Jan. 1, 2005, through Dec. 31, 2006. The first column lists the top spenders who were elected or re-elected in the 2006 election.

Name, Party, State (District)	Expenditures	Opponent	Expenditures
Vern Buchanan, R-Fla. (13)	$8,112,752	Christine Jennings, D	$3,002,798
Thomas M. Reynolds, R-N.Y. (26)	$5,275,474	Jack Davis, D	$2,386,358
J. Dennis Hastert, R-Ill. (14)	$5,206,105	John Laesch, D	$306,072
Heather A. Wilson, R-N.M. (1)	$4,906,596	Patricia Madrid, D	$3,386,200
Deborah Pryce, R-Ohio (15)	$4,696,772	Mary Jo Kilroy, D	$2,749,231
Melissa Bean, D-Ill. (8)	$4,299,589	David McSweeney, R	$5,140,109
Geoff Davis, R-Ky. (4)	$4,255,379	Ken Lucas, D	$1,469,555
Ron Klein, D-Fla. (22)	$4,185,922	E. Clay Shaw Jr., R	$5,226,161
Christopher Shays, R-Conn. (4)	$3,804,187	Diane Farrell, D	$2,961,500
Nick Lampson, D-Texas (22)	$3,578,097	Shelley Sekula-Gibbs, R (write-in)	$912,977

CAMPAIGN FINANCE

10 Least-Expensive Winning House Campaigns

The chart is based on expenditures from Jan. 1, 2005, through Dec. 31, 2006, for contested elections.

Name, Party, State (Dist.)	Expenditures	Name, Party, State (Dist.)	Expenditures
Diane Watson, D-Calif. (33)	$181,051	Robert C. Scott, D-Va. (3)	$307,440
Wayne Gilchrest, R-Md. (1)	$182,375	José E. Serrano, D-N.Y. (16)	$314,380
Rob Bishop, R-Utah (1)	$262,727	Luis V. Gutierrez, D-Ill. (4)	$315,779
Jeff Flake, R-Ariz. (6)	$272,420	Grace F. Napolitano, D-Calif. (38)	$317,822
Carol Shea-Porter, D-N.H. (1)	$291,663	Gene Taylor, D-Miss. (5)	$320,183

CAMPAIGN FINANCE

Winners Outspent by Opponents

General-election winners in 2006 who spent less than their opponents. Totals cover the period Jan. 1, 2005, through Dec. 31, 2006. Losing incumbents are in italics.

(in order of spending margin)

Senate

Name, Party, State	Expenditures	Opponent	Expenditures
Bob Casey, D-Pa.	$17,592,212	*Rick Santorum, R*	$25,832,567
Jim Webb, D-Va.	$8,558,861	*George Allen, R*	$16,071,564
Ben Nelson, D-Neb.	$7,492,134	Pete Ricketts, R	$13,417,690
Sherrod Brown, D-Ohio	$10,751,765	*Mike DeWine, R*	$14,161,402
Joseph I. Lieberman, I-Conn.	$17,210,710	Ned Lamont, D	$20,614,353
Jon Tester, D-Mont.	$5,588,292	*Conrad Burns, R*	$8,516,022
Claire McCaskill, D-Mo.	$11,705,967	*Jim Talent, R*	$14,340,762
Bernard Sanders, I-Vt.	$6,004,222	Rich Tarrant, R	$7,300,392
Amy Klobuchar, D-Minn.	$9,155,313	Mark Kennedy, R	$10,308,273

House

Name, Party, State (Dist.)	Expenditures	Opponent	Expenditures
Ciro D. Rodriguez, D-Texas (23)	$963,647	*Henry Bonilla, R*	$3,821,285
Heath Shuler, D-N.C. (11)	$1,804,365	*Charles H.Taylor, R*	$4,425,482
Christopher S. Murphy, D-Conn. (5)	$2,486,251	*Nancy L. Johnson, R*	$5,106,462
Jerry McNerney, D-Calif. (11)	$2,423,295	*Richard W. Pombo, R*	$4,629,983
Joe Donnelly, D-Ind. (2)	$1,561,420	*Chris Chocola, R*	$3,415,742
Peter Roskam, R-Ill. (6)	$3,302,702	Tammy Duckworth, D	$4,556,495
John Yarmuth, D-Ky. (3)	$2,224,248	*Anne M. Northup, R*	$3,421,281
Jason Altmire, D-Pa. (4)	$1,091,584	*Melissa A. Hart, R*	$2,235,952
Harry E. Mitchell, D-Ariz. (5)	$1,933,184	*J. D. Hayworth, R*	$3,000,381
Ron Klein, D-Fla. (22)	$4,185,922	*E. Clay Shaw, R*	$5,226,161
Brian P. Bilbray, R-Calif. (50) *	$2,619,848	Francine Busby, D *	$3,596,185
John Hall, D-N.Y. (19)	$1,626,670	*Sue W. Kelly, R*	$2,519,164
Melissa Bean, D-Ill. (8)	$4,299,589	David McSweeney, R	$5,140,109
Baron P. Hill, D-Ind. (9)	$1,888,695	*Mike Sodrel, R*	$2,724,285
Kirsten Gillibrand, D-N.Y. (20)	$2,595,659	*John E. Sweeney, R*	$3,425,841
Carol Shea-Porter, D-N.H. (1)	$291,663	*Jeb Bradley, R*	$1,062,132
Christopher Carney, D-Pa. (10)	$1,555,004	*Don Sherwood, R*	$2,334,743
Joe Courtney, D-Conn. (2)	$2,410,306	*Rob Simmons, R*	$3,177,694
Patrick J. Murphy, D-Pa. (8)	$2,410,530	*Michael G. Fitzpatrick, R*	$3,174,384
Jim Gerlach, R-Pa. (6)	$3,492,402	Lois Murphy, D	$4,097,663
Michele Bachmann, R-Minn. (6)	$2,694,789	Patty Wetterling, D	$3,179,222
Tim Walz, D-Minn. (1)	$1,281,136	*Gil Gutknecht, R*	$1,723,707
Brad Miller, D-N.C. (13)	$1,766,708	Vernon L. Robinson, R	$2,179,456
Nancy Boyda, D-Kan. (2)	$726,738	*Jim Ryun, R*	$1,075,223
Bruce Braley, D-Iowa (1)	$2,235,245	Mike Whalen, R	$2,385,532
Jim Marshall, D-Ga. (8)	$1,849,155	Mac Collins, R	$1,981,928
Mark Souder, R-Ind. (3)	$642,282	Thomas Hayhurst, D	$708,181
Dave Loebsack, D-Iowa (2)	$488,385	*Jim Leach, R*	$533,734
John R. "Randy" Kuhl Jr., R-N.Y. (29)	$1,475,289	Eric Massa, D	$1,501,716
William J. Jefferson, D-La. (2)	$1,238,408	Karen Carter, D	$1,258,965

* Includes special-election expenditures.

Campaign Finance

Figures are given for all members of Congress and their general election opponents as reported by the Federal Election Commission (FEC). If only one candidate is listed, either that candidate was unopposed or the second-leading vote-getter did not raise at least $5,000.

For House members, figures are for the 2006 elections. For senators, figures are for their most recent election.

The campaign finance data covers the receipts and expenditures of each candidate during the two-year election cycle. Data for 2006 covers the period Jan. 1, 2005, to Dec. 31, 2006. Data for 2004 covers the period Jan. 1, 2003, to Dec. 31, 2004, although spending on runoffs or special elections later in 2004 for a few candidates is also included. Data for 2002 covers the period Jan. 1, 2001, to Nov. 6, 2002. Some figures may include amended filings.

The figures for political action committee receipts are based on the FEC summary report for each candidate. Amounts listed include contributions from both PACs and candidate committees, but not party committees.

Candidates who ran in special elections in the two-year cycle are marked with †. In these cases, campaign finance figures include money spent on the special elections.

The FEC is constantly receiving amended reports. The figures listed were the latest available, as of April 2007.

Alabama

	RECEIPTS	FROM PACS	EXPENDITURES
SENIOR SENATOR - 2004			
Shelby (R)	$6,610,117	$1,480,707 (22%)	$1,922,646
JUNIOR SENATOR - 2002			
Sessions (R)	$4,635,963	$1,018,184 (22%)	$5,070,766
Parker (D)	$1,191,848	$178,820 (15%)	$1,185,718
DISTRICT 1			
Bonner (R)	$1,060,001	$353,672 (33%)	$875,364
Beckerle (D)	$14,885	$2,500 (17%)	$13,211
DISTRICT 2			
Everett (R)	$698,389	$381,954 (55%)	$330,375
James (D)	$1,182	$0 (0%)	$5,292
DISTRICT 3			
Rogers (R)	$1,435,191	$590,882 (41%)	$1,046,764
Pierce (D)	$7,709	$0 (0%)	$7,674
Layfield (I)	$5,041	$0 (0%)	$4,951
DISTRICT 4			
Aderholt (R)	$715,803	$291,600 (41%)	$622,248
DISTRICT 5			
Cramer (D)	$895,212	$470,000 (53%)	$589,469
DISTRICT 6			
Bachus (R)	$1,638,815	$1,028,133 (63%)	$1,893,917
DISTRICT 7			
Davis (D)	$764,141	$566,743 (74%)	$579,160

Alaska

	RECEIPTS	FROM PACS	EXPENDITURES
SENIOR SENATOR - 2002			
Stevens (R)	$2,718,907	$967,202 (36%)	$2,093,021
Vondersaar (D)	$1,050	$0 (0%)	$1,049
JUNIOR SENATOR - 2004			
Murkowski (R)	$5,702,709	$1,991,677 (35%)	$5,429,904
Knowles (D)	$5,834,694	$784,870 (13%)	$5,767,707
Millican (NON)	$187,850	$0 (0%)	$190,379
Sykes (GREEN)	$15,247	$0 (0%)	$8,771
AT LARGE			
Young (R)	$1,919,782	$707,822 (37%)	$1,959,806
Benson (D)	$199,579	$0 (0%)	$198,225

Arizona

	RECEIPTS	FROM PACS	EXPENDITURES
SENIOR SENATOR - 2004			
McCain (R)	$3,419,717	$658,093 (19%)	$2,140,807
Starky (D)	$12,956	$7,000 (54%)	$12,716
JUNIOR SENATOR - 2006			
Kyl (R)	$14,123,880	$2,802,011 (20%)	$15,571,727
Pederson (D)	$14,707,261	$422,057 (3%)	$14,703,074
DISTRICT 1			
Renzi (R)	$2,110,744	$1,099,829 (52%)	$2,246,790
Simon (D)	$1,514,960	$125,700 (8%)	$1,514,638
Schlosser (LIBERT)	$29,550	$0 (0%)	$30,628
DISTRICT 2			
Franks (R)	$440,591	$184,083 (42%)	$474,707
Thrasher (D)	$37,620	$0 (0%)	$37,231
DISTRICT 3			
Shadegg (R)	$1,078,942	$486,215 (45%)	$1,167,473
Paine (D)	$102,521	$2,500 (2%)	$96,976
DISTRICT 4			
Pastor (D)	$1,092,996	$519,198 (48%)	$763,931
DISTRICT 5			
Mitchell (D)	$1,954,180	$445,567 (23%)	$1,933,184
Hayworth (R)	$2,947,388	$1,402,368 (48%)	$3,000,381
DISTRICT 6			
Flake (R)	$543,620	$148,350 (27%)	$272,420
DISTRICT 7			
Grijalva (D)	$623,493	$265,824 (43%)	$662,758
Drake (R)	$182,037	$17,000 (9%)	$180,158
DISTRICT 8			
Giffords (D)	$2,583,799	$624,519 (24%)	$2,442,119
Graf (R)	$1,368,136	$230,654 (17%)	$1,341,943
Nolan (LIBERT)	$22,211	$2,000 (9%)	$20,768
Quick (IND)	$58,311	$0 (0%)	$53,019

Arkansas

	RECEIPTS	FROM PACS	EXPENDITURES
SENIOR SENATOR - 2004			
Lincoln (D)	$5,489,103	$2,427,554 (44%)	$5,816,913
Holt (R)	$153,628	$7,000 (5%)	$148,682
JUNIOR SENATOR - 2002			
Pryor (D)	$4,442,708	$843,572 (19%)	$4,365,349
Hutchinson (R)	$4,858,117	$1,693,422 (35%)	$4,942,828

DISTRICT 1			
Berry (D)	$1,295,565	$650,024 (50%)	$1,320,295
Stumbaugh (R)	$98,110	$6,770 (7%)	$93,107
DISTRICT 2			
Snyder (D)	$659,814	$221,750 (34%)	$643,531
Mayberry (R)	$99,035	$1,600 (2%)	$98,845
DISTRICT 3			
Boozman (R)	$575,628	$306,210 (53%)	$651,611
Anderson (D)	$362,689	$8,500 (2%)	$361,155
DISTRICT 4			
Ross (D)	$1,334,109	$769,402 (58%)	$1,254,480

California

	RECEIPTS	FROM PACS	EXPENDITURES
SENIOR SENATOR - 2006			
Feinstein (D)	$8,238,616	$1,327,479 (16%)	$8,030,489
Mountjoy (R)	$198,630	$3,360 (2%)	$195,265
Chretien (GREEN)	$61,549	$0 (0%)	$59,435
JUNIOR SENATOR - 2004			
Boxer (D)	$14,301,289	$1,290,551 (9%)	$14,886,426
Jones (R)	$7,766,693	$559,414 (7%)	$7,774,352
Gray (LIBERT)	$251,832	$9,500 (4%)	$250,244
DISTRICT 1			
Thompson (D)	$1,747,991	$696,480 (40%)	$1,382,639
Jones (R)	$100,146	$1,000 (1%)	$64,164
DISTRICT 2			
Herger (R)	$689,944	$411,128 (60%)	$711,849
Sekhon (D)	$199,382	$0 (0%)	$157,449
DISTRICT 3			
Lungren (R)	$1,062,692	$470,685 (44%)	$633,991
Durston (D)	$318,664	$25,517 (8%)	$313,766
DISTRICT 4			
Doolittle (R)	$2,354,786	$813,135 (35%)	$2,449,428
Brown (D)	$1,713,863	$351,258 (20%)	$1,650,458
DISTRICT 5 †			
Matsui (D)	$2,297,570	$1,054,766 (46%)	$2,463,336
Kravitz (GREEN)	$13,339	$0 (0%)	$12,632
Chernay (R)	$16,620	$0 (0%)	$16,619
Flynn (R)	$46,532	$1,000 (2%)	$46,542
Padilla (D)	$37,401	$0 (0%)	$37,400
DISTRICT 6			
Woolsey (D)	$1,400,103	$480,405 (34%)	$1,443,910
Hooper (R)	$12,156	$0 (0%)	$12,156
DISTRICT 7			
Miller (D)	$667,494	$464,418 (70%)	$719,639
DISTRICT 8			
Pelosi (D)	$1,679,511	$1,117,899 (67%)	$1,853,040
DeNunzio (R)	$149,842	$2,600 (2%)	$149,248
Keefer (GREEN)	$31,325	$0 (0%)	$32,091
DISTRICT 9			
Lee (D)	$965,875	$213,424 (22%)	$1,054,307
denDulk (R)	$39,030	$0 (0%)	$38,769
DISTRICT 10			
Tauscher (D)	$930,129	$572,372 (62%)	$830,579
Linn (R)	$4,004	$0 (0%)	$7,366
DISTRICT 11			
McNerney (D)	$2,462,894	$386,887 (16%)	$2,423,295
Pombo (R)	$4,547,779	$1,801,011 (40%)	$4,629,983
DISTRICT 12			
Lantos (D)	$1,029,421	$175,345 (17%)	$695,534
DISTRICT 13			
Stark (D)	$430,320	$311,689 (72%)	$645,573
Bruno (R)	$25,188	$0 (0%)	$24,061
DISTRICT 14			
Eshoo (D)	$1,036,470	$554,164 (53%)	$1,069,186
Brouillet (GREEN)	$7,228	$0 (0%)	$7,194
DISTRICT 15			
Honda (D)	$761,703	$353,685 (46%)	$763,242
Chukwu (R)	$46,275	$0 (0%)	$46,274
DISTRICT 16			
Lofgren (D)	$624,136	$322,127 (52%)	$622,369
DISTRICT 17			
Farr (D)	$773,188	$402,641 (52%)	$678,902
DISTRICT 18			
Cardoza (D)	$1,076,223	$526,601 (49%)	$952,158
Kanno (R)	$155,439	$0 (0%)	$138,766
DISTRICT 19			
Radanovich (R)	$1,147,987	$448,669 (39%)	$1,197,702
Cox (D)	$886,175	$18,750 (2%)	$886,086
DISTRICT 20			
Costa (D)	$901,164	$474,550 (53%)	$722,335
DISTRICT 21			
Nunes (R)	$1,156,518	$511,600 (44%)	$991,874
Haze (D)	$154,180	$0 (0%)	$154,339
DISTRICT 22			
McCarthy (R)	$1,152,444	$491,043 (43%)	$682,340
Beery (D)	$27,206	$1,000 4%)	$27,673
DISTRICT 23			
Capps (D)	$874,676	$409,808 (47%)	$922,774
Tognazzini (R)	$74,092	$0 (0%)	$79,530
DISTRICT 24			
Gallegly (R)	$645,820	$134,298 (21%)	$944,852
Martinez (D)	$134,371	$16,059 (12%)	$131,905
DISTRICT 25			
McKeon (R)	$1,253,498	$580,600 (46%)	$1,370,664
Rodriguez (D)	$237,844	$8,000 (3%)	$230,516
DISTRICT 26			
Dreier (R)	$2,357,846	$1,047,936 (44%)	$2,540,691
Matthews (D)	$54,484	$1,987 (4%)	$17,182
DISTRICT 27			
Sherman (D)	$1,610,334	$467,210 (29%)	$851,404
Hankwitz (R)	$47,479	$0 (0%)	$42,311
DISTRICT 28			
Berman (D)	$914,914	$274,385 (30%)	$954,004
De Lear (GREEN)	$81,035	$0 (0%)	$68,714
DISTRICT 29			
Schiff (D)	$1,200,905	$487,845 (41%)	$900,377
Paparian (GREEN)	$50,058	$200 (0%)	$44,441
DISTRICT 30			
Waxman (D)	$648,175	$473,500 (73%)	$553,049
Jones (R)	$23,558	$0 (0%)	$21,825
DISTRICT 31			
Becerra (D)	$838,454	$581,850 (69%)	$762,409
DISTRICT 32			
Solis (D)	$809,643	$488,328 (60%)	$882,866

DISTRICT 33			
Watson (D)	$182,018	$91,763 (50%)	$181,051
DISTRICT 34			
Roybal-Allard (D)	$589,538	$285,876 (48%)	$658,270
DISTRICT 35			
Waters (D)	$795,431	$163,893 (21%)	$759,619
DISTRICT 36			
Harman (D)	$922,972	$301,510 (33%)	$1,176,771
Gibson (R)	$11,316	$1,897 (17%)	$12,049
Smith (PFP)	$7,469	$0 (0%)	$8,436
DISTRICT 37			
Millender -McDonald (D)	$315,374	$239,746 (76%)	$355,784
DISTRICT 38			
Napolitano (D)	$329,193	$226,350 (69%)	$317,822
Street (R)	$8,703	$800 (9%)	$8,704
DISTRICT 39			
Sánchez (D)	$645,970	$353,523 (55%)	$639,354
Andion (R)	$20,636	$0 (0%)	$19,095
DISTRICT 40			
Royce (R)	$1,520,392	$514,784 (34%)	$1,317,274
Hoffman (D)	$143,706	$56,500 (39%)	$140,406
DISTRICT 41			
Lewis (R)	$1,384,486	$893,200 (65%)	$1,806,532
DISTRICT 42			
Miller (R)	$671,006	$327,875 (49%)	$365,812
DISTRICT 43			
Baca (D)	$686,650	$359,730 (52%)	$744,228
Folkens (R)	$17,104	$500 (3%)	$16,597
DISTRICT 44			
Calvert (R)	$922,444	$352,580 (38%)	$857,529
Vandenberg (D)	$8,668	$1,500 (17%)	$3,154
DISTRICT 45			
Bono (R)	$1,496,456	$504,597 (34%)	$1,528,130
Roth (D)	$725,020	$175,800 (24%)	$722,765
DISTRICT 46			
Rohrabacher (R)	$294,370	$74,045 (25%)	$354,651
Brandt (D)	$77,764	$5,000 (6%)	$80,078
DISTRICT 47			
Sanchez (D)	$1,366,455	$577,348 (42%)	$1,829,971
Nguyen (R)	$547,564	$0 (0%)	$547,646
DISTRICT 48 †			
Campbell (R)	$2,290,958	$725,152 (32%)	$2,254,028
Young (D)	$435,083	$49,825 (11%)	$434,792
Gilchrist (AMI)	$1,125,524	$17,301 (2%)	$1,105,006
Udall (R)	$15,235	$0 (0%)	$17,489
DISTRICT 49			
Issa (R)	$908,837	$490,149 (54%)	$1,102,601
Criscenzo (D)	$90,050	$9,550 (11%)	$88,834
DISTRICT 50 †			
Bilbray (R)	$2,559,241	$1,137,172 (44%)	$2,619,848
Busby (D)	$3,636,717	$609,758 (17%)	$3,596,185
Earnest (R)	$985,983	$0 (0%)	$985,981
Hauf (R)	$1,577,810	$0 (0%)	$1,577,808
Kaloogian (R)	$515,729	$23,320 (5%)	$514,810
Morrow (R)	$535,454	$26;249 (5%)	$540,817
Orren (R)	$9,701	$0 (0%)	$9,701
Roach (R)	$2,917,044	$0 (0%)	$2,916,957
Turner (R)	$80,785	$0 (0%)	$79,941
Uke (R)	$1,332,463	$0 (0%)	$1,326,898
Young (D)	$15,726	$5,000 (32%)	$15,711
DISTRICT 51			
Filner (D)	$1,805,969	$652,140 (36%)	$2,001,750
Miles (R)	$69,300	$0 (0%)	$66,656
DISTRICT 52			
Hunter (R)	$1,063,228	$488,650 (46%)	$1,042,928
Rinaldi (D)	$80,480	$3,885 (5%)	$80,423
DISTRICT 53			
Davis (D)	$343,916	$149,375 (43%)	$430,945
Woodrum (R)	$93,226	$1,250 (1%)	$90,750

Colorado

	RECEIPTS	FROM PACS	EXPENDITURES
SENIOR SENATOR - 2002			
Allard (R)	$5,163,810	$1,940,956 (38%)	$5,077,481
Strickland (D)	$5,164,823	$784,890 (15%)	$5,048,097
Stanley (LIBERT)	$14,504	$0 (0%)	$14,283
JUNIOR SENATOR - 2004			
Salazar (D)	$9,925,778	$1,018,212 (10%)	$9,886,551
Coors (R)	$7,879,182	$1,301,667 (17%)	$7,858,598
DISTRICT 1			
DeGette (D)	$635,208	$343,555 (54%)	$642,405
DISTRICT 2			
Udall (D)	$1,512,865	$484,489 (32%)	$932,188
Mancuso (R)	$15,150	$0 (0%)	$14,748
DISTRICT 3			
Salazar (D)	$2,028,066	$1,037,269 (51%)	$2,033,671
Tipton (R)	$821,303	$117,350 (14%)	$819,314
DISTRICT 4			
Musgrave (R)	$3,160,640	$1,004,123 (32%)	$3,212,143
Paccione (D)	$1,977,177	$422,212 (21%)	$1,951,180
Eidsness (REF)	$26,983	$9,940 (37%)	$31,808
DISTRICT 5			
Lamborn (R)	$1,026,182	$356,654 (35%)	$997,973
Fawcett (D)	$673,385	$118,387 (18%)	$669,520
DISTRICT 6			
Tancredo (R)	$1,781,975	$61,984 (3%)	$1,754,235
Winter (D)	$807,011	$140,810 (17%)	$806,518
DISTRICT 7			
Perlmutter (D)	$2,996,171	$808,633 (27%)	$2,945,170
O'Donnell (R)	$2,818,132	$661,882 (23%)	$2,771,913

Connecticut

	RECEIPTS	FROM PACS	EXPENDITURES
SENIOR SENATOR - 2004			
Dodd (D)	$4,676,379	$1,368,210 (29%)	$3,938,132
Orchulli (R)	$1,476,876	$800 (0%)	$1,462,401
JUNIOR SENATOR - 2006			
Lieberman (CFL)	$18,996,689	$2,324,109 (12%)	$17,210,710
Lamont (D)	$20,524,133	$53,599 (0%)	$20,614,353
Schlesinger (R)	$221,019	$5,650 (3%)	$204,113
DISTRICT 1			
Larson (D)	$983,926	$568,675 (58%)	$953,971
DISTRICT 2			
Courtney (D)	$2,457,906	$617,460 (25%)	$2,410,306

Simmons (R)	$3,112,876	$1,468,491 (47%)	$3,177,694
DISTRICT 3			
DeLauro (D)	$819,470	$471,435 (58%)	$860,821
DISTRICT 4			
Shays (R)	$3,827,216	$1,078,339 (28%)	$3,804,187
Farrell (D)	$3,044,909	$530,426 (17%)	$2,961,500
Maymin (LIBERT)	$40,967	$4,888 (12%)	$41,066
DISTRICT 5			
Murphy (D)	$2,536,953	$568,655 (22%)	$2,486,251
Johnson (R)	$4,055,866	$2,211,881 (55%)	$5,106,462

Delaware

	RECEIPTS	FROM PACS	EXPENDITURES
SENIOR SENATOR - 2002			
Biden (D)	$2,726,583	$0 (0%)	$2,991,862
Clatworthy (R)	$1,871,163	$13,100 (1%)	$1,804,123
JUNIOR SENATOR - 2006			
Carper (D)	$3,177,275	$1,564,498 (49%)	$2,632,478
Ting (R)	$212,766	$5,700 (3%)	$212,765
O'Donnell (X)	$62,575	$0 (0%)	$63,629
AT LARGE			
Castle (R)	$1,267,040	$497,264 (39%)	$1,112,716
Berg (GREEN)	$37,771	$0 (0%)	$37,969

Florida

	RECEIPTS	FROM PACS	EXPENDITURES
SENIOR SENATOR - 2006			
Nelson (D)	$15,355,490	$1,804,712 (12%)	$16,116,224
Harris (R)	$9,341,803	$277,500 (3%)	$9,334,232
Moore (I)	$16,234	$0 (0%)	$12,177
Tanner (X)	$13,000	$0 (0%)	$12,968
JUNIOR SENATOR - 2004			
Martinez (R)	$12,856,384	$2,245,433 (17%)	$12,837,220
Castor (D)	$11,645,379	$880,326 (8%)	$11,472,071
Bradley (VET)	$15,793	$1,552 (10%)	$15,794
DISTRICT 1			
Miller (R)	$329,210	$120,718 (37%)	$322,726
Roberts (D)	$62,141	$5,000 (8%)	$48,383
DISTRICT 2			
Boyd (D)	$1,042,491	$675,564 (65%)	$615,784
DISTRICT 3			
Brown (D)	$491,300	$286,435 (58%)	$476,775
DISTRICT 4			
Crenshaw (R)	$1,223,900	$217,975 (18%)	$1,202,193
Harms (D)	$42,797	$0 (0%)	$42,727
DISTRICT 5			
Brown-Waite (R)	$794,360	$456,991 (58%)	$784,889
Russell (D)	$90,230	$12,387 (14%)	$88,703
DISTRICT 6			
Streams (R)	$835,493	$506,697 (61%)	$455,531
Bruderly (D)	$139,020	$10,650 (8%)	$150,508
DISTRICT 7			
Mica (R)	$794,268	$359,088 (45%)	$665,785
Chagnon (D)	$21,056	$50 (0%)	$11,282
DISTRICT 8			
Keller (R)	$1,285,096	$601,395 (47%)	$1,691,408
Stuart (D)	$1,040,161	$168,303 (16%)	$998,271
Hoaglund (X)	$12,686	$0 (0%)	$12,742
DISTRICT 9			
Bilirakis (R)	$2,656,746	$609,783 (23%)	$2,574,356
Busansky (D)	$1,424,355	$347,814 (24%)	$1,419,414
DISTRICT 10			
Young (R)	$635,223	$317,350 (50%)	$506,473
Simpson (D)	$40,246	$3,500 (9%)	$39,744
DISTRICT 11			
Castor (D)	$1,373,273	$343,235 (25%)	$1,221,825
Adams (R)	$28,005	$2,000 (7%)	$27,990
DISTRICT 12			
Putnam (R)	$1,078,377	$532,192 (49%)	$991,101
Viscusi (X)	$37,271	$0 (0%)	$36,935
Bowlin (X)	$14,827	$0 (0%)	$14,833
DISTRICT 13			
Buchanan (R)	$8,123,186	$343,541 (4%)	$8,112,752
Jennings (D)	$3,268,396	$856,649 (26%)	$3,002,798
DISTRICT 14			
Mack (R)	$1,149,296	$328,362 (29%)	$973,082
Neeld (D)	$43,084	$0 (0%)	$41,314
DISTRICT 15			
Weldon (R)	$791,682	$271,061 (34%)	$925,951
Bowman (D)	$119,155	$1,650 (1%)	$115,380
DISTRICT 16			
Mahoney (D)	$2,838,536	$567,090 (20%)	$2,783,045
Foley (R)	$1,657,680	$645,140 (39%)	$2,178,197
Negron (R)	$872,199	$274,874 (32%)	$814,562
DISTRICT 17			
Meek (D)	$1,008,007	$428,299 (42%)	$976,658
DISTRICT 18			
Ros-Lehtinen (R)	$1,190,331	$325,501 (27%)	$1,439,441
Patlak (D)	$75,999	$3,000 (4%)	$75,698
DISTRICT 19			
Wexler (D)	$789,946	$240,077 (30%)	$793,904
DISTRICT 20			
Wasserman-Schultz (D)	$1,036,924	$533,938 (51%)	$828,658
DISTRICT 21			
Diaz-Balart (R)	$839,373	$271,045 (32%)	$926,106
DISTRICT 22			
Klein (D)	$4,186,909	$666,762 (16%)	$4,185,922
Shaw (R)	$4,707,676	$1,676,114 (36%)	$5,226,161
Evangelista (X)	$12,800	$2,200 (17%)	$6,749
DISTRICT 23			
Hastings (D)	$343,108	$164,595 (48%)	$427,924
DISTRICT 24			
Feeney (R)	$1,375,589	$728,071 (53%)	$1,571,417
Curtis (D)	$104,633	$7,000 (7%)	$84,804
DISTRICT 25			
Diaz-Balart (R)	$696,022	$297,180 (43%)	$697,936
Calderin (D)	$35,292	$500 (1%)	$35,161

Georgia

	RECEIPTS	FROM PACS	EXPENDITURES
SENIOR SENATOR - 2002			
Chambliss (R)	$7,422,836	$1,282,955 (17%)	$7,475,943

Cleland (D)	$8,146,827	$1,827,709 (22%)	$9,055,254
Thomas (LIBERT)	$11,109	$0 (0%)	$11,108
JUNIOR SENATOR - 2004			
Isakson (R)	$8,577,130	$1,713,570 (20%)	$8,038,200
Majette (D)	$2,084,294	$602,604 (29%)	$2,470,272
Buckley (LIBERT)	$42,377	$0 (0%)	$42,376
DISTRICT 1			
Kingston (R)	$1,129,762	$476,934 (42%)	$1,237,548
Nelson (D)	$118,173	$11,800 (10%)	$120,771
DISTRICT 2			
Bishop (D)	$818,301	$454,800 (56%)	$745,257
Hughes (R)	$29,174	$2,000 (7%)	$27,142
DISTRICT 3			
Westmoreland (R)	$1,238,598	$448,309 (36%)	$936,111
McGraw (D)	$76,838	$15,000 (20%)	$55,060
DISTRICT 4			
Johnson (D)	$797,997	$267,552 (34%)	$786,158
Davis (R)	$234,444	$5,950 (3%)	$230,444
DISTRICT 5			
Lewis (D)	$631,102	$406,000 (64%)	$702,246
DISTRICT 6			
Price (R)	$2,172,054	$826,292 (38%)	$2,281,556
Sinton (D)	$98,356	$11,250 (11%)	$104,821
DISTRICT 7			
Linder (R)	$737,202	$343,800 (47%)	$398,794
Burns (D)	$33,792	$3,500 (10%)	$33,213
DISTRICT 8			
Marshall (D)	$1,953,070	$774,236 (40%)	$1,849,155
Collins (R)	$2,085,957	$623,200 (30%)	$1,981,928
DISTRICT 9			
Deal (R)	$1,107,572	$812,676 (73%)	$959,845
Bradbury (D)	$15,770	$643 (4%)	$15,737
DISTRICT 10			
Norwood (R)	$1,453,284	$642,638 (44%)	$1,158,294
Holley (D)	$28,453	$5,000 (18%)	$31,821
DISTRICT 11			
Gingrey (R)	$1,360,287	$357,320 (26%)	$1,011,322
Pillion (D)	$3,203	$3,000 (94%)	$3,318
DISTRICT 12			
Barrow (D)	$2,491,085	$1,185,949 (48%)	$2,265,762
Burns (R)	$2,200,493	$765,518 (35%)	$2,173,231
DISTRICT 13			
Scott (D)	$1,241,679	$803,896 (65%)	$1,364,825
Honeycutt (R)	$1,339,777	$11,000 (1%)	$1,319,909

Hawaii

	RECEIPTS	FROM PACS	EXPENDITURES
SENIOR SENATOR - 2004			
Inouye (D)	$2,788,703	$957,571 (34%)	$1,768,886
Cavasso (R)	$57,514	$8,500 (15%)	$57,122
JUNIOR SENATOR - 2006			
Akaka (D)	$2,648,898	$921,664 (35%)	$2,651,026
Thielen (R)	$356,419	$15,253 (4%)	$356,413
DISTRICT 1			
Abercrombie (D)	$1,074,345	$555,330 (52%)	$823,229
Hough (R)	$17,728	$0 (0%)	$16,551
DISTRICT 2			
Hirono (D)	$1,430,359	$383,925 (27%)	$1,374,988
Hogue (R)	$232,672	$11,500 (5%)	$230,411

Idaho

	RECEIPTS	FROM PACS	EXPENDITURES
SENIOR SENATOR - 2002			
Craig (R)	$3,012,333	$1,065,581 (35%)	$2,933,495
Blinken (D)	$2,173,286	$97,000 (4%)	$2,149,333
JUNIOR SENATOR - 2004			
Crapo (R)	$1,948,398	$1,241,988 (64%)	$1,031,912
DISTRICT 1			
Sali (R)	$1,088,175	$477,158 (44%)	$1,061,340
Grant (D)	$779,766	$155,239 (20%)	$768,324
Hedden-Nicely (NL)	$20,085	$0 (0%)	$20,084
DISTRICT 2			
Simpson (R)	$539,784	$378,840 (70%)	$571,630
Hansen (D)	$163,750	$200 (0%)	$162,639

Illinois

	RECEIPTS	FROM PACS	EXPENDITURES
SENIOR SENATOR - 2002			
Durbin (D)	$5,174,051	$1,228,196 (24%)	$4,870,737
Durkin (R)	$795,941	$102,478 (13%)	$770,458
JUNIOR SENATOR - 2004			
Obama (D)	$15,096,157	$1,205,724 (8%)	$14,532,493
Keyes (R)	$2,687,483	$50,608 (2%)	$2,545,325
DISTRICT 1			
Rush (D)	$575,304	$384,844 (67%)	$684,692
DISTRICT 2			
Jackson (D)	$1,084,135	$246,350 (23%)	$946,736
DISTRICT 3			
Lipinski (D)	$371,989	$206,700 (56%)	$414,167
DISTRICT 4			
Gutierrez (D)	$161,593	$104,750 (65%)	$315,779
DISTRICT 5			
Emanuel (D)	$1,287,804	$638,525 (50%)	$1,380,457
White (R)	$40,630	$20,311 (50%)	$31,038
DISTRICT 6			
Roskam (R)	$3,443,597	$1,147,705 (33%)	$3,302,702
Duckworth (D)	$4,563,409	$748,800 (16%)	$4,556,495
DISTRICT 7			
Davis (D)	$542,153	$277,516 (51%)	$414,881
DISTRICT 8			
Bean (D)	$4,337,073	$1,498,972 (35%)	$4,299,589
McSweeney (R)	$5,140,197	$460,258 (9%)	$5,140,109
Scheurer (X)	$47,429	$35,000 (74%)	$46,299
DISTRICT 9			
Schakowsky (D)	$1,138,224	$317,925 (28%)	$1,134,762
DISTRICT 10			
Kirk (R)	$3,168,367	$644,130 (20%)	$3,512,971
Seals (D)	$1,918,167	$177,795 (9%)	$1,882,795
DISTRICT 11			
Weller (R)	$1,993,355	$1,167,012 (59%)	$1,906,882
Pavich (D)	$601,284	$76,905 (13%)	$593,310

DISTRICT 12			
Costello (D)	$1,180,687	$460,854 (39%)	$757,056
DISTRICT 13			
Biggert (R)	$920,056	$455,081 (49%)	$1,014,819
Shannon (D)	$216,819	$8,473 (4%)	$225,842
DISTRICT 14			
Hastert (R)	$5,064,847	$2,400,128 (47%)	$5,206,105
Laesch (D)	$310,214	$18,885 (6%)	$306,072
DISTRICT 15			
Johnson (R)	$342,316	$219,532 (64%)	$493,982
Gill (D)	$235,909	$15,075 (6%)	$234,168
DISTRICT 16			
Manzullo (R)	$1,173,279	$616,326 (53%)	$1,334,337
Auman (D)	$107,801	$8,550 (8%)	$105,581
Borling (X)	$106,900	$0 (0%)	$89,832
DISTRICT 17			
Hare (D)	$864,114	$498,210 (58%)	$808,792
Zinga (R)	$427,875	$67,335 (16%)	$405,650
DISTRICT 18			
LaHood (R)	$1,174,538	$467,881 (40%)	$1,262,225
DISTRICT 19			
Shimkus (R)	$1,212,017	$748,111 (62%)	$826,242
Stover (D)	$171,504	$24,658 (14%)	$166,732

Indiana

SENIOR SENATOR - 2006			
Lugar (R)	$2,925,923	$771,820 (26%)	$3,133,830
JUNIOR SENATOR - 2004			
Bayh (D)	$4,820,160	$1,583,913 (33%)	$2,250,428
Scott (R)	2,265,166	$6,450 0%)	$2,242,526
DISTRICT 1			
Visclosky (D)	$1,373,882	$444,486 (32%)	$1,207,585
Leyva (R)	$10,940	$0 (0%)	$10,899
DISTRICT 2			
Donnelly (D)	$1,554,571	$563,725 (36%)	$1,561,420
Chocola (R)	$3,247,573	$1,483,299 (46%)	$3,415,742
DISTRICT 3			
Souder (R)	$622,034	$274,025 (44%)	$642,282
Hayhurst (D)	$708,182	$43,700 (6%)	$708,181
DISTRICT 4			
Buyer (R)	$744,682	$571,855 (77%)	$536,985
Sanders (D)	$136,352	$5,835 (4%)	$133,260
DISTRICT 5			
Burton (R)	$527,819	$202,145 (38%)	$781,677
Carr (D)	$13,287	$7,741 (58%)	$12,956
DISTRICT 6			
Pence (R)	$1,535,469	$587,246 (38%)	$1,319,503
Welsh (D)	$51,755	$2,127 (4%)	$45,424
DISTRICT 7			
Carson (D)	$476,139	$230,250 (48%)	$604,962
Dickerson (R)	$79,591	$6,000 (8%)	$74,288
DISTRICT 8			
Ellsworth (D)	$1,769,955	$744,875 (42%)	$1,742,341
Hostettler (R)	$598,400	$88,500 (15%)	$580,161
DISTRICT 9			
Hill (D)	$1,906,651	$808,129 (42%)	$1,888,695
Sodrel (R)	$2,730,270	$1,266,415 (46%)	$2,724,285
Schansberg (LIBERT)	$26,765	$5,000 (19%)	$22,120

Iowa

	RECEIPTS	FROM PACS	EXPENDITURES
SENIOR SENATOR - 2004			
Grassley (R)	$5,655,068	$2,146,135 (38%)	$6,403,445
Small (D)	$140,204	$1,200 (1%)	$135,503
JUNIOR SENATOR - 2002			
Harkin (D)	$7,016,840	$1,441,247 (21%)	$6,727,132
Ganske (R)	$5,426,297	$779,685 (14%)	$5,334,084
DISTRICT 1			
Braley (D)	$2,485,489	$728,897 (29%)	$2,235,245
Whalen (R)	$2,390,693	$681,844 (29%)	$2,385,532
DISTRICT 2			
Loebsack (D)	$521,636	$173,991 (33%)	$488,385
Leach (R)	$490,858	$0 (0%)	$533,734
DISTRICT 3			
Boswell (D)	$2,147,051	$1,278,314 (60%)	$2,060,474
Lamberti (R)	$2,003,871	$577,546 (29%)	$1,994,605
DISTRICT 4			
Latham (R)	$1,131,896	$563,211 (50%)	$1,125,580
Spencer (D)	$482,166	$30,738 (6%)	$478,932
DISTRICT 5			
King (R)	$612,291	$363,744 (59%)	$620,071
Schulte (D)	$73,327	$6,200 (8%)	$73,262
Nielsen (X)	$150,841	$0 (0%)	$149,777

Kansas

	RECEIPTS	FROM PACS	EXPENDITURES
SENIOR SENATOR - 2004			
Brownback (R)	$2,730,682	$893,588 (33%)	$2,476,585
Jones (D)	$71,102	$32,000 (45%)	$31,147
JUNIOR SENATOR - 2002			
Roberts (R)	$1,408,528	$787,087 (56%)	$1,012,747
DISTRICT 1			
Moran (R)	$970,213	$486,686 (50%)	$723,063
Doll (D)	$63,887	$0 (0%)	$62,274
DISTRICT 2			
Boyda (D)	$760,761	$108,000 (14%)	$726,738
Ryun (R)	$1,132,890	$618,216 (55%)	$1,075,223
DISTRICT 3			
Moore (D)	$2,240,158	$1,240,777 (55%)	$1,851,895
Ahner (R)	$469,609	$6,000 (1%)	$433,456
DISTRICT 4			
Tiahrt (R)	$1,104,585	$533,250 (48%)	$1,078,321
McGinn (D)	$28,048	$500 (2%)	$25,612

Kentucky

	RECEIPTS	FROM PACS	EXPENDITURES
SENIOR SENATOR - 2002			
McConnell (R)	$4,735,540	$1,192,388 (25%)	$5,241,832
Weinberg (D)	$2,239,125	$198,101 (9%)	$2,189,846
JUNIOR SENATOR - 2004			
Bunning (R)	$5,120,291	$1,903,137 (37%)	$6,075,399
Mongiardo (D)	$3,127,490	$484,365 (15%)	$3,104,981

	RECEIPTS	FROM PACS	EXPENDITURES
DISTRICT 1			
Whitfield (R)	$1,052,012	$576,629 (55%)	$1,063,078
Barlow (D)	$127,550	$6,100 (5%)	$113,495
DISTRICT 2			
Lewis (R)	$1,707,710	$1,011,613 (59%)	$1,975,693
Weaver (D)	$912,881	$328,934 (36%)	$883,819
DISTRICT 3			
Yarmuth (D)	$2,250,298	$183,000 (8%)	$2,224,248
Northup (R)	$3,397,906	$1,215,561 (36%)	$3,421,281
DISTRICT 4			
Davis (R)	$4,198,788	$1,518,827 (36%)	$4,255,379
Lucas (D)	$1,469,554	$565,990 (39%)	$1,469,555
DISTRICT 5			
Rogers (R)	$1,072,946	$365,208 (34%)	$916,202
DISTRICT 6			
Chandler (D)	$1,115,946	$497,972 (45%)	$723,278

Louisiana

	RECEIPTS	FROM PACS	EXPENDITURES
SENIOR SENATOR - 2002			
Landrieu (D)	$6,770,029	$2,614,362 (39%)	$7,326,155
Cooksey (R)	$1,899,166	$65,225 (3%)	$1,835,326
Terrell (R)	$3,387,167	$820,277 (24%)	$2,760,276
Perkins (R)	$639,258	$39,681 (6%)	$634,270
JUNIOR SENATOR - 2004			
Vitter (R)	$7,743,804	$1,182,643 (15%)	$7,206,714
John (D)	$4,893,113	$1,065,880 (22%)	$4,868,165
Kennedy (D)	$1,919,879	$122,570 (6%)	$1,919,774
Morrell (D)	$68,653	$12,050 (18%)	$67,214
DISTRICT 1			
Jindal (R)	$2,976,542	$664,315 (22%)	$3,573,673
Gereighty (D)	$15,240	$0 (0%)	$18,139
Tallitsch (D)	$36,699	$1,000 (3%)	$37,041
Beary (LIBERT)	$5,800	$0 (0%)	$5,800
DISTRICT 2			
Jefferson (D)	$1,162,795	$489,783 (42%)	$1,238,408
K. Carter (D)	$1,290,191	$131,737 (10%)	$1,258,965
Shepherd (D)	$511,527	$300 (0%)	$462,787
Lavigne (R)	$317,750	$0 (0%)	$291,129
T. Carter (D)	$178,072	$0 (0%)	$171,850
Bartholomew (D)	$45,875	$250 (1%)	$45,842
Edwards (D)	$9,465	$0 (0%)	$7,511
Mendoza (D)	$23,200	$100 (0%)	$22,152
DISTRICT 3			
Melancon (D)	$2,691,846	$1,261,025 (47%)	$2,596,270
Romero (R)	$1,925,381	$143,300 (7%)	$1,936,495
Breech (D)	$11,635	$0 (0%)	$11,557
DISTRICT 4			
McCrery (R)	$2,606,023	$1,734,600 (67%)	$2,246,203
Cash (D)	$11,294	$0 (0%)	$7,619
Kelley (R)	$87,875	$0 (0%)	$79,783
DISTRICT 5			
Alexander (R)	$1,311,468	$551,149 (42%)	$1,199,376
Hearn (D)	$156,083	$0 (0%)	$155,823
DISTRICT 6			
Baker (R)	$1,408,132	$836,376 (59%)	$1,604,762
DISTRICT 7			
Boustany (R)	$1,738,745	$791,005 (45%)	$1,623,340
Stagg (D)	$63,876	$0 (0%)	$57,011

Maine

	RECEIPTS	FROM PACS	EXPENDITURES
SENIOR SENATOR - 2006			
Snowe (R)	$3,434,635	$1,247,685 (36%)	$2,773,431
Bright (D)	$127,767	$12,382 (10%)	$126,823
Slavick (I)	$1,931	$0 (0%)	$5,580
JUNIOR SENATOR - 2002			
Collins (R)	$4,007,560	$1,511,332 (38%)	$3,945,683
Pingree (D)	$3,865,577	$340,306 (9%)	$3,741,905
DISTRICT 1			
Allen (D)	$1,058,725	$353,093 (33%)	$656,455
Curley (R)	$185,766	$35,251 (19%)	$181,764
Kamilewicz (I)	$41,581	$0 (0%)	$43,930
DISTRICT 2			
Michaud (D)	$737,082	$486,785 (66%)	$724,232
D'Amboise (R)	$28,808	$7,000 (24%)	$18,526

Maryland

	RECEIPTS	FROM PACS	EXPENDITURES
SENIOR SENATOR - 2004			
Mikulski (D)	$5,911,959	$1,133,700 (19%)	$5,997,093
Pipkin (R)	$2,313,360	$16,310 (1%)	$2,298,709
JUNIOR SENATOR - 2006			
Cardin (D)	$8,770,424	$1,480,090 (17%)	$8,676,056
Steele (R)	$8,432,622	$1,212,942 (14%)	$8,219,686
Zeese (GREEN)	$68,909	$0 (0%)	$68,908
DISTRICT 1			
Gilchrest (R)	$351,704	$3,570 (1%)	$182,375
Corwin (D)	$29,704	$1,500 (5%)	$29,701
DISTRICT 2			
Ruppersberger (D)	$854,594	$406,783 (48%)	$590,984
Mathis (R)	$8,449	$0 (0%)	$8,448
DISTRICT 3			
Sarbanes (D)	$1,463,575	$208,250 (14%)	$1,396,582
White (R)	$476,345	$5,000 (1%)	$471,185
DISTRICT 4			
Wynn (D)	$799,324	$474,875 (59%)	$980,863
DISTRICT 5			
Hoyer (D)	$2,354,470	$1,705,074 (72%)	$2,360,627
Warner (GREEN)	$3,978	$0 (0%)	$10,424
DISTRICT 6			
Bartlett (R)	$362,819	$126,131 (35%)	$417,097
Duck (D)	$212,913	$43,750 (21%)	$210,533
Kozak (GREEN)	$5,435	$0 (0%)	$5,404
DISTRICT 7			
Cummings (D)	$882,989	$462,035 (52%)	$560,956
DISTRICT 8			
Van Hollen (D)	$1,686,584	$452,737 (27%)	$676,816
Stein (R)	$31,844	$0 (0%)	$31,845

Massachusetts

	RECEIPTS	FROM PACS	EXPENDITURES
SENIOR SENATOR - 2006			
Kennedy (D)	$8,931,742	$1,012,376 (11%)	$7,043,877
Chase (R)	$873,982	$0 (0%)	$853,730
JUNIOR SENATOR - 2002			
Kerry (D)	$8,605,482	$16,200 (0%)	$5,971,092
Cloud (LIBERT)	$199,740	$50 (0%)	$199,476
DISTRICT 1			
Olver (D)	$660,116	$302,585 (46%)	$670,481
Szych (X)	$47,154	$0 (0%)	$49,283
DISTRICT 2			
Neal (D)	$715,000	$371,168 (52%)	$552,127
DISTRICT 3			
McGovern (D)	$755,594	$218,107 (29%)	$705,491
DISTRICT 4			
Frank (D)	$1,872,924	$806,114 (43%)	$1,159,692
DISTRICT 5			
Meehan (D)	$1,057,917	$0 (0%)	$452,780
DISTRICT 6			
Tierney (D)	$654,168	$185,720 (28%)	$497,514
Barton (R)	$66,772	$3,650 (5%)	$65,648
DISTRICT 7			
Markey (D)	$942,520	$420,035 (45%)	$913,564
DISTRICT 8			
Capuano (D)	$836,728	$347,684 (42%)	$626,795
DISTRICT 9			
Lynch (D)	$1,170,450	$321,975 (28%)	$868,163
Robinson (R)	$125,112	$0 (0%)	$130,634
DISTRICT 10			
Delahunt (D)	$1,133,495	$288,535 (25%)	$974,422
Beatty (R)	$106,012	$7,950 (7%)	$74,271
White (I)	$4,803	$400 (8%)	$4,709

Michigan

	RECEIPTS	FROM PACS	EXPENDITURES
SENIOR SENATOR - 2002			
Levin (D)	$5,090,498	$838,109 (16%)	$4,099,215
Raczkowski (R)	$1,096,368	$0 (0%)	$819,356
JUNIOR SENATOR - 2006			
Stabenow (D)	$9,211,206	$1,566,316 (17%)	$11,220,506
Bouchard (R)	$6,065,160	$709,826 (12%)	$6,050,148
Sole (GREEN)	$5,527	$0 (0%)	$5,508
DISTRICT 1			
Stupak (D)	$805,653	$519,250 (64%)	$833,135
Hooper (R)	$5,316	$0 (0%)	$5,362
DISTRICT 2			
Hoekstra (R)	$720,728	$323,522 (45%)	$676,667
Kotos (D)	$15,498	$0 (0%)	$9,622
DISTRICT 3			
Ehlers (R)	$458,404	$185,170 (40%)	$458,540
Rinck (D)	$24,132	$8,000 (33%)	$24,124
DISTRICT 4			
Camp (R)	$1,215,951	$840,738 (69%)	$1,111,769
Huckleberry (D)	$66,490	$13,513 (20%)	$62,030
DISTRICT 5			
Kildee (D)	$556,803	$261,310 (47%)	$593,816
DISTRICT 6			
Upton (R)	$1,237,450	$664,163 (54%)	$972,296
Clark (D)	$145,295	$3,000 (2%)	$145,039
DISTRICT 7			
Walberg (R)	$1,260,111	$294,596 (23%)	$1,225,137
Renier (D)	$55,682	$18,950 (34%)	$55,794
Schwarz (R)	$1,608,497	$884,637 (55%)	$1,688,277
DISTRICT 8			
Rogers (R)	$1,487,893	$820,331 (55%)	$1,863,914
Marcinkowski (D)	$552,157	$121,310 (22%)	$552,220
DISTRICT 9			
Knollenberg (R)	$2,652,836	$880,854 (33%)	$3,105,161
Skinner (D)	$422,382	$80,270 (19%)	$403,726
DISTRICT 10			
Miller (R)	$860,582	$433,742 (50%)	$692,651
Denison (D)	$14,076	$7,500 (53%)	$14,077
DISTRICT 11			
McCotter (R)	$871,572	$349,526 (40%)	$875,708
Trupiano (D)	$83,418	$20,450 (25%)	$134,142
DISTRICT 12			
Levin (D)	$626,413	$439,387 (70%)	$742,094
DISTRICT 13			
Kilpatrick (D)	$460,445	$309,585 (67%)	$551,497
DISTRICT 14			
Conyers (D)	$1,069,653	$470,210 (44%)	$913,514
Miles (R)	$6,963	$0 (0%)	$6,963
DISTRICT 15			
Dingell (D)	$1,557,064	$1,167,035 (75%)	$1,400,145

Minnesota

	RECEIPTS	FROM PACS	EXPENDITURES
SENIOR SENATOR - 2002			
Coleman (R)	$9,912,726	$1,735,858 (18%)	$9,648,999
Mondale (D)	$2,728,910	$380,004 (14%)	$1,731,176
Moore (INDC)	$49,503	$200 (0%)	$45,611
JUNIOR SENATOR - 2006			
Klobuchar (D)	$9,202,052	$905,058 (10%)	$9,155,313
Kennedy (R)	$10,211,119	$2,245,415 (22%)	$10,308,273
Fitzgerald (INDC)	$13,652	$0 (0%)	$13,350
Cavlan (GREEN)	$9,378	$0 (0%)	$8,544
DISTRICT 1			
Walz (D)	$1,304,192	$365,558 (28%)	$1,281,136
Gutknecht (R)	$1,364,284	$598,454 (44%)	$1,723,707
DISTRICT 2			
Kline (R)	$1,495,470	$605,496 (40%)	$1,478,465
Rowley (D)	$692,476	$76,960 (11%)	$690,132
DISTRICT 3			
Ramstad (R)	$1,028,886	$612,045 (59%)	$1,424,365
Wilde (D)	$67,887	$12,000 (18%)	$67,861
DISTRICT 4			
McCollum (D)	$562,752	$272,185 (48%)	$611,908
Sium (R)	$79,223	$2,000 (3%)	$75,617
DISTRICT 5			
Ellison (D)	$795,047	$230,294 (29%)	$786,127
Fine (R)	$198,319	$800 (0%)	$198,621

Lee (INDC)	$228,938	$14,750 (6%)	$226,398
Pond (GREEN)	$9,102	$0 (0%)	$9,103
DISTRICT 6			
Bachmann (R)	$2,771,661	$832,314 (30%)	$2,694,789
Wetterling (D)	$3,153,303	$502,777 (16%)	$3,179,222
Binkowski (INDC)	$18,297	$0 (0%)	$17,261
DISTRICT 7			
Peterson (D)	$938,128	$720,025 (77%)	$645,285
Barrett (R)	$41,378	$8,000 (19%)	$41,375
DISTRICT 8			
Oberstar (D)	$1,368,865	$800,703 (58%)	$1,422,123
Grams (R)	$468,730	$99,550 (21%)	$546,121
Welty (UNT)	$5,677	$0 (0%)	$5,398

Mississippi

	RECEIPTS	FROM PACS	EXPENDITURES
SENIOR SENATOR - 2002			
Cochran (R)	$1,688,273	$824,510 (49%)	$1,432,856
JUNIOR SENATOR - 2006			
Lott (R)	$2,810,405	$1,356,049 (48%)	$2,088,465
Fleming (D)	$43,157	$10,200 (24%)	$38,495
DISTRICT 1			
Wicker (R)	$845,748	$366,600 (43%)	$746,938
Hurt (D)	$17,299	$0 (0%)	$16,398
DISTRICT 2			
Thompson (D)	$1,375,701	$817,281 (59%)	$1,393,496
Brown (R)	$122,984	$31,300 (25%)	$122,769
DISTRICT 3			
Pickering (R)	$1,253,264	$811,998 (65%)	$726,303
DISTRICT 4			
Taylor (D)	$428,332	$256,919 (60%)	$320,183

Missouri

	RECEIPTS	FROM PACS	EXPENDITURES
SENIOR SENATOR - 2004			
Bond (R)	$8,093,952	$2,098,125 (26%)	$7,848,506
Farmer (D)	$3,600,882	$512,409 (14%)	$3,548,116
JUNIOR SENATOR - 2006			
McCaskill (D)	$11,935,806	$1,058,519 (9%)	$11,705,967
Talent (R)	$14,098,563	$3,472,930 (25%)	$14,340,762
Lewis (PRO)	$5,937	$0 (0%)	$5,938
DISTRICT 1			
Clay (D)	$443,363	$307,158 (69%)	$464,665
Byrne (R)	$74,994	$2,400 (3%)	$68,419
DISTRICT 2			
Akin (R)	$857,416	$289,343 (34%)	$698,050
DISTRICT 3			
Carnahan (D)	$1,263,763	$644,460 (51%)	$1,184,962
Bertelsen (R)	$8,301	$0 (0%)	$8,300
DISTRICT 4			
Skelton (D)	$1,050,907	$662,163 (63%)	$1,044,003
Noland (R)	$21,028	$600 (3%)	$21,027
DISTRICT 5			
Cleaver (D)	$669,497	$344,152 (51%)	$617,748
Turk (R)	$31,321	$0 (0%)	$31,796
DISTRICT 6			
Graves (R)	$1,218,347	$596,893 (49%)	$1,215,978
Shettles (D)	$131,570	$55,149 (42%)	$130,313
DISTRICT 7			
Blunt (R)	$3,162,484	$1,880,294 (59%)	$3,301,391
DISTRICT 8			
Emerson (R)	$1,166,412	$668,434 (57%)	$1,129,359
Hambacker (D)	$66,788	$5,939 (9%)	$60,412
DISTRICT 9			
Hulshof (R)	$1,425,467	$755,042 (53%)	$1,363,653
Burghard (D)	$258,616	$5,582 (2%)	$253,380

Montana

	RECEIPTS	FROM PACS	EXPENDITURES
SENIOR SENATOR - 2002			
Baucus (D)	$5,945,541	$2,620,108 (44%)	$6,106,052
Taylor (R)	$1,798,533	$77,237 (4%)	$1,793,389
JUNIOR SENATOR - 2006			
Tester (D)	$5,588,548	$565,531 (10%)	$5,588,292
Burns (R)	$8,057,326	$2,586,600 (32%)	$8,516,022
AT LARGE			
Rehberg (R)	$1,205,015	$451,946 (38%)	$1,132,530
Lindeen (D)	$518,137	$99,966 (19%)	$512,425

Nebraska

	RECEIPTS	FROM PACS	EXPENDITURES
SENIOR SENATOR - 2002			
Hagel (R)	$1,609,967	$883,266 (55%)	$1,350,307
Chase (I)	$24,321	$0 (0%)	$24,293
JUNIOR SENATOR - 2006			
Nelson (D)	$6,451,279	$2,683,758 (42%)	$7,492,134
Ricketts (R)	$13,424,896	$197,700 (1%)	$13,417,690
DISTRICT 1			
Fortenberry (R)	$1,144,271	$569,505 (50%)	$1,134,332
Moul (D)	$995,381	$273,225 (27%)	$994,032
DISTRICT 2			
Terry (R)	$1,116,825	$579,473 (52%)	$998,578
Esch (D)	$412,554	$2,500 (1%)	$420,010
DISTRICT 3			
Smith (R)	$1,259,119	$418,754 (33%)	$1,242,661
Kleeb (D)	$1,048,426	$219,659 (21%)	$975,392

Nevada

	RECEIPTS	FROM PACS	EXPENDITURES
SENIOR SENATOR - 2004			
Reid (D)	$7,015,254	$2,103,980 (30%)	$7,040,588
Ziser (R)	$648,792	$9,343 (1%)	$647,500
JUNIOR SENATOR - 2006			
Ensign (R)	$5,305,606	$1,851,877 (35%)	$4,456,881
Carter (D)	$2,266,273	$186,856 (8%)	$2,264,708
DISTRICT 1			
Berkley (D)	$1,742,767	$520,671 (30%)	$1,674,409
Wegner (R)	$96,582	$0 (0%)	$96,534

DISTRICT 2			
Heller (R)	$1,699,942	$434,149 (26%)	$1,674,281
Derby (D)	$1,610,549	$521,969 (32%)	$1,594,051
DISTRICT 3			
Porter (R)	$3,015,397	$1,278,630 (42%)	$3,036,311
Hafen (D)	$1,497,306	$512,197 (34%)	$1,501,465

New Hampshire

	RECEIPTS	FROM PACS	EXPENDITURES
SENIOR SENATOR - 2004			
Gregg (R)	$2,982,530	$1,654,297 (55%)	$1,897,466
Haddock (D)	$177,594	$0 (0%)	$177,199
JUNIOR SENATOR - 2002			
Sununu (R)	$3,622,980	$1,232,534 (34%)	$3,507,470
Shaheen (D)	$5,823,007	$999,209 (17%)	$5,791,661
DISTRICT 1			
Shea-Porter (D)	$360,380	$51,056 (14%)	$291,663
Bradley (R)	$1,111,590	$576,960 (52%)	$1,062,132
DISTRICT 2			
Hodes (D)	$1,648,323	$372,035 (23%)	$1,638,729
Bass (R)	$1,228,541	$741,666 (60%)	$1,237,271

New Jersey

	RECEIPTS	FROM PACS	EXPENDITURES
SENIOR SENATOR - 2002			
Lautenberg (D)	$3,109,237	$413,075 (13%)	$2,844,020
Forrester (R)	$10,604,219	$484,793 (5%)	$10,540,687
Glick (GREEN)	$39,421	$0 (0%)	$28,318
JUNIOR SENATOR - 2006			
Menendez (D)	$11,950,586	$2,151,084 (18%)	$13,328,665
Kean (R)	$7,879,050	$1,250,612 (16%)	$7,762,370
Flynn (LIBERT)	$5,172	$0 (0%)	$5,632
DISTRICT 1			
Andrews (D)	$2,203,661	$696,985 (32%)	$1,450,582
DISTRICT 2			
LoBiondo (R)	$1,549,238	$599,709 (39%)	$1,648,220
Thomas-Hughes (D)	$24,828	$3,681 (15%)	$26,903
DISTRICT 3			
Saxton (R)	$1,364,031	$440,509 (32%)	$1,314,846
Sexton (D)	$161,187	$11,291 (7%)	$161,186
DISTRICT 4			
Smith (R)	$482,374	$187,288 (39%)	$471,992
Gay (D)	$95,189	$21,398 (22%)	$94,172
DISTRICT 5			
Garrett (R)	$1,158,306	$438,277 (38%)	$1,081,990
Aronsohn (D)	$576,274	$121,550 (21%)	$549,555
DISTRICT 6			
Pallone (D)	$2,279,563	$676,700 (30%)	$874,194
Bellew (R)	$17,751	$1,425 (8%)	$15,289
DISTRICT 7			
Ferguson (R)	$2,932,480	$1,231,871 (42%)	$3,043,589
Stender (D)	$1,932,564	$445,816 (23%)	$1,926,891
DISTRICT 8			
Pascrell (D)	$1,389,546	$482,422 (35%)	$1,098,407
Sandoval (R)	$232,483	$2,000 (1%)	$234,505
DISTRICT 9			
Rothman (D)	$1,544,024	$495,129 (32%)	$912,808
Micco (R)	$53,730	$1,975 (4%)	$52,114
DISTRICT 10			
Payne (D)	$603,477	$324,206 (54%)	$492,949
DISTRICT 11			
Frelinghuysen (R)	$1,054,826	$386,197 (37%)	$1,187,427
Wyka (D)	$26,856	$0 (0%)	$12,107
DISTRICT 12			
Holt (D)	$1,465,207	$326,663 (22%)	$1,055,244
DISTRICT 13 †			
Sires (D)	$1,901,805	$300,121 (16%)	$1,884,679

New Mexico

	RECEIPTS	FROM PACS	EXPENDITURES
SENIOR SENATOR - 2002			
Domenici (R)	$4,195,731	$939,490 (22%)	$4,115,919
Tristani (D)	$732,304	$140,478 (19%)	$834,607
JUNIOR SENATOR - 2006			
Bingaman (D)	$3,310,009	$1,609,084 (49%)	$2,628,276
McCulloch (R)	$559,138	$10,230 (2%)	$555,511
DISTRICT 1			
Wilson (R)	$4,904,809	$1,871,677 (38%)	$4,906,596
Madrid (D)	$3,381,176	$649,181 (19%)	$3,386,200
DISTRICT 2			
Pearce (R)	$1,474,360	$557,622 (38%)	$1,338,921
Kissling (D)	$185,716	$4,900 (3%)	$183,160
DISTRICT 3			
Udall (D)	$515,102	$181,995 (35%)	$396,860
Dolin (R)	$23,573	$0 (0%)	$23,572

New York

	RECEIPTS	FROM PACS	EXPENDITURES
SENIOR SENATOR - 2004			
Schumer (D)	$11,921,568	$928,698 (8%)	$15,467,530
Mills (R)	$632,319	$51,350 (8%)	$629,170
Hirschfeld (BLD)	$702,000	$0 (0%)	$87,293
O'Grady (C)	$47,143	$0 (0%)	$15,628
McReynolds (GREEN)	$14,275	$0 (0%)	$7,209
Silberger (LIBERT)	$9,999	$0 (0%)	$9,594
JUNIOR SENATOR - 2006			
Clinton (D)	$39,833,526	$1,543,092 (4%)	$34,358,255
Spencer (R)	$5,849,610	$27,696 (0%)	$5,660,688
Russell (LIBERT)	$9,809	$0 (0%)	$9,807
Hawkins (GREEN)	$48,044	$201 (0%)	$45,871
DISTRICT 1			
Bishop (D)	$1,400,902	$484,895 (35%)	$1,065,866
Zanzi (R)	$343,335	$19,075 (6%)	$321,495
DISTRICT 2			
Israel (D)	$1,498,557	$583,804 (39%)	$1,167,026
DISTRICT 3			
King (R)	$1,474,660	$657,100 (45%)	$2,075,502
Mejias (D)	$916,407	$189,296 (21%)	$908,135
DISTRICT 4			
McCarthy (D)	$1,441,801	$521,340 (36%)	$1,368,799
Blessinger (R)	$112,165	$600 (1%)	$112,122

DISTRICT 5			
Ackerman (D)	$754,367	$323,555 (43%)	$844,526
DISTRICT 6			
Meeks (D)	$819,726	$575,971 (70%)	$935,949
DISTRICT 7			
Crowley (D)	$1,738,323	$1,040,755 (60%)	$1,505,477
DISTRICT 8			
Nadler (D)	$758,666	$248,035 (33%)	$764,960
DISTRICT 9			
Weiner (D)	$639,777	$164,235 (26%)	$837,956
DISTRICT 10			
Towns (D)	$1,330,386	$750,598 (56%)	$1,339,964
DISTRICT 11			
Clarke (D)	$649,814	$149,927 (23%)	$622,247
McClean (FDM)	$24,954	$0 (0%)	$22,111
DISTRICT 12			
Velázquez (D)	$766,762	$431,685 (56%)	$698,615
DISTRICT 13			
Fossella (R)	$1,488,053	$749,748 (50%)	$1,639,598
Harrison (D)	$138,952	$23,360 (17%)	$132,454
DISTRICT 14			
Maloney (D)	$1,179,894	$180,121 (15%)	$1,030,382
Maio (R)	$82,425	$0 (0%)	$82,425
DISTRICT 15			
Rangel (D)	$1,995,574	$1,134,175 (57%)	$2,047,116
DISTRICT 16			
Serrano (D)	$312,397	$147,125 (47%)	$314,380
DISTRICT 17			
Engel (D)	$862,882	$442,317 (51%)	$945,640
DISTRICT 18			
Lowey (D)	$1,344,129	$276,553 (21%)	$1,555,658
Hoffman (R)	$65,754	$6,999 (11%)	$65,824
DISTRICT 19			
Hall (D)	$1,681,117	$222,883 (13%)	$1,626,670
Kelly (R)	$2,293,809	$1,299,602 (57%)	$2,519,164
DISTRICT 20			
Gillibrand (D)	$2,634,157	$566,438 (22%)	$2,595,659
Sweeney (R)	$2,956,197	$1,405,648 (48%)	$3,425,841
DISTRICT 21			
McNulty (D)	$482,264	$286,945 (59%)	$562,751
DISTRICT 22			
Hinchey (D)	$664,148	$211,448 (32%)	$685,751
DISTRICT 23			
McHugh (R)	$561,841	$419,600 (75%)	$744,416
Johnson (D)	$161,770	$4,170 (3%)	$160,193
DISTRICT 24			
Arcuri (D)	$2,233,065	$726,987 (33%)	$2,197,558
Meier (R)	$1,635,397	$853,296 (52%)	$1,586,397
DISTRICT 25			
Walsh (R)	$1,396,424	$708,780 (51%)	$1,787,552
Maffei (D)	$958,295	$298,300 (31%)	$918,270
DISTRICT 26			
Reynolds (R)	$4,337,295	$1,777,245 (41%)	$5,275,474
Davis (D)	$2,403,310	$64,850 (3%)	$2,386,358
DISTRICT 27			
Higgins (D)	$1,206,490	$646,958 (54%)	$846,790
DISTRICT 28			
Slaughter (D)	$510,564	$303,325 (59%)	$675,787
Donnelly (R)	$36,274	$11,200 (31%)	$24,468
DISTRICT 29			
Kuhl (R)	$1,450,864	$946,476 (65%)	$1,475,289
Massa (D)	$1,511,535	$329,199 (22%)	$1,501,716

North Carolina

	RECEIPTS	FROM PACS	EXPENDITURES
SENIOR SENATOR - 2002			
Dole (R)	$13,681,111	$1,432,111 (10%)	$13,555,960
Bowles (D)	$13,304,804	$523,128 (4%)	$13,273,188
JUNIOR SENATOR - 2004			
Burr (R)	$12,951,226	$2,796,484 (22%)	$12,853,110
Bowles (D)	$13,405,743	$822,974 (6%)	$13,357,851
DISTRICT 1			
Butterfield (D)	$387,424	$271,105 (70%)	$359,758
DISTRICT 2			
Etheridge (D)	$907,474	$444,105 (49%)	$919,522
Mansell (R)	$61,692	$2,000 (3%)	$61,689
DISTRICT 3			
Jones (R)	$553,971	$292,217 (53%)	$674,917
Weber (D)	$56,908	$0 (0%)	$48,371
DISTRICT 4			
Price (D)	$931,155	$364,994 (39%)	$800,298
Acuff (R)	$55,680	$3,900 (7%)	$54,247
DISTRICT 5			
Foxx (R)	$1,408,198	$488,165 (35%)	$797,491
Sharpe (D)	$138,998	$6,300 (5%)	$97,747
DISTRICT 6			
Coble (R)	$457,914	$388,950 (85%)	$552,271
Blake (D)	$14,670	$0 (0%)	$14,004
DISTRICT 7			
McIntyre (D)	$901,698	$400,031 (44%)	$1,006,381
Davis (R)	$26,224	$0 (0%)	$41,222
DISTRICT 8			
Hayes (R)	$2,438,745	$1,165,158 (48%)	$2,475,169
Kissell (D)	$806,242	$175,675 (22%)	$804,010
DISTRICT 9			
Myrick (R)	$1,287,147	$580,948 (45%)	$1,262,588
Glass (D)	$13,760	$1,350 (10%)	$11,692
DISTRICT 10			
McHenry (R)	$1,464,716	$776,554 (53%)	$1,339,776
Carsner (D)	$22,726	$0 (0%)	$22,724
DISTRICT 11			
Shuler (D)	$1,850,365	$587,068 (32%)	$1,804,365
Taylor (R)	$4,397,723	$681,147 (15%)	$4,425,482
DISTRICT 12			
Watt (D)	$503,513	$446,813 (89%)	$535,743
Fisher (R)	$444,042	$0 (0%)	$446,779
DISTRICT 13			
Miller (D)	$1,771,007	$698,630 (39%)	$1,766,708
Robinson (R)	$2,048,421	$12,750 (1%)	$2,179,456

North Dakota

	RECEIPTS	FROM PACS	EXPENDITURES
SENIOR SENATOR - 2006			
Conrad (D)	$4,664,878	$2,033,240 (44%)	$3,532,732

Grotberg (R)	$259,080	$125 (0%)	$259,081
JUNIOR SENATOR - 2004			
Dorgan (D)	$2,941,662	$1,410,617 (48%)	$2,676,756
Liffrig (R)	$380,351	$12,299 (3%)	$381,125
AT LARGE			
Pomeroy (D)	$1,591,806	$1,193,435 (75%)	$1,378,061

Ohio

	RECEIPTS	FROM PACS	EXPENDITURES
SENIOR SENATOR - 2004			
Voinovich (R)	$7,326,196	$1,670,976 (23%)	$8,956,380
Fingerhut (D)	$1,171,554	$97,837 (8%)	$1,166,538
JUNIOR SENATOR - 2006			
Brown (D)	$8,937,004	$1,471,968 (16%)	$10,751,765
DeWine (R)	$12,094,898	$2,906,920 (24%)	$14,161,402
DISTRICT 1			
Chabot (R)	$2,669,976	$1,380,081 (52%)	$2,991,572
Cranley (D)	$2,024,604	$495,057 (24%)	$2,021,495
DISTRICT 2 †			
Schmidt (R)	$2,087,434	$852,951 (41%)	$2,078,564
Wulsin (D)	$1,089,095	$238,480 (22%)	$1,041,185
Condit (X)	$21,028	$0 (0%)	$21,027
Hackett (D)	$868,952	$66,596 (8%)	$868,951
DISTRICT 3			
Turner (R)	$1,043,686	$451,428 (43%)	$1,112,107
Chema (D)	$418,050	$35,300 (8%)	$417,577
DISTRICT 4			
Jordan (R)	$1,408,770	$413,512 (29%)	$1,348,197
Siferd (D)	$163,615	$12,951 (8%)	$161,767
DISTRICT 5			
Gillmor (R)	$568,949	$470,500 (83%)	$723,408
Weirauch (D)	$117,478	$21,475 (18%)	$115,664
DISTRICT 6			
Wilson (D)	$1,860,494	$678,817 (36%)	$1,800,909
Blasdel (R)	$1,105,652	$533,159 (48%)	$1,066,716
DISTRICT 7			
Hobson (R)	$1,960,807	$823,997 (42%)	$2,157,850
Conner (D)	$17,505	$4,000 (23%)	$17,119
DISTRICT 8			
Boehner (R)	$3,200,084	$1,936,911 (61%)	$2,952,525
DISTRICT 9			
Kaptur (D)	$505,050	$289,505 (57%)	$495,351
DISTRICT 10			
Kucinich (D)	$635,097	$191,850 (30%)	$622,699
Dovilla (R)	$70,919	$3,325 (5%)	$70,343
DISTRICT 11			
Jones (D)	$754,168	$402,203 (53%)	$781,721
DISTRICT 12			
Tiberi (R)	$2,277,594	$1,093,348 (48%)	$2,985,858
Shamansky (D)	$1,688,254	$43,610 (3%)	$1,639,175
DISTRICT 13			
Sutton (D)	$1,285,421	$473,565 (37%)	$1,278,960
Foltin (R)	$652,041	$222,259 (34%)	$650,595
DISTRICT 14			
LaTourette (R)	$1,605,878	$878,767 (55%)	$1,446,269
Katz (D)	$236,038	$4,850 (2%)	$227,286
DISTRICT 15			
Pryce (R)	$4,278,439	$2,437,580 (57%)	$4,696,772
Kilroy (D)	$2,780,726	$539,526 (19%)	$2,749,231
DISTRICT 16			
Regula (R)	$1,027,709	$369,743 (36%)	$1,016,885
DISTRICT 17			
Ryan (D)	$609,009	$376,289 (62%)	$642,773
DISTRICT 18			
Space (D)	$1,638,828	$505,909 (31%)	$1,611,369
Padgett (R)	$852,588	$532,826 (62%)	$851,149

Oklahoma

	RECEIPTS	FROM PACS	EXPENDITURES
SENIOR SENATOR - 2002			
Inhofe (R)	$2,992,267	$1,069,350 (36%)	$2,955,965
Walters (D)	$2,085,102	$389,927 (19%)	$2,042,689
JUNIOR SENATOR - 2004			
Coburn (R)	$5,106,058	$895,428 (18%)	$5,078,647
Carson (D)	$6,345,497	$1,016,490 (16%)	$6,256,444
DISTRICT 1			
Sullivan (R)	$875,469	$481,871 (55%)	$767,488
Gentges (D)	$44,519	$200 (0%)	$40,223
Wortman (I)	$6,900	$0 (0%)	$6,785
DISTRICT 2			
Boren (D)	$1,314,638	$549,472 (42%)	$1,000,638
DISTRICT 3			
Lucas (R)	$559,459	$338,089 (60%)	$507,637
Barton (D)	$37,211	$0 (0%)	$26,556
DISTRICT 4			
Cole (R)	$1,020,035	$336,973 (33%)	$1,059,124
Spake (D)	$29,344	$2,700 (9%)	$31,091
DISTRICT 5			
Fallin (R)	$1,734,537	$287,800 (17%)	$1,629,550
Hunter (D)	$409,692	$19,500 (5%)	$400,837

Oregon

	RECEIPTS	FROM PACS	EXPENDITURES
SENIOR SENATOR - 2004			
Wyden (D)	$3,802,681	$1,111,758 (29%)	$2,817,706
King (R)	$33,012	$5,250 (16%)	$32,930
Keane (I)	$9,940	$0 (0%)	$8,511
JUNIOR SENATOR - 2002			
Smith (R)	$5,250,893	$1,543,784 (29%)	$5,530,479
Bradbury (D)	$2,127,941	$326,694 (15%)	$2,104,194
Mabon (CNSTP)	$30,899	$0 (0%)	$30,853
DISTRICT 1			
Wu (D)	$1,432,946	$387,910 (27%)	$1,130,617
Kitts (R)	$139,048	$18,000 (13%)	$144,469
DISTRICT 2			
Walden (R)	$1,349,417	$658,208 (49%)	$1,399,112
Voisin (D)	$65,685	$1,500 (2%)	$65,266
DISTRICT 3			
Blumenauer (D)	$789,369	$372,424 (47%)	$676,028
DISTRICT 4			
DeFazio (D)	$793,123	$373,969 (47%)	$753,011
Feldkamp (R)	$472,893	$46,983 (10%)	$473,235

	RECEIPTS	FROM PACS	EXPENDITURES
DISTRICT 5			
Hooley (D)	$1,819,523	$1,043,390 (57%)	$2,030,646
Erickson (R)	$1,799,744	$34,700 (2%)	$1,798,733

Pennsylvania

	RECEIPTS	FROM PACS	EXPENDITURES
SENIOR SENATOR - 2004			
Specter (R)	$14,952,496	$2,605,116 (17%)	$20,307,099
Hoeffel (D)	$4,556,417	$405,686 (9%)	$4,540,209
Clymer (CNSTP)	$218,996	$4,500 (2%)	$212,896
JUNIOR SENATOR - 2006			
Casey (D)	$17,941,270	$1,328,861 (7%)	$17,592,212
Santorum (R)	$24,796,718	$4,007,539 (16%)	$25,832,567
DISTRICT 1			
Brady (D)	$694,747	$250,350 (36%)	$564,660
DISTRICT 2			
Fattah (D)	$1,080,364	$323,896 (30%)	$688,698
DISTRICT 3			
English (R)	$1,342,820	$816,590 (61%)	$1,390,914
Porter (D)	$81,102	$10,050 (12%)	$63,034
DISTRICT 4			
Altmire (D)	$1,146,418	$283,250 (25%)	$1,091,584
Hart (R)	$2,124,719	$1,192,802 (56%)	$2,235,952
DISTRICT 5			
Peterson (R)	$645,371	$313,939 (49%)	$668,336
DISTRICT 6			
Gerlach (R)	$3,353,282	$1,717,641 (51%)	$3,492,402
Murphy (D)	$4,120,102	$650,208 (16%)	$4,097,663
DISTRICT 7			
Sestak (D)	$3,285,954	$509,365 (16%)	$3,075,719
Weldon (R)	$2,752,353	$1,132,632 (41%)	$2,940,608
DISTRICT 8			
Murphy (D)	$2,420,915	$474,920 (20%)	$2,410,530
Fitzpatrick (R)	$3,049,018	$1,463,083 (48%)	$3,174,384
DISTRICT 9			
Shuster (R)	$1,110,998	$462,016 (42%)	$1,168,741
Barr (D)	$56,212	$3,400 (6%)	$60,019
DISTRICT 10			
Carney (D)	$1,542,917	$423,054 (27%)	$1,555,004
Sherwood (R)	$2,130,829	$903,224 (42%)	$2,334,743
DISTRICT 11			
Kanjorski (D)	$1,073,773	$717,158 (67%)	$652,549
Leonardi (R)	$9,631	$763 (8%)	$9,882
DISTRICT 12			
Murtha (D)	$2,760,857	$801,618 (29%)	$3,254,226
Irey (R)	$858,483	$38,600 (4%)	$852,811
DISTRICT 13			
Schwartz (D)	$2,788,236	$564,204 (20%)	$2,248,091
Bhakta (R)	$478,271	$14,999 (3%)	$477,960
DISTRICT 14			
Doyle (D)	$923,775	$473,862 (51%)	$829,745
DISTRICT 15			
Dent (R)	$1,282,680	$582,955 (45%)	$1,284,757
Dertinger (D)	$90,172	$18,900 (21%)	$88,920
DISTRICT 16			
Pitts (R)	$506,238	$289,551 (57%)	$579,161
Herr (D)	$316,422	$16,545 (5%)	$320,016
Murphy (I)	$12,460	$0 (0%)	$13,731
DISTRICT 17			
Holden (D)	$1,093,747	$679,611 (62%)	$649,165
Wertz (R)	$12,400	$0 (0%)	$12,463
DISTRICT 18			
Murphy (R)	$1,609,248	$761,642 (47%)	$1,482,467
Kluko (D)	$95,320	$15,500 (16%)	$81,321
DISTRICT 19			
Platts (R)	$313,948	$0 (0%)	$374,579
Avillo (D)	$181,944	$4,250 (2%)	$174,531

Rhode Island

	RECEIPTS	FROM PACS	EXPENDITURES
SENIOR SENATOR - 2002			
Reed (D)	$2,322,852	$863,064 (37%)	$1,707,655
JUNIOR SENATOR - 2006			
Whitehouse (D)	$6,580,257	$746,035 (11%)	$6,426,874
Chafee (R)	$4,782,343	$1,349,397 (28%)	$5,381,488
DISTRICT 1			
Kennedy (D)	$1,963,055	$474,425 (24%)	$2,155,761
Scott (R)	$9,730	$0 (0%)	$9,542
DISTRICT 2			
Langevin (D)	$839,351	$369,389 (44%)	$829,178
Driver (I)	$192,019	$0 (0%)	$178,488

South Carolina

	RECEIPTS	FROM PACS	EXPENDITURES
SENIOR SENATOR - 2002			
Graham (R)	$6,207,367	$1,639,451 (26%)	$6,147,640
Sanders (D)	$4,284,388	$564,259 (13%)	$4,183,141
JUNIOR SENATOR - 2004			
DeMint (R)	$9,040,100	$2,347,943 (26%)	$9,036,086
Tenenbaum (D)	$6,275,269	$644,938 (10%)	$6,156,183
Tyndall (CNSTP)	$13,319	$0 (0%)	$13,318
DISTRICT 1			
Brown (R)	$783,026	$199,896 (26%)	$606,499
Maatta (D)	$114,937	$8,000 (7%)	$79,774
DISTRICT 2			
Wilson (R)	$943,411	$386,341 (41%)	$848,938
DISTRICT 3			
Barrett (R)	$1,043,520	$459,741 (44%)	$857,922
Ballenger (D)	$54,328	$1,500 (3%)	$27,891
DISTRICT 4			
Inglis (R)	$556,556	$179,330 (32%)	$397,946
Griffith (D)	$57,541	$0 (0%)	$53,481
Cobin (LIBERT)	$22,731	$0 (0%)	$23,009
DISTRICT 5			
Spratt (D)	$2,315,149	$1,326,864 (57%)	$2,665,535
Norman (R)	$1,441,234	$371,282 (26%)	$1,431,802
DISTRICT 6			
Clyburn (D)	$1,134,696	$824,590 (73%)	$988,405
McLeod (R)	$6,444	$0 (0%)	$3,155

South Dakota

	RECEIPTS	FROM PACS	EXPENDITURES
SENIOR SENATOR - 2002			
Johnson (D)	$5,524,580	$2,065,663 (37%)	$6,092,770
Thune (R)	$5,487,625	$1,312,130 (24%)	$5,918,310
JUNIOR SENATOR - 2004			
Thune (R)	$16,103,023	$1,183,602 (7%)	$14,666,225
Daschle (D)	$19,333,685	$2,807,562 (15%)	$19,975,170
AT LARGE			
Herseth-Sandlin (D)	$1,525,606	$941,699 (62%)	$1,332,097
Whalen (R)	$150,447	$17,387 (12%)	$147,967

Tennessee

	RECEIPTS	FROM PACS	EXPENDITURES
SENIOR SENATOR - 2002			
Alexander (R)	$5,841,364	$900,059 (15%)	$3,440,187
Clement (D)	$2,790,653	$660,672 (24%)	$2,791,905
JUNIOR SENATOR - 2006			
Corker (R)	$16,831,072	$1,599,958 (10%)	$18,565,935
Ford (D)	$14,306,467	$1,503,653 (11%)	$15,302,455
DISTRICT 1			
Davis (R)	$585,957	$209,285 (36%)	$518,037
Trent (D)	$78,906	$0 (0%)	$78,185
Reeves (I)	$9,509	$0 (0%)	$9,389
DISTRICT 2			
Duncan (R)	$731,810	$416,269 (57%)	$568,762
DISTRICT 3			
Wamp (R)	$1,326,997	$330,900 (25%)	$1,439,487
Benedict (D)	$19,590	$3,000 (15%)	$19,588
DISTRICT 4			
Davis (D)	$916,145	$631,552 (69%)	$810,397
DISTRICT 5			
Cooper (D)	$772,293	$298,727 (39%)	$732,657
Welsch (I)	$25,505	$0 (0%)	$25,605
DISTRICT 6			
Gordon (D)	$1,060,081	$702,070 (66%)	$939,722
DISTRICT 7			
Blackburn (R)	$1,204,671	$519,958 (43%)	$855,071
Morrison (D)	$68,038	$18,500 (27%)	$68,807
DISTRICT 8			
Tanner (D)	$1,001,398	$903,906 (90%)	$804,767
DISTRICT 9			
Cohen (D)	$748,876	$217,287 (29%)	$619,935
Ford (I)	$169,096	$1,000 (1%)	$169,084
White (R)	$227,452	$0 (0%)	$227,222

Texas

	RECEIPTS	FROM PACS	EXPENDITURES
SENIOR SENATOR - 2006			
Hutchison (R)	$6,378,589	$1,023,385 (16%)	$5,734,146
Radnofsky (D)	$1,482,207	$49,890 (3%)	$1,432,107
JUNIOR SENATOR - 2002			
Cornyn (R)	$9,615,872	$1,627,531 (17%)	$9,513,548
Kirk (D)	$9,517,001	$931,555 (10%)	$9,315,171
DISTRICT 1			
Gohmert (R)	$1,057,369	$228,552 (22%)	$955,344
DISTRICT 2			
Poe (R)	$1,020,015	$383,432 (38%)	$781,959
Binderim (D)	$16,189	$2,400 (15%)	$14,945
DISTRICT 3			
Johnson (R)	$1,167,853	$659,599 (56%)	$974,859
Dodd (D)	$40,475	$5,735 (14%)	$40,491
DISTRICT 4			
Hall (R)	$907,158	$462,250 (51%)	$942,635
Melancon (D)	$61,846	$4,260 (7%)	$63,897
DISTRICT 5			
Hensarling (R)	$1,472,926	$585,739 (40%)	$1,129,059
Thompson (D)	$22,670	$1,000 (4%)	$19,753
DISTRICT 6			
Barton (R)	$3,164,154	$1,826,166 (58%)	$2,351,932
Harris (D)	$28,421	$4,500 (16%)	$26,993
DISTRICT 7			
Culberson (R)	$718,882	$253,000 (35%)	$734,383
Henley (D)	$121,341	$2,000 (2%)	$122,145
DISTRICT 8			
Brady (R)	$515,795	$398,590 (77%)	$527,711
DISTRICT 9			
Green (D)	$431,655	$283,200 (66%)	$392,972
DISTRICT 10			
McCaul (R)	$1,155,543	$387,345 (34%)	$1,111,980
Ankrum (D)	$72,061	$2,050 (3%)	$64,633
Badnarik (LIBERT)	$439,678	$600 (0%)	$439,010
DISTRICT 11			
Conaway (R)	$1,005,167	$419,928 (42%)	$737,564
DISTRICT 12			
Granger (R)	$1,274,755	$433,881 (34%)	$1,350,752
Morris (D)	$13,709	$3,000 (22%)	$13,708
DISTRICT 13			
Thornberry (R)	$631,023	$146,350 (23%)	$551,841
Waun (D)	$27,417	$13,158 (48%)	$27,384
DISTRICT 14			
Paul (R)	$1,508,073	$31,740 (2%)	$1,469,488
Sklar (D)	$556,108	$150,850 (27%)	$552,798
DISTRICT 15			
Hinojosa (D)	$681,521	$371,025 (54%)	$497,420
Zamora (R)	$13,169	$0 (0%)	$13,841
DISTRICT 16			
Reyes (D)	$701,687	$354,271 (50%)	$681,551
DISTRICT 17			
Edwards (D)	$3,194,165	$1,493,323 (47%)	$3,138,215
Taylor (R)	$2,589,364	$233,845 (9%)	$2,515,527
DISTRICT 18			
Jackson-Lee (D)	$395,014	$136,650 (35%)	$502,818
DISTRICT 19			
Neugebauer (R)	$1,402,333	$537,090 (38%)	$1,203,930
Ricketts (D)	$88,833	$4,808 (5%)	$88,830
DISTRICT 20			
Gonzalez (D)	$761,665	$497,556 (65%)	$694,162
DISTRICT 21			
Smith (R)	$1,328,200	$421,676 (32%)	$1,632,039
Courage (D)	$368,118	$78,625 (21%)	$352,243

Calvert (I)	$28,700	$0 (0%)	$33,755
Strohm (LIBERT)	$9,387	$0 (0%)	$8,803
DISTRICT 22 †			
Lampson (D)	$3,730,044	$765,637 (21%)	$3,578,097
Sekula-Gibbs (R)	$993,529	$293,042 (29%)	$912,977
Smither (LIBERT)	$63,378	$0 (0%)	$54,117
Richardson (R)	$13,500	$0 (0%)	$39,375
Reasbeck (R)	$9,125	$0 (0%)	$8,442
DISTRICT 23			
Rodriguez (D)	$1,046,200	$321,554 (31%)	$963,647
Bonilla (R)	$3,600,091	$1,733,012 (48%)	$3,821,285
Uresti (D)	$56,830	$15,000 (26%)	$56,313
Gilliland (D)	$1,055,572	$1,000 (0%)	$1,055,818
Beltran (D)	$24,900	$0 (0%)	$23,626
Bolanos (D)	$28,064	$1,000 (4%)	$29,293
DISTRICT 24			
Marchant (R)	$748,190	$430,023 (57%)	$554,709
Page (D)	$11,166	$0 (0%)	$10,135
DISTRICT 25			
Doggett (D)	$1,089,095	$299,335 (27%)	$570,699
Rostig (R)	$7,274	$500 (7%)	$7,074
DISTRICT 26			
Burgess (R)	$839,913	$572,947 (68%)	$942,669
Barnwell (D)	$17,516	$3,750 (21%)	$16,612
DISTRICT 27			
Ortiz (D)	$702,750	$195,807 (28%)	$712,499
Vaden (R)	$142,200	$0 (0%)	$102,011
DISTRICT 28			
Cuellar (D)	$1,718,752	$586,556 (34%)	$1,674,231
Enriquez (D)	$405,775	$0 (0%)	$408,762
DISTRICT 29			
Green (D)	$728,000	$569,156 (78%)	$703,804
Story (R)	$28,058	$250 (1%)	$27,434
DISTRICT 30			
Johnson (D)	$411,189	$153,350 (37%)	$410,117
Aurbach (R)	$73,700	$0 (0%)	$73,614
DISTRICT 31			
Carter (R)	$876,895	$384,585 (44%)	$908,827
Harrell (D)	$207,441	$11,700 (6%)	$207,294
DISTRICT 32			
Sessions (R)	$1,878,156	$820,122 (44%)	$1,762,182
Pryor (D)	$491,942	$29,295 (6%)	$460,074

Utah

	RECEIPTS	FROM PACS	EXPENDITURES
SENIOR SENATOR - 2006			
Hatch (R)	$4,880,281	$1,765,142 (36%)	$3,340,902
Price (PC)	$6,172	$200 (3%)	$1,375
Bradley (CNSTP)	$24,733	$0 (0%)	$8,225
JUNIOR SENATOR - 2004			
Bennett (R)	$2,755,838	$1,093,642 (40%)	$2,649,234
Van Dam (D)	$118,226	$18,750 (16%)	$116,959
DISTRICT 1			
Bishop (R)	$364,797	$190,000 (52%)	$262,727
Olsen (D)	$60,115	$2,500 (4%)	$60,103
Hudson (CNSTP)	$6,368	$0 (0%)	$6,340
DISTRICT 2			
Matheson (D)	$1,860,573	$1,163,671 (63%)	$1,624,165
Christensen (R)	$865,800	$23,484 (3%)	$834,661
DISTRICT 3			
Cannon (R)	$1,168,740	$739,264 (63%)	$1,159,603
Burridge (D)	$62,396	$10,000 (16%)	$69,753
Noorlander (CNSTP)	$26,602	$0 (0%)	$26,454

Vermont

	RECEIPTS	FROM PACS	EXPENDITURES
SENIOR SENATOR - 2004			
Leahy (D)	$2,292,393	$1,500 (0%)	$1,531,833
McMullen (R)	$731,028	$2,100 (0%)	$736,126
JUNIOR SENATOR - 2006			
Sanders (I)	$6,179,359	$551,038 (9%)	$6,004,222
Tarrant (R)	$7,315,854	$0 (0%)	$7,300,392
AT LARGE			
Welch (D)	$2,066,308	$571,539 (28%)	$1,737,958
Rainville (R)	$1,133,132	$297,806 (26%)	$1,132,968

Virginia

	RECEIPTS	FROM PACS	EXPENDITURES
SENIOR SENATOR - 2002			
Warner (R)	$2,617,764	$887,268 (34%)	$1,674,292
Spannaus (I)	$65,529	$500 (1%)	$65,550
Hornberger (I)	$62,406	$0 (0%)	$61,838
JUNIOR SENATOR - 2006			
Webb (D)	$8,590,412	$468,957 (5%)	$8,558,861
Allen (R)	$14,994,264	$2,843,031 (19%)	$16,071,564
Parker (IGREEN)	$22,784	$0 (0%)	$19,992
DISTRICT 1			
Davis (R)	$578,103	$275,782 (48%)	$636,419
O'Donnell (D)	$112,960	$18,700 (17%)	$89,531
Pixton (I)	$9,275	$2,000 (22%)	$10,097
DISTRICT 2			
Drake (R)	$2,350,037	$1,214,196 (52%)	$2,348,983
Kellam (D)	$1,687,128	$472,000 (28%)	$1,703,424
DISTRICT 3			
Scott (D)	$336,423	$211,258 (63%)	$307,440
DISTRICT 4			
Forbes (R)	$650,871	$244,352 (38%)	$566,651
DISTRICT 5			
Goode (R)	$996,385	$284,276 (29%)	$1,064,515
Weed (D)	$607,808	$18,500 (3%)	$577,982
DISTRICT 6			
Goodlatte (R)	$1,212,609	$687,378 (57%)	$1,029,538
Peery (I)	$8,284	$0 (0%)	$8,140
DISTRICT 7			
Cantor (R)	$3,310,828	$1,702,925 (51%)	$3,499,247
Nachman (D)	$108,060	$4,525 (4%)	$108,061
Blanton (I)	$54,863	$0 (0%)	$57,488
DISTRICT 8			
Moran (D)	$1,339,440	$439,930 (33%)	$1,054,506
O'Donoghue (R)	$119,276	$3,633 (3%)	$115,167
Hurysz (I)	$16,628	$0 (0%)	$16,576
DISTRICT 9			
Boucher (D)	$1,422,762	$936,074 (66%)	$1,249,993
Carrico (R)	$71,256	$19,058 (27%)	$69,980

	RECEIPTS	FROM PACS	EXPENDITURES
DISTRICT 10			
Wolf (R)	$1,735,555	$531,675 (31%)	$1,793,567
Feder (D)	$1,580,461	$231,105 (15%)	$1,573,523
Wood (LIBERT)	$10,252	$853 (8%)	$9,817
Nigam (I)	$2,050	$0 (0%)	$8,213
DISTRICT 11			
Davis (R)	$2,784,636	$898,052 (32%)	$3,301,041
Hurst (D)	$357,394	$4,200 (1%)	$360,563

Washington

	RECEIPTS	FROM PACS	EXPENDITURES
SENIOR SENATOR - 2004			
Murray (D)	$11,081,050	$1,691,587 (15%)	$11,556,148
Nethercutt (R)	$8,011,311	$1,326,952 (17%)	$7,726,296
JUNIOR SENATOR - 2006			
Cantwell (D)	$13,725,773	$55,514 (0%)	$14,013,932
McGavick (R)	$10,853,230	$978,417 (9%)	$10,842,132
Guthrie (LIBERT)	$1,255,235	$0 (0%)	$1,243,606
Dixon (GREEN)	$87,749	$0 (0%)	$87,118
Adair (I)	$16,199	$0 (0%)	$16,079
DISTRICT 1			
Inslee (D)	$885,876	$424,418 (48%)	$929,507
Ishmael (R)	$43,733	$0 (0%)	$43,036
DISTRICT 2			
Larsen (D)	$1,456,945	$688,063 (47%)	$1,550,524
Roulstone (R)	$695,344	$169,050 (24%)	$698,209
DISTRICT 3			
Baird (D)	$834,004	$372,737 (45%)	$735,464
Messmore (R)	$150,237	$0 (0%)	$147,274
DISTRICT 4			
Hastings (R)	$567,224	$250,949 (44%)	$621,673
Wright (D)	$298,242	$13,260 (4%)	$293,969
DISTRICT 5			
Rodgers (R)	$1,851,062	$864,528 (47%)	$1,931,501
Goldmark (D)	$1,204,878	$202,855 (17%)	$1,198,156
DISTRICT 6			
Dicks (D)	$975,071	$445,139 (46%)	$995,770
DISTRICT 7			
McDermott (D)	$888,559	$222,391 (25%)	$496,250
Beren (R)	$22,826	$0 (0%)	$22,032
Noreen (I)	$79,864	$0 (0%)	$79,946
DISTRICT 8			
Reichert (R)	$3,045,766	$1,168,872 (38%)	$3,051,918
Burner (D)	$3,080,927	$567,771 (18%)	$3,048,902
DISTRICT 9			
Smith (D)	$739,885	$411,784 (56%)	$642,549
Cofchin (R)	$39,838	$0 (0%)	$43,043

West Virginia

	RECEIPTS	FROM PACS	EXPENDITURES
SENIOR SENATOR - 2006			
Byrd (D)	$5,114,217	$1,158,555 (23%)	$4,944,546
Raese (R)	$3,163,848	$128,184 (4%)	$3,147,967
JUNIOR SENATOR - 2002			
Rockefeller (D)	$2,466,775	$1,010,101 (41%)	$2,158,227
Wolfe (R)	$136,410	$3,742 (3%)	$136,373
DISTRICT 1			
Mollohan (D)	$1,622,991	$588,150 (36%)	$1,726,707
Wakim (R)	$766,204	$254,142 (33%)	$729,046
DISTRICT 2			
Capito (R)	$2,440,788	$848,902 (35%)	$2,349,741
Callaghan (D)	$620,626	$35,000 (6%)	$626,876
DISTRICT 3			
Rahall (D)	$565,269	$275,236 (49%)	$648,642
Wolfe (R)	$48,006	$1,000 (2%)	$44,188

Wisconsin

	RECEIPTS	FROM PACS	EXPENDITURES
SENIOR SENATOR - 2006			
Kohl (D)	$6,438,431	$450 (0%)	$6,347,126
Lorge (R)	$175,772	$0 (0%)	$176,987
Vogeler (WG)	$49,733	$227 (0%)	$48,669
JUNIOR SENATOR - 2004			
Feingold (D)	$8,377,885	$684,717 (8%)	$9,239,908
Michels (R)	$5,547,838	$397,532 (7%)	$5,542,087
DISTRICT 1			
Ryan (R)	$1,462,674	$697,273 (48%)	$1,316,881
Thomas (D)	$20,581	$0 (0%)	$20,581
DISTRICT 2			
Baldwin (D)	$1,565,234	$331,897 (21%)	$1,617,301
Magnum (R)	$969,832	$12,750 (1%)	$985,933
DISTRICT 3			
Kind (D)	$933,903	$480,552 (51%)	$780,394
Nelson (R)	$244,439	$9,100 (4%)	$247,922
DISTRICT 4			
Moore (D)	$565,396	$342,800 (61%)	$668,855
Rivera (R)	$19,805	$0 (0%)	$19,723
DISTRICT 5			
Sensenbrenner (R)	$774,141	$527,711 (68%)	$831,766
Kennedy (D)	$339,667	$74,350 (22%)	$353,166
Levis (WG)	$19,475	$0 (0%)	$19,474
DISTRICT 6			
Petri (R)	$645,367	$434,400 (67%)	$913,108
DISTRICT 7			
Obey (D)	$1,207,763	$698,763 (58%)	$1,400,489
Reid (R)	$217,845	$5,750 (3%)	$211,609
DISTRICT 8			
Kagen (D)	$3,239,730	$316,700 (10%)	$3,187,330
Gard (R)	$2,831,675	$992,709 (35%)	$2,831,522

Wyoming

	RECEIPTS	FROM PACS	EXPENDITURES
SENIOR SENATOR - 2006			
Thomas (R)	$1,622,792	$977,474 (60%)	$1,392,057
Groutage (D)	$141,899	$5,000 (4%)	$141,164
JUNIOR SENATOR - 2002			
Enzi (R)	$1,175,276	$791,568 (67%)	$850,095
Corcoran (D)	$8,488	$1,275 (15%)	$8,467
AT LARGE			
Cubin (R)	$1,254,499	$845,983 (67%)	$1,265,862
Trauner (D)	$985,453	$148,018 (15%)	$940,182

House Committees

House standing and select committees are listed alphabetically. Membership is in order of seniority on the panel. Subcommittee membership is listed in order of seniority. Partisan committees are on page 1194.

On full committee rosters, members of the majority party, Democrats, are shown in roman type; members of the minority party, Republicans, are shown in *italic* type. Independents are labeled. A vacancy indicates that a committee or subcommittee seat had not been filled at press time, April 2007. Subcommittee vacancies do not necessarily indicate vacancies on full committees or vice versa.

The telephone area code for Washington, D.C., is 202. The ZIP code for all House office buildings is 20515.

AGRICULTURE

225-2171 1301 Longworth
Party Ratio: D 25-R 21
Collin C. Peterson, D-Minn., chairman

Tim Holden, Pa.
Mike McIntyre, N.C.
Bob Etheridge, N.C.
Leonard L. Boswell, Iowa
Joe Baca, Calif.
Dennis Cardoza, Calif.
David Scott, Ga.
Jim Marshall, Ga.
Stephanie Herseth-Sandlin, S.D.
Henry Cuellar, Texas
Jim Costa, Calif.
John Salazar, Colo.
Brad Ellsworth, Ind.
Nancy Boyda, Kan.
Zack Space, Ohio
Tim Walz, Minn.
Kirsten Gillibrand, N.Y.
Steve Kagen, Wis.
Earl Pomeroy, N.D.
Lincoln Davis, Tenn.
John Barrow, Ga.
Nick Lampson, Texas
Joe Donnelly, Ind.
Tim Mahoney, Fla.

Robert W. Goodlatte, Va.
Terry Everett, Ala.
Frank D. Lucas, Okla.
Jerry Moran, Kan.
Robin Hayes, N.C.
Timothy V. Johnson, Ill.
Sam Graves, Mo.
Jo Bonner, Ala.
Mike D. Rogers, Ala.
Steve King, Iowa
Marilyn Musgrave, Colo.
Randy Neugebauer, Texas
Charles Boustany Jr., La.
John R. "Randy" Kuhl Jr., N.Y.
Virginia Foxx, N.C.
K. Michael Conaway, Texas
Jeff Fortenberry, Neb.
Jean Schmidt, Ohio
Adrian Smith, Neb.
Kevin McCarthy, Calif.
Tim Walberg, Mich.

CONSERVATION, CREDIT, ENERGY & RESEARCH

Holden, chairman

Democrats: Herseth-Sandlin, Cuellar, Costa, Ellsworth, Space, Walz, Scott, Salazar, Boyda, Gillibrand, Cardoza, Boswell, Kagen
Republicans: Lucas, Rogers, King, Fortenberry, Schmidt, Walberg, Everett, Moran, Hayes, Graves, Bonner, Musgrave

GENERAL FARM COMMODITIES & RISK MANAGEMENT

Etheridge, chairman

Democrats: Scott, Marshall, Salazar, Boyda, Herseth-Sandlin, Ellsworth, Space, Walz, Pomeroy
Republicans: Moran, Johnson, Graves, Boustany, Conaway, Lucas, Neugebauer, McCarthy

HORTICULTURE & ORGANIC AGRICULTURE

Cardoza, chairman

Democrats: Etheridge, Davis, Mahoney, Barrow, Gillibrand
Republicans: Neugebauer, Kuhl, Foxx, McCarthy, Conaway

LIVESTOCK, DAIRY & POULTRY

Boswell, chairman

Democrats: Gillibrand, Kagen, Holden, Baca, Cardoza, Lampson, Donnelly, Costa, Mahoney
Republicans: Hayes, Rogers, King, Foxx, Conaway, Schmidt, Smith, Walberg

OPERATIONS, OVERSIGHT, NUTRITION & FORESTRY

Baca, chairman

Democrats: Pomeroy, Davis, Lampson, Kagen, Boyda
Republicans: Bonner, Moran, King, Neugebauer, Boustany

SPECIALTY CROPS, RURAL DEVELOPMENT & FOREIGN AGRICULTURE

McIntyre, chairman

Democrats: Marshall, Cuellar, Salazar, Barrow, Pomeroy
Republicans: Musgrave, Everett, Smith, Fortenberry, Hayes

APPROPRIATIONS

225-2771 H-218 Capitol
Party Ratio: D 37-R 29
David R. Obey, D-Wis., chairman

John P. Murtha, Pa.
Norm Dicks, Wash.
Alan B. Mollohan, W.Va.
Marcy Kaptur, Ohio
Peter J. Visclosky, Ind.
Nita M. Lowey, N.Y.
José E. Serrano, N.Y.
Rosa DeLauro, Conn.
James P. Moran, Va.
John W. Olver, Mass.
Ed Pastor, Ariz.
David E. Price, N.C.
Chet Edwards, Texas
Robert E. "Bud" Cramer, Ala.
Patrick J. Kennedy, R.I.
Maurice D. Hinchey, N.Y.
Lucille Roybal-Allard, Calif.
Sam Farr, Calif.
Jesse L. Jackson Jr., Ill.
Carolyn Cheeks Kilpatrick, Mich.
Allen Boyd, Fla.
Chaka Fattah, Pa.
Steven R. Rothman, N.J.
Sanford D. Bishop Jr., Ga.
Marion Berry, Ark.
Barbara Lee, Calif.
Tom Udall, N.M.
Adam B. Schiff, Calif.
Michael M. Honda, Calif.
Betty McCollum, Minn.
Steve Israel, N.Y.
Tim Ryan, Ohio
C.A. Dutch Ruppersberger, Md.
Ben Chandler, Ky.
Debbie Wasserman-Schultz, Fla.
Ciro D. Rodriguez, Texas

Jerry Lewis, Calif.
C.W. Bill Young, Fla.
Ralph Regula, Ohio
Harold Rogers, Ky.
Frank R. Wolf, Va.
James T. Walsh, N.Y.
David L. Hobson, Ohio
Joe Knollenberg, Mich.
Jack Kingston, Ga.
Rodney Frelinghuysen, N.J.
Roger Wicker, Miss.
Todd Tiahrt, Kan.
Zach Wamp, Tenn.
Tom Latham, Iowa
Robert B. Aderholt, Ala.
Jo Ann Emerson, Mo.
Kay Granger, Texas
John E. Peterson, Pa.
Virgil H. Goode Jr., Va.
Ray LaHood, Ill.
Dave Weldon, Fla.
Mike Simpson, Idaho
John Culberson, Texas
Mark Steven Kirk, Ill.
Ander Crenshaw, Fla.
Denny Rehberg, Mont.
John Carter, Texas
Rodney Alexander, La.
Ken Calvert, Calif.

AGRICULTURE
DeLauro, chairwoman

Democrats: Hinchey, Farr, Boyd, Bishop, Kaptur, Jackson, Rothman
Republicans: Kingston, Latham, Emerson, LaHood, Alexander

COMMERCE-JUSTICE-SCIENCE
Mollohan, chairman

Democrats: Kennedy, Fattah, Ruppersberger, Schiff, Honda, DeLauro, Price
Republicans: Frelinghuysen, Culberson, Rogers, Latham, Aderholt

DEFENSE
Murtha, chairman

Democrats: Dicks, Visclosky, Moran, Kaptur, Cramer, Boyd, Rothman, Bishop
Republicans: Young, Hobson, Frelinghuysen, Tiahrt, Wicker, Kingston

ENERGY-WATER
Visclosky, chairman

Democrats: Edwards, Pastor, Berry, Fattah, Israel, Ryan, Serrano, Olver
Republicans: Hobson, Wamp, Emerson, Simpson, Granger, Vacancy

FINANCIAL SERVICES
Serrano, chairman

Democrats: Kilpatrick, Ruppersberger, Wasserman-Schultz, Visclosky, Moran, Cramer, Hinchey
Republicans: Regula, Latham, Kirk, Rehberg, Alexander

HOMELAND SECURITY
Price, chairman

Democrats: Serrano, Kilpatrick, Rodriguez, Lowey, Edwards, Roybal-Allard, Farr, Fattah
Republicans: Rogers, Carter, Aderholt, Granger, Peterson, Culberson

INTERIOR-ENVIRONMENT
Dicks, chairman

Democrats: Moran, Hinchey, Olver, Mollohan, Udall, Chandler, Pastor
Republicans: Tiahrt, Peterson, Emerson, Goode, Vacancy

LABOR-HHS-EDUCATION
Obey, chairman

Democrats: Lowey, DeLauro, Jackson, Kennedy, Roybal-Allard, Lee, Udall, Honda, McCollum, Ryan
Republicans: Walsh, Regula, Peterson, Weldon, Simpson, Rehberg

LEGISLATIVE BRANCH
Wasserman-Schultz, chairwoman

Democrats: Lee, Udall, Honda, McCollum, Ruppersberger
Republicans: Wamp, LaHood, Vacancy

MILITARY CONSTRUCTION-VA
Edwards, chairman

Democrats: Farr, Dicks, Mollohan, Kennedy, Boyd, Bishop, Berry
Republicans: Wicker, Crenshaw, Young, Carter, Granger

STATE-FOREIGN OPERATIONS
Lowey, chairwoman

Democrats: Jackson, Schiff, Israel, Chandler, Rothman, Lee, McCollum
Republicans: Wolf, Knollenberg, Kirk, Crenshaw, Weldon

TRANSPORTATION-HUD
Olver, chairman

Democrats: Pastor, Rodriguez, Kaptur, Price, Cramer, Roybal-Allard, Berry
Republicans: Knollenberg, Wolf, Aderholt, Walsh, Goode

SELECT INTELLIGENCE OVERSIGHT *
Holt, chairman

Democrats: Obey, Murtha, Reyes, Dicks, Lowey, Cramer, Schiff
Republicans: LaHood, Lewis, Young, Hoekstra, Frelinghuysen

** The panel's required designees from the Select Intelligence Committee are Peter Hoekstra, R-Mich., Rush D. Holt, D-N.J., and Silvestre Reyes, D-Texas.*

ARMED SERVICES

225-4151 2120 Rayburn
Party Ratio: D 34-R 28
Ike Skelton, D-Mo., chairman

John M. Spratt Jr., S.C.
Solomon P. Ortiz, Texas
Gene Taylor, Miss.
Neil Abercrombie, Hawaii
Martin T. Meehan, Mass.
Silvestre Reyes, Texas
Vic Snyder, Ark.
Adam Smith, Wash.
Loretta Sanchez, Calif.
Mike McIntyre, N.C.
Ellen O. Tauscher, Calif.
Robert A. Brady, Pa.
Robert E. Andrews, N.J.
Susan A. Davis, Calif.
Rick Larsen, Wash.
Jim Cooper, Tenn.
Jim Marshall, Ga.
Madeleine Z. Bordallo, Guam
Mark Udall, Colo.
Dan Boren, Okla.
Brad Ellsworth, Ind.
Nancy Boyda, Kan.
Patrick J. Murphy, Pa.
Hank Johnson, Ga.
Carol Shea-Porter, N.H.
Joe Courtney, Conn.
Dave Loebsack, Iowa
Kirsten Gillibrand, N.Y.
Joe Sestak, Pa.
Gabrielle Giffords, Ariz.
Elijah E. Cummings, Md.
Kendrick B. Meek, Fla.
Kathy Castor, Fla.

Duncan Hunter, Calif.
H. James Saxton, N.J.
John M. McHugh, N.Y.
Terry Everett, Ala.
Roscoe G. Bartlett, Md.
Howard P. "Buck" McKeon, Calif.
William M. "Mac" Thornberry, Texas
Walter B. Jones, N.C.
Robin Hayes, N.C.
Jo Ann Davis, Va.
Todd Akin, Mo.
J. Randy Forbes, Va.
Jeff Miller, Fla.
Joe Wilson, S.C.
Frank A. LoBiondo, N.J.
Tom Cole, Okla.
Rob Bishop, Utah
Michael R. Turner, Ohio
John Kline, Minn.
Candice S. Miller, Mich.
Phil Gingrey, Ga.
Mike D. Rogers, Ala.
Trent Franks, Ariz.
Bill Shuster, Pa.
Thelma Drake, Va.
Cathy McMorris Rodgers, Wash.
K. Michael Conaway, Texas
Geoff Davis, Ky.

AIR & LAND FORCES
Abercrombie, chairman

Democrats: Spratt, Ortiz, Reyes, Smith, McIntyre, Tauscher, Brady, Marshall, Boren, Johnson, Sestak, Giffords, Meek, Castor
Republicans: Saxton, McKeon, Miller (Fla.), Wilson, LoBiondo, Cole, Bishop, Turner, Miller (Mich.), Gingrey, Rodgers, Davis (Ky.), Akin

MILITARY PERSONNEL
Snyder, chairman

Democrats: Meehan, Sanchez, Davis (Calif.), Boyda, Murphy, Shea-Porter
Republicans: McHugh, Kline, Drake, Jones, Wilson

OVERSIGHT & INVESTIGATIONS
Meehan, chairman

Democrats: Spratt, Snyder, Sanchez, Tauscher, Andrews, Davis (Calif.), Cooper, Sestak
Republicans: Akin, Bartlett, Jones, Miller (Fla.), Gingrey, Conaway, Davis (Ky.)

READINESS
Ortiz, chairman

Democrats: Taylor, Reyes, Sanchez, Brady, Marshall, Bordallo, Udall, Boren, Boyda, Shea-Porter, Courtney, Loebsack, Giffords, Cummings
Republicans: Davis (Va.), Jones, Forbes, Rogers, McHugh, McKeon, Hayes, LoBiondo, Cole, Bishop, Miller (Mich.), Franks, Rodgers

SEAPOWER & EXPEDITIONARY FORCES
Taylor, chairman

Democrats: Abercrombie, Larsen, Bordallo, Ellsworth, Courtney, Gillibrand, Sestak
Republicans: Bartlett, Everett, Davis (Va.), Forbes, Wilson, Vacancy

STRATEGIC FORCES
Tauscher, chairwoman

Democrats: Spratt, Reyes, Larsen, Cooper, Johnson, Loebsack
Republicans: Everett, Franks, Thornberry, Turner, Rogers

TERRORISM, UNCONVENTIONAL THREATS & CAPABILITIES
Smith, chairman

Democrats: McIntyre, Andrews, Cooper, Marshall, Udall, Ellsworth, Gillibrand, Castor
Republicans: Thornberry, Hayes, Kline, Drake, Conaway, Saxton, Vacancy

BUDGET

226-7200 207 Cannon
Party Ratio: D 22-R 17
John M. Spratt Jr., D-S.C., chairman

Rosa DeLauro, Conn.
Chet Edwards, Texas
Jim Cooper, Tenn.
Tom Allen, Maine
Allyson Y. Schwartz, Pa.
Marcy Kaptur, Ohio
Xavier Becerra, Calif.
Lloyd Doggett, Texas
Earl Blumenauer, Ore.
Marion Berry, Ark.
Allen Boyd, Fla.
Jim McGovern, Mass.
Betty Sutton, Ohio
Robert E. Andrews, N.J.
Robert C. Scott, Va.
Bob Etheridge, N.C.
Darlene Hooley, Ore.
Brian Baird, Wash.
Dennis Moore, Kan.
Timothy H. Bishop, N.Y.
Gwen Moore, Wis.

Paul D. Ryan, Wis.
J. Gresham Barrett, S.C.
Jo Bonner, Ala.
Scott Garrett, N.J.
Mario Diaz-Balart, Fla.
Jeb Hensarling, Texas
Dan Lungren, Calif.
Mike Simpson, Idaho
Patrick T. McHenry, N.C.
Connie Mack, Fla.
K. Michael Conaway, Texas
John Campbell, Calif.
Pat Tiberi, Ohio
Jon Porter, Nev.
Rodney Alexander, La.
Adrian Smith, Neb.
Vacancy

EDUCATION & LABOR

225-3725 2181 Rayburn
Party Ratio: D 27-R 22
George Miller, D-Calif., chairman

Dale E. Kildee, Mich.
Donald M. Payne, N.J.
Robert E. Andrews, N.J.
Robert C. Scott, Va.
Lynn Woolsey, Calif.
Rubén Hinojosa, Texas
Carolyn McCarthy, N.Y.
John F. Tierney, Mass.
Dennis J. Kucinich, Ohio
David Wu, Ore.
Rush D. Holt, N.J.
Susan A. Davis, Calif.
Danny K. Davis, Ill.
Raúl M. Grijalva, Ariz.
Timothy H. Bishop, N.Y.
Linda T. Sánchez, Calif.
John Sarbanes, Md.
Joe Sestak, Pa.
Dave Loebsack, Iowa
Mazie K. Hirono, Hawaii
Jason Altmire, Pa.
John Yarmuth, Ky.
Phil Hare, Ill.
Yvette D. Clarke, N.Y.
Joe Courtney, Conn.
Carol Shea-Porter, N.H.

Howard P. "Buck" McKeon, Calif.
Tom Petri, Wis.
Peter Hoekstra, Mich.
Michael N. Castle, Del.
Mark Souder, Ind.
Vernon J. Ehlers, Mich.
Judy Biggert, Ill.
Todd R. Platts, Pa.
Ric Keller, Fla.
Joe Wilson, S.C.
John Kline, Minn.
Cathy McMorris Rodgers, Wash.
Kenny Marchant, Texas
Tom Price, Ga.
Luis Fortuño, P.R.
Charles Boustany Jr., La.
Virginia Foxx, N.C.
John R. "Randy" Kuhl Jr., N.Y.
Rob Bishop, Utah
David Davis, Tenn.
Tim Walberg, Mich.
Dean Heller, Nev.

EARLY CHILDHOOD, ELEMENTARY & SECONDARY EDUCATION

Kildee, chairman

Democrats: Scott, Kucinich, Davis (Calif.), Davis (Ill.), Grijalva, Payne, Holt, Sánchez, Sarbanes, Sestak, Loebsack, Hirono, Hare, Woolsey, Hinojosa
Republicans: Castle, Hoekstra, Souder, Ehlers, Biggert, Fortuño, Bishop, Platts, Keller, Wilson, Boustany, Kuhl, Heller

HEALTH, EMPLOYMENT, LABOR & PENSIONS

Andrews, chairman

Democrats: Miller, Kildee, McCarthy, Tierney, Wu, Holt, Sánchez, Sestak, Loebsack, Hare, Clarke, Courtney
Republicans: Kline, McKeon, Marchant, Boustany, Davis (Tenn.), Hoekstra, Rodgers, Price, Foxx, Walberg

HEALTHY FAMILIES & COMMUNITIES

McCarthy, chairwoman

Democrats: Clarke, Shea-Porter, Kucinich, Grijalva, Sarbanes, Altmire, Yarmuth
Republicans: Platts, McKeon, Marchant, Fortuño, Davis, Heller

HIGHER EDUCATION, LIFELONG LEARNING & COMPETITIVENESS

Hinojosa, chairman

Democrats: Miller, Tierney, Wu, Bishop, Altmire, Yarmuth, Courtney, Andrews, Scott, Davis (Calif.), Davis (Ill.), Hirono
Republicans: Keller, Petri, Rodgers, Foxx, Kuhl, Walberg, Castle, Souder, Ehlers, Biggert

WORKFORCE PROTECTIONS

Woolsey, chairwoman

Democrats: Payne, Bishop, Shea-Porter, Hare
Republicans: Wilson, Price, Kline

ENERGY & COMMERCE

225-2927 2125 Rayburn
Party Ratio: D 31-R 26
John D. Dingell, D-Mich., chairman

Henry A. Waxman, Calif.
Edward J. Markey, Mass.
Rick Boucher, Va.
Edolphus Towns, N.Y.
Frank Pallone Jr., N.J.
Bart Gordon, Tenn.
Bobby L. Rush, Ill.
Anna G. Eshoo, Calif.
Bart Stupak, Mich.
Eliot L. Engel, N.Y.
Albert R. Wynn, Md.
Gene Green, Texas
Diana DeGette, Colo.
Lois Capps, Calif.
Mike Doyle, Pa.
Jane Harman, Calif.
Tom Allen, Maine
Jan Schakowsky, Ill.
Hilda L. Solis, Calif.
Charlie Gonzalez, Texas
Jay Inslee, Wash.
Tammy Baldwin, Wis.
Mike Ross, Ark.
Darlene Hooley, Ore.
Anthony Weiner, N.Y.
Jim Matheson, Utah
G.K. Butterfield, N.C.
Charlie Melancon, La.
John Barrow, Ga.
Baron P. Hill, Ind.

Joe L. Barton, Texas
Ralph M. Hall, Texas
J. Dennis Hastert, Ill.
Fred Upton, Mich.
Cliff Stearns, Fla.
Nathan Deal, Ga.
Edward Whitfield, Ky.
Barbara Cubin, Wyo.
John Shimkus, Ill.
Heather A. Wilson, N.M.
John Shadegg, Ariz.
Charles W. "Chip" Pickering Jr., Miss.
Vito J. Fossella, N.Y.
Steve Buyer, Ind.
George Radanovich, Calif.
Joe Pitts, Pa.
Mary Bono, Calif.
Greg Walden, Ore.
Lee Terry, Neb.
Mike Ferguson, N.J.
Mike Rogers, Mich.
Sue Myrick, N.C.
John Sullivan, Okla.
Tim Murphy, Pa.
Michael C. Burgess, Texas
Marsha Blackburn, Tenn.

COMMERCE, TRADE & CONSUMER PROTECTION

Rush, chairman

Democrats: Schakowsky, Butterfield, Barrow, Hill, Markey, Boucher, Towns, DeGette, Gonzalez, Ross, Hooley, Weiner, Matheson, Melancon
Republicans: Stearns, Hastert, Whitfield, Pickering, Fossella, Radanovich, Pitts, Bono, Terry, Myrick, Burgess, Blackburn

ENERGY & AIR QUALITY
Boucher, chairman

Democrats: Butterfield, Melancon, Barrow, Waxman, Markey, Wynn, Doyle, Harman, Allen, Gonzalez, Inslee, Baldwin, Ross, Hooley, Weiner, Matheson
Republicans: Hastert, Hall, Upton, Whitfield, Shimkus, Shadegg, Pickering, Buyer, Bono, Walden, Rogers, Myrick, Sullivan, Burgess

ENVIRONMENT & HAZARDOUS MATERIALS
Wynn, chairman

Democrats: Pallone, Stupak, Capps, Allen, Solis, Baldwin, Butterfield, Barrow, Hill, DeGette, Weiner, Waxman, Green, Schakowsky
Republicans: Shimkus, Stearns, Deal, Wilson, Shadegg, Fossella, Radanovich, Pitts, Terry, Rogers, Sullivan, Murphy

HEALTH
Pallone, chairman

Democrats: Waxman, Towns, Gordon, Eshoo, Green, DeGette, Capps, Allen, Baldwin, Engel, Schakowsky, Solis, Ross, Hooley, Weiner, Matheson
Republicans: Deal, Hall, Cubin, Wilson, Shadegg, Buyer, Pitts, Ferguson, Rogers, Myrick, Sullivan, Murphy, Burgess, Blackburn

OVERSIGHT & INVESTIGATIONS
Stupak, chairman

Democrats: DeGette, Melancon, Waxman, Green, Doyle, Schakowsky, Inslee
Republicans: Whitfield, Walden, Ferguson, Murphy, Burgess, Blackburn

TELECOMMUNICATIONS & THE INTERNET
Markey, chairman

Democrats: Doyle, Harman, Gonzalez, Inslee, Hill, Boucher, Towns, Pallone, Gordon, Rush, Eshoo, Stupak, Engel, Green, Capps, Solis
Republicans: Upton, Hastert, Stearns, Deal, Cubin, Shimkus, Wilson, Pickering, Fossella, Radanovich, Bono, Walden, Terry, Ferguson

FINANCIAL SERVICES

225-4247 2129 Rayburn
Party Ratio: D 37-R 33
Barney Frank, D-Mass., chairman

Paul E. Kanjorski, Pa.
Maxine Waters, Calif.
Carolyn B. Maloney, N.Y.
Luis V. Gutierrez, Ill.
Nydia M. Velázquez, N.Y.
Melvin Watt, N.C.
Gary L. Ackerman, N.Y.
Julia Carson, Ind.
Brad Sherman, Calif.
Gregory W. Meeks, N.Y.
Dennis Moore, Kan.
Michael E. Capuano, Mass.
Rubén Hinojosa, Texas
William Lacy Clay, Mo.
Carolyn McCarthy, N.Y.
Joe Baca, Calif.
Stephen F. Lynch, Mass.
Brad Miller, N.C.
David Scott, Ga.
Al Green, Texas
Emanuel Cleaver II, Mo.
Melissa Bean, Ill.
Gwen Moore, Wis.
Lincoln Davis, Tenn.
Albio Sires, N.J.
Paul W. Hodes, N.H.
Keith Ellison, Minn.
Ron Klein, Fla.
Tim Mahoney, Fla.
Charlie Wilson, Ohio
Ed Perlmutter, Colo.
Christopher S. Murphy, Conn.
Joe Donnelly, Ind.
Robert Wexler, Fla.
Jim Marshall, Ga.
Dan Boren, Okla.

Spencer Bachus, Ala.
Richard H. Baker, La.
Deborah Pryce, Ohio
Michael N. Castle, Del.
Peter T. King, N.Y.
Ed Royce, Calif.
Frank D. Lucas, Okla.
Ron Paul, Texas
Paul E. Gillmor, Ohio
Steven C. LaTourette, Ohio
Donald Manzullo, Ill.
Walter B. Jones, N.C.
Judy Biggert, Ill.
Christopher Shays, Conn.
Gary G. Miller, Calif.
Shelley Moore Capito, W.Va.
Tom Feeney, Fla.
Jeb Hensarling, Texas
Scott Garrett, N.J.
Ginny Brown-Waite, Fla.
J. Gresham Barrett, S.C.
Jim Gerlach, Pa.
Steve Pearce, N.M.
Randy Neugebauer, Texas
Tom Price, Ga.
Geoff Davis, Ky.
Patrick T. McHenry, N.C.
John Campbell, Calif.
Adam H. Putnam, Fla.
Michele Bachmann, Minn.
Peter Roskam, Ill.
Kenny Marchant, Texas
Thaddeus McCotter, Mich.

CAPITAL MARKETS, INSURANCE & GSES
Kanjorski, chairman

Democrats: Ackerman, Sherman, Meeks, Moore (Kan.), Capuano, Hinojosa, McCarthy, Baca, Lynch, Miller, Scott, Velázquez, Bean, Moore (Wis.), Davis, Sires, Hodes, Klein, Mahoney, Perlmutter, Murphy, Donnelly, Wexler, Marshall, Boren
Republicans: Pryce, Baker, Shays, Gillmor, Castle, King, Lucas, Manzullo, Royce, Capito, Putnam, Barrett, Brown-Waite, Feeney, Garrett, Gerlach, Hensarling, Davis, Campbell, Bachmann, Roskam, Marchant, McCotter

DOMESTIC & INTERNATIONAL MONETARY POLICY, TRADE & TECHNOLOGY
Gutierrez, chairman

Democrats: Maloney, Waters, Kanjorski, Sherman, Moore (Wis.), Meeks, Moore (Kan.), Clay, Ellison, Wilson, Wexler, Marshall, Boren
Republicans: Paul, Castle, Lucas, LaTourette, Manzullo, Jones, Hensarling, Price, McHenry, Bachmann, Roskam, Marchant

FINANCIAL INSTITUTIONS & CONSUMER CREDIT
Maloney, chairwoman

Democrats: Watt, Ackerman, Sherman, Gutierrez, Moore (Kan.), Kanjorski, Waters, Carson, Hinojosa, McCarthy, Baca, Green, Clay, Miller, Scott, Cleaver, Bean, Davis, Hodes, Ellison, Klein, Mahoney, Wilson, Perlmutter
Republicans: Gillmor, Price, Baker, Pryce, Castle, King, Royce, LaTourette, Jones, Biggert, Capito, Feeney, Hensarling, Garrett, Brown-Waite, Barrett, Gerlach, Pearce, Neugebauer, Davis, McHenry, Campbell

HOUSING & COMMUNITY OPPORTUNITY
Waters, chairwoman

Democrats: Velázquez, Carson, Lynch, Cleaver, Green, Clay, Maloney, Moore (Wis.), Sires, Ellison, Wilson, Murphy, Donnelly
Republicans: Biggert, Pearce, King, Gillmor, Shays, Miller, Capito, Garrett, Neugebauer, Davis, Campbell, McCotter

OVERSIGHT & INVESTIGATIONS
Watt, chairman

Democrats: Gutierrez, Waters, Lynch, Cleaver, Velázquez, Capuano, McCarthy, Klein, Mahoney, Wexler
Republicans: Miller, McHenry, Royce, Paul, LaTourette, Barrett, Price, Bachmann, Roskam

FOREIGN AFFAIRS

225-5021 2170 Rayburn
Party Ratio: D 27-R 23
Tom Lantos, D-Calif., chairman

Democrats	Republicans
Howard L. Berman, Calif.	*Ileana Ros-Lehtinen, Fla.*
Gary L. Ackerman, N.Y.	*Christopher H. Smith, N.J.*
Eni F.H. Faleomavaega, Am. Samoa	*Dan Burton, Ind.*
Donald M. Payne, N.J.	*Elton Gallegly, Calif.*
Brad Sherman, Calif.	*Dana Rohrabacher, Calif.*
Robert Wexler, Fla.	*Donald Manzullo, Ill.*
Eliot L. Engel, N.Y.	*Ed Royce, Calif.*
Bill Delahunt, Mass.	*Steve Chabot, Ohio*
Gregory W. Meeks, N.Y.	*Tom Tancredo, Colo.*
Diane Watson, Calif.	*Ron Paul, Texas*
Adam Smith, Wash.	*Jeff Flake, Ariz.*
Russ Carnahan, Mo.	*Jo Ann Davis, Va.*
John Tanner, Tenn.	*Mike Pence, Ind.*
Gene Green, Texas	*Joe Wilson, S.C.*
Lynn Woolsey, Calif.	*John Boozman, Ark.*
Sheila Jackson-Lee, Texas	*J. Gresham Barrett, S.C.*
Rubén Hinojosa, Texas	*Connie Mack, Fla.*
Joseph Crowley, N.Y.	*Jeff Fortenberry, Neb.*
David Wu, Ore.	*Michael McCaul, Texas*
Brad Miller, N.C.	*Ted Poe, Texas*
Linda T. Sánchez, Calif.	*Bob Inglis, S.C.*
David Scott, Ga.	*Luis Fortuño, P.R.*
Jim Costa, Calif.	*Gus Bilirakis, Fla.*
Albio Sires, N.J.	
Gabrielle Giffords, Ariz.	
Ron Klein, Fla.	

AFRICA & GLOBAL HEALTH
Payne, chairman

Democrats: Watson, Woolsey, Jackson-Lee, Smith, Miller
Republicans: Smith, Tancredo, Boozman, Fortenberry, McCaul

ASIA, THE PACIFIC & THE GLOBAL ENVIRONMENT
Faleomavaega, chairman

Democrats: Smith, Ackerman, Meeks, Watson, Hinojosa, Sires
Republicans: Manzullo, Burton, Rohrabacher, Royce, Chabot, Flake

EUROPE
Wexler, chairman

Democrats: Tanner, Hinojosa, Miller, Sánchez, Costa, Engel, Sires
Republicans: Gallegly, Wilson, Poe, Inglis, Fortuño, Vacancy

INTERNATIONAL ORGANIZATIONS, HUMAN RIGHTS & OVERSIGHT
Delahunt, chairman

Democrats: Carnahan, Payne, Meeks, Crowley
Republicans: Rohrabacher, Paul, Flake

MIDDLE EAST & SOUTH ASIA
Ackerman, chairman

Democrats: Berman, Scott, Costa, Klein, Sherman, Wexler, Engel, Carnahan, Jackson-Lee
Republicans: Pence, Chabot, Davis, Wilson, Barrett, Fortenberry, Inglis, Mack, Vacancy

TERRORISM, NONPROLIFERATION & TRADE
Sherman, chairman

Democrats: Wu, Scott, Klein, Green, Crowley
Republicans: Royce, Boozman, Poe, Manzullo, Tancredo

WESTERN HEMISPHERE
Engel, chairman

Democrats: Meeks, Sánchez, Sires, Giffords, Faleomavaega, Payne, Delahunt, Klein, Green
Republicans: Burton, Mack, McCaul, Fortuño, Smith, Gallegly, Paul, Davis

HOMELAND SECURITY

226-2616 H2-176 Ford
Party Ratio: D 19-R 15
Bennie Thompson, D-Miss., chairman

Democrats	Republicans
Loretta Sanchez, Calif.	*Peter T. King, N.Y.*
Edward J. Markey, Mass.	*Lamar Smith, Texas*
Norm Dicks, Wash.	*Christopher Shays, Conn.*
Jane Harman, Calif.	*Mark Souder, Ind.*
Peter A. DeFazio, Ore.	*Thomas M. Davis III, Va.*
Nita M. Lowey, N.Y.	*Dan Lungren, Calif.*
Eleanor Holmes Norton, D.C.	*Mike D. Rogers, Ala.*
Zoe Lofgren, Calif.	*Bobby Jindal, La.*
Sheila Jackson-Lee, Texas	*Dave Reichert, Wash.*
Donna M.C. Christensen, Virgin Is.	*Michael McCaul, Texas*
Bob Etheridge, N.C.	*Charlie Dent, Pa.*
Jim Langevin, R.I.	*Ginny Brown-Waite, Fla.*
Henry Cuellar, Texas	*Gus Bilirakis, Fla.*
Christopher Carney, Pa.	*David Davis, Tenn.*
Yvette D. Clarke, N.Y.	*Kevin McCarthy, Calif.*
Al Green, Texas	
Ed Perlmutter, Colo.	
Vacancy	

BORDER, MARITIME & GLOBAL COUNTERTERRORISM
Sanchez, chairwoman

Democrats: Harman, Lofgren, Jackson-Lee, Langevin, Cuellar, Green
Republicans: Souder, Jindal, Reichert, McCaul, Bilirakis

EMERGENCY COMMUNICATIONS
Cuellar, chairman

Democrats: Sanchez, Dicks, Lowey, Norton, Christensen, Etheridge
Republicans: Dent, Souder, Rogers, Jindal, Davis (Tenn.)

EMERGING THREATS
Langevin, chairman

Democrats: Lofgren, Christensen, Etheridge, Green, Vacancy
Republicans: McCaul, Lungren, Brown-Waite, McCarthy

INTELLIGENCE, INFORMATION SHARING & TERRORISM RISK ASSESSMENT
Harman, chairwoman

Democrats: Dicks, Langevin, Carney, Perlmutter
Republicans: Reichert, Shays, Dent

MANAGEMENT & OVERSIGHT
Carney, chairman

Democrats: DeFazio, Clarke, Perlmutter, Vacancy
Republicans: Rogers, Davis (Va.), McCaul

TRANSPORTATION SECURITY & INFRASTRUCTURE PROTECTION
Jackson-Lee, chairwoman

Democrats: Markey, DeFazio, Norton, Clarke, Perlmutter
Republicans: Lungren, Brown-Waite, Bilirakis, McCarthy

HOUSE ADMINISTRATION

225-2061 1309 Longworth
Party Ratio: D 6-R 3
Robert A. Brady, D-Pa., chairman

Zoe Lofgren, Calif.	*Vernon J. Ehlers, Mich.*
Michael E. Capuano, Mass.	*Dan Lungren, Calif.*
Charlie Gonzalez, Texas	*Kevin McCarthy, Calif.*
Susan A. Davis, Calif.	
Artur Davis, Ala.	

CAPITOL SECURITY
Brady, chairman

Democrat: Capuano
Republican: Lungren

ELECTIONS
Lofgren, chairwoman

Democrats: Gonzalez, Davis (Calif.), Davis (Ala.)
Republicans: Ehlers, McCarthy

TASKFORCE ON CONTESTED ELECTION (FLORIDA 13)
Gonzalez, chairman

Democrats: Lofgren
Republicans: McCarthy

JUDICIARY

225-3951 2138 Rayburn
Party Ratio: D 23-R 17
John Conyers Jr., D-Mich., chairman

Howard L. Berman, Calif.	*Lamar Smith, Texas*
Rick Boucher, Va.	*F. James Sensenbrenner Jr., Wis.*
Jerrold Nadler, N.Y.	*Howard Coble, N.C.*
Robert C. Scott, Va.	*Elton Gallegly, Calif.*
Melvin Watt, N.C.	*Robert W. Goodlatte, Va.*
Zoe Lofgren, Calif.	*Steve Chabot, Ohio*
Sheila Jackson-Lee, Texas	*Dan Lungren, Calif.*
Maxine Waters, Calif.	*Chris Cannon, Utah*
Martin T. Meehan, Mass.	*Ric Keller, Fla.*
Bill Delahunt, Mass.	*Darrell Issa, Calif.*
Robert Wexler, Fla.	*Mike Pence, Ind.*
Linda T. Sánchez, Calif.	*J. Randy Forbes, Va.*
Steve Cohen, Tenn.	*Steve King, Iowa*
Hank Johnson, Ga.	*Tom Feeney, Fla.*
Luis V. Gutierrez, Ill.	*Trent Franks, Ariz.*
Brad Sherman, Calif.	*Louie Gohmert, Texas*
Tammy Baldwin, Wis.	*Jim Jordan, Ohio*
Anthony Weiner, N.Y.	
Adam B. Schiff, Calif.	
Artur Davis, Ala.	
Debbie Wasserman-Schultz, Fla.	
Keith Ellison, Minn.	

COMMERCIAL & ADMINISTRATIVE LAW
Sánchez, chairwoman

Democrats: Conyers, Johnson, Lofgren, Delahunt, Watt, Cohen
Republicans: Cannon, Jordan, Keller, Feeney, Franks

CONSTITUTION, CIVIL RIGHTS & CIVIL LIBERTIES
Nadler, chairman

Democrats: Davis, Wasserman-Schultz, Ellison, Conyers, Scott, Watt, Cohen
Republicans: Franks, Pence, Issa, King, Jordan

COURTS, THE INTERNET & INTELLECTUAL PROPERTY
Berman, chairman

Democrats: Conyers, Boucher, Meehan, Wexler, Watt, Jackson-Lee, Cohen, Johnson, Sherman, Weiner, Schiff, Lofgren
Republicans: Coble, Feeney, Sensenbrenner, Gallegly, Goodlatte, Chabot, Cannon, Keller, Issa, Pence, Smith

CRIME, TERRORISM & HOMELAND SECURITY
Scott, chairman

Democrats: Waters, Delahunt, Nadler, Johnson, Weiner, Jackson-Lee, Meehan, Davis, Baldwin
Republicans: Forbes, Gohmert, Sensenbrenner, Coble, Chabot, Lungren

IMMIGRATION, CITIZENSHIP, REFUGEES, BORDER SECURITY & INTERNATIONAL LAW
Lofgren, chairwoman

Democrats: Gutierrez, Berman, Jackson-Lee, Waters, Meehan, Delahunt, Sánchez, Davis, Ellison
Republicans: King, Gallegly, Goodlatte, Lungren, Forbes, Gohmert

ANTI-TRUST TASKFORCE
Conyers, chairman

Democrats: Berman, Boucher, Lofgren, Jackson-Lee, Waters, Cohen, Weiner, Davis, Wasserman-Schultz
Republicans: Chabot, Keller, Smith, Sensenbrenner, Goodlatte, Cannon, Issa, Forbes, King

NATURAL RESOURCES
225-6065 1324 Longworth
Party Ratio: D 27-R 22
Nick J. Rahall II, D-W.Va., chairman

Dale E. Kildee, Mich.	*Don Young, Alaska*
Eni F.H. Faleomavaega, Am. Samoa	*H. James Saxton, N.J.*
Neil Abercrombie, Hawaii	*Elton Gallegly, Calif.*
Solomon P. Ortiz, Texas	*John J. "Jimmy" Duncan Jr., Tenn.*
Frank Pallone Jr., N.J.	*Wayne T. Gilchrest, Md.*
Donna M.C. Christensen, Virgin Is.	*Chris Cannon, Utah*
Grace F. Napolitano, Calif.	*Tom Tancredo, Colo.*
Rush D. Holt, N.J.	*Jeff Flake, Ariz.*
Raúl M. Grijalva, Ariz.	*Steve Pearce, N.M.*
Madeleine Z. Bordallo, Guam	*Henry E. Brown Jr., S.C.*
Jim Costa, Calif.	*Luis Fortuño, P.R.*
Dan Boren, Okla.	*Cathy McMorris Rodgers, Wash.*
John Sarbanes, Md.	*Bobby Jindal, La.*
George Miller, Calif.	*Louie Gohmert, Texas*
Edward J. Markey, Mass.	*Tom Cole, Okla.*
Peter A. DeFazio, Ore.	*Rob Bishop, Utah*
Maurice D. Hinchey, N.Y.	*Bill Shuster, Pa.*
Patrick J. Kennedy, R.I.	*Dean Heller, Nev.*
Ron Kind, Wis.	*Bill Sali, Idaho*
Lois Capps, Calif.	*Doug Lamborn, Colo.*
Jay Inslee, Wash.	*Mary Fallin, Okla.*
Mark Udall, Colo.	*Kevin McCarthy, Calif.*
Joe Baca, Calif.	
Hilda L. Solis, Calif.	
Stephanie Herseth-Sandlin, S.D.	
Heath Shuler, N.C.	

ENERGY & MINERAL RESOURCES
Costa, chairman

Democrats: Faleomavaega, Ortiz, Holt, Boren, Hinchey, Kennedy, Solis
Republicans: Pearce, Jindal, Gohmert, Shuster, Heller, Sali

FISHERIES, WILDLIFE & OCEANS
Bordallo, chairwoman

Democrats: Kildee, Faleomavaega, Abercrombie, Ortiz, Pallone, Kennedy, Kind, Capps
Republicans: Brown, Saxton, Gilchrest, Rodgers, Jindal, Cole, Sali

INSULAR AFFAIRS
Christensen, chairwoman

Democrats: Faleomavaega, Grijalva, Bordallo
Republicans: Fortuño, Gallegly, Flake

NATIONAL PARKS, FORESTS & PUBLIC LANDS
Grijalva, chairman

Democrats: Kildee, Abercrombie, Christensen, Holt, Boren, Sarbanes, DeFazio, Hinchey, Kind, Capps, Inslee, Udall, Herseth-Sandlin, Shuler
Republicans: Bishop, Duncan, Cannon, Tancredo, Flake, Pearce, Brown, Gohmert, Cole, Heller, Sali, Lamborn, Vacancy

WATER & POWER
Napolitano, chairwoman

Democrats: Costa, Miller, Udall, Baca, Solis
Republicans: Rodgers, Heller, Lamborn, Vacancy

OVERSIGHT & GOVERNMENT REFORM
225-5051 2157 Rayburn
Party Ratio: D 23-R 18
Henry A. Waxman, D-Calif., chairman

Tom Lantos, Calif.	*Thomas M. Davis III, Va.*
Edolphus Towns, N.Y.	*Dan Burton, Ind.*
Paul E. Kanjorski, Pa.	*Christopher Shays, Conn.*
Carolyn B. Maloney, N.Y.	*John M. McHugh, N.Y.*
Elijah E. Cummings, Md.	*John L. Mica, Fla.*
Dennis J. Kucinich, Ohio	*Mark Souder, Ind.*
Danny K. Davis, Ill.	*Todd R. Platts, Pa.*
John F. Tierney, Mass.	*Chris Cannon, Utah*
William Lacy Clay, Mo.	*John J. "Jimmy" Duncan Jr., Tenn.*
Diane Watson, Calif.	*Michael R. Turner, Ohio*
Stephen F. Lynch, Mass.	*Darrell Issa, Calif.*
Brian Higgins, N.Y.	*Kenny Marchant, Texas*
John Yarmuth, Ky.	*Lynn Westmoreland, Ga.*
Bruce Braley, Iowa	*Patrick T. McHenry, N.C.*
Eleanor Holmes Norton, D.C.	*Virginia Foxx, N.C.*
Betty McCollum, Minn.	*Brian P. Bilbray, Calif.*
Jim Cooper, Tenn.	*Bill Sali, Idaho*
Chris Van Hollen, Md.	*Jim Jordan, Ohio*
Paul W. Hodes, N.H.	
Christopher S. Murphy, Conn.	
John Sarbanes, Md.	
Peter Welch, Vt.	

DOMESTIC POLICY
Kucinich, chairman

Democrats: Lantos, Cummings, Watson, Murphy, Davis, Tierney, Higgins, Braley
Republicans: Issa, Burton, Shays, Mica, Souder, Cannon, Bilbray

FEDERAL WORKFORCE, POSTAL SERVICE & THE DISTRICT OF COLUMBIA
Davis, chairman

Democrats: Norton, Sarbanes, Cummings, Kucinich, Clay, Lynch
Republicans: Marchant, McHugh, Mica, Issa, Vacancy

GOVERNMENT MANAGEMENT, ORGANIZATION & PROCUREMENT
Towns, chairman

Democrats: Kanjorski, Murphy, Welch, Maloney
Republicans: Bilbray, Platts, Duncan

INFORMATION POLICY, CENSUS & NATIONAL ARCHIVES
Clay, chairman

Democrats: Kanjorski, Maloney, Yarmuth, Hodes
Republicans: Turner, Cannon, Sali

NATIONAL SECURITY & FOREIGN AFFAIRS
Tierney, chairman

Democrats: Maloney, Lynch, Higgins, Yarmuth, Braley, McCollum, Cooper, Van Hollen, Hodes, Welch, Lantos
Republicans: Shays, Burton, McHugh, Platts, Duncan, Turner, Marchant, Westmoreland, McHenry, Foxx

RULES

225-9091 H-312 Capitol
Party Ratio: D 9-R 4
Louise M. Slaughter, D-N.Y., chairwoman

Jim McGovern, Mass.	*David Dreier, Calif.*
Alcee L. Hastings, Fla.	*Lincoln Diaz-Balart, Fla.*
Doris Matsui, Calif.	*Doc Hastings, Wash.*
Dennis Cardoza, Calif.	*Pete Sessions, Texas*
Peter Welch, Vt.	
Kathy Castor, Fla.	
Michael Arcuri, N.Y.	
Betty Sutton, Ohio	

LEGISLATIVE & BUDGET PROCESS
Hastings, chairman

Democrats: Cardoza, Welch, Sutton, Slaughter
Republicans: Diaz-Balart, Dreier

RULES & THE ORGANIZATION OF THE HOUSE
McGovern, chairman

Democrats: Matsui, Castor, Arcuri, Slaughter
Republicans: Hastings, Sessions

SCIENCE & TECHNOLOGY

225-6375 2320 Rayburn
Party Ratio: D 24-R 20
Bart Gordon, D-Tenn., chairman

Jerry F. Costello, Ill.	*Ralph M. Hall, Texas*
Eddie Bernice Johnson, Texas	*F. James Sensenbrenner Jr., Wis.*
Lynn Woolsey, Calif.	*Lamar Smith, Texas*
Mark Udall, Colo.	*Dana Rohrabacher, Calif.*
David Wu, Ore.	*Roscoe G. Bartlett, Md.*
Brian Baird, Wash.	*Vernon J. Ehlers, Mich.*
Brad Miller, N.C.	*Frank D. Lucas, Okla.*
Daniel Lipinski, Ill.	*Judy Biggert, Ill.*
Nick Lampson, Texas	*Todd Akin, Mo.*
Gabrielle Giffords, Ariz.	*Jo Bonner, Ala.*
Jerry McNerney, Calif.	*Tom Feeney, Fla.*
Paul E. Kanjorski, Pa.	*Randy Neugebauer, Texas*
Darlene Hooley, Ore.	*Bob Inglis, S.C.*
Steven R. Rothman, N.J.	*Dave Reichert, Wash.*
Michael M. Honda, Calif.	*Michael McCaul, Texas*
Jim Matheson, Utah	*Mario Diaz-Balart, Fla.*
Mike Ross, Ark.	*Phil Gingrey, Ga.*
Ben Chandler, Ky.	*Brian P. Bilbray, Calif.*
Russ Carnahan, Mo.	*Adrian Smith, Neb.*
Charlie Melancon, La.	*Vacancy*
Baron P. Hill, Ind.	
Harry E. Mitchell, Ariz.	
Charlie Wilson, Ohio	

ENERGY & ENVIRONMENT
Lampson, chairman

Democrats: Costello, Woolsey, Lipinski, Giffords, McNerney, Udall, Baird, Kanjorski
Republicans: Inglis, Bartlett, Biggert, Akin, Neugebauer, McCaul, Diaz-Balart

INVESTIGATIONS & OVERSIGHT
Miller, chairman

Democrats: Costello, Johnson, Hooley, Rothman, Baird
Republicans: Sensenbrenner, Rohrabacher, Feeney, McCaul

RESEARCH & SCIENCE EDUCATION
Baird, chairman

Democrats: Johnson, Lipinski, McNerney, Hooley, Carnahan, Hill
Republicans: Ehlers, Bartlett, Lucas, Neugebauer, Bilbray

SPACE & AERONAUTICS
Udall, chairman

Democrats: Wu, Lampson, Rothman, Ross, Chandler, Melancon
Republicans: Feeney, Rohrabacher, Lucas, Bonner, Vacancy

TECHNOLOGY & INNOVATION
Wu, chairman

Democrats: Matheson, Mitchell, Wilson, Chandler, Ross, Honda
Republicans: Gingrey, Ehlers, Biggert, Bonner, Smith (Neb.)

SELECT ENERGY INDEPENDENCE & GLOBAL WARMING

225-4012 2108 Rayburn
Party Ratio: D 9-R 6
Edward J. Markey, D-Mass., chairman

Earl Blumenauer, Ore.
Jay Inslee, Wash.
John B. Larson, Conn.
Hilda L. Solis, Calif.
Stephanie Herseth-Sandlin, S.D.
Emanuel Cleaver II, Mo.
John Hall, N.Y.
Jerry McNerney, Calif.

F. James Sensenbrenner Jr., Wis.
John Shadegg, Ariz.
Greg Walden, Ore.
John Sullivan, Okla.
Marsha Blackburn, Tenn.
Candice S. Miller, Mich.

SELECT INTELLIGENCE

225-7690 H-405 Capitol
Party Ratio: D 12-R 9
Silvestre Reyes, D-Texas, chairman

Alcee L. Hastings, Fla.
Leonard L. Boswell, Iowa
Robert E. "Bud" Cramer, Ala.
Anna G. Eshoo, Calif.
Rush D. Holt, N.J.
C.A. Dutch Ruppersberger, Md.
Mike Thompson, Calif.
Jan Schakowsky, Ill.
Jim Langevin, R.I.
Patrick J. Murphy, Pa.

Peter Hoekstra, Mich.
Terry Everett, Ala.
Heather A. Wilson, N.M.
William M. "Mac" Thornberry, Texas
John M. McHugh, N.Y.
Todd Tiahrt, Kan.
Mike Rogers, Mich.
Darrell Issa, Calif.
Elton Gallegly, Calif.

INTELLIGENCE COMMUNITY MANAGEMENT
Eshoo, chairwoman

Democrats: Holt, Ruppersberger, Thompson, Murphy
Republicans: Issa, Thornberry, Tiahrt

OVERSIGHT & INVESTIGATIONS
Cramer, chairman

Democrats: Hastings, Tierney, Schakowsky, Ruppersberger
Republicans: Wilson, McHugh, Vacancy

TECHNICAL & TACTICAL INTELLIGENCE
Ruppersberger, chairman

Democrats: Cramer, Langevin, Holt, Murphy
Republicans: Wilson, Everett, Thornberry

TERRORISM, HUMAN INTELLIGENCE, ANALYSIS & COUNTERINTELLIGENCE
Thompson, chairman

Democrats: Boswell, Langevin, Murphy, Hastings
Republicans: Rogers, Everett, McHugh

SMALL BUSINESS

225-4038 2361 Rayburn
Party Ratio: D 18-R 15
Nydia M. Velázquez, D-N.Y., chairwoman

William J. Jefferson, La.
Heath Shuler, N.C.
Charlie Gonzalez, Texas
Rick Larsen, Wash.
Raúl M. Grijalva, Ariz.
Michael H. Michaud, Maine
Melissa Bean, Ill.
Henry Cuellar, Texas
Daniel Lipinski, Ill.
Gwen Moore, Wis.
Jason Altmire, Pa.
Bruce Braley, Iowa
Yvette D. Clarke, N.Y.
Brad Ellsworth, Ind.
Hank Johnson, Ga.
Joe Sestak, Pa.
Vacancy

Steve Chabot, Ohio
Roscoe G. Bartlett, Md.
Sam Graves, Mo.
Todd Akin, Mo.
Bill Shuster, Pa.
Marilyn Musgrave, Colo.
Steve King, Iowa
Jeff Fortenberry, Neb.
Lynn Westmoreland, Ga.
Louie Gohmert, Texas
Dean Heller, Nev.
David Davis, Tenn.
Mary Fallin, Okla.
Vern Buchanan, Fla.
Jim Jordan, Ohio

CONTRACTING & TECHNOLOGY
Braley, chairman

Democrats: Jefferson, Cuellar, Moore, Clarke, Sestak
Republicans: Davis, Bartlett, Graves, Akin, Fallin

FINANCE & TAX
Bean, chairwoman

Democrats: Grijalva, Michaud, Johnson, Sestak, Ellsworth
Republicans: Heller, Buchanan, Jordan, Shuster, King

INVESTIGATIONS & OVERSIGHT
Altmire, chairman

Democrats: Gonzalez, Grijalva, Vacancy
Republicans: Gohmert, Westmoreland

REGULATIONS, HEALTHCARE & TRADE
Gonzalez, chairman

Democrats: Lipinski, Jefferson, Larsen, Altmire, Bean, Moore, Sestak
Republicans: Westmoreland, King, Fallin, Musgrave, Buchanan, Jordan

RURAL & URBAN ENTREPRENEURSHIP
Shuler, chairman

Democrats: Larsen, Ellsworth, Michaud, Moore, Clarke, Johnson
Republicans: Fortenberry, Musgrave, Bartlett, Heller, Davis

STANDARDS OF OFFICIAL CONDUCT

225-7103 HT-2 Capitol
Party Ratio: D 5-R 5
Stephanie Tubbs Jones, D-Ohio, chairwoman

Gene Green, Texas
Lucille Roybal-Allard, Calif.
Mike Doyle, Pa.
Bill Delahunt, Mass.

Doc Hastings, Wash.
Jo Bonner, Ala.
J. Gresham Barrett, S.C.
John Kline, Minn.
Michael McCaul, Texas

TRANSPORTATION & INFRASTRUCTURE

225-4472 2165 Rayburn
Party Ratio: D 41-R 34
James L. Oberstar, D-Minn., chairman

Nick J. Rahall II, W.Va.
Peter A. DeFazio, Ore.
Jerry F. Costello, Ill.
Eleanor Holmes Norton, D.C.
Jerrold Nadler, N.Y.
Corrine Brown, Fla.
Bob Filner, Calif.
Eddie Bernice Johnson, Texas
Gene Taylor, Miss.
Elijah E. Cummings, Md.
Ellen O. Tauscher, Calif.
Leonard L. Boswell, Iowa
Tim Holden, Pa.
Brian Baird, Wash.
Rick Larsen, Wash.
Michael E. Capuano, Mass.
Julia Carson, Ind.
Timothy H. Bishop, N.Y.
Michael H. Michaud, Maine
Brian Higgins, N.Y.
Russ Carnahan, Mo.
John Salazar, Colo.
Grace F. Napolitano, Calif.
Daniel Lipinski, Ill.
Doris Matsui, Calif.
Nick Lampson, Texas
Zack Space, Ohio
Mazie K. Hirono, Hawaii
Bruce Braley, Iowa
Jason Altmire, Pa.
Tim Walz, Minn.
Heath Shuler, N.C.
Michael Arcuri, N.Y.
Harry E. Mitchell, Ariz.
Christopher Carney, Pa.
John Hall, N.Y.
Steve Kagen, Wis.
Steve Cohen, Tenn.
Jerry McNerney, Calif.
Vacancy

John L. Mica, Fla.
Don Young, Alaska
Tom Petri, Wis.
Howard Coble, N.C.
John J. "Jimmy" Duncan Jr., Tenn.
Wayne T. Gilchrest, Md.
Vernon J. Ehlers, Mich.
Steven C. LaTourette, Ohio
Richard H. Baker, La.
Frank A. LoBiondo, N.J.
Jerry Moran, Kan.
Gary G. Miller, Calif.
Robin Hayes, N.C.
Henry E. Brown Jr., S.C.
Timothy V. Johnson, Ill.
Todd R. Platts, Pa.
Sam Graves, Mo.
Bill Shuster, Pa.
John Boozman, Ark.
Shelley Moore Capito, W.Va.
Jim Gerlach, Pa.
Mario Diaz-Balart, Fla.
Charlie Dent, Pa.
Ted Poe, Texas
Dave Reichert, Wash.
Connie Mack, Fla.
John R. "Randy" Kuhl Jr., N.Y.
Lynn Westmoreland, Ga.
Charles Boustany Jr., La.
Jean Schmidt, Ohio
Candice S. Miller, Mich.
Thelma Drake, Va.
Mary Fallin, Okla.
Vern Buchanan, Fla.

AVIATION

Costello, chairman

Democrats: Filner, Boswell, Larsen, Carnahan, Salazar, Lipinski, Lampson, Space, Braley, Mitchell, Hall, Kagen, Cohen, Rahall, DeFazio, Norton, Brown, Johnson, Tauscher, Holden, Capuano, Matsui, Hirono, Vacancy
Republicans: Petri, Coble, Duncan, Ehlers, LaTourette, LoBiondo, Moran, Hayes, Graves, Boozman, Capito, Gerlach, Diaz-Balart, Dent, Poe, Reichert, Mack, Kuhl, Westmoreland, Fallin, Buchanan

COAST GUARD & MARITIME TRANSPORTATION

Cummings, chairman

Democrats: Taylor, Larsen, Brown, Higgins, Baird, Bishop, Vacancy
Republicans: LaTourette, Young, Coble, Gilchrest, LoBiondo, Poe

ECONOMIC DEVELOPMENT, PUBLIC BUILDINGS & EMERGENCY MANAGEMENT

Norton, chairwoman

Democrats: Michaud, Altmire, Arcuri, Carney, Walz, Cohen
Republicans: Graves, Shuster, Capito, Dent, Kuhl

HIGHWAYS & TRANSIT

DeFazio, chairman

Democrats: Rahall, Nadler, Tauscher, Holden, Capuano, Carson, Bishop, Michaud, Higgins, Napolitano, Hirono, Altmire, Walz, Shuler, Arcuri, Carney, McNerney, Filner, Cummings, Baird, Lipinski, Matsui, Cohen, Space, Braley, Mitchell, Vacancy
Republicans: Duncan, Young, Petri, Coble, Baker, Miller (Calif.), Hayes, Brown, Johnson, Platts, Boozman, Capito, Gerlach, Diaz-Balart, Dent, Poe, Reichert, Boustany, Schmidt, Miller (Mich.), Drake, Fallin, Buchanan

RAILROADS, PIPELINES & HAZARDOUS MATERIALS

Brown, chairwoman

Democrats: Nadler, Boswell, Carson, Napolitano, Lampson, Space, Braley, Walz, Rahall, DeFazio, Costello, Johnson (Texas), Cummings, Michaud, Lipinski
Republicans: Shuster, Petri, Gilchrest, LaTourette, Moran, Miller (Calif.), Brown, Johnson, Platts, Graves, Gerlach, Diaz-Balart, Westmoreland

WATER RESOURCES & ENVIRONMENT

Johnson, chairwoman

Democrats: Taylor, Baird, Matsui, Costello, Bishop, Higgins, Carnahan, Salazar, Hirono, Shuler, Mitchell, Hall, Kagen, McNerney, Norton, Filner, Tauscher, Capuano, Napolitano, Arcuri
Republicans: Baker, Duncan, Gilchrest, Ehlers, LoBiondo, Miller (Calif.), Hayes, Brown, Platts, Shuster, Boozman, Mack, Kuhl, Boustany, Schmidt, Miller (Mich.), Drake

VETERANS' AFFAIRS

225-9756 335 Cannon
Party Ratio: D 16-R 13
Bob Filner, D-Calif., chairman

Corrine Brown, Fla.
Vic Snyder, Ark.
Michael H. Michaud, Maine
Stephanie Herseth-Sandlin, S.D.
Harry E. Mitchell, Ariz.
John Hall, N.Y.
Phil Hare, Ill.
Mike Doyle, Pa.
Shelley Berkley, Nev.
John Salazar, Colo.
Ciro D. Rodriguez, Texas
Joe Donnelly, Ind.
Jerry McNerney, Calif.
Zack Space, Ohio
Tim Walz, Minn.

Steve Buyer, Ind.
Cliff Stearns, Fla.
Jerry Moran, Kan.
Richard H. Baker, La.
Henry E. Brown Jr., S.C.
Jeff Miller, Fla.
John Boozman, Ark.
Ginny Brown-Waite, Fla.
Michael R. Turner, Ohio
Brian P. Bilbray, Calif.
Doug Lamborn, Colo.
Gus Bilirakis, Fla.
Vern Buchanan, Fla.

DISABILITY ASSISTANCE & MEMORIAL AFFAIRS

Hall, chairman

Democrats: Rodriguez, Hare, Berkley
Republicans: Lamborn, Turner, Bilirakis

ECONOMIC OPPORTUNITY
Herseth-Sandlin, chairwoman

Democrats: Donnelly, McNerney, Hall
Republicans: Boozman, Baker, Moran

HEALTH
Michaud, chairman

Democrats: Brown, Snyder, Hare, Doyle, Berkley, Salazar
Republicans: Miller, Stearns, Moran, Baker, Brown

OVERSIGHT & INVESTIGATIONS
Mitchell, chairman

Democrats: Space, Walz, Rodriguez
Republicans: Brown-Waite, Stearns, Bilbray

WAYS & MEANS

225-3625 1102 Longworth
Party Ratio: D 24-R 17
Charles B. Rangel, D-N.Y., chairman

Pete Stark, Calif.
Sander M. Levin, Mich.
Jim McDermott, Wash.
John Lewis, Ga.
Richard E. Neal, Mass.
Michael R. McNulty, N.Y.
John Tanner, Tenn.
Xavier Becerra, Calif.
Lloyd Doggett, Texas
Earl Pomeroy, N.D.
Stephanie Tubbs Jones, Ohio
Mike Thompson, Calif.
John B. Larson, Conn.
Rahm Emanuel, Ill.
Earl Blumenauer, Ore.
Ron Kind, Wis.
Bill Pascrell Jr., N.J.
Shelley Berkley, Nev.
Joseph Crowley, N.Y.
Chris Van Hollen, Md.
Kendrick B. Meek, Fla.
Allyson Y. Schwartz, Pa.
Artur Davis, Ala.

Jim McCrery, La.
Wally Herger, Calif.
Dave Camp, Mich.
Jim Ramstad, Minn.
Sam Johnson, Texas
Phil English, Pa.
Jerry Weller, Ill.
Kenny Hulshof, Mo.
Ron Lewis, Ky.
Kevin Brady, Texas
Thomas M. Reynolds, N.Y.
Paul D. Ryan, Wis.
Eric Cantor, Va.
John Linder, Ga.
Devin Nunes, Calif.
Pat Tiberi, Ohio
Jon Porter, Nev.

HEALTH
Stark, chairman

Democrats: Doggett, Thompson, Emanuel, Becerra, Pomeroy, Jones, Kind
Republicans: Camp, Johnson, Ramstad, English, Hulshof

INCOME SECURITY & FAMILY SUPPORT
McDermott, chairman

Democrats: Stark, Davis, Lewis, McNulty, Berkley, Van Hollen, Meek
Republicans: Weller, Herger, Camp, Porter, English

OVERSIGHT
Lewis, chairman

Democrats: Tanner, Neal, Becerra, Jones, Kind, Pascrell, Crowley
Republicans: Ramstad, Cantor, Linder, Nunes, Tiberi

SELECT REVENUE MEASURES
Neal, chairman

Democrats: Doggett, Thompson, Larson, Schwartz, McDermott, Emanuel, Blumenauer
Republicans: English, Reynolds, Cantor, Linder, Ryan

SOCIAL SECURITY
McNulty, chairman

Democrats: Levin, Pomeroy, Schwartz, Davis, Becerra, Doggett, Jones
Republicans: Johnson, Lewis, Brady, Ryan, Nunes

TRADE
Levin, chairman

Democrats: Tanner, Larson, Blumenauer, Pascrell, Berkley, Crowley, Van Hollen, Meek
Republicans: Herger, Weller, Lewis, Brady, Reynolds, Hulshof

Partisan House Committees

DEMOCRATIC LEADERS

Speaker . . . . Nancy Pelosi
Majority Leader . . . . Steny H. Hoyer
Majority Whip . . . . James E. Clyburn
Caucus Chairman . . . . Rahm Emanuel
Caucus Vice Chairman . . . . John B. Larson
Assistant to the Speaker . . . . Xavier Beccera

Chief Deputy Whips: John Lewis (senior), G.K. Butterfield, Joseph Crowley, Diana DeGette, Ed Pastor, Jan Schakowsky, John Tanner, Debbie Wasserman-Schultz, Maxine Waters

Regional Whips: Shelley Berkley, Emanuel Cleaver II, Lincoln Davis, Al Green, Maurice D. Hinchey, Rubén Hinojosa, Ron Kind, Stephen F. Lynch, Jim Langevin, Rick Larsen, Betty McCollum, Brad Miller, Patrick J. Murphy, Bill Pascrell Jr., Bobby L. Rush, Tim Ryan, David Scott, Vic Snyder, Hilda L. Solis, Ellen O. Tauscher, Diane Watson, Anthony Weiner, Lynn Woolsey, Albert R. Wynn

DEMOCRATIC CONGRESSIONAL CAMPAIGN COMMITTEE

863-1500 430 S. Capitol St. S.E. 20003

Chairman . . . . Chris Van Hollen
Chairman's Council Chairman . . . . John D. Dingell
Executive Board Chairman . . . . Charles B. Rangel
Business Council Chairman . . . . Joseph Crowley
Frontline Democrats Chairwoman. . . . . Debbie Wasserman-Schultz
Recruitment Chairman . . . . Artur Davis
Women LEAD Chairwoman . . . . Allyson Y. Schwarz
National Jewish Outreach Chairman . . . . Steve Israel

Recruitment Chairmen: Russ Carnahan, Mike Doyle, Rahm Emanuel, Steve Israel, Ron Kind, Jim Matheson, Betty McCollum, Mike Ross, Tim Ryan, Adam B. Schiff, Hilda L. Solis, Debbie Wasserman-Schultz

Ex-Officio Members: James E. Clyburn, Steny H. Hoyer, Patrick J. Kennedy, Nancy Pelosi

HOUSE DEMOCRATIC STEERING & POLICY COMMITTEE

225-0100 H-204 Capitol

Chairwoman . . . . Nancy Pelosi
Co-Chairwoman . . . . Rosa DeLauro
Co-Chairman . . . . George Miller
Vice Chairman. . . . . Marion Berry
Vice Chairwoman . . . . Hilda L. Solis
Vice Chairwoman . . . . Maxine Waters

Members: Tammy Baldwin, G.K. Butterfield, Michael E. Capuano, Dennis Cardoza, Kathy Castor, James E. Clyburn, Jim Cooper, Jerry F. Costello, Joseph Crowley, Artur Davis, Diana DeGette, John D. Dingell, Lloyd Doggett, Rahm Emanuel, Barney Frank, Kirsten Gillibrand, Gene Green, Rush D. Holt, Steny H. Hoyer, Marcy Kaptur, John B. Larson, John Lewis, Doris Matsui, Jerry McNerney, Kendrick B. Meek, Gregory W. Meeks, Charlie Melancon, David R. Obey, Ed Pastor, Charles B. Rangel, Tim Ryan, C.A. Dutch Ruppersberger, Loretta Sanchez, Jan Schakowsky, Brad Sherman, Louise M. Slaughter, John M. Spratt Jr., John Tanner, Gene Taylor, Mike Thompson, John F. Tierney, Tom Udall, Nydia M. Velázquez, Debbie Wasserman-Schultz, Maxine Waters

REPUBLICAN LEADERS

Minority Leader. . . . . John A. Boehner
Minority Whip. . . . . Roy Blunt
Conference Chairman . . . . Adam H. Putnam
Conference Vice Chairwoman . . . . Kay Granger
Conference Secretary . . . . John Carter
Chief Deputy Whip. . . . . Eric Cantor

NATIONAL REPUBLICAN CONGRESSIONAL COMMITTEE

479-7070 320 First St. S.E. 20003

Chairman . . . . Tom Cole
Executive Committee Chairman. . . . . . . Thomas A. Davis III
Management Chairman . . . . John Kline
Finance Chairman . . . . Eric Cantor
Finance Vice Chairman & IE Task Force . . Patrick T. McHenry
Communications Chairwoman . . . . Marsha Blackburn
Audit Chairman . . . . K. Michael Conaway
Candidate Recruitment Chairwoman . . . . . Candice S. Miller
Incumbent Retention Chairman . . . . . . Robert W. Goodlatte

Members: J. Gresham Barrett, John A. Boehner, Roy Blunt, Ginny Brown-Waite, John Carter, Michael N. Castle, Mary Fallin, Luis Fortuño, Virginia Foxx, Phil Gingrey, Kay Granger, J. Dennis Hastert, Jeb Hensarling, Darrell Issa, John Linder, Kevin McCarthy, Thaddeus McCotter, Howard P. "Buck" McKeon, Jeff Miller, Devin Nunes, Jon Porter, Adam H. Putnam, Thomas M. Reynolds, Cathy McMorris Rodgers, Pete Sessions, Bill Shuster, Pat Tiberi, Jerry Weller, Lynn Westmoreland, Roger Wicker

POLICY COMMITTEE

225-6168 2471 Rayburn

Chairman . . . . Thaddeus McCotter

HOUSE REPUBLICAN STEERING COMMITTEE

225-2204 H-232 Capitol

Chairman. . . . . John A. Boehner

Members: Joe L. Barton, Roy Blunt, Ken Calvert, Dave Camp, Eric Cantor, John Carter, Tom Cole, David Dreier, Kay Granger, J. Dennis Hastert, Doc Hastings, Ray LaHood, Jerry Lewis, John Linder, Kevin McCarthy, Thaddeus McCotter, Jim McCrery, John M. McHugh, Adam H. Putnam, Ralph Regula, Thomas M. Reynolds, Cathy McMorris Rodgers, Harold Rogers, Lamar Smith, Lee Terry, Don Young, C.W. Bill Young

Senate Committees

The standing and select committees of the U.S. Senate are listed below in alphabetical order. The listings include a telephone number, room number and party ratio for each full committee. Membership is given in order of seniority on the committee. Subcommittee membership is listed in order of seniority.

On full committee rosters, members of the majority party, Democrats, are shown in roman type; members of the minority party, Republicans, are shown in *italic* type.

The word "vacancy" indicates that a committee or subcommittee seat had not been filled at press time, April 2007. Subcommittee vacancies do not necessarily indicate vacancies on full committees or vice versa.

The telephone area code for Washington, D.C., is 202. The ZIP code for all Senate offices is 20510.

Partisan committees are listed on page 1202.

AGRICULTURE, NUTRITION & FORESTRY

224-2035 328A Russell
Party Ratio: D 11-R 10
Tom Harkin, D-Iowa, chairman

Patrick J. Leahy, Vt.	*Saxby Chambliss, Ga.*
Kent Conrad, N.D.	*Richard G. Lugar, Ind.*
Max Baucus, Mont.	*Thad Cochran, Miss.*
Blanche Lincoln, Ark.	*Mitch McConnell, Ky.*
Debbie Stabenow, Mich.	*Pat Roberts, Kan.*
Ben Nelson, Neb.	*Lindsey Graham, S.C.*
Ken Salazar, Colo.	*Norm Coleman, Minn.*
Sherrod Brown, Ohio	*Michael D. Crapo, Idaho*
Bob Casey, Pa.	*John Thune, S.D.*
Amy Klobuchar, Minn.	*Charles E. Grassley, Iowa*

DOMESTIC & FOREIGN MARKETING
Baucus, chairman

Democrats: Conrad, Stabenow, Nelson, Salazar, Casey
Republicans: Graham, McConnell, Roberts, Crapo, Thune

ENERGY, SCIENCE & TECHNOLOGY
Conrad, chairman

Democrats: Nelson, Salazar, Brown, Casey, Klobuchar
Republicans: Thune, Lugar, Graham, Coleman, Grassley

NUTRITION & FOOD ASSISTANCE
Leahy, chairman

Democrats: Lincoln, Stabenow, Brown, Casey, Klobuchar
Republicans: Coleman, Lugar, Cochran, McConnell, Crapo

PRODUCTION, INCOME PROTECTION & PRICE SUPPORT
Lincoln, chairwoman

Democrats: Leahy, Conrad, Baucus, Brown, Klobuchar
Republicans: Roberts, Cochran, Coleman, Thune, Grassley

RURAL REVITALIZATION, CONSERVATION, FORESTRY & CREDIT
Stabenow, chairwoman

Democrats: Leahy, Baucus, Lincoln, Nelson, Salazar
Republicans: Crapo, Lugar, Cochran, McConnell, Graham

APPROPRIATIONS

224-7363 S-131 Capitol
Party Ratio: D 15-R 14
Robert C. Byrd, D-W.Va., chairman

Daniel K. Inouye, Hawaii	*Thad Cochran, Miss.*
Patrick J. Leahy, Vt.	*Ted Stevens, Alaska*
Tom Harkin, Iowa	*Arlen Specter, Pa.*
Barbara A. Mikulski, Md.	*Pete V. Domenici, N.M.*
Herb Kohl, Wis.	*Christopher S. Bond, Mo.*
Patty Murray, Wash.	*Mitch McConnell, Ky.*
Byron L. Dorgan, N.D.	*Richard C. Shelby, Ala.*
Dianne Feinstein, Calif.	*Judd Gregg, N.H.*
Richard J. Durbin, Ill.	*Robert F. Bennett, Utah*
Tim Johnson, S.D.	*Larry E. Craig, Idaho*
Mary L. Landrieu, La.	*Kay Bailey Hutchison, Texas*
Jack Reed, R.I.	*Sam Brownback, Kan.*
Frank R. Lautenberg, N.J.	*Wayne Allard, Colo.*
Ben Nelson, Neb.	*Lamar Alexander, Tenn.*

AGRICULTURE
Kohl, chairman

Democrats: Harkin, Dorgan, Feinstein, Durbin, Johnson, Nelson, Reed
Republicans: Bennett, Cochran, Specter, Bond, McConnell, Craig, Brownback

COMMERCE-JUSTICE-SCIENCE
Mikulski, chairwoman

Democrats: Inouye, Leahy, Kohl, Harkin, Dorgan, Feinstein, Reed, Lautenberg
Republicans: Shelby, Gregg, Stevens, Domenici, McConnell, Hutchison, Brownback, Alexander

DEFENSE
Inouye, chairman

Democrats: Byrd, Leahy, Harkin, Dorgan, Durbin, Feinstein, Mikulski, Kohl, Murray
Republicans: Stevens, Cochran, Specter, Domenici, Bond, McConnell, Shelby, Gregg, Hutchison

ENERGY-WATER
Dorgan, chairman

Democrats: Byrd, Murray, Feinstein, Johnson, Landrieu, Inouye, Reed, Lautenberg
Republicans: Domenici, Cochran, McConnell, Bennett, Craig, Bond, Hutchison, Allard

FINANCIAL SERVICES
Durbin, chairman

Democrats: Murray, Landrieu, Lautenberg, Nelson
Republicans: Brownback, Bond, Shelby, Allard

HOMELAND SECURITY
Byrd, chairman

Democrats: Inouye, Leahy, Mikulski, Kohl, Murray, Landrieu, Lautenberg, Nelson
Republicans: Cochran, Gregg, Stevens, Specter, Domenici, Shelby, Craig, Alexander

INTERIOR-ENVIRONMENT
Feinstein, chairwoman

Democrats: Byrd, Leahy, Dorgan, Mikulski, Kohl, Johnson, Reed, Nelson
Republicans: Craig, Stevens, Cochran, Domenici, Bennett, Gregg, Allard, Alexander

LABOR-HHS-EDUCATION
Harkin, chairman

Democrats: Inouye, Kohl, Murray, Landrieu, Durbin, Reed, Lautenberg
Republicans: Specter, Cochran, Gregg, Craig, Hutchison, Stevens, Shelby

LEGISLATIVE BRANCH
Landrieu, chairwoman

Democrats: Durbin, Nelson
Republicans: Allard, Alexander

MILITARY CONSTRUCTION-VA
Johnson, chairman

Democrats: Inouye, Landrieu, Byrd, Murray, Reed, acting chairman, Nelson
Republicans: Hutchison, Craig, Brownback, Allard, McConnell, Bennett

STATE-FOREIGN OPERATIONS
Leahy, chairman

Democrats: Inouye, Harkin, Mikulski, Durbin, Johnson, Landrieu, Reed
Republicans: Gregg, McConnell, Specter, Bennett, Bond, Brownback, Alexander

TRANSPORTATION-HUD
Murray, chairwoman

Democrats: Byrd, Mikulski, Kohl, Durbin, Dorgan, Leahy, Harkin, Feinstein, Johnson, Lautenberg
Republicans: Bond, Shelby, Specter, Bennett, Hutchison, Brownback, Stevens, Domenici, Alexander, Allard

ARMED SERVICES

224-3871 228 Russell
Party Ratio: D 13-R 12
Carl Levin, D-Mich., chairman

Edward M. Kennedy, Mass.	*John McCain, Ariz.*
Robert C. Byrd, W.Va.	*John W. Warner, Va.*
Joseph I. Lieberman, I-Conn.	*James M. Inhofe, Okla.*
Jack Reed, R.I.	*Jeff Sessions, Ala.*
Daniel K. Akaka, Hawaii	*Susan Collins, Maine*
Bill Nelson, Fla.	*John Ensign, Nev.*
Ben Nelson, Neb.	*Saxby Chambliss, Ga.*
Evan Bayh, Ind.	*Lindsey Graham, S.C.*
Hillary Rodham Clinton, N.Y.	*Elizabeth Dole, N.C.*
Mark Pryor, Ark.	*John Cornyn, Texas*
Jim Webb, Va.	*John Thune, S.D.*
Claire McCaskill, Mo.	*Mel Martinez, Fla.*

AIRLAND
Lieberman, chairman

Democrats: Akaka, Bayh, Clinton, Pryor, Webb, McCaskill
Republicans: Cornyn, Warner, Inhofe, Sessions, Ensign, Chambliss

EMERGING THREATS & CAPABILITIES
Reed, chairman

Democrats: Kennedy, Byrd, Nelson (Fla.), Nelson (Neb.), Bayh, Clinton
Republicans: Dole, Warner, Collins, Graham, Cornyn, Martinez

PERSONNEL
Nelson (Neb.), chairman

Democrats: Kennedy, Lieberman, Webb, McCaskill
Republicans: Graham, Collins, Chambliss, Dole

READINESS & MANAGEMENT SUPPORT
Akaka, chairman

Democrats: Byrd, Bayh, Clinton, Pryor, McCaskill
Republicans: Ensign, Inhofe, Sessions, Chambliss, Dole

SEAPOWER
Kennedy, chairman

Democrats: Lieberman, Reed, Akaka, Nelson (Fla.), Webb
Republicans: Thune, Warner, Collins, Ensign, Martinez

STRATEGIC FORCES
Nelson (Fla.), chairman

Democrats: Nelson (Neb.), Byrd, Reed, Pryor
Republicans: Sessions, Inhofe, Graham, Thune

BANKING, HOUSING & URBAN AFFAIRS

224-7391 534 Dirksen
Party Ratio: D 11-R 10
Christopher J. Dodd, D-Conn., chairman

Tim Johnson, S.D.	*Richard C. Shelby, Ala.*
Jack Reed, R.I.	*Robert F. Bennett, Utah*
Charles E. Schumer, N.Y.	*Wayne Allard, Colo.*
Evan Bayh, Ind.	*Michael B. Enzi, Wyo.*
Thomas R. Carper, Del.	*Chuck Hagel, Neb.*
Robert Menendez, N.J.	*Jim Bunning, Ky.*
Daniel K. Akaka, Hawaii	*Michael D. Crapo, Idaho*
Sherrod Brown, Ohio	*John E. Sununu, N.H.*
Bob Casey, Pa.	*Elizabeth Dole, N.C.*
Jon Tester, Mont.	*Mel Martinez, Fla.*

ECONOMIC POLICY

Carper, chairman

Democrat: Brown
Republican: Bunning

FINANCIAL INSTITUTIONS

Johnson, chairman

Democrats: Tester, Menendez, Akaka, Reed, Schumer, Bayh, Carper
Republicans: Hagel, Bennett, Allard, Sununu, Bunning, Crapo, Dole

HOUSING, TRANSPORTATION & COMMUNITY DEVELOPMENT

Schumer, chairman

Democrats: Akaka, Casey, Reed, Carper, Brown, Tester, Menendez
Republicans: Crapo, Dole, Martinez, Allard, Enzi, Hagel, Sununu

SECURITIES, INSURANCE & INVESTMENT

Reed, chairman

Democrats: Menendez, Johnson, Schumer, Bayh, Casey, Akaka, Tester
Republicans: Allard, Enzi, Sununu, Bennett, Hagel, Bunning, Crapo

SECURITY & INTERNATIONAL TRADE

Bayh, chairman

Democrats: Brown, Johnson, Casey, Dodd
Republicans: Martinez, Enzi, Dole, Bennett

BUDGET

224-0642 624 Dirksen
Party Ratio: D 12-R 11
Kent Conrad, D-N.D., chairman

Patty Murray, Wash.	*Judd Gregg, N.H.*
Ron Wyden, Ore.	*Pete V. Domenici, N.M.*
Russ Feingold, Wis.	*Charles E. Grassley, Iowa*
Robert C. Byrd, W.Va.	*Wayne Allard, Colo.*
Bill Nelson, Fla.	*Michael B. Enzi, Wyo.*
Debbie Stabenow, Mich.	*Jeff Sessions, Ala.*
Robert Menendez, N.J.	*Jim Bunning, Ky.*
Frank R. Lautenberg, N.J.	*Michael D. Crapo, Idaho*
Benjamin L. Cardin, Md.	*John Ensign, Nev.*
Bernard Sanders, I-Vt.	*John Cornyn, Texas*
Sheldon Whitehouse, R.I.	*Lindsey Graham, S.C.*

COMMERCE, SCIENCE & TRANSPORTATION

224-5115 508 Dirksen
Party Ratio: D 12-R 11
Daniel K. Inouye, D-Hawaii, chairman

John D. Rockefeller IV, W.Va.	*Ted Stevens, Alaska*
John Kerry, Mass.	*John McCain, Ariz.*
Byron L. Dorgan, N.D.	*Trent Lott, Miss.*
Barbara Boxer, Calif.	*Kay Bailey Hutchison, Texas*
Bill Nelson, Fla.	*Olympia J. Snowe, Maine*
Maria Cantwell, Wash.	*Gordon H. Smith, Ore.*
Frank R. Lautenberg, N.J.	*John Ensign, Nev.*
Mark Pryor, Ark.	*John E. Sununu, N.H.*
Thomas R. Carper, Del.	*Jim DeMint, S.C.*
Claire McCaskill, Mo.	*David Vitter, La.*
Amy Klobuchar, Minn.	*John Thune, S.D.*

AVIATION OPERATIONS, SAFETY & SECURITY

Rockefeller, chairman

Democrats: Kerry, Dorgan, Boxer, Nelson, Cantwell, Lautenberg, Pryor, Carper, McCaskill, Klobuchar
Republicans: Lott, McCain, Hutchison, Snowe, Smith, Ensign, Sununu, DeMint, Vitter, Thune

CONSUMER AFFAIRS, INSURANCE & AUTOMOTIVE SAFETY

Pryor, chairman

Democrats: Rockefeller, Nelson, Cantwell, Lautenberg, Carper, McCaskill, Klobuchar
Republicans: Sununu, McCain, Lott, Snowe, Smith, Vitter, Thune

INTERSTATE COMMERCE, TRADE & TOURISM

Dorgan, chairman

Democrats: Rockefeller, Kerry, Boxer, Cantwell, Pryor, McCaskill
Republicans: DeMint, McCain, Snowe, Smith, Ensign, Sununu

OCEANS, ATMOSPHERE, FISHERIES & COAST GUARD

Cantwell, chairwoman

Democrats: Kerry, Boxer, Nelson, Lautenberg, Carper, Klobuchar
Republicans: Snowe, Lott, Smith, Sununu, DeMint, Vitter

SCIENCE, TECHNOLOGY & INNOVATION

Kerry, chairman

Democrats: Rockefeller, Dorgan, Boxer, Cantwell, Pryor, McCaskill, Klobuchar
Republicans: Ensign, McCain, Hutchison, Smith, Sununu, DeMint, Thune

SPACE, AERONAUTICS & RELATED SCIENCES

Nelson, chairman

Democrats: Kerry, Dorgan, Pryor
Republicans: Hutchison, Lott, Sununu

SURFACE TRANSPORTATION AND MERCHANT MARINE
Lautenberg, chairman

Democrats: Rockefeller, Kerry, Dorgan, Cantwell, Pryor, Carper, McCaskill, Klobuchar
Republicans: Smith, McCain, Lott, Hutchison, Snowe, DeMint, Vitter, Thune

ENERGY & NATURAL RESOURCES

224-4971 304 Dirksen
Party Ratio: D 12-R 11
Jeff Bingaman, D-N.M., chairman

Daniel K. Akaka, Hawaii	*Pete V. Domenici, N.M.*
Byron L. Dorgan, N.D.	*Larry E. Craig, Idaho*
Ron Wyden, Ore.	*Craig Thomas, Wyo.*
Tim Johnson, S.D.	*Lisa Murkowski, Alaska*
Mary L. Landrieu, La.	*Richard M. Burr, N.C.*
Maria Cantwell, Wash.	*Mel Martinez, Fla.*
Ken Salazar, Colo.	*Gordon H. Smith, Ore.*
Robert Menendez, N.J.	*Jim Bunning, Ky.*
Blanche Lincoln, Ark.	*Jim DeMint, S.C.*
Bernard Sanders, I-Vt.	*Bob Corker, Tenn.*
Jon Tester, Mont.	*Jeff Sessions, Ala.*

ENERGY
Dorgan, chairman

Democrats: Akaka, Wyden, Johnson, Landrieu, Cantwell, Menendez, Sanders, Tester
Republicans: Murkowski, Craig, Burr, DeMint, Corker, Sessions, Bunning, Martinez

NATIONAL PARKS
Akaka, chairman

Democrats: Dorgan, Landrieu, Salazar, Menendez, Lincoln, Sanders, Tester
Republicans: Thomas, Murkowski, Burr, Corker, Sessions, Smith, Martinez

PUBLIC LANDS & FORESTS
Wyden, chairman

Democrats: Akaka, Johnson, Landrieu, Cantwell, Salazar, Menendez, Lincoln, Sanders
Republicans: Burr, Craig, Thomas, Murkowski, DeMint, Sessions, Smith, Bunning

WATER & POWER
Johnson, chairman

Democrats: Dorgan, Wyden, Cantwell, Salazar, Lincoln, Tester
Republicans: Corker, Craig, Thomas, DeMint, Smith, Bunning

ENVIRONMENT & PUBLIC WORKS

224-8832 456 Dirksen
Party Ratio: D 10-R 9
Barbara Boxer, D-Calif., chairwoman

Max Baucus, Mont.	*James M. Inhofe, Okla.*
Joseph I. Lieberman, I-Conn.	*John W. Warner, Va.*
Thomas R. Carper, Del.	*George V. Voinovich, Ohio*
Hillary Rodham Clinton, N.Y.	*Johnny Isakson, Ga.*
Frank R. Lautenberg, N.J.	*David Vitter, La.*
Benjamin L. Cardin, Md.	*Larry E. Craig, Idaho*
Bernard Sanders, I-Vt.	*Lamar Alexander, Tenn.*
Amy Klobuchar, Minn.	*Craig Thomas, Wyo.*
Sheldon Whitehouse, R.I.	*Christopher S. Bond, Mo.*

CLEAN AIR & NUCLEAR SAFETY
Carper, chairman

Democrats: Lieberman, Clinton, Sanders
Republicans: Voinovich, Isakson, Alexander

PRIVATE SECTOR & CONSUMER SOLUTIONS TO GLOBAL WARMING AND WILDLIFE PROTECTION
Lieberman, chairman

Democrats: Baucus, Lautenberg, Sanders
Republicans: Warner, Thomas, Isakson

PUBLIC SECTOR SOLUTIONS TO GLOBAL WARMING & CHILDREN'S HEALTH PROTECTION
Boxer, chairwoman

Democrats: Lieberman, Carper, Klobuchar, Whitehouse
Republicans: Alexander, Craig, Bond, Thomas

SUPERFUND & ENVIRONMENTAL HEALTH
Clinton, chairwoman

Democrats: Baucus, Lautenberg, Cardin
Republicans: Craig, Vitter, Bond

TRANSPORTATION & INFRASTRUCTURE
Baucus, chairman

Democrats: Carper, Clinton, Cardin, Sanders
Republicans: Isakson, Warner, Voinovich, Vitter

TRANSPORTATION SAFETY, INFRASTRUCTURE SECURITY & WATER QUALITY
Lautenberg, chairman

Democrats: Cardin, Klobuchar, Whitehouse
Republicans: Vitter, Bond, Voinovich

FINANCE

224-4515 219 Dirksen
Party Ratio: D 11-R 10
Max Baucus, D-Mont., chairman

John D. Rockefeller IV, W.Va.	*Charles E. Grassley, Iowa*
Kent Conrad, N.D.	*Orrin G. Hatch, Utah*
Jeff Bingaman, N.M.	*Trent Lott, Miss.*
John Kerry, Mass.	*Olympia J. Snowe, Maine*
Blanche Lincoln, Ark.	*Jon Kyl, Ariz.*
Ron Wyden, Ore.	*Craig Thomas, Wyo.*
Charles E. Schumer, N.Y.	*Gordon H. Smith, Ore.*
Debbie Stabenow, Mich.	*Jim Bunning, Ky.*
Maria Cantwell, Wash.	*Michael D. Crapo, Idaho*
Ken Salazar, Colo.	*Pat Roberts, Kan.*

ENERGY, NATURAL RESOURCES & INFRASTRUCTURE

Bingaman, chairman

Democrats: Conrad, Kerry, Lincoln, Wyden, Cantwell, Salazar
Republicans: Thomas, Smith, Hatch, Bunning, Lott, Crapo

HEALTH CARE

Rockefeller, chairman

Democrats: Kerry, Bingaman, Lincoln, Wyden, Stabenow, Cantwell, Salazar
Republicans: Hatch, Grassley, Snowe, Kyl, Thomas, Roberts, Bunning

INTERNATIONAL TRADE & GLOBAL COMPETITIVENESS

Lincoln, chairwoman

Democrats: Baucus, Rockefeller, Bingaman, Stabenow, Schumer
Republicans: Smith, Crapo, Snowe, Thomas, Roberts

SOCIAL SECURITY, PENSIONS & FAMILY POLICY

Kerry, chairman

Democrats: Rockefeller, Conrad, Schumer
Republicans: Bunning, Lott, Kyl

TAXATION, IRS OVERSIGHT & LONG-TERM GROWTH

Conrad, chairman

Democrats: Baucus, Wyden, Cantwell, Schumer, Stabenow, Salazar
Republicans: Kyl, Lott, Roberts, Snowe, Crapo, Hatch

FOREIGN RELATIONS

224-4651 439 Dirksen
Party Ratio: D 11-R 10
Joseph R. Biden Jr., D-Del., chairman

Christopher J. Dodd, Conn.	*Richard G. Lugar, Ind.*
John Kerry, Mass.	*Chuck Hagel, Neb.*
Russ Feingold, Wis.	*Norm Coleman, Minn.*
Barbara Boxer, Calif.	*Bob Corker, Tenn.*
Bill Nelson, Fla.	*John E. Sununu, N.H.*
Barack Obama, Ill.	*George V. Voinovich, Ohio*
Robert Menendez, N.J.	*Lisa Murkowski, Alaska*
Benjamin L. Cardin, Md.	*Jim DeMint, S.C.*
Bob Casey, Pa.	*Johnny Isakson, Ga.*
Jim Webb, Va.	*David Vitter, La.*

AFRICAN AFFAIRS

Feingold, chairman

Democrats: Nelson, Obama, Cardin, Webb
Republicans: Sununu, Coleman, Vitter, Hagel

EAST ASIAN & PACIFIC AFFAIRS

Boxer, chairwoman

Democrats: Kerry, Feingold, Obama, Webb
Republicans: Murkowski, Isakson, Vitter, Hagel

EUROPEAN AFFAIRS

Obama, chairman

Democrats: Dodd, Menendez, Cardin, Casey
Republicans: DeMint, Voinovich, Corker, Murkowski

INTERNATIONAL DEVELOPMENT

Menendez, chairman

Democrats: Kerry, Boxer, Obama, Casey
Republicans: Hagel, Corker, Murkowski, DeMint

INTERNATIONAL OPERATIONS & ORGANIZATIONS

Nelson, chairman

Democrats: Feingold, Menendez, Casey, Webb
Republicans: Vitter, Voinovich, DeMint, Isakson

NEAR EASTERN & SOUTH & CENTRAL ASIAN AFFAIRS

Kerry, chairman

Democrats: Dodd, Feingold, Boxer, Cardin
Republicans: Coleman, Hagel, Sununu, Voinovich

WESTERN HEMISPHERE, PEACE CORPS & NARCOTICS AFFAIRS

Dodd, chairman

Democrats: Kerry, Nelson, Menendez, Webb
Republicans: Corker, Isakson, Coleman, Sununu

HEALTH, EDUCATION, LABOR & PENSIONS

224-5375 428 Dirksen
Party Ratio: D 11-R 10
Edward M. Kennedy, D-Mass., chairman

Christopher J. Dodd, Conn.	*Michael B. Enzi, Wyo.*
Tom Harkin, Iowa	*Judd Gregg, N.H.*
Barbara A. Mikulski, Md.	*Lamar Alexander, Tenn.*
Jeff Bingaman, N.M.	*Richard M. Burr, N.C.*
Patty Murray, Wash.	*Johnny Isakson, Ga.*
Jack Reed, R.I.	*Lisa Murkowski, Alaska*
Hillary Rodham Clinton, N.Y.	*Orrin G. Hatch, Utah*
Barack Obama, Ill.	*Pat Roberts, Kan.*
Bernard Sanders, I-Vt.	*Wayne Allard, Colo.*
Sherrod Brown, Ohio	*Tom Coburn, Okla.*

CHILDREN & FAMILIES

Dodd, chairman

Democrats: Bingaman, Murray, Reed, Clinton, Obama, Sanders
Republicans: Alexander, Gregg, Murkowski, Hatch, Roberts, Allard

EMPLOYMENT & WORKPLACE SAFETY
Murray, chairwoman

Democrats: Dodd, Harkin, Mikulski, Clinton, Obama, Brown
Republicans: Isakson, Burr, Murkowski, Roberts, Allard, Coburn

RETIREMENT & AGING
Mikulski, chairwoman

Democrats: Harkin, Bingaman, Reed, Sanders, Brown
Republicans: Burr, Gregg, Alexander, Isakson, Hatch

HOMELAND SECURITY & GOVERNMENTAL AFFAIRS

224-2627 340 Dirksen
Party Ratio: D 9-R 8
Joseph I. Lieberman, I-Conn., chairman

Democrats	Republicans
Carl Levin, Mich.	*Susan Collins, Maine*
Daniel K. Akaka, Hawaii	*Ted Stevens, Alaska*
Thomas R. Carper, Del.	*George V. Voinovich, Ohio*
Mark Pryor, Ark.	*Norm Coleman, Minn.*
Mary L. Landrieu, La.	*Tom Coburn, Okla.*
Barack Obama, Ill.	*Pete V. Domenici, N.M.*
Claire McCaskill, Mo.	*John W. Warner, Va.*
Jon Tester, Mont.	*John E. Sununu, N.H.*

DISASTER RECOVERY
Landrieu, chairwoman

Democrats: Carper, Pryor
Republicans: Stevens, Domenici

FEDERAL FINANCIAL MANAGEMENT
Carper, chairman

Democrats: Levin, Akaka, Obama, McCaskill, Tester
Republicans: Coburn, Stevens, Voinovich, Domenici, Sununu

OVERSIGHT OF GOVERNMENT MANAGEMENT
Akaka, chairman

Democrats: Levin, Carper, Pryor, Landrieu
Republicans: Voinovich, Stevens, Coburn, Warner

PERMANENT INVESTIGATIONS
Levin, chairman

Democrats: Carper, Pryor, Obama, McCaskill, Tester
Republicans: Coleman, Coburn, Domenici, Warner, Sununu

STATE, LOCAL & PRIVATE SECTOR PREPAREDNESS
Pryor, chairman

Democrats: Akaka, Landrieu, Obama, McCaskill, Tester
Republicans: Sununu, Voinovich, Coleman, Domenici, Warner

INDIAN AFFAIRS

224-2251 838 Hart
Party Ratio: D 8-R 7
Byron L. Dorgan, D-N.D., chairman

Democrats	Republicans
Daniel K. Inouye, Hawaii	*Craig Thomas, Wyo.*
Kent Conrad, N.D.	*John McCain, Ariz.*
Daniel K. Akaka, Hawaii	*Lisa Murkowski, Alaska*
Tim Johnson, S.D.	*Tom Coburn, Okla.*
Maria Cantwell, Wash.	*Pete V. Domenici, N.M.*
Claire McCaskill, Mo.	*Gordon H. Smith, Ore.*
Jon Tester, Mont.	*Richard M. Burr, N.C.*

JUDICIARY

224-7703 224 Dirksen
Party Ratio: D 10-R 9
Patrick J. Leahy, D-Vt., chairman

Democrats	Republicans
Edward M. Kennedy, Mass.	*Arlen Specter, Pa.*
Joseph R. Biden Jr., Del.	*Orrin G. Hatch, Utah*
Herb Kohl, Wis.	*Charles E. Grassley, Iowa*
Dianne Feinstein, Calif.	*Jon Kyl, Ariz.*
Russ Feingold, Wis.	*Jeff Sessions, Ala.*
Charles E. Schumer, N.Y.	*Lindsey Graham, S.C.*
Richard J. Durbin, Ill.	*John Cornyn, Texas*
Benjamin L. Cardin, Md.	*Sam Brownback, Kan.*
Sheldon Whitehouse, R.I.	*Tom Coburn, Okla.*

ADMINISTRATIVE OVERSIGHT & THE COURTS
Schumer, chairman

Democrats: Feinstein, Feingold, Whitehouse
Republicans: Sessions, Grassley, Graham

ANTITRUST, COMPETITION POLICY & CONSUMER RIGHTS
Kohl, chairman

Democrats: Leahy, Biden, Feingold, Schumer, Cardin
Republicans: Hatch, Specter, Grassley, Brownback, Coburn

CONSTITUTION
Feingold, chairman

Democrats: Kennedy, Feinstein, Durbin, Cardin
Republicans: Brownback, Specter, Graham, Cornyn

CRIME & DRUGS
Biden, chairman

Democrats: Kennedy, Kohl, Feinstein, Feingold, Schumer, Durbin
Republicans: Graham, Specter, Hatch, Grassley, Sessions, Coburn

HUMAN RIGHTS & THE LAW
Durbin, chairman

Democrats: Kennedy, Biden, Feingold, Cardin, Whitehouse
Republicans: Coburn, Kyl, Graham, Cornyn, Brownback

IMMIGRATION, REFUGEES & BORDER SECURITY
Kennedy, chairman

Democrats: Biden, Feinstein, Schumer, Durbin
Republicans: Cornyn, Grassley, Kyl, Sessions

TERRORISM, TECHNOLOGY & HOMELAND SECURITY

Feinstein, chairwoman

Democrats: Kennedy, Biden, Kohl, Schumer, Durbin, Cardin
Republicans: Kyl, Hatch, Sessions, Cornyn, Brownback, Coburn

RULES & ADMINISTRATION

224-6352 305 Russell
Party Ratio: D 10-R 9
Dianne Feinstein, D-Calif., chairwoman

Robert C. Byrd, W.Va.	*Robert F. Bennett, Utah*
Daniel K. Inouye, Hawaii	*Ted Stevens, Alaska*
Christopher J. Dodd, Conn.	*Mitch McConnell, Ky.*
Charles E. Schumer, N.Y.	*Thad Cochran, Miss.*
Richard J. Durbin, Ill.	*Trent Lott, Miss.*
Ben Nelson, Neb.	*Kay Bailey Hutchison, Texas*
Harry Reid, Nev.	*Saxby Chambliss, Ga.*
Patty Murray, Wash.	*Chuck Hagel, Neb.*
Mark Pryor, Ark.	*Lamar Alexander, Tenn.*

SELECT ETHICS

224-2981 220 Hart
Party Ratio: D 3-R 3
Tim Johnson, D-S.D., chairman

Barbara Boxer, Calif., acting chairwoman	*John Cornyn, Texas*
Mark Pryor, Ark.	*Pat Roberts, Kan.*
Ken Salazar, Colo.	*Craig Thomas, Wyo.*

SELECT INTELLIGENCE

224-1700 211 Hart
Party Ratio: D 8-R 7
John D. Rockefeller IV, D-W.Va., chairman

Dianne Feinstein, Calif.	*Christopher S. Bond, Mo.*
Ron Wyden, Ore.	*John W. Warner, Va.*
Evan Bayh, Ind.	*Chuck Hagel, Neb.*
Barbara A. Mikulski, Md.	*Saxby Chambliss, Ga.*
Russ Feingold, Wis.	*Orrin G. Hatch, Utah*
Bill Nelson, Fla.	*Olympia J. Snowe, Maine*
Sheldon Whitehouse, R.I.	*Richard M. Burr, N.C.*

SMALL BUSINESS & ENTREPRENEURSHIP

224-5175 428A Russell
Party Ratio: D 10-R 9
John Kerry, D-Mass., chairman

Carl Levin, Mich.	*Olympia J. Snowe, Maine*
Tom Harkin, Iowa	*Christopher S. Bond, Mo.*
Joseph I. Lieberman, I-Conn.	*Norm Coleman, Minn.*
Mary L. Landrieu, La.	*David Vitter, La.*
Maria Cantwell, Wash.	*Elizabeth Dole, N.C.*
Evan Bayh, Ind.	*John Thune, S.D.*
Mark Pryor, Ark.	*Bob Corker, Tenn.*
Benjamin L. Cardin, Md.	*Michael B. Enzi, Wyo.*
Jon Tester, Mont.	*Johnny Isakson, Ga.*

SPECIAL AGING

224-5364 G31 Dirksen
Party Ratio: D 11-R 10
Herb Kohl, D-Wis., chairman

Ron Wyden, Ore.	*Gordon H. Smith, Ore.*
Blanche Lincoln, Ark.	*Richard C. Shelby, Ala.*
Evan Bayh, Ind.	*Susan Collins, Maine*
Thomas R. Carper, Del.	*Mel Martinez, Fla.*
Bill Nelson, Fla.	*Larry E. Craig, Idaho*
Hillary Rodham Clinton, N.Y.	*Elizabeth Dole, N.C.*
Ken Salazar, Colo.	*Norm Coleman, Minn.*
Bob Casey, Pa.	*David Vitter, La.*
Claire McCaskill, Mo.	*Bob Corker, Tenn.*
Sheldon Whitehouse, R.I.	*Arlen Specter, Pa.*

VETERANS' AFFAIRS

224-9126 412 Russell
Party Ratio: D 8-R 7
Daniel K. Akaka, D-Hawaii, chairman

John D. Rockefeller IV, W.Va.	*Larry E. Craig, Idaho*
Patty Murray, Wash.	*Arlen Specter, Pa.*
Barack Obama, Ill.	*Richard M. Burr, N.C.*
Bernard Sanders, I-Vt.	*Johnny Isakson, Ga.*
Sherrod Brown, Ohio	*Lindsey Graham, S.C.*
Jim Webb, Va.	*Kay Bailey Hutchison, Texas*
Jon Tester, Mont.	*John Ensign, Nev.*

Partisan Senate Committees

DEMOCRATIC LEADERS

President Pro Tempore . . . . Robert C. Byrd
Majority Leader. . . . . Harry Reid
Majority Whip . . . . Richard J. Durbin
Caucus Vice Chairman . . . . Charles E. Schumer
Conference Secretary . . . . Patty Murray
Committee Outreach Chairman . . . . Jeff Bingaman
Cmte. Outreach Vice Chairwoman . . Hillary Rodham Clinton
Rural Outreach Chairwoman . . . . Blanche Lincoln
Chief Deputy Whip . . . . Barbara Boxer
Deputy Whips: Sherrod Brown, Benjamin L. Cardin, Thomas R. Carper, Russ Feingold, Amy Klobuchar, Claire McCaskill, Patty Murray, Bill Nelson, Mark Pryor, Ken Salazar, Ron Wyden

DEMOCRATIC SENATORIAL CAMPAIGN COMMITTEE

224-2447 120 Maryland Ave. N.E. 20002

Chairman . . . . Charles E. Schumer

POLICY COMMITTEE

224-3232 419 Hart

Chairman . . . . Byron L. Dorgan
Regional Chairmen: Evan Bayh, Jack Reed, Ken Salazar, Mary L. Landrieu
Members: Daniel K. Akaka, Sherrod Brown, Thomas R. Carper, Russ Feingold, Dianne Feinstein, Tim Johnson, Frank R. Lautenberg, Joseph I. Lieberman, Blanche Lincoln, Barbara A. Mikulski, Bill Nelson, Harry Reid, John D. Rockefeller IV, Charles E. Schumer, Ron Wyden
Ex-Officio Members: . . . . . Richard J. Durbin, Patty Murray

STEERING AND OUTREACH COMMITTEE

224-9048 712 Hart

Chairwoman . . . . Debbie Stabenow

REPUBLICAN LEADERS

President . . . . Vice President Dick Cheney
Minority Leader . . . . Mitch McConnell
Minority Whip . . . . Trent Lott
Conference Chairman . . . . Jon Kyl
Conference Vice Chairman . . . . John Cornyn
Counsel & Adviser to the Leader. . . . . Robert F. Bennett
Chief Deputy Whip . . . . John Thune
Deputy Whips: Richard M. Burr, Norm Coleman, Larry E. Craig, James M. Inhofe, Olympia J. Snowe, John E. Sununu, David Vitter

NATIONAL REPUBLICAN SENATORIAL COMMITTEE

675-6000 425 Second St. N.E. 20002

Chairman . . . . John Ensign
Program Chairmen: Christopher S. Bond, Saxby Chambliss, Jim DeMint, James M. Inhofe, Johnny Isakson, Mitch McConnell, Lisa Murkowski

POLICY COMMITTEE

224-2946 347 Russell

Chairwoman. . . . . Kay Bailey Hutchison

COMMITTEE ON COMMITTEES

224-6142 239 Dirksen

Chairman . . . . Michael D. Crapo

Committees by the Numbers

75 **Members on the House Transportation and Infrastructure panel**, the largest committee in this Congress. The biggest Senate panel is Appropriations, with 29 seats.

21 **House gavels held by Californians**, more than any other state. New Yorkers have 14; Massachusetts lawmakers, nine; Texans, nine; Pennsylvanians, eight; North Carolinians, six.

16 **Subcommittees** in either chamber **with** the word **"oversight" in their name**. There are 13 with the word "health" or "healthy" in the name, nine with "energy," eight with "environment" or "environmental" and eight with "international."

15 **Freshmen on the House Transportation and Infrastructure Committee**, or one-fifth of the panel membership. No other committee in the 110th Congress has more freshmen.

6 **Members on the Senate Ethics Committee**, the smallest panel in Congress. The smallest in the House is House Administration, with nine members.

2 **Senators from a state** serving together on a committee : Agriculture (Iowa and Minnesota); Armed Services (Florida and Virginia); Budget (New Jersey); Energy and Natural Resources (Oregon and New Mexico); Finance (Oregon); Indian Affairs (North Dakota and Hawaii); Judiciary (Wisconsin); Small Business (Louisiana); Special Aging (Florida, Pennsylvania and Oregon); Rules and Administration (Mississippi and Nebraska).

Joint Committees

JOINT ECONOMIC
224-5171 G-01 Dirksen
Charles E. Schumer, N.Y., chairman

Senate Members
Democrats: Edward M. Kennedy, Mass., Jeff Bingaman, N.M., Amy Klobuchar, Minn., Bob Casey, Pa., Jim Webb, Va.
Republicans: Robert F. Bennett, Utah, Sam Brownback, Kan., John E. Sununu, N.H., Jim DeMint, S.C.
House Members
Democrats: Carolyn B. Maloney, N.Y., Maurice D. Hinchey, N.Y., Baron P. Hill, Ind., Loretta Sanchez, Calif., Elijah E. Cummings, Md., Lloyd Doggett, Texas
Republicans: H. James Saxton, N.J., Kevin Brady, Texas, Phil English, Pa., Ron Paul, Texas

JOINT LIBRARY
224-6352 305 Russell
Dianne Feinstein, Calif., chairwoman

Senate Members
Democrats: Christopher J. Dodd, Conn., Charles E. Schumer, N.Y.
Republicans: Robert F. Bennett, Utah, Ted Stevens, Alaska
House Members
Democrats: Zoe Lofgren, Calif., Debbie Wasserman-Schultz, Fla., Vacancy
Republicans: Vernon J. Ehlers, Mich., Dan Lungren, Calif.

JOINT PRINTING
225-2061 1309 Longworth
Robert A. Brady, Pa., chairman

Senate Members
Democrats: Dianne Feinstein, Calif., Daniel K. Inouye, Hawaii, Patty Murray, Wash.
Republicans: Robert F. Bennett, Utah, Saxby Chambliss, Ga.
House Members
Democrats: Michael E. Capuano, Mass., Vacancy
Republicans: Vernon J. Ehlers, Mich., Kevin McCarthy, Calif.

JOINT TAXATION
225-3621 1015 Longworth
Charles B. Rangel, N.Y., chairman

Senate Members
Democrats: Max Baucus, Mont., John D. Rockefeller IV, W.Va., Kent Conrad, N.D.
Republicans: Charles E. Grassley, Iowa, Orrin G. Hatch, Utah
House Members
Democrats: Pete Stark, Calif., Sander M. Levin, Mich.
Republicans: Jim McCrery, La., Wally Herger, Calif.

Better Know a Chairman

Who is the most senior Democratic senator who does not chair a committee?

That would be Maryland's **Barbara A. Mikulski**, who was elected in 1986.

Who is the most junior senator who is a committee chairman?

It's **Charles E. Schumer** of New York, who chairs the Joint Economic Committee. Schumer was elected in 1998.

Which senator has the most committee gavels?

There's a five-way tie. Hawaii's **Daniel K. Akaka,** North Dakota's **Byron L. Dorgan**, South Dakota's **Tim Johnson,** and **John Kerry** of Massachusetts each chair a full panel and three subcommittees. **Dianne Feinstein** of California is chairwoman of a full committee, a joint committee and two subcommittees.

Name the most senior House Democrat who is not a full committee chairman.

California's **Pete Stark**, who was elected in 1972, chairs the Ways and Means Health Subcommittee, but does not preside over a full committee.

Who is the most senior House Democrat, not in the leadership, who doesn't wield a full panel or subcommittee gavel?

That's **Marcy Kaptur** of Ohio, who is in her 13th term, but doesn't have a chairmanship in the 110th Congress.

Who is the most junior House Democrat who chairs a committee?

Stephanie Tubbs Jones of Ohio, who was elected in 1998, chairs the Standards of Official Conduct panel.

Did You Know?

It's common knowledge that Hillary Rodham Clinton was the First Lady and John McCain was a prisoner of war in Vietnam, but many other members of Congress also have noteworthy and occasionally quirky backgrounds. These unique experiences and interests can provide insight into his or her behavior as a member.

Tom Harkin, for instance, has long been interested in legislation affecting people with disabilities. His inspiration for that was his brother, Frank, who was deaf.

A lawmaker's past often provides clues to why they got into politics in the first place. For example, three members – Patty Murray, Darlene Hooley and Betty McCollum – all can point to their dissatisfaction with the way their local officials dealt with playground equipment. For others, it's in the genes: 29 current lawmakers have followed their parents into Congress.

And sometimes these personal tidbits offer a fascinating humanizing touch. For example, did you know that:

Rep. **Gary L. Ackerman**, D-N.Y., used to live on a houseboat named "Unsinkable." It sank.

Pennsylvania Democratic Rep. **Jason Altmire** was a walk-on football player at Florida State University, where he played wide receiver and was sometimes aligned in practice against future NFL star Deion Sanders.

Rep. **Roscoe G. Bartlett**, R-Md., holds 20 patents including ones for components in breathing equipment used by pilots, astronauts and rescue workers.

As a young man, Sen. **Max Baucus**, D-Mont., hitchhiked around Europe with Gypsies and says that he had an epiphany to enter public service while traveling in the Belgian Congo.

One of Sen. **Evan Bayh**'s, D-Ind., babysitters was Lynda Bird Johnson, the president's daughter.

The four-member Arkansas House delegation is well-versed in the medical field: **Marion Berry**, D, is a pharmacist; **John Boozman**, R, is an optometrist; **Mike Ross**, D, owns a pharmacy; and **Vic Snyder**, D, is a doctor.

Kentucky Republican Sen. **Jim Bunning** is a member of the Baseball Hall of Fame. He is the first pitcher to record 100 wins and 1,000 strikeouts in each league.

North Carolina Republican Sen. **Richard M. Burr** is descended from Aaron Burr, the New York senator and vice president, who survived a famous duel in U.S. history.

Rep. **Dave Camp** has a rack of several dozen men's neckties in his Washington office. The Michigan Republican began the collection when The Detroit News reported that he arrived in Congress with just three ties and invited readers to help.

To pay for his education at the University of Maryland, Rep. **William Lacy Clay**, D-Mo., was a U.S. House of Representatives doorman for seven years.

Rep. **James E. Clyburn**, D-S.C., is the first African-American elected to Congress from South Carolina since 1896, when his great-uncle, George Washington Murray, was in the House.

Rep. **Steve Cohen**, D-Tenn., was diagnosed with polio as a child, but was too young to take the same vaccine that his father, a doctor, was helping Jonas Salk test.

An aunt of Florida GOP Reps. **Lincoln Diaz-Balart** and **Mario Diaz-Balart**, who are brothers, was once married to Fidel Castro.

When Rep. **Anna G. Eshoo**, D-Calif., was in high school in Connecticut, President Harry S Truman gave her a ride home from school.

California's Rep. **Sam Farr** is the only current member of Congress born on July Fourth. The Democrat celebrates his birthday by attending mass-naturalization ceremonies for immigrants who have earned U.S. citizenship.

Rep. **Rahm Emanuel**, D-Ill., took a ballet class to improve his soccer agility and liked it so much that he continued to study dance while working on his college degree.

Rep. **Chaka Fattah**, D-Pa., was born Arthur Davenport. Fattah's mother changed his name when she married community activist David Fattah. She called him "Chaka" in honor of a Zulu warrior.

Rep. **Rodney Frelinghuysen**, R-N.J., is the sixth member of his family to serve in Congress.

Republican **Luis Fortuño**, the resident commissioner from Puerto Rico, is the only member of Congress with a four-year term.

Rep. **Gabrielle Giffords**, D-Ariz., chose U2's "Beautiful Day" to be played as a wake-up call for her fiancé, NASA astronaut Mark Kelly, when he was on a 2006 space mission.

When the famously feisty Rep. Henry B. Gonzalez of Texas retired from the House after 37 years, he refused to endorse his son, **Charlie Gonzalez**, in a seven-way Democratic primary to succeed him in 1998. He said he wanted his son to stand on his own. Charlie Gonzalez won.

Sen. **Charles E. Grassley**, R-Iowa, works on the family farm on weekends, and tucks a cell phone inside his cap while driving the tractor so he will feel the vibrations of an incoming call.

Sen. **Judd Gregg**, R-N.H., Rep. **F. James Sensenbrenner Jr.**, R-Wis., and Rep. **Kevin McCarthy**, R-Calif., are all lottery winners. Gregg donated some of his $853,492 to charity, Sensenbrenner put his $250,000 toward charities and investments and McCarthy invested the $5,000 from his scratch-off ticket to open "Kevin O's Deli."

New York Democratic Rep. **John Hall** was the lead singer of the 1970s rock-and-roll band Orleans when he penned the pop standard "Still the One," which hit No. 2 on the Billboard charts.

As a young Hill aide on a 1969 trip to Vietnam, Sen. **Tom Harkin**, D-Iowa, discovered the "tiger cages," squalid underground cells where the South Vietnamese government secretly kept prisoners of war. Harkin's revelations got worldwide attention.

Sen. **Orrin G. Hatch**, R-Utah, has written songs and movie soundtracks performed by the Osmonds and Gladys Knight; He often scribbles song lyrics between Senate votes, and has produced several discs of religious, romantic and patriotic songs.

Rep. **Rush D. Holt**, D-N.J., a physicist, is a former champion on the TV quiz show "Jeopardy." Sen. **Charles E. Schumer** appeared on the high school quiz program "It's Academic" in 1967 and was captain of his team. Fellow New York Democrat, Sen. **Hillary Rodham Clinton**, was an alternate for her high school team in 1964-65 but never got on the air.

In 1993, Oklahoma Republican Sen. **James M. Inhofe** became the only member of Congress to fly an airplane around the world. He retraced Wiley Post's journey, the first solo flight around the world.

Sen. **Daniel K. Inouye**, D-Hawaii, was awarded a Medal of Honor in 2000 for heroism in World War II. A member of the famed all-Nisei "Go for Broke" 442nd Regimental Combat Team, he lost his right arm when he advanced alone to take out a machine gun that had pinned down his men.

Rep. **Jesse L. Jackson Jr.**, D-Ill., vacuums his office carpet for relaxation.

Louisiana Republican Rep. **Bobby Jindal**'s third child was born with little advance warning, so Jindal delivered the baby himself at home. He tied off the umbilical cord with a shoelace before paramedics arrived. "I tried to do everything you see in the movies," Jindal said.

Rep. **Sam Johnson**, R-Texas, spent almost seven years in a North Vietnamese prison camp. For a brief stretch, he shared a cell with with fellow prisoner of war Sen. **John McCain**, R-Ariz.

Rep. **Paul E. Kanjorski**, D-Pa., a licensed attorney since 1966, never graduated from law school. He didn't graduate from college, either.

University of Georgia graduate **Jack Kingston**, R-Ga., was the only House member to oppose a 2006 resolution commending the Bulldogs' arch-rival University of Florida Gators for winning the college football championship.

During his service in the Marine Corps, Minnesota Republican Rep. **John Kline** carried the "football" — the briefcase with nuclear war codes — for Presidents Jimmy Carter and Ronald Reagan and flew the presidential helicopter, Marine One.

Ohio Democratic Rep. **Dennis J. Kucinich** was so unpopular as mayor of Cleveland that he wore a bulletproof vest to throw out the first pitch at an Indians game.

Rep. **Tom Lantos**, D-Calif., fought with the Hungarian resistance against the Nazis. He escaped from a Nazi work camp.

Connecticut Independent Sen. **Joseph I. Lieberman** taught freshman Democratic Sens. **Sherrod Brown** of Ohio and **Amy Klobuchar** of Minnesota in separate seminar classes at Yale University. Klobuchar's program was about the Democratic Party.

The first bill that Iowa Democratic Rep. **Dave Loebsack** introduced was to name a federal building in Davenport after the man he defeated to win his House seat, Republican Jim Leach.

Rep. **Stephen F. Lynch**, D-Mass., donated more than half his liver to his brother.

In 2000, Georgia Democratic Rep. **Jim Marshall** was running for the House when Senate Majority Leader **Trent Lott** of Mississippi threatened to move military contracts out of Georgia. Marshall brought a live donkey to a press conference, and said, "I just want to invite Sen. Lott to kiss my donkey."

Reps. **George Miller**, D-Calif., and **Bill Delahunt**, D-Mass., and Sens. **Charles E. Schumer**, D-N.Y., and **Richard J. Durbin**, D-Ill., all share a Capitol Hill rowhouse of such notorious disarray that it merited a New York Times write-up and a visit from an ABC News television crew in early 2007.

Rep. **Dennis Moore**, D-Kan., has played guitar since high school, and once shared the stage at a Farm Aid concert with Willie Nelson and David Crosby. Pennsylvania GOP Rep. **Tim Murphy** taught himself to play guitar and once opened for banjo legend Earl Scruggs. And Idaho Republican Rep. **Bill Sali**, on drums, has opened for the likes of Toby Keith, Billy Ray Cyrus and Waylon Jennings.

Rep. **Patrick J. Murphy**, D-Pa., is the only Iraq War veteran in Congress. Rep. **Heather A. Wilson**, R-N.M., is the only female military veteran currently in Congress.

In high school, Democratic Rep. **John P. Murtha** of Pennsylvania acted in school plays; his most memorable moment was as a professor in "Little Women" when he split his pants and never turned his back to the audience.

2008 Democratic presidential contenders **Barack Obama** of Illinois and **Hillary Rodham Clinton** of New York have each won a Grammy award for best spoken word album.

Rep. **Collin C. Peterson**, D-Minn., is the lead singer of a country rock band called "The Second Amendments" that also includes Reps. **Jon Porter**, R-Nev.; **Dave Weldon,** R-Fla.; **Kenny Hulshof**, R-Mo.; and **Thaddeus McCotter,** R-Mich. They have performed for U.S. troops in Iraq, Pakistan and Afghanistan. **McCotter** once played in a band called Sir Funk-a-Lot.

Rep. **Candice S. Miller**, R-Mich., earned the honorary title "Old Goat" in 2001 when she competed in her 25th Port Huron to Mackinac Island sailboat race.

Rep. **Harry E. Mitchell**, D-Ariz., was such a popular mayor in his hometown of Tempe that city officials established the Harry E. Mitchell Government Complex and erected a 35-foot abstract steel statue of him near city hall.

Sen. **Lisa Murkowski**, R-Alaska, is the first woman to represent Alaska. She is also the first person ever appointed to the Senate by her father.

Rep. **Randy Neugebauer**, R-Texas, was so skilled at back flips, twists and other moves that while at Texas Tech he joined the Flying Matadors trampoline troupe.

Of the 48 House votes in the 109th Congress (2005-06) on which there was a solitary no, Rep. **Ron Paul**, R-Texas, cast that vote 31 times.

As a girl, Speaker **Nancy Pelosi**, D-Calif., slept above stacks of the Congressional Record. Her father, Thomas D'Alesandro Jr., was a Maryland congressman and stored them under her bed in their Baltimore rowhouse.

Republican Rep. **Tom Petri**'s first job was hosting a radio show called "Teen Time," a weekly program that made him the Badger State's youngest on-air personality.

Political science professor and now Rep. **David E. Price**, D-N.C., helped judge Illinois Democratic Rep. **Daniel Lipinski**'s doctoral thesis at Duke University.

Every Congress, Rep. **Ralph Regula**, R-Ohio, sponsors a bill stopping Alaska from changing the name of Mount McKinley to the original Native Alaskan word Denali, meaning "high one." The 25th president, William McKinley, was born in Regula's district.

Rep. **Dave Reichert**, R-Wash., was the original lead detective in the Green River serial killer task force. Almost 20 years later, as the King County sheriff, he announced the arrest of Gary Ridgway in 2001.

Sen. **Harry Reid**, D-Nev., took on organized crime as chairman of the Nevada Gaming Commission. A bomb was once found under the hood of his car.

Arizona Republican Rep. **Rick Renzi** and his wife, Roberta, have 12 children, more than any other congressional family. And all of the kids' names begin with the letter "R."

Rep. **Dana Rohrabacher**, R-Calif., says John Wayne taught him how to drink tequila.

Illinois Democratic Rep. **Bobby L. Rush** is a former Black Panther who served six months in prison on a weapons charge.

Rep. **José E. Serrano**, D-N.Y., learned to speak English by listening to Frank Sinatra records.

Retired Navy Vice Admiral **Joe Sestak**, D-Pa., is the highest-ranking military officer ever elected to Congress or to serve in the House.

Rep. **Jean Schmidt**, R-Ohio, has participated in 10 Boston marathons.

In the 1960s, Sen. **Arlen Specter,** D-Pa., as a top aide to the Warren Commission, helped devise the "single bullet" theory that a lone gunman was responsible for the 1963 assassination of President John F. Kennedy.

Rep. **Pete Stark**, a California Democrat, is recognized by the American Humanist Association as the highest-ranking U.S. official and the first member of Congress to proclaim that he is an atheist. Stark says he's a Unitarian who does not believe in a supreme being.

A former junior high school teacher, Rep. **Tom Tancredo**, R-Colo., first ran for the state House on a dare from his students.

Sen. **Craig Thomas**, R-Wyo., occupies the "candy desk," an aisle seat at the rear of the Senate chamber on the GOP side. In 1965, Republican George Murphy of California originated the practice of stashing candy in the desk to share with colleagues. Thomas took over the seat in 2007 from defeated Sen. Rick Santorum, R-Pa.

Colorado's Rep. **Mark Udall** keeps a pair of his father's size 15, white high-top sneakers, a reminder that he has big shoes to fill. The Democrat's father is the late, legendary Rep. Morris K. "Mo" Udall of Arizona, who served in the House for 30 years.

In 1983, while working as a White House aide, Rep. **Fred Upton**, R-Mich., proposed to his wife during a Baltimore Orioles baseball game, hiring an airplane to fly overhead with a banner reading, "Amey this is the inning to say yes."

In 1967, Virginia Democratic Sen. **Jim Webb**, as a student at the U.S. Naval Academy, lost a boxing championship to Oliver L. North, who would later become a household name for his role in the Iran-Contra affair.

Rep. **Lynn Woolsey**, D-Calif., went on welfare after a divorce left her on her own with three young children and no job skills. Wisconsin Democratic Rep. **Gwen Moore** was on welfare while pregnant and going to college to receive her undergraduate degree.

Rep. **Charlie Wilson**, D-Ohio, received a certificate in mortuary sciences and was president of the Ohio Funeral Directors Association. Pennsylvania Republican Rep. **Tim Murphy** dug graves to earn money for college.

Index

A

Abercrombie, Neil, D-Hawaii (1), **305**
Ackerman, Gary L., D-N.Y. (5), **691**
Aderholt, Robert B., R-Ala. (4), **13**
Akaka, Daniel K., D-Hawaii, 302, **303**, 307
Akin, Todd, R-Mo. (2), **579**
Alexander, Lamar, R-Tenn., 199, 561, 564, **924**, 1026
Alexander, Rodney, R-La. (5), **440**
Allard, Wayne, R-Colo., **178**, 605, 947
Allen, Tom, D-Maine (1), 451, **452**
Altmire, Jason, D-Pa. (4), **858**
Andrews, Robert E., D-N.J. (1), 637, **639**
Arcuri, Michael, D-N.Y. (24), **726**

B

Baca, Joe, D-Calif. (43), 133, 147, **154**, 162
Bachmann, Michele, R-Minn. (6), **552**
Bachus, Spencer, R-Ala. (6), 11, **17**, 405, 442
Baird, Brian, D-Wash. (3), **1072**
Baker, Richard H., R-La. (6), 17, **442**
Baldwin, Tammy, D-Wis. (2), **1106**, 1110
Barrett, J. Gresham, R-S.C. (3), **906**
Barrow, John, D-Ga. (12), 288, 292, **295**
Bartlett, Roscoe G., R-Md. (6), **471**, 674
Barton, Joe L., R-Texas (6), 115, 279, 290, 371, 537, 761, 948, **961**
Baucus, Max, D-Mont., 384, **597**, 602, 1091
Bayh, Evan, D-Ind., 52, 55, **364**
Bean, Melissa, D-Ill. (8), **337**
Becerra, Xavier, D-Calif. (31), **131**, 138
Bennett, Robert F., R-Utah, **1019**
Berkley, Shelley, D-Nev. (1), **620**, 623
Berman, Howard L., D-Calif. (28), **125**, 130, 1074
Berry, Marion, D-Ark. (1), **56**, 277
Biden, Joseph R. Jr., D-Del., 6, **210**, 212, 215, 322, 505, 606
Biggert, Judy, R-Ill. (13), **347**
Bilbray, Brian P., R-Calif. (50), 120, **168**, 175
Bilirakis, Gus, R-Fla. (9), **239**
Bingaman, Jeff, D-N.M., 667, **668**, 961
Bishop, Rob, R-Utah (1), **1021**
Bishop, Sanford D. Jr., D-Ga. (2), 275, **277**
Bishop, Timothy H., D-N.Y. (1), **683**
Blackburn, Marsha, R-Tenn. (7), 243, **939**
Blumenauer, Earl, D-Ore. (3), 837, **839**
Blunt, Roy, R-Mo. (7), 40, 106, 112, 121, 229, 341, 392, 407, 522, 576, **589**, 591, 623, 691, 794, 802, 882, 929, 969, 973, 1052, 1130
Boehner, John A., R-Ohio (8), 40, 112, 119, 133, 214, 229, 347, 369, 375, 392, 407, 522, 589, 593, 623, 727, 792, **794**, 802, 906, 929, 961, 1052, 1081, 1114, 1130
Bond, Christopher S., R-Mo., **573**, 590, 593, 818, 1029
Bonner, Jo, R-Ala. (1), **7**
Bono, Mary, R-Calif. (45), **158**, 246, 874
Boozman, John, R-Ark. (3), **60**
Bordallo, Madeleine Z., D-Guam (AL), **1129**
Boren, Dan, D-Okla. (2), 15, **822**, 1005
Boswell, Leonard L., D-Iowa (3), **390**
Boucher, Rick, D-Va. (9), 1051, **1056**
Boustany, Charles Jr., R-La. (7), **444**
Boxer, Barbara, D-Calif., 70, **71**, 73, 84, 122, 134, 163, 668, 800, 816, 1031
Boyd, Allen, D-Fla. (2), **225**
Boyda, Nancy, D-Kan. (2), **404**
Brady, Kevin, R-Texas (8), **965**
Brady, Robert A., D-Pa. (1), **852**, 854
Braley, Bruce, D-Iowa (1), **388**
Brown, Corrine, D-Fla. (3), **227**
Brown, Henry E. Jr., R-S.C. (1), **902**
Brown, Sherrod, D-Ohio, **780**, 804, 1039
Brown-Waite, Ginny, R-Fla. (5), **231**
Brownback, Sam, R-Kan., **398**, 402, 407, 1105
Buchanan, Vern, R-Fla. (13), **245**, 989
Bunning, Jim, R-Ky., **413**
Burgess, Michael C., R-Texas (26), **1001**, 1007
Burr, Richard M., R-N.C., **741**, 752, 1123
Burton, Dan, R-Ind. (5), 129, 136, **373**, 1054
Butterfield, G.K., D-N.C. (1), **743**
Buyer, Steve, R-Ind. (4), 170, 171, 227, **371**
Byrd, Robert C., D-W.Va., 24, 210, 301, 479, 547, 559, 635, 818, **1088**, 1090, 1093, 1097

C

Calvert, Ken, R-Calif. (44), **156**
Camp, Dave, R-Mich. (4), **515**
Campbell, John, R-Calif. (48), **164**
Cannon, Chris, R-Utah (3), 1020, **1025**
Cantor, Eric, R-Va. (7), 522, 589, 973, **1052**
Cantwell, Maria, D-Wash., **1066**
Capito, Shelley Moore, R-W.Va. (2), 137, 358, **1094**
Capps, Lois, D-Calif. (23), **115**, 1076
Capuano, Michael E., D-Mass. (8), **497**, 700
Cardin, Benjamin L., D-Md., **460**, 465, 466, 470, 476, 530
Cardoza, Dennis, D-Calif. (18), **106**
Carnahan, Russ, D-Mo. (3), **581**
Carney, Christopher, D-Pa. (10), **867**
Carper, Thomas R., D-Del., 52, **212**, 924
Carson, Julia, D-Ind. (7), **377**
Carter, John, R-Texas (31), 951, **1011**
Casey, Bob, D-Pa., 543, 679, **850**, 874
Castle, Michael N., R-Del. (AL), 182, 213, **214**, 547, 709, 942
Castor, Kathy, D-Fla. (11), **242**
Chabot, Steve, R-Ohio (1), **782**
Chambliss, Saxby, R-Ga., **271**, 274, 276, 289, 400
Chandler, Ben, D-Ky. (6), **424**
Christensen, Donna M.C., D-Virgin Is. (AL), **1131**
Clarke, Yvette D., D-N.Y. (11), **703**
Clay, William Lacy, D-Mo. (1), **577**
Cleaver Emanuel II, D-Mo. (5), **585**
Clinton, Hillary Rodham, D-N.Y., 32, 72, 196, 322, 364, 458, 481, 490, 532, 536, 619, 679, **681**, 688, 716, 729, 850, 1089
Clyburn, James E., D-S.C. (6), 182, 332, 474, 532, **912**, 1005
Coble, Howard, R-N.C. (6), 100, **753**
Coburn, Tom, R-Okla., 23, 322, **818**, 822, 917, 1103
Cochran, Thad, R-Miss., 5, 150, **559**, 562, 567, 666
Cohen, Steve, D-Tenn. (9), **943**
Cole, Tom, R-Okla. (4), **826**, 1013, 1060
Coleman, Norm, R-Minn., 460, **540**, 543, 739
Collins, Susan, R-Maine, 199, 448, **450**, 453
Conaway, K. Michael, R-Texas (11), **971**, 988
Conrad, Kent, D-N.D., 627, **770**, 773, 775, 910
Conyers, John Jr., D-Mich. (14), 532, **534**, 722, 764
Cooper, Jim, D-Tenn. (5), **935**
Corker, Bob, R-Tenn., **926**

D

E

F

G

H

I

J

K

L

M

N

O

P

R

S

T

U

V

W

Y